McDougal Littell

THE LANGUAGE OF LITERATURE

BRITISH LITERATURE

TEACHER'S EDITION

McDougal Littell
A HOUGHTON MIFFLIN COMPANY
Evanston, Illinois • Boston • Dallas

ISBN 0-395-93189-4

Printed in the United States of America.

2 3 4 5 6 7 8 9 – DWO – 04 03 02 01 00 99

You teach many types of students with different personalities and abilities. *The Language of Literature* lets you share your passion for literature with all of them. A variety of unique strategies for approaching the selections helps you meet the diverse needs of your students.

THE LANGUAGE OF LITERATURE

Share Your Passion!

"Passion, I see, is catching."

—William Shakespeare

Unique features that engage and motivate students:

Author Studies
Share your favorite authors—their lives, times, and works—with your students. Every in-depth study contains historical background, a variety of selections, and student projects.

Related Readings
Provide exciting opportunities for students to relate what they read to the larger world—and to their own lives—with these additional readings and primary sources.

Preparing to Read
Prepare students for the selections with literary elements, active reading strategies, important vocabulary, and personal connections to the literature.

Thinking Through the Literature
Encourage reflection and analysis through personal responses, critical thinking, and literary analysis.

Author Study

OVERVIEW

Objectives
- appreciate the craft of England's most famous playwright.
- interpret the possible influences of the historical context on *Macbeth.*
- gain information about Shakespeare by reading nonfiction.

This Author Study offers a unique opportunity for students to focus on the work of a major writer. In addition, students can gather information about the life of Shakespeare, gaining insight into the real person behind his now famous literary works.

Reading Skills and Strategies
Establishing a Purpose for Reading
Have students scan pages 314–322 and establish a purpose or purposes for reading. Discuss the array of material on these pages.

Author Study
WILLIAM SHAKESPEARE

OVERVIEW

"He was not of an age, but for all time!"
—Ben Jonson

HIS LIFE
HIS TIMES

Master Playwright and Poet

With his brilliant poetic language and keen insight into human nature, William Shakespeare is generally regarded as the world's greatest writer in the English language. His plays are more widely translated than any other works except the Bible. Yet his life remains something of a mystery, with many details lost in the swirl of time.

1564–1616

"I COULD A TALE UNFOLD" Shakespeare was born in Stratford-upon-Avon, a busy market town on the Avon River, northwest of London. Though the precise date of his birth is not known, church records indicate that he was baptized on April 26, 1564. Unlike most other writers of his era, he did not come from a noble family with close ties to the English court. The Shakespeares were what today we would call middle class, although his father, a glove maker, once served as the equivalent of mayor of Stratford.

Though no record of Shakespeare's schooling survives, it is assumed that he attended the local grammar school in Stratford. Again unlike most other writers of his day, Shakespeare did not

go on to a u
the age of 1
Hathaway,
have three c
birth, the d
Shakespeare
blank for se
was in Lonc
noticed as a

"THIS REA
Shakespeare
as a major
the powerfu
Spanish inv
victory, Lor
The arts,
as well. The
celebrated li
Spenser and
royal court.
the more so
Attracted b
people from
London, a l
first public
suburban S
became avic

1564 **Is born in Stratford-upon-Avon**
Tudor house in Stratford
1572 **Family suffers a decline in fortune, loses most land holdings**

1560 1565 1570 1575 158

1558 **Elizabeth I becomes queen; England returns to the Protestant faith.**
Elizabeth I
1572 **Protestants massacred in Paris on St. Bartholomew's Day.**
1577–80 **English explorer Sir Francis Drake sails around the world.**

314

...ns. Critical Thinking. Grammar. Vocabulary. Writing. Assessment.

The Language of Literature gives you many ways to help students catch your passion for literature. In-depth **Author Studies**, engaging **Literature in Performance** videos, **Related Readings**, **Preparing to Read** activities, and other features motivate students to read while helping them connect great literature to their own lives.

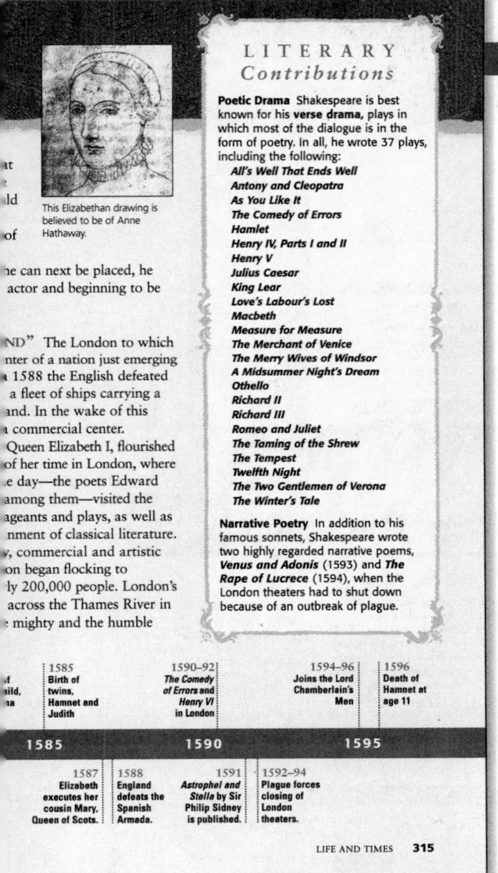

...at
...e
...ld
...of

This Elizabethan drawing is believed to be of Anne Hathaway.

...he can next be placed, he ...actor and beginning to be

...ND" The London to which ...nter of a nation just emerging ... 1588 the English defeated ... a fleet of ships carrying a ...and. In the wake of this ... a commercial center. ...Queen Elizabeth I, flourished ...of her time in London, where ...e day—the poets Edward ...among them—visited the ...ageants and plays, as well as ...nment of classical literature. ..., commercial and artistic ...on began flocking to ...ly 200,000 people. London's ...across the Thames River in ... mighty and the humble

LITERARY *Contributions*

Poetic Drama Shakespeare is best known for his **verse drama**, plays in which most of the dialogue is in the form of poetry. In all, he wrote 37 plays, including the following:

All's Well That Ends Well
Antony and Cleopatra
As You Like It
The Comedy of Errors
Hamlet
Henry IV, Parts I and II
Henry V
Julius Caesar
King Lear
Love's Labour's Lost
Macbeth
Measure for Measure
The Merchant of Venice
The Merry Wives of Windsor
A Midsummer Night's Dream
Othello
Richard II
Richard III
Romeo and Juliet
The Taming of the Shrew
The Tempest
Twelfth Night
The Two Gentlemen of Verona
The Winter's Tale

Narrative Poetry In addition to his famous sonnets, Shakespeare wrote two highly regarded narrative poems, ***Venus and Adonis*** (1593) and ***The Rape of Lucrece*** (1594), when the London theaters had to shut down because of an outbreak of plague.

1585 Birth of twins, Hamnet and Judith
1590–92 *The Comedy of Errors* and *Henry VI* in London
1594–96 Joins the Lord Chamberlain's Men
1596 Death of Hamnet at age 11

1585 | 1590 | 1595

1587 Elizabeth executes her cousin Mary, Queen of Scots.
1588 England defeats the Spanish Armada.
1591 *Astrophel and Stella* by Sir Philip Sidney is published.
1592–94 Plague forces closing of London theaters.

LIFE AND TIMES 315

LIFE AND TIMES

World Culture
Ⓐ If Shakespeare received a traditional education, his experience would have been similar to that of students in schools and colleges throughout Renaissance Europe. The standard curriculum used in these institutions was inherited from the Roman Empire. It consisted of the *trivium* (grammar, logic, and rhetoric) and the *quadrivium* (arithmetic, geometry, astronomy, and music). Courses were conducted in Latin.

History
Ⓑ After 1560, a wave of immigrants swept into England. Many of these newcomers, who practiced a variety of trades and professions, were Protestants who fled mainland Europe to escape persecution by Catholics. Although most English people supported the idea of asylum for these people, the English in general were suspicious of these "strangers."

Science
Ⓒ Medical knowledge during Shakespeare's time offered little hope to the sick. Most doctors believed that health was based on four humors, or bodily fluids: blood, phlegm, black bile, and yellow bile. The four humors were supposed to correspond to four elementary qualities: hot, cold, dry, and moist. The prevailing belief was that too much or too little of a particular humor caused illness. As a result, Doctors often treated people with such practices as bleeding, which was thought to restore the proper balance.

LIFE AND TIMES 315

Passionate Video Performances

Capture students' interest and give them a new perspective on the selections. The *Literature in Performance* video series features a wide variety of compelling performances of great literature. British Literature includes **Orson Welles** in *Macbeth*, **Sir John Gielgud** in *The Pardoner's Tale*, **Charlotte Cornwell** reading *The Lady of Shalott*, and other moving performances of great literature.

THE LANGUAGE OF LITERATURE

ar. Vocabulary. Writing. Assessment. Reading. Motivation. Conne

"Only connect the prose and the passion,

Writing Workshops Present students with standards for successful writing, along with models that show the standards in action,and skills for revising and editing.

Vocabulary in Action Develop students' vocabulary with prereading and postreading activities, as well as specific strategies for vocabulary development.

Sentence Crafting Use excerpts from the literature to highlight ways in which writers make effective use of grammatical structures.

Building Vocabulary

Objectives

- research word origins
- understand how to use Greek and Latin roots to determine meanings and build word families
- use etymology as an aid to expand vocabulary

EXERCISE

1. *resolute*
   Latin root: *solvere*
   Meaning: to release or set free
   Word Family: resolution; resolve; resoluble; resolvent
2. *prediction*
   Latin root: *dicere*
   Meaning: to say
   Word Family: dictionary; diction; dictum; edict
3. *conspires*
   Latin root: *spirare*
   Meaning: to breathe together
   Word Family: conspirator; respiration
4. *metaphysical*
   Greek root: *physis*
   Meaning: nature
   Word Family: physics; physique
5. *rhinoceros*
   Greek root: *keras*
   Meaning: nose-horned
   Word Family: rhinal; rhinology

432 UNIT TWO PART 2

Building Vocabulary — Analyzing Word Parts—Roots

Core Meanings

> **Boundless** intemperance
> **In nature is a tyranny. . . .**
> —William Shakespeare, *Macbeth*, Act 4, Scene 3

English speakers regularly borrow words from other languages to add to their own. Greek and Latin in particular have been fertile sources of roots for building English words. (A **root** is a core part of a word, to which other word parts, such as prefixes and suffixes, can be added to create new words.) Consider, for instance, the word *intemperance* in the sentence above from *Macbeth*. The Latin root *temper* means "to moderate," the prefix *in-* means "not" or "without," and the suffix *-ance* indicates a condition or action. By putting the meanings of the parts together you can infer that *intemperance* probably means something like "action that is without moderation."

Strategies for Building Vocabulary

If you know some common Greek and Latin roots and their meanings, you can figure out the meaning of unknown words—even without a dictionary.

Use the Meanings of Roots to Build Word Families You can expand your knowledge of roots by noting the etymologies of words that you look up in the dictionary. Read the etymology of *horrific* below. What insight into the meaning of the English word does it provide?

[Latin *horrificus* : *horrēre*, to tremble + *-ficus*,

Greek Root	Meaning	Word Family
arche	primitive, ancient	archaic, archetype, archaize, archaeologist
bibl	book	bibliography, Bible
cosm	world	cosmic, cosmopolitan,
gnos	know	Gnostic, agnostic, diagnosis
mania	madness	maniac, kleptomania
path	feeling	pathetic, sympathy

Latin Root	Meaning	Word Family
belli	war	bellicose, antebellum,

Writing Workshop — Personality Profile

Objectives

- write a Personality Profile
- use a written text as a model for writing
- revise a draft to add details
- use commas to add clarity to complex phrases and sentences

Introducing the Workshop

(A) **Personality Profile** Many television and film documentaries also include personality profiles. These profiles are popular because they acquaint us with celebrities and other notable people that we might never meet face to face. Have students name a few people they have read about in profiles. Point out that through writing a personality profile, students, too, will be able to "introduce" their readers to fascinating individuals that we might otherwise never encounter.

Establish some criteria for what makes one person fascinating to another. Students may be interested in celebrities who possess exceptional intellectual, musical, or athletic abilities. Some, like the student writer of the model, may be fascinated by a relative or close friend who is special in some way.

Basics in a Box

(B) **Using the Graphic** Like the tiles in a mosaic, the items in a personality profile work together to create an overall impression. The graphic offers suggestions for pieces that students can use to draft an effective essay.

(C) **Presenting the Rubric** To better understand the assignment, students can refer to the Standards for Writing a Successful Personality Profile. You may also want to share with them the complete rubric, which describes several levels of proficiency.

Use the complete rubric to evaluate student writing; stress the importance of producing an error-free final draft.

See the Skills Trace at the beginning of the unit for information on TEKS covered in this lesson.

200 UNIT ONE PART 2

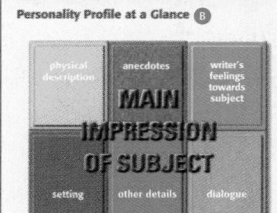

Writing Workshop — Personality Profile

Describing a Fascinating Person . . .

From Reading to Writing Good descriptive writing takes the reader inside the writer's world. Chaucer's remarkable character portraits in *The Canterbury Tales*, for example, transport the modern reader to the Middle Ages. Through carefully chosen details, Chaucer creates living personalities on the page—fascinating as individuals and for their universal human qualities. The same techniques are also applied to writing a **personality profile**, a common feature in newspapers and magazines. A personality profile combines compelling information and vivid language to describe a person. (A)

For Your Portfolio

WRITING PROMPT Write a personality profile of a person of your choice.

Purpose: To make readers feel like they know the person

Audience: Your peers, family, or general readers

Basics in a Box

Personality Profile at a Glance (B)

physical description | anecdotes | writer's feelings towards subject

MAIN IMPRESSION OF SUBJECT

setting | other details | dialogue

RUBRIC Standards for Writing (C)

A successful personality profile should

- use lively descriptions, details, anecdotes, and/or dialogue to create a vivid impression of the person
- put the person in a context that helps reveal the subject's personality
- convey why the person is important to the writer
- paint a word portrait that shows the person's character
- create a unified tone and impression
- capture the reader's interest at the beginning and give a sense of completeness at the end

200 UNIT ONE PART 2: REFLECTIONS ON EVERYDAY LIFE

LESSON SUPPORT

USING PRINT RESOURCES
Unit One Resource Book
- Prewriting, p. 51
- Drafting, p. 52
- Peer Response, p. 53
- Revising, p. 54
- Editing and Proofreading, p. 55
- Student Models, pp. 56–58
- Rubric, p. 63

Writing Transparencies and Copymasters
- Personality Profile Template, p. 25
- Sensory Word List, p. 14

USING MEDIA RESOURCES
LaserLinks
Writing Springboards
See Teacher's SourceBook p. 114 for bar codes.
Writing Coach CD-ROM
Visit our website:
www.mcdougallittell.com

ns. Critical Thinking. Grammar. Vocabulary. Writing. Assessment

*The **Language of Literature** helps you teach it all with assessment instruction and skills instruction that naturally flow from the literature. **Sentence Crafting** and **Vocabulary** activities, **Writing Workshops**, **Reading and Writing for Assessment** practice, and other skills features help put the passion into action.*

Reading&Writing for Assessment

OVERVIEW

The Reading and Writing for Assessment feature provides practice in taking standardized tests. As students work through this lesson, they will learn strategies for reading comprehension questions, multiple-choice questions, and essay and short-answer questions. Boxed strategies located alongside the text will help guide students through the activities. These strategies model processes students can use as they take standardized tests.

This feature is based on and will help students prepare for state assessments as well as end-of-course assessments. It will also prepare students for the reading comprehension questions used on such college entrance examinations as the Scholastic Aptitude Test (SAT) and the American College Test (ACT).

Objectives

- understand and apply strategies for reading a test selection
- recognize literary techniques in a test selection
- understand and apply strategies for answering multiple-choice questions about a test selection
- respond to a writing prompt and to present ideas in a logical order
- understand and apply strategies for revising and proofreading a test response

Reading&Writing for Assessment

Throughout high school, you will be tested on your ability to read and understand many different kinds of reading selections. These tests will assess your basic understanding of ideas and knowledge of vocabulary. They will also check your ability to analyze and evaluate both the message of the text and the techniques the writer uses in getting that message across.

The following pages will give you test-taking strategies. Practice applying these strategies by working through each of the models provided.

PART 1 How to Read a Test Selection

In many tests, you will read a passage and then answer multiple-choice questions about it. Applying the basic test-taking strategies that follow, taking notes, and highlighting or underscoring passages as you read can help you focus on the information you will need to know.

STRATEGIES FOR READING A TEST SELECTION

- **Before you begin reading, skim the questions that follow the passage.** These can help focus your reading.
- **Use your active reading strategies such as analyzing, predicting, and questioning.** Make notes in the margin or highlight key words and passages to help you focus your reading. You may do this only if the test directions allow you to mark on the test itself.
- **Think about the title.** What does it suggest about the overall message or theme of the selection?
- **Look for main ideas.** These are often stated at the beginnings or ends of paragraphs. Sometimes they are implied, not stated. After reading each paragraph, ask "What was this passage about?"
- **Note the literary elements and techniques used by the writer.** You might consider the writer's introduction, use of quotations, or descriptive language. Then ask yourself what effect the writer achieves with each choice.
- **Unlock word meanings.** Use context clues and word parts to help you unlock the meaning of unfamiliar words.
- **Think about the message or theme.** What larger lesson can you draw from the passage? Can you infer anything or make generalizations about other similar situations, human beings, or life in general?

508

Assessment

Customize assessment to match your teaching style and your students' needs with flexible assessment options, including:

- *Reading and Writing for Assessment* provides guidelines, models, and strategies for reading an assessment prompt and responding to the kinds of questions included in state tests.
- *Vocabulary Assessment Practice* lets students demonstrate knowledge of vocabulary in various standardized test formats.
- *Reflect and Assess* helps students review and reflect upon what they have learned in the course of the unit.
- *Assessment Practice: Revising and Editing* offers standardized test practice at the end of every Writing Workshop

THE LANGUAGE OF LITERATURE
Share Your Passion!

and both will be exalted..." —E. M. Forster

Resources to help you share your passion!

Teacher's Resource Package

Unit Resource Books
Complete resources for each selection, including reading, vocabulary, grammar, writing, and literature support plus annotated models with rubrics for evaluation

Students Acquiring English

Teacher's Sourcebook for Language Development

Spanish Study Guide
Selection summaries and SkillBuilder pages in Spanish

Assessment

Teacher's Guide to Assessment and Portfolio Use
Portfolio Assessment, Writing Rubrics, and other open-ended forms of assessment

Formal Assessment
Selection Tests, Standardized Test Practice, Writing Prompts, Scoring Rubrics

Integrated Assessment

Professional Development and Planning Guide
Includes lesson plans for regular and block scheduling

Skills Transparencies and Copymasters
- Writing
- Grammar
- Vocabulary
- Communications (includes transparencies for Speaking and Listening and for Viewing and Representing Fine Art)
- Literary Analysis
- Reading and Critical Thinking

For in-depth instruction and practice in writing, grammar, usage, and mechanics, use McDougal Littell's ***Language Network.***

Technology Resources

Literature in Performance
Video Series
Literature comes alive in these compelling and famous performances.

British Literature Contents:
- *Beowulf*—The Battle with Grendel
- *The Pardoner's Tale* (starring **Sir John Gielgud**)
- *Macbeth* (starring **Orson Welles**)
- *Macbeth* (performed by the **Royal Shakespeare Company**)
- *Kubla Khan*
- *Lady of Shalott* (read by **Charlotte Cornwell**)
- *The Rocking-Horse Winner* (with **John Mills**)

Website: www.mcdougallittell.com
A treasury of on-line resources, including selection support, links, activities, and more.

NetActivities (CD-ROM) Helps students extend their learning and explore favorite authors in greater depth through interactive activities and links to the Internet.

Audio Library (audio CD and cassette)

LaserLinks (videodisc)

Writing Coach (CD-ROM)

Electronic Teacher Tools (CD-ROM)

Test Generator (CD-ROM)

Electronic Library (CD-ROM)

THE LANGUAGE OF LITERATURE
Share Your Passion!

McDougal Littell

THE LANGUAGE OF LITERATURE

BRITISH LITERATURE

Arthur N. Applebee
Andrea B. Bermúdez
Sheridan Blau
Rebekah Caplan
Peter Elbow
Susan Hynds
Judith A. Langer
James Marshall

McDougal Littell
A HOUGHTON MIFFLIN COMPANY
Evanston, Illinois • Boston • Dallas

Acknowledgments

A. P. Watt Ltd.: "The Ant and the Grasshopper" by W. Somerset Maugham, from *The Collected Stories of W. Somerset Maugham.* Reprinted by permission of A. P. Watt Limited on behalf of the Royal Literary Fund.

Unit One

Dutton Signet: Excerpts from *Beowulf,* translated by Burton Raffel. Translation Copyright © 1963 by Burton Raffel, Afterword © 1963 by New American Library. "Fifth Day, Ninth Story" retitled "Federigo's Falcon," from *The Decameron* by Giovanni Boccaccio, translated by Mark Musa and Peter Bondanella, Translation copyright © 1982 by Mark Musa and Peter Bondanella.

From *Le Morte D'Arthur* by Sir Thomas Malory, translated by Keith Baines. Translation copyright © 1962 by Keith Baines, renewed © 1990 by Francesca Evans. Introduction © 1962 by Robert Graves, renewed © 1990 by Beryl Graves. Used by permission of Dutton Signet, a division of Penguin Putnam Inc.

The New York Times: "A Collaboration Across 1,200 Years" by D. J. R. Bruckner, from *The New York Times,* July 22, 1997. Copyright © 1997 by *The New York Times.* Reprinted by permission.

Doubleday: Excerpts from *The Iliad* by Homer, translated by Robert Fitzgerald. Copyright © 1974 by Robert Fitzgerald. Used by permission of Doubleday, a division of Bantam Doubleday Dell Publishing Group, Inc.

Yale University Press: "The Seafarer" and "The Wanderer," from *Poems and Prose from the Old English,* translated by Burton Raffel. Copyright © 1997 by Yale University Press. Used by permission of Yale University Press.

Continued on page 1451

ISBN 0-395-93182-7

Printed in the United States of America.

2 3 4 5 6 7 8 9 – DWO – 05 04 03 02 01 00 99

iv

Senior Consultants

The senior consultants guided the conceptual development for *The Language of Literature* series. They participated actively in shaping prototype materials for major components, and they reviewed completed prototypes and/or completed units to ensure consistency with current research and the philosophy of the series.

Arthur N. Applebee Professor of Education, State University of New York at Albany; Director, Center for the Learning and Teaching of Literature; Senior Fellow, Center for Writing and Literacy

Andrea B. Bermúdez Professor of Studies in Language and Culture; Director, Research Center for Language and Culture; Chair, Foundations and Professional Studies, University of Houston-Clear Lake

Sheridan Blau Senior Lecturer in English and Education and former Director of Composition, University of California at Santa Barbara; Director, South Coast Writing Project; Director, Literature Institute for Teachers; Vice President, National Council of Teachers of English

Rebekah Caplan Coordinator, English Language Arts K-12, Oakland Unified School District, Oakland, California; Teacher-Consultant, Bay Area Writing Project, University of California at Berkeley; served on the California State English Assessment Development Team for Language Arts

Peter Elbow Professor of English, University of Massachusetts at Amherst; Fellow, Bard Center for Writing and Thinking

Susan Hynds Professor and Director of English Education, Syracuse University, Syracuse, New York

Judith A. Langer Professor of Education, State University of New York at Albany; Co-director, Center for the Learning and Teaching of Literature; Senior Fellow, Center for Writing and Literacy

James Marshall Professor of English and English Education, University of Iowa, Iowa City

Contributing Consultants

Tommy Boley Associate Professor of English, University of Texas at El Paso

Jeffrey N. Golub Assistant Professor of English Education, University of South Florida, Tampa

William L. McBride, Ph.D. Reading and Curriculum Specialist; former middle and high school English instructor

Sharon Sicinski-Skeans, Ph.D. Assistant Professor of Reading, University of Houston-Clear Lake

v

Multicultural Advisory Board

The multicultural advisors reviewed literature selections for appropriate content and made suggestions for teaching lessons in a multicultural classroom.

Julie A. Anderson, English Department Chairperson, Dayton High School, Dayton, Oregon

Vikki Pepper Ascuena, Meridian High School, Meridian, Idaho

Dr. Joyce M. Bell, Chairperson, English Department, Townview Magnet Center, Dallas, Texas

Linda F. Bellmore, Livermore High School, Livermore, California

Dr. Eugenia W. Collier, Author; lecturer; Chairperson, Department of English and Language Arts; Teacher of Creative Writing and American Literature, Morgan State University, Maryland

Dr. Bill Compagnone, English Department Chairperson, Lawrence High School, Lawrence, Massachusetts

Kathleen S. Fowler, President, Palm Beach County Council of Teachers of English, Boca Raton Middle School, Boca Raton, Florida

Jan Graham, Cobb Middle School, Tallahassee, Florida

Janna Rigby, Clovis High School, Clovis, California

Continued on page 1467

Teacher Review Panels

The following educators provided ongoing review during the development of the tables of contents, lesson design, and key components of the program.

TEXAS

Anita Arnold, English Department Chairperson, Thomas Jefferson High School, San Antonio Independent School District

Gilbert Barraza, J. M. Hanks High School, Ysleta Independent School District

Continued on page 1467

Manuscript Reviewers

The following educators reviewed prototype lessons and tables of contents during the development of *The Language of Literature* program.

David Adcox, Trinity High School, Euless, Texas

Carol Alves, English Department Chairperson, Apopka High School, Apopka, Florida

Jacqueline Anderson, James A. Foshay Learning Center, Los Angeles, California

Continued on page 1469

vi

Student Board

The student board members read and evaluated selections to assess their appeal for 12th-grade students.

Daniel Birdsall, Muhlenberg High School, Reading, Pennsylvania

Shane M. Cummins, Loudoun County High School, Leesburg, Virginia

Carrie Mitchell, Butler Traditional High School, Shively, Kentucky

Jennifer Schwab, MacArthur High School, San Antonio, Texas

Sarah Marie Slezak, Union High School, Grand Rapids, Michigan

Staci Talis Smith, Ramsay Alternative High School, Birmingham, Alabama

Eve E. Tanner, Justin F. Kimball High School, Dallas, Texas

vii

OVERVIEW

viii

Literature Connections

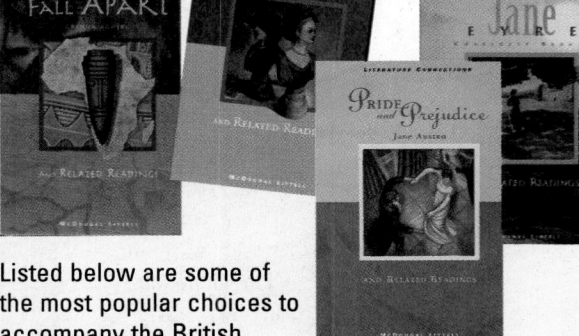

Each of the books in the *Literature Connections* series combines a novel or play with related readings—poems, stories, plays, personal essays, articles—that add new perspectives on the theme or subject matter of the long work.

Hamlet
WILLIAM SHAKESPEARE

WITH THESE RELATED READINGS

David Bevington	***from* Introduction to Hamlet**
Stanley Kunitz	**Father and Son**
Arthur Rimbaud	**Ophelia**
Bharati Mukherjee	**The Management of Grief**
Juan Rulfo	**Tell Them Not to Kill Me!**
Yevgeny Vinokurov	**Hamlet**
Toshio Mori	**Japanese Hamlet**

Listed below are some of the most popular choices to accompany the British literature anthology.

Pride and Prejudice
JANE AUSTEN

Jane Eyre
CHARLOTTE BRONTË

Tess of the d'Urbervilles
THOMAS HARDY

Pygmalion
GEORGE BERNARD SHAW

Great Expectations
CHARLES DICKENS

A Tale of Two Cities
CHARLES DICKENS

Beowulf

The Canterbury Tales
GEOFFREY CHAUCER

1984
GEORGE ORWELL

Things Fall Apart
CHINUA ACHEBE

Nervous Conditions
TSITSI DANGAREMBGA

When Rain Clouds Gather
BESSIE HEAD

ix

UNIT ONE
PAGE 14

The Anglo-Saxon and Medieval Periods
449–1485

x

xi

xii

UNIT TWO The English Renaissance 1485–1660

PAGE 272

xiii

PART 2 A Passion for Power 313

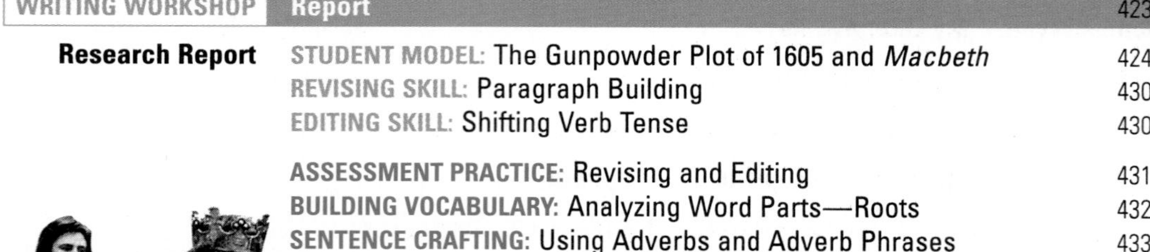

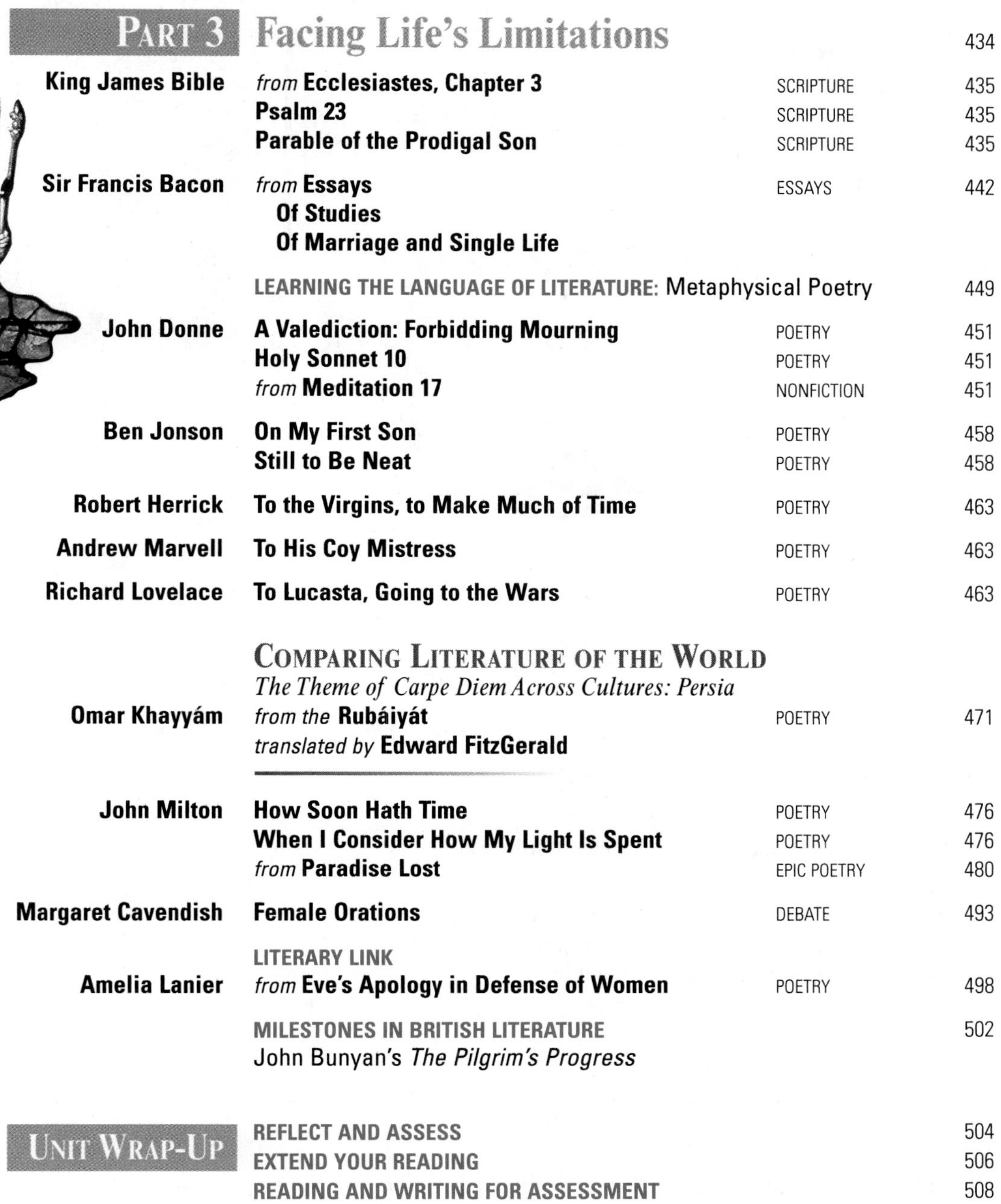

PART 3 Facing Life's Limitations 434

xv

UNIT THREE
PAGE 514

The *Restoration* and *Enlightenment*
1660–1798

xvii

PART 3 Revelations About Human Nature

xviii

UNIT FOUR
PAGE 696

The Flowering of Romanticism

1798–1832

xix

William Wordsworth

Author Study
England's Greatest Nature Poet

xx

PART 2 Embracing the Imagination

xxi

UNIT FIVE
PAGE 828

The *Victorians* 1832–1901

xxii

xxiii

UNIT SIX
PAGE 978

Emerging Modernism
1901–1950

xxv

xxvi

UNIT SEVEN
PAGE 1188

Contemporary Voices
1950–PRESENT

xxvii

PART 2 Culture and Conflict

Student *Resource Bank*

xxix

Selections by Genre

Epic

Romance

Scripture

Fiction

Nonfiction

xxx

Poetry

xxxi

xxxii

Drama

Electronic Library

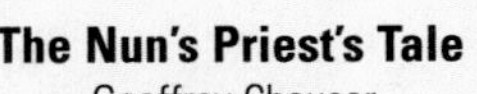

The *Electronic Library* is a CD-ROM that contains additional fiction, nonfiction, poetry, and drama for each unit in *The Language of Literature*. Here is a sampling from the 47 titles included in Grade 12.

The Nun's Priest's Tale
Geoffrey Chaucer

Everyman
Anonymous

My True Love Hath My Heart
Sir Philip Sidney

Easter-Wings
George Herbert

Sonnet 73
William Shakespeare

L'Allegro
John Milton

To a Mouse
Robert Burns

London, 1802
William Wordsworth

A Dissertation upon Roast Pig
Charles Lamb

Ode to a Nightingale
John Keats

The Blessed Damozel
Dante Gabriel Rossetti

The Darkling Thrush
Thomas Hardy

Terence, This Is Stupid Stuff
A. E. Housman

Professions for Women
Virginia Woolf

The Horse Dealer's Daughter
D. H. Lawrence

The Wild Swans at Coole
William Butler Yeats

The Boarding House
James Joyce

The Shield of Achilles
W. H. Auden

Miss Brill
Katherine Mansfield

A Voyage to Cythera
Margaret Drabble

xxxiii

Special Features in This Book

Author Study

Learning the Language of Literature

Comparing Literature of the World

Related Readings

Milestones in British Literature

Writing Workshops

Communication Workshops

Building Vocabulary

Sentence Crafting

Assessment Pages

Timeless Stories

What do Beowulf, Star Wars, *and* Frankenstein *have in common? Each tells a powerful story that for generations has held readers or moviegoers spellbound. And each contains characters, themes, and conflicts similar to those in hundreds of other stories. Read the following comments about these classic tales:*

"One of the most frequent questions asked by students is 'Why do we study this stuff, especially *Beowulf,* an epic story of Vikings and monsters? What place does it hold in today's society?' My response is, 'If it is so out of date, why do so many blockbuster films of today resemble the plot and the characteristics portrayed in *Beowulf?*'"

Richard L. Cameron III
Teacher

"*Star Wars* has always struck a chord with people. There are issues of loyalty, of friendship, of good and evil. . . . The themes came from stories and ideas that have been around for thousands of years. . . ."

George Lucas
Movie Director

"Mary Shelley, whose 200th birthday is this year, completed her novel *Frankenstein* 180 years ago. The book has never been out of print.... Cinematic attempts to piece together a family for Frankenstein have spawned a bride (1935), a son (1957), and a daughter who, in the rebellious '60s, joined up with Jesse James."

Lee Neville, Journalist

- **Why do some stories survive through the centuries?**
- **How do people living in today's technology-filled world find ways to connect to classic tales about monsters and heroic quests?**
- **How can YOU find relevance in literature from centuries ago?**

The answers lie on the next few pages.

Get Involved with the Literature

Think of any activity you enjoy—sports, music, traveling, painting. How did you really learn to understand and appreciate it? By watching others, or by participating yourself? Just about any activity is richer, more interesting, and more exciting when you are actively involved. The same is true with literature. You can't simply sit back and absorb the words on a page. You have to jump into the stories and participate.

Your Reader's Notebook

Almost any kind of notebook can be used to help you interact with literature. Use your Reader's Notebook to keep track of what's going on inside your mind as you read. Here are three ways to interact.

❶ Record Your Thoughts

In your READER'S NOTEBOOK, jot down ideas, responses, connections, and questions before, while, and after you read a selection. (See "Strategies for Reading," page 7.) Summarize important passages, and include sketches and charts, too, if they will help. If you wish, compare your ideas with those of a classmate.

"The Ant and the Grasshopper"
by W. Somerset Maugham

(page 9) The narrator says, "in an imperfect world industry is rewarded and giddiness punished." Why does he say "in an imperfect world"?

<u>Important Idea</u>
This story really got me thinking about myself. I remember when I first learned the fable "The Ant and The Grasshopper." The moral was quite clear to me: those who play may seem to be getting the most out of life, but in the end those who work will be rewarded while those who play will suffer for their irresponsibility.

READING MODEL

Alongside "The Ant and the Grasshopper" are comments made by two 12th-grade students, Christopher Domm and Marcy Ellis, while they were reading the story. Their comments provide a glimpse into the minds of readers actively engaged in the process of reading. You'll notice that Chris and Marcy quite naturally used the Strategies for Reading that were introduced on page 5. You'll also note that these readers responded differently to the story—no two readers think about or relate to a literary work in exactly the same way.

To benefit from this model of active reading, read the story first, jotting down your responses in your reading log. Then read Chris's and Marcy's comments and compare theirs with your own. The more you actively engage in reading and sharing ideas, the more you'll learn about yourself and others.

The Ant and the Grasshoppe[r]

W. SOMERSET MAUGHAM

STRATEGIES FOR READING

The Brothers Bernheim-Jeune, Art Dealers and Publishers (early 20th century), Pierre Bonnard, Musée d'Orsay, Paris, France, Erich Lessing/Art Resource, New York.

❷ Improve Your Reading Skills

Complete the specific **READER'S NOTEBOOK** activity on the first page of each literature lesson. This activity will help you apply an important skill as you read the selection.

"The Ant and the Grasshopper"
by W. Somerset Maugham

Writing Idea

- I could also write a modern-day story based on a fable.
- My uncle is a lot like the character Tom. I could write a fable about him.

When I was a very small boy I was made to learn by heart certain of the fables of La Fontaine, and the moral of each was carefully explained to me. Among those I learnt was *The Ant and The Grasshopper,* which is devised to bring home to the young the useful lesson that in an imperfect world industry is rewarded and giddiness punished. In this admirable fable (I apologize for telling something which everyone is politely, but inexactly, supposed to know) the ant spends a laborious summer gathering its winter store, while the grasshopper sits on a blade of grass singing to the sun. Winter comes and the ant is comfortably provided for, but the grasshopper has an empty larder: he goes to the ant and begs for a little food. Then the ant gives him her classic answer:

"What were you doing in the summer time?"

"Saving your presence, I sang, I sang all day, all night."

"You sang. Why, then go and dance."

I do not ascribe it to perversity on my part, but rather to the inconsequence of childhood, which is deficient in moral sense, that I could never quite reconcile myself to the lesson. My sympathies were with the grasshopper and for some time I never saw an ant without putting my foot on it. In this summary (and as I have discovered since, entirely human) fashion I sought to express my disapproval of prudence and common sense.

I could not help thinking of this fable when the other day I saw George Ramsay lunching by himself in a restaurant. I never saw anyone wear an expression of such deep gloom. He was staring into space. He looked as though the burden of the whole world sat on his shoulders. I was sorry for him: I suspected at once that his unfortunate brother had been causing trouble again. I went up to him and held out my hand.

"How are you?" I asked.

"I'm not in hilarious spirits," he answered.

"Is it Tom again?"

He sighed.

"Yes, it's Tom again."

"Why don't you chuck him? You've done everything in the world for him. You must know by now that he's quite hopeless."

I suppose every family has a black sheep. Tom had been a sore trial to his for twenty years. He had begun life decently enough: he went into business, married, and had two children. The Ramsays were perfectly respectable people and there was every reason to suppose that Tom Ramsay would have a useful and honorable career. But one day, without warning, he announced that he didn't like work and that he wasn't suited for marriage. He wanted to enjoy himself. He would listen to no expostulations. He left his wife and his office. He had a little money and he spent two happy years in the various capitals of Europe. Rumors of his doings reached his relations from time to time and they were

***Chris:** I like this line right here—I think people can relate that to their own lives.*
EVALUATING

***Chris:** I can imagine the ant with a stern look on her face and the grasshopper being all happy-go-lucky.*
VISUALIZING

***Marcy:** Wow! I always looked down on the grasshopper. It surprises me that the narrator looks down on the ant.*
CONNECTING/CLARIFYING

***Marcy:** I don't know what the connection is going to be between the fable and whatever this story is about. I'll need to keep the fable in mind as I read on.*
MONITORING

***Chris:** "Why don't you chuck him?" I don't really understand what he means.*
QUESTIONING

***Marcy:** "Chuck him"? That's weird language!*
QUESTIONING/EVALUATING

***Marcy:** I'm seeing the parallel between the brother and the grasshopper. He'll probably be like him and fail.*
CLARIFYING/PREDICTING

THE ANT AND THE GRASSHOPPER 9

❸ Collect Ideas for Writing

Be aware of intriguing themes, passages, and thoughts of your own as you read or complete follow-up activities. In a special section of your **READER'S NOTEBOOK**, jot down anything that may later be a springboard to your own writing.

Your Working Portfolio

Artists and writers keep portfolios in which they store works in progress or the works they are most proud of. Your portfolio can be a folder, a box, or a notebook—the form doesn't matter. Just make sure to keep adding to it—with drafts of your writing experiments, summaries of your projects, and your own goals and accomplishments as a reader and writer. Later in this book, on the Reflect and Assess pages, you will choose your best or favorite work to place in a ***Presentation Portfolio.***

5

Become an Active Reader

The strategies you need to become an active reader are already within your grasp. In fact, you use them every day to make sense of the images and the events in your world. And you really exercise them when you are watching a television program or a movie!

Take a look at this shot from a film version of *Gulliver's Travels*. The four strategies shown here—Question, Predict, Clarify, and Connect—are among those you can use to understand and interpret the situation. These and the other reading strategies listed on the next page can help you interact with literature as well.

Question *What in the world is happening here? Where are these people? And WHO are they?*

Clarify *It looks like the little people have tied the big guy up and are questioning him.*

Predict *I bet he'll pop the ropes and scare off the little people.*

Connect *I remember situations where I've felt as out of place as this guy looks.*

Strategies for Reading

Following are specific reading strategies that are introduced and applied throughout this book. Use them when you read and interact with the various literature selections. Occasionally **monitor** how well the strategies are working for you and, if desired, modify them to suit your needs.

PREDICT Try to figure out what will happen next and how the selection might end. Then read on to see how accurate your guesses were.

VISUALIZE Visualize characters, events, and setting to help you understand what's happening. When you read nonfiction, pay attention to the images that form in your mind as you read.

CONNECT Connect personally with what you're reading. Think of similarities between the descriptions in the selection and what you have personally experienced, heard about, and read about.

QUESTION Question what happens while you read. Searching for reasons behind events and characters' feelings can help you feel closer to what you are reading.

CLARIFY Stop occasionally to review what you understand, and expect to have your understanding change and develop as you read on. Reread and use resources to help you clarify your understanding. Also watch for answers to questions you had earlier

EVALUATE Form opinions about what you read, both while you're reading and after you've finished. Develop your own ideas about characters and events.

On the next page, you will see how two readers applied these strategies to the story "The Ant and the Grasshopper."

Go Beyond the Text If you really become an active reader, your involvement doesn't stop with the last line of the text. Decide what else you'd like to know. Discuss your ideas with others, do some research, or jump on the Internet.

More Online
www.mcdougallittell.com

7

READING MODEL

Alongside "The Ant and the Grasshopper" are comments made by two 12th-grade students, Christopher Domm and Marcy Ellis, while they were reading the story. Their comments provide a glimpse into the minds of readers actively engaged in the process of reading. You'll notice that Chris and Marcy quite naturally used the Strategies for Reading that were introduced on page 5. You'll also note that these readers responded differently to the story—no two readers think about or relate to a literary work in exactly the same way.

To benefit from this model of active reading, read the story first, jotting down your responses in your reading log. Then read Chris's and Marcy's comments and compare theirs with your own. The more you actively engage in reading and sharing ideas, the more you'll learn about yourself and others.

The Ant and the Grasshopper

W. SOMERSET MAUGHAM

The Brothers Bernheim-Jeune, Art Dealers and Publishers (early 20th century), Pierre Bonnard, Musée d'Orsay, Paris, France, Erich Lessing/Art Resource, New York.

8 STRATEGIES FOR READING

When I was a very small boy I was made to learn by heart certain of the fables of La Fontaine, and the moral of each was carefully explained to me. Among those I learnt was *The Ant and The Grasshopper,* which is devised to bring home to the young the useful lesson that in an imperfect world industry is rewarded and giddiness punished. In this admirable fable (I apologize for telling something which everyone is politely, but inexactly, supposed to know) the ant spends a laborious summer gathering its winter store, while the grasshopper sits on a blade of grass singing to the sun. Winter comes and the ant is comfortably provided for, but the grasshopper has an empty larder: he goes to the ant and begs for a little food. Then the ant gives him her classic answer:

"What were you doing in the summer time?"

"Saving your presence, I sang, I sang all day, all night."

"You sang. Why, then go and dance."

I do not ascribe it to perversity on my part, but rather to the inconsequence of childhood, which is deficient in moral sense, that I could never quite reconcile myself to the lesson. My sympathies were with the grasshopper and for some time I never saw an ant without putting my foot on it. In this summary (and as I have discovered since, entirely human) fashion I sought to express my disapproval of prudence and common sense.

I could not help thinking of this fable when the other day I saw George Ramsay lunching by himself in a restaurant. I never saw anyone wear an expression of such deep gloom. He was staring into space. He looked as though the burden of the whole world sat on his shoulders. I was sorry for him: I suspected at once that his unfortunate brother had been causing trouble again. I went up to him and held out my hand.

"How are you?" I asked.

"I'm not in hilarious spirits," he answered.

"Is it Tom again?"

He sighed.

"Yes, it's Tom again."

"Why don't you chuck him? You've done everything in the world for him. You must know by now that he's quite hopeless."

I suppose every family has a black sheep. Tom had been a sore trial to his for twenty years. He had begun life decently enough: he went into business, married, and had two children. The Ramsays were perfectly respectable people and there was every reason to suppose that Tom Ramsay would have a useful and honorable career. But one day, without warning, he announced that he didn't like work and that he wasn't suited for marriage. He wanted to enjoy himself. He would listen to no expostulations. He left his wife and his office. He had a little money and he spent two happy years in the various capitals of Europe. Rumors of his doings reached his relations from time to time and they were

Chris: *I like this line right here—I think people can relate that to their own lives.*
EVALUATING

Chris: *I can imagine the ant with a stern look on her face and the grasshopper being all happy-go-lucky.*
VISUALIZING

Marcy: *Wow! I always looked down on the grasshopper. It surprises me that the narrator looks down on the ant.*
CONNECTING/CLARIFYING

Marcy: *I don't know what the connection is going to be between the fable and whatever this story is about. I'll need to keep the fable in mind as I read on.*
MONITORING

Chris: *"Why don't you chuck him?" I don't really understand what he means.*
QUESTIONING

Marcy: *"Chuck him"? That's weird language!*
QUESTIONING/EVALUATING

Marcy: *I'm seeing the parallel between the brother and the grasshopper. He'll probably be like him and fail.*
CLARIFYING/PREDICTING

THE ANT AND THE GRASSHOPPER 9

profoundly shocked. He certainly had a very good time. They shook their heads and asked what would happen when his money was spent. They soon found out: he borrowed. He was charming and unscrupulous. I have never met anyone to whom it was more difficult to refuse a loan. He made a steady income from his friends and he made friends easily. But he always said that the money you spent on necessities was boring; the money that was amusing to spend was the money you spent on luxuries. For this he depended on his brother George. He did not waste his charm on him. George was a serious man and insensible to such enticements. George was respectable. Once or twice he fell to Tom's promises of amendment and gave him considerable sums in order that he might make a fresh start. On these Tom bought a motorcar and some very nice jewelry. But when circumstances forced George to realize that his brother would never settle down and he washed his hands of him, Tom, without a qualm, began to blackmail him. It was not very nice for a respectable lawyer to find his brother shaking cocktails behind the bar of his favorite restaurant or to see him waiting on the box seat of a taxi outside his club. Tom said that to serve in a bar or to drive a taxi was a perfectly decent occupation, but if George could oblige him with a couple of hundred pounds he didn't mind for the honor of the family giving it up. George paid.

Once Tom nearly went to prison. George was terribly upset. He went into the whole discreditable affair. Really Tom had gone too far. He had been wild, thoughtless, and selfish, but he had never before done anything dishonest, by which George meant illegal; and if he were prosecuted he would assuredly be convicted. But you cannot allow your only brother to go to jail. The man Tom had cheated, a man called Cronshaw, was vindictive. He was determined to take the matter into court; he said Tom was a scoundrel and should be punished. It cost George an infinite deal of trouble and five hundred pounds to settle the affair. I have never seen him in such a rage as when he heard that Tom and Cronshaw had gone off together to Monte Carlo the moment they cashed the check. They spent a happy month there.

For twenty years Tom raced and gambled, philandered with the prettiest girls, danced, ate in the most expensive restaurants, and dressed beautifully. He always looked as if he had just stepped out of a bandbox. Though he was forty-six you would never have taken him for more than thirty-five. He was a most amusing companion and though you knew he was perfectly worthless you could not but enjoy his society. He had high spirits, an unfailing gaiety, and incredible charm. I never grudged the contributions he regularly levied on me for the necessities of his existence. I never lent him fifty pounds without feeling that I was in his debt. Tom Ramsay knew everyone and everyone knew Tom Ramsay. You could not approve of him, but you could not help liking him.

Marcy: *He reminds me of the father in* As I Lay Dying. *The guy in* As I Lay Dying *thought that if he sweated, he would die. So he was always asking people to do things for him. Tom is always asking his friends for money and depending on his friends. They won't refuse him.*
CONNECTING

Marcy: *This would be hard for me—to wash my hands of my family. I understand why he felt he had to, but I couldn't do it.*
CONNECTING

Chris: *Tom's taking advantage of his brother's friendship. It's probably going to come back to him further down the line.*
PREDICTING

Chris: *This reminds me of the brothers' relationship in* A River Runs Through It. *The one brother is always out having fun . . . always taking advantage of the other brother.*
CONNECTING/EVALUATING

Marcy: *Oh, they went out together! They were in cahoots. I would be mad, too.*
CLARIFYING/CONNECTING

Marcy: *46—that's too old to be so irresponsible.*
EVALUATING

Poor George, only a year older than his scapegrace brother, looked sixty. He had never taken more than a fortnight's holiday in the year for a quarter of a century. He was in his office every morning at nine-thirty and never left it till six. He was honest, industrious, and worthy. He had a good wife, to whom he had never been unfaithful even in thought, and four daughters to whom he was the best of fathers. He made a point of saving a third of his income and his plan was to retire at fifty-five to a little house in the country where he proposed to cultivate his garden and play golf. His life was blameless. He was glad that he was growing old because Tom was growing old too. He rubbed his hands and said:

"It was all very well when Tom was young and good-looking, but he's only a year younger than I am. In four years he'll be fifty. He won't find life so easy then. I shall have thirty thousand pounds by the time I'm fifty. For twenty-five years I've said that Tom would end in the gutter. And we shall see how he likes that. We shall see if it really pays best to work or be idle."

Poor George! I sympathized with him. I wondered now as I sat down beside him what infamous thing Tom had done. George was evidently very much upset.

"Do you know what's happened now?" he asked me.

I was prepared for the worst. I wondered if Tom had got into the hands of the police at last. George could hardly bring himself to speak.

"You're not going to deny that all my life I've been hardworking, decent, respectable, and straightforward. After a life of industry and thrift I can look forward to retiring on a small income in gilt-edged securities. I've always done my duty in that state of life in which it has pleased Providence to place me."

"True."

"And you can't deny that Tom has been an idle, worthless, dissolute, and dishonorable rogue. If there were any justice he'd be in the workhouse."

"True."

George grew red in the face.

"A few weeks ago he became engaged to a woman old enough to be his mother. And now she's died and left him everything she had. Half a million pounds, a yacht, a house in London, and a house in the country."

George Ramsay beat his clenched fist on the table.

"It's not fair, I tell you, it's not fair. Damn it, it's not fair."

I could not help it. I burst into a shout of laughter as I looked at George's wrathful face, I rolled in my chair, I very nearly fell on the floor. George never forgave me. But Tom often asks me to excellent dinners in his charming house in Mayfair, and if he occasionally borrows a trifle from me, that is merely from force of habit. It is never more than a sovereign.

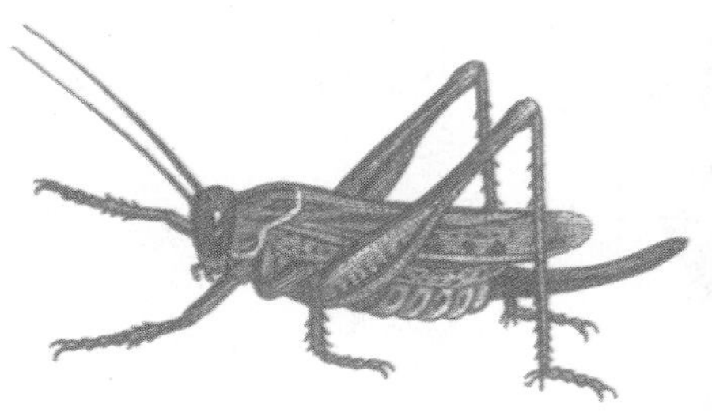

Chris: *I think George is jealous of Tom's life.*
EVALUATING

Chris: *I think this is funny right here. Tom's brother was so reserved and watched everything he did. Tom, on the other hand, took a chance in life. He didn't worry about the future; he just enjoyed life.*
EVALUATING/CLARIFYING

Chris: *Usually the fable holds true to life, but this time it didn't.*
CLARIFYING

Marcy: *It's not fair! I'd be upset. Of course George will still have his money—his retirement—but that's not much. Maybe Tom will share with George, but I don't think so. I doubt if he'll even pay back the money George gave him.*
CLARIFYING/EVALUATING/PREDICTING

THE ANT AND THE GRASSHOPPER 11

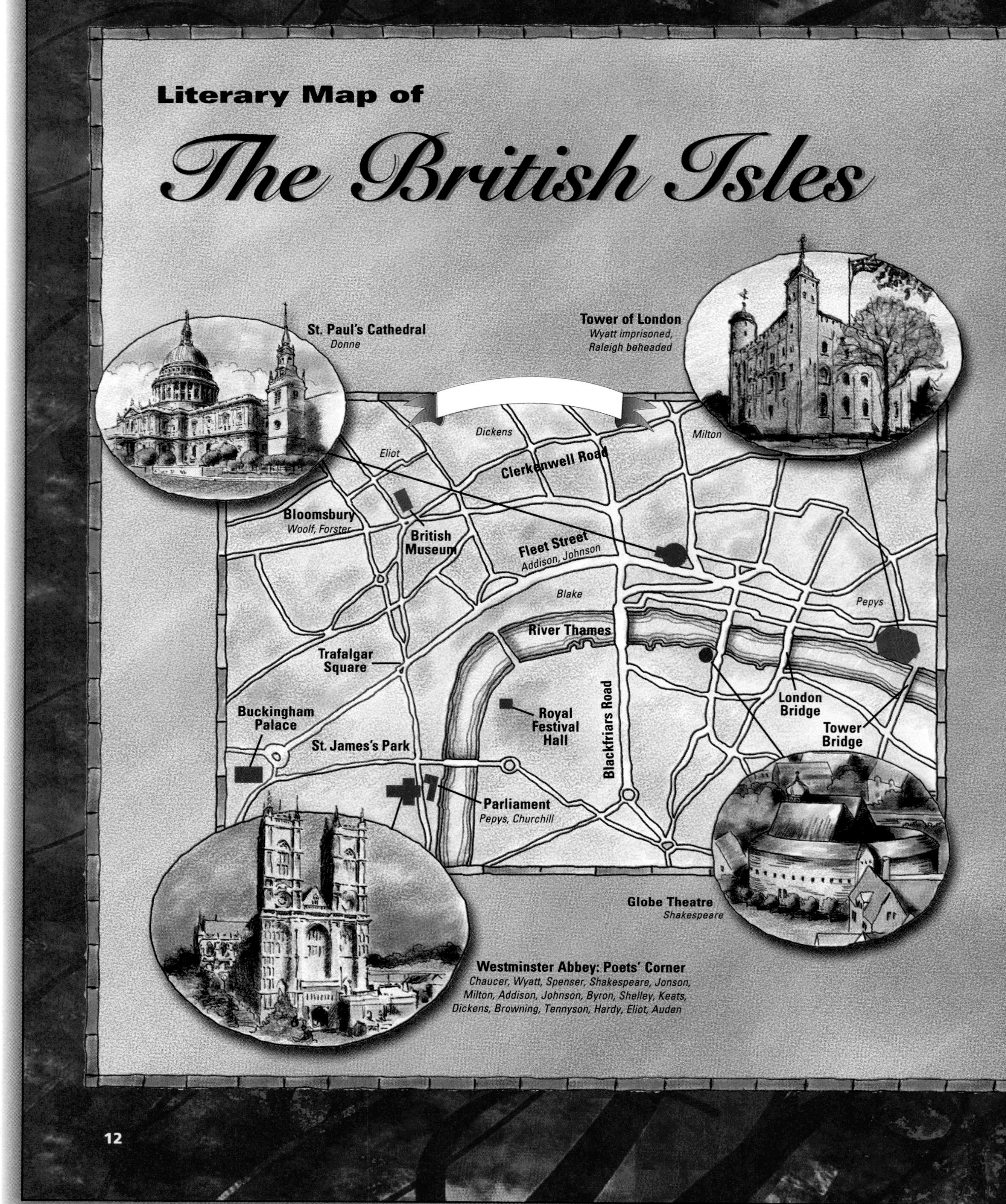
Literary Map of
The British Isles
St. Paul's Cathedral
Donne
Tower of London
Wyatt imprisoned,
Raleigh beheaded
Dickens
Milton
Eliot
Clerkenwell Road
Bloomsbury
Woolf, Forster
British Museum
Fleet Street
Addison, Johnson
Blake
Pepys
River Thames
Trafalgar Square
Buckingham Palace
Royal Festival Hall
Blackfriars Road
London Bridge
Tower Bridge
St. James's Park
Parliament
Pepys, Churchill
Globe Theatre
Shakespeare
Westminster Abbey: Poets' Corner
Chaucer, Wyatt, Spenser, Shakespeare, Jonson,
Milton, Addison, Johnson, Byron, Shelley, Keats,
Dickens, Browning, Tennyson, Hardy, Eliot, Auden
12

John o'Groats
Outer Hebrides
Inner Hebrides
Inverness
Macbeth at Dunsinane, Shakespeare
Dunsinane
Birnam Woods
Glasgow
Edinburgh
Boswell, Spark
SCOTLAND
N. IRELAND
Belfast
Heaney
Sligo
IRELAND
Galway
Dublin
Swift, Yeats, Lady Gregory, Joyce, Bowen
Doneraile
Spenser
Wexford
County Cork
Trevor
Dove Cottage, home of the Wordsworths
Grasmere
Jarrow
Bede
ENGLAND
Haworth
York
Auden
Yorkshire moors, where the Brontës lived
Manchester
Gaskell
Somersby
Tennyson
St. Asaph
Hopkins
Newstead Abbey
Byron
Norwich
Pastons
Cambridge
Spenser, Marlowe, Bacon, Milton, Pepys, Gray, Wordsworth, Coleridge, Tennyson, Brooke, Sassoon, Hughes
Stratford-upon-Avon
Shakespeare
WALES
Sutton Hoo ship burial, Beowulf
Hampstead
Keats, Mansfield, Lawrence, Orwell
Swansea
Dylan Thomas
Tintern
Oxford
Raleigh, Donne, Lovelace, Addison, Johnson, Arnold, Hopkins, Housman, Brittain, Huxley, Auden, Lively
LONDON
Twickenham
Pope
Canterbury
Chawton
Austen
Nether Stowey
Coleridge
Dorchester
Hardy
Dean Prior
Herrick
Land's End
Ruins of Tintern Abbey, inspiration for Wordsworth
St. Thomas à Becket, from stained glass window in Canterbury Cathedral, Chaucer

The Anglo-Saxon and Medieval Periods

The selections in Unit One present a portrayal of courage, glory, and honor in the medieval world. The unit is divided into three sections to better represent the public and private lives of the people of the era.

Part 1

Tests of Courage This part of the unit focuses on epic Anglo-Saxon poetry. The verse selections celebrate the deeds of heroic figures and examine eternal human problems, such as the struggle between good and evil. Real-life spiritual challenges of Anglo-Saxons are encountered in an excerpt from a history of England, written during the time period. The epic poem used for **Comparing Literature** describes a legendary hero of a different culture—Greece.

Part 2

Reflections of Everyday Life The tales and ballads in this section unveil how people lived in medieval England. An **Author Study** on Geoffrey Chaucer brings together some of the most vivid pictures of such life. Further light on the age is shed by letters sent between members of an upper-class English family. The **Comparing Literature** selection recounts courtly love in medieval Italy.

Part 3

Attempts at Perfection The selections in this part of the unit explore religious ideals and the code of chivalric behavior. By adhering to strict codes of discipline, the people and characters in these worlds seek to achieve perfection. The **Comparing Literature** selection forges thematic connections between the literary traditions of England and India.

THE ANGLO-SAXON AND

The Bayeux tapestry (late 11th century–early 12th century). Musée de la Tapisserie, Bayeux, France. Giraudon/Art Resource New York.

Viewing and Representing

The Bayeux tapestry, anonymous

ART APPRECIATION

Instruction Created near the turn of the 12th century, the Bayeux (bī-yo͞o′) tapestry illustrates, through about 75 continuous scenes, the story of the Norman conquest of England in 1066. The tapestry is more accurately an embroidery, for its figures are sewn with a needle onto a linen fabric rather than being woven into it. Also, at 230 feet long but just 20 inches high, the tapestry is as much a gigantic frieze as it is a wall covering. It resides in the town of Bayeux, in northwest France; however, most scholars agree that it was created in England. The tapestry has been nearly destroyed many times.

This tapestry is comprised of hundreds of persons, animals, ships, and buildings. The scene above is near the end of the tapestry, showing the Battle of Hastings. The foot soldiers of England's King Harold are enduring a two-sided cavalry and archery attack of William's Normans.

449-1485

MEDIEVAL PERIODS

IN READING GREAT LITERATURE, I BECOME A THOUSAND MEN AND YET REMAIN MYSELF.

C.S. LEWIS
NOVELIST AND ESSAYIST

15

Making Connections

To help students explore the connections among the art, the quotation, and the unit title found in this unit-opening spread, have them consider the following questions:

Ask: **How do you define "great literature"?**
Possible Response: Great literature is writing that endures throughout the ages because it reveals universal truths about human nature and the human condition.

C.S. (Clive Staples) Lewis (1898–1963) was an Irish-born British novelist and essayist and is most remembered for his novel in letter form, *The Screwtape Letters,* and his children's story about the land of Narnia, *The Lion, the Witch, and the Wardrobe.*
Ask: **How would you paraphrase C.S. Lewis's quotation?**
Possible Response: Great literature lets readers experience the lives of countless people almost as if the readers were living them.

Ask: **Based on the art, quotation, and unit title, what do you think the selections in this unit might be about?**
Possible Response: The selections will describe heroic battles of the past as well as timeless myths and legends that concern the eternal values of honor, glory, and courage.

VIDEODISC **LaserLinks**
Historical Literary Connection: The Anglo-Saxon and Medieval Periods
This film highlights representative art, architecture, and music of this period. Tapestries, illuminated manuscripts, cathedrals, and castles are among the images presented. This montage helps students understand the world of Anglo-Saxon and medieval England.
See Teacher's SourceBook p. 6 for bar codes.

Use the following questions to help develop students visual literacy.
Ask: **What do you learn from the tapestry's bottom panel?**
Possible Response: The carnage indicates that the battle was fierce.
Ask: **What values do you think were important to the cultures involved?**
Possible Responses: physical confrontation, the conquering of enemies, heroism, skill in battle.

UNIT ONE
PART 1 SKILLS TRACE

Features and Selections	Literary Analysis	Reading and Critical Thinking	Writing Opportunities	
The Anglo-Saxon and Medieval Periods **Time Line** **Historical Background/Essay**				
Learning the Language of Literature The Epic	The Epic 28, 29	Epic Across Cultures, 29 Strategies for Reading, 86		
EPIC POETRY *from* Beowulf **Literary Link** A Collaboration Across 1,200 Years	Alliteration, 30, 63 Informal Assess., 39 Nonfiction: critical review, 61	Making Judgments, 30, 63 Test Practice, 51 Informal Assess., 60 Analyze Review, 62	Warrior's Letter, 64 Director's Notes, 64 News Story, 64 Comparison, 64	
EPIC POETRY **Comparing Literature of the World** *from the* Iliad	Simile, 66, 81 Review Epic, 81	Classifying Characters, 66, 81 Comparing Epics, 66 Points of Comparison, 81	Letter of Commendation, 82 Character Sketch, 82 Alternative Outline, 82 Points of Comparison, 82 Informal Assess., 79	
POETRY *from the* Exeter Book The Seafarer The Wanderer The Wife's Lament	Kenning, p 84, 96 Review Alliteration, 96	Interpreting Details, 84, 96 Test Practice, 92 Informal Assess., 93	Diary Entry, 97 Exploration, 97 Informal Assess., 89	
HISTORICAL WRITING *from* A History of the English Church and People	Historical Writing, 98, 104	Author's Purpose, 98, 104 Using Text Organizers, 104	Simile for Life, 105	

UNIT ONE
PART 2 SKILLS TRACE

AUTHOR STUDY
Geoffrey Chaucer

Features and Selections	Literary Analysis	Reading and Critical Thinking	Writing Opportunities	
POETRY *from* The Canterbury Tales The Prologue	Tone, 111, 137	Characterization, 111, 137 Comparing Literature, 111	Character Analysis, 138 Sketch of Pilgrim,138 Informal Assess.,124 Informal Assess., 136	
NONFICTION *from* The Life and Times of Chaucer	Comparing Texts, 140			

LEGEND PE instruction shown in black
TE Mini Lessons shown in green
CCL indicates a Cross-Curricular Link
DLS indicates Daily Language SkillBuilder

Speaking and Listening Viewing and Representing	Inquiry and Research	Grammar, Usage, and Mechanics	Vocabulary
Art Appreciation,15, 20			Suffixes, 19 Word Origins, 22
Cartoon Hero, 64 ***Beowulf* Aloud, 64** **A Video Scop, 64** Dramatic Reading, 37 Description, 46 Art Appreciation, 34 Helmet, 40 Viking Sword, 49	**Religious Beliefs, 64** **Sutton Who? 64**	DLS, 31 Parts of Speech, 32	**Context Clues, 65** Word Origins, 31 Using a Thesaurus, 41 Multiple Meaning, 56
Dramatic Reading, 82 **Dance Interpretation, 82** **Heroic Mural, 82** **Homeric Epithets, 82** Analyzing Performance, 77 Art Appreciation, 67, 76	**Digging Up Troy, 82** **Translations of Homer, 82** Digging Up Troy, 82	DLS, 66 Parts of Speech, 75	**Related Words, 83** Antonyms, 68, 69 Test Practice, 74 Using a Dictionary, 80
Weather Map, 97 **TV Interview, 97** Dramatic Reading, 99 Art Appreciation, 95	**Everyday Anglo-Saxons, 97** Topic Questions, 97	DLS, 84 Simple Sentences, 87	Word Origins *Solus,* 86
Sketch of a Dream, 105 Art Appreciation, 101	**Routes to Rome, 105** Sources, 105	DLS, 98 **Complete Sentences, 102, 103**	**Assessment Practice, 105** Using a Dictionary, 99
Pilgrimage Poster, 138 **Pilgrim Predictions, 138** Art Appreciation, 113, 122, 132 Dramatic Reading, 120	**Medieval Inns, 138**	DLS, 111 Pronoun Cases, 118 Pronoun-Antecedent Agreement, 123	**Context Clues/Assessment Practice, 138** Context Clues, 112 Antonyms, 117 Homonyms and Homographs, 134

PART 2 SKILLS TRACE

Features and Selections	Literary Analysis	Reading and Critical Thinking	Writing Opportunities
POETRY *from* The Canterbury Tales *from* The Pardoner's Tale	Moral Tale, 141, 152 Informal Assess., 151	Predicting, 141, 152 Test Practice, 147	Ye Olde News,153 Personification,153 Moral Tale,153
POETRY *from* The Canterbury Tales The Wife of Bath's Tale	Narrator, 154, 167	Analyzing Structure, 154, 167	Pilgrim Dialogue, 169 Comparing Knights, 169 Informal Assess., 163 Informal Assess., 166
The Author's Style Author Study Project	Analysis of Style, 168		Imitating Style, 168
TALE **Comparing Literature of the World** *from* The Decameron Federigo's Falcon	Plot, 171, 177 Author Activity, 179	Cause and Effect, 171, 177	Diary, 178 Frame Story, 178 Points of Comparison, 178 Informal Assess., 176
LETTER *from* The Paston Letters	Conflict, 180, 190 Review: Tone	Credibility of Sources, 180, 190	Margery Paston's Diary, 191 Opinion Paragraph, 191 Business Letters, 182 Informal Assess., 189
BALLAD Barbara Allan Sir Patrick Spens Get Up and Bar the Door	Ballads, 192, 198	Strategies for Reading Ballads, 192, 198	Barbara Allan, 199 In Memoriam, 199 Ballad, 199 Descriptive Paragraph, 199 Test Practice, 197
Writing Workshop: **Personality Profile** **Assessment Practice** Building Vocabulary Sentence Crafting		Analyzing a Student Model, 201	Personality Profile, 200

LEGEND **PE instruction shown in black** **TE Mini Lessons shown in green** **CCL indicates a Cross-Curricular Link** **DLS indicates Daily Language SkillBuilder**

Speaking and Listening Viewing and Representing	Inquiry and Research	Grammar, Usage, and Mechanics	Vocabulary
Oral Retelling, 153 Video Adaptation, 153 Ballad Version, 153 Art Appreciation, 143, 150	Plague, 153	DLS, 141 Indefinite Pronouns, 149	Context Clues/Meaning Clues, 153 Using a Dictionary, 142 Word Origins, 144
Gender Debate, 169 Medieval Manuscript, 169 Costume Drawings, 169 Woman's Roles, 169 Art Appreciation, 159, 160	Medieval Justice, 169 Bath, 169	DLS, 154 Pronouns, 164 Kinds of Sentences, 169	Synonyms/Antonyms, 170 Using a Dictionary, 156 Denotation and Connotation, 162
Speaking and Listening, 168 Illustrating Style, 168 Mock Interviews, 170			
Wedding Gift, 178 Pantomime Presentation, 178 Dramatic Presentation, 174	The Art of Falconry, 178 Love Traditions, 178		Synonyms/Antonyms, 178 Context Clues, 172 Preteaching Vocabulary, 173 Suffixes, 175
Map Mileage Scale, 191 Illustrated Fashions, 191 Dramatic Presentation, 191 Panel Discussion, 191 Oral History, 187	Life Spans, 191 15th Century History, 191	DLS, 181 Imperative Sentences, 188	Researching Word Origins, 181
Illustrated Tragedy, 199 Dance Interpretation, 199 Ballad Role Play, 199 Dramatic Recital, 195	Blues Music, 199 Popularity of Tragedy, 199 History or Legend? 199	DLS, 192 Subjects and Predicates, 196	
Text Structure, 201		Editing and Proofing, 204 Run-on Sentences, 205 Revising and Editing, 205 Inverting Word Order, 207	Using Word Origins, 206

PART 3 SKILLS TRACE

Features and Selections	Literary Analysis	Reading and Critical Thinking	Writing Opportunities
POETRY *from* Sir Gawain and the Green Knight	Romance, 209, 222 Author Activity, 224 Review: Conflict 222 Intended Meaning, 215	Narrative Poem, 209, 222	Questions for Green Knight, 223 New Story, 223 Essay on Romance, 223 TV News Report, 223 Speech , 223
ROMANCE *from* Le Morte d'Arthur **Related Reading** Le Morte d'Arthur	Characterization, 225, 237 Review: Romance, 237 Primary Source	Characterization, 225, 237 Paraphrasing and Summarizing, 239	Essay on Virtues, 238 Informal Assess., 236
EPIC POETRY **Comparing Literature of the World** *from the* Ramayana	Supernatural Elements, 240, 250 Review: Epic, 250	Classifying Characters, 240, 250 Informal Assess., 249	Rama's Speech, 251 Points of Comparison, 251
AUTOBIOGRAPHY *from* The Book of Margery Kempe	Autobiography, 252, 256	Autobiography, 252, 256	Dialog Script, 257 Narrative on Survival, 257
Writing Workshop: **Application Essay** **Assessment Practice** Building Vocabulary Sentence Crafting			Application Essay, 260 Analyzing a Student Model, 261
Reflect and Assess	Reviewing Literary Concepts, 269		Comparing Challenges, 268

LEGEND **PE instruction shown in black** **CCL indicates a Cross-Curricular Link**
TE Mini Lessons shown in green **DLS indicates Daily Language SkillBuilder**

Speaking and Listening Viewing and Representing	Inquiry and Research	Grammar, Usage, and Mechanics	Vocabulary
Computer Game Challenge, 223 **Dramatic Presentation, 223** **Special Effects Diagram, 223** **Set for a Play, 223** **Storyboard Scene, 223** Contracts, 218 Dramatic Interpretation, 221	**Weapons of War, 223** **Honorable Pursuits, 223**	DLS, 209 Compound Predicates, 213 Compound Subjects, 217	**Analogies, 224** Using Synonyms, 210 Prefixes, 216
News Report, 234		DLS, 225 Active and Passive Voice, 230 Irregular Verbs, 238	Context Clues, 238 Using Context Clues, 226 Test Practice, 228 Root Words, 235
Illustrated Battle, 251 **Battle Scene Soundtrack, 251** Press Conference, 247	**Hidden Temple, 251**	DLS, 240 Subject and Predicate, 243	**Context Clues, 251** Using a Thesaurus, 241 Context Clues, 244
Visionary Art, 57 **Book Jacket, 257**	**Medieval Medical Care, 257** **Author Activity, 257**	DLS , 252 Compound and Complex Structures, 254	
Text Structure, 262		**Editing and Proofreading, 263, 264** **Active Voice/Subject Verb Agreement, 264** **Revising and Editing, 265** **Compound and Complex Sentences, 267** Active and Passive Voice, 264	**Multiple Meanings, 266**
Resetting the Scene, 268 **Role Playing, 268** **Building Your Portfolio, 269**			

UNIT ONE
RESOURCE MANAGEMENT GUIDE
PART 1

To introduce the theme/literary period of this unit, use Fine Art Transparencies T17–19 in the Communications Transparencies and Copymasters.

Selection	Unit Resource Book	Assessment	Integrated Technology and Media	Additional Support: Literary Analysis Transparencies
from **Beowulf** *pp. 30–65*	• Summary p. 8 • Active Reading p. 9 • Literary Analysis p. 10 • Words to Know p. 11 • Selection Quiz p. 12	• Selection Test, Formal Assessment pp. 7–8 Test Generator	Audio Library LaserLinks, Teacher's SourceBook pp. 6–7 Video: Literature in Performance, Video Resource Book pp. 3–8 Research Starter www.mcdougallittell.com	• Alliteration T3
from the **Iliad** *pp. 66–83*	• Summary p. 13 • Active Reading p. 14 • Literary Analysis p. 15 • Words to Know p. 16 • Selection Quiz p. 17	• Selection Test, Formal Assessment pp. 9–10 Test Generator	Audio Library LaserLinks, Teacher's SourceBook p. 8 Research Starter www.mcdougallittell.com	• Poetic Devices T16
from the **Exeter Book, The Seafarer / The Wanderer / The Wife's Lament,** *pp. 84–97*	• Active Reading p. 18 • Literary Analysis p. 19	• Selection Test, Formal Assessment pp. 11–12 Test Generator	Audio Library	• Poetic Devices T16
from **A History of the English Church and People** *pp. 98–105*	• Summary p. 20 • Active Reading p. 21 • Literary Analysis p. 22 • Words to Know p. 23 • Selection Quiz p. 24	• Selection Test, Formal Assessment pp. 13–14 Test Generator	Audio Library LaserLinks, Teacher's SourceBook p. 9	
		Unit Assessment	***Unit Technology***	
		• Unit One, Part 1 Test, Formal Assessment pp. 15–16 Test Generator • Unit One Integrated Test, Integrated Assessment pp. 1–10	ClassZone www.mcdougallittell.com Electronic Teacher Tools Electronic Library	

UNIT ONE
PART 2

To introduce the theme/literary period of this unit, use Fine Art Transparencies T17–19 in the Communications Transparencies and Copymasters.

Selection	Unit Resource Book	Assessment	Integrated Technology and Media	Additional Support: Literary Analysis Transparencies
from **The Canterbury Tales The Prologue** *pp. 111–138*	• Summary p. 25 • Active Reading p. 26 • Literary Analysis p. 27 • Words to Know p. 28 • Selection Quiz p. 29	• Selection Test, Formal Assessment pp. 17–18 Test Generator	Audio Library LaserLinks, Teacher's SourceBook pp. 9–10 NetActivities	• Style, Tone, and Mood T24
from **The Pardoner's Tale** *pp. 141–153*	• Summary p. 30 • Active Reading p. 31 • Literary Analysis p. 32 • Words to Know p. 33 • Selection Quiz p. 34	• Selection Test, Formal Assessment pp. 19–20 Test Generator	Audio Library LaserLinks, Teacher's SourceBook pp. 9–10 Video: Literature in Performance, Video Resource Book pp. 9–14 NetActivities	• The Moral Tale, Ballad, Fable, and Folk Tale T23
The Wife of Bath's Tale *pp. 154–170*	• Summary p. 35 • Active Reading p. 36 • Literary Analysis p. 37 • Words to Know p. 38 • Selection Quiz p. 39	• Selection Test, Formal Assessment pp. 21–22 Test Generator	Audio Library LaserLinks, Teacher's SourceBook pp. 9–10 NetActivities	

T = Transparency C = Copymaster

Reading and Critical Thinking Transparencies	Grammar Transparencies and Copymasters	Vocabulary Transparencies and Copymasters	Writing Transparencies and Copymasters	Communications Transparencies and Copymasters
• Making Judgments T5 • Observation Chart T47 • Venn Diagram T51	• Daily Language SkillBuilder T1 • Diagnostic: Parts of Speech C61	• Personal Word List C17 • Using a Thesaurus C18 • Words with Multiple Meanings C19	• Showing, Not Telling T22 • Compare-Contrast C34	• Reading Aloud T11
• Using an Outline T44 • Organizational Chart: Horizontal T52	• Daily Language SkillBuilder T1 • Parts of Speech C62	• Using a Dictionary C20	• Showing, Not Telling T22 • Compare-Contrast C34	• Dramatic Reading T12
• Visualizing T8 • Cluster Diagram T49	• Daily Language SkillBuilder T1 • Simple Sentences C75	• Word Origins C21	• Showing, Not Telling T22 • Literary Interpretation C33	• Interviewing T9
• Determining Author's Purpose and Audience T20 • Determining Author's Bias: Effect of Stance and Tone on Structure T23 • Organizing and Interpreting Information on Bar Graphs T38	• Daily Language SkillBuilder T2 • Sentence Fragments T42 • Run-on Sentences T43 • Complete Sentences C76		• Figurative Language and Sound Devices T15	• Formal Presentations T10

STUDENTS ACQUIRING ENGLISH

The **Spanish Study Guide,** pp. 1–15, includes language support for the following pages:

- Family and Community Involvement (per unit)
- Selection Summaries and Vocabulary
- Active Reading
- Literary Analysis

Reading and Critical Thinking Transparencies	Grammar Transparencies and Copymasters	Vocabulary Transparencies and Copymasters	Writing Transparencies and Copymasters	Communications Transparencies and Copymasters
• Organizational Chart: Horizontal T52	• Daily Language SkillBuilder T2 • Pronouns–Personal, Reflexive, and Intensive T39 • Pronouns–Correct Case T41 • Pronoun-Antecedent Agreement T48 • Types of Pronouns I C64 • Types of Pronouns II C65	• Antonyms C22 • Homonyms and Homographs C23	• Organizing Your Writing T11 • Literary Interpretation C33	• Evaluating Roles in Groups T8
• Predicting Outcomes T2	• Daily Language SkillBuilder T3 • Indefinite Pronouns T40 • Indefinite Pronouns as Antecedents C146	• Word Origins C24	• Achieving Unity T7	
• Analyzing Text Structure T17 • Venn Diagram T51	• Daily Language SkillBuilder T3 • Pronouns–Correct Case T41 • Pronoun Cases II C67 • Kinds of Sentences C77	• Denotation and Connotation C25	• The Uses of Dialogue T24 • Compare-Contrast C34	• Impromptu Speaking: Debate T15

UNIT ONE PART 2 CONTINUED

	Unit Resource Book	Assessment	Integrated Technology and Media	Additional Support: Literary Analysis Transparencies
from **The Decameron Federigo's Falcon** *pp. 171–179*	• Summary p. 40 • Active Reading p. 41 • Literary Analysis p. 42 • Words to Know p. 43 • Selection Quiz p. 44	• Selection Test, Formal Assessment pp. 23–24 Test Generator	Audio Library LaserLinks, Teacher's SourceBook p. 11 Research Starter www.mcdougallittell.com	• Plot T10
from **The Paston Letters** *pp. 180–191*	• Summary p. 45 • Active Reading p. 46 • Literary Analysis p. 47 • Selection Quiz p. 48	• Selection Test, Formal Assessment pp. 25–26 Test Generator	Audio Library Research Starter www.mcdougallittell.com	• External Conflicts/ Social Conflicts T20
Barbara Allan / Sir Patrick Spens / Get Up and Bar the Door, *pp. 192–199*	• Active Reading p. 49 • Literary Analysis p. 50	• Selection Test, Formal Assessment pp. 27–28 Test Generator	Audio Library LaserLinks, Teacher's SourceBook p. 12 Research Starter www.mcdougallittell.com	• The Moral Tale, Ballad, Fable, and Folk Tale T23

Writing Workshop: Personality Profile

Unit One Resource Book
- Prewriting p. 51
- Drafting and Elaboration p. 52
- Peer Response Guide pp. 53–54
- Revising, Editing, and Proofreading p. 55
- Student Models pp. 56–58
- Rubric for Evaluation p. 59

Writing Coach

Writing Transparencies and Copymasters T11, T19, C25

Teacher's Guide to Assessment and Portfolio Use

Unit Assessment
- Unit One, Part 2 Test, Formal Assessment pp. 29–30
- Test Generator
- Unit One Integrated Test, Integrated Assessment pp. 1–10

Unit Technology
- ClassZone www.mcdougallittell.com
- Electronic Teacher Tools
- Electronic Library

UNIT ONE PART 3

To introduce the theme/literary period of this unit, use Fine Art Transparencies T17–19 in the Communications Transparencies and Copymasters.

	Unit Resource Book	Assessment	Integrated Technology and Media	Additional Support: Literary Analysis Transparencies
from **Sir Gawain and the Green Knight** *pp. 209–224*	• Summary p. 62 • Active Reading p. 63 • Literary Analysis p. 64 • Words to Know p. 65 • Selection Quiz p. 66	• Selection Test, Formal Assessment pp. 31–32 Test Generator	Audio Library LaserLinks, Teacher's SourceBook pp. 12–13 Research Starter www.mcdougallittell.com	
from **Le Morte d'Arthur** *pp. 225–238*	• Summary p. 67 • Active Reading p. 68 • Literary Analysis p. 69 • Words to Know p. 70 • Selection Quiz p. 71	• Selection Test, Formal Assessment pp. 33–34 Test Generator	Audio Library LaserLinks, Teacher's SourceBook p. 14	• Characterization T21
from **the Ramayana** *pp. 240–251*	• Summary p. 72 • Active Reading p. 73 • Literary Analysis p. 74 • Words to Know p. 75 • Selection Quiz p. 76	• Selection Test, Formal Assessment pp. 35–36 Test Generator	Audio Library LaserLinks, Teacher's SourceBook p. 15 Research Starter www.mcdougallittell.com	• Characteristics of the Epic T1
from **The Book of Margery Kempe,** *pp. 252–257*	• Summary p. 77 • Active Reading p. 78 • Literary Analysis p. 79 • Selection Quiz p. 80	• Selection Test, Formal Assessment p. 37 Test Generator	Audio Library	

Writing Workshop: Application Essay

Unit One Resource Book
- Prewriting p. 81
- Drafting and Elaboration p. 82
- Peer Response Guide pp. 83–84
- Revising, Editing, and Proofreading p. 85
- Student Models pp. 86–91
- Rubric for Evaluation p. 92

Writing Coach

Writing Transparencies and Copymasters T11, T19, C26

Teacher's Guide to Assessment and Portfolio Use

Unit Assessment
- Unit One, Part 3 Test, Formal Assessment pp. 39-40
- Test Generator
- Unit One Integrated Test, Integrated Assessment pp. 1-10

Unit Technology
- ClassZone www.mcdougallittell.com
- Electronic Teacher Tools
- Electronic Library

T = Transparency   C = Copymaster

Reading and Critical Thinking Transparencies	Grammar Transparencies and Copymasters	Vocabulary Transparencies and Copymasters	Writing Transparencies and Copymasters	Communications Transparencies and Copymasters
• Sequence Chain T50	• Daily Language SkillBuilder T5 • Conjunctions C73	• Suffixes C26	• Compare-Contrast C34 • Autobiographical Incident C36	• Giving and Using Feedback to Improve Performance T16
• Evaluating Credibility of Information Sources T43	• Daily Language SkillBuilder T4 • Simple Subjects and Simple Predicates C79	• Researching Word Origins C27	• Compare-Contrast C34 • Opinion Statement C35	• Impromptu Speaking: Dialogue, Role-Play T14
• Visualizing T8 • Paraphrasing and Summarizing T42	• Daily Language SkillBuilder T4 • Complete Subjects and Complete Predicates C78		• Effective Language T13 • Showing, Not Telling T22	• Impromptu Speaking: Dialogue, Role-Play T14

STUDENTS ACQUIRING ENGLISH

The **Spanish Study Guide,** pp. 16-33, includes language support for the following pages:

- Family and Community Involvement (per unit)
- Selection Summaries and Vocabulary
- Active Reading
- Literary Analysis

Reading and Critical Thinking Transparencies	Grammar Transparencies and Copymasters	Vocabulary Transparencies and Copymasters	Writing Transparencies and Copymasters	Communications Transparencies and Copymasters
• Noting Details T9 • Interviewing T40	• Daily Language SkillBuilder T5 • Compound Predicates C81 • Compound Subjects C82	• Prefixes C28	• Transitional Words T9 • Sensory Word List T14 • Opinion Statement C35	• Dramatic Reading T12 • Identifying and Analyzing Artistic Elements in Literary Texts T13
• Cluster Diagram T49	• Daily Language SkillBuilder T5 • Verbs–Using Correct Verb Forms T45 • Correct Forms of Irregular Verbs C129 • Active and Passive Voice II C135	• Roots C29	• Topic Sentences and Thesis Statements T6 • Subject Analysis C30	
• Compare and Contrast T15 • Classification Tree T59	• Diagramming Subjects, Verbs, and Modifiers T58 • Finding the Subject and Predicate C83	• Context Clues C30	• Opinion Statement C35	• Formal Presentations T10
• Analyzing Text T18	• Daily Language SkillBuilder T6 • Diagramming Complements and Appositives T59 • Compound and Complex Sentences C123	• Word Origins C31	• The Uses of Dialogue T24 • Autobiographical Incident C36	• Formal Presentations T10

STUDENTS ACQUIRING ENGLISH

The **Spanish Study Guide,** pp. 34–45, includes language support for the following pages:

- Family and Community Involvement (per unit)
- Selection Summaries and Vocabulary
- Active Reading
- Literary Analysis

DAILY LANGUAGE SKILLBUILDERS

Selection	SkillBuilder Sentences	Suggested Answers
from Beowulf	**1.** It wasn't until several centuries after the poems action—between AD 500 and 600 that Beowulf was written down.	**1.** It wasn't until several centuries after the poem's action—between A.D. 500 and 600—that **Beowulf** was written down.
	2. Before it was recorded the poem as spoken aloud or sang by a poet, also known as a scop.	**2.** Before it was recorded, the poem **was** spoken aloud or sung by a poet, also known as a **scop**.
from the Iliad	**1.** The two greek epics, titled the iliad and the Odyssey, are atributed to a poet named homer.	**1.** The two **G**reek epics titled the **Iliad** and the **Odyssey** are at**t**ributed to a poet named **H**omer.
	2. Many greeks believed that the poet had been blind. Perhaps because a character in the Odyssey a bard called Demodokos is blind.	**2.** Many **G**reeks believed that **Homer** had been blind**, p**erhaps because a character in the **Odyssey,** a bard called Demodokos, is blind.
from the Exeter Book The Seafarer The Wanderer The Wife's Lament	**1.** The Exeter Book, one of the most important sources of Old english literature s a collection of poems that includes The Seafarer The Wanderer and The Wifes Lament.	1. **The Exeter Book**, one of the most important sources of Old **E**nglish literature**, is** a collection of poems that includes "The Seafarer," "The Wanderer," and "The Wife's Lament."
	2. the book also contains a famous collection of riddles and several, longer religious poems.	**2.** **T**he book also contains a famous collection of riddles and several longer religious poems.
from A History of the English Church and People	**1.** Bede is the auther of many works his History of the English Church and People is said to be the most informative and artful account produced in medieval England.	1. Bede is the auth**o**r of many works**, but** his **History of the English Church and People** is said to be the most informative and artful account produced in medieval England.
	2. His book gives a detailed account of the changes that took place in England, both religious and political, during the spread of Christianity.	**2.** His book gives a detailed account of the **religious and political** changes that took place in England during the spread of Christianity.
from The Canterbury Tales The Prologue	**1.** In the fourteenth century England had a population of about 2,500,000.	1. In the fourteenth century**,** England had a population of about 2,500,000.
	2. Small Market towns which were seldom populated by more than 150 person dotted the English Countryside.	**2.** Small **m**arket towns**,** which were seldom populated by more than 150 persons**,** dotted the English **c**ountryside.

Selection	SkillBuilder Sentences	Suggested Answers
from The Canterbury Tales *from* The Pardoner's Tale	**1.** Of all the pilgrems in The canterbery tails, the pardoner is one of the most complex figures **2.** We no he is'nt stupid because his knowlege and use of pychology demonstrate his inteligennce.	**1.** Of all the pilgr**i**ms in **The Canterbury Tales**, the **P**ardoner is one of the most complex figures**.** **2.** We **know** he is**n't** stupid because his knowledge and use of psychology demonstrate his intellig**ence**.
from The Canterbury Tales The Wife of Bath's Tale	**1.** Inn chauser's time, riters offen maligned womens in stories buy portraying them as week charcters. **2.** The wife of bath holds all that has been charged aginst women in litrature, but she openley glories inn her posession of those charactristics.	1. **In C**haucer's time, **w**riters often maligned women in stories **by** portraying them as we**a**k characters. **2.** The **W**ife of **B**ath holds all that has been charged ag**a**inst women in lit**e**rature, but she open**ly** glories **in** her possession of those charact**e**ristics.
from The Decameron Federigo's Falcon	**1.** What does <u>The arabian Nights</u>, <u>Aesop's Fables</u>, Boccaccios <u>Decameron</u>, chaucer's <u>Canterbury Tales</u>, <u>Grimm's Fairy Tales</u>, and "Jack and the Beanstalk" have in common? **2.** Well, they can all be traced back—believe it or not to the same begining: ancient indian litrature.	1. What do <u>The **A**rabian Nights</u>, <u>Aesop's Fables</u>, Boccaccio's <u>Decameron</u>, **C**haucer's <u>Canterbury Tales</u>, <u>Grimm's Fairy Tales</u>, and "Jack and the Beanstalk" have in common? **2.** Well, they can all be traced back—believe it or not—to the same begin**n**ing: ancient **I**ndian literature.
from The Paston Letters	**1.** The Wars of the Roses were a conflict between two nobel families the yorks and the lancasters. **2.** Niether family was ultimately victorious Henry Tudor, a distant relative of the Lancaster's claimed the throne and ended it.	1. The Wars of the Roses **was** a conflict between two nob**le** families**,** the **Y**orks and the **L**ancasters. **2.** Neither family was ultimately victorious**.** Henry Tudor, a distant relative of the Lancaste**rs,** claimed the throne and ended **the war**.
Barbara Allan Sir Patrick Spens Get Up and Bar the Door	**1.** Barbara Allan hurryed to town to get help for sir John but her efforts were in vane. **2.** Most ballads are about lifes tradjedies, real or fictional, and many deal with dissappointed love.	1. Barbara Allan hurr**ie**d to town to get help for Sir John**,** but her efforts were in **vain**. **2.** Most ballads are about life**'**s tra**g**edies, real or fictional, and many deal with disappointed love.

DAILY LANGUAGE SKILLBUILDERS, continued

Selection	SkillBuilder Sentences	Suggested Answers
from Sir Gawain and the Green Knight	**1.** King Arthur and his Round table have been the basis for stories for centurys. **2.** one famous versions is TH White's book, "The Once and Future King."	**1.** King Arthur and his Round **T**able have been the basis for stories for centur**ies**. **2.** **O**ne famous version is T.H. White's book, **The Once and Future King**.
from Le Morte d'Arthur	**1.** Whom is imdisputably the best known literary hero of all time. **2.** No one knows for sure whether Arthur was a real person or not some say he was military man while others think he was member of Royalty.	**1.** **Who** is indisputably the best known literary hero of all time**?** **2.** No one knows for sure whether Arthur was a real person or not**. S**ome say he was **a** military man**,** while others think he was **a** member of **r**oyalty.
from The Book of Margery Kempe	**1.** Students please note the change in peoples attitudes toward women during the Middle Ages women in literature asended to a new level. **2.** Perhaps influenced by fasinating arabian tales in which women were idealized, french and Provencal poets began relating tales of romance and courtly love.	**1.** Students**,** please note the change in people**'**s attitudes toward women during the Middle Ages**. W**omen in literature ascended to a new level. **2.** Perhaps influenced by fas**c**inating **A**rabian tales in which women were idealized, **F**rench and Provencal poets began relating tales of romance and courtly love.

INTEGRATING GRAMMAR AND LITERATURE: GRAMMAR PLANNER

	Unit One	Unit Two	Unit Three	Unit Four	Unit Five	Unit Six	Unit Seven
Grammar Focus by Unit	Parts of a Sentence	Phrases, Part I	Phrases, Part II	Clauses, Part I	Clauses, Part II	Rhetorical Grammar, Part I	Rhetorical Grammar, Part II

The Language of Literature offers several options for integrating grammar instruction and literature.

- Each literature unit has a grammar focus. The Teacher's Edition includes Mini Lessons for each selection that help develop the grammar focus for the unit and spring from the content of the specific literature.
- The Pupil Edition includes several full-page lessons on Sentence Crafting. These lessons are related to both the literature and the grammar focus for the unit and help students use grammar in their own writing.
- Daily Language SkillBuilders in the Teacher's Edition provide students with ongoing proofreading practice and reinforce punctuation, spelling, grammar and usage, and capitalization.
- Grammar Copymasters and Transparencies, which may be used to complement or extend lessons in the Teacher's Edition, present grammar in a traditional, systematic sequence. References to appropriate copymasters or transparencies are included at point of use in the Teacher's Edition Mini Lessons.

TE Mini Lessons shown in green
PE instruction shown in black

Part 1

Parts of Speech

Diagnostic
from *Beowulf*, p. 33

Overview
from the *Iliad*, p. 75

Parts of the Sentence

Simple Sentences
"The Seafarer," "The Wanderer," "The Wife's Lament," p. 87

Complete Sentences
from *A History of the English Church and People*, p. 102

Part 2

Parts of Speech

Pronoun Cases
"The Prologue," from *The Canterbury Tales*, pp. 118–119"
"The Wife of Bath's Tale," from *The Canterbury Tales*, p. 164

Types of Conjunctions
"Federigo's Falcon," p. 179

Parts of the Sentence

Kinds of Sentences
"The Wife of Bath's Tale," from *The Canterbury Tales*, p. 169

Complete Subjects and Complete Predicates
Ballads, p. 196

Imperative Sentences and the Understood Subject
from *The Paston Letters*, p. 188

Using Clauses

Run-on Sentences
Writing Workshop, p. 205

Subject-Verb Agreement

Sentence Crafting, p. 207

Pronoun Usage

Pronoun-Antecedent Agreement
"The Prologue," from *The Canterbury Tales*, p. 123

Indefinite Pronouns as Antecedent
"The Pardoner's Tale," from *The Canterbury Tales*, pp. 148–149

End Marks and Commas

Correcting Comma Splices
Writing Workshop, p. 205

Other Punctuation

Punctuation: Forming Singular Possessives

Punctuating Dialogue
Writing Workshop, p. 205

Style

Word Order Variation
Sentence Crafting, p. 207

Part 3

Parts of the Sentence

Compound Predicates
from *Sir Gawain and the Green Knight*, p. 213

Compound Subjects
from *Sir Gawain and the Green Knight*, p. 217

Finding the Subject and Predicate
from the *Ramayana*, p. 243

Using Clauses

Compound and Complex Sentences
from *The Book of Margery Kempe*, p. 255
Sentence Crafting, p. 267

Verb Usage

Using Correct Form of Irregular Verbs
from *Le Morte d'Arthur*, p. 238

Verbs: Avoiding Unnecessary Shifts in Tense
Writing Workshop, p. 265

Active and Passive Voice
from *Le Morte d'Arthur*, p. 230
Writing Workshop, p. 265

Subject-Verb Agreement

Writing Workshop, p. 265

End Marks and Commas

Correcting Comma Splices
Sentence Crafting, p. 267

This time line shows some major events in the history of Britain from the Anglo-Saxon period to the end of the Middle Ages. Encourage students to refer back to this timeline as they read the literature in this unit. Doing so will help them understand the historical context in which literary works were written. Additional information about selected people and events is provided below.

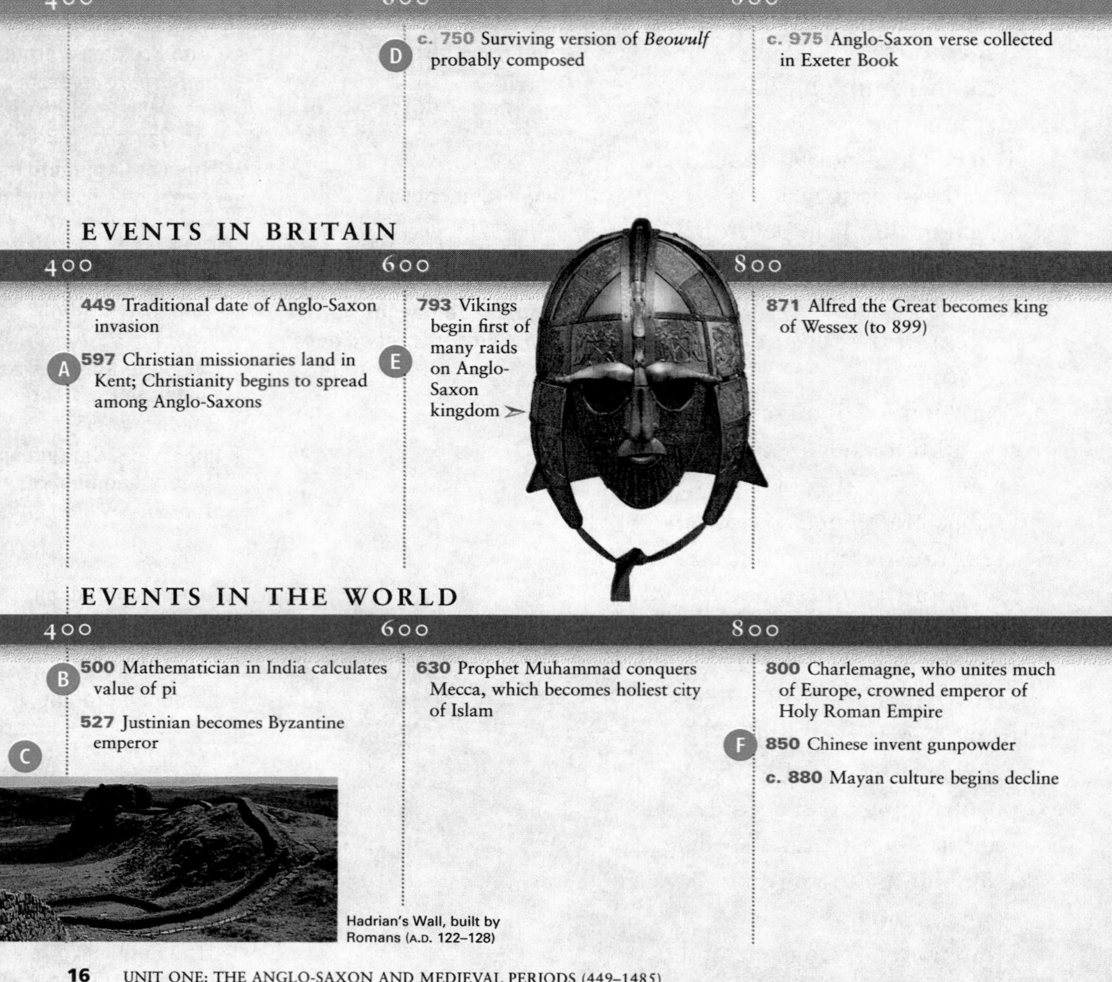

TIME LINE 449-1485

THE ANGLO-SAXON AND MEDIEVAL PERIODS

EVENTS IN BRITISH LITERATURE

400 | 600 | 800

(D) **c. 750** Surviving version of *Beowulf* probably composed

c. 975 Anglo-Saxon verse collected in Exeter Book

EVENTS IN BRITAIN

400 | 600 | 800

449 Traditional date of Anglo-Saxon invasion

(A) **597** Christian missionaries land in Kent; Christianity begins to spread among Anglo-Saxons

(E) **793** Vikings begin first of many raids on Anglo-Saxon kingdom ➢

871 Alfred the Great becomes king of Wessex (to 899)

EVENTS IN THE WORLD

400 | 600 | 800

(B) **500** Mathematician in India calculates value of pi

527 Justinian becomes Byzantine emperor

(C)

630 Prophet Muhammad conquers Mecca, which becomes holiest city of Islam

800 Charlemagne, who unites much of Europe, crowned emperor of Holy Roman Empire

(F) **850** Chinese invent gunpowder

c. 880 Mayan culture begins decline

Hadrian's Wall, built by Romans (A.D. 122–128)

16 UNIT ONE: THE ANGLO-SAXON AND MEDIEVAL PERIODS (449–1485)

Britain: 597

(A) According to the Venerable Bede, the pagan Anglo-Saxons were impressed by the missionaries' certainty of an afterlife.

World: 500

(B) India at this time boasted some of the world's most advanced mathematicians. Indian contributions from this time period include modern numerals, the zero, and the decimal system. For example, an Indian named Aryabhata calculated the value of pi to four decimal places and the length of the solar year to 365.3586805 days.

World: Hadrian's Wall

(C) The Roman emperor Hadrian (A.D. 76–138) personally surveyed with his architects the stretch of land across which the wall was built. The wall, built between A.D. 122–128 across one of the narrowest parts of northern Britain, was 73 miles long and had fortresses at intervals of one Roman mile (slightly shorter than the modern mile), with smaller towers in between. The Romans left Britain in 407 to help defend the city of Rome, which came under attack successively by Visigoths, Huns, and Vandals. The latter sacked Rome in 455.

Literature: c. 750

(D) *Beowulf* is believed to have been written by a Christian, since it contains passages that suggest a Christian world view.

Britain: 793

(E) After sailing across the North Sea to Britain, the Viking raiders established bases at the mouths of rivers, from which they sailed upstream, plundering monasteries and towns. By the time of Alfred the Great in 871, however, the Vikings had become more interested in settling on the island than in raiding it.

World: 850

(F) Around this time, great leaps in technology were being made in China. Among other things, the Chinese invented the mechanical clock, the printing block, and gunpowder. First used only for fireworks, gunpowder soon became used for weapons. This invention spread slowly west over the next 500 years and found its way into English warfare for the first time around 1325.

Roman sandals

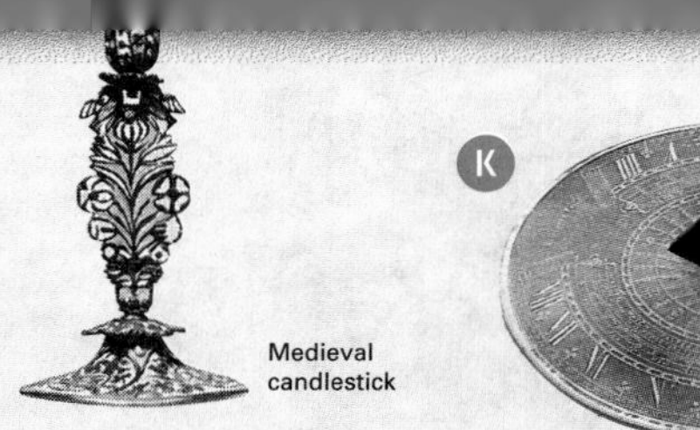

Medieval candlestick

(K) Sundial for telling time

1000 · 1200 · 1400

- **c. 1000** Surviving version of *Beowulf* written out by monks
- **c. 1375** *Sir Gawain and the Green Knight* composed
- **c. 1386** Chaucer begins *The Canterbury Tales*
- **c. 1420** Earliest surviving Paston letter written
- (L) **1485** William Caxton prints Sir Thomas Malory's *Le Morte d'Arthur*

The Prioress

1000 · 1200 · 1400

- **1016** Canute, a Dane, becomes king of England (to 1035)
- (G) **1066** Norman Conquest—William the Conqueror defeats Harold at Hastings and becomes king of England
- **1166** Henry II institutes judge-and-jury system throughout England
- **1170** Thomas à Becket murdered
- **1171** Henry II declares himself lord of Ireland, beginning centuries of English-Irish conflict
- (H) **1215** King John signs Magna Carta
- **1282** England conquers Wales
- **1295** Model Parliament assembled under Edward I
- **1301** Edward II becomes first prince of Wales, a title thereafter given to male heirs of British throne
- (I) **1337** Hundred Years' War with France begins (to 1453) ➤
- **c. 1430** Modern English develops from Middle English
- **c. 1476** Caxton establishes first printing press in Britain; prints first dated book in English language (1477)

1000 · 1200 · 1400

- **1054** Christian Church divides into east and west branches
- **1095** First of "holy wars" called Crusades begins (to 1272)
- **1192** Japanese emperor takes title of shogun
- **1206** Genghis Khan begins Mongol conquest of much of Asia (to 1227)
- **1235** West African kingdom of Mali emerges
- **1271** Marco Polo arrives in China
- **c. 1300** Renaissance begins in northern Italy
- **1325** Aztecs establish Tenochtitlan, site of present Mexico City
- (J) **1347** Bubonic plague reaches Europe, soon killing millions
- **1431** Joan of Arc burned at stake
- (M) **1453** Ottomans conquer Constantinople
- **1455** Gutenberg Bible produced on printing press

(G) William the Conqueror defeated Harold at Hastings, on England's southeast coast. To meet William's threat at Hastings, Harold had to lead his weary army on a forced march from near York, in northern England, where only 20 days previously he had defeated his brother Tostig and Harold III of Norway, who had also contested his right to the English throne.

Britain: 1215

(H) Rebelling nobles forced King John to sign the Magna Carta ("Great Charter"). It was originally drafted to protect only nobles' rights but eventually came to guarantee basic rights to all English citizens. Because King John was so unpopular, he is the only king whose name is not given to potential heirs to the English throne.

Britain: 1337

(I) The Hundred Years' War changed the English social structure because it led to a partnership of knights and barons in Parliament as well as in battle. Many noblemen also amassed great fortunes during the war.

World: 1347

(J) The bubonic plague, spread by rats carrying infected fleas, arrived in England on trading ships. In all, nearly 25 million Europeans died, as well as millions more in China and North Africa. The labor shortage caused by the bubonic plague accelerated the change from serfdom to freeholding of land.

Period Pieces

(K) Sundials are among the oldest of scientific instruments: the earliest known examples are Egyptian and date from the 15th century B.C. Sundials continued in use through ancient times and the Middle Ages, and into modern times. Although large garden dials, like the one shown, are best known today, small, hand-held dials were popular before the mid-19th century.

Literature: 1485

(L) Caxton (c. 1421–1491) was himself a prolific translator who learned the art of printing in order to meet the demand for copies of his translation of a French romance about the Trojan War. Besides *Le Morte d'Arthur* and his own translations, he also printed works by Chaucer and others, as well as many devotional works.

World: 1453

(M) The city of Constantinople (modern Istanbul) was all the territory that remained of the Byzantine Empire, the eastern branch of the Christian Church, at the time it fell to the Ottoman Muslims.

UNIT ONE
HISTORICAL BACKGROUND

OVERVIEW

Introduction
By providing an overview of the major historical events of the Anglo-Saxon and medieval periods, this article complements and expands the time line. In conjunction with the article there are sidebar commentaries on the simultaneous emergence of the English language and the development of literary forms. The latter permits students to interpret the possible influences of historical contexts on literary works.

Teaching Nonfiction

Reading Skills and Strategies

ESTABLISHING A PURPOSE FOR READING
Explain that this introductory article introduces students to the thousand-year period of British history beginning at about the time of the end of Roman rule. Have students preview the article and establish a purpose for reading. *(students will be reading to find out about the history of the Anglo-Saxon and Medieval periods.)*

ANALYZING TEXT STRUCTURE
As students scan the article, have them find out how it is organized. Specifically, they should look at the headings and notice that the time period is divided into two main parts, with subsections offering significant characteristics of each part. The article presents the time period in chronological order.

IDENTIFYING MAIN IDEAS
The headings in this article form sections that become the main ideas of the article. Have students approach the article by reading one section at a time, identifying its main idea, and noting the supporting ideas and then thinking about how its idea is developed through important and less important details.

NOTETAKING
Encourage students to take notes while they read, jotting down important concepts, vocabulary, and terms. They may also construct graphic organizers that create visual connections that can help them more easily remember concepts.

THE ANGLO-SAXON AND MEDIEVAL PERIODS

449-1485

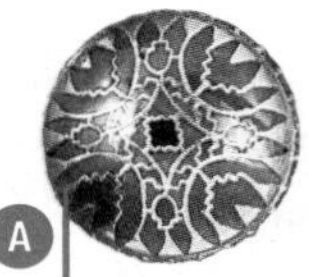

A

The British Isles, just off the west coast of continental Europe, enter recorded history in the writings of the Roman general Julius Caesar. In 55 B.C., fresh from his conquest of Celtic peoples known as Gauls, Caesar sailed from what is now France to Britain, largest of the British Isles, to assert Rome's authority over it. There he encountered a Celtic people called the Britons, from whom the island takes its name. Also living on Britain were Picts, remnants of a pre-Celtic civilization, and farther west, on Ireland (the next-largest British island) was another group of Celtic speakers, the Gaels.

The Britons had a thriving culture by most standards of the day. They were skilled in agriculture and metalwork, traded with their Celtic neighbors overseas, and had an oral tradition of literature and learning preserved by a priestly class known as druids. They were, however, no match for the Romans. About a century after Caesar's visit, Roman armies returned to Britain to make good his claim. Despite resistance, they rapidly conquered the Britons and drove the war-

B

Detail of a Celtic container

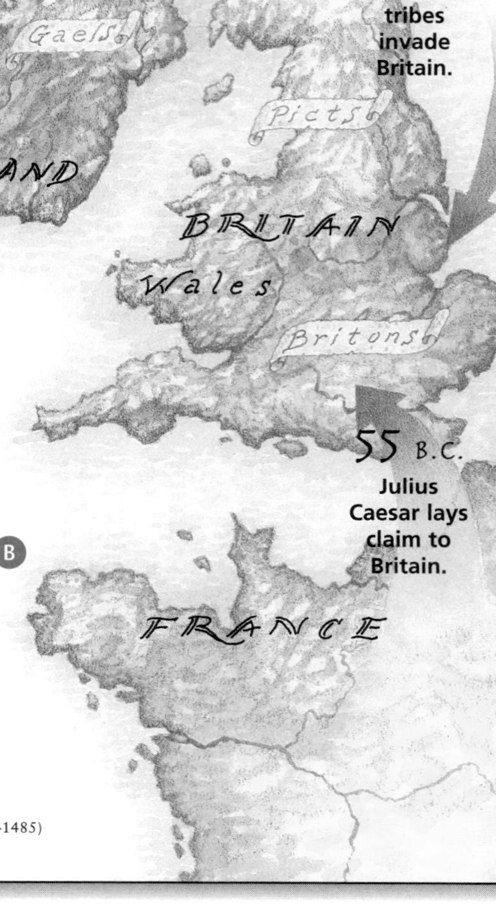

Development of the English Language

SUFFIXES
Tell students that evidence that many British cities developed from Roman military camps survives in town names ending in *-caster* and *-chester* (such as Lancaster and Manchester), both of which derive from Latin *castra*, "camp."

Have students work in pairs to find place names in the United States that include a suffix or second word stemming from a non-English word meaning "town," "city," or "farm." (Latin, as well as Old English and German, has contributed common suffixes such as *-town (-*ton), *-ville*, *-burg* (-berg, -bourg), *-borough*, and the like.)

like Picts northward to what is now Scotland.

Britain became a province of the great Roman Empire, and the Romans introduced cities, fine stone roads, written scholarship, and eventually Christianity to the island. As they adapted to a more urban way of life, the "Romanized" Britons came to depend on the Roman military for protection; but early in the fifth century, with much of their empire being overrun by invaders, the Roman armies abandoned Britain to defend the city of Rome. It was not long before Britain too became the target of invasion.

Above: Celtic cross

The Anglo-Saxon Period
449-1066

In an invasion traditionally assigned to the year A.D. 449 but actually taking place over several decades, Angles, Saxons, and other Germanic peoples (such as Jutes and Frisians) left their northern European homelands and began settling on Britain's eastern and southern shores. The Britons—perhaps led by a Christian commander named Arthur—fought a series of legendary battles in an effort to stop the invasion. Eventually, however, they were driven to seek refuge in Cornwall and Wales on the western fringes of the island; in the northern area now called Scotland, where Gaels from Ireland were also settling; and in an area on the west coast of continental Europe that would come to be known as Britanny. In southern and central Britain, Celtic culture all but disappeared. The Germanic tribes eventually organized themselves into a confederation

Development of the English Language

Just as Britain's fifth-century invaders eventually united into a nation called England, their closely related Germanic dialects evolved over time into a distinct language called English—today usually called Old English to distinguish it from later forms of the language. Old English was very different from the English we speak today. Harsher in sound, it was written phonetically, with no silent letters. Grammatically, it was more complex than modern English, with words changing form to indicate different functions, so that word order was more flexible than it is now. The most valuable characteristic of the language, how- ever, was its ability to change and grow, adopting new words as the need arose.

Literary History

Although the early Anglo-Saxons did have a writing system, called the runic alphabet, they used it mainly for inscriptions on coins, monuments, and the like. Their literature was composed and transmitted orally rather than in writing. In the mead halls of kings and nobles, where the Anglo-Saxons gathered to eat, drink, and socialize, oral poets called scops celebrated the deeds of heroic warriors in long **epic poems.** They also sang shorter, **lyric poems.** In some of these, deaths or other losses are mourned in the mood of bleak fatalism characteristic of early Anglo-Saxon times. Many of the lyrics composed after the advent of Christianity express religious faith or offer moral instruction. Others reflect a more playful nature: the brief Anglo-Saxon **riddles,** for example, describe familiar objects, like a ship or a bird, in ways that force the audience to guess their identity.

Making Connections

Literature

A Julius Caesar (100–44 B.C.) was not only a brilliant and charismatic general and politician but also one of the greatest prose stylist of his day. His contemporaries considered him second only to Cicero as an orator. For centuries, Caesar's *Commentaries on the Gallic War* (c. 55–44 B.C.) was used to introduce English schoolchildren to the Latin language and its literature. Book IV of the *Commentaries* covers Caesar's first expedition to Britain.

History

B The druids served not only as priests but also as judges and counselors. They educated the sons of chiefs and preserved religious and cultural traditions. According to Julius Caesar, the druids knew how to use the Greek alphabet but did not allow writing, since they wanted to preserve their culture by means of the oral tradition.

Anthropology

C Celtic languages and culture live on in modern times. Many Celtic regions preserve ancient traditions, such as the playing of bagpipes in Scotland, Ireland, and Galicia (in Spain). People continue to speak Celtic languages in Wales, Scotland, and Brittany. In the Republic of Ireland, Irish, not English, is the first official language.

Performance Art

D To help them create their poems, scops probably carried in their heads a large store of stock phrases and verbal patterns. However, they still needed to be improvisers, since they did not memorize poems word for word but clothed their stories in words as they sang—in effect presenting a unique version with every performance.

Teaching Nonfiction

SUMMARIZING

When students have finished reading this article, have them use their notes to help them write a summary of the major points of "The Anglo-Saxon and Medieval Periods, 449–1485." Remind them that a summary includes the main ideas and supporting details, but does not include their opinions.

MAIN IDEA AND SUPPORTING DETAILS

Though the article as a whole reflects organization by chronological order, smaller sections such as "The Growth of Christianity" are organized on the principle of main idea and supporting details. Ask students to find details supporting the idea of Christianity's growth in the British Isles.

Possible Response: Patrick converted Ireland's Gaels to Christianity in the 5th century. Missionaries from Iona spread Christianity to the Picts and Angles in the north British Isles. Augustine established a Roman monastery at Canterbury, from where Christianity then spread to all of Britain by the end of the 7th century.

of seven kingdoms called the Heptarchy. In the southeast was Kent, kingdom of the Jutes. Further west were the Saxon kingdoms of Sussex, Essex, and Wessex. To the north were the kingdoms of the Angles—East Anglia, Mercia, and Northumbria. Perhaps because the Angles were dominant in the early history of the Heptarchy, the area of Germanic settlement became known as Angle-land, or England, and its people came to be called the English. Modern scholars, however, usually employ the term *Anglo-Saxon* to refer to the people and culture of this period of English history.

Like all cultures, that of the Anglo-Saxons changed over time. The early invaders were seafaring wanderers
A whose lives were bleak, violent, and short. With them, they brought their pagan religion—marked by a strong belief in *wyrd,* or fate—and their admiration for heroic warriors whose *wyrd* it was to prevail in battle. As they settled into their new land, however, the Anglo-Saxons became an agricultural people—less violent, more secure, more civilized. One of the most important civilizing forces was the Christianity they began accepting late in the sixth century.

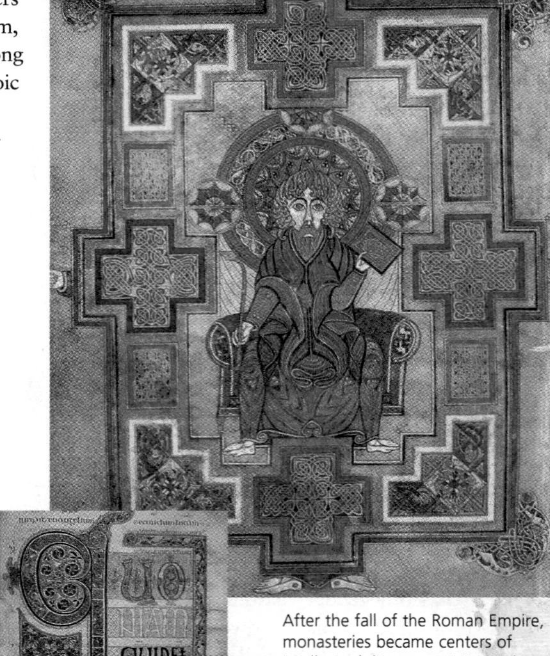

On Lindisfarne, a tiny island off the Northumbrian coast, monks produced the beautiful Bible manuscript known as the Lindisfarne Gospels.

After the fall of the Roman Empire, monasteries became centers of intellectual, literary, artistic, and social activity. The Book of Kells is an illuminated gospel book begun in an Irish monastery in the late eighth century.

The Growth of Christianity

Despite the collapse of Roman power there, Christianity had never completely died out in the British Isles. Early in the fifth century a Romanized Briton named Patrick
B had converted Ireland's Gaels to Christianity. When the Gaels began colonizing Scotland, they brought Christianity in their wake. From the isle of Iona off the Scottish coast, missionaries spread the faith among the Picts and Angles in the north. Later, in 597, a Roman missionary named Augustine arrived in the kingdom of Kent, where he established a monastery at
C Canterbury. From there, Christianity spread so rapidly that by 690 all of Britain was at least nominally Christian.

Mini Lesson: Viewing and Representing

The Book of Kells, anonymous

ART APPRECIATION

Instruction Written on prepared calfskin, the Book of Kells has been described by a 13th century historian as "the work, not of men, but of angels." It is a large-format, 680-page manuscript of the Latin text of the Biblical gospels and was designed for use on the altar. (Kells, known today as Ceanannus, is an urban district about 35 miles northwest of Dublin.) It is the major work in the style produced by monks who let their imaginations run riot with decorative illuminations such as brightly colored geometric shapes and intricate designs and patterns. Here a seated St. John holds the tools of a scribe: a stylized quill pen in one hand and his gospel book in the other. Near his right foot is an inkpot, apparently carved from a cow horn and stuck in the ground. Use the following questions to help develop students' visual literacy.

The Danish Invasions

In the 790s, a new group of northern European invaders—the Danes, also known as the Vikings—began to devastate Northumbria's flourishing culture. Coming at first to loot monasteries, the Danes in time gained control of much of (D) northern and eastern England. They were less successful in the south, where their advance was halted by a powerful king of Wessex, Alfred the Great. After inflicting defeats on the Danes in 878 and 886, Alfred forced them to agree to a truce and to accept Christianity.

Although Alfred's reign was a high point in Anglo-Saxon civilization, the tug-of-war with the Danes resumed after his death. In 1016 a Dane named Canute even managed to become king of all England; he proved a successful ruler and won the support of many Anglo-Saxon noblemen. Less successful was the deeply religious Edward the Confessor, who came to the throne in 1042. Edward, who had no children, had once sworn an oath making William, duke of Normandy, his heir—or so William claimed. Later, Edward was persuaded to name Harold, earl of Wessex, as his heir. When Edward died in 1066, the English witan (an advisory council of nobles and church officials) supported Harold's claim. Incensed, William led his Normans in what was to be the last successful invasion of the island of Britain: the Norman Conquest. Harold was killed at the Battle of Hastings, and on Christmas Day of 1066, a triumphant William—who would go down in history as William the Conqueror—was crowned king of England.

Ornamental pin commissioned by Alfred the Great

Literary History

The spread of Christianity in Britain was accompanied by a spread of literacy and by the introduction of the Roman alphabet in place of the runic alphabet. Though poetry remained primarily an oral art, poems were now more likely to get written down. In this age before printing, however, the only books were manuscripts that scribes copied by hand. Thus, only a fraction of Anglo-Saxon poetry has survived, in manuscripts produced centuries after the poems were composed. The most famous survivor is the epic *Beowulf,* about a legendary hero of the northern European past. A manuscript known as the Exeter Book contains many of the surviving Anglo-Saxon lyrics, including "The Seafarer," "The Wife's Lament," and over 90 riddles.

Most Old English poems are anonymous. One of the few poets known by name is a monk called Caedmon,

described by the Venerable Bede in his famous eighth-century history of England. Like most scholars of his day, Bede wrote in Latin, the language of the church. (E) It was not until the reign of Alfred the Great that writing in English began to be widespread. In 891, Alfred initiated the compiling of the *Anglo-Saxon Chronicle,* a historic record in poetry and prose that was added to, on and off, until early Norman times. He also encouraged English translations of portions of the Bible and other Latin works.

Inset above: Detail from an illuminated Bible

Ask: What would you say makes the seated figure of St. John so attention-grabbing?

Possible Response: St. John has a wide-eyed stare, and his head is surrounded by highly decorative haloes. The seated figure itself is surrounded by an assortment of red, blue, and yellow geometric patterns and interwoven designs that invite closer inspection.

Making Connections

Sociology

(A) Early Anglo-Saxon society centered on ancestral tribes or clans, each ruled by a chieftain surrounded by a group of warriors who served him in return for rewards and protection. Not surprisingly, loyalty to the chieftain and love of battle figure as prominent themes in Anglo-Saxon poems.

Culture

(B) Ironically, much Latin learning was preserved in Ireland, which had never been part of the Roman Empire.

Concurrent History

(C) At the time that Christianity was spreading throughout Britain, a new religion, Islam, was working its way into Europe. Islam was founded in the early 600s by Muhammad. By the time of Muhammad's death in 632, most of the Arabian Peninsula was united under Islam. In the century that followed, his followers—Muslims—settled in parts of India and conquered North Africa and Spain. Their progress north brought them to within 100 miles of Paris before being halted at the Battle of Tours in 732. The Muslims then settled back into southern Spain.

Concurrent History

(D) While the Vikings were beginning their raids in England, Charlemagne (742?–814), the ruler of a Germanic people known as Franks, was uniting western and central Europe, from the North to the Mediterranean seas. Only the Iberian peninsula, where the Muslims had settled after the Battle of Tours, escaped his control. Charlemagne's empire spread Christianity and laid the foundations of the Holy Roman Empire.

Literature

(E) Alfred the Great (849–899) knew Latin and encouraged the average person to learn to read and write. Beyond that, his main achievement is considered the promoting of Old English literary prose. Like Charlemagne, Alfred surrounded himself with scholars and made his court a center of learning. Because the Vikings had destroyed so many monasteries, much of his scholars' time was spent in recovering and copying existing works instead of producing new ones. Alfred himself may have helped to translate Bede's *History of the English Church and People.*

Making Connections

Economics

A In 1085, to ensure his tax revenues and a continuous flow of funds, William ordered the compilation of a detailed survey of the land and population of England, including every piece of property, the number of workers and animals on it, and the name of its owner. This so-called Domesday Book, completed in 1086, gives modern scholars an invaluable picture of English society at the time. (*Domesday* is a variant of the word *doomsday,* meaning "day of judgment," and is pronounced the same way.)

Sociology

B In feudal society, the position of a woman depended on that of her husband or father. A woman and her property were always under the custody of a man—if she was widowed, under that of her eldest son or her husband's overlord. Women's principal occupation was the running of their households; their other activities included such tasks as spinning, weaving, and sewing. Although always subservient to her husband, a woman held the same rank in society as he. When her husband was absent from home, she controlled not only the household but also whatever land he owned. Thus, her responsibilities could include authority over hundreds of people.

Architecture

C The surviving Norman cathedrals are among the most important examples of Romanesque architecture. Some churches were built in gratitude to God, some as acts of penitence—such as Battle Abbey, which William ordered built near Hastings. Other churches were built on pilgrimage routes. The construction on the great cathedrals of Ely, Durham, Lincoln, Peterborough, and Winchester all began in Norman times, with many of them taking decades, some even centuries, to complete. In all, after 1070, the Normans built hundreds of parish churches. Massive in size and richly decorated, these churches were modeled on Roman basilicas but anticipated techniques of the later Gothic architecture.

The Medieval Period
1066–1485

Like the Danes of Britain, the Normans (whose name means "north men") had originally been Viking raiders from northern Europe. However, after settling in the region that became known as Normandy, just northeast of Britanny on the coast of France, the Normans had adopted French ways. Now William introduced these practices to England, beginning the medieval (or middle) period in English history.

A Probably the most significant of William's introductions was feudalism, a political and economic system in which the hierarchy of power was based on the premise that the king owned all the land in the kingdom. Keeping a fourth for himself and granting a fourth to the church, William parceled out the rest of England to loyal nobles—mostly Norman barons—who, in return, either paid him or supplied him with warriors called knights. The barons swore allegiance to the king, the knights to their barons, and so on down the social ladder. B At the bottom of the ladder were the conquered Anglo-Saxons, many of whom were serfs—peasants bound to land they could not own. To protect Norman interests, barons were encouraged to build strong castles from which they could dominate the countryside and defend the realm from attack; at the same time, great cathedrals and abbeys were erected on the new church lands. C

Because William's successors were less strong and organized than he, power struggles among the barons

Hoping to influence the church, Henry II appointed his friend Thomas à Becket archbishop of Canterbury. When the archbishop began favoring church interests over those of the crown, Henry's sharp criticisms prompted four loyal knights to murder Becket. Henry quickly proclaimed his innocence and reconciled with the church; Becket was declared a saint, his shrine at Canterbury becoming a popular destination for Christian pilgrims.

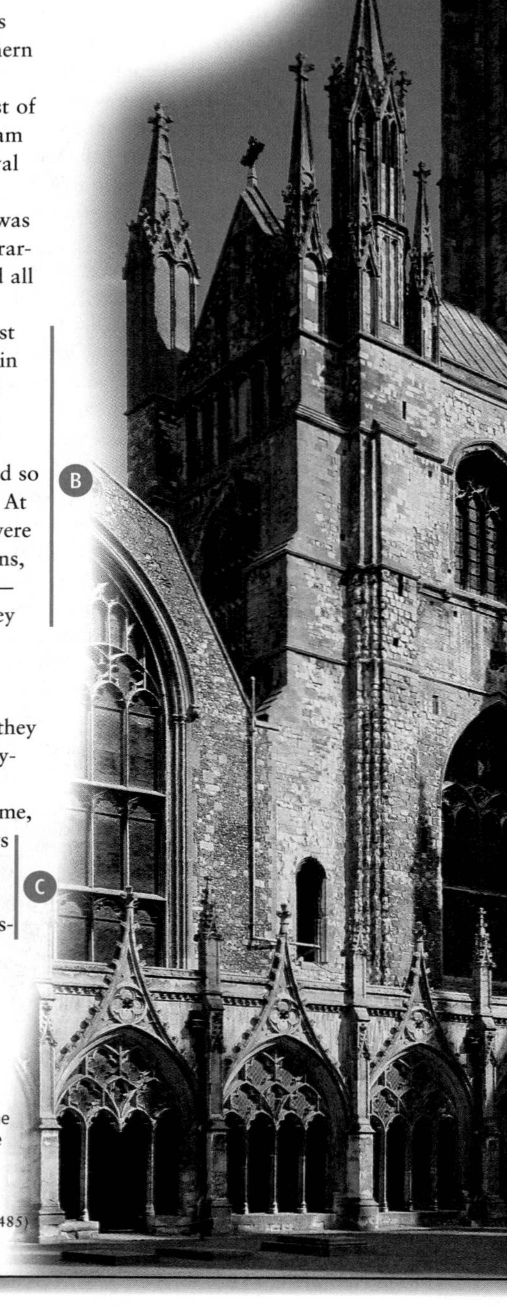

Canterbury Cathedral, begun in the 11th century, reflects the influence of Norman architecture.

Mini Lesson Development of the English Language

WORD ORIGINS

Make certain that students understand that the "evil" that they hear pronounced at the end of *medieval* does not come from the word *evil.* The medieval era is not "a time of evil." Its nickname "the Dark Ages" is an overreaction and refers mainly to the years before 1000. Have students work in pairs to research the origin of *medieval,* breaking the word down into its two parts. Ask students to describe how the two roots set up the word's meaning. (Latin, *medium,* middle; *aevum,* age)

were common in the decades after his death. When William's son Henry I died in 1135, the barons took sides in a violent struggle for power between Henry's daughter Matilda and his nephew Stephen. The near anarchy ended in 1154, when Matilda's son Henry Plantagenet took the throne as Henry II. One of medieval England's most memorable rulers, Henry reformed the judicial system, instituting royal courts throughout the country, establishing a system of juries, and initiating the formation of English common law out of a patchwork of centuries-old practices.

At least as colorful as Henry II was his wife, Eleanor of Aquitaine, a former French queen who had brought as her dowry vast landholdings in (D) France. From French court circles she also brought the ideals of chivalry, a code of honor intended to govern knightly behavior. The code encouraged knights to honor and protect ladies and to go on holy quests—like the Crusades, the military expeditions in (E) which European Christians attempted to wrest the holy city of Jerusalem from Moslem control.

Henry's son Richard I, called Richard the Lion-Hearted, spent much of his ten-year reign fighting in the Crusades and in France, where English possessions were threatened. During his absence, his treacherous brother John—the villain of many Robin Hood legends—plotted against him. When Richard died and John became king, he found that the royal

Jousting knights

Development of the English Language

The Norman Conquest led to great changes in the English language. Despite their Viking origins, by 1066 the Normans spoke a dialect of Old French, which they brought to England with them. Norman French became the language of the English court, of government business, of the new nobility, and of the scholars, cooks, and craftspeople that the Norman barons brought with them to serve their more "refined" needs. The use of English became confined to the conquered, mostly peasant population. Ever adaptable, however, English soon incorporated thousands of words and many grammatical conventions from Norman French. These changes led to the development of Middle English, a form much closer than Old English to the language we speak today.

Literary History

As English became the language of a mostly illiterate peasantry, the common folk again relied on the oral tradition to tell their stories and express their feelings. Many of their compositions were folk ballads, brief narrative poems sung to musical accompaniment. The later Middle Ages saw the flowering of **mystery** and **miracle plays,** which dramatized episodes from the Bible and from saints' lives, and **morality plays,** which taught (F) moral lessons. From these simple plays, intended to convey religious truths to an audience only partly literate, arose the great tradition of English drama.

Making Connections

Humanities

(D) Eleanor (c. 1122–1204) was arguably the most powerful woman in the 12th century. She was also a great patroness of troubadours—poets who principally wrote song of courtly love but also wrote poems about religion and politics. One of the tenets of the chivalric code was that love of a lady ennobled a man, making him a better knight or a better poet. Of course, the greater the lady's rank, the higher the prestige for her lover; so great ladies tended to collect admirers. When her husband, Henry II, imprisoned her in Winchester Castle in 1174 for siding with her sons against him, Eleanor's situation was much lamented in song.

History

(E) The Crusades (1096–1270) were the Christian response to the expansion of Islam. The eight major expeditions established the leadership of the Roman Catholic Church and were a powerful expression of the growing energy of the Christian civilization of western Europe. For the knights who participated, the Crusades were a combination of pilgrimage and holy war. However, some knights, especially in the later Crusades, participated in the quests for personal gain, believing the eastern Mediterranean area to be a region of great wealth ripe for plunder.

Literary History

(F) Mystery, miracle, and morality plays were tremendously popular until Shakespeare's time, when Protestant opposition put an end to them. Town guilds were often responsible for producing miracle plays, and a guild would often choose to represent a subject connected with its members' occupation. Carpenters or shipwrights, for example, might stage the story of Noah's ark.

Making Connections

Law

(A) The king's Great Council, which had come to be called Parliament, was a meeting of the barons to deal with legal cases, military issues, and taxation. Perhaps because he wanted the general public to understand and approve of his taxes, Edward I called knights and town representatives, as well as nobles and clergy, to Parliament. This set a precedent for making Parliament a more representative body.

Economics

(B) The Crusades fostered the development of a money economy. New methods of taxation had to be developed to finance them, and the capture of wealthy Islamic cities exposed the Crusaders to a finer way of life. As Europeans developed a taste for Eastern products and the market for these grew, so did trade and banking.

Government

(C) Because every town was located on some lord's lands, its inhabitants were subject to the taxes and laws he imposed. One of the important functions of the guilds was to fight the lord's control. By the 12th century, however, towns were obtaining royal charters that gave them the right to maintain their own municipal governments, law courts, and systems of taxation. Although the towns' citizens still had to pay fees and taxes to their lords, they did so collectively, thus avoiding personal harassment. Farsighted lords, eager for the revenues that towns and their markets could generate, founded towns themselves.

Right: Flexible body armor called mail was made from iron links.

treasury had been bankrupted by overseas warfare. In 1215 he was forced to sign the Magna Carta ("Great Charter"), which limited royal authority by granting more power to the barons and thus was an early step on the road to democracy. During the reign of John's son Henry III, an advisory council of barons—now called a parliament—began to meet regularly. Under his successor, Edward I, the Model Parliament of 1295 established the inclusion of commoners (eventually to become the House of Commons) as well as barons (the "House of Lords") in the council. (A)

The Decline of Feudalism

The growth of the commoners' power went hand in hand with the growth of medieval towns, a result of an increase in trade that was stimulated in part by the Crusades. (B) In the towns, merchants and craftspeople formed organizations called guilds to control the flow and price of goods and to set up rules for advancing from apprentice to master craftsman. (C) The

King Philip II of France *(above),* along with Richard the Lion-Hearted and Frederick I of Germany, was a leader of the forces attempting to recapture Jerusalem in the Third Crusade (1189–1192).

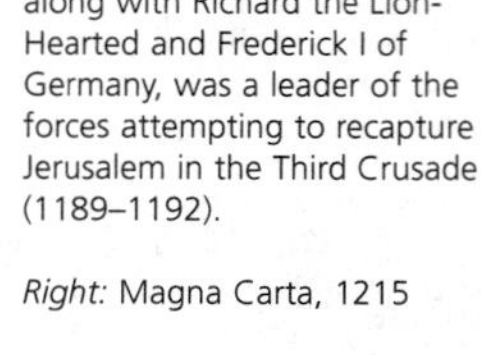

Right: Magna Carta, 1215

Wool, an important product in medieval commerce, was shipped from sheep farms to market towns, where merchants exchanged money for goods.

The spread of ideas was greatly assisted by a landmark innovation in 15th-century Europe—the printing press.

growth of towns meant the decline of feudalism, since wealth was no longer based exclusively on land ownership. On the other hand, the crowding of townspeople in conditions of poor sanitation ensured that diseases like plague could spread rapidly.

D As towns were becoming centers of commerce, universities were becoming England's chief centers of learning. At Oxford University, 13th-century scholars like Roger Bacon advanced the study of science and mathematics. A century later, an Oxford scholar named John Wycliffe led an effort to end widespread church corruption. Though his followers, the Lollards, were suppressed, his ideas spread to John Huss in central Europe and through him influenced the later religious reformer Martin Luther.

The Hundred Years' War

Wycliffe's reform efforts took place during the Hundred Years' War, a long struggle between England and France that had begun in 1337 during the reign of Edward III. As the war continued on and off for more than a century, England also had to weather several domestic crises, including a great epidemic of plague known as the Black Death, which killed a third of England's popu-

Literary History

Religious faith was a vital element of medieval English life and literature. One of the most distinctive products of the age is the long poem known as Piers Plowman, a dream vision that explores Christianity's spiritual mysteries. Religious devotion is also the key concern of *The Book of Margery Kempe,* an autobiography in which Kempe focuses on her spiritual growth. In contrast, far more worldly attitudes are expressed in the surviving correspondence of the Paston family. These remarkable letters, written from about 1420 to 1500 and discovered centuries later by one of the Pastons' descendants, provide fascinating glimpses of life in later medieval times.

E Especially popular in the Middle Ages were **romances**—tales of chivalric knights, many of which feature King Arthur and the members of his court. For centuries the oral poets of the Britons in Wales had celebrated their legendary hero Arthur just as Anglo-Saxon scops had celebrated Beowulf. Then, about 1135, the monk Geoffrey of Monmouth produced a Latin "history" based on the old Welsh legends. Geoffrey's book caught the fancy of French, German, and English writers, who soon produced their own versions of the legends, updating them to reflect then-current notions of chivalry. In about 1375, an anonymous English poet produced *Sir Gawain and the Green Knight,* recounting the marvelous adventures of a knight of Arthur's court. A century later, in *Le Morte d'Arthur,* Sir Thomas Malory retold a number of the French Arthurian tales in Middle English.

Making Connections

Education

D As the written word came into increasing use in government, the church, and the courts, education became necessary for advancement, and students gathered wherever teachers were to be found. The term *university* was originally synonymous with *guild* and referred to any organized group. Some universities were organized by students to protect themselves from having to pay excessive rents for classrooms and exorbitant rates for food and lodging; some, such as Oxford University, were originally organizations of teachers. Others were outgrowths of municipal schools or of schools that cathedrals maintained for the education of the clergy. After mastering the seven liberal arts (grammar, rhetoric, astronomy, logic, geometry, arithmetic, and music), a student could receive a license to teach anywhere or could go on to study civil law, medicine, or theology.

Literary History

E Also popular in Europe were tales of Charlemagne's knights, or paladins. Characters such as Oliver, Archbishop Turpin, Astolfo, Rinaldo, and the evil Ganelon—whom Dante placed in hell and Chaucer cited as an exemplar of treachery in "The Nun's Priest's Tale"—figured in many poems. The greatest of Charlemagne's legendary warriors was Roland, or Orlando, who became the hero of the French epic *La Chanson de Roland,* and of the Italian romances *Orlando Innamorato* and *Orlando Furioso.*

HISTORICAL BACKGROUND 25

Making Connections

Language

A After the English lost Normandy in 1204, English gradually became the language of trade and government in the country. In 1362, English became the official language of the courts of law by royal decree. The Middle English romances and the work of Chaucer further bolstered the status of English by legitimizing it as a literary language.

Literary History

B As a teenager, Chaucer (1340/43–1400) joined King Edward III's army to fight the French in the Hundred Years' War. He was captured in 1359 during an unsuccessful siege on the fortified northern French town of Reims, and the king himself ransomed him. A few years later Chaucer began his writings, producing such major works as *The House of Fame, The Parliament of Fowls,* and the great love poem *Troilus and Criseyde* between 1369 and 1387. At that time he began his epic *The Canterbury Tales,* which was incomplete at the time of his death 13 years later.

History

C On his mother's side, Henry, son of Edmund Tudor, was a direct descendant of John of Gaunt, duke of Lancaster, by John's morganatic marriage to Katharine Roet. Ever a practical man, Henry married Elizabeth of York to settle the question of inheritance and bring the Wars of the Roses to an end. Henry was the first monarch of the Tudor dynasty.

Development of the English Language

A As warfare with France dragged on, English not only survived but triumphed. Among England's upper class it came to seem unpatriotic to use the language of the nation's number one enemy, especially since the Anglo-Norman variety of French was ridiculed by the "real" French speakers across the English Channel. By the end of the Hundred Years' War, English had once again become the first language of most of the English nobility.

Literary History

B In the rebirth of English as a language of literature, no writer was more important than the 14th-century poet Geoffrey Chaucer, the towering figure of Middle English letters. Chaucer's masterpiece, *The Canterbury Tales,* is a collection of tales supposedly narrated by a group of pilgrims traveling from London to Canterbury to visit the shrine of Thomas à Becket. The pilgrims, who come from all walks of medieval life—the castle, the farm, the church, the town—are introduced in the famous "Prologue," where Chaucer weaves a vivid and charming tapestry of English life in the later Middle Ages.

26

lation; the Peasants' Revolt of 1381; and Richard II's forced abdication in 1399, which brought Henry IV to the English throne. The war itself had many famous episodes—like Henry V's great victory over the French at Agincourt and the French army's lifting of the siege of Orléans under the inspired leadership of the young peasant woman Joan of Arc. When the war finally ended in 1453, England had lost nearly all of its French possessions. It was also on the verge of a conflict in which two rival families claimed the throne—the house of York, whose symbol was a white rose, and the house of Lancaster, whose symbol was a red rose. The fighting, C known as the Wars of the Roses, ended in 1485, when the Lancastrian Henry Tudor killed the Yorkist king Richard III at Bosworth Field and took the throne as Henry VII. This event is usually taken as marking the end of the Middle Ages in England.

In medieval art, the Black Death was often portrayed as a skeleton.

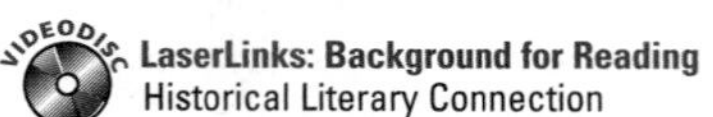

LaserLinks: Background for Reading
Historical Literary Connection

During the Hundred Years' War, the use of the longbow helped the English to inflict heavy casualties on the French, who were armed with the less efficient crossbow.

Cross Curricular Link Humanities

Use **Fine Art Transparencies** pp. 17, 18, and 19 in **Communication Transparencies and Copymasters** to acquaint students with art of the period.

PART 1 Tests of Courage

The Anglo-Saxon and medieval periods were ones of turmoil and change—times when people's courage was frequently put to the test. Amid this turmoil, the tests of courage often took the form of physical challenges, such as confronting a dreaded foe or battling to survive on the high seas. Other tests of courage involved spiritual or emotional challenges, such as standing up for one's religious beliefs or enduring the absence of a loved one. As you read about tests of courage in this part of Unit One, try to place yourself in the distant past and imagine how you would respond to similar challenges.

27

OVERVIEW

Objectives
- understand the following literary terms:
  - epic
  - stock epithet
  - kenning
- recognize shared characteristics of cultures through reading
- recognize themes across cultures

Teaching the Lesson

In this unit students will be reading epics written hundreds of years ago. This lesson will give them some background on the epic as a literary form and on literary concepts related to the epic.

Introducing the Concepts
In times past, listeners were held spellbound by the power of the epic. Probably no two performances of an epic were exactly alike. Today's epic heroes may not be exactly like Beowulf or Achilles, but they share some important similarities. As students read the epics in this unit, have them consider the following questions:

What modern professions are most similar to the professions of epic heroes such as Beowulf, Ramayana, or Achilles?
Possible Responses: state leaders, soldiers

In traditional epics, heroes are generally male. What roles do women play? How does the role change in some modern epic prose?
Possible Responses: Women generally are in the background in supporting roles. In some modern epic literature, women play roles similar to those played by men: starship commanders, warrior princesses.

As they finish reading epic selections, students can write reactions to these questions and keep their responses in their Working Portfolios.

LEARNING the Language of Literature

The Epic

Oral Heroic Narrative—An Epic Task

Imagine that you're performing with an improvisational theater group. First, you are asked to pretend that you're an Automated Teller Machine (ATM) that intentionally tries people's patience. Easy, you think. Next, you must play a butcher who can't stand the sight of meat. No problem. Then a scholarly-looking man asks you to recite a long narrative poem about the heroic struggles of a legendary figure who uses strength, cunning, and help from the gods to survive perilous trials—and you have to use elevated, solemn language throughout. You're speechless, uncomprehending, until it hits you—the man wants an epic.

What Is an Epic?

An **epic** is a long narrative poem that celebrates a hero's deeds. The earliest epic tales survived for centuries as oral traditions before they were finally written down. They came into existence as spoken words and were retold by poet after poet from one generation to the next. Most orally composed epics date back to preliterate periods—before the cultures that produced them had developed written forms of their languages.

Many epics are based in historical fact, so that their public performance by poets (known in different cultures by such names as *scops* or *bards)* provided both entertainment and education for the audience. Oral poets had to be master improvisers, able to compose verse in their heads while simultaneously singing or chanting it. These poets didn't make up their stories from scratch, however; they drew on existing songs and legends, which they could embellish or combine with original material.

One characteristic feature of oral poetry is the repetition of certain words, phrases, or even lines. Two of the most notable examples of repeated elements are stock epithets and kennings.

Stock epithets are adjectives that point out special traits of particular persons or things. In Homer, stock epithets are often compound adjectives, such as the "swift-footed" used to describe Achilles.

Kennings are poetic synonyms found in Germanic poems, such as the Anglo-Saxon epic *Beowulf.* Rather than being an adjective, like an epithet, a kenning is a descriptive phrase or compound word that substitutes for a noun. For example, in *Beowulf* "the Almighty's enemy" and "sin-stained demon" are two kennings that are used in place of Grendel's name.

Stock epithets and kennings were building blocks that a poet could recite while turning his attention to the next line or stanza. Epithets had an added advantage—they were designed to fit metrically into specific parts of the lines of verse. In skillful hands, these "formulas" helped to establish tone and reinforce essentials of character and setting.

Characteristics of an Epic

Epics from different languages and time periods do not always have the same characteristics. Kennings, for example, are not found in Homer's epics. However, the following characteristics are shared by most epics, whether they were composed orally or in

Presenting the Concepts
Read through the strategies on page 29 aloud or project them on a transparency. Using the Characteristics of an Epic, also listed on page 29, identify a piece of prose, a popular adventure novel, or a movie that would be considered epic in its scale. Model how to use the strategies to analyze and evaluate the story.
Possible Response: The movie *Braveheart,* set in early 14th Century Scotland, might be considered a story told on an epic scale. Its hero, William Wallace, is extremely courageous, leading thousands of Scotsmen to revolt against English rule. The theme of the story is "No price is too high to pay for a country's freedom," the lines between good and evil are clearly drawn, and even under torture, Wallace doesn't give up his cry for freedom.

 Use **Literary Analysis Transparencies** pp. 1, 2 to project these sentences.

writing, in the Middle Ages or last year, in Old English or in Slovak:

- The hero, generally a male, is of noble birth or high position, and often of great historical or legendary importance.
- The hero's character traits reflect important ideals of his society.
- The hero performs courageous—sometimes even superhuman—deeds that reflect the values of the era.
- The actions of the hero often determine the fate of a nation or group of people.
- The setting is vast in scope, often involving more than one nation.
- The poet uses formal diction and a serious tone.
- Major characters often deliver long, formal speeches.
- The plot is complicated by supernatural beings or events and may involve a long and dangerous journey through foreign lands.
- The poem reflects timeless values, such as courage and honor.
- The poem treats universal themes, such as good and evil or life and death.

The Epic Across Cultures

The epic is not a dead form. Although epics were sung by Sumerians as far back as the third millennium B.C., new oral epics continue to be created and recited in places like the Balkans and Southeast Asia. Many poets around the world still write poems in the epic tradition, and the epic spirit animates many prose works, such as J. R. R. Tolkien's *The Lord of the Rings,* a popular fantasy novel. Many contemporary films are also cast in an epic mold, including such Hollywood hits as the *Star Wars* trilogy, which features an intergalactic struggle between the forces of good and evil.

YOUR TURN What evidence of epic features might you expect to find in the *Star Wars* trilogy?

Strategies for Reading: The Epic

1. Notice which characteristics of epics appear in the poem you are reading.
2. Decide what virtues the hero embodies.
3. Decide if the epic's values are still held today.
4. Determine the hero's role in bringing about any changes in fortune for the characters.
5. Use a list or diagram to keep track of the characters.
6. If a passage confuses you, go back and summarize the main idea of the passage.
7. When reading *Beowulf* (page 32) or the *Iliad* (page 67), use the accompanying Guide for Reading to help you clarify the language and form your own interpretation.
8. Monitor your reading strategies and modify them when your understanding breaks down. Remember to use your Strategies for Active Reading: **predict, visualize, connect, question, clarify,** and **evaluate.**

Making Connections

Epic Heroes Across Cultures

Many cultures developed epics celebrating the glories of their heroes. Share the descriptions of these heroes.

Sunjata (Mali, Africa)
Sunjata is the lame son of an Old Mali king and his second wife. Willing himself to walk, Sunjata becomes so strong and powerful that he kills a beast that has been terrorizing the kingdom. When his father's first wife plots to kill him, Sunjata is forced into a seven-year exile. During his exile, an evil sorcerer-king conquers Sunjata's homeland. Sunjata returns home to defeat the sorcerer-king and reclaim the Manding throne. Under Sunjata's leadership, the kingdom grows and its people live in peace.

Mwindo (Zaire, Africa)
Mwindo's father, a village chief, tries repeatedly to kill his son because he has forbidden his wives to give birth to a male child. The clever and powerful Mwindo, however, earns his father's respect and half his kingdom. Mwindo slays a dragon and travels from the underworld to the heavens. Mwindo returns to teach his people that all forms of life are good and deserve respect and equal consideration. His teachings stress also the importance of being kind and forgiving.

Maui (Polynesia)
No one can get anything done because the sun travels so quickly across the sky. Maui, the trickster-hero, is angry that his mother must rush and work so hard each day to prepare their meals and make their clothing. Maui makes special nooses in which he traps the sun's rays. When the sun tries to burn Maui, Maui attacks him and persuades the sun to travel more slowly for just half the year. During the part of the year when the sun moves slowly, the days become longer.

As students read *Beowulf*, the *Iliad*, and *Ramayana*, have them compare the heros with Sunjata, Mwindo, and Maui.

OVERVIEW

An excerpt of this selection is included in the **Grade 12 InterActive Reader.**

Objectives

1. appreciate a classic **epic (Literary Analysis)**
2. identify **alliteration** and appreciate its effects **(Literary Analysis)**
3. **make judgments** about *Beowulf* as an epic **(Active Reading)**

Summary

Each night for 12 years, the monster Grendel has come out of the darkness to terrorize the Danes. Beowulf, a young prince of the Geats, travels to the Danish shore and offers to kill Grendel with his bare hands. The Danish king Hrothgar gratefully accepts. A fierce battle between Beowulf and the monster ends with the mortal injury of Grendel. When Grendel's mother comes to seek revenge, Beowulf pursues her into the depths of a lake, battles with her, and kills her. Years later, when Beowulf is the aged king of the Geats, he fights a dragon. Beowulf defeats the beast but is mortally wounded during the battle. Beowulf's devoted followers build a tower in his memory.

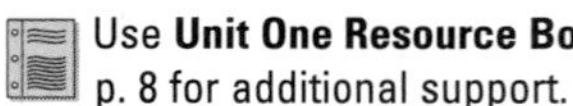
Use **Unit One Resource Book,** p. 8 for additional support.

Thematic Link

Like many epic heroes, Beowulf faces several **tests of courage** during his life. By demonstrating unusual physical strength and skill as well as bravery in the battles with Grendel, Grendel's mother, and the dragon, he earns great respect and honor.

from Beowulf

Epic Poetry by the BEOWULF POET
Translated by BURTON RAFFEL

Comparing Literature of the World

Beowulf and the *Iliad*

This lesson and the one that follows present an opportunity for comparing the epic heroes in *Beowulf* and the *Iliad.* Specific points of comparison in the *Iliad* lesson will help you contrast Beowulf's heroism with that of characters in Homer's epic poem.

Connect to Your Life

Brave Heart According to *The American Heritage Dictionary of the English Language,* a traditional hero is someone "endowed with great courage and strength" and "celebrated for his bold exploits." Are courage, strength, and boldness qualities you look for in a modern hero? Would you say that a hero's deeds have to be celebrated, or at least widely known? Think about people in today's world that you consider heroic. Then, in a cluster diagram like the one shown, jot down the qualities that make these people heroes in your eyes. Use your ideas to help you formulate your own definition of *hero.*

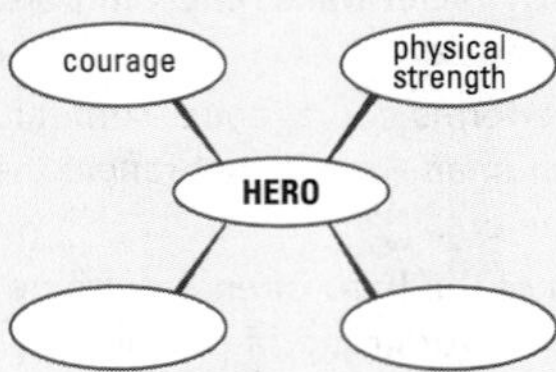

WORDS TO KNOW
Vocabulary Preview

- affliction
- cowering
- fetter
- gorge
- infamous
- lament
- livid
- loathsome
- murky
- pilgrimage
- purge
- relish
- talon
- taut
- writhing

Focus Your Reading

LITERARY ANALYSIS **ALLITERATION** **Alliteration** is the repetition of consonant sounds at the beginning of words. Poets frequently use alliteration to emphasize particular words or images, heighten moods, or create musical effects. In works of the oral tradition, alliteration was also used to aid memorization. In his translation of *Beowulf,* Burton Raffel has used alliteration to suggest the sound and style of the Old English poem.

The ancient blade broke, bit into
The monster's skin, drew blood . . .

Look for other examples of alliteration as you read the excerpts from *Beowulf.*

ACTIVE READING **MAKING JUDGMENTS** On pages 28–29, you were introduced to the characteristics shared by many **epics.** Look for evidence of these characteristics in *Beowulf,* and, on the basis of the evidence you find, **make judgments** about the ways in which the poem resembles and differs from other epics.

READER'S NOTEBOOK Use the information provided on pages 28–29 to create a chart in which you list common characteristics of epics. Then, as you read the excerpts from *Beowulf,* record evidence of the presence or absence of those characteristics in the poem. In your judgment, is *Beowulf* a typical epic?

LESSON RESOURCES

UNIT ONE RESOURCE BOOK, pp. 8–12

ASSESSMENT RESOURCES

Formal Assessment, pp. 7–8
Teacher's Guide to Assessment and Portfolio Use
Test Generator

SKILLS TRANSPARENCIES AND COPYMASTERS

Literary Analysis
- Alliteration, T3 (for Literary Analysis, p. 63)

Reading and Critical Thinking
- Making Judgments, T5 (for Think Critically 6, p. 63)

Grammar
- Diagnostic: Parts of Speech, C61 (for Mini Lesson, p. 32)

Vocabulary
- Using a Thesaurus, C18 (for Mini Lesson, p. 41)
- Words with Multiple Meanings, C19 (for Mini Lesson, p. 56)

Writing
- Showing, Not Telling, T22 (for Writing Option 1, p. 64)
- Compare-Contrast, C34 (for Writing Option 4, p. 64)

Communications
- Reading Aloud, T11 (for Activities & Explorations 2, p. 64)

INTEGRATED TECHNOLOGY

LaserLinks
- Historical Connection: Anglo-Saxon Warriors and *Beowulf*
- Storyteller: Syd Lieberman Tells *Beowulf.* See **Teacher's SourceBook,** p. 6.

Audio Library
Video: Literature in Performance
- *The Battle with Grendel.* See **Video Resource Book,** pp. 3–8

Internet: Research Starter
Visit our website:
www.mcdougallittell.com

Build Background

The Birth of the *Beowulf* Epic After the fall of the Western Roman Empire to Germanic tribes in the fifth century A.D., Europe entered a chaotic period of political unrest and economic and cultural decline. Among the Germanic-speaking tribes of northern Europe, life was dominated by frequent bloody warfare, which drove some of them to abandon their homes for foreign shores. These tribes included groups of Angles, Saxons, and Jutes who settled on the island of Britain, where they established what is now called Anglo-Saxon civilization. Their famous tale of the great hero Beowulf, however, takes place on the European mainland, among two related tribes, the Danes of what is now Denmark and the Geats (gēts or gā-əts) of what is now Sweden.

Beowulf is a Geat warrior who crosses the sea to aid the Danes and later returns to Sweden to succeed his uncle Hygelac (the Higlac of this translation) as king of the Geats. While we cannot be sure whether Beowulf ever really lived, we do know that Hygelac was a historical figure who led a military raid some time around the year 525. The action of *Beowulf* is presumably set not long afterward.

At that time, the northern Germanic societies had not yet adopted Christianity. Their warrior culture celebrated loyalty and deeds of great strength and courage. For entertainment the people gathered in mead halls, large wooden buildings where they feasted, drank mead (an alcoholic beverage), and listened to tales of heroic achievements. Such tales were presented both in the form of long epic poems and in the form of shorter verse narratives. Poet-singers—called scops (shōps) in Anglo-Saxon society—recited the poems in a chanting voice, usually accompanying themselves on a harp.

Old English Text *Beowulf* is the most famous of the early Germanic heroic poems that survive. The form of the poem that has come down to us dates from sometime between the eighth and tenth centuries—after the Anglo-Saxons' conversion to Christianity. It is written in Old English, the language spoken in Britain in the Anglo-Saxon period. As the lines shown below illustrate, Old English neither looks nor sounds like Modern English, and it must therefore be translated for most modern readers.

Old English poetry has a strong rhythm, with each line divided into two parts by a pause, called a **caesura** (sĭ-zhŏŏr′ə). In the Old English text printed here, the caesuras are indicated by extra space in the lines. In his translation, Burton Raffel has often used punctuation to reproduce the effect of the caesuras.

Routes of Anglo-Saxon Invaders

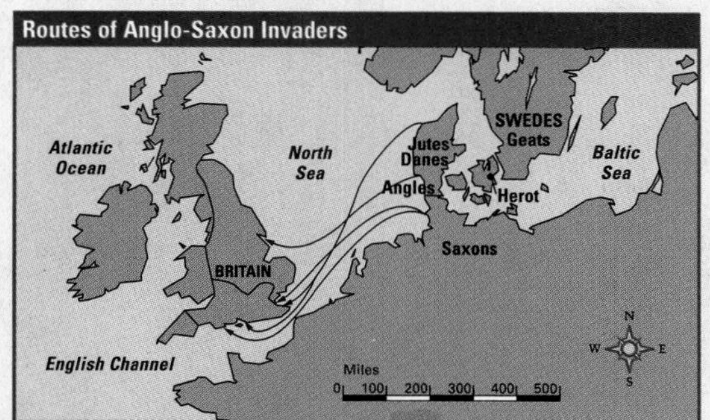

Lines from *Beowulf* in Old English

Ða com of more under misthleoþum
grendel gongan— godes yrre bær;
mynte se manscaða manna cynnes
sumne besyrwan in sele þam hean.

Modern English translation by Burton Raffel

Out from the marsh, from the foot of misty
Hills and bogs, bearing God's hatred,
Grendel came, hoping to kill
Anyone he could trap on this trip to high Herot.

LaserLinks: Background for Reading
Historical Connection

5-Minute Warm-Up

Daily Language SkillBuilder

Have students **proofread** the display sentences on page 15k and write them correctly. The sentences also appear on Transparency 1 of **Grammar Transparencies and Copymasters.**

Mini Lesson Preteaching Vocabulary

RESEARCHING WORD ORIGINS

Instruction Explain that the Germanic languages spoken during the time of *Beowulf* are the roots of Modern English. Although English is considered a Germanic language, many of its words have their origins in Latin and French. In this lesson, students will use dictionaries to find the definitions and word origins of the Words to Know.

Model Write the following example definition and word origin on the board:

affliction 1 A condition of pain, suffering, or distress. **2** A cause of pain, suffering, or distress. From the ME *afflighten* < Lat. *affligere,* to cast down.

Point out to students how they can use the dictionary entry to see that the word *affliction* comes most recently from the Middle English (ME) word *afflighten,* derived from the Latin *affligere.*

Activity Have students copy the definitions and word origins of the remaining Words to Know. Ask them to put checkmarks by the words with Old English or Scandinavian origins. (*cower, fetter, loathsome, writhing*) Forms of these words were used in northern Europe during the time of *Beowulf.*

Use **Unit One Resource Book,** p. 11 for additional support.**Edition.**

TEACHING THE LITERATURE

Reading and Analyzing

Active Reading MAKING JUDGMENTS

A Ask students if they think the opening lines of this passage are gripping, and why. Is the monster a compelling character? Do the opening lines gain their attention? Will a story about a monster and warriors be exciting? What does the presence of a monster suggest about epic poetry? Have students offer their evaluations based on the above questions.

Possible Responses: Students will likely consider the opening lines to be engaging because of the monster's power, pain, and impatience, which suggest an upcoming conflict between the monster and the celebrating warriors.

Use **Unit One Resource Book,** p. 9 for additional support.

Literary Analysis ALLITERATION

B Have students cite examples of the repetition of consonant sounds at the beginning of words.

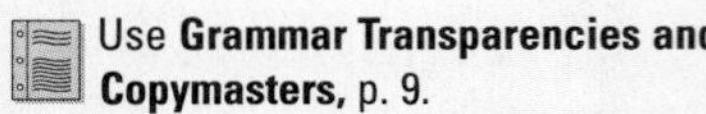
Use **Grammar Transparencies and Copymasters,** p. 9.

Possible Response: Students may note the *l* sound in *land, light, lovely, leaves,* and *life*; the *h* sound in *Hrothgar's, happy,* and *hall.*

Literary Analysis: GENRE

Have students prepare a chart like the one below. As they read, students can look for examples of each characteristic to list in the second column.

Characteristics of Poetry from an Oral Tradition	Examples in *Beowulf*
Strong rhythm	lines 1–7, 233–235, 736–740
Repetition of sounds	all alliteration
Repetition of words and phrases	lines 3, 18–19
Repetition of ideas	lines 16, 273
Parallel grammatical structures	lines 76–78 and 233–234

from BEO

32

Teaching Options

Grammar

DIAGNOSTIC: PARTS OF SPEECH

Instruction Parts of speech—nouns, pronouns, verbs, adjectives, adverbs, prepositions, conjunctions, and interjections—are the building blocks of the English language.

Activity Write the eight parts of speech and the three sentences shown below on the chalkboard. Underline the *mean* in each sentence.

Grendel was not just a mean monster but a fierce and powerful one. (*adj*)

What does Beowulf mean when he says, "Grendel's name has echoed in our land?" (*v*)

The king needs Beowulf's help because the average number—or the mean—of victims falling prey to Grendel's attacks is increasing. (*n*)

Explain that the way a word is used in a sentence determines its part of speech. Have students explain how the word *mean* is used in each sentence. Have them identify the part of speech for each use.

Diagnostic Exercise Have students write the part of speech for each underlined word as it is used in the poem.

WULF

Hrothgar (hrôth'gär'), king of the Danes, has built a wonderful mead hall called Herot (hĕr'ət), where his subjects congregate and make merry. As this selection opens, a fierce and powerful monster named Grendel invades the mead hall, bringing death and destruction.

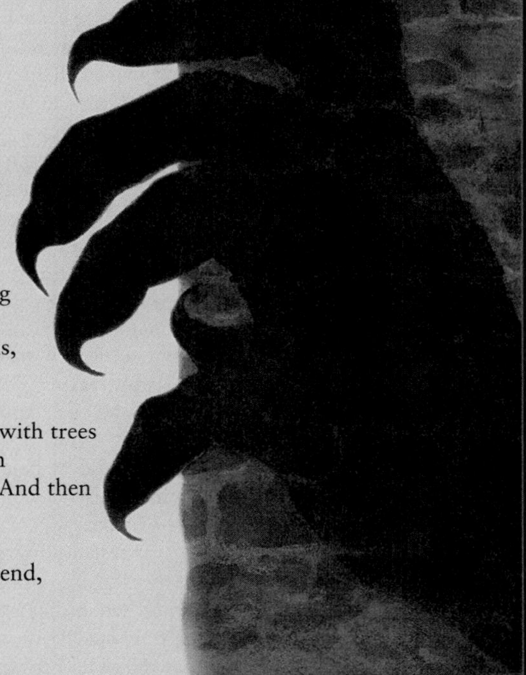

GRENDEL

A powerful monster, living down
(A) In the darkness, growled in pain, impatient
As day after day the music rang
Loud in that hall, the harp's rejoicing
Call and the poet's clear songs, sung
Of the ancient beginnings of us all, recalling
The Almighty making the earth, shaping
These beautiful plains marked off by oceans,
Then proudly setting the sun and moon
To glow across the land and light it;
(B) The corners of the earth were made lovely with trees
And leaves, made quick with life, with each
Of the nations who now move on its face. And then
As now warriors sang of their pleasure:
So Hrothgar's men lived happy in his hall
Till the monster stirred, that demon, that fiend,

33

Customizing Instruction

Less Proficient Readers

- To give students an overall view of the passage, have them scan the selection, noting the illustrations and reading the italicized introductions to each section.
- After students read the introduction and the first 15 lines, have them imagine the types of activities that occur in the mead hall, and have them predict how the appearance of Grendel would affect them. Ask students to read to find out if their predictions are accurate.

Students Acquiring English

- Introduce *Beowulf* by outlining the events in the passage. Most cultures have stories that recount great battles between heroes and monsters. Have students share similar tales from their culture of origin.
- This selection is especially challenging because of the long descriptive sentences and irregular line breaks. Work with students to paraphrase long passages.

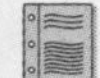

Use **Spanish Study Guide** for additional support, pp. 4–6.

Gifted and Talented

As students read the selection, have them consider what *Beowulf* reveals about Anglo-Saxon attitudes toward the following topics: courage; fate; the span of life; the deceased. When students have finished reading, have them write a short essay comparing some of these attitudes and customs with those practiced today.

"Then Wulfgar went to the door and addressed
The waiting seafarers with soldier's words:
"My lord, the great king of the Danes, commands me
To tell you that he knows of your noble birth
And that having come to him from over the open
Sea you have come bravely and are welcome.
Now go to him as you are, in your armor and helmets,
But leave your battle-shields here, and your spears,
Let them lie waiting for the promises your words
May make."

Use the results of this diagnostic mini lesson to plan grammar instruction.

Use **Grammar Transparencies and Copymasters,** p. 61.

Reading and Analyzing

GUIDE FOR READING

A Grendel was descended from Cain by way of a pair of monsters.

Literary Analysis ALLITERATION

B Note that Old English verse traditionally repeated a particular initial consonant sound in each line. Ask students what initial consonant sound dominates line 31 (*w* sound), line 32 (*d* sound), and line 33 (*s* sound). Then challenge students to locate lines that contain repeated consonant sounds that are **not** all initial consonants. What effect do these repeated sounds have?
Possible Response: For example, line 52 contains four *s* sounds. The repetition creates a hissing effect that may remind some readers of the evil serpent found in the Book of Genesis.

Literary Analysis: FIGURATIVE LANGUAGE

C Have students explain the meaning of "His misery leaped/The seas."
Possible Response: His misery was so terrible that people all over the world heard about it.

Grendel, who haunted the moors, the wild
Marshes, and made his home in a hell
Not hell but earth. He was spawned in that slime,
Conceived by a pair of those monsters born
Of Cain, murderous creatures banished
By God, punished forever for the crime
Of Abel's death. The Almighty drove
Those demons out, and their exile was bitter,
Shut away from men; they split
Into a thousand forms of evil—spirits
And fiends, goblins, monsters, giants,
A brood forever opposing the Lord's
Will, and again and again defeated.

Then, when darkness had dropped, Grendel
Went up to Herot, wondering what the warriors
Would do in that hall when their drinking was done.
He found them sprawled in sleep, suspecting
Nothing, their dreams undisturbed. The monster's
Thoughts were as quick as his greed or his claws:
He slipped through the door and there in the silence
Snatched up thirty men, smashed them
Unknowing in their beds and ran out with their bodies,
The blood dripping behind him, back
To his lair, delighted with his night's slaughter.
At daybreak, with the sun's first light, they saw
How well he had worked, and in that gray morning
Broke their long feast with tears and laments
For the dead. Hrothgar, their lord, sat joyless
In Herot, a mighty prince mourning
The fate of his lost friends and companions,
Knowing by its tracks that some demon had torn
His followers apart. He wept, fearing
The beginning might not be the end. And that night
Grendel came again, so set
On murder that no crime could ever be enough,
No savage assault quench his lust
For evil. Then each warrior tried
To escape him, searched for rest in different
Beds, as far from Herot as they could find,
Seeing how Grendel hunted when they slept.
Distance was safety; the only survivors
Were those who fled him. Hate had triumphed.
So Grendel ruled, fought with the righteous,

GUIDE FOR READING

17 moors (mo͝orz): broad, open regions with patches of bog.

19 spawned: born.

21 Cain: the eldest son of Adam and Eve. According to the Bible (Genesis 4), he murdered his younger brother Abel.

19–29 Who were Grendel's earliest ancestors? How did he come to exist?

40 lair: the den of a wild animal.

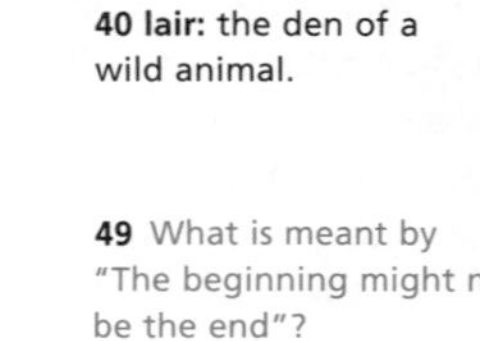

49 What is meant by "The beginning might not be the end"?

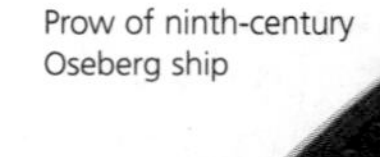

58 In what way has hate triumphed?

Prow of ninth-century Oseberg ship

WORDS TO KNOW **lament** (lə-mĕnt′) *n.* an audible expression of grief; wail

34

Teaching Options

Mini Lesson Viewing and Representing

Prow of Ninth-Century Oseberg Ship

ART APPRECIATION In the early 1900s in Oseberg, Norway, archaeologists discovered a Viking ship that dated to the ninth century. The ship contained a collection of artifacts that have provided scholars with valuable information about medieval life in northern Europe.

Instruction Have students study the photograph of the prow. If necessary, point out how elaborately the prow is carved.

Application Have students speculate about the meaning or purpose of such ornamental design. What does it suggest about the values and practices of medieval society?

Possible Responses: The intricacy and detail of the prow suggests that its builders were also artists, and that the Viking sailors must have taken great pride in their ships. Sailing was important to many people. People living in the Middle Ages probably enjoyed the line, shape, and texture of beautiful objects and ornaments.

One against many, and won; so Herot
Stood empty, and stayed deserted for years,
Twelve winters of grief for Hrothgar, king
Of the Danes, sorrow heaped at his door
By hell-forged hands. His misery leaped
The seas, was told and sung in all
Men's ears: how Grendel's hatred began,
How the monster relished his savage war
On the Danes, keeping the bloody feud
Alive, seeking no peace, offering
No truce, accepting no settlement, no price
In gold or land, and paying the living
For one crime only with another. No one
Waited for reparation from his plundering claws:
That shadow of death hunted in the darkness,
Stalked Hrothgar's warriors, old
And young, lying in waiting, hidden
In mist, invisibly following them from the edge
Of the marsh, always there, unseen.
So mankind's enemy continued his crimes,
Killing as often as he could, coming
Alone, bloodthirsty and horrible. Though he lived
In Herot, when the night hid him, he never
Dared to touch king Hrothgar's glorious
Throne, protected by God—God,
Whose love Grendel could not know. But Hrothgar's
Heart was bent. The best and most noble
Of his council debated remedies, sat
In secret sessions, talking of terror
And wondering what the bravest of warriors could do.
And sometimes they sacrificed to the old stone gods,
Made heathen vows, hoping for Hell's
Support, the Devil's guidance in driving
Their affliction off. That was their way,
And the heathen's only hope, Hell
Always in their hearts, knowing neither God
Nor His passing as He walks through our world, the Lord
Of Heaven and earth; their ears could not hear
His praise nor know His glory. Let them
Beware, those who are thrust into danger,
Clutched at by trouble, yet can carry no solace
In their hearts, cannot hope to be better! Hail
To those who will rise to God, drop off
Their dead bodies and seek our Father's peace!

64 What does the phrase "hell-forged hands" suggest about Grendel?

73 reparation: something done to make amends for loss or suffering. In Germanic society, someone who killed another person was generally expected to make a payment to the victim's family as a way of restoring peace.

84 The reference to God shows the influence of Christianity on the Beowulf Poet. What does Grendel's inability to know God's love suggest about him?

91 heathen (hē'*th*ən): pagan; non-Christian. Though the Beowulf Poet was a Christian, he recognized that the characters in the poem lived before the Germanic tribes were converted to Christianity, when they still worshiped "the old stone gods."

WORDS TO KNOW
relish (rĕl'ĭsh) *v.* to enjoy keenly
affliction (ə-flĭk'shən) *n.* a cause of pain or distress

35

Customizing Instruction

Less Proficient Readers

1 Use the following questions to assess students' comprehension of Grendel's background and his effect on the Danes.

- What people does Grendel attack for 12 years?
  Answer: The Danes.
- What is Grendel's attitude toward the Danes?
  Answer: He wants to destroy their lives and their happiness.
- What universal idea does Grendel stand for?
  Answer: Evil.
- **Set a Purpose** Have students read to find out what kind of person will try to stop Grendel from terrorizing Herot.

Multiple Learning Styles

Auditory Learners

2 To demonstrate the effect of oral poetry, read lines 79–103 aloud two or three times. Use a different tone for each reading (sad, angry, and preachy, for example). Discuss the different effects with students.

Multicultural Link: Oral Poets

Explain that scops, the oral poet-singers of Anglo-Saxon civilization, have their equivalents in many other cultures of the world.

- Among the Celtic peoples of Britain and Ireland, oral poets known as bards preserved tales of great heroes. One of the best-known tales sung by the bards was that of King Arthur.
- Among the people of West Africa, oral historians known as griots preserved and passed on legends of heroic deeds and events. The African epic *Sundiata* is probably the best-known hero tale preserved over the centuries by griots.

Reading and Analyzing

Active Reading **MAKING JUDGMENTS**

(A) The Beowulf Poet uses exaggeration (or *hyperbole*) in lines 110–111 to help emphasize Beowulf's heroism and to give a strong first impression of Beowulf. Ask: What effect does this kind of exaggeration have on epic poetry?
Possible Response: Exaggeration helps create a larger-than-life image of the epic hero.

Reading Skills and Strategies:
DRAWING CONCLUSIONS

(A) (B) (C) Ask students to read lines 110–111, 115–116, and 127–130. Have them make inferences from the lines and draw conclusions about the characteristics of an epic hero. Have them support their conclusions with textual evidence and experience.
Possible Response: Students may say that an epic hero is strong, generous, helpful, of noble birth, and brave.

Literary Analysis:
FIGURATIVE LANGUAGE

(D) Ask students to explain what the poet means by "Light and life fleeing together."
Possible Response: At night, sunlight disappears, and the people leave the mead hall in fear of Grendel.

BEOWULF

So the living sorrow of Healfdane's son
Simmered, bitter and fresh, and no wisdom
Or strength could break it: that agony hung
On king and people alike, harsh
And unending, violent and cruel, and evil.
In his far-off home Beowulf, Higlac's
Follower and the strongest of the Geats—greater
And stronger than anyone anywhere in this world— (A)
Heard how Grendel filled nights with horror
And quickly commanded a boat fitted out,
Proclaiming that he'd go to that famous king,
Would sail across the sea to Hrothgar,
Now when help was needed. None (B)
Of the wise ones regretted his going, much
As he was loved by the Geats: the omens were good,
And they urged the adventure on. So Beowulf
Chose the mightiest men he could find,
The bravest and best of the Geats, fourteen
In all, and led them down to their boat;
He knew the sea, would point the prow
1 Straight to that distant Danish shore.

104 Healfdane's son: Hrothgar.

109–110 Higlac's follower: warrior loyal to Higlac (hĭg′lăk′), king of the Geats (and Beowulf's uncle).

Beowulf and his men sail over the sea to the land of the Danes to offer help to Hrothgar. They are escorted by a Danish guard to Herot, where Wulfgar, one of Hrothgar's soldiers, tells the king of their arrival. Hrothgar knows of Beowulf and is ready to welcome the young prince and his men.

Then Wulfgar went to the door and addressed
The waiting seafarers with soldier's words:
"My lord, the great king of the Danes, commands me
To tell you that he knows of your noble birth
And that having come to him from over the open (C)
Sea you have come bravely and are welcome.
Now go to him as you are, in your armor and helmets,
But leave your battle-shields here, and your spears,
Let them lie waiting for the promises your words
May make."
Beowulf arose, with his men
Around him, ordering a few to remain
With their weapons, leading the others quickly

Teaching Options

Cross Curricular Link **Geography**

CROSSING THE NORTH SEA Using a map or globe, point out northern Europe. Show the locations of England and Denmark. Explain that the sea across which Beowulf and his men sailed is now known as the North Sea and that their journey of about three hundred miles probably lasted a week.

2 Along under Herot's steep roof into Hrothgar's
Presence. Standing on that prince's own hearth,
Helmeted, the silvery metal of his mail shirt
Gleaming with a smith's high art, he greeted
The Danes' great lord:
"Hail, Hrothgar!
Higlac is my cousin and my king; the days
3 Of my youth have been filled with glory. Now Grendel's
Name has echoed in our land: sailors
Have brought us stories of Herot, the best
Of all mead-halls, deserted and useless when the moon
Hangs in skies the sun had lit,
Light and life fleeing together.
My people have said, the wisest, most knowing
And best of them, that my duty was to go to the Danes'
Great king. They have seen my strength for themselves,

139 mail shirt: flexible body armor made of metal links or overlapping metal scales.

140 smith's high art: the skilled craft of a blacksmith (a person who fashions objects from iron).

D **142 cousin:** here, a general term for a relative. Beowulf is actually Higlac's nephew.

Front view of a wooden Viking house in Trelleborg, Denmark, that serves today as an outdoor museum. Such houses had a main door at each end and contained a huge central room where a great fire burned.

Customizing Instruction

Less Proficient Readers

1 To help students **monitor** their own reading strategies, ask them to summarize the opening passage about Beowulf (lines 104–141).

Possible Response: In his distant home, Beowulf, the strongest of the Geats, hears tales of Grendel's brutality. Beowulf decides to sail across the sea and help the suffering Hrothgar and his people. Upon his arrival, he is welcomed by one of Hrothgar's soldiers and then invited into Herot to greet Hrothgar himself.

If students are unable to summarize their reading, have them **modify** their strategies, possibly by summarizing the events described in each section.

Multiple Learning Styles

Visual Learners

2 Before reading Beowulf's speech beginning on page 37 at line 141, invite students to set the scene at Herot by commenting on the picture of the Viking mead hall. What may the interior have looked like?

Possible Response: Students may say that the interior was probably spacious, with high, pitched ceilings and a large, open center space.

Students Acquiring English

3 Beowulf's speech contains many long, complex sentences and elaborate imagery. You may want to pair students and have them work through parts of the speech together, paraphrasing each sentence.

Mini Lesson Speaking and Listening

DRAMATIC READING

Instruction Help students prepare an oral presentation of Beowulf's speech by sharing the following suggestions with the class.

- Read the material several times to be sure you understand it. Check unfamiliar words in a dictionary, and clarify ideas by discussing them with others.
- Focus on the emotions you are trying to convey. Use body language, as well as your voice, to convey feelings.
- Be aware of and use rhyme, rhythm, and any other musical devices.
- Don't pause at the end of a line unless it makes sense to do so. Use the poem's meaning and its punctuation, if any, to decide when to pause.
- Rehearse your presentation.
- Tape-record your rehearsal for self-evaluation.

Present Have students take turns reading Beowulf's speech (lines 141–189).

BLOCK SCHEDULING This activity is particularly well-suited for longer class periods.

Reading and Analyzing

GUIDE FOR READING

A He believes in a fair fight; he daringly tempts fate in order to show his courage; he believes a true hero will not give himself an advantage over his adversary.

Reading Skills and Strategies:
SUMMARIZING

B Ask students to summarize the events leading up to Edgetho's departure for the land of the Danes.
Possible Response: Edgetho, Beowulf's father, once started a feud with the Wulfing tribe by killing one of their warriors. His people turned him away from his homeland, fearing that his presence would cause a war to break out. So Edgetho set sail for the land of the Danes.

GUIDE FOR READING

C Hrothgar came to Edgetho's rescue by sending treasures to Edgetho's enemies, the Wulfings, thus buying peace between the tribes.

Literary Analysis ALLITERATION

D Hrothgar's account of the damage Grendel has done (lines 210–222) provides many examples of alliteration. Have students locate lines that contain the repetition of an initial consonant sound.
Answer: All lines except 212.
Then read the entire passage aloud as students follow along. Ask students to listen for the consonant sound that dominates the passage.
Answer: The *s* sound.

Have watched me rise from the darkness of war,
Dripping with my enemies' blood. I drove
Five great giants into chains, chased
All of that race from the earth. I swam
In the blackness of night, hunting monsters
Out of the ocean, and killing them one
By one; death was my errand and the fate
They had earned. Now Grendel and I are called
Together, and I've come. Grant me, then,
Lord and protector of this noble place,
A single request! I have come so far,
Oh shelterer of warriors and your people's loved friend,
That this one favor you should not refuse me—
That I, alone and with the help of my men,
May purge all evil from this hall. I have heard,
Too, that the monster's scorn of men
Is so great that he needs no weapons and fears none.
Nor will I. My lord Higlac
Might think less of me if I let my sword
Go where my feet were afraid to, if I hid
Behind some broad linden shield: my hands
Alone shall fight for me, struggle for life
Against the monster. God must decide
Who will be given to death's cold grip.
Grendel's plan, I think, will be
What it has been before, to invade this hall
And gorge his belly with our bodies. If he can,
If he can. And I think, if my time will have come,
There'll be nothing to mourn over, no corpse to prepare
For its grave: Grendel will carry our bloody
Flesh to the moors, crunch on our bones
And smear torn scraps of our skin on the walls
Of his den. No, I expect no Danes
Will fret about sewing our shrouds, if he wins.
And if death does take me, send the hammered
Mail of my armor to Higlac, return
The inheritance I had from Hrethel, and he
From Wayland. Fate will unwind as it must!"

Hrothgar replied, protector of the Danes:
"Beowulf, you've come to us in friendship,
and because

172 linden shield: shield made from the wood of a linden tree.

172–174 Beowulf insists on fighting Grendel without weapons. **A** Why do you think this is so important to him?

185 shrouds: cloths in which dead bodies are wrapped.

188 Hrethel (hrĕth'əl): a former king of the Geats—Higlac's father and Beowulf's grandfather.

189 Wayland: a famous blacksmith and magician.

WORDS TO KNOW
purge (pûrj) *v.* to cleanse or purify
gorge (gôrj) *v.* to stuff with food

Teaching Options

Assessment Informal Assessment

CHARACTERISTICS OF EPIC POETRY
You can informally assess students' initial understanding of epic poetry by having them write a list of characteristics of epic poetry based on their reading so far. For each characteristic, ask them to provide an example from the text of *Beowulf.*
Possible Response: Students may say that the epic poem features an epic hero who is courageous, sometimes superhuman, generous, and so forth; it treats universal themes such as good against evil; the setting is vast, including more than one nation or geographical area; and major characters often deliver long, formal speeches.

RUBRIC

3 **Full Accomplishment** Writing reflects understanding of characteristics of epic poetry and includes strong, relevant examples of each characteristic.

2 **Substantial Accomplishment** Writing reflects a general understanding of the characteristics of epic poetry, but not all examples are strong.

3 **Little or Partial Accomplishment** Writing displays little comprehension of the characteristics of epic poetry and includes some inappropriate examples from the text.

Of the reception your father found at our court.
Edgetho had begun a bitter feud,
Killing Hathlaf, a Wulfing warrior:
Your father's countrymen were afraid of war,
If he returned to his home, and they turned him away.
Then he traveled across the curving waves
To the land of the Danes. I was new to the throne,
Then, a young man ruling this wide
Kingdom and its golden city: Hergar,
My older brother, a far better man
Than I, had died and dying made me,
Second among Healfdane's sons, first
In this nation. I bought the end of Edgetho's
Quarrel, sent ancient treasures through the ocean's
Furrows to the Wulfings; your father swore
He'd keep that peace. My tongue grows heavy,
And my heart, when I try to tell you what Grendel
Has brought us, the damage he's done, here
In this hall. You see for yourself how much smaller
Our ranks have become, and can guess what we've lost
To his terror. Surely the Lord Almighty
Could stop his madness, smother his lust!
How many times have my men, glowing
With courage drawn from too many cups
Of ale, sworn to stay after dark
And stem that horror with a sweep of their swords.
And then, in the morning, this mead-hall glittering
With new light would be drenched with blood, the benches
Stained red, the floors, all wet from that fiend's
Savage assault—and my soldiers would be fewer
Still, death taking more and more.
But to table, Beowulf, a banquet in your honor:
Let us toast your victories, and talk of the future."
Then Hrothgar's men gave places to the Geats,
Yielded benches to the brave visitors
And led them to the feast. The keeper of the mead
Came carrying out the carved flasks,
And poured that bright sweetness. A poet
Sang, from time to time, in a clear
Pure voice. Danes and visiting Geats
Celebrated as one, drank and rejoiced.

B

193 Edgetho (ĕj'thō): Beowulf's father.

194 Wulfing: a member of another Germanic tribe.

C **191–206** What service did Hrothgar perform for Beowulf's father?

D

Customizing Instruction

Students Acquiring English

Make sure students understand the meanings of the following idioms and metaphors:

- "My tongue grows heavy, /And my heart . . ." (lines 207–208)
  Possible Response: I grow sad and can say nothing.
- "Let us toast your victories . . ." (line 224)
  Possible Response: Let us praise your victories.

BEOWULF 39

Reading and Analyzing

GUIDE FOR READING

A The rhythm created by the midline punctuation (commas) reinforces Grendel's stealth and cunning as he creeps up from the marsh to Herot.

Literary Analysis: KENNINGS

B Point out that the Beowulf Poet uses kennings, descriptive phrases or compound words that substitute for nouns. For example, "strong-hearted wakeful sleeper," line 270, is a kenning for Beowulf. When memorized, kennings served as aids in oral recitation. Ask students what the kenning "shepherd of evil" (line 273) might imply about Grendel?
Possible Response: Evil follows him; he nurtures and protects evil.

Active Reading MAKING JUDGMENTS

C Epic heroes display larger-than-life qualities. What epic quality does Beowulf display in these lines?
Possible Response: Beowulf displays superhuman strength in grasping Grendel's claws.

Literary Analysis ALLITERATION

D Ask students to identify the alliteration in lines 283–285 and to tell how alliteration contributes to meaning.
Possible Response: The repetition of the *c* sound brings the cracking sound to life.

Reconstruction of helmet from Sutton Hoo ship burial

After the banquet, Hrothgar and his followers leave Herot, and Beowulf and his warriors remain to spend the night. Beowulf reiterates his intent to fight Grendel without a sword and, while his followers sleep, lies waiting, eager for Grendel to appear.

THE BATTLE WITH GRENDEL

1

Out from the marsh, from the foot of misty
Hills and bogs, bearing God's hatred,
Grendel came, hoping to kill
Anyone he could trap on this trip to high Herot.
He moved quickly through the cloudy night,
Up from his swampland, sliding silently
Toward that gold-shining hall. He had visited Hrothgar's
Home before, knew the way—
But never, before nor after that night,
Found Herot defended so firmly, his reception

A **233–235** The translator uses punctuation to convey the effect of the midline pauses in the original Old English verses. How does the rhythm created by the midline punctuation reinforce the account of the action here?

Teaching Options

Viewing and Representing

Helmet from Sutton Hoo Ship Burial

In 1939, archaeologists in Suffolk, England, found evidence of an ancient buried ship. Though the wood had rotted, the shape remained.
Instruction Among the artifacts taken from the entombment, known as the Sutton Hoo Ship Burial, was this helmet. Its elaborate decorations indicate that its owner was an important figure.

Application Ask students how an opponent might react when facing the wearer of such a helmet.
Possible Response: Most people would react with fear.

Then ask students if the helmet reminds them of any contemporary epics or epic characters.
Possible Response: Students might see the resemblance between the Sutton Hoo helmet and that of *Star Wars'* Darth Vader.)

So harsh. He journeyed, forever joyless,
Straight to the door, then snapped it open,
Tore its iron fasteners with a touch
And rushed angrily over the threshold.
He strode quickly across the inlaid
Floor, snarling and fierce: his eyes
Gleamed in the darkness, burned with a gruesome
Light. Then he stopped, seeing the hall
Crowded with sleeping warriors, stuffed
With rows of young soldiers resting together.
And his heart laughed, he relished the sight,
Intended to tear the life from those bodies
By morning; the monster's mind was hot
With the thought of food and the feasting his belly
Would soon know. But fate, that night, intended
Grendel to gnaw the broken bones
Of his last human supper. Human
Eyes were watching his evil steps,
Waiting to see his swift hard claws.
Grendel snatched at the first Geat
He came to, ripped him apart, cut
His body to bits with powerful jaws,
Drank the blood from his veins and bolted 2
Him down, hands and feet; death
And Grendel's great teeth came together,
Snapping life shut. Then he stepped to another
Still body, clutched at Beowulf with his claws,
Grasped at a strong-hearted wakeful sleeper
—And was instantly seized himself, claws
Bent back as Beowulf leaned up on one arm.
B
That shepherd of evil, guardian of crime,
Knew at once that nowhere on earth
Had he met a man whose hands were harder;
His mind was flooded with fear—but nothing
Could take his <u>talons</u> and himself from that tight
Hard grip. Grendel's one thought was to run
From Beowulf, flee back to his marsh and hide there:
This was a different Herot than the hall he had emptied.
C
But Higlac's follower remembered his final
Boast and, standing erect, stopped
The monster's flight, fastened those claws
In his fists till they cracked, clutched Grendel
Closer. The <u>infamous</u> killer fought
D

246 threshold: the strip of wood or stone at the bottom of a doorway.

WORDS TO KNOW
talon (tăl'ən) *n.* a claw
infamous (ĭn'fə-məs) *adj.* having a bad reputation; notorious

41

Customizing Instruction

Students Acquiring English

Visual Learners

1 Remind students that in literature, spatial details may have symbolic meanings. Ask students to visualize Grendel's progression from the marsh toward Herot. In what direction is he moving?

Answer: Upwards.

What might the location of the marsh in relation to the location of Herot symbolize?

Possible Response: The low-lying marsh symbolizes Grendel's evil, while Herot's high position symbolizes its goodness; the low-lying marsh represents Hell, while the high, "gold-shining hall" represents heaven.

Multiple Learning Styles

2 Help students understand the meaning of difficult expressions. "Bolted / Him down" describes how Grendel ate the man. Define *bolt* as "to swallow suddenly."

Mini Lesson Vocabulary Strategy

USING A THESAURUS

Instruction Write the following lines from the poem (276–278) on the chalkboard: ". . . but nothing / Could take his talons and himself from that tight / Hard grip." Demonstrate for students how to use a thesaurus to find a synonym for the word *talon.* Ask them why the *Beowulf* translator might have used the word *talon* instead of *claw* in this particular line. (Note that *claws* is used later, in line 283.)

Answer: The word *talon* alliterates with the words *take* and *tight.*

Activity Have students use a thesaurus or a synonym finder to locate synonyms for the remaining Words to Know (*infamous, writhing, cowering,* and *taut*). Ask students to write down two or three synonyms for each word. Then guide the class to speculate on why the translator chose the words he did. Have students be prepared to discuss precise word meanings.

Use **Vocabulary Transparencies and Copymasters,** p. 18.

Reading and Analyzing

GUIDE FOR READING

A He has never before met a human who could match his strength and realizes that Beowulf is capable of killing him.

Literary Analysis:
FIGURATIVE LANGUAGE

B Ask students why the poet may have chosen to use figurative language "to open / A path for his evil soul," rather than simply saying "to kill."
Possible Responses: The phrase tells something more about Grendel—he has an evil soul; the phrase fits the rhythm of the poetry.

GUIDE FOR READING

C He has cast a spell that makes all weapons useless against him.

Reading Skills and Strategies:
MAKING INFERENCES

D Have students explain who the "still worse fiends" might be. Have them support their inferences with textual evidence.
Possible Response: This may refer to fiends in hell or devil.

GUIDE FOR READING

E **Possible Responses:** He does this to prove his victory; he is using it as a trophy of war.

Literary Analysis: IMAGERY

F Have students cite and analyze vivid sensory images that help the reader experience what Grendel's death was like. Also, ask them to indicate the senses to which each image appeals.
Answer: "staggering tracks," sight and touch; "bloody footprints," sight; "dragged his corpselike way," sight and touch; "pounding waves," sight, hearing, and touch.

For his freedom, wanting no flesh but retreat,
Desiring nothing but escape; his claws
Had been caught, he was trapped. That trip to Herot
Was a miserable journey for the writhing monster!
 The high hall rang, its roof boards swayed,
And Danes shook with terror. Down
The aisles the battle swept, angry
And wild. Herot trembled, wonderfully
Built to withstand the blows, the struggling
Great bodies beating at its beautiful walls;
Shaped and fastened with iron, inside
And out, artfully worked, the building
Stood firm. Its benches rattled, fell
To the floor, gold-covered boards grating
As Grendel and Beowulf battled across them.
Hrothgar's wise men had fashioned Herot
To stand forever; only fire,
They had planned, could shatter what such skill had put
Together, swallow in hot flames such splendor
Of ivory and iron and wood. Suddenly
The sounds changed, the Danes started
In new terror, cowering in their beds as the terrible
Screams of the Almighty's enemy sang
In the darkness, the horrible shrieks of pain
And defeat, the tears torn out of Grendel's
Taut throat, hell's captive caught in the arms
Of him who of all the men on earth
Was the strongest.

 That mighty protector of men
Meant to hold the monster till its life
Leaped out, knowing the fiend was no use
To anyone in Denmark. All of Beowulf's
Band had jumped from their beds, ancestral
Swords raised and ready, determined
To protect their prince if they could. Their courage
Was great but all wasted: they could hack at Grendel
From every side, trying to open
A path for his evil soul, but their points
Could not hurt him, the sharpest and hardest iron
Could not scratch at his skin, for that sin-stained demon
Had bewitched all men's weapons, laid spells
That blunted every mortal man's blade.

A **278–289** Up to this point Grendel has killed his human victims easily. Why might he be trying to run away from Beowulf?

C **322–326** Why do you think no weapons can hurt Grendel?

WORDS TO KNOW
writhing (rī'thĭng) *adj.* twisting and turning in pain **writhe** *v.*
cowering (kou'ər-ĭng) *adj.* cringing in fear **cower** *v.*
taut (tôt) *adj.* pulled tight

42

Teaching Options

BLOCK SCHEDULING: MANAGING TIME

If your schedule requires that you cover the lesson objectives in a shorter time, use . . .

- Preparing to Read, pp. 30–31
- Thinking Through the Literature, p. 63
- Vocabulary in Action, p. 65

If you want to take advantage of longer class time, use . . .

- TE Teaching Options: Vocabulary, pp. 31, 41, 56; Grammar, p. 32; Viewing and Representing, pp. 34, 40, 49, 61; Multicultural Link, pp. 35, 55; Cross Curricular Link, pp. 36, 48, 54; Speaking and Listening Mini Lessons, pp. 37, 46; Informal Assessment, pp. 38, 60; Workplace Link, p. 44; Standardized Test Practice, p. 50
- Choices & Challenges: Writing Options, Activities & Explorations, Inquiry & Research, p. 64

And yet his time had come, his days
Were over, his death near; down
To hell he would go, swept groaning and helpless
To the waiting hands of still worse fiends.
Now he discovered—once the afflictor
Of men, tormentor of their days—what it meant
To feud with Almighty God: Grendel
Saw that his strength was deserting him, his claws
Bound fast, Higlac's brave follower tearing at
His hands. The monster's hatred rose higher,
But his power had gone. He twisted in pain,
And the bleeding sinews deep in his shoulder
Snapped, muscle and bone split
And broke. The battle was over, Beowulf
Had been granted new glory: Grendel escaped,
But wounded as he was could flee to his den,
His miserable hole at the bottom of the marsh,
Only to die, to wait for the end
Of all his days. And after that bloody
Combat the Danes laughed with delight.
He who had come to them from across the sea,
Bold and strong-minded, had driven affliction
Off, purged Herot clean. He was happy,
Now, with that night's fierce work; the Danes
Had been served as he'd boasted he'd serve them; Beowulf,
A prince of the Geats, had killed Grendel,
Ended the grief, the sorrow, the suffering
Forced on Hrothgar's helpless people
By a bloodthirsty fiend. No Dane doubted
The victory, for the proof, hanging high
From the rafters where Beowulf had hung it, was the monster's
Arm, claw and shoulder and all.

And then, in the morning, crowds surrounded
Herot, warriors coming to that hall
From faraway lands, princes and leaders
Of men hurrying to behold the monster's
Great staggering tracks. They gaped with no sense
Of sorrow, felt no regret for his suffering,
Went tracing his bloody footprints, his beaten
And lonely flight, to the edge of the lake
Where he'd dragged his corpselike way, doomed
And already weary of his vanishing life.

338 sinews (sĭn'yo͞oz): the tendons that connect muscles to bones.

355–358 Why do you think Beowulf hangs Grendel's arm from the rafters?

Customizing Instruction

Less Proficient Readers

1 Ask students why making this trip to Herot was a "miserable journey" for Grendel.

Possible Response: He realized he had met his match; he was afraid and wanted to flee but could not.

Students Acquiring English

2 Make sure students understand the meaning of *purge* ("to free or rid of something bad").

Gifted and Talented

3 Have students contrast the behavior of the Danes and Beowulf's band and then offer a theory explaining the difference.

Possible Response: Beowulf's band shows courage and loyalty, while the Danes show fear and cowardice. The Danes may behave this way because, after 12 years of Grendel's violence, their spirits have been squelched; Beowulf's band, on the other hand, is made up of newcomers with fresh spirits and no prior exposure to Grendel.

BEOWULF 43

Reading and Analyzing

GUIDE FOR READING

A As described in lines 389–396, the poet seems to play the role of a craftsperson or artist, skillfully "weav[ing] a net of words" and "tying the knot of his verses / Smoothly, swiftly, into place." His "Quick skill" also connects the poet with the epic hero himself.

B **Possible Responses:** She takes the claw as a symbolic act of revenge; because she knows how highly it is valued by Beowulf and the Danes; because it was her son's and she is grieving his death; because she is too cowardly to stay and seek real revenge.

Thinking Through the Literature

1. Grendel is fierce, cunning, strong, and murderous.
2. Accept all reasonable responses.
3. Possible Responses: jealousy of their happiness; desire to do harm; evil nature.
4. Possible Responses: to win fame; to pit himself against a powerful foe; to help a related Germanic tribe; to help King Hrothgar, who helped Beowulf's family members in the past.

The water was bloody, steaming and boiling
In horrible pounding waves, heat
Sucked from his magic veins; but the swirling
Surf had covered his death, hidden
Deep in murky darkness his miserable
End, as hell opened to receive him.
    Then old and young rejoiced, turned back
From that happy pilgrimage, mounted their hard-hooved
Horses, high-spirited stallions, and rode them
Slowly toward Herot again, retelling
Beowulf's bravery as they jogged along.
And over and over they swore that nowhere
On earth or under the spreading sky
Or between the seas, neither south nor north,
Was there a warrior worthier to rule over men.
(But no one meant Beowulf's praise to belittle
Hrothgar, their kind and gracious king!)
    And sometimes, when the path ran straight and clear,
They would let their horses race, red
And brown and pale yellow backs streaming
Down the road. And sometimes a proud old soldier
Who had heard songs of the ancient heroes
And could sing them all through, story after story,
Would weave a net of words for Beowulf's
Victory, tying the knot of his verses
Smoothly, swiftly, into place with a poet's
Quick skill, singing his new song aloud
While he shaped it, and the old songs as well. . . .

A **389–396** What role do poets seem to play in Beowulf's society?

Thinking Through the Literature

1. **Comprehension Check** What characteristics does Grendel have that make him particularly terrifying to the Danes?
2. What impressions of Beowulf do you have after reading this part of the poem?
3. What do you think causes Grendel to attack human beings?

   THINK ABOUT
   - his relatives and ancestors
   - his actions and attitudes
   - the Danish warriors' reactions to him
4. Why do you think Beowulf offers to help a tribe other than his own, in spite of the danger?

WORDS TO KNOW
murky (mur'kē) *adj.* cloudy; gloomy
pilgrimage (pĭl'grə-mĭj) *n.* a journey to a sacred place or with a lofty purpose

44

Teaching Options

Workplace Link: Writing a Proposal

Beowulf visits the Danes to offer his services. He is thus an early example of a freelancer, which originally was a warrior for hire but today is any person who sells his or her services to employers without making a long-term commitment. Freelancers, contractors, and other self-employed people often write proposals for the jobs they want to perform. Such proposals include:

1. a statement of the goal
2. a list of steps necessary to achieve the goal
3. a timetable showing how long each step should take
4. a list of any special supplies or facilities
5. an estimate of all the costs involved

Application Have students work in small groups to write a proposal for a task such as painting a house or cleaning up a trash-filled area.

BLOCK SCHEDULING This activity is particularly well-suited for longer class periods.

Although one monster has died, another still lives. From her lair in a cold and murky lake, where she has been brooding over her loss, Grendel's mother emerges, bent on revenge.

GRENDEL'S MOTHER

So she reached Herot,
Where the Danes slept as though already dead;
Her visit ended their good fortune, reversed
The bright vane of their luck. No female, no matter
How fierce, could have come with a man's strength,
Fought with the power and courage men fight with,
Smashing their shining swords, their bloody,
Hammer-forged blades onto boar-headed helmets,
Slashing and stabbing with the sharpest of points.
The soldiers raised their shields and drew
Those gleaming swords, swung them above
The piled-up benches, leaving their mail shirts
And their helmets where they'd lain when the terror took
hold of them.
To save her life she moved still faster,
Took a single victim and fled from the hall,
Running to the moors, discovered, but her supper
Assured, sheltered in her dripping claws.
She'd taken Hrothgar's closest friend,
The man he most loved of all men on earth;
She'd killed a glorious soldier, cut
A noble life short. No Geat could have stopped her:
Beowulf and his band had been given better
Beds; sleep had come to them in a different
Hall. Then all Herot burst into shouts:
She had carried off Grendel's claw. Sorrow
Had returned to Denmark. They'd traded deaths,
Danes and monsters, and no one had won,
Both had lost!

400 vane: a device that turns to show the direction the wind is blowing—here associated metaphorically with luck, which is as changeable as the wind.

404 boar-headed helmets: Germanic warriors often wore helmets bearing the images of wild pigs or other fierce creatures in the hope that the images would increase their ferocity and protect them against their enemies.

B **421** Why do you think Grendel's mother takes his claw?

Customizing Instruction

Less Proficient Readers

1 Make sure students understand the outcome of the battle between Beowulf and Grendel.

- How is the outcome of this battle different from Grendel's other battles?
  Answer: He loses.
- How is Grendel's behavior different after he encounters Beowulf?
  Possible Response: He becomes fearful, recognizing he has met his match.
- What seems to motivate Beowulf to fight Grendel?
  Possible Response: He wants to help people in trouble; to rid the world of evil; to win fame and glory.

Students Acquiring English

2 Explain to students that a *vane* is a pointer, often an arrow, that pivots on a rooftop to indicate the direction of the wind. Show students a picture of a vane, if possible.

3 Make sure students understand that, in lines 400–405, the poet is **not** describing the battle between Grendel's mother and the Danes. Instead, he makes the point that all women (even monster women) are weaker warriors than men, and then describes, as a point of comparison, the actions of courageous men doing battle.

Less Proficient Readers

4 Ask students why they think the Beowulf Poet has Grendel's mother seize Hrothgar's closest friend.
Possible Response: Students may say that was done to increase the justification for revenge and to give Beowulf an honorable cause for which to fight.

Reading and Analyzing

GUIDE FOR READING

A It is unpleasant dark, windy, stormy.

Literary Analysis: EPIC POETRY

B What characteristic of an epic hero does Beowulf display in these lines?

Possible Response: He performs superhuman actions.

Literary Analysis: SETTING

C Ask students how they feel as they imagine following Beowulf to the bottom of the lake.

Possible Responses: Anxious, apprehensive.

Ask: How does the underwater setting contribute to the mood of the scene?

Possible Response: It helps create a sense of urgency and suspense—how will Beowulf fare in enemy territory?

Devastated by the loss of his friend, Hrothgar sends for Beowulf and recounts what Grendel's mother has done. Then Hrothgar describes the dark lake where Grendel's mother has dwelt with her son.

"They live in secret places, windy
Cliffs, wolf-dens where water pours
From the rocks, then runs underground, where mist
Steams like black clouds, and the groves of trees
Growing out over their lake are all covered
With frozen spray, and wind down snakelike
Roots that reach as far as the water
And help keep it dark. At night that lake
Burns like a torch. No one knows its bottom,
No wisdom reaches such depths. A deer,
Hunted through the woods by packs of hounds, **A**
A stag with great horns, though driven through the forest
From faraway places, prefers to die
On those shores, refuses to save its life
In that water. It isn't far, nor is it
A pleasant spot! When the wind stirs
And storms, waves splash toward the sky,
As dark as the air, as black as the rain
That the heavens weep. Our only help,
Again, lies with you. Grendel's mother
Is hidden in her terrible home, in a place

You've not seen. Seek it, if you dare! Save us,
Once more, and again twisted gold,
Heaped-up ancient treasure, will reward you
For the battle you win!"

425–432 What sort of place is the underwater lair of Grendel's mother? How does the translator's use of alliteration make this description more effective?

447–449 Germanic warriors placed great importance on amassing treasure as a way of acquiring fame and temporarily defeating fate.

Teaching Options

Mini Lesson Speaking and Listening

LISTENING TO DESCRIPTION

Instruction Because many epic poems such as *Beowulf* were originally composed for listening audiences, they contain poetic expressions and devices (such as alliteration) that are particularly pleasing to the ear.

Prepare Invite a volunteer to prepare a dramatic reading of Hrothgar's description of the dark lake (lines 425–449). Before the performance, explain to listening students that the volunteer will do two readings of the passage.

Present During the first reading, have listeners close their eyes and listen for meaning and mood. Then, during the second reading, have listeners jot down any repeated sounds they hear and any particularly striking images. After both readings, discuss students' reactions and impressions. Ask students how Beowulf might have felt upon hearing the description, and, following it, Hrothgar's invitation to "Seek it, if you dare!"

BLOCK SCHEDULING This activity is particularly well-suited for longer class periods

Bronze matrix for pressed foil, cast with carved details. Björnhovda, Torslunda, Öland. 7th century A.D.

Beowulf accepts Hrothgar's challenge, and the king and his men accompany the hero to the dreadful lair of Grendel's mother. Fearlessly, Beowulf prepares to battle the terrible creature.

The Battle with Grendel's Mother

He leaped into the lake, would not wait for anyone's
Answer; the heaving water covered him
Over. For hours he sank through the waves;
At last he saw the mud of the bottom.
And all at once the greedy she-wolf
Who'd ruled those waters for half a hundred
Years discovered him, saw that a creature
From above had come to explore the bottom
Of her wet world. She welcomed him in her claws,
Clutched at him savagely but could not harm him,
Tried to work her fingers through the tight
Ring-woven mail on his breast, but tore
And scratched in vain. Then she carried him, armor
And sword and all, to her home; he struggled
To free his weapon, and failed. The fight
Brought other monsters swimming to see
Her catch, a host of sea beasts who beat at
His mail shirt, stabbing with tusks and teeth
As they followed along. Then he realized, suddenly,
That she'd brought him into someone's battle-hall,
And there the water's heat could not hurt him,
Nor anything in the lake attack him through

Customizing Instruction

Less Proficient Readers

1 Have students predict Beowulf's response to Hrothgar's challenge.

Possible Response: He will accept the challenge and defeat Grendel's mother in battle.

BEOWULF 47

Reading and Analyzing

GUIDE FOR READING

A It is very important; at this point, Beowulf's desire for fame seems to be the only thing that keeps him from giving up.

Literary Analysis: SETTING

B Point out that the action moves from under the water, where Beowulf cuts off Grendel's head, to the edge of the lake, where the elders discuss what might be happening. Then the setting once again switches to the scene at the bottom of the lake. Such changes in setting are indicated with paragraph indentations and, in line 561 (on page 50), a dash. How do these changes in setting heighten the sense of suspense in the narrative?

Possible Response: The readers know that Beowulf is victorious and are anxious for the onlookers to realize that they have misinterpreted the bloody water.

The building's high-arching roof. A brilliant
1 Light burned all around him, the lake
Itself like a fiery flame.
Then he saw
The mighty water witch, and swung his sword,
His ring-marked blade, straight at her head;
The iron sang its fierce song,
Sang Beowulf's strength. But her guest 2
Discovered that no sword could slice her evil
Skin, that Hrunting could not hurt her, was useless
Now when he needed it. They wrestled, she ripped
And tore and clawed at him, bit holes in his helmet,
3 And that too failed him; for the first time in years
Of being worn to war it would earn no glory;
It was the last time anyone would wear it. But Beowulf
Longed only for fame, leaped back
Into battle. He tossed his sword aside,
Angry; the steel-edged blade lay where
He'd dropped it. If weapons were useless he'd use
His hands, the strength in his fingers. So fame
Comes to the men who mean to win it
And care about nothing else! He raised
His arms and seized her by the shoulder; anger
Doubled his strength, he threw her to the floor.
She fell, Grendel's fierce mother, and the Geats'
Proud prince was ready to leap on her. But she rose
At once and repaid him with her clutching claws,
Wildly tearing at him. He was weary, that best
And strongest of soldiers; his feet stumbled
4 And in an instant she had him down, held helpless.
Squatting with her weight on his stomach, she drew
A dagger, brown with dried blood, and prepared
To avenge her only son. But he was stretched
On his back, and her stabbing blade was blunted
By the woven mail shirt he wore on his chest.
The hammered links held; the point
Could not touch him. He'd have traveled to the bottom of the earth,
Edgetho's son, and died there, if that shining
Woven metal had not helped—and Holy
God, who sent him victory, gave judgment
For truth and right, Ruler of the Heavens,
Once Beowulf was back on his feet and fighting.

476 his ring-marked blade: For the battle with Grendel's mother, Beowulf has been given an heirloom sword with an intricately etched blade.

480 Hrunting (hrŭn'tĭng): the name of Beowulf's sword. (Germanic warriors' swords were possessions of such value that they were often given names.)

A **490–492** How important is fame to Beowulf?

Teaching Options

Cross Curricular Link History

FAME Direct students' attention to lines 485–487 ("But Beowulf / Longed only for fame, leaped back / Into battle"). Explain that fame was vitally important to a warrior because of its practical rewards, such as wealth and the loyalty of both kinspeople and other tribes. However, fame had an added importance in cultures whose religion offered no hope for an afterlife. Then, it was only through fame that a person could hope to achieve immortality. The poet who sang the story of the hero, therefore, was the agent upon whom the hero's immortality depended. For this reason, scops and bards held important positions in the royal courts of northern Europe for centuries.

Then he saw, hanging on the wall, a heavy
Sword, hammered by giants, strong
And blessed with their magic, the best of all weapons
But so massive that no ordinary man could lift
Its carved and decorated length. He drew it
From its scabbard, broke the chain on its hilt,
And then, savage, now, angry
4 And desperate, lifted it high over his head
And struck with all the strength he had left,
Caught her in the neck and cut it through,
Broke bones and all. Her body fell
To the floor, lifeless, the sword was wet
With her blood, and Beowulf rejoiced at the sight.
The brilliant light shone, suddenly,
As though burning in that hall, and as bright as Heaven's
Own candle, lit in the sky. He looked
At her home, then following along the wall
Went walking, his hands tight on the sword,
His heart still angry. He was hunting another
Dead monster, and took his weapon with him
For final revenge against Grendel's vicious
Attacks, his nighttime raids, over
And over, coming to Herot when Hrothgar's
Men slept, killing them in their beds,
Eating some on the spot, fifteen
Or more, and running to his loathsome moor
With another such sickening meal waiting
In his pouch. But Beowulf repaid him for those visits,
Found him lying dead in his corner,
Armless, exactly as that fierce fighter
Had sent him out from Herot, then struck off
His head with a single swift blow. The body
Jerked for the last time, then lay still.
The wise old warriors who surrounded Hrothgar,
Like him staring into the monsters' lake,
Saw the waves surging and blood
B Spurting through. They spoke about Beowulf,
All the graybeards, whispered together
And said that hope was gone, that the hero
Had lost fame and his life at once, and would never
Return to the living, come back as triumphant
As he had left; almost all agreed that Grendel's
Mighty mother, the she-wolf, had killed him.

Viking sword

550 graybeards: old men.

WORDS TO KNOW **loathsome** (lōth′səm) *adj.* disgusting; hateful

Customizing Instruction

Students Acquiring English

Explain to students the meanings of the following symbol and idiom.

1 ". . . the lake / Itself like a fiery flame" (lines 473–474) *(The fiery lake symbolizes Hell.)*

2 "The iron sang its fierce song, / Sang Beowulf's strength" (lines 477–478) *(The sword made a loud noise as it struck Grendel's mother.)*

Less Proficient Readers

3 Ask students what motivates Beowulf in these lines.
Possible Response: He is motivated by his desire for fame and glory and also by his anger.

Then ask how these lines help create suspense in the narrative.
Possible Response: For the first time, we see Beowulf in a vulnerable position—his sword and his helmet have both failed him.

4 Have students summarize the action in lines 489–525.
Possible Response: Beowulf uses his bare hands to throw Grendel's mother to the floor. They struggle. She pins him down but his mail shirt protects him from her dagger. Beowulf gets up, grabs a massive sword off the wall, and cuts Grendel's mother through the neck. She falls; Beowulf rejoices.

Mini Lesson Viewing and Representing

Viking Sword

Instruction The term *Viking* refers to the seafaring Scandinavians who plundered the coasts of northern and western Europe (including the British Isles) from the eighth through the tenth centuries. The artifacts found in their ships include loot from most parts of Europe. Though Beowulf and the Geats predated the Vikings, they shared similar backgrounds.

Application Have students examine the sword closely. Then ask them to describe the kind of person they imagine might have owned and used the sword.
Possible Response: Someone who needed a weapon in everyday life.

Ask what they think the sword might have meant to its owner.
Possible Responses: It probably meant a great deal to its owner because it was a main source of protection; because it gave the owner courage; or because it was a symbol of victory over an enemy.

Reading and Analyzing

Literary Analysis: VISUALIZING

A Have students close their eyes and visualize this passage (lines 589–605) as you read it aloud. Suggest they draw or describe two scenes that show Beowulf's great strength.

Possible Response: Four warriors struggle to carry Grendel's head on a spear; however, Beowulf himself carries it by the hair.

GUIDE FOR READING

B Grendel's skull is Beowulf's trophy; it serves as proof that the battle with Grendel is over.

Literary Analysis ALLITERATION

C Point out the repeated *w* sound in these lines. Demonstrate that, when saying the *w* sound, the mouth is formed in an "o" shape—a shape also expressive of surprise and wonder. Have students suggest how this might affect the appearance of a scop giving an oral performance of the piece.

Gold torque (a collar or necklace) from Snettisham in Norfolk in eastern England, made sometime in the middle of the first century B.C.

The sun slid over past noon, went further
Down. The Danes gave up, left
The lake and went home, Hrothgar with them.
The Geats stayed, sat sadly, watching,
Imagining they saw their lord but not believing
They would ever see him again.
—Then the sword 1
Melted, blood-soaked, dripping down
Like water, disappearing like ice when the world's
Eternal Lord loosens invisible
Fetters and unwinds icicles and frost
As only He can, He who rules
Time and seasons, He who is truly
God. The monsters' hall was full of
Rich treasures, but all that Beowulf took
Was Grendel's head and the hilt of the giants'
Jeweled sword; the rest of that ring-marked
Blade had dissolved in Grendel's steaming
Blood, boiling even after his death.
And then the battle's only survivor
Swam up and away from those silent corpses;
The water was calm and clean, the whole
Huge lake peaceful once the demons who'd lived in it
Were dead.
Then that noble protector of all seamen
Swam to land, rejoicing in the heavy
Burdens he was bringing with him. He

578 that noble protector of all seamen: Beowulf, who will be buried in a tower that will serve as a navigational aid to sailors.

WORDS TO KNOW

fetter (fĕt'ər) *n.* a shackle or chain; restraint

50

Teaching Options

Assessment Standardized Test Practice

CHOOSING THE BEST SUMMARY For some standardized tests, students will be asked to choose the best summary of a passage. To provide students with some practice in choosing the best summary, read aloud or write on the chalkboard the following question:

Which of the following statements best summarizes lines 578–605 (Beowulf's return to Herot)?

A. While the lake turns red with blood, Beowulf swims to the shore and walks with his men back to the mead hall.

B. The weight of Grendel's skull is so enormous that Beowulf's men stagger; Beowulf himself ends up carrying the ugly head into the mead hall.

C. Beowulf and his men, triumphant, return to the mead hall, where they present Hrothgar with the head of Grendel.

Lead students through the process of choosing the best summary. Consider each choice. Point out that, while all of the statements contain accurate information, the best summary should include the most important information. For that reason, **C** is the best choice.

And all his glorious band of Geats
Thanked God that their leader had come back unharmed;
They left the lake together. The Geats
Carried Beowulf's helmet, and his mail shirt.
Behind them the water slowly thickened
As the monsters' blood came seeping up.
They walked quickly, happily, across
Roads all of them remembered, left
The lake and the cliffs alongside it, brave men
Staggering under the weight of Grendel's skull,
Too heavy for fewer than four of them to handle—
Two on each side of the spear jammed through it—
Yet proud of their ugly load and determined
That the Danes, seated in Herot, should see it.
Soon, fourteen Geats arrived
At the hall, bold and warlike, and with Beowulf,

Their lord and leader, they walked on the mead-hall
Green. Then the Geats' brave prince entered
Herot, covered with glory for the daring
Battles he had fought; he sought Hrothgar
To salute him and show Grendel's head.
He carried that terrible trophy by the hair,
Brought it straight to where the Danes sat,
Drinking, the queen among them. It was a weird
And wonderful sight, and the warriors stared.

B **593–594** Why do you think the Geats want the Danes to see the monster's skull?

C

604 queen: Welthow, wife of Hrothgar.

Thinking Through the Literature

1. **Comprehension Check** What heroic action does Beowulf perform in this part of the poem?
2. Do you think you would have enjoyed living among the Danes of Beowulf's day? Why or why not?
3. What qualities does Beowulf display in this second battle?

   THINK ABOUT
   - the description of Grendel's mother and her actions
   - the details describing her lair
   - Beowulf's motives and actions
4. Are Beowulf's words and deeds those of a traditional **epic hero?** Support your opinion with evidence from the poem.
5. Does the behavior of Grendel's mother seem as wicked or unreasonable as Grendel's behavior? Explain your answer.

Customizing Instruction

Less Proficient Readers

1 Use the following questions to check students' comprehension of events.

- What conclusion do the warriors come to as they watch the surface of the lake?
  Answer: They think that Beowulf has been slain.
- Why do you think the sword dissolves after Beowulf decapitates Grendel?
  Possible Response: It has come in contact with evil blood; its dissolution symbolizes the completion of Beowulf's battle.

Thinking Through the Literature

1. He battles with and vanquishes Grendel's mother.
2. Accept all reasonable responses. Students should base their opinions on evidence they have encountered in the text.
3. Among Beowulf's qualities that students may mention are bravery, resourcefulness, physical strength, and perseverance.
4. Possible Responses: Beowulf is a traditional epic hero in his desire for fame. Fame means that he will be remembered after he goes to his fate, or death; fame, or being remembered, is his one way of outliving his fate. He is also a traditional epic hero in his high social status, heroic actions, and deeds that determine the fate of whole groups of people.
5. Those students who find her as wicked as Grendel may point to her murderous violence. Those who find her less wicked may suggest that she has more reasonable motives for her actions than Grendel did, since she is motivated by grief over the death of her son and a desire to avenge that death.

Reading and Analyzing

Literary Analysis: FORESHADOWING

A Ask students what these lines foreshadow about the outcome of Beowulf's last battle.

Possible Response: The lines hint that Beowulf will lose the battle and die.

Literary Analysis: CHARACTERIZATION

B Ask students what Beowulf's remarks reveal about his personality and attitude toward danger.

Possible Response: He is courageous and stoic; he believes he is fated to meet the dragon; he accepts his fate without question.

Reading Skills and Strategies: ANALYZING

C Briefly discuss the use of *still* in line 633. Ask why some might have expected Beowulf to be brave and strong no longer.

Possible Response: Beowulf is much older than he was at the time of his battles with Grendel and Grendel's mother.

With Grendel's mother destroyed, peace is restored to the land of the Danes, and Beowulf, laden with Hrothgar's gifts, returns to the land of his own people, the Geats. After his uncle and cousin die, Beowulf becomes king of the Geats and rules in peace and prosperity for 50 years. One day, however, a fire-breathing dragon that has been guarding a treasure for hundreds of years is disturbed by a thief, who enters the treasure tower and steals a cup. The dragon begins terrorizing the Geats, and Beowulf, now an old man, takes on the challenge of fighting it.

Viking cup, silver and gilt

Beowulf's Last Battle

And Beowulf uttered his final boast:
"I've never known fear, as a youth I fought
In endless battles. I am old, now,
But I will fight again, seek fame still,
If the dragon hiding in his tower dares
To face me."
Then he said farewell to his followers,
Each in his turn, for the last time:
"I'd use no sword, no weapon, if this beast
Could be killed without it, crushed to death
Like Grendel, gripped in my hands and torn
Limb from limb. But his breath will be burning
Hot, poison will pour from his tongue.
I feel no shame, with shield and sword
And armor, against this monster: when he comes to me

I mean to stand, not run from his shooting
Flames, stand till fate decides
Which of us wins. My heart is firm,
My hands calm: I need no hot
Words. Wait for me close by, my friends.
We shall see, soon, who will survive
This bloody battle, stand when the fighting
Is done. No one else could do
What I mean to, here, no man but me
Could hope to defeat this monster. No one
Could try. And this dragon's treasure, his gold
And everything hidden in that tower, will be mine
Or war will sweep me to a bitter death!"
Then Beowulf rose, still brave, still strong,
And with his shield at his side, and a mail shirt on his breast,
Strode calmly, confidently, toward the tower, under
The rocky cliffs: no coward could have walked there!
And then he who'd endured dozens of desperate
Battles, who'd stood boldly while swords and shields
Clashed, the best of kings, saw
Huge stone arches and felt the heat
Of the dragon's breath, flooding down
Through the hidden entrance, too hot for anyone
To stand, a streaming current of fire
And smoke that blocked all passage. And the Geats'
Lord and leader, angry, lowered
His sword and roared out a battle cry,
A call so loud and clear that it reached through
The hoary rock, hung in the dragon's
Ear. The beast rose, angry,
Knowing a man had come—and then nothing
But war could have followed. Its breath came first,
A steaming cloud pouring from the stone,
Then the earth itself shook. Beowulf
Swung his shield into place, held it
In front of him, facing the entrance. The dragon
Coiled and uncoiled, its heart urging it
Into battle. Beowulf's ancient sword
Was waiting, unsheathed, his sharp and gleaming
Blade. The beast came closer; both of them
Were ready, each set on slaughter. The Geats'
Great prince stood firm, unmoving, prepared

648 hoary (hôr'ē): gray with age.

Customizing Instruction

Less Proficient Readers

1 Explain that "hot words" (lines 623-624) is an idiom for bold, angry, or unkind words, or words that have no meaning or substance.

2 Ask students to speculate on why Beowulf wants his friends to stay "close by."

Possible Responses: He wants his friends to see him perform heroic deeds; he wants their moral support; he isn't as sure of himself as he says he is, and wants help to be nearby if he needs it.

3 Explain that when a noise "hangs" in someone's ear, it lingers or echoes there. Point out that the word has a negative connotation—something that hangs can also be considered a weight or a burden. The use of idiom in lines 648–649, therefore, suggests that the dragon was not happy to hear Beowulf's call.

Reading and Analyzing

GUIDE FOR READING

A He has a heroic reputation to maintain; he is a man of action who never gives up; he is a man of courage who faces death as squarely as he has always faced danger.

Reading Skills and Strategies:

DRAWING CONCLUSIONS

B Ask students what they conclude about the poet's attitude toward the behavior of Beowulf's comrades other than Wiglaf.

Possible Responses: Critical, disapproving.

Have them explain which text details led them to their conclusion.

Possible Responses: Students may say that the remark about Wiglaf's remembering, "As a good man must, what kinship should mean" implies that the others have forgotten about loyalty and courage.

Active Reading MAKING JUDGMENTS

C Ask what heroic quality Wiglaf represents and champions in his speech.

Possible Response: Loyalty.

Then ask if students think Wiglaf himself qualifies as an epic hero.

Possible Responses: Students' responses will vary. Some may say yes, based on his bravery and loyalty. Some may say no, because he hesitates before helping Beowulf.

GUIDE FOR READING

D Wiglaf is loyal to Beowulf and remembers what he owes to his lord.

E Wiglaf suggests that Beowulf has grown old and has lost some of his strength.

Behind his high shield, waiting in his shining
Armor. The monster came quickly toward him,
Pouring out fire and smoke, hurrying
To its fate. Flames beat at the iron
Shield, and for a time it held, protected
Beowulf as he'd planned; then it began to melt,
And for the first time in his life that famous prince
Fought with fate against him, with glory
Denied him. He knew it, but he raised his sword
And struck at the dragon's scaly hide.
The ancient blade broke, bit into
The monster's skin, drew blood, but cracked
And failed him before it went deep enough, helped him
Less than he needed. The dragon leaped
With pain, thrashed and beat at him, spouting
Murderous flames, spreading them everywhere.
And the Geats' ring-giver did not boast of glorious
Victories in other wars: his weapon
Had failed him, deserted him, now when he needed it
Most, that excellent sword. Edgetho's
Famous son stared at death,
Unwilling to leave this world, to exchange it
For a dwelling in some distant place—a journey
Into darkness that all men must make, as death
Ends their few brief hours on earth.
Quickly, the dragon came at him, encouraged
As Beowulf fell back; its breath flared,
And he suffered, wrapped around in swirling
Flames—a king, before, but now
A beaten warrior. None of his comrades
Came to him, helped him, his brave and noble
Followers; they ran for their lives, fled
Deep in a wood. And only one of them
Remained, stood there, miserable, remembering,
As a good man must, what kinship should mean.

His name was Wiglaf, he was Wexstan's son
And a good soldier; his family had been Swedish,
Once. Watching Beowulf, he could see
How his king was suffering, burning. Remembering
Everything his lord and cousin had given him,
Armor and gold and the great estates
Wexstan's family enjoyed, Wiglaf's

A 670–671 Why do you think Beowulf keeps fighting?

678 ring-giver: king; lord. When a man swore allegiance to a Germanic lord in return for his protection, the lord typically bestowed a ring on his follower to symbolize the bond.

Teaching Options

Cross Curricular Link History

RING-GIVERS Generosity was a quality much admired by the Anglo-Saxons. Their leaders were often noted for giving generous gifts to their followers. Kings often bestowed gold rings on those who swore loyalty to them, and were often referred to as "ring-givers."

Mind was made up; he raised his yellow
Shield and drew his sword. . . .
And Wiglaf, his heart heavy, uttered
The kind of words his comrades deserved:
"I remember how we sat in the mead-hall, drinking
And boasting of how brave we'd be when Beowulf
Needed us, he who gave us these swords
And armor: all of us swore to repay him,
When the time came, kindness for kindness
—With our lives, if he needed them. He allowed us to join him,
Chose us from all his great army, thinking
Our boasting words had some weight, believing
Our promises, trusting our swords. He took us
For soldiers, for men. He meant to kill
This monster himself, our mighty king,
Fight this battle alone and unaided,
3 As in the days when his strength and daring dazzled
Men's eyes. But those days are over and gone
And now our lord must lean on younger
Arms. And we must go to him, while angry
Flames burn at his flesh, help
Our glorious king! By almighty God,
I'd rather burn myself than see
Flames swirling around my lord.
And who are we to carry home
Our shields before we've slain his enemy
And ours, to run back to our homes with Beowulf
So hard-pressed here? I swear that nothing
He ever did deserved an end
Like this, dying miserably and alone,
Butchered by this savage beast: we swore
That these swords and armor were each for us all!"

D **694–705** How is Wiglaf unlike Beowulf's other subjects?

717–723 What does Wiglaf suggest is the reason Beowulf has failed to defeat the dragon?

Customizing Instruction

Less Proficient Readers

1 Point out that in these lines, the dragon is the aggressor, the first to attack. Ask students what this suggests about how the battle may proceed.

Possible Response: The dragon has the upper hand from the beginning, and will probably keep it.

2 Ask students what these lines reveal about early Anglo-Saxon attitudes toward life.

Possible Response: The Anglo-Saxons were fatalistic and viewed life as both short and fragile.

Multiple Learning Styles

Auditory Learners

3 Explain that an exhortation is a speech given to motivate or rouse someone to take action. Do a dramatic reading of Wiglaf's exhortation (or invite a volunteer to do one). Then have listeners explain which part of the speech they found most motivating, and why.

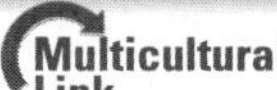

Praise Poems of Africa

Explain that songs or poems of praise are a popular form of traditional literature the world over. Praise poems are common in the traditional literatures of sub-Saharan Africa, where they go by such terms as *oridi* (Yoruba), *izibongo* (Zulu), and *lithoko* (Basuto). African praise poems offer tribute not only to heroes, monarchs, gods, and others of high stature, but also to animals, plants, and places important to a people or their history. In its simplest form, a praise poem strings together a series of "praise-names," epithets detailing positive qualities. If the subject is a person, the string often includes acknowledgment of high birth or noble forbears. Because the poems are composed and performed in the oral tradition, the actual details widely vary from performer to performer. Performances may be sung or chanted to musical accompaniment.

Reading and Analyzing

Literary Analysis: RHYTHM

A Point out that the rhythm used in Old English verse typically contained a strong midline pause, or *caesura*, and that lines 736–740 are a good illustration of several midline pauses in a row. You might read them aloud, slightly emphasizing the pause, or have a volunteer do so. Have students analyze the effect of the rhythm.

Literary Analysis: FIGURATIVE LANGUAGE

B Have students consider the remark that Beowulf has "unwound / His string of days on earth" (lines 737–738). Ask what the expression means.

Possible Response: It indicates that Beowulf has come to the end of his life.

Discuss with students why the figurative language is more moving and memorable than a literal statement, such as "Beowulf's life was over."

GUIDE FOR READING

C Life is of a certain length and no longer; once unwound, it can't be rewound.

D His speech reveals his concern with honor and family, as well as treasure.

Wiglaf joins Beowulf, who again attacks the dragon single-handed; but the remnant of his sword shatters, and the monster wounds him in the neck. Wiglaf then strikes the dragon, and he and Beowulf together finally succeed in killing the beast. Their triumph is short-lived, however, because Beowulf's wound proves to be mortal.

The Death of Beowulf

A
Beowulf spoke, in spite of the swollen,
Livid wound, knowing he'd unwound
His string of days on earth, seen **B**
As much as God would grant him; all worldly
Pleasure was gone, as life would go,
Soon:
"I'd leave my armor to my son,
Now, if God had given me an heir,
A child born of my body, his life
Created from mine. I've worn this crown
For fifty winters: no neighboring people
Have tried to threaten the Geats, sent soldiers
Against us or talked of terror. My days
Have gone by as fate willed, waiting
For its word to be spoken, ruling as well
As I knew how, swearing no unholy oaths,
Seeking no lying wars. I can leave
This life happy; I can die, here,
Knowing the Lord of all life has never
1 Watched me wash my sword in blood
Born of my own family. Belovèd
Wiglaf, go, quickly, find
The dragon's treasure: we've taken its life,
But its gold is ours, too. Hurry,
Bring me ancient silver, precious
Jewels, shining armor and gems,
Before I die. Death will be softer,
Leaving life and this people I've ruled
So long, if I look at this last of all prizes."

C **737–738** What view of fate does the image of the unwinding string convey?

D **741–763** What values are reflected in Beowulf's speech?

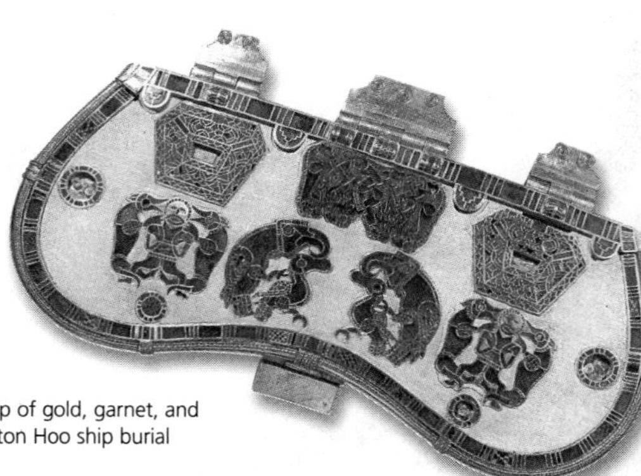

Viking purse clip of gold, garnet, and glass, from Sutton Hoo ship burial

WORDS TO KNOW **livid** (lĭv'ĭd) *adj.* discolored; black and blue

56

Teaching Options

Vocabulary Strategy

MULTIPLE MEANING WORDS

Instruction Write the following sentence on the board: "Beowulf spoke, in spite of the swollen, livid wound." Point out the definition of the word *livid* at the bottom of page 58 ("discolored; black and blue"). Then explain to students that *livid* can also mean "ashen or pallid, as from anger," or "extremely angry; furious." Guide students to realize that, in the context of this sentence, *livid* must mean "discolored," since a wound cannot be angry, nor is a wound typically thought of as being ashen or pale.

Exercise Have students read the following sentence, consider the context, and choose the correct meaning for the word *taut.*

The coach's mouth was pulled into a taut, grim line; she was not pleased with the loss. **(A)**

A. pulled or drawn tight; not slack
B. strained; tense
C. kept in trim shape; neat; tidy

Use **Vocabulary Transparencies and Copymasters,** p. 19.

A lesson on multiple meaning words appears on p. 266 in the Pupil's Edition.

Gold buckle from Sutton Hoo ship burial, showing animals, snakes, and birds

Then Wexstan's son went in, as quickly
As he could, did as the dying Beowulf
Asked, entered the inner darkness
Of the tower, went with his mail shirt and his sword.
Flushed with victory he groped his way,
A brave young warrior, and suddenly saw
Piles of gleaming gold, precious
Gems, scattered on the floor, cups
And bracelets, rusty old helmets, beautifully
Made but rotting with no hands to rub
And polish them. They lay where the dragon left them;
It had flown in the darkness, once, before fighting
Its final battle. (So gold can easily
Triumph, defeat the strongest of men,
No matter how deep it is hidden!) And he saw,
2 Hanging high above, a golden
Banner, woven by the best of weavers
And beautiful. And over everything he saw
A strange light, shining everywhere,
On walls and floor and treasure. Nothing
Moved, no other monsters appeared;
He took what he wanted, all the treasures
That pleased his eye, heavy plates
And golden cups and the glorious banner,
Loaded his arms with all they could hold.
Beowulf's dagger, his iron blade,
Had finished the fire-spitting terror
That once protected tower and treasures
Alike; the gray-bearded lord of the Geats
Had ended those flying, burning raids
Forever.

Customizing Instruction

Students Acquiring English

1 Students may have trouble following Beowulf's speech in this passage. You may wish to read it aloud, explaining the following difficult phrases:

- "waiting / For its word to be spoken" (lines 748–749) *(waiting for fate to decide what will happen)*
- "swearing no unholy oaths" (line 750) *(making no promises to do evil deeds)*
- "Seeking no lying wars" (line 751) *(not using lies, treachery, or deceit to start wars)*
- "wash my sword in blood / Born of my own family" (lines 754–755) *(kill or injure a relative)*
- "Death will be softer" (line 761) *(I will more easily welcome death.)*

Less Proficient Readers

2 Have students describe the interior of the dragon's tower (lines 764–794).
Possible Response: The outer regions are dark, but deep within there are piles of gleaming gold, jewels, and other treasures. A gold banner hangs above, and a strange light shines over all. It is still and deserted, except for Wiglaf.

BEOWULF 57

Reading and Analyzing

Active Reading MAKING JUDGMENTS

A Ask students if they agree or disagree that Beowulf sold his life well.
Possible Responses: Agree—he sold his life to protect his people and gain treasure for them, as a good Anglo-Saxon leader should; he was getting old, and it was better to die in battle than to die of old age. Disagree—No one's life is worth treasure; he was needed to lead his people.

Reading Skills and Strategies:
MAKING INFERENCES

B What do Beowulf's gifts to Wiglaf suggest about Wiglaf's future? Have students support their opinions with text evidence.
Possible Response: He will become the next king of the Geats.

GUIDE FOR READING

C His tomb will serve as a beacon.

D They failed to come to Beowulf's aid in his fight with the dragon.

Reading Skills and Strategies:
CONNECTING

E Ask students to name the pre-Christian, Anglo-Saxon concept that is comparable to the God Beowulf describes in these lines.
Answer: Fate.

Literary Analysis ALLITERATION

F Have students identify the repeated consonant sound in these lines.
Answer: Students should notice the *g* sound.
Ask how the alliteration enhances this description of Beowulf's death.
Possible Response: The harsh, guttural sounds give the description dignity, solemnity, a somber rhythm.

Then Wiglaf went back, anxious
To return while Beowulf was alive, to bring him
Treasure they'd won together. He ran,
Hoping his wounded king, weak
And dying, had not left the world too soon.
Then he brought their treasure to Beowulf, and found
His famous king bloody, gasping
For breath. But Wiglaf sprinkled water
Over his lord, until the words
Deep in his breast broke through and were heard.
Beholding the treasure he spoke, haltingly:
"For this, this gold, these jewels, I thank
Our Father in Heaven, Ruler of the Earth—
For all of this, that His grace has given me,
Allowed me to bring to my people while breath
Still came to my lips. I sold my life
For this treasure, and I sold it well. Take
What I leave, Wiglaf, lead my people,
Help them; my time is gone. Have
The brave Geats build me a tomb,
When the funeral flames have burned me, and build it
Here, at the water's edge, high
On this spit of land, so sailors can see
This tower, and remember my name, and call it
Beowulf's tower, and boats in the darkness
And mist, crossing the sea, will know it."
Then that brave king gave the golden
Necklace from around his throat to Wiglaf,
Gave him his gold-covered helmet, and his rings,
And his mail shirt, and ordered him to use them well:
"You're the last of all our far-flung family.
Fate has swept our race away,
Taken warriors in their strength and led them
To the death that was waiting. And now I follow them."
The old man's mouth was silent, spoke
No more, had said as much as it could;
He would sleep in the fire, soon. His soul
Left his flesh, flew to glory. . . .
And when the battle was over Beowulf's followers
Came out of the wood, cowards and traitors,
Knowing the dragon was dead. Afraid,
While it spit its fires, to fight in their lord's

816 spit: a narrow point of land extending into a body of water.

C **805–819** How will Beowulf continue to aid his people after his death?

D **833** In what sense are Beowulf's followers traitors? Whom or what have they betrayed?

Defense, to throw their javelins and spears,
They came like shamefaced jackals, their shields
In their hands, to the place where the prince lay dead,
And waited for Wiglaf to speak. He was sitting
Near Beowulf's body, wearily sprinkling
Water in the dead man's face, trying
To stir him. He could not. No one could have kept
Life in their lord's body, or turned
Aside the Lord's will: world
E And men and all move as He orders,
And always have, and always will.
  Then Wiglaf turned and angrily told them
What men without courage must hear.
Wexstan's brave son stared at the traitors,
His heart sorrowful, and said what he had to:
  "I say what anyone who speaks the truth
Must say. . . .
Too few of his warriors remembered
To come, when our lord faced death, alone.
And now the giving of swords, of golden
Rings and rich estates, is over,
Ended for you and everyone who shares
Your blood: when the brave Geats hear
How you bolted and ran none of your race
2 Will have anything left but their lives. And death
Would be better for them all, and for you, than the kind
Of life you can lead, branded with disgrace!"
      Then the warriors rose,
Walked slowly down from the cliff, stared
3 At those wonderful sights, stood weeping as they saw
Beowulf dead on the sand, their bold
Ring-giver resting in his last bed;
He'd reached the end of his days, their mighty
F War-king, the great lord of the Geats,
Gone to a glorious death. . . .

836 javelins (jăv′lĭnz): light spears used as weapons.

837 jackals (jăk′əlz): doglike animals that sometimes feed on the flesh of dead beasts.

859 bolted: ran away; fled.

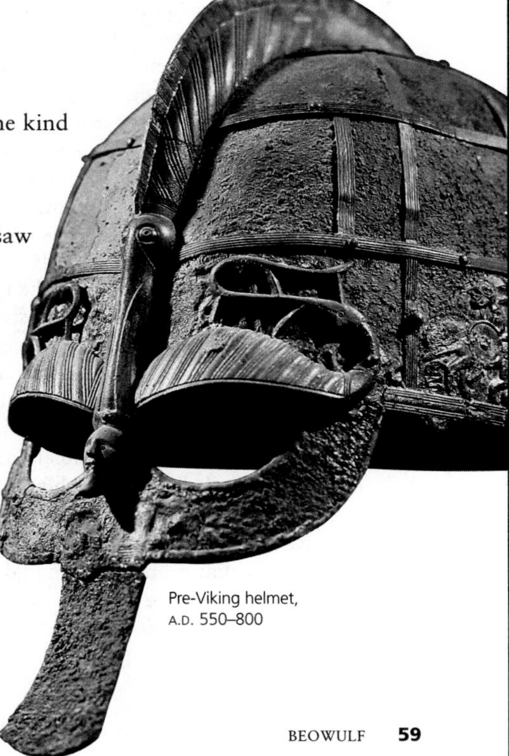

Pre-Viking helmet, A.D. 550–800

Customizing Instruction

Less Proficient Readers

1 To help students **clarify** the meaning of lines 801–803, have them explain to whom *his* refers in line 802 and to whom it refers in line 803.
Answer: Wiglaf; Beowulf.

2 Ask students what consequence the warriors' cowardice will have for the rest of the Geat tribe, according to Wiglaf.
Possible Response: It will dishonor and disgrace the entire community.

Students Acquiring English

3 Explain that here "wonderful" means "capable of exciting wonder; astonishing."

BEOWULF **59**

Reading and Analyzing

GUIDE FOR READING

A Explain that *mild* in this context means something like "considerate" or "merciful."

MOURNING BEOWULF

Then the Geats built the tower, as Beowulf
Had asked, strong and tall, so sailors
Could find it from far and wide; working
For ten long days they made his monument,
Sealed his ashes in walls as straight
And high as wise and willing hands
Could raise them. And the riches he and Wiglaf
Had won from the dragon, rings, necklaces,
Ancient, hammered armor—all
The treasures they'd taken were left there, too,
Silver and jewels buried in the sandy
Ground, back in the earth, again
And forever hidden and useless to men.
And then twelve of the bravest Geats
Rode their horses around the tower,
Telling their sorrow, telling stories
Of their dead king and his greatness, his glory,
Praising him for heroic deeds, for a life
As noble as his name. So should all men
Raise up words for their lords, warm
With love, when their shield and protector leaves
His body behind, sends his soul
On high. And so Beowulf's followers
Rode, mourning their belovéd leader,

Crying that no better king had ever
Lived, no prince so mild, no man
So open to his people, so deserving of praise.

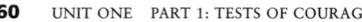

Ornamental bird used as decoration on a shield, from the Sutton Hoo ship burial

896 mild: gentle or kindly. Do you agree that Beowulf was a mild ruler? Why or why not?

Teaching Options

Assessment Informal Assessment

BIOGRAPHICAL ENTRY Provide students copies of biographical dictionaries or other biographical reference books. To informally assess your students' understanding of the selection, have them write a similar brief biography of Beowulf.
Include information about his background, experiences, and achievements.

RUBRIC

3 Full Accomplishment Students exhibit clear understanding of Beowulf's character and goals. They accurately and concisely describe events in the selection, placing them in the correct order.

2 Substantial Accomplishment Students exhibit some understanding of Beowulf's character. They correctly order most of the events in the selection and describe them accurately.

1 Little or Partial Accomplishment Student biographies indicate some confusion about the events in the selection, missing some or placing them in incorrect sequence.

A Collaboration Across 1,200 Years

Review by D. J. R. Bruckner

A Modern Scop *Listening to the story of* Beowulf *sung by a scop playing a harp is no longer an experience confined to the past. American musician and medieval scholar Benjamin Bagby has begun performing* Beowulf *in the original Anglo-Saxon to enthusiastic audiences. Bagby likens* Beowulf *to a "campfire ghost story" and compares his performances to rap and jazz, both of which involve improvisation and spontaneity. The following review, written in 1997, captures the excitement of Bagby's* Beowulf.

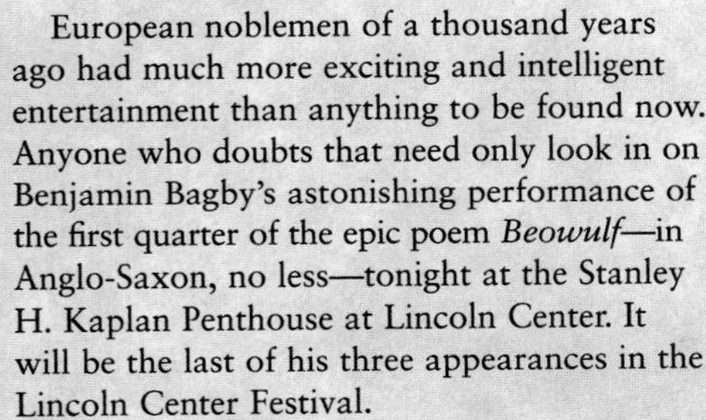

B European noblemen of a thousand years ago had much more exciting and intelligent entertainment than anything to be found now. Anyone who doubts that need only look in on Benjamin Bagby's astonishing performance of the first quarter of the epic poem *Beowulf*—in Anglo-Saxon, no less—tonight at the Stanley H. Kaplan Penthouse at Lincoln Center. It will be the last of his three appearances in the Lincoln Center Festival.

From the moment he strode on stage on Sunday for the opening night, silencing the audience with that famous first word, "Hwaet!" ("Pay attention!"), until hell swallowed the "pagan soul" of the monster's maw, there were bursts of laughter, mutters and sighs, and when Mr. Bagby's voice stopped at the end, as abruptly as it had begun, there was an audible rippling gasp before a thunderclap of applause from cheering people who called him back again and again, unwilling to let him go.

Mr. Bagby—a Midwesterner who fell in love with *Beowulf* at 12 and who now is co-director of a medieval music ensemble, Sequentia, in Cologne, Germany—accompanies himself on a six-string lyre modeled on one C found in a seventh-century tomb near Stuttgart. This surprisingly facile instrument underscores the meter of the epic verses and is counterpoint to Mr. Bagby's voice as he recites, chants and occasionally sings the lines.

On the whole, this is a restrained presentation. The performer captures listeners at once simply by letting us feel his conviction that he has a tale to tell that is more captivating than

LITERARY LINK

Reading Skills and Strategies:
MAKING INFERENCES

B Discuss with students the role that a bard or scop must have played at royal houses during the ninth century. What kind of greeting would the entertainers have received?

Reading Skills and Strategies:
CLARIFYING

C The original lyre found in the tomb, upon which Mr. Bagby's model is based, was made from oak. Explain that the lyre is a harp-like stringed instrument.

Viewing and Representing

LITERATURE IN PERFORMANCE

STORYTELLER Syd Lieberman weaves the legendary tale of Beowulf's battle with the monster Grendel.

"It's the first story in our language," says Lieberman, explaining his interest in the tale, "and, of all things, it's a monster story. There's something about scary tales that people love. *Beowulf* has all the ingredients of a wonderful tale—blood and gore, drama, good versus evil."

Lieberman enjoys bringing this ancient story alive for audiences: "I try to have the audience imagine they are around a camp fire or in a mead hall."

VIDEO

Literature in Performance

Reading and Analyzing

Reading Skills and Strategies: COMPARING

Ask students to compare the review of Bagby's presentation of *Beowulf* with their own responses to the written text.

any other story in the world. He avoids histrionic gestures, letting the majestic rhythms of the epic seize our emotions and guide them through the action. Gradually the many voices that fill the great poem emerge and the listener always knows who is speaking: a warrior, a watchman, a king, a sarcastic drunk. A translation is handed out to the audience, but after a while one notices people are following it less and just letting the sound of this strange and beautiful language wash over them. Perhaps not so strange, after all—enough phrases begin to penetrate the understanding that one finally knows deep down that, yes, this is where English came from.

How authentic is all this? Well, we know from many historical sources that in the first millennium at royal or noble houses a performer called a scop would present epics. Mr. Bagby has lived with this epic for many years, as well as with ancient music, and his performance is his argument that *Beowulf* was meant to be heard, not read, and that this is the way we ought to hear it. It is a powerful argument, indeed. The test of it is that when he has finished, you leave with the overwhelming impression that you know the anonymous poet who created *Beowulf* more than a dozen centuries ago, that you have felt the man's personality touch you. That is a much too rare experience in theater.

Teaching Options

Speaking and Listening

ANALYZING A PERFORMANCE REVIEW

Instruction Tell students that analyzing a review of a performance will give them insights into both the performer and the literary work.

Prepare Tell students the following criteria may be used to analyze a written review of a performance.

- identifies its subject at the beginning
- opens with a general opinion
- includes enough facts, examples, and specifics to support the general opinion
- displays logical organization
- quickly establishes a tone

Present Have students read and discuss the performance review. Then have students analyze and evaluate the review using the above criteria.

Additional Activity Show students the video "The Battle with Grendel." Have them write a review of the performance using the performance review as a model. Encourage them to share their reviews and compare them with their own responses.

Connect to the Literature

1. **What Do You Think?** How do you think you would have reacted to Beowulf's death if you had been one of his subjects?

Comprehension Check
- Who is the only person to help Beowulf battle the dragon?
- What happens to Beowulf as a result of the battle?
- What happens to the dragon and its treasure?

Think Critically

2. How would you describe Wiglaf's **character traits?**
3. Beowulf is able to defeat evil in the form of Grendel and Grendel's mother, yet he loses his life. What **theme** does this suggest about the struggle between good and evil?
4. In your opinion, what view of youth and old age does *Beowulf* convey? In answering, consider not only the details in the last part of the poem but also the earlier portrayals of Beowulf and Hrothgar.
5. On the basis of your reading of *Beowulf,* what qualities or values do you think the Anglo-Saxons admired?

THINK ABOUT
- Beowulf's reputation, position, and wealth
- Beowulf's behavior before and during his battles
- the behavior of other characters

6. ACTIVE READING MAKING JUDGMENTS According to the evidence that you recorded in the chart in your  READER'S NOTEBOOK, how well does *Beowulf* conform to the characteristics of a typical **epic?**

Extend Interpretations

7. **Critic's Corner** In his famous essay "Beowulf: The Monsters and the Critics," the author and scholar J.R.R. Tolkien wrote, "*Beowulf* is in fact so interesting as poetry, in places so powerful, that this quite overshadows the historical content, and is largely independent even of the most important facts . . . that research has discovered." Do you think Burton Raffel's verse translation captures that poetic power, or do you think this selection's greatest value is in its depiction of early Germanic tribal life? Explain your opinion.
8. **Connect to Life** In today's society we have our own kinds of "monsters" that threaten our safety or way of life. Who or what are today's monsters, and what threats do they pose?

Literary Analysis

ALLITERATION Old English poetry is often called alliterative verse because of the poets' extensive use of **alliteration**—the repetition of consonant sounds at the beginning of words. In modern poetry, alliteration may be used to emphasize certain words or images, heighten moods, or create musical effects. In Old English poetry, it was an integral part of the structure of the verse itself, like rhyme in much later European poetry.

Even if you can't understand these Old English lines from *Beowulf,* you can tell that the repeated sound is *w* in the first line, *g* in the second, and *f* in the third:

Wod under wolcnum to þæs he winreced,
goldsele gumena, gearwost wisse,
fættum fahne. . . .

In translating *Beowulf,* Burton Raffel could not reproduce the original alliteration, but he did use alliteration whenever possible. In this translation of the Old English lines above, notice how Raffel uses repeated *k* and *s* sounds to reinforce the image of Grendel's movement:

He moved quickly through the cloudy night,
Up from his swampland, sliding silently
Toward that gold-shining hall. . . .

Paired Activity Work with a partner to identify more examples of alliteration in Raffel's translation of *Beowulf.* Then explain what image, mood, or idea the alliteration helps to emphasize in each case.

Extend Interpretations

Critic's Corner This question is well suited for gifted students. **If you wish to make the question easier,** allow students to discuss it in small groups. Good responses will include either specific elements of the translation's poetic power (such as alliteration, or figurative language), or details related to early Germanic tribal life.

Connect to Life Students may mention diseases, natural or economic disasters, crime, bigotry, substance abuse, and environmental problems.

Literary Analysis

Paired Activity Students might extend the activity by writing sentences or lines of poetry that contain examples of alliteration.

GUIDING STUDENT RESPONSE

Connect to the Literature

1. **What Do You Think?**
Guidelines for student response: Students are likely to describe emotions and actions that mirror those of Beowulf's subjects as they mourn and pay respects to their dead leader. Good responses to the question will reflect students' understanding of epic heroes. For example, students may say that Beowulf was courageous and generous, that he fought evil to help his people, and that others were loyal to him.

Comprehension Check
- Wiglaf
- He dies.
- The dragon also dies; the treasure is buried with Beowulf's ashes in the tower.

 Use Selection Quiz in **Unit One Resource Book,** p. 12.

Think Critically

2. Wiglaf is courageous, loyal, respectful, honorable, and sincere.
3. Some students may say that the theme is death—death is inevitable in the struggle between good and evil. Others may say the theme is sacrifice—the death of a hero while conquering evil allows others to live without the threat of the evil force.
4. Students may point out that most heroic deeds are accomplished in youth or that youth is a time of strength and courage. With old age comes the wisdom, respect, and fame a person earned in his or her younger, bolder days.
5. Students' responses should include some or all of the following: fame, leadership, honorably earned wealth, courage, honesty, loyalty, generosity. They may point to Beowulf's position as prince and, later, as king; to his bravery and skill during his battles with Grendel, Grendel's mother, and the dragon; and to the respectful treatment that he received from his kinspeople and allies.
6. Most students will reply that *Beowulf* conforms well to the characteristics of a typical epic (as listed on page 29). Responses should include examples from the story of each characteristic.

Writing Options

1. A Warrior's Letter Imagine that you are one of Hrothgar's warriors. Write a letter to a comrade, in which you describe Grendel, his nightly visits, and your fears about what might happen.

2. Director's Notes Imagine that you are a movie director about to shoot scenes involving the three monsters that Beowulf fights: Grendel, his mother, and the fire-breathing dragon. To help you direct the scenes, make notes about each monster's motives, actions, strengths, and weaknesses and about the outcome of the monster's battle with Beowulf.

3. Anglo-Saxon News Story Write a news story describing one of Beowulf's three battles. Include details from the selection and statements from imaginary witnesses to the event.

4. Comparison Essay In an essay, compare and contrast Beowulf with a hero from popular culture, such as Indiana Jones, Batman, or Luke Skywalker. What makes each character heroic? You might organize your ideas in a Venn diagram like the one shown here. Place the essay in your **Working Portfolio.**

Beowulf | Batman | Luke Skywalker

Writing Handbook
See page 1367: Compare and Contrast.

Activities & Explorations

1. Cartoon Hero Choose one of Beowulf's three battles and turn it into a comic strip in which the action is largely or entirely conveyed by means of the illustrations that you draw. (If you prefer, you can use a pad of paper to create a flipbook version of the battle, so that the characters will appear to move.) ~ **ART**

2. Beowulf Aloud Divide up the selection with a small group of classmates so that each of you is responsible for a different portion. Then, imagining that you are scops of old, present *Beowulf* in a series of oral recitations, in which the reciter or another member of the group strums a harp, a guitar, or another stringed instrument as musical accompaniment. ~ **SPEAKING AND LISTENING**

3. A Video Scop View the video of a storyteller telling the legendary tale of Beowulf's battle with the monster Grendel. What did you like most about this interpretation? Least? How did it affect your understanding of the character of Beowulf? Choose a passage from the epic and develop your own storytelling version of it. ~ **VIEWING AND REPRESENTING**

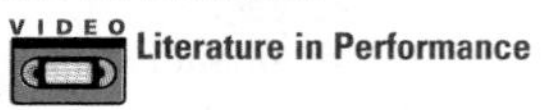

Inquiry & Research

1. Religious Beliefs Find out more about the religious beliefs of the Germanic peoples in Beowulf's day and of the Anglo-Saxons after they adopted Christianity. Who were the pre-Christian Germanic gods? What role did fate play in pre-Christian Germanic beliefs? When were the various Germanic peoples converted to Christianity? What role did Christianity play in the Anglo-Saxons' daily life? Present your findings in a written report.

Shoulder clasps from the Sutton Hoo burial

2. Sutton Who? Investigate the discovery of the ship burial at Sutton Hoo in Suffolk, England. Who was buried there, and when was he most likely buried? Why was he buried in a ship? What have the artifacts found at the site revealed about Anglo-Saxon culture? Share your research with the rest of the class.

More Online: Research Starter
www.mcdougallittell.com

Writing Options

1. **A Warrior's Letter** Students' letters should include words and images that capture an overall mood or atmosphere in keeping with the warrior's emotional response.
2. **Director's Notes** Students' notes should include accurate details relating to each monster's behavior and how it contributes to the outcome of its battle with Beowulf.
3. **Anglo-Saxon News Story** Information should tell who, what, where, when, how, and why. The most important information should appear in the opening paragraphs.
4. **Comparison Essay** Good responses will clearly identify several heroic qualities, explain which of the qualities each hero exhibits, and provide relevant details.

Activities & Explorations

1. **Cartoon Hero** Students might research animation before they begin. Those who create a flipbook might videotape it on fast speed and then show it at a slower speed.
2. ***Beowulf* Aloud** The mini-lesson on page 37 provides tips on preparing students for dramatic readings.
3. **A Video Scop** Responses should reflect students' understanding that reading aloud is an act of interpretation. It should also include supportable opinions about the video performance they viewed.

Inquiry & Research

Some students may prefer to work with a group to find source materials. Suggest that they visit the school library, a local library, or look on the Internet. Remind students to keep an accurate record of bibliographical information. If students search for information online, be sure that they use reliable sources.

1. **Religious Beliefs** To make the activity easier, have students write a separate answer for each question.
2. **Sutton Who?** Suggest that students interested in including graphics in their reports choose the **Sutton Who?** activity. Have them include sketches or annotated photocopies of the artifacts.

Vocabulary in Action

EXERCISE A: CONTEXT CLUES On your paper, write the vocabulary word that best completes each sentence.

1. With each razor-sharp ________, Grendel tore his victim's flesh.
2. Grendel loved evil and seemed to ________ his nightly visits to Herot.
3. After the battle, Grendel was left ________ in agony on the floor.
4. The Danes rejoiced when Beowulf was finally able to ________ Herot of Grendel.
5. Grendel and his mother lived in the ________ depths of a dark lake.
6. Many people went on the ________ to see the lake where Grendel had died.
7. Beowulf was not one of the warriors ________ in fear of the monsters.

EXERCISE B: WORD MEANING On your paper, write *T* for each true statement and *F* for each false statement.

1. Grendel's visits were an **affliction** for the Danish people.
2. Grendel liked to **gorge** on Danish people, not pastry.
3. During their battle, Grendel tore flesh out of Beowulf's **taut** throat.
4. Grendel lost his claw because Beowulf locked it in tight **fetters**.
5. Grendel's mother was another **loathsome** monster.
6. Beowulf's fight with the dragon left him with a swollen, **livid** wound that would prove fatal.
7. To the Geats, Beowulf was an **infamous** king.
8. Not one **lament** was sung at Beowulf's funeral.

WORDS TO KNOW					
affliction	gorge	livid	pilgrimage	talon	
cowering	infamous	loathsome	purge	taut	
fetter	lament	murky	relish	writhing	

Building Vocabulary
For an in-depth study of context clues, see page 938.

The Beowulf Poet
About 750?

An Anonymous Author Nothing is known about the author of *Beowulf* except what can be inferred from the poem itself. Clearly the author was an educated person familiar with Christianity and the Bible; details in the poem also suggest that he knew something of ancient epics, such as Virgil's *Aeneid.* From their study of the poem's language and ideas, some scholars have concluded that the poet lived in northern England in the eighth century A.D. Others, however, dispute that conclusion, maintaining that he probably lived in southwestern England two centuries later. Whenever he lived, he drew on an oral tradition of poems celebrating the hero Beowulf.

A Famous Manuscript Only one copy of *Beowulf* has survived from Anglo-Saxon times. Dating from about the year 1000, it is the work of Christian monks who preserved the literature of the past by copying manuscripts. After escaping destruction several times, the *Beowulf* manuscript is now safely housed in the British Library in London.

The Electronic Beowulf Today, the most up-to-date technology is being used to preserve the fragile manuscript. The Electronic Beowulf Project is creating detailed digital images of every page so that scholars can study them on computers, without handling the actual manuscript.

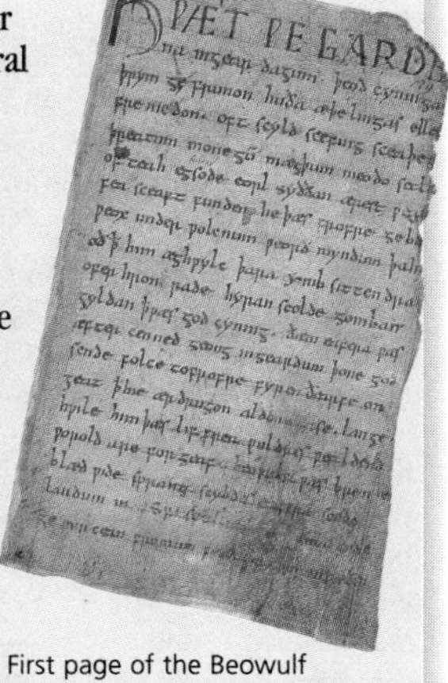

First page of the Beowulf manuscript, showing fire damage

LaserLinks: Background for Reading
Storyteller

Vocabulary in Action

Exercise A
1. talon
2. relish
3. writhing
4. purge
5. murky
6. pilgrimage
7. cowering

Exercise B
1. T
2. T
3. F
4. T
5. T
6. T
7. F
8. F

OVERVIEW

Objectives

1. **compare** two of the world's great epics
2. appreciate the author's use of **similes** and **epic similes (Literary Analysis)**
3. identify and **classify characters** to understand the epic poem **(Active Reading)**

Summary

The Greek hero Achilles vows to avenge the death of his friend, Patroclus, who has been killed by the Trojan warrior Hector. When Achilles and Hector duel, Achilles stabs Hector in the neck and then refuses Hector's dying request to return his body to the Trojan people. Achilles next ties Hector's corpse to his chariot and drags it to the Greek camp. Hector's father—Priam, king of Troy—goes to the Greek camp to beg for his son's body. Moved by the old man's grief and prompted by the gods, Achilles agrees to return Hector's body to the Trojans.

Use **Unit One Resource Book,** p. 13 for additional support.

Thematic Link

Both Achilles and Hector face **tests of courage** in this epic story. Achilles must overcome despair over the death of his friend in order to seek revenge. Hector must summon the courage first to confront his foe and then to die boldly rather than dishonorably.

5-Minute Warm-Up

Daily Language SkillBuilder

Have students **proofread** the display sentences on page 15k and write them correctly. The sentences also appear on Transparency 1 of **Grammar Transparencies and Copymasters.**

Preteaching Vocabulary

If you would like to preteach the WORDS TO KNOW for this selection, use the Mini Lesson pp. 68–69.

PREPARING to *Read*

from the Iliad

Epic Poetry by HOMER
Translated by ROBERT FITZGERALD

Comparing Literature of the World

The Epic Hero Across Cultures

Comparing *Beowulf* and the *Iliad* The *Iliad* was written centuries before *Beowulf.* Nonetheless, there are many similarities between the two poems.

Points of Comparison

As you read the following excerpt from the *Iliad,* compare the heroes Hector and Achilles with Beowulf. Consider the following characteristics of an epic hero as you make your comparisons:

- heroic actions that determine the fate of nations or groups of people
- heroic deeds and actions that reflect the values of the age
- the hero's interaction with supernatural beings and events

Build Background

When Greeks and Trojans War The *Iliad* is an epic poem believed to be the work of a Greek poet named Homer in the eighth century B.C. The setting of the poem is the Trojan War, a conflict between Greeks and Trojans at the ancient city of Troy in Asia Minor. Most historians believe that some type of conflict involving Greeks and Trojans did in fact occur around 1200 B.C. According to Homer's poem, the Trojan War resulted when Paris, a prince of Troy, kidnapped Helen, the world's most beautiful woman, from her Greek home. This action naturally offended her husband, King Menelaus (mĕn'ə-lā'əs), who gathered an army of Greeks and set out to invade Troy and bring Helen home. Under the leadership of his brother Agamemnon (ăg'ə-mĕm'nŏn'), the Greeks laid siege to the walled city of Troy for ten years before finally achieving victory. The *Iliad* relates events that took place in the final year of that siege. The excerpts in the following selection show the grim results of clashing loyalties.

WORDS TO KNOW
Vocabulary Preview

abstain	flouting
clamor	havoc
defile	ponderous
destitute	quell
elude	scourge
evade	vulnerable
evocation	whetted
exult	

Focus Your Reading

LITERARY ANALYSIS SIMILE AND EPIC SIMILE

A simile is a figure of speech that uses *like* or *as* to make a comparison between two things. For example, when the poet says, "Now like a lion at one bound Achilles left the room," he uses a simile to compare the Greek warrior to a lion in his speed and strength. An **epic simile** is a long figurative comparison in an epic poem that often continues for a number of lines. An example can be found in lines 89–92 of the *Iliad.* As you read this selection from the *Iliad*, look for other examples of similes and epic similes.

ACTIVE READING CLASSIFYING CHARACTERS

The *Iliad* is a complex story involving many characters—both human and divine. In order to understand what is happening in the epic, it is important to keep track of these various characters.

READER'S NOTEBOOK Create a list of the following characters: Achilles, Hector, Thetis, Zeus, Patroclus, Pallas Athena, Apollo, Hermes, and Priam. As you read, use the notes that accompany the text to help you classify each character as a Greek, a Trojan, or a god. For each god, indicate whether he or she is helping the Greeks or the Trojans. Jot down the important actions and characteristics of each character.

LESSON RESOURCES

UNIT ONE RESOURCE BOOK, pp. 13–17

ASSESSMENT RESOURCES
Formal Assessment, pp. 9–10
Teacher's Guide to Assessment and Portfolio Use
Test Generator

SKILLS TRANSPARENCIES AND COPYMASTERS
Literary Analysis
- Poetic Devices, T16 (for Literary Analysis, p. 81)

Reading and Critical Thinking
- Using an Outline, T44 (for Writing Option 3, p. 82)

Grammar
- Parts of Speech, C62 (for Mini Lesson, p. 75)

Vocabulary
- Using a Dictionary, C20 (for Mini Lesson, p. 80)

Writing
- Showing, Not Telling, T22 (for Writing Option 2, p. 82)
- Compare-Contrast, C34 (for Writing Option 4, p. 82)

Communications
- Dramatic Reading, T12 (for Activities & Explorations 1, p. 82)

INTEGRATED TECHNOLOGY
Audio Library
LaserLinks
- Art Gallery: Art of the Trojan War. See **Teacher's SourceBook,** p. 8.

Internet: Research Starter
Visit our website:
www.mcdougallittell.com

from THE ILIAD

HOMER

While the Greeks are laying siege to Troy, a quarrel breaks out between Agamemnon and his greatest warrior Achilles (ə-kĭl'ēz). As a result, the angry Achilles decides to remain in his tent and let the Greeks fight without him. With Achilles off the battlefield, the Trojans, under the leadership of Hector, are able to drive the Greeks back to the sea. During the battle, Hector kills Achilles' best friend, Patroclus (pə-trō'kləs). While grieving for his friend, Achilles is visited by his mother, Thetis (thē'tĭs), a goddess of the sea.

Death of Hector, sixth-century B.C. Corinthian bowl painting

from Book 18

THE IMMORTAL SHIELD

Bending near
her groaning son, the gentle goddess wailed
and took his head between her hands in pity,
saying softly:

"Child, why are you weeping?
What great sorrow came to you? Speak out,

TEACHING THE LITERATURE

Customizing Instruction

Less Proficient Readers
Have students review the characteristics of epics explained on pages 28 and 29. As they read the *Iliad* they can write examples of each characteristic in their Reader's Notebooks.

Gifted and Talented
As students read the selection, have them compare the roles of women in the *Iliad* and *Beowulf.* They can read further in each of the epics to widen their familiarity with characters.

Students Acquiring English
Help students understand the modern idiom *Achilles' heel.* When Achilles was born, Thetis dipped him in the River Styx to make him invulnerable, but the water never touched the heel by which she held him. After the events described in this selection, the Trojan prince Paris shoots Achilles with an arrow, mortally wounding him in his only vulnerable spot—hence the expression *Achilles' heel,* referring to someone's weak spot.

Use **Spanish Study Guide** for additional support, pp. 7–9

Mini Lesson Viewing and Representing

Death of Hector, **anonymous**

ART APPRECIATION

Instruction The bowl on which this painting appears was produced in the ancient Greek city of Corinth, which was founded in Homeric times. The bowl was made in the sixth century B.C.

Application Ask students what the two figures standing over Hector's body might be trying to do.

Possible Responses: They are guarding the body; participating in a funeral; trying to move the body.

ILIAD 67

Reading and Analyzing

Literary Analysis SIMILE

A Point out that the figurative language in lines 48–50 uses *than* and *like* to state a comparison. Ask students what anger is being compared to in these lines.

Possible Response: It is compared to honey and smoke.

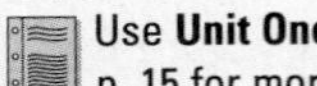
Use **Unit One Resource Book,** p. 15 for more exercises

Literary Analysis: CHARACTERIZATION

B You might point out that the hero Heracles is perhaps better known to students by his Roman name, Hercules. Ask students to name the characteristic for which Hercules is known.

Answer: He is known for his great strength.

GUIDE FOR READING

C **Possible Response:** He is resigned to his fate and does not seem concerned about meeting his death.

Active Reading
CLASSIFYING CHARACTERS

D Ask students who the god Apollo protects. Then ask who the goddess Pallas Athena is helping when she persuades him to fight Achilles.

Answer: Apollo protects the Trojans. Athena is helping Achilles and the Greeks.

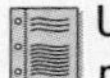
Use **Unit One Resource Book,** p. 14 for more practice.

do not conceal it. Zeus
did all you asked: Achaean troops,
for want of you, were all forced back again
upon the ship sterns, taking heavy losses
none of them could wish."

The great runner
groaned and answered:

"Mother, yes, the master
of high Olympus brought it all about,
but how have I benefited? My greatest friend
is gone: Patroclus, comrade in arms, whom I
held dear above all others—dear as myself—
now gone, lost; Hector cut him down, despoiled him
of my own arms, massive and fine, a wonder
in all men's eyes. The gods gave them to Peleus
that day they put you in a mortal's bed—
how I wish the immortals of the sea
had been your only consorts! How I wish
Peleus had taken a mortal queen! Sorrow
immeasurable is in store for you as well,
when your own child is lost: never again
on his homecoming day will you embrace him!
I must reject this life, my heart tells me,
reject the world of men,
if Hector does not feel my battering spear
tear the life out of him, making him pay
in his own blood for the slaughter of Patroclus!"

Letting a tear fall, Thetis said:

"You'll be
swift to meet your end, child, as you say:
your doom comes close on the heels of Hector's own."

Achilles the great runner ground his teeth
and said:

"May it come quickly. As things were,
I could not help my friend in his extremity.
Far from his home he died; he needed me
to shield him or to parry the death stroke.
For me there's no return to my own country.

GUIDE FOR READING

6–7 Previously Achilles asked Thetis to persuade Zeus (zo͞os), ruler of the gods, to turn the tide of battle against the Greeks so that they would see how much they needed him.

7 Achaean (ə-kē′ən): Greek.

12 Olympus (ə-lĭm′pəs): the highest mountain in Greece, on whose peak the Greek gods and goddesses were thought to dwell.

16–17 Patroclus wore Achilles' armor to frighten the Trojans. "Despoiled him of my own arms" refers to Hector's taking the armor from Patroclus' corpse.

18 Peleus (pē′lē-əs): Achilles' human father.

38 parry: to turn aside the thrust of a sword.

Teaching Options

Preteaching Vocabulary

ANTONYMS

Instruction Call students' attention to the list of WORDS TO KNOW. Explain that in this lesson they will be learning the definitions of the WORDS TO KNOW and then choosing the best antonym for each one.

Model Write the following example on the chalk board.

abstain **A.** purify **B.** surrender **C.** indulge

Abstain is a verb meaning "to hold oneself back deliberately." If necessary have students look up the definitions of *purify, surrender,* and *indulge.* Discuss why *indulge* is the best antonym for *abstain.*

Exercise Have students use dictionaries to find the definitions of the WORDS TO KNOW. Then ask them to choose the best antonym for each word.

1. clamor
   A. silence **B.** dryness **C.** fear
2. defile
   A. disorganize **B.** protect **C.** murder
3. destitute
   A. wealthy **B.** immoral **C.** free

Not the slightest gleam of hope did I
afford Patroclus or the other men
whom Hector overpowered. Here I sat,
my weight a useless burden to the earth,
and I am one who has no peer in war
among Achaean captains—
though in council
there are wiser. Ai! let strife and rancor
perish from the lives of gods and men,
with anger that envenoms even the wise
A and is far sweeter than slow-dripping honey,
clouding the hearts of men like smoke: just so
the marshal of the army, Agamemnon,
moved me to anger. But we'll let that go,
though I'm still sore at heart; it is all past,
and I have quelled my passion as I must.

Now I must go to look for the destroyer
of my great friend. I shall confront the dark
drear spirit of death at any hour Zeus
and the other gods may wish to make an end.
Not even Heracles escaped that terror
B though cherished by the Lord Zeus. Destiny
and Hera's bitter anger mastered him.
Likewise with me, if destiny like his
awaits me, I shall rest when I have fallen!
Now, though, may I win my perfect glory
and make some wife of Troy break down,
or some deep-breasted Dardan woman sob
and wipe tears from her soft cheeks. They'll know then
how long they had been spared the deaths of men,
while I abstained from war!
Do not attempt to keep me from the fight,
though you love me; you cannot make me listen."

46 rancor (răng'kər): bitter, long-lasting ill will.

48 envenoms (ĕn-vĕn'əmz): fills with poison.

59–61 Heracles (hĕr'ə-klēz'): the greatest legendary hero of ancient Greece, son of Zeus and a mortal woman named Alcmena (ălk-mē'nə). Zeus' wife, the goddess Hera (hîr'ə), hated and persecuted Heracles until his death.

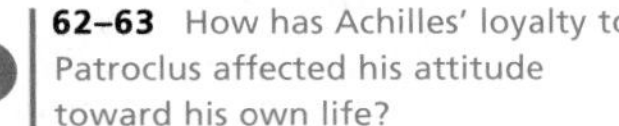

C **62–63** How has Achilles' loyalty to Patroclus affected his attitude toward his own life?

66 Dardan (där'dn): Trojan.

D **Achilles seeks to avenge Patroclus by slaughtering Trojans. Apollo, a god who protects Troy, opens the gates of the city so that the Trojans can rush to safety inside the walls. Only Hector is left outside. Achilles chases him around the walls of Troy three times. Finally the goddess Pallas Athena** (păl'əs ə-thē'nə)**, disguised as Hector's brother Deiphobus** (dē-ĭf'ə-bəs)**, appears to Hector and persuades him to fight Achilles.** 1

WORDS TO KNOW

quell (kwĕl) *v.* to quiet; suppress
abstain (ăb-stān') *v.* to hold oneself back deliberately

69

Customizing Instruction

Less Proficient Readers

1 Make sure students understand what Achilles plans to do.

- Who was Patroclus?
  Answer: He was Achilles' best friend.
- How did Patroclus die, and why was Achilles not present?
  Answer: Patroclus was killed by the Trojan warrior Hector during a battle; Achilles did not fight because he was angry with his commander.
- What does Achilles plan to do?
  Answer: He plans to avenge Patroclus' death.
- **Set a Purpose** Ask students to read to find out whether Achilles will satisfy his vengeance.

4. elude
A. shout **B.** memorize **C.** encounter

5. evade
A. confront **B.** promise **C.** forget

6. evocation
A. speech **B.** repression **C.** reminiscence

7. ponderous
A. jolly **B.** light **C.** bold

8. quell
A. express **B.** write **C.** tremble

9. scourge
A. preference **B.** reward **C.** compliment

Use **Unit One Resource Book,** p. 16 for more practice.

Reading and Analyzing

Literary Analysis EPIC SIMILE

A Note that a characteristic style element of the *Iliad* is the use of long, figurative comparisons. An example of one of these comparisons, or epic similes, can be found in lines 89–92. Ask students what Achilles might mean by this comparison.

Possible Responses: He and Hector are natural enemies; he will make no pacts with Hector.

Reading Skills and Strategies: ANALYZING

B Ask students to identify Achilles' emotions during his exchange with Hector.

Possible Response: Students may say that his responses include anger, hatred, bitterness, vengefulness.

Active Reading CLASSIFYING CHARACTERS

C Ask students who Zeus favors now, and who he has favored in the past.

Answer: Now he favors the Greeks; in the past he has favored the Trojans.

Ask: What does this information reveal about Zeus's character?

Possible Responses: He is fickle; he uses his power randomly; he is not dependable; he probably had a good reason to switch allegiance.

from Book 22

DESOLATION BEFORE TROY

And when at last the two men faced each other,
Hector was the first to speak. He said:

"I will no longer fear you as before,
son of Peleus, though I ran from you
round Priam's town three times and could not face you.
Now my soul would have me stand and fight,
whether I kill you or am killed. So come,
we'll summon gods here as our witnesses,
none higher, arbiters of a pact: I swear
that, terrible as you are,
I'll not insult your corpse should Zeus allow me
victory in the end, your life as prize.
Once I have your gear, I'll give your body
back to Achaeans. Grant me, too, this grace."

But swift Achilles frowned at him and said:

"Hector, I'll have no talk of pacts with you,
forever unforgiven as you are.
As between men and lions there are none,
no concord between wolves and sheep, but all
hold one another hateful through and through,
so there can be no courtesy between us,
no sworn truce, till one of us is down
and glutting with his blood the wargod Ares.
Summon up what skills you have. By god,
you'd better be a spearman and a fighter!
Now there is no way out. Pallas Athena
will have the upper hand of you. The weapon
belongs to me. You'll pay the reckoning
in full for all the pain my men have borne,
who met death by your spear."

He twirled and cast
his shaft with its long shadow. Splendid Hector,
keeping his eye upon the point, eluded it
by ducking at the instant of the cast,

76 Priam (prī′əm): the king of Troy.

80 arbiters (är′bĭ-tərz): judges; referees.

84–85 The Greeks and Trojans generally returned the bodies of the slain to their commanders or companions.

90 concord (kŏn′kôrd′): peace or harmony.

94 glutting with his blood the wargod Ares (âr′ēz): satisfying Ares, the god of war, by bleeding to death.

97–98 Pallas Athena, the goddess of wisdom, favors the Greeks.

WORDS TO KNOW **elude** (ĭ-lo͞od′) *v.* to avoid or escape

70

Teaching Options

Epic Traditions

The world's oldest surviving epic is from ancient Mesopotamia (now part of Iraq), a region between the Tigris and Euphrates rivers. Predating the *Iliad* by over a thousand years, the *Epic of Gilgamesh* tells of a Sumerian king who ruled the city-state of Uruk between 3000 and 2000 B.C.

According to the epic, Gilgamesh is part god, part human, and very arrogant, although he is also valiant and strong. Scholars believe that the epic was well-known in Greece and may have traveled there via the ancient Hittites of Asia Minor (now part of Turkey).

so shaft and bronze shank passed him overhead
and punched into the earth. But unperceived
by Hector, Pallas Athena plucked it out
and gave it back to Achilles. Hector said:

2 "A clean miss. Godlike as you are,
you have not yet known doom for me from Zeus.
You thought you had, by heaven. Then you turned
into a word-thrower, hoping to make me lose
my fighting heart and head in fear of you.
You cannot plant your spear between my shoulders
while I am running. If you have the gift,
just put it through my chest as I come forward.
Now it's for you to dodge my own. Would god
you'd give the whole shaft lodging in your body!
War for the Trojans would be eased
if you were blotted out, bane that you are."

With this he twirled his long spearshaft and cast it,
hitting his enemy mid-shield, but off
and away the spear rebounded. Furious
that he had lost it, made his throw for nothing,
Hector stood bemused. He had no other.
Then he gave a great shout to Deiphobus
to ask for a long spear. But there was no one
near him, not a soul. Now in his heart
the Trojan realized the truth and said:

"This is the end. The gods are calling deathward.
I had thought
a good soldier, Deiphobus, was with me.
He is inside the walls. Athena tricked me.
Death is near, and black, not at a distance,
not to be evaded. Long ago
this hour must have been to Zeus's liking
and to the liking of his archer son.
They have been well disposed before, but now
the appointed time's upon me. Still, I would not
die without delivering a stroke,
or die ingloriously, but in some action
memorable to men in days to come."

Achilles dragging the body of Hector around the walls of Troy (about 520 B.C.), attributed to the Antiope Group. Attic black figure hydria, courtesy of the Museum of Fine Arts, Boston, William Francis Warden Fund.

120 bane: a cause of distress, death, or ruin.

125 bemused (bĭ-myo͞ozd'): dazed; confused.

135–139 Zeus' "archer son" is Apollo, god of the sun, whose arrows may represent the sun's rays. Until now, Zeus and Apollo have assisted the Trojans.

WORDS TO KNOW **evade** (ĭ-vād') *v.* to escape by cleverness or deception

Customizing Instruction

Students Acquiring English

1 Define *pact* as "an agreement." Ask students what pact Hector wants to make with Achilles.

Answer: He wants Achilles to agree that whoever wins will return the body of the other to his people.

Less Proficient Readers

2 Ask students to paraphrase line 110.

Possible Response: Zeus has not yet helped you to harm me.

BLOCK SCHEDULING: MANAGING TIME

If your schedule requires that you cover the lesson objectives in a shorter time, use . . .

- Preparing to Read, p. 66
- Thinking Through the Literature, p. 81
- Vocabulary in Action, p. 83

If you want to take advantage of longer class time, use . . .

- TE Teaching Options: Viewing and Representing, pp. 67, 76; Vocabulary, pp. 68, 80; Multicultural Link, pp. 70, 73; Cross Curricular Links, pp. 72, 78; Standardized Test Practice, p. 74; Grammar, p. 75; Speaking and Listening, p. 77; Informal Assessment, p. 79
- Choices & Challenges, p. 82

Reading and Analyzing

Literary Analysis EPIC SIMILE

A Ask students to what Hector and Achilles are being compared in lines 145–147.

Answer: Hector is compared to an eagle about to strike a victim; Achilles is compared to a lamb or cowering hare.

Ask: Are the comparisons valid?

Possible Responses: The comparison to the eagle is appropriate, but the one to the lamb or hare is not, since Achilles is not a weak or easily intimidated man.

Literary Analysis: CHARACTERIZATION

B Remind students that characters often reveal their personality traits in their speeches. Then ask students to tell what Achilles reveals about himself in his speech to the dying Hector.

Possible Response: He is boastful, proud, loyal to his friend, and capable of intense hatred.

Literary Analysis: METAPHOR

C Have students explain the meaning of the image in lines 204–205.

Possible Response: Achilles' heart is as hard and unyielding as iron.

With this he drew the <u>whetted</u> blade that hung
upon his left flank, <u>ponderous</u> and long,
collecting all his might the way an eagle
narrows himself to dive through shady cloud
and strike a lamb or cowering hare: so Hector
lanced ahead and swung his whetted blade.
Achilles with wild fury in his heart
pulled in upon his chest his beautiful shield—
his helmet with four burnished metal ridges
nodding above it, and the golden crest
Hephaestus locked there tossing in the wind.
Conspicuous as the evening star that comes,
amid the first in heaven, at fall of night,
and stands most lovely in the west, so shone
in sunlight the fine-pointed spear
Achilles poised in his right hand, with deadly
aim at Hector, at the skin where most
it lay exposed. But nearly all was covered
by the bronze gear he took from slain Patroclus,
showing only, where his collarbones
divided neck and shoulders, the bare throat
where the destruction of a life is quickest.
Here, then, as the Trojan charged, Achilles
drove his point straight through the tender neck,
but did not cut the windpipe, leaving Hector
able to speak and to respond. He fell
aside into the dust. And Prince Achilles
now <u>exulted</u>:

"Hector, had you thought
that you could kill Patroclus and be safe?
Nothing to dread from me; I was not there.
All childishness. Though distant then, Patroclus'
comrade in arms was greater far than he—
and it is I who had been left behind
that day beside the deepsea ships who now
have made your knees give way. The dogs and kites
will rip your body. His will lie in honor
when the Achaeans give him funeral."

Hector, barely whispering, replied:

153 Hephaestus (hĭ-fĕs'təs): the god of fire and blacksmith of the gods, who made Achilles' new armor.

160–161 Hector is wearing the armor of Achilles that he took from Patroclus' body.

177 kites: hawklike birds of prey.

178 "His [body]" refers to that of Patroclus.

WORDS TO KNOW

whetted (hwĕt'ĭd) *adj.* sharpened **whet** *v.*
ponderous (pŏn'dər-əs) *adj.* very heavy
exult (ĭg-zŭlt') *v.* to feel great joy, especially in conquest or triumph

72

Teaching Options

Cross Curricular Link **History**

GREEK INFLUENCE ON ROME Point out to students that ancient Greece heavily influenced the culture of ancient Rome, which flourished several centuries later. For example, the Romans adopted much of Greek mythology, often translating the Greek names into Roman ones. Therefore, most Roman gods and goddesses have earlier Greek equivalents. These include the following examples:

Greek	Roman
Zeus	Jupiter
Athena	Minerva
Aphrodite	Venus
Hermes	Mercury
Hephaestus	Vulcan

"I beg you by your soul and by your parents,
do not let the dogs feed on me
in your encampment by the ships. Accept
the bronze and gold my father will provide
as gifts, my father and her ladyship
my mother. Let them have my body back,
so that our men and women may accord me
decency of fire when I am dead."

Achilles the great runner scowled and said:

[3] "Beg me no beggary by soul or parents,
whining dog! Would god my passion drove me
to slaughter you and eat you raw, you've caused
such agony to me! No man exists
who could defend you from the carrion pack—
not if they spread for me ten times your ransom,
twenty times, and promise more as well;
aye, not if Priam, son of Dardanus,
tells them to buy you for your weight in gold!
You'll have no bed of death, nor will you be
laid out and mourned by her who gave you birth.
Dogs and birds will have you, every scrap."

Then at the point of death Lord Hector said:

"I see you now for what you are. No chance
to win you over. Iron in your breast
your heart is. Think a bit, though: this may be [4]
a thing the gods in anger hold against you
on that day when Paris and Apollo
destroy you at the Gates, great as you are."

Even as he spoke, the end came, and death hid him;
spirit from body fluttered to undergloom,
bewailing fate that made him leave his youth
and manhood in the world. And as he died
Achilles spoke again. He said:

"Die, make an end. I shall accept my own
whenever Zeus and the other gods desire."

At this he pulled his spearhead from the body,
laying it aside, and stripped

185–186 Hector's father is Priam, and his mother is Hecuba (hĕk'yə-bə).

188 Burning the bodies of the dead was customary. Truces were often arranged for this purpose.

194 carrion (kăr'ē-ən) **pack:** the wild animals that feed on dead flesh.

197 Dardanus (där'dn-əs): the founder of the line of Trojan kings. Here "son" means "descendant."

205–208 Although Achilles is still alive as the *Iliad* ends, other tales of the Trojan War tell how he is eventually killed by Hector's brother Paris, with the aid of Apollo.

Replica of Trojan Horse

Customizing Instruction

Multiple Learning Styles

1 Visual Learners Lines 149–164 include detailed information about how each warrior looks and positions himself just before Achilles launches his fatal attack against Hector. Have visual learners sketch this moment.

Students Acquiring English

2 Help students understand the comparison of Achilles' spear to the first evening star (lines 154–160) by reading the sentence aloud slowly. Then reread the sentence, pausing at each comma, and have students restate the phrase you just said in their own words.

Less Proficient Readers

3 Ask students to paraphrase the following: "Beg me no beggary by soul or parents."

Possible Response: Don't ask me for mercy by invoking my morals or thoughts of my parents.

Ask: What earlier line of Hector's does this one refer to?

Answer: "I beg you by your soul and by your parents."

Students Acquiring English

4 Ask students to restate the following in standard word order: "Iron in your breast your heart is."

Possible Response: Your heart is iron in your breast.

Point out that this is an example of inverted word order. Encourage students to look for other examples of inverted word order in the *Iliad.*

Multicultural Link: Mythology

Explain that a culture's myths often deal with or explain its deities.

- In Egyptian mythology, the supreme deity is the sun god known as Ra or Re; Osiris is the god of death and renewal; Osiris's wife and sister, Isis, is the goddess of fertility.
- Among the pre-Christian Germanic tribes, the chief god was Wotan (called Odin by the Norse, or Vikings); his wife is the goddess Fricka; and the god of strength and thunder is Donner (Thor to the Norse).
- According to Ashanti mythology, a god called Nyame created the universe. Many of Nyame's descendants are gods and goddesses who protect specific regions, represent geographic features, or are associated with particular occupations or crafts.

Reading and Analyzing

Reading Skills and Strategies: SPECULATING

A Ask students why the Greek soldiers all want to stab Hector's body.

Possible Response: Students may say that they want to take revenge on an enemy, to gloat over their victory, or to break the spirit of any Trojans who might be watching.

Literary Analysis: EPITHET

B Have students explain how Achilles has earned the descriptive phrase "the great master of pursuit."

Possible Response: He pursued and killed Hector.

GUIDE FOR READING

C Priam is willing to humble himself before his enemy and to expose himself to personal harm in order to recover Hector's body. In this, he shows great loyalty to his family. Some students may believe he is honorable to seek to end the mistreatment of Hector's body; others may feel that his loyalty to his son has overcome his sense of honor.

Active Reading

CLASSIFYING CHARACTERS

D If students are using a character chart to track which gods help the Greeks and which the Trojans, have them add Hermes at this point. Then ask students who Zeus seems to favor now.

Answer: He seems to favor the Trojans.

the bloodstained shield and cuirass from his shoulders.
Other Achaeans hastened round to see
A Hector's fine body and his comely face,
and no one came who did not stab the body.
Glancing at one another they would say:

"Now Hector has turned vulnerable, softer
than when he put the torches to the ships!"

B And he who said this would inflict a wound.
When the great master of pursuit, Achilles,
had the body stripped, he stood among them,
saying swiftly:

"Friends, my lords and captains
of Argives, now that the gods at last have let me
bring to earth this man who wrought
havoc among us—more than all the rest—
come, we'll offer battle around the city,
to learn the intentions of the Trojans now.
Will they give up their strongpoint at this loss?
Can they fight on, though Hector's dead?

But wait:
why do I ponder, why take up these questions?
Down by the ships Patroclus' body lies
unwept, unburied. I shall not forget him
while I can keep my feet among the living.
If in the dead world they forget the dead,
I say there, too, I shall remember him,
my friend. Men of Achaea, lift a song!
Down to the ships we go, and take this body,
our glory. We have beaten Hector down,
to whom as to a god the Trojans prayed."

Indeed, he had in mind for Hector's body
outrage and shame. Behind both feet he pierced
the tendons, heel to ankle. Rawhide cords
he drew through both and lashed them to his chariot,
letting the man's head trail. Stepping aboard,
bearing the great trophy of the arms,
he shook the reins, and whipped the team ahead

218 cuirass (kwĭ-răs'): an armored breastplate.

224 Hector's torching of the ships occurred when the Trojans forced the Greeks (fighting without Achilles) back to the sea.

228–229 captains of Argives (är'jīvz'): Greek officers.

240 The "dead world" is the house of Hades, or the underworld, where the Greeks believed the shades of the dead to reside.

WORDS TO KNOW

vulnerable (vŭl'nər-ə-bəl) *adj.* open to attack; easily hurt
havoc (hăv'ək) *n.* widespread destruction

74

Teaching Options

Assessment Standardized Test Practice

ANALOGIES

Instruction Explain that analogies in standardized tests are double comparisons that follow the pattern A : B :: C : D, which can be read, "A is to B as C is to D." Students are usually given one pair of words and asked to complete a second pair so that it expresses a similar relationship; for example:

helmet : head :: cuirass : _____

A. foot **B.** chest **C.** knee **D.** hand

The answer is **B.** chest: just as a helmet protects the head, a cuirass protects the chest. Analogies can show many other types of relationships, including synonyms, antonyms, cause and effect, and part to whole.

Exercise Have students select the letter of the word that best completes each analogy. Remind them to begin by identifying the relationship between the first two words.

1. destitute : needy :: vulnerable : _____
   A. weak **B.** strong **C.** foolish **D.** peaceful
2. cuirass : armor :: chariot : _____
   A. wheel **B.** trophy **C.** ship **D.** vehicle
3. spear : wound :: scourge : _____
   A. mire **B.** clamor **C.** surfeit **D.** havoc

into a willing run. A dustcloud rose
above the furrowing body; the dark tresses
flowed behind, and the head so princely once
lay back in dust. Zeus gave him to his enemies
to be <u>defiled</u> in his own fatherland.
So his whole head was blackened. Looking down,
his mother tore her braids, threw off her veil,
and wailed, heartbroken to behold her son.
Piteously his father groaned, and round him
lamentation spread throughout the town,
most like the <u>clamor</u> to be heard if Ilion's
towers, top to bottom, seethed in flames.
1 They barely stayed the old man, mad with grief,
from passing through the gates. Then in the mire
he rolled, and begged them all, each man by name:

263 Ilion (ĭl'ē-ən): another name for Troy.

2 "Relent, friends. It is hard; but let me go
out of the city to the Achaean ships.
I'll make my plea to that demonic heart.
He may feel shame before his peers, or pity
my old age. His father, too, is old.
Peleus, who brought him up to be a <u>scourge</u>
to Trojans, cruel to all, but most to me,
so many of my sons in flower of youth
he cut away. And, though I grieve, I cannot
mourn them all as much as I do one,
for whom my grief will take me to the grave—
and that is Hector. Why could he not have died
where I might hold him? In our weeping, then,
his mother, now so <u>destitute</u>, and I
might have had surfeit and relief of tears."

C **268–270** Think about Priam's decision to approach Achilles. What does this reveal about his sense of honor and loyalty?

282 surfeit (sûr'fĭt): more than enough for satisfaction.

D **Achilles and his warriors return to their camp and carry out the burial rites for Patroclus. Three times, Achilles drags Hector's body behind his chariot around Patroclus' grave. Afterwards, the gods cleanse and restore the body, and Zeus asks Thetis to tell Achilles to return the body to the Trojans. Priam sets out for the Greek camp, accompanied only by an old servant, to ask Achilles to return the body. He is not aware that the god Hermes** (hûr'mēz) **helps him by putting the sentries to sleep and opening the gates. Hermes leads Priam to Achilles' tent and then vanishes.** 3

WORDS TO KNOW

defile (dĭ-fīl') *v.* to make filthy; violate the honor of
clamor (klăm'ər) *n.* a loud, confused noise or outcry
scourge (skûrj) *n.* a source of great suffering or destruction
destitute (dĕs'tĭ-to͞ot') *adj.* lacking in resources; bereft

Customizing Instruction

Students Acquiring English

1 Point out to students that *mad* has more than one meaning. In line 265, *mad* means *crazed,* not *angry.* Ask students why Priam, who is grieving, might be described as *mad?*

Possible Response: Grieving people act irrationally; Priam tries to leave the safety of the city to go to his son's body.

Multiple Learning Styles

Auditory Learners

2 Some students may benefit from hearing Priam's speech read aloud. You might want to have two volunteers prepare dramatic readings, one expressing anger, the other sorrow. After the readings, discuss with students the differences between the two. Which one did students find more effective? Why?

Less Proficient Readers

3 Make sure students understand what takes place between Achilles and Hector.

- Which god or goddess helps Achilles kill Hector?
  Answer: Pallas Athena, disguised as Hector's brother, convinces Hector to fight Achilles.
- What is Hector's dying request?
  Answer: He asks that his body be returned to Troy.
- Why does Achilles refuse his request?
  Answer: He is angry with Hector for killing Patroclus.
- **Set a Purpose** Have students read to find out if Priam changes Achilles' mind.

Mini Lesson Grammar

OVERVIEW: PARTS OF SPEECH

Instruction The most basic elements of the English language are nouns and verbs. Nouns name people, places, things, qualities, and actions. Verbs express an action, condition, or state of being.

Activity Write this sentence on the chalkboard.

"Achilles wept."

Have students identify the noun and verb in the sentence. Then review the other parts of speech:

- **pronouns** replace nouns
- **adjectives** modify nouns or pronouns
- **adverbs** modify verbs, adjectives, or adverbs
- **conjunctions** connect words, phrases, or clauses
- **interjections** express strong feelings
- **prepositions** show relationship between a noun or a pronoun and another word.

Have students find the pronouns *(his),* adjectives *(best),* adverb *(bitterly),* in the following sentence.

Achilles wept bitterly for his best friend, Patroclus.

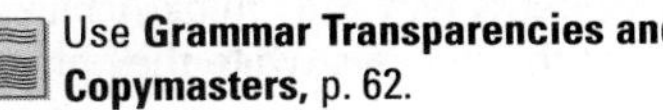

Use **Grammar Transparencies and Copymasters,** p. 62.

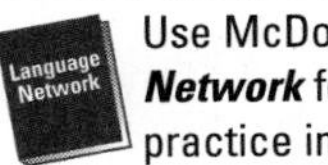

Use McDougal Littell's ***Language Network*** for more instruction and practice in parts of speech.

Reading and Analyzing

Literary Analysis: CHARACTERIZATION

A Ask students what Priam's actions reveal about him.

Possible Responses: He is a loyal and loving father; he is deeply grieved by his son's death; he is willing to risk danger for his son's sake.

Literary Analysis EPIC SIMILE

B Ask students to summarize the comparison made in the simile in lines 287–291.

Possible Response: The Greeks regard Priam with the same awe as people do when they encounter someone who has committed murder and is living in exile.

Ask students whether they find the comparison appropriate.

Possible Responses: Yes, because Priam is a kind of exile in the enemy's camp; no, because the comparison implies that Priam is guilty of something.

Literary Analysis: EPITHET

C Point out the phrase "killer of men" used to characterize Hector. Ask students whether they think the epithet is appropriate here.

Possible Responses: It is inappropriate, because the epithet jars with Priam's grief; it is appropriate, because it reminds the reader of Hector's achievements in war and the cause of Achilles' vengefulness.

GUIDE FOR READING

D **Possible Response:** Initially, Achilles' hatred made him vengeful and inflexible. Now that he has been moved to sympathy by Priam's pleas, he seems more human.

from Book 24

A GRACE GIVEN IN SORROW

Priam,
the great king of Troy, passed by the others,
(A) knelt down, took in his arms Achilles' knees,
and kissed the hands of wrath that killed his sons.

When, taken with mad Folly in his own land,
a man does murder and in exile finds
(B) refuge in some rich house, then all who see him
stand in awe.
So these men stood.
Achilles
gazed in wonder at the splendid king,
and his companions marveled too, all silent,
with glances to and fro. Now Priam prayed
to the man before him:

"Remember your own father,
Achilles, in your godlike youth: his years
like mine are many, and he stands upon
the fearful doorstep of old age. He, too,
is hard pressed, it may be, by those around him,
there being no one able to defend him
from bane of war and ruin. Ah, but he
may nonetheless hear news of you alive,
and so with glad heart hope through all his days
for sight of his dear son, come back from Troy,
while I have deathly fortune.

Noble sons
I fathered here, but scarce one man is left me.
Fifty I had when the Achaeans came,
nineteen out of a single belly, others
born of attendant women. Most are gone.
Raging Ares cut their knees from under them.
And he who stood alone among them all,
their champion, and Troy's, ten days ago
you killed him, fighting for his land, my prince,
Hector.

It is for him that I have come
among these ships, to beg him back from you,
and I bring ransom without stint.

316 stint: limitation.

Teaching Options

Viewing and Representing

Ajax and Achilles Playing Dice, **by Exekias**

ART APPRECIATION Exekias was a Greek artist who perfected the technique of painting figures in black over the natural colors of the clay vase. This vase painting from about 530 B.C. shows two legendary Greek warriors gambling, a popular activity among the Greek troops.

Application Ask students why they think Achilles and Ajax are holding their spears while they play.

Possible Response: They are holding their spears because they want to be ready for a sudden attack and because their spears are symbols of their courage and behavior.

Ask: Is this representation consistent with what they know about Achilles' personality?

Possible Response: Yes; Achilles is very defensive, quick to fight.

Achilles,
be reverent toward the great gods! And take
pity on me, remember your own father.
Think me more pitiful by far, since I
have brought myself to do what no man else
has done before—to lift to my lips the hand
of one who killed my son."

Now in Achilles
the evocation of his father stirred
new longing, and an ache of grief. He lifted
the old man's hand and gently put him by.
Then both were overborne as they remembered:
the old king huddled at Achilles' feet
wept, and wept for Hector, killer of men,
while great Achilles wept for his own father
as for Patroclus once again; and sobbing
filled the room.

But when Achilles' heart
had known the luxury of tears, and pain
within his breast and bones had passed away,
he stood then, raised the old king up, in pity
for his grey head and greybeard cheek, and spoke
in a warm rush of words:

"Ah, sad and old!
Trouble and pain you've borne, and bear, aplenty.
Only a great will could have brought you here
among the Achaean ships, and here alone
before the eyes of one who stripped your sons,
your many sons, in battle. Iron must be
the heart within you. Come, then, and sit down.
We'll probe our wounds no more but let them rest,
though grief lies heavy on us. Tears heal nothing,
drying so stiff and cold. This is the way
the gods ordained the destiny of men,
to bear such burdens in our lives, while they
feel no affliction. At the door of Zeus
are those two urns of good and evil gifts
that he may choose for us; and one for whom
the lightning's joyous king dips in both urns
will have by turns bad luck and good. But one

326 overborne: overcome; overwhelmed.

Ajax and Achilles playing dice, Greek vase painting

336–348 Compare the impression of Achilles you got from lines 87–94 with the impression you get from these lines.

WORDS TO KNOW **evocation** (ĕv'ə-kā'shən) *n.* a bringing to mind

77

Customizing Instruction

Multiple Learning Styles

1 You may want to encourage students who enjoy drawing or writing poetry to express their ideas and feelings about the scene between Achilles and Priam. Students may wish to share their artworks with the class.

Students Acquiring English

2 Help students understand the meaning of the idiom "to put someone by" (line 325). *(to put someone to one's side, to establish space between two people)*

Mini Lesson Speaking and Listening

ANALYZING A LITERARY PERFORMANCE

Instruction Tell students that developing good listening skills will help them appreciate a literary performance.

Prepare Suggest that students use this criteria for analyzing, evaluating, and critiquing a performance:

- use of voice (volume and tone) to establish mood and convey meaning
- use of movement and gesture to establish mood and convey meaning
- use of facial expressions to establish mood and convey meaning

Present Have students take turns presenting and observing performances. Have students use the above criteria to analyze, evaluate, and critique each performance.

BLOCK SCHEDULING This activity is particularly well-suited for longer class periods.

Reading and Analyzing

Reading Skills and Strategies: ANALYZING

A Point out that in line 363 and elsewhere Achilles intimates that he expects to die soon. Other characters, including Thetis (lines 32–34) and Hector (lines 207–208), also seem to know when and how Achilles will die. Ask students how these characters might have gained this knowledge about the future.

Possible Responses: One of the gods might have told them; they might guess Achilles will die young because he is such a reckless soldier.

Ask: What effects do these predictions and hints about future events have on the reader?

Possible Responses: They spoil the surprise; they stress the power and control of the gods; they whet audience interest in how a predicted event will unfold.

Literary Analysis: CHARACTERIZATION

B Ask students to explain what Achilles' reply to Priam reveals about his personality.

Possible Responses: It reveals that Achilles has a violent temper that he must struggle to control; it reveals that he doesn't like to be pressured; it reveals that his moods change suddenly and without warning.

Literary Analysis SIMILE

C Have students identify the comparison in lines 399–400 and the feelings or qualities it conveys about Achilles.

Possible Response: Achilles leaves the room in one bound, like a lion; the comparison conveys Achilles' decisiveness, abruptness, ferocity, strength, ability to inspire fear or awe.

to whom he sends all evil—that man goes
contemptible by the will of Zeus; ravenous
hunger drives him over the wondrous earth,
unresting, without honor from gods or men.
Mixed fortune came to Peleus. Shining gifts
at the gods' hands he had from birth: felicity,
wealth overflowing, rule of the Myrmidons,
a bride immortal at his mortal side.
But then Zeus gave afflictions too—no family
of powerful sons grew up for him at home,
A but one child, of all seasons and of none.
Can I stand by him in his age? Far from my country
I sit at Troy to grieve you and your children.
You, too, sir, in time past were fortunate,
we hear men say. From Macar's isle of Lesbos
northward, and south of Phrygia and the Straits,
no one had wealth like yours, or sons like yours.
Then gods out of the sky sent you this bitterness:
the years of siege, the battles and the losses.
Endure it, then. And do not mourn forever
for your dead son. There is no remedy.
You will not make him stand again. Rather
await some new misfortune to be suffered."

The old king in his majesty replied:

"Never give me a chair, my lord, while Hector
lies in your camp uncared for. Yield him to me
now. Allow me sight of him. Accept
the many gifts I bring. May they reward you,
and may you see your home again.
You spared my life at once and let me live."

Achilles, the great runner, frowned and eyed him
under his brows:

"Do not vex me, sir," he said.
"I have intended, in my own good time,
to yield up Hector to you. She who bore me,
the daughter of the Ancient of the sea,
1 has come with word to me from Zeus. I know
in your case, too—though you say nothing, Priam—
that some god guided you to the shipways here.

358 felicity (fĭ-lĭs'ĭ-tē): happiness; good fortune.

359 Myrmidons (mûr'mə-dŏnz'): a people of Thessaly in Greece, subjects of Achilles' father, Peleus.

363 "Of all seasons and of none" suggests that Achilles expects an early death for himself.

367–368 Lesbos (lĕz'bŏs) . . . **Phrygia** (frĭj'ē-ə) . . . **the Straits:** Lesbos is an island off the western coast of Asia Minor; Phrygia was an ancient kingdom in western Asia Minor; the Straits are the Dardanelles.

387 "The Ancient of the sea" is the sea god Nereus (nîr'ē-əs), father of Thetis.

Teaching Options

Cross Curricular Link History

DEATH AND BURIAL IN ANCIENT GREECE The ancient Greeks believed that a person's soul would wander the earth in eternal misery if he or she had not received a proper funeral. Sometimes the funeral consisted of a burial, and other times the body was cremated (as suggested by Hector's plea in lines 187–188 on page 73: "accord me / decency of fire when I am dead"). Whether buried or burned, the body was typically accompanied by possessions (sometimes including animals and slaves) that the ancient Greeks believed were needed in the afterlife.

No strong man in his best days could make entry
into this camp. How could he pass the guard,
or force our gateway?
Therefore, *let me be.*
Sting my sore heart again, and even here,
B under my own roof, suppliant though you are,
I may not spare you, sir, but trample on
the express command of Zeus!"

When he heard this,
the old man feared him and obeyed with silence.
Now like a lion at one bound Achilles
C left the room. Close at his back the officers
Automedon and Alcimus went out—
comrades in arms whom he esteemed the most
after the dead Patroclus. They unharnessed
mules and horses, led the old king's crier
2 to a low bench and sat him down.
Then from the polished wagon
they took the piled-up price of Hector's body.
One chiton and two capes they left aside
as dress and shrouding for the homeward journey.
Then, calling to the women slaves, Achilles
ordered the body bathed and rubbed with oil—
but lifted, too, and placed apart, where Priam
could not see his son—for seeing Hector
he might in his great pain give way to rage,
and fury then might rise up in Achilles
to slay the old king, flouting Zeus's word.
So after bathing and anointing Hector
3 they drew the shirt and beautiful shrouding over him.
Then with his own hands lifting him, Achilles
laid him upon a couch, and with his two
companions aiding, placed him in the wagon.
Now a bitter groan burst from Achilles,
who stood and prayed to his own dead friend:

"Patroclus,
do not be angry with me, if somehow
4 even in the world of Death you learn of this—
that I released Prince Hector to his father.
The gifts he gave were not unworthy. Aye,
and you shall have your share, this time as well."

395 suppliant (sŭp'lē-ənt): one who begs or pleads earnestly.

401 Automedon (ô-tŏm'ə-dn) . . . **Alcimus** (ăl'sə-məs).

408 chiton (kīt'n): a shirtlike garment; tunic.

WORDS TO KNOW **flouting** (flout'ĭng) *adj.* disregarding in a contemptuous way; scorning **flout** *v.*

Customizing Instruction

Less Proficient Readers

1 Ask students whether they think Achilles made his decision only because of the gods' intervention or whether Priam's words had anything to do with it.

Possible Responses: Some students may feel that Priam's appeal for sympathy moves Achilles, as illustrated by his remarks on page 77. Others may feel that his decision is based solely on the demands of the gods and that he finds Priam's appeals vexing, as lines 384 and 393–397 indicate.

Students Acquiring English

2 Help students understand the meaning of the word *crier* (line 404).

Answer: One who makes announcements, usually by shouting them in a public place such as a street.

3 Explain that *anointing* means "applying oil, especially in a religious ceremony."

Less Proficient Readers

4 Have students paraphrase lines 423–428.

Possible Response: Achilles is asking Patroclus not to be angry with him for accepting Priam's offered gifts in exchange for the body of Hector, Patroclus' murderer.

Assessment Informal Assessment

CASTING NOTES To assess students' understanding of the selection, you might offer them the following scenario: *You are the casting director for a dramatization of this selection. Create a casting note for each of the main characters (including gods and goddesses) describing his or her personality traits, behavior, and relationship to the rest of the cast.*

RUBRIC

3 **Full Accomplishment** Students accurately and concisely describe each character's personality, behavior, and relationship to others.

2 **Substantial Accomplishment** Students accurately describe characters' personalities, behavior, and relationships, but descriptions are not concise.

1 **Little or Partial Accomplishment** Students have difficulty describing the characters and their actions, omitting or misrepresenting details.

Reading and Analyzing

Active Reading

CLASSIFYING CHARACTERS

Remind students that characterization is the combination of techniques a writer uses to guide readers' impressions of characters. A writer may develop a character by describing his or her physical appearance; by presenting the character's actions, words, and thoughts; by presenting the actions, words, and thoughts of other characters, and by presenting direct comments about the character's nature.

After students have read the entire selection, you might want to have them complete a chart such as the one below.

Characters	Character's Words/ Actions	Personality Traits
Achilles		
Priam		
Hector		

The Prince Achilles turned back to his quarters.
He took again the splendid chair that stood
against the farther wall, then looked at Priam
and made his declaration:

"As you wished, sir,
the body of your son is now set free.
He lies in state. At the first sight of Dawn
you shall take charge of him yourself and see him.
Now let us think of supper. We are told
that even Niobe in her extremity
took thought for bread—though all her brood had perished,
her six young girls and six tall sons. Apollo,
making his silver longbow whip and sing,
shot the lads down, and Artemis with raining
arrows killed the daughters—all this after
Niobe had compared herself with Leto,
the smooth-cheeked goddess.
She has borne two children,
Niobe said, How many have I borne!
But soon those two destroyed the twelve.
Besides,
nine days the dead lay stark, no one could bury them,
for Zeus had turned all folk of theirs to stone.
The gods made graves for them on the tenth day,
and then at last, being weak and spent with weeping,
Niobe thought of food. Among the rocks
of Sipylus' lonely mountainside, where nymphs
who race Achelous river go to rest,
she, too, long turned to stone, somewhere broods on
the gall immortal gods gave her to drink.

Like her we'll think of supper, noble sir.
Weep for your son again when you have borne him
back to Troy; there he'll be mourned indeed."

Priam and Achilles agree to an 11-day truce. During that time, the Trojans will mourn Hector's body before its burial.

436–455 The mortal woman Niobe (nī′ə-bē) claimed that having so many children made her superior to the goddess Leto (lē′tō), who had only two. Leto's son and daughter, Apollo and Artemis (är′tə-mĭs), punished Niobe by killing all her children. After many days of grieving, Niobe asked the gods to relieve her by turning her to stone.

452 Sipylus (sĭp′ə-ləs): a mountain in west central Asia Minor.

453 Achelous (ăk′ə-lō′əs): a river near Mount Sipylus.

455 gall: bitterness; bile.

Teaching Options

Vocabulary Strategy

USING A DICTIONARY

Instruction Explain that *Achilles' heel* and *Trojan horse* are just two of many terms that come from ancient Greek literature. Such terms are usually defined in dictionaries; however, if the term consists of two or more words, it may be listed at the end of an entry for a key word, rather than alphabetically under its first word. For example, *Trojan horse* may be listed under *t* or found at the end of the dictionary's entry for *horse.*

Activity Ask students to use a dictionary to find the precise meaning and origin of the following terms from Greek literature:

narcissistic *("excessively vain," from* Narcissus, *a youth who fell in love with his own reflection)*

odyssey *("long journey," from Odysseus' wanderings home from Troy, recounted in the* Odyssey)

Pandora's box *("source of unforeseen troubles," from the myth of Pandora, who out of curiosity opened a box containing all the world's ills)*

Use **Vocabulary Transparencies and Copymasters,** p. 20.

Connect to the Literature

1. **What Do You Think?** What is your impression of Achilles? Share your thoughts with a classmate.

Comprehension Check
- What does Achilles refuse to promise the dying Hector?
- What does Achilles do with Hector after he kills him?
- Identify the character who pleads for the return of Hector's body.

Think Critically

2. In your opinion, does Achilles' loyalty to his friend Patroclus justify the way he treats Hector? Explain your answer.
3. How would you describe the relationship between Achilles and Priam?

- Achilles' killing of Hector
- the dialogue between the two men
- why Achilles gives Hector's body to Priam

4. To what extent do Achilles and Hector correspond to your idea of a **hero?**

- the kind of warrior each man is
- Hector's speech that begins "This is the end. . . ." (line 130, page 00)
- Achilles' treatment of Hector's body
- Achilles' response to Priam

5. How might your impression of Achilles be different if he refused to give Hector's body to Priam?
6. ACTIVE READING CLASSIFYING CHARACTERS Look back at the list you made in your READER'S NOTEBOOK and compare Achilles, Hector, and Priam. In your opinion, which **character** is the most courageous? Why?

Extend Interpretations

7. **Connect to Life** Achilles and Hector fight one-on-one. Do you think leaders of rival nations, tribes, or groups should settle differences between themselves without involving their followers? Is it possible or practical to settle conflicts this way? Support your responses.
8. **Points of Comparison** Compare and contrast Achilles and Beowulf. Consider their actions and the reasons for those actions. Think about how they are alike and how they are different. Who behaves more like a true **epic hero?**

Literary Analysis

SIMILE AND EPIC SIMILE A **simile** is a figure of speech that makes a comparison between two things that are actually unlike yet have something in common. The comparison is expressed by means of the word *like* or *as.* "Silent as death" and "John went down like a stone" are examples of similes. **Epic similes** are long comparisons that often continue for a number of lines. The epic simile in lines 145–148 of this selection compares Hector to an eagle. (In a translation, the word *like* or *as* may not appear; in the lines cited, *as* could be substituted for "the way.") What does the simile suggest about Hector's character?

Paired Activity Now analyze the simile in lines 154–158. What two things are being compared in the simile? How do the epic similes in lines 145–148 and lines 154–158 contribute to the telling of the story? With a classmate, make a list of all the similes that you can find in the poem.

REVIEW EPIC As you may recall, an **epic** is a long narrative poem on a serious subject, presented in an elevated or formal style. It usually traces the adventures of a great hero. Both *Beowulf* and the *Iliad* are epics. What similarities and differences do you see between the two poems?

GUIDING STUDENT RESPONSE

Connect to the Literature

1. **What Do You Think?** Some students may say that Achilles is hot-tempered, violent, and selfish, while others find him a charismatic hero.

Comprehension Check
- Achilles refuses to promise Hector that his body will be returned to the Trojans for proper funeral.
- He ties the body to a chariot and drags it around the walls of Troy.
- Priam, Hector's father and king of the Trojans, pleads for the return of Hector's body.

Use Selection Quiz in **Unit One Resource Book,** p. 17.

Think Critically

2. Possible Responses: Achilles' actions are justified because Hector killed his friend; Achilles' actions are not justified because killing Hector is revenge enough without also defiling the body.
3. Possible Responses: Priam regards Achilles with fear and awe, but the young soldier also reminds him of his own slain son; Achilles regards Priam first as an opponent but then finds that the old man reminds him of his own father.
4. Possible Responses: Achilles is heroic because he is strong, victorious, heedless of death, loyal to his friend, and able to overcome his vengefulness. Hector is heroic because he faces death bravely, shows concern for his people, and treats his foe with respect.
5. Most students will reply that if Achilles had refused to return Hector's body he would have seemed heartless.
6. Possible Responses: Achilles is most courageous because he seeks revenge and then later yields to Priam's pleas; Hector, because he fights bravely, even knowing that he will die; Priam, because he ventures into the enemy's camp on behalf of his son's honor.

Extend Interpretations

Connect to Life These questions are well suited for gifted students. **If you wish to make the questions easier,** have students discuss the questions in small groups. Most students will believe that followers or citizens should be involved in some way in the settlement of conflicts.

Points of Comparison Possible Responses: Achilles exhibits commitment to ideals, and humane response to Priam; Beowulf exhibits superhuman powers, concern for the welfare of other people (the Danes), bravery, and generosity.

Literary Analysis

Paired Activity The spear of Achilles is compared to the evening star in lines 154–158.

Writing Options

1. **Letter of Commendation** Letters will vary, but students' opinions about Achilles or Hector should be supported with events and details from the selection.
2. **Character Sketch** Students' sketches will vary, but should reflect Achilles' changing regard for Priam, first as an enemy and later as a father who is concerned for his son. **To make this assignment more challenging,** have students write an additional character sketch describing Achilles from Priam's point of view.
3. **Alternative Outline** Students' outlines will vary, but should show a logical progression from event to event and should remain true to the personalities and tendencies of the human characters.
4. **Points of Comparison** Essays will vary. Good responses will reflect an understanding of the concepts of fate and ambition in each selection and will include relevant support from the texts.

Activities & Explorations

1. **Dramatic Reading** Students' readings should convey various emotions appropriate to the words each character speaks. Encourage students to rehearse their dramatic readings, perhaps tape-recording rehearsals to evaluate their performances. See the mini-lesson on page 77 for tips on analyzing, evaluating, and critiquing dramatic readings.
2. **Dance Interpretation** You might make this a cooperative activity and group students who have a background in dance or music with those who do not.
3. **Heroic Mural** Suggest that students arrange their murals to reflect the sequence of events in the narrative. Students can appoint an "art director" to ensure cohesiveness among the scenes.
4. **Homeric Epithets** Students' epithets should reflect celebrities' outstanding skills or personality traits. Encourage students to be creative.

Choices & CHALLENGES

Writing Options

1. **Letter of Commendation** As either a Greek or a Trojan general, write a letter of commendation for Achilles or Hector. Explain why you are awarding him your army's highest medal. Place the letter in your **Working Portfolio.**

2. **Character Sketch** Think again about the relationship between Achilles and Priam. Then write a character sketch of Priam from Achilles' point of view.

3. **Alternative Outline** Imagine events as they might have occurred without the gods and goddesses. Write an outline for a version of the poem in which the human characters determine their own fate.

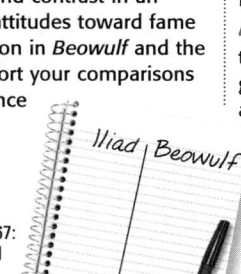

4. **Points of Comparison** Compare and contrast in an essay the attitudes toward fame and ambition in *Beowulf* and the *Iliad.* Support your comparisons with evidence from the selections.

Writing Handbook
See page 1367: Compare and Contrast.

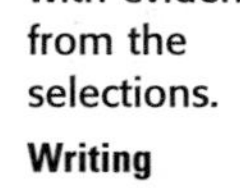

Activities & Explorations

1. **Dramatic Reading** With a classmate, give a dramatic reading of the encounter between Achilles and Priam. Use your voices and facial expressions to convey emotions such as sorrow, anger, desperation, compassion, and fear. ~ **SPEAKING AND LISTENING**

2. **Dance Interpretation** Create a dance interpretation of the battle between Hector and Achilles. Choose appropriate music to accompany it, and perform your dance for the class.
~ **DANCE / MUSIC**

3. **Heroic Mural** With a group of classmates, using large sheets of paper, sketch or paint a series of scenes from the *Iliad* and put them together to form a mural for your classroom. ~ **ART**

4. **Homeric Epithets** In line 10, the reference to Achilles as "the great runner" is an example of an **epithet,** a brief phrase that refers to a characteristic of a particular person or thing. Other examples are the references to Hector as "killer of men" and Priam as "great king of Troy." With a group of classmates, have one member of the group call out the names of current sports figures or other celebrities and then have the other members call out possible epithets for that person.
~ **SPEAKING AND LISTENING**

Inquiry & Research

1. **Digging Up Troy** Find out more about the real city of Troy. Where was it located? What have archaeologists discovered about the city? Present your findings to the class in an outline for a television documentary about Troy.

More Online: Research Starter
www.mcdougallittell.com

2. **Translations of Homer** There have been many translations of Homer into English. The 18th-century poet Alexander Pope, for example, translated both the *Iliad* and the *Odyssey.* With classmates, find three modern translations of the *Iliad* in addition to the one you just read. Choose a brief passage and compare its treatment in the three versions. Then in class read the three translations of the passage aloud. Discuss the differences with your classmates.

Inquiry & Research

1. **Digging Up Troy** Have students work in small groups, with each group focusing on a different aspect of ancient Troy, including its geography, its history, archaeological findings, and its daily life. Encourage students to use general reference sources such as encyclopedias to find print and non-print information, but also to look at specialized books and online databases. After students have completed their research, have each student prepare a topic outline detailing his or her research. Groups can then combine their outlines to create an outline for the complete documentary.
2. **Translations of Homer** Translations students may find and compare include those by Michael Reck (1994), Robert Fagles (1990), and Richmond Lattimore (1951). Students may also benefit from listening to recorded translations, such as that by Ennis Rees (1987). When comparing selections, encourage students to think about word choice, tone, and format (i.e., verse or prose).

Vocabulary in Action

EXERCISE: RELATED WORDS Write the letter of the word that is not related in meaning to the other words in each set.

1. (a) face, (b) meet, (c) evade, (d) confront
2. (a) ponderous, (b) swift, (c) weighty, (d) hefty
3. (a) clamor, (b) peacefulness, (c) silence, (d) calmness
4. (a) dirty, (b) cleanse, (c) defile, (d) corrupt
5. (a) strong, (b) vulnerable, (c) weak, (d) defenseless
6. (a) dodge, (b) capture, (c) elude, (d) escape
7. (a) destruction, (b) disaster, (c) havoc, (d) protection
8. (a) whetted, (b) dull, (c) blunt, (d) rounded
9. (a) disobey, (b) flout, (c) punish, (d) disregard
10. (a) promise, (b) exult, (c) rejoice, (d) celebrate
11. (a) defender, (b) guardian, (c) protector, (d) scourge
12. (a) act, (b) abstain, (c) proceed, (d) perform
13. (a) remembrance, (b) calendar, (c) reminder, (d) evocation
14. (a) soothe, (b) quell, (c) scold, (d) hush
15. (a) destitute, (b) needy, (c) deprived, (d) injured

WORDS TO KNOW				
abstain	destitute	evocation	havoc	scourge
clamor	elude	exult	ponderous	vulnerable
defile	evade	flouting	quell	whetted

Building Vocabulary
For an in-depth lesson on how to expand your vocabulary, see page 1182.

Homer

800–600 B.C.

Who Was Homer? Little is known about the Greek poet Homer. In fact, for centuries scholars have debated whether such a man ever really existed. Today, most agree that the author of two equally famous epics, the *Iliad* and the *Odyssey,* was indeed a man named Homer, who lived sometime between 800 and 600 B.C. Evidence of his life and authorship has been gathered indirectly from other writings of ancient Greece, from historical references, and from his poems. It seems likely that the mysterious poet was born either in western Asia Minor or on one of the nearby Aegean islands.

The Blind Bard According to legend, Homer was blind; however, some scholars believe that this legend is not likely to be literally true. They point out that the typical ancient Greek portrayal of a sage or philosopher was of a blind man with exceptional inner vision. Ancient Greeks viewed the *Iliad* and the *Odyssey* as works that revealed all-important truths about human beings and their place in the universe. Often, Greek children were required to memorize portions of the epics and to model their behavior on the heroic code set forth by their author. With the possible exception of Shakespeare, no other poet in the Western world has been quoted more often than Homer.

Oral Poetry Homer's poems probably had a long oral history before they were written down. It is believed that they were composed in verse partly because the meter made them easier to memorize. According to modern scholars, Homer was probably illiterate, living as he did at a time when writing was just being introduced among the Greeks. In his old age, the poet may have recited his epics for someone else to record.

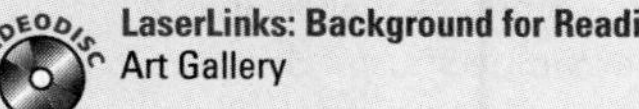

LaserLinks: Background for Reading
Art Gallery

Vocabulary in Action

ANSWERS

1. c
2. b
3. a
4. b
5. a
6. b
7. d
8. a
9. c
10. a
11. d
12. b
13. b
14. c
15. d

ILIAD 83

OVERVIEW

Objectives

1. understand and appreciate **lyric poetry (Literary Analysis)**
2. appreciate the poets' use of **kennings (Literary Analysis)**
3. understand how **interpreting details** aids comprehension **(Active Reading)**

Summary

"The Seafarer" first describes the miseries and attractions of life at sea, and then reflects upon earthly kingdoms, human pleasures, and the impermanence of life. The poem ends with a prayer that humans turn all thoughts to Heaven. "The Wanderer" tells of the hardships of a man who has lost his lord, presumably in battle. As a result, he travels the seas, homeless. The narrator mourns the passing of his life as a warrior. "The Wife's Lament" is the sorrowful song of an exiled woman. After her husband's men successfully plotted to separate the two, her husband banished her to the woods. There, she lives in a cave, alone, angry, and resentful.

Thematic Link

The seafarer, the wanderer, and the wife all face **tests of courage**. The seafarer and the wanderer battle the harsh sea, while the wife makes her life in the dark, remote woods. All three suffer from extreme loneliness and struggle against the odds to keep their spirits alive.

5-Minute Warm-Up

Daily Language SkillBuilder

Have students **proofread** the display sentences on page 15k and write them correctly. The sentences also appear on Transparency 1 of **Grammar Transparencies and Copymasters.**

PREPARING to *Read*

The Seafarer / The Wanderer / The Wife's Lament

Poetry from the EXETER BOOK

Connect to Your Life

Lonely Times Remember a time when you felt lonely or isolated. Perhaps you were separated from your friends or family as a result of a move or a vacation, or maybe you simply felt alone. How did you react to the situation—with anger or with sadness? What helped you cope with the situation? With a partner, discuss your personal definition of loneliness.

Build Background

Leaving Loved Ones Behind Life in Anglo-Saxon times was filled with hardships that separated people from their loved ones for long periods—or permanently. Outbreaks of disease, attacks by wild animals, and natural disasters such as storms and floods killed many before their time. Frequent warfare wreaked havoc on small communities, bringing untimely death to some and scattering others, who might be forced into permanent exile if their communities' protectors had been slain in the fighting.

Also facing the hardship of separation were the men who left behind their families and communities to travel the sea. Sailing the ocean in primitive boats and in all kinds of weather, these seafarers had to face both physical danger and intense loneliness. The women and children they left behind endured months and even years without knowing whether their husbands and fathers would ever return.

The three Old English poems you are about to read reflect the uncertainty of life in Anglo-Saxon times, as well as the Anglo-Saxons' human needs and desires. Each deals, in one way or another, with the effects of separation.

Focus Your Reading

LITERARY ANALYSIS | **KENNING** A prominent characteristic of Old English poetry is the use of **kennings**—descriptive compound words and phrases—in place of simple nouns. Common kennings include *ring-giver* for a king or lord and *helmet bearer* for a warrior. Kennings are often metaphorical, like *heaven's candle* for the sun. The following lines from "The Wife's Lament" contain a kenning for the sea:

> ***First my lord went out away from his people over***
> ***the wave-tumult.***

Look for other examples of kennings as you read the three poems.

ACTIVE READING | **INTERPRETING DETAILS** These poems from the Exeter Book are filled with **details** that can help you **visualize** the scenes, objects, and people being described. Interpreting these details will help you decide what ideas, **moods,** and attitudes the poems convey. For example, "lonely dawns" and "frozen waves" in "The Wanderer" suggest emptiness and desolation.

READER'S NOTEBOOK As you read each poem, create a cluster diagram like the one below to help you organize the **descriptive details** in the poem. Jot down the ideas, moods, or attitudes that the details seem to convey.

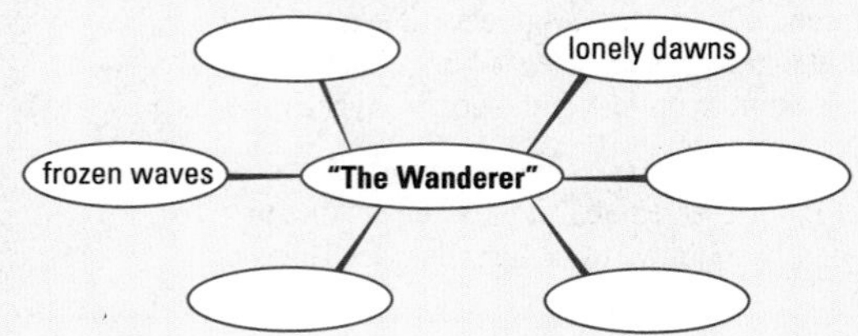

LESSON RESOURCES

UNIT ONE RESOURCE BOOK, pp. 18–19

ASSESSMENT RESOURCES
Formal Assessment, pp. 11–12
Teacher's Guide to Assessment and Portfolio Use
Test Generator

SKILLS TRANSPARENCIES AND COPYMASTERS
Literary Analysis
• Poetic Devices, T16 (for Literary Analysis, p. 96)
Reading and Critical Thinking
• Visualizing, T8 (for Writing Option 1, p. 97)
Grammar
• Simple Sentences, C75 (for Mini Lesson, p. 87)
Vocabulary
• Word Origins, C21 (for Mini Lesson, p. 86)
Writing
• Showing, Not Telling, T22 (for Writing Option 1, p. 97)
• Literary Interpretation, C33 (for Writing Option 2, p. 97)
Communications
• Interviewing, T9 (for Activities & Explorations 2, p. 97)

INTEGRATED TECHNOLOGY
Audio Library
LaserLinks
Visit our website:
www.mcdougallittell.com

GUIDE FOR READING

Ⓐ He took many journeys and saw much suffering.

from The Seafarer

This tale is true, and mine. It tells
How the sea took me, swept me back
And forth in sorrow and fear and pain,
Showed me suffering in a hundred ships,
In a thousand ports, and in me. It tells
Of smashing surf when I sweated in the cold
Of an anxious watch, perched in the bow
As it dashed under cliffs. My feet were cast
In icy bands, bound with frost,
With frozen chains, and hardship groaned
Around my heart. Hunger tore
At my sea-weary soul. No man sheltered
On the quiet fairness of earth can feel
How wretched I was, drifting through winter
On an ice-cold sea, whirled in sorrow,
Alone in a world blown clear of love,
Hung with icicles. The hailstorms flew.
The only sound was the roaring sea,
The freezing waves. The song of the swan
Might serve for pleasure, the cry of the sea-fowl,
The death-noise of birds instead of laughter,

GUIDE FOR READING

A | **2–3** Did the sea literally sweep the speaker back and forth? If not, what might he mean?

TEACHING THE LITERATURE

Customizing Instruction

Less Proficient Readers
Suggest that students create a chart such as the one shown for each of the three poems. As they read, they can fill in descriptive details and the feeling, or mood, each one conveys.

Poem Title: The Seafarer	
Descriptive Details	**Mood Conveyed**
"smashing surf" (line 6)	violent, harsh

Students Acquiring English
Have students read the poem aloud so that they can hear the rhythm of the language. If any students are familiar with poems or songs about the sea in their primary language, ask them to share these with the class.

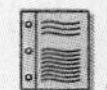 Use **Spanish Study Guide** for additional support, pp. 10–12.

Gifted and Talented
Explain that some scholars believe that "The Seafarer" and "The Wanderer" were each composed by more than one person—that each was added to many years after its creation. As students read, have them look for evidence to support this theory.
Possible Response: Both contain hopeful, pious endings that are inconsistent with the poems' pessimistic outlook and tone.

BLOCK SCHEDULING: MANAGING TIME

If your schedule requires that you cover the lesson objectives in a shorter time, use . . .
- Preparing to Read, p. 84
- Thinking Through the Literature, p. 96

If you want to take advantage of longer class time, use . . .
- TE Teaching Options: Vocabulary, p. 86; Grammar, p. 87; Cross Curricular Links, pp. 88, 91, 94; Informal Assessment, pp. 89, 93; Speaking and Listening, p. 90; Standardized Test Practice, p. 92; Viewing and Representing, p. 95
- Choices & Challenges, p. 97

Reading and Analyzing

GUIDE FOR READING

A The speaker is stressing his loneliness—his only company is the gulls.

Literary Analysis KENNING

B Remind students that kennings are descriptive compound words or phrases that stand for simple nouns. Ask them to identify the kenning in line 33.
Answer: "coldest seeds," which refers to hail.

Ask how the kenning enhances the noun "hail."
Possible Response: It emphasizes hail's coldness and texture.

Have students find other examples of kennings on pages 86 and 87.
Possible Responses: "Summer's sentinel," line 53; "the whales' / Home," lines 59–60; and "givers of gold," line 83.

Use **Unit One Resource Book,** p. 19 for additional support.

GUIDE FOR READING

C **Possible Response:** His own youth, when he served a powerful lord.

Active Reading
INTERPRETING DETAILS

D Ask students to paraphrase lines 94–96.
Possible Response: A dead person cannot taste, feel, move, or think.
Ask how details included by the poet affect the reader.
Possible Response: It names particular tastes, feelings, and movements, which makes it easier for the reader to picture death.

Use **Unit One Resource Book,** p. 18 for additional support.

The mewing of gulls instead of mead.
Storms beat on the rocky cliffs and were echoed
By icy-feathered terns and the eagle's screams;
No kinsman could offer comfort there,
To a soul left drowning in desolation.
   And who could believe, knowing but
The passion of cities, swelled proud with wine
And no taste of misfortune, how often, how wearily,
I put myself back on the paths of the sea.
Night would blacken; it would snow from the north;
Frost bound the earth and hail would fall,
The coldest seeds. And how my heart
Would begin to beat, knowing once more
The salt waves tossing and the towering sea!
The time for journeys would come and my soul
Called me eagerly out, sent me over
The horizon, seeking foreigners' homes.
   But there isn't a man on earth so proud,
So born to greatness, so bold with his youth,
Grown so brave, or so graced by God,
That he feels no fear as the sails unfurl,
Wondering what Fate has willed and will do.
No harps ring in his heart, no rewards,
No passion for women, no worldly pleasures,
Nothing, only the ocean's heave;
But longing wraps itself around him.
Orchards blossom, the towns bloom,
Fields grow lovely as the world springs fresh,
And all these admonish that willing mind
Leaping to journeys, always set
In thoughts travelling on a quickening tide.
So summer's sentinel, the cuckoo, sings
In his murmuring voice, and our hearts mourn
As he urges. Who could understand,
In ignorant ease, what we others suffer
As the paths of exile stretch endlessly on?
   And yet my heart wanders away,
My soul roams with the sea, the whales'
Home, wandering to the widest corners
Of the world, returning ravenous with desire,
Flying solitary, screaming, exciting me
To the open ocean, breaking oaths
On the curve of a wave.

22 mead: an alcoholic beverage made from fermented honey, frequently drunk in Anglo-Saxon gatherings. In contrasting mead with "the mewing of gulls," what is the speaker stressing?

24 terns: sea birds similar to gulls.

28 The "cities" of the seafarer's day were far smaller than modern cities—more like villages and encampments.

50 admonish (ăd-mŏn′ĭsh): criticize or caution.

53 sentinel (sĕn′tə-nəl): guard; watchman.

Teaching Options

Vocabulary Strategy

RESEARCHING WORD ORIGINS: *SOLUS*

Instruction Tell students that the word *solitary* (line 62) is based upon the Latin root *solus,* which means "alone." The seafarer leads a solitary life, facing the dangers of life at sea. Other words based on the same root are *solitude, solipsism, soliloquy,* and *solo.*

Activity Have students work in pairs to find the meaning of *solitude, solipsism, soliloquy,* and *solo.* Ask them to use each word in a sentence. Ask students to describe how they can use knowledge of the root word *solus* to remember the meanings of these words.

Use **Vocabulary Transparencies and Copymasters,** p. 21.

A lesson on reading word origins appears on p. 206 of the Pupil's Edition.

Thus the joys of God
Are fervent with life, where life itself
Fades quickly into the earth. The wealth
Of the world neither reaches to Heaven nor remains.
No man has ever faced the dawn
Certain which of Fate's three threats
Would fall: illness, or age, or an enemy's
Sword, snatching the life from his soul.
The praise the living pour on the dead
Flowers from reputation: plant
An earthly life of profit reaped
Even from hatred and rancor, of bravery
Flung in the devil's face, and death
Can only bring you earthly praise
And a song to celebrate a place
With the angels, life eternally blessed
In the hosts of Heaven.
The days are gone
When the kingdoms of earth flourished in glory;
Now there are no rulers, no emperors,
No givers of gold, as once there were,
When wonderful things were worked among them
And they lived in lordly magnificence.
Those powers have vanished, those pleasures are dead,
The weakest survives and the world continues,
Kept spinning by toil. All glory is tarnished,
The world's honor ages and shrinks,
Bent like the men who mold it. Their faces
Blanch as time advances, their beards
Wither and they mourn the memory of friends,
The sons of princes, sown in the dust.
The soul stripped of its flesh knows nothing
Of sweetness or sour, feels no pain,
Bends neither its hand nor its brain. A brother
Opens his palms and pours down gold
On his kinsman's grave, strewing his coffin
With treasures intended for Heaven, but nothing
Golden shakes the wrath of God
For a soul overflowing with sin, and nothing
Hidden on earth rises to Heaven.
We all fear God. He turns the earth,
He set it swinging firmly in space,
Gave life to the world and light to the sky.
Death leaps at the fools who forget their God.
He who lives humbly has angels from Heaven

2 3 4

75 rancor (răng'kər): bitter, long-lasting ill will.

80 hosts of Heaven: bands of angels.

C **80–85** To what glorious era might the speaker be referring?

91 blanch: turn white.

D

Customizing Instruction

Less Proficient Readers

1 Ask students what two competing opinions the speaker expresses in these lines.

Possible Response: He says that life at sea is a life of exile and discomfort, but that he longs for the freedom he feels when on the open ocean.

Students Acquiring English

2 Have students paraphrase lines 64–66.

Possible Response: Being happy about God's creations can fill you with life, but life itself is very short.

Less Proficient Readers

3 Help students break this long sentence into smaller parts and then to paraphrase each part.

Possible Response: "The praise the living pour on the dead / Flowers from reputation"—The dead are praised because of the good reputations they earned during their lives; "plant / An earthly life of profit . . . Flung in the devil's face"—If you lead a good life, then in spite of hatred or foolishness; "and death / Can only bring you . . . Heaven"—those still alive will praise you and exalt you when you are dead.

Multiple Learning Styles

Auditory Learners

4 Reading aloud or listening to difficult passages such as this one may help students understand the complex imagery and syntax of the poem.

Grammar

SIMPLE SENTENCES

Instruction A sentence is a group of words that expresses a complete thought. Every sentence has two parts: a subject and a predicate. The subject is the person, place, thing, or idea about which something is said. The predicate tells what the subject does or what happens to the subject.

Activity Write these sentences about "The Seafarer" on the chalkboard. Underline the subjects.

The seafarer's feet became numb from the cold.

The sound of the roaring sea broke the silence.

Ask if each underlined word is a subject or predicate. *(subject)* Then have students find the predicate in each sentence. *(became; broke)*

Exercise For each of the following sentences, have students underline the subject once and the predicate twice.

1. The seafarer endured the fierce winter storm. *(seafarer, endured)*
2. Which bird's song gave the seafarer pleasure? *(song, gave)*

Use **Grammar Transparencies and Copymasters**, p. 126.

Use McDougal Littell's ***Language Network*** for more instruction and practice in (different in every selection).

THE SEAFARER 87

Reading and Analyzing

Reading Skills and Strategies: COMPARING AND CONTRASTING

A Have students recall the main characters' attitudes toward revenge in *Beowulf* and the *Iliad.*

Possible Response: Both Beowulf and Achilles felt that avenging a death was honorable.

Then have students read lines 109–115. Ask how "The Seafarer" poet's attitude toward revenge differs from that of Beowulf and Achilles.

Possible Response: Unlike Beowulf and Achilles, the poet believes that revenge is wrong, even when a person feels hatred toward another.

Literary Analysis: METAPHOR

B Guide students to conclude that Heaven is being compared to home in these lines. Ask why the poet might have chosen this metaphor to describe Heaven.

Possible Response: Students may say that it reflects the theme of the poem—the seafarer's wandering far from home on the open sea.

If this metaphor implies that Heaven is the seafarer's ultimate home, to what might the sea be compared?

Possible Response: It may be compared to our earthly life.

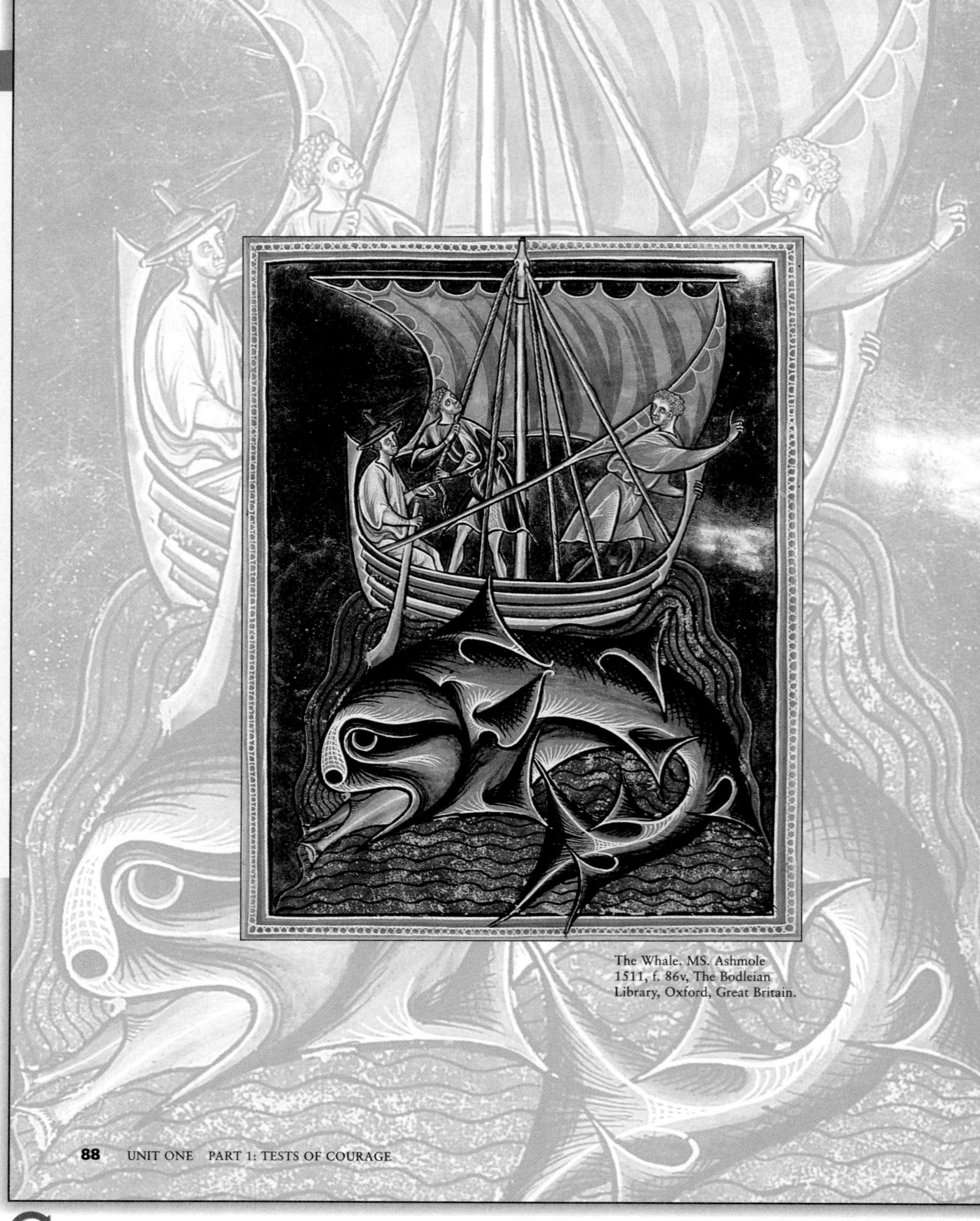

The Whale. MS. Ashmole 1511, f. 86v, The Bodleian Library, Oxford, Great Britain.

88 UNIT ONE PART 1: TESTS OF COURAGE

Teaching Options

Cross Curricular Link **History**

THE GOKSTAD SHIP In 1880, a Viking ship dating to about A.D. 900 was discovered at Gokstad, Norway. Because the clay in which it had been buried was airtight, the ship was almost totally preserved, lacking only the mast and some upper parts of the stern. The ship measures about 76 feet long and 17 feet wide and is equipped for 16 pairs of oars. Its keel, or backbone, had been taken from a single oak tree that must have measured 80 feet in height. (Trees of such a height no longer exist in Norway.) The deck planking was not nailed down, because loose planks allowed for easy access to stored items down below—weapons, food, and other equipment.

Not only did the discovery at Gokstad provide scholars with definitive information about the seafaring Vikings, but it also captured the imaginations of people worldwide—so much so that, in 1893, a replica of the ship was built and launched toward America in an ambitious reenactment of Columbus's voyage to the New World. The voyage was a success and proved that much of the folklore surrounding Viking ships was, in fact, true.

To carry him courage and strength and belief.
A man must conquer pride, not kill it,
Be firm with his fellows, chaste for himself,
Treat all the world as the world deserves,
With love or with hate but never with harm,
Though an enemy seek to scorch him in hell,
Or set the flames of a funeral pyre
Under his lord. Fate is stronger
And God mightier than any man's mind.
Our thoughts should turn to where our home is,
Consider the ways of coming there,
Then strive for sure permission for us
To rise to that eternal joy,
That life born in the love of God
And the hope of Heaven. Praise the Holy
Grace of He who honored us,
Eternal, unchanging creator of earth. Amen.

Translated by Burton Raffel

110 chaste (chāst): pure in thought and deed.

114 funeral pyre (pīr): a bonfire for burning a corpse.

Thinking Through the Literature

1. **Comprehension Check** What conflicting emotions does the seafarer feel when he sets off on a sea voyage?
2. What **images** remain with you after reading this poem? Describe the images, or draw a sketch of them.
3. Why do you think the seafarer chose a life at sea in spite of its hardships?

   THINK ABOUT
   - the feelings he expresses in lines 58–64
   - the problems recounted in lines 81–102
   - the view of fate expressed in the final lines
4. Why do you think the seafarer tells about his life and its hardships? Cite details from the poem to support your opinion.

Customizing Instruction

Less Proficient Readers

1 To aid their understanding of this long sentence, have students paraphrase lines 109–115.

Possible Response: People must overcome pride, use discipline with others and themselves, and be just but not vengeful—even when wrong is being done to them.

Multiple Learning Styles

Auditory Learners

2 To encourage students to pause at a period, rather than at the end of each line, you may want to suggest that partners take turns reading each sentence on this page aloud.

Thinking Through the Literature

1. Possible Response: excitement and fear
2. Accept any reasonable response.
3. Possible Response: The Seafarer is drawn by the sea, by the freedom he feels on the open waves. He feels that the sea was fated to be his home. The Seafarer is also disgusted by the hypocrisy he sees on land.
4. Accept any reasonable response.

Assessment Informal Assessment

A LETTER HOME You can informally assess students' understanding of the selection by having them rewrite the poem as a letter to a loved one who has been left behind. Encourage students to begin by paraphrasing each paragraph of the poem, and then to write their letter using the paraphrases as a guide. Remind students to try to capture the same tones, or moods, expressed by the speaker at various points in the poem, and also to include some of the details or images they find most striking.

RUBRIC

3 Full Accomplishment Student writing reflects a full understanding of the feelings and thoughts of the speaker and includes relevant details from the poem.

2 Substantial Accomplishment Student writing shows a general understanding of the speaker's reflections, but details may be lacking or not relevant.

1 Little or Partial Accomplishment Student writing displays little understanding of the speaker's reflections and provides few or no relevant details.

Reading and Analyzing

Active Reading

INTERPRETING DETAILS

A Ask students to identify details in the opening lines that help the reader picture the traveler's state of mind.
Possible Response: Students may mention the grief that hangs on his heart and follows the sea foam; his ship, which sails endlessly and aimlessly; or the image of his slaughtered kinsmen.

Have students look for other details on pages 90–91 that bring the traveler's sorrow to life. Challenge them to tell which sense (sight, hearing, touch, taste, or smell) each detail appeals to.
Possible Responses: "I've drunk too many lonely dawns," line 8; "Fate blows hardest on a bleeding heart," line 16; "How cruel a journey / I've travelled, sharing my bread with sorrow," lines 28–29; "And I open my eyes . . . the hail and the snow," lines 44–48; "They fade away, / Swimming soundlessly out of sight," lines 52–53; "How loathsome become / The frozen waves to a weary heart," lines 54–55.

GUIDE FOR READING

B The wanderer's kinsmen were slaughtered and, as if returning to the same port time after time, he remembers this event over and over.

C Students may say that the "brown sea-billows" are the waves or the wake behind the ship.

D Their riches; their lives.

The Wanderer

A This lonely traveler longs for grace,
For the mercy of God; grief hangs on
His heart and follows the frost-cold foam
He cuts in the sea, sailing endlessly,
Aimlessly, in exile. Fate has opened
A single port: memory. He sees
His kinsmen slaughtered again, and cries: 1
"I've drunk too many lonely dawns,
Grey with mourning. Once there were men 2
To whom my heart could hurry, hot
With open longing. They're long since dead.
My heart has closed on itself, quietly
Learning that silence is noble and sorrow
Nothing that speech can cure. Sadness
Has never driven sadness off;
Fate blows hardest on a bleeding heart.
So those who thirst for glory smother
Secret weakness and longing, neither
Weep nor sigh nor listen to the sickness
In their souls. So I, lost and homeless,
Forced to flee the darkness that fell
On the earth and my lord.

GUIDE FOR READING

5–7 What has happened to the wanderer's kinsmen? How might his memory be like a port? How has fate limited him to a "single port"?

Teaching Options

Speaking and Listening

DRAMATIC READING

Have students work in **cooperative groups** to prepare a dramatic interpretation of "The Wanderer." Explain to students that dramatic readings can be enhanced with lighting, sound effects, and pantomime. For example, a reading of "The Wanderer" might be accompanied by the sound of a pounding hammer (line 16), a suddenly darkened room (line 21), and the sound of footsteps (line 31). Or, it might feature a spotlit narrator and traveler who describe the action as it is simultaneously pantomimed by other actors.

Activity Encourage students to use simple props, motions, and sound effects to bring the action and mood of the poem to life. After each performance, have audience members comment on the most effective aspect of the performance.

BLOCK SCHEDULING This activity is particularly well-suited for longer class periods.

Leaving everything,
Weary with winter I wandered out
On the frozen waves, hoping to find
A place, a people, a lord to replace
My lost ones. No one knew me, now, **3**
No one offered comfort, allowed
Me feasting or joy. How cruel a journey
I've travelled, sharing my bread with sorrow
Alone, an exile in every land, **4**
Could only be told by telling my footsteps.
For who can hear: "friendless and poor,"
And know what I've known since the long cheerful nights
When, young and yearning, with my lord I yet feasted
Most welcome of all. That warmth is dead.
He only knows who needs his lord
As I do, eager for long-missing aid;
He only knows who never sleeps
Without the deepest dreams of longing.
Sometimes it seems I see my lord,
Kiss and embrace him, bend my hands
And head to his knee, kneeling as though
He still sat enthroned, ruling his thanes.
And I open my eyes, embracing the air,
And see the brown sea-billows heave, **5**
See the sea-birds bathe, spreading
Their white-feathered wings, watch the frost
And the hail and the snow. And heavy in heart
I long for my lord, alone and unloved.
Sometimes it seems I see my kin
And greet them gladly, give them welcome,
The best of friends. They fade away,
Swimming soundlessly out of sight,
Leaving nothing.
How loathsome become
The frozen waves to a weary heart.
In this brief world I cannot wonder
That my mind is set on melancholy,
Because I never forget the fate
Of men, robbed of their riches, suddenly
Looted by death—the doom of earth,
Sent to us all by every rising
Sun. Wisdom is slow, and comes

31 telling: counting.

43 thanes: followers of a lord.

C **45** What are the "brown sea-billows"?

D **60 looted:** robbed by force. What was taken from the men who were "looted by death"?

Customizing Instruction

Less Proficient Readers

Make sure students understand the events leading up to the traveler's sea journey.

1 What has become of the traveler's fellow warriors and his lord?

Answer: They have been killed, probably in battle.

Students Acquiring English

2 Help students understand the metaphor in lines 8–9. If necessary, explain that the Wanderer is not physically drinking the dawn, nor is he drunk. Ask students whether they think "grey with mourning" describes the dawn or the Wanderer himself, and why.

Less Proficient Readers

3 Why has the traveler taken to the sea?

Answer: He is in search of a new home.

4 Has he been well received in other lands?

Answer: No.

How do you know?

Possible Response: He has traveled a "cruel" journey; he is "an exile in every land"; at some point he has been referred to as "friendless and poor."

5 Does the traveler literally "see" his lord (line 40) and his kin (line 50)?

Possible Answer: No; he is daydreaming or remembering them.

What usually interferes with the traveler's daydreams or visions?

Possible Answer: The visions are usually interrupted by things he can actually see—"the brown sea-billows," "the sea-birds," "the frost / And the hail and the snow," "The frozen waves."

Cross Curricular Link History

MEDIEVAL KINGSHIP Medieval kingship was not characterized by the distance and formality that later royal courts were known for. Instead, the king, or lord, was the active leader of a small, intimate household. The king's followers were called retainers, or thanes (from the Anglo-Saxon word *thegn*); they were expected to defend their lord in battle and to sacrifice their own lives to protect his. In the centuries before the many Anglo-Saxon kingdoms were unified by the strong arm of Alfred the Great (849–899), kingdoms were formed and disbanded very rapidly. It was difficult for any king to keep his power for long: power depended on military might, military might was secured by gift-giving, gift-giving was possible only through wealth, and wealth was obtained through military conquest. The predicament of the wanderer—a nobleman in exile from his own kin and in search of generous or receptive lords—was quite common. Until this fragmented society was forced to unify in response to the Viking invasions of the late eighth and early ninth centuries, the Anglo-Saxon kingship remained an unstable and often dangerous office.

Reading and Analyzing

GUIDE FOR READING

A **Possible Response:** Some were killed in battle; others drowned; some died of disease; and others died natural deaths and were buried by loved ones.

Literary Analysis KENNING

B Have students identify the kennings in these lines.
Answer: war-steed, war-lord, feasting-places.

Then ask why they think the poet used the term "war-steed" instead of "horse."
Possible Response: "War-steed" helps preserve the rhythm and alliteration in these lines.

Active Reading
INTERPRETING DETAILS

C Ask students to identify details describing the outer world. What do these details reveal about the speaker's feelings or state of mind?
Possible Response: "These rocky slopes are beaten by storms," line 99—The wanderer is beaten down by ill fortune; "This earth pinned down by driving snow . . . in the shadows of night," lines 100–102—The wanderer is pinned down by hopelessness and frozen with loneliness.

Literary Analysis: ALLITERATION

D Have students identify the repeated *h* sound in line 103; the repeated *e* sound in line 104; and the repeated *f* sound in lines 105–106. Then ask how this intense alliteration adds to the poem's fatalistic mood.
Possible Response: The sounds sweep or pull the reader along.

But late. He who has it is patient;
He cannot be hasty to hate or speak,
He must be bold and yet not blind,
Nor ever too craven, complacent, or covetous,
1 Nor ready to gloat before he wins glory. 2
The man's a fool who flings his boasts
Hotly to the heavens, heeding his spleen
And not the better boldness of knowledge.
What knowing man knows not the ghostly,
Waste-like end of worldly wealth:
See, already the wreckage is there,
The wind-swept walls stand far and wide,
The storm-beaten blocks besmeared with frost,
The mead-halls crumbled, the monarchs thrown down
And stripped of their pleasures. The proudest of warriors
Now lie by the wall: some of them war
Destroyed; some the monstrous sea-bird
Bore over the ocean; to some the old wolf
Dealt out death; and for some dejected
Followers fashioned an earth-cave coffin.
Thus the Maker of men lays waste
This earth, crushing our callow mirth.
And the work of old giants stands withered and still."

He who these ruins rightly sees,
And deeply considers this dark twisted life,
Who sagely remembers the endless slaughters
Of a bloody past, is bound to proclaim:
"Where is the war-steed? Where is the warrior? Where is
his war-lord?
Where now the feasting-places? Where now the mead-hall
pleasures?
Alas, bright cup! Alas, brave knight!
Alas, you glorious princes! All gone,
Lost in the night, as you never had lived.
And all that survives you a serpentine wall,
Wondrously high, worked in strange ways.
Mighty spears have slain these men,
Greedy weapons have framed their fate.
These rocky slopes are beaten by storms,
This earth pinned down by driving snow,
By the horror of winter, smothering warmth
In the shadows of night. And the north angrily

66 craven (krā′vən): cowardly; **complacent** (kəm-plā′sənt): self-satisfied; **covetous** (kŭv′ĭ-təs): greedy.

69 spleen: bad temper. (The spleen is a body organ that was formerly thought to be the seat of strong emotions.)

A **77–82** In what different ways have the warriors met their fate?

84 callow mirth: childish joy.

95 serpentine: winding or twisting, like a snake.

Teaching Options

Assessment Standardized Test Practice

IDENTIFYING THE MAIN IDEA For some standardized tests, students will be asked to choose the best main idea for a passage. To give students some practice choosing the best main idea, read aloud or write on the chalkboard the following question.

Which of the following statements best expresses the main idea of "The Wanderer"?

A. A person who goes to sea in winter often must battle loneliness, harsh conditions, and feelings of hopelessness.
B. Even when we have lost all that we value, we can take great comfort in the beauty of the world that surrounds us.
C. Everything in this world is fleeting—relationships, wealth, even life itself.
D. If you lead a selfish, boastful life, you are likely to die in misery.

Lead students through the process of choosing the best main idea (C). Consider each choice. Point out that, although answers A and D are supported by the poem, they are not the poem's main concern, and that answer B is incorrect because it is inconsistent with the poem's harsh portrait of nature.

Hurls its hailstorms at our helpless heads.
Everything earthly is evilly born,
Firmly clutched by a fickle Fate.
Fortune vanishes, friendship vanishes,
Man is fleeting, woman is fleeting,
And all this earth rolls into emptiness."
So says the sage in his heart, sitting alone with
His thought.
It's good to guard your faith, nor let your grief come forth
Until it cannot call for help, nor help but heed
The path you've placed before it. It's good to find your
grace
In God, the heavenly rock where rests our every hope.

Translated by Burton Raffel

Thinking Through the Literature

1. **Comprehension Check** What happened to cause the poem's title **character** to become a wanderer?
2. What emotion does this poem chiefly evoke in you? Share your reaction with classmates.
3. How would you describe the wanderer's present life and his feelings about it?

- the experiences he describes in lines 8–22
- the life he led before he became a wanderer
- his remarks in lines 90–108

4. Do you agree with the attitude toward grief expressed in lines 12–16? Why or why not?

Customizing Instruction

Less Proficient Readers

1 What is the tone of these lines?

Possible Response: Students may say that the tone of the lines is bitter, regretful, ironic, angry, or resentful.

What do these lines suggest about the wanderer's own past?

Possible Response: The lines suggest that the wanderer behaved in a foolish, boastful, and hotheaded manner.

Students Acquiring English

2 Help students understand the meaning of *gloat*.

Answer: to feel malicious pleasure or self-satisfaction.

Also remind students of the definition of *mead-hall,* which they learned about reading *Beowulf.*

Less Proficient Readers

3 Ask students to compare the wanderer's closing lines (104–108) with those of the narrator (lines 110–113). How do they differ?

Possible Response: The speaker is totally pessimistic; he believes that life amounts to nothing. The narrator believes that in God there is hope.

Thinking Through the Literature

1. Possible Response: His lord and home were attacked and his friends and kinsmen were killed.
2. Accept any reasonable response.
3. Possible Response: The Wanderer's present life is hard and lonely and he does not have any hope. Before, he was happy and wealthy and had many friends.
4. Accept any well-supported response.

Assessment Informal Assessment

VENN DIAGRAMS To help students assess their own understanding of "The Seafarer" and "The Wanderer," have them make a Venn diagram that compares and contrasts the two poems. (Alternatively, they may want to compare and contrast the two speakers of the poems.)
Have students consider the following questions:

- What facts do we know about each speaker's past?
- What has each speaker lost?
- What is each speaker's attitude toward his current situation?
- Do the poems contain any similar images or details?
- What unique images or details does each poem contain?

When they are finished, have students discuss their diagram with a partner and revise it if necessary.

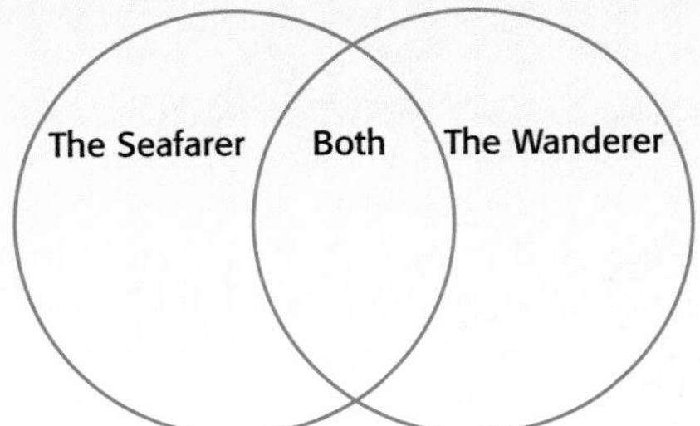

THE WANDERER 93

Reading and Analyzing

Literary Analysis: CAESURA

A Remind students that caesura is a common feature of Old English poetry, and that the space in the center of each line indicates a pause. Read aloud the first stanza, pausing for a second or two at each caesura. Then ask students what effect the pauses have on the poem's mood.
Possible Response: The pauses create a sense of sadness and weariness.

GUIDE FOR READING

B Students may say that the kenning helps the poet depict the dangers of life at sea.

Reading Skills and Strategies: SPECULATING

C Ask why the husband's kin might have tried to divide them.
Possible Response: They didn't want to support her while he was gone.

GUIDE FOR READING

D Students may say that her home is a cavelike dwelling.

Literary Analysis: IMAGERY

E Remind students that imagery refers to words and phrases that appeal to one or more of the five senses. Have students identify images in lines 30–53 and describe the effect they create.
Possible Responses: Images include: dark valleys, high hills, the yard overgrown and bitter with briars. Discuss that these images create a sense of the home's joylessness. Other images, such as "rocky cliff," "rimed with frost," "dreary in spirit," "drenched with water," and "ruined hall," suggest a sense of desolation.

The Wife's Lament

Poverty carrying a sack of wheat to the mill reaches a dangerous bridge (about 1450–1475). Rene I d'Anjou, King of Naples. From *Le Mortifiement de vaine plaisance,* M.705, f. 38v.

A
I make this song   about me full sadly
my own wayfaring.   I a woman tell
what griefs I had   since I grew up
new or old   never more than now.
Ever I know   the dark of my exile. **1**

First my lord went out   away from his people
over the wave-tumult.   I grieved each dawn
wondered where my lord   my first on earth might be.
Then I went forth   a friendless exile
to seek service   in my sorrow's need.
C
My man's kinsmen   began to plot
by darkened thought   to divide us two
so we most widely   in the world's kingdom
lived wretchedly   and I suffered longing.

My lord commanded me   to move my dwelling here.
I had few loved ones   in this land
2
or faithful friends.   For this my heart grieves:
that I should find the man   well matched to me
hard of fortune   mournful of mind
hiding his mood   thinking of murder.

GUIDE FOR READING

1 To show the rhythmic structure of Old English poetry, this translator has divided each line into two units with a break called a caesura (sĭ-zhŏŏr′ə). The caesuras signal places where the scop, or poet-singer, probably paused for breath while reciting the poem.

2 wayfaring: journeying.

6 my lord: the speaker's husband.

B **7 wave-tumult:** the sea. Why might the poet have used this kenning?

19 hard . . . mind: having a hard life and feeling sad.

Teaching Options

Cross Curricular Link History

GENDER ROLES Feudal society was organized for war, and was therefore a fundamentally masculine society. Women were afforded few legal rights. A woman was essentially the property of the male head of her household—her father, brother, or husband—and was legally required to obey his commands. A woman typically had little or no input in decisions that affected her life. It was common for a girl to enter an arranged marriage at the age of twelve or so, although, on occasion, an older (and usually widowed) woman could purchase from her feudal lord the right to choose her own husband.

Blithe was our bearing often we vowed
that but death alone would part us two
naught else. But this is turned round
now . . . as if it never were
our friendship. I must far and near
bear the anger of my beloved.
The man sent me out to live in the woods
under an oak tree in this den in the earth.
Ancient this earth hall. I am all longing.

The valleys are dark the hills high
the yard overgrown bitter with briars
a joyless dwelling. Full oft the lack of my lord
seizes me cruelly here. Friends there are on earth
living beloved lying in bed
while I at dawn am walking alone
under the oak tree through these earth halls.
There I may sit the summerlong day
there I can weep over my exile
my many hardships. Hence I may not rest
from this care of heart which belongs to me ever
nor all this longing that has caught me in this life.

May that young man be sad-minded always
hard his heart's thought while he must wear
a blithe bearing with care in the breast
a crowd of sorrows. May on himself depend
all his world's joy. Be he outlawed far
in a strange folk-land— that my beloved sits
under a rocky cliff rimed with frost
a lord dreary in spirit drenched with water
in a ruined hall. My lord endures
much care of mind. He remembers too often
a happier dwelling. Woe be to them
that for a loved one must wait in longing.

Translated by Ann Stanford

29 "Earth hall" refers to the speaker's living quarters. What kind of place do you think it is?

42–50 In these lines, the speaker seems to wish for her husband the same sad, lonely life that he has forced her to endure.

Customizing Instruction

Students Acquiring English

1 Explain to students that *exile* means "the state of being sent away from one's country or home."

Less Proficient Readers

2 Have students explain what saddens the speaker.
Possible Response: Her husband, once a good companion, has become gloomy and violent.

3 Ask students to identify what the husband first did to upset the wife and what later command also upset her.
Possible Response: First he went away; then he made her move to a strange land.

4 Ask what is contradictory about the wife's feelings for her husband.
Possible Response: She loves him yet wants him to suffer.

Ask how her feelings are like those expressed in "The Seafarer."
Possible Response: They are mixed, like the seafarer's feelings for the sea.

Gifted and Talented Students

Have students discuss what the poem reveals about the society in which the wife lived.

Viewing and Representing

Poverty carrying a sack of wheat to the mill reaches a dangerous bridge, **unknown artist**

ART APPRECIATION

Instruction Explain that the strong symbolism here is typical of later medieval art and literature, in which characters often represent abstract ideas like poverty, faith, and hope.

Application Ask students what chief feeling or emotion this work conveys.

Possible Responses: It conveys a sense of hopelessness, weariness, or exhaustion.

Then ask how similar emotions are conveyed in "The Wife's Lament."

Possible Responses: The wife has lost faith in her husband; her lonely life in exile has made her tired and downtrodden.

GUIDING STUDENT RESPONSE

Connect to the Literature

1. What Do You Think?
Guidelines for student response: Good responses will include details from the poem to support students' reactions and opinions. Most students will sympathize with the wife and find her husband's (and his kinsmen's) treatment of her unfair.

Comprehension Check

- The wife mourned the husband's absence; the husband's kinsmen plotted to turn her husband against her.
- The husband and the wife live apart because he sent her into exile.
- The wife wishes her husband to suffer the same loneliness and sorrow that she does.

Think Critically

2. Answers will vary. Some students may feel that the wife has led a hard life, forced to endure her husband's going off to sea, his kin's attempts to separate them, and exile from her home. Others may feel that the wife's loneliness has colored her perception of events.
3. Answers will vary. Students will probably reply that the wife blames her husband for her misery; that she thinks him selfish; and that she wants him to suffer.
4. Answers will vary. Students may point out that the husband does his best in trying to provide for her; that she should have known in advance what marriage to a seafarer would be like; that he is as lonely as she and far less safe.
5. Answers will vary slightly, but most students will identify the mood of the poems as lonely, desolate, sorrowful, mournful, regretful, hopeless, gloomy, harsh, or cold.

Literary Analysis

Cooperative Learning Activity Possible Responses: city—people hive; journey—crow's flight; ship—floating tree; tree—stout warrior; war—clash of giants.

Thinking through the LITERATURE

Connect to the Literature

1. **What Do You Think?** What is your reaction to the story told in "The Wife's Lament"?

Comprehension Check
- What happened after the wife's husband went to sea?
- Why do the husband and the wife live apart?
- What does the wife wish her husband to feel?

Think Critically

2. Evaluate the kind of life the wife has led. Support your evaluation with details from the poem.
3. How would you describe the wife's opinion of her husband's behavior?

THINK ABOUT
- the influence of her husband's kinsmen
- the vow that the husband and the wife made to each other
- the wife's thoughts in lines 42–50

4. In your opinion, how might the husband respond to his wife's accusations?
5. ACTIVE READING INTERPRETING DETAILS Get together with a partner and discuss the cluster diagrams of **descriptive details** you created in your  READER'S NOTEBOOK. What **moods** do the details help convey?

Extend Interpretations

6. **What If?** Suppose that the husband of the speaker in "The Wife's Lament" returned to her. Describe their reunion.
7. **Comparing Texts** Compare the plights of the three poems' title characters. Who do you think faces the most difficult hardships? What makes you think this way? Defend your opinion.
8. **Connect to Life** In the modern world, many refugees leave their countries to escape dangers, not knowing when or if they will ever return to the homelands and people they love. How do you think the loneliness and other hardships they face compare with those endured in Anglo-Saxon times? Cite evidence from the poems to support your opinion.

Literary Analysis

KENNING Anglo-Saxon poets made frequent use of **kennings,** descriptive terms and phrases substituted for simple nouns. In a translation of Old English poetry, a kenning may appear as a compound word, like *wave-tumult,* used for the sea in "The Wife's Lament." A kenning may also appear as a group of two or more words, like *swan road,* another common kenning for the sea. The name *Beowulf* itself can be interpreted as "bee-wolf," a kenning for a bear (because bears like honey and so are often found around beehives).

Cooperative Learning Activity Identify two more kennings in the poems and explain what they mean. Then copy the chart below and try creating your own kennings for the words in the first column. Discuss your ideas and complete the chart with a small group of classmates.

Term	Kenning
city	
journey	
ship	
tree	
war	

REVIEW ALLITERATION Besides rhythm, the most important element of sound in Old English poetry is **alliteration,** the repetition of initial consonant sounds. Look for examples in all three poems.

Extend Interpretations

What If? Good responses will draw logical conclusions from the details and information given in the poem. Some students will imagine that the wife becomes so overjoyed by the reunion that she forgives her husband and welcomes him home. Others will describe a reunion in which the wife expresses her displeasure and anger or in which the husband apologizes for his behavior. **If you wish to make this question more difficult,** have students write a dialogue that might take place between the husband and the wife upon their reunion.

Comparing Texts Some students may feel that the seafarer's or the wanderer's plight is the worst because they face more physical dangers. Others may feel the wife's plight is the worst because she has less freedom than the men do.

Connect to Life Some students may feel that improvements in transportation, communications, and physical conditions make the modern situations easier to bear. Others may point out that loss of culture or homeland is still devastating.

Choices & CHALLENGES

Writing Options

1. **Diary Entry** Imagine that you are the title character of one of the poems. Write a diary entry describing a typical day in your life—for "The Seafarer," for example, you might describe a typical day at sea. Place the entry in your **Working Portfolio.**

2. **Exploration** Write a paragraph in which you explore the inner conflict of the title character in one of the poems. State the conflict that you perceive, and then support your statement with details from the poem.

Writing Handbook
See page 1359: Paragraphs.

Activities & Explorations

1. **Weather Map** Research the weather patterns over the waters surrounding Britain. Then draw a map showing the places where an Anglo-Saxon sailor may have encountered weather-related dangers and the types of dangers he may have faced. ~ SCIENCE

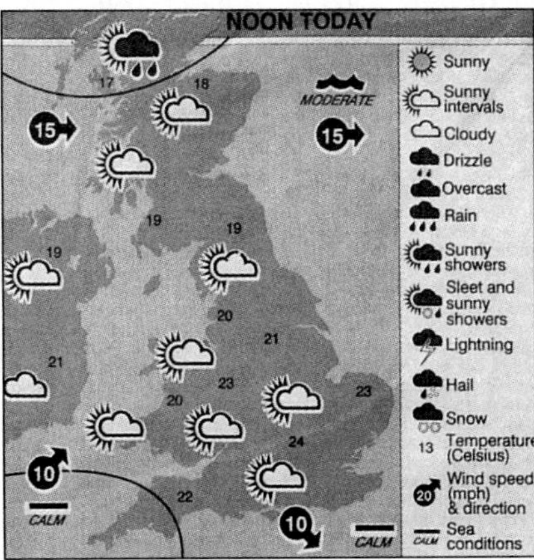

2. **TV Interview** With a group of classmates, stage a TV talk show in which a host interviews the title characters of the poems. The host should encourage the guests to discuss their hopes and plans for the future as well as their past experiences. ~ SPEAKING AND LISTENING

Inquiry & Research

Everyday Anglo-Saxons Use history books and other reliable sources to find out more about the Anglo-Saxons. Go beyond the accounts of historic events to investigate the lifestyles of the various classes of Anglo-Saxon society—women and farmers as well as kings and warriors. Prepare a written report on your findings.

Stained glass window depicting a farmer sowing seeds by hand

The Authors

Surviving Anonymity Nothing is known about the authors of "The Seafarer," "The Wanderer," and "The Wife's Lament." All three poems survive in the Exeter Book, a manuscript produced by scribes around A.D. 950. Leofric, the first bishop of Exeter in England, had this collection of Anglo-Saxon poems in his personal library. After he donated it to the Exeter Cathedral library sometime between 1050 and 1072, the Exeter Book was neglected and abused for centuries because few people were able to read the Old English language in which it was written. The original binding and an unknown number of pages were lost. Other pages were badly stained or scorched. Today the Exeter Book is handled with great care and treasured as one of the few surviving poetic manuscripts from the Anglo-Saxon period.

Mini Lesson Inquiry and Research

CREATING AND NARROWING A LIST OF TOPIC QUESTIONS

Introduce Suggest that before students begin their research into Anglo-Saxon life, they make a list of relevant, interesting, and researchable questions. To help them get started, suggest they brainstorm a list of topics they would like to explore and develop questions for each topic. Students should pick the topic and questions that interest them the most.

Practice Have students take their narrowed list of questions to the library for an overview search. Encourage them to do subject searches on the on-line catalog, to browse through encyclopedias and history books, and to search the Internet. Once they get a sense of how much information is available on each of their questions, they can decide on the single question they want to research.

Writing Options

1. **Diary Entry** **To make this assignment more challenging,** have students write two diary entries, one by a title character from one of the poems and another by a loved one the character has been separated from.
2. **Exploration** Students writing about the seafarer may discuss the conflict between his love for the sea and his loneliness. Students writing about the wanderer may discuss the conflict between those memories he cherishes and those he regrets. Students writing about the wife may discuss the conflict between her love for her husband and her hatred of what he has done to her.

Activities & Explorations

1. **Weather Map** Students might obtain information not only from the usual reference books but also from publications for sailors or tourists. Other sources might include the Internet, television, or radio.
2. **TV Interview** Have students work in groups of five or six, with one student serving as director, one as the host, two as guest speakers, and one or more as writers. Suggest that students work together to make a general outline of what will be said in the performance.

Inquiry & Research

Everyday Anglo-Saxons Encourage students to think first about their own hobbies and interests, and then to jot down related questions about life in the Middle Ages. If possible, give students the Web site addresses for museums with medieval collections, or direct them to general works on medieval England such as *The Anglo-Saxons,* edited by James Campbell (Ithaca: Cornell University Press, 1982).

OVERVIEW

Objectives

1. understand and appreciate **historical writing (Literary Analysis)**
2. evaluate **historical writing** and understand its characteristics **(Literary Analysis)**
3. analyze the **author's purpose (Active Reading)**

Summary

In the first excerpt, King Edwin asks his ministers whether he should become a Christian. They advise him to do so. The high priest, Coifi, then destroys the shrines of the old faith. The second excerpt tells the story of Caedmon, an aged cowherd. A man comes to Caedmon in a dream gives him the gift of being able to sing God's praises. Caedmon is received into a monastic community and he writes more hymns of praise.

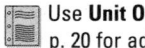

Use **Unit One Resource Book,** p. 20 for additional support.

Thematic Link

King Edwin and the high priest Coifi each face a **test of courage** when they are asked to reject their old faith and embrace a new religion. Caedmon, an elderly peasant, must face the challenge of a new life when he is invited to join a monastery as a poet.

5-Minute Warm-Up

Daily Language SkillBuilder

Have students **proofread** the display sentences on page 15k and write them correctly. The sentences also appear on Transparency 2 of **Grammar Transparencies and Copymasters.**

PREPARING to *Read*

from A History of the English Church and People

Historical Writing by THE VENERABLE BEDE

"We know nothing of what went before this life, and what follows."

Connect to Your Life

Accepting Challenges, Making Changes Think about a time when you were challenged to make a major change in your life and you took on that challenge. How did the change affect the way you think or live? Share your experience with a group of classmates.

Build Background

The Christian Challenge The Venerable Bede, regarded as the father of English history, lived and worked in a monastery in northern Britain during the late seventh and early eighth centuries. His most famous work, *A History of the English Church and People,* is a major source of information about life in Britain from the first successful Roman invasion, about A.D. 46, to A.D. 731. Bede was a careful and thorough historian for his time. He sought out original documents and reliable eyewitness accounts on which to base his writing.

Bede's *History* is filled with stories about the spread of Christianity among the English between A.D. 597 and 731. Christianity had been introduced into Britain during the Roman occupation and had flourished for a time. The Anglo-Saxon tribes who began invading around A.D. 450, however, were pagans and brought their religion with them. By the late sixth century, Christianity had been abandoned in many areas. In A.D. 597, missionaries from Rome began arriving in Britain to persuade the Anglo-Saxons to reject their pagan beliefs and accept the challenge of the Christian faith.

WORDS TO KNOW
Vocabulary Preview

aspire	prudent
desecrate	render
devout	renounce
effectual	secular
profess	zealous

Focus Your Reading

LITERARY ANALYSIS | HISTORICAL WRITING **Historical writing** is a systematic account, often in narrative form, of the past of a nation or a group of people. Historical writing generally has the following characteristics: (1) it is concerned with real events, (2) the events are treated in chronological order, and (3) it is usually an objective retelling of facts rather than a personal interpretation. Which of these characteristics are evident in this passage from Bede's *History?*

> ***Then, full of joy at his knowledge of the worship of the true God, he told his companions to set fire to the temple and its enclosures and destroy them. The site where these idols once stood is still shown . . . and is known as Goodmanham.***

As you read the selection from Bede's chronicle, consider whether it displays the characteristics of historical writing.

ACTIVE READING | ANALYZING AN AUTHOR'S PURPOSE An author may write to **inform,** to **describe,** to **narrate,** to **entertain,** or to **persuade.** Frequently an author writes to accomplish two or more of these purposes. To help you identify the Venerable Bede's purpose for composing his *History,* notice the following as you read:

- incidents the author recounts
- people the author describes
- descriptions that convey the author's stance or position
- the author's **tone** throughout the selection

READER'S NOTEBOOK Jot down details that suggest the author's purpose.

LESSON RESOURCES

UNIT ONE RESOURCE BOOK, pp. 20–24

ASSESSMENT RESOURCES
Formal Assessment, pp. 13–14
Teacher's Guide to Assessment and Portfolio Use
Test Generator

SKILLS TRANSPARENCIES AND COPYMASTERS
Reading and Critical Thinking
- Determining Author's Purpose and Audience, T20 (for Active Reading, p. 98)

Grammar
- Sentence Fragments, T42 (for Mini Lesson, pp. 102–103)
- Run-on Sentences, T43 (for Mini Lesson, pp. 102–103)
- Complete Sentences, C76 (for Mini Lesson, pp. 102–103)

Writing
- Figurative Language and Sound Devices, T15 (for Writing Options, p. 105)

Communications
- Formal Presentations, T10 (for Inquiry & Research, p. 105)

INTEGRATED TECHNOLOGY
Audio Library
LaserLinks
- Author Background: The Venerable Bede. See **Teacher's SourceBook,** p. 9.

Visit our website:
www.mcdougallittell.com

from *A History of the English Church and People*

The Venerable BEDE

King Edwin was a powerful ruler of Northumbria—a kingdom in northern Britain—during the early seventh century. Although a pagan, Edwin married a Christian, Ethelberga of Kent, and allowed her to practice her Christian faith. Ethelberga's chaplain, Paulinus, challenged her new husband to convert to Christianity.

When Paulinus had spoken, the king answered that he was both willing and obliged to accept the Faith which he taught, but said that he must discuss the matter with his principal advisers and friends, so that if they were in agreement, they might all be cleansed together in Christ the Fount of Life. Paulinus agreed, and the king kept his promise. He summoned a council of the wise men, and asked each in turn his opinion of this new faith and new God being proclaimed.

Portrait of the scribe Eadwine

Coifi, the High Priest, replied without hesitation: "Your Majesty, let us give careful consideration to this new teaching, for I frankly admit that, in my experience, the religion that we have hitherto professed seems valueless and powerless. None of your subjects has been more devoted to the service of the gods than myself, yet there are many to whom you show greater favor, who receive greater honors, and who are more successful in all their undertakings. Now, if the

WORDS TO KNOW
profess (prə-fĕs') *v.* to claim belief in or allegiance to

TEACHING THE LITERATURE

Customizing Instruction

Students Acquiring English
The archaic language and formal style of this selection may challenge students. Read certain sections aloud to help clarify meaning.

Use **Spanish Study Guide** for additional support, pp. 13–15.

Less Proficient Readers
Set a Purpose Have students read to find out about how an early English ruler became converted to Christianity.

Gifted and Talented Students
Bede's work is called *A History of the English Speaking People* yet it is written in Latin. Ask the students to consider the context in which Bede's history was written and explain why it might have been written in Latin.

Mini Lesson: Preteaching Vocabulary

USING A DICTIONARY TO FIND PRECISE MEANING
Most of the WORDS TO KNOW for this selection are used in a religious context–that is, they are used to refer to religious ideas, attitudes, or behaviors.

Instruction The word *profess* is defined: *"to claim belief in or allegiance to."* Have students locate the sentence in the selection. *(" ... in my experience, the religion that we have hitherto professed seems valueless and powerless"; page 99)* Ask students to use the definition on the chalkboard to paraphrase the sentence.

Possible Response: the religion that we formerly believed in . . .

Activity Have students use a dictionary to look up the precise meanings of the WORDS TO KNOW. Ask students to write down the full definition of each word, followed by one sentence that uses the word in a religious context and one sentence that uses the word in a non-religious context.

Use **Unit One Resource Book** p. 23 for additional support.

Reading and Analyzing

Active Reading

ANALYZING AN AUTHOR'S PURPOSE

A Explain that Bede had several purposes when writing the *History*. One was to record historical facts. Another may have been to persuade people to convert to Christianity. Ask students which purpose is reflected in these lines.

Possible Responses: These lines record the fact that Edwin's advisors recommended conversion to Christianity; the lines are meant to be persuasive. The phrase "under God's guidance" implies that God rewards or guides those who do His will.

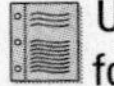
Use **Unit One Resource Book** p. 21 for more practice.

Literary Analysis

HISTORICAL WRITING

Historical writing is about real events told in chronological order and with objectivity. Use the following prompt to help students evaluate Bede's objectivity. Consider how Bede reports the story of Caedmon. Does the historian seem objective?

Possible Responses: Bede gives only one perspective on Caedmon—a very pro-Christian story. His explanation is based not only on verifiable events, but on Caedmon's own account of what he perceived was a gift from God.

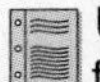
Use **Unit One Resource Book** p. 22 for more exercises.

gods had any power, they would surely have favored myself, who have been more zealous in their service. Therefore, if on examination these new teachings are found to be better and more effectual, let us not hesitate to accept them."

Another of the king's chief men signified his agreement with this prudent argument, and went on to say: "Your Majesty, when we compare the present life of man with that time of which we have no knowledge, it seems to me like the swift flight of a lone sparrow through the banqueting-hall where you sit in the winter months to dine with your thanes[1] and counselors. Inside there is a comforting fire to warm the room; outside, the wintry storms of snow and rain are raging. This sparrow flies swiftly in through one door of the hall, and out through another. While he is inside, he is safe from the winter storms; but after a few moments of comfort, he vanishes from sight into the darkness whence he came. Similarly, man appears on earth for a little while, but we know nothing of what went before this life, and what follows. Therefore if this new teaching can reveal any more certain knowledge, it seems only right that we should follow it." The other elders and counselors of the king, under God's guidance,
A gave the same advice.

Coifi then added that he wished to hear Paulinus' teaching about God in greater detail; and when, at the king's bidding, this had been given, the High Priest said: "I have long realized that there is nothing in what we worshiped, for the more diligently I sought after truth in our religion, the less I found. I now publicly confess that this teaching clearly reveals truths that will
1 afford us the blessings of life, salvation, and eternal happiness. Therefore, Your Majesty, I submit that the temples and altars that we have dedicated to no advantage be immediately desecrated and burned." In short, the king granted blessed Paulinus full permission to preach, renounced idolatry, and professed his acceptance of the Faith of Christ. And when he asked the High Priest who should be the first to profane[2] the altars and shrines of the idols, together with the enclosures that surrounded
them, Coifi replied: "I will do this myself, for **2**
now that the true God has granted me knowledge, who more suitably than I can set a public example, and destroy the idols that I worshiped in ignorance?" So he formally renounced his empty superstitions, and asked the king to give him arms and a stallion—for hitherto it had not been lawful for the High Priest to carry arms, or to ride anything but a mare—and, thus equipped, he set out to destroy the idols. Girded with a sword and with a spear in his hand, he mounted the king's stallion and rode up to the idols. When the crowd saw him, they thought he had gone mad, but without hesitation, as soon as he reached the temple, he cast a spear into it and profaned it. Then, full of joy at his knowledge of the worship of the true God, he told his companions to set fire to the temple and its enclosures and destroy them. The site where these idols once stood is still shown, not far east of York, beyond the river Derwent, and is known as Goodmanham. Here it was that the High Priest, inspired by the true God, desecrated and destroyed the altars that he had himself dedicated.

1. **thanes:** freemen attached to the household of an Anglo-Saxon lord, serving as his personal band of warriors.
2. **profane:** desecrate.

WORDS TO KNOW

zealous (zĕl'əs) *adj.* filled with enthusiasm; eager
effectual (ĭ-fĕk'cho͞o-əl) *adj.* able to produce a desired effect
prudent (pro͞od'nt) *adj.* showing wisdom or good judgment
desecrate (dĕs'ĭ-krāt') *v.* to violate the sacredness of
renounce (rĭ-nouns') *v.* to give up or reject

100

Teaching Options

Multicultural Link: Early Histories

Note that the effort of the monk-scholar Bede to create a written record of his people's history has parallels in other cultures. Much of what we know of the Aztecs comes from the writings of late 16th-century Roman Catholic friars and missionaries who tried to record events from earlier times. The most famous of these efforts are the *General History of the Things of New Spain* by Fray Bernardino de Sahagún and *The History of the Indies of New Spain* by Fray Diego Durán. A friar in Mexico City, Sahagún wrote his *General History* in both Spanish and the Aztec language Nahuatl. Preserved in a complete copy in Florence, Italy, known as the *Florentine Codex,* the work includes speeches, songs, legends, and descriptions of Aztec religious ceremonies, as well as a history of the Spanish conquest. Durán, who grew up in Texcoco, Mexico, was also a friar. His *History,* prepared around 1580, is the best known of several Spanish versions of a lost Nahuatl legendary history known as the *Crónica X.*

A page from the Venerable Bede's *History of the English Church and People.* The Granger Collection, New York.

Customizing Instruction

Multiple Learning Styles

Visual/Kinesthetic Learners

Encourage students interested in art to copy a paragraph of Bede's *History* and then to decorate, or "illuminate," it.

Students Acquiring English

1 Help students recognize that *afford* in this context means "to provide" rather than "to be able to pay for." Point out that the latter definition takes only a direct object, whereas *afford* meaning "to provide" often takes an indirect object as well. Have students identify the direct object and indirect object.

Answer: blessings, us.

Less Proficient Readers

2 Make sure students understand the substance of the council's advice.

- What criticism of the old religion does Coifi make?
  Possible Response: He complains that faithful adherents are not suitably rewarded.
- Why does the second advisor recommend conversion to Christianity?
  Possible Response: It may reveal certain knowledge of what precedes and follows life on earth.
- Who volunteers to destroy the altars of the old faith?
  Answer: Coifi.

Set a Purpose Tell students to continue reading to learn about another early Anglo-Saxon Christian, the poet Caedmon.

Mini Lesson Viewing and Representing

A page from the Venerable Bede's *History of the English Church and People*

ART APPRECIATION Until the spread of Christianity, English artistry was expressed mainly in the form of small, portable objects such as ornate weapons, purses, and jewelry. The Christian culture imported from Rome introduced a new form of artistic expression: the illumination of liturgical books. These masterpieces combine the decorative tradition of Anglo-Saxon culture with the complex geometrical art of the Mediterranean. A common characteristic of medieval illumination is the tightly compacted design seen in the segmented panels of the large letter in the page from Bede's *History* shown above. When combined with rich yet cool colors—often shades of gold, red, green, and blue—these designs seem to shimmer on the page.

Instruction An illuminated page is typically decorated with ornamental designs, miniatures, or lettering in brilliant colors.

Application Ask how the illustrator used color to make this page appear "illuminated." What illumination or source of light might Bede want to convey to his readers? Possible Responses: He may have wanted to depict God as a symbolic source of light.

Reading and Analyzing

Literary Analysis: SIMILE

A Ask students what the heavens, or sky, is being compared to.

Possible Response: The sky is compared to a roof.

Have students look for another example of simile on this page.

Possible Response: "So Caedmon . . . like an animal chewing the cud, turned it into such melodious verse. . . ." (p. 103, second column)

Active Reading

ANALYZING AN AUTHOR'S PURPOSE

B Ask students what they think Bede's purpose was in telling this story.

Possible Responses: Students may say it was to entertain; to describe a miracle; to persuade people that the Christian God is powerful and generous.

Ask: From the last six lines of the story, what do you learn about Bede's values and beliefs?

Possible Response: We learn that he prefers love and goodness to wickedness; that he values religion, humility, discipline, and the rejection of evil.

Caedmon (kăd′mən) is the earliest English poet known to us by name. According to Bede, Caedmon composed many poems; however, only his first poem, a hymn to God the Creator, has survived. In the following account, Bede describes how Caedmon, who was an illiterate cowherd, became an accomplished poet.

Friars singing in choir, miniature from the Psalter of Henry VI (detail). Cotton Domitian A. XVII, f. 122v, by permission of The British Library.

In this monastery of Whitby there lived a brother[3] whom God's grace made remarkable. So skillful was he in composing religious and devotional songs, that he could quickly turn whatever passages of Scripture were explained to him into delightful and moving poetry in his own English tongue. These verses of his stirred the hearts of many folk to despise the world and aspire to heavenly things. Others after him tried to compose religious poems in English, but none could compare with him, for he received this gift of poetry as a gift from God and did not acquire it through any human teacher. For this reason he
1 could never compose any frivolous or profane verses, but only such as had a religious theme fell fittingly from his devout lips. And although he followed a secular occupation until well advanced in years, he had never learned anything about poetry: indeed, whenever all those present at a feast took it in turns to sing and

3. **brother:** a man who lives in or works for a religious community but is not a priest or monk.

WORDS TO KNOW
aspire (ə-spīr′) *v.* to strive to attain
devout (dĭ-vout′) *adj.* showing religious devotion and piety
secular (sĕk′yə-lər) *adj.* unrelated to religion

102

Teaching Options

Grammar

COMPLETE SENTENCES

Instruction A complete sentence has a subject and a predicate and expresses a complete thought. When a writer combines two or more sentences without using a conjunction and/or the correct punctuation, a run-on sentence is created.

Activity Write the following sentence on the chalkboard.

I enjoyed reading this story by the Venerable Bede it made history come alive.

Have students identify the two complete thoughts in this run-on sentence. Show students ways to fix this run-on sentence.

- Make two separate sentences. *(. . . Bede. It . . .)*
- Create a compound sentence using a comma and a coordinating conjunction. *(. . . Bede, for it . . .)*
- Create a compound sentence using a semicolon. *(. . . Bede; it . . .)*
- Create a compound sentence with a semicolon, a conjunctive adverb, and a comma. *(. . . Bede; moreover, it . . .)*

Exercise Ask students to fix each run-on sentence.

entertain the company, he would get up from table and go home directly he saw the harp[4] approaching him.

On one such occasion he had left the house in which the entertainment was being held and went out to the stable, where it was his duty to look after the beasts that night. He lay down there at the appointed time and fell asleep, and in a dream he saw a man standing beside him who called him by name. "Caedmon," he said, "sing me a song." "I don't know how to sing," he replied. "It is because I cannot sing that I left the feast and came here." The man who addressed him then said: "But you shall sing to me." "What should I sing about?" he replied. "Sing about the Creation of all things," the other answered. And Caedmon immediately began to sing verses in praise of God the Creator that he had never heard before, and their theme ran thus: "Let us praise the Maker of the kingdom of heaven, the power and purpose of our Creator, and the acts of the Father of glory. Let us sing how the eternal God, the Author of all marvels, first created the A heavens for the sons of men as a roof to cover them, and how their almighty Protector gave them the earth for their dwelling place." This is the general sense, but not the actual words that Caedmon sang in his dream; for however excellent the verses, it is impossible to translate them from one language into another[5] without losing much of their beauty and dignity. When Caedmon awoke, he remembered everything that he had sung in his dream, and soon added more verses in the same style to the glory of God.

Early in the morning he went to his superior the reeve,[6] and told him about this gift that he had received. The reeve took him before the abbess,[7] who ordered him to give an account of his dream and repeat the verses in the presence of many learned men, so that they might decide their quality and origin. All of them agreed that Caedmon's gift had been given him by our Lord, and when they had explained to him a passage of scriptural history or doctrine, they asked him to render it into verse if he could. He promised to do this, and returned next morning with excellent verses as they had ordered him. The abbess was delighted that God had given such grace to the man, and advised him to abandon secular life and adopt the monastic state. And when she had admitted him into the Community as a brother, she ordered him to be instructed in the events of sacred history.[8] So Caedmon stored up in his memory all that he learned, and like an animal chewing the cud, turned it into such melodious 2 verse that his delightful renderings turned his instructors into his audience. He sang of the creation of the world, the origin of the human race, and the whole story of Genesis. He sang of Israel's departure from Egypt, their entry into the land of promise, and many other events of scriptural history. He sang of the Lord's Incarnation, Passion, Resurrection, and Ascension into heaven, the coming of the Holy Spirit, and the teaching of the Apostles. He also made many poems on the terrors of the Last Judgment, the horrible pains of Hell, and the joys of the kingdom of heaven. In addition to these, he composed several others on the blessings and judgments of God, by which he sought to turn his hearers from delight in wickedness, and to inspire them to love and do good. For Caedmon was a deeply religious man, who humbly submitted to B regular discipline,[9] and firmly resisted all who tried to do evil, thus winning a happy death. ❖ 3

4. **harp:** In Anglo-Saxon times, poetry was often recited to the accompaniment of a small harp.
5. **translate . . . another:** Caedmon's verses were composed in Old English, but Bede wrote in Latin.
6. **reeve:** the officer who oversaw the monastery's farms.
7. **abbess** (ăb′ĭs): a woman in charge of a convent or monastery. The abbess of Whitby at this time was named Hilda.
8. **sacred history:** the narratives in the Bible.
9. **regular discipline:** the rules of monastic life.

WORDS TO KNOW **render** (rĕn′dər) *v.* to express in another language or form

103

Customizing Instruction

Students Acquiring English

1 Help students understand the meaning of unfamiliar words. *Frivolous* means silly or of little importance. *Profane* means not related to religion.

2 Explain that the *cud* is food that a cow has partially digested and then brought up for further chewing. Then ask students how Caedmon is like an animal "chewing the cud."
Possible Response: He turns the biblical information over in his mind until he produces a poem about it.

Less Proficient Readers

3 Have students describe Caedmon's experience. Ask them to explain why it might be considered miraculous.
Possible Response: He has no poetic talents until inspired by a divine vision.

Gifted and Talented Students

Have students explain the Christian Anglo-Saxon attitude toward miracles, based on these excerpts.
Possible Response: The transformations of Coifi and Caedmon suggest a belief in the ability of divine power to change people in a dramatic way.

Have students meet in cooperative groups to compare the methods they use to fix each run-on sentence. Tell them to suggest alternate remedies for the problem.

1. In this story the king met with Paulinus, the king said that he would discuss the change in religion with his advisors. *(Possible answer—compound: . . . Paulinus; moreover, the king . . .)*
2. Coifi was accepting of the new religion, he was unhappy with the gods he served. *(Possible answer—complex: . . . religion, since he . . .)*
3. Ethelberga's Christianity eventually brought about this change in religion her husband, Edwin, was a pagan. *(Possible answer—two sentences: . . . religion. Her . . .)*
4. The Venerable Bede worked in a monastery he is a noted historical writer. *(Possible answer—compound: . . . monastery; he . . .)*

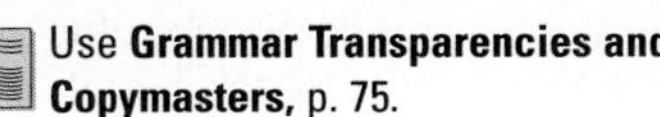
Use **Grammar Transparencies and Copymasters,** p. 75.

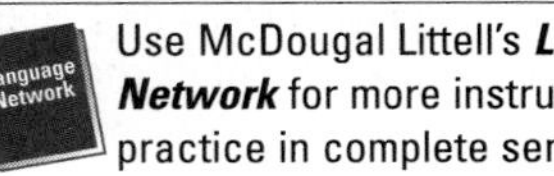

Use McDougal Littell's ***Language Network*** for more instruction and practice in complete sentences.

GUIDING STUDENT RESPONSE

Connect to the Literature

1. **What Do You Think?** Students' reactions will vary, but should be supported by details and examples from the selections. Many students will find the miracle described in the second selection less believable than the events described in the first selection.

Comprehension Check

- Coifi was willing to consider the Christian faith because he was not being rewarded for practicing his non-Christian religion.
- The abbess advised Caedmon to adopt the monastic state because she felt that his gift was from God.

Use Selection Quiz in **Unit One Resource Book** p. 24.

Think Critically

2. Answers will vary. Some students will reply that the king trusts his counselors. Others will observe that the decision to convert is a momentous one.
3. Answers will vary. Some students will reply that Coifi shows courage in rejecting familiar beliefs for an unknown religion; others will find Coifi lacking in courage, since his position as high priest protects him.
4. Answers will vary slightly. Some students will respond that Bede's purpose was to inform people about events in the early English church and will find him objective and largely credible. Others will recognize Bede's investment in converting people to Christianity and will find him less credible because of his bias.

Literary Analysis

Paired Activity You might display in the classroom the bar graphs created by students.

Active Reading Using Text Organizers You might make a chart listing different text organizers on the chalkboard.

Connect to the Literature

1. **What Do You Think?** What is your reaction to the type of events Bede describes? Explain.

Comprehension Check

- Why was Coifi willing to consider the faith professed by Paulinus?
- Why did the abbess advise Caedmon to abandon secular life and adopt the monastic state?

Think Critically

2. Why do you think the king seeks the advice of his counselors before responding to the challenge to accept Christianity?
3. In your opinion, does Coifi's destruction of the temples show great courage?

THINK ABOUT
- Coifi's position as high priest
- his role as adviser to the king
- the crowd's reaction at the temple

4. **ACTIVE READING** ANALYZING AN AUTHOR'S PURPOSE Use the details you wrote in your READER'S NOTEBOOK to determine the Venerable Bede's **purpose.** How does his purpose affect the credibility of the events he relates?

Extend Interpretations

5. **What If?** What do you think life would have been like for Caedmon if, after having his dream, he had chosen not to compose poetry?
6. **Critic's Corner** In the introduction to his translation of Bede's *History,* Leo Sherley-Price writes, "Such is the interest of the subject matter and the vividness of Bede's characteristic style that the scenes and folk of long ago live again." Comment on whether the excerpts you have read support this view of Bede's subject matter and **style.**
7. **Comparing Texts** Contrast the portrayals of life in Bede's *History* and in *Beowulf.* What aspects of Anglo-Saxon culture are emphasized in each work? What might account for the differences between the two portrayals?
8. **Connect to Life** The decisions and actions of King Edwin and Coifi hastened the spread of Christianity throughout England in a relatively short time, producing a major shift in the entire society. Think of another time in history when a political decision or some significant event or development has had a great effect on a whole nation or culture. How did people respond to the challenges to their way of life?

Literary Analysis

HISTORICAL WRITING

The characteristics of **historical writing** include a concern with real events and a chronological and objective narration of the events. Of these three characteristics, objectivity is the hardest to achieve. In Bede's account, some of his statements and choice of details may reflect his feelings and opinions. For example, Coifi's assertion that "I have long realized that there is nothing in what we worshiped" could be a reflection of the author's own opinion rather than an objective retelling of an event.

Paired Activity Choose three passages from the selection. With a partner, create a bar graph like the one shown and rate the objectivity of each passage on a scale of 1 to 10, with 1 being the least objective and 10 being the most.

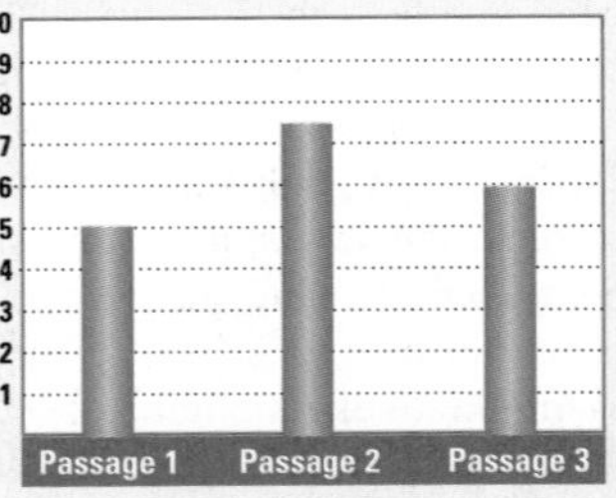

ACTIVE READING USING TEXT ORGANIZERS This **historical narrative** by the Venerable Bede uses text organizers, such as different type sizes, colors, and styles, to help clarify and structure ideas. Go back to the beginning of the selection and note the use of different treatments of type, especially in the paragraphs set off on pages 99 and 102. Identify the text organizers and note the purposes they serve in clarifying ideas.

Extend Interpretations

What If? Students may say that Caedmon would have lived in obscurity if he hadn't chosen to be a poet, or that he would have felt guilty or unfulfilled.

Critic's Corner Students' comments should be supported with examples and details from the text. Students may observe that Bede's narrative style is akin to storytelling. **To make this activity more difficult,** have students imitate Bede's style to write a narrative based on an event in their own life.

Comparing Texts Students may point out that *Beowulf* emphasizes warfare and heroism and that it is more of a legend (or a song) than a historical narrative. They may say that Bede's *History* focuses on religion, is concerned with real events, and is written as a historical narrative.

Connect to Life Responses will vary. Good responses will be supported by historical facts and sound reasons.

Choices & CHALLENGES

Writing Options

Simile for Life One of the king's advisers uses a simile, comparing human life to the flight of a sparrow. Write your own simile for life and explain your comparison.

Activities & Explorations

Sketch of a Dream Recall Caedmon's dream. Then create a sketch or painting of the man who appeared to Caedmon and inspired him to write poetry. ~ ART

Inquiry & Research

Routes to Rome Research travel between Rome and Britain during the time of Bede. Find a map showing Europe as it was in the seventh and eighth centuries. Trace the probable routes from Rome to Britain. What means of travel were used? How long would a trip from Rome to Britain have taken? What dangers would travelers have faced? Record your findings and share them in an oral report.

Vocabulary in Action

EXERCISE: ASSESSMENT PRACTICE

Decide whether the words in each of the following pairs are more nearly synonyms or antonyms. On your paper, write *S* for *Synonyms* or *A* for *Antonyms.*

1. zealous—enthusiastic
2. renounce—abandon
3. prudent—unwise
4. effectual—effective
5. devout—pious
6. desecrate—honor
7. aspire—desire
8. secular—religious
9. render—interpret
10. profess—deny

The Venerable Bede
673?–735

Other Works
History of the Abbots
On the Reckoning of Time

Leaving Home At the age of seven, Bede was taken by his parents to a monastery at Wearmouth, on the northeast coast of Britain, where he was left in the care of the abbot, Benedict Biscop (bĭsh'əp). It is not known why the boy's parents left him or whether he ever saw them again. When he was nine years old, Bede was moved a short distance to a new monastery at Jarrow, where he was to spend the rest of his life.

A Devout Child Bede seems to have been a naturally devout and studious child. He read widely in the monastery libraries, studied Latin and perhaps a little Greek, and participated fully in the religious life of the monastery. He was exposed to the art and learning of Europe through the paintings, books, and religious objects brought from Rome by Abbot Benedict. Bede became a deacon of the church at the age of 19, 6 years earlier than normal, and was ordained to the priesthood when he was 30.

A Gifted Scholar Bede was a brilliant scholar and a gifted writer and teacher. He wrote about 40 books, including works on spelling, grammar, science, history, and religion. In addition, he popularized the dating of events from the birth of Christ, the system still in use today.

Lasting Reputation Bede's reputation as a scholar and a devout monk spread throughout Europe during his lifetime and in the centuries following. (The title "Venerable" was probably first applied to him during the century after his death.) Although Bede was influenced by the outlook of his time—as is evident in the miracle stories he included in his *History*—his carefulness and integrity are still respected and valued by scholars today, almost 1,300 years later.

LaserLinks: Background for Reading
Author Background

Writing Options

Simile for Life Similes will vary. Accept all similes that have a logical connection to the life process and that are elaborated with details.

Activities & Explorations

Sketch of a Dream Sketches or paintings should incorporate selection details and try to capture the dreamy, spiritual mood of Caedmon's vision.

Inquiry & Research

Routes to Rome **As an alternate activity,** have students create maps that show place names associated with the selection, its accompanying art, or its author. Locations include Northumbria, Canterbury, Kent, York, the Derwent River, and Whitby.

Vocabulary in Action

ANSWERS

1.	S	6.	A
2.	S	7.	S
3.	A	8.	A
4.	S	9.	S
5.	S	10.	A

Mini Lesson Inquiry & Research

PRIMARY AND SECONDARY SOURCES Explain to students that historical writing involves some research. Explain that research for historical writing may be based on two kinds of sources.

- **Primary sources** provide firsthand information about a historical period. They include original documents, such as legal papers and inventories, as well as diaries, letters, poems, interviews, and other oral accounts or writings of participants or eyewitnesses.
- **Secondary sources** are based on primary sources. They summarize and often interpret historical events. They include histories, biographies, and other accounts by writers who did not witness or participate in events.

Explain that Bede's *History* is a secondary source of information on the early Anglo-Saxons, since he studied primary sources to write about events that he himself did not witness.

ACTIVITY Have students choose a historical event within the last two hundred years. Ask them to visit the school or local library and to locate one primary source and one secondary source containing information about the event. Have students share their findings with the class.

PART 2 Reflections of Everyday Life

What was life like for people in the Middle Ages? What made them laugh or cry? How did they carry out the business of living from day to day? In this part of Unit One, you will read selections that give insights into the nature of people's lives in the 14th and 15th centuries. The era will come alive for you as characters reveal their strengths and weaknesses, hopes and fears, joys and sorrows. Despite the hundreds of years that separate us from these interesting personalities, our similarities are quite astonishing.

Author Study

Geoffrey Chaucer

OVERVIEW

"There was never a man who was more of a Maker than Chaucer. . . . He came very near to making a nation."

—G. K. Chesterton

England's First Great Writer

Geoffrey Chaucer made an enormous mark on the language and literature of England. Writing in an age when French was widely spoken in educated circles, Chaucer was among the first writers to show that English could be a respectable literary language. Today, his work is considered a cornerstone of English literature.

The facts that are known about Chaucer's life paint a portrait of a man as colorful as any of the characters he created. Explore the life and times of this groundbreaking English author.

1340?–1400

BEFRIENDED BY ROYALS Chaucer was born sometime between 1340 and 1343, probably in London, in an era when expanding commerce was helping to bring the Middle Ages to a close. His family, though not noble, was fairly well off, having made money in the wine and leather trades—(the name *Chaucer* itself comes from the French word for a shoemaker.) Chaucer's parents were able to place him in the household of the wife of Prince Lionel, a son of King Edward III, where he

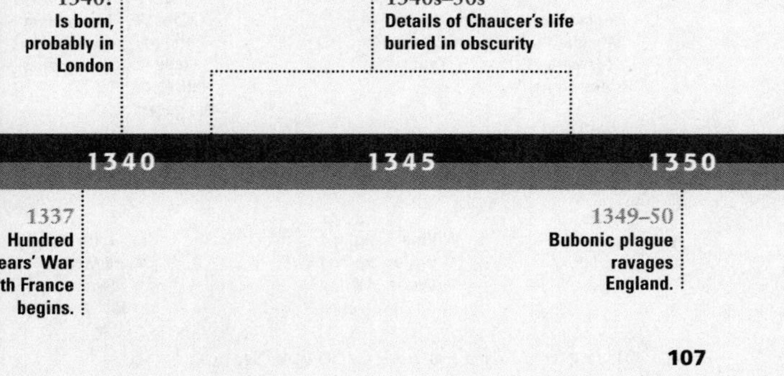

1340? Is born, probably in London
1340s–50s Details of Chaucer's life buried in obscurity
HIS LIFE
HIS TIMES
1340
1345
1350
1337 Hundred Years' War with France begins.
1349–50 Bubonic plague ravages England.

107

Author Study

OVERVIEW

Objectives

- appreciate the craft of one of England's first great writers.
- interpret the significance of world events on selections from *The Canterbury Tales.*
- gain information about Chaucer by reading nonfiction.

This Author Study offers a unique opportunity for students to focus on the work of a major writer. In addition, students can gather information about the life of Chaucer, gaining insight into the real person behind his now famous literary works.

As students read the selections, encourage them occasionally to refer to this time line and note any influences the historical context had on Chaucer's writing.

TEKS

See the Skills Trace at the beginning of the unit for information on TEKS covered in this lesson.

History

A The large English Army was very short of supplies as it moved through France in 1859. The landscape was empty of peasants. Houses, wheat fields, and even entire towns had been burned before the arrival of the English army. Chaucer took part in foraging expeditions that ventured far from the army to find food. It was on one of these expeditions that Chaucer was ambushed, captured by the French, and held for ransom.

World Culture

B Chaucer's travels in Italy exposed him to more than just Italian literature. England was characterized by quaint architecture of stone, wood, and plaster. During the Renaissance, Italy was a center of magnificent art and architecture and sophisticated music. Chaucer's trip to Italy was a turning point in his career, both as a poet and a servant to the king.

Architecture

C Chaucer's home above Aldgate, where he lived for eleven years, was a grand house, containing splendid furnishings and an enormous library (for the time) of sixty books. As controller of customs and subsidies, Chaucer was given a rent-free lease for the house.

served as an attendant. Such a position was a vital means of advancement, teaching the young Chaucer the customs of upper-class life and bringing him into contact with influential people. It may have been during this period that Chaucer met Lionel's younger brother John of Gaunt, who would become Chaucer's lifelong patron and a leading political figure of the day.

While still a teenager, Chaucer joined the king's army to fight against the French in what we now call the Hundred Years' War. He was captured by the French during the siege of Rheims, and the king himself contributed to his ransom. Chaucer later served as a royal messenger, and he would be given more important diplomatic missions in years to come. His royal contacts also led to his marriage to Philippa, a lady in waiting to the queen, and his appointment as comptroller of customs for London in 1374.

EARLY INSPIRATIONS Chaucer's diplomatic travels to the European mainland exposed him to the latest in French and Italian literature—works that would stimulate his own writing. In Italy, for example, he discovered the works of Dante, Petrarch, and Boccaccio. Chaucer's earliest major writing effort was probably an English translation of part of *The Romance of the Rose,* a famous medieval French verse romance. Not long afterward, he produced his first important original work, *The Book of the Duchess,* a long narrative poem paying tribute to Blanche, John of Gaunt's first wife, who died of plague in 1369. It was followed a few years later by *The House of Fame,* a humorous narrative about the instability of renown.

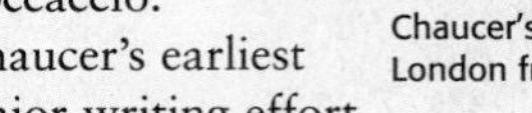

Chaucer's home above Aldgate in London from 1374–1385

TURBULENT TIMES Despite his writing successes, Chaucer's primary career remained one of politics and diplomacy. Unlike many other courtiers of the era, Chaucer continued to enjoy royal favor throughout the turbulent reign of Richard II, who was still only a boy when he became England's king in 1377. Chaucer's next major work, *The Parliament of Fowls,* was probably written to commemorate Richard's

1355 — 1360 — 1365 — 1370 — 1375

- 1357 **Becomes an attendant to the wife of Prince Lionel**
- 1359–60 **Captured in the Hundred Years' War**
- 1362? **William Langland writes the first version of *Piers Plowman.***
- 1364 **King John II of France dies in the Tower of London.**
- 1365? **Marries Philippa, lady in waiting to the queen**
- 1366 **Makes first diplomatic mission**
- 1369? **Writes *The Book of the Duchess***
- 1372 **Visits Italy; discovers Boccaccio's work**

Boccaccio

- 1377 **Edward III dies; Richard II becomes king.**

marriage to Anne of Bohemia in 1382. Four years later, Chaucer was appointed a knight of the shire and became a member of Parliament. In the 1390s he continued to enjoy various royal appointments, including those of clerk of the king's works and subforester of a royal park. D

Meanwhile, Richard II's reign was marked by conflict at home and abroad, including a peasants' revolt led by Wat Tyler and heightened agitation by the Lollards, a group of church reformers led by John Wycliffe. Finally, while Richard was off attempting to quell a rebellion in Ireland in 1399, his popular cousin Henry Bolingbroke wrested the throne from his control and was crowned as King Henry IV. The change of monarch did not affect Chaucer's political fortunes, since Henry was the son of Chaucer's longtime patron John of Gaunt. However, the writer had little time to enjoy the favor of the new monarch, for he died only a year after Henry came to the throne.

FRUITFUL YEARS The last two decades of Chaucer's life saw his finest literary achievements—the brilliant verse romance *Troilus and Criseyde* and his masterpiece, *The Canterbury Tales,* a collection of verse and prose tales of many different kinds. To join the stories together, Chaucer decided to pretend they are told by members of a group of travelers journeying from London to Canterbury. Though he may have written some of the stories earlier, most scholars think that he began organizing *The Canterbury Tales* about 1387. The work

LITERARY *Contributions*

Considered the greatest English writer before Shakespeare, Chaucer was praised in his lifetime and widely imitated after his death, when a group of 15th-century poets adopted his writing style. Later in the 15th century, when the printing press was introduced into England, *The Canterbury Tales* was among the first works to be printed.

Longer Poetic Works Chaucer is best known for his verse narratives. These include the following:

The Book of the Duchess
The House of Fame
The Parliament of Fowls
Troilus and Criseyde
The Legend of Good Women
The Canterbury Tales

Short Poems Chaucer also wrote several shorter poems, including these:

"Complaint to His Empty Purse"
"Words, to Adam, His Own Scrivener"
"Truth"
"Fortune"
"Gentilesse [Nobility]**"**
"Envoy [Message] **to Scogan"**
"Envoy [Message] **to Bukton"**

Prose As outgrowths of his scholarly interests, Chaucer produced these prose works:

The Consolation of Philosophy (translated from the Latin of Boethius)
E ***Treatise on the Astrolabe***

1386 Becomes a member of Parliament

1387 Begins to plan *The Canterbury Tales*

1389 Appointed clerk of the king's works

1400 Dies and is buried in Westminster Abbey

1380 1385 1390 1395 1400

1381 Peasants' Revolt breaks out.

1382 Richard II marries Anne of Bohemia.

1388 Opponents of Richard II execute eight of his friends.

1395 Lollards petition for church reform.

1399 Richard II is deposed; Henry IV becomes king.

Chaucer's Workplace

D As clerk of the king's works, Chaucer was the official in charge of most of the king's large building projects. He hired architects, oversaw the buying and transporting of materials, and finally inspected the finished work.

Science

E Chaucer's interest in astronomy led him to write his *Treatise on the Astrolabe.* Astrolabes, which date back to the 6th century, enable the user to measure the height of a star or other celestial body above the horizon. By the middle of the 15th century, mariners were using astrolabes to navigate on the high seas.

More About Chaucer

A The cause of Chaucer's death is not known. He may have succumbed to the plague, which recurred in Europe in the year of his death. He was buried in Westminster Abbey not because of his literary achievements, but rather because of his service to the king. Other famous poets buried in Poets' Corner include John Dryden, Tennyson, Robert Browning and John Masefield.

Link to History

B Medieval pilgrims generally began their journeys with a priest's blessing. They wore clothing identifying them as pilgrims and stayed at roadside hospices that catered specifically to pilgrims. Travel time, whether one walked or rode a horse, depended on road conditions. English roads became pools of mud when wet. Upon reaching a shrine, a pilgrim could buy as a souvenir a small badge of cast pewter.

Chaucer's London

Originally a walled town built by the Romans, London had become a bustling commercial city by Chaucer's day. Its walls enclosed a semicircular area of roughly a square mile, extending along the Thames River from the Tower of London to the Fleet River. On this small patch of land lived about 35,000 people, plus rats and other vermin, crowded together in noisy, unsanitary conditions. A marsh outside the city's north wall, although little more than an open sewer, nevertheless afforded excellent diversion when frozen over in winter.

A was still unfinished at the time of his death; Chaucer had penned nearly 20,000 lines, but many more tales were planned.

B **UNCOMMON HONOR** When he died in 1400, Chaucer was accorded an honor rare for a commoner—burial in London's Westminster Abbey. In 1566 an admirer erected an elaborate marble tomb for his remains. This was the beginning of Westminster Abbey's famous Poets' Corner, where many other great English writers have since been buried.

Chaucer's attitude toward his great subsequent renown would probably be one of humility and amusement. In *The Canterbury Tales,* he portrayed himself as a short, plump, slightly foolish pilgrim who commands no great respect. Yet from the mind of this gentle poet came a host of memorable characters and some of the finest poetry ever created in the English language.

More Online: Author Link
www.mcdougallittell.com

LaserLinks: Background for Reading
Cultural Connection
Author Background

The Shrine of Canterbury

The travelers in *The Canterbury Tales* are making a pilgrimage to the popular shrine of Saint Thomas à Becket in Canterbury. Becket was appointed archbishop of Canterbury by his friend King Henry II in 1162. However, after the two quarreled bitterly over the rights of the church, four of Henry's loyal knights murdered the archbishop in his own cathedral in 1170. Three years later, Becket was declared a saint by the Roman Catholic Church.

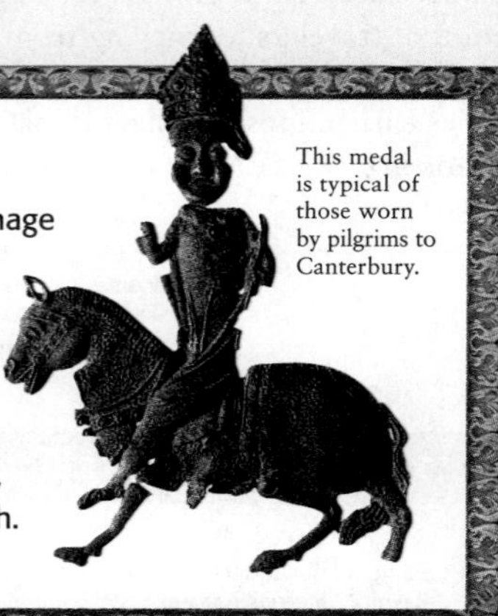

This medal is typical of those worn by pilgrims to Canterbury.

The Prologue

from The Canterbury Tales

Poetry by GEOFFREY CHAUCER
Translated by NEVILL COGHILL

Comparing Literature of the World

The Canterbury Tales and *The Decameron*

If you wish to compare the storytelling tradition across cultures, you might read "Federigo's Falcon," the excerpt from *The Decameron* that follows the three excerpts from *The Canterbury Tales.* Points of Comparison between Chaucer's and Boccaccio's tales include the narrative structure of the frame story and the authors' focus on stories with love themes.

Connect to Your Life

Story Time Recall a time when you and some friends told funny stories about growing up. What situations inspire people to tell stories? What role does an audience play in making the telling of a story more interesting? Share your thoughts in a class discussion.

Build Background

Medieval Story Time In the "Prologue," or introduction, from *The Canterbury Tales,* a group of travelers from various walks of life gather in an inn outside London to make a pilgrimage to the shrine of Saint Thomas à Becket in the city of Canterbury. At the suggestion of the innkeeper (the Host), the group decides to hold a storytelling competition to pass the time as they travel. The portion of *The Canterbury Tales* that follows the "Prologue" consists mainly of the stories that various pilgrims tell.

WORDS TO KNOW **Vocabulary Preview**

accrue	disdain	mode
agility	dispatch	personable
courtliness	eminent	repine
defer	frugal	sedately
diligent	malady	wield

Focus Your Reading

LITERARY ANALYSIS TONE The **tone** of a literary work expresses the writer's attitude toward the work's subject or characters. A tone, for example, may be formal or informal, amused or impatient. In the "Prologue" the narrator uses a detached, **ironic** tone, often understating his criticisms or saying the opposite of what he really thinks. For example, in the following lines Chaucer reveals his attitude toward a Friar who dispenses God's forgiveness ("absolution") freely, as long as he receives a donation—an attitude he probably expects the reader to share.

Sweetly he heard his penitents at shrift
With pleasant absolution, for a gift.

ACTIVE READING ANALYZING CHARACTERIZATION
Characterization is the means by which a writer develops a **character**'s personality. A writer can use a number of techniques:

- description of the character's physical appearance
- presentation of the character's speech, thoughts, feelings, and actions
- presentation of other characters' speech, thoughts, feelings, and actions as they relate to the character

READER'S NOTEBOOK As you read the "Prologue," jot down words or phrases that convey the personalities of some of the characters the **narrator** describes, as well as the narrator himself. Be sure to include the Pardoner and the Wife of Bath.

OVERVIEW

An excerpt of this selection is included in the **Grade 12 InterActive Reader.**

Objectives

1. understand and appreciate a **narrative poem (Literary Analysis)**
2. identify the **tone** of a literary work **(Literary Analysis)**
3. analyze the author's use of **characterization (Active Reading)**

Summary

From all over Britain, pilgrims make their way to Canterbury to receive the blessings of St. Thomas à Becket. At an inn, the narrator (Chaucer) joins twenty-nine pilgrims bound for Canterbury. At the suggestion of the inn's Host, the pilgrims decide to exchange stories to pass the time as they travel. In this prologue, Chaucer describes the other pilgrims. The description of the group provides insight into the larger society as a whole.

Use **Unit One Resource Book,** p. 25 for additional support.

Thematic Link

Storytelling, historically a common diversion, provides the means through which Chaucer shares the details of people's **everyday lives.**

5-Minute Warm-Up

Daily Language SkillBuilder

Have students **proofread** the display sentences on page 15k and write them correctly. The sentences also appear on Transparency 2 of **Grammar Transparencies and Copymasters.**

Mini Lesson **Preteaching Vocabulary**

To preteach the WORDS TO KNOW for this selection, use the Mini Lesson on p. 114.

LESSON RESOURCES

UNIT ONE RESOURCE BOOK, pp. 25–29

ASSESSMENT RESOURCES
Formal Assessment, pp. 17–18
Teacher's Guide to Assessment and Portfolio Use
Test Generator

SKILLS TRANSPARENCIES AND COPYMASTERS
Literary Analysis
- Style, Tone, and Mood, T24 (for Literary Analysis, p. 111)

Reading and Critical Thinking
- Organizational Chart: Horizontal, T52 (for Active Reading, p. 111)

Grammar
- Pronouns—Correct Case, T41 (for Mini Lesson, pp. 118–119)
- Pronoun-Antecedent Agreement, T48 (for Mini Lesson, pp. 123)

Vocabulary
- Antonyms, C22 (for Mini Lesson, p. 116)

Writing
- Organizing Your Writing, T11 (for Writing Option 1, p. 138)

Communications
- Evaluating Roles in Groups, T8 (for Activities & Explorations 2, p. 138)

INTEGRATED TECHNOLOGY
Audio Library
LaserLinks
- Cultural Connection: The Pilgrimage.
- Author Background: Geoffrey Chaucer. See **Teacher's SourceBook,** pp. 9–10.

Net Activities
Visit our website:
www.mcdougallittell.com

TEACHING THE LITERATURE

Reading and Analyzing

Active Reading

ANALYZING CHARACTERIZATION

One of the techniques Chaucer uses to develop characters is description of their physical appearance. As students read this section, have them list the pilgrims and one or two words about the physical appearance of each. They can construct a table to organize this information. Getting a good idea about what characters look like will help students distinguish among characters.

CHARACTER	APPEARANCE
Friar	
Pardoner	

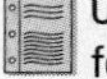 Use **Unit One Resource Book** p. 26 for more practice.

Literary Analysis TONE

The tone of a literary work conveys the writer's attitude towards characters or events. At the beginning of the prologue, Chaucer says, "But none the less, while I have time and space, Before my story takes a further pace, It seems a reasonable thing to say what their condition was, their full array." Ask how Chaucer seems to feel about his own writing.

Possible Response: He seems to view his work with humor; he doesn't take himself too seriously.

 Use **Unit One Resource Book** p.27 for more exercises.

GUIDE FOR READING

A The wind signals the coming of spring.

Chaucer on horseback. From the Ellesmere manuscript, EL 26 c. 9, fol. 153v, The Huntington Library, San Marino, California.

Teaching Options

Viewing and Representing

The Ellesmere Manuscript

ART APPRECIATION This illuminated, or artfully decorated, manuscript containing *The Canterbury Tales,* is considered by some to be the most beautiful of all English manuscripts. It was named for Sir Thomas Edgerton, first Baron Ellesmere, who added the manuscript to what became the oldest and largest family library in England. The manuscript is beautifully illustrated with descriptive images of the characters in *The Canterbury Tales,* as seen in this illustration of Geoffrey Chaucer on horseback.

Instruction Point out to students that medieval art, while not very realistic in its treatment of human form, often attended to certain details so clearly as to reveal the subject's social position, trade, and even attitude. Illuminated manuscripts like this one were filled with gold or silver gilding, brilliantly colored designs, and miniature pictures.

Application As students analyze the image on this page, ask them who the man in the drawing is. Point out the caption if necessary. *(The man in the drawing is Chaucer.)* Ask students how further illustrations from the manuscript might help them

The Prologue

When in April the sweet showers fall
And pierce the drought of March to the root, and all
The veins are bathed in liquor of such power
As brings about the engendering of the flower,
When also Zephyrus with his sweet breath
Exhales an air in every grove and heath
Upon the tender shoots, and the young sun
His half-course in the sign of the *Ram* has run,
And the small fowl are making melody
That sleep away the night with open eye
(So nature pricks them and their heart engages)
Then people long to go on pilgrimages
And palmers long to seek the stranger strands
Of far-off saints, hallowed in sundry lands,
And specially, from every shire's end
Of England, down to Canterbury they wend
To seek the holy blissful martyr, quick
To give his help to them when they were sick.

It happened in that season that one day
In Southwark, at *The Tabard,* as I lay
Ready to go on pilgrimage and start
For Canterbury, most devout at heart,
At night there came into that hostelry
Some nine and twenty in a company
Of sundry folk happening then to fall
In fellowship, and they were pilgrims all
That towards Canterbury meant to ride.

GUIDE FOR READING

5 Zephyrus (zĕf'ər-əs): the Greek god of the west wind (the blowing of which is viewed as a sign of spring). What detail or details in line 1 are reinforced here? **A**

8 the Ram Aries—one of the 12 groups of stars through which the sun appears to move in the course of the year. The sun completes its passage through Aries in mid-April.

13 palmers: people journeying to religious shrines; pilgrims; **strands:** shores.

14 sundry (sŭn'drē): various.

15 shire's: county's.

17 martyr: St. Thomas à Becket.

20 Southwark (sŭ*th*'ərk): in Chaucer's day, a town just south of London (now part of the city itself). The Tabard was an actual inn in Southwark.

23 hostelry (hŏs'təl-rē): inn.

Customizing Instruction

Less Proficient Readers

Explain that a narrative poem tells a story and, like a short story or a novel, has a setting, characters, plot, and point of view. As students read, encourage them to identify these elements in the poem.

Students Acquiring English

Explain that the language used in 14th-century **narrative poems** was more formal than that used today. Read aloud some examples, such as "And the small fowl are making melody That sleep away the night with open eye," and model paraphrasing to give the modern equivalent. *(Small birds, which sleep with one eye open, are singing.)* Guide students to identify additional formal phrases and to discuss their modern equivalents.

Use **Spanish Study Guide** for additional support, pp. 16–18.

Gifted and Talented

Explain that pilgrims traveled from Southwark to Canterbury, as well as to other holy places such as Glastonbury, Walsingham, and Salisbury. Ask students to locate each of these holy places on a map of England. Invite them to use a variety of reference sources, including the Internet, to research the social and spiritual aspects of such pilgrimages, past and present. When students have completed reading the selection, have them compare and contrast the purpose and meaning of such journeys for people in 14th-century England and for people today.

better understand each character.
Possible Response: The illustrations provide visual clues about character traits, positions in society, and personalities. Have students look at the illustrations throughout *The Prologue.* Each illustration is taken from the Ellesmere manuscript and is representative of a different character presented *in The Canterbury Tales.* Ask students what details they note in each illustration that give clues to the social status or profession of the character.
Possible Response: For example: the illustration of the Cook on page 123 shows him riding a horse and carrying a meat hook. Exposed on his knee is an ulcer. In Chaucer's day, such an ulcer was often a result of a skin disease caused by poor diet and careless hygiene.

Reading and Analyzing

Reading Skills and Strategies:
COMPREHENDING

Ask students why this group of people is gathered at the Tabard Inn.

Possible Response: They are pilgrims going to Canterbury together.

A Have students explain how it comes about that the narrator travels with the twenty-nine pilgrims to Canterbury.

Possible Response: They visit during the evening of their arrival at the inn and become friends. Since he had planned to go anyway, the narrator agrees to travel with them.

GUIDE FOR READING

B He is going to describe each pilgrim before they all begin telling their stories.

Active Reading

ANALYZING CHARACTERIZATION

C Ask the students what the description of the Knight's clothing reveals about his character.

Possible Response: His clothes are coarse and simple, showing signs of his work, suggesting he is an honest and unpretentious man.

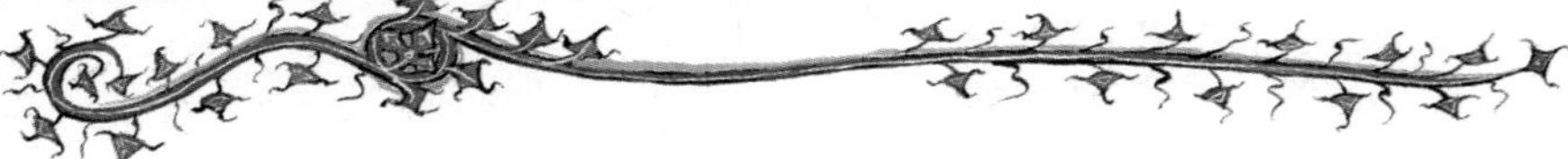

The rooms and stables of the inn were wide;
They made us easy, all was of the best.
And, briefly, when the sun had gone to rest,
I'd spoken to them all upon the trip
And was soon one with them in fellowship,
Pledged to rise early and to take the way
To Canterbury, as you heard me say.

But none the less, while I have time and space,
Before my story takes a further pace,
It seems a reasonable thing to say
What their condition was, the full array
Of each of them, as it appeared to me,
According to profession and degree,
And what apparel they were riding in;
And at a Knight I therefore will begin.
There was a *Knight,* a most distinguished man,
Who from the day on which he first began
To ride abroad had followed chivalry,
Truth, honor, generousness and courtesy.
He had done nobly in his sovereign's war
And ridden into battle, no man more,
As well in Christian as in heathen places,
And ever honored for his noble graces.

When we took Alexandria, he was there.
He often sat at table in the chair
Of honor, above all nations, when in Prussia.
In Lithuania he had ridden, and Russia,
No Christian man so often, of his rank.
When, in Granada, Algeciras sank
Under assault, he had been there, and in
North Africa, raiding Benamarin;
In Anatolia he had been as well
And fought when Ayas and Attalia fell,
For all along the Mediterranean coast
He had embarked with many a noble host.
In fifteen mortal battles he had been
And jousted for our faith at Tramissene
Thrice in the lists, and always killed his man.
This same distinguished knight had led the van
Once with the Bey of Balat, doing work

B **35–41** What is the narrator going to take time and space to do? What is he interrupting?

45 chivalry (shĭv'əl-rē): the code of behavior of medieval knights, which stressed the values listed in line 46.

51 Alexandria: a city in Egypt, captured by European Christians in 1365. All the places named in lines 51–64 were scenes of conflicts in which medieval Christians battled Muslims and other non-Christian peoples.

64 jousted: fought with a lance in an arranged battle against another knight.

65 thrice: three times; **lists:** fenced areas for jousting.

66 van: vanguard—the troops foremost in an attack.

67 Bey of Balat: a Turkish ruler.

Teaching Options

Preteaching Vocabulary

USING CONTEXT CLUES Call students' attention to the list of WORDS TO KNOW on p. 111. Demonstrate the strategy of using context clues using the following model.

Model Sentence The owner of the restaurant was so *personable* that customers came back often just to visit with her.

Instruction

- Write the model sentence on the chalkboard.
- Ask a volunteer to paraphrase the meaning of the sentence.
- Have students use the meaning of the sentence to suggest meanings for the word *personable.*
- Ask a volunteer to use the word *personable* in a sentence.

Exercise Read the following sentences. Ask students to use context clues to determine the meanings of the italicized terms.

1. By continuing to charge items that you can't afford, you *accrue* a lot of debt.
2. She runs with such *agility* that her stride resembles that of a deer in motion.

A lesson on using context clues appears on p. 939 of the Pupil's Edition.

Use **Unit One Resource Book** p. 28 for more exercises.

For him against another heathen Turk;
He was of sovereign value in all eyes.
And though so much distinguished, he was wise
And in his bearing modest as a maid.
He never yet a boorish thing had said
In all his life to any, come what might;
He was a true, a perfect gentle-knight.

C Speaking of his equipment, he possessed
Fine horses, but he was not gaily dressed.
He wore a fustian tunic stained and dark
With smudges where his armor had left mark;
Just home from service, he had joined our ranks
To do his pilgrimage and render thanks.

2 He had his son with him, a fine young *Squire,*
A lover and cadet, a lad of fire
With locks as curly as if they had been pressed.
He was some twenty years of age, I guessed.
In stature he was of a moderate length,
With wonderful agility and strength.
He'd seen some service with the cavalry
In Flanders and Artois and Picardy
And had done valiantly in little space
Of time, in hope to win his lady's grace.
He was embroidered like a meadow bright
And full of freshest flowers, red and white.
Singing he was, or fluting all the day;
He was as fresh as is the month of May.
Short was his gown, the sleeves were long and wide;
He knew the way to sit a horse and ride.
He could make songs and poems and recite,
Knew how to joust and dance, to draw and write.
He loved so hotly that till dawn grew pale
He slept as little as a nightingale.
Courteous he was, lowly and serviceable,
And carved to serve his father at the table.

There was a *Yeoman* with him at his side,
No other servant; so he chose to ride.

77 fustian (fŭs'chən): a strong cloth made of linen and cotton.

81 Squire: a young man attending on and receiving training from a knight.

82 cadet: soldier in training.

88 Flanders and Artois (är-twä') **and Picardy** (pĭk'ər-dē): areas in what is now Belgium and northern France.

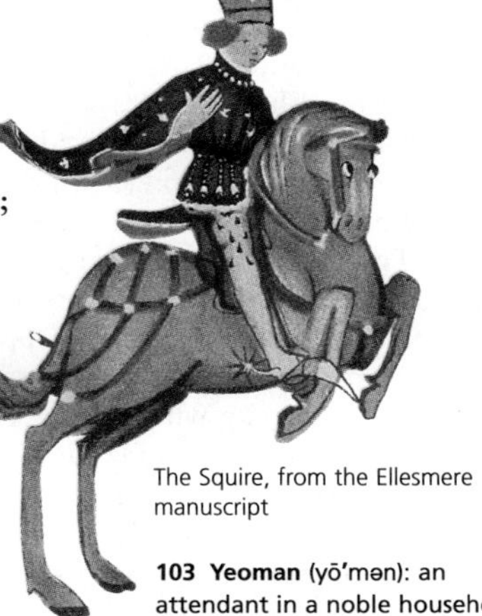

The Squire, from the Ellesmere manuscript

103 Yeoman (yō'mən): an attendant in a noble household; **him:** the Knight.

WORDS TO KNOW **agility** (ə-jĭl'ĭ-tē) *n.* an ability to move quickly and easily; nimbleness

115

Students Acquiring English

1 Help students understand the meaning of difficult terms. Point out that *heathen,* in line 49, refers to people who are not Christian. The use of the word here describes the people the Knight had fought against.

Less Proficient Readers

2 Make sure students understand the differences between the Knight and the Squire. Ask the following questions.

- Who is older, the Knight or the Squire?
  Answer: *Knight.*
- Which one plays a flute, sings, and writes and recites poetry?
  Answer: *Squire.*

Multiple Learning Styles

Visual or Spatial Learners

Suggest that students draw a series of connected boxes of characters introduced by the narrator. As they read "The Prologue," they can sequentially enter the names of the characters and write an interesting detail about each one in the boxes of their diagram.

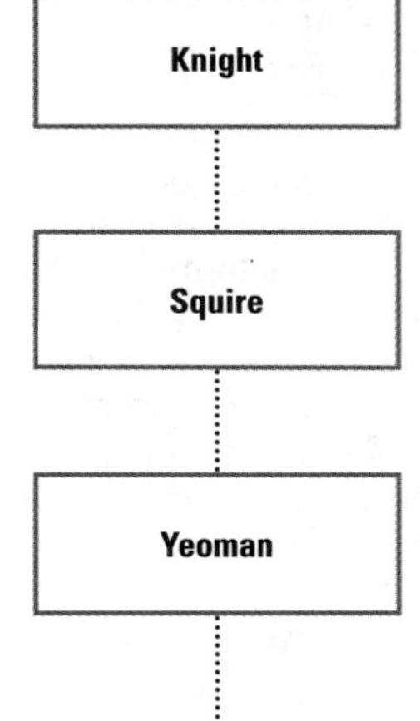

BLOCK SCHEDULING: MANAGING TIME

If your schedule requires that you cover the lesson objectives in a shorter time, use . . .

- Preparing to Read, p. 111
- Thinking Through the Literature, p. 137
- Vocabulary in Action, p. 138

If you want to take advantage of longer class time, use . . .

- TE Teaching Options: Viewing and Representing, p. 112, 122, 132; Vocabulary, pp. 114, 116, 134; Grammar, pp. 118, 123; Speaking and Listening, pp. 120, 130; Informal Assessment, pp. 124, 128, 136; Multicultural Link, p. 126; Workplace Link, p. 129
- Choices & Challenges, p. 138

Reading and Analyzing

Literary Analysis: IRONY

A Irony is a contrast between expectation and reality. Verbal irony occurs when what is said is not what is meant. Have students explain how this passage might be an example of verbal irony: "He was a proper forester, I guess."

Possible Response: The narrator, after noting the obvious attributes of a proper forester, questions his own appraisal.

GUIDE FOR READING

B The French spoken there was probably more provincial.

Reading Skills and Strategies: PARAPHRASING

C Explain that a summary is a short restatement of a writer's main ideas.

Paraphrasing helps readers understand and remember what they have read. Invite a volunteer to model the strategy by summarizing the information in lines 150–154.

Possible Response: Based on her kind actions toward her pet dogs, the nun can be said to have a tender heart.

Active Reading

ANALYZING CHARACTERIZATION

D At the time Chaucer wrote this work, coral, worn as jewelry, was considered an earthly love charm. Ask students what this information might reveal about the nun's character.

Possible Response: Wearing a coral love charm, an indication of an interest in secular things, seems out of character for the nun, who is described as spiritual and dignified.

GUIDE FOR READING

E The Monk did not live strictly according to the rules of religion.

This Yeoman wore a coat and hood of green,
And peacock-feathered arrows, bright and keen
And neatly sheathed, hung at his belt the while
—For he could dress his gear in yeoman style,
His arrows never drooped their feathers low—
And in his hand he bore a mighty bow.
His head was like a nut, his face was brown.
He knew the whole of woodcraft up and down.
A saucy brace was on his arm to ward
It from the bow-string, and a shield and sword
Hung at one side, and at the other slipped
A jaunty dirk, spear-sharp and well-equipped.
A medal of St Christopher he wore
Of shining silver on his breast, and bore
A hunting-horn, well slung and burnished clean,
A That dangled from a baldrick of bright green.
He was a proper forester, I guess.

There also was a *Nun,* a Prioress,
Her way of smiling very simple and coy.
Her greatest oath was only "By St. Loy!"
And she was known as Madam Eglantyne.
And well she sang a service, with a fine
Intoning through her nose, as was most seemly,
And she spoke daintily in French, extremely,
After the school of Stratford-atte-Bowe;
French in the Paris style she did not know.
At meat her manners were well taught withal;
No morsel from her lips did she let fall,
Nor dipped her fingers in the sauce too deep;
But she could carry a morsel up and keep
The smallest drop from falling on her breast.
For <u>courtliness</u> she had a special zest,
And she would wipe her upper lip so clean
That not a trace of grease was to be seen
Upon the cup when she had drunk; to eat,
She reached a hand <u>sedately</u> for the meat.
She certainly was very entertaining,
Pleasant and friendly in her ways, and straining
To counterfeit a courtly kind of grace,
A stately bearing fitting to her place,

113 saucy: jaunty; stylish; **brace:** a leather arm-guard worn by archers.

116 dirk: small dagger.

117 St. Christopher: the patron saint of foresters and travelers.

120 baldrick: shoulder strap.

122 Prioress: a nun ranking just below the abbess (head) of a convent.

124 St. Loy: St. Eligius (known as St. Eloi in France).

B **129 Stratford-atte-Bowe:** a town (now part of London) near the Prioress's convent. How do you think the French spoken there differed from that spoken in Paris?

131 at meat: when dining; **withal:** moreover.

The Prioress

WORDS TO KNOW

courtliness (kôrt'lē-nĭs) *n.* refined behavior; elegance

sedately (sĭ-dāt'lē) *adv.* in a composed, dignified manner; calmly

Teaching Options

Vocabulary Strategy

ANTONYMS

Instruction Words that have opposite or almost opposite meanings are called **antonyms.** Antonyms in context can offer clues to meanings of unfamiliar words or terms. *Work with students to model the process of finding the meaning of a word by using its antonym.*

Activity Have students use the following sentence to suggest a meaning for *sedately. The Nun reached <u>sedately</u> for a piece of the meat, while the Yeoman energetically filled his plate.*

Model Sentence

The <u>courtliness</u> of the Knight's behavior contrasted with the <u>rudeness</u> of his brothers'.

From the model sentence students can understand that *courtliness* is the opposite of rudeness. Therefore, *courtliness* implies politeness.

Use **Vocabulary Transparencies and Copymasters,** p. 22.

And to seem dignified in all her dealings.
As for her sympathies and tender feelings,
She was so charitably solicitous
She used to weep if she but saw a mouse
Caught in a trap, if it were dead or bleeding.
And she had little dogs she would be feeding
With roasted flesh, or milk, or fine white bread.
(C) And bitterly she wept if one were dead
Or someone took a stick and made it smart;
She was all sentiment and tender heart.
Her veil was gathered in a seemly way,
Her nose was elegant, her eyes glass-grey;
Her mouth was very small, but soft and red,
Her forehead, certainly, was fair of spread,
Almost a span across the brows, I own;
She was indeed by no means undergrown.
Her cloak, I noticed, had a graceful charm.
(D) She wore a coral trinket on her arm, [1]
A set of beads, the gaudies tricked in green,
Whence hung a golden brooch of brightest sheen
On which there first was graven a crowned A,
And lower, *Amor vincit omnia.*

Another *Nun*, the secretary at her cell,
Was riding with her, and *three Priests* as well.

A *Monk* there was, one of the finest sort
Who rode the country; hunting was his sport.
A manly man, to be an Abbot able;
Many a dainty horse he had in stable.
[2] His bridle, when he rode, a man might hear
Jingling in a whistling wind as clear,
[3] Aye, and as loud as does the chapel bell
Where my lord Monk was Prior of the cell.
The Rule of good St. Benet or St. Maur
As old and strict he tended to ignore;
He let go by the things of yesterday
And took the modern world's more spacious way.
He did not rate that text at a plucked hen
Which says that hunters are not holy men
And that a monk uncloistered is a mere
Fish out of water, flapping on the pier,

The Monk

159 span: a unit of length equal to nine inches. A broad forehead was considered a sign of beauty in Chaucer's day.

163 gaudies: the larger beads in a set of prayer beads.

166 *Amor vincit omnia* (ä'môr wĭn'kĭt ôm'nē-ə): Latin for "Love conquers all things."

171 Abbot: the head of a monastery.

172 dainty: excellent.

176 Prior of the cell: head of a subsidiary group of monks.

177 St. Benet . . . St. Maur: St. Benedict, who established a strict set of rules for monks' behavior, and his follower St. Maurus, who introduced those rules into France.

(E) **180** What does the narrator mean by "the modern world's more spacious way"?

Customizing Instruction

Students Acquiring English

1 Explain to students that Chaucer's physical descriptions of his characters often reveal character trait. For example, the Prioress's graceful—and probably expensive—cloak and jewelry suggest that she is vain about her appearance.

2 Ask students to paraphrase what is meant by lines 173–174, "His bridle, when he rode, a man might hear / Jingling in a whistling wind as clear."
Possible Response: His bridle made a clear, jingling sound as he rode.

Less Proficient Readers

Check students' comprehension by asking these questions.

- How many nuns and priests are in the group of travelers?
  Answer: Two nuns, three priests.
- What conclusions can you draw about the Nun from Chaucer's description?
  Possible Response: She is a good and dignified woman, nice to be around, with perhaps some hidden qualities that make her unpredictable and interesting.

Multiple Learning Styles

Auditory Learners

3 Invite a volunteer to read aloud lines 169–176. Ask students how Chaucer's choice of sensory words, such as *jingling* and *whistling,* helps them imagine what is being described. Encourage students to be aware of other examples of words that help them hear what is happening.

THE CANTERBURY TALES 117

Reading and Analyzing

Literary Analysis: NARRATIVE POEM
Review with students the elements of a narrative that Chaucer has introduced thus far. What elements have not been introduced?
Possible Response: The setting, narrator's point of view, and some of the characters have been introduced; the plot has not yet begun to unfold.

GUIDE FOR READING
A The people pay the Friar for absolution from their sins.

Active Reading
ANALYZING CHARACTERIZATION
Explain that the Nun, the Monk, and the Friar have characters that are very different. In a discussion, have students compare and contrast characteristics of these three pilgrims, based on the way they are described by the narrator. Then ask students to decide which one they would like to spend time with, and tell why. You may wish to draw a diagram on the board to help guide the discussion.

	Nun	Monk	Friar
Physical description			
Actions			
Narrator's comment			

That is to say a monk out of his cloister.
That was a text he held not worth an oyster;
And I agreed and said his views were sound;
Was he to study till his head went round
Poring over books in cloisters? Must he toil
As Austin bade and till the very soil?
Was he to leave the world upon the shelf?
Let Austin have his labor to himself.

This Monk was therefore a good man to horse;
Greyhounds he had, as swift as birds, to course.
Hunting a hare or riding at a fence
Was all his fun, he spared for no expense.
I saw his sleeves were garnished at the hand
With fine grey fur, the finest in the land,
And on his hood, to fasten it at his chin
He had a wrought-gold cunningly fashioned pin;
Into a lover's knot it seemed to pass.
His head was bald and shone like looking-glass;
So did his face, as if it had been greased.
He was a fat and personable priest;
His prominent eyeballs never seemed to settle.
They glittered like the flames beneath a kettle;
Supple his boots, his horse in fine condition.
He was a prelate fit for exhibition,
He was not pale like a tormented soul.
He liked a fat swan best, and roasted whole.
His palfrey was as brown as is a berry.

There was a *Friar,* a wanton one and merry,
A Limiter, a very festive fellow.
In all Four Orders there was none so mellow,
So glib with gallant phrase and well-turned speech.
He'd fixed up many a marriage, giving each
Of his young women what he could afford her.
He was a noble pillar to his Order.
Highly beloved and intimate was he
With County folk within his boundary,
And city dames of honor and possessions;
For he was qualified to hear confessions,
Or so he said, with more than priestly scope;

190 Austin: St. Augustine of Hippo, who recommended that monks engage in hard agricultural labor.

194 to course: for hunting.

208 prelate (prĕl′ĭt): high-ranking member of the clergy.

211 palfrey (pôl′frē): saddle horse.

212 Friar: a member of a religious group sworn to poverty and living on charitable donations; **wanton** (wŏn′tən): playful; jolly.

213 Limiter: a friar licensed to beg for donations in a limited area.

214 Four Orders: the four groups of friars—Dominican, Franciscan, Carmelite, and Augustinian.

222 confessions: church rites in which penitents (people seeking absolution, or formal forgiveness, for their sins) confess their sins to members of the clergy, who usually require the penitents to perform certain tasks, called penances, as a condition of the forgiveness. Only certain friars were licensed to hear confessions.

WORDS TO KNOW **personable** (pûr′sə-nə-bəl) *adj.* pleasing in behavior and appearance

Teaching Options

Grammar

PRONOUN CASES
Instruction In English there are three cases: nominative, objective, and possessive. The case of a pronoun depends on its function in a sentence. For example, pronouns used as subjects are in the nominative case; those used as direct objects are in the objective case, and those that show ownership are in the possessive case.

Look at the following chart. Notice how the pronoun forms change according to case.

	Nominative	Objective	Possessive
Singular	I, you, he, she, it	me, you, him, her, it	my, mine, your, yours, his, her, hers, its
Plural	we, you, they	us, you, them	our, ours, your, yours their, theirs

He had a special license from the Pope.
Sweetly he heard his penitents at shrift
With pleasant absolution, for a gift.
He was an easy man in penance-giving
Where he could hope to make a decent living;
1 It's a sure sign whenever gifts are given
To a poor Order that a man's well shriven,
And should he give enough he knew in verity
The penitent repented in sincerity.
For many a fellow is so hard of heart
He cannot weep, for all his inward smart.
Therefore instead of weeping and of prayer
One should give silver for a poor Friar's care.
He kept his tippet stuffed with pins for curls,
And pocket-knives, to give to pretty girls.
And certainly his voice was gay and sturdy,
For he sang well and played the hurdy-gurdy.
At sing-songs he was champion of the hour.
His neck was whiter than a lily-flower
But strong enough to butt a bruiser down.
He knew the taverns well in every town
And every innkeeper and barmaid too
Better than lepers, beggars and that crew,
For in so eminent a man as he
It was not fitting with the dignity
Of his position, dealing with a scum
Of wretched lepers; nothing good can come
Of commerce with such slum-and-gutter dwellers,
But only with the rich and victual-sellers.
But anywhere a profit might accrue
Courteous he was and lowly of service too.
Natural gifts like his were hard to match.
He was the finest beggar of his batch,
And, for his begging-district, paid a rent;
His brethren did no poaching where he went.
For though a widow mightn't have a shoe,
So pleasant was his holy how-d'ye-do
He got his farthing from her just the same
Before he left, and so his income came
To more than he laid out. And how he romped,
Just like a puppy! He was ever prompt

225 shrift: confession.

230 well shriven: completely forgiven through the rite of confession. A What role does money seem to play in the confessions that the Friar hears?

231 verity: truth.

237 tippet: an extension of a hood or sleeve, used as a pocket.

240 hurdy-gurdy: a stringed musical instrument, similar to a lute, played by turning a crank while pressing down keys.

The Friar

252 victual (vĭt′l): food.

261 farthing: a coin of small value used in England until recent times.

WORDS TO KNOW

eminent (ĕm′ə-nənt) *adj.* standing out above others; high-ranking; prominent
accrue (ə-kro͞o′) *v.* to come as gain; accumulate

Customizing Instruction

Less Proficient Readers

Read aloud the following lines to guide students in a discussion about the **irony** Chaucer uses in describing the Friar's **character.**

- "For he was qualified to hear confessions, / Or so he said, with more than priestly scope" (lines 222–223).
  Possible Response: Inserting humor, the narrator questions the Friar's claim that he is qualified. Suggesting he is curious about the affairs of others.
- "For though a widow mightn't have a shoe, / So pleasant was his holy how-d'ye-do / He got his farthing from her just the same / Before he left, and so his income came" (lines 259–262).
  Possible Response: Inserting humor and playfulness, the narrator mocks the Friar's greeting; then he points out the Friar's insincere way of getting money from the widow.

Multiple Learning Styles

Auditory Learners

1 Have students listen and clap to the rhythm of iambic pentameter as you read these lines (223–235) aloud. Have them note that the lines are not all end-stopped; that is, to get the sense, it is often necessary to read on to the next line.

Activity Write these sentences on the chalkboard. Have students identify the case of each pronoun.

Geoffrey Chaucer was born in England around 1340. His family was well-off, having made money in the wine and leather trades. When he was young, they placed him as an attendant in Prince Lionel's household. It was this initial position that gave him the influential contacts that he needed later on in his life. *(poss; nom; nom; obj; nom; obj; nom; poss;)*

Exercise Ask students to choose the correct pronoun to complete each sentence. Then have them identify the case of the pronoun.

1. In *The Canterbury Tales,* Chaucer tells of pilgrimages that were common in ______ (he, him, his) time. *(his, poss.)*
2. ______ (I, me, my) read this story in ______ (I, me, my) fourth period class. *(I, nom.; my, poss.)*
3. The Knight brought ______ (he, his, him) son with ______ (he, his, him). *(his, poss.; him, obj.)*

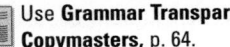

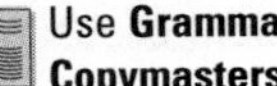
Use **Grammar Transparencies and Copymasters,** p. 64.

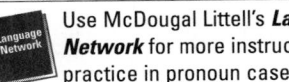

Use McDougal Littell's ***Language Network*** for more instruction and practice in pronoun cases.

Reading and Analyzing

Literary Analysis 

Ⓐ Tone is the expression of a writer's attitude toward the subject of the work and can be figured out from the writer's word choice and the kinds of statements the writer makes. The writer's choice of details helps establish the tone, which might be serious, humorous, sarcastic, playful, ironic, bitter, or objective. Have students reread the description of the Merchant in lines 288–290 to determine the narrator's tone.

Possible Responses: humorous, ironic, playful.

GUIDE FOR READING

Ⓑ The Merchant is obviously a shrewd businessman who is not unwilling to take a risk.

Ⓒ The clerk is dedicated to learning and not to material prosperity.

Reading Skills and Strategies: PARAPHRASING

Ⓓ Readers sometimes paraphrase, or restate a passage in their own words, to help them better understand or remember material. A good paraphrase includes essentially the same information, but it is expressed in a different way. Have students paraphrase lines 326–332 aloud, giving the main idea and supporting details in their own words.

Possible Response: The Sergeant at the Law was so well educated and had such good recall that he earned respect and a lot of money, but he led people to think that he was busier and wiser than he really was.

GUIDE FOR READING

Ⓔ He is officious and yet also efficient.

To arbitrate disputes on settling days
(For a small fee) in many helpful ways,
Not then appearing as your cloistered scholar
With threadbare habit hardly worth a dollar,
But much more like a Doctor or a Pope.
Of double-worsted was the semi-cope
Upon his shoulders, and the swelling fold
About him, like a bell about its mold
When it is casting, rounded out his dress.
He lisped a little out of wantonness
To make his English sweet upon his tongue.
When he had played his harp, or having sung,
His eyes would twinkle in his head as bright
As any star upon a frosty night.
This worthy's name was Hubert, it appeared.

There was a *Merchant* with a forking beard
And motley dress; high on his horse he sat,
Upon his head a Flemish beaver hat
And on his feet daintily buckled boots.
1 He told of his opinions and pursuits
In solemn tones, he harped on his increase
Of capital; there should be sea-police
(He thought) upon the Harwich-Holland ranges;
He was expert at dabbling in exchanges.
Ⓐ This estimable Merchant so had set
His wits to work, none knew he was in debt,
He was so stately in administration,
In loans and bargains and negotiation.
He was an excellent fellow all the same;
To tell the truth I do not know his name.

An *Oxford Cleric,* still a student though,
One who had taken logic long ago,
Was there; his horse was thinner than a rake,
And he was not too fat, I undertake,
But had a hollow look, a sober stare;
The thread upon his overcoat was bare.
He had found no preferment in the church
And he was too unworldly to make search
For secular employment. By his bed
He preferred having twenty books in red

265 settling days: days on which disputes were settled out of court. Friars often acted as arbiters in the disputes and charged for their services, though forbidden by the church to do so.

270 double-worsted (wŏŏs'tĭd): a strong, fairly costly fabric made from tightly twisted yarn; **semi-cope:** a short cloak.

281 motley: multicolored.

282 Flemish: from Flanders, an area in what is now Belgium and northern France.

287 Harwich-Holland ranges: shipping routes between Harwich (hăr' ĭj), a port on England's east coast, and the country of Holland.

288 exchanges: selling foreign currency at a profit. Ⓑ From his dabbling in this practice, which was illegal in Chaucer's day, what can you conclude about the Merchant?

295 Cleric: a clergyman—here, a student preparing for the priesthood.

301 preferment: advancement; promotion.

303 secular (sĕk'yə-lər): outside the church.

Teaching Options

Speaking and Listening

DRAMATIC READING

Instruction Explain that, even though the "Prologue" is written in third person, from the narrator's point of view, it can be retold in first person, from each character's point of view.

Prepare Point out that specific ironic passages may take on a different tone when conveyed from a first-person point of view. Have students work in **cooperative groups,** with each student choosing a character in the "Prologue" to dramatize aloud, in first person rather than third person.

Present Students should prepare for their performances by writing them first and then reciting them to each other.

BLOCK SCHEDULING This activity is particularly well-suited for longer class periods.

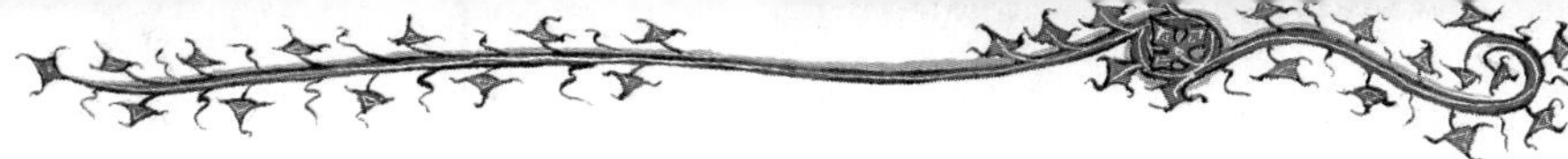

2 And black, of Aristotle's philosophy,
Than costly clothes, fiddle or psaltery.
Though a philosopher, as I have told,
He had not found the stone for making gold.
Whatever money from his friends he took
He spent on learning or another book
And prayed for them most earnestly, returning
Thanks to them thus for paying for his learning.
His only care was study, and indeed
He never spoke a word more than was need,
Formal at that, respectful in the extreme,
Short, to the point, and lofty in his theme.
A tone of moral virtue filled his speech
And gladly would he learn, and gladly teach.

A *Sergeant at the Law* who paid his calls,
Wary and wise, for clients at St. Paul's
There also was, of noted excellence.
Discreet he was, a man to reverence,
Or so he seemed, his sayings were so wise.
He often had been Justice of Assize
By letters patent, and in full commission.
His fame and learning and his high position
Had won him many a robe and many a fee.
D There was no such conveyancer as he;
All was fee-simple to his strong digestion,
Not one conveyance could be called in question.
Though there was nowhere one so busy as he,
He was less busy than he seemed to be.
He knew of every judgement, case and crime
Ever recorded since King William's time.
He could dictate defenses or draft deeds;
No one could pinch a comma from his screeds
And he knew every statute off by rote.
He wore a homely parti-colored coat,
Girt with a silken belt of pin-stripe stuff;
Of his appearance I have said enough.

305 Aristotle's philosophy: the writings of Aristotle, a famous Greek philosopher of the fourth century B.C.

306 psaltery (sôl'tə-rē): a stringed instrument.

C **307–308 Though a philosopher . . . stone for making gold:** Practitioners of the false science of alchemy often sought the "philosopher's stone," supposedly capable of turning common metals into gold. What does the narrator mean by this statement?

319 Sergeant at the Law: a lawyer appointed by the monarch to serve as a judge.

320 St. Paul's: the cathedral of London, outside which lawyers met clients when the courts were closed.

324 Justice of Assize: a judge who traveled about the country to hear cases.

325 letters patent: royal documents commissioning a judge.

328 conveyancer: lawyer specializing in conveyances (deeds) and property disputes.

329 fee-simple: property owned without restrictions.

E **331–332** Explain the apparent contradiction here. How would you sum up the skill and work habits of the Sergeant at the Law?

334 King William's time: the reign of William the Conqueror.

336 screeds: documents.

Customizing Instruction

Less Proficient Readers

Use the following questions to guide students to understand that the Oxford Cleric is one of the most admired people on the pilgrimage.

- On what does the Oxford clerk spend money he has obtained from his friends?
  Answer: He spends it on learning and books.
- What was his response to his friends' generosity?
  Answer: He thanked them.
- How do you know that he was a quiet and humble man?
  Answer: He never spoke more than was necessary; he was as eager to learn from others as he was to teach.

Set a Purpose Have students read on to learn about the rest of the pilgrims.

Multiple Learning Styles

Visual Learners

Have students draw a sketch of the Merchant, the Oxford Cleric, and/or the Sergeant at the Law, based on their descriptions in the text. Then ask pairs of students to compare their drawings of the same character to observe different interpretations of the story.

Students Acquiring English

1 Help students understand the meaning of difficult words. The word *harped* in line 285 means that the merchant talked a lot about getting rich.

2 Say *psaltery* aloud for students and have them repeat after you. Remind them that, in English, a *p* before *n, s,* or *t* is silent.

THE CANTERBURY TALES **121**

Reading and Analyzing

Reading Skills and Strategies: QUESTIONING

Encourage students to be aware of questions they form in their reading. Tell them to keep these questions in mind as they read further to find the answers. Looking for reasons behind events and characters' feelings can help students feel closer to what they are reading. Noting confusing words or statements, and keeping them in mind also helps. Encourage students to be aware of questions they have about the Franklin as they read.

Literary Analysis: IRONY

A Have students reread lines 405–410 to understand the **irony** of Chaucer's tone. Ask these questions:

- What is ironic about the "excellent" Skipper's behavior toward the trader?
  Possible Response: The skipper stole wine while the trader was asleep.
- How would you explain the irony in "He sent his prisoners home; they walked the plank."
  Possible Response: Chaucer ironically uses home to mean "to their death."

GUIDE FOR READING

B The Skipper seems hearty and companionable.

The Franklin

There was a *Franklin* with him, it appeared;
White as a daisy-petal was his beard.
A sanguine man, high-colored and benign,
He loved a morning sop of cake in wine.
He lived for pleasure and had always done,
For he was Epicurus' very son,
In whose opinion sensual delight
Was the one true felicity in sight.
As noted as St. Julian was for bounty
He made his household free to all the County.
His bread, his ale were finest of the fine
And no one had a better stock of wine.
His house was never short of bake-meat pies,
Of fish and flesh, and these in such supplies
It positively snowed with meat and drink
And all the dainties that a man could think.
According to the seasons of the year
Changes of dish were ordered to appear.
He kept fat partridges in coops, beyond,
Many a bream and pike were in his pond.
Woe to the cook unless the sauce was hot
And sharp, or if he wasn't on the spot!
And in his hall a table stood arrayed
And ready all day long, with places laid.
As Justice at the Sessions none stood higher;
He often had been Member for the Shire.
A dagger and a little purse of silk
Hung at his girdle, white as morning milk.
As Sheriff he checked audit, every entry.
He was a model among landed gentry.

341 Franklin: a wealthy landowner.

343 sanguine (săng′gwĭn): In medieval science, the human body was thought to contain four "humors" (blood, phlegm, yellow bile, and black bile), the relative proportions of which determined a person's temperament. A sanguine person (one in whom blood was thought to predominate) was cheerful and good-natured.

346 Epicurus' very son: someone who pursues pleasure as the chief goal in life, as the ancient Greek philosopher Epicurus was supposed to have recommended.

349 St. Julian: the patron saint of hospitality; **bounty:** generosity.

365 Sessions: local court proceedings.

366 Member for the Shire: his county's representative in Parliament.

368 girdle: belt.

369 Sheriff: a royal tax collector.

370 landed gentry (jĕn′trē): well-born, wealthy landowners.

Teaching Options

Mini Lesson: Viewing and Representing

The Franklin, The Cook

ART APPRECIATION

Instruction Explain that illustrations can tell a lot about characters that may or may not be obvious in the words of the story. Beyond illustrating physical attributes, these visual clues can offer the reader details that reveal such things as economic status and demeanor.

Application Ask students to analyze the illustrations of the Cook and the Franklin, looking for visual clues that offer hints about the character of each. Specifically, direct students to notice the hand gestures, the type and condition of the clothing, and the ages of the Cook and the Franklin as they form an opinion of each. Encourage groups of students to discuss their ideas.

A *Haberdasher*, a *Dyer*, a *Carpenter*,
A *Weaver* and a *Carpet-maker* were
Among our ranks, all in the livery
Of one impressive guild-fraternity.
They were so trim and fresh their gear would pass
For new. Their knives were not tricked out with brass
But wrought with purest silver, which avouches
A like display on girdles and on pouches.
Each seemed a worthy burgess, fit to grace
A guild-hall with a seat upon the dais.
Their wisdom would have justified a plan
To make each one of them an alderman;
They had the capital and revenue,
Besides their wives declared it was their due.
And if they did not think so, then they ought;
To be called *"Madam"* is a glorious thought,
And so is going to church and being seen
Having your mantle carried, like a queen.

They had a *Cook* with them who stood alone
For boiling chicken with a marrow-bone,
Sharp flavoring-powder and a spice for savor.
He could distinguish London ale by flavor,
And he could roast and seethe and broil and fry,
Make good thick soup and bake a tasty pie.
But what a pity—so it seemed to me,
That he should have an ulcer on his knee.
As for blancmange, he made it with the best.

There was a *Skipper* hailing from far west;
He came from Dartmouth, so I understood.
He rode a farmer's horse as best he could,
In a woolen gown that reached his knee.
A dagger on a lanyard falling free
Hung from his neck under his arm and down.
The summer heat had tanned his color brown,
And certainly he was an excellent fellow.
Many a draft of vintage, red and yellow,
He'd drawn at Bordeaux, while the trader snored.
The nicer rules of conscience he ignored.
If, when he fought, the enemy vessel sank,
He sent his prisoners home; they walked the plank.

371 Haberdasher: a seller of hats and other clothing accessories.

373–374 livery . . . guild-fraternity: uniform of a social or religious organization.

379 burgess (bûr′jĭs): citizen of a town.

382 alderman: town councilor.

388 mantle: cloak.

The Cook

397 blancmange (blə-mänj′): in Chaucer's day, a thick chicken stew with almonds.

399 Dartmouth (därt′məth): a port in southwestern England.

402 lanyard (lăn′yərd): a cord worn as a necklace.

405 What might the narrator mean by calling the Skipper "an excellent fellow"?

406 vintage: wine.

407 Bordeaux (bôr-dō′): a region of France famous for its wine.

Customizing Instruction

Less Proficient Readers

1 Explain that guilds were organizations of tradespeople who taught their apprentices a type of work. The guilds controlled the quality and prices of the goods they made, and they held power in the community. Ask students to answer these questions to help them better understand the guild members:

- How would you describe the way they dress?
  Answer: impeccably and with great pride.
- Would you say they are impressed with themselves? Explain.
  Possible Response: Yes, they have a high opinion of their own wisdom and income.

Students Acquiring English

Discuss the different professions described in the "Prologue" with students. Point out that many of these professions are also common surnames in English. Ask students which, if any, professions in their primary languages are common surnames.

Mini Lesson Grammar

PRONOUN-ANTECEDENT AGREEMENT

Instruction An antecedent is the noun or pronoun to which a pronoun refers. When students use pronouns they must match the antecedent's number (singular or plural), gender (masculine, feminine, or neuter), and person (first, second, or third).

Activity Write these sentences on the chalkboard. Underline the words as shown.

Every traveler will tell his or her own story.
The travelers settled into their seats.

Have students determine the antecedents for each underlined pronoun. Point out that in the first sentence the antecedent *traveler* is third-person singular and could be masculine or feminine. In the second sentence the antecedent *travelers* is third-person plural and could be masculine or feminine.

Exercise Have students identify the antecedent in this sentence. Have them choose the correct form of the pronoun to complete the sentence.
The Squire and the Yeoman ride ______ (he, his, their) horses. *(Squire and Yeoman; their)*

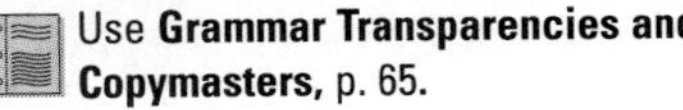

Use **Grammar Transparencies and Copymasters**, p. 65.

Use McDougal Littell's ***Language Network*** for more instruction and practice in pronoun-antecedent agreement.

Reading and Analyzing

Active Reading
ANALYZING CHARACTERIZATION

A What does Chaucer reveal about the Doctor's personality through his description?
Possible Response: He is greedy and motivated by money; he does not enjoy common pleasures of food and drink, but he indulges himself by wearing fine clothing.

Reading Skills and Strategies:
SUMMARIZING

Ask students to summarize the characteristics of the woman from Bath. They should identify a main idea or impression about her and then details that support this impression.
Possible Responses: The Wife of Bath seems to be a very formidable figure. She is an accomplished weaver who has trouble hearing. She is worldly, having been married five times and having had relationships prior to her marriages. She has traveled widely and is good and entertaining company. She has offered her knowledge and skills to women who found themselves in various forms of trouble resulting from love affairs.

GUIDE FOR READING

B This shows that all of her marriages were performed according to the rules of religion and the Church; this shows she is a respectable member of society.

As for his skill in reckoning his tides,
Currents and many another risk besides,
Moons, harbors, pilots, he had such dispatch
That none from Hull to Carthage was his match.
Hardy he was, prudent in undertaking;
His beard in many a tempest had its shaking,
And he knew all the havens as they were
From Gottland to the Cape of Finisterre,
And every creek in Brittany and Spain;
The barge he owned was called *The Maudelayne*.

A *Doctor* too emerged as we proceeded;
No one alive could talk as well as he did
On points of medicine and of surgery,
For, being grounded in astronomy,
He watched his patient closely for the hours
When, by his horoscope, he knew the powers
Of favorable planets, then ascendent,
Worked on the images for his dependant.
The cause of every malady you'd got
He knew, and whether dry, cold, moist or hot;
He knew their seat, their humor and condition.
He was a perfect practicing physician.
These causes being known for what they were,
He gave the man his medicine then and there.
All his apothecaries in a tribe
Were ready with the drugs he would prescribe
And each made money from the other's guile;
They had been friendly for a goodish while.
He was well-versed in Aesculapius too
And what Hippocrates and Rufus knew
And Dioscorides, now dead and gone,
Galen and Rhazes, Hali, Serapion,
Averroes, Avicenna, Constantine,
Scotch Bernard, John of Gaddesden, Gilbertine.
In his own diet he observed some measure;
There were no superfluities for pleasure,
Only digestives, nutritives and such.
He did not read the Bible very much.
In blood-red garments, slashed with bluish grey
And lined with taffeta, he rode his way;

414 Hull . . . Carthage: ports in England and in Spain. The places named in lines 414–419 show that the Skipper is familiar with all the western coast of Europe.

416 tempest: violent storm.

424 astronomy: astrology.

430 dry, cold, moist . . . hot: in medieval science, the four basic qualities that were thought to combine in various ways to form both the four elements of the world (fire, air, water, and earth) and the four humors of the human body (see the note at line 343). An excess of any of these qualities in a person could lead to illness.

435 apothecaries (ə-pŏth'ĭ-kĕr'ēz): druggists.

439–444 Aesculapius (ĕs'kyə-lā'pē-əs) **. . . Gilbertine:** famous ancient and medieval medical experts.

446 superfluities (so͞o'pər-flo͞o'ĭ-tēz): excesses.

450 taffeta (tăf'ĭ-tə): a stiff, smooth fabric.

WORDS TO KNOW
dispatch (dĭ-spăch') *n.* promptness; efficiency
malady (măl'ə-dē) *n.* a disease or disorder; ailment

Teaching Options

Assessment Informal Assessment

WRITING A SELF-DESCRIPTION Have students imagine that they are members of the pilgrimage to Canterbury and that the narrator has asked them to write a description of themselves to enter into the "Prologue." Each third-person description should include the following information about the character: (1) physical traits, (2) behavioral traits, and (3) an ironic twist about the character from the narrator's point of view.

RUBRIC

3 **Full Accomplishment** Students accurately convey substantial information describing physical and behavioral traits of character, as well as ironic twist about character.

2 **Substantial Accomplishment** Student writing shows general description of physical and behavioral traits character, but is lacking in development of ironic twist.

1 **Little or Partial Accomplishment** Student writing displays incomplete description with no ironic twist.

Yet he was rather close as to expenses
And kept the gold he won in pestilences.
Gold stimulates the heart, or so we're told.
He therefore had a special love of gold.

A worthy *woman* from beside *Bath* city
Was with us, somewhat deaf, which was a pity.
In making cloth she showed so great a bent
She bettered those of Ypres and of Ghent.
In all the parish not a dame dared stir
Towards the altar steps in front of her,
And if indeed they did, so wrath was she
As to be quite put out of charity.
Her kerchiefs were of finely woven ground;
I dared have sworn they weighed a good ten pound,
The ones she wore on Sunday, on her head.
Her hose were of the finest scarlet red
And gartered tight; her shoes were soft and new.
Bold was her face, handsome, and red in hue.
A worthy woman all her life, what's more
She'd had five husbands, all at the church door,
Apart from other company in youth;
No need just now to speak of that, forsooth.
And she had thrice been to Jerusalem,
Seen many strange rivers and passed over them;
She'd been to Rome and also to Boulogne,
St. James of Compostella and Cologne,
And she was skilled in wandering by the way.
She had gap-teeth, set widely, truth to say.
Easily on an ambling horse she sat
Well wimpled up, and on her head a hat
As broad as is a buckler or a shield;
She had a flowing mantle that concealed
Large hips, her heels spurred sharply under that.
In company she liked to laugh and chat
And knew the remedies for love's mischances,
An art in which she knew the oldest dances.

A holy-minded man of good renown
There was, and poor, the *Parson* to a town,
Yet he was rich in holy thought and work.

452 pestilences: plagues.

455 Bath: a city in southwestern England.

458 Ypres (ē′prə) **. . . Ghent** (gĕnt): Flemish cities famous in the Middle Ages for manufacturing fine wool fabrics.

461 wrath (răth): angry.

463 ground: a textured fabric.

466 hose: stockings.

470 all at the church door: In medieval times, a marriage was performed outside or just within the doors of a church; afterwards, the marriage party went inside for mass. Why might the narrator feel it necessary to mention that all five weddings were church weddings?

472 forsooth: in truth; indeed.

473–476 Jerusalem . . . Rome . . . Boulogne (bo͞o-lōn′), **St. James of Compostella and Cologne** (kə-lōn′): popular goals of religious pilgrimages in the Middle Ages.

480 wimpled: with her hair and neck covered by a cloth headdress.

481 buckler: small round shield.

Customizing Instruction

Gifted and Talented

Satire is a literary technique in which ideas, customs, behaviors, or institutions are ridiculed for the purpose of bringing about social reform. Satire may be gently witty, mildly abrasive, or bitterly critical, and it often uses exaggeration to force readers to see something in a more critical light. Have students discuss Chaucer's attitude towards the Doctor. Ask them to explain how the depiction of the Doctor is satirical.

Possible Response: Although Chaucer says the doctor is an esteemed physician, it is clear to Chaucer—and to the reader—that the Doctor gains financially from his patients' illnesses. His motivation is profit, rather than kindliness.

Less Proficient Readers

Have students think of words to describe the Wife of Bath's character.

Possible Responses: bold, confident, brave, fearless, intelligent, straightforward, etc.

THE CANTERBURY TALES 125

Reading and Analyzing

Active Reading
ANALYZING CHARACTERIZATION

A Remind students that one way to develop characterization is by describing actions of a character. Ask them to identify actions showing that the Parson is a good priest.
Possible Response: The Parson stayed with his parish, even though he could have earned more money in the city; he showed kindness, spoke softly, and was fair in his dealings.

B Ask students how they would describe the economic status of the Parson.
Answer: He is poor.

Have them reread the Parson's passage to determine whether, based on what they know of Chaucer's tone and values, they think he approves or disapproves of the Parson's economic status.
Possible Response: Students may say he approves, since he has portrayed other impoverished characters as being virtuous, and the Parson is "rich in holy thought and work."

GUIDE FOR READING

C The figurative language means that if priests turn to evil, common people will turn even more to bad deeds.

D He could hate the sin and love the sinner.

E They might share similar ideas, values, and business practices.

He also was a learned man, a clerk,
Who truly knew Christ's gospel and would preach it
Devoutly to parishioners, and teach it.
Benign and wonderfully diligent,
And patient when adversity was sent
A (For so he proved in much adversity)
He hated cursing to extort a fee,
Nay rather he preferred beyond a doubt
Giving to poor parishioners round about
Both from church offerings and his property;
B He could in little find sufficiency.
Wide was his parish, with houses far asunder,
Yet he neglected not in rain or thunder,
In sickness or in grief, to pay a call
On the remotest, whether great or small,
Upon his feet, and in his hand a stave.
This noble example to his sheep he gave
That first he wrought, and afterwards he taught;
And it was from the Gospel he had caught
Those words, and he would add this figure too,
That if gold rust, what then will iron do?
For if a priest be foul in whom we trust
No wonder that a common man should rust;
And shame it is to see—let priests take stock—
A shitten shepherd and a snowy flock.
The true example that a priest should give
Is one of cleanness, how the sheep should live.
He did not set his benefice to hire
And leave his sheep encumbered in the mire
Or run to London to earn easy bread
By singing masses for the wealthy dead,
Or find some Brotherhood and get enrolled.
He stayed at home and watched over his fold
So that no wolf should make the sheep miscarry.
He was a shepherd and no mercenary.
Holy and virtuous he was, but then
Never contemptuous of sinful men,
Never disdainful, never too proud or fine,
But was discreet in teaching and benign.
His business was to show a fair behavior
And draw men thus to Heaven and their Savior,
Unless indeed a man were obstinate;

490 clerk: scholar.

500 sufficiency: enough to get by on.

501 asunder: apart.

505 stave: staff.

507 wrought (rôt): worked.

C **509 figure:** figure of speech. What does the figure of speech in line 510 mean?

517 set his benefice (bĕn′ə-fĭs) **to hire:** pay someone to perform his parish duties for him.

WORDS TO KNOW **diligent** (dĭl′ə-jənt) *adj.* painstaking; hard-working

126

Teaching Options

Multicultural Link: Pilgrimages

Religious pilgrimages were a widespread phenomenon among European Christians during the Middle Ages. Today, journeys are made by the devout to such sites as Jerusalem, Rome, and the shrine at Lourdes, France. Perhaps the most widely followed pilgrimage today is that of Moslems to Mecca, the city in Saudi Arabia where Mohammed received the Koran from Allah. The Koran decrees that a trip to Mecca is one of the five Pillars of Faith for Moslems. This pilgrimage is a once-in-a-lifetime journey that a believer may make at any time in his or her life. The Arabic word for the pilgrimage is *hajj,* and a person who has made the pilgrimage is thereafter addressed by the honorific *hajji.* Invite students to tell about pilgrimages that they know of from their own backgrounds.

And such, whether of high or low estate,
He put to sharp rebuke, to say the least.
I think there never was a better priest.
He sought no pomp or glory in his dealings,
No scrupulosity had spiced his feelings.
Christ and His Twelve Apostles and their lore
He taught, but followed it himself before.

There was a *Plowman* with him there, his brother;
Many a load of dung one time or other
He must have carted through the morning dew.
He was an honest worker, good and true,
Living in peace and perfect charity,
And, as the gospel bade him, so did he,
1 Loving God best with all his heart and mind
And then his neighbor as himself, repined
At no misfortune, slacked for no content,
For steadily about his work he went
To thrash his corn, to dig or to manure
Or make a ditch; and he would help the poor
For love of Christ and never take a penny
If he could help it, and, as prompt as any,
He paid his tithes in full when they were due
On what he owned, and on his earnings too.
He wore a tabard smock and rode a mare.

There was a *Reeve,* also a *Miller,* there,
A College *Manciple* from the Inns of Court,
A papal *Pardoner* and, in close consort,
A Church-Court *Summoner,* riding at a trot,
And finally myself—that was the lot.

The *Miller* was a chap of sixteen stone,
A great stout fellow big in brawn and bone.
He did well out of them, for he could go
And win the ram at any wrestling show.
Broad, knotty and short-shouldered, he would boast
He could heave any door off hinge and post,
Or take a run and break it with his head.
His beard, like any sow or fox, was red

536 scrupulosity (skrōō'pyə-lŏs'ĭ-tē): excessive concern with fine points of behavior. D How would a lack of scrupulosity add to the Parson's effectiveness?

553 tithes (tīthz): payments to the church, traditionally one-tenth of one's annual income.

555 tabard smock: a short loose jacket made of a heavy material.

556 Reeve: an estate manager.

557 Manciple: a servant in charge of purchasing food; **Inns of Court:** London institutions for training law students.

558–559 Pardoner: a church official authorized to sell people pardons for their sins; **Summoner:** a layman with the job of summoning sinners to church courts. E Why might the Pardoner and the Summoner be riding together as friends?

561 stone: a unit of weight equal to 14 pounds.

WORDS TO KNOW
repine (rĭ-pīn') *v.* to complain; fret

Customizing Instruction

Multiple Learning Styles

Interpersonal Learners

Students may wish to dramatize lines 486–538 (the Parson) and 539–555 (the Plowman). Ask students to work together in cooperative groups to discuss the following questions:

- What praiseworthy qualities do the Parson and the Plowman share?
  Possible Response: They are spiritual, nonmaterialistic, generous, and giving.
- What other character have you read about in the "Prologue" who also shares these qualities?
  Answer: the Cleric.

Students Acquiring English

1 Help students point out that *bade* (line 544) is the past tense of *bid,* meaning "to command."

Gifted and Talented

Ask students to write a paper contrasting the characters of the Parson and the Plowman. Encourage students to build background by researching educational backgrounds and skills required for people in medieval times with these professions.

And broad as well, as though it were a spade;
And, at its very tip, his nose displayed
A wart on which there stood a tuft of hair
Red as the bristles in an old sow's ear.
His nostrils were as black as they were wide.
He had a sword and buckler at his side,
His mighty mouth was like a furnace door.
A wrangler and buffoon, he had a store
Of tavern stories, filthy in the main.
His was a master-hand at stealing grain.
He felt it with his thumb and thus he knew
Its quality and took three times his due—
A thumb of gold, by God, to gauge an oat!
He wore a hood of blue and a white coat.
He liked to play his bagpipes up and down
And that was how he brought us out of town.

The *Manciple* came from the Inner Temple;
All caterers might follow his example
In buying victuals; he was never rash
Whether he bought on credit or paid cash.
He used to watch the market most precisely
And got in first, and so he did quite nicely.
Now isn't it a marvel of God's grace
That an illiterate fellow can outpace
The wisdom of a heap of learned men?
His masters—he had more than thirty then— **A** **1**
All versed in the abstrusest legal knowledge,
Could have produced a dozen from their College
Fit to be stewards in land and rents and game
To any Peer in England you could name,
And show him how to live on what he had
Debt-free (unless of course the Peer were mad)
Or be as frugal as he might desire,
And make them fit to help about the Shire
In any legal case there was to try;
And yet this Manciple could wipe their eye.

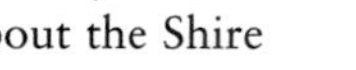

The *Reeve* was old and choleric and thin; **B**
His beard was shaven closely to the skin,
His shorn hair came abruptly to a stop

576 wrangler (răng′glər): a loud, argumentative person; **buffoon** (bə-fo͞on′): a fool.

577 in the main: for the most part.

581 thumb of gold: a reference to a proverb, "An honest miller has a golden thumb"—perhaps meaning that there is no such thing as an honest miller.

585 Inner Temple: one of the Inns of Court.

594 his masters: the lawyers that the Manciple feeds.

595 abstrusest: most scholarly and difficult to understand.

597–598 stewards . . . Peer: estate managers for any nobleman.

604 wipe their eye: outdo them.

605 choleric (kŏl′ə-rĭk): having a temperament in which yellow bile predominates (see the note at line 343), and therefore prone to outbursts of anger.

WORDS TO KNOW **frugal** (fro͞o′gəl) *adj.* careful with money; thrifty

Reading and Analyzing

Active Reading

ANALYZING CHARACTERIZATION

A Ask students to describe how the Manciple has become so successful.

Possible Response: The Manciple is a steward for a law school in London, and he is responsible for purchasing the food. Although not as highly educated as the attorneys, he is so astute in purchasing that he has been able to set aside a nice sum of money for himself.

B Ask students to summarize lines 605–610.

Possible Response: The Reeve is a skinny old man.

GUIDE FOR READING

C His master trusts the Reeve; if he were unscrupulous, he might cheat his master.

Literary Analysis: IRONY

D Explain that the duty of a Reeve in the Middle Ages was to oversee the holdings of the manor and to charge workers fines if he found anything wrong. Ask students to review lines 621–630 and discuss the irony Chaucer intends.

Possible Response: While the Reeve treats the poor people who work for him harshly and demands every penny they owe him, he lavishly entertains and provides gifts for his wealthy lord.

Teaching Options

Assessment Informal Assessment

POINTING OUT PASSAGES You can continue an informal assessment of students' understanding of the "Prologue" by asking them to point out passages that contain examples of irony and to paraphrase specific passages.

The Reeve

Above his ears, and he was docked on top
Just like a priest in front; his legs were lean,
Like sticks they were, no calf was to be seen.
He kept his bins and garners very trim;
No auditor could gain a point on him.
And he could judge by watching drought and rain
The yield he might expect from seed and grain.
His master's sheep, his animals and hens,
Pigs, horses, dairies, stores and cattle-pens
Were wholly trusted to his government.
He had been under contract to present
The accounts, right from his master's earliest years.
No one had ever caught him in arrears.
No bailiff, serf or herdsman dared to kick,
He knew their dodges, knew their every trick;
Feared like the plague he was, by those beneath.
He had a lovely dwelling on a heath,
Shadowed in green by trees above the sward.
A better hand at bargains than his lord,
He had grown rich and had a store of treasure
Well tucked away, yet out it came to pleasure
His lord with subtle loans or gifts of goods,
To earn his thanks and even coats and hoods.
When young he'd learnt a useful trade and still
He was a carpenter of first-rate skill.
The stallion-cob he rode at a slow trot
Was dapple-grey and bore the name of Scot.
He wore an overcoat of bluish shade
And rather long; he had a rusty blade
Slung at his side. He came, as I heard tell,
From Norfolk, near a place called Baldeswell.
His coat was tucked under his belt and splayed.
He rode the hindmost of our cavalcade.

608 docked: clipped short.

611 garners: buildings for storing grain.

617 government: authority. What opinion of the Reeve does his employer seem to hold? How might the Reeve take advantage of his position?

620 in arrears: with unpaid debts.

621 bailiff: farm manager; **serf:** farm laborer.

625 sward: grassy plot.

633 stallion-cob: a thickset, short-legged male horse.

638 Norfolk (nôr′fək): a county in eastern England.

Customizing Instruction

Multiple Learning Styles

1 Auditory Learners Have students clap the rhythm of the description of the Manciple as they read it aloud.

Less Proficient Readers

2 Ask students to reread lines 635–639 and then to paraphrase the physical description of the Reeve.

Workplace Link: Demonstrating Leadership

Instruction Discuss the Host's leadership abilities. Elicit from students the skills and methods he uses to organize the storytelling activity. These are as follows:

1. Defines the problem or needs of the group and identifies the goal
2. Requests, rather than demands, cooperation
3. Explains his plan and the process for carrying it out
4. Clearly states the rules, penalties, and rewards
5. Takes personal responsibility for his role
6. Participates as well as directs

Application Have students imagine that they are starting a small business, such as mowing lawns, painting houses, or walking dogs. To get started, they need partners. Ask them to list specific steps that they, as leaders of this enterprise, might take to recruit partners and to organize the business.

THE CANTERBURY TALES 129

Reading and Analyzing

Active Reading

ANALYZING CHARACTERIZATION

(A) Ask students what Chaucer wants the reader to understand about the Summoner based on his description of the Summoner's skin conditions.

Possible Response: Chaucer wants the reader to know that the Summoner is neither an upstanding nor a likable character.

Reading Skills and Strategies:
PARAPHRASING

Ask each student to select three or four lines to paraphrase. Students may choose to read aloud a passage from the original text and then clarify the passage by paraphrasing it.

GUIDE FOR READING

(B) His learning is superficial.

(C) Sinner would have to pay for absolution.

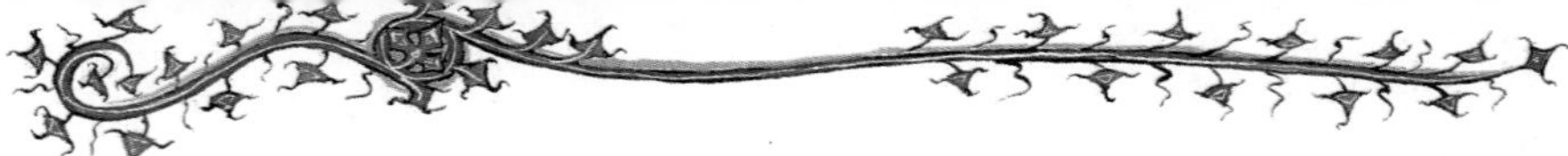

The Summoner

There was a *Summoner* with us at that Inn,
His face on fire, like a cherubin,
For he had carbuncles. His eyes were narrow,
He was as hot and lecherous as a sparrow.
Black scabby brows he had, and a thin beard.
Children were afraid when he appeared.
No quicksilver, lead ointment, tartar creams,
No brimstone, no boracic, so it seems,
Could make a salve that had the power to bite,
Clean up or cure his whelks of knobby white
Or purge the pimples sitting on his cheeks.
Garlic he loved, and onions too, and leeks,
And drinking strong red wine till all was hazy.
Then he would shout and jabber as if crazy,
And wouldn't speak a word except in Latin
When he was drunk, such tags as he was pat in;
He only had a few, say two or three,
That he had mugged up out of some decree;
No wonder, for he heard them every day.
And, as you know, a man can teach a jay
To call out "Walter" better than the Pope.
But had you tried to test his wits and grope
For more, you'd have found nothing in the bag.
Then "*Questio quid juris*" was his tag.
He was a noble varlet and a kind one,
You'd meet none better if you went to find one.
Why, he'd allow—just for a quart of wine—
Any good lad to keep a concubine

642 cherubin (chĕr′ə-bĭn′): a type of angel—in the Middle Ages often depicted with a fiery red face.

643 carbuncles (kär′bŭng′kəlz): big pimples, considered a sign of drunkenness and lechery in the Middle Ages.

647–648 quicksilver . . . boracic (bə-răs′ĭk): substances used as skin medicines in medieval times.

650 whelks (hwĕlks): swellings.

656 tags: brief quotations.

658 mugged up: memorized.

660 jay: a bird that can be taught to mimic human speech without understanding it. What does the narrator's statement in lines 660–661 imply about the Summoner?

664 *Questio quid juris* (kwĕs′tē-ō kwĭd yŏŏr′ĭs): Latin for "The question is, What part of the law (is applicable)?"—a statement often heard in medieval courts.

Teaching Options

Speaking and Listening

VOICING AN OPINION

Instruction Explain that scholars have found that the Cook was a real-life host of an inn called the Tabard in Southwark, and that Dartmouth (home of the Skipper) was known for its piracy. Some accounts maintain that the Pardoner may have been inspired by a real-life pardoner from a real-life hospital in England.

Prepare Invite students to discover further information about the Parson, Plowman, Reeve, Miller, Manciple, Summoner, and Pardoner by researching those categories of characters in other reference sources. Have them jot down their findings, then discuss them in small groups.

Present Finally, based on information shared in small groups, invite each student to voice an opinion about whether the characters were real-life acquaintances of the author.

BLOCK SCHEDULING This activity is particularly well-suited for longer class periods.

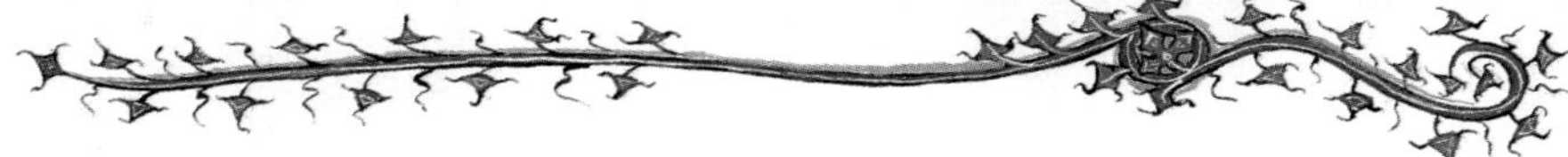

A twelvemonth and dispense him altogether!
And he had finches of his own to feather:
And if he found some rascal with a maid
He would instruct him not to be afraid
In such a case of the Archdeacon's curse
(Unless the rascal's soul were in his purse)
For in his purse the punishment should be.
"Purse is the good Archdeacon's Hell," said he.
But well I know he lied in what he said;
A curse should put a guilty man in dread,
For curses kill, as shriving brings, salvation.
We should beware of excommunication.
Thus, as he pleased, the man could bring duress
On any young fellow in the diocese.
He knew their secrets, they did what he said.
He wore a garland set upon his head
Large as the holly-bush upon a stake
Outside an ale-house, and he had a cake,
A round one, which it was his joke to <u>wield</u>
As if it were intended for a shield.

He and a gentle *Pardoner* rode together,
A bird from Charing Cross of the same feather,
Just back from visiting the Court of Rome.
He loudly sang, "*Come hither, love, come home!*"
The Summoner sang deep seconds to this song,
No trumpet ever sounded half so strong.
This Pardoner had hair as yellow as wax,
Hanging down smoothly like a hank of flax.
In driblets fell his locks behind his head
Down to his shoulders which they overspread;
Thinly they fell, like rat-tails, one by one.
He wore no hood upon his head, for fun;
The hood inside his wallet had been stowed,
He aimed at riding in the latest <u>mode</u>;
But for a little cap his head was bare
And he had bulging eye-balls, like a hare.
He'd sewed a holy relic on his cap;
His wallet lay before him on his lap,
Brimful of pardons come from Rome, all hot.
He had the same small voice a goat has got.

673 Archdeacon's curse: excommunication—an official exclusion of a person from participating in the rites of the church. (An archdeacon is a high church official.)

675 How could a sinner's punishment be "in his purse"?

681 duress (dŏŏ-rĕs'): compulsion by means of threats.

682 diocese (dī'ə-sĭs): the district under a bishop's supervision.

685–686 the holly-bush . . . ale-house: Since few people could read in the Middle Ages, many businesses identified themselves with symbols. Outside many taverns could be found wreaths of holly on stakes.

690 Charing Cross: a section of London.

696 flax: a pale grayish yellow fiber used for making linen cloth.

701 wallet: knapsack.

705 holy relic: an object revered because of its association with a holy person.

WORDS TO KNOW
wield (wēld) *v.* to handle skillfully
mode (mōd) *n.* a current fashion or style

Customizing Instruction

Less Proficient Readers

Ask students to answer these questions about the Summoner:

- In line 664, why does the Summoner ask the Latin phrase *"Questio quid juris?"*
  Possible Response: He wants to stall for time to think of a response to the testing of his wits.
- Paraphrase the meaning of line 683.
  Possible Response: The Summoner blackmailed people to do his bidding by threatening to tell what he knew about them.
- Based on lines 695–706, summarize the physical description of the Pardoner.
  Possible Responses: He has long blond hair, which falls in thin ringlets over his shoulders. He is conscious of fashion and, in keeping with the latest mode, chooses not to wear a cap.

Set a Purpose Have students read to find out more about the actions of The Pardoner.

Reading and Analyzing

Active Reading
ANALYZING CHARACTERIZATION

A Remind students that one technique of developing characterization is for the author to use the character's words to reveal something about the character's personality. Have students reread lines 714–718 and, keeping the background material in mind, determine what the Pardoner's words reveal about him.

Possible Responses: He is perhaps lying about possessing holy artifacts in order to make people think his connection with the church is strong. He is probably dishonest in his dealings with others, encouraging them to believe that the pardons he offers are of great value.

Literary Analysis TONE

B Ask students to identify Chaucer's tone in lines 735–739 and to explain their reasoning.

Possible Response: The tone is humorous, ironic, and playful, as in "at that high-class hostelry."

GUIDE FOR READING

C So that he can use strong language and have some latitude in telling his tales.

His chin no beard had harbored, nor would harbor,
Smoother than ever chin was left by barber.
I judge he was a gelding, or a mare.
As to his trade, from Berwick down to Ware
There was no pardoner of equal grace,
For in his trunk he had a pillow-case
Which he asserted was Our Lady's veil.
He said he had a gobbet of the sail
Saint Peter had the time when he made bold
To walk the waves, till Jesu Christ took hold.
He had a cross of metal set with stones
And, in a glass, a rubble of pigs' bones.
And with these relics, any time he found
Some poor up-country parson to astound,
In one short day, in money down, he drew
More than the parson in a month or two,
And by his flatteries and prevarication
Made monkeys of the priest and congregation.
But still to do him justice first and last
In church he was a noble ecclesiast.
How well he read a lesson or told a story!
But best of all he sang an Offertory,
For well he knew that when that song was sung
He'd have to preach and tune his honey-tongue
And (well he could) win silver from the crowd.
That's why he sang so merrily and loud.

Now I have told you shortly, in a clause,
The rank, the array, the number and the cause
Of our assembly in this company
In Southwark, at that high-class hostelry
Known as *The Tabard,* close beside *The Bell.*
And now the time has come for me to tell
How we behaved that evening; I'll begin
After we had alighted at the Inn,
Then I'll report our journey, stage by stage,
All the remainder of our pilgrimage.
But first I beg of you, in courtesy,
Not to condemn me as unmannerly
If I speak plainly and with no concealings
And give account of all their words and dealings,
Using their very phrases as they fell.

711 gelding (gĕl'dĭng): a castrated horse—here, a eunuch.

712 Berwick (bĕr'ĭk) . . . **Ware:** towns in the north and the south of England.

715 Our Lady's veil: the kerchief of the Virgin Mary.

716 gobbet: piece.

717–718 when he . . . took hold: a reference to an incident in which Jesus extended a helping hand to Peter as he tried to walk on water (Matthew 14:29–31).

725 prevarication (prĭ-văr'ĭ-kā'shən): lying.

728 ecclesiast (ĭ-klē'zē-ăst'): clergyman.

730 Offertory: a chant accompanying the ceremonial offering of bread and wine to God in a mass.

739 The Bell: another inn.

Teaching Options

Viewing and Representing

Pilgrims leaving Canterbury, English manuscript illumination

ART APPRECIATION

Instruction This illustration was painted during the early 16th century, more than 100 years after Chaucer's death. It is an early illustration showing some of the pilgrims leaving the cathedral and the town, having completed their pilgrimage. One of the characters is the English poet John Lydgate, in whose volume of poems this illustration appears.

Application Ask students to identify some of the characters in this illustration as those they have read about in the "Prologue." Ask students what they think the travelers in the illustration might be thinking or discussing and the elements of the illustration that inspired their conclusions.

Possible Response: The travelers may be thinking about the long journey home; they could also be looking forward to hearing new tales as they journey home.

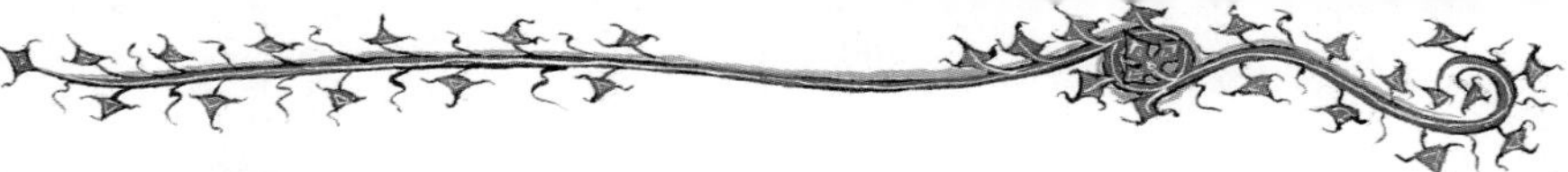

Pilgrims leaving Canterbury (about 1400). English manuscript illumination, The Granger Collection, New York.

For certainly, as you all know so well,
He who repeats a tale after a man
Is bound to say, as nearly as he can,
Each single word, if he remembers it,
However rudely spoken or unfit,
Or else the tale he tells will be untrue,
The things pretended and the phrases new.
He may not flinch although it were his brother,
He may as well say one word as another.
And Christ Himself spoke broad in Holy Writ,
Yet there is no scurrility in it,
And Plato says, for those with power to read,

745–756 The narrator apologizes in advance for using the exact words of his companions. Why might he make such an apology?

759 broad: bluntly; plainly.

760 scurrility (skə-rĭl′ĭ-tē): vulgarity; coarseness.

761 Plato (plā′tō): a famous philosopher of ancient Greece.

Customizing Instruction

Multiple Learning Styles

Visual Learners

Encourage students to develop a visual image of how the group of pilgrims might have appeared as they set off on their journey. On a sheet of paper, have students draw, paint, or make a collage showing characters who might be going ahead of or following behind those in the illustration. If you want students to work in groups, have them create a mural showing the party of pilgrims, with each character drawn in a way that reflects her or his description in the "Prologue."

Have students compare and contrast the illustration presented here with the individual characters from the Ellesmere manuscript that are pictured throughout the selection. Students should discuss the similarities and differences between the illustrations.

Possible Response: The illustrations were important because they provide the only pictorial representation of the pilgrimage and the people and places of the time period.

Have students consider how they might visually represent the Canterbury pilgrims. What medium would they use to chronicle a journey of this length and importance?

Possible Response: Students may suggest a variety of options from simple photographs to web pages to a documentary film.

Reading and Analyzing

Active Reading

ANALYZING CHARACTERIZATION

A Ask how Chaucer develops the Host's character.

Possible Response: Chaucer describes the Host's actions as well as his speech and appearance.

What kind of person is the Host?

Possible Response: He is a jovial and generous fellow with an enormous amount of self-confidence—all good qualities for one whose business requires him to interact favorably with others.

Reading Skills and Strategies: PARAPHRASING

B Ask students to paraphrase the Host's proposition to the pilgrims.

Possible Response: Since the journey can be boring, they should spend the time entertaining one another by telling stories. He would come along and serve as the judge, determining which story was most entertaining. The winner would be provided with a free meal upon their return to the inn.

GUIDE FOR READING

C He seems likeable and the proposal sounds like fun.

"The word should be as cousin to the deed."
Further I beg you to forgive it me
If I neglect the order and degree
And what is due to rank in what I've planned.
I'm short of wit as you will understand.

Our *Host* gave us great welcome; everyone
Was given a place and supper was begun.
He served the finest victuals you could think,
The wine was strong and we were glad to drink.
A very striking man our Host withal,
And fit to be a marshal in a hall.
His eyes were bright, his girth a little wide; **A**
There is no finer burgess in Cheapside.
Bold in his speech, yet wise and full of tact,
There was no manly attribute he lacked,
What's more he was a merry-hearted man.
After our meal he jokingly began
To talk of sport, and, among other things
After we'd settled up our reckonings,
He said as follows: "Truly, gentlemen,
You're very welcome and I can't think when
—Upon my word I'm telling you no lie—
I've seen a gathering here that looked so spry,
No, not this year, as in this tavern now.
I'd think you up some fun if I knew how.
And, as it happens, a thought has just occurred
To please you, costing nothing, on my word.
You're off to Canterbury—well, God speed!
Blessed St. Thomas answer to your need!
And I don't doubt, before the journey's done
You mean to while the time in tales and fun.
Indeed, there's little pleasure for your bones
Riding along and all as dumb as stones.
So let me then propose for your enjoyment,
Just as I said, a suitable employment.
And if my notion suits and you agree **B**
And promise to submit yourselves to me
Playing your parts exactly as I say
Tomorrow as you ride along the way,
Then by my father's soul (and he is dead)
If you don't like it you can have my head!
Hold up your hands, and not another word."

767 Host: the innkeeper of the Tabard.

772 marshal in a hall: an official in charge of arranging a nobleman's banquet.

774 Cheapside: the main business district of London in Chaucer's day.

780 settled up our reckonings: paid our bills.

790 St. Thomas: St. Thomas à Becket, to whose shrine the pilgrims are traveling.

794 dumb: silent.

Teaching Options

Mini Lesson

Vocabulary Strategy

HOMONYMS AND HOMOGRAPHS

Instruction Homonyms are two or more words with the same pronunciation and often the same spelling, but with different meanings and derivations.

Examples:

die: to cease living

die: a device used for cutting, forming, and stamping material

Homographs are two or more words that are spelled the same but have different meanings and are pronounced differently.

bow: front of the boat

bow: hair accessory

Advise students that they can use context to determine appropriate meanings of homonyms and homographs.

Practice Have a volunteer locate the word *harbor* (line 709) in a dictionary. Discuss how the reader knows which definition is the correct one in this context. *(The word is used as a verb, not as a noun. Of the definitions offered for the verb form, the one that makes sense is "to be the home of.")*

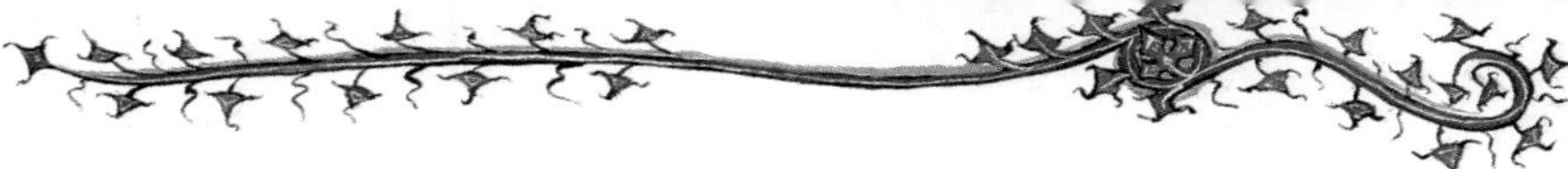

Well, our opinion was not long deferred,
It seemed not worth a serious debate;
We all agreed to it at any rate
And bade him issue what commands he would.
"My lords," he said, "now listen for your good,
And please don't treat my notion with disdain.
This is the point. I'll make it short and plain.
Each one of you shall help to make things slip
By telling two stories on the outward trip
To Canterbury, that's what I intend,
And, on the homeward way to journey's end
Another two, tales from the days of old;
And then the man whose story is best told,
That is to say who gives the fullest measure
Of good morality and general pleasure,
He shall be given a supper, paid by all,
Here in this tavern, in this very hall,
When we come back again from Canterbury.
And in the hope to keep you bright and merry
I'll go along with you myself and ride
All at my own expense and serve as guide.
I'll be the judge, and those who won't obey
Shall pay for what we spend upon the way.
Now if you all agree to what you've heard
Tell me at once without another word,
And I will make arrangements early for it."

Of course we all agreed, in fact we swore it
Delightedly, and made entreaty too
That he should act as he proposed to do,
Become our Governor in short, and be
Judge of our tales and general referee,
And set the supper at a certain price.
We promised to be ruled by his advice
Come high, come low; unanimously thus
We set him up in judgement over us.
More wine was fetched, the business being done;
We drank it off and up went everyone
To bed without a moment of delay.

807 bade him: asked him to. C Why do you think the pilgrims are so quick to agree to the innkeeper's proposal?

831 made entreaty: begged.

WORDS TO KNOW
defer (dĭ-fûr') *v.* to postpone
disdain (dĭs-dān') *n.* a show of contempt; scorn

135

Customizing Instruction

Multiple Learning Styles

Interpersonal Learners

1 Have students reread lines 804–841, in which the host proposes that each Pilgrim tell two stories on the road to Canterbury. Ask students to work in cooperative groups to role-play the scene, using their own words, as they imagine the situation might occur if it happened today.

Less Proficient Readers

2 Lead students to understand the irony in lines 819–820. Explain that the Host suggests a plan wherein the Pilgrims will be paying for a culminating meal, which will bring profit to the Host and his inn.

Have students locate other examples of homonyms or homographs on this page and, using context, determine which meaning of each word is applicable. Encourage them to use this process throughout their reading.

Use **Vocabulary Transparencies and Copymasters,** p. 22.

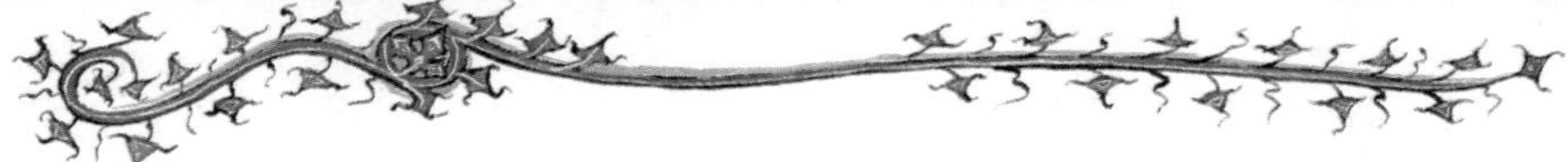

Reading and Analyzing

Literary Analysis: SIMILE

Have students identify the simile in this passage.

Answer: "roused us like a cock," line 843.

Then ask them how this simile is extended in the next line.

Possible Response: The Host is a rooster and the pilgrims are his flock of hens.

Encourage students to look back over the "Prologue" and find other similes.

Early next morning at the spring of day
Up rose our Host and roused us like a cock,
Gathering us together in a flock,
And off we rode at slightly faster pace
Than walking to St. Thomas' watering-place;
And there our Host drew up, began to ease
His horse, and said, "Now, listen if you please,
My lords! Remember what you promised me.
If evensong and matins will agree
Let's see who shall be first to tell a tale.
And as I hope to drink good wine and ale
I'll be your judge. The rebel who disobeys,
However much the journey costs, he pays.
Now draw for cut and then we can depart;
The man who draws the shortest cut shall start."

843 cock: rooster (whose cry rouses people from sleep).

846 St. Thomas' watering-place: a brook about two miles from London.

850 if evensong and matins (măt'nz) **will agree:** if what you said last night is what you will do this morning. (Evensong and matins are evening and morning prayer services.)

855 draw for cut: draw lots.

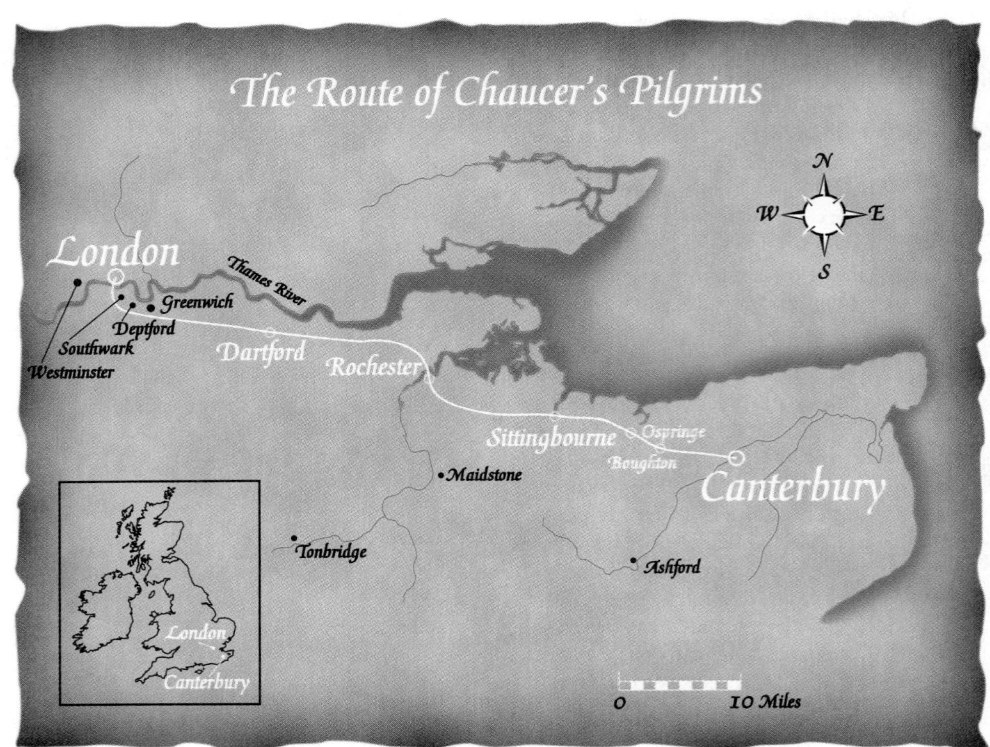

Teaching Options

 Assessment **Informal Assessment**

ALTERNATIVE ENDING You can informally assess students' understanding of the selection by having them brainstorm and then write alternative endings to the "Prologue." For example, students might suggest an ending in which some of the characters object to the Host's suggestions that he lead them to Canterbury. Students' writing could take the form of testimony by one or more of the characters stating why they think the Host's offer should be refused. Testimonies should reflect character's personalities in the "Prologue."

RUBRIC

3 **Full Accomplishment** Student writing reflects full understanding of character of the Host, as well as full understanding of other characters selected for writing.

2 **Substantial Accomplishment** Student writing shows general understanding of the character of Host and other characters selected for writing.

1 **Little or Partial Accomplishment** Student writing displays little understanding of the character of Host or of other characters selected for writing.

Connect to the Literature

1. **What Do You Think?** Would you like traveling with this group of people? Why or why not?

Comprehension Check
- In what month is the group making its pilgrimage?
- With what high-ranking person does the narrator open his descriptions?
- Who will judge the storytelling contest, and what will the prize be?

Think Critically

2. Consider the opening details about the season. Why would spring make people "long to go on pilgrimages"?
3. **ACTIVE READING** **ANALYZING CHARACTERIZATION** As you read, study the cluster diagrams you created in your **READER'S NOTEBOOK.** According to the information you gathered, which of the pilgrims does the narrator admire most? Which does he admire least?
4. How would you describe the **narrator**'s values?

THINK ABOUT
- his varied view of medieval life
- the characters he admires and those he criticizes
- his descriptions of himself

5. What impression does the narrator give of the church in his day? Cite details from his portrayals of religious figures to support your answer.
6. Why do you think the Host proposes the storytelling contest?

Extend Interpretations

7. **Critic's Corner** In 1700, John Dryden made a famous observation about Chaucer's characterization: "All his pilgrims are severally [individually] distinguished from each other; and not only in their inclinations, but in their very physiognomies [faces] and persons." Do you agree that Chaucer was able to create a number of distinctive characters? Explain.
8. **Connect to Life** Think of modern professions for some of the characters in the "Prologue." What might be the modern equivalent of the Knight? the Squire? the Pardoner? Explain your choices.

Literary Analysis

TONE In the "Prologue," much of the humor springs from the narrator's **tone,** which is detached and **ironic.** Instead of openly criticizing the scoundrels of his age for their greed and hypocrisy, he understates his opinions about them or says the opposite of what he really thinks. His seemingly impersonal attitude forces readers to draw their own conclusions.

In lines 208–211, for example, the narrator describes the Monk:

He was a prelate fit for exhibition,
He was not pale like a tormented soul.
He liked a fat swan best, and roasted whole.
His palfrey was as brown as is a berry.

The narrator's tone reinforces the discrepancies between the Monk's life and the ideal monastic life of humility and self-sacrifice.

Paired Activity Working with a partner, identify passages that reveal the narrator's tone. Look for evidence in the form of particular words and phrases. Organize your ideas in a chart like this one.

Character	What Narrator Says	What Narrator Means
Friar	Natural gifts like his were hard to match. (line 255)	He was a greedy flatterer.

GUIDING STUDENT RESPONSE

Connect to the Literature

1. **What Do You Think?** Guidelines for student response: Based on student responses, you might make a chart on the chalkboard of reasons for and against traveling with the pilgrims.

Comprehension Check
- April
- the Knight
- the Host, or proprietor of the Tabard Inn; a free meal at the Tabard

Use Selection Quiz in **Unit One Resource Book** p. 29.

Think Critically

2. Possible Response: Spring is the season of nature's rebirth and a time when people might enjoy traveling. Easter, the holiday celebrating Christ's resurrection, might also inspire Christians to make holy pilgrimages.
3. Possible Responses: He most admires the Knight, the Oxford Cleric, the Parson, and the Plowman. He least admires the Friar, the Summoner, and the Pardoner.
4. Students may suggest that the narrator values honesty, courage, piety, charity, scholarship, good times, and storytelling.
5. Possible Response: While some members of the church are corrupt, hypocritical, and overly materialistic, others are pious, charitable, and honorable.
6. Possible Responses: to make the traveling time pass more pleasantly; to appear hospitable and encourage future business at his inn; because he enjoys storytelling and likes this particular group

Extend Interpretations

Critic's Corner Accept all reasonable responses supported by sufficient and relevant details from the "Prologue."

Connect to Life Possible Responses: the Knight, a decorated member of the military; the Squire, a lower-ranking soldier traveling with him; the Yeoman, a forest ranger; the Friar, a fundraiser for charity; the Oxford Cleric, a poor student at a university or seminary; the Sergeant at the Law, a lawyer with a government job; the Franklin, a rich property owner and politician; the Haberdasher, a clothing-store owner or tailor who also makes hats; the Weaver, owner of a small garment factory; the Skipper, a steamship captain or member of the merchant marine; the Plowman, a small farmer; the Reeve, caretaker or groundskeeper of an estate; the Manciple, a food-service administrator at a law school or similar institution; the Summoner and Pardoner, hucksters or con artists of some kind.

Literary Analysis

Paired Activity You might display student charts on a wall in the classroom.

Writing Options

1. **Character Analysis** Students' statements should make use of details from the "Prologue."
2. **Sketch of a New Pilgrim** Students' sketches should capture details of contemporary life in order to bring the modern-day person to life.

Activities & Explorations

1. **Pilgrimage Poster** Posters should include notable spots in Canterbury. They might include a map as well.
2. **Pilgrimage Predictions** Stress to students that predictions should be plausibly grounded in the text.

Inquiry & Research

Medieval Inns Paul Johnson in his book *The Offshore Islanders* (New York: Holt, p. 110) has some amusing information about English attitudes in the period toward foreigners, their inns, and how Englishman should conduct themselves in such establishments. If students are not interested in this topic, encourage them to select a topic of their own for your approval.

Vocabulary in Action

ACTIVITY A Reasons may vary but should show an understanding of the meaning of each vocabulary word.

1. Yes, bad weather could postpone a journey.
2. Yes, by definition a fashionable person would adopt a modern style, or current mode, or dress.
3. Yes, a knight generally handles a sword in battle.
4. No, the Parson is not contemptuous of his rural parish and in fact is quite solicitous of the people's needs.
5. No, many of the pilgrims were not famous, respected figures but were simply everyday English men and women.
6. No, while similar in sound to the phrase, "my lady," the word *malady* means disease.
7. No, according to the narrator, the Summoner is among the least pleasant of the travelers.

Choices & CHALLENGES

Writing Options

1. **Character Analysis** Write a short analysis of one of the characters in the "Prologue." Consider his or her appearance, personality, and motives. Support your general statements about the character with specific details from the "Prologue." You might organize your ideas in an outline like this:

Character: ________

I. General quality or motive
   A. Supporting detail
   B. Supporting detail

II. General quality or motive
   A. Supporting detail
   B. Supporting detail

Writing Handbook
See page 1369: Analysis.

2. **Sketch of a New Pilgrim** Imagine how Chaucer would describe a modern-day person. Write a character sketch of that person, identifying his or her social role or profession. Use prose instead of rhymed lines of poetry if you prefer. Place your sketch in your **Working Portfolio.**

Activities & Explorations

1. **Pilgrimage Poster** Design a poster advertising a pilgrimage to Canterbury. If you like, you can use a computer drawing program. ~ **ART**

2. **Pilgrim Predictions** With a group, make predictions about the characters introduced in the "Prologue." Which ones will get along? Which will not? Which will tell the best stories? Record your predictions to share with the class. ~ **SPEAKING AND LISTENING**

Inquiry & Research

Medieval Inns Find out more about English medieval inns by consulting books about the history of society and travel. What role did inns play in Chaucer's day? Alternatively, explore the signs used to identify the inns, many of which featured symbols rather than words. Present your findings in a written report.

Vocabulary in Action

EXERCISE A: CONTEXT CLUES On your paper, answer the following questions, giving a reason for each answer. Your reason should show an understanding of the meaning of the boldfaced word.

1. Could bad weather **defer** the pilgrims' journey?
2. Would a fashionable pilgrim dress according to the **mode?**
3. Might the Knight **wield** a sword in battle?
4. Does the Parson show **disdain** for his rural parish by treating the parishioners well?
5. Were Chaucer's pilgrims all **eminent** figures of the day?
6. Would others call the pleasant Prioress a **malady?**
7. Was the Summoner, who was feared by children, a **personable** individual?

EXERCISE B: ASSESSMENT PRACTICE On your paper, indicate whether the words in each pair are synonyms or antonyms.

1. agility—clumsiness
2. dispatch—inefficiency
3. sedately—frantically
4. frugal—thrifty
5. repine—praise
6. accrue—accumulate
7. diligent—lazy
8. courtliness—elegance

WORDS TO KNOW					
accrue	defer	dispatch	malady	repine	
agility	diligent	eminent	mode	sedately	
courtliness	disdain	frugal	personable	wield	

Building Vocabulary
Most of the Words to Know in this lesson come from Latin. For an in-depth study of word origins, see page 206.

ACTIVITY B

1. antonyms
2. antonyms
3. antonyms
4. synonyms
5. antonyms
6. synonyms
7. antonyms
8. synonyms

Preparing to Read

Build Background

John Gardner was a popular novelist as well as a medieval scholar. Among the best-known of his works of fiction is the novel *Grendel,* which tells the story of Beowulf's battle in Herot from the monster's point of view. *The Life and Times of Chaucer* is a lively nonfiction account of Chaucer and his age. The passage on these pages provides a horrifying glimpse into the administration of justice—and injustice—in London during the Middle Ages.

from

The Life and Times of CHAUCER

Nonfiction by JOHN GARDNER

IT HARDLY NEEDS SAYING THAT THE WORLD INTO WHICH GEOFFREY CHAUCER WAS BORN WAS NOT LIKE OURS. After careful thought, if we were given the choice of living then or now, we might well decide to scrap our modern world; but on first transportation to Chaucer's time, we would probably have hated it—its opinions and customs, its superstitions, its cruelty, its hobbled intellect, in some respects its downright madness. One need not talk of such blood-curdling horrors as public hangings, beheadings, burnings-at-the-stake, drawing-and-quarterings,[1] public whippings, blindings, . . . or of imprisonments in chains and darkness without hope of deliverance; or of trials by combat,[2] or of torturings . . . —all these were common,

1. **drawing-and-quarterings:** executions in which the criminals' arms and legs were tied to four horses, which were then driven in different directions.
2. **trials by combat:** procedures in which disputants (or people selected by them) would fight to the death in order to determine who was in the right.

Teaching Nonfiction

Build Background

Though mainly a novelist, John Gardner (1933–1982) was becoming a noted scholar in Old and Middle English poetry at the time of his sudden death. Critics have described his study *The Life and Times of Chaucer* (1977) as an "investigative biography," in which the American author "wears his mortarboard in a rakish tilt."

This excerpt gives a broad picture of Chaucer's day. Gardner's book later delves into specific examples of the schizophrenia of the times. For one, there is the church of the Pardoner: violence was officially abhorred, and saints were models of virtue. Yet, in reality, Jewish ghettos were burned, and the Crusades killed thousands. Then there is the idealized courtly respect for women, as found in the Wife of Bath's tale. In reality, women in Chaucer's day were supposedly "the source and symbol of all human wickedness," and wife-beating was legal.

Reading Skills and Strategies:
EXAMINING AUTHOR'S PURPOSE

An author's purpose in writing may be to inform, to influence, to express opinions, or to entertain. Although one purpose is usually the most important, a writer can be motivated by two or more.

Students read this excerpt to be informed about Chaucer's times, and that is one of Gardner's purposes in writing this book. Ask students to identify Gardner's second purpose. Have them support their responses with evidence from the text.

Possible Responses: Students may say that Gardner also expresses his opinions. Evidence is in the first paragraph, where he says that if people were transported to Chaucer's time, they would hate it.

IDENTIFYING MAIN IDEAS

Ask students which sentence they think expresses Gardner's main, or most important, idea about life in Chaucer's day. Then ask what details he uses to support his main idea.

Possible Responses: the first sentence; several statements support the idea that living in Chaucer's time was very different from living in ours

See the Skills Trace at the beginning of the unit for information on TEKS covered in this lesson.

Thinking Through the Literature

1. Responses will vary. Students might suggest some of the following adjectives: *cruel, barbaric, unfair, uncivilized.*
2. Students should take a position—Chaucer does or does not ignore the negative side of medieval life—and use elements of the "Prologue" to defend their positions. To support the idea that Chaucer does not ignore the negative side, students may pick out couplets containing these portraits of medieval life: the monk is less than pious, the friar is greedy, and the doctor makes money off people's pain and suffering in the pestilence.
3. Responses will vary. In their answers, students will **recognize and discuss connections that cross cultures** as they compare medieval society with the modern world. Students can choose an injustice that is similar to an injustice in the "Prologue" or in Gardner's selection. For example, they might consider capital punishment to be as much of an injustice in our time as it was in Chaucer's. Whatever they may choose, encourage them to consider what Chaucer might have disliked about the modern injustice.

the unavoidable experience of any man who had eyes to see or ears not deaf to the victims' shrieks; and if far less common in England than in France or, worse yet, Italy, where the family of Malatesta ("Badhead") filled a deep well with the severed heads of victims, the difference would strike a modern visitor as trifling. England's great poet of gentleness and compassion walked every day in a city where the fly-bitten, bird-scarred corpses of hanged criminals—men and women, even children—draped their shadows across the crowded public square. If the crime was political, the corpse was tarred to prevent its decaying before the achievement of the full measure of its shame. As Chaucer strolled across London Bridge, making up intricate ballades[3] in his head, counting beats on his fingers, he could see, if he looked up, the staked heads of wrongdoers hurried away by earnest Christians to their presumed eternal torment. With our modern sensibilities we would certainly object and perhaps interfere—as Chaucer never did—and for the attempt to undermine the king's peace, not to mention God's, our severed heads would go up on the stakes beside those others.

3. **ballades** (bə-lädz′): poems usually consisting of three 7-, 8-, or 10-line stanzas (with the same rhymes in each) along with an envoy, or closing stanza. Several of Chaucer's ballades have survived, and he probably composed a number of others.

Thinking Through the Literature

1. In the light of the information Gardner presents, what adjectives would you use to describe the world into which Chaucer was born?
2. **Comparing Texts** Compare and contrast the world that Chaucer presents in the "Prologue" with the world that Gardner describes. Would you say that Chaucer entirely ignores the negative side of medieval life? Cite evidence to support your evaluation.
3. What are some of the brutalities or injustices to which people in the modern world often close their eyes? What do you think Chaucer might have disliked if he had been transported forward in time to our world?

from The Pardoner's Tale

from The Canterbury Tales

Poetry by GEOFFREY CHAUCER
Translated by NEVILL COGHILL

Connect to Your Life

Roots of Evil "The love of money is the root of all evil," the Bible tells us. In a group discussion, share thoughts about the desire for money and the ways in which it influences human behavior. In what situations is the desire for money evil or harmful? When does the desire seem normal or legitimate to you?

Build Background

Begging Pardon Among the more memorable of the Canterbury pilgrims is the Pardoner, described in lines 689–734 of the "Prologue" (pages 131–132). Licensed by the church to grant indulgences (documents forgiving peoples' sins), pardoners were in theory supposed to grant them only to people who showed great charity. In practice, however, many pardoners simply sold their pardons to make money for the church or for themselves. To spur sales, unethical pardoners often threatened reluctant buyers with eternal doom. Chaucer's Pardoner encourages buyers with a story that illustrates the dangers of the love of money.

WORDS TO KNOW
Vocabulary Preview

adversary	parley
avarice	saunter
castigate	transcend
covetousness	vermin
pallor	wary

Focus Your Reading

LITERARY ANALYSIS **MORAL TALE** A **moral tale** teaches a lesson about what is right and wrong in human behavior. In a moral tale, good characters usually triumph and evil characters come to a bad end. These outcomes send a message, or **moral** (which is often stated explicitly in the tale). In "The Pardoner's Tale," the moral is the biblical observation that "the love of money is the root of all evil." The Pardoner states this moral in Latin, the language of the medieval Roman Catholic Church:

Radix malorum est cupiditas.

As you read this tale, pay close attention to the actions of the characters, as well as those of the Pardoner, the teller of the tale.

ACTIVE READING **PREDICTING** To make reasonable **predictions** about what will happen next and what will happen in the end, take the following into account:

- the characters, settings, and events presented in the story
- **foreshadowing,** or hints about what is going to happen
- your own knowledge of human behavior and experiences
- what you know of other literary works with similar characters, settings, or events

My Prediction	Lines It's Based On	Actual Outcome

READER'S NOTEBOOK As you read, jot down your predictions in a chart like this one. Continue reading to see if the events match your predictions.

OVERVIEW

Objectives

1. understand and appreciate a **moral tale** that provides insights into life during the Middle Ages **(Literary Analysis)**
2. make **predictions** to enrich understanding and appreciation of a narrative poem **(Active Reading)**

Summary

Three young men set out to find and slay Death, who has killed a townsman. On the way, they meet an extremely old and mysterious man, who points them toward Death's path, where they find eight bushels of gold. Two of the men plot against the third, and he plots against them. He secretly poisons the wine, but the other two kill him first; they then drink the poisoned wine, and die.

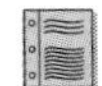
Use **Unit One Resource Book,** p. 30 for additional support.

Thematic Link

In "The Pardoner's Tale," Chaucer examines hypocrisy and deceit motivated by greed. News stories today commonly reveal how these elements of human weakness motivate the actions of misguided individuals in **everyday life,** just as they did during Chaucer's time.

5-Minute Warm-Up

Daily Language SkillBuilder

Have students **proofread** the display sentences on page 151 and write them correctly. The sentences also appear on Transparency 3 of **Grammar Transparencies and Copymasters.**

LESSON RESOURCES

UNIT ONE RESOURCE BOOK, pp. 30–34

ASSESSMENT RESOURCES
Formal Assessment, pp. 19–20
Teacher's Guide to Assessment and Portfolio Use
Test Generator

SKILLS TRANSPARENCIES AND COPYMASTERS
Literary Analysis
- The Moral Tale, Ballad, Fable, and Folk Tale, T23 (for Literary Analysis, p. 141)

Reading and Critical Thinking
- Predicting Outcomes, T2 (for Active Reading, p. 141)

Grammar
- Indefinite Pronouns, T40 (for Mini Lesson, pp. 148–149)
- Indefinite Pronouns as Antecedents, C146 (for Mini Lesson, pp. 148–149)

Vocabulary
- Word Origins, C24 (for Mini Lesson, p. 144)

Writing
- Achieving Unity, T7 (for Writing Option 3, p. 153)

INTEGRATED TECHNOLOGY
Audio Library
Video: Literature in Performance
- "The Pardoner's Tale," a film adaptation. See **Video Resource Book,** pp. 9–14.

Net Activities
Visit our website:
www.mcdougallittell.com

Mini Lesson **Preteaching Vocabulary**

If you would like to preteach the WORDS TO KNOW for this selection, use the Mini Lesson on p. 142.

Editor's Note This selection contains material or language that may be considered objectionable.

TEACHING THE LITERATURE

Reading and Analyzing

GUIDE FOR READING

A The Pardoner seems contemptuous toward those to whom he preaches.

Literary Analysis MORAL TALE

B Call students' attention to lines 56–57. Point out that "The Pardoner's Tale" is a moral tale. Explain that in the Middle Ages, moral tales were used to dramatize moral conflicts through allegory. Many of the characters in these tales were allegorical figures, such as Vice, Mercy, Death, and Good Deeds. Over time, these dramatic tales (and the corresponding morality plays) became increasingly elaborate and popular, and some were told well into the Renaissance period.

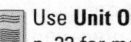

Use **Unit One Resource Book,** p. 32 for more practice.

Active Reading PREDICTING

Have students write their predictions in their Reader's Notebook. As students read, they can compare their predictions with the actual events. Were students surprised by any of the events? Discuss how surprise keeps a reader's interest high.

Use **Unit One Resource Book,** p. 31 for more practice.

Literary Analysis: FRAME STORY

"The Pardoner's Tale" is an example of one story within the frame story *The Canterbury Tales.* In "The Prologue," the narrator (Chaucer) establishes a frame within which other tales will be told.

from The Pardoner's Prologue

"My lords," he said, "in churches where I preach
I cultivate a haughty kind of speech
And ring it out as roundly as a bell;
I've got it all by heart, the tale I tell.
I have a text, it always is the same
And always has been, since I learnt the game,
Old as the hills and fresher than the grass,
Radix malorum est cupiditas.

I preach, as you have heard me say before,
And tell a hundred lying mockeries more.
I take great pains, and stretching out my neck
To east and west I crane about and peck
Just like a pigeon sitting on a barn.
My hands and tongue together spin the yarn
And all my antics are a joy to see.
The curse of avarice and cupidity
Is all my sermon, for it frees the pelf.
Out come the pence, and specially for myself,
For my exclusive purpose is to win
And not at all to castigate their sin.
Once dead what matter how their souls may fare?
They can go blackberrying, for all I care!

The Pardoner

GUIDE FOR READING

8 ***Radix malorum est cupiditas*** (rä'dĭks mä-lôr'əm ĕst' ko͞o-pĭd'ĭ-täs'): Latin for "The love of money is the root of all evil"—a quotation from the Bible (1 Timothy 6:10).

10 mockeries: false tales.

16 cupidity (kyo͞o-pĭd'ĭ-tē): excessive desire for something, especially for money.

17 pelf: riches, especially those that are acquired dishonestly.

18 pence: pennies.

19–22 What is the Pardoner's attitude toward those who listen to him preach?

WORDS TO KNOW

avarice (ăv'ə-rĭs) *n.* an excessive desire for wealth; greed
castigate (kăs'tĭ-gāt') *v.* to criticize harshly

142

Teaching Options

Mini Lesson Preteaching Vocabulary

USING A DICTIONARY TO FIND PRECISE MEANINGS

Instruction Dictionaries often supply more than one meaning for a word. Sometimes historical context can help students choose among different meanings to find the appropriate meaning of a word. For example, in 14th-century England, *avarice* was considered one of the seven deadly sins that could doom a sinner's soul eternally unless the sin was confessed to a pardoner.

Activity Have students work in **cooperative groups** to find the meaning for the Words to Know. Ask them to consider the historical context as they choose among the dictionary entries.

Use **Unit One Resource Book,** p. 33 for more practice.

A lesson on precision in language appears on p. 574 of the Pupil's Edition.

And thus I preach against the very vice
I make my living out of—avarice.
And yet however guilty of that sin
Myself, with others I have power to win
Them from it, I can bring them to repent;
But that is not my principal intent.
<u>Covetousness</u> is both the root and stuff
Of all I preach. That ought to be enough.

"Well, then I give examples thick and fast
From bygone times, old stories from the past.
A yokel mind loves stories from of old,
Being the kind it can repeat and hold.
What! Do you think, as long as I can preach
And get their silver for the things I teach,
That I will live in poverty, from choice?
That's not the counsel of my inner voice!
No! Let me preach and beg from kirk to kirk
And never do an honest job of work,
No, nor make baskets, like St. Paul, to gain
A livelihood. I do not preach in vain.
There's no apostle I would counterfeit;
I mean to have money, wool and cheese and wheat
Though it were given me by the poorest lad
Or poorest village widow, though she had
A string of starving children, all agape.
No, let me drink the liquor of the grape
And keep a jolly wench in every town!

"But listen, gentlemen; to bring things down
To a conclusion, would you like a tale?
Now as I've drunk a draft of corn-ripe ale,
By God it stands to reason I can strike
On some good story that you all will like.
For though I am a wholly vicious man
Don't think I can't tell moral tales. I can!
Here's one I often preach when out for winning. . . ."

39 kirk: church.

WORDS TO KNOW
covetousness (kŭv'ĭ-təs-nĭs) *n.* an excessive desire for wealth or possessions

Customizing Instruction

Less Proficient Readers

As you introduce students to this selection, write the following questions on the board. Have students copy them on note cards, leaving space to write answers as they read.

- Which character tells this story?
  Answer: The Pardoner.
- Who are the three main characters?
  Answer: Main characters are three men, along with an extremely old man.
- What is the setting?
  Answer: The story takes place in a tavern and under a tree.
- Describe the conflict.
  Possible Response: Three men's greed tests their friendship.

Students Acquiring English

A prologue is the introduction to a larger literary work—in this case, the story that begins on page 144. Then have students discuss fables they have read. Ask them to compare the structure of those stories with "The Pardoner's Tale" as they read.

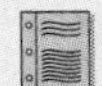
Use **Spanish Study Guide** for additional support, pp. 19–21

Gifted and Talented

"The Pardoner's Tale" is packed with irony. Have students note as they read the different levels of irony in the story. Then have them write a description of how the use of irony both strengthens the author's position with regard to the Pardoner and makes the story more enjoyable to read.

Mini Lesson: Viewing and Representing

***The Pardoner,* from the Ellesmere Manuscript**

ART APPRECIATION

Instruction Have students note details, such as clothing, props, gestures, and posture, that offer clues about the Pardoner's position in society.

Application Ask what the illustration says about the Pardoner's profession and personality. As they read the Pardoner's "Prologue," have them consider whether he would consider the illustration a good representation of himself. If the Pardoner were going to advertise his skills on a brochure, would he include this illustration? Why or why not?

Reading and Analyzing

Literary Analysis: PERSONIFICATION

A Remind students that writers sometimes attribute human qualities to an object, animal, or idea—a technique known as personification. Ask them to discuss Chaucer's personification of Death in lines 72–80.

- What is the general feeling about Death?
  Possible Response: People are afraid of him.
- What has Death done to deserve this reputation?
  Possible Response: He kills individuals in various ways and has killed a thousand people through a plague.

Active Reading PREDICTING

B Point out that foreshadowing, a device which can add suspense, is a technique an author uses to prepare a reader for an event/action that is to happen later in the story. Then direct students' attention to lines 79–81, which warns the rioters about the danger of meeting up with Death. Ask students to interpret these lines as foreshadowing and to predict the event/action that is to come.

GUIDE FOR READING

C Both their judgment and behavior, undermined by their drinking, have become erratic.

from The Pardoner's Tale

It's of three rioters I have to tell
Who, long before the morning service bell,
Were sitting in a tavern for a drink.
And as they sat, they heard the hand-bell clink
Before a coffin going to the grave;
One of them called the little tavern-knave
And said "Go and find out at once—look spry!—
Whose corpse is in that coffin passing by;
And see you get the name correctly too."
"Sir," said the boy, "no need, I promise you;
Two hours before you came here I was told.
He was a friend of yours in days of old,
And suddenly, last night, the man was slain,
Upon his bench, face up, dead drunk again.
There came a privy thief, they call him Death,
Who kills us all round here, and in a breath
He speared him through the heart, he never stirred.
And then Death went his way without a word.
A He's killed a thousand in the present plague,
And, sir, it doesn't do to be too vague
If you should meet him; you had best be wary.
Be on your guard with such an adversary,
Be primed to meet him everywhere you go, **B**
That's what my mother said. It's all I know."

58 rioters: rowdy people; revelers.

61–62 hand-bell . . . grave: In Chaucer's time, a bell was carried beside the coffin in a funeral procession.

63 tavern-knave (nāv): a serving boy in an inn.

72 privy (prĭv′ē): hidden; secretive.

72–81 Death is personified as a thief in the night, who slays his victims and then flees. Bubonic plague killed at least a quarter of the population of Europe in the mid-14th century.

WORDS TO KNOW
wary (wâr′ē) *adj.* cautious; on one's guard
adversary (ăd′vər-sĕr′ē) *n.* an enemy; opponent

144

Teaching Options

Vocabulary Strategy

RESEARCHING WORD ORIGINS

Instruction Explain that early versions of the Bible were translated from Hebrew into Latin. Ask students to read the English translation of the Latin verse, *Radix malorum est cupiditas,* in side note 8: "The love of money is the root of all evil."

Practice Point out the similarities between *cupidity* (line 16) and *cupiditas* (line 8). Have students read side note 16 for the meaning of cupidity. Explain that the English word *cupidity* is derived from the Latin word *cupiditas.*

Have students research in a dictionary the Latin origins of the following words: *avarice, adversary, pallor, vermin, transcend (avaritia, adversus, pallere, vermin-vermen, transcendere).* Ask them to take notes about the Latin root words to help them determine the meanings of related English words.

 Use **Grammar Transparencies and Copymasters,** p. 23.

A lesson on researching word origins appears on p. 206 of the Pupil's Edition.

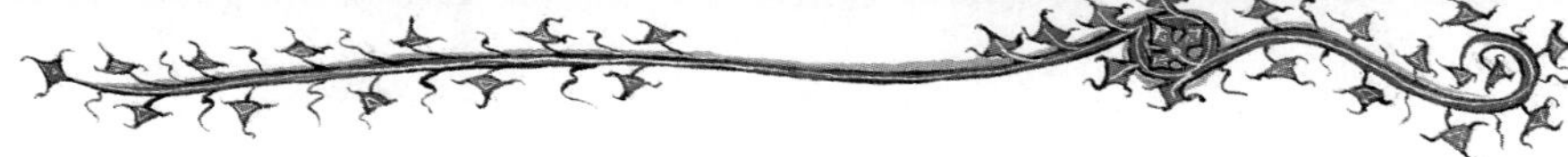

The publican joined in with, "By St. Mary,
What the child says is right; you'd best be wary,
This very year he killed, in a large village
A mile away, man, woman, serf at tillage,
Page in the household, children—all there were.
Yes, I imagine that he lives round there.
It's well to be prepared in these alarms,
He might do you dishonor." "Huh, God's arms!"
The rioter said, "Is he so fierce to meet?
I'll search for him, by Jesus, street by street.
God's blessed bones! I'll register a vow!
Here, chaps! The three of us together now,
Hold up your hands, like me, and we'll be brothers
In this affair, and each defend the others,
And we will kill this traitor Death, I say!
Away with him as he has made away
With all our friends. God's dignity! Tonight!"

They made their bargain, swore with appetite,
These three, to live and die for one another
As brother-born might swear to his born brother.
And up they started in their drunken rage
And made towards this village which the page
And publican had spoken of before.
Many and grisly were the oaths they swore,
Tearing Christ's blessed body to a shred;
"If we can only catch him, Death is dead!"

When they had gone not fully half a mile,
Just as they were about to cross a stile,
They came upon a very poor old man
Who humbly greeted them and thus began,
"God look to you, my lords, and give you quiet!"
To which the proudest of these men of riot
Gave back the answer, "What, old fool? Give place!
Why are you all wrapped up except your face?
Why live so long? Isn't it time to die?"

The old, old fellow looked him in the eye
And said, "Because I never yet have found,
Though I have walked to India, searching round

82 publican: innkeeper; tavern owner.

86 page: boy servant.

C **99–107** How might the rioters' drinking be affecting their judgment and behavior?

109 stile: a stairway used to climb over a fence or wall.

Customizing Instruction

Less Proficient Readers

Make sure students understand that the three rioters are acting fearlessly probably because they are drunk. Ask the following questions.

- What are the rioters doing together in the beginning?
  Possible Response: Sitting in a tavern drinking.
- Why do they tell the tavern-knave to go at once to inquire?
  Possible Response: They want to know who has died.
- What does the tavern-knave tell them about Death?
  Possible Response: Death is killing people, and they should stay clear of him.

Students Acquiring English

1 Ask students to reread lines 94–95. Explain that gestures can enhance language, and they are often similar across languages. Ask students to demonstrate gestures they have used to indicate alliance or friendship; then have them compare their gestures to the hand gesture described in the story.

Reading and Analyzing

Literary Analysis: IRONY

A Remind students that irony is a contrast between expectation and reality. Dramatic irony occurs when the reader understands meanings that one or more characters do not. Verbal irony occurs when what is said is not what is meant. Have students identify the dramatic irony in line 146.

Possible Response: The reader suspects, but the rioter does not, that the extremely old man is warning of impending Death.

GUIDE FOR READING

B He accuses the old man of killing the younger folk.

C No—the opposite is likely to occur.

Reading Skills and Strategies: PARAPHRASING

Remind students that **paraphrasing** can help them better comprehend what they have read. Ask them to select several lines from pages 146–147, and to restate them in their own words. They should include both the main idea and supporting details of the passage.

Literary Analysis: PERSONIFICATION

Have students identify and then discuss the effect of two examples of personification (excluding Death) on pages 146 and 147.

Possible Response: Mother, the earth; Fortune, fate.

Village and city on my pilgrimage,
One who would change his youth to have my age.
And so my age is mine and must be still
Upon me, for such time as God may will.

"Not even Death, alas, will take my life;
So, like a wretched prisoner at strife
Within himself, I walk alone and wait
About the earth, which is my mother's gate,
Knock-knocking with my staff from night to noon
And crying, 'Mother, open to me soon!
Look at me, mother, won't you let me in?
See how I wither, flesh and blood and skin!
Alas! When will these bones be laid to rest?
Mother, I would exchange—for that were best—
The wardrobe in my chamber, standing there
So long, for yours! Aye, for a shirt of hair
To wrap me in!' She has refused her grace,
Whence comes the pallor of my withered face.

"But it dishonored you when you began
To speak so roughly, sir, to an old man,
Unless he had injured you in word or deed.
It says in holy writ, as you may read,
'Thou shalt rise up before the hoary head
And honor it.' And therefore be it said
'Do no more harm to an old man than you,
Being now young, would have another do
When you are old'—if you should live till then.
And so may God be with you, gentlemen,
For I must go whither I have to go."

"By God," the gambler said, "you shan't do so,
You don't get off so easy, by St. John!
I heard you mention, just a moment gone,
A certain traitor Death who singles out
And kills the fine young fellows hereabout.
And you're his spy, by God! You wait a bit.
Say where he is or you shall pay for it,
By God and by the Holy Sacrament!

129 The old man addresses the earth as his mother (compare the familiar expressions "Mother Earth" and "Mother Nature").

135 shirt of hair: a rough shirt made of animal hair, worn to punish oneself for one's sins.

142 hoary: gray or white with age.

WORDS TO KNOW **pallor** (păl′ər) *n.* a lack of color; extreme paleness

146

Teaching Options

BLOCK SCHEDULING: MANAGING TIME

If your schedule requires that you cover the lesson objectives in a shorter time, use . . .

- Preparing to Read, p. 141
- Thinking Through the Literature, p. 152
- Vocabulary in Action, p. 153

If you want to take advantage of longer class time, use . . .

- TE Teaching Options: Vocabulary, pp. 142, 144; Viewing and Representing, pp. 143, 150; Standardized Test Practice, p. 147; Grammar, p. 148; Informal Assessment, p. 151
- Choices & Challenges, p. 153

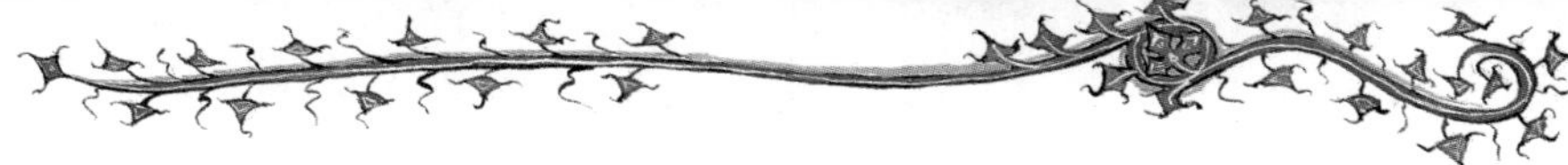

I say you've joined together by consent
To kill us younger folk, you thieving swine!"

"Well, sirs," he said, "if it be your design
To find out Death, turn up this crooked way
Towards that grove, I left him there today
Under a tree, and there you'll find him waiting.
He isn't one to hide for all your prating.
You see that oak? He won't be far to find.
And God protect you that redeemed mankind,
Aye, and amend you!" Thus that ancient man.

At once the three young rioters began
To run, and reached the tree, and there they found
A pile of golden florins on the ground,
2 New-coined, eight bushels of them as they thought.
No longer was it Death those fellows sought,
For they were all so thrilled to see the sight,
The florins were so beautiful and bright,
That down they sat beside the precious pile.
The wickedest spoke first after a while.
"Brothers," he said, "you listen to what I say.
I'm pretty sharp although I joke away.
It's clear that Fortune has bestowed this treasure
To let us live in jollity and pleasure.
Light come, light go! We'll spend it as we ought.
God's precious dignity! Who would have thought
This morning was to be our lucky day?

"If one could only get the gold away,
Back to my house, or else to yours, perhaps—
For as you know, the gold is ours, chaps—
We'd all be at the top of fortune, hey?
But certainly it can't be done by day.
People would call us robbers—a strong gang,
So our own property would make us hang.
No, we must bring this treasure back by night
Some prudent way, and keep it out of sight.
And so as a solution I propose
3 We draw for lots and see the way it goes;
The one who draws the longest, lucky man,
Shall run to town as quickly as he can

B **154–158** What accusations against the old man does the young man make?

169 florins: coins.

C **178** "Fortune" here means "fate." Do you think the young men will be blessed by Fortune?

The Three Living, from the *Psalter and Prayer Book of Bonne of Luxembourg, Duchess of Normandy.*

Customizing Instruction

Less Proficient Readers

1 Have students explain why the old man's face is so pale and white.

Possible Response: He is Death personified.

Multiple Learning Styles

Visual and Tactile Learners

2 Have students reread lines 167–174, visualizing the scenario. Explain that florins were coins worth 24 pence (the plural of penny). Then have students gather props to represent the tree and about eight bushels of golden and bright florins. Ask them to use the props to help them imagine or role-play the rioters' response when they see this amount of money under the tree.

Students Acquiring English

3 Be certain that second language students understand the idiom of drawing for lots (lines 193–194). Explain that a *lot* is an object used as a counter in determining a question by chance, often used to help people decide something. Point out that, in this case, whoever draws the longest lot will be asked to run to town to get food and drink.

Assessment Standardized Test Practice

CHOOSING THE BEST SUMMARY Some standardized tests require students to find the best summary of a passage. To help students practice this skill, read aloud the following:

Which of the following statements best summarizes the physical and emotional state of the old man, as he addresses the earth as his mother? (lines 129–137)

A. The old man is upset because his flesh and blood are withering.

B. The old man desperately wants Mother Earth to take his tired and worn-out body.

C. The old man would like to trade Mother Earth a shirt of punishment for his own clothing.

Guide students to understand that, although all sentences pertain to the passage, only **B** summarizes the most important information.

THE CANTERBURY TALES 147

To fetch us bread and wine—but keep things dark—
While two remain in hiding here to mark
Our heap of treasure. If there's no delay,
When night comes down we'll carry it away,
All three of us, wherever we have planned."

He gathered lots and hid them in his hand
Bidding them draw for where the luck should fall.
It fell upon the youngest of them all,
And off he ran at once towards the town.

As soon as he had gone the first sat down
And thus began a parley with the other:
"You know that you can trust me as a brother;
Now let me tell you where your profit lies;
You know our friend has gone to get supplies
And here's a lot of gold that is to be
Divided equally amongst us three.
Nevertheless, if I could shape things thus
(A) So that we shared it out—the two of us— (B)
Wouldn't you take it as a friendly act?"

"But how?" the other said. "He knows the fact
That all the gold was left with me and you;
What can we tell him? What are we to do?"

"Is it a bargain," said the first, "or no?
For I can tell you in a word or so
What's to be done to bring the thing about."
"Trust me," the other said, "you needn't doubt
My word. I won't betray you, I'll be true."

"Well," said his friend, "you see that we are two,
And two are twice as powerful as one.
Now look; when he comes back, get up in fun
To have a wrestle; then, as you attack,
I'll up and put my dagger through his back
While you and he are struggling, as in game;
Then draw your dagger too and do the same.
Then all this money will be ours to spend,

196 keep things dark: act in secret, without giving away what has happened.

(C) **225–229** What does the young man's plan suggest about human nature and the desire for money?

WORDS TO KNOW

parley (pär′lē) *n.* a discussion or conference

148

Reading and Analyzing

Active Reading PREDICTING

(A) Ask students to read line 214, "Wouldn't you take it as a friendly act?" to help them predict what might happen to the relationship of the two rioters in conversation.

Possible Response: Students should recognize that if the man will turn against one friend, he might turn against the other, as well.

Reading Skills and Strategies: QUESTIONING

(B) Refer students again to line 214. Ask them to question the speaker's motivation. Is he asking for help because the third rioter has been unfair? Does he dislike the third rioter? Why does he favor the rioter in conversation over the other one? Have students give reasons for their answers on the basis of earlier passages. Encourage them to pose additional questions they can answer by reading further.

GUIDE FOR READING

(C) The young man's plan suggests that people can be greedy and treacherous.

Reading Skills and Strategy: PARAPHRASING

(D) Ask students to paraphrase lines 236–242. Remind them to include only the most important information.

GUIDE FOR READING

(E) His evil thoughts and deeds put him in the Devil's power.

Teaching Options

Grammar

INDEFINITE PRONOUNS AS ANTECEDENTS

Instruction Some indefinite pronouns, such as *anybody, each, either, no one,* and *someone,* are singular. When a singular indefinite pronoun is an antecedent, then the possessive pronoun in the sentence is also singular.

Activity Write this sentence on the chalkboard.

Each of the rioters believed his plan would work.

Ask students to find the pronoun antecedent. (*Each*) Point out that even though the prepositional phrase has a plural noun, the pronoun *his* is singular because the antecedent *Each* is singular. *Both, few, many,* and *several* are plural indefinite pronouns. *All, some, many, most,* and *none* may be singular or plural depending on their context. Have students identify the antecedent in each of these sentences. Discuss whether the possessive pronoun is singular or plural.

Few would be rude to their elders. (*Few; plural*)
None of the rioters thought about his death. (*None; singular*)

Exercise Ask students to underline the pronoun antecedent and choose the correct form of the

Divided equally of course, dear friend.
Then we can gratify our lusts and fill
The day with dicing at our own sweet will."
Thus these two miscreants agreed to slay
The third and youngest, as you heard me say.

233 dicing: gambling with dice.

234 miscreants (mĭs'krē-ənts): evildoers; villains.

D
The youngest, as he ran towards the town,
Kept turning over, rolling up and down
Within his heart the beauty of those bright
New florins, saying, "Lord, to think I might
Have all that treasure to myself alone!
Could there be anyone beneath the throne
Of God so happy as I then should be?"

And so the Fiend, our common enemy,
Was given power to put it in his thought
That there was always poison to be bought,
And that with poison he could kill his friends.
To men in such a state the Devil sends
Thoughts of this kind, and has a full permission
To lure them on to sorrow and perdition;
For this young man was utterly content
To kill them both and never to repent.

243 Fiend: the Devil; Satan.

249 perdition: damnation; hell.

E **243–251** Why does the Devil have influence over the young man?

1
And on he ran, he had no thought to tarry,
Came to the town, found an apothecary
And said, "Sell me some poison if you will,
I have a lot of rats I want to kill
And there's a polecat too about my yard
That takes my chickens and it hits me hard;
But I'll get even, as is only right,
With vermin that destroy a man by night."

The chemist answered, "I've a preparation
Which you shall have, and by my soul's salvation
If any living creature eat or drink
A mouthful, ere he has the time to think,
Though he took less than makes a grain of wheat,
You'll see him fall down dying at your feet;
Yes, die he must, and in so short a while

WORDS TO KNOW **vermin** (vûr'mĭn) *n.* small animals that are destructive or carriers of disease

Customizing Instruction

Less Proficient Readers

1 Invite students to discuss the thoughts and actions of the younger rioter.

- Describe his thoughts as he runs toward the town.
  Possible Response: His rationalizing and deceitfulness escalate to the point at which he is fully absolved of guilt, in his own mind.
- Why does the young rioter lie to the pharmacist?
  Possible Response: He wants to get some poison to kill the other two rioters.

Gifted and Talented

Have students conduct research to compare and contrast modern-day pharmacists with 14th-century chemists. Encourage them to include information about training, responsibilities, and so forth. Then have students write a paper or create a chart illustrating their findings.

possessive pronoun to complete each sentence. In cooperative groups have students construct sentences with *all, some, many, most,* and *none* as the antecedent. The sentences should show both singular and plural forms of the possessive pronoun.

1. One of the travelers began ______ (his, their) tale. (*One*; *his*)
2. The pardoner said that many met ______ (his or her, their) end as a result of the plague. (*many*; *their*)
3. The old man was looking for somebody who would trade ______ (his or her, their) youth for old age. (*somebody*; *his* or *her*)
4. All of those gold florins tempted the rioters with ______ (its, their) promise. (*All*; *their*)
5. No one felt the least bit of loyalty to ______ (his, their) companions. (*No one*; *his*)

Use McDougal Littell's ***Language Network*** for more instruction in indefinite pronouns.

Reading and Analyzing

Literary Analysis: FORESHADOWING

A Refer students to lines 284–285. Ask them what the lines might foreshadow regarding the fate of the remaining two rioters. Ask them what clues they used as a basis for their speculations.

Possible Response: The rioters are happy now, but they are about to drink the poisoned wine, after which there will be more than one corpse to bury.

GUIDE FOR READING

B Because each planned to commit murder, they deserved to die painful deaths.

C He wants the other pilgrims to worry that they might die with their sins unforgiven, which might send them to Hell for all eternity. He wants them to pay him to forgive their sins.

You'd hardly have the time to walk a mile,
The poison is so strong, you understand."

This cursed fellow grabbed into his hand
The box of poison and away he ran
Into a neighboring street, and found a man
Who lent him three large bottles. He withdrew
And deftly poured the poison into two.
He kept the third one clean, as well he might,
For his own drink, meaning to work all night
Stacking the gold and carrying it away.
And when this rioter, this devil's clay,
Had filled his bottles up with wine, all three,
Back to rejoin his comrades sauntered he.

Why make a sermon of it? Why waste breath?
Exactly in the way they'd planned his death
They fell on him and slew him, two to one.
Then said the first of them when this was done,
A "Now for a drink. Sit down and let's be merry,
For later on there'll be the corpse to bury."
And, as it happened, reaching for a sup,
He took a bottle full of poison up
And drank; and his companion, nothing loth,
Drank from it also, and they perished both.

There is, in Avicenna's long relation
Concerning poison and its operation,
Trust me, no ghastlier section to transcend
What these two wretches suffered at their end.
Thus these two murderers received their due,
So did the treacherous young poisoner too.

O cursed sin! O blackguardly excess!
1 O treacherous homicide! O wickedness!
O gluttony that lusted on and diced!

Dearly beloved, God forgive your sin
And keep you from the vice of avarice!

The Three Dead, from the *Psalter and Prayer Book of Bonne of Luxembourg, Duchess of Normandy* (14th century), fol.322r. Grisaille, color, gilt, and brown ink on vellum (4 15/16" x 3 9/16"). French, Paris. The Metropolitan Museum of Art, New York. The Cloisters Collection

288 nothing loth: not at all unwilling.

290 Avicenna's (ăv'ĭ-sĕn'əz) **long relation:** a medical text written by an 11th-century Islamic physician; it includes descriptions of various poisons and their effects.

 **294** Why does the Pardoner say that the young men "received their due"?

296 blackguardly: worthy of a scoundrel; villainous.

299 The Pardoner is now addressing his fellow pilgrims.

WORDS TO KNOW

saunter (sôn'tər) *v.* to walk in a slow and leisurely manner; stroll
transcend (trăn-sĕnd') *v.* to go beyond; surpass

150

Teaching Options

Viewing and Representing

The Three Dead, from an illuminated manuscript

ART APPRECIATION

Instruction Explain that visual clues, such as illustrations, help readers better understand the text. In Chaucer's day, when few people could read, illustrations were especially critical for comprehension.

Application Ask students to compare and contrast "The Three Dead," above, with "The Three Living," on page 147, by responding to these prompts:

- Discuss the following elements of each drawing: body gesture, facial expression, clothing, movement, and background.
- Tell what you think the artist was saying.
- Do the illustrations enhance your understanding and enjoyment of the selection? Why or why not?

My holy pardon frees you all of this,
Provided that you make the right approaches,
That is with sterling, rings, or silver brooches.
Bow down your heads under this holy bull!
Come on, you women, offer up your wool!
I'll write your name into my ledger; so!
Into the bliss of Heaven you shall go.
For I'll absolve you by my holy power,
You that make offering, clean as at the hour
When you were born. . . . That, sirs, is how I preach.
And Jesu Christ, soul's healer, aye, the leech
Of every soul, grant pardon and relieve you
Of sin, for that is best, I won't deceive you.

One thing I should have mentioned in my tale,
Dear people. I've some relics in my bale
And pardons too, as full and fine, I hope,
As any in England, given me by the Pope.
If there be one among you that is willing
To have my absolution for a shilling
Devoutly given, come! and do not harden
Your hearts but kneel in humbleness for pardon;
Or else, receive my pardon as we go.
You can renew it every town or so
Always provided that you still renew
Each time, and in good money, what is due.
It is an honor to you to have found
A pardoner with his credentials sound
Who can absolve you as you ply the spur
In any accident that may occur.
For instance—we are all at Fortune's beck—
Your horse may throw you down and break your neck.
What a security it is to all
To have me here among you and at call
With pardon for the lowly and the great
When soul leaves body for the future state!
And I advise our Host here to begin,
The most enveloped of you all in sin.
Come forward, Host, you shall be the first to pay,
And kiss my holy relics right away.
Only a groat. Come on, unbuckle your purse!"

304 bull: an official document from the pope.

311 leech: physician.

319 shilling: a coin worth twelve pence.

C **330–331** The Pardoner reminds the other pilgrims that death may come to them at any time. Why does he emphasize this point?

340 groat: a silver coin worth four pence.

Customizing Instruction

Less Proficient Readers

1 Define the word *dice* in this context as a game of chance played with death. Point out that by using the word *diced,* the author emphasizes the carelessness by which the rioters conducted their very serious business with each other and the old man.

Gifted and Talented

2 Have students read the Pardoner's lines 307 and 308, "Into the bliss of Heaven you shall go. / For I'll absolve you by my holy power." Point out that all three rioters also make references to religion. Ask students to speculate on why the Pardoner would have the rioters mention religion periodically, even though their actions were criminal.
Possible Response: Perhaps he is mirroring, and even condoning, his own behavior.

Students Acquiring English

3 Help students understand the meaning of difficult terms, such as *absolution,* in this passage. The Pardoner consistently tries to elicit the confessions of the pilgrims by promising a remission of their sins, an absolution, in exchange for their money.

Assessment Informal Assessment

INTERPRETING THE TALE

Explain that "The Pardoner's Tale" can be interpreted on many levels. Ask students to work in small groups to discuss the story in the following ways:

- as an example of dramatic and verbal irony
- as a moral tale
- as a personality study of the Pardoner
- as a commentary on the human condition

Have each group then select one of these genres and share their interpretation with the class.

RUBRIC

3 **Full Accomplishment** Student contributes to both small group and class discussion, supporting interpretation with relevant details.

2 **Substantial Accomplishment** Student contributes to only one form of discussion, supporting interpretation with some relevant details.

1 **Little or Partial Accomplishment** Student displays little understanding of story and does not participate in discussion.

Connect to the Literature

1. **What Do You Think?**
Guidelines for student response: Students will summarize the events at the end of the tale. Good discussions should touch upon the concepts of poetic justice and irony.

Comprehension Check
- After seeing the funeral procession of an old friend, the rioters decide to find and "kill this traitor Death."
- The rioters expect to find Death sitting under the tree, but instead they find a pile of gold coins.
- The youngest rioter is killed by the other two, who want to split the money. The remaining two die when they unknowingly drink the poison the youngest rioter intended to use to kill them.

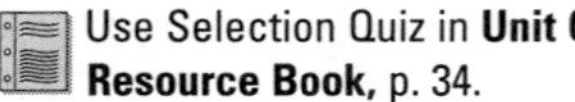
Use Selection Quiz in **Unit One Resource Book,** p. 34.

Think Critically

2. Possible Responses: What happened to the rioters was not surprising because Chaucer characterizes them as drunkards; he describes one of them as "wicked," and certainly calling them "the rioters" indicates they are not virtuous citizens; the ending was surprising because the rioters could have benefited greatly if they had acted in a reasonable manner.
3. Possible Responses: Having seen so many people submit to Death, they fear for their lives; they seek the prestige and glory of triumphing over such a formidable adversary; in their revelry, they get caught up in the thrill of engaging in such a dangerous pursuit.
4. What they do find under the tree (the money) causes them to behave in ways that lead to their own demise—death.
5. Possible Responses: Though death is usually feared and seen as frightening, the old man's lament that "Not even Death . . . will take my life" shows another side of things.
6. The Pardoner reveals in the "Prologue" that he is primarily concerned with accruing wealth. He then tells a tale warning against greed.

Connect to the Literature

1. **What Do You Think?** Discuss with a partner your reaction to the ending of this tale.

Comprehension Check
- Why are the three rioters looking for Death?
- What do they expect to find under the tree, and what do they actually find?
- What happens to the rioters?

Think Critically

2. **ACTIVE READING** **PREDICTING** Look back at the predictions you made in your **READER'S NOTEBOOK**. Were you surprised by the tale's ending? If not, explain what details led you to **predict** the ending. If you were surprised, explain what details led you to predict a different ending.

3. Why do you think the rioters set out to kill Death?

- what they learn from the boy and the innkeeper
- their view of themselves
- other factors that may influence their judgment

4. In what sense is the old man's statement that the rioters can find Death under the oak tree true?

5. Why do you think the **character** of the old man is included in the tale?

- the story of his life
- his views about Death
- his directions for finding Death

6. In the light of the Pardoner's true **motives**, as revealed in the "Prologue," why is the moral of this tale **ironic?**

Extend Interpretations

7. **What If?** If the Pardoner hadn't revealed so much information about his practices, how might the other pilgrims have responded to his tale?

8. **Connect to Life** Do you think this story could serve as an effective warning against greed to people today? Why or why not?

Literary Analysis

MORAL TALE "The Pardoner's Tale" is a **moral tale,** a story that teaches a lesson about good and evil or about what is right and wrong in human behavior. In it, the Pardoner teaches that "the love of money is the root of all evil" by showing how characters who suffer from the sin of avarice, or love of money, destroy themselves in the end.

Paired Activity Working with a partner, analyze how the story's elements work together to teach the moral. Among the elements to consider are the events of the plot, the personalities and motives of the characters, and the details of the setting. You might organize the elements in a chart like this one.

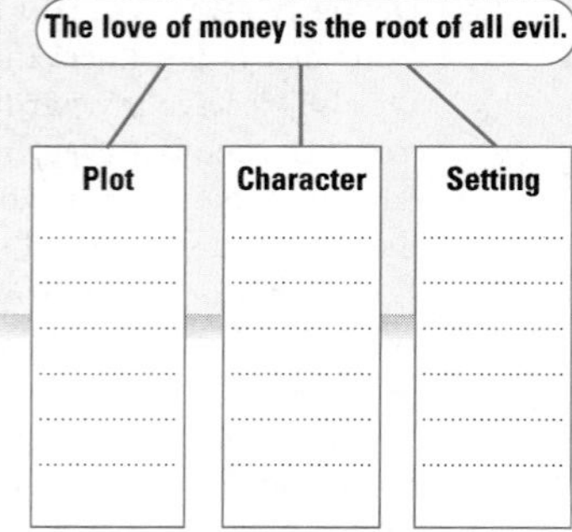

Extend Interpretations

What If? Had the Pardoner not so clearly stated his desire to sell relics and other forms of "religious insurance" to people, the other pilgrims might have taken his tale about the sin of avarice more to heart.

Connect to Life Some students may respond that greed today can still often produce disastrous results. Others may think that greed is condoned and rewarded in today's society.

Literary Analysis

Paired Activity Possible Response: Plot—the youngest rioter buys poison while he is in town, in order to kill the other men and keep the money for himself. Character—this man is so driven by his love for money that he is willing to murder his friends. Setting—the fact that the money is found on a hillside in the country, away from town, enables the youngest rioter to separate from the others and buy the poison to kill them.

Writing Options

1. Ye Olde News Write a news article about the discovery of the rioters' bodies and the events that led up to it. Include interviews with characters.

2. Personification Paragraph Write a paragraph explaining the personification of death in "The Pardoner's Tale." First explain the reasons why the Pardoner may have decided to personify death (turn death into a figure with human qualities). Then explain the effects you think this device has on readers. You might organize your ideas in a cause-and-effect diagram like this one.

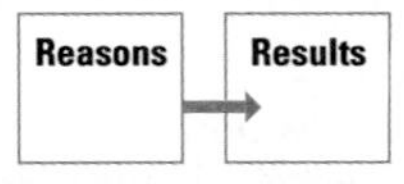

Writing Handbook
See page 1368: Cause and Effect.

3. Moral Tale Think of other proverbs or quotations about good and evil or right and wrong human behavior—for example, "Cheaters never prosper" or "What goes around, comes around." Then write a brief moral tale with that as its moral. You might state the moral at the start or the end of the tale.

Activities & Explorations

1. Oral Retelling Simplify the language and details of the tale to suit an audience of younger children. Arrange to tell the tale at a library or an elementary school. ~ **SPEAKING AND LISTENING**

2. Video Adaptation View the performance of "The Pardoner's Tale." Focus on the portrayals of the characters, particularly that of the old man. Then, in a class discussion, compare the portrayals with Chaucer's descriptions. ~ **VIEWING AND REPRESENTING**

Literature in Performance

3. Ballad Version Turn "The Pardoner's Tale" into a ballad set to music. The music can be original or borrowed from an existing song. Perform the ballad live or audiotape it. ~ **MUSIC**

Inquiry & Research

Plague Write a brief research paper on the outbreak of plague in mid-14th-century Europe. Include information about its origins and its effects on European life and culture. Be sure to document your sources.

Vocabulary in Action

EXERCISE A: CONTEXT CLUES On your paper, fill in each blank with the vocabulary word that best completes the sentence.

1. Filled with distrust, the rioters were ________ of one another.
2. Did the rioter ________, or did he walk swiftly?
3. Death brought a ________ to her once-rosy face.
4. Does the Pardoner tell the tale to ________ sinners?
5. It is hard to ________ our sinful impulses, but we should try to move beyond them.

EXERCISE B: MEANING CLUES On your paper, indicate whether each statement is true or false. Give a reason for your choice.

1. Guests at the inn most likely ordered **vermin** for dinner.
2. Someone who counts his or her money all the time may be guilty of **avarice**.
3. Giving money away is a sign of **covetousness**.
4. You should expect an **adversary** to agree with you.
5. A **parley** might lead to peace between warring factions.

WORDS TO KNOW

adversary	pallor	vermin
avarice	parley	wary
castigate	saunter	
covetousness	transcend	

Building Vocabulary
Several Words to Know in this lesson contain prefixes and suffixes. For an in-depth study of word parts, see page 1104.

Writing Options

1. **Ye Olde News** Student articles should be well organized and answer the basic questions: who, what, where, when, how, and why. Students should provide as much detail as possible in their articles to make them more lively.
2. **Personification Paragraph** Student paragraphs should deal with the issue of whether the personification of death makes it more frightening. **To make this assignment more challenging,** suggest that students write a paragraph explaining how another abstract concept, such as greed, might be personified in the story.
3. **Moral Tale** Other quotations that students might use include "Honesty is the best policy" or "Do unto others as you would have them do unto you."

Activities & Explorations

1. **Oral Retelling** Have students write a paraphrase of the events in the tale. Have them use their summaries of the story as the basis for their retelling in simpler language.
2. **Video Adaptation** You might wish to broaden this discussion to include screen adaptations of other books with which students are familiar.
3. **Ballad Version** Students can use melodies such as those drawn from traditional folk songs, or melodies from contemporary music.

Inquiry & Research

Plague If students are not interested in this topic, encourage them to choose their own, with your approval. You might suggest to students that they use the Internet to obtain information, as well as standard reference works in the library.

Vocabulary in Action

Exercise A	Exercise B
1. wary	1. False
2. saunter	2. True
3. pallor	3. False
4. castigate	4. False
5. transcend	5. True

OVERVIEW

Objectives

1. understand and appreciate a **narrative poem (Literary Analysis)**
2. analyze the author's use of a **narrator** to tell a story **(Literary Analysis)**
3. analyze the structure of a story and understand how the use of a frame story affects plot **(Active Reading)**

Summary

In the prologue, the Wife of Bath explains that she will offer a tale about the tribulations of married life. She then tells the tale of a knight who raped a young maiden and, in punishment for breaking the rules of chivalry, was given one year to find out what women most desire—or else die. He searches unsuccessfully, but finally comes upon an ugly Old Lady, who agrees to tell him the answer, providing he grant her a favor. He agrees, she tells him that women desire sovereignty over their husbands, and the queen acquits the knight.

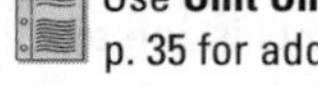

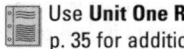

Use **Unit One Resource Book,** p. 35 for additional support.

Thematic Link

"The Wife of Bath's Tale" addresses the timeless and universal topic of love and marriage, exploring what married women and men expect in **everyday life.**

5-Minute Warm-Up

Daily Language SkillBuilder

Have students **proofread** the display sentences on page 15l and write them correctly. The sentences also appear on Transparency 3 of **Grammar Transparencies and Copymasters.**

Preteaching Vocabulary

If you would like to preteach the WORDS TO KNOW for this selection, use the Mini Lesson for p. 156.

"What is the thing that women most desire?"

The Wife of Bath's Tale
from The Canterbury Tales

Poetry by GEOFFREY CHAUCER
Translated by NEVILL COGHILL

Connect to Your Life

Love and Marriage You are probably familiar with the phrase "the battle of the sexes." This expression suggests that romantic relationships have an aspect of conflict, in which one party attempts to gain the upper hand. What are your own opinions on the subject? Would you say that a good marriage is basically an equal partnership, or do you think that one person needs to be the decision maker? Explain your opinions in a class discussion.

Build Background

Romance and Chivalry "The Wife of Bath's Tale" belongs to the so-called Marriage Group of *The Canterbury Tales,* in which different pilgrims offer stories that express their philosophies of love and marriage. Set in the days of Britain's legendary King Arthur, the story qualifies as a medieval **romance**—an adventure tale of knights and chivalry, in which the code of ideal knightly behavior (loyalty, faith, honor, and courtesy, especially to women) is stressed. In this story, however, a knight breaks the rules of chivalry and, as punishment, must undertake a quest.

WORDS TO KNOW
Vocabulary Preview

abominably	implore
bequeath	maim
concede	prowess
contemptuous	rebuke
cosset	statute
crone	temporal
dejected	tribulation
ecstasy	

Focus Your Reading

LITERARY ANALYSIS NARRATOR Whether a story is told in prose or verse, the **narrator** is the person or voice that tells the story. In *The Canterbury Tales,* the narrator of the "Prologue" introduces the characters who will serve as narrators of the tales that follow. Reread lines 455–486 of the "Prologue" (page 125), which introduce the Wife of Bath. Then try to predict the view of love and marriage that she might present in her tale.

ACTIVE READING ANALYZING STRUCTURE **Structure** is the way in which the parts of a literary work are put together. A **frame story** is a story that serves as a narrative setting or frame for one or more other stories. *The Canterbury Tales* as a whole has a frame structure, in which the story of the pilgrims serves as a frame within which the pilgrims tell their stories. The structure of "The Wife of Bath's Tale" features a main **plot** with several interruptions. For example, in the opening lines the Wife of Bath interrupts the main plot with a passage in which she criticizes friars. This particular interruption stems from the Wife's ongoing quarrel with the Friar as they travel to Canterbury.

READER'S NOTEBOOK As you read "The Wife of Bath's Tale," use a chart similar to the one shown to keep track of the interruptions to the main story.

Interruption	Reason
criticism of friars	Wife of Bath's quarrel with Friar in frame story

LESSON RESOURCES

UNIT ONE RESOURCE BOOK, pp. 35–39

ASSESSMENT RESOURCES
Formal Assessment, pp. 21–22
Teacher's Guide to Assessment and Portfolio Use
Test Generator

SKILLS TRANSPARENCIES AND COPYMASTERS
Reading and Critical Thinking
- Analyzing Text Structure, T17 (for Active Reading, p. 154)

Grammar
- Pronouns—Correct Case, T41 (for Mini Lesson, pp. 164–165)
- Pronoun Cases II, C67 (for Mini Lesson, pp. 164–165)
- Kinds of Sentences, C77 (for Mini Lesson, p. 169)

Vocabulary
- Denotation and Connotation, C25 (for Mini Lesson, p. 162)

Writing
- The Uses of Dialogue, T24 (for Writing Option 1, p. 169)
- Compare-Contrast, C34 (for Writing Option 2, p. 169)

Communications
- Impromptu Speaking: Debate, T15 (for Activities & Explorations 1, p. 169)

INTEGRATED TECHNOLOGY
Audio Library
Net Activities
Visit our website:
www.mcdougallittell.com

from The Wife of Bath's Prologue

The Pardoner started up, and thereupon
"Madam," he said, "by God and by St. John,
That's noble preaching no one could surpass!
I was about to take a wife; alas!
Am I to buy it on my flesh so dear?
There'll be no marrying for me this year!"

"You wait," she said, "my story's not begun.
You'll taste another brew before I've done;
You'll find it doesn't taste as good as ale;
And when I've finished telling you my tale
Of tribulation in the married life
In which I've been an expert as a wife,
That is to say, myself have been the whip.
So please yourself whether you want to sip
At that same cask of marriage I shall broach.
Be cautious before making the approach,
For I'll give instances, and more than ten.
And those who won't be warned by other men,
By other men shall suffer their correction,
So Ptolemy has said, in this connection.
You read his *Almagest;* you'll find it there."

"Madam, I put it to you as a prayer,"
The Pardoner said, "go on as you began!
Tell us your tale, spare not for any man.
Instruct us younger men in your technique."
"Gladly," she said, "if you will let me speak,
But still I hope the company won't reprove me
Though I should speak as fantasy may move me,
And please don't be offended at my views;
They're really only offered to amuse. . . ."

The Wife of Bath

3 noble preaching: In the passage preceding this excerpt, the Wife of Bath has spoken at length about her view of marriage.

15 cask: barrel; **broach:** tap into.

20 Ptolemy (tŏl'ə-mē): a famous astronomer of the second century A.D. The *Almagest,* his most famous work, does not, however, contain the proverb cited in lines 18–19.

WORDS TO KNOW

tribulation (trĭb'yə-lā'shən) *n.* suffering; great distress

TEACHING THE LITERATURE

Customizing Instruction

Less Proficient Readers

As you begin teaching the selection, write the following questions on the chalkboard. Have students copy the questions on a note card to keep in mind, answering them as they read.

- How does the Wife of Bath feel about marriage?
- How does the knight feel about marrying the old woman in the first part of the story?
- How does the knight feel about marrying the old woman in the last part of the story?

Gifted and Talented

Explain that throughout this story, the Wife of Bath interrupts the storyline with smaller stories to illustrate her point. As students read, they may draw and label a graphic organizer in the shape of imbedded frames to show the construction of the story as it unfolds from beginning to end. Remind them to begin with the largest frame, *The Canterbury Tales.*

BLOCK SCHEDULING: MANAGING TIME

If your schedule requires that you cover the lesson objectives in a shorter time, use . . .

- Preparing to Read, p. 154
- Thinking Through the Literature, p. 167
- Vocabulary in Action, p. 170

If you want to take advantage of longer class time, use . . .

- TE Teaching Options: Vocabulary, pp. 156, 162; Viewing and Representing, pp. 158, 160; Multicultural Link, p. 161; Informal Assessment, pp. 163, 166; Grammar, pp. 164, 169
- Choices & Challenges, p. 169
- The Author's Style, p. 168
- Author Study Project, p. 170

Reading and Analyzing

Literary Analysis NARRATOR

Remind students that *The Canterbury Tales* is a poem that tells a story—a narrative poem—with familiar elements: characters, setting, plot, and point of view, all of which combine to develop a theme.

Explain that the narrator is the person or voice that tells the story. It can be a character in the story or a voice outside the action. In this story, the narrator is the Wife of Bath.

 Use **Unit One Resource Book,** p. 37 for more exercises.

Active Reading

ANALYZING STRUCTURE

A Remind students that structure is the way in which the parts of a literary work are put together. Ask them to read the poem with the development of the main plot in mind, and to remain flexible as the narrator shifts focus to elaborate on extraneous information. For example, have students discuss lines 39–56, in which the narrator builds background while asserting, through verbal irony, her disregard for friars.

 Use **Unit One Resource Book,** p. 36 for more practice.

GUIDE FOR READING

B She thinks friars are more a curse than a blessing. She facetiously suggests that their constant blessing results in the demise of fairies. Furthermore, the monks break their vows of chastity.

C They demand the knight's death, but the king grants final judgment to the queen.

The Wife of Bath's Tale

When good King Arthur ruled in ancient days
(A king that every Briton loves to praise)
This was a land brim-full of fairy folk.
The Elf-Queen and her courtiers joined and broke
Their elfin dance on many a green mead,
Or so was the opinion once, I read,
Hundreds of years ago, in days of yore.
But no one now sees fairies any more.
For now the saintly charity and prayer
Of holy friars seem to have purged the air;
They search the countryside through field and stream
As thick as motes that speckle a sun-beam,
Blessing the halls, the chambers, kitchens, bowers,
Cities and boroughs, castles, courts and towers,
Thorpes, barns and stables, outhouses and dairies,
And that's the reason why there are no fairies.
A Wherever there was wont to walk an elf
To-day there walks the holy friar himself
As evening falls or when the daylight springs,
Saying his matins and his holy things,
Walking his limit round from town to town.
Women can now go safely up and down
By every bush or under every tree;
There is no other incubus but he,
So there is really no one else to hurt you
And he will do no more than take your virtue.

1 Now it so happened, I began to say,
Long, long ago in good King Arthur's day,
There was a knight who was a lusty liver.
One day as he came riding from the river
He saw a maiden walking all forlorn
Ahead of him, alone as she was born.
And of that maiden, spite of all she said,
By very force he took her maidenhead.

This act of violence made such a stir,
So much petitioning to the king for her,
That he condemned the knight to lose his head
By course of law. He was as good as dead

35 mead: meadow.

42 motes: specks of dust.

43 bowers: bedrooms.

45 thorpes: villages; **outhouses:** sheds.

47 wherever . . . elf: wherever an elf was accustomed to walk.

51 limit: the area to which a friar was restricted in his begging for donations.

54 incubus (ĭn'kyə-bəs): an evil spirit believed to descend on women while they sleep.

 **39–56** What seems to be the Wife of Bath's attitude toward friars?

61 forlorn: sad and lonely.

63–64 of that maiden . . . maidenhead: in spite of the maiden's protests, he robbed her of her virtue.

Teaching Options

Preteaching Vocabulary

USING A DICTIONARY Call students' attention to the list of WORDS TO KNOW. Tell them reference materials, such as a dictionary, can help them determine precise word meanings and usage.

Instruction Write the following list of guidelines on the board. Point out the word *abominably* in the list on page 154. Tell students to find it in the dictionary, and demonstrate how to use the guidelines.

- Find the origins of the word.
- Study the order of meanings from most common to least common.
- Determine which, if any, meanings are out-of-date.
- Read examples of how the word is used in illustrative sentences.
- Take note of synonyms and antonyms.

Remind students that using this process when they encounter an unfamiliar word will help them determine precise word meanings and usage.

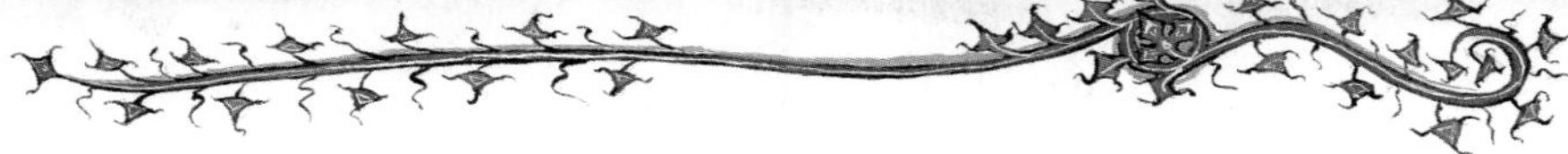

(It seems that then the statutes took that view)
But that the queen, and other ladies too,
2 Implored the king to exercise his grace
So ceaselessly, he gave the queen the case
And granted her his life, and she could choose
Whether to show him mercy or refuse.

The queen returned him thanks with all her might,
And then she sent a summons to the knight
At her convenience, and expressed her will:
"You stand, for such is the position still,
In no way certain of your life," said she,
"Yet you shall live if you can answer me:
What is the thing that women most desire?
Beware the axe and say as I require.

"If you can't answer on the moment, though,
I will concede you this: you are to go
A twelvemonth and a day to seek and learn
Sufficient answer, then you shall return.
I shall take gages from you to extort
Surrender of your body to the court."

Sad was the knight and sorrowfully sighed,
But there! All other choices were denied,
And in the end he chose to go away
And to return after a year and day
Armed with such answer as there might be sent
To him by God. He took his leave and went.

He knocked at every house, searched every place,
Yes, anywhere that offered hope of grace.
What could it be that women wanted most?
But all the same he never touched a coast,
3 Country or town in which there seemed to be
Any two people willing to agree.

Some said that women wanted wealth and treasure,
"Honor," said some, some "Jollity and pleasure,"

71 grace: mercy; clemency.

65–74 What punishment do the king and the law demand? To whom does the king grant the final judgment?

87 gages: pledges.

WORDS TO KNOW	
	statute (stăch'o͞ot) *n.* a law
	implore (ĭm-plôr') *v.* to plead; beg
	concede (kən-sēd') *v.* to grant or acknowledge, often unwillingly

Customizing Instruction

Students Acquiring English

1 Explain that the description of the knight as a "lusty liver," or one who lives in a lusty way, refers to the knight's intense desire for beautiful women.

Tell students that the title in this story refers to a married woman from the city of Bath (Băth), west of London and on the Avon River. It is a well-known health resort with three mineral springs, founded by the Romans.

Use **Spanish Study Guide** for additional support, pp. 22–24

Less Proficient Readers

2 Invite students to discuss the king's reaction to the knight's crime. Use the following questions:

- What is the king's response?
  Answer: He condemns the knight to lose his head.
- Who changes the king's mind?
  Answer: The queen and other ladies beg him to reconsider.
- How does the king resolve the problem?
  Answer: He turns it over to the queen.

Gifted and Talented

3 Ask students to identify the conflict established in lines 98–100.
Possible Response: No two people agree.

Then ask them to discuss in small groups some strategies they might use to lead people to agree.

Activity Have students write the following abbreviated guidelines beneath each word in the WORDS TO KNOW. Then have them use the dictionary to find this information for each word.

1. Word origins
2. Order of meanings
3. Out-of-date meanings
4. Usage
5. Synonyms
6. Antonyms

Use **Unit One Resource Book,** p. 38 for additional support.

Reading and Analyzing

Active Reading

ANALYZING STRUCTURE

A Lead students to notice in lines 127–129 the structural shift the narrator takes as she introduces the story of King Midas. Remind them to be prepared to return to the plot of the story about the knight.

Literary Analysis: ALLUSION

B An allusion is a reference to a historical or fictional person, place, or event. Understanding allusions can give readers a better understanding of a work. Here there are two allusions, one to Midas (fictional) and one to Ovid (historical). Be on the lookout for allusions as you read.

GUIDE FOR READING

C The comparison suggests that her whisper was no whisper at all but was loud and could be overheard.

Reading Skills and Strategies: COMPREHENDING

D Ask students to answer these questions:

1. What does the knight feel dejected?
   Possible Response: He has been unsuccessful in finding a common response.
2. What sight does he see at the edge of the woods?
   Answer: He sees more than twenty-four ladies dancing on the leafy ground.
3. What happens to the dancers when he approaches them?
   Answer: All except one disappear.
4. What does the old woman claim?
   Answer: She says that she might have the answer to his question.

Some "Gorgeous clothes" and others "Fun in bed,"
"To be oft widowed and remarried," said
Others again, and some that what most mattered
Was that we should be cosseted and flattered.
That's very near the truth, it seems to me;
A man can win us best with flattery.
To dance attendance on us, make a fuss,
Ensnares us all, the best and worst of us.

Some say the things we most desire are these:
Freedom to do exactly as we please,
With no one to reprove our faults and lies,
Rather to have one call us good and wise. **1**
Truly there's not a woman in ten score
Who has a fault, and someone rubs the sore,
But she will kick if what he says is true;
You try it out and you will find so too.
However vicious we may be within
We like to be thought wise and void of sin.
Others assert we women find it sweet
When we are thought dependable, discreet
And secret, firm of purpose and controlled,
Never betraying things that we are told.
But that's not worth the handle of a rake;
Women conceal a thing? For Heaven's sake!
A Remember Midas? Will you hear the tale?

B Among some other little things, now stale,
Ovid relates that under his long hair
The unhappy Midas grew a splendid pair **2**
Of ass's ears; as subtly as he might,
He kept his foul deformity from sight;
Save for his wife, there was not one that knew.
He loved her best, and trusted in her too.
He begged her not to tell a living creature
That he possessed so horrible a feature.
And she—she swore, were all the world to win,
She would not do such villainy and sin
As saddle her husband with so foul a name;
Besides to speak would be to share the shame.
Nevertheless she thought she would have died
Keeping this secret bottled up inside;

115 ten score: 200.

117 but she will: who will not.

120 void of sin: sinless.

127 Midas: a legendary king of Phrygia in Asia Minor.

129 Ovid (ŏv'ĭd): an ancient Roman poet whose *Metamorphoses* is a storehouse of Greek and Roman legends. According to Ovid, it was a barber, not Midas's wife, who told the secret of his donkey's ears.

133 save: except.

WORDS TO KNOW **cosset** (kŏs'ĭt) *v.* to treat like a pet; pamper

Teaching Options

Viewing and Representing

Sir Gawain, from an illuminated manuscript

ART APPRECIATION The illustration on p. 159 by an unknown artist depicts Sir Gawain, a hero from Arthurian legend, who is credited with discovering the Grail.

Instruction Have students discuss Sir Gawain's equipment and armor. Point out that he is wearing chainmail, not plate mail, which was invented later.

Application Have students discuss why they think the artist chose those colors for Sir Gawain's tunic and shield. Then have students research the term *heraldry* and find out what creature is shown on Sir Gawain's shield and why that creature might be significant for the English.

It seemed to swell her heart and she, no doubt,
Thought it was on the point of bursting out.

Fearing to speak of it to woman or man,
Down to a reedy marsh she quickly ran
And reached the sedge. Her heart was all on fire
And, as a bittern bumbles in the mire,
She whispered to the water, near the ground,
"Betray me not, O water, with thy sound!
To thee alone I tell it: it appears
My husband has a pair of ass's ears!
Ah! My heart's well again, the secret's out!
I could no longer keep it, not a doubt."
And so you see, although we may hold fast
A little while, it must come out at last,
We can't keep secrets; as for Midas, well,
Read Ovid for his story; he will tell.

This knight that I am telling you about
3 Perceived at last he never would find out
What it could be that women loved the best.
Faint was the soul within his sorrowful breast,
As home he went, he dared no longer stay;
His year was up and now it was the day.

As he rode home in a dejected mood
Suddenly, at the margin of a wood,
He saw a dance upon the leafy floor
Of four and twenty ladies, nay, and more.
Eagerly he approached, in hope to learn
Some words of wisdom ere he should return;
But lo! Before he came to where they were,
D Dancers and dance all vanished into air!
There wasn't a living creature to be seen
Save one old woman crouched upon the green.
A fouler-looking creature I suppose
Could scarcely be imagined. She arose
And said, "Sir knight, there's no way on from here.
Tell me what you are looking for, my dear,
For peradventure that were best for you;
We old, old women know a thing or two."

147 sedge: marsh grasses.

C **148 bumbles in the mire:** booms in the swamp. (The bittern, a wading bird, is famous for its loud call.) What does this comparison suggest about the queen's whisper?

Sir Gawain, from an illuminated manuscript

179 peradventure: perhaps.

WORDS TO KNOW **dejected** (dĭ-jĕk′tĭd) *adj.* sad; depressed

Customizing Instruction

Less Proficient Readers

1 Help students understand information the narrator gives about what women want by listing their various responses on the board. Discuss any unfamiliar terms, and then have students restate in their own words what it is women want.

Students Acquiring English

2 Be certain that students understand that *ass* is a synonym for *donkey.* Ask them why the king might want to hide his ears and keep them a secret.

Multiple Learning Styles

Interpersonal Learners

3 Explain that the knight's finding no consensus among women is probably what would actually happen if the story were real. Ask students to speculate in small groups as to why so many women each had a different response.
Possible Response: Everyone has her own individual wants and needs.

Next have students compose a list of five subjective questions to pose to other students in the school. Have them record the responses and compare them for consensus or for variety of responses.

Reading and Analyzing

GUIDE FOR READING

A Possible Response: A woman's power over a lover might be based on his infatuation; a wife's power over her husband might be based on companionability and mutuality of interests.

Literary Analysis: IRONY

B Ask students to reread lines 217–218. Remind them that verbal irony occurs when someone says one thing but means another. Have students identify the verbal irony of this passage.
Possible Response: The last thing the knight wants is to die; however, he graciously leaves the decision up to the queen.

Literary Analysis NARRATOR

C Have students reread lines 249–252. Point out that the narrator, or Wife, has returned to the narration, in that she provides a bridge, or transition, to the next phase of the story through this brief first-person narrative.

"Dear Mother," said the knight, "alack the day!
I am as good as dead if I can't say
What thing it is that women most desire;
If you could tell me I would pay your hire."
"Give me your hand," she said, "and swear to do
Whatever I shall next require of you
—If so to do should lie within your might—
And you shall know the answer before night."
"Upon my honor," he answered, "I agree."
"Then," said the crone, "I dare to guarantee
Your life is safe; I shall make good my claim.
Upon my life the queen will say the same.
Show me the very proudest of them all
In costly coverchief or jewelled caul
That dare say no to what I have to teach.
Let us go forward without further speech."
And then she crooned her gospel in his ear
And told him to be glad and not to fear.

They came to court. This knight, in full array,
Stood forth and said, "O Queen, I've kept my day
And kept my word and have my answer ready."

There sat the noble matrons and the heady
Young girls, and widows too, that have the grace
Of wisdom, all assembled in that place,
And there the queen herself was throned to hear
And judge his answer. Then the knight drew near
And silence was commanded through the hall.

The queen gave order he should tell them all
What thing it was that women wanted most.
He stood not silent like a beast or post,
But gave his answer with the ringing word
Of a man's voice and the assembly heard:

"My liege and lady, in general," said he,
"A woman wants the self-same sovereignty
Over her husband as over her lover,
And master him; he must not be above her.

181 alack the day: an exclamation of sorrow, roughly equivalent to "Woe is me!"

The Knight and the Old Lady

194 coverchief: kerchief; **caul** (kaul): an ornamental hair-net.

197 gospel: message.

199 in full array: in all his finery.

202 heady: giddy; impetuous.

203 grace: gift.

213 liege (lēj): lord.

214 sovereignty (sŏv'ər-ĭn-tē): rule; power.

214–215 How might a woman's power over a lover differ from her power over a husband?

WORDS TO KNOW **crone** (krōn) *n.* an ugly old woman; hag

Teaching Options

Viewing and Representing

The Knight and the Old Lady

ART APPRECIATION

Instruction Explain that illustrations of two or more people can help readers better understand the relationship between the characters.

Practice Call students' attention to the illustration above, *The Knight and the Old Lady,* as they appeared when they first met. Ask students to respond to the following questions:

- Which character appears to admire the other? Explain.
  Possible Response: The Old Lady does, in that she leans forward and looks upward.
- Which character appears to have something urgent to say?
  Possible Response: The Old Lady seems intent upon speaking, as her posture and facial expression indicate.

Invite students to draw or paint another image showing the knight and his horse as though the knight were in conversation with a beautiful young woman.

B That is your greatest wish, whether you kill
Or spare me; please yourself. I wait your will."

In all the court not one that shook her head
Or contradicted what the knight had said;
Maid, wife and widow cried, "He's saved his life!"

And on the word up started the old wife,
The one the knight saw sitting on the green,
And cried, "Your mercy, sovereign lady queen!
Before the court disperses, do me right!
'Twas I who taught this answer to the knight,
For which he swore, and pledged his honor to it,
That the first thing I asked of him he'd do it,
So far as it should lie within his might.
Before this court I ask you then, sir knight,
To keep your word and take me for your wife;
For well you know that I have saved your life.
If this be false, deny it on your sword!"

"Alas!" he said, "Old lady, by the Lord
I know indeed that such was my behest,
But for God's love think of a new request,
Take all my goods, but leave my body free."
"A curse on us," she said, "if I agree!
I may be foul, I may be poor and old,
Yet will not choose to be, for all the gold
That's bedded in the earth or lies above,
Less than your wife, nay, than your very love!"

"My love?" said he. "By heaven, my damnation!
1 Alas that any of my race and station
Should ever make so foul a misalliance!"
Yet in the end his pleading and defiance
All went for nothing, he was forced to wed.
He takes his ancient wife and goes to bed.

C Now peradventure some may well suspect
A lack of care in me since I neglect
To tell of the rejoicing and display
Made at the feast upon their wedding-day.
I have but a short answer to let fall;
I say there was no joy or feast at all,

235 behest (bĭ-hĕst'): promise.

244 race and station: family and rank.

245 misalliance (mĭs'ə-lī'əns): an unsuitable marriage.

Customizing Instruction

Less Proficient Readers

1 Explain that lines 244–245 refer to the knight's objection to his marrying the old woman.

- Why does the knight think he should not marry the old woman?
  Possible Response: She is not appealing to him, and he thinks his high social standing in society should merit him someone much better than an old woman.
- What does "so foul a misalliance" mean?
  Possible Response: It refers to an extremely unpleasant and unsuitable marriage.
- Why is the knight upset with the old woman's proposal of matrimony?
  Possible Response: He thinks she has tricked him into something he might otherwise never have agreed to.

THE CANTERBURY TALES 161

Reading and Analyzing

Literary Analysis NARRATOR

A Remind students that Chaucer takes liberties with the structure of this story. Have students reread lines 255–263, taking into account the presence of the narrator's voice. In line 263, the narrator reintroduces the dialogue between the old woman and the knight. Invite students to discuss whether they like this structure, in which the narrator's voice is interspersed with the dialogue.

Reading Skills and Strategies: PARAPHRASING

B Remind students that paraphrasing can help them understand the meaning of a specific passage. Ask them to restate in their own words the meaning of lines 285–300.

Possible Response: True gentility cannot be inherited from one's ancestors but must be earned through virtuous acts.

Active Reading
ANALYZING STRUCTURE

Point out that the structure of the story changes even more, albeit more subtly, between lines 287 and 321. The lines in between are dedicated solely to the old woman's monologue about the virtues and history of gentility. During this time, the reader's attention is diverted away from the knight and the dialogue between himself and the old woman; his presence is not acknowledged again until line 321.

GUIDE FOR READING

C He does good works. "Gentle birth" here means the birth through baptism, and "gentleness" means goodness, mercy, and generosity.

Nothing but heaviness of heart and sorrow.
He married her in private on the morrow
And all day long stayed hidden like an owl,
It was such torture that his wife looked foul.

256 **the morrow:** the next day.

A

Great was the anguish churning in his head
When he and she were piloted to bed;
He wallowed back and forth in desperate style.
His ancient wife lay smiling all the while;
At last she said, "Bless us! Is this, my dear,
How knights and wives get on together here?
Are these the laws of good King Arthur's house?
Are knights of his all so contemptuous?
I am your own beloved and your wife,
And I am she, indeed, that saved your life;
And certainly I never did you wrong.
2 Then why, this first of nights, so sad a song?
You're carrying on as if you were half-witted.
Say, for God's love, what sin have I committed?
I'll put things right if you will tell me how."

260 **piloted:** led. (In the Middle Ages, it was customary for the wedding party to escort the bride and groom to their bedchamber.)

261 **wallowed** (wŏl'ōd): rolled around; thrashed about.

"Put right?" he cried. "That never can be now!
Nothing can ever be put right again!
You're old, and so abominably plain,
So poor to start with, so low-bred to follow;
It's little wonder if I twist and wallow!
God, that my heart would burst within my breast!"

"Is that," said she, "the cause of your unrest?"

"Yes, certainly," he said, "and can you wonder?"

"I could set right what you suppose a blunder,
That's if I cared to, in a day or two,
If I were shown more courtesy by you.
Just now," she said, "you spoke of gentle birth,
Such as descends from ancient wealth and worth.
B If that's the claim you make for gentlemen
Such arrogance is hardly worth a hen.
Whoever loves to work for virtuous ends,

Dante and his Poem, Domenico di Michelino

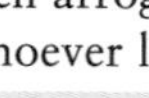

WORDS TO KNOW
contemptuous (kən-tĕmp'cho͞o-əs) *adj.* scornful; openly disrespectful
abominably (ə-bŏm'ə-nə-blē) *adv.* unpleasantly; terribly

Teaching Options

Vocabulary Strategy

DENOTATION AND CONNOTATION

Instruction Explain that synonyms can have different shades of meaning. Invite students to examine the **denotation,** the dictionary definition or explicit meaning, of a pair of synonyms and the **connotation,** or the meaning conveyed by attitudes and emotions, of the pair.

Model Read aloud line 261, and discuss the meaning of *wallow.* Point out that *wallow* and *roll* have the same denotative meanings in the dictionary. Then write these sentences on the board:

- The toddler *rolled* in the pile of leaves.
- The toddler *wallowed* in the pile of leaves.

Explain that *wallowed* can have a negative connotation, as in *He wallowed in self-pity.*

Activity Have students identify the denotative meanings shared by each pair of words. Then have them use each word in a sentence that reflects its connotative meaning.

1. disrespectful; contemptuous
2. unpleasant; abominable

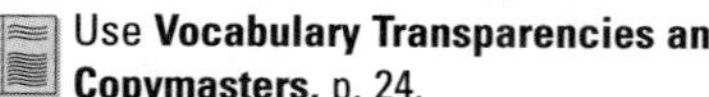

Use **Vocabulary Transparencies and Copymasters,** p. 24.

A lesson on identifying denotation and connotation appears on p. 645 of the Pupil's Edition.

Public and private, and who most intends
To do what deeds of gentleness he can,
Take him to be the greatest gentleman.
Christ wills we take our gentleness from Him,
Not from a wealth of ancestry long dim,
Though they bequeath their whole establishment
By which we claim to be of high descent.
Our fathers cannot make us a bequest
Of all those virtues that became them best
And earned for them the name of gentlemen,
But bade us follow them as best we can.

285–292 What does the old woman think is the chief qualification of a gentleman? How would you define "gentle birth" and "gentleness" as used in this passage?

"Thus the wise poet of the Florentines,
Dante by name, has written in these lines,
For such is the opinion Dante launches:
'Seldom arises by these slender branches
Prowess of men, for it is God, no less,
Wills us to claim of Him our gentleness.'
For of our parents nothing can we claim
Save temporal things, and these may hurt and maim.

301 Florentines: the people of Florence, Italy.

302 Dante (dän'tā): a famous medieval Italian poet. The quotation in lines 304–306 is a paraphrase of a passage in Dante's most famous work, *The Divine Comedy,* which he completed in 1321.

"But everyone knows this as well as I;
For if gentility were implanted by
The natural course of lineage down the line,
Public or private, could it cease to shine
In doing the fair work of gentle deed?
No vice or villainy could then bear seed.

310 gentility (jĕn-tĭl'ĭ-tē): the quality possessed by a gentle, or noble, person.

"Take fire and carry it to the darkest house
Between this kingdom and the Caucasus,
And shut the doors on it and leave it there,
It will burn on, and it will burn as fair
As if ten thousand men were there to see,
For fire will keep its nature and degree,
I can assure you, sir, until it dies.

316 Caucasus (kô'kə-səs): a region of western Asia, between the Black and Caspian seas.

"But gentleness, as you will recognize,
Is not annexed in nature to possessions.
Men fail in living up to their professions;
But fire never ceases to be fire.

324 professions: beliefs; ideals.

WORDS TO KNOW

bequeath (bĭ-kwēth') *v.* to leave in a will; give as an inheritance
prowess (prou'ĭs) *n.* superior skill; great ability
temporal (tĕm'pər-əl) *adj.* of the material world; not eternal
maim (mām) *v.* to disable or permanently wound

163

Customizing Instruction

Gifted and Talented

1 Call students attention to the simile "[he] stayed hidden like an owl" in line 257. Remind them that a simile is a figure of speech that compares two things, using the word *like* or *as,* that are basically unlike yet have something in common. Challenge students to write three of their own similes to describe the knight and the Wife based on other passages from pages 162 and 163.

Students Acquiring English

2 Ask students to reread line 271. Explain that "half-witted" refers to someone who does not exhibit intelligence.

Less Proficient Readers

3 Lead students to understand the analogy drawn between fire and gentility in lines 315–321.

Possible Response: Like fire, the spirit of true gentility shines brightly in all circumstances, not just when others can witness it.

Assessment Informal Assessment

ALTERNATIVE STRUCTURE OF THE PLOT

You can informally assess students' understanding of the selection by having them imagine an **alternative structure of the plot** with only the **narrator's** voice. Ask them to write a **summary** of everything the knight and the Wife have said to this point. Students' writing could take the form of a short story told in the third person

RUBRIC

3 **Full Accomplishment** Student writing reflects full understanding of events in story and of Wife and knight.

2 **Substantial Accomplishment** Student writings shows general understanding of events but may not fully reflect knowledge of one or both characters.

1 **Little or Partial Accomplishment** Student writing displays little understanding of events or of Wife and knight.

Reading and Analyzing

GUIDE FOR READING

A A person's station, or class, determined whether he or she was "gentle" or "churlish," not a person's behavior.

Reading Skills and Strategies: PARAPHRASING

B Ask students to paraphrase lines 361–364 by briefly restating the text in their own words.

Literary Analysis: IRONY

C Point out the **irony** in lines 383–386. The Wife chides the knight for claiming to adhere to a code of honor that demands respect for old age and wisdom while rejecting her for these very characteristics.

Active Reading

ANALYZING STRUCTURE

Point out that on pages 164 and 165, the plot progresses without any interruptions from the knight or digressions by the narrator. Ask students these questions:

- Why do you think Chaucer provides the old woman a forum to present her concerns?
  Possible Response: She is emotional and has something important to say.
- What reaction do you think the knight has during her lengthy monologue?
  Possible Response: He is probably still and quiet, intent upon listening.
- How would you describe the tone of the speaker's voice during this lengthy speech?
  Possible Response: It is probably heated and persuasive.

God knows you'll often find, if you enquire,
Some lording full of villainy and shame.
If you would be esteemed for the mere name
Of having been by birth a gentleman
And stemming from some virtuous, noble clan,
And do not live yourself by gentle deed
Or take your father's noble code and creed,
You are no gentleman, though duke or earl.
Vice and bad manners are what make a churl.

"Gentility is only the renown
For bounty that your fathers handed down,
Quite foreign to your person, not your own;
Gentility must come from God alone.
That we are gentle comes to us by grace
And by no means is it bequeathed with place.

"Reflect how noble (says Valerius)
Was Tullius surnamed Hostilius,
Who rose from poverty to nobleness.
And read Boethius, Seneca no less,
Thus they express themselves and are agreed:
'Gentle is he that does a gentle deed.'
And therefore, my dear husband, I conclude
That even if my ancestors were rude,
Yet God on high—and so I hope He will—
Can grant me grace to live in virtue still,
A gentlewoman only when beginning
To live in virtue and to shrink from sinning.

"As for my poverty which you reprove,
Almighty God Himself in whom we move,
Believe and have our being, chose a life
Of poverty, and every man or wife,
Nay, every child can see our Heavenly King
Would never stoop to choose a shameful thing.
No shame in poverty if the heart is gay,
As Seneca and all the learned say.
B He who accepts his poverty unhurt
I'd say is rich although he lacked a shirt.
But truly poor are they who whine and fret
And covet what they cannot hope to get.
And he that, having nothing, covets not,

327 lording: lord; nobleman.

334 churl (chûrl): low-class person; boor. Why might the sentiment expressed in this line have been viewed as fairly radical in the Wife of Bath's day?

341 Valerius (və-lîr'ē-əs): Valerius Maximus, a Roman writer of the first century A.D. who compiled a collection of historical anecdotes.

342 Tullius (tŭl'ē-əs) **surnamed Hostilius** (hŏ-stĭl'ē-əs): Tullus Hostilius—in Roman legend, the third king of the Romans.

344 Boethius (bō-ē'thē-əs): a Christian philosopher of the Dark Ages; **Seneca** (sĕn'ĭ-kə): an ancient Roman philosopher, writer, teacher, and politician.

Teaching Options

Grammar

PRONOUNS: CASE

Instruction A pronoun takes one of three cases, depending on its function in a sentence. Pronouns that are subjects or predicate nominatives take the nominative case, those that are objects take the objective case, and those that show possession take the possessive case. Remind students that paying attention to a pronoun's function in a sentence will help them avoid making errors in case. The following chart contains helpful reminders for students.

	Nominative	Objective	Possessive
First	I, we	me, us	my, mine, our, ours
Second	you	you	your, yours
Third	he, she, it, they	him, her, it, them	his, her, hers, its, their, theirs

Activity Suggest students refer to the chart above as they identify the function of each underlined pronoun in the following sentences. Have them write the pronoun in its correct form.

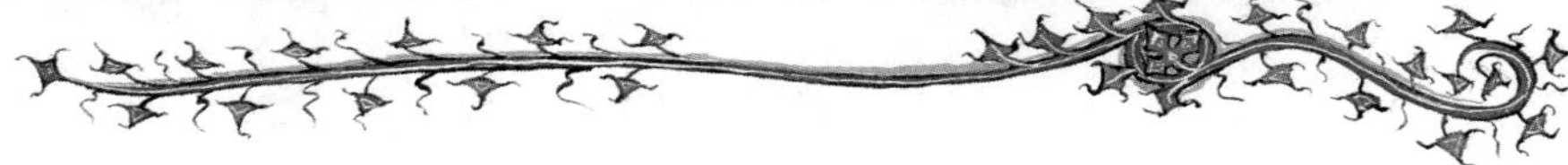

Is rich, though you may think he is a sot.

"True poverty can find a song to sing.
Juvenal says a pleasant little thing:
'The poor can dance and sing in the relief
Of having nothing that will tempt a thief.'
Though it be hateful, poverty is good,
A great incentive to a livelihood,
And a great help to our capacity
For wisdom, if accepted patiently.
Poverty is, though wanting in estate,
A kind of wealth that none calumniate.
Poverty often, when the heart is lowly,
Brings one to God and teaches what is holy,
Gives knowledge of oneself and even lends
A glass by which to see one's truest friends. **2**
And since it's no offense, let me be plain;
Do not rebuke my poverty again.

"Lastly you taxed me, sir, with being old.
Yet even if you never had been told
By ancient books, you gentlemen engage,
Yourselves in honor to respect old age.
To call an old man 'father' shows good breeding,
And this could be supported from my reading.

"You say I'm old and fouler than a fen.
You need not fear to be a cuckold, then.
Filth and old age, I'm sure you will agree,
Are powerful wardens over chastity.
Nevertheless, well knowing your delights,
I shall fulfil your worldly appetites.

"You have two choices; which one will you try?
To have me old and ugly till I die,
But still a loyal, true, and humble wife
That never will displease you all her life,
Or would you rather I were young and pretty
And chance your arm what happens in a city
Where friends will visit you because of me,
Yes, and in other places too, maybe.

366 sot: fool.

368 Juvenal (jo͞o'və-nəl): an ancient Roman satirist.

375 wanting in estate: lacking in grandeur.

376 calumniate (kə-lŭm'nē-āt'): criticize with false statements; slander.

389 fen: marsh.

390 cuckold (kŭk'əld): a husband whose wife is unfaithful.

400 chance your arm: take your chance on.

WORDS TO KNOW **rebuke** (rĭ-byo͞ok') *v.* to criticize

Customizing Instruction

Less Proficient Readers

1 Ask students to reread lines 367–370. Ask these questions:

- What does the old woman mean when she says that poverty can sing?
  Possible Response: She means that being poor can have its advantages.
- Why can the poor dance and sing with relief?
  Possible Response: They have no material possessions to be stolen.

Students Acquiring English

2 Explain that "A glass by which to see one's truest friends," line 380, refers to a magnifying glass. The speaker is saying that poverty allows a person to clearly assess the loyalty and motives of others.

Gifted and Talented

Ask students to apply the old woman's definition of *gentility* to her own character. Would they qualify her as a gentle person? Challenge students to support both a "yes" and a "no" answer and then to determine which answer they could most strongly support.
Possible Response: She seems ungentle in that she tricks the knight into marrying her; however, her compassion for his life and happiness appear to be gentle in nature.

Michael and her gave a reading from "The Wife of Bath's Tale." We enjoyed them acting out the different parts. Liz and me think they should join Drama Club. (*subject, shows possession, subject; she, their, I*)

Exercise Ask students to choose the correct form of the pronoun to complete each sentence and to identify its function and case.

1. When the queen summoned him, the knight wondered if there was any chance of (him, his) being freed. (*his; shows possession; possessive*)
2. The knight hoped (him, his) questioning of as many people as possible would provide an answer. (*his; shows possession; possessive*)
3. Planning to speak to the dancers, the knight was dismayed at (them, their) disappearing. (*their; shows possession; possessive*)
4. The knight consulted the crone, and it was (she, her) who finally gave him the answer. (*she; predicate nominative; nominative*)
5. The knight and (she, her) returned to the court. (*she; subject; nominative*)

Use **Grammar Transparencies and Copymasters,** p. 64.

Use McDougal Littell's ***Language Network*** for more instruction and practice in pronouns.

Reading and Analyzing

GUIDE FOR READING

A He has given the power of decision-making to his wife, showing her that he wants to make her happy.

Active Reading

ANALYZING STRUCTURE

B Have students identify the structural shift, the point at which the narrator once again intercedes and concludes the story.

Which would you have? The choice is all your own."

The knight thought long, and with a piteous groan
At last he said, with all the care in life,
"My lady and my love, my dearest wife,
I leave the matter to your wise decision.
You make the choice yourself, for the provision
Of what may be agreeable and rich
In honor to us both, I don't care which;
Whatever pleases you suffices me."

404 piteous (pĭt'ē-əs): pitiable; pathetic.

411 suffices (sə-fī'səz): satisfies.

A How does the knight's statement relate to what he has learned about "the thing that women most desire"?

"And have I won the mastery?" said she,
"Since I'm to choose and rule as I think fit?"
"Certainly, wife," he answered her, "that's it."
"Kiss me," she cried. "No quarrels! On my oath
And word of honor, you shall find me both,
That is, both fair and faithful as a wife;
May I go howling mad and take my life
Unless I prove to be as good and true
As ever wife was since the world was new!
And if to-morrow when the sun's above
I seem less fair than any lady-love,
Than any queen or empress east or west,
Do with my life and death as you think best.
Cast up the curtain, husband. Look at me!"

B
And when indeed the knight had looked to see,
Lo, she was young and lovely, rich in charms.
In ecstasy he caught her in his arms,
His heart went bathing in a bath of blisses
And melted in a hundred thousand kisses,
And she responded in the fullest measure
With all that could delight or give him pleasure.

The Lover and the Lady, from an illuminated manuscript

So they lived ever after to the end
In perfect bliss; and may Christ Jesus send
Us husbands meek and young and fresh in bed,
And grace to overbid them when we wed.
And—Jesu hear my prayer!—cut short the lives
Of those who won't be governed by their wives;
And all old, angry niggards of their pence,
God send them soon a very pestilence!

439 niggards: misers.

WORDS TO KNOW

ecstasy (ĕk'stə-sē) *n.* intense joy or delight; bliss

166

Teaching Options

Assessment Informal Assessment

ALTERNATIVE ENDING

You can informally assess students' understanding of the selection by having them imagine an alternative ending in which the old woman does not turn into a young and lovely woman. Students' writing could take the form of testimony by the knight.

RUBRIC

3 **Full Accomplishment** Student writing reflects full understanding of events in story that lead up to ending, and of characters of old woman and knight.

2 **Substantial Accomplishment** Student writing shows general understanding of events, but may not fully reflect one or both of main characters.

1 **Little or Partial Accomplishment** Student writing displays little understanding of events or of either of main characters.

Connect to the Literature

1. **What Do You Think?** Were you surprised by the outcome of the knight's quest? Why or why not?

Comprehension Check
- What change does the queen make in the knight's sentence?
- What information does the old woman give the knight?
- What happens to the old woman after the knight agrees to abide by her decision?

Think Critically

2. In what way is the question that the queen poses to the knight related to the crime that he has committed?
3. What **theme,** or message, about marriage would you say the tale conveys? Do you agree with the message? Why or why not?
4. ACTIVE READING ANALYZING STRUCTURE Look over your chart in your  READER'S NOTEBOOK and review the reasons you inferred. What do the interruptions tell you about what matters to the Wife of Bath?
5. Consider the **narrator** of the "Prologue." How would you describe his values?

THINK ABOUT
- his characterizations of people like the Summoner, the Pardoner, and the Wife of Bath
- his opinions of their actions
- his description of himself as "short of wit" in line 766 of the "Prologue" (page 134)

Extend Interpretations

6. **Comparing Texts** Which part of *The Canterbury Tales*—the "Prologue" or the two tales—did you find the most enjoyable or interesting? Give reasons for your choice.
7. **Critic's Corner** One critic has described Chaucer as "a modern writer," one whose work can be appreciated by every generation of readers. Do you agree with this observation? Cite specific passages of *The Canterbury Tales* to back up your opinion.
8. **Connect to Life** Do you see any similarities between the attitudes of the Wife of Bath and the old woman in "The Wife of Bath's Tale" and the attitudes of modern American women? Cite details to support your answer.

Literary Analysis

NARRATOR The teller of a story in prose or verse is known as the story's **narrator.** The narrator may be a character in the story or a voice outside the action. In the "Prologue" from *The Canterbury Tales,* a narrator (whom Chaucer identifies as himself) introduces several characters, who then narrate the various tales.

Cooperative Learning Activity In a small-group discussion, consider how the portrait of the Wife of Bath in lines 455–486 of the "Prologue" (page 125) relates to the tale that she tells. Then work with the group to create a chart in which you list details about the Wife of Bath as you can. Include details about her appearance, skills, social position, personality, attitudes, and motives.

Detail	Evidence
worthy	"Prologue," lines 455 and 469
somewhat deaf	"Prologue," line 456

GUIDING STUDENT RESPONSE

Connect to the Literature

1. **What Do You Think?** Guidelines for student response: Whether they were surprised or not surprised by the outcome, students should provide evidence from the text to support their opinions.

Comprehension Check
- She commutes his death sentence and instead sends him on a yearlong quest to discover what women most desire.
- She tells him that women most want the same sovereignty over their husbands as over their lovers.
- She transforms into a lovely young woman who is also faithful to the knight.

Use Selection Quiz in **Unit One Resource Book** p. 39

Think Critically

2. Possible Response: Having acted badly towards women, he must seek to understand what women do want.
3. Possible Responses: Women should have the upper hand, or at least wield considerable power, in marriage; husbands who try to please their wives have happy marriages. Students' opinions will vary but should be supported by examples and logical reasons.
4. Possible Response: The interruptions indicate that the Wife of Bath thinks that women should not hide what it is they want—mastery in marriage.
5. Possible Responses: The narrator is concerned with morality and virtue, based on his disapproval of the actions of the Summoner and the Pardoner. His ironic use of language may demonstrate a quick-witted and biting sarcasm. His facility with language shows intelligence, but he is modest and rather self-deprecating (describing himself as "short of wit").

Literary Analysis

Cooperative Learning Activity A much-married woman who prefers younger men and also likes having the upper hand in marriage, the Wife of Bath tells a tale in which a woman in her situation triumphs. Students' details should be supported by evidence in the General Prologue or the Wife of Bath's prologue or tale.

Extend Interpretations

Comparing Texts Some students may prefer the variety of characters and portraits provided in the "Prologue," others may prefer the strong story line of "The Pardoner's Tale," and still others may prefer the humor of "The Wife of Bath's Tale." Whichever part students find most enjoyable and interesting, they should provided evidence from the text to support their opinions.

Critic's Corner Students agreeing with this assessment might cite the timelessness of certain themes that Chaucer addresses—greed, love, sin, etc. Accept all responses for which students use the text to support their ideas.

Connect to Life Accept all reasonable responses. Some students may comment on the egalitarian attitudes of the Wife of Bath and be of the opinion that her views seems relatively contemporary in the ongoing "battle of the sexes."

The Author's Style

Beyond the techniques of rhyming couplets and metrical patterns is the consideration of Chaucer's style, which helps make his picture of medieval life lucid and memorable. Students will be made aware of Chaucer's style through the "Key Aspects of Chaucer's Style" chart and then find examples of the four points in the excepts in the right margin.

Analysis of Style

A First activity

irony: the Doctor's greed in growing rich from pestilences; the cherubic Summoner having carbuncles; women who are thought discreet actually being betrayers of secrets

vivid imagery: the Prioress's table manners; the Summoner's fearsome appearance; the deaths of the murderers compared to a ghastly medical text

clear differentiation between characters: the discreet Prioress; the greedy Doctor; the Summoner's fearsome appearance

characters' "voices": the oily demeanor ("trust me") coming through the Pardoner's formal language; the comical, earthy language ("not worth the handle of a rake") of the Wife of Bath

B Second activity

amusing examples include the Prioress's "zest" for courtliness and etiquette; the "medical" idea that gold stimulates the heart; the Summoner being frightening to children; the Wife of Bath's revelation of a "discreet" woman being a tattletale

C Third activity

There are many examples of the **key aspects** of Chaucer's style throughout *The Canterbury Tales.* For example, in the "Prologue," Chaucer uses the irony of a monk with refined tastes and habits to expose a monk's faults and humanity.

The Author's Style

Chaucer's Realism as Entertainment

Chaucer's enduring appeal as a poet stems in part from the humor and realism of his characterizations. Chaucer had no illusions about humanity, yet he showed a genuine fondness for human beings—warts and all. His combination of detachment and sympathy distinguishes his writing style.

Key Aspects of Chaucer's Style

- a gentle irony that exposes characters' faults while emphasizing their essential humanity
- a use of vivid but spare imagery and figurative language in describing characters' physical appearance
- a clear differentiation between characters
- a stylistic appropriateness of the tales to their narrators (Each character has a particular "voice.")

Analysis of Style

On the right are five excerpts from *The Canterbury Tales.* Study the chart above and read the excerpts carefully. Then,

- A • find examples of the listed aspects of Chaucer's style
- B • explain what, if anything, is amusing about each excerpt and identify which aspects of style contribute to this effect
- C • go back through the selections from *The Canterbury Tales* and find other examples of these key aspects of Chaucer's style

Applications

1. Speaking and Listening With a partner, study the description of either the Pardoner or the Wife of Bath in the "Prologue." Then read aloud selected passages from the character's tale in the way that the character might have told it. Have your partner critique your oral interpretation and suggest improvements.

2. Illustrating Style Choose one of Chaucer's pilgrims whose physical appearance is vividly described. Then draw a picture of the character, based on Chaucer's description.

3. Imitating Style In poetry or prose, create a character (preferably from a modern profession) and describe him or her with the mixture of detachment and sympathy that Chaucer used to such advantage.

from the **Prologue**

About the Prioress:

For courtliness she had a special zest,
And she would wipe her upper lip so clean
That not a trace of grease was to be seen
Upon the cup when she had drunk; to eat,
She reached a hand sedately for the meat.

About the Doctor:

Yet he was rather close as to expenses
And kept the gold he won in pestilences.
Gold stimulates the heart, or so we're told.
He therefore had a special love of gold.

About the Summoner:

There was a Summoner with us at that Inn,
His face on fire, like a cherubin,
For he had carbuncles. His eyes were narrow,
He was as hot and lecherous as a sparrow.
Black scabby brows he had, and a thin beard.
Children were afraid when he appeared.

from **The Pardoner's Tale**

There is, in Avicenna's long relation
Concerning poison and its operation,
Trust me, no ghastlier section to transcend
What these two wretches suffered at their end.
Thus these two murderers received their due,
So did the treacherous young poisoner too.

from **The Wife of Bath's Tale**

Others assert we women find it sweet
When we are thought dependable, discreet
And secret, firm of purpose and controlled,
Never betraying things that we are told.
But that's not worth the handle of a rake;
Women conceal a thing? For Heaven's sake!

Applications

1. **Speaking and Listening** Have students use the following criteria to critique oral interpretation. The student:
   - makes and supports a valid interpretation of how the character might tell the tale.
   - uses voice (volume and tone) to establish mood and convey meaning
   - uses movement and gestures to establish mood and convey meaning
   - use facial expressions to establish mood and convey meaning

   As a conclusion to this activity, have the class identify and analyze the effect Chaucer's development of the character has on the interpretation.
2. **Illustrating Style** Students will find that Chaucer's descriptions are detailed enough for them to draw many physical features.
3. **Imitating Style** Remind students to revisit the Key Aspects box on the page before beginning their creations.

See the Skills Trace at the beginning of the unit for information on TEKS covered in this lesson.

Writing Options

1. Pilgrim Dialogue How might the other pilgrims have reacted to the "The Wife of Bath's Tale"? Write a dialogue in which at least two pilgrims, as well as the Wife of Bath herself, comment on the story and its message about men's and women's roles. Try to keep the comments true to the personalities and attitudes of the pilgrims as conveyed in the "Prologue."

2. Comparing Knights The Knight on the Canterbury pilgrimage, described in lines 43–80 of the "Prologue" (pages 114–115) is usually considered a model of chivalry. Write a short compare-and-contrast essay in which you compare the Knight with the knight in "The Wife of Bath's Tale." You might organize your ideas in a Venn diagram. Put your essay in your **Working Portfolio.**

Writing Handbook
See page 1367: Compare and Contrast.

Activities & Explorations

1. Gender Debate Conduct a debate about the key ingredients in healthy relationships. Your debate might focus on the differing expectations and responsibilities of men and women in life and in relationships.
~ **SPEAKING AND LISTENING**

2. Medieval Manuscript Create your own manuscript page of a passage from "The Wife of Bath's Tale" or another tale by Chaucer. Include the text of the passage, an appropriate illustration, and a decorative border for the page. ~ **ART**

3. Costume Drawings Imagine a live performance of one of the tales. Find or draw pictures that show how the characters might be dressed.
~ **ART**

4. Woman's Roles Find out more about the roles of women in Chaucer's day. Was the Wife of Bath representative of her sex? Did widows like her have more independence than married or single women? What was life like for noble women? for women affiliated with the church? Answer these questions in an oral report. ~ **HISTORY**

5. Medieval Justice The justice meted out in "The Wife of Bath's Tale" may seem unusual by modern standards. Find out more about justice in medieval England. What influence did the monarch have over the courts of justice? What role did the church play in justice? What exactly is English common law? What were trial by combat and trial by ordeal, and when did they cease to be used? How did the jury system evolve? How were lawyers trained? Research the answer to one of these questions or a related question, then share your findings in a written report.
~ **HISTORY**

Inquiry & Research

Bath The city of Bath in England (pictured below) has a history that dates back to Roman times. Research this city, the home of the Wife of Bath. Present your findings in an illustrated time line entitled "Bath Yesterday and Today."

Scene from Bath today

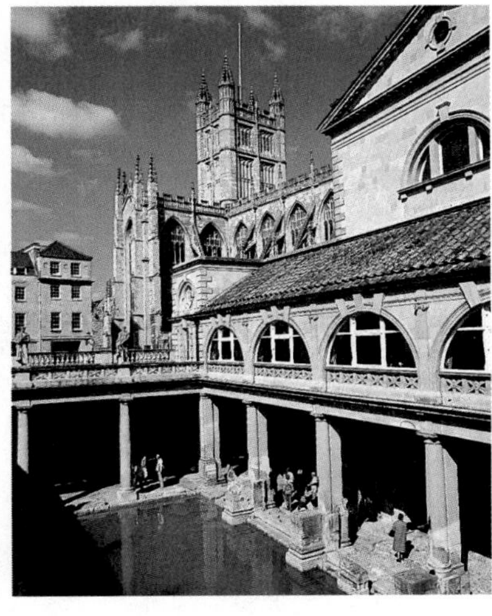

Writing Options

1. **Pilgrim Dialogue** You might suggest to students that they use the Squire in their dialogues. He is described in this way: "He loved so hotly that till dawn grew pale / He slept as little as a nightingale."
2. **Comparing Knights** Emphasize to students that their comparison-and-contrast essay should mention qualities unique to each knight as well as qualities they have in common.

Activities & Explorations

1. **Gender Debate** You might want to choose three students for each side in the debate or ask for volunteers. Have the rest of the students record key points made by each speaker. Then ask students to summarize the important points made by each side in the debate.
2. **Medieval Manuscript** Have students display their illuminated manuscript pages on a wall in the classroom.
3. **Costume Drawings** Set aside an area in the classroom to display students' costume drawings.
4. **Woman's Roles** Direct students to book-length studies of these issues, as well as to the standard encyclopedias in the school or local library. Students might also research these topics on the Internet.
5. **Medieval Justice** You might help students narrow down which question they wish to research. A narrowly focused topic is more likely to produce a decent report.

Inquiry & Research

Bath You might bring a picture book of Bath to class to spark interest among students. Students will find pictures, diagrams, and reconstructions of the ancient Roman baths and ruins especially interesting.

If students are not interested in this topic, encourage them to select another appropriate for this selection.

Grammar

KINDS OF SENTENCES

Instruction There are four kinds of sentences: declarative, interrogative, imperative, and exclamatory. A declarative sentence states a fact, wish, intent, or feeling. It ends with a period. An interrogative sentence asks a question and ends with a question mark. An imperative sentence gives a command, request, or direction and ends with either a period or an exclamation point. An exclamatory sentence expresses strong feeling or excitement and ends with an exclamation point.

Activity Write the following sentences from "The Wife of Bath's Tale" on the chalkboard.

"Am I to buy it on my flesh so dear? There'll be no marrying for me this year!"(lines 5–6)

"Madam, I put it to you as a prayer," The Pardoner said, "go on as you began! Tell us your tale, spare not for any man."(lines 22–24)

Have students identify each kind of sentence. Ask volunteers to give examples of declarative sentences.

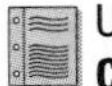
Use **Grammar Transparencies and Copymasters,** p. 76.

Use McDougal Littell's ***Language Network*** for more instruction and practice in (different in every selection).

Vocabulary in Action

Exercise A
1. grant
2. regulation
3. talent
4. indulge
5. beseech
6. hag
7. awfully
8. heal

Exercise B
1. peace
2. inherit
3. praise
4. elated
5. spiritual
6. misery
7. respectful

Author Study Project

MOCK INTERVIEWS

The interviewer should ask questions to elicit particular responses as well as to encourage a lively discussion. Remind students to use *who, what, where, when,* and *how* questions. Those who feel they know their medieval person's life well enough may want to extend the activity by submitting themselves to the rest of the class for an impromptu interview session.

Primary/Secondary Print Sources
Help students locate appropriate print and nonprint information by using text resources such as books and encyclopedias as well as technical resources such as databases and the Internet.

Another good secondary print source is *Daily Life in Chaucer's England* by Jeffrey Singman and Will McLean (Greenwood Press, 1995).

MULTIMEDIA PROJECT
Students can turn their mock interviews into a multimedia project by working in groups of six or seven, with one student serving as director, one as the host-interviewer, two as medieval interviewees, one as a locator and presenter of period-appropriate background music, and one or more a writer. They can create a mock television studio and videotape their interviews, possibly even wearing appropriate costumes for both the interviewer and the medieval person.

Vocabulary in Action

EXERCISE A: SYNONYMS On your paper, write the word that is closest in meaning to the boldfaced word.

1. **concede:** follow, grant, start, end
2. **statute:** regulation, remark, area, sculpture
3. **prowess:** stress, talent, front, back
4. **cosset:** release, urge, indulge, intrude
5. **implore:** beget, beseech, believe, belittle
6. **crone:** murmur, wizard, hag, scream
7. **abominably:** awfully, feebly, unwisely, easily

EXERCISE B: ANTONYMS On your paper, write the word whose meaning is most nearly opposite the meaning of the boldfaced word.

1. **tribulation:** criticism, sorrow, peace, anger
2. **bequeath:** gain, argue, doubt, inherit
3. **rebuke:** praise, predict, question, answer
4. **dejected:** depressed, elated, inserted, wise
5. **temporal:** harsh, timely, worldly, spiritual
6. **ecstasy:** misery, fury, confusion, bliss
7. **contemptuous:** proud, kind, new, respectful
8. **maim:** scar, scorn, infect, heal

WORDS TO KNOW			
	abominably	crone	prowess
	bequeath	dejected	rebuke
	concede	ecstasy	statute
	contemptuous	implore	temporal
	cosset	maim	tribulation

Building Vocabulary
Several Words to Know in this lesson derive from Old or Middle English. For an in-depth study of word origins, see page 206.

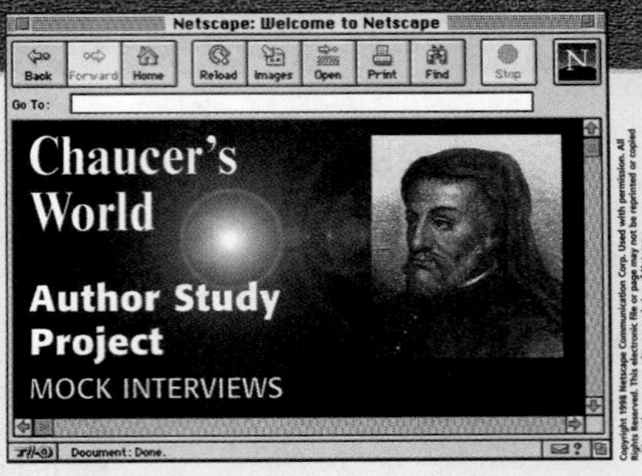

Research and present a series of mock interviews with English men and women of Chaucer's day. Begin by brainstorming a list of possible interviewees with the entire class. Consider the characters in the "Prologue" of *The Canterbury Tales* and the professions mentioned in the biographical information about Chaucer. Then get together with a partner and research one of the medieval people or lifestyles. Use your findings to prepare questions and discussion points for a mock interview in which one member of your pair takes on the role of interviewer and the other portrays a medieval person.

Primary Print Sources Consider reading letters and diaries from the era, as well as more of *The Canterbury Tales*. A brief general survey of English literature, such as one found in an encyclopedia, might help you locate appropriate medieval sources.

Secondary Print Sources Social histories, which focus on people's daily lives, may prove to be valuable sources. Biographies of Chaucer and other people of his day should also be useful. Consider books that combine biography and social history, such as John Gardner's *The Life and Times of Chaucer*.

Web Sites Search for the Web sites of Chaucer and Middle English societies, medieval museums, and British castles. Also use the Web to locate medieval studies departments at British and American universities.

More Online: Research Starter
www.mcdougallittell.com

Federigo's Falcon

from The Decameron

Tale by GIOVANNI BOCCACCIO (jō-vä'nē bō-kä'chē-ō')

Comparing Literature of the World

The Storytelling Tradition Across Cultures

The Canterbury Tales* and *The Decameron The 14th-century Italian collection of tales known as *The Decameron,* by Giovanni Boccaccio, greatly influenced Chaucer's writing of *The Canterbury Tales*.

Points of Comparison As you read one of Boccaccio's famous tales, compare it with Chaucer's work in terms of **narrative structure** and **themes** relating to love and human nature.

Build Background

Plagued by Love Boccaccio lived during the Italian Renaissance—a time of great achievements in art, music, and literature. Like Chaucer's *Canterbury Tales, The Decameron* is a collection of tales set within a frame story. The frame, or outer story, is about ten characters who flee to the country to escape a plague that is ravaging Florence, Italy. For ten days they amuse themselves by telling stories, each day selecting a "king" or "queen" who presides over the storytelling. Their 100 tales make up the bulk of *The Decameron.* As this selection begins, the queen of the day decides that it is time to tell her own story.

"Federigo's Falcon" is a tale of courtly love. In medieval times, marriages were often arranged. As a result, couples sometimes looked outside marriage for romantic attachments. This practice was not considered scandalous as long as the love remained idealized. Federigo is devoted to a married woman, Monna Giovanna (mō'nä jō'vä'nä), and will sacrifice anything to gain her love.

WORDS TO KNOW **Vocabulary Preview**

anguish, commend, compel, deign, discretion, legitimate, meagerly, oblige, presumption, reproach

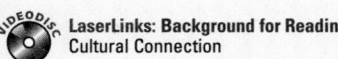

LaserLinks: Background for Reading
Cultural Connection

Focus Your Reading

LITERARY ANALYSIS PLOT The **plot** of a literary work consists of all the actions and events in the work. A plot moves forward because of a **conflict**—a struggle between opposing forces. As you read the story, notice how the plot develops around the main conflict.

ACTIVE READING ANALYZING CAUSE AND EFFECT In a well-crafted story, a single event often has an effect that becomes the cause of still another effect and so on. To identify true cause-and-effect relationships in "Federigo's Falcon," make sure the relationship between events is causal by connecting them with the word *because.* If the sentence makes sense, the relationship is causal.

READER'S NOTEBOOK As you read this story about love and its sacrifices, try to keep track of the relationships between events by making a cause-and-effect diagram like the one started here.

Federigo falls in love with Monna Giovanna. → He spends all of his money to impress her. → He is left with only a small farm and his falcon. → [ ]

OVERVIEW

Objectives

1. compare the selection to stories in *The Canterbury Tales* by analyzing the themes and structures of both works **(Critical Thinking)**
2. identify **conflicts** contributing to a story's **plot (Literary Analysis)**
3. analyze **cause and effect (Active Reading)**

Summary

Monna Giovanna's son becomes seriously ill, and he asks his mother for one thing only—Federigo's falcon. She goes to Federigo's farm. Because Federigo has nothing worthy to serve so great a woman, he roasts his falcon and serves it to her. Federigo learns the true purpose of the visit too late—and soon afterward the child dies. After a period of mourning, Monna Giovanna is urged to remarry. She will have only one man—Federigo.

Use **Unit One Resource Book,** p. 40 for additional support.

Thematic Link

This tale of courtly love illustrates the kind of storytelling that provided entertainment for many people during medieval times. It reveals the timeless qualities of love and the sacrifices people make for it in **everyday life.**

Mini Lesson Preteaching Vocabulary

If you would like to preteach the WORDS TO KNOW for this selection, use the Mini Lesson on p. 172.

5-Minute Warm-Up

Daily Language SkillBuilder

Have students **proofread** the display sentences on page 15l and write them correctly. The sentences also appear on Transparency 5 of **Grammar Transparencies and Copymasters.**

LESSON RESOURCES

UNIT ONE RESOURCE BOOK, pp. 40–44

ASSESSMENT RESOURCES
Formal Assessment, pp. 23–24
Teacher's Guide to Assessment and Portfolio Use
Test Generator

SKILLS TRANSPARENCIES AND COPYMASTERS
Literary Analysis
- Plot, T10 (for Literary Analysis, p. 171)

Reading and Critical Thinking
- Sequence Chain, T50 (for Active Reading, p. 171)

Grammar
- Conjunctions, C73 (for Mini Lesson, pp. 178–179)

Vocabulary
- Suffixes, C26 (for Mini Lesson, p. 175)

Writing
- Compare-Contrast, C34 (for Writing Option 3, p. 178)
- Autobiographical Incident, C36 (for Writing Option 1, p. 178)

Communications
- Giving and Using Feedback to Improve Performance, T16 (for Activities & Explorations 2, p. 178)

INTEGRATED TECHNOLOGY
Audio Library
Laser Links
- Cultural Connection: The World of *The Decameron*
- Science Connection: The Falcon. See **Teacher's Sourcebook,** p. 11.

Internet: Research Starter
Visit our website:
www.mcdougallittell.com

TEACHING THE LITERATURE

Reading and Analyzing

Active Reading

ANALYZING CAUSE AND EFFECT

A Tell students that analyzing cause and effect can help them follow the plot and better understand what is happening in a story. Ask them what causes Federigo to spend far beyond his means.

Possible Response: He is trying to impress Monna Giovanna.

Have them identify the effect of his efforts on his immediate financial situation.

Answer: He loses his wealth and is left with only his farm and one falcon.

Use **Unit One Resource Book,** p. 41 for more practice.

Literary Analysis PLOT

B Explain that plot is the sequence of actions and events in a narrative story. Stress that some kind of conflict is central to any plot. Point out that some conflicts are external, such as those between opposing characters or between characters and nature. Internal conflicts exist when a character struggles with opposing motivations or emotions. Have students describe the conflict between Federigo and Monna Giovanna and identify it as internal or external.

Possible Response: Federigo can't please Monna Giovanna; external.

Use **Unit One Resource Book,** p. 42 for additional support.

Federigo's FALCON

GIOVANNI BOCCACCIO

Filomena had already finished speaking, and when the Queen saw there was no one left to speak except for Dioneo,[1] who was exempted because of his special privilege, she herself with a cheerful face said:

It is now my turn to tell a story and, dearest ladies, I shall do so most willingly with a tale similar in some respects to the preceding one, its purpose being not only to show you how much power your beauty has over the gentle heart, but also so that you yourselves may learn, whenever it is fitting, to be the donors of your favors instead of always leaving this act to the whim of Fortune,[2] who, as it happens, on most occasions bestows such favors with more abundance than discretion.

You should know, then, that Coppo di Borghese Domenichi,[3] who once lived in our city and perhaps still does, a man of great and respected authority in our times, one most illustrious and worthy of eternal fame both for his way of life and his ability much more than for the nobility of his blood, often took delight, when he was an old man, in discussing things from the past with his neighbors and with others. He knew how to do this well, for he was more logical and had a better memory and a more eloquent style of speaking than any other man. Among the many beautiful tales he told, there was one he would often tell about a young man who once lived in Florence named Federigo, the son of Messer Filippo Alberighi,[4] renowned above all other men in Tuscany for his prowess in arms and for his courtliness.

As often happens to most men of gentle breeding, he fell in love, with a noble lady named Monna Giovanna, in her day considered to be one of the most beautiful and most charming ladies that ever there was in Florence; and in order to win her love, he participated in jousts and tournaments, organized and gave banquets, spending his money without restraint; **A** but she, no less virtuous than beautiful, cared little for these things he did on her behalf, nor did she care for the one who did them. Now, as Federigo was spending far beyond his means and getting nowhere, as can easily happen, he lost his wealth and was reduced to poverty, and was left with nothing to his name but his little farm **B** (from whose revenues he lived very meagerly) and one falcon, which was among the finest of its kind in the world.

More in love than ever, but knowing that he would never be able to live the way he wished to in the city, he went to live at Campi, where his farm was. There he passed his time hawking whenever he could, imposing on no one, and enduring his poverty patiently. Now one day, during the time that Federigo was reduced to these extremes, it happened that the husband of Monna Giovanna fell ill, and realizing death was near, he made his last will: he was very rich, and he left everything to his son, who was just

1. **Dioneo** (dē′ô-nā′ō).
2. **Fortune:** a personification of the power that supposedly distributes good and bad luck to people.
3. **Coppo di Borghese Domenichi** (kôp′pō dē bōr-gā′zĕ dō-mĕ′nē-kē).
4. **Messer Filippo Alberighi** (mās′sĕr fē-lēp′pō äl′bĕ-rē′gē).

WORDS TO KNOW

discretion (dĭ-skrĕsh′ən) *n.* a sense of carefulness and restraint in one's actions or words

meagerly (mē′gər-lē) *adv.* poorly; scantily

172

Teaching Options

Preteaching Vocabulary

USING CONTEXT CLUES Call students' attention to the list of WORDS TO KNOW. Remind them that sometimes they can understand the meaning of an unfamiliar word by examining the context in which the word is used. Then read the following excerpt from page 172 aloud: "He knew how to do this well, for he was more logical and had a better memory and a more *eloquent* style of speaking than any other man." Ask students to summarize the meaning of *eloquent* based on its use in the sentence.

Demonstrate the strategy for them using the following model.

Model Sentence He *anguished* over the difficult decision until his head began to ache.

Instruction

- Write the model sentence on the chalkboard.
- Ask a volunteer to summarize the meaning of the sentence.
- Have students use the meaning of the sentence to suggest meanings for the word *anguished.*

La Pia de Tolommei (1868–1880), Dante Gabriel Rossetti. Oil on canvas, Spencer Museum of Art, University of Kansas.

growing up, and since he had also loved Monna Giovanna very much, he made her his heir should his son die without any legitimate children; and then he died.

Monna Giovanna was now a widow, and every summer, as our women usually do, she would go to the country with her son to one of their estates very close by to Federigo's farm. Now this young boy of hers happened to become more and more friendly with Federigo and he began to enjoy birds and dogs; and after seeing Federigo's falcon fly many times, it made him so happy that he very much wished it were his own, but he did not dare to ask for it, for he could see how precious it was to Federigo. During this time, it happened that the young boy took ill, and his mother was much grieved, for he was her only child and she loved him dearly; she would spend the entire day by his side, never ceasing to comfort him, asking him time and again if there was anything he wished, begging him to tell her what it might be, for if it was possible to obtain

WORDS TO KNOW

legitimate (lə-jĭt'ə-mĭt) *adj.* born of parents who are legally married to each other

Customizing Instruction

Students Acquiring English

Boccaccio's complex, lengthy sentence structure may challenge students. Encourage them to break sentences into comprehensible sections in order to grasp the meaning.

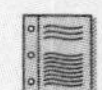 Use **Spanish Study Guide** for additional support, pp. 25–27

Less Proficient Readers

Encourage students to talk about any large birds they have seen in captivity or in the wild. Then have them read to discover the importance of the falcon mentioned in the title.

Gifted and Talented

Have students consider what "Federigo's Falcon" sets forth as proper behavior between men and women. Ask them to compare roles endorsed for men and women with those described in *The Canterbury Tales*.

- Ask a volunteer to use *anguished* in a sentence.

Exercise Write the following sentences on the chalkboard. Ask students to use context clues to determine the meanings of the underlined words.

1. You have worked very hard on this project; I commend your efforts.
2. If it's against the law, it can't be legitimate!
3. Having only a bed and a chair, the struggling artist furnished the room meagerly.
4. She did him a favor, so he is obliged to help her now.
5. Your presumption about the future is based only on hearsay.

 Use **Unit One Resource Book,** p. 43 for more practice.

A lesson on using context clues appears on p. 939 of the Pupil's Edition.

Reading and Analyzing

Literary Analysis: IRONY

Remind students that irony is a contrast between expectation and reality.

A Ask students to identify the irony in Federigo's chivalrous claim that he is not aware the lady has ever harmed him.

Possible Response: His pursuit of her has impoverished him.

B Have students identify the dramatic irony as Monna Giovanna finally explains the reason for her visit.

Possible Response: The reader knows, but the lady does not, that she has eaten the bird she is requesting as a gift.

She knew that Federigo had been in love with her for some time now.

it, she would certainly do everything in her power to get it. After the young boy had heard her make this offer many times, he said:

1 "Mother, if you can arrange for me to have Federigo's falcon, I think I would get well quickly."

When the lady heard this, she was taken aback for a moment, and then she began thinking what she could do about it. She knew that Federigo had been in love with her for some time now, but she had never deigned to give him a second look; so, she said to herself:

"How can I go to him, or even send someone, and ask for this falcon of his, which is, as I have heard tell, the finest that ever flew, and furthermore, his only means of support? And how can I be so insensitive as to wish to take away from this nobleman the only pleasure which is left to him?"

And involved in these thoughts, knowing that she was certain to have the bird if she asked for it, but not knowing what to say to her son, she stood there without answering him. Finally the love she bore her son persuaded her that she should make him happy, and no matter what the consequences might be, she would not send for the bird, but rather go herself to fetch it and bring it back to him; so she answered her son:

"My son, cheer up and think only of getting well, for I promise you that first thing tomorrow morning I shall go and fetch it for you."

The child was so happy that he showed some improvement that very day. The following morning, the lady, accompanied by another woman, as if they were out for a stroll, went to Federigo's modest little house and asked for him. Since the weather for the past few days had not been right for hawking, Federigo happened to be in his orchard attending to certain tasks, and when he heard that Monna Giovanna was asking for him at the door, he was so surprised and happy that he rushed there; as she saw him coming, she rose to greet him with womanly grace, and once Federigo had welcomed her most courteously, she said:

"How do you do, Federigo?" Then she continued, "I have come to make amends for the harm you have suffered on my account by loving me more than you should have, and in token of this, I intend to have a simple meal with you and this companion of mine this very day."

To this Federigo humbly replied: "Madonna,[5] I have no recollection of ever suffering any harm because of you; on the contrary: so much good have I received from you that if ever I was worth anything, it was because of your worth and the love I bore for you; and your generous visit is certainly so very dear to me that I would spend all over again all that I spent in the past, but you have come to a poor host." A

And having said this, he humbly led her through the house and into his garden, and because he had no one there to keep her company, he said:

"My lady, since there is no one else, this good woman, who is the wife of the farmer here, will keep you company while I see to the table."

Though he was very poor, Federigo until now had never realized to what extent he had wasted his wealth; but this morning, the fact that he had nothing in the house with which he could honor the lady for the love of whom he had in the past entertained countless people, gave him cause to reflect: in great anguish, he cursed himself and his fortune, and like someone out of his senses he started running here and there throughout the house, but unable to find either money or anything he might be able to pawn, and since it

5. **Madonna:** Italian for "my lady," a polite form of address used in speaking to a married woman. "Monna" is a contraction of this term.

WORDS TO KNOW

deign (dān) *v.* to consider worthy of one's dignity; condescend
anguish (ăng'gwĭsh) *n.* agony

174

Teaching Options

Speaking and Listening

DRAMATIC PRESENTATION

Instruction Help students prepare a dramatic presentation using the pattern of a frame story.

Prepare Have them work in **cooperative groups** to think of ideas and to develop their stories. Remind them to agree upon a setting for their frame story before they begin to work. Challenge students to include examples of **irony** in their individual stories.

Present Allow **cooperative groups** to be creative in deciding how to make their dramatic presentations. One group may choose to improvise a story, while members of another group may wish to read aloud a story they have composed. Invite students to respond to each other's presentations.

BLOCK SCHEDULING This activity is particularly well-suited for longer class periods.

was getting late and he was still very much set on serving this noble lady some sort of meal, but unwilling to turn for help to even his own farmer (not to mention anyone else), he set his eyes upon his good falcon, which was sitting on its perch in a small room, and since he had nowhere else to turn, he took the bird, and finding it plump, he decided that it would be a worthy food for such a lady. So, without giving the matter a second thought, he wrung its neck and quickly gave it to his servant girl to pluck, prepare, and place on a spit to be roasted with care; and when he had set the table with the whitest of tablecloths (a few of which he still had left), he returned, with a cheerful face, to the lady in his garden and announced that the meal, such as he was able to prepare, was ready.

The lady and her companion rose and went to the table together with Federigo, who waited upon them with the greatest devotion, and they ate the good falcon without knowing what it was they were eating. Then, having left the table and spent some time in pleasant conversation, the lady thought it time now to say what she had come to say, and so she spoke these kind words to Federigo:

Peregrine Falcon. Raja Serfogee of Tanjore Collection, by permission of The British Library.

"Federigo, if you recall your former way of life and my virtue, which you perhaps mistook for harshness and cruelty, I have no doubt at all that you will be amazed by my presumption when you hear what my main reason for coming here is; but if you had children, through whom you might have experienced the power of parental love, I feel certain that you would, at least in part, forgive me. But, just as you have no child, I do have one, and I cannot escape the
2 laws common to all mothers; the force of such laws compels me to follow them, against my own will and against good manners and duty,
B and to ask of you a gift which I know is most precious to you; and it is naturally so, since your extreme condition has left you no other delight, no other pleasure, no other consolation; and this gift is your falcon, which my son is so taken by that if I do not bring it to him, I fear his sickness will grow so much worse that I may lose him. And therefore I beg you, not because of the love that you bear for me, which does not oblige you in the least, but because of your own nobleness, which you have shown to be greater than that of all others in practicing courtliness, that you be pleased to give it to me, so that I may say that I have saved the life of my son by means of this

WORDS TO KNOW

presumption (prĭ-zŭmp'shən) *n.* bold or outrageous behavior
compel (kəm-pĕl') *v.* to urge irresistibly; constrain
oblige (ə-blīj') *v.* to make it one's duty to act

175

Customizing Instruction

Less Proficient Readers

1 Make sure students understand why Monna Giovanna meets Federigo. Ask students the following questions.

- What happens to Monna Giovanna's son?
  Answer: He becomes ill.
- Why does the boy ask for the falcon?
  Possible Response: He believes it will make him better; he covets the bird.
- What does Monna Giovanna decide to do?
  Possible Response: She decides to go to Federigo to ask for the bird.

Set a Purpose Have students finish the story to find out if Monna Giovanna gets the falcon for her son.

Students Acquiring English

2 As students read Monna Giovanna's speech to Federigo, lead them to understand that she is not speaking of laws in the legal sense but of the laws of nature that compel a mother's love for her child.

Mini Lesson Vocabulary Strategy

UNDERSTANDING SUFFIXES

Instruction The suffixes *-ion, -tion,* and *-ation* are examples of an affix, a word part attached to a base word to make a new word. These suffixes can indicate action, a result, or a state.

Activity Write the words *conversation, presumption,* and *consolation* on the board and have students identify the base words and suffixes. Have them explain the change in the word's function or meaning when the suffix is added.

conversation	converse	-ation
presumption	presume	-tion
consolation	console	-ation

Ask students to look up the etymology of *companion* and explain why the word is not included in the list.

Use **Vocabulary Transparencies and Copymasters,** p. 25.

A lesson on the parts of a word appears on p. 1104 of the Pupil's Edition.

Reading and Analyzing

Literary Analysis PLOT

A Have students identify the falling action, or the part of the story in which the loose ends are tied up.

Possible Response: The part from the paragraph beginning "After the period of her mourning" to the end of the story.

Active Reading

ANALYZING CAUSE AND EFFECT

B Ask students what causes Monna Giovanna to marry Federigo.

Possible Response: Her brothers urge her to marry, and she admires Federigo for his kind actions.

Have students discuss the effect of the marriage on the lives of both characters.

Possible Response: They lived happily together.

Reading Skills and Strategies: COMPREHENDING

Check students' comprehension of the story ending by asking questions such as these:

- Why does Monna Giovanna commend Federigo for his deed?
  Possible Response: Because she understands it was a noble and generous gesture on his part to kill the falcon.
- What does Monna Giovanna mean when she says, "I would much rather have a man who lacks money than money that lacks a man"?
  Possible Response: She would rather have a poor man with good character than a wealthy man who lacks good qualities.

gift, and because of it I have placed him in your debt forever."

When he heard what the lady requested and knew that he could not oblige her because he had given her the falcon to eat, Federigo began to weep in her presence, for he could not utter a word in reply. The lady at first thought his tears were caused more by the sorrow of having to part with the good falcon than by anything else, and she was on the verge of telling him she no longer wished it, but she held back and waited for Federigo's reply once he stopped weeping. And he said:

"My lady, ever since it pleased God for me to place my love in you, I have felt that Fortune has been hostile to me in many ways, and I have complained of her, but all this is nothing compared to what she has just done to me, and I shall never be at peace with her again, when I think how you have come here to my poor home, where, when it was rich, you never deigned to come, and how you requested but a small gift, and Fortune worked to make it impossible for me to give it to you; and why this is so I shall tell you in a few words. When I heard that you, out of your kindness, wished to dine with me, I considered it only fitting and proper, taking into account your excellence and your worthiness, that I should honor you, according to my possibilities, with a more precious food than that which I usually serve to other people. So I thought of the falcon for which you have just asked me and of its value and I judged it a food worthy of you, and this very day I had it roasted and served to you as best I could. But seeing now that you desired it another way, my sorrow in not being able to serve you is so great that never shall I be able to console myself again."

And after he had said this, he laid the feathers, the feet, and the beak of the bird before her as proof. When the lady heard and saw this, she first reproached him for having killed a falcon such as this to serve as a meal to a woman. But then to herself she commended the greatness of his spirit, which no poverty was able, or would be able, to diminish; then, having lost all hope of getting the falcon and thus, perhaps, of improving the health of her son, she thanked Federigo both for the honor paid to her and for his good intentions, and then left in grief to return to her son. To his mother's extreme sorrow, whether in disappointment in not having the falcon or because his illness inevitably led to it, the boy passed from this life only a few days later.

After the period of her mourning and her bitterness had passed, the lady was repeatedly urged by her brothers to remarry, since she was very rich and still young; and although she did not wish to do so, they became so insistent that remembering the worthiness of Federigo and his last act of generosity—that is, to have killed such a falcon to do her honor—she said to her brothers: **A**

"I would prefer to remain a widow, if only that would be pleasing to you, but since you wish me to take a husband, you may be sure that I shall take no man other than Federigo degli Alberighi."

In answer to this, her brothers, making fun of her, replied:

"You foolish woman, what are you saying? How can you want him? He hasn't a penny to his name."

To this she replied: "My brothers, I am well aware of what you say, but I would much rather have a man who lacks money than money that lacks a man." **B**

Her brothers, seeing that she was determined and knowing Federigo to be of noble birth, no matter how poor he was, accepted her wishes and gave her with all her riches in marriage to him; when he found himself the husband of such a great lady, whom he had loved so much and who was so wealthy besides, he managed his financial affairs with more prudence than in the past and lived with her happily the rest of his days. ❖

Translated by Mark Musa and Peter Bondanella

WORDS TO KNOW
reproach (rĭ-prōch') *v.* to express disapproval of or disappointment in
commend (kə-mĕnd') *v.* to express approval of; praise

Teaching Options

Assessment **Informal Assessment**

OMITTING IRONIC TWISTS You can informally assess students' understanding of the selection by having them speculate on how the course of the story would differ if its ironic twists were omitted.

RUBRIC

3 Full Accomplishment Student writing reflects full understanding of events of story. Possible response: Monna Giovanna would have immediately asked Federigo for live falcon; he probably would have given it to her; the gift would not have saved boy's life; lady would not have married Federigo.

2 Substantial Accomplishment Student writing shows general understanding of events but may not insightfully describe how events might have differed without ironic twists.

1 Little or Partial Accomplishment Student writing displays little understanding of events or of effect of irony on plot.

Connect to the Literature

1. **What Do You Think?** What is your reaction to the events in this story?

Comprehension Check
- How does Federigo lose his fortune?
- What happens during Monna Giovanna's visit to Federigo's house?

Think Critically

2. **ACTIVE READING** ANALYZING CAUSE AND EFFECT Get together with a classmate and compare your cause-and-effect diagrams in your READER'S NOTEBOOK. What does the story's chain of events suggest about the relationship between Federigo and Monna Giovanna?

3. Do you think Federigo acts nobly or foolishly? Use evidence to support your answer.

4. What is your opinion of Monna Giovanna?

THINK ABOUT
- her response to Federigo's love for her
- her visit to Federigo's house
- her response when Federigo tells her of the bird's fate
- her reason for taking Federigo as her husband

5. What do you think is the most important **theme,** or message about human nature, conveyed by this story?

Extend Interpretations

6. **What If?** Imagine that Monna Giovanna had explained the purpose for her visit as soon as she arrived at Federigo's house. What impact, if any, would this earlier disclosure have had on Monna Giovanna's son? on Federigo? on Monna Giovanna's decision to remarry?

7. **Connect to Life** In Boccaccio's time, women of Monna Giovanna's social class were expected to be married. Do women today feel the same pressure to marry? Are women and men under equal pressure to marry? Support your opinions with examples.

8. **Points of Comparison** Money plays an important role in both "Federigo's Falcon" and Chaucer's "The Pardoner's Tale." Compare Federigo's response to money with that of the "three rioters" in Chaucer's tale. What do the characters' reactions reveal about their personalities?

Literary Analysis

PLOT A narrative's **plot** can often be traced by identifying the following four basic elements:

- **exposition,** in which the characters are introduced, the setting is established, and the major conflict is identified
- **rising action,** in which suspense builds as the conflict intensifies and complications arise
- **a climax,** or turning point, which often occurs when a main character makes an important discovery or decision
- **falling action,** which shows the results of the climax and ties up loose ends

The events that make up the plot are driven by **conflict.** In "Federigo's Falcon," the main conflict is that between Federigo and Monna Giovanna. Federigo's attempts to make Monna Giovanna fall in love with him and her indifference to him are at the heart of each element of the plot.

Cooperative Learning Activity Use the cause-and-effect diagram you made on page 171 to help you decide which events make up the exposition, the rising action, the climax, and the falling action of "Federigo's Falcon." Discuss your decisions with a group of your classmates. Then label and briefly describe the story's plot elements on a diagram like the one below.

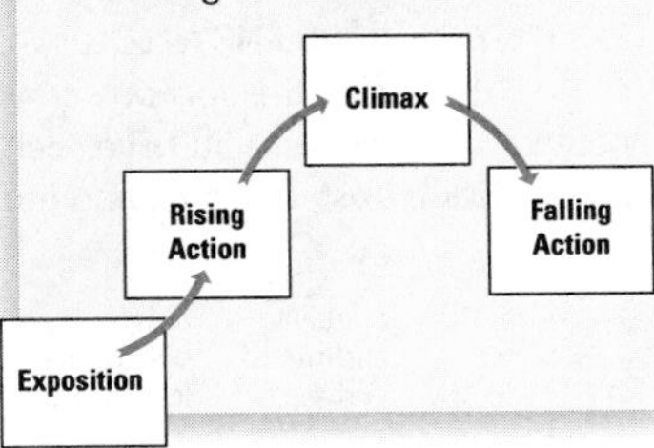

GUIDING STUDENT RESPONSE

Connect to the Literature

1. **What Do You Think?**
Guidelines for student response: Perhaps the best way into this discussion with students is the path provided by the pervasive irony in the story. If the characters knew what the reader knows, then everything might have been different. You might discuss with students the various misapprehensions and misunderstandings that contribute to the plot of this story.

Comprehension Check
- In order to win the love of Monna Giovanna, Federigo spends huge sums on banquets and tournaments, which gain him only a life of poverty.
- He serves her the roasted falcon and then learns that she had intended to ask him for the falcon as a gift for her son.

Use Selection Quiz in **Unit One Resource Book** p. 44.

Think Critically

2. Encourage students to note whether they used all information available to them when they made their cause-and-effect diagrams. Students' conclusions will vary according to their opinions of Federigo and Monna Giovanna. For example, students who find Federigo foolish may believe that each of his decisions makes his situation worse.
3. Possible Responses: nobly, because of his indifference to material wealth, his loyalty to his beloved, and his generosity; foolishly, because Monna Giovanna does not encourage his pursuit.
4. Possible Responses: Some students may find Monna Giovanna a cold, manipulative person who does not deserve Federigo's sacrifices. Others may find her a loving mother and an independent woman who, in the end, recognizes Federigo's worth.
5. Possible Responses: Students may mention a variety of possible themes, such as compassion, love, loyalty, thoughtfulness, nobility of character, purity of motive, and so forth.

Extend Interpretations

What If? Good responses will include that the son might have lived longer; that Federigo might not have had the opportunity to marry Monna Giovanna; that Monna Giovanna might not have had a change of heart to remarry.

Connect to Life Have students choose partners. The partners can discuss ideas, focusing on present-day views of love and commitment.

Points of Comparison Students' writings may reflect that although Federigo sacrificed the falcon, his most prized possession, and gained love and social position in return, the rioters demonstrated extreme greed that resulted in their deaths.

Literary Analysis

Cooperative Learning Activity Student diagrams may be displayed in the classroom.

Writing Options

1. Monna Giovanna's Diary Imagine Monna Giovanna's feelings when she discovers that she has dined on the falcon. Write a diary entry that she might compose to express her thoughts and feelings about the incident.

2. Frame Story Develop an idea for your own frame story. Using *The Decameron* as a model, determine the characters and setting of your frame, a reason for the characters to tell stories, and the duration of their storytelling. Share your ideas with other students.

3. Points of Comparison In a draft of an essay, compare and contrast Monna Giovanna's views about love and marriage with those portrayed in Chaucer's "The Wife of Bath's Tale." Include specific examples from both stories.

Writing Handbook
See page 1367: Compare and Contrast.

Activities & Explorations

1. Wedding Gift Think of the perfect wedding gift from Federigo to Monna Giovanna or from Monna Giovanna to Federigo. Then create the gift itself, or make a model or illustration of it. Keep in mind the giver's personality and financial status.
~ ART

2. Pantomime Presentation With a classmate, create a pantomime depicting Monna Giovanna's visit to Federigo's home. Make sure that your facial expressions and gestures reflect emotions appropriate to the actions.
~ PERFORMING

Inquiry & Research

1. The Art of Falconry Find out more about falcons and falconry. How does a falcon go after its prey? How is a falcon trapped and trained for sport?

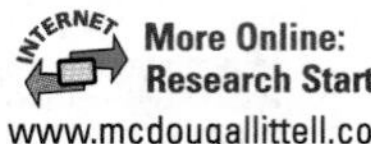

More Online: Research Starter
www.mcdougallittell.com

2. Long Ago Love Traditions Prepare an oral report on the traditions of courtly love during the Middle Ages and the Italian Renaissance. Include information on what men did to woo their ladies and how the ladies were expected to respond. You might even suggest other things Federigo might have done to win Monna Giovanna's love.

Vocabulary in Action

EXERCISE A: SYNONYMS AND ANTONYMS Classify the words in each of the following pairs as synonyms or antonyms.

1. legitimate—lawful
2. commend—blame
3. compel—force
4. reproach—compliment
5. discretion—recklessness
6. presumption—impudence
7. oblige—release
8. anguish—sorrow
9. meagerly—abundantly
10. deign—refuse

EXERCISE B: WORD KNOWLEDGE Work with a small group of classmates to devise a game show, using the vocabulary words as either clues or answers. Think about popular game shows you have seen to help you decide on a format. From your group, pick a host, a helper, and judges, and then play your game with the class.

WORDS TO KNOW				
anguish	deign	meagerly	presumption	
commend	discretion	oblige	reproach	
compel	legitimate			

Building Vocabulary
For an in-depth lesson on how to expand your vocabulary, see page 1182.

Writing Options

1. **Monna Giovanna's Diary** Students may wish to prewrite by jotting down brief responsive notes as they reread the scene.
2. **Frame Story** The students' frame stories should adapt elements from "Federigo's Falcon" into a convincing and perhaps contemporary form.
3. **Points of Comparison** Students' drafts should contrast Monna Giovanna's changing views about love and marriage with those of the Wife of Bath, who consistently wished to be married throughout her life.

Activities & Explorations

1. **Wedding Gift** Allow latitude in the choice of the gift. Students may choose a contemporary gift or a gift associated with the characters' era.
2. **Pantomime Presentation** Casting will have a major impact on the tone of the pantomime; allow parodies and more serious approaches.

Inquiry & Research

1. **The Art of Falconry** Have students conduct their research in teams, first discussing ways of finding the information. Team members should divide research tasks. Have each team decide how to present its information—in a written report, an illustrated talk, a poster, a videotape, or some other form.
2. **Long Ago Love Traditions** After students have divided the tasks and completed their research, they can meet in groups to share their findings. Encourage groups to prepare an oral report on courtly love to present to the class.

Vocabulary in Action

1. synonyms
2. antonyms
3. synonyms
4. antonyms
5. antonyms
6. synonyms
7. antonyms
8. synonyms
9. antonyms
10. antonyms

Teaching Options

Grammar

TYPES OF CONJUNCTIONS

Instruction Conjunctions connect words, phrases, and clauses. Coordinating conjunctions, such as *and, but,* and *or,* connect words or groups of words that have the same function in a sentence. Correlative conjunctions, such as *both . . . and, neither . . . nor,* and *whether . . . or,* are always used in pairs and connect parallel elements in a sentence. Other types of conjunctions are subordinating conjunctions, such as *since, where, because,* and *that,* and conjunctive adverbs, such as *nevertheless* and *furthermore.*

Activity Write these sentences on the chalkboard. Have students identify each conjunction and name its type.

- Federigo spent all his money on banquets and tournaments. (*and; coordinating*)
- While visiting Federigo, the young boy began to enjoy both birds and dogs. (*both, and; correlative*)
- The boy cried out with joy when the falcon soared through the air. (*when; subordinating*)
- Monna Giovanna was uncomfortable visiting Federigo; nevertheless she did it for her son. (*nevertheless; conjunctive adverb*)

Giovanni Boccaccio

1313–1375

Other Works
"Elegy for Fiammetta"
"Treatise in Praise of Dante"

An Overbearing Father Although Giovanni Boccaccio began writing poetry as a child, his early talent was not rewarded. Instead, his merchant father demanded that his son forget about writing and learn business. While still a teenager, he was sent from his home in Tuscany to Naples, where he was apprenticed to a banker. When he failed at banking, his father arranged for him to study religious law. Boccaccio was unsuccessful at law too, and after about 12 years in Naples, he returned home to seek other employment. None of his jobs were very satisfactory, however, and he often lived on the brink of poverty.

A Source of Inspiration Fortunately, Boccaccio had continued to write in spite of his father's objections, and even during his unsuccessful venture in Naples, he produced an abundance of prose and poetry. It was also in Naples that he may have met his beloved "Fiammetta," a young woman who became the subject of much of his early writing and whose name he used for the narrator of "Federigo's Falcon" in *The Decameron.* The real identity of this woman has never been discovered.

An Influential Poet Boccaccio complained that because his father "strove to bend" his talent, he was unable to become "a distinguished poet." Eventually, of course, he did achieve distinction as a great poet, storyteller, and scholar. Along with his friend Petrarch, an Italian poet whose writings you will encounter in Unit Two, Boccaccio helped to set new directions for Italian literature and for the study of the classical poets of ancient Rome. With the publication of *The Decameron,* he became an international celebrity. In addition to his contemporary, Chaucer, many later poets writing in English—including Shakespeare, Dryden, Keats, Longfellow, and Tennyson—have been influenced by his work.

LaserLinks: Background for Reading
Science Connection

Author Activity

Love Story Read another story about love from Boccaccio's *The Decameron.* What does the story demonstrate about love or human nature? How is the theme similar to or different from the theme of "Federigo's Falcon"?

Author Activity

Love Story Answers will vary, depending on the story selected.

Exercise Ask students to write one of the following conjunctions in each blank. Then have them identify the type of conjunction they used.

And	both	but	furthermore
nor	or	since	neither

1. Federigo was known throughout Tuscany for his fighting abilities _____ his manners. (*and; coordinating*)
2. Monna Giovanna, _____ beautiful _____ charming, was unimpressed by Federigo's exploits. (*both, and; correlative*)
3. _____ he wasted his fortune in his quest, Federigo lived in poverty at his farm in Campi. (*Since; subordinating*)
4. Monna Giovanna lost her husband; _____, she was about to lose her child. (*furthermore; conjunctive adverb*)
5. Monna Giovanna stated that she would marry no man _____ Federigo. (*but; coordinating*)

Use **Grammar Transparencies and Copymasters,** p. 73.

Use McDougal Littell's ***Language Network*** for more instruction and practice in (different in every selection).

OVERVIEW

Objectives

1. understand and appreciate **personal letters** written by landowners in 15th-century England **(Literary Analysis)**
2. identify and understand **external** and **internal conflict (Literary Analysis)**
3. evaluate the **credibility of sources (Active Reading)**

Summary

In her first letter, Margaret Paston explains to her husband, John, that she has fled the family estate at Gresham after learning that it may be attacked. In the next two letters, Margaret describes events at another Paston estate, Hellesdon. The next pair of letters concern the engagement of Margery Paston (Margaret and John's daughter) to Richard Calle, the manager of the Paston estate. The last three letters, written by Margaret and her two oldest sons, discuss financial and physical difficulties and the grim news of a rapidly spreading plague.

Use **Unit One Resource Book,** p. 45 for additional support.

Thematic Link

Amid this turmoil and uncertainty, the members of the Paston family contend with drastic changes in their **everyday lives,** such as attacks and invasions, separation from one another, and injury and illness. The letters reveal their reactions to and feelings about these challenges.

from The Paston Letters

by the PASTON FAMILY

"I beg you with all my heart that you will be kind enough to send me word how you are."

Connect to Your Life

Person to Person Make a list of the various methods you use to communicate with other people. Also list the kinds of information you exchange by each of the methods. Which method do you use most often? Might one form of communication be better than the others in a particular instance? Share your thoughts with classmates.

Focus Your Reading

LITERARY ANALYSIS CONFLICT **Conflict** is a struggle between opposing forces that moves a narrative forward. Conflict may be **external,** with a character being pitted against some outside force, or it may be **internal,** occurring within a character. In the following excerpt from a letter by Margaret to her husband, notice how she and her husband seem to be involved in a deadly dispute with enemies:

> ***I beg you with all my heart, for reverence of God, beware of Lord Moleyns and his men, however pleasantly they speak to you, and do not eat or drink with them; for they are so false that they cannot be trusted.***

As you read these letters, be aware of the various conflicts the writers experience, both in their dealings with the world as well as in their own feelings about people and events.

ACTIVE READING CREDIBILITY OF SOURCES Primary sources such as letters provide valuable insights into the thinking of people directly involved in the events they describe. As you read, you must take the writers' motives and objectivity into account when evaluating the credibility, or believability, of primary sources such as the Paston letters. Here are a couple of things to keep in mind.

- **Writer's Motives** Most of these letters deal with marriage and property. All of the people involved had different interests, both inside and outside the family. How might their interests have affected their interpretations and descriptions of people and events? For example, think about how the Pastons' views on marriage and property might influence the letters about the marriage of Margery to Richard Calle.
- **Objectivity** Is the information presented in the letters fact, opinion, or a mix of both? In reading about the disagreements between parents and child about a suitable marriage partner, for example, you must decide which statements are fact and which are opinion. Further, you must decide what motives a writer might have for holding a particular opinion.

READER'S NOTEBOOK As you read these letters, write down examples of ways in which each writer's motives might have influenced his or her description of people and events. Think about how the writer's level of objectivity might have influenced his or her interpretation of the facts.

LESSON RESOURCES

UNIT ONE RESOURCE BOOK, pp. 45–48

ASSESSMENT RESOURCES

Formal Assessment, pp. 25–26

Teacher's Guide to Assessment and Portfolio Use

Test Generator

SKILLS TRANSPARENCIES AND COPYMASTERS

Literary Analysis

- External Conflicts/Social Conflicts, T20 (for Literary Analysis, p. 180)

Reading and Critical Thinking

- Evaluating Credibility of Information Sources, T43 (for Active Reading, p. 180)

Grammar

- Simple Subjects and Simple Predicates, C79 (for Mini Lesson, p. 188)

Vocabulary

- Researching Word Origins, C27 (for Mini Lesson, p. 181)

Writing

- Compare-Contrast, C34 (for Activities & Explorations 4, p. 191)
- Opinion Statement, C35 (for Writing Option 2, p. 191)

Communications

- Impromptu Speaking: Dialogue, Role-Play, T14 (for Activities & Explorations 3, p. 191)

INTEGRATED TECHNOLOGY

Audio Library

Internet: Research Starter

Visit our website:
www.mcdougallittell.com

Build Background

Landowners and Letters The 15th century in England was a period of great unrest and lawlessness. Landowners often attacked their neighbors' estates and betrayed their political allies. The Wars of the Roses, a conflict between two royal families for control of the kingdom, ravaged England between 1455 and 1485. In addition, several outbreaks of the plague devastated many English families during the century.

A firsthand record of this turbulent era survives in the more than 1,000 surviving documents and letters of the Pastons, an English landowning family. During the early 1400s, William Paston, a lawyer, began accumulating property in Norfolk, a county of eastern England, both through purchases and through his acquisition of estates inherited by his wife, Agnes Berry. William's extensive landholdings and growing prosperity, however, made him a number of enemies. Some even challenged his claim to certain properties and brought grief to William's descendants for many years.

Business Matters In their letters, the Pastons exchanged information about their legal disputes and other problems in considerable detail. Although writing letters had become an important means of communication by the 15th century, sending the letters was not easy. They had to be delivered by hand, often by a servant or even a total stranger. Weeks might pass before a letter reached its destination, and many never arrived. Consequently, the matters discussed in letters were seldom frivolous, usually being confined to important business or family news. Despite these limitations, the Pastons wrote hundreds of letters over the course of 90 years, leaving an invaluable source of information about the social and political conditions of the times.

Family Tree A family tree traces genealogy—that is, the relationships of birth and descent in a family. The family tree on this page shows three generations of the Paston family. Before you read the letters, take some time to study these relationships. The names in red are those of the writers and recipients of the letters you will read.

Notice that William Paston and Agnes Berry had five children. The oldest, John I, inherited much of the family property when his father died in 1444, and his marriage to Margaret Mautby led to the acquisition of even more property from his wife's family. Like his father, John I was a lawyer, possessed of skills that were much needed in his constant legal battles over claims to various properties. His many legal disputes required John I to stay in London for long periods of time, leaving Margaret to manage the Paston estates. Notice also that John and Margaret's large family included two sons named John. After the death of John I, his oldest son, John II, became responsible for much of the family business, even though Margaret was still living.

As you read the letters, refer often to the Paston family tree. Doing so may help you keep in mind that the people who communicated through these letters were real human beings who had many of the same needs, hopes, and fears that people have today.

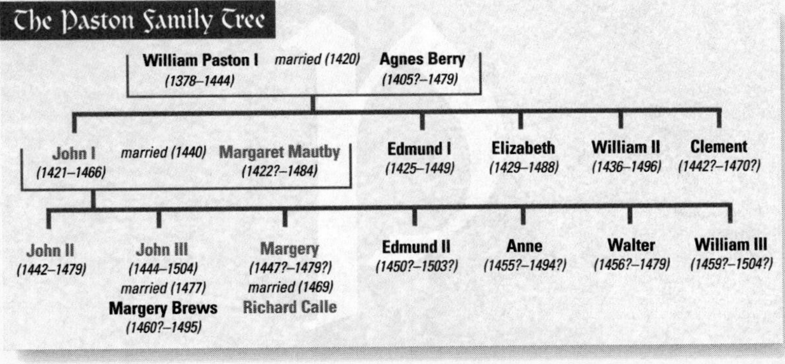

5-Minute Warm-Up

Daily Language SkillBuilder

Have students **proofread** the display sentences on page 15l and write them correctly. The sentences also appear on Transparency 4 of **Grammar Transparencies and Copymasters.**

Vocabulary Strategy

RESEARCHING WORD ORIGINS

Instruction Have students study the dictionary entry for the word *tenant* (page 185). Point out the bracketed information, which tells about the origins of the word. Ask what languages *tenant* is derived from (Old French, Latin).

Application Have students use dictionaries to determine the derivations of the words below.

1. **stuff** *(from the Old French word* estoffe, *to equip)*
2. **enquire** *(from the Old French word* enquerrer, *to seek)*
3. **alderman** *(from the Old English words* ealdorman, *meaning chief, and* eald, *meaning old)*
4. **brazier** *(from the Old English word* broesen (or broes), *meaning brass)*
5. **writ** *(an Old English word meaning a written order issued by a court, derived from the Old English verb* writan, *to write)*

Use **Vocabulary Transparencies and Copymasters,** p. 27.

A lesson on researching word origins appears on p. 206 of the Pupil's Edition.

TEACHING THE LITERATURE

Reading and Analyzing

Literary Analysis CONFLICT

A Ask students what struggles Margaret Paston describes in the first paragraph of her letter to her husband. Encourage students to identify struggles involving other people (external conflicts) and those occurring within the writer (internal conflicts).

Possible Responses: external conflicts—Margaret versus Lord Moleyns's men, the Pastons versus Lord Moleyns; internal conflicts—Margaret's fear of angering her husband versus her fear of the kidnappers, Margaret's concern for her husband versus her displeasure at not hearing from him.

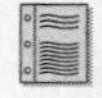

Use **Unit One Resource Book,** p. 47 for more exercises.

Active Reading

EVALUATING CREDIBILITY OF SOURCES

Discuss with students whether the following statements are facts or opinions:

- "They let me know that various of Lord Moleyns' men said that if they could get their hands on me they would carry me off and keep me in the castle."
  Possible Response: Margaret describes an ally's opinion about what may happen to Margaret. Remind students that a factual event must have already taken place.
- "Nobody in the place knew that I was leaving except the lady of the house, until an hour before I went."
  Possible Response: Students will probably consider this to be a fact. Details are specific and verifiable.

Use **Unit One Resource Book,** p. 46 for more practice.

Women defending castle

from THE PASTON LETTERS

Margaret Paston, in the absence of her husband, John I, was able to deal equally well with small housekeeping problems and with family disasters, including attacks against the Paston manors. While she was living at the Paston estate of Gresham, it was attacked by a Lord Moleyns, who claimed rights to the property and ejected Margaret from her home. Margaret first escaped to a friend's house about a mile away; but later, fearing that Moleyns's band of men might kidnap her, she fled to the city of Norwich, where she wrote the following letter to her husband.

Teaching Options

Workplace Link — Business Letters

Because the Pastons were landowners, their primary business was the management of their property. This concern dominates their correspondence. Written communication between people engaged in business has been important for hundreds of years, though the method of transmittal has evolved from messengers on foot to horseback riders to mail carriers to fax machines and, most recently, to electronic mail.

On the chalkboard, outline the standard form for business letters. (Remind students that the format for electronic mail can be more informal but that faxed letters should be in standard form.) Have students work in pairs to compose a business letter and a reply. Review with students various kinds of business letters, such as letters that request information about a product or service, letters expressing satisfaction or dissatisfaction with a product or service, and job application letters. Remind students to write in a clear, simple style and to use a formal, polite tone.

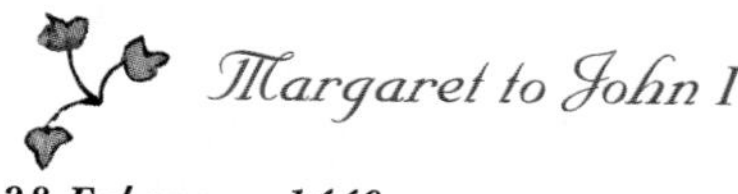

Margaret to John I

28 February 1449

A *Right worshipful husband,* I commend myself to you, wishing with all my heart to hear that you are well, and begging that you will not be angry at my leaving the place where you left me. On my word, such news was brought to me by various people who are sympathetic to you and me that I did not dare stay there any longer. I will tell you who the people were when you come home. They let me know that various of Lord Moleyns' men said that if they could get their hands on me they would carry me off and keep me in the castle. They wanted you to get me out again, and said that it would not cause you much heart-ache. After I heard this news, I could not rest easy until I was here, and I did not dare go out of the place where I was until I was ready to ride away. Nobody in the place knew that I was leaving except the lady of the house, until an hour before I went. And I told her that I would come here to have clothes made for myself and the children, which I wanted made, and said I thought I would be here a fortnight[1] or three weeks. Please keep the reason for my departure a secret until I talk to you, for those who warned me do not on any account want it known.

I spoke to your mother as I came this way, and she offered to let me stay in this town, if you agree. She would very much like us to stay at her place, and will send me such things as she can spare so that I can set up house until you can get a place and things of your own to set up a household. Please let me know by the man who brings this what you would like me to do. I would be very unhappy to live so close to Gresham as I was until this matter is completely settled between you and Lord Moleyns.

Barow[2] told me that there was no better evidence in England than that Lord Moleyns has for [his title to] the manor of Gresham. I told him that I supposed the evidence was of the kind that William Hasard said yours was, and that the seals were not yet cold.[3] That, I said, was what I expected his lord's evidence to be like. I said I knew that your evidence was such that no one could have better evidence, and the seals on it were two hundred years older than he was. Then Barow said to me that if he came to London while you were there he would have a drink with you, to quell any anger there was between you. He said that he only acted as a servant, and as he was ordered to do. Purry[4] will tell you about the conversation between Barow and me when I came from Walsingham. I beg you with all my heart, for reverence of God, beware of Lord Moleyns and his men, however pleasantly they speak to you, and do not eat or drink with them; for they are so false that they cannot be trusted. And please take care when you eat or drink in any other men's company, for no one can be trusted.

I beg you with all my heart that you will be kind enough to send me word how you are, and how your affairs are going, by the man who brings this. I am very surprised that you do not send me more news than you have done. . . .

1. **fortnight:** two weeks.
2. **Barow:** one of Lord Moleyns's men.
3. **seals . . . cold:** A seal, often made by impressing a family emblem on hot wax, was placed on a document to show its authenticity. Margaret is suggesting that Lord Moleyns's documents are recent forgeries.
4. **Purry:** perhaps a servant or tenant of the Pastons.

Customizing Instruction

Less Proficient Readers

Have students create a chart for each letter in the selection and fill in the charts as they read.

Writer/ Receiver of Letter	Summary of Information in the Letter	Conflicts Described in the Letter

Students Acquiring English

Explain that the language used in 15th-century letters was more formal than that used today. Read aloud some examples, such as "I beg you with all my heart that you will be kind enough to send me word how you are," and have students give the modern equivalent.

Possible Response: How are you? Please let me know if you're all right.

Guide students to identify additional formal phrases and to discuss their modern equivalents.

Use **Spanish Study Guide** for additional support, pp. 28–30

Gifted and Talented

As students read the Paston letters, ask them to imagine that the Pastons live in the contemporary world and that they own a successful business. What similar problems would they face in modern society? What new problems would they encounter? How would modern life affect relationships within the family? Have students rewrite one of the letters using a contemporary setting and point of view.

Cross Curricular Link History

SEALS AND STAMPS Ask students what they have learned from Margaret's letter about mail delivery in late 15th-century England.

Possible Response: Servants carried letters back and forth between sender and recipient.

Explain that great care was taken to prevent a letter from being opened by someone other than the addressee. The letter was folded, fastened by a paper strap, wrapped once with silk thread or string, and then sealed with wax. Well-to-do families often used custom-made stamps to apply wax to their letters. These stamps featured unique designs—a coat of arms, for example—that identified the sender's family. Such seals were decorative, but, more important, they functioned as a safeguard against unauthorized reading. If broken by an outsider, the family seal could not be restored without the original stamp.

Reading and Analyzing

Literary Analysis CONFLICT

(A) Ask students what new struggles are revealed or suggested in the second paragraph.

Possible Response: The number of enemies conspiring against the Pastons seems to be growing. Margaret seems to have been attacked, although the nature of the attack—verbal or physical—remains unclear.

Then ask students how Margaret's account of these new threats affects their impression of her.

Possible Response: She seems brave, but also more lonely and vulnerable.

Literary Analysis: WRITER'S CRAFT

(B) Remind students that a writer's craft, also known as style, is not *what* is said but *how* it is said. Many elements contribute to style, including word choice, sentence structure, figurative language, and point of view.

Ask students to describe the style of Margaret Paston's writing as it is demonstrated in her plea to her husband to obtain an order for the release of Robert Lovegold.

Possible Response: Plain, matter-of-fact, businesslike.

Literary Analysis: TONE

(C) Review with students that tone is the writer's attitude toward a character, a subject, or the reader. Ask students how Margaret's repeated use of the phrase "For the reverence of God," in the letter on page 185, affects the tone of her letter.

Possible Responses: It makes the message seem very urgent and serious; it suggests that Margaret is growing more impatient with her husband.

In 1465, in still another property dispute, the Paston estate of Hellesdon was attacked by the duke of Suffolk, who had gained the support of several local officials. Although Margaret and John were not living at Hellesdon at the time, many of their servants and tenants suffered from the extensive damage. In the following two letters, Margaret tells her husband about the devastation.

Margaret to John I

17 October 1465

. . . On Tuesday morning John Botillere, also John Palmer, Darcy Arnald your cook and William Malthouse of Aylsham were seized at Hellesdon by the bailiff[5] of Eye, called Bottisforth, and taken to Costessey,[6] and they are being kept there still without any warrant or authority from a justice of the peace; and they say they will carry them off to Eye prison and as many others of your men and tenants as they can get who are friendly towards you or have supported you, and they threaten to kill or imprison them.

(A) The duke came to Norwich at 10 o'clock on Tuesday with five hundred men and he sent for the mayor, aldermen and sheriffs, asking them in the king's name that they should enquire of the constables of every ward within the city which men had been on your side or had helped or supported your men at the time of any of these gatherings and if they could find any they should take them and arrest them and punish them; which the mayor did, and will do anything he can for him and his men. (B) At this the mayor has arrested a man who was with me, called Robert Lovegold, a brazier,[7] and threatened him that he shall be hanged by the neck. So I would be glad if you could get a writ sent down for his release, if you think it can be done. He was only with me when Harlesdon[8] and others attacked me at Lammas.[9] He is very true and faithful to you, so I would like him to be helped. I have no one attending me who dares to be known, except Little John. William Naunton is here with me, but he dares not be known because he is much threatened. I am told that the old lady and the duke have been frequently set against us by what Harlesdon, the bailiff of Costessey, Andrews and Doget the bailiff's son and other false villains have told them, who want this affair pursued for their own pleasure; there are evil rumors about it in this part of the world and other places.

As for Sir John Heveningham, Sir John Wyndefeld and other respectable men, they have been made into their catspaws,[10] which will not do their reputation any good after this, I think. . . .

The lodge and remainder of your place was demolished on Tuesday and Wednesday, and the duke rode on Wednesday to Drayton and then to Costessey while the lodge at Hellesdon was being demolished. Last night at midnight Thomas Slyford, Green, Porter and John Bottisforth the bailiff of Eye and others got a cart and took away the featherbeds and all the stuff of ours that was left at the parson's and Thomas Water's house for safe-keeping. I will send you lists later, as accurately as I can, of the things we have lost. Please let me know what you want me to do, whether you want me to stay at Caister[11] or come to you in London.

I have no time to write any more. God have you in his keeping. Written at Norwich on St. Luke's eve.[12]

M.P.

5. **bailiff:** the manager of an estate.
6. **Costessey:** an estate owned by the duke of Suffolk.
7. **brazier** (brā′zhər): person who makes articles of brass.
8. **Harlesdon:** one of the duke of Suffolk's men.
9. **Lammas:** a religious feast that was celebrated on August 1.
10. **catspaws:** people who are deceived and used as tools by others.
11. **Caister:** one of the Paston estates.
12. **St. Luke's eve:** the eve of St. Luke's Day, a religious feast. Writers often dated letters in this way instead of using days and months.

Teaching Options

BLOCK SCHEDULING: MANAGING TIME

If your schedule requires that you cover the lesson objectives in a shorter time, use . . .

- Preparing to Read, pp. 180–181
- Thinking Through the Literature, p. 190

If you want to take advantage of longer class time, use . . .

- TE Teaching Options: Vocabulary, p. 181; Workplace Link, p. 182; CrossCurricular Links, pp. 183; 185; 186; Speaking and Listening, p. 187; Grammar, p. 188; Informal Assessment, p. 189
- Choices and Challenges, p. 191

Margaret to John I

27 October 1465

. . . I was at Hellesdon last Thursday and saw the place there, and indeed no one can imagine what a horrible mess it is unless they see it. Many people come out each day, both from Norwich and elsewhere, to look at it, and they talk of it as a great shame. The duke would have done better to lose £1000 than to have caused this to be done, and you have all the more goodwill from people because it has been done so foully. And they made your tenants at Hellesdon and Drayton, and others, help them to break down the walls of both the house and the lodge: God knows, it was against their will, but they did not dare do otherwise for fear. I have spoken with your tenants both at Hellesdon and Drayton, and encouraged them as best I can.

The duke's men ransacked the church, and carried off all the goods that were left there, both ours and the tenants, and left little behind; they stood on the high altar and ransacked the images, and took away everything they could find. They shut the parson out of the church until they had finished, and ransacked everyone's house in the town five or six times. The ringleaders in the thefts were the bailiff of Eye and the bailiff of Stradbroke, Thomas Slyford. And Slyford was the leader in robbing the church and, after the bailiff of Eye, it is he who has most of the proceeds of the robbery. As for the lead, brass, pewter, iron, doors, gates, and other household stuff, men from Costessey and Cawston have got it, and what they could not carry they hacked up in the most spiteful fashion. If possible, I would like some reputable men to be sent for from the king, to see how things are both there and at the lodge, before any snows come, so that they can report the truth, because otherwise it will not be so plain as it is now. For reverence of God, finish your business now, for the expense and trouble we have each day is horrible, and it will be like this until you have finished; and your men dare not go around collecting your rents, while we keep here every day more than twenty people to save ourselves and the place; for indeed, if the place had not been strongly defended, the duke would have come here. . . . C

For the reverence of God, if any respectable and profitable method can be used to settle your business, do not neglect it, so that we can get out of these troubles and the great costs and expenses we have and may have in future. It is thought here that if my lord of Norfolk would act on your behalf, and got a commission to enquire into the riots and robberies committed on you and others in this part of the world, then the whole county will wait on him and do as you wish, for people love and respect him more than any other lord, except the king and my lord of Warwick. . . .

Please do let me know quickly how you are and how your affairs are going, and let me know how your sons are. I came home late last night, and will be here until I hear from you again. Wykes came home on Saturday, but he did not meet your sons.

God have you in his keeping and send us good news from you. Written in haste on the eve of St. Simon and St. Jude.

By yours, M.P.

Customizing Instruction

Less Proficient Readers

Monitor comprehension Make sure that students understand the content of the letters between Margaret and John I. Use the following questions:

- What event prompted Margaret to write this letter to her husband?
  Possible Response: The family estate of Hellesdon had been attacked.
- What did the attackers do to the estate and to the people living there?
  Possible Response: Buildings were destroyed; valuables and furnishings were stolen; people were imprisoned.
- How do you think the raids on the Paston estates made Margaret feel?
  Possible Response: Afraid, angry.

Students Acquiring English

As students read, help them identify the antecedents of personal pronouns in the passage. In this sentence, *them* refers to the tenants on the Paston estates.

This letter contains lengthy sentences that may be confusing to students. Help them break down long, complex sentences into a series of short, simple sentences, paraphrasing when necessary.
Possible Response: Perhaps my lord of Norfolk would act on your behalf and look into the riots and robberies committed on you and others here. The whole county may then wait on him and do as you wish. After all, people love and respect him more than any other lord except the king and my lord of Warwick . . .

Cross Curricular Link Economics

THE VALUE OF MONEY Direct students' attention to Margaret's comment that "The duke would have done better to lose £1000 than to have caused this [destruction to our estate] to be done. . . ." Explain that one thousand pounds was a vast sum in the 15th century. Even in Victorian times, 400 years later, it would have constituted a respectable yearly income for a middle-class professional or a minor member of the aristocracy.

Cross Curricular Link History

LORD OF THE MANOR Under the feudal system, land was owned by the lord of a manor, or estate. The local church and village, including private dwellings, were typically situated on manor lands and therefore considered the landowner's property. Thus, as part of his attack on the Paston estate, the duke of Suffolk directs his men to ransack the church and the houses in town.

Reading and Analyzing

Active Reading

EVALUATING CREDIBILITY OF SOURCES

Guide students to evaluate Richard Calle's credibility by asking the following questions:

- What are some of Richard's motives for writing to Margery?
  Possible Responses: He wants to express his love for her; he wants to assure her that he has been trying to communicate with her; he wants to receive reassurance that she loves him; he wants her to tell her mother the truth about their relationship.
- Do you think Richard's letter contains objective information? Why or why not?
  Possible Response: Students may find that his letter appeals to Margery's emotions rather than to her intelligence. Students will also note that the letter is full of exaggeration.

Reading Strategy:
MAKING INFERENCES

A Explain to students that, during the Middle Ages, a woman became the property of the man she married. If her parents approved of the marriage, they would give the new husband a dowry consisting of money and often property. It was important, therefore, for a son to marry a wealthy woman if the family hoped to gain financially from the union. Have students explain the meaning of the sentence "Also their honor does not depend on your marriage, but in their own marriage [that is, John II's]." Then ask students what this statement suggests about marriage in the medieval period.
Possible Response: It was more important for the son, as bearer of the family name and the inheritor of his wife's dowry, to marry well.

During the fifteenth century, most marriages among the upper classes were arranged by families, usually to strengthen economic or political ties. The Paston family was greatly alarmed, therefore, when they learned that Margery, a daughter of Margaret and John I, had secretly become engaged to the Paston bailiff Richard Calle. Eventually, the two were married in spite of bitter opposition from Margery's family. In the following letter to Margery—the only piece of their correspondence to survive—Richard expresses his feelings about their predicament. The next letter is the response of Margery's mother, Margaret, to the situation, written to her son, John II.

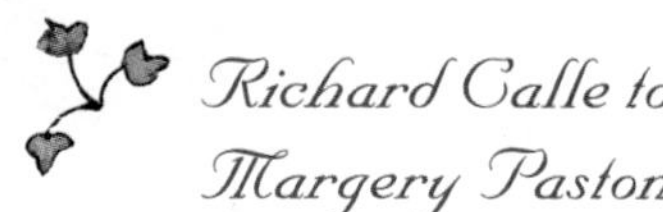

Richard Calle to Margery Paston

Spring-Summer 1469

My own lady and mistress, and indeed my true wife before God,[13] I commend myself to you with a very sad heart as a man who cannot be cheerful and will not be until things stand otherwise with us than they do now. This life that we lead now pleases neither God nor the world, considering the great bond of matrimony that is made between us, and also the great love that has been, and I trust still is, between us, and which for my part was never greater. So I pray that Almighty God will comfort us as soon as it pleases him, for we who ought by rights to be most together are most apart; it seems a thousand years since I last spoke to you. I would rather be with you than all the wealth in the world. Alas, also, good lady, those who keep us apart like this, scarcely realize what they are doing: those who hinder matrimony are cursed in church four times a year. It makes many men think that they can stretch a point of conscience in other matters as well as this one. But whatever happens, lady, bear it as you have done and be as cheerful as you can, for be sure, lady, that God in the long run will of his righteousness help his servants who mean to be true and want to live according to his laws.

I realize, lady, that you have had as much sorrow on my account as any gentlewoman has ever had in this world; I wish to God that all the sorrow you have had had fallen on me, so that you were freed of it; for indeed, lady, it kills me to hear that you are being treated otherwise than you should be. This is a painful life we lead; I cannot imagine that we live like this without God being displeased by it.

You will want to know that I sent you a letter from London by my lad, and he told me he could not speak to you, because so great a watch was kept on both you and him. He told me that John Thresher came to him in your name, and said that you had sent him to my lad for a letter or token which you thought I had sent you; but he did not trust him and would not deliver anything to him. After that he brought a ring, saying that you sent it to him, commanding him to deliver the letter or token to him, which I gather since then from my 1
lad was not sent by you, but was a plot of my mistress [i.e., Margaret Paston] and James Gloys.[14] Alas, what do they intend? I suppose they think we are not engaged; and if this is the case I am very surprised, for they are not being sensible, remembering how plainly I told my mistress about everything at the beginning, and I think you have told her so too, if you have done as you should. And if you have denied it, as I have been told you have done, it was done neither with a good conscience nor to the pleasure of God, unless you did it for fear and to please those who were with you at the time. If this was the reason you did it, it was justified, considering how insistently you were

13. **my true wife before God:** In the 1400's, the spoken vow of a man and woman, even without a witness, was regarded as an official marriage.
14. **James Gloys:** the Paston family chaplain.

Teaching Options

Cross Curricular Link History

COURTSHIP Students may be struck by the intense ardor expressed in Richard Calle's letter to Margery. Explain that excessive flattery and hyperbole—"I would rather be with you than all the wealth in the world"—was a convention of courtship during the Middle Ages. Students may be familiar with the term "courtly love," in which a lady is wooed, usually from a distance, by a suitor who regards himself as the lady's "servant" and who idealizes—even worships—the object of his love. Point out that, in the case of Richard and Margery, the suitor is of a lower social class than his beloved, and therefore defers to her all the more. Still, women, even those of the nobility, had far fewer rights than men. Wives, for example, were considered the property of their husbands, and many men gained wealth through marriage: parents who approved of their daughter's marriage would offer a dowry of money and property to their new son-in-law. Because Margery's parents disapproved of the marriage, Margery surrendered her privilege, wealth, and social status as a landowner's daughter.

called on to deny it; and you were told many untrue stories about me, which, God knows, I was never guilty of.

My lad told me that your mother asked him if he had brought any letter to you, and she accused him falsely of many other things; among other things, she said to him in the end that I would not tell her about it at the beginning, but she expected that I would at the ending. As for that, God knows that she knew about it first from me and no one else. I do not know what my mistress means, for in truth there is no other gentlewoman alive who I respect more than her and whom I would be more sorry to displease, saving only yourself who by right I ought to cherish and love best, for I am bound to do so by God's law and will do so while I live, whatever may come of it. I expect that if you tell them the sober truth, they will not damn their souls for our sake. Even if I tell them the truth they will not believe me as much as they would you. And so, good lady, for reverence of God be plain with them and tell the truth, and if they will not agree, let it be between them, God and the devil; and as for the peril we should be in, I pray God it may lie on them and not on us. I am very sad and sorry when I think of their attitude. God guide them and send them rest and peace.

I am very surprised that they are as concerned about this affair as I gather that they are, in view of the fact that nothing can be done about it, and that I deserve better; from any point of view there should be no obstacles to it. Also their honor does not depend on your marriage, but in their own marriage [i.e., John II's]; I pray God send them a marriage which will be to their honor, to God's pleasure and to their heart's ease, for otherwise it would be a great pity.

Mistress, I am frightened of writing to you, for I understand that you have showed the letters that I have sent you before to others, but I beg you, let no one see this letter. As soon as you have read it, burn it, for I would not want anyone to see it. You have had nothing in writing from me for two years, and I will not send you any more: so I leave everything to your wisdom. 2

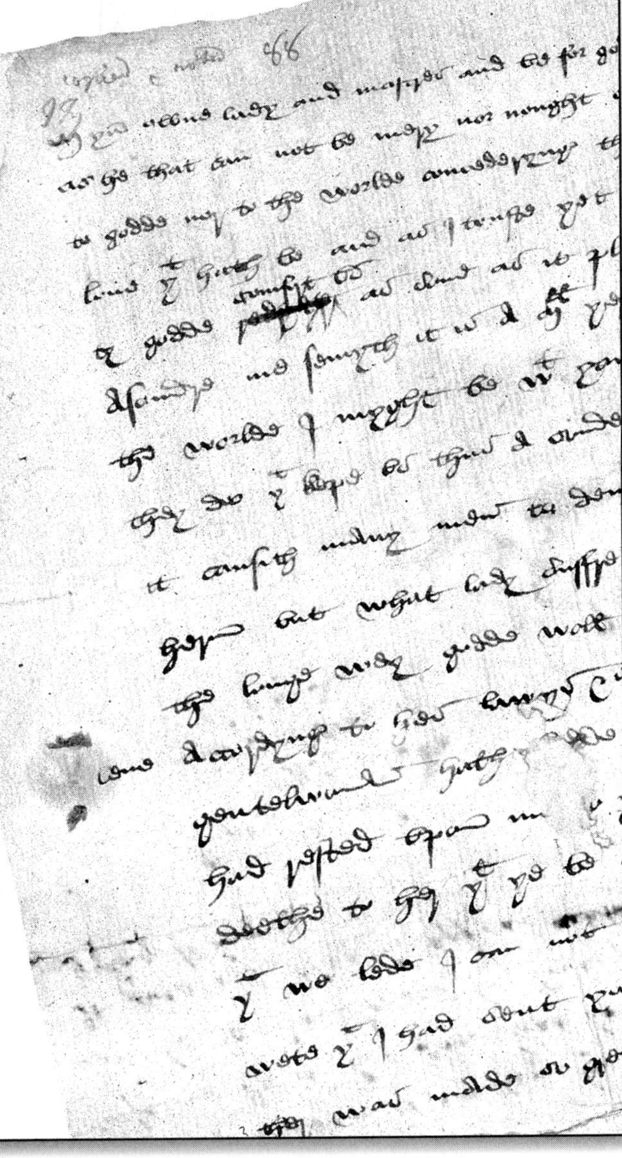

Letter from Richard Calle to Margery Paston, 1469

Customizing Instruction

Students Acquiring English

1 Students may be confused by the sequence of events described in this passage. Guide students to understand that Margaret Paston's "plot" was apparently designed to intercept Richard's letter to Margery. Help students see the distinction between the use of "plot" in this passage and the meaning of "plot" in a literary work.

Multiple Learning Styles

Auditory Learners

Invite several students to prepare readings of the letter's last three paragraphs. Assign each student a different tone of voice or attitude, or allow them to choose one of their own. (Some possible tones include sarcastic, timid, suspicious, and loving.) Have students perform dramatic readings for the class.

Less Proficient Readers

2 Prompt students to discuss the situation and series of events Richard Calle describes in his letter. Use these questions:

- How long have Richard and Margery been apart?
  Answer: Two years.
- Richard claims to have sent a letter to Margery from London. What happened to the letter? Was it answered?
  Possible Response: Margery was being too closely watched for Richard's servant to deliver the letter; one of the Pastons' men came to Richard's servant with a letter and then with a ring, claiming that they were from Margery; the servant denied the tokens, believing them to be sent by Margaret Paston as a trick.

Mini Lesson Speaking and Listening

ORAL HISTORY

Instruction Explain that today recording oral history is a good way to store firsthand information about an event or a historical period. This information can be gathered by interviewing people who lived through an event or a period. The interviewer prepares a list of questions designed to elicit detailed responses. Then he or she sits down with the eyewitness and records the interview, either by taking notes or by using a tape recorder.

Prepare Invite students to collect information on their own family or neighborhood histories. Have them interview at least one family member, asking questions about family life in the past.

Present Have students make a brief presentation describing how listening to the stories of others helped them understand their family or neighborhood histories.

BLOCK SCHEDULING This activity is particularly well-suited for longer class periods.

Reading and Analyzing

Reading Skills and Strategies: SPECULATING

A Remind students that Margery's marriage to Richard, an employee of the Pastons, would, in Margaret and John Paston's view, bring dishonor to their daughter and to her family. Then ask students why Margaret is so angry with her daughter.

Possible Responses: Margaret may have just learned that Margery and Richard are engaged; Margaret may be angry because Margery has received a letter from Richard.

What might Margaret mean when she refers to "the day in question"?

Possible Response: Margery's wedding day.

Active Reading

EVALUATING CREDIBILITY OF SOURCES

After students have read Margaret's letters to John II, discuss students' evolving opinions of Margaret. Have her motives become clearer? Have they changed? Have her values shifted? Does she seem more or less credible than she did in her first letter to her husband? Why?

Possible Response: Students may find Margaret more self-centered and desperate in these later letters. They may observe that what appeared earlier to be an admirable desire to protect her family has now become a selfish desire to retain her possessions and maintain her social status.

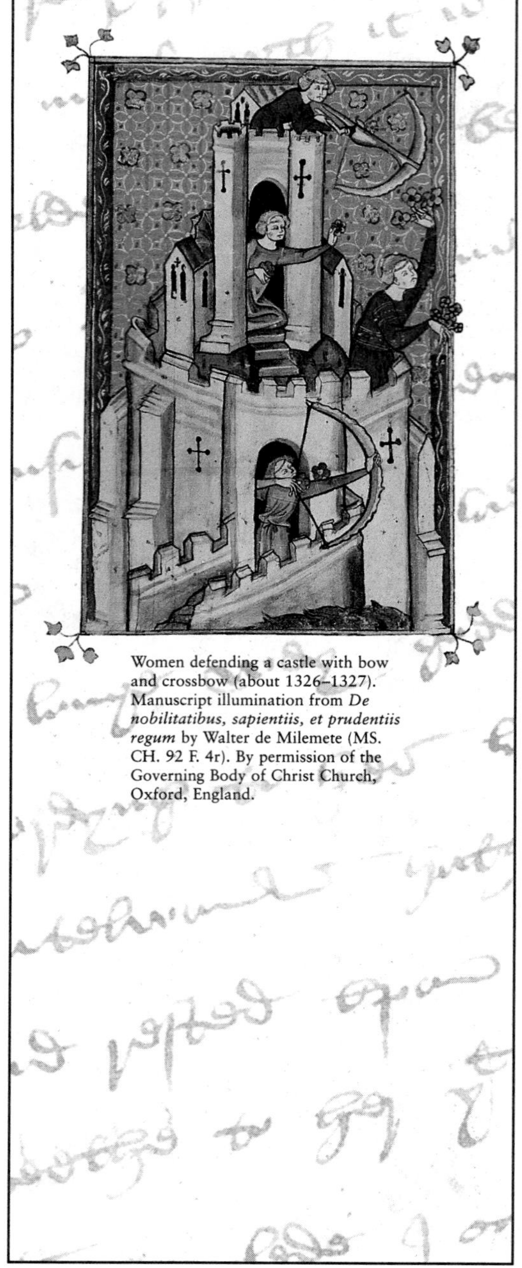

Women defending a castle with bow and crossbow (about 1326–1327). Manuscript illumination from *De nobilitatibus, sapientiis, et prudentiis regum* by Walter de Milemete (MS. CH. 92 F. 4r). By permission of the Governing Body of Christ Church, Oxford, England.

Almighty Jesu preserve, keep and give you your heart's desire, which I am sure will please God. This letter was written with as great difficulty as I ever wrote anything in my life, for I have been very ill, and am not yet really recovered, may God amend it.

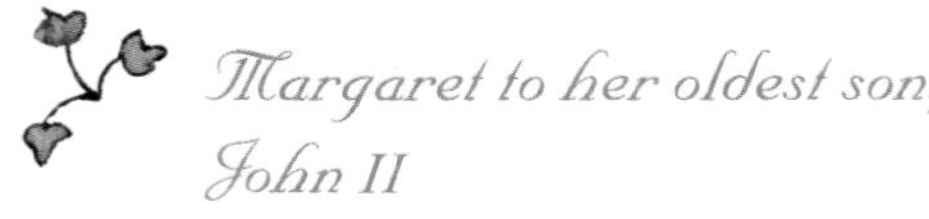

Margaret to her oldest son, John II

10 September 1469

. . . When I heard how she [Margery] had behaved, I ordered my servants that she was not to be allowed in my house. I had warned her, and she might have taken heed if she had been well-disposed. I sent messages to one or two others that they should not let her in if she came. She was brought back to my house to be let in, and James Gloys told those who brought her that I had ordered them all that she should not be allowed in. **A** So my lord of Norwich has lodged her at Roger Best's, to stay there until the day in question; God knows it is much against his will and his wife's, but they dare not do otherwise. I am sorry that they are burdened with her, but I am better off with her there than somewhere else, because he and his wife are sober and well-disposed to us, and she will not be allowed to play the good-for-nothing there.

Please do not take all this too hard, because I know that it is a matter close to your heart, as it is to mine and other people's; but remember, as I do, that we have only lost a good-for-nothing in her, and take it less to heart: if she had been any good, whatever might have happened, things would not have been as they are, for even if he[15] were dead now, she would never be as close to me as she was. . . . You can be sure that she will regret her foolishness afterwards, and I pray to God that she does. Please, for my sake, be cheerful about all this. I trust that God will help us; may he do so in all our affairs. . . .

15. **he:** Richard Calle.

Teaching Options

Mini Lesson Grammar

IMPERATIVE SENTENCES AND THE UNDERSTOOD SUBJECT

Instruction An imperative sentence gives a command, request, or direction. The subject of such a sentence is usually not stated but is understood to be the pronoun *you.* Provide students with these examples:

Stated subject: You should pay more attention to your expenses.

Understood subject: Pay more attention to your expenses.

Exercise Have students scan the Paston letters for imperative sentences.

Activity: Write the sentences they find on the chalkboard. Then have students rewrite the following as imperative sentences with understood subjects:

1. You should not take all this too hard, because I know that it is a matter close to your heart. *(Do not take all this too hard. I know that it is a matter close to your heart.)*
2. For my sake, I want you to be cheerful about all this. *(For my sake, be cheerful about all this.)*

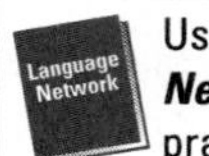

Use McDougal Littell's ***Language Network*** for more instruction and practice in (different in every selection).

Although the Pastons were considered wealthy, they faced continual struggles. They even experienced occasional financial difficulties, particularly after the death of John I in 1466. John II, though frequently in London to deal with family legal matters, seems at times to have paid more attention to his own interests. The Pastons were also affected by the ravages of warfare and disease. The following three letters deal with some of their hardships.

Margaret to John II

28 October 1470

. . . Unless you pay more attention to your expenses, you will bring great shame on yourself and your friends, and impoverish them so that none of us will be able to help each other, to the great encouragement of our enemies.

Those who claim to be your friends in this part of the world realize in what great danger and need you stand, both from various of your friends and from your enemies. It is rumored that I have parted with so much to you that I cannot help either you or any of my friends, which is no honor to us and causes people to esteem us less. At the moment it means that I must disperse my household and lodge somewhere, which I would be very loath to do if I were free to choose. It has caused a great deal of talk in this town and I would not have needed to do it if I had held back when I could. So for God's sake pay attention and be careful from now on, for I have handed over to you both my own property and your father's, and have held nothing back, either for myself or for his sake. . . .

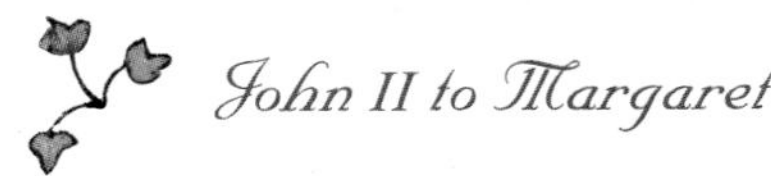

John II to Margaret

April 1471

Mother, I commend myself to you and let you know, blessed be God, my brother John is alive and well, and in no danger of dying. Nevertheless he is badly hurt by an arrow in his right arm below the elbow, and I have sent a surgeon to him, who has dressed the wound; and he tells me that he hopes he will be healed within a very short time. John Mylsent is dead. God have mercy on his soul; William Mylsent is alive and all his other servants seem to have escaped. . . .

John II to John III

15 September 1471

. . . Please send me word if any of our friends or well-wishers are dead, for I fear that there is great mortality in Norwich and in other boroughs and towns in Norfolk: I assure you that it is the most widespread plague I ever knew of in England, for by my faith I cannot hear of pilgrims going through the country nor of any other man who rides or goes anywhere, that any town or borough in England is free from the sickness. May God put an end to it, when it please him. So, for God's sake, get my mother to take care of my younger brothers and see that they are not anywhere where the sickness is prevalent, and that they do not amuse themselves with other young people who go where the sickness is. If anyone has died of the sickness, or is infected with it, in Norwich, for God's sake let her send them to some friend of hers in the country; I would advise you to do the same. I would rather my mother moved her household into the country. . . . ❖

Customizing Instruction

Less Proficient Readers

Ask these questions to check students' comprehension of the letters about Margery Paston and Richard Calle.

- Why must Margery and Richard live apart?
  Answer: Margery's parents oppose their engagement.
- Why doesn't Richard plan to write any more letters to Margery?
  Possible Responses: He's afraid the letters will be intercepted by Margery's parents; he wants Margery to tell her parents the truth about their relationship.
- Why does Margaret call Margery a "good-for-nothing" in her letter to her son?
  Possible Response: Margaret has found out about her daughter's engagement.

Students Acquiring English

Use these questions to help students understand Margaret's relationship with her son John II.

- Why does Margaret have to disperse her household?
  Answer: She has given so much money to her son that she cannot afford to maintain a large house.
- Why does John II want his mother to move to the country?
  Answer: To escape the plague.

Gifted and Talented

Invite students to research the plague in late 15th-century England. Then challenge them to write a letter of response from John III to John II. Ask them to include in the letter several facts they discovered in their research.

Assessment: Informal Assessment

WRITE A LETTER Have students imagine that they are members of the Paston family living two or more generations after the letter writers. They have discovered the letters in a box. Ask each student to write a letter to another latter-generation member of the Paston family (a cousin, for example). In each letter, the writer should (1) elaborate on what he or she has learned, (2) list remaining questions, and (3) offer an opinion of the credibility of the old letters and of those who wrote them.

RUBRIC

3 Full Accomplishment Students accurately convey substantial information gained from the letters, provide intriguing questions and opinions, and give a valid assessment of the letters' and letter-writers' credibility.

2 Substantial Accomplishment Students convey a moderate amount of accurate information. Questions, opinions, and evaluation of credibility are relevant but unoriginal.

1 Little or Partial Accomplishment Students convey little precise information from the letters, include few cogent questions and opinions, and offer an unsupported evaluation of credibility.

Connect to the Literature

1. **What Do You Think?** What is your impression of the events described in the Paston family letters?

Comprehension Check
- What did the duke of Suffolk do when he arrived at the Paston estate of Hellesdon?
- Why did Margery Paston's family oppose her marriage to Richard Calle?

Think Critically

2. How would you describe Margaret Paston?

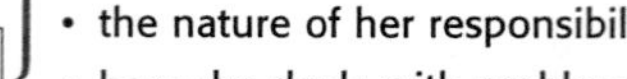

THINK ABOUT
- the **tone** she communicates in her letters
- the nature of her responsibilities
- how she deals with problems
- her relationships with her husband and her children

3. What advice might you give Richard Calle and Margery Paston for dealing with their predicament?

4. ACTIVE READING CREDIBILITY OF SOURCES Look back at the examples you wrote in your READER'S NOTEBOOK. On the basis of your reading of these letters, how reliable do you think the Pastons' accounts are? Give reasons for your answer that address issues of **motive** and **objectivity.**

Extend Interpretations

5. **Critic's Corner** Virginia Woolf wrote of the Paston letters that "in all this there is no writing for writing's sake; no use of the pen to convey pleasure or amusement." What does this observation suggest about the lives of the people who wrote these letters?

6. **Connect to Life** Margaret Paston was forced to take care of family business while her husband was away. How do you think a contemporary businesswoman would view Margaret's handling of these matters?

Literary Analysis

CONFLICT Because of the turbulent times in which the Pastons lived, their letters present a number of **conflicts,** or struggles between opposing forces. In fiction, a conflict usually reaches a point of resolution; in a series of real letters, however, many of the conflicts described may necessarily remain unresolved.

In both fiction and nonfiction, the term **external conflict** is used to describe a situation in which a person is pitted against an outside force (such as another person, a physical obstacle, nature, or society). The term **internal conflict** refers to a struggle that takes place within a person.

Cooperative Learning Activity With a group of classmates, go through the letters, creating a list of the various conflicts that are described by each writer. Decide whether each conflict is external or internal. Then choose one conflict and write an imaginative description of how it might have been resolved. Share your group's work with the rest of the class.

REVIEW TONE **Tone** is the expression of a writer's attitude toward his or her subject. Analyze the general tone of these letters. Think about the writers' purposes, the language used, the details included, and the recipients of the letters. Then try to come up with a one-word description of their tone.

GUIDING STUDENT RESPONSE

Connect to the Literature

1. What Do You Think?
Guidelines for student response: Students' responses are likely to vary widely, although most students will observe how difficult life was during the period, based on the events described. Students who are less sensitive to the social constraints of the period (such as the expectation that a wealthy young girl would marry "well") may judge the Paston family—especially Margaret—harshly. Other students will be sympathetic to the family's financial trials, Margaret's strength under duress, and the family's constant fear of attack and illness. Good responses to the question will acknowledge the dangers of applying today's standards and conventions to events that occurred long ago.

Comprehension Check
- He destroyed property and imprisoned servants and tenants of the estate.
- The marriage would bring neither money nor power to the Paston family.

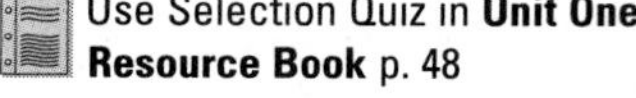

Use Selection Quiz in **Unit One Resource Book** p. 48

Think Critically

2. Students' descriptions of Margaret Paston will vary. Some may find her strong-willed in her defense of the family fortune; others may find her selfish and hard-hearted, particularly in her reaction to Margery's engagement.
3. Many students will advise Richard and Margery to follow their hearts' desires in spite of social convention. Others may advise less secrecy and more tact and honesty. Still others may advise the couple to abandon the hopeless relationship in favor of social and financial security.
4. Answers will vary. Some students will consider the letters credible because the writers are so well-known to their immediate audiences and because the letters seem sincere, businesslike, and fact-based. Others will observe that some letters, such as Richard Calle's, may have been written with other readers in mind or with the motive of self-interest.

Extend Interpretations

Critic's Corner Answers will vary, but Woolf probably means that the pressures of the Pastons' lives prevented them from sending letters casually; the arrival of a letter implied a crisis.

Connect to Life Answers will vary. A businesswoman of today might feel that Margaret should have made more decisions herself, but she also might admire Margaret for having been as independent as a married woman of her era could have been.

Literary Analysis

Conflict Volunteers from each group might read their description aloud to the rest of the class.

Tone Use students' words to draw a word web on the chalkboard.

Writing Options

1. Margery Paston's Diary Imagine that you are Margery Paston. Write a diary entry in which you express your thoughts about your mother's reaction to your marriage plans.

2. Opinion Paragraph In a paragraph, tell which of the persons mentioned in the Paston letters you would judge as the most interesting and which the least interesting. Explain your choices. Place the paragraph in your **Working Portfolio.**

Activities & Explorations

1. Map Mileage Scale On the map shown, locate the estate at Paston. Then use the mileage scale to estimate the distances between Paston and three other estates or towns mentioned in the letters you have read.
~ **GEOGRAPHY**

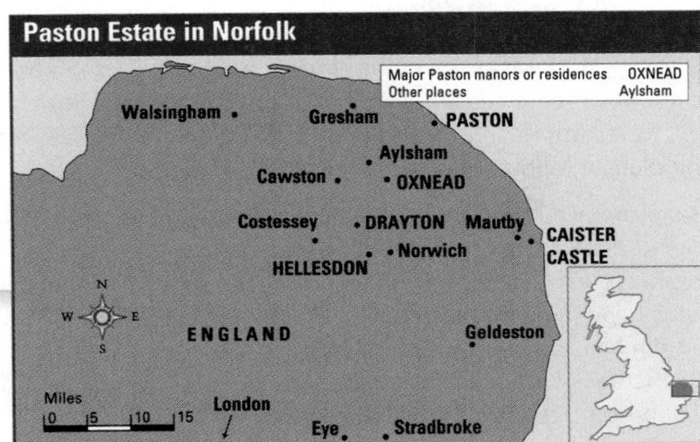

2. Illustrated Fashions Research the fashions of 15th-century England. Then make an illustration showing clothing that would have been appropriate for a man or woman of the Paston family.
~ **ART**

3. Dramatic Presentation With several other students, give a short dramatic presentation of one of the letters.
~ **SPEAKING AND LISTENING**

4. Panel Discussion Think about the limitations of communicating only through letters. If faster or easier methods of communication had been available to the Pastons, how might their lives have been different? With classmates, conduct a panel discussion in which you explore this question. ~ **SPEAKING AND LISTENING**

Inquiry & Research

1. Life Spans Using dates from the Paston family tree on page 181, calculate the life span of each person shown in the diagram. For this activity, assume that all approximate dates are exact. What was the average life span of the men? of the women?

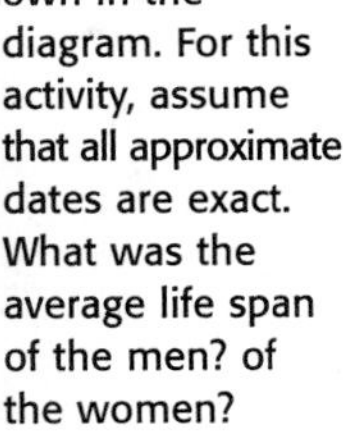

2. 15th-Century History With three classmates, investigate one of these topics related to the 15th century: the Wars of the Roses, courtship and marriage, education, religion, medicine and life expectancy, the role of women, art and music, or life on a medieval manor. Present your findings to the class.

More Online: Research Starter
www.mcdougallittell.com

Writing Options

1. **Margery Paston's Diary** Students' entries will vary. (You may want to invite your male students to write from the point of view of one of Margaret's sons who has decided to marry one of the Paston's female servants.)
2. **Opinion Paragraph** Students' evaluations will vary. Many may find Richard Calle the most interesting, as his interests and emotional remarks are similar to those of many adolescents. Less interesting figures are likely to be the sons of Margaret and John Paston.

Activities & Explorations

1. **Map Mileage Scale** Have students work in pairs. Invite each student to estimate the distances independently and write the answers on a sheet of paper. Partners can then exchange papers and check the measurements.
2. **Illustrated Fashions** Have interested students go to the library to find books containing illustrations of 15th-century English fashions. Skilled artists in your class may want to extend the activity by designing contemporary clothes inspired by clothing of the late Middle Ages.
3. **Dramatic Presentation** Have the members of each group select a letter and discuss ways of dramatizing it. For example, students might alternate speakers, speak in unison, or combine the techniques.
4. **Panel Discussion** Invite five or six volunteers to sit on the panel and appoint a moderator, who will ensure that everyone has a chance to speak and who will be responsible for clarifying or paraphrasing discussion points. Suggest that students start the discussion by letting each panelist have a turn to speak. After that, encourage a free flow of discussion.

Inquiry & Research

1. **Life Spans** The average for men is 44; the average for women is 50. You might suggest, as an additional activity, that students make a time line showing the births and deaths of Paston family members as well as important events in the Pastons' lives.
2. **15th-Century History** Have each group meet to select a topic and construct a research plan. To further prepare for the project, students should break broad topics into more specific subtopics. For instance, subtopics for "medicine and life expectancy" might include disease, infant mortality, and surgical techniques. Have students generate a list of researchable questions for their topics. Have each student research and compile information on one or two subtopics. During the presentation, invite each member to speak on the subtopics he or she researched.

OVERVIEW

Objectives

1. understand and appreciate three traditional **ballads (Literary Analysis)**
2. understand and identify folk ballads and characteristics of the ballad stanza **(Literary Analysis)**
3. use strategies for reading ballads such as reading aloud, paraphrasing, and rereading **(Active Reading)**

Summary

"Barbara Allan" tells the story of a tragic love. "Sir Patrick Spens" describes the loss at sea of a Scottish ship, its commander, and the crew. "Get Up and Bar the Door" tells the humorous story of a strong-willed husband and wife locked in an argument.

Thematic Link

"Barbara Allan"deals with the themes of unfulfilled love and impending doom, common ones in ballads of the time. "Sir Patrick Spens" deals with the dangers faced by men venturing out to sea in the days of sailing ships. "Get Up and Bar the Door" treats the theme of marital discord in a humorous way. All three ballads deal with problems encountered in **everyday life.**

5-Minute Warm-Up

Daily Language SkillBuilder

Have students **proofread** the display sentences on page 151 and write them correctly. The sentences also appear on Transparency 4 of **Grammar Transparencies and Copymasters.**

PREPARING to *Read*

Barbara Allan / Sir Patrick Spens / Get Up and Bar the Door

Anonymous Ballads

"Since my love died for me today, / I'll die for him tomorrow."

Connect to Your Life

What's Sad and What's Funny? What comes to mind when you hear the word *tragedy?* Natural disasters? Wars? Lost loves? What about when you hear the word *comedy?* Do you think of mistaken identities, slapstick, silly arguments? With a group of classmates, brainstorm a variety of associations with the words.

Build Background

Songs That Tell a Story Throughout history, many of life's tragedies and comedies, real or fictional, have been depicted in song. Narrative songs called **ballads** were popular in England and Scotland during the medieval period, particularly among the common people, many of whom could not read or write. Minstrels traveled about, singing these narratives to entertain their listeners with dramatic stories about ordinary people. The best of the early ballads were passed on orally from one generation to the next and sometimes from country to country. Stories often changed in the retelling, sometimes resulting in dozens of versions of the same ballad. Most composers of these popular, or folk, ballads remained anonymous, and the songs themselves were not written down before the 18th century.

LaserLinks: Background for Reading
Literary Connection

Focus Your Reading

LITERARY ANALYSIS | BALLADS The early popular **ballads** share certain characteristics common to oral traditions. The typical ballad focuses on a single incident, beginning in the middle of a crisis and proceeding directly to the resolution, with only the most sketchy background information, character development, and descriptive detail. Popular subjects of these early ballads include tragic love, domestic conflict, crime, war, and shipwreck. As you read the three ballads in this lesson, note which treat tragic subjects and which treat comic matters.

ACTIVE READING | STRATEGIES FOR READING BALLADS In the ballads you are about to read, certain words of Scottish **dialect** appear—*rase* and *guid,* for example. In order to help you understand the ballads, including dialect, follow these steps.

- Read each ballad through once, using the notes to help you decipher dialect and other difficult passages.
- **Paraphrase** each stanza as you read to make sure you understand what is happening in the story.
- Read the ballad again without referring to the notes.
- Read the ballad aloud, allowing the sounds of the words to help you appreciate the texture and flavor of the poems.

READER'S NOTEBOOK As you read, jot down notes about which strategies and steps you find most useful in helping you to understand the ballads.

Strategies
paraphrasing
rereading

LESSON RESOURCES

UNIT ONE RESOURCE BOOK, pp. 49–50

ASSESSMENT RESOURCES

Formal Assessment, pp. 27–28

Teacher's Guide to Assessment and Portfolio Use

Test Generator

SKILLS TRANSPARENCIES AND COPYMASTERS

Literary Analysis

- The Moral Tale, Ballad, Fable, and Folk Tale, T23 (for Literary Analysis, p. 192)

Reading and Critical Thinking

- Visualizing, T8 (for Activities & Explorations 1, p. 199)

Grammar

- Complete Subjects and Complete Predicates, C78 (for Mini Lesson, p. 196)

Writing

- Effective Language, T13 (for Writing Option 2, p. 199)
- Showing, Not Telling, T22 (for Writing Option 4, p. 199)

Communications

- Impromptu Speaking: Dialogue, Role-Play, T14 (for Activities & Explorations 3, p. 199)

INTEGRATED TECHNOLOGY

Audio Library

LaserLinks

- Literary Connection: Scenes from the Ballad. See **Teacher's SourceBook,** p. 12.

Internet: Research Starter

Visit our website:
www.mcdougallittell.com

Barbara Allan

It was in and about the Martinmas time,
When the green leaves were a-fallin';
That Sir John Graeme in the West Country
Fell in love with Barbara Allan.

He sent his man down through the town
To the place where she was dwellin':
"O haste and come to my master dear,
Gin ye be Barbara Allan."

O slowly, slowly rase she up,
To the place where he was lyin',
And when she drew the curtain by:
"Young man, I think you're dyin'."

"O it's I'm sick, and very, very sick,
And 'tis a' for Barbara Allan."
"O the better for me ye sal never be,
Though your heart's blood were a-spillin'.

"O dinna ye mind, young man," said she,
"When ye the cups were fillin',
That ye made the healths gae round and round,
And slighted Barbara Allan?"

He turned his face unto the wall,
And death with him was dealin':
"Adieu, adieu, my dear friends all,
And be kind to Barbara Allan."

And slowly, slowly, rase she up,
And slowly, slowly left him;
And sighing said she could not stay,
Since death of life had reft him.

She had not gane a mile but twa,
When she heard the dead-bell knellin',
And every jow that the dead-bell ga'ed
It cried, "Woe to Barbara Allan!"

"O mother, mother, make my bed,
O make it soft and narrow:
Since my love died for me today,
I'll die for him tomorrow."

1 Martinmas: November 11 (St. Martin's Day).

8 gin (gĭn): if.

9 rase (rāz): rose.

15 sal: shall.

17 dinna ye mind: don't you remember.

19 healths: toasts; **gae** (gā): go.

28 reft: deprived.

29 gane (gān): gone; **twa:** two.

30 dead-bell: a church bell rung to announce a person's death.

31 jow (jou): stroke; **ga'ed:** gave.

TEACHING THE LITERATURE

Customizing Instruction

Less Proficient Readers

Set a Purpose: Ask students to think of some modern songs that tell a story and to identify their subjects. Then, have students read to discover what happens to Barbara Allan, Sir Patrick Spens, and the couple in "Get Up and Bar the Door."

Students Acquiring English

Emphasize to students that the dialect in these stories poses problems for all readers. Make sure they use the side notes to get the meaning of the more obscure examples of dialect.

Use **Spanish Study Guide** for additional support, pp. 31–33

Gifted and Talented

After students have read the ballads, ask them to write one of their own about some person or situation that they think would lend itself to the ballad form. Volunteers might read their ballads to the class.

Cross Curricular Link Music

FOLK SONGS AND INSTRUMENTS Ask students to think about how folk music in the Americas is closely associated with the guitar. Encourage the class to offer examples of folk songs from the United States and South and Central America that are often sung to a guitar accompaniment.

Minstrels in medieval times used the lute to accompany their singing of ballads such as the ones in this section. *Lute* is the generic name for stringed instruments such as the lute itself, the mandolin, and the modern-day guitar. All of these instruments have a body, a neck, and strings that stretch across the instrument.

The sitar, the primary stringed instrument of India, is also a type of lute. Like the guitar, it, too, is sometimes used to accompany folk singers as they retell the ballads common to their culture.

Reading and Analyzing

Active Reading

STRATEGIES FOR READING BALLADS

A Discuss with students the advantages and disadvantages of the traditional ballad format of beginning a story in the middle of a crisis, with only minimal background information about the conflict, setting, or characters. Then, focus on the sound structure of "Sir Patrick Spens." Ask students to chart the rhyme scheme of the first two stanzas (abcb, defe).

Discuss how rhyme and repetition of sounds enabled minstrels to recall ballads, which were not written down. For comparative purposes, point out how rhyme and repeated patterns of sounds enhance their recall.

Use **Unit One Resource Book,** p. 49 for more practice.

Literary Analysis BALLADS

B Alliteration is a characteristic of the ballad form. Review with students the definition of alliteration. Be sure they understand that it refers to repeated initial consonant sounds, not to spelling.

Ask students to identify the repeated consonant sound in lines 7 and 8.

Possible Response: The movements of the sea; waves.

C Repetition is another device characteristic of the traditional ballad form. It is a literary technique in which a word or group of words is repeated throughout a work, sometimes with a slight variation.

Ask students to find examples of repetition in "Sir Patrick Spens."

Possible Responses: "this deed,/ This ill deed"; "lang, lang"; "Half o'er, half o'er."

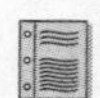
Use **Unit One Resource Book,** p. 50 for more exercises.

Sir Patrick Spens

The king sits in Dumferline town,
Drinking the blude-reid wine:
A "O whar will I get a guid sailor
To sail this ship of mine?"

Up and spak an eldern knicht,
Sat at the king's richt knee:
"Sir Patrick Spens is the best sailor
That sails upon the sea." **B**

1 Dumferline: the town of Dumferline in Scotland, site of a favorite residence of Scottish kings.
2 blude-reid (blo͝od'rēd'): blood-red.
3 guid (go͝od): good.
5 eldern knicht (knĭKHt): elderly knight.
6 richt (rĭKHt): right.

Teaching Options

BLOCK SCHEDULING: MANAGING TIME

If your schedule requires that you cover the lesson objectives in a shorter time, use . . .
- Preparing to Read, p. 192
- Thinking Through the Literature, p. 198

If you want to take advantage of longer class time, use . . .
- Teacher's Edition Teaching Options: Cross Curricular Link, p. 193; Speaking and Listening, p. 195; Grammar, p. 196; Standardized Test Practice, p. 197
- Choices & Challenges, p. 199

The king has written a braid letter
And signed it wi' his hand,
And sent it to Sir Patrick Spens,
Was walking on the sand.

The first line that Sir Patrick read,
A loud lauch lauched he;
The next line that Sir Patrick read,
The tear blinded his ee.

"O wha is this has done this deed,
This ill deed done to me,
To send me out this time o' the year,
To sail upon the sea?

"Make haste, make haste, my mirry men all,
Our guid ship sails the morn."
"O say na sae, my master dear,
For I fear a deadly storm.

"Late late yestre'en I saw the new moon
Wi' the auld moon in her arm,
And I fear, I fear, my dear master,
That we will come to harm."

O our Scots nobles were richt laith
To weet their cork-heeled shoon,
But lang owre a' the play were played
Their hats they swam aboon.

O lang, lang may their ladies sit,
Wi' their fans into their hand,
Or e'er they see Sir Patrick Spens
Come sailing to the land.

O lang, lang may the ladies stand,
Wi' their gold kembs in their hair,
Waiting for their ain dear lords,
For they'll see thame na mair.

Half o'er, half o'er to Aberdour
It's fifty fadom deep,
And there lies guid Sir Patrick Spens,
Wi' the Scots lords at his feet.

9 braid (brād): broad; emphatic.

14 lauch (loukh): laugh.

16 ee: eye.

17 wha: who.

23 na sae (nä sā): not so.

25 yestre'en (yĕ-strēn'): yesterday evening.

25–26 the new moon . . . arm: a thin crescent moon with the rest of the moon's disk faintly illuminated by light reflected from the earth.

26 auld (ould): old.

29 laith (lāth): loath; unwilling.

30 weet: wet; **shoon:** shoes.

31 lang owre a' (läng our ä): long before all.

32 aboon (ə-bo͞on'): above (them).

35 or e'er (ôr îr): before ever.

38 kembs: combs.

39 ain (ān): own.

40 na mair (nä mâr): no more.

41 half o'er: halfway over; **Aberdour:** a small town on the Scottish coast.

42 fadom (fä'dəm): fathoms.

Customizing Instruction

Students Acquiring English

Ask students what "Up and spak" in line 5 means.

Answer: Spoke up.

Then, ask them to identify the tense of the word *spak.*

Answer: The past tense of *speak.*

Less Proficient Readers

Make sure students understand the tragic tale that this ballad tells. Ask: What vision does Sir Patrick have before the ship sets sail?

Answer: The new moon carrying the old moon in her arms.

Set a Purpose Have students read on to find out what happens to the ship that Sir Patrick Spens sails for the king.

Mini Lesson Speaking and Listening

DRAMATIC RECITAL

Instruction Ballads offer an excellent opportunity for students to memorize and recite poetry.

Prepare Have students form small **cooperative groups** to memorize the ballads. Half the groups should work on "Barbara Allan" and the other half on "Sir Patrick Spens." Assign each student in a group the role of one character in the group's ballad. Have the student memorize lines for that character only. For both ballads, you may want to designate one or more students as narrator(s) to memorize descriptive and narrative sections.

Present Have the groups take turns reciting the ballads for the class. When all the groups have finished their recitations, discuss the presentations with the class. Have the students point out differences in tone of voice, emphasis, and pace of delivery and try to analyze how these factors affected each group's interpretation of the ballad.

BLOCK SCHEDULING This activity is particularly well-suited for longer class periods.

Reading and Analyzing

Literary Analysis BALLADS

Discuss with students the usual rhyme scheme for ballad form, using stanzas two and three as models. Chart the *abcb* rhyme scheme on the chalkboard. Ask students what conclusions we can draw about changes in the English language through the off-rhymes of "then/pan" (lines 2,4), "sure/door" (lines 14, 16), and "black/spake" (lines 26, 28).

Possible Response: Chances are that the words in each pair had the same vowel sound hundreds of years ago and did not become distinct, separate sounds until the period of Modern English (sixteenth century to present).

Literary Analysis: CHARACTERIZATION

Ask the class what kinds of character traits the man and the woman exhibit. Have them support their opinions with references to the text.

Possible Responses: Encourage responses such as *stubbornness* (lines 23–24 and 27–28) and *pride* (lines 39–40).

Ask whether these characterizations are believable and represent qualities that we see in real people.

Get *Up* and *Bar* the Door

It fell about the Martinmas time,
And a gay time it was then,
When our goodwife got puddings to make,
And she's boild them in the pan.

The wind sae cauld blew south and north,
And blew into the floor;
Quoth our goodman to our goodwife,
"Gae out and bar the door."

The Peasant Couple Dancing (1514), Albrecht Dürer. Engraving, The Metropolitan Museum of Art, New York, Fletcher Fund, 1919 (19.73.102).

Teaching Options

Grammar

COMPLETE SUBJECTS AND COMPLETE PREDICATES

Instruction A complete subject includes all the words that modify the subject—adjectives, adverbs, articles, and prepositional phrases. Likewise, the complete predicate includes all of the words that tell what the subject did, or what happened to the subject.

Activity Write the following sentence on the chalkboard.

An anguished Barbara Allan heard the tolling of the death bell.

Have students identify the simple subject and simple predicate. *(Barbara Allan; heard)* Ask students to find the complete subject. *(An anguished Barbara Allan)* Then have students identify the complete predicate. *(heard the tolling of the death bell)*

Exercise Ask students to underline the complete subject once and the complete predicate twice.

1. A dying Sir John Graeme summoned Barbara Allan to his side.
2. Barbara Allan foolishly rejected his love because of an imagined slight.

Use **Grammar Transparencies and Copymasters,** p. 77 for more exercises.

"My hand is in my hussyfskap,
Goodman, as ye may see;
An it shoud nae be barrd this hundred year,
It's no be barrd for me."

They made a paction tween them twa,
They made it firm and sure,
That the first word whae'er shoud speak,
Shoud rise and bar the door.

Then by there came two gentlemen,
At twelve o'clock at night,
And they could neither see house nor hall,
Nor coal nor candle-light.

"Now whether is this a rich man's house,
Or whether is it a poor?"
But ne'er a word wad ane o' them speak,
For barring of the door.

And first they ate the white puddings,
And then they ate the black;
Tho muckle thought the goodwife to hersel,
Yet ne'er a word she spake.

Then said the one unto the other,
"Here, man, tak ye my knife;
Do ye tak aff the auld man's beard,
And I'll kiss the goodwife."

"But there's nae water in the house,
And what shall we do than?"
"What ails ye at the pudding-broo,
That boils into the pan?"

O up then started our goodman,
An angry man was he:
"Will ye kiss my wife before my een,
And scad me wi' pudding-bree?"

Then up and started our goodwife,
Gied three skips on the floor:
"Goodman, you've spoken the foremost word,
Get up and bar the door."

9 hussyfskap: household chores.

13 paction: agreement.

15 whae'er: whoever.

27 muckle: a great deal.

35–36 What . . . pan?: What's wrong with using the broth the puddings are boiling in?

40 scad: scald; **bree:** broth.

Customizing Instruction

Less Proficient Readers

Make certain that students understand the cause-and-effect relationships that move the plot along. Write the following questions on the board and have students write the answers on their own papers.

- What causes the man to ask his wife to get up and close the door?
  Answer: A strong wind blew open the door.
- Why does the woman refuse to close the door?
  Answer: She says she is busy with her household chores.
- What pact do they make?
  Answer: The first person to speak has to get up and close the door.
- How is the pact broken?
  Possible Response: The man speaks when two men enter and threaten to cut off the man's beard, using the pudding broth for water, and kiss the woman. His wife then demands that he get up and bar the door.

Multiple Learning Styles

Visual Learners

To help students follow the cause-effect sequence of events related to the pact the couple makes, have students draw brief sketches depicting each of the following events from the ballad: the wind blowing open the door, the two men entering and threatening the couple, the man jumping up to speak, and the woman skipping around the room. Have students identify what important pieces of information a purely visual representation of the ballad omits.

Assessment Standardized Test Practice

WRITING SHORT ANSWERS Often, students are expected to draw upon their own experience and opinions to interpret literature. Have students work in pairs to write answers to the following questions. When they have finished, have them share answers with the class.

1. One comment frequently made about Sir John in "Barbara Allan" is that he is spineless and gives her up much too easily. Do you agree? Why or why not?

Possible Response: It is hard to tell from the ballad alone exactly what has happened in the relationship between Sir John and Barbara Allan, and therefore it would probably be difficult to say that he is spineless in his treatment of her.

2. Through the character of Sir Patrick Spens, we get a picture of medieval ideas of responsibility and honor. What are these ideas? How are they similar to or different from our own?

Possible Responses: Unquestioning loyalty to king. We believe more in making own decisions.

As students share their answers, point out that different points of view are the basis for literary analysis.

GET UP AND BAR THE DOOR 197

GUIDING STUDENT RESPONSE

Connect to the Literature

1. **What Do You Think?**
   Guidelines for Student Response: Accept all reasonable responses. Encourage students to provide specific reasons (characterization, sound, plot) as to why they prefer one ballad to the other.

Comprehension Check
- Because her lover is dead
- Because he realizes that he and his men will not return alive from the trip the king has ordered
- She says she is too busy with her household chores.

Think Critically

2. Possible Response: They apparently had a romantic relationship that was broken off when Sir John slighted Barbara. However, they still seem to love each other.
3. Possible Response: because he is a knight and is known as a great sailor, he feels obliged to obey the king.
4. "Get Up and Bar the Door" is humorous rather than tragic.
5. Possible Responses: "Barbara Allan" is more tragic because the characters realize too late that they love each other. "Sir Patrick Spens" is more tragic because the sailors know their lives are doomed.
6. Encourage students to evaluate their comments. Have them note which strategies helped them the most.

Literary Analysis

Cooperative Learning Activity All three ballads have a similar rhyme scheme and number of metrical feet per line.

Connect to the Literature

1. **What Do You Think?** Which ballad would you say told the most interesting story? Share your thoughts with a classmate.

Comprehension Check
- Why does Barbara Allan want to die?
- Why does Sir Patrick Spens shed a tear when he reads the king's letter?
- What reason does the woman give for not barring the door?

Think Critically

2. What is your opinion of the relationship between Barbara Allan and Sir John Graeme?

- his request to see her
- the reason for his illness
- her statement "I'll die for him tomorrow" (line 36)

3. Why do you think Sir Patrick Spens chooses to sail the ship in spite of the risk?

- the elderly knight's opinion of him (lines 7–8)
- his reaction to the king's letter (lines 13–22)
- the warning from one of his men (lines 23–28)

4. How does the **tone** of "Get Up and Bar the Door" differ from that of the other two ballads?
5. In your opinion, which of the two tragic ballads tells the sadder story? Explain your opinion.
6. **ACTIVE READING** **STRATEGIES FOR READING BALLADS** Consult the notes in your **READER'S NOTEBOOK**. Which strategy did you find most useful in helping you to understand the ballad?

Extend Interpretations

7. **Comparing Texts** Both Sir Patrick Spens and the **speaker** of "The Seafarer" (pages 85–89) go off to sea despite anticipated danger. Compare and contrast their motives and attitudes.
8. **Connect to Life** Recall your responses to the words *tragedy* and *comedy* in Connect to Your Life on page 192. What types of **tragedies** and **comedies** might you expect to find described in ballads written today?

Literary Analysis

BALLADS Typically, a **ballad** consists of four-line stanzas, or **quatrains,** with the second and fourth lines of each stanza rhyming. Each stanza has a strong rhythmic pattern, usually with four stressed syllables in the first and third lines and three stressed syllables in the second and fourth lines. Most ballads also contain **dialogue** and repetitions of sounds, words, and phrases for emphasis. Notice the patterns of **rhyme, rhythm,** and **repetition** in the following stanza from "Barbara Allan."

O slowly, slowly rase she up,
To the place where he was lyin',
And when she drew the curtain by:
"Young man, I think you're dyin'."

Cooperative Learning Activity Select a stanza from "Sir Patrick Spens" or "Get Up and Bar the Door" and determine whether its patterns of **rhyme** and **rhythm** are the same as those in the stanza from "Barbara Allan." Then look for examples of **dialogue** and **repetition** in the three ballads. What effects are created by the use of these four elements? Share your findings with the class.

Extend Interpretations

Comparing Texts Students might respond that the speaker of "The Seafarer" goes willingly and repeatedly to sea; he sees it as his destiny, his love of the sea and of exotic places motivating him to continue his journey. Sir Patrick, on the other hand, undertakes this voyage because his king has commanded him to do so and Spens realizes the loyalty he owes to his ruler.

Connect to Life Students might still expect to find ballads about lost love, but ballads about plane crashes, fires, or earthquakes might be more common today than ballads about shipwrecks. Comic ballads would probably still cover human weaknesses, such as stubbornness, and could still center around domestic situations, such as a husband and wife arguing.

Choices & CHALLENGES

Writing Options

1. Story of Barbara Allan Draft a short story in which you give a more detailed account of the relationship between Barbara Allan and Sir John Graeme. You might, for example, present events that may have occurred earlier in their relationship.

2. In Memoriam Create appropriate epitaphs for Barbara Allan and Sir Patrick Spens—brief statements, in prose or verse, that might be placed on their tombstones to memorialize their deaths.

3. Contemporary Ballad Try to write your own ballad on a contemporary subject. Focus on events leading up to the climax of a comic or tragic situation.

4. Descriptive Paragraph Think of an event you have heard or read about that you would call a tragedy—an accident resulting in death, for example, or a relationship ending in separation. Write a paragraph describing this event. Would this event be a good subject for a modern-day ballad?

Writing Handbook
See page 1363: Descriptive Writing.

Activities & Explorations

1. Illustrated Tragedy Imagine the exact circumstances of Sir Patrick Spens's death. Then create a drawing or painting of the incident. ~ **ART**

Buddy Guy performing at the Chicago Blues Festival

2. Dance Interpretation Choreograph a dance that portrays the action of one of these ballads. Perform your dance for the class. ~ **VIEWING AND REPRESENTING**

3. Ballad Role Play In most medieval ballads, the speaker has no personal involvement in the story. How might each of these ballads be different if it were told from the point of view of someone affected by the events—for example, the mother of Barbara Allan, a woman whose husband was lost at sea with Sir Patrick Spens, or one of the two gentlemen who disturb the peace of the goodman and goodwife? Assume the point of view of someone other than the main characters in one of these ballads and then tell the story to the class from that point of view.

Inquiry & Research

1. Blues Music Research contemporary blues music and find examples of songs that combine characteristics of ballads with traditional tragic themes. Play recordings of these blues songs for your classmates.

INTERNET **More Online: Research Starter** www.mcdougallittell.com

2. The Popularity of Tragedy Tragedy is still a common theme in contemporary forms of entertainment, such as plays, television dramas, soap operas, and documentaries. Discuss possible reasons for the popularity of tragic and comic subjects throughout human history.

3. History or Legend? The ballad of "Sir Patrick Spens" may have a basis in historical fact. Do some research to find out whether or not such a person existed and what historical voyage the ballad may indirectly commemorate.

Writing Options

1. **Story of Barbara Allan** Point out that the story might be narrated from a third-person point of view or from the first-person point of view of either character. Suggest that students explore the social class, personality traits, and emotions of the characters.
2. **In Memoriam** Suggest that students write each epitaph in the form of a rhymed couplet. They may, of course, write brief prose epitaphs if they choose. Remind students that an epitaph typically emphasizes a person's most memorable trait.
3. **Contemporary Ballad** Suggest that students imitate the four-line stanzas of old ballads, with an *abcb* rhyme scheme and three-beat iambic lines.
4. **Descriptive Paragraph** You might suggest that students review recent news reports for contemporary events appropriate for this assignment.

Activities & Explorations

1. **Illustrated Tragedy** Invite students to look again at the illustration on page 194. They should try to imagine the effects of a terrible storm on such a vessel.
2. **Dance Interpretation** Students might want to select music to accompany their dance.
3. **Ballad Role Play** This can be effective as an individual or cooperative-learning activity. Have students make a chart on which they list at least three possible narrators for each ballad.

Inquiry & Research

1. **Blues Music** To find possible songs, students might look at brief biographies of blues artists such as Billie Holiday or at capsule histories of jazz.
2. **The Popularity of Tragedy** Ask students to discuss movies or television shows they have seen recently that had tragic themes. Then, ask why tragic subjects are popular. By way of contrast, discuss the elements of comedy, perhaps by asking students what or who makes them laugh. Usually, people are in far more agreement about what is tragic than about what is comic.
3. **History or Legend?** Have students share their information with the class.

BARBARA ALLAN / SIR PATRICK SPENS / GET UP AND BAR THE DOOR 199

Objectives
- write a Personality Profile
- use a written text as a model for writing
- revise a draft to add details
- use commas to add clarity to complex phrases and sentences

Introducing the Workshop

(A) Personality Profile Many television and film documentaries also include personality profiles. These profiles are popular because they acquaint us with celebrities and other notable people that we might never meet face to face. Have students name a few people they have read about in profiles. Point out that through writing a personality profile, students, too, will be able to "introduce" their readers to fascinating individuals that we might otherwise never encounter.

Establish some criteria for what makes one person fascinating to another. Students may be interested in celebrities who possess exceptional intellectual, musical, or athletic abilities. Some, like the student writer of the model, may be fascinated by a relative or close friend who is special in some way.

Basics in a Box

(B) Using the Graphic Like the tiles in a mosaic, the items in a personality profile work together to create an overall impression. The graphic offers suggestions for pieces that students can use to draft an effective essay.

(C) Presenting the Rubric To better understand the assignment, students can refer to the Standards for Writing a Successful Personality Profile. You may also want to share with them the complete rubric, which describes several levels of proficiency.

Use the complete rubric to evaluate student writing; stress the importance of producing an error-free final draft.

Writing Workshop
Personality Profile

Describing a Fascinating Person . . .

From Reading to Writing Good descriptive writing takes the reader inside the writer's world. Chaucer's remarkable character portraits in *The Canterbury Tales,* for example, transport the modern reader to the Middle Ages. Through carefully chosen details, Chaucer creates living personalities on the page—fascinating as individuals and for their universal human qualities. The same techniques are also applied to writing a **personality profile,** a common feature in newspapers and magazines. A personality profile combines compelling information and vivid language to describe a person. (A)

For Your Portfolio

WRITING PROMPT Write a personality profile of a person of your choice.

Purpose: To make readers feel like they know the person

Audience: Your peers, family, or general readers

Basics in a Box

Personality Profile at a Glance (B)

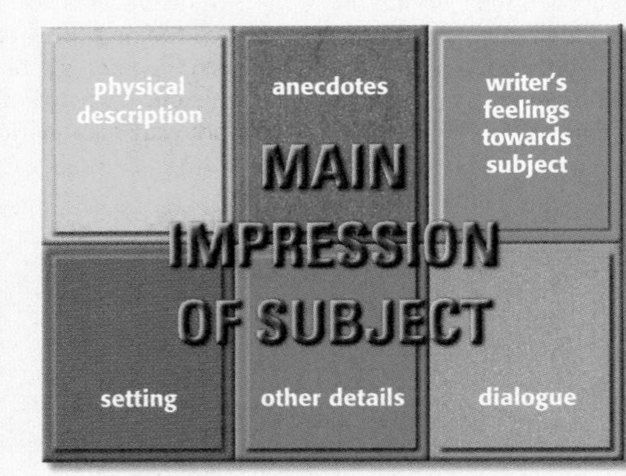

RUBRIC Standards for Writing (C)

A successful personality profile should
- use lively descriptions, details, anecdotes, and/or dialogue to create a vivid impression of the person
- put the person in a context that helps reveal the subject's personality
- convey why the person is important to the writer
- paint a word portrait that shows the person's character
- create a unified tone and impression
- capture the reader's interest at the beginning and give a sense of completeness at the end

LESSON RESOURCES

USING PRINT RESOURCES

Unit One Resource Book
- Prewriting, p. 51
- Drafting, p. 52
- Peer Response, p. 53
- Revising, p. 54
- Editing and Proofreading, p. 55
- Student Models, pp. 56–58
- Rubric, p. 63

Writing Transparencies and Copymasters
- Personality Profile Template, p. 25
- Sensory Word List, p. 14

USING MEDIA RESOURCES

LaserLinks
Writing Springboards
See Teacher's SourceBook p. 114 for bar codes.

Writing Coach CD-ROM

Visit our website:
www.mcdougallittell.com

For a complete view of Lesson Resources, see page 15i.

Analyzing a Student Model

Jenny Yu
Niskayuna High School

Her Three-Inch Feet D

She is different. Not just different, her presence in this big city seems anachronistic, misplaced. She has a benign grandmotherly smile; skin like a piece of crumbled lined-paper flattened out with lines revealing her age; a petite, almost childlike, body; and tiny bound feet* only three inches long.

It is difficult to get a close look at her feet since she likes to move about constantly. She can never and will never stay in one place long enough. For most of her life, Great-Aunt Yeung worked diligently—first for her parents, then her husband, and later her children. In the seventy-six years she has lived, her life has been burdened by responsibility. And because of the challenges life has presented her, Great-Aunt Yeung possesses vigor that exceeds a teenager's.

However, if you have seen her feet, you will never forget them. They are small and pale. They are like two pieces of sponge cake that have been accidentally mushed and tortured. They are painful to look at, for one thinks how excruciating it must be to walk on them; yet, they are fascinating. They represent the ancient world of the East, a place of a thousand emperors and fabled dragons.

It is always a treat for me to visit Great-Aunt Yeung, though it means a three-hour drive to New York City. She lives on Mott Street, only three blocks from the heart of Chinatown. Her apartment isn't very big, and appears somewhat cluttered if compared to the typical Niskayuna four-bedroom colonial. It only has one bedroom, one bath, and a small space that one might call a living room. There isn't much to see in the living room, just a chair, a few pieces of furniture which she might have gotten from garage sales (since they don't quite match), a 13-inch TV, and a table.

But it's not just a table: it's the table of Chinese gods. The burning incense on it perfumes the whole apartment. The twice-daily ritual of worship consists of kneeling, lighting the incense, then bowing to the gods while holding up the incense with both hands above the head. It is quite a lovely scene. I like to watch her and pretend to be lost in the world of yin and yang, Confucius, and fortune cookies. But deep down, I know I can never be a part of that inscrutable world.

That is how I feel about my Great-Aunt Yeung. The combination of her and New York City is as odd as eating rice topped with rocky road ice cream. She prefers bamboo mats over soft mattresses, medicinal tea over creamy cappuccino, and cooked vegetables over raw salads. Great-Aunt Yeung will always have her own ways. The East and the West will always remain apart, and the best proof of that is seeing Great-Aunt Yeung plod the streets of New York in her size-one black-cloth shoes.

* Refers to the defunct Chinese custom of foot-binding, which produced small, deformed feet in women.

RUBRIC IN ACTION

1. The writer immediately establishes interest and tone with intriguing language and lively description details
   Other Options:
   - Start with a revealing anecdote.
   - Describe the setting.
2. The writer focuses on various concrete details and uses figurative language to create a word portrait.
   Other Options:
   - Show the person interacting with others.
   - Use dialogue.
3. Puts the person in a context
4. Reveals the writer's own feelings
5. Uses lively figurative language to fill out the picture
6. Ends with an image that reinforces the main tone and impression

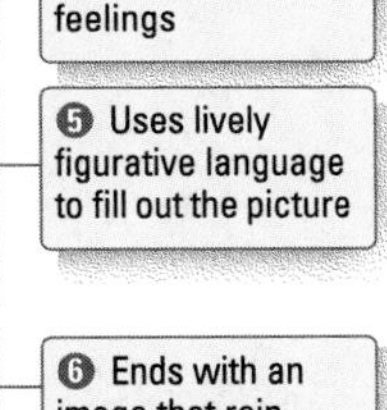

Teaching the Lesson

Analyzing the Model

"Her Three-Inch Feet"

D Before students read the model, explain that the writer uses unconventional sentence structure and punctuation as part of her own unique style. The student model introduces the reader to a 76-year-old Chinese woman with bound feet, a person that the writer affectionately calls Great-Aunt Yeung.

Explain that in parts of China, small feet were at one time considered beautiful. A girl's feet were broken and wrapped tightly in cloths so her feet wouldn't grow. This painful custom is no longer practiced. Have students read the model aloud. Then ask them what the bound feet of Great-Aunt Yeung might symbolize.

Possible Response: Great-Aunt Yeung's bound feet represent a past way of life for some Chinese women.

ANALYZING CLEAR TEXT

After students have read the model, have them evaluate the text for conciseness, correctness, and completeness. In addition have them evaluate how well the text meets the rubric for a successful personality profile.

1. Have students suggest an alternate opening based on the other options listed.
   Possible Response: She plods through the streets of New York's Chinatown in her size-one black-cloth shoes.
3. Ask students what the setting tells them about Great-Aunt Yeung.
   Possible Response: Since she lives near the heart of Chinatown in New York City, she most likely identifies with the Chinese culture. She is probably not wealthy since she lives in a small apartment with simple, worn possessions.
4. Point out that the writer's feelings towards a subject are important components in personality profiles. In other kinds of writing, the writer's feelings are less important.

Use McDougal Littell's ***Language Network,*** Chapter 18, for more instruction on writing a personality profile.

To engage students visually, use **Power Presentation** 1, Personality Profile.

Guiding Student Writing

Prewriting

Choosing a Subject

If after reading the Idea Bank students are having difficulty choosing their subjects, suggest they try the following:

- Find a photograph of a friend or relative. Freewrite about the photograph. Consider questions such as the following: What is the person doing? What is the setting of the picture? Why did someone take a picture of the event shown?
- Collect feature articles about personalities from newspapers, sports magazines, or TV and movie reviews.
- Watch a home video of friends, teammates, or family at an event at school or home. Describe one of the people during that event.

Planning the Personality Profile

1. Have students work in **writing pairs** to clarify their feelings about the subject. Allow three minutes for the first student to describe his or her feelings about the subject. The listener should ask questions to clarify what the speaker is feeling. After three minutes, tell students to switch roles, having the speaker become the listener/questioner.
2. Visual students may find it helpful to sketch out their subject in his or her surroundings.
3. Have students prepare a list of questions to ask in their interview. Tell them to prepare the kinds of questions that, when answered, will reveal what things in life are important to the person they are profiling.
4. Have students choose 3-4 ideas they'd like to share about their subjects. They can prioritize these ideas to set goals.

IDEA Bank

1. Your Working Portfolio
Look for ideas in the Writing Options you completed earlier in this unit:

- **Comparing Knights,** p. 169
- **Opinion Paragraph,** p. 191

2. Brainstorm
Discuss with classmates the kinds of people you admire and the traits of these people that stand out to you.

3. Match People and Categories
Think of qualities you admire, and then try to think of people to match those categories; for example, "The bravest person I can think of is ________."

Writing a Personality Profile

1 Prewriting

Choose a person you want to write about. Try **making a list** of people you consider your heroes or admire in some way. They don't have to be famous. In fact, you may feel more comfortable writing about someone that you know well:

- a favorite relative
- a neighbor
- a teacher
- a coach

What comes to mind when you think about these people? Write a few words or phrases to describe each one. You also might try **writing a simile** to summarize each person. ("Listening to this person is like drinking sunshine.") See the **Idea Bank** in the margin for more suggestions. After you select a person you want to write about, follow the steps below.

Planning Your Personality Profile

1. **Explore your attitude towards the subject.** How do you feel about the person? Why is the person important to you? What details or incidents can you describe that show the importance of the subject to you?
2. **Picture your subject in a typical setting.** Try visualizing your subject in his or her usual surroundings. What stands out about your subject? You might make a chart like this one to record details.

Personality Characteristics			
Physical	What Person Says	How Person Acts	How Others React

3. **Research or interview to gather information.** You can research a historical or famous figure using library resources or the Internet. For a profile of a lesser-known person, interviewing is the best method of getting information. Interviewing the subject and other people who know the subject well may give you information that is not available anywhere else.
4. **Set your goal for writing.** What impression of the subject do you want to leave in the minds of your readers? Analyze your subject to find an angle—a dominant impression or theme that captures the essence of the person. Then look for special details that help a reader picture the person.

Viewing and Representing

PICTURING TEXT STRUCTURE

Instruction Word choice and ideas are important parts of effective writing. However, the structure of a text—the way in which the words and ideas are organized—also adds to the effectiveness of a written piece.

Activity: Have students analyze the text structure of the student model by constructing an image such as a graphic organizer. While the graphic organizer on page 200 shows the basic features of a personality profile, the graphic students construct should reflect how the student writer has organized her piece. Students might first write a note about each paragraph to see how the paragraphs relate to one another and to the whole profile.
See sample graphic.

❷ Drafting

Make visible what, without you, might never have been seen.
Robert Bresson

Start drafting by simply getting your ideas down on paper. Keep your overall goal in mind as you try to get into the flow of your writing. Set down everything you want to say. Later you can cut what you don't need and add what you forgot.

Organizing Your Draft

Once you've gotten it all down, look for a way to organize what you want to say. As you rework your draft you are beginning your revision process. Here are some ways a personality profile might be organized.

- **In Chronological Order.** Narrate incidents in the time sequence in which they occurred. You might even focus on a day in your subject's life.
- **By Category.** Analyze different aspects of your subject's personality—such as characteristics, actions, and traits—one at a time.
- **By Setting.** Show your subject interacting in various settings or situations.
- **In Order of Importance.** Begin the essay with the most important incident or detail.

Choose one of these ways or any other way of developing your profile that works for you. Be sure to tie the incidents and descriptions you relate together with appropriate transitions.

Beginnings and Endings

Begin with something that will capture the reader's interest—a remarkable detail about the person or setting, some dialogue, or a good anecdote. You might end with a memorable detail or your personal reflections on the subject. Your ending should give a sense of completeness.

Elaborating on Ideas

Work to create a profile of your subject as a whole person, not just a one-dimensional figure. Lace your descriptions with details, specific scenes, and quotations or dialogue that indicate how the person you portray interacts with others. It should also be clear from your writing what things are important to the person you are profiling.

As you draft and refine your essay, be sure to consider the **purpose, audience,** and **occasion.** For example, if you are describing a situation in your school, include background information that a reader would need to know.

Have a Question?

See the **Writing Handbook**
Introductions, p.1358
Descriptive Writing, pp. 1363–1364

Ask Your Peer Reader

- What dominant impression did you get of my subject?
- How would you describe my attitude towards the person?
- What details are particularly vivid or memorable?
- What details, if any, distracted from the picture I was trying to present?
- What more would you like to know about my subject?

Drafting

Organizing the Draft

The student model represents one approach to writing a personality profile. Have students create their own structure. Students may begin their own writing by outlining their draft or by drawing a graphic organizer that helps them visualize how details may be grouped. For a sample graphic organizer, you may wish to revisit the graphic on page TE 201. You might share this graphic with students if you have not already done so.

Point out that there is no one "right" choice. For example, the writer of the student model could have organized her personality profile in chronological order. She might have begun by describing Great-Aunt Yeung's childhood, having her feet bound, her arrival in the United States, a specific time when she prayed, and a specific time when she went out into the streets of New York. Have students suggest how organization by chronological order would change the effect of the student model.

Beginnings and Endings

If students want to write a beginning that grabs the readers' interest, have them write two or three possible beginnings and read them to their writing partner. They can use the partner's response to choose an opening.

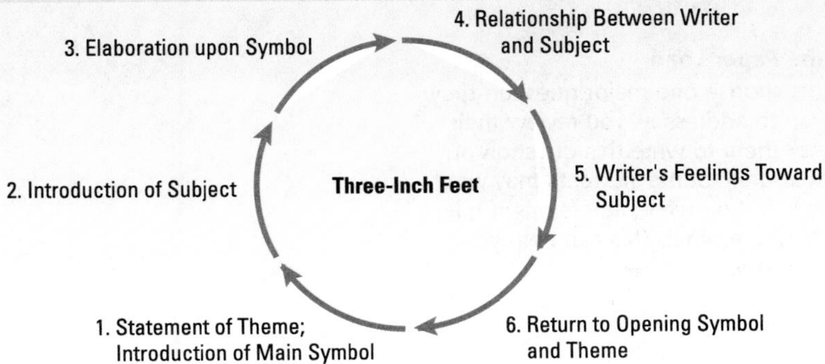

Revising

ADDING DETAIL

You might do a simple activity to guide students through the process of adding detail. Ask a volunteer to create a very simple sentence (Subject, predicate, adjective) describing the classroom. Then have students suggest additional modifiers, phrases, or precise verbs that create a more detailed description. Have students compare the initial simple sentence with the final sentence.

Editing and Proofreading

COMMA SPLICES

Remind students that when a comma is incorrectly used to separate two sentences, the error that results is a run-on sentence. A run-on sentence is confusing because it fails to indicate where one idea ends and the next begins. Show students that there are several ways to correct a run-on sentence. The method they choose may depend on the meaning of the sentence. See the Grammar Mini-Lesson on TE 205 for more information on correcting run-on sentences.

Other errors include the following: *East* and *West* are capitalized because they name hemispheres of the world. *Great-Aunt, size-one,* and *black-cloth* are hyphenated because they are compound adjectives. Hyphenating *size-one* and *black-cloth* also helps to avoid confusion in reading the last sentence. Although a comma could be used between *size-one* and *black-cloth,* leaving out the comma is a matter of style. The words seem to echo the sound of Great-Aunt Yeung's feet plodding through the streets of New York City.

Reflecting

Encourage students to recognize and evaluate the way in which they approached the writing assignment. Which prewriting strategies were most helpful? How did the praise or suggestions of their peer readers help them improve their personality profiles? Have them add these self-evaluations to their working portfolios.

Need revising help?

Review the **Rubric,** p. 200.

Consider **peer reader** comments.

Check **Revision Guidelines,** p. 1355.

3 Revising

TARGET SKILL ▶ ADDING DETAIL In descriptive writing, concrete details and examples help the reader envision the scene. They *show* the subject's personality traits in action rather than just naming them. Remember, however, to add details selectively so that they build a coherent impression.

> But it's not just a table: it's the table of Chinese gods. The burning incense on it ~~fills~~ *perfumes* the whole apartment. ~~Twice a day she kneels and lights~~ *The twice-daily ritual of worship consists of kneeling, lighting* the incense*, then bowing to the gods while holding up the incense with both hands above the head*. It is quite a lovely scene.

Confused by comma splices?

See the **Grammar Handbook,** pp. 1396–1429.

4 Editing and Proofreading

TARGET SKILL ▶ COMMA SPLICES With elaboration, you often have to link together several strings of ideas into more complex phrases and sentences. Commas, used carefully, add clarity to sentences and enable the reader to grasp how the parts relate. However, used incorrectly they can be distracting or confusing. One common error is the comma splice (or comma fault), in which the writer separates two sentences with a comma instead of the correct end mark.

> Great-Aunt Yeung will always have her own ways. The East and the West will always remain apart. The best proof of that is seeing Great-Aunt Yeung plod the streets of New York in her size-one black-cloth shoes.

Publishing IDEAS

- Collect the class profiles in a booklet to distribute in your school, to local libraries, or to senior citizen centers in your community.
- Submit your profile to a student-writing Web site.

More Online: Publishing Options
www.mcdougallittell.com

5 Reflecting

FOR YOUR WORKING PORTFOLIO What did you discover about your subject while completing the personality profile? What did you learn about yourself or about life from this experience? Attach your answers to these questions to your finished personality profile. Save your personality profile in your **Working Portfolio.**

Option

Managing the Paper Load

Have students choose one major question they would like you to address as you review their first drafts. Ask them to write this question on the top of their draft. Some students may want help with organization while others might have questions about grammar. This can help you focus your first review.

Assessment Practice Revising & Editing

Read this opening from the first draft of a personality profile. The underlined sections include the following kinds of errors:

- **unsupported ideas**
- **run-on sentences**
- **incorrect possessives**
- **punctuation errors**

For each underlined phrase or sentence, choose the revision that most improves the writing.

Her nickname is 'Mique, don't believe it. (1) Chamique Holdsclaw is anything but meek. She's a powerhouse. She has been called "the greatest women's basketball player of all time," yet she always strives to be better. (2)

Holdsclaws' (3) intensity helps to motivate her teammates. "Once I get it up, it filters through the team" she (4) says. Her team is the Tennessee Lady Volunteers the team won three consecutive championships. (5) Holdsclaw is definitely the heart and fire of the team. Her determination helps her live up to her favorite saying. (6)

1. **A.** Her nickname is 'Mique don't believe it.
   B. Just because her nickname is 'Mique don't believe it.
   C. Her nickname is 'Mique, but don't believe it.
   D. Correct as is.
2. **A.** She has been called "the greatest women's basketball player of all time." Yet she always strives to be better.
   B. She has been called "the greatest women's basketball player of all time," or she always strives to be better.
   C. Although she has been called "the greatest women's basketball player of all time," yet she always strives to be better.
   D. Correct as is.
3. **A.** Holdsclaw's
   B. Holdsclaws
   C. Holdsclaws's
   D. Correct as is.
4. **A.** team, "she
   B. team." She
   C. team," she
   D. team". She
5. **A.** Because Holdsclaw plays for the Tennessee Lady Volunteers, the team won three consecutive championships.
   B. Her team is the Tennessee Lady Volunteers and the team won three consecutive championships.
   C. Her team is the Tennessee Lady Volunteers, winner of three consecutive championships.
   D. Correct as is.
6. **A.** Her determination helped her live up to her favorite saying.
   B. Her determination helps her live up to her favorite saying, which she follows every day.
   C. Her determination helps her live up to her favorite saying: "Don't Dream it. Be it".
   D. Correct as is.

Need extra help?

See the **Grammar Handbook**
Run-on sentences, p. 1414
Punctuation, pp. 1418–1419
Possessives, p. 1319

Assessment Practice

Demonstrate how students can eliminate incorrect choices for the first question.

A. The first choice is a run-on sentence, therefore it isn't correct.
B. This sentence should include a comma to add clarity.
C. This choice is an improvement on the original sentence. By adding the conjunction, *but,* the writer links two ideas in one strong compound sentence.
D. This is a run-on sentence.

Answers
1. C; 2. D; 3. A; 4. C; 5. C; 6. C

Grammar

RUN-ON SENTENCES

Instruction A run-on sentence is made up of two or more sentences written as though they were one sentence.

Activity Write these run-on sentences on the chalkboard. Discuss why they are hard to read. Then have volunteers correct the sentences.

Great-Aunt Yeung lives in New York City, her apartment is located near the heart of Chinatown.

Great-Aunt Yeung's feet were bound to prevent them from growing this custom is no longer practiced in China.

Correct Great-Aunt Yeung lives in New York City. Her apartment is located near the heart of Chinatown. (with a period and a capital letter)

Correct Great-Aunt Yeung lives in New York City; her apartment is located near the heart of Chinatown. (with a semicolon)

Correct Great-Aunt Yeung's feet were bound to prevent them from growing; however, this custom is no longer practiced in China. (with a semicolon, a conjunctive adverb, and a comma)

Objectives
- research word origins as an aid to understanding word meaning, derivations, and influences on the English language
- understand how to use word parts and word families to build vocabulary
- use etymology as an aid in spelling

EXERCISE
Have students give their answers in the style of the column headed **Modern English.** Students' etymology traces will vary depending on the detail presented in the dictionaries that they consult. Samples are shown here.

companion—Middle English *compaignyon;* from Old French *compaignon;* from Vulgar Latin *companio, companion-:* from Latin *com-,* with + *panis,* bread.
diversion—Late Latin *diversio, diversion-,* act of turning aside; from Latin *diversus,* past participle of *divertere,* to divert.
entertain—Middle English *entertinen,* to maintain; from Old French *entretenir;* from Medieval Latin *intertenere:* Latin *inter,* among + *tenere,* to hold.
haughty—Middle English *haut;* from Old French *haut, halt;* alteration of Latin *altus,* high.
melody—Middle English *melodie;* from Old French; from Late Latin *melodia;* from Greek *meloidia,* singing choral song: *melos,* tune + *aiode,* song.
mischief—Middle English *mischef;* from Old French *meschief,* misfortune; from *meschever,* to end badly: *mes-,* badly + *chever,* to happen, come to an end.
pain—Middle English; from Old French *peine;* from Latin *poena,* penalty; from Greek *poine,* penalty.
solution—Middle English; from Old French; from Latin *solutio, solution-;* from *solutus,* past participle of *solvere,* to loosen.
technique—French, technical, technique; from Greek *tekhnikos,* technical.
traitor—Middle English; from Old French; from Latin *traditor, traditor-;* from *traditus,* past participle of *tradere,* to betray.

The Origins of English Words

The English language is growing and changing constantly. Notice the differences between this passage from *The Canterbury Tales* in Middle English and a modern English translation of the same lines.

> **And smale foweles maken melodyë**
> **That slepen al the nyght with open yë**
> —Chaucer, *The Canterbury Tales*
>
> **And the small fowl are making melody**
> **That sleep away the night with open eye**
> —*The Canterbury Tales,* translated by Nevill Coghill

Modern English evolved from Middle English, which evolved from Old English. Along the way, words from other languages, including Latin and Greek, were added to English. One way to build your vocabulary is to explore the **etymology,** or history and origins, of words.

Etymology Information in Dictionaries Learning about how Modern English words came to be can help you understand their meanings. You can find information about the etymology of a word like *prologue* in most kinds of dictionaries. Examine the following dictionary entry to see how this word developed from words in other languages.

pro•logue (prō′lôg′) *n.* the preface or introduction to a story or play. [Middle English *prolog,* from Old French *prologue,* from Latin *prologus* preface to a play, from Greek *prologos,* part of a Greek play preceding the entry of the chorus, from *pro-* before + *logos* speech]

Modern English
prologue
Middle English
prolog
Old French
prologue
Latin
prologus
Greek
prologos
pro- + *logos*
(before) + (speech)

Strategies for Building Vocabulary

❶ Word Parts Now that you have studied the word *prologue,* you know that the meaning of the word part *logue* involves speech. Suppose you later come across the word *epilogue.* You can assume that this word also has something to do with speech because it contains *logue.* If you also know that the prefix *epi-* can mean "after," then you can predict that the meaning of *epilogue* is somehow related to "after speech."

epi- + *logue* = *epilogue*
(after) (speech) (concluding section in a literary work)

❷ Word Families Groups of words that contain the same word parts are called **word families.** Knowing the meaning of one word in a family can help you predict the meanings of related words. The table in the next column shows a family of words that contain *logue* and are derived from the Greek word *logos.* Notice how the meanings of the words are related.

English Words Derived from Greek *logos*

English Word	Meaning
prologue	the preface or introduction to a story or play
monologue	the speech of a character who is alone on stage, voicing his or her thoughts
dialogue	a conversation between two or more characters
epilogue	a concluding section in a literary work, often dealing with the future of the characters

❸ Spelling Learning the etymology of *prologue* can help you remember how to spell it and words related to it. For example, once you realize that *monologue, dialogue,* and *epilogue* all contain the word part *logue,* you may find it easier to remember the unusual spelling of the last syllable.

EXERCISE Use a dictionary to trace the etymology of these words from *The Canterbury Tales.*

companion	haughty	pain	technique
diversion	melody	solution	traitor
entertain	mischief		

Inverting Word Order for Sentence Variety

Grammar from Literature

Writers vary sentence structure in both prose and poetry for a variety of reasons.

- To add interest.
- To shift the emphasis in a sentence.
- To achieve a poetic effect.

One way to vary sentence structure is by inverting, or reversing, the order of the subject and the verb.

Subject first

subject ... verb

Those two urns of good and evil gifts are at the door of Zeus.

Inverted

verb ... subject

At the door of Zeus are those two urns of good and evil gifts.

—Homer, the *Iliad*

The subject can also come after other sentence parts.

adverb subject verb

Eagerly he approached, in hope to learn.

—*The Canterbury Tales*

prepositional phrases ... subject verb

At daybreak, with the sun's first light, they saw
How well he had worked.

—*Beowulf*

direct object ... subject verb

A medal of St. Christopher he wore.

—*The Canterbury Tales*

As you look at your own writing, ask yourself these questions to see if you should consider using inverted word order:

- Are my sentences too similar in structure or length?
- Do I want to emphasize certain words or ideas?
- Would changing the order of some of the words create an interesting rhythm?

Usage Tip When you place a verb before a subject, make sure you choose the correct verb form to match the subject. Plural subjects need plural verbs; singular subjects need singular verbs.

Incorrect

verb ... subject

Near the smoldering wreck stands the dazed victims.

Correct

verb ... subject

Near the smoldering wreck stand the dazed victims.

Punctuation Tip When you invert word order by moving a sequence of prepositional phrases from the end of a sentence to the beginning of a sentence, remember to put a comma after the last prepositional phrase in the sequence.

In the hall of Hrothgar, Grendel murdered many men.
On the road to Canterbury, the people told tales.

WRITING EXERCISE Change the structure of each of the following sentences by moving the underlined words to a different position within the sentence. Remember to punctuate correctly.

1. Grendel's mother goes to Herot to seek revenge the night after Beowulf defeats Grendel.
2. Beowulf fights bravely as the monster claws at him.
3. The pilgrims set off on a journey from Southwark.
4. The seafarer drifted through winter on an ice-cold sea.
5. Barbara Allan is a cruel woman.

PROOFREADING EXERCISE Rewrite the sentences below, correcting any errors in punctuation and usage.

1. Into Canterbury rides the 29 travelers and the innkeeper.
2. To Caedmon's account of his amazing dream listens the abbess and the reeve.
3. In the tale of Beowulf we learn about the heroism of a Geatish warrior.
4. Before the terrible monster lies the bodies of those who fell.
5. Outside the walls of Troy Achilles and Hector fight to the death.

Sentence Crafting

Objectives

- use varied sentence structure to express meanings and achieve desired effect
- revise drafts by rethinking content organization and style

WRITING EXERCISE

1. The night after Beowulf defeats Grendel, Grendel's mother goes to Herot to seek revenge.
2. Bravely Beowulf fights as the monster claws at him.
3. From Southwark the pilgrims set off on a journey.
4. Through winter drifted the seafarer on an ice-cold sea.
5. A cruel woman is Barbara Allan.

PROOFREADING EXERCISE

1. Into Canterbury ride the 29 travelers and the innkeeper.
2. To Caedmon's account of his amazing dream listen the abbess and the reeve.
3. In the tale of Beowulf, we learn about the heroism of a Geatish warrior.
4. Before the terrible monster lie the bodies of those who fell.
5. Outside the walls of Troy, Achilles and Hector fight to the death.

PART 3 Attempts at Perfection

Like the people of any age, those of the medieval period lived in an imperfect world. Nevertheless, they dreamed of what their lives could be. Some people looked to religion to teach them how to live virtuously. Others sought an idealized world in literature. Tales of chivalry, popular in this era, recount the adventures of heroic knights who live by a strict code of behavior. In this part of Unit One, you will read about characters who strive for—but don't quite attain—perfection. As you read, consider how your attitude toward them would be different if they were perfect.

208

PREPARING to *Read*

from Sir Gawain and the Green Knight

Romance by THE GAWAIN POET
Translated by JOHN GARDNER

Connect to Your Life

A Person of Honor Suppose that you hear someone say, "The student-council president should be a person of honor." What qualities or ideals come to mind? Create a word web like the one shown, jotting down words or phrases that you think describe an honorable person.

Build Background

An Ideal World Medieval aristocrats relished tales of adventure, especially stories of brave and gallant knights. Although real knights were far from perfect, the knights of legend strove continually to obey a code of chivalry, a set of rules for gentlemanly and heroic behavior. Their code represented a combination of Christian and military ideals, including faith, modesty, loyalty, courtesy, bravery, and honor. The ideal knight respected and vigorously defended his church, his king, his country, and victims of injustice.

Especially popular during the medieval period were legends of King Arthur and his heroic knights of the Round Table. The popularity of these tales was due in part to the idealized world in which they were set. It was a world of castles, heroes, courtly love, and magical spells—a world quite unlike the real medieval England, with its plagues, political battles, and civil unrest. Although Launcelot was often presented as the greatest and most distinguished of Arthur's knights, in early tales that role was given to Arthur's nephew Gawain (gə-wän'), who was famous for his courage and for his unfailing chivalry.

WORDS TO KNOW
Vocabulary Preview

aghast	pivot
amended	renown
chagrin	reproof
daunt	respite
efficacious	uncanny
flinch	unwieldy
heft	wince
ingeniously	

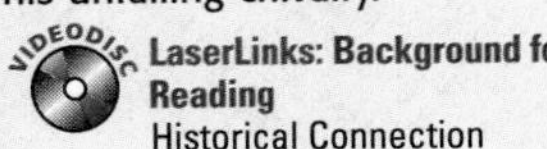

LaserLinks: Background for Reading
Historical Connection

Focus Your Reading

LITERARY ANALYSIS ROMANCE The **romance** has been a popular narrative form since the Middle Ages. Generally, the term *romance* refers to any imaginative adventure concerned with noble heroes, gallant love, a chivalric code of honor, and daring deeds. Romances usually have faraway settings, depict events unlike those of ordinary life, and idealize their heroes as well as the eras in which the heroes lived. Medieval romances are also often lighthearted in tone and involve fantasy. Be aware of the characteristics of romance as you read the excerpt from *Sir Gawain and the Green Knight.*

ACTIVE READING READING A NARRATIVE POEM Like all narrative poems, *Sir Gawain and the Green Knight* contains the same elements as a short story—**setting, characters,** and **plot.** These elements combine to develop one or more **themes.** With any narrative poem, it is important to identify details of setting, character, and plot as you read.

READER'S NOTEBOOK Keep track of the plot by writing brief notes about the actions of each character. Note the ways in which honor plays a role in the course of events.

OVERVIEW

Objectives

1. understand and appreciate a medieval **romance** form **(Literary Analysis)**
2. describe the development of **plot** and identify conflicts **(Literary Analysis)**
3. use reading strategies such as **reading a narrative poem (Active Reading)**

Summary

A huge knight, dressed all in green, appears at Camelot on New Year's Eve. The Green Knight challenges any man in the court to strike his bare neck with an ax, provided that the Green Knight may do the same to the man in a year and a day. Sir Gawain accepts the challenge and severs the Green Knight's head with one blow. The Green Knight retrieves his head and rides off. One year later, on the way to keep his appointment with the Green Knight, Gawain reaches a castle, the lord and lady who reside there invite him to stay for a few days. The lady attempts to seduce Gawain, but he resists her advances. After leaving the castle, Gawain faces the Green Knight. The Knight nicks Gawain's neck, thus fulfilling the pact. The Green Knight explains that he himself had been Gawain's host and had arranged for his wife to test Gawain's honor.

 Use **Unit One Resource Book,** p. 62 for additional support.

Thematic Link

Gawain, in his **attempts at perfection**, presents a model for the ideal behavior expected of a Knight of the Round Table.

5-Minute Warm-Up

Daily Language SkillBuilder

Have students **proofread** the display sentences on page 15m and write them correctly. The sentences also appear on Transparency 5 of **Grammar Transparencies and Copymasters.**

Preteaching Vocabulary

If you would like to preteach the WORDS TO KNOW for this selection, use the Mini Lesson p. 210.

LESSON RESOURCES

UNIT ONE RESOURCE BOOK, pp. 62–66

ASSESSMENT RESOURCES
Formal Assessment, pp. 31–32
Teacher's Guide to Assessment and Portfolio Use
Test Generator

SKILLS TRANSPARENCIES AND COPYMASTERS
Reading and Critical Thinking
- Noting Details, T9 (for Think Critically 4, p. 222)

Grammar
- Compound Predicates, C81 (for Mini Lesson, p. 213)
- Compound Subjects, C82 (for Mini Lesson, p. 217)

Vocabulary
- Prefixes, C28 (for Mini Lesson, p. 216)

Writing
- Transitional Words, T9 (for Writing Option 4, p. 223)
- Sensory Word List, T14 (for Writing Option 2, p. 223)
- Opinion Statement, C35 (for Writing Option 3, p. 223)

Communications
- Dramatic Reading, T12 (for Activities & Explorations 2, p. 223)
- Identifying and Analyzing Artistic Elements in Literary Texts, T13 (for Activities & Explorations 3, 4, p. 223)

INTEGRATED TECHNOLOGY
Audio Library
LaserLinks
- Historical Connection: The World of Medieval Knights. See **Teacher's SourceBook,** p. 12.

Internet: Research Starter
Visit our website:
www.mcdougallittell.com

TEACHING THE LITERATURE

Reading and Analyzing

Reading Skills and Strategies: PREVIEW

Have students scan the selection before they begin reading. They can pay special attention to headings, pieces of art, and called-out quotations. Discuss what students anticipate as they begin reading. Have students support their predictions with evidence and experience.

Active Reading

READING A NARRATIVE POEM

Ask students to note as they read details of setting, character, and plot. Where is the story taking place? What time of year is it? What sort of behavior might be expected from a knight errant? Have them monitor and modify their strategies as they read.

Use **Unit One Resource Book,** p. 64 for more practice.

Literary Analysis ROMANCE

The word *romance*, as generally used today, refers to courtship and love. However, in literary terms, a romance is any imaginative adventure story concerned with noble heroes, gallant love, a chivalric code of honor, and daring deeds.

Use **Unit One Resource Book,** p. 65 for more exercises.

Literary Analysis: CONFLICT

A Ask what conflict is established through the two-sentence introduction that precedes the narrative itself.

Possible Response: Answers will vary but should include the Green Knight's intrusive actions.

As the poem begins, Arthur and his knights are gathered to celebrate Christmas and the new year with feasting and revelry. In the midst of their festivities, an enormous man—who is entirely green—bounds through the door. A

Splendid that knight errant stood in a splay of green,
And green, too, was the mane of his mighty destrier;
Fair fanning tresses enveloped the fighting man's shoulders,
And over his breast hung a beard as big as a bush;
The beard and the huge mane burgeoning forth from his head
Were clipped off clean in a straight line over his elbows,
And the upper half of each arm was hidden underneath
As if covered by a king's chaperon, closed round the neck.
The mane of the marvelous horse was much the same,
Well crisped and combed and carefully pranked with knots,
Threads of gold interwoven with the glorious green,
Now a thread of hair, now another thread of gold;
The tail of the horse and the forelock were tricked the same way,
And both were bound up with a band of brilliant green
Adorned with glittering jewels the length of the dock,
Then caught up tight with a thong in a criss-cross knot
Where many a bell tinkled brightly, all burnished gold.
So monstrous a mount, so mighty a man in the saddle
Was never once encountered on all this earth
till then;
His eyes, like lightning, flashed,
And it seemed to many a man,
That any man who clashed
With him would not long stand.

GUIDE FOR READING

1 knight errant (ĕr′ənt): a knight who wanders about, searching for adventure in order to prove his chivalry; **splay:** display.

2 destrier (dĕs′trē-ər): war horse.

5 burgeoning (bûr′jə-nĭng): growing.

8 chaperon (shăp′ə-rōn′): hood.

10 pranked with knots: decorated with bows.

13 forelock: the part of a horse's mane that falls forward between the ears.

15 dock: the fleshy part of an animal's tail.

Teaching Options

Mini Lesson Preteaching Vocabulary

USING SYNONYMS

Instruction Call students' attention to the list of WORDS TO KNOW. Remind them that supplying familiar synonyms in connection with new words often helps people learn the new words.

Activity Write the following words on the chalkboard and have the students copy them in a single column on their papers: *shocked, corrected, embarrassment, dismay, effective, lift up, recoil, cleverly, turn, fame, criticism, rest (n.), eerie, unmanageable, spring back.*

As students proceed through the selection, have them enter the appropriate Word To Know next to the correct synonym. Have students interpret the connotative difference.

Monitor students' work periodically, perhaps by calling upon students to share their entries with the class. Encourage more capable students to supply an additional synonym for words such as *uncanny, respite,* and *heft.*

Use **Unit One Resource Book,** p. 66 for more practice.

Green Knight

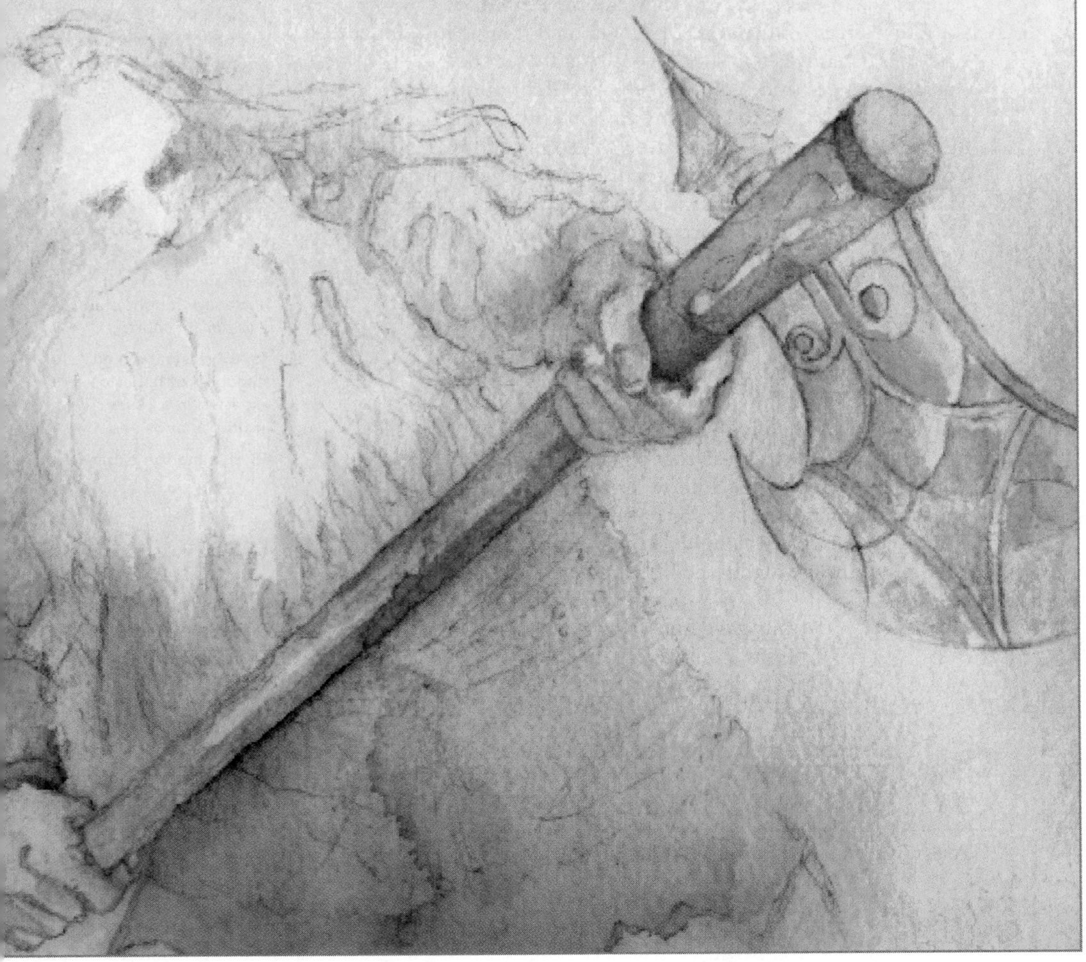

Customizing Instruction

Less Proficient Readers

Encourage students to page through the selection to observe that it is divided into sections separated by brief narratives that summarize connecting material. Point out that these narratives will help them keep track of how much time has passed between sections.

Gifted and Talented Students

Encourage students to identify some of the symbols used in the selection and explain their significance.

Possible Responses: Holly, representing everlasting life through Christ; green, representing spring and the regeneration of life; the cut Gawain receives, representing his lapse; green sash, representing Gawain's fall and redemption.

Students Acquiring English

The long, complex sentences in this selection may challenge many students. Encourage those who are having difficulty to read this piece as if it were prose. Emphasize the importance of reading to punctuation marks, not to the end of a poetic line.

 Use **Spanish Study Guide** for additional support, pp. 34–36

Reading and Analyzing

Literary Analysis ROMANCE

A Ask students to identify the selection's setting.

Answer: Camelot, King Arthur's court.

Also, ask how the appearance of the Green Knight exhibits characteristics of romance.

Possible Response: He is a giant and both he and his horse are all green.

Then, ask students what they know or have heard about Camelot. Why isn't King Arthur afraid of the Green Knight?

Possible Response: He is heroic and brave; he lives according to a chivalric code of behavior.

GUIDE FOR READING

B The Green Knight's tone seems arrogant.

Literary Analysis: CONFLICT

C Review with students the basic components of plot: initiating incident, exposition, rising action, climax, falling action, resolution. Also review the concept that every plot is based upon some type of conflict, or problem to solve. Explain that the Green Knight's challenge completes the exposition of the plot. Ask students what important information the story has established so far.

Possible Response: A strange knight has appeared and issued a challenge to Arthur's knights.

GUIDE FOR READING

D The Green Knight dares any of Arthur's knights to exchange strokes with an ax.

E Arthur is angry because the Green Knight has insulted his knights.

But the huge man came unarmed, without helmet or hauberk,
No breastplate or gorget or iron cleats on his arms;
He brought neither shield nor spearshaft to shove or to smite,
But instead he held in one hand a bough of the holly
That grows most green when all the groves are bare
And held in the other an ax, immense and unwieldy,
A pitiless battleblade terrible to tell of.

King Arthur stared down at the stranger before the high dais
And greeted him nobly, for nothing on earth frightened him.
And he said to him, "Sir, you are welcome in this place;
I am the head of this court. They call me Arthur.
Get down from your horse, I beg you, and join us for dinner,
And then whatever you seek we will gladly see to."
But the stranger said, "No, so help me God on high,
My errand is hardly to sit at my ease in your castle!
But friend, since your praises are sung so far and wide,
Your castle the best ever built, people say, and your barons
The stoutest men in steel armor that ever rode steeds,
Most mighty and most worthy of all mortal men
And tough devils to toy with in tournament games,
And since courtesy is in flower in this court, they say,
All these tales, in truth, have drawn me to you at this time.
You may be assured by this holly branch I bear
That I come to you in peace, not spoiling for battle.
If I'd wanted to come in finery, fixed up for fighting,
I have back at home both a helmet and a hauberk,
A shield and a sharp spear that shines like fire,
And other weapons that I know pretty well how to use.
But since I don't come here for battle, my clothes are mere cloth.
Now if you are truly as bold as the people all say,
You will grant me gladly the little game that I ask
as my right."
Arthur gave him answer
And said, "Sir noble knight,
If it's a duel you're after,
We'll furnish you your fight."

"Good heavens, I want no such thing! I assure you, Sire,
You've nothing but beardless babes about this bench!
If I were hasped in my armor and high on my horse,
You haven't a man that could match me, your might is so feeble.

25 hauberk (hô′bərk): a coat of chain mail (a type of armor).

26 breastplate or gorget (gôr′jĭt) **or iron cleats:** armor for the chest, the throat, or the shoulders and elbows.

32 dais (dā′ĭs): a raised platform where honored guests are seated.

34 this place: Camelot, Arthur's favorite castle and the site of his court of the Round Table.

44 In medieval tournaments, knights on horseback fought one another for sport.

45 courtesy: the high standards of behavior expected in a king's court; **in flower:** at its best.

48 spoiling for: eager for.

63 hasped: fastened.

B **61–64** What is the Green Knight's tone as he addresses King Arthur?

WORDS TO KNOW

unwieldy (ŭn-wēl′dē) *adj.* so large, heavy, or oddly shaped as to be difficult to hold or use

212

Teaching Options

BLOCK SCHEDULING: MANAGING TIME

If your schedule requires that you cover the lesson objectives in a shorter time, use . . .

- Preparing to Read, p. 209
- Thinking Through the Literature, p. 222
- Vocabulary in Action, p. 224

If you want to take advantage of longer class time, use . . .

- TE Teaching Options: Vocabulary, pp. 210, 216; Grammar, pp. 213, 217; Multicultural Link, p. 214; Workplace Link, p. 218; Standardized Test Practice, p. 215; Viewing and Representing, p. 220
- Choices and Challenges and Author Activity, pp. 223–224

And so all I ask of this court is a Christmas game,
For the Yule is here, and New Year's, and here sit young men;
If any man holds himself, here in this house, so hardy,
So bold in his blood—and so brainless in his head—
That he dares to stoutly exchange one stroke for another,
I shall let him have as my present this lovely gisarme,
This ax, as heavy as he'll need, to handle as he likes,
And I will abide the first blow, bare-necked as I sit.
C If anyone here has the daring to try what I've offered,
Leap to me lightly, lad; lift up this weapon;
I give you the thing forever—you may think it your own;
And I will stand still for your stroke, steady on the floor,
Provided you honor my right, when my inning comes,
to repay.
But let the respite be
A twelvemonth and a day;
Come now, my boys, let's see
What any here can say."

70 gisarme (gĭ-zärm'): a battle-ax with a long shaft and a two-edged head.

D **67–82** What challenge does the Green Knight offer?

If they were like stone before, they were stiller now,
Every last lord in the hall, both the high and the low;
The stranger on his destrier stirred in the saddle
And ferociously his red eyes rolled around;
He lowered his grisly eyebrows, glistening green,
And waved his beard and waited for someone to rise;
When no one answered, he coughed, as if embarrassed,
And drew himself up straight and spoke again:
"What! Can this be King Arthur's court?" said the stranger,
"Whose renown runs through many a realm, flung far and wide?
What has become of your chivalry and your conquest,
Your greatness-of-heart and your grimness and grand words?
Behold the radiance and renown of the mighty Round Table
Overwhelmed by a word out of one man's mouth!
You shiver and blanch before a blow's been shown!"
And with that he laughed so loud that the lord was distressed;
In chagrin, his blood shot up in his face and limbs
so fair;
More angry he was than the wind,
And likewise each man there;
And Arthur, bravest of men,
Decided now to draw near.

97 blanch: turn white.

E **99–101** Why is King Arthur so angry?

WORDS TO KNOW

respite (rĕs'pĭt) *n.* a period of rest or delay
renown (rĭ-noun') *n.* fame
chagrin (shə-grĭn') *n.* a feeling of embarrassment caused by humiliation or failure

Customizing Instruction

Multiple Learning Styles

Visual Learners

Encourage students to visualize the Green Knight with his holly bough, ax, and fiery steed. Ask them to draw the knight, if they wish. Invite them to visualize other descriptive passages and action scenes in the selection as well.

Have students draw a chart with two heads: Plot Elements and Events. Under the first heading, have them list the main elements of plot: initiating incident, exposition, rising action, climax, falling action, resolution. Then, under the second heading, have them list events in the story that fulfill the specific plot function. For example, the initiating incident is the Green Knight's entrance into Camelot.

Students Acquiring English

1 Explain to students that the Green Knight carries a holly branch as a symbol of his peaceful intentions. Tell them the white dove is another symbol of peace for many Western cultures. Then, ask students what plants or animals symbolize peace in their home cultures. Encourage them to draw comparisons and contrasts between their cultural symbols and images such as the dove or holly branch.

Gifted and Talented

Encourage students to explore the differences between being confident and being egotistical. Which term do they think best describes the Green Knight?

Mini Lesson Grammar

COMPOUND PREDICATES

Instruction Write this excerpt from "Sir Gawain and the Green Knight" on the chalkboard.

"King Arthur stared down at the stranger before the high dais and greeted him nobly. . . ." (lines 32–33)

Ask students to identify the subject of the sentence. (*King Arthur*) Then ask them to identify the predicate. (*stared and greeted*) Point out that this is a compound predicate. A compound predicate consists of two or more verbs that share the same subject and are joined by a conjunction. In this case, the verbs are joined by the conjunction *and*.

Activity Have students create other sentences with compound predicates that have King Arthur as the subject.

Exercise Ask students to identify the compound predicate in the following sentence.

The Green Knight leaped from his horse, gave Arthur his sword, and bared his neck for the blow. (*leaped, gave, bared*)

Use **Grammar Transparencies and Copymasters,** p. 79.

Use McDougal Littell's ***Language Network*** for more instruction in compound predicates.

Reading and Analyzing

Reading Skills and Strategies: MAKING INFERENCES

A Ask students to explain why King Arthur accepts the Green Knight's challenge. Have them support their opinion with evidence and experience.
Possible Response: He feels his position as leader requires him to do so.

GUIDE FOR READING

B Gawain is modest and loyal.

Literary Analysis ROMANCE

C Ask students what element of fantasy has been introduced into the story.
Possible Response: The Green Knight's head has been chopped off, but he remains unharmed.

Ask why Sir Gawain will probably seek out the Green Knight on the appointed day.
Possible Responses: because he promised; because his allegiance to the chivalric code requires it.

Literary Analysis: CONFLICT

D The surprising moment when the decapitated Green Knight picks up his own head is a major event propelling the rising action. Ask how this complicates the conflict between Sir Gawain and the Green Knight.
Possible Responses: The Green Knight has supernatural powers; Gawain realizes he probably will be killed.

GUIDE FOR READING

E Since he struck the Green Knight with an ax, Gawain must accept a similar blow.

And he said, "By heaven, sir, your request is strange;
But since you have come here for folly, you may as well find it.
I know no one here who's aghast of your great words.
Give me your gisarme, then, for the love of God,
And gladly I'll grant you the gift you have asked to be given."
Lightly the King leaped down and clutched it in his hand;
Then quickly that other lord alighted on his feet.
Arthur lay hold of the ax, he gripped it by the handle,
And he swung it up over him sternly, as if to strike.
The stranger stood before him, in stature higher
By a head or more than any man here in the house;
Sober and thoughtful he stood there and stroked his beard,
And with patience like a priest's he pulled down his collar,
No more unmanned or dismayed by Arthur's might
Than he'd be if some baron on the bench had brought him a glass
of wine.
Then Gawain, at Guinevere's side,
Made to the King a sign:
"I beseech you, Sire," he said,
"Let this game be mine.

"Now if you, my worthy lord," said Gawain to the King,
"Would command me to step from the dais and stand with you there,
That I might without bad manners move down from my place
(Though I couldn't, of course, if my liege lady disliked it)
I'd be deeply honored to advise you before all the court;
For I think it unseemly, if I understand the matter,
That challenges such as this churl has chosen to offer
Be met by Your Majesty—much as it may amuse you—
When so many bold-hearted barons sit about the bench:
No men under Heaven, I am sure, are more hardy in will
Or better in body on the fields where battles are fought;
I myself am the weakest, of course, and in wit the most feeble;
My life would be least missed, if we let out the truth.
Only as you are my uncle have I any honor,
For excepting your blood, I bear in my body slight virtue.
And since this affair that's befallen us here is so foolish,
And since I have asked for it first, let it fall to me.
If I've reasoned incorrectly, let all the court say,
without blame."
The nobles gather round
And all advise the same:
"Let the King step down
And give Sir Gawain the game!"

106 folly: dangerous and foolish activity.

118 unmanned: deprived of manly courage.

121 Guinevere: King Arthur's wife.

128 liege (lēj) **lady:** a lady to whom one owes loyalty and service; here used by Gawain to refer to Queen Guinevere.

131 churl: rude, uncouth person.

B **136–139** How does Gawain's description of himself reflect a knight's code of chivalry?

WORDS TO KNOW **aghast** (ə-găst') *adj.* struck with terror or amazement; shocked

214

Teaching Options

Multicultural Link: Chivalric Tales

Romances about King Arthur and the members of his court were told and retold in various medieval European cultures, including those of England, France, and Germany, and have become part of the common heritage of Western civilization. In Japan, tales of the samurai, a warrior class whose code of unquestioning loyalty is similar to the code of chivalry, are the basis of numerous poems, plays, and films. Although most chivalric tales exalt their heroes, *Don Quixote,* by Spanish writer Miguel de Cervantes, takes a satiric look at the knight's code of chivalry. One of the greatest works of all literature, the novel tells the story of a middle-aged Spanish landowner who imagines himself a knight in armor and sets out to perform heroic deeds.

The figure of the chivalrous knight has descendants in later literary genres as well, including science fiction, westerns, detective thrillers, and gothic romances. You might ask students to compare their favorite contemporary heroes from one of these genres with Sir Gawain and the code of chivalry.

Arthur grants Gawain's request to take on the Green Knight's challenge. The Green Knight asks Gawain to identify himself, and the two agree on their pact. Gawain then prepares to strike his blow against the Green Knight.

On the ground, the Green Knight got himself into position,
His head bent forward a little, the bare flesh showing,
His long and lovely locks laid over his crown
So that any man there might note the naked neck.
Sir Gawain laid hold of the ax and he hefted it high,
His pivot foot thrown forward before him on the floor,
And then, swiftly, he slashed at the naked neck;
The sharp of the battleblade shattered asunder the bones
And sank through the shining fat and slit it in two,
And the bit of the bright steel buried itself in the ground.
The fair head fell from the neck to the floor of the hall
And the people all kicked it away as it came near their feet.
The blood splashed up from the body and glistened on the green,
But he never faltered or fell for all of that,
But swiftly he started forth upon stout shanks
And rushed to reach out, where the King's retainers stood,
Caught hold of the lovely head, and lifted it up,
And leaped to his steed and snatched up the reins of the bridle,
Stepped into stirrups of steel and, striding aloft,
He held his head by the hair, high, in his hand;
And the stranger sat there as steadily in his saddle
As a man entirely unharmed, although he was headless
on his steed.
He turned his trunk about,
That baleful body that bled,
And many were faint with fright
When all his say was said.

He held his head in his hand up high before him,
Addressing the face to the dearest of all on the dais;
And the eyelids lifted wide, and the eyes looked out,
And the mouth said just this much, as you may now hear:
"Look that you go, Sir Gawain, as good as your word,
And seek till you find me, as loyally, my friend,
As you've sworn in this hall to do, in the hearing of the knights.
Come to the Green Chapel, I charge you, and take
A stroke the same as you've given, for well you deserve
To be readily requited on New Year's morn.

162 shanks: legs.

163 retainers: servants or attendants.

172 baleful: threatening evil; sinister.

184 requited: paid back.

E For what does Gawain deserve to be requited? How do you expect this will be done?

WORDS TO KNOW

heft (hĕft) *v.* to lift up; hoist

pivot (pĭv′ət) *adj.* acting as a center around which something turns

Customizing Instruction

Less Proficient Readers

Check to make sure students understand what has happened in King Arthur's court.

- What is the Green Knight's challenge?
  Answer: He offers to exchange ax blows to the neck with any knight.
- How do the knights react to the challenge?
  Possible Response: At first the knights are aghast, and then Arthur answers the challenge; finally, Gawain takes Arthur's place.

Then, have students set a purpose for reading. Have students read to see what will happen when Gawain strikes his blow. Encourage them to speculate about why the Green Knight is so fearless. Help them see the relationship between the supernatural aspects of the Knight and his seeming invincibility.

Students Acquiring English

1 Make sure students understand what "gift" Arthur is referring to in line 109 *(the blow to the Green Knight's neck).* To help students understand poetic language such as alliteration, have them supply words from their native language that are alliterative. Then, ask them to translate these words into English and to note which ones retain alliteration (or can be made to, with close translations) and which ones do not. Often, words that come from an Indo-European language retain alliteration more so than words from other language families.

Assessment Standardized Test Practice

IDENTIFYING A WRITER'S INTENDED MEANING

Have students compare the descriptions of the Green Knight on pages 212 and 213 (lines 1–30 and lines 85–88) to that on page 215 (148–164). Ask them why the poet chose the descriptive words he did. How did he want the audience to visualize the Green Knight in these two different scenes? If necessary, focus their attention on words such as *grisly* and *ferociously* (lines 86–87) and *fair* (line 158) and *lovely* (line 164). Students should note that the first two descriptions of the Green Knight emphasize his barbaric qualities and are intended to frighten the audience. The later description presents the Green Knight as more of a martyr; instead of being huge and ferocious, he is fair and completely unarmed.

Reading and Analyzing

Reading Skills and Strategies:
MAKING INFERENCES

A Ask students why they think the king and Gawain laugh after the Green Knight departs.
Possible Responses: to release tension; to conceal their fear; to show they think the situation preposterous.

Literary Analysis: SIMILE

B Review the concept of simile with students, then ask them to note the similes in lines 199 and 200. Discuss what these similes add to our understanding and picture of Gawain's situation.

Literary Analysis ROMANCE

C The chivalrous knight's idealistic devotion to his lady is a major element in this medieval adventure. Ask students what other principles guide Gawain's behavior.
Possible Responses: loyalty to his king; Christian moral codes; ideals of courage and fairness.

Also point out, however, that the woman is taking the initiative here, a behavior not usually seen in women in medieval romances.

GUIDE FOR READING

D Because it might help protect him against the blow struck by the Green Knight.

Active Reading
READING A NARRATIVE POEM

E Ask students what Sir Gawain's agreement to remain silent about the gift suggests about his character.
Possible Responses: Gawain isn't perfect; he respects his lady's wishes; he fears the consequences if he tells his host the truth.

Many men know me, the Knight of the Green Chapel;
Therefore if you seek to find me, you shall not fail.
Come or be counted a coward, as is fitting."
Then with a rough jerk he turned the reins
And haled away through the hall-door, his head in his hand,
And fire of the flint flew out from the hooves of the foal.
To what kingdom he was carried no man there knew,
No more than they knew what country it was he came from.
What then?
The King and Gawain there
Laugh at the thing and grin; **A**
And yet, it was an affair
Most marvelous to men.

As the end of the year approaches, Gawain leaves on his quest to find the Green Chapel and fulfill his pledge. After riding through wild country and encountering many dangers, he comes upon a splendid castle. The lord of the castle welcomes Gawain and invites him to stay with him and his lady for a few days.

1 The lord proposes that he will go out to hunt each day while Gawain stays at the castle. At the end of the day, they will exchange what they have won. **2** While the lord is out hunting, the lady attempts to seduce Gawain. Gawain resists her, however, and on the first two days accepts only kisses, which he gives to the lord at the end of each day in exchange for what the lord has gained in the hunt. On the third day Gawain continues to resist the lady, but she presses him to accept another gift.

She held toward him a ring of the yellowest gold
And, standing aloft on the band, a stone like a star **B**
From which flew splendid beams like the light of the sun;
And mark you well, it was worth a rich king's ransom. **3**
But right away he refused it, replying in haste,
"My lady gay, I can hardly take gifts at the moment;
Having nothing to give, I'd be wrong to take gifts in turn."
She implored him again, still more earnestly, but again
He refused it and swore on his knighthood that he could take nothing.
Grieved that he still would not take it, she told him then: **C**
"If taking my ring would be wrong on account of its worth,
And being so much in my debt would be bothersome to you,
I'll give you merely this sash that's of slighter value."
She swiftly unfastened the sash that encircled her waist,
Tied around her fair tunic, inside her bright mantle;
It was made of green silk and was marked of gleaming gold

205 implored: begged.

212 tunic: a shirtlike garment worn by both men and women; **mantle:** a sleeveless cloak worn over the tunic.

Teaching Options

Vocabulary Strategy

PREFIXES

Instruction Point out the words *encountered* (page 210, line 19) and *encircled* (page 216, line 211). Explain that these words are formed by the addition of the prefix *en-* to the words *countered* and *circled.*

Explain that *en-* changes word meaning in different ways because it has more than one meaning. Write this definition of *en-* on the chalkboard.

1. To put, or go, into or onto. **2.** To cover or provide with. **3.** To cause to be or happen. **4.** Completely.

Activity Write the words *encrust, envenom, ensure, enroot,* and *enthrone* on the chalkboard. Have students use dictionaries to find the definitions of the roots of the words. Then, have them meet with partners to look up the definitions of the prefixed words. Have them discuss the way in which *en-* has changed each word root's meaning.

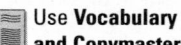

Use **Vocabulary Transparencies and Copymasters,** p. 27.

A lesson on the parts of a word appears on p. 1104 of the Pupil's Edition.

Embroidered along the edges, ingeniously stitched.
This too she held out to the knight, and she earnestly begged him
To take it, trifling as it was, to remember her by.
But again he said no, there was nothing at all he could take,
Neither treasure nor token, until such time as the Lord
Had granted him some end to his adventure.
"And therefore, I pray you, do not be displeased,
But give up, for I cannot grant it, however fair
or right.
I know your worth and price,
And my debt's by no means slight;
I swear through fire and ice
To be your humble knight."

"Do you lay aside this silk," said the lady then,
"Because it seems unworthy—as well it may?
Listen. Little as it is, it seems less in value,
But he who knew what charms are woven within it
Might place a better price on it, perchance.
For the man who goes to battle in this green lace,
As long as he keeps it looped around him,
No man under Heaven can hurt him, whoever may try,
For nothing on earth, however uncanny, can kill him."
The knight cast about in distress, and it came to his heart
This might be a treasure indeed when the time came to take
The blow he had bargained to suffer beside the Green Chapel.
If the gift meant remaining alive, it might well be worth it;
So he listened in silence and suffered the lady to speak,
And she pressed the sash upon him and begged him to take it,
And Gawain did, and she gave him the gift with great pleasure
And begged him, for her sake, to say not a word,
And to keep it hidden from her lord. And he said he would,
That except for themselves, this business would never be known
to a man.
He thanked her earnestly,
And boldly his heart now ran;
And now a third time she
Leaned down and kissed her man.

216 trifling: of little value.

D **242** Why do you think Gawain finally accepts the green sash?

When the lord returns at the end of the third day, Gawain gives him a kiss but does not reveal the gift of the sash.

WORDS TO KNOW

ingeniously (ĭn-jēn′yəs-lē) *adv.* in a way marked by skill and imagination; cleverly

uncanny (ŭn-kăn′ē) *adj.* frighteningly unnatural or supernatural; mysterious

Customizing Instruction

Students Acquiring English

1 What agreement does Gawain make with the lord of the castle?
Answer: To exchange each day whatever they have won.

2 What does the lady of the castle attempt to do?
Answer: To seduce Gawain.

3 Explain to students that a ransom is money paid to guarantee a hostage's safety or to deliver the hostage from danger. Then, ask them how much they think a "king's ransom" (line 201) might be.
Answer: A huge sum of money.

Less Proficient Readers

Make sure students understand what happens while Gawain stays in the country castle.

4 Why does Gawain break his agreement and keep the sash hidden from his host?
Possible Response: He believes the sash will protect him, so he does not want to surrender it; the lady begs him not to tell; he is afraid of the lord's reaction.

5 **Set a Purpose** Have students predict what will happen when Gawain meets the Green Knight.

Mini Lesson Grammar

COMPOUND SUBJECTS

Instruction A compound subject consists of two or more subjects that share the same verb and are joined by a conjunction.

Activity Write the following sentence on the chalkboard.

King Arthur and his knights were startled by the Green Knight's challenge.

Ask students to find the compound subject—the two persons, places, things, or ideas that the sentence is about. *(King Arthur, knights)* Then ask them to identify the conjunction. *(and)* Tell students that the subject, the predicate, or both can be compound in a sentence. Write the following sentence on the chalkboard.

King Arthur and his knights were startled and silenced by the Green Knight's challenge.

Have students analyze the change to the sentence and then identify the compound subject and the compound predicate. *(King Arthur, knights; startled, silenced)* Have students circle the conjunctions. *(and, and)*

Use **Grammar Transparencies and Copymasters,** p. 80.

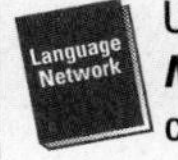

Use McDougal Littell's ***Language Network*** for more instruction in compound subjects.

Reading and Analyzing

Reading Skills and Strategies: **MAKING INFERENCES**

A Ask students what response the Green Knight wants to elicit when he mocks Sir Gawain.

Possible Responses: Anger, shame, a display of bravery.

GUIDE FOR READING

B Unlike the Green Knight, if Gawain's head is chopped off it cannot be fixed, and so Gawain shows greater courage than the Green Knight in facing the ax.

Literary Analysis: **CONFLICT**

C Remind students that the climax is the conflict's turning point; it is the "point of no return" in the action. Then, ask them to identify the climax in this selection.

Possible Responses: The moment when the Green Knight finally brings down the ax on Gawain; when Gawain does not flinch at the anticipated blow.

Literary Analysis: **DIALOGUE**

D Draw students' attention to the exchange between Sir Gawain and the Green Knight. You might have students read the exchange aloud. Ask them what effect the knights' bantering has on the action.

Possible Responses: The bantering retards the forward movement of the plot, thereby increasing suspense for the readers and for Gawain; the unexpected humor also increases suspense. What does the dialogue reveal about Gawain's character?

GUIDE FOR READING

E He might explain it as a miracle, involving divine intervention, or possibly as magic.

1 On New Year's Day Gawain must go to meet the Green Knight. Wearing the green sash, he sets out before dawn. Gawain arrives at a wild, rugged place, where he sees no chapel but hears the sound of a blade being sharpened. Gawain calls out, and the Green Knight appears with a huge ax. The Green Knight greets Gawain, who, with pounding heart, bows his head to take his blow.

Quickly then the man in the green made ready,
Grabbed up his keen-ground ax to strike Sir Gawain;
With all the might in his body he bore it aloft
And sharply brought it down as if to slay him;
Had he made it fall with the force he first intended
He would have stretched out the strongest man on earth.
But Sir Gawain cast a side glance at the ax
As it glided down to give him his Kingdom Come,
And his shoulders jerked away from the iron a little,
And the Green Knight caught the handle, holding it back,
And mocked the prince with many a proud reproof:
"*You* can't be Gawain," he said, "who's thought so good,
A man who's never been daunted on hill or dale!
For look how you flinch for fear before anything's felt!
I never heard tell that Sir Gawain was ever a coward!
I never moved a muscle when *you* came down;
In Arthur's hall I never so much as winced.
My head fell off at my feet, yet I never flickered;
But you! You tremble at heart before you're touched!
I'm bound to be called a better man than you, then,
my lord."
Said Gawain, "I shied once:
No more. You have my word.
But if my head falls to the stones
It cannot be restored.

"But be brisk, man, by your faith, and come to the point!
Deal out my doom if you can, and do it at once,
For I'll stand for one good stroke, and I'll start no more
Until your ax has hit—and that I swear."
"Here goes, then," said the other, and heaves it aloft
And stands there waiting, scowling like a madman;
He swings down sharp, then suddenly stops again,
Holds back the ax with his hand before it can hurt,
And Gawain stands there stirring not even a nerve;

258 his Kingdom Come: his death and entry into the afterlife; a reference to the sentence "Thy kingdom come" in the Lord's Prayer.

B **274–275** The Green Knight has proclaimed himself a better man than Gawain. How does Gawain dispute that idea in these lines?

WORDS TO KNOW
reproof (rĭ-pro͞of′) *n.* an expression of disapproval; criticism
daunt (dônt) *v.* to destroy the courage of; dismay
flinch (flĭnch) *v.* to pull back from something unpleasant or surprising
wince (wĭns) *v.* to spring back involuntarily, as in pain

218

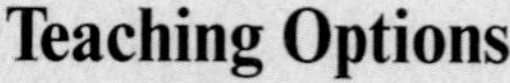

Teaching Options

Workplace Link: Contracts

Instruction Point out that in this selection Sir Gawain and the Green Knight form many agreements. Agreements and contracts, written or oral, are essential in any field of work. A common kind of contract is one between employer and employee. For example, a contract may include details such as the work involved, the hours required to do the work, the conditions under which the work will be done, and the amount of money the worker will receive.

Activity Have students work with a partner to agree upon a contract for a specific task. One student should act as the employer and the other as the employee. Have each student write a list of requirements that he or she would like to see met. After the partners have created their lists, have them draft a mutually agreeable contract.

He stood there still as a stone or the stock of a tree
That's wedged in rocky ground by a hundred roots.
O, merrily then he spoke, the man in green:
"Good! You've got your heart back! Now I can hit you.
May all that glory the good King Arthur gave you
Prove efficacious now—if it ever can—
And save your neck." In rage Sir Gawain shouted,
"*Hit* me, hero! I'm right up to here with your threats!
Is it *you* that's the cringing coward after all?"
C "Whoo!" said the man in green, "he's wrathful, too!
No pauses, then; I'll pay up my pledge at once,
I vow!"
He takes his stride to strike
And lifts his lip and brow;
It's not a thing Gawain can like,
For nothing can save him now!

He raises that ax up lightly and flashes it down,
And that blinding bit bites in at the knight's bare neck—
But hard as he hammered it down, it hurt him no more
Than to nick the nape of his neck, so it split the skin;
The sharp blade slit to the flesh through the shiny hide,
And red blood shot to his shoulders and spattered the ground.
And when Gawain saw his blood where it blinked in the snow
He sprang from the man with a leap to the length of a spear;
He snatched up his helmet swiftly and slapped it on,
Shifted his shield into place with a jerk of his shoulders,
And snapped his sword out faster than sight; said boldly—
And, mortal born of his mother that he was,
There was never on earth a man so happy by half—
"No more strokes, my friend; you've had your swing!
I've stood one swipe of your ax without resistance;
D If you offer me any more, I'll repay you at once
With all the force and fire I've got—as you
will see.
I take one stroke, that's all,
For that was the compact we
Arranged in Arthur's hall;
But now, no more for me!"

The Green Knight remained where he stood, relaxing on his ax—
Settled the shaft on the rocks and leaned on the sharp end—
And studied the young man standing there, shoulders hunched,

E **314–322** At this moment, how do you think Gawain would explain the fact that he has received only a slight cut from the Green Knight's ax?

WORDS TO KNOW **efficacious** (ĕf'ĭ-kā'shəs) *adj.* effective

Customizing Instruction

Less Proficient Readers

1 Make certain that students have read the transitional narrative paragraph that introduces this section. Have them note the amount of time that has passed since the beginning of the story. Set a purpose for reading. Have students read to find out what happens when Sir Gawain sets out to fulfill his pledge.

Gifted and Talented

Have students think about how the surface conflict between Gawain and the Green Knight represents multiple conflicts beneath the surface. Among these are the questions of when to tell the "whole truth," what is courage and what is cowardice, what is the real honor of a knight of the Round Table, and, ultimately, whether Sir Gawain is truly a chivalrous knight worthy of Arthur's respect.

Multiple Learning Styles

Visual Learners

Have students prepare a timeline that charts the events of the story. Have them place the opening incident with the correct time of year (banquet, Christmas) at the left end, and then write in the anticipated ending incident (a year and a day later) at the right end. Then, have them fill in the major events of the plot at appropriate intervals.

And considered that staunch and doughty stance he took,
Undaunted yet, and in his heart he liked it;
And then he said merrily, with a mighty voice—
With a roar like rushing wind he reproved the knight—
"Here, don't be such an ogre on your ground!
Nobody here has behaved with bad manners toward you
Or done a thing except as the contract said.
I owed you a stroke, and I've struck; consider yourself
Well paid. And now I release you from all further duties.
If I'd cared to hustle, it may be, perchance, that I might
Have hit somewhat harder, and then you might well be cross!
1 The first time I lifted my ax it was lighthearted sport,
I merely feinted and made no mark, as was right,
For you kept our pact of the first night with honor
And abided by your word and held yourself true to me,
Giving me all you owed as a good man should.
I feinted a second time, friend, for the morning
You kissed my pretty wife twice and returned me the kisses;
And so for the first two days, mere feints, nothing more severe.

2 A man who's true to his word,
There's nothing he needs to fear;
You failed me, though, on the third
Exchange, so I've tapped you here.

"That sash you wear by your scabbard belongs to me;
My own wife gave it to you, as I ought to know.
I know, too, of your kisses and all your words
And my wife's advances, for I myself arranged them.
It was I who sent her to test you. I'm convinced
You're the finest man that ever walked this earth.
C As a pearl is of greater price than dry white peas,
So Gawain indeed stands out above all other knights.
But you lacked a little, sir; you were less than loyal;
But since it was not for the sash itself or for lust
But because you loved your life, I blame you less."
Sir Gawain stood in a study a long, long while,
So miserable with disgrace that he wept within,
And all the blood of his chest went up to his face
And he shrank away in shame from the man's gentle words.
The first words Gawain could find to say were these:
"Cursed be cowardice and covetousness both,
Villainy and vice that destroy all virtue!"
He caught at the knots of the girdle and loosened them
And fiercely flung the sash at the Green Knight.

326 staunch: firm; **doughty** (dou'tē): brave.

338 feinted (fān'tĭd): pretended to attack.

A **337–343** What does the Green Knight reveal about himself?

350 scabbard (skăb'ərd): a sheath for a dagger or sword.

B **354** What was the Green Knight's test?

368 girdle: sash.

Reading and Analyzing

GUIDE FOR READING

A The Green Knight reveals that out of respect for Gawain he pulled his punches.

B The Green Knight sent his wife to test Gawain's virtue.

Literary Analysis: SIMILE/ANALOGY

C Review the definition of a simile. Then, point out that the simile in lines 356–357 creates an analogy, or an extended comparison. Ask students to restate the analogy.
Possible Response: Gawain is to other knights as a pearl is to white peas.
Then, ask them what images or ideas the simile conveys about Gawain.
Possible Response: Conveys idea that even though Gawain may seem to be like other knights, he is far more worthy.

Also ask students what the statement shows about the Green Knight's estimation or opinion of Gawain.
Possible Response: shows that he recognizes Gawain's integrity.

GUIDE FOR READING

D He means that he was led to abandon the code of chivalry and knighthood.

Literary Analysis: PLOT

E Ask students how the ending resolves the conflict between Gawain and the Green Knight
Possible Response: The Green Knight admires Gawain for his honesty.

GUIDE FOR READING

F The Green Knight gives Gawain the sash to remind him of their struggle.

Teaching Options

Speaking and Listening

DRAMATIC INTERPRETATION Have students work in small groups to write and act out a short play based on the excerpt. Students should assign the roles of Gawain, the Green Knight, the Green Knight's wife, and King Arthur. They might also have a narrator who reads the bridging portions and provides background information from the poem. Each group should create dialogue that reflects the characters' emotions and motivations.

"There, there's my fault! The foul fiend vex it!
Foolish cowardice taught me, from fear of your stroke,
To bargain, covetous, and abandon my kind,
The selflessness and loyalty suitable in knights;
Here I stand, faulty and false, much as I've feared them,
Both of them, untruth and treachery; may they see sorrow
and care!
I can't deny my guilt;
My works shine none too fair!
Give me your good will
And henceforth I'll beware."

E
At that, the Green Knight laughed, saying graciously,
"Whatever harm I've had, I hold it amended
Since now you're confessed so clean, acknowledging sins
And bearing the plain penance of my point;
I consider you polished as white and as perfectly clean
As if you had never fallen since first you were born.
And I give you, sir, this gold-embroidered girdle,
For the cloth is as green as my gown. Sir Gawain, think
On this when you go forth among great princes;
Remember our struggle here; recall to your mind
This rich token. Remember the Green Chapel.
And now, come on, let's both go back to my castle
And finish the New Year's revels with feasting and joy,
not strife,
I beg you," said the lord,
And said, "As for my wife,
She'll be your friend, no more
A threat against your life."

"No, sir," said the knight, and seized his helmet
And quickly removed it, thanking the Green Knight,
"I've reveled too well already; but fortune be with you;
May He who gives all honors honor you well."

And so they embraced and kissed and commended each other
To the Prince of Paradise, and parted then
in the cold;
Sir Gawain turned again
To Camelot and his lord;
And as for the man in green,
He went wherever he would.

370 vex: harass; torment.

D **371–372** What does Gawain mean when he says, "Foolish cowardice taught me . . . to bargain . . . and abandon my kind"?

384 penance: punishment accepted by a person to show sorrow for wrongdoing; **point:** blade.

382–386 The Green Knight is saying that Gawain has paid for his fault by admitting it and offering his head to the ax.

F **387–388** Why do you think the Green Knight gives Gawain the sash?

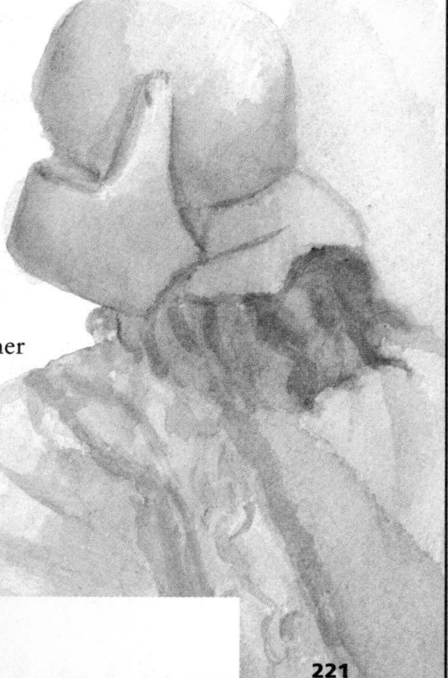

WORDS TO KNOW

amended (ə-mĕn′dĭd) *adj.* corrected **amend** *v.*

221

Customizing Instruction

Gifted and Talented Students

Ask students how the initial depiction of the Green Knight's lady contrasts with the chivalric ideal of women.

Possible Responses: Responses will vary but probably will focus on her taking the initiative to suggest a relationship with Gawain and on her seeming to be an unfaithful wife.

Why is the idea of her as an unfaithful wife ultimately ironic?

Possible Response: She tempts Gawain not because she is disloyal to her husband, but because she is testing Gawain's character.

Less Proficient Readers

Use the following questions to gauge students' understanding of the meeting between Gawain and the Green Knight:

1 What happens the first two times Gawain bows his head to receive the blow?

Answer: Gawain flinches, and the Green Knight does not follow through.

2 Why did the Green Knight cut Gawain on the third stroke?

Possible Responses: Because Gawain deceived the Green Knight; because receiving a blow was part of the original agreement.

GUIDING STUDENT RESPONSE

Connect to the Literature

1. What Do You Think?
Guidelines for student response: You might have students focus on the concepts of chivalry and knighthood in their reactions to the romance.

Comprehension Check
- He will allow a knight to strike him on the neck with an ax and will return the blow in a year and a day.
- He raises it once for each time the Green Knight's wife has tempted Gawain.

 Use Selection Quiz in **Unit One Resource Book** p. 67

Think Critically

2. Responses will vary. Make certain that students clearly show a cause-effect relationship between a particular action and the concept of honor.
3. Possible Responses: Gawain is innately brave; he feels obligated to defend the honor of the Round Table; he is shamed into it by the Green Knight's ridicule.
4. Some students may say Gawain fulfilled the Green Knight's challenge because he submitted to the ax blow on the appointed day. Others may say he did not fulfill the pledge because his actions betrayed his fear.
5. Some students may say that the test was unfair because the host and hostess conspired against Gawain. Others may say it was fair because it revealed Gawain's true nature.
6. You might have students discuss whether there are any groups today who follow a code of honor similar to that of Gawain.

Literary Analysis

Cooperative Learning Activity Have students present their "modern romance" to the class, either as dramatic presentation, panel discussion, or reading.

Conflict Be sure students discuss how conflicts are addressed and resolved.

Connect to the Literature

1. **What Do You Think?** What is your reaction to this romance?

Comprehension Check
- What challenge does the Green Knight present to Arthur and his knights?
- Why does the Green Knight raise his ax three times over Gawain's neck?

Think Critically

2. ACTIVE READING **READING A NARRATIVE POEM** Review the notes you took in your  READER'S NOTEBOOK about the actions of Sir Gawain and the Green Knight. What do these actions reveal about each character's sense of honor?

3. Why do you think Gawain requests to take up the Green Knight's challenge?

   THINK ABOUT
   - the Green Knight's behavior
   - the response of the other knights
   - the code of chivalry

4. In your opinion, how well does Gawain fulfill the Green Knight's challenge? Use details from the poem to support your opinion.

5. Think about the way in which the Green Knight tests Gawain's virtues at the castle. Do you think the test is fair? Why or why not?

6. Look again at the word web you created for Connect to Your Life on page 209. Compare and contrast your own concept of honor with that of Gawain.

Extend Interpretations

7. **What If?** What might have happened if Gawain had refused to accept the sash? Explain your answer.

8. **Comparing Texts** Compare and contrast Gawain and Beowulf. In your opinion, who is the more honorable **character?**

9. **Connect to Life** King Arthur and his knights were judged by their conduct, specifically by how well they followed the code of chivalry. Do you think today's leaders are judged by a specific code of conduct? If so, what is it?

Literary Analysis

ROMANCE Set in a faraway time and place, a **romance** involves noble heroes who perform daring deeds according to a strict code of honor. In *Sir Gawain and the Green Knight*, for example, the noble Gawain accepts the Green Knight's deadly challenge to uphold the honor of Arthur's court. Like other medieval romances, the story is filled with extraordinary events and fantastic scenes, including this description of the Green Knight just before he addresses Sir Gawain:

He held his head by the hair, high,
in his hand;
And the stranger sat there as
steadily in his saddle
As a man entirely unharmed,
although he was headless. . . .

Although Gawain berates himself for not fully measuring up to his own ideals, his struggle for perfection is typical of the **hero** of romance.

Cooperative Learning Activity Get together in a group and discuss how a modern story or event could be retold as a romance. You might consider retelling a current news story or the plot of a realistic film. Use as many elements of romance as you can as you develop your story's setting, characters, and plot.

REVIEW CONFLICT A **conflict** is a struggle between opposing forces that moves a plot forward. What would you say are the key conflicts in *Sir Gawain and the Green Knight*? Note whether they are **external** or **internal.**

Extend Interpretations

What If? Responses will vary. Encourage students to support their answers with evidence from the text.

Comparing Texts Some students may say that Beowulf is more honorable, as he faces danger and self-sacrifice unflinchingly. Others may suggest that Gawain, a fallible human with real fears and temptations, is more honorable for facing his fears and resisting his temptations.

Connect to Life Accept all reasonable, well-supported responses. You might have students broaden the discussion by considering how leaders in other countries (such as Japan) behave and what code of conduct they seem to follow.

Writing Options

1. Questions for the Green Knight Prepare a list of questions that you would ask the Green Knight in an interview for your school paper.

Questions for the Green Knight
1
2
3

2. New Story Ending Suppose that Gawain failed to meet the Green Knight in 12 months and a day. In prose, write a new story ending to show what you think might happen.

3. Essay on Romance You have read that *Sir Gawain and the Green Knight* is a medieval romance. In a short essay, explain why you think the romance remains a popular narrative form.

4. Television News Report Write a television news story in which you report the Green Knight's intrusion into Arthur's court. You might interview one of the knights at the Round Table for his eyewitness account of the strange event.

5. Speech Honoring Gawain Imagine that you are King Arthur presiding over the Round Table. Write the speech that you would make upon Gawain's safe return to Camelot.

Activities & Explorations

1. Computer Game Challenge Devise a computer game based on the Green Knight's challenge. Make one or more drawings to illustrate the way the game would be played. ~ **TECHNOLOGY**

2. Dramatic Presentation With a small group of classmates, prepare a dramatic interpretation of a scene from the poem. After deciding on roles, lines, and actions, rehearse your performance before presenting it to the class. ~ **VIEWING AND REPRESENTING**

3. Special Effects Diagram Investigate the techniques used to create special effects in movies. Then draw a diagram that illustrates the technique you would use to film the beheading of the Green Knight. ~ **ART**

4. A Set for a Play Imagine that you are producing a play based on this selection. Choose a scene and design a miniature set for it, depicting the scenery, the props, and the characters. ~ **ART/DRAMA**

5. Storyboard Scene Create a storyboard, or sequence of sketches, depicting the Green Knight's appearance and speech before Arthur and his knights. Write a brief caption or explanatory note for each sketch. ~ **ART**

Inquiry & Research

1. Weapons of War Find out more about the armor and weaponry used in medieval England. How did real-life warriors typically prepare for battle? What were their weapons? If you have access to a CD-ROM encyclopedia or an on-line encyclopedia, you might use a computer to start your research.

More Online: Research Starter www.mcdougallittell.com

2. Honorable Pursuits Research the activities of real knights. How were they appointed? Who were they expected to defend? What, if anything, did they have to do to prove their bravery and strength?

Writing Options

1. **Questions for the Green Knight** Remind students to focus on who, what, when, where, why, and how questions.
2. **New Story Ending** Encourage students to think about what the new story ending might reveal about Gawain's character.
3. **Essay on Romance** Suggest that students prewrite by noting what they enjoy about romance.
4. **Television News Report** Encourage students to capture the sense of immediacy and urgency that might accompany such an event.
5. **Speech Honoring Gawain** Have students reread Arthur's speeches in lines 35–37, 58–60, and 105–109 to remind themselves of his regal style.

Activities & Explorations

1. **Computer Game Challenge** Encourage students to work in groups, outlining the game's details (pathways, enemies, weapons, obstacles, levels, and shortcuts) on poster board.
2. **Dramatic Presentation** Use Mini Lesson p. 221.
3. **Special Effects Diagram** Refer students to the film glossary *The Video Resource Book* for general information on techniques.
4. **A Set for a Play** Students could use dollhouse toys or construct miniature sets out of cardboard or small pieces of wood.
5. **Storyboard Scene** Display students' storyboards.

Inquiry & Research

If students are not interested in either of these topics, encourage them to select their own topic, with your approval.

1. Weapons of War Have students research individually, if possible. Note, however, that students unfamiliar with electronic resources may need help from peer tutors. Encourage students to illustrate their reports with fine art or their own drawings.

2. Honorable Pursuits Have students share their information with their classmates. Encourage them to draw real-life parallels between the "job description" of a knight and that of any contemporary profession that requires similar attributes.

SIR GAWAIN AND THE GREEN KNIGHT 223

Vocabulary in Action

1. b 2. c 3. b 4. c 5. c 6. a 7. c 8. b 9. a 10. a 11. c 12. c 13. b 14. b 15. c

Author Activity

The surviving copy of the manuscript of *Sir Gawain and the Green Knight* is in the British Museum in London. Of the other poems in the manuscript, *Purity* and *Patience* are highly regarded biblical homilies, and *Pearl,* which many critics consider the poet's masterpiece, is a dream allegory.

Vocabulary in Action

EXERCISE: ANALOGIES Write the letter of the pair of terms that express the relationship closest to that of the capitalized pair.

1. RENOWN : FAME :: (a) greed : cowardice, (b) courtesy : politeness, (c) friendship : conflict
2. DAUNT : ENCOURAGE :: (a) notify : warn, (b) neglect : leave, (c) rejoice : mourn
3. WEIGHT LIFTER : HEFT :: (a) pianist : piano, (b) artist : draw, (c) actor : applaud
4. ERROR : AMENDED :: (a) accident : avoided, (b) storm : predicted, (c) crack : repaired
5. PAINFUL : WINCE :: (a) proud : succeed, (b) satisfied : eat, (c) funny : laugh
6. RESPITE : WEEKEND :: (a) exercise : jogging, (b) failure : victory, (c) problem : food
7. AGHAST : SHOCKED :: (a) angry : jealous, (b) surprised : shy, (c) cautious : careful
8. GHOST : UNCANNY :: (a) comedian : serious, (b) scholar : intelligent, (c) volunteer : numerous
9. EFFICACIOUS : USELESS :: (a) loyal : unfaithful, (b) honest : wise, (c) important : significant
10. FLINCH : UNSHAKABLE :: (a) perspire : cold, (b) gamble : daring, (c) smile : friendly
11. MANAGEABLE : UNWIELDY :: (a) wide : deep, (b) lost : crumpled, (c) light : heavy
12. INGENIOUSLY : CLEVERLY :: (a) slowly : speedily, (b) joyfully : nicely, (c) carelessly : recklessly
13. PIVOT : TURNING :: (a) vehicle : moving, (b) axis : rotating, (c) crosswalk : stopping
14. CHAGRIN : UNPLEASANT :: (a) regret : amused, (b) bliss : joyful, (c) impatience : calm
15. REPROOF : APPROVE :: (a) hatred : oppose, (b) assistance : encourage, (c) recognition : ignore

WORDS TO KNOW					
aghast	daunt	heft	renown	uncanny	
amended	efficacious	ingeniously	reproof	unwieldy	
chagrin	flinch	pivot	respite	wince	

Building Vocabulary
For an in-depth lesson on analogies, see page 1317.

The Gawain Poet

Mystery Man The identity of the author of *Sir Gawain and the Green Knight* is unknown. The only surviving early manuscript of the poem, produced by an anonymous copyist around 1400, contains three other poems—*Pearl, Purity,* and *Patience*—that are believed to be the work of the same man. (Since *Pearl* is the most technically brilliant of the four poems, their author is also known as the Pearl Poet.) The Gawain Poet's descriptions and language suggest that he wrote in the second half of the 14th century and was therefore a contemporary of Chaucer. His dialect, however, indicates that he was not a Londoner like Chaucer but lived somewhere in the northwestern part of England.

Man for All Seasons The Gawain Poet's works reveal that he was widely read in French and Latin and had some knowledge of law and theology. Although he was familiar with many details of medieval aristocratic life, his descriptions and metaphors also show a love of the countryside and rural life. Because of his rich imagination, sophisticated technique, and wide knowledge, he is considered one of the greatest of medieval English poets.

Author Activity

Locate a translation of *Pearl* and read excerpts from it. Then compare its themes and characteristics with those in *Sir Gawain and the Green Knight.* Share your findings with your classmates.

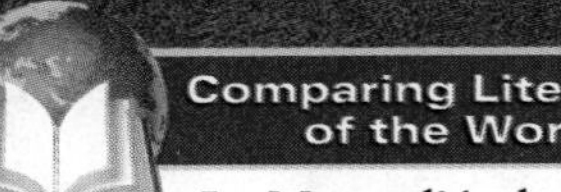

from Le Morte d'Arthur

Romance by SIR THOMAS MALORY
Retold by KEITH BAINES

Comparing Literature of the World

Le Morte d'Arthur and the Ramayana

This lesson and the one that follows present an opportunity for comparing legendary deeds in *Le Morte d'Arthur* and the *Ramayana.* Specific points of comparison in the *Ramayana* lesson will help you contrast characters and scenes in *Le Morte d'Arthur* with those in Valmiki's epic.

Connect to Your Life

A Second Chance Have you ever done or said something that you later regretted? If so, why did you regret it? Given a second chance, how would you have behaved differently? Share your thoughts with your classmates.

Build Background

Arthurian Legends The legend of King Arthur is one of the most popular and enduring legends in Western culture. Some historians believe that the fictional Arthur was modeled on a real fifth- or sixth-century Celtic military leader whose cavalry defended Britain against the invading Anglo-Saxons. However, the historical Arthur was undoubtedly very different from the king of later legend, who ruled an idealized world of romance, chivalry, and magic.

Since the sixth century, there have been many variations of the stories celebrating King Arthur. Most English-speaking readers have been introduced to the Arthurian legends through Thomas Malory's *Le Morte d'Arthur* or one of its many adaptations. Malory's work consists of a number of interwoven tales that chronicle the rise and fall of the Arthurian world. These tales are based on earlier English and French stories about Arthur's court and are populated by such famous characters as Merlin the magician, Queen Gwynevere (also spelled Guinevere), and a host of knights, including Sir Launcelot, Sir Gawain—whom you encountered in the previous selection—Sir Tristram, and Sir Galahad. Although the title *Le Morte d'Arthur* ("The Death of Arthur") perhaps applies best to the last section of Malory's work, it is by this title that the entire work has come to be known.

WORDS TO KNOW **Vocabulary Preview**

acquiesce	ensue	ravage
assail	entreaty	redress
depredation	forbearance	reeling
dissuade	guile	succor
dwindle	incumbent	usurp

Focus Your Reading

LITERARY ANALYSIS CHARACTERIZATION

Characterization is the way in which writers guide readers' impressions of characters. Malory combines details of appearance, speech, thoughts, and actions with comments on the characters to establish the essential nature of his characters.

> ***During the absence of King Arthur from Britain, Sir Modred, already vested with sovereign powers, had decided to usurp the throne. Accordingly, he had false letters written—announcing the death of King Arthur in battle—and delivered to himself.***

As you read this story, be aware of details of appearance, behavior, and action that contribute to characterization.

ACTIVE READING UNDERSTANDING CHARACTERIZATION

In describing Malory's **characterizations,** one critic has said that Launcelot always seems noble in spite of his faults. As you read the selection, note Launcelot's words and actions and those of other characters in response to him. Think about whether these details of characterization support the view of Launcelot as flawed but noble.

READER'S NOTEBOOK Use a cluster diagram to record examples of Launcelot's speech and behavior, as well as the words and acts of others, that contribute to Malory's characterization of him.

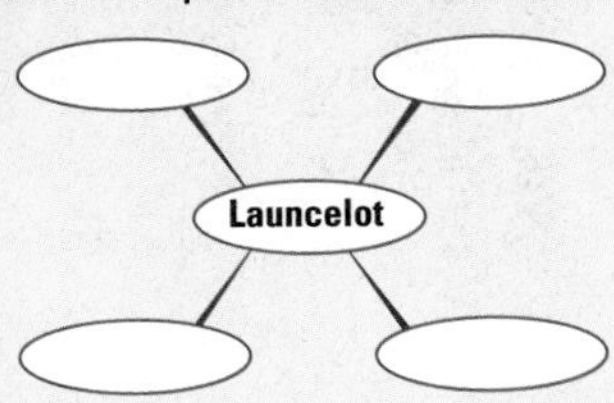

OVERVIEW

Objectives

1. understand and appreciate a classic written in the **medieval romance** genre **(Literary Analysis)**
2. identify and **understand** a writer's use of **characterization (Active Reading)**
3. review **romance (Literary Analysis)**

Summary

King Arthur and his army have besieged Sir Launcelot in the fortified city of Benwick. Meanwhile, Sir Modred has seized Arthur's throne and attempts to persuade Queen Gwynevere to marry him. Arthur sails back to Britain to regain his throne, and Gawain is injured as they fight their way ashore. Before dying, Gawain writes to Launcelot, begging him to help Arthur. In a vision, Gawain also warns Arthur that he will be killed if he battles Modred before Launcelot's return. Arthur makes peace with Modred, but fighting erupts at the signing of the treaty. Modred is killed, and Arthur is mortally wounded. A barge takes the dead Arthur away to the land of Avalon, and no one sees him in Britain again.

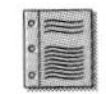

Use **Unit One Resource Book,** p. 67 for additional support.

Thematic Link

King Arthur has come to represent the best of chivalry and of courtly behavior. The Arthurian legend describes a king who held to these principles in an **attempt at perfection.**

5-Minute Warm-Up

Daily Language SkillBuilder

Have students **proofread** the display sentences on page 15m and write them correctly. The sentences also appear on Transparency 5 of **Grammar Transparencies and Copymasters.**

LESSON RESOURCES

UNIT ONE RESOURCE BOOK, pp. 67–71

ASSESSMENT RESOURCES

Formal Assessment, pp. 33–34

Teacher's Guide to Assessment and Portfolio Use

Test Generator

SKILLS TRANSPARENCIES AND COPYMASTERS

Literary Analysis

- Characterization, T21 (for Literary Analysis, p. 225)

Reading and Critical Thinking

- Cluster Diagram, T49 (for Active Reading, p. 225)

Grammar

- Verbs—Using Correct Verb Forms, T45 (for Mini Lesson, p. 238)
- Correct Forms of Irregular Verbs, C129 (for Mini Lesson, p. 238)
- Active and Passive Voice II, C135 (for Mini Lesson, pp. 230–231)

Vocabulary

- Roots, C29 (for Mini Lesson, p. 235)

Writing

- Topic Sentences and Thesis Statements, T6 (for Writing Options, p. 238)
- Subject Analysis, C30 (for Writing Options, p. 238)

INTEGRATED TECHNOLOGY

Audio Library

LaserLinks

- Author Background: Sir Thomas Malory. See **Teacher's SourceBook,** p. 14.

Visit our website:
www.mcdougallittell.com

Preteaching Vocabulary

If you would like to preteach the WORDS TO KNOW for this selection, use the Mini Lesson on page 226.

TEACHING THE LITERATURE

Reading and Analyzing

Active Reading

UNDERSTANDING CHARACTERIZATION

A Point out to students how the words spoken by each of Launcelot's counselors serve to characterize them. Sir Bors comes across as bold and aggressive. Sir Lyonel seems cautious and wise. King Bagdemagus advises action.

Use **Unit One Resource Book** p. 69 for more practice.

Literary Analysis

CHARACTERIZATION

B Mention that one way a writer develops a character is by presenting his or her speech, thoughts, feelings, and actions. Ask students what Sir Launcelot's speech reveals about his personality.

Possible Response: Launcelot is fair, reasonable, loyal.

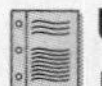

Use **Unit One Resource Book** p. 70 for more exercises.

Literary Analysis: ROMANCE

Ask students if they have heard of any of the following: King Arthur *(a famous English king of long ago)*; the Round Table *(a gathering place for King Arthur's knights)*; Excalibur *(the sword that only King Arthur can pull from the stone)*; Merlin *(a magician and tutor to Arthur)*; Gwynevere *(King Arthur's beautiful wife)*; Sir Launcelot *(a noble knight torn between his allegiance to King Arthur and his love for Gwynevere).* All these people or things are commonly referred to in our modern culture. They all come from the tales of King Arthur, the most famous version of which is the medieval romance *Le Morte d' Arthur* by Sir Thomas Malory.

KING ARTHUR'S FAVORITE KNIGHT, **SIR LAUNCELOT,** HAS FALLEN **IN LOVE** WITH THE KING'S WIFE, **GWYNEVERE.** THE SECRET LOVE **AFFAIR** IS EXPOSED BY SIR MODRED, ARTHUR'S SON BY **ANOTHER** WOMAN, AND GWYNEVERE IS **SENTENCED** TO **BURN** AT THE STAKE. WHILE RESCUING THE **IMPRISONED** GWYNEVERE, LAUNCELOT SLAYS TWO **KNIGHTS** WHO, UNKNOWN TO HIM AT THE TIME, ARE THE BROTHERS OF **SIR GAWAIN,** A FAVORITE NEPHEW OF ARTHUR'S. AFTER A **RECONCILIATION,** LAUNCELOT RETURNS **GWYNEVERE** TO ARTHUR TO BE REINSTATED AS **QUEEN.** AT THE URGING OF SIR GAWAIN, WHO STILL WANTS **REVENGE** ON LAUNCELOT, THE KING BANISHES LAUNCELOT TO **FRANCE,** WHERE THE FOLLOWING EXCERPT **BEGINS.**

Detail of Arthur from the Nine Heroes Tapestries (about 1385), probably Nicolas Bataille. The Metropolitan Museum of Art, New York, The Cloisters Collection, Munsey Fund, 1932 (32.130.3a).

Teaching Options

Preteaching Vocabulary

USING CONTEXT CLUES

Instruction The Words to Know for this selection are used in the context of warfare. Write the word *ravage* on the chalkboard, along with its definition: "to cause great damage to; devastate." Then read the sentence in which the word appears. *("Sir Launcelot, I understand that it is out of courtesy that you permit the king to ravage your lands, but where will this courtesy end?" page 227)* Ask a volunteer to explain what *ravage* means using sentence context.

Then ask students to think of a sentence that uses the word in a context other than war. (For example, *The disease will continue to ravage the population unless a vaccine can be found.)*

Activity Have students write the meanings of the Words to Know. Have them write in their Vocabulary notebooks a sentence that uses the word in a contemporary context other than war.

Use **Unit One Resource Book** p. 70 for additional support.

A lesson using context clues appears on p. 939 of the Pupil's Edition.

SIR THOMAS MALORY

from LE MORTE D'ARTHUR

T

When Sir Launcelot had established dominion over France, he garrisoned the towns and settled with his army in the fortified city of Benwick, where his father King Ban had held court.

King Arthur, after appointing Sir Modred ruler in his absence, and instructing Queen Gwynevere to obey him, sailed to France with an army of sixty thousand men, and, on the advice of Sir Gawain, started laying waste[1] all before him.

News of the invasion reached Sir Launcelot, and his counselors advised him. Sir Bors spoke first:

"My lord Sir Launcelot, is it wise to allow King Arthur to lay your lands waste when sooner or later he will oblige you to offer him battle?"

Sir Lyonel spoke next: "My lord, I would recommend that we remain within the walls of our city until the invaders are weakened by cold and hunger, and then let us sally forth[2] and destroy them."

Next, King Bagdemagus: "Sir Launcelot, I understand that it is out of courtesy that you permit the king to ravage your lands, but where will this courtesy end? If you remain within the city, soon everything will be destroyed."

Then Sir Galyhud: "Sir, you command knights of royal blood; you cannot expect them to remain meekly within the city walls. I pray you, let us encounter the enemy on the open field, and they will soon repent of their expedition."

And to this the seven knights of West Britain all muttered their assent. Then Sir Launcelot spoke:

"My lords, I am reluctant to shed Christian blood in a war against my own liege;[3] and yet I do know that these lands have already suffered depredation in the wars between King Claudas and my father and uncle, King Ban and King Bors. Therefore I will next send a messenger to King Arthur and sue[4] for peace, for peace is always preferable to war."

1. **laying waste:** destroying.
2. **sally forth:** rush out suddenly in an attack.
3. **liege** (lēj): a lord or ruler to whom one owes loyalty and service.
4. **sue:** appeal; beg.

WORDS TO KNOW

ravage (răv'ĭj) *v.* to cause great damage to; devastate

depredation (dĕp'rĭ-dā'shən) *n.* destruction caused by robbery or looting

Customizing Instruction

Less Proficient Readers

Set a Purpose Ask students what they already know about King Arthur and the Round Table from books and film. Then have students read to find out what happens when Sir Gawain confronts Sir Launcelot.

Gifted and Talented Students

As students read, ask them to consider how chance affects a sequence of events. Have them identify some of the instances in which chance plays a determining role in the narrative.

Students Acquiring English

Ask students if the title of the selection looks like English. Point out that the title of the selection is in French. In English it means "The Death of Arthur."

Use **Spanish Study Guide** for additional support, pp. 37–39

BLOCK SCHEDULING: MANAGING TIME

If your schedule requires that you cover the lesson objectives in a shorter time, use . . .

- Preparing to Read, p. 225
- Thinking Through the Literature, p. 237
- Vocabulary in Action, p. 238

If you want to take advantage of longer class time, use . . .

- Teacher's Edition Teaching Options: Vocabulary, pp. 226, 235; Standardized Test Practice, p. 228; Grammar, pp. 230, 238; Multicultural Link, p. 232; Cross Curricular Link, p. 233; Speaking and Listening, p. 234; Informal Assessment, p. 236
- Choices & Challenges, p. 238

Reading and Analyzing

Literary Analysis: DIALOGUE

A Have students discuss what the dialogue between Arthur and Gawain reveals about the personalities of the two men.

Possible Response: Arthur appears rather weak-willed—perhaps as a result of his love for both Gawain and Launcelot. Gawain is proud and holds grudges.

Literary Analysis
CHARACTERIZATION

B Throughout most of the Arthurian cycle, Gawain and Launcelot have been staunch allies. Ask students to describe the relationship of the two knights in this selection and justify their descriptions.

Possible Response: Gawain says he is Launcelot's implacable enemy. He will not let Arthur entertain Launcelot's overtures for peace.

Reading Skills and Strategies: EVALUATING

C Ask students how the revelation of Gawain's secret might influence their attitude toward the knight.

Possible Responses: makes the reader sympathize more with Launcelot; makes the reader feel as if Gawain is cheating in some way.

Accordingly a young noblewoman accompanied by a dwarf was sent to King Arthur. They were received by the gentle knight Sir Lucas the Butler.

"My lady, you bring a message from Sir Launcelot?" he asked.

"My lord, I do. It is for the king."

"Alas! King Arthur would readily be reconciled to Sir Launcelot, but Sir Gawain forbids it; and it is a shame, because Sir Launcelot is certainly the greatest knight living."

The young noblewoman was brought before the king, and when he had heard Sir Launcelot's entreaties for peace he wept, and would readily have accepted them had not Sir Gawain spoken up:

"My liege, if we retreat now we will become a laughingstock, in this land and in our own. Surely our honor demands that we pursue this war to its proper conclusion."

"Sir Gawain, I will do as you advise, although reluctantly, for Sir Launcelot's terms are
A generous and he is still dear to me. I beg you make a reply to him on my behalf."

Sir Gawain addressed the young noblewoman:

1 "Tell Sir Launcelot that we will not bandy words with him, and it is too late now to sue for peace. Further that I, Sir Gawain, shall not cease to strive against him until one of us is killed."

The young noblewoman was escorted back to Sir Launcelot, and when she had delivered Sir Gawain's message they both wept. Then Sir Bors spoke:

"My lord, we beseech you, do not look so dismayed! You have many trustworthy knights behind you; lead us onto the field and we will put an end to this quarrel."

"My lords, I do not doubt you, but I pray you, be ruled by me: I will not lead you against our liege until we ourselves are endangered; only then can we honorably sally forth and defeat him."

Sir Launcelot's nobles submitted; but the next day it was seen that King Arthur had laid siege to the city of Benwick. Then Sir Gawain rode before the city walls and shouted a challenge:

"My lord Sir Launcelot: have you no knight who will dare to ride forth and break spears with me? It is I, Sir Gawain."

Sir Bors accepted the challenge. He rode out of the castle gate, they encountered, and he was wounded and flung from his horse. His comrades helped him back to the castle, and then Sir Lyonel offered to joust. He too was overthrown and helped back to the castle.

Thereafter, every day for six months Sir Gawain rode before the city and overthrew whoever accepted his challenge. Meanwhile, as a result of skirmishes, numbers on both sides were beginning to dwindle. Then one day Sir Gawain challenged Sir Launcelot:

"My lord Sir Launcelot: traitor to the king and to me, come forth if you dare and meet your mortal foe, instead of lurking like a coward in your castle!" **B**

Sir Launcelot heard the challenge, and one of his kinsmen spoke to him:

"My lord, you must accept the challenge, or be shamed forever."

"Alas, that I should have to fight Sir Gawain!" said Sir Launcelot. "But now I am obliged to."

Sir Launcelot gave orders for his most powerful courser[5] to be harnessed, and when he had armed, rode to the tower and addressed King Arthur:

"My lord King Arthur, it is with a heavy heart that I set forth to do battle with one of your own blood; but now it is incumbent upon my honor to do so. For six months I have suffered your majesty to lay my lands waste and to besiege me in my own city. My courtesy is repaid with insults, so deadly and shameful that now I must by force of arms seek redress."

"Have done, Sir Launcelot, and let us to battle!" shouted Sir Gawain.

5. **courser:** a horse trained for battle.

WORDS TO KNOW
entreaty (ĕn-trē′tē) *n.* an earnest request; plea
dwindle (dwĭn′dl) *v.* to become steadily less
incumbent (ĭn-kŭm′bənt) *adj.* required as a duty or obligation
redress (rĭ-drĕs′) *n.* repayment for a wrong or injury

Teaching Options

Assessment **Standardized Test Practice**

ANALOGIES

Instruction Explain to students that an analogy measures someone's understanding of the relationship between words. The pairs of words are alike in that the relationship between the two words in the first pair is the same as the relationship between the two words in the second pair. Write the following example on the board:

INCH : FOOT ::

a. quart : container
b. weight : bushel
c. ounce : pound
d. height : weight

Read the analogy aloud: "Inch is to foot as . . ." Discuss with students the relationship between *inch* and *foot* (both are units of measurement, with inch being a division of foot). The only word that expresses the same relationship to *ounce* is *pound.*

Emphasize that in analogies dealing with vocabulary, both sets of words are usually in the same form: for example, if the first pair is two verbs, chances are the correct answer will also be two verbs.

Sir Launcelot rode from the city at the head of his entire army. King Arthur was astonished at his strength and realized that Sir Launcelot had not been boasting when he claimed to have acted with forbearance. "Alas, that I should ever have come to war with him!" he said to himself.

It was agreed that the two combatants should fight to the death, with interference from none. Sir Launcelot and Sir Gawain then drew apart and galloped furiously together, and so great was their strength that their horses crashed to the ground and both riders were overthrown.

A terrible sword fight commenced, and each felt the might of the other as fresh wounds were inflicted with every blow. For three hours they fought with scarcely a pause, and the blood seeped out from their armor and trickled to the ground. Sir Launcelot found to his dismay that Sir Gawain, instead of weakening, seemed to increase in strength as they proceeded, and he began to fear that he was battling not with a knight but with a fiend incarnate.[6] He decided to fight defensively and to conserve his strength.

It was a secret known only to King Arthur and to Sir Gawain himself that his strength increased for three hours in the morning, reaching its zenith[7] at noon, and waning again. This was due to an enchantment that had been cast over him by a hermit[8] when he was still a youth. Often in the past, as now, he had taken advantage of this.

Thus when the hour of noon had passed, Sir Launcelot felt Sir Gawain's strength return to normal, and knew that he could defeat him.

A TERRIBLE **SWORD** FIGHT COMMENCED, AND EACH FELT THE **MIGHT** OF THE OTHER.

"Sir Gawain, I have endured many hard blows from you these last three hours, but now beware, for I see that you have weakened, and it is I who am the stronger."

Thereupon Sir Launcelot redoubled his blows, and with one, catching Sir Gawain sidelong on the helmet, sent him reeling to the ground. Then he courteously stood back.

"Sir Launcelot, I still defy you!" said Sir Gawain from the ground. "Why do you not kill me now? for I warn you that if ever I recover I shall challenge you again."

"Sir Gawain, by the grace of God I shall endure you again," Sir Launcelot replied, and then turned to the king:

"My liege, your expedition can find no honorable conclusion at these walls, so I pray you withdraw and spare your noble knights. Remember me with kindness and be guided, as ever, by the love of God."

"Alas!" said the king, "Sir Launcelot scruples[9] to fight against me or those of my blood, and once more I am beholden to him."

Sir Launcelot withdrew to the city and Sir Gawain was taken to his pavilion, where his wounds were dressed. King Arthur was doubly grieved, by his quarrel with Sir Launcelot and by the seriousness of Sir Gawain's wounds.

For three weeks, while Sir Gawain was recovering, the siege was relaxed and both sides skirmished only halfheartedly. But once recovered,

6. **fiend incarnate:** devil in human form.
7. **zenith:** highest point; peak.
8. **hermit:** a person living in solitude for religious reasons.
9. **scruples:** hesitates for reasons of principle.

WORDS TO KNOW

forbearance (fôr-bâr'əns) *n.* self-control; patient restraint
reeling (rē'lĭng) *adj.* falling back **reel** *v.*

Customizing Instruction

Students Acquiring English

1 Ask students to use context clues to determine the meaning of the phrases *bandy words* and *strive against him.*

Possible Responses: Exchange meaningless words; fight him.

Gifted and Talented Students

Have students work in small groups to talk about how *Sir Gawain and the Green Knight* and the excerpt from *Le Morte d' Arthur* both exhibit the characteristics of a romance. How are they similar? How are they different?

Exercise Write the following analogies on the board and have students work independently or in pairs to complete these analogies:

1. acquiesce : disagree ::
- a. design : draw
- b. grade : succeed
- c. trick : fool
- d. cease : start

2. succor : assistance ::
- a. deputy : aide
- b. pet : dog
- c. groove : grudge
- d. growth : decay

3. forbearance : patience ::
- a. balance : weight
- b. suspicion : trust
- c. remark : comment
- d. erase : include

4. ensue : precede
- a. alert : lazy
- b. weave : separate
- c. mistake : error
- d. experienced : amateur

Reading and Analyzing

Literary Analysis
CHARACTERIZATION

(A) Invite students to discuss the techniques used to reveal Launcelot's and Gawain's personalities during their combat.
Possible Response: Dialogue and the characters' actions.

Then ask students what the scene reveals about the combatants' personalities.
Possible Responses: Launcelot is chivalrous and fair; Gawain is proud, brave, vengeful, and unrelenting.

(B) Ask students what Modred's actions reveal about his personality.
Possible Responses: evil, scheming, gullible.

What do Gwynevere's actions reveal about her?
Possible Responses: smart, resourceful, courageous, tricky.

Reading Skills and Strategies:
DRAWING CONCLUSIONS

(C) Point out that in the passage where Modred appeals for the barony's support, the narrator directly comments on the action. Ask students what effect these comments have on the reader.
Possible Response: They guide or manipulate the reader's sympathies.

Sir Gawain rode up to the castle walls and challenged Sir Launcelot again:

"Sir Launcelot, traitor! Come forth, it is Sir Gawain who challenges you."

"Sir Gawain, why these insults? I have the measure of your strength and you can do me but little harm."

"Come forth, traitor, and this time I shall make good my revenge!" Sir Gawain shouted.

"Sir Gawain, I have once spared your life; should you not beware of meddling with me again?"

Sir Launcelot armed and rode out to meet him. They jousted and Sir Gawain broke his spear and was flung from his horse. He leaped up immediately, and putting his shield before him, called on Sir Launcelot to fight on foot.

"The issue[10] of a mare has failed me; but I am the issue of a king and a queen and I shall not fail!" he exclaimed.

As before, Sir Launcelot felt Sir Gawain's strength increase until noon, during which period he defended himself, and then weaken again.

"Sir Gawain, you are a proved knight, and with the increase of your strength until noon you must have overcome many of your opponents, but now your strength has gone, and once more you are at my mercy."

Sir Launcelot struck out lustily and by chance reopened the wound he had made before. Sir Gawain fell to the ground in a faint, but when he came to he said weakly:

"Sir Launcelot, I still defy you. Make an end of me, or I shall fight you again!"

"Sir Gawain, while you stand on your two feet I will not gainsay[11] you; but I will never strike a knight who has fallen. God defend me from such dishonor!" (A)

Sir Launcelot walked away and Sir Gawain continued to call after him: "Traitor! Until one of us is dead I shall never give in!"

For a month Sir Gawain lay recovering from his wounds, and the siege remained; but then, as Sir Gawain was preparing to fight Sir Launcelot once more, King Arthur received news which caused him to strike camp and lead his army on a forced march to the coast, and thence to embark for Britain.

10. **issue:** offspring.
11. **gainsay:** deny.

Teaching Options

Grammar

ACTIVE AND PASSIVE VOICE

Instruction When the subject of the sentence does the action, the verb is in the active voice. When the subject of the sentence receives the action, the verb is in the passive voice.

Activity Write the following excerpt from "Le Morte d'Arthur" on the chalkboard.

"... Sir Lyonel offered to joust. He too was overthrown and helped back to the castle."

Underline the subject of each sentence. Ask students to identify the verbs and to tell whether Sir Lyonel did something or whether something was done to him. Point out that in the first sentence, Sir Lyonel "offered." He did something, so the verb *offered* is in the active voice. In the second sentence, the verbs *was overthrown* and *helped* indicate that Sir Lyonel didn't do the overthrowing or helping. These things were done to him; thus, the verbs are in the passive voice.

During the absence of King Arthur from Britain, Sir Modred, already vested with sovereign powers,[12] had decided to usurp the throne. Accordingly, he had false letters written—announcing the death of King Arthur in battle—and delivered to himself. Then, calling a parliament, he ordered the letters to be read and persuaded the nobility to elect him king. The coronation took place at Canterbury and was celebrated with a fifteen-day feast.

Sir Modred then settled in Camelot and made overtures to Queen Gwynevere to marry him. The queen seemingly acquiesced, but as soon as she had won his confidence, begged leave to make a journey to London in order to prepare her trousseau.[13] Sir Modred consented, and the queen rode straight to the Tower which, with the aid of her loyal nobles, she manned and provisioned for her defense.

Sir Modred, outraged, at once marched against her, and laid siege to the Tower, but despite his large army, siege engines, and guns, was unable to effect a breach. He then tried to entice the queen from the Tower, first by guile and then by threats, but she would listen to neither. Finally the Archbishop of Canterbury came forward to protest:

"Sir Modred, do you not fear God's displeasure? First you have falsely made yourself king; now you, who were begotten by King Arthur on his aunt, try to marry your father's wife! If you do not revoke your evil deeds I shall curse you with bell, book, and candle."[14]

"Fie on you! Do your worst!" Sir Modred replied.

"Sir Modred, I warn you take heed! or the wrath of the Lord will descend upon you."

"Away, false priest, or I shall behead you!"

The Archbishop withdrew, and after excommunicating Sir Modred, abandoned his office and fled to Glastonbury. There he took up his abode as a simple hermit, and by fasting and prayer sought divine intercession[15] in the troubled affairs of his country.

Sir Modred tried to assassinate the Archbishop, but was too late. He continued to assail the queen with entreaties and threats, both of which failed, and then the news reached him that King Arthur was returning with his army from France in order to seek revenge.

Sir Modred now appealed to the barony to support him, and it has to be told that they came forward in large numbers to do so. Why? it will be asked. Was not King Arthur, the noblest sovereign Christendom had seen, now leading his armies in a righteous cause? The answer lies in the people of Britain, who, then as now, were fickle. Those who so readily transferred their allegiance to Sir Modred did so with the excuse that whereas King Arthur's reign had led them into war and strife, Sir Modred promised them peace and festivity.

Hence it was with an army of a hundred thousand that Sir Modred marched to Dover to battle against his own father, and to withhold from him his rightful crown.

As King Arthur with his fleet drew into the harbor, Sir Modred and his army launched forth

12. **vested with sovereign powers:** given the authority of a king.
13. **trousseau** (trōō′sō): clothes and linens that a bride brings to her marriage.
14. **I shall curse you with bell, book, and candle:** The archbishop is threatening to excommunicate Modred—that is, to deny him participation in the rites of the church. In the medieval ritual of excommunication, a bell was rung, a book was shut, and a candle was extinguished.
15. **divine intercession:** assistance from God.

WORDS TO KNOW
- **usurp** (yōō-sûrp′) *v.* to seize unlawfully by force
- **acquiesce** (ăk′wē-ĕs′) *v.* to agree or give in without protest
- **guile** (gīl) *n.* clever trickery; deceit
- **assail** (ə-sāl′) *v.* to attack, either with blows or with words

231

Customizing Instruction

Less Proficient Readers

Ask students the following questions to make sure they understand the sequence of events leading up to the siege of Benwick:

- Why does Sir Gawain advise Arthur to pursue war against Sir Launcelot?
  Possible Response: Gawain wants to avenge the deaths of his brothers.
- Why is Arthur reluctant to follow Gawain's advice?
  Possible Response: He still loves Launcelot.
- What happens when Gawain and Launcelot face each other on the battlefield?
  Possible Response: Launcelot twice defeats Gawain; Gawain challenges Launcelot to kill him, but Launcelot refuses.

Students Acquiring English

1 Encourage students to use context clues to determine the meaning of the terms *laid siege, siege engines, effect a breach,* and *entice.* If students are still confused, ask a volunteer to read the passage aloud and paraphrase it for the class.

Gifted and Talented Students

Have pairs of students choose any scene from the selection and create dialogue to further develop the action.

Exercises Ask students to underline the verbs in the following sentences and to tell whether they are in the active or passive voice. Have students meet in cooperative groups to discuss strategies for determining whether a verb is in the active or passive voice.

1. Sir Launcelot decided to send a messenger to King Arthur and sue for peace. *(decided: active; sue: active)*
2. A young noblewoman was chosen to bring the message to King Arthur. *(was chosen: passive)*
3. Sir Launcelot and Sir Gawain fought for over three hours, and each was wounded many times. *(fought: active; was wounded: passive)*
4. Sir Launcelot returned to the city, and Sir Gawain was helped to his pavilion. *(returned: active; was helped: passive)*

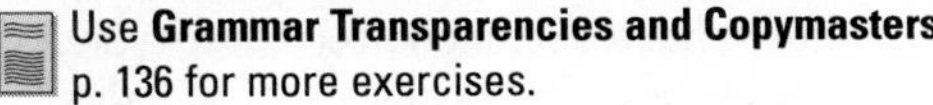
Use **Grammar Transparencies and Copymasters,** p. 136 for more exercises.

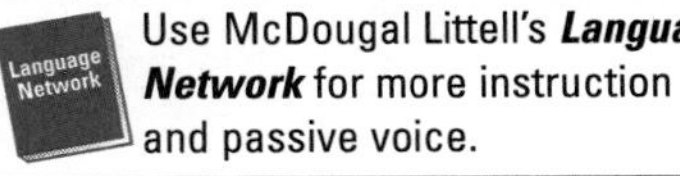

Use McDougal Littell's ***Language Network*** for more instruction in active and passive voice.

Reading and Analyzing

Literary Analysis
CHARACTERIZATION

A Have students contrast the wounded Gawain's speech to King Arthur with his earlier remarks about Launcelot. What causes Gawain's change in attitude?

Possible Responses: Imminent death puts their old enmity in perspective. Launcelot appears to advantage next to Modred.

How might Gawain be perceived if he had cursed Launcelot with his dying breath?

Possible Response: He would appear less sympathetic, less tragic.

Why is it important to Gawain that he attribute his death to Launcelot's blow?

Possible Response: It soothes his pride to think that he was killed by the greatest knight, not one of Modred's men.

Literary Analysis: MOOD

B Ask students how Arthur's vision of Gawain helps dispel the mood created by his strange dream.

Possible Response: Gawain and the ladies appear like angelic emissaries from heaven. The vision provides relief since it offers a means of escape from the destiny suggested by the hellish nightmare.

Reading Skills and Strategies: PREDICTING

C Ask students to predict what will happen at the signing of the treaty, and why. Have them use evidence and experience to support their answers.

Possible Response: Treachery, given the title's reference to Arthur's death and the fearful content of Arthur's dream.

in every available craft, and a bloody battle ensued in the ships and on the beach. If King Arthur's army were the smaller, their courage was the higher, confident as they were of the righteousness of their cause. Without stint[16] they battled through the burning ships, the screaming wounded, and the corpses floating on the bloodstained waters. Once ashore they put Sir Modred's entire army to flight.

The battle over, King Arthur began a search for his casualties, and on peering into one of the ships found Sir Gawain, mortally wounded. Sir Gawain fainted when King Arthur lifted him in his arms; and when he came to, the king spoke:

"Alas! dear nephew, that you lie here thus, mortally wounded! What joy is now left to me on this earth? You must know it was you and Sir Launcelot I loved above all others, and it seems that I have lost you both."

"My good uncle, it was my pride and my stubbornness that brought all this about, for had I not urged you to war with Sir Launcelot your subjects would not now be in revolt. Alas, that Sir Launcelot is not here, for he would soon drive them out! And it is at Sir Launcelot's hands that I suffer my own death: the wound which he dealt me has reopened. I would not wish it otherwise, because is he not the greatest and gentlest of knights?

A "I know that by noon I shall be dead, and I repent bitterly that I may not be reconciled to Sir Launcelot; therefore I pray you, good uncle, give me pen, paper, and ink so that I may write to him."

YOU MUST KNOW IT WAS YOU AND SIR LAUNCELOT I LOVED ABOVE ALL OTHERS.

A priest was summoned and Sir Gawain confessed; then a clerk brought ink, pen, and paper, and Sir Gawain wrote to Sir Launcelot as follows:

"Sir Launcelot, flower of the knighthood: I, Sir Gawain, son of King Lot of Orkney and of King Arthur's sister, send you my greetings!

"I am about to die; the cause of my death is the wound I received from you outside the city of Benwick; and I would make it known that my death was of my own seeking, that I was moved by the spirit of revenge and spite to provoke you to battle.

"Therefore, Sir Launcelot, I beseech you to visit my tomb and offer what prayers you will on my behalf; and for myself, I am content to die at the hands of the noblest knight living.

"One more request: that you hasten with your armies across the sea and give succor to our noble king. Sir Modred, his bastard son, has usurped the throne and now holds against him with an army of a hundred thousand. He would have won the queen, too, but she fled to the Tower of London and there charged her loyal supporters with her defense.

"Today is the tenth of May, and at noon I shall give up the ghost; this letter is written partly with my blood. This morning we fought our way ashore, against the armies of Sir Modred, and that is how my wound came to be reopened. We won the day, but my lord King Arthur needs you, and I too, that on my tomb you may bestow your blessing." 1

16. **stint:** holding back.

WORDS TO KNOW
ensue (ĕn-sōō′) *v.* to occur as a result; follow
succor (sŭk′ər) *n.* aid in a time of need; relief

Teaching Options

Multicultural Link: Myths and Legends

The group of romances revolving around King Arthur and the Knights of the Round Table is the great national legend of England; the noble ideals and dashing characters of that legend still stir patriotic pride in British people. Many cultures have national epics that stir similar pride, and some of them have become known far beyond the boundaries of their native lands. The Indian *Ramayana* (see page 240) and *Mahabharata,* the Greek *Iliad* (see page 66), the Aztec legend of Quetzalcoatl, the Norse *Eddas,* the German *Nibelungenlied,* the epic of Sundiata from the African nation of Mali, the Persian epic *Shahname,* the French *Song of Roland,* the Old Testament narratives of the patriarchs and of David—all these are stories in which heroes give shape to a cultural identity.

Sir Gawain fainted when he had finished, and the king wept. When he came to he was given extreme unction,[17] and died, as he had anticipated, at the hour of noon. The king buried him in the chapel at Dover Castle, and there many came to see him, and all noticed the wound on his head which he had received from Sir Launcelot.

Then the news reached Arthur that Sir Modred offered him battle on the field at Baron Down. Arthur hastened there with his army, they fought, and Sir Modred fled once more, this time to Canterbury.

When King Arthur had begun the search for his wounded and dead, many volunteers from all 2 parts of the country came to fight under his flag, convinced now of the rightness of his cause. Arthur marched westward, and Sir Modred once more offered him battle. It was assigned for the Monday following Trinity Sunday, on Salisbury Down.

Sir Modred levied fresh troops from East Anglia and the places about London, and fresh volunteers came forward to help Arthur. Then, on the night of Trinity Sunday, Arthur was vouchsafed[18] a strange dream:

He was appareled in gold cloth and seated in a chair which stood on a pivoted scaffold. Below him, many fathoms deep, was a dark well, and in the water swam serpents, dragons, and wild beasts. Suddenly the scaffold tilted and Arthur was flung into the water, where all the creatures struggled toward him and began tearing him limb from limb.

Arthur cried out in his sleep and his squires hastened to waken him. Later, as he lay between B waking and sleeping, he thought he saw Sir Gawain, and with him a host of beautiful noblewomen. Arthur spoke:

"My sister's son! I thought you had died; but now I see you live, and I thank the lord Jesu! I pray you, tell me, who are these ladies?"

"My lord, these are the ladies I championed[19] in righteous quarrels when I was on earth. Our lord God has vouchsafed that we visit you and plead with you not to give battle to Sir Modred tomorrow, for if you do, not only will you yourself be killed, but all your noble followers too. We beg you to be warned, and to make a treaty with Sir Modred, calling a truce for a month, and granting him whatever terms he may demand. In a month Sir Launcelot will be here, and he will defeat Sir Modred."

Thereupon Sir Gawain and the ladies vanished, and King Arthur once more summoned his squires and his counselors and told them his vision. Sir Lucas and Sir Bedivere were commissioned to make a treaty with Sir Modred. They were to be accompanied by two bishops and to grant, within reason, whatever terms he demanded.

The ambassadors found Sir Modred in command of an army of a hundred thousand and unwilling to listen to overtures of peace. However, the ambassadors eventually prevailed on him, and in return for the truce granted him suzerainty[20] of Cornwall and Kent, and succession to the British throne when King Arthur died. The treaty was to be signed by King Arthur and Sir C Modred the next day. They were to meet between the two armies, and each was to be accompanied by no more than fourteen knights.

Both King Arthur and Sir Modred suspected the other of treachery, and gave orders for their armies to attack at the sight of a naked sword. When they met at the appointed place the treaty was signed and both drank a glass of wine.

---

17. **extreme unction:** a ritual in which a priest anoints and prays for a dying person.
18. **vouchsafed:** granted.
19. **championed:** defended or fought for.
20. **suzerainty** (so͞o′zər-ən-tē): the position of feudal lord.

Customizing Instruction

Students Acquiring English

1 Tell students that "I shall give up the ghost" is an idiom in English that means "I shall die."

Gifted and Talented

2 Ask students why volunteers are now convinced that Arthur is right. What events could have led them to that conclusion?

Possible Responses: Arthur just won a major battle at Baron Down; Modred was excommunicated and therefore must be guilty of terrible sins; Because of Arthur's search for casualties, more people became aware of the war between Arthur and Modred.

Cross Curricular Link History

WARS OF THE ROSES The motif of civil war between two opposing claimants to the English throne parallels the Wars of the Roses, in which Malory himself was a participant. The Wars of the Roses (1455–1485) was a struggle for supremacy between two houses that originally stemmed from one family, the Plantagenets, which had ruled England since 1154. The House of Lancaster fought the House of York for possession of the throne until 1485, when the Lancastrians defeated the Yorkist king Richard III at the Battle of Bosworth. The war was named for the emblems of the two houses: the white rose of York and the red rose of Lancaster.

LE MORTE D'ARTHUR 233

Reading and Analyzing

Reading Skills and Strategies: MAKING INFERENCES

A Ask students why Arthur insists on killing Modred.

Possible Response: Because of the vision, Arthur knows he will die; he wants to die knowing he has killed Modred.

Literary Analysis: MOOD

B Ask students what details the writer uses to create a dark, frightening mood in the scene following Arthur's battle with Modred.

Possible Responses: Camp followers murdering the wounded; descriptions of Arthur's and Lucas's wounds.

Then, by chance, one of the soldiers was bitten in the foot by an adder[21] which had lain concealed in the brush. The soldier unthinkingly drew his sword to kill it, and at once, as the sword flashed in the light, the alarums[22] were given, trumpets sounded, and both armies galloped into the attack.

1 "Alas for this fateful day!" exclaimed King Arthur, as both he and Sir Modred hastily mounted and galloped back to their armies. There followed one of those rare and heartless battles in which both armies fought until they were destroyed. King Arthur, with his customary valor, led squadron after squadron of cavalry into the attack, and Sir Modred encountered him unflinchingly. As the number of dead and wounded mounted on both sides, the active combatants continued dauntless until nightfall, when four men alone survived.

King Arthur wept with dismay to see his beloved followers fallen; then, struggling toward him, unhorsed and badly wounded, he saw Sir Lucas the Butler and his brother, Sir Bedivere.

"Alas!" said the king, "that the day should come when I see all my noble knights destroyed! I would prefer that I myself had fallen. But what has become of the traitor Sir Modred, whose evil ambition was responsible for this carnage?"

Looking about him King Arthur then noticed Sir Modred leaning with his sword on a heap of the dead.

"Sir Lucas, I pray you give me my spear, for I have seen Sir Modred."

"Sire, I entreat you, remember your vision—how Sir Gawain appeared with a heaven-sent message to dissuade you from fighting Sir Modred. Allow this fateful day to pass; it is ours, for we three hold the field, while the enemy is broken."

A "My lords, I care nothing for my life now! And while Sir Modred is at large I must kill him: there may not be another chance."

"God speed you, then!" said Sir Bedivere.

When Sir Modred saw King Arthur advance with his spear, he rushed to meet him with drawn sword. Arthur caught Sir Modred below the shield and drove his spear through his body; Sir Modred, knowing that the wound was mortal, thrust himself up to the handle of the spear, and then, brandishing his sword in both hands, struck Arthur on the side of the helmet, cutting through it and into the skull beneath; then he crashed to the ground, gruesome and dead. 2

King Arthur fainted many times as Sir Lucas and Sir Bedivere struggled with him to a small chapel nearby, where they managed to ease his wounds a little. When Arthur came to, he thought he heard cries coming from the battlefield.

"Sir Lucas, I pray you, find out who cries on the battlefield," he said.

Wounded as he was, Sir Lucas hobbled painfully to the field, and there in the moonlight saw the camp followers stealing gold and jewels from the dead, and murdering the wounded. He returned to the king and reported to him what he had seen, and then added:

"My lord, it surely would be better to move you to the nearest town?"

"My wounds forbid it. But alas for the good Sir Launcelot! How sadly I have missed him today! And now I must die—as Sir Gawain warned me I would—repenting our quarrel with my last breath."

Sir Lucas and Sir Bedivere made one further attempt to lift the king. He fainted as they did so. Then Sir Lucas fainted as part of his intestines broke through a wound in the stomach. When the king came to, he saw Sir Lucas lying dead with foam at his mouth. B

"Sweet Jesu, give him succor!" he said. "This noble knight has died trying to save my life—alas that this was so!"

Sir Bedivere wept for his brother.

21. **adder:** a poisonous snake.

22. **alarums:** calls to arms.

WORDS TO KNOW **dissuade** (dĭ-swād') *v.* to divert from a course of action by persuasion

234

Teaching Options

Speaking and Listening

NEWS REPORT

Instruction Tell students that a good newscast usually presents a story by answering who, what, where, when, why, and how questions.

Prepare Newscasters strive to report the facts accurately, but they sometimes introduce their own opinions in a report as well. Have students write a news report on events from *Le Morte d' Arthur.*

Present Have students present their reports to the class. Have listening students write down facts and opinions that they hear and make note of what the speaker does well and what could be improved. Then have students work in small groups to discuss fact vs. opinion and to give each other constructive criticism. Encourage students to write down the comments they received so that they can improve their next presentation.

This activity is particularly well-suited for longer class periods.

Illustration from an illuminated manuscript showing a wounded Arthur in the foreground waiting for Sir Bedivere, who watches a hand appear from the lake to take King Arthur's sword, Excalibur.

"Sir Bedivere, weep no more," said King Arthur, "for you can save neither your brother nor me; and I would ask you to take my sword Excalibur to the shore of the lake and throw it in the water. Then return to me and tell me what you have seen."

"My lord, as you command, it shall be done."

Sir Bedivere took the sword, but when he came to the water's edge, it appeared so beautiful that he could not bring himself to throw it in, so instead he hid it by a tree, and then returned to the king.

"Sir Bedivere, what did you see?"

"My lord, I saw nothing but the wind upon the waves."

"Then you did not obey me; I pray you, go swiftly again, and this time fulfill my command."

Sir Bedivere went and returned again, but this time too he had failed to fulfill the king's command.

"Sir Bedivere, what did you see?"

"My lord, nothing but the lapping of the waves."

"Sir Bedivere, twice you have betrayed me! And for the sake only of my sword: it is unworthy of you! Now I pray you, do as I command, for I have not long to live."

This time Sir Bedivere wrapped the girdle around the sheath and hurled it as far as he could into the water. A hand appeared from below the surface, took the sword, waved it thrice, and disappeared again. Sir Bedivere re-

Customizing Instruction

Less Proficient Readers

1 Ask students to explain why King Arthur calls the day of the battle a "fateful" day.

Possible Response: The outcome was fated, foretold in Arthur's two dreams.

Gifted and Talented Students

2 Have students compare the fighting styles of Gawain and Arthur with those of Launcelot and Modred.

Possible Responses: Gawain and Arthur are both willing to fight to the death; Launcelot fights fairly, but Modred is a vicious warrior.

Less Proficient Readers

Make sure students understand what happens when King Arthur returns to Britain.

- Why do Arthur and his army return to Britain?
  Answer: Modred is attempting to usurp Arthur's throne.
- What fate befalls Sir Gawain?
  Answer: The wound dealt him by Launcelot is reopened while fighting Modred's army. Gawain dies.
- Why does Gawain appear to Arthur in a vision?
  Answer: To warn him not to fight Modred.
- Why is Arthur taken to Avalon?
  Possible Responses: To have his wound healed; to die.

Mini Lesson Vocabulary Strategy

ROOT WORDS: *Mort*

Instruction The Latin root *mort-* means "death." The relationship between the French word for death, *morte,* and the original Latin root is apparent through spelling and pronunciation. Words with the root *mort* include *mortal* and *mortuary.*

Activity Have students work in small groups to compile a list of words deriving from the Latin root *mort-*. Have them find at least five words (other than the ones discussed in class) stemming from this root. Make certain that they do not confuse the roots *mor-* (meaning "custom," as in *morality*), *morb-* (meaning "illness," as in *morbid*), or *mord-* or *mors-* (meaning "bite," as in *mordant* or *morsel*). Have students share their findings with the class, explaining how the current English word is related to the idea of death.

 Use **Vocabulary Transparencies and Copymasters,** p. 28 for more exercises.

A lesson on root words appears on p. 432 of the Pupil's Edition.

Reading and Analyzing

Literary Analysis: MOOD

A Ask students to describe the mood created by the scene at the lake.
Possible Response: Sorrowful.

What details help set this mood?
Possible Response: The weeping ladies, their black hoods, the "piteous lament," Sir Bedivere's weeping and his expression of loneliness.

B Ask students to describe the mood of the last portion of the selection, beginning with Bedivere's arrival at the hermitage.
Possible Responses: respectful, mysterious, legendary.

Literary Analysis
CHARACTERIZATION

C Ask students to tell what Sir Bedivere's last line of dialogue means and what it tells us about his character.
Possible Responses: He remains devoted to King Arthur. He wants only to remain near him and to serve him even in death.

Reading Skills and Strategies: SUMMARIZING

D Ask students to describe the site of King Arthur's burial. What is the place like? What effect is created by the place?
Possible Responses: It is a secluded, small shrine lit by candles. The Archbishop and Sir Bedivere are continuous mourners at the tomb, which is inscribed with a Latin inscription of noble words. The effect created is one of reverence and nobility.

turned to the king and told him what he had seen.

"Sir Bedivere, I pray you now help me hence, or I fear it will be too late."

Sir Bedivere carried the king to the water's edge, and there found a barge in which sat many beautiful ladies with their queen. All were wearing black hoods, and when they saw the king, they raised their voices in a piteous lament.

"I pray you, set me in the barge," said the king.

Sir Bedivere did so, and one of the ladies laid the king's head in her lap; then the queen spoke to him:

A "My dear brother, you have stayed too long: I fear that the wound on your head is already cold."

Thereupon they rowed away from the land and Sir Bedivere wept to see them go.

"My lord King Arthur, you have deserted me! I am alone now, and among enemies."

"Sir Bedivere, take what comfort you may, for my time is passed, and now I must be taken to Avalon[23] for my wound to be healed. If you hear of me no more, I beg you pray for my soul."

The barge slowly crossed the water and out of sight while the ladies wept. Sir Bedivere walked alone into the forest and there remained for the night.

B In the morning he saw beyond the trees of a copse[24] a small hermitage. He entered and found a hermit kneeling down by a fresh tomb. The hermit was weeping as he prayed, and then Sir Bedivere recognized him as the Archbishop of Canterbury, who had been banished by Sir Modred.

"Father, I pray you, tell me, whose tomb is this?"

"My son, I do not know. At midnight the body was brought here by a company of ladies. We buried it, they lit a hundred candles for the service, and rewarded me with a thousand bezants."[25]

"Father, King Arthur lies buried in this tomb."

Sir Bedivere fainted when he had spoken, and when he came to he begged the Archbishop to allow him to remain at the hermitage and end his days in fasting and prayer.

C "Father, I wish only to be near to my true liege."

"My son, you are welcome; and do I not recognize you as Sir Bedivere the Bold, brother to Sir Lucas the Butler?"

Thus the Archbishop and Sir Bedivere remained at the hermitage, wearing the habits of hermits and devoting themselves to the tomb with fasting and prayers of contrition.[26]

Such was the death of King Arthur as written down by Sir Bedivere. By some it is told that there were three queens on the barge: Queen Morgan le Fay, the Queen of North Galys, and the Queen of the Waste Lands; and others include the name of Nyneve, the Lady of the Lake who had served King Arthur well in the past, and had married the good knight Sir Pelleas.

D In many parts of Britain it is believed that King Arthur did not die and that he will return to us and win fresh glory and the Holy Cross of our Lord Jesu Christ; but for myself I do not believe this, and would leave him buried peacefully in his tomb at Glastonbury, where the Archbishop of Canterbury and Sir Bedivere humbled themselves, and with prayers and fasting honored his memory. And inscribed on his tomb, men say, is this legend:

HIC IACET **ARTHURUS,**
REX **QUONDAM** REXQUE FUTURUS.[27]

23. **Avalon:** an island paradise of Celtic legend, where heroes are taken after death.
24. **copse** (kŏps): a grove of small trees.
25. **bezants** (bĕz′ənts): gold coins.
26. **contrition** (kən-trĭsh′ən): sincere regret for wrongdoing.
27. ***Hic iacet Arthurus, rex quondam rexque futurus*** (hĭk yä′kĕt är-tōō′rŏŏs rāks kwôn′däm rāk′skwĕ fŏŏ-tōō′rŏŏs) *Latin:* Here lies Arthur, the once and future king.

Teaching Options

Assessment Informal Assessment

RETELL EVENTS Ask students to retell the events presented in the selection from the first-person viewpoint of one of the characters. They may choose a major character, such as Arthur, Gawain, or Launcelot, or a secondary character, such as the Archbishop of Canterbury. Remind students that their writing should reflect the personality, viewpoint, and thoughts of their character. Students may carry out this activity individually, in pairs, or in small groups.

RUBRIC

3 Full Accomplishment Student's story retells legend accurately from consistent narrative viewpoint.

2 Substantial Accomplishment Student's story recounts legend accurately, but point of view is not consistently maintained.

1 Little or Partial Accomplishment Student's story does not recount legend accurately and does not maintain consistent point of view.

Connect to the Literature

1. **What Do You Think?** What thoughts were in your mind as you finished reading this selection? Share them with the class.

Comprehension Check
- What happens when Gawain and Launcelot meet on the field of battle?
- What is Gawain's secret weakness in combat?
- What warning does Sir Gawain give to Arthur in a vision?

Think Critically

2. In your opinion, which character in the selection is most admirable, and which is least admirable?

THINK ABOUT
- the ways in which Launcelot shows loyalty and disloyalty to the king
- Arthur's willingness to forget his loyalty to Launcelot and follow Gawain's advice
- Modred's seizure of the throne
- Gwynevere's involvement with Launcelot

3. How much choice do you think Arthur has in determining his own fate?

THINK ABOUT
- the importance of chivalry to his followers
- the consequences of his long stay in France
- the warnings he receives in his dreams

4. If Arthur, Launcelot, and Gawain were given a second chance to resolve their conflicts, what do you think they might do differently?

5. **ACTIVE READING** UNDERSTANDING CHARACTERIZATION
Look again at your READER'S NOTEBOOK. What did you discover about the characterization of Launcelot as you recorded examples of his words and behavior in the cluster diagram?

Extend Interpretations

6. **What If?** Suppose that Sir Launcelot had arrived with his army in time to help Arthur battle Modred. How might things have turned out differently for the major characters?

7. **Connect to Life** Would you say that the forces that end Arthur's reign are the same forces that bring down governments in the real world? Support your answer with examples from local, national, or world history.

Literary Analysis

CHARACTERIZATION The way in which writers guide readers' impressions of characters is called **characterization.** There are four basic methods of developing a character: (1) description of the character's physical appearance; (2) presentation of the character's speech, thoughts, feelings, and actions; (3) presentation of other characters' speech, thoughts, feelings, and actions; and (4) direct comments about the character.

Cooperative Learning Activity With a group of classmates, look back through this selection, identifying passages that help create readers' impressions of Launcelot, Arthur, Gawain, Modred, and Gwynevere. In a chart, record the character, passage, method of characterization, and the qualities of character that are revealed in the passage.

Character	Passage	Method	Qualities
Launcelot	"I will not lead you against . . .	Launcelot's own words	Nobility and honor
Arthur			

REVIEW ROMANCE The term **romance** refers to an imaginative adventure concerned with noble heroes, gallant love, a chivalric code of honor, and daring deeds. Romances usually have far-away settings, depict events unlike those of ordinary life, and idealize heroes as well as the eras in which the heroes lived. What characteristics of romance can you find in this excerpt?

GUIDING STUDENT RESPONSE

Connect to the Literature

1. **What Do You Think?**
Guidelines for student response: Students might choose to address a number of themes in the selection, such as the nature of courage, loyalty, friendship, and wise government. Ask students to provide details from the text to illustrate their thoughts.

Comprehension Check
- Launcelot overcomes Gawain but refuses to kill him.
- Gawain's secret weakness is that his strength wanes in the afternoon.
- Sir Gawain warns Arthur that if he fights Modred, they will both die.

Use Selection Quiz in **Unit One Resource Book** p. 72

Think Critically

2. Possible Responses: Students may say that Launcelot is most admirable because he tries to maintain peace; students may say that Modred is least admirable because he betrays his father.
3. Possible Responses: little choice, because he is bound by conflicting loyalties; much choice, because he is king.
4. Possible Response: Arthur and Gawain might not leave England to battle Launcelot.
5. Accept all reasonable responses. Students should also have recorded in their cluster diagrams examples of the words and deeds of others as well as those of Launcelot.

Literary Analysis

Cooperative Learning Activity Display student charts in the classroom.
Review: Romance Remind students of the following characteristics of romance: noble heroes, faraway setting, fantasy.

Extend Interpretations

What If? Many students will think that King Arthur would have defeated Modred and ruled England in peace and justice. Some may think that Arthur would have forgiven Launcelot and had him remain; others may think that Launcelot would have left England. Accept all reasonable responses.

Connect to Life Many students will find similar forces at work today: thirst for power, interpersonal rivalry, failures of common sense, greed, and betrayal of principle. Accept all appropriate examples.

Writing Options

Essay on Virtues Have students brainstorm as a class for a list of virtues. Write their responses on the chalkboard, then ask them to focus on two or three that are of most personal value.

Vocabulary in Action

Activity: context clues

1. assail
2. forbearance
3. usurp
4. dissuade
5. entreaty
6. guile
7. acquiesce
8. incumbent
9. redress
10. ensue
11. ravage
12. dwindle
13. reeling
14. succor
15. depredation

Sir Thomas Malory

The son of a knight, Thomas Malory inherited his father's lands in 1433. During the Wars of the Roses, he supported his patron, the Earl of Warwick, who switched from the Yorkist to the Lancastrian side. In 1450, Malory was accused of ambushing and attempting to murder a duke and of raping or seizing the wife of another man; the following year, he was accused of twice robbing an abbey. He was imprisoned eight times and escaped twice, but while in Newgate prison he wrote energetically and read from the library of a nearby monastery.

Choices & CHALLENGES

Writing Options

Essay on Virtues Many virtues are portrayed in this excerpt from Malory. Write a two-or-three paragraph essay in which you explain which virtues of Malory's characters are most important to you in your life. Place the essay in your **Working Portfolio.**

Sir Thomas Malory
1405?–1471

An Active Life A son of prosperous parents, the Thomas Malory who many scholars think to be the author of *Le Morte d'Arthur* led a surprisingly unsettled life that ended in prison. A native of Warwickshire, England, he fought in the Hundred Years' War, was knighted around 1442, and was elected to Parliament in 1445. Malory then became embroiled in the violent political conflicts that preceded the outbreak of the Wars of the Roses.

Political Turmoil A staunch supporter of the house of Lancaster and its claim to the throne, Malory was imprisoned repeatedly by the Yorkist government on a variety of charges, including robbery, cattle rustling, bribery, and attempted murder. He pleaded innocent to all the charges, and his guilt was never proven. It is possible that his outspoken opposition to the ruling family provoked enemies to accuse him falsely in some instances.

Prisoner and Writer Malory seems to have written *Le Morte d'Arthur* while he served a series of prison terms that began in 1451. He finished the book about two years before his death in 1471. William Caxton, who introduced the art of printing to England, published the first edition of Malory's work in 1485, giving the book the title by which it is known today. *Le Morte d'Arthur* remains the most complete English version of the Arthurian legends and has been the source of many later adaptations of the tales.

LaserLinks: Background for Reading
Author Background

Vocabulary in Action

EXERCISE: CONTEXT CLUES Choose the word that could be substituted for the italicized word or phrase in each sentence below.

1. The king's followers began to *attack* his honor.
2. Everyone marveled at the *patience* with which he reacted to the attacks.
3. The king's enemies tried to *unlawfully take over* the throne.
4. The king hoped to *discourage* them from doing harm.
5. The enemies ignored the king's *plea* for peace.
6. They used *trickery* and threats against him.
7. The king had to agree *without protest* to a declaration of war.
8. He felt that it was *laid as a duty* on him to fight for his honor.
9. His army sought *repayment* for crimes against the king.
10. The king knew that after he issued his challenge, a full-scale war would *follow.*
11. His advisers warned that the war would *greatly damage* the land.
12. The number of healthy soldiers began to *decline.*
13. Wounded soldiers were seen *falling back* all over the battlefield.
14. Other kingdoms were asked to give *assistance* to the weakened army.
15. The plundering soldiers caused *damage* and sorrow throughout the land.

WORDS TO KNOW

acquiesce	entreaty	reeling
assail	forbearance	succor
depredation	guile	usurp
dissuade	incumbent	
dwindle	ravage	
ensue	redress	

Building Vocabulary
For an in-depth study of context clues, see page 938.

Mini Lesson **Grammar**

USING THE CORRECT FORM OF IRREGULAR VERBS

Instruction Verbs have different tenses to show when an action occurs. Tenses are formed by using the principle parts of a verb and combining them as necessary with auxiliary verbs such as *be* and *have*. The principle parts of a verb are the present, the present participle, the past, and the past participle. Most verbs, called "regular verbs," form their past and past participle by adding *–d* or *–ed* to the present.

A few verbs, called "irregular verbs," form their past and past participle in other ways.

Activity Write on the chalkboard the following sentence from *Le Morte d' Arthur.*

"Sir Launcelot *rode* from the city at the head of his entire army." (p. 229)

Underline the verb *rode*. Point out that it is an irregular verb, with the forms *ride* (present tense), *rode* (past tense), and *had ridden* (past perfect tense). The past perfect tense is formed by combining *had* with the past participle *ridden*.

Use **Grammar Transparencies and Copymasters,** p. 131.

Use McDougal Littell's ***Language Network*** for more instruction in irregular verbs.

from

PREFACE TO THE FIRST EDITION

Le Morte d' Arthur

William Caxton, the first English printer, had a significant impact on the literature of his day. In his preface to the first edition of Malory's *Le Morte d'Arthur,* published in 1485, Caxton describes his anticipated audience and reveals his purpose in publishing the work.

1 I have, after the simple cunning that God hath sent to me, under the favor and correction of all noble lords and gentlemen, enprised to enprint a book of the noble histories of the said King Arthur and of certain of his knights, after a copy unto me delivered, which copy Sir Thomas Malory did take out of certain books of French and reduced it into English.

2 And I, according to my copy, have done set it in enprint to the intent that noble men may see and learn the noble acts of chivalry, the gentle and virtuous deeds that some knights used in tho[se] days, by which they came to honor, and how they that were vicious were punished and oft put to shame and rebuke; humbly beseeching all noble lords and ladies with all other estates, of what estate or degree they been of, that shall see and read in this said book and work, that
3 they take the good and honest acts in their remembrance, and to follow the same; wherein they shall find many joyous and pleasant histories and noble and renowned acts of humanity, gentleness, and chivalries. For herein may be seen noble chivalry, courtesy, humanity, friendliness, hardiness, love, friendship, cowardice, murder, hate, virtue and sin. Do after the good and leave the evil, and it shall bring you to good fame.

Reading for Information

The **preface** to a literary work typically sheds light on why the author wrote the work. Imagine that you are a printer at a time when books are scarce. What might you want to include in your preface to a first edition?

PARAPHRASING AND SUMMARIZING

As you might expect, Caxton's language and syntax are typical of 15th-century English. To unlock the meanings of such challenging texts, you can use the skills of paraphrasing and summarizing. Review the primary source as you complete these activities:

1. **Paraphrase,** or restate in your own words, the first paragraph. What sources does Caxton suggest Malory used?
2. Refer to your paraphrase of the second paragraph. What was Caxton's purpose in publishing *Le Morte d'Arthur?* What virtues does it portray? Who does Caxton expect will be his audience?
3. Look at your paraphrase of "that they take the good and honest acts in their remembrance, and to follow the same." What is Caxton hoping his readers will do?

Summarizing With a partner, summarize Caxton's main points. How has reading Caxton's words affected your understanding of *Le Morte d'Arthur.* In what ways, if any, has your reaction to characters such as Sir Gawain changed?

RELATED *Reading*

Primary Source

Objectives

- read and analyze primary sources
- read to recognize logical modes of persuasion in text
- understand the function of a preface to a literary work

Further Background

While a source is any book, document, or person from which information is obtained, a **primary source** is a book, document, or person that provides original, firsthand information about a topic.

The text of Caxton's preface begins underneath the large, fancy typographic symbol that appears nearly halfway down the sheet. This symbol is called a printer's device—a personal, decorative identifying mark. In this example, Caxton's initials "W" and "C" are used.

Reading for Information

Students may suggest that as a printer during a time of book scarcity, they would try to impress readers with the uniqueness of what they hold in their hands and the benefits of treating it with respect.

Paraphrasing

1. **Possible Response:** "I have used my talents, under the guidance of noble gentlemen, to print a book about King Arthur and his knights. I have worked from a copy that was given to me by Sir Thomas Malory, who translated it from French books into English." Caxton suggests that Malory read French sources of the King Arthur stories. (Have students continue on to paraphrase paragraph two.)
2. **Possible Response:** Caxton published *Le Morte d'Arthur* to serve as a good example. It portrays such virtues as chivalry, courtesy, humanity, friendliness, hardiness, love, and friendship. Caxton probably expects only "noble men," lords, and ladies—educated classes of the day—to read his book.
3. **Possible Response:** Caxton hopes his readers will remember the good deeds in the book and imitate them.

Summarizing

Possible Response: The preface implies that the story of King Arthur should be understood as a lesson for life. The characters seemed less lifelike when viewed as examples of virtuous behavior.

OVERVIEW

Objectives

1. compare **legendary deeds** across cultures **(Points of Comparison)**
2. understand and appreciate an **epic** written in India **(Literary Analysis)**
3. identify and evaluate the use of **supernatural elements** as factors in a story **(Literary Analysis)**
4. improve comprehension by **classifying characters (Active Reading)**

Summary

Rama is waging a fierce battle against the ten-headed demon Ravana because Ravana has abducted Sita, Rama's wife. After several skirmishes between the opposing forces, Rama wounds Ravana but allows him to leave the battlefield. Humiliated and outraged, Ravana awakens his mighty brother Kumbakarna and enlists his aid. Kumbakarna destroys thousands of Rama's monkey warriors but is finally killed by Rama. The gods send Rama a special chariot, and the battle takes to the sky. When Ravana is unable to destroy Rama with arrows and trickery, he unsuccessfully tries to enlist supernatural forces. Rama then cuts off Ravana's heads, but they all grow back. At last Rama kills Ravana with a special weapon aimed at his heart. As the demon lies dead, Rama praises what Ravana might have been, had he not been evil.

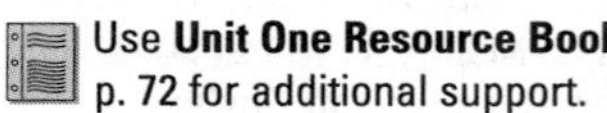

Use **Unit One Resource Book,** p. 72 for additional support.

Thematic Link

The epic *Ramayana* shows how people everywhere **attempt to reach perfection** through word and deed.

5-Minute Warm-Up

Daily Language SkillBuilder

Have students **proofread** the display sentences on page 21i and write them correctly. The sentences also appear on Transparency 1 of **Grammar Transparencies and Copymasters.**

PREPARING to *Read*

from the Ramayana

Epic by VALMIKI
Translated and adapted by R. K. NARAYAN

Comparing Literature of the World

Legendary Deeds Across Cultures

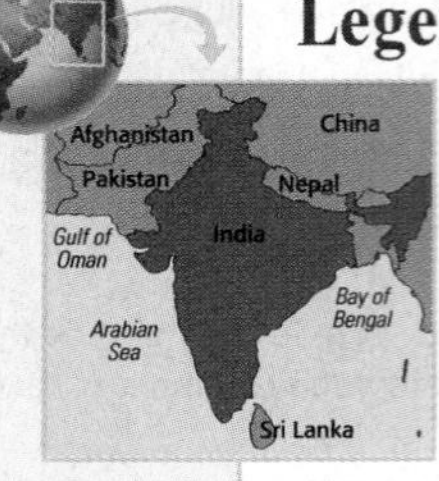

Le Morte d'Arthur **and the** ***Ramayana*** The *Ramayana* was written hundreds of centuries before *Le Morte d'Arthur.* However, both tales contain chivalric **heroes** who clash with their adversaries during **epic battles.** In both cases, the combatants are aided by supernatural elements that enhance their power.

Points of Comparison As you read the *Ramayana,* compare its **characters,** battles, and turn of events with those you recall from *Le Morte d'Arthur.*

Build Background

Epic Proportions The great Indian **epic** *Ramayana* was composed in verse by the poet Valmiki, probably between 300 and 200 B.C. Like epics of other cultures, the *Ramayana* celebrates the achievements of both human heroes and divine beings. It is the story of Rama (rä'mə), a royal prince who is the seventh incarnation, or embodiment, of the god Vishnu (vĭsh'nōō). The epic describes Rama's life, love, battles, and hardships. At the point of the story where this excerpt begins, Rama's wife Sita (sē'tä) has been kidnapped by Ravana (rä'və-nə), the 10-headed, 20-armed demon-king of the island of Lanka (ləng'kä). Hanuman (hə'nōō-män), a flying monkey in Rama's army, has located Sita and helped build a bridge to Lanka so that all of Rama's forces can cross over and rescue her.

WORDS TO KNOW
Vocabulary Preview

esoteric	incarnation
formidable	invincibility
impervious	parrying
imprecation	primordial
incantation	rampart

LaserLinks:
Background for Reading
Literary/Cultural Connection

Focus Your Reading

LITERARY ANALYSIS SUPERNATURAL ELEMENTS

Epics often journey into the realm of the supernatural. Supernatural elements include any beings, powers, or events that are unexplainable by the known forces or laws of nature. In the *Ramayana,* for example, Ravana's son Indrajit is a supernatural being, as this passage suggests.

> ***He also created a figure resembling Sita, carried her in his chariot, took her before Rama's army and killed her within their sight.***

Be aware of other supernatural elements as you read this excerpt from the *Ramayana.*

ACTIVE READING CLASSIFYING CHARACTERS In this selection, the hero Rama and his followers engage in a major battle with the demon-king Ravana and his allies. As the battle progresses, it will be important for you to keep track of characters by **classifying** them as belonging on either Rama's or Ravana's side of the **conflict.**

READER'S NOTEBOOK As you read, list the participants in groups according to their loyalty to Rama or to Ravana. Beside each name, write down something that will help you remember the **character**—a physical description, a personality trait, or his or her role in the **epic.**

LESSON RESOURCES

UNIT ONE RESOURCE BOOK, pp. 72–76

ASSESSMENT RESOURCES
Formal Assessment, pp. 35–36
Teacher's Guide to Assessment and Portfolio Use
Test Generator

SKILLS TRANSPARENCIES AND COPYMASTERS
Literary Analysis
- Characteristics of the Epic, T1 (for Literary Analysis, p. 240)

Reading and Critical Thinking
- Compare and Contrast, T15 (for Writing Option 2, p. 251)

Grammar
- Diagramming Subjects, Verbs, and Modifiers, T58 (for Mini Lesson, p. 243)
- Finding the Subject and Predicate, C83 (for Mini Lesson, p. 243)

Vocabulary
- Context Clues, C30 (for Mini Lesson, pp. 244–245)

Writing
- Opinion Statement, C35 (for Writing Option 2, p. 251)

Communications
- Formal Presentations, T10 (for Mini Lesson, p. 247)

INTEGRATED TECHNOLOGY
Audio Library
LaserLinks
- Literary/Cultural Connection: Scenes from the *Ramayana.* See **Teacher's SourceBook,** p. 15.

Internet: Research Starter
Visit our website:
www.mcdougallittell.com

from the RAMAYANA

THE SIEGE OF LANKA

Sculpture of Hanuman

Ravana deployed the pick of his divisions to guard the approaches to the capital and appointed his trusted generals and kinsmen in special charge of key places. Gradually, however, his world began to shrink. As the fight developed he lost his associates one by one. No one who went out returned.

He tried some devious measures in desperation. He sent spies in the garb of Rama's monkey army across to deflect and corrupt some of Rama's staunchest supporters, such as Sugreeva,[1] on whom rested the entire burden of this war. He employed sorcerers to disturb the mind of Sita, hoping that if she yielded, Rama would ultimately lose heart. He ordered a sorcerer to create a decapitated head resembling Rama's and placed it before Sita as evidence of Rama's defeat. Sita, although shaken at first, very soon recovered her composure and remained unaffected by the spectacle.

1. **Sugreeva** (so͝o-grē′və).

TEACHING THE LITERATURE

Customizing Instruction

Multiple Learning Style

Interpersonal Learners

Encourage students to read and discuss the selection in small groups, helping one another keep track of the characters and plot. You might invite the groups to devise a board game based on the story elements.

Students Acquiring English

Explain that this selection is a modern translation and adaptation of a very old story from India. Since this version does not contain very many unusual or archaic words and phrases, most students should be able to follow the story's events without too much difficulty.

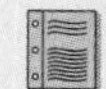 Use **Spanish Study Guide** for additional support, pp. 40–42.

Less Proficient Readers

Tell students that Ravana, the villain of this epic, has mighty allies with whom he battles Rama. You might have the students make a chart of the characters' names with a brief descriptive or identifying phrase next to each. This technique should enable students to keep the characters straight.

Gifted and Talented Students

Encourage students to investigate the Hindu religion: its principal beliefs, its pantheon of deities, and its other scriptures, such as the *Vedas* and the *Mahabharata*. Ask a volunteer to give a brief talk on Hinduism.

Mini Lesson Preteaching Vocabulary

USING A THESAURUS

Instruction Explain that the synonyms in a thesaurus are only close approximations of similar meanings. On the chalkboard write the words *happy* and *pleased.* Have students offer their comments on the similarities and differences in meaning between the two words. Point out that each is listed as a synonym for the other in a thesaurus and, while the two are close in meaning, they are not exact equivalents.

Emphasize that, often, trying to replace one word with another from a list of synonyms may result in a slight change in meaning. Also point out, however, that supplying familiar synonyms for new words helps us increase our vocabulary.

Activity Have students use a thesaurus to find and write down at least two synonyms for each of the Words To Know. After the students have compiled their lists, you might have them quiz each other by supplying the synonym and asking a classmate for the correct word from the Words To Know list.

Use **Unit One Resource Book** p. 76 for more practice.

Reading and Analyzing

Active Reading

CLASSIFYING CHARACTERS

Students might make use of a chart such as the one below to keep track of the characters in this selection. As they read, they can add the names of followers of either Rama or Ravana to the chart.

Rama	Ravana
Sugreeva	Indrajit
Sita	Kumakarna

Use **Unit One Resource Book** p. 74 for more practice.

Literary Analysis

SUPERNATURAL ELEMENTS

A Ask students to recount the details that indicate that Indrajit is a supernatural being.
Possible Response: He is the son of a demon-king; he has the power to remain invisible; he creates illusions.

Use **Unit One Resource Book** p. 75 for more exercises.

Literary Analysis: CHARACTERIZATION

B Ask students what Ravana's words upon hearing of his son's death tell about Ravana's character.
Possible Response: He is quick to blame others when he himself is at fault; he is vengeful.

At length a messenger from Rama arrived, saying, "Rama bids me warn you that your doom is at hand. Even now it is not too late for you to restore Sita and beg Rama's forgiveness. You have troubled the world too long. You are not fit to continue as King. At our camp, your brother, Vibishana,[2] has already been crowned the King of this land, and the world knows all people will be happy under him."

Ravana ordered the messenger to be killed instantly. But it was more easily said than done, the messenger being Angada,[3] the son of mighty Vali.[4] When two rakshasas[5] came to seize him, he tucked one of them under each arm, rose into the sky, and flung the rakshasas down. In addition, he kicked and broke off the tower of Ravana's palace, and left. Ravana viewed the broken tower with dismay.

Rama awaited the return of Angada, and, on hearing his report, decided that there was no further cause to hope for a change of heart in Ravana and immediately ordered the assault on Lanka.

As the fury of the battle grew, both sides lost sight of the distinction between night and day. The air was filled with the cries of fighters, their challenges, cheers, and imprecations; buildings and trees were torn up and, as one of his spies reported to Ravana, the monkeys were like a sea overrunning Lanka. The end did not seem to be in sight.

At one stage of the battle, Rama and Lakshmana[6] were attacked by Indrajit,[7] and the serpent darts employed by him made them swoon on the battlefield. Indrajit went back to his father to proclaim that it was all over with Rama and Lakshmana and soon, without a leader, the monkeys would be annihilated.

Ravana rejoiced to hear it and cried, "Did not I say so? All you fools believed that I should surrender." He added, "Go and tell Sita that Rama and his brother are no more. Take her high up in Pushpak Vimana,[8] my chariot, and show her their bodies on the battlefield." His words were obeyed instantly. Sita, happy to have a chance to glimpse a long-lost face, accepted the chance, went high up, and saw her husband lying dead in the field below. She broke down. "How I wish I had been left alone and not brought up to see this spectacle. Ah, me . . . Help me to put an end to my life."

Trijata,[9] one of Ravana's women, whispered to her, "Don't lose heart, they are not dead," and she explained why they were in a faint.

In due course, the effect of the serpent darts was neutralized when Garuda,[10] the mighty eagle, the born enemy of all serpents, appeared on the scene; the venomous darts enveloping Rama and Lakshmana scattered at the approach of Garuda and the brothers were on their feet again.

From his palace retreat Ravana was surprised to hear again the cheers of the enemy hordes outside the ramparts; the siege was on again. Ravana still had about him his commander-in-chief, his son Indrajit, and five or six others on whom he felt he could rely at the last instance. He sent them one by one. He felt shattered when news came of the death of his commander-in-chief.

"No time to sit back. I will myself go and destroy this Rama and his horde of monkeys," he said and got into his chariot and entered the field.

At this encounter Lakshmana fell down in a faint, and Hanuman hoisted Rama on his shoulders and charged in the direction of Ravana.

2. **Vibishana** (vĭ-bē′shə-nə).
3. **Angada** (əng′gə-də).
4. **Vali** (və′lē): king of the monkeys.
5. **rakshasas** (räk′shə-səz): demons.
6. **Lakshmana** (lək′shmə-nə).
7. **Indrajit** (ĭn′drə-jēt): Ravana's son.
8. **Pushpak Vimana** (pŏŏsh′pək vĭ-mä′nə).
9. **Trijata** (trĭ′jə-tä).
10. **Garuda** (gə-rōō′də).

WORDS TO KNOW

imprecation (ĭm′prĭ-kā′shən) *n.* a curse
rampart (răm′pärt′) *n.* an embankment or wall for defense against attack

Teaching Options

BLOCK SCHEDULING: MANAGING TIME

If your schedule requires that you cover the lesson objectives in a shorter time, use . . .
- Preparing to Read, p. 240
- Thinking Through the Literature, p. 250
- Vocabulary in Action, p. 251

If you want to take advantage of longer class time, use . . .
- TE Teaching Options: Vocabulary, pp. 241, 244; Grammar, p. 243; Multicultural Link, p. 246; Speaking and Listening, p. 247; Informal Assessment, p.248
- Choices & Challenges, p. 251

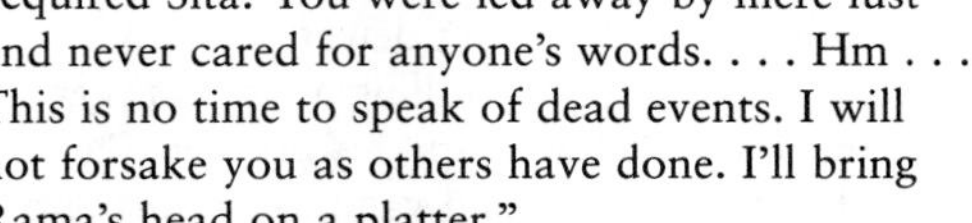

The main combatants were face to face for the first time. At the end of this engagement Ravana was sorely wounded, his crown was shattered, and his chariot was broken. Helplessly, bare-handed, he stood before Rama, and Rama said, "You may go now and come back tomorrow with fresh weapons." For the first time in his existence of many thousand years, Ravana faced the humiliation of accepting a concession, and he returned crestfallen to his palace.

He ordered that his brother Kumbakarna,[11] famous for his deep sleep, should be awakened. He could depend upon him, and only on him now. It was a mighty task to wake up Kumbakarna. A small army had to be engaged. They sounded trumpets and drums at his ears and were ready with enormous quantities of food and drink for him, for when Kumbakarna awoke from
1 sleep, his hunger was phenomenal and he made a meal of whomever he could grab at his bedside. They cudgelled, belaboured, pushed, pulled, and shook him, with the help of elephants; at last he opened his eyes and swept his arms about and crushed quite a number among those who had stirred him up. When he had eaten and drunk, he was approached by Ravana's chief minister and told, "My lord, the battle is going badly for us."

"Which battle?" he asked, not yet fully awake.

And they had to refresh his memory. "Your brother has fought and has been worsted; our enemies are breaking in, our fort walls are crumbling. . . ."

Kumbakarna was roused. "Why did not anyone tell me all this before? Well, it is not too late; I will deal with that Rama. His end is come." Thus saying, he strode into Ravana's chamber and said, "Don't worry about anything any more. I will take care of everything."

Ravana spoke with anxiety and defeat in his voice. Kumbakarna, who had never seen him in this state, said, "You have gone on without heeding anyone's words and brought yourself to this pass. You should have fought Rama and acquired Sita. You were led away by mere lust and never cared for anyone's words. . . . Hm . . . This is no time to speak of dead events. I will not forsake you as others have done. I'll bring Rama's head on a platter."

Kumbakarna's entry into the battle created havoc. He destroyed and swallowed hundreds and thousands of the monkey warriors and came very near finishing off the great Sugreeva himself. Rama himself had to take a hand at destroying this demon; he sent the sharpest of his arrows, which cut Kumbakarna limb from limb; but he fought fiercely with only inches of his body remaining intact. Finally Rama severed his head with an arrow. That was the end of Kumbakarna.

When he heard of it, Ravana lamented, "My right hand is cut off."

One of his sons reminded him, "Why should you despair? You have Brahma's[12] gift of invincibility. You should not grieve." Indrajit told him, "What have you to fear when I am alive?"

Indrajit had the power to remain invisible and fight, and accounted for much destruction in the invader's camp. He also created a figure resembling Sita, carried her in his chariot, took her before Rama's army and killed her within their sight. A

This completely demoralized the monkeys, who suspended their fight, crying, "Why should we fight when our goddess Sita is thus gone?" They were in a rout until Vibishana came to their rescue and rallied them again.

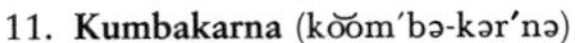

Indrajit fell by Lakshmana's hand in the end. When he heard of his son's death, Ravana shed bitter tears and swore, "This is the time to kill that woman Sita, the cause of all this misery."

11. **Kumbakarna** (ko͝om′bə-kər′nə).

12. **Brahma's** (brä′məz): given by Brahma—in the Hindu religion, the creator of the universe and one of a trinity of gods that make up the Supreme God.

WORDS TO KNOW **invincibility** (ĭn-vĭn′sə-bĭl′ĭ-tē) *n.* a state of being unbeatable

Customizing Instruction

Less Proficient Readers

1 After students read this passage, check their comprehension by having them describe the awakening of Kumbakarna in their own words.

Multiple Learning Styles

Visual Learners

Students may have a difficult time envisioning the strange-looking Ravana. You might assign students to draw Ravana, using descriptive details given in the text. Let students compare their different interpretations of Ravana's appearance and discuss the reasons for the possible differences in their drawings.

Mini Lesson Grammar

FINDING THE SUBJECT AND PREDICATE

Instruction To add details, build interest, and provide rhythm and variety to their writing, writers sometimes begin sentences with adverbs, phrases, or clauses. They may also insert adverbs, phrases, or clauses that separate the subject and predicate. This can make locating the subject and predicate more challenging.

Activity Write these excerpts from the Ramayana on the chalkboard.

"' . . . Surely (adv.) before this day is done, (adv. clause) one of them (prep. phrase) will be a widow.'"

"One who had spent a lifetime in destruction, (adj. clause) now (adv.) found the gory spectacle intolerable."

Have students find each sentence's subject and verb. Discuss the placement of the subject and verb in each sentence and the adverbs, phrases, or clauses that interrupt them.

Use **Grammar Transparencies and Copymasters,** p. 81.

Use McDougal Littell's ***Language Network*** for more instruction and practice in subjects and predicates.

Reading and Analyzing

Literary Analysis: CHARACTERIZATION

A Invite students to discuss how this section makes them feel about Ravana.

Possible Responses: Many may say that compassion and adherence to ritual reveal his potential goodness and former glory; others may say that he seems hypocritical.

Ask students what Rama's orders to his driver emphasize about his character.

Possible Responses: He is a master strategist who fully understands his opponent's weakness; he is calm and poised under pressure.

Have students describe Mahodara as a person and as a soldier.

Possible Response: He is reckless and only concerned with gaining honor for himself.

Literary Analysis: METAPHOR

B A metaphor is a figure of speech that compares two things that are dissimilar yet have something in common. For example, "Ravana sent a shower of arrows on Rama." In this metaphor, the arrows, falling thick and fast from the sky, are compared to rain. Ask students how this metaphor adds to their understanding of the battle.

Possible Response: Using the word *shower* gives a vivid picture of how thickly and how fast the arrows must have been falling.

A few encouraged this idea, but one of his councillors advised, "Don't defeat your own purpose and integrity by killing a woman. Let your anger scorch Rama and his brother. Gather all your armies and go and vanquish Rama and Lakshmana, you know you can, and then take Sita. Put on your blessed armour and go forth."

A RAMA AND RAVANA IN BATTLE

Every moment, news came to Ravana of fresh disasters in his camp. One by one, most of his commanders were lost. No one who went forth with battle cries was heard of again. Cries and shouts and the wailings of the widows of warriors came over the chants and songs of triumph that his courtiers arranged to keep up at a loud pitch in his assembly hall. Ravana became restless and abruptly left the hall and went up on a tower, from which he could obtain a full view of the city. He surveyed the scene below but could not stand it. One who had spent a lifetime in destruction, now found the gory spectacle intolerable. Groans and wailings reached his ears with deadly clarity; and he noticed how the monkey hordes revelled in their bloody handiwork. This was too much for him. He felt a terrific rage rising within him, mixed with some admiration for Rama's valour. He told himself, "The time has come for me to act by myself again."

He hurried down the steps of the tower, returned to his chamber, and prepared himself for the battle. He had a ritual bath and performed special prayers to gain the benediction of Shiva; donned his battle dress, matchless armour, armlets, and crowns. He had on a protective armour for every inch of his body. He girt his sword-belt and attached to his body his accoutrements for protection and decoration.

When he emerged from his chamber, his heroic appearance was breathtaking. He summoned his chariot, which could be drawn by horses or move on its own if the horses were hurt or killed. People stood aside when he came out of the palace and entered his chariot. "This is my resolve," he said to himself: "Either that woman Sita, or my wife Mandodari,[13] will soon have cause to cry and roll in the dust in grief. Surely, before this day is done, one of them will be a widow."

The gods in heaven noticed Ravana's determined move and felt that Rama would need all the support they could muster. They requested Indra to send down his special chariot for Rama's use. When the chariot appeared at his camp, Rama was deeply impressed with the magnitude and brilliance of the vehicle. "How has this come to be here?" he asked.

"Sir," the charioteer answered, "my name is Matali.[14] I have the honour of being the charioteer of Indra. Brahma, the four-faced god and the creator of the Universe, and Shiva, whose power has emboldened Ravana now to challenge you, have commanded me to bring it here for your use. It can fly swifter than air over all obstacles, over any mountain, sea, or sky, and will help you to emerge victorious in this battle."

Rama reflected aloud, "It may be that the rakshasas have created this illusion for me. It may be a trap. I don't know how to view it." Whereupon Matali spoke convincingly to dispel the doubt in Rama's mind. Rama, still hesitant, though partially convinced, looked at Hanuman 1
and Lakshmana and asked, "What do you think of it?" Both answered, "We feel no doubt that this chariot is Indra's; it is not an illusory creation."

Rama fastened his sword, slung two quivers full of rare arrows over his shoulders, and climbed into the chariot.

The beat of war drums, the challenging cries of soldiers, the trumpets, and the rolling chariots speeding along to confront each other, created a deafening mixture of noise. While Ravana had

13. **Mandodari** (mən-dō'də-rē).
14. **Matali** (mä'tə-lē).

Teaching Options

Vocabulary Strategy

USING CONTEXT CLUES

Instruction Explain to students that they can often find the meanings of strange words or words used in unfamiliar ways by examining the context—the surrounding words, phrases, and sentences. Point out the word *girt* (page 244, paragraph 2). This word is most likely unfamiliar to students, but they can probably figure out its meaning of "fastened" from the context: a description of a warrior dressing for battle. Also point out the word *arrest* (page 247, paragraph 1). From the context, it is plain that *arrest* has a meaning different from the one with which they are most likely familiar. The meaning here is simply "to stop."

Activity Have the students make a chart on their own paper. They should have three columns, labeled *Word, My Definition,* and *Dictionary Definition.* Write the following words and citations on the chalkboard:

horde (page 242, paragraph 10)
engagement (page 243, paragraph 1)
demoralized (page 243, paragraph 12)
vanquish (page 244, paragraph 1)

instructed his charioteer to speed ahead, Rama very gently ordered his chariot-driver, "Ravana is in a rage; let him perform all the antics he desires and exhaust himself. Until then be calm; we don't have to hurry forward. Move slowly and calmly, and you must strictly follow my instructions; I will tell you when to drive faster."

Ravana's assistant and one of his staunchest supporters, Mahodara[15]—the giant among giants in his physical appearance—begged Ravana, "Let me not be a mere spectator when you confront Rama. Let me have the honour of grappling with him. Permit me to attack Rama."

"Rama is my sole concern," Ravana replied. "If you wish to engage yourself in a fight, you may fight his brother Lakshmana."

Noticing Mahodara's purpose, Rama steered his chariot across his path in order to prevent Mahodara from reaching Lakshmana. Whereupon Mahodara ordered his chariot-driver, "Now dash straight ahead, directly into Rama's chariot."

The charioteer, more practical-minded, advised him, "I would not go near Rama. Let us keep away." But Mahodara, obstinate and intoxicated with war fever, made straight for Rama. He wanted to have the honour of a direct encounter with Rama himself in spite of Ravana's advice; and for this honour he paid a heavy price, as it was a moment's work for Rama to destroy him, and leave him lifeless and shapeless on the field. Noticing this, Ravana's anger mounted further. He commanded his driver, "You will not slacken now. Go." Many ominous signs were seen now—his bow-strings suddenly snapped; the mountains shook; thunders rumbled in the skies; tears flowed from the horses' eyes; elephants with decorated foreheads moved along dejectedly. Ravana, noticing them, hesitated only for a second, saying, "I don't care. This mere mortal Rama is of no account, and these omens do not concern me at all." Meanwhile, Rama paused for a moment to consider his next step; and suddenly turned towards the armies supporting Ravana, which stretched away to the horizon, and destroyed them. He felt that this might be one way of saving Ravana. With his armies gone, it was possible that Ravana might have a change of heart. But it had only the effect of spurring Ravana on; he plunged forward and kept coming nearer Rama and his own doom.

Rama's army cleared and made way for Ravana's chariot, unable to stand the force of his approach. Ravana blew his conch[16] and its shrill challenge reverberated through space. Following it another conch, called "Panchajanya,"[17] which belonged to Mahavishnu[18] (Rama's original form before his present incarnation), sounded of its own accord in answer to the challenge, agitating the universe with its vibrations. And then Matali picked up another conch, which was Indra's, and blew it. This was the signal indicating the commencement of the actual battle. Presently Ravana sent a shower of arrows on Rama; and Rama's followers, unable to bear the sight of his body being studded with arrows, averted their heads. Then the chariot horses of Ravana and Rama glared at each other in hostility, and the flags topping the chariots—Ravana's ensign of the Veena[19] and Rama's with the whole universe on it—clashed, and one heard the stringing and twanging of bow-strings on both sides, over-powering in volume all other sound. Then followed a shower of arrows from Rama's own bow. Ravana stood gazing at the chariot sent by Indra and swore, "These gods, instead of supporting me, have gone to the support of this

B

2

15. **Mahodara** (mə-hō′də-rä).
16. **conch** (kŏngk): a large spiral seashell, used as a trumpet.
17. **Panchajanya** (pän′chə-jən′yə).
18. **Mahavishnu** (mə-hä′vĭsh′no͞o): the Supreme God in Hinduism, who divides himself into the trinity of Brahma, Vishnu, and Shiva.
19. **Veena** (vē′nə): a stringed musical instrument.

WORDS TO KNOW **incarnation** (ĭn′kär-nā′shən) *n.* a bodily form taken on by a spirit

Customizing Instruction

Multiple Learning Styles

Interpersonal Learners

1 Have four students role-play the scene in which Rama is helped to determine the true nature of the chariot. Provide help with the dialogue as needed.

Visual Learners

2 The fascinating image of the flag with the entire universe pictured on it might present a welcome challenge. Invite students to draw or paint what the flag might look like. Display the results.

Less Proficient Readers

Ask students to summarize "The Siege of Lanka."

- Why are Ravana and Rama enemies?
  Answer: Ravana has kidnapped Rama's wife, Sita.
- Whom do Rama and his brother Lakshmana kill?
  Answer: Rama kills Kumbakarna, Ravana's brother; Lakshmana kills Indrajit, Ravana's son.

Set a Purpose Have students continue to find out how Ravana is affected by the deaths of his brother and son.

Instruct the students to write the words in their *Words* column. Then, have them find the words in the text. Using each word's context, students should come up with a meaning for the word and write it in the *My Definition* column. Once they have done this for all five words, have the students look up the words in a dictionary and write the appropriate definitions in the *Dictionary Definition* column. (You should probably remind students to look at all the numbered definitions of each word.) Have them compare their own definitions to the dictionary's. You might let students discuss any particular surprises or discoveries.

Use **Vocabulary Transparencies and Copymasters,** p. 29.

A lesson on using context clues appears on p. 939 of the Pupil's Edition.

Reading and Analyzing

Literary Analysis
SUPERNATURAL ELEMENTS

A The battle so far has involved both natural and supernatural weapons. How has the battle now changed?
Possible Response: Now it rises to a purely supernatural level, involving asthras and incantations.

Literary Analysis: SYMBOLISM

B Have students analyze the weapons that Rama and Ravana use at this stage of the battle.
Possible Responses: Ravana creates illusions that Rama counteracts with wisdom or perception; Ravana creates darkness that Rama defeats with insight or understanding.

What do these weapons symbolize?
Possible Responses: Most students will agree that the weapons stand for moral or spiritual qualities that divide people and cause conflict.

Have students compare and contrast the natural omens associated with the battle exploits of Ravana and Rama.
Possible Responses: The omens for Ravana are bad—shaking mountains, rumbling thunder, crying horses, and dejected elephants; the omen for Rama is good—the divine eagle perched on its flag post.

Point out that the omens also function as symbols of the good and evil forces in the battle.

petty human being. I will teach them a lesson. He is not fit to be killed with my arrows but I shall seize him and his chariot together and fling them into high heaven and dash them to destruction." Despite his oath, he still strung his bow and sent a shower of arrows at Rama, raining in thousands, but they were all invariably shattered and neutralized by the arrows from Rama's bow, which met arrow for arrow. Ultimately Ravana, instead of using one bow, used ten with his twenty arms, multiplying his attack tenfold; but Rama stood unhurt.

Ravana suddenly realized that he should change his tactics and ordered his charioteer to fly the chariot up in the skies. From there he attacked and destroyed a great many of the monkey army supporting Rama. Rama ordered Matali, "Go up in the air. Our young soldiers are being attacked from the sky. Follow Ravana, and don't slacken."

There followed an aerial pursuit at dizzying speed across the dome of the sky and rim of the earth. Ravana's arrows came down like rain; he was bent upon destroying everything in the world. But Rama's arrows diverted, broke, or neutralized Ravana's. Terror-stricken, the gods watched this pursuit. Presently Ravana's arrows struck Rama's horses and pierced the heart of Matali himself. The charioteer fell. Rama paused for a while in grief, undecided as to his next step. Then he recovered and resumed his offensive. At that moment the divine eagle Garuda was seen perched on Rama's flagpost, and the gods who were watching felt that this could be an auspicious sign.

After circling the globe several times, the duelling chariots returned, and the fight continued over Lanka. It was impossible to be very clear about the location of the battleground as the fight occurred here, there, and everywhere. Rama's arrows pierced Ravana's armour and made him wince. Ravana was so insensible to pain and impervious to attack that for him to wince was a good sign, and the gods hoped that this was a turn for the better. But at this moment, Ravana suddenly changed his tactics. Instead of merely shooting his arrows, which were powerful in themselves, he also invoked several supernatural forces to create strange effects: He was an adept in the use of various asthras[20] which could be made dynamic with special incantations. At this point, the fight became one of attack with supernatural powers, and parrying of such an attack with other supernatural powers. **A**

Ravana realized that the mere aiming of shafts with ten or twenty of his arms would be of no avail because the mortal whom he had so contemptuously thought of destroying with a slight effort was proving formidable, and his arrows were beginning to pierce and cause pain. Among the asthras sent by Ravana was one called "Danda," a special gift from Shiva, capable of pursuing and pulverizing its target. When it came flaming along, the gods were struck with fear. But Rama's arrow neutralized it.

Now Ravana said to himself, "These are all petty weapons. I should really get down to proper business." And he invoked the one called "Maya"—a weapon which created illusions and confused the enemy.

With proper incantations and worship, he sent off this weapon and it created an illusion of reviving all the armies and its leaders—Kumbakarna and Indrajit and the others—and bringing them back to the battlefield. Presently Rama found all those who, he thought, were no **B**

20. **asthras** (əs'thrəz): arrows or other weapons powered by supernatural forces.

WORDS TO KNOW
impervious (ĭm-pûr'vē-əs) *adj.* incapable of being penetrated; unaffected
incantation (ĭn'kăn-tā'shən) *n.* a chant intended to bring forth supernatural powers; magic spell
parrying (păr'ē-ĭng) *n.* warding off or turning aside **parry** *v.*
formidable (fôr'mĭ-də-bəl) *adj.* hard to handle or overcome

Teaching Options

Multicultural Link

Reverence for Life

In India, animals are treated with special respect because many of the people believe that all living creatures have souls. Many animals are associated with gods. The bull is revered because Shiva is believed to ride on a bull. The elephant is a symbol of the god of learning. Because birds inhabit the sky, they are thought to transmit messages from the gods to mortals or between lovers. The monkey-god Hanuman, friend and servant of Rama, is able to fly "like an arrow through space." A monkey called the *hanuman langur,* common to southern Asia, is a symbol of self-sacrifice throughout India. Legends say its black face and hands were scorched in a fire when the langur helped a friend. As students progress through the *Ramayana,* have them consider why this monkey is named after the god Hanuman.

B

more, coming on with battle cries and surrounding him. Every man in the enemy's army was again up in arms. They seemed to fall on Rama with victorious cries. This was very confusing and Rama asked Matali, whom he had by now revived, "What is happening now? How are all these coming back? They were dead." Matali explained, "In your original identity you are the creator of illusions in this universe. Please know that Ravana has created phantoms to confuse you. If you make up your mind, you can dispel them immediately." Matali's explanation was a great help. Rama at once invoked a weapon called "Gnana"[21]—which means "wisdom" or "perception." This was a very rare weapon, and he sent it forth. And all the terrifying armies who seemed to have come on in such a great mass suddenly evaporated into thin air.

Ravana then shot an asthra called "Thama," whose nature was to create total darkness in all the worlds. The arrows came with heads exposing frightening eyes and fangs, and fiery tongues. End to end the earth was enveloped in total darkness and the whole of creation was paralysed. This asthra also created a deluge of rain on one side, a rain of stones on the other, a hail-storm showering down intermittently, and a tornado sweeping the earth. Ravana was sure that this would arrest Rama's enterprise. But Rama was able to meet it with what was named "Shivasthra."[22] He understood the nature of the phenomenon and the cause of it and chose the appropriate asthra for counteracting it.

Ravana now shot off what he considered his deadliest weapon—a trident[23] endowed with extraordinary destructive power, once gifted to Ravana by the gods. When it started on its journey there was real panic all round. It came on flaming toward Rama, its speed or course unaffected by the arrows he flung at it.

When Rama noticed his arrows falling down

Rama and Lakshmana fight the demoness Taraka (1587–1598, India, Mughal, school of Akbar), Mushfiq. Leaf from a manuscript, opaque colors and gold on paper, 27.5 cm x 15.2 cm, courtesy of the Freer Gallery of Art, Smithsonian Institution, Washington, D.C. (07.217 35v).

21. **Gnana** (gnä'nə).
22. **Shivasthra** (shĭ-vəs'thrə).
23. **trident** (trīd'nt): a spear with three prongs.

Customizing Instruction

Gifted and Talented Students

Have students read another epic such as the *Odyssey, Gilgamesh,* or *Sundiata* and compare Rama to the heroes of these ancient epics. Have students describe each hero in terms of the following characteristics:

- He is of noble birth or high social position.
- He reflects values important to his society.
- His actions consist of courageous, even superhuman, deeds.
- He must often battle supernatural forces.

Mini Lesson Speaking and Listening

PRESS CONFERENCE

Instruction Explain that presidents and other officials give press conferences to explain their policies and actions to the public. At the beginning of a conference, the official may read a prepared statement. He or she may also have established rules on the types or number of questions the press is allowed to ask.

Prepare Have students hold a press conference that Rama may have held after defeating Ravana. Have them work in cooperative groups. Student reporters should prepare their questions beforehand.

Present One student should be Rama's press secretary, making a brief introduction and delivering a laudatory statement. Rama should give a brief statement and then answer questions. Finally, the dean of the press corps should exclaim, "Thank you, Prince Rama," at which point the press conference ends.

BLOCK SCHEDULING This activity is particularly well-suited for longer class periods.

Reading and Analyzing

Literary Analysis
SUPERNATURAL ELEMENTS

(A) Have students identify the supernatural elements displayed as Ravana's head and arms are severed.
Possible Response: Every time a head or arm is cut off, another grows in its place; devils and demons feast on the flesh.

Active Reading
CLASSIFYING CHARACTERS

(B) Ask: Who does the character Matali support in the conflict?
Answer: Rama.

Literary Analysis: SYMBOLISM

(C) Rama sends Brahmasthra, "aiming at his [Ravana's] heart rather than his head." What does Ravana's vulnerability signify?
Possible Response: Ravana's weakness lies not in his learning or in his weaponry but in his moral shortcomings or in his emotions.

Ask: What is the symbolism of Ravana's transformation in death?
Possible Response: The transformation symbolizes the possibility that all people in their "pristine form" have the potential for good, though this potential may be corrupted during life.

Reading Skills and Strategies: CONNECTING

(D) Have students explain the superficial "layers of dross" that Rama's arrows burn off.
Possible Response: The "layers of dross" are Ravana's faults ("anger, conceit, cruelty, lust, and egotism") that when burned away reveal a noble nature underneath.

ineffectively while the trident sailed towards him, for a moment he lost heart. When it came quite near, he uttered a certain mantra[24] from the depth of his being and while he was breathing out that incantation, an esoteric syllable in perfect timing, the trident collapsed. Ravana, who had been so certain of vanquishing Rama with his trident, was astonished to see it fall down within an inch of him, and for a minute wondered if his adversary might not after all be a divine being although he looked like a mortal. Ravana thought to himself, "This is, perhaps, the highest God. Who could he be? Not Shiva, for Shiva is my supporter; he could not be Brahma, who is four faced; could not be Vishnu, because of my immunity from the weapons of the whole trinity. Perhaps this man is the primordial being, the cause behind the whole universe. But whoever he may be, I will not stop my fight until I defeat and crush him or at least take him prisoner."

With this resolve, Ravana next sent a weapon which issued forth monstrous serpents vomiting fire and venom, with enormous fangs and red eyes. They came darting in from all directions.

Rama now selected an asthra called "Garuda" (which meant "eagle"). Very soon thousands of eagles were aloft, and they picked off the serpents with their claws and beaks and destroyed them. Seeing this also fail, Ravana's anger was roused to a mad pitch and he blindly emptied a quiverful of arrows in Rama's direction. Rama's arrows met them half way and turned them round so that they went back and their sharp points embedded themselves in Ravana's own chest.

Ravana was weakening in spirit. He realized that he was at the end of his resources. All his learning and equipment in weaponry were of no avail and he had practically come to the end of his special gifts of destruction. While he was going down thus, Rama's own spirit was soaring up. The combatants were now near enough to grapple with each other and Rama realized that this was the best moment to cut off Ravana's heads. He sent a crescent-shaped arrow which sliced off one of Ravana's heads and flung it far into the sea, and this process continued; but every time a head was cut off, Ravana had the benediction of having another one grown in its place. Rama's crescent-shaped weapon was continuously busy as Ravana's heads kept cropping up. Rama lopped off his arms but they grew again and every lopped-off arm hit Matali and the chariot and tried to cause destruction by itself, and the tongue in a new head wagged, uttered challenges, and cursed Rama. On the cast-off heads of Ravana devils and minor demons, who had all along been in terror of Ravana and had obeyed and pleased him, executed a dance of death and feasted on the flesh. (A)

Ravana was now desperate. Rama's arrows embedded themselves in a hundred places on his body and weakened him. Presently he collapsed in a faint on the floor of his chariot. Noticing his state, his charioteer pulled back and drew the chariot aside. Matali whispered to Rama, "This is the time to finish off that demon. He is in a faint. Go on. Go on." (B)

But Rama put away his bow and said, "It is not fair warfare to attack a man who is in a faint. I will wait. Let him recover," and waited.

When Ravana revived, he was angry with his charioteer for withdrawing, and took out his sword, crying, "You have disgraced me. Those who look on will think I have retreated." But his charioteer explained how Rama suspended the fight and forebore to attack when he was in a faint. Somehow, Ravana appreciated his explanation and patted his back and resumed his attacks. Having exhausted his special weapons, in desperation Ravana began to throw on Rama

24. **mantra** (măn′trə): a word, sound, or phrase used as a prayer or spell.

WORDS TO KNOW
esoteric (ĕs′ə-tĕr′ĭk) *adj.* understood only by a chosen few
primordial (prī-môr′dē-əl) *adj.* first existing; original

Teaching Options

Assessment Informal Assessment

STORY MAPS Have students work in pairs or small groups to create story maps that include: Exposition; Rising Action; Climax; Falling Action.

RUBRIC

3 **Full Accomplishment** Story map is completely and accurately filled in. Sequence is correct.
2 **Substantial Accomplishment** Story map contains minor errors or inconsistencies. Sequence is correct.
1 **Little or Partial Accomplishment** Story map contains major errors or omissions. Sequence is not correct.

STORY MAP

Setting:	Indian island of Lanka
Main Characters:	Rama, a prince who is an incarnation of Vishnu; Ravana, a demon
Exposition:	Ravana has kidnapped Rama's wife, Sita; Rama lays siege to Lanka.

all sorts of things such as staves, cast-iron balls, heavy rocks, and oddments he could lay hands on. None of them touched Rama, but glanced off and fell ineffectually. Rama went on shooting his arrows. There seemed to be no end of this struggle in sight.

Now Rama had to pause to consider what final measure he should take to bring this campaign to an end. After much thought, he decided to use "Brahmasthra,"[25] a weapon specially designed by the Creator Brahma on a former occasion, when he had to provide one for Shiva to destroy Tripura,[26] the old monster who assumed the forms of flying mountains and settled down on habitations and cities, seeking to destroy the world. The Brahmasthra was a special gift to be used only when all other means had failed. Now Rama, with prayers and worship, invoked its fullest power and sent it in Ravana's direction, aiming at his heart rather than his head; Ravana being vulnerable at heart. While he had prayed for indestructibility of his several heads and arms, he had forgotten to strengthen his heart, where the Brahmasthra entered and ended his career.

Rama watched him fall headlong from his chariot face down onto the earth, and that was the end of the great campaign. Now one noticed Ravana's face aglow with a new quality. Rama's arrows had burnt off the layers of dross,[27] the anger, conceit, cruelty, lust, and egotism which had encrusted his real self, and now his personality came through in its pristine form—of one who was devout and capable of tremendous attainments. His constant meditation on Rama, although as an adversary, now seemed to bear fruit, as his face shone with serenity and peace. Rama noticed it from his chariot above and commanded Matali, "Set me down on the ground." When the chariot descended and came to rest on its wheels, Rama got down and commanded Matali, "I am grateful for your services to me. You may now take the chariot back to Indra."

Surrounded by his brother Lakshmana and Hanuman and all his other war chiefs, Rama approached Ravana's body, and stood gazing on it. He noted his crowns and jewellery scattered piecemeal on the ground. The decorations and the extraordinary workmanship of the armour on his chest were blood-covered. Rama sighed as if to say, "What might he not have achieved but for the evil stirring within him!"

At this moment, as they readjusted Ravana's blood-stained body, Rama noticed to his great shock a scar on Ravana's back and said with a smile, "Perhaps this is not an episode of glory for me as I seem to have killed an enemy who was turning his back and retreating. Perhaps I was wrong in shooting the Brahmasthra into him." He looked so concerned at this supposed lapse on his part that Vibishana, Ravana's brother, came forward to explain. "What you have achieved is unique. I say so although it meant the death of my brother."

"But I have attacked a man who had turned his back," Rama said. "See that scar."

Vibishana explained, "It is an old scar. In ancient days, when he paraded his strength around the globe, once he tried to attack the divine elephants that guard the four directions. When he tried to catch them, he was gored in the back by one of the tuskers and that is the scar you see now; it is not a fresh one though fresh blood is flowing on it."

Rama accepted the explanation. "Honour him and cherish his memory so that his spirit may go to heaven, where he has his place. And now I will leave you to attend to his funeral arrangements, befitting his grandeur." ❖

---

25. **Brahmasthra** (brə-məs′thrə).
26. **Tripura** (trĭ-po͞o′rə).
27. **dross:** waste matter; impurities.

Customizing Instruction

Less Proficient Readers
Have students summarize the battle strategies of the combatants and the supernatural weapons each employs. Ask students what point about good and evil they think the epic makes.
Possible Response: Good is ultimately stronger than evil.

Rising Action: Ravana sends spies to Rama's army; Rama sends a messenger, whom Ravana tries to kill; Rama orders battle; Ravana goes to face Rama and is defeated but released; Ravana wakes his brother Kumbakarna.

Climax: Rama kills Ravana with the Brahmasthra.

Falling Action: Ravana is beautifully transformed in death; Rama orders a funeral honoring Ravana's former grandeur.

GUIDING STUDENT RESPONSE

Connect to the Literature

1. **What Do You Think?** Guidelines for student response: Students might describe the battle in terms of some of the other epic struggles they have seen in this unit in the excerpts from *Beowulf* and the *Iliad*.

Comprehension Check

- Ravana has kidnapped Sita, Rama's wife.
- He has a sorcerer create the illusion of Rama's severed head and of the revival of his own dead armies.
- He honors Ravana.

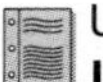
Use Selection Quiz in **Unit One Resource Book** p. 77

Think Critically

2. Possible Responses: Rama has divine support; he is a better strategist; he is cooler under pressure; his motives are pure and heroic.
3. Possible Response: Rama is brave, honest, fair, and magnanimous. He tries to end the conflict peacefully, refusing to fight the unarmed Ravana. He is concerned about possibly having wounded Ravana in the back.
4. Possible Response: Ravana is not heroic because he fights unfairly and relies on spies, illusion, and trickery. Ravana had the potential for heroism, as shown in his transformation after death and his observance of ritual in preparation for direct battle with Rama.
5. Encourage students to substantiate their interpretations of characters with specific reference to the literature and their own experience. Make certain that they are making generalizations about character *(Ravana is noble)* rather than about actions *(Ravana did noble deeds).*

Literary Analysis

Cooperative Learning Activity Have groups of students perform or read their rewritten scenes for the class.

Thinking through the LITERATURE

Connect to the Literature

1. **What Do You Think?** What is your reaction to the battle between Rama and Ravana?

Comprehension Check
- Why does Rama lay siege to Ravana's island?
- Name some ways in which Ravana uses illusion as a weapon.
- How does Rama treat Ravana after killing him?

Think Critically

2. Ravana, with his 10 heads and 20 arms, would seem to have an advantage over Rama. Why do you think Rama is able to defeat him?
3. How would you describe Rama's **heroic code** of conduct?

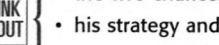

   THINK ABOUT
   - the offer he sends to Ravana by messenger
   - the two chances he gives Ravana to recover
   - his strategy and behavior in battle
   - what he tells Ravana's brother after Ravana has been killed

4. Do you think that Ravana is heroic? Use evidence from the epic to support your answer.
5. **ACTIVE READING** CLASSIFYING CHARACTERS Look over your chart in your READER'S NOTEBOOK and discuss the **characters** with a partner. What generalizations can you make about the characters on each side? Remember that you can form a generalization about a character by making broad judgments based on evidence in the story.

Extend Interpretations

6. **What If?** Suppose that Trijata had let Sita believe that Rama and his brother had been killed. What do you think Sita would have done? What impact might her actions have had on Rama and the battle with Ravana?
7. **Connect to Life** In India, Rama has been celebrated as a **hero** for centuries. Compare Rama's heroic qualities with those displayed by heroes of your own country.
8. **Points of Comparison** Compare Sir Launcelot's refusal to strike Sir Gawain after he falls to the ground in *Le Morte d'Arthur* with Rama's insistence on halting the fight until Ravana comes out of a faint. What does their behavior suggest about their character and code of honor?

Literary Analysis

SUPERNATURAL ELEMENTS

Both Rama and Ravana use **supernatural elements** to try to defeat the other. Supernatural elements go beyond the bounds of reality by involving beings, powers, or events that cannot be explained by the laws of nature. Some of the supernatural elements in this excerpt from the *Ramayana* include the following:

- Indra's chariot, which has the power to "fly swifter than air over all obstacles"
- the ominous signs—mountains shaking, tears flowing from horses' eyes—that herald Ravana's attack on Rama
- asthras—arrows powered by supernatural forces

Supernatural elements are found in the literatures of nearly all cultures. In **epics,** in particular, these elements help make the characters' attributes larger-than-life.

Cooperative Learning Activity With a group of classmates, discuss the supernatural elements in this excerpt from the *Ramayana.* Then think about how the epic would be affected if it didn't include supernatural elements. Choose a scene and rewrite it, deleting those elements. What is lost? What, if anything, is gained?

REVIEW EPIC An **epic** is a long narrative poem, presented in an elevated or formal style, that traces the adventures of a great hero. *Beowulf* and the *Iliad* are two other epics you have read. What characteristics do these poems share with the *Ramayana?*

Extend Interpretations

What If? Accept all reasonable responses that are based on valid readings of the literature.

Connect to Life Accept all reasonable, well-supported responses.

Points of Comparison To get the students started on their comparison, discuss the relationship between behavior and character. Ask them whether good people do bad things, and, conversely, whether bad people do good things.

Writing Options

1. Rama's Speech Compose a speech that Rama might deliver to his people following his victory at Lanka. The speech should focus on Rama's own actions, courage, and faith in the face of Ravana's onslaught. Place the entry in your **Working Portfolio.**

2. Points of Comparison Compare the supernatural powers Ravana uses to trick his enemy with those Sir Launcelot wields against Sir Gawain. Then answer the following question in a brief essay: Do you think Ravana and Launcelot would have been able to defeat their opponents if they could have traded supernatural powers? Why or why not?

Activities & Explorations

1. Illustrated Battle Illustrate a battle scene described in the excerpt. You might depict the scene in one illustration or in a series of sketches. ~ **ART**

2. Battle Scene Soundtrack Using sound effects, voices, and passages from recordings, create a soundtrack that captures the mood of a battle scene or other event in the excerpt. ~ **SPEAKING AND LISTENING**

Inquiry & Research

Hidden Temple The sculpture shown on page 241 adorns Angkor Wat, a group of temples in Cambodia that were constructed in the 1100s. Long hidden by forest growth, Angkor Wat was discovered by a French naturalist in 1860. Research to find out more about the history and art of Angkor Wat. Present your findings to the class.

More Online: Research Starter www.mcdougallittell.com

Vocabulary in Action

EXERCISE: CONTEXT CLUES Write the word that best fits in each blank.

Zing, the hero of the Zoori nation, was an ___1___ of Erg, the god of energy. According to legend, Zing was a ___2___ being, the first and greatest of the Zoori man-gods. He fought bravely from behind a ___3___ when attacked by Zud, the six-fisted demon. The nasty Zud, with his superior weapons, was a ___4___ opponent. Because of his many fists and scaly skin, Zud seemed ___5___ to harm. Zing recited an ___6___, seeking aid from his divine protectors. His words were ___7___ and meant only for heavenly ears. An army of sacred zebras arrived to help Zing ___8___ the many swords and spears of his foe. Zing and his army proved their ___9___, easily overpowering Zud and his evil followers. Zud shouted a hateful ___10___, shook his six fists, and retired from the battlefield.

WORDS TO KNOW

esoteric	incarnation
formidable	invincibility
impervious	parrying
imprecation	primordial
incantation	rampart

Building Vocabulary
For an in-depth study of context clues, see page 938.

Valmiki

First Poet of India According to current versions of the *Ramayana,* the story of Rama was told to the wise man Valmiki by the divine sage Narada. Although little is known about the poet, some scholars believe that Valmiki was indeed a man of genius. They regard him as the "first poet" of India and the inventor of the *sloka,* the poetic meter used in the *Ramayana* and popular in later Indian poetry.

Influential Epic The *Ramayana* pervades the culture of India. Over the centuries, it has been translated and adapted by many authors, including the 20th-century writer R. K. Narayan. According to Narayan, "Everyone of whatever age, outlook, education, or station in life knows the essential part of the epic and adores the main figures in it."

Writing Options

1. **Rama's Speech** Have students work on their speeches with a partner. Encourage them to have a specific purpose in mind: to persuade the audience of the rightness of Rama's actions; to inform the audience of what transpired.
2. **Points of Comparison** Have students begin by making a chart with column heads for each character or by mapping out ideas. Then, have them evaluate which character seems to rely the most on supernatural elements.

Activities & Explorations

1. **Illustrated Battle** Encourage students to include only the details suggested or stated in the passage.
2. **Battle Scene Soundtrack** Students might pair up with those doing battle scene drawings and provide the soundtracks and commentary for their peers' work.

Inquiry & Research

Hidden Temple Students not familiar with electronic research methods may need help from peer tutors.

Vocabulary in Action

Context Clues

1. incarnation
2. primordial
3. rampart
4. formidable
5. impervious
6. incantation
7. esoteric
8. parrying
9. invincibility
10. imprecation

OVERVIEW

Objectives
1. understand and appreciate an **autobiography (Literary Analysis)**
2. research word origins as an aid to understanding meaning **(Vocabulary)**

Summary
In this excerpt, Kempe recounts the troubled period before and after the birth of her first child. After her child was born, Kempe, thinking that she was about to die, wanted to confess something that had long troubled her. As she began to confess, her confessor passed judgment on her, so she would say no more. Soon after, Kempe "went out of her mind," having visions of devils and performing wicked and self-destructive acts. After many months, she said Christ appeared to her in the likeness of a man, assuring her that he had never forsaken her. Afterward, Kempe grew calm and, with the help of her husband, resumed her normal daily life.

Use **Unit One Resource Book,** p. 77 for additional support.

Thematic Link
Like the other characters in this section, Margery Kempe **attempted to achieve perfection** in her life. Her autobiography provides a female perspective on the rigors of life in the Middle Ages.

5-Minute Warm-Up
Daily Language SkillBuilder

Have students **proofread** the display sentences on page 15m and write them correctly. The sentences also appear on Transparency 6 of **Grammar Transparencies and Copymasters.**

"Daughter, why have you forsaken me, and I never forsook you?"

from The Book of Margery Kempe

Autobiography by MARGERY KEMPE

Connect to Your Life
Handling Stress Think of a time when you experienced a great deal of stress or anxiety—perhaps a time when you were facing a serious illness or a major change in your life. How did you handle the experience? Did you do anything special to help yourself cope?

Build Background
Religion and the Middle Ages During the Middle Ages, religion influenced all aspects of life, and the clergy was a powerful force in both spiritual and political matters. Like the rest of medieval society, the religious hierarchy was controlled by men. A woman who wished to pursue a spiritual calling was expected to join a convent or to live as a recluse. Margery Kempe did neither. Although a wife and mother, she was determined to devote her life to Christ and, at the age of 40, became a religious visionary, traveling and preaching extensively in England, Europe, and the Holy Land. In the 1430s, Kempe's story of her spiritual life, *The Book of Margery Kempe,* was first set down in manuscript. Kempe dictated the story of her spiritual life to two different scribes, who then wrote it down. It is the earliest surviving autobiography in the English language. Kempe's account begins with the birth of her first child and describes a deeply troubling experience that would affect the course of her life.

Focus Your Reading
LITERARY ANALYSIS AUTOBIOGRAPHY

An **autobiography** is an account of a writer's own life, told in his or her own words. An autobiography provides revealing insights into the following subjects:

- the writer's character
- the writer's attitudes
- the writer's motivations
- the society in which the writer lived

As you read this autobiographical excerpt, be aware of details that suggest how Margery Kempe views herself and her experience.

ACTIVE READING STRATEGIES FOR READING AUTOBIOGRAPHY

Typically, writers of autobiographies recount their experiences in the first person, using the pronouns *I* and *me.* Margery Kempe, however, tells her story in the third person, referring to herself as "this creature" and using the pronouns *she* and *her.*

READER'S NOTEBOOK As you read Kempe's account of her experience, think of reasons why she might have chosen to use the third-person point of view and to use such phrases as "this creature." Jot down notes to indicate the effect this has on you as a reader.

LESSON RESOURCES

UNIT ONE RESOURCE BOOK, pp. 77–80

ASSESSMENT RESOURCES
Formal Assessment, p. 37
Teacher's Guide to Assessment and Portfolio Use
Test Generator

SKILLS TRANSPARENCIES AND COPYMASTERS
Reading and Critical Thinking
- Analyzing Text, T18 (for Active Reading, p. 252)

Grammar
- Diagramming Complements and Appositives, T59 (for Mini Lesson, pp. 254–255)
- Compound and Complex Sentences, C123 (for Mini Lesson, pp. 254–255)

Vocabulary
- Word Origins, C31 (for Author Activity, p. 257)

Writing
- The Uses of Dialogue, T24 (for Writing Option 1, p. 257)
- Autobiographical Incident, C36 (for Writing Option 2, p. 257)

Communications
- Formal Presentations, T10 (for Inquiry & Research, p. 257)

INTEGRATED TECHNOLOGY
Audio Library
Visit our website:
www.mcdougallittell.com

from The Book of Margery Kempe

Chapter One Illness and Recovery

Woman tending fire and reading, from an illuminated manuscript

When this creature was twenty years of age, or somewhat more, she was married to a worshipful burgess[1] [of Lynn] and was with child within a short time, as nature would have it. And after she had conceived, she was troubled with severe attacks of sickness until the

1. **burgess** (bûr′jĭs): a citizen of an English town.

TEACHING THE LITERATURE

Customizing Instruction

Students Acquiring English
Point out that "this creature" in the opening sentence is Margery herself; she is writing in third-person point of view, rather than in the first person that is more typical of autobiographies.

Use **Spanish Study Guide** for additional support, pp. 43–45.

Less Proficient Readers
Ask students to think of a time in their lives when they were discouraged or sad. Tell them to keep their own experiences in mind as they read about Margery Kempe.

Gifted and Talented
Invite students to consider what the excerpt reveals about the contradictions in Margery Kempe's character.
Possible Responses: She is strong and independent but also especially vulnerable to self-doubt and disapproval from others; she is very religious but also susceptible to temptation.

BLOCK SCHEDULING: MANAGING TIME

If your schedule requires that you cover the lesson objectives in a shorter time, use . . .
- Preparing to Read, p. 252
- Thinking Through the Literature, p. 256

If you want to take advantage of longer class time, use . . .
- TE Teaching Options: Grammar, p. 254
- Choices & Challenges and Author Activity, p. 257

Reading and Analyzing

Active Reading

STRATEGIES FOR READING AUTOBIOGRAPHY

Review two main categories of point of view, first person and third person. Distinguish between an omniscient third-person narrator (one who knows all) and a limited third-person narrator (one who tells the point of view of only one person). Remind students that although most autobiographies are written in the first person, Margery Kempe wrote about herself in the third person.

 Use **Unit One Resource Book,** p. 79 for more practice.

Literary Analysis **AUTOBIOGRAPHY**

Review the definition of autobiography: a personal account of one's own life. An autobiography provides insights into the writer's own character, as well as some understanding of the time period in which the writer lived.

A Suggest that internal and external conflicts drive Kempe to nervous exhaustion and mental illness. Foremost among these conflicts are her fear of damnation and the encounter with her confessor.

Ask students what purpose might have compelled Kempe to write an account of her life.

Possible Responses: Therapy; as a warning to herself and others; as a record of a remarkable spiritual journey.

 Use **Unit One Resource Book,** p. 80 for more exercises.

child was born. And then, what with the labor-pains she had in childbirth and the sickness that had gone before, she despaired of her life, believing she might not live. Then she sent for her confessor,[2] for she had a thing on her conscience which she had never revealed before that time in all her life. For she was continually hindered by her enemy—the devil—always saying to her while she was in good health that she didn't need to confess but to do penance by herself alone, and all should be forgiven, for God is merciful enough. And therefore this creature often did great penance in fasting on bread and water, and performed other acts of charity with devout prayers, but she would not reveal that one thing in confession.

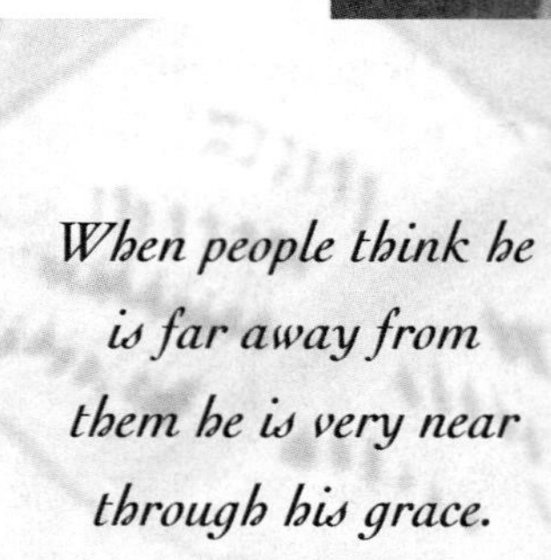

When people think he is far away from them he is very near through his grace.

And when she was at any time sick or troubled, the devil said in her mind that she should be damned, for she was not shriven[3] of that fault. Therefore, after her child was born, and not believing she would live, she sent for her confessor, as said before, fully wishing to be
A shriven of her whole lifetime, as near as she could. And when she came to the point of saying that thing which she had so long concealed, her confessor was a little too hasty and began sharply to reprove her before she had fully said what she meant, and so she would say no more in spite of anything he might do. And soon after, because of the dread she had of damnation on the one hand, and his sharp reproving of her on the other, this creature went out of her mind and was amazingly disturbed and tormented with spirits for half a year, eight weeks and odd days.

And in this time she saw, as she thought, devils opening their mouths all alight with burning
flames of fire, as if they would **1**
have swallowed her in, sometimes pawing at her, sometimes threatening her, sometimes pulling her and hauling her about both night and day during the said time. And also the devils called out to her with great threats, and bade her that she should forsake her Christian faith and belief, and deny her God, his mother, and all the saints in heaven, her good works and all good virtues, her father, her mother, and all her friends. And so she did. She slandered her husband, her friends, and her own self. She spoke many sharp and reproving words; she recognized no virtue nor goodness; she desired all wickedness; just as the spirits tempted her to say and do, so she said and did. She would

2. **confessor:** spiritual adviser; the priest to whom Margery confessed her sins.

3. **shriven:** absolved; forgiven.

Teaching Options

Grammar

COMPOUND AND COMPLEX SENTENCES

Instruction A clause is a group of words that has a subject and a predicate. There are two types of clauses: independent and subordinate. An independent clause is a clause that can stand alone as a sentence. When two or more independent clauses are joined together, they form a compound sentence. The independent clauses may be joined with a comma and a coordinating conjunction; with a semicolon; or with a semicolon, conjunctive adverb, and a comma.

Unlike an independent clause, a subordinate clause cannot stand alone as a sentence; it is dependent. A complex sentence has one independent clause and one or more subordinate clauses.

Activity Write these examples on the chalkboard.

Compound Sentence

<u>Margery Kempe withstood much ridicule</u>, yet <u>her faith in her mission was strong</u>.

Complex Sentence

<u>After we read Margery Kempe's autobiography</u>, <u>we discussed her spiritual experiences</u>.

In the first example, have students identify the

have killed herself many a time as they stirred her to, and would have been damned with them in hell, and in witness of this she bit her own hand so violently that the mark could be seen for the rest of her life. And also she pitilessly tore the skin on her body near her heart with her nails, for she had no other implement, and she would have done something worse, except that she was tied up and forcibly restrained both day and night so that she could not do as she wanted.

And when she had long been troubled by these and many other temptations, so that people
2 thought she should never have escaped from them alive, then one time as she lay by herself and her keepers were not with her, our merciful Lord Christ Jesus—ever to be trusted, worshiped be his name, never forsaking his servant in time of need—appeared to his creature who had forsaken him, in the likeness of a man, the most seemly, most beauteous, and most amiable that ever might be seen with man's eye, clad in a mantle of purple silk, sitting upon her bedside, looking upon her with so blessed a countenance that she was strengthened in all her spirits, and he said to her these words: "Daughter, why have you forsaken me, and I never forsook you?"

And as soon as he had said these words, she saw truly how the air opened as bright as any lightning, and he ascended up into the air, not hastily and quickly, but beautifully and gradually, so that she could clearly behold him in the air until it closed up again.

And presently the creature grew as calm in her wits and her reason as she ever was before, and asked her husband, as soon as he came to her, if she could have the keys of the buttery[4] to get her food and drink as she had done before. Her maids and her keepers advised him that he should not deliver up any keys to her, for they said she would only give away such goods as there were, because she did not know what she was saying, as they believed.

Nevertheless, her husband, who always had tenderness and compassion for her, ordered that they should give her the keys. And she took food and drink as her bodily strength would allow her, and she once again recognized her friends and her household, and everybody else who came to her in order to see how our Lord Jesus Christ had worked his grace in her—blessed may he be, who is ever near in tribulation.[5] When people think he is far away from them he is very near through his grace. Afterwards this creature performed all her responsibilities wisely and soberly enough, except that she did not truly know our Lord's power to draw us to him.[6] ❖

4. **buttery:** pantry.
5. **tribulation:** suffering or distress.
6. **did not . . . power:** did not feel the full attraction of God's grace. Kempe is saying that her total devotion to the Lord did not come until later.

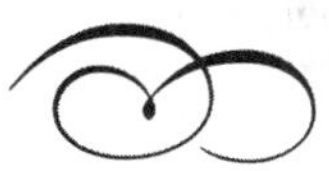

Customizing Instruction

Gifted and Talented

1 Ask students how the devil and Christ are portrayed in Kempe's autobiography.

Possible Response: As immediate and personal, as real characters in her drama.

What do these portrayals tell us about Kempe's attitude toward her religion?

Possible Response: Her religion is real and tangible to her, not just a collection of philosophical theories and attitudes.

Less Proficient Readers

2 Direct students to the first full paragraph on page 255 ("And when she had long . . ."). Point out that the paragraph is only one sentence. Have students work in pairs to identify the subject and verb of the first clause:

Answer: Lord Christ Jesus/appeared.

Have them identify the subject and verb of the second clause:

Answer: he/said.

Use the following questions to check students' understanding of Kempe's experiences:

- What causes Kempe's mental disturbance?
  Answer: Her dread of damnation and the priest's scolding.
- What do the devils in Kempe's visions tell her to do?
  Answer: Forsake her faith.
- How is she healed?
  Answer: A vision of Jesus reassures her.

independent clauses. Point out the comma and coordinating conjunction (*yet*) that join these clauses. In the second example, underline the subordinate clause twice and the independent clause once. Ask students to differentiate between the two types of clauses.

Exercise Ask students to label each sentence as compound or complex. Have students underline each independent clause once and each subordinate clause twice.

1. When Margery Kempe was twenty years old, she married John Kempe, who was a tax collector from the town of Lynn in Norfolk county. *(complex: one independent clause and two subordinate clauses)*
2. Margery called for her confessor, and she prepared to reveal her most secret sin. *(compound: two independent clauses)*

Use **Grammar Transparencies and Copymasters,** p. 121 for more exercises.

Use McDougal Littell's ***Language Network*** for more instruction in compound and complex sentences.

GUIDING STUDENT RESPONSE

Connect to the Literature

1. **What Do You Think?** Guidelines for student response: Students' empathy with Margery's condition might be manifested in a number of ways, including an understanding of emotional distress and a sympathy for the loss of mental balance.

Comprehension Check

- She thinks she might die.
- Devils tell her to kill herself.
- She realizes that Christ has not forsaken her.

Use Selection Quiz in **Unit One Resource Book,** p.81.

Think Critically

2. Possible Responses: She is an independent-minded woman whose faith and underlying stability allow her to endure emotional distress; she is an unstable, frail woman whose illness reflects the ideology of her culture.
3. Some students may point to the details Kempe uses to support the accuracy of her account. Others may claim that the details are exaggerated.
4. Possible Responses: Kempe's society knew little about the causes and treatment of mental or emotional illness. People tended to blame devils for severe emotional distress. People may have believed that religion offered the only hope for recovery.
5. Possible Responses: Third person allows the narrator to look at herself more objectively; third person allows the narrator to "hide" behind another identity; in Kempe's world, perhaps women were encouraged to be modest and not to think of themselves, so third person might seem more natural for the time period. First-person narration allows the writer to speak more easily of personal feelings and behavior; also, autobiography seems more naturally suited to first-person rather than third-person narration.

Literary Analysis

Paired Activity Reasons for writing autobiography: desire for fame, to be remembered, to understand past events, to help others, self-analysis or self-evaluation.

Thinking through the LITERATURE

Connect to the Literature

1. **What Do You Think?** How did Margery Kempe's description of her illness affect you? Share your thoughts with the class.

Comprehension Check

- Why does Kempe send for her confessor?
- Why does Kempe tear her skin and bite herself?
- Why does the vision of Christ restore her senses?

Think Critically

2. On the basis of your reading, how would you describe Margery Kempe?

THINK ABOUT
- her reasons for talking to a confessor
- the way she handles stress and anxiety
- her response to the spiritual vision

3. Do you think Kempe's account of her illness and recovery is believable? Why or why not?
4. What does Kempe's experience tell you about her society's attitude toward mental illness?
5. **ACTIVE READING** **STRATEGIES FOR READING AUTOBIOGRAPHY** Look at your notes in your **READER'S NOTEBOOK.** What might be some of the advantages and disadvantages of writing an autobiography in the third person?

Extend Interpretations

6. **Critic's Corner** A critic has said that Margery Kempe exhibits contradictory qualities, appearing to be both humble and forceful, both devout and arrogant. What evidence do you see in the selection of these contradictory qualities? Be specific in your answer.
7. **Different Perspectives** Assume the role of Margery Kempe's husband and describe her experience from his point of view. What additional information do you think his account might contain?
8. **Connect to Life** Think about modern attitudes toward mental illness. How do you think Margery Kempe's experiences would be viewed today? Explain your opinion.

Literary Analysis

AUTOBIOGRAPHY

An **autobiography** is a writer's account of his or her own life. Autobiographies often convey profound insights as writers recount past events from the perspective of greater understanding and distance.

Paired Activity With a partner, list various reasons why someone might be inspired to write an autobiography. Then decide which of those reasons—or what other possible reasons—might have prompted Kempe to record her life story. Share your ideas with the class.

Extend Interpretations

Critic's Corner Possible responses: Kempe is humble and devout because she repeatedly refers to herself as a "creature" and credits Christ and religion for restoring her senses. They might say she is forceful and arrogant because she considers her story worth sharing at a time when most women remained in obscurity.

Different Perspectives You might consider pairing students to role-play John and Margery Kempe before the class begins the assignment. Remind students to consider Margery's illness from John's point of view. Thus, John would be able to describe Margery's actions and his anxieties about his wife's mental state but might not fathom her inner turmoil.

Connect to Life Accept all reasonable, well-supported responses. Students might make comparisons between the understanding of the causes of mental illness in Margery's world and today's world, as well as between the different attitudes toward, and treatments for, mental illness in the medieval and modern worlds.

Writing Options

1. Dialogue Script Write a script for a dialogue in which Kempe and her husband discuss her recovery after more than eight months of mental disturbances.

2. Narrative on Survival Think about a time when you recovered from an illness or survived a bad experience in your life. What kept you going during this difficult time? What attitudes and strategies did you use to survive? Write a personal narrative in which you describe the qualities you possess that helped you endure. Place the narrative in your **Working Portfolio.**

Activities & Explorations

1. Visionary Art Make a drawing or painting of one of the visions Kempe experienced during her illness. ~ **ART**

2. Book Jacket Design and create a book jacket for Kempe's autobiography. Use images from the selection.
~ **ART**

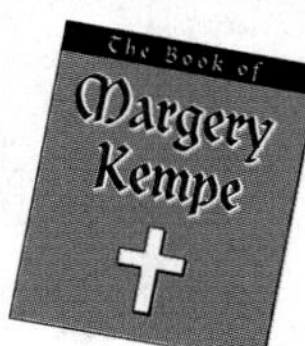

Inquiry & Research

Medieval Medical Care Investigate the nature of medical care during the 14th and 15th centuries. Present your findings in an oral report to the class.

Margery Kempe
1373?–1439?

First Religious Stirrings Margery Kempe was born about 1373 in Lynn—a town in the county of Norfolk, England—where her father served five terms as mayor. Although born to a prominent family, Kempe, like most women of her time, received little education. Around the age of 20, she married John Kempe, a tax collector, with whom she had 14 children. At around the age of 40, Margery Kempe decided to become a "bride of Christ"—to live in chastity and preach her visions to the world. As a vocal, outgoing speaker she was quite an oddity at a time when most women remained at home as wives and mothers. Although many men and women she met considered her a model of human compassion and devotion, many others disapproved of her lifestyle.

A Religious Life Once Kempe had made her commitment to God, she began a series of religious pilgrimages to Jerusalem, Spain, Italy, and Germany. It was in Jerusalem that she received her "gift" of weeping. She would fall into violent fits of crying at unpredictable times throughout the rest of her life, often during church services. Both the clergy and the common people found her hysterical crying at best annoying, at worst heretical. As a result, Kempe encountered a good deal of persecution and ridicule, although she maintained that her tears were a special gift from God, a physical token of her special worth in his eyes. She was also censured by many for dressing all in white, which at the time was a symbol of both chastity and piety.

Her Life Story Her autobiography, *The Book of Margery Kempe,* is important for several reasons. The work serves as a sort of time capsule, preserving for the reader the social customs, speech, and attitudes of the day. It also reveals the singular character of Kempe herself, a strong woman of faith who lived by her convictions despite intense social criticism and opposition. Finally, as an autobiography it is unique in its purpose: Kempe felt her story to be worth the telling not as a record of her life, which she probably thought too unimportant to merit a written account, but as a testament to God's power and his wonderful dealings with "this creature" Margery Kempe.

Author Activity

Words into Print Margery Kempe's autobiography has had an unusual publishing history. Check an encyclopedia, biography, the Internet, or some other reference source to find out how her words made their way into print.

Writing Options

1. **Dialogue Script** Students may work individually or with a partner, each writing the dialogue for one character. You might have students perform their dialogues for the class.
2. **Narrative on Survival** To help generate ideas, encourage students to remember what the illness or experience prevented them from doing or enjoying. Encourage them to recall their emotions as well as the event itself.

Activities & Explorations

1. **Visionary Art** Invite students to reread Kempe's detailed descriptions of her visions to help them make their drawings. Particularly effective are her visions of the devils.
2. **Book Jacket** Point out that students can adapt drawings and paintings from the earlier activity as part of a book jacket design. You might tell students that the illustration on page 253 was used on the book jacket of an edition of *The Book of Margery Kempe.*

Inquiry & Research

Medieval Medical Care Have students work in small groups, each student investigating a separate aspect of medical care. Topics might include the presence of women physicians, physician training, surgery, the use of medicinal herbs, and the treatment of disease. After completing the research, each student should write his or her section. Once group members have finished writing, they should organize the sections into a cohesive report that they can present to the class.

Author Activity

Words into Print Although Kempe in the 1430s dictated to two different scribes the story of her spiritual life, *The Book of Margery Kempe* was not published in a modernized version in its entirety until 1936. A version in the original Middle English was not published until 1940.

After the fall of the Roman Empire, dramatic performances virtually disappeared in the Western world, primarily because of church opposition to such public entertainments. Ironically, it was in the church itself that drama was reborn, as the clergy began to introduce dramatic elements into the liturgy and to create plays for the instruction of illiterate laypeople. During the 11th–15th centuries, as drama slowly moved from the church to the streets, plays began to feature humor (even farce), historical and everyday characters, and plot development leading to a climax—characteristics that were to blossom in the comedies, tragedies, and history plays of the Elizabethan age.

Additional Background

Medieval Drama Liturgical drama first appeared about the 10th century, when clergymen began including brief dramatic dialogues and representations in the religious ceremony called the Mass. By the 11th century, fully developed religious dramas with sets, costumes, and props had appeared. During the 1200s and 1300s, these plays became separated from religious services: they began to be presented in the churchyard and marketplace and to be performed in the vernacular by lay actors.

Another form of theater—the interlude—developed in the late 1400s, perhaps as banquet entertainment. Interludes treated morality-play subjects intellectually rather than religiously, reflecting the humanistic stirrings of the Renaissance and a shift from instruction to entertainment. An example is John Heywood's The Four P's, in which a palmer, a pardoner, a 'pothecary, and a peddler compete to see who can tell the biggest lie.

In the early 1500s, companies of professional actors supported by English noble families had begun appearing. Traveling performers were active too, as they had been throughout the Middle Ages, but they were often regarded as rogues and vagabonds; restrictions on their activities were in effect through Shakespeare's time.

Above: *Watercolor of the Last Judgment, a subject frequently dramatized in mystery cycles*

Above right: *Miniature from a manuscript of* Li Romans d'Alixandre *(about 1340), showing people wearing animal masks, perhaps for an entertainment at court*

Mystery, Miracle, & Morality *Plays*

During the early Middle Ages, in order to make church teachings accessible to the common people, clergymen began to dramatize stories from the Bible and episodes from the lives of saints. The clerics themselves played the roles in the dramas, bringing sacred history to life as part of church services. These dramatized stories soon became a popular part of church life.

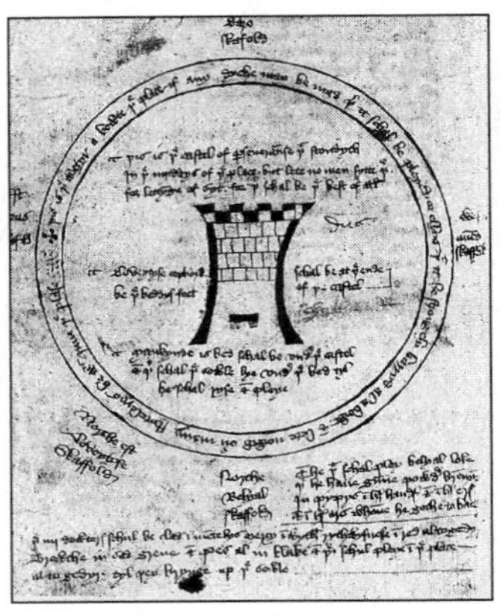

Staging diagram for The Castle of Perseverance, *one of the earliest surviving English morality plays*

As time passed, these plays developed into more elaborate productions, known as **mystery plays** (the biblical dramas) and **miracle plays** (the dramas of saints' lives), that were unsuitable for performance inside a church. The job of presenting the mystery plays was taken over by trade and craft guilds, or unions. Each guild took responsibility for one or two plays, building a pageant wagon and making costumes, props, and scenery. On a feast day, the guilds would load their props and scenery onto their wagons, form a procession, and take turns performing the plays at prearranged sites. Together, the plays formed what is called a mystery cycle, covering the whole history of the world, from the creation of Adam and Eve to the Last Judgment.

The mystery cycles were fabulous events. They often ran from sunrise to sunset, sometimes for three or more days, and included music, dance, comedy skits, and special effects to create the illusion of rain, lightning, and flying. These spectacular productions whetted the English appetite for drama. By the 1400s, professional acting troupes were traveling the countryside, performing plays of their own—called **morality plays**—that dealt with the moral struggles of everyday people.

Morality plays dramatized the inner conflicts of characters such as Everyman, an average man who is summoned by Death. Everyman tries to soften his fate by appealing to friends with names like Kindred and Fellowship, but in the face of Death they desert him. He can bring only Good Deeds along with him to the grave.

The message, of course, was crystal clear, but the play *Everyman* was more than a sermon or fable. To a large extent, morality plays such as this represented a step away from the religious drama and toward a popular English secular drama. By the 1500s, morality plays were a regular part of street pageants and began to adopt elements of court entertainments, such as mummers plays (pantomimes), tournaments, and masquerades.

As morality plays grew more varied and sophisticated, their popularity increased. The English people became a nation of theatergoers, and a wide range of dramatic entertainments became part of England's cultural life. In this way, the morality plays—like the mystery and miracle plays before them—set the stage for Elizabethan drama and the genius of playwrights like William Shakespeare.

Above:
Woodcut illustrating John Skot's edition of Everyman *(about 1503)*

Left:
In a mystery cycle, a trade or craft guild might produce a play related to its members' occupation. A shipbuilders' guild, for example, might produce a play about Noah's ark.

LITERARY CHRONOLOGY

Although much medieval drama has been lost, the following are some notable landmarks:

c. 1000 *Quem quaeritis* [Whom do you seek?], a dramatic trope in Latin, performed as part of the Easter liturgy

c. 1110 miracle play about St. Catherine performed in Dunstable, England

1300–1450 development of mystery cycles, including the four surviving English cycles: the 48 York plays, the 32 Towneley (or Wakefield) plays, the 24 Chester plays, and the 43 so-called *Ludus Coventriae* (or N Town) plays

c. 1425 *The Castle of Perseverance,* one of the earliest known English morality plays

c. 1500 *Everyman,* the most famous English morality play, probably based on a Dutch play, *Elckerlyc; Fulgens and Lucrece* by Henry Medwall, an interlude that is the earliest surviving English secular drama

c. 1520 *The Four P's* by John Heywood

Objectives
- write an Application Essay
- use a written text as a model for writing
- revise a draft to use the active voice
- check a draft for subject-verb agreement

Introducing the Workshop

A Application Essay Discuss with students what it means to present themselves positively. If a school or potential employer asks them for an essay, they should think of the essay as a letter of recommendation for themselves. Writing a strong application essay will increase their chances of getting a job or being accepted at a school.

It would be impossible for students to tell everything about themselves in an application essay, but it isn't necessary. Instead, students can reveal a great deal about themselves by focusing on a significant experience or achievement and explaining what it means to them.

Basics in a Box
B Using the Graphic
The graphic illustrates the basic structure of the application essay—introduction, body, and conclusion. The introduction pulls the reader into the essay with an interesting detail. The body focuses on the details of the student's experience and accentuates the positive elements of that experience. Here the student clearly emerges as the *star* of the essay. The conclusion wraps up the essay by explaining the importance of the experience in the writer's life.

C Presenting the Rubric
To help students grasp the basic concept of an application essay, review the Standards for Writing a Successful Application Essay. You may also wish to share with students the complete rubric, which describes several levels of proficiency.

Writing Workshop
Application Essay

Presenting yourself positively . . .

A **From Reading to Writing** *Le Morte d'Arthur* and *Sir Gawain and the Green Knight* reflect the ideal medieval virtues of honor, courage, and loyalty. Although the characters in these legends do not always achieve their goals, they are generally portrayed in a positive light. One way to present yourself in a positive way is through an **application essay,** often part of applying to college or for a job. Writing an application essay gives you an opportunity to reflect on the meaning of a significant experience in your life and to reveal your interests, achievements, and abilities for others to judge.

For Your Portfolio
WRITING PROMPT Write an application essay in which you reflect on the significance of an important experience or achievement that has special meaning to you.
Purpose: To present information about yourself that would encourage a college to admit you
Audience: Members of a college admissions committee

Basics in a Box

Application Essay at a Glance B

Introduction
Begins with a hook, or attention-grabbing detail

Body
- Tells about your significant experience
- Reveals your qualities, interests, and abilities
- Shows that you can organize thoughts and express yourself

Conclusion
Summarizes the effects of the experience on your life

C **RUBRIC Standards for Writing**
A successful application essay should
- reflect a thoughtful response to the application prompt
- identify and describe a significant experience or achievement
- explain what the experience or achievement means to you
- be written honestly in your own voice and from your personal experience
- have an engaging introduction
- reflect careful attention to grammar, style, and organization

LESSON RESOURCES

USING PRINT RESOURCES
Unit One Resource Book
- Prewriting, p. 81
- Drafting, p. 82
- Peer Response, p. 83
- Revising, p. 84
- Editing and Proofreading, p. 85
- Student Models, pp. 86–91
- Rubric, p. 92

Writing Transparencies and Copymasters
- Application Essay Template, p. 26
- Showing, Not Telling, p. 22
- Strategies for Proofreading, p. 4

USING MEDIA RESOURCES
LaserLinks
Writing Springboards
See Teacher's SourceBook p. 114 for bar codes.
Writing Coach CD-ROM
Visit our website:
www.mcdougallittell.com

For a complete view of Lesson Resources, see page 15i.

Analyzing a Student Model

Jennifer Talon
Truman High School

Whomp!

My friends and I have a special word to perfectly describe an "ah hah experience." The word is *Whomp!* We use this word to describe what happens when something really hits us hard. For example: "I left my accounting project at home, and, Whomp!, Mrs. Winslow gave me *six* extra assignments as a consequence!" Or, "I couldn't believe he took her out. Whomp! It's really over between us."

Okay. I hope you now have an idea of the significance of the word. With that as background I can tell you about the biggest Whomp! of my life. It happened early in October of my junior year. I was with a group of friends at a cabin in the hills of eastern Iowa. While I was standing on a balcony approximately thirty-five feet above the rocky terrain, the supports under the balcony gave way. Luckily for me, the ground broke D my fall; unluckily, my leg did the same. One minute I was a healthy, mobile sixteen-year-old and, Whomp!, the next I had a leg in about fourteen different pieces, with some of those pieces protruding through a gaping wound.

My memories of the next few days are rather hazy. I can remember my mother's worried face hovering over me from time to time. I remember being told that I'd been through surgery and that they'd (the wondrous orthopedists) packed the bones together and fastened them at each end with pins. "Cool. You'll beep the airport metal detectors, Jen," my brother told me. Well, I'd also have sore armpits (crutches became my best friend and worst brother), and a cast up to my hip for six months. It seemed like an eternity.

Physical pain was the least of my worries. Whomp! People stared at me now. I couldn't take a shower. I couldn't go jogging. I couldn't stand for very long. I couldn't be on the track team. I couldn't get down to the newspaper room at school. I could watch TV—small compensation. I felt totally helpless and very frustrated at times. I needed help getting dressed, and getting to class, and getting into the car. . . .

RUBRIC IN ACTION

❶ The writer begins with an unusual hook that sets an engaging, humorous tone.

Other Options:
- Begin with a general concept (such as a quote or proverb) that will be tested or proved by your own experience
- Open with a dramatic thesis statement

❷ The writer focuses on the details of one incident, described chronologically.

Other Options:
- Tell several anecdotes that highlight your different qualities
- Describe more recent events first, then tell what led up to them

❸ Uses vivid details and narrative techniques to draw readers into the scene

❹ Brings up extracurricular activities by weaving them into the story

Teaching the Lesson

Analyzing the Model

"Whomp"

D Explain that the student model relates a difficult experience in the life of the writer—an experience that causes her to be more sensitive to the needs of others. After students have read the model, discuss the Rubric in Action.

1. Have students suggest an alternative opening.
   Possible Response: Sometimes your whole world can drop from under you within a matter of seconds. That is what happened to me as I stood on the balcony of a cabin thirty-five feet above the rocky terrain of eastern Iowa.
2. To help students feel comfortable with the application essay, point out the narrative features in this paragraph—it has a main character, the narrator; it has a setting, a cabin in eastern Iowa; and it has a plot that begins with the accident.
3. Call students' attention to the writer's humorous use of dialogue to present a character, Jennifer's brother.
4. Naming these extracurricular activities is one way students can communicate their interests. Another way would be to focus on an incident that highlights one of these interests.

Use McDougal Littell's ***Language Network,*** Chapter 17, for more instruction on writing an application essay.

To engage students visually, use **Power Presentation** 2, Application Essay.

5. From a sudden awareness of her own physical limitations, the writer becomes aware of the needs of others and is motivated to initiate a change.
6. Ask students how the essay would be affected if the writer did not include the example of David's reaction to Peer Advocates.
   Possible Response: The essay would be weaker and less interesting. David's reaction *shows* rather than *tells* that Peer Advocates was a good idea.
7. Repetition of the word "Whomp!" neatly ties the ideas in the essay together.

Wait a minute, this cast is only going to be on for six more months. Whomp! Some people are like this for their entire life. Some people have much worse problems that they must deal with every day of their existence with no light at the end of a six-month tunnel.

This really got me thinking. What would it be like to be physically disabled? Dependent your whole life? These insights made me want to get involved. They made me want to do something to make a difference.

> ❺ Repeats the hook to create a transition into the major accomplishment described next

Now it's my senior year. Students with disabilities (trainable mentally retarded kids, some with physical disabilities, too) have been brought to Westside for their Special Education classes. I went to see the Department Head of Special Education. Together we devised a club called Peer Advocates, which is like a buddy system between the regular education and special-education kids. We have tried to pair the non-disabled with the disabled students according to interests and personalities. Each pair is required to spend at least four hours a month together. We are also planning several group field trips to places like the zoo and the bowling alley.

Organizing this group has been one of the most meaningful things I've ever done. Now kids of two totally different lifestyles are going out to lunch together and learning things about each other that they could never have learned from reading a book or studying disabilities. We are all learning compassion and tolerance and understanding. As for myself, I feel as though I'm doing something extremely worthwhile. For example, one morning, after a breakfast meeting of the group, a boy with Down's Syndrome named David walked up to me with a huge smile and gave me a great bear hug. He told me that he was so happy to have a special friend at Westside and thanked me. That was all I needed to know that the idea had been a good one.

> ❻ *Shows* through an example that she cares about her subject *and* that the experience was important to her

Breaking my leg and its aftermath of pain and frustration was one experience I'd never want to go through again. But what it taught me was invaluable and I wouldn't change it for the world. It was a definite Whomp!

> ❼ Concludes with a brief summary of her main point

Viewing and Representing

PICTURING TEXT STRUCTURE

Instruction In writing an application essay, students must present themselves in a positive way. The way in which the essay is written is an important part of its effectiveness. Have students analyze the way the student writer organizes her model.

Activity Have students visualize the text structure of the student model by constructing a graphic organizer. The graphic students construct should illustrate how the student writer organized her essay. Students might begin by rereading the model and jotting down the main idea of each paragraph. From their notes they can construct a graphic organizer that shows how the ideas relate to each other as well as to the whole. Students should analyze the structure and explain how it influenced their understanding.

Writing Your Application Essay

❶ Prewriting

One writes out of one thing only—one's own experience.
James Baldwin

Begin with the directions on your application. Many college-essay prompts invite you to tell about how something or someone affected your life. Try listing turning points in your life and people who have influenced you along the way. See the **Idea Bank** in the margin for more topic suggestions.

Choose a topic that you truly care about, then consider how you can best use it to represent yourself to the application committee. The important thing is to write about your experiences meaningfully and demonstrate how they contributed to your personal growth. You are more likely to write a forceful, engaging essay if you stay true to your interests and experience.

Planning Your Application Essay

1. **Carefully consider the prompt.** What information should be included in the response? Note that the prompt on page 260 asks you to reflect on the significance of an important experience—not just retell it.
2. **Examine your strengths.** What personal qualities, talents, and accomplishments are you most proud of? What experiences have had special meanings for you?
3. **Think about your experience.** Why is it important to you? What meaning or significance can you draw from it?
4. **Determine a focus.** What is the overall point you want to make? Which of your achievements or experiences best supports your reflections on your own learning and growth?

❷ Drafting

There are many approaches you can take in writing a reflective essay. Like the writer of the student model, you could focus on a particular event and use it to reveal an aspect of yourself. Or, you could show how several similar events have influenced you in significant ways. Whatever the approach, keep it focused—don't try to tell everything about yourself.

As you draft your essay, include **details, description,** and **dialogue,** if appropriate to engage the readers. Give extra attention to writing a strong beginning. The opening should be engaging and informative without sounding contrived. It needs to catch the interest of an admissions officer, who has to read a stack of applications.

Ask Your Peer Reader

- What experience or achievement is my essay about?
- Why is the experience I talk about important to me?
- What is the most important thing you learn about me from this essay?
- In what places can I improve my voice to avoid sounding contrived?

IDEABank

1. Your Working Portfolio
Build on the Writing Options you completed earlier in this unit:

- **Essay On Virtues,** p. 238
- **Rama's Speech,** p. 251
- **Narrative on Survival,** p. 257

2. Time Line
Make a time line of your life, listing important events and accomplishments in your past. Look at the time line and identify major turning points.

3. Notebook
Write down the essay prompt (or prompts) in a notebook or on an index card. Keep this with you for several days, and write down ideas as you think about the essay.

Have a Question?

See the **Writing Handbook**
Elaboration, p. 1361
Descriptive Writing, pp. 1363–1364

Guiding Student Writing

Prewriting

Choosing a Subject

Have students begin by reviewing their working portfolios and considering the other suggestions in the Idea Bank. If students need more help in choosing a subject, you might suggest the following activities:

1. Obtain samples of college essay questions from your school guidance office.
2. Make a list of experiences in which you had difficulties or setbacks as well as successes. From this list choose an experience that changed you in some way.

Planning Your Application Essay

1. Students may respond either to the essay prompt on an actual college application or to the writing prompt on page 260.
2. To help students recognize their own strengths, have them make a quick list of their activities and achievements. They might ask a friend to remind them of any special strengths or skills they possess.
4. Emphasize that colleges look for applicants with the capacity to learn, grow, and change. Sometimes they can reveal their strengths through an incident that at first seems unimportant.

Drafting

Organizing the Draft

Individual students will use one type of organization in their application essay. The organization they choose will depend on their subject.

Explain that specific details and description help the reader picture the people in the essay. Dialogue reveals character by allowing the reader to hear what the people say. Have students consider which techniques will best fit the ideas they want to communicate.

Definition of Keyword—"Whomp!"
↓
Significant experience—breaking her leg
↙ ↘
Awareness of own physical limitations | Awareness of the needs of others with disabilities
↘ ↙
Significance of the experience

Revising

USING THE ACTIVE VOICE

If students need help with active and passive voice, use the Grammar Mini-Lesson.

In the first unrevised sentence, the verb, *is planned,* is in the passive voice. The subject, *lesson,* is the receiver of the action. In the revised sentence the verb, *plan,* is in the active voice. The subject, *counselors,* is the performer of the action.

The second unrevised sentence has a subordinate clause, *if a conflict between two campers was revealed.* The clause has a subject, *conflict,* and a verb, *was revealed.*

- *Was revealed* is in the passive voice. The subject, *conflict,* is the receiver of the action.
- The verb, *might be done,* is in the passive voice. The subject, *activity,* is the receiver of the action.

In the revised sentence, the verb of the subordinate clause, *arose,* is in the active voice. The subject, *conflict,* is the performer of the action; the verb, *might organize,* is in the active voice. The subject, *staff,* is the performer of the action.

Editing and Proofreading

SUBJECT-VERB AGREEMENT

The subject of the first sentence is *group*. Although the group is made up of more than one person, the noun *group* is a collective singular noun. Since *group* is singular, choose the singular verb *learns*.

In the second sentence, point out that sometimes words come between a subject and the verb. However, these intervening words do not affect subject-verb agreement. The verb *receives* should agree with the subject. *I* not with *staff,* the noun closest to the verb.

Reflecting

Have students write a brief note addressing their writing experience. They can clip their assessment to the essay itself and place both in their Working Portfolios.

Need help with active and passive voice?

See the **Grammar Handbook,** pp. 1396–1429.

3 Revising

TARGET SKILL ▶ USING THE ACTIVE VOICE Writing sentences in the active voice produces a more lively and engaging style, which helps draw readers in. It also helps place the focus on you as the main achiever in your story. While the passive voice is sometimes necessary, choosing the active voice can make your writing stronger and more fluent.

Each day, *[the counselors plan]* a new lesson ~~is planned~~ based on events that occurred the previous day. For example, if a conflict *[arose]* between two campers ~~was revealed~~, *[the staff might organize]* a trust activity ~~might be done~~ for the next day.

Uncertain about agreement?

See the **Grammar Handbook,** pp. 1396–1429.

4 Editing and Proofreading

TARGET SKILL ▶ SUBJECT-VERB AGREEMENT When rewriting from passive to active voice, be sure to check that your subjects and verbs agree, particularly when a word or phrase separates the subject from the verb. Also, keep in mind that a college essay should be a polished piece of work—so edit and proofread everything carefully.

[Each day] ~~U~~under my guidance, a special group of kids learn*[s]* the basics of swimming. In return, I, along with the rest of the staff, receive~~s~~ a valuable lesson in courage and perseverance.

Publishing IDEAS

- Submit your essay to the college of your choice.
- In a group, read your essays aloud, then role-play the response of an application review committee.

More Online: Publishing Options www.mcdougallittell.com

5 Reflecting

FOR YOUR WORKING PORTFOLIO What did you discover about yourself while completing your application essay? How did writing about yourself help you understand your strengths better? Attach your answer to your finished essay. Save your application essay in your **Working Portfolio.**

Mini Lesson Viewing and Representing

ACTIVE AND PASSIVE VOICE

Instruction A verb is in the active voice if the subject performs the action. A verb is in the passive voice if the subject receives the action.

Activity: Write these two sentences on the chalkboard. Then explain how to identify the active or passive voice in each sentence.

The club was organized to help students in Special Education feel comfortable in our high school.

We organized the club to help students in Special Education feel comfortable in our high school.

(In the first sentence, the verb, *was organized,* is in the passive voice. The subject, *club,* is the receiver of the action. In the second sentence, the verb, *organized,* is in the active voice. The subject, *we,* is the performer of the action.)

Assessment Practice Revising & Editing

Read this opening from the first draft of an application essay. The underlined sections include the following kinds of errors:

- **using active and passive voice**
- **subject-verb agreement**
- **verb tense errors**
- **sentence fragments**

For each underlined phrase or sentence, choose the revision that most improves the writing.

> It just took two little words to change everything: "We're moving." One simple sentence was uprooting (1) my whole life. How could I have anticipated the challenges? Never predicted the rewards. (2)
>
> Of course, at the beginning I loathe (3) the idea. I was overwhelmed by even the thought of moving. (4) Fourteen years are (5) a long time to live in one house. It was hard to imagine coming home to a strange house or doing homework in a foreign kitchen. You see, change still made me nervous then. (6)

1. **A.** had been uprooting
   B. uprooted
   C. will uproot
   D. Correct as is
2. **A.** How could I have anticipated the challenges or predicted the rewards?
   B. I could never have anticipated the challenges. Never predicted the rewards.
   C. How could I have anticipated the challenges, predicted the rewards.
   D. Correct as is
3. **A.** loathes
   B. loathed
   C. was loathing
   D. had loathed
4. **A.** I had been overwhelmed by even the thought of moving.
   B. I was being overwhelmed by even the thought of moving.
   C. Even the thought of moving overwhelmed me.
   D. Correct as is
5. **A.** is
   B. is being
   C. are being
   D. will be
6. **A.** You see. Change still made me nervous then.
   B. Then, you see, I was still made nervous by change.
   C. You see, change is still making me nervous then.
   D. Correct as is

Need extra help?

See the **Grammar Handbook:**
Active and passive voice, p. 1402
Subject-verb agreement, p. 1415–1417
Verb tenses, p. 1401
Sentence fragments, p. 1414

Assessment Practice

Demonstrate how students can eliminate incorrect choices for the first question.

A. This verb tense is incorrect because it is past perfect progressive and indicates ongoing action when the action was completed in the past.

C. Future tense is incorrect because it shows action that has not yet occurred.

D. Past progressive tense is incorrect because it shows ongoing action.

B. This verb tense is correct because the sentence requires a past-tense verb.

Answers

1. B; **2.** A; **3.** B; **4.** C; **5.** A; **6.** D

Building Vocabulary

Objectives

- rely on context to determine the meanings of words such as multiple meaning words
- use reference materials such as a dictionary to determine precise word meanings

EXERCISE

Have students identify the word or words in the sentence that helped them determine the meaning of the unfamiliar word.

1. offspring
2. to greet or welcome
3. sad or burdened
4. to need or require
5. to make a petition; appeal; beseech

Matching Meanings to Contexts

Language is constantly evolving to meet the needs of those who use it. As a result, many words have acquired more than one meaning. One such word is *craft,* which comes from the Old English word *cræft,* meaning "strength." Compare the ways in which *craft* is used in the sentences on the right.

In the first sentence, *craft* means "skill in deception or evasion"; in the second, *craft* refers to a boat or small ship. *Craft* can also mean "proficiency, skill, and dexterity" or "to make in a skillful manner by hand." Note that over time the original meaning of the word—"strength"—was extended to refer to various kinds of skill.

With craft and guile, Sir Modred persuaded the people to turn against their king.

As King Arthur with his fleet drew into the harbor, Sir Modred and his army launched forth in every available craft.

—Sir Thomas Malory, *Le Morte d'Arthur,* retold by Keith Baines

Strategies for Building Vocabulary

As you read, be alert to words that do not mean what you'd expect. Then use the following strategies to increase your understanding of the new words.

❶ Use Context Clues to Determine Meaning When you encounter a word that is used in an unexpected way, begin by using the sense of the sentences that surround the word to figure out the word's meaning. Read the passage below.

> **"Sir Gawain, why these insults? I have the measure of your strength and you can do me but little harm."**
>
> **"Come forth, traitor, and this time I shall make good my revenge!" Sir Gawain shouted.**
>
> —*Le Morte d'Arthur*

You can tell from the context that the two men have met before and that the first speaker is not concerned about the abilities of the second. These clues help you determine that in this context, *measure* means "a knowledge of the limits of the other's strength and skill," and that *make good* means "to fulfill."

❷ Look Up the Word in a Dictionary Sometimes you may need more help than context clues provide. To determine the appropriate meaning of a word with multiple definitions, locate the word in a dictionary and read through the definitions in order to identify the one that makes the most sense in the sentence.

Occasionally you will discover that a word appears to have two entries in the dictionary. These are actually separate words called **homonyms**—words with the same pronunciation and spelling but different meanings and origins. One such word is *pale.* What meaning does it have in each sentence below?

> Sir Lancelot was banished because his actions were beyond the *pale.*
>
> As a ruler, Sir Modred was a *pale* substitute for King Arthur.

Be aware that writers, especially poets, may intentionally use words in ways that evoke both literal and symbolic meanings. Note the double meaning of *age* in this quote "Every age has its pleasures." *Age* can be taken to mean the stages in a person's life or a time period in history.

EXERCISE Use a dictionary or context clues to define each underlined word in these passages from *Le Morte d'Arthur.*

1. "The issue of a mare has failed me; but I am the issue of a king and a queen and I shall not fail!" he exclaimed.
2. They were received by the gentle knight Sir Lucas the Butler.
3. "My lord King Arthur, it is with a heavy heart that I set forth to do battle."
4. "Surely our honor demands that we pursue this war to its proper conclusion."
5. "It is too late now to sue for peace."

Grammar from Literature

Expert writers craft sentences that express ideas as efficiently and effectively as possible. Using more advanced sentence structures can help add variety to your writing and show relationships between ideas.

A **compound sentence** is used to connect two ideas of equal importance. It consists of two independent clauses, which are clauses that can stand alone as sentences. The independent clauses in a compound sentence are separated by a semicolon or by a comma and coordinating conjunction such as *and, but,* and *or.*

independent clause / semicolon / independent clause

"Sir Gawain, I have once spared your life; should you not beware of meddling with me again?"

—Sir Thomas Malory, *Le Morte d'Arthur*

independent clause / conjunction / independent clause

I know your worth and price, and my debt's by no means slight.

—*Sir Gawain and the Green Knight*

A **complex sentence** consists of one independent clause and at least one subordinate clause. The independent clause contains the main idea, and the subordinate clause contains a related, less important idea. A subordinate clause is a clause that cannot stand alone as a sentence. A subordinate clause often begins with a subordinating conjunction, such as *if* and *when.*

subordinate clause / independent clause

If you remain within the city, soon everything will be destroyed.

—*Le Morte d'Arthur*

independent clause / subordinate clause

I never moved a muscle when you came down.

—*Sir Gawain and the Green Knight*

The following example shows how you can combine two simple sentences into one complex sentence by adding the subordinating conjunction *when.*

SEPARATE

King Arthur leaves Britain to fight Sir Launcelot. Modred decides to take control of the throne.

COMBINED

When King Arthur leaves Britain to fight Sir Launcelot, Modred decides to take control of the throne.

Usage Tip If you use a comma between the two independent clauses in a compound sentence, you must also include a coordinating conjunction. Not using a coordinating conjunction results in a type of run-on sentence known as a comma splice.

INCORRECT

no conjunction

The Green Knight's head was cut off, it didn't seem to bother him much.

CORRECT

conjunction

The Green Knight's head was cut off, but it didn't seem to bother him much.

Punctuation Tip When a complex sentence begins with a subordinate clause, a comma should appear at the end of the subordinate clause. If the subordinate clause appears at the end of the sentence, it is not preceded by a comma.

After she gave birth to her first child, Margery Kempe became seriously ill.

Margery Kempe became seriously ill after she gave birth to her first child.

WRITING EXERCISE Rewrite each sentence or pair of sentences below, following the directions that appear at the end of each exercise.

1. The Green Knight has a big bushy beard. His war horse has a green mane. (Make a compound sentence that includes a conjunction.)
2. The Green Knight issues a challenge. King Arthur's knights at first do not know what to do. (Make a complex sentence that includes the word *when.*)
3. Arthur runs Modred through with a spear. However, then Modred mortally wounds Arthur. (Make a compound sentence, replacing one of the words with the word *but.*)
4. Sir Bedivere must throw Excalibur into the lake, or King Arthur will not be taken to Avalon. (Make a complex sentence beginning with the word *if,* replacing the word *must* with different words and omitting *or.*)
5. If Margery Kempe does not stop seeing demons, she will not be able to take care of her child. (Make a compound sentence by omitting some words and adding the words *or else.*)

Sentence Crafting

Objectives

- use varied sentence structure to express meanings and achieve desired effect
- revise drafts by rethinking content organization and style to better accomplish the task

WRITING EXERCISE

1. The Green Knight has a big bushy beard, and his war horse has a green mane.
2. When the Green Knight issues a challenge, King Arthur's knights at first do not know what to do.
3. Arthur runs Modred through with a spear, but then Modred mortally wounds Arthur.
4. If Sir Bedivere does not throw Excalibur into the lake, King Arthur will not be taken to Avalon.
5. Margery Kempe must stop seeing demons, or else she will not be able to take care of her child.

Possible Objectives
- reflect on and assess understanding of the unit
- compare text events with experiences
- provide examples of themes that cross texts
- compare across texts elements of texts such as conflicts and characterization
- assess and build portfolios

Reflecting on the Unit

OPTION 1

A successful response will
- select one character from each of the three parts in Unit 1 and identify the characters as real or fictitious.
- note examples of challenges faced by each of the characters.
- describe how each character responds to the challenge.
- evaluate whether or not the response would be useful today.

OPTION 2

A successful response will
- recreate a realistic scene that involves two or more characters.
- contain dialogue among characters as well as narration to communicate the setting and the personality of the characters.
- entertain and interest the audience.

OPTION 3

To get students started, have them choose a moderator and assign roles of heroic characters. The group can work together drafting questions for the moderator to ask. Students portraying heroic figures can consider the questions beforehand so they can respond in character.

Self-Assessment
Ask students to identify the preconceptions they had about people of the Anglo-Saxon and medieval periods before they read the selections. Ask them to explain how characters or situation affected their preconceptions.

The Anglo-Saxon and Medieval Periods

How has reading the selections in this unit added to your understanding of the Anglo-Saxon and medieval periods? What new insights did you gain into life during these times, and how does it compare with life as you know it? Explore these questions by completing one or more options in each of the following sections.

Reflecting on the Unit

OPTION 1

Comparing Challenges Many of the people you have encountered in this unit—both real and fictitious—endure physical, spiritual, and emotional challenges. Select an individual from each of the three parts of the unit, and then write a few paragraphs comparing the ways in which the three people confront their challenges. Explain which person's methods of coping with adversity might be most useful in today's society.

OPTION 2

Resetting the Scene With a small group of classmates, discuss which selections in this unit stand out in your mind as being most representative of life in medieval times. Then choose a scene from one of these selections and perform it as a short skit for the rest of the class. If possible, use costumes and background music to help you convey the feeling of the period.

OPTION 3

Role-Playing With four or five classmates, hold a "meeting of the minds" in which you role-play several heroic individuals from this unit who sit down to reflect on their lives and times. You may wish to have them praise, criticize, or question one another's actions as they are depicted in the selections.

Self ASSESSMENT

READER'S NOTEBOOK
Make a list of the impressions you had about people of the Anglo-Saxon and medieval periods before you read the selections in Unit One. Then note whether your reading has confirmed these preconceptions or proved them wrong.

Reviewing Literary Concepts

OPTION 1

Understanding the Epic Across Cultures This unit contains excerpts from three epics, each originating in a different culture: *Beowulf* (Anglo-Saxon culture), the *Iliad* (Ancient Greek culture), and the *Ramayana* (Indian culture). Look back at the list of characteristics that most epics share (page 29). In terms of these characteristics, what do the three epics have in common? How would you explain these similarities?

Character	Main Conflict	Type of Conflict
Beowulf	He must battle with Grendel and the fire dragon.	External

OPTION 2

Assessing Conflict The individuals portrayed in this unit become involved in a variety of conflicts, both external and internal. In a chart similar to the one shown, list at least six characters or historical figures from the unit. Describe the main conflict that each faces, and note whether that conflict is external or internal. Are most of the conflicts external, or internal? What kinds of problems would you say the people of these times were concerned with?

Self ASSESSMENT

READER'S NOTEBOOK

On a sheet of paper, copy the following list of literary terms introduced in this unit. Put a question mark next to each term that you do not fully understand. Consult the **Glossary of Literary Terms** (page 1328) to clarify the meanings of the terms you've marked with question marks.

alliteration
simile
epic simile
historical writing
kenning
tone
moral tale
narrator
plot
conflict
ballad
romance
characterization
supernatural elements
autobiography

Building Your Portfolio

- **Writing Options** Many of the Writing Options in this unit asked you to assume the identities of characters and people depicted in the selections. From your responses, choose two that you think are particularly successful at conveying the individuals' personalities. In a cover note, explain what you think makes each piece of writing so effective. Then add the pieces and the cover notes to your **Presentation Portfolio.**
- **Writing Workshops** In this unit, you wrote a Personality Profile based on a person of interest and an Application Essay in which you focused on a way to present yourself in a positive light. Reread these pieces and assess the quality of the writing. Would you like to keep either or both of these pieces for inclusion in your **Presentation Portfolio?** If so, attach a note indicating the strengths and weaknesses of the writing.
- **Additional Activities** Think back to any of the assignments you completed under **Activities & Explorations** and **Inquiry & Research.** Keep a record in your portfolio of any assignments that you think are representative of your best work.

Self ASSESSMENT

Review the pieces you have chosen to include so far in your **Presentation Portfolio.** What generalizations can you make about your writing strengths and interests?

Setting GOALS

As you work through the reading and writing activities in the unit, you probably became aware of areas in which your work could use some improvement. After thinking over the work you did for this unit, create a list of skills or concepts that you would like to work on in the next unit.

Reviewing Literary Concepts

OPTION 1

To expand this assignment, have students note examples from the unit of each literary term.

OPTION 2

Use the Unit One Resource Book, p. 95, to provide students a ready-made, full-depth chart for recording the conflicts of their six characters.

Building Your Portfolio

For more information on using, writing, and assessing portfolios, see the *Teacher's Guide to Assessment and Portfolio Use,* p. 53.

The *Electronic Library* is a CD-ROM that contains additional fiction, nonfiction, poetry, and drama for each unit in *The Language of Literature.*

These are the additional selections found in Unit 1 of the *Electronic Library:*

Geoffrey Chaucer
from **The Canterbury Tales**
The Nun's Priest's Tale

Anonymous
Everyman

UNIT ONE Extend Your *Reading*

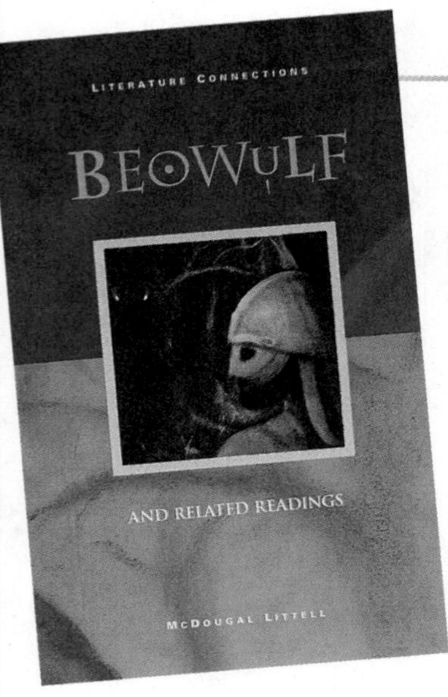

LITERATURE CONNECTIONS

Beowulf

ANONYMOUS, TRANSLATED BY BURTON RAFFEL

Read this epic masterpiece in its entirety to find out more about the exploits of the great Anglo-Saxon warrior. Swords and shields, monsters and dragons, sailing ships and spears play an important part in this powerful tale of heroism. Beowulf sails the seas in search of adventure, and by doing great deeds he wins honor and fame for himself and his people. Beowulf and his adventures reveal how the Anglo-Saxons viewed good and evil, life and death.

These thematically related readings are provided along with *Beowulf:*

The Wanderer
ANONYMOUS, TRANSLATED BY BURTON RAFFEL

Beowulf
BY RICHARD WILBUR

from **Grendel**
BY JOHN GARDNER

Beowulf
BY MAURICE SAGOFF

from **Gilgamesh**
ANONYMOUS, TRANSLATED BY HERBERT MASON

David and Goliath
from **The King James Bible**

Anger *from* **The Seven Deadly Sins**
BY LINDA PASTAN

from **A Gathering of Heroes**
BY GREGORY ALAN-WILLIAMS

And Even *More* . . .

Grendel

JOHN GARDNER

This modern retelling of the *Beowulf* story from Grendel's point of view provides an inside look at the mind of a monster. Told with equal parts of humor and horror, the tale makes the point that even monsters have a story to tell.

Books

Beowulf
GEORGE CLARK
A recent, widely available critical study.

Eaters of the Dead
MICHAEL CRICHTON
The popular author resets *Beowulf* among 10th-century Vikings in a novel disguised as nonfiction.

The Life and Times of Chaucer
JOHN GARDNER
A lively biography of the poet by the author of *Grendel.*

LITERATURE CONNECTIONS

from The Canterbury Tales

GEOFFREY CHAUCER

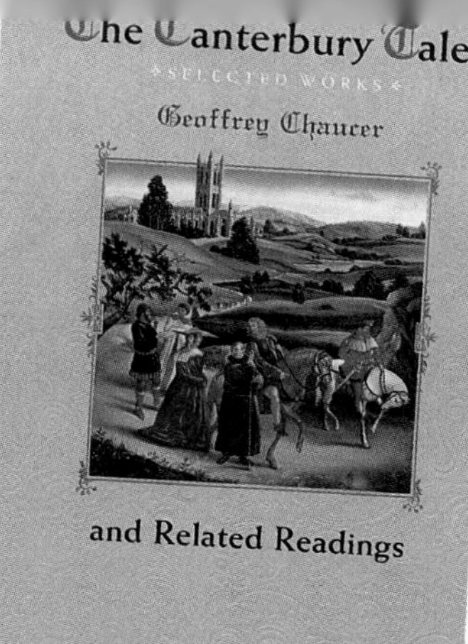

The Canterbury Tales
SELECTED WORKS
Geoffrey Chaucer
and Related Readings

A matchless array of humanity passes before the reader's eyes in Chaucer's brilliant collection of related stories, *The Canterbury Tales.* Chaucer views his pilgrims with a wise tolerance and a gentle humor that communicate his deep understanding of the paths, both crooked and straight, taken by different people. This book expands your enjoyment of Chaucer by offering several more of his classic tales.

These thematically related readings are provided along with *The Canterbury Tales:*

***from* The Life and Times of Chaucer**
BY JOHN GARDNER

from* The Author's Introduction to *The Decameron
BY GIOVANNI BOCCACCIO, TRANSLATED BY MARK MUSA AND PETER E. BONDANELLA

***from* The Art of Courtly Love**
BY ANDREAS CAPELLANUS, TRANSLATED BY JOHN JAY PARRY

Laüstic (the Nightingale)
BY MARIE DE FRANCE

***from* The Romance of Reynard the Fox**
ANONYMOUS FABLE, TRANSLATED BY D. D. R. OWEN

The Second Shepherds' Play *from* The Wakefield Mystery Cycle
EDITED BY MARTIAL ROSE

***from* The Autobiography of Malcolm X**
BY MALCOLM X, WITH ALEX HALEY

Chaucer Aboard a Spaceship
BY NAOSHI KORIYAMA

The Hobbit
J.R.R. TOLKIEN
This famous fantasy of Middle Earth draws on the author's profound knowledge of Anglo-Saxon life and literature.

The Aeneid
VIRGIL, TRANSLATED BY ROBERT FITZGERALD
This epic poem about the founding of Rome by the hero Aeneas was modeled on Homer's *Iliad* and *Odyssey.* Virgil's poem illustrates the ancient virtues of heroism, filial devotion, piety, and dedication to Rome.

Other Media

Beowulf
Old English poetry, including "The Wanderer" and passages from *Beowulf.*
(AUDIOCASSETTE)

The Canterbury Tales
Tim Pigott-Smith, Prunella Scales, and other British actors read "The Prologue," "The Pardoner's Tale," and "The Wife of Bath's Tale," as well as other tales in modern English.
(AUDIOCASSETTES)

The Dark Ages: Europe After the Fall of Rome
Includes reenactments of dramatic moments in the development of Medieval Europe.
(VIDEOCASSETTE)

A Prologue to Chaucer
Originally produced in 1986 by the University of California, Berkeley, this video relates characters and themes of *The Canterbury Tales* to everyday life in late 14th-century England.
(VIDEOCASSETTE)

EXTEND YOUR READING 271

The English Renaissance

The selections in Unit Two show the great flowering of literary, artistic, and intellectual development in England in the 16th and 17th centuries. The unit is divided into three sections to capture more fully this great explosion of cultural energy.

Part 1

Aspects of Love The first half of the unit presents some of the best love poetry of the English Renaissance. These lyric poems and sonnets reveal the growing importance of the individual during the Renaissance. Two sonnets by Francesco Petrarch, one of the leading lights of the Italian Renaissance, comprise the **Comparing Literature** feature.

Part 2

A Passion for Power An **Author Study** on William Shakespeare comprises the entirety of this section. An article on the English Renaissance theater prefaces *The Tragedy of Macbeth.* Two excerpts from *Holinshed's Chronicles* present primary source materials that Shakespeare used for his plays. A modern murder mystery humorously comments on the obsession some people have with the murders in *Macbeth.*

Part 3

Facing Life's Limitations This section presents a different view of the Renaissance, shown through scripture, poetry, and prose. These selections take a more serious look at life, death, and the importance of using time wisely. Taking the idea of *carpe diem,* or "seize the day," across cultures, **Comparing Literature** features the appearance of this theme in the verse of the Persian poet and tentmaker Omar Khayyám.

UNIT TWO

No man is an island,
entire of itself;
every man is a piece of the
continent,
a part of the main.

John Donne
poet

1485–1660

The ENGLISH Renaissance

272

Viewing and Representing

Detail of the altarpiece of the
Virgin of the Navigators
by Alejo Fernández

ART APPRECIATION

Instruction Alejo Fernández (c. 1475–1545) was a Spanish painter who lived in Seville after 1508. Between the years c. 1531–1536, he (and possibly some of his pupils) painted the *Virgin of the Navigators* for the chapel of Seville's *Casa de la Contratación* (Trade House), which coordinated Spain's overseas expeditions. Above the detail shown, the figure of the Virgin floats over the water, her mantle protecting a group of Spanish explorers that includes Columbus and Cortés. The large ship in the detail is a *nao,* a vessel designed to withstand long, often stormy ocean voyages. From the end of the 16th to the beginning of the 17th century, 200 ships, with 8,000 crewmen, left annually from Seville.

Detail of the altarpiece of the *Virgin of the Navigators* (16th century). Alejo Fernández. Seville, Spain, Reales Alcázares.

Making Connections

To help students explore the connections among the art, the quotation, and the unit title found in this unit-opening spread, have them consider the following questions:

Ask: What do you think John Donne means when he says "No man is an island"?
Possible Response: No person is separate from the rest of humanity.

Ask: How can people be a "piece of the continent, a part of the main[land]"?
Possible Response: The "continent" or "main[land]" is humankind. By virtue of being a human being, everyone is bonded to everyone else.

Ask: Do you agree with Donne's comment? Why or why not?
Possible Response: Agree, because no one truly lives alone; disagree, because people can survive apart from all society.
Have students study the detail from the *Virgin of the Navigators* altarpiece.

Ask: How does the image of the 16th-century vessel reinforce Donne's message?
Possible Response: The emergence of ship travel, for good and for bad—to explore and to conquer—was the driving force that made Donne's words of the interrelationship of humankind ring true.

Ask: Based on the unit title, quotation, and painting, what sort of selections might you expect to read in this unit?
Possible Response: Selections displaying an increasing awareness of others and a desire to connect with them

LaserLinks
Historical Literary Connection: The English Renaissance
See Teacher's SourceBook p. 18 for bar codes.

UNIT TWO
PART 1 SKILLS TRACE

Features and Selections	Literary Analysis	Reading and Critical Thinking	Writing Opportunities
The English Renaissance **Time Line** **Historical Background/Essay**			
POETRY My Lute, Awake! On Monsieur's Departure	Rhyme Scheme, 283, 287	Clarifying Meaning, 283, 287	Letter from a Queen, 288
POETRY The Passionate Shepherd to His Love The Nymph's Reply to the Shepherd	Pastoral, 289, 293 Informal Assess., 294	Comparing Speakers, 289, 293	Modern Parody, 294
POETRY **Learning the Language of Literature:** Sonnet Form Sonnet 30 Sonnet 75	Spenserian Sonnet, 297, 300 Review: Alliteration, 300	Major Ideas, 297, 300	Natural Comparison, 301
POETRY Sonnet 29 Sonnet 116 Sonnet 130	Shakespearean Sonnet, 302, 306 Figurative Language, 306 Informal Assess., 305	Analyzing Sensory Language, 302, 306	Love Poem, 307 Character Sketch, 307 Letter to Speaker, 307 Opinion Essay, 307
POETRY **Comparing Literature of the World:** Sonnet 169 Sonnet 292	Italian Sonnet, 308, 311	Major Ideas, 308, 311	Soap-Opera Outline, 312 Points of Comparison, 312

UNIT TWO
PART 2 SKILLS TRACE

AUTHOR STUDY
William Shakespeare

Features and Selections	Literary Analysis	Reading and Critical Thinking	Writing Opportunities
Learning the Language of Literature Shakespearean Tragedy	Reading Strategies, 322		
VERSE DRAMA The Tragedy of Macbeth Act One	Soliloquy/Aside, 324, 346 Blank Verse, 324 Dramatic Irony, 324 Foreshadowing, 324 Theme, 324 Review Characterization, 346 CCL: Government, 331	Reading Drama, 325 Shakespeare's Language, 325, 346	Informal Assess., 338
VERSE DRAMA The Tragedy of Macbeth Act Two	Blank Verse, 362 Figurative Language, 362 Informal Assess, 353	Reading Drama, 362	

LEGEND **PE instruction shown in black** **TE Mini Lessons shown in green** **CCL indicates a Cross-Curricular Link** **DLS indicates Daily Language SkillBuilder**

Speaking and Listening Viewing and Representing	Inquiry and Research	Grammar, Usage, and Mechanics	Vocabulary
Art Appreciation, 276			
Mood Music, 288 Poems as Songs, 284		DLS, 283 Prepositional Phrases, 286	Test Practice, 285
Telephone Dialogue, 294 Drawing Shepherds, 294 Art Appreciation, 290		DLS, 289 Appositive Phrases, 292	Origins of *Pastoral,* 291
Opinion Poll, 301 Poetry Reading, 299	Courtship and Marriage, 301	DLS, 297 Infinitives, 301	Using Context, 298
Talk Show, 307 Love's Scrapbook, 307 A Reading of Sonnets, 307 List of Resources, 307 Debate, 304	Portraits of Women, 307 What is Love? 307 Illustrating Poetry, 307	DLS, 302 Participial Phrases, 303	
Dance Interpretation, 312	Italian Renaissance, 312 Author Activity, 312	DLS, 308 Gerund Phrases, 310	Denotation and Connotation, 309
View and Compare, p. 347 Film Analysis, 332 Collage, 337 Dramatic Reading, 340		DLS, 323 Modifiers, 344	Using Dictionary, 330 Test Practice, 336 Expand Vocabulary, 343
Art Appreciation, 347 Media Techniques, 349 Dramatic Presentation, 358		Adjectives, 360	Expanding Vocabulary, 352 Word Origins, 356

UNIT TWO
PART 2 SKILLS TRACE

Features and Selections	Literary Analysis	Reading and Critical Thinking	Writing Opportunities
VERSE DRAMA The Tragedy of Macbeth Act Three	Dramatic Irony, 381	Shakespeare's Language, 381	Informal Assess., 367 Diary Entry, 375
VERSE DRAMA The Tragedy of Macbeth Act Four	Foreshadowing, 399	Reading Drama, 399 Test Practice, 397	Informal Assess., 387
VERSE DRAMA The Tragedy of Macbeth Act Five	Theme, 420 Review Conflict, 420	Reading Drama, 420 Film and Review, 416	News Coverage, 422 Modern Version, 422 Obituary, 422
SHORT STORY The Macbeth Murder Mystery			
The Author's Style Author Study Project			Changing Style, 421 Imitating Style, 421
Writing Workshop: **Research Report** **Assessment Practice** Building Vocabulary Sentence Crafting		Analyzing a Student Model, 424	Research Report, 426

UNIT TWO
PART 3 SKILLS TRACE

Features and Selections	Literary Analysis	Reading and Critical Thinking	Writing Opportunities
SCRIPTURE *from* Ecclesiastes, Chapter 3 Psalm 23 Parable of the Prodigal Son	Repetition, 435, 440 Parable, p. 440	Making Inferences, 435, 440	Parable Sequel, 441 Modern Parable, 441 Editorial, 441 Spiritual Essay, 441
ESSAY *from* Essays	Essay, 442, 447	Evaluating Opinion, 442, 447	Letter to Bacon, 448 Persuasive Essay, 448 Marriage Questions, 448
POETRY AND NONFICTION A Valediction: Forbidding Mourning Holy Sonnet 10 *from* Meditation 17	Extended Metaphor, 451, 456	Interpreting Language Structures, 451, 456	Extended Metaphor, 457 Metaphysical Conceits, 455

LEGEND **PE instruction shown in black** **TE Mini Lessons shown in green** **CCL indicates a Cross-Curricular Link** **DLS indicates Daily Language SkillBuilder**

Speaking and Listening Viewing and Representing	Inquiry and Research	Grammar, Usage, and Mechanics	Vocabulary
Film Analysis, 366, 369 Director's Plan, 373		Adverbs, 371	Using Context, 372
View and Compare, 400 Art Appreciation, 382, 385, 389		Double Comparisons, 394	Words Coined, 386 Using a Dictionary, 390
Actors' Workshop, 422 Video, 422 Art Appreciation, 400, 403, 411, 413 Dramatic Reading, 405	History, 422	Illogical Comparisons, 406	Using Context, 414 Denotation and Connotation, 415
Art Appreciation, 418			
Speaking, Listening, 421	Creating a Magazine, 422		
	Research Report, 426	Paragraph Building/ Shifting Verb Tense, 430 Revising & Editing, 431 Adverb Phrases, 433 Incorrect Verb Tenses, 431	Word Parts—Roots, 432
Calendar Design, 441 Dramatic Soliloquy, 441 Biblical Collage, 441 Art Connection, 441	Language Chart, 441 Music and the Bible, 441	DLS, 435 Infinitive Phrases, 436	
Image Collection, 448 Opinion Poll, 448 Parallelism, 446	Brain Calisthenics, 448 Author Activity, 448	DLS, 442 Placement of Phrases, 445	
Mood Painting, 457 Dramatic Reading, 457	A Modern Novel, 457 Author Activity, 457	DLS, 451 Modifiers, 452	Meaning in Context, 454

UNIT TWO
PART 3 SKILLS TRACE

Features and Selections	Literary Analysis	Reading and Critical Thinking	Writing Opportunities
POETRY On My First Son Still to Be Neat	Epitaph, 458, 461 Review: Repetition, 461	Comparing Speakers, 458, 461	Condolence Note, 462 Poetic Parody, 462
POETRY To the Virgins, to Make Much of Time To His Coy Mistress To Lucasta, Going to the Wars	Hyperbole, 463, 468 Review: Theme, 468 Metaphor, 468	Comparing Speakers, 463, 468	Comparing Poems, 469 Exaggerated Speech, 469 Letter in Wartime, 469 Tone, 467
POETRY **Comparing Literature of the World** *from the* Rubáiyát	Theme and Metaphor, 471, 474	Drawing Conclusions About Tone, 471, 474	Explanation, 475 Letter to Omar, 475 Points of Comparison, 475
POETRY How Soon Hath Time When I Consider How My Light Is Spent	Allusion, 476, 479 Review: Sonnet, 479	Sentence Meaning, 476, 479	
EPIC POETRY Paradise Lost	Diction, 480, 491 Review: Blank Verse, 491	Meaning, 480, 491 Informal Assess., 489	Psychological Profile, 492 Description, 492
DEBATE Female Orations	Argumentation, 493, 500	Structure of Arguments, 493, 500 Writer's Motivation and Text Structure, 500 Informal Assess., 497	Argument Outline, 501
Reflect and Assess	Figurative Language, 505 Shakespearean Drama, 505	Important Issues, 504	Drafting an Essay, 504 Interpreting a Quotation, 504
Reading & Writing for Assessment			

LEGEND **PE instruction shown in black** **TE Mini Lessons shown in green** **CCL indicates a Cross-Curricular Link** **DLS indicates Daily Language SkillBuilder**

Speaking and Listening Viewing and Representing	Inquiry and Research	Grammar, Usage, and Mechanics	Vocabulary
Monument Design, 462 Pictorial Essay, 462	Fashion Sense, 462 Fashion Sense, 462	DLS, 458 Verbs: Moods, 459	
Carpe Diem Banner, 469 Quotations Booklet, 469 Cartoons and Poetry, 469 Matching the Mood, 469	The Reign of Charles I, 469	DLS, 463 Verbs: Participles, 465	Connotation and Denotation, 464
Philosophy Report, 475	Omar's Culture, 475 Author Activity, 475	DLS, 471 AbsoluPhrases, 473	
		DLS, 476	Multiple Meanings, 477
Paradise Lost Illustrated, 492 Accompaniment, 492 Author Activity, 492 Art Appreciation, 482, 484 Dramatic Reading, 485	Researching Angels, 492	Prepositional Phrases, 490	Using a Thesaurus, 481 Test Practice, 486
Mural Design, 501 Art Appreciation, 498	Women in the 17th Century, 501	DLS, 493 Prepositional Phrases, 496	Context Clues, 501 Latin Roots, 494
		Test-Taking Strategies, 508–513	

UNIT TWO
RESOURCE MANAGEMENT GUIDE
PART 1

To introduce the theme/literary period of this unit, use Fine Art Transparencies T20–22 in the Communications Transparencies and Copymasters.

Selection	Unit Resource Book	Assessment	Integrated Technology and Media	Additional Support: Literary Analysis Transparencies
My Lute, Awake! **On Monsieur's Departure** *pp. 283–288*	• Active Reading p. 4 • Literary Analysis p. 5	• Selection Test, Formal Assessment pp. 41–42 Test Generator	Audio Library LaserLinks, Teacher's SourceBook pp. 19–20	
The Passionate Shepherd to His Love **The Nymph's Reply to the Shepherd,** *pp. 289–294*	• Active Reading p. 6 • Literary Analysis p. 7	• Selection Test, Formal Assessment p. 43 Test Generator	Audio Library LaserLinks, Teacher's SourceBook pp. 21–22	
Spenser, *pp. 297–301* **Sonnet 30** **Sonnet 75**	• Active Reading p. 8 • Literary Analysis p. 9	• Selection Test, Formal Assessment pp. 45–46 Test Generator	Audio Library LaserLinks, Teacher's SourceBook p. 23	• Petrarchan, Shakespearean, and Spenserian Sonnets T4
Shakespeare, *pp. 302–307* **Sonnet 29** **Sonnet 116** **Sonnet 30**	• Active Reading p. 10 • Literary Analysis p. 11	• Selection Test, Formal Assessment pp. 47–48 Test Generator	Audio Library LaserLinks, Teacher's SourceBook p. 24 Research Starter www.mcdougallittell.com	• Petrarchan, Shakespearean, and Spenserian Sonnets T4 • Sonnets T5
Petrarch, *pp. 308–312* **Sonnet 169** **Sonnet 292**	• Active Reading p. 12 • Literary Analysis p. 13	• Selection Test, Formal Assessment p. 49 Test Generator	Audio Library LaserLinks, Teacher's SourceBook p. 25	• Petrarchan, Shakespearean, and Spenserian Sonnets T4 • Sonnets T5
		Unit Assessment	***Unit Technology***	
		• Unit Two, Part 1 Test, Formal Assessment pp. 51–52 Test Generator • Unit Two Integrated Test, Integrated Assessment pp. 11–18	ClassZone www.mcdougallittell.com Electronic Teacher Tools Electronic Library	

UNIT TWO
PART 2

To introduce the theme/literary period of this unit, use Fine Art Transparencies T20–22 in the Communications Transparencies and Copymasters.

Selection	Unit Resource Book	Assessment	Integrated Technology and Media	Additional Support: Literary Analysis Transparencies
Macbeth • **Act One** • **Act Two** • **Act Three** • **Act Four** • **Act Five** *pp. 323–422*	• Summary pp. 14, 18, 22, 26, 30 • Active Reading pp. 15, 19, 23, 27, 31 • Literary Analysis pp. 16, 20, 24, 28, 32 • Selection Quiz pp. 17, 21, 25, 29, 33	• Selection Test, Formal Assessment pp. 53–62 Test Generator	Audio Library Video: Literature in Performance, Video Resource Book pp. 15–22 Research Starter www.mcdougallittell.com	• Dramatic Irony in Shakespeare T6 • Foreshadowing in Shakespeare T7 • Characteristics of Tragedy T8
		Unit Assessment	***Unit Technology***	
		• Unit Two, Part 2 Test, Formal Assessment pp. 63–64 Test Generator • Unit Two Integrated Test, Integrated Assessment pp. 11–18	ClassZone www.mcdougallittell.com Electronic Teacher Tools Electronic Library	

Writing Workshop: Research Report

Unit One Resource Book
- Prewriting p. 34
- Drafting and Elaboration p. 35
- Peer Response Guide pp. 36–37
- Revising, Editing, and Proofreading p. 38
- Student Models pp. 39–44
- Rubric for Evaluation p. 45

Writing Coach

Writing Transparencies and Copymasters T11, T19, C27

Teacher's Guide to Assessment and Portfolio Use

T = Transparency C = Copymaster

Reading and Critical Thinking Transparencies	Grammar Transparencies and Copymasters	Vocabulary Transparencies and Copymasters	Writing Transparencies and Copymasters	Communications Transparencies and Copymasters
• Analyzing Text T18 • Paraphrasing and Summarizing T42	• Daily Language SkillBuilder T6 • Diagramming Subjects, Verbs, and Modifiers T58 • Prepositional Phrases C85		• Effective Language T13	
• Compare and Contrast T15 • Determining Author's Purpose and Audience T20	• Daily Language SkillBuilder T6 • Diagramming Complements and Appositives T59 • Appositives C95	• Word Origins C32	• Identifying Writing Variables T2	• Impromptu Speaking: Dialogue, Role-Play T14
• Paraphrasing and Summarizing T42 • Organizational Chart: Horizontal T52	• Daily Language SkillBuilder T7 • Diagramming Verbal Phrases T60 • Verbals and Verbal Phrases T94	• Using Context to Determine Meaning C33	• Compare-Contrast C34	
• Observation Chart T47	• Daily Language SkillBuilder T7 • Avoiding Misplaced Modifiers T51 • Participles and Participial Phrases C99		• Figurative Language and Sound Devices T15 • Opinion Statement C35	• Reading Aloud T11 • Impromptu Speaking: Dialogue, Role-Play T14
• Paraphrasing and Summarizing T42 • Using an Outline T44	• Daily Language SkillBuilder T7 • Gerunds and Gerund Phrases C103	• Denotation and Connotation C34	• Compare-Contrast C34	

STUDENTS ACQUIRING ENGLISH

The **Spanish Study Guide,** pp. 46–63, includes language support for the following pages:

- Family and Community Involvement (per unit)
- Selection Summaries and Vocabulary
- Active Reading
- Literary Analysis

Reading and Critical Thinking Transparencies	Grammar Transparencies and Copymasters	Vocabulary Transparencies and Copymasters	Writing Transparencies and Copymasters	Communications Transparencies and Copymasters
• Summarizing T10 • Locating Information Using Databases and the Internet T35 • Paraphrasing and Summarizing T42	• Daily Language SkillBuilder T8 • Comparison of Regular and Irregular Adjectives and Adverbs T52 • Identifying Adjectives C68 • Identifying Adverbs C70 • Modifiers C152 • Avoiding Double Comparisons C155 • Avoiding Illogical Comparisons C156	• Using a Dictionary and Context to Determine Meaning C35 • Word Origins C38 • Connotation C39 • Using Context to Determine Meaning C40 • Words Coined by Shakespeare C41 • Using a Dictionary C42 • Using Context to Determine Meaning C43 • Denotation and Connotation C44	• Showing, Not Telling T22 • Personality Profile C25	• Dramatic Reading T12 • Giving and Using Feedback to Improve Performance T16

STUDENTS ACQUIRING ENGLISH

The **Spanish Study Guide,** pp. 64–78, includes language support for the following pages:

- Family and Community Involvement (per unit)
- Selection Summaries and Vocabulary
- Active Reading
- Literary Analysis

RESOURCE MANAGEMENT GUIDE PART 3

To introduce the theme/literary period of this unit, use Fine Art Transparencies T20–22 in the Communications Transparencies and Copymasters.

Selection	Unit Resource Book	Assessment	Integrated Technology and Media	Additional Support: Literary Analysis Transparencies
The King James Bible *from* **Ecclesiastes, Chapter 3** **Psalm 23** **Parable of the Prodigal Son,** *pp. 435–441*	• Summary p. 48 • Active Reading p. 49 • Literary Analysis p. 50 • Selection Quiz p. 51	• Selection Test, Formal Assessment pp. 65–66 Test Generator	Audio Library LaserLinks, Teacher's SourceBook p. 26	
from **Essays** *pp. 442–448*	• Summary p. 52 • Active Reading p. 53 • Literary Analysis p. 54 • Selection Quiz p. 55	• Selection Test, Formal Assessment p. 67 Test Generator	Audio Library Research Starter www.mcdougallittell.com	• Characteristics of the Essay T11
A Valediction: Forbidden Mourning **Holy Sonnet 10** *from* **Meditation 17** *pp. 451–457*	• Summary p. 56 • Active Reading p. 57 • Literary Analysis p. 58 • Selection Quiz p. 59	• Selection Test, Formal Assessment pp. 69–70 Test Generator	Audio Library LaserLinks, Teacher's SourceBook p. 27 Research Starter www.mcdougallittell.com	• Theme T9
On My First Son **Still to Be Neat** *pp. 458–462*	• Active Reading p. 60 • Literary Analysis p. 61	• Selection Test, Formal Assessment p. 71 Test Generator	Audio Library	• Theme T9
To the Virgins, to Make Much of Time **To His Coy Mistress** **To Lucasta, Going to the Wars,** *pp. 463–470*	• Active Reading p. 62 • Literary Analysis p. 63	• Selection Test, Formal Assessment pp. 73–74 Test Generator	Audio Library LaserLinks, Teacher's SourceBook p. 28 Research Starter www.mcdougallittell.com	• Theme T9
from **The Rubaiyat** *pp. 471–475*	• Active Reading p. 64 • Literary Analysis p. 65	• Selection Test, Formal Assessment p. 75 Test Generator	Audio Library	• Theme T9
How Soon Hath Time **When I Consider How My Light is Spent** *pp. 476–479*	• Active Reading p. 66 • Literary Analysis p. 67	• Selection Test, Formal Assessment pp. 77–78 Test Generator	Audio Library LaserLinks, Teacher's SourceBook p. 29	• Figurative Language T22
from **Paradise Lost** *pp. 480–492*	• Summary p. 68 • Active Reading p. 69 • Literary Analysis p. 70 • Selection Quiz p. 71	• Selection Test, Formal Assessment pp. 79–80 Test Generator	Research Starter www.mcdougallittell.com	• Figurative Language T22
Female Orations *pp. 493–501*	• Summary p. 72 • Active Reading p. 73 • Literary Analysis p. 74 • Words to Know p. 75 • Selection Quiz p. 76	• Selection Test, Formal Assessment pp. 81–82 Test Generator	Audio Library	
		Unit Assessment	***Unit Technology***	
		• Unit Two, Part 3 Test, Formal Assessment pp. 83–84 Test Generator • Unit Two Integrated Test, Integrated Assessment pp. 11–18	ClassZone www.mcdougallittell.com Electronic Teacher Tools Electronic Library	

T = Transparency C = Copymaster

Reading and Critical Thinking Transparencies	Grammar Transparencies and Copymasters	Vocabulary Transparencies and Copymasters	Writing Transparencies and Copymasters	Communications Transparencies and Copymasters
• Paraphrasing and Summarizing T42	• Daily Language SkillBuilder T8 • Diagramming Verbal Phrases T60 • Infinitive Phrase Used as Adverb C97		• Identifying Writing Variables T2 • Opinion Statement C35	• Dramatic Reading T12
• Analyzing Text Structure T17 • Determining Author's Purpose and Audience T20 • Organizational Chart: Horizontal T52	• Daily Language SkillBuilder T9 • Avoiding Misplaced and Dangling Modifiers T51 • Placement of Phrases C88		• Opinion Statement C35	• Interviewing T9
• Analyzing Text T18 • Comparing Authors' Views T24	• Daily Language SkillBuilder T9 • Diagramming Complements and Appositives T59 • Modifiers That Follow Verbs C72	• Meaning in Context C46	• Figurative Language and Sound Devices T15	• Dramatic Reading T12
• Comparing Authors' Views T24 • Venn Diagram T51	• Daily Language SkillBuilder T9 • Indicative and Imperative Mood C137 • Subjunctive Mood C138		• Identifying Writing Variables T2	
• Compare and Contrast T15 • Comparing Authors' Views T24	• Daily Language SkillBuilder T10 • Verbs–Using Correct Verb Forms T45 • Verbs: Present and Past Participles C128	• Denotation and Connotation C47	• Figurative Language and Sound Devices T15 • Compare-Contrast C34	
• Compare and Contrast T15 • Comparing Authors' Views T24 • Organizational Chart: Horizontal T52	• Daily Language SkillBuilder T10 • Absolute Phrases C92		• Organizing Your Writing T11	• Formal Presentations T10
• Paraphrasing and Summarizing T42	• Daily Language SkillBuilder T11	• Words with Multiple Meanings C48		
• Visualizing T8 • Analyzing Text T18	• Daily Language SkillBuilder T11 • Diagramming Subjects, Verbs, and Modifiers T58 • Prepositional Phrases C85	• Using a Thesaurus C49	• Effective Language T13 • Personality Profile C25	
• Analyzing Text Structure T17 • Determining Author's Bias T23 • Using an Outline T44	• Daily Language SkillBuilder T11 • Prepositional Phrases Used as Adverbs C87		• Levels of Language T12	• Impromptu Speaking: Debate T15

STUDENTS ACQUIRING ENGLISH

The **Spanish Study Guide,** pp. 79–107, includes language support for the following pages:

- Family and Community Involvement (per unit)
- Selection Summaries and Vocabulary
- Active Reading
- Literary Analysis

DAILY LANGUAGE SKILLBUILDERS

Selection	SkillBuilder Sentences	Suggested Answers
My Lute, Awake! On Monsieur's Departure	**1.** Elizabeth I the daughter of King Henry VIII ruled england for almost half a century. **2.** Sir Thomas Wyatt trained to be a musician also wrote poetry	**1.** Elizabeth I**,** the daughter of King Henry VIII**,** ruled **E**ngland for almost half a century. **2.** Sir Thomas Wyatt**,** trained to be a musician**,** also wrote poetry**.**
The Passionate Shepherd to His Love The Nymph's Reply to the Shepherd	**1.** In writing pastoral poetry the words must be selected for musical quality as well as meaning. **2.** While reading a poem by Christopher Marlowe, my glasses slipped down my nose.	**1.** In writing pastoral poetry**, one must select** the words for musical quality as well as meaning. **2.** While **I was** reading a poem by Christopher Marlowe, my glasses slipped down my nose.
Sonnet 30 Sonnet 75	**1.** A product off sixteenth century London Edmund Spenser knew the city the court and the univesity. **2.** Edmund the son of John Spenser a cloth maker attended the merchant taylors school.	**1.** A product of **16th-**century London**,** Edmund Spenser knew the city**,** the court**,** and the university. **2.** Edmund**,** the son of John Spenser**,** a cloth maker**,** attended the **M**erchant **T**aylors**'** school.
Sonnet 29 Sonnet 116 Sonnet 130	**1.** William Shakespeare wrote two long poems venus and adonis and the rape of lucrece. **2.** William Shakespeare, and Ann Hathaway were married, in 1582.	**1.** William Shakespeare wrote two long poems**,** **"V**enus and **A**donis**"** and **"**The **R**ape of **L**ucrece.**"** **2.** William Shakespeare and Ann Hathaway were married in 1582.
Sonnet 169 Sonnet 292	**1.** Francescso Petrarch is a 14th century poet whom established the sonnet as a major form. **2.** A beautifull women named Laura was Petrarchs inspiration.	**1.** France**sco** Petrarch is a 14th-century poet **who** established the sonnet as a major form. **2.** A beautifu**l** woman named Laura was Petrarch's inspiration.

Selection	SkillBuilder Sentences	Suggested Answers
The Tragedy of Macbeth	1. shakespeere found the histerical episodes and charcters for MacBeth in a kronicle wrote by Raphael Holinshed. 2. He folowed the storyes from the chronicle closly, although he combind some charactrs and changed some other facts	1. **S**hakespe**a**re found the hist**o**rical episodes and char**a**cters for **<u>Macbeth</u>** in a **ch**ronicle **written** by Raphael Holinshed. 2. He fol**l**owed the stor**i**es from the chronicle clos**e**ly, although he combin**e**d some charact**e**rs and changed some other facts**.**
from Ecclesiastes, Chapter 3 Psalm 23 Parable of the Prodigal Son	1. In its' three parts the trinity covers many aspects of christianity. 2. The Puritans were never to busy read there bibles.	1. In **its** three parts**,** the **T**rinity covers many aspects of **C**hristianity. 2. The Puritans were never **too** busy **to** read **their** **B**ibles.
from Essays Of Studies Of Marriage and Single Life	1. Alexander Popes an essay on criticism is actually a series of rhymed couplets. 2. Have you read the essay by Robert Burton titled the anatomy of melancholy?	1. Alexander Pope**'**s **"A**n **E**ssay on **C**riticism**"** is actually a series of rhymed couplets. 2. Have you read the essay by Robert Burton titled **"**The **A**natomy of **M**elancholy**"**?
A Valediction: Forbidding Mourning Holy Sonnet 10 *from* Meditation 17	1. John Donne was born in london england in 1572. 2. After his father died in 1576 his mother married dr. John Syminges.	1. John Donne was born in **L**ondon**, E**ngland**,** in 1572. 2. After his father died in 1576**,** his mother married **D**r. John Syminges.
On My First Son Still to Be Neat	1. Writing plays and poetry, Ben Jonson's reputation was made. 2. Young Ben Jonson could often be seen by his mother while writing in the kitchen.	1. Ben Jonson **made his** reputation writing plays and poetry. 2. Ben **Jonson's mother** often **saw** young Ben writing in the kitchen.

UNIT TWO
DAILY LANGUAGE SKILLBUILDERS, continued

Selection	SkillBuilder Sentences	Suggested Answers
To the Virgins, to Make Much of Time To His Coy Mistress To Lucasta, Going to the Wars	**1.** King Charles I a Stuart king descended from the Scots inherited the throne of england from his father James I. who was also james VI of Scotland. **2.** King James wanted his sun to marry a Spainish princess in order to bring Spain and England closer but Charles married a French princess instead.	**1.** King Charles I**,** a Stuart king descended from the Scots**,** inherited the throne of **E**ngland from his father**,** James I**,** who was also **J**ames VI of Scotland. **2.** King James wanted his s**o**n to marry a Sp**an**ish princess in order to bring Spain and England closer**,** but Charles married a French princess instead.
from the Rubáiyát	**1.** When we examine stanzas 63–64–68–69 we see that the riter of these quatrains seem's to be preoccupied with the lack of control humens can exercise over their own lifes. **2.** For instance in one stanza he compares people to peaces on a checker board moved by the hand of an unseen player.	**1.** When we examine stanzas 63**,** 64**,** 68**,** and 69**,** we see that the **w**riter of these quatrains see**ms** to be preoccupied with the lack of control hum**a**ns can exercise over their own li**ve**s. **2.** For instance**,** in one stanza he compares people to p**ie**ces on a checker board moved by the hand of an unseen player.
How Soon Hath Time When I Consider How My Light Is Spent	**1.** John Milton the author of many sonnets' and of Paradise Lost was a supporter of Oliver Cromwell the head of Englands government during the Commonwealth period. **2.** When the monarchy was restored in 1660 Milton was considered to be a political enemy of the government because of his past association's.	**1.** John Milton**,** the author of many sonnets and of **Paradise Lost**, was a supporter of Oliver Cromwell**,** the head of England**'**s government during the Commonwealth period. **2.** When the monarchy was restored in 1660**,** Milton was considered to be a political enemy of the government because of his past associatio**ns**.
from Paradise Lost	**1.** One of the ways we know the power of a book are it's influence on other speakers and writers. **2.** Unconscious quotations, from Paridise Lost, occur in the everyday speech of people.	**1.** One of the ways we know the power of a book **is its** influence on other speakers and writers. **2.** Unconscious quotations from **Paradise Lost** occur in the everyday speech of people.
Female Orations	**1.** Margaret Lucas Cavendish, one of the earliest woman writers in english spent part of her life in france. **2.** As a young women, she acompanied the Queen of England to Paris, in 1645.	**1.** Margaret Lucas Cavendish, one of the earliest wom**e**n writers in **E**nglish**,** spent part of her life in **F**rance. **2.** As a young wom**a**n, she accompanied the Queen of England to Paris in 1645.

INTEGRATING GRAMMAR AND LITERATURE: GRAMMAR PLANNER

	Unit One	Unit Two	Unit Three	Unit Four	Unit Five	Unit Six	Unit Seven
Grammar Focus by Unit	Parts of a Sentence	Phrases, Part I	Phrases, Part II	Clauses, Part I	Clauses, Part II	Rhetorical Grammar, Part I	Rhetorical Grammar, Part II

The Language of Literature offers several options for integrating grammar instruction and literature.

- Each literature unit has a grammar focus. The Teacher's Edition includes Mini Lessons for each selection that help develop the grammar focus for the unit and spring from the content of the specific literature.
- The Pupil Edition includes several full-page lessons on Sentence Crafting. These lessons are related to both the literature and the grammar focus for the unit and help students use grammar in their own writing.
- Daily Language SkillBuilders in the Teacher's Edition provide students with ongoing proofreading practice and reinforce punctuation, spelling, grammar and usage, and capitalization.
- Grammar Copymasters and Transparencies, which may be used to complement or extend lessons in the Teacher's Edition, present grammar in a traditional, systematic sequence. References to appropriate copymasters or transparencies are included at point of use in the Teacher's Edition Mini Lessons.

TE Mini Lessons shown in green
PE instruction shown in black

Part 1

Using Phrases

Prepositional Phrases
"My Lute, Awake!" "On Monsieur's Departure," p. 286

Appositives and Appositive Phrases
"The Passionate Shepherd to His Love," "The Nymph's Reply to the Shepherd," p. 292

Verb Phrases: Infinitives
Spenser sonnets, p. 301

Verb Phrases: Participles and Participial Phrases
Shakespeare sonnets, p. 303

Verb Phrases: Gerunds and Gerund Phrases
Petrarch sonnets, p. 310

Part 2

Parts of Speech

Modifiers: Adjectives
Macbeth, Act Two, p. 360

Modifiers: Adverbs
Macbeth, Act Three, p. 371
Sentence Crafting, p. 433

Using Phrases

Prepositional Phrases Used as Adverbs
Sentence Crafting, p. 433

Verb Usage

Verbs: Avoiding Unnecessary Shifts in Tense
Writing Workshop, p. 431

Using Modifiers

Understanding Modifiers
Macbeth, Act One, p. 344

Modifiers: Avoiding Double Comparisons
Macbeth, Act Four, p. 394

Modifiers: Avoiding Illogical Comparisons
Macbeth, Act Five, pp. 406–407

Capitalization

Proper Nouns and Proper Adjectives
Writing Workshop, p. 431

Style

Adverbials: Function and Placement
Sentence Crafting, p. 433

Part 3

Parts of Speech

Modifiers That Follow Verbs
Donne poems, from "Meditation 17," p. 452

Using Phrases

Prepositional Phrases
from *Paradise Lost,* p. 490

Prepositional Phrases Used as Adverbs
"Female Orations," p. 496

Placement of Phrases
"Of Studies," "Of Marriage and Single Life," p. 445

Absolute Phrases
from the *Rubáiyát,* p. 473

Infinitive Phrase Used as an Adverb
King James Bible, p. 436

Verb Usage

Principle Parts: Present and Past Participles
Herrick, Marvell, Lovelace poems, p. 465

This time line shows some major events occurring during the English Renaissance. Further information about selected people and events is provided below.

Britain: 1485

A The death of the Yorkist king Richard III ended the 30-year English civil war known as the War of the Roses. It was the struggle for the English throne between two noble houses, each symbolized by a rose—red (Lancaster) and white (York). After the war, the victorious Lancastrian king Henry Tudor married Elizabeth, daughter of the former Yorkist king Edward IV. This united the two houses, establishing the Tudor royal family. The latter's symbol became a red rose superimposed upon a white rose. The appearance of the Tudor dynasty effectively ended feudalism in England.

Literature: 1516

B The scholar-statesman Sir Thomas More played a leading role in the early Renaissance in England. Although More served as Henry VIII's chancellor from 1529 to 1532, he refused to support the king's break with Roman Catholicism. Dismissed from his post, imprisoned, and beheaded for his stance on this issue, More was canonized by the Roman Catholic Church 400 years later.

Britain: 1534

C Henry VIII's actions created the Church of England, with the king as its "only supreme head on earth." Protestants gained influence as monasteries were closed.

World: 1520

D The Ottoman Empire (modern-day Turkey) reached its zenith under Suleiman I (1494–1566), called by his own people Suleiman the Lawgiver and known in the West as Suleiman the Magnificent. He created panic in Central Europe when his forces reached as far into the continent as Hungary and Austria before being stopped at the outskirts of Vienna in 1529. His Ottoman Empire was a model of governmental efficiency and social organization, and the arts and literature flourished under his rule.

Britain: 1558

E Elizabeth I was the third child of Henry VIII. Her predecessor and half-sister, Mary I, had returned the English Church to Roman Catholic rule in 1554, and many Protestants were killed. Elizabeth I, however, turned England again to Protestantism. She avoided further bloodshed, though, by founding a state church, with provisions for both Catholics and Protestants.w

World: 1526

F The Muslim leader Babur (1483–1530) inherited a small kingdom in central Asia in 1494 as an 11-year-old. By 1504, he had established the kingdom of Afghanistan. In 1526, he invaded Hindu India, conquering nearly all of the north region. He thus founded the Mughal Empire that lasted in India until 1857.

TIME LINE 1485–1660

The ENGLISH Renaissance

EVENTS IN BRITISH LITERATURE

c. 1495 Everyman, earliest morality play, written anonymously (printed c. 1530)

B **1516** Thomas More publishes *Utopia*, written in Latin (published in English c. 1551) ➢

1557 Tottel's anthology *Miscellany*, originally *Songs and Sonnets*, published, containing 97 poems attributed to Sir Thomas Wyatt

c. 1576 Edmund Spenser writes his first poetry

EVENTS IN BRITAIN

1450 | 1500 | 1550

A **1485** Henry Tudor defeats Richard III and takes throne as Henry VII

1509 Reign of Henry VIII begins (to 1547) ➢

C **1534** At insistence of Henry VIII, Parliament passes Act of Supremacy, completing England's break with Roman Catholic Church

1536 Henry VIII unites England and Wales

1547 Reign of Edward VI begins

1553 Reign of Mary I begins

E **1558** Reign of Elizabeth I begins (to 1603) ➢

EVENTS IN THE WORLD

1450 | 1500 | 1550

1492 Columbus sails to Bahamas in Western Hemisphere

c. 1502 First slaves exported from Africa for work in Americas

1517 Martin Luther begins Reformation, creating Protestant Christians

D **1520** Suleiman I begins reign as Ottoman sultan (to 1566)

1521 Cortés conquers Aztecs in Mexico

1522 Magellan's crew sails around world

F **1526** Babur begins reign of Mughal Empire in India

Period Pieces

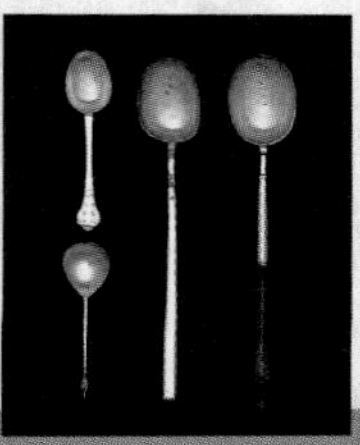

Household items

Early microscope

K Engraved filoral cloc from mid-17th century

- c. **1587** Christopher Marlowe's tragedy *Tamburlaine the Great,* which introduced blank verse, produced
- c. **1590** Shakespeare, settled in London, begins career as playwright
- **1597** First edition of Bacon's Essays published
- I **1604** King James appoints committee of scholars that begins creating new translation of Bible
- **1606** Shakespeare's *Macbeth* produced
- **1633** John Donne's Poems published anonymously
- **1643** John Milton's pamphlet *Areopagitica* attacks press censorship
- **1658** Milton begins composing *Paradise Lost*

1600 1650

- **1580** Sir Francis Drake brings great treasures back to England after sailing around world
- G **1588** English navy defeats Spanish Armada
- **1603** James VI of Scotland becomes king of England as James I (to 1625)
- J **1605** Gunpowder Plot uncovered, saving life of James I
- **1607** English establish Jamestown colony in Virginia
- **1620** English Pilgrims establish colony in Plymouth, Massachusetts
- **1625** Reign of Charles I begins
- L **1642** English civil war begins (to 1649)
- **1649** Charles I beheaded
- **1660** Monarchy restored with accession of Charles II

1600 1650

- H **1543** Theory of Polish astronomer, Nicolaus Copernicus, that earth and other planets revolve around sun, published
- **1549** Ivan the Terrible seizes power in Russia, becoming first czar (to 1584)
- **1590** Dutch eyeglass-maker Zacharias Janssen invents microscope
- **1603** Japan's Tokugawa regime begins (to 1868)
- **1609** Italian scientist Galileo Galilei studies heavens with telescope
- **1631** Mughal emperor Shah Jahan begins construction of Taj Mahal
- **1633** Galileo condemned by Inquisition for supporting Copernicus' theory
- **1643** Louis XIV begins 72-year reign in France
- M **1644** Ming Dynasty collapses, replaced by the Qing Dynasty, China's last (to 1912)

G The Catholic king of Spain attacked Elizabeth I's Protestant England with 130 ships—the Spanish Armada—carrying about 30,000 sailors and soldiers into the English Channel. However, the Spanish were met by an English naval force with superior, heavier guns and faster ships. Bad weather also took its toll on Spanish ships. The defeat cost Spain control of the high seas and opened the Americas to exploration by other European countries.

World: 1543

H The Age of Exploration brought the Scientific Revolution, in which people questioned scientific and religious beliefs. After 25 years of study, Copernicus reasoned that the sun, not the earth, was at the center of the universe. This idea still took nearly 200 more years to be accepted.

Literature: 1604

I The King James version of the Bible, first printed in 1611, replaced earlier, poorer English-language versions. The new translation was a powerful argument in favor of the English language. Soon, large numbers of ancient and contemporary works were being translated into English.

Britain: 1605

J The Gunpowder Plot was a plan to blow up the Parliament building, kill King James I, and incite a Catholic uprising. The plot was uncovered before being carried out, and one of the conspirators, Guy Fawkes, became memorialized. Bonfires burn all over England on the night of November 5—Guy Fawkes' Day—and children go "trick-or-treating" with the cry "A penny for the guy!" This tradition is referred to in literary works, including T. S. Eliot's poem "The Hollow Men" (1925).

Period Pieces

K With the introduction of coiled springs as the motive power in clocks (c. 1500), it became possible to build less bulky, more elegant timepieces, like the one shown here. In the 1650s, Dutch scientist Christiaan Huygens was the first to use pendulums in clocks.

Britain: 1625

L With the reign of Charles I came further civil war in England, between the king's supporters (Royalists) and opponents (Puritans). The Puritans finally prevailed, and they tried Charles for treason and beheaded him. Never before had a sitting monarch been tried in public and executed.

World: 1644

M The Ming Dynasty in China (1368–1644) drove out its Mongol rulers and united the country and largely withdrew into self-sufficient isolation after 1433. However, ineffective rulers and corrupt officials eventually weakened the country and caused it to fall to Manchu invaders from the north. The new rulers founded a Qing Dynasty that brought Taiwan, Mongolia, and Tibet into China and lasted into the 20th century.

OVERVIEW

Introduction
This article provides a historical and literary context for the English Renaissance writings presented in this unit.

Teaching Nonfiction

Reading Skills and Strategies
ESTABLISHING A PURPOSE FOR READING
Have students scan the article to establish a purpose for reading. Remind them to adjust their purpose if they need to.

USING TEXT ORGANIZERS
If students need more support, ask them what they can learn about the article's content by looking at the title, subheads and images. Ask them what information they would expect to find in the side notes. Ask students what they imagine the nearly page-and-a-half of text preceding the first heading wll consist of. Ask students what they imagine the nearly page-and-a-half of an introduction to the main article that reflects on the shift from Britain's medieval society to the acceptance of Renaissance ideas.

Remind students they should use text organizers to locate and categorize information when they research for independent project.

ANALYZING TEXT STRUCTURE
Ask students how the information in this article is presented. (*in chronological order*) Discuss how this structure influences the way they read and understand material and the skills they should use while reading. (*identifying main ideas and noretaking*)

NOTETAKING
Encourage students to take notes while they read, jotting down important concepts, vocabulary, and terms. They may also want to create graphic organizers to serve as visual connections back to the text.

The ENGLISH Renaissance
1485–1660

At certain points in history, factors converge to cause dramatic shifts in human values and perceptions. One such shift, beginning in 14th-century Italy, launched the period of European history known as the Renaissance ("rebirth"). During the [A] Renaissance, the medieval world view, focused on religion and the afterlife, was replaced by a more modern view, stressing human life here on earth. Renaissance Europeans delighted in the arts and literature, in the beauty of nature, in human impulses, and in a new sense of mastery over the world. They reinterpreted [B] Europe's pre-Christian past, using the arts and philosophies of ancient Greece and Rome as models for their own achievements. Surging with creative energy, they expanded the scientific, geographical, and philosophical boundaries of the medieval world, often questioning timeworn truths and challenging authority. A new emphasis was placed on the individual and [C] on the development of human potential. The ideal "Renaissance man" was a many-faceted person who cultivated his innate talents to the fullest.

In England, political instability delayed the advent of Renaissance ideas, but they began to penetrate English society after 1485, when the Wars of the Roses ended and Henry Tudor took the throne as Henry VII. A shrewd if colorless monarch, Henry exercised strong authority at home and negotiated favorable commercial treaties abroad. He built up the nation's merchant fleet and financed expeditions that established English claims in the New World. He also engineered a clever political alliance by arranging

Above: Henry VIII
Right: Self-portrait of Leonardo da Vinci, artistic and scientific genius of the Italian Renaissance

Mini Lesson: Viewing and Representing

Portrait of Henry VIII
by Hans Holbein

ART APPRECIATION
Instruction The portrait of Henry VIII is attributed to Hans Holbein, the younger (c. 1497–1543), a northern Renaissance master. (Some scholars believe that the portrait was actually created in Holbein's studio by a follower.) Two years earlier, Holbein had been hired to paint the members of the Tudor family, in whose service he remained until his death, possibly of plague, at age 46. The painting of the infant Edward on page 278 is from his Tudor series.

In 1537, Henry VIII's third wife died, and Henry wished to marry again. He was attracted to physical beauty, and Holbein was sent to the continent to paint the likeness of each candidate being considered for his hand. Holbein did this for two years, and based on Holbein's portrait of her, Anne of Cleves was selected in 1539 as Henry's next wife.

Ask: How would you characterize Henry VIII from his portrait?

Possible response: Henry VIII seems confident, all powerful, and distant—his expression lacks warmth.

for his eldest son, Arthur, to marry Catherine of Aragon, daughter of King Ferdinand and Queen Isabella of Spain, England's greatest New World rival. When Arthur died unexpectedly, the pope granted a special dispensation allowing Arthur's younger brother Henry, the new heir to the throne, to marry Catherine. The marriage would have startling consequences.

Stained-glass panels depicting Henry VIII and Catherine of Aragon

The Reign of Henry VIII

Henry VIII succeeded his father in 1509. A true Renaissance prince, Henry was a skilled athlete, poet, and musician, well educated in French, Italian, and Latin. During his reign, the Protestant Reformation was sweeping northern Europe, propelled by discontent with church abuses and a growing nationalism that resented the influence of Rome. While many in England sympathized with Protestant reforms, Henry at first remained loyal to Rome. However, after 18 years of marriage he had only one child, Mary, and he became obsessed with producing a male heir. Insisting that the papal dispensation had been a mistake, he requested that his marriage be annulled so that he could wed Catherine's court attendant Anne Boleyn. When the pope refused to comply, Henry broke with Rome and in 1534 declared himself head of the Church of England, or Anglican Church.

Anne Boleyn

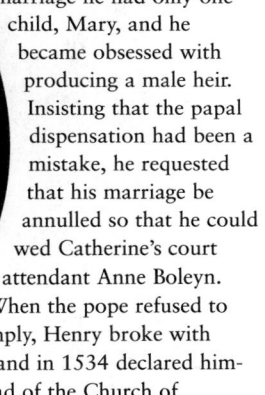

Development of the English Language

During the 1400s, the pronunciation of most English long vowels changed, in what is referred to as the Great Vowel Shift. In addition, the final *e* in words like *take* was no longer pronounced. By 1500, Middle English had evolved into an early form of the modern English spoken today. In spite of the changes in pronunciation, however, early printers continued to use Middle English spellings— retaining, for example, the *k* and *e* in *knave,* even though the letters were no longer pronounced. This practice resulted in many of the inconsistent spellings for which modern English is known.

Printing helped stabilize the language, so that the differences between Renaissance English and our own are comparatively minor. Nevertheless, there are some differences. In the Renaissance, *thou, thee, thy,* and *thine* were used for familiar address, while *you, your,* and *yours* were reserved for more formal and impersonal situations. Renaissance speakers and writers also distinguished between "this tree" (near), "that tree" (farther), and "yon tree" (even farther). They used the verb ending *-est* or *-st* with the second-person singular subject *thou* ("thou leadest," "thou canst") and *-eth* or *-th* with third-person singular subjects ("she looketh," "he doth"). They also used fewer helping verbs, especially in questions ("Saw you the bird?").

The English vocabulary grew as new ideas and discoveries demanded new words. The Renaissance interest in the classics gave rise to new formations from Greek and Latin roots. Trade brought English speakers into contact with languages such as Spanish, Portuguese, Italian, Dutch, and Arabic—as well as various African, Indian, and American languages—and English borrowed words from all of them. The Renaissance spirit also encouraged writers to coin new words. Shakespeare is credited with some 2000 coinages, many involving the use of nouns as verbs and verbs as nouns.

Making Connections

Economics

A During the Renaissance, Europe's economy changed from a rural, self-sustaining system based in manor farms and villages to an international trading economy concentrated in the growing number of towns and cities. Gold and silver from the New World made money more available, and bankers developed the practices of investment, loans, and credit. Merchants who had made great fortunes in trade rivaled the landed gentry in political importance and as supporters of literature and the arts.

Literary History

B After the breakup of the Western Roman Empire in the fifth century A. D., a number of classical texts fell into oblivion, surviving only as a few manuscripts in the libraries of medieval monasteries. Some Greek and Roman works (such as Virgil's *Aeneid* and Ovid's *Amores)* were copied and recopied, but many lay untouched for centuries. Ironically, the names of the 14th-century Italian humanists who began bringing these texts to light are largely unremembered today.

Sociology

C The sharp contrast between the medieval and Renaissance world views is evident in the differences between the morality play *Everyman,* written in the last years of the 15th century, and Christopher Marlowe's *Tamburlaine the Great,* produced fewer than 90 years later. In *Everyman,* the protagonist belatedly recognizes the need for repentance, whereas Marlowe's protagonist is driven by boundless ambition to try to conquer the world.

Sociology

D Change was the order of the day. Martin Luther's challenge to the Roman Catholic Church in 1517 led to the Protestant Reformation. National governments and new churches became alternative sources of authority and power. Latin, the universal language of learning, was challenged by developing European languages, in which great works of literature were being written. The printing press greatly increased the speed with which new ideas could be spread.

Law

E While the invention of printing from movable type was of incalculable importance in the Renaissance, printing in England was restricted, largely because of the fear that it could fuel religious dissent and sedition against the government. After the incorporation by royal charter of the Stationers' Company in 1557, no one could print a document for sale without a special privilege or patent, and all printed documents had to be registered.

Teaching Nonfiction

OUTLINING
Have students research and prepare an outline of English rule during this period. They should begin with the 1485 creation of Tudor reign. Following this are the reigns of the House of Stuart, the Commonwealth (with Oliver Cromwell as virtual dictator), the Protectorate (with Oliver and then his son Richard Cromwell at the helm), and finally the reestabishment of the monarchy with the return of the House of Stuart in 1660. You might have interested students research the short reign of Lady Jane Grey.

F Growing English nationalism and the spread of Protestant ideas brought popular support for Henry's action; those who openly opposed it frequently paid with their lives.

Ironically, Anne Boleyn produced only a daughter, Elizabeth, and eventually Anne was executed on a charge of adultery. A third marriage finally gave Henry his long-sought son, the frail and sickly Edward VI, who in 1547, at the age of nine, succeeded his father. During his six-year reign, the Church of England became more truly Protestant, clarifying its beliefs and establishing its rituals in a landmark publication, the Book of Common Prayer. When Edward died, however, his half-sister Mary took the throne and tried to reintroduce Roman Catholicism. The move was unpopular, as was her marriage to her cousin Philip II of Spain, and her persecution of Protestants earned her the nickname Bloody Mary. On her death in 1558, most welcomed the succession of her half-sister Elizabeth.

Top to bottom: Edward, Prince of Wales, son of Henry VIII and Jane Seymour; Mary, daughter of Henry VIII and Catherine of Aragon; Elizabeth I, daughter of Henry VIII and Anne Boleyn

The Elizabethan Era

G Elizabeth I, the unwanted daughter of Henry VIII and Anne Boleyn, proved to be one of the ablest monarchs in English history. During her long reign, the English Renaissance reached its full flower, and England enjoyed a time of unprecedented prosperity and international prestige. A practical and disciplined ruler, Elizabeth loved pomp and ceremony but was nevertheless frugal and intent on balancing the national budget. She was also a consummate politician, exercising absolute authority while remaining sensitive to public opinion and respectful of Parliament. In religious matters she steered a middle course. Reestablishing the independent Church of England, she made it a buffer between Roman Catholics and radical Protestants, now often called Puritans because they sought to "purify" the church of all remaining Roman Catholic practices.

H In foreign policy, Elizabeth was a shrewd strategist who kept England out of costly wars and ended the unpopular Spanish alliance. Though she never married, for 20 years she used the possibility of her marriage to utmost advantage, feigning interest in one European prince after another. Convinced by advisers that the path to national prosperity lay in New World riches, she encouraged overseas ventures, including Sir Francis Drake's circumnavigation of the globe and Sir Walter Raleigh's attempt to establish a colony in Virginia. I In secret, she funded pirate raids against the ships of Spain, while publicly denouncing such "unlawful acts" of plunder.

The quarrel with Catholic Spain intensified in 1587, when Elizabeth reluctantly executed her cousin Mary Stuart, the Roman Catholic queen of Scotland, for conspiracy. Catholics, who questioned the legitimacy of Elizabeth's parents' marriage, had believed Mary to be the rightful heir to the English throne and had participated in a number of foreign-backed plots against Elizabeth. A year after Mary's execution, Spain's Philip II sent a great armada, or fleet of warships, to challenge the English navy. Aided by a violent storm, the smaller, more maneuverable English ships defeated the Spanish Armada, making Elizabeth the undisputed leader of a great military power. J

The Rise of the Stuarts

With Elizabeth's death in 1603, the powerful Tudor dynasty came to an end, and the rule of England fell into the hands of the weaker house of Stuart. Elizabeth was succeeded by her cousin James VI of Scotland, son of Mary Stuart, who ascended

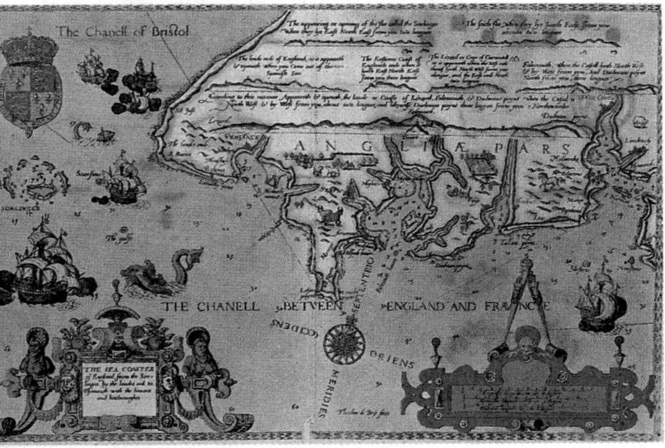

Map published in 1588, depicting the approach of the Spanish Armada

Literary History

Although the zenith of English Renaissance literature was not reached until Elizabeth's reign, a number of earlier writers paved the way. Among them were Sir Thomas Wyatt and Henry Howard, earl of Surrey, court poets of Henry VIII's reign who introduced into England the Italian verse form called the **sonnet.** During Elizabethan times, the sonnet became the most popular form of love lyric. Sonnets were often published in sequences, such as Edmund Spenser's *Amoretti,* addressed to his future wife. William Shakespeare's magnificent sonnets do not form a clear sequence, but several address a mysterious figure known as the Dark Lady, who some scholars think may have been the poet Amelia Lanier.

Shakespeare left an even clearer mark on drama, which came of age in the Renaissance. Although most plays of medieval times had treated religious themes, Renaissance drama was concerned with the complexities of human life here on earth. Plays were often staged at court, in the homes of wealthy nobles, and in inn yards, where spectators could sit on the ground in front of the stage or in balconies overlooking it. A similar plan was used in England's first theaters, like the famous Globe Theater in London. Most of the plays were written mainly or entirely in verse. Among the era's finest playwrights other than Shakespeare were Christopher Marlowe and Ben Jonson. Jonson was influential in shaping English drama on the basis of classical models, distinguishing clearly between **tragedies,** which end with their heroes' downfall, and **comedies,** which end happily.

Making Connections

Economics

F Once he had broken with Rome and founded the Church of England, Henry dissolved the English monasteries and distributed their landholdings to his courtiers so that the monastic properties could never be returned to the Roman Catholic Church.

History

G Elizabeth's eventual ascension to the throne was anything but a foregone conclusion. Just before her mother was executed, three-year-old Elizabeth was declared illegitimate. However, eight years later Parliament restored her succession as third in line after her half brother, Edward, and half sister, Mary. Then, raised a Protestant, Elizabeth had to be extremely self-controlled and discreet so as not to run afoul of Mary once the latter became queen, for Mary was an ardent Catholic who sometimes burned Protestants.

History

H Elizabeth exploited the possibility of her marriage both to influence her courtiers at home and to gain diplomatic leverage in dealings with foreign powers. The "virgin queen" also enjoyed a semilegendary status in the literature produced by some of the period's greatest writers, such as Spenser and Raleigh. Gloriana—the central figure in Spenser's *The Faerie Queene,* the greatest English romance of the high Renaissance—is in part an idealization of Elizabeth.

Biography

I Sir Walter Raleigh was a warrior and explorer who helped introduce the crops tobacco and potatoes into Ireland. He also engaged in chemical research, contributed to English prose with his *History of the World,* and wrote fine love poetry. Raleigh was alternately in and out of Elizabeth's favor, and after her death his life became even more difficult. Under James I, he was tried on charges of treason, imprisoned in the famous Tower of London for many years, released in 1616 to hunt for gold in South America, arrested again for disobeying orders, and finally executed in 1618.

Military History

J The 1588 defeat of the Spanish Armada was one of the watersheds in Elizabeth's reign. The invading expedition consisted of 130 ships and a force of nearly 30,000 men. After the decisive sea battle in the English Channel, the remaining Spanish ships, outmaneuvered by the smaller and faster English vessels, were forced by storms to make their way home on a course around Scotland and Ireland.

HISTORICAL BACKGROUND 279

Making Connections

History

K Like Elizabeth, James I was an exceptionally learned monarch. His written works included *True Law of Free Monarchies* (1598), in which he defended the divine right of kings; *Basilikan Doron* (1599), in which he set forth, for his son's benefit, precepts of governing; and poems in Scots, Latin, and English. Several aspects of Shakespeare's *Macbeth* may have been influenced by James I; the king had a strong interest in witches, for example, and was also said to be a descendant of Banquo, one of Macbeth's victims.

Law

L The Star Chamber was named for the stars painted on the ceiling of the council's original meeting place in Westminster palace. Starting in the 15th century, the council had gradually extended its jurisdiction over criminal matters.

Science

M Despite the political turbulence of this period, British science took great strides in the first two-thirds of the 17th century. In addition to William Harvey's discovery of the circulation of the blood, notable advances included the botanical treatises of John Parkinson, the invention of a balance spring for watches by Robert Hooke, the first description of typhoid fever by Thomas Willis, and the publication of *The Sceptical Chymist* (1661) by Robert Boyle, who would later be celebrated as the discoverer of Boyle's law (relating the volume and pressure of gases). In 1645, London scientists held preliminary meetings that would lead, almost two decades later, to the founding of the Royal Society.

K the throne of England as James I. Separated from his mother in childhood, James was happy to support the Church of England, but both Roman Catholic and Protestant extremists expected otherwise—Catholics because he was Mary Stuart's son, Puritans because he was king of Presbyterian Scotland. Problems with Roman Catholics arose early in his reign, when a group including Guy Fawkes conspired to kill him and blow up Parliament in the unsuccessful Gunpowder Plot of 1605. Later, James had greater difficulties with the Puritans, and these problems only worsened when his son Charles I took the throne in 1625.

James and Charles lacked the political savvy and frugality of Elizabeth, and both aroused opposition by their belief in the divine right of kings, considering themselves God's representatives in all civil and religious matters. Their contempt for Parliament and their shocking extravagance met with much hostility in the House of Commons, now dominated by Puritans. Even more offensive to the Puritans was the kings' preference for "High-Church" rituals in the Anglican Church—rituals that seemed to smack of Roman Catholicism.

In 1629, with the situation deteriorating, Charles I dismissed Parliament, refusing to summon it again for 11 years. During this time he took strong measures against his political opponents through the royal L Courts of the Star Chamber, which operated without trial by jury. The result of these oppressive measures was a deepening of religious, political, and economic unrest. Thousands of English citizens—especially Puritans—emigrated to North America, making the Stuart years England's first period of major colonial expansion. Then, in 1637, Charles's attempt to introduce Anglican prayers and practices in Scotland's Presbyterian churches led to open rebellion there. In need of funds to suppress the Scots, Charles was forced to reconvene Parliament. In a session known as the Long Parliament, many of his powers were M stripped. He responded with a show of military force, and England was soon plunged into civil war.

Top: James I
Bottom: Charles I, depicted as a knight on horseback

The Pilgrims begin their voyage to the New World after living in the Netherlands for 12 years.

Oliver Cromwell in his military finery

The Defeat of the Monarchy

The English civil war pitted the Royalists, or supporters of the monarchy—mainly Roman Catholics, Anglicans, and members of the nobility—against the supporters of Parliament, consisting principally of Puritans, smaller landowners, and middle-class town dwellers. Under the skilled leadership of General Oliver Cromwell, the devout, disciplined Puritan army soundly defeated the Royalists in 1645, and the king surrendered a year later. Cromwell's army, now in control of Parliament, ordered stiff retaliatory measures against the Royalists. In 1649, the king himself was executed.

The members of Parliament had difficulty in deciding on an alternative to monarchy. At first they established a commonwealth with Cromwell as head; later they made him "lord protector" for life. Under the Puritan-dominated government, England's theaters were closed and most forms of recreation suspended; Sunday became a day of prayer, when even walking for pleasure was forbidden. A reluctant but able politician, Cromwell curbed quarrels among members of the military, religious leaders, and discontented government officials. When Cromwell died in 1658, his son inherited his title. Richard Cromwell, however, showed little of his father's ability to control the country's political wrangling and increasingly unruly public. Puritan government had proved no less autocratic than the Stuart reign, and in 1660 a new Parliament invited Charles II, son of Charles I, to return from exile and assume the throne. His reign ushered in a new chapter in English history, known as the Restoration.

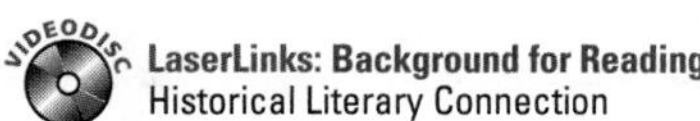

LaserLinks: Background for Reading
Historical Literary Connection

Literary History

Like Shakespeare, Marlowe and Jonson were fine lyric poets. Marlowe's "The Passionate Shepherd to His Love" is a famous example of **pastoral verse,** which praises the simple joys of rural life. Jonson's lyrics influenced many of the younger poets of the age, such as Robert Herrick and Richard Lovelace. Jonson's contemporary, John Donne, broke with poetic conventions, employing unusual imagery and elaborate metaphors to produce what came to be called **metaphysical poetry.** His blend of passion and intellect was especially influential among younger religious poets, such as George Herbert. (N)

The English Renaissance was also a high point in the history of epic poetry. Edmund Spenser dedicated his action-packed romantic epic *The Faerie Queene* to Elizabeth I. Some decades later, the Puritan poet John Milton penned the lofty epic *Paradise Lost,* retelling the story of the fall of Adam and Eve in the Garden of Eden. (O) The Bible, Milton's main source of inspiration, had been made accessible to all English people in 1611, with the publication of the magnificent King James Bible—the culmination of years of effort by many translators, most notably the Protestant reformer William Tyndale. Although this translation rivals Shakespeare's plays in its use of memorable poetic language, most sections are in fact prose. Among the era's other influential prose works are the essays of Sir Francis Bacon, who pioneered the essay form in English, and the sermons and meditations of John Donne.

Making Connections

Link to Literature

(N) The name "metaphysical poets" was bestowed on Donne and his followers by Samuel Johnson in the 18th century, as a reference to the esoteric learning they displayed in their poems. In addition to elaborate and unexpected metaphors, which are sometimes called conceits, the hallmarks of the metaphysical style include intellectual complexity, wit, irony, paradox, and irregular rhythms that reflect the accents of natural speech. During the 1920s and 1930s, T. S. Eliot helped to reawaken interest in the metaphysical poets, especially Donne and Andrew Marvell.

Biography

(O) In addition to the inspiration he derived from the Bible, Milton drew on his vast knowledge of Greek and Latin literature in virtually all his works. His great predecessors in the art of the epic, whom he simultaneously venerated and strove to surpass, were Homer, Virgil, and Dante. Throughout *Paradise Lost,* many structural devices and verbal allusions bear witness to the influence of these poets on Milton.

HISTORICAL BACKGROUND 281

PART 1 Aspects of Love

The Renaissance was a time of rapid change in the arts, literature, and learning. New ideas were embraced, and old ones–including the concept of love–were examined from different perspectives. In sonnets and other forms of verse, English poets of the period explored the many aspects of love: unrequited love, constant love, timeless love, and love that is subject to change. As you read the poems in this part of Unit Two, compare your own ideas about love with those expressed in these works.

PREPARING to *Read*

My Lute, Awake!

Poetry by
SIR THOMAS WYATT

On Monsieur's Departure

Poetry by
ELIZABETH I

Connect to Your Life

Dealing with Rejection Suppose that you loved or liked someone who did not return your love or your friendship. How would you react? In your reader's notebook, write a short paragraph describing the effect that such a rejection might have on you.

Build Background

Court Poets and Courtly Love Sir Thomas Wyatt, a diplomat in the service of King Henry VIII, traveled widely and was responsible for introducing various forms of Italian lyric poetry to England. Although this achievement was of great importance to the development of English poetry, many of Wyatt's best poems—including "My Lute, Awake!"—are in the style of the native English dance song, or ballet (băl′ət). The ballet was a lively and forceful kind of verse written to be sung to the accompaniment of the lute, a stringed instrument popular in the 16th century.

The writer of "On Monsieur's Departure," Elizabeth I, was a daughter of Henry VIII and queen of England during the flowering of the English Renaissance. Elizabeth was unusually well educated for a woman of her time and wrote several poems, all of which seem to have been based on events in her life.

One of the popular themes of love poetry in the 16th century was unrequited love—love that is ignored or rejected. In the tradition of earlier European poems of courtly love, such poetry portrayed the rejected lover as desolate and anguished, totally in the power of the beloved. These poems by Wyatt and Elizabeth I are both concerned with the theme of unrequited love. The individuality of each poem lies in the way the poet works subtle variations on the traditional situations and responses.

Focus Your Reading

LITERARY ANALYSIS RHYME SCHEME A **rhyme scheme** is the pattern of end rhyme in a poem. Notice the pattern of end rhyme in this stanza from "My Lute, Awake!"

Proud of the spoil that thou hast got
Of simple hearts, thorough love's shot;
By whom, unkind, thou hast them won,
Think not he hath his bow forgot,
Although my lute and I have done.

As you read both poems, be aware of their different rhyme schemes.

ACTIVE READING CLARIFYING MEANING Poetry of the Renaissance can be challenging to modern readers. If you find the syntax or the order of the words hard to follow, you can use the following strategies to increase your understanding:

- Use the text annotations and the dictionary to help you define difficult words or phrases.
- Reread the poem several times—aloud and silently.
- Try **paraphrasing** the lines until the sense becomes clear. For example, read these lines from "On Monsieur's Departure."

I grieve and dare not show my discontent,
I love and yet am forced to seem to hate, . . .

You might paraphrase the lines as follows: "I must hide my grief and disguise my love."

READER'S NOTEBOOK As you read these poems, try to paraphrase lines that seem difficult to you.

OVERVIEW

Objectives

1. understand and appreciate two **lyric poems (Literary Analysis)**
2. identify and examine a poem's **rhyme scheme (Literary Analysis)**
3. use strategies for **clarifying meaning** in a lyric poem **(Active Reading)**

Summary

Both Sir Thomas Wyatt and Elizabeth I write about unrequited love. Wyatt has been rejected by his love and feels ill-treated and angry. Elizabeth I, however, has rejected her love and seeks peace from her painful emotions. Each poet reacts differently to the situation: Wyatt declares his angry feelings to his beloved; Elizabeth I remains quiet and hides her feelings from everyone.

Thematic Link

"My Lute, Awake!" and "On Monsieur's Departure" are examples of courtly love poetry and express a common **aspect of love**—dejection over the loss of a great love. Although the poems are quite different in tone, the feelings expressed are very similar. Both poets suffer from feelings of helplessness.

5-Minute Warm-Up

Daily Language SkillBuilder

Have students **proofread** the display sentences on page 273k and write them correctly. The sentences also appear on Transparency 6 of **Grammar Transparencies and Copymasters.**

LESSON RESOURCES

UNIT TWO RESOURCE BOOK, pp. 4–5

ASSESSMENT RESOURCES
Formal Assessment, pp. 41–42
Teacher's Guide to Assessment and Portfolio Use
Test Generator

SKILLS TRANSPARENCIES AND COPYMASTERS
Reading and Critical Thinking
- Analyzing Text, T18 (for Active Reading, p. 283)

Grammar
- Diagramming Subjects, Verbs, and Modifiers, T58 (for Mini Lesson, p. 286)
- Prepositional Phrases, C85 (for Mini Lesson, p. 286)

Writing
- Effective Language, T13 (for Writing Options, p. 288)

INTEGRATED TECHNOLOGY
Audio Library
LaserLinks
- Author Background: Elizabeth I
- Music Connection: Music During the English Renaissance. See **Teacher's SourceBook,** pp. 19–20.

Visit our website:
www.mcdougallittell.com

TEACHING THE LITERATURE

Reading and Analyzing

Active Reading CLARIFYING MEANING

Ask students to read to discover the attitude of the rejected suitor toward his beloved. How does the speaker describe his beloved?

Possible Responses: cruel, arrogant, flirtatious.

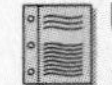
Use **Unit Two Resource Book,** p. 4 for more practice.

Literary Analysis RHYME SCHEME

A Rhyme scheme is the pattern of end rhyme in a poem. The rhyme scheme is noted by assigning a letter of the alphabet, beginning with "a," to each line. Lines that rhyme are given the same letter—For example, in "My Lute, Awake!" the rhyme scheme of each stanza is *aabab*.

Use **Unit Two Resource Book,** p. 5 for more exercises.

Thinking Through the Literature

1. The speaker has been rejected by the subject of the poem and is expressing anger and disappointment.
2. Accept all reasonable responses.
3. The speaker feels bitter and angry.
4. She would be neglected by someone she loves and become lonely.
5. He is probably not sincere at this point because he seems to be obsessed with the woman and not yet willing to forget her and try to find another love.

My Lute, Awake!

Sir Thomas Wyatt

My lute, awake! Perform the last
Labor that thou and I shall waste, **A**
And end that I have now begun;
For when this song is sung and past,
My lute, be still, for I have done.

As to be heard where ear is none,
As lead to grave in marble stone,
My song may pierce her heart as soon.
Should we then sigh or sing or moan?
No, no, my lute, for I have done.

6–8 as to be heard . . . as soon: My song's having an effect on her emotions is as unlikely as sound being heard without an ear or soft lead carving hard marble.

The rocks do not so cruelly
Repulse the waves continually
As she my suit and affection.
So that I am past remedy,
Whereby my lute and I have done.

13 suit: wooing; courtship.

Proud of the spoil that thou hast got
Of simple hearts, thorough love's shot;
By whom, unkind, thou hast them won,
Think not he hath his bow forgot,
Although my lute and I have done.

17 thorough love's shot: through the arrow of Cupid, the god of love.

Teaching Options

Speaking and Listening

LYRIC POEMS AS SONGS

Instruction Many English Renaissance lyric poems were written to be sung, and because their purpose was to express the author's feelings, the rhythm and tone of the poem is often a function of their sound as well as their sense.

Prepare Ask students to practice reading aloud the following examples: line 4 "song is sung" and line 10 "no, no"; line 12 "repulse" (*sound quality and negative connotation*); line 19 "Think not he hath his bow forgot" (*long* o *sounds suggest seriousness and possible sadness*); line 21 "shall fall" (*short monosyllabic internal rhyme for dramatic effect*); line 26 "withered" (*connotation and sound quality*); line 35 "wish and want" and lines 36–37 "last / Labor" (*alliteration*).

Present Have students read aloud the rehearsed lines and discuss the sound qualities of the word choices. Point out to students that in a poem in which a musical instrument is personified and apostrophized, the reader should expect the word choices to be especially melodic and alliterative.

BLOCK SCHEDULING This activity is particularly well-suited for longer class periods.

Vengeance shall fall on thy disdain
That makest but game on earnest pain.
Think not alone under the sun
Unquit to cause thy lovers plain,
Although my lute and I have done.

Perchance thee lie withered and old
The winter nights that are so cold,
Plaining in vain unto the moon.
Thy wishes then dare not be told.
Care then who list, for I have done.

And then may chance thee to repent
The time that thou hast lost and spent
To cause thy lovers sigh and swoon.
Then shalt thou know beauty but lent,
And wish and want as I have done.

Now cease, my lute. This is the last
Labor that thou and I shall waste,
And ended is that we begun.
Now is this song both sung and past;
My lute, be still, for I have done.

23–24 think not . . . plain: Do not think that you alone under the sun will escape unrevenged for causing your lovers to lament.

30 list: likes; wishes.

Thinking Through the Literature

1. **Comprehension Check** What has happened between the speaker and the subject of the poem?
2. What is your impression of this poem?
3. How would you describe the speaker's attitude toward the woman who is the subject of the poem?
4. If the speaker's wishes came true, what do you think would happen to the woman? Explain your answer.
5. Do you think the speaker is sincere when he says "I have done"? Why or why not?

Customizing Instruction

Less Proficient Readers

Have students discuss briefly the feelings that might be expressed in a poem written by a rejected lover. Encourage students to jot down some of their ideas and look for them as they read each poem. Students may compare their ideas to the ideas expressed in each poem.

Students Acquiring English

Point out some of the similes in the poems and discuss possible meanings: the comparison of the woman's rejection of the speaker and the rock's repulsion of the waves in lines 11–13 of "My Lute, Awake!"

 Use **Spanish Study Guide** for additional support, pp. 49–51

Gifted and Talented

Ask students to compare how the speaker in each poem reacts to rejection. What do their reactions suggest about their social and political positions and the social and political positions of their respective loved ones?

Possible Response: Wyatt describes his beloved and is obviously surprised by her rejection. The woman is probably of his same social class. Elizabeth I does not describe her lover and leads the reader to think that acknowledgment is not possible because he is beneath her socially and politically.

✓ Assessment Standardized Test Practice

IDENTIFYING MEANINGS Since many English Renaissance lyric poems were written to be sung as songs, the regular repetition of a refrain, word, or line was common. Sometimes the repeated words or lines were presented in contexts that changed their meaning. Ask students to examine the repetition of "I have done" in the last line of every stanza in "My Lute, Awake!" and identify at least two different meanings "I have done" could have. Remind students to refer to specific lines from the poem in their answers.

RUBRIC

3 Full Accomplishment Student accurately identifies two different meanings of repeated phrase within context of poem and refers to specific lines from poem for support.

2 Substantial Accomplishment Student accurately identifies two meanings of phrase but does not provide specific support from poem.

1 Little or Partial Accomplishment Student shows little understanding of meaning of poem.

Reading and Analyzing

Literary Analysis RHYME SCHEME

A Have students identify the rhyme scheme of the poem.

Answer: ababcc.

Literary Analysis: SIMILE

B **Simile** is a figure of speech, generally using *like* or *as,* that compares two dissimilar things that have something in common. Point out examples of similes in "On Monsieur's Departure" and discuss them with students before reading the poem. Line 7 contains one example: "My care is like my shadow in the sun."

Active Reading

CLARIFYING MEANING

As students read the poem, have them paraphrase each sentence to clarify the poem's meaning. Then have them compare their paraphrased sentences to those in the poem. Ask the following questions:

- What are the differences between the sentences?
- How does this strategy help you understand the poem's message?

Possible Response: The paraphrased sentences are more straightforward and use contemporary language. In order to paraphrase, students need to understand the meaning of the poem.

ELIZABETH I

On Monsieur's Departure

Young Elizabeth

I grieve and dare not show my discontent,
I love and yet am forced to seem to hate,
I do, yet dare not say I ever meant,
I seem stark mute but inwardly do prate.
I am and not, I freeze and yet am burned,
Since from myself another self I turned. A

B My care is like my shadow in the sun,
Follows me flying, flies when I pursue it,
Stands and lies by me, doth what I have done.
His too familiar care doth make me rue it.
No means I find to rid him from my breast,
Till by the end of things it be suppressed.

Some gentler passion slide into my mind,
For I am soft and made of melting snow;
Or be more cruel, love, and so be kind.
Let me or float or sink, be high or low.
Or let me live with some more sweet content,
Or die and so forget what love ere meant.

4 prate: chatter.

6 another self: The man referred to in this poem is thought by some to be a French duke who had been involved in negotiations for marriage to Elizabeth; by others, to be the earl of Essex, a favorite courtier of Elizabeth's who was executed for treason in 1601.

7 care: sorrow.

9 doth . . . done: does all that I do.

10 his too familiar care . . . it: His too easy and superficial sorrow makes me regret my own feelings of sorrow.

286 UNIT TWO PART 1: ASPECTS OF LOVE

Teaching Options

Grammar

PREPOSITIONAL PHRASES

Instruction A prepositional phrase includes a preposition, its object, and any modifiers of the object that are part of the phrase. Prepositional phrases can function as adjectives or adverbs. Adjective phrases modify nouns or pronouns. Adverb phrases modify verbs, adjectives, or other adverbs; they tell where, when, how, why, or to what extent.

Activity Write the following sentence on the chalkboard.

"No means I find to rid him from my breast,
Till by the end of things it be suppressed."

Underline the prepositional phrases as shown. Have students identify the types of prepositional phrases and the word or words that each modifies. *(adverb, rid; adjective, end)* Point out that the adverb phrase *from my breast* tells where, and the adjective phrase *of things* modifies *end,* the object of a prepositional phrase.

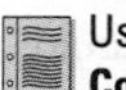

Use **Grammar Transparencies and Copymasters,** p. 83.

Use McDougal Littell's ***Language Network*** for more instruction and practice in prepositional phrases.

Connect to the Literature

1. **What Do You Think?** Do you feel sympathy for the speaker of "On Monsieur's Departure"? Why or why not?

Comprehension Check
- How does the speaker in "On Monsieur's Departure" feel about the man she refers to?
- How does the speaker hope to conquer her painful emotions?

Think Critically

2. What **conflicts** does the speaker in "On Monsieur's Departure" seem to be experiencing?

   THINK ABOUT
   - the contrasts she presents in lines 1–5
   - what she says in line 6
   - the references to her care and "his too familiar care"

3. Do you think the **speaker** is responsible for the situation she finds herself in? Why or why not?
4. How would you explain the speaker's wish in the last stanza?
5. How does knowing that this poem was written by Queen Elizabeth I affect your interpretation of it?
6. ACTIVE READING CLARIFYING MEANING Choose two lines that you paraphrased in your READER'S NOTEBOOK as you read the poems. Compare your paraphrase with that of a classmate. What additional understanding did you gain through comparing your work?

Extend Interpretations

7. **Comparing Texts** Compare the portrayals of unrequited love in "My Lute, Awake!" and "On Monsieur's Departure." Think about the attitudes and actions of the man and the woman in each poem, the **tone** of each poem, and the traditional portrayal of unrequited love in courtly-love poetry.
8. **Connect to Life** How is unrequited love portrayed in literature and film today? How do modern **characters** react when they are rejected?

Literary Analysis

RHYME SCHEME The pattern of end rhyme in a poem determines the poem's **rhyme scheme.** The rhyme scheme is charted by assigning a letter of the alphabet, beginning with *a*, to each line. Lines that rhyme are given the same letter. Notice that in "My Lute, Awake!," for example, the rhyme scheme of each stanza is *aabab.*

Proud of the spoil that thou hast got *a*
Of simple hearts, thorough love's shot; *a*
By whom, unkind, thou hast them won, *b*
Think not he hath his bow forgot, *a*
Although my lute and I have done. *b*

Be aware, however, that the rhyme may not always be exact. In the first stanza of "My Lute, Awake!" the word waste is meant to rhyme with last and past.

Paired Activity Working with a partner, use the letters *a, b,* and *c* to chart the rhyme scheme of the stanzas of "On Monsieur's Departure."

GUIDING STUDENT RESPONSE

Connect to the Literature

1. **What Do You Think?**
   Guidelines for student response: Accept all reasonable responses. Students might think of other situations involving separation in order to gain insight into the emotions experienced by the speaker of the poem.

Comprehension Check
- The speaker was in love with the man about whom the poem is written, but apparently cannot express her love due to political responsibilities, class differences, or other circumstances beyond her control.
- The speaker hopes to replace her feelings with some less painful, milder emotions or forget them through death.

Think Critically

2. Possible Responses: public duties vs. private concerns, outer strength vs. true feelings, warm emotions vs. coldness
3. Some students may feel that she was forced to reject her suitor because of political responsibilities or other factors beyond her control; others may interpret line 6 to mean that rejecting him was a personal decision that she now questions.
4. Possible Responses: She wants her unsettled feelings to be soothed; she exaggerates her desire for calm to stress her turmoil.
5. Possible Response: It helps explain the conflict between public show and private feelings and the possible reasons for the rejection of the suitor.
6. Responses will vary.

Literary Analysis

Paired Activity The rhyme scheme is *ababcc.* If students wished to plot out the whole poem, the rhyme scheme would be as follows: *dedeff / ghghaa.*

Extend Interpretations

Comparing Texts Possible response: Both speakers suffer great unhappiness for their lost loves. Wyatt's speaker is bitter and vengeful and places all blame on his beloved; Elizabeth's speaker agonizes and indicates that she has done the rejecting.

Connect to Life Responses will vary. Students should cite examples from current books and films to support their answers.

Writing Options

Letter from a Queen Accept all reasonable responses. Students' letters should contain detailed references to Wyatt's poem.

Activities & Explorations

Mood Music Before students listen to the recordings, encourage them to determine what mood their chosen poem creates and what instruments or sounds would best reflect that mood.

Choices & CHALLENGES

Writing Options

Letter from a Queen Imagine that you are Elizabeth I and have just read "My Lute, Awake!" Write a letter to a friend, expressing your reaction to Wyatt's poem.

Activities & Explorations

Mood Music Listen to some recordings of Renaissance music, both vocal and instrumental. Select a group of pieces that you think reflect the mood of either "My Lute, Awake!" or "On Monsieur's Departure." Then make a tape recording of the pieces and play it for the class. Explain your choices, and ask for feedback from your classmates.
~ **MUSIC**

Sir Thomas Wyatt
1503–1542

Other Works
"Whoso List to Hunt"
"Blame Not My Lute"
"My Galley Charged with Forgetfulness"

At the King's Service As a courtier and diplomat for Henry VIII, Sir Thomas Wyatt was alternately in and out of favor with the whimsical king. Henry ordered Wyatt imprisoned twice, once for quarreling with a duke and once for treason, both times threatening him with execution. Each time, however, Wyatt was pardoned and accepted back into the king's service.

Lyrics for the Lute A skilled musician and amateur poet, Wyatt wrote lyrics in his leisure time to amuse himself and other courtiers. As was usual during the Renaissance, his poems were circulated privately, and only a few were published during his lifetime. Critical opinion of Wyatt's poems varies—some think their rhythm too irregular and rough, while others consider them fresh and vigorous. Most critics agree, however, that his most inventive work is to be found in the songs he wrote for lute accompaniment and that his introduction of the Italian sonnet form into English was a significant contribution to English literature.

Elizabeth I
1533–1603

Other Works
"The Doubt of Future Foes"
"Speech to the Troops at Tilbury"

Lonely Childhood Elizabeth I, daughter of King Henry VIII and Anne Boleyn, had an unsettling and probably lonely childhood. Her father, hoping for a male heir, was disappointed at Elizabeth's birth and two years later ordered her mother executed, supposedly for treason. Despite his bitterness at not having a son, Henry provided Elizabeth with the rigorous education normally given only to boys. She learned Latin, Greek, French, Italian, history, and theology, and her literary output includes speeches, translations, and a small collection of poems focusing on events in her personal life.

Glorious Reign Elizabeth ascended the throne in 1558 and ruled for 45 years. Her reign was a glorious period in English history, a time of great prosperity, artistic achievement, and international prestige. Although she considered a number of marriage proposals, Elizabeth rejected all of them, ignoring the advisers who hoped she would marry and provide an heir to the throne.

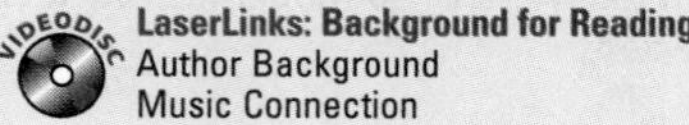

LaserLinks: Background for Reading
Author Background
Music Connection

The Passionate Shepherd to His Love

Poetry by CHRISTOPHER MARLOWE

The Nymph's Reply to the Shepherd

Poetry by SIR WALTER RALEIGH

Connect to Your Life

Imagining Paradise Close your eyes and think of a beautiful place you have visited. What images make up your mental picture of the place? Create a cluster diagram similar to the one shown, identifying the place in the center oval and surrounding it with words and phrases that describe the images you associate with the place. Which of your images do you consider realistic? Which would you describe as romantic or idealized?

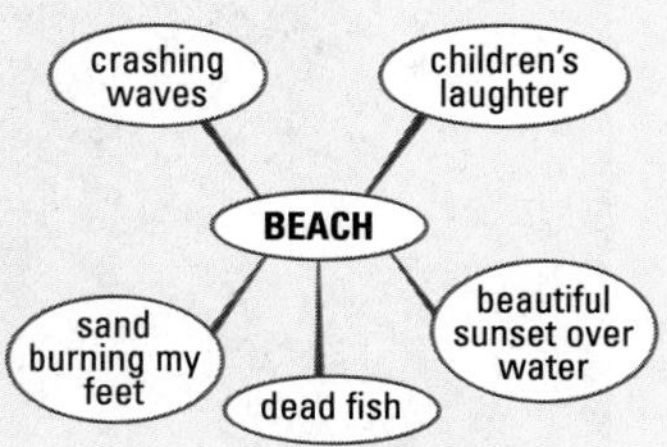

Build Background

Renaissance Poetry The Renaissance was a time in which knowledge and skills were cultivated in a broad range of fields, from music, art, and literature to science and athletics. According to writers of the time, the ideal "Renaissance man" should develop himself in every possible way.

Included in the ranks of the true Renaissance men were two kindred spirits, Christopher Marlowe and Sir Walter Raleigh. During his short life, Marlowe studied religion, became a talented and recognized poet and playwright, conducted secret government business, and engaged in philosophical discussions with his friend Raleigh. As a statesman, writer, soldier, scientist, adventurer, and explorer, Raleigh lived a life of action as well as contemplation.

Marlowe's poem "The Passionate Shepherd to His Love" became so famous that other poets wrote responses to it. The most notable of these is "The Nymph's Reply to the Shepherd," written by Raleigh. Together, the two poems enact a debate about the realities of love.

LaserLinks: Background for Reading
Cultural/Biographical Connection

Focus Your Reading

LITERARY ANALYSIS **PASTORAL** Renaissance poets used **pastorals** to convey their own thoughts and feelings about love and other subjects. A pastoral is a poem presenting shepherds in rural settings that are usually idealized. Notice the images from a country setting in the following lines:

And we will sit upon the rocks,
Seeing the shepherds feed their flocks.

As you read these poems, notice examples of pastoral life involving shepherds and their rural existence.

ACTIVE READING **COMPARING SPEAKERS IN POETRY** The two speakers in these poems—the shepherd and the nymph—have very different perspectives on the topic of love. To identify the differences, consider the following:

- each speaker's choice of words when addressing the other person
- evidence of each speaker's motivation
- each speaker's attitude about life

READER'S NOTEBOOK As you read these poems, jot down details that point out the differences between the two speakers on the subject of romantic love.

LESSON RESOURCES

UNIT TWO RESOURCE BOOK, pp. 6–7

ASSESSMENT RESOURCES
Formal Assessment, p. 43
Teacher's Guide to Assessment and Portfolio Use
Test Generator

SKILLS TRANSPARENCIES AND COPYMASTERS
Reading and Critical Thinking
- Compare and Contrast, T15 (for Active Reading, p. 289)

Grammar
- Diagramming Complements and Appositives, T59 (for Mini Lesson, p. 292)
- Appositives, C95 (for Mini Lesson, p. 292)

Vocabulary
- Word Origins, C32 (for Mini Lesson, p. 291)

Writing
- Identifying Writing Variables, T2 (for Informal Assessment, p. 294)

Communications
- Impromptu Speaking: Dialogue, Role-Play, T14 (for Activities & Explorations 1, p. 294)

INTEGRATED TECHNOLOGY
Audio Library
LaserLinks
- Cultural/Biographical Connection: Sir Walter Raleigh
- Literary Connection: Pastorals. See **Teacher's SourceBook,** pp. 21–22.

Visit our website:
www.mcdougallittell.com

OVERVIEW

Objectives

1. understand and appreciate two **pastoral** poems **(Literary Analysis)**
2. use strategies for **comparing speakers** in poetry **(Active Reading)**

Summary

"The Passionate Shepherd to His Love" extols the virtues of country life and idealizes the world of nature. The shepherd pleads with his love (the shepherdess) to live a life filled with eternal spring, happiness, and pleasure.

"The Nymph's Reply to the Shepherd" is more practical. The nymph has a better grasp of reality and is skeptical of the shepherd's flowery promises. The nymph thinks that love based on beauty and youth will wither and die, and she turns down the shepherd's proposal.

Thematic Link

These two poems exemplify different aspects of love. The shepherd is idealistic and full of hope about love. The nymph, however, believes that pleasures and spring are not eternal, and neither is love that is based on these ideals.

5-Minute Warm-Up

Daily Language SkillBuilder

Have students **proofread** the display sentences on page 273k and write them correctly. The sentences also appear on Transparency 6 of **Grammar Transparencies and Copymasters.**

TEACHING THE LITERATURE

Reading and Analyzing

Literary Analysis PASTORAL
Pastoral is a conventional form of lyric poetry that presents an idealized picture of nature and rural life. Ask students what overall picture of rural life is conveyed by the "The Passionate Shepherd to His Love."
Possible Response: simple, beautiful, pleasant, idealized.

 Use **Unit Two Resource Book,** p. 7 for more exercises.

Active Reading
COMPARING SPEAKERS IN POETRY
Have students note key words and phrases that portray the shepherd's view of love. Remind students to keep their notes to compare the shepherd's point of view to the nymph's.

 Use **Unit Two Resource Book,** p. 60 for more practice.

Literary Analysis: ALLITERATION
A Alliteration is the repetition of consonant sounds at the beginning of words. Alliteration can create mood and reinforce meaning. Have students find examples of alliteration in lines 17–20.
Answer: b in line 17, c in line 18, th and m in line 19, l in line 20.

Thinking Through the Literature

1. Accept all reasonable responses.
2. Possible Responses: not very serious, as so many details are fanciful; serious in wanting to give his love the best of everything.
3. Possible Response: because the natural images are so romantic.

Christopher Marlowe

THE PASSIONATE SHEPHERD *to* HIS LOVE

The Hireling Shepherd (1851), William Holman Hunt. Manchester (U.K.) City Art Gallery/A.K.G., Berlin/Superstock.

Come live with me and be my love,
And we will all the pleasures prove
That valleys, groves, hills, and fields,
Woods, or steepy mountain yields.

And we will sit upon the rocks,
Seeing the shepherds feed their flocks,
By shallow rivers to whose falls
Melodious birds sing madrigals.

2 prove: experience.

8 madrigals: songs of a type popular during the Renaissance.

Teaching Options

Viewing and Representing

The Hireling Shepherd **by William Holman Hunt**

ART APPRECIATION In this painting, Hunt (1827–1910) sought to portray a real pair of working people against a realistic landscape.
Instruction Discuss with students the relationship of tone in art and music with tone in poetry. Have students share what they know about artistic styles such as Impressionism and Romanticism.
Possible Response Impressionists concentrated on the realism of light and color rather than realism of form; they sought to reproduce the actual impression an object made on their eyes. Romantics emphasized emotion rather than intellect and subjective rather than objective visions. They felt free to invent their own dream worlds.
Application Have students discuss and compare their impressions of *The Hireling Shepherd.* Ask students to decide: Do you find the painting realistic or idealistic; impressionistic or romantic? Have students use multiple sources to research this or another painting of their choice to see how closely their impressions of the painting matched the artist's intentions. What impression did the artist hope to evoke.

And I will make thee beds of roses
And a thousand fragrant posies,
A cap of flowers, and a kirtle
Embroidered all with leaves of myrtle;

A gown made of the finest wool
Which from our pretty lambs we pull;
Fair lined slippers for the cold,
With buckles of the purest gold;

A
A belt of straw and ivy buds,
With coral clasps and amber studs:
And if these pleasures may thee move,
Come live with me, and be my love.

The shepherds' swains shall dance and sing
For thy delight each May morning:
If these delights thy mind may move,
Then live with me and be my love.

11 kirtle: skirt.

21 swains: youths.

Thinking Through the Literature

1. What is your opinion of the gifts that the shepherd offers to his beloved?
2. How serious or realistic do you think the shepherd's offer is?
   THINK ABOUT
   - the way he describes the setting
   - the gifts he promises
3. Why do you think Marlowe chose the setting described in the poem?

Customizing Instruction

Less Proficient Readers

Provide students with copies of the two poems side by side so that students can compare and contrast the poems line by line. The poems have the same number of lines with the same number of syllables per line; Raleigh repeats some of Marlowe's language in each stanza. The different attitudes about love expressed by the speakers will become apparent in a line-by-line comparison.

Students Acquiring English

Help students understand the meanings of *groves* (line 3), *myrtle* (line 12), and *coral* and *amber* (line 18) in "The Passionate Shepherd to His Love."

Answer: groves, "small forests"; myrtle, "a type of shrub"; coral, "a marine creature that secretes a rocklike skeleton"; amber, "a hard, translucent fossil resin." Showing students pictures may be the most effective way of defining these words.

Use **Spanish Study Guide** for additional support, pp. 52–54

Multiple Learning Styles

Visual/Kinesthetic Learners

Have visual learners use a Venn diagram to compare the two poems. Elements such as speaker, main point, and tone could be included in each circle. Students should include similarities between the poems in the overlapping area of the diagram.

Mini Lesson

Vocabulary Strategy

ORIGINS OF THE WORD *PASTORAL*

Instruction Explain that pastoral poems are songlike poems that praise the pleasures of a simple country life. The word *pastoral* means "rural" and "having to do with the rustic life of shepherds." *Pastoral* also refers to a pastor and his work. The pastoral epistles addressed to Timothy and Titus in the New Testament are so called because they deal with pastorship. The concept of *pastoral* also applies to painting (shepherds in idealized rustic scenes) and music (pastorale—an opera or other vocal composition based on a rural theme or subject; pastoral—an instrumental composition with a tender melody in a moderately slow rhythm suggestive of idyllic rural life).

Activity Have students research and write a definition of *pastoral* as used in either poetry, music, or art. Students should be able to share with the class at least two examples of the genre.

Use **Vocabulary Transparencies and Copymasters,** p. 15.

Reading and Analyzing

Active Reading

COMPARING SPEAKERS IN POETRY

A Ask students what line 2 implies about the nymph's attitude toward Marlowe's shepherd.

Possible Response: She thinks he may be dishonest.

Have students refer to the notes they took when reading Marlowe's poem. What do the speakers imply about their feelings toward the idea of love?

Possible Response: The shepherd is in love with the idea of love; the nymph is more practical and realizes that love based solely on beauty and youth will not last.

Literary Analysis: ALLITERATION

B Ask students to find examples of alliteration in lines 9–12.

Answer: f in line 9, w in line 10, h in line 11, f and s in line 12.

Literary Analysis PASTORAL

C Ask students which aspect of the ideal rural life the nymph rebuts in her reply to the shepherd.

Possible Response: The shepherd talks only of May and the beauty of spring. The nymph enjoys spring but reminds the shepherd that winter can be very difficult and that living in the country is hard work.

Sir Walter Raleigh

The Nymph's Reply *to* the Shepherd

A

If all the world and love were young,
And truth in every shepherd's tongue,
These pretty pleasures might me move
To live with thee and be thy love.

Time drives the flocks from field to fold
When rivers rage and rocks grow cold,
And Philomel becometh dumb;
The rest complains of cares to come.

B

The flowers do fade, and wanton fields
To wayward winter reckoning yields;
A honey tongue, a heart of gall,
Is fancy's spring, but sorrow's fall.

Thy gowns, thy shoes, thy beds of roses,
Thy cap, thy kirtle, and thy posies
Soon break, soon wither, soon forgotten—
In folly ripe, in reason rotten.

Thy belt of straw and ivy buds,
Thy coral clasps and amber studs,
All these in me no means can move
To come to thee and be thy love.

C

But could youth last and love still breed,
Had joys no date nor age no need,
Then these delights my mind might move
To live with thee and be thy love.

5 fold: a pen for animals, especially sheep.

7 Philomel: the nightingale; **dumb:** silent.

9 wanton: producing abundant crops; luxuriant.

22 date: ending.

Teaching Options

Grammar

APPOSITIVES AND APPOSITIVE PHRASES

Instruction An appositive is a noun or a pronoun that provides added detail about the word. When the appositive has modifiers, such as a word, phrase, or clause, then the appositive and all the modifiers are called an appositive phrase.

Activity Write these lines on the chalkboard.

"Thy belt of straw and ivy buds,
Thy coral clasps and amber studs,
All these in me no means can move
To come to thee and be thy love."

Underline the word *All* in the passage. Ask students what the pronoun *all* refers to in that passage. *(belt, clasps, studs)* Point out that here the appositive comes before the pronoun for which it provides detail.

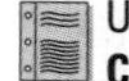

Use **Grammar Transparencies and Copymasters,** p. 95.

Use McDougal Littell's ***Language Network*** for more instruction in appositives.

Connect to the Literature

1. **What Do You Think?** Were you surprised by the nymph's response in "The Nymph's Reply to the Shepherd"? Share your thoughts with a classmate.

Comprehension Check

- What images in Marlowe's poem are repeated in Raleigh's poem?
- Does the nymph in Raleigh's poem agree or disagree with the shepherd's arguments in Marlowe's poem?

Think Critically

2. How would you describe the nymph's attitude toward life?

- the connection she makes between youth and love
- her descriptions of the effects of time

3. Do you agree with the nymph's reasons for not accepting the shepherd's offer? Why or why not?

4. On the basis of the first and last **stanzas,** what do you think might convince the nymph to accept the shepherd's offer?

5. **ACTIVE READING** **COMPARING SPEAKERS IN POETRY** Look back at the details you noted in your READER'S NOTEBOOK about the speakers' perspectives. What is the debate between the two **speakers** of these poems all about? Which of the two speakers' attitudes is closer to your own attitude?

Extend Interpretations

6. **Comparing Texts** Who do you think would be more likely to share the shepherd's attitude toward love—the speaker of Wyatt's "My Lute, Awake!" or the speaker of Elizabeth I's "On Monsieur's Departure"? Explain your opinion.

7. **Connect to Life** Think about the different ways love is depicted in current music. Do these depictions usually reflect a romantic or realistic view of love?

Literary Analysis

PASTORAL A **pastoral** is a poem presenting shepherds in rural settings, usually in an idealized manner. The style of pastorals may seem unnatural, since the supposedly simple, rustic characters tend to use very formal, courtly language; however, Renaissance poets were drawn to this form not as a means of accurately portraying rustic life but as a means of conveying their own emotions and ideas in an artistic way. Marlowe's "The Passionate Shepherd to His Love" is a perfect example of a pastoral.

Paired Activity With a partner, decide on the **mood** that the pastoral evokes in you. What are the details that the poet provides to create a pastoral feeling or atmosphere? How do these details help to create the mood? Use a chart like the one below to organize your ideas. Compare your findings with those of your classmates.

	Details	Mood
"The Passionate Shepherd to His Love"		
"The Nymph's Reply to the Shepherd"		

GUIDING STUDENT RESPONSE

Connect to the Literature

1. **What Do You Think?**
Guidelines for student response: Accept all reasonable responses. If students were surprised, ask them to explain what response they expected from the nymph.

Comprehension Check

- Raleigh repeats "to live with thee, and be thy love" in the first, fifth, and last stanzas which is where Marlowe repeats "come live with me, and be my love." Raleigh also talks about the flocks and rocks, the belt of straw, ivy buds, coral clasps, and amber studs where Marlowe does in stanzas two and five.
- The nymph disagrees with the shepherd's arguments. She seems to think that the shepherd is impractical.

Think Critically

2. Possible Responses: realistic, unsentimental, cynical
3. Students who agree may find the offer too rosy or dishonest. Those who disagree may believe that the nymph is too cynical or feel that her attitude discourages love.
4. Possible Response: a more realistic or honest approach
5. The speakers are debating the nature of love. The shepherd offers a life of pleasures, eternal spring, and happiness. The nymph is more practical and thinks that love will fade just as spring and summer fade into winter and just as youth and beauty fade.

Literary Analysis

Paired Activity You might display charts made by students in the classroom, or you might ask volunteers to read the details and moods they have recorded on their chart to the rest of the class.

Extend Interpretations

Comparing Texts Accept all reasonable answers. One possible answer would be that the speaker of "On Monsieur's Departure" would be more likely to agree with the shepherd because the speaker of "My Lute, Awake!" is very bitter and angry about love.

Connect to Life Accept all reasonable answers. Ask students to give examples from contemporary music to support their opinions.

Writing Options

A Modern Parody Before students begin, have them identify the poem's rhyme scheme *(aabb)* and describe the regular rhythm, or meter, in terms of beats or stressed syllables per line (four). Encourage students to develop a tone that is appropriate to the speaker. Each poem should also refer to some of the items the speaker would use in his or her job.

Activities & Explorations

1. **Telephone Dialogue** Tell students to use contemporary English and modern references but to express sentiments and ideas similar to those in the two poems.
2. **Drawing Shepherds and Nymphs** You might make this a cooperative activity in which you pair students who have an art background with those who do not and have them both contribute to the drawing or painting.

Choices & CHALLENGES

Writing Options

A Modern Parody Write a parody, or humorous imitation, of "The Passionate Shepherd to His Love." In place of the shepherd, substitute a person with a different job (for example, an accountant, a truck driver, a plumber, or a chef) and select an appropriate setting. Place the parody in your **Working Portfolio.**

Activities & Explorations

1. **Telephone Dialogue** With a partner, act out a modern phone conversation in which the shepherd tries to persuade the nymph to accept his offer. ~ **SPEAKING AND LISTENING**
2. **Drawing Shepherds and Nymphs** Create a single drawing or painting that depicts the contrasting scenes described in the two poems. ~ **ART**

Christopher Marlowe
1564–1593

Other Works
The Tragedy of Dido, Queen of Carthage
Edward II
Hero and Leander

Talent and Intrigue Christopher Marlowe is best remembered for writing plays in which his use of what Ben Jonson dubbed his "mighty line," or blank verse, transformed the British theater. The son of a shoemaker, Marlowe attended Cambridge University on a scholarship but was almost denied his master's degree because he was suspected of conspiring against the queen. A letter from the queen's Privy Council excused the young man, hinting that he was active in Elizabeth's secret service.

Brief but Influential Life Marlowe wrote his first successful play, *Tamburlaine the Great,* at the age of 23. He lived only six more years but wrote five plays during that time, including *The Jew of Malta* and *Dr. Faustus,* works that would profoundly influence the development of Elizabethan drama. Like his friend Sir Walter Raleigh, Marlowe was a freethinker who was suspected of treasonous and antichurch sentiment. In 1593, at the age of 29, Marlowe was murdered in a tavern, allegedly during an argument over the bill.

Sir Walter Raleigh
1552?–1618

Other Works
"Epitaph of Sir Philip Sidney"
The History of the World

An Active Life Sir Walter Raleigh was a man of action and intellect. He attended Oxford University, studied law, and was widely read in chemistry, mathematics, and medicine. He also wrote history and poetry. By helping to quell an Irish rebellion in 1580, he won the affection of Queen Elizabeth. As the queen's favorite, he was granted land, made a vice-admiral, knighted, and appointed governor of Jersey, an island in the English Channel.

Exploration and Imprisonment Raleigh fell out of favor with the queen in 1592 but continued to pursue ambitious projects. Among his activities were the establishment of the short-lived Roanoke colony in North America and the leading of an expedition to South America in search of gold. In 1603, during the reign of James I, he was charged with treason and imprisoned for 13 years. Afterward, Raleigh led another expedition to South America but fell into disfavor once again when his soldiers burned a local settlement. On his return to London, he was imprisoned and executed.

LaserLinks: Background for Reading
Literary Connection

Teaching Options

Assessment Informal Assessment

ANALYZING PASTORALS Pastoral poems can be analyzed in the areas of tone, setting, characterization, language devices, and musical/tonal qualities. Have students list aspects of each quality and cite examples from "The Passionate Shepherd to His Love" and "The Nymph's Reply to the Shepherd." Then have students write a definition of pastoral poems using at least four of the qualities listed here and giving examples from the poems.

RUBRIC

3 Full Accomplishment Student writes accurate definition of pastoral poems using four qualities of pastoral and giving evidence from poems.

2 Substantial Accomplishment Student writes accurate definition of pastoral poems using qualities of pastoral but fails to provide support from poems.

1 Little or Partial Accomplishment Student shows little understanding of definition of pastoral poems.

Sonnet Form

Origins of the Sonnet

A **sonnet** is a 14-line lyric poem with a complicated rhyme scheme and a defined structure. Because of the technical skill required to write a sonnet, the form has challenged English poets ever since it was introduced into England almost 500 years ago.

The sonnet originated in Italy in the 13th century (the word *sonnet* comes from the Italian for "little song"). The great Italian poet Petrarch (1304–1374) perfected the **Italian sonnet**, which is often called the **Petrarchan sonnet** in his honor. Petrarch felt that the sonnet, with its brevity and musical rhymes, was a perfect medium for the expression of emotion, especially love. Although the Italian sonneteers did not restrict themselves to love as a subject, Petrarch wrote over 300 sonnets detailing his devotion to a beautiful but unobtainable lady, whom he called Laura.

The English Sonnet Develops

The story of the English sonnet begins, not surprisingly, with another lovelorn poet, Sir Thomas Wyatt (1503–1542). A diplomat in the court of King Henry VIII, Wyatt was rumored to be in love with the ill-fated queen Anne Boleyn. In the 1530s, Wyatt translated some of Petrarch's love sonnets and wrote a few of his own in a slight modification of the Italian form. By this time, the Renaissance had at last reached England, accompanied by an awakening of interest in Italian literature. Henry VIII, although brutal to his wives, encouraged the poetry of courtly love and so welcomed the sonnet as a poetic form. Another English poet who deserves credit for popularizing the sonnet in England is Henry Howard, earl of Surrey (1517–1547). Building on Wyatt's modifications, Surrey changed the rhyme scheme of the sonnet to adapt it to the rhyme-poor English language. Surrey's innovations distinguished the English sonnet from the Italian sonnet. The English form ultimately became known as the **Shakespearean sonnet** because William Shakespeare used it with such distinction.

By 1609, when Shakespeare's sonnets were published, the conventions of love sonnets had been firmly established, most notably by Sir Philip Sidney's *Astrophel and Stella* (1591) and Edmund Spenser's *Amoretti* (1595). Surrey's rhyme scheme allowed Shakespeare more freedom in his versification, and he used this freedom to expand sonnet conventions. In some of his sonnets, for example, the object of the speaker's affection is not a divinely beautiful woman but one with all-too-human defects. Instead of limiting himself to the subject of love, he introduced deep philosophical issues and perplexing ironies. Because of his mastery of the sonnet's form and broadening of its content, Shakespeare remains the undisputed master of the English sonnet.

What Makes a Poem a Sonnet?	
Length	14 lines
Subject(s)	a lyrical nature—a focus on personal feelings and thoughts
Meter	iambic pentameter lines (lines containing five metrical units, each consisting of an unstressed syllable followed by a stressed syllable)
Structure and rhyme scheme	a particular structure and rhyme scheme, Petrarchan or Shakespearean (that of the sonnet or another variation)

LEARNING the Language of LITERATURE

OVERVIEW

Objectives

- understand the following literary terms:
  - Sonnet
  - Octave
  - Sestet
  - Quatrain
  - Couplet
- appreciate shared characteristics of literature across cultures.
- recognize themes across cultures.

Teaching the Lesson

As they read the literature in Unit 2, students will encounter sonnets. This lesson will give them some background on the sonnet as a literary form.

Introducing the Concepts

Few contemporary poets use the sonnet form. However, today's pop songs are filled with lyrics concerning love and other personal feelings. Although the form may have changed from that of the sonnet, the popularity of lyrics expressing deep emotions has not. As students read the sonnets in this unit, have them consider the following questions:

What themes do these sonnets have in common with modern love songs or poems?

What images in these sonnets are also found in modern love songs or poems?

Presenting the Concepts

Read aloud or project a transparency of the Strategies for Reading on page 296. To introduce the first sonnet in the unit, project or write on the chalkboard Spenser's sonnet. Have students note the characteristics present in the sonnet. Model how to use the strategies to analyze a poem.

Making Connections

Sonnets Across Cultures

The sonnet form was developed in Italy during the 13th century and was used extensively during the Renaissance. The sonnet then spread to many other countries. Share with students the history of poetry and the sonnet in these countries.

Japan

In 1882, the publication of some English and American poems translated into Japanese, including a few by Shakespeare, provided writers in Japan with new literary models. As a result, some of these Japanese writers adopted Western literary forms, including the sonnet.

Spain

The poetry of Spain during the Renaissance was heavily influenced by Italian writers. The great Spanish poet Garcilaso de la Vega adopted Italian forms, including the sonnet, which came to be the dominant form of Spanish poetry of the time. Unlike Italian sonnets, however, some Spanish sonnets had religious themes.

Chile

In the 20th century, the sonnet flourished in Chile. The Nobel Prize-winning Chilean poet Pablo Neruda (1904–1973) wrote in many different forms, including the sonnet. One of Neruda's books of poetry is titled *One Hundred Love Sonnets (Cien sonnetos de amor).*

Sonnet Structure

The Petrarchan Form What distinguishes the Italian sonnet is its two-part structure: an **octave** (the first eight lines), usually rhyming *abbaabba,* followed by a **sestet** (the last six lines) with the rhyme scheme *cdcdcd* or *cdecde*. Typically, the octave establishes the speaker's situation, and the sestet resolves, draws conclusions about, or expresses a reaction to that situation. The Petrarchan sonnet has been called "organic" in its unity—like an acorn in its cup, the octave and sestet fit together perfectly. Unity is also produced by the rhyme scheme, which involves only four or five different rhyming sounds. The resulting need for many rhyming words makes the Petrarchan sonnet difficult to write in English. Still, plenty of English poets have written them, including John Milton, William Wordsworth, and John Keats to name just a few.

The Shakespearean Form The English sonnet is divided into three **quatrains** (groups of four lines) and a rhyming **couplet** (two lines).

Generally, the first quatrain introduces a situation, which is explored in the next two quatrains.

Often, a turn, or shift in thought, occurs at the third quatrain or at the couplet.

The couplet resolves the situation. The rhyme scheme follows the pattern: *abab cdcd efef gg.*

That time of year thou mayst in me behold
When yellow leaves, or none, or few, do hang
Upon those boughs which shake against the cold,
Bare ruined choirs, where late the sweet birds sang.
In me thou see'st the twilight of such day
As after sunset fadeth in the west;
Which by and by black night doth take away,
Death's second self, that seals up all in rest.
In me thou see'st the glowing of such fire,
That on the ashes of his youth doth lie,
As the deathbed whereon it must expire,
Consumed with that which it was nourished by.
This thou perceiv'st, which makes thy love more strong,
To love that well which thou must leave ere long.

—Shakespeare, *Sonnet 73*

Notice that each quatrain elaborates on a particular image: autumn in the first quatrain, twilight in the second, and the embers of a fire in the third. The final couplet is a concise statement that pulls the sonnet together by shedding new light on the situation developed in the three quatrains. Think of the closing couplet in a Shakespearean sonnet as a "punch line" that gives meaning to the whole.

Strategies for Reading: Sonnet Form

1. Read the sonnet several times.
2. Use letters to label like-sounding words at the end of lines.
3. Identify the major units of thought or feeling.
4. Describe the situation introduced in the first part of the sonnet.
5. Paraphrase the speaker's final resolution of, conclusions about, or reaction to the situation.
6. Study the imagery and figurative language for clues to the emotions expressed.
7. **Monitor** your reading strategies and modify them when your understanding breaks down. Remember to use your Strategies for Active Reading: **predict, visualize, connect, question, clarify,** and **evaluate.**

Sonnet 30 / Sonnet 75

Poetry by EDMUND SPENSER

Comparing Literature of the World

Sonnets of Spenser, Shakespeare, and Petrarch

This lesson and the two that follow present an opportunity for you to compare the work of three sonnet masters: Spenser, Shakespeare, and Petrarch. Specific points of comparison contained in these lessons will help you understand the similarities and differences among sonnet forms and themes.

Connect to Your Life

Romantic Responses Romantic love can generate a variety of intense feelings and conflicting emotions. Recall a character in a book or a movie—or perhaps someone you know—who has seemed to respond to romantic love in an unusually intense way. With a group of classmates, briefly discuss the emotions and reactions of that individual, explaining why you think the individual reacted as he or she did.

Build Background

Tokens of Love During the 16th century, the **sonnet** became one of the most popular poetic forms in England. Originally developed in Italy in the 13th century, the sonnet was used to convey deep and intense amorous feelings, often expressing an idealized love typical of the courtly love of the Middle Ages. In many Renaissance sonnets, the speaker—typically a man—tells of his intense love and of the anxiety and distress he feels as his beloved remains aloof and unreachable.

"Sonnet 30" and "Sonnet 75" by Edmund Spenser are part of a collection of sonnets, or **sonnet sequence,** that he named *Amoretti,* which can be translated roughly as "intimate little tokens of love." Published in 1595, the sonnets in *Amoretti* are arranged in a narrative progression that simulates the ritual and emotions of a courtship. Many of them were written during Spenser's courtship of his second wife, Elizabeth Boyle, and the details and emotions they present are thought to be in part autobiographical.

Focus Your Reading

LITERARY ANALYSIS | **SPENSERIAN SONNET** The **Spenserian sonnet** is a variation of the English sonnet, which was introduced on page 295. Both consist of three 4-line units, called **quatrains,** followed by a **couplet** (two rhymed lines), but the Spenserian sonnet has an interlocking **rhyme scheme** linking the quatrains *(abab bcbc cdcd ee)* by the use of rhyming lines.

As you read each of Spenser's sonnets, think about the relationship between the quatrains and couplet and watch for the interlocking rhymes.

ACTIVE READING | **SUMMARIZING MAJOR IDEAS IN POETRY** You can understand the sonnets' **major ideas** by breaking each poem down into its three quatrains and couplet and **summarizing** the meaning expressed in each of the parts.

READER'S NOTEBOOK For each poem, create a chart like the one shown. Jot down the major idea expressed in each part of the sonnet.

"Sonnet 30"	
Part of Poem	Major Idea
1st quatrain	
2nd quatrain	
3rd quatrain	
couplet	

OVERVIEW

Objectives

1. understand and appreciate **Spenserian sonnets (Literary Analysis)**
2. understand and examine the **sonnet form (Literary Analysis)**
3. use strategies for **summarizing major ideas in poetry (Active Reading)**

Summary

These sonnets express idealized, courtly love. "Sonnet 30" reflects on how the speaker's beloved turns colder and colder as his love heats up. He speculates that love can be as surprising as his love's apparent ability to break the rules of nature for fire and ice. In "Sonnet 75," Spenser seeks to immortalize his beloved. Although his beloved argues that she is only mortal and will disappear, Spenser chooses to believe that his poem will make her immortal.

Thematic Link

Spenser's sonnets represent more examples of courtly, romantic love. The sonnets express intense **aspects of love.** A recurrent theme in the love poems presented to this point is that the women to whom the poems are written do not seem to be as enamored as the men who are writing the poems.

5-Minute Warm-Up

Daily Language SkillBuilder

Have students **proofread** the display sentences on page 273k and write them correctly. The sentences also appear on Transparency 7 of **Grammar Transparencies and Copymasters.**

LESSON RESOURCES

UNIT TWO RESOURCE BOOK, pp. 8–9

ASSESSMENT RESOURCES

Formal Assessment, pp. 45–46

Teacher's Guide to Assessment and Portfolio Use

Test Generator

SKILLS TRANSPARENCIES AND COPYMASTERS

Literary Analysis
- Petrarchan, Shakespearean, and Spenserian Sonnets, T4 (for Literary Analysis, p. 297)

Reading and Critical Thinking
- Paraphrasing and Summarizing, T42 (for Active Reading, p. 297)

Grammar
- Diagramming Verbal Phrases, T60 (for Mini Lesson, p. 301)
- Verbals and Verbal Phrases, T94 (for Mini Lesson, p. 301)

Vocabulary
- Using Context to Determine Meaning, C33 (for Mini Lesson, p. 298)

Writing
- Compare-Contrast, C34 (for Writing Options, p. 301)

INTEGRATED TECHNOLOGY

Audio Library

LaserLinks
- Author Background: Edmund Spenser and *The Faerie Queen*. See **Teacher's SourceBook,** p. 23.

Visit our website: www.mcdougallittell.com

TEACHING THE LITERATURE

Reading and Analyzing

Literary Analysis
SPENSERIAN SONNET

Have students recall the structure and rhyme scheme of the Spenserian sonnet. Point out the three quatrains and the rhymed couplet. Also point out the rhyme scheme that links the quatrains *(abab bcbc cdcd ee).*

Use **Unit Two Resource Book,** pp. 00–00 for additional support.

Active Reading
SUMMARIZING MAJOR IDEAS IN POETRY

A Quatrains one and two of "Sonnet 30" are in the form of questions, with the last quatrain and the couplet supplying an "answer." Have students summarize the questions in quatrains one and two.

Possible Response: Why is the poet's beloved so cold when his love is so hot? Why is the poet's fire not cooled by his love's coldness?

Then have students summarize the answer in quatrain three and the "emphatic conclusion" in the couplet.

Possible Response: The poet finds it ironic that his love's fire is not melting his beloved's ice, but that only shows that love can also take an unexpected course.

Use **Unit Two Resource Book,** p. 8 for additional support.

Thinking Through the Literature

1. Accept all reasonable responses.
2. Possible Response: Love is full of surprises.
3. Accept all reasonable responses.

SONNET 30

Edmund Spenser

A

My love is like to ice, and I to fire;
How comes it then that this her cold so great
Is not dissolved through my so hot desire,
But harder grows the more I her entreat?
Or how comes it that my exceeding heat
Is not delayed by her heart-frozen cold:
But that I burn much more in boiling sweat,
And feel my flames augmented manifold?
What more miraculous thing may be told
That fire which all things melts, should harden ice:
And ice which is congealed with senseless cold,
Should kindle fire by wonderful device.
Such is the pow'r of love in gentle mind,
That it can alter all the course of kind.

4 entreat: plead with.

8 augmented manifold: greatly increased.

11 congealed: solidified.

14 kind: nature.

Thinking Through the Literature

1. What are your reactions to the speaker's feelings about love?
2. Why do you think Spenser chose to use the **images** of fire and ice?
   THINK ABOUT
   - the characteristics usually associated with fire and ice
   - the characteristics of fire and ice in this sonnet
3. Is this poem a believable description of a love relationship? Explain your opinion.

Teaching Options

Mini Lesson Vocabulary Strategy

USING CONTEXT TO DETERMINE MEANING

Instruction Remind students that contextual analysis is a word identification process that uses words and phrases in the surrounding text to determine the meaning of a word. Lyric poets utilized familiar words, but they often depended on unfamiliar or obscure definitions to convey meaning in their poetry. Read aloud line 11 from "Sonnet 30" and ask students to discuss the context that surrounds the words *congealed* and *senseless.*

Activity Write on the board the words given here. Then, in small groups, have students analyze the passages to determine the best meaning of each word. Encourage students to jot down the context clues they used to determine a word's meaning. Have each group briefly share their analysis.

Sonnet 30	Sonnet 75
line 12: device	line 1: strand
line 14: kind	line 5: vain
	line 8: eke

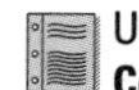
Use **Vocabulary Transparencies and Copymasters,** p. 16.

SONNET 75

Edmund Spenser

One day I wrote her name upon the strand,
But came the waves and washéd it away:
Again I wrote it with a second hand,
But came the tide, and made my pains his prey.
"Vain man," said she, "that dost in vain assay,
A mortal thing so to immortalize.
For I myself shall like to this decay,
And eke my name be wipéd out likewise."
"Not so," quod I, "let baser things devise
To die in dust, but you shall live by fame:
My verse your virtues rare shall eternize,
And in the heavens write your glorious name,
Where whenas death shall all the world subdue,
Our love shall live, and later life renew."

1 **strand:** beach.

5 **assay:** try.

8 **eke:** also.

9 **quod:** said.

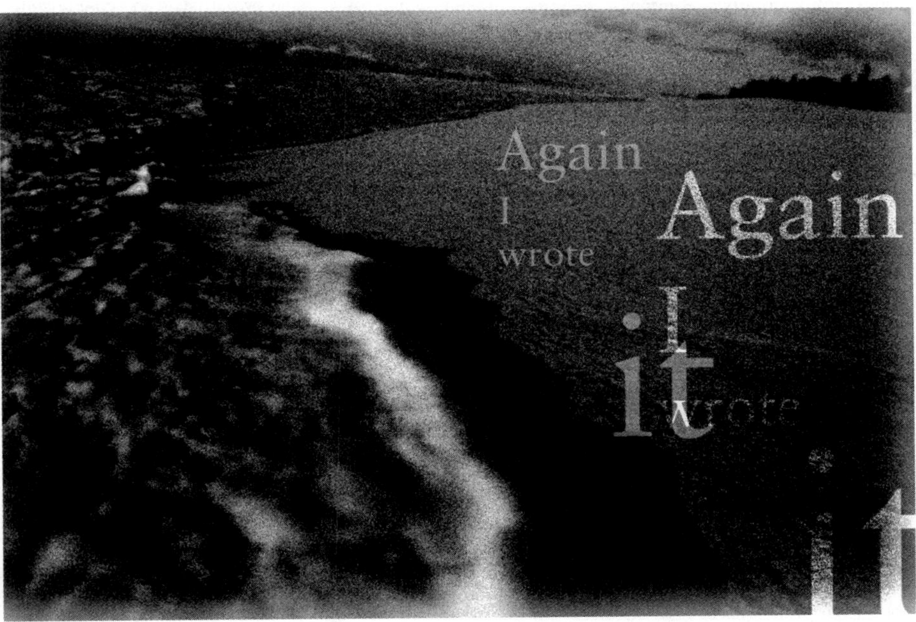

Customizing Instruction

Less Proficient Readers

Have students read each sonnet and discuss the differences between the speaker and his beloved.

Possible Response: The speaker in "Sonnet 30" finds it ironic that the heat and passion of his love only serves to make his beloved colder and more unloving; the speaker in "Sonnet 75" wants to immortalize his beloved, but she realizes that she is mortal and will eventually disappear.

Students Acquiring English

Note that conventional word order is often modified in Elizabethan verse to fit the meter. Have students restate lines in the sonnets in conventional order. For example, lines 2 and 3 in "Sonnet 30" would be read *Then why is her coldness not dissolved by the heat of my desire?* Lines 3 and 4 of "Sonnet 75" could also be restated in a more conventional word order.

 Use **Spanish Study Guide** for additional support, pp. 55–57.

Gifted and Talented

Ask students whether they think the poems' conclusions are logical.

Possible Response: "Sonnet 30" moves logically from specific to general but it is based on a somewhat illogical comparison; "Sonnet 75" presents a more logical conclusion although it is still based on love and not logic.

Mini Lesson: Speaking and Listening

POETRY READING

Instruction Remind students that oral interpretation of a poem demands that the reader use voice without the benefit of props or movement to interpret the lines being read. Tell students that they are going to work with a partner to practice reading the sonnets aloud.

Prepare Before students begin reading the sonnets aloud, have them choose one and make a copy of it. Then have them mark the end of each sentence and any groups of words that go together. A colored pencil would probably be useful. Also have students mark any words that need emphasis, such as questions or exclamations, and places to pause.

Present Allow time for practice, then have students read the sonnets aloud to their partners. Partners should listen to share praise and suggestions until each reader feels satisfied with his or her own performance. Encourage volunteers to read their sonnets for the entire class.

BLOCK SCHEDULING This activity is particularly well-suited for longer class periods.

GUIDING STUDENT RESPONSE

Connect to the Literature

1. What Do You Think?
Guidelines for student response: You might list on the chalkboard all the images that students come up with.

Comprehension Check
- The woman says that it is useless for the poet to try to immortalize her because she is mortal and will disappear, just like her name written in the sand.
- The speaker thinks their love will endure because his poem will forever immortalize his love.

Think Critically

2. Possible Responses: as a gift to show his love; to celebrate her rare virtues; to inspire future lovers
3. Some students may feel that love can overcome death if its memory becomes an inspiration; others may feel that the memory of love can never replace the actual experience.
4. The main idea of "Sonnet 30" is that love is full of surprises and can take an unexpected course. The main idea of "Sonnet 75" is that the speaker plans to immortalize his beloved with his poem. Accept all reasonable, well-supported titles for each poem.

Literary Analysis

Paired Activity Have students read their sonnets to the rest of the class.
Review Alliteration Possible Response: The alliteration makes the poem more musical by capturing the sound of waves.

Connect to the Literature

1. What Do You Think? What **images** remain in your mind after your reading of "Sonnet 75"?

Comprehension Check
- How does the woman in the poem react when the speaker writes her name in the sand?
- Why does the speaker believe that their love will endure?

Think Critically

2. Why do you think the **speaker** in "Sonnet 75" wants to immortalize his love? Explain your thinking.

3. Reread lines 13 and 14. Do you agree with the speaker that love can overcome death?

- the woman's statement that she and her name will be "wiped out"
- the speaker's assertion in line 11
- your own observations about love

4. **ACTIVE READING** SUMMARIZING MAJOR IDEAS IN POETRY
With a partner, compare the charts you created in your READER'S NOTEBOOK and then discuss what you think are the **major ideas** in each of Spenser's poems. Collaborate on creating a title for each poem, choosing words or phrases that summarize the major ideas and reflect the thoughts and intense feelings of each speaker.

Extend Interpretations

5. **Comparing Texts** Compare Spenser's "Sonnet 30" with Elizabeth I's "On Monsieur's Departure," paying particular attention to similarities and differences in the poets' uses of opposites in their descriptions of love relationships.

6. **Different Perspectives** Suppose that the object of the speaker's love in either "Sonnet 30" or "Sonnet 75" wrote a reply. What do you think would be her view of the speaker and his ideas about love?

7. **Connect to Life** Think back to the character or person you recalled in Connect to Your Life on page 297. Which of the two sonnets most closely expresses how this character or person responded to romantic love?

Literary Analysis

SPENSERIAN SONNET The **Spenserian sonnet,** like the English sonnet, consists of 14 lines of **iambic pentameter** divided into three **quatrains** followed by a **couplet.** However, while the typical **rhyme scheme** of an English sonnet is *abab cdcd efef gg,* a Spenserian sonnet uses the interlocking rhyme scheme *abab bcbc cdcd ee.* This rhyme scheme reinforces the relationship of ideas between the quatrains.

Paired Activity Notice the progression of the speaker's thoughts about the intensity of love in each of Spenser's sonnets. Note, too, the progression of the relationship between the man and woman from one poem to the next. With a partner, write notes for a Spenserian sonnet that might bridge the gap between "Sonnet 30" and "Sonnet 75." Jot down images you could use to express intense feelings of love. Use your notes to write the sonnet, applying the interlocking rhyme scheme as effectively as possible.

REVIEW ALLITERATION
Alliteration is the repetition of consonant sounds at the beginnings of words. Read "Sonnet 75" aloud, paying particular attention to the use of alliteration. What effect do you think these repetitions of sounds create?

Extend Interpretations

Comparing Texts Possible Responses: Both poems focus on love's contradictions and even use some similar imagery. The opposites in "Sonnet 30" are between the speaker and his beloved; however, those in Elizabeth I's poem are within the speaker herself.

Different Perspectives Accept all reasonable responses. Remind students of the dialogue between Marlowe's poem and Raleigh's reply as a parallel to keep in mind as they frame their answer.
Connect to Life Accept all reasonable responses.

Choices & CHALLENGES

Writing Options

Natural Comparison In "Sonnet 30," Spenser compares his feelings to fire. Write a paragraph in which you make your own comparison between love and some aspect of nature. Explain the reasons for your comparison.

Writing Handbook
See page 1367: Compare and Contrast.

Activities & Explorations

Opinion Poll Conduct an opinion poll in which you ask ten or more participants to complete the sentence "Love is like . . ." Record their responses on tape or in your notebook. Share any unusual responses with the class.
~ **SPEAKING AND LISTENING**

Inquiry & Research

Renaissance Courtship and Marriage Find out about more typical courtship and marriage customs of the English Renaissance by answering these questions: What was the average age of the courters? Was love an essential component of the relationship? How long did a typical engagement last?

Edmund Spenser

1552?–1599

Other Works
"Sonnet 26"
"Sonnet 67"
"Sonnet 71"
"Sonnet 72"

Early Ambitions Born to a relatively poor London family, Edmund Spenser was able to work his way through Cambridge University as a "poor scholar." He read extensively, becoming acquainted with Latin, Greek, French, and Italian literature. His earliest publication was of translations of several French poems, written when he was 16 years old. While at Cambridge, Spenser established literary friendships and showed that he had ambitious plans for a poetic career.

Influences and Experimentation After receiving his master of arts degree in 1576, Spenser served as secretary to several influential men, including the earl of Leicester. His employment in Leicester's household was important, for it was there that he met and developed a friendship with Sir Philip Sidney and other court writers who were promoting the new English poetry of the Elizabethan Age. In his own poetry, Spenser often experimented with verse forms and used archaic language for its rustic and musical effect. He was respected and imitated by his contemporaries, as he has been by many later poets.

Literary Achievements One year after publishing his first major work, *The Shepheardes Calender,* which he dedicated to Sidney, Spenser moved to Ireland, where he held various minor government jobs and continued his writing. It was there that he wrote one of the greatest poetic romances in English literature, *The Faerie Queene.* Spenser spent most of his remaining life in Ireland, but after his home near Dublin was destroyed during a civil war, he returned to England, where he died a few years later almost impoverished despite his many years of service to nobility. In honor of his great literary achievements, Spenser was buried near Geoffrey Chaucer—one of his favorite poets—in what is now called the Poets' Corner of Westminster Abbey.

Author Activity

Mystery Queen To learn more about *The Faerie Queene,* find a copy of the work and read a few passages. Investigate its background and structure. To whom did Spenser dedicate the romance? How long is the poem? What, in brief, is it about?

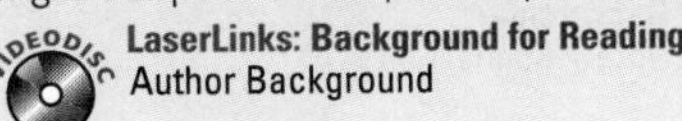
LaserLinks: Background for Reading
Author Background

Writing Options

Natural Comparison Suggest that students start with a basic comparison and then expand it or elaborate on it point by point.

Activities & Explorations

Opinion Poll Have students work in groups of three, with one conducting the interviews, another in charge of recording the responses, and a third in charge of reporting unusual responses back to classmates.

Inquiry & Research

Renaissance Courtship and Marriage Arrange for students to visit the library or provide class time for them to use Internet resources. You may want to have students focus on one aspect of courtship and marriage customs, such as how matches were made.

Author Activity

Mystery Queen Spenser's long poems in the pastoral tradition include the wedding poems *Prothalamion* and *Epithalamion;* the latter celebrates his 1594 marriage to Elizabeth Boyle and was published a year later with the *Amoretti* sonnets. *The Faerie Queene,* Spenser's best-known work, combines elements of the epic and the poetic romance; its glorious title figure is a tribute to Elizabeth I.

Grammar

VERB PHRASES: INFINITIVES

Instruction A verb shows action or a state of being. Verbs can also be used as nouns, adjectives, or adverbs and, as such, are called verbals. One kind of verbal is an infinitive. An infinitive usually has two parts: the word *to* and the base form of a verb.

Activity Write the following on the chalkboard.

In "Sonnet 75," to immortalize his love is the poet's aim.

Underline the infinitive. Point out the two parts of the infinitive. Discuss with students whether this infinitive is a noun, adjective, or adverb. *(noun)* Have students identify its function in the sentence. *(subject)*

Explain that an infinitive can have modifiers and complements. Together they form an infinitive phrase. Have students identify the infinitive phrase and classify its complement. *(to immortalize his love; direct object)*

Point out that not all infinitives include the word *to.* Students can decide if a verbal is an infinitive by rereading and mentally inserting the word *to;* for example, "I don't dare [to] jump off the dock."

Use McDougal Littell's ***Language Network*** for more instruction and practice in infinitives.

OVERVIEW

This selection is included in the **Grade 12 InterActive Reader.**

Objectives

1. understand and appreciate classic **Shakespearean sonnets (Literary Analysis)**
2. identify and examine similes and metaphors as examples of **figurative language (Literary Analysis)**
3. use strategies for **analyzing sensory language (Active Reading)**

Summary

In "Sonnet 29," the speaker's mood changes from one of despair, discontent, and envy to a mood of joy when he thinks upon his love. "Sonnet 116" voices the conviction that love is unalterable, an anchor in the changing sea of time. In an amusing twist on the subject of a woman's beauty, the speaker in "Sonnet 130" observes that his love, like most real women, does not have the beauty of a goddess, but she is still beautiful.

Thematic Link

This group of Shakespeare's sonnets addresses the **aspects of love** as an antidote to negative thoughts and emotions and expresses the ideal that love should last forever. Shakespeare also says that love should be based on more than just a physical attraction.

5-Minute Warm-Up

Daily Language SkillBuilder

Have students **proofread** the display sentences on page 273k and write them correctly. The sentences also appear on Transparency 7 of **Grammar Transparencies and Copymasters.**

Sonnet 29 / Sonnet 116 / Sonnet 130

Poetry by WILLIAM SHAKESPEARE

Comparing Literature of the World

Sonnets of Spenser, Shakespeare, and Petrarch

This lesson, as well as the one before on Spenser and the one following on Petrarch, presents an opportunity for you to compare the work of three sonnet masters: Spenser, Shakespeare, and Petrarch. Specific points of comparison contained in these lessons will help you understand the similarities and differences among sonnet forms and themes.

Connect to Your Life

True Love Think about two people you know who have a strong love relationship that has lasted for many years. Consider the qualities of each of the persons involved in the relationship. Do you think those qualities help explain the strength of the relationship? Share your thoughts with classmates.

Build Background

Shakespeare's Sonnets William Shakespeare, best known for his plays, also wrote nondramatic poetry, including a series of 154 sonnets. In the 1590s many English poets wrote **sonnet sequences,** groups of sonnets related through an overall narrative structure, usually addressed to an idealized but unattainable woman. Typical themes included the woman's great beauty, her coldness and disdain, the suffering of the poet-lover, and the immortality of poetry. Shakespeare almost certainly wrote his sonnets—which were not published until 1609—during the 1590s too, but they differ in some ways from the sonnets written by other poets. First, they are addressed to at least three different people: a young man, whom the poet urges to marry and have children; a "dark lady," who is unlike the ideal beautiful woman of the time; and a rival poet. Second, the themes of Shakespeare's sonnets are more complex and less predictable than those of other poets' sonnets. Shakespeare writes, for example, of time, change, and death as well as of love and beauty. Third, Shakespeare developed the structure of the sonnet form to its highest artistic level; today, the English sonnet is often referred to as the **Shakespearean sonnet.**

VIDEODISC **LaserLinks: Background for Reading**
Author Background
Contemporary Connection

Focus Your Reading

LITERARY ANALYSIS SHAKESPEAREAN SONNET

Like Spenser, Shakespeare uses the structure of three **quatrains** and a **couplet** in his sonnets. However, he uses the **rhyme scheme** *abab cdcd efef gg* instead of the interlocking Spenserian pattern *(abab bcbc cdcd ee).* As you read these three **Shakespearean sonnets,** discuss with your classmates how the rhyme scheme contributes to the meaning and appeal of each poem.

ACTIVE READING ANALYZING SENSORY LANGUAGE

In his sonnets, Shakespeare often chose words that would appeal to the reader's senses. As you read the poems, you will notice language used by the poet that appeals to the five senses: sight, hearing, touch, smell, and taste.

READER'S NOTEBOOK Make a chart like the one shown. As you read each poem, record words or phrases that appeal to one or more of the senses. Note whether any of the senses are not used. Also note that some poems may have more **sensory language** than others.

	Sonnet 29	Sonnet 116	Sonnet 130
Sight			
Hearing			
Touch			
Smell			
Taste			

LESSON RESOURCES

UNIT TWO RESOURCE BOOK, pp. 10–11

ASSESSMENT RESOURCES

Formal Assessment, pp. 47–48

Teacher's Guide to Assessment and Portfolio Use

Test Generator

SKILLS TRANSPARENCIES AND COPYMASTERS

Literary Analysis

- Petrarchan, Shakespearean, and Spenserian Sonnets, T4 (for Literary Analysis, p. 302)

Reading and Critical Thinking

- Observation Chart, T47 (for Active Reading, p. 302)

Grammar

- Avoiding Misplaced Modifiers, T51 (for Mini Lesson, p. 303)
- Participles and Participial Phrases, C99 (for Mini Lesson, p. 303)

Writing

- Figurative Language and Sound Devices, T15 (for Writing Option 1, p. 307)
- Opinion Statement, C35 (for Writing Option 4, p. 307)

Communications

- Reading Aloud, T11 (for Activities & Explorations 3, p. 307)
- Impromptu Speaking: Dialogue, Role-Play, T14 (for Activities & Explorations 1, p. 307)

INTEGRATED TECHNOLOGY

Audio Library

LaserLinks

- Author Background: An Afternoon at the Globe Theater
- Contemporary Connections: Shakespeare Today. See **Teacher's SourceBook,** p. 24.

Internet: Research Starter

Visit our website:
www.mcdougallittell.com

SONNET 29

WILLIAM SHAKESPEARE

When in disgrace with Fortune and men's eyes
I all alone beweep my outcast state,
And trouble deaf heaven with my bootless cries,
And look upon myself and curse my fate,
Wishing me like to one more rich in hope,
Featur'd like him, like him with friends possess'd,
Desiring this man's art, and that man's scope,
With what I most enjoy contented least;
Yet in these thoughts myself almost despising,
Haply I think on thee, and then my state,
Like to the lark at break of day arising
From sullen earth, sings hymns at heaven's gate,
  For thy sweet love rememb'red such wealth brings,
  That then I scorn to change my state with kings.

2 state: condition.

3 bootless: futile; useless.

6 featur'd like him: with his features—that is, handsome.

7 scope: intelligence.

11 lark: the English skylark, noted for its beautiful singing while soaring in flight.

Thinking Through the Literature

1. **Comprehension Check** What changes the speaker's mood in "Sonnet 29"?
2. Can you identify in any way with the speaker of this poem? Share your thoughts with classmates.
3. What do you think are the speaker's strongest feelings in this sonnet? Cite lines from the poem to support your answer.

TEACHING THE LITERATURE

Customizing Instruction

Less Proficient Readers
Have students discuss the importance of love in the modern world. As students read these sonnets, have them look for Shakespeare's views on love and its effects.

Students Acquiring English
Suggest that students use the sonnets' punctuation to break the long sentences into smaller, more manageable phrases. Encourage students to paraphrase the lines in their own words.

Use **Spanish Study Guide** for additional support, pp. 59–60.

Gifted and Talented
Point out that in Shakespeare's time love poems were a common way to express love. Have students consider how we express love today—with flowers and other small gifts and by fax, phone, or computer messages. What do these methods say about our society in comparison with Shakespeare's?

Thinking Through the Literature

1. He thinks about his loved one.
2. Accept all reasonable responses.
3. Possible Responses: depression, since more lines are devoted to it *(lines 1–8)*; joy, because the couplet obliterates the despair described in the preceding lines.

Grammar

VERB PHRASES: PARTICIPLES AND PARTICIPIAL PHRASES

Instruction A verbal is a form of a verb that is used as a noun, adjective, or adverb. Participles are verbals that function as adjectives. They modify nouns and pronouns. Like other verbal forms, participles can have modifiers and complements, and these participial phrases also act as adjectives.

Activity Have students look through the three sonnets and identify participles and participial phrases. *[Sample answers–Sonnet 29: "Desiring this man's art, . . . "(participial phrase); Sonnet 116: "Within his bending sickle's compass come, . . . " (participle); Sonnet 130: ". . . a far more pleasing sound;" (participle)]*

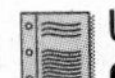
Use **Grammar Transparencies and Copymasters,** p. 100.

Reading and Analyzing

Active Reading

STRATEGY ANALYZING SENSORY LANGUAGE

Have students chart the use of the five senses in "Sonnet 130." Students can work in groups and list the five senses on one side of a chart and the corresponding language from the sonnet on the other side of the chart. For example:

Sight *no roses I see in her cheeks*
Smell *perfumes*
Sound *music*

Use **Unit Two Resource Book,** p. 10 for more practice.

Literary Analysis

SHAKESPEAREAN SONNET

Most sonnets are written in iambic pentameter, a pattern in which a typical line has five unstressed syllables alternating with five stressed syllables:

I néver wrít, nor nó man éver lóved

The English or Shakespearean sonnet consists of three four-line units, called quatrains, followed by a couplet. The three quatrains express three different but related thoughts, with the couplet providing the conclusion.

Use **Unit Two Resource Book,** p. 11 for more exercises.

Thinking Through the Literature

1. Accept all reasonable responses.
2. Possible Responses: young, idealistic person; older, experienced person
3. Possible Responses: realistic—time cannot change true love; unrealistic—time can cause people to fall out of love.

SONNET 116

WILLIAM SHAKESPEARE

Let me not to the marriage of true minds
Admit impediments; love is not love
Which alters when it alteration finds,
Or bends with the remover to remove.
O no, it is an ever-fixéd mark
That looks on tempests and is never shaken;
It is the star to every wand'ring bark,
Whose worth's unknown, although his height be taken.
Love's not Time's fool, though rosy lips and cheeks
Within his bending sickle's compass come,
Love alters not with his brief hours and weeks,
But bears it out even to the edge of doom.
    If this be error and upon me proved,
    I never writ, nor no man ever loved.

2 impediments: obstacles. The traditional marriage service reads in part, "If any of you know cause or just impediment why these persons should not be joined together . . ."

5 mark: seamark—a landmark that can be seen from the sea and used as a guide in navigation.

7 bark: sailing ship.

8 whose . . . height be taken: a reference to the star, whose value is measureless even though its altitude is measured by navigators.

10 within . . . compass: within the range of his curving sickle.

12 bears it out: endures; **doom:** Doomsday; Judgment Day.

Anne of Gonzaga, Nathaniel Hatch. Victoria & Albert Museum, London/Art Resource, New York.

Thinking Through the Literature

1. What is your response to the description of love in this poem?
2. What kind of person might the speaker be?
   THINK ABOUT
   - the likely age of such a person
   - the experiences that such a person might have had
3. Do you think the speaker's concept of love is realistic? Why or why not?

Teaching Options

Mini Lesson: Speaking and Listening

DEBATE

Instruction Explain that a debate is a formal argument in which two teams take opposite sides of a question. In developing one side of an argument, a team should anticipate the opposing side's arguments. Each team will be expected to rebut the arguments of its opponent.

Prepare Time limits are set for the presentation of opening arguments and rebuttal of opposing arguments.

Divide the class into teams to interpret Shakespeare's sonnets and then to debate the question of whether those sonnets express the elation and the melancholy of love as well as today's music does.

Present After students have prepared their arguments, including a clear thesis, supporting points and evidence, and rhetorical strategies, stage the debate. Students who are not arguing the question can be judges, taking notes about and assessing the effectiveness of arguments and rebuttals. Allow for a ten-minute question and answer period to conclude the debate. These students can then lead a discussion of which points and counterpoints were the most convincing.

This activity is particularly well-suited for longer class periods.

SONNET 130

WILLIAM SHAKESPEARE

Catherine Howard, John Hoskins. Victoria & Albert Museum, London/Art Resource, New York.

My mistress' eyes are nothing like the sun;
Coral is far more red than her lips' red;
If snow be white, why then her breasts are dun;
If hairs be wires, black wires grow on her head.
I have seen roses damask'd, red and white,
But no such roses see I in her cheeks,
And in some perfumes is there more delight
Than in the breath that from my mistress reeks.
I love to hear her speak, yet well I know
That music hath a far more pleasing sound;
I grant I never saw a goddess go,
My mistress when she walks treads on the ground.
And yet, by heaven, I think my love as rare
As any she belied with false compare.

3 dun: tan.

5 damask'd: with mingled colors.

8 reeks: is exhaled (used here without the word's present reference to offensive odors).

11 go: walk.

14 as . . . compare: as any woman misrepresented by exaggerated comparisons.

Customizing Instruction

Students Acquiring English

1 Have students explain in their own words what the final couplet means.

Possible Response: If you can prove that I am wrong, then I'm no writer and no one has ever been in love.

What does the couplet suggest about the speaker?

Possible Response: He is certain he is right about the nature of love.

Less Proficient Readers

Have students discuss the views of love expressed in these three sonnets. What attitudes toward love are expressed in these sonnets?

Possible Response: "Sonnet 29"—Love brings comfort in time of despair, "Sonnet 116"—Love is constant, not mutable; "Sonnet 130"—The object of one's love is a real person.

Multiple Learning Styles

Visual/Interpersonal Learners

Encourage students to work in pairs to read the sonnets together and create a chart of what love is and what love is not, according to Shakespeare. In a two-column chart, students can list everything Shakespeare says love is in the first column and everything Shakespeare says love is not in the second column.

Informal Assessment

UNDERSTANDING CLICHES Have students define the word *cliché* (a trite or overused expression or image). Give several examples ("dumb as an ox," "old as the hills," etc.). Have students list the clichés that Shakespeare refers to in "Sonnet 130." After they list the clichés (eyes like the sun, lips like coral, etc.), ask students to write a brief essay that explains how the couplet relates to the clichés mentioned in the rest of the sonnet. Have students evaluate the effectiveness of this couplet as an ending to the sonnet. Remind students to use examples from the sonnet to support their positions.

RUBRIC

3 **Full Accomplishment** Students show in-depth understanding of clichés as presented in sonnet and how they relate to theme expressed in couplet. They support opinions with details from poem.

2 **Substantial Accomplishment** Students show good understanding of clichés as presented in sonnet and how they relate to theme expressed in couplet.

1 **Little or Partial Accomplishment** Students show little understanding of sonnet and have difficulty supporting ideas with details.

GUIDING STUDENT RESPONSE

Connect to the Literature

1. What Do You Think?
Guidelines for student response: Most students will probably be aware that the poet is turning upside down the conventions of love poetry in order to present a more accurate description of his beloved. Nonetheless, the realism of his description might startle some readers.

Comprehension Check
- dark *(line 4)*
- No; the speaker believes his love is a real woman and he does not need to flatter her with false comparisons.

Think Critically

2. Possible Responses: realistic, since he recognizes that she is not a goddess; loving, since he claims she is "rare." Have students amplify their response by taking the Think About into account.
3. Possible Responses: to mock the unrealistic ideas contained in more traditional love poems; to show that beauty is in the eye of the beholder.
4. Realistic.
5. Accept all reasonable, well-supported answers. Most students will probably state that "Sonnet 130" contains the most sensory language.

Literary Analysis

Shakespearean Sonnet: Paired Activity
In "Sonnet 29," the turn occurs between the second and third quatrains. The mood of the poem changes from rather dark and somber to happy and bright. "Sonnet 116" does not have a distinctive turn. Each quatrain offers another proof of the timelessness of love, and the couplet is almost an oath that everything said in the poem is true. The turn in "Sonnet 130" comes between the third quatrain and the couplet. The quatrains reveal the shortcomings of physical beauty of the speaker's beloved, and the couplet declares that the speaker's beloved is a real woman. She may have flaws, but he loves her anyway.

Figurative Language Volunteers might read their explications of the similes and metaphors they have chosen to the class.

Thinking through the LITERATURE

Connect to the Literature

1. **What Do You Think?** Were you surprised by the **description** in "Sonnet 130"? Share your reactions with your classmates.

Comprehension Check
- Is the speaker's mistress dark or fair?
- Do the flaws pointed out by the speaker affect his love for the woman described?

Think Critically

2. In "Sonnet 130," what do you think is the **speaker's** attitude toward the woman he loves?

THINK ABOUT
- his descriptions of her physical characteristics
- his description of her voice
- his conclusion in the **couplet**

3. What do you think might have been Shakespeare's **purpose** in writing this sonnet?
4. Does this poem present a realistic or idealized portrait of the beloved?
5. **ACTIVE READING** **ANALYZING SENSORY LANGUAGE** Review the chart you prepared for your READER'S NOTEBOOK. Which sonnet contains the most **sensory language?** How does this language suit the subject? Cite examples in your answer.

Extend Interpretations

6. **Critic's Corner** One critic, Hallett Smith, has called Shakespeare's sonnets "explorations of the human spirit." Discuss ways in which this interpretation applies to the three sonnets you have read. Use details from the poems to support your conclusions.
7. **Connect to Life** Renaissance sonnets often focus on the great beauty of the beloved. How important is physical beauty or attractiveness in today's society?
8. **Points of Comparison** The speaker of "Sonnet 130," like the speaker of Spenser's "Sonnet 75," uses the word *rare* to describe his beloved. Compare the thoughts and emotions of the two **speakers.** Whom would you more likely enjoy meeting? Why?

Literary Analysis

SHAKESPEAREAN SONNET The **Shakespearean sonnet,** also called the English or Elizabethan sonnet, consists of 14 lines of **iambic pentameter** divided into three **quatrains,** or four-line units, and a final **couplet.** The typical **rhyme scheme** is *abab cdcd efef gg.* The couplet provides a final commentary on the subject developed in the three quatrains. There is also usually a **turn,** or shift in thought, in the poem, occurring most often at the couplet or at the beginning of the third quatrain.

Paired Activity With a partner, decide where the turn occurs in each of the three Shakespeare sonnets. In which poem does the turn occur between the second and third quatrains? Does the turn occur at the couplet in any of the poems? What is the effect of each turn?

FIGURATIVE LANGUAGE **Figurative language** is language that conveys meaning beyond the literal meanings of the words. **Similes** and **metaphors** are types of figurative language. A simile uses the word *like* or *as* to make a comparison between things. A metaphor makes a comparison without using those words.

Simile: Her hair was bright as gold.

Metaphor: Hope is a light in the dark.

Activity Choose one simile or one metaphor from each of the three sonnets. Explain the comparison and its effect.

Extend Interpretations

Critic's Corner Some students may say that Shakespeare only deals with love in these sonnets; others may say that he uses love to explore all aspects of the human spirit. Have students support their deductive reasoning with evidence from the text.

Connect to Life Some students may feel that most people today realize beauty is only skin deep. Others may feel that physical beauty sometimes helps ensure success or happiness.

Points of Comparison Possible responses: Speaker of "Sonnet 130," because he seems to have a sense of humor and to appreciate people for who they are; speaker of "Sonnet 75" because he immortalizes his beloved.

Writing Options

1. Love Poem Write a Shakespearean sonnet describing someone you love or greatly admire. Use at least one simile or metaphor. Place the sonnet in your **Working Portfolio.** 

2. Character Sketch As the speaker of "Sonnet 116," write a character sketch of the ideal partner in a strong love relationship. Make sure to identify various qualities the person would need to possess.

3. Letter to the Speaker Imagine that you are the woman described in "Sonnet 130." In a letter to the speaker, give your opinion of his description.

4. Opinion Essay Which of the three sonnets do you think expresses the strongest commitment to a love relationship? Write a two- or three-paragraph essay explaining your opinion.

Writing Handbook
See page 1369–1370: Analysis.

Activities & Explorations

1. Television Talk Show With a partner, stage a television talk show in which the host interviews William Shakespeare about the meaning of love.
~ **SPEAKING AND LISTENING**

2. Love's Scrapbook Prepare a scrapbook of items—such as photos, drawings, poems, and sayings—that express your conception of a strong love relationship. ~ **ART**

3. A Reading of Sonnets With a small group of classmates, investigate some of Shakespeare's other sonnets. Have each group member prepare a reading of his or her favorite sonnet. Discuss the feelings and ideas expressed in each poem, and compare it with one or more of the three sonnets you have read in this lesson.
~ **SPEAKING AND LISTENING**

4. List of Resources Reread each of the three sonnets, and choose your favorite. Think of films, novels, short stories, works of art, and musical compositions that in some way represent the mood of the poem or the ideas and images in it. List these resources, and share the list with the class.
~ **VIEWING AND REPRESENTING**

Inquiry & Research

1. Portraits of Women Find books of English Renaissance painting showing portraits of women of the time. Look at several of the portraits and think about whether they seem idealized or realistic. How does the portrayal of women in painting of the period compare with the portrayal of women in Renaissance poetry?

2. What Is Love? For most people, love is one of the most important aspects of life. Investigate some of the definitions and analyses of love in the writings of contemporary psychologists. Share what you find with the class, and discuss any relationships you can see between Shakespeare's views of love and the psychologists' views.

More Online: Research Starter
www.mcdougallittell.com

Art Connection

Illustrating Poetry Look again at the two small portraits of women on pages 304–305. Why do you think they were chosen to illustrate "Sonnet 116" and "Sonnet 130"? Look for other paintings that you think could be used to illustrate the two poems.

A biography of William Shakespeare appears on pages 314–317.

Writing Options

1. **Love Poem** Have students look at the similes and metaphors they chose in the Figurative Language Activity on the facing page and use them as models for their sonnets.
2. **Character Sketch** Have students work in pairs to brainstorm the qualities of their ideal partners before they begin drafting.
3. **Letter to the Speaker** Suggest that students write a brief character sketch or draw a picture of this woman to help them understand her point of view.
4. **Opinion Essay** Have students make an outline for their essays as a prewriting activity. The essays should provide evidence from the sonnets.

Activities & Explorations

1. **Television Talk Show** Have students work in groups of four, taking on the roles of director, question writer, interviewer, and Shakespeare.
2. **Love's Scrapbook** Note that greeting cards and books of quotations may provide suitable sayings; the former may also supply suitable pictures.
3. **A Reading of Sonnets** Suggest sonnets 18, 30, 55, 71, 73, and 106 as candidates for oral reading.
4. **List of Resources** Have students work in pairs. Tell them to be prepared to explain how each source they list reflects the mood, ideas, or images of the sonnet.

Inquiry & Research

1. **Portraits of Women** If you cannot easily locate books of English Renaissance painting, you might bring a standard art history book such as H. W. Janson's classic study *A History of Art* to class to show students Renaissance portraits of women.
2. **What Is Love?** You might point out to students that Sigmund Freud, a great psychological thinker, observed that the great creative artists such as Shakespeare and Michelangelo achieved great and profound psychological insights into human behavior that were explored and developed later by psychologists and others.

Art Connection

Illustrating Poetry Possible response: The first portrays a timeless beauty, reinforcing the timelessness of the love described in "Sonnet 116." The second shows a curly-haired, rather plain woman, reflecting the realistic view of love in "Sonnet 130."

OVERVIEW

Objectives

1. understand and appreciate classic **Italian sonnets (Literary Analysis)**
2. **summarize major ideas** in poems **(Active Reading)**
3. recognize and discuss connections that cross cultures

Summary

In "Sonnet 169" the speaker struggles with his feelings of love, vacillating between fleeing or seeking his beloved's company and between telling her of his love or keeping silent. In "Sonnet 292" the speaker recounts those details about his love that gave him joy. With her death, the speaker's source of inspiration is gone.

Thematic Link

These sonnets deal with different **aspects of love,** specifically, the traditional themes of unrequited love and love lost. "Sonnet 292" also touches on the idea that love can inspire artistic expression.

5-Minute Warm-Up

Daily Language SkillBuilder

Have students **proofread** the display sentences on page 273k and write them correctly. The sentences also appear on Transparency 7 of **Grammar Transparencies and Copymasters.**

PREPARING to *Read*

Sonnet 169 / Sonnet 292

Poetry by FRANCESCO PETRARCH (frän-chās′ kō pē′trärk′)

Comparing Literature of the World

The Sonnet Across Cultures

Sonnets of Spenser, Shakespeare, and Petrarch Long before Spenser and Shakespeare's time, the Italian poet Petrarch played an influential role in the development of the structure as well as the content of the **sonnet.** A brilliant man of the 14th-century Italian Renaissance, Petrarch perfected the sonnet style that 200 years later was used and adapted by Spenser, Shakespeare, and other English poets. Because of this, you will find in Petrarch's writing the same love **themes** that were explored by his followers: unrequited love, desperate love, eternal love, and tragic love.

Points of Comparison As you read these sonnets by Petrarch, compare the poet's treatment of love with that seen in Spenser's and Shakespeare's sonnets.

Build Background

The Sonnet Takes Shape Although sonnets had been written in Italy for nearly 100 years before Petrarch wrote his, it was he who established the **sonnet** as a major poetic form. In addition to his impact on the Elizabethans, Petrarch had a considerable influence on such poets as Michelangelo, Ronsard, and Lope de Vega.

Petrarch's sonnets, the output of a lifetime of work, show his longing for a woman named Laura, with whom he reportedly fell passionately in love on Good Friday, April 6, 1327, after seeing her in church. Even though Laura did not return his love, she was the inspiration for over 300 of Petrarch's poems. Like many of Petrarch's contemporaries, Laura died in the plague that devastated much of Europe in the mid-14th century. "Sonnet 292" was written after her death.

Focus Your Reading

LITERARY ANALYSIS ITALIAN SONNET The **Italian sonnet** used by Petrarch is different in form from the English sonnet. The 14 lines of the Italian sonnet are divided into these two parts:

- an octave (the first eight lines)
- a sestet (the last six lines)

Generally, the octave tells a story, introduces a situation, or raises a question. In the sestet, the speaker comments on the story, situation, or question.

As you read these sonnets, notice the relationship between their structure and content.

ACTIVE READING SUMMARIZING MAJOR IDEAS IN POEMS The ideas expressed in a poem can be hard to understand because the language of poetry may be difficult to decipher. The following steps are strategies you can use to determine the major ideas in Petrarch's sonnets:

- Reread the poem two or three times.
- Look for the major idea in each stanza.
- Identify the story or situation introduced in the octave.
- Determine the comment made by the speaker in the sestet.

READER'S NOTEBOOK **Summarize** the major idea of each stanza in the two sonnets.

LESSON RESOURCES

UNIT TWO RESOURCE BOOK, pp. 12–13

ASSESSMENT RESOURCES
Formal Assessment, p. 49
Teacher's Guide to Assessment and Portfolio Use
Test Generator

SKILLS TRANSPARENCIES AND COPYMASTERS
Literary Analysis
- Petrarchan, Shakespearean, and Spenserian Sonnets, T4 (for Literary Analysis, p. 308)

Reading and Critical Thinking
- Paraphrasing and Summarizing, T42 (for Active Reading, p. 308)

Grammar
- Gerunds and Gerund Phrases, C103 (for Mini Lesson, pp. 310–311)

Vocabulary
- Denotation and Connotation, C34 (for Mini Lesson, p. 309)

Writing
- Compare-Contrast, C34 (for Writing Option 2, p. 312)

INTEGRATED TECHNOLOGY
Audio Library
LaserLinks
- Author Background: Francesco Petrarch. See **Teacher's SourceBook,** p. 25.

Visit our website:
www.mcdougallittell.com

FRANCESCO PETRARCH

ONNET 169

Rapt in the one fond thought that makes me stray
from other men and walk this world alone,
sometimes I have escaped myself and flown
to seek the very one that I should flee;

so fair and fell I see her passing by
that the soul trembles to take flight again,
so many arméd sighs are in her train,
this lovely foe to Love himself and me!

And yet, upon that high and clouded brow
I seem to see a ray of pity shine,
shedding some light across the grieving heart:

so I call back my soul, and when I vow
at last to tell her of my hidden pain,
I have so much to say I dare not start.

Translated by Anthony Mortimer

1 rapt: deeply absorbed.

5 fell: cruel.

7 train: a group of people following in attendance.

Thinking Through the Literature

1. What are your thoughts about the feelings the speaker expresses in this poem?
2. How would you describe the relationship between the speaker and his beloved?

THINK ABOUT
- the **conflict** the speaker expresses in lines 3–4
- his description of how his soul "trembles to take flight again" (line 6)
- his use of contradictory phrases in describing the beloved, such as "fair and fell" (line 5) and "lovely foe" (line 8)
- the needs he suggests in lines 12–14

TEACHING THE LITERATURE

Customizing Instruction

Less Proficient Readers
Remind students to use punctuation, not line breaks, to understand the units of thought in these two poems.

Students Acquiring English
Ask students if they have ever translated something from their primary language into English, or from English into their primary language. Discuss the difficulties posed by translation and students' experiences with translated text.

Use **Spanish Study Guide** for additional support, pp. 61–63.

Gifted and Talented Students
Explain to students that the plague, often called the Black Death, was caused by a bacterial infection known today as the bubonic plague. The plague ravaged the population of Europe and Asia during the Middle Ages. Have students research the effects of the Black Death on medieval European society.

Thinking Through the Literature

1. Accept all reasonable responses.
2. Possible Responses: one-sided; idealized; secret.

Mini Lesson Vocabulary Strategy

DENOTATION AND CONNOTATION

Instruction Denotation is the explicit meaning of a word. Connotation refers to attitudes or emotions that a word evokes. A word suggests these ideas or feelings without their being part of the literal meaning.

Model Have students look up the definition of *rapt* in a dictionary.

Then have students discuss the images that the word *rapt* evokes.

rapt (line 1) deeply absorbed; engrossed; reaction to something magical or amazing, which could be either positive or negative.

Activity Have students examine each of the words below in the context of the sonnet. Then have them list for each word the dictionary definition that best fits the context, a synonym, and its connotations.

 Use **Vocabulary Transparencies and Copymasters,** p. 17.

Reading and Analyzing

Literary Analysis ITALIAN SONNET

Sonnet is from the Italian for "little song." The Italian, or Petrarchan, sonnet achieves its music in part through rhyme. Petrarch also established conventions of love sonnets, including the use of conceits (such as the elaborate comparisons to ice and fire in Spencer's "Sonnet 30"), the topic of unrequited love for a woman, and the exaggeration of her many beauties (mocked in Shakespeare's "Sonnet 130").

Have students examine "Sonnet 292" to determine how well the rhyme has been maintained in the translation from Italian to English. Ask what near rhymes the translator uses to maintain the rhyme scheme in the octave.

Possible Responses: burn/men; shone/gone; rays/paradise.

Use **Unit Two Resource Book,** p. 13 for more exercises.

Active Reading

SUMMARIZING MAJOR IDEAS IN POEMS

(A) Before students begin reading the sonnet, have them put themselves in Petrarch's place. Remind them that all around him people are dying of a terrible plague. For many years Petrarch has written poems about a woman who did not return his love; now she too is dead from the plague. Then have students read the poem and write down the major ideas it contains.

Possible Response: Petrarch's love was a beautiful woman who made the earth a paradise. Now she is dead, and he feels utterly alone and abandoned. His inspiration is gone, so he will turn from poetry to grief.

Use **Unit Two Resource Book,** p. 12 for more practice.

FRANCESCO PETRARCH

(A)

Sonnet 292

Portrait of a Man and Woman at a Casement (about 1440–1445), Fra Filippo Lippi. Tempera on wood, 25¼" × 16½", The Metropolitan Museum of Art, New York, gift of Henry G. Marquand, 1889, Marquand Collection (89.15.19).

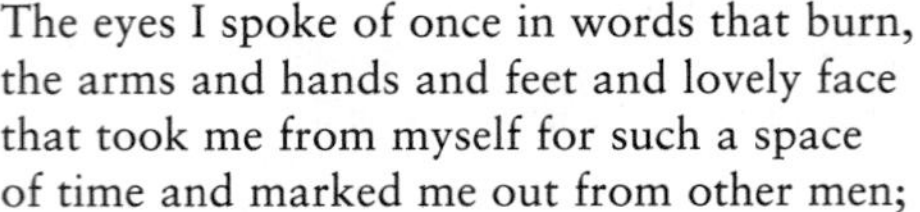

The eyes I spoke of once in words that burn,
the arms and hands and feet and lovely face
that took me from myself for such a space
of time and marked me out from other men;

the waving hair of unmixed gold that shone,
the smile that flashed with the angelic rays
that used to make this earth a paradise,
are now a little dust, all feeling gone;

and yet I live, grief and disdain to me,
left where the light I cherished never shows,
in fragile bark on the tempestuous sea.

Here let my loving song come to a close,
the vein of my accustomed art is dry,
and this, my lyre, turned at last to tears.

Translated by Anthony Mortimer

11 bark: sailing ship; **tempestuous:** stormy.

14 lyre (līr): a stringed musical instrument of the harp family, used in ancient Greece.

Teaching Options

Grammar

VERB PHRASES: GERUNDS AND GERUND PHRASES

Instruction A gerund is a verb form that uses only the *–ing* form of the verb and is always used as a noun. A gerund phrase consists of a gerund and its modifiers and complements.

Activity Write the following lines from "Sonnet 292" on the chalkboard.

"… the waving hair of unmixed gold that shone,
the smile that flashed with the angelic rays
that used to make this earth a paradise,
are now a little dust, all feeling gone; …"

Underline *waving* and *feeling* in the passage. Tell students that one of the underlined words is a gerund and one is a participle. Have students discuss which part of speech each word is and how each word fits its definition. *(waving: participle, form of* wave *used as an adjective modifying* hair*; feeling: gerund, form of* feel *used as a noun that is the subject of the verb* gone.*)*

Connect to the Literature

1. **What Do You Think?** What type of music would convey the overall **mood** of "Sonnet 292"?

Comprehension Check
- What has happened to the woman in the poem?
- Who or what is meant by "fragile bark" and "tempestuous sea"?

Think Critically

2. How would you describe the speaker's feelings over the loss of love?

THINK ABOUT
- his description of his beloved's physical attributes
- his attitude toward his own life (lines 9–11)
- what he means by "the vein of my accustomed art is dry" (line 13)

3. ACTIVE READING SUMMARIZING MAJOR IDEAS IN POEMS Review the summaries for each stanza that you created in your  READER'S NOTEBOOK. How would you describe what happens in each poem? Compare your ideas with those of a partner.

Extend Interpretations

4. **Critic's Corner** Edgar Quinet, a 19th-century French critic, said that "Petrarch's originality consists in having realized, for the first time, that every moment of our existence contains in itself the substance of a poem." Read Petrarch's sonnets again. Do you agree that everyday incidents can in themselves be poetic? Explain your opinion.

5. **Connect to Life** Think again about the two situations presented in these poems. Do you think it is more difficult to cope with a love that is hopeless or with the death of someone you love? Explain your answer.

6. Points of Comparison Compare the attitude toward the beloved in Petrarch's "Sonnet 292" with that in Shakespeare's "Sonnet 130." How does each speaker view his beloved?

7. Points of Comparison Compare the treatment of love in Petrarch's "Sonnet 169" with that in Spenser's "Sonnet 30." How are the two poems similar? How do they differ?

Literary Analysis

ITALIAN SONNET The 14 lines of the Italian sonnet are divided into two parts: an octave (the first eight lines) and a sestet (the last six lines). The usual rhyme scheme for the octave is *abbaabba*. The rhyme scheme for the sestet may be *cdecde, cdccdc,* or a similar variation. The octave generally presents a problem or raises a question, and the sestet resolves or comments on the question.

Cooperative Learning Activity Reread the sonnets by Spenser and those by Shakespeare in this part of Unit Two. Then compare the form of these Italian sonnets with those of Spenser's and Shakespeare's sonnets. Which form do you think gives the writer more liberties? Which seems to you to fit more situations or themes? Jot down your ideas in a chart like the one shown below. Then compare your conclusions with those of your classmates.

Sonnets:		
Spenser's	Shakespeare's	Petrarch's

GUIDING STUDENT RESPONSE

Connect to the Literature

1. **What Do You Think?**
Guidelines for student response: Responses will vary. Accept all reasonable responses. Students should cite examples of the kinds of music they think would work to convey the overall mood.

Comprehension Check
- She has died.
- Possible Response: "Fragile bark" is Petrarch's own body. "Tempestuous sea" is life itself.

Think Critically

2. Possible Responses: grief-stricken, bereft, devastated.
3. Summaries will vary but should be logical interpretations of the text.

Extend Interpretations

Critic's Corner Encourage students to expand their discussion of the poetic value of everyday incidents to include other poems and poets.

Connect to Life Responses will vary.

Points of Comparison Possible Response: The speaker in "Sonnet 292" worships his beloved as if she were a goddess. She served as the inspiration for his poetry, and, her beauty made earth a paradise. In contrast, the speaker in "Sonnet 130" sees his mistress as a real, imperfect woman.

Points of Comparison Possible Response: The two poems are similar because they both address the topic of unrequited love. In "Sonnet 169," however, the speaker avoids the object of his love because it is torment to be near her. "Sonnet 30" is about the continual pursuit of the beloved.

Literary Analysis

Cooperative Learning Activity Have each group present its conclusions to the class. Students can make a composite chart on posterboard.

Exercise Ask students to write each gerund and underline the gerund phrase, then to compose five of their own sentences using gerunds.

1. Petrarch's writing of sonnets predates Shakespeare's sonnets by 200 years. *(writing)*
2. Even without looking at Petrarch, Laura pierces his senses as she passes by. *(looking)*
3. His cherishing of Laura's memory is evidenced in Petrarch's "Sonnet 292." *(cherishing)*
4. Petrarch wrote 300 sonnets expressing his longing for his only love Laura. *(longing)*
5. Even after dying, Laura inspires Petrarch's loving devotion. *(dying)*

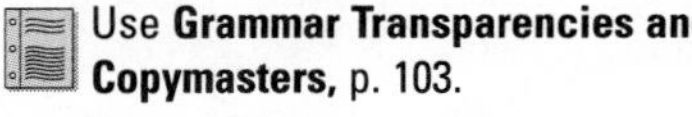
Use **Grammar Transparencies and Copymasters,** p. 103.

Use McDougal Littell's ***Language Network*** for more instruction in verb phrases.

Writing Options

1. **Soap-Opera Outline** To get students started, allow them to work together and brainstorm an outline. Tell students to be prepared to cite details from the poems to support their outlines.
2. **Points of Comparison** Encourage students to reread all the sonnets before deciding which approach they identify with the most. Have students cite lines from the sonnets in their letters to lend support to their positions.

Activities & Explorations

Dance Interpretation Have students work in small groups, with those interested or experienced in dance grouped with classmates who are less experienced.

Inquiry & Research

Italian Renaissance If possible, bring art history books to class that have color photos of paintings by Renaissance artists such as Fra Filippo Lippi. Direct students to appropriate sources on the World Wide Web.

Author Activity

Lady Muse Students may participate more equally if they research the three questions together. Then students could divide the responsibilities for the presentation among group members. For example, one person could prepare a visual aid, another could write a script, and the third could prepare a bibliography of the sources the group used.

Writing Options

1. **Soap-Opera Outline** Write an outline for a series of soap-opera episodes based on Petrarch's two sonnets. Describe the speaker and the woman he loves. Add details to explain the speaker's "hidden pain" and grief. Place the outline in your **Working Portfolio.**

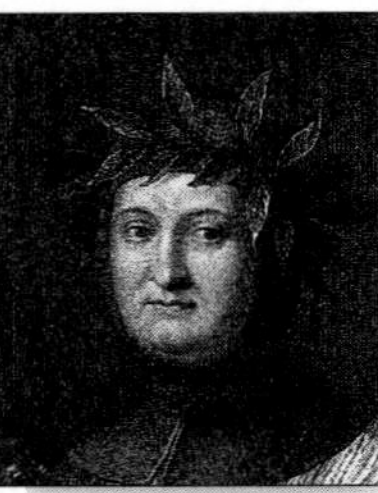

2. **Points of Comparison** Compare the attitude toward love conveyed in the sonnets you have read by Spenser, Shakespeare, and Petrarch. Which approach do you identify with the most? Write a letter to the poet explaining why you appreciate his attitude.

Activities & Explorations

Dance Interpretation Choreograph a dance interpretation of one of Petrarch's sonnets. Create different movements to express the speaker's thoughts and emotions. Perform your dance for the class. ~ **PERFORMING**

Inquiry & Research

Italian Renaissance Research the Italian Renaissance to find out what impact the art and writing of the period had on Europe. What artists and writers led the Renaissance? What themes and ideas were typical of the period?

Francesco Petrarch
1304–1374

Early Years Although born in Italy, Petrarch moved with his family to France, where his father had accepted a job. It was in France that Petrarch, on his father's insistence, began his study of law, later returning to Italy to continue his education. After his father's death in 1326, however, Petrarch abandoned law, a subject for which he had little inclination, to study Greek and Latin literature and to write poetry.

Renaissance Man In the spirit of the Renaissance, Petrarch had varied interests, ranging from the scholarly and literary to a love of and fascination with nature. In 1336, together with his brother, he climbed Mt. Ventoux in the Alps; the climb was quite unusual in an age that showed little interest in nature. He also had a deep interest in religious studies, which led him to join the clergy. The church positions he held provided him not only with a modest means of income but also with much free time to devote to literature. He studied, wrote, and traveled extensively and was highly regarded as a literary and cultural leader of his time.

Wreathed in Laurels In 1340, Petrarch received invitations from both Paris and Rome to become poet laureate. He chose Rome, and in 1341 received the honor of being its first poet laureate since ancient times. Most of the 366 poems in the *Canzoniere* ("Book of Songs"), Petrarch's poetic masterpiece, are written about his love for Laura, who also appears in his *Trionfi* ("Triumphs"). Petrarch never lost his love of writing. He spent the last years of his life composing and revising his literary works, and he died in his study, at work at his desk.

Author Activity

Lady Muse Get together with a small group of classmates and find out what you can about Laura. Divide the following questions among the group members: When did Laura die? Why was the date significant? What else can you find out about her? Present your findings to the class.

LaserLinks: Background for Reading
Author Background

PART 2 A Passion for Power

During Shakespeare's lifetime there were frequent struggles for political control in and around the court of Elizabeth I and her successor, James I. Many of Shakespeare's history plays as well as his tragedies deal with political conflict and the never-ending struggle to achieve a balance between power, justice, and legitimate authority in society. Shakespeare's play *Macbeth* is one of the definitive studies of the effect of power and ambition on the mind and soul. Who should be king and how political power should be first gained and then secured are among the issues addressed in this play.

OVERVIEW

Objectives

- appreciate the craft of England's most famous playwright.
- interpret the possible influences of the historical context on *Macbeth.*
- gain information about Shakespeare by reading nonfiction.

This Author Study offers a unique opportunity for students to focus on the work of a major writer. In addition, students can gather information about the life of Shakespeare, gaining insight into the real person behind his now famous literary works.

Reading Skills and Strategies

Establishing a Purpose for Reading
Have students scan pages 314–322 and establish a purpose or purposes for reading. Discuss the array of material on these pages.

Author Study

WILLIAM SHAKESPEARE

OVERVIEW

"He was not of an age, but for all time!"
—*Ben Jonson*

Master Playwright and Poet

With his brilliant poetic language and keen insight into human nature, William Shakespeare is generally regarded as the world's greatest writer in the English language. His plays are more widely translated than any other works except the Bible. Yet his life remains something of a mystery, with many details lost in the swirl of time.

1564–1616

"I COULD A TALE UNFOLD" Shakespeare was born in Stratford-upon-Avon, a busy market town on the Avon River, northwest of London. Though the precise date of his birth is not known, church records indicate that he was baptized on April 26, 1564. Unlike most other writers of his era, he did not come from a noble family with close ties to the English court. The Shakespeares were what today we would call middle class, although his father, a glove maker, once served as the equivalent of mayor of Stratford.

Though no record of Shakespeare's schooling survives, it is assumed that he attended the local grammar school in Stratford. Again unlike most other writers of his day, Shakespeare did not

HIS LIFE
HIS TIMES

1564 **Is born in Stratford-upon-Avon**

Tudor house in Stratford

1572 **Family suffers a decline in fortune, loses most land holdings**

1560 1565 1570 1575

1558 **Elizabeth I becomes queen; England returns to the Protestant faith.**

Elizabeth I

1572 **Protestants massacred in Paris on St. Bartholomew's Day.**

314

go on to a university; instead, at the age of 18, he married Anne Hathaway, with whom he would have three children. After their birth, the documentary record of Shakespeare's life is once again blank for several years. When he can next be placed, he was in London, working as an actor and beginning to be noticed as a playwright.

This Elizabethan drawing is believed to be of Anne Hathaway.

"THIS REALM, THIS ENGLAND" The London to which Shakespeare came was at the center of a nation just emerging as a major European power. In 1588 the English defeated the powerful Spanish Armada, a fleet of ships carrying a Spanish invasion force to England. In the wake of this victory, London flourished as a commercial center.

The arts, with the support of Queen Elizabeth I, flourished as well. The queen spent much of her time in London, where celebrated literary figures of the day—the poets Edward Spenser and Sir Philip Sidney, among them—visited the royal court. She also enjoyed pageants and plays, as well as the more sophisticated entertainment of classical literature. Attracted by England's vitality, commercial and artistic people from other countries soon began flocking to London, a bustling city of nearly 200,000 people. London's first public theaters sprung up across the Thames River in suburban Southwark. Both the mighty and the humble became avid theatergoers.

LITERARY *Contributions*

Poetic Drama Shakespeare is best known for his **verse drama,** plays in which most of the dialogue is in the form of poetry. In all, he wrote 37 plays, including the following:

All's Well That Ends Well
Antony and Cleopatra
As You Like It
The Comedy of Errors
Hamlet
Henry IV, Parts I and II
Henry V
Julius Caesar
King Lear
Love's Labour's Lost
Macbeth
Measure for Measure
The Merchant of Venice
The Merry Wives of Windsor
A Midsummer Night's Dream
Othello
Richard II
Richard III
Romeo and Juliet
The Taming of the Shrew
The Tempest
Twelfth Night
The Two Gentlemen of Verona
The Winter's Tale

Narrative Poetry In addition to his famous sonnets, Shakespeare wrote two highly regarded narrative poems, ***Venus and Adonis*** (1593) and ***The Rape of Lucrece*** (1594), when the London theaters had to shut down because of an outbreak of plague.

1582 **Marries Anne Hathaway**

1583 **Birth of first child, Susanna**

1585 **Birth of twins, Hamnet and Judith**

1590–92 ***The Comedy of Errors* and *Henry VI* in London**

1594–96 **Joins the Lord Chamberlain's Men**

1596 **Death of Hamnet at age 11**

1580 1585 1590 1595

1577–80 **English explorer Sir Francis Drake sails around the world.**

1587 **Elizabeth executes her cousin Mary, Queen of Scots.**

1588 **England defeats the Spanish Armada.**

1591 ***Astrophel and Stella* by Sir Philip Sidney is published.**

1592–94 **Plague forces closing of London theaters.**

LIFE AND TIMES

World Culture

A If Shakespeare received a traditional education, his experience would have been similar to that of students in schools and colleges throughout Renaissance Europe. The standard curriculum used in these institutions was inherited from the Roman Empire. It consisted of the *trivium* (grammar, logic, and rhetoric) and the *quadrivium* (arithmetic, geometry, astronomy, and music). Courses were conducted in Latin.

History

B After 1560, a wave of immigrants swept into England. Many of these newcomers, who practiced a variety of trades and professions, were Protestants who fled mainland Europe to escape persecution by Catholics. Although most English people supported the idea of asylum for these people, the English in general were suspicious of these "strangers."

Science

C Medical knowledge during Shakespeare's time offered little hope to the sick. Most doctors believed that health was based on four humors, or bodily fluids: blood, phlegm, black bile, and yellow bile. The four humors were supposed to correspond to four elementary qualities: hot, cold, dry, and moist. The prevailing belief was that too much or too little of a particular humor caused illness. As a result, Doctors often treated people with such practices as bleeding, which was thought to restore the proper balance.

History

D Unlike most Renaissance artists, Shakespeare relied more on his popularity with Londoners than on any single wealthy patron for financial support. The practice of patronage began in the Middle Ages when actors traveled from place to place performing their shows. These travelers needed the protection of a powerful person, or patron. In Elizabethan times, patronage gave actors and artists a recognized place in the social structure, allowing them to enjoy the status of gentlemen.

World Culture

E When Shakespeare obtained a coat of arms for his family, it was more than a status symbol. From the time of King Henry V (1387–1422), using a coat of arms in England was illegal without the approval of the English Court of Chivalry. Also, heralds monitored the use of coats of arms in most European countries. The symbols used in a coat of arms placed the owner in a strict social hierarchy, and certain marks even indicated a person's order of birth within the family.

History

F Although the theater was popular during Shakespeare's time, not everyone approved of it. High-ranking Puritan officials passed regulations regarding actors and theaters. For example, some Puritan officials enacted laws stating that no plays could be performed during times of worship or when there was plague in London. Despite Puritan opposition, Queen Elizabeth I and King James I supported and protected theaters and actors. King James even allowed the King's Men, Shakespeare's company, to wear his livery.

LaserLinks
Background for Reading
Use Teacher's SourceBook p. 102 for bar code.

"ALL THE WORLD'S A STAGE" The first extant mention of William Shakespeare's presence on London's literary scene is in a 1592 pamphlet mocking his dramatic efforts. Already famous enough to be criticized (the rival dramatist Robert Greene referred to Shakespeare bitterly as an "upstart crow"), he became a member of the Lord Chamberlain's Men, a company of actors whose patron was an influential member of Elizabeth's court. Shakespeare's plays helped to make the company successful—so successful that the queen herself attended its productions. Although the precise dating of Shakespeare's plays is uncertain, his early masterpieces include *Richard III, The Comedy of Errors, The Taming of the Shrew,* and *Romeo and Juliet.* By 1598, one scholar was praising Shakespeare as England's finest playwright: "As Plautus and Seneca are accounted the best for Comedy and Tragedy among the Latins," wrote Francis Meres, "so Shakespeare among the English is the most excellent in both kinds for the stage."

D Shakespeare's fame was accompanied by a financial success that allowed him to become a partner in London's new Globe Theatre and to purchase a fine home, called New Place, in E Stratford. He also paid to obtain a coat of arms for his father, perhaps in an effort to improve his family's social position.

When Elizabeth's Scottish cousin James succeeded her in 1603, the Lord Chamberlain's F Men became the King's Men, and the company's domination of the London stage continued. In 1608, Shakespeare and the other leading members of the King's Men even leased a second London theater, the Blackfriars, which was better equipped for winter performances.

"OUR REVELS NOW ARE ENDED" After 1608, Shakespeare curtailed his theatrical activities and spent more time back in Stratford. He wrote no plays after 1613; his last complete dramas are believed to be *The Winter's Tale, The Tempest,* and *Henry VIII.* He died in 1616 and was buried in his parish church in Stratford. His famous epitaph, which he may have written himself, reads:

Good friend, for Jesus' sake forbear
To dig the dust enclosed here.
Blest be the man that spares these stones,
And curst be he that moves my bones.

More Online: Author Link
www.mcdougallittell.com

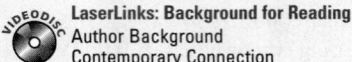

LaserLinks: Background for Reading
Author Background
Contemporary Connection

1603 Receives royal license for the King's Men

1605–6 First performances of *King Lear* and *Macbeth*

1608 Leases London's Blackfriars Theatre

1611–12 First performance of *The Tempest*

1616 Dies on April 23

1600 — 1605 — 1610 — 1615

1600 East India Company receives a royal charter.

1603 Elizabeth I dies; James VI of Scotland becomes James I of England.

James I

1611 King James translation of the Bible appears.

To Be or Not to Be *Shakespeare*

Because documentary evidence of his life is scanty and his origins and education were relatively humble, some people have for centuries (G) speculated that Shakespeare did not write the works attributed to him. Such theories persist even though they have no basis in solid fact and many scholars dispute them. Here are some of the nearly 60 people who have been offered by various sources as the real Shakespeare.

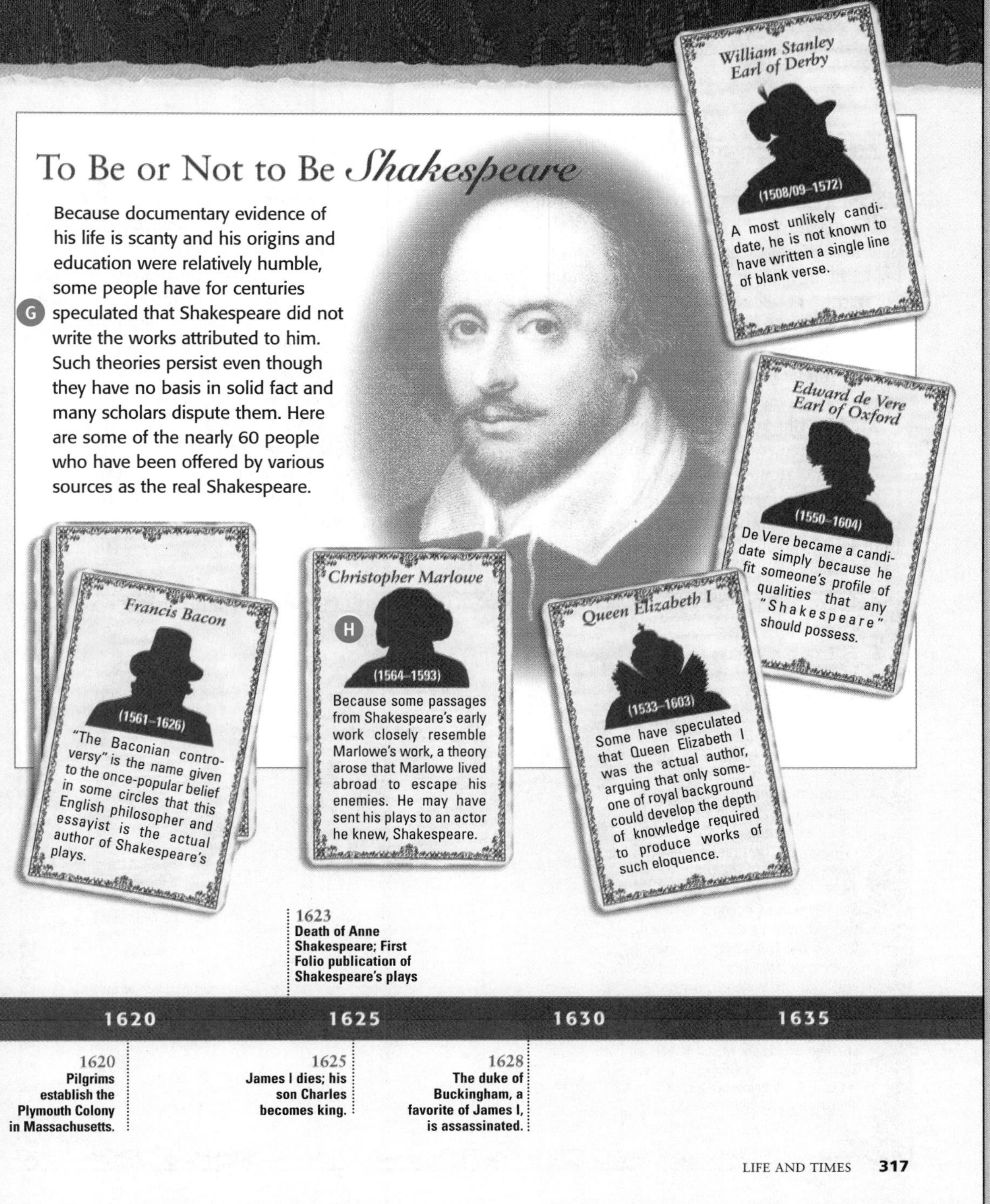

William Stanley Earl of Derby
(1508/09–1572)
A most unlikely candidate, he is not known to have written a single line of blank verse.
Edward de Vere Earl of Oxford
(1550–1604)
De Vere became a candidate simply because he fit someone's profile of qualities that any "Shakespeare" should possess.
Francis Bacon
(1561–1626)
"The Baconian controversy" is the name given to the once-popular belief in some circles that this English philosopher and essayist is the actual author of Shakespeare's plays.
Christopher Marlowe
(H)
(1564–1593)
Because some passages from Shakespeare's early work closely resemble Marlowe's work, a theory arose that Marlowe lived abroad to escape his enemies. He may have sent his plays to an actor he knew, Shakespeare.
Queen Elizabeth I
(1533–1603)
Some have speculated that Queen Elizabeth I was the actual author, arguing that only someone of royal background could develop the depth of knowledge required to produce works of such eloquence.

1623
Death of Anne Shakespeare; First Folio publication of Shakespeare's plays

1620 | 1625 | 1630 | 1635

1620
Pilgrims establish the Plymouth Colony in Massachusetts.

1625
James I dies; his son Charles becomes king.

1628
The duke of Buckingham, a favorite of James I, is assassinated.

History

(G) Some of those thought to be the "real Shakespeare" were members of the royal court. A Renaissance court was made up of a ruler, the ruler's family, and the support people needed to help the ruler govern. A typical court included guards, escorts, patrols, scribes, secretaries, major-domos (they arranged meetings), cooks, musicians, stable workers, artists, historians, poets, and others. Some courts consisted of 1,500 to 2,000 people. Before the mid-16th century, most courts traveled with their rulers. For example, Queen Elizabeth I moved throughout England attracting supporters.

History

(H) Christopher Marlowe was born in 1564, the same year as Shakespeare. Marlowe was one of the first playwrights to adapt the ancient form of the tragedy to the Elizabethan stage. The heroes of his plays possess the tragic flaw of hubris, and Marlowe also used rich language in his dialogue. His plays had a strong influence on Shakespeare, who further developed Elizabethan tragedy.

World Culture

I Renaissance acting companies such as Shakespeare's developed from groups of players who traveled Europe performing morality plays in churches, inn yards, and noblemen's houses. These players were usually accompanied by jugglers, dancers, and other entertainers. Eventually, Oxford colleges and clubs in France, the Netherlands, and Italy began paying actors to perform secular plays in their halls. These shows laid the foundation for the creation of new, secular plays, which would be produced in large, enclosed settings.

Science/Technology

J Theaters of the Renaissance used a variety of "machines" to achieve special effects. One was a device similar to a crane, which lowered actors playing gods from above the stage. Another effect involved scenes that were supposed to take place in another room or setting. Elements of the scene were put on wheels and pushed out into the view of the audience. Lightning could be imitated by painting flashes of lightning on planks with dark backgrounds and dropping them into the audience's view.

The English Renaissance Theater

From the Courtyard to the Globe

The Renaissance brought to England a heightened interest in drama—at first in the universities, then in the royal court, and finally among the public at large. Although, small private stage productions might be held indoors, in schools, royal palaces, and noblemen's homes, public performances demanded more space and access.

I Most of the earliest public performances were held in the courtyards of inns, with the spectators watching from the surrounding balconies. The permanent public theater was designed to resemble one of these courtyards. Built by James Burbage, it opened in 1576 in the London suburb of Shoreditch and was called simply the Theatre. Later two other theaters, the Rose and the Swan, opened in the Bankside area of Southwark, just south of central London. This location proved popular, and in 1599 the original Theatre was torn down and rebuilt in the Bankside area as the Globe. By 1600, London had more playhouses than any other European capital.

Because the Globe—which Shakespeare referred to as "this Wooden O" in *Henry V*—was home to the Lord Chamberlain's Men, the acting company with which Shakespeare was affiliated, it is the best-known of the Elizabethan public theaters.

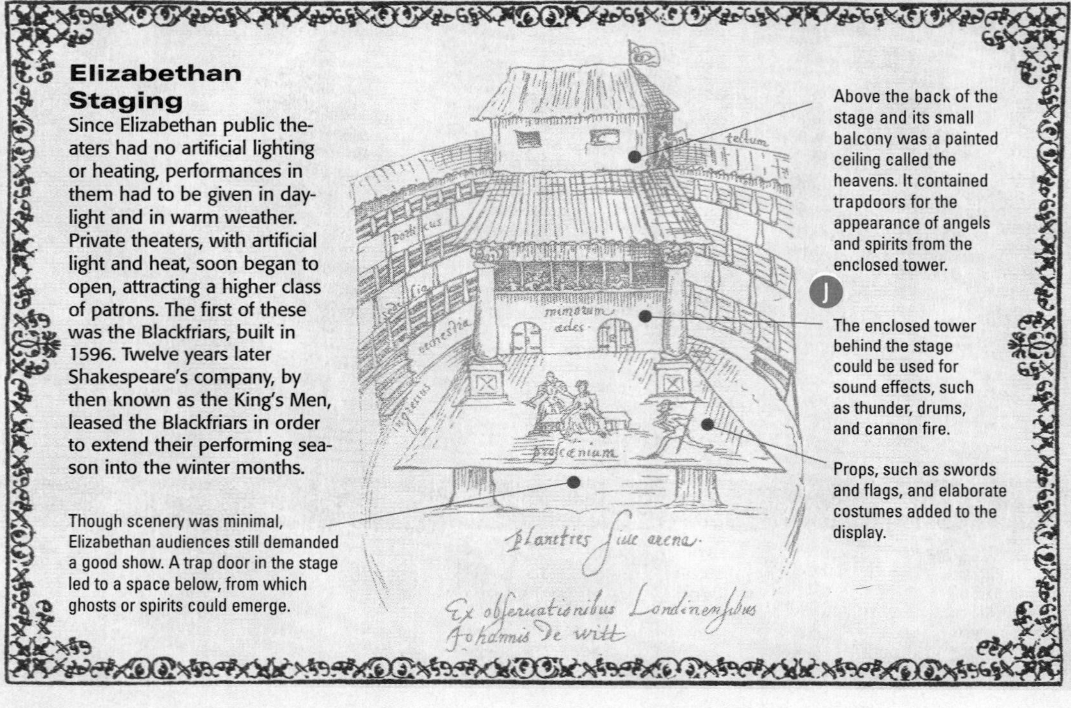

Elizabethan Staging

Since Elizabethan public theaters had no artificial lighting or heating, performances in them had to be given in daylight and in warm weather. Private theaters, with artificial light and heat, soon began to open, attracting a higher class of patrons. The first of these was the Blackfriars, built in 1596. Twelve years later Shakespeare's company, by then known as the King's Men, leased the Blackfriars in order to extend their performing season into the winter months.

Though scenery was minimal, Elizabethan audiences still demanded a good show. A trap door in the stage led to a space below, from which ghosts or spirits could emerge.

Above the back of the stage and its small balcony was a painted ceiling called the heavens. It contained trapdoors for the appearance of angels and spirits from the enclosed tower.

J The enclosed tower behind the stage could be used for sound effects, such as thunder, drums, and cannon fire.

Props, such as swords and flags, and elaborate costumes added to the display.

"THIS WOODEN O" The Globe Theatre was a three-story wooden structure that could hold as many as 3,000 people. Plays were performed in the open air on a platform stage that jutted out into a roofless courtyard in the theater's center, where the poorer patrons, or "groundlings," stood to watch the performance. Except for the part directly behind the stage, the theater building consisted of covered galleries where wealthier patrons sat, protected from the elements.

A 17th century drawing of the Globe Theater in its London neighborhood

ELIZABETHAN ACTORS It wasn't easy being an actor in Shakespeare's time. Besides having to memorize their lines, actors had to be able to sing and dance, wrestle and fence, clown and weep. They also had to be able to convey subtle messages with simple gestures or minor changes in voice. Because the stage had no front curtain, the actors always walked on and off the stage in full view of the audience. Plays had to be written so that any character who died on stage could be unobtrusively hauled off.

Actors worked in close proximity to the audience, who either stood around the stage, eating and drinking, or watched from the galleries. If audience members disapproved of certain characters or lines, they would let the actors know by jeering or throwing food. The large crowds also attracted pickpockets and other ruffians. The rowdiness of the audiences caused many towns to label actors as vagrants, lumping them together with rogues, vagabonds, and other undesirables.

Because of the scandalous nature of the Elizabethan theater, women were not allowed to perform. All the actors were male, with young boys usually playing the female roles, from aging matrons to young lovers. Shakespeare himself was an actor as well as a playwright, although it was in the latter capacity that he won fame. The leading tragic actor in Shakespeare's company was Richard Burbage, the son of the man who had built London's first theater.

THE FATE OF THE GLOBE In 1613, the K Globe's roof caught fire during a performance of *Henry VIII,* and the theater was destroyed. It was quickly rebuilt at the same location, however this time with a tiled gallery roof. Only 30 years later, Oliver Cromwell and the Puritans suppressed what they considered a frivolous form of entertainment by closing the theater's doors. The Globe was torn down in 1644 and replaced with tenement housing. A lively period in London's history had come to a close.

History

K The Globe Theater was the first to be owned in part by the actors who played there. On the afternoon of June 29, 1613, the Globe was presenting Shakespeare's *Henry VIII*. During a battle scene, a spark from the burning fuse on a cannon ignited the thatch roof. No one was injured, but the resulting fire destroyed the theater. The same group of actors and businessmen rebuilt the Globe but covered the interior roof with tiles to prevent future fires.

LIFE AND TIMES 319

Science

(L) In order to excavate the site of the Globe Theater, archaeologists first made maps of the site. They then divided the area into small squares to record the exact location of each object found. Archaeologists then classified the objects by typology— matching it to a type of known object—or seriation—matching it with a series of styles of a particular object type. The ages of objects were determined by radiocarbon dating or potassium-argon dating. Both methods measure the decay of certain chemicals in an object.

The Rebirth of the Globe

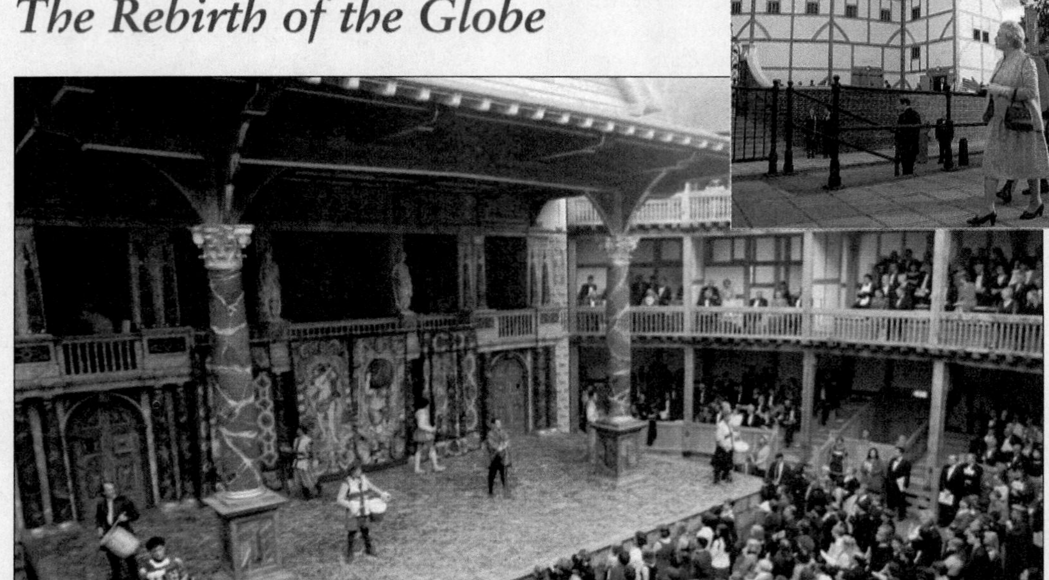

One of the first performances in the newly restored Globe Theater; *inset:* Queen Elizabeth II views the exterior of the new Globe Theater, 1997.

After more than 300 years, a new Globe Theatre now stands only 200 yards from the original site. A pet project of the American actor Sam (L) Wanamaker and a product of much historical and archaeological research, it opened in June 1997 with a performance of *Henry V.* The new Globe features three levels of wooden benches surrounding an open yard and a platform stage. It seats 1,500 theatergoers—substantially fewer than the 3,000 that the original theater held—because today's audiences prefer not to be crowded as close together as Elizabethan audiences were.

As in its Elizabethan namesake, no formal sets, microphones, or spotlights are used in productions at today's Globe. And another Elizabethan tradition continues: contemporary audiences often mimic their 16th-century predecessors by voicing their reactions, sometimes quite loudly and energetically, to events on the stage.

Shakespearean Tragedy

Renaissance Drama

During the Middle Ages, English drama focused mainly on religious themes, teaching moral lessons or retelling Bible stories to a populace that by and large could not read. With the Renaissance, however, came a rebirth of interest in the dramas of ancient Greece and Rome. First at England's universities and then among graduates of those universities, plays imitating classical models became increasingly popular. These plays fell into two main categories: **comedies** and **tragedies.**

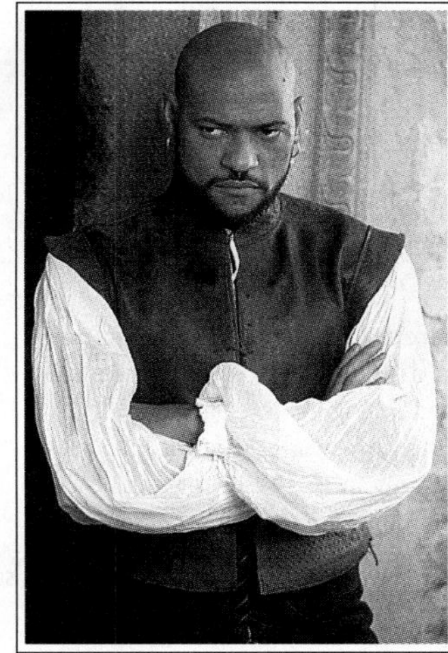

Laurence Fishburne as Othello in the 1995 film directed by Oliver Parker

In Renaissance England, comedy was broadly defined as a dramatic work with a happy ending; many comedies contained humor, but humor was not required. A tragedy, in contrast, was a work in which the main character, or tragic hero, came to an unhappy end. In addition to comedies and tragedies, Shakespeare wrote several plays classified as histories—these present stories about England's earlier monarchs. Of all Shakespeare's plays, however, his tragedies are the ones most often cited as his greatest.

The Greek Origins of Tragedy

In the Western tradition, both comedies and tragedies arose in ancient Greece, where they were performed as part of elaborate outdoor festivals. According to the definition of the famous ancient Greek philosopher Aristotle, tragedy arouses pity and fear in the audience—pity for the hero and fear for all human beings, who are subject to character flaws and an unknown destiny. Seeing a tragedy unfold produces a catharsis, or cleansing, of these emotions, for by the end the audience is watching in awe as the hero faces defeat with great courage and dignity.

In ancient Greek tragedies, the heroes' tragic flaw was often hubris—an excessive pride that led a tragic hero to challenge the gods. Angered by such hubris, the gods unleashed their retribution, or nemesis, on the hero. Ancient Greek tragedies also made use of a chorus, a group of performers who stood outside the action and commented on the events and characters in a play, often hinting at the doom to come and stressing the fatalistic aspect of the hero's downfall. By Shakespeare's day, the chorus consisted of only one person—a kind of narrator—or was dispensed with entirely.

Characteristics of Tragedy

Shakespearean tragedy differs somewhat from classic Greek tragedy in that Shakespeare's works are not unrelentingly serious. For example, he often eased the intensity of the action by using the device of **comic relief**—the following of a serious scene with a lighter, mildly humorous one. Nevertheless, the following general characteristics are shared by Shakespearean tragedy and classic Greek tragedy:

- The main character, called the **tragic hero,** comes to an unhappy or miserable end.
- The tragic hero is generally a person of importance in society, such as a king or a queen.
- The tragic hero exhibits extraordinary abilities but also a **tragic flaw,** a fatal error in judgment or weakness of character, that leads directly to his or her downfall.

OVERVIEW

Objectives

- understand the following literary terms:
  - Comedy
  - Tragedy
  - Comic relief
  - Tragic hero
  - Tragic flaw
  - Antagonist
  - Catastrophe
- recognize shared characteristics of literature across cultures.
- recognize themes across cultures.

Teaching the Lesson

Introducing the Concepts

As students read *Macbeth,* have them consider the following questions:

If someone wrote Macbeth's story today, would he be the hero or the villain?

Possible Response: He could be viewed as a villain for whom the audience has sympathy.

If you were to rewrite *Macbeth* in a modern setting, what might Macbeth's job be?

Possible Response: *Macbeth* could possibly be written in a corporate setting with Macbeth holding the top position in a large company.

As they finish reading the play, students can write reactions to these questions and keep their responses in their Writing Portfolios.

Presenting the Concepts

Monitoring and Modifying Reading Strategies

Have students read through the strategies for reading Shakespearean Tragedy on page 322. Encourage them to apply these strategies in their understanding of *Macbeth* breaks down. By developing a repertoire of strategies, students will become more flexible and responsive readers.

Making Connections

Tragedy Across Cultures

Writers across Europe wrote tragedies similar to those of the ancient Greeks. Some of these tragedies were based on Greek plays and myths, while others made use of historical events. Share the following information about Renaissance tragedies with students.

Spain

Spanish tragedies of the Renaissance, like those of Shakespeare, were often based on events in Europe. Two Spanish playwrights, Damián Salucio del Poyo and Antonio Mira de Amescua, wrote tragedies about Spanish court favorite Don Álvaro de Luna. Spanish tragedies were also written about the 6th-century Byzantine hero Belisarius, the 16th-century Portuguese general Duarte Pacheco Pereira, the French dukes Biron and Montmorency, and Queen Elizabeth's favorite, the earl of Essex.

France

The great French tragedian Corneille (1625–1709) wrote tragedies based on Greek plays such as *Medea* and *Oedipus Rex*, but his masterpiece was *El Cid.* It is based on a Spanish story about a man whose honor demands that he avenge an insult to his father made by the father of his own beloved. Corneille's rival, Racine (1639–1699), also wrote a mixture of Greek-based and more historically based tragedies.

Italy

Italian writers of tragedy also drew from Greek myths, such as that of Ulysses. However, the Italian dramatist Tasso (1544–1595) wrote a tragedy called *Il re Torrismondo* that, like Shakespeare's *Hamlet,* told the story of a Scandinavian prince during the Middle Ages.

- Outside forces may also contribute to the hero's downfall. If so, the person or force with whom the hero battles is called the **antagonist.**
- A series of causally related events lead inevitably to the **catastrophe,** or tragic resolution. This final stage of the plot usually involves the death of the hero, but other characters may also be affected.
- The tragic hero usually recognizes his or her tragic flaw by the end and so gains the audience's sympathy.
- The tragic hero meets his or her doom with courage and dignity, reaffirming the grandeur of the human spirit.

Shakespeare on the Big Screen

Leonardo DiCaprio and Clare Danes as Romeo and Juliet, 1997

Romeo and Juliet, Shakespeare's first great tragedy, is a tale of teenaged lovers from two feuding families in medieval Verona, Italy. A 1997 film version featured Leonardo Di Caprio and Clare Danes.

Julius Caesar focuses on Roman emperor Brutus, a close friend of Julius Caesar's who reluctantly joins the plot to assassinate him. Marlon Brando played Mark Anthony in the 1953 version.

Hamlet tells the story of a prince of Denmark whose procrastination leads to disaster. Kenneth Branagh directed and starred in the 1996 epic film that uses all of Shakespeare's original script.

Othello focuses on a North African soldier whose great flaw "is the green-eyed monster," jealousy. In 1995, Laurence Fishburne appeared in the title role.

King Lear tells of an aged monarch who fails to distinguish honesty from flattery. *A Thousand Acres,* an update of the King Lear story, became a film in 1997.

Macbeth, which appears in this book (see page 323), is a powerful drama of ambition and murder. Several images appearing throughout the selection are from Orson Welles's 1948 version and Roman Polanski's 1971 version.

YOUR TURN Why do you think that so many of Shakespeare's plays have been adapted to film?

Strategies for Reading: Shakespearean Tragedy

1. Trace the plot's main events, especially the causes and effects that lead to the catastrophe. Watch for the first event that sets the series in motion. At what point is there no turning back?
2. Sort out the antagonists in the play. Who is against whom, and what are the conflicts?
3. Identify the tragic hero. Make sure that you can justify your choice with reasons.
4. Determine the hero's admirable character traits as well as his or her tragic flaw.
5. Analyze how the tragic hero faces destiny. Does he or she show courage and dignity in defeat?
6. **Monitor** your reading strategies and modify them when your understanding breaks down. Remember to use your Strategies for Active Reading: **predict, visualize, connect, question, clarify,** and **evaluate.**

The Tragedy of Macbeth

Verse drama by WILLIAM SHAKESPEARE

"Fair is foul, and foul is fair."

Connect to Your Life

Ambitious Goals Lazy people are often blamed for having too little ambition. At the same time, many overachievers are criticized for excessive single-mindedness or for doing the wrong things to achieve their goals. Think about your own ambitions and the people you would describe as ambitious. When is ambition good? When is it undesirable or even evil? Share your ideas in a class discussion.

Build Background

A Scottish Clan Ambition is a driving force in *Macbeth.* The title character is based to some extent on a historical Macbeth, a king of 11th-century Scotland who seized the monarchy after killing his predecessor, Duncan I. The play was written to please King James I, who had been the King of Scotland (as James VI) before the death of his cousin Elizabeth in 1603 brought him to the English throne. King James became the patron, or chief sponsor, of Shakespeare's acting company, thereafter known as the King's Men. *The Tragedy of Macbeth* was probably first performed in the summer of 1606, with James I and the visiting king of Denmark in attendance.

Shakespeare's desire to please King James may account for the prominence of witchcraft in *Macbeth.* The new king was quite interested in the subject, having himself written a book on witchcraft, called *Demonology,* which was published in 1597. Belief in witchcraft was widespread in Shakespeare's day, particularly among less educated people. Members of the nobility, whether or not they truly believed in witches, at times used accusations of witchcraft as a way to get rid of political enemies.

OVERVIEW

An excerpt of this selection is included in the **Grade 12 InterActive Reader.**

Objectives

1. understand and appreciate a classic Shakespearean tragedy **(Literary Analysis)**
2. identify and examine **soliloquies and asides** in a tragedy **(Literary Analysis)**
3. identify and examine **theme** in a tragedy **(Literary Analysis)**
4. identify and examine **blank verse (Literary Analysis)**
5. identify and examine **dramatic irony (Literary Analysis)**
6. identify and examine **foreshadowing** in a classic tragedy **(Literary Analysis)**
7. use strategies for understanding **Shakespeare's language (Active Reading)**
8. use strategies for reading **drama (Active Reading)**
9. expand vocabulary by listening, using context, discussing **(Vocabulary)**

Summary

The Tragedy of Macbeth, first performed in 1606, opens with the triggering of latent ambitions held by the Scottish noble Macbeth, thane of Cawdor, as he comes upon three witches, who hail him as king of Scotland. Spurred on by his ruthless wife, Lady Macbeth, he murders King Duncan and usurps the throne. The couple is haunted by the bloody deed. Lady Macbeth loses her mind and dies; tormented by ghosts, Macbeth is slain by the noble Macduff. The throne is restored to Duncan's son Malcolm.

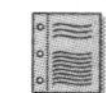

Use **Unit Two Resource Book,** pp. 14, 18, 22, and 30 for additional support.

Thematic Link

The overriding theme of crime and consequence as a result of **a passion for power** pervades this tragedy as Macbeth, a brave and intelligent man, deliberately murders his king, a deed that escalates into more murders and, eventually, his own violent death.

LESSON RESOURCES

UNIT TWO RESOURCE BOOK, pp. 14–33

ASSESSMENT RESOURCES

Formal Assessment, pp. 53–62

Teacher's Guide to Assessment and Portfolio Use

Test Generator

SKILLS TRANSPARENCIES AND COPYMASTERS

Literary Analysis

- Dramatic Irony in Shakespeare, T6 (for Literary Analysis, p. 324)
- Foreshadowing in Shakespeare, T7 (for Literary Analysis, p. 324)
- Characteristics of Tragedy, T8 (for Shakespearean Tragedy, p. 321)

Reading and Critical Thinking

- Summarizing, T10 (for Active Reading, p. 324)

Grammar

- Comparison of Regular and Irregular Adjectives and Adverbs, T52 (for Mini Lesson, p. 344)
- Identifying Adjectives, C68 (for Mini Lesson, p. 344)
- Identifying Adverbs, C70 (for Mini Lesson, p. 370)
- Avoiding Double Comparisons, C155 (for Mini Lesson, p. 394)
- Avoiding Illogical Comparisons, C156 (for Mini Lesson, p. 406)

Vocabulary

- Using a Dictionary and Context to Determine Meaning, C35 (for Mini Lesson, p. 330)
- Word Origins, C38 (for Mini Lesson, p. 356)
- Connotation, C39 (for Mini Lesson, p. 415)

TEACHING THE LITERATURE

Reading and Analyzing

Literary Analysis SOLILOQUY/ASIDE

A Arrange students in small groups. Have them review the characteristics of the soliloquy and the aside on p. 324. Then have each group write a brief scene in which one character performs a soliloquy while 2 or 3 other characters make asides to the audience and each other. The students may make their scenes humorous if they wish. You might allow them to assign parts and perform their scenes.

Literary Analysis BLANK VERSE

B Have students read aloud the example given for blank verse on p. 324: "So fair and foul a day I have not seen." Remind them that blank verse consists of unrhymed lines of iambic pentameter, and ask them to clap the rhythm as they reread the line aloud. Then, ask for volunteers to identify and read aloud several lines of blank verse from Macbeth.

Literary Analysis THEME

C To ensure that students understand the meaning of each topic, ask them to work in small groups to discuss definitions of the topics listed. Encourage students to use a dictionary to help them with any unfamiliar terms. Have students prepare possible themes related to the topics. Have them name stories they have read that have these themes.

Active Reading
SHAKESPEARE'S LANGUAGE

D As a prereading exercise, students may work in small groups, practicing the four steps listed on p. 325 to help them understand Shakespeare's language. Have each group select one or two pages of *Macbeth* on which to explore the four steps. Encourage students to take turns reading aloud and discussing the four steps. Remind students to monitor their strategies and modify them as necessary by the suggested strategies.

Focus Your Reading: Literary Analysis

A

LITERARY ANALYSIS SOLILOQUY/ASIDE Authors of plays rely on certain conventions to give the audience more information about the characters. Two such conventions are the soliloquy and the aside.

- A **soliloquy** is a speech that a character makes while alone on stage, to reveal his or her thoughts to the audience.
- An **aside** is a remark that a character makes in an undertone to the audience or another character but that others on stage are not supposed to hear. A stage direction clarifies that a remark is an aside; unless otherwise specified, the aside is to the audience. Here is an example:

  Macbeth. [*Aside*] Glamis, and Thane of Cawdor!
  The greatest is behind.—[*To* Ross *and* Angus] Thanks for your pains.
  [*Aside to* Banquo] Do you not hope your children shall be kings . . . ?

B

LITERARY ANALYSIS BLANK VERSE Like most plays written before the 20th century, *Macbeth* is a **verse drama,** a play in which the dialogue consists almost entirely of poetry with a fixed pattern of rhythm, or **meter.** Many English verse dramas are written in blank verse, or unrhymed iambic pentameter, a meter in which the normal line contains five stressed syllables, each preceded by an unstressed syllable:

Sŏ fóul ănd fáir ă dáy Ĭ háve nŏt séen.

Blank verse has been a popular medium for drama because it easily accommodates the rhythms of spoken English.

LITERARY ANALYSIS DRAMATIC IRONY **Irony** is based on a contrast between appearance or expectation and reality. In **dramatic irony,** what appears true to one or more characters in a play is seen to be false to the audience. The audience has a more complete picture of the action, because it knows more details. In Act One of *Macbeth,* dramatic irony can be found in Duncan's words to Lady Macbeth upon his arrival at the Macbeths' castle.

Conduct me to mine host. We love him highly
And shall continue our graces toward him.

Duncan is sure of Macbeth's loyalty and says that he will continue to honor Macbeth with marks of his favor. However, the audience knows that Macbeth is planning to murder Duncan to increase his own power. The audience recognizes the irony of Duncan's trusting remarks.

LITERARY ANALYSIS FORESHADOWING **Foreshadowing** is a writer's use of hints or clues to suggest what events will occur later in a work. The witches' prophesies are the most explicit hints of what is going to happen in the play. As you read *Macbeth,* list examples of foreshadowing and the events you think they hint at.

Act, Scene, Lines	What the Lines Hint At
Act Two, Scene 1, lines 62–64	Macbeth will murder Duncan.

C

LITERARY ANALYSIS THEME A **theme** is a central idea conveyed by a work of literature. Not to be confused with the work's subject (what it is about in a literal sense), a theme is a general perception about life or human nature. Longer works like *Macbeth* usually contain several themes. As you read the play, take notes about what it has to say about the following topics:

- ambition
- impulses and desires
- marriage
- fate and our efforts to control it
- appearance versus reality
- loyalty
- the supernatural
- reason and mental stability

LESSON RESOURCES, continued

- Using Context to Determine Meaning, C40 (for Mini Lesson, p. 372)
- Words Coined by Shakespeare, C41 (for Mini Lesson, p. 386)
- Using a Dictionary, C42 (for Mini Lesson, p. 390)
- Using Context to Determine Meaning, C43 (for Mini Lesson, p. 336)
- Denotation and Connotation, C44 (for Mini Lesson, p. 415)

Writing

- Showing, Not Telling, T22 (for Writing Option 1, p. 422)
- Personality Profile, C25 (for Inquiry & Research, p. 422)

Communications

- Dramatic Reading, T12 (for Mini Lesson, p. 404)
- Giving and Using Feedback to Improve Performance, T16 (for Activities & Explorations, p. 422)

INTEGRATED TECHNOLOGY

Audio Library

LaserLinks

- Author Background: An Afternoon at the Globe Theater
- Contemporary Connection: Shakespeare Today. See **Teacher's SourceBook,** p. 24.

Video: Literature in Performance

- from *Macbeth,* two film adaptations. See **Video Resource Book,** pp. 15–22.

Internet: Research Starter
Visit our website:
www.mcdougallittell.com

Focus Your Reading: Active Reading Skills

Using Your READER'S NOTEBOOK
As you read *Macbeth,* record any of your questions or comments about Shakespeare's use of dramatic conventions or language. For specific suggestions, refer to the Active Reading strategies that follow.

ACTIVE READING | READING DRAMA The printed text of Shakespeare's *Macbeth,* like that of any drama, consists mainly of **dialogue** spoken by the characters (with labels that show who is speaking) and **stage directions** that specify settings (times and places) and tell how characters behave and speak. The play is divided into **acts,** which are themselves divided into **scenes.** The beginning of a new scene usually involves a change in setting.

Strategies for Reading *Macbeth*

1. Read the opening list of characters—the dramatis personae, to familiarize yourself with the characters.
2. Study the plot summary and stage directions at the beginning of each scene. Try to develop a mental picture of the setting of the scene's action.
3. Pay attention to the labels that show who is speaking and to stage directions that indicate to whom the characters are speaking. Try to envision what each character might look and sound like if you were seeing the play performed on a stage.
4. To get a better sense of what the dialogue might sound like, try reading some of it aloud.

ACTIVE READING | SHAKESPEARE'S LANGUAGE
Though Shakespeare wrote in modern English, the language of his time was quite different from today's English. Here are some major differences:

- **Grammatical forms:** In Shakespeare's day, people still commonly used the pronouns *thou, thee, thy, thine,* and *thyself* in place of forms of *you.* Verb forms that are now outdated were also in use—*art* for *are* and *cometh* for *comes,* for example.
- **Grammatical structures:** Helping verbs were used far less than they are today. For example, instead of saying "Don't you know he has?" Lady Macbeth says "Know you not he has?"
- **Unusual word order:** Shakespeare often puts verbs before subjects, objects before verbs, and other sentence parts in positions that now seem unusual. For instance, Lady Macbeth says "O, never shall the sun that morrow see!" instead of "O, the sun shall never see that morrow!"
- **Unfamiliar vocabulary:** Shakespeare's vocabulary included many words no longer in use (like *seeling* meaning "blinding") or with meanings different from their meanings today (like *choppy* meaning "chapped"). Shakespeare also coined new words, some of which (like *assassination*) have become a permanent part of the language. The Guide for Reading notes accompanying the play will clarify the meanings of many of the unfamiliar words.

D

Strategies for Reading Shakespeare's Language

As you read *Macbeth,* you may find it helpful to go through the scenes several times to improve your understanding of the language.

1. Skim each scene quickly to get a general sense of what is going on.
2. Study the Guide for Reading notes for help with the unfamiliar vocabulary and phrasing.
3. Go through the scene again, paraphrasing the lines in your head to clarify their meaning.
4. Read through the scene—or at least the important speeches—one more time, focusing on the figurative language and sensory images (imagery that appeals to the five senses) and the clues they contain about the characters and themes.
5. Focus on the wording of the dialogue, especially asides or soliloquies, to make inferences about the characters' their feelings, attitudes, thoughts, and motives.

BLOCK SCHEDULING: MANAGING TIME

If your schedule requires that you cover the lesson objectives in a shorter time, use . . .

- Preparing to Read, pp. 323–325
- Thinking Through the Literature, p. 346

If you want to take advantage of longer class time, use . . .

- TE Teaching Options: Viewing and Representing, pp. 332, 337; Cross Curricular Links, pp. 328, 331; Vocabulary Strategy, pp. 330, 342; Multicultural Links, p. 333; Speaking and Listening, p. 340; Standardized Test Practice, p. 336; Informal Assessment, p. 338; Grammar, p. 344

Reading and Analyzing

Active Reading
SHAKESPEARE'S LANGUAGE

Review with students that they will encounter unusual grammatical forms and structures, word order, and vocabulary in Shakespeare's play. In the cast of characters listed on page 327, for example, students may not be familiar with the phrase "attending on" (that is, *serving* or *waiting upon*).

Use **Unit Two Resource Book** p. 15 for more practice.

Literary Analysis **SOLILOQUY/ASIDE**

Remind students that soliloquies and asides are dramatic conventions used to convey information to the audience. Actors acknowledge the audience through asides, while they seem to ignore the audience during a soliloquy. Encourage students to make notes on when soliloquies and asides are used during the play (in moments of conflict, when new information or characters are introduced, and so on). Have students comment on which technique seems more realistic.

Use **Unit Two Resource Book** p. 16 for more exercises.

Orson Welles as Macbeth
(film, directed by Orson Welles, 1948)

Macbeth

William Shakespeare

 CHARACTERS 

Duncan, king of Scotland

His sons
- **Malcolm**
- **Donalbain**

Noblemen of Scotland
- **Macbeth**
- **Banquo**
- **Macduff**
- **Lennox**
- **Ross**
- **Menteith** (mĕn-tēth')
- **Angus**
- **Caithness** (kāth'nĭs)

Fleance (flā'əns), son to Banquo

Siward (syōō'ərd), earl of Northumberland, general of the English forces

Young Siward, his son

Seyton (sā'tən), an officer attending on Macbeth

Son, to Macduff

An English Doctor

A Scottish Doctor

A Porter

An Old Man

Three Murderers

Lady Macbeth

Lady Macduff

A Gentlewoman attending on Lady Macbeth

Hecate (hĕk'ĭt), goddess of witchcraft

Three Witches

Apparitions

Lords, Officers, Soldiers, Messengers, and Attendants

THE TIME: THE ELEVENTH CENTURY
THE PLACE: SCOTLAND AND ENGLAND

Customizing Instruction

Less Proficient Readers

As you begin teaching the selection, write the following questions on the chalkboard. Have students copy the questions on a sheet of paper, leaving several lines of space between each question; have them answer the questions as they read.

- Who are the characters in the story?
- What is the setting of each act?
- What is the main conflict?
- How would you describe the climax?

Students Acquiring English

Have students look at the photo images throughout the selection and discuss how the images offer clues about the characters.

 Use **Spanish Study Guide** for additional support, pp. 64–66

Gifted and Talented

As you introduce students to this selection, explain that it is a story about an otherwise decent man who becomes corrupt. Ask them to analyze Macbeth's actions as they read and to jot down their thoughts about reasons for his declining behavior.

Possible Responses: greedy ambition—perhaps he's trying to impress Lady Macbeth and others; desire for power—he doesn't feel strong enough in his current position; desperate need for attention—he wants others to notice him more, etc.

Reading and Analyzing

Literary Analysis: FORESHADOWING

A Remind students that foreshadowing builds a sense of what is to come and often ties this future action to a theme. Point out the following instances of foreshadowing:

- The thunder and lightning in the stage directions.
- "When the hurlyburly's done / When the battle's lost and won" (lines 3–4).
- "Fair is foul, and foul is fair" (line 10).

Ask students what these three examples have in common.

Possible Responses: They all refer to frightening or violent events; they all refer to a disturbance of nature.

Literary Analysis: THEME

Remind students that foreshadowing often ties future action to a theme. Ask students what themes are present in Act One.

Possible Responses: Supernatural forces can intervene in human affairs; appearances can distort reality.

Reading Skills and Strategies: PREDICTING

Discuss with students the impressions they get of the characters, and use the examples of foreshadowing referred to above to make predictions about what might happen to the characters in the play. They should support their predictions with evidence from the text and personal experience.

Possible Responses: Macbeth may not be the loyal hero he appears; the apparent outcome of the battle may be deceptive.

GUIDE FOR READING

B It suggests that he is a brave and formidable soldier.

Act 1

SCENE 1

An open place in Scotland.

The play opens in a wild and lonely place in medieval Scotland. Three witches enter and speak of what they know will happen this day: The civil war will end, and they will meet Macbeth, one of the generals. Their meeting ends when their demon companions, in the form of a toad and a cat, call them away.

[*Thunder and lightning. Enter three* Witches.]

First Witch. When shall we three meet again
In thunder, lightning, or in rain?

Second Witch. When the hurlyburly's done,
When the battle's lost and won.

Third Witch. That will be ere the set of sun.

First Witch. Where the place?

A **Second Witch.** Upon the heath.

Third Witch. There to meet with Macbeth.

First Witch. I come, Graymalkin!

Second Witch. Paddock calls.

Third Witch. Anon!

All. Fair is foul, and foul is fair.
Hover through the fog and filthy air.

[*Exeunt.*]

3 hurlyburly: turmoil; uproar.

8–9 Graymalkin . . . Paddock: two demon helpers in the form of a cat and a toad; **anon:** at once.

10 Fair . . . fair: The witches delight in the confusion of good and bad, beauty and ugliness.

[Stage Direction] ***Exeunt*** *Latin:* They leave (the stage).

Opening scene, *Macbeth* (film, directed by Roman Polanski, 1971)

328

Teaching Options

Cross Curricular Link **History**

A KING'S SUCCESSOR Determining a king's successor was a difficult issue in early Scotland. Before the kingdom of Alba became Scotland, kings were not succeeded by their eldest sons, but by their nearest male relatives. King Kenneth II (971–995), however, made his son Malcolm his heir. King Kenneth was killed, and Malcolm's claim to the throne was disregarded. Malcolm eventually killed the usurpers and ruled as Malcolm II. Malcolm II passed the crown to his grandson Duncan, who united under his rule most of the territory of modern Scotland. This first Scottish king was killed in 1040 by Macbeth, the mormaer (chief) of Moray, who ruled for seventeen peaceful years before Duncan's sons defeated and killed him in battle. Macbeth, a relative of Duncan, was a member of the branch of the family that was dispossessed of the throne by Malcolm's untraditional choice of successor.

SCENE 2

King Duncan's camp near the battlefield.

Duncan, the king of Scotland, waits in his camp for news of the battle. He learns that one of his generals, Macbeth, has been victorious in several battles. Not only has Macbeth defeated the rebellious Macdonwald, but he has also conquered the armies of the king of Norway and the Scottish traitor, the thane of Cawdor. Duncan orders the thane of Cawdor's execution and announces that Macbeth will receive the traitor's title.

[*Alarum within. Enter* Duncan, Malcolm, Donalbain, Lennox, *with* Attendants, *meeting a bleeding* Captain.]

Duncan. What bloody man is that? He can report,
1 As seemeth by his plight, of the revolt
The newest state.

Malcolm. This is the sergeant
Who like a good and hardy soldier fought
'Gainst my captivity. Hail, brave friend!
Say to the King the knowledge of the broil
As thou didst leave it.

Captain. Doubtful it stood,
As two spent swimmers that do cling together
And choke their art. The merciless Macdonwald
(Worthy to be a rebel, for to that
The multiplying villainies of nature
Do swarm upon him) from the Western Isles
2 Of kerns and gallowglasses is supplied;
And Fortune, on his damned quarrel smiling,
Showed like a rebel's whore. But all's too weak;
For brave Macbeth (well he deserves that name),
Disdaining Fortune, with his brandished steel,
Which smoked with bloody execution
(Like valor's minion), carved out his passage
3 Till he faced the slave;
Which ne'er shook hands nor bade farewell to him
Till he unseamed him from the nave to the chops
And fixed his head upon our battlements.

4 **Duncan.** O valiant cousin! worthy gentleman!

Captain. As whence the sun 'gins his reflection
Shipwracking storms and direful thunders break,
So from that spring whence comfort seemed to come
Discomfort swells. Mark, King of Scotland, mark.
No sooner justice had, with valor armed,
Compelled these skipping kerns to trust their heels

[Stage Direction] **alarum within:** the sound of a trumpet offstage, a signal that soldiers should arm themselves.

5 'gainst my captivity: to save me from capture.
6 broil: battle.

7–9 Doubtful . . . art: The two armies are compared to two exhausted swimmers who cling to each other and thus cannot swim.

9–13 The officer hates Macdonwald, whose evils (**multiplying villainies**) swarm like insects around him. His army consists of soldiers (**kerns and gallowglasses**) from the Hebrides (**Western Isles**).

19 valor's minion: the favorite of valor, meaning the bravest of all.

22 unseamed him . . . chops: split him open from the navel to the jaw. What does this act suggest about Macbeth? B

25–28 As whence . . . discomfort swells: As the rising sun is sometimes followed by storms, a new assault on Macbeth began.

Customizing Instruction

Students Acquiring English

1 In many of Shakespeare's sentences, a prepositional phrase is placed before the direct object it modifies. Show students how to switch the direct object and the prepositional phrase for a more modern sentence pattern. *(Example: "He can report, as seemeth by his plight, the newest state of the revolt.")*

As students read, help them to identify the direct object of each sentence.

Less Proficient Readers

The captain uses figurative language to describe the battle and Macbeth's actions. Use the following questions to make sure students understand the facts and actions described.

2 Which side in the battle did Fortune favor?
Answer: the side of the rebel Macdonwald.

3 Who is "the slave" in line 20?
Answer: the rebel Macdonwald.

4 What did Macbeth do that pleased Duncan?
Answer: He killed Macdonwald.

Ask students why Shakespeare has the captain use figurative rather than plain language.
Possible Response: to make the battle, and Macbeth's fighting, sound more dramatic and glorious.

Multiple Learning Styles

Auditory or Interpersonal Learners

Ask students to prepare a short TV news-style report of the events in Scene 2 and to present it to the class. Suggest different approaches they might take to the story, such as a patriotic view of the battle, an antiwar commentary, or a "man of the year" profile of Macbeth.

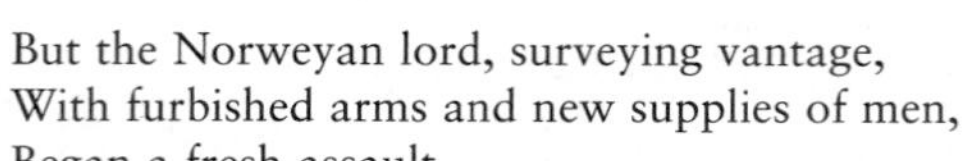

Reading and Analyzing

Literary Analysis: ANALOGY

Help students understand the following analogies employed by the captain to describe Macbeth and Banquo:

- "Yes, as sparrows eagles, or the hare the lion" (lines 34–35).
  Possible Response: Macbeth and Banquo were as dismayed by the attack as eagles are by sparrows or as lions are by rabbits.
- ". . . [T]hey were as cannons overcharged with double cracks. . . ." (lines 36–37).
  Possible Response: Macbeth and Banquo were like cannons loaded with extra ammunition; they became twice as deadly as before.

Literary Analysis: BLANK VERSE

A Ask students to mark the stresses in the line "As spárrows eágles, or the háre the líon" (line 35). Then have students think about how the meter of the line might have influenced word order.
Possible Response: The most important words receive the most emphasis.

Have students rearrange the word order to see how the effect is different.
Possible Response: "As eagles sparrows, or the lion the hare" has less dramatic impact.

GUIDE FOR READING

C The title of Thane of Cawdor.

But the Norweyan lord, surveying vantage,
With furbished arms and new supplies of men,
Began a fresh assault.

Duncan. Dismayed not this
Our captains, Macbeth and Banquo?

Captain. Yes,
A As sparrows eagles, or the hare the lion.
If I say sooth, I must report they were
As cannons overcharged with double cracks, so they
Doubly redoubled strokes upon the foe.
Except they meant to bathe in reeking wounds,
Or memorize another Golgotha,
I cannot tell—
But I am faint; my gashes cry for help.

Duncan. So well thy words become thee as thy wounds
They smack of honor both. Go get him surgeons.

[*Exit* Captain, *attended.*]

[*Enter* Ross *and* Angus.]

Who comes here?

Malcolm. The worthy Thane of Ross.

Lennox. What a haste looks through his eyes! So should he look
That seems to speak things strange.

Ross. God save the King!

Duncan. Whence cam'st thou, worthy thane?

Ross. From Fife, great King,
Where the Norweyan banners flout the sky
And fan our people cold. Norway himself,
With terrible numbers,
Assisted by that most disloyal traitor
The Thane of Cawdor, began a dismal conflict,
Till that Bellona's bridegroom, lapped in proof,
Confronted him with self-comparisons,
Point against point, rebellious arm 'gainst arm,
Curbing his lavish spirit; and to conclude,
The victory fell on us.

Duncan. Great happiness!

Ross. That now
Sweno, the Norways' king, craves composition;
Nor would we deign him burial of his men
Till he disbursed, at Saint Colme's Inch,
Ten thousand dollars to our general use.

Duncan. No more that Thane of Cawdor shall deceive

31–33 the Norweyan . . . assault: The king of Norway took an opportunity to attack.

36 sooth: the truth.

37 double cracks: a double load of ammunition.

39–40 Except . . . memorize another Golgotha: The officer's admiration leads to exaggeration. He claims he cannot decide whether **(except)** Macbeth and Banquo wanted to bathe in blood or make the battlefield as famous as Golgotha, the site of Christ's crucifixion.

45 Thane: a Scottish noble, similar in rank to an English earl.

48–58 Ross has arrived from Fife, where Norway's troops had invaded and frightened the people. There the king of Norway, along with the thane of Cawdor, met Macbeth (described as the husband of **Bellona,** the goddess of war). Macbeth, in heavy armor **(proof),** challenged the enemy, and achieved victory.

59 craves composition: wants a treaty.

60 deign: allow.

61 disbursed, at Saint Colme's Inch: paid at Saint Colme's Inch, an island in the North Sea.

Teaching Options

Vocabulary Strategy

USING DICTIONARY AND CONTEXT TO DETERMINE PRECISE WORD MEANING

Instruction Point out to students that although many of the words used in Shakespeare's time are used today, they are often used differently.

Activity Ask students to look up the primary meaning of each of the words below in a dictionary, and then have students use context to determine how the words are used in the play.

- memorize (line 40)
  Possible Response: Today it means "to commit to memory," while Shakespeare uses it to mean "to make memorable to others."
- become (line 43)
  Possible Response: Today it usually means "to grow or come to be," while Shakespeare uses it to mean "to suit."
- present (line 64)
  Possible Response: Today it means "existing or happening now" or "in attendance," but Shakespeare uses it to mean "immediate."

4 Our bosom interest. Go pronounce his present death
And with his former title greet Macbeth.

5 **Ross.** I'll see it done.

6 **Duncan.** What he hath lost noble Macbeth hath won.

[*Exeunt.*]

63–64 deceive our bosom interest: betray our friendship; **present death:** immediate execution.

65 What reward has the king decided to give to Macbeth? 

SCENE 3

A bleak place near the battlefield.

While leaving the battlefield, Macbeth and Banquo meet the witches, who are gleefully discussing the trouble they have caused. The witches hail Macbeth by a title he already holds, thane of Glamis. Then they prophesy that he will become both thane of Cawdor and king. When Banquo asks about his future, they speak in riddles, saying that he will be the father of kings but not a king himself.

After the witches vanish, Ross and Angus arrive to announce that Macbeth has been named thane of Cawdor. The first part of the witches' prophecy has come true, and Macbeth is stunned. He immediately begins to consider the possibility of murdering King Duncan to fulfill the rest of the witches' prophecy to him. Shaken, he turns his thoughts away from this "horrid image."

[*Thunder. Enter the three* Witches.]

7 **First Witch.** Where hast thou been, sister?

Second Witch. Killing swine.

Third Witch. Sister, where thou?

First Witch. A sailor's wife had chestnuts in her lap
And mounched and mounched and mounched. "Give me," quoth I.
"Aroint thee, witch!" the rump-fed ronyon cries.
Her husband's to Aleppo gone, master o' the "Tiger";
But in a sieve I'll thither sail
And, like a rat without a tail,
I'll do, I'll do, and I'll do.

Second Witch. I'll give thee a wind.

First Witch. Th' art kind.

Third Witch. And I another.

First Witch. I myself have all the other,
And the very ports they blow,
All the quarters that they know
I' the shipman's card.

2 Killing swine: Witches were often accused of killing people's pigs.

5 mounched: munched.

6 "Aroint thee, witch!" . . . ronyon cries: "Go away, witch!" the fat-bottomed **(rump-fed)**, ugly creature **(ronyon)** cries.

7–8 The woman's husband, the master of a merchant ship **(the "Tiger")**, has sailed to Aleppo, a famous trading center in the Middle East. The witch will pursue him. Witches, who could change shape at will, were thought to sail on strainers **(sieve)**.

Customizing Instruction

Less Proficient Readers

Use the following questions to make sure students understand the passage:

1 Who attacks Macbeth and Banquo and how do they react?
Answer: The king of Norway attacks them; they fight harder.

2 What news does Ross bring?
Answer: Macbeth's defeat of the Norwegian forces.

3 Why did the king of Norway pay ten thousand dollars to the Scottish army?
Answer: so he would be allowed to bury his dead soldiers.

4 What actions are taken against the Thane of Cawdor? Why?
Answer: He is sentenced to death and stripped of his title for treason against the king.

5 How does the king reward Macbeth's success in battle?
Answer: He makes him Thane of Cawdor.

Students Acquiring English

Point out that Elizabethan English was inflected slightly differently from current English. Some verbs, such as "have," changed their forms for the second and third person singular. Direct students to the following forms of "have":

6 "What he hath lost noble Macbeth hath won." The *-th* form agrees with third-person singular nouns.

7 "Where hast thou been, sister?" The *-st* form agrees with second-person singular nouns.

Multiple Learning Styles

Visual Learners

Have students draw a network tree to show the hierarchical relationships of the members of King Duncan's court (Duncan, Malcolm, Lennox, Ross, Macbeth, Banquo).

Cross Curricular Link Government

INTERNATIONAL LAW Point out to students that the Scottish army forces the Norwegian king to pay for the right to bury his dead soldiers. Discuss the international laws and groups that might forbid such an action today, such as the Geneva Convention, which was first signed in 1864 and was most recently revised in 1977, or the United Nations. Ask students whether they think contemporary warfare is more civilized than the warfare depicted in Macbeth. What might have happened if there had been UN peacekeepers in Macbeth's day?

Reading and Analyzing

Reading Skills and Strategies:
READING SIDE NOTES

Explain to students that side notes are the easiest way for an editor to give readers the meanings of archaic or unusual words. Ask students what they thought the following words meant before they read the side notes.

- penthouse lid
- posters
- aught
- choppy
- fantastical

GUIDE FOR READING

A He notices that they may be supernatural.

B He only possesses the title of Thane of Glamis; the other two, as far as he knows, do not belong to him.

View and Compare

In what ways do each of these images convey the eerie nature of the witches' scene?

Act 1, Scene 3: Macbeth and Banquo meet one of the witches, *The Throne of Blood* (film, directed by Akira Kurosawa, Japan, 1957)

Act 1, Scene 3: Banquo and the Witches (film, 1961)

332

Teaching Options

Viewing and Representing

FILM ANALYSIS

Orson Welles's film of *Macbeth* was shot in 23 days on a small budget. Despite the lack of time and money, the critic Jean Cocteau said that "Orson Welles's *Macbeth* has a kind of crude, irreverent power."

Instruction Show students film clips of Macbeth with the witches from Orson Welles's and the Royal Shakespeare Company's versions of *Macbeth*. Have students compare the two versions. Discuss lighting, camera angles, costumes, music, and the delivery of lines. Ask which version is closer to the way they imagined the scene, and why. Ask students whether they think the director of the Royal Shakespeare Company would agree with Orson Welles's interpretation and why.

Application Have students watch and respond to the video, which is part of the Literature in Performance series. Use **Literature in Performance Resource Book**.

I'll drain him dry as hay.
Sleep shall neither night nor day
Hang upon his penthouse lid.
He shall live a man forbid.
Weary sev'nights, nine times nine,
Shall he dwindle, peak, and pine.
Though his bark cannot be lost,
Yet it shall be tempest-tost.
Look what I have.

Second Witch. Show me! Show me!

First Witch. Here I have a pilot's thumb,
Wracked as homeward he did come.

[*Drum within.*]

Third Witch. A drum, a drum!
Macbeth doth come.

All. The Weird Sisters, hand in hand,
Posters of the sea and land,
Thus do go about, about,
Thrice to thine, and thrice to mine,
And thrice again, to make up nine.
Peace! The charm's wound up.

[*Enter* Macbeth *and* Banquo.]

Macbeth. So foul and fair a day I have not seen.

Banquo. How far is't called to Forres? What are these,
So withered, and so wild in their attire,
That look not like the inhabitants o' the earth,
And yet are on't? Live you? or are you aught
That man may question? You seem to understand me,
By each at once her choppy finger laying
Upon her skinny lips. You should be women,
And yet your beards forbid me to interpret
That you are so.

Macbeth. Speak, if you can. What are you?

First Witch. All hail, Macbeth! Hail to thee, Thane of Glamis!

Second Witch. All hail, Macbeth! Hail to thee, Thane of Cawdor!

Third Witch. All hail, Macbeth, that shalt be King hereafter!

1 **Banquo.** Good sir, why do you start and seem to fear
Things that do sound so fair? I' the name of truth,
Are ye fantastical, or that indeed
Which outwardly ye show? My noble partner
You greet with present grace and great prediction

14–23 The witch is going to torture the woman's husband. She controls where the winds blow, covering all points of a compass (**shipman's card**). She will make him sleepless, keeping his eyelids (**penthouse lid**) from closing. Thus, he will lead an accursed (**forbid**) life for weeks (**sev'nights**), wasting away with fatigue.

33 posters: quick riders.

36 Nine was considered a magical number by superstitious people.

42–46 aught: anything; **choppy:** chapped; **your beards:** Beards on women identified them as witches. Banquo vividly describes the witches. What does he notice about them? A

48–50 What is surprising about the three titles the witches use to greet Macbeth? B

53 Are ye fantastical: Are you (the witches) imaginary?

Customizing Instruction

Less Proficient Readers

1 Direct students' attention to Banquo's line, "Good sir, why do you start and seem to fear things that do sound so fair?" (lines 51–52). Make sure they understand that Banquo is speaking this sentence to Macbeth. Ask students to describe Macbeth's reaction in their own words.

Possible Response: Accept any response that indicates Macbeth is startled or frightened.

Ask students why Macbeth might react in this way.

Possible Response: Macbeth already has an idea of what he might do to become king.

Reading and Analyzing

Literary Analysis: PLOT

Remind students that the plot of a drama consists of exposition, rising action, climax, and denouement. To what part of the plot do the first three scenes of Macbeth belong?
Answer: exposition.

What is the purpose of exposition in a play?
Possible Responses: to familiarize the audience with the characters and situation; to introduce themes.
What devices does Shakespeare use to accomplish these purposes?
Possible Response: He familiarizes audiences with the characters and situation through dialogue. He introduces themes in dialogue by the choice of words the characters speak and by using soliloquies and asides.

GUIDE FOR READING

A That he will be the father of kings, but not one himself. Accept all reasonable responses for student predictions.

Reading Skills and Strategies: SKIMMING

B Explain to students that courtiers in Shakespeare's day used very elaborate language, especially on important occasions. Ask students to skim the meeting between Ross and Angus and Macbeth and Banquo (lines 89–116).

- What is the main point of the dialogue?
  Answer: The king has made Macbeth Thane of Cawdor and wants to see him in person.
- Discuss with students what kind of people use elaborate language today.
  Possible Responses: politicians, doctors, businesspeople.

Of noble having and of royal hope,
That he seems rapt withal. To me you speak not.
If you can look into the seeds of time
And say which grain will grow and which will not,
Speak then to me, who neither beg nor fear
Your favors nor your hate.

First Witch. Hail!

Second Witch. Hail!

Third Witch. Hail!

First Witch. Lesser than Macbeth, and greater.

Second Witch. Not so happy, yet much happier.

Third Witch. Thou shalt get kings, though thou be none.
So all hail, Macbeth and Banquo!

First Witch. Banquo and Macbeth, all hail!

Macbeth. Stay, you imperfect speakers, tell me more!
By Sinel's death I know I am Thane of Glamis,
But how of Cawdor? The Thane of Cawdor lives,
A prosperous gentleman; and to be King
Stands not within the prospect of belief,
No more than to be Cawdor. Say from whence
You owe this strange intelligence, or why
Upon this blasted heath you stop our way
With such prophetic greeting. Speak, I charge you.

[Witches *vanish.*]

Banquo. The earth hath bubbles, as the water has,
And these are of them. Whither are they vanished?

Macbeth. Into the air, and what seemed corporal melted
As breath into the wind. Would they had stayed!

Banquo. Were such things here as we do speak about?
Or have we eaten on the insane root
That takes the reason prisoner?

Macbeth. Your children shall be kings.

Banquo. You shall be King.

Macbeth. And Thane of Cawdor too. Went it not so?

Banquo. To the selfsame tune and words. Who's here?

[*Enter* Ross *and* Angus.]

Ross. The King hath happily received, Macbeth,
The news of thy success; and when he reads
Thy personal venture in the rebels' fight,
His wonders and his praises do contend

54–57 My noble partner . . . . rapt withal: The witches' prophecies of noble possessions (**having**)—the lands and wealth of Cawdor—and kingship (**royal hope**) have left Macbeth dazed (**rapt withal**). Look for evidence that shows what Macbeth thinks of the prophecies.

65–68 The witches speak in riddles. Though Banquo will be less fortunate (**happy**) than Macbeth, he will be father to (**get**) future kings. What do the witches predict for Banquo? What do you think their predictions mean?

75–76 whence: where. Macbeth wants to know where the witches received their knowledge (**strange intelligence**).

80 whither: where.

81 corporal: physical; real.

84 insane root: A number of plants were believed to cause insanity when eaten.

92–93 His wonders . . . Silenced with that: King Duncan hesitates between awe (**wonders**) and gratitude (**praise**) and is, as a result, speechless.

Which should be thine or his. Silenced with that,
In viewing o'er the rest o' the selfsame day,
He finds thee in the stout Norweyan ranks,
Nothing afeard of what thyself didst make,
Strange images of death. As thick as hail
Came post with post, and every one did bear
Thy praises in his kingdom's great defense
And poured them down before him.

Angus. We are sent
To give thee from our royal master thanks;
Only to herald thee into his sight,
Not pay thee.

Ross. And for an earnest of a greater honor,
He bade me, from him, call thee Thane of Cawdor;
In which addition, hail, most worthy Thane!
For it is thine.

Banquo. What, can the devil speak true?

Macbeth. The Thane of Cawdor lives. Why do you dress me
In borrowed robes?

Angus. Who was the Thane lives yet,
But under heavy judgment bears that life
Which he deserves to lose. Whether he was combined
With those of Norway, or did line the rebel
With hidden help and vantage, or that with both
He labored in his country's wrack, I know not;
But treasons capital, confessed and proved,
Have overthrown him.

Macbeth. [*Aside*] Glamis, and Thane of Cawdor!
The greatest is behind.—[*To* Ross *and* Angus] Thanks for
your pains.
[*Aside to* Banquo] Do you not hope your children shall
be kings,
When those that gave the Thane of Cawdor to me
Promised no less to them?

Banquo. [*Aside to* Macbeth] That, trusted home,
Might yet enkindle you unto the crown,
Besides the Thane of Cawdor. But 'tis strange!
And oftentimes, to win us to our harm,
The instruments of darkness tell us truths,
Win us with honest trifles, to betray's
In deepest consequence.—
Cousins, a word, I pray you.

96–97 nothing afeard . . . of death: Although Macbeth left many dead (**strange images of death**), he obviously did not fear death himself.

104 earnest: partial payment.

106 addition: title.

111–116 Whether he was . . . overthrown him: The former thane of Cawdor may have been secretly allied (**combined**) with the king of Norway, or he may have supported the traitor Macdonwald (**did line the rebel**). But he is guilty of treasons that deserve the death penalty (**treasons capital**), having aimed at the country's ruin (**wrack**).

116 aside: a stage direction that means Macbeth is speaking to himself, beyond hearing.

120 home: fully; completely.

121 enkindle you unto: inflame your ambitions.

123–126 to win us . . . consequence: Banquo warns that evil powers often offer little truths to tempt people. The witches may be lying about what matters most (**in deepest consequence**).

Customizing Instruction

Less Proficient Readers

Point out the following words:

1 *whence*

2 *whither*

Explain that in Shakespeare's time *here, there,* and *where* had special forms indicating direction:

To: hither, thither, whither

From: hence, thence, whence

Reading and Analyzing

Reading Skills and Strategies: REREADING

A Ask students to reread Macbeth's aside to improve their understanding of the passage. Discuss nuances they might have missed the first time.

Possible Responses: Macbeth's confusion over whether the witches' prophecy is good or evil; the effects on Macbeth's body of his thoughts of murder; and his statement that "nothing is / But what is not."

Ask students to read a third time to interpret Macbeth's state of mind. Discuss with students whether or not Macbeth is in his right mind.

Possible Responses: He is in his right mind because he uses the witches' accurate prophecy about the title Thane of Cawdor to try to convince himself that he will also be king; Macbeth is not in his right mind because he thinks ". . . nothing is / But what is not."

Literary Analysis: DRAMATIC IRONY

B Remind students of the definition of dramatic irony. Ask students what they as readers know that Duncan does not in lines 14–21.

Answer: Duncan doesn't know that Macbeth is thinking of killing him.

Macbeth. [*Aside*] Two truths are told,
As happy prologues to the swelling act
Of the imperial theme.—I thank you, gentlemen.—
[*Aside*] This supernatural soliciting
Cannot be ill; cannot be good. If ill,
Why hath it given me earnest of success,
Commencing in a truth? I am Thane of Cawdor.
A If good, why do I yield to that suggestion
Whose horrid image doth unfix my hair
And make my seated heart knock at my ribs
Against the use of nature? Present fears
Are less than horrible imaginings.
My thought, whose murder yet is but fantastical,
Shakes so my single state of man that function
Is smothered in surmise and nothing is
But what is not.

Banquo. Look how our partner's rapt.

Macbeth. [*Aside*] If chance will have me King, why chance may crown me,
Without my stir.

Banquo. New honors come upon him,
Like our strange garments, cleave not to their mold
But with the aid of use.

Macbeth. [*Aside*] Come what come may,
Time and the hour runs through the roughest day.

Banquo. Worthy Macbeth, we stay upon your leisure.

Macbeth. Give me your favor. My dull brain was wrought
With things forgotten. Kind gentlemen, your pains
Are registered where every day I turn
The leaf to read them. Let us toward the King.
[*Aside to* Banquo] Think upon what hath chanced, and, at more time,
The interim having weighed it, let us speak
Our free hearts each to other.

Banquo. [*Aside to* Macbeth] Very gladly.

Macbeth. [*Aside to* Banquo] Till then, enough.—Come, friends.
[*Exeunt.*]

144 my stir: my doing anything.

146–147 Come what . . . roughest day: The future will arrive no matter what.

148 stay: wait.

150–152 your pains . . . read them: I will always remember your efforts. The metaphor refers to keeping a diary and reading it regularly.

153–155 at more time . . . other: Macbeth wants to discuss the prophecies later, after he and Banquo have had time to think about them.

Teaching Options

Assessment **Standardized Test Practice**

USING CONTEXT TO DETERMINE MEANING OF WORDS AND PHRASES For some standardized tests, students will be asked to use the context of a passage to determine the meaning of words with multiple meanings, unfamiliar and uncommon words and phrases, and figurative language. To provide students with practice in using context, write the following lines on the board or read them aloud:

Banquo [about Macbeth]:
New honors come upon him,
Like our strange garments, cleave not to their mold
But with the aid of use. (lines 144–46)

Help students understand the context of these lines, which is that Macbeth has just received the honor of a new title from the king, and then have them identify the parts of the metaphor. Students should understand that Macbeth's new honor is being compared to strange or new clothes, which don't fit well until they begin to conform to the body after prolonged use. Point out that *cleave* has two contradictory meanings: *to adhere firmly* and *to split.* Have students decide on the appropriate meaning in this context.

SCENE 4

A room in the king's palace at Forres.

King Duncan receives news of the execution of the former thane of Cawdor. As the king is admitting his bad judgment concerning the traitor, Macbeth enters with Banquo, Ross, and Angus. Duncan expresses his gratitude to them and then, in a most unusual action, officially names his own son Malcolm as heir to the throne. To honor Macbeth, Duncan decides to visit Macbeth's castle at Inverness. Macbeth, his thoughts full of dark ambition, leaves to prepare for the king's visit.

[*Flourish. Enter* Duncan, Lennox, Malcolm, Donalbain, *and* Attendants.]

Duncan. Is execution done on Cawdor? Are not
Those in commission yet returned?

Malcolm. My liege,
They are not yet come back. But I have spoke
With one that saw him die; who did report
That very frankly he confessed his treasons,
Implored your Highness' pardon, and set forth
A deep repentance. Nothing in his life
Became him like the leaving it. He died
As one that had been studied in his death
1 To throw away the dearest thing he owed
As 'twere a careless trifle.

Duncan. There's no art
To find the mind's construction in the face.
He was a gentleman on whom I built
An absolute trust.

[*Enter* Macbeth, Banquo, Ross, *and* Angus.]

O worthiest cousin,
The sin of my ingratitude even now
Was heavy on me! Thou art so far before
B That swiftest wing of recompense is slow
To overtake thee. Would thou hadst less deserved,
That the proportion both of thanks and payment
Might have been mine! Only I have left to say,
More is thy due than more than all can pay.

Macbeth. The service and the loyalty I owe,
In doing it pays itself. Your Highness' part
Is to receive our duties; and our duties

2 those in commission: those who have the responsibility for Cawdor's execution.

6 set forth: showed.

8–11 He died as . . . trifle: He died as if he had rehearsed **(studied)** the moment. Though losing his life **(the dearest thing he owed)**, he behaved with calm dignity.

14–21 O worthiest . . . pay: The king feels that he cannot repay **(recompense)** Macbeth enough. Macbeth's qualities and accomplishments are of greater value than any thanks or payment Duncan can give.

Customizing Instruction

Multiple Learning Styles

Kinesthetic/Interpersonal Learners

1 Discuss why a playwright might choose to have an action simply reported by a character rather than dramatizing it on the stage.

Possible Responses: The action is not important enough to show; there isn't enough time; it would be too difficult to create the stage set.

Ask students to act out the scene of Cawdor's death. They will have to imagine some of the details for themselves.

Gifted and Talented

Explain to students that predictions and riddles are plot devices often used in tragedy. Ask students to make a list of the predictions and riddles that have appeared in the play so far. Suggest that students read Sophocles' *Oedipus Rex* and notice the function of the oracle in that tragedy. How do oracles and prophecies reinforce the tragic themes of fate and appearance vs. reality in both plays?

Possible Responses: Oracles and prophecies are the voice of Fate. The tragic hero brings about his fated ruin by acting on oracles or prophecies at face value, only later to discover their deeper meanings.

Mini Lesson: Viewing and Representing

Use this activity to help students use viewing and representing skills. Ask students to create collages using photographs, paintings, or original drawings to represent Macbeth's state of mind as he thinks about killing Duncan.

Activity Have students explain to the class why they think their collages are representative of Macbeth's thoughts and feelings. Suggest that they address the following considerations:

- images
- color
- shapes
- order or disorder

Reading and Analyzing

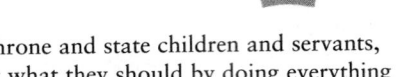

Reading Skills and Strategies:
CLARIFYING ARCHAIC WORD FORMS

Point out to students the pronoun usages on these pages. Note that Duncan calls Macbeth and Banquo "thee," while Macbeth and Banquo call Duncan "you." Discuss with students why this might be. Explain that, like many modern languages, Elizabethan English had two forms of the second-person pronoun, an intimate form ("thee") and a respectful form ("you"). Point out also that Duncan uses the "royal we"—that he always refers to himself in the plural.

GUIDE FOR READING

A He may be thinking that he is to be richly rewarded by Duncan's kindness.

B Macbeth might resent Malcolm.

Literary Analysis ASIDE

C Remind students of the definition of an aside (a remark that a character makes in an undertone to the audience or another character but that those on stage are not supposed to hear). Have students read Macbeth's aside in lines 48–53. Ask students the following questions about the aside:

- Why did Shakespeare put in this aside?
  Possible Response: because he couldn't have Macbeth voice his feelings in dialogue.
- Ask students to think about how this aside might be presented in a film of Macbeth.
  Possible Responses: The filmmaker might do a close-up of Macbeth in which he mutters these words to himself; the filmmaker might have a voice-over speaking Macbeth's thoughts.

Are to your throne and state children and servants,
Which do but what they should by doing everything
Safe toward your love and honor.

Duncan. Welcome hither.
I have begun to plant thee and will labor
To make thee full of growing. Noble Banquo,
That hast no less deserved, nor must be known
No less to have done so, let me infold thee
And hold thee to my heart.

Banquo. There if I grow,
The harvest is your own.

Duncan. My plenteous joys,
Wanton in fullness, seek to hide themselves
In drops of sorrow. Sons, kinsmen, thanes,
And you whose places are the nearest, know
We will establish our estate upon
Our eldest, Malcolm, whom we name hereafter
The Prince of Cumberland; which honor must
Not unaccompanied invest him only,
But signs of nobleness, like stars, shall shine
On all deservers. From hence to Inverness,
And bind us further to you.

Macbeth. The rest is labor, which is not used for you.
I'll be myself the harbinger, and make joyful
The hearing of my wife with your approach;
So, humbly take my leave.

Duncan. My worthy Cawdor!

C **Macbeth.** [*Aside*] The Prince of Cumberland! That is a step
On which I must fall down, or else o'erleap,
For in my way it lies. Stars, hide your fires!
Let not light see my black and deep desires.
The eye wink at the hand; yet let that be,
Which the eye fears, when it is done, to see. [*Exit.*]

Duncan. True, worthy Banquo: he is full so valiant,
And in his commendations I am fed;
It is a banquet to me. Let's after him,
Whose care is gone before to bid us welcome.
It is a peerless kinsman.

[*Flourish. Exeunt.*]

28–29 I have . . . growing: The king plans to give more honors to Macbeth. What might Macbeth be thinking now? A

33–35 My plenteous . . . sorrow: The king is crying tears of joy.

39 Prince of Cumberland: the title given to the heir to the Scottish throne. Now that Malcolm is heir, how might Macbeth react? B

42 Inverness: site of Macbeth's castle, where the king has just invited himself, giving another honor to Macbeth.

45 harbinger: a representative sent before a royal party to make proper arrangements for its arrival.

52–53 The eye . . . to see: Macbeth hopes for the king's murder, although he does not want to see it.

Teaching Options

Assessment Informal Assessment

OUTLINE You can assess students' understanding of the first four scenes by having them make an outline of the main events so far. Have them use the scene numbers as the first-level heading.

RUBRIC

3 **Full Accomplishment** Outline contains all important events of first four scenes arranged in correct sequence.

2 **Substantial Accomplishment** Outline contains most important events of first four scenes.

1 **Little or Partial Accomplishment** Outline contains only a few of important events of first four scenes, and/or events are incorrectly organized by scene.

SCENE 5

Macbeth's castle at Inverness.

Lady Macbeth reads a letter from her husband that tells her of the witches' prophecies, one of which has already come true. She is determined that Macbeth will be king. However, she fears that he lacks the courage to kill Duncan. After a messenger tells her the king is coming, she calls on the powers of evil to help her do what must be done. When Macbeth arrives, she tells him that the king must die that night but reminds him that he must appear to be a good and loyal host.

[*Enter* Lady Macbeth *alone, with a letter.*]

Lady Macbeth. [*Reads*] "They met me in the day of success; and I have learned by the perfect'st report they **2** have more in them than mortal knowledge. When I burned in desire to question them further, they made themselves air, into which they vanished. Whiles I stood rapt in the wonder of it, came missives from the King, **3** who all-hailed me Thane of Cawdor, by which title, before, these Weird Sisters saluted me, and referred me to the coming on of time with 'Hail, King that shalt be!' This have I thought good to deliver thee, my **4** dearest partner of greatness, that thou mightst not lose the dues of rejoicing by being ignorant of what greatness is promised thee. Lay it to thy heart, and farewell."

Glamis thou art, and Cawdor, and shalt be
What thou art promised. Yet do I fear thy nature.
It is too full o' the milk of human kindness
To catch the nearest way. Thou wouldst be great;
Art not without ambition, but without
The illness should attend it. What thou wouldst highly,
That wouldst thou holily; wouldst not play false,
And yet wouldst wrongly win. Thou'ldst have, great Glamis,
That which cries "Thus thou must do," if thou have it;
And that which rather thou dost fear to do
Than wishest should be undone. Hie thee hither,
That I may pour my spirits in thine ear
And chastise with the valor of my tongue
All that impedes thee from the golden round
Which fate and metaphysical aid doth seem
To have thee crowned withal.

[*Enter* Messenger.]

16–21 Yet do . . . holily: Lady Macbeth fears her husband is too good (**too full o' the milk of human kindness**) to seize the throne by murder (**the nearest way**). Lacking the necessary wickedness (**illness**), he wants to gain power virtuously (**holily**).

Customizing Instruction

Students Acquiring English

Explain that in Shakespeare's time the rules of English were more flexible than they are today. As a result, some of Shakespeare's usages are incorrect by modern standards. Point out the following usages, and ask students what the correct contemporary form would be.

1 "It"
Answer: He.

2 "perfect'st"
Answer: most perfect.

3 "came missives"
Answer: there came missives.

4 "deliver thee"
Answer: deliver to thee.

Reading and Analyzing

GUIDE FOR READING

A Accept all reasonable responses. Ask students to support their opinions with evidence from the text.

Reading Skills and Strategies: PARAPHRASING TO UNDERSTAND UNUSUAL WORD ORDER

Ask students to paraphrase the following sentence with unusual word order.

B "O, never / Shall sun that morrow see!"

Possible Response: Oh, tomorrow will never see the sun!

GUIDE FOR READING

C Students should support their answers with evidence from the text.

Literary Analysis: RHYME

D Point out to students that Shakespeare's lines rarely rhyme, and ask students to find the lines that rhyme on page 341.

Answer: lines 69 and 70, lines 72 and 73.

Discuss what effect these rhymes have on the reader.

Possible Responses: The rhymes make these lines stand out; the rhymes make them seem persuasive; these couplets put emphasis on this couple bent on murder.

What is your tidings?

Messenger. The King comes here tonight.

Lady Macbeth. Thou'rt mad to say it!
Is not thy master with him? who, were't so,
Would have informed for preparation.

Messenger. So please you, it is true. Our Thane is coming.
One of my fellows had the speed of him,
Who, almost dead for breath, had scarcely more
Than would make up his message.

Lady Macbeth. Give him tending;
He brings great news.

[*Exit* Messenger.]

1

The raven himself is hoarse
That croaks the fatal entrance of Duncan
Under my battlements. Come, you spirits
That tend on mortal thoughts, unsex me here,
And fill me, from the crown to the toe, top-full
Of direst cruelty! Make thick my blood;
Stop up the access and passage to remorse,
That no compunctious visitings of nature
Shake my fell purpose nor keep peace between
The effect and it! Come to my woman's breasts
And take my milk for gall, you murd'ring ministers,
Wherever in your sightless substances
You wait on nature's mischief! Come, thick night,
And pall thee in the dunnest smoke of hell,
That my keen knife see not the wound it makes,
Nor heaven peep through the blanket of the dark
To cry "Hold, hold!"

[*Enter* Macbeth.]

Great Glamis! worthy Cawdor!
Greater than both, by the all-hail hereafter!
Thy letters have transported me beyond
This ignorant present, and I feel now
The future in the instant.

Macbeth My dearest love,
Duncan comes here tonight.

Lady Macbeth. And when goes hence?

Macbeth. Tomorrow, as he purposes.

B

Lady Macbeth. O, never
Shall sun that morrow see!
Your face, my Thane, is as a book where men
May read strange matters. To beguile the time,

35 had the speed of him: rode faster than he.

38 raven: The harsh cry of the raven, a bird symbolizing evil and misfortune, was supposed to indicate an approaching death.

40–54 Lady Macbeth calls on the spirits of evil to rid her of feminine weakness (**unsex me**) and to block out guilt. She wants no normal pangs of conscience (**compunctious visitings of nature**) to get in the way of her murderous plan. She asks that her mother's milk be turned to bile (**gall**) by the unseen evil forces (**murd'ring ministers, sightless substances**) that exist in nature. Furthermore, she asks that the night wrap (**pall**) itself in darkness as black as hell so that no one may see or stop the crime. Do you think Lady Macbeth could actually kill Duncan? **A**

Teaching Options

Speaking and Listening

DRAMATIC READING

Instruction Discuss with students the impact an actor's performance can have on an audience's interpretation of a play. Explain that emotions and feelings are not found in the text itself but rather in the choices made by actors as they decide how to bring their dramatic characters to life.

Prepare Ask two students to perform dramatic readings of Lady Macbeth's soliloquy. Instruct one student to play her as sympathetically, and the other as unsympathetically, as possible.

Present Have the class analyze the difference between the two performances. What was the effect of different tones of voice, facial expressions, and word emphasis? What other versions of Lady Macbeth might be created by another interpretation?

BLOCK SCHEDULING This activity is particularly well-suited for longer class periods.

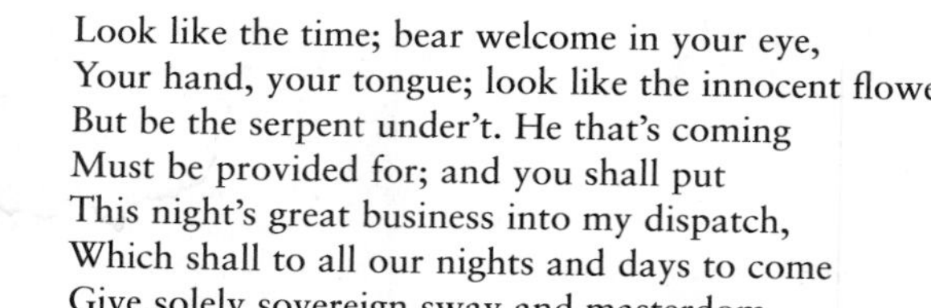

Look like the time; bear welcome in your eye,
2 Your hand, your tongue; look like the innocent flower,
But be the serpent under't. He that's coming
Must be provided for; and you shall put
This night's great business into my dispatch,
Which shall to all our nights and days to come
Give solely sovereign sway and masterdom.

D **Macbeth.** We will speak further.

Lady Macbeth. Only look up clear.
To alter favor ever is to fear.
Leave all the rest to me.

[*Exeunt.*]

63–66 To beguile . . . under't: To fool (**beguile**) everyone, act as expected at such a time, that is, as a good host. Who is more like a serpent, Lady Macbeth or her husband? C

68 my dispatch: my management.

70 give solely sovereign sway: bring absolute royal power.

72 To alter . . . fear: To change your expression (**favor**) is a sign of fear.

SCENE 6

In front of Macbeth's castle.

King Duncan and his party arrive, and Lady Macbeth welcomes them. Duncan is generous in his praise of his hosts and eagerly awaits the arrival of Macbeth.

[*Hautboys and torches. Enter* Duncan, Malcolm, Donalbain, Banquo, Lennox, Macduff, Ross, Angus, *and* Attendants.]

[Stage Direction] **hautboys:** oboes.

Duncan. This castle hath a pleasant seat. The air
Nimbly and sweetly recommends itself
Unto our gentle senses.

1 seat: location.

Banquo. This guest of summer,
The temple-haunting martlet, does approve
By his loved mansionry that the heaven's breath
3 Smells wooingly here. No jutty, frieze,
Buttress, nor coign of vantage, but this bird
Hath made his pendent bed and procreant cradle.
Where they most breed and haunt, I have observed
The air is delicate.

[*Enter* Lady Macbeth.]

Duncan. See, see, our honored hostess!
The love that follows us sometime is our trouble,
Which still we thank as love. Herein I teach you
How you shall bid God 'ield us for your pains
And thank us for your trouble.

Lady Macbeth. All our service
In every point twice done, and then done double

3–10 This guest . . . delicate: The martin (**martlet**) usually built its nest on a church (**temple**), where every projection (**jutty**), sculptured decoration (**frieze**), support (**buttress**), and convenient corner (**coign of vantage**) offered a good nesting site. Banquo sees the presence of the martin's hanging (**pendent**) nest, a breeding (**procreant**) place, as a sign of healthy air.

Customizing Instruction

Less Proficient Readers

Make sure students have read the side notes by asking them to tell the main points of the following lines.

1 Lines 38–54
Possible Response: Lady Macbeth wants to be made ruthless and protected from her conscience.

2 Lines 64–66
Possible Response: Lady Macbeth is asking Macbeth to pretend to welcome Duncan.

3 Lines 3–10
Possible Response: Banquo thinks the fact that martins have built their nests on Macbeth's castle proves that the air is healthful there.

Reading and Analyzing

GUIDE FOR READING

A To lull him into a false sense of security.

Literary Analysis SOLILOQUY

B Remind students that a soliloquy is a speech in a dramatic work in which a character speaks his or her thoughts aloud. Shakespeare's soliloquies are particularly memorable for their poetic language and psychological insight. Discuss the subtleties of Macbeth's character that are revealed in this soliloquy.
Possible Responses: his fear of unintended consequences; his awareness that Duncan doesn't deserve to die; his real admiration for Duncan.

Were poor and single business to contend
Against those honors deep and broad wherewith
Your Majesty loads our house. For those of old,
And the late dignities heaped up to them,
We rest your hermits.

Duncan. Where's the Thane of Cawdor?
We coursed him at the heels and had a purpose
To be his purveyor; but he rides well,
And his great love, sharp as his spur, hath holp him
To his home before us. Fair and noble hostess,
We are your guest tonight.

Lady Macbeth. Your servants ever
Have theirs, themselves, and what is theirs, in compt,
To make their audit at your Highness' pleasure,
Still to return your own.

Duncan. Give me your hand;
Conduct me to mine host. We love him highly
And shall continue our graces towards him.
By your leave, hostess.

[*Exeunt.*]

16 single business: weak service. Lady Macbeth claims that nothing she or her husband can do will match Duncan's generosity.

20 we rest your hermits: we can only repay you with prayers. The wealthy used to hire hermits to pray for the dead.

21 coursed him at the heels: followed him closely.

22 purveyor: one who makes advance arrangements for a royal visit.

23 holp: helped.

25–28 Legally, Duncan owned everything in his kingdom. Lady Macbeth politely says that they hold his property in trust (**compt**), ready to return it (**make their audit**) whenever he wants. Why do you think Lady Macbeth is being especially gracious to Duncan? **A**

Act 1, Scene 6: Duncan at Macbeth's castle (film, 1971)

342

Teaching Options

Mini Lesson Vocabulary Strategy

EXPAND VOCABULARY BY LISTENING

Instruction Have students list the following words from Macbeth's soliloquy:
- trammel up
- surcease
- faculties
- meek
- taking-off

Activity Read the soliloquy aloud, and ask students to write down meanings for these words as they listen. Repeat the sentences that contain them if necessary. Then discuss students' answers and compare them with the words' meanings listed here: trammel up—"restrain"; surcease—"cessation, death"; faculties—"powers"; meek—"gentle"; taking-off—"departure, death."

Use **Vocabulary Transparencies and Copymasters,** p. 18.

SCENE 7

A room in Macbeth's castle.

Macbeth has left Duncan in the middle of dinner. Alone, he begins to have second thoughts about his murderous plan. Lady Macbeth enters and discovers that he has changed his mind. She scornfully accuses him of cowardice and tells him that a true man would never back out of a commitment. She reassures him of success and explains her plan. She will make sure that the king's attendants drink too much. When they are fast asleep, Macbeth will stab the king with the servants' weapons.

[*Hautboys. Torches. Enter a* Sewer, *and divers* Servants *with dishes and service over the stage. Then enter* Macbeth.]

Macbeth. If it were done when 'tis done, then 'twere well
It were done quickly. If the assassination
Could trammel up the consequence, and catch,
With his surcease, success, that but this blow
Might be the be-all and the end-all here, **1**
But here, upon this bank and shoal of time,
We'ld jump the life to come. But in these cases
We still have judgment here, that we but teach
Bloody instructions, which, being taught, return
To plague the inventor. This even-handed justice **2**
Commends the ingredience of our poisoned chalice
To our own lips. He's here in double trust:
First, as I am his kinsman and his subject,
Strong both against the deed; then, as his host,
Who should against his murderer shut the door, **B**
Not bear the knife myself. Besides, this Duncan
Hath borne his faculties so meek, hath been
So clear in his great office, that his virtues
Will plead like angels, trumpet-tongued, against
The deep damnation of his taking-off;
And pity, like a naked new-born babe,
Striding the blast, or heaven's cherubin, horsed
Upon the sightless couriers of the air,
Shall blow the horrid deed in every eye,
That tears shall drown the wind. I have no spur
To prick the sides of my intent, but only
Vaulting ambition, which o'erleaps itself
And falls on the other—

[*Enter* Lady Macbeth.]

How now? What news?

[Stage Direction] **Sewer:** the steward, the servant in charge of arranging the banquet and tasting the King's food; **divers:** various.

1–10 Again, Macbeth argues with himself about murdering the king. If it could be done without causing problems later, then it would be good to do it soon. If Duncan's murder would have no negative consequences and be successfully completed with his death (**surcease**), then Macbeth would risk eternal damnation. He knows, however, that terrible deeds (**bloody instructions**) often backfire.

12–28 Macbeth reminds himself that he is Duncan's relative, subject, and host and that the king has never abused his royal powers (**faculties**). In fact, Duncan is such a good person that there is no possible reason for his murder except Macbeth's own driving ambition.

Customizing Instruction

Students Acquiring English

Help students understand the following idiomatic phrases:

1 "the be-all and the end-all"
Answer: something which is complete in itself.

2 "even-handed"
Answer: fair; dealing with everyone in the same way.

Reading and Analyzing

Literary Analysis: TRAGEDY

Have students review the characteristics of tragedy on pp. 321–322. Discuss with students how Macbeth fits the definition of a tragedy so far.

Possible Responses: Macbeth is a man of great importance in society—first a noble and then king; Macbeth is an extraordinarily brave and able man with a tragic flaw—his ambition.

Literary Analysis: CHARACTERIZATION

Point out that in plays, characters are defined by their appearance, actions, and words. Ask students to examine the characterization of Lady Macbeth. They should support their opinions with experience and evidence from the text.

- What seems to motivate Lady Macbeth?
  Possible Response: ambition.
- Does Shakespeare describe Lady Macbeth as a feminine woman?
  Answer: Words spoken by her and by Macbeth describe Lady Macbeth as a masculine woman.
- How would the play be different if she did not exist, or did not know of her husband's plans?
  Possible Responses: Macbeth might abandon his idea of murdering Duncan; Macbeth might seem like a worse character, since he would be the only character who means anyone harm.

GUIDE FOR READING

A He seems to decide against murdering Duncan.

B Students should support their opinion with evidence from the text.

Act 1, Scene 7: Orson Welles as Macbeth and Jeanette Nolan as Lady Macbeth (film, 1948)

1 **Lady Macbeth.** He has almost supped. Why have you left the
chamber?

Macbeth. Hath he asked for me?

Lady Macbeth. Know you not he has?

Macbeth. We will proceed no further in this business.
He hath honored me of late, and I have bought
Golden opinions from all sorts of people,
Which would be worn now in their newest gloss,
Not cast aside so soon.

Lady Macbeth. Was the hope drunk
Wherein you dressed yourself? Hath it slept since?
And wakes it now to look so green and pale
At what it did so freely? From this time
Such I account thy love. Art thou afeard
To be the same in thine own act and valor
As thou art in desire? Wouldst thou have that
Which thou esteem'st the ornament of life,
And live a coward in thine own esteem,
Letting "I dare not" wait upon "I would,"
Like the poor cat i' the adage?

2 **Macbeth.** Prithee peace!
I dare do all that may become a man.

32–35 I have . . . so soon: The praises that Macbeth has received are, like new clothes, to be worn, not quickly thrown away. What has Macbeth decided? **A**

35–38 Was the hope drunk . . . freely: Lady Macbeth sarcastically suggests that Macbeth's ambition must have been drunk, because it now seems to have a hangover (**to look so green and pale**).

39–45 Such I . . . adage: Lady Macbeth criticizes Macbeth's weakened resolve to secure the crown (**ornament of life**) and calls him a coward. She compares him to a cat in a proverb (**adage**) who wouldn't catch fish because it feared wet feet.

Teaching Options

Grammar

UNDERSTANDING MODIFIERS

Instruction Adjectives are words that change or limit nouns and pronouns. An adjective often comes before the word it modifies and that it answers one of the following questions: Which one?, What kind?, How many?, or How much? Explain that a predicate adjective is an adjective that follows a linking verb, such as *is, feels, looks,* and *seems,* and modifies the noun or pronoun subject of the sentence. Add that adverbs modify verbs, adjectives, or other adverbs and they answer the questions: Where?, When?, How?, or To what extent?

Activity Write the passage on the chalkboard. Underline the words as shown and have students identify the adjectives *(human, nearest),* adverbs *(too, not, highly, holily, not, false, wrongly),* and the predicate adjective *(great).*

"It is too full o' the milk of human kindness
To catch the nearest way. Thou wouldst be great;
Art not without ambition, but without
The illness should attend it. What thou wouldst highly,
That wouldst thou holily; wouldst not play false,

Who dares do more is none.

Lady Macbeth. What beast was't then
[3] That made you break this enterprise to me?
When you durst do it, then you were a man; [4]
And to be more than what you were, you would
Be so much more the man. Nor time nor place
Did then adhere, and yet you would make both.
They have made themselves, and that their fitness now
Does unmake you. I have given suck, and know
How tender 'tis to love the babe that milks me.
I would, while it was smiling in my face,
Have plucked my nipple from his boneless gums
And dashed the brains out, had I so sworn as you
Have done to this.

Macbeth. If we should fail?

Lady Macbeth. We fail?
But screw your courage to the sticking place,
And we'll not fail. When Duncan is asleep
[5] (Whereto the rather shall his day's hard journey
Soundly invite him), his two chamberlains
Will I with wine and wassail so convince
That memory, the warder of the brain,
Shall be a fume, and the receipt of reason
A limbeck only. When in swinish sleep
Their drenched natures lie as in a death,
What cannot you and I perform upon
The unguarded Duncan? what not put upon
His spongy officers, who shall bear the guilt
Of our great quell?

Macbeth. Bring forth men-children only,
For thy undaunted mettle should compose
Nothing but males. Will it not be received,
When we have marked with blood those sleepy two
Of his own chamber and used their very daggers,
That they have done't?

Lady Macbeth. Who dares receive it other,
As we shall make our griefs and clamor roar
Upon his death?

Macbeth. I am settled and bend up
Each corporal agent to this terrible feat.
Away, and mock the time with fairest show;
False face must hide what the false heart doth know.

[Exeunt.]

54 I have given suck: I have nursed a baby.

60 but . . . place: When each string of a guitar or lute is tightened to the peg (**sticking place**), the instrument is ready to be played.

65–67 that memory . . . a limbeck only: Memory was thought to be at the base of the brain, to guard against harmful vapors rising from the body. Lady Macbeth will get the guards so drunk that their reason will become like a still (**limbeck**), producing confused thoughts.

72 quell: murder.

72–74 Bring forth . . . males: Your bold spirit (**undaunted mettle**) is better suited to raising males than females. Do you think Macbeth's words express admiration?

79–82 I am settled . . . know: Now that Macbeth has made up his mind, every part of his body (**each corporal agent**) is tightened like a bow. He and Lady Macbeth will return to the banquet and deceive everyone (**mock the time**), hiding their evil intent with gracious faces.

Customizing Instruction

Less Proficient Readers

Make sure students understand the following archaic forms and words:

1. *supped* (eaten supper; dined)
2. *prithee* (I pray thee; please)
3. *was't* (was it)
4. *durst* (dared)
5. *whereto* (to which)

And yet wouldst wrongly win. . . ."

Exercise Ask students to write the adjectives, adverbs, or predicate adjectives in each sentence and label each with its part of speech.

1. Macbeth seems to be deeply troubled by the prophesy of the three witches. *(deeply: adverb; troubled: predicate adjective; three: adjective)*
2. Macbeth's heroic defense during the Norwegian attack was reported to Duncan by the bloodied Captain. *(Macbeth's, heroic, Norwegian, bloodied; adjectives)*
3. Shakespeare's play, *Macbeth*, is based on actual events in the life of an 11th-century king of Scotland. *(Shakespeare's, actual, 11th-century: adjectives)*

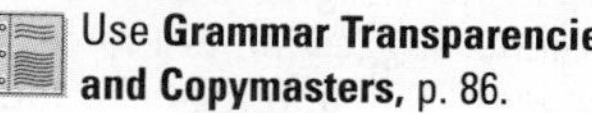

Use **Grammar Transparencies and Copymasters,** p. 86.

Use McDougal Littell's ***Language Network*** for more information in understanding modifiers.

GUIDING STUDENT RESPONSE

Connect to the Literature

1. What Do You Think?
Guidelines for student response: Accept all reasonable responses that are supported with evidence from the text.

Comprehension Check
- He will be Thane of Cawdor and king hereafter.
- kill the current king
- He will be lesser than Macbeth and be greater; he will be less happy than Macbeth, yet happier; he won't be king himself, but he will beget kings.

 Use Selection Quiz in **Unit Two Resource Book** p. 17.

Think Critically

2. Possible motives include ambition, lust for power, love of spouse.
3. Students who name Lady Macbeth may say that she is the prime mover prodding Macbeth to action. Students who name Macbeth may say that he actually performs the murder.
4. Accept all reasonable responses. Students who think the witches control Macbeth's future may mention that their predictions do indeed come true or that they are evil forces in which people at the time believed. Students who think Macbeth controls his own future may say that the witches do not compel him to take action.
5. Possible Responses: Banquo may prove himself to be a greater and happier man than the worldly Macbeth. Banquo will not be king himself, but his descendants will be.
6. Possible Response:
   - If I'm to kill the king, the time is now. I fear the unforeseen consequences of my actions.
   - the trust of a subject owing loyalty to the king and of a host offering refuge and hospitality to a guest.
   - Possible responses: meek, virtuous, innocent, good
   - Possible responses: My motive is ambition, moving me to action which may prove self-destructive; this ambition is compared to the spur that drives a horse to vault an obstacle, misjudge the distance, and overleap, falling on itself.

Connect to the Literature

1. **What Do You Think?** At this point, what are your impressions of Macbeth and his wife?

Comprehension Check
- What predictions do the three witches make about Macbeth's future?
- What do Macbeth and his wife plan to do to make the last prediction come true?
- What predictions do the witches make about Banquo?

Think Critically

2. What values do you think motivate Macbeth?
3. At this point in the play, who would you say is the more forceful character, Macbeth or Lady Macbeth? Why?

   THINK ABOUT
   - their ambitions and fears
   - their attitudes toward Duncan
   - their attitudes toward murder
   - their attitudes toward each other
4. Do you think Macbeth would have formed his murderous plan if the witches hadn't made their predictions to him? Explain who you think controls Macbeth's fate.
5. What might the witches' predictions about Banquo mean?
6. ACTIVE READING SHAKESPEARE'S LANGUAGE In Act One, Scene 7, what does Macbeth mean in the final sentence of his **soliloquy,** lines 25–28? You may want to refer to your  READER'S NOTEBOOK for notes you took on the Strategies for Reading Shakespeare's Language.

Extend Interpretations

7. **What If?** Imagine that you are a friend and adviser of Macbeth and his wife. What advice would you give them? What would you tell them about the three witches' predictions?
8. **Critic's Corner** According to the critic L. C. Knights, "*Macbeth* defines a particular kind of evil—the evil that results from a lust for power." On the basis of what you have read so far, do you agree? Is excessive ambition the only source of Macbeth's "evil"? Support your opinion with details from Act One.

Literary Analysis

SOLILOQUY/ASIDE A **soliloquy** is a speech that reveals a character's private thoughts to the audience. An **aside** is a character's remark that others on the stage are not supposed to hear. Although unrealistic, the soliloquy and the aside allow playwrights to reveal characters' thoughts and motives that would otherwise remain hidden.

Paired Activity Working with a partner, identify revealing soliloquies and asides in Act One of *Macbeth,* and explain the thoughts and motives that they reveal. You might fill in a chart like the one below.

Act, Scene, Lines	Soliloquy or Aside?	What It Reveals
Act One, Scene 3, lines 116–117	Aside	Macbeth's ambition and his belief in the witches' prophecies

REVIEW CHARACTERIZATION Consider Duncan's speeches and actions, as well as the remarks that Macbeth and others make about him. What sort of person does Duncan seem to be? How good a king is he?

Extend Interpretations

What If? Accept all reasonable responses that show an awareness of the play's events and characterization.

Critic's Corner Students who disagree may feel that supernatural elements suggest an evil force manipulating the Macbeths' fate and may cite the validity of the witches' predictions as evidence. Those who agree may say that the predictions merely show the way for the Macbeths to act upon their lust for power and may cite remarks by the Macbeths illustrating such ambitions.

Literary Analysis

Paired Activity You might display students' charts in the classroom or ask volunteers to read the information they have recorded on their charts.

View and Compare

What aspects of Macbeth's character do these images convey?

Laurence Olivier, Memorial Theatre, Stratford-upon-Avon, England (1955)

John Gielgud, Piccadilly Theatre, London (1942)

Toshiro Mifune as Macbeth, *The Throne of Blood* (film, 1957)

Raul Julia, New York Shakespeare Festival

347

Mini Lesson: Viewing and Representing

View and Compare

ART APPRECIATION

Instruction Laurence Olivier's Macbeth was motivated in the later acts of the play by a growing frustration at not being able to enjoy his crown in peace. Some critics felt that Olivier's Macbeth was definitive. Olivier himself said he wanted to play Macbeth as "the kind of man whose arm you would not take as you crossed the street."

Application Have students compare and contrast the images of Macbeth presented above. What characteristics of the king are illustrated in each of the images? What do the facial expressions of the actors reveal about the character of Macbeth? Do any of the images present Macbeth sympathetically? Have students clarify their interpretations by discussing which representations make the strongest impact on them.

TEACHING THE LITERATURE

Reading and Analyzing

Literary Analysis BLANK VERSE

Macbeth is written in blank verse, unrhymed poetry written in iambic pentameter. Because iambic pentameter resembles the natural rhythm of spoken English, it has been considered the most suitable meter for dramatic verse in English.

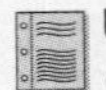

Use **Unit Two Resource Book,** p. 20 for additional support.

Active Reading READING DRAMA

Explain that students can better understand the meaning of a play by using strategies for reading drama. Write the following strategies on the board:

1. Read the play silently.
2. Determine what is happening in this act by reading the set descriptions and introduction to the plot.
3. Pay close attention to stage directions.
4. Think of the characters as though you know them.
5. Write a two- or three-sentence summary of the events of each scene.
6. Read the play aloud.

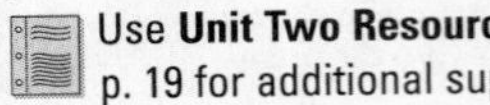

Use **Unit Two Resource Book,** p. 19 for additional support.

GUIDE FOR READING

A Students will probably not believe Macbeth is sincere because he has been thinking about killing the king.

B Macbeth is probably annoyed that Banquo is being so loyal and ethical.

C He could be revealing the first signs of the guilt-induced dementia that surfaces at later points in the play.

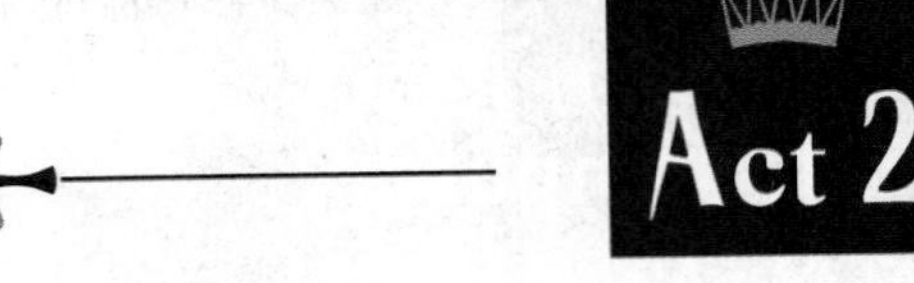

Act 2

SCENE 1

The court of Macbeth's castle.

It is past midnight, and Banquo and his son Fleance cannot sleep. When Macbeth appears, Banquo tells of his uneasy dreams about the witches. Macbeth promises that they will discuss the prophecies later, and Banquo goes to bed. Once alone, Macbeth imagines a dagger leading him toward the king's chamber. When he hears a bell, the signal from Lady Macbeth, he knows it is time to go to Duncan's room.

[*Enter* Banquo, *and* Fleance *with a torch before him.*]

Banquo. How goes the night, boy?

Fleance. The moon is down; I have not heard the clock.

Banquo. And she goes down at twelve.

Fleance. I take't, 'tis later, sir.

Banquo. Hold, take my sword. There's husbandry in heaven;
Their candles are all out. Take thee that too.
A heavy summons lies like lead upon me,
And yet I would not sleep. Merciful powers,
Restrain in me the cursed thoughts that nature
Gives way to in repose!

[*Enter* Macbeth, *and a* Servant *with a torch.*]

Give me my sword.
Who's there?

Macbeth. A friend.

1 **Banquo.** What, sir, not yet at rest? The King's abed.
He hath been in unusual pleasure and
Sent forth great largess to your offices.
This diamond he greets your wife withal
By the name of most kind hostess, and shut up
In measureless content.

Macbeth. Being unprepared,
Our will became the servant to defect,
Which else should free have wrought.

Banquo. All's well.
2 I dreamt last night of the three Weird Sisters.
To you they have showed some truth.

Macbeth. I think not of them.
Yet when we can entreat an hour to serve,

4–5 There's husbandry . . . all out: The heavens show economy (**husbandry**) by keeping the lights (**candles**) out—it is a starless night.

6 heavy summons: desire for sleep.

14 largess to your offices: gifts to the servants' quarters.

16 shut up: went to bed.

17–19 Being . . . wrought: Because we were unprepared, we could not entertain the king as we would have liked. Do you believe in Macbeth's sincerity here? **A**

22 can entreat an hour: both have the time.

Teaching Options

BLOCK SCHEDULING: MANAGING TIME

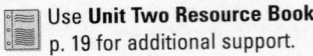

If your schedule requires that you cover the lesson objectives in a shorter time, use . . .

- Preparing to Read, pp. 323–325
- Thinking Through the Literature, p. 362

If you want to take advantage of longer class time, use . . .

- Viewing and Representing, p. 349; Speaking and Listening, p. 358; Multicultural Link, p. 350; Vocabulary Strategy, pp. 352, 356; Informal Assessment, pp. 353, 359; Cross Curricular Links, p. 354; Grammar, p. 360

We would spend it in some words upon that business,
If you would grant the time.

Banquo. At your kind'st leisure.

Macbeth. If you shall cleave to my consent, when 'tis,
It shall make honor for you.

Banquo. So I lose none
In seeking to augment it but still keep
My bosom franchised and allegiance clear,
I shall be counseled.

Macbeth. Good repose the while!

Banquo. Thanks, sir. The like to you!

[*Exeunt* Banquo *and* Fleance.]

Macbeth. Go bid thy mistress, when my drink is ready,
She strike upon the bell. Get thee to bed.

[*Exit* Servant.]

Is this a dagger which I see before me,
The handle toward my hand? Come, let me clutch thee!
I have thee not, and yet I see thee still.
Art thou not, fatal vision, sensible
To feeling as to sight? or art thou but
A dagger of the mind, a false creation,
Proceeding from the heat-oppressed brain?
I see thee yet, in form as palpable
As this which now I draw.
Thou marshal'st me the way that I was going,
And such an instrument I was to use.

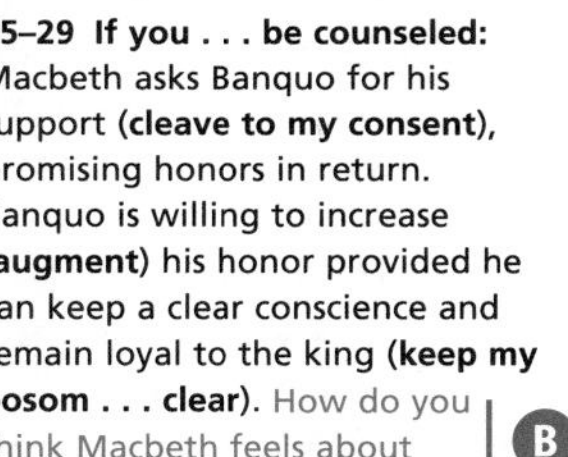

25–29 If you . . . be counseled: Macbeth asks Banquo for his support (**cleave to my consent**), promising honors in return. Banquo is willing to increase (**augment**) his honor provided he can keep a clear conscience and remain loyal to the king (**keep my bosom . . . clear**). How do you think Macbeth feels about Banquo's virtuous stand?

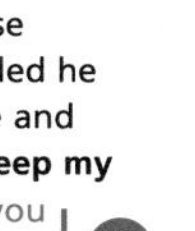

B

33–43 Is this a dagger . . . to use: Macbeth sees a dagger hanging in midair before him and questions whether it is real (**palpable**) or the illusion of a disturbed (**heat-oppressed**) mind. The floating, imaginary dagger, which leads (**marshal'st**) him to Duncan's room, prompts him to draw his own dagger. Is Macbeth losing his mind? C

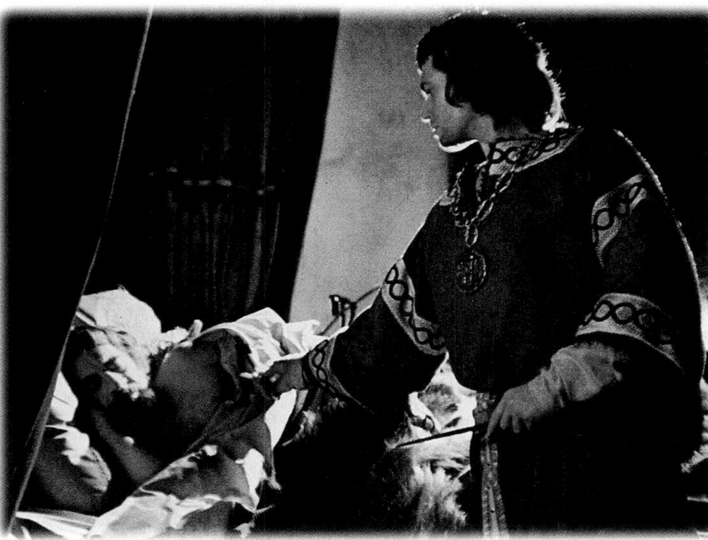

Act 2, Scene 2: Duncan's murder, Jon Finch as Macbeth (film, 1971)

Customizing Instruction

Students Acquiring English

1 Explain that people today say that someone is "in bed," rather than "abed." Some words with the introductory *a* still exist, however, such as *atop, abroad, aloft,* and *aghast.*

Less Proficient Readers

2 Invite students to discuss Banquo's worries about his dream. Use the following questions:

- Whom did Banquo dream about?
  Answer: He dreamed about the three weird sisters.
- Why is Banquo troubled about the dream?
  Answer: He is worried about the meaning of the witches' prophecies for Macbeth.
- What is Macbeth's reaction to Banquo's concern?
  Answer: He shrugs off Banquo's worries, saying he thinks "not of them the weird sisters."

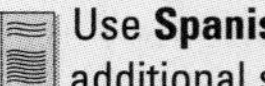

Use **Spanish Study Guide** for additional support, pp. 67–69

Mini Lesson Viewing and Representing

RECOGNIZING MEDIA TECHNIQUES

Instruction Encourage students to reread the stage directions for clues about lighting on the original stages of Shakespeare's theater. Ask them to imagine the effects of torches and dark, moonless nights—without the assistance of modern-day stage lights. Explain that in the Renaissance many plays were performed during the day precisely because of a lack of light.

Application Students may keep a list of stage directions that affect lighting, music, and special effects throughout *Macbeth,* referencing page number and line. Ask them to compare a director's use of lighting, music, and special effects with Shakespeare's stage directions.

Reading and Analyzing

Literary Analysis: FORESHADOWING

A Remind students that foreshadowing is a device a writer uses to prepare readers for an event or action that is to happen later in the story. Foreshadowing takes the form of hints—or bits of information—that suggest what is to come. This device adds suspense to the story of *Macbeth.* Ask students the following questions:

- What is Macbeth referring to in lines 49–50, "Now o'er the one half-world / Nature seems dead"?

Answer: One half of the world is darkened by night, seemingly lifeless.

- Do his words give you a feeling that something ominous is about to happen? Explain.

Possible Response: Yes. The reference to death suggests that perhaps someone is about to die.

Reading Skills and Strategies: VISUALIZING SCENES

Macbeth's soliloquy (lines 33–64) in which he sees an imaginary dagger floating in front of him presents unique problems to the actor, who must make decisions about how much "interaction" to have with the vision of the knife. Have students visualize Macbeth's speech—does he merely talk to himself or does he actually address the hallucination? Does he clutch and grab at the knife that isn't there? Students may choose to illustrate what they've envisioned by performing the scene for the class.

Mine eyes are made the fools o' the other senses,
Or else worth all the rest. I see thee still;
And on thy blade and dudgeon gouts of blood,
Which was not so before. There's no such thing.
It is the bloody business which informs
Thus to mine eyes. Now o'er the one half-world
Nature seems dead, and wicked dreams abuse
The curtained sleep. Witchcraft celebrates
Pale Hecate's offerings; and withered murder,
Alarumed by his sentinel, the wolf,
Whose howl's his watch, thus with his stealthy pace,
With Tarquin's ravishing strides, towards his design
Moves like a ghost. Thou sure and firm-set earth,
Hear not my steps which way they walk, for fear
Thy very stones prate of my whereabout
And take the present horror from the time,
Which now suits with it. Whiles I threat, he lives;
Words to the heat of deeds too cold breath gives.

[*A bell rings.*]

I go, and it is done. The bell invites me.
Hear it not, Duncan, for it is a knell
That summons thee to heaven, or to hell.

[*Exit.*]

44–45 Mine eyes . . . the rest: Either his eyes are mistaken **(fools)** or his other senses are.

46 on thy blade . . . blood: drops of blood on the blade and handle.

60–61 Whiles I . . . gives: Talk **(threat)** delays action **(deeds)**.

63 knell: funeral bell.

SCENE 2

Macbeth's castle.

As Lady Macbeth waits for her husband, she explains how she drugged Duncan's servants. Suddenly a dazed and terrified Macbeth enters, carrying the bloody daggers that he used to murder Duncan. He imagines a voice that warns, "Macbeth shall sleep no more" and is too afraid to return to the scene of the crime. Lady Macbeth takes the bloody daggers back so that the servants will be blamed. Startled by a knocking at the gate, she hurries back and tells Macbeth to wash off the blood and change into his nightclothes.

[*Enter* Lady Macbeth.]

Lady Macbeth. That which hath made them drunk hath made me bold;
What hath quenched them hath given me fire. Hark! Peace!
It was the owl that shrieked, the fatal bellman
Which gives the stern'st good-night. He is about it.
The doors are open, and the surfeited grooms
Do mock their charge with snores. I have drugged their possets,

3 fatal bellman: town crier.

5 surfeited grooms: drunken servants.

6 possets: drinks.

Teaching Options

Multicultural Link: Samurai

Akiro Kurosawa'a *The Throne of Blood* (1957) was one of the many films he made about the samurai. The samurai were members of the warrior class that dominated the Japanese government until the 19th century. The ideal samurai was supposed to follow a code of conduct called *Bushido.* This code emphasized bravery, frugal living, kindness, honesty, filial piety, and, above all, loyalty to one's lord. The best-known illustration of bushido is the true story of the 47 ronin, or masterless samurai.

In the early 18th century, a young lord named Asano was given an important position. A high-ranking official named Kira was sent to advise him. However, Kira took every opportunity to insult Lord Asano in public. Asano lost his temper, drew his sword, and wounded Kira. For this offense, he was forced to commit seppuku, or ritual suicide. Asano's samurai became ronin as a result of their lord's death and swore to avenge him. Forty-seven of Asano's most loyal warriors killed Kira after a battle with his armed guards. The shogun (Asano's superior in noble rank) was impressed by the ronins' loyalty to their dead lord,

View and Compare

In the scene portraying Duncan's murder, how do you interpret the dynamics between Macbeth and Lady Macbeth in each photo?

Act 2, Scene 2: After Duncan's murder, Derek Jacobi as Macbeth and Cheryl Campbell as Lady Macbeth, Royal Shakespeare Company (1993)

Act 2, Scene 2: After Duncan's murder, Toshiro Mifune as Macbeth and Isuzu Yamada as Lady Macbeth, *The Throne of Blood* (film, 1957)

Customizing Instruction

Less Proficient Readers

1 Students may not understand why Macbeth is standing around talking to himself. Point out the phrases that Macbeth uses to describe his situation: "gouts of blood" (line 46), "bloody business" (line 49), "Nature seems dead" (line 50), "wicked dreams" (line 50), "Witchcraft" (line 51), "withered murder" (line 52), "stealthy pace" (line 54), "ravishing strides" (line 55), "Moves like a ghost" (line 56). Ask students what they think is the overall impression given by these phrases?
Possible Responses: horror; guilt.
What, then, might be Macbeth's reason for engaging in this long soliloquy?
Possible Response: He is horrified by what he is planning to do, and is procrastinating.

Students Acquiring English

2 Help students understand the meaning of difficult imagery, and guide them to visualize passages such as the one in lines 56–60 by showing them how Macbeth's footsteps across the "firm-set earth" demonstrate his regained sense of purpose. He also doesn't want the earth (that is, "nature") to notice where he's walking, because he's going to commit a horrible crime.

Multiple Learning Styles

Auditory Learners

Give each student a single poetic line from the soliloquy to recite. Place students in a circle, seated or standing; then have each say his or her line in order. The goal is the even flow of a single voice. When this has been done, vary the instructions: Have students shout their lines or whisper their lines.

but he could not let them go unpunished. All but the youngest ronin committed seppuku.

Today, the sacrifice of these men is celebrated in a play called *Chusingura,* and thousands of Japanese visit their gravesite each year to pay homage to their dedication to bushido.

Reading and Analyzing

Active Reading READING DRAMA

Ask students to consider the structure of the play in relation to the following elements: exposition, rising action, climax, and denouement. Point out that the exposition was established in Act One, whereas Act Two deals mostly with rising action. As they read Act Two, students may write events on their diagrams that they think contribute to the rising action of the play.

GUIDE FOR READING

(A) She's afraid he'll wake up their other guests.

(B) He's afraid that he's beyond the reach of prayer and of God, and so has damned his soul with his immoral acts.

Literary Analysis:
FIGURATIVE LANGUAGE

(C) Remind students that a figurative expression is not literally true, but rather creates an impression in the reader's mind. Ask students to discuss the meaning of the personification given in line 37: "Sleep that knits up the raveled sleave of care . . ."
Possible Response: Sleep relieves the burdens of everyday work and worries.

GUIDE FOR READING

(D) Macbeth is concerned that his guilt will get the better of him, and that because he is not "innocent" he will no longer enjoy the comfort of sleep; his conscience will never rest again.

(E) Lady Macbeth does not shy away from the blood of the murders, while Macbeth appears almost frightened of it once he's killed Duncan.

That death and nature do contend about them
Whether they live or die.

Macbeth. [*Within*] Who's there? What, ho?

Lady Macbeth. Alack, I am afraid they have awaked,
And 'tis not done! The attempt, and not the deed,
Confounds us. Hark! I laid their daggers ready;
He could not miss 'em. Had he not resembled
My father as he slept, I had done't.

[*Enter Macbeth.*]

My husband!

Macbeth. I have done the deed. Didst thou not hear a noise?

Lady Macbeth. I heard the owl scream and the crickets cry.
Did not you speak?

Macbeth. When?

Lady Macbeth. Now.

Macbeth. As I descended?

Lady Macbeth. Ay.

Macbeth. Hark!
Who lies i' the second chamber?

Lady Macbeth. Donalbain.

Macbeth. This is a sorry sight.

Lady Macbeth. A foolish thought, to say a sorry sight.

1 **Macbeth.** There's one did laugh in's sleep, and one cried
"Murder!"
That they did wake each other. I stood and heard them.
But they did say their prayers and addressed them
Again to sleep.

2 **Lady Macbeth.** There are two lodged together.

Macbeth. One cried "God bless us!" and "Amen!" the other,
As they had seen me with these hangman's hands,
List'ning their fear. I could not say "Amen!"
When they did say "God bless us!"

Lady Macbeth. Consider it not so deeply.

Macbeth. But wherefore could not I pronounce "Amen"?
I had most need of blessing, and "Amen"
Stuck in my throat.

Lady Macbeth. These deeds must not be thought
After these ways. So, it will make us mad.

Macbeth. Methought I heard a voice cry "Sleep no more!
Macbeth does murder sleep"—the innocent sleep,

9–10 Why does the sound of Macbeth's voice make his wife so afraid? (A)

11 confounds: destroys. If Duncan survives, they will be killed (as his attempted murderers)

27–28 as they . . . fear: He imagines that the sleepers could see him listening to their exclamations of fear, with his hands bloody like those of an executioner.

28–33 Why is Macbeth so troubled by the fact that he cannot say "Amen"? (B)

Teaching Options

Vocabulary Strategy

EXPANDING VOCABULARY BY DISCUSSING

Instruction Remind students that they can better understand unfamiliar words by discussing them with each other. Review with the class several of the strategies they have learned by writing the strategies on the board: looking for context clues, differentiating between connotation and denotation, and researching the meanings of idioms.

Activity Have students work in small groups to discuss the following words. Ask them to use the strategies on the board to determine intended meanings and to write down their own definitions.

- "Alack" (line 9)
Answer: "Oh no;" a sound of dismay.
- "Methought" (line 35)
Answer: "It seemed to me."
- "Balm" (line 39)
Answer: Something that soothes or comforts.
- "Infirm" (line 52)
Answer: weak or yielding.
- "gild" (line 56)
Answer: to decorate or cover.

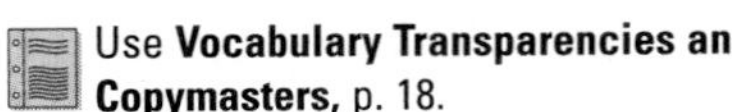

Use **Vocabulary Transparencies and Copymasters,** p. 18.

C Sleep that knits up the raveled sleave of care,
The death of each day's life, sore labor's bath,
Balm of hurt minds, great nature's second course,
Chief nourisher in life's feast.

Lady Macbeth. What do you mean?

Macbeth. Still it cried "Sleep no more!" to all the house;
"Glamis hath murdered sleep, and therefore Cawdor
Shall sleep no more! Macbeth shall sleep no more!"

Lady Macbeth. Who was it that thus cried? Why, worthy Thane,
You do unbend your noble strength to think
3 So brainsickly of things. Go get some water
And wash this filthy witness from your hand.
Why did you bring these daggers from the place?
They must lie there. Go carry them and smear
The sleepy grooms with blood.

Macbeth. I'll go no more.
I am afraid to think what I have done;
Look on't again I dare not.

Lady Macbeth. Infirm of purpose!
Give me the daggers. The sleeping and the dead
Are but as pictures. 'Tis the eye of childhood
That fears a painted devil. If he do bleed,
I'll gild the faces of the grooms withal,
For it must seem their guilt. [*Exit. Knocking within.*]

Macbeth. Whence is that knocking?
How is't with me when every noise appals me?
What hands are here? Ha! they pluck out mine eyes!
Will all great Neptune's ocean wash this blood
4 Clean from my hand? No. This my hand will rather
The multitudinous seas incarnadine,
Making the green one red. [*Enter* Lady Macbeth.]

Lady Macbeth. My hands are of your color, but I shame
To wear a heart so white. [*Knock.*] I hear a knocking
At the south entry. Retire we to our chamber.
A little water clears us of this deed.
How easy is it then! Your constancy
Hath left you unattended. [*Knock.*] Hark! more knocking.
Get on your nightgown, lest occasion call us
And show us to be watchers. Be not lost
So poorly in your thoughts.

Macbeth. To know my deed, 'twere best not know myself.
[*Knock.*]
Wake Duncan with thy knocking! I would thou couldst!
[*Exeunt.*]

36–40 the innocent sleep . . . life's feast: Sleep eases worries (**knits up the raveled sleave of care**), relieves the aches of physical work (**sore labor's bath**), soothes the anxious (**hurt minds**), and nourishes like food. Why is Macbeth so concerned about sleep? D

47 this filthy witness: the evidence, that is, the blood.

56–57 I'll gild . . . guilt: She'll cover (**gild**) the servants with blood, blaming them for the murder. How is her attitude toward blood different from her husband's? E

61–63 This my hand . . . one red: The blood on my hand will redden (**incarnadine**) the seas.

68–69 Your constancy . . . unattended: Your courage has left you.

70–71 lest . . . watchers: in case we are called for and found awake (**watchers**), which would look suspicious.

73 To know . . . myself: To come to terms with what I have done, I must forget about my conscience.

Customizing Instruction

Multiple Learning Styles

Auditory Learners

1 In lines 22–43, Macbeth describes the sounds he heard after he murdered Duncan. Have students make a tape recording—complete with distinct voices and sound effects—of what Macbeth heard. Encourage them to be creative and to make it as realistic as possible.

Gifted and Talented

Encourage students to consider the very different reactions to the murder that Macbeth and Lady Macbeth have. Have the students discuss whose reaction they find more admirable or acceptable, and why. Have them look especially at lines 44–75.

Possible Response: Macbeth's reaction is more acceptable, as he at least seems to realize the enormity of what he has done and to feel remorse; Lady Macbeth's reaction is more acceptable, as she faces up to what has been done and does not flinch.

Students Acquiring English

2 Help students understand the meaning of "lodged together" in line 26. Explain that the term indicates the two were sleeping in the same room.

Less Proficient Readers

Ask students these questions about the washing of hands:

3 Why does Lady Macbeth tell her husband to wash his hands?

Answer: She wants him to wash away the evidence of the murder.

4 Why does Macbeth say that he cannot get his hands clean?

Possible Response: He feels that his guilt is so great that he cannot get rid of it so easily.

Assessment Informal Assessment

IDENTIFYING CAUSE-AND-EFFECT RELATIONSHIPS

You can informally assess students' understanding of the selection up to this point by having them list the main events that have occurred in Act Two, as well as the causes for those events. From their lists, students can write a brief summary of what has happened in the plot.

RUBRIC

3 **Full Accomplishment** Student writing reflects full understanding of main events in Act Two and their causes.

2 **Substantial Accomplishment** Student writing shows general understanding of some of main events, but causes unclear.

1 **Little or Partial Accomplishment** Student writing displays little understanding of main events or their causes.

MACBETH: ACT TWO 353

Reading and Analyzing

Active Reading READING DRAMA

Remind students that learning to read a dramatic play involves paying close attention to stage directions, which are instructions for the actors and descriptions of the scenery. Have students visualize how the stage looks and picture the actions in their minds. Encourage them to imagine they are watching a performance. Direct students' attention to the stage directions on pages 354–355 and ask them these questions:

- Name the characters who enter the scene on pages 354–355.

Answer: a Porter, Macduff, Lennox, and Macbeth.

- In lines 1–21, how does the knocking sound, as indicated in the stage directions, affect the drama of the play?

Possible Response: It gives the porter subject matter for an amusing monologue, thereby lending the play some comic relief.

Literary Analysis: COMIC RELIEF

(A) Explain that in most of Shakespeare's plays, comic episodes interrupt the plot to relieve the main action. The Porter's prose, exemplifies the element of comic relief in an otherwise tragic story line. Ask students how humor is helpful at this point and why.

Possible Response: The last scene was horrifying and intense, and the audience probably needs a break before moving on to the next emotional scene.

SCENE 3

Within Macbeth's castle, near the gate.

The drunken porter staggers across the courtyard to answer the knocking. After Lennox and Macduff are let in, Macbeth arrives to lead them to the king's quarters. Macduff enters Duncan's room and discovers his murder. Lennox and Macbeth then go to the scene, and Macbeth, pretending to be enraged, kills the two servants. Amid all the commotion, Lady Macbeth faints. Duncan's sons, Malcolm and Donalbain, fearing for their lives, quietly leave, hoping to escape the country.

[*Enter a* Porter. *Knocking within.*]

Porter. Here's a knocking indeed! If a man were porter of hell gate, he should have old turning the key. [*Knock.*] Knock, knock, knock! Who's there, i' the name of Belzebub? Here's a farmer that hanged himself on the expectation of plenty. Come in time! Have napkins enow about you; here you'll sweat for't. [*Knock.*] Knock, knock! Who's there, in the other devil's name? Faith, here's an equivocator, that could swear in both the scales against either scale; who committed treason enough for God's sake, yet could not equivocate to heaven. O, come in, equivocator! [*Knock.*] Knock, knock, knock! Who's there? Faith, here's an English

2 old turning the key: plenty of key turning. Hell's porter would be busy because so many people are ending up in hell these days.

4 Belzebub: a devil.

Act 2, Scene 3: The porter (right), with Lennox and Macduff, in a stage production of *Macbeth* (1948)

354

Teaching Options

Cross Curricular Link History

EQUIVOCATORS *Macbeth* is rarely discussed without some mention of James I. James's reign is probably referred to in the Porter scene when the Porter welcomes an equivocator into hell. An Elizabethan audience would be familiar with equivocators (those who make statements having two possible meanings to be purposely deceptive) because of the Gunpowder Plot (1605). Henry Garnet, a Jesuit, and Guy Fawkes, a soldier, plotted along with three others to blow up the houses of Parliament and assassinate King James I in order to place a Catholic monarch on the throne. The plan was foiled and the men were arrested and later executed. However, at the trial in 1606, Garnet in his defense invoked the Doctrine of Equivocation, which he claimed permitted him to commit perjury in a morally acceptable cause. The cause he referred to was maintaining the sanctity of the confessional, where he supposedly *first* heard of the murderous plot. He claimed that he could not report what he heard because of the confidentiality of the confessional. Protestant England was appalled by what it perceived as a maneuver around the law.

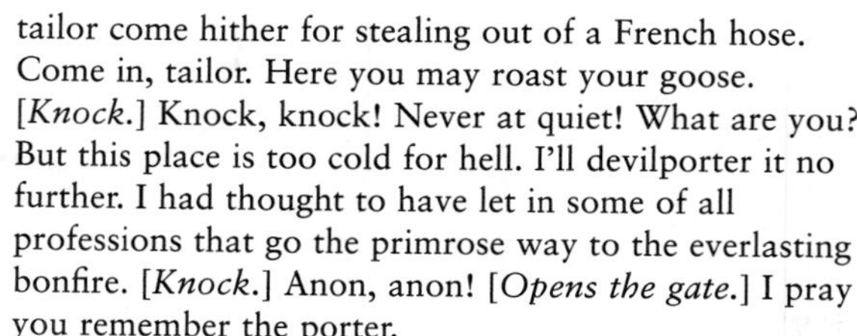

A tailor come hither for stealing out of a French hose. Come in, tailor. Here you may roast your goose. [*Knock.*] Knock, knock! Never at quiet! What are you? But this place is too cold for hell. I'll devilporter it no further. I had thought to have let in some of all professions that go the primrose way to the everlasting bonfire. [*Knock.*] Anon, anon! [*Opens the gate.*] I pray you remember the porter.

[*Enter* Macduff *and* Lennox.]

Macduff. Was it so late, friend, ere you went to bed,
That you do lie so late?

Porter. Faith, sir, we were carousing till the second cock; and drink, sir, is a great provoker of three things.

Macduff. What three things does drink especially provoke?

Porter. Marry, sir, nose-painting, sleep, and urine. Lechery, sir, it provokes, and unprovokes: it provokes the desire, but it takes away the performance. Therefore much drink may be said to be an equivocator with lechery: it makes him, and it mars him; it sets him on, and it takes him off; it persuades him, and disheartens him; makes him stand to, and not stand to; in conclusion, equivocates him in a sleep, and, giving him the lie, leaves him.

Macduff. I believe drink gave thee the lie last night.

Porter. That it did, sir, i' the very throat on me; but I requited him for his lie; and, I think, being too strong for him, though he took up my legs sometime, yet I made a shift to cast him.

1 **Macduff.** Is thy master stirring?

[*Enter* Macbeth.]

Our knocking has awaked him; here he comes.

Lennox. Good morrow, noble sir.

Macbeth. Good morrow, both.

Macduff. Is the King stirring, worthy Thane?

Macbeth. Not yet.

2 **Macduff.** He did command me to call timely on him;
I have almost slipped the hour.

Macbeth. I'll bring you to him.

Macduff. I know this is a joyful trouble to you;
But yet 'tis one.

4–13 The porter pretends he is welcoming a farmer who killed himself after his schemes to get rich (**expectation of plenty**) failed, a double talker (**equivocator**) who perjured himself yet couldn't talk his way into heaven, and a tailor who cheated his customers by skimping on material (**stealing out of a French hose**).

23 second cock: early morning, announced by the crow of a rooster.

28–35 The porter jokes that alcohol stimulates lust (**lechery**) but makes the lover a failure.

36–40 More jokes about alcohol, this time described as a wrestler finally thrown off (**cast**) by the porter, who thus paid him back (**requited him**) for disappointment in love. *Cast* also means "to vomit" and "to urinate," two other ways of dealing with alcohol.

45 timely: early.

46 slipped the hour: missed the time.

Customizing Instruction

Students Acquiring English

1 Explain to students that *stirring* in lines 41 and 44 means "awake." Ask students what the common definition of *stir* is.

Answer: to mix, shake, or move something.

Then ask students why *stirring* might be an appropriate term for someone who is awake.

Possible Response: unlike someone who is asleep, someone awake moves around.

Less Proficient Readers

2 Help students understand the exchange between Macduff and Macbeth (lines 43–48) by asking them why Macbeth offers to take Macduff to the chamber of the man Macbeth murdered in the night.

Possible Response: By doing so, Macbeth makes it seem as though he does not know about the murder.

MACBETH: ACT TWO 355

Reading and Analyzing

A Point out Macbeth's statement in lines 90–95. Ask students to explain how this statement contains both verbal irony and dramatic irony. You might want to remind students that this play is a tragedy; therefore, the reader already knows that things will not end well for Macbeth.

Possible Response: The statement contains verbal irony because Macbeth believes that Duncan's death will improve Macbeth's lot in life, although he is saying the opposite. The dramatic irony stems from the fact that the reader knows that what Macbeth says is most likely the truth, although Macbeth does not know it.

GUIDE FOR READING

B Although he is pretending to be innocent, he probably also really feels some regret for his crime.

Literary Analysis: IRONY

C Remind students of the definitions of verbal and dramatic irony.

Answers: a dramatic effect achieved when the intended meaning of words is the opposite of their usual meaning; a dramatic effect achieved when what appears to be true to one or more characters is not true to readers.

Then, ask how the conversation between Lennox and Macbeth in lines 100–107 shows both verbal and dramatic irony.

Possible Response: Dramatic irony is created by Lennox's belief that Duncan's grooms killed the King, while the reader knows that Macbeth killed Duncan. Verbal irony is created by Macbeth's assertion that he regrets killing the grooms in "fury," when he actually killed the grooms in cold blood in order to protect himself.

Macbeth. The labor we delight in physics pain.
This is the door.

Macduff. I'll make so bold to call,
For 'tis my limited service. [*Exit.*]

Lennox. Goes the King hence today?

Macbeth. He does; he did appoint so.

Lennox. The night has been unruly. Where we lay,
Our chimneys were blown down, and, as they say,
Lamentings heard i' the air, strange screams of death,
And prophesying, with accents terrible,
Of dire combustion and confused events
New hatched to the woeful time. The obscure bird
Clamored the livelong night. Some say the earth
Was feverous and did shake.

Macbeth. 'Twas a rough night.

Lennox. My young remembrance cannot parallel
A fellow to it.

[*Enter* Macduff.]

Macduff. O horror, horror, horror! Tongue nor heart
Cannot conceive nor name thee!

Macbeth and Lennox. What's the matter?

Macduff. Confusion now hath made his masterpiece!
Most sacrilegious murder hath broke ope
The Lord's anointed temple and stole thence
The life o' the building!

Macbeth. What is't you say? the life?

Lennox. Mean you his majesty?

Macduff. Approach the chamber, and destroy your sight
With a new Gorgon. Do not bid me speak.
See, and then speak yourselves.

[*Exeunt* Macbeth *and* Lennox.]

Awake, awake!
Ring the alarum bell. Murder and treason!
Banquo and Donalbain! Malcolm! awake!
Shake off this downy sleep, death's counterfeit,
And look on death itself! Up, up, and see
The great doom's image! Malcolm! Banquo!
As from your graves rise up and walk like sprites
To countenance this horror! Ring the bell!

[*Bell rings.*]

[*Enter Lady* Macbeth.]

49 physics: cures.

51 limited service: appointed duty.

53–60 Lennox discusses the strange events of the night, from fierce winds to the continuous shrieking (**strange screams of death**) of an owl (**obscure bird**). The owl's scream, a sign of death, bodes more (**new hatched**) uproar (**combustion**) and confusion.

65–68 Macduff mourns Duncan's death as the destruction (**confusion**) of order and as sacrilegious, violating all that is holy. In Shakespeare's time the king was believed to be God's sacred representative on earth.

71 new Gorgon: Macduff compares the shocking sight of the corpse to a Gorgon, a monster of Greek mythology with snakes for hair. Anyone who saw a Gorgon turned to stone.

75 counterfeit: imitation.

77 great doom's image: a picture like the Last Judgment, the end of the world.

78 sprites: spirits. The spirits of the dead were supposed to rise on Judgment Day.

Teaching Options

Vocabulary Strategy

RESEARCHING WORD ORIGINS

Instruction Many words that are now in regular English usage were first used in print by Shakespeare. The popularity of Shakespeare's works helped bring these new words into everyday use. Some of these words are based on foreign words, others are formed from compounding English words, and still others are formed from the addition of affixes to common English words. Tell students that all of the following words were coined by Shakespeare. Write the words on the chalkboard: *leapfrog, mountaineer, alligator, lonely, watchdog.*

Activity Have students write the words on their own paper. Then have them look up each word in a dictionary. Next to each word, they should write its definition and then indicate whether the word is of foreign origin, a compound, or formed with an affix. If the word is of foreign origin they should write the language of origin and the word as it appears in that language.

Use **Vocabulary Transparencies and Copymasters,** p. 35.

A lesson on word origins appears on page 206 in the Pupil's Edition.

Lady Macbeth. What's the business,
That such a hideous trumpet calls to parley
The sleepers of the house? Speak, speak!

Macduff. O gentle lady,
'Tis not for you to hear what I can speak!
The repetition in a woman's ear
Would murder as it fell.
[*Enter* Banquo.]
O Banquo, Banquo,
Our royal master's murdered!

Lady Macbeth. Woe, alas!
What, in our house?

Banquo. Too cruel anywhere.
Dear Duff, I prithee contradict thyself
And say it is not so.

[*Enter* Macbeth, Lennox, *and* Ross.]

Macbeth. Had I but died an hour before this chance,
I had lived a blessed time; for from this instant
There's nothing serious in mortality;
All is but toys; renown and grace is dead;
The wine of life is drawn, and the mere lees
Is left this vault to brag of.

[*Enter* Malcolm *and* Donalbain.]

Donalbain. What is amiss?

Macbeth. You are, and do not know't.
The spring, the head, the fountain of your blood
Is stopped, the very source of it is stopped.

Macduff. Your royal father's murdered.

Malcolm. O, by whom?

Lennox. Those of his chamber, as it seemed, had done't.
Their hands and faces were all badged with blood;
So were their daggers, which unwiped we found
Upon their pillows.
They stared and were distracted. No man's life
Was to be trusted with them.

Macbeth. O, yet I do repent me of my fury
That I did kill them.

Macduff. Wherefore did you so?

Macbeth. Who can be wise, amazed, temp'rate, and furious,
Loyal and neutral, in a moment? No man.
The expedition of my violent love

81 trumpet calls to parley: She compares the clanging bell to a trumpet used to call two sides of a battle to negotiation.

91–95 for from . . . brag of: From now on, nothing matters (**there's nothing serious**) in human life (**mortality**); even fame and grace have been made meaningless. The good wine of life has been removed (**drawn**), leaving only the dregs (**lees**). Is Macbeth being completely insincere, or does he regret his crime?

101 badged: marked.

Customizing Instruction

Less Proficient Readers

1 Ask students to reread lines 88–89, "Dear Duff, I prithee contradict thyself / And say it is not so." Then ask the following questions:

- Who is Duff?

Answer: This is a nickname, an endearment, for Macduff.

- What does *prithee* mean?

Answer: It means "pray thee," or "please," as in asking a favor.

- What is Banquo asking Macduff?

Answer: "Please say that what you've just said isn't true."

Gifted and Talented

Point out the situation in Act Two—a prominent ruler has been murdered. Ask students to speculate about the reaction today if a prominent leader of their country were assassinated. What would be the immediate concerns of those who found the assassinated leader? Take into account current methods of selecting leaders and the presence of news media. Have students get into groups. Have each group assemble a list of the actions performed by Lennox, Macduff, Macbeth, Lady Macbeth, Banquo, Malcolm, and Donalbain. Have them evaluate each action as appropriate or inappropriate in a modern setting, and then come up with an appropriate action if necessary.

MACBETH: ACT TWO 357

Reading and Analyzing

GUIDE FOR READING

(A) Lady Macbeth is probably trying to divert attention from her husband, whose behavior has suddenly become overly dramatic, thus potentially revealing his guilt.

Reading Skills and Strategies: PREDICTING

(B) Ask students to predict what will happen to Malcolm and Donalbain as a result of their departure.

Possible Responses: They are blamed for the murder, pursued, and killed; they raise an army and come back to defeat Macbeth.

GUIDE FOR READING

(C) Students should support their answers with evidence from the text.

Literary Analysis: THEME

(D) Have students reread the dialogue between Ross and the Old Man (Scene 4, lines 1–20). Ask them to summarize it. Then, have students reread similar descriptions of the evening of Duncan's murder in Scene 1, lines 4–9 and Scene 3, lines 53–60.

Ask students what topics identified in prereading are illustrated by these descriptions and have them support their answers. Ask students if they can state themes that relate to those topics.

Possible Responses: Supernatural forces can make nature behave contrary to its laws; the breakdown of loyalty (symbolized by the well-treated horses' sudden disobedience) is part of the disruption of the natural order; ambition (shown by the owl that kills the hawk) disrupts the natural order.

Outrun the pauser, reason. Here lay Duncan,
His silver skin laced with his golden blood,
And his gashed stabs looked like a breach in nature
For ruin's wasteful entrance; there, the murderers,
Steeped in the colors of their trade, their daggers
Unmannerly breeched with gore. Who could refrain
That had a heart to love and in that heart
Courage to make's love known?

Lady Macbeth. Help me hence, ho!

Macduff. Look to the lady.

Malcolm. [*Aside to* Donalbain] Why do we hold our tongues,
That most may claim this argument for ours?

(B) **Donalbain.** [*Aside to* Malcolm] What should be spoken here,
Where our fate, hid in an auger hole,
May rush and seize us? Let's away,
Our tears are not yet brewed.

Malcolm. [*Aside to* Donalbain] Nor our strong sorrow
Upon the foot of motion.

Banquo. Look to the lady.

[Lady Macbeth *is carried out.*]

And when we have our naked frailties hid,
That suffer in exposure, let us meet
And question this most bloody piece of work,
To know it further. Fears and scruples shake us.
In the great hand of God I stand, and thence
Against the undivulged pretense I fight
Of treasonous malice.

Macduff. And so do I.

All. So all.

Macbeth. Let's briefly put on manly readiness
And meet i' the hall together.

All. Well contented.

[*Exeunt all but* Malcolm *and* Donalbain.]

Malcolm. What will you do? Let's not consort with them.
To show an unfelt sorrow is an office
Which the false man does easy. I'll to England.

[1] **Donalbain.** To Ireland I. Our separated fortune
Shall keep us both the safer. Where we are,
There's daggers in men's smiles; the near in blood,
The nearer bloody.

110–111 The . . . reason: He claims his emotions overpowered his reason, which would have made him pause to think before he killed Duncan's servants.

113 breach: a military term to describe a break in defenses, such as a hole in a castle wall.

118 Lady Macbeth faints. Is she only pretending? (A)

119–120 Why do . . . ours: Malcolm wonders why he and Donalbain are silent, since they have the most right to discuss the topic (**argument**) of their father's death.

126–129 Banquo suggests that they all meet to discuss the murder after they have dressed (**our naked frailties hid**), since people are shivering in their nightclothes (**suffer in exposure**).

129–132 Though shaken by fears and doubts (**scruples**), he will fight against the secret plans (**undivulged pretense**) of the traitor. Do you think Banquo suspects Macbeth? 

135–137 Malcolm does not want to join (**consort with**) the others because one of them may have plotted the murder.

Teaching Options

Speaking and Listening

DRAMATIC PRESENTATION

Instruction Performers use the following techniques to stress ideas and convey emotions:

- changes in volume, or loudness, of speech
- changes in speed of delivery
- changes in tone of voice
- facial expressions
- gestures or other body language

Have students work in groups to prepare and present part of a scene. Have students practice their listening skills while their classmates present their dramatic readings. Encourage them to take notes during each reading, jotting down the techniques the performers use to stress ideas and convey emotions. After the reading, invite students to share their suggestions for improvement with the performers.

This activity is particularly well-suited for longer class periods.

Malcolm. This murderous shaft that's shot
Hath not yet lighted, and our safest way
Is to avoid the aim. Therefore to horse!
And let us not be dainty of leave-taking
But shift away. There's warrant in that theft
Which steals itself when there's no mercy left.
[*Exeunt.*]

145–146 There's . . . left: There's good reason (**warrant**) to steal away from a situation that promises no mercy.

SCENE 4

Outside Macbeth's castle.

[*Enter* Ross *with an* Old Man.]

Old Man. Threescore and ten I can remember well;
Within the volume of which time I have seen
Hours dreadful and things strange; but this sore night
Hath trifled former knowings.

Ross. Ah, good father,
Thou seest the heavens, as troubled with man's act,
Threaten his bloody stage. By the clock 'tis day,
And yet dark night strangles the traveling lamp.
Is't night's predominance, or the day's shame,
That darkness does the face of earth entomb
When living light should kiss it?

2

Old Man. 'Tis unnatural,
Even like the deed that's done. On Tuesday last
A falcon, tow'ring in her pride of place,
Was by a mousing owl hawked at and killed.

Ross. And Duncan's horses (a thing most strange and certain),
Beauteous and swift, the minions of their race,
Turned wild in nature, broke their stalls, flung out,
Contending 'gainst obedience, as they would make
War with mankind.

Old Man. 'Tis said they eat each other.

Ross. They did so, to the amazement of mine eyes
That looked upon't.
[*Enter* Macduff.]
Here comes the good Macduff.
How goes the world, sir, now?

Macduff. Why, see you not?

Ross. Is't known who did this more than bloody deed?

1–4 Nothing the old man has seen in seventy years (**threescore and ten**) has been as strange and terrible (**sore**) as this night. It has made other times seem trivial (**hath trifled**) by comparison.

6–10 By the clock . . . kiss it: Though daytime, an unnatural darkness blots out the sun (**strangles the traveling lamp**).

12–13 a falcon . . . and killed: The owl would never be expected to attack a high-flying (**tow'ring**) falcon, much less defeat one.

15 minions: best or favorites.

17 contending 'gainst obedience: The well-trained horses rebelliously fought against all constraints.

Customizing Instruction

Less Proficient Readers

1 Explain that an important element of any writer's style is diction, or choice of words. Diction includes both vocabulary (individual words) and syntax (the order or arrangement of words). Diction can be formal or informal, technical or ordinary, abstract or concrete. The diction in *Macbeth* is formal.

- Have students look at "To Ireland I" (line 138). Ask students how they would say this in current, everyday diction.

Possible Response: I'll go to Ireland.

- Have students locate other syntax now considered formal and perhaps even old-fashioned and put it into current, informal diction.

Possible Response: "And let us not be dainty of leave-taking / But shift away" [lines 144–145]—"let's not bother to leave politely; let's go quickly."

Students Acquiring English

2 Remind students of the technique called personification as you ask them to reread lines 6–10, page 359. Help them understand the meaning of the passage by asking the following questions:

- What is the meaning of "dark night strangles the traveling lamp"?

Possible Response: The sun is hidden by darkness.

- What is meant by "darkness does the face of earth entomb / when living light should kiss it?"

Possible Response: The earth is dark when it should be light.

Assessment Informal Assessment

ALTERNATIVE ENDING

You can informally assess students' understanding of the selection by having them imagine an alternative ending to Act Two in which Macbeth's hideous crime is discovered by his colleagues. Remind students to take into account Macbeth's character in their description of the discovery. Tell them to ask themselves whether Macbeth would confess, deny the allegations, flee, or react in some other way.

RUBRIC

3 **Full Accomplishment** Student writing reflects full understanding of events in story and of character of Macbeth.

2 **Substantial Accomplishment** Student writing shows general understanding of events, but may not fully reflect character of Macbeth.

1 **Little or Partial Accomplishment** Student writing displays little understanding of either events or character of Macbeth.

Reading and Analyzing

Reading Skills and Strategies: TRACING MAIN EVENTS

Ask students to trace the main events of the plot in Act Two by giving in their own words a shortened version of the most important information.

Possible Response: Macbeth murders Duncan, and he and Lady Macbeth frame the King's grooms for the crime. When Duncan's corpse is discovered in the morning, Macbeth, feigning a fit of rage, kills the two grooms. Fearing that they will also be killed, Duncan's sons Malcolm and Donalbain flee to England and Ireland, respectively. Ominous supernatural sights are reported. Macbeth, Duncan's nearest relative after his sons, goes to Scone to receive the kingship.

Literary Analysis: DICTION

Explain to students that a writer's choice of diction can affect the mood and impact of a piece. Not only *what* is said, but also *how* it is said is important for conveying meaning. Have students reread Shakespeare's description of Macbeth's meeting with the witches (Act One, Scene 3, lines 30–85), and then have them read Holinshed's account of the same event on p. 361. Ask students to analyze the choice of language in each selection and compare the effect each has on the audience.

Possible Responses: The rhythm makes the witches' speech seem more like the chanting of spells; The more imaginative language usually found in verse helps the scene feel eerier.

Macduff. Those that Macbeth hath slain.

Ross. Alas, the day!
What good could they pretend?

Macduff. They were suborned.
Malcolm and Donalbain, the King's two sons,
Are stol'n away and fled, which puts upon them
Suspicion of the deed.

Ross. 'Gainst nature still!
Thriftless ambition, that will raven up
Thine own live's means! Then 'tis most like
The sovereignty will fall upon Macbeth.

Macduff. He is already named, and gone to Scone
To be invested.

Ross. Where is Duncan's body?

Macduff. Carried to Colmekill,
The sacred storehouse of his predecessors
And guardian of their bones.

Ross. Will you to Scone?

Macduff. No, cousin, I'll to Fife.

Ross. Well, I will thither.

Macduff. Well, may you see things well done there. Adieu,
Lest our old robes sit easier than our new!

Ross. Farewell, father.

Old Man. God's benison go with you, and with those
That would make good of bad, and friends of foes!

[*Exeunt omnes.*]

24 What . . . pretend: Ross wonders what the servants could have hoped to achieve (**pretend**) by killing; **suborned:** hired or bribed.

27–29 He is horrified by the thought that the sons could act contrary to nature (**'gainst nature still**) because of wasteful (**thriftless**) ambition and greedily destroy (**raven up**) their father, the source of their own life (**thine own live's means**).

31–32 to Scone . . . invested: Macbeth went to the traditional site (**Scone**) where Scotland's kings were crowned.

40–41 The old man gives his blessing (**benison**) to Macduff and all those who would restore good and bring peace to the troubled land.

Teaching Options

Grammar

MODIFIERS: ADJECTIVES

Instruction An adjective modifies a noun or pronoun, and a predicate adjective follows a linking verb and modifies the subject. A proper adjective is formed from a proper noun and is always capitalized. Explain that articles—*the, a,* and *an*—are the most commonly used adjectives. *The* is a definite article (it refers to one specific person, place, or thing), and *a* and *an* are indefinite articles (the nouns they modify are only one of many). Nouns, pronouns, and verbals (e. g., *traveling*) can also be used as adjectives.

Activity Write these lines on the chalkboard.
"There's comfort yet; they are <u>assailable</u>,
Then be thou jocund. Ere <u>the</u> bat hath flown
<u>His</u> cloistered flight, ere to <u>black Hecate's</u> summons
The shard-borne beetle with his drowsy hums
Hath rung night's yawning peal, there shall be done
A deed of dreadful note."

from
HOLINSHED'S CHRONICLES

Preparing to Read

Build Background

One of Shakespeare's favorite sources for his plays was the *Chronicles* (1577), a collection of histories and descriptions of the British Isles written by Raphael Holinshed and others. The following passage reveals Macbeth's involvement in Duncan's murder.

It fortuned, as Macbeth and Banquo journeyed toward Forres, where the King then lay, they went sporting by the way together without other company save only themselves, passing through the woods and fields, when suddenly, in the midst of a laund,[1] there met them three women in strange and wild apparel, resembling creatures of elder[2] world; whom when they attentively beheld, wondering much at the sight, the first of them spoke and said, "All hail, Macbeth, Thane of Glamis!" (for he had lately entered into that dignity and office by the death of his father Sinel). The second of them said, "Hail, Macbeth, Thane of Cawdor!" But the third said, "All hail, Macbeth, that hereafter shalt be King of Scotland!"

Then Banquo. "What manner of women," saith he, "are you, that seem so little favorable unto me, whereas to my fellow here, besides high offices, ye assign also the kingdom, appointing forth nothing for me at all?" "Yes," saith the first of them, "we promise greater benefits unto thee than unto him, for he shall reign indeed, but with an unlucky end; neither shall he leave any issue behind him to succeed in his place, where contrarily thou indeed shalt not reign at all, but of thee those shall be born which shall govern the Scottish kingdom by long order of continual descent." Herewith the foresaid women vanished immediately out of their sight. . . . Shortly after, the Thane of Cawdor being condemned at Forres of treason against the King committed, his lands, livings, and offices were given of the King's liberality to Macbeth. . . .

Shortly after it chanced that King Duncan, having two sons by his wife (which was the daughter of Siward Earl of Northumberland), he made the elder of them (called Malcolm) Prince of Cumberland, as it were thereby to appoint him his successor in the kingdom immediately after his decease. Macbeth, sore troubled herewith, for that he saw by this means his hope sore hindered . . . he began to take counsel how he might usurp the kingdom by force, having a just quarrel[3] so to do (as he took the matter), for that Duncan did what in him lay to defraud him of all manner of title and claim which he might, in time to come, pretend[4] unto the crown.

The words of the three Weird Sisters also (of whom before ye have heard) greatly encouraged him hereunto; but specially his wife lay sore upon him[5] to attempt the thing, as she that was very ambitious, burning in unquenchable desire to bear the name of a queen. At length, therefore, communicating his purposed intent with his trusty friends, amongst whom Banquo was the chiefest, upon confidence of their promised aid he slew the King at Inverness or (as some say) at Bothgowanan, in the sixth year of his reign.

1. **laund:** glade.
2. **elder:** ancient.
3. **quarrel:** cause.
4. **pretend:** claim.
5. **lay sore upon him:** pressed him hard.

Teaching the Literature

Build Background

Raphael Holinshed arrived in London around 1560 and began working for publisher Reginald Wolfe, who was preparing a history of Great Britain and Ireland. Wolfe appointed Holinshed editor-in-chief. When Wolfe died in 1573, the project was taken over by three other publishers.

Holinshed wrote a history of England for this project—called the *Chronicles.* However, the accuracy and reliability of some of his material and sources were openly called into question at the time, and some of it was even expurgated.

Chronicles, however, was not famous for its history, but for the writers who used its ideas for their novels, poems, and plays. The great British poet Sir Edmund Spenser once said that "Master Holinshed hath much furthered and advantaged me."

Reading Skills and Strategies

DRAWING CONCLUSIONS

Drawing conclusions involves combining text information with prior knowledge. When they draw conclusions, students gain insight into a piece of writing.

Students can read this excerpt of *Chronicles* to get an idea of how Shakespeare used it as a basis for his plays. Ask students to conclude why Macbeth murdered Duncan.

Possible Response: Macbeth probably murdered Duncan out of jealousy. Because the Weird Sisters told Macbeth he would be king, he was upset when Malcolm was named the successor.

Underline the adjectives as shown and have students identify the type of adjective for each. *(predicate adjective; definite article; pronoun; adjective; proper adjective)* Ask students to find other adjectives in the passage and identify their type and the words they modify.

Exercise Ask students to write *adjective, predicate adjective, proper adjective, pronoun,* or *article* to characterize the underlined word in each sentence. Then have students meet in cooperative groups to find and identify by type other adjectives in each sentence.

1. Banquo's uneasy dreams of the three witches have him walking restlessly in the starry night. *(proper adjective)*
2. Macbeth, suspicious and murderous, seeks Banquo's allegiance. *(adjective)*
3. Is Lady Macbeth innocent or culpable in Duncan's murder? *(predicate adjective)*
4. Who is the third murderer? *(article)*
5. In his torment, Macbeth imagines that Banquo's ghost has taken his place at the table. *(pronoun)*

Use **Grammar Transparencies and Copymasters,** p. 8.

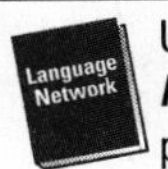

Use McDougal Littell's ***Language Network*** for more instruction and practice in adjectives.

GUIDING STUDENT RESPONSE

Connect to the Literature

1. **What Do You Think?**
Guidelines for student response: Accept all reasonable responses. Have volunteers share the words and phrases they jotted down with the class.

Comprehension Check
- Duncan's grooms
- They flee Scotland.
- Macbeth

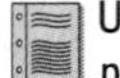 Use **Unit Two Resource Book,** p. 21 for additional support.

Think Critically

2. Possible Response: The time—midnight, a time traditionally associated with the supernatural—and the lack of visible moon and stars create an oppressive, eerie atmosphere.
3. Possible Response: His guilt and fear become visible in the shape of the weapon he will use to commit his crime. Students should support their response with evidence from the text.
4. Accept all responses that aim for eerieness, suspense, or other appropriate effects, given the events of Act Two.
5. Possible Responses: Macbeth is a sinner. Macbeth's greed for power and fame are like the farmer's greed; for him, as for the equivocator, foul seems fair; he steals power as the tailor steals riches.
6. Possible Response: Lady Macbeth is more ruthless and ambitious than her husband. She is less horrified by the murder; she has more presence of mind to cover up the crime; she has less imagination and depth than her husband and fails to envision the repercussions of the crime.
7. Accept all reasonable responses that students can support with experience and/or evidence from the text. Students who think the Macbeths are likely to continue killing may identify Malcolm as a future target, since he would be king of Scotland had he not fled and since he may wish to avenge his father's murder. Others may identify Banquo and any of his offspring, since he knows the witches' predictions and seems likely to be suspicious of Macbeth in the future, and since the witches predicted that Banquo's descendants would one day rule Scotland.

Connect to the Literature

1. **What Do You Think?** What mental picture from this act lingers most in your mind? Jot down words and phrases to describe it.

Comprehension Check
- Whom do Macbeth and his wife plan to take the blame for Duncan's murder?
- What prompts people to think that Malcolm and Donalbain may be guilty of killing their father?
- In the absence of Malcolm and Donalbain, who will become king?

Think Critically

2. How does the nocturnal setting of Act Two, Scene 1, contribute to the scene's overall **mood,** or atmosphere?

THINK ABOUT
- the time of night at which the events take place
- Banquo's observations about the night
- Macbeth's remarks about the night

3. Why do you think Macbeth imagines that he sees a dagger at the end of Act Two, Scene 1?

4. **ACTIVE READING** **READING DRAMA** Review any questions about or reactions to stage directions in your  READER'S NOTEBOOK. What effect do you think each of the following **sound effects** might have on the audience?
- the bell at the end of Scene 1
- the owl referred to in Scene 2
- the knocking that ends Scene 2 and continues in Scene 3
- the "alarum bell" in Scene 3

5. Consider the porter's humorous comments on the types of people who wind up at the gates of hell. How is Macbeth like or unlike the sinners that the porter describes?

6. How does Lady Macbeth compare with her husband at this point in the play? Cite evidence to support your opinion.

7. Do you think the Macbeths are finished with their killing? If so, why? If not, whom do you think they might kill next?

Extend Interpretations

8. **What If?** Do you think Macbeth would have killed Duncan if his wife had not urged him to do so? Cite evidence from the first two acts to support your opinion.

Literary Analysis

BLANK VERSE One of the most popular verse forms in English, **blank verse** consists of unrhymed iambic pentameter, in which the normal line contains five stressed syllables, each preceded by an unstressed syllable:

Wĭll áll grĕat Néptŭne's ócĕan wásh thĭs blóod

Paired Activity Working with a partner, copy a representative passage from *Macbeth,* marking the unstressed (˘) and stressed (´) syllables. Then discuss the following questions:
- Shakespeare sometimes introduces rhyming pairs of lines for emphasis or as signals to the actors, indicating entrances or changes of scene. What are some examples in Act Two?
- Shakespeare sometimes has characters speak in prose. Why do you think he uses prose for the porter's opening remarks in Act Two, Scene 3?

REVIEW **FIGURATIVE LANGUAGE** Find examples of figurative language that help convey Macbeth's fears and doubts before the murder of Duncan, his horror of the act itself, and the guilt he feels afterward.

Extend Interpretations

What If? Accept all reasonable, well-supported responses. Students should cite evidence from the text to support their opinions.

Literary Analysis

Paired Activity Examples of rhymed couplets include: Scene 1, lines 64–65; Scene 3, lines 145–146; Scene 4, lines 40–41.

Possible Response: The porter is a comic fellow whose scene is meant to contrast with the tragedy of the rest of the play.

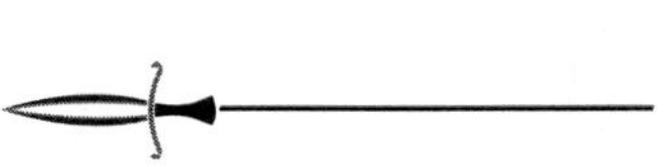

Act 3

SCENE 1

Macbeth's palace at Forres.

Banquo voices his suspicions of Macbeth but still hopes that the prophecy about his own children will prove true. Macbeth, as king, enters to request Banquo's presence at a state banquet. Banquo explains that he will be away during the day with his son Fleance but that they will return in time for the banquet. Alone, Macbeth expresses his fear of Banquo, because of the witches' promise that Banquo's sons will be kings. He persuades two murderers to kill Banquo and his son before the banquet.

[*Enter* Banquo.]

Banquo. Thou hast it now—King, Cawdor, Glamis, all,
As the Weird Women promised; and I fear
Thou play'dst most foully for't. Yet it was said
It should not stand in thy posterity,
But that myself should be the root and father
Of many kings. If there come truth from them
(As upon thee, Macbeth, their speeches shine),
Why, by the verities on thee made good,
May they not be my oracles as well
And set me up in hope? But, hush, no more!

[*Sennet sounded. Enter* Macbeth, *as King;* Lady Macbeth, *as Queen;* Lennox, Ross, Lords, *and* Attendants.]

Macbeth. Here's our chief guest.

1 **Lady Macbeth.** If he had been forgotten, 2
It had been as a gap in our great feast,
And all-thing unbecoming.

Macbeth. Tonight we hold a solemn supper, sir,
And I'll request your presence.

Banquo. Let your Highness
Command upon me, to the which my duties
Are with a most indissoluble tie
For ever knit.

Macbeth. Ride you this afternoon?

Banquo. Ay, my good lord.

Macbeth. We should have else desired your good advice
(Which still hath been both grave and prosperous)

3–4 it was said . . . posterity: it was predicted that the kingship would not remain in your family.

6–10 If . . . in hope: Banquo is impressed by the truth **(verities)** of the prophecies. He hopes the witches' prediction for him will come true too **(be my oracles as well)**.

[Stage Direction] **sennet sounded:** A trumpet is sounded.

14–15 A king usually uses the royal pronoun *we.* Notice how Macbeth switches to *I,* keeping a personal tone with Banquo.

15–18 Banquo says he is duty-bound to serve the king. Do you think his tone is cold or warm here? A

21 grave and prosperous: thoughtful and profitable.

TEACHING THE LITERATURE

Customizing Instruction

Less Proficient Readers

1 Show students that "It had been as a gap in our great feast" is really the same as the modern conditional past verb form ("It would have been as a gap in our great feast"). Caution students that the contemporary construction is "would have been," not "would *of* been."

Students Acquiring English

2 Help students understand the unusual usage "all-thing." Explain that this is an archaic phrase meaning "wholly." Have them paraphrase lines 11-13.

Possible Response: If he had not been invited, it would have been a great gap in our feast, and would have been wholly unbecoming.

Use **Spanish Study Guide** for additional support, pp. 70–72

GUIDE FOR READING

A Although some students might think the tone is warm because Banquo is trying to maintain a friendly relationship with Macbeth, many students will find the tone cold and even ironic, because Banquo means he's tied to Macbeth in matters that stretch beyond an obligatory dinner party.

Reading and Analyzing

Literary Analysis DRAMATIC IRONY

A Review with students the definitions of verbal irony (the effect achieved when a speaker says the opposite of what he or she means) and dramatic irony (the effect achieved when the audience has information that a character doesn't have). When they have finished Act Three, have students analyze the irony of Macbeth's request in line 27.

Possible Response: Verbal irony occurs because Macbeth knows that, by his own arrangement, Banquo will be dead before the feast. Dramatic irony occurs because Banquo thinks Macbeth is being friendly, while we (and Macbeth) know that he is plotting murder.

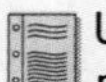
Use **Unit Two Resource Book,** p. 24 for more exercises.

GUIDE FOR READING

B They might be accusing Macbeth of killing their father.

C He must fight Fate because Fate seems to be preferring others to him, even though he's trying desperately to control his and his family's fate with his bloody acts.

Active Reading
SHAKESPEARE'S LANGUAGE

D Tell students that in Shakespeare's time, the word *without* could mean "outside." Have them look for other examples of archaic language and give the modern equivalent.

Possible Response: *clept* (line 93) means "called."

Use **Unit Two Resource Book,** p. 24 for amore practice.

In this day's council; but we'll take tomorrow.
Is't far you ride?

Banquo. As far, my lord, as will fill up the time
'Twixt this and supper. Go not my horse the better,
I must become a borrower of the night
For a dark hour or twain.

A **Macbeth.** Fail not our feast.

Banquo. My lord, I will not.

Macbeth. We hear our bloody cousins are bestowed
In England and in Ireland, not confessing
Their cruel parricide, filling their hearers
With strange invention. But of that tomorrow,
When therewithal we shall have cause of state
Craving us jointly. Hie you to horse. Adieu,
Till you return at night. Goes Fleance with you?

Banquo. Ay, my good lord. Our time does call upon's.

Macbeth. I wish your horses swift and sure of foot,
And so I do commend you to their backs.
Farewell.

[*Exit* Banquo.]

Let every man be master of his time
Till seven at night. To make society
The sweeter welcome, we will keep ourself
Till supper time alone. While then, God be with you!

[*Exeunt all but* Macbeth *and a* Servant.]

Sirrah, a word with you. Attend those men
Our pleasure?

Servant. They are, my lord, without the palace gate.

Macbeth. Bring them before us.

[*Exit* Servant.]

Macbeth. To be thus is nothing,
But to be safely thus. Our fears in Banquo
Stick deep, and in his royalty of nature
Reigns that which would be feared. 'Tis much he dares,
And to that dauntless temper of his mind
He hath a wisdom that doth guide his valor
To act in safety. There is none but he
Whose being I do fear; and under him
My genius is rebuked, as it is said
Mark Antony's was by Caesar. He chid the Sisters
When first they put the name of King upon me,
And bade them speak to him. Then, prophet-like,

25–27 Go not . . . twain: If his horse goes no faster than usual, he'll be back an hour or two (**twain**) after dark.

29 bloody cousins: murderous relatives (Malcolm and Donalbain); **bestowed:** settled.

32 strange invention: lies; stories they have invented. What kinds of stories might they be telling? **B**

33–34 when . . . jointly: when matters of state will require the attention of us both.

40 be master of his time: do what he wants.

43 while: until.

44–45 sirrah: a term of address to an inferior; **Attend . . . pleasure:** Are they waiting for me?

47–48 To be thus . . . safely thus: To be king is worthless unless my position as king is safe.

51 dauntless temper: fearless temperament.

55–56 my genius . . . Caesar: Banquo's mere presence forces back (**rebukes**) Macbeth's ruling spirit (**genius**). In ancient Rome, Octavius Caesar, who became emperor, had the same effect on his rival, Mark Antony.

Teaching Options

BLOCK SCHEDULING: MANAGING TIME

If your schedule requires that you cover the lesson objectives in a shorter time, use . . .
- Preparing to Read, pp. 323–325
- Thinking Through the Literature, p. 381

If you want to take advantage of longer class time, use . . .
- TE Teaching Options: Cross Curricular Links, p. 365; Viewing and Representing, pp. 366, 368, 373; Informal Assessment, pp. 367, 375; Vocabulary Strategy, p. 372; Grammar, p. 371

They hailed him father to a line of kings.
Upon my head they placed a fruitless crown
And put a barren scepter in my gripe,
Thence to be wrenched with an unlineal hand,
No son of mine succeeding. If't be so,
For Banquo's issue have I filed my mind;
For them the gracious Duncan have I murdered;
Put rancors in the vessel of my peace
Only for them, and mine eternal jewel
Given to the common enemy of man
To make them kings, the seed of Banquo kings!
Rather than so, come, Fate, into the list,
And champion me to the utterance! Who's there?

[*Enter* Servant *and two* Murderers.]

Now go to the door and stay there till we call.

[*Exit* Servant.]

Was it not yesterday we spoke together?

Murderers. It was, so please your Highness.

Macbeth. Well then, now
Have you considered of my speeches? Know
1 That it was he, in the times past, which held you
So under fortune, which you thought had been
Our innocent self. This I made good to you
In our last conference, passed in probation with you
How you were borne in hand, how crossed; the instruments; 
Who wrought with them; and all things else that might
To half a soul and to a notion crazed
Say "Thus did Banquo."

First Murderer. You made it known to us.

Macbeth. I did so; and went further, which is now
Our point of second meeting. Do you find
Your patience so predominant in your nature
That you can let this go? Are you so gospeled
To pray for this good man and for his issue,
Whose heavy hand hath bowed you to the grave
And beggared yours for ever?

3 **First Murderer.** We are men, my liege.

Macbeth. Ay, in the catalogue ye go for men,
As hounds and greyhounds, mongrels, spaniels, curs,
Shoughs, water-rugs, and demi-wolves are clept D
All by the name of dogs. The valued file
Distinguishes the swift, the slow, the subtle,
The housekeeper, the hunter, every one

60–69 They gave me a childless (**fruitless, barren**) crown and scepter, which will be taken away by someone outside my family (**unlineal**). It appears that I have committed murder, poisoned (**filed**) my mind, and destroyed my soul (**eternal jewel**) all for the benefit of Banquo's heirs.

70–71 Rather . . . utterance: Rather than allowing Banquo's heirs to become kings, he calls upon Fate itself to enter the combat arena (**list**) so that he can fight it to the death (**utterance**). Why does he feel that he needs to fight Fate? C

75–83 Macbeth supposedly proved (**passed in probation**) Banquo's role, his deception (**how you were borne in hand**), his methods, and his allies. Even a half-wit (**half a soul**) or a crazed person would agree that Banquo caused their trouble.

87–90 He asks whether they are so influenced by the gospel's message of forgiveness (**so gospeled**) that they will pray for Banquo and his children despite his harshness, which will leave their own families beggars.

Customizing Instruction

Less Proficient Readers

1 Help students understand the meaning of Macbeth's speech in lines 74–78. Point out that *he* in line 76 refers back to the unrecorded conversation of the previous day when Banquo's name was uttered and that *he,* therefore, is Banquo.

2 Explain that the sentence that runs from lines 78 to 83 has clauses in line 80 with passive constructions. Also point out that the subject ("Banquo") is understood in these constructions. Have students change this sentence to active voice.
Answer: I made it clear to you in our last conference how Banquo bore you in hand, how he crossed you, and what means he used. . . .

3 Use the following questions to make sure students understand tone and characterization.

- What tone and style of argument in lines 85–107 does Macbeth use to ensure that the murderers are bound to their task?
  Possible Response: His tone is condescending; he plays on their sense of manhood, comparing many types of dogs to many types of men, suggesting that they are not fully men.
- Why would this be an effective argument with men of the murderers' station in life?
  Possible Response: They seek to prove to the king that they are men worthy of serving him.
- Where else does Macbeth use their sense of pride to manipulate them?
  Answer: In lines 75–83, he convinces them that Banquo is the reason they are "So under fortune."

Cross Curricular Link History

PRIMOGENITURE Preference given to the firstborn son in inheritance of titles and property is called *primogeniture.* While the laws restricting the inheritance of property to the eldest son changed in 1540 when the passage of the English Statute of Wills made it possible to pass estates to others, hereditary kingship that is passed down to the oldest son still exists today in England. It is important to know that primogeniture was *not* in effect in Scotland in Macbeth's time, and Duncan's naming of Malcolm as his successor in Act One was actually illegal on two counts. Not only did a law exist that restricted the succession to those who had reached adulthood (which Malcolm had not), but another law explicitly prohibited a son from succeeding his father on the throne. The throne was supposed to alternate between different branches of the royal family, with the inheritor of the throne leading the king's army while awaiting his accession. The man who actually had been next in line for the throne after Duncan was Lady Macbeth's son by an earlier marriage, but he was murdered to prevent his becoming king.

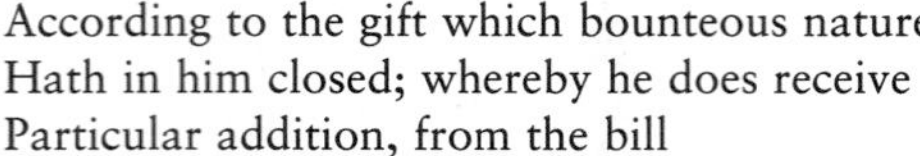

Reading and Analyzing

Reading Skills and Strategies: EVALUATING

Have students evaluate Macbeth as a motivator of men.

- Ask what the murderers want to prove to Macbeth.
  Possible Response: that they are men prepared to exact revenge and serve their king.
- Ask students how Macbeth, a king, makes his request seem appealing to these men.
  Answer: He says he feels like they do and asks for assistance. What tone should then be taken when the passage is read aloud?

Reading Skills and Strategies: CLARIFYING

A Macbeth is describing his options and explaining his two courses of action. Ask them to reread the passage and clarify Macbeth's explanation.
Possible Response: Macbeth could kill Banquo himself and feel justified in doing it. Yet because friends of both Macbeth and Banquo would be upset by Banquo's death, Macbeth prefers to use hired killers and keep his involvement secret.

GUIDE FOR READING

B His death is important because the witches prophesied that Banquo would be the father of kings. Because Macbeth is interested in the elimination of any threat to his own throne, he's interested in whether Fleance lives.

According to the gift which bounteous nature
Hath in him closed; whereby he does receive
Particular addition, from the bill
That writes them all alike; and so of men.
Now, if you have a station in the file,
Not i' the worst rank of manhood, say't;
And I will put that business in your bosoms
Whose execution takes your enemy off,
Grapples you to the heart and love of us,
Who wear our health but sickly in his life,
Which in his death were perfect.

91–100 The true worth of a dog can be measured only by examining the record (**valued file**) of its special qualities (**particular addition**).

103–107 Macbeth will give them a secret job (**business in your bosoms**) that will earn them his loyalty (**grapples you to the heart**) and love. Banquo's death will make this sick king healthy.

Act 3, Scene 1: Macbeth with the murderers (film 1971)

Teaching Options

Viewing and Representing

FILM ANALYSIS

Instruction Have students think about the various factors that go into producing a film version of a stage play. Filmmakers must first have an expert understanding of the play they are producing. Remind students that choices must be made about which scenes to dramatize, what kind of costumes to use, and what camera angles and shots will be most effective.

Application Ask students which line of the scene they think this still photo depicts. Have students comment on the composition of the scene as it is revealed in this shot. How does this camera angle contribute to the meaning of the line?

Possible Response: Line 139: Macbeth is looking over his shoulder as he prepares to leave. When he cuts off the First Murderer's speech in line 127, it shows his eagerness to get away, now that the business has been concluded.

Second Murderer. I am one, my liege,
Whom the vile blows and buffets of the world
have so incensed that I am reckless what
I do to spite the world.

First Murderer. And I another,
So weary with disasters, tugged with fortune,
That I would set my life on any chance,
To mend it or be rid on't.

Macbeth. Both of you
Know Banquo was your enemy.

Murderers. True, my lord.

Macbeth. So is he mine, and in such bloody distance
That every minute of his being thrusts
Against my near'st of life; and though I could
With barefaced power sweep him from my sight
And bid my will avouch it, yet I must not,
For certain friends that are both his and mine, A
Whose loves I may not drop, but wail his fall
Who I myself struck down. And thence it is
That I to your assistance do make love,
Masking the business from the common eye
For sundry weighty reasons.

Second Murderer. We shall, my lord,
Perform what you command us.

First Murderer. Though our lives—

Macbeth. Your spirits shine through you. Within this hour
at most
I will advise you where to plant yourselves,

Acquaint you with the perfect spy o' the time,
The moment on't; for't must be done tonight,
And something from the palace (always thought
That I require a clearness), and with him,
To leave no rubs nor botches in the work,
Fleance his son, that keeps him company,
Whose absence is no less material to me
Than is his father's, must embrace the fate
Of that dark hour. Resolve yourselves apart;
I'll come to you anon.

Murderers. We are resolved, my lord.

Macbeth. I'll call upon you straight. Abide within.
[*Exeunt* Murderers.]

111 tugged with: knocked about by.

115–117 Banquo is near enough to draw blood, and like a menacing swordsman, his mere presence threatens (**thrusts against**) Macbeth's existence.

119 bid my will avouch it: justify it as my will.

127 Your spirits shine through you: Your courage is evident.

131–132 and something . . . clearness: The murder must be done away from the palace so that I remain blameless (**I require a clearness**).

135 absence: death. Why is the death of Fleance so important? B

137 Resolve yourselves apart: Decide in private.

139 straight: soon.

Customizing Instruction

Less Proficient Readers

1 Explain to readers that there are some lines and phrases in Shakespeare that scholars interpret differently. For example, in line 129, the "perfect spy o' the time" is thought to be a person (perhaps a lookout) or to mean "precise timing" or perhaps "precise information." After students have read Act Three, Scene 3, return to this line and inform students that among scholars who think that the "perfect spy" is a person, there are some who believe that he is the third murderer. Ask them for their reactions.

Possible Response: Responses will vary. Students may or may not accept that explanation of the line. Ask students to support their opinions with evidence from the text.

Assessment Informal Assessment

WRITING CHRONOLOGICALLY Have students write a letter from Banquo to a trusted friend. Students are to write as if Banquo suspects that he will be murdered. Instruct them to include the events that lead to Banquo's murder and to address them in chronological order.

RUBRIC

3 Full Accomplishment Student includes events leading to Banquo's murder in well-organized, chronological fashion.

2 Substantial Accomplishment Student presents most events leading to Banquo's murder with fair understanding of chronology of events.

1 Little or Partial Accomplishment Student presents few events leading to Banquo's murder with little or no understanding of chronology of events.

MACBETH: ACT THREE 367

Reading and Analyzing

Literary Analysis: RHYME

A Shakespeare's main characters tend to speak in blank verse poetry rather than rhymed verse. However, point out Lady Macbeth's lines 4–7 and have students turn to passages involving the witches. Ask them what similarity they notice.

Answer: The witches speak in rhymed couplets, just as Lady Macbeth does here.

Ask students to draw conclusions about why Shakespeare may have placed this rhyming passage where he did.

Possible Response: The unhappiness she complains of is a direct result of things prophesied by the witches, and the rhyme serves to link her complaint to the prophecy.

GUIDE FOR READING

B No, she has just been thinking about Duncan's murder.

Reading Skills and Strategies: EVALUATING

C Call students' attention to the imagery involving snakes. Ask them to explain the context of the following quote, about whom or what the analogy is made, and what the imagery is conveying.

- "We have scotched the snake, not killed it . . . whilst our poor malice / Remains in danger of her former tooth" (Act Three, Scene 2, lines 13–14).

  Answer: Macbeth is speaking to Lady Macbeth about Duncan's murder. The analogy refers to Duncan's family. The image conveys danger.

It is concluded. Banquo, thy soul's flight,
If it find heaven, must find it out tonight.
[*Exit.*]

SCENE 2

Macbeth's palace at Forres.

Lady Macbeth and her husband discuss the troubled thoughts and bad dreams they have had since Duncan's murder. However, they agree to hide their dark emotions at the night's banquet. Lady Macbeth tries to comfort the tormented Macbeth, but her words do no good. Instead, Macbeth hints at some terrible event that will occur that night.

[*Enter* Lady Macbeth *and a* Servant

Lady Macbeth. Is Banquo gone from court?

Servant. Ay, madam, but returns again tonight.

Lady Macbeth. Say to the King I would attend his leisure
For a few words.

Servant. Madam, I will.

[*Exit.*]

Lady Macbeth. Naught's had, all's spent,
(A) Where our desire is got without content.
'Tis safer to be that which we destroy
Than by destruction dwell in doubtful joy.

4–7 Nothing (**naught**) has been gained; everything has been wasted (**spent**). It would be better to be dead like Duncan than to live in uncertain joy.

[*Enter* Macbeth.]

How now, my lord? Why do you keep alone,
Of sorriest fancies your companions making,
Using those thoughts which should indeed have died
With them they think on? Things without all remedy
Should be without regard. What's done is done.

8–12 Does Lady Macbeth follow her own advice about forgetting Duncan's murder? (B)

(C) **Macbeth.** We have scotched the snake, not killed it.
She'll close and be herself, whilst our poor malice
Remains in danger of her former tooth.
(1) But let the frame of things disjoint, both the worlds suffer,
Ere we will eat our meal in fear and sleep
In the affliction of these terrible dreams
That shake us nightly. Better be with the dead,
Whom we, to gain our peace, have sent to peace,
Than on the torture of the mind to lie
In restless ecstasy. Duncan is in his grave;
After life's fitful fever he sleeps well.
Treason has done his worst: nor steel nor poison,

16–22 He would rather have the world fall apart (**the frame of things disjoint**) than be afflicted with such fears and nightmares. Death is preferable to life on the torture rack of mental anguish (**restless ecstasy**).

Teaching Options

Viewing and Representing

FILM ANALYSIS

Instruction Roman Polanski's 1971 production of *Macbeth* is representative both of his radical film-making style and of the era. Polanski's Macbeth and Lady Macbeth were cast as much younger than the Macbeths of previous productions. Polanski wanted to portray a protagonist seduced into a murderous plot by a wife and his own ambition. Crucial to the director's vision was the foolishness of youth, for an older, wiser man would not, in Polanski's view, enter into so reckless a plan nor be so fundamentally transformed into a tyrant; nor would an older, more mature woman concoct such a radical and risky scheme.

Application Have students discuss the apparent ages of the Macbeths in the clips above. Does age affect the staging of this scene? Does age affect the believability of the characters? Ask students what the positions of the Macbeths says about their relationship. Based on these clips, how would they compare the characters? Which Macbeth seems more disturbed? Which Lady Macbeth seems more concerned?

Then have students work in groups of four to

View and Compare

Compare the facial expressions of these two Lady Macbeths. Which better fits your idea of her attitude as she tries to persuade Macbeth to forget about Duncan?

Act 3, Scene 2: Jon Finch as Macbeth and Francesca Annis as Lady Macbeth (film, 1971)

Act 3, Scene 2: Laurence Olivier as Macbeth and Vivian Leigh as Lady Macbeth, Memorial Theatre, Stratford-upon-Avon, England (1955)

369

Customizing Instruction

Less Proficient Readers

1 Explain to students that what Macbeth means by "both the worlds" is the material world and the spiritual world. Ask students how Macbeth weighs the suffering of both worlds against his own recurrent nightmares.

Possible Response: Macbeth would rather have both worlds suffer than to endure his dreams. He feels it's better to be dead and peaceful than alive in "restless ecstasy."

stage Scene 2. Students need not memorize lines; it is sufficient for them to paraphrase the speeches in modern English. They should concentrate on blocking (the placement of actors on the "stage") and body language. If time and equipment permit, encourage students to wear costumes and play background music appropriate for the scene. Three students will portray Macbeth, Lady Macbeth, and the servant. The fourth student will take care of props, lighting, and/or sound.

Reading and Analyzing

Literary Analysis DRAMATIC IRONY

A Ask students to explain the dramatic irony in Macbeth's speech (lines 29–35).

Possible Response: Lady Macbeth takes the speech at face value while Macbeth and the reader/audience know that Macbeth has arranged Banquo's murder and does not expect him to be present at the feast.

Literary Analysis: PERSONIFICATION

B Have students identify two examples of the personification of night and day.

Possible Responses: lines "Come, seeling night, / Scarf up the tender eye of pitiful day" (46–47); "Good things of day begin to droop and drowse, / Whiles night's black agents to their preys do rouse" (lines 52–53).

Malice domestic, foreign levy, nothing,
Can touch him further.

Lady Macbeth. Come on.
Gentle my lord, sleek o'er your rugged looks;
Be bright and jovial among your guests tonight.

Macbeth. So shall I, love; and so, I pray, be you.
Let your remembrance apply to Banquo;
Present him eminence both with eye and tongue:
Unsafe the while, that we
Must lave our honors in these flattering streams
And make our faces vizards to our hearts,
Disguising what they are.

Lady Macbeth You must leave this.

Macbeth. O, full of scorpions is my mind, dear wife!
Thou know'st that Banquo, and his Fleance, lives.

Lady Macbeth. But in them Nature's copy's not eterne.

Macbeth. There's comfort yet; they are assailable.
Then be thou jocund. Ere the bat hath flown
His cloistered flight, ere to black Hecate's summons
The shard-borne beetle with his drowsy hums
Hath rung night's yawning peal, there shall be done
A deed of dreadful note.

Lady Macbeth. What's to be done?

Macbeth. Be innocent of the knowledge, dearest chuck,
Till thou applaud the deed. Come, seeling night,
Scarf up the tender eye of pitiful day,
And with thy bloody and invisible hand
Cancel and tear to pieces that great bond
Which keeps me pale! Light thickens, and the crow
Makes wing to the rooky wood.
Good things of day begin to droop and drowse,
Whiles night's black agents to their preys do rouse.
Thou marvell'st at my words; but hold thee still:
Things bad begun make strong themselves by ill.
So prithee go with me.

[*Exeunt.*]

27 sleek: smooth.

31 present him eminence: pay special attention to him.

33 lave . . . streams: wash **(lave)** our honor in streams of flattery—that is, falsify our feelings.

34 vizards: masks.

38 in them . . . not eterne: Nature did not give them immortality.

40–44 jocund: cheerful; merry; **Ere the bat . . . note:** Before nightfall, when the bats and beetles fly, something dreadful will happen.

45 chuck: chick (a term of affection).

46 seeling: blinding.

49 great bond: Banquo's life.

51 rooky: gloomy; also, filled with crows (rooks).

55 Things brought about through evil need additional evil to make them strong.

Teaching Options

Grammar

MODIFIERS: ADVERBS

Instruction Adverbs modify verbs, adjectives, and other adverbs. Many adverbs are formed by adding *-ly* to an adjective, for example, *gracious* and *graciously.* Adverbs modify a verb by telling where, when, how, or to what extent (e.g., *went quickly*).

Tell students that two types of adverbs are intensifiers and directive adverbs. Intensifiers add emphasis to adjectives or adverbs. Examples are *too, very,* and *really.* Directive adverbs tell where about the verb—they indicate place or direction. Examples are *out* and *in.*

Activity Write these lines on the chalkboard.

". . . Things have been strangely borne.
The gracious Duncan
Was pitied of Macbeth. Marry, he was dead!
And the right valiant Banquo walked too late;
Whom, you may say (if't please you) Fleance killed,
For Fleance fled. . . ."

Have students underline the adverbs in the

SCENE 3

1 *A park near the palace.*

The two murderers, joined by a third, ambush Banquo and Fleance, killing Banquo. Fleance manages to escape in the darkness.

[*Enter three* Murderers.]

First Murderer. But who did bid thee join with us?

Third Murderer. Macbeth.

Second Murderer. He needs not our mistrust, since he delivers
Our offices, and what we have to do,
To the direction just.

First Murderer. Then stand with us.
The west yet glimmers with some streaks of day.
Now spurs the lated traveler apace
To gain the timely inn, and near approaches
The subject of our watch.

Third Murderer. Hark! I hear horses.

Banquo. [*Within*] Give us a light there, ho!

Second Murderer. Then 'tis he! The rest
That are within the note of expectation
Already are i' the court.

First Murderer. His horses go about.

Third Murderer. Almost a mile; but he does usually,
So all men do, from hence to the palace gate
Make it their walk.

[*Enter* Banquo, *and* Fleance *with a torch.*]

Second Murderer. A light, a light!

Third Murderer. 'Tis he.

First Murderer. Stand to't.

Banquo. It will be rain tonight.

2 **First Murderer.** Let it come down!

[*They set upon* Banquo.]

Banquo. O, treachery! Fly, good Fleance, fly, fly, fly!
Thou mayst revenge. O slave!

[*Dies.* Fleance *escapes.*]

Third Murderer. Who did strike out the light?

First Murderer. Was't not the way?

Third Murderer. There's but one down; the son is fled.

Second Murderer. We have lost

2–4 He needs . . . just: Macbeth should not be distrustful, since he gave us the orders (**offices**) and we plan to follow his directions exactly.

6 lated: tardy; late.

9 Give us a light: Banquo, nearing the palace, calls for servants to bring a light.

9–11 Then 'tis . . . court: It must be Banquo, since all the other expected guests are already in the palace.

15 Stand to't: Be prepared.

18 Thou mayst revenge: You might live to avenge my death.

19 Was't not the way: Isn't that what we were supposed to do? Apparently, one of the murderers struck out the light, thus allowing Fleance to escape.

Customizing Instruction

Multiple Learning Styles

Kinesthetic/Interpersonal Learners

1 Act Three, Scene 3 contains few lines yet is crucial to the drama. In groups, have students block this scene and then perform it for the class. Remind students that the Globe Theater did not have the lighting facilities a modern theater does. Make sure they address lighting, weather, the murder, and the body left on the stage at the scene's conclusion.

Students Acquiring English

2 Point out that "Let it come down!" (the second half of line 16) has a double meaning. While it is ostensibly a reply to Banquo's remark about rain *("Let the rain come down!")*, it is at the same time the signal to commit murder *("Let your murderous blows come down upon Banquo and Fleance.")*

passage. *(strangely, too, late)* Ask students to identify the word that each modifies and how it is modified. *(strangely: borne, how; too: late, intensifier; late: walked, when)*

Exercise Ask students to write the adverb(s) in each sentence. Have students identify the word modified, and name the way in which each word is modified.

1. During his soliloquy Macbeth speaks hauntingly of the dagger he sees before his eyes. *(hauntingly: speaks, how)*
2. Lady Macbeth chides her husband for being so distraught immediately after the murder. *(so: distraught, intensifier; immediately: distraught, when)*
3. Shakespeare added comic relief to Act 2, Scene 3, with the porter's rather ungracious remarks about people who would knock at that hour. *(rather: ungracious; intensifier)*

Use **Grammar Transparencies and Copymasters,** p. 10.

Use McDougal Littell's ***Language Network*** for more instruction and practice in adverbs. See also conflicting style on p. 687

Reading and Analyzing

Literary Analysis: ASIDE

A Remind students that an aside allows insight into a character's thoughts. Have students analyze Macbeth's aside in lines 22–26. What is he saying?

Possible Response: He thought that with this latest assassination all his problems would be solved, but his doubts and fears still haunt him.

What does this reveal to the reader about the tragic hero's progressive downfall?

Possible Response: Macbeth uses the words "perfect" and "whole" to describe what his situation would be if the murders of Banquo and Fleance had been successful, which indicates how far from social mores he has fallen.

GUIDE FOR READING

B He claims not to be too worried about Fleance's escape, but privately he is deeply troubled.

Best half of our affair.

First Murderer. Well, let's away, and say how much is done.

[*Exeunt.*]

SCENE 4

The hall in the palace.

As the banquet begins, one of the murderers reports on Banquo's death and Fleance's escape. Macbeth is disturbed by the news and even more shaken when he returns to the banquet table and sees the bloody ghost of Banquo. Only Macbeth sees the ghost, and his terrified reaction startles the guests. Lady Macbeth explains her husband's strange behavior as an illness from childhood that will soon pass. Once the ghost disappears, Macbeth calls for a toast to Banquo, whose ghost immediately reappears. Because Macbeth begins to rant and rave, Lady Macbeth dismisses the guests, fearful that her husband will reveal too much. Macbeth, alone with his wife, tells of his suspicions of Macduff, absent from the banquet. He also says he will visit the witches again and hints at bloody deeds yet to happen.

[*Banquet prepared. Enter* Macbeth, Lady Macbeth, Ross, Lennox, Lords, *and* Attendants.]

Macbeth. You know your own degrees, sit down. At first
And last the hearty welcome.

Lords. Thanks to your Majesty.

Macbeth. Ourself will mingle with society
And play the humble host.
Our hostess keeps her state, but in best time
We will require her welcome.

Lady Macbeth. Pronounce it for me, sir, to all our friends,
For my heart speaks they are welcome.

[*Enter* First Murderer *to the door.*]

Macbeth. See, they encounter thee with their hearts' thanks.
Both sides are even: here I'll sit i' the midst.
Be large in mirth; anon we'll drink a measure
The table round. [*Moves toward* Murderer *at door.*]
There's blood upon thy face.

Murderer. 'Tis Banquo's then.

Macbeth. 'Tis better thee without than he within.
Is he dispatched?

Murderer. My lord, his throat is cut. That I did for him.

Macbeth. Thou art the best o' the cutthroats! Yet he's good
That did the like for Fleance. If thou didst it,

1 your own degrees: where your rank entitles you to sit.

5 keeps her state: sits on her throne rather than at the banquet table.

11 measure: toast. Macbeth keeps talking to his wife and guests as he casually edges toward the door to speak privately with the murderer.

16 dispatched: killed.

Teaching Options

Vocabulary Strategy

USING CONTEXT TO DETERMINE MEANING

Instruction Read the sentence that runs through lines 30–32 aloud. Remind students of Macbeth's use of a snake metaphor in Act Three, Scene 2, Lines 13–15 to represent the forces that oppose him. Explain that Macbeth is again using snake metaphors to describe his situation. Here, the immediate context is a conversation about Banquo's death and Fleance's escape.

Activity Have students use context to paraphrase the metaphor. You may need to encourage students to think about who the "grown serpent" and the "worm" would be in this context.

Possible Response: There Banquo lies. Fleance, who has fled, will come to be dangerous to me when he grows up, but right now he poses no threat.

Then have students work in pairs or individually to write their own metaphor to describe the situation they paraphrased.

Possible Response: The great bear lies dead. The cub has run away and will someday be strong enough to be a danger, but for now his claws are too small to harm me.

Use **Vocabulary Transparencies and Copymasters,** p. 37.

Thou art the nonpareil.

Murderer. Most royal sir,
Fleance is scaped.

Macbeth. [*Aside*] Then comes my fit again. I had else been perfect;
Whole as the marble, founded as the rock,
As broad and general as the casing air.
But now I am cabined, cribbed, confined, bound in
To saucy doubts and fears.—But Banquo's safe?

Murderer. Ay, my good lord. Safe in a ditch he bides,
With twenty trenched gashes on his head,
The least a death to nature.

Macbeth. Thanks for that!
There the grown serpent lies; the worm that's fled
Hath nature that in time will venom breed,
No teeth for the present. Get thee gone. Tomorrow
We'll hear ourselves again.

[*Exit* Murderer.]

Lady Macbeth. My royal lord,
You do not give the cheer. The feast is sold
That is not often vouched, while 'tis a-making,
'Tis given with welcome. To feed were best at home.
From thence, the sauce to meat is ceremony;
Meeting were bare without it.

[*Enter the Ghost of* Banquo, *and sits in* Macbeth's *place.*]

20 nonpareil: best.

22 fit: fever of fear.

24 casing: surrounding.

30 worm: little serpent, that is, Fleance.

32 no teeth for the present: too young to cause harm right now. Contrast this comment with his privately expressed fears.

33 hear ourselves: talk together.

Act 3, Scene 4: Orson Welles as Macbeth faces Banquo's ghost (film, 1948)

Customizing Instruction

Students Acquiring English

Explain to students that Shakespeare has characters shorten or not fully enunciate all words, much like people today do in conversation. Point out "scaped" (line 21), meaning "escaped," and "bides" (line 27), meaning "abides" ("dwells"). Show students that Shakespeare often does this to maintain line rhythm (for example in line 15: "'Tis [It is] better thee without than he within"). Ask students to give examples of words that can be shortened in this way from their first languages.

Mini Lesson Viewing and Representing

THE DIRECTOR'S PLAN

Instruction Orson Welles is widely considered one of the geniuses of American filmmaking. He was both an actor and a director, and he kept tight creative control over productions. He actually released two versions of his 1948 *Macbeth.* One runs 105 minutes, and the other 86 minutes. Some reviewers criticize the shorter version for its pared-down presentation. Welles himself said he was not physically well suited for Macbeth; he thought he was better made to be an Othello or Lear.

Application Based on the picture above, have students anticipate how the haunting banquet scene with Banquo is played by Welles in his rapidly paced 1948 film. Ask students if they have any feeling for whether Welles is physically right for this lead role since he himself expressed doubts. After students have looked at the scene from the point of view of Welles-as-Director, have students themselves take on a directorial outlook. What parts of the text of the play thus far could be cut, edited, or done as a voice-over? What scenes do the students feel must be present? How would their directorial visions differ from Welles's in this scene?

Reading and Analyzing

Reading Skills and Strategies: DIALOGUE

A Shakespeare included very few stage directions. Modern editions of his plays usually have stage directions that editors have deduced from the dialogue. Ask students how a reader can know strictly from the dialogue where Banquo's ghost is?

Possible Response: Lines 44–52 indicate that Banquo's ghost is in the chair reserved for Macbeth.

GUIDE FOR READING

B She doesn't want them to think he's insane or to suspect that he's been involved in all the murders.

C Although some students might think that her appeals will work because she seems so strong in the face of his emotional behavior, most will probably think they won't work, because he's beginning to see that he's doomed by his previous actions.

Macbeth. Sweet remembrancer!
Now good digestion wait on appetite,
And health on both!

Lennox. May't please your Highness sit.

Macbeth. Here had we now our country's honor, roofed,
Were the graced person of our Banquo present;
Who may I rather challenge for unkindness
Than pity for mischance!

Ross. His absence, sir,
Lays blame upon his promise. Please't your Highness
To grace us with your royal company?

Macbeth. The table's full.

Lennox. Here is a place reserved, sir.

Macbeth. Where?

Lennox. Here, my good lord. What is't that moves your
Highness?

Macbeth. Which of you have done this?

Lords. What, my good lord?

Macbeth. Thou canst not say I did it. Never shake
Thy gory locks at me.

Ross. Gentlemen, rise. His Highness is not well.

Lady Macbeth. Sit, worthy friends. My lord is often thus,
And hath been from his youth. Pray you keep seat.
The fit is momentary; upon a thought
He will again be well. If much you note him,
You shall offend him and extend his passion.
Feed, and regard him not.—Are you a man?

Macbeth. Ay, and a bold one, that dare look on that
Which might appal the devil.

Lady Macbeth. O proper stuff!
This is the very painting of your fear.
This is the air-drawn dagger which you said
Led you to Duncan. O, these flaws and starts
(Impostors to true fear) would well become
A woman's story at a winter's fire,
Authorized by her grandam. Shame itself!
Why do you make such faces? When all's done,
You look but on a stool.

Macbeth. Prithee see there! behold! look! lo! How say you?
Why, what care I? If thou canst nod, speak too.
If charnel houses and our graves must send

33–38 Macbeth must not forget his duties as host. A feast will be no different from a meal that one pays for unless the host gives his guests courteous attention (**ceremony**), the best part of any meal.

38 sweet remembrancer: a term of affection for his wife, who has reminded him of his duty.

41–44 The best people of Scotland would all be under Macbeth's roof if Banquo were present too. He hopes Banquo's absence is due to rudeness rather than to some accident (**mischance**).

47 Macbeth finally notices that Banquo's ghost is present and sitting in the king's chair. As you read about this encounter, consider how Macbeth's reaction affects his guests.

52 gory: bloody.

54–59 Sit . . . not: Lady Macbeth tries to calm the guests by claiming her husband often has such fits. She says the attack will pass quickly (**upon a thought**) and that looking at him will only make him worse (**extend his passion**). Why does Lady Macbeth make up a story to tell the guests?

61–69 She dismisses his hallucination as utter nonsense (**proper stuff**). His outbursts (**flaws and starts**) are the product of imaginary fears (**impostors to true fear**) and are unmanly, the kind of behavior described in a woman's story. Do you think her appeal to his manhood will work this time?

Teaching Options

✓ Assessment Informal Assessment

WRITING A DIARY ENTRY Have your students write a diary entry from the point of view of one of the guests at the banquet in Scene 4. Tell them to be sure to include all the details of Macbeth's strange behavior, as well as their own reactions to him and Lady Macbeth.

RUBRIC

3 Full Accomplishment Student demonstrates full understanding of action of scene and supplies appropriate reactions to events in scene.

2 Substantial Accomplishment Student demonstrates basic understanding of scene and supplies appropriate reactions to most events in scene.

1 Little or Partial Accomplishment Student demonstrates little or no understanding of action of scene and supplies few or inappropriate reactions to events in scene.

Those that we bury back, our monuments
Shall be the maws of kites.

[*Exit* Ghost.]

Lady Macbeth. What, quite unmanned in folly?

Macbeth. If I stand here, I saw him.

Lady Macbeth. Fie, for shame!

Macbeth. Blood hath been shed ere now, i' the olden time
Ere humane statue purged the gentle weal;
Ay, and since too, murders have been performed
Too terrible for the ear. The time has been
That, when the brains were out, the man would die,
And there an end! But now they rise again,
With twenty mortal murders on their crowns,
And push us from our stools. This is more strange
Than such a murder is.

Lady Macbeth. My worthy lord,
Your noble friends do lack you.

Macbeth. I do forget.
Do not muse at me, my most worthy friends.
I have a strange infirmity, which is nothing
To those that know me. Come, love and health to all!
Then I'll sit down. Give me some wine, fill full.

[*Enter* Ghost.]

I drink to the general joy o' the whole table,
And to our dear friend Banquo, whom we miss.
Would he were here! To all, and him, we thirst,
And all to all.

1

Lords. Our duties, and the pledge.

Macbeth. Avaunt, and quit my sight! Let the earth hide thee!
Thy bones are marrowless, thy blood is cold;
Thou hast no speculation in those eyes
Which thou dost glare with!

Lady Macbeth. Think of this, good peers,
But as a thing of custom. 'Tis no other.
Only it spoils the pleasure of the time.

Macbeth. What man dare, I dare.
Approach thou like the rugged Russian bear,
The armed rhinoceros, or the Hyrcan tiger;
Take any shape but that, and my firm nerves
Shall never tremble. Or be alive again
And dare me to the desert with thy sword.

72–74 If burial vaults (**charnel houses**) give back the dead, then we may as well throw our bodies to the birds (**kites**), whose stomachs (**maws**) will become our tombs (**monuments**).

76–79 Macbeth desperately tries to justify his murder of Banquo. Murder has been common from ancient times to the present, though laws (**humane statute**) have tried to rid civilized society (**gentle weal**) of violence.

86 muse: wonder.

92–93 To all . . . to all: Macbeth toasts everyone, including Banquo.

94–97 avaunt: go away. Macbeth sees Banquo again. He tells Banquo that he is only a ghost, with unreal bones, cold blood, and no consciousness (**speculation**).

Customizing Instruction

Less Proficient Readers

1 In order for students to recognize the irony of line 92, followed by the reappearance of the ghost in line 94, it is necessary for them to recognize that the subjunctive construction "Would he were here!" indicates a wish. Explain that the sentence could be rephrased as "I wish he were here!" Ask students why this situation is an example of dramatic irony.

Possible Response: While Macbeth laments Banquo's absence, the audience knows that Banquo is present in the form of a ghost.

MACBETH: ACT THREE 375

Reading and Analyzing

GUIDE FOR READING

A He is worried that Macduff has turned against him and might return to challenge him.

Reading Skills and Strategies: PARAPHRASING

B Ask students to paraphrase Hecate's speech in Scene 5, lines 2–35, in order to understand her complaints.

Possible Response: In their dealings with Macbeth, the witches have gone beyond their prerogatives and usurped Hecate's role; they also have bestowed favor on Macbeth, who is committed to his goals rather than theirs.

If trembling I inhabit then, protest me
The baby of a girl. Hence, horrible shadow!
Unreal mock'ry, hence!

[*Exit* Ghost.]

Why, so! Being gone,
I am a man again. Pray you sit still.

Lady Macbeth. You have displaced the mirth, broke the good meeting
With most admired disorder.

Macbeth. Can such things be,
And overcome us like a summer's cloud
Without our special wonder? You make me strange
Even to the disposition that I owe,
When now I think you can behold such sights
And keep the natural ruby of your cheeks
When mine is blanched with fear.

Ross. What sights, my lord?

Lady Macbeth. I pray you speak not. He grows worse and worse;
Question enrages him. At once, good night.
Stand not upon the order of your going,
But go at once.

Lennox. Good night, and better health
Attend his Majesty!

Lady Macbeth. A kind good night to all!

[*Exeunt* Lords *and* Attendants.]

Macbeth. It will have blood, they say: blood will have blood.
Stones have been known to move and trees to speak;
Augures and understood relations have
By maggot-pies and choughs and rooks brought forth
The secret'st man of blood. What is the night?

Lady Macbeth. Almost at odds with morning, which is which.

Macbeth. How say'st thou that Macduff denies his person
At our great bidding?

Lady Macbeth. Did you send to him, sir?

Macbeth. I hear it by the way; but I will send.
There's not a one of them but in his house
I keep a servant feed. I will tomorrow
(And betimes I will) to the Weird Sisters.
More shall they speak; for now I am bent to know
By the worst means the worst. For mine own good
All causes shall give way. I am in blood
Stepped in so far that, should I wade no more,

100–108 Macbeth would be willing to face Banquo in any other form, even his living self. **If trembling . . . girl:** If I still tremble, call me a girl's doll.

111 admired: astonishing.

111–117 Macbeth is bewildered by his wife's calm. Her reaction makes him seem a stranger to himself (**strange even to the disposition that I owe**): she seems to be the one with all the courage, since he is white (**blanched**) with fear.

120 Stand . . . going: Don't worry about the proper formalities of leaving.

123–127 Macbeth fears that Banquo's murder (**it**) will be revenged by his own murder. Stones, trees, or talking birds (**maggot-pies and choughs and rooks**) may reveal the hidden knowledge (**augures**) of his guilt.

129–130 How say'st . . . bidding: What do you think of Macduff's refusal to come? Why do you think Macbeth is suddenly so concerned about Macduff? **A**

132–133 There's . . . feed: Macbeth has paid (**feed**) household servants to spy on every noble, including Macduff.

134 betimes: early.

135 bent: determined.

136–141 For mine . . . scanned: Macbeth will do anything to protect himself. He has stepped so far into a river of blood that it would make no sense to turn back. He will act upon his unnatural (**strange**) thoughts without having examined (**scanned**) them.

Returning were as tedious as go o'er.
Strange things I have in head, that will to hand,
Which must be acted ere they may be scanned.

Lady Macbeth. You lack the season of all natures, sleep.

Macbeth. Come, we'll to sleep. My strange and self-abuse
Is the initiate fear that wants hard use.
We are yet but young in deed.

[*Exeunt.*]

142 season: preservative.

143–145 His vision of the ghost (**strange and self-abuse**) is only the result of a beginner's fear (**initiate fear**), to be cured with practice (**hard use**).

SCENE 5

A heath.

The goddess of witchcraft, Hecate, scolds the three witches for dealing independently with Macbeth. She outlines their next meeting with him, planning to cause his downfall by making him overconfident. (Experts believe this scene was not written by Shakespeare but rather was added later.)

[*Thunder. Enter the three* Witches, *meeting* Hecate.]

1 **First Witch.** Why, how now, Hecate? You look angerly.

Hecate. Have I not reason, beldams as you are,
Saucy and overbold? How did you dare 2
B To trade and traffic with Macbeth
In riddles and affairs of death;
And I, the mistress of your charms,
The close contriver of all harms,
Was never called to bear my part
Or show the glory of our art?
And, which is worse, all you have done
Hath been but for a wayward son,
Spiteful and wrathful, who, as others do,
Loves for his own ends, not for you.
But make amends now. Get you gone
And at the pit of Acheron
Meet me i' the morning. Thither he
Will come to know his destiny.
Your vessels and your spells provide,
Your charms and everything beside.
I am for the air. This night I'll spend
Unto a dismal and a fatal end.
Great business must be wrought ere noon.
Upon the corner of the moon
There hangs a vap'rous drop profound.
I'll catch it ere it come to ground;

2 beldams: hags.

7 close contriver: secret inventor.

13 loves . . . you: cares only about his own goals, not about you.

15 Acheron: a river in hell, according to Greek mythology. Hecate plans to hold their meeting in a hellish place.

20–21 This . . . end: Tonight I'm working for a disastrous (**dismal**) and fatal end for Macbeth.

Customizing Instruction

Multiple Learning Styles

Auditory Learners

1 Have students find passages containing the witches' dialogue. Then have them read the witches' and Hecate's lines aloud. Have students contrast the way the witches speak with the way Hecate speaks. What do the differences in their styles suggest about their relationship?

Possible Response: Hecate's longer speech, elevated diction, and use of rhymed couplets indicate that she occupies a higher position than the witches, and therefore has power over them.

Students Acquiring English

2 Help students understand that "saucy" is used idiomatically and means "impertinent" or "flippant." Point out that Shakespeare positions these adjectives ("saucy" and "overbold") behind the noun they modify ("beldams"), which is an irregular word order.

MACBETH: ACT THREE 377

Reading and Analyzing

Reading Skills and Strategies:
EVALUATING

A Ask students to paraphrase Hecate's generalization about people.
Possible Response: When people feel they are safe, they are most vulnerable.
Then ask them to consider whether this statement is true of people in general and whether it is true in regard to Macbeth. Have them explain their opinions.
Possible Responses: It is true of people in general because when people feel safe, they tend to let their guard down; it is true of Macbeth because he thought he was safe from Banquo and was therefore terrorized by the appearance of Banquo's ghost.

Active Reading
SHAKESPEARE'S LANGUAGE

B Have students examine Lennox's questions in lines 7–14. Ask students why Shakespeare has Lennox use questions rather than statements to make his point. What effect is created?
Possible Response: By having Lennox ask questions, Shakespeare makes the audience think carefully in order to answer those questions. This kind of rhetorical strategy produces an ironic effect, because Lennox is skirting the issues that really concern him.

And that, distilled by magic sleights,
Shall raise such artificial sprites
As by the strength of their illusion
Shall draw him on to his confusion.
He shall spurn fate, scorn death, and bear
His hopes 'bove wisdom, grace, and fear;
And you all know security
Is mortals' chiefest enemy.
[*Music and a song within. "Come away, come away," etc.*]
Hark! I am called. My little spirit, see,
Sits in a foggy cloud and stays for me.
[*Exit.*]

First Witch. Come, let's make haste. She'll soon be back again.
[*Exeunt.*]

23–29 Hecate will obtain a magical drop from the moon, treat it with secret art, and so create spirits (**artificial sprites**) that will lead Macbeth to his destruction (**confusion**).

34–35 Like the other witches, Hecate has a demon helper (**my little spirit**). At the end of her speech, she is raised by pulley to the "Heavens" of the stage.

SCENE 6

The palace at Forres.

Lennox and another Scottish lord review the events surrounding the murders of Duncan and Banquo, indirectly suggesting that Macbeth is both a murderer and a tyrant. It is reported that Macduff has gone to England, where Duncan's son Malcolm is staying with King Edward and raising an army to regain the Scottish throne. Macbeth, angered by Macduff's refusal to see him, is also preparing for war.

[*Enter* Lennox *and another* Lord.]

Lennox. My former speeches have but hit your thoughts,
Which can interpret farther. Only I say
Things have been strangely borne. The gracious Duncan
Was pitied of Macbeth. Marry, he was dead!
And the right valiant Banquo walked too late;
Whom, you may say (if't please you) Fleance killed,
For Fleance fled. Men must not walk too late.
Who cannot want the thought how monstrous
It was for Malcolm and for Donalbain
To kill their gracious father? Damned fact!
How it did grieve Macbeth! Did he not straight,
In pious rage, the two delinquents tear,
That were the slaves of drink and thralls of sleep?
Was not that nobly done? Ay, and wisely too!
For 'twould have angered any heart alive
To hear the men deny't. So that I say
He has borne all things well; and I do think

1–3 My former . . . borne: Lennox and the other lord have shared suspicions of Macbeth.

6–7 whom . . . Fleance fled: Lennox is being ironic when he says that fleeing the scene of the crime must make Fleance guilty of his father's death.

8–10 who . . . father: He says that everyone agrees on the horror of Duncan's murder by his sons. But Lennox has been consistently ironic, claiming to believe in what is obviously false. His words indirectly blame Macbeth.

12 pious: holy.

15–16 For 'twould . . . deny't: Again, he is being ironic. If the servants had lived, Macbeth might have been discovered.

That, had he Duncan's sons under his key
(As, an't please heaven, he shall not), they should find
What 'twere to kill a father. So should Fleance.
But peace! for from broad words, and 'cause he failed
His presence at the tyrant's feast, I hear
Macduff lives in disgrace. Sir, can you tell
Where he bestows himself?

Lord. The son of Duncan,
From whom this tyrant holds the due of birth,
Lives in the English court, and is received
Of the most pious Edward with such grace
That the malevolence of fortune nothing
Takes from his high respect. Thither Macduff
1 Is gone to pray the holy King upon his aid
To wake Northumberland and warlike Siward;
That by the help of these (with Him above
To ratify the work) we may again
Give to our tables meat, sleep to our nights,
Free from our feasts and banquets bloody knives,
Do faithful homage and receive free honors—
All which we pine for now. And this report
Hath so exasperate the King that he
Prepares for some attempt of war.

Lennox. Sent he to Macduff?

Lord. He did; and with an absolute "Sir, not I!"
2 The cloudy messenger turns me his back
And hums, as who should say, "You'll rue the time
That clogs me with this answer."

Lennox. And that well might
Advise him to a caution t' hold what distance
His wisdom can provide. Some holy angel
Fly to the court of England and unfold
His message ere he come, that a swift blessing
May soon return to this our suffering country
Under a hand accursed!

Lord. I'll send my prayers with him.

[*Exeunt.*]

21 from broad words: because of his frank talk.

24 bestows himself: is staying.

25 from . . . birth: Macbeth keeps Malcolm from his birthright. As the eldest son of Duncan, Malcolm should be king.

27 Edward: Edward the Confessor, king of England from 1042 to 1066, a man known for his virtue and religion.

28–29 that . . . respect: Though Malcolm suffers from bad fortune (the loss of the throne), he is respectfully treated by Edward.

29–37 Thither . . . for now: Macduff wants the king to persuade the people of Northumberland and their earl, Siward, to join Malcolm's cause.

40–43 The messenger, fearing Macbeth's anger, was unhappy (**cloudy**) with Macduff's refusal to cooperate. Because Macduff burdens (**clogs**) him with bad news, he will not hurry back.

Customizing Instruction

Less Proficient Readers

1 Students may have trouble understanding why Macduff is in England. Explain to them that "the holy king" (line 30) is the king of England, and then have them read lines 29–43, with the side notes. Have them summarize the passage.

Possible Response: Macduff is in England, trying to get the king to convince Lord Siward of Northumbria to fight against Macbeth for Malcolm. Macbeth is also preparing for war, and summoned Macduff. Macduff refused.

Students Acquiring English

2 In line 41, point out that *turns me* is a colloquialism meaning simply "turns." Explain that the Lord is delivering this account of Macduff's refusal secondhand, because he wasn't with the messenger.

MACBETH: ACT THREE **379**

Thinking Through the Literature

1. Possible Responses: It was convoluted, with many conspiracies. It relied on violence and murder as a means of settling political differences and determining who would lead. It was more complicated than Macbeth suggests. Have students support their conclusions with experience and/or evidence from the text.
2. Possible Responses: It reflects the beliefs of its times (witches, magic, etc.), and so may contain elements that seem impossible to 20th-century readers. However, these elements might not affect its credibility as an information source; it recounts legends that mix imaginative elements with fact.
3. Comparing Texts Similar characters include Macbeth, Lady Macbeth, Duncan, Malcolm, Banquo, Fleance, and the three Weird Sisters; similar events include the forest encounter with the Weird Sisters, whose predictions of Macbeth's future elevations of rank encourage his plotting to kill Duncan; Macbeth's frustration on hearing that Duncan has designated Malcolm as his heir to the throne; the fact that Lady Macbeth encourages her husband; the killing of Duncan; and the killing of Banquo on the way to Macbeth's banquet. Holinshed's Chronicles differ from the play by including some apparent validity to Macbeth's claim of kingship and some indication of others supporting his claims and being in on the plot to kill Duncan. Most students are likely to feel that Shakespeare chose to show Banquo in a more flattering light precisely because Banquo was King James's relative, and Shakespeare did not want to risk offending the king.

from HOLINSHED'S CHRONICLES

Preparing to Read

Build Background

As this passage from the *Chronicles* begins, Macbeth has been courting the favor of the people. As you read, follow the reasoning that leads Macbeth to murder.

This was but a counterfeit zeal of equity[1] showed by him, partly against his natural inclination, to purchase thereby the favor of the people. Shortly after, he began to show what he was, instead of equity practicing cruelty. For the prick of consciene (as it chanceth ever in tyrants and such as attain to any estate by unrighteous means) caused him ever to fear lest he should be served of the same cup as he had ministered to his predecessor. The words also of the three Weird Sisters would not out of his mind, which as they promised him the kingdom, so likewise did they promise it at the same time unto the posterity of Banquo. He willed therefore the same Banquo, with his son named Fleance, to come to a supper that he had prepared for them; which was indeed, as he had devised, present death at the hands of certain murderers whom he hired to execute that deed, appointing them to meet with the same Banquo and his son without the palace, as they returned to their lodgings, and there to slay them, so that he would not have his house slandered but that in time to come he might clear himself if anything were laid to his charge upon any suspicion that might arise.

It chanced by the benefit of the dark night that, though the father were slain, yet the son, by the help of almighty God reserving him to better fortune, escaped that danger; and afterward, having some inkling (by the admonition of some friends which he had in the court) how his life was sought no less than his father's, who was slain not by chance-medley[2] (as by the handling of the matter Macbeth would have had it to appear) but even upon a prepensed[3] device, whereupon to avoid further peril he fled into Wales.

1. **equity**: fairness.
2. **chance-medley**: accidental homicide.
3. **prepensed**: premeditated.

Thinking Through the Literature

1. Based on this and the preceding selection from Holinshed's *Chronicles*, what can you conclude about politics and power in Macbeth's Scotland?
2. What does the inclusion of the three witches suggest about the historical accuracy of Holinshed's *Chronicles*?
3. **Comparing Texts** Compare the information from Holinshed's *Chronicles* with the **plot** and **characters** so far in *Macbeth.* What events and characters are similar? What differences do you detect? Why do you think Shakespeare portrays King James's ancestor Banquo in a more flattering light than he appears in the *Chronicles*?

Connect to the Literature

1. **What Do You Think?** How has your impression of Macbeth and Lady Macbeth changed?

Comprehension Check

- What suspicions does Banquo voice?
- Why does Macbeth fear Banquo?
- What happens to Fleance when Banquo is killed?
- Where does Banquo's ghost appear?

Think Critically

2. **ACTIVE READING** SHAKESPEARE'S LANGUAGE Summarize what Macbeth and Lady Macbeth say to each other in Act Three, Scene 2. What notes did you take in your  READER'S NOTEBOOK about what these **characters** discuss? How would you restate Lady Macbeth's soliloquy lines 4-7 in contemporary language?

3. How has the relationship between Macbeth and his wife changed since the death of Duncan?

THINK ABOUT
- Macbeth's view of Duncan's murder
- Lady Macbeth's view of Duncan's murder
- Macbeth's refusal to tell his wife about his plan to murder Banquo
- Macbeth's "fit" at the banquet and his wife's reaction to it

4. Why aren't Macbeth and Lady Macbeth happy being king and queen? Cite evidence to support your opinion.

5. Why is the escape of Fleance significant in the light of the witches' earlier predictions?

Extend Interpretations

6. **Critic's Corner** In Act Three, Scene 1, Macbeth meets with two murderers, but three murderers take part in the actual murder in Scene 3. Critics have speculated about the identity of the third murderer, with some thinking that it may be Macbeth himself. How do you explain this situation?

7. **Comparing Texts** What do Macbeth and his wife have in common with the villainous characters in "The Pardoner's Tale" from Chaucer's *Canterbury Tales* (page 141)?

8. **Connect to Life** Think about present-day explanations of the behavior of criminals. In what ways might Macbeth's state of mind and behavior in Act Three be similar to those of criminals today? Cite evidence to explain your response.

Literary Analysis

DRAMATIC IRONY Writers introduce **irony** into their works when they convey a contrast or discrepancy between appearance and reality—between the way things seem and the way they really are. In **dramatic irony,** what appears true to one or more characters in a play is seen to be false by the audience.

Cooperative Learning Activity With a small group of classmates, focus on one of the first three acts of *Macbeth* and analyze at least two remarks or incidents that create dramatic irony. Explain why the remarks or incidents are ironic, detailing the contrast between what characters think and what the audience knows. Then consider how the irony affects your enjoyment of the play. Before presenting your group's ideas to the class, organize your thoughts in a chart.

What Characters Think	What Audience Knows

GUIDING STUDENT RESPONSE

Connect to the Literature

1. **What Do You Think?** Guidelines for student response: Students should provides examples from the text of the ways in which the two characters have changed.

Comprehension Check

- He suspects the means by which Macbeth has fulfilled the witches' final prediction about Macbeth's becoming king.
- Banquo knows the witches' predictions, and the witches also predicted that his descendants would rule Scotland one day.
- Fleance escapes.
- in Macbeth's chair at a banquet

 Use Selection Quiz in **Unit Two Resource Book, p. 25**

Think Critically

2. Possible summary should include main idea and supporting details. Lady Macbeth, noting her husband's guilty conscience and fears, tries to strengthen his resolve. Possible restatement: Nothing is gained and everything is wasted when achieving our desires doesn't make us happy.
3. Possible Response: Macbeth seems more independent, having plotted Banquo's murder without her help. Aside from that, the dynamic between the two characters remains much the same.
4. Possible Response: They have to be suspicious of everyone to protect what they have illicitly gained, and their guilt becomes debilitating.
5. Possible Response: Fleance's escape is significant because the witches predicted that Banquo's descendants would become kings of Scotland.

Extend Interpretations

Critic's Corner Some students may say that there is no discrepancy; the third murderer simply was not present at the earlier meeting. Others may say that Shakespeare just made a mistake and confused the number of murderers in the two scenes.

Comparing Texts Among the similarities with Chaucer's villains are excessive self-interest, willingness to kill to obtain their desires, and willingness to break God's and society's laws.

Connect to Life Students who see similarities may mention that Macbeth's initial crime has started him on a life of crime. Students who do not see similarities may feel that he shows a guilty conscience instead of rationalizing his crimes, as some criminals seem to do today.

Literary Analysis

Cooperative Learning Students might make up a composite chart that reflects the main findings of the various groups.

TEACHING THE LITERATURE

Reading and Analyzing

Active Reading READING DRAMA

Have students look at lines 10–11, 20–21, and 35–36. Tell students that such a repeated set of lines is called a refrain. Ask them whether it reminds them of anything they hear in everyday life.

Possible Response: Students will probably say that it is like the chorus of a song.

Explain that the refrain has the same purpose as a song's chorus: it simultaneously provides a break from the verses and unifies them.

 Use **Unit Two Resource Book,** p. 27 for more practice.

Literary Analysis FORESHADOWING

A Review with students that foreshadowing is hints or clues that let the audience know what is going to happen later in the work. Point out lines 44–47 and the stage direction after line 47. What comment do these lines make about Macbeth?

Possible Response: Macbeth is identified as "wicked."

What does this suggest about the action in the rest of the play?

Possible Response: The lines indicate that Macbeth will continue performing evil acts.

 Use **Unit Two Resource Book,** p. 28 for more exercises.

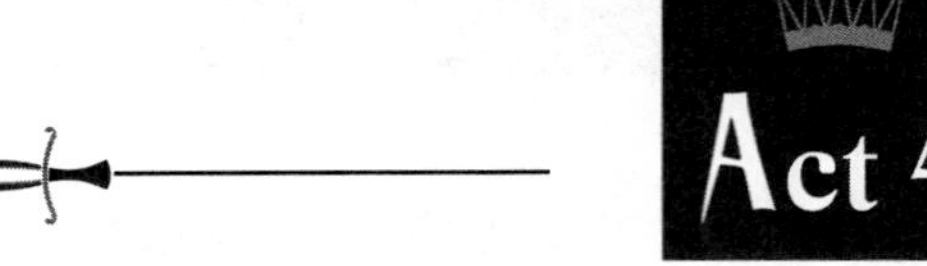

Act 4

SCENE 1

A cave. In the middle, a boiling cauldron.

1 *The three witches prepare a potion in a boiling kettle. When Macbeth arrives, demanding to know his future, the witches raise three apparitions. The first, an armed head, tells him to beware of Macduff. Next, a bloody child assures Macbeth that he will never be harmed by anyone born of woman. The third apparition tells him that he will never be defeated until the trees of Birnam Wood move toward his castle at Dunsinane. Macbeth, now confident of his future, asks about Banquo's son. His confidence fades when the witches show him a line of kings who all resemble Banquo, suggesting that Banquo's sons will indeed be kings. Macbeth curses the witches as they disappear.*

Lennox enters the cave and tells Macbeth that Macduff has gone to the English court. Hearing this, Macbeth swears to kill Macduff's family.

[*Thunder. Enter the three* Witches.]

2 **First Witch.** Thrice the brinded cat hath mewed.
Second Witch. Thrice, and once the hedge-pig whined.
Third Witch. Harpier cries; 'tis time, 'tis time.
First Witch. Round about the cauldron go;
In the poisoned entrails throw.
Toad, that under cold stone
Days and nights has thirty-one
Swelt'red venom sleeping got,

1–3 Magical signals and the call of the third witch's attending demon (**Harpier**) tell the witches to begin.

The Three Witches (1783), Henry Fuseli. Oil on canvas, Royal Shakespeare Theatre Collection, London.

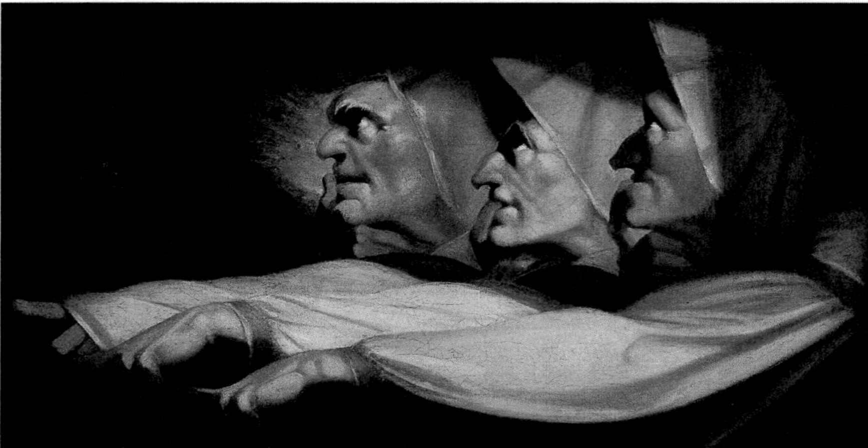

382

Teaching Options

Mini Lesson Viewing and Representing

The Three Witches
by Henry Fuseli

ART APPRECIATION Henry Fuseli (1741–1825) was a Swiss-born history painter whose work demonstrates the horrific, heroic, and dramatic qualities of early Romanticism. Working for Boydell's Shakespeare Gallery in England, he painted scenes from many of the plays, including several from *Macbeth,* that contain his characteristically distorted figures.

Instruction Artists in the Western tradition have always derived inspiration from history, legends, and stories. *Macbeth* is all three of these, and like so many of Shakespeare's works, it has held sway over the imagination of artists and audience since its creation.

Application Encourage students to explore the content and emotion of this first scene in Act IV in a different medium from oil. Suggest a drawing, an abstract painting, or a clay sculpture. Give artistic license, but then have students explain their motivation and what they are trying to convey about the scene in the play.

Boil thou first i' the charmed pot.

All. Double, double, toil and trouble;
Fire burn, and cauldron bubble.

Second Witch. Fillet of a fenny snake,
In the cauldron boil and bake;
Eye of newt, and toe of frog,
Wool of bat, and tongue of dog,
Adder's fork, and blindworm's sting,
Lizard's leg, and howlet's wing;
For a charm of pow'rful trouble
Like a hell-broth boil and bubble.

All. Double, double, toil and trouble;
Fire burn, and cauldron bubble.

Third Witch. Scale of dragon, tooth of wolf,
Witch's mummy, maw and gulf
Of the ravined salt-sea shark,
Root of hemlock, digged i' the dark;
Liver of blaspheming Jew,
Gall of goat, and slips of yew
Slivered in the moon's eclipse;
Nose of Turk and Tartar's lips;
Finger of birth-strangled babe
Ditch-delivered by a drab:
Make the gruel thick and slab.
Add thereto a tiger's chaudron
For the ingredience of our cauldron.

All. Double, double, toil and trouble;
Fire burn, and cauldron bubble.

Second Witch. Cool it with a baboon's blood,
Then the charm is firm and good.

[*Enter* Hecate *and the other three* Witches.]

3 **Hecate.** O, well done! I commend your pains,
And every one shall share i' the gains.
And now about the cauldron sing
Like elves and fairies in a ring,
Enchanting all that you put in.

[*Music and a song, "Black spirit," etc.*]

Second Witch. By the pricking of my thumbs,
Something wicked this way comes.
A Open locks,
Whoever knocks!

[*Enter* Macbeth.]

4–34 The witches are stirring up a magical stew to bring trouble to humanity. Their recipe includes intestines (**entrails, chaudron**), a slice (**fillet**) of snake, eye of salamander (**newt**), snake tongue (**adder's fork**), a lizard (**blindworm**), a baby owl's (**howlet's**) wing, a shark's stomach and gullet (**maw and gulf**), the finger of a baby strangled by a prostitute (**drab**), and other gruesome ingredients. They stir their brew until it is thick and slimy (**slab**).

[Stage Direction] **Enter Hecate . . .** : Most experts believe that the entrance of Hecate and three more witches was not written by Shakespeare. The characters were probably added later to expand the role of the witches, who were favorites of the audience.

Customizing Instruction

Less Proficient Readers

1 Ask students how this extended section dealing with the witches and supernatural phenomena affects the atmosphere of the play. The play is at once a story of Scottish political intrigue and a gothic tale of mystery and magic. Have students comment on how these two aspects of the play work together.

2 Point out to students that *brinded* in line 1 is an archaic form of the word *brindled.* Have students define *brindled* by using the dictionary.
(Answer: *brindled—a color of an animal's coat that is gray or fawn with dark streaks or flecks*)

3 Explain to students that *pains* in line 39 means *efforts.* Hecate is not saying that she is glad the witches are in physical pain, but rather that she is impressed with the efforts they have taken with their potion and spell.

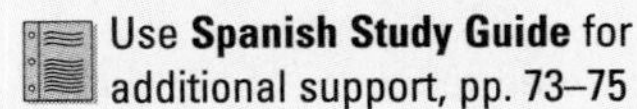
Use **Spanish Study Guide** for additional support, pp. 73–75

Reading and Analyzing

Literary Analysis: THEME

A Remind students of the topics listed in the **Preparing to Read** section. Which of these is present as Macbeth implores the witches to answer his question?

Possible Responses: ambition; impulse or desire; fate and our efforts to control it; the supernatural.

How might the apparent meaning of the witches' statements not correspond with reality?

Possible Responses: Their statements are subject to different interpretations, pointing out the discrepancy between appearance and reality.

GUIDE FOR READING

B Initially, he was suspicious of them and uneasy about their predictions; now he's bold, demanding, and relentless in his quest for information from them.

C The armed head perhaps represents the armed rebellion of Macduff.

D The bloody child probably signifies Macduff, who was "untimely ripped," (see Act Five, Scene 8, lines 15–16) from his mother's womb.

E Macbeth will become even more arrogant and have even more illusions that he is invincible.

F The crowned child probably represents Malcolm; the tree he holds foreshadows the final battle in which Malcolm and his troops approach Dunsinane carrying boughs as camouflage.

Macbeth. How now, you secret, black, and midnight hags?
What is't you do?

All. A deed without a name.

Macbeth. I conjure you by that which you profess
(Howe'er you come to know it), answer me.
Though you untie the winds and let them fight
Against the churches; though the yesty waves
Confound and swallow navigation up;
Though bladed corn be lodged and trees blown down; **A**
Though castles topple on their warders' heads;
Though palaces and pyramids do slope
Their heads to their foundations; though the treasure
Of nature's germens tumble all together,
Even till destruction sicken—answer me
To what I ask you.

First Witch. Speak.

Second Witch. Demand.

Third Witch. We'll answer.

First Witch. Say, if th' hadst rather hear it from our mouths
Or from our masters.

Macbeth. Call 'em! Let me see 'em.

First Witch. Pour in sow's blood, that hath eaten
Her nine farrow; grease that's sweaten
From the murderer's gibbet throw
Into the flame.

All. Come, high or low;
Thyself and office deftly show!

[*Thunder.* First Apparition, *an Armed Head.*]

Macbeth. Tell me, thou unknown power—

First Witch. He knows thy thought.
Hear his speech, but say thou naught.

First Apparition. Macbeth! Macbeth! Macbeth! Beware Macduff;
Beware the Thane of Fife. Dismiss me. Enough.

[*He descends.*]

Macbeth. Whate'er thou art, for thy good caution thanks!
Thou hast harped my fear aright. But one word more—

First Witch. He will not be commanded. Here's another,
More potent than the first.

[*Thunder.* Second Apparition, *a Bloody Child.*]

Second Apparition. Macbeth! Macbeth! Macbeth!

Macbeth. Had I three ears, I'ld hear thee.

50–61 Macbeth calls upon (**conjure**) the witches in the name of their dark magic (**that which you profess**). Though they unleash winds to topple churches and make foaming (**yesty**) waves to destroy (**confound**) ships, though they flatten wheat (**corn**) fields, destroy buildings, and reduce nature's order to chaos by mixing all seeds (**germens**) together, he demands an answer to his question. How has Macbeth's attitude toward the witches changed from his earlier meetings? **B**

63 masters: the demons whom the witches serve.

65–66 farrow: newborn pigs; **grease . . . gibbet:** grease from a gallows where a murderer was hung.

[Stage Direction] Each of the three apparitions holds a clue to Macbeth's future. What do you think is suggested by the armed head? **C**

74 harped: guessed. The apparition has confirmed Macbeth's fears of Macduff.

[Stage Direction] Whom or what might the bloody child represent? **D**

Teaching Options

BLOCK SCHEDULING: MANAGING TIME

If your schedule requires that you cover the lesson objectives in a shorter time, use . . .

- Preparing to Read, pp. 323–325
- Thinking Through the Literature, p. 399

If you want to take advantage of longer class time, use . . .

- TE Teaching Options: Viewing and Representing, pp. 382, 385, 388, 400; Vocabulary Strategy, pp. 386, 390; Informal Assessment, p. 387; Grammar, p. 394; Standardized Test Practice, p. 396

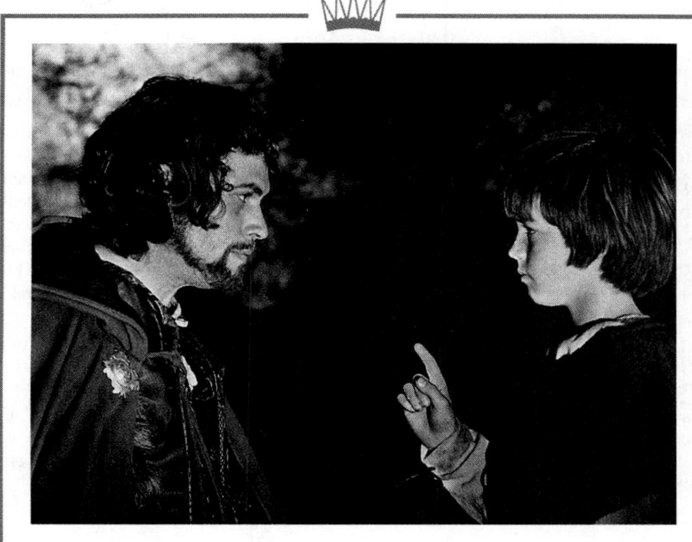

Act 4, Scene 1: Macbeth meets the second apparition (film 1971)

Second Apparition. Be bloody, bold, and resolute; laugh to scorn
The pow'r of man, for none of woman born
Shall harm Macbeth.

[*Descends.*]

Macbeth. Then live, Macduff. What need I fear of thee?
But yet I'll make assurance double sure
And take a bond of fate. Thou shalt not live!
1 That I may tell pale-hearted fear it lies
And sleep in spite of thunder.

[*Thunder.* Third Apparition, *a Child Crowned, with a tree in his hand.*]

What is this
That rises like the issue of a king
And wears upon his baby-brow the round
And top of sovereignty?

All. Listen, but speak not to't.

2 **Third Apparition.** Be lion-mettled, proud, and take no care
Who chafes, who frets, or where conspirers are.
Macbeth shall never vanquished be until
Great Birnam Wood to high Dunsinane Hill
Shall come against him. [*Descends.*]

Macbeth. That will never be.

79–81 How do you think this prophecy will affect Macbeth? E

83–84 Despite the prophecy's apparent promise of safety, Macbeth decides to seek double insurance. The murder of Macduff will give Macbeth a guarantee (**bond**) of his fate and put his fears to rest.

[Stage Direction] Whom or what might the child crowned represent? F

87 issue: child.

88–89 the round and top: the crown.

90–94 The third apparition tells Macbeth to take courage. He cannot be defeated unless Birnam Wood travels the 12-mile distance to Dunsinane Hill, where his castle is located.

Customizing Instruction

Less Proficient Readers

1 Explain to students that visualizing can help them interpret this figure of speech. Ask students to think of someone trying to sleep during a thunderstorm. Ask them to think about what kinds of difficulties the person might have.

Possible Response: The noise of the thunder, the light from the lightning, and fear of injury might keep the person awake.

Who is actually able to sleep under such conditions? Ask them to speculate on the personality attributes that such a person might possess.

Possible Responses: a deep sense of security; courage; a feeling of invincibility.

Have students now paraphrase the passage from "Thou shalt . . ." (line 84) through ". . . in spite of thunder" (line 86).

Possible Response: Macduff will be killed so that I may tell myself that there is nothing to fear and so that I may sleep in spite of the things that now keep me awake.

Students Acquiring English

2 Explain to students that in Western culture, animals are often associated with stereotyped traits. The peacock is associated with pride, the owl with wisdom, the fox with cleverness, and the dog with loyalty. The lion is characteristically associated with courage or bravery. Ask students to give examples of animals and their associated traits from their cultures. Then explain that *mettle* means "quality of character." Ask students what "lion-mettled" means.

Possible Responses: brave; courageous.

Mini Lesson Viewing and Representing

Act 4, Scene 1: Macbeth meets the second apparition (film 1971)

ART APPRECIATION In this still shot from Roman Polanski's *Macbeth,* Jon Finch as Macbeth reacts to the second apparition.

Instruction Act IV, Scene 1 is full of disturbing imagery, and perhaps most disturbing is that of the apparition of a bloody child. Shakespeare includes few stage directions to indicate how an actor is to behave when confronted with a character, comment, or event.

Application Have students examine the still photo above. Ask them how Macbeth appears to react to the second apparition. Do students find it appropriate?

Possible Response: Answers will vary but students should support their opinions with reasons.

Have students draw their own versions of Macbeth reacting to this apparition. Students need not depict Macbeth as he appears in the photo, and the apparition need not be in the drawing.

Reading and Analyzing

Active Reading READING DRAMA

Explain to students that Act Four of most of Shakespeare's plays falls between the rising action of the first three acts and the concluding events of the fifth. As students read, have them keep a log of the significant events of Act Four. When they have finished the act, have them review their logs and ask them whether Act Four is essential to the progress of the play or whether it is a placeholder that merely gives the play its requisite number of acts.

Possible Responses: It is important to the play because Macbeth is still engaging in evil acts and further securing his downfall; it is not essential because all of Macbeth's enemies have been made and his downfall has been assured by the end of Act Three.

GUIDE FOR READING

A Macbeth is probably worried that the witches' first prophecy will come true and Banquo's descendants will occupy the throne.

B Macbeth wants to prove his resolve, and he also wants to make sure that Macduff's immediate family and future descendants can't hurt him.

Who can impress the forest, bid the tree
Unfix his earth-bound root? Sweet bodements, good!
Rebellious dead rise never till the Wood
Of Birnam rise, and our high-placed Macbeth
Shall live the lease of nature, pay his breath
To time and mortal custom. Yet my heart
Throbs to know one thing. Tell me, if your art
Can tell so much—shall Banquo's issue ever
Reign in this kingdom?

All. Seek to know no more.

Macbeth. I will be satisfied. Deny me this,
And an eternal curse fall on you! Let me know.
Why sinks that cauldron? and what noise is this?
[*Hautboys.*]

First Witch. Show!

Second Witch. Show!

Third Witch. Show!

All. Show his eyes, and grieve his heart!
Come like shadows, so depart!

[*A show of eight Kings, the eighth with a glass in his hand, and* Banquo *last.*]

Macbeth. Thou art too like the spirit of Banquo. Down!
Thy crown does sear mine eyeballs. And thy hair,
Thou other gold-bound brow, is like the first.
A third is like the former. Filthy hags!
Why do you show me this? A fourth? Start, eyes!
What, will the line stretch out to the crack of doom?
Another yet? A seventh? I'll see no more.
And yet the eighth appears, who bears a glass
Which shows me many more; and some I see
That twofold balls and treble scepters carry.
Horrible sight! Now I see 'tis true;
For the blood-boltered Banquo smiles upon me
And points at them for his. [Apparitions *descend.*] What?
Is this so?

First Witch. Ay, sir, all this is so. But why
Stands Macbeth thus amazedly?
Come, sisters, cheer we up his sprites
And show the best of our delights.
I'll charm the air to give a sound
While you perform your antic round,
That this great king may kindly say
Our duties did his welcome pay.

95 impress: force into service.

96 bodements: prophecies.

97–100 Rebellious . . . custom: Macbeth boasts that he will never again be troubled by ghosts (**rebellious dead**) and that he will live out his expected life span (**lease of nature**). He believes he will die (**pay his breath**) by natural causes (**mortal custom**).

106 Why . . . this: The cauldron is sinking from sight to make room for the next apparition.

[Stage Direction] **A show . . . :** Macbeth next sees a procession (**show**) of eight kings, the last carrying a mirror (**glass**). According to legend, Fleance escaped to England, where he founded the Stuart family. James I of England, the king when this play was first performed, was the eighth Stuart king, the first to rule over both England and Scotland.

112–124 Macbeth is outraged that all eight kings in the procession look like Banquo. The mirror held by the last one shows a future with many more Banquo look-alikes as kings. The twofold balls and treble scepters pictured in the mirror foretell the union of Scotland and England in 1603, the year that James became king of both realms. Banquo, his hair matted (**boltered**) with blood, claims all the kings as his descendants. What do you think is going through Macbeth's mind? **A**

Teaching Options

Vocabulary Strategy

RESEARCHING WORDS COINED BY SHAKESPEARE

Instruction Tell students that the word *bodements* (line 96) is a word coined by Shakespeare. Inform students that many words now in common usage were first put into print in Shakespeare's works. Tell them that these words are used by English speakers of all walks of life.

Activity Arrange students into small groups, and have them look up the definitions of the words in the following list. For each word, have students list an occupation in which that word would likely be used on a daily basis.

recoil (*Macbeth,* Act Four, Scene 3)
multitudinous (*Macbeth,* Act Two, Scene 2)
dislocate (*King Lear,* Act Four, Scene 2)
accommodation (*Othello,* Act One, Scene 3)

Possible Response: *dislocate*—physical therapist.

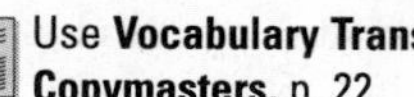

Use **Vocabulary Transparencies and Copymasters,** p. 22.

[*Music. The* Witches *dance, and vanish.*]

Macbeth. Where are they? Gone? Let this pernicious hour
Stand aye accursed in the calendar!
Come in, without there!

[*Enter* Lennox.]

Lennox. What's your Grace's will?

Macbeth. Saw you the Weird Sisters?

Lennox. No, my lord.

Macbeth. Came they not by you?

Lennox. No indeed, my lord.

Macbeth. Infected be the air whereon they ride,
And damned all those that trust them! I did hear
The galloping of horse. Who was't came by?

Lennox. 'Tis two or three, my lord, that bring you word
Macduff is fled to England.

Macbeth. Fled to England?

Lennox. Ay, my good lord.

Macbeth. [*Aside*] Time, thou anticipat'st my dread exploits.
The flighty purpose never is o'ertook
Unless the deed go with it. From this moment
The very firstlings of my heart shall be
The firstlings of my hand. And even now,
1 To crown my thoughts with acts, be it thought and done!
The castle of Macduff I will surprise,
Seize upon Fife, give to the edge o' the sword
His wife, his babes, and all unfortunate souls
That trace him in his line. No boasting like a fool!
This deed I'll do before this purpose cool.
But no more sights!—Where are these gentlemen?
Come, bring me where they are.

[*Exeunt.*]

133–135 pernicious: deadly, destructive; **aye:** always. After the witches vanish, Macbeth hears noises outside the cave and calls out.

144–156 Frustrated in his desire to kill Macduff, Macbeth blames his own hesitation, which gave his enemy time to flee. He concludes that one's plans (**flighty purpose**) are never achieved (**o'ertook**) unless carried out at once. From now on, Macbeth promises, he will act immediately on his impulses (**firstlings of my heart**) and complete (**crown**) his thoughts with acts. He will surprise Macduff's castle at Fife and kill his wife and children. Why does Macbeth decide to kill Macduff's family?

Customizing Instruction

Gifted and Talented

1 Point out that, traditionally, thought and action are only seen as identical in acts of gods, for example, in creating the world. This line can be read as showing the height of Macbeth's arrogance in aspiring to have control over life and death and the history of Scotland.

Students familiar with *Hamlet* might also be asked to compare and contrast the protagonists' approach to action after encounters with ghosts and strange auguries.

Possible Response: Macbeth will crown thoughts with acts, while Hamlet says of his "dull revenge . . . Of thinking too precisely on th' event – / A thought which, quartered, hath but one part wisdom / And ever three parts coward —I do not know / Why yet I live to say, 'This thing's to do . . .'" (Act Four, Scene 4, lines 33, 41–44).

What conclusion can be drawn about the type of character these men possess because of their contrasting actions?

Possible Response: Student responses will vary but should be rooted in the text.

Assessment Informal Assessment

PREDICTING OUTCOME You can informally assess students' understanding of the selection by having them imagine the rest of Act Four and the content of Act Five, including the outcome of Macbeth's plans.

RUBRIC

3 **Full Accomplishment** Student writing reflects full understanding of significance of fate and choice in play and of character of Macbeth.

2 **Substantial Accomplishment** Student writing may not reflect character of Macbeth or may not show understanding of interplay between Macbeth and other forces at work in play.

1 **Little or Partial Accomplishment** Student writing displays little understanding of Macbeth and context in which he acts.

Reading and Analyzing

Reading Skills and Strategies: EVALUATING

A Ask students to decide whether wisdom or fear could have motivated Macduff's departure from Scotland and explain their choice.

Possible Responses: It could stem from wisdom if Macduff thinks it will secure the means to overthrow Macbeth or prevent the murder of his family because Macbeth will leave the family alone and just go after Macduff; it could stem from fear if Macduff is so scared of Macbeth that he abandons his family to save himself.

Literary Analysis: ANALOGY

B Ask students to explain the analogy Lady Macduff is drawing between the wren and Macduff.

Possible Response: Both the wren's and Macduff's families are vulnerable to attack.

Why is the analogy incomplete?

Possible Response: The wren fights to protect its family, but Macduff has fled.

GUIDE FOR READING

C Lady Macduff is grief-stricken to think that her husband would leave her unprotected, and she expresses her feeling of abandonment. Lady Macduff is speaking metaphorically; she means that her husband's absence amounts to death, because she is left alone to raise and defend her family.

SCENE 2

Macduff's castle at Fife.

Ross visits Lady Macduff to assure her of her husband's wisdom and courage. Lady Macduff cannot be comforted, believing that he left out of fear. After Ross leaves she tells her son, who is still loyal to his father, that Macduff was a traitor and is now dead. A messenger warns them to flee but is too late. Murderers sent by Macbeth burst in, killing both wife and son.

[*Enter* Lady Macduff, *her* Son, *and* Ross.]

Lady Macduff. What had he done to make him fly the land?

Ross. You must have patience, madam.

Lady Macduff. He had none.
His flight was madness. When our actions do not,
Our fears do make us traitors.

Ross. You know not
A Whether it was his wisdom or his fear.

Lady Macduff. Wisdom? To leave his wife, to leave his babes,
His mansion, and his titles, in a place
From whence himself does fly? He loves us not,
He wants the natural touch. For the poor wren,
B (The most diminutive of birds) will fight,
Her young ones in her nest, against the owl. 
All is the fear, and nothing is the love,
As little is the wisdom, where the flight
So runs against all reason.

Ross. My dearest coz,
I pray you school yourself. But for your husband,
He is noble, wise, judicious, and best knows
The fits o' the season. I dare not speak much further;
But cruel are the times, when we are traitors
And do not know ourselves; when we hold rumor
From what we fear, yet know not what we fear,
But float upon a wild and violent sea
Each way and move—I take my leave of you.
Shall not be long but I'll be here again. **2**
Things at the worst will cease, or else climb upward
To what they were before.—My pretty cousin,
Blessing upon you!

Lady Macduff. Fathered he is, and yet he's fatherless.

Ross. I am so much a fool, should I stay longer,
It would be my disgrace and your discomfort.

3–4 When our . . . traitors: Macduff's wife is worried that others will think her husband a traitor because his fears made him flee the country (**our fears do make us traitors**), though he was guilty of no wrongdoing.

9 wants the natural touch: lacks the instinct to protect his family.

12–14 All . . . reason: Lady Macduff believes her husband is motivated entirely by fear, not by love of his family. His hasty flight is contrary to reason.

14–15 coz: cousin (a term used for any close relation); **school:** control; **for:** as for.

17 fits o' the season: disorders of the present time.

18–22 But . . . upon you: Ross laments the cruelty of the times that made Macduff flee. In such times, people are treated like traitors for no reason. Their fears make them believe (**hold**) rumors, though they do not know what to fear and drift aimlessly like ships tossed by a tempest.

Teaching Options

Viewing and Representing

Macduff's Castle (film, 1948)

ART APPRECIATION

Instruction Explain to students that plays must be staged differently depending on whether they are being performed live on a stage in a theater or filmed in various locations for a movie. Film directors have more options than stage directors when it comes to setting a scene. Scenes shot outdoors or in real buildings for a film would have a different atmosphere, and perhaps a different meaning, if they were staged in a theater.

Application Based on details in the still photo, have students suggest how the intimacy of the dialogue between Lady Macduff and her son fits or contrasts with the tableau in this particular photograph. Then ask them to describe how they would set this scene. If students wish, they may draw the set rather than describing it. Have students decide whether they are designing for a movie set or a theater stage.

Macduff's Castle (film, 1948)

I take my leave at once. [*Exit.*]

Lady Macduff. Sirrah, your father's dead;
And what will you do now? How will you live?

3 **Son.** As birds do, mother.

Lady Macduff. What, with worms and flies?

Son. With what I get, I mean; and so do they.

Lady Macduff. Poor bird! thou'dst never fear the net nor lime,

28–30 Moved by pity for Macduff's family, Ross is near tears (**my disgrace**). He will leave before he embarrasses himself.

30–31 Why does Lady Macduff tell her son that his father is dead, though the boy heard her discussion with Ross?

Customizing Instruction

Students Acquiring English

1 Point out the irregular syntax in lines 9–11 and show students that "her young ones in her nest" is a dependent clause that interrupts the main phrase describing the wren. Make sure they understand that the wren is not fighting the "young ones in her nest." Have students recast the sentence into a more common sentence structure.

Possible Response: For the poor wren, (the most diminutive of birds) will fight against the owl when her young ones are in her nest.

2 The sentence structure in line 23 might look awkward to some students, because Shakespeare omits a word in order to maintain correct meter. Help students identify the missing word.

Answer: "it" at the beginning of the sentence.

Also point out that *but* in this context means *before.* Help students paraphrase this sentence into more standard English.

Possible Response: It shall not be long before I'll be here again.

Less Proficient Readers

3 Point out that Shakespeare continues to use the bird imagery he began in Lady Macduff's wren metaphor (lines 9–11) with her son's remarks that begin at line 32. Have students consider why Shakespeare might use such imagery with the Macduffs in this scene.

Possible Response: Lady Macduff and her son are birdlike themselves, because their home becomes a cage in which they are trapped by the murderers. And like many birds, they become prey for the larger "animals" that come to kill them. Using animal metaphors also heightens the beastly nature of their murders.

MACBETH: ACT FOUR 389

Reading and Analyzing

Reading Skills and Strategies: EVALUATING

A Ask students what sort of relationship they think Lady Macduff and her son have, judging from their conversation.

Possible Responses: They are comfortable with one another and enjoy joking with each other; the son cheers up Lady Macduff when she is upset.

B Ask students to **compare or contrast** Lady Macduff's mention of "womanly defense" with Lady Macbeth's call of "unsex me" (Act One, Scene 5, line 41).

Possible Responses: Comparison—both women see "female" responses to pressing situations as weak and ineffectual; contrast—Lady Macduff is lamenting that she has no defense against those who might charge her with treason that she did not commit, while Lady Macbeth is expressing her desire to commit treason.

GUIDE FOR READING

C The son admires and loves his father and is quick to defend Macduff's reputation, even against overwhelming odds.

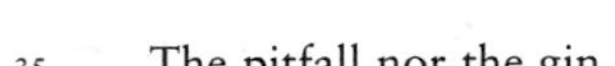

(A) The pitfall nor the gin.

Son. Why should I, mother? Poor birds they are not set for.
My father is not dead, for all your saying.

Lady Macduff. Yes, he is dead. How wilt thou do for a father?

Son. Nay, how will you do for a husband?

Lady Macduff. Why, I can buy me twenty at any market.

Son. Then you'll buy 'em to sell again.

Lady Macduff. Thou speak'st with all thy wit; and yet, i' faith,
With wit enough for thee.

Son. Was my father a traitor, mother?

Lady Macduff. Ay, that he was!

Son. What is a traitor?

Lady Macduff. Why, one that swears, and lies.

Son. And be all traitors that do so?

Lady Macduff. Every one that does so is a traitor and must be hanged.

Son. And must they all be hanged that swear and lie?

Lady Macduff. Every one.

Son. Who must hang them?

Lady Macduff. Why, the honest men.

Son. Then the liars and swearers are fools; for there are liars and swearers enow to beat the honest men and hang up them.

Lady Macduff. Now God help thee, poor monkey! But how wilt thou do for a father?

Son. If he were dead, you'ld weep for him. If you would not, it were a good sign that I should quickly have a new father.

Lady Macduff. Poor prattler, how thou talk'st!

[*Enter a* Messenger.]

Messenger. Bless you, fair dame! I am not to you known,
Though in your state of honor I am perfect.
I doubt some danger does approach you nearly.
If you will take a homely man's advice,
Be not found here. Hence with your little ones!
To fright you thus methinks I am too savage;
To do worse to you were fell cruelty,
Which is too nigh your person. Heaven preserve you!
I dare abide no longer. [*Exit.*]

Lady Macduff. Whither should I fly?
I have done no harm. But I remember now

32–35 The spirited son refuses to be defeated by their bleak situation. He will live as birds do, taking whatever comes his way. His mother responds in kind, calling attention to devices used to catch birds: nets, sticky birdlime (**lime**), snares (**pitfall**), and traps (**gin**).

40–43 Lady Macduff and her son affectionately joke about her ability to find a new husband. She expresses admiration for his intelligence (**with wit enough**).

44–54 Continuing his banter, the son asks if his father is a traitor. Lady Macduff, understandably hurt and confused by her husband's unexplained departure, answers yes.

55–63 Her son points out that traitors outnumber honest men in this troubled time. The mother's terms of affection, *monkey* and *prattler* (childish talker), suggest that his playfulness has won her over.

64–72 The messenger, who knows Lady Macduff is an honorable person (**in your state of honor I am perfect**), delivers a polite but desperate warning, urging her to flee immediately. While he apologizes for scaring her, he warns that she faces a deadly (**fell**) cruelty, one dangerously close (**too nigh**).

Teaching Options

Vocabulary Strategy

USING A DICTIONARY TO DETERMINE WORD USAGE

Instruction Tell students that the word *homely* has a number of meanings. As an adjective, it can mean "belonging to the home or household"; "familiar"; kind; unsophisticated; not beautiful. Reading the *Oxford English Dictionary* entry (the best source for exact meaning of Shakespearean usage) for *homely* clearly identifies the meaning as "unsophisticated" because the line from *Macbeth* is actually quoted there.

Activity Have students make a list of five words from the play, the meanings of which they cannot precisely define. Have them use the *OED* to look up the words, checking for the actual line from the play, but also for the first usage date for each meaning, and the range of meaning. Have them share what they find out with the class.

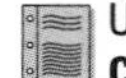

Use **Vocabulary Transparencies and Copymasters,** p. 8.

I am in this earthly world, where to do harm
Is often laudable, to do good sometime
Accounted dangerous folly. Why then, alas,
Do I put up that womanly defense
To say I have done no harm?—What are these faces?

[*Enter* Murderers.]

Murderer. Where is your husband?

Lady Macduff. I hope, in no place so unsanctified
Where such as thou mayst find him.

Murderer. He's a traitor.

Son. Thou liest, thou shag-eared villain!

Murderer. What, you egg!

[*Stabbing him.*]

Young fry of treachery!

Son. He has killed me, mother.
Run away, I pray you! [*Dies.*]

[*Exit* Lady Macduff, *crying "Murder!" followed by* Murderers.]

80 unsanctified: unholy.

82 shag-eared: long-haired. Note how quickly the son reacts to the word *traitor.* How do you think he feels about his father?

83 young fry: small fish.

SCENE 3

England. Before King Edward's palace.

Macduff urges Malcolm to join him in an invasion of Scotland, where the people suffer under Macbeth's harsh rule. Since Malcolm is uncertain of Macduff's motives, he tests him to see what kind of king Macduff would support. Once convinced of Macduff's honesty, Malcolm tells him that he has ten thousand soldiers ready to launch an attack. Ross arrives to tell them that some revolts against Macbeth have already begun. Reluctantly, Ross tells Macduff about the murder of his family. Wild with grief, Macduff vows to confront Macbeth and avenge the murders.

[*Enter* Malcolm *and* Macduff.]

Malcolm. Let us seek out some desolate shade, and there
Weep our sad bosoms empty.

Macduff. Let us rather
Hold fast the mortal sword and, like good men,
Bestride our downfall'n birthdom. Each new morn
New widows howl, new orphans cry, new sorrows
Strike heaven on the face, that it resounds
As if it felt with Scotland and yelled out
Like syllable of dolor.

Customizing Instruction

Students Acquiring English

1 Point out that *you* (and associated forms) and *thou* (and associated forms) both mean "you" as we understand it in modern English. Have students review the usages of these terms in Scene 2 up to page 390 and try to determine the difference in usage. (See, for instance, lines 2, 4, 15, and 39; and 34, 38, 58, and 60.) Help students see that *you* forms are used between adults (Ross and Lady Macduff) and by child to parent (son to Lady Macduff) and seem formal and respectful, while *thou* is used by Lady Macduff to her son and seems to be familiar usage, or the usage between a superior and an inferior. From this we would guess that children would address adults with *you* forms. However, we find that both Lady Macduff and her son address the murderers with *thou* forms. Using this form probably adds to the insult of the son's remark. Even as he kills the son, the murderer uses the *you* form to address him (line 82). Ask students why they think he has used *you* rather than *thou.*
Possible Response: The son is the murderer's social superior, and Shakespeare wanted to emphasize the difference between their social stations.

MACBETH: ACT FOUR 391

Reading and Analyzing

Reading Skills and Strategies: MAKING INFERENCES

A Ask students why Macduff does not answer Malcolm's question in lines 26–28. Have them support their opinions with evidence from the text.
Possible Responses: He feels guilty about his decision; he is insulted by the question because he feels that Malcolm should trust him.

Literary Analysis: THEME

Have students review the list of topics on p. 324. Ask students to list the topics that are touched on in this exchange between Malcolm and Macduff. Have them explain why they chose each topic.
Possible Responses: appearance vs. reality—Malcolm is pretending to be the kind of tyrant that he is not; loyalty—Malcolm is testing Macduff's loyalty to Scotland.

How might these topics relate to the theme of the violation of the natural order?
Possible Response: Tyranny, disloyalty, dissembling all symbolize the overturning of the natural order.

GUIDE FOR READING

B Malcolm's sins will not necessarily be controlled after he becomes king, even though it may be easier for him to indulge his appetites.

Malcolm. What I believe, I'll wail;
What know, believe; and what I can redress,
As I shall find the time to friend, I will.
What you have spoke, it may be so perchance.
This tyrant, whose sole name blisters our tongues,
Was once thought honest; you have loved him well;
He hath not touched you yet. I am young; but something
You may discern of him through me, and wisdom
To offer up a weak, poor, innocent lamb
T' appease an angry god.

Macduff. I am not treacherous.

Malcolm. But Macbeth is.
A good and virtuous nature may recoil
In an imperial charge. But I shall crave your pardon.
That which you are, my thoughts cannot transpose.
Angels are bright still, though the brightest fell.
Though all things foul would wear the brows of grace,
Yet grace must still look so.

Macduff. I have lost my hopes.

Malcolm. Perchance even there where I did find my doubts.
A Why in that rawness left you wife and child,
Those precious motives, those strong knots of love,
Without leave-taking? I pray you,
Let not my jealousies be your dishonors,
But mine own safeties. You may be rightly just,
Whatever I shall think.

Macduff. Bleed, bleed, poor country!
Great tyranny, lay thou thy basis sure,
For goodness dare not check thee! Wear thou thy wrongs;
The title is affeered! Fare thee well, lord.
I would not be the villain that thou think'st
For the whole space that's in the tyrant's grasp
And the rich East to boot.

Malcolm. Be not offended.
I speak not as in absolute fear of you.
I think our country sinks beneath the yoke;
It weeps, it bleeds, and each new day a gash
Is added to her wounds. I think withal
There would be hands uplifted in my right;
And here from gracious England have I offer
Of goodly thousands. But, for all this,
When I shall tread upon the tyrant's head
Or wear it on my sword, yet my poor country
Shall have more vices than it had before,

1–8 In response to Malcolm's depression about Scotland, Macduff advises that they grab a deadly (**mortal**) sword and defend their homeland (**birthdom**). The anguished cries of Macbeth's victims strike heaven and make the skies echo with cries of sorrow (**syllable of dolor**).

8–15 Malcolm will strike back only if the time is right (**as I shall find the time to friend**). Macduff may be honorable (**honest**), but he may be deceiving Malcolm to gain a reward from Macbeth (**something you may discern of him through me**).

18–24 Malcolm further explains the reasons for his suspicions. Even a good person may fall (**recoil**) into wickedness because of a king's command (**imperial charge**). If Macduff is innocent, he will not be harmed by these suspicions, which cannot change (**transpose**) his nature (**that which you are**). Virtue cannot be damaged even by those who fall into evil, like Lucifer (the **brightest** angel), and disguise themselves as virtuous (**wear the brows of grace**).

25–31 Malcolm cannot understand how Macduff could leave his family, a source of inspiration (**motives**) and love, in an unprotected state (**rawness**). He asks him not to be insulted by his suspicions (**jealousies**); Malcolm is guarding his own safety.

34 affered: confirmed.

More suffer and more sundry ways than ever,
By him that shall succeed.

Macduff. What should he be?

Malcolm. It is myself I mean; in whom I know
All the particulars of vice so grafted
That, when they shall be opened, black Macbeth
Will seem as pure as snow, and the poor state
Esteem him as a lamb, being compared
With my confineless harms.

Macduff. Not in the legions
Of horrid hell can come a devil more damned
In evils to top Macbeth.

Malcolm. I grant him bloody,
Luxurious, avaricious, false, deceitful,
Sudden, malicious, smacking of every sin
That has a name. But there's no bottom, none,
In my voluptuousness. Your wives, your daughters,
1 Your matrons, and your maids could not fill up
The cistern of my lust; and my desire
All continent impediments would o'erbear
That did oppose my will. Better Macbeth
Than such an one to reign.

Macduff. Boundless intemperance
In nature is a tyranny. It hath been
The untimely emptying of the happy throne
And fall of many kings. But fear not yet
To take upon you what is yours. You may
Convey your pleasures in a spacious plenty,
And yet seem cold—the time you may so hoodwink.
We have willing dames enough. There cannot be
That vulture in you to devour so many
As will to greatness dedicate themselves,
Finding it so inclined.

Malcolm. With this there grows
In my most ill-composed affection such
A stanchless avarice that, were I King,
I should cut off the nobles for their lands,
Desire his jewels, and this other's house,
And my more-having would be as a sauce
To make me hunger more, that I should forge
Quarrels unjust against the good and loyal,
Destroying them for wealth.

46–49 yet my . . . succeed: To test Macduff's honor and loyalty, Malcolm begins a lengthy description of his own fictitious vices. He suggests that Scotland may suffer more under his rule than under Macbeth's.

50–55 Malcolm says that his own vices are so plentiful and deeply planted (**grafted**) that Macbeth will seem innocent by comparison.

58 luxurious: lustful.

59 sudden: violent; **smacking:** tasting.

61 voluptuousness: lust.

63 cistern: large storage tank.

63–65 His lust is so great that it would overpower (**o'erbear**) all restraining obstacles (**continent impediments**).

66–76 Macduff describes uncontrolled desire (**boundless intemperance**) as a tyrant of human nature that has caused the early (**untimely**) downfall of many kings. When Malcolm is king, however, his lustful appetite (**vulture in you**) can be satisfied by the many women willing to give (**dedicate**) themselves to a king.  Do you think Macduff's prediction is accurate?

76–78 Malcolm adds insatiable greed (**stanchless avarice**) to the list of evils in his disposition (**affection**).

Customizing Instruction

Students Acquiring English

1 Help students differentiate among the words for women used in this scene. *Matron* (line 62) refers to a married woman, while a *maid* (line 62) is unmarried. Here, *dames* (line 73) is used as a general term to refer to all women, regardless of marital status.

Multiple Learning Styles

Visual, Kinesthetic, and Auditory Learners

Have students reread the dialogue between Macduff and Malcolm. Knowing that Malcolm is not truthful, how do students suppose an actor would play this scene? How would Macduff's confusion be realistically conveyed? Have students assign parts for the passage from lines 1–139, practice it, and then present it to the class through video or live performance.

MACBETH: ACT FOUR 393

Reading and Analyzing

Active Reading READING DRAMA

Remind students of the elements of plot: exposition, rising action, climax, and denouement. Ask students at what stage of the plot they are now.
Answer: denouement.

GUIDE FOR READING

A Students might agree with Macduff and think that having inherent virtues, such as mercy and patience, can offset the vice of avarice, because avarice can be satisfied relatively easily with material goods. It's less easy to correct vices that keep you from the "king-becoming graces."

GUIDE FOR READING

B He cannot speak because everything seemed so hopeless only moments before with the thought of such a wicked man being king, and now things are better than he could have hoped.

Literary Analysis: FOIL

C A foil is a character whose personality or actions are in striking contrast to those of another character, allowing an author to highlight a main character's traits. How might Edward the Confessor be a foil to Macbeth?
Possible Response: Edward heals his subjects of a debilitating disease and has the gift of prophecy from heaven; Macbeth has his subjects murdered and must visit evil witches for prophecies.

Macduff. This avarice
Sticks deeper, grows with more pernicious root
Than summer-seeming lust; and it hath been
The sword of our slain kings. Yet do not fear.
Scotland hath foisons to fill up your will
Of your mere own. All these are portable,
With other graces weighed.

Malcolm. But I have none. The king-becoming graces,
As justice, verity, temp'rance, stableness,
Bounty, perseverance, mercy, lowliness,
Devotion, patience, courage, fortitude,
I have no relish of them, but abound
In the division of each several crime,
Acting it many ways. Nay, had I pow'r, I should
Pour the sweet milk of concord into hell,
Uproar the universal peace, confound
All unity on earth.

Macduff. O Scotland, Scotland!

Malcolm. If such a one be fit to govern, speak.
I am as I have spoken.

Macduff. Fit to govern?
No, not to live. O nation miserable,
With an untitled tyrant bloody-scept'red,
When shalt thou see thy wholesome days again,
Since that the truest issue of thy throne
By his own interdiction stands accursed
And does blaspheme his breed? Thy royal father
Was a most sainted king; the queen that bore thee,
1 Oft'ner upon her knees than on her feet,
Died every day she lived. Fare thee well!
These evils thou repeat'st upon thyself
Have banished me from Scotland. O my breast,
Thy hope ends here!

Malcolm. Macduff, this noble passion,
Child of integrity, hath from my soul
Wiped the black scruples, reconciled my thoughts
To thy good truth and honor. Devilish Macbeth
By many of these trains hath sought to win me
Into his power; and modest wisdom plucks me
From over-credulous haste; but God above
Deal between thee and me! for even now
I put myself to thy direction and
Unspeak mine own detraction, here abjure

84–90 Macduff recognizes that greed is a deeper-rooted problem than lust, which passes as quickly as the summer (**summer-seeming**). But the king's property alone (**of your mere own**) offers plenty (**foisons**) to satisfy his desire. Malcolm's vices can be tolerated (**are portable**). Do you think Macduff's position is sensible? **A**

91–95 Malcolm claims that he lacks all the virtues appropriate to a king (**king-becoming graces**). His list of missing virtues includes truthfulness (**verity**), consistency (**stableness**), generosity (**bounty**), humility (**lowliness**), and religious devotion.

102–114 Macduff can see no prospect of relief for Scotland's suffering under a tyrant who has no right to the throne (**untitled**). The rightful heir (**truest issue**), Malcolm, bans himself from the throne (**by his own interdiction**) because of his evil. Malcolm's vices slander his parents (**blaspheme his breed**)—his saintly father and his mother who renounced the world (**died every day**) for the sake of her religion. Since Macduff will not help an evil man to become king, he will not be able to return to Scotland.

Teaching Options

Grammar

MODIFIERS: AVOIDING DOUBLE COMPARISONS

Instruction Adjectives and adverbs have three forms, or degrees: positive, comparative, and superlative.

Activity Write these lines on the chalkboard.

"... Gracious England hath
Lent us good Siward and ten thousand men.
An older and a better soldier none
That Christendom gives out." <396–397>

Point out that *good* describes Siward generally, or in the positive degree, and that *older* and *better* show the comparative degree—a comparison of two things. In the comparative degree, *old* becomes *older,* and *good* becomes *better.* The comparative is usually formed by adding either *–er* or *more/less.*

Superlatives compare more than two things and are formed by adding either *-est* or *most/least.* Point out that double comparisons are incorrect. Either add *-er* or *more/less,* but not both. Tell students that comparatives and superlatives of some words are made with new words (e.g., *good, better, best*), and that these should not get double comparatives either: use *best,* not *more better.*

The taints and blames I laid upon myself
For strangers to my nature. I am yet
Unknown to woman, never was forsworn,
Scarcely have coveted what was mine own,
At no time broke my faith, would not betray
The devil to his fellow, and delight
No less in truth than life. My first false speaking
Was this upon myself. What I am truly,
Is thine and my poor country's to command;
Whither indeed, before thy here-approach,
Old Siward with ten thousand warlike men
Already at a point was setting forth.
Now we'll together; and the chance of goodness
Be like our warranted quarrel! Why are you silent?

Macduff. Such welcome and unwelcome things at once
'Tis hard to reconcile.

[*Enter a* Doctor.]

Malcolm. Well, more anon. Comes the King forth, I pray you?

Doctor. Ay, sir. There are a crew of wretched souls
That stay his cure. Their malady convinces
The great assay of art; but at his touch,
Such sanctity hath heaven given his hand,
They presently amend.

Malcolm. I thank you, doctor.

[*Exit* Doctor.]

Macduff. What's the disease he means?

Malcolm. 'Tis called the evil:
A most miraculous work in this good king,
Which often since my here-remain in England
I have seen him do. How he solicits heaven
Himself best knows; but strangely-visited people,
All swol'n and ulcerous, pitiful to the eye,
The mere despair of surgery, he cures,
Hanging a golden stamp about their necks,
Put on with holy prayers; and 'tis spoken,
To the succeeding royalty he leaves
The healing benediction. With this strange virtue,
He hath a heavenly gift of prophecy,
And sundry blessings hang about his throne
C That speak him full of grace.

[*Enter* Ross.]

114–125 Macduff has finally convinced Malcolm of his honesty. Malcolm explains that his caution (**modest wisdom**) resulted from his fear of Macbeth's tricks. He takes back his accusations against himself (**unspeak mine own detraction**) and renounces (**abjure**) the evils he previously claimed.

133–137 Malcolm already has an army, 10,000 troops belonging to old Siward, the earl of Northumberland. Now that Macduff is an ally, he hopes the battle's result will match the justice of their cause (**warranted quarrel**). Why is Macduff left speechless by Malcolm's revelation? B

141–159 Edward the Confessor, king of England, could reportedly heal the disease of scrofula (**the evil**) by his saintly touch. The doctor describes people who cannot be helped by medicine's best efforts (**the great assay of art**) waiting for the touch of the king's hand. Edward has cured many victims of this disease. Each time, he hangs a gold coin around their necks and offers prayers, a healing ritual that he will teach to his royal descendants (**succeeding royalty**).

Customizing Instruction

Less Proficient Readers

1 Explain to students that "upon her knees" refers to her kneeling in prayer. Ask students what sort of image of Malcolm's mother Macduff is trying to convey with this reference to her prayer habits.

Possible Response: a holy, pious woman.

Exercise Ask students to rewrite each sentence using the correct form of the adjective or adverb. If the form of the modifier is correct, have them write *correct.* Ask students to work in cooperative groups and look through Act 4, Scene 3, for examples of comparative and superlative forms of modifiers.

1. *Macbeth* is possibly Shakespeare's most greatest play. *(greatest, not most greatest)*
2. Her attendant worries that Lady Macbeth seems most disturbed. *(correct)*
3. Macbeth believes that the most worst is over when he sees the three apparitions. *(worst, not most worst)*
4. Malcolm tests Macduff's loyalty by telling him lies about himself—each lie more viler than the last. *(more vile, or viler, not more viler)*
5. Macbeth, in his fight with Macduff, believes that the least probable prophesy is still to be realized. *(correct)*

Use **Grammar Transparencies and Copymasters,** p. 89.

Use McDougal Littell's ***Language Network*** for more instruction and practice in double comparisons.

Reading and Analyzing

Literary Analysis: VERBAL IRONY

A Ask students to explain the irony of Ross's statement.

Possible Response: The literal meaning of the statement is opposite the real meaning, which is that they have not been left alone but have, in fact, been killed.

Reading Skills and Strategies: CONNECTING

B Ask students whether they agree with Malcolm's advice to "give sorrow words."

Possible Response: Yes, it's better to share your grief with someone else whom you trust.

Literary Analysis: DRAMATIC DIALOGUE

C Have students analyze the effect of Macduff's repeated questions.

Possible Response: They emphasize his inability to take in what he is being told.

Reading Skills and Strategies: MAKING INFERENCES

D Explain to students that some critics think this line refers to Malcolm, not Macbeth. Ask them to speculate about what it would mean if it referred to Malcolm.

Possible Response: It could be Macduff's explanation of why Malcolm would, before Macduff has even fully understood the horrible news that Ross is giving him, tell Macduff to "be comforted," which probably seems ludicrous to Macduff at the time.

Macduff. See who comes here.
Malcolm. My countryman; but yet I know him not.
Macduff. My ever gentle cousin, welcome hither.
Malcolm. I know him now. Good God betimes remove
The means that makes us strangers!
Ross. Sir, amen.
Macduff. Stands Scotland where it did?
Ross. Alas, poor country,
Almost afraid to know itself! It cannot
Be called our mother, but our grave; where nothing,
But who knows nothing, is once seen to smile;
Where sighs and groans, and shrieks that rent the air,
Are made, not marked; where violent sorrow seems
A modern ecstasy. The dead man's knell
Is there scarce asked for who; and good men's lives
Expire before the flowers in their caps,
Dying or ere they sicken.
Macduff. O, relation
Too nice, and yet too true!
Malcolm. What's the newest grief?
Ross. That of an hour's age doth hiss the speaker;
Each minute teems a new one.
Macduff. How does my wife?
Ross. Why, well.
Macduff. And all my children?
Ross. Well too.
Macduff. The tyrant has not battered at their peace?
A **Ross.** No, they were well at peace when I did leave 'em.
Macduff. Be not a niggard of your speech. How goes't?
Ross. When I came hither to transport the tidings
Which I have heavily borne, there ran a rumor
Of many worthy fellows that were out;
Which was to my belief witnessed the rather
For that I saw the tyrant's power afoot.
Now is the time of help. Your eye in Scotland
Would create soldiers, make our women fight
To doff their dire distresses.
1 **Malcolm.** Be't their comfort
We are coming thither. Gracious England hath

162–163 Good God . . . strangers: May God remove Macbeth, who is the cause **(means)** of our being strangers.

164–173 Ross describes Scotland's terrible condition. In a land where screams have become so common that they go unnoticed **(are made, not marked)**, violent sorrow becomes a commonplace emotion **(modern ecstasy)**. So many have died that people no longer ask for their names, and good men die before their time.

173–174 relation too nice: news that is too accurate.

175–176 If the news is more than an hour old, listeners hiss at the speaker for being outdated; every minute gives birth to a new grief.

179 well at peace: Ross knows about the murder of Macduff's wife and son, but the news is too terrible to report.

181–188 Notice how Ross avoids the subject of Macduff's family. He mentions the rumors of nobles who are rebelling **(out)** against Macbeth. Ross believes the rumors because he saw Macbeth's troops on the march **(tyrant's power afoot)**. The presence **(eye)** of Malcolm and Macduff in Scotland would help raise soldiers and remove **(doff)** Macbeth's evil **(dire distresses)**.

Teaching Options

Assessment Standardized Test Practice

CHOOSING THE BEST ANSWER For some standardized tests, students will be asked to answer multiple-choice questions. To provide students with some help in working with these questions, read aloud or write on the chalkboard the following question:

What does Malcolm mean when he says, "Ne'er pull your hat upon your brows"?

A. Pay more attention to fashion!
B. Don't be so sad!
C. You're ruining your hat by scrunching it!
D. Do not hide yourself in your grief!

Lead students through the process of choosing the *best* answer. Have them consider each choice. Point out that A is absurd and can be rejected immediately. C is possibly true, but inconsequential considering the situation. B is a possible answer in the situation but doesn't have the force that the situation deserves. D is the best answer.

Lent us good Siward and ten thousand men.
An older and a better soldier none
2 That Christendom gives out.

Ross. Would I could answer
This comfort with the like! But I have words
That would be howled out in the desert air,
Where hearing should not latch them.

Macduff. What concern they?
The general cause? or is it a fee-grief
Due to some single breast?

Ross. No mind that's honest
But in it shares some woe, though the main part
Pertains to you alone.

Macduff. If it be mine,
Keep it not from me, quickly let me have it.

Ross. Let not your ears despise my tongue for ever,
Which shall possess them with the heaviest sound
That ever yet they heard.

Macduff. Humh! I guess at it.

Ross. Your castle is surprised; your wife and babes
Savagely slaughtered. To relate the manner
Were, on the quarry of these murdered deer,
To add the death of you.

Malcolm. Merciful heaven!
What, man! Ne'er pull your hat upon your brows.
B Give sorrow words. The grief that does not speak
Whispers the o'erfraught heart and bids it break.

C

Macduff. My children too?

Ross. Wife, children, servants, all
That could be found.

Macduff. And I must be from thence?
My wife killed too?

Ross. I have said.

Malcolm. Be comforted.
Let's make us med'cines of our great revenge
To cure this deadly grief.

D **Macduff.** He has no children. All my pretty ones?
Did you say all? O hell-kite! All?
What, all my pretty chickens and their dam
At one fell swoop?

194 would: should.

195 latch: catch.

196 fee-grief: private sorrow.

197–198 No mind . . . woe: Every honorable (**honest**) person shares in this sorrow.

205–207 To relate . . . of you: Ross won't add to Macduff's sorrow by telling him how his family was killed. He compares Macduff's dear ones to the piled bodies of killed deer (**quarry**).

209–210 The grief . . . break: Silence will only push an overburdened heart to the breaking point.

212 Macduff laments his absence from the castle.

216–219 He has no children: possibly a reference to Macbeth, who has no children to be killed for revenge. Macduff compares Macbeth to a bird of prey (**hell-kite**) who kills defenseless chickens and their mother.

Customizing Instruction

Less Proficient Readers

1 Point out that, unlike Macduff's remarks in which he calls upon Scotland, this is not an apostrophe to England; rather it is referring to the ruler, King Edward, treating him as England personified.

Students Acquiring English

2 Students may need to be told that *Christendom* refers to all the parts of the world that follow the Christian religion.

MACBETH: ACT FOUR 397

Reading and Analyzing

Literary Analysis: FOIL

Remind students of the definition of *foil* (a character who, by contrast, emphasizes one or more characteristics of another) and have them consider ways in which Macduff is a foil for Macbeth.

Possible Responses: Macduff's chief concern is for Scotland, while Macbeth's chief concern is for himself; Macduff reveres Duncan, whom Macbeth killed.

Reading Skills and Strategies: CLARIFYING

A What is Macduff trying to convey to Malcolm?

Possible Response: The appropriate response to the murder of Macduff's family has two parts—first, the human response of grief and mourning, and second, the demand for revenge—and they must be dealt with in that order.

Literary Analysis: CONFLICT

B Remind students that conflicts can be external (against outside forces) or internal (against oneself). Ask students which kind of conflict Macduff is facing in lines 220–227 and what that conflict is.

Possible Response: internal—he must get through his grief so that he may get to his revenge.

Malcolm. Dispute it like a man.

Macduff. I shall do so;
But I must also feel it as a man.
I cannot but remember such things were
That were most precious to me. Did heaven look on
And would not take their part? Sinful Macduff,
They were all struck for thee! Naught that I am,
Not for their own demerits, but for mine,
Fell slaughter on their souls. Heaven rest them now!

Malcolm. Be this the whetstone of your sword. Let grief
Convert to anger; blunt not the heart, enrage it.

Macduff. O, I could play the woman with mine eyes
And braggart with my tongue! But, gentle heavens,
Cut short all intermission. Front to front
Bring thou this fiend of Scotland and myself.
Within my sword's length set him. If he scape,
Heaven forgive him too!

Malcolm. This tune goes manly.
Come, go we to the King. Our power is ready;
Our lack is nothing but our leave. Macbeth
Is ripe for shaking, and the pow'rs above
Put on their instruments. Receive what cheer you may.
The night is long that never finds the day.

[*Exeunt.*]

225 naught: nothing.

228 whetstone: grindstone used for sharpening.

230–235 O, I could play . . . him too: Macduff won't act like a woman by crying or like a braggart by boasting. He wants no delay (**intermission**) to keep him from face-to-face combat with Macbeth. Macduff ironically swears that if Macbeth escapes, he deserves heaven's mercy.

236–240 Our troops are ready to attack, needing only the king's permission (**our lack is nothing but our leave**). Like a ripe fruit, Macbeth is ready to fall, and heavenly powers are preparing to assist us. The long night of Macbeth's evil will be broken.

Teaching Options

Multicultural Link: Themes Across Cultures

VENGEANCE Vengeance is a common cross-cultural theme in literature. Shakespeare wrote many plays with themes of vengeance—*Romeo and Juliet, Hamlet, Julius Caesar,* and *Othello,* just to name a few. The Bedouin poet Ta`abbata Sharran wrote a "Song of Revenge" for his uncle in pre-Islamic times. The Maori have a special chant form called *kaioraora.* These chants promise terrible revenge and insult the enemy and are accompanied by formalized gestures.

Most societies have institutions designed to prevent (or reduce) the loss of life and property that result from revenge. Among Anglo-Saxon tribes, *wergild,* or blood money, was paid by members of the killer's family to the family of the victim. Blood payment was also common among many Native Americans of the Pacific Northwest. Regulated combat was a substitute for revenge among Australian Aborigines.

Thinking through the LITERATURE

Connect to the Literature

1. **What Do You Think?** Do you have any sympathy for Macbeth at this point in the play? Why or why not?

Comprehension Check
- What three messages does Macbeth receive from the three apparitions?
- What happens to Lady Macduff and her children?
- After learning of his family fate, what does Macduff vow to do?

Think Critically

2. ACTIVE READING | READING DRAMA Envision Act Four, Scene 1, as it might be performed on a stage. Also, review any notes about this scene that you may have recorded in your READER'S NOTEBOOK. What sights and sounds (and perhaps smells) would you expect the **audience** to experience?
3. How would you describe the attitude toward the supernatural expressed in this play?
4. Why do you think Macbeth is so interested in learning about the future?
5. Consider Macduff's reaction to the news of his family's murder. Do you find his behavior realistic? Why or why not?
6. What do you think will happen when Malcolm and Macduff confront Macbeth?

   THINK ABOUT
   - the predictions of the three apparitions
   - the motives of all three men
   - Macduff's pledge to fight Macbeth
7. Do you think Malcolm would make a good king? Why or why not?

Extend Interpretations

8. **Comparing Texts** Recall the views of vengeance, heroism, and kingship expressed in *Beowulf* (page 30). Which **characters** in *Macbeth* would you say are most like Beowulf? Which would you say are more like the monsters? Cite details from the two works as support.
9. **Connect to Life** Consider the methods present-day politicians use to gauge public response to their actions and to shape their policies. On which of these methods might Macbeth rely if he were a leader today?

Literary Analysis

FORESHADOWING One way that writers heighten their audiences' interest is by foreshadowing upcoming events. **Foreshadowing** is a writer's use of hints or clues to suggest what events will occur later in a work.

Activity Create a third column in the chart you've been using to keep track of foreshadowing. In the new column, indicate whether each instance of foreshadowing you have listed has actually hinted at what you thought it did, at least as far as you know at this point in the play.

Act, Scene, Lines	What the Lines Hint At	Accurate?
Act Two, Scene 1, lines 62–64	Macbeth will murder Duncan.	yes

Extend Interpretations

Comparing Texts Possible responses: Macbeth is like Beowulf in his strength; Malcolm is like Beowulf in his concern for his kingdom; Banquo, Malcolm, and Macduff are like Beowulf in their virtue. The Macbeths are like the monsters in their violence and willingness to do evil.

Connect to Life Students might mention public opinion polls, demographic studies, and town-hall meetings, among other predictors.

Literary Analysis

Activity You might have volunteers share their comments about foreshadowing.

GUIDING STUDENT RESPONSE

Connect to the Literature

1. **What Do You Think?**
   Guidelines for student response: Accept all reasonable responses that are supported by evidence from the text.

Comprehension Check
- Macbeth should beware Macduff; no one born of woman can harm Macbeth; and Macbeth will not be defeated until Birnam Wood goes to Dunsinane Hill.
- They are murdered by Macbeth's henchmen.
- avenge their deaths by killing Macbeth; help Malcolm rid Scotland of Macbeth

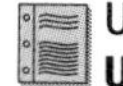
Use Selection Quiz in **Unit Two Resource Book,** p. 29

Think Critically

2. Accept all responses that show a reasonable understanding of the mood. Among other things, students may suggest steam from the boiling cauldron, the *glug-glug* sound of its boiling brew, and perhaps an unpleasant odor emanating from it.
3. Possible Response: The play relies on the assumption that supernatural events have an effect on human lives.
4. Students should support their responses with evidence from the text and/or their experience. Possible Response: The earlier prediction that Banquo's children would rule makes Macbeth eager to know how things will happen so that he can try to reshape events in his favor.
5. Accept all responses that recognize Macduff's deep grief and his desire to avenge the murder of his family.
6. Accept all reasonable responses.
7. Accept all reasonable responses. Students who think he would make a good king may contrast him with Macbeth or may mention his decisiveness, willingness to fight for what is right, willingness to work with others, and/or concern with virtue. Students who think he will not make a good king may mention his hasty flight from Scotland after the murder of Duncan and/or the deviousness of his testing of Macduff.

Reading and Analyzing

GUIDE FOR READING

A She's worried that she might sound treasonous if she reveals that she knows about Lady Macbeth's crimes; if she had witnesses, she would have someone to corroborate her suspicions against the queen.

B She's afraid of the dark and of sleep, because she'll be haunted by her conscience.

View and Compare

What characteristics—costuming, posture, facial expressions—link these images of Lady Macbeth? What qualities set them apart?

Judith Anderson as Lady Macbeth

Francesca Annis as Lady Macbeth (film, 1971)

Isuzu Yamada as Lady Macbeth, *The Throne of Blood* (film, 1957)

Ellen Terry as Lady Macbeth (1889), John Singer Sargent, National Portrait Gallery, London

Teaching Options

Viewing and Representing

ART APPRECIATION

Instruction Akira Kurosawa's 1957 *Throne of Blood (The Castle of the Spider's Web)* is not a translation of Shakespeare's *Macbeth,* but a work inspired by that play. Some consider it, interestingly enough, the finest Shakespearean film ever made. Kurosawa's story is told in the Noh drama style of his home country Japan. The acting is mimelike, with gestures conveying the meaning. Each of the characters in this production has a mask with a frozen expression that represents his or her character. An expressionless face, whitened with makeup, stands for Death itself.

Application Have students make masks to mirror the emotion or character of one of the characters in the play. An extended assignment might call for them to act out a scene using the masks.

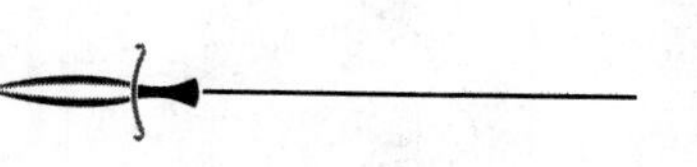

Act 5

SCENE 1

Macbeth's castle at Dunsinane.

A sleepwalking Lady Macbeth is observed by a concerned attendant, or gentlewoman, and a doctor. Lady Macbeth appears to be washing imagined blood from her hands. Her actions and confused speech greatly concern the doctor, and he warns the attendant to keep an eye on Lady Macbeth, fearing that she will harm herself.

[*Enter a* Doctor of Physic *and a* Waiting Gentlewoman.]

Doctor. I have two nights watched with you, but can perceive no truth in your report. When was it she last walked?

Gentlewoman. Since his Majesty went into the field I have seen her rise from her bed, throw her nightgown upon her, unlock her closet, take forth paper, fold it, write upon't, read it, afterwards seal it, and again return to bed; yet all this while in a most fast sleep.

Doctor. A great perturbation in nature, to receive at once the benefit of sleep and do the effects of watching! In this slumb'ry agitation, besides her walking and other actual performances, what (at any time) have you heard her say?

Gentlewoman. That, sir, which I will not report after her.

Doctor. You may to me, and 'tis most meet you should.

Gentlewoman. Neither to you nor any one, having no witness to confirm my speech.

[*Enter* Lady Macbeth, *with a taper.*]

Lo you, here she comes! This is her very guise, and, upon my life, fast asleep! Observe her; stand close.

Doctor. How came she by that light?

Gentlewoman. Why, it stood by her. She has light by her continually. 'Tis her command.

Doctor. You see her eyes are open.

1 **Gentlewoman.** Ay, but their sense is shut.

Doctor. What is it she does now? Look how she rubs her hands.

Gentlewoman. It is an accustomed action with her, to

4 went into the field: went to battle.

9–10 A great . . . of watching: To behave as though awake (**watching**) while sleeping is a sign of a greatly troubled nature.

15 meet: appropriate.

A **16–17** The attendant won't repeat what Lady Macbeth has said, because there are no other witnesses to confirm her report. What is she worried about?

18–19 guise: usual manner; **stand close:** hide yourself.

20 that light: her candle.

B **21–22** Why might Lady Macbeth want a light by her at all times?

TEACHING THE LITERATURE

Customizing Instruction

Less Proficient Readers

Remind students that even in a drama written in blank verse some characters speak in prose, and point out that the gentlewoman and the doctor are two such characters. Ask students why they think these characters speak in prose rather than verse.

Possible Response: They are commoners rather than aristocracy.

Students Acquiring English

1 Help students understand the meaning of "their sense is shut." *Sense* could mean "power of sight" (her eyes are open but she doesn't actually see what or who is in front of her). *Sense* here could also refer to "sense of reason" meaning that her eyes are open but she's acting irrationally and is unaware of what she's doing.

 Use **Spanish Study Guide** for additional support, pp. 76–78.

Gifted and Talented

Lady Macbeth presents a troubling and perhaps pitiful image as she lapses deeper into guilt-induced insanity. Invite students to write an essay comparing the Lady Macbeth of Act Five to the Lady Macbeth of the first four acts. Do they feel sympathy for her or do they feel she's getting what she deserves?

MACBETH: ACT FIVE **401**

Reading and Analyzing

Active Reading DIALOGUE

Remind students that drama depends on dialogue rather than description to convey character, motivation, etc. Ask students what has become of Lady Macbeth's character, judging from the dialogue in Scene 1.

Possible Response: The guilt she feels for her participation in the murders is driving her insane.

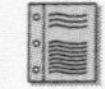 Use **Unit Two Resource Book,** p. 31 for more practice.

Literary Analysis THEME

Have students review the topics listed on p. 324. Ask students which topics are addressed in Scene 1, and why they think so.

Possible Response: reason or mental stability—Lady Macbeth is acting as though she has gone insane.

How might mental instability relate to the theme of the overturning of this natural order?

Possible Response: Reason is unseated from its natural place at the center of human action and morality, reflecting the perversion of natural order.

 Use **Unit Two Resource Book,** p. 32 for more exercises.

GUIDE FOR READING

Ⓐ He now knows that she was involved in causing the deaths of Duncan, the Macduff family, and Banquo.

View and Compare

Which of these portrayals of Lady Macbeth's madness do you find more intriguing?

Diana Rigg as Lady Macbeth, National Theatre, London

Isuzu Yamada as Lady Macbeth in *The Throne of Blood* (film, 1957)

402

Teaching Options

BLOCK SCHEDULING: MANAGING TIME

If your schedule requires that you cover the lesson objectives in a shorter time, use . . .

- Preparing to Read, pp. 323–325
- Thinking Through the Literature, p. 420

If you want to take advantage of longer class time, use . . .

- TE Teaching Options: Viewing and Representing, pp. 403, 410, 413, 418; Cross Curricular Links, p. 408; Speaking and Listening, p. 404; Grammar, p. 406; Multicultural Link, p. 412; Vocabulary Strategy, pp. 414, 415

seem thus washing her hands. I have known her continue in this a quarter of an hour.

Lady Macbeth. Yet here's a spot.

Doctor. Hark, she speaks! I will set down what comes from her, to satisfy my remembrance the more strongly.

Lady Macbeth. Out, damned spot! out, I say! One; two. Why then 'tis time to do't. Hell is murky. Fie, my lord, fie! a soldier, and afeard? What need we fear who knows it, when none can call our pow'r to accompt? Yet who would have thought the old man to have had so much blood in him?

Doctor. Do you mark that?

Lady Macbeth. The Thane of Fife had a wife. Where is she now? What, will these hands ne'er be clean? No more o' that, my lord, no more o' that! You mar all with this starting.

Doctor. Go to, go to! You have known what you should not.

Gentlewoman. She has spoke what she should not, I am sure of that. Heaven knows what she has known.

Lady Macbeth. Here's the smell of the blood still. All the perfumes of Arabia will not sweeten this little hand. Oh, oh, oh!

Doctor. What a sigh is there! The heart is sorely charged.

Gentlewoman. I would not have such a heart in my bosom for the dignity of the whole body.

1 **Doctor.** Well, well, well.

Gentlewoman. Pray God it be, sir.

2 **Doctor.** This disease is beyond my practice. Yet I have known those which have walked in their sleep who have died holily in their beds.

Lady Macbeth. Wash your hands, put on your nightgown, look not so pale! I tell you yet again, Banquo's buried. He cannot come out on's grave.

Doctor. Even so?

Lady Macbeth. To bed, to bed! There's knocking at the gate. Come, come, come, come, give me your hand! What's done cannot be undone. To bed, to bed, to bed!

[*Exit.*]

Doctor. Will she go now to bed?

Gentlewoman. Directly.

32–35 Lady Macbeth refers to hell's darkness, and then she relives how she persuaded her husband to murder Duncan; she had believed that their power would keep them from being held accountable (**accompt**).

39–42 Lady Macbeth shows guilt about Macduff's wife. Then she addresses her husband, as if he were having another ghostly fit (**starting**).

50 sorely charged: heavily burdened.

51–52 The gentlewoman says that she would not want Lady Macbeth's heavy heart in exchange for being queen.

55 practice: skill.

60 on's: of his.

61 What has the doctor learned so far from Lady Macbeth's ramblings?

Customizing Instruction

Less Proficient Readers

1 Point out to students the double understanding of "Well, well, well." The Doctor says it as a kind of filler, expressing his amazement and distress at Lady Macbeth's revelations. The Gentlewoman, however, thinks of the denotative value of the word ("good; "satisfactory") and prays God that all will be "well."

Students Acquiring English

2 Remind students that pronouns were used differently in Shakespeare's time than in ours. The pronoun *which,* which we consider impersonal, is used here to refer to people. Point out that in current usage, we would use *who* in this construction.

Mini Lesson Viewing and Representing

Diana Rigg as Lady Macbeth, National Theatre, London; Isuzu Yamada as Lady Macbeth in *The Throne of Blood* (film, 1957)

ART APPRECIATION

Instruction Point out that the images given here not only are references to two different cultures (Japanese and English) but that they represent two different media (film and stage). Makeup is one theatrical component that would probably change depending on the cultural tradition and medium of production.

Application Have students compare the faces of the two Lady Macbeths in the photos above. Point out how the eyebrows of the Japanese Lady Macbeth have been "moved" and her face whitened to give her a masklike appearance. Instruct students to draw their own pictures of Lady Macbeth as they imagine her in this scene. Tell them to pay particular attention to facial features that should convey Lady Macbeth's state of mind.

Reading and Analyzing

Literary Analysis THEME

A Have students review the list of topics on p. 324. Then, direct students to the Doctor's final comments in lines 67–75. Upon what themes do these topics touch?

Possible Responses: the supernatural with "unnatural troubles"; reason or mental stability with "Infected minds"; loyalty with his willingness not to speak of this event.

Reading Skills and Strategies: REREADING

When students have finished Scene 2, have them reread Act One, Scene 7, lines 47–59. Ask them how Lady Macbeth's attitude toward murder has changed from Act One to Act Five.

Possible Response: In Act One she is remorseless, but in Act Five she is tormented by guilt.

Literary Analysis: STYLE

B The use of symbols and repetition of imagery is an effective part of Shakespeare's style. Direct students to Scene 2, line 17, and then have them look again at Scene 1, lines 40, 47–48, and 58. Ask students to explain the connection between the images in these lines from Scene 1 and the line from Scene 2.

Answer: All deal with unclean hands. Have students look back through the play to find earlier uses of this image.

Possible Responses: Act Two, Scene 2, lines 27, 46–47, 59–65.

Ask students what purpose the repetition of this image serves.

Possible Response: It ties the murders more firmly to their consequences; it provides an easily envisioned symbol of the Macbeths' guilt.

Doctor. Foul whisp'rings are abroad. Unnatural deeds
Do breed unnatural troubles. Infected minds
To their deaf pillows will discharge their secrets.
A More needs she the divine than the physician.
God, God forgive us all! Look after her;
Remove from her the means of all annoyance,
And still keep eyes upon her. So good night.
My mind she has mated, and amazed my sight.
I think, but dare not speak.

Gentlewoman. Good night, good doctor.

[*Exeunt.*]

67 Foul whisp'rings are abroad: Rumors of evil deeds are circulating.

70 She needs a priest more than a doctor.

72 annoyance: injury. The doctor may be worried about the possibility of Lady Macbeth's committing suicide.

74 mated: astonished.

SCENE 2

The country near Dunsinane.

The Scottish rebels, led by Menteith, Caithness, Angus, and Lennox, have come to Birnam Wood to join Malcolm and his English army. They know that Dunsinane has been fortified by a furious and brave Macbeth. They also know that his men neither love nor respect him.

[*Drum and Colors. Enter* Menteith, Caithness, Angus, Lennox, Soldiers.]

Menteith. The English pow'r is near, led on by Malcolm,
His uncle Siward, and the good Macduff.
Revenges burn in them; for their dear causes
Would to the bleeding and the grim alarm
Excite the mortified man.

Angus. Near Birnam Wood
Shall we well meet them; that way are they coming.

Caithness. Who knows if Donalbain be with his brother?

Lennox. For certain, sir, he is not. I have a file
Of all the gentry. There is Siward's son
And many unrough youths that even now
Protest their first of manhood.

Menteith. What does the tyrant?

Caithness. Great Dunsinane he strongly fortifies.
Some say he's mad; others, that lesser hate him,
Do call it valiant fury; but for certain
He cannot buckle his distempered cause
Within the belt of rule.

Angus. Now does he feel
B His secret murders sticking on his hands.

3–5 for their dear . . . man: The cause of Malcolm and Macduff is so deeply felt that a dead (**mortified**) man would respond to their call to arms (**alarm**).

10–11 many . . . manhood: many soldiers who are too young to grow beards (**unrough**)—that is, who have hardly reached manhood.

15–16 Like a man so swollen with disease (**distempered**) that he cannot buckle his belt, Macbeth cannot control his evil actions.

Teaching Options

Speaking and Listening

DRAMATIC READING

Instruction Act Five, Scene 3 is particularly demanding because of the sarcastic humor that characterizes Macbeth's lines and the interruptions, which must be well timed in order to be effective.

Prepare Help students prepare a dramatic presentation of Act 5, Scene 3. Have students consider Macbeth's voice: its tone, pitch, volume, and speed. Discuss what vocal qualities convey sarcasm. Then have them work in cooperative groups of four to take turns playing Macbeth, Servant, Seyton, and the Doctor in order to learn more about conveying sarcastic humor and dramatic interruptions.

Present Student groups can choose their favorite casting and present their interpretation to their classmates.

BLOCK SCHEDULING This activity is particularly well-suited for longer class periods.

Now minutely revolts upbraid his faith-breach.
Those he commands move only in command,
Nothing in love. Now does he feel his title
Hang loose about him, like a giant's robe
Upon a dwarfish thief.

Menteith. Who then shall blame
His pestered senses to recoil and start,
When all that is within him does condemn
Itself for being there?

Caithness. Well, march we on
To give obedience where 'tis truly owed.
Meet we the med'cine of the sickly weal;
And with him pour we in our country's purge
Each drop of us.

Lennox. Or so much as it needs
To dew the sovereign flower and drown the weeds.
Make we our march towards Birnam.

[*Exeunt, marching.*]

18 Every minute, the revolts against Macbeth shame him for his treachery (**faith-breach**).

22–25 Macbeth's troubled nerves (**pestered senses**)—the product of his guilty conscience—have made him jumpy.

25–29 Caithness and the others will give their loyalty to the only help (**med'cine**) for the sick country (**weal**). They are willing to sacrifice their last drop of blood to cleanse (**purge**) Scotland.

29–31 Lennox compares Malcolm to a flower that needs the blood of patriots to water (**dew**) it and drown out weeds like Macbeth.

SCENE 3

Dunsinane. A room in the castle.

Macbeth awaits battle, confident of victory because of what he learned from the witches. After hearing that a huge army is ready to march upon his castle, he expresses bitter regrets about his life. While Macbeth prepares for battle, the doctor reports that he cannot cure Lady Macbeth, whose illness is mental, not physical.

[*Enter* Macbeth, Doctor, *and* Attendants.]

Macbeth. Bring me no more reports. Let them fly all!
Till Birnam Wood remove to Dunsinane,
1 I cannot taint with fear. What's the boy Malcolm?
Was he not born of woman? The spirits that know
All mortal consequences have pronounced me thus:
"Fear not, Macbeth. No man that's born of woman
Shall e'er have power upon thee." Then fly, false thanes,
2 And mingle with the English epicures.
The mind I sway by and the heart I bear
Shall never sag with doubt nor shake with fear.

[*Enter* Servant.]

The devil damn thee black, thou cream-faced loon!
Where got'st thou that goose look?

Servant. There is ten thousand—

Macbeth. Geese, villain?

1 Macbeth wants no more news of thanes who have gone to Malcolm's side.

2–10 Macbeth will not be infected (**taint**) with fear, because the witches (**spirits**), who know all human events (**mortal consequences**), have convinced him that he is invincible. He mocks the self-indulgent English (**English epicures**), then swears that he will never lack confidence.

11–12 **loon:** stupid rascal; **goose look:** look of fear.

Customizing Instruction

Less Proficient Readers

1 Point out that this sentence uses *taint* in an active form where today we would use it in a passive form and say, "I cannot be tainted by fear."

Gifted and Talented

2 Explain to students that eponymous words are words that come from someone's name. Point out that *epicure* is an eponym because it comes from the name of the Greek philosopher Epicurus. Mention some other eponyms, such as the unusual eponym *sideburn* (from General Ambrose Everett Burnside) and *sandwich* (from John Montagu, Earl of Sandwich). Encourage students to be on the lookout for eponyms.

MACBETH: ACT FIVE 405

Reading and Analyzing

GUIDE FOR READING

A Although some students may think that Macbeth probably does share his wife's feelings of guilt because he is able to describe her troubled conscience so well, others may think that his arrogance in this scene belies a sense of guilt.

B Macbeth seems to think there might actually be something the doctor can do to help his wife, which complements the invincible mood he projects.

Literary Analysis: DRAMATIC IRONY

C Ask students how, since we know that this play is a tragedy, this statement (lines 59–60) is an example of dramatic irony.

Possible Response: Macbeth is convinced that he is invincible, but the audience knows that he will be defeated and killed.

Reading Skills and Strategies: MAKING INFERENCES

D Ask students why they think the doctor has such an aversion to Dunsinane. Have them ground their opinions in text evidence and experience.

Possible Response: He has learned of the Macbeths' crimes and is horrified by them; he is not convinced of Macbeth's invincibility and thinks that defeat is inevitable.

Act 5, Scene 3: Orson Welles as Macbeth with Edgar Barrier as the Servant (film, 1948)

Servant. Soldiers, sir.

Macbeth. Go prick thy face and over-red thy fear,
Thou lily-livered boy. What soldiers, patch?
Death of thy soul! Those linen cheeks of thine
Are counselors to fear. What soldiers, whey-face?

Servant. The English force, so please you.

Macbeth. Take thy face hence.

[*Exit* Servant.]

Seyton!—I am sick at heart,
When I behold—Seyton, I say!—This push
Will cheer me ever, or disseat me now.
I have lived long enough. My way of life
Is fallen into the sere, the yellow leaf;
And that which should accompany old age,
As honor, love, obedience, troops of friends,
I must not look to have; but, in their stead,
Curses not loud but deep, mouth-honor, breath,
Which the poor heart would fain deny, and dare not.
Seyton!

[*Enter* Seyton.]

Seyton. What's your gracious pleasure?

Macbeth. What news more?

14–17 Macbeth suggests that the servant cut his face so that blood will hide his cowardice. He repeatedly insults the servant, calling him a coward (**lily-livered**) and a clown (**patch**) and making fun of his white complexion (**linen cheeks, whey-face**).

20–28 This push . . . dare not: The upcoming battle will either make Macbeth secure (**cheer me ever**) or dethrone (**disseat**) him. He bitterly compares his life to a withered (**sere**) leaf. He cannot look forward to old age with friends and honor, but only to curses and empty flattery (**mouth-honor, breath**) from those too timid (**the poor heart**) to tell the truth.

Teaching Options

Mini Lesson Grammar

MODIFIERS: AVOIDING ILLOGICAL COMPARISONS

Instruction A comparison has to be logical to be clearly understood. Write the following on the chalkboard.

> Macbeth, as fierce as any <u>other</u> tyrant England had known, plotted the death of Macduff. Trusting in the prophesy that no man born of woman could kill him, Macbeth believed he was <u>invincible</u>, but his understanding of this prophesy was as mistaken <u>as,</u> if not more mistaken than, his understanding of the prophesy about Birnam Wood.

Point out that one way to make a clear comparison is to use the words *other* or *else* when comparing one member with the rest of the group. Have students read the first sentence with and without the word *other* and decide which makes a clearer comparison.

Ask students to read the second sentence, which contains an absolute. Explain that absolutes, such as *invincible, impossible,* and *unique,* don't

Seyton. All is confirmed, my lord, which was reported.

Macbeth. I'll fight, till from my bones my flesh be hacked.
Give me my armor.

Seyton. 'Tis not needed yet.

Macbeth. I'll put it on.
Send out mo horses, skirr the country round;
Hang those that talk of fear. Give me mine armor.
How does your patient, doctor?

Doctor. Not so sick, my lord,
As she is troubled with thick-coming fancies
That keep her from her rest.

Macbeth. Cure her of that!
Canst thou not minister to a mind diseased,
Pluck from the memory a rooted sorrow,
Raze out the written troubles of the brain,
And with some sweet oblivious antidote
Cleanse the stuffed bosom of that perilous stuff
Which weighs upon the heart?

Doctor. Therein the patient
Must minister to himself.

Macbeth. Throw physic to the dogs, I'll none of it!—
Come, put mine armor on. Give me my staff.
Seyton, send out.—Doctor, the thanes fly from me.—
Come, sir, dispatch.—If thou couldst, doctor, cast
The water of my land, find her disease,
And purge it to a sound and pristine health,
I would applaud thee to the very echo,
That should applaud again.—Pull't off, I say.—
What rhubarb, senna, or what purgative drug,
Would scour these English hence? Hear'st thou of them?

Doctor. Ay, my good lord. Your royal preparation
Makes us hear something.

Macbeth. Bring it after me!
C I will not be afraid of death and bane
Till Birnam Forest come to Dunsinane.

D **Doctor.** [*Aside*] Were I from Dunsinane away and clear,
Profit again should hardly draw me here.

[*Exeunt.*]

35 mo: more; **skirr:** scour.

39–45 Macbeth asks the doctor to remove the sorrow from Lady Macbeth's memory, to erase (**raze out**) the troubles imprinted on her mind, and to relieve her overburdened heart (**stuffed bosom**) of its guilt (**perilous stuff**).

A Do you think Macbeth shares his wife's feelings of guilt?

B **47–56** Macbeth has lost his faith in the ability of medicine (**physic**) to help his wife. As he struggles into his armor, he says that if the doctor could successfully search the kingdom (**cast . . . land**) to find a cure for Lady Macbeth's disease, Macbeth would never stop praising him. What kind of mood is Macbeth in?

58–60 Macbeth leaves for battle, telling Seyton to bring the armor. He declares his fearlessness before death and destruction (**bane**).

Customizing Instruction

Less Proficient Readers

Help students to understand Macbeth's two speeches by telling them the meanings of these words:

- *oblivious* (line 43)—able to make someone forget
- *purge* (line 52)—to remove undesirable things
- *pristine* (line 52)—pure
- *purgative* (line 55)—something that purges
- *rhubarb* (line 55)—a plant that looks like reddish celery and is used as a purgative
- *senna* (line 55)—pods of a plant used as a purgative

have comparative or superlative forms. It is not logical to be *most invincible* or *more unique.*

Exercise Ask students to rewrite each sentence so that the comparison is logical. If the comparison is already logical, have them write *correct.*

1. Shakespeare is considered to be as brilliant a writer as any English writer ever has been. *(. . . as any other English writer . . .)*
2. Most people enjoy reading *Macbeth*—its plot of murder and intrigue is better, or at least as good, as any modern thriller. *(. . . is better than, or at least as good as, . . .)*
3. It is most impossible to judge exactly the influence Shakespeare has had on modern writing. *(It is impossible . . .)*
4. As a villain, Lady Macbeth is almost perfect—she is villainous in her actions and seeks redemption in her dreams. *(correct)*

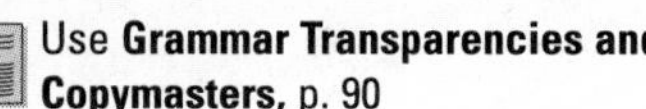

Use **Grammar Transparencies and Copymasters,** p. 90

Use McDougal Littell's ***Language Network*** for more instruction and practice in avoiding illogical comparisons.

Reading and Analyzing

Literary Analysis: DRAMATIC IRONY

A Remind students that dramatic irony has its effect because something is known to one party that is not known to another. Ask them to identify what is ironic about this passage (line 4–7).

Answer: We know that Malcolm and his men are fulfilling the witches' prophecy to Macbeth, but they do not know this.

GUIDE FOR READING

B Students should begin to understand that Malcolm's men are disguised with leaves and branches as they approach Dunsinane, and so the prophecy will be fulfilled even thought the actual forest isn't moving (which is how Macbeth interprets the prophecy).

Active Reading READING DRAMA

C Have students review Characteristics of Tragedy on p. 321, paying special attention to what it has to say about tragic flaw. Then ask them to consider what flaw in Macbeth's character is made manifest in this speech.

Possible Responses: overconfidence; arrogance.

GUIDE FOR READING

D Responses will vary, but students should try to think of their feelings toward Macbeth over the course of the play as they consider their answers.

SCENE 4

The country near Birnam Wood.

The rebels and English forces have met in Birnam Wood. Malcolm orders each soldier to cut tree branches to camouflage himself. In this way Birnam Wood will march upon Dunsinane.

[*Drum and Colors. Enter* Malcolm, Siward, Macduff, Siward's Son, Menteith, Caithness, Angus, Lennox, Ross, *and* Soldiers, *marching.*]

Malcolm. Cousins, I hope the days are near at hand
That chambers will be safe.

Menteith. We doubt it nothing.

Siward. What wood is this before us?

Menteith. The wood of Birnam.

Malcolm. Let every soldier hew him down a bough
A And bear't before him. Thereby shall we shadow
The numbers of our host and make discovery
Err in report of us.

Soldiers. It shall be done.

Siward. We learn no other but the confident tyrant
Keeps still in Dunsinane and will endure
Our setting down before't.

Malcolm. 'Tis his main hope;
For where there is advantage to be given,
Both more and less have given him the revolt;
And none serve with him but constrained things,
Whose hearts are absent too.

Macduff. Let our just censures
Attend the true event, and put we on
Industrious soldiership.

Siward. The time approaches
That will with due decision make us know
What we shall say we have, and what we owe.
Thoughts speculative their unsure hopes relate,
But certain issue strokes must arbitrate;
Towards which advance the war.

[*Exeunt, marching.*]

B **4–7** Malcolm orders his men to cut down tree branches to camouflage themselves. This will conceal (**shadow**) the size of their army and confuse Macbeth's scouts. Consider the prophecy about Birnam Wood. What do you now think the prophecy means?

10 setting down: siege.

10–14 Malcolm says that men of all ranks (**both more and less**) have abandoned Macbeth. Only weak men who have been forced into service remain with him.

14–16 Macduff warns against overconfidence and advises that they attend to the business of fighting.

16–21 Siward says that the approaching battle will decide whether their claims will match what they actually possess (**owe**). Right now, their hopes and expectations are the product of guesswork (**thoughts speculative**); only fighting (**strokes**) can settle (**arbitrate**) the issue.

Teaching Options

History

WARFARE IN THE 11TH CENTURY

In lines 1–3 of Scene 5, Macbeth refers to the "outward walls" and praises his castle's ability to withstand a siege. The 11th century was the time at which the structure recognized as a typical medieval castle came into being. A building with multiple walls, towers at the corners, and a moat, the castle included storage areas for food so that inhabitants were well prepared to outlast a siege.

SCENE 5

Dunsinane. Within the castle.

Convinced of his powers, Macbeth mocks the enemy; his slaughters have left him fearless. News of Lady Macbeth's death stirs little emotion, only a comment on the emptiness of life. However, when a messenger reports that Birnam Wood seems to be moving toward the castle, Macbeth grows agitated. Fearing that the prophecies have deceived him, he decides to leave the castle to fight and die on the battlefield.

[*Enter* Macbeth, Seyton, *and* Soldiers, *with Drum and Colors.*]

Macbeth. Hang out our banners on the outward walls.
The cry is still, "They come!" Our castle's strength
Will laugh a siege to scorn. Here let them lie
Till famine and the ague eat them up.
Were they not forced with those that should be ours,
We might have met them dareful, beard to beard,
And beat them backward home.

[*A cry within of women.*]

What is that noise?

Seyton. It is the cry of women, my good lord. [*Exit.*]

C **Macbeth.** I have almost forgot the taste of fears.
The time has been, my senses would have cooled
To hear a night-shriek, and my fell of hair
Would at a dismal treatise rouse and stir
As life were in't. I have supped full with horrors.
Direness, familiar to my slaughterous thoughts,
Cannot once start me.

[*Enter* Seyton.]

Wherefore was that cry?

Seyton. The Queen, my lord, is dead.

1 **Macbeth.** She should have died hereafter;
There would have been a time for such a word.
Tomorrow, and tomorrow, and tomorrow
Creeps in this petty pace from day to day
To the last syllable of recorded time;
And all our yesterdays have lighted fools
The way to dusty death. Out, out, brief candle!
Life's but a walking shadow, a poor player,
That struts and frets his hour upon the stage
And then is heard no more. It is a tale
Told by an idiot, full of sound and fury,
Signifying nothing.

4 ague: fever.

5–7 Macbeth complains that the attackers have been reinforced (**forced**) by deserters (**those that should be ours**), which has forced him to wait at Dunsinane instead of seeking victory on the battlefield.

9–15 There was a time when a scream in the night would have frozen Macbeth in fear and a terrifying tale (**dismal treatise**) would have made his hair (**fell**) stand on end. But since he has fed on horror (**direness**), it cannot stir (**start**) him anymore.

17–23 Macbeth wishes that his wife had died later (**hereafter**), when he would have had time to mourn her. He is moved to express despair about his own meaningless life: the future promises monotonous repetition (**tomorrow, and tomorrow, and tomorrow**), and the past merely illustrates death's power. He wishes his life could be snuffed out like a candle.

D **24–28** Macbeth compares life to an actor who only briefly plays a part. Life is senseless, like a tale told by a raving idiot. Do you feel sorry for Macbeth here?

Customizing Instruction

Gifted and Talented

1 Point out to students that this speech on the futility of life is made up entirely of figures of speech, chiefly metaphor and personification. Have students write their own speeches on life, expressing their own feelings about it and using vivid figures of speech throughout. Ask students to read their speeches to the class.

MACBETH: ACT FIVE **409**

Reading and Analyzing

Active Reading

SHAKESPEARE'S LANGUAGE

A Draw students' attention to lines 38–41, particularly the word "sooth." Have students use context clues to define this word, which is an archaic term that means "true." Help them understand the analogy implied by the parallel sentence structure—If thou speak'st false :: If thy speech be sooth (that is, "true").

[*Enter a* Messenger.]

Thou com'st to use thy tongue. Thy story quickly!

Messenger. Gracious my lord,
I should report that which I say I saw,
But know not how to do't.

Macbeth. Well, say, sir!

Messenger. As I did stand my watch upon the hill,
I looked toward Birnam, and anon methought
The wood began to move.

Macbeth. Liar and slave!

Messenger. Let me endure your wrath if't be not so.
Within this three mile may you see it coming;
I say, a moving grove.

A

Macbeth. If thou speak'st false,
Upon the next tree shalt thou hang alive,
Till famine cling thee. If thy speech be sooth,
I care not if thou dost for me as much.
I pull in resolution, and begin
To doubt the equivocation of the fiend,
That lies like truth. "Fear not, till Birnam Wood
Do come to Dunsinane!" and now a wood
Comes toward Dunsinane. Arm, arm, and out!
If this which he avouches does appear,
There is nor flying hence nor tarrying here.
I 'gin to be aweary of the sun,
And wish the estate o' the world were now undone.
Ring the alarum bell! Blow wind, come wrack,
At least we'll die with harness on our back!

[*Exeunt.*]

38–52 The messenger's news has dampened Macbeth's determination (**resolution**); Macbeth begins to fear that the witches have tricked him (**to doubt the equivocation of the fiend**). His fear that the messenger tells the truth (**avouches**) makes him decide to confront the enemy instead of staying in his castle. Weary of life, he nevertheless decides to face death and ruin (**wrack**) with his armor (**harness**) on.

SCENE 6

Dunsinane. Before the castle.

Malcolm and the combined forces reach the castle, throw away their camouflage, and prepare for battle.

[*Drum and Colors. Enter* Malcolm, Siward, Macduff, *and their Army, with boughs.*]

1

Malcolm. Now near enough. Your leavy screens throw down
And show like those you are. You, worthy uncle,
Shall with my cousin, your right noble son,
Lead our first battle. Worthy Macduff and we
Shall take upon's what else remains to do,

Teaching Options

Viewing and Representing

Act 5, Scene 6: The attack on Dunsinane Castle (film, 1961)

ART APPRECIATION

Instruction Since students are often fascinated by warfare, the picture on page 411 could be used as a catalyst for research in that area. Have students study the photo and make a list of items they see that are essential to fighting this battle.

Application Students probably will have categories such as armor, weapons, clothing, castle defenses, perhaps even combat strategy. Have students research the components of warfare in 11th-century Europe, using multiple sources, and then sketch their interpretation of the scene depicted in the photograph, appropriate for the time and place. How historically accurate is the photo?

Act 5, Scene 6: The attack on Dunsinane Castle (film, 1961)

According to our order.
Siward. Fare you well.
Do we but find the tyrant's power tonight,
Let us be beaten if we cannot fight.
Macduff. Make all our trumpets speak, give them all breath,
Those clamorous harbingers of blood and death.
[*Exeunt. Alarums continued.*]

1–6 Malcolm commands the troops to put down their branches (**leavy screens**) and gives the battle instructions.

7 power: forces.

10 harbingers: announcers.

SCENE 7

Another part of the battlefield.

Macbeth kills young Siward, which restores his belief that he cannot be killed by any man born of a woman. Meanwhile, Macduff searches for the hated king. Young Siward's father reports that Macbeth's soldiers have surrendered and that many have even joined their attackers.

[*Enter* Macbeth.]

Macbeth. They have tied me to a stake. I cannot fly,
But bearlike I must fight the course. What's he
That was not born of woman? Such a one
Am I to fear, or none.

1–4 Macbeth compares himself to a bear tied to a post (a reference to the sport of bearbaiting, in which a bear was tied to a stake and attacked by dogs).

Customizing Instruction

Students Acquiring English

1 Students may be confused when they see the word *leavy* in line 1. You may want to take this opportunity to point out that we would use *leafy* in current English and to review words in which *f* changes to *v* when a suffix is added and words in which *f* does not change.

MACBETH: ACT FIVE **411**

Reading and Analyzing

Literary Analysis: CONFLICT

A The conflict between Macbeth and Young Siward may seem frivolous to students, since Young Siward is a very minor character. Explain to them that the fight is more important to our feelings about Macbeth than to our feelings about Siward. Ask them how the fight affects their perceptions of Macbeth. What character traits does it bring out?

Possible Response: The conflict brings out Macbeth's arrogance because he still believes himself invincible despite the surprise regarding Birnam Wood.

GUIDE FOR READING

B Responses will vary. Some may think that he should be expecting the revelation of the trick in the prophecy regarding his nemesis who is "not of woman born," because the other prophecies are fulfilled; others may think that he is still managing to cheat death and so should be confident.

Reading Skills and Strategies: PARAPHRASING

C Have students paraphrase lines 14–16 to check comprehension.

Possible Response: The noise is coming from that direction. Don't hide from me, Macbeth! If you are killed by someone else, I will feel that I have not avenged my family, and my guilt will remain with me.

[*Enter* Young Siward.]

Young Siward. What is thy name?

Macbeth. Thou'lt be afraid to hear it.

Young Siward. No; though thou call'st thyself a hotter name
Than any is in hell.

Macbeth. My name's Macbeth.

Young Siward. The devil himself could not pronounce a title
More hateful to mine ear.

Macbeth. No, nor more fearful.

Young Siward. Thou liest, abhorred tyrant! With my sword
I'll prove the lie thou speak'st.

[*Fight, and* Young Siward *slain.*]

Macbeth. Thou wast born of woman.
But swords I smile at, weapons laugh to scorn,
Brandished by man that's of a woman born. [*Exit.*]

[*Alarums. Enter* Macduff.]

Macduff. That way the noise is. Tyrant, show thy face!
If thou beest slain and with no stroke of mine,
My wife and children's ghosts will haunt me still.
I cannot strike at wretched kerns, whose arms
Are hired to bear their staves. Either thou, Macbeth,
Or else my sword with an unbattered edge
I sheathe again undeeded. There thou shouldst be.
By this great clatter one of greatest note
Seems bruited. Let me find him, Fortune!
And more I beg not.

[*Exit. Alarums.*]

[*Enter* Malcolm *and* Siward.]

Siward. This way, my lord. The castle's gently rendered:
The tyrant's people on both sides do fight;
The noble thanes do bravely in the war;
The day almost itself professes yours,
And little is to do.

Malcolm. We have met with foes
That strike beside us.

Siward. Enter, sir, the castle.

[*Exeunt. Alarum.*]

B **11–13** Do you think Macbeth is justified in his confidence?

14–20 Macduff enters alone. He wants to avenge the murders of his wife and children and hopes to find Macbeth before someone else has the chance to kill him. Macduff does not want to fight the miserable hired soldiers (**kerns**), who are armed only with spears (**staves**). If he can't fight Macbeth, Macduff will leave his sword unused (**undeeded**).

20–23 After hearing sounds suggesting that a person of great distinction (**note**) is nearby, Macduff exits in pursuit of Macbeth.

24 gently rendered: surrendered without a fight.

27 You have almost won the day.

28–29 During the battle many of Macbeth's men deserted to Malcolm's army.

Teaching Options

Fate

The concept of fate pervades Western tragedies. In *MacBeth,* fate drives the action of the story, inexorably moving the protagonist toward his or her destruction. Fate is unchangeable; even if steps are taken to avoid it. This concept is derived from Greek mythology, which had the three fates (or Moirai) and their mother, Ananke. These female figures have parallels in other cultures as well. In Germanic mythology, a group of supernatural beings called the Norns wove the fates of human beings. They were often depicted as three young women. The Ajivikas, members of a Hindu sect, also believed that fate (or *niyati*) was unchangeable and that human beings had no control over their own lives.

Not all cultures have such a deterministic view of fate. Among the Ijo peoples of the Niger Delta, God (who is female) allows a person to choose his or her own fate before birth. Most Christian denominations also believe in free will and the ability to control one's future.

View and Compare

Which portrayal of Macbeth's death better captures the mood of the scene as you interpret it?

The fallen Macbeth in *The Throne of Blood* (film, 1957)

Macduff and Macbeth fight (film, 1971)

Customizing Instruction

Students Acquiring English

1 Point out the use of the possessive pronoun *mine* instead of the *my* of contemporary English. Explain to students that in Shakespeare's time, *mine* was used before words beginning with vowel sounds and my was used before words beginning with consonant sounds; today, however, *my* is used before any noun, and *mine* is used only when it stands alone. You may wish to review current rules of usage for pronouns.

Mini Lesson Viewing and Representing

View and Compare

ART APPRECIATION

Instruction Have students examine both photographs above and discuss how meaning is produced differently depending on the characters' postures (one is cramped and cornered; the others are in full movement as they fight) and their facial expressions (one is agonized and almost frantic; the others are focused on their duel). Students should understand that such staging and acting choices are not arbitrarily enacted but are chosen to convey specific interpretations of the text.

Application Point out once again that filmed productions and live performances differ when it comes to making meaning through performance. Explain that even though Macbeth finally dies, we never see that death in Shakespeare's text. Have students consider Macbeth's death, including his fight with Macduff, his death offstage, and Macduff's presentation of the slain king's head, and present their ideas for how to stage this scene. Students need to decide whether they are filming the scene or presenting it live on stage. How does the medium (film or stage) affect how they interpret this part of the play?

Reading and Analyzing

Literary Analysis: CATASTROPHE

Inform students that the resolution of a classic tragic play includes catastrophe, the final action that completes the unraveling of the plot. It is not surprising that the current common use of the word denotes widespread disaster, for in tragedies most of the main characters die. (Remind students of *Romeo and Juliet,* with which they are probably familiar.)

Ask students to explain how Act Five, Scene 8 is catastrophic.

Possible Response: Macbeth is killed in a way that accords with prophecies about him, so Malcolm becomes king, which resolves the plot.

GUIDE FOR READING

A Some students may think that Macbeth still believes he is invincible and so doesn't want to fight and kill Macduff, because he regrets killing Macduff's family.

B Many students will find Macbeth's pride foolish and irrational, although some could see his perseverance as courageous.

C Some students may think old Siward's attitude is practical and appropriate for a soldier; others may find his response cold and dismissive of his son's sacrifice.

SCENE 8

Another part of the battlefield.

Macduff finally hunts down Macbeth, who is reluctant to fight because he has already killed too many Macduffs. The still-proud Macbeth tells his enemy that no man born of a woman can defeat him, only to learn that Macduff was ripped from his mother's womb, thus not born naturally. Rather than face humiliation, Macbeth decides to fight to the death. After their fight takes them elsewhere, the Scottish lords, now in charge of Macbeth's castle, discuss young Siward's noble death. Macduff returns carrying Macbeth's bloody head, proclaiming final victory and declaring Malcolm king of Scotland. The new king thanks his supporters and promises rewards, while asking for God's help to restore order and harmony.

[*Enter* Macbeth.]

Macbeth. Why should I play the Roman fool and die
On mine own sword? Whiles I see lives, the gashes
Do better upon them.

[*Enter* Macduff.]

Macduff. Turn, hellhound, turn!

Macbeth. Of all men else I have avoided thee.
But get thee back! My soul is too much charged
With blood of thine already.

Macduff. I have no words;
My voice is in my sword, thou bloodier villain
Than terms can give thee out!

[*Fight. Alarum.*]

Macbeth. Thou losest labor.
As easy mayst thou the intrenchant air
With thy keen sword impress as make me bleed.
Let fall thy blade on vulnerable crests.
I bear a charmed life, which must not yield
To one of woman born.

Macduff. Despair thy charm!
And let the angel whom thou still hast served
1 Tell thee, Macduff was from his mother's womb
Untimely ripped.

Macbeth. Accursed be that tongue that tells me so,
For it hath cowed my better part of man!
And be these juggling fiends no more believed,
That palter with us in a double sense,

1–3 Macbeth vows to continue fighting, refusing to commit suicide in the style of a defeated Roman general.

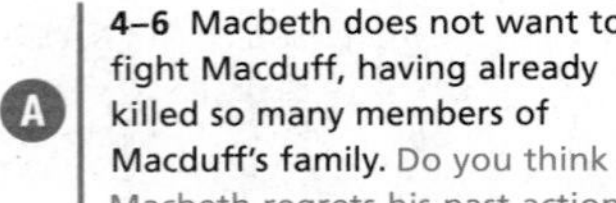

A **4–6** Macbeth does not want to fight Macduff, having already killed so many members of Macduff's family. Do you think Macbeth regrets his past actions?

8–13 Macbeth says that Macduff is wasting his effort. Trying to wound Macbeth is as useless as trying to wound the invulnerable **(intrenchant)** air. Macduff should attack other, more easily injured foes, described in terms of helmets **(crests)**.

15–16 Macduff . . . untimely ripped: Macduff was a premature baby delivered by cesarean section, an operation that removes the child directly from the mother's womb.

18 cowed my better part of man: made my spirit, or soul, fearful.

Teaching Options

Mini Lesson Vocabulary Strategy

USING CONTEXT TO DETERMINE MEANINGS

Instruction Ask students to share their initial interpretation of the witches' words to Macbeth that "no man of woman born" could harm him. Explain to students that while we might see the possibility of the sentence not excluding a woman or child from harming Macbeth, in the Elizabethan usage, *man* meant "person" regardless of gender.

Application Macbeth interpreted the statement to mean that *no one* could harm him because everyone is born of woman. However, technically, the word *born* means "given birth to naturally." Macduff, who was born by a surgical operation known as a cesarean section, was actually not "born" in the one sense, and thus, though a man, was able to fulfill the prophecy.

Use **Vocabulary Transparencies and Copymasters,** p. 23.

That keep the word of promise to our ear
And break it to our hope! I'll not fight with thee!

Macduff. Then yield thee, coward,
And live to be the show and gaze o' the time!
We'll have thee, as our rarer monsters are,
Painted upon a pole, and underwrit
"Here may you see the tyrant."

Macbeth. I will not yield,
To kiss the ground before young Malcolm's feet
And to be baited with the rabble's curse.
Though Birnam Wood be come to Dunsinane,
And thou opposed, being of no woman born,
Yet I will try the last. Before my body
I throw my warlike shield. Lay on, Macduff,
And damned be him that first cries "Hold, enough!"

[*Exeunt fighting. Alarums.*]

[*Retreat and flourish. Enter, with Drum and Colors,* Malcolm, Siward, Ross, Thanes, *and* Soldiers.]

Malcolm. I would the friends we miss were safe arrived.

Siward. Some must go off; and yet, by these I see,
So great a day as this is cheaply bought.

Malcolm. Macduff is missing, and your noble son.

Ross. Your son, my lord, has paid a soldier's debt.
He only lived but till he was a man,
The which no sooner had his prowess confirmed
In the unshrinking station where he fought
But like a man he died.

Siward. Then he is dead?

Ross. Ay, and brought off the field. Your cause of sorrow
Must not be measured by his worth, for then
It hath no end.

Siward. Had he his hurts before?

Ross. Ay, on the front.

Siward. Why then, God's soldier be he!
Had I as many sons as I have hairs,
I would not wish them to a fairer death.
And so his knell is knolled.

Malcolm. He's worth more sorrow,
And that I'll spend for him.

Siward. He's worth no more.
They say he parted well and paid his score,
And so, God be with him! Here comes newer comfort.

19–22 The cheating witches **(juggling fiends)** have tricked him **(palter with us)** with words that have double meanings.

B **23–27** Macduff scornfully tells Macbeth to surrender so that he can become a public spectacle **(the show and gaze o' the time)**. Macbeth's picture will be hung on a pole **(painted upon a pole)** as if he were part of a circus sideshow.

27–34 Macbeth cannot face the shame of surrender and public ridicule. He prefers to fight to the death **(try the last)** against Macduff, even though he knows all hope is gone. What is your opinion of Macbeth's attitude?

[Stage Direction] **Retreat . . . :** The first trumpet call **(retreat)** signals the battle's end. The next one **(flourish)** announces Malcolm's entrance.

36–37 Though some must die **(go off)** in battle, Siward can see that their side does not have many casualties.

44–46 Ross tells old Siward that if he mourns his son according to the boy's value, his sorrow will never end.

46 hurts before: wounds before his battle with Macbeth, which would give further evidence of his courage.

C **50 knell is knolled:** Young Siward's death bell has already rung, meaning there is no need to mourn him further. What do you think of old Siward's refusal to grieve for his son?

Customizing Instruction

Multiple Learning Styles

Visual Learners

Rather than having students write a summary of the action in Scenes 7 and 8, have them create an illustrated account of the conclusion of the play. The account should be drawn over six panels, each one depicting a different portion of the conclusion, in chronological order. Stress accuracy of sequence, not artistic excellence. To keep students referring to the text, you can also have them provide an apropos quote for a caption on each picture.

Gifted and Talented

1 It is unusual that Macduff was born by cesarean section in medieval Scotland. Have students speculate on Shakespeare's motivation for including it as a characteristic for the man who defeated Macbeth.

Possible Responses: It makes possible Macbeth's defeat in compliance with the prophecies of the witches.

Mini Lesson Vocabulary Strategy

DENOTATION AND CONNOTATION

Instruction Remind students that each word has a literal meaning—its denotation—and many have a connotation, or emotional impact, that they carry as well. Tell students that the word *rabble* has many synonyms, including *crowd, mob, gang, group,* and *bunch.* Point out that every synonym has a different shade of meaning, which is related to its connotation.

Activity For each of the synonyms in the preceding paragraph, have students determine the denotative and the connotative meaning. Have them discuss the power of various connotations.

Use **Vocabulary Transparencies and Copymasters,** p. 24.

Reading and Analyzing

Literary Analysis: TRAGIC HERO

Have students review the defining points of a tragic hero given on pp. 321 and 322. Ask them in what ways Macbeth qualifies as a tragic hero.

Possible Response: Macbeth dies miserably, with his wife dead and his hopes dashed; he is a person of great importance, first a thane, then a king; he shows extraordinary qualities in his courage and martial skill, but his pride and ambition lead to his downfall; outside forces—Malcolm, Macduff, Siward, and rebellious Scottish thanes—also contribute to his downfall.

[*Enter* Macduff, *with* Macbeth's *head.*]

Macduff. Hail, King! for so thou art. Behold where stands
The usurper's cursed head. The time is free.
I see thee compassed with thy kingdom's pearl,
That speak my salutation in their minds;
Whose voices I desire aloud with mine—
Hail, King of Scotland!

All. Hail, King of Scotland!

[*Flourish.*]

Malcolm. We shall not spend a large expense of time
Before we reckon with your several loves
And make us even with you. My Thanes and kinsmen,
Henceforth be Earls, the first that ever Scotland
In such an honor named. What's more to do
Which would be planted newly with the time—
As calling home our exiled friends abroad
That fled the snares of watchful tyranny,
Producing forth the cruel ministers
Of this dead butcher and his fiendlike queen,
Who (as 'tis thought) by self and violent hands
Took off her life—this, and what needful else
That calls upon us, by the grace of Grace
We will perform in measure, time, and place.
So thanks to all at once and to each one,
Whom we invite to see us crowned at Scone.

[*Flourish. Exeunt omnes.*]

[Stage Direction] Macduff is probably carrying Macbeth's head on a pole.

55–56 The time . . . pearl: Macduff declares that the age (**time**) is now freed from tyranny. He sees Malcolm surrounded by Scotland's noblest men (**thy kingdom's pearl**).

60–75 Malcolm promises that he will quickly reward his nobles according to the devotion (**several loves**) they have shown. He gives the thanes new titles (**henceforth be Earls**) and declares his intention, as a sign of the new age (**planted newly with the time**), to welcome back the exiles who fled Macbeth's tyranny and his cruel agents (**ministers**). Now that Scotland is free of the butcher Macbeth and his queen, who is reported to have killed herself, Malcolm asks for God's help to restore order and harmony. He concludes by inviting all present to his coronation.

Teaching Options

Viewing and Representing

FILM AND FILM REVIEW

Show one of the films of *Macbeth* that is referred to in the student edition. The *Literature in Performance* video shows excerpts from two film adaptations of *Macbeth*—the version directed by Orson Welles and that produced by the Royal Shakespeare Festival.

Have students locate and analyze reviews of one or both of the films. In a class discussion, have students compare their own reactions to the film with those of the reviewer. Use the Teacher's SourceBook accompanying the video for additional support.

THE MACBETH MURDER MYSTERY

by James Thurber

Preparing to Read

Build Background

Ohio-born author James Thurber (1894–1961) had a long association with the literary magazine *The New Yorker,* to which he contributed not only stories and other humorous pieces but also comical drawings. Thurber, in his writings, often portrayed an average person attempting to function as normally as possible in a perplexing, modern-day world.

Focus Your Reading

ESSAY | HUMOR "The Macbeth Murder Mystery" ridicules certain ideas or customs. As you read, think about what Thurber is making fun of and to what purpose.

"It was a stupid mistake to make," said the American woman I had met at my hotel in the English lake country, "but it was on the counter with the other Penguin books—the little sixpenny ones, you know, with the paper covers—and I supposed of course it was a detective story. All the others were detective stories. I'd read all the others, so I bought this one without really looking at it carefully. You can imagine how mad I was when I found it was Shakespeare." I murmured something sympathetically. "I don't see why the Penguin-books people had to get out Shakespeare's plays in the same size and everything as the detective stories," went on my companion. "I think they have different-colored jackets," I said. "Well, I didn't notice that," she said. "Anyway, I got real comfy in bed that night and all ready to read a good mystery story and here I had 'The Tragedy of Macbeth'—a book for high-school students. Like 'Ivanhoe.'" "Or 'Lorna Doone,'" I said. "Exactly," said the American lady. "And I was just crazy for a good Agatha Christie, or something. Hercule Poirot is my favorite detective." "Is he the rabbity one?" I asked. "Oh, no," said my crime-fiction expert. "He's the Belgian one. You're thinking of Mr. Pinkerton, the one that helps Inspector Bull. He's good, too."

Over her second cup of tea my companion began to tell the plot of a detective story that had fooled her completely—it seems it was the old family doctor all the time. But I cut in on her. "Tell me," I said. "Did you read 'Macbeth'?" "I *had* to read it," she said. "There wasn't a scrap of anything else to read in the whole room." "Did you like it?" I asked. "No, I did not," she said, decisively. "In the first place, I don't think for a moment that Macbeth did it." I looked at her blankly. "Did what?" I asked. "I don't think for a moment that he killed the King," she said. "I don't think the Macbeth woman was mixed up in it, either.

Teach the Literature

Build Background

James Thurber's works include essays, short stories, fables, and children's books. He often depicts middle-class domestic situations. One of his most popular stories is "The Secret Life of Walter Mitty," a story about a confused man who reacts to everyday life by fantasizing about himself in heroic roles. One literary critic compared Thurber's writing favorably to that of Ernest Hemingway, Henry James, and J.D. Salinger.

Thurber was also a prolific cartoonist—he illustrated many of his stories, including "The Macbeth Murder Mystery." Before his drawings caught official attention though, he often filled pads with casual sketches and even drew on the walls of *The New Yorker* offices. One day a co-worker urged Thurber to submit his drawings to the magazine for publication, but he declined. That co-worker later took some of Thurber's discarded drawings to the art editor, who accepted them. One critic complimented his style saying that his cartoon characters "have the outer semblance of unbaked cookies."

Reading: Skills and Strategies
EXAMINING HUMOR

Humor is the quality that makes something seem funny or amusing. Writers can create humor with exaggeration, amusing descriptions, sarcasm, and witty dialogue.

There are three basic types of humor in literature: humor of situation, which is developed from the plot of the story; humor of character, which is based on the quirks of the characters' personalities; and humor of language, which includes the use of sarcasm, exaggeration, or irony. Ask students to identify what kinds of humor Thurber uses in "The Macbeth Murder Mystery."

Possible Responses: Thurber uses humor of character to depict the American woman who disdains Shakespeare for murder-mysteries. Humor of situation and humor of language are evident as Thurber weaves exaggeration and sarcasm in the exchanges between the American woman and the person with whom she is conversing.

READING AND ANALYZING

Literary Analysis: DIALOGUE

A Ask students to explain how Thurber makes this dialogue realistic. Do they find the nonstandard dialogue format, with no indentation for a new speaker, effective? Why or why not?

Possible Responses: He uses a typical grammatical error—*who* instead of *whom*—and an expletive in the narrator's speech; his nonstandard dialogue format is effective because it conveys the quick pace with which the conversation probably happened. However, it's confusing because it's difficult to identify the speaker.

Literary Analysis: HUMOR

B Encourage students to notice the humor of the misapplied criteria. Have students find examples in which the woman continues to apply her rules for solving mysteries to reading the tragedy.

Possible Responses: She explains Banquo's murder as being necessary because he was the first person she suspected, and the first suspect should be the second murder victim; she doesn't suspect Malcolm and Donalbain because their flight looks "too suspicious."

C In order to prevent the "misapplied criteria" humor from getting stale, Thurber applies a new twist. Ask students to identify it.

Possible Response: The narrator now begins to apply the same standards that the woman used and beats her at her own game.

You suspect them the most, of course, but those are the ones that are never guilty—or shouldn't be, anyway." "I'm afraid," I began, "that I—" "But don't you see?" said the American lady. "It would spoil everything if you could figure out right away who did it. Shakespeare was too smart for that. I've read that people never *have* figured out 'Hamlet,' so it isn't likely Shakespeare would have made 'Macbeth' as simple as it seems." I thought this over while I filled my pipe. "Who do you suspect?" I asked, **A** suddenly. "Macduff," she said, promptly. "Good God!" I whispered, softly.

"Oh, Macduff did it, all right," said the murder specialist. "Hercule Poirot would have got him easily." "How did you figure it out?" I demanded. "Well," she said, "I didn't right away. At first I suspected Banquo. And then, of course, he was the second person killed. That was good right in there, that part. The person you suspect of the first murder should always be the second victim." "Is that so?" I murmured. "Oh, yes," said my informant. "They have to keep surprising you. Well, after the second murder I didn't know *who* the killer was for a while." "How about Malcolm and Donalbain, the King's sons?" I asked. "As I remember it, they fled right after the first murder. That looks suspicious." **B** "Too suspicious," said the American lady. "Much too suspicious. When they flee, they're never guilty. You can count on that." "I believe," I said, "I'll have a brandy," and I summoned the waiter. My companion leaned toward me, her eyes bright, her teacup quivering. "Do you know who discovered Duncan's body?" she demanded. I said I was sorry, but I had forgotten. "Macduff discovers it," she said, slipping into the historical present. "Then he comes running downstairs and shouts, 'Confusion has broke open the Lord's anointed temple' and 'Sacrilegious murder has made his masterpiece' and on and on like that." The good lady tapped me on the knee. "All that stuff was *rehearsed*," she said. "You wouldn't say a lot of stuff like that, offhand, would you—if you had found a body?" She fixed me with a glittering eye. "I—" I began. "You're right!" she said. "You wouldn't! Unless you had practiced it in advance. 'My God, there's a body in here!' is what an innocent man would say." She sat back with a confident glare.

I thought for a while. "But what do you make of the Third Murderer?" I asked. "You know, the Third Murderer has puzzled 'Macbeth' scholars for three hundred years." "That's because they never thought of Macduff," said the American lady. "It was Macduff, I'm certain. You couldn't have one of the victims murdered by two ordinary thugs—the murderer always has to be somebody important." "But what about the banquet scene?" I asked, after a moment. "How do you account for Macbeth's guilty actions there, when Banquo's ghost came in and sat in his chair?" The lady leaned forward and tapped me on the knee again. "There wasn't any ghost," she said. "A big, strong man like that doesn't go around seeing ghosts—especially in a brightly lighted banquet hall with dozens of people around. Macbeth was *shielding somebody!*" "Who was he shielding?" I asked. "Mrs. Macbeth, of course," she said. "He thought she did it and he was going to take the rap himself. The husband always does that when the wife is suspected." "But what," I demanded, "about the sleepwalking scene, then?" "The same thing, only the other way around," said my companion. "That time *she* was shielding *him*. She wasn't asleep at all. Do you remember where it says, 'Enter Lady Macbeth with a taper'?" "Yes," I said. "Well, people who walk in their sleep *never carry lights!*" said my fellow-traveler. "They have a second sight. Did you ever hear of a sleepwalker carrying a light?" "No," I said, "I never did." "Well, then, she wasn't asleep. She was acting guilty to shield Macbeth." "I think," I said, "I'll have another brandy," and I called the waiter. When he brought it, I drank it rapidly and rose to go. "I believe," I said, "that you have got hold of something. Would you lend me that 'Macbeth'? I'd like to look it over tonight. I don't feel, somehow, as if I'd ever really read it." "I'll get it for you," she said. "But you'll find that I am right."

Teaching Options

Viewing and Representing

Illustration **by James Thurber**

ART APPRECIATION

Instruction The illustration above is typical of Thurber's style. His cartoonlike sketches, characterized by his use of shape and line, often accompany his stories and essays. Have students identify the lightheartedness of this picture and its elements of exaggeration that are a reflection of those same tones found in the story.

Application Have students draft on paper or use a computer drawing program to create their own cartoon sketches to accompany the "new" *Macbeth* that the American woman and the narrator have created. Students should pick one of the scenes they describe in their revision, perhaps even using an appropriate line from that scene for a caption.

Illustration by James Thurber

"I've found out," I said, triumphantly, "the name of the murderer!"

I read the play over carefully that night, and the next morning, after breakfast, I sought out the American woman. She was on the putting green, and I came up behind her silently and took her arm. She gave an exclamation. "Could I see you alone?" I asked, in a low voice. She nodded cautiously and followed me to a secluded spot. "You've found out something?" she breathed. "I've found out," I said, triumphantly, "the name of the murderer!" "You mean it wasn't Macduff?" she said. "Macduff is as innocent of those murders," I said, "as Macbeth and the Macbeth woman." I opened the copy of the play, which I had with me, and turned to Act II, Scene 2. "Here," I said, "you will see where Lady Macbeth says, 'I laid their daggers ready. He could not miss 'em. Had he not resembled my father as he slept, I had done it.' Do you see?" "No," said the American woman, bluntly, "I don't." "But it's simple!" I exclaimed. "I wonder I didn't see it years ago. The reason Duncan resembled Lady Macbeth's father as he slept is that *it actually was her father!*" "Good God!" breathed my companion, softly. "Lady Macbeth's father killed the King," I said, "and, hearing someone coming, thrust the body under the bed and crawled into the bed himself." "But," said the lady, "you can't have a murderer who only appears in the story once. You can't have that."

"I know that," I said, and I turned to Act II, Scene 4. "It says here, 'Enter Ross with an old Man.' Now, that old man is never identified and it is my contention he was old Mr. Macbeth, whose ambition it was to make his daughter Queen. There you have your motive." "But even then," cried the American lady, "he's still a minor character!" "Not," I said, gleefully, "when you realize that he was also *one of the weird sisters in disguise!*" "You mean one of the three witches?" "Precisely," I said. "Listen to this speech of the old man's. 'On Tuesday last, a falcon towering in her pride of place, was by a mousing owl hawk'd at and kill'd.' Who does that sound like?" "It sounds like the way the three witches talk," said my companion, reluctantly. "Precisely!" I said again. "Well," said the American woman, "maybe you're right, but—" "I'm sure I am," I said. "And do you know what I'm going to do now?" "No," she said. "What?" "Buy a copy of 'Hamlet,'" I said, "and solve *that!*" My companion's eyes brightened. "Then," she said, "you don't think Hamlet did it?" "I am," I said, "absolutely positive he didn't." "But who," she demanded, "do you suspect?" I looked at her cryptically. "Everybody," I said, and disappeared into a small grove of trees as silently as I had come.

Thinking Through the Literature

1. What do you think of the American woman's solution to the centuries-old mystery of the third murderer and her explanation of the sleepwalking scene? Would you say that she has a thorough understanding of *Macbeth?* Explain.
2. What is Thurber poking fun at in his **satire,** and why?
3. **Comparing Texts** Recall murder mysteries you have read or seen on TV and in movies. What characteristics of murder mysteries does the woman's attitude toward *Macbeth* reveal?

Thinking Through the Literature

1. **Possible Response:** Her solution is ludicrous and humorous. No, she treats a great tragedy like a popular murder mystery.
2. Students who feel that Thurber pokes fun at mysteries may say that he is mocking their far-fetched, least-likely-suspect solutions or their tendency to feature formulaic plots. Students who think he pokes fun at *Macbeth* may say that he is mocking the play's excessive violence or Macbeth's melodramatic means of rising to power.
3. **Possible Responses:** their predictability and adherence to formula; their abandonment of character depth and human insight.

Connect to the Literature

1. **What Do You Think?** Guidelines for student response: Accept all reasonable responses that are supported by evidence from the text.

Comprehension Check

- She breaks down mentally; she sleepwalks and expresses feelings of guilt; she dies.
- Macduff does kill Macbeth; he proves to be not of woman born because he was delivered by cesarean section; the boughs of Birnam Wood are used as a disguise by Malcolm's forces, making it seem as though the wood itself is coming to Dunsinane.
- Malcolm

Use Selection Quiz in **Unit Two Resource Book,** p. 33.

Think Critically

2. Once so sure of herself that she mocked Macbeth's guilty conscience and fears, she is driven to madness and suicide by her own guilt.
3. Accept all reasonable responses that show an understanding of the eerie tension of the scene.
4. Possible Response: Things that seem good are evil, and vice versa. For example, the Macbeths think it will be fair or pleasant to be king and queen, but it proves foul.
5. Students who name "fate" may mention the predictions and the supernatural elements behind them. Students who name Macbeth's ambition may say that he has the choice of committing or not committing his crimes.
6. Possible Response: Macbeth is a person of high position with exceptional bravery and battle skill who is flawed by unhealthy ambition and arrogance.
7. Possible Response: Lady Macbeth shares many of her husband's tragically heroic qualities: she is well positioned in society, her courage and devotion to purpose are normally positive characteristics that become warped when used for immoral ends, and she comes to a miserable end. She is, however, a woman, which according to Aristotle immediately disqualifies her from being considered a tragic hero. Some students might also say that she doesn't recognize her tragic flaw or meet her doom with dignity.

Extend Interpretations

Critic's Corner Accept all opinions that students support with evidence from the play.

Connect To Life Accept all reasonable responses. For example, some students may see Lady Macbeth as contemporary in her failing to foresee the consequences of her actions and failing to recognize her own weaknesses.

Literary Analysis

Cooperative Learning Activity Working in groups, students could divide the topics among them and work together on revising their thematic statements and sharing the evidence they found for each theme.

Review Conflict External conflicts include Macbeth vs. Macduff, Macbeth vs. Malcolm, and Macbeth vs. his fate or the supernatural. Internal conflicts include Macbeth's guilt and fears vs. his ambition and lust for power and Macbeth's desire for self-preservation vs. his guilty conscience. Accept any student connections of conflicts to themes that are reasonable and supported by the text.

Connect to the Literature

1. **What Do You Think?** Were you surprised by the outcome of events for the Macbeths? Why or why not?

Comprehension Check

- What happens to Lady Macbeth in Act Five?
- How do the apparitions' three predictions in Act Four come true?
- Who becomes king of Scotland after Macbeth is killed?

Think Critically

2. How does Lady Macbeth change during the play?

- her early ambition
- her remarks in the sleepwalking scene (Act Five, Scene 1)
- the remarks of the doctor and the gentlewoman as they observe her in the scene

3. **ACTIVE READING** **READING DRAMA** Some playwrights use numerous **stage directions,** but Shakespeare does not. Imagine Lady Macbeth's sleepwalking scene as it might appear on a stage. In what type and color of garment might Lady Macbeth be dressed? How might she speak and move? You may want to refer to any notes you have taken about Lady Macbeth in your
4. In the play's opening scene, the witches say "Fair is foul, and foul is fair." How is this **paradox,** or apparent contradiction, manifested in Act Five?
5. Do you think Macbeth's downfall is more a result of fate or of his own ambition? Support your response.
6. Even though Macbeth is a villain, how is he also a **tragic hero?** Review the characteristics of tragedy listed on page 321, and use examples of Macbeth's character traits as support.
7. Do you think Lady Macbeth can be considered a **tragic hero?** Why or why not?

Extend Interpretations

8. **Critic's Corner** In a famous assessment of Shakespeare's plays, the poet and critic Samuel Taylor Coleridge wrote, "The interest in the **plot** is always . . . on account of the **characters,** not vice versa." Do you agree that *Macbeth's* runover from side column ıan its plot? Explain.
9. **Connect to Life** What aspects of *Macbeth* make it relevant to readers and audiences today? Support your answer.

Literary Analysis

THEME A work of literature usually conveys a central idea about life or human nature, called a **theme.** Longer works like *Macbeth* usually contain several themes.

Cooperative Learning Activity Review your notes about the possible themes you discovered as you read *Macbeth*. Then, with a small group of classmates, discuss what ideas the play conveys about the following topics:

- ambition
- appearance versus reality
- fate and our efforts to control it
- impulses and desires
- loyalty
- marriage
- reason and mental stability
- the supernatural

Then write a sentence stating each theme, and cite specific evidence from the play to support it.

REVIEW **CONFLICT** Identify an external conflict in any act of the play. Then find an example of an internal conflict. How does the outcome of each conflict help convey one or more of the play's themes?

The Author's Style

Shakespeare's Poetic Language

Style refers to the particular way in which a work is written. It reflects a writer's unique way of communicating ideas. Shakespeare was a poet as well as a playwright. He is as famous for his powerful poetic language as for his universal themes and keen insight into human behavior.

Key Aspects of Shakespeare's Style

- precise and sometimes lofty diction, or word choice
- coinage of new words (often by using one part of speech as another) and use of words with double meanings
- inversions of word order for poetic effect
- restatements of ideas for emphasis
- vivid imagery and pairs of images that appeal to more than one of the senses
- imaginative figurative language, including personifications, metaphors, similes, and hyperboles

Analysis of Style

At the right are four excerpts from *Macbeth*. Study the list above, and read each excerpt carefully. Then do the following:

A • Identify an example of each aspect of Shakespeare's style in the excerpts. Notice, for example, the two instances of personification in the first line of the second excerpt (sleep's having the ability to knit and care's having a raveled sleeve).

B • Look through the play to find three or four additional examples of Shakespeare's stylistic devices.

C • Try drawing or describing the images in the examples you identified.

Applications

1. Speaking and Listening Share your examples of Shakespeare's stylistic devices by reading them aloud to a small group of classmates. Then discuss how the examples illustrate different aspects of Shakespeare's style.

2. Changing Style Choose a famous soliloquy or another famous passage from *Macbeth*, then rewrite it in informal, contemporary language that expresses the same ideas. Share your rewritten version with classmates.

3. Imitating Style Working with a partner, write an additional scene for *Macbeth*—one that takes place just after the actual end of the play. Try to imitate Shakespeare's style. If humor is your strength, try parodying Shakespeare's style in your new scene.

from **Act One, Scene 5**

. . . Come, thick night,
And pall thee in the dunnest smoke of hell,
That my keen knife see not the wound it makes,
Nor heaven peep through the blanket of the dark
To cry "Hold, hold!". . .

from **Act Two, Scene 2**

Sleep that knits up the raveled sleave of care,
The death of each day's life, sore labor's bath,
Balm of hurt minds, great nature's second course,
Chief nourisher in life's feast.

from **Act Two, Scene 2**

You do unbend your noble strength to think
So brainsickly of things. . . .

from **Act Five, Scene 5**

Tomorrow, and tomorrow, and tomorrow
Creeps in this petty pace from day to day
To the last syllable of recorded time;
And all our yesterdays have lighted fools
The way to dusty death. Out, out, brief candle!
Life's but a walking shadow, a poor player,
That struts and frets his hour upon the stage
And then is heard no more. It is a tale
Told by an idiot, full of sound and fury,
Signifying nothing.

The Author's Style

Analysis of Style

A First activity

diction: the dunnest smoke of hell; To the last syllable of recorded time.

new words: dunnest; nourisher; brainsickly

inverted word order: my keen knife see not; And then is heard no more

restatement: my keen knife see not the wound it makes/Nor heaven peep through the blanket of the dark; sore labor's bath/Balm of hurt minds

vivid imagery: Creeps in this petty pace from day to day; That struts and frets his hour upon the stage; Sleep that knits up the reveled sleave of care

figurative language: That my keen knife see not the wound it makes; Life's but a walking shadow, a poor player

B Second activity

additional examples: Out, damned spot!; He cannot buckle his distempered cause within the belt of rule; [Macbeth and Banquo were dismayed] As sparrows [dismay] eagles, or the hare [dismays] the lion; Where the Norweyan banners flout the sky;

C Third activity

Students should choose 3–4 images to depict.

Applications

1. Speaking and Listening Have students use the following criteria to critique oral interpretation.

- makes and supports a valid interpretation of how the character might voice those lines
- uses voice (volume and tone) to establish mood and convey meaning
- uses movement and gestures to establish mood and convey meaning
- uses facial expressions to establish mood and convey meaning

2. Changing Style Ask students to focus on making the language contemporary as well as keeping the tone consistent with *Macbeth.*

3. Imitating Style Students will have an easier time with the assignment if they spend some time planning the scene, taking into consideration when it takes place, who is present, and how the scene unfolds. Students should also note the Key Aspects box on the page before beginning their assignment.

Choices & CHALLENGES

Writing Options

1. **News Coverage** To make this assignment more challenging, encourage students to include interviews, illustrations with captions, and feature stories to create an entire newspaper.
2. **Modern Version** Students might begin by brainstorming the cultural elements of the play that can be translated into a modern idiom. Remind students that a synopsis carries only the major points and plot developments of a story.
3. **Obituary** Be sensitive to personal experiences that may make this a difficult assignment for students (for example, a recent death among family, friends, or neighbors or an experience with a life-threatening illness or injury).

Activities & Explorations

1. **Actors' Workshop** Students may wish to watch other productions first to get some ideas of possibilities. Encourage students to choose scenes in which parts are fairly evenly distributed. It may be desirable to ask young women who wish to do so to take male parts, or have young men cast as the witches.
2. **Video** Encourage students to create a list of criteria before they compare the two versions. Suggest that they take into account, if possible, the budgets of the different versions.

Inquiry & Research

History In addition to looking for specific information on Macbeth, Duncan, and Banquo, have students make preliminary categories and use general sources to look for background information on the characters. They may pick categories like Scottish royalty, a general history of the Scottish nation, Scotland's historical relationship to England, castles of Scotland like Dunsinane.

Writing Options

1. **News Coverage** Write three or four news articles covering different events in *Macbeth,* such as Duncan's murder, Macbeth's odd behavior after Banquo's death, and Lady Macbeth's mental breakdown.

Writing Handbook
See page 1368: Cause and Effect.

2. **Modern Version** Write a synopsis of a modernized version of the play. Focus on keeping the play's major themes while modernizing its plot, setting, and characters. For example, in what present-day arenas might Macbeth compete for higher status?
3. **Obituary** Write an obituary for one of the victims in *Macbeth.* You might write in the persona of one of the surviving characters.

Activities & Explorations

1. **Actors' Workshop** With a small group of classmates, perform a scene from *Macbeth*. As in Shakespeare's day, keep the scenery simple, but feel free to use props and costumes. Afterwards, discuss how each actor's interpretation of a character helped to shape the performance. ~ **PERFORMING**
2. **Video** View the movie segment of Act One, Scenes 1 and 3, of *Macbeth* and the videotaped play segment from Act One. Then get together with your classmates to compare the presentations. Which depiction of the witches was more interesting? Create a comparison diagram to record your classmates' opinions. ~ **VIEWING AND REPRESENTING**

Literature in Performance

Inquiry & Research

History Research Scottish history to learn about the real figures on whom such characters as Macbeth, Duncan, and Banquo were based. Share your findings in a written report. Put the report in your **Working Portfolio.**

Shakespeare's London Life

Work with a group of classmates to research the London of Shakespeare's day, then present your findings in a special-edition magazine called *London Life.* Your magazine should include illustrations, maps, and articles that provide information about different aspects of London life—for example, religion and politics; theater and literature; science, health, and hygiene; upper-class life; and the London poor. Organize the work equitably, with some group members concentrating on illustrations, others on research, others on writing and editing, and so on.

Primary Sources Investigate editions of letters, diaries, pamphlets, and other writings by people of the time.

Secondary Sources Consult general histories, social histories, and biographies of Shakespeare. Especially useful are books that combine biography and social history, such as Marchette Chute's *Shakespeare of London.* Also consult books on specific subjects, such as the history of the English theater.

World Wide Web Sites Reliable Web sites can provide a wealth of detail, including addresses to which you can write for more information. Consider searching for keywords such as *Shakespeare, Elizabethan society, theater museums,* and *London tourist information.* Also look at the Web sites of English and drama departments at major universities.

More Online: Research Starter
www.mcdougallittell.com

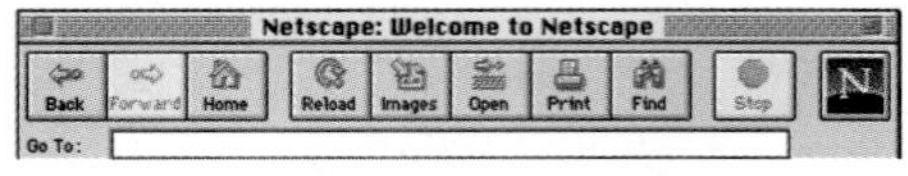

Author Study Project

CREATING A MAGAZINE

Students should be able to evaluate the appropriateness and credibility of their print and electronic sources. Also, remind students that once they have pulled together sources, they should record and organize information in a systematic way. If this project doesn't interest them, perhaps students can choose their own topics.

MULTIMEDIA PROJECT

Students could adapt *London Life* into a video news magazine in which each member of the group could be an expert brought onto the show to discuss different aspects of Elizabethan life. Students could also design a Web page that would illustrate different aspects of life in London.

Writing Workshop Research Report

Exploring a topic in depth . . .

From Reading to Writing As you read *Macbeth,* several questions probably came to mind. Was Macbeth a real person? Was treason a serious threat to the monarch in Shakespeare's day? Did Banquo's descendants ever rule Scotland? Out of these questions you might develop a topic for a **research report.** A research report is an academic paper in which you present information you have gathered and synthesized in exploring a subject. The skills you acquire in writing a research report can help you outside of school, too, whether deciding which brand of a particular product to buy or investigating a college or career.

For Your Portfolio

WRITING PROMPT Write a research report on a literary topic or another topic that intrigues you.

Purpose: To share information and draw a conclusion about your topic

Audience: Your classmates, teacher, or someone who shares your interest in the topic

Basics in a Box

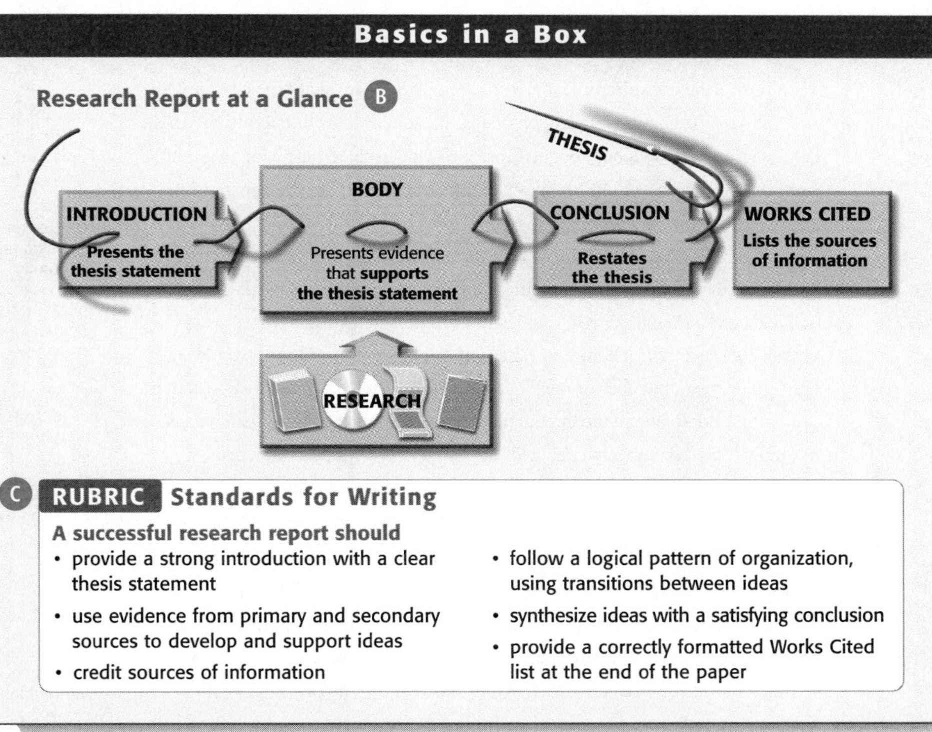

RUBRIC Standards for Writing

A successful research report should

- provide a strong introduction with a clear thesis statement
- use evidence from primary and secondary sources to develop and support ideas
- credit sources of information
- follow a logical pattern of organization, using transitions between ideas
- synthesize ideas with a satisfying conclusion
- provide a correctly formatted Works Cited list at the end of the paper

LESSON RESOURCES

USING PRINT RESOURCES

Unit Two Resource Book
- Prewriting, p. 34
- Peer Response, pp. 36–37
- Revising/Editing, p. 38
- Student Models, pp. 39–44
- Rubric for Evaluation, p. 45

USING MEDIA RESOURCES

LaserLinks
Writing Springboards
See Teacher's SourceBook p. 114 for bar codes.

Writing Coach CD-ROM

Visit our website:
www.mcdougallittell.com

For a complete view of Lesson Resources, see page 273g.

Writing Workshop
Personality Profile

Objectives
- write a Research Report
- use a written text as a model for writing
- revise a draft to build paragraphs
- control verb tenses to correctly show actions in relation to other actions

Introducing the Workshop

A Research Reports
Research reports require the writer to synthesize information from various print and nonprint sources. This skill is useful in many professions such as teaching, law, psychology, science, and business, in which writers must draw on source information to support claims and develop analyses. Citing one's sources is important because it establishes credibility and provides a foundation of factual information upon which to base claims and draw conclusions.

Establish criteria for what makes a claim authoritative. Readers may consider a claim more valid if its source is considered credible. A source should demonstrate expertise, knowledge, credentials, objectivity, and character.

Basics in a Box

B Using the Graphic
Although the writer presents the evidence to support the thesis statement in the body of the research paper, all the parts of the paper—the introduction, body, conclusion, and works cited—must be tied together to create a unified paper.

C Presenting the Rubric
To better understand the assignment, students can refer to the Standards for Writing a Successful Research Report. You may wish to discuss with them the complete rubric, which describes several levels of proficiency.

Use McDougal Littell's ***Language Network,*** Chapter 24, for more instruction on writing a research report.

To engage students visually, use **Power Presentation** 3, Research Report.

Teaching the Lesson

Analyzing the Model

"The Gunpowder Plot of 1605 and Macbeth"

D The student model begins with a factual retelling of the events, motives, and outcome of The Gunpowder Plot.

Explain that although the primary subject of this paper is *Macbeth*, a literary text, the writer begins with intriguing historical facts. Ask students why the writer would choose to open the paper this way.
Possible Response: In addition to grabbing the reader's immediate attention, this introduction provides background information on the Gunpowder Plot. Readers will need that historical information in order to understand references to the Gunpowder Plot in *Macbeth.*

Students can take turns reading aloud the Rubric in Action. Point out the key words and phrases in the student model that correspond to the elements mentioned in the Rubric in Action.

1 Have students suggest an alternative introduction based on the other options given. Discuss pros or cons of each alternative.
2 Discuss whether the purpose of this thesis statement is to inform.
Possible Responses: Its primary purpose is to inform and, to a lesser degree, persuade.
3 In an extended paper such as this, it is important to provide readers with structural clues indicating relationships between parts. Ask students how this transitional sentence serves to connect the two topics.
Possible Response: The words *"in order to understand"* indicate that the historical background must be established before the larger claims can be demonstrated.

Analyzing a Student Model

Tom Mendozza
Ms. Forrest
English IV
May 15

Mendozza 1

The Gunpowder Plot of 1605 and Macbeth

On the night of November 4, 1605, an Englishman named Guy Fawkes was found with 36 barrels of gunpowder in a cellar beneath the palace of Westminster (Nicholls 8–9). His intention was to blow up King James I, along with the queen, their eldest son Henry, and the House of Lords during the opening session of Parliament the very next day. Before Fawkes could carry out this plan, he was captured and interrogated by the English government. Under torture, Fawkes revealed that he was part of a conspiracy of English Catholics to murder the king and restore Catholicism to England. This conspiracy came to be known as The Gunpowder Plot (Fraser, Faith and Treason 189).

The attempted assassination of King James and the subsequent trials and executions of the conspirators were widely publicized in Shakespeare's day (Wills 15–19). It is in this highly charged atmosphere of political intrigue that Shakespeare's play Macbeth opened in 1606. Shakespeare was well aware of these political goings-on. In Macbeth, he makes reference to the events of the Gunpowder Plot to add drama to his play.

In order to understand these references in Macbeth, it is first necessary to be aware of the details surrounding the Gunpowder Plot. According to official sources at the time, King James himself helped avert the tragedy. On October 26, several days before the attempted assassination was to take place, Lord Monteagle, a member of the House of Lords, received an anonymous letter warning him not to attend the upcoming session of Parliament. The letter stated that "though there be no appearance of any stir, yet I say they shall receive a terrible blow this Parliament; and yet they shall not see who hurts them" (Faith 150). Monteagle took the letter to Robert Cecil, the chief minister to King James. Cecil did not immediately show the letter to the king, who was away on a hunting expedition at the time. On November 1, the day after King James returned from hunting, Cecil gave Monteagle's letter to the king. James suspected that the warning referred to an explosion because his own father was killed in a plot involving gunpowder (Faith 161; King James 19).

RUBRIC IN ACTION

1 This writer begins with an engaging fact to capture the reader's attention.
Other Options:
- Begin with an intriguing question
- Start with a quotation

2 Presents the thesis statement

3 Uses a transitional sentence between paragraphs to connect ideas

4 This writer uses a direct quotation to support an idea.
Other Options:
- Paraphrase a quotation
- Summarize the information

5 Credits the sources of information

Viewing and Representing

CREATING A FLOW CHART

Writing a research report is a complex process that involves specific stages. Students will probably be more successful if they complete the project in stages, following a systematic plan.

A flow chart is a good tool for organizing a complex writing task.

Have students create a flow chart that includes space for describing each task to be completed, a due date for completion, and a place to check off when the task has been completed. As they read further, a sample flow chart might follow this setup:

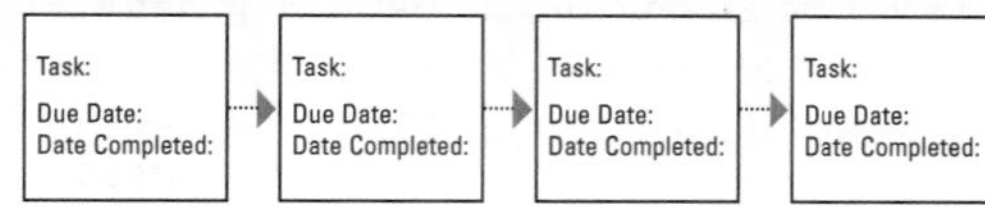

Mendozza 2

On the night of November 4, the king's officials searched the building of Parliament and noticed an unusually large pile of firewood in a storehouse beneath the House of Lords. They reported their findings to the king, who ordered a second, more thorough search. This time the king's officials uncovered the gunpowder and apprehended Guy Fawkes, who was found lurking on the premises. At first, Fawkes gave his name as John Johnson, but after days of interrogation by the English government, he revealed his true identity and eventually named his fellow conspirators (Nicholls 8–9; Parkinson 75–76).

One connection to the Gunpowder Plot and Macbeth involves the use of

> **6** This writer presents information chronologically.
>
> **Another Option:**
> - Arrange ideas by order of importance

Mendozza 13

Works Cited

Boot, Jeremy. Gunpowder Plot: High Treason in 1605. 16 May 1998 <http://www.innotts.co.uk/~asperges/fawkes/>.

Fraser, Antonia. Faith and Treason: The Story of the Gunpowder Plot. New York: Doubleday, 1996.

Fraser, Antonia. King James VI of Scotland, I of England. New York: Knopf, 1974.

Greaves, Richard L. "Gunpowder Plot." The World Book Encyclopedia. 1996 ed.

Greenblatt, Stephen. "Toil and Trouble." New Republic 14 Nov. 1994: 32-37.

"Gunpowder Plot." Britannica Online. Vers. 98.2 Apr. 1998. Encyclopaedia Britannica. 16 May 1998 <http://www.eb.com:180>.

Nicholls, Mark. Investigating Gunpowder Plot. Manchester, England: Manchester UP, 1991.

Parkinson, C. Northcote. Gunpowder, Treason and Plot. New York: St. Martin's, 1976.

Wills, Garry. Witches and Jesuits: Shakespeare's Macbeth. New York: Oxford UP, 1995.

> **Works Cited**
> - Identifies sources of information used in researching a paper
> - Alphabetizes entries by author's last name
> - Lists complete publication information
> - Punctuates entries correctly
> - Follows a preferred style

Need help with Works Cited?

See page 1376 in the **Writing Handbook**.

4 Ask students what is gained here by using a direct quotation rather than a summary or paraphrase.
Possible Response: It involves the reader in the immediate action in a way that a paraphrase cannot. The letter also hints at the impending disaster to come.

5 Have students map the in-text citation to the Works Cited list to see how the two are coordinated.

6 Have students list key words that indicate chronological order.
Possible Response: Key words include: *On the night of, This time, At first, but after days, and eventually.*

Works Cited Explain that each entry has three parts—author information, title information, and publication information—and that each part ends with a period.

Works Cited Tip

The 4th edition of the *MLA Handbook for Writers of Research Papers* was used in preparing the print citations that appear on the Works Cited page. Information on how to cite Internet sources came from the MLA online-site at www.mla.org/set_stl.htm. With regard to citing Internet sources, the MLA site differs somewhat from their guidelines in the 4th edition of the *MLA Handbook.*

WRITING WORKSHOP 425

Guiding Student Writing

Prewriting

Choosing a Subject

If after reading the Idea Bank students are having difficulty choosing their subjects, suggest they try the following:

- Read recent newspapers and news magazines looking for problems or controversies in world events. A "problem-solution" essay can be a good form for a research report.
- Explain to students that a question is usually the foundation of a research report. That is, the writer conducts research for the purpose of answering a question.

Planning the Research Report

2. Students may need to conduct a preliminary search in books or on the Internet to see if their topic is too broad. Looking at tables of contents and indexes can provide tips on how a topic can be divided into a smaller part.
5. Have each student write his or her controlling purpose on a 3 X 5 card and tape it in a prominent place. This visual reminder will help students stay focused. Remind students that as they discover new aspects of the topic through research, their purpose may change. They should remain flexible and open to new ideas.

Researching

Students should not feel limited by the library. Encourage them to seek out interviews or use television and radio programs as a source of information. The Internet also provides unique sources; however, students must first determine whether a source on the Internet is reliable before they use the information in their report.

Research Tip:

You might suggest that students review the table of contents and the index of each book they find on their topic. The table of contents and the index can direct students toward useful sections of the book.

IDEABank

1. Your Working Portfolio
Build on the Inquiry & Research activity you completed earlier in this unit:
- **History,** p. 422

2. Reading Literature
What authors or literary works made a strong impression on you? Are you drawn to certain writers or the subjects they address? Choose one as a starting point for your research.

3. Surfing the Net
Browse the Internet for topics that interest you. Explore frequently visited sites or do a subject search using various search engines. Choose one topic and explore it further.

Writing Your Research Report

Writing, like life itself, is a voyage of discovery.
Henry Miller

1 Prewriting and Exploring

To explore topics, you might begin by looking through the magazine section of the library. Skim several periodicals and jot down interesting subjects. Think of movies you've seen or books you've read. Generate a list of interesting and researchable questions. As you read and write about a topic, you will understand it better. See the **Idea Bank** in the margin for further suggestions on finding a topic.

The steps below will help you choose and narrow your topic and define your goal.

Planning Your Research Report

1. **Choose a topic.** What topic appeals to you most? What would you like to learn about it? You might make a cluster map with a general topic area in the center. Connect related ideas with lines and circles radiating outward.

air traffic controllers
new airports
aviation
accidents
aircraft noise

2. **Narrow your topic.** Is your topic too broad to cover in the research report you plan to write? How can you divide it into smaller subtopics? You may need to do some preliminary research as you narrow your topic.
3. **Set your goal.** What do you want your writing to accomplish? Do you want simply to learn more about your subject, to prove a point, or to elicit a strong response from your audience?
4. **Identify your purpose.** Will your main purpose be to inform, to examine cause and effect, to compare and contrast, to analyze, or a combination of these?
5. **Write a statement of controlling purpose.** What will you focus on in your paper? Your controlling purpose will guide your research and give you direction as you work. Your controlling purpose should be flexible, so you can revise it as you continue your research.

ResearchTIP

Use primary sources when they are available and easy to read. **Use secondary sources** to explain difficult or hard-to-read material from primary sources.

2 Researching

Research is the process of gathering information on a topic from reliable sources. The best place to begin your search for reliable information is the library. Consider making a list of questions about your topic that will help to guide your research. The information you find will either be in primary or secondary sources. **Primary sources** furnish eyewitness accounts of events. Primary sources include letters, journals, diaries, and historical documents. **Secondary sources** present information that is derived or compiled from other sources. Encyclopedias, many books, newspapers, and magazine articles are examples of secondary sources.

Evaluate Your Sources

Some sources of information are better than others. Use these guidelines to evaluate your sources.

- **To what extent is the author's viewpoint biased**—that is, influenced by his or her political position, gender, or ethnic background? Be sure to read material from a variety of viewpoints.
- **Is the source up-to-date?** Certain fields such as science, technology, and medicine change rapidly. Use recent information when researching these fields.
- **Is the source reliable?** Supermarket tabloid newspapers, for example, are not reliable sources of information.
- **What is the intended audience?** Is the source written for young people, for the general public, or for experts in a particular field?

Internet Tip

Not all sites on the Internet are reliable. Evaluate information found on the Internet as you would print material. Generally, information from a government agency (.gov) or an educational institution (.edu) will be reputable. Material posted to someone's personal web page may or may not be reliable.

Make Source Cards

When you have found information that is relevant to your topic, you will need to make source cards. Use index cards, like those at the right, to record publishing information for each source you decide to use. Follow the format for each type of source card. Number each source card and refer to it when you take notes. You will use these source cards to credit sources in your report and to write your Works Cited page.

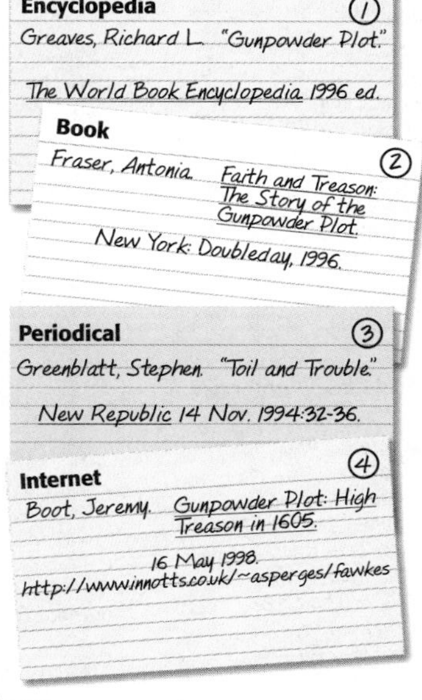

Take Notes

Keeping your controlling purpose in mind, take notes on pertinent information. Use a separate index card for each piece of information and write the number of the source on each note card. You need not document general knowledge—that is, information that is widely known and that your readers would not question. The example below shows ways of noting information.

Paraphrase. Restate the material in your own words. Paraphrasing is a good choice when your notes need to be detailed.

Source Number.

Quotation. Copy the original text word for word, including all punctuation. Use quotations marks to indicate the beginning and end of the quotation. Use this form to emphasize a point or when the author's words are well phrased.

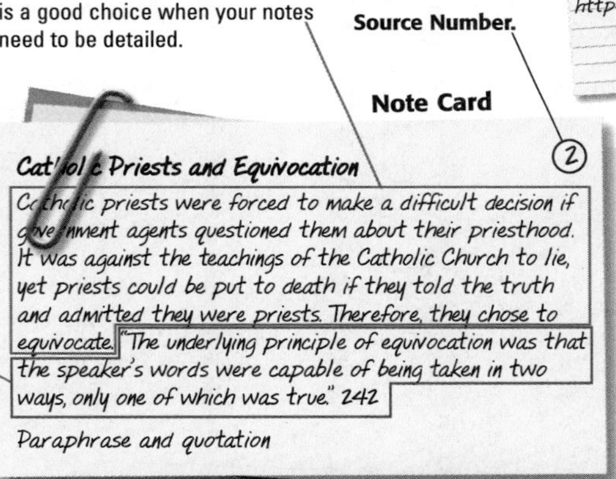

More Online: Research Starter
www.mcdougallittell.com

Evaluate Your Sources

Have students determine whether an author is an authority on a given subject by looking in a collection of brief biographies. Many fields have their own *Who's Who,* which can be found in the reference section of most libraries.

Make Source Cards

Have examples of a book, encyclopedia, and periodical in the classroom so that students can compare each type of sample card to the actual object. Demonstrate where students can find each piece of information they will need to put on a source card. If your classroom is connected to the Internet, you might also demonstrate how students can find the information they will need in order to make a source card for an Internet site.

Have students consult the *MLA Handbook for Writers of Research Papers* for information on how to document other types of sources, such as a live interview, or a foreword or afterward from a book.

Teaching Tip: Making Source Cards

Advise students to copy complete publication information for each source they might use. If they plan to return to the library at a later time for this information, they may find that the books or magazines they need are checked out or in use.

Take Notes

Students will have an easier time writing their research papers if they paraphrase and summarize on their note. Warn students against overusing quotations. Choosing a few well-phrased quotations and placing them in strategic places in their research report will be more effective than sprinkling their paper with several weak quotes.

Organize Your Material

Extra time spent at this stage of the project is time well spent. Set aside time to confer with students on the logic of their outline and report. Students might have gaps in their information and will need to do additional research. Other students may have information on their outlines that is interesting but unrelated to their controlling purpose. Still others may need to reorganize the information they have in order to present it more effectively. Have students revise topic outlines several times until they are tight and logically coherent.

Organize Your Material

Once you have gathered the information from your sources, you can begin to organize your notes. One way to do this is to make a topic outline. Begin by grouping your note cards into stacks of related material. Determine the main idea of each stack. Next, think about the best way to arrange your stacks of note cards. Chronological order works well for historical or biographical information, although you may wish to try other organizational patterns, such as comparison-and-contrast order or cause-and-effect order. Write your outline based on the order of the main ideas and subpoints in your stacks of notes.

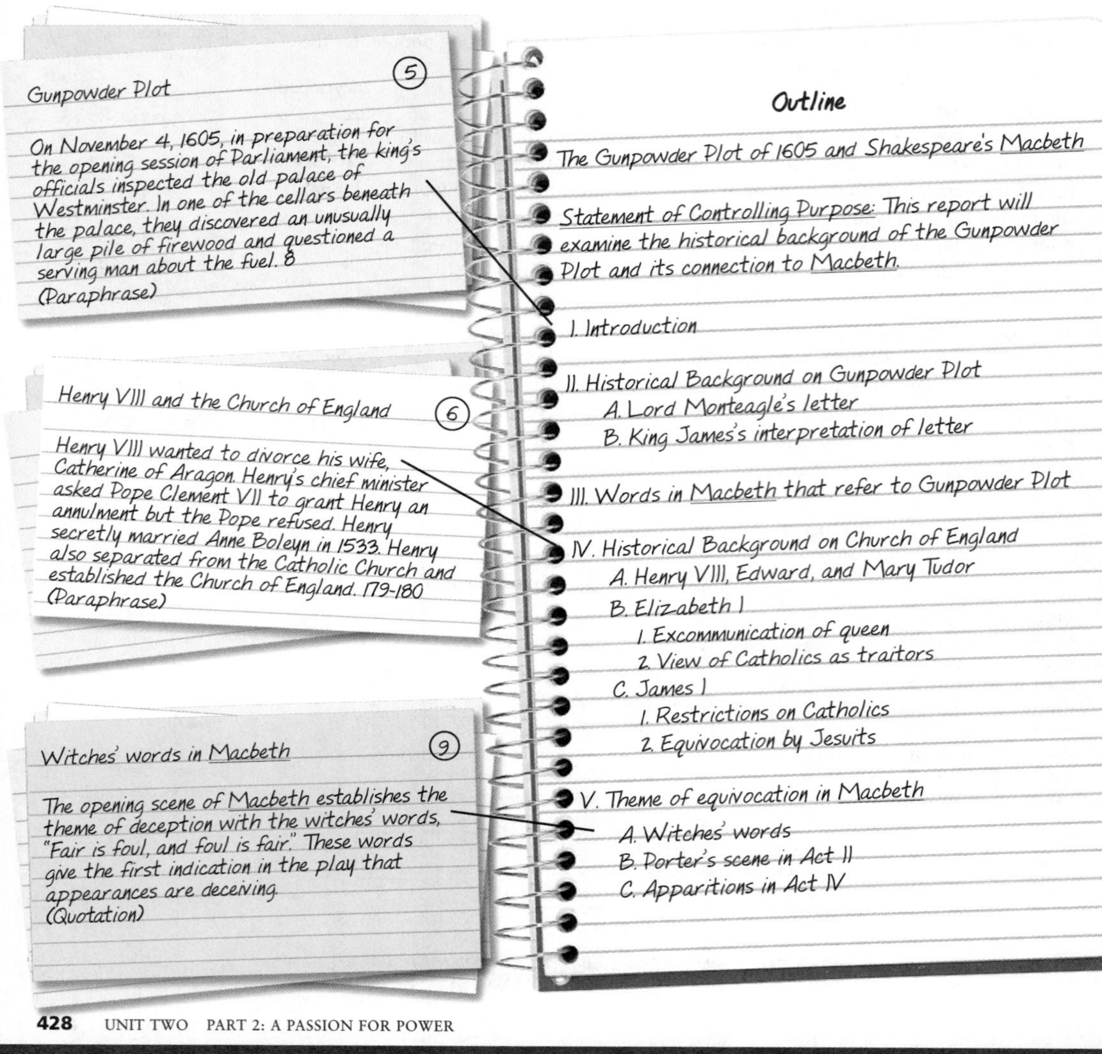

Gunpowder Plot (5)

On November 4, 1605, in preparation for the opening session of Parliament, the king's officials inspected the old palace of Westminster. In one of the cellars beneath the palace, they discovered an unusually large pile of firewood and questioned a serving man about the fuel. 8
(Paraphrase)

Henry VIII and the Church of England (6)

Henry VIII wanted to divorce his wife, Catherine of Aragon. Henry's chief minister asked Pope Clement VII to grant Henry an annulment but the Pope refused. Henry secretly married Anne Boleyn in 1533. Henry also separated from the Catholic Church and established the Church of England. 179-180
(Paraphrase)

Witches' words in Macbeth (9)

The opening scene of Macbeth establishes the theme of deception with the witches' words, "Fair is foul, and foul is fair." These words give the first indication in the play that appearances are deceiving.
(Quotation)

Outline

The Gunpowder Plot of 1605 and Shakespeare's Macbeth

Statement of Controlling Purpose: This report will examine the historical background of the Gunpowder Plot and its connection to Macbeth.

I. Introduction

II. Historical Background on Gunpowder Plot
- A. Lord Monteagle's letter
- B. King James's interpretation of letter

III. Words in Macbeth that refer to Gunpowder Plot

IV. Historical Background on Church of England
- A. Henry VIII, Edward, and Mary Tudor
- B. Elizabeth I
  - 1. Excommunication of queen
  - 2. View of Catholics as traitors
- C. James I
  - 1. Restrictions on Catholics
  - 2. Equivocation by Jesuits

V. Theme of equivocation in Macbeth
- A. Witches' words
- B. Porter's scene in Act II
- C. Apparitions in Act IV

❸ Drafting

Your report, like many other essays, will begin with an introduction that states your thesis and will end with a conclusion that restates this thesis and summarizes your main points. The largest part of your report, the body, should explain and support your topic.

Develop a Thesis Statement

When you finish your research, you should have a good idea of what you want your report to accomplish. Rework your statement of controlling purpose into a **thesis statement** that expresses the main idea of your report.

Write Your Draft

In the drafting stage, concentrate on getting your ideas on paper using your own voice. Follow your outline and refer to your note cards as you write.

Support your thesis. Use the information from your sources creatively, analyzing, synthesizing, making inferences, and interpreting evidence to reach a conclusion. Use facts, quotations, statistics, and examples from your research to support your thesis. While writing, you may discover that you need to do further research on your topic.

Document your sources. After each quotation, paraphrase, or summary in your paper, write in parentheses the author's name (or the source title, if no name is given) and the page number. Use your note cards and source cards to identify the sources of information used in your report. Failure to credit your sources constitutes **plagiarism**—the unlawful use of another's words or ideas as your own. The Works Cited page at the end of your report will provide complete publishing information for each source used in your report.

Evaluate Your Draft

Think about these questions as you review your draft.

- How could I make my thesis statement clearer?
- What additional support for my thesis can I provide in the body of the report?
- What material can I delete?
- How can I organize my material more effectively?
- What material could I paraphrase rather than quote directly?
- What facts and documentation do I need to check?
- How can I better accomplish my purpose?

Drafting Tip

Remember that your outline is only a tool. Feel free to reorganize your material at any time or collect new information as needed.

Need help documenting sources?

See the **Writing Handbook**, p. 1376.

Ask Your Peer Reader

- What did you like most about my paper?
- What was the most memorable thing you learned about my topic?
- Which parts, if any, seemed confusing or unclear?
- What would you like to know more about?

Drafting

To prevent students from becoming overwhelmed by their task, encourage them to set realistic goals focused on one section of the outline at a time. As they complete each section, have them check it off on the flow chart they created.

Develop a Thesis Statement

Review the difference between a statement of controlling purpose and a thesis statement. Point out that the controlling purpose in the student outline establishes the purpose of the report and guides the student research. The thesis statement in the research report reflects the conclusions the writer drew after finishing his or her research. Have students note how the thesis statement is worked into the introduction of the research report.

Have students work in pairs to revise their statements of controlling purpose and write a thesis statement that reflects the conclusions they have drawn about their topic.

Teaching Tip: Drawing Conclusions

Many students will need guidance in drafting a paper that goes beyond the gathered facts to synthesize information and draw conclusions. Have volunteers share some of the conclusions they have drawn from their research. Discuss how they reached these conclusions.

Write Your Draft

Remind students that their goal is to synthesize the information they researched. The body of the report should not be a quilt work of documented sources. Their ideas and interpretations should be most evident.

Revising

Paragraph Building

Have a volunteer discuss the main idea in the sample paragraph. Discuss why the final sentence does not belong.

Next, have students work with a fresh copy of their draft and underline the topic sentence in each paragraph. Then have them reread the same paragraphs to check that each sentence in the paragraph helps to develop the topic sentence.

Editing

Shifting Verb Tense

Before students can edit for shifting verb tense, have them decide on a predominant verb tense for their paper. They should then revise one paragraph at a time for consistency with that verb tense.

Making a Works Cited List

Point out that the Works Cited list contains only sources that have actually been cited, i.e., quoted, paraphrased, or summarized in the research report.

Remind students that the entries should be in alphabetical order; they should leave a double-space between entries; and the first line of each entry should begin at the left margin with subsequent lines indented.

Reflecting

Encourage students to think about how their controlling purpose evolved as they conducted their research. They might also consider how the process of writing a research paper differed from the processes they used in other types of writing. Did they do enough planning before beginning to write? Have students add these self-evaluations to their working portfolios.

Need revising help?

Review the **Rubric,** p. 423

Consider **peer reader** comments

Check **Revision Guidelines,** p. 1355

4 Revising

TARGET SKILL ▶ PARAGRAPH BUILDING Writing has unity when all the sentences in a paragraph support its central idea. As you revise your research report, delete any unrelated ideas.

> At the time of Elizabeth I's death in 1603, many penalties were imposed against English Catholics. Catholics were prohibited from celebrating Mass anywhere in England. Those who violated this restriction were fined and jailed, and some priests were executed. ~~Phillip II, the Catholic king of Spain, wanted to restore Catholicism to England.~~

5 Editing

TARGET SKILL ▶ SHIFTING VERB TENSE Keep in mind that writers generally avoid shifting verb tense in a paper. However, not all shifts in verb tense are incorrect. A shift in tense may be needed to show when an action occurred in relation to another action.

> Father Garnet ~~wrote~~ *had written* a Treatise of Equivocation before the English government tried and executed him for conspiracy in ~~T~~the Gunpowder Plot. In this treatise, Garnet claim~~s~~*ed* that a person may, under certain circumstances, avoid telling the complete truth.

6 Making a Works Cited List

When you have finished revising and editing your report, make a **Works Cited list** and attach it to the end of your paper. See pages 1376–1378 in the **Writing Handbook** for the correct format.

Publishing IDEAS

- Share your paper with the class as an oral presentation.

More Online: Publishing Options
www.mcdougallittell.com

7 Reflecting

FOR YOUR PORTFOLIO What did you learn about yourself as you worked through the process of writing a research report? Is there anything more you would like to know about your topic? Draw relevant questions for further study from your findings. Attach them to your research report and save them in your **Working Portfolio.**

Assessment Practice Revising & Editing

Read this opening from the first draft of a research report. The underlined sections may include the following kinds of errors:

- **unrelated ideas in a paragraph**
- **incorrect verb tenses**
- **capitalization errors**
- **comma errors**

For each underlined phrase or sentence, choose the revision that most improves the writing.

> You shouldn't judge a book by its cover, but you shouldn't ignore the cover either. The dust jacket copy is important, too. (1) One of the most famous book covers in American fiction appeared on the first edition of F. Scott Fitzgerald's the *Great Gatsby*. (2) Fitzgerald was so pleased with the art that he writes the image into his book. (3) The mysterious artwork was created by Spanish-born artist Francis Cugat. (4) It shows a woman's sad face floating, above bright and gaudy city lights. (5) A single green tear drops from one eye. This poignant design is often reprinted. (6)

1. **A.** The dust-jacket copy is important, too.
   B. It is important to judge the dust jacket copy, too.
   C. Delete sentence
   D. Correct as is
2. **A.** First Edition of F. Scott Fitzgerald's *The Great Gatsby.*
   B. first edition of F. Scott Fitzgerald's *The Great Gatsby.*
   C. first edition of F. Scott Fitzgerald's *the Great Gatsby.*
   D. Correct as is
3. **A.** Fitzgerald is so pleased with the art that he wrote the image into his book.
   B. Fitzgerald was so pleased with the art that he had written the image into his book.
   C. Fitzgerald was so pleased with the art that he wrote the image into his book.
   D. Correct as is
4. **A.** Spanish-Born artist Francis Cugat.
   B. Spanish-Born Artist Francis Cugat.
   C. spanish-born artist Francis Cugat.
   D. Correct as is
5. **A.** floating above bright and gaudy city lights.
   B. floating above bright, and gaudy city lights.
   C. floating, above bright, and gaudy, city lights.
   D. Correct as is
6. **A.** As a result, this poignant design is often reprinted.
   B. Because this poignant design beautifully reflects the book's content, it is often reprinted on modern editions.
   C. Cugat often reprints this poignant design.
   D. Correct as is

Need extra help?

See the **Grammar Handbook**

Verb tenses, p. 1401

Capitalization, p. 1420

Commas, pp. 1418–1419

Assessment Practice

Before students begin to identify errors in the passage, review the types of errors the passage contains. Remind students to carefully read the entire passage before correcting the errors.

Answers:
1. C; **2.** B; **3.** C; **4.** D; **5.** A; **6.** B

Grammar

AVOIDING INCONSISTENT VERB TENSES

Instruction Avoid switching unnecessarily from one tense to another. Choose a dominant verb tense and stay with it.

Activity Write the following sentences on the chalkboard. Discuss the tense shift in each. Then have volunteers correct the sentences.

1. The teacher asked a question, and I decide to answer. (decided)
2. Al gives the dog a pat on the head, and the dog wagged its tail. (wags)
3. The dog liked to run, and loves to go to the park. (likes)
4. The man parks in front of the gate and opened his car door. (opens)
5. I sang the song, and it hurts everyone's ears. (hurt)

Building Vocabulary

Objectives
- research word origins
- understand how to use Greek and Latin roots to determine meanings and build word families
- use etymology as an aid to expand vocabulary

EXERCISE

1. *resolute*
   Latin root: *solvere*
   Meaning: to release or set free
   Word Family: resolution; resolve; resoluble; resolvent
2. *prediction*
   Latin root: *dicere*
   Meaning: to say
   Word Family: dictionary; diction; dictum; edict
3. *conspires*
   Latin root: *spirare*
   Meaning: to breathe together
   Word Family: conspirator; respiration
4. *metaphysical*
   Greek root: *physis*
   Meaning: nature
   Word Family: physics; physique
5. *rhinoceros*
   Greek root: *keras*
   Meaning: nose-horned
   Word Family: rhinal; rhinology

Building Vocabulary Analyzing Word Parts—Roots

Core Meanings

> **Boundless intemperance**
> **In nature is a tyranny. . . .**
> —William Shakespeare, *Macbeth,* Act 4, Scene 3

English speakers regularly borrow words from other languages to add to their own. Greek and Latin in particular have been fertile sources of roots for building English words. (A **root** is a core part of a word, to which other word parts, such as prefixes and suffixes, can be added to create new words.) Consider, for instance, the word *intemperance* in the sentence above from *Macbeth.* The Latin root *temper* means "to moderate," the prefix *in-* means "not" or "without," and the suffix *-ance* indicates a condition or action. By putting the meanings of the parts together you can infer that *intemperance* probably means something like "action that is without moderation."

Strategies for Building Vocabulary

If you know some common Greek and Latin roots and their meanings, you can figure out the meaning of unknown words—even without a dictionary.

Use the Meanings of Roots to Build Word Families You can expand your knowledge of roots by noting the etymologies of words that you look up in the dictionary. Read the etymology of *horrific* below. What insight into the meaning of the English word does it provide?

[Latin *horrificus : horrēre,* to tremble + *-ficus,* -fic (causing).]

Once you understand the meaning of the root, you can use it to help you understand other unfamiliar words that also contain that root. The illustration below shows one Greek root, *chron,* and its word family.

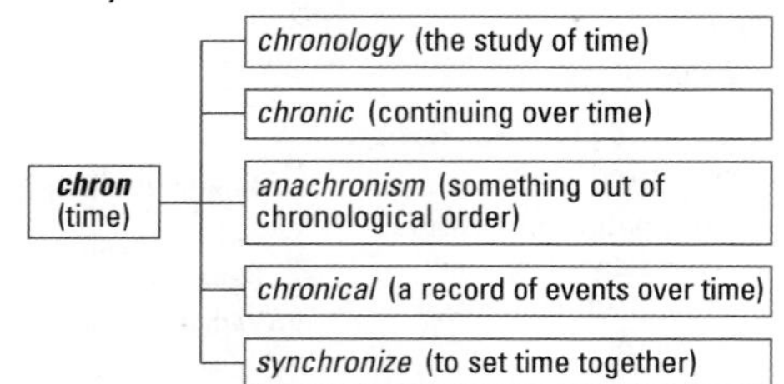

Study the charts that follow to learn the meanings of some other Greek and Latin roots that have given rise to English word families.

Greek Root	Meaning	Word Family
arche	primitive, ancient	archaic, archetype, archaize, archaeologist
bibl	book	bibliography, Bible
cosm	world	cosmic, cosmopolitan,
gnos	know	Gnostic, agnostic, diagnosis
mania	madness	maniac, kleptomania
path	feeling	pathetic, sympathy

Latin Root	Meaning	Word Family
belli	war	bellicose, antebellum, belligerent
cede, ceed	go	proceed, exceed, recede
cide	kill	homicide, insecticide
cla(i)m	shout	proclaim, clamor, exclaim
imag	likeness	image, imagine, imagery
ment	mind	mental, demented, mentality
mor(t)	death	moribund, mortal, mortified
optim	best	optimum, optimist, optimize
sanit	health	sanitary, insanity, sanitarium
viv, vit	alive, life	vital, survive, vivid, vivacious

EXERCISE Use a dictionary to identify the meaning and root of each of these words from *Macbeth.* Use the information you find to create charts like the ones above for the words' Greek and Latin roots.

1. resolute
2. prediction
3. conspirers
4. metaphysical
5. rhinoceros

Using Adverbs and Adverb Phrases

Grammar from Literature

Look at the lines below from *Macbeth.* Notice the information that the highlighted adverbs add to each sentence.

SINGLE-WORD ADVERBS

She has light by her continually. (time)

Was not that nobly done? Ay, and wisely too! (manner, manner)

ADVERB PREPOSITIONAL PHRASES

Is this a dagger which I see before me? (location)

He's worth more sorrow, and that I'll spend for him. (purpose)

I would applaud thee to the very echo. (degree)

Writers use adverbs to tell how, when, or where. These uses are also sometimes referred to as manner, time, location, purpose, and degree.

Adverbs modify verbs, adjectives, and other adverbs. You will notice from the examples above that adverbs can take the form of single words or of phrases.

Using Adverbs in Your Writing You can make your writing more precise by using adverbs to establish details about the how, when, or where of scenes, events, or people's actions. You can also add precision and accuracy by using adverbs to qualify or limit your ideas. Such qualification can improve accuracy.

The following examples show the two different ways you can use adverbs.

ADD DETAIL

Ross says the king has received news of Macbeth's success.

Ross says the king has happily received news of Macbeth's success.

ADD DETAIL

Macduff rejoices that his kingdom is free.

In the final scene, Macduff rejoices that his kingdom is finally free from tyranny.

QUALIFY OR LIMIT

The conflict in Shakespeare's plays centers on how characters resolve moral issues.

The conflict in Shakespeare's plays often centers on how characters resolve moral issues.

Usage Tip Placement of adverbs can affect meaning. If you misplace an adverb, your sentence may not say what you want it to say.

INCORRECT

Before 1603 Shakespeare only wrote four tragedies.

CORRECT

Before 1603 Shakespeare wrote only four tragedies.

The first example says that Shakespeare did nothing but write tragedies. Placing *only* next to *four* correctly indicates that he wrote a limited number of tragedies.

WRITING EXERCISE Rewrite the following sentences, following the instructions given in parentheses.

1. The three witches appear to Macbeth. (Add one or more single-word adverbs that tell how, when, or where the witches appeared.)
2. Lady Macbeth urges her husband to commit crimes. (Add a prepositional phrase that tells how, when, or where.)
3. Macduff vows to kill Macbeth. (Add a prepositional phrase that indicates purpose.)
4. Shakespeare is called the "bard of Avon" and the "swan of Avon." (Add a single-word adverb or an adverb prepositional phrase to qualify this statement and make it more accurate.)
5. Shakespeare is considered the greatest dramatist of all time. (Add an adverb or an adverb prepositional phrase to qualify this statement and make it more accurate.)

Sentence Crafting

WRITING EXERCISE
Suggested answers are shown. Answers may vary.

1. The three witches suddenly appear to Macbeth.
2. With evil intent Lady Macbeth urges her husband to commit crimes.
3. For his own reasons Macduff vows to kill Macbeth.
4. Shakespeare is sometimes called the "bard of Avon" and the "swan of Avon."
5. Shakespeare is considered the greatest dramatist of all time by many scholars.

PART 3 Facing Life's Limitations

Many people of the Renaissance sought answers to questions about life's limitations. Some found comfort in the lessons of the Bible. Others read works in which writers reflected on love, death, and the role of men and women. You may find that the questions posed are still relevant today.

434

"To every thing there is a season, and a time to every purpose under the heaven."

King James Bible
from Ecclesiastes, Chapter 3
Psalm 23
Parable of the Prodigal Son

Connect to Your Life

Time Line Think about events that have occurred in your life. Which of these events stand out in your mind as being particularly important? Create a time line, charting significant events and phases. If appropriate, include times when you made major changes in your attitude and times when you learned valuable lessons about life.

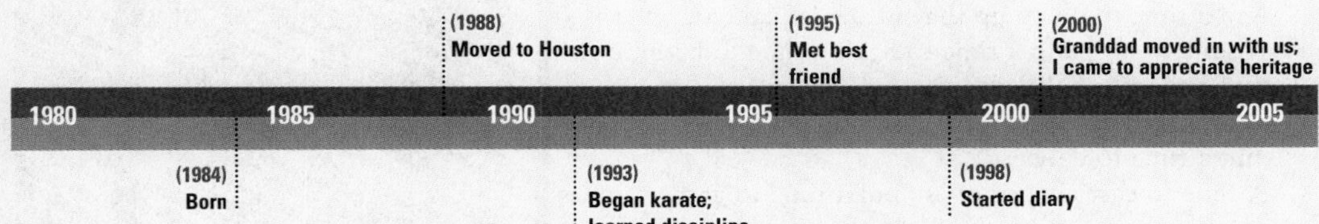

(1988) Moved to Houston
(1995) Met best friend
(2000) Granddad moved in with us; I came to appreciate heritage
1980
1985
1990
1995
2000
2005
(1984) Born
(1993) Began karate; learned discipline
(1998) Started diary

Build Background

The King James Version of the Bible When James I, the successor of Elizabeth I, became king of England in 1603, Puritan leaders petitioned him to support a new translation of the Bible. Although he bore no great love for the Puritans, he agreed that English worshipers needed a translation better than the ones in popular use. In 1604, the king appointed 54 distinguished scholars and clergymen to create a new translation—one that would be more accurate than previous English versions and more beautiful in its use of language. The result—the King James Bible—was the main Protestant Bible in English for over 300 years. Even today, although many other translations are available, it remains the most important and influential of all versions.

The following passages from the King James Bible illustrate different types of scriptural writing, each designed to impart spiritual lessons about life. The selection from Ecclesiastes is an example of what is called wisdom literature—literature intended to help human beings find the meaning of life. The second selection is a psalm, or song of praise. The last is a parable, a brief story that is meant to teach a moral or religious lesson.

Focus Your Reading

LITERARY ANALYSIS REPETITION

Repetition is a technique in which a word or group of words is repeated throughout a selection. As you read the following excerpts from the Bible, notice examples of repetition and the effect they have.

ACTIVE READING MAKING INFERENCES In order to be able to understand and interpret passages from the Bible, it is important to be able to make inferences from the text about the spiritual lesson being taught. Inferences are ideas and meanings not directly stated in the material. **Making inferences** often means reading between the lines to understand the main idea.

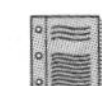 READER'S NOTEBOOK As you read each excerpt from the Bible, try to infer the spiritual lesson or main idea, and then briefly **summarize** it.

OVERVIEW

Objectives

1. understand and appreciate **parables** from scripture **(Literary Analysis)**
2. identify **repetition** and examine its effects **(Literary Analysis)**
3. **make inferences** to understand spiritual message **(Active Reading)**

Summary

The excerpt from "Ecclesiastes," an example of wisdom literature, asserts that there is a proper time and season for everything that happens in life. "Psalm 23," a biblical song of praise, presents God as a shepherd to his flock, humankind.

In the "Parable of the Prodigal Son," a man's younger son leaves home and squanders his share of the family wealth. When a famine arises, the hungry son returns home, planning to beg for a place as a hired servant. When he arrives, his father greets him joyfully and prepares a feast.

Use **Unit Two Resource Book,** p. 48 for additional support.

Thematic Link

These excerpts from the King James Bible teach important lessons about **facing life's limitations.**

5-Minute Warm-Up

Daily Language SkillBuilder

Have students **proofread** the display sentences on page 273l and write them correctly. The sentences also appear on Transparency 8 of **Grammar Transparencies and Copymasters.**

LESSON RESOURCES

UNIT TWO RESOURCE BOOK, pp. 48–51

ASSESSMENT RESOURCES

Formal Assessment, pp. 65–66

Teacher's Guide to Assessment and Portfolio Use

Test Generator

SKILLS TRANSPARENCIES AND COPYMASTERS

Reading and Critical Thinking
- Paraphrasing and Summarizing, T42 (for Active Reading, p. 435)

Grammar
- Diagramming Verbal Phrases, T60 (for Mini Lesson, p. 436)
- Infinitive Phrases Used as Adverbs, C97 (for Mini Lesson, p. 436)

Writing
- Identifying Writing Variables, T2 (for Writing Option 2, p. 441)
- Opinion Statement, C35 (for Writing Option 3, p. 441)

Communications
- Dramatic Reading, T12 (for Activities & Explorations 2, p. 441)

INTEGRATED TECHNOLOGY

Audio Library

LaserLinks
- Art Gallery: Biblical Art. See **Teacher's SourceBook,** p. 26.

Visit our website:
www.mcdougallittell.com

TEACHING THE LITERATURE

Reading and Analyzing

Active Reading MAKING INFERENCES

A Remind students that inferences are ideas and meanings not directly stated in the text. Ask students what spiritual lesson they infer from this excerpt from Ecclesiastes. Remind them that they must be able to support their inferences with textured evidence and experience.
Possible Response: Everything in life happens for a purpose and in its own good time.

Use **Unit Two Resource Book,** p. 49 for additional support.

Literary Analysis REPETITION

B Point out the repetition of the word *time* and the parallel grammatical structure repeated throughout much of the excerpt from Ecclesiastes. Ask how the rhythmic effect of this repetition emphasizes the selection's theme.
Possible Response: The regular rhythm reinforces the idea that things happen in a particular pattern.

Use **Unit Two Resource Book,** p. 50 for additional support.

Literary Analysis: Metaphor

C Have students identify the opening metaphor in Psalm 23.
Answer: The Lord is compared to a shepherd.

Thinking Through the Literature

1. Responses will vary.
2. Some students may find the advice realistic or comforting; others may find it too fatalistic.
3. Accept all reasonable, well-supported responses. Students may note the contemporary resonance of the lines concerning war and peace.

from the King James Bible

Month of July from *Très riches heures du duc de Berry* (about 1415), Limbourg brothers. Musée Condé, Chantilly, France. Giraudon/Art Resource, New York.

A *from* Ecclesiastes, Chapter 3

B
1 To every thing there is a season, and a time to every purpose under the heaven:
2 A time to be born, and a time to die; a time to plant, and a time to pluck up that which is planted;
3 A time to kill, and a time to heal; a time to break down, and a time to build up;
4 A time to weep, and a time to laugh; a time to mourn, and a time to dance;
5 A time to cast away stones, and a time to gather stones together; a time to embrace, and a time to refrain from embracing;
6 A time to get,[1] and a time to lose; a time to keep, and a time to cast away;
7 A time to rend,[2] and a time to sew; a time to keep silence, and a time to speak;
8 A time to love, and a time to hate; a time of war, and a time of peace.

1. **get:** gain; win.
2. **rend:** tear or rip.

Thinking Through the Literature

1. What is your overall reaction to this excerpt from Ecclesiastes?
2. Do you agree with the message conveyed in this excerpt?

THINK ABOUT
- the meaning of the statement "To every thing there is a season" (line 1)
- the contrasting examples given throughout the excerpt

3. Which lines do you think have special relevance to contemporary life?

Teaching Options

Mini Lesson **Grammar**

INFINITIVE PHRASE USED AS ADVERB

Instruction An adverb, which modifies a verb, tells where, when, how, or to what extent the action is happening. Point out that infinitives—verbals formed with the word *to* and a verb form—can also function as adverbs.

Activity Write the excerpt on the chalkboard.

"And he went and joined himself to a citizen of that country; and he sent him into his fields to feed swine."

Have students underline the infinitive phrase in the sentence. *(to feed swine)* The infinitive phrase modifies the verb *sent;* therefore, the infinitive phrase functions as an adverb in the sentence.

Exercise Ask students to underline the infinitive phrase that is used as an adverb in each sentence and to write the verb that the phrase modifies.

1. The fifty-four scholars hired by King James I to translate the Bible created an English version of the Bible that has maintained dominance for more than 300 years. *(to translate the Bible; hired)*

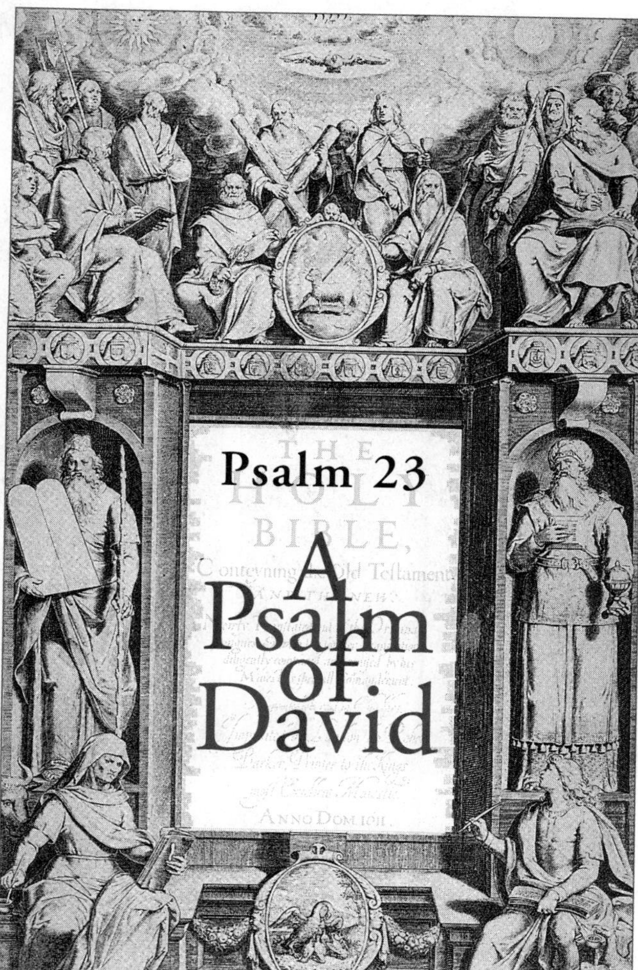

Psalm 23

A Psalm of David

Title page of the first edition of the King James Bible, London, 1611. The Granger Collection, New York.

1 The Lord is my shepherd; I shall not want.[1]

2 He maketh me to lie down in green pastures: he leadeth me beside the still waters.

3 He restoreth my soul: he leadeth me in the paths of righteousness for his name's sake.

4 Yea, though I walk through the valley of the shadow of death, I will fear no evil: for thou art with me; thy rod and thy staff they comfort me.

5 Thou preparest a table before me in the presence of mine enemies: thou anointest my head with oil; my cup runneth over.[2]

6 Surely goodness and mercy shall follow me all the days of my life: and I will dwell in the house of the Lord for ever.

---

1. **want:** be in need.
2. **Thou preparest . . . runneth over:** In this verse, the Lord is presented as a generous host who offers his guest food, oil for grooming, and an overflowing cup of wine. In ancient times, olive oil was used as a cleansing agent and was quite expensive.

Thinking Through the Literature

1. What **images** are you left with after reading this psalm?
2. In your opinion, how might this psalm affect someone trying to cope with life's difficulties or limitations?
3. Psalm 23 is part of a group of psalms often called "songs of trust." Why do you think it is included in this group?

Customizing Instruction

Less Proficient Readers

Remind students that the ending *-(e)th* on verbs can be replaced with *-s* in modern English. Point out as well the use of *thou* and *thy,* which are *you* and *your* in modern English.

For "Psalm 23," help students understand that "the / valley of the shadow of death" is the temptation and danger that people face every day.

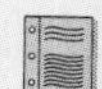

Use **Spanish Study Guide** for additional support, pp. 79–81.

Gifted and Talented

Have students rewrite the passages in contemporary prose. They should customize the messages presented in these selections for our modern world. Encourage them to use metaphors and images appropriate to modern society.

Thinking Through the Literature

1. Accept all reasonable responses.
2. Possible Response: It might give a person strength or courage to face problems.
3. Possible Responses: It expresses trust in the Lord and suggests that those who trust in the Lord need not fear death or the afterlife.

2. In the "Parable of the Prodigal Son," one son begs to be given a share of his father's estate. *(to be given a share of his father's estate; begs)*
3. The father rushes to embrace his son—for him forgiveness is not an issue. *(to embrace his son; rushes)*
4. The elder brother speaks with his father to express his hurt and frustration at the celebration. *(to express his hurt and frustration at the celebration; speaks)*
5. A person who reads the excerpt from Ecclesiastes to find wisdom and the meaning of life discovers the seasons used as a metaphor for the cycle of human events. *(to find wisdom and the meaning of life; reads)*

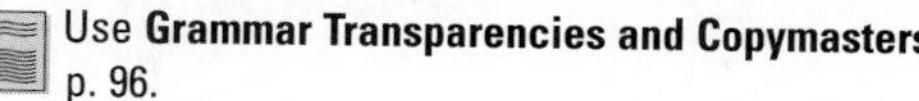

Use **Grammar Transparencies and Copymasters,** p. 96.

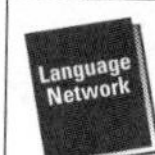

Use McDougal Littell's ***Language Network*** for more instruction and practice in infinitive phrases used as adverbs.

Reading and Analyzing

Literary Analysis REPETITION

A Have students consider reasons for the repetition of the son's words.
Possible Response: It stresses his contrite, sinful state.

Active Reading MAKING INFERENCES

Ask what values the parable suggests are important.
Possible Responses: mercy, forgiveness, love.
Ask students who the father and the son in the parable symbolize.
Answer: God and a wayward sinner.
Who does the older son symbolize?
Answer: A faithful follower who questions why the sinner should be welcomed back with such rejoicing.

Literary Analysis: PARABLE

Explain that parables usually have the following characteristics:

- They teach a moral lesson in a short and focused format.
- They are a type of allegory, a work in which the characters and events stand for abstract ideas and principles.

Ask students to explain these characteristics of parable in the parable of the prodigal son.
Possible Responses: It teaches that we should rejoice when someone returns to a righteous life; the father and son symbolize God and a wayward sinner.

Return of the Prodigal Son (1667–1668), Rembrandt van Rijn. The Hermitage Museum, St. Petersburg, Russia. Bridgeman Art Library, London/Superstock.

from Luke, Chapter 15

Parable of the Prodigal Son

11 And he said, A certain man had two sons:
12 And the younger of them said to his father, Father, give me the
portion of goods that falleth to me. And he divided unto them
his living.
13 And not many days after the younger son gathered all together,
and took his journey into a far country, and there wasted his
substance with riotous living.
14 And when he had spent all, there arose a mighty famine in that
land; and he began to be in want.

15 And he went and joined himself to a citizen of that country; and he[1] sent him into his fields to feed swine.
16 And he would fain[2] have filled his belly with the husks that the swine did eat: and no man gave unto him.
17 And when he came to himself, he said, How many hired servants of my father's have bread enough and to spare, and I perish with hunger!
18 I will arise and go to my father, and will say unto him, Father, I have sinned against heaven, and before thee,
19 And am no more worthy to be called thy son: make me as one of thy hired servants.
20 And he arose, and came to his father. But when he was yet a great way off, his father saw him, and had compassion, and ran, and fell on his neck, and kissed him.
21 And the son said unto him, Father, I have sinned against heaven, and in thy sight, and am no more worthy to be called thy son.
22 But the father said to his servants, Bring forth the best robe, and put it on him; and put a ring on his hand, and shoes on his feet:
23 And bring hither the fatted calf, and kill it; and let us eat, and be merry:
24 For this my son was dead, and is alive again; he was lost, and is found. And they began to be merry.
25 Now his elder son was in the field: and as he came and drew nigh to the house, he heard musick and dancing.
26 And he called one of the servants, and asked what these things meant.
27 And he said unto him, Thy brother is come; and thy father hath killed the fatted calf, because he hath received him safe and sound.
28 And he was angry, and would not go in: therefore came his father out, and intreated[3] him.
29 And he answering said to his father, Lo, these many years do I serve thee, neither transgressed[4] I at any time thy commandment: and yet thou never gavest me a kid,[5] that I might make merry with my friends:
30 But as soon as this thy son was come, which hath devoured thy living with harlots, thou hast killed for him the fatted calf.
31 And he said unto him, Son, thou art ever with me, and all that I have is thine.
32 It was meet[6] that we should make merry, and be glad: for this thy brother was dead, and is alive again; and was lost, and is found.

1. **he:** the citizen.
2. **fain:** gladly.
3. **intreated:** entreated; urged.
4. **transgressed:** violated; broke.
5. **kid:** young goat.
6. **meet:** fitting; proper.

Customizing Instruction

Less Proficient Readers

Have students use the description of the son's actions to infer what *prodigal* means.

Possible Responses: extravagantly wasteful, dissipated.

Students Acquiring English

Explain that *fatted* means "fattened up" so as to serve as a good meal. Then ask what the expression "to kill the fatted calf," which is used in this parable, might mean.

Possible Response: to make a feast of celebration.

THE KING JAMES BIBLE 439

GUIDING STUDENT RESPONSE

Connect to the Literature

1. What Do You Think?
Guidelines for student response: Students should be able to discuss, with evidence from the text, the three main characters in the parable—the father, the elder son, and the prodigal son.

Comprehension Check
- happy
- angry, resentful

 Use **Unit Two Resource Book,** p. 51 for additional support.

Think Critically

2. Students who agree with the father may feel that a parent must be grateful for a child's safe return, and that the repentant son deserves forgiveness. Those who disagree may feel that the son will revert to his sinful ways, or that the father is unfair to his loyal elder son.
3. Possible Responses: We should forgive repentant sinners. We should celebrate people's good qualities and not dwell on their faults.
4. Accept all thorough and reasonable responses that students support with evidence from the text and their own experiences.

Literary Analysis

Activity Responses will vary. Students may note that in Ecclesiastes, there is formal repetition in the presentation of the antithetical activities ("a time" to do this, and "a time" to do that). In the parable, the repetition of certain lines (such as the prodigal son's admissions of sin) enforces the moral lesson.

Parable Have students write brief character sketches of each of the main characters. They should note what each character represents (the father is "God the father," for example). As a way of thinking about the efficacy of a parable as moral instruction, have students discuss whether they relate to the characters' behavior and responses in the story.

Thinking through the LITERATURE

Connect to the Literature

1. **What Do You Think?** How did you respond to the three **characters** in the parable of the prodigal son?

Comprehension Check
- How does the father feel about the prodigal son's return?
- How does the elder son feel about the return of the prodigal son?

Think Critically

2. If you were in the father's place, would you react to the younger son's return as he does?

THINK ABOUT
- the father's reaction to the words spoken by the younger son upon his return
- the father's explanation to his older son
- your own feelings about forgiveness

3. In your opinion, what is the message or lesson of this **parable?**

4. ACTIVE READING MAKING INFERENCES Look back at your  READER'S NOTEBOOK for your summary of the spiritual lesson of the parable. What details from the text support your summary? Compare your ideas with those of your classmates.

Extend Interpretations

5. **Comparing Texts** Look again at the excerpt from *The Book of Margery Kempe* (page 252). Which of the three selections from the Bible do you think would offer the greatest comfort to Kempe?

6. **Different Perspectives** How might readers of different ages—for example, a teenager and an elderly person—differ in their reactions to the selection from Ecclesiastes, to Psalm 23, or to the parable?

7. **Connect to Life** Think about the different spiritual lessons presented in the passages from Ecclesiastes, Psalm 23, and the parable of the prodigal son. Do you think it is difficult to put these lessons into practice today? Discuss your ideas.

Literary Analysis

REPETITION Used in both poetry and prose, **repetition** is a technique in which a word or group of words is repeated throughout a selection. Repetition of words and phrases often helps to reinforce meaning and to create an appealing rhythm.

Activity Find examples of repetition in the excerpt from Ecclesiastes and in the parable of the prodigal son. Record them in a chart like the one shown. In which selection do you think repetition plays a more important role? Discuss your conclusions with your classmates.

	Examples of Repetition
Ecclesiastes	
Parable of the Prodigal Son	

PARABLE A **parable** is a brief story that is intended to teach a lesson or illustrate a moral truth. Although the characters, action, and dialogue are simple and direct, they point to fundamental ideas about how humans should live. Think again about the parable of the prodigal son. Do you think a parable is an effective way to present moral teachings?

Extend Interpretations

Comparing Texts Possible Responses: Kempe would find comfort in Ecclesiastes's reminder of the cycle of the seasons; she would find comfort in Psalm 23's reminder of God's love; she would find comfort in the parable's reminder of the love and forgiveness of fellow human beings.

Different Perspectives Students may say that a teenager might be impatient with the message of the excerpt from Ecclesiastes and that an elderly person might derive comfort from it.

Connect to Life Some students may say yes, because life is more complicated today. Others may say no, because people are still basically the same.

Choices & CHALLENGES

Writing Options

1. **Parable Sequel** Decide what might happen next in the parable of the prodigal son. Write a sequel to the story.

2. **Modern Parable** Think of a simple lesson about life that you would like to teach others. Then write a modern parable, in either a serious or a humorous style, to convey the lesson. Place the parable in your **Working Portfolio.**

3. **Newspaper Editorial** Pretend that you work for your local newspaper. Write an editorial relating the message of one of these selections to contemporary life. Tell how a local or world situation might be improved if people took the message to heart.

Writing Handbook
See pages 1369–1370: Analysis.

4. **Spiritual Essay** The philosopher George Santayana once said that "there is no cure for birth and death save to enjoy the interval." How does his reflection on life compare with the spiritual lessons taught in these three selections? Draft an essay to answer this question, using specific lines or sentences from the three selections to support your opinion.

Activities & Explorations

1. **Calendar Design** Design a 12-month calendar that contains your favorite lines from the selections. Choose one line for each month. Then find appropriate art to accompany the texts, or use a computer to make your own illustrations. ~ **ART**

2. **Dramatic Soliloquy** Imagine that you are the older son in the parable of the prodigal son. Rehearse and perform a dramatic soliloquy—a speech revealing your innermost thoughts—about events in your life. ~ **PERFORMING**

3. **Biblical Collage** Create a collage of images that reflects your understanding of the excerpt from Ecclesiastes. You may use fine art, photographs, illustrations, or a combination of the three. ~ **ART**

Inquiry & Research

1. **Language Chart** Note that the King James Bible contains verb forms ending in *-eth* and *-est.* Look up these endings in a dictionary. How far back do they go in the history of the language? Which ending is used for the second person, and which for the third person? In most dictionaries, terms such as *colloquial, slang, poetic,* and *archaic* are used to describe certain words. Which term is applied to these endings?

2. **Music and the Bible** Find and share with classmates the Byrds' 1966 recording of the song "Turn, Turn, Turn." Compare the lyrics of the song with the passage from Ecclesiastes that you have read. Then discuss the significance of the song's title.

Art Connection

Looking at Rembrandt One critic has stated that Rembrandt's *Return of the Prodigal Son* (page 438) represents the artist's idea of Christian forgiveness and mercy. Look closely at the painting. In addition to the subject matter, what qualities of the painting do you think express the idea of mercy or forgiveness?

LaserLinks:
Background for Reading
Art Gallery

Writing Options

1. **Parable Sequel** Ask students to base their continuations on details from the parable as well as their own experience.
2. **Modern Parable** Have students brainstorm for ideas about the lesson they want to teach. Then have students review the characteristics of a parable on page 443 before completing this activity.
3. **Newspaper Editorial** Encourage students to examine actual newspaper editorials and to use them as models for their own editorials.
4. **Spiritual Essay** Divide students into groups and have them discuss this question before drafting their essays. Encourage them to list the aspects of life that the three selections emphasize and those emphasized by the quote. Students can refer to these lists as they write their essays.

Activities & Explorations

1. **Calendar Design** Remind students that the art on page 436 was used to illustrate a medieval calendar. Ask students to choose lines that have seasonal references to particular months.
2. **Dramatic Soliloquy** Have students expand on the older son's words and other details about his behavior that appear in the parable. Remind students to think about and represent specific emotions at appropriate moments in their performances.
3. **Biblical Collage** Encourage students to illustrate both the positive and the negative aspects of life mentioned in the excerpt.

Art Connection

Looking at Rembrandt Possible Responses: Students may mention the father's facial expression, the embrace, the physical postures of the characters, and the warm colors in the painting.

Inquiry & Research

1. **Language Chart** Point out that this material actually refers to the translator's style. Students will find that the endings go back to Old English; *-eth* was used with third-person subjects; *-est,* with second-person. Both are now archaic.
2. **Music and the Bible** Recordings of this song by various performers are readily available on audiocassette and CD. You might play different versions in class to spark discussion. Ask students whether the addition of music changes the meaning of the lines. Does music affect the tone of the lines? If so, how?

OVERVIEW

Objectives

1. understand and appreciate classic **essays (Literary Analysis)**
2. use the strategy of **evaluating opinion (Active Reading)**

Summary

Studies, according to Bacon, have three purposes. Privately, they provide delight; in society, they ornament conversation; in business, they aid judgment. In all areas, however, an excessive dependence on them is harmful. Single men, according to Bacon, enjoy liberty and opportunities for great enterprises. Those who are married and have children, however, often show the greatest concern for the future, because their descendants will have to live in it.

 Use **Unit Two Resource Book,** p. 52 for additional support.

Thematic Link

"Of Studies" explores the nature of study as a means to self-improvement with an admonition for moderation and right purpose. "Of Marriage and Single Life" addresses the various benefits and limitations of marriage. Both essays deal with ways in which people **face life's limitations.**

5-Minute Warm-Up

Daily Language SkillBuilder

Have students **proofread** the display sentences on page 273l and write them correctly. The sentences also appear on Transparency 9 of **Grammar Transparencies and Copymasters.**

PREPARING to *Read*

from Essays

By SIR FRANCIS BACON

"Reading maketh a full man, conference a ready man, and writing an exact man."

Connect to Your Life

Burning Issues Most people have strong opinions about certain topics or issues. Think about an issue that concerns you—perhaps something that affects you personally, such as a school policy or a community problem, or a more universal issue, such as crime, the protection of the environment, or individual rights. Then get together with a group of classmates and explain your stand on the issue, citing reasons that support your position.

Build Background

Opinions on Life Sir Francis Bacon is often called the father of the English **essay.** In 1597, he published ten essays, the first examples of that literary form to gain popularity in England. Bacon actually borrowed the title and concept for his *Essays* from the French author Michel de Montaigne, who had published a similar work, titled *Essais,* in 1580. In contrast with Montaigne's writing—which is light and personal, revealing glimpses of the author's own life and personality—Bacon's essays are more philosophical, offering opinions on the nature of human behavior and motivation and generalizing about what humans do and ought to do. In writing his essays, Bacon had a single purpose in mind—to give instruction and advice to young men who were ambitious to succeed. His first collection included "Of Studies," one of the essays presented on the following pages. His final collection was published in 1625, a year before his death, and included 58 essays on subjects ranging from love, friendship, and beauty to superstition, death, and revenge.

Focus Your Reading

LITERARY ANALYSIS ESSAY An **essay** is a brief work of nonfiction that offers an opinion on a subject. The purpose of an essay may be to express ideas and feelings, to inform, to entertain, or to persuade. The main point of an essay is often presented in the opening sentences, as in the first sentence of "Of Studies."

Studies serve for delight, for ornament, and for ability.

As you read the two essays, pay particular attention to the examples, facts, and reasons Bacon uses to support his main points.

ACTIVE READING EVALUATING OPINION When you are reading nonfiction, it is important to **evaluate opinions** as you encounter them.

READER'S NOTEBOOK Make two charts like the one shown, one for each of Bacon's essays. As you read each essay, look for statements of opinion. Write each statement in your chart and use a check to indicate whether you agree or disagree with it.

Opinion	Agree	Disagree
To spend too much time in studies is sloth.		

LESSON RESOURCES

UNIT TWO RESOURCE BOOK, pp. 52–55

ASSESSMENT RESOURCES

Formal Assessment, p. 67

Teacher's Guide to Assessment and Portfolio Use

Test Generator

SKILLS TRANSPARENCIES AND COPYMASTERS

Literary Analysis

- Characteristics of the Essay, T11 (for Literary Analysis, p. 442)

Reading and Critical Thinking

- Analyzing Text Structure, T17 (for Active Reading, p. 442)

Grammar

- Avoiding Misplaced and Dangling Modifiers, T51 (for Mini Lesson, pp. 444–445)
- Placement of Phrases, C88 (for Mini Lesson, pp. 444–445)

Writing

- Opinion Statement, C35 (for Writing Option 2, p. 448)

Communications

- Interviewing, T9 (for Activities & Explorations 2, p. 448)

INTEGRATED TECHNOLOGY

Audio Library

Internet: Research Starter

Visit our website: www.mcdougallittell.com

Of Studies

Sir Francis Bacon

wise men use them

Crafty men contemn studies

Abeunt studia in mores

natural abilities are like natural plants

Reading maketh a full man

Some books are to be tasted

simple men admire them

Detail of *Still Life with Old Books* (17th century), unknown French artist. Courtesy of the Musée de Brou, Bourg-en-Bresse, France.

Studies serve for delight, for ornament, and for ability. Their chief use for delight is in privateness and retiring; for ornament, is in discourse;[1] and for ability, is in the judgment and disposition of business. For expert men can execute, and perhaps judge of particulars, one by one; but the general counsels, and the plots and marshaling of affairs, come best from those that are learned. To spend too much time in studies is sloth; to use them too much for ornament is affectation;[2] to make judgment wholly by their rules is the humor[3] of a scholar. They perfect

1. **discourse:** conversation.
2. **affectation:** something done just for show or to give a false impression.
3. **humor:** whim; temperament.

TEACHING THE LITERATURE

Customizing Instruction

Less Proficient Readers

Set a Purpose Have students read the selections to discover Bacon's most important points about the value of education.

Student Acquiring English

Point out that in parallel structures, repeated words are often omitted as understood. Ask what words are omitted in the phrases following "History make men wise."

Answer: "make men."

Use **Spanish Study Guide** for additional support, pp. 82–84.

BLOCK SCHEDULING: MANAGING TIME

If your schedule requires that you cover the lesson objectives in a shorter time, use . . .

- Preparing to Read, p. 442
- Thinking Through the Literature, p. 447

If you want to take advantage of longer class time, use . . .

- TE Teaching Options: Grammar, p. 444; Speaking and Listening, p. 446
- Choices & Challenges and Author Activity, p. 448

Reading and Analyzing

Active Reading EVALUATING OPINION

Remind students that opinions are statements that are not verifiable but instead represent a person's attitudes, beliefs, or feelings about an issue. Have students identify Bacon's opinion about books.

Possible Response: He thinks books are beneficial if used with judgment and thought.

 Use **Unit Two Resource Book,** p. 53 for additional support.

Literary Analysis ESSAY

A The listing of sports and the ailments they are said to cure may seem an unnecessary digression to students. Tell students that such seemingly unfocused arguments typify informal essays. Ask students to explain why Bacon might have provided this information about sports.

Possible Responses: to give parallel examples of what benefits the body before giving examples of what benefits the mind; to add interest for those who are sports-minded.

 Use **Unit Two Resource Book,** p. 54 for additional support.

Thinking Through the Literature

1. They could overdo it and become lazy or put on affectations; they could rely too much on others' judgment.
2. Accept all reasonable responses.
3. Some students may feel that different studies develop different skills or types of learning—visual, kinesthetic, and so on. Others may feel that all studies develop the same basic critical-thinking skills.
4. Accept all reasonable responses.

nature, and are perfected by experience; for natural abilities are like natural plants, that need pruning by study; and studies themselves do give forth directions too much at large, except they be bounded in by experience. Crafty men contemn[4] studies, simple men admire them, and wise men use them, for they teach not their own use; but that is a wisdom without them, and above them, won by observation. Read not to contradict and confute,[5] nor to believe and take for granted, nor to find talk and discourse, but to weigh and consider. Some books are to be tasted, others to be swallowed, and some few to be chewed and digested; that is, some books are to be read only in parts; others to be read, but not curiously;[6] and some few to be read wholly, and with diligence and attention. Some books also may be read by deputy and extracts made of them by others, but that would be only in the less important arguments and the meaner sort of books; else[7] distilled[8] books are like common distilled waters,[9] flashy[10] things. Reading maketh a full man, conference[11] a ready man, and writing an exact man. And therefore, if a man write little, he had need have a great memory; if he confer little, he had need have a present wit;[12] and if he read little, he had need have much cunning, to seem to know that he doth not. Histories make men wise; poets, witty; the mathematics, subtle; natural philosophy, deep; moral, grave; logic and rhetoric, able to contend. *Abeunt studia in mores.*[13] Nay, there is no stond[14] or impediment in the wit but may be wrought out by fit studies, like as diseases of the body may have appropriate exercises. Bowling is good for the stone and reins,[15] shooting for the lungs and breast, gentle walking for the stomach, riding for the head, and the like. So if a man's wit be wandering, let him study the mathematics; for in demonstrations, if his wit be called away never so little, he must begin again. If his wit be not apt to distinguish or find differences, let him study the schoolmen,[16] for they are *cumini sectores.*[17] If he be not apt to beat over[18] matters and to call up one thing to prove and illustrate another, let him study the lawyer's cases. So every defect of the mind may have a special receipt.[19] ❖ **A**

4. **contemn:** view with contempt, hate.
5. **confute:** prove wrong.
6. **curiously:** carefully or thoroughly.
7. **else:** in other respects.
8. **distilled:** having only the important elements extracted or taken out.
9. **common distilled waters:** herbal home remedies.
10. **flashy:** tasteless; dull.
11. **conference:** conversation.
12. **present wit:** active intelligence.
13. ***Abeunt studia in mores*** (ä′bĕ-o͝ont sto͞o′dē-ä ĭn mō′rāz) *Latin:* Studies show themselves in manners.
14. **stond:** stoppage.
15. **the stone and reins:** kidney stones and other kidney disorders.
16. **schoolmen:** medieval scholastic philosophers.
17. ***cumini sectores*** (ko͞o′mĭ-nē sĕk-tō′rāz) *Latin:* cutters of herbs—that is, people who make extremely fine distinctions; hairsplitters.
18. **beat over:** reason through.
19. **receipt:** remedy; prescription.

Thinking Through the Literature

1. **Comprehension Check** According to Bacon, why should men avoid being too influenced by their studies?
2. What was your first reaction to Bacon's views on studies?
3. Do you think that different kinds of studies can have different effects on you? Give reasons for your opinion.
4. Have Bacon's opinions changed your attitude toward studies or toward the reading of books? Explain your answer.

Teaching Options

Grammar

PLACEMENT OF PHRASES

Instruction Writers usually place phrases near the word the phrase modifies to make the relationship clear.

Activity Write this sentence on the chalkboard.

"He that hath wife and children hath given hostages to fortune; for they are impediments to great enterprises, <u>either of virtue or mischief.</u>"

Underline the phrase as shown. Ask students to name the word being modified. *(enterprises)* Have them explain why it isn't *impediments* that is modified. (The phrase is located immediately after the word *enterprises.*)

Two of the errors that writers sometimes make when placing phrases are called misplaced modifiers and dangling modifiers. A misplaced modifier is placed so far away from the word it modifies that the meaning of the sentence is unclear, or even funny. Example: "Hopping slowly across the yard, I saw a toad."

A dangling modifier, often found at the beginning of a sentence, does not clearly modify any noun or pronoun in the sentence. Example: "Having failed to show up for the performance, the part was played by John." To correct dangling

Of Marriage and Single Life

Sir Francis Bacon

Vetulam suam praetulit immortalitati

single men . . . are more cruel and hard-hearted

single life is liberty

It is often seen that BAD husbands have very *good* wives

Unmarried men are best friends . . . but not always best subjects

wife and children are a kind of discipline of humanity

. . . those that have children should have greatest care of future times

Customizing Instruction

Less Proficient Readers

Set a Purpose Tell students to read the next essay to discover Bacon's ideas about the benefits and drawbacks of marriage.

Students Acquiring English

Point out that Bacon makes a number of remarks about wives and children. Help students follow Bacon's argument by having students list Bacon's opinions about the relative merits of wives and children.

Have students work together to answer the following questions from the two essays.

1. What does Bacon say must temper studies?

Answer: experience.

2. What does he say "maketh an exact man?"

Answer: writing.

3. What kind of people does he feel make better clergymen? Better soldiers?

Answer: single; married.

modifiers, students need to make sure the sentence names the thing being modified.

Exercise Ask students to rewrite each sentence to correct any dangling or misplaced modifiers. If the sentence is correct, have students write correct.

1. Sir Francis Bacon published essays that were meant to help young men be successful beginning in 1597. *(. . . published essays beginning in 1597 that were . . .)*
2. Borrowing the form of the essay from a French writer, the essay was transformed from a light personal piece into a philosophical study. *(. . . French writer, Bacon transformed the essay from a light . . .)*
3. If you believe that there are three reasons to study—to be entertained, to show off, or to learn—then you and Sir Francis Bacon share an opinion. *(correct)*

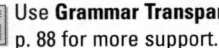

Use **Grammar Transparencies and Copymasters,** p. 88 for more support.

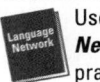

Use McDougal Littell's ***Language Network*** for more instruction and practice in placement of phrases.

Reading and Analyzing

Literary Analysis: APHORISM

A An aphorism is a concise, pointed statement that expresses a general observation about life in a clever or forceful way. Have students identify aphorisms in the essay that seem memorable enough to appear in a book of quotations.

Possible Response: Unmarried men are best friends, best masters, best servants, but not always best subjects . . .

Reading Skills and Strategies: STATING YOUR OPINION

B Ask if students agree that the unmarried are likely to make better friends.

Possible Responses: Yes, since family demands one's time or concern; no, since family ties teach love and loyalty.

He that hath wife and children hath given hostages to fortune; for they are impediments to great enterprises, either of virtue or mischief. Certainly the best works, and of greatest merit for the public, have proceeded from the unmarried or childless men, which both in affection and means have married and endowed the public. Yet it were great reason that those that have children should have greatest care of future times, unto which they know they must transmit their dearest pledges. Some there are who, though they lead a single life, yet their thoughts do end with themselves, and account future times impertinences.[1] Nay, there are some other that account wife and children but as bills of charges. Nay more, there are some foolish rich covetous men that take a pride in having no children, because they may be thought so much the richer. For perhaps they have heard some talk, "Such an one is a great rich man," and another except to it, "Yea, but he hath a great charge of children"; as if it were an abatement[2] to his riches. But the most ordinary cause of a single life is liberty, especially in certain self-pleasing and humorous[3] minds, which are so sensible of every restraint, as they will go near to think their girdles and garters to be bonds and shackles. Unmarried men are best friends, best masters, best servants, but not always best subjects, for they are light to run away, and almost all fugitives are of that condition. A single life doth well with churchmen, for charity will hardly water the ground where it must first fill a pool. It is indifferent for judges and magistrates, for if they be facile[4] and corrupt, you shall have a servant five times worse than a wife. For soldiers, I find the generals commonly in their hortatives[5] put men in mind of their wives and children; and I think the despising of marriage amongst the Turks maketh the vulgar[6] soldier more base. Certainly wife and children are a kind of discipline of humanity; and single men, though they be many times more charitable, because their means are less exhaust,[7] yet, on the other side, they are more cruel and hard-hearted (good to make severe inquisitors), because their tenderness is not so oft called upon. Grave natures, led by custom, and therefore constant, are commonly loving husbands, as was said of Ulysses, *Vetulam suam praetulit immortalitati.*[8] Chaste women are often proud and froward,[9] as presuming upon the merit of their chastity. It is one of the best bonds, both of chastity and obedience, in the wife if she think her husband wise, which she will never do if she find him jealous. Wives are young men's mistresses, companions for middle age, and old men's nurses, so as a man may have a quarrel[10] to marry when he will. But yet he was reputed one of the wise men that made answer to the question when a man should marry: "A young man not yet, an elder man not at all." It is often seen that bad husbands have very good wives; whether it be that it raiseth the price of their husbands' kindness when it comes, or that the wives take a pride in their patience. But this never fails, if the bad husbands were of their own choosing, against their friends' consent; for then they will be sure to make good their own folly. ❖

A single life doth well with churchmen

Wives are young men's mistresses, . . . and old men's nurses

1. **impertinences** (ĭm-pûr′tn-ən-səz): irrelevant concerns; things not worthy of attention.
2. **abatement** (ə-bāt′mənt): a reduction.
3. **humorous:** whimsical.
4. **facile** (făs′əl): easily influenced or persuaded.
5. **hortatives** (hôr′tə-tĭvz): speeches to encourage troops before battle.
6. **vulgar:** common; ordinary.
7. **exhaust:** depleted; drained.
8. ***Vetulam suam praetulit immortalitati*** (vĕ′tŏŏ-läm sŏŏ′äm prī′tŏŏ-lĭt ĭm-môr-tä′lĭ-tä′tē) *Latin:* He preferred his aged wife to immortality.
9. **froward** (frō′wərd): stubborn.
10. **quarrel:** reason; excuse.

Teaching Options

Speaking and Listening

RECOGNIZING PARALLELISM

Instruction Bacon often uses identical grammatical structures to express related ideas. This technique, called parallelism, is illustrated in the statement "Crafty men contemn studies, simple men admire them." Explain to students that parallelism helps make statements more memorable and allows the writer to omit repeated words.

Prepare Have students find other examples of parallelism in the essay, such as "Studies serve for delight, for ornament, and for ability."

Present Students should share their examples with the class by reading them aloud to emphasize the rhythm created by using parallelism.

BLOCK SCHEDULING This activity is particularly well-suited for longer class periods.

Connect to the Literature

1. **What Do You Think?** Did any of the statements in "Of Marriage and Single Life" surprise you? Explain why.

Comprehension Check
- According to Bacon, which professions are best suited to unmarried men?
- Describe the importance of marriage to men at different times in their lives.

Think Critically

2. Which do you think Bacon respects more, the married life or the single life? Support your answer with details from the **essay.**

3. How would you describe Bacon's views of men and of women?

THINK ABOUT
- the assumptions he makes about men and about women
- the different roles he assigns to men and women
- his opinion of the relationship between men and women

4. Think about the aspects of marriage that Bacon describes in his essay. In your opinion, why has he failed to mention love?

5. ACTIVE READING EVALUATING OPINION Study the opinion charts you completed in your READER'S NOTEBOOK as you read the two essays. Beside each statement you disagreed with, write down your own opinion on the subject. Discuss your opinions with a partner.

Extend Interpretations

6. **What If?** Suppose that Bacon had addressed his essays to young women. What specific advice do you think he would offer?

7. **Different Perspectives** What advice do you think a female contemporary of Bacon's would give to young men on marriage?

8. **Connect to Life** Today there is a great deal of discussion about what makes a good marriage. Do you think any of Bacon's views are relevant to contemporary ideas about marriage? Provide supporting details for your conclusions.

Literary Analysis

ESSAY In an **essay,** a writer offers an opinion on a subject. Bacon's essays are **persuasive,** designed to convince the reader to accept his ideas. Some of Bacon's statements are well supported with examples, facts, and reasons. For example, in "Of Marriage and Single Life," Bacon claims that single men produce the best works because they can devote all their energies to a particular task. A married man's wife and children, he suggests, are "impediments to great enterprises." On the other hand, some of Bacon's statements are unsubstantiated. His declaration that chaste women are often proud and stubborn, for instance, is unsupported by any reasons or examples.

Cooperative Learning Activity Remember that one of Bacon's main purposes in writing his essays was to give advice to young men of the time who wanted to succeed in life. As a class, divide into two groups. With your group, make a list of guidelines from each essay that could be included in a book of "rules for success." Share your list with the class.

GUIDING STUDENT RESPONSE

Connect to the Literature

1. **What Do You Think?** Guidelines for student response: Students should provide evidence from the text in their explanations.

Comprehension Check
- servants, churchmen
- Young men desire their wives; men in middle age have companionable wives; old men have wives to nurse them.

 Use **Unit Two Resource Book,** p. 55 for additional support.

Thinking Critically

2. Students who answer "the single life" may cite Bacon's calling a wife and children impediments to success. Those who answer "the married life" may mention his suggestion that single men are irresponsible. Some students may feel that he balances the pros and cons equally.
3. Possible responses: Bacon views men as achievers and leaders but sees women only in domestic roles; he recognizes good and bad qualities in men but dwells on negative qualities in women.
4. Possible responses: His focus is on society, not the individual; he is a pragmatist, not a romantic; he lived at a time when marriages were often made for practical reasons.
5. Accept all well-supported, reasonable responses.

Extend Interpretations

What If? Bacon might suggest that women combine more obedience and amiability with their chastity to produce "the best bonds."

Different Perspectives A woman writing to the young men might caution them to appreciate their wives' attention and patience. She might also remind them that because women take care of many domestic responsibilities (such as raising children) men are able to pursue their more public duties and enjoy more personal freedom.

Connect to Life Responses will vary. Some students might think Bacon's view that children enrich a man's life is an important sentiment in any era. Others may find Bacon's rather dismissive attitude toward women and wives incompatible with contemporary notions of a good marriage.

Literary Analysis

Cooperative Learning Activity Some students might serve as drafters, pooling ideas and creating a tentative list. Others might be judges, voting on whether to include each item on the list. Still others can be writers, polishing the list into a final product. Finally, one student should serve as overall manager of the group project.

Writing Options

1. **Letter to Bacon** Students' letters will be similar to persuasive essays, so they should support generalizations and opinions with facts, examples, and reasons.
2. **Persuasive Essay** Again, remind students to support their ideas. You might ask them to try to include some aphorisms, using parallelism to make the statements memorable.
3. **Marriage Questionnaire** Students can work in small groups to complete this assignment and pool their ideas. Students will want to include queries from both the male and female point of view, keeping in mind that the questions might challenge as well as reflect Bacon's ideas.

Activities & Explorations

1. **Image Collection** Students might work in pairs to create their collections using personal photographs, pictures from magazines, prints of paintings, or original drawings. Students viewing the collections should try to explain how the images relate to the chosen passage.
2. **Opinion Poll** Students should try to poll both married and unmarried people, men and women, and people of various ages. Have students poll fellow classmates, family members, and other adults, and share their opinions with the class.

Choices & CHALLENGES

Writing Options

1. **Letter to Bacon** Select one of Bacon's statements with which you disagree. In a letter to the author, give reasons why you do not share his opinion.

2. **Persuasive Essay** Draft a persuasive essay about the issue you named for the Connect to Your Life on page 442. State your opinion regarding the issue, and give reasons for it. Place the persuasive essay in your **Working Portfolio.**

3. **Marriage Questionnaire** Create a list of questions for an opinion poll on marriage. Include questions that reflect Bacon's ideas.

Activities & Explorations

1. **Image Collection** Put together a collection of images—either paintings or photographs—that could be used to illustrate some of the ideas and impressions in "Of Studies" or in "Of Marriage and Single Life." Show your collection to the class and ask them what passage they think each image is related to. Discuss the reasons for your choices. ~ **VIEWING AND REPRESENTING**

2. **Opinion Poll** With a partner, conduct the opinion poll described in the third activity under "Writing Options." Question both students and adults, and videotape their responses if possible. Show your video to the class. ~ **SPEAKING AND LISTENING**

Inquiry & Research

Brain Calisthenics In Bacon's opinion, a variety of studies is needed to stimulate the different functions of the brain. Investigate current research on the brain and its functions. Report on two or three of the functions, listing activities that can strengthen each of them.

More Online: Research Starter
www.mcdougallittell.com

Sir Francis Bacon

1561–1626

Other Works
"Of Truth"
"Of Great Place"

Rise and Fall Like Marlowe and Raleigh, Francis Bacon was a Renaissance man. His interests extended from law and public service to philosophy and science. Although he entered Cambridge University at the age of 12, he stayed there just two years. He began his legal studies only when faced with financial difficulties, but he became an ambitious public servant and rose steadily in royal service, acting as legal counsel both to Elizabeth I and to James I. Bacon was eventually knighted and in 1618 was appointed to the highest judicial position in England. Three years later, his career ended in scandal when he was charged with—and admitted—accepting bribes.

Deadly Experimentation Banished from public service, Bacon directed his full attention to other interests. He was a prolific writer and produced, in addition to his famous essays, many philosophical and scientific treatises. Unfortunately, his avid interest in scientific discovery led ultimately to his death. Curious about the preservative effects of refrigeration, Bacon killed a hen and carefully stuffed it with snow. Chilled by the experiment, he developed bronchitis, from which he died on April 9, 1626.

Author Activity

Is Bacon the Bard? Some people have claimed that Francis Bacon is actually the author of plays attributed to William Shakespeare. Research these claims and draw your own conclusions. Share your results with the class.

Inquiry & Research

Brain Calisthenics Have students use a medical dictionary to familiarize themselves with terms related to the brain before moving on to more specialized journals of science and medicine. Students might want to draw diagrams or use illustrations from other sources to accompany their reports. They might do their research individually, prepare notes, and then share their findings in a panel discussion.

Author Activity

Is Bacon the Bard? Have students narrow their field of inquiry and focus on one or two of the claims made in favor of Bacon as the bard. Students should do research on both Shakespeare and Bacon before drawing conclusions. They might also want to read more of Shakespeare's work (the sonnets, for example) and more of Bacon's essays to develop their own sense of the authors' styles.

Metaphysical Poetry

Leaving the Elizabethans Behind

Portrait of John Donne as a young man (artist unknown)

If you found the intricacies of the sonnet form and the musical language of Elizabethan love poetry artificial, you aren't alone. During the 17th century, a number of poets rejected the highly ornamented style of late-Elizabethan lyric poetry. They wrote what became known as **metaphysical poetry.**

Metaphysical poetry was written in the manner of everyday speech—the everyday speech, that is, of someone deeply introspective and slightly irreverent. (*Metaphysical* in this usage refers to abstract or theoretical reasoning.) Such a personality is evident throughout the works of John Donne, who is considered the movement's central figure. His down-to-earth yet philosophical approach also characterizes the works of the other metaphysical poets, including Andrew Marvell, George Herbert, Richard Crashaw, and Henry Vaughan.

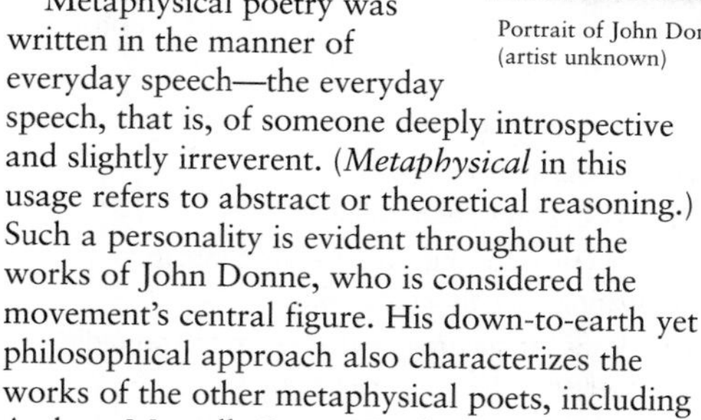

Riddles from Donne

YOUR TURN Try to figure out these comparisons from Donne (answers appear below):

That swimming college, and free hospitall
Of all mankind; that cage and vivary
Of fowls, and beasts . . .

* * * * *

In which as in a gallery this mouse
Walk'd, and surveyed the rooms of this vast house,
And to the brain, the souls bedchamber, went,
And gnaw'd the life cords there.

Answers: Noah's ark; Mouse enters elephant through trunk.

Experiments with Language

When you first read metaphysical poetry, the ideas expressed in it may seem confusing. The metaphysical poets experimented with language in imaginative ways. One device they used was the **metaphysical conceit,** an extended metaphor that makes a surprising connection between two quite dissimilar things. An example is Donne's description in "A Valediction: Forbidding Mourning" of how two lovers' souls are connected, despite their physical distance:

> **If they be two, they are two so**
> **As stiff twin compasses are two;**
> **Thy soul, the fixed foot, makes no show**
> **To move, but doth, if th' other do.**
>
> **—John Donne, "A Valediction: Forbidding Mourning"**

The speaker likens the lovers' souls to the legs of a compass used for drawing circles. One lover is the "fixed foot" that remains home, while the other is the foot that journeys away—but always in a circle. The conceit suggests that, though the lovers are not together, their souls are so joined that they will always be in sympathy with each other. The metaphysical poets' use of such fanciful and extended conceits led the writer and critic Samuel Johnson to complain about their "violent yoking together of heterogeneous ideas."

Another characteristic of metaphysical poetry is **paradox**—a statement that seems contradictory but nevertheless suggests a truth. In his poem "A Fever," Donne ties together the contradictory concepts of love and hate in a startling way:

LEARNING the language of LITERATURE

OVERVIEW

Objectives

- understand the following literary terms:
  - Metaphysical poetry
  - Metaphysical conceit
  - Paradox
- recognize themes across cultures.

Teaching the Lesson

This lesson will give students some background on the metaphysical poem as a literary form.

Introducing the Concepts

To spark interest in metaphysical poetry, ask students which popular songs treat the topic love.

After students have suggested the names of songs, ask which songs have words comparing love or a lover to something else.

Possible Response: Love might be compared to a deep ocean; a lover might be compared to rain falling on hardened ground.

As students read, have them keep in mind similarities and differences between modern expressions of feelings and the feelings expressed by metaphysical poets.

Presenting the Concepts

Read through the strategies aloud or project them on a transparency. Using the Elements of Metaphysical Poetry listed on page 450, compare metaphysical poetry with the sonnet. Model how to use the strategies to analyze the poems.

Making Connections

Metaphysical Poetry Across Cultures

The metaphysical poets were a small group in England, but traditions of introspective, philosophical poems using simple language were well established in a number of cultures by the 13th century. Share the following poetic traditions with students.

Japan
Since the sixth century, Japanese followers of Zen, a Buddhist philosophy, have written poems to express their spiritual enlightenment. Poems by Dogen, a Zen master of the 13th century, use simple descriptions of nature to express spiritual truths.

China
Orthodox Confucians in China thought one of the most important purposes of poetry was to give moral instruction and to inspire people to do their duty. Like Japanese Zen poets, Chinese poets of the 13th century often used descriptions of nature to express spiritual truths. Unlike the Zen poets, they expressed their ideas and feelings directly.

Persia
In Persia (modern-day Iran), Sufi mystics sought to express their union with God in poetry. The most famous Sufi poet was Jalalu'l-Din Rūmī, who lived in the 13th century. His poems express spiritual truths directly, as well as through metaphors.

Oh do not die, for I shall hate
All women so when thou art gone,
That thee I shall not celebrate
When I remember, thou wast one.

—John Donne, "A Fever"

The speaker's feelings reveal a paradox: he loves a woman so much that he will not praise her if she dies.

YOUR TURN With a partner, come up with a paradox or a conceit of your own using objects from everyday life.

Another characteristic of Donne's poetry is his disruption of poetic meter (the regular pattern of stressed and unstressed syllables). Violating the poetic meter occurs frequently in poetry, but in the eyes of many critics, Donne used this poetic technique too often. Poet Ben Jonson once declared that "Donne, for not keeping of accent, deserved hanging." However, Jonson had to admit that he greatly admired Donne as a poet.

The Critics Respond

As Jonson's comment reveals, metaphysical poetry did have its detractors. In fact, the label "metaphysical poetry" was originally meant as a criticism. In the late 1700s, Samuel Johnson named the group metaphysical poets because he thought that they used their poetry merely to show off their knowledge. Earlier, the writer John Dryden had made a similar criticism of Donne's poetry. Donne, Dryden wrote, "affects the metaphysics . . . [even] in his amorous verses, where nature only should reign."

The metaphysical poets experienced a revival in the early 20th century, thanks in part to poet and critic T. S. Eliot. In a famous essay, Eliot praised the metaphysical poets' ability to unify experience—in particular, to "feel their thought as immediately as the odor of a rose."

Elements of Metaphysical Poetry

Although every metaphysical poet had a unique style, their poetry shares several traits:

- simple, conversational diction
- complex sentence patterns
- themes that are often philosophical
- metaphysical conceits, or extended metaphors comparing very dissimilar things
- paradoxes, or statements that seem to contradict themselves
- disruptions of poetic meter
- witty and imaginative plays on words

Strategies for Reading: Metaphysical Poetry

1. Use the notes that accompany the poems to help you better understand the metaphysical poets' use of language.
2. Study each metaphysical conceit and identify the things being compared.
3. Look for paradoxes and try to determine what deeper meanings they convey.
4. Identify the subject and verb of any problematic clause, and then try to determine the functions of surrounding words or phrases.
5. Paraphrase any dense passages.
6. **Monitor** your reading strategies and modify them when your understanding breaks down. Remember to use your Strategies for Active Reading: **predict, visualize, connect, question, clarify,** and **evaluate.**

"No man is an island, entire of itself."

A Valediction: Forbidding Mourning
Holy Sonnet 10
from Meditation 17

Poetry and Nonfiction by JOHN DONNE

Connect to Your Life

The Meaning of Life Many writers struggle with life's difficult questions and try to come to terms with their own doubts and fears by writing about them. Think about how you strive to find answers to your most challenging questions about life. How do you express your thoughts and concerns? Share your reflections with others.

Build Background

Poet and Preacher As a young man, John Donne wrote passionate love poems and sought the admiration of numerous women. Later in life, Donne made a notable change. He married, fathered 12 children, entered the ministry, and authored over 160 sermons. "Jack" Donne, the spirited young Renaissance man, became Dr. John Donne, a highly respected preacher and the dean of St. Paul's Cathedral in London.

Donne was an intellectual who contemplated life's most perplexing questions, particularly those involving death—a common literary theme of the time. During the Renaissance, medical knowledge was limited, and effective medicines were rare. It was not unusual for people to die well before the age of 50. Donne's own wife died at the age of 33, shortly after giving birth to their 12th child. Two of his children were stillborn, and others died at the ages of 3, 7, and 19.

"A Valediction: Forbidding Mourning" was written prior to the poet's departure for France in 1611. The poem was intended to console his wife, who was distressed over her husband's impending long absence. "Holy Sonnet 10" reflects Donne's concerns about spiritual matters, particularly death and salvation. Donne wrote "Meditation 17" in 1623 while recovering from a serious illness. He was inspired in part by hearing the ringing of church bells to announce a person's death.

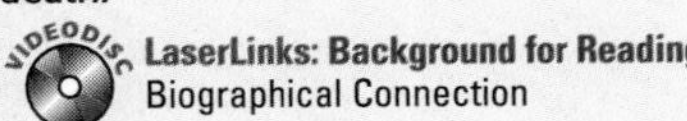

LaserLinks: Background for Reading
Biographical Connection

Focus Your Reading

LITERARY ANALYSIS EXTENDED METAPHOR

An **extended metaphor,** or **conceit,** compares two unlike things at length and in a number of ways. In "Meditation 17," for example, Donne uses an extended metaphor to compare humanity to a book in which each person makes up a chapter. As you read these selections, be aware of other examples of extended metaphors employed by the writer.

ACTIVE READING INTERPRETING LANGUAGE STRUCTURES

In his writing, Donne frequently uses **paradox** (a statement that seems to contradict itself but reveals some element of truth), unusual **imagery,** and surprising **comparisons.** By identifying these elements, you can gain insight into the main ideas in a work and the relationship between those ideas.

READER'S NOTEBOOK As you read these selections by Donne, identify and list unusual images, paradoxes, and comparisons in each work.

OVERVIEW

Objectives

1. understand and appreciate **metaphysical poetry and prose (Literary Analysis)**
2. identify and examine **extended metaphors (Literary Analysis)**
3. use strategies for interpreting language structures **(Active Reading)**

Summary

In "A Valediction: Forbidding Mourning," the speaker urges his love not to mourn his absence, because their love is spiritually strong and can endure the physical separation. He compares their love to twin compasses with one lover remaining stationary, while the other revolves around its center, making a perfect circle.

In "Holy Sonnet 10," the speaker claims not to fear death. He commands it not to be proud, because those who die live on eternally, while Death itself shall die.

Donne states in "Meditation 17" that because all people are creations of God, they are connected to one another like the limbs of a single body. Therefore, what affects one person affects everyone.

Use **Unit Two Resource Book,** p. 56 for additional support.

Thematic Link

In these selections Donne reflects on **facing life's limitations,** such as separation from a loved one, illness, and death. At the same time he affirms the power of the human spirit—the strength of love, the immortal soul, and the ties of the human family.

5-Minute Warm-Up

Daily Language SkillBuilder

Have students **proofread** the display sentences on page 273l and write them correctly. The sentences also appear on Transparency 9 of **Grammar Transparencies and Copymasters.**

LESSON RESOURCES

UNIT TWO RESOURCE BOOK, pp. 56–59

ASSESSMENT RESOURCES

Formal Assessment, pp. 69–70
Teacher's Guide to Assessment and Portfolio Use
Test Generator

SKILLS TRANSPARENCIES AND COPYMASTERS

Literary Analysis
- Theme, T9 (for Extend Interpretations 5, p. 456)

Reading and Critical Thinking
- Analyzing Text, T18 (for Think Critically, p. 456)

Grammar
- Diagramming Complements and Appositives, T59 (for Mini Lesson, p. 452)
- Modifiers that Follow Verbs, C72 (for Mini Lesson, p. 452)

Vocabulary
- Meaning in Context, C46 (for Mini Lesson, p. 454)

Writing
- Figurative Language and Sound Devices, T15 (for Writing Option 1, p. 457)

Communications
- Dramatic Reading, T12 (for Activities & Explorations 2, p. 457)

INTEGRATED TECHNOLOGY

Audio Library
LaserLinks
- Biographical Connection: John Donne. See **Teacher's SourceBook,** p. 27.

Internet: Research Starter
Visit our website:
www.mcdougallittell.com

TEACHING THE LITERATURE

Reading and Analyzing

Literary Analysis: SIMILE

A Have students summarize the comparison in lines 1–6.

Possible Response: Let us part quietly, as virtuous souls do when they die.

Ask students to describe what kind of parting this might be because it is compared to death.

Possible Responses: serious; painful; a long absence.

Literary Analysis
EXTENDED METAPHOR

B Remind students that extended metaphors compare two unlike things at length. Have students explain the types of love contrasted here (lines 13–20) and the implied comparison to stanza 3.

Possible Response: Just as earthquakes cause harm but heavenly motion does not, partings upset earthbound lovers but not more spiritual lovers such as the speaker and his beloved.

Use **Unit Two Resource Book,** p. 58 for more exercises.

Active Reading
INTERPRETING LANGUAGE STRUCTURES

C Remind students that the use of unusual imagery is common in Donne's poetry. Have students paraphrase the image comparing the couples' souls to beaten gold.

Possible Response: Gold doesn't disappear but merely stretches when it is beaten thin; this image mirrors the couple's souls, which are so in sympathy that they are more connected than diminished when they're apart.

Use **Unit Two Resource Book,** p. 57 for more practice.

A Valediction: Forbidding Mourning

John Donne

A

As virtuous men pass mildly away,
    And whisper to their souls to go,
Whilst some of their sad friends do say
    The breath goes now, and some say, No;

So let us melt, and make no noise,
    No tear-floods, nor sigh-tempests move,
'Twere profanation of our joys
    To tell the laity our love.

Moving of th' earth brings harms and fears,
    Men reckon what it did and meant;
But trepidation of the spheres,
    Though greater far, is innocent.

5 melt: part; dissolve our togetherness.
7 profanation (prŏf'ə-nā'shən): an act of contempt for what is sacred or respected.
8 laity (lā'ĭ-tē): persons without understanding of the "religion" of love.
9 moving of th' earth: an earthquake.
11 trepidation of the spheres: apparently irregular movements of heavenly bodies.
12 innocent: harmless.

Teaching Options

Grammar

MODIFIERS THAT FOLLOW VERBS

Instruction Action verbs express an action, condition, or state of being; linking verbs link a subject to its complement; and adverbs and adjectives are modifiers that can follow verbs. An adverb or adverb phrase can modify an action verb by telling where, when, how, and to what extent. A predicate adjective comes after a linking verb and modifies the subject of the sentence.

Point out that some linking verbs, such as *looked, appeared,* and *feel,* can also be action verbs, so students must use the correct form—adjective or adverb—following the verb. Remind students that participles can also be predicate adjectives.

Practice Write the following on the chalkboard.

"Perchance he for whom this bell tolls may be so ill as that he knows not it tolls for him; . . ."

Have students decide whether each underlined word or phrase is an adverb or a predicate adjective and identify the word that is modified. *(ill: predicate adjective, he; not: adverb, knows; for him: adverb phrase, tolls)*

Exercise Ask students to write the correct form of

B

Dull sublunary lovers' love
 (Whose soul is sense) cannot admit
Absence, because it doth remove
 Those things which elemented it.

But we by a love so much refined
 That our selves know not what it is,
Inter-assuréd of the mind,
 Care less, eyes, lips, and hands to miss.

C

Our two souls therefore, which are one,
 Though I must go, endure not yet
A breach, but an expansion,
 Like gold to airy thinness beat.

If they be two, they are two so
 As stiff twin compasses are two;
Thy soul, the fixed foot, makes no show
 To move, but doth, if th' other do.

And though it in the center sit,
 Yet when the other far doth roam,
It leans and hearkens after it,
 And grows erect, as that comes home.

Such wilt thou be to me, who must
 Like th' other foot, obliquely run;
Thy firmness makes my circle just,
 And makes me end where I begun.

13 sublunary (sŭb'lo͞o-nĕr'ē) **lovers' love:** the love of earthly lovers, which, like all things beneath the moon, is subject to change and death.
14 soul: essence; **sense:** sensuality.
16 elemented: composed.

19 inter-assuréd of the mind: confident of each other's love.

22 endure not yet: do not, nevertheless, suffer.

26 twin compasses: the two legs of a compass used for drawing circles.

32 as that comes home: when the moving foot returns to the center as the compass is closed.

34 obliquely (ō-blēk'lē): not in a straight line.
35 firmness: constancy; **just:** perfect.

Thinking Through the Literature

1. **Comprehension Check** To what does the poem compare the speaker and his love?
2. What **image** in this poem made the greatest impression on you? Why did it impress you?
3. How do you think the speaker would define true love?
   THINK ABOUT
   - his description of "sublunary lovers' love" (lines 13–16)
   - the comparison in lines 25–36
   - the title of the poem
4. In your opinion, is the message of this poem still relevant? Explain your answer.

Customizing Instruction

Less Proficient Readers

Set a Purpose Have students read the poem to discover how Donne feels about leaving his wife.

Students Acquiring English

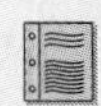

Use **Spanish Study Guide** for additional support, pp. 85–87.

Gifted and Talented

Ask students to consider the philosophical content of the three selections as they read. Have them compare the speaker's attitudes toward love and death to the attitudes of Shakespeare and Spenser. Has there been a philosophical shift in the generation between these writers?

Thinking Through the Literature

1. The poem compares their souls to two twin compasses.
2. Accept all reasonable responses.
3. Some students will say the speaker defines true love as mental and emotional rather than merely physical. Others will say he sees true love as a deep mutual understanding.
4. Those students who find it relevant will speak of love's universality. Other students will cite rapid transportation and communications that make separations less lengthy.

the word for each sentence and to write *adverb* or *predicate adjective* to describe the function of the word. Have students work in cooperative groups to find adverbs and predicate adjectives in a selection by Donne.

1. In "A Valediction: Forbidding Mourning" John Donne seems (fervent, fervently) in his belief that true love is steady regardless of distance. *(fervent; predicate adjective)*
2. Donne's wife felt (bad, badly) about her husband being away from her for long periods of time. *(badly; adverb)*
3. In "Holy Sonnet 10" the poet appears (real, really) absorbed in the subject of death. *(really; adverb)*
4. The bell tolled (slow, slowly) to mark the passing of life. *(slowly; adverb)*
5. John Donne's work seems (current, currently) because many of his phrases and themes have inspired recent works of prose or song. *(current; predicate adjective)*

Use **Grammar Transparencies and Copymasters,** p. 12.

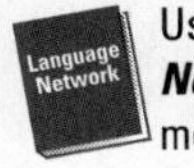

Use McDougal Littell's ***Language Network*** for more instruction in modifiers that follow verbs.

Reading and Analyzing

Active Reading

INTERPRETING LANGUAGE STRUCTURES

A Have students paraphrase the apparent paradoxes in lines 3 and 4 of "Holy Sonnet 10."

Possible Responses: Those whom Death thinks it kills actually do not die; Death cannot kill me.

Then ask how these seeming contradictions might be true in some way.

Possible Responses: Those who die find eternal life in Heaven; those who die live on in memory; poets live through their poetry.

Literary Analysis

EXTENDED METAPHOR

B Have students identify the basic metaphor upon which these lines elaborate.

Answer: "All mankind is of one author and is one volume."

Then ask what the basic metaphor implies about humanity.

Possible Responses: All humans are God's creatures; humans are more alike than different; humans share common experiences.

Thinking Through the Literature

1. Accept all reasonable responses.
2. Possible Responses: The speaker lacks fear of death; addressing death as a person makes death seem less powerful.
3. Possible Responses: In heaven death ceases to exist; once we know eternal life, we will no longer fear death.

Detail of Nativity of Christ. Stained glass, Abbey Ste. Foy, Conques, France. Giraudon/Art Resource, New York.

Holy Sonnet 10

John Donne

Death, be not proud, though some have callèd thee 1
Mighty and dreadful, for thou art not so;
A For those whom thou think'st thou dost overthrow
Die not, poor Death, nor yet canst thou kill me.
From rest and sleep, which but thy pictures be,
Much pleasure; then from thee much more must flow,
And soonest our best men with thee do go,
Rest of their bones, and soul's delivery.
Thou art slave to fate, chance, kings, and desperate men,
And dost with poison, war, and sickness dwell,
And poppy or charms can make us sleep as well
And better than thy stroke; why swell'st thou then?
One short sleep past, we wake eternally
And death shall be no more; Death, thou shalt die. 2

5–6 From rest . . . flow: Since we derive pleasure from rest and sleep, which are only likenesses of death, we should derive much more from death itself.

8 soul's delivery: the freeing of the soul from the body.

11 poppy: opium, a narcotic drug made from the juice of the poppy plant.

12 swell'st: swell with pride.

Thinking Through the Literature

1. What are your thoughts about the **speaker's** attitude toward death? Share your response with your classmates.
2. Why do you think the speaker addresses death as a person?
3. How do you interpret the speaker's statement, "Death, thou shalt die"? Explain your response.

Teaching Options

Vocabulary Strategy

USING CONTEXT TO DETERMINE MEANING

Instruction Remind students that using context is helpful in determining the meaning of figurative language, which includes language that is connotative (*connotation* is the associated attitudes or emotions that a word evokes). Have students note Donne's use of figurative language, even though he uses many simple one-syllable words.

Activity Divide students into groups and have them examine Donne's poetry and prose for words that have strong connotations and/or are used figuratively. Have students use context clues to determine precise word meanings. They might also find it useful to paraphrase the figurative language to enforce meaning.

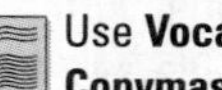

Use **Vocabulary Transparencies and Copymasters,** p. 26.

A lesson on using context clues appears on p. 939 of the Pupil's Edition.

from

Meditation 17

John Donne

Perchance he for whom this bell tolls may be so ill as that he knows not it tolls for him; and perchance I may think myself so much better than I am, as that they who are about me and see my state may have caused it to toll for me, and I know not that. The church is catholic,[1] universal, so are all her actions; all that she does belongs to all. When she baptizes a child, that action concerns me; for that child is thereby connected to that body which is my head too, and ingrafted into that body whereof I am a member.[2] And when she buries a man, that
B action concerns me: all mankind is of one author and is one volume;
when one man dies, one chapter is not torn out of the book, but
translated into a better language; and every chapter must be so
3 translated. God employs several translators; some pieces are
translated by age, some by sickness, some by war, some by justice;
4 but God's hand is in every translation, and his hand shall bind up all
our scattered leaves again for that library where every book shall lie
open to one another. As therefore the bell that rings to a sermon calls not upon the preacher only, but upon the congregation to come, so this bell calls us all; but how much more me, who am brought so near the door by this sickness. . . . Who casts not up his eye to the sun when it rises? but who takes off his eye from a comet when that breaks out? Who bends not his ear to any bell which upon any occasion rings? but who can remove it from that bell which is passing a piece of himself out of this world? No man is an island, entire of itself; every man is a piece of the continent, a part of the main.[3] If a clod be washed away by the sea, Europe is the less, as well as if a promontory[4] were, as well as if a manor of thy friend's or of thine own were. Any man's death diminishes me because I am involved in mankind, and therefore never send to know for whom the bell tolls; it tolls for thee. ❖

Nunc lento

sonitu dicunt,

Now this bell tolling

morieris.

softly

for another,

says to me,

Thou must

die.

1. **is catholic:** embraces all humankind.
2. **body which is my head . . . member:** Donne likens the church to the head, which controls every part of the body, and to the body itself, because it is made up of interconnected parts (the individuals who compose it).
3. **main:** mainland.
4. **promontory** (prŏm′ən-tôr′ē): a ridge of land jutting out into a body of water.

Customizing Instruction

Students Acquiring English

1 Note that the first four words in line 1 comprise a command. Have students reword the command in contemporary English.
Answer: Death, don't be proud.

Less Proficient Readers

Set a Purpose Ask students to read these two selections to learn more about Donne's religious and philosophical beliefs.

2 Ask students to describe the speaker's tone toward Death in "Holy Sonnet 10."
Possible Response: He is defiant, confident, and bold.

3 Ask students who Donne believes is the single author of the "book" of humanity in "Meditation 17."
Answer: God.

Students Acquiring English

4 Help students understand Donne's metaphor of God as "translator," and have them explain what the speaker means by saying "some pieces are translated by age . . ."
Possible Responses: God decides when people will move from an earthly life to eternal life: some people die from old age, and some from sickness, war, or just punishment.

Assessment Informal Assessment

METAPHYSICAL CONCEITS Remind students that a metaphysical conceit deals with both subject matter (the metaphysical: experience beyond rational thought) and technique (the conceit: an elaborate or unusual comparison).
Have students write a brief paper in which they define metaphysical conceit, then give examples from the three works studied.

RUBRIC

3 **Full Accomplishment** Definitions will be clear and precise, and examples will be detailed, appropriate, and drawn from each of three selections.

2 **Substantial Accomplishment** Definitions will be adequate, and examples will be appropriate, although perhaps not drawn from each work.

1 **Little or Partial Accomplishment** Definitions will be inaccurate or incomplete, and examples will either be incomplete or incorrect.

GUIDING STUDENT RESPONSE

Connect to the Literature

1. What Do You Think?
Guidelines for student response: Students should provide evidence from the text to support their choice.

Comprehension Check
- someone's impending death
- We should be moved.

 Use Selection Quiz in **Unit Two Resource Book** p. 59

Think Critically

2. Possible Responses: Some students will say that Donne is saying that the life of every individual is important to all humanity. Others will say that no individual can live and die without being connected in some way to others.
3. Possible Responses: Some students will say that Donne means that people will find eternal life in heaven. Others will say that he means that people will be remembered for their virtues or positive achievements.
4. Possible Responses: Some students will believe that Donne's religious faith offers hope in times of sorrow. Others will think that the idea that humans are interconnected shows that one need not cope with life's limitations alone.

Literary Analysis

Cooperative Learning Activity Divide students into groups to discuss the poem. Possible interpretations might include viewing the lovers as connected over time and space just as the compass legs are connected across space on the drafter's paper. Have the groups share their findings with the class.

Thinking through the LITERATURE

Connect to the Literature

1. **What Do You Think?** Which part of the excerpt from Donne's "Meditation 17" did you find most thought-provoking? Discuss your choice with your classmates.

Comprehension Check
- What does the ringing church bell announce?
- Does the writer suggest we should be moved or unmoved by the fate of others?

Think Critically

2. **ACTIVE READING** **INTERPRETING LANGUAGE STRUCTURES**
What do you think Donne is saying in the last three sentences of "Meditation 17"? You may want to review your list of unusual **images, paradoxes,** and **comparisons** from your  **READER'S NOTEBOOK.**

3. Donne says that when a person dies, the person's "chapter is not torn out of the book, but translated into a better language." What do you think he means by this statement?

4. In your opinion, how might the thoughts recorded in this meditation help someone to cope with life's limitations?

THINK ABOUT
- Donne's statements about how people are connected
- his views of God and the church

Extend Interpretations

5. **Critic's Corner** The scholar C. S. Lewis commented that much of Donne's writing deals with rather grim **themes.** On the basis of your understanding of these three selections, do you agree or disagree with Lewis? Give evidence to support your answer.

6. **Comparing Texts** Compare Donne's depiction of love in "A Valediction: Forbidding Mourning" with Shakespeare's depiction of love in "Sonnet 116." Do the two speakers appear to agree or to disagree? Explain your opinion.

7. **Connect to Life** In their writings, Donne and many of his contemporaries tried to unravel the mysteries of death. Do you think the level of interest in death is as great in today's society? Why or why not?

Literary Analysis

EXTENDED METAPHOR Donne's writing contains several types of figurative language, including extended metaphors, or **conceits.** Like any metaphor, an **extended metaphor** is a comparison between two essentially unlike things that does not contain the word *like* or *as.* A metaphor becomes extended when the two things are compared at length and in a number of ways—perhaps throughout a stanza, a paragraph, or even an entire work.

Cooperative Learning Activity The comparison of two lovers to the two feet of a draftsman's compass in "A Valediction: Forbidding Mourning" is one of the most famous **conceits** in metaphysical poetry. With classmates, draw up a list of interpretations of what the metaphor might mean.

Extend Interpretations

Critic's Corner First have students propose themes that apply to two or more selections. Then have them discuss whether they agree or disagree with C. S. Lewis. Some students may agree that themes like separation and death are grim, while others may think that Donne's faith in love and God make his views about these themes comforting and uplifting.

Comparing Texts Students who find that the speakers agree may feel that both show a strong love beyond the physical or that both use fanciful figures of speech to convey that love. Those who take the opposite view may feel that the different rhyme schemes and meters give the two poems very different moods.

Connect to Life Some students may think that medical research has revealed some of death's mysteries, which will diminish our interest in death. Others may think that our increased knowledge about preventing death makes us even more interested in the topic.

Writing Options

1. **Extended Metaphor** Create your own extended metaphor, or conceit, to depict either love or death. You may choose to write your metaphor in the form of a paragraph or a short poem.
2. **Poem of Farewell** Using the title "A Valediction," write a poem of your own in which you describe your thoughts about going away and leaving someone you love behind. Place your poem in your **Working Portfolio.**

Activities & Explorations

1. **Mood Painting/Collage** Using appropriate colors, shapes, and images, create an abstract or representational painting or collage that reflects the mood conveyed by one of the Donne selections. ~ **ART**
2. **Dramatic Reading** With a partner, prepare a reading of "A Valediction: Forbidding Mourning." Take turns reading, with one person taking the odd-numbered and the other the even-numbered stanzas. ~ **SPEAKING AND LISTENING**

Inquiry & Research

A Modern Novel An important American writer of this century has used a phrase from this meditation of Donne's as the title of one of his novels. Discover the writer, the title of the novel, the year of its publication, and the subject of the book. Then, by reading a summary of the novel, try to figure out the relevance of the title to the subject of the book.

More Online: Research Starter
www.mcdougallittell.com

John Donne

1572–1631

Other Works
"The Canonization"
"The Flea"
"Holy Sonnet 7"

Early Years John Donne was born into a Roman Catholic family at a time when the Protestant majority had no tolerance for religious ideas different from their own. Although he attended Oxford University for several years, he was not eligible for a degree because of his religious beliefs. In 1593, his only brother died while imprisoned for sheltering a Jesuit priest.

Public Career At the age of 25, Donne became the personal secretary of Sir Thomas Egerton, a distinguished official of the royal court. A few years later, he married Egerton's niece, Ann More, secretly and without seeking permission. When the marriage was discovered, Donne lost his job. He was left nearly penniless and battled poverty for many years thereafter. Eventually, King James I recruited the struggling poet to the cause of Protestantism, and Donne became an Anglican priest in 1615. Within six years, he was named dean of St. Paul's Cathedral, a position he held until his death. Donne was hailed as a dynamic preacher who incorporated wit and poetic language into his sermons.

A Master of Paradox Donne, whose writing is filled with paradoxes, was something of a paradox himself—a poet turned preacher, a sensualist and a scholar, a doubter and a believer. He was both dramatic and introspective, worldly and spiritual. Steeped in medieval learning, he was at the same time open to the fresh currents of 17th-century science and discovery. It is said that Donne "married passion to reason," and his example has influenced writers from his own time to the 20th century.

Author Activity

A Burial Shroud Near the end of his life, Donne had his portrait painted while dressed in his burial shroud. There is also a statue of him in this shroud. Investigate one of these portrayals of Donne and find out how and why he had it made.

Writing Options

1. **Extended Metaphor** Suggest that students begin with a basic metaphor, then elaborate.
2. **Poem of Farewell** Students may draw on personal experience or might imagine a scenario that involves leave-taking. Ask students to try to include images and figurative language in their poems.

Activities & Explorations

1. **Mood Painting/Collage** You might make this a cooperative activity in which you pair students who have a background in art with those who do not.
2. **Dramatic Reading** You might consider pairing students acquiring English or less proficient readers with a partner whose reading skills are strong. Remind students to follow punctuation cues for pausing and to use inflection as they read.

Inquiry & Research

A Modern Novel Have students reread the selection and note any famous lines that might be likely candidates for the novel's title. Direct students to collections of American literature and online links. Students should eventually discover that Ernest Hemingway wrote *For Whom the Bell Tolls.*

Author Activity

A Burial Shroud Direct students to biographies of Donne that might discuss his reasons for representing himself in his shroud and might also include pictures of the painting or statue. Students might also look at books of 17th-century art for representations of Donne's shroud or of other paintings or sculpture of people in their burial attire. For wider context, students might investigate whether Donne's activity was common in his day.

OVERVIEW

Objectives

1. understand and appreciate two **lyric poems (Literary Analysis)**
2. evaluate an **epitaph (Literary Analysis)**
3. use strategies for **comparing the speakers in poetry (Active Reading)**

Summary

The speaker of "On My First Son" memorializes his son, who died at the age of seven, and observes that his son is now free of life's sorrows.

The speaker of "Still to Be Neat" claims that a more natural look captures the heart, not just the eye.

Thematic Links

In these poems, Jonson addresses two very different issues, both dealing with **life's limitations.**

5-Minute Warm-Up

Daily Language SkillBuilder

Have students **proofread** the display sentences on page 273l and write them correctly. The sentences also appear on Transparency 9 of **Grammar Transparencies and Copymasters.**

Reading and Analyzing

Active Reading

COMPARING SPEAKERS IN POETRY

Although authors are often the speakers in their poems, often they are not. Ask students if they think Jonson is the speaker in this poem.

Possible Response: Yes, because the subject is so personal.

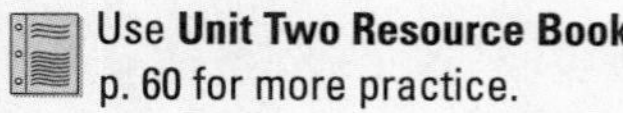

Use **Unit Two Resource Book,** p. 60 for more practice.

Literary Analysis EPITAPH

(A) Point out that the quotation resembles a tombstone inscription. Ask what calling the son Jonson's "best piece of poetry" implies.

Possible Response: His son is his finest creation.

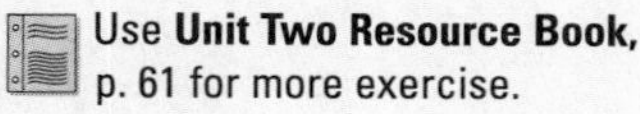

Use **Unit Two Resource Book,** p. 61 for more exercise.

PREPARING to *Read*

On My First Son / Still to Be Neat

Poetry by BEN JONSON

"Here doth lie / Ben Jonson his best piece of poetry."

Connect to Your Life

Invalid Assumptions Most of us make various assumptions as we go through life. For example, we might assume that certain events will happen as we have planned or that people will behave as we expect. Do you tend to make assumptions about yourself and others? Can you remember a time when something did not happen the way you assumed it would? With your classmates, discuss assumptions you have made about yourself or others. Which assumptions were valid? Which ones were not?

Build Background

Literary Lion Ben Jonson was a literary giant who knew most of London's important writers, including Francis Bacon, John Donne, and William Shakespeare. Like Shakespeare, Jonson has been remembered chiefly as a great playwright—in fact, his influence on English drama may have been equal to that of his more celebrated contemporary. However, Jonson also wrote some of the finest poetry in the English language.

The selections on the following pages show two of Jonson's varied poetic styles. Each poem deals with a speaker's assumptions about life and people. "On My First Son" is the poet's response to the death of his son, Benjamin. Like John Donne and others in his society, Jonson was forced on more than one occasion to experience the anguish of an untimely death. Both of his children died at very young ages, his son at the age of seven, a victim of the plague, and his daughter, Mary, in infancy. The second poem, "Still to Be Neat," is a song from one of Jonson's major plays, the comedy *Epicene; or, The Silent Woman.* In it, the speaker shares his assumptions about a "neat" woman.

Focus Your Reading

LITERARY ANALYSIS EPITAPH An **epitaph** is an inscription placed on a tomb or monument to honor the memory of the person buried there. The term *epitaph* has also been used more loosely to describe a verse, such as "On My First Son," which commemorates someone who has died. Notice the serious tone and somber mood of this line from the poem, as Jonson memorializes his dead son.

Farewell, thou child of my right hand, and joy;
My sin was too much hope of thee, loved boy. . . .

As you read the poem, determine which other lines are especially deserving of the label *epitaph.*

ACTIVE READING COMPARING SPEAKERS IN POETRY The speaker in a poem is often thought to be the writer, but in many cases this assumption is not valid. Though a writer may speak with his or her own voice in a poem, the speaker is often a voice or character made up by the writer. Two poems by the same writer may therefore have very different speakers.

READER'S NOTEBOOK As you read these poems by Ben Jonson, note the differences in the two speakers. You might use a Venn diagram to list the speakers' similarities and differences.

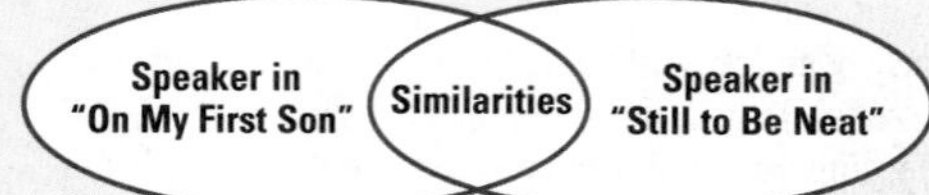

LESSON RESOURCES

UNIT TWO RESOURCE BOOK, pp. 60–61

ASSESSMENT RESOURCES

Formal Assessment, p. 71

Teacher's Guide to Assessment and Portfolio Use

Test Generator

SKILLS TRANSPARENCIES AND COPYMASTERS

Literary Analysis

- Theme, T9 (for Think Critically 2, p. 461)

Reading and Critical Thinking

- Comparing Authors' Views, T24 (for Extend Interpretations 5, p. 461)

Grammar

- Indicative and Imperative Mood, C137 (for Mini Lesson, p. 459)
- Subjunctive Mood, C138 (for Mini Lesson, p. 459)

Writing

- Identifying Writing Variables, T2 (for Writing Option 2, p. 462)

INTEGRATED TECHNOLOGY

Audio Library

Visit our website: www.mcdougallittell.com

ON MY FIRST SON

Ben Jonson

Farewell, thou child of my right hand, and joy;
My sin was too much hope of thee, loved boy:
Seven years thou wert lent to me, and I thee pay,
Exacted by thy fate, on the just day.
O could I lose all father now! for why
Will man lament the state he should envy,
To have so soon 'scaped world's and flesh's rage,
And, if no other misery, yet age?
A Rest in soft peace, and asked, say, "Here doth lie
Ben Jonson his best piece of poetry."
For whose sake henceforth all his vows be such
As what he loves may never like too much.

1 child of my right hand: The Hebrew name *Benjamin* means "son of the right hand."

4 just: required.

5 lose all father: lose the feeling of being a father.

Detail of *The Graham Children* (1742), William Hogarth. Oil on canvas. The Granger Collection, New York.

Thinking Through the Literature

1. What is your attitude toward the **speaker** after reading the poem?
2. In your opinion, what are some of the emotions and issues the speaker is grappling with as a result of his son's death?

THINK ABOUT
- the "sin" he describes in line 2
- the comparison he makes in lines 3–4
- his resolve in lines 11–12

3. The English poet Alfred, Lord Tennyson, once wrote, "'Tis better to have loved and lost / Than never to have loved at all." How do you think Jonson would have responded to Tennyson's statement?

TEACHING THE LITERATURE

Customizing Instruction

Less Proficient Readers
Have students read both selections to discover how the speaker feels about his son in "On My First Son," and how he feels about the woman he is addressing in "Still to Be Neat."

Students Acquiring English

Use **Spanish Study Guide** for additional support, pp. 88–90

Thinking Through the Literature

1. Accept all reasonable responses.
2. Some students will say he feels guilt for placing too much hope in his son. Others will say he feels pain at his loss.
3. Some students will say that Jonson's recognition of his son's value, as in lines 9–10, supports the quotation. Others will say lines 2 and 11–12 contradict it.

Mini Lesson Grammar

VERBS: INDICATIVE AND IMPERATIVE MOOD

Instruction *Mood* is a grammar term that describes how a verb is used to express an idea. Most of the writing and speaking people do is in the indicative mood or in the imperative mood. The indicative mood states a fact or asks a question; the imperative mood gives a command or makes a request. In the imperative mood, the verb is always second person present tense.

Activity Write these lines on the chalkboard.

"Will man lament the state he should envy,
To have so soon 'scaped world's and flesh's rage,
And, if no other misery, yet age?
Rest in soft peace, and asked, say, 'Here doth lie
Ben Jonson his best piece of poetry.'"

This excerpt includes both indicative and imperative moods. Have students name the parts of the excerpt that show each mood. *(Will . . . age?: indicative; Rest . . . poetry: imperative; Here . . . poetry: indicative)*

Use **Grammar Transparencies and Copymasters,** p. 137.

Use McDougal Littell's ***Language Network*** for more instruction in verb moods.

ON MY FIRST SON 459

Reading and Analyzing

Literary Analysis: REPETITION

(A) Remind students that repetition of a sound, word, phrase, or line is used for emphasis or unity. Repetition can reinforce meaning and create an appealing rhythm. What does Jonson's repetition of *still* suggest in the first stanza of "Still to Be Neat"?

Possible Response: The woman's appearance is relentlessly managed and artificial.

Literary Analysis: LYRIC POETRY

Explain that lyric poetry has compact lines; precise, polished language; and an overall musical effect. Have students find examples of these characteristics in the two poems.

Possible Responses: "Give me a look, give me a face / That makes simplicity a grace" is both musical and succinct; the first two lines of "On My First Son" contain precise language.

Reading Skills and Strategies: USING A VENN DIAGRAM

Remind students to fill in the Venn diagrams they began in their Reader's Notebooks. If necessary, guide students to see that the speaker in each poem seems to have a negative attitude toward life. Some students may also believe that both speakers are sensitive.

Portrait of Frances Howard, Countess of Essex and Somerset, Isaac Oliver. Victoria & Albert Museum, London/Art Resource, New York.

STILL TO BE NEAT

BEN JONSON

Still to be neat, still to be dressed,
As you were going to a feast;
(A) Still to be powdered, still perfumed;
Lady, it is to be presumed,
Though art's hid causes are not found,
All is not sweet, all is not sound.

Give me a look, give me a face
That makes simplicity a grace;
Robes loosely flowing, hair as free;
Such sweet neglect more taketh me
Than all th'adulteries of art.
They strike mine eyes, but not my heart.

1 still: always.

11 adulteries: impurities; debasements.

Connect to the Literature

1. **What Do You Think?** Do you agree with the ideas expressed by the speaker of "Still to Be Neat"?

Comprehension Check
- Why does the speaker object to the lady's "neat" appearance?
- What look does the speaker in the poem claim to prefer?

Think Critically

2. What do you think the **speaker** assumes about the "powdered" and "perfumed" woman?

THINK ABOUT
- his reference to "art's hid causes" (line 5)
- what he means by "All is not sweet, all is not sound" (line 6)
- his use of the word "adulteries" to describe the ways in which a woman tries to improve her appearance (line 11)

3. On the basis of your reading of the poem, what is your opinion of the speaker of "Still to Be Neat"?

4. ACTIVE READING COMPARING SPEAKERS IN POETRY Look again at the Venn diagram you completed in your READER'S NOTEBOOK. How are the speakers similar? How do they differ? Discuss your ideas with a partner.

Extend Interpretations

5. **Comparing Texts** Reread lines 5–8 of "On My First Son." Then compare Jonson's attitude toward death with that of John Donne in "Holy Sonnet 10."

6. **What If?** How do you think the woman addressed in "Still to Be Neat" might respond to the poem's speaker? Consider why she uses powder and perfume and what effect she hopes to achieve.

7. **Connect to Life** Do you think "Still to Be Neat" could have been written about a contemporary woman? Explain your opinion, keeping in mind the values of today's society.

Literary Analysis

EPITAPH In literature, an **epitaph** is used to describe any verse commemorating someone who has died. Although a few humorous epitaphs have been composed, most are serious in tone. "On My First Son" is considered an epitaph. In Jonson's poem, phrases such as "O could I lose all father now!" and "Rest in soft peace" reflect the poet's deep grief over the death of his son. Such lines effectively convey the poet's sadness to the reader.

Paired Activity With a partner, reread the poem and decide which lines would be the best epitaph to inscribe on a gravestone for Jonson's son, or adapt the poem's language and tone and write your own epitaph for the boy.

REVIEW REPETITION Find examples of **repetition** in "Still to Be Neat." Discuss why Jonson might have chosen to repeat certain words. How does the repetition affect your reading of the poem? You might want to use a chart like the one below to organize your thoughts.

Repeated Words	Reasons for Repetition	Effects on Reader

GUIDING STUDENT RESPONSE

Connect to the Literature

1. **What Do You Think?** Guidelines for student response: Accept all reasonable responses. Students should provide examples from contemporary life to support their opinion.

Comprehension Check
- It is not a natural look.
- a more natural look

Think Critically

2. Possible Responses: He assumes she is hiding some flaw behind her painted exterior; he assumes she is as false or artificial in character as she is in appearance.
3. Some students will feel that he is critical and suspicious of others. Others will say he values simplicity and dislikes artifice. Still others will say he is perhaps not as honest with himself as the speaker of "On My First Son" is.
4. Possible Responses: Both speakers use precise language to convey their feelings, but their tones differ: One is sad and serious, and the other is playfully critical.

Literary Analysis

Paired Activity Some students might choose the first line, while others may say that lines 9–10 are most appropriate. Encourage students to mirror Jonson's particular expressions of sadness (such as his lament that his son died so young) when writing their epitaphs for the boy.

Review Examples include "still to be" in lines 1 and 3, "all is not" in line 6, "give me a" in line 7, and "art" in lines 5 and 11. Students may suggest that the repetition contributes to the poem's musical quality; helps tie ideas together; and, in stanza 1, suggests a tedium that reflects the speaker's negative feelings toward the woman's artifice.

Extend Interpretations

Comparing Texts Possible response: Both authors express their faith in an afterlife and explore their subjects seriously and thoughtfully. Donne's poem expresses strong religious faith; Jonson's is sadder and shows more mixed feelings toward death. Donne deals with death in general (which he personifies), while Jonson deals with the specific and untimely death of his young son.

What If? Possible response: The woman might claim that she is embellishing her appearance in order to be more attractive to men. She might feel that men judge women's characters by how perfect they look; thus, a disheveled appearance would suggest loose morals.

Connect to Life Some students may think that the issues addressed in the poem are outdated, because today we look beyond superficial appearances. Others may feel that there is still much attention paid to a woman's appearance and that the "natural" versus "cosmetics" debate is still current.

Writing Options

1. **Message of Condolence** Encourage students to study the biographical information on Jonson on pages 458 and 462 before they write their notes.
2. **Poetic Parody** Tell students that a good parody makes clear the material that is being imitated, usually by picking up words and/or style elements.

Activities & Explorations

1. **Monument Design** Students may find it helpful to study actual or photographed tombstones and monuments before beginning this activity.
2. **Pictorial Essay** Ask students to use magazine or newspaper cuttings, copies of book illustrations, posters, photographs, and product labels.

Choices & CHALLENGES

Writing Options

1. **Message of Condolence** Write a sympathy note to Ben Jonson, offering him advice or comfort on the occasion of the death of his son. You may refer to his poem "On My First Son" in your note and try to help him with some of the issues he raises.

2. **Poetic Parody** Think of a quality or trait that you particularly dislike in a person. Using that trait as your subject, write a parody, or imitation, of the first stanza of "Still to Be Neat."

Activities & Explorations

1. **Monument Design** Create a sketch of a tombstone or monument that Jonson might have erected in memory of his son. ~ **ART**

2. **Pictorial Essay** Put together a pictorial essay depicting the contrast between natural beauty and the "adulteries of art." ~ **VIEWING AND REPRESENTING**

Inquiry & Research

Fashion Sense In "Still to Be Neat," Jonson refers to a woman's efforts to dress for a "feast." Find out what cosmetics and clothes women of the Elizabethan Age wore to a formal gathering. To what extent, if any, did hygiene influence what was worn? Share your findings with the class.

Ben Jonson

1572–1637

Other Works
"Song, to Celia"
"To the Memory of My Beloved, the Author Master William Shakespeare"
"Epitaph on Elizabeth, L. H."

Eclectic Careers In spite of a quarrelsome nature, Ben Jonson was a leader in the literary world and was greatly admired by a group of young poets—including Robert Herrick and Sir John Suckling—who proudly called themselves the "sons of Ben." Although well-educated as a child, Jonson never attended a university. He worked a short time as a bricklayer and then joined the British army. While aiding the Dutch in their war against Spain, Jonson killed the enemy's best soldier in single combat. Returning to England, he pursued a career in the theater, faring poorly as an actor but gaining extensive popularity as a playwright.

Close Calls A man of great bulk, with what he described as a "mountain belly" and a "rocky face," Jonson lived life with gusto. Unfortunately, his volcanic temperament led to occasional scrapes with the law. Once, he barely escaped hanging after killing a fellow actor in a duel. Because a knowledge of Latin was largely confined to clergymen in Renaissance England, Jonson eluded death by reading a "neck verse"—a passage from the Latin Bible—so that he could be tried by a church court rather than a more harsh criminal court. He was, however, branded on the thumb as a convicted felon. He was also twice imprisoned when he offended authorities with his plays.

Literary Works Satire, which was just emerging as a popular dramatic form, was well suited to Jonson's combative nature and scathing wit. He gained fame for his satiric comedies, two of which, *Volpone* and *The Alchemist,* are still staged in theaters today. Many of his plays were performed at the Globe Theater, and Shakespeare himself acted in Jonson's first comedy, *Every Man in His Humor.* In 1616, Jonson published a volume of his plays and poems under the title *Works.* At that time, only more intellectual subjects, such as history and theology, were considered important enough to be presented as "works." The volume therefore became quite controversial, as Jonson undoubtedly had hoped. In his later years, Jonson wrote elaborate entertainments for the royal court and was rewarded with a sizable pension. His tombstone in Westminster Abbey bears the epitaph "O rare Ben Jonson."

Inquiry & Research

Fashion Sense Have students refer to several books and other sources on the history of fashion and costume. Have them make categories, such as "clothes," "cosmetics," and "wigs or hairstyle," to help focus their research. As they compile sources, they should look for detailed descriptions and pictures of Elizabethan fashion and also for any repercussions of various practices (for example, the lead in many cosmetics was poisonous). How did the expense of clothes and cosmetics affect women of various social classes in this period? Have students present their findings via a Web page, slide show, or videotaped speech, if possible.

To the Virgins, to Make Much of Time

Poetry by ROBERT HERRICK

To His Coy Mistress

Poetry by ANDREW MARVELL

To Lucasta, Going to the Wars

Poetry by RICHARD LOVELACE

Comparing Literature of the World

The Lyrics of the Cavalier Poets and Omar Khayyám

This lesson and the one that follows present an opportunity for you to compare the lyrics of the Cavalier poets with the poems of Omar Khayyám. Specific points of comparison in the Khayyám lesson will help you note similarities and differences in the writers' treatments of the *carpe diem* theme.

Connect to Your Life

"Gather Ye Rosebuds While Ye May" The Latin expression *carpe diem* (kär'pĕ dē'ĕm)—"seize the day"—comes from a poem in which the Roman poet Horace advocates enjoying life fully because death is inevitable. This philosophy of life has been embraced by various individuals over the centuries and is still popular with some people today. With a group of classmates, discuss your opinion of this approach to life.

Build Background

The Cavalier Poets The Stuart king Charles I—successor to James I—believed that he had a divine right to rule, independent of Parliament. Tension grew between Charles and members of the legislative body, and in 1629 the king suspended Parliament. Thirteen years later, in 1642, England erupted in a civil war between those who supported the monarchy, who were called Cavaliers, and those who supported Parliament, known as Roundheads. The Cavaliers included a group of poets whose musical, lighthearted verse was popular among members of the royal court. The Cavalier poets focused on themes of love, war, honor, and courtly behavior and frequently advocated the philosophy of *carpe diem*, or living for the moment.

Prominent among the Cavalier poets were Robert Herrick and Richard Lovelace. Another 17th-century poet, Andrew Marvell, although not a Cavalier in political sympathies, is often grouped with the Cavaliers because of his poetic style. His combination of the intellectual depth and wit of the metaphysical poets with the lighthearted and melodious style of the Cavaliers makes him difficult to categorize.

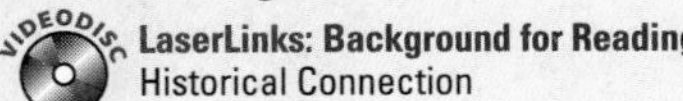

LaserLinks: Background for Reading
Historical Connection

Focus Your Reading

LITERARY ANALYSIS **HYPERBOLE** Figurative language that greatly exaggerates facts or ideas for humorous effect or for emphasis is called **hyperbole** (hī-pûr′ bə-lē). For example, in "To His Coy Mistress," the speaker talks about loving someone for 30,000 years. Look for other instances of hyperbole in Marvell's poem.

ACTIVE READING **COMPARING SPEAKERS IN POETRY** Each of the speakers in these three poems has a slightly different attitude toward love and life. As you read, compare the speakers' feelings as reflected in their words. Remember these points:

- the speaker is the voice in a poem that talks to the reader
- the speaker can be a distant observer or an intimate participant
- the speaker and the poet are not necessarily the same

READER'S NOTEBOOK As you read these poems, jot down a few words or phrases for each that seem to capture the speaker's attitude toward love and life.

OVERVIEW

Objectives

1. understand and appreciate three lyric poems **(Literary Analysis)**
2. identify and examine **hyperbole (Literary Analysis)**
3. use strategies for **comparing speakers in poetry (Active Reading)**

Summary

These three lyric poems address the subjects of love and youth. Herrick urges people to marry while they are young to avoid facing old age alone. Marvell's poem is an appeal to action. Lovelace speaks of the paradox of participating in war while being in love.

Thematic Link

The three poems address questions of love and **facing life's limitations.** Herrick and Marvell address the idea of *carpe diem,* while Lovelace considers the effect of honor on love.

5-Minute Warm-Up

Daily Language SkillBuilder

Have students **proofread** the display sentences on page 273m and write them correctly. The sentences also appear on Transparency 10 of **Grammar Transparencies and Copymasters.**

LESSON RESOURCES

UNIT TWO RESOURCE BOOK, pp. 62–63

ASSESSMENT RESOURCES

Formal Assessment, pp. 73–74

Teacher's Guide to Assessment and Portfolio Use

Test Generator

SKILLS TRANSPARENCIES AND COPYMASTERS

Literary Analysis

- Theme, T9 (for Extend Interpretations 7, p. 468)

Reading and Critical Thinking

- Compare and Contrast, T15 (for Think Critically 5, p. 468)

Grammar

- Verbs–Using Correct Verb Forms, T45 (for Mini Lesson, p. 465)
- Verbs: Present and Past Participles, C128 (for Mini Lesson, p. 465)

Vocabulary

- Denotation and Connotation, C47 (for Mini Lesson, p. 464)

Writing

- Figurative Language and Sound Devices, T15 (for Writing Option 2, p. 469)
- Compare-Contrast, C34 (for Writing Option 1, p. 469)

INTEGRATED TECHNOLOGY

Audio Library

LaserLinks

- Historical Connection: The English Civil War, 1642–1651. See **Teacher's SourceBook,** p. 28.

Internet: Research Starter

Visit our website:
www.mcdougallittell.com

TEACHING THE LITERATURE

Reading and Analyzing

Active Reading

COMPARING SPEAKERS IN POETRY

Have students consider the intended audiences of the three poems. How does the intended audience affect each speaker's tone?

Possible Response: Herrick's audience is the virgins. His tone is friendly but not intimate. Marvell's audience is his mistress. His tone is intimate and intense. Lovelace's audience is Lucasta. His tone is intimate and gentle.

 Use **Unit Two Resource Book** p. 62 for more practice.

Literary Analysis HYPERBOLE

Ask students whether Marvell uses hyperbole for emphasis or for humor in lines 7–8 of "To His Coy Mistress": "I would / Love you ten years before the flood . . ."

Possible Response: Marvell uses hyperbole for emphasis, to show how long he would love his mistress.

 Use **Unit Two Resource Book** p. 63 for more exercises.

GUIDE FOR READING

A He thinks life gets worse as we age. Opinions will vary.

B They urge the maidens to make the most of life and youth.

C To show the distances over which they could court. He use exaggeration to make his point.

Thinking Through the Literature

1. Accept all reasonable responses.
2. Possible Responses: Life is short; time passes quickly.
3. Yes—youth is a time of idealism, strong passions, expanding horizons, and better health. No—the young lack foresight, experience, stability, wisdom, and independence.

TO THE VIRGINS, TO MAKE MUCH OF TIME

Robert Herrick

Gather ye rosebuds while ye may,
    Old time is still a-flying;
And this same flower that smiles today
    Tomorrow will be dying.

The glorious lamp of heaven, the sun,
    The higher he's a-getting,
The sooner will his race be run,
    And nearer he's to setting.

That age is best which is the first,
    When youth and blood are warmer;
But being spent, the worse, and worst
    Times still succeed the former.

Then be not coy, but use your time,
    And, while ye may, go marry;
For, having lost but once your prime,
    You may forever tarry.

GUIDE FOR READING

9–12 How does the speaker appear to feel about old age? Do you agree with his opinion? 

13 coy: hesitant; modest.

15–16 How do these lines reflect the philosophy of *carpe diem?* 

16 tarry: wait.

Thinking Through the Literature

1. What was your overall reaction to this poem? Record your response in your notebook.
2. How would you describe the **speaker's** thoughts about time? Be sure to use examples from the poem to help explain your opinion.
3. Do you agree or disagree with the speaker's idea that "that age is best which is the first" (line 9)? Why or why not?

Teaching Options

Vocabulary Strategy

CONNOTATION AND DENOTATION

Instruction Call students' attention to the phrase "vegetable love" in Marvell's poem. *Vegetable* carries with it not only its literal meaning but also connotative meanings, meanings which are carried with a word because of its associations rather than its literal definition.

Activity Have students consider the connotations of the following word. Then have them find a synonym and substitute it in the poem. *nunnery,* line 2 of "To Lucasta . . ."

Possible Response: *Nunnery* brings to mind a safe place secluded from the cares and vices of the world. A synonym is *convent*. *Convent* has roughly the same connotations as *nunnery,* although it does not have such strong female associations.

 Use **Vocabulary Transparencies and Copymasters,** p. 27.

A lesson on connotation and denotation appears on p. 645 in the Pupil's Edition.

The Proposal (1872), Adolphe-William Bouguereau. Oil on canvas, 64⅜″ × 44″, The Metropolitan Museum of Art, New York, gift of Mrs. Elliot L. Kamen in memory of her father, Bernard R. Armour, 1960 (60.122).

TO HIS COY MISTRESS

Andrew Marvell

Had we but world enough, and time,
This coyness, lady, were no crime.
We would sit down, and think which way
To walk, and pass our long love's day.
Thou by the Indian Ganges' side
Shouldst rubies find; I by the tide
Of Humber would complain. I would
Love you ten years before the flood,
And you should, if you please, refuse

GUIDE FOR READING

5 Ganges (găn′jēz′): a great river of northern India.

7 Humber: a river of northern England, flowing through Marvell's hometown; **complain:** sing melancholy love songs.

5–7 Why do you think the speaker chooses to place his lover at the Ganges and himself at the Humber? What is his argument and his objective? C

8 flood: the biblical Flood.

Customizing Instruction

Less Proficient Readers

Set a Purpose Have students read to learn more about the philosophy of *carpe diem.* Suggest that they consider what advice they would give to their friends if they were advocates of this philosophy.

1 In stanza 2, Herrick describes in detail the sun's movement across the sky. To what is Herrick comparing the sun's movement?

Answer: person's lifetime.

Students Acquiring English

Have students think of songs from their native culture or in their native language that have a theme of *carpe diem.* Ask them to describe the song's message in their own words.

In "To the Virgins . . ." have students look up the meanings for *race* (line 7) and *spent* (line 11). What meanings does Herrick intend?

Answer: *Race* means "the sun's course"; *spent* means "having come to an end."

 Use **Spanish Study Guide** for additional support, pp. 91–93

Gifted and Talented

Have students work in pairs to create a debate about Herrick's argument. Students might compare the opportunities available to women in the 17th century with those available to women today.

Mini Lesson Grammar

VERBS: PRESENT AND PAST PARTICIPLES

Instruction Verbs have different forms constructed using the four principal parts of the verb. The present infinitive is the base form of any verb.

Activity Write these lines on the chalkboard.

"Gather ye rosebuds while ye may,
Old time is still a-flying
And this same flower that smiles today
Tomorrow will be dying."

Underline the verb *gather.* Explain that this is the present form. To form the present participle, the ending *-ing* must be added to the verb as well as an auxiliary verb such as *is, are,* or another form of the verb *be.* Point out that the present participle of *gather* is *(is) gathering.* Have students find a present participle in the excerpt. *([will be] dying)* Most verbs are regular—they form the past by adding *-d* or *-ed. Gather* is regular, so its past form is *gathered.*

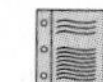 Use **Grammar Transparencies and Copymasters,** p. 70.

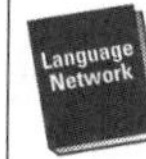

Use McDougal Littell's ***Language Network*** for more instruction in present and past participles.

Reading and Analyzing

GUIDE FOR READING

A Playful, flattering, exaggerated.

B It has become more serious, harsher.

C He tries to enjoy life while he can.

D He flies from Lucasta's arms to the arms (or weapons) of the enemy in war.

E Honor and patriotism.

Active Reading

COMPARING SPEAKERS IN POETRY

F After students have read Lovelace's poem, have them summarize the speaker's attitude toward life and love.

Possible Response: The speaker believes that honor is the most important thing in life. Being honorable enables him to love more truly and faithfully.

Ask students to compare the speakers' attitudes in the poems by Lovelace and Marvell.

Possible Response: The speaker in Marvell's poem believes that love is the most important thing in life. His attitude toward life is one of *carpe diem*, which lends his poem a sense of urgency that is not present in "To Lucasta, Going to the Wars."

Thinking Through the Literature

1. Accept all reasonable responses.
2. Those students finding it convincing may cite the use of imagery. Others may cite flaws in logic or morality.
3. Some students may feel that he is insincere and wants to seduce her; others may feel that he is sincere and exaggerates to stress his feelings.

Till the conversion of the Jews.
My vegetable love should grow
Vaster than empires and more slow;
An hundred years should go to praise
Thine eyes, and on thy forehead gaze;
Two hundred to adore each breast,
But thirty thousand to the rest;
An age at least to every part,
And the last age should show your heart.
For, lady, you deserve this state,
Nor would I love at lower rate.
But at my back I always hear
Time's wingéd chariot hurrying near;
And yonder all before us lie
Deserts of vast eternity.
Thy beauty shall no more be found,
Nor, in thy marble vault, shall sound
My echoing song; then worms shall try
That long-preserved virginity,
And your quaint honor turn to dust,
And into ashes all my lust:
The grave's a fine and private place,
But none, I think, do there embrace.
Now therefore, while the youthful hue
Sits on thy skin like morning dew,
And while thy willing soul transpires
At every pore with instant fires,
Now let us sport us while we may,
And now, like amorous birds of prey,
Rather at once our time devour
Than languish in his slow-chapped power.
Let us roll all our strength and all
Our sweetness up into one ball,
And tear our pleasures with rough strife
Thorough the iron gates of life:
Thus, though we cannot make our sun
Stand still, yet we will make him run.

10 till . . . Jews: In Marvell's day, Christians believed that all Jews would convert to Christianity just before the Last Judgment and the end of the world.

11 vegetable love: a love that grows like a plant (an oak tree, for example)—slowly but with the power to become very large.

19 state: dignity.

20 How would you describe the speaker's tone up to this point? 

32 Has the speaker's tone changed? B

35 transpires: breathes.

37–40 Consider the title of this part of Unit Two, "Facing Life's Limitations." How is the speaker trying to deal with life's limitations? C

40 slow-chapped: slow-jawed.

44 thorough: through.

Thinking Through the Literature

1. How do you picture the **speaker** in the poem?
2. Do you think the speaker's argument about time is convincing? Explain your opinion, using support from the poem.
3. In your opinion, is the speaker sincere in his description of the way he would go about loving his mistress if he had more time?

Teaching Options

Multicultural Link: Carpe Diem

Tell students that Horace (65–8 B.C.) was one of the greatest poets of ancient Rome. His message *Carpe diem, quam minimum credula postero* ("Seize the day, put no trust in tomorrow!") concludes one of the odes he published in 23 B.C. A similar sentiment is expressed in the Bible (Isaiah 21:11): "Let us eat and drink; for tomorrow we shall die." In religious writings, however, such a message usually goes on to suggest preparing for the afterlife, not merely enjoying life while one can. The philosophy of *carpe diem* is especially strong in the *Rubáiyát* of the 12th-century Persian poet Omar Khayyám (refer students to the selection from the *Rubáiyát* on page 471). It also occurs in several poems by the great 8th-century Chinese poet Li Bo. In 20th-century America the theme has been explored in works such as Robert Frost's poem "Carpe Diem" and in Saul Bellow's novel *Seize the Day.*

To Lucasta, GOING TO THE WARS

Tell me not, Sweet, I am unkind
That from the nunnery
Of thy chaste breast and quiet mind, **1**
To war and arms I fly.

True, a new mistress now I chase,
The first foe in the field;
And with a stronger faith embrace
A sword, a horse, a shield.

Yet this inconstancy is such
As you too shall adore;
F I could not love thee, Dear, so much,
Loved I not honor more. **2**

RICHARD
LOVELACE

GUIDE FOR READING

4 Think about the speaker's use of the word *arms.* Why is it especially appropriate for the speaker to talk about flying to arms? **D**

7 What is the "stronger faith" the speaker mentions in this line? **E**

Sir Philip Sidney (about 1576), unknown artist. The Granger Collection, New York.

Customizing Options

Students Acquiring English

1 Have students look up *nunnery* (line 2) and *chaste* (line 3). According to the description given in Stanza 1, what sort of woman is Lucasta?

Answer: a pure, thoughtful, calm person.

The speaker assumes that Lucasta will appreciate his putting honor before love. Do you think he is right in making this assumption?

Possible Response: Chastity, a quality Lucasta possesses, is a virtue. Since honor is also a virtue, she would probably appreciate his argument.

Gifted and Talented

2 Discuss the concept of honor. Then, ask what kind of honor is required on the battlefield. What kind of honor is required in love? Do you agree with the speaker's argument in the last two lines? Why or why not?

Possible Response: Students may recognize that acting honorably, whether on the battlefield or in love, is a great thing.

Assessment Informal Assessment

WRITING ABOUT TONE Remind students that tone refers to the attitude a writer or speaker expresses toward his or her subject. In poetry, tone is largely determined by diction, or word choice; musical devices such as rhythm and rhyme; sentence types such as questions, commands, and exclamations; and the images and figurative language used. Have students write an essay about how these four elements were used to express tone in either "To the Virgins, to Make Much of Time," "To His Coy Mistress," or "To Lucasta, Going to the Wars."

RUBRIC

3 **Full Accomplishment** Student clearly explains how each of four elements was used in poem to express tone. Student demonstrates good understanding of elements and poem.

2 **Substantial Accomplishment** Student explains how three elements were used in poem to express tone. Student demonstrates adequate understanding of elements and poem.

1 **Little or Partial Accomplishment** Student fails to address two or more elements. Demonstrates little understanding of elements or poem.

GUIDING STUDENT RESPONSE

Connect to the Literature

1. **What Do You Think?**
Guidelines for student response: Student responses may range from admiring to hostile. Ask students to identify the values underlying their choices.

Comprehension Check

- Lucasta seems to be jealous that the speaker has a new "mistress," and she has called him "unkind."
- honor

Think Critically

2. Some students may think that the speaker prefers war, citing his willingness to leave Lucasta in order to fight. Others may think that he prefers love, citing his description of Lucasta. Still others may perceive that his chief preference is for honor, which dictates his actions regarding love and war.
3. Students may notice that all these words have to do with relations between men and women, and that these terms help the speaker draw a comparison between his love of Lucasta and his love of honor.
4. Students will respond in a variety of ways, depending on their assessment of the speaker's argument.
5. Accept all reasonable responses. Students should support their opinions of the speakers' attitudes toward women with evidence from the text.

Literary Analysis

Cooperative Learning Activity Students might make up a master list of examples found by all the groups.

Review Theme Have students propose themes that cross two or three of the poems.

Review Metaphor List examples of striking metaphors on the chalkboard.

Thinking through the LITERATURE

Connect to the Literature

1. **What Do You Think?** Jot down words or phrases that convey your impression of the speaker of "To Lucasta, Going to the Wars." Share them with a partner.

Comprehension Check
- How does Lucasta feel about the speaker going off to war?
- What does the speaker love most?

Think Critically

2. Which do you think the speaker prefers, love or war?

THINK ABOUT
- his description of Lucasta
- what he means by "stronger faith" in line 7
- his thoughts about honor

3. Why do you think the speaker uses words like *mistress, embrace, inconstancy,* and *adore* in referring to his duty?

4. If you were the speaker's beloved, how might you react to lines 11–12?

5. ACTIVE READING COMPARING SPEAKERS IN POETRY Review the words and phrases reflecting the speakers' attitudes that you jotted down in your  READER'S NOTEBOOK. Then think about the ways in which women are described in "To the Virgins, to Make Much of Time," "To His Coy Mistress," and "To Lucasta, Going to the Wars." Do you think the **speakers** share the same attitude toward women? Explain your opinion.

Extend Interpretations

6. **Comparing Texts** In your opinion, what would each of the speakers of these poems think of the kind of love described in Donne's "A Valediction: Forbidding Mourning"?

7. **Different Perspectives** What if the speaker in "To His Coy Mistress" were the speaker in "To Lucasta, Going to the Wars"? What differences do you think there would be in **theme** and **tone?**

8. **Connect to Life** Think about the philosophy of *carpe diem* as it is expressed in these poems. Are there popular songs today that express the same idea as "seize the day" or "Gather ye rosebuds while ye may"?

Literary Analysis

HYPERBOLE "Saying goodbye felt like the end of the world" is an example of **hyperbole,** figurative language that greatly exaggerates facts or ideas for humorous effect or for emphasis.

Cooperative Learning Activity What examples of hyperbole can you find in "To His Coy Mistress"? How do they help the speaker develop his argument? In a small group, list all the examples of hyperbole you can find in the poem. Then compare your list with those of other groups.

REVIEW THEME Recall that a **theme** is a central idea or message in a work of literature. Sometimes the theme is directly stated; at other times, it is implied. What would you say is the theme in each of the three poems?

REVIEW METAPHOR Recall that a **metaphor** is a figure of speech that makes a comparison between two things that are basically unlike but have something in common. In Andrew Marvell's poem "To His Coy Mistress," the phrase "time's wingéd chariot" is a metaphor in which the swift passage of time is compared to a speeding chariot. Look for other striking metaphors in the poems.

Extend Interpretations

Comparing Texts Student responses will vary but should draw on the personas of the three poems' speakers to support the opinions they express about Donne's "A Valediction: Forbidding Mourning."

Different Perspectives Student responses will vary, but may suggest that the new theme would be *carpe diem,* endorsing making the most of the time they have before the speaker goes to war, and that the tone would be lighter and more comic.

Connect to Life Ask students to bring to class recordings of contemporary songs that capture the idea of the theme.

Writing Options

1. **Comparison of Poems** Draft a short comparison-contrast essay in which you compare the poems "To His Coy Mistress" and "To the Virgins, to Make Much of Time," concentrating on their speakers, themes, and styles.

Writing Handbook
See page 1367: Compare and Contrast

2. **Exaggerated Speech** Write a speech in which you use your own examples of hyperbole to convince your listeners to "seize the day" **Working Portfolio.**

3. **Letter in Time of War** Write a letter from Lucasta to her lover after he's left for the war. Be sure to mention how you feel about his choice to leave you and go fight in a war.

Activities & Explorations

1. ***Carpe Diem* Banner** Arrange images and words to create a classroom banner on the *carpe diem* theme. ~ **VIEWING AND REPRESENTING**

2. **Booklet of Quotations** Prepare a booklet of quotations about the fleeting nature of time. Be sure to include Marvell's reference to "time's wingéd chariot." ~ **LITERATURE**

3. **Cartoons and Poetry** Draw single-panel cartoons depicting some of the ideas and objects that are personified in the poems—for example, "old time . . . still a-flying." ~ **ART**

Inquiry & Research

The Reign of Charles I Find out more about life during the reign of Charles I—include court life, the lifestyle of the Cavalier poets, and the events that led up to the civil war.

More Online: Research Starter
www.mcdougallittell.com

Art Connection

Matching the Mood Look again at Adolphe-William Bouguereau's painting *The Proposal* on page 465. In your opinion, does this painting capture the mood of Marvell's poem "To His Coy Mistress"? Give reasons for your answer.

Robert Herrick
1591–1674

Other Works
"Corinna's Going A-Maying"
"Delight in Disorder"
"The Argument of His Book"

Youth and Man-About-Town As a young man, Robert Herrick tried his hand at goldsmithing, the family trade, before going off to Cambridge University. There he received two degrees and, a few years later, was ordained a priest. An ardent admirer of Ben Jonson, Herrick was one of the "sons of Ben" and an active member of London society. He loved the city and was disappointed when assigned to a rural church in Devonshire. Because of his loyalty to the king, he was deprived of this post for 15 years under the Parliamentary government but was reassigned to Devonshire when the monarchy was restored.

Poet and Priest While in London in 1648, Herrick published his only book, *Hesperides,* which contained over 1,400 poems on both worldly and religious themes. Unfortunately, because of the civil war, society was not very interested in Herrick's light, playful verse, and his work was not much appreciated until the 19th century. After returning to the country, Herrick settled down to his life as a country priest, spending his days in enjoyment of nature and the quiet life and writing no more poetry. Herrick's poetry is greatly appreciated today, and he has been called "the greatest songwriter ever born of English race."

Writing Options

1. **Comparison of Poems** Students may organize their essays either by the suggested topics or by poems. In either case, remind students to support their ideas with quotations from the poems.
2. **Exaggerated Speech** Students are invited to use their imaginations in this exercise and should be given credit for creativity.
3. **Letters in Time of War** Letters should reflect an understanding of the issues of love and honor.

Activities & Explorations

1. ***Carpe Diem* Banner** Bring old magazines and newspapers to be used in creating the banner.
2. **Booklet of Quotations** Remind students that time has many measurements. Geologic time has its fleeting moments, too, although they may occupy thousands or millions of years. Thus, the quotations do not have to be limited to sayings about youth and old age.
3. **Cartoons and Poetry** Ask contributors to introduce their cartoons and to ask for classroom responses.

Inquiry and Research

The Reign of Charles I Have students share their findings with the class. Let them discuss where their sympathies lie—with the King's supporters or with the Puritans, and why.

Art Connection

Matching the Mood You might have students suggest other paintings or illustrations that they think better capture the mood of the poem.

Andrew Marvell

1621–1678

Other Works
"The Mower's Song"
"The Garden"
"On a Drop of Dew"

Student and Tutor During his lifetime, Andrew Marvell was known for his political activities rather than his poetry. After receiving a degree from Cambridge University, he traveled abroad for several years before returning to England in 1650 to tutor the daughter of the Parliamentary general Lord Fairfax. It was while living at the Fairfax estate that he wrote most of his nonsatirical poetry. Three years later, Marvell became tutor to Oliver Cromwell's ward, William Dutton.

A Political Poet Marvell wrote a number of poems about Cromwell, including "An Horatian Ode upon Cromwell's Return from Ireland," perhaps the greatest political poem in English. In 1657 he became an assistant to John Milton, the Latin secretary for the Parliamentary government, and in 1659 was himself elected to membership in Parliament, an office he held until his death. After the Restoration, he seems to have been influential in securing Milton's deliverance from prison and from possible execution. During this time he also wrote many political satires attacking the king's policies. Marvell's poetry was not published until after his death, and his true talent as a poet was not fully recognized until the 20th century.

Richard Lovelace

1618–1657

Other Works
"To Amarantha, That She Would Dishevel Her Hair"
"To Lucasta, Going Beyond the Seas"
"To Althea, from Prison"

The Perfect Cavalier A courtier, soldier, poet, lover, connoisseur of the arts, and reputedly one of the most handsome men in England—Richard Lovelace had all of the qualities of the perfect Cavalier. He was born into a wealthy military family and was educated at Oxford. On a visit to the university, the king and queen admired him so much that they granted him a master's degree on the spot. Naturally, he fought for the monarchy during the civil war.

Prisoner and Poet Lovelace was imprisoned twice, once for petitioning Parliament in the king's favor and again for his involvement in an uprising against the legislative body. It was while he was imprisoned that he wrote his best and most famous poems, "To Althea, from Prison" and "To Lucasta, Going to the Wars." In 1646, he was badly wounded while fighting the Spanish in France. Lovelace depleted most of his fortune trying to help the king and spent the last years of his life dependent on the charity of friends. During his lifetime, Lovelace's poems were popular and even set to music, but after his death they were forgotten for over 100 years.

from the Rubáiyát (rōō′ bē-yät′)

Poetry by OMAR KHAYYÁM (ō′ mär kī-yäm′)
Translated by EDWARD FITZGERALD

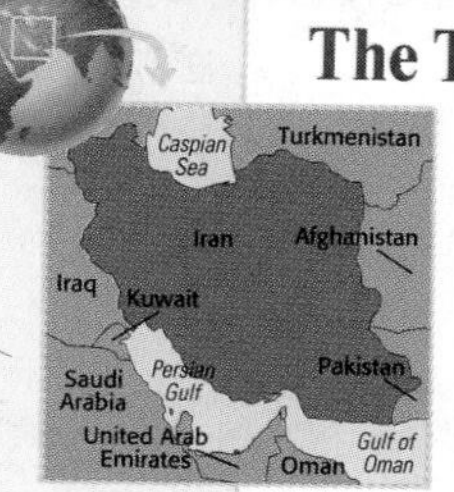

Comparing Literature of the World

The Theme of *Carpe Diem* Across Cultures

Poems by Herrick, Marvell, Lovelace, and Omar Khayyám The theme of *carpe diem*—"seize the day"—is dominant in the *Rubáiyát,* just as it is in the poems of the English Cavalier poets and Andrew Marvell. Many of the poems by Herrick, Marvell, Lovelace, and Omar Khayyám feature speakers who warn about the fleeting nature of time and urge their audiences to live in the present. These poets also use metaphors to convey their themes.

Points of Comparison As you read the poems from the *Rubáiyát,* compare their **themes** and **metaphors** with those you encountered in the poems by Herrick, Marvell, and Lovelace.

Build Background

Persian Poetry The *Rubáiyát* is probably the work of Persian literature best known in the West. It has been translated into almost every major language of the world. The word *rubáiyát* is the plural form of *ruba'i,* the name of a Persian poetic form. A ruba'i is a quatrain, or four-line poem, in which the first, second, and fourth lines rhyme.

In its entirety, the *Rubáiyát* contains more than 400 of these quatrains. Each quatrain conveys a single thought about a subject such as beauty, love, death, or the fleeting nature of time. Although at one time all 400 poems were attributed to the 12th-century Persian poet Omar Khayyám, scholars now believe that he perhaps wrote no more than 250.

In 1859, the British writer Edward FitzGerald translated 75 of the poems into English. FitzGerald tried to remain true to Omar's expression of his philosophy of life by respecting the poems' form and individual themes, but he did modify the images to fit the tastes of his Victorian audience. Because the original quatrains were disconnected, FitzGerald rearranged them into a more unified and continuous sequence.

Focus Your Reading

LITERARY ANALYSIS **THEME AND METAPHOR** As you know, the **theme** of a literary work is a message or insight about life or human nature that the writer wishes to communicate to the reader. You will also recall that a **metaphor** is a comparison that does not contain the word *like* or *as.* This comparison may be stated directly, as in "Life is a broken-winged bird," or it may be implied, as in "the Bird of Time." Metaphors can be an effective means of conveying theme in a literary work. As you read these poems from the *Rubáiyát,* look for metaphors that are used to express theme.

ACTIVE READING **DRAWING CONCLUSIONS ABOUT TONE** Frequently, a writer relies on **imagery**—words and phrases that appeal to the senses—to convey his or her **tone,** or attitude, toward a subject. The writer's tone, in turn, usually reflects his or her philosophy of life.

READER'S NOTEBOOK As you read these poems, look for imagery that helps establish the tone. Keep track of the images you find by using a chart like the one shown.

Poem	Imagery
1	Field of Night, Shaft of Light
7	
12	

LESSON RESOURCES

UNIT TWO RESOURCE BOOK, pp. 64–65

ASSESSMENT RESOURCES
Formal Assessment, p. 75
Teacher's Guide to Assessment and Portfolio Use
Test Generator

SKILLS TRANSPARENCIES AND COPYMASTERS
Literary Analysis
- Theme, T9 (for Literary Analysis, p. 471)

Reading and Critical Thinking
- Compare and Contrast, T15 (for Extend Interpretations 8, p. 474)

Grammar
- Absolute Phrases, C92 (for Mini Lesson, p. 472)

Writing
- Organizing Your Writing, T11 (for Writing Option 2, p. 475)

Communications
- Formal Presentations, T10 (for Activities & Explorations 1, p. 475)

INTEGRATED TECHNOLOGY
Audio Library
Visit our website:
www.mcdougallittell.com

OVERVIEW

Objectives
1. understand and appreciate a selection from **Persian poetry (Literary Analysis)**
2. identify and examine **themes** and **metaphors (Literary Analysis)**
3. recognize and discuss connections that cross cultures
4. use strategies for **drawing conclusions** about **tone (Active Reading)**

Summary
In these four-line poems (quatrains), Omar Khayyám declares that people should enjoy life during youth and appreciate nature. He uses vivid imagery to create metaphors about the brevity of life, the swiftness of time, and the impotence of human beings. Many of the poems seem to be addressed to a lover.

Thematic Link
Like the poets Marvell and Herrick, Omar Khayyám believes that humanity must become conscious of the waste of postponing until tomorrow the possibilities of today. This exuberant theme of *carpe diem* is underscored by the poet's feeling that human beings are the pawns and playthings of an indifferent God, powerless to change their fate as they **face life's limitations**.

5-Minute Warm-Up
Daily Language SkillBuilder

Have students **proofread** the display sentences on page 273m and write them correctly. The sentences also appear on Transparency 10 of **Grammar Transparencies and Copymasters.**

TEACHING THE LITERATURE

Reading and Analyzing

Literary Analysis

THEME AND METAPHOR

Omar Khayyám uses metaphors in almost every quatrain to express the themes of the poems. Have students identify the theme in each quatrain and write that theme in the center of a word web. Then, have them write the metaphors and images in ovals around the theme.

Ask students to share their word webs with the class. Discuss the meaning of each metaphor to ensure students' understanding.

 Use **Unit Two Resource Book,** pp. 65 for more exercises.

Active Reading

DRAWING CONCLUSIONS ABOUT TONE

Tone is the way in which an author's attitude toward his subject is expressed. Omar deals with serious subject matter in these quatrains. Is his attitude serious or light-hearted?
Possible Response: His attitude is serious but not glum.
What images and metaphors are more serious, and which more light-hearted?
Possible Response: The image of Time as a bird is relatively light-hearted, but the metaphor of God playing with humans as if they were chess pieces is more serious.

 Use **Unit Two Resource Book,** pp. 64 for more practice.

FROM THE

Rubáiyát

Omar Khayyám

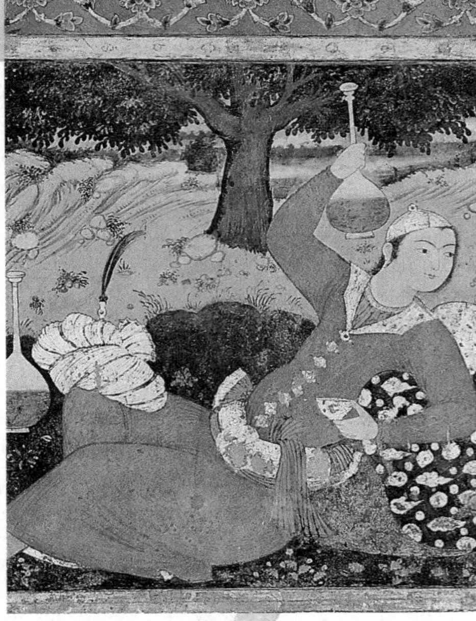

Joy of Wine fresco. Chehel Sotün Palace, Isfahan, Iran. Photo by Roloff Beny, courtesy of the National Archives of Canada (PA-1986-009).

1

Wake! For the Sun, who scatter'd into flight
The Stars before him from the Field of Night,
    Drives Night along with them from Heav'n, and strikes
The Sultán's Turret with a Shaft of Light.

4 Sultán's Turret: a tower in the palace of a Moslem ruler.

7

Come, fill the Cup, and in the fire of Spring
Your Winter-garment of Repentance fling:
    The Bird of Time has but a little way
To flutter—and the Bird is on the Wing.

Teaching Options

Grammar

ABSOLUTE PHRASES

Instruction An absolute phrase is a sentence part that describes the rest of the sentence in which it appears. It contains both a participle and the noun or pronoun modified by the participle.

Activity Write the following sentence on the chalkboard.

> His scientific genius being recognized, Omar Khayyám was asked to help design an observatory in the city of Isfahan.

Have students underline the participle and the noun it modifies. *(being recognized; genius)* Point out that the absolute phrase adds detail to the independent clause. Absolutes are *almost* complete sentences. You can make any absolute a sentence by adding a form of *to be,* such as *is, are, was,* or *were.* Ask students to make the absolute phrase in the sample sentence into a sentence that could stand alone. *(His scientific genius was being recognized.)*

Tell students that writers sometimes use absolute phrases to add detail without creating run-on sentences. They combine connected sentences by changing the verb in one sentence to a participle.

12

A Book of Verses underneath the Bough,
A Jug of Wine, a Loaf of Bread—and Thou
Beside me singing in the Wilderness—
Oh, Wilderness were Paradise enow!

12 enow: enough.

63

Oh, threats of Hell and Hopes of Paradise!
One thing at least is certain—*This* Life flies;
One thing is certain and the rest is Lies;
The Flower that once has blown for ever dies.

64

Strange, is it not? that of the myriads who
Before us pass'd the door of Darkness through,
Not one returns to tell us of the Road,
Which to discover we must travel too.

17 myriads (mĭr′ē-ədz): countless numbers (of people).

68

We are no other than a moving row
Of Magic Shadow-shapes that come and go
Round with the Sun-illumined Lantern held
In Midnight by the Master of the Show;

69

But helpless Pieces of the Game He plays
Upon this Checker-board of Nights and Days;
Hither and thither moves, and checks, and slays,
And one by one back in the Closet lays.

27 hither and thither: here and there.

96

Yet Ah, that Spring should vanish with the Rose!
That Youth's sweet-scented manuscript should close!
The Nightingale that in the branches sang,
Ah, whence, and whither flown again, who knows!

99

Ah, Love! could you and I with Him conspire
To grasp this sorry Scheme of Things entire,
Would not we shatter it to bits—and then
Re-mold it nearer to the Heart's Desire!

Customizing Instruction

Less Proficient Readers

Explain to students that a lantern show is an early projection technique whereby still images are projected onto a wall by the light of a lantern.

Students Acquiring English

Have students look at line 16 and use the context to explain the meaning of *blown.*

Answer: bloomed.

Use **Spanish Study Guide** for additional support, pp. 94-96.

Gifted and Talented

Have students write a quatrain responding to a poem in this selection. They could write an answer to one of Omar's invitations, like Sir Walter Raleigh's reply to "The Passionate Shepherd to His Love," or they could write an argument against one of the ideas or themes presented in a quatrain.

Multiple Learning Styles

Visual/Kinesthetic Learners

Have students sketch a drawing based on the images presented in the first quatrain. Suggest they replace the Sultán's Turret with a building more familiar to them, perhaps from their own town or city.

Explain that to check for absolute phrases, students can apply the reverse process.

Exercise The following sentences contain images from the *Rubáiyát.* Ask students to underline the absolute phrase, and then write the participle and the noun it modifies. Have students work in cooperative groups to write two related sentences, and then combine them by writing an absolute phrase.

1. The sun, its light scattering the stars from the sky, drives the night away. *(scattering, light)*
2. The Bird of Time, its wings carrying it swiftly along, has but a little way to go. *(carrying, wings)*
3. He met her beneath the giant oak, his hands clutching a jug of wine and a loaf of bread. *(clutching, hands)*
4. Its sweet song silenced, the nightingale has flown away. *(silenced, song)*

Use **Grammar Transparencies and Copymasters,** p. 32.

Use McDougal Littell's ***Language Network*** for more instruction and practice in (different in every selection).

RUBÁIYÁT 473

GUIDING STUDENT RESPONSE

Connect to the Literature

1. What Do You Think?
Guidelines for student response: Students may find Omar too pessimistic. Others may say they wish they could follow his advice but they have to work hard to get into college or find a good job. Some students may agree with Omar about life being here and now, with no prospect of an afterlife; others may disagree.

Comprehension Check
- death
- companionship, food and drink, leisure, poetry, a beautiful spring or summer day in the natural world

Think Critically

2. Student responses will vary but should be based on the content of the selection. You might require students to refer to specific passages to support their answers.
3. Possible Response: As the "Master of the Show" in poem 68 and the chess player in stanza 69, God is the master who controls human beings.
4. Students may notice that although the conclusions may seem fatalistic, the tone is not depressed and is even lighthearted in many places.
5. Responses will vary, but students should draw on the content of the quatrains to explain their answers.

Literary Analysis

Paired Activity Have pairs share the metaphors they have identified. You might draw on the chalkboard a chart similar to the one shown here and fill it in with examples provided by the students.

Connect to the Literature

1. What Do You Think? Freewrite about the thoughts you had after reading these poems.

Comprehension Check
- According to the speaker, what one thing in life is certain?
- What would make life like a paradise for the speaker?

Think Critically

2. How would you describe the philosophy of life expressed by the **speaker?**

THINK ABOUT
- what he compares time to in poem 7
- the actions he advocates in poems 1, 7, and 12
- his view of death in poems 63 and 64
- what he compares human beings to in poems 68 and 69

3. How do you think the speaker views the relationship between human beings and God?

4. ACTIVE READING DRAWING CONCLUSIONS ABOUT TONE
Look back at the **imagery** chart you kept in your READER'S NOTEBOOK as you read. What conclusions can you draw about the **tone** in each poem?

5. Which **theme** expressed in the poems seems to come closest to your own philosophy of life? Explain your response.

Extend Interpretations

6. **Critic's Corner** One critic, Gordon S. Haight, stated that the *Rubáiyát* "will always attract some readers by its dark philosophy." What do you think Haight meant by "dark philosophy"? Explain your interpretation.

7. **Connect to Life** The speaker suggests that happiness can be achieved very simply, with "a Book of verses . . . a Jug of Wine, a Loaf of Bread—and Thou." Do you think most people can be satisfied with such simple pleasures? Give reasons for your opinion.

8. Points of Comparison Which of these poems from the *Rubáiyát* seem most closely related to the ideas expressed in Robert Herrick's "To the Virgins, to Make Much of Time" (page 464)? What theme do they share with Herrick's poem?

Literary Analysis

THEME AND METAPHOR In poetry, **metaphors** often help convey **themes.** For example, in poem 7, time is compared to a bird that has already completed part of a short journey. This comparison reflects the theme that time is limited and passes quickly.

Paired Activity With a partner, identify at least five other metaphors in these poems. Determine what theme or themes the metaphors help convey.

Poem Number	Metaphor	Theme
1		
7		
12		
63		
64		
68		
69		
96		
99		

Extend Interpretations

Critic's Corner Students may say that Haight meant that Omar seems not to believe in an afterlife and that he advocates casting off repentance. These philosophies at odds with the redemptive ideals in most religions.

Connect to Life Students may take this list literally, in which case they would find it lacking. Some may see it as synecdoche, as in the phrase "Give us this day our daily bread," in which bread represents sustenance. In that case, students may find the list satisfactory or even attractive because it implies a worry-free lifestyle.

Points of Comparison Possible response: Stanzas 7, 63, and 96 are most closely related to Herrick's poem because of their references to flowers. The poems share the theme of *carpe diem.*

Choices & CHALLENGES

Writing Options

1. Paragraph of Explanation In a paragraph, identify the person whom you think the speaker is addressing in these poems. Give reasons for your opinion.

I think the speaker is addressing . . .

2. Letter to Omar Select one poem with which you strongly agree or disagree. Write a letter to Omar Khayyám, explaining your thoughts about his ideas. Place the letter in your **Working Portfolio.**

3. Points of Comparison Compare the metaphors used in the *Rubáiyát* with those in Marvell's "To His Coy Mistress." Then write your own metaphor to express your philosophy of life.

Writing Handbook
See page 1367: Compare and Contrast.

Activities & Explorations

1. Philosophy Report Read other poems from the *Rubáiyát* and choose two to share with classmates. In a brief oral report, tell how you think each poem reflects the speaker's philosophy of life. ~ **SPEAKING AND LISTENING**

2. Poetic Mural Create a mural depicting images or ideas presented in some or all of the poems. ~ **ART**

Inquiry & Research

Omar's Culture Investigate the culture of 12th-century Persia—the culture in which Omar Khayyám wrote his poems. Find information on religion, education, or government, and report your findings to the class.

Omar Khayyám

1050?–1123?

Omar the Tentmaker Omar Khayyám lived in Persia, the region now occupied by the nation of Iran. During his lifetime, he was more famous for his work as a scientist than for his poetry. The name Khayyám means "tentmaker"; thus, the author of the *Rubáiyát* is sometimes called Omar the Tentmaker. It is possible that Omar briefly engaged in this line of work before going on to more scholarly pursuits; however, it is more likely that his father was the tentmaker.

Man of Science Omar was an exceptionally brilliant man who mastered the subjects of mathematics, astronomy, philosophy, history, medicine, and law. He was the author of important works on astronomy, geometry, and algebra as well as poetry. Because of his scientific genius, Omar was asked to make the astronomical calculations that were needed to reform the calendar in use at the time. He was later asked to help in the design and building of an observatory in the city of Isfahan. Despite his many scientific contributions, however, Omar's worldwide reputation is based mainly on his poetry.

Author Activity

Counting the Days Working with a partner or in a small group, find out about the calendar that Omar helped reform. What was the old calendar based on? What changes were made to the new one? How does the reformed calendar compare with the calendar used today in the Western

Writing Options

1. **Paragraph of Explanation** Students may think the speaker is addressing a lover, adopting the seductive tone of Marvell. Others may imagine a more general audience.
2. **Letter to Omar** Students may disagree with Khayyám's concept of mortality or with his apparent idea that no moderation is possible.
3. **Points of Comparison** Responses will vary. Students may point out that the lovers in Marvell's poem can influence their sun, whereas Omar Khayyám's people are at the mercy of the sun. The difference is crucial to the poets' different views of human life and agency. Student metaphors may show people as relatively powerful or completely at the mercy of unnamed forces.

Activities & Explorations

1. **Philosophy Report** If materials are not available in the school library, you may have to bring samples of your own.
2. **Poetic Mural** Students may draw or paint their own murals, or they may cut out images from newspapers and magazines.

Author Activity

Counting the Days The Gregorian calendar numbers years from the birth of Jesus and uses the designation A.D. (anno Domini). The Muslim calendar on which Omar Khayyám worked begins with the year in which Mohammed, the prophet of Islam, fled from Mecca to Medina (A.D. 622); years are numbered from the emigration (anno Hegira). Furthermore, the calendar of Omar Khayyám is lunar, not solar. While there are twelve months in a year, the year is only 355 days long.

Inquiry & Research

Omar's Culture Remind students that the modern name of Persia is Iran, but that the language is still called Persian. Persian, unlike English, has not undergone many changes, and it is still possible for a modern Iranian to read old texts such as the *Rubáiyát* with relative ease. However, for an English-speaking person, a translation is necessary. Just as the work of Omar Khayyám depends upon the British translator Edward FitzGerald in order to reach English speakers, so poets such as Rumi have their translators in American authors such as Coleman Barks. Students may wish to look into other poets writing in Persian whose work is available to Americans today. As students investigate 12th century Persia, ask them to interpret the influence that historical context had on the content or style of the *Rubáiyát*.

OVERVIEW

Objectives

1. understand and examine **allusion** in poetry **(Literary Analysis)**
2. use strategies for **clarifying sentence meaning (Active Reading)**

Summary

These two sonnets were written at times in Milton's life when he was questioning his life and his relationship to "the will of Heaven" and his "Maker." The Puritans of Milton's time believed they had a direct, personal relationship with their creator and that their task was to discover the "Taskmaster's" will for them. To be unproductive created a crisis for Milton because it suggested that he might have chosen the wrong vocation. Additionally, becoming blind caused him to wonder whether he had offended the maker whom he wished to serve.

Thematic Link

Milton expresses the view of many Puritans that a person's limitations were determined by his relationship with God. **Facing life's limitations** meant accepting the will of God.

5-Minute Warm-Up

Daily Language SkillBuilder

Have students **proofread** the display sentences on page 273m and write them correctly. The sentences also appear on Transparency 11 of **Grammar Transparencies and Copymasters.**

PREPARING to *Read*

How Soon Hath Time
When I Consider How My Light Is Spent

Poetry by JOHN MILTON

"They also serve who only stand and wait."

Connect to Your Life

A Dream Deferred Think about someone you know or have read about—such as a musician or an athlete—who has suffered disappointment in trying to reach a desired goal or realize a dream. Discuss your impressions of how that person reacted to disappointment and how he or she carried on afterward.

Build Background

Life's Disappointments Studious and devout even as a child, John Milton devoted his life to writing about religious issues and dreamed of producing great poetry that would explore humanity's relationship with God. Though he ultimately realized this ambition, his life was marked by a series of disappointments, not the least of which was the political downfall of the Puritans, the faction he supported in the civil warfare that racked mid-17th-century England. The two famous sonnets you will read explore two other disappointments in the writer's life. In the first, composed to mark the occasion of his 23rd birthday, Milton examines the meagerness of his creative output. In the second, he reveals his feelings about his loss of sight at the age of 43.

Focus Your Reading

LITERARY ANALYSIS ALLUSION An **allusion** is a brief reference to a historical or fictional person, place, event, or thing with which the reader is assumed to be familiar. A devout Puritan who often wrote on religious topics, Milton frequently alluded to material in the Bible. As you read these sonnets, look for examples of biblical allusions.

ACTIVE READING CLARIFYING SENTENCE MEANING Like many other poets, Milton sometimes used unusual word order to make his ideas fit particular patterns of **rhythm** or **rhyme** and to make his lines more memorable. For example, instead of writing "that I am arrived so near to manhood," he wrote:

That I to manhood am arrived so near

READER'S NOTEBOOK As you read these sonnets, be alert to the order of words in Milton's sentences. When the word order in a sentence seems odd, try **paraphrasing** the sentence in a way that sounds more natural and makes sense to you. Record your paraphrases in your notebook.

Milton's sentence:
"...who best/Bear his mild yoke, they serve him best."
My paraphrase:

LESSON RESOURCES

UNIT TWO RESOURCE BOOK, pp. 66–67

ASSESSMENT RESOURCES
Formal Assessment, pp. 77–78
Teacher's Guide to Assessment and Portfolio Use
Test Generator

SKILLS TRANSPARENCIES AND COPYMASTERS
Literary Analysis
- Figurative Language, T22 (for Literary Analysis, p. 476)

Reading and Critical Thinking
- Paraphrasing and Summarizing, T42 (for Think Critically 3, p. 479)

Vocabulary
- Words with Multiple Meanings, C48 (for Mini Lesson, p. 477)

INTEGRATED TECHNOLOGY
Audio Library
LaserLinks
- Author Background: John Milton. See **Teacher's SourceBook,** p. 29.

Visit our website:
www.mcdougallittell.com

How Soon Hath Time

JOHN MILTON

How soon hath Time, the subtle thief of youth,
Stoln on his wing my three and twentieth year!
My hasting days fly on with full career,
But my late spring no bud or blossom show'th.
Perhaps my semblance might deceive the truth,
That I to manhood am arrived so near,
And inward ripeness doth much less appear,
That some more timely-happy spirits endu'th.
Yet be it less or more, or soon or slow,
It shall be still in strictest measure even
To that same lot, however mean or high,
Toward which Time leads me, and the will of Heaven;
All is, if I have grace to use it so,
As ever in my great Taskmaster's eye.

3 career: speed.

5 semblance: outward appearance.

8 more timely-happy spirits: people who have accomplished more at an early age; **endu'th:** endows.

10 still: always; **even:** adequate.

11 lot: fate.

14 ever: eternally.

Thinking Through the Literature

1. Does this poem seem optimistic or pessimistic to you? Explain your impression.
2. Do you think the 23-year-old speaker would characterize himself as a youth or as a man? Consider the evidence.

   THINK ABOUT
   - his statement that "no bud or blossom show'th"
   - his reference to his appearance in line 5
   - the "inward ripeness" he mentions in line 7
3. What conclusions does the speaker reach by the poem's end?

TEACHING THE LITERATURE

Customizing Options

Students Acquiring English
Before students read "When I Consider How My Light Is Spent," explain that a yoke is a wooden frame placed around an animal's neck to allow it to pull a plow.

Use **Spanish Study Guide** for additional support, pp. 97–99.

Gifted and Talented
Have students compare the images of time and youth in the poetry of Marvell, Herrick, Omar Khayyàm and Milton.

Thinking Through the Literature

1. Responses will vary. Students should support their answers with evidence from the poem.
2. Possible Response: He sees himself as a man in years but a youth in achievements and wisdom.
3. Possible Response: He concludes that God will guide his destiny regardless of how much or how fast he works; he will achieve whatever God wills.

Mini Lesson: Vocabulary Strategy

MULTIPLE-MEANING WORDS

Instruction Explain to students that English is a living language; consequently, words can develop new meanings at almost any time, even while the old meanings continue to be valid. An example is the word *hack.* This word is now used to describe breaking into someone else's computer system. However, *hack* has retained its old meanings of "to cut or chop" and "to cough loudly." The phenomenon of multiple-meaning words is the basis of many puns.

Activity Have students consult dictionaries to find additional meanings for the following words. Have students apply these meanings to the poem to see if it might enrich their understanding of the poem:

career, "How Soon Hath Time," line 3
grace, "How Soon Hath Time," line 13
dark, "When I Consider How My Light Is Spent," line 2
talent, "When I Consider How My Light Is Spent," line 3
serve, "When I Consider How My Light Is Spent," line 14

Use **Vocabulary Transparencies and Copymasters,** p. 28.

Reading and Analyzing

Literary Analysis ALLUSION

Read to students the parable of the talents in the Bible. Have students paraphrase the parable. In "When I Consider How My Light Is Spent," to which servant does Milton compare himself? Why?

Answer: the third, because he feels he has failed to make something out of his "talent."

What might be the significance to Milton of verse 30: "And cast the worthless servant into the outer darkness"?

Possible Response: He might consider his blindness to be a sign of having been cast into the "outer darkness."

Use **Unit Two Resource Book,** pp. 67 for more exercises.

Active Reading

CLARIFYING SENTENCE MEANING

Milton occasionally uses phrases that seem awkward to our ears. This awkwardness is sometimes necessary to maintain the meter or rhyme; at other times it serves to emphasize certain ideas. For example, in line 6 of "How Soon Hath Time," Milton emphasizes *manhood* and assures the rhyme by moving the phrase "to manhood" forward in the line. Have students work in pairs or small groups to rephrase the following lines: in "How Soon Hath Time" line 4, lines 9–12; in "When I Consider" lines 1–6, Patience's reply in lines 9–11.

Use **Unit Two Resource Book,** pp. 66 for more practice.

Literary Analysis: PERSONIFICATION

Personification is a literary device whereby something non-human is described as having human qualities. What is being personified in "How Soon Hath Time?"

Answer: time.

What human qualities does Milton attribute to time?

Answer: It steals; it leads.

Illustration (about 1856), Birket Foster.

WHEN I CONSIDER HOW MY LIGHT IS SPENT

John Milton

When I consider how my light is spent
    Ere half my days, in this dark world and wide,
    And that one talent which is death to hide,
    Lodged with me useless, though my soul more bent
To serve therewith my Maker, and present
    My true account, lest he returning chide;
    "Doth God exact day-labor, light denied?"
    I fondly ask; but Patience to prevent
That murmur, soon replies, "God doth not need
    Either man's work or his own gifts; who best
    Bear his mild yoke, they serve him best. His state
Is kingly. Thousands at his bidding speed
    And post o'er land and ocean without rest:
    They also serve who only stand and wait."

3 talent: a reference to the biblical parable of the talents (Matthew 25:14–30), in which a servant who has hidden his one talent (a sum of money) in the earth is reprimanded for not putting it to good use.

8 fondly: foolishly.

12 thousands: here, thousands of angels.

Connect to the Literature

1. **What Do You Think?** What are your thoughts about the last line of "When I Consider How My Light Is Spent"? Share your reaction with classmates.

Comprehension Check
- What is the speaker's problem?
- What does the speaker ask about God?

Think Critically

2. What seems to trouble the speaker most about his loss of sight?

THINK ABOUT
- the **image** conveyed by "this dark world" in line 2
- the reference to his "talent" in lines 3–4
- the question he "fondly" asks in line 8

3. ACTIVE READING CLARIFYING SENTENCE MEANING Look again at the sentences you paraphrased in your READER'S NOTEBOOK. How would you **paraphrase** Patience's statements in lines 9–14 in everyday English? What would you say is the main point of Patience's speech?

4. Do you think the speaker will be able to follow the advice of Patience? Why or why not?

Extend Interpretations

5. **Comparing Texts** Compare and contrast the speakers' attitudes in "How Soon Hath Time" and "When I Consider How My Light Is Spent." Pay particular attention to their feelings about their talent and their relationship with God.

6. **What If?** If Milton had been deaf rather than blind, how might his writing have been different?

7. **Connect to Life** In what specific situations do you think the advice in either sonnet might be useful to people today? Explain your opinion.

Literary Analysis

ALLUSION Writers often use **allusions** to make their works more meaningful to readers. An allusion is a brief reference to a historical or fictional person, place, event, or thing with which the reader is assumed to be familiar. In "When I Consider How My Light Is Spent," Milton alludes to a biblical parable in which a master praises two servants who have made good use of the talents entrusted to them and criticizes a servant who has buried his one talent instead of using it. The first two servants are given rewards, but the third has his talent taken away.

Activity
- Explain the two meanings of the word *talent* in the poem. What, specifically, might the speaker's "one talent" be?
- Explain how the allusion to the biblical parable of the talents adds to the meaning of the poem.

REVIEW SONNET These two poems follow the **Italian sonnet** form: an **octave** (eight lines) followed by a **sestet** (six lines). The **rhyme scheme** in the octave is *abbaabba;* in the sestet, it is *cdedce* or *cdecde*. For each of the two sonnets, explain the relationship between the content of the octave and the content of the sestet.

GUIDING STUDENT RESPONSE

Connect to the Literature

1. **What Do You Think?** Guidelines for student response: Students may be confused about what it means to "stand and wait." Suggest that they consider figurative meanings. Remind them that Milton is writing in a context in which this life is merely preparation for eternal life after death.

Comprehension Check
- He is blind.
- How can the speaker serve God, now that the speaker is blind?

Think Critically

2. Possible Response: Some students will believe that he is most troubled by his inability to serve God fully; others will say his inability to write.
3. Possible Response: "God does not need your services. What is more important is your readiness to serve." Patience is telling the speaker that he can serve God no matter what his condition.
4. Possible Responses: No, he has a strong ambition to serve God by writing; yes, his strong faith will allow him to "stand and wait."

Literary Analysis

Activity The speaker's "one talent" might be writing. The Biblical parable adds another layer of meaning to the poem.

Review Sonnet In both poems the sestet provides a kind of resolution.

Extend Interpretations

Comparing Texts Both poems express concern about the speaker's ability to use his talents and resolve those concerns by putting faith in God's will. In the first poem the speaker seems confident that he will succeed in time; in the second he expresses doubt about what he can achieve in the future. He perceives a strict, exacting God in the first poem and a merciful one in the second.

What If? Students may want to discuss whether sight or hearing is more heavily relied upon by poets. Others may want to discuss which of our senses is more likely to disturb concentration by introducing distractions.

Connect to Life Students may know of friends who consider themselves to be behind in some goal they had planned to accomplish. Some may relate to Milton's concern with his standing in God's eyes. Some may look upon the age of twenty-three as really old, and agree that he has every right to be worried.

OVERVIEW

An excerpt of this selection is included in the **Grade 12 InterActive Reader.**

Objectives

1. understand and appreciate a classic epic poem **(Literary Analysis)**
2. identify and examine diction in an epic poem **(Literary Analysis)**
3. use strategies for clarifying meaning **(Active Reading)**

Summary

Milton's epic poem relates the history of God's attempt to banish Satan, once an angel like Michael and Gabriel. Satan sets up his own underworld kingdom, with its palace called Pandemonium, and plots his revenge.

Use **Unit Two Resource Book,** p. 68 for additional support.

Thematic Link

In *Paradise Lost,* Milton not only justifies "the ways of God to men," but he also shows his characters **facing life's limitations.**

Editor's Note:

This selection contains material or language that may be considered objectionable.

PREPARING to *Read*

from Paradise Lost

Epic poetry by JOHN MILTON

Connect to Your Life

Masterpiece Imagine that you are a writer, a filmmaker, or a creative artist of some other kind and that you are planning to create your finest work ever. What subject might you choose to explore in your masterpiece? On what great works of the past might you draw? What themes might you hope to express? Jot down ideas for your masterpiece. You might organize them in a cluster diagram like this one.

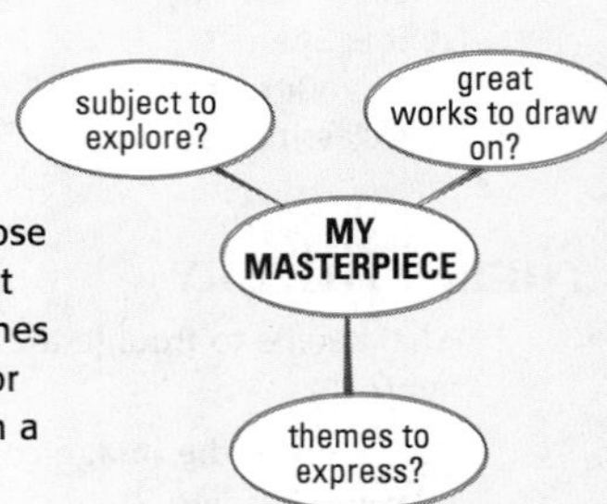

Focus Your Reading

LITERARY ANALYSIS DICTION **Diction** is another term for word choice. In *Paradise Lost,* Milton employs the lofty, elevated diction that his exalted **subject** and **themes** demand. Notice how, in the following passage, powerful nouns and verbs are juxtaposed with eloquent adjectives to convey the majestic nature of the event described:

. . . Him the Almighty Power
Hurled headlong flaming from th' ethereal sky
With hideous ruin and combustion down
To bottomless perdition, there to dwell
In adamantine chains and penal fire

As you read the selection, look for other examples of elevated diction.

ACTIVE READING CLARIFYING MEANING Milton's long, sweeping sentences and elevated diction take some time to appreciate. Here are some obstacles you may encounter, along with suggestions on how to **clarify meaning:**

- **Archaic verb and pronoun forms** (like *dost* for *does* and *thou* for *you*): Think of a familiar word that resembles the unfamiliar form and see if it makes sense in the context; if it does not, consult a dictionary.
- **Obsolete or unfamiliar vocabulary:** See if you can determine meanings from context or from information in the Guide for Reading notes; consult a dictionary when necessary.
- **Allusions** (mainly to people, places, and events in the Bible and in ancient mythology): Use the Guide for Reading notes to help you understand the allusions and their significance.
- **Long, sweeping sentences:** Mentally break each sentence down into parts you can understand; focus on key words, such as the subject and the verb, to get the gist of the sentence's meaning before taking account of qualifiers and interrupters.
- **Unusual word order:** Mentally reorder the words in the sentences so that they sound more natural and make sense to you.

READER'S NOTEBOOK As you encounter difficult passages in this selection, use the strategies suggested above to improve your understanding of them. Write down definitions and explanations to help you remember the meanings of complex lines.

LESSON RESOURCES

UNIT TWO RESOURCE BOOK, pp. 68–71

ASSESSMENT RESOURCES

Formal Assessment, pp. 79–80
Teacher's Guide to Assessment and Portfolio Use
Test Generator

SKILLS TRANSPARENCIES AND COPYMASTERS

Literary Analysis
- Figurative Language, T22 (for Literary Analysis, p. 480)

Reading and Critical Thinking
- Visualizing, T8 (for Active Reading, p. 480)

Grammar
- Diagramming Subjects, Verbs, and Modifiers, T58 (for Mini Lesson, p. 490)
- Prepositional Phrases, C85 (for Mini Lesson, p. 490)

Vocabulary
- Using a Thesaurus, C49 (for Mini Lesson, p. 484)

Writing
- Effective Language, T13 (for Writing Option 2, p. 492)
- Personality Profile, C25 (for Writing Option 1, p. 492)

INTEGRATED TECHNOLOGY

Audio Library
LaserLinks
- Author Background: John Milton. See **Teacher's SourceBook,** p. 29.

Internet: Research Starter
Visit our website:
www.mcdougallittell.com

Build Background

Epic Proportions In 1658, when he had been blind for almost a decade, John Milton undertook the composition of his masterpiece, a poem in which he would achieve "things unattempted yet in prose or rhyme." The poem he hoped to create was one that he had had in mind since he was 19, a great Christian epic that would "justify the ways of God to men." It was his hope "that by labor and intent study (which I take to be my portion in this life), joined with the strong propensity of nature, I might perhaps leave something so written to aftertimes, as they should not willingly let it die." In a sense, his whole life was a preparation for this task.

Using the biblical account in Genesis as his basic source, he mentally constructed long, flowing sentences in rhythmic blank verse, which he then dictated, 20 or 30 lines at a time, to paid assistants, friends, and relatives, including his three daughters. For seven painstaking years he worked on his ambitious project. The result, *Paradise Lost,* is widely considered to be the finest epic poem in the English language. In it Milton probes the relationships between free will and destiny and between freedom and responsibility. His treatment of these themes is appropriately grand, in the tradition of the ancient epics—Homer's *Iliad* and *Odyssey* and Virgil's *Aeneid*—that were his models.

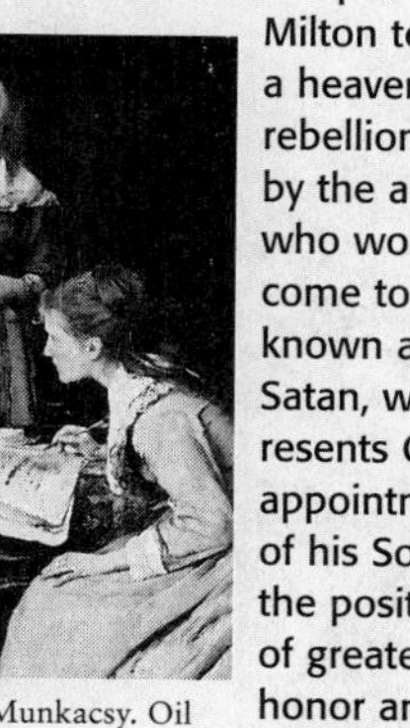

The Blind Milton Dictating to his Daughters (1878), Mihaly von Munkacsy. Oil on canvas, The Granger Collection, New York

Rebellion and Its Aftermath Divided into 12 books, *Paradise Lost* is vast in its scope. Milton tells of a heavenly rebellion led by the angel who would come to be known as Satan, who resents God's appointment of his Son to the position of greatest honor and power in Heaven. After the rebel angels are defeated and cast into Hell, Satan vows to corrupt God's latest creation, humanity. This he accomplishes by tempting the first woman, Eve, to disobey God by eating the fruit of the Tree of Knowledge in the Garden of Eden. When Eve and her mate, Adam, realize that they have disobeyed God, they are overcome with grief and despair. Yet they experience God's mercy as well as his wrath and by the end of the epic have some hope for the future: though they have been banished from the Garden of Eden, their exile has been softened by the promise of a Messiah. Milton's *Paradise Regained,* an epic sequel to *Paradise Lost,* presents the fulfillment of that promise.

5-Minute Warm-Up

Daily Language SkillBuilder

Have students **proofread** the display sentences on page 273m and write them correctly. The sentences also appear on Transparency 11 of **Grammar Transparencies and Copymasters.**

Mini Lesson Viewing and Representing

The Blind Milton Dictating to His Daughters
by Mihaly von Munkacsy
ART APPRECIATION

Instruction A popular subgenre of historical paintings of the 19th century was the theatrical reconstruction of the surroundings of creative geniuses. Such works were the specialty of Hungary's most notable painter, Mihaly von Munkacsy (1844–1900), who lived in Paris from 1872 until his death. He painted Mozart and many others but won international art fame with his costume drama of the sightless Milton dictating *Paradise Lost* to his daughters.

Application Point out that the painting was made over two hundred years after Milton wrote *Paradise Lost.* What does the painting suggest about the painter's view of Milton's later life? Have students examine other resources to analyze how well the painting depicts Milton and what strategies he used to compose.

Possible Response: In later life, Milton came to rely increasingly on others, but retained his literary ambitions.

TEACHING THE LITERATURE

Reading and Analyzing

Literary Analysis DICTION

A Read aloud lines 19–23 beginning with "thou from the first . . ." Have students note the change in diction that comes halfway through line 22. Ask students why Milton may have made this change. You might also have students look up the meanings of *illumine.*

Use **Unit Two Resource Book,** p. 70 for more exercises.

Active Reading

CLARIFYING MEANING

- **Archaic verb and pronoun forms** *Thee, thy,* and *thine* can be read as *you, your,* and *yours.* Milton rarely uses *ye* for *you. Doth* and *dost* are merely forms of the verb *do.*
- **Obsolete or unfamiliar vocabulary** Many obsolete words look like words with which students are familiar. For example, *seed* in line 8, meaning "offspring" or "progeny," and *fast* in line 12, meaning "near," may confuse students.
- **Allusions** You may wish to review the story of the expulsion of Adam and Eve from the Garden of Eden from the Book of Genesis to help students with the poet's allusions.
- **Long, sweeping sentences** Suggest that students pay attention to end punctuation in its various forms: the period, the semicolon, and the colon.
- **Unusual word order** Suggest that students move the words "Sing, Heavenly Muse" from line 6 to the poem's beginning.

Use **Unit Two Resource Book,** p. 69 for more practice.

Engraving from Dante's *Inferno* by Gustave Doré (1861).

482

Teaching Options

Viewing and Representing

Engraving **by Gustave Doré**

ART APPRECIATION

Instruction The engravings by Gustave Doré here and on pp. 488 and 490 capture an event that Milton chronicles: Satan's expulsion from Heaven and consignment to Hell.

Application Ask students to describe the engravings by referring to specific uses of line, color, shape, and space on pages 482, 488, and 490 and then to explain the emotion expressed and how it is achieved. Ask them to analyze whether the engravings represent Hell as they have pictured it based on Milton's descriptions. Have them make their own black-and-white drawings of Milton's Hell as they imagine it, letting them choose whether to include Satan and/or his companions.

John Milton

from Paradise Lost

In this excerpt—the opening of Book I—Milton begins his epic like the ancient epics that were his models, with an invocation of, or call upon, a Muse, in which the speaker asks for inspiration and sets forth the subject and themes of the poem. (In Greek mythology, the Muses were goddesses of learning and the creative arts.) There follows a summary of how Satan, once among the most powerful of God's angels, was cast out of Heaven for leading a rebellion against God's rule. Awakening in Hell alongside Beëlzebub (bē-ĕl′zə-bŭb′), *another fallen angel, Satan considers what he has lost and reaffirms his defiance of God.*

Of man's first disobedience, and the fruit
Of that forbidden tree whose mortal taste
Brought death into the world, and all our woe,
With loss of Eden, till one greater Man
Restore us, and regain the blissful seat,
Sing, Heavenly Muse, that on the secret top
Of Oreb, or of Sinai, didst inspire
That shepherd who first taught the chosen seed
In the beginning how the heavens and earth
Rose out of Chaos: or, if Sion hill
Delight thee more, and Siloa's brook that flowed
Fast by the oracle of God, I thence
Invoke thy aid to my adventurous song,
That with no middle flight intends to soar
Above th' Aonian mount, while it pursues
Things unattempted yet in prose or rhyme.
And chiefly thou, O Spirit, that dost prefer
Before all temples th' upright heart and pure,
Instruct me, for thou know'st; thou from the first
Wast present, and with mighty wings outspread

Dovelike sat'st brooding on the vast abyss,
And mad'st it pregnant: what in me is dark
Illumine; what is low, raise and support;

GUIDE FOR READING

4 one greater Man: Jesus Christ.

6 Heavenly Muse: the divine source of Milton's poetic inspiration—here identified with the Spirit of God that the Bible says spoke to Moses (the "shepherd" of line 8).

7 Oreb . . . Sinai: Mounts Horeb and Sinai, on which Moses heard the voice of God.

8 the chosen seed: the Jews.

10–11 Sion Hill . . . Siloa's brook: places in Jerusalem, the holy city of the Jews.

12 fast by the oracle of God: near the Jews' temple in Jerusalem.

15 Aonian (ā-ō′nē-ən) **mount:** Mount Helicon in Greece, which in ancient times was considered sacred to the Muses.

20–22 with mighty wings . . . pregnant: In the Bible, the Spirit of God is described as hovering over the primeval "deep" during the creation of the universe.

Customizing Instruction

Less Proficient Readers

Use the following questions to guide students to understand the development of Satan's attitude toward Heaven.

- Why has Satan fallen to Hell?
  Answer: God sends him to Hell for leading an uprising in heaven.
- What does Satan say he has not lost?
  Answer: He has not lost his strong will, his desire for revenge, or his courage.
- How does Beëlzebub account for their having fallen to Hell with their strength intact
  Answer: Perhaps God wants them to suffer more, or perhaps he has errands in mind for them.
- How does Satan answer Beëlzebub?
  Answer: He says that they will take revenge by doing evil.

Students Acquiring English

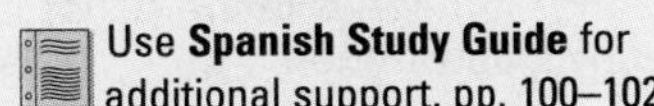
Use **Spanish Study Guide** for additional support, pp. 100–102

Gifted and Talented

Have students research one or more of these references in this selection: Mount Horeb, Mount Sinai, Aonian mount, Palestine, the Titans, Mount Etna, the river Styx, the river Lethe. Have students discuss how these references affect their response to the poetry.

BLOCK SCHEDULING: MANAGING TIME

If your schedule requires that you cover the lesson objectives in a shorter time, use . . .

- Preparing to Read, pp. 480–481
- Thinking Through the Literature, p. 491

If you want to take advantage of longer class time, use . . .

- TE Teaching Options: Vocabulary Strategy, p. 484; Viewing and Representing, pp. 481, 482; Speaking and Listening, p. 485; Standardized Test Practice, p. 486; Multicultural Link, pp. 487, 488; Informal Assessment, p. 489; Grammar, p. 490
- Choices & Challenges and Author Activity, p. 492

Reading and Analyzing

GUIDE FOR READING

A He assumes that he is capable of understanding God's thoughts and actions.

B Serpentlike; envious and revengeful; deceitful; proud; ambitious; rebellious. Satan views God as a rival power, not as a sovereign to be obeyed.

C God throws him out of Heaven into Hell.

D He is even more angry at God; he is not repentant.

Active Reading

CLARIFYING MEANING

E To help them understand lines 56–60, students should use a dictionary and the Guide for Reading. Point out the word *ken* in line 59, an obsolete verb meaning "can see." Ask students what contextual clue might help with understanding *ken.*
Answer: the word *views* in the clause immediately following *ken.*

GUIDE FOR READING

F Full of light, hope, peace, joy.

G Satan is speaking here to another rebel angel, Beëlzebub.

H He refuses to change his original intent to oppose God ("fixed mind and high disdain")

I God.

That to the height of this great argument
I may assert Eternal Providence,
And justify the ways of God to men.
   Say first (for Heaven hides nothing from thy view,
Nor the deep tract of Hell), say first what cause
Moved our grand parents, in that happy state,
Favored of Heaven so highly, to fall off
From their Creator, and transgress his will
For one restraint, lords of the world besides?
Who first seduced them to that foul revolt?
   Th' infernal serpent; he it was, whose guile,
Stirred up with envy and revenge, deceived
The mother of mankind, what time his pride
Had cast him out from Heaven, with all his host
Of rebel angels, by whose aid aspiring
To set himself in glory above his peers,
He trusted to have equaled the Most High,
If he opposed; and with ambitious aim
Against the throne and monarchy of God
Raised impious war in Heaven and battle proud,
With vain attempt. Him the Almighty Power
Hurled headlong flaming from th' ethereal sky
With hideous ruin and combustion down
To bottomless perdition, there to dwell
In adamantine chains and penal fire,
Who durst defy th' Omnipotent to arms.
      Nine times the space that measures day and night
To mortal men, he with his horrid crew
Lay vanquished, rolling in the fiery gulf
Confounded though immortal. But his doom
Reserved him to more wrath; for now the thought
Both of lost happiness and lasting pain
Torments him; round he throws his baleful eyes,
That witnessed huge affliction and dismay,
Mixed with obdùrate pride and steadfast hate.
At once, as far as angels ken, he views
The dismal situation waste and wild:
A dungeon horrible, on all sides round
As one great furnace flamed; yet from those flames
No light, but rather darkness visible
Served only to discover sights of woe,
Regions of sorrow, doleful shades, where peace
And rest can never dwell, hope never comes
That comes to all, but torture without end
Still urges, and a fiery deluge, fed

24 argument: subject.

25 Providence: God's plan for the universe.

26 justify: show the justice of. Milton states his purpose in this line. **A** What assumptions does he make about his own abilities?

29 our grand parents: Adam and Eve.

31 transgress: overstep the limits set by.

32 for: on account of; **besides:** otherwise.

34 th' infernal serpent: Satan, who in the Bible is referred to as "that old serpent" (Revelation 20:2). Later in the poem, it will be in the form of a serpent that Satan will tempt Eve to eat the fruit of the Tree of Knowledge.

36 what time: when.

43 impious (ĭm′pē-əs): showing disrespect for God; sacrilegious.

B **34–44** These lines introduce the figure of Satan. What is your first impression of him? How does he view God?

45 th' ethereal (ĭ-thîr′ē-əl) **sky:** Heaven.

47 perdition: damnation.

48 adamantine (ăd′ə-măn′tēn′): indestructible; unbreakable.

C **44–49** What has happened to Satan?

53–54 his doom . . . wrath: fate had more punishment in store for him.

D **53–56** What is Satan's reaction to his punishment?

58 obdurate (ŏb′dŏŏ-rĭt): stubborn; unyielding.

62–63 Milton conveys the desolation of hell through a horrifying paradox: flames that give no light, only "darkness visible."

Teaching Options

Vocabulary Strategy

USING A THESAURUS TO FIND SYNONYMS

Instruction Students may find a thesaurus useful for understanding the vocabulary of this poem. Explain that a thesaurus is chiefly a source of synonyms. To begin finding a synonym, students should determine the part of speech of the word. Explain that they may also need to determine the root word. For example, in line 21, the word *brooding* itself would not appear in a thesaurus. Students need to know that the root word here is a verb, *brood.* By searching for *brood* as a verb, they will be led to choices such as "to meditate morbidly" and "to incubate." Using context clues, students can decide which is the appropriate synonym.

Activity Have students work in pairs to determine synonyms for the following words.

line 28, *tract,* noun
line 31, *transgress,* verb
line 34, *foul,* adjective
line 37, *host,* noun
line 48, *penal,* adjective

Use **Vocabulary Transparencies and Copymasters,** p. 45 for more exercises.

With ever-burning sulphur unconsumed:
Such place Eternal Justice had prepared
For those rebellious; here their prison ordained
In utter darkness and their portion set
As far removed from God and light of Heaven
As from the center thrice to th' utmost pole.
O how unlike the place from whence they fell!
There the companions of his fall, o'erwhelmed
With floods and whirlwinds of tempestuous fire,
He soon discerns; and, weltering by his side,
One next himself in power, and next in crime,
2 Long after known in Palestine, and named
Beëlzebub. To whom th' arch-enemy,
And thence in Heaven called Satan, with bold words
Breaking the horrid silence thus began:
"If thou beëst he—but O how fallen! how changed
From him who in the happy realms of light
Clothed with transcendent brightness didst outshine
Myriads, though bright! if he whom mutual league,
United thoughts and counsels, equal hope
And hazard in the glorious enterprise,
Joined with me once, now misery hath joined
In equal ruin; into what pit thou seest
From what height fallen, so much the stronger proved
He with his thunder: and till then who knew
The force of those dire arms? Yet not for those,
Nor what the potent Victor in his rage
Can else inflict, do I repent or change,
Though changed in outward luster, that fixed mind
And high disdain, from sense of injured merit,
That with the Mightiest raised me to contend,
And to the fierce contention brought along
Innumerable force of spirits armed,
That durst dislike his reign, and me preferring,
His utmost power with adverse power opposed
In dubious battle on the plains of Heaven,
And shook his throne. What though the field be lost?
All is not lost: the unconquerable will,
And study of revenge, immortal hate,
And courage never to submit or yield:
And what is else not to be overcome?
That glory never shall his wrath or might
Extort from me. To bow and sue for grace
With suppliant knee, and deify his power
Who from the terror of this arm so late

73–74 as far . . . utmost pole: a reference to a passage in Virgil's *Aeneid,* which states that Tartarus (hell) is twice as far below the surface of the earth as the heavens are above it.

F **75** What must Heaven be like if it is the opposite of Hell?

78 weltering: writhing; thrashing about.

80 Palestine (păl'ĭ-stīn'): here, the land of the Phoenicians, who worshiped the god Baal.

81 Beëlzebub: a powerful demon, called "the prince of the devils" in the Bible (Matthew 12:24) and identified with the Phoenician god Baal.

81–82 th' arch-enemy . . . Satan: The name *Satan* comes from a Hebrew word meaning "adversary," or "enemy."

84 Who is speaking here, and to whom is he speaking?

94–99 What does Satan refuse to change?

107 study: pursuit.

110 To whom does "his" refer here?

112 with suppliant (sŭp'lē-ənt) **knee:** kneeling in a begging posture.

Customizing Instruction

Less Proficient Readers

1 Ask students to look at lines 27–49 and to create a list of all the ways Milton refers to God by noticing words that are capitalized even though they are not the first words of lines. Students may want to work in teams.
Answer: Other names for God are Heaven, Creator, Most High, Almighty Power, and Omnipotent.

Students Acquiring English

2 Read lines 78–82 aloud. Ask students what *next* means in line 79.
Answer: second in order.
Then, ask what four things we learn about Beëlzebub here.
Answer: He is writhing beside Satan; he is second only to Satan in power; he is second only to Satan in crime; he is later known in Palestine.

Speaking and Listening

DRAMATIC READING
Instruction Between lines 83 and 84, the narrative undergoes a change of speaker from the voice of the poet to the voice of Satan.
Prepare Ask students to work in pairs to present a dramatic reading involving two voices: that of the narrator and that of Satan addressing Beëlzebub. The narrator might start at line 59 or line 75; Satan might go to line 94 or to line 111. Students should show the ways in which the speakers contrast in tone and mood.
Present Ask those students who are in the audience to discuss how hearing the lines read aloud influences their understanding of the speakers. Have students discuss which voice has a stronger presence and why. Encourage a comparison of the performers' interpretations of the poem as well as the audience's reactions to the readings.

Reading and Analyzing

Literary Analysis: EPIC POETRY

The elements of an epic poem include supernatural characters, warriors, love, war, and a journey of descent. Have students apply each element to the selection.

Answer: supernatural characters: God, Satan, Beëlzebub, other angels; warriors: Satan, Beëlzebub, other angels; love: Satan's love for himself, Beëlzebub's love of Satan; war: Satan's battle with God; a descent: Satan and his army descending into Hell.

GUIDE FOR READING

A Beëlzebub.

Active Reading

CLARIFYING MEANING

B Satan makes an important declaration in lines 159–160. Ask students to rephrase this statement for clarity.

Possible Response: "Our task will be not to do anything good, but to enjoy doing bad."

GUIDE FOR READING

C God has ended the fiery and thunderous attack on the rebel angels.

D Satan proposes that the disorganized rebel angels retreat to a nearby plain and plot their next strategy against God.

Doubted his empire—that were low indeed;
That were an ignominy and shame beneath
This downfall; since, by fate, the strength of gods
And this empyreal substance cannot fail;
Since, through experience of this great event,
In arms not worse, in foresight much advanced,
We may with more successful hope resolve
To wage by force or guile eternal war,
Irreconcilable to our grand Foe,
Who now triùmphs, and in th' excess of joy
Sole reigning holds the tyranny of Heaven."
So spake th' apostate angel, though in pain,
Vaunting aloud, but racked with deep despair;
And him thus answered soon his bold compeer:
"O prince, O chief of many thronèd powers,
That led th' embattled seraphim to war
Under thy conduct, and in dreadful deeds
Fearless, endangered Heaven's perpetual King,
And put to proof his high supremacy,
Whether upheld by strength, or chance, or fate!
Too well I see and rue the dire event
That with sad overthrow and foul defeat
Hath lost us Heaven, and all this mighty host
In horrible destruction laid thus low,
As far as gods and heavenly essences
Can perish: for the mind and spirit remains
Invincible, and vigor soon returns,
Though all our glory extinct, and happy state
Here swallowed up in endless misery.
But what if he our Conqueror (whom I now
Of force believe almighty, since no less
Than such could have o'erpowered such force as ours)
Have left us this our spirit and strength entire,
Strongly to suffer and support our pains,
That we may so suffice his vengeful ire,
Or do him mightier service as his thralls
By right of war, whate'er his business be,
Here in the heart of Hell to work in fire,
Or do his errands in the gloomy deep?
What can it then avail though yet we feel
Strength undiminished, or eternal being
To undergo eternal punishment?"
Whereto with speedy words th' arch-fiend replied:
"Fallen cherub, to be weak is miserable,
Doing or suffering: but of this be sure,
B To do aught good never will be our task,

114 doubted: feared for.

115 ignominy (ĭg'nə-mĭn'ē): disgrace.

117 this empyreal (ĕm-pîr'ē-əl) **substance:** the heavenly material of which the angels' bodies are made.

125 apostate (ə-pŏs'tāt'): renegade.

126 vaunting: boasting.

127 compeer (kəm-pîr'): companion of equal rank.

A 128 Who begins speaking here?

129 seraphim (sĕr'ə-fĭm): an order of angels.

144 of force: necessarily.

148 suffice (sə-fīs'): satisfy fully.

149 thralls: slaves.

143–155 Beëlzebub suggests that God has left the fallen angels their strength so that their suffering will be increased or so that he can use them for his own purposes. Then Beëlzebub asks what use in that case ("what can it then avail") the fallen angels' strength and eternal life will be to them.

157 cherub: angel.

Teaching Options

Assessment Standardized Test Practice

CHOOSING THE BEST MULTIPLE CHOICE ANSWER

Have students answer the following questions.

1. What is the meaning of *arms* as it is used in line 49?
   A. upper limbs of the body
   B. branches
   C. warfare
   D. anger
2. What is the meaning of *arms* as it is used in line 94?
   A. upper limbs of the body
   B. branches
   C. warfare
   D. anger

1. The answer is C. *Arms* in this line refers to lines 42–43: "Against the throne and monarchy of God / Raised impious war in Heaven and battle proud. . . ."
2. The answer is A. God has cast Satan and his minions into hell; this line implies he has literally thrown them down.

But ever to do ill our sole delight,
As being the contrary to his high will
Whom we resist. If then his providence
Out of our evil seek to bring forth good,
Our labor must be to pervert that end,
And out of good still to find means of evil;
Which ofttimes may succeed, so as perhaps
Shall grieve him, if I fail not, and disturb
His inmost counsels from their destined aim.
But see! the angry Victor hath recalled
His ministers of vengeance and pursuit
Back to the gates of Heaven; the sulphurous hail,
Shot after us in storm, o'erblown hath laid
The fiery surge that from the precipice
Of Heaven received us falling; and the thunder,
Winged with red lightning and impetuous rage,
Perhaps hath spent his shafts, and ceases now
To bellow through the vast and boundless deep.
Let us not slip th' occasion, whether scorn
Or satiate fury yield it from our Foe.
Seest thou yon dreary plain, forlorn and wild,
The seat of desolation, void of light,
Save what the glimmering of these livid flames
Casts pale and dreadful? Thither let us tend
From off the tossing of these fiery waves;
There rest, if any rest can harbor there;
And reassembling our afflicted powers,
Consult how we may henceforth most offend
Our enemy, our own loss how repair,
How overcome this dire calamity,
What reinforcement we may gain from hope,
If not, what resolution from despair."
    Thus Satan talking to his nearest mate
With head uplift above the wave, and eyes
That sparkling blazed; his other parts besides
1 Prone on the flood, extended long and large
Lay floating many a rood, in bulk as huge
As whom the fables name of monstrous size,
Titanian or Earth-born, that warred on Jove,
Briareos or Typhon, whom the den
By ancient Tarsus held, or that sea beast
Leviathan, which God of all his works
Created hugest that swim th' ocean-stream.
Him, haply, slumbering on the Norway foam,
The pilot of some small night-foundered skiff,
Deeming some island, oft, as seamen tell,

167 fail not: am not mistaken.

172 laid: calmed.

175 impetuous (ĭm-pĕch′o͞o-əs): violently forceful.

C **171–177** What change is Satan describing in these lines?

178 slip th' occasion: miss the chance.

179 satiate (sā′shē-īt): satisfied.

186 powers: troops.

190 reinforcement: increase of strength.

180–191 What does Satan propose?

196 rood: a unit of measure, between six and eight yards.

197–200 as whom . . . Tarsus held: In Greek mythology, both the huge Titans—of whom Briareos was one—and the earth-born giant Typhon battled unsuccessfully against Jove (Zeus), just as Satan rebelled against God. Zeus defeated Typhon in Asia Minor, near the town of Tarsus.

201 Leviathan (lə-vī′ə-thən): a huge sea beast mentioned in the Bible—here identified with the whale by Milton.

204 night-foundered: overtaken by the darkness of night.

Customizing Instruction

Multiple Learning Styles

Visual Learners

1 Have students read the description of Satan lying on the burning lake. Then, have them create drawings of the scene using details from the selection.

Multicultural Link: Epic Poetry

Nearly every culture has its own epic poetry—narrative poetry characterized by length and an elevated heroic mood. Epic poetry can be either oral or written; some of the most famous examples originated from traditions of oral storytelling. Scholars believe that rhyme was used to help storytellers remember the words. The Greek stories of the *Odyssey* and the *Iliad* probably originated as oral tales but were later written down. On the other hand, Virgil wrote his *Aeneid* without reference to an oral version. All epics from the *Ramayana* to *Beowulf* combine the exaggeration of events into heroic proportion and the fusion of history with folk tale and imagination. The purpose of epic seems to be to keep past glory alive for today's appreciation and tomorrow's inspiration.

PARADISE LOST 487

One attribute of epic literature is the heroic, "larger than life" quality of the events and people. What attributes of Satan seem exaggerated and of epic proportions?

Possible Response: Students may mention his size, his strength, the power of his emotions, and the force of his will.

GUIDE FOR READING

A Satan is compared to a Greek Titan and to a leviathan.

B Despite Satan's intentions and motivations, he can do only what God allows. God will ultimately use Satan's actions to produce good in the world while bringing condemnation of Satan himself (in Christian theology, the defeat of Satan by Christ).

Active Reading

CLARIFYING MEANING

C Satan and Beëlzebub have been thrashing about in a burning lake. Satan then takes wing, "till on dry land/He lights." Explain to students that *lights* has a meaning here with which they may not be familiar. Have them look up *light* in a dictionary and select the meaning that is most appropriate for the context. Then, have them paraphrase "till on dry land/He lights."

Possible Response: "until he lands on dry land."

GUIDE FOR READING

D They suppose—falsely—that they can operate independently of God's power and control.

Engraving from Dante's *Inferno* by Gustave Doré (1861).

488

Teaching Options

Multicultural Link: Angels

Angels are found in the literature of Judaism, Christianity, and Islam. In general, angels are believed to be intermediaries between God and mankind. In the Old Testament, angels constitute God's heavenly court, and in his name fight Israel's battles. Angels are given specific tasks and often appear in human form throughout the Bible. The representation of angels has changed over the years. It is generally believed that Egyptian and Assyrian sculptures of winged beasts guarding the royal palaces were a major influence in early representations of angels as the mighty cherubim of Yahweh's throne. By the 4th century, angels were depicted as men or youths clad in white tunics with wings and halos. Child angels, cherubs, began to be depicted in the 12th century. Cupid, the winged messenger of romantic love, is their pagan model. Female angels made their first appearance in the Renaissance.

With fixèd anchor in his scaly rind
Moors by his side under the lee, while night
Invests the sea, and wishèd morn delays:
So stretched out huge in length the arch-fiend lay,
Chained on the burning lake; nor ever thence
Had risen or heaved his head, but that the will
And high permission of all-ruling Heaven
Left him at large to his own dark designs,
That with reiterated crimes he might
Heap on himself damnation, while he sought
Evil to others, and enraged might see
How all his malice served but to bring forth
Infinite goodness, grace, and mercy shown
On man by him seduced, but on himself
Treble confusion, wrath, and vengeance poured.
Forthwith upright he rears from off the pool
His mighty stature; on each hand the flames
Driven backward slope their pointing spires, and rolled
In billows, leave i' th' midst a horrid vale.
Then with expanded wings he steers his flight
Aloft, incumbent on the dusky air,
That felt unusual weight; till on dry land
He lights, if it were land that ever burned
With solid, as the lake with liquid fire,
And such appeared in hue; as when the force
Of subterranean wind transports a hill
Torn from Pelorus or the shattered side
Of thundering Etna, whose combustible
And fuelèd entrails thence conceiving fire,
Sublimed with mineral fury, aid the winds,
And leave a singèd bottom all involved
With stench and smoke: such resting found the sole
Of unblest feet. Him followed his next mate,
Both glorying to have 'scaped the Stygian flood
As gods, and by their own recovered strength,
Not by the sufferance of supernal power.
"Is this the region, this the soil, the clime,"
Said then the lost archangel, "this the seat
That we must change for Heaven? this mournful gloom
For that celestial light? Be it so, since he
Who now is sovereign can dispose and bid
What shall be right: farthest from him is best,
Whom reason hath equaled, force hath made supreme
Above his equals. Farewell, happy fields,
Where joy forever dwells! Hail, horrors! hail,
Infernal world! and thou, profoundest Hell,

208 invests: covers.

A **196–209** An **epic simile** is a comparison that extends over a number of lines. What two comparisons does Milton make in these lines?

214 reiterated (rē-ĭt'ə-rā'tĭd): repeated.

220 treble: three times as much.

B **210–220** What do these lines suggest about how much control Satan has over his own destiny?

226 incumbent on: resting upon.

230–231 the force . . . transports a hill: It was formerly thought that earthquakes were caused by underground winds.

232 Pelorus (pə-lôr'əs): a cape on the coast of Sicily.

233 Etna: a volcano near Pelorus.

235 sublimed: vaporized.

236–237 involved with: wrapped in.

239 the Stygian (stĭj'ē-ən) **flood:** the river Styx—in Greek mythology, one of the rivers of the underworld.

D **241 sufferance:** permission. How do Satan and Beëlzebub view their own power in relation to God's power?

Customizing Instruction

Multiple Learning Styles

Visual Learners

Ask students to map the underworld that Milton has so far described. What are its physical features?

Possible Response: There is a fiery river or lake as well as dry land, but everything is burning with a fire that does not give off light.

Students Acquiring English

1 Point out to students that *hail* means "welcome." What is it that Satan welcomes?

Answer: horrors, Hell.

What has he left behind?

Answer: joy

Assessment Informal Assessment

FINDING EVIDENCE IN THE TEXT

Have students answer the following question. Remind them to support their response with evidence from the text.

If he had it to do all over again, do you think Satan would try to overthrow God?

RUBRIC

3 **Full Accomplishment** The text implies Satan would try to overthrow God again because he believes that God uses power unjustly. However, accept any well-reasoned response supported with evidence from text.

2 **Substantial Accomplishment** Student demonstrates understanding of Satan's character and provides adequate support from text.

1 **Little or Partial Accomplishment** Student demonstrates little or no understanding of Satan's character or fails to provide support from text.

Reading and Analyzing

GUIDE FOR READING

Literary Analysis: ALLUSION

A *Paradise Lost* was written in 1667, roughly sixty years after Shakespeare's *Hamlet.* Compare lines 254–255 of *Paradise Lost* with this one from *Hamlet:* "There's nothing good nor bad but thinking makes it so." In what way are these two statements similar?
Possible Response: Hamlet and Satan seem to agree that ideas of Heaven and good are relative, depending on the values of the speaker.

B To assert his superiority to his circumstances and environment.

Literary Analysis: EPIC POETRY

In an epic poem, the heroes are portrayed as larger-than-life. Have students read again lines 254 to the end. Satan has just said good-bye to the "happy fields" of Heaven. Now he is building an argument. What is he convincing himself of and how does he do it?
Possible Response: Satan convinces himself that he can be a great ruler of Hell. He argues that the mind is itself wherever it is; that he is the same even in Hell; that he is free and God won't bother him; that being a ruler is a great ambition; and, therefore, that it is better to rule in Hell than to serve in Heaven.

Ask students whether they find Satan's logic to be sound. Is he a true hero? Why or why not?
Possible Responses: His logic is sound, and he is a true hero because he is not letting adversity stand in the way of his ambition; his logic is unsound, and he is not a hero because all of his ambition focuses on his own glory.

Receive thy new possessor, one who brings
A mind not to be changed by place or time.
A The mind is its own place, and in itself
Can make a Heaven of Hell, a Hell of Heaven.
What matter where, if I be still the same,
And what I should be, all but less than he
Whom thunder hath made greater? Here at least
We shall be free; th' Almighty hath not built
Here for his envy, will not drive us hence.
Here we may reign secure; and in my choice
To reign is worth ambition, though in Hell:
Better to reign in Hell than serve in Heaven.
But wherefore let we then our faithful friends,
Th' associates and copartners of our loss,
Lie thus astonished on th' oblivious pool,
And call them not to share with us their part
In this unhappy mansion, or once more
With rallied arms to try what may be yet
Regained in Heaven, or what more lost in Hell?"

B **254–255** Why do you think Satan makes this statement?

257 all but less than: second only to.

264 wherefore: why.

266 astonished: stunned; **th' oblivious pool:** the river Lethe—in Greek mythology, a river of the underworld that causes forgetfulness.

268 mansion: dwelling place.

Engraving from Dante's *Inferno* by Gustave Doré (1861).

490

Teaching Options

Grammar

PREPOSITIONAL PHRASES

Instruction A preposition shows the relationship between a noun or pronoun and another word in the sentence. Point out to students that a preposition generally indicates location *(beside, under),* direction *(down, toward),* or association *(like, without).*

Activity Write the following excerpt from "Paradise Lost" on the chalkboard.

". . . Stirred up with envy and revenge, deceived
The mother of mankind, what time his pride
Had cast him out from Heaven, . . ."

Have students identify the prepositions. Underline each one as it is identified. Point out that a prepositional phrase consists of a preposition, its objects, and the object's modifiers. Have students identify the object of each preposition. *(with, envy and revenge; of, mankind; from, Heaven)* Then put two lines under each object. Explain that the underlined words are prepositional phrases.

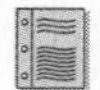

Use **Grammar Transparencies and Copymasters,** p. 24 for exercises.

Use McDougal Littell's ***Language Network*** for more instruction in prepositional phrases.

Connect to the Literature

1. **What Do You Think?** What is your overall impression of Satan?

Comprehension Check
- Where do the fallen angels find themselves after their rebellion?
- Whom does Satan talk to?

Think Critically

2. **ACTIVE READING | CLARIFYING MEANING** Whom is the **speaker** addressing in lines 1–26? In order to answer this question, review the suggestions for **clarifying meaning** in the Active Reading feature on page 480. Take special note of the technique for breaking down long, sweeping sentences.

3. Do the **details** in the opening invocation give you the impression that the poet is humble, ambitious, or both? Cite details to explain your evaluation.

4. What human characteristics does Satan display?

THINK ABOUT
- his past actions
- his attitude toward God
- his views of Heaven and Hell

5. In the light of their past, why would Satan and Beëlzebub find Hell especially painful and horrible?

6. Do you think Satan actually believes the statement he makes in line 263? Why or why not?

Extend Interpretations

7. **Critic's Corner** In an essay on Milton, the Victorian historian and literary critic Thomas Babington Macaulay observed, "Poetry which relates to the beings of another world ought to be at once mysterious and picturesque. That of Milton is so." Do you agree? Cite details from the selection to support your evaluation.

8. **Comparing Texts** Compare and contrast Satan with an **epic hero** (such as Beowulf) and with a **tragic hero** (such as Shakespeare's Macbeth). With which **character** would you say he has more in common? Why?

9. **Connect to Life** Satan is greedy for total power in his world. What historical figures have had a similar kind of greed? What are the effects of such greed?

Literary Analysis

DICTION In *Paradise Lost,* Milton employed the powerful, elevated **diction,** or word choice, that his lofty subject and themes demanded. Consider, for example, lines 230–235 of the selection:

. . . as when the force
Of subterranean wind transports
    a hill
Torn from Pelorus or the shattered
    side
Of thundering Etna, whose
    combustible
And fuelèd entrails thence
    conceiving fire,
Sublimed with mineral fury . . .

Milton could have used words less imposing and elevated than those underlined in the lines above. Instead, he chose words that eloquently convey the majesty of his subject and themes.

Paired Activity Choose a passage from *Paradise Lost,* such as the summary of Satan's fall in lines 34–49 or Satan's speech in lines 242–270. In a chart, list words that exemplify Milton's diction in that passage. Then write a synonym of each word you listed. Discuss how Milton's word choice contributes to his powerful, lofty style.

	Milton's Words	Synonyms
Nouns	clime (l. 242)	climate
Verbs	dispose (l. 246)	
Modifiers	celestial (l. 245)	

REVIEW | BLANK VERSE Milton's long, sweeping sentences are cast in the form of blank verse—unrhymed iambic pentameter. Do you find this verse form appropriate for his lofty subject and themes? Explain.

GUIDING STUDENT RESPONSE

Connect to the Literature

1. **What Do You Think?**
Guidelines for student response: Satan is envious of God and resolves that if he can't have what he wants, he will want what he has. He is a strong, forceful creature whose defeat has not taught him respect.

Comprehension Check
- The fallen angels find themselves in a lake of magical fire that burns without consuming itself or giving off light.
- Satan talks to his lieutenant, Beëlzebub.

Use Selection Quiz in **Unit Two Resource Book,** p. 71.

Think Critically

2. The speaker addresses the Holy Spirit, whom he calls "Heavenly Muse."
3. Possible Response: The poet describes himself as adventurous, endowed with a pure and upright heart, and in need of instruction and illumination. He seems both humble and ambitious.
4. Possible Response: Satan is proud and unrepentant. He does not concede defeat.
5. Possible Response: They were among the most beautiful and favored of the angels, and now they are cut off from God and banished to a desolate place.
6. Answers may vary; students should defend their answers with evidence from the text.

Literary Analysis

Paired Activity Ask volunteers to read examples that they charted of Milton's diction and the synonyms for each. When students discuss Milton's diction, have them discuss the effect his word choice has on them.

Extend Interpretations

Critic's Corner Students should use details from the text to support their positions.

Comparing Texts Beowulf is like Satan in that he is an undaunted fighter. However, Beowulf fights to protect others and Satan fights for selfish reasons. Macbeth, on the other hand, allows his ambition to overrule his conscience, with the result that he is ultimately defeated. Satan is more like Macbeth in that he destroys his fortune by his own acts.

Connect to Life Answers will vary, but some historical figures with a greed for total power include Attila the Hun, the last Chinese emperors, Julius Caesar, the Pharaohs, Kaiser Wilhelm, Czar Nicholas, Hitler, Pol Pot, Spain's General Franco, and Emperor Hirohito. The effects of their greed include much pain and suffering and a place in history.

PARADISE LOST 491

Writing Options

1. **Psychological Profile** Satan is resilient and strong-minded. He is driven by vengeance and resents authority; the speaker of "How Soon Hath Time" is critical of himself and unhappy with his artistic development. He is, however, a person of faith and will endure his frustration for as long as he feels God will require it of him; the speaker of "When I Consider How My Light Is Spent" is frustrated with his disability, but is a person of faith and will endure his unhappiness as long as God will require it of him.
2. **Descriptive Paragraph** Encourage students to use the visual details supplied by Milton to extrapolate smells, sounds, and tactile sensations. Students might describe how the dark, flickering flames of the lake of fire give off the rotten smell of sulphur; the hard, barren dry land bakes with heat that scorches the soles of one's feet; the shadowy, roaring, stinking desolation stretches into the distance beyond the range of vision.

Activities & Explorations

1. ***Paradise Lost* Illustrated** Details might include his relative size, his wings, his strength. Challenge students to examine the stereotyped, comic-strip Satan. Does Milton's Satan have horns and a tail? Does he carry a trident? (No to both questions. Details about Satan's physical attributes are limited, so students will have a great deal of room for interpretation. Pictures should, however, reflect the mood and tone of the excerpt, depicting Satan as imposing and powerful.)
2. **Musical Accompaniment** Students should make an effort to match the mood of the music with that of the sonnet.

Choices & CHALLENGES

Writing Options

1. **Psychological Profile** Write a psychological profile of Satan as he is presented in the excerpt from *Paradise Lost* or of the speaker of either of the two sonnets. Briefly describe your subject's personality traits and attitudes.
2. **Descriptive Paragraph** Write a paragraph in which you describe Hell as it is presented in the excerpt from *Paradise Lost.*

Activities & Explorations

1. ***Paradise Lost* Illustrated** Paint or draw a picture of Satan as he is depicted in the excerpt from *Paradise Lost.* ~ **ART**
2. **Musical Accompaniment** Set either of Milton's two sonnets to music—either your original composition or a recording that you find suitable. Perform your musical version of the sonnet in class, or record it on audiotape. ~ **MUSIC**

Inquiry & Research

Researching Angels Research an aspect of the Judeo-Christian concept of angels touched on in *Paradise Lost.* For example, you might find out more about the different orders of angels (seraphim, cherubim, and so on) or about the idea of the fall of rebellious angels led by Satan. Present your findings in an oral report.

More Online: Research Starter
www.mcdougallittell.com

John Milton

1608–1674

Other Works
Comus
"Lycidas"
"L'Allegro"
"Il Penseroso"
Areopagitica

Youthful Dreams A devout youth of scholarly bent, Milton seemed destined for the clergy but instead, while still a teenager, decided to become a writer. He dreamed of producing important poetry dealing with religious themes. To that end, he studied Latin, Greek, Hebrew, and most of the modern European languages. His knowledge of Italian allowed him to read *The Divine Comedy,* the great 14th-century Christian poem by Dante Alighieri.

A Contentious Puritan Milton attended Cambridge University, where he was critical of the curriculum and at one point was briefly suspended for arguing with his tutor. He had adversaries in the political arena as well. When civil war erupted in 1642, he devoted his energies to writing political pamphlets for the Puritan faction, or Roundheads, who supported Parliament over the king. For a time the Roundheads triumphed under Oliver Cromwell, and Milton accepted the post of Cromwell's Latin secretary; but after Cromwell's death and the restoration of the monarchy, Milton was arrested for his earlier political activities. He avoided execution or lengthy imprisonment, however—in part through the intercession of his former protégé, the poet Andrew Marvell.

Crowning Achievements By this time, Milton's progressive blindness had become total, but he still managed to complete his masterpiece, *Paradise Lost.* A 10-book version of the poem was published in 1667, and a revised version, in which the poem was divided into 12 books, appeared in 1674, the year of Milton's death. Milton also composed a sequel, *Paradise Regained,* and a drama, *Samson Agonistes,* which was patterned on the tragedies of ancient Greece.

Author Activity

Courtly Entertainment Milton's *Comus* is a masque, a form of drama popular in the Renaissance. Find out why *Comus* was written, what it is about, and where it was first performed.

LaserLinks: Background for Reading
Author Background

Inquiry & Research

Researching Angels Students should be alerted to the fact that the appearance of angels in literature, beginning with the Old Testament, is different from the representation of angels in art many hundreds of years later and that Milton would have been working from the older, literary sources. You might also allow students to research angels in Islamic tradition and compare them to the angels in *Paradise Lost.*

Author Activity

Courtly Entertainment Students may need help locating materials for research. Help them become familiar with the school library's resources, or direct them to a school librarian. Have students write an outline or script for their oral reports. Students should practice and revise their oral reports before presenting to the class.

Female Orations

Debate by MARGARET CAVENDISH, DUCHESS OF NEWCASTLE

"Let us hawk, hunt, race, and do the like exercises that men have."

Connect to Your Life

Privileged Gender? Have you ever felt that members of the opposite sex have special privileges or advantages not available to members of your sex? Have you ever engaged in a dialogue or debate about this subject with members of your own or the opposite sex? Draw up a list of some of the advantages that you think each sex possesses. Then share your list with the class.

Build Background

A Feminist Pioneer Margaret Cavendish lived at a time when female writers were few and tended to concentrate on such subjects as family, religion, romance, and the responsibilities of keeping a household. Modesty was highly valued as a feminine virtue, so most women writers of the time never published their work. Cavendish was keenly aware of the limitations placed on women in her society, yet she published her unorthodox writings despite them. She became the subject of considerable criticism and scorn for publishing her thoughts on subjects that were considered off-limits to female interpretation. In "Female Orations" she records an imaginary debate between women with differing points of view on the role of women in society.

WORDS TO KNOW
Vocabulary Preview
demeanor
eloquently
enticing
subsistence
unconscionable

Focus Your Reading

LITERARY ANALYSIS **ARGUMENTATION** Speech or writing intended to convince an audience that a proposal should be adopted or rejected is called **argumentation.** An argument may be developed in an essay, in a speech, or in a debate like that in "Female Orations." As you read this work, look for the arguments Cavendish presents for and against women's rights.

ACTIVE READING **ANALYZING THE STRUCTURE OF ARGUMENTS** The overall structure of "Female Orations" is an imaginary debate in which seven women express different points of view. The arguments of the individual speakers, however, contain examples of other structures. For example, the first speaker uses a **comparison-contrast structure,** comparing the conditions of men and women. The fourth speaker uses a **problem-and-solution structure,** arguing that lack of strength and wit can be overcome by means of exercise and conversation.

READER'S NOTEBOOK As you read "Female Orations," take note of the argument set forth by each speaker. Also note other examples of comparison-contrast and problem-solution structures that you find.

OVERVIEW

Objectives

1. understand and appreciate **argumentation (Literary Analysis)**
2. use strategies for analyzing the structure of arguments **(Active Reading)**

Summary

In this series of seven orations, Margaret Cavendish presents arguments for and against women's rights.

 Use **Unit Two Resource Book,** p. 72 for additional support.

Thematic Link

In "Female Orations," Margaret Cavendish **faces life's limitations** for women. "Eve's Apology in Defense of Women" is an argument for absolving Eve for humanity's expulsion from the Garden of Eden.

5-Minute Warm-Up

Daily Language SkillBuilder

Have students **proofread** the display sentences on page 273m and write them correctly. The sentences also appear on Transparency 11 of **Grammar Transparencies and Copymasters.**

Mini Lesson Preteaching Vocabulary

If you would like to preteach the WORDS TO KNOW for this selection, use the Mini Lesson p. 494.

Editor's Note: This selection contains material that may be considered objectionable.

LESSON RESOURCES

UNIT TWO RESOURCE BOOK, pp. 72–76

ASSESSMENT RESOURCES
Formal Assessment, pp. 81–82
Teacher's Guide to Assessment and Portfolio Use
Test Generator

SKILLS TRANSPARENCIES AND COPYMASTERS
Reading and Critical Thinking
• Analyzing Text Structure, T17 (for Active Reading, p. 493)

Grammar
• Prepositional Phrases Used as Adverbs, C87 (for Mini Lesson, p. 496)

Writing
• Levels of Language, T12 (for Writing Option 1, p. 501)

Communications
• Impromptu Speaking: Debate, T15 (for Informal Assessment, p. 497)

INTEGRATED TECHNOLOGY
Audio Library
Visit our website:
www.mcdougallittell.com

TEACHING THE LITERATURE

Reading and Analyzing

Literary Analysis ARGUMENTATION

As students read, have them write down each speaker's argument. Then discuss whether the speakers seem to represent two "sides" or whether they represent a variety of overlapping positions.

 Use **Unit Two Resource Book,** p. 74 for more exercises.

Active Reading
ANALYZING THE STRUCTURE OF ARGUMENTS

Speaker I compares and contrasts the condition of men and women. Ask students to create a chart with two columns, one headed MEN and one WOMEN. What qualities go in each column?

Answer: Women: live as beasts, as if produced from beasts, miserable, restless with labor, easeless with pain, melancholy for want of pleasures, helpless for want of power, die in oblivion. Men: free, happy, famous, possess ease, rest, pleasure, wealth, power, unconscionable and cruel.

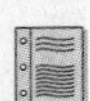 Use **Unit Two Resource Book,** p. 73 for more practice.

Literary Analysis: TONE

Tone is the mood or attitude created by the speaker. Each speaker in "Female Orations" strikes a different tone; some even change their tone during their speech. Have students work in pairs or small groups to create a chart showing the speakers' tones. The chart should include quotes to support each tone.

Female Orations

MARGARET CAVENDISH,
DUCHESS OF NEWCASTLE

Young Woman Standing at a Virginal (about 1670), Jan Vermeer. The Granger Collection, New York.

Teaching Options

Mini Lesson Preteaching Vocabulary

WORDS BASED ON LATIN ROOTS

Instruction Explain to students that many English words originally come from other languages. Point out that learning the origin of a word may make it easier to remember, and it will reinforce what students have learned about root words.

Activity Have students work in pairs to determine the origins of the WORDS TO KNOW. All the WORDS TO KNOW can be traced back to Latin, although many dictionaries extend the etymology only back to French or Old French. Students may need to go to the library and look for other resources to trace the words back to Latin.

1. demeanor–*minari* (lead, conduct)
2. eloquently–*eloqui* (speak out)
3. enticing–*intitiare* (from titius, firebrand)
4. subsistence–*subsistere* (support)
5. unconscionable–*conscire* (be conscious of)

Have students list other words in English derived from the same Latin roots. (for example: *demeanor: menace)*

 Use **Unit Two Resource Book,** p. 75 for more practice.

I

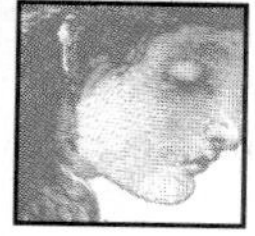

Ladies, gentlewomen, and other inferior women, but not less worthy: I have been industrious to assemble you together, and wish I were so fortunate as to persuade you to make frequent assemblies, associations, and combinations amongst our sex, that we may unite in prudent counsels, to make ourselves as free, happy, and famous as men; whereas now we live and die as if we were produced from beasts, rather than from men; for men are happy, and we women are miserable; they possess all the ease, rest, pleasure, wealth, power, and fame; whereas women are restless with labor, easeless with pain, melancholy for want of pleasures, helpless for want of power, and die in oblivion, for want of fame. Nevertheless, men are so unconscionable and cruel against us that they endeavor to bar us of all sorts of liberty, and will not suffer us freely to associate amongst our own sex; but would fain[1] bury us in their houses or beds, as in a grave. The truth is, we live like bats or owls, labor like beasts, and die like worms.

II

Ladies, gentlewomen, and other inferior women: The lady that spoke to you hath spoken wisely and eloquently, in expressing our unhappiness; but she hath not declared a remedy, or showed us a way to come out of our miseries; but, if she could or would be our guide, to lead us out of the labyrinth men have put us into, we should not only praise and admire her, but adore and worship her as our goddess: but alas! men, that are not only our tyrants but our devils, keep us in the hell of subjection, from whence I cannot perceive any redemption or getting out; we may complain and bewail our condition, yet that will not free us; we may murmur and rail against men, yet they regard not what we say. In short, our words to men are as empty sounds; our sighs, as puffs of winds; and our tears, as fruitless showers; and our power is so inconsiderable, that men laugh at our weakness.

III

Ladies, gentlewomen, and other inferior women: The former orations were exclamations against men, repining[2] at their condition and mourning for our own; but we have no reason to speak against men, who are our admirers and lovers; they are our protectors, defenders, and maintainers; they admire our beauties, and love our persons; they protect us from injuries, defend us from dangers, are industrious for our subsistence, and provide for our children; they swim great voyages by sea, travel long journeys by land, to get us rarities and curiosities; they dig to the center of the earth for gold for us; they dive to the bottom of the sea for jewels for us: they build to the skies houses for us: they hunt, fowl, fish, plant, and reap for food for us. All which, we could not do ourselves; and yet we complain of men, as if they were our enemies, whenas[3] we could not possibly live without them, which shows we are as ungrateful as inconstant.

1. **fain:** gladly.
2. **repining:** complaining.
3. **whenas:** when in fact.

WORDS TO KNOW

unconscionable (ŭn-kŏn′shə-nə-bəl) *adj.* showing no conscience; shockingly unreasonable or unjust
eloquently (ĕl′ə-kwənt-lē) *adv.* with powerful and persuasive words
subsistence (səb-sĭs′təns) *n.* the obtaining of the necessities of life; livelihood

495

Customizing Instruction

Less Proficient Readers

Ask students to draw a thermometer with a range of cold, cool, warm, hot, and scalding—representing the emotional force of each of the seven speakers. Then, ask them to place speakers 1 through 7 on this scale. Remind students that emotional tone is different from point of view; speakers may be equally excited but on different sides of an argument. Students may want to work in teams or small groups on this assignment.

Students Acquiring English

Remind students that a semicolon signals the end of a complete thought. Have them mentally replace each semicolon with a period as they read "Female Orations."

Use **Spanish Study Guide** for additional support, pp. 103–105

Gifted and Talented

Have students compare the forms of address of each of the speakers. Remind them that Cavendish is a member of the aristocracy serving the queen. What might each speaker mean by the phrase "inferior women"? How is this phrase adapted by each speaker to show her point of view?

BLOCK SCHEDULING: MANAGING TIME

If your schedule requires that you cover the lesson objectives in a shorter time, use . . .

- Preparing to Read, p. 493
- Thinking Through the Literature, p. 500
- Vocabulary in Action, p. 501

If you want to take advantage of longer class time, use . . .

- TE Teaching Options: Preteaching Vocabulary, p. 494; Grammar, p. 496; Informal Assessment, p. 497; Viewing and Representing, p. 498; Cross Curricular Link, p. 499

Reading and Analyzing

Literary Analysis ARGUMENTATION

Speakers IV and VI both arrive at the conclusion that it is good for women to become more masculine. Ask students to compare and contrast the reasoning by which they arrive at this conclusion.

Possible Response: Speaker IV reasons that women should become more masculine to prove to men and to themselves that they are not weak and foolish. She argues that improving the mind and body will make women more powerful. Speaker VI argues that women should become more masculine because men are superior, and it is only natural and right to strive for improvement.

Active Reading

ANALYZING THE STRUCTURE OF ARGUMENTS

Ask students to characterize the structure of Speaker V's argument as either problem–and–solution or comparison–contrast and support their answer with evidence from the text.

Possible Response: Speaker V's speech has a comparison–contrast structure. She says that if women become more masculine, they will be unnatural and corrupt; but if women strive to perfect the female virtues, which she lists, then they will be praised by men and blessed by Heaven.

But we have more reason to murmur against Nature, than against men, who hath made men more ingenious, witty,[4] and wise than women; more strong, industrious, and laborious than women; for women are witless and strengthless, and unprofitable creatures, did they not bear children. Wherefore, let us love men, praise men, and pray for men; for without men, we should be the most miserable creatures that Nature hath made or could make.

IV

Noble ladies, gentlewomen, and other inferior women: The former oratoress says we are witless and strengthless; if so, it is that we neglect the one and make no use of the other, for strength is increased by exercise, and wit is lost for want of conversation. But to show men we are not so weak and foolish as the former oratoress doth express us to be, let us hawk, hunt, race, and do the like exercises that men have; and let us converse in camps,[5] courts, and cities; in schools, colleges, and courts of judicature; in taverns, brothels, and gaming houses; all of which will make our strength and wit known, both to men and to our own selves, for we are as ignorant of ourselves as men are of us. And how should we know ourselves, when we never made a trial of ourselves? Or how should men know us, when they never put us to the proof? Wherefore my advice is, we should imitate men; so will our bodies and minds appear more masculine, and our power will increase by our actions.

V

Noble, honorable, and virtuous women: The former oration was to persuade us to change the custom of our sex, which is a strange and unwise persuasion, since we cannot change the nature of our sex, nor make ourselves men; and to have female bodies, and yet to act masculine parts, will be very preposterous and unnatural. In truth, we shall make ourselves like the defects of Nature, and be hermaphroditical,[6] neither perfect women, nor perfect men, but corrupt and imperfect creatures. Wherefore let me persuade you, since we cannot alter the nature of our persons, not to alter the course of our lives; but to rule so our lives and behaviors that we be acceptable and pleasing to God and men; which is, to be modest, chaste, temperate, humble, patient, and pious; also, be housewifely, cleanly, and of few words. All which will gain us praise from men and blessing from Heaven; love in this world and glory in the next.

VI

Worthy women: The former oratoress's oration endeavored to persuade us that it would not only be a reproach and disgrace, but unnatural, for women in their actions and behavior to imitate men: we may as well say it will be a reproach, disgrace, and unnatural to imitate the gods, which imitation we are commanded both by the gods and their ministers; and shall we neglect the imitation of men, which is more easy and natural than the imitation of the gods? For how can terrestrial[7] creatures imitate celestial deities?[8] Yet one terrestrial may imitate another, although in different sorts of creatures. Wherefore, since all terrestrial imitations ought to ascend to the

4. **witty:** intelligent.
5. **camps:** military encampments.
6. **hermaphroditical** (hər-măf′rə-dĭt′ĭ-kəl): having both male and female characteristics in one body.
7. **terrestrial:** earthly.
8. **celestial deities:** heavenly gods.

Teaching Options

Mini Lesson Grammar

PREPOSITIONAL PHRASES USED AS ADVERBS

Instruction An adverb modifies a verb, an adjective, or another adverb by indicating *where, when, why, how,* or *to what extent.* An adverb phrase is a prepositional phrase that functions as an adverb. It includes the preposition, its object, and any modifiers of the object in the phrase.

Activity Write the following on the chalkboard.

> ". . . they protect us from injuries, defend us from dangers, are industrious for our subsistence, and provide for our children; they swim great voyages by sea, travel long journeys by land, to get us rarities and curiosities; . . . ."

Underline the adverb phrase as shown. Point out that this adverb phrase tells how they are protected. Ask students to underline other adverb phrases in the passage and to determine which word each phrase modifies and how it modifies the word. *(from dangers, defend; for our subsistence, industrious; for our children, provide; by sea, swim; by land, travel)*

Use **Grammar Transparencies and Copymasters,** p. 26.

Use McDougal Littell's ***Language Network*** for more instruction and practice in prepositional phrases used as adverbs.

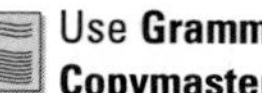

better and not to descend to the worse, women ought to imitate men, as being a degree in nature more perfect than they themselves; and all masculine women ought to be as much praised as effeminate men to be dispraised; for the one advances to perfection, the other sinks to imperfection; that so, by our industry, we may come, at last, to equal men, both in perfection and power.

1 VII

Noble ladies, honorable gentlewomen, and worthy female-commoners: The former oratoress's speech was to persuade us out of ourselves and to be that which Nature never intended us to be, to wit, masculine. But why should we desire to be masculine, since our own sex and condition is far the better? For if men have more courage, they have more danger; and if men have more strength, they have more labor than women have; if men are more eloquent in speech, women are more harmonious in voice; if men be more active, women are more graceful; if men have more liberty, women have more safety; for we never fight duels nor battles; nor do we go long travels or dangerous voyages; we labor not in building nor digging in mines, quarries, or pits, for metal, stone, or coals; neither do we waste or shorten our lives with university or scholastical studies, questions, and disputes; we burn not our faces with smiths' forges or chemists'[9] furnaces; and hundreds of other actions which men are employed in; for they would not only fade the fresh beauty, spoil the lovely features, and decay the youth of women, causing them to appear old, when they are young; but would break their small limbs, and destroy their tender lives. Wherefore women have no reason to complain against Nature or the god of Nature, for although the gifts are not the same as they have given to men, yet those gifts they have given to women are much better; for we women are much more favored by Nature than men, in giving us such beauties, features, shapes, graceful demeanor, and such insinuating and enticing attractives, that men are forced to admire us, love us, and be desirous of us; insomuch that rather than not have and enjoy us, they will deliver to our disposals their power, persons, and lives, enslaving themselves to our will and pleasures; also, we are their saints, whom they adore and worship; and what can we desire more than to be men's tyrants, destinies, and goddesses? ❖ 2

9. **chemists'**: alchemists'.

WORDS TO KNOW

demeanor (dĭ-mē′nər) *n.* a way of behaving; manner
enticing (ĕn-tī′sĭng) *adj.* tempting **entice** *v.*

Customizing Instruction

Less Proficient Readers

1 Speaker VII argues that women have received gifts that are superior to men's. What are they?

Answer: Women are harmonious in voice, graceful, and beautiful.

Students Acquiring English

Help students understand the unfamiliar terms and occupations mentioned by Speaker VII. Duels were fought one-on-one, usually over a point of honor; quarries are open pits from which stone is dug; smiths' forges are the hearths or ovens in which metal is heated in order to be worked; chemists' furnaces are used to heat medicines or chemicals.

Gifted and Talented Students

2 Have students work in small groups to explain what Speaker VII means by "tyrants, destinies, and goddesses."

Possible Response: By *tyrants* she means that women rule the men; by *destinies* she means that it is men's fate to have women to serve; by *goddesses* she means that women are better endowed with virtues than men. Then have students consider whether these roles are desirable or even realized today.

Multiple Learning Styles

Visual or Kinesthetic Learners

Have students choose *tyrant, destiny,* or *goddess* and create a collage representing that role using images from advertising.

Assessment Informal Assessment

SUPPORTING AN ARGUMENT After students have read all the orations, have them answer the following question.

Which speaker best represents Cavendish's point of view? Support your answer with evidence from the selection.

RUBRIC

3 **Full Accomplishment** Student makes clear argument supported by evidence from selection. Student may take into account Cavendish's social standing, clues in salutations, and tone of each speaker.

2 **Substantial Accomplishment** Student makes clear argument supported by some evidence from selection.

1 **Little or Partial Accomplishment** Student makes vague argument or does not support argument with evidence from selection.

Reading and Analyzing

Reading Skills and Strategies:
ANALYZING POETIC STRUCTURE

Ask students how the subject of each stanza changes and how the punctuation between the stanzas provides clues to the relationship of each to the others.

Possible Response: Stanza 1 introduces the relative culpability of Adam and Eve; stanza 2 describes Adam; the comma between the two shows that stanza 2 is a continuation of stanza 1. Stanza 3 takes up the case of Eve, again in relation to Adam (the semicolon unites them). The end punctuation after stanza 3 announces that stanza 4 will make its own, independent statement.

Literary Analysis ARGUMENTATION

Have students consider what would make this poem persuasive to Lanier's audience. Would the poem or Cavendish's "Orations" be more persuasive?

Possible Response: Women would find the poem persuasive because it removes blame from their sex for humankind's expulsion from Eden. Men might find the poem persuasive because the argument is logical and inoffensive; although the poem places blame on Adam, it does not vilify men in general. More men and women would find the poem persuasive than "Female Orations" because the argument is less extreme. It does not propose that either women or men change their roles or their habits.

from Eve's Apology in Defense of Women

Amelia Lanier

Adam Tempted by Eve (1517), Hans Holbein the Younger. Öffentliche Kunstsammlung Basel, Switzerland (313).

In the biblical Book of Genesis, Eve is tempted by a serpent to eat the fruit of the forbidden tree of knowledge, and she, in turn, offers it to Adam. As a result of their disobedience, God expels them from the Garden of Eden, taking away the gift of human immortality. These stanzas are from Amelia Lanier's defense of Eve, in which the poet (1570?–1640?) adopts a position that was quite radical in its time.

Teaching Options

Mini Lesson: Viewing and Representing

Adam Tempted by Eve
by Hans Holbein the Younger

ART APPRECIATION

Instruction Holbein (1497?–1543) was born in Germany but spent most of his career in England. This painting of Adam and Eve was done when Holbein was 20, before he traveled to England.

Application Ask students to analyze the painting as they answer the following questions.

- What details in the painting help bring the story of Adam and Eve to life?

Possible Response: Eve has already taken a bite out of the apple and seems to be offering it to Adam. The tilt of his head and the direction of his gaze indicate that he is considering whether he should eat the apple or not.

- What does Adam's expression reveal about his thoughts and feelings toward Eve?

Possible Response: Adam is looking not at Eve but upward, as if at God. His forehead appears furrowed, as if he is concentrating or worried. Adam seems torn between the temptation of the apple and the fear of God.

But surely Adam cannot be excused;
Her fault though great, yet he was most to blame.
What weakness offered, strength might have refused;
Being lord of all, the greater was his shame;
Although the serpent's craft had her abused,
God's holy word ought all his actions frame;
1 For he was lord and king of all the earth,
Before poor Eve had either life or breath,

Who being framed by God's eternal hand
The perfectest man that ever breathed on earth,
And from God's mouth received that strait command,
The breach whereof he knew was present death;
Yea, having power to rule both sea and land,
Yet with one apple won to lose that breath
Which God had breathèd in his beauteous face,
Bringing us all in danger and disgrace;

And then to lay the fault on patience's back,
That we (poor women) must endure it all;
We know right well he did discretion lack,
Being not persuaded thereunto at all.
If Eve did err, it was for knowledge sake;
The fruit being fair persuaded him to fall.
No subtle serpent's falsehood did betray him;
If he would eat it, who had power to stay him?

Not Eve, whose fault was only too much love,
Which made her give this present to her dear,
That what she tasted he likewise might prove,
Whereby his knowledge might become more clear;
He never sought her weakness to reprove
With those sharp words which he of God did hear;
Yet men will boast of knowledge, which he took
From Eve's fair hand, as from a learned book.

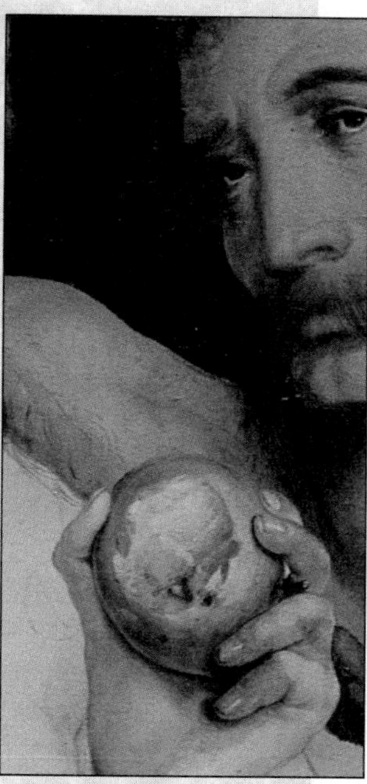

Customizing Options

Less Proficient Readers

1 What powers does the poet attribute to Adam?
Answer: lord and king of all the earth.
Which lines of Stanza 1 describe him?
Answer: lines 4 and 7.
Ask students to search Stanza 2 for additional information.

Students Acquiring English

Some words are used in unfamiliar ways: *frame* appears in both lines 6 and 9, but with the meaning "create"; *strait* in line 11, meaning "direct"; and *breach* in line 12, meaning "break."

Gifted and Talented Students

Have students rephrase Lanier's argument in a paragraph. Then, have them discuss, in writing, how the poem might be received today.

Cross Curricular Link Sociology

WOMEN'S LIVES IN THE 17TH CENTURY
Scholars have come to think that the deadly plague of the 16th century contributed to the rise of the middle class in Europe because, for the first time, food was in abundance. By examining portraits of 17th century women, we begin to see an abundance of detail in the clothing of upper-class women that goes far beyond any utilitarian purpose. Fabrics such as velvet come into vogue, and dresses are adorned with lavish embroidery and insets of lace. These are not the clothes of women who must work in the mud and dust. At the same time, a woman's place was to bear children, and we read of men taking first, second, and even third wives to replace those who had died in childbirth. Throughout most of Europe, women received no schooling and could not own property in their own names: The death of a husband without a male heir could mean that, in England at least, the widow had to find another home or beg for food and clothing.

Connect to the Literature

1. **What Do You Think?** Which of the seven speakers makes the most sense to you?

Comprehension Check
- What is the third speaker's attitude toward men?
- Does the seventh speaker regard women as inferior or superior to men?

Think Critically

2. How does the third speaker's **argument** compare with those of the two preceding speakers?

3. What seems to have been the role of women in the society of the time?

THINK ABOUT
- public life
- family life
- household management
- political and military affairs

4. Why do you think Cavendish presented a variety of viewpoints?

5. **ACTIVE READING** **ANALYZING THE STRUCTURE OF ARGUMENTS** Look back at the notes you took in your READER'S NOTEBOOK. What examples of comparison-contrast and problem-solution structures did you find?

Extend Interpretations

6. **Comparing Texts** Consider the view of the relationship between men and women expressed in the excerpt from "Eve's Apology in Defense of Women." How is it similar to or different from the view of one or more of the speakers in "Female Orations"?

7. **Different Perspectives** How might a male speaker have responded to the speeches in "Female Orations"?

8. **Connect to Life** Do you think Cavendish believed in equality of the sexes as we understand it today? Support your opinion.

Literary Analysis

ARGUMENTATION

Argumentation is speech or writing intended to convince an audience that a proposal should be adopted or rejected. Most arguments begin with a statement of an idea or opinion, which is then supported with logical evidence. Another technique of argumentation is the anticipation and rebuttal of opposing views. In "Female Orations," Cavendish presents a number of different arguments through the mouths of the seven speakers.

Cooperative Learning Activity With six classmates, read aloud to the rest of the class the seven speeches that make up this imaginary debate. Try to make your reading sound like a real debate, with each speaker directing her response to the preceding speaker.

ACTIVE READING **WRITER'S MOTIVATION AND TEXT STRUCTURE**

A writer's motivation can affect the form, or structure, he or she uses to express ideas. Cavendish examines ideas and arguments about the roles and rights of women in the form of a debate between seven speakers, who voice a variety of opinions. Think about Cavendish's possible motivation for writing about the position of women. Think also about the society in which she lived. Why do you think she cast the orations as debates?

GUIDING STUDENT RESPONSE

Connect to the Literature

1. **What Do You Think?**
Guidelines for student response: The answer will depend on the student's values and experience.

Comprehension Check
- The third speaker thinks that men work hard to make women happy.
- superior

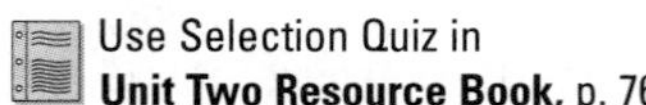

Use Selection Quiz in **Unit Two Resource Book,** p. 76.

Think Critically

2. The first speaker argues that although men have all the advantages, they treat women cruelly. The second speaker adds that men fail to listen to women. The third speaker argues from a different premise: that men do care for women and work hard to please them.
3. Women seem to have been asked to be responsible for family and household, but they had little to do with public life, nothing to do with the military, and only indirect influence on political life.
4. Student answers will vary but should be supported by details from the selection.
5. Accept any responses that demonstrate thoughtful consideration of the topic. The arguments of speakers I, III, V, and VII have the most obvious comparison–contrast structure. The argument of speaker IV has the most obvious problem–solution structure.

Literary Analysis

Cooperative Learning Activity The audience might ask the seven speakers questions after the reading.

Active Reading Possibly to show there are many sides to an issue.

Extend Interpretations

Comparing Texts Possible Response: Most of the speakers in "Female Orations" are addressing the topic of how women are inherently different from men and what might be done about it. Only one, Speaker II, talks about "the labyrinth men have put us into." In this way she resembles Lanier, who addresses the world's view of women as having brought on the fall from grace.

Different Perspectives Answers will vary. Students should demonstrate an understanding of the arguments in "Female Orations."

Connect to Life To write about this question, students will need to consider which of the voices seems to come closest to Cavendish's own or whether hers is a composite of two or more.

Writing Options

Argument Outline Imagine that you are an eighth speaker in this debate. Write an outline of the main points of your response to the seven speakers who have preceded you. What additional points, not touched on by them, might you wish to address?

Activities & Explorations

Mural Design Sketch a design for a wall mural showing the roles of women in society today. ~ **ART**

Inquiry & Research

Women in the 17th Century Do some research to find out about famous women of the 17th century. What did they do to achieve fame? Choose a woman who interests you and write a two- or three-paragraph summary of her life and achievements.

Vocabulary in Action

EXERCISE: CONTEXT CLUES Read each sentence below. On your paper, indicate whether the boldfaced word is used correctly or incorrectly.

1. One of the speakers in Cavendish's imaginary debate says that the preceding speaker spoke **eloquently** and intelligently.
2. Another of the speakers admires men for their kind and **unconscionable** behavior.
3. There must have been a large **subsistence** of women who were dissatisfied with their lives.
4. Cavendish pitied women whose sole purpose in life was to appear **enticing** to men.
5. In the 17th century, men were sometimes willing to listen to a woman's **demeanor.**

WORDS TO KNOW	demeanor	subsistence
	eloquently	unconscionable
	enticing	

Building Vocabulary
For an in-depth study of context clues, see page 938.

Margaret Cavendish
1623?–1674

Early Years Born Margaret Lucas, Margaret Cavendish was two years old when her father died. Her mother, who assumed control of the family's extensive estate, was regarded as a shrewd and ambitious businessperson and, as a result, was not well liked by her neighbors. The Lucas family further alienated their neighbors by allying themselves with the monarchy during the conflicts between the king and Parliament. Margaret became an attendant to the queen, whom she accompanied to Paris in 1645. There she met and married William Cavendish, the duke of Newcastle.

Civil War and Exile As an English nobleman and supporter of the monarchy, the duke had voluntarily fled to France during England's civil war. As the new duchess of Newcastle, Margaret Cavendish was forced to live in exile as well, and in poverty, until the monarchy was restored. It was during her exile that the childless Cavendish began writing with the intent of publishing her work.

After the Restoration After the restoration of the monarchy, Cavendish and her husband returned to England, where she began to pursue a literary career in earnest. Cavendish wrote about science, mathematics, and philosophy—subjects considered beyond the capacities of women in the 17th century—and produced numerous works of poetry, prose, and drama. Her bold writings and strange manner earned her the nickname Mad Madge of Newcastle. Her husband, however, supported her throughout and at her death wrote that "This Dutches was a wise, wittie and learned Lady, which her many Bookes do well testifie."

CHOICES & CHALLENGES

Writing Options

Argument Outline Students may wish to defend men, or they may approach the topic from the standpoint of a single woman. Students may also wish to write from the point of view of a man.

Activities & Explorations

Mural Design An instructive mural might be made of photos from advertisements. Students might ask themselves, "Do these photographs depict real women today or a fantasy that women struggle to live up to? Who creates the media? How do the media preach to women today about their lifestyles and physical appearance?"

Vocabulary in Action

1. correctly
2. incorrectly
3. incorrectly
4. correctly
5. incorrectly

Inquiry & Research

Women in the 17th Century After the reign of Elizabeth I, who died in 1603, 17th-century England produced no more female monarchs, although the queen's influence continued to be felt. Among authors, Aphra Behn (1640–1689) emerged as a playwright. She is commended by Virginia Woolf as the first woman to earn her living as an author. Emilia Lanier (1570?–1640?), writer of religious poems, belonged to an Italian family living in London. Because of the attention given to women's studies, research is now available on these writers, as well as on Margaret Cavendish, who was known to Samuel Pepys and was dismissed by him as "mad, conceited, and ridiculous."

MILESTONES IN BRITISH LITERATURE

John Bunyan's *The Pilgrim's Progress from This World to That Which is to Come* is a two-part religious story that was once second only to the Bible in popularity. Bunyan presents the first part as a dream in which the main character, Christian, journeys to salvation—from the City of Destruction. It's a metaphor comparing life to a journey. *Pilgrim's Progress* contains characteristics of the 18th-century novel with its humor and realistic portrayal of such characters as Mr. Worldly Wiseman, Faithful, Hopeful, Pliant, and Obstinate. In the second part (1684), Bunyan tells the story of Christian's wife and sons as they try to join him.

Additional Background

JOHN BUNYAN

In his day the writing of John Bunyan (1628–1688) was found in every English home, and he was known by every ordinary reader. Raised in the English Midlands, he went to fight in the English Civil War in 1644 in Oliver Cromwell's army, and this brought him into contact with some left-wing religious groups. This exposed him to a variety of religious ideas and probably helped cause his eventual conversion to Puritanism. The Restoration of Charles II ended 20 years of relative religious freedom, and in 1660 Bunyan was jailed for 12 years for holding a service that did not conform to the Church of England. Bunyan's greatness was recognized by such literary giants as Jonathan Swift and Samuel Johnson, but nothing marks his work more than its ability to evoke responses from a wide range of readers.

John Bunyan

The Pilgrim's Progress

"This Book will make a Traveller of thee." So claims John Bunyan in the Author's Apology to *The Pilgrim's Progress* (1678). The author's promise is all the more striking because he wrote much of this prose masterpiece while in prison. However, the "travel" Bunyan had in mind was not literal: it was a spiritual journey that reflected the author's own religious experiences and beliefs.

These beliefs were formed during a turbulent period in English history—the time of the English civil war and of Oliver Cromwell's Puritan-dominated government, which ruled after the defeat of the monarchy in 1649. During this time, Bunyan, a traveling mender of pots and pans who had little formal education, plunged into a lengthy spiritual crisis. He emerged a devout Christian and lay preacher. When the monarchy was restored in 1660 and Charles II sought to suppress religious dissent, Bunyan was imprisoned for "preaching without a license." He was jailed twice, for a total of nearly 12 years. While in prison, Bunyan worked on his allegorical "travel guide." *The Pilgrim's Progress* dramatizes the process of religious salvation by tracing the progress of a wayfarer named Christian on his journey through a fallen world. Christian's pilgrimage begins when he leaves the City of Destruction without his wife and relatives, all of whom ridicule his visions of a coming apocalypse. He is urged on by Evangelist, a godly man who directs him to keep his eyes on "yonder shining light."

This wood engraving from a 19th-century edition of The Pilgrim's Progress *shows Christian setting out from the City of Destruction.*

Christian encounters a series of characters who embody outlooks that are obstacles to salvation. Mr. Worldly Wiseman, for example, gives Christian short-sighted advice to quit his "desperate venture" and move into the village of Morality, which offers the safety and friendship of such men as Legality and Civility.

The allegorical nature of Christian's struggles is clear. At one point he and a companion named Hopeful fall asleep on the grounds of Doubting Castle. They are discovered by Giant Despair and locked in the dungeon. Christian is almost driven to suicide, but eventually he opens the door with a key called Promise. Such symbolism can be traced back to the morality plays of the Middle Ages.

Bunyan's rendering of characters and events, however, is so natural and lifelike that his tale "thrilled many generations of children who did not recognize the allegory," according to the 20th-century English critic W. W. Robson. Bunyan's descriptive details about everyday life and his ear for dialogue reflect the rural England of his time, and the beauty of his language and imagery often transcends his allegorical purpose.

The direct, vivid style and the sense of spiritual urgency in *The Pilgrim's Progress* contributed to its instant success with all social classes. It was so popular, in fact, that six years later Bunyan wrote and published a second part, which portrays the journey to salvation of Christian's wife and children.

In all, Bunyan wrote nearly 60 works, mostly doctrinal tracts. He remains best known for *The Pilgrim's Progress,* which was one of the most widely read works in the English language for over two centuries.

Above:
William Blake's portrayal of the encounter between Christian and Mr. Worldly Wiseman. Illustrations to John Bunyan's "The Pilgrim's Progress" *(1824–7) by William Blake. The Frick Collection, New York*

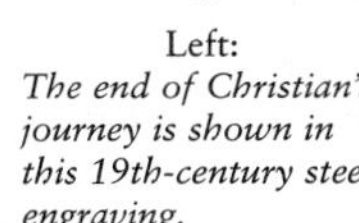

Left:
The end of Christian's journey is shown in this 19th-century steel engraving.

LITERARY CHRONOLOGY

The following are the publication dates of some of Bunyan's most important works:

1656 *Some Gospel Truths Opened*

1657 *A Vindication of Some Gospel Truths Opened*

1666 *Grace Abounding to the Chief of Sinners*

1671 *A Confession of My Faith*

1678 *Pilgrim's Progress from This World to the World Which Is to Come*

1680 *The Life and Death of Mr. Badman*

1684 *Pilgrim's Progress (second part)*

1686 *A Book for Boys and Girls*

MILESTONES IN BRITISH LITERATURE 503

Objectives

- reflect on and assess the understanding of the unit
- compare text events with the readers' own experiences
- provide examples of themes that cross texts
- compare across texts elements of texts, such as themes, conflicts, and other issues
- assess and build portfolios

Reflecting on the Unit

Option 1

A successful response will
- select works which the student finds most relevant to today.
- include an explanation of how the particular work relates to the students. The selections describing infatuation, unrequited love, lost love, bereavement, and bonds between parent and child will probably be most appealing.
- demonstrate how the selections' subjects and themes are relevant to modern life.

Option 2

A successful response will
- identify the main issues—topics, events, enthusiasms, fears, and convictions—with which English Renaissance writers were concerned.
- list generalizations and select a line and an image from a selection that symbolizes it.
- have the groups combine their quotations and images.
- create a class collage that conveys the spirit of the English Renaissance.

Option 3

A successful response will
- select two favorite writers in this unit other than Donne.
- examine what the writer's reaction to the quotation might be.
- create a diary entry for each writer.
- include your thoughts about what the quotation means to you.

The English Renaissance

From reading this unit, what have you learned about the interests and problems of people who lived during the English Renaissance? What connections have you discovered between life then and your life now? Explore these questions by completing one or more options in each of the following sections.

Reflecting on the Unit

OPTION 1

Drafting an Essay Many of the works in this unit deal with various aspects of the theme of love. Which of these works did you find the most meaningful for life today? Explore this question in a brief essay, drawing connections between the works and experiences you have had, heard about, or witnessed.

OPTION 2

Focusing on Important Issues After reading the selections in this unit, you should be able to identify some of the main issues with which English Renaissance writers were concerned. Develop a list of generalizations about concerns that can be inferred from the selections. To illustrate each generalization, quote a sentence or a line of poetry from the unit. Then, working with your classmates, combine the quotations with appropriate images to create a collage that conveys the spirit of the English Renaissance.

OPTION 3

Interpreting a Quotation Recall the quotation from John Donne at the beginning of this unit: "No man is an island, entire of itself; every man is a piece of the continent, a part of the main." Choose your two favorite writers in this unit (other than Donne himself). Create a diary entry for each of them in which you explore what the writer's reaction to the quotation might be. Then jot down your thoughts about what the quotation means to you.

Self ASSESSMENT

To explore how your understanding of the English Renaissance has developed over the course of the unit, jot down words and phrases that come to mind when you think of this historical period. Then circle at least three words and phrases that you think describe the English Renaissance most accurately. Get together with a partner and compare what the two of you have noted. Feel free to make changes in your own list on the basis of your partner's ideas.

Reviewing Literary Concepts

OPTION 1

Identifying Figurative Language Most of the poetry you have read in this unit contains figurative language, including metaphor, simile, personification, and hyperbole. In a chart like the one shown, name at least two poems in each part of the unit that contain figurative language. Quote an example of figurative language from each poem, and note what type of figurative language it is. When you have completed the chart, identify the example of figurative language you find the most interesting or appealing, as well as your reasons for finding it so.

Poems	Example of Figurative Language	Type of Figurative Language
"My Lute, Awake!"	"Perform the last / Labor that thou and I shall waste" (ll. 1–2)	Personification

OPTION 2

Shakespearean Drama Review the definitions of *soliloquy, aside, dramatic irony,* and *foreshadowing* on pages 323–325. Then look back through *Macbeth* and find one or two examples of each of these literary techniques. Get together with a partner and compare the examples you chose.

Self ASSESSMENT

Copy the following list of literary terms introduced in this unit. Rank the terms to show your understanding of their meanings, from 1 (the term that you feel you understand most fully) to 17 (the term you understand the least). Your ranking should help you decide which concepts you need to review.

rhyme scheme
pastoral
sonnet
Spenserian sonnet
Shakespearean sonnet
figurative language
Italian sonnet
repetition
essay
extended metaphor
epitaph
hyperbole
theme
metaphor
allusion
diction
argumentation

Building Your Portfolio

- **Writing Options** Several of the Writing Options in this unit asked you to analyze attitudes and ideas presented in the selections. Choose two pieces of writing that you think represent your best attempts at analyzing the literature in this unit. Write a cover note supporting your choices, then add the note and the two pieces to your **Working Portfolio.**
- **Writing Workshop** Earlier in this unit, you worked on a Research Report that had you investigate a topic that intrigued you. Look over your report and evaluate your work on the basis of the following:

  Did your writing stay focused on your thesis statement?

  Was your information organized?

  Were your conclusions supported by thorough research?

  Write the answers to these questions on a note that you attach to your report. Then place the report in your **Working Portfolio.**
- **Additional Activities** Reflect on the various assignments you completed under **Activities & Explorations** and **Inquiry & Research.** Which activities proved to be the most rewarding? Write a note that explains your choice, and add it to your **Working Portfolio.**

Self ASSESSMENT

Now that you have a handful of writing pieces in your portfolio, look them over and decide which are examples of your strongest work. Are there any pieces that you consider weak and may wish to replace as the year goes on?

Setting GOALS

As you worked through the reading and writing activities in this unit, you probably became more aware of your interests and abilities. Are there any skills on which you feel you still need improvement? Are there any particular writers or genres that you would like to investigate further? Create a list of these skills and interests.

Reviewing Literary Concepts

Option 1

Use the Unit 2 Resource Book p. 77 to provide students a ready-made, full-depth chart for recording examples of figurative language in all the poems.

Option 2

After students have reviewed the definitions of soliloquy, aside, dramatic irony, and foreshadowing, conduct a class discussion in which students are asked to provide examples of the terms from their own lives.

Building Your Portfolio

Students will use their Presentation Portfolios to file what they consider their highest quality work—the very best projects and activities from their Working Portfolios.

For more information on using writing and assessing portfolios, see the *Teacher's Guide to Assessment and Portfolio,* p. 53.

The *Electronic Library* is a CD-ROM that contains additional fiction, nonfiction, poetry, and drama for each unit in *The Language of Literature.*

These are the additional selections found in Unit 2 of the *Electronic Library:*

Sir Philip Sidney
My True Love Hath My Heart

George Herbert
Virtue
Easter-Wings

Sir John Suckling
The Constant Lover
Song

William Shakespeare
Sonnet 30
Sonnet 73
Sonnet 77

John Milton
L'Allegro
Il Penseroso

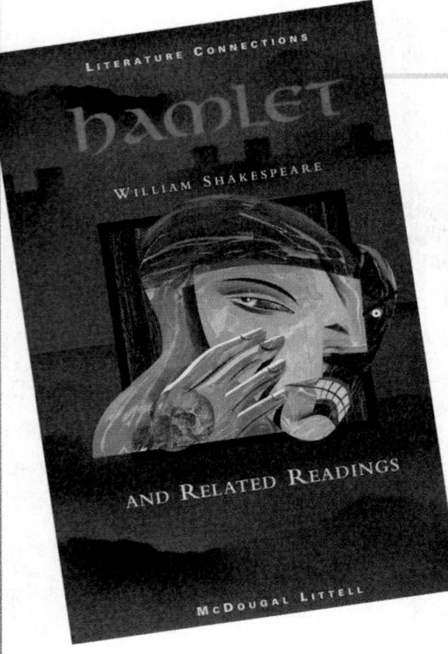

LITERATURE CONNECTIONS

Hamlet

WILLIAM SHAKESPEARE

Hamlet, Shakespeare's best-known and most frequently performed play, is a tragedy of revenge, betrayal, and inner conflict. Like *Macbeth,* the play involves the murder of a king and the seizing of the crown by an unlawful usurper. Hamlet seeks revenge against his father's murderer in a story involving sword fights, poison, and duels.

These thematically related readings are provided along with *Hamlet:*

***from* Introduction to Hamlet**
BY DAVID BEVINGTON

Father and Son
BY STANLEY KUNITZ

Ophelia
BY ARTHUR RIMBAUD

The Management of Grief
BY BHARATI MUKHERJEE

Tell Them Not to Kill Me!
BY JUAN RULFO

Hamlet
BY YEVGENY VINOKUROV

Japanese Hamlet
BY TOSHIO MORI

And Even *More* . . .

Mary Queen of Scots

ANTONIA FRASER

This heartwarming biography of a queen caught in the political and religious turmoil of Elizabethan England provides not only a vivid picture of the context of Mary's life but a clear portrait of her as a person. Mary was next in line to succeed to the throne of England, held at the time by her cousin, Elizabeth I. Elizabeth suspected Mary of treason and a fatal struggle ensued.

Books

The Succession: A Novel of Elizabeth and James
GEORGE GARRETT
A fictionalized account of political events in England at the time that Shakespeare was writing his plays.

Shakespeare: His Life, Work, and Era
DENNIS KAY
Excellent account of Shakespeare's life, with extensive background.

Light Thickens
NGAIO MARSH
Detective story involving a production of *Macbeth* that is truly cursed.

LITERATURE CONNECTIONS

A Midsummer Night's Dream

WILLIAM SHAKESPEARE

The line between illusion and reality blurs in this fun-filled comedy featuring the escapades of mischievous fairies and spellbound young lovers in an enchanted forest. After a wild night of love potions, magical transformations, and confusion, harmony is restored, love is set right, and weddings are celebrated.

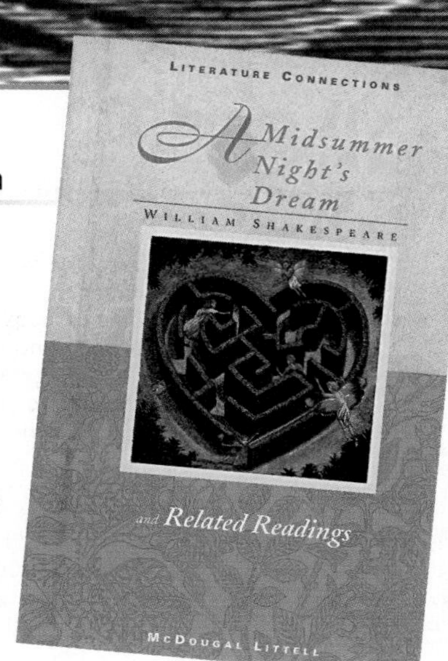

These thematically related readings are provided along with *A Midsummer Night's Dream:*

A Midsummer Night's Dream
BY NORRIE EPSTEIN

The Song of Wandering Aengus
BY WILLIAM BUTLER YEATS

The Sweet Miracle / El Dulce Milagro
BY JUANA DE IBARBOUROU

April Witch
BY RAY BRADBURY

Come. And Be My Baby
BY MAYA ANGELOU

Love's Initiations
BY THOMAS MOORE

The Sensible Thing
BY F. SCOTT FITZGERALD

***from* Love and Marriage**
BY BILL COSBY

A Preface to Milton
LOIS POTTER
The author examines Milton's life and work to show his commitment to intellectual freedom and love of learning.

Witches & Jesuits: Shakespeare's *Macbeth*
GARY WILLS
A discussion of the theological and political crises that formed the backdrop for *Macbeth,* in particular the Gunpowder Plot of 1605.

Other Media

English Literature on Video: Shakespeare and the Globe
An educational program that retraces Shakespeare's life and work. Films for the Humanities.
(VIDEOCASSETTE)

Macbeth
This version stars Orson Welles, Jeanette Nolan, and Roddy McDowall. Directed by Orson Welles. NTA Home Entertainment.
(VIDEOCASSETTE)

Metaphysical and Devotional Poetry
Films for the Humanities & Sciences.
(VIDEOCASSETTE)

Shakespeare's Sonnets
Films for the Humanities & Sciences.
(VIDEOCASSETTE)

Throne of Blood
Excellent Japanese film adaptation with a Samurai setting. Directed by Akira Kurosawa. Rental: Films, Inc. Lease: Macmillan Films.
(VIDEOCASSETTE)

Reading&Writing
for Assessment

OVERVIEW

The Reading and Writing for Assessment feature provides practice in taking standardized tests. As students work through this lesson, they will learn strategies for reading comprehension questions, multiple-choice questions, and essay and short-answer questions. Boxed strategies located alongside the text will help guide students through the activities. These strategies model processes students can use as they take standardized tests.

This feature is based on and will help students prepare for state assessments as well as end-of-course assessments. It will also prepare students for the reading comprehension questions used on such college entrance examinations as the Scholastic Aptitude Test (SAT) and the American College Test (ACT).

Objectives

- understand and apply strategies for reading a test selection
- recognize literary techniques in a test selection
- understand and apply strategies for answering multiple-choice questions about a test selection
- respond to a writing prompt and to present ideas in a logical order
- understand and apply strategies for revising and proofreading a test response

Reading&Writing for Assessment

Throughout high school, you will be tested on your ability to read and understand many different kinds of reading selections. These tests will assess your basic understanding of ideas and knowledge of vocabulary. They will also check your ability to analyze and evaluate both the message of the text and the techniques the writer uses in getting that message across.

The following pages will give you test-taking strategies. Practice applying these strategies by working through each of the models provided.

PART 1 How to Read a Test Selection

In many tests, you will read a passage and then answer multiple-choice questions about it. Applying the basic test-taking strategies that follow, taking notes, and highlighting or underscoring passages as you read can help you focus on the information you will need to know.

STRATEGIES FOR READING A TEST SELECTION

- **Before you begin reading, skim the questions that follow the passage.** These can help focus your reading.
- **Use your active reading strategies such as analyzing, predicting, and questioning.** Make notes in the margin or highlight key words and passages to help you focus your reading. You may do this only if the test directions allow you to mark on the test itself.
- **Think about the title.** What does it suggest about the overall message or theme of the selection?
- **Look for main ideas.** These are often stated at the beginnings or ends of paragraphs. Sometimes they are implied, not stated. After reading each paragraph, ask "What was this passage about?"
- **Note the literary elements and techniques used by the writer.** You might consider the writer's introduction, use of quotations, or descriptive language. Then ask yourself what effect the writer achieves with each choice.
- **Unlock word meanings.** Use context clues and word parts to help you unlock the meaning of unfamiliar words.
- **Think about the message or theme.** What larger lesson can you draw from the passage? Can you infer anything or make generalizations about other similar situations, human beings, or life in general?

Reading Selection

Network Helps Children Cope With Serious Illness
by Catherine Greenman

1 When 16-year-old Thricia DrePaul logged onto Starbright World, a computer network for hospitalized children, she usually chose to be a silver pony, her favorite character of the 40 offered. Although she was comfortable trading messages with any of the other children roaming the three-dimensional landscape, the idea of entering the network's video-conferencing and talking face to face with someone was intimidating to her.

2 ❷ But two weeks after her kidney transplant, Thricia decided to give it a shot. She propped herself up in her bed at Mount Sinai Medical Center in New York to look at a computer monitor and exchange a few words with Chris, a 13-year-old asthma patient at Children's Hospital of Pittsburgh. "I don't know what to say," she whispered to Karen Marcinczyk, a therapist in the Child Life program at Mount Sinai who pointed a video camera toward Thricia and handed her a small microphone. "Why don't you say 'Hi,' and ask him what his name is?" she coaxed.

3 Chris, no stranger to Starbright's video-conferencing, stared into his monitor and called out an introduction. He had already met children on line from hospitals in Dallas, Minneapolis, and Seattle. "Hi, I'm Chris," he said. "What are you in the hospital for?" Thricia told him, and he admired a stuffed animal he spotted on her pillow. With slight delays after each giddy sentence, Thricia and Chris continued a conversation that spanned the weather, hospital food, and how long each would be in the hospital. Then Thricia had to say goodbye to have her blood pressure taken. Afterward, she said she was glad she had tried video-conferencing and that she might try to find someone else to talk to the next day.

4 Encounters like this, as well as text- and audio-only chats, occur about 30 times a day within Starbright World, a password-protected service started by the Starbright Foundation. . . . ❸ The goal of the network is to create a community on line for seriously ill children that will educate them and help them cope with the difficulties of hospitalization. . . .

5 Because most hospitals in the program have three to five computer terminals in their children's wards to dedicate to Starbright World, computer time is allotted to the children with the most acute needs. "In some cases, such as when a child is in isolation, we roll the computer into the hospital room on a cart, and it stays there for the entire isolation period," said Merri Fishman, manager of the Child Life program at Mount Sinai. Otherwise, the children go to the hospital schoolroom or playroom to log on.

STRATEGIES IN ACTION

❶ Think about the title.

ONE STUDENT'S THOUGHTS

"If I hadn't read the title I would think this selection was going to be about Thricia DrePaul—but the title suggests it will be about a computer network."

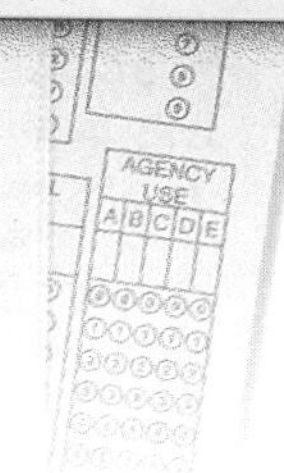

❷ Notice the writer's technique at the beginning.

"By telling me Thricia's story, the writer creates a strong introduction."

YOUR TURN

What other techniques does the writer use to keep you interested?

❸ Look for main ideas.

"This selection is about Starbright World and how it helps seriously ill children."

YOUR TURN

What other key ideas have been introduced so far?

Strategies in Action

1 Begin by previewing the text. Note the title and identify the subject of the reading selection. Read through the questions and prompts at the end of the text. Ask students what they will need to look for as they read.

Possible Response: Students should look for how Starbright World helps children, how the writer uses anecdotes and quotations, and what details the writer uses to show the isolation of the children in the hospital.

2 The introduction is an extended example of the service described in the title. Ask students how the introduction (paragraphs 1–3) gives them information they might need to answer the test questions.

YOUR TURN The writer uses visual details and quotations. The writer also tells the anecdote from Thricia's point of view, including her thoughts and feelings. Point out to students that these details help the reader to empathize with Thricia and other children in similar situations.

3 Students are more likely to be tested on the main ideas in the selection rather than specific details. Ask students which ideas in this paragraph do they think are important enough to be included on a test.

YOUR TURN Being hospitalized for long periods of time is difficult for children. Starbright World provides interaction for hospitalized children across the United States.

4 Students can save time by checking their own understanding as they read. Ask students to make an inference about the selection's theme based on what they have read so far. What larger lesson about life might the writer intend to convey?
Possible Response: To overcome adversity you need support from your peers.

5 Many reading comprehension tests include not only questions about a selection's main ideas but questions about the literary techniques used by the writer. Students can save time if they notice these literary techniques.

YOUR TURN The quotations provide information, make the selection more interesting, and show the sources of information the writer used for the article.

Customizing for Less Proficient Readers

6 Use the following questions to understand what is meant by a "community of peers."

- What does the word *peer* mean?
  Possible Response: Someone who is the same age or is in the same position in life.
- Who are the peers of a child in the hospital?
  Possible Response: Other children or other patients.

7 Most reading comprehension tests assess literal comprehension and students' ability to analyze and interpret the selection.

YOUR TURN Starbright World can provide information about illnesses in databases that children can access. They can also help children connect with children who are not in the hospital but who share similar interests. They can also help children use on-line resources during their stay in the hospital.

6 Though enough personal computers are not always available, the prospect of communicating with someone in Starbright World can help motivate a child to get out of bed and walk down the hall. Ms. Fishman remembered a time last year when two patients on the same hall started chatting with each other over the network. ❹ "Although they were both immobilized and couldn't meet for a long time, they were really able to cheer each other on," she said.

7 Diane Rode, director of the Child Life program at Mount Sinai, agreed that Starbright World gave hospitalized children a sense of connectedness and a forum for self-expression, but she emphasized the importance of giving them a context in which to express themselves. ❺ "Hooking kids up with other kids in similar situations is not a new idea for us," she said. "It's existed in support groups and over the phone for years. After the initial thrill of seeing and talking to someone on a computer screen goes away, it helps if the kids can share a sense of purpose."

8 For this reason, Ms. Rode uses computer technology in the same way she uses art, music or any other therapeutic medium. "I take issue with, 'Here's a sick child; we'll give him a computer and make his life better,' " she said. "It treats the patient as an object of pity who needs to be given something to make it all better. Any child has absolutely no interest in that idea at all. Whether it's a computer, a box of watercolors, or a musical instrument, they want to learn how to master it and say something meaningful about themselves with it."

9 Based on feedback received from children who have used the network . . . , the Starbright Foundation will introduce a new version of Starbright World. . . . ❻ "Creating a community of peers is by far the most important element of Starbright World," said Nancy Hayes, chief executive of the Starbright Foundation, based in Los Angeles. "So with the new version, we're trying to facilitate as many opportunities for connection between the kids as possible." . . .

10 ❼ "If a child is about to undergo chemotherapy, he or she will be able to enter a chat room and hear what to expect from a child who has gone through it," she said. Another new component, Find a Friend, will match two children of similar age who have similar illnesses. Young patients will be able to view videos about procedures like getting a blood test or being hooked up to an intravenous line.

11 "Kids want more information on health care topics in their own language, not doctor-speak," Ms. Hayes said.

12 The children using Starbright World want contacts with more children on line, so the foundation is working on expanding the network.

13 "After we expand Starbright World, our long-term goal is to make the network accessible to kids after they leave the hospital, by using a password to log on at home," Ms. Hayes said.

❹ Think about the message.
"Kids in the hospital are pretty isolated. I guess using a computer doesn't so much improve their computer skills as give them a way to talk to other kids."

❺ Note techniques used by the writer.
"This quote helps me to visualize why Starbright World is important—it helps kids meet each other's needs for support."

YOUR TURN
Look at the other quotations in the selection. What purpose does each quotation serve?

❻ Skim the questions that follow the passage.
"What is a 'community of peers'? I have to figure out what Ms. Hayes means to answer question 4."

❼ Read actively—analyze.
"If kids who have the same illness talk to each other, they can learn more about what to expect."

YOUR TURN
How else might Starbright World be able to help seriously ill children?

Check Your Understanding

Have students use the following questions to test their own understanding of the selection before they answer the questions in their texts.

- What were the main ideas in the selection?
- How does the writer encourage readers to care about the information in the article?
- What structure does the writer use for the selection?
- Did the selection answer all your questions about the subject? If not, what questions remain unanswered?

PART 2 How to Answer Multiple-Choice Questions

Use the strategies in the box and the notes in the side column to help you answer the questions below and on the following pages.

Based on the selection you have just read, choose the best answer for each of the following questions.

1. According to the writer, how does Starbright World help children?
   - **A.** It gives them a way to communicate with other children at a time when they may be physically isolated.
   - **B.** It gives them a way to continue their education at a time when they cannot go to school.
   - **C.** It entertains them at a time when they need cheering up.
   - **D.** It provides them with access to medical sites on the Internet.
2. How does the anecdote in paragraphs 1, 2, and 3 entice readers to read on?
   - **A.** It discusses the services of Starbright World.
   - **B.** It makes readers realize that they themselves might one day need Starbright World.
   - **C.** It adds human interest to the selection.
   - **D.** all of the above
3. How does the writer of this selection use quotations?
   - **A.** to provide information
   - **B.** to add interest
   - **C.** to support the selection's message
   - **D.** all of the above
4. In paragraph 9, the writer quotes Nancy Hayes who says, "Creating a community of peers is by far the most important element of Starbright World." What does she mean?
   - **A.** Learning computer skills helps hospitalized children.
   - **B.** Reaching out to other children and sharing experiences helps hospitalized children.
   - **C.** Hospitalized children need to connect to the local community.
   - **D.** Children need to express feelings about their illnesses.
5. The primary technique this writer uses to keep the reader's interest is to include
   - **A.** comparisons.
   - **B.** descriptive language.
   - **C.** quotations.
   - **D.** chronological structure.

STRATEGIES FOR ANSWERING MULTIPLE-CHOICE QUESTIONS

- Ask questions that help you eliminate some of the choices.
- Pay attention to choices such as "all of the above" or "none of the above." To eliminate them, all you need to find is one answer that doesn't fit.
- Skim your notes. Details you noticed as you read may provide answers.

STRATEGIES IN ACTION

Pay attention to choices such as "all of the above."

ONE STUDENT'S THOUGHTS

"The anecdote doesn't discuss the services of Starbright World—it gives an example of one child who used them. So I can eliminate choice A—and that means I can also eliminate choice D. "

YOUR TURN

Which other choice doesn't make sense?

Skim your notes.

ONE STUDENT'S THOUGHTS

"I also noticed the word 'community' in paragraph 4. I don't think learning computer skills is the purpose of Starbright World. I can eliminate choice A."

YOUR TURN

How can you choose the best answer from the three choices that remain?

Guilding Student Response

Multiple Choice Questions

1. A
2. C

YOUR TURN Choice B does not apply because the selection does not attempt to predict who will use Starbright World.

3. D
4. B

YOUR TURN Choices C and D may be true. However, the quotation uses the words *community* and *peers.* This suggests that Hayes is referring to children connecting with other children, a process that is described in choice B.

5. C

STRATEGIES IN ACTION

Short-Answer Question

The writer shows that children are isolated by mentioning that they sometimes must stay in one room, that the computer sometimes has to be rolled in on a cart, and sometimes children who are in the same hospital are only able to meet on-line.

YOUR TURN Two children on the same floor of one hospital couldn't meet for a long time and could only communicate through Starbright World.

Essay Question

Starbright World offers services that help hospitalized children connect with each other. Through Starbright, children can communicate using chat rooms or video conferences. They can learn what to expect from their illness from other children who have it. Isolated children can become lonely, and Starbright gives them a way to bring other children into their hospital rooms—on-line.

YOUR TURN Text and audio chats with other children on-line, matches with other children who have the same illness through "Find a Friend," and videos about hospital procedures.

PART 3 How to Respond in Writing

You may also be asked to write answers to questions about a reading passage. Short-answer questions usually ask you to answer in a sentence or two. Essay questions require a fully developed piece of writing.

Short-Answer Question

STRATEGIES FOR RESPONDING TO SHORT-ANSWER QUESTIONS

- **Identify the key words** in the writing prompt that tell you the ideas to discuss. Make sure you know what is meant by each.
- **State your response directly** and to the point.
- **Support your ideas** by using evidence from the selection.
- **Use correct grammar.**

Sample Question

Answer the following question in one or two sentences.

How does the writer show that children in the hospital are isolated? What details does the writer use as evidence?

STRATEGIES IN ACTION

Support your ideas using evidence from the selection.

ONE STUDENT'S THOUGHTS

"The prompt asks for *details* that show how *isolated* children are when they are in the hospital. For example, I remember that sometimes a computer has to be rolled into a child's room on a cart."

YOUR TURN

What other detail in the selection shows that hospitalized children are isolated?

Essay Question

STRATEGIES FOR ANSWERING ESSAY QUESTIONS

- **Look for direction words** in the writing prompt, such as *essay, analyze, describe,* or *compare* and *contrast,* that tell you how to respond directly to the prompt.
- **List the points** you want to make before beginning to write.
- **Write an interesting introduction** that presents your main point.
- **Develop your ideas** by using evidence from the selection that supports the statements you make. Present the ideas in a logical order.
- **Write a conclusion** that summarizes your points.
- **Check your work** for correct grammar.

Sample Prompt

How does Starbright World help children cope with their illnesses? Write an essay in which you describe the services offered by Starbright World and analyze how these services could make a difference to a child during his or her recovery.

Look for direction words.

ONE STUDENT'S THOUGHTS

"The key words are *describe* and *analyze.* First I will describe the services that Starbright provides. Then, I will *analyze* how a sick child could benefit from Starbright's services."

YOUR TURN

List the services that Starbright offers to children.

512

PART 4 How to Revise and Edit a Test Selection

Here is a student's first draft in response to the writing prompt at the bottom of page 512. Read it and answer the multiple-choice questions that follow.

> Starbright World offers services that help children in the hospital to connect with other children. Through Starbright, children can talk to other children in several ways. They can use chat rooms. They can use video conferences. They can learn what to expect about their illness from other children who have it, too.
>
> They can become lonely if they spend most of their time alone. Starbright gives children a way to bring other children into their hospital rooms with them—on line. Starbright also makes being sick less scary giving children a chance to talk to other children with the same illness.

1. What is the BEST way to combine the three sentences in lines 2–4 ("Through Starbright . . . conferences.")?

A. Through Starbright, children can talk to other children using chat rooms or video conferences.

B. Chat rooms and video conferences, through Starbright are ways children can talk to other children in several ways.

C. Several ways that Starbright has can help children to talk to each other, chat rooms or video conferences.

D. Talking to other children in several ways through Starbright, children can use chat rooms or video conferences.

2. The meaning of the sentence in lines 7–8 ("They . . . alone.") can BEST be improved by changing *They* to

A. These children

B. Those children

C. Children in the hospital

D. Children using chat rooms

3. What is the BEST change, if any, to make to the sentence in lines 9–11 ("Starbright also . . . same illness.")?

A. Insert the word *by* between *scary* and *giving.*

B. Delete the word *giving* between *scary* and *children.*

C. Insert a period after *scary* and capitalize the first letter of *giving.*

D. Make no change.

STRATEGIES FOR REVISING, EDITING, AND PROOFREADING

- **Read the passage carefully.**
- **Note the parts that are confusing** or don't make sense. What kinds of errors would that signal?
- **Look for errors** in grammar, usage, spelling, and capitalization. Common errors include:
  - run-on sentences
  - sentence fragments
  - lack of subject-verb agreement
  - unclear pronoun antecedents
  - lack of transition words

Answers
1. A; **2.** B; **3.** A

Check Your Understanding

Have students re-read their own responses to the short-answer and essay questions. Then have students use the following questions to guide themselves as they revise and edit their own work.

- Have I responded directly to the direction words in the writing prompt?
- Have I supported my ideas with evidence from the selection?
- Have I presented my ideas in a logical order?
- Have I included an introduction and a conclusion?
- Have I used correct grammar?

The Restoration and Enlightenment

The selections in Unit Three reflect Britain's efforts in the 18th century to reestablish a sense of order and security after the great political, religious, and social upheavals of the previous era. The unit is divided into three sections to better represent the people's public and private lives.

Part 1

Views of Society The selections in this part of the unit reflect the social and cultural concerns of the late 17th and early 18th centuries. The essays, poems, and letters present a revealing look at the manners and attitudes of the time. Two French humorous moral tales make up the **Comparing Literature** feature.

Part 2

Arguments for Change While arguing for social change, the writers in this section reveal their faith in reason as well as their intelligence, education, and sense of discipline. An **Author Study** on Jonathan Swift takes particular aim at social injustices. The **Comparing Literature** selection contrasts Swift's satire with that of France's Voltaire.

Part 3

Revelations About Human Nature The works in this section tap the roots of the pre-Romantic movement. These writers herald the beginning of the reaction against the Enlightenment's emphasis on reason and intellect. The **Comparing Literature** selection traces a common outlook between French and English thinkers.

UNIT THREE

Spring Gardens, Ranelagh, Thomas Rowlandson. Victoria & Albert Museum, London/Superstock.

Viewing and Representing

Spring Gardens, Ranelagh
by Thomas Rowlandson

ART APPRECIATION

Instruction Thomas Rowlandson (1756–1827) was an English artist and caricaturist. When he was 24 years old, he turned his attention to illustration. One writer noted that Rowlandson came to see that "the lives of the people embraced unlovely elements—irony, tragedy, hypocrisy, self-seeking, frustration, deception, and defeat," and he wanted to "capture" this "whimsical *tableaux* fashioned by fate."

Many of Rowlandson's comic portraits became familiar stereotypes to his 18th-century audience. The pen-and-watercolor sketch above from c. 1785–90 shows people at the Spring Gardens entrance to the Ranelagh (răʹ-nĭl-ə) amusement center in the London borough of Chelsea. A figure at the left carries an umbrella, a part of stylish outdoor attire in 18th-century Europe.

The Restoration *and* Enlightenment

1660—1798

Let observation with extensive view,
Survey mankind, from China to Peru;
Remark each anxious toil, each eager strife
And watch the busy scenes of crowded life.

SAMUEL JOHNSON
critic and scholar

Making Connections

To help students explore this unit-opening spread, have them consider the following questions:

Have students study the title of this unit. Ask: **What do you think "Restoration" means? Who or what might have been restored?**
Possible Responses: The word *restoration* means "the act of reintroducing, reviving, or bringing back something"; "Restoration" refers to the return of the monarchy, which in turn signaled a return to social and political stability.

Ask: **What do you think "Enlightenment" means? How can people be enlightened?**
Possible Responses: The word *enlightenment* means "the act of educating, informing, or bringing knowledge." People are enlightened by considering new ideas or by looking at things in a new way. "Enlightenment" refers to the philosophical movement of the 18th century that emphasized the use of reason.

LaserLinks
Historical Literary Connection: The Restoration and Enlightenment
Key historical events and representative artwork of the period are highlighted in this film. Pictures of the return of Charles II and of a Newton experiment, paintings by John Constable and Sir Joshua Reynolds, and architecture by Robert Adams are among the images presented. Use this video to help students develop an understanding of Enlightenment themes and of English society in the Age of Reason.

See Teacher's SourceBook p. 32 for bar codes.

Ask: **What details in the painting suggest that the Restoration and Enlightenment was a time of prosperity and stability?**
Possible Response: The people appear to be well dressed, relaxed, and carefree.

PART 1 SKILLS TRACE

Features and Selections	Literary Analysis	Reading and Critical Thinking	Writing Opportunities
The Restoration and Enlightenment **Time Line** **Historical Background/Essay**			
DIARY *from* The Diary of Samuel Pepys	Diary, 525, 532	Making Inferences, 525, 532 Evaluating Sources, 532	Problem-Solving Essay, 533
POETRY *from* An Essay on Man Epigrams, *from* An Essay on Criticism	Heroic couplet, 534, 538	Analyzing Ideas, 534, 538	Epigram, 539 Essay, 539
FABLE Comparing Literature of the World The Acorn and the Pumpkin The Value of Knowledge	Fable, 540, 544	Society Across Cultures, 540 Making Judgments, 540, 544	An Original Fable, 545 Points of Comparison, 545
Learning the Language of Literature Nonfiction in the 18th Century	Essay, 546 Other Forms of Nonfiction, 547	Strategies for Reading, 547	
INFORMAL ESSAY *from* The Spectator	Informal Essay, 548, 552	Author's Purpose, 548, 552	Newspaper Column, 553
from Letters to His Son Letter to Her Daughter	Parallelism, 554, 564	Generalizations, 554, 564 Author's Purpose, Main Ideas, and Details, 557	Essay, 565 Business Letter, 561 Informal Assess., 563
Writing Workshop: Proposal Assessment Practice Building Vocabulary Sentence Crafting		Analyzing Persuasive Messages, 569	Proposal, 571, 572

LEGEND PE instruction shown in black
TE Mini Lessons shown in green
CCL indicates a Cross-Curricular Link
DLS indicates Daily Language SkillBuilder

Speaking and Listening Viewing and Representing	Inquiry and Research	Grammar, Usage, and Mechanics	Vocabulary
Art Appreciation, 514 Art Appreciation, 522			
A Movie Set, 533 Art Appreciation, 526	Commonwealth and Restoration, 533	DLS, 525 Adjective Phrases, 530	Word Origins, 527
Character List, 539	Reasonable Ideas, 539	DLS, 534 Adjective Prepositional Phrases, 537	Denotation and Connotation, 536
Debate, 545 Comic Strip, 545	Other Writers of Fables, 545 Author Activity, 545	DLS, 540 Prepositional Phrases, 542	Suffixes, 541
	Your Turn, 547		
Illustrated Excerpts, 553	Author Activity, 553	DLS, 548 Compound Adjectives, 551	Synonyms/Meaning Clues, 553 Analogies, 549
Art Appreciation, 560 Writer's Viewpoint, 562	CCL: Social Science, 565	DLS, 554 Commas, 558	Clues and Idioms, 565 Synonyms, 555
Text Structure, 570 Springboard, 572		Revising and Editing, 573 Adjectives and Adjective Phrases, 575 Adjectives and Adverbs, 573	Precision in Language, 574

UNIT THREE
PART 2 SKILLS TRACE

Features and Selections	Literary Analysis	Reading and Critical Thinking	Writing Opportunities
ESSAY *from* An Academy for Women	Persuasive Essay, 577, 582	Analyzing an Argument, 577, 582	Persuasive Letter, 582 Informal Assess., 581
Learning the Language of Literature Satire	Satire, 584	Reading Strategies, 585	
AUTHOR STUDY **Jonathan Swift**			
FICTION *from* Gulliver's Travels	Fantasy, 590, 607 Satire, 607	Visualizing, 590, 607 Test Practice, 593	Satiric Fantasy, 608 Creating Another Land, 608 Informal Assess., 597 Informal Assess., 606
ESSAY A Modest Proposal	Irony, 611, 620	Drawing Conclusions, 611, 620 Test Practice, 616 Informal Assess., 619	Editorial Memo, 622 Ironic Rebuttal, 622 Another Proposal, 622
The Author's Style Author Study Project	Analysis of Style, 621		Imitation of Style, 621
FICTION Comparing Literature of the World *from* Candide	Humor, 624, 629	Satirical Commentary, 624 Drawing Conclusions, 624, 629	Points of Comparison, 630
ESSAY *from* A Vindication of the Rights of Women	Argumentation, 631, 637	Logical Persuasion, 631, 637	Opinion Paper, 638 Questions and Answers, 638
Writing Workshop: Satire Assessment Practice Building Vocabulary Sentence Crafting			Satire, 642, 643

LEGEND PE instruction shown in black
TE Mini Lessons shown in green
CCL indicates a Cross-Curricular Link
DLS indicates Daily Language SkillBuilder

Speaking and Listening Viewing and Representing	Inquiry and Research	Grammar, Usage, and Mechanics	Vocabulary
Advertisement, 583 Interview with Defoe, 583	Educational Opportunities, 583	DLS, 577 Infinitives, 583	Antonyms, 583
Scene Performance, 608 Lilliput on Video, 608 Comparing Size, 608 Roundtable Discussion, 601 Art Appreciation, 605	Literary History, 608 CCL: History, 598	DLS, 590	Context Clues/Synonyms and Antonyms, 608 Synonyms, 591 Suffixes, 600
Town Meeting, 622 Political Cartoon, 622 "Modest" Diagrams, 622 Art Appreciation, 613 Panel Discussion, 617 Preparing a Monologue, 618	Literary History, 622 Irish History, 622 Swift Biography, 622 Swift Online, 622	DLS, 611 Gerunds and Gerund Phrases, 620	Synonyms and Antonyms, 623 Synonyms and Antonyms, 612
Changing Style, 621 Speaking and Listening, 621	Producing a Talk Show, 623		
	Enlightened Ideas, 630	DLS, 624 Participles, Gerunds, and Verbs, 626	Context Clues, 630 Context Clues, 625
		DLS, 631 Verbals and Verbal Phrases, 634	Meaning Clues, 638 Thesaurus, 632 Root Words, 636
		Revising and Editing, 644 Elements in a Series, 646	Denotations and Connotations, 645

PART 3 SKILLS TRACE

Features and Selections	Literary Analysis	Reading and Critical Thinking	Writing Opportunities
ESSAYS On Spring from The Rambler On Idleness from The Idler	Aphorism, 648, 656 Informal Essay, 656	Strategies for Clarifying Meaning, 648, 656	Anecdote, 657
Related Reading: *from* A Dictionary of the English Language			
BIOGRAPHY from The Life of Samuel Johnson	Biography, 659, 664	Biographer's Perspective, 659, 644 Evaluating Sources, 664	Biography Outline, 665
POETRY Elegy Written in a Country Churchyard	Personification, 666, 672 Elegy, 672	Making Inferences, 666, 672	Paragraph, 673 Alternative Title, 673 Informal Assess., 671
DIARY *from* The Diary and Letters of Madame d'Arblay	Dialogue, 674, 679	Word Choice, 674, 679	Party Script, 680 Diary Entry, 680
Comparing Literature of the World: from Memoirs of Madame Vigée-Lebrun	Description, 681, 690 Evaluating Sources, 690	Personal Narratives, 681 Interpreting Details, 681, 690	Points of Comparison, 691
Reflect and Assess	Form and Content, 692 Irony and Satire, 693	Evaluating the Issues, 692 Analyzing Essays, 693	Gaining Insights, 692 Building Your Portfolio, 693

LEGEND PE instruction shown in black · TE Mini Lessons shown in green · CCL indicates a Cross-Curricular Link · DLS indicates Daily Language SkillBuilder

Speaking and Listening Viewing and Representing	Inquiry and Research	Grammar, Usage, and Mechanics	Vocabulary
Caricature, 657 Mood in Art, 651 Art Appreciation, 653		DLS, 648 Verbs, 654	**Context Clues, 657** Context Clues, 649 Analogies, 652
			Denotation and Connotation, 658
Pantomime, 665 Dialogue, 665		DLS, 659 Verbs, 662	**Context Clues, 665** Context Clues, 660
Background Music, 673 **Author Activity, 673**	**King Charles I, 673**	DLS, 666	Dictionary, 667 Multiple Meaning Words, 669
Caricature, 680 **Photo Essay, 680** Summary, 678	**Literary Ladies, 680**	DLS, 674 Subject and Verb Agreement, 677	**Idioms, 680** Context Clues, 676
Art Appreciation, 685 Art Appreciation, 688		DLS, 681 Verbs, 686	**Context Clues, 691** Dictionary, 682 Suffixes, 684

UNIT THREE
RESOURCE MANAGEMENT GUIDE
PART 1

To introduce the theme/literary period of this unit, use Fine Art Transparencies T23–25 in the Communications Transparencies and Copymasters.

	Unit Resource Book	Assessment	Integrated Technology and Media	Additional Support: Literary Analysis Transparencies
from The Diary of Samuel Pepys *pp. 525–533*	• Summary p. 4 • Active Reading p. 6 • Literary Analysis p. 7 • Selection Quiz p. 8	• Selection Test, Formal Assessment pp. 85–86 Test Generator	Audio Library LaserLinks, Teacher's SourceBook pp. 32–33 Research Starter www.mcdougallittell.com	
from An Essay on Man Epigrams from An Essay on Criticism, *pp. 534–539*	• Active Reading p. 9 • Literary Analysis p. 10	• Selection Test, Formal Assessment pp. 87–88 Test Generator	Audio Library LaserLinks, Teacher's SourceBook pp. 33–34	• Characteristics of the Essay T11
The Acorn and the Pumpkin The Value of Knowledge *pp. 540–545*	• Active Reading p. 11 • Literary Analysis p. 12	• Selection Test, Formal Assessment pp. 89–90 Test Generator	Audio Library Research Starter www.mcdougallittell.com	• The Moral Tale, Ballad, Fable, and Folk Tale T23
from The Spectator *pp. 548-553*	• Summary p. 13 • Active Reading p. 14 • Literary Analysis p. 15 • Words to Know p. 16 • Selection Quiz p. 17	• Selection Test, Formal Assessment pp. 91–92 Test Generator	Audio Library LaserLinks, Teacher's SourceBook p. 35	
from Letters to His Son Letter to Her Daughter *pp. 554–565*	• Summary pp. 18, 19 • Active Reading p. 20 • Literary Analysis p. 21 • Words to Know p. 22 • Selection Quiz p. 23	• Selection Test, Formal Assessment pp. 93–94 Test Generator	Audio Library	

Writing Workshop: Proposal

Unit Three Resource Book
- Prewriting p. 24
- Drafting and Elaboration p. 25
- Peer Response Guide pp. 26–27
- Revising, Editing, and Proofreading p. 28
- Student Models pp. 29–34
- Rubric for Evaluation p. 35

Writing Coach

Writing Transparencies and Copymasters T11, T19, C28

Teacher's Guide to Assessment and Portfolio Use

Unit Assessment
- Unit Three, Part 1 Test, Formal Assessment pp. 95–96
  Test Generator
- Unit Three Integrated Test, Integrated Assessment pp. 19–28

Unit Technology

ClassZone www.mcdougallittell.com
Electronic Teacher Tools
Electronic Library

UNIT THREE
PART 2

To introduce the theme/literary period of this unit, use Fine Art Transparencies T23–25 in the Communications Transparencies and Copymasters.

	Unit Resource Book	Assessment	Integrated Technology and Media	Additional Support: Literary Analysis Transparencies
from An Academy for Women *pp. 577–583*	• Summary p. 38 • Active Reading p. 39 • Literary Analysis p. 40 • Words to Know p. 41 • Selection Quiz p. 42	• Selection Test, Formal Assessment pp. 97–98 Test Generator	Audio Library LaserLinks, Teacher's SourceBook p. 36	• Characteristics of the Essay T11
from Gulliver's Travels *pp. 590–608*	• Summary p. 43 • Active Reading p. 44 • Literary Analysis p. 45 • Words to Know p. 46 • Selection Quiz p. 47	• Selection Test, Formal Assessment pp. 99–100 Test Generator	Audio Library NetActivities	• Horatian vs. Juvenalian Satire T12
A Modest Proposal *pp. 611–623*	• Summary p. 48 • Active Reading p. 49 • Literary Analysis p. 50 • Words to Know p. 51 • Selection Quiz p. 52	• Selection Test, Formal Assessment pp. 101–102 Test Generator	Audio Library LaserLinks, Teacher's SourceBook p. 37 NetActivities	• Horatian vs. Juvenalian Satire T12

T = Transparency C = Copymaster

Reading and Critical Thinking Transparencies	Grammar Transparencies and Copymasters	Vocabulary Transparencies and Copymasters	Writing Transparencies and Copymasters	Communications Transparencies and Copymasters
• Evaluating Credibility of Information Sources T43 • Organizational Chart: Horizontal T52 • Problem-Solution Chart T57	• Daily Language SkillBuilder T12 • Diagramming Subjects, Verbs, and Modifiers T58 • Types of Adjective Phrases C90	• Word Origins C50	• Proposal C28	
• Compare and Contrast T15	• Daily Language SkillBuilder T12 • Adjective Prepositional Phrases C86	• Denotation and Connotation C51	• Achieving Conciseness T21 • Proposal C28	
• Making Judgments T5 • Comparing Authors' Views T24	• Daily Language SkillBuilder T13 • Placement of Prepositional Phrases C89	• Prefixes, Suffixes, and Roots C52	• Compare-Contrast C34	• Impromptu Speaking: Debate T15
• Determining Author's Purpose and Audience T20 • Organizational Chart: Horizontal T52	• Daily Language SkillBuilder T13 • Compound Adjectives C69		• Proposal C28	
• Organizational Chart: Horizontal T52 • Problem-Solution Chart T57	• Daily Language SkillBuilder T13 • Punctuating Elements in a Series T54 • Commas in a Series of Phrases C160		• Proposal C28	

STUDENTS ACQUIRING ENGLISH

The **Spanish Study Guide,** pp. 108–127, includes language support for the following pages:

- Family and Community Involvement (per unit)
- Selection Summaries and Vocabulary
- Active Reading
- Literary Analysis

Reading and Critical Thinking Transparencies	Grammar Transparencies and Copymasters	Vocabulary Transparencies and Copymasters	Writing Transparencies and Copymasters	Communications Transparencies and Copymasters
• Main Idea and Supporting Details T12 • Organizational Chart: Vertical T53	• Daily Language SkillBuilder T14 • Diagramming Verbal Phrases T60 • Infinitives C96		• Opinion Statement C35	• Interviewing T9
• Visualizing T8 • Compare and Contrast T15 • Locating Information Using Databases and the Internet T35	• Daily Language SkillBuilder T14 • Avoiding Misplaced and Dangling Modifiers T51 • Dangling Participles C102	• Suffixes C53	• Satire C29	• Appreciative Listening T2 • Dramatic Reading T12
• Organizational Chart: Horizontal T52 • Problem-Solution Chart T57	• Daily Language SkillBuilder T15 • Diagramming Verbal Phrases T60 • Gerund and Gerund Phrases II C104		• Proposal C28 • Satire C29	• Evaluating Roles in Groups T8

UNIT THREE, PART 2 CONTINUED

	Unit Resource Book	Assessment	Integrated Technology and Media	Additional Support: Literary Analysis Transparencies
from **Candide** *pp. 624–630*	• Summary p. 53 • Active Reading p. 54 • Literary Analysis p. 55 • Words to Know p. 56 • Selection Quiz p. 57	• Selection Test, Formal Assessment pp. 103–104 Test Generator	Audio Library	
from **A Vindication of the Rights of Woman** *pp. 631–638*	• Summary p. 58 • Active Reading p. 59 • Literary Analysis p. 60 • Words to Know p. 61 • Selection Quiz p. 62	• Selection Test, Formal Assessment p. 105 Test Generator	Audio Library	
Writing Workshop: Satire	**Unit Three Resource Book** • Prewriting p. 63 • Drafting and Elaboration p. 64 • Peer Response Guide pp. 65–66 • Revising, Editing, and Proofreading p. 67 • Student Models pp. 68–73 • Rubric for Evaluation p. 74 **Writing Coach** **Writing Transparencies and Copymasters** T11, T19, C29 **Teacher's Guide to Assessment and Portfolio Use**	***Unit Assessment*** • Unit Three, Part 2 Test, Formal Assessment pp. 107–108 Test Generator • Unit Three Integrated Test, Integrated Assessment pp. 19–28	***Unit Technology*** ClassZone www.mcdougallittell.com Electronic Teacher Tools Electronic Library	

UNIT THREE PART 3

To introduce the theme/literary period of this unit, use Fine Art Transparencies T23–25 in the Communications Transparencies and Copymasters.

	Unit Resource Book	Assessment	Integrated Technology and Media	Additional Support: Literary Analysis Transparencies
from **The Rambler On Spring** *from* **The Idler On Idleness,** *pp. 648–657*	• Summary pp. 77-78 • Active Reading p. 79 • Literary Analysis p. 80 • Words to Know p. 81 • Selection Quiz p. 82	• Selection Test, Formal Assessment pp. 109–110 Test Generator	Audio Library LaserLinks, Teacher's SourceBook p. 38	
from **The Life of Samuel Johnson** *pp. 659–665*	• Summary p. 83 • Active Reading p. 85 • Literary Analysis p. 86 • Words to Know p. 87 • Selection Quiz p. 88	• Selection Test, Formal Assessment pp. 111–112 Test Generator	Audio Library	
Elegy Written in a Country Churchyard *pp. 666–673*	• Active Reading p. 89 • Literary Analysis p. 90	• Selection Test, Formal Assessment p. 113 Test Generator	Audio Library LaserLinks, Teacher's SourceBook p. 39 Research Starter www.mcdougallittell.com	
from **The Diary and Letter of Madame d'Arblay,** *pp. 674–680*	• Summary p. 91 • Active Reading p. 92 • Literary Analysis p. 93 • Words to Know p. 94 • Selection Quiz p. 95	• Selection Test, Formal Assessment pp. 115–116 Test Generator	Audio Library	
from **Memoirs of Madame Vigée-Lebrun** *pp. 681–691*	• Summary p. 96 • Active Reading p. 97 • Literary Analysis p. 98 • Words to Know p. 99 • Selection Quiz p. 100	• Selection Test, Formal Assessment pp. 117–118 Test Generator	Audio Library LaserLinks, Teacher's SourceBook pp. 40–41	
		Unit Assessment • Unit Three, Part 3 Test, Formal Assessment pp. 119–120 • Mid-Year Test, Formal Assessment pp. 121–124 Test Generator • Unit Three Integrated Test, Integrated Assessment pp. 19–28	***Unit Technology*** ClassZone www.mcdougallittell.com Electronic Teacher Tools Electronic Library	

T = Transparency C = Copymaster

Reading and Critical Thinking Transparencies	Grammar Transparencies and Copymasters	Vocabulary Transparencies and Copymasters	Writing Transparencies and Copymasters	Communications Transparencies and Copymasters
• Visualizing T8 • Compare and Contrast T15 • Organizational Chart: Horizontal T52	• Daily Language SkillBuilder T15 • Diagramming Verbal Phrases T60 • Distinguishing Participles, Gerunds, and Verbs C93		• Compare-Contrast C34	
• Evaluating Argumentation I T21 • Identifying Persuasive Techniques T25 • Analyzing Persuasive Techniques T26	• Daily Language SkillBuilder T16 • Diagramming Verbal Phrases T60 • Verbals and Verbal Phrases C94	• Roots C54	• Opinion Statement C35	• Interviewing T9

STUDENTS ACQUIRING ENGLISH

The **Spanish Study Guide,** pp. 128–142, includes language support for the following pages:

- Family and Community Involvement (per unit)
- Selection Summaries and Vocabulary
- Active Reading
- Literary Analysis

Reading and Critical Thinking Transparencies	Grammar Transparencies and Copymasters	Vocabulary Transparencies and Copymasters	Writing Transparencies and Copymasters	Communications Transparencies and Copymasters
• Reading for Details T16 • Notetaking T41 • Paraphrasing and Summarizing T42	• Daily Language SkillBuilder T16 • Commonly Confused Verbs C139	• Synonyms and Antonyms C55	• Showing, Not Telling T22 • Personality Profile C25	
• Determining Author's Bias T23 • Evaluating Credibility of Information Sources T43 • Using an Outline T44	• Daily Language SkillBuilder T16 • Progressive Verb Forms C132 • Subject-Verb Agreement I C140		• Personality Profile C25	• Identifying and Analyzing Artistic Elements in Literary Texts T13
• Making Inferences T7 • Noting Details T9	• Daily Language SkillBuilder T17 • Verbs–Using Correct Verb Forms T45 • Emphatic Verb Forms C131	• Using a Dictionary C56 • Words with Multiple Meanings C57	• Literary Interpretation C33	• Appreciative Listening T2 • Reading Aloud T11
• Analyzing Emotional Appeals T19	• Daily Language SkillBuilder T17 • Agreement of Subject and Verb T47 • Subject-Verb Agreement I C140		• Effective Language T13 • The Uses of Dialogue T24 • Dramatic Scene C31	
• Evaluating Credibility of Information Sources T43 • Organizational Chart: Horizontal T52	• Daily Language SkillBuilder T17 • Active and Passive Voice II C135	• Suffixes C58	• Compare-Contrast C34	

STUDENTS ACQUIRING ENGLISH

The **Spanish Study Guide,** pp. 143–159, includes language support for the following pages:

- Family and Community Involvement (per unit)
- Selection Summaries and Vocabulary
- Active Reading
- Literary Analysis

UNIT THREE
DAILY LANGUAGE SKILLBUILDERS

Selection	SkillBuilder Sentences	Suggested Answers
from The Diary of Samuel Pepys	1. One of the most energetic diarists of all time are, i believe, Samuel Pepys his diary covers the years 1660 to 1669. **2.** Your going to find this hard to believe: Mr Pepys wrote his diary in a well known form of shorthand. In addition he disguised private passages by using a Spanish-based code.	1. One of the most energetic diarists of all time **is,** **I** believe, Samuel Pepys**;** his diary covers the years 1660 to 1669. **2.** You'**re** going to find this hard to believe: Mr**.** Pepys wrote his diary in a well**-**known form of shorthand. In addition**,** he disguised private passages by using a Spanish-based code.
from An Essay on Man	**1.** The writing of Alexander Pope has influenced many writers not merely in England, but also abroad. **2.** One poem, with the suggestive title of "the rape of the lock" tells the story of a women who's hair is cut against her will while she is innocently sipping coffee.	1. The writing of Alexander Pope has influenced many writers**,** not merely in England but also abroad. 2. One poem, with the suggestive title of "**T**he **R**ape of the **L**ock" tells the story of a wom**a**n **whose** hair is cut against her will while she is innocently sipping coffee.
The Acorn and the Pumpkin The Value of Knowledge	**1.** Fables have been written by many authors' around the world. **2.** The word fable is derived from a latin word meaning to speak.	**1.** Fables have been written by many authors around the world. **2.** The word **<u>fable</u>** is derived from a **L**atin word meaning **"**to speak.**"**
from The Spectator	**1.** Addison and Richard Steele, they is the ones whom wrote the spectator and the tatler; london newspapers. **2.** Addison the author of these essays were the most conservative of the too.	**1.** Addison and Richard Steele **wrote <u>The Tatler</u>** and **<u>The Spectator</u>, L**ondon newspapers. **2.** Addison**,** the author of these essays**,** was the more conservative of the t**w**o.
Letters to His Son Letter to Her Daughter	**1.** Philip Dormer Stanhope: 4th earl of Chesterfield, was a great admiror of French manners and culture. **2.** He was ambassador to holland from 1728–1732.	**1.** Philip Dormer Stanhope**, fourth** earl of Chesterfield, was a great admir**e**r of French manners and culture. **2.** He was ambassador to **H**olland from 1728 **to** 1732.

Selection	SkillBuilder Sentences	Suggested Answers
from An Academy for Women	**1.** Daniel Defoe is widly reconized as the man who put prose fiction on the Birtish literary map, he however did not make it respectible. **2.** Despite his devout Presbyterian beleifs, Defoe wrote storys about theives, rebels, and lose women.	**1.** Daniel Defoe is widely reco**g**nized as the man who put prose fiction on the B**ri**tish literary map**;** **however, he** did not make it respect**a**ble. **2.** Despite his devout Presbyterian bel**ie**fs, Defoe wrote stories about th**ie**ves, rebels, and lo**o**se w**o**men.
from Gulliver's Travels	**1.** Although Jonathan Swift had wrote many satires criticizing Human behavior, he had many close friendships, with men and women. **2.** Swift was a member of the anglican church and he was raised to a position of authority in the church in Ireland.	**1.** Although Jonathan Swift wrote many satires criticizing **h**uman behavior, he had many close friendships with men and women. **2.** Swift was a member of the **A**nglican **C**hurch**,** and he was raised to a position of authority in the **C**hurch in Ireland.
A Modest Proposal	**1.** Satire, which form was used frequent in eighteenth century england, often made people mad. **2.** Jonathan Swift who was a freind of Alexander Pope wrote the greater satires of the period.	**1.** Satire, **a** form used frequent**ly** in **18th**-century **E**ngland, often made people mad. **2.** Jonathan Swift**,** who was a fr**ie**nd of Alexander Pope**,** wrote the great**est** satires of the period.
from Candide	**1.** Candide is an honest boy who was rose up in the barons castle. **2.** Candide and his teacher tryed to get away but they were catched and put in prisen.	**1.** Candide is an honest boy who was **raised** in the baron's castle. **2.** Candide and his teacher tr**ie**d to get away**,** but they were **caught** and put in pris**o**n.
from A Vindication of the Rights of Woman	**1.** In england during the eighteenth century women have less opportunitys than men. **2.** Because men were physically stronger then women people assumed they was mentally weaker too.	**1.** In **E**ngland during the **18th**-century**,** women **had fewer** opportuniti**e**s than men **had.** **2.** Because men were physically stronger th**a**n women**,** people assumed **that men were** mentally **superior,** too.

DAILY LANGUAGE SKILLBUILDERS, continued

Selection	SkillBuilder Sentences	Suggested Answers
from The Rambler On Spring *from* The Idler On Idleness	**1.** Samuel Johnson—weve learned this in English Class is the best-known writer of eighteenth century england. **2.** Although Johnson wanted to be a playwrite the only play he wrote was not very popular.	**1.** Samuel Johnson—we've learned this in English **c**lass—is the best-known writer of **18th**-century **E**ngland. **2.** Although Johnson wanted to be a playwri**ght,** the only play he wrote was not very popular.
from A Dictionary of the English Language	**1.** James Boswell who was from scotland when very young met Samuel Johnson in a Book Store. **2.** On May 16 1763, Boswell succeeded in meeting Johnson, however he didn't show no liking for him at first.	**1.** James Boswell**,** who was from **S**cotland**, was** very young when **he** met Samuel Johnson in a **bookstore**. **2.** On May 16**,** 1763, Boswell succeeded in meeting Johnson**;** however**,** Johnson showed no liking for Boswell at first.
from The Life of Samuel Johnson Elegy Written in a Country Churchyard	**1.** Them peasants in Grays' poem worked hard and obscurely and they died quiet. **2.** Charles I was a king, whom treated the upperclasses good.	**1.** **Those** peasants in Gray**'s** poem worked hard and **in obscurity,** and they died quiet**ly**. **2.** Charles I was a king **who** treated the **upper classes well**.
from The Diary and Letters of Madame d'Arblay	**1.** The Art of conversation was important in the 1700s, people were judged by how good they were speaking. **2.** Many women who were intelligent witty and wealthy had parties so that thier guests could meet and talk and listen to music.	**1.** The **a**rt of conversation was important in the 1700s, **and** people were judged by how **well** they **spoke**. **2.** Many women who were intelligent**,** witty**,** and wealthy had parties so that their guests could meet**,** talk, and listen to music.
from Memoirs of Madame Vigée-Lebrun	**1.** The french painter madame Vigee-Lebrun, excepted the queen's invitation to visit the palace in Paris france. **2.** The common people, which Vigee-Lebrun felt afraid of, were watching the Aristocracy and their expenses were excessive with resentment.	**1.** The **F**rench painter **M**adame Vigee-Lebrun **ac**cepted the queen's invitation to visit the palace in Paris**,** **F**rance. **2.** The common people, **whom** Vigee-Lebrun felt afraid of, watch**ed** the **a**ristocracy, **whose** expenses were excessive**,** with resentment.

INTEGRATING GRAMMAR AND LITERATURE: GRAMMAR PLANNER

Grammar Focus by Unit

Unit One	Unit Two	Unit Three	Unit Four	Unit Five	Unit Six	Unit Seven
Parts of a Sentence	Phrases, Part I	Phrases, Part II	Clauses, Part I	Clauses, Part II	Rhetorical Grammar, Part I	Rhetorical Grammar, Part II

The Language of Literature offers several options for integrating grammar instruction and literature.

- Each literature unit has a grammar focus. The Teacher's Edition includes Mini Lessons for each selection that help develop the grammar focus for the unit and spring from the content of the specific literature.
- The Pupil Edition includes several full-page lessons on Sentence Crafting. These lessons are related to both the literature and the grammar focus for the unit and help students use grammar in their own writing.
- Daily Language SkillBuilders in the Teacher's Edition provide students with ongoing proofreading practice and reinforce punctuation, spelling, grammar and usage, and capitalization.
- Grammar Copymasters and Transparencies, which may be used to complement or extend lessons in the Teacher's Edition, present grammar in a traditional, systematic sequence. References to appropriate copymasters or transparencies are included at point of use in the Teacher's Edition Mini Lessons.

TE Mini Lessons shown in green
PE instruction shown in black

Part 1

Parts of Speech

Modifiers: Adjectives
Sentence Crafting, p. 575

Compound Adjectives
from *The Spectator,* p. 551

Using Phrases

Adjective Prepositional Phrases
from *An Essay on Man,* from *An Essay on Criticism,* p. 537

Placement of Prepositional Phrases
"The Acorn and the Pumpkin," "The Value of Knowledge," pp. 542–543

Types of Adjective Phrases
from *The Diary of Samuel Pepys,* pp. 530–531

Participial Phrases Used as Adjectives
Sentence Crafting, p. 575

Using Clauses

Run-on Sentences
Writing Workshop, p. 573

Verb Usage

Avoiding Unnecessary Shifts in Tense
Writing Workshop, p. 573

Using Modifiers

Understanding Modifiers
Writing Workshop, p. 573

Misplaced and Dangling Modifiers
Sentence Crafting, p. 575

End Marks and Commas

Commas in a Series of Phrases
from *Letters to His Son,* Letter to Her Daughter, p. 558

Part 2

Parts of the Sentence

Complete Sentences
Writing Workshop, p. 644

Using Phrases

Distinguishing Participles, Gerunds, and Verbs
from *Candide,* p. 626

Verbs and Verbal Phrases
from *A Vindication of the Rights of Woman,* p. 634

Verb Phrases: Infinitives
from *An Academy for Women,* p. 583

Dangling Participles
from *Gulliver's Travels,* pp. 602–603

Verb Phrases: Gerunds and Gerund Phrases
"A Modest Proposal," p. 620

Pronoun Usage

Pronoun-Antecedent Agreement
Writing Workshop, p. 644

Using Modifiers

Misplaced and Dangling Modifiers
Writing Workshop, p. 644

End Marks and Punctuation

Commas in a Series of Phrases
Sentence Crafting, p. 646

Other Punctuation

Using Dashes to Introduce an Explanation
Sentence Crafting, p. 646

Style

Cohesion: Parallelism
Sentence Crafting, p. 646

Part 3

Verb Usage

Emphatic Forms
"Elegy Written in a Country Churchyard," p. 673

Using the Progressive Form
from *The Life of Samuel Johnson,* p. 662

Active and Passive Voice
from *Memoirs of Madame Vigée-Lebrun,* p. 686

Commonly Confused Verbs
"On Spring," "On Idleness," p. 654

Subject-Verb Agreement
from *The Diary and Letters of Madame d'Arblay,* p. 677

This time line shows important events in the period extending from the Restoration to the end of the 18th century. Further information about some people and events is provided below. Discuss with students the historical context in which British literary events occurred.

1663

One of Charles II's first acts upon his Restoration in 1660 was to revive theatrical entertainment, which Puritan rule had banned. Theater companies were founded, and in 1663 the Drury Lane Theatre opened for dramas and social satires. Now, for the first time, actresses played female roles that had earlier been played by boys.

Literature: 1668

A The title of "poet laureate" honors a person for poetic achievement. The recipient becomes a salaried member of the British royal household. Since Dryden's appointment, the position has been filled automatically when made vacant. Laureates often write poems to celebrate national and royal events.

Britain: 1666

B The Great Fire of London culminated a short period of disasters for the city. First, a flea-and-rat-borne plague the year before had taken about 100,000 lives. Then a fire broke out in a baker's shop and spread throughout London's mainly wooden structures. About 75 percent of the city was destroyed. In his diary, Samuel Pepys wrote that "all over the Thames, with one's face in the wind you were almost burned with a shower of firedrops." The heat destroyed St. Paul's Cathedral, melting its lead roof.

World: 1661

C The Palace of Versailles, residence of kings of France until 1789, is more than a quarter-mile long and has nearly 1,300 rooms. Its opulence is unrivaled. For instance, bedrooms are adorned with gold-covered wood and decorated with rare antiques. The garden and park of its grounds cover about 250 acres. Construction of the palace took more than 40 years. Today the palace, 12 miles from Paris, is a museum.

TIME LINE 1660-1798

The Restoration *and* Enlightenment

EVENTS IN BRITISH LITERATURE

1650 — 1700

1660 Samuel Pepys begins diary

A **1668** John Dryden first official poet laureate

1671 John Milton's *Paradise Regained* published

1690 John Locke publishes essay *Two Treatises on Civil Government* stating natural rights of life, liberty, and property

D **1695** End of prepublication censorship a victory for press freedom

1709 Richard Steele begins periodical *The Tatler,* to which Joseph Addison contributes articles

1711 Addison and Steele begin *The Spectator*

1719 Daniel Defoe's narrative chronicle *Robinson Crusoe* published, considered by many the first novel in English

EVENTS IN BRITAIN

1650 — 1700

1665 Great Plague of London kills thousands

B **1666** Four-day Great Fire of London destroys large section of city

1685 Reign of James II begins (to 1688) ➢

1687 Sir Isaac Newton publishes law of gravity

1689 Parliament passes English Bill of Rights

E **1702** Reign of Anne, last Stuart monarch, begins (to 1714) ➢

1707 England and Scotland united as Great Britain

1714 Reign of George I, first Hanoverian monarch, begins (to 1727)

EVENTS IN THE WORLD

1650 — 1700

C **1661** Louis XIV begins building grand palace at Versailles near Paris

1699 After 17-year war, Austria negotiates control of east-central Europe, ending Turkish presence in region

1703 Peter the Great begins building city of St. Petersburg

1707 Mughal Empire in India breaks into patchwork of independent states

1721 Edo (Tokyo) becomes world's largest city

F **1722** Safavid Empire of Persia collapses from Afghan and Ottoman assaults

Literature: 1695

D The English government had always reviewed, before publication, all manuscripts. Milton and others argued for years against such a practice. The dropping of "prior restraint" was viewed as a great victory for freedom of the press, even though the government retained the right to hold criminal prosecutions after publication of texts voicing "forbidden sentiments."

Britain: 1702

E Under Queen Anne, the rise of the middle class produced a demand for newspapers, magazines, and lending libraries. Rather than depending on the support of aristocratic patrons, writers began to be paid by the booksellers who published their works. The practices of modern publishing, the use of copyright, and royalty fees began to emerge in London at this time.

Period Pieces

Personal cleanliness began to assume more importance. Pictured is a drawing of an 18th-century washstand.

Day-bed, c. 1695

Painted watch dial from latter half of the 18th century

K

1750

1722 Defoe publishes *A Journal of the Plague Year,* fictional narrative of London's deadly plague of 1665–66

1726 Jonathan Swift arranges anonymous delivery of manuscript of *Gulliver's Travels* to London printer

1740 Samuel Richardson's *Pamela* published, considered by others first novel in English

I 1746 Samuel Johnson signs contract to prepare *A Dictionary of the English Language* (published 1755)

1763 James Boswell meets Samuel Johnson, forming 21-year friendship

1768 Publication of *Encyclopaedia Britannica* begins in Scotland

L 1784 William Blake creates "illuminated printing" technique for combining text and illustration

1791 Boswell issues two-volume *Life of Samuel Johnson*

1750

G 1721 Robert Walpole, first political leader to be called prime minister, takes office

1727 Reign of George II begins (to 1760)

1757 British rule over India begins (to 1947)

1760 Reign of George III begins (to 1820)

1763 Britain defeats France in Seven Years' (French and Indian) War, acquiring French Canada

1775 War with colonies in North America begins (to 1781)

1781 American independence acknowledged after Yorktown battle

1784 Religious reformer John Wesley, founder of Methodism, officially splits with Church of England

1788 First British settlement in Australia

1793 War with revolutionary France begins (to 1815)

1750

H 1736 Eventually to lead China to its greatest prosperity, Qian-long becomes emperor (to 1795)

1740 Maria Theresa becomes queen of Austria, Bohemia, and Hungary (to 1780)

1756 Frederick the Great of Prussia starts Seven Years' War fought in Europe, North America, and India

1762 Catherine the Great begins rule of Russia (to 1796)

J 1789 French Revolution starts (to 1794)

1791 Austrian composer genius Wolfgang Amadeus Mozart dies at age 35

1793 French King Louis XVI executed by guillotine

1795 Napoleon Bonaparte's defense of National Convention delegates from rebels makes him savior of French republic

World: 1722

F The Safavids, of Iranian origin, claimed to be descended from the prophet Muhammad. By 1501, they occupied most of modern-day Iran. Their empire's golden age occurred during Abbas the Great's reign (1587–1628). Eventually, weak leadership allowed Ottomans from the west and Afghans from the east to overrun the Safavids.

Britain: 1721

G Though the title *premier ministre* existed in 17th-century France, it was Walpole's appointment as prime minister in England that made the office what it is today. As it has evolved, a prime minister is the chief executive of government in countries with a parliamentary system.

World: 1736

H With its rich ancient culture, isolationist China looked down on foreigners. In 1793, Qian-long received an ambassador from England, who brought gifts such as clocks and musical instruments. In a letter to King George III, Qian-long dismissed these "strange objects," saying that China had no need for England's "manufactures."

Literature: 1746

I The *Dictionary,* compiled almost single-handedly by Johnson, contained definitions for 40,000 words that were accompanied by thousands of quotations to illustrate usage.

World: 1789

J Most historians agree that Enlightenment ideas of individualism and liberty contributed to the revolt, but a more immediate cause was France's bankruptcy. By mid-July, Parisians were going hungry. Soon people demanded guns along with bread. On July 14, agitated by aggressive reformers, crowds of Parisians marched on the Bastille, a Paris prison, looking for gunpowder. In October, bread riots caused thousands of Parisians to march on Versailles and force the king and his family to Paris as prisoners.

Period Pieces

K Watches became so prominent a part of dress that fashionable Englishmen wore one in each vest pocket as a means of displaying their ornate watch fobs, chains, and decorative seals.

Literature: 1784

L Blake pioneered "illuminated printing," a technique of relief etching that engraved text (usually poems) and illustrations on the same metal plate. The printed pages were then usually colored by hand.

OVERVIEW

Introduction
This article provides a historical and literary context for the writings presented in Unit Three. This article describes how the return of the monarchy paved the way for renewed learning and luxury as well as relative stability.

Teaching Nonfiction

Reading Skills and Strategies

ESTABLISHING A PURPOSE FOR READING
Explain that this introductory article introduces students to the period of British history referred to as the Restoration and the Enlightenment. Have students preview the article and establish a purpose for reading.

ANALYZING TEXT STRUCTURE AND USING TEXT ORGANIZERS
Have students scan the article to get a feeling for the period's opulence and attention to learning. Specifically, they should look at the headings and notice that the time period falls into two sections: the concerns of royalty and the advancements brought on by the age of reason. Ask students what they imagine the nearly page-and-a-half of text preceding the first heading will concentrate on.
Possible Response: an introduction to the main article that sets the stage for the reappearance of royal rule into Britain.

IDENTIFYING MAIN IDEAS AND SUMMARIZING
Point out that the headings form sections that become the main ideas of the article. Have students approach the article by reading one section at a time and then thinking about how its idea is developed through important and less important details, and summarizing these main ideas and details.

NOTETAKING
Encourage students to take notes while they read, jotting down important concepts, vocabulary, and terms. They may also want to create graphic organizers to serve as visual connections back to the text.

The Restoration and Enlightenment

1660–1798

The palace and grounds of Versailles, residence of the French king Louis XIV

Charles II wearing finery inspired by the French fashions he saw during his exile

Left: Hand bells were rung to warn of approaching carts filled with victims of the Great Plague of 1665.

[C] *Below:* Sir Christopher Wren designed the new St. Paul's Cathedral (completed 1710) to replace one that had been destroyed by the Great Fire of London in 1666.

After the restoration of the monarchy in 1660, England turned its back on the grim era of Puritan rule and entered a lively period in which the glittering Stuart court set the tone for upper-class social and political life. Charles II had spent much of his long exile in France, absorbing the glamour, elegance, and intrigue of the court of Louis XIV, and after his return to England he and his courtiers tried to emulate the French court's [A] sophistication and splendor. Lords and ladies dressed in rich silks and lace-trimmed finery, wearing elaborate wigs and sparkling jewels. They performed intricate, stately dances at elegant balls and flocked to London's newly reopened theaters. Like Louis XIV, Charles was a patron of the arts and sciences, appointing England's first official poet laureate [B] and chartering the scientific organization known as the Royal Society. Clever and cynical, the king was also extremely self-indulgent, and his excesses both shocked and titillated the English public.

With the Restoration came a return to Anglicanism as England's state religion and a realization that future monarchs would have to share their authority with Parliament, whose influence had increased substantially. An astute

politician, Charles at first won widespread support in Parliament, weathering a series of disasters that included the Great Plague of 1665 and the Great Fire of London a year later. Soon, however, old political rivalries resurfaced, creating two factions that became the nation's chief political parties: the Tories and the Whigs. (D) The Tory party—supporters of royal authority—consisted mainly of landowning aristocrats and conservative Anglicans, who had little tolerance for Protestant dissenters and no desire for war with France. The Whigs, who wanted to limit royal authority, included several powerful nobles as well as wealthy merchants and financiers. Suspicious of the king's Catholic advisers and his pro-French sympathies, the Whigs favored leniency toward Protestant dissenters and sought to curb French expansion in Europe and North America, which they saw as a threat to England's commercial interests.

William and Mary

Political conflict increased when Charles, who had no legitimate children, was succeeded in 1685 by his Catholic brother, James. A blundering, tactless statesman, James II was determined to restore Roman Catholicism as England's state religion, thereby losing the support even of many Tories. As a result, the Whigs in Parliament met with little opposition when they began negotiating to replace James with his Protestant daughter Mary and her husband, the Dutch nobleman William of Orange. In 1688, James was forced to abdicate, and William and Mary took the English throne peacefully in what would become known as the Glorious (or Bloodless)

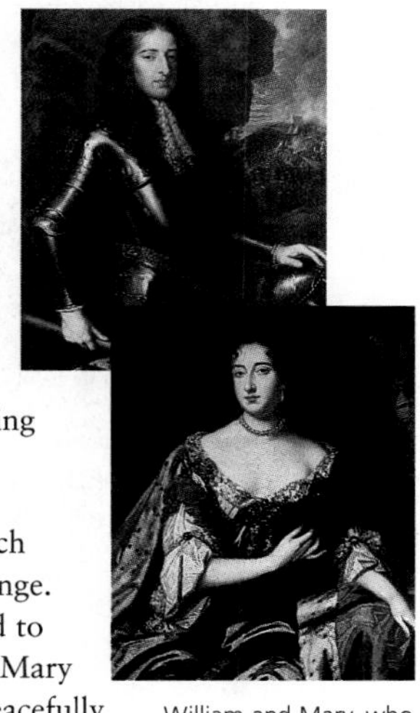

William and Mary, who ruled England jointly after the Glorious Revolution

Development of the English Language

During the Enlightenment, emphasis on reason and logic led to efforts to stabilize and systematize the English language. In 1693 the influential writer John Dryden complained, "We have yet no prosodia, not so much as a tolerable dictionary or grammar, so that our language is in a manner barbarous," and over the next decades scholars worked to remedy the situation. One such scholar was Samuel Johnson, whose *Dictionary of the English Language* was published in 1755. Although Johnson recognized that language is always changing, he also recognized the importance of a standard for pronunciation, usage, and spelling. Seven years later Robert Lowth published *A Short Introduction to English Grammar,* in which he attempted to establish a system of rules for judging correctness in matters under dispute. Since early grammarians like Lowth based their ideas on Latin, however, their rules often proved inappropriate for English. For example, they considered the infinitive form of an English verb to consist of two words ("to stun"); but because Latin infinitives are single words, they deemed it incorrect to "split" an English infinitive with an adverb ("to completely stun"), thus creating a puzzling "rule" that has bedeviled generations of schoolchildren.

Despite the Enlightenment scholars' search for uniformity and stability, overseas colonization was bringing variety and growth to English. New environments demanded new vocabulary, often borrowed from the native languages of the regions (like *raccoon* and *chipmunk* from Native American tongues and kangaroo from the language of Australian Aborigines). (E) In addition, the great distance of the colonies from the homeland and the slow methods of communication allowed differences between the colonists' English and that spoken in Britain to grow.

Making Connections

Social Strata

(A) To reward those who remained loyal during his exile, Charles II was generous in bestowing titles and in elevating nobles to higher ranks (making barons earls, for example). Many members of Britain's upper aristocracy trace their earldoms and dukedoms to Restoration times.

History

(B) The Royal Society received its charter from Charles II in 1662. Taking all human knowledge as its province, it numbered among its members the writer John Dryden, the scientist Robert Boyle (considered the father of modern chemistry), and Isaac Newton, who formulated theories of gravitation, motion, and optics.

Architecture

(C) From 1670 to 1711, Sir Christopher Wren designed 53 London churches. Most are still standing. He helped found the Royal Society, and he is buried in the crypt of St. Paul's. An inscription above his tombstone, put there by his son, reads *Si monumentum requiris, circumspice* ("If you are seeking his monument, look around you").

Politics

(D) Tories and Whigs are ancestors of England's modern political parties. The term *Tory* was first used for Catholic outlaws in Ireland. It was used as a derogatory political name around 1679 for conservative supporters of James II. The Tory Party dissipated after 1832, but members of the modern Conservative Party are sometimes still labeled Tories.

The term *Whig* was a derogatory term for Scottish Presbyterians of the 1600s. It was applied around 1679 to opponents of the succession of Charles II. The Whig Party evolved into the Liberal Party around 1850.

Language

(E) As a result of about 400 years of borrowing foreign words, modern English contains examples of words from most of the languages of the world.

HISTORICAL BACKGROUND 519

Making Connections

Religion

F The Bloodless Revolution was not bloodless in Ireland, where James II found support among Irish Catholics. In 1690, his forces were defeated by those of King William. The Irish Protestants, who lived mainly in the northern countries of the island, became known as Orangemen because they sided with William of Orange. The defeat signaled the beginning of Protestant domination in Ireland, which continues in Northern Ireland to the present day.

Literature

G The reign of Queen Anne was the height of the Augustan Age, when neo-classical writers stressed order and harmony and generally praised the stability and wisdom of the queen's rule. With Anne's death and the advent of the house of Hanover, some of these writers fell from favor and turned to satire to express their dissatisfaction with the changed political scene.

Music

H Though the Hanoverian connection was disruptive for British politics, it was fortuitous for British music. In 1710, while ruler of Hanover, George I had hired George Frideric Handel as his personal music director. Handel then moved to Britain in 1712 for an annual pension under Queen Anne. Soon after George I was installed as king there in 1714, he tripled his former employee's pension. Handel stayed in Britain the rest of his life. It was for George I that Handel composed his famous *Water Music* suite in 1717, and it was under George II, another former Hanoverian ruler, that he composed his masterpiece, *Messiah,* in 1741. Handel became the musical toast of Britain and is buried in Westminster Abbey.

History

I Because the first four monarchs of the house of Hanover were all named George, the period during which they reigned is sometimes called the Georgian era.

Revolution—a triumph of Parliamentary rule over the divine right of kings. The next year, Parliament passed the English Bill of Rights, which put specific limits on royal authority. The remaining supporters of James II—and later those who supported the [F] royal claims of his Catholic son, James Edward Stuart—were known as Jacobites (from *Jacobus,* the Latin form of *James*).

As a Dutchman and a Protestant, King William (who ruled alone after Mary died) was a natural enemy of Catholic France and its expansionist threats to Holland. From the first year of his reign, with Whig support, he took every opportunity to oppose the ambitions of Louis XIV with English military power, beginning a series of wars with France that some historians consider a "Second Hundred Years' War." A year before William's death, Parliament passed the Act of Settlement, which permanently barred Catholics from the throne. In 1702, therefore, the crown passed to Mary's Protestant sister, Anne, a somewhat stodgy but undemanding ruler who faithfully tended to her royal duties. During her reign, Scotland officially united with England to form Great Britain, and war with France continued— [G] although Anne, unlike William, sided with the Tories who opposed it. A peace treaty arranged by her Tory ministers, or advisers, in 1713 procured what was to be only a brief lull in British-French antagonisms.

German-born George I was the first Hanoverian ruler of England.

Portrait of George III with his wife Charlotte and the first 6 of their 15 children

The House of Hanover

Outliving all 16 of her children, Anne was the last monarch of the house of Stuart. With her death in 1714, the crown passed to a distant cousin of hers—the ruler of Hanover in Germany—who as George I became the first ruler of [H] Britain's house of Hanover. The new king spoke no English and was viewed with contempt by many Tories, some of whom supported James Edward

Stuart's bid for the throne in the unsuccessful Jacobite rebellion of 1715. The Whigs, on the other hand, favored the Hanoverian succession and won the new king's loyalty. Because of the language barrier, George I relied heavily on his Whig ministers; and Robert Walpole, the head of the Whig party, emerged as the king's "prime minister" (the first official to be so called)—a position he continued to hold under George II, who succeeded his father in 1727. Toward the end of George II's reign, another able prime minister, William Pitt (the Elder), arose on the political scene. Pitt led the nation to victory over France in the Seven Years' War (called the French and Indian War in America), which resulted in Britain's acquisition of French Canada.

The Seven Years' War was still being fought when George III, grandson of George II, succeeded to the throne in 1760. The first British-born monarch of the house of Hanover, George III sought a more active role in governing the country, but his highhanded ways soon antagonized many. [J] Scornful of the Whigs, George had trouble working with nearly everyone, partly because he suffered from a mental illness that [K] grew worse over the years. During the first few decades of his 60-year reign, he led Britain into a series of political blunders that ultimately resulted in the loss of the American colonies.

In 1770, British soldiers attacked American colonists in the Boston Massacre, one of the events leading to the American Revolution.

Literary History

The literary style that prevailed from the Restoration nearly to the end of the 18th century is called neoclassicism ("new classicism"). Neoclassical writers modeled their works on those of ancient Greece and Rome—especially those of Rome—emulating the supposed restraint, rationality, and dignity of classical writing. Neoclassicists stressed balance, order, logic, sophisticated wit, and emotional restraint, focusing on society and the human intellect and avoiding personal feelings. The neoclassical era in English literature is often divided into three periods: the Restoration (1660–1700), the Augustan Age (1700–1750), and the Age of Johnson (1750–1784).

During the Restoration, drama flourished in England's newly reopened theaters. Influenced by the French "comedy of manners," witty Restoration comedies portrayed and often satirized the artificial, sophisticated society centered in the Stuart court. Equally popular were heroic dramas, tragedies or tragicomedies featuring idealized heroes, dastardly villains, exciting action, and spectacular staging. Although many of the comedies were in prose, the heroic dramas were usually written in heroic couplets (iambic pentameter lines rhyming in pairs), the dominant verse form of the neoclassical period.

Both the Restoration comedies and the heroic dramas appealed primarily to the elite. Attracting a much wider audience was *The Pilgrim's Progress* (1678), a prose allegory by the Puritan John Bunyan, in which he extolled the virtues [L] of faith, hope, and charity and condemned the shallow inhabitants of a worldly place called Vanity Fair. Another great Restoration prose work was the personal diary of Samuel Pepys, not published until 1825.

Making Connections

Politics

J When George III took the throne, the political parties were in a state of flux, and the new king seemed bent on abolishing them altogether. Eventually the Tories emerged as the more organized party; the Whigs, plagued by conflicting views of the French Revolution and Napoleon. remained factionalized for decades.

Medicine

K Some scholars now believe that George III suffered not from mental illness but from porphyria, a genetic abnormality that could not have been diagnosed in his day. Among the symptoms of porphyria are blistering and scarring of the skin and extreme sensitivity to light, along with nervousness, weakness, and paralysis. The 1994 British film *The Madness of King George* portrayed George III's torment with wit and poignancy.

Biography

L One critic has said that except for the Bible and possibly *Robinson Crusoe,* no other book in the English language has been as popular worldwide as *The Pilgrim's Progress.* The non-Puritan world was slow to accept its literary merits, even though Swift and Johnson praised it. Puritans, however, embraced it early as a substitute for the secular literature and theatergoing that strict Puritanism forbade.

HISTORICAL BACKGROUND 521

Making Connections

Philosophy

M To justify the Glorious Revolution, Locke argued that there existed a social contract between governments and the people they governed, guaranteeing the "natural rights" of life, liberty, and property and that any government that failed to uphold those rights should be changed or overthrown. His ideas were echoed nearly a century later in the American colonies' Declaration of Independence.

Crafts/Design

N The fine craftsmanship of the Georgian era is exemplified by the elegant furniture of Chippendale, Hepplewhite, and Sheraton; the classically inspired interiors designed by the Adam brothers; and the work of the landscape architect "Capability" Brown, who thought nothing of moving hills or creating artificial lakes in the attempt to fashion "natural" vistas.

Fashion

O When Parliament was not in session, the most fashionable resort for much of the 18th century was Bath, an architectural gem in southwestern Britain built over mineral springs whose waters were thought to be healthful for drinking and bathing. Toward the end of the century, when doctors began recommending sea bathing, the coastal town of Brighton in southeastern Britain also became a fashionable summertime destination.

Pastimes

P Boxing, cricket, and horseracing became popular sports in the 18th century.

The Age of Reason

Despite recurring warfare with France and the disaster of the American Revolution, the 18th century was a time of relative stability in Britain. The thought of the time was heavily influenced by the Enlightenment, a philosophical movement inspired by the works of such late-17th-century figures as John Locke, the political philosopher who had provided a logical justification for the Glorious Revolution, and Sir Isaac Newton, the scientist who had provided rational explanations of gravity and motion. Order, balance, logic, and reason were the paramount ideals of the day—so much so that the 18th century is often called the Age of Reason. The methods of scientific inquiry were applied to everything from farming to politics. Religion, the source of so much bloodshed a century earlier, became a far less emotional issue, although John Wesley did lead an evangelical revival that gave rise not only to the new Methodist groups but also to a revivalist movement within the Church of England.

Many British citizens lived well during the 18th century, and a few lived sumptuously. Wealthy aristocrats built lavish country estates filled with furnishings of exquisite craftsmanship and surrounded by beautifully tended lawns and gardens. When Parliament was in session, members relocated to their London townhouses on the spacious new streets and squares that had been laid out after the Great Fire. Writers, artists, politicians, and other educated members of society gathered daily in London's coffeehouses to exchange ideas, conduct business, and gossip. Educated women sometimes held salons, or private gatherings, where they too could participate in the nation's intellectual life.

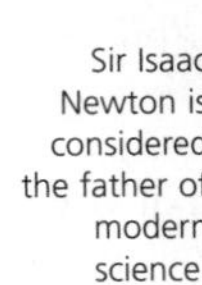

Sir Isaac Newton is considered the father of modern science.

Women at a salon, about 1780

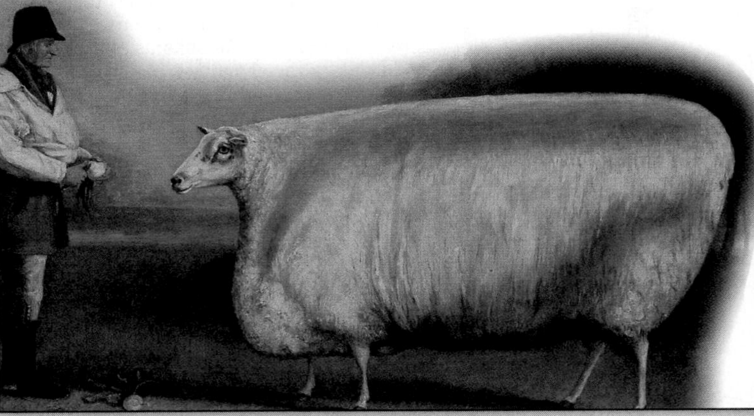

By producing larger animals, breeding experiments led to an improved diet, with more meat for more people.

Mini Lesson: Viewing and Representing

Mr. Healey's Sheep
by W. H. Davis

ART APPRECIATION

Instruction The sheep was painted in 1838 by William Henry Davis (c. 1786–1865), one of the most prolific livestock painters of the mid-19th century. A farmer named Healey feeds his sheep turnips. The sheep is a long-wooled New Leicester, specially bred to produce more meat. Such sheep were so overfed and fat that they could scarcely walk, and their stomachs nearly touched the ground. They looked ridiculous with their tiny heads and very short legs. However, even given the fact that this sheep may have had its coat fluffed and teased before the portrait, the painting of this bloated creature is considered an accurate rendering.

Advances and Changes

The spirit of the Enlightenment led to many improvements in living conditions. Early in the century, Lady Mary Wortley Montagu, the wife of a British ambassador, brought back from Turkey the idea of inoculation to prevent smallpox, and by the end of the 1700s, Edward Jenner had developed an effective smallpox vaccination. Dramatic advances in agriculture helped improve Britain's food supply as wealthy landowners developed more productive methods of cultivating and harvesting crops. Breeding experiments resulted in larger animals: by the end of the century, the average weight of sheep and cattle had more than doubled. Unfortunately, putting these improvements into practice drove thousands of peasant farmers off the land. Increasingly, the open fields that had formerly been available to villagers for livestock grazing were being enclosed into large, separate tracts, held by the prosperous landowners who could then make use of the agricultural innovations. Although this enclosure of the land improved farming efficiency and output, it destroyed the traditional way of life of the English village. Q

Many of the villagers forced off the land sought jobs at the factories that had begun to dot the landscape. Britain, with its wealth of inventions, ample coal and iron, and ready colonial markets, was becoming a pioneer in the use of machines and steam power to manufacture goods that had formerly been made by hand. This Industrial Revolution changed the very fabric of British life. Sleepy towns in the north and west, near the sources of coal, iron, and water power, were transformed into grimy manufacturing centers in which workers—many of them women and children—labored long hours for low pay. By the end of the century, Britain had produced not only a solid commercial and industrial base but also a growing mass of restless, impoverished workers. The stability that had marked 18th-century life was beginning to crumble. R S

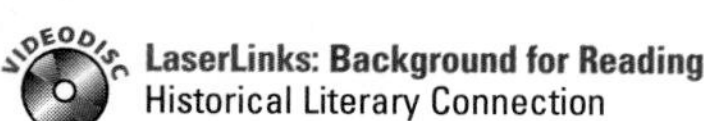

LaserLinks: Background for Reading
Historical Literary Connection

Literary History

Neoclassicism reached its zenith in the Augustan Age—so named because its writers likened their society to that of Rome in the prosperous, stable reign of the emperor Augustus, when the finest Roman literature was produced. An alternative name for the period is the Age of Pope, because Alexander Pope dominated the literary world of the day with his epigrammatic and satiric verses. Satire also characterized the poetry and prose of Jonathan Swift and the essays of Joseph Addison and Richard Steele, which appeared in the early English magazines *The Tatler* and *The Spectator.*

The 18th century also saw the birth of novels as we know them. Early examples of these works of fiction include Daniel Defoe's episodic tale of adventure *Robinson Crusoe,* the sentimental stories of Samuel Richardson, and the comic works of Tobias Smollett and Henry Fielding.

The name "Age of Johnson" is a tribute to Samuel Johnson, Britain's most influential man of letters in the second half of the 18th century. Johnson was at the center of a circle that included his biographer James Boswell, the historian Edward Gibbon, the novelist and diarist Fanny Burney, and the comic dramatist Richard Brinsley Sheridan. Though Johnson and most of his associates affirmed neoclassical ideals, during this time poetry entered a transitional stage in which poets began writing simpler, freer lyrics on subjects close to the human heart. The reflective poetry of Oliver Goldsmith and Thomas Gray and the lyrical songs of Scotland's Robert Burns anticipate the first stirrings of romanticism at the very end of the century. T

Making Connections

Medicine

Q Smallpox—an often fatal, highly infectious disease—is marked by high fever and skin lesions similar to but deeper than those of chickenpox. The method of inoculation introduced by Lady Mary Wortley Montagu was replaced by Jenner's more effective vaccination, which gave the inoculated person the related but nonfatal disease of cowpox, thereby rendering him or her immune to smallpox.

Technology

R James Hargreave's spinning jenny (which twisted and wound cotton or wool fibers into 8 to 11 threads at once) and James Watt's improvements to the steam engine were among the most significant of the many new technologies spurring the Industrial Revolution in Britain.

Technology

S After 1860, new turnpikes helped producers bring their goods to market and substantially reduced transportation costs. The cheapest and fastest way to move goods, however, was by water: Natural inland waterways were supplemented by artificial ones, beginning with the Duke of Bridgewater's canal, which opened in 1761 to transport coal from the Worsley mines to Manchester.

Literature

T Gibbon's masterpiece, *The History of the Decline and Fall of the Roman Empire* (1776–1788), is often cited as the greatest historical work in the English language. Sheridan's stage comedies include *The Rivals* (1775), with its famous character of Mrs. Malaprop, whose humorous misuse of sound-alike words ("Illiterate him . . . from your memory") is enshrined in the term *malapropism.*

PART 1 Views of Society

In the late 17th and early 18th centuries, English writers sought to make sense of their world by observing human society and reflecting on both its positive and negative attributes. In this part of Unit Three, some of the writers of the time offer their views on the restored monarchy, human nature, the proper behavior of children, and the role of women in society. As you read the selections, decide what these observations reveal about English society of this era.

524

"By and by Jane comes and tells me that she hears that above 300 houses have been burned down tonight by the fire we saw."

from The Diary of Samuel Pepys

By SAMUEL PEPYS (pēps)

Connect to Your Life

Exaggeration and Honesty Many people exaggerate when relating stories about themselves. Think of people you know who exaggerate their own qualities and experiences. Which do they tend to exaggerate most—their good qualities or their bad ones? Do you know any people who always describe their experiences honestly, giving a balanced, candid portrayal of themselves and their activities? Discuss these questions with classmates.

Build Background

Public and Private Events Few descriptions of daily life in any period of history are as vivid as those found in *The Diary of Samuel Pepys*—a rare firsthand account of events that occurred over 300 years ago. Begun in 1660, the historic year of the Restoration, the **diary** not only records the drama of public events but also provides a candid portrayal of the social and domestic life of a middle-class Londoner. Although Samuel Pepys wrote his diary in shorthand to ensure the privacy of his thoughts, he was undoubtedly aware of its immense value to future generations, since he eventually bequeathed his library, including the diary, to Cambridge University.

Pepys had an intimate view of some of the most dramatic events of his time. As personal secretary to a British admiral, he was aboard the ship on which King Charles II returned to England after a long exile in France. He also witnessed the Great Fire of London in 1666, which destroyed more than 13,000 homes, at least 80 churches, and most of London's government buildings.

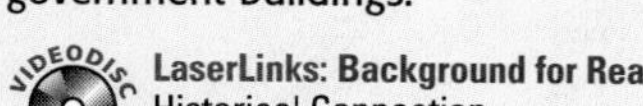

LaserLinks: Background for Reading
Historical Connection

Focus Your Reading

LITERARY ANALYSIS DIARY A **diary** is a writer's personal day-to-day account of his or her experiences and impressions. *The Diary of Samuel Pepys* is an example of a well-written diary of great historical interest. As you read these excerpts from the diary, note how Pepys discusses matters of both personal and public concern.

ACTIVE READING MAKING INFERENCES ABOUT CHARACTER TRAITS In reading a diary, one of the things you can **make inferences** about is the dominant **character traits** of the writer of the diary. As you read, certain qualities or characteristics of the person will come to seem particularly important. To make inferences about Pepys's character, note details about his words and actions that seem to reveal something about his character.

READER'S NOTEBOOK Use a chart like the one shown to list the character traits that you think Samuel Pepys possessed. Cite evidence from the selection to support the traits you identify.

Traits	Evidence

LESSON RESOURCES

UNIT THREE RESOURCE BOOK, pp. 4–8

ASSESSMENT RESOURCES
Formal Assessment, pp. 85–86
Teacher's Guide to Assessment and Portfolio Use
Test Generator

SKILLS TRANSPARENCIES AND COPYMASTERS
Reading and Critical Thinking
- Evaluating Credibility of Information Sources, T43 (for Active Reading, p. 532)

Grammar
- Diagramming Subjects, Verbs, and Modifiers, T58 (for Mini Lesson, p. 530)
- Types of Adjective Phrases, C90 (for Mini Lesson, p. 530)

Vocabulary
- Word Origins, C50 (for Mini Lesson, p. 527)

Writing
- Proposal, C28 (for Writing Options, p. 533)

INTEGRATED TECHNOLOGY
Audio Library
LaserLinks
- Historical Connection: The London of Samuel Pepys. See **Teacher's SourceBook,** pp. 32–33.

Internet: Research Starter
Visit our website:
www.mcdougallittell.com

OVERVIEW

Objectives
1. understand and appreciate excerpts from a **diary** that explores life in 17th-century London **(Literary Analysis)**
2. identify and understand the purposes and characteristics of a **diary (Literary Analysis)**
3. **make inferences** about **character traits** based upon details in a diary **(Active Reading)**

Summary
Samuel Pepys's diary includes eyewitness accounts of the restoration of the monarchy in 1660, the coronation of Charles II in 1661, and the Great Fire of London in 1666. Pepys also describes personal social activities, such as giving a dinner party and attending a church service, a theatrical performance, and a prize fight. He further describes a difficult scene between himself and his wife, who suspects him of infidelity.

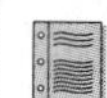

Use **Unit Three Resource Book,** pp. 4–5 for additional support.

Thematic Link
Pepys was a keen observer of the world around him, of his home life, of life in London, and of the greater political life of England. His curiosity led him not just to keep a diary in which he recorded his **views of society,** but to study every subject available to him.

5-Minute Warm-Up
Daily Language SkillBuilder

Have students **proofread** the display sentences on page 515k and write them correctly. The sentences also appear on Transparency 12 of **Grammar Transparencies and Copymasters.**

EDITOR'S NOTE
This selection contains material that may be considered objectionable.

TEACHING THE LITERATURE

Reading and Analyzing

Literary Analysis DIARY

Writing daily accounts of events is bound to contrast with writing that summarizes longer periods of time. What details of Pepys's account would probably be omitted from histories of Charles II written after his coronation?

Possible Response: Subsequent writers would not report the sensory details of colors, etc. They would be more focused on developing an idea about the king's reign.

 Use **Unit Three Resource Book,** p. 7 for more exercises.

Active Reading

MAKING INFERENCES ABOUT CHARACTER TRAITS

A Why is Pepys surprised to find the king walking about upon his return to England? Why do you think that Pepys thought the king would be less active or less visible? What inferences can be drawn about the king's character from the fact that he behaves as he does?

Possible Response: Pepys may have imagined the king to be older or more aloof than he turns out to be. However, the king seems to want to engage with his subjects and seems to have been invigorated by his adventures.

 Use **Unit Three Resource Book,** p. 6 for more practice.

from

THE DIARY OF Samuel Pepys

Samuel Pepys (1666), John Hayls. Oil on canvas. The Granger Collection, New York. *Frame:* The last page of Pepys's diary. Courtesy of The Master and Fellows, Magdalene College, Cambridge, U.K.

SAMUEL PEPYS

Teaching Options

Viewing and Representing

Samuel Pepys **by John Hayls**

ART APPRECIATION In his diary, Pepys recalls his satisfaction with this portrait that he commissioned. He is wearing a rented Indian robe and holding a piece of music he composed.

Instruction Portraits are always the products of composition; that is, they represent an agreement between the patron and the artist. During the 17th century, portraits were increasingly commissioned by individuals to influence how they wished to be perceived. Setting was important, for it told the viewer how the subject saw his role in society and something about his interests, intentions, and values. Backgrounds converted ideas into objects, which were read by the viewer as symbols.

Application Ask students to describe Samuel Pepys. What ideas does Pepys convey about himself in this portrait which he commissioned of John Hayls? (The manuscript used as a background for Pepys's portrait is the actual last page of his diary. However, the diary itself was unknown to Pepys's contemporaries, and was not completely deciphered until 1825.)

The Restoration of Charles II

1660

March 16. . . . To Westminster Hall, where I heard how the Parliament had this day dissolved themselves[1] and did pass very cheerfully through the Hall and the Speaker without his mace.[2] The whole Hall was joyful thereat, as well as themselves; and now they begin to talk loud of the King. . . .

May 22. . . . News brought that the two dukes are coming on board, which, by and by they did in a Dutch boat, the Duke of York in yellow trimming, the Duke of Gloucester in gray and red. My Lord[3] went in a boat to meet them, the captain, myself, and others standing at the entering port. . . .

A *May 23.* . . . All the afternoon the King walking here and there, up and down (quite contrary to
1 what I thought him to have been), very active and stirring. Upon the quarter-deck he fell in discourse of his escape from Worcester.[4] Where it made me ready to weep to hear the stories that he told of his difficulties that he had passed through. As his traveling four days and three nights on foot, every step up to his knees in dirt, with nothing but a green coat and a pair of country breeches on and a pair of country shoes, that made him so sore all over his feet that he could scarce stir. Yet he was forced to run away from a miller and other company that took them for rogues. His sitting at table at one place, where the master of the house, that had not seen him in eight years, did know him but kept it private; when at the same table there was one that had been of his own regiment at Worcester, could not know him but made him drink the King's health and said that the King was at least four fingers higher than he. Another place, he was by some servants of the house made to drink, that they might know him not to be a Roundhead,[5] which they swore he was. In another place, at his inn, the master of the house, as the King was standing with his hands upon the back of a chair by the fire-side, he kneeled down and kissed his hand privately, saying that he would not ask him who he was, but bid God bless him whither that he was going. . . .

The Coronation of the King

1661

April 23. . . . About 4 in the morning I rose. . . . And got to the Abbey,[6] . . . where with a great deal of patience I sat from past 4 till 11 before the King came in. And a pleasure it was to see the Abbey raised in the middle, all covered with red and a throne (that is a chair) and footstool on the top of it. And all the officers of all kinds, so much as the very fiddlers, in red vests. At last comes in the dean and prebends of Westminster with the bishops (many of them in cloth-of-gold copes[7]); and after them the nobility all in their parliament-robes, which was a most magnificent sight. Then

1. **Parliament . . . themselves:** This Parliament abolished the government established by Oliver Cromwell and restored the monarchy under Charles II, who had been living in exile in France.
2. **mace:** a staff used as a symbol of authority.
3. **my Lord:** Sir Edward Montagu, Pepys's employer, who was in command of the fleet that brought Charles II back to England.
4. **his escape from Worcester** (wo͝os'tər): Charles II, at the head of a Scottish army, had been defeated by Cromwell's troops at the Battle of Worcester in 1651. He had gone into hiding, journeyed secretively to the coast, and escaped to France.
5. **Roundhead:** a supporter of Cromwell's Puritan government.
6. **Abbey:** Westminster Abbey, the London church where monarchs are crowned.
7. **copes:** long robes worn by church officials while performing services or rites.

Customizing Instruction

Less Proficient Readers

Samuel Pepys's diary contains entries that describe history-making events from a personal point of view. Invite students to discuss some more recent history-making events from their point of view. Encourage them to discuss where they were, what they thought, and whether the event had an immediate or long-term impact on their lives. Remind students to keep their feelings in mind as they read Pepys's accounts of events recorded in his diary.

Students Acquiring English

1 The informal writing of a diary may break some of the rules of formal writing. For example, Pepys writes in sentence fragments, using participles only. Note his entry for May 23: "the King walking . . . his traveling, . . . his sitting. . . ." Urge students to complete these sentences as they read to enhance their comprehension.

Use **Spanish Study Guide** for additional support, pp. 109–112.

Gifted and Talented

Have students consider the following questions as they read: What might the reception of Pepys's diary have been had it been published during his lifetime? What is the value of his diary today? Have students keep in mind that Pepys wrote in shorthand, which was not common in his day, to hide any potentially objectionable material.

Mini Lesson Vocabulary Strategy

WORD ORIGINS Have students research the word origins of the following words as an aid to understanding meaning: *mace, prebend, cope, scepter, mond.* Students may also choose to illustrate a mace, a scepter, and a mond; or they may choose to seek examples of these in art from the 17th century.

1. *mace*—an ornamental staff modeled after a heavy, often spiked club used in the Middle Ages to break armor, from the Latin *mateola*, mallet
2. *prebend*—clergy who receive a stipend, from the Latin *praebendus,* to offer
3. *cope*—a long, enveloping ecclesiastical gown, from the Latin *cappa*, head covering
4. *scepter*—a staff borne by a sovereign as a symbol of authority, from the Latin *sceptrum*, scepter
5. *mond*—the orb, a sphere with a cross on top, used first in the coronation of Charles II, from the French *monde*, world

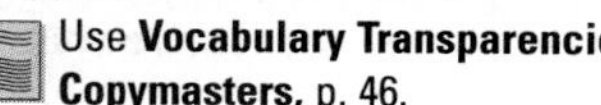

Use **Vocabulary Transparencies and Copymasters,** p. 46.

Reading and Analyzing

Literary Analysis DIARY

Ask students how Pepys's diary entry about the fire conveys a sense of the devastation and personal loss. Invite students to share specific sentences, phrases, or passages that they find particularly revealing.

Possible Responses: ". . . above 300 houses have been burned . . .", "Everybody endeavoring to remove their goods, . . .", "seeing people almost distracted and no manner of means to quench the fire."

Active Reading

MAKING INFERENCES ABOUT CHARACTER TRAITS

A After students have read the section on the Great Fire, have them make a chart of Pepys's responses to the disaster and what these responses suggest about his personal qualities.

RESPONSE	PERSONAL QUALITY
After looking out the window, he returns to bed.	imperturbable

Reading Skills and Strategies

MAKING INFERENCES

Ask students to interpret the reason that Lord Albemarle went to the kitchen and ate a bit of the first dish that was to go to the king's table.

Possible Response: Lord Albemarle may have been the king's taster; it would have been his duty to taste the king's food to make sure it had not been altered in some way that could harm the king.

the duke and the King with a scepter (carried by my Lord of Sandwich) and sword and mond[8] before him, and the crown too.

The King in his robes, bare-headed, which was very fine. And after all had placed themselves—there was a sermon and the service. And then in the choir at the high altar he passed all the ceremonies of the coronation—which, to my very great grief, I and most in the Abbey could not see. The crown being put upon his head, a great shout begun. And he came forth to the throne and there passed more ceremonies: as, taking the oath and having things read to him by the bishop, and his lords (who put on their caps as soon as the King put on his crown) and bishops came and kneeled before him. And three times the king-at-arms[9] went to the three open places on the scaffold and proclaimed that if any one could show any reason why Ch. Stuart[10] should not be King of England, that now he should come and speak. And a general pardon also was read by the Lord Chancellor; and medals flung up and down by my Lord Cornwallis—of silver; but I could not come by any.

But so great a noise, that I could make but little of the music; and indeed, it was lost to everybody. . . . I went out a little while before the King had done all his ceremonies and went round the Abbey to Westminster Hall, all the way within rails, and 10,000 people, with the ground covered with blue cloth—and scaffolds all the way. Into the hall I got—where it was very fine with hangings and scaffolds, one upon another, full of brave ladies. And my wife in one little one on the right hand. Here I stayed walking up and down; and at last, upon one of the side-stalls, I stood and saw the King come in with all the persons (but the soldiers) that were yesterday in the cavalcade; and a most pleasant sight it was to see them in their several robes. And the King came in with his crown on and his scepter in his hand—under a canopy borne up by six silver staves, carried by barons of the Cinque Ports[11]—and little bells at every end.

And after a long time he got up to the farther end, and all set themselves down at their several tables—and that was also a rare sight. And the King's first course carried up by the Knights of the Bath. And many fine ceremonies there was of the heralds leading up people before him and bowing; and my Lord of Albemarle going to the kitchen and ate a bit of the first dish that was to go to the Kings's table. . . . **1**

The Great London Fire

1666

A

September 2. (Lord's day) Some of our maids sitting up late last night to get things ready against our feast today, Jane called us up, about 3 in the morning, to tell us of a great fire they saw in the city. So I rose, and slipped on my nightgown and went to her window, and thought it to be on the back side of Mark Lane at the furthest; but being unused to such fires as followed, I thought it far enough off, and so went to bed again and to sleep. About 7 rose again to dress myself, and there looked out at the window and saw the fire not so much as it was, and further off. So to my closet to set things to rights after yesterday's cleaning. By and by Jane comes and tells me that she hears that above 300 houses have been burned down tonight by the fire we saw, and that it was now burning down all Fish Street by London Bridge. So I made myself ready presently, and walked to the Tower[12] and there got up upon one of the high places, Sir J. Robinson's little son

8. **mond:** a sphere with a cross on top, used as a symbol of royal power and justice.
9. **king-at-arms:** one of the chief heralds assigned to make official proclamations.
10. **Ch. Stuart:** Charles Stuart. (Charles II was one of the Stuart line of English monarchs.)
11. **Cinque** (sĭngk) **Ports:** a group of seaports of southeastern England that formed a defensive association.
12. **Tower:** the Tower of London, a group of buildings built as a fortress and later used as a royal residence and a prison for political offenders.

Teaching Options

Assessment **Standardized Test Practice**

IDENTIFYING A WRITER'S PURPOSE, POINT OF VIEW, AND INTENDED MEANING For some standardized tests, students will be asked to analyze content and phrasing to determine a writer's opinion or point of view. To provide students with some help in identifying the writer's opinion or point of view, read aloud or write on the chalkboard the following question.

Which of the following details best illustrates Samuel Pepys's view that, although the fire was obviously large and spreading through London, there was no danger to him or his household?

A. Pepys walked to the Tower where he could get a better view of the fire.

B. Pepys looked out the window and speculated that the fire was a good distance from his house.

C. Pepys arose at 7:00 to dress and then set about arranging his closet after it had been cleaned.

D. Pepys said that he was not used to such fires, which indicates he did not realize that there may have been danger to his house.

The Great Fire of London (1666), Dutch school. The Granger Collection, New York.

going up with me; and there I did see the houses at that end of the bridge all on fire, and an infinite great fire on this and the other side the end of the bridge—which, among other people, did trouble me for poor little Michell and our Sarah on the bridge.[13] So down, with my heart full of trouble, to the Lieutenant of the Tower, who tells me that it begun this morning in the King's baker's house in Pudding Lane, and that it hath burned down St. Magnus Church and most part of Fish Street already. So I down to the water-side and there got a boat and through bridge, and there saw a lamentable fire. Poor Michell's house, as far as the Old Swan, already burned that way and the fire running further, that in a very little time it got as far as the steelyard while I was there. Everybody endeavoring to remove their goods, and flinging into the river or bringing them into lighters that lay off. Poor people staying in their houses as long as till the very fire touched them, and then running into boats or clambering from one pair of stair by the water-side to another. And among other things, the poor pigeons I perceive were loath to leave their houses, but hovered about the windows and balconies till they were some of them burned, their wings, and fell down.

. . . At last met my Lord Mayor in Canning Street, like a man spent, with a handkerchief about his neck. To the King's message, he cried like a fainting woman, "Lord, what can I do? I am spent. People will not obey me. I have been pull[ing] down houses. But the fire overtakes us faster than we can do it." That he needed no more soldiers; and that for himself, he must go and refresh himself, having been up all night. So he left me, and I him, and walked home—seeing people all almost distracted and no manner of means used to quench the fire. The houses too, so very thick thereabouts, and full of matter for burning, as pitch and tar, in Thames Street—and warehouses of oil and wines and brandy and other things. . . .

13. **on the bridge:** in one of the houses on Old London Bridge. (London was so crowded that this bridge bore an entire superstructure of houses and shops.)

Customizing Instruction

Less Proficient Readers

Invite students to describe an important ceremony they have observed in person or on television. Then, have them read the description of King Charles's coronation. Encourage students to discuss how King Charles's coronation might be covered in a television news special.

Students Acquiring English

1 Explain that *rare* here means not just "unique or unusual" but also "excellent or fine." What are the "rare sights" that Pepys mentions?

Possible Response: The nobility in their parliament robes; the king, bareheaded and in his robes; the decorated hall; the procession into the hall; the king and his entourage at their tables; the knights carrying the first course; the bowing.

Gifted and Talented

Have students choose someone that was at the coronation and write diary entries as that character to describe the coronation. Students should keep in mind that participants in the coronation will have a very different perspective of the ceremony from the citizens observing on the sidelines. Students may choose to do some research on Charles II and on the coronation ceremony of the time.

Multiple Learning Styles

Auditory Learners

Play court music of the 17th century, such as pieces by Michael Praetorious or Henry Purcell, for students. Have them describe the atmosphere created by this music.

Lead students through the process of choosing the best response. Consider each choice and point out that each statement contains accurate information from the selection. The best choice should contain the most revealing information about Pepys's attitude toward the danger of the fire. Therefore, C is the best choice because Pepys chose to rise at his normal time, dress, and then arrange his closet. If Pepys perceived any danger, it seems unlikely that he would have bothered to put his closet in order before fleeing from the fire.

Reading and Analyzing

Reading Skills and Strategies: NOTING DETAILS

Draw up a floor plan of the Pepys house, based on the entries of January 13, 1663, and January 12, 1669.

Possible Response: The Pepys house seems to have more than one fireplace—one in each of the chambers and one in the kitchen. The kitchen seems to be downstairs and the dining room above. Mrs. Pepys seems to have her own bedroom.

Reading Skills and Strategies: EVALUATING CREDIBILITY OF SOURCES

Discuss disasters and the way people respond during a disaster. Are people completely reliable witnesses? Why or why not? Discuss Pepys's description of the Great Fire. Is he a reliable witness? Why or why not?

Possible Response: Students may find that he is reliable in regard to what he describes.

Could a historian depend solely on Pepys's descriptions? Why or why not?

Possible Response: Pepys did not have access to all aspects of the disaster, but he could be, and is today, relied upon for what he did record.

Having seen as much as I could now, I away to Whitehall[14] by appointment, and there walked to St. James's Park, and there met my wife and Creed and Wood and his wife and walked to my boat, and there upon the water again, and to the fire up and down, it still increasing and the wind great. So near the fire as we could for smoke; and all over the Thames,[15] with one's face in the wind you were almost burned with a shower of firedrops—this is very true—so as houses were burned by these drops and flakes of fire, three or four, nay five or six houses, one from another. When we could endure no more upon the water, we to a little alehouse on the bankside over against the Three Cranes, and there stayed till it was dark almost and saw the fire grow; and as it grew darker, appeared more and more, and in corners and upon steeples and between churches and houses, as far as we could see up the hill of the city, in a most horrid malicious bloody flame, not like the fine flame of an ordinary fire. Barbary and her husband away before us. We stayed till, it being darkish, we saw the fire as only one entire arch of fire from this to the other side the bridge, and in a bow up the hill, for an arch of above a mile long. It made me weep to see it. The churches, houses, and all on fire and flaming at once, and a horrid noise the flames made, and the cracking of houses at their ruin. So home with a sad heart, and there find everybody discoursing and lamenting the fire. . . .

September 3. About 4 o'clock in the morning, my Lady Batten sent me a cart to carry away all my money and plate and best things to Sir W. Rider's at Bethnal Green; which I did, riding myself in my nightgown in the cart; and Lord, to see how the streets and the highways are crowded with people, running and riding and getting of carts at any rate to fetch away thing[s]. . . .

September 8. . . . I met with many people undone, and more that have extraordinary great losses. People speaking their thoughts variously about the beginning of the fire and the rebuilding of the city. . . .

September 20. . . . In the afternoon out by coach, my wife with me (which we have not done several weeks now), through all the ruins to show her them, which frets her much—and is a sad sight indeed. . . .

September 25. . . . So home to bed—and all night still mightily troubled in my sleep with fire and houses pulling down.

Domestic Affairs

1663

January 13. So my poor wife rose by 5 o'clock in the morning, before day, and went to market and bought fowl and many other things for dinner—with which I was highly pleased. And the chine of beef was down also before 6 o'clock, and my own jack,[16] of which I was doubtful, doth carry it very well. Things being put in order and the cook come, I went to the office, where we sat till noon; and then broke up and I home—whither by and by comes Dr. Clerke and his lady—his sister and a she-cousin, and Mr. Pierce and his wife, which was all my guest[s].

I had for them, after oysters—at first course, a hash of rabbits and lamb, and a rare chine of beef—next, a great dish of roasted fowl, cost me about 30*s*, and a tart; and then fruit and cheese. My dinner was noble and enough. I had my house mighty clean and neat, my room below with a good fire in it—my dining-room above, and my chamber being made a withdrawing-chamber, and my wife's a good fire also. I find my new table very proper, and will hold nine or ten people well, but eight with great room. After dinner, the women to cards in my wife's chamber and the doctor [and] Mr. Pierce in mine, because the dining-room smokes unless I keep a good charcoal fire, which I was not then provided with. . . .

14. **Whitehall:** a wide road in London, the location of many government offices.
15. **Thames** (tĕmz): the principal river flowing through London.
16. **jack:** a device for roasting meat.

Teaching Options

Grammar

TYPES OF ADJECTIVE PHRASES

Instruction Just like adjectives, certain types of phrases—prepositional, participial, and infinitive—modify nouns and pronouns. These phrases are called adjective phrases.

Activity Write on the chalkboard the following excerpt from Samuel Pepys's diary. Underline the phrases as shown here.

> **"September 3.** About 4 o'clock in the morning, my Lady Batten sent me a cart to carry away all my money and plate and best things to Sir W. Rider's at Bethnal Green; which I did, riding myself in my nightgown in the cart; and Lord, to see how the streets and the highways are crowded with people, running and riding and getting of carts at any rate to fetch away thing[s]. . . ."

Identify for the students the types of adjective phrases underlined in the examples. *(prepositional phrase; infinitive phrase; participial phrase)* Ask them to name the preposition, infinitive, or participle that begins its respective phrase. *(in; to carry; running and riding and getting)* Then ask them to identify the noun or pronoun that each one modifies. *(4 o'clock, cart, people)*

October 21. This evening after I came home, I begun to enter my wife in arithmetic, in order to her studying of the globes,[17] and she takes it very well—and I hope with great pleasure I shall bring her to understand many fine things. 3

1667

January 7. . . . To the duke's house and saw *Macbeth;* which though I saw it lately, yet appears a most excellent play in all respects, but especially in divertisement,[18] though it be a deep tragedy; which is a strange perfection in a tragedy, it being most proper here and suitable. . . .

1 *May 26.* (Lord's day) . . . After dinner, I by water alone to Westminster . . . toward the parish church. . . . I did entertain myself with my perspective glass[19] up and down the church, by which I had the great pleasure of seeing and gazing a great many very fine women; and what with that and sleeping, I passed away the time till sermon was done. . . .

2 *May 27.* . . . Stopped at the Bear Garden[20] stairs, there to see a prize fought; but the house so full, there was no getting in there; so forced to [go] through an alehouse into the pit where the bears are baited, and upon a stool did see them fight, which they did very furiously, a butcher and a waterman. The former had the better all along, till by and by the latter dropped his sword out of his hand, and the butcher, whether not seeing his sword dropped or I know not, but did give him a cut over the wrist, so as he was disabled to fight any longer. But Lord, to see how in a minute the whole stage was full of watermen to revenge the foul play, and the butchers to defend their fellow, though most blamed him; and there they all fell to it, to knocking down and cutting many of each side. It was pleasant to see, but that I stood in the pit and feared that in the tumult I might get some hurt. At last the rabble broke up, and so I away. . . .

1669

January 12. . . . This evening I observed my wife mighty dull; and I myself was not mighty fond, because of some hard words she did give me at noon, out of a jealousy at my being abroad this morning; when, God knows, it was upon the business of the office unexpectedly; but I to bed, not thinking but she would come after me; but waking by and by out of a slumber, which I usually fall into presently after my coming into the bed, I found she did not prepare to come to bed, but got fresh candles and more wood for her fire, it being mighty cold too. At this being troubled, I after a while prayed her to come to bed, all my people being gone to bed; so after an hour or two, she silent, and I now and then praying her to come to bed, she fell out into a fury, that I was a rogue and false to her. . . . At last, about 1 o'clock, she came to my side of the bed and drew my curtain open, and with the tongs, red hot at the ends, made as if she did design to pinch me with them; at which in dismay I rose up, and with a few words she laid them down and did by little and little, very sillily, let all the discourse fall; and about 2, but with much seeming difficulty, came to bed and there lay well all night. . . .

17. **the globes:** geography (the terrestrial globe) and astronomy (the celestial globe).
18. **divertisement** (dĭ-vûr′tĭs-mənt): diversion; amusement.
19. **perspective glass:** small telescope.
20. **Bear Garden:** an establishment in which bears were chained to a post and tormented by dogs as a form of entertainment. It was also the site of scheduled fights between men.

Customizing Instruction

Less Proficient Readers

1 Have students reread the entry. What two things did Pepys do during the sermon?

Answer: look at women, sleep.

What is Pepys's attitude toward his own behavior?

Possible Response: He is quite pleased with himself.

Students Acquiring English

2 Point out to students that Pepys is hard to follow in the description of the fight. He seems to be saying he saw the bears fight, but he is clearly describing two men fighting, the butcher and the waterman.

Gifted and Talented

Ask students to compare the forms of entertainment mentioned in Pepys's diary. What do these different activities reveal about life in London during the Restoration? What do the activities reveal about the status of women in society?

Multiple Learning Styles

Visual or Kinesthetic Learners

3 Have students create a cartoon strip showing the development of relations between Pepys and his wife. Students may choose to add dialogue to what is already in the entry.

Exercise For each underlined phrase, have students name what type of adjective phrase it is, and note which noun or pronoun it modifies. Students can meet in pairs or cooperative groups to find additional prepositional phrases used as adjectives.

1. Pepys's diary is a historical record about public and private events in London in the late 1600s. *(prepositional phrase; "record")*
2. Pepys was not one to avoid public events. *(infinitive phrase; "one")*
3. Witnessing the Great London Fire as he did, Pepys was awed by how fast it spread from house to house. *(participial phrase;* "Pepys")
4. The fire caused chaos in the streets with people riding and rushing carts in every direction. *(participial phrase; "people")*
5. To show his wife the aftermath of the fire, he drove her in a coach through the streets of London. *(prepositional phrase; "aftermath")*

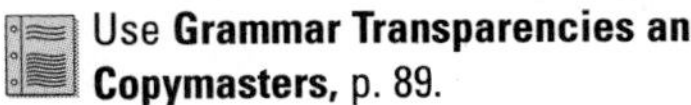
Use **Grammar Transparencies and Copymasters,** p. 89.

Use McDougal Littell's ***Language Network*** for more instruction in adjective phrases.

GUIDING STUDENT RESPONSE

Connect to the Literature

1. What Do You Think?
Guidelines for student response: Students should explain their answers with examples from the selection.

Comprehension Check
- Pepys is full of sympathy for the king, who is only three years older than Pepys. He rejoices in his stories of narrow escape and the splendor with which the monarchy has made its return.
- He portrays them sympathetically, troubled by the refugees from the fire, their distress, and the energy they must expend to save their things.

 Use Selection Quiz **Unit Three Resource Book,** p. 8.

Think Critically

2. Possible Response: Pepys's purpose must be related to his sense that the restoration of the monarchy was a great moment in English history and that, being part of it, he was a witness to the life in an important capital city.
3. Be sure students support their response with personal experience and evidence from the text. Pepys is curious, loyal to the monarchy, interested in sights, not very interested in serious content of sermons or plays, attracted to women, and pleased with himself.
4. Various answers are possible. The choices are not mutually exclusive. To the extent that he exaggerates his best qualities, he might be considered exceptionally candid, if one believes that people should practice modesty.

Connect to the Literature

1. **What Do You Think?** Which of Pepys's entries was the most interesting?

Comprehension Check
- What is Pepys's attitude toward the return of King Charles II?
- How does Pepys portray the victims of the fire?

Think Critically

2. What do you think might have been Pepys's **purpose** in keeping his diary?

THINK ABOUT
- the variety of events he describes
- what types of people he chooses to describe
- whether his observations are primarily objective or subjective

3. ACTIVE READING MAKING INFERENCES ABOUT CHARACTER TRAITS On the basis of the entries you have read, what would you say are Pepys's main **character traits?** Support your answer with evidence from the selection. You may want to refer to the chart of personality traits of Pepys that you developed in your  READER'S NOTEBOOK.

4. Does Pepys seem to you to give a candid portrayal of himself, or do you think he exaggerates his best qualities? Explain your answer.

Extend Interpretations

5. **Critic's Corner** The author Virginia Woolf once said that the "chief delight" of Pepys's diary might be its revelation of "those very weaknesses and idiosyncrasies which in our own case we would die rather than reveal." What do you think Woolf meant? What effect do Pepys's "weaknesses" have on you as you read the diary?

6. **Different Perspectives** Imagine that the Lord Mayor of London were writing his account of the great fire and his encounter with Pepys while the fire raged. How might the mayor's account of their conversation differ from Pepys's account?

7. **Connect to Life** Suppose that Pepys were living today and had witnessed a recent memorable event—for example, an inauguration, a meeting of world leaders, or a natural disaster, such as a hurricane, an earthquake, or a flood. What aspects of the event would he most likely highlight in his **diary?**

Literary Analysis

DIARY Most diaries are private and not intended to be shared. Some, however, have been published because they are well written and provide useful perspectives on historical events or on the everyday life of particular eras. In the following passage from Pepys's diary, notice the glimpse into the writer's domestic life even as he reports the Great Fire of London:

Some of our maids sitting up late last night to get things ready against our feast today, Jane called us up, about 3 in the morning, to tell us of a great fire they saw in the city.

Paired Activity What unique insights into a public event might be found in a diary but not in a more formal account of the event? With a partner, draw up a list of the kinds of insights that might be found in a diary. Include examples from Pepys's diary. Share your list with the class.

ACTIVE READING EVALUATING CREDIBILITY OF SOURCES
Diaries can be valuable sources of information about the period in which they are written. To evaluate the credibility of a diary, you need to consider the writer's motivation, the objectivity of observations and descriptions, and the relationship of the diary to other sources of information about the period. How would you describe Pepys's motivation for writing his diary? Do you think the diary would be a reliable source of information about life in England in the late 17th century?

Literary Analysis

Paired Activity Students might make up a composite list to display in the classroom.

Active Reading You might mention other famous diaries that students can look at for the purposes of comparison. Jonathan Swift and Fanny Burney, two other writers in this unit, also kept diaries.

Extend Interpretations

Critic's Corner Woolf may have thought that few people would admit they went to church to look at attractive members of the opposite sex and sleep through the sermon. Reading Pepys may have different effects on different students, depending on whether they think all writing about historical events must be serious and thesis-driven, or whether they make room for the candor of "ordinary" people.

Different Perspectives Possible Response: The mayor would probably describe people's predicaments as well as his efforts to help and might castigate people like Pepys who stood around rubbernecking.

Connect to Life Students may imagine that, witnessing a recent event, Pepys would write down his personal experience, highlighting vividly the spectacle and color.

Writing Options

Problem-Solving Essay Write an essay in which you recommend possible solutions to the threat of fires in London. Discuss issues of overcrowding, materials used in construction, fire prevention techniques, and general proposals for reducing the outbreak of fires. You might also suggest strategies for dealing with fires once they occur. Place the essay in your **Working Portfolio.**

Fire Prevention
1. ______
2. ______
3. ______

Writing Handbook
See page 1369: Problem-Solution.

Activities & Explorations

A Movie Set Design a set for a movie depiction of the Great Fire of London. Be sure to include specific details from Pepys's description. ~ **ART**

Inquiry & Research

Commonwealth and Restoration Investigate the events that led to the downfall of the Puritan Commonwealth and the restoration of the English monarchy under Charles II. What was the mood of the people? How was the Parliamentary government overthrown?

INTERNET **More Online: Research Starter**
www.mcdougallittell.com

Samuel Pepys
1633–1703

An Insatiable Curiosity The son of a tailor, Samuel Pepys received a scholarship to Cambridge University, where he earned both a bachelor's and a master's degree. Pepys had an insatiable curiosity and strove to learn all that he could about every subject. His interests ranged from music and theater to science, history, and mathematics. It was undoubtedly this fascination with life that inspired him, at the age of 26, to begin keeping the diary in which he would eventually set down more than 1.2 million words. After faithfully making entries for nine years, he was forced to abandon his diary because of poor eyesight.

The Royal Navy Shortly after starting the diary, Pepys became a clerk in the Royal Navy office, where he decided to prove his own worth by becoming a naval expert. His hard work and honesty, as well as his saving of the navy office during the Great Fire of London, led eventually to his appointment as secretary of the admiralty. In that capacity, he doubled the number of battleships and restored the previously weakened Royal Navy as a major sea power.

A Public Life During his years of public service, Pepys enjoyed an active social life amid a circle of friends that included such notables as Sir Isaac Newton and John Dryden. However, Pepys also made enemies in his rise to power. In 1678, some of his adversaries tried unsuccessfully to ruin his reputation. They first tried to implicate Pepys in the murder of a London official, then falsely accused him of treason. Although Pepys was imprisoned briefly, the intervention of King Charles II kept him from further punishment, and in 1683 he returned once again to public service. One tragedy marred Pepys's middle years. His wife, Elizabeth, died in 1669 of a fever. Pepys never remarried.

In Retirement Pepys lived in retirement for the last 14 years of his life. He spent his time amassing a large personal library, collecting material for a history of the navy—which he unfortunately never completed—and corresponding with various artists and scholars. He died at the home of his friend and former servant, William Hewer.

Writing Options

Problem-Solving Essay Pepys supplies some clues to the problem: crowded housing ("houses very thick"), lack of dedicated water supply for fire fighting, no plan for evacuation of the area, an abundance of combustible material. Students can consult with their local fire fighting departments for insights in dealing with these problem.

Activities & Explorations

A Movie Set Students might use several of the vistas Pepys describes to design their set. For example, the "arch of fire" at night or the sight of London Bridge with all of its attendant shops and houses would be visually arresting. Material for close-ups from Pepys's diary might include the carts streaming down the streets, boats on the Thames, and windowsills with frightened pigeons.

Inquiry & Research

Commonwealth and Restoration
Knowledge of some specialized vocabulary will help students in their research:

Covenanters The name for Scottish Presbyterians who sought to preserve the reformed Church of Scotland and who signed the Scottish National Covenant of 1638.

Levellers A dissenting group declaring that both Cromwell and the king should recognize that the franchise belonged to every man, not just to men of property, and calling for the establishment of religious toleration, freedom from impressment, and equality before the law.

Interregnum A designation of the period between the fall of Charles I in 1649 and the restoration of Charles II in 1660. Literally, the period between reigns or regimes.

Protectorate A designation for the government of the Commonwealth. In 1653, Oliver Cromwell refused to take the title of king, choosing instead the title Lord Protector.

Rump Parliament The Parliament that was left after it was purged of all those of noble birth or in disagreement with the Puritans.

Stuart The name of the royal house that governed England from the death of Elizabeth I to the accession of William and Mary.

OVERVIEW

Objectives

1. understand and appreciate excerpts from two **verse essays** that explore the contradictions in human nature **(Literary Analysis)**
2. identify and understand **heroic couplets (Literary Analysis)**
3. **analyze the author's ideas** to appreciate and understand two verse essays **(Active Reading)**

Summary

Pope's *An Essay on Man,* of which this is an excerpt, consists of four letters addressed to Henry St. John, Lord Bolingbroke. The purpose of the verse essay is to vindicate the ways of God to man and to prove that the scheme of the universe is the best possible one in spite of appearances of evil: our failure to see the perfection of the whole is due to our limited vision. In *An Essay on Criticism,* Pope writes in an epigrammatic style about wit, Nature, and the moral guidelines for criticism.

Thematic Link

Pope brought an observant and well-read perspective to issues such as the relationship between Nature and Reason. His couplets present **views of society** that are typical of the neoclassical age in England.

5-Minute Warm-Up

Daily Language SkillBuilder

Have students **proofread** the display sentences on page 515k and write them correctly. The sentences also appear on Transparency 12 of **Grammar Transparencies and Copymasters.**

PREPARING to *Read*

from An Essay on Man

Epigrams, *from* An Essay on Criticism

Poetry by ALEXANDER POPE

Comparing Literature of the World

Poetry of Alexander Pope and Jean de La Fontaine

This lesson and the one that follows present an opportunity for comparing Pope's observations on society with those of French poet Jean de La Fontaine. Specific Points of Comparison in the La Fontaine lesson will help you note similarities and differences in the two poets' perspectives and themes.

Connect to Your Life

Social Graces Recall some recent social events in which you have participated—parties or dances, perhaps, or more informal get-togethers with friends. Jot down words that describe your attitude or behavior in each situation. Were you friendly or sympathetic on one occasion and hostile or insensitive on another? Did you act wisely one time and foolishly another? If so, how do you account for the contradictions in your behavior?

Build Background

Classic Ideals In England, the literary movement of neoclassicism began about 1660 and persisted throughout much of the 18th century. Neoclassical writers modeled their works on the literature of ancient Greece and Rome, which they believed contained universal truths and rules of form important in writing. Neoclassicists emphasized reason, common sense, good taste, simplicity, emotional restraint, order, and balance. Many writers exposed the contradictions and weaknesses of society; some gave moral instruction.

Two concepts important to neoclassicists were nature and wit. *Nature* generally referred to the universal principles of truth underlying the structure of the world. Nature was viewed as a source of order and harmony both in society and in individual behavior. The word *wit* had a number of meanings, ranging from "intellect" to "imagination" to "cleverness."

Alexander Pope was a neoclassical writer in both thought and style; the two verse essays *An Essay on Man* and *An Essay on Criticism* reflect many of the neoclassical ideals. In *An Essay on Criticism,* which Pope began writing when he was just 17, he made use of the **epigram,** a literary form that had originated in ancient Greece. The epigram developed from simple inscriptions on monuments into a literary genre—a short poem or saying characterized by conciseness, balance, clarity, and wit.

Focus Your Reading

LITERARY ANALYSIS HEROIC COUPLET A **heroic couplet** consists of two rhyming lines written in **iambic pentameter**—a metrical pattern of five feet (units), each of which is made up of two syllables, the first unstressed and the second stressed. The following lines are an example of a heroic couplet:

Ăvóid ĕxtrémes; ănd shún thĕ fáult ŏf súch,
Whŏ stíll ăre pléased tŏo lítlle ŏr tóo múch.

As you read, be aware of the meter and content of the heroic couplets in Pope's poetry.

ACTIVE READING ANALYZING AN AUTHOR'S IDEAS In his verse essays, Pope uses contrasting words and statements to express his opinion about weaknesses and contradictions in human nature.

READER'S NOTEBOOK For each poem, create a diagram like the one shown here. As you read, use the diagrams to record the contrasts that Pope presents in each poem. Underline contrasts that point out contradictions in human nature.

An Essay on Man

	Contrasts	
1. darkly 2. <u>lord</u> 3.	⟷	1. wise 2. <u>prey</u> 3.

LaserLinks: Background for Reading
Literary Connection

LESSON RESOURCES

UNIT THREE RESOURCE BOOK, pp. 9–10

ASSESSMENT RESOURCES
Formal Assessment, pp. 87–88
Teacher's Guide to Assessment and Portfolio Use
Test Generator

SKILLS TRANSPARENCIES AND COPYMASTERS
Literary Analysis
- Characteristics of the Essay, T11 (for Think Critically 4, p. 538)

Reading and Critical Thinking
- Compare and Contrast, T15 (for Active Reading, p. 534)

Grammar
- Adjective Prepositional Phrases, C86 (for Mini Lesson, p. 537)

Vocabulary
- Denotation and Connotation, C51 (for Mini Lesson, p. 536)

Writing
- Proposal, T21 (for Writing Option 2, p. 539)
- Achieving Conciseness, C28 (for Writing Option 2, p. 539)

INTEGRATED TECHNOLOGY
Audio Library
LaserLinks
- Literary Connection: English Neoclassicism
- Historical Connection: The Age of Reason. See **Teacher's SourceBook,** p. 33.

Visit our website:
www.mcdougallittell.com

FROM
AN ESSAY ON MAN

ALEXANDER POPE

Know then thyself, presume not God to scan;
The proper study of mankind is man.
Placed on this isthmus of a middle state,
A being darkly wise, and rudely great:
With too much knowledge for the Skeptic side,
With too much weakness for the Stoic's pride,
He hangs between; in doubt to act, or rest;
In doubt to deem himself a god, or beast;
In doubt his mind or body to prefer;
Born but to die, and reasoning but to err;
Alike in ignorance, his reason such,
Whether he thinks too little, or too much:
Chaos of thought and passion, all confused;
Still by himself abused, or disabused;
Created half to rise, and half to fall;
Great lord of all things, yet a prey to all;
Sole judge of truth, in endless error hurled:
The glory, jest, and riddle of the world!

3 isthmus (ĭs′mes): a narrow strip of land connecting larger bodies of land.

4 rudely: in a rough or clumsy way.

5 Skeptic side: the Greek philosophy of skepticism, whose adherents held that sure knowledge is unattainable.

6 Stoic's (stō′ĭks) **pride:** the haughty behavior of an adherent of the Greek philosophy of Stoicism, which taught that human beings should be indifferent to all pleasure and pain.

8 deem: judge; consider.

Thinking Through the Literature

1. **Comprehension Check** Identify two examples of contradictions in the poem.
2. What is your reaction to Pope's **style** and manner of writing? Take a few moments to discuss your impressions.
3. Why do you think Pope says that human beings are continually "in doubt" (lines 7–9)? Use evidence from the poem to support your ideas.

TEACHING THE LITERATURE

Customizing Instruction

Less Proficient Readers

Before they read the essays, have students describe a situation in which they felt doubt about what to do. After reading the excerpt from *An Essay on Man,* have students look back at lines 7–9. Ask them why Pope says that humans are always in doubt.

Possible Response: They never know whether to follow the instincts of the body or the logic of the mind.

Students Acquiring English

The unusual word order in these selections may be problematic for students. Have students rearrange difficult sentences to put them in natural word order. Direct them first to find the verb and then to identify the subject. Remind them that the subject may not be the noun or pronoun closest to the verb and that the subject of imperative verbs is understood to be *you.*

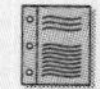
Use **Spanish Study Guide** for additional support, pp. 113–115

Gifted and Talented

Remind students that a paradox states an apparent contradiction, then ask them to find the paradoxes in the passage from *An Essay on Man.*

Encourage interested students to research the nine Muses and their roles in various myths. Have students write their own myths about one of the Muses.

Thinking Through the Literature

1. Possible Responses: too much knowledge—too much weakness; god—beast; lord—prey.
2. Accept all reasonable responses.
3. Possible Response: Pope believes that people do not know whether to succumb to the instincts of the body or the logic of the mind.

Reading and Analyzing

Literary Analysis HEROIC COUPLET

Review the elements of a heroic couplet as described on page 534. Tell students that punctuation is an important clue to rhythm. A comma within a line changes the rhythm without affecting the meter, while a semicolon or colon at the end of a closed couplet draws the reader along more rapidly than a period. Have students identify places where Pope uses semicolons and colons and explain how the punctuation serves the meaning.

Use **Unit Three Resource Book** p. 10 for more exercises.

Active Reading ANALYZING AN AUTHOR'S IDEAS

A Ask students whether they agree with Pope's statements about true ease in writing coming from art, not chance. What does he mean by the phrase "true ease"? Writing that is easy for the writer or writing that is graceful? How does line 36 add to the meaning of the couplet?

Possible Response: "True ease" means that writing will be easy for the writer and sound natural to the reader. Line 36 makes this meaning clear; someone who has learned to dance will move more easily or gracefully because dancing improves coordination, flexibility, and grace.

Use **Unit Three Resource Book** p. 9 for more practice.

Literary Analysis: EPIGRAMS

An epigram is a short, memorable saying that is characterized by conciseness, balance, clarity, and wit. Explain that these elements, along with rhyme and meter, help make the epigrams memorable. Have students think of other epigrams, such as "A stitch in time saves nine" and "You can lead a horse to water but you can't make him drink."

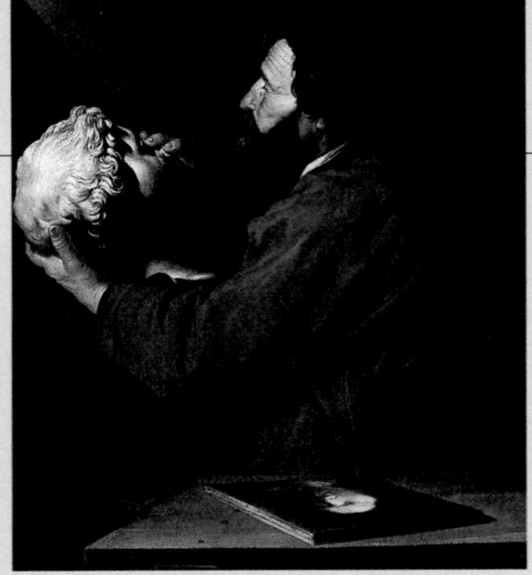

The Sense of Touch (about 1615–1616), Jusepe de Ribera. Oil on canvas, 45 ⅝" × 34 ¾", The Norton Simon Foundation, Pasadena, California.

EPIGRAMS

from AN ESSAY ON CRITICISM

ALEXANDER POPE

First follow Nature, and your judgment frame
By her just standard, which is still the same:
Unerring Nature, still divinely bright,
One clear, unchanged, and universal light,
Life, force, and beauty, must to all impart,
At once the source, and end, and test of art.

■

Of all the causes which conspire to blind
Man's erring judgment, and misguide the mind,
What the weak head with strongest bias rules,
Is pride, the never-failing vice of fools.

■

Pride, where wit fails, steps in to our defense,
And fills up all the mighty void of sense.
If once right reason drives that cloud away,
Truth breaks upon us with resistless day.
Trust not yourself; but your defects to know,
Make use of every friend—and every foe.
A little learning is a dangerous thing;
Drink deep, or taste not the Pierian spring:
There shallow draughts intoxicate the brain,
And drinking largely sobers us again.

■

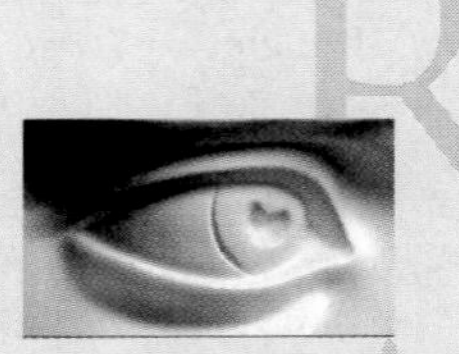

12 void: emptiness; vacuum.

18 Pierian (pī-ĭr'ē-ən) **spring:** a spring sacred to the Muses and therefore considered a source of inspiration. (In Greek mythology, the Muses—nine daughters of Zeus and Memory—were the goddesses of all artistic and intellectual pursuits.)

19 draughts (drăfts): gulps or swallows.

1

Teaching Options

Vocabulary Strategy

DENOTATION AND CONNOTATION

Instruction *Denotation* generally refers to the literal, naming function of words. *Connotation* refers to the values, secondary ideas, and associated attributes that are conveyed by a word. The denotative meaning of the word *beast,* for example, is a *wild animal.* The connotative meaning, however, is colored by a feeling that beasts are without conscience and that their lives consist of feeding and reproducing.

Activity Have students look up and write the denotation of the following words. Then have them write the connotation for each word as it is used in context.

1. *darkly* (line 4 from *An Essay on Man*)
   Possible Response: denotation: sullenly, gloomily, mysteriously; connotation: lacking the best intentions, ignorantly.
2. *judgment* (line 1 from *An Essay on Criticism*)
   Possible Response: denotation: considered opinion; connotation: morals, values

Use **Vocabulary Transparencies and Copymasters,** p. 47.

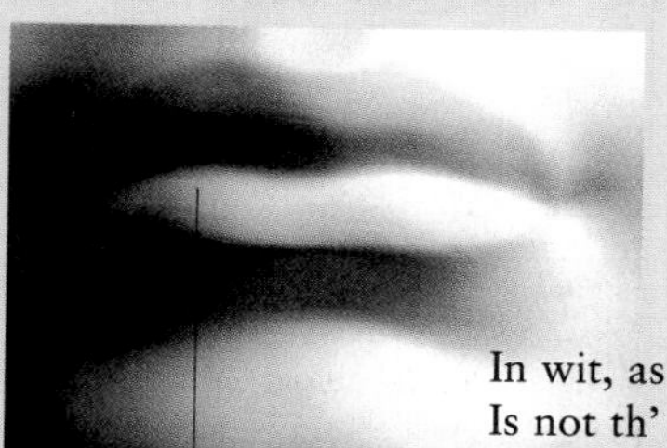

In wit, as Nature, what affects our hearts
Is not th' exactness of peculiar parts;
'Tis not a lip, or eye, we beauty call,
But the joint force and full result of all.

22 peculiar: individual.

■

Whoever thinks a faultless piece to see,
Thinks what ne'er was, nor is, nor e'er shall be.
In every work regard the writer's end,
Since none can compass more than they intend;
And if the means be just, the conduct true,
Applause, in spite of trivial faults, is due.

27 end: goal or intention.

28 compass: accomplish.

■

True wit is Nature to advantage dressed,
What oft was thought, but ne'er so well expressed;
Something, whose truth convinced at sight we find,
That gives us back the image of our mind.

■

True ease in writing comes from art, not chance,
As those move easiest who have learned to dance.
'Tis not enough no harshness gives offense,
The sound must seem an echo to the sense.

■

Avoid extremes; and shun the fault of such,
Who still are pleased too little or too much.

■

Regard not then if wit be old or new,
But blame the false, and value still the true.

■

Good nature and good sense must ever join;
To err is human, to forgive, divine.

Customizing Instruction

Less Proficient Readers

1 Remind students to refer to the note in the margin about the allusion to the Pierian spring. What does Pope really mean?

Possible Response: He means that knowing a little can cause people to act foolishly, whereas knowing a great deal causes them to act more wisely.

Multiple Learning Styles

Auditory Learners

Have students work in small groups to prepare a choral reading of one of the epigrams. Explain that a choral reading takes advantage of the qualities of each person's voice. Students may want to assign serious lines to those with deep voices and more light-hearted lines to those with lighter voices. Students may also wish to employ gestures to emphasize the meaning of the epigram.

Gifted and Talented

Explain to students that the paintings and engravings of English artist William Hogarth (1697–1764) reveal a social conscience and attitudes not unlike those of his contemporary, Alexander Pope. Hogarth was interested in his social surroundings and was highly critical of what he saw. Read students these lines, which Pope addressed to Hogarth:

Were but you and I acquainted
Every figure should be painted.
Draw them so that we may trace
All the soul in every face.

Ask students to find examples of Hogarth's work and to ask whether he successfully reveals "all the soul in every face."

Mini Lesson Grammar

ADJECTIVE PREPOSITIONAL PHRASES

Instruction A prepositional phrase begins with a preposition and ends with its object. A prepositional phrase may also include any modifiers of its object. When a prepositional phrase modifies a noun or a pronoun, the phrase itself acts as an adjective and is called an adjective phrase.

Activity Write on the chalkboard the following excerpt from Pope's "An Essay on Man."

"With too much knowledge for the Skeptic side,
With too much weakness for the Stoic's pride,
He hangs between; . . . "

Call students' attention to the four underlined prepositional phrases. Ask students to identify the preposition that begins each phrase. (With; for; With; for) Tell students that these are all adjective phrases. Then ask students to identify the noun or pronoun each phrase modifies. (With–He; for–knowledge; With–He; for–weakness)

Exercise Ask students to identify the prepositional phrase used as an adjective in the following sentence. Tell students to name the noun or pronoun the phrase modifies.

Many would agree that the human race, in constant confusion, either uses its brain too much, or too little. (in constant confusion; "race")

Use **Grammar Transparencies and Copymasters,** p. 85.

Use McDougal Littell's ***Language Network*** for more instruction in placement of phrases.

EPIGRAMS 537

GUIDING STUDENT RESPONSE

Connect to the Literature

1. What Do You Think?
Guidelines for student response: Responses will vary. Ask students to explain why they have chosen their epigrams. What in particular appeals to them about the epigrams they have chosen?

Comprehension Check

- One should avoid light or superficial learning: "drink deep."
- If the purpose and the means are honest and truthful, then writing should be praised despite minor flaws.

Think Critically

2. Possible Responses: Pope is concerned with how people should regard and use nature, art, and wit. He wants people to improve themselves by looking to nature for guidance, avoiding pride, and gaining knowledge.
3. Answers will vary depending on which contrasts students recorded. Pope uses contradictions to demonstrate the conflicts inherent in the human condition. Have students discuss the effect the contradictions had on them as readers. Were they effective?
4. Answers will vary. Pope seems to regard human nature as a mixture of elements, capable of great wisdom or great folly and so there are elements of both pessimism and optimism in his view of human nature.

Literary Analysis

Activity You might ask volunteers to explicate for the class the epigrams they have chosen, paying attention to versification and effectiveness.

Connect to the Literature

1. **What Do You Think?** Write down two of your favorite epigrams from *An Essay on Criticism,* and share them with another student.

Comprehension Check

- According to Pope, how should one approach learning?
- How should the reader evaluate a writer's work?

Think Critically

2. What seem to be some of Pope's main concerns in these **epigrams?**

THINK ABOUT
- his references to nature, art, and wit
- what he says about pride
- his statements "the sound must seem an echo to the sense" (line 38) and "blame the false, and value still the true" (line 42)

3. **ACTIVE READING** ANALYZING AN AUTHOR'S IDEAS Look back in your  READER'S NOTEBOOK at the diagrams you used to record contrasts in the poems. What ideas about human nature does Pope convey through contrasting words and statements in these epigrams? How does he use contradictions in the epigrams?

4. Do you think Pope is optimistic or pessimistic about human behavior? Support your opinion with details from the poems.

Extend Interpretations

5. **Comparing Texts** How might the descriptions of events in *The Diary of Samuel Pepys* (page 526) be used to illustrate the contradiction Pope suggests in his statement that a human being is "great lord of all things, yet a prey to all"?

6. **Art Connection** Look again at the reproduction of the painting *The Sense of Touch* on page 536. Notice that the man's eyes are shut and that a portrait is lying on the table. In what ways might the painting reflect some of the concerns Pope expresses in the epigrams?

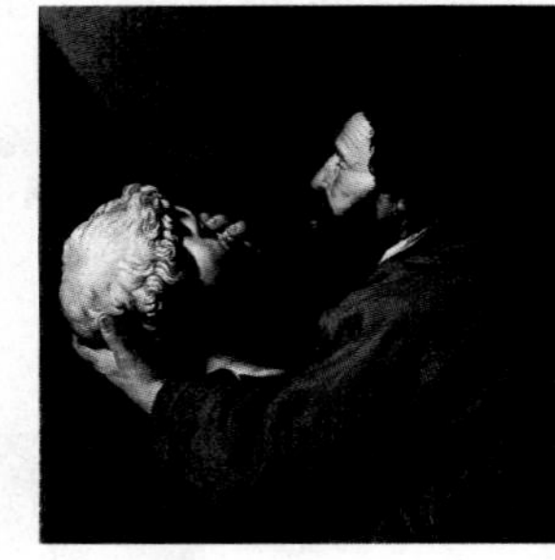

7. **Connect to Life** Compare the views of human nature expressed in the excerpts from *An Essay on Man* and *An Essay on Criticism* with modern views. Do you think Pope's viewpoints are similar to those held today?

Literary Analysis

HEROIC COUPLET Two rhyming lines written in **iambic pentameter** are referred to as a **heroic couplet.** The couplet is called *heroic* because English poems written in iambic pentameter often have heroic themes and elevated style. Heroic couplets are especially well suited to writing epigrams. Notice the elevated style of this epigram from *An Essay on Criticism.*

Good nature and good sense must ever join;
To err is human, to forgive, divine.

Activity Choose one epigram from *An Essay on Criticism* and note Pope's use of the heroic couplet in it. Read the epigram aloud and then mark the unstressed and stressed syllables. Is the pattern of stresses strictly iambic, or are there some variations? How effective is the form of the heroic couplet in this epigram?

Extend Interpretations

Comparing Texts The material from Pepys's diary that illustrates Pope's epigram can include descriptions of the king having to run for his life, as well as the descriptions of people of all stations fleeing from the fire.

Art Connection Possible response: The artist portrays a man using his sense of touch to appreciate the structure of a face beyond its visual appearance. Pope would approve: the man's actions reflect his charge to expand one's understanding, and to use one's reason and analytical skills vigorously.

Connect to Life Answers will vary. Have students defend their answers by expressing as clearly as possible what differences or similarities they see between Pope's views and those of modern artists and thinkers.

Writing Options

1. Epigram on Human Nature
Convey your own message about human nature in an epigram consisting of one or more heroic couplets.

2. Essay on a Social Problem
Address a social problem or failing raised by Pope in *An Essay on Criticism* and write an essay in which you provide your own solution to the problem. Place the essay in your **Working Portfolio.**

Writing Handbook
See page 1369: Problem-Solution.

Activities & Explorations

Character List Make a list of TV or movie characters who exhibit some of the contradictory qualities suggested in the excerpt from *An Essay on Man.*
~ **INTERPRETING**

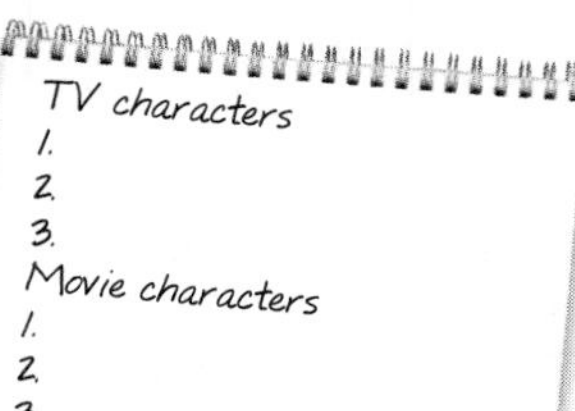

Inquiry & Research

Reasonable Ideas In the history of Western thought, the 18th century is often referred to as the Age of Reason or the Enlightenment. Most of the philosophers of the time considered reason to be the only road to truth and were therefore particularly interested in the methods and laws of science and mathematics. Investigate some of the ideas of the Age of Reason, and share your findings with the class. Pay particular attention to ideas that you see reflected in Pope's work.

Alexander Pope
1688–1744

Other Works
The Rape of the Lock
"Epistle to Miss Blount"

Physical Limitations From childhood, Alexander Pope was plagued by ill health. As a result of tuberculosis of the spine, he suffered constant physical pain and grew to a height of only four feet six inches. Although he was therefore severely limited in his physical activities, it is likely that these limitations may have contributed to his early devotion to reading and writing and to his ultimate success as a writer.

Early Genius Pope was raised as a Roman Catholic during a period in England's history when only Protestants could obtain a university education or hold public office. For this reason, he was largely self-taught. He was an exceptional child, however, and his genius as a poet was recognized at an early age. Pope maintained that he began writing verse before the age of 12. By the time he was 17, his poems were being read and admired by many of England's best literary critics. Unlike most of his predecessors in the literary world, Pope was able to prosper with writing as his sole career. His prosperity was achieved primarily through his translations of Homer's *Iliad* and *Odyssey,* products of an enormous amount of work for which he was handsomely rewarded.

Friends and Enemies Pope's friends included the distinguished writers Richard Steele, Joseph Addison, Jonathan Swift, and John Gay. Along with Swift and Gay, he was a member of the Scriblerus Club, a group devoted to the writing of satires. Because of his sharp tongue, Pope was often the object of criticism by less talented writers, with several of whom he engaged in lifelong feuds.

Author Activity

Roasted and Skewered Read some of the satires Pope wrote as a member of the Scriblerus Club. Who or what were the objects of his satiric wit? What form did his satires take? How did Pope's victims react to his attacks?

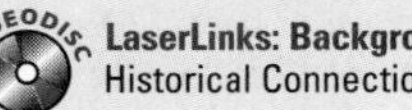

LaserLinks: Background for Reading
Historical Connection

Writing Options

1. **Epigram on Human Nature** Encourage students to use a prewriting technique such as freewriting or clustering to identify an aspect of human nature. They could also read the advice columns in the paper for ideas. Responses should follow iambic pentameter and have an *aa, bb,* etc. rhyme scheme.
2. **Essay on a Social Problem** Have students address possible arguments against or concerns about their solution. Encourage students to read and discuss each other's essays.

Activities & Explorations

Character List Get students started by giving them an example such as Clark Kent/Superman, who embodies both the timid and the heroic sides of human nature. Encourage them to recall and comment on other TV or movie characters with contradictory qualities.

Inquiry & Research

Reasonable Ideas Ask students to form three groups to investigate 18th-century thought in the fields of science, mathematics, and philosophy. Each group might list major thinkers in each domain, such as Newton, Descartes, and Voltaire. Have students generate questions to research.
Individual students could then do research in encyclopedias and histories of the period to find out the contribution of each major figure. Finally, representatives from each group might share their group's findings in a round-table discussion of Enlightenment thought.

Author Activity

Roasted and Skewered There are many excellent biographies of Pope that students might read to gain more information about Pope, including *Alexander Pope: A Life* by Maynard Mack. This biography provides extensive information about the objects of Pope's satire and their reactions to his attacks.

OVERVIEW

Objectives

1. understand and appreciate **verse fables (Literary Analysis)**
2. appreciate the author's use of **fable** to teach lessons about life **(Literary Analysis)**
3. **make judgments** to appreciate and understand La Fontaine's fables **(Active Reading)**

Summary

In each of these fables, a main character makes a mistake about the world, but subsequent events point out the error. In each case, the fabulist leads us to a broad, general conclusion.

Thematic Link

Like Pope, La Fontaine is a keen observer of human foibles. He wrote his fables as a way of teaching others about the flaws he saw in his **views of society.**

5-Minute Warm-Up

Daily Language SkillBuilder

Have students **proofread** the display sentences on page 515k and write them correctly. The sentences also appear on Transparency 13 of **Grammar Transparencies and Copymasters.**

The Acorn and the Pumpkin
The Value of Knowledge

Fables by JEAN DE LA FONTAINE (zhän də lə fōN-tān′)

Comparing Literature of the World

Observing Society Across Cultures

Pope's Verse Essays and La Fontaine's Fables Jean de La Fontaine wrote his poetry in France in the 17th century, and Alexander Pope wrote his poetry in England in the 18th century, but they had a common goal: to observe human nature and society and comment on the manners and morals of their times.

Points of Comparison As you read the following fables by La Fontaine, compare them with Pope's poems in terms of the observations made about human behavior and society.

Build Background

Neoclassicism and Fables In France, the neoclassical movement began around 1600, roughly 60 years before the advent of English neoclassicism. Jean de La Fontaine and other 17th-century French writers, like their later English counterparts, placed great emphasis on reason, intellect, order, and simplicity in thought and actions. Many focused on the flaws in human nature, pointing out society's weaknesses and giving moral instruction.

Like the English writers of the late 1600s, La Fontaine was inspired by his reading of ancient authors; he borrowed ideas for many of his fables from the tales traditionally ascribed to Aesop, a Greek slave who lived around 600 B.C. In his masterful verse retellings of Aesop's fables, La Fontaine employed a natural, relaxed style that made the tales more appealing to readers, often using humor to reveal human shortcomings and to convey meaningful messages about life. The two poems you are about to read are from his Fables, a collection of over 200 moral tales that have entertained readers for centuries.

Focus Your Reading

LITERARY ANALYSIS FABLE A brief tale, in either prose or verse, told to illustrate a moral or teach a lesson is a **fable.** In the following opening lines from "The Acorn and the Pumpkin," La Fontaine makes it clear that the story he is about to tell will teach a lesson:

The Lord knows best what He's about.
No need to search for proof throughout
The Universe. Look at the pumpkin.
It gives us all the proof we need.

As you read these fables, be aware of how the details of each tale contribute to the moral, or lesson, the writer seems to be conveying.

ACTIVE READING MAKING JUDGMENTS A **fable** persuades or convinces the reader of its moral not by presenting logical arguments but by illustrating the lesson in a brief, entertaining tale. To judge the effectiveness of a fable, use the following criteria:

- Is the tale entertaining?
- How well does the tale illustrate the moral?
- Are you persuaded or convinced by the moral?

READER'S NOTEBOOK Briefly **summarize** the story that is being told by each poem, and then note the moral of each.

LESSON RESOURCES

UNIT THREE RESOURCE BOOK, pp. 11–12

ASSESSMENT RESOURCES

Formal Assessment, pp. 89–90

Teacher's Guide to Assessment and Portfolio Use

Test Generator

SKILLS TRANSPARENCIES AND COPYMASTERS

Literary Analysis

- The Moral Tale, Ballad, Fable, and Folk Tale, T23 (for Literary Analysis, p. 544)

Reading and Critical Thinking

- Making Judgments, T5 (for Active Reading, p. 540)

Grammar

- Placement of Prepositional Phrases, C89 (for Mini Lesson, pp. 542–543)

Vocabulary

- Prefixes, Suffixes, and Roots, C52 (for Mini Lesson, p. 541)

Writing

- Compare-Contrast, C34 (for Writing Option 2, p. 545)

Communications

- Impromptu Speaking: Debate, T15 (for Activities & Explorations 1, p. 545)

INTEGRATED TECHNOLOGY

Audio Library

Visit our website:
www.mcdougallittell.com

The Acorn and the Pumpkin

Jean de La Fontaine

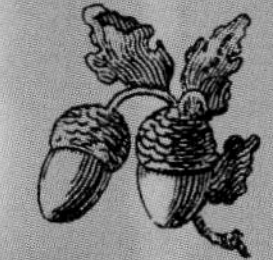

The Lord knows best what He's about.
No need to search for proof throughout
The universe. Look at the pumpkin.
It gives us all the proof we need. To wit:
The story of a village bumpkin—
Garo by name—who found one, gazed at it,
And wondered how so huge a fruit could be
Hung from so slight a stem: "It doesn't fit!
God's done it wrong! If He'd asked me,
He'd hang them from those oaks. Big fruit, big tree.
Too bad someone so smart and strong—
1 At least that's what the vicar's always saying
With all his preaching and his praying—
Didn't have me to help His work along!
I'd hang the acorn from this vine instead . . .
No bigger than my nail . . . It's like I said:
God's got things backwards. It's all wrong . . .
Well, after all that weighty thought I'd best
Take me a nap. We thinkers need our rest."
No sooner said than done. Beneath an oak
Our Garo laid his head in sweet repose.
Next moment, though, he painfully awoke:
An acorn, falling, hit him on the nose.
Rubbing his face, feeling his bruises,
He finds it still entangled in his beard.
"A bloody nose from this?" he muses.
"I must say, things aren't quite what they appeared.
My goodness, if this little nut
Had been a pumpkin or a squash, then what?
God knows His business after all, no question!
It's time I changed my tune!" With that suggestion,
Garo goes home, singing the praise
Of God and of His wondrous ways.

Translated by Norman R. Shapiro

4 to wit: that is to say (used to introduce an explanation or example).

26 muses: thinks to himself; ponders.

Thinking Through the Literature

1. How did you react to the story of Garo?
2. What is your opinion of the logic that Garo uses? Explain your response.
3. What message do you think the speaker is trying to convey? Support your opinion.

TEACHING THE LITERATURE

Customizing Instruction

Less Proficient Readers
Have students create a chart for each fable. In the first box, have students state the main character's point of view. In the middle boxes, students should summarize the process by which the moral is reached. The moral should appear in the last box.

Students Acquiring English
1 Tell students that a *vicar* is a parish priest. In 17th-century Europe, the vicar would have been the best-educated member of a village community.

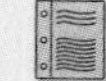
Use **Spanish Study Guide** for additional support, pp. 116–118

Gifted and Talented
Have students read other fables by La Fontaine and share the stories with the class either by retelling them or by illustrating them.

Thinking Through the Literature

1. Accept all reasonable responses.
2. Possible Responses: Garo uses sound reasoning, since a large plant looks as if it should have large fruit; Garo is so influenced by appearances that he does not think about possible results.
3. Accept all reasonable, well-supported responses.

Mini Lesson Vocabulary Strategy

SUFFIXES

Instruction The English language derives much of its strength from the ease with which words may be made more versatile by a change in their grammatical identity. Nouns, for example, may become verbs or adjectives with the addition of one or more suffixes to the base word or root.

Activity Have students mix and match the list of words in the chart with the list of suffixes. Then discuss with them the impact the addition of the suffix has on the root or base word in terms of part of speech and meaning.

WORDS	SUFFIXES
think	*-er*
suggest	*-ion or tion*
home	*-less*
book	*-ish*
foolhardy	*-hood*

Use **Vocabulary Transparencies and Copymasters,** p. 48.

Reading and Analyzing

Active Reading MAKING JUDGMENTS

A Ask students to identify the two speakers in the fable.
Answer: The narrator, the rich burgher.

Ask students to identify and describe the two characters in the fable.
Possible Response: The rich burgher, who is vain and boorish; the poor burgher, who is humble, witty, and learned.

Then have students suggest reasons that the voice of the scholar is not heard.
Possible Response: The two speakers are the narrator and the rich burgher. The fabulist seems to have enjoyed imitating the comic excesses of the burgher in creating his caricature.

 Use **Unit Three Resource Book,** p. 11 for more practice.

Literary Analysis FABLE

B Discuss the moral of the fable. Ask students what the rich burgher thinks gives a person power.
Answer: money.

Ask what power the poor burgher has.
Answer: wit.

Ask students how, according to La Fontaine, "knowledge is power."
Possible Response: The poor burgher has knowledge; he is witty and interesting; people like to be around him.

Ask students if La Fontaine is making a strict comparison of wealth and knowledge, and have them support their position with evidence from the text.
Possible Response: La Fontaine is not making a strict comparison; in lines 10–11 La Fontaine argues that wealth without worth is not enough, though worth without wealth is.

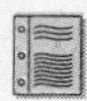 Use **Unit Three Resource Book** p. 12 for more exercises.

THE VALUE of KNOWLEDGE

Jean de La Fontaine

Betwixt two burghers there arose
A row. One, quick of wit, was poor;
The other, rich, but much the boor.
A The latter, twitting, clucks and crows: **1**
Surely his bookish rival owes
The likes of him respect, and should—
If he, indeed, had any sense—
Pay homage to his opulence.
("Sense"? Hardly! Rather say "foolhardihood"!
For why revere mere wealth without
B Real worth? It's meaningless.) "So, brother,"
Brashly the lout would taunt and flout
The other;
"Doubtless you think yourself my better; but
How often do you have your friends to dinner?
What good are books? Will reading fill their gut?
The wretches just grow poorer, thinner;
Up in their garrets, garbed all year the same;
No servants but their shadows! Fie! For shame!
The body politic has little use
For those who never buy. Wealth and excess—
Luxury, in a word—produce
The greatest deal of human happiness.
Our pleasures set the wheel a-turning:
Earning and spending; spending, earning.

1 burghers: citizens of a town.

3 boor (bo͝or): a rude, ill-mannered person.

4 twitting: mocking; ridiculing.

8 opulence: wealth.

10 revere: regard with great respect; honor.

12 flout: show contempt for; scorn.

18 garrets: rooms on the top floor of buildings; attics.

19 fie: an interjection used to express disapproval or distaste.

20 body politic: the people of a nation or state.

Teaching Options

Grammar

PLACEMENT OF PREPOSITIONAL PHRASES

Instruction A prepositional phrase may modify a noun, pronoun, verb, or group of words acting as a noun. Usually it is placed just before or after the word or words it modifies in a sentence. Sometimes the position of a prepositional phrase can be changed in order to control rhythm and emphasis within a sentence.

Activity Write on the chalkboard the following lines from "The Acorn and the Pumpkin."

"Too bad someone so smart and strong—
At least that's what the vicar's always saying
With all his preaching and his praying—
Didn't have me to help His work along!"

" . . . With that suggestion,
Garo goes home, singing the praise
Of God and of His wondrous ways."

Point out the underlined prepositional phrases in the excerpts and their respective positions within each poetic "sentence" *(middle; beginning; end).* Explain that, in the first example, the poet has placed the prepositional phrase immediately after

Each of us, Heaven knows, must play his part:
Spinners and seamsters, fancy beaus and belles
Who buy the finery the merchant sells;
And even you, who with your useless art,
Toady to patrons ever quick to pay."
Our bookman doesn't deign respond:
There's much too much that he might say.
But still, revenge is his, and far beyond
Mere satire's meager means. For war breaks out,
And Mars wreaks havoc round about.
Homeless, our vagabonds must beg their bread.
Scorned everywhere, the boor meets glare and glower;
Welcomed, the wit is plied with board and bed.

So ends their quarrel. Fools take heed: knowledge is power!

Translated by Norman R. Shapiro

27 beaus (bōz) **and belles** (bĕlz): fashionable men and women.

30 toady: act in a subservient way, using flattery to get what one wants.

31 Our bookman . . . respond: Our scholar thinks it beneath his dignity to reply.

35 Mars wreaks (rēks) **havoc:** war causes great destruction. (In Roman mythology, Mars was the god of war.)

38 plied: continually supplied.

Engraving by Gustave Doré.

Customizing Instruction

Students Acquiring English

Suggest that students make a list of unfamiliar words such as *betwixt, lout, garbed, finery, deign, meager, vagabonds, glower.* Have students work in pairs or small groups to determine the meaning of the words. Students should note which words have fallen out of usage and suggest words currently in usage to replace them.

Answer: betwixt, between; garbed, dressed.

Less Proficient Readers

1 Point out that "quick of wit" has more than one possible meaning. Guide students in a brief discussion of the meaning as used here *(possessing practical intelligence, good sense).* Lead students to realize that the contrast in line 3 that describes the other burgher is what determines the best meaning in this context.

the verb it modifies *([is] . . . saying)*—although he could have chosen to place it *before* the verb (for example: ". . . that's what, with all his preaching and his praying, the vicar's always saying . . .").

In the second excerpt, point out that prepositional phrases both begin and conclude the sentence. The poet has placed the first one before the verb it modifies *(goes).* The concluding prepositional phrase is placed right after the noun it describes *(praise).*

Exercise Ask students to underline each prepositional phrase and note its placement in the sentence. Have students meet in cooperative groups to discuss whether any prepositional phrase could be placed elsewhere within its sentence.

1. A fable is a short tale written in either prose or verse. *(in either prose or verse, placement after the verb "written")*
2. The purpose of a fable is to teach a lesson. *(of a fable, placement after the noun "purpose")*

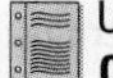

Use **Grammar Transparencies and Copymasters,** p. 87.

Use McDougal Littell's ***Language Network*** for more instruction and practice in prepositional phrases.

GUIDING STUDENT RESPONSE

Connect to the Literature

1. **What Do You Think?**
Guidelines for student response: Students may have heard the final statement before; others may disagree with it.

Comprehension Check
- Reading does not put food on the table, and there are plenty of smart people who live in garrets, do not have enough to eat, and own only one set of clothes.
- as a man of "mere wealth without real worth"

Think Critically

2. Possible Response: The boor was unpleasant in his prosperity and has no friends to turn to, while the wit is welcomed for his entertaining stories and useful knowledge. When the war breaks out, the boor loses the one thing people sought him out for—his wealth. Knowledge is the power that will help people survive a crisis.
3. Encourage a wide range of views. Possible Responses: Some material comfort is desirable; purchasing goods can help the economy.
4. Possible Response: Mental achievements are more valuable than material possessions. The poem seems sharply to divide humans into only two camps, but other categories are possible.
5. Ask students to refer to their notes with reference to the three criteria suggested in the activity.

Literary Analysis

Paired Activity Possible Response: The bumpkin is humorous and entertaining in his discovery of a flaw in God's plan. He is very serious in his thinking that he must explain the error concerning the acorn and the pumpkin to the vicar—as if somehow the mistake might be corrected. "The Value of Knowledge" is more serious in its tone. The two characters are presented in an entertaining manner, but their speech and the moral of the fable is more realistic than "The Acorn and the Pumpkin."

Thinking through the LITERATURE

Connect to the Literature

1. **What Do You Think?** Were you satisfied with the way "The Value of Knowledge" ended? Share your thoughts with the class.

Comprehension Check
- Why does the wealthy burgher say that books serve no purpose?
- How does the poor burgher view the rich burgher?

Think Critically

2. Why do you think the wit is welcomed and the boor rejected at the end of the poem?

THINK ABOUT
- the description of the boor
- the conditions after the outbreak of war
- what the speaker means by the statement that "knowledge is power"

3. Do you agree with any of the rich burgher's opinions? Explain your response.
4. What messages about human nature do you think the poem expresses?
5. ACTIVE READING MAKING JUDGMENTS Review the summaries and notes you made earlier in your READER'S NOTEBOOK. Which of the two tales do you think illustrates its moral more effectively? Explain your answer with reference to the criteria on page 540.

Extend Interpretations

6. **Connect to Life** Do you agree or disagree with the morals of these two **fables?** Defend your position with examples from modern life.
7. Points of Comparison Compare La Fontaine's poetic fables with the epigrams from Pope's *An Essay on Criticism* (page 536). How do fables and epigrams differ in **style?** in **tone?** Can you think of any situations in which one of these forms of moral instruction might be preferable to the other? Explain your thoughts.

Literary Analysis

FABLE A **fable** is a brief tale, in either prose or verse, told to illustrate a moral or teach a lesson. Often, the moral of a fable appears in a distinct and memorable statement near the tale's beginning or end. Because they draw a clear lesson from a single episode, fables generally contain simple narratives and exaggerated characters. **Humor** is a prominent feature of many fables.

Paired Activity Which of the following elements do you think contribute to the humorous **tone** of these fables? In a chart like the one shown, make a note of any examples you find of the following:

- humorous situations
- exaggerated characters
- humorous language

Then discuss with your partner whether the humorous elements contribute to the lesson each fable is trying to teach. Explain your answer.

Humorous Situations	Exaggerated Characters	Humorous Language

Extend Interpretations

Connect to Life You might guide students to consider the broader point of whether the morals or lessons taught by old fables as well as other literature of the past have continued relevance to modern life. Have them discuss themes or connections that cross cultures.

Points of Comparison Students should be able to detect the contrast between the formality of Pope's writing and the informality or conversational quality of the fables. La Fontaine's stories are laced with humor, while Pope's epigrams seem ultimately serious. La Fontaine's verse fables are more simple and down-to-earth than Pope's elegant epigrams. Both use rhyme and alliteration, but La Fontaine's form is looser and he is more entertaining as he presents his moral.

Writing Options

1. An Original Fable Think of a familiar saying or proverb you know, such as "Haste makes waste." Compose an original fable to illustrate the saying. Include it as the moral of your fable.

2. Points of Comparison Write an essay comparing the views of human nature and society found in the excerpt from Pope's *Essay on Man* with the views found in one of La Fontaine's fables.

Writing Handbook
See page 1367: Compare and Contrast.

Activities & Explorations

1. Debate on Lifestyles With several of your classmates, present a debate on the pros and cons of the lifestyles of the two characters in "The Value of Knowledge." Include visual aids, such as charts or diagrams, to help you illustrate your points. Ask the class to vote on which side presents the most logical and effective argument.
~ **SPEAKING AND LISTENING**

2. Comic Strip Create a comic strip based on the story of Garo in "The Acorn and the Pumpkin."
~ **ART**

Inquiry & Research

Other Writers of Fables Fables are a popular form of literature. They have their roots in folklore and are found in nearly every culture. Important writers of fables, in addition to La Fontaine and the Greek Aesop, are John Gay in England, Gotthold Lessing in Germany, and Ivan Krylov in Russia. Do some research about the fables written by Gay, Lessing, and Krylov. Share your findings with the class.

More Online: Research Starter
www.mcdougallittell.com

Jean de La Fontaine
1621–1695

Other Works
"The Crow and the Fox"
"The Stag Who Saw Himself in the Water"
"The Hen Who Laid Golden Eggs"

Youth and Student As a young man, Jean de La Fontaine was rather restless, with no apparent goals in life and little inclination to work. Born into a middle-class family in the Champagne region of France, La Fontaine began studying for the priesthood at the age of 19 but after a very short time switched to the study of law. His father, an inspector of waterways and forests, arranged for his son to take over his position, one that La Fontaine was to occupy—with little interest or attention—for almost 20 years.

A Writing Career Although he read a great deal of poetry, especially the works of classical authors, La Fontaine did not begin writing original poems until he was in his mid-30s. In 1656, he moved to Paris, where for several years the financial support of a succession of wealthy patrons enabled him to devote his time to writing. He also frequented Parisian literary circles, becoming acquainted with such important French writers as Molière and Racine.

The Fables La Fontaine produced great quantities of prose and poetry, but his lasting fame depends chiefly on his *Fables.* These poetic tales are an important part of French culture and are enjoyed by people of all ages, from small schoolchildren to world-renowned scholars.

Author Activity

The Kindness of Patrons Throughout his career, La Fontaine was able to gain the support of wealthy patrons such as Nicolas Fouquet, the superintendent of finance. Find out what other patrons La Fontaine had. Draw up a list of the names of his more important patrons, along with a little information about each one.

Writing Options

1. **An Original Fable** Suggested sayings or proverbs: "What goes around, comes around," "Know thyself," the Golden Rule, "A rolling stone gathers no moss." Suggest that students study comic strips to see the ways that certain animals are used to represent different types of humans. Animals may be substituted for human characters in telling their stories.
2. **Points of Comparison** Recommend that students write out the observations they developed under Extend Interpretations.

Activities & Explorations

1. **Debate on Lifestyles** Encourage students to develop criteria for judging the effectiveness of the debaters, such as clarity of speech, use of body language, appeal to emotion, and appeal to logic. Have each team use this feedback to set goals for future debates and presentations.
2. **Comic Strip** Garo is a simple-minded anti-hero of the type that is frequently found in comic strips. *Blondie* and *Peanuts* are two examples students might refer to in creating their Garo strip. Have students first plan what Garo will be doing in each panel of their strip. Suggest that they try out each finished strip on someone who has not read the poem to be sure the point of the fable comes across.

Author Activity

The Kindness of Patrons Other patrons of La Fontaine included the dowager Duchess of Orleans and Mme de La Sabliere.

Inquiry & Research

Other Writers of Fables John Gay, Gotthold Lessing, and Ivan Krylov are fabulists influenced by La Fontaine. Krylov, a Russian (1769–1844), became interested in fables after translating the work of La Fontaine. He went on to create many fables of his own which are prized by the Russian people today. John Gay, an Englishman, wrote widely, and is probably best known for "The Beggar's Opera," which was reinterpreted in 1923 by the German Berthold Brecht as "The Threepenny Opera." Without his patron, the duke of Queensbury, the fables of John Gay might have been lost. Gotthold Lessing, a German dramatist (1729–1781), is notable for suggesting in his critical writing that Germans read Shakespeare and English literature for good models.

OVERVIEW

Objectives

- understand the following literary terms:
  - essay
  - letter
  - diary
  - biography
- appreciate shared characteristics of literature across cultures
- recognize themes across cultures

Teaching the Lesson

This lesson provides background on nonfiction as a literary form.

Motivating the Students
Nonfiction is the most influential literary form in contemporary society. The media broadcast nonfiction on television and radio and publish it in magazines, in newspapers, and on the Internet. As students read the nonfiction pieces in this unit, have them consider the following questions:

How were the lives of 17th- and 18th-century women different from the lives of women today?
Possible Responses: Women today have more independence and are taken more seriously.

What beliefs did people of the 17th and 18th centuries have about young people? Are those beliefs still current?
Possible Responses: Adults believed that young people needed to be coached in acquiring ambition and on how to choose friends and behave in good society. Basically, these beliefs are still current.

What did people value in the 17th and 18th centuries? Do we value the same things today?
Possible Responses: People at that time valued appearances, manners, and social standing. These things seem to be valued still today, though the definitions of what constitute these things has changed.

As they finish reading these nonfiction pieces, students can write reactions to these questions and keep their responses in their Writing Portfolios.

Nonfiction in the 18th Century

New Ways of Knowing

In recent years, as the pace of technological innovation has seemed to carry with it a promise of continued progress, many people have come to view the future with enthusiasm. A similar enthusiasm was evident among English people as they entered the 18th century. They were seized by a spirit of curiosity and experimentation—a spirit fueled by the movement known as the Enlightenment. In England, the movement was ushered in by the writings of two major political thinkers, John Locke and Thomas Hobbes, who inspired citizens to rethink all aspects of society. The English people found themselves questioning accepted beliefs, exploring new ideas, and applying close scrutiny to nature and society. Other English writers quickly capitalized on this new spirit.

Isaac Biekerstaff, the mythical editor of *The Tatler*

The Growth of Nonfiction

In this rich environment of ideas, **nonfiction** writing became a favored literary form. Though the aristocracy was the primary audience of the Enlightenment writers, the vitality of the period also touched the middle and lower classes. A spread of education in the 17th century had caused the literacy rate in England to soar. The newly literate public's appetite for information grew, and London became home to a number of periodicals. (See the time line below.)

The Development of the Essay

Most of the contents of 18th-century periodicals consisted of essays. The **essay** is a short work of nonfiction that offers a writer's opinion on a particular subject. The essay form became popular after the 16th-century French philosopher Michel de Montaigne published a collection of writings

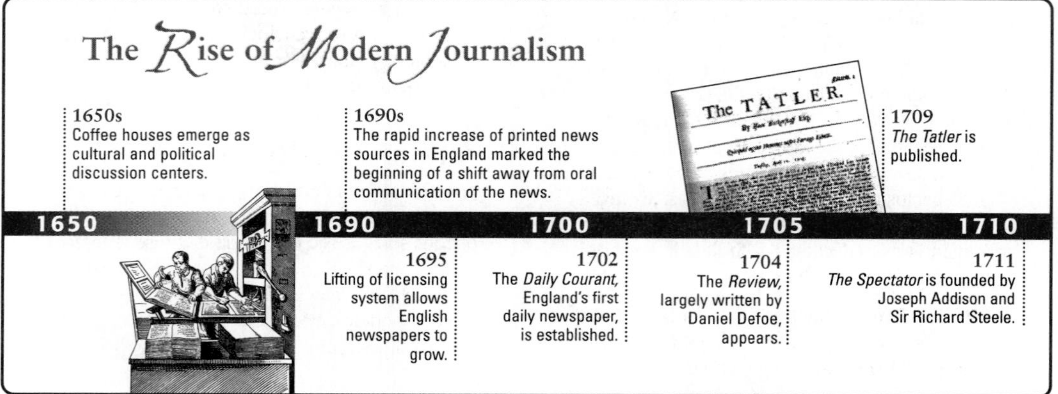

The Rise of Modern Journalism
1650s
Coffee houses emerge as cultural and political discussion centers.
1690s
The rapid increase of printed news sources in England marked the beginning of a shift away from oral communication of the news.
The TATLER.
1709
The Tatler is published.
1650
1690
1700
1705
1710
1695
Lifting of licensing system allows English newspapers to grow.
1702
The Daily Courant, England's first daily newspaper, is established.
1704
The Review, largely written by Daniel Defoe, appears.
1711
The Spectator is founded by Joseph Addison and Sir Richard Steele.

Presenting the Concepts
Read through the strategies aloud or project them on a transparency. Using the descriptions of different forms of nonfiction, ask students which forms of nonfiction are still popular today. Then have them list contemporary programs or publications that might publish or broadcast each form of nonfiction. As students read, model how to use the strategies to analyze the nonfiction pieces.

with the title *Essais,* which means "attempts." In 1597, Francis Bacon became the first prominent English essayist, when he published the first edition of his *Essays*. Works labeled essays were even written in verse, as Alexander Pope's *An Essay on Criticism* shows. The essay became a popular means of expression, a way for English writers to air their views on public matters and to promote social reform.

Informal essays are essays in which writers express their opinions without adopting a completely serious or formal tone. An informal essay can include humor and may deal with an unconventional topic, like these examples:

- Joseph Addison's witty and entertaining commentaries on the morals and manners of the day
- Samuel Johnson's powerfully personal essays in *The Rambler*

Formal essays explore topics in a more serious, thorough, and organized manner than informal essays. Eighteenth-century examples include

- Daniel Defoe's persuasive analysis of female education in "An Academy for Women"
- Mary Wollstonecraft's argument against injustice in *A Vindication of the Rights of Woman*

Other Forms of Nonfiction

Letters and **diaries** often provide personal details of everyday life at the time they were written. You have already read excerpts from Samuel Pepys's diary. This work is important as a record by someone who observed life in its smallest details and then meditated on the meaning of what he had witnessed. Other examples are

- the letters of Lord Chesterfield and Lady Mary Wortley Montagu, which are candid and serious
- the letters in Fanny Burney's *The Diary and Letters of Madame d'Arblay*

Biography is nonfiction in which a writer recounts the events of another person's life. Memoirs, a form of autobiography, are works in which people recall significant events in their own lives. Eighteenth-century examples of these forms include

- James Boswell's biography *The Life of Samuel Johnson,* which gives a full and vivid picture of a great literary figure
- Élisabeth Vigée-Lebrun's memoirs, which tell of her experiences during the upheaval of the French Revolution.

YOUR TURN Find and examine a few modern-day equivalents of any of the nonfiction forms discussed.

Strategies for Reading: Nonfiction

1. Take note of the kind of document you are reading. Is it a formal essay, or is it an informal work with a loose structure?
2. Draw conclusions about the writer's purpose. Was the writer addressing a social problem? What solutions does he or she suggest?
3. Connect to the work by putting yourself in the place and time of the work's original audience.
4. If the writer is giving advice to the reader, consider its value at the time the work was published and its relevance today.
5. Summarize the main ideas of the work in your own words when you have finished reading it.
6. **Monitor** your reading strategies and modify them when your understanding breaks down. Remember to use your Strategies for Active Reading: **predict, visualize, connect, question, clarify,** and **evaluate.**

Making Connections

Nonfiction Across Cultures

As Europeans of the 18th century established trade with lands around the globe, they also spread the idea of the newspaper. Share the following accounts of the development of the newspaper across cultures.

Egypt

When French troops under Napoleon Bonaparte invaded Egypt in 1798, the Egyptian ruler Muhammad Ali was impressed with Bonaparte's use of printed bulletins to influence public opinion. In 1815, Muhammad Ali sent 15-year-old Niquila Musabiki to Milan to learn the art of printing. On his return, Muhammad Ali established the first Arabic periodical, *Jurnal al-Khidiw.* Neither this journal nor the newspaper begun shortly after was circulated to the average citizen. Both were intended for government and military officials, as well as teachers and students in the newly formed schools.

India

An Englishman named James Augustus Hickey took the art of printing to India. On January 29, 1780, he printed the first issue of the *Bengal Gazette.* Within twenty years, 28 other newspapers were started in Calcutta. The English East India Company, which ruled India, was uneasy with the press. On May 13, 1799, less than twenty years after the first Indian newspaper was published, Lord Wellesley, the British governor general of India, issued regulations for censorship of the press.

Japan

In the 17th century, Japanese rulers relied for news of the outside world on Dutch traders, who published annual reports called the *Dutch Book of Rumors.* As Japan became more open to trade, groups of foreigners living in Japan published newspapers in their own languages. In the 1860s, a group of Japanese scholars called *Kaiyakukai* published over a dozen newspapers in Japanese. One member of this group, Fukuchi, published editorials against the government and became the first journalist imprisoned in Japan.

OVERVIEW

Objectives

1. understand and appreciate 18th-century newspaper **essays (Literary Analysis)**
2. appreciate the author's use of the **informal essay** to explore the manners and morals of the day **(Literary Analysis)**
3. **understand the author's purpose** in order to appreciate the informal essay **(Active Reading)**

Summary

These five excerpts reveal Addison's polished, witty style and his worldview. In the first, he describes his purpose—to prompt philosophical discussions in everyday life as people read and talk about his work. The second pokes fun at the overly polite manners of country gentlemen. The third advocates careful inspection of a potential spouse for flaws and blindness to the flaws of the person you have already committed yourself to in marriage. In the fourth, he chides people who seem committed to being melancholy, and, in the last, he reflects on the joy of having children.

 Use **Unit Three Resource Book,** p. 13 for additional support.

Thematic Link

Addison applies the Enlightenment ideals of order, balance, logic, and reason to everyday life. These pieces are noteworthy for a style that embodies the very ideals that are being advocated—Addison presents his **views of society** in a balanced and reasonable manner.

5-Minute Warm-Up

Daily Language SkillBuilder

Have students **proofread** the display sentences on page 515k and write them correctly. The sentences also appear on Transparency 13 of **Grammar Transparencies and Copymasters.**

"It is with much satisfaction that I hear this great city inquiring day by day after these my papers."

from The Spectator

Informal Essays by JOSEPH ADDISON

Connect to Your Life

Popular Bylines Most major newspapers publish daily or weekly feature columns by noted journalists. Many of these columns are extremely popular. Think of some columnists whose articles you have read. What kinds of topics do they usually discuss? Are they concerned with everyday life, or do they focus on other issues? Discuss why these columnists enjoy such a wide readership.

Build Background

Everyday Issues In the late 1600s, England's growing middle class became increasingly concerned with the morals and manners of English society. Responding to this concern, certain writers began to offer moral instruction in periodicals, displaying a casual, good-natured approach to society's ills.

Although hundreds of these periodicals were published before the 18th century, none enjoyed the popularity of those written by Joseph Addison and his friend Richard Steele in the early 1700s. Together, Addison and Steele created a form of writing that has remained popular for nearly three centuries—a predecessor of the articles in modern newsmagazines.

The pair jointly launched *The Spectator,* a periodical dealing with issues of everyday life. It was distributed six days a week for nearly two years. Addison and Steele were the first journalists to write deliberately for women as well as men and to publish letters from both male and female readers.

WORDS TO KNOW **Vocabulary Preview**

assiduous	laudable	scruple	temper
disconsolate	lugubrious	speculation	
indulge	reprobate	superficial	

 **LaserLinks: Background for Reading**
Cultural Connection

Focus Your Reading

LITERARY ANALYSIS INFORMAL ESSAY Through their periodicals, Addison and Steele increased the popularity of the informal essay. An **informal essay** presents an opinion on a subject, but not in a completely serious or formal tone. Characteristics of this type of essay include

- humor
- a personal or confidential approach
- a loose and sometimes rambling style
- a surprising or unconventional topic

As you read the excerpts from *The Spectator,* look for these characteristics of the informal essay.

ACTIVE READING UNDERSTANDING AUTHOR'S PURPOSE An **author's purpose** may be to **entertain,** to **inform,** to **express opinions,** or to **persuade.** An author may fulfill more than one purpose in a piece of writing, but one purpose is usually the most important. To help you understand Addison's purposes, be aware of the following as you read these excerpts:

- the author's **tone**
- the main subject
- the supporting details the author uses to develop his ideas

READER'S NOTEBOOK Use a chart like the one shown to jot down Addison's purposes and the details that support each one.

Title of Excerpt	Purpose(s)	Details Supporting Purpose(s)

LESSON RESOURCES

UNIT THREE RESOURCE BOOK, pp. 13–17

ASSESSMENT RESOURCES

Formal Assessment, pp. 91–92
Teacher's Guide to Assessment and Portfolio Use
Test Generator

SKILLS TRANSPARENCIES AND COPYMASTERS

Reading and Critical Thinking
- Determining Author's Purpose and Audience, T20 (for Active Reading, p. 548)

Grammar
- Compound Adjectives, C69 (for Mini Lesson, p. 551)

Writing
- Proposal, C28 (for Writing Options, p. 553)

INTEGRATED TECHNOLOGY

Audio Library
LaserLinks
- Cultural Connection: The Advent of the Periodical. See **Teacher's SourceBook,** p. 35.

Visit our website:
www.mcdougallittell.com

from The SPECTATOR

JOSEPH ADDISON

PLAN *and* PURPOSE

It is with much satisfaction that I hear this great city inquiring day by day after these my papers, and receiving my morning lectures with a becoming seriousness and attention. My publisher tells me that there are already three thousand of them distributed every day. . . . Since I have raised to myself so great an audience, I shall spare no pains to make their instruction agreeable, and their diversion useful. For which reasons I shall endeavor to enliven morality with wit, and to temper wit with morality, that my readers may, if possible, both ways find their account in the speculation of the day. . . . The mind that lies fallow[1] but a single day, sprouts up in follies that are only to be killed by a constant and assiduous culture. It was said of Socrates, that he brought philosophy down from heaven to inhabit among men; and I shall be ambitious to have it said of me, that I have brought philosophy out of closets and libraries, schools and colleges, to dwell in clubs and assemblies, at tea tables and in coffeehouses.

I would therefore in a very particular manner recommend these my speculations to all well-regulated families, that set apart an hour in every morning for tea and bread and butter; and would earnestly advise them for their good to order this paper to be punctually served up and to be looked upon as a part of the tea equipage. . . .[2]

1. **lies fallow:** is uncultivated, like a field in which no crops have been sown.
2. **equipage:** equipment.

WORDS TO KNOW
temper (tĕm′pər) *v.* to make less intense; moderate
speculation (spĕk′yə-lā′shən) *n.* a consideration of a subject
assiduous (ə-sĭj′o͞o-əs) *adj.* steadily and carefully attentive

549

TEACHING THE LITERATURE

Customizing Instruction

Less Proficient Readers

Set a purpose As students approach each excerpt, they should note the heading to predict what subject the selection will cover. After reading each selection, they can evaluate their predictions.

Students Acquiring English

Explain that Addison used long, well-balanced sentences that sounded both amiably chatty (i.e., conversational) and learned at the same time. Help students manage the difficult language by finding statements in each essay that relate to the stated topic.

Use **Spanish Study Guide** for additional support, pp. 119–210.

Gifted and Talented

Ask students to describe how Addison's syntax and diction affect the essay's tone.

Possible Response: Humorously didactic.

Students should ask themselves how Addison views himself and his readers. Have them write an informal essay that tries to predict the kind of response Addison (or a journalist with his purpose) would receive today. Encourage them to share their conclusions and to modify their essays if they change their opinions.

Mini Lesson Preteaching Vocabulary

ANALOGIES Explain that analogies are statements that identify the relationship between a pair of words. Analogies are often easiest to decipher if they are put in the form of a sentence that explains the relationship.

Model

ASSIDUOUS : INATTENTIVE would be rewritten as "ASSIDUOUS is the opposite of INATTENTIVE."

Instruction Ask students to explain the relationship between the two terms. Write *analogy* on the board or an overhead transparency.

Exercise Ask students to form sentences that explain the following analogies:

1. TEMPER : INTENSIFY *opposites*
2. SPECULATION : THEORY *same*
3. DISCONSOLATE : PERKY *opposites*
4. INDULGE : REFRAIN *opposites*
5. IMMORAL : REPROBATE *characteristic*

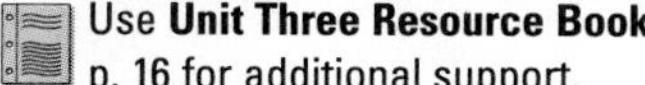
Use **Unit Three Resource Book,** p. 16 for additional support.

A lesson on analogies appears on p. 1317 of the Pupil's Edition.

Reading and Analyzing

Literary Analysis INFORMAL ESSAY

Ask students to pause as they read each essay to consider whether the informality of Addison's essays undercut the fundamental seriousness of his points.

Possible Response: The humor and informality make them seem more relevant to the readers; his light treatment of the subjects trivialize his topics.

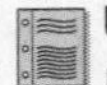 Use **Unit Three Resource Book,** p. 15 for more exercises.

Active Reading UNDERSTANDING AUTHOR'S PURPOSE

Have students evaluate how well each essay accomplishes **Addison's purpose** (as stated in the first excerpt: to bring philosophy into the everyday world). Help them establish criteria for making judgments.

Possible Criteria: Is the essay morally instructive? Is it entertaining?

Remind them to look for details that support their judgments. Students who have identified each essay's purpose in a chart for the Reader's Notebook can evaluate how consistent this essay's purpose is with Addison's general purpose.

 Use **Unit Three Resource Book,** p. 14 for more practice.

Literary Analysis: TONE

A Ask students how Addison reveals his opinion of lugubrious people in this opening sentence.

Possible Response: Words like "mistaken" and "weakness" are not neutral descriptions of lugubrious people; they show that he disapproves of them.

COUNTRY MANNERS

The first and most obvious reflections which arise in a man who changes the city for the country are upon the different manners of the people whom he meets with in those two different scenes of life. By manners I do not mean morals, but behavior and good breeding, as they show themselves in the town and in the country. . . .

1 Rural politeness is very troublesome to a man of my temper, who generally takes the chair that is next me and walks first or last, in the front or in the rear, as chance directs. I have known my friend Sir Roger's dinner almost cold before the company could adjust the ceremonial and be prevailed upon to sit down. . . . Honest Will Wimble, who I should have thought had been altogether uninfected with ceremony, gives me abundance of trouble in this particular. Though he has been fishing all the morning, he will not help himself at dinner till I am served. When we are going out of the hall, he runs behind me; and last night, as we were walking in the fields, stopped short at a stile[3] till I came up to it, and upon my making signs to him to get over, told me, with a serious smile, that sure I believed they had no manners in the country. . . .

Patience in a Punt (1792), Henry William Bunbury. Watercolor, 8″ × 12⅜″, The Paul Mellon Collection, Upperville, Virginia.

On COURTSHIP *and* MARRIAGE

Before marriage we cannot be too inquisitive and discerning in the faults of the person beloved, nor after it too dim-sighted and superficial. However perfect and accomplished the person appears to you at a distance, you will find many blemishes and imperfections in her humor,[4] upon a more intimate acquaintance, which you never discovered or perhaps suspected. Here therefore discretion and good nature are to show their strength; the first will hinder your thoughts from dwelling on what is disagreeable, the other will raise in you all the tenderness of compassion and humanity, and by degrees soften those very imperfections into beauties. . . .

3. **stile:** a set of steps for climbing over a fence.
4. **humor:** disposition; temperament.

WORDS TO KNOW **superficial** (so͞o′pər-fĭsh′əl) *adj.* showing little attention to detail; shallow

Teaching Options

BLOCK SCHEDULING: MANAGING TIME

If your schedule requires that you cover the lesson objectives in a shorter time, use . . .
- Preparing to Read, p. 548
- Thinking Through the Literature, p. 552
- Vocabulary in Action, p. 553

If you want to take advantage of longer class time, use . . .
- TE Teaching Options: Preteaching Vocabulary, p. 549; Grammar, p. 551; Informal Assessment, p. 553
- Choices & Challenges and Author Activity, p. 553

LUGUBRIOUS PEOPLE

A There are many persons, who, by a natural uncheerfulness of heart, mistaken notions of piety, or weakness of understanding, love to indulge this uncomfortable way of life, and give up themselves a prey to grief and melancholy. Superstitious fears, and groundless scruples, cut them off from the pleasures of conversation, and all those social entertainments which are not only innocent but laudable; as if mirth was made for reprobates, and cheerfulness of heart denied those who are the only persons that have a proper title to it.

Sombrius is one of these sons of sorrow. He thinks himself obliged in duty to be sad and disconsolate. He looks on a
2 sudden fit of laughter, as a breach of his baptismal vow. An innocent jest startles him like blasphemy. Tell him of one who is advanced to a title of honor, he lifts up his hands and eyes; describe a public ceremony, he shakes his head. . . . All the little ornaments of life are pomps and vanities. Mirth is wanton,[5] and wit profane. He is scandalized at youth for being lively, and at childhood for being playful. He sits at a Christening, or a marriage feast, as at a funeral; sighs at the conclusion of a merry story; and grows devout when the rest of the company grow pleasant. . . .

ADVANTAGES *of* MARRIAGE

There is another accidental advantage in marriage, which has likewise fallen to my share; I mean having a multitude of children. These I cannot but regard as very great blessings. When I see my little troop before me, I rejoice in the additions which I have made to my species, to my country, and to my religion, in having produced such a number of reasonable creatures, citizens, and Christians. I am pleased to see myself thus perpetuated, and as there is no production comparable to that of a human creature, I am more proud of having been the occasion of ten such glorious productions, than if I had built a hundred pyramids at my own expense, or published as many volumes of the finest wit and learning. . . . ❖

5. **wanton:** immoral or impure.

WORDS TO KNOW

lugubrious (lo͝o-go͞o'brē-əs) *adj.* dismal or gloomy to an exaggerated degree
indulge (ĭn-dŭlj') *v.* to yield to; devote oneself to
scruple (skro͞o'pəl) *n.* an uneasiness about the rightness of an action
laudable (lô'də-bəl) *adj.* praiseworthy
reprobate (rĕp'rə-bāt') *n.* an immoral person; one without principles
disconsolate (dĭs-kŏn'sə-lĭt) *adj.* unable to be comforted; cheerless and gloomy

551

Customizing Instruction

Students Acquiring English

1 Ask students to determine the meaning of *temper* by using context clues.
Answer: disposition.

2 Ask volunteers familiar with the rite of baptism to explain what a "baptismal vow" is.
Possible Response: a formal renunciation of sin.

Less Proficient Readers

Ask students to reflect upon the predictions they made about the excerpts' content based upon the headings. Have them discuss how well Addison chose each title in light of the success (or lack of it) they had with their predictions.

Gifted and Talented

Attic is a term derived from classical Greece that is associated with a clear, polished, witty style. Ask students to find examples of contemporary writing that displays qualities of purity, simplicity, and elegance and share their examples with the class.

Mini Lesson Grammar

COMPOUND ADJECTIVES

Instruction A compound adjective is made up of two adjectives that work together to express a single thought. Such adjectives are linked by a hyphen, as shown in the examples.

Activity Write on the chalkboard the following excerpt from "The Spectator" and underline the compound adjective. Ask students to identify the word the compound adjective modifies. *(families)*

"I would therefore in a very particular manner recommend these my speculations to all well-regulated families . . ."

Exercise Have students rewrite the following sentence, creating compound adjectives wherever possible. Ask them to underline the compound adjectives in their rewritten sentence. (NOTE: Tell students that usually no hyphen is used when the compound adjective follows a linking verb.)

According to Addison, time that is well spent is time that is well planned. *(According to Addison, well-spent time is well-planned time.)*

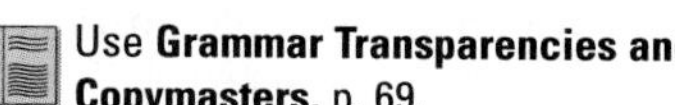

Use **Grammar Transparencies and Copymasters,** p. 69.

Use McDougal Littell's ***Language Network*** for more instruction in compound adjectives.

GUIDING STUDENT RESPONSE

Connect to the Literature

1. What Do You Think?
Guidelines for student response: Students should note the writer's overall tone of reasonableness and moderation in their responses, although in their impressions they may interpret this calmness and temperance as either tepidness or good sense.

Comprehension Check

- They are "troublesome"—forced and impractical.
- Look for faults in beloved before marriage; ignore faults after marriage.

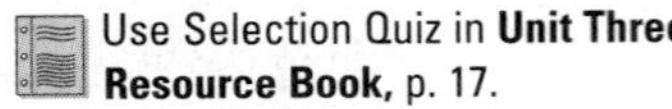
Use Selection Quiz in **Unit Three Resource Book,** p. 17.

Think Critically

2. Possible Responses: Addison was worried about the cultivation of the rising middle classes and liked to advise them. He had a sense of humor about life; he had a tolerant attitude toward human failings.
3. Possible Responses: His purposes were to make instruction in morals and manners more widespread than it had been in the past; to wryly suggest the superiority of "city" manners over the more traditional "country" ones; to give hints on creating marital bliss; to gently chide those who refuse to enjoy life; and to celebrate children and domesticity.
4. Possible Responses: that good sense and cheerfulness are desirable traits; that absurdity and overseriousness are to be avoided.
5. His audience wanted advice on manners and moral guidance, and they enjoyed his witty, thought-provoking ideas about everyday life.

Thinking through the LITERATURE

Connect to the Literature

1. **What Do You Think?** What is your overall impression of these excerpts from *The Spectator?*

Comprehension Check

- Why does Addison object to some practices stemming from "rural politeness"?
- According to Addison, how should you regard your beloved before marriage? after marriage?

Think Critically

2. On the basis of these excerpts, how would you describe Addison?

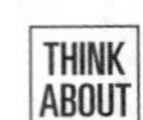
THINK ABOUT
- his goals, as stated under "Plan and Purpose"
- the kinds of topics he addresses
- his **tone,** or attitude toward the topics

3. **ACTIVE READING** **UNDERSTANDING AUTHOR'S PURPOSE** With a small group of classmates, discuss Addison's purposes in these excerpts. Consider each possible **purpose,** providing reasons and details from the excerpts to support it. Then come to a group consensus on Addison's main purpose in each essay. During the discussion, you may want to refer to the chart you made in your **READER'S NOTEBOOK.**

4. What messages about everyday life do you think Addison hoped to convey to his readers?

THINK ABOUT
- the lifestyles and manners he praises
- the types of behavior he criticizes

5. Considering the popularity of Addison's writing when it first appeared, what can you conclude about his **audience?** Give evidence to support your conclusions.

Extend Interpretations

6. **Comparing Texts** Compare the third and fifth excerpts from Addison's essays with Sir Francis Bacon's essay "Of Marriage and Single Life" (page 445). What similarities and differences in subject matter and **tone** do you notice?

7. **Connect to Life** Do you think any of the opinions expressed in the excerpts could be applied to contemporary life? Explain your answer and, if appropriate, support it with examples.

Literary Analysis

INFORMAL ESSAY An **informal essay** presents an opinion on a subject, usually in a light or humorous tone. Other characteristics of this type of essay include a personal approach, a loose rambling style, and often a surprising or unconventional topic. All of these aspects are evident in the following lines from "Lugubrious People":

Sombrius is one of these sons of sorrow. . . . He sits at a Christening, or a marriage feast, as at a funeral; sighs at the conclusion of a merry story; and grows devout when the rest of the company grow pleasant. . . .

Paired Activity With a partner, find other examples from Addison's essays that contain the characteristics mentioned above. List the examples and the characteristics they contain in a chart like the one shown. Then discuss the following question: Why do you think the informal essay was particularly suited to Addison's purpose?

Examples	Characteristics
"Rural politeness is very troublesome to a man of my temper. . . ."	humorous tone, personal approach

Literary Analysis

Paired Activity Humorous anecdotes and a rambling style are clearly observable characteristics of "Country Manners" and "Lugubrious People." All the essays have a personal tone, especially "Advantages of Marriage," in which Addison congratulates himself on his ten children. Unconventional topics include his mildly satirical treatment of overly gloomy and self-consciously polite people. These features help Addison achieve his purpose by permitting him to instruct without being heavy-handed or preachy.

Extend Interpretations

Comparing Texts Possible responses: Both give serious advice about marriage. Bacon looks at its effects on society and a man's career. Addison looks at it as a personal happiness issue, praising the joys of marriage and family.

Connect to Life Accept any reasoned and well-supported response. Addison's observations on courtship and marriage may be seen to have the most relevance to contemporary life.

Choices & CHALLENGES

Writing Options

Newspaper Column Write a newspaper column about a problem in your school or community, presenting your solution to the problem. Place the column in your **Working Portfolio.**

Writing Handbook
See page 1369: Problem-Solution.

Activities & Explorations

Illustrated Excerpts Illustrate the excerpts from *The Spectator.* You might draw your own sketches or find cartoons or other finished pieces that represent the excerpts. ~ **ART**

Vocabulary in Action

EXERCISE A: SYNONYMS Write the letter of the word that is a synonym of the boldfaced word.

1. **temper:** (a) modify, (b) gratify, (c) explain
2. **assiduous:** (a) critical, (b) diligent, (c) flexible
3. **disconsolate:** (a) forlorn, (b) argumentative, (c) separated
4. **lugubrious:** (a) huge, (b) difficult, (c) mournful
5. **indulge:** (a) praise, (b) submit, (c) ruin

EXERCISE B: MEANING CLUES For each phrase in the first column, write the letter of the rhyming phrase in the second column that has a similar meaning.

1. shame the villain
2. distinct and admirable
3. a shallow administrator
4. greatly increase your ethics
5. a pondering about the economy

a. quadruple your **scruples**
b. humiliate the **reprobate**
c. a **speculation** on inflation
d. audible and **laudable**
e. a **superficial** official

Building Vocabulary
For an in-depth lesson on how to expand your vocabulary, see page 1182.

Joseph Addison
1672–1719

Inseparable Friends Joseph Addison's name is inseparably linked with that of his friend Richard Steele because of their collaboration on *The Spectator.* Addison and Steele's long friendship began when they were teenagers at the same London school. Both attended Oxford University and later became strong supporters of the liberal political party known as the Whigs.

Poet and Statesman At Oxford, Addison received a master's degree and distinguished himself as a master of Latin verse. He later served as a member of the British and Irish parliaments and held several important government posts, including that of secretary of state.

Coffeehouse Philosophy Addison was successful in his attempt to bring philosophy "out of closets and libraries . . . and in[to] coffeehouses," partly because the light, humorous style of *The Spectator* made its moral content acceptable to 18th-century readers. By praising marriage, honesty, and simplicity while ridiculing hypocrisy and pride, Addison and Steele sought to improve the morals and manners of their audience; and by writing about the events and scenes of everyday life, they have given future generations a good idea of how people lived in their time.

Author Activity

More Words of Wisdom Read some other articles written by Addison for *The Spectator.* Select a favorite article and present a summary of it to the class.

Writing Options

Newspaper Column Look at different newspaper columnists with your students to examine styles. Draw their attention to the explanation of need for action, the framing of the thesis, and the presentation of the solutions. Have students brainstorm issues and solutions.

Activities & Explorations

Illustrated Excerpts Illustrations should relate to the subject of each excerpt and, ideally, reflect the tone and purpose of the excerpt. History and art history books in a library are good places to start explorations.

Author Activity

More Words of Wisdom There are a number of recurring characters in the periodical essays of Addison. These include two of those briefly mentioned in these excerpts: Will Wimble, a gentleman of leisure, and Sir Roger de Coverley, a country squire, as well as Sir Andrew Freeport, Captain Sentry, and Will Honeycomb.

Vocabulary in Action

Exercise A

1. a
2. b
3. a
4. c
5. b

Exercise B

1. b
2. d
3. e
4. a
5. c

Assessment Informal Assessment

COMPARING AND CONTRASTING

Have students choose an editorial or commentary from the newspaper, then write an essay that finds similarities and differences in Addison's and the modern journalist's style, subject matter, and tone. Students should conclude with an evaluation of the changes 300 years have brought.

RUBRIC

3 **Full Accomplishment** Students insightfully treat style, subject, and tone of both writers and effectively evaluate cultural connections in essay.

2 **Substantial Accomplishment** Students' essays show general understanding but are less well written and thorough.

1 **Little or Partial Accomplishment** Student writing treats only one or two literary elements and fails to note cultural changes.

OVERVIEW

Objectives

1. understand and appreciate **personal letters** that provide insight into 18th-century English society **(Literary Analysis)**
2. appreciate the authors' use of **parallelism (Literary Analysis)**
3. **make generalizations** about personal letters **(Active Reading)**

Summary

In his first letter, Lord Chesterfield discusses problems caused by social "awkwardness." In the second letter, he urges his son to flatter women, since they are socially influential, but not to deal with them seriously.

Lady Montagu advises her daughter on the education of Lady Mary, a granddaughter. She recommends learning as a substitute for marriage and as a remedy for the isolation and loneliness many women face.

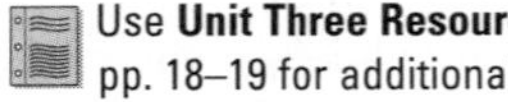

Use **Unit Three Resource Book,** pp. 18–19 for additional support.

Thematic Link

In the course of imparting advice to their children, both Chesterfield and Montagu provide their **views of society.** The letters themselves give cogent and, in many ways, contrasting views of the roles and prospects of women of the time.

5-Minute Warm-Up

Daily Language SkillBuilder

Have students **proofread** the display sentences on page 515k and write them correctly. The sentences also appear on Transparency 13 of **Grammar Transparencies and Copymasters.**

from Letters to His Son

By PHILIP STANHOPE, LORD CHESTERFIELD

Letter to Her Daughter

By LADY MARY WORTLEY MONTAGU

Connect to Your Life

Let Me Give You Some Advice Most parents feel that they have a responsibility to advise their children and attempt to do so in various ways. Think about your own response to advice from parents or older family members. What is the most important or helpful advice that a parent can give a child?

Build Background

Collections of Correspondence The popularity of letter writing during the 1700s resulted in collections of correspondence that have become an important part of English literary tradition. Among the most notable are the **letters** written by Philip Stanhope, Lord Chesterfield, to his son and godson and those written by Lady Mary Wortley Montagu to her husband, sister, and daughter. Because these letters were personal and meant to be read only by their recipients, they offer unique perspectives on 18th-century society.

Chesterfield wrote letters nearly every day for more than 30 years, most of them dealing with matters of etiquette and social awareness. An able statesman, he was known as a man of wit and elegance. The published correspondence of Montagu, who traveled widely and was a leading figure in society, consists of almost 900 letters. In them she reveals her views on society, focusing on the lives and education of women. Also the author of poems and essays, Montagu was encouraged in her pursuits by her friend Mary Astell, who argued for a woman's right to a challenging and balanced education.

WORDS TO KNOW
Vocabulary Preview

contrive	inveterate
controverted	inviolably
diverting	mortification
edifice	prepossess
implacable	scrupulous

Focus Your Reading

LITERARY ANALYSIS PARALLELISM **Parallelism** is the use of similar grammatical constructions to express ideas that are related or equal in importance.

No entertainment is so cheap as reading, nor any pleasure so lasting.

In this example, there are a number of parallel items. *No* is balanced by *nor; entertainment* is balanced by *pleasure; so cheap* is balanced by *so lasting.* As you read these letters, be aware of the writers' use of parallelism.

ACTIVE READING MAKING GENERALIZATIONS A **generalization** is a broad statement based on several examples. In these letters, the two writers present many details about life in 18th-century England—particularly education, the roles of women and men, and manners of the time. Think about what generalizations you might make about 18th-century English society based on the details you find.

READER'S NOTEBOOK As you read these letters, record evidence about education, the roles of men and women, and manners of the day in a chart like the one shown. Make one generalization for each topic.

Topic	Details from Chesterfield Letters	Details from Montagu Letter	Generalization
1. Education			
2. Roles of men and women			
3. Manners of the day			

LESSON RESOURCES

UNIT THREE RESOURCE BOOK, pp. 18–23

ASSESSMENT RESOURCES

Formal Assessment, pp. 93–94
Teacher's Guide to Assessment and Portfolio Use
Test Generator

SKILLS TRANSPARENCIES AND COPYMASTERS

Reading and Critical Thinking
- Organizational Chart: Horizontal, T52 (for Active Reading, p. 554)

Grammar
- Punctuating Elements in a Series, T54 (for Mini Lesson, pp. 558–559)
- Commas in a Series of Phrases, C160 (for Mini Lesson, pp. 558–559)

Writing
- Proposal, C28 (for Writing Options, p. 565)

INTEGRATED TECHNOLOGY

Audio Library
Visit our website: www.mcdougallittell.com

George Morland (about 1785–1810), Thomas Rowlandson. British Museum, London, Bridgeman/Art Resource.

from Letters to His Son

PHILIP STANHOPE,
LORD CHESTERFIELD

SPA, JULY 25, 1741

Dear Boy,

I have often told you in my former letters (and it is most certainly true) that the strictest and most scrupulous honor and virtue can alone make you esteemed and valued by mankind; that parts and learning can alone make you admired and celebrated by them; but that the possession of lesser talents was most absolutely necessary towards making you liked, beloved, and sought after in private life. Of these lesser talents, good-breeding is the principal and most necessary one, not only as it is very important in itself; but as it adds great luster to the more solid advantages both of the heart and the mind.

I have often touched upon good-breeding to you before; so that this letter shall be upon the next necessary qualification to it, which is a genteel, easy manner and carriage, wholly free from those odd tricks, ill habits, and awkwardnesses, which even very many worthy and sensible people have in their behavior. However trifling a genteel manner may sound, it is of very great consequence towards pleasing in private life, especially the women; which, one time or other, you will think worth pleasing; and I have known many a man, from his awkwardness, give people such a dislike of him at first, that all his merit could not get the better of it afterwards. Whereas a genteel manner prepossesses people in your favor, bends them towards you, and makes them wish to like you.

WORDS TO KNOW

scrupulous (skrōō'pyə-ləs) *adj.* showing great strictness and care, especially in matters of right and wrong

prepossess (prē'pə-zĕs') *v.* to influence beforehand; prejudice

TEACHING THE LITERATURE

Customizing Instruction

Less Proficient Readers

Set a Purpose Ask students to discuss the advice they have received from their elders. Then have them compare that advice with Lord Chesterfield's in the first letter.

Students Acquiring English

Allow students adequate time to read the letters, as the density of the text and the difficulty of the language may be discouraging. Have students discuss difficult passages or vocabulary after reading each paragraph.

Help students understand the meanings of *genteel, carriage, consequence,* and *awkwardness.*

Answer: polite, refined in manner; posture, bearing; importance; clumsy, lacking grace.

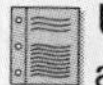 Use **Spanish Study Guide** for additional support, pp. 122–125.

Gifted and Talented

Have students research American colonial society at this time. Were Americans as concerned with manners? What was the general opinion of women? What issues were important to the colonists?

Preteaching Vocabulary

SYNONYMS

Instruction Synonyms are words that have similar meanings. Because no two words have exactly the same meaning, it is important to understand the connotations that each word carries.

Activity Have students work with a partner to think of a synonym for each WORD TO KNOW. The synonym should not appear in the definition given for the word in the textbook. If students have difficulty thinking of a synonym, have them look up the WORD TO KNOW in a thesaurus or synonym finder. Then have students look up the definition of the synonym in a dictionary. Have students discuss the connotative differences between the two words.

Possible Responses: contrive–scheme; controverted–contradicted; diverting–pleasing; edifice–structure; implacable–remorseless; inveterate–entrenched; inviolably–guardedly; mortification–chagrin; prepossess–bias; scrupulous–careful.

 Use **Unit Three Resource Book,** p. 22 for more practice.

Reading and Analyzing

Literary Analysis PARALLELISM

Tell students that parallelism uses matching grammatical constructions to create forceful, balanced writing. Explain that parallelisms are easily recognized if students look for the repetition of words, phrases, or syntax. These elements are often linked by correlative conjunctions (either/or, neither/nor, not only/but also). Ask students to find parallelisms in Chesterfield's first letter.

Possible Response: First sentence at top of page 556.

How do the parallelisms affect the writing?

Possible Responses: connect ideas; sentences flow logically; writing has rhythm.

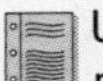

Use **Unit Three Resource Book,** p. 21 for more exercises.

Active Reading

MAKING GENERALIZATIONS

Chesterfield makes the general statement that awkwardness proceeds from two causes. Ask students what they are.

Answer: not having kept good company or not having observed good company carefully enough.

What examples does Chesterfield give of awkwardness?

Possible Response: He gives many examples of an awkward man's boorish behavior in company, including poor table manners and clumsy gestures.

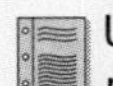

Use **Unit Three Resource Book,** p. 20 for more practice.

Reading Skills and Strategies: MAKING INFERENCES

Ask students what Chesterfield might mean by "little passion(s)."

Possible Response: He might mean emotions such as jealousy, irritation, indignation, or excitement.

Awkwardness can proceed but from two causes; either from not having kept good company, or from not having attended to it. As for your keeping good company, I will take care of that; do you take care to observe their ways and manners, and to form your own upon them. Attention is absolutely necessary for this, as indeed it is for everything else; and a man without attention is not fit to live in the world. When an awkward fellow first comes into a room, it is highly probable that his sword gets between his legs, and throws him down, or makes him stumble at least; when he has recovered this accident, he goes and places himself in the very place of the whole room where he should not; there he soon lets his hat fall down; and, taking it up again, throws down his cane; in recovering his cane, his hat falls a second time; so that he is a quarter of an hour before he is in order again. If he drinks tea or coffee, he certainly scalds his mouth, and lets either the cup or the saucer fall, and spills the tea or coffee in his breeches. At dinner, his awkwardness distinguishes itself particularly, as he has more to do: there he holds his knife, fork, and spoon differently from other people; eats with his knife to the great danger of his mouth, picks his teeth with his fork, and puts his spoon, which has been in his throat twenty times, into the dishes again. If he is to carve, he can never hit the joint; but, in his vain efforts to cut through the bone, scatters the sauce in everybody's face. He generally daubs himself with soup and grease, though his napkin is commonly stuck through a button-hole, and tickles his chin. When he drinks, he infallibly coughs in his glass, and besprinkles the company. Besides all this, he has strange tricks and gestures; such as snuffing up his nose, making faces, putting his fingers in his nose, or blowing it and looking afterwards in his handkerchief, so as to make the company sick. His hands are troublesome to him, when he has not something in them, and he does not know where to put them; but they are in perpetual motion between his bosom and his breeches: he does not wear his clothes, and in short does nothing, like other people. All this, I own, is not in any degree criminal; but it is highly disagreeable and ridiculous in company, and ought most carefully to be avoided by whoever desires to please.

AWKWARDNESS CAN PROCEED BUT FROM TWO CAUSES; EITHER FROM NOT HAVING KEPT GOOD COMPANY, OR FROM NOT HAVING ATTENDED TO IT.

From this account of what you should not do, you may easily judge what you should do; and a due attention to the manners of people of fashion, and who have seen the world, will make it habitual and familiar to you.

There is, likewise, an awkwardness of expression and words, most carefully to be avoided; such as false English, bad pronunciation, old sayings, and common proverbs; which are so many proofs of having kept bad and low company. For example: if, instead of saying that tastes are different, and that every man has his own peculiar one, you should let off a proverb, and say, That what is one man's meat is another man's poison; or else, Every one as they like, as the good man said when he kissed his cow; everybody would be persuaded that you had never kept company with anybody above footmen and housemaids.

Attention will do all this; and without attention nothing is to be done: want of attention, which is really want of thought, is either folly or madness. You should not only have attention to everything, but a quickness of attention, so as to observe, at

Teaching Options

BLOCK SCHEDULING: MANAGING TIME

If your schedule requires that you cover the lesson objectives in a shorter time, use . . .

- Preparing to Read, p. 554
- Thinking Through the Literature, p. 564
- Vocabulary in Action, p. 565

If you want to take advantage of longer class time, use . . .

- TE Teaching Options: Preteaching Vocabulary, p. 555; Standardized Test Practice, p. 557; Grammar, p. 558; Viewing and Representing, p. 560; Link to Workplace, p. 561; Speaking and Listening, p. 562; Informal Assessment, p. 563; Cross Curricular Link, p. 565

once, all the people in the room; their motions, their looks, and their words; and yet without staring at them, and seeming to be an observer. This quick and unobserved observation is of infinite advantage in life, and is to be acquired with care; and, on the contrary, what is called absence, which is a thoughtlessness, and want of attention about what is doing, makes a man so like either a fool or a madman, that, for my part, I see no real difference. A fool never had thought; a madman has lost it; and an absent man is, for the time, without it.

Adieu! Direct your next to me, *chez Monsieur*
1 *Chabert, Banquier, à Paris;*[1] and take care that I find the improvements I expect at my return.

LONDON, SEPTEMBER 5, 1748

Dear Boy,

. . . As women are a considerable, or at least a pretty numerous part, of company; and as their suffrages[2] go a great way towards establishing a man's character in the fashionable part of the world (which is of great importance to the fortune and figure he proposes to make in it), it is necessary to please them. I will therefore, upon this subject, let you into certain *arcana,*[3] that will be very useful for you to know, but which you must, with the utmost care, conceal, and never seem to know.

2 Women, then, are only children of a larger growth; they have an entertaining tattle and sometimes wit; but for solid, reasoning good-sense, I never in my life knew one that had it, or who reasoned or acted consequentially[4] for four-and-twenty hours together. Some little passion or humor always breaks in upon their best resolutions. Their beauty neglected or controverted, their age increased, or their supposed understandings depreciated, instantly kindles their little passions, and overturns any system of consequential conduct, that in their most reasonable moments they might have been capable of forming. A man of sense only trifles with them, plays with them, humors and flatters them, as he does with a sprightly, forward child; but he neither consults them about, nor trusts them with, serious matters; though he often makes them believe that he does both; which is the thing in the world that they are proud of; for they love mightily to be dabbling in business (which by the way, they always spoil); and being justly distrustful, that men in general look upon them in a trifling light, they almost adore that man, who talks more seriously to them, and who seems to consult and trust them; I say, who seems, for weak men really do, but wise ones only seem to do it. No flattery is either too high or too low for them. They will greedily swallow the highest, and gratefully accept of the lowest; and you may safely flatter any woman, from her understanding down to the exquisite taste of her fan.

Women who are either indisputably beautiful, or indisputably ugly, are best flattered upon the score of their understandings; but those who are in a state of mediocrity, are best flattered upon their beauty, or at least their graces; for every woman who is not absolutely ugly, thinks herself handsome; but, not hearing often that she is so, is the more grateful and the more obliged to the few who tell her so; whereas a decided and conscious beauty looks upon every tribute paid to her beauty, only as her due; but wants to shine, and to be considered on the side of her understanding; and a woman who is ugly enough to know that she is so, knows that she has nothing left for it but her understanding, which is consequently (and probably in more senses than one) her weak side.

But these are secrets which you must keep inviolably, if you would not, like Orpheus, be torn

1. *chez* (shā) . . . *à Paris* (ä pä-rē′) *French:* at the house of . . . in Paris. (Chesterfield is giving the address where he can be reached.)
2. **suffrages** (sŭf′rĭ-jĭz): signs of approval.
3. ***arcana*** (är-kā′nə) *Latin:* secrets; mysteries.
4. **consequentially:** in a logically consistent manner.

WORDS TO KNOW

controverted (kŏn′trə-vûr′tĭd) *adj.* disputed; denied **controvert** *v.*
inviolably (ĭn-vī′ə-lə-blē) *adv.* with absolute security

Customizing Instruction

Gifted and Talented

1 Have students speculate about what sort of improvements Chesterfield wants to find in his son. Then have them write a letter from the son in response to this letter from Lord Chesterfield. Would the son be insulted by this advice or take it seriously? Tell students that, at this time, Chesterfield's son was 9 years old.

Less Proficient Readers

Use the following questions to lead a discussion of Chesterfield's letters:

- What does Chesterfield consider the most appealing, genteel manner?
  Answer: one that shows social grace.
- Why does Chesterfield tell his son to manage, please, and flatter women?
  Answer: to advance socially.

2 Check students' understanding with the following questions.

- How does Chesterfield describe women?
  Answer: as children with little good sense.
- How does he tell his son to treat women?
  Possible Response: like children, tricking them into thinking they are involved in business and other serious matters, asking them for advice but not paying attention to what they say.

Students Acquiring English

Encourage students to use punctuation to break the long, difficult sentences into shorter, more easily understood phrases. Advise students that "the fashionable part of the world" refers to the rich and influential people in society.

Ask them to suggest synonyms for *fortune* and *figure.*

Possible Responses: *fortune:* attainments/success; *figure:* image/reputation.

Assessment Standardized Test Practice

IDENTIFYING AUTHOR'S PURPOSE, MAIN IDEAS, AND DETAILS

1. Why is Lord Chesterfield writing this letter?
   A. to tell him that women are childlike
   B. to tell him how to find a good wife
   C. to tell him how to handle women
   D. to tell him that women are socially important
2. Which of the following details does not support the main idea in the second paragraph?
   A. Women will believe any piece of flattery.
   B. Women are incapable of sustained thought.
   C. Women always spoil a business venture.
   D. Women are distrustful of men.

Of the four choices in question 1, all but **B** are actually addressed in the letter. **A** and **D** are main ideas presented in the letter, but only one paragraph is dedicated to each. **C** best describes the purpose of the entire letter.

In question 2, the main idea of the paragraph is that women, who are inferior to men, should be patronized. All four choices are details cited in the paragraph, but **D** does not support the main idea.

Reading and Analyzing

Reading Skills and Strategies: MAKING INFERENCES

A Ask students why Chesterfield says that "Those who laugh with you then will, upon reflection, fear . . . you." Students should support their inferences with evidence from the text and from their experience.

Possible Response: Even if you have not insulted those people, they will conclude from your behavior that you might insult them one day. They will fear you because they will believe that you would humiliate them out of spite or the desire to impress others.

B Ask students to explain why they think Lady Montagu includes these bits of family history in her letter.

Possible Responses: to pass on family heritage, to establish a platform for her opinions.

Thinking Through the Literature

1. Accept all reasonable responses.
2. Possible Responses: Chesterfield is most concerned with social success; he wants his son to have every social grace and to please women, who can affect a man's prospects in society.
3. Possible Response: The father is somewhat overbearing and very ambitious for his son. He says that he will see that his son keeps good company, which implies that he will choose his son's friends. His ambition is obvious in the amount of advice he gives his son about how to behave in good society.

to pieces by the whole sex;[5] on the contrary, a man who thinks of living in the great world, must be gallant, polite, and attentive to please the women. They have, from the weakness of men, more or less influence in all Courts; they absolutely stamp every man's character in the *beau monde*,[6] and make it either current, or cry it down, and stop it in payments. It is, therefore, absolutely necessary to manage, please, and flatter them; and never to discover the least marks of contempt, which is what they never forgive; but in this they are not singular, for it is the same with men; who will much sooner forgive an injustice than an insult. Every man is not ambitious, or covetous, or passionate; but every man has pride enough in his composition to feel and resent the least slight and contempt. Remember, therefore, most carefully to conceal your contempt, however just, wherever you would not make an implacable enemy. Men are much more unwilling to have their weaknesses and their imperfections known, than their crimes; and, if you hint to a man that you think him silly, ignorant, or even ill-bred or awkward, he will hate you more, and longer, than if you tell him plainly that you think him a rogue. Never yield to that temptation, which to most young men is very strong, of exposing other people's weaknesses and infirmities, for the sake either of diverting the company, or of showing your own superiority. You may get the laugh on your side by it, for the present; but you will make enemies by it for ever; and even those who laugh with you then will, upon reflection, fear, and consequently hate you; besides that, it is ill-natured, and a good heart desires rather to conceal than expose other people's weaknesses or misfortunes. If you have wit, use it to please, and not to hurt: you may shine like the sun in the temperate zones, without scorching. Here it is wished for: under the line[7] it is dreaded. **A**

These are some of the hints which my long experience in the great world enables me to give you; and which, if you attend to them, may prove useful to you in your journey through it. I wish it may be a prosperous one; at least, I am sure that it must be your own fault if it is not.

Make my compliments to Mr. Harte, who, I am very sorry to hear, is not well. I hope by this time he is recovered. ❖

Adieu!

5. **like Orpheus** (ôr'fē-əs) . . . **sex:** a reference to a Greek myth in which the musician Orpheus is torn limb from limb by maenads—women frenzied under the influence of the god Dionysus.
6. ***beau monde*** (bō môɴd) *French:* the fashionable world; high society.
7. **line:** equator.

Thinking Through the Literature

1. What is your reaction to Chesterfield after reading his letters?
2. What attitudes and behavior seem to be most important to Chesterfield? Consider the evidence.

   THINK ABOUT
   - the kind of advice he offers and the examples he gives
   - what he hopes to accomplish
   - his views of men and women
3. How would you describe Chesterfield's relationship with his son? Support your ideas with evidence from the letters.

WORDS TO KNOW

implacable (ĭm-plăk'ə-bəl) *adj.* impossible to appease; unforgiving

diverting (dĭ-vûr'tĭng) *n.* entertaining; amusing **divert** *v.*

558

Teaching Options

Grammar

COMMAS IN A SERIES OF PHRASES

Instruction Commas are used to separate the elements in a series that consist of three or more words, phrases, or clauses. In a series a comma is usually placed before the conjunction that connects the last element.

Activity Write the following sentences on the chalkboard.

According to Lady Montagu true knowledge is a matter of knowing things, not just words. It consists of understanding ideas, of grasping facts, and of articulating them.

Ask students to name the phrases that are written in a series. *(of understanding ideas, of grasping facts, and of articulating them)* Next ask them to identify the type of phrases that they are. *(prepositional phrases)*

Exercise Ask students to rewrite each sentence, adding commas where needed and underlining the phrases in a series. Have students meet in pairs to identify the types of phrases that are written in a series.

1. Lord Chesterfield says a man must take care to dominate women to pretend admiration of

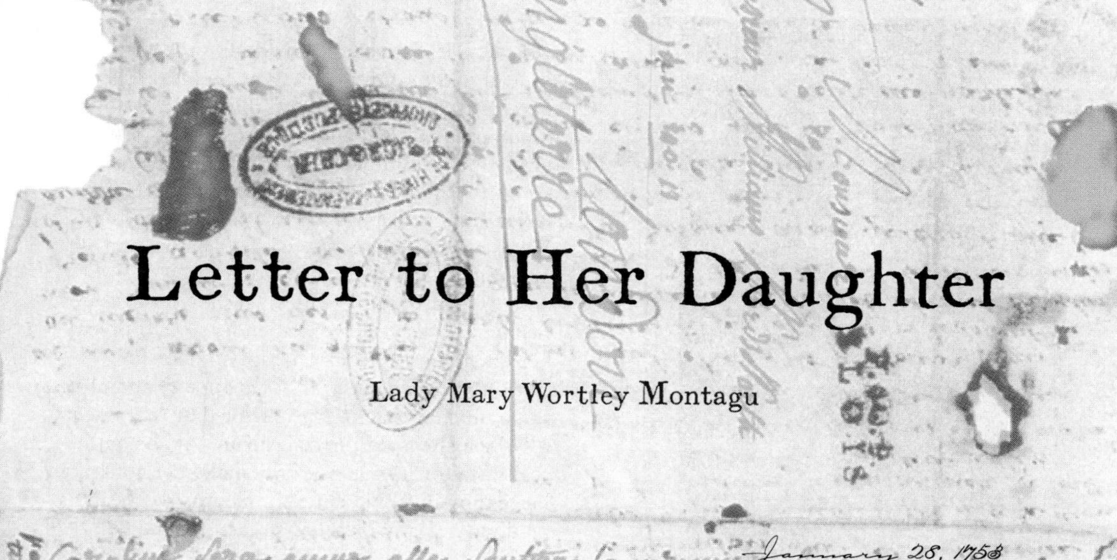

Letter to Her Daughter

Lady Mary Wortley Montagu

January 28, 1753

Dear Child,

You have given me a great deal of satisfaction by your account of your eldest daughter. I am particularly pleased to hear she is a good arithmetician; it is the best proof of understanding. The knowledge of numbers is one of the chief distinctions between us and brutes. If there is anything in blood you may reasonably expect your children should be endowed with an uncommon share of good sense. Mr. Wortley's family and mine have both produced some of the greatest men that have been born in England. I mean Admiral Sandwich, and my great-grandfather who was distinguished by the name of Wise William. I have heard Lord Bute's father mentioned as an extraordinary genius (though he had not many opportunities of showing it), and his uncle the present Duke of Argyle has one of the best heads I ever knew.

B

Customizing Instruction

Less Proficient Readers

Set a Purpose Ask students to read Lady Montagu's letter with an eye on the differences between the view of women in this letter and in Chesterfield's letter.

Students Acquiring English

Make sure students understand that Montagu's letter is to her daughter and concerns her granddaughter. The name of Lady Mary Wortley Montagu's daughter is not mentioned in the letter. The Lady Mary mentioned in the letter is Montagu's granddaughter.

Gifted and Talented

Remind students that Chesterfield's view of women was typical of his class and time. Ask students to consider whether reading Montagu's letter would change his opinion of women. What would he make of her obvious wit and learning?

their ideas and to flatter them at all times. *(Lord Chesterfield says a man must take care to dominate women, to pretend admiration of their ideas, and to flatter them at all times.—infinitive phrases)*

2. For her granddaughter to find happiness in life, Lady Montagu recommends learning languages, and reading books and studying arithmetic. *(No commas are necessary. The gerund phrases are all connected by the conjunction "and.")*
3. In Lady Montagu's day women must have wished for more professional opportunities for more freedom of expression and for more freedom to be themselves. *(In Lady Montagu's day, women must have wished for more professional opportunities, for more freedom of expression, and for more freedom to be themselves.—prepositional phrases)*

Use **Grammar Transparencies and Copymasters,** p. 154.

Use McDougal Littell's ***Language Network*** for more instruction and practice in commas in phrases.

Reading and Analyzing

Active Reading

MAKING GENERALIZATIONS

A Ask students what generalizations they can make about 18th-century views of education and marriage based on Lady Mary Montagu's observations.

Possible Response: Only attractive, wealthy young women with good personalities could hope to receive the best marriage offers.

Literary Analysis: TONE

Ask students how they would characterize the tone of this letter.

Possible Responses: confiding, rather self-satisfied, analytical.

Then ask students, given the social status of women at the time, if they think the letter is practical and thoughtful or cold-hearted. Would they follow this advice for their own daughter?

Answer: Responses will vary.

Reading Skills and Strategies: MAKING INFERENCES

B Ask students why they think Montagu assumes that her granddaughter will live a quiet life rather than attain a high place in society.

Possible Response: She is ill or plain and/or without funds.

C Ask students what the anecdote about the poem reveals about Montagu.

Possible Response: She is proud of her knowledge and protective of her friends.

What is the message or lesson here?

Possible Response: Knowledge will prevent a woman from being duped easily.

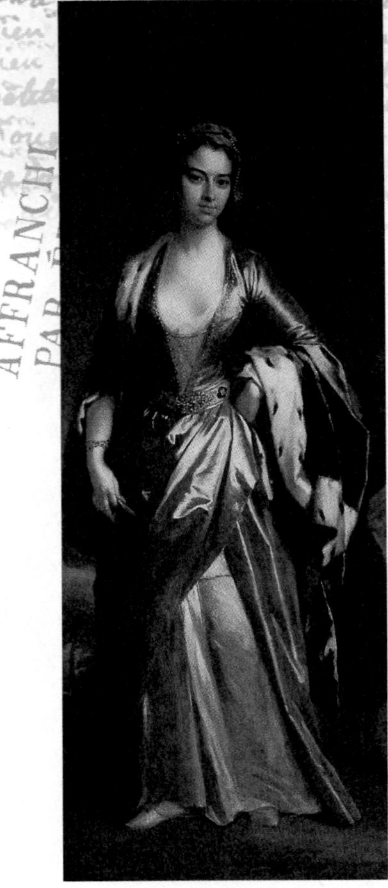

Lady Mary Wortley Montagu (about 1725), Jonathan Richardson. Private collection, courtesy of the Earl of Harrowby.

I will therefore speak to you as supposing Lady Mary not only capable but desirous of learning. In that case, by all means let her be indulged in it. You will tell me, I did not make it a part of your education. Your prospect was very different from hers, as you had no defect either in mind or person to hinder, and much in your circumstances to attract, the highest offers. It seemed your business to learn how to live in the **A**

world, as it is hers to know how to be easy out of it. It is the common error of builders and parents to follow some plan they think beautiful (and perhaps is so) without considering that nothing is beautiful that is misplaced. Hence we see so many edifices raised that the raisers can never inhabit, being too large for their fortunes. Vistas are laid open over barren heaths, and apartments contrived for a coolness very agreeable in Italy but killing in the north of Britain. Thus every woman endeavors to breed her daughter a fine lady, qualifying her for a station in which she will never appear, and at the same time incapacitating her for that retirement to which she is destined. Learning (if she has a real taste for it) will not only make her contented but happy in it. No entertainment is so cheap as reading, nor any pleasure so lasting. She will not want new fashions nor regret the loss of expensive diversions or variety of company if she can be amused with an author in her closet. To render this amusement extensive, she should be permitted to learn the languages. I have heard it lamented that boys lose so many years in mere learning of words. This is no objection to a girl, whose time is not so precious. She cannot advance herself in any profession, and has therefore more hours to spare; and as you say her memory is good she will be very agreeably employed this way. **B** **1**

There are two cautions to be given on this subject: first, not to think herself learned when she can read Latin or even Greek. Languages are more properly to be called vehicles of learning than learning itself, as may be observed in many schoolmasters, who though perhaps critics in grammar are the most ignorant fellows upon earth. True knowledge consists in knowing things, not words. I would wish her no further a linguist than to enable her to read books in their originals, that are often corrupted and always injured by translations. Two hours application every morning will bring this about much sooner

WORDS TO KNOW

edifice (ĕd'ə-fĭs) *n.* a building, especially a large and impressive one

contrive (kən-trīv') *v.* to plan cleverly; devise

560

Teaching Options

Mini Lesson: Viewing and Representing

Lady Mary Wortley Montagu **by Jonathan Richardson**

ART APPRECIATION

Instruction This portrait of Lady Mary by Jonathan Richardson was painted in 1725 when she was 36. Lady Montagu had lived in Turkey from 1716 to 1718 while her husband served as ambassador. The dress she is wearing in this portrait shows a touch of that Eastern influence in the fabric's color and texture.

Application Ask students what impression of Lady Montagu they get from this portrait. Would they guess that she was a woman of learning who had traveled widely and had knowledge of other customs and cultures? Why or why not? Ask students to explain what they would change to make her attributes more evident.

than you can imagine, and she will have leisure enough beside to run over the English poetry, which is a more important part of a woman's education than it is generally supposed. Many a young damsel has been ruined by a fine copy of verses, which she would have laughed at if she had known it had been stolen from Mr. Waller.[1] I remember when I was a girl I saved one of my companions from destruction, who communicated to me an epistle[2] she was quite charmed with. As she had a natural good taste she observed the lines were not so smooth as Prior's or Pope's,[3] but had more thought and spirit than any of theirs. She was wonderfully delighted with such a demonstration of her lover's sense and passion, and not a little pleased with her own charms, that had force enough to inspire such elegancies. In the midst of this triumph I showed her they were taken from Randolph's *Poems,* and the unfortunate transcriber was dismissed with the scorn he deserved. To say truth, the poor plagiary[4] was very unlucky to fall into my hands; that author, being no longer in fashion, would have escaped anyone of less universal reading than myself. You should encourage your daughter to talk over with you what she reads, and as you are very capable of distinguishing, take care she does not mistake pert folly for wit and humor, or rhyme for poetry, which are the common errors of young people, and have a train of ill consequences.

Christie's Images.

The second caution to be given her (and which is most absolutely necessary) is to conceal whatever learning she attains, with as much solicitude as she would hide crookedness or lameness. The parade of it can only serve to draw on her the envy, and consequently the most inveterate hatred of all he and she fools, which will certainly be at least three parts in four of all her acquaintance. The use of knowledge in our sex (beside the amusement of solitude) is to moderate the passions and learn to be contented with a small expense, which are the certain effects of a studious life and, it may be, preferable even to that fame which men have engrossed to themselves and will not suffer us to share. You will tell me I have not observed this rule myself, but you are mistaken; it is only inevitable accident that has given me any reputation that way. I have always carefully avoided it, and ever thought it a misfortune.

The explanation of this paragraph would occasion a long digression, which I will not trouble you with, it being my present design only to say what I think useful for the instruction of my granddaughter, which I have much at heart. If she has the same inclination (I should say passion) for learning that I was born with, history, geography, and philosophy will furnish her with materials to pass away cheerfully a longer life than is allotted to mortals. I believe there are few heads capable of making Sir Isaac Newton's calculations, but the result of them is not difficult to be understood by a moderate capacity. Do not fear this should make her affect the character of Lady———, or Lady————, or Mrs.———. Those women are ridiculous not because they have learning but because they have

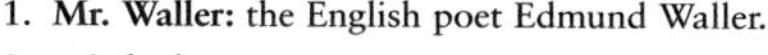

1. **Mr. Waller:** the English poet Edmund Waller.
2. **epistle:** letter.
3. **as Prior's or Pope's:** as those of Matthew Prior or Alexander Pope, both English poets.
4. **plagiary:** plagiarist—one who copies someone else's writing and presents it as his or her own.

WORDS TO KNOW **inveterate** (ĭn-vĕt′ər-ĭt) *adj.* firmly established and deep-rooted

561

Customizing Instruction

Less Proficient Readers

Encourage students to stop every few sentences and paraphrase what they've just read.

1 Ask students to explain the comparison Montagu makes between builders and parents. How can an overambitious builder and an overambitious parent be similar?

Possible Response: Both proceed on the basis of unrealistic assumptions: The builder constructs an enormous edifice when something modest is called for; the parent prepares the child for a place in society he or she will never achieve, not the modest station they are most likely to assume.

Students Acquiring English

Help students understand the sense of "would occasion a long digression, which I will not trouble you with."

Answer: It would take too long to explain why I believe this to be true so I won't bother you with it.

Gifted and Talented

Encourage students to discuss Lady Montagu's admonition to hide what you know, to avoid envy and hatred. Can they think of any time in their lives when it would be or has been better to conceal their learning?

Answer: Responses will vary.

Workplace Link: Writing a Business Letter

Instruction Remind students that business letters have a different audience and purpose than personal letters. Business letters are usually written to people (an audience) with whom the writer has little or no personal relationship. They always have a practical purpose—such as ordering an item, making an appointment, filing a complaint, requesting information, or negotiating a contract.

Activity Ask students to discuss the appropriate tone for business letters and how this tone would differ from that of a personal letter. Then ask them to write the business letter that either Lord Chesterfield or Lady Montagu might have written to a prospective tutor for a young relative.

Reading and Analyzing

Literary Analysis PARALLELISM

Ask students what is the effect of the parallelism in the second sentence.

Possible Responses: helps create rhythmic flow; emphasizes the balance she would like to see given to sewing, drawing, and books.

Reading Skills and Strategies:
DRAWING CONCLUSIONS

Point out to students that Montagu distinguishes between true knowledge and the mere appearance of knowing, accusing women with very little education of taking themselves too seriously. If, as she states earlier, "true knowledge consists in knowing things, not words," what things does she say in this letter that you think she would consider true knowledge?

Possible Responses: the insight that true knowledge is different from the appearance of knowledge; that people should prepare themselves to be happy in the life that they are most likely to lead.

it not. One thinks herself a complete historian after reading Echard's *Roman History*,[5] another a profound philosopher having got by heart some of Pope's unintelligible essays, and a third an able divine[6] on the strength of Whitefield's sermons.[7] Thus you hear them screaming politics and controversy. It is a saying of Thucydides:[8] Ignorance is bold, and knowledge reserved. Indeed it is impossible to be far advanced in it without being more humbled by a conviction of human ignorance than elated by learning.

At the same time I recommend books I neither exclude work nor drawing. I think it as scandalous for a woman not to know how to use a needle, as for a man not to know how to use a sword. I was once extreme fond of my pencil, and it was a great mortification to me when my father turned off my master,[9] having made a considerable progress for the short time I learned. My over-eagerness in the pursuit of it had brought a weakness on my eyes that made it necessary to leave it off, and all the advantage I got was the improvement of my hand. I see by hers that practice will make her a ready writer. She may attain it by serving you for a secretary when your health or affairs make it troublesome to you to write yourself, and custom will make it an agreeable amusement to her. She cannot have too many for that station in life which will probably be her fate. The ultimate end of your education was to make you a good wife (and I have the comfort to hear that you are one); hers ought to be, to make her happy in a virgin state. I will not say it is happier, but it is undoubtedly safer than any marriage. In a lottery where there is (at the lowest computation) ten thousand blanks to a prize it is the most prudent choice not to venture.

I have always been so thoroughly persuaded of this truth that notwithstanding the flattering views I had for you (as I never intended you a sacrifice to my vanity) I thought I owed you the justice to lay before you all the hazards attending matrimony. You may recollect I did so in the strongest manner. Perhaps you may have more success in the instructing your daughter. She has so much company at home she will not need seeking it abroad, and will more readily take the notions you think fit to give her. As you were alone in my family, it would have been thought a great cruelty to suffer you no companions of your own age, especially having so many near relations, and I do not wonder their opinions influenced yours. I was not sorry to see you not determined on a single life, knowing it was not your father's intention, and contented myself with endeavoring to make your home so easy that you might not be in haste to leave it.

I am afraid you will think this a very long and insignificant letter. I hope the kindness of the design will excuse it, being willing to give you every proof in my power that I am your most affectionate mother,

M. Wortley

5. **Echard's *Roman History*:** a book by Lawrence Echard, an English historian.
6. **able divine:** knowledgeable religious scholar.
7. **Whitefield's sermons:** the printed sermons of George Whitefield, a famous English preacher.
8. **Thucydides** (thoo-sĭd′ĭ-dēz′): an ancient Greek historian.
9. **turned off my master:** discharged my art instructor.

WORDS TO KNOW **mortification** (môr′tə-fĭ-kā′shən) *n.* extreme embarrassment; humiliation

562

Teaching Options

Mini Lesson: Speaking and Listening

PRESENTING A WRITER'S VIEWPOINT

Instruction Have students adopt the personas of Lord Chesterfield and Lady Montagu to stage an improvised skit portraying their views.

Prepare Have students work in pairs to study the characters' voices, lives, and views, then practice role-playing them.

Present Let students stage a five-minute discussion in character about a topic addressed in the letters. The rest of the class should listen to share feedback about each performer's dialogue and interpretation. What lines in the text support the performance? Ask students how a modern conversation on this topic might differ from the one they imagined between Lord Chesterfield and Lady Montagu.

BLOCK SCHEDULING This activity is particularly well-suited for longer class periods.

from

Some Reflections upon Marriage

Mary Astell

1 According to the rate that young women are educated, according to the way their time is spent, they are destined to folly and impertinence, to say no worse, and, which is yet more inhuman, they are blamed for that ill conduct they are not suffered to avoid, and reproached for those faults they are in a manner forced into; so that if Heaven has bestowed any sense on them, no other use is made of it, than to leave them without excuse. So much, and no more, of the world is shown them, than serves to weaken and corrupt their minds, to give them wrong notions, and busy them in mean pursuits; to disturb, not to regulate their passions; to make them timorous and dependent, and, in a word, fit for nothing else but to act a farce for the diversion of their governors.

LITERARY LINK

Customizing Instruction

Less Proficient Readers

To get the sense of the excerpt by Mary Astell, students will need to understand the basis of her complaint as laid out in the first two clauses; namely, that young women receive too little education to achieve "true knowledge" (Montagu's term) and are not given any outlets to express constructively what they do know.

Students Acquiring English

1 The length of this sentence may be daunting to students acquiring English. Have them break it up into intelligible units, paying particular attention to parallelisms.

Answer: According to . . . according to; blamed for that . . . they are not . . . reproached for those . . . they are . . .

Point out the string of infinitive phrases in the next sentence.

Gifted and Talented

Ask students to describe similarities and differences between this excerpt by Mary Astell and the letter by Lady Mary Wortley Montagu.

Possible Response: They voice many of the same concerns, but Astell is more combative, less resigned to women accepting a fate that can only be made moderately happy.

Assessment Informal Assessment

WRITING AN ESSAY Have students write an essay comparing the three writers' attitudes toward education, the roles of men and women, and manners of the day. Tell students to support their answers with quotations from the texts.

RUBRIC

3 **Full Accomplishment** Student clearly describes each writer's attitude toward three issues. The comparisons are reasonable and supported with quotations from three texts.

2 **Substantial Accomplishment** Student describes each writer's attitude toward three issues. Student's treatment of one of the issues may be sketchy. Comparisons are reasonable and supported with quotations or other evidence from texts.

1 **Little or Partial Accomplishment** Student addresses only two of three writers or describes each writer's attitude toward only one or two of the issues. The comparisons may demonstrate faulty reasoning or be unsupported with evidence from texts.

GUIDING STUDENT RESPONSE

Connect to the Literature

1. What Do You Think?
Guidelines for student response: Students should support their opinions of Montagu with evidence from the text.

Comprehension Check
- She does not expect her to marry and thinks she should prepare herself to be happy living a life removed from society.
- True knowledge lies in an awareness of larger issues, such as the vastness of what a person has yet to learn.

Use Selection Quiz in **Unit Three Resource Book,** p. 23.

Think Critically

2. Accept all reasonable responses. Students should reveal a detailed knowledge of Montagu's views on education and marriage in their own opinions. Ask them to support their opinions with evidence drawn from the text.
3. Possible Responses: she fears that her granddaughter would never find a husband; her own marriage was unhappy.
4. Possible Responses: interested, insulted, grateful, stimulated to learn.
5. Possible Response: Answers will vary, but most students will probably feel that appearances and manner mattered a very great deal. They should point to examples from both letter writers to prove it is a generalization. Sound inferential thinking is an essential backdrop for good generalizations.

Literary Analysis

Paired Activity You might have pairs of volunteers read their letters aloud to the class.

Connect to the Literature

1. **What Do You Think?** Does Montagu strike you as an appealing person? Explain your opinion.

Comprehension Check
- What kind of future does Montagu expect for her granddaughter?
- What advice does Montagu give on distinguishing true knowledge from the mere appearance of knowing?

Think Critically

2. What is your opinion of Montagu's views on education and marriage for women? Explain your opinion.
3. What factors do you think might have influenced Montagu to give this kind of advice about the raising of her granddaughter?
4. How do you think Montagu's granddaughter might have felt about her grandmother's advice?
5. **ACTIVE READING** **MAKING GENERALIZATIONS** Look back at the chart and the **generalizations** you made about 18th-century society in your READER'S NOTEBOOK. What generalization can you make about how much appearances and manners mattered in 18th-century England?

Extend Interpretations

6. **Comparing Texts** Reread the excerpt from *Some Reflections upon Marriage* on page 563. In what ways might the **letters** of Chesterfield and Montagu be used to support Astell's claims about the treatment of women? Be specific in your answer.
7. **What If?** Suppose Montagu's granddaughter had no "defect either in mind or person." How do you think Montagu's letter would be different? What advice would she impart regarding her granddaughter?
8. **Connect to Life** What do you think Montagu and Chesterfield would make of the role of women in society today? Discuss with your classmates.

Literary Analysis

PARALLELISM **Parallelism**—the use of similar grammatical constructions to express ideas that are related or equal in importance—may involve words, phrases, sentences, or paragraphs. The following sentence from Chesterfield's second letter, for example, repeats both words and phrases:

Women who are either indisputably beautiful, or indisputably ugly, are best flattered upon the score of their understandings; but those who are in a state of mediocrity, are best flattered upon their beauty. . . .

There are many such examples in these letters of parallel constructions that reflect the relationship between ideas.

Paired Activity With a partner, exchange letters on a subject of interest to you both—sports or movies, for example—in which you employ parallelism to express your thoughts.

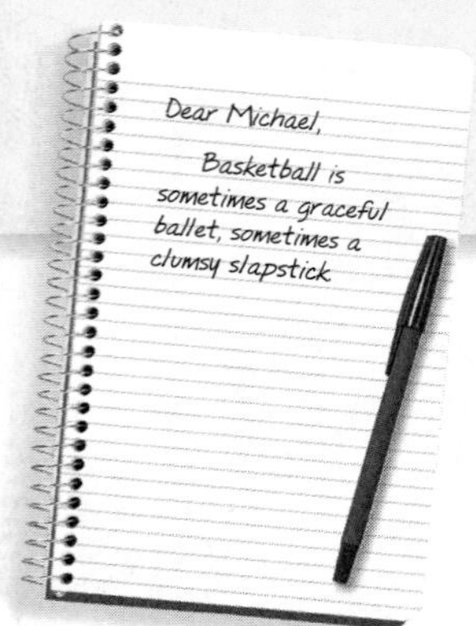

Dear Michael,
Basketball is sometimes a graceful ballet, sometimes a clumsy slapstick

Extend Interpretations

Comparing Texts Possible response: Chesterfield's description of 18th-century women as silly, irrational, and obsessed with trivialities is similar to Astell's (if less sympathetic). Montagu, likewise, describes the hazards of providing women with too little education. In addition, the letters of both Chesterfield and Montagu give ample evidence of the narrow prospects young women had.

What If? Answers may vary. Most obvious response: She wouldn't ascribe as much importance to education, since she had not found it to be as important for the mother, who had no "defects."

Connect to Life Chesterfield would be surprised at the attainments of many of them. Montagu would probably be heartened by their increased opportunities, although she might think too many of them are married (given her feeling that marriage is a gamble, or "lottery" for women).

Writing Options

Essay on Awkwardness
Chesterfield addresses the problem of awkwardness in social relations and proposes ways of dealing with it. Write an essay in which you suggest solutions to social awkwardness in today's world. Place the essay in your **Working Portfolio.**

Writing Handbook
See page 1368: Cause and Effect.

Vocabulary in Action

EXERCISE: CLUES AND IDIOMS
On your paper, write the vocabulary words that are suggested by the phrases in items 1–5 and by the groups of idioms in items 6–10.

1. how secrets should be kept and deep friendships preserved
2. what you do when you make a friend expect a blind date to be terrific
3. what the White House and Buckingham Palace are examples of
4. the kind of behavior that is so habitual that it can never be changed
5. what inventors, architects, and schemers do
6. nearly die of shame, blow one's cool, be red as a beet, feel like two cents
7. dotting all the i's, being as good as one's word, taking pains, following through
8. no way, on the contrary, have a bone to pick
9. just for laughs, take a break, live a little
10. carry a grudge, heart of stone, hard as nails

Building Vocabulary
Several Words to Know in this lesson contain prefixes and suffixes. For an in-depth study of word parts, see page 1104.

WORDS TO KNOW			
contrive	implacable	prepossess	
controverted	inveterate	scrupulous	
diverting	inviolably		
edifice	mortification		

Philip Stanhope, Lord Chesterfield
1694–1773

Diplomat, Writer, Patron of the Arts Philip Stanhope was raised and educated by his grandmother and largely ignored by his aristocratic father. He studied briefly at Cambridge University, then left the university to travel abroad, where he eagerly observed and imitated French manners and culture. He became a capable statesman and diplomat, eventually serving as secretary of state. Chesterfield was a friend of Pope, Swift, and Voltaire, and as a patron of the arts he gave financial assistance to many struggling writers. Although he contributed numerous essays to periodicals, he is remembered chiefly for his letters to his son and godson.

Lady Mary Wortley Montagu
1689–1762

An Adventurous Life Lady Mary Wortley Montagu, a gifted poet and essayist, was acquainted with many literary figures, including Pope, Addison, and Steele. Her first published work was an essay contributed to *The Spectator.* A daughter of London aristocrats, Montagu educated herself in her father's library. In 1712, to escape an arranged marriage, she eloped with Edward Wortley Montagu. When Edward was appointed ambassador to Turkey, Lady Mary accompanied him to Constantinople, where she wrote more than 50 letters describing Turkish culture. Her Turkish letters were published in 1763, but a full edition of her letters was not available until 1967.

Writing Options

Essay on Awkwardness Remind students that their essays should have a strong thesis and convincing supporting evidence for their ideas. Encourage them to attempt the use of parallelisms.

Vocabulary in Action

1. inviolably
2. prepossess
3. edifice
4. inveterate
5. contrive
6. mortification
7. scrupulous
8. controvert
9. diverting
10. implacable

Cross Curricular Link Social Science

MANNERS Remind your students that Lord Chesterfield implies that good manners are the products of paying attention and emulating the behavior of those who have social graces. But is it that easy? Ask your students if their ideas of proper behavior are the same as those of their grandparents—or the same as those of someone in Saudi Arabia or Japan or France or ancient Rome. Ask students to form small groups and research one of the following topics of their own choosing, using multiple sources. They can, with your approval, report their findings to the class in a skit or graphic presentation.

- Compare/contrast manners of two cultures, looking at specific features such as table manners, driving etiquette, proper clothing, courtship.
- Pick a time period, and show the similarities and differences between that time and now.
- Look at two 20th-century experts on manners (Miss Manners, Emily Post, Martha Stewart, Elsa Maxwell) for differences.

As support for the research process, refer students to the following resources: Writing Handbook: Research Report Writing, pp. 1373–1378 Communication Handbook: Research and Inquiry, pp. 1381–1390

MILESTONES IN BRITISH LITERATURE

Robinson Crusoe (full title: *The Life and Strange Surprising Adventures of Robinson Crusoe of York, Mariner*) was instantly acclaimed upon publication in 1719. It is widely considered the first important English novel, and one critic has even classified it as among the "dozen immortal books in English." Detailing a shipwreck, a far-away desert island, and a struggle for survival by using one's wits, *Robinson Crusoe* is a classic adventure story, and its combination of romance and realism set the tone for much fiction that followed it.

Additional Background

Daniel Defoe (Foe before he changed his name about 1703) apparently had a compulsive need to express his opinions in print. In his first book, *An Essay on Projects* (1697), he argued for such projects as the "academy for women" proposed in Part 2 of this unit. His ironic treatment of religious intolerance in *The Shortest Way with the Dissenters* (1702) got him imprisoned and pilloried. After Defoe's release from prison in 1703, he became a pamphleteer (and government spy) for Robert Harley, the earl of Oxford, who later became Prime Minister. After 1704, he continued writing satire and political opinion on a broad scale.

Defoe was almost 60 when he began a new career—that of a writer of fiction. *Robinson Crusoe* (1719) was his first novel, and many of his other popular books, such as *Moll Flanders* (1722) and *Roxana* (1724), followed quickly. His novels, all written in the first person and based on real events and people, are notable for their portrayals of ordinary humans who survive unusual circumstances with courage and ingenuity. His remarkable *Journal of the Plague Year* (1722), told by a fictional "eyewitness," is so realistic in its reconstruction of London's devastating killer plague of 1664–65 that it is often considered a more authentic view of the tragedy than nonfiction accounts such as *The Diary of Samuel Pepys.*

MILESTONES IN BRITISH LITERATURE

Daniel Defoe

Robinson Crusoe

If you were marooned on a remote and wild island, how would you respond to the challenges of nature? What would you eat? Where would you sleep? Would you go mad from isolation—or use the experience as a chance to grow? These are some of the issues confronted by the hero of Daniel Defoe's masterful adventure story *Robinson Crusoe.*

The plot of *Robinson Crusoe* is based on the true story of Alexander Selkirk, a sailor who had been stranded for 52 months on an uninhabited island near Chile. Defoe capitalized on public interest in Selkirk by producing a memoir of a fictional castaway—Robinson Crusoe—using the first-person narrative, exact details, and precise chronology that would be found in the journal of a seasoned seafarer. The resulting story was so popular that unscrupulous publishers scrambled to produce and sell their own editions. Even today, the book is available in many editions, some lavishly illustrated, and the story of Robinson Crusoe is used as a basis for comic books, feature films, and science fiction adventures.

In his 28 years on the island, Crusoe learns how to make tools, plant seeds, and domesticate animals. Slowly, he turns the untamed land into a secure and productive homestead.

566 UNIT THREE PART 1: VIEWS OF SOCIETY

In addition to chronicling the adventures of a castaway, Defoe explored the social and moral values of his time. For example, he portrays Crusoe as a willful son whose disregard for the wishes of his parents leads him into danger, slavery, and shipwreck. He also shows how the experience of life alone on the island leads Crusoe to appreciate the moral and social values back home. Only when Crusoe begins to apply these values, along with his native talents, does he begin to prosper. He teaches himself carpentry, pottery, agriculture, and animal husbandry. He learns the geography of his island. He rescues from cannibals a man whom he names Friday and who becomes his devoted servant. Finally, he saves the captain of a passing ship from mutineers. Leaving the mutineers on the island, Crusoe and the captain sail with Friday to England, where Crusoe assumes a place in English society.

At one time or another, almost everyone has wondered what it would be like to have to survive in a wilderness. In *Robinson Crusoe,* Defoe presents a man who not only survives but thrives—who transforms the wilderness into an expression of humanity. The result is a story that appeals to everyone who yearns for adventure.

Left:
Despite ominous mishaps, including a severe storm, Robinson Crusoe is determined to make his fortune at sea.

Center:
Crusoe, the disheveled castaway

Right:
For 26 of his years on the island, Crusoe's only companions are a dog, some cats, a goat, and his parrot, which he teaches to say "Poor Robin Crusoe! Where are you?"

LITERARY CHRONOLOGY

The following are publication dates of some of Defoe's most famous writings:

1697 *An Essay on Projects*

1701 *The True-born Englishman*

1702 *The Shortest Way with the Dissenters*

1719 *Robinson Crusoe*

1722 *Moll Flanders*
A Journal of the Plague Year
Colonel Jack

1724 *Roxana*

MILESTONES IN BRITISH LITERATURE 567

Objectives
- write a Proposal
- use a written text as a model for writing
- revise a draft to establish transitions
- use adverbs correctly

Introducing the Workshop

A Proposal By making proposals, individuals formally present detailed solutions to existing problems. The proposal writer's main goal is to convince readers to implement a recommended plan of action. Proposal writing is a practical skill with many applications in the business world, in the academic professions, and in community service.

Ask students to recount times they have proposed changes in the way things were done. What techniques did they use to present their ideas and persuade others to act on their suggestions? Which techniques worked and which did not? The skills students will learn in this workshop will help them identify a problem, present a detailed solution, and rebut possible objections to their proposal.

Basics in a Box

B Using the Graphic The graphic suggests two essential elements to a successful proposal: a clear statement of the problem or need and a detailed presentation of the solution and its benefits. Point out that establishing that a problem exists can sometimes be a detailed task in itself.

C Presenting the Rubric To better understand the assignment, students can refer to the Standards for Writing a Successful Proposal. You may wish to discuss with them the complete rubric, which describes several levels of proficiency. Use the rubric to evaluate the writing of student proposals.

Use McDougal Littell's ***Language Network,*** Chapter 21, for more instruction on writing a proposal.

To engage students visually, use **Power Presentation** 4, Proposal.

Writing Workshop

Proposal

Recommending a Solution . . .

From Reading to Writing In the second half of the 17th century, English writers sought to make sense of their world by observing society and addressing problems that they saw. People today are just as observant and concerned, and they often make (A) suggestions on improving their communities in the form of proposals. A **proposal** is a document or speech that identifies a problem or need, and offers a plan of action to solve the problem or meet the need. You can write a proposal to address issues affecting your family, school, or community.

For Your Portfolio

WRITING PROMPT Write a proposal recommending a solution to a problem or a need.

Purpose: To convince a group or organization to put your plan into practice

Audience: The decision-makers who will be evaluating your proposal

Basics in a Box

Proposal at a Glance

(B)

Summary of Proposal
Briefly states the purpose of the proposal

Need
- Defines the problem or need
- States why addressing it is important

Proposed Solution
- Presents a detailed solution
- Explains its benefits
- Restates the problem or need and the benefits of the solution

(C) **RUBRIC Standards for Writing**

A successful proposal should
- target a specific audience
- clearly define a problem or state a need
- present a clear solution, using evidence to demonstrate that the plan is workable
- show how the plan will be implemented and what resources will be required
- demonstrate clearly that the advantages of the plan outweigh possible objections to it

LESSON RESOURCES

USING PRINT RESOURCES

Unit Three Resource Book
- Prewriting, p. 24
- Drafting, p. 25
- Peer Response, pp. 26–27
- Revising, Editing, and Proofreading, p. 28
- Student Models, pp. 29–34
- Rubric, p. 35

Writing Transparencies and Copymasters
- Writing Process Transparencies, pp. 3, 4
- Writing Structure Transparencies, p. 9
- Writing Template Copymasters, p. 28

USING MEDIA RESOURCES

LaserLinks
Writing Springboards
See Teacher's SourceBook p. 114 for bar codes.

Writing Coach CD-ROM

Visit our website:
www.mcdougallittell.com

For a complete view of Lesson Resources, see page 515g.

Analyzing a Student Model

Simona Ioffe
Stevenson High School

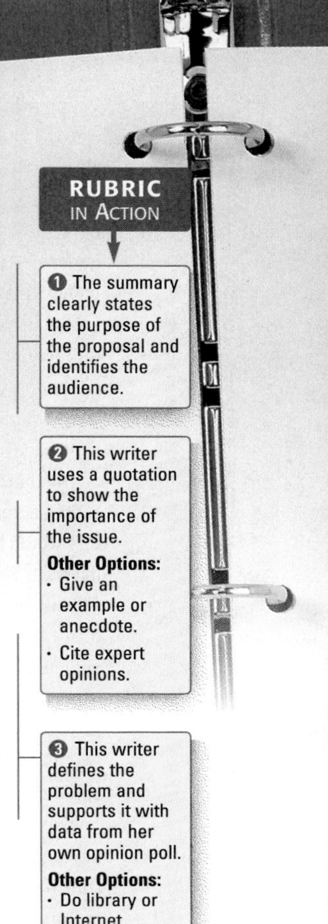

RUBRIC IN ACTION

❶ The summary clearly states the purpose of the proposal and identifies the audience.

❷ This writer uses a quotation to show the importance of the issue.

Other Options:
- Give an example or anecdote.
- Cite expert opinions.

❸ This writer defines the problem and supports it with data from her own opinion poll.

Other Options:
- Do library or Internet research.
- Consult authorities.

❹ Points out the weaknesses of a current plan

A Proposal to Enhance Arts Education at Stevenson High School

Summary

This proposal requests approval and support from the faculty and administration of Stevenson High School for creating an arts festival. This festival will increase students' awareness of and appreciation for the arts and will give them a more fully rounded education.

Need

An understanding of the arts is vital because it broadens the horizons of every individual. The Association for the Advancement of Arts Education (AAAE) states that "the arts are necessary at all grade levels for many aspects of students' success in school and in life, as in their careers." The Association further states that "all of the arts help students develop emotionally and socially."

D Stevenson High School currently addresses this need by offering several courses in the areas of art and music and by sponsoring student drama and dance clubs. However, many students do not take advantage of these opportunities. A random poll of 50 senior students at Stevenson High School showed that 40 percent had not taken any arts courses throughout their years at the school. Some even stated that "only people who will become actors need to participate in the arts." Other disturbing comments included "the fine arts are a waste of time" and "it's boring!" This poll clearly shows the need for the school to develop a plan that will give all students at least a basic appreciation for the arts.

To solve this problem, members of the faculty have suggested creating an arts requirement for graduation. This idea meets the problem head-on. However, it will take time to plan and may require a restructuring of the arts department. For example, a new survey class covering visual art, theater, music, and dance will have to be developed. Although this would be a good long-term solution, students need an opportunity to experience the arts as soon as possible—and not by reading about them in a textbook.

Teaching the Lesson

Analyzing the Model

"A Proposal to Enhance Arts Education at Stevenson High School"

D The student model proposes the implementation of a two-day arts festival at the writer's high school. Have students read the model and analyze its effectiveness. Then discuss the Rubric in Action. Point out key words and phrases in the student model that correspond to the elements mentioned in the Rubric in Action.

2. Explain that using expert opinion or expert testimony can be an effective way to lend credibility to a claim. By citing a source, the writer gains authority and adds persuasive power to her proposal.
3. Ask students to consider the credibility of the writer's opinion poll. What effect does her opinion poll have on readers? How might the writer's motivation affect their evaluation of the poll and the writer's credibility? **Possible Response:** Although the opinion poll lacks scientific credibility, it seems reliable enough to support the conclusion the writer draws from it. However the writer's motivation might make the reader question the poll design and results.
4. Ask students how the writer both disputes and endorses the opposition's point in this paragraph. **Possible Response:** The writer deals effectively with the competing proposal. She confronts it head on and points out its immediate weaknesses but then acknowledges its long-term benefits.

Mini Lesson: Viewing and Representing

PICTURING TEXT STRUCTURE

Instruction Explain that a proposal has a specific structure for presenting information. That structure entails summarizing the problem; presenting the need; and stating clear, concise solutions to the problem.

Activity Have students analyze the text structure of the student model by constructing a graphic organizer. The graphic should illustrate how the student writer organized her proposal. Students might begin by rereading the model and jotting down the main idea in each paragraph. From their notes they can construct a graphic organizer that shows how the ideas relate to each other as well as to the whole. Students should conclude by discussing how the text structure influences their understanding. A sample graphic organizer is shown.

Summary
- create an arts festival at Stevenson H.S.

↓

Need
- random poll shows a need for arts education

↓

Proposed Solution
- create an arts festival in the spring
- implement with help of entire school community

↓

Rebuttal of Objection
- school days will be lost but arts festival offers other benefits

5. An arts festival at Stevenson High School would be comprised of performances, visual presentations, exhibits, classes, and workshops that would provide hands-on experience in the arts. Students would gain a broad exposure to all four genres of the arts.
6. Explain that a proposal must be realistic if it is to be accepted. Readers need to know how the plan will be implemented. Ask students what suggestions the writer makes for implementing her plan. **Possible Responses:** The proposal calls for school community involvement. The writer specifically assigns roles to various groups and provides suggestions in dealing with costs.
7. Have students determine the tone the writer uses to persuade her audience in the last paragraph. **Possible Response:** The writer's tone is factual rather than emotional. She acknowledges the accuracy and validity of the opposition and then reasons *around* their objection.

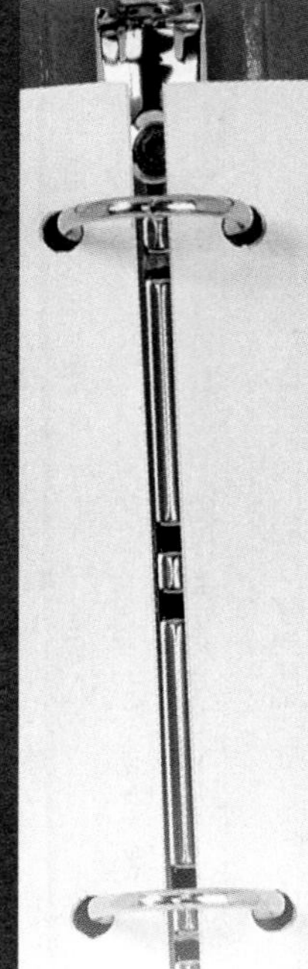

Proposed Solution

My solution is to create an arts festival this spring. The festival would allow students to participate in the arts firsthand and would be a school-wide event involving the entire student body, faculty, and staff. During the two-day festival, Stevenson High School would be completely transformed into a learning facility for the arts. The festival would include performances, visual presentations, and hands-on experiences for every student. Exhibits, classes, workshops, and activities would be held throughout the building.

Students would be allowed to select the events to participate in, but they would be required to experience all four genres of art. The mix of genres and formats would give students broad exposure to the arts.

❺ Explains the details of the solution

Implementing this plan would require commitment from the entire school community. The arts department faculty would need to plan events that would be interesting and beneficial for students and manageable for the staff. The administration would handle scheduling and legal issues. The maintenance staff would need to organize the acquisition and distribution of chairs, tables, and other necessary furniture. Student volunteers would do much of the work of making the festival run smoothly. Most of the funding for the fair could probably come from the regular budgets of the administration and art department. However, local businesses could be asked to donate materials; and if necessary, students and faculty could hold fundraising activities such as bake sales or car washes.

❻ This writer describes the general resources needed to implement the plan.

Other Options
- Spell out the steps involved in putting the plan into action
- Identify people who will back or fund the plan
- Estimate the costs

Even though an arts festival would shorten the school year by two days, Stevenson High School would be responding to the needs of students. Writer Marcel Proust said, "Only through art can we get outside of ourselves and know another's view of the universe. . . ." An arts festival would give students the opportunity to explore new ways of understanding and experiencing the world.

❼ Explains how the advantages of the plan outweigh the disadvantages

Speaking and Listening

ANALYZING PERSUASIVE MESSAGES
Have students present their proposals and have the audience analyze, evaluate, and critique the presentations.

Instruction Ask students to use this criteria for analyzing, evaluating, and critiquing the proposal presentations. The speaker:
- has a clear goal or argument
- supports the argument with convincing facts
- uses sound logic in developing the argument
- uses voice, facial expressions, and gestures effectively
- holds the audience's attention

Application Have students use the criteria to analyze (examine in detail) and evaluate (judge) the presentation of each proposal. Students can critique (review or discuss critically) orally or in writing.

Note: Refer students to Speaking and Listening in the Communication Handbook on pp. 1386–1388.

Writing Your Proposal

❶ Prewriting

Begin by choosing a problem to be solved or identifying a need to be filled. You might make a **list** of ideas for improving your school or community. You could also try **brainstorming** problems or needs with a group of friends. See the **Idea Bank** in the margin for more suggestions. After you have selected the topic for your proposal, follow the steps below.

Planning your Proposal

1. **Think about your proposal.** Why is the issue important? How will your proposal meet the need?
2. **Consider your audience.** Who will evaluate your proposal? What do they care about? What will persuade them to accept your proposal?
3. **List the details.** What steps are involved? What resources are needed?
4. **Evaluate the workability of your proposal.** How hard will it be to put your plan into effect? What are some of the arguments against it?
5. **Plan your research.** What information will help support the proposal? Where can you find information? Can you conduct some of your own research?

❷ Drafting

A problem well stated is a problem half solved.
Charles Kettering, inventor

You can begin drafting your proposal anywhere—with the summary, the problem or need, or the solution. No matter where you begin, though, you eventually will have to address all these points. As you draft, remember to show both why addressing the problem or need is important and how your proposed solution accomplishes that. Be sure to support your statements with facts, statistics, or expert opinions. Also, define any technical terms your audience might not know and think about objections they might have to your plan. You can improve your draft later with input from your peer readers.

Ask Your Peer Reader

- What other evidence would convince people there is a real problem or need?
- How can obstacles to implementing my plan be overcome?
- What other resources are needed to support my plan?
- Who is likely to oppose my plan and why?

IDEABank

1. Your Working Portfolio
Build on one of the Writing Options you completed earlier in this unit:

- **Problem-Solving Essay,** p. 533
- **Essay on a Social Problem,** p. 539
- **Newspaper Column,** p. 553
- **Essay on Awkwardness,** p. 565

2. Community Issues
Study recent issues of your school or community newsletters to find problems that need solutions.

3. A Friend in Need
Interview friends or neighbors to find out what neighborhood problem bothers them most. What can you think of that would help solve this problem? Choose one solution as the focus for your proposal.

Adding an appendix

Include supporting material such as charts, copies of published articles, letters of support, and other information at the end of your proposal in a section called the appendix.

Guiding Student Writing

Prewriting

Choosing a Topic

If after reading the Idea Bank students are having difficulty choosing their topics, suggest they try the following:

- Divide a piece of paper in two columns. In the left-hand column, list all groups, organizations, and communities to which they belong. In the right-hand column, list any problems that each group experiences.
- Construct a chart similar to the one above focusing on problems in the workplace. List problems perceived from an employer's or a customer's perspective.

Planning the Proposal

1. Have students work with a partner to evaluate their topics and describe the solutions they propose.
2. Proposal writers must carefully consider the needs of their audience because they are depending on their audience to help them carry out their ideas.
3. Have students develop a plan of action to implement the proposal. Suggest they write down steps, resources, and potential problems in the solution as they now see them.
4. Have students share their proposal with someone who is opposed to the solution being proposed. Tell students to ask the other person to explain his or her objections.
5. Suggest that students pursue research in the library or talk with knowledgeable community members to identify support for their solution.

Drafting

Organizing the Draft

You might share the following guide to organizing a standard proposal with students:

A. Summary of proposal
B. Statement of need, supported by examples, testimony, and data, when appropriate
C. Description of plan of action, detailing steps to be taken and describing benefits of the plan and how benefits will outweigh any disadvantages
D. Description of request: exactly what money or other resources are needed and how they will be used

As students begin drafting, ask them to look for ways to incorporate facts, data, evidence, or expert opinion through direct quotation. The beginning and ending of the essay are both good places to use quotes because those are the places where a first and last impression is created. An "authoritative" voice can help persuade readers.

Revising

TRANSITION WORDS

Explain that the use of transitional words helps make writing coherent. Transitional words can be used both within a paragraph and between paragraphs to indicate relationships between ideas. Point out that in the model, words like *however* and *although* show contrast and signal that the writer is refuting an objection to her plan. Other words that students might use to signal contrast in their own essays include *nevertheless, on the other hand, but, yet,* and *still.*

Editing and Proofreading

USING ADVERBS CORRECTLY

To help students distinguish between adjectives and adverbs in the example, ask them to identify the word that *smooth* is modifying. Once students determine that *smooth* is meant to modify the verb *run,* they can see that an adverb is needed, not an adjective. In the second sentence, *probable* is meant to modify the verb *could come;* therefore, the correct choice is the adverb *probably.* Also, encourage students to consult a manual of style as needed. Students should produce an error-free final draft of the proposal.

Reflecting

You might also have students consider the following questions as they reflect on their writing: Are the problems they've addressed in their proposal universal or limited to a small group? Do their solutions create more problems? Have them briefly respond to these questions and attach their response to their proposal.

Need revising help?

Review the **Rubric,** p. 568

Consider **peer reader** comments

Check **Revision Guidelines,** p. 1355.

3 Revising

TARGET SKILL ▶ TRANSITION WORDS Transition words or phrases show how the ideas in your proposal are related and so make your writing more convincing. You can also use transitions to signal that you are refuting an objection to your plan.

> This poll clearly shows the need for the school to develop a plan that will give all students at least a basic appreciation for the arts. *To solve this problem,* ~~M~~members of the faculty have suggested creating an arts requirement for graduation. This idea meets the problem head-on. *However,* ~~I~~it will take time and may require a restructuring of the arts department. *For example,* ~~A~~a new survey class covering visual art, theater, music, and dance will have to be developed. *Although* ~~T~~this would be a good long-term solution, students need an opportunity to experience the fine arts as soon as possible—and not by reading about them in a textbook.

Stumped by adverbs?

See the **Grammar Handbook,** p. 1403

4 Editing and Proofreading

TARGET SKILL ▶ USING ADVERBS CORRECTLY As you edit your proposal, check to see that you have used adverbs correctly. Do not use an adjective when an adverb is needed.

> Student volunteers would do much of the work of making the festival run smooth*ly*. Most of the funding for the ~~fare~~ *fair* could probabl~~e~~*y* come from the regular budgets of the admin*i*stration and art department.

Publishing IDEAS

- Present your proposal orally to the audience for which it was intended.
- Submit your proposal to a school or local newspaper to bring it to the attention of a wider audience.

More Online: Publishing Options
www.mcdougallittell.com

5 Reflecting

FOR YOUR WORKING PORTFOLIO In what ways did your initial idea change during the writing of your proposal? What influences led to the changes? Attach your answer to your proposal. Save your proposal in your **Working Portfolio.**

Assessment Practice Revising & Editing

Read this introduction from the first draft of a student essay. The underlined sections may include the following kinds of errors:

- **run-on sentences**
- **incorrect plural forms**
- **incorrectly used adverb and adjective modifiers**
- **verb tense errors**

For each underlined section, choose the revision that most improves the writing.

> Nelson Park played an important role in our region's history; therefore, the park should be granted (1) landmark status by the community board. Without this recognition, commercial development will sure destroy (2) the park. Although small in size, it was (3) loaded with history. In the early part of this century, Susan B. Anthony has led (4) important suffragist rallies at Nelson Park. Later in the century, the park became a focus for the civil rights movement. Many peaceful assemblys (5) took place there. Nelson Park has a proud history it should also have a strong future. (6)

1. **A.** be granting
   B. granted
   C. have granted
   D. Correct as is
2. **A.** will, for sure, destroy
   B. sure will destroy
   C. will surely destroy
   D. Correct as is
3. **A.** is
   B. were
   C. am
   D. Correct as is
4. **A.** had led
   B. led
   C. leads
   D. Correct as is
5. **A.** assembles
   B. assembling
   C. assemblies
   D. Correct as is
6. **A.** Nelson Park has a proud history, it should also have a strong future.
   B. Nelson Park has a proud history. It should also have a strong future.
   C. Nelson Park has a proud, history it should also have a strong, future.
   D. Correct as is

Need extra help?

See the **Grammar Handbook**
Writing Complete Sentences, p. 1414
Modifiers, pp. 1403–1404
Nouns, p. 1397
Verbs, pp. 1400–1401

Assessment Practice
Have students read the entire passage first before they correct the errors.

Answers:
1. D; **2.** C; **3.** A; **4.** B; **5.** C; **6.** B

Grammar

ADJECTIVES AND ADVERBS

Instruction An adjective modifies a noun or pronoun and answers the questions *which one? what kind? how many?* or *how much?* An adverb modifies a verb, an adjective, or another adverb. Adverbs tell *when, where, how,* and *to what extent* about the words they modify. Many adverbs end in *–ly.*

Activity Write the following sentences on the chalkboard. Have students identify the adverbs and adjectives in each sentence.

1. The young man eats breakfast here often. [*young*—adjective; *here*—adverb; *often*—adverb]
2. The outfielder quickly threw the ball to the alert catcher. [*quickly*—adverb; *alert*—adjective]
3. Two spotted turtles slowly crawled away from the rocky shore. [*two*—adjective; *spotted*—adjective; *slowly*—adverb; *away*—adverb; *rocky*—adjective]
4. The play was quite unusual. [*quite*—adverb; *unusual*—adjective]

Building Vocabulary

Objectives
- expand vocabulary
- use reference materials such as a thesaurus and dictionary to determine precise usage

Strategies for Building Vocabulary

EXERCISE
Students' listings of parts of speech and meanings for each word will depend on the detail presented in the dictionaries that they consult. Synonyms will vary according to the part of speech used for some of the words and depending on the completeness of the thesaurus consulted. Sample sentences are shown below.

1. That was the most beautiful [delicate] Monet painting I've seen.
2. The object [goal] of this training to be make you a better athlete.
3. To sell my car was a profitable [lucrative] move.
4. Are all of these demands on my time fair [justifiable]?
5. There is nothing like a home run to animate [exhilarate] a crowd.

Expanding Word Choice

Before the 18th century, people lacked many of the reference tools we use to help us in our writing. There was no way to look up unfamiliar English words, no way to determine words' correct usages, and no standard for spelling. Amid this confusion, Samuel Johnson began work on his *Dictionary of the English Language*. When the book was published in 1755, it became an instant bestseller.

Today, many reference tools are available both in print and on-line. One of the most helpful reference tools for writers is a book of synonyms and related words that is called a **thesaurus.**

When to Use a Thesaurus If you are looking for just the right word to express an idea or if you simply want to vary your word choices, a thesaurus can be even more useful than a dictionary. A dictionary entry will give you the meanings of a word, often accompanied by some synonyms (words with similar meanings), but a thesaurus will usually provide you with a more thorough listing of the word's synonyms. Compare the following thesaurus entry for *valuable* with the dictionary entry in your dictionary.

valuable *adjective*

Of great value: *valuable Georgian silver.*	***Syns:*** costly, inestimable, invaluable, precious, priceless, worthy. —*Idioms* beyond price, of great price. ***Near-syns:*** dear, expensive, pricey; prized, treasured, valued. ***Ants:*** valueless, worthless.

—*Roget's II: The New Thesaurus*

The dictionary entry may detail more of the word's shades of meaning, but the thesaurus entry lists a number of synonyms, near synonyms, and antonyms (words opposite in meaning).

Strategies for Building Vocabulary

A thesaurus can help you spice up your writing and speaking and can help you build your vocabulary.

❶ Find the Precise Word If you tend to overuse certain words or if you want to make your writing more vivid, a thesaurus can help you convey your thoughts more precisely. Suppose you are looking for a verb to replace *use* in the sentence "Use your brain if you want to succeed in life!" A thesaurus can help. Look at this entry for *use* from *Roget's II: The New Thesaurus.*

use *verb*

1. To put into action or use: *Use the utmost caution at intersections. He used the money to pay off debts. I used the brakes as quickly as possible. We want to use her talents to our advantage.*	1. ***Syns:*** actuate, apply, employ, exercise, exploit, implement, practice, utilize. —*Idioms* bring into play, bring to bear, make use of, put into practice, put to use.
2. To control or direct the functioning of.	2. OPERATE.
3. *Informal.* To take advantage of unfairly.	3. ABUSE *verb.*
4. To be depleted.	4. GO *verb.*

Begin by reading the left-hand column to find the meaning that you want to employ. Then refer to the right-hand column for synonyms that reflect that meaning. Which synonym would you choose?

❷ Use Available Technology Some word-processing programs have built-in thesauruses. Besides offering a list of synonyms, an electronic thesaurus may also provide other information, such as lists of antonyms and words with similar spellings. Most such thesauruses can also insert into your document any synonym you choose.

❸ Develop Your Options Take time to study a thesaurus, jotting down words you find interesting. Try to use those words in conversation until they become part of your vocabulary.

EXERCISE Use a dictionary to determine what parts of speech each of these words can serve as, as well as the word's possible meanings. Write a sentence containing the word; then use a thesaurus to find a synonym that can replace the word in the sentence.

1. beautiful
2. object
3. profitable
4. fair
5. animate

Using Adjectives and Adjective Phrases

Grammar from Literature

Writers use adjectives for a variety of reasons:

- To add sensory detail such as description of size, color, and kind.
- To make characters and settings more realistic.
- To make explanations more precise.

Look at the passage below about Lord Chesterfield's views of a person's composition, or personality. Notice how the highlighted adjectives add information to this passage and the other passages below.

> single-word adjectives
> **Every man is not ambitious, or covetous, or passionate; but every man has pride enough in his composition to feel and resent the least slight and contempt.**
> —Lord Chesterfield, *Letters to His Son*

> adjective prepositional phrases
> **The knowledge of numbers is one of the chief distinctions between us and brutes.**
> —Lady Mary Wortley Montagu, letter to her daughter

> participial phrase
> **I hear this great city inquiring day by day after these my papers.**
> —Joseph Addison, *The Spectator*

You may recall that a participle is a verb form that functions as an adjective. A participial phrase consists of a participle and any words that modify the participle.

Using Adjectives in Your Writing Look for places in your writing where you can make the picture in your reader's mind clearer and more accurate. Include adjectives that capture the sights, smells, tastes, and experiences you are recording.

> **Can you imagine yourself stranded on an uninhabited island? Everything around you is strange and unfamiliar. Will that curious orange prickly fruit be your supper tonight, or is it poisonous? This is the situation Robinson Crusoe found himself in.**

Usage Tip Place adjectives as close as possible to the words they modify. Misplaced modifiers can be confusing and at times even humorous.

> INCORRECT
> **Lord Albemarle smelled the fish going to the kitchen.**
> CORRECT
> **Going to the kitchen, Lord Albemarle smelled the fish.**

> INCORRECT
> **The helpful librarian pointed out the copy of Pepys's diary to the boy on the shelf.**
> CORRECT
> **The helpful librarian pointed out the copy of Pepys's diary on the shelf to the boy.**

Punctuation Tip Use a comma after an introductory participial phrase.

> **Reading Pepys's diary, we discover an earlier era.**

WRITING EXERCISE Rewrite these sentences, following the directions in parentheses.

1. The ceremonies surrounding the king's coronation impressed Samuel Pepys. (Add a single-word adjective describing the ceremonies.)
2. I did see the houses and warehouses all on fire. (Add one or more prepositional phrases that tell what kind of houses or warehouses or their location.)
3. According to Chesterfield, ^men look upon women as somewhat silly. The men are being justly distrustful. (Combine the two sentences, inserting the information in the second sentence into the first sentence at the caret as a participle. Delete the underlined words.)
4. ________ and ________, the survivors of the fire wandered the streets. (Fill in the blanks with two participles or participial phrases.)
5. People make little show of what they know. These people are truly educated. (Insert the information from the second sentence into the first as a participle. Delete words if necessary.)

GRAMMAR EXERCISE Rewrite the sentences, correcting errors in punctuation and usage.

1. Spectators saw many tragic sights walking the streets of London after the fire.
2. Considered distinguished Montagu's grandfather was known as Wise William.
3. Having a passion for learning Lady Montagu supported education for women.
4. Pope wrote many famous epigrams blessed with a remarkable brain.
5. A lugubrious person takes no joy in life having a sour personality.

Sentence Crafting

Objectives

- understand what adjectives are and how to use them to make writing more rich, realistic, and precise
- compose increasingly more involved sentences that contain participles

WRITING EXERCISE

1. **Possible Response:** The elaborate ceremonies surrounding the king's coronation impressed Samuel Pepys.
2. **Possible Response:** I did see the houses of the poor and warehouses on the wharf all on fire.
3. According to Chesterfield, being justly distrustful, men look upon women as somewhat silly.
4. **Possible Response:** Weeping and wringing their hands, the survivors of the fire wandered the streets.
5. Truly educated people make little show of what they know.

GRAMMAR EXERCISE

1. Walking the streets of London after the fire, spectators saw many tragic sights.
2. Considered distinguished, Montagu's grandfather was known as Wise William.
3. Having a passion for learning, Lady Montagu supported education for women.
4. Blessed with a remarkable brain, Pope wrote many famous epigrams.
5. Having a sour personality, a lugubrious person takes no joy in life.

PART 2 Arguments for Change

Social and economic conditions improved for many people during the Enlightenment. However, the wealth and privilege enjoyed by the middle and upper classes contrasted strikingly with the poverty suffered by the rest of the people. Many writers fought against the injustices they perceived by arguing in favor of social reforms. Some, including several of the essayists in this part of Unit Three, supported equal opportunities for women. Others penned stinging satires attacking the treatment of the poor. As you read the selections, think about what changes you would promote in today's society.

576

"A woman well-bred and well taught . . . is a creature without comparison."

from An Academy for Women

Essay by DANIEL DEFOE

Connect to Your Life

Limits on Learning In the 17th and early 18th centuries, the only females who received an education were those whose families could afford private lessons, and even they were taught only a few subjects and were barred from attending universities. On the basis of your understanding of history and social customs, why do you think females were prevented from receiving the same education as males? Record your thoughts.

Build Background

Women's Rights Although the education of females in 17th-century England was not entirely neglected, the only schooling available to them was private tutoring, which was usually shared with siblings or cousins. Such tutoring was an option only for the upper classes, and then only if the father or husband allowed it. Despite their limited education, a few women began to express themselves publicly in books, pamphlets, and essays during the 1600s. Some called for more rights for women, including the right to an education. In most circles, however, such ideas were ignored or ridiculed.

Following the Restoration, England experienced a period of growth in social awareness as well as in industry and commerce. More and more individuals looked for practical ways to correct what they perceived as society's flaws. One of those individuals was Daniel Defoe. Best known today as a novelist, Defoe was also involved in both commerce and social reform. One of his first publications, written in 1697, was *An Essay on Projects*, a series of proposals advocating, among other things, the establishment of banks, insurance companies, and credit unions—and, in "An Academy for Women," the education of females.

LaserLinks: Background for Reading
Cultural Connection

WORDS TO KNOW
Vocabulary Preview
cloister
degenerate
manifest
retentive
vie

Focus Your Reading

LITERARY ANALYSIS **PERSUASIVE ESSAY** In a **persuasive essay,** a writer attempts to convince readers to adopt a particular opinion or to perform a certain action. In the first sentence of his essay, Defoe introduces a general opinion that he hopes to persuade his readers to adopt:

> ***I have often thought of it as one of the most barbarous customs in the world . . . that we deny the advantages of learning to women.***

As you read the essay, look for statements of opinion and pay particular attention to the ways in which Defoe supports his opinions.

ACTIVE READING **ANALYZING A FORMAL ARGUMENT**
In a formal argument, a writer makes a proposal and then presents facts, reasons, and examples to support it. The proposal is generally a call to action and usually appears near the beginning of the argument.

READER'S NOTEBOOK Make a chart like the one shown, and as you read this selection on the education of females, use it to record Defoe's main proposal and supporting details.

Proposal	Supporting Details
	1.
	2.
	3.
	4.

OVERVIEW

Objectives

1. understand and appreciate a piece written in the **essay genre (Literary Analysis)**
2. appreciate the author's use of a **persuasive essay** to explore arguments for the education of women **(Literary Analysis)**
3. **analyze a formal argument (Active Reading)**

Summary

Defoe describes the paltry education most 18th-century women receive and proposes an academy where they can learn music, dancing, foreign languages, and the art of conversation. He would have women read books, especially history, so they could understand the world and make sound judgments. A well-bred woman, he claims, is angelic, but a woman robbed of an education "degenerates to be turbulent" and "nasty." Creatures so glorious, he states, cannot have been created only to be slaves.

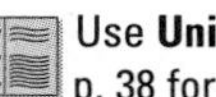

Use **Unit Three Resource Book,** p. 38 for additional support.

Thematic Link

The lack of importance put on the education of women is increasingly anomalous in an age that places a high value on balance and social harmony. Defoe's **argument for change** suggests that better-educated women would make for a better, more harmonious society.

5-Minute Warm-Up

Daily Language SkillBuilder

Have students **proofread** the display sentences on page 515l and write them correctly. The sentences also appear on Transparency 14 of **Grammar Transparencies and Copymasters.**

Preteaching Vocabulary

If you would like to preteach the WORDS TO KNOW for this selection, use the Mini Lesson p. 578.

LESSON RESOURCES

UNIT THREE RESOURCE BOOK, pp. 38–42

ASSESSMENT RESOURCES
Formal Assessment, pp. 97–98
Teacher's Guide to Assessment and Portfolio Use
Test Generator

SKILLS TRANSPARENCIES AND COPYMASTERS
Literary Analysis
- Characteristics of the Essay, T11 (for Literary Analysis, p. 582)

Reading and Critical Thinking
- Main Idea and Supporting Details, T12 (for Active Reading, p. 577)

Grammar
- Diagramming Verbal Phrases, T60 (for Mini Lesson, p. 583)
- Infinitives, C96 (for Mini Lesson, p. 583)

Writing
- Opinion Statement, C35 (for Writing Options, p. 583)

Communications
- Interviewing, T9 (for Activities & Explorations 2, p. 583)

INTEGRATED TECHNOLOGY
Audio Library
LaserLinks
- Cultural Connection: 18th-Century Upper-Class Women. See **Teacher's SourceBook,** p. 36.

Visit our website:
www.mcdougallittell.com

TEACHING THE LITERATURE

Reading and Analyzing

Literary Analysis

PERSUASIVE ESSAY

Remind students that a persuasive essay is an attempt by the author to convince readers to adopt a particular opinion or to take a certain action. Have students note how Defoe structures this persuasive essay: he introduces the problem, explains its complications, presents a solution, and concludes with an urgent call for action. Have students consider how text structure influences their understanding.

 Use **Unit Three Resource Book,** p. 40 for more exercises.

Active Reading

ANALYZING A FORMAL ARGUMENT

Tell students that a formal argument should be supported by reasons, facts, and examples. Defoe indulges in some unsupported expressions of opinion in "An Academy for Women." Point out to students that although Defoe's statements usually contradict negative stereotypes and readers might agree with his point of view, he does not always provide reasons, facts, or examples as support. Have students make note of which arguments Defoe supports with examples or facts and which arguments lack support. When students have finished reading the selection, have them rewrite unsupported arguments to include examples or facts. Students may have to do some research to discover the achievements of women during Defoe's time.

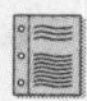 Use **Unit Three Resource Book,** p. 39 for more practice.

FROM An Academy *for* WOMEN

Daniel Defoe

I have often thought of it as one of the most barbarous customs in the world, considering us as a civilized and a Christian country, that we deny the advantages of learning to women. We reproach the sex every day with folly and impertinence, while I am confident, had they the advantages of education equal to us, they would be guilty of less than ourselves.

One would wonder, indeed, how it should happen that women are conversible[1] at all, since they are only beholden to natural parts for all their knowledge. Their youth is spent to teach them to stitch and sew or make baubles. They are taught to read indeed, and perhaps to write their names or so, and that is the height of a woman's education. And I would but ask any who slight the sex for their understanding, what is a man (a gentleman, I mean) good for that is taught no more? . . .

The soul is placed in the body like a rough diamond, and must be polished, or the luster of it will never appear: and it is manifest that as the rational soul distinguishes us from brutes, so education carries on the distinction and makes some less brutish than others. This is too evident to need any demonstration. But why then should women be denied the benefit of instruction? If knowledge and understanding had been useless additions to the sex, God Almighty would never have given them capacities, for He made nothing needless. Besides, I would ask such what they can see in ignorance that they should think it a necessary ornament to a woman? or how much worse is a wise woman than a fool? or what has the woman done to forfeit the privilege of being taught? Does she plague us with her pride and impertinence? Why did we not let her learn, that she might have had more wit? Shall we upbraid women with folly,[2] when it is only the error of this inhuman custom that hindered them being made wiser?

The capacities of women are supposed to be greater and their senses quicker than those of the men; and what they might be capable of being
bred to is plain from some instances of female wit, 1
which this age is not without; which upbraids us with injustice, and looks as if we denied women the advantages of education for fear they should vie with the men in their improvements.

To remove this objection, and that women might have at least a needful opportunity of

1. **conversible:** able to carry on a conversation.
2. **upbraid women with folly:** scold women for foolishness.

WORDS TO KNOW

manifest (măn′ə-fĕst′) *adj.* obvious; clear
vie (vī) *v.* to compete

578

Teaching Options

Mini Lesson: Preteaching Vocabulary

USING A DICTIONARY TO DETERMINE PRECISE MEANINGS Have students work in small groups to find the meanings of each WORD TO KNOW. Students should record the definitions in their vocabulary notebooks. When they find the term in the selection, they can determine which meaning fits the context.

 Use **Unit Three Resource Book,** p. 41 for more exercises.

A lesson on precision in language appears on p. 574 of the Pupil's Edition.

Portrait of a Young Woman, called Mademoiselle Charlotte du Val d'Ognes (about 1800), unknown French artist. Oil on canvas, 63½″ × 50⅝″, The Metropolitan Museum of Art, bequest of Isaac D. Fletcher, 1917. Mr. and Mrs. Isaac D. Fletcher Collection (17.120.204). Copyright © 1989 The Metropolitan Museum of Art.

Customizing Instruction

Less Proficient Readers

Set a Purpose Encourage pairs, or small groups, of students to fill in the Proposal column of their Reading Connection charts after reaching the second paragraph of page 578 and to keep adding to the Supporting Details column.

Students Acquiring English

Tell students that this essay from the 1700s contains some words that are no longer commonly used.

1 Explain that *bred to* really means "taught to accomplish." Help students find an equivalent for *upbraids us with injustice.*

Possible Response: blames us for being unfair.

Use **Spanish Study Guide** for additional support, pp. 126–128.

Gifted and Talented

Invite students to make a critical evaluation of Defoe's proposed curriculum, with the goal of recommending their own ideal curriculum for both sexes.

Reading and Analyzing

ACTIVE READING

A ANALYZE Possible Response: Women should receive an education so that they may be capable of all sorts of conversation and sensible in what they say, so that their judgment will be improved, and so that their understanding of the world increased.

ACTIVE READING

B QUESTION Possible Response: External beauty is no guarantee of inner beauty.

Literary Analysis

PERSUASIVE ESSAY

C Invite students to evaluate the effectiveness of the passage about the "very fine woman" and ask if they can name two persuasive devices Defoe uses here.

Answer: an example; a quotation.

education in all sorts of useful learning, I propose the draft of an academy for that purpose. . . .

The academy I propose should differ but little from public schools, wherein such ladies as were willing to study should have all the advantages of learning suitable to their genius. . . .

The persons who enter should be taught all sorts of breeding suitable to both their genius and their quality, and in particular music and dancing, which it would be cruelty to bar the sex of, because they are their darlings; but besides this, they should be taught languages, as particularly French and Italian; and I would venture the injury of giving a woman more tongues than one.

They should, as a particular study, be taught all the graces of speech and all the necessary air of conversation, which our common education is so defective in that I need not expose it. They should be brought to read books, and especially history, and so to read as to make them understand the world, and be able to know and judge of things when they hear of them.

ACTIVE READING

A **ANALYZE** What reasons does Defoe present to support his **formal argument**?

To such whose genius would lead them to it I would deny no sort of learning; but the chief thing in general is to cultivate the understandings of the sex, that they may be capable of all sorts of conversation; that their parts and judgments being improved, they may be as profitable in their conversation as they are pleasant.

Women, in my observation, have little or no difference in them, but as they are or are not distinguished by education. Tempers indeed may in some degree influence them, but the main distinguishing part is their breeding.

The whole sex are generally quick and sharp. I believe I may be allowed to say generally so, for you rarely see them lumpish and heavy when they are children, as boys will often be. If a woman be well-bred, and taught the proper management of her natural wit, she proves generally very sensible and retentive; and without partiality, a woman of sense and manners is the finest and most delicate part of God's creation; the glory of her Maker, and the great instance of His singular regard to man, His darling creature, to whom He gave the best gift either God could bestow or man receive. And it is the sordidest[3] piece of folly and ingratitude in the world to withhold from the sex the due luster which the advantages of education gives to the natural beauty of their minds.

The great distinguishing difference which is seen in the world between men and women is in their EDUCATION.

A woman well-bred and well taught, furnished with the additional accomplishments of knowledge and behavior, is a creature without comparison; her society is the emblem of sublimer[4] enjoyments; her person is angelic and her conversation heavenly; she is all softness and sweetness, peace, love, wit, and delight. She is every way suitable to the sublimest wish, and the man that has such a one to his portion has nothing to do but to rejoice in her and be thankful.

On the other hand, suppose her to be the very same woman, and rob her of the benefit of

3. **sordidest:** most meanly selfish.
4. **sublimer:** more noble or exalted.

WORDS TO KNOW **retentive** (rĭ-tĕn′tĭv) *adj.* able to retain knowledge or information easily

BLOCK SCHEDULING: MANAGING TIME

If your schedule requires that you cover the lesson objectives in a shorter time, use . . .
- Preparing to Read, p. 577
- Thinking Through the Literature, p. 582
- Vocabulary in Action, p. 583

If you want to take advantage of longer class time, use . . .
- TE Teaching Options: Preteaching Vocabulary, p. 578; Informal Assessment, p. 581; Grammar Mini Lesson, p. 583

education, and it follows thus:

If her temper be good, want of education makes her soft and easy.

Her wit, for want of teaching, makes her impertinent and talkative.

Her knowledge, for want of judgment and experience, makes her fanciful and whimsical.

If her temper be bad, want of breeding makes her worse, and she grows haughty, insolent, and loud.

If she be passionate, want of manners makes her termagant[5] and a scold, which is much at one with lunatic.

If she be proud, want of discretion (which still is breeding) makes her conceited, fantastic, and ridiculous.

And from these she degenerates to be turbulent, clamorous, noisy, nasty, and the devil.

Methinks mankind for their own sakes, since, say what we will of the women, we all think fit one time or other to be concerned with them, should take some care to breed them up to be suitable and serviceable, if they expected no such thing as delight from them. Bless us! what care do we take to breed up a good horse and to break him well, and what a value do we put upon him when it is done, and all because he should be fit for our use; and why not a woman? Since all her ornaments and beauty without suitable behavior is a cheat in nature, like the false tradesman who puts the best of his goods uppermost that the buyer may think the rest are of the same goodness. . . .

ACTIVE READING

QUESTION What point is Defoe making in his simile of the false tradesman?

But to come closer to the business, the great distinguishing difference which is seen in the world between men and women is in their education, and this is manifested by comparing it with the difference between one man or woman and another.

And herein it is that I take upon me to make such a bold assertion that all the world are mistaken in their practice about women; for I cannot think that God Almighty ever made them so delicate, so glorious creatures, and furnished them with such charms, so agreeable and so delightful to mankind, with souls capable of the same accomplishments with men, and all to be only stewards of our houses, *cooks and slaves.*

. . . I remember a passage which I heard from a very fine woman; she had wit and capacity enough, an extraordinary shape and face, and a great fortune, but had been cloistered up all her time, and for fear of being stolen, had not had the liberty of being taught the common necessary knowledge of women's affairs; and when she came to converse in the world, her natural wit made her so sensible of the want of education, that she gave this short reflection on herself: "I am ashamed to talk with my very maids," says she, "for I don't know when they do right or wrong. I had more need to go to school than be married." C

I need not enlarge on the loss the defect of education is to the sex, nor argue the benefit of the contrary practice; it is a thing will be more easily granted than remedied. This chapter is but an essay at the thing, and I refer the practice to those happy days, if ever they shall be, when men shall be wise enough to mend it. ❖ 1

5. **termagant** (tûr′mə-gənt): a quarrelsome woman.

WORDS TO KNOW

degenerate (dĭ-jĕn′ə-rāt′) *v.* to sink to a lower condition; deteriorate

cloister (kloi′stər) *v.* to confine or seclude, as in a convent

Customizing Instruction

Less Proficient Readers

Invite students to list the main points Defoe makes in the essay. Does Defoe think women are the equal of men?

Answer: Accept all reasonable, well-supported responses.

Students Acquiring English

1 Help students paraphrase the statement "it is a thing will be more easily granted than remedied."

Possible Response: It is easier to concede that discriminatory attitudes are wrong than it will be to change them.

Gifted and Talented

Invite students to make a critical evaluation of Defoe's proposed curriculum with the goal of proposing an ideal curriculum of their own that meets the needs of students (of both sexes) in the 21st century.

Assessment Informal Assessment

PROVIDING EXAMPLES Tell students that Defoe's proposal of a practical and an academic education for women was ahead of the traditional thinking of his day. Have them read through the selection and look specifically for statements that exemplify Defoe as thinking ahead of his time. Then have students write their own essays that provide examples of Defoe's forward-thinking attitude and examples of how his attitude contrasted with the mindset of the day. Remind students to give support from the selection.

RUBRIC

3 Full Accomplishment Students present examples from essay that show Defoe thinking ahead of his time and contrast with examples of typical mindset of day.

2 Substantial Accomplishment Students present some examples of Defoe's thinking but provide little supporting evidence from essay or do not contrast Defoe's views with typical mindset of day.

1 Little or Partial Accomplishment Students fail to recognize Defoe's thinking as ahead of its time.

GUIDING STUDENT RESPONSE

Connect to the Literature

1. What Do You Think?
Accept all reasonable responses.

Comprehension Check

- music, art, speech, reading (especially history), and foreign languages (especially French and Italian)
- They allow women to reach their full potential and make them better, happier, more agreeable partners.

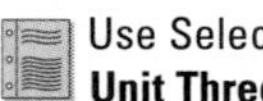

Use Selection Quiz in **Unit Three Resource Book,** p. 42.

Think Critically

2. Some students may say that Defoe is ahead of his time in recognizing the intellectual potential of women; others may fault him for regarding women as adjuncts to or ornaments for men; for others, the studies he proposes might seem lightweight and his descriptions of uneducated women hostile.
3. Students should be able to
   - summarize Defoe's proposal and the details that support the main idea;
   - discuss their opinion about his argument.

   Their response should include an evaluation of his argument and its effect on them.

Literary Analysis

Paired Activity Student response should distinguish between those supporting details that appeal to logic (logical arguments) and those that appeal to emotions (deceptive arguments).

Thinking through the LITERATURE

Connect to the Literature

1. **What Do You Think?** What thoughts came to mind when you finished reading this **essay?**

Comprehension Check

- What courses would be taught at Defoe's academy?
- Why does Defoe believe that these areas of study are necessary?

Think Critically

2. How would you describe Defoe's attitude toward women?

THINK ABOUT

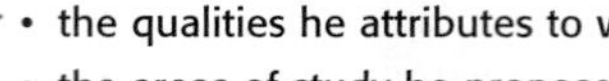

- the qualities he attributes to women
- the areas of study he proposes for them
- his description of an uneducated woman
- the possible motives behind his proposal

3. **ACTIVE READING** **ANALYZING A FORMAL ARGUMENT** Refer to the chart you created in your **READER'S NOTEBOOK.** In your opinion, does Defoe present a convincing **argument?** Defend your answer.

Extend Interpretations

4. **Different Perspectives** How might a contemporary defender of women's rights respond to Defoe's essay?
5. **Comparing Texts** Compare Defoe's opinions on the education of women with those expressed by Lady Mary Wortley Montagu in her **letter** to her daughter (page 559). What opinions do Defoe and Montagu seem to share? On what issues might they disagree?
6. **Connect to Life** Do you think that any issues related to the education or training of women are still controversial? Explain your answer.
7. **Art Connection** Look closely at the portrait of Mademoiselle Charlotte du Val d'Orgnes on page 579. In your opinion, what specific elements of the painting reflect ideas presented in this selection?

Literary Analysis

PERSUASIVE ESSAY When writing a **persuasive essay,** a writer tries to influence readers to accept an idea, adopt an opinion, or perform an action. The body of evidence a writer uses to convince readers includes the facts, reasons, or examples that support his or her opinion or proposal.

In Defoe's essay, the writer proposes the establishment of an educational academy for women. Statements such as the following support his proposal:

If knowledge and understanding had been useless additions to the sex, God Almighty would never have given them capacities. . . .

If a woman be well-bred, and taught the proper management of her natural wit, she proves generally very sensible and retentive. . . .

Effective persuasion appeals to both the intelligence and the emotions of its intended audience.

Paired Activity With a partner, reread Defoe's essay, looking for details that support his proposal. Of the supporting details that you find, which ones do you think appeal to readers' intelligence? Which appeal to their emotions?

Extend Interpretations

Different Perspectives Students' responses are likely to parallel those to the previous question: A contemporary feminist might honor Defoe for being an early champion of women's rights but regret that he saw women as appendages of men.
Comparing Texts Both writers believe that women need to be educated. Lady Montagu sees it as a means of making a woman's life happier, but only because she is resigned to women living cloistered lives; Defoe wants to make women more worldly, but as much of his essay is spent arguing the benefits of this to men as to women.
Connect to Life Possible responses: Some people believe girls are steered away from math and science as teenagers. Equity in athletics also remains controversial.
Art Connection Possible responses: Young woman is drawing or painting, as if this is a self-portrait; she is graceful and well-bred, things of which Defoe approves. Her clothing connects her to classical culture.

Writing Options

Persuasive Letter Imagine that you are an educated 17th-century woman. Write a letter in which you try to convince educated 17th-century men to support Defoe's proposal. Use humor to persuade your audience. Place the letter in your **Working Portfolio.**

Activities & Explorations

1. **Advertisement for the Academy** Create an advertisement for Defoe's proposed academy that would encourage women to enroll. ~ ART
2. **Interview with Defoe** With a partner, conduct an interview between Defoe and a contemporary female television or radio talk-show host. ~ SPEAKING AND LISTENING

Inquiry & Research

Educational Opportunities Investigate the education of women in England after 1700. What types of formal education were offered to females? What subjects were taught? When were women's colleges founded in the major universities?

Vocabulary in Action

EXERCISE: ANTONYMS For each group of words below, write the letter of the word that is an antonym of the boldfaced word.

1. **degenerate:** (a) produce, (b) improve, (c) accelerate
2. **retentive:** (a) forgetful, (b) selfish, (c) graceful
3. **vie:** (a) startle, (b) cooperate, (c) lose
4. **cloister:** (a) free, (b) organize, (c) praise
5. **manifest:** (a) hurtful, (b) questionable, (c) timid

Building Vocabulary
For an in-depth lesson on how to use a thesaurus to find a word's synonyms and antonyms, see page 574.

Daniel Defoe
1660–1731

Other Works
Moll Flanders
Roxana
Colonel Jack

Rich Man, Poor Man "No man has tasted differing fortunes more, / And thirteen times I have been rich and poor." In this self-description, Daniel Defoe summarized the many ups and downs of his career. Fascinated with the world of trade, Defoe became a merchant, dealing at different times in an assortment of products, from bricks to insurance. Although he amassed great wealth in many of his ventures, occasional bad investments led him to bankruptcy.

Popular Opinions Defoe wrote many political pamphlets, one of which led to his imprisonment. A devout Presbyterian, his interest in politics stemmed largely from his desire to "purify" the Church of England. His imprisonment included time in the pillory, a wooden device with holes for the prisoner's head and hands. Prisoners in the pillory were usually pelted with rotten fruit and vegetables by onlookers, but Defoe's views were so popular that the public drank to his health and threw flowers instead. One of his political poems, *The True-Born Englishman,* reportedly sold more copies than any poem published in England before that time.

Novel Approach Today Defoe is most recognized for his novels, which he did not begin writing until he was in his late 50s. His most famous novel, *Robinson Crusoe,* was the first book other than the Bible to be widely read by members of all levels of English society.

Writing Options

Persuasive Letter Students' letters will vary, but each should be well developed and contain elements of humor or irony.

Activities & Explorations

1. **Advertisement for the Academy** Have students explain how their choices of color, images, and words would attract their audience and convince them to enroll.
2. **Interview with Defoe** Base assessment on relevancy of discussion; that is, on whether discussion demonstrates a thorough understanding of the issues raised by Defoe's essay.

Inquiry & Research

Educational Opportunities Have students report their findings in an oral report or graphic presentation.

Vocabulary in Action

1. b
2. a
3. b
4. a
5. b

Mini Lesson Grammar

INFINITIVES

Instruction An infinitive is a verb form made up of the word *to* plus the base form of a verb. Sometimes an auxiliary verb form of *be* or *have* is added to the present infinitive. An infinitive may function as a noun, an adjective, or an adverb.

Activity Write the following examples on the chalkboard. Underline the infinitive phrases.

Noun
To be educated is a woman's right as much as a man's right.

Adjective
The point to make is that women should not be considered "cooks and slaves."

Adverb
"Defoe believes society's attitudes will be hard to change.

The infinitive *to be educated* is the subject of the sentence and acts as a noun. *To make* modifies the noun *point; to change* modifies the predicate adjective *hard.*

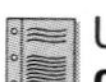
Use **Grammar Transparencies and Copymasters,** p. 99.

Use McDougal Littell's ***Language Network*** for more instruction and practice in infinitives.

OVERVIEW

Objectives

- understand the following literary terms:
  - Horatian satire
  - Juvenalian satire
- appreciate shared characteristics of literature across cultures
- recognize themes across cultures

Teaching the Lesson

This lesson provides information on satire as a literary form.

Motivating the Students
Satire is entertaining, but it also helps people see themselves and their lives in a different way. The insight gained from this outside view can bring about social and personal change. As students read the satires in this unit, have them consider the following questions:

How do the targets of satire in the 17th and 18th centuries compare to the targets of satire today?
Possible Responses: Surprisingly, many of the targets have remained the same: the wealthy, the ruling classes, politics, writers, personal vanity, and corruption. However several common targets of satire today include situations and people in professions that did not exist centuries ago: political systems, urban congestion, professional athletes and other entertainers, and the like.

What do you think the presence of abundant political satire indicates about the stability of a country?
Possible Responses: Many students should see that the presence of wide-ranging political satire is an indication of the general stability of a country. A good and strong political system tolerates and may even promote the critical examination that satire brings to politics.

As they finish reading the satires, students can write reactions to these questions and keep their responses in their Writing Portfolios.

Satire

Laughter as a Weapon

Satire is a literary technique in which behaviors or institutions are ridiculed for the purpose of improving society. What sets satire apart from other forms of social and political protest is humor. Satirists use irony and exaggeration to poke fun at human faults and foolishness in order to correct human behavior.

A famous example of satire is Alexander Pope's brilliant mock epic *The Rape of the Lock* (1714). The poem, which satirizes the trivial pursuits of the idle wealthy, echoes the openings of ancient epics in its famous first lines:

Gulliver in Lilliput. Illustration by H. J. Ford for an 1891 edition of Swift's *Gulliver's Travels*

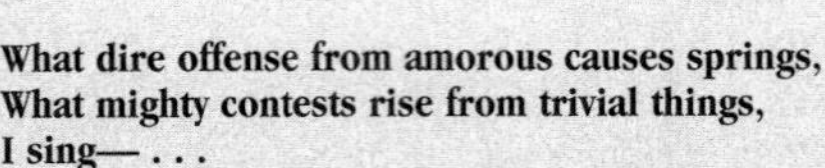

What dire offense from amorous causes springs,
What mighty contests rise from trivial things,
I sing— . . .

—Alexander Pope, *The Rape of the Lock*

In the poem, a young lord is so smitten by a lady's beauty that he secretly cuts off a lock of her hair. The lady's offense at this violation takes on epic—or mock-epic—proportions:

Then flashed the living lightning from her eyes,
And screams of horror rend the affrighted skies.
Not louder shrieks to pitying heaven are cast,
When husbands, or when lapdogs breathe their last;

—Alexander Pope, *The Rape of the Lock*

The exaggeration of the lady's response, plus the ironic aside equating the death of husbands with the death of favorite pets, typifies this satire's charm.

For the most part, a satirist attempts to bring about change by exposing an oddity or a problem in an imaginative, often humorous way. The target is often a social or political one.

A Historical Perspective

Satire began with the ancient Greeks but came into its own in ancient Rome, where the "fathers" of satire, Horace and Juvenal, had their names given to the two basic types of satire:

- **Horatian satire** is playfully amusing and seeks to correct vice or foolishness with gentle laughter and understanding. Alexander Pope's satire is Horatian.
- **Juvenalian satire** provokes a darker kind of laughter. It is often bitter and criticizes corruption or incompetence with scorn and outrage. Swift, in *Gulliver's Travels,* tended toward Juvenalian satire.

The next great flourishing of satire began in Europe in the second half of the 17th century and continued throughout the 18th century. In England, this "golden age" of satire encompassed the talents of the Restoration dramatists, as well as Dryden, Pope, Swift and Samuel Johnson.

The 18th century was dominated by satiric poetry, prose, and drama. Satirists, as guardians of the culture, sought to protect their highly developed civilization from corruption by attacking hypocrisy, arrogance, greed, vanity, and stupidity. "The satirist is to be regarded as our physician, not our enemy," wrote Henry Fielding.

Presenting the Strategies
Read through the strategies aloud or project them on a transparency. As an option, you might ask students to use the descriptions on page 584 to write a short Horatian satire and a short Juvenalian satire on the same subject. Students should direct their strategies to a specific audience. Model how to use the strategies on page 585 to analyze the satires.

Satire Since 1800

With a few notable exceptions—namely, Lord Byron, William Makepeace Thackeray, and Samuel Butler in England and Mark Twain in America—the popularity of satire faded in the 19th century.

Much of the satire of the 20th century, reacting to warfare and complex social issues, has been Juvenalian in the extreme. George Orwell's political satire *Animal Farm* (1945) departed from this gloomy pattern through the use of fantasy. This seemingly simple animal fable satirizes political systems that claim to be democracies but oppress their citizens. Like *Gulliver's Travels*, *Animal Farm* portrays a fantasy world with similarities to our own. But unlike Swift's work, some modern satires lack humorous elements to raise them from bleakness and despair.

YOUR TURN Identify other examples of satire in the 20th century that you have read or know about. Add your examples to a class list.

Satire Today

Although some critics lament the scarcity of good literary satire, today satire has permeated all forms of popular culture. Political cartoons, with their caricatures of leaders and parodies of contemporary issues, have always been hallmarks of satire. The satiric spirit also pervades many of today's popular comic strips, such as *Doonesbury, Dilbert,* and *Cathy.* Many national magazines either devote themselves entirely to satire *(National Lampoon* and *Spy)* or dedicate part of their pages to satirizing contemporary life (*The New Yorker* and *Esquire).*

You can also find satire on TV—on programs such as *The Simpsons* and the Saturday late-night comedy shows—and in movie theaters all across the United States. Future historians may look back on the end of the 20th century as the dawn of another great age of satire.

Strategies for Reading: Satire

1. Determine the object of the satire. A writer who encourages you to laugh at a custom, or a person, probably thinks that the object of laughter is an undesirable part of society.
2. Use your knowledge of what the satirist criticizes to infer what he or she believes is right and proper.
3. Watch for irony, which often points directly to the object of the satire.
4. Evaluate whether the satire is more Horatian (playful and sympathetic) or Juvenalian (bitter and critical).
5. Enjoy the humor. Pay attention to what makes you laugh or what sounds ridiculous.
6. **Monitor** your reading strategies and modify them when your understanding breaks down. Remember to use your Strategies for Active Reading: **predict, visualize, connect, question, clarify,** and **evaluate.**

Making Connections

Satire Across Cultures

Share the following information about satire across cultures with students.

The Ashanti

The Ashanti people of Africa had a ceremony called the *Apo.* This ceremony was held in the middle of April, and during the time it lasted, everyone was free to make fun of whomever he or she wished. The most popular targets were chiefs and nobles.

Native American

Native American peoples also have ceremonies of ritual satire. In southern Mexico these rituals have become associated with Christian holidays. The men who are chosen to be entertainers for the fiesta use humorous poems called *bombas* to make fun of a variety of social misbehaviors. The "buffoons" of the Pueblo culture, in the southwestern United States, are given free rein to satirize sacred ceremonies.

European

In the Middle Ages and later, fool societies, or *sociétés joyeuses,* flourished in France. On holidays, these highly organized societies held satirical processions and performed humorous plays called *sotties.* The Polish fool society called the Babinian Republic was founded in 1568. The Republic invited people who had done foolish things to be members. Nearly all church and government officials were willing members of the Republic.

SATIRE 585

OVERVIEW

Objectives

- appreciate the craft of one of England's greatest satirists
- interpret the interaction between satire and the society in which it is produced
- gain information about Swift by reading nonfiction

The Author Study offers a unique opportunity for students to focus on the work of a major writer. In addition, students can gather information about the life of Swift, gaining insight into the person who wrote such influential satires.

Reading Skills and Strategies

Establish and Modify Purposes for Reading

Have students scan pages 586 through 589 and establish a purpose or purposes for reading. Preview the array of materials on these pages. Ask students to suggest how they might adjust their purposes for reading as they encounter different formats such as time lines.

Author Study

Jonathan Swift

"[Swift] stood solitary on the peak of his nature, his scornful eyes raking mankind."

-Carl Van Doren

Jonathan Swift

HIS LIFE
HIS TIMES

The Great Satirist

1667–1745

Jonathan Swift has been called the greatest satirist in the English language. Readers have enjoyed him and critics have argued about him for centuries. He is one of the few great writers who appeals to children as well as adults.

This Author Study will introduce you to this complicated man—a clergyman and political writer as well as a satirist—who delighted readers even in his bitterest moments.

Early Life Swift was born of English parents in Dublin. Although his family wasn't rich, the young Swift received the best education available. After graduating from Trinity College, he moved to Surrey in England to accept a position as secretary to a retired diplomat, Sir William Temple.

Swift worked on and off for Temple for approximately ten years—a crucial time in his intellectual and social development. It was also at Temple's estate that Swift met eight-year-old Esther Johnson, whom he nicknamed Stella. She would become Swift's lifelong friend and confidante. By the time Temple died in 1699, Swift had been ordained as an Anglican priest and

1667 **Is born Nov. 30 in Dublin**

1678 **Roman Catholics in England are excluded from serving in Parliament.**

1686 **Receives B.A. degree from Trinity College, Dublin**

1670

1680

A 1665 **The Great Plague begins in London and eventually kills over 65,000.**

1679 **English political parties, Whig and Tory, are formed.**

1683 **Antony van Leeuwenhoek first observes bacteria under a microscope.**

586

become a full-fledged satirist, with two completed works ready for publication.

Satire and Politics Swift supported himself as a clergyman and political writer for the Whig party, while he tried out his satire on the public. His first two satires, *The Battle of the Books* and *A Tale of a Tub*, established Swift's biting style. Whether lampooning modern thinkers and scientists (John Locke and Isaac Newton among them), religious abuses, or humans at large, Swift raged at the arrogance, phoniness, and shallowness he saw infecting contemporary intellectual and moral life. He stood for justice, order, moral rectitude, and rational thought. B

Both satires were published anonymously. However, as Swift became known for his venomous political writing and his witty contributions to *The Tatler* and *The Spectator*, people recognized Swift's style and ascribed the authorship unofficially to him.

When the Whigs lost power to the Tories in 1710, the Tories courted Swift to join their side. Swift was by nature conservative and so worked enthusiastically for the Tory cause. As a man of principle and a strict moralist, he eventually found himself temperamentally unsuited to the compromises and manipulations of politics. When Queen Anne died in 1714 and the Whigs returned to power, Swift left England a bitter and disappointed man.

LITERARY *Contributions*

The Satirist's Edge Swift stands out even among his 18th-century contemporaries in the great Age of Satire. The darkness and savagery of his satire is unequaled in English literature. In addition to *Gulliver's Travels* (1726) and "A Modest Proposal" (1729), here are two more examples of Swift's prose satire as its best:

The Battle of the Books (1704)
A Tale of a Tub (1704)

The Personal Side Swift's personal warmth and kindness found expression in private letters to his many friends in Ireland and England. The most famous of his correspondence is *Journal to Stella.* Not published until after Swift's death, this journal consists of letters Swift wrote to Esther Johnson in Ireland while he was in London promoting the Tory cause.

C **The Poetic Side** Swift also wrote poetry, much of it witty or satirical. Here are two examples:

"Cadenus and Vanessa" (1726)
"Verses on the Death of Dr. Swift" (1739)

1689 **In England, becomes secretary to Sir William Temple; first meets Esther Johnson (Stella)**

1695 **Ordained as Anglican priest**

1702 **Receives D.D. (doctor of divinity) degree from Trinity College, Dublin**

1707 **Petitions Queen Anne on behalf of Ireland; becomes friends with Joseph Addison**

1690 — 1700

1688 **Glorious Revolution overthrowing James II begins; William and Mary become monarchs (1689).**

1690 **England's population reaches 5 million; John Locke publishes "An Essay Concerning Human Understanding."**

1702 **The first daily newspaper, *The Daily Courant,* is founded in England.**

587

LIFE AND TIMES

Science

A At the time, people realized that objects as well as people can carry infection. During the Great Plague, doctors protected themselves by wearing special suits that covered their whole bodies. At the time, people believed that bad smells could cause infection. For this reason, some of the protective suits were made with a long nose covering stuffed with sweet herbs.

History

B Sir Isaac Newton not only introduced mankind to the laws of motion and a theory of gravitation that was accepted for generations; he also discovered why things appear to be different colors and that sunlight is composed of all colors. Newton's ideas made the industrial revolution possible. John Locke's key ideas helped start the Age of Reason, or Enlightenment. He believed that all of a person's ideas are derived from his or her experience, that every person has natural rights and duties, and that the purpose of government is to protect people's rights of life, liberty, and property.

World Culture

C Swift was an avid supporter of the Anglican Church, the state church of England. In the decade prior to 1710, the ruling Whig party advocated relaxing church rules that required all office-holders in England to take Sacrament according to Anglican rites. This would have given Roman Catholics and Protestant Dissenters access to political power. Swift considered these groups fanatics who would lead England back to a period of civil war. Thus Swift joined the Tories.

Sociology

D Swift's long-standing affair with Stella had begun in 1701 when he convinced her and her companion, Rebecca Dingley, to move to Ireland. (Though Stella acted as Swift's hostess, he never saw Stella outside the company of Rebecca, and even his *Letters to Stella* were addressed to both women together.) This was complicated when another Esther ("Vanessa") fell in love in 1710 with Swift. Vanessa saw him socially in Ireland for years and died weeks after throwing a jealous fit over Stella in 1723. Swift was always loyal to Stella and was profoundly affected by her death in 1728.

History

E Between the 15th and 18th centuries, England took political control of Ireland. Irish livestock exports were taxed highly, and Irish weavers were forbidden from exporting their wares. These actions contributed to the impoverishment of Ireland.

Politics

F In the early 18th century, political commentary such as Swift's was available from several types of publications. Newspapers were relatively expensive but could be read for no extra charge at coffee houses. In addition, there were papers devoted to political commentary. Longer commentaries were published in pamphlets of 16 to 96 pages.

Literature

G *Gulliver's Travels* is unique in its impact nearly 300 years later. Since 1945 alone, more than 500 books and articles assessing Gulliver have been published. It is considered by many critics both the "most misread classic" and "finest prose satire" in the English language.

History

H From September 1727 on, Swift never left Ireland. His status as a hero grew quickly to the point where his birthday was celebrated each year in Ireland with ringing bells and bonfires.

IRISH PATRIOT Before Queen Anne died, Swift was appointed dean of St. Patrick's Cathedral in Dublin. Stung by his political defeats and far from his London friends—such as John Arbuthnot, Alexander Pope, and John Gay—Swift at first felt exiled in Ireland. He maintained a quiet life of church administration and visits with his friends, who included at that time both Stella and Esther Vanhomrigh (nicknamed Vanessa), a young woman who had fallen in love with him in London and followed him to Ireland. After about ten years, however, Swift grew interested in politics again—Irish politics, this time. **D**

E Ireland had been reduced to a state of poverty and dependence by England's repressive policies. The Catholic majority could not vote, hold public office, buy land, or receive an education. In addition, Ireland was restricted from trade with the American colonies. Angered by such tyranny, Swift fought back in a series of publications collectively called *The Drapier's Letters:* "Were not the people of Ireland born as free as those of England? . . . Am I a freeman in England, and do I become a slave in six hours by crossing the channel?" Although the letters were published anonymously, most people recognized Swift's indignant voice. Rhetoric such as this had never been raised by an Anglo-Irish voice against the English. For Irish Catholics and Protestants alike, Swift became a hero. **F**

GULLIVER'S SUCCESS

Swift's reputation for fierce satire was now legendary in both Ireland and England. Although such impassioned writing won him loyal friends, it also earned him bitter enemies. Two years after *The Drapier's Letters,* Swift anonymously published his masterful satire *Gulliver's Travels.* **G**

The narration of a fictional voyager allowed Swift to vent his fury at political corruption and his annoyance with the general worthlessness of human beings. "Drown the world!" he exclaimed. "I am not content with despising it, but I would anger it if I could with safety." Anger is what he hoped to achieve with *Gulliver's Travels,* which gets increasingly pessimistic with each voyage. Swift expected the book to offend people; he wanted "to vex the world rather than divert it." Instead, in an ironic twist that Swift himself must have appreciated, the book diverted—entertained—almost everyone.

1710 **Begins political activity and writing for the Tory government in London; becomes friends with John Gay, Alexander Pope, John Arbuthnot, and Esther Vanhomrigh (Vanessa)**

1713 **Appointed dean of St. Patrick's Cathedral in Dublin**

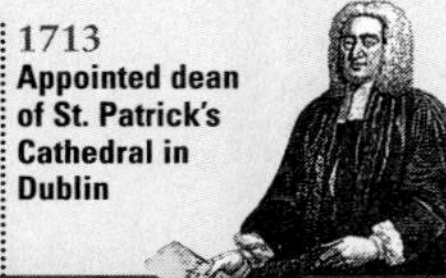

1714 **Alexander Pope publishes "The Rape of the Lock."**

1717 **Lady Mary Wortley Montagu introduces smallpox inoculation in England.**

1719 **Ireland is declared inseparable from England; Daniel Defoe publishes *Robinson Crusoe.***

1720

H 1724 **Publishes *The Drapier's Letters;* gains reputation as Irish hero**

1726 **Publishes *Gulliver's Travels* in London**

The Literary Coffee House

Coffee houses such as this one were popular with educated men like Swift, who often dined at a coffee house in the evening with his literary friends and political associates. Coffee houses were the center of cultural and political life in London from 1650 to 1860.

THE HATE BEHIND THE HUMOR Swift's humor is so light that many readers miss the deep vein of rage that runs throughout his work. In his words: "I have ever hated all nations, professions, and communities, and all my love is towards individuals. . . . But principally I hate and detest that animal called man." Swift's misanthropy, (I) his hatred of humankind, may have grown from his religious conviction. He saw humans as fallen victims of original sin, not the rational creatures that many Enlightenment thinkers believed in.

Swift's last major work about Ireland, "A Modest Proposal," is an outrageous attack on those who mistreated Ireland's poor. Once again, his ferocious satire made people laugh.

THE GREATEST EPITAPH Swift outlived most of his friends. Before succumbing to mental decline, he arranged to be buried next to Esther (J) Johnson in St. Patrick's. He left his remaining fortune to go toward building a mental hospital.

W. B. Yeats, the great 20th-century Irish poet, maintained that "Swift sleeps under the greatest epitaph in history." Composed by Swift in Latin, the epitaph is translated as follows:

Here lies the body of
Jonathan Swift, D.D., Dean of this Cathedral.
He has gone where fierce indignation
can lacerate his heart no more.
Go, traveler, and imitate if you can
a man who was an undaunted
champion of liberty.

1728 Long-time friend Esther Johnson (Stella) dies.

1729 Publishes "A Modest Proposal"

1731 Composes "Verses on the Death of Dr. Swift" (published in 1739)

1745 Dies Oct. 19 and is buried in St. Patrick's Cathedral

1730

1740

1729 Johann Sebastian Bach composes "St. Matthew Passion."

1732 Benjamin Franklin publishes *Poor Richard's Almanack.*

1741 George Frederick Handel composes "The Messiah."

1742 Swift is declared by court to be "of unsound mind and memory" (K)

Sociology

(I) As seen through *Gilliver's Travels,* Swift was especially upset by human pride, treating the vanity of the book's hero with caustic irony.

Medicine

(J) Swift's mental decline has been traced back to his 23rd year when he first suffered the symptoms of what modern medicine has diagnosed as Ménière's disease, or vertigo—an incurable inner-ear disturbance. Soon, he was experiencing giddiness, nausea, and noises in his head. After 1738, he became increasingly affected by the disorder, becoming more and more hard of hearing. In 1742 he lapsed into dementia and never recovered, though he lived another three years.

Science/Technology

(K) It is ironic that Swift was declared mentally unsound before his death. Like most people of the time, Swift thought people with mental problems were sinful and targeted them in satire. Treatment for mental illness consisted of "taming" the patient through discipline. Many mental patients were locked up in asylums such as London's infamous Bethlehem Hospital, known as Bedlam. For a small fee, visitors were allowed to amuse themselves by watching the inmates.

OVERVIEW

Objectives

1. understand and appreciate a **satire (Literary Analysis)**
2. appreciate the author's use of **fantasy (Literary Analysis)**
3. use **visualizing** to appreciate the fantasy in *Gulliver's Travels* **(Active Reading)**

Summary

Lemuel Gulliver, a ship's surgeon and captain, recounts his four voyages to remote parts of the world. Gulliver's first voyage to Lilliput, a land populated by six-inch people who are also small-minded, is followed by a visit to Brobdingnag, where Gulliver is the diminutive visitor next to the magnanimous giants.

 Use **Unit Three Resource Book,** p. 43 for additional support.

Thematic Link

Considered Swift's most extended satirical treatment of human faults and vices, *Gulliver's Travels* stands out in an age known for its great satires. The whimsical tales of Gulliver's journeys to foreign lands are rich with Swift's ironic perspective on the corrupt nature of human beings, and his story is filled with critical, often hilarious portraits of pride, arrogance, dullness, and depravity. Swift's satire constitutes an **argument for change.**

5-Minute Warm-Up

Daily Language SkillBuilder

Have students **proofread** the display sentences on page 515l and write them correctly. The sentences also appear on Transparency 14 of **Grammar Transparencies and Copymasters.**

PREPARING *to Read*

from Gulliver's Travels

Fiction by JONATHAN SWIFT

Comparing Literature of the World

Gulliver's Travels, "A Modest Proposal," and *Candide*

To compare satirical writing across cultures, read the excerpt from *Candide* on page 625. Specific points of comparison between the works of Swift and Voltaire will help you examine how each author satirizes 18th-century society.

Connect to Your Life

Giant Size Recall a time when you found yourself in an unfamiliar country or culture. How did you react? Were you frightened and uncomfortable, or did you find the experience exciting? How did people from that country or culture react to you? Write about what your experience as a stranger in an unfamiliar place was like.

Build Background

Out of Place Lilliput, a kingdom of six-inch people, is the first place described in Jonathan Swift's satiric masterpiece *Gulliver's Travels*—originally titled *Travels into Several Remote Nations of the World, in Four Parts, by Lemuel Gulliver, First a Surgeon, and Then a Captain of Several Ships.* Gulliver's second voyage brings him to Brobdingnag, where he finds himself in the opposite position: he is the diminutive human among giants.

Gulliver's Travels is not only a comedy about an ordinary man's adventures in some extraordinary places, but also a **satire** of English society in Swift's day and of humankind in general. Use Strategies for Reading: Satire on page 585 to help you recognize the objects of Swift's satire. You will notice that Gulliver himself is often an object of satire, for his uncritical narration of what he sees reveals that he is naive and, true to his name, totally gullible.

WORDS TO KNOW **Vocabulary Preview**

censure	infallibly	prostrating
civility	morose	recapitulate
conjecture	panegyric	retinue
dexterity	perfidiousness	schism
diminutive	pernicious	solicitation

Focus Your Reading

LITERARY ANALYSIS FANTASY **Fantasy** is literature in which the limits of reality are purposely disregarded. The aim of fantasy may be to entertain, to make a serious comment about society and human nature, or both. For Swift, the humorous fantasy of *Gulliver's Travels* is a perfect vehicle for his **satire.** What aspects of society could Swift criticize through a fantasy that places a normal human in a country where everyone else is only six inches tall? How might Swift use an opposite fantasy—a normal-sized person living among 70-foot giants—to satirize different qualities of humanity?

ACTIVE READING VISUALIZING Forming a mental picture from a verbal or written description—something you do every day—is called **visualizing.** For example, vivid details about a character in a story help the reader form an idea or "picture" of that character. Swift helps readers visualize the setting, characters, and events in *Gulliver's Travels* by providing a number of realistic details.

READER'S NOTEBOOK As you read, keep track of key details that help you visualize by filling in a graphic like the one shown. You might also sketch some scenes that Swift describes.

His Behavior and Treatment	Key Details
How he is confined	Body (including hair) is tied by strings and pegs to the ground
What he eats and drinks; in what amounts	

LESSON RESOURCES

UNIT THREE RESOURCE BOOK, pp. 43–47

ASSESSMENT RESOURCES

Formal Assessment, pp. 99–100

Teacher's Guide to Assessment and Portfolio Use

Test Generator

SKILLS TRANSPARENCIES AND COPYMASTERS

Literary Analysis
- Horatian vs. Juvenalian Satire, T12 (for Review, p. 607)

Reading and Critical Thinking
- Visualizing, T8 (for Active Reading, p. 607)

Grammar
- Avoiding Misplaced and Dangling Modifiers, T51 (for Mini Lesson, pp. 602–603)
- Dangling Participles, C102 (for Mini Lesson, pp. 602–603)

Vocabulary
- Suffixes, C53 (for Mini Lesson, p. 600)

Writing
- Satire, C29 (for Writing Option 1, p. 608)

Communications
- Appreciative Listening, T2 (for Activities & Explorations 1, p. 608)
- Dramatic Reading, T12 (for Activities & Explorations 1, p. 608)

INTEGRATED TECHNOLOGY

Audio Library

Net Activities

Visit our website: www.mcdougallittell.com

Jonathan Swift

from Gulliver's Travels

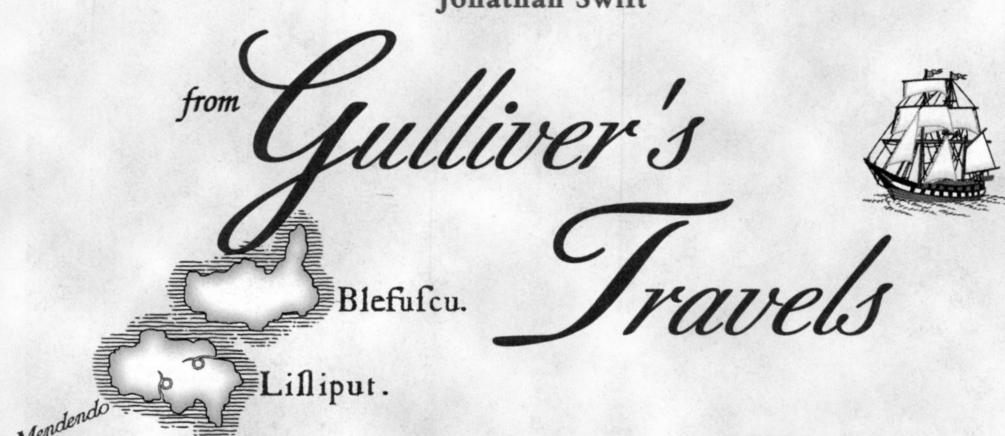

Map of Lilliput from the first edition of *Gulliver's Travels,* 1726

from PART 1. A Voyage to Lilliput

The first part of Gulliver's Travels *describes his adventures in Lilliput. After going to sea as a ship's doctor, Gulliver faces disaster as his ship breaks apart in a storm. He swims toward land, reaches shore, and falls exhausted on the ground.*

I lay down on the grass, which was very short and soft, where I slept sounder than ever I remember to have done in my life, and as I reckoned, above nine hours; for when I awaked, it was just daylight. I attempted to rise, but was not able to stir: for as I happened to lie on my back, I found my arms and legs were strongly fastened on each side to the ground; and my hair, which was long and thick, tied down in the same manner. I likewise felt several slender ligatures[1] across my body, from my armpits to my thighs. I could only look upwards; the sun began to grow hot, and the light offended my eyes. I heard a confused noise about me, but in the posture I lay, could see nothing except the sky. In a little time I felt something alive moving on my left leg, which advancing gently forward over my breast, came almost up to my chin; when bending my eyes downwards as much as I could, I perceived it to be a human creature not six inches high, with a bow and arrow in his hands, and a quiver[2] at his back. In the meantime, I felt at least forty more of the same kind (as I conjectured) following the first. I was in the utmost astonishment, and roared so loud, that they all ran back in a fright; and some of them, as I was afterwards told, were hurt with the falls they got by leaping from my sides upon the ground. However, they soon returned; and one of them, who ventured so far as to get a full sight of my face, lifting up his hands and eyes by way of admiration, cried out in a shrill, but distinct voice, *Hekinah Degul:* the others repeated the same words several times, but I then knew not what they meant.

I lay all this while, as the reader may believe, in great uneasiness; at length, struggling to get loose, I had the fortune to break the strings, and wrench out the pegs that fastened my left arm to the ground; for, by lifting it up to my face, I discovered the methods they had taken to bind

1. **ligatures** (lĭg′ə-cho͝orz′): cords used to tie something up.
2. **quiver:** a case for carrying arrows.

TEACHING THE LITERATURE

Customizing Instruction

Less Proficient Readers

Set a Purpose Have students read to discover what kind of people populate the lands of Lilliput and Brobdingnag. Encourage them to keep notes as they learn more about each country and its people.

Students Acquiring English

Explain to students that Swift presents Gulliver's experiences as though they actually happened in real places. Ask students what details Swift includes to make the story seem more real.

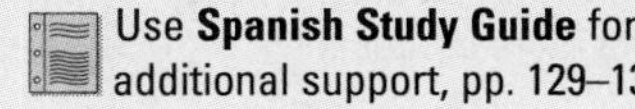
Use **Spanish Study Guide** for additional support, pp. 129–131.

Gifted and Talented

Invite students to consider how Swift treats Gulliver himself as an object of satire. What aspects of human nature does Swift satirize through Gulliver's behavior?

SYNONYMS Synonyms are words with similar meanings. Reading and understanding synonyms helps expand vocabulary.

Activity

1. Have students find a synonym for each of the WORDS TO KNOW, using a dictionary and a thesaurus if necessary.
2. Students should write sentences using the synonyms, recognizing the connotative differences between the word pairs.

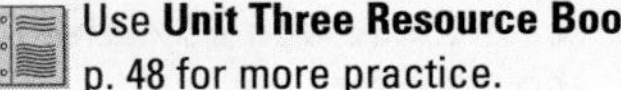
Use **Unit Three Resource Book,** p. 48 for more practice.

GULLIVER'S TRAVELS 591

Reading and Analyzing

Reading Skills and Strategies: QUESTIONING

(A) What effect is produced when Gulliver quotes the Lilliputian language?
Possible Responses: The story seems more realistic; Swift has created an entire fantasy world, complete with language.

Active Reading VISUALIZING

(B) Visualizing helps clarify a verbal or written description. Have students visualize the structure built next to Gulliver's ear. What is it like and why was it built?

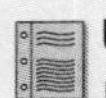 Use **Unit Three Resource Book,** p. 44 for more practice.

Literary Analysis FANTASY

A writer can satirize elements of real life by using a fantasy world as a point of comparison, but such a fantasy world needs to be at least somewhat believable to be effective. How does Swift construct his Lilliputian world to make it seem believable?
Possible Responses: He gives them a language; they have politicians and a government; he describes their food.

 Use **Unit Three Resource Book,** p. 45 for more exercises.

Ted Danson as Gulliver (*Gulliver's Travels,* NBC, 1996). Photofest.

me; and, at the same time, with a violent pull, which gave me excessive pain, I a little loosened the strings that tied down my hair on the left side; so that I was just able to turn my head about two inches. But the creatures ran off a second time, before I could seize them;
1 whereupon there was a great shout in a very shrill accent; and after it ceased, I heard one of
A them cry aloud, *Tolgo phonac*; when in an instant I felt above an hundred arrows discharged on my left hand, which pricked me like so many needles; and besides they shot another flight into the air, as we do bombs in Europe, whereof many, I suppose, fell on my body (though I felt them not) and some on my face, which I immediately covered with my left hand. When this shower of arrows was over, I fell a groaning with grief and pain; and then striving again to get loose, they discharged another volley[3] larger than the first, and some of them attempted with spears to stick me in the sides; but, by good luck, I had on me a buff jerkin[4], which they could not pierce. I thought it
2 the most prudent method to lie still; and my design was to continue so till night, when, my left hand being already loose, I could easily free myself: and as for the inhabitants, I had reason to believe I might be a match for the greatest armies they could bring against me, if they were all of the same size with him that I saw. But fortune disposed otherwise of me.

When the people observed I was quiet, they discharged no more arrows: but by the noise increasing, I knew their numbers were greater; and about four yards from me, over-against my
right ear, I heard a knocking for above an hour, B
like people at work; when turning my head that way, as well as the pegs and strings would permit me, I saw a stage erected about a foot and a half from the ground, capable of holding four of the inhabitants, with two or three ladders to mount it: from whence one of them, who seemed to be a person of quality,[5] made me a long speech, whereof I understood not one syllable. But I should have mentioned, that before the principal

3. **volley:** a group of missiles—in this case, arrows—fired simultaneously.
4. **buff jerkin:** a leather jacket.
5. **person of quality:** a high-ranking person.

Teaching Options

BLOCK SCHEDULING: MANAGING TIME

If your schedule requires that you cover the lesson objectives in a shorter time, use . . .
- Preparing to Read, p. 590
- Thinking Through the Literature, p. 607
- Vocabulary in Action, p. 608

If you want to take advantage of longer class time, use . . .
- TE Teaching Options: Preteaching Vocabulary, p. 591; Standardized Test Practice, p. 593; Speaking and Listening, p. 601; Informal Assessment, pp. 596, 606; Cross Curricular Links, p. 598; Grammar, p. 602; Viewing and Representing, p. 604

person began his oration, he cried out three times, *Langro Dehul san:* (these words and the former were afterwards repeated and explained to me). Whereupon immediately about fifty of the inhabitants came, and cut the strings that fastened the left side of my head, which gave me the liberty of turning it to the right, and of observing the person and gesture of him who was to speak. He appeared to be of a middle age, and taller than any of the other three who attended him; whereof one was a page[6] who held up his train, and seemed to be somewhat longer than my middle finger; the other two stood one on each side to support him. He acted every part of an orator, and I could observe many periods of threatenings, and others of promises, pity and kindness. I answered in a few words, but in the most submissive manner, lifting up my left hand and both my eyes to the sun, as calling him for a witness; and being almost famished with hunger, having not eaten a morsel for some hours before I left the ship, I found the demands of nature so strong upon me, that I could not forbear showing my impatience (perhaps against the strict rules of decency) by putting my finger frequently on my mouth, to signify that I wanted food.

The *Hurgo* (for so they call a great lord, as I afterwards learned) understood me very well. He descended from the stage, and commanded that several ladders should be applied to my sides, on which above an hundred of the inhabitants mounted, and walked towards my mouth, laden with baskets full of meat, which had been provided and sent thither by the King's orders upon the first intelligence[7] he received of me. I observed there was the flesh of several animals, but could not distinguish them by the taste. There were shoulders, legs, and loins shaped like those of mutton, and very well dressed, but smaller than the wings of a lark. I eat them by two or three at a mouthful, and took three loaves at a time, about the bigness of musket bullets. They supplied me as fast as they could, showing a thousand marks of wonder and astonishment at my bulk and appetite. I then made another sign that I wanted drink. They found by my eating that a small quantity would not suffice[8] me; and being a most ingenious people, they slung up with great dexterity one of their largest hogsheads;[9] then rolled it towards my hand, and beat out the top; I drank it off at a draft,[10] which I might well do, for it hardly held half a pint, and tasted like a small wine of Burgundy, but much more delicious. They brought me a second hogshead, which I drank in the same manner, and made signs for more, but they had none to give me. When I had performed these wonders, they shouted for joy, and danced upon my breast, repeating several times as they did at first, *Hekinah Degul.* They made me a sign that I should throw down the two hogsheads, but first warned the people below to stand out of the way, crying aloud, *Borach Mivola*, and when they saw the vessels in the air, there was an universal shout of *Hekinah Degul.*

I confess I was often tempted, while they were passing backwards and forwards on my body, to seize forty or fifty of the first that came in my reach, and dash them against the ground. But **3** the remembrance of what I had felt, which probably might not be the worst they could do; and the promise of honor I made them, for so I interpreted my submissive behavior, soon drove out those imaginations. Besides, I now considered myself as bound by the laws of hospitality to a people who had treated me with so much expense and magnificence. However, in my thoughts I could not sufficiently wonder at the intrepidity[11] of these diminutive mortals, who

6. **page:** a youth serving as a personal attendant.
7. **intelligence:** news; information.
8. **suffice:** satisfy.
9. **hogsheads:** large barrels used to store liquids, such as wine or ale.
10. **draft:** a swallow or gulp.
11. **intrepidity** (ĭn-trə-pĭd′ĭ-tē): boldness; courage.

WORDS TO KNOW **diminutive** (dĭ-mĭn′yə-tĭv) *adj.* tiny

Customizing Options

Students Acquiring English

1 Point out, or have students guess, the meanings of archaic words such as *whereupon* (then, at that point); *whence* (where), *whereof* (of which), and *thither* (there).

Less Proficient Readers

2 Ask students to explain what Gulliver plans to do as he is being showered with arrows.

Answer: He seems to be planning to wait until nightfall and then fight.

3 Have students explain in their own words why Gulliver does not "seize forty or fifty" Lilliputians and dash them to the ground.

Possible Responses: He remembers how badly the arrows hurt and realizes that they might be able to do even more; he feels that it would be dishonorable to do anything to them.

Assessment Standardized Test Practice

IDENTIFYING PURPOSE AND MEANING
For some standardized tests, students will be asked to identify the writer's purpose, point of view, and intended meaning. Read the following statements aloud to help students pick the most accurate expression of Swift's purpose and intended meaning in *Gulliver's Travels.*

A. Swift's purpose was to criticize human nature and social institutions with no aim to reform them.

B. Swift wanted to write a thoroughly negative and serious story that pessimistically criticized human nature and society.

C. Swift wanted to present a humorous and satirically critical work about the faults of human beings and their potential for improvement.

Remind students that while more than one statement may be *partially* true, the best choice will reflect the author's purpose most completely; for that reason, **C** is the best answer.

Reading and Analyzing

Reading Skills and Strategies: PARAPHRASING

A Paraphrasing is useful when readers are taking notes and can be used as a comprehension aid with any difficult text or passage. Have students paraphrase the passage from "His Excellency" to "be conveyed," in which an official from the Emperor meets Gulliver.

Possible Response: Even though this tiny official has to crawl up Gulliver's leg even to speak to him, His Excellency still insists on showing his power and authority. He brings his entourage, a royal seal, and an order for transporting Gulliver to the capital city.

Literary Analysis FANTASY

B Ask students what kind of person Swift might be satirizing by presenting the fantastical image of the six-inch representative of the king who claims royal authority over a giant twelve times his size.

Possible Response: people who have an inflated sense of their own importance.

Literary Analysis: CHARACTER

C Ask students what impressions they have of Gulliver in this passage. How does he describe himself?

Possible Response: He's proud of being so well liked by the Lilliputians and is rather self-satisfied that he's learned their language so quickly.

Reading Skills and Strategies: QUESTIONING

D Why do the politicians dance on the rope for the king?

Answer: because they want political favors and preferment.

---

durst[12] venture to mount and walk on my body, while one of my hands was at liberty, without
1 trembling at the very sight of so prodigious a creature as I must appear to them.

After some time, when they observed that I made no more demands for meat, there appeared before me a person of high rank from his Imperial **A** Majesty. His Excellency, having mounted on the small of my right leg, advanced forwards up to my face, with about a dozen of his retinue. And producing his credentials under the Signet Royal,[13] which he applied close to my eyes, spoke about ten minutes, without any signs of anger, but with **B** a kind of determinate resolution; often pointing forwards, which, as I afterwards found, was towards the capital city, about half a mile distant, whither it was agreed by his Majesty in council that I must be conveyed. I answered in a few words, but to no purpose, and made a sign with my hand that was loose, putting it to the other (but over his Excellency's head, for fear of hurting him or his train) and then to my own head and body, to signify that I desired my liberty. It appeared that he understood me well enough; for he shook his head by way of disapprobation,[14] and held his hand in a posture to show that I must be carried as a prisoner. However, he made other signs to let me understand that I should have meat and drink enough, and very good treatment. Whereupon I once more thought of attempting to break my bonds; but again, when I felt the smart of their arrows upon my face and hands, which were all in blisters, and many of the darts still sticking in them; and observing likewise that the number of my enemies increased; I gave tokens to let them know that they might do with me what they pleased. Upon this the *Hurgo* and his train withdrew, with much civility and cheerful countenances.[15] Soon after I heard a general shout, with frequent repetitions of the words, *Peplom Selan,* and I felt great numbers of the people on my left side relaxing the cords to such a degree, that I was able to turn upon my right, and to ease myself. . . .

C My gentleness and good behavior had gained so far on the Emperor and his court, and indeed upon the army and people in general, that I began to conceive hopes of getting my liberty in 2
a short time. I took all possible methods to cultivate this favorable disposition. The natives came by degrees to be less apprehensive of any danger from me. I would sometimes lie down, and let five or six of them dance on my hand. And at last the boys and girls would venture to come and play at hide-and-seek in my hair. I had now made a good progress in understanding and speaking their language. The Emperor had a mind one day to entertain me with several of the country shows; wherein they exceed all nations I have known, both for dexterity and magnificence. I was diverted with none so much as that of the rope-dancers,[16] performed upon a slender white thread, extended about two foot,

The boys and girls would venture to come and play at hide-and-seek in my hair.

12. **durst:** dared.
13. **Signet Royal:** the official seal of a king or queen.
14. **disapprobation** (dĭs-ăp′rə-bā′shən): disapproval.
15. **countenances:** facial expressions.
16. **rope-dancers:** acrobats who perform on a tightrope. Here the rope-dancers represent Whig Party politicians at the court of George I, whose "acrobatics"—political maneuverings—were intended to increase their power. (Swift supported the opposing party, the Tories.)

WORDS TO KNOW
retinue (rĕt′n-o͞o′) *n.* a group of people accompanying an important person
civility (sĭ-vĭl′ĭ-tē) *n.* politeness; courtesy
dexterity (dĕk-stĕr′ĭ-tē) *n.* skill and quickness of bodily movement

and twelve inches from the ground. Upon which I shall desire liberty, with the reader's patience, to enlarge a little.

This diversion is only practiced by those persons who are candidates for great

D employments, and high favor, at court. They are trained in this art from their youth, and are not always of noble birth, or liberal education. When a great office is vacant either by death or disgrace (which often happens) five or six of those candidates petition the Emperor to entertain his Majesty and the court with a dance on the rope; and whoever jumps the highest without falling, succeeds in the office. Very often the chief ministers themselves are commanded to show their skill, and to convince the Emperor that they have not lost their faculty. Flimnap, The Treasurer,[17] is allowed to cut a caper on the strait rope, at least an inch higher than any other lord in the whole empire. I have seen him do the summerset[18] several times together upon a trencher[19] fixed on the rope, which is no thicker than a common packthread[20] in England. My friend Reldresal, Principal Secretary for Private Affairs, is, in my opinion, if I am not partial, the second after the Treasurer; the rest of the great officers are much upon a par.

These diversions are often attended with fatal accidents, whereof great numbers are on record. I myself have seen two or three candidates break a limb. But the danger is much greater when the ministers themselves are commanded to show their dexterity; for, by contending to excel themselves and their fellows, they strain so far, that there is hardly one of them who hath not received a fall; and some of them two or three. I was assured, that a year or two before my

3 arrival, Flimnap would have infallibly broke his neck, if one of the King's cushions, that accidentally lay on the ground, had not weakened the force of his fall.

There is likewise another diversion, which is only shown before the Emperor and Empress, and first minister, upon particular occasions. The Emperor lays on a table three fine silken threads of six inches long. One is blue, the other red, 4

and the third green.[21] These threads are proposed as prizes for those persons whom the Emperor hath a mind to distinguish by a peculiar mark of his favor. The ceremony is performed in his Majesty's great chamber of state; where the candidates are to undergo a trial of dexterity very different from the former, and such as I have not observed the least resemblance of in any other country of the old or the new world. The Emperor holds a stick in his hands, both ends parallel to the horizon, while the candidates, advancing one by one, sometimes leap over the stick, sometimes creep under it backwards and forwards several times, according as the stick is advanced or depressed. Sometimes the Emperor holds one end of the stick, and his first minister the other; sometimes the minister has it entirely to himself. Whoever performs his part with most agility, and holds out the longest in *leaping* and *creeping,* is rewarded with the blue-colored silk; the red is given to the next, and the green to the third, which they all wear girt[22] twice round about the middle; and you see few great persons about this court who are not adorned with one of these girdles. . . .

I had sent so many memorials and petitions for my liberty, that his Majesty at length mentioned the matter first in the cabinet, and

17. **Flimnap, The Treasurer:** a character representing the Whig leader and statesman Sir Robert Walpole, who served as first lord of the treasury from 1715 to 1717 and from 1721 to 1742.
18. **summerset:** somersault.
19. **trencher:** a tray or platter for serving food.
20. **packthread:** a strong twine for tying packages.
21. **three fine silken . . . third green:** The three colored threads represent the Order of the Garter, the Order of the Bath, and the Order of the Thistle—honorary societies revived by Walpole.
22. **girt:** wrapped.

WORDS TO KNOW

infallibly (ĭn-făl'ə-blē) *adv.* without fail; certainly

Customizing Options

Students Acquiring English

1 Have students use context clues to comprehend the meaning of *prodigious,* which was a common word in the 18th century.

Answer: enormous; exciting wonder.

Less Proficient Readers

2 Have students paraphrase the sentences "My gentleness and good behavior had gained so far on the Emperor and his court" and "I took all possible methods to cultivate this favorable disposition."

Possible Response: My gentle and proper behavior made a good impression on the Emperor and his court; I tried very hard to stay on their good side.

3 Point out the reference to Flimnap falling on one of the king's cushions. Ask students to explain this reference in terms of general political activity.

Possible Response: A politician who becomes unpopular or loses office can be protected and restored to power by those in authority.

Gifted and Talented

4 Invite students to research the real honors represented by the Lilliputians' blue, red, and green threads (the Order of the Garter, the Order of the Bath, and the Order of the Thistle). Have students find out the status these honorary societies had during Swift's time.

Reading and Analyzing

Active Reading VISUALIZING

A Have students visualize the description of the Lilliputian manner of swearing an oath ("... hold my right foot in my left hand ..."). Why does Swift create such a ridiculous ritual?

Possible Response: Swift is satirizing the meaningless or absurd ceremonies of state business; he's making fun of Gulliver for taking such silly behavior seriously.

Literary Analysis: SATIRE

B Gulliver's articles of freedom begin with a tribute to the "most mighty Emperor of Lilliput." What is ironic about Swift's description of the king in this preamble, and how does his irony contribute to the satire on the Lilliputians?

Possible Responses: The tiny king is described as "taller than the sons of men," whose "head strikes against the sun." Swift uses exaggeration to ridicule self-aggrandizing rhetoric and inflated egos.

Literary Analysis FANTASY

C Gulliver reports that the Lilliputians use detailed calculations to figure his food and drink allowance. Why would Swift include such concrete details in a fantasy?

Possible Responses: The facts and figures sound plausible, which makes the tale believable rather than merely ridiculous.

then in a full council; where it was opposed by none, except Skyresh Bolgolam, who was pleased, without any provocation, to be my mortal enemy. But it was carried against him by the whole board, and confirmed by the Emperor. That minister was *Galbet,* or Admiral of the Realm; very much in his master's confidence, and a person well versed in affairs, but of a morose
1 and sour complexion. However, he was at length persuaded to comply; but prevailed that the articles and conditions upon which I should be set free, and to which I must swear, should be drawn up by himself. These articles were brought to me by Skyresh Bolgolam in person, attended by two under-secretaries, and several persons of distinction. After they were read, I was demanded to swear to the performance of them; first in the manner of my own country, and afterwards in the method prescribed by their
A laws; which was to hold my right foot in my left hand, to place the middle finger of my right hand on the crown of my head, and my thumb on the tip of my right ear. But because the reader may perhaps be curious to have some idea of the style and manner of expression peculiar to that people, as well as to know the articles upon which I recovered my liberty, I have made a translation of the whole instrument, word for word, as near as I was able; which I here offer to the public.

GOLBASTO MOMAREN EVLAME GURDILO SHEFIN
B MULLY ULLY GUE, most mighty Emperor of Lilliput, delight and terror of the universe, whose dominions extend five thousand blustrugs (about twelve miles in circumference) to the extremities of the globe; Monarch of all Monarchs; taller than the sons of men; whose feet press down to the center, and whose head strikes against the sun; at whose nod the princes of the earth shake their knees; pleasant as the spring, comfortable as the summer, fruitful as autumn, dreadful as winter. His most sublime Majesty proposeth to the Man-Mountain, lately arrived at our celestial dominions, the following articles, which by a solemn oath he shall be obliged to perform.

Ted Danson as Gulliver in Lilliput (NBC, 1996). Photofest.

First, the Man-Mountain shall not depart from our dominions, without our license under our great seal.

Secondly, He shall not presume to come into our metropolis, without our express order; at which time the inhabitants shall have two hours warning, to keep within their doors.

Thirdly, The said Man-Mountain shall confine his walks to our principal high roads; and not offer to walk or lie down in a meadow, or field of corn.

Fourthly, As he walks the said roads, he shall take the utmost care not to trample upon the bodies of any of our loving subjects, their horses, or carriages, nor take any of our said subjects into his hands, without their own consent.

Fifthly, If an express require extraordinary dispatch, the Man-Mountain shall be obliged to

WORDS TO KNOW **morose** (mə-rōs') *adj.* gloomy

Teaching Options

Assessment **Informal Assessment**

WRITING A SUMMARY The Lilliputians finally remove Gulliver's chains after he agrees to certain restrictions on his movements and activities and signs a document to that effect. Have students write a summary of the conditions under which Gulliver is given his freedom in Lilliput.

RUBRIC

3 **Full Accomplishment** Students cover all conditions and clearly summarize main idea of each.

2 **Substantial Accomplishment** Students cover most conditions and adequately summarize main idea of each.

1 **Little or Partial Accomplishment** Students cover few conditions and offer incomplete or inaccurate summaries of main ideas.

carry in his pocket the messenger and horse, a six days' journey once in every moon, and return the said messenger back (if so required) safe to our Imperial Presence.

Sixthly, He shall be our ally against our enemies in the island of Blefuscu, and do his utmost to destroy their fleet, which is now preparing to invade us.

Seventhly, That the said Man-Mountain shall, at his times of leisure, be aiding and assisting to our workmen, in helping to raise certain great stones, towards covering the wall of the principal park, and other our royal buildings.

Eighthly, That the said Man-Mountain shall, in two moons' time, deliver in an exact survey of the circumference of our dominions by a computation of his own paces round the coast.

Lastly, That upon his solemn
C oath to observe all the above articles, the said Man-Mountain shall have a daily allowance of meat and drink sufficient for the support of 1,728 of our subjects;
2 with free access to our Royal Person, and other marks of our favor. Given at our palace at Belfaborac the twelfth day of the ninety-first moon of our reign.

I made my acknowledgements by prostrating myself at his Majesty's feet.

I swore and subscribed[23] to these articles with great cheerfulness and content . . . whereupon my chains were immediately unlocked, and I was at full liberty: the Emperor himself in person did me the honor to be by at the whole ceremony. I made my acknowledge-
3 ments by prostrating myself at his Majesty's feet: but he commanded me to rise; and after many gracious expressions, which, to avoid the censure of vanity, I shall not repeat, he added, that he hoped I should prove a useful servant, and well deserve all the favors he had already conferred upon me, or might do for the future.

The reader may please to observe, that in the last article for the recovery of my liberty, the Emperor stipulates to allow me a quantity of meat and drink, sufficient for the support of 1,728 Lilliputians. Some time after, asking a friend at court how they came to fix on that determinate number, he told me, that his Majesty's mathematicians, having taken the height of my body by the help of a quadrant,[24] and finding it to exceed theirs in the proportion of twelve to one, they concluded from the similarity of their bodies, that mine must contain at least 1,728 of theirs, and consequently would require as much food as was necessary to support that number of Lilliputians. By which, the reader may conceive an idea of the ingenuity of that people, as well as the prudent and exact economy of so great a prince. One morning, about a fortnight after I had obtained my liberty, Reldresal, Principal Secretary (as they style him) of Private Affairs, came to my house, attended only by one servant. He ordered his coach to wait at a distance, and desired I would give him an hour's audience; which I readily consented to, on account of his quality, and personal merits, as well as of the many good offices he had done me during my solicitations at court. I offered to lie down, that he might the more conveniently reach my ear; but he chose rather to let me hold him in my hand during our conversation. He began with compliments on my liberty, said he might pretend to some merit in it; but, however, added, that if it had not been for the present situation of things at court, perhaps I might not have obtained it so soon. For, said he, as flourishing a

23. **subscribed:** signed my name.

24. **quadrant:** an instrument for measuring altitudes.

WORDS TO KNOW	
	prostrating (prŏs'trā'tĭng) *v.* kneeling or bowing down **prostrate** *v.*
	censure (sĕn'shər) *n.* criticism; blame
	solicitation (sə-lĭs'ĭ-tā'shən) *n.* a plea or request

Customizing Options

Students Acquiring English

1 Point out the word *complexion,* and explain that it doesn't always mean the hue or appearance of the skin. Have students use context clues to determine the meaning of *complexion* here.

Answer: attitude or inclination.

Less Proficient Readers

2 Gulliver's terms of release say he has "free access to our Royal Person." Ask students what this phrase means. Why is the plural pronoun *our* used?

Possible Response: He can visit the king any time he wants; since the king represents all the people in the kingdom, he uses plural pronouns.

3 As k students to explain why Gulliver's display of respect—"I made my acknowledgements by prostrating myself at his Majesty's feet"—is ironic.

Possible Response: Gulliver, who is huge in comparison, is bowing down to a tiny king. Perhaps Swift is taking a swipe at royal authority by implying that subjects are often greater than their king.

Reading and Analyzing

Reading Skills and Strategies: SUMMARIZING

A Have students summarize the conflicts between the High-Heels and the Low-Heels and between the Big-Endians and the Little-Endians. Students should include in their summaries the main ideas and supporting details.

Possible Responses: The Low-Heels are the party in the Emperor's favor and therefore have more power than the more numerous High-Heels. The Little-Endians open their eggs at the small end, in accord with Lilliputian law. Big-Endians are a dissenting faction of Lilliputians who open their eggs at the large end. They are supported by the government of Blefescu.

Reading Skills and Strategies: QUESTIONING

B Why are the Lilliputians at war with Blefescu? What real countries do Lilliput and Blefescu represent?

Possible Responses: because Blefescu supports the Big-Endians; Lilliput represents England, and Blefescu represents France.

condition as we appear to be in to foreigners, we labor under two mighty evils; a violent faction at home, and the danger of an invasion by a most potent enemy from abroad. As to the first, you are to understand, that for above seventy moons past, there have been two struggling parties in the empire, under the names of *Tramecksan,* and *Slamecksan,*[25] from the high and low heels on their shoes, by which they distinguish themselves.

It is alleged indeed, that the high heels are (A) most agreeable to our ancient constitution: but however this be, his Majesty hath determined to make use of only low heels in the administration of the government and all offices in the gift of the crown; as you cannot but observe; and particularly, that his Majesty's imperial heels are lower at least by a *drurr* than any of his court; (*drurr* is a measure about the fourteenth part of an inch). The animosities between these two parties run so high, that they will neither eat nor drink, nor talk with each other. We compute the *Tramecksan,* or High-Heels, to exceed us in number, but the power is wholly on our side. We apprehend his Imperial Highness, the heir to the crown, to have some tendency towards the High-Heels; at least we can plainly discover one of his heels higher than the other, which gives him a hobble in his gait.[26] Now, in the midst of these intestine[27] disquiets, we are threatened with an invasion from the island of Blefuscu,[28] which is the other great empire of the universe, almost as large and powerful as this of his Majesty. For as to what we have heard you affirm, that there are other kingdoms and states in the world, inhabited by human creatures as large as yourself, our philosophers are in much doubt; and would rather conjecture that you dropped from the moon, or one of the stars; because it is certain, that an hundred mortals of your bulk would, in a short time, destroy all the fruits and cattle of his Majesty's dominions. Besides, our histories of six thousand moons make no mention of any other regions, than the two great empires of Lilliput and Blefuscu. Which two mighty powers have, as I was going to tell you, been engaged in a most obstinate war for six and thirty moons past. It began upon the following occasion.

It is allowed on all hands, that the primitive way of breaking eggs before we eat them, was upon the larger end: but his present Majesty's grandfather, while he was a boy, going to eat an egg, and breaking it according to the ancient practice, happened to cut one of his fingers. Whereupon the Emperor his father published an edict, commanding all his subjects, upon great penalties, to break the smaller end of their eggs. The people so highly resented this law, that our histories tell us there have been six rebellions raised on that account; wherein one emperor lost his life, and another his crown.[29] These civil commotions were constantly (B) fomented by the monarchs of Blefuscu; and when they were quelled, the exiles always fled for refuge to that empire. It is computed, that eleven thousand persons have, at several times, suffered death, rather than submit to break their eggs at the smaller end. Many hundred large volumes have been published upon this

25. **Tramecksan, and Slamecksan . . . shoes:** The "high heel" party corresponds to the Tory Party, which promoted the "High-Church" (Catholic) aspects of Anglicanism; the "low heel" party corresponds to the Whig Party, which promoted the "Low-Church" (Protestant) aspects.
26. **his Imperial Highness . . . hobble in his gait:** The Prince of Wales, who later reigned as George II, had both Tory and Whig friends.
27. **intestine:** internal.
28. **Blefuscu:** an imaginary country that represents France, Britain's main political rival at the time.
29. **six rebellions . . . his crown:** The dispute over egg breaking corresponds to the conflict between Roman Catholics and Protestants in 17th-century England. The "emperor" who lost his life in the conflict was King Charles I; the one who lost his crown was James II, who fled into exile.

WORDS TO KNOW **conjecture** (kən-jĕk'chər) *v.* to guess or infer

598

Teaching Options

Cross Curricular Link History

SEVENTEENTH-CENTURY POLITICS Swift packs a great deal of complicated religious and political history into his allegory of the Big-Endians and Little-Endians. In this allegory, the Big-Endians represent Roman Catholics. The Lilliputian monarch who decrees that his subjects must break their eggs at the smaller end is clearly Henry VIII, the English king who broke with the Roman Catholic Church. Thus, the Little-Endians are Protestants, and Blefescu is France, the traditional enemy of Protestant England and ally of Catholics who wanted to reclaim the English crown. France provided a safe haven for these Catholics after the time of Henry VIII, and harbored a number of religious and political exiles during the English Civil War (1642–1652) and the subsequent period of rule by Oliver Cromwell (1653–1658). Swift also refers to the Test Act, which was passed during the Restoration. Have students research the Test Act and this time period to interpret possible influences on Swift's satire. Students could share their research and conclusions in writing or orally.

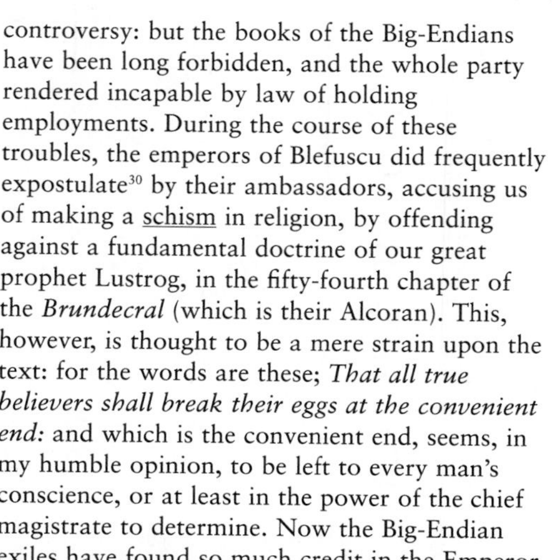

controversy: but the books of the Big-Endians have been long forbidden, and the whole party rendered incapable by law of holding employments. During the course of these troubles, the emperors of Blefuscu did frequently expostulate[30] by their ambassadors, accusing us of making a schism in religion, by offending against a fundamental doctrine of our great prophet Lustrog, in the fifty-fourth chapter of the *Brundecral* (which is their Alcoran). This, however, is thought to be a mere strain upon the text: for the words are these; *That all true believers shall break their eggs at the convenient end:* and which is the convenient end, seems, in my humble opinion, to be left to every man's conscience, or at least in the power of the chief magistrate to determine. Now the Big-Endian exiles have found so much credit in the Emperor of Blefuscu's court, and so much private assistance and encouragement from their party here at home, that a bloody war hath been carried on between the two empires for six and thirty moons with various success; during which time we have lost forty capital ships, and a much greater number of smaller vessels, together with thirty thousand of our best seamen and soldiers; and the damage received by the enemy is reckoned to be somewhat greater than ours. However, they have now equipped a numerous fleet, and are just preparing to make a descent upon us; and his Imperial Majesty, placing great confidence in your valor and strength, hath commanded me to lay this account of his affairs before you.

I desired the Secretary to present my humble duty to the Emperor, and to let him know, that I thought it would not become me, who was a foreigner, to interfere with parties; but I was ready, with the hazard of my life, to defend his person and state against all invaders.

30. **expostulate** (ĭk-spŏs′chə-lāt′): raise objections.

Thinking Through the Literature

1. What situation or **character** from Gulliver's adventures in Lilliput did you find especially amusing or interesting? Explain your choice.
2. What is your opinion of the diminutive Lilliputians? Think of three words to describe them and give three examples of their behavior to support your opinion.
3. Name some characteristics of human societies that Swift may be **satirizing** through the Lilliputians.

   THINK ABOUT
   - how the Emperor of Lilliput sees himself
   - how the Emperor selects people for political offices and favors
   - what divides the Lilliputians from each other and from neighboring Blefuscu
   - how the Lilliputians treat Gulliver
4. Considering that Gulliver is physically capable of destroying Lilliput ("I might be a match for the greatest armies they could bring against me"), why do you think he acts so submissively?
5. What do you think of Gulliver at this point in the story? Explain your opinion of him as a person and as a narrator of his travels.

WORDS TO KNOW
schism (sĭz′əm) *n.* a split or division, especially one within a religious group

Customizing Options

Students Acquiring English

1 Help students understand the meaning of the phrase "It is allowed on all hands." Have them paraphrase the idiom.
Answer: everybody agrees that.

2 Heflp students use context clues to determine the meaning of *fomented.*
Answer: incited; roused.

Help them find the antonym of *fomented* in the next part of the sentence.
Answer: quelled.

Less Proficient Readers

Explain that Swift is referring to a great deal of complicated British history in his stories about conflicts that seem harmless and silly—who wears high or low heels and how people break their eggs. Have students discuss their impressions of Swift's localized satire. Does it add to or detract from the story?
Possible Response: It adds depth and a serious tone, but it makes the story hard to follow if the reader is not familiar with the contemporary issues being satirized.

Thinking Through the Literature

1. Accept all responses for which students provide reasons or explanations.
2. Possible words to describe the Lilliputians may include *curious, generous, formal,* and *proud.* Details from the story that would support such a characterization include the Lilliputians' amazement at Gulliver and their desire to learn more about him, their generosity in providing for his care, their love of ceremony and their seeming adherence to elaborate rules of conduct, and the king's self-aggrandizing language.
3. Possible Responses: the self-importance of rulers or ruling bodies; the sometimes nonsensical criteria by which people are selected for political office; prejudices; fear of the unfamiliar.
4. Possible Responses: Gulliver realizes that he stands to gain nothing by destroying Lilliput; he feels that it would be dishonorable to fight them after seeking their trust.
5. Accept all responses that indicate an understanding of the events of the story and Swift's characterization of Lemuel Gulliver.

Reading and Analyzing

Reading Skills and Strategies: QUESTIONING

A What is your first clue that Gulliver has landed in another fantasy world?
Possible Response: He casually remarks that the corn is 40 feet high.

Active Reading VISUALIZING

B Have students use information from the text (the height of the corn, hedges, and steps; the length of the giant's stride) to estimate the height of the Brobdingnagians.

Literary Analysis FANTASY

C What familiar features of human society does Swift include in his initial description of Brobdingnag?
Possible Response: They cultivate land; they have roads; there is some kind of social hierarchy.

Map of Brobdingnag from the first edition of *Gulliver's Travels,* 1726

from PART 2. A Voyage to Brobdingnag

The second part of Gulliver's Travels describes his adventures in Brobdingnag. As the story opens, Gulliver has again gone to sea as a ship's doctor. The ship has been blown off course by a storm. When the ship comes in sight of land, the captain sends ashore a boatload of men (including Gulliver) to look for drinking water. While exploring the island, Gulliver is separated from the others, and when he returns to the boat he sees his shipmates rowing in a panic back to the ship, in flight from a huge monster who is chasing them. Gulliver turns back into the interior to hide from the giant.

I fell into a highroad, for so I took it to be, although it served to the inhabitants only as a footpath through a field of barley. Here I walked on for some time, but could see little on either side, it being now near harvest, and the **A** corn rising at least forty foot. I was an hour walking to the end of this field, which was fenced in with a hedge of at least one hundred and twenty foot high, and the trees so lofty that I could make no computation of their altitude. There was a stile[31] to pass from this field into the next: it had four steps, and a stone to cross over when you came to the utmost. It was impossible for me to climb this stile, because every step was six foot high, and the upper stone above twenty. I was endeavoring to find some gap in the hedge when I discovered one of the inhabitants in the next field advancing towards the stile, of the same size with him whom I saw in the sea pursuing our boat. He appeared as tall as an ordinary spire-steeple, and took about ten yards **B** at every stride, as near as I could guess. I was struck with the utmost fear and astonishment, and ran to hide myself in the corn, from whence I saw him at the top of the stile, looking back into the next field on the right hand; and heard him call in a voice many degrees louder than a speaking trumpet; but the noise was so high in **1** the air that at first I certainly thought it was thunder. Whereupon seven monsters like himself came towards him with reaping hooks in their hands, each hook about the largeness of six scythes. These people were not so well clad as the first, whose servants or laborers they seemed to be. **C**

31. **stile:** a set of steps for climbing over a hedge or fence.

Teaching Options

Vocabulary Strategy

SUFFIXES

Instruction Suffixes are word parts added to the end of a word to change the part of speech of that word. They can help students recognize what part of speech an unfamiliar word is. This can be a useful first step in figuring out the meaning of a word from its context.

Activity

1. Have students find the words in the WORDS TO KNOW list that have suffixes and write them in the first column of a chart. Have them analyze each word to determine its root word and suffix.

Words to Know	Root	Suffix
civility	civil	–ity

2. Have students add other suffixes to each root word to see what other forms they can generate. Have students discuss the effect each new suffix has on the word's meanings.

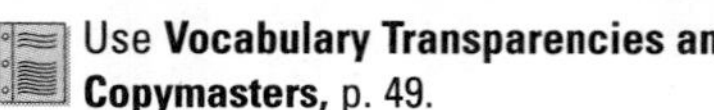
Use **Vocabulary Transparencies and Copymasters,** p. 49.

Richard Redgrave, *Gulliver Exhibited to the Brobdingnag Farmer;* Victoria and Albert Museum, London.

For, upon some words he spoke, they went to reap the corn in the field where I lay. I kept from them at as great a distance as I could, but was forced to move with extreme difficulty, for the stalks of the corn were sometimes not above a foot distant, so that I could hardly squeeze my
2 body betwixt them. However, I made a shift to go
3 forward till I came to a part of the field where the corn had been laid by the rain and wind; here it was impossible for me to advance a step, for the stalks were so interwoven that I could not creep through, and the beards of the fallen ears so strong and pointed that they pierced through my clothes into my flesh. At the same time I heard the reapers not above an hundred yards behind me. Being quite dispirited with toil, and wholly overcome by grief and despair, I lay down between two ridges and heartily wished I might there end my days. I bemoaned my desolate widow and fatherless children; I lamented my own folly and willfulness in attempting a second voyage against the advice of all my friends and relations. In this terrible agitation of mind, I could not forbear[32] thinking of Lilliput, whose inhabitants looked upon me as the greatest prodigy that ever appeared in the world; where I was able to draw an imperial fleet in my hand, and perform those other actions which will be recorded forever in the chronicles of that empire, while posterity shall hardly believe them,

32. **forbear:** refrain from; resist.

Customizing Options

Less Proficient Readers

Set a Purpose Have students read to discover the characteristics of the inhabitants of Brobdingnag.

Students Acquiring English

1 Help students use context clues to understand what a *speaking trumpet* does.

Possible Response: A speaking trumpet is a megaphone, which is used to intensify or direct the voice.

2 Point out the archaic word *betwixt.* Have students give the modern equivalent.

Answer: between.

3 Help students understand the idiom *I made a shift to go forward.* Have them paraphrase the sentence.

Possible Response: I made a great attempt to go forward.

Speaking and Listening

ROUNDTABLE DISCUSSION

Instruction Popular formats on news programs that feature political issues and current events, roundtable discussions allow for the presentation of a variety of perspectives. Although they are informal, they still demand effective arguments and valid support for claims.

Prepare Have students plan a discussion roundtable with representatives from Lilliput, Brobdingnag, and England. A moderator should also be one of the participants.

Present Remind students to respond appropriately to others' views and questions. Afterwards, have students discuss the problem of trying to present an "objective" description of their own cultures.

BLOCK SCHEDULING This activity is particularly well-suited for longer class periods.

GULLIVER'S TRAVELS 601

Reading and Analyzing

Active Reading VISUALIZING

A Have students visualize and describe what Gulliver must look like to the giant when the giant first picks him up in the field.

Possible Response: He probably looks like a little animal—a mouse or a lizard—as the giant holds him between two fingers.

Literary Analysis: CHARACTER

B How is Gulliver made to look ridiculous when he first presents himself to the farmer?

Possible Response: He doesn't see that he couldn't run away if he tried; the Brobdingnagians would have little use for the relatively tiny amount of money he "humbly" offers them.

Literary Analysis: SATIRE

C Remind students that satire ridicules human foolishness or vice for the sake of improving society. Have students identify the targets of satire in the exchange between Gulliver and the king about English culture.

Possible Response: England's image of itself; the condescension of those who are larger or more powerful; human nature itself.

D How is Gulliver the object of Swift's satire in his response to the king's unflattering description of the English?

Possible Response: Gulliver is being ridiculed for his blind admiration or for ignoring his country's faults.

although attested by millions. I reflected what a mortification it must prove to me to appear as inconsiderable in this nation as one single Lilliputian would be among us. But this I conceived was to be the least of my misfortunes; for as human creatures are observed to be more savage and cruel in proportion to their bulk, what could I expect but to be a morsel in the mouth of the first among these enormous barbarians who should happen to seize me? Undoubtedly philosophers are in the right when they tell us that nothing is great or little otherwise than by comparison. It might have pleased fortune to let the Lilliputians find some nation where the people were as diminutive with respect to them as they were to me. And who knows but that even this prodigious race of mortals might be equally overmatched in some distant part of the world, whereof we have yet no discovery?

Scared and confounded as I was, I could not forbear going on with these reflections; when one of the reapers approaching within ten yards of the ridge where I lay, made me apprehend that with the next step I should be squashed to death under his foot, or cut in two with his reaping hook. And therefore when he was again about to move, I screamed as loud as fear could make me. Whereupon the huge creature trod short, and looking round about under him for some time, at last espied me as I lay on the ground. He considered a while with the caution of one who **A** endeavors to lay hold on a small dangerous animal in such a manner that it shall not be able either to scratch or to bite him, as I myself have sometimes done with a weasel in England. At length he ventured to take me up behind by the middle between his forefinger and thumb, and brought me within three yards of his eyes, that he might behold my shape more perfectly. . . .

He ventured to take me up behind by the middle between his forefinger and thumb.

Lifting up the lappet[33] of his coat, he put me gently into it, and immediately ran along with me to his master, who was a substantial farmer, and the same person I had first seen in the field.

The farmer having (as I supposed by their talk) received such an account of me as his servant could give him, took a piece of a small straw about the size of a walking staff, and therewith lifted up the lappets of my coat, which it seems he thought to be some kind of covering that nature had given me. He blew my hairs aside to take a better view of my face. He called his hinds[34] about him, and asked them (as I afterwards learned) whether they had ever seen in the fields any little creature that resembled me. He then placed me softly on **B** the ground upon all four; but I got immediately up, and walked slowly backwards and forwards, to let those people see I had no intent to run away. They all sat down in a circle about me, the better to observe my motions. I pulled off my hat, and made a low bow towards the farmer; I fell on my knees, and lifted up my hands and eyes, and spoke several words as loud as I could; I took a purse of gold out of my pocket, and humbly presented it to him. . . .

The farmer by this time was convinced I must be a rational creature. He spoke often to me, but the sound of his voice pierced my ears like that of a water mill, yet his words were articulate enough. I answered as loud as I could in several languages, and he often laid his ear within two yards of me, but all in vain, for we were wholly unintelligible to each other. He then sent his servants to their work, and taking his

33. **lappet:** flap or fold.

34. **hinds:** farm servants.

Teaching Options

Grammar

DANGLING PARTICIPLES

Instruction Explain that a participle is a type of verbal that functions as an adjective in a sentence. If it does not clearly modify any noun or pronoun, it is called a dangling participle.

Activity Write the following sentences on the chalkboard. Underline the participial phrases.

Incorrect

Known for his satirical style, *Gulliver's Travels* became legendary.

Correct

Known for his satirical style, Jonathan Swift became legendary after writing *Gulliver's Travels.*

Correct

Jonathan Swift, known for his satirical style, became legendary after writing Gulliver's Travels.

Point out the participial phrases in the sentences. Then ask students why the first example is incorrect. *(The reader doesn't know who is known for his satirical style.)* Tell students that to correct a dangling participle make sure the sentence names the noun or pronoun it modifies and be sure to place the participle close to the word it modifies. Otherwise, the phrase will modify the wrong word or appear to have no logical connection to the rest of the sentence.

handkerchief out of his pocket, he doubled and spread it on his hand, which he placed flat on the ground with the palm upwards, making me a sign to step into it, as I could easily do, for it was not above a foot in thickness. I thought it my part to obey, and for fear of falling, laid myself at full length upon the handkerchief, with the remainder of which he lapped me up to the head for further security, and in this manner carried me home to his house. . . .

Gulliver lives with the farmer and his family and grows especially close to the farmer's daughter, Glumdalclitch. After a number of adventures in the farmer's house, including an attack on Gulliver by two ferocious rats, he is taken to the metropolis where he is purchased from the farmer by the queen of Brobdingnag, who presents him to the king. Glumdalclitch remains with Gulliver at the royal court as his nurse and instructor. Gulliver becomes a favorite of the king and queen.

C It is the custom that every Wednesday (which, as I have before observed, was their Sabbath) the King and Queen, with the royal issue of both sexes, dine together in the apartment of his Majesty, to whom I was now become a favorite; and at these times my little chair and table were placed at his left hand, before one of the salt-cellars. This prince took a pleasure in conversing with me, inquiring into the manners, religion, laws, government, and learning of Europe; wherein I gave him the best account I was able. His apprehension was so clear, and his judgment so exact, that he made very wise reflections and observations upon all I said. But I confess that after I had been a little too copious[35] in talking of my own beloved country, of our trade and wars by sea and land, of our schisms in religion and parties in the state, the prejudices of his education prevailed so far that he could not forbear taking me up in his right hand, and stroking me gently with the other, after an hearty fit of laughing, asked me whether I were a Whig or a Tory. Then turning to his first minister, who waited behind him with a white staff, near as tall as the mainmast of the *Royal Sovereign,*[36] he observed how contemptible a thing was human grandeur, **1** which could be mimicked by such diminutive insects as I: "and yet," said he, "I dare engage, these creatures have their titles and distinctions of honor; they contrive little nests and burrows, that they call houses and cities; they make a figure in dress and equipage; they love, they fight, they dispute, they cheat, they betray." And thus he continued on, while my color came and went several times with indignation to hear our noble **D** country, the mistress of arts and arms, the scourge of France, the arbitress of Europe, the seat of virtue, piety, honor, and truth, the pride and envy of the world, so contemptuously treated.

But as I was not in a condition to resent injuries, so, upon mature thoughts, I began to doubt whether I were injured or no. For, after having been accustomed several months to the sight and converse of this people, and observed every object upon which I cast my eyes to be of proportionable magnitude, the horror I had first conceived from their bulk and aspect was so far **2** worn off that if I had then beheld a company of English lords and ladies in their finery and birthday clothes,[37] acting their several parts in the most courtly manner of strutting and bowing and prating,[38] to say the truth, I should have been strongly tempted to laugh as much at them as this **3** King and his grandees did at me. Neither indeed could I forbear smiling at myself when the Queen used to place me upon her hand towards a looking glass, by which both our persons appeared before me in full view together; and there could be nothing more ridiculous than the comparison; so that I really began to imagine myself dwindled many degrees below my usual size. . . .

35. **copious** (kō′pē-əs): wordy; verbose.

36. ***Royal Sovereign:*** at the time, one of the largest ships of the British navy.

37. **birthday clothes:** elaborate costumes worn by courtiers on the monarch's birthday.

38. **prating** (prā′tĭng): chattering; talking foolishly.

Customizing Options

Less Proficient Readers

1 Help students paraphrase the difficult passage in Gulliver's account of the king's remarks: ". . . he observed how contemptible a thing was human grandeur, which could be mimicked by such diminutive insects as I."

Possible Response: He observed how human grandeur was worthy of contempt if little insects like Gulliver could attempt to imitate it.

Students Acquiring English

2 Help students determine the meaning of *bulk* and *aspect* from their context.

Answer: What is it about Brobdingnagians that makes Gulliver feel horror? Their *size* and *appearance.* Help them determine the meaning of *finery* by studying the context and the root word.

Answer: He is obviously referring to things they are wearing, and these are *fine* things.

Gifted and Talented

3 Invite students to consider how Gulliver's perception of himself and his country changes according to his environment.

Possible Responses: When he's bigger than everyone else in Lilliput, he is the accomplished and grand representative of England; when he's the tiny one among giants, he reveals the petty side of his culture, and he feels smaller than he really is.

Exercise Have students underline each participial phrase and identify if it is dangling. Then have students work individually to rewrite each sentence with a dangling participle. Discuss their revisions in cooperative groups.

1. Breaking apart in the storm, Gulliver watches from shore. *(dangling participial phrase; possible answer: From shore Gulliver watches his ship breaking apart in the storm.)*
2. Bending his eyes downward, a bow and arrow come into full view. *(dangling participial phrase; possible answer: Bending his eyes downward, Gulliver sees a bow and arrow come into full view.)*
3. Gulliver is soon covered with human creatures standing no more than six inches tall. *(no dangling participles)*

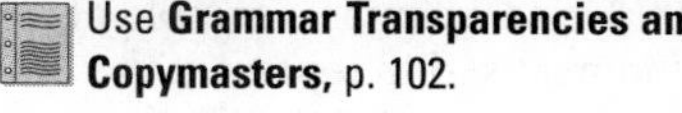

Use **Grammar Transparencies and Copymasters,** p. 102.

Use McDougal Littell's ***Language Network*** for more instruction and practice in dangling participles.

Reading and Analyzing

Literary Analysis: CHARACTER

A Gulliver has many vexing encounters with animals and insects in Brobdingnag. How does setting Gulliver in contests with animals affect our sense of his character?

Possible Response: We can see that, despite his tiny size and the ridiculousness of being involved in mortal combat with insects, Gulliver takes pride in his bravery and values his dignity.

Active Reading VISUALIZING

B Have students provide concrete estimates of the size of the flies and wasps that Gulliver encounters, since Gulliver's descriptions—"as big as a Dunstable lark" (5 to 9 inches long) and "as large as a partridge" (about 12 inches long)—may not be clear to them. Ask students to estimate the size of other everyday Brobdingnagian items.

Reading Skills and Strategies: SUMMARIZING

C Have students summarize the setting and content of Gulliver's private conversations with the Brobdingnagian king about English government. Students should include all main ideas and supporting details.

Possible Response: The king and Gulliver sit face-to-face, and the king listens to his explanations and commentary on English government, just in case there is something positive to emulate.

I was frequently rallied by the Queen upon
A account of my fearfulness, and she used to ask me whether the people of my country were as great cowards as myself. The occasion was this. The kingdom is much pestered with flies in summer, and these odious insects, each of them
B as big as a Dunstable lark, hardly gave me any rest while I sat at dinner, with their continual humming and buzzing about my ears. They
1 would sometimes alight upon my victuals, and leave their loathsome excrement or spawn behind, which to me was very visible, although not to the natives of that country, whose large optics were not so acute as mine in viewing smaller objects. Sometimes they would fix upon my nose or forehead, where they stung me to the quick, smelling very offensively; and I could easily trace that viscous[39] matter, which our naturalists tell us enables those creatures to walk with their feet upwards upon a ceiling. I had much ado to defend myself against these detestable animals, and could not forbear starting when they came on my face. It was the common practice of the dwarf to catch a number of these insects in his hand, as schoolboys do among us, and let them out suddenly under my nose, on purpose to frighten me, and divert the Queen. My remedy was to cut them in pieces with my knife as they flew in the air, wherein my dexterity was much admired.

I remember one morning when Glumdalclitch had set me in my box upon a window, as she usually did in fair days to give me air (for I
2 durst not venture to let the box be hung on a nail out of the window, as we do with cages in
3 England), after I had lifted up one of my sashes, and sat down at my table to eat a piece of sweet cake for my breakfast, above twenty wasps, allured by the smell, came flying into the room, humming louder than the drones of as many bagpipes. Some of them seized my cake, and carried it piecemeal away; others flew about my head and face, confounding me with the noise, and putting me in the utmost terror of their stings. However, I had the courage to rise and draw my hanger, and attack them in the air. I dispatched four of them, but the rest got away, and I presently shut my window. These insects were as large as partridges; I took out their stings, found them an inch and a half long, and as sharp as needles. I carefully preserved them all, and having since shown them with some other curiosities in several parts of Europe, upon my return to England I gave three of them to Gresham College,[40] and kept the fourth for myself. . . .

The King, who, as I before observed, was a C prince of excellent understanding, would frequently order that I should be brought in my box and set upon the table in his closet. He would then command me to bring one of my chairs out of the box, and sit down within three yards distance upon the top of the cabinet, which brought me almost to a level with his face. In this manner I had several conversations with him. . . . He desired I would give him as exact an account of the government of England as I possibly could; because, as fond as princes commonly are of their own customs (for so he conjectured of other monarchs, by my former discourses), he should be glad to hear of anything that might deserve imitation. . . .

He wondered to hear me talk of such chargeable and extensive wars; that certainly we must be a quarrelsome people, or live among very bad neighbors, and that our generals must needs be richer than our kings.[41] He asked what business we had out of our own islands, unless upon the

39. **viscous** (vĭs′kəs): thick and sticky.

40. **Gresham** (grĕsh′əm) **College:** a London college that was the meeting place of the Royal Society (the principal British scientific organization of Swift's day).

41. **our generals . . . our kings:** a reference to the wealth of the Duke of Marlborough, a former general whose palace was larger than the king's.

Teaching Options

Viewing and Representing

Gulliver with the King of Brobdingnag. Illustration from a 19th century edition of *Gulliver's Travels*

ART APPRECIATION

Instruction *Gulliver's Travels* has intrigued readers, artists, and performers for years, and the art shown throughout this selection is a sample of the various visual forms used to represent the story since it was published in 1726. Still photographs from a television movie, a painting, and an illustration show the wide range of media used to bring Gulliver to life over the past several hundred years.

Application Have students produce their own representations of a scene from *Gulliver's Travels.* Encourage them to pick a scene they can clearly visualize, and have them make notes of what features from the text they particularly want to represent. Students might use various media and materials in their productions: They might draw or paint; they might make a collage using photographs from magazines; they might stage a scene with props and costumes and photograph or videotape it. Have students share their Gulliver projects for group discussion.

Gulliver with the king of Brobdingnag. Illustration from a 19th-century edition of *Gulliver's Travels.*

Customizing Options

Students Acquiring English

1 Point out the word *victual,* and explain that it is pronounced "vittle." Help students use the context to determine its meaning.

Answer: food or provisions.

Less Proficient Readers

Have students list what hazards Gulliver encounters during his stay in Brobdingnag.

Possible Response: He is attacked by rats, flies, and wasps; a dwarf torments him; he's in danger of falling great distances.

Students Acquiring English

2 Have students determine the meaning of *durst* and give its modern equivalent.

Answer: dared.

3 Help students understand the multiple meanings of *sashes, hanger,* and *closet.* Ask them to determine the more common meanings before working on the less common usages presented here.

Answer: as used here: *sashes*—the framework of a window; *hanger*—a small sword; *closet*—private sitting room.

Reading and Analyzing

Literary Analysis FANTASY

A How does Swift use his fantasy world in this paragraph to deliver his satire on England's interest in war?

Possible Response: Swift satirizes England's policies through the unflattering conclusions drawn by the outsider who, in contrast to the English, appears rational and ethical.

Literary Analysis: SATIRE

B Have students list Swift's targets and discuss his satirical comments. What message is Swift sending through the Brobdingnagian king?

Possible Responses: His tone becomes more serious and savage; among Swift's targets are legislators, priests, and the government, and his comments are deeply critical of current English behavior; Swift articulates the message that England has strayed from and perverted its original ideals through the scornful remarks of the king.

Literary Analysis: CHARACTER

C Have students discuss their impressions of Gulliver as they read the Brobdingnagian king's assessment of English culture and society. Are their opinions of Gulliver changed by the king's biting criticism?

Possible Responses: Some students may adopt Swift's satirical point of view and see Gulliver as the contemptible representative of the corrupt English nation; others might think the king's harsh views don't apply to Gulliver, because Gulliver spends so much time away at sea.

score of trade or treaty or to defend the coasts with our fleet. **A** Above all, he was amazed to hear me talk of a mercenary standing army in the midst of peace, and among a free people. He said if we were governed by our own consent in the persons of our representatives, he could not imagine of whom we were afraid, or against whom we were to fight; and would hear my opinion whether a private man's house might not better be defended by himself, his children, and family, than by half a dozen rascals picked up at a venture[42] in the streets for small wages, who might get an hundred times more by cutting their throats. . . .

B He was perfectly astonished with the historical account I gave him of our affairs during the last century, protesting it was only an heap of conspiracies, rebellions, murders, massacres, revolutions, banishments, the very worst effects that avarice, faction, hypocrisy, perfidiousness, cruelty, rage, madness, hatred, envy, lust, malice, or ambition could produce.

His Majesty in another audience was at the pains to recapitulate the sum of all I had spoken; compared the questions he made with the answers I had given; then taking me into his hands, and stroking me gently, delivered himself in these words, which I shall never forget, nor the manner he spoke them in: "My little friend **C** Grildrig, you have made a most admirable panegyric upon your country. You have clearly proved that ignorance, idleness, and vice are the proper ingredients for qualifying a legislator. That laws are best explained, interpreted, and applied by those whose interests and abilities lie in perverting, confounding, and eluding them. I observe among you some lines of an institution which in its original might have been tolerable; but these half erased, and the rest wholly blurred and blotted by corruptions. It doth not appear from all you have said how any one virtue is required towards the procurement of any one station among you; much less that men are ennobled on account of their virtue, that priests are advanced for their piety or learning, soldiers for their conduct or valor, judges for their integrity, senators for the love of their country, or counselors for their wisdom. As for yourself," continued the King, "who have spent the greatest part of your life in traveling, I am well disposed to hope you may hitherto have escaped many vices of your country. But by what I have gathered from your own relation, and the answers I have with much pains wringed and extorted from you, I cannot but conclude the bulk of your natives to be the most pernicious race of little odious vermin that nature ever suffered to crawl upon the surface of the earth." ❖

42. **at a venture:** at random.

WORDS TO KNOW

perfidiousness (pər-fĭd'ē-əs-nĭs) n. treachery; betrayal
recapitulate (rē'kə-pĭch'ə-lāt') *v.* to repeat in concise form; summarize
panegyric (păn'ə-jĭr'ĭk) *n.* a public speech of praise
pernicious (pər-nĭsh'əs) *adj.* destructive; wicked

Teaching Options

Assessment Informal Assessment

WRITING A RESPONSE

Have students write two or three paragraphs in which they agree or disagree with the following statement. Remind them to support their response with evidence from the selection.

Although Gulliver travels to amazing places, he remains essentially unchanged by his experiences.

RUBRIC

3 Full Accomplishment Student's response is logical, well organized, and supported with evidence from selection.

2 Substantial Accomplishment Student's response is well organized and supported with evidence from selection.

1 Little or Partial Accomplishment Student's response is vague and may lack evidence from selection.

Connect to the Literature

1. **What Do You Think?** What impressed you most about Gulliver's adventures in Brobdingnag?

Comprehension Check
- What dangers does Gulliver face in Brobdingnag?
- In general, how do the Brobdingnagians treat Gulliver?
- What is the king's opinion of England?

Think Critically

2. What changes of feelings or attitudes does Gulliver experience in Brobdingnag because of his diminutive size?
3. How does Gulliver's opinion of the Brobdingnagians change?
4. What can you infer about the Brobdingnagians and their society from the king's reaction to Gulliver's account of English society?

THINK ABOUT
- why the king is curious about England
- what he thinks about English warfare
- what he thinks about English history

5. **ACTIVE READING VISUALIZING** Review the chart of details and any sketches you made in your READER'S NOTEBOOK as you read. In your opinion, what is the overall effect of such detailed descriptions of Gulliver's experiences?

Extend Interpretations

6. **Comparing Texts** Compare the Lilliputians with the Brobdingnagians. Then write a sentence stating the major difference between the two societies.
7. **Critic's Corner** Swift claimed that he was a misanthrope, one who hates humanity. Critics have debated this issue for centuries, some defending Swift as more moralistic than misanthropic. What do you think? Cite evidence from these excerpts from *Gulliver's Travels* to support Swift's assertion or to argue against it.
8. **Connect to Life** If you had been lost in Lilliput and Brobdingnag, in what ways would you have felt or acted differently than Gulliver did? How would you have felt or acted differently than what you described about your own reactions in Connect to Your Life?

Literary Analysis

FANTASY As you know, a **fantasy** is a work of fiction that stretches the limits of reality. However, fantasies often do explore genuine ideas about human life—in fact, effective fantasies usually contain enough realistic details to make them believable.

In *Gulliver's Travels,* for example, Gulliver remains recognizably human. Moreover, his fantasy account of strange lands was not unlike the authentic accounts of foreign cultures published in Swift's time. Swift's talent lay in making his fantasy both strange and familiar.

Cooperative Learning Activity Some of the events and feelings described in *Gulliver's Travels* seem realistic—it's no surprise that a stranger in an unfamiliar land would be treated with suspicion, for example. However, the element of fantasy becomes clear when Swift describes just *who* has made Gulliver captive. Working in a small group, use a chart similar to this one to sort out the real and fantasy aspects of Gulliver's experiences.

Event/Reaction	Real qualities	Fantasy qualities
Gulliver awakens in Lilliput.	Gulliver is taken captive by inhabitants.	Captors are six inches tall.

REVIEW SATIRE Which do you think is the major kind of satire in *Gulliver's Travels*—Horatian satire, which is playful and sympathetic, or Juvenalian satire, which is bitter and critical? Give examples from the text.

GUIDING STUDENT RESPONSE

Connect to the Literature

1. What Do You Think?
Guidelines for student response: Accept all responses for which students provide reasons or explanations. You might ask students what they would like most and fear most as a tiny creature in a land of giants.

Comprehension Check
- He is almost scythed by a farm laborer; he is attacked by flies and wasps.
- They seem fascinated by him and generally treat him well; they even seem to develop an affection for him.
- The king believes it is a backward and corrupt place filled with "the most pernicious race of little odious vermin" on Earth.

Use Selection Quiz in **Unit Three Resource Book,** p. 47.

Think Critically

2. Because of the threat his small size poses to his safety, Gulliver is initially quite frightened by the Brobdingnagians. He consequently seems more timid, meek, and passive than he did in Lilliput.
3. While Gulliver is at first afraid of the Brobdingnagians, he becomes fond of them and regards them with respect and admiration.
4. Students might infer that the Brobdingnagians are always looking for ways to improve their society and government, are peaceful, and are opposed to intrigue and political maneuvering. Students should support their response with evidence from the text.
5. Possible Responses: Although the experiences described in *Gulliver's Travels* are fantastic, the detailed account draws the reader in and creates a feeling of authenticity. Since *Gulliver's Travels* is a fantasy, such details are essential to enabling the reader to imagine what is happening.

Literary Analysis

Cooperative Learning Activity Students should supply at least two events each from Lilliput and Brobdingnag. Students should clearly demonstrate the ability to distinguish realistic elements from fantastic elements.

Extend Interpretations

Comparing Texts Possible responses: The Brobdingnagians are peaceful, while Lilliputian society is riddled with conflict. Lilliputians are preoccupied with status, which is not of great concern to the Brobdingnagians, who would see those concerns as shallow.

Critic's Corner Students who agree that Swift was a misanthrope might argue that Gulliver says nothing positive about humans; all of his descriptions are of human flaws. In Gulliver's conversation with the King of Brobdingnag, Swift, speaking through the king, writes that English society illustrates "the very worst effects that avarice, faction, hypocrisy, perfidiousness, cruelty, rage, madness, hatred, envy, lust, malice, or ambition could produce." Students who find Swift more moralistic than misanthropic might note the affection that seems to grow between both Gulliver and the Lilliputians and Gulliver and the Brobdingnagians.

Connect to Life Accept all thoughtful responses.

Writing Options

1. **Satiric Fantasy** Encourage students to decide on a topic and then write in a voice and style appropriate to their audience and purpose. Students might adopt Swift's technique of having a well-meaning character who is also a target of the satire.
2. **Creating Another Land** Invite students to create all the necessary components of another world: language, culture, geography (perhaps a map), and precise and often mathematical descriptions of the environment. The tone of a journal entry will necessarily be informal, but the essay should still be precise in language and detail.

Activities & Explorations

1. **Scene Performance** Have students pay attention to performance details such as cues for entrances and exits, notes for blocking the scene, and suggestions for expressive delivery of dialogue.
2. **Lilliput on Video** Responses will vary. Some students will appreciate the literalization of the scene, because it presents a visual picture of the verbal description. Others will find the visual representation intrusive, because it presents a view of the scene different from the picture they had in mind.
3. **Comparing Size** Gulliver is 12 times as tall as a Lilliputian. They figure that Gulliver's body could hold 1,728 Lilliputians ($12 \times 12 \times 12 = 1{,}728$), so they provide food for him equal to the amount it would take to feed 1,728 of them. A Brobdingnagian is 12 times as tall as Gulliver, so 1,728 Gullivers would eat as much as one Brobdingnagian.

Inquiry & Research

Literary History *Gulliver's Travels* was a success when it was first published. In addition to Swift's correspondence and biographies of the writer, students might follow up on any references to 18th-century newspapers or periodicals that mention the publication and reception of the book.

Choices & CHALLENGES

Writing Options

1. **Satiric Fantasy** Using the excerpts from *Gulliver's Travels* as a model, draft a satiric fantasy on a topic of your choice. Think of an issue or experience you want to make fun of—for example, you might satirize the process of applying to colleges or interviewing for a job. Possible formats might include a travel narrative, a children's story, or a comic book.

2. **Creating Another Land** Create your own fantasy land for Gulliver to visit. Write a journal entry in which you describe this new land.

Writing Handbook
See page 1367: Compare and Contrast.

Activities & Explorations

1. **Scene Performance** With a partner, choose a scene from *Gulliver's Travels* to perform for the class. Possible scenes: the early communication between Gulliver and the lords of Lilliput or Gulliver's arrival in Brobdingnag. You may need to create additional dialogue based on Gulliver's account. ~ **SPEAKING AND LISTENING**

2. **Lilliput on Video** Watch the video segment of the Lilliputians' first encounter with Gulliver. Discuss how the camera angles convey both Gulliver's and the Lilliputians' points of view. Do the special effects enhance or detract from Swift's descriptions of the encounter? ~ **VIEWING AND REPRESENTING**

VIDEO **Literature in Performance**

3. **Comparing Size** Find details in the story to figure out how tall Gulliver is. How does Swift figure that Gulliver eats as much as 1,728 Lilliputians? Next, calculate how tall the Brobdingnagians are. How many Gullivers would it take to eat as much as one Brobdingnagian? Make a **diagram** of this information and explain it to your classmates. ~ **MATH**

Inquiry & Research

Literary History How did people react to *Gulliver's Travels* when it was first published? Read letters to Swift dated November 1726, a month after the book was published, to find out. Look up letters by John Arbuthnot, Alexander Pope, and John Gay in *The Correspondence of Jonathan Swift,* edited by Harold Williams. Report your findings to the class.

Vocabulary in Action

EXERCISE A: CONTEXT CLUES On your paper, write the word from the list below that is most clearly related to the topic of each sentence.

censure **prostrating** **retinue**
panegyric **recapitulate**

1. Gulliver's speech describing the glories of his native land was received with great amusement.
2. The members of the royal court followed their monarch like sheep behind a shepherd.
3. As the emperor appeared, thousands of his subjects fell to the ground in awe and submission.
4. The crowd was so delighted by the story that the sailor was forced to tell it again and again.
5. Gulliver feared that some would criticize him for being too vain.

EXERCISE B: ASSESSMENT PRACTICE On your paper, identify each pair of words as synonyms or antonyms.

1. **morose**—sad
2. **schism**—unification
3. **solicitation**—appeal
4. **diminutive**—huge
5. **civility**—rudeness
6. **pernicious**—evil
7. **infallibly**—doubtfully
8. **perfidiousness**—loyalty
9. **conjecture**—guess
10. **dexterity**—clumsiness

Building Vocabulary
For an in-depth study of context clues, see page 938.

Vocabulary in Action

Exercise A
1. panegyric
2. retinue
3. prostrating
4. recapitulate
5. censure

Exercise B
1. synonym
2. antonym
3. synonym
4. antonym
5. antonym
6. synonym
7. antonym
8. antonym
9. synonym
10. antonym

Letter from Richard Sympson

PSEUDONYM OF JONATHAN SWIFT

Preparing to Read

Build Background

Because Swift thought the political satire in *Gulliver's Travels* would offend powerful people, especially his political enemies, he took the precaution of having it published anonymously. In August of 1726, Swift sent part of the manuscript by messenger to a London publisher. The manuscript contained the following cover letter written under the fictitious name of "Richard Sympson," supposedly Lemuel Gulliver's cousin, friend, and manager.

Focus Your Reading

PRIMARY SOURCES LETTER

As you read this letter, notice the questions Swift/Sympson raises about the manuscript and the cautious nature of his business negotiations.

London, August 8, 1726

Sir,

My cousin, Mr. Lemuel Gulliver, entrusted me some years ago with a copy of his travels, whereof that which I here send you is about a fourth part, for I shortened them very much, as you will find in my Preface to the Reader. I have shown them to several persons of great judgment and distinction, who are confident they will sell very well; and, although some parts of this and the following volumes may be thought in one or two places to be a little satirical, yet it is agreed they will give no offence; but in that you must judge for yourself, and take the advice of your friends, and if they or you be of another opinion, you may let me know it when you return these papers, which I expect shall be in three days at furthest. The good report I have received of you makes me put so great a trust into your hands, which I hope you will give me no reason to repent, and in that confidence I require that you will never suffer these papers to be once out of your sight.

As the printing these Travels will probably be of great value to you, so, as a manager for my friend and cousin, I expect you will give a due consideration for it, because I know the author intends the profit

This portrait of Lemuel Gulliver, printed in the 1726 edition of *Gulliver's Travels,* was part of the effort to make people think that Gulliver was a real person.

Teaching the Literature

Build Background

Discuss with students the different masks that Swift adopts in presenting his satire to the public. Not only does he adopt the personas of different characters such as Gulliver and the King of Brobdingnag in writing his fiction, but he also constructs a fictitious person to deliver his manuscript to the world.

Reading Skills and Strategies

TONE AND WRITER'S MOTIVATION

Tell students that a deliberate tone—such as humor, bitterness, or seriousness, to name a few—is an element in all writing. Discuss with students how a writer's motivation may affect the tone of a text. What is Swift's motivation? What tone has he chosen? What does this tone communicate? Which words and phrases set the tone?

Possible Responses: Swift wants to get the manuscript published anonymously. Swift has chosen a cautious, slightly anxious tone. This seriousness creates an image of a man a bit nervous in seeking out a publisher for this possibly controversial manuscript. However, this tone also adds an air of believability to the manuscript enclosed with the letter. Phrases such as the following volumes may be thought . . . to be a little satirical and you will never suffer these papers to be once out of your sight help to set the tone.

Thinking Through the Literature

1. In the very first sentence, Swift indicates that the manuscript contains observations based on Lemuel Gulliver's travels, and later in the letter he states that some of the observations may be considered satiric.
2. Swift clearly realized that some people would perhaps be offended by the work's biting tone, which he believed would be the only possible reason it might be rejected by publishers.
3. Possible Response: His willingness to repay the sum if sales were disappointing indicates that his primary wish was simply to have his work published.
4. Possible Response: Have students review the historical context in which Gulliver's Travels wqs written by referring to the opening essay and time line on pp. 586–589. The discussion that Gulliver has with the king might very well have offended people for its unrestrained criticism of English society. The upper class and individuals involved in government would likely have been the most offended.

for the use of poor seamen, and I am advised to say that two hundred pounds is the least sum I will receive on his account; but if it shall happen that the sale will not answer, as I expect and believe, then whatever shall be thought too much, even upon your own word, shall be duly repaid.

Perhaps you may think this a strange way of proceeding to a man of trade, but since I begin with so great a trust to you, whom I never saw, I think it not hard that you should trust me as much; therefore, if after three days' reading and consulting these papers you think it proper to stand to my agreement, you may begin to print them, and the subsequent parts shall be all sent you one after another in less than a week, provided that immediately upon your resolution to print them you do within three days deliver a bank-bill of two hundred pounds, wrapped up so as to make a parcel, to the hand from whence you receive this, who will come in the same manner exactly at nine o'clock at night on Thursday, which will be the IIth instant.

If you do not approve of this proposal, deliver these papers to the person who will come on Thursday. If you choose rather to send the papers, make no other proposal of your own, but just barely write on a piece of paper that you do not accept my offer. I am, Sir,

Your humble servant,

Richard Sympson

Richard Sympson

Thinking Through the Literature

1. What does Swift as Sympson say about the manuscript that gives a clue to its content?
2. What doubts about the manuscript does he reveal?
3. Swift asked for and eventually received £200 (less than his annual earnings as Dean of St. Patrick's) for *Gulliver's Travels.* That was the only money he ever earned from his writing. How do you think he felt about this payment based on the financial arrangements he stipulates in this letter?
4. **Comparing Texts** Look back over the excerpts from *Gulliver's Travels.* Which sections do you think might have been offensive? Who might have been offended?

"I can think of no one objection that will possibly be raised against this proposal."

A Modest Proposal

Essay by JONATHAN SWIFT

Connect to Your Life

Reacting to Injustice Has there ever been a situation that you witnessed or read about that upset or angered you? How did you react? What did you do? Discuss with classmates ways other people have called attention to a bad situation or an injustice.

Build Background

Ireland in Swift's Day By 1700, Ireland was so completely dominated by England that it seemed like a conquered territory. All the laws governing Ireland came from the English Parliament. The English also strangled the country economically by restricting Irish trade and agriculture so that few jobs were available. Even in the best years, life was harsh for Ireland's poor. When crops failed—as they did several years during the 1720s—many faced starvation. Religious and class divisions fostered by the English added to Ireland's political and economic woes. The vast majority of Irish were Roman Catholics, who according to English law could not own land and consequently had to pay high rents. Most of the landowners and officeholders were Anglo-Irish Anglicans—people like Swift who were of English ancestry and members of the Protestant Church of England.

While he served as dean of St. Patrick's Cathedral in Dublin, Swift wrote several pamphlets to attack English injustices toward Ireland and to encourage the Irish to resist oppression. In 1729, three years after the success of *Gulliver's Travels,* Swift wrote his most famous piece about Ireland, "A Modest Proposal." Instead of reason and argumentation, Swift used savage satire well-suited to the desperation he saw around him.

WORDS TO KNOW
Vocabulary Preview

animosity	expedient
deference	perpetual
deplorable	prodigious
emulation	proficiency
encumbrance	rudiment

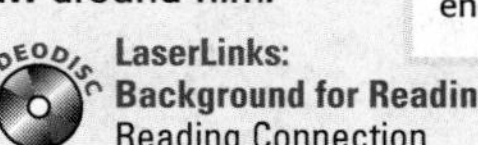

LaserLinks:
Background for Reading
Reading Connection

Focus Your Reading

LITERARY ANALYSIS IRONY An important element of satire is **irony,** the contrast between what is expected and what actually happens. For example, it is ironic that the tiny Lilliputians act so aggressively, whereas the giant Gulliver is meek as a kitten. One type of irony that is typical of satirical prose is **verbal irony.** Verbal irony occurs when what is said is not exactly what is meant—as when someone says "Nice day, isn't it?" during a rainstorm. As you read Swift's proposal, watch for the irony in his rational arguments.

ACTIVE READING DRAWING CONCLUSIONS How can you tell what an author really means? One way is to **draw conclusions** by using information you already know. For instance, you know that Swift is a **satirist,** so you can expect him to be ironic. Another way to draw conclusions about an author's purpose is to look for the deeper meaning beneath the surface details.

READER'S NOTEBOOK As you read, use a chart like the one below to record your reactions to Swift's statements in "A Modest Proposal." In the first column, write down a statement from the selection that seems important or surprising to you. In the second column, record your response to that statement.

Statement	My Comments/Reactions
"a boy or girl before twelve years old is no salable commodity"	• The Irish didn't have slaves. • Earlier, Swift wrote about "breeders"—as if people were like livestock.

OVERVIEW

This selection is included in the **Grade 12 InterActive Reader.**

Objectives

1. understand and appreciate a classic **satiric essay** that explores the need for reform in 18th-century Ireland **(Literary Analysis)**
2. appreciate the author's use of **irony (Literary Analysis)**
3. **draw conclusions** in order to appreciate and understand satire **(Active Reading)**

Summary

Swift ironically suggests that the terrible problems of poverty and starvation in Ireland could be solved by the simple expedient of slaughtering the majority of Irish children and using them for food. This would decrease greatly the number of mouths to be fed while providing nutrition for those remaining. He enumerates additional benefits of the plan and points out its superiority to other remedies, such as taxing the absentee landlords or teaching them to have mercy on their tenants.

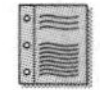

Use **Unit Three Resource Book,** p. 48 for additional support.

Thematic Link

Far from modest, Swift's proposal is a ghastly, outlandish "solution"—or **argument for change**—to very real and serious problems in Ireland.

5-Minute Warm-Up

Daily Language SkillBuilder

Have students **proofread** the display sentences on page 515l and write them correctly. The sentences also appear on Transparency 15 of **Grammar Transparencies and Copymasters.**

Preteaching Vocabulary

If you would like to preteach the WORDS TO KNOW for this selection, use the Mini Lesson p. 612.

EDITOR'S NOTE: This selection contains material that may be considered objectionable.

LESSON RESOURCES

UNIT THREE RESOURCE BOOK, pp. 48–52

ASSESSMENT RESOURCES
Formal Assessment, pp. 101–102
Teacher's Guide to Assessment and Portfolio Use
Test Generator

SKILLS TRANSPARENCIES AND COPYMASTERS
Literary Analysis
- Horatian vs. Juvenalian Satire, T12 (for Think Critically, item 4, p. 620)

Reading and Critical Thinking
- Organizational Chart: Horizontal, T52 (for Active Reading, p. 611)

Grammar
- Diagramming Verbal Phrases, T60 (for Mini Lesson, p. 620)
- Gerund and Gerund Phrases II, C104 (for Mini Lesson, p. 620)

Writing
- Proposal, C28 (for Writing Option 3, p. 622)
- Satire, C29 (for Writing Option 2, p. 622)

Communications
- Evaluating Roles in Groups, T8 (for Activities & Explorations 1, p. 622)

INTEGRATED TECHNOLOGY
Audio Library
Net Activities
LaserLinks
- Reading Connection: Understanding Satire. See **Teacher's SourceBook,** p. 37.

Visit our website:
www.mcdougallittell.com

TEACHING THE LITERATURE

Reading and Analyzing

Literary Analysis IRONY

A Remind students that verbal irony is saying the opposite of what is meant. Ask students to explain why the title and subtitle of Swift's work are examples of verbal irony.

Possible Responses: The proposal isn't "modest"—it's extreme; eating children isn't making them "beneficial to the public"—it's an act of barbarism.

Use **Unit Three Resource Book,** p. 50 for more exercises.

Active Reading DRAWING CONCLUSIONS

B Ask students to conclude, on the basis of the opening paragraph, what issues are of concern to the speaker.

Possible Responses: poverty in Ireland; overpopulation; the desperate state of beggars.

Use **Unit Three Resource Book,** p. 49 for more practice.

Literary Analysis: SATIRIC ESSAY

Explain that there are two types of satire, named for the Roman satirists Horace and Juvenal. Horatian satire is playful and seeks to correct vice and foolishness gently and sympathetically. Juvenalian satire, on the other hand, is dark and biting. It criticizes social injustice and corruption with scorn and outrage. As students read, have them think about whether "A Modest Proposal" is Horatian or Juvenalian satire.

Answer: Juvenalian.

A Modest PROPOSAL

FOR PREVENTING THE CHILDREN OF POOR PEOPLE IN IRELAND FROM BEING A BURDEN TO THEIR PARENTS OR COUNTRY, A AND FOR MAKING THEM BENEFICIAL TO THE PUBLIC

Jonathan Swift

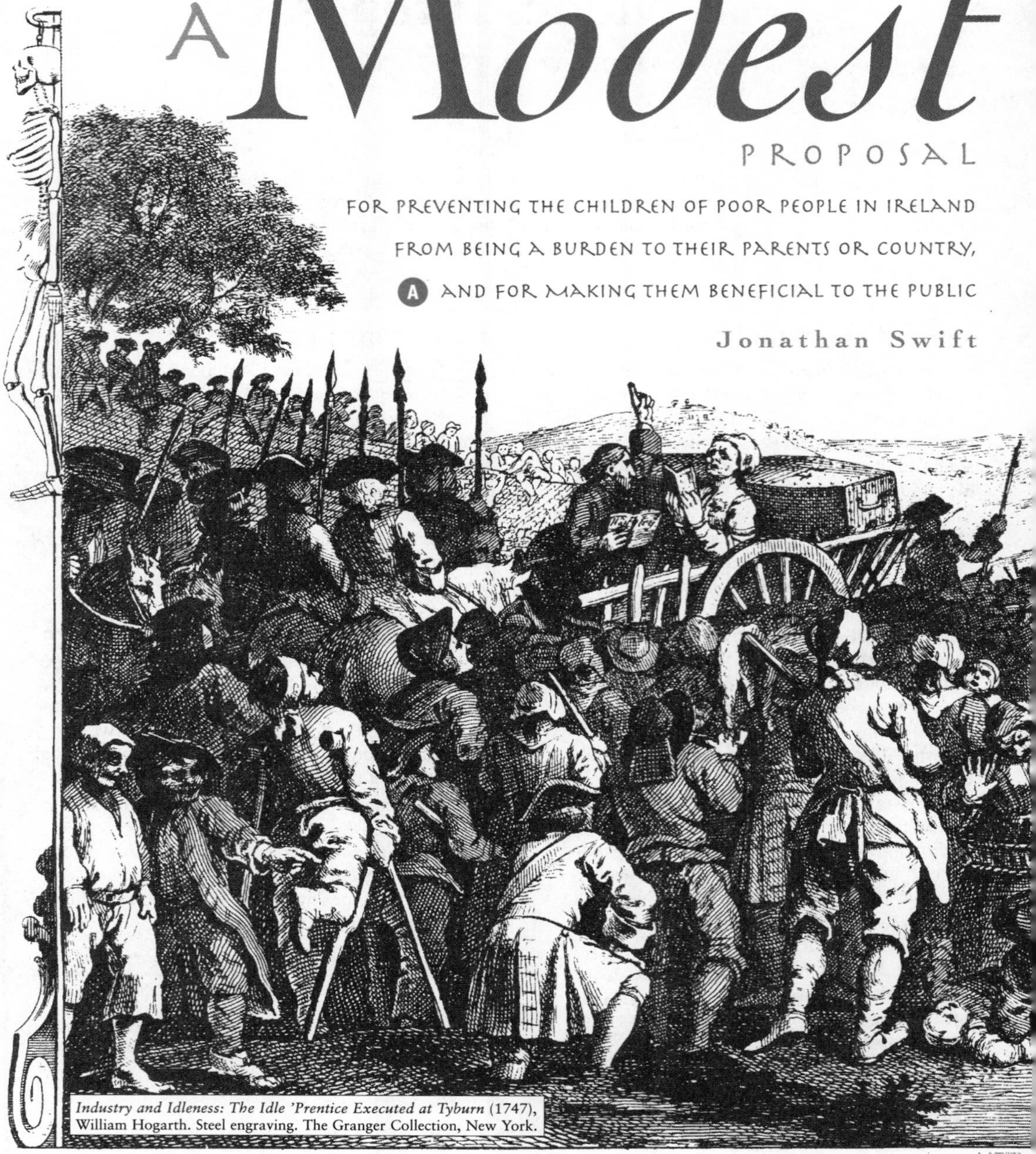

Industry and Idleness: The Idle 'Prentice Executed at Tyburn (1747), William Hogarth. Steel engraving. The Granger Collection, New York.

Teaching Options

Mini Lesson Preteaching Vocabulary

SYNONYMS AND ANTONYMS

Instruction Synonyms are words that have similar meanings. Learning synonyms for unfamiliar words can help expand vocabulary and increase comprehension.

Antonyms are words that have opposite meanings. Studying antonyms can help reinforce the learning of the original words.

Activity

1. Have students prepare a chart with the WORDS TO KNOW in one column, a synonym for each word in a second column, and an antonym for each word in a third column, using a dictionary or thesaurus if necessary.
2. Remind students that the pairs of synonyms do not have exactly the same meaning, and that they should pay attention to the subtle differences between them.
3. As students read the selection, they should substitute the synonym for the word from the WORDS TO KNOW list. Have them discuss how the substitution changes the meaning.

Use **Unit Three Resource Book,** p. 51 for more practice.

It is a melancholy object to those who walk through this great town[1] or travel in the country, when they see the streets, the roads, and cabin doors, crowded with beggars of the female sex, followed by three, four, or six children, all in rags and importuning every passenger for an alms. These mothers, instead of being able to work for their honest livelihood, are forced to employ all their time in strolling to beg sustenance for their helpless infants, who, as they grow up, either turn thieves for

B want of work, or leave their dear native country

1. this great town: Dublin.

Customizing Instruction

Less Proficient Readers

Have students identify the proposal set forth by the speaker. Encourage them to write down "translations" of ironic statements.

Students Acquiring English

Provide background for this selection by explaining that the author makes the outrageous suggestion that people eat small children as a solution to the problem of starvation in Ireland. Identify this kind of writing as *satire,* and explain that Jonathan Swift uses it to make people think about more humane solutions.

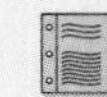

Use **Spanish Study Guide** for additional support, pp. 132–134.

Gifted and Talented

Ask students to use Swift's essay to make generalizations about the life of the poor in Ireland. In addition, direct students to look for the serious solutions to Irish poverty that Swift proposes in his essay. Have students think about how these solutions could be implemented.

Mini Lesson Viewing and Representing

Industry and Idleness: The Idle 'Prentice Executed at Tyburn (1747) **by William Hogarth**

ART APPRECIATION The painter and engraver William Hogarth (1697–1764) was the first British artist to achieve a significant reputation in continental Europe.

Instruction The engraving *The Idle 'Prentice* (apprentice) is typically Hogarthian in its subject matter: a public execution, a hurly-burly crowd scene, and a moral comment. To the left of the center of the picture, a coffin, being prayed over by two people, is drawn through the crowd.

Application Divide students into groups of four or five. Have each group produce a detailed reading of the print. Then have each group present its analysis to the class for further discussion. Students should consider the following points:

1. What kind of people are in the crowd?
2. What does such a large crowd at a public hanging tell you about 18th-century culture?
3. What impression do such details as the distressed woman with the baby in her arms, the mistreated dog, and the fruit vendor give you about the value of life in the 18th century?
4. Why would Hogarth place skeletons on the border of his engraving?

Reading and Analyzing

Literary Analysis IRONY

A Have students identify phrases in this paragraph that seem to express compassion.

Possible Responses: "sacrificing the poor innocent babes"; "move tears and pity in the most savage and inhuman breast."

After students have read the next page, in which the speaker reveals his plan, have them reread this paragraph. How do the speaker's words of compassion strike them now?

Possible Responses: as ironic; his proposal is supremely inhuman, recommending the actual sacrifice of "poor innocent babes."

ACTIVE READING

B **EVALUATE**
reasonable, scientific, analytical, objective

Active Reading
DRAWING CONCLUSIONS

C Ask students to conclude, on the basis of the advice of the "American acquaintance," what the stereotype of Americans might have been among the British in 1729.

Possible Response: Americans were considered backwoods barbarians.

ACTIVE READING

D **QUESTION** **Possible Response:** The landlords have figuratively devoured the parents by subjecting them to often fatal conditions of poverty and oppression.

to fight for the Pretender[2] in Spain, or sell themselves to the Barbadoes.[3]

I think it is agreed by all parties that this prodigious number of children in the arms, or on the backs, or at the heels of their mothers, and frequently of their fathers, is in the present deplorable state of the kingdom a very great additional grievance; and therefore whoever could find out a fair, cheap, and easy method of making these children sound, useful members of the commonwealth would deserve so well of the public as to have his statue set up for a preserver of the nation.

But my intention is very far from being confined to provide only for the children of professed beggars; it is of a much greater extent, and shall take in the whole number of infants at a certain age who are born of parents in effect as little able to support them as those who demand our charity in the streets.

As to my own part, having turned my thoughts for many years upon this important subject, and maturely weighed the several schemes of other projectors, I have always found them grossly mistaken in their computation. It is true, a child just dropped from its dam[4] may be supported by her milk for a solar year, with little other nourishment; at most not above the value of two shillings, which the mother may certainly get, or the value in scraps, by her lawful occupation of begging; and it is exactly at one year old that I propose to provide for them in such a manner as instead of being a charge upon their parents or the parish, or wanting food and raiment for the rest of their lives, they shall on the contrary contribute to the feeding, and partly to the clothing, of many thousands.

There is likewise another great advantage in my scheme, that it will prevent those voluntary abortions, and that horrid practice of women murdering their bastard children, alas, too frequent among us, sacrificing the poor innocent babes, I doubt, more to avoid the expense than the shame, which would move tears and pity in the most savage and inhuman breast. **A**

The number of souls in this kingdom being usually reckoned one million and a half, of these I calculate there may be about two hundred thousand couple whose wives are breeders; from which number I subtract thirty thousand couples who are able to maintain their own children, although I apprehend there cannot be so many under the present distresses of the kingdom; but this being granted, there will remain an hundred and seventy thousand breeders. I again subtract fifty thousand for those women who miscarry, or whose children die by accident or disease within the year. There only remain an hundred and twenty thousand children of poor parents annually born. The question therefore is, how this number shall be reared and provided for, which, as I have already said, under the present situation of affairs, is utterly impossible by all the methods hitherto proposed. For we can neither employ them in handicraft or agriculture; we neither build houses (I mean in the country) nor cultivate land. They can very

ACTIVE READING

EVALUATE What tone is conveyed by the speaker's mathematical calculations? **B**

2. **Pretender:** James Edward Stuart—the "pretender," or claimant, to the English throne, from which his father, James II, had been deposed in 1688. Because he was Roman Catholic, the common people of Ireland were loyal to him.
3. **sell . . . the Barbadoes** (bär-bā′dōz): To escape extreme poverty, some of the Irish migrated to the West Indies, obtaining money for their passage by agreeing to work in servitude on plantations there for a set time.
4. **dam:** female parent (used almost exclusively of farm animals).

WORDS TO KNOW
prodigious (prə-dĭj′əs) *adj.* enormous
deplorable (dĭ-plôr′ə-bəl) *adj.* miserable; woeful

614

BLOCK SCHEDULING: MANAGING TIME

If your schedule requires that you cover the lesson objectives in a shorter time, use . . .
- Preparing to Read, p. 611
- Thinking Through the Literature, p. 620
- Vocabulary in Action, p. 623

If you want to take advantage of longer class time, use . . .
- TE Teaching Options: Preteaching Vocabulary, p. 612; Viewing and Representing, p. 613; Cross Curricular Links, p. 615; Standardized Test Practice, p. 616; Speaking and Listening, pp. 617, 618; Informal Assessment, p. 619; Grammar, 620
- Choices and Challenges, p. 622
- Author Study Project, p. 623

seldom pick up a livelihood by stealing till they arrive at six years old, except where they are of towardly parts;[5] although I confess they learn the rudiments much earlier, during which time they can however be looked upon only as probationers, as I have been informed by a principal gentleman in the county of Cavan, who protested to me that he never knew above one or two instances under the age of six, even in a part of the kingdom so renowned for the quickest proficiency in that art.

I am assured by our merchants that a boy or girl before twelve years old is no salable commodity; and even when they come to this age they will not yield above three pounds, or three pounds and half a crown at most on the Exchange; which cannot turn to account either to the parents or the kingdom, the charge of nutriment and rags having been at least four times that value.

I shall now therefore humbly propose my own thoughts, which I hope will not be liable to the least objection.

C I have been assured by a very knowing American of my acquaintance in London, that a young healthy child well nursed is at a year old a most delicious, nourishing, and wholesome food, whether stewed, roasted, baked, or boiled; and I make no doubt that it will equally serve in a fricassee or a ragout.[6]

I do therefore humbly offer it to public consideration that of the hundred and twenty thousand children, already computed, twenty
1 thousand may be reserved for breed, whereof only one fourth part to be males, which is more than we allow to sheep, black cattle, or swine; and my reason is that these children are seldom the fruits of marriage, a circumstance not much regarded by our savages, therefore one male will be sufficient to serve four females. That the remaining hundred thousand may at a year old be offered in sale to the persons of quality and fortune through the kingdom, always advising the mother to let them suck plentifully in the last month, so as to render them plump and fat for a good table. A child will make two dishes at an entertainment for friends; and when the family dines alone, the fore or hind quarter will make a reasonable dish, and seasoned with a little pepper or salt will be very good boiled on the fourth day, especially in winter.

I have reckoned upon a medium that a child 2
just born will weigh twelve pounds, and in a solar year if tolerably nursed increaseth to twenty-eight pounds.

I grant this food will be somewhat dear, and therefore very proper for landlords, who, as they have already devoured most of the parents, seem to have the best title to the children.

ACTIVE READING

QUESTION What is your reaction to the speaker's statement about "landlords, who . . . have already devoured most of the parents"?

Infant's flesh will be in season throughout the year, but more plentiful in March, and a little D before and after. For we are told by a grave author, an eminent French physician,[7] that fish being a prolific[8] diet, there
are more children born in Roman Catholic 3
countries about nine months after Lent than at any other season; therefore, reckoning a year after Lent, the markets will be more glutted than usual, because the number of popish[9] infants is at least three to one in this kingdom; and therefore it will have one other collateral advantage, by lessening the number of Papists[10] among us.

I have already computed the charge of nursing a beggar's child (in which list I reckon all

---

5. **are of towardly parts:** have a promising talent.
6. **fricassee** (frĭk′ə-sē′) . . . **ragout** (ră-gōō′): types of meat stews.
7. **grave . . . physician:** François Rabelais (1494?–1553), a French satirist.
8. **prolific:** promoting fertility.
9. **popish** (pō′pĭsh): Roman Catholic.
10. **Papists** (pā′pĭsts): Roman Catholics.

WORDS TO KNOW

rudiment (rōō′də-mənt) *n.* a basic principle or skill
proficiency (prə-fĭsh′ən-sē) *n.* competence; expertise

615

Customizing Instruction

Less Proficient Readers

1 Point out the use of the phrase *for breed,* and ask students what the speaker means.
Answer: Some male and female children will be spared so that they can produce more offspring.

Have students discuss why he compares poor people to farm animals. What point is Swift trying to make?
Possible Response: that poor people live no better than animals.

Students Acquiring English

2 Explain that the phrase *reckoned upon a medium* means "come up with an average." Point out the old-fashioned verb form *increaseth,* and ask students for the modern equivalent.
Answer: increases.

3 Based on this paragraph, what prejudices does the speaker have about Roman Catholics?
Possible Response: They have too many children; decreasing their number would be a good thing.

Cross Curricular Link Social Studies

RELIGION Explain to students that Lent is a 40-day period of penance and prayer among Christians, beginning on Ash Wednesday and lasting until Easter. Roman Catholics pay special attention to Lenten observances. Abstinence from meat is one of these observances; in the past, meat was not eaten at all during Lent (or on Fridays throughout the year) by devout Roman Catholics, so fish was the dish of choice during this season. Through the years, the observance has become less strict, but still today many Roman Catholics do not eat meat on Fridays during Lent. Remind students that although Ireland is a predominantly Catholic country, many Irish are members of the Protestant Anglican Church, as was Swift.

Reading and Analyzing

Reading Skills and Strategies: MAKING INFERENCES

A Ask students what inferences they can make about the intensity of Swift's feelings against the landowners in Ireland based on the graphic passage that ends the first section of the essay.

Possible Response: It must be very intense, as he is comparing them to butchers.

Literary Analysis IRONY

B Lead students to see that the narrator's hesitancy about eating 12-to-14-year-old girls because it is "a little bordering upon cruelty" is ironic, in view of the extreme cruelty of what he has already proposed.

C Ask students whom the speaker calls the enemy here.

Answer: the "papists."

Whom does he praise?

Answer: the Protestants.

Does Swift agree with what he's saying? Who is really being criticized here?

Answer: No; he is criticizing the absentee landlords.

Literary Analysis: SATIRE

D Ask what Swift is satirizing in the phrase "the goods being entirely of our own growth and manufacture."

Answer: the ridiculous practicality of the speaker, through his idea that a "homegrown" crop of children will encourage the local economy and alleviate poverty.

cottagers, laborers, and four fifths of the farmers), to be about two shillings per annum, rags included; and I believe no gentleman would repine to give ten shillings for the carcass of a good fat child, which, as I have said, will make four dishes of excellent nutritive meat, when he hath only some particular friend or his own family to dine with him. Thus the squire will learn to be a good landlord, and grow popular among the tenants; the mother will have eight shillings net profit, and be fit for work till she produces another child.

Those who are more thrifty (as I must confess the times require) may flay the carcass; the skin of which artificially dressed will make admirable gloves for ladies, and summer boots for fine gentlemen.

As to our city of Dublin, shambles[11] may be
A appointed for this purpose in the most convenient parts of it, and butchers we may be assured will not be wanting; although I rather recommend buying the children alive, and dressing them hot from the knife as we do roasting pigs.

1 A very worthy person, a true lover of his country, and whose virtues I highly esteem, was lately pleased in discoursing on this matter to offer a refinement upon my scheme. He said that many gentlemen of this kingdom, having of late destroyed their deer, he conceived that the want of venison might be well supplied by the bodies of young lads and maidens, not exceeding fourteen years of age nor under twelve, so great a number of both sexes in every county being now ready to starve for want of work and service; and these to be disposed of by their parents, if alive, or otherwise by their nearest relations. But with due deference to so excellent a friend and so deserving a patriot, I cannot be altogether in his sentiments; for as to the males, my American acquaintance assured me from frequent experience that their flesh was generally tough and lean, like that of our schoolboys, by continual exercise, and their taste disagreeable; and to fatten them would not answer the charge. Then as to the females, it would, I think with humble submission, be a loss to the public, because they soon would become breeders themselves; and besides, it is not improbable that some scrupulous people might be apt to censure such a practice (although
indeed very unjustly) as a little bordering upon B
cruelty; which, I confess, hath always been with me the strongest objection against any project, how well soever intended.

But in order to justify my friend, he confessed that this expedient was put into his head by the famous Psalmanazar,[12] a native of the island Formosa, who came from thence to London above twenty years ago, and in conversation told my friend that in his country when any young person happened to be put to death, the executioner sold the carcass to persons of quality as a prime dainty; and that in his time the body of a plump girl of fifteen, who was crucified for an attempt to poison the emperor, was sold to his Imperial Majesty's prime minister of state, and other great mandarins of the court, in joints from the gibbet,[13] at four hundred crowns. Neither indeed can I deny that if the same use were made of several plump young girls in this town, who without one single groat[14] to their fortunes cannot stir abroad without a chair, and appear at the playhouse and assemblies in foreign fineries which they never will pay for, the kingdom would not be the worse.

Some persons of a desponding spirit are in great concern about that vast number of poor people

11. **shambles:** slaughterhouses.
12. **Psalmanazar** (săl′mə-năz′ər): a French impostor in London, who called himself George Psalmanazar and pretended to be from Formosa (now Taiwan)—where, he said, cannibalism was practiced.
13. **gibbet** (jĭb′ĭt): gallows.
14. **groat:** an old British coin worth four pennies.

WORDS TO KNOW
deference (dĕf′ər-əns) *n.* courteous regard or respect
expedient (ĭk-spē′dē-ənt) *n.* a means to an end

Teaching Options

Assessment Standardized Test Practice

CHOOSING THE BEST ANSWER Have students read the two paragraphs beginning "A very worthy person . . ." on p. 616. Then have them answer the following question.

Which statement best describes the point that Swift is trying to make?

A. People should eat adolescent boys and girls.
B. People from Formosa are liars.
C. The lack of work and food for young boys and girls is terrible.
D. Cannibalism should be illegal.

Because Swift's tone in this essay is ironic, **A** is the opposite of his opinion. **B** is an unsupported generalization that is unrelated to the subject of the two paragraphs. Although **D** is logical, the legality of cannibalism is not the focus of the paragraphs. Therefore, the correct answer is **C.** Swift mentions in both paragraphs young boys' and girls' lack of work, food, and money.

who are aged, diseased, or maimed, and I have been desired to employ my thoughts what course may be taken to ease the nation of so grievous an encumbrance. But I am not in the least pain upon that matter, because it is very well known that they are every day dying and rotting by cold and famine, and filth and vermin, as fast as can be reasonably expected. And as to the younger laborers, they are now in almost as hopeful a condition. They cannot get work, and conse-
2 quently pine away for want of nourishment to a degree that if at any time they are accidentally hired to common labor, they have not strength to perform it; and thus the country and themselves are happily delivered from the evils to come.

3 I have too long digressed, and therefore shall return to my subject. I think the advantages by the proposal which I have made are obvious and many, as well as of the highest importance.

C For first, as I have already observed, it would greatly lessen the number of Papists, with whom we are yearly overrun, being the principal breeders of the nation as well as our most dangerous enemies; and who stay at home on purpose to deliver the kingdom to the Pretender, hoping to take their advantage by the absence of so many good Protestants, who have chosen rather to leave their country than stay at home and pay tithes against their conscience to an Episcopal curate.[15]

Secondly, the poorer tenants will have something valuable of their own, which by law may be made liable to distress,[16] and help to pay their landlord's rent, their corn and cattle being already seized and money a thing unknown.

Thirdly, whereas the maintenance of an hundred thousand children, from two years old and upwards, cannot be computed at less than ten shillings a piece per annum, the nation's stock will be thereby increased fifty thousand pounds per annum, besides the profit of a new dish introduced to the tables of all gentlemen of fortune in the kingdom who have any refinement in taste. And the money will circulate among ourselves, the goods being entirely of our own D
growth and manufacture.

Fourthly, the constant breeders, besides the gain of eight shillings sterling per annum by the sale of their children, will be rid of the charge of maintaining them after the first year.

Fifthly, this food would likewise bring great custom to taverns, where the vintners will certainly be so prudent as to procure the best receipts for dressing it to perfection, and consequently have their houses frequented by all the fine gentlemen, who justly value themselves upon their knowledge in good eating; and a skillful cook, who understands how to oblige his guests, will contrive

15. **Protestants . . . curate:** Swift is referring to Anglo-Irish landowners who lived—and spent the income from their property—in England.

16. **distress:** seizure for the payment of debts.

WORDS TO KNOW **encumbrance** (ĕn-kŭm′brəns) *n.* a burden

617

Customizing Instruction

Less Proficient Readers

1 The narrator describes his friend who suggests eating 14-year-old boys as "a true lover of his country" and "a patriot." What is ironic about these descriptions?

Possible Response: A true patriot wouldn't want to kill his own countrymen, especially if they were children.

Encourage students to note the major details of the proposal as they read and to determine the targets of Swift's satire.

Students Acquiring English

2 Point out the phrase *pine away,* and ask students to use context clues to determine its meaning. Help students find the effect of pining away later in the sentence ("they have not the strength to perform [labor]").

Answer: languish; to lose health and flesh; to waste away.

3 Ask students to use context clues to determine the meaning of *digressed.* Help them see the contrast in the sentence indicated by the conjunction *therefore* ("return to my subject" is the opposite of "digressed").

Answer: wandered from the subject.

Gifted and Talented

Invite students to consider the author's proposal from the perspective of the poor. How would they respond to its "advantages"? How would they describe their lives? What alternatives might they offer to the narrator's proposal?

Mini Lesson Speaking and Listening

HOLDING A PANEL DISCUSSION

Instruction Explain to students that the rules for a panel discussion are more flexible than those for a debate. There is usually a moderator who introduces the participants and the topic, asks questions, and monitors the etiquette of the discussion. Participants are likely to represent a spectrum of views or areas of expertise.

Prepare Mention that it is common for panel members to take notes and rebut what previous speakers have said in order to advance their own points of view. Invite small groups of students to hold panel discussions on possible remedies for poverty and hunger in today's world.

Present Suggest that each member represent a particular aspect of the topic or a particular point of view. Encourage students to prepare for the discussion by doing some library research for facts and figures. They might look for examples of proposals that have been successful and those that have been unsuccessful. Have them use their notes in the discussion.

BLOCK SCHEDULING This activity is particularly well-suited for longer class periods.

Reading and Analyzing

Literary Analysis IRONY

A Discuss the irony of the speaker's claim that raising babies for food would make mothers more caring and husbands fonder of their wives. What real prejudice, satirized here by Swift, underlies the obviously tongue-in-cheek claim?
Possible Responses: Swift is satirically criticizing the abuse of women and children; Swift underscores the English tendency to see the Irish as less than human by suggesting that the Irish have no love for their families.

ACTIVE READING

B EVALUATE **Possible Response:** He is trying to shock, amuse, and rouse readers to outrage about poverty in the hope that they will be inspired to find a genuine solution.

Reading Skills and Strategies: MAKING INFERENCES

C Ask students what inferences they can make from the speaker's comment that the carcasses of Irish children would be sold cheaper in "the rest of the kingdom" (that is, in England).
Possible Response: The English don't value the lives of the Irish.

ACTIVE READING

D QUESTION They might come from Swift's own ideas or from other thinkers of his time.

to make it as expensive as they please.

Sixthly, this would be a great inducement to marriage, which all wise nations have either encouraged by rewards or enforced by laws and penalties. It would increase the care and tenderness of mothers toward their children, when they were sure of a settlement for life to the poor babes, provided in some sort by the public, to their annual profit instead of expense. We should see an honest emulation among the married women, which of them could bring the fattest child to the market. Men would become as fond of their wives during the time of their pregnancy as they are now of their mares in foal, their cows in calf, or sows when they are ready to farrow; nor offer to beat or kick them (as is too frequent a practice) for fear of a miscarriage. **A**

ACTIVE READING

B EVALUATE What effect is the speaker trying to create by listing the advantages of the proposal?

Many other advantages might be enumerated. For instance, the addition of some thousand carcasses in our exportation of barreled beef, the propagation of swine's flesh, and improvement in the art of making good bacon, so much wanted among us by the great destruction of pigs, too frequent at our tables, which are no way comparable in taste or magnificence to a well-grown, fat, yearling child, which roasted whole will make a considerable figure at a lord mayor's feast or any other public entertainment. But this and many others I omit, being studious of brevity.

Supposing that one thousand families in this city would be constant customers for infants' flesh, besides others who might have it at merry meetings, particularly weddings and christenings, I compute that Dublin would take off annually about twenty thousand carcasses, and the rest of the kingdom (where probably they will be sold somewhat cheaper) the remaining eighty thousand. **C**

I can think of no one objection that will possibly be raised against this proposal, unless it should be urged that the number of people will be thereby much lessened in the kingdom. This I freely own, and it was indeed one principal design in offering it to the world. I desire the reader will observe, that I calculate my remedy for this one individual kingdom of Ireland and for no other that ever was, is, or I think ever can be upon earth. Therefore let no man talk to me of other expedients: of taxing our absentees at five shillings a pound: of using neither clothes nor household furniture except what is of our own growth and manufacture: of utterly rejecting the materials and instruments that promote foreign luxury: of curing the expensiveness of pride, vanity, idleness, and gaming in our women: of introducing a vein of parsimony,[17] prudence, and temperance: of learning to love our country, in the want of which we differ even from Laplanders and the inhabitants of Topinamboo:[18] of quitting our animosities and factions, nor acting any longer like the Jews, who were murdering one another at the very moment their city was taken:[19] of being a little cautious not to sell our country and conscience for nothing: of teaching landlords to have at least one degree of

17. **parsimony** (pär′sə-mō′nē): frugality; thrift.
18. **Topinamboo** (tŏp′ĭ-năm′bo͞o): an area in Brazil.
19. **Jews . . . taken:** In A.D. 70, during a Jewish revolt against Roman rule, the inhabitants of Jerusalem, by fighting among themselves, made it easier for the future Roman emperor Titus to capture the city.

WORDS TO KNOW
emulation (ĕm′yə-lā′shən) *n.* an effort to equal or outdo another person; rivalry
animosity (ăn′ə-mŏs′ĭ-tē) *n.* hostility; hatred

618

Teaching Options

Speaking and Listening

PERFORMING A MONOLOGUE

Instruction Have students select a passage that is approximately one third of a page in length to read as a monologue to the class.

Prepare When selecting a passage, students should consider whether it has a logical beginning and ending and a complete argument. The introductory passage is well-suited for a monologue, as are many of the opening paragraphs in each section. Have students write their monologues on note cards and rehearse them several times, practicing their diction and pacing.

Present Encourage students to use props or wear costumes. As students listen to each monologue, have them consider the following points.

1. Does the speaker make eye contact occasionally?
2. Is the speaker reading too fast or too slow?
3. Is the speaker reading with tone and inflection?

After several students have read their monologues, discuss how well the speakers performed. Have students make general comments rather than singling out individuals. How did each presenter's choice of diction, pacing, and props affect the interpretation?

mercy toward their tenants: lastly, of putting a spirit of honesty, industry, and skill into our shopkeepers; who, if a resolution could now be taken to buy only our native goods, would immediately unite to cheat and exact upon us in the price, the measure, and the goodness, nor could ever yet be brought to make one fair proposal of just dealing, though often and earnestly invited to it.

D **ACTIVE READING**

QUESTION What might be the speaker's source for the "other expedients" he lists?

Therefore I repeat, let no man talk to me of these and the like expedients,[20] till he hath at least some glimpse of hope that there will ever be some hearty and sincere attempt to put them in practice.

But as to myself, having been wearied out for many years with offering vain, idle, visionary thoughts, and at length utterly despairing of success, I fortunately fell upon this proposal, which, as it is wholly new, so it hath something solid and real, of no expense and little trouble, full in our own power, and whereby we can incur no danger in disobliging England. For this kind of commodity will not bear exportation, the flesh being of too tender a consistence to admit a long continuance in salt, although perhaps I could name a country which would be glad to

eat up our whole nation without it.

After all, I am not so violently bent upon my own opinion as to reject any offer proposed by wise men, which shall be found equally innocent, cheap, easy, and effectual. But before something of that kind shall be advanced in contradiction to my scheme, and offering a better, I desire the author or authors will be pleased maturely to consider two points. First, as things now stand, how they will be able to find food and raiment for an hundred thousand useless mouths and backs. And secondly, there being a round million of creatures in human figure throughout this kingdom, whose sole subsistence put into a common stock would leave them in debt two millions of pounds sterling, adding those who are beggars by profession to the bulk of farmers, cottagers, and laborers, with their wives and children who are beggars in effect; I desire those politicians who dislike my overture, and may perhaps be so bold to attempt an answer, that they will first ask the parents of these mortals whether they would not at this day think it a great happiness to have been sold for food at a year old in the manner I prescribe, and thereby have avoided such a perpetual scene of misfortunes as they have since gone through by the oppression of landlords, the impossibility of paying rent without money or trade, the want of common sustenance, with neither house nor clothes to cover them from the inclemencies of the weather, and the most inevitable prospect of entailing the like or greater miseries upon their breed forever.

I profess, in the sincerity of my heart, that I have not the least personal interest in endeavoring to promote this necessary work, having no other motive than the public good of my country, by advancing our trade, providing for infants, relieving the poor, and giving some pleasure to the rich. I have no children by which I can propose to get a 2
single penny; the youngest being nine years old, and my wife past childbearing. ❖

20. **let no man . . . expedients:** Swift had, in his writings, suggested the "other expedients" without success.

WORDS TO KNOW **perpetual** (pər-pĕch′o͞o-əl) *adj.* everlasting; continual

Less Proficient Readers

1 Ask students what country the speaker is referring to when he says he "could name a country which would be glad to eat up our whole nation."

Answer: England.

Ask students the following questions about the essay:

- Whom or what is Swift actually satirizing?
  Answer: England's policies toward Ireland; those who enrich themselves at the expense of the Irish.
- Why does the speaker claim that some of the poor might "think it a great happiness" to have been sold for food at a year old?
  Answer: because then they would have avoided much misfortune.

2 Why does the speaker mention that he has no children of his own that he could sell at the end of the essay?

Possible Responses: He wants to appear altruistic rather than self-interested, and he wants his proposal to sound unbiased and legitimate; since he has no children, he'll make no money from his scheme.

Assessment Informal Assessment

CHECKING COMPREHENSION Have students check their comprehension by discussing the following questions:

1. What problem does Swift's "modest proposal" discuss solving?
   Answer: the poverty in Ireland.
2. What is the proposal?
   Answer: that Irish infants be raised for food.
3. Name two or more courses of action that, according to Swift, are available to poor Irish people.
   Possible Responses: begging, stealing, emigration, indentured servitude.
4. When is Swift most serious in the essay?
   Answer: when he lists the real remedies for the situation, pretending to reject them.

GUIDING STUDENT RESPONSE

Connect to the Literature

1. **What Do You Think?**
Students will probably experience a gradual realization that the proposal made by the narrator in Swift's satire is not taken seriously.

Comprehension Check
- that poor Irish children should be raised for food
- the problem of the growing number of children born in poverty
- controlling the Catholic population in Ireland, providing poor people with a means of paying off debts, stimulating economic growth.

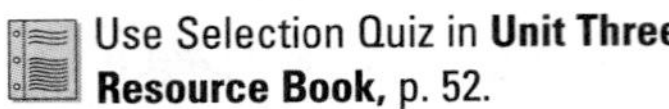
Use Selection Quiz in **Unit Three Resource Book,** p. 52.

Think Critically

2. Possible Response: Swift's purpose was to draw people's attention to a serious problem. He did so by
   - describing problem from unacceptable viewpoint
   - suggesting an outlandish solution
   - discussing miserable alternatives for the Irish
   - proposing reasonable solutions and then rejecting them
3. Possible Responses: Swift hoped to draw attention to the plight of the Irish poor; by outraging readers, he hoped to make them take action.
4. Possible Response: Swift's satire is particularly powerful when he enumerates the other expedients because, in this passage, he provides workable solutions to the problem, but presents them as unreasonable.
5. Be sure that students do not confuse the speaker with Swift himself. Possible responses might include "cruel," "upper class," "methodical," or "obtuse."
6. The other expedients Swift proposes are more reasonable suggestions.

Extend Interpretations

Comparing Texts Swift adopts an ironic stance toward both Gulliver and the speaker in "A Modest Proposal," but neither Gulliver nor the speaker is himself ironic toward the problems he faces.

Connect to Life Present-day topics might include immigration, welfare reform, education reform, poverty, racism, or war.

Connect to the Literature

1. **What Do You Think?** What was your first reaction to the proposal offered in this essay?

Comprehension Check
- What is Swift's proposal?
- What problem in Ireland does the proposal pretend to solve?
- Name one advantage that the speaker sees in this solution.

Think Critically

2. ACTIVE READING DRAWING CONCLUSIONS Use the chart you created in your READER'S NOTEBOOK to review the statements from "A Modest Proposal" and your responses to their meanings. What can you conclude was Swift's **purpose** in suggesting such a horrible solution? Support your conclusion with evidence from the selection.
3. What response do you think Swift hoped to get from readers of "A Modest Proposal"?
4. Go back through the essay and find at least two places where you think Swift's **satire** is particularly powerful. Explain your choices.
5. How would you describe the **speaker** in the essay? Use details to support your answer.
6. In your opinion, why did Swift have the speaker list "other expedients" to solve Ireland's problems?

THINK ABOUT
- the types of proposals the speaker mentions
- the contrast between those proposals and the "modest proposal"
- Swift's overall purpose for writing the essay

Extend Interpretations

7. **Comparing Texts** What major similarities and differences do you see between Gulliver and the speaker in this essay? Support your response with examples from the two works.
8. **Connect to Life** Poverty and starvation in 18th-century Ireland inspired Swift to write "A Modest Proposal." What are some of the social and political issues that might inspire satirists today? Give reasons for your choices.

Literary Analysis

IRONY **Irony** is the contrast between expectation and reality. **Verbal irony** is a specific kind of irony in which what is said is not what is meant. The title of Swift's essay is an example of verbal irony, for the proposal is hardly "modest"—it's totally outrageous. The verbal irony in the title points to the ironic tone of the essay as a whole. But Swift's irony is not an end in itself; he used it to expose what he saw as deep truths.

Cooperative Learning Activity Work with a small group of classmates to find at least three ironic statements in "A Modest Proposal" that reveal important facts about Ireland's condition in Swift's time. Use graphics like those below to organize your ideas.

Ironic Statement
1. "I am assured by our merchants that a boy or girl before twelve years old is no salable commodity." (p. 615)

Truth Revealed
1. Irish children are not seen as human beings but as worthless objects.

Ironic Statement
2. "This food will be . . . very proper for landlords, who, as they have already devoured most of the parents, seem to have the best title to the children." (p. 615)

Truth Revealed

REVIEW SATIRE What kind of person is Swift satirizing with the speaker in this essay?

Mini Lesson

Grammar

GERUNDS AND GERUND PHRASES

Instruction A gerund is a verb form that ends in -*ing* and always acts as a noun in a sentence, such as *Writing stimulates the mind.* Here *Writing,* used as a noun, functions as the subject of the sentence. When a gerund has modifiers and complements it is called a gerund phrase, as in the sentence *Writing a critical essay stimulates the mind.*

Activity Write on the chalkboard the following excerpt from "A Modest Proposal."

"I profess, in the sincerity of my heart, that I have not the least personal interest in endeavoring to promote this necessary work, having no other motive than the public good of my country, by advancing our trade, providing for infants, relieving the poor, and giving some pleasure to the rich.

Ask students to identify the five gerunds in this excerpt. *(endeavoring, advancing, providing, relieving, giving)*

Use **Grammar Transparencies and Copymasters,** p. 103.

Use McDougal Littell's ***Language Network*** for more instruction in gerunds and gerund phrases.

The Author's Style
Swift's Savage Wit

Jonathan Swift's signature style in his great satiric works sets him apart from his more lighthearted contemporaries, such as Alexander Pope, and even from most satirists today. An uncompromising moralist, Swift was continually disappointed by what he saw as humankind's corruption. His passion made him bitter, but his irony gave his bitterness a clever twist.

Key Aspects of Swift's Style

- the use of a persona—a narrator or speaker other than Swift—as an object of satire
- words, phrases, and situations that are shocking or disturbing
- ironic statements and situations that point out human shortcomings and faults
- use of understatement to expose a mindless acceptance of surface facts without regard to their deeper meaning

Analysis of Style

Study the aspects of Swift's style in the chart above. Then read the excerpts at right and complete the following activities:

A • Find examples of each stylistic device in the excerpts. Explain who you think is the object of the satire in each excerpt.

B • Explain what, if anything, you think is funny about each excerpt, and identify which stylistic device best contributes to this effect.

C • Go back through the selections in this Author Study and identify other examples of Swift's satiric style.

Applications

1. **Imitation of Style** Try imitating Swift's style in a written commentary on some human weaknesses that you see around you. Use at least two of his techniques from the chart above.
2. **Changing Style** Go through the selections and paraphrase two or three of Swift's ideas in a straightforward way, without irony. Read your paraphrases along with Swift's original wording to your classmates. Discuss how the use of irony makes a difference.
3. **Speaking and Listening** How do you think Gulliver, the world traveler, would react to "A Modest Proposal"? Working with a partner, create and perform an interview with Gulliver for the amusement of your classmates.

from **A Tale of a Tub**

Last week I saw a woman flayed [skinned], and you will hardly believe how much it altered her person for the worse.

from the preface to **The Battle of the Books**

Satire is a sort of glass, wherein beholders do generally discover everybody's face but their own; which is the chief reason for that kind of reception it meets in the world, and that so very few are offended with it.

from **Gulliver's Travels**

The learning of this people [the Brobdingnagians] is very defective, consisting only in morality, history, poetry, and mathematics, wherein they must be allowed to excel. But the last of these is wholly applied to what may be useful in life, to the improvement of agriculture and all mechanical arts; so that among us it would be little esteemed.

from **"A Modest Proposal"**

I rather recommend buying the children alive, and dressing them hot from the knife as we do roasting pigs.

from **"Verses on the Death of Dr. Swift"**

My female Friends, whose tender Hearts,
Have better learn'd to Act their Parts,
Receive the News in *doleful Dumps*,
"The Dean is Dead, *(and what is Trumps?)*
Then Lord have Mercy on his Soul."

The Author's Style

Swift seems never very far from using words and phrases that might shock or offend his readers, and this became the trademark of his style.

Analysis of Style

A First activity

persona: In the *Gulliver* excerpt, the uncomprehending narrator is the object of satire.

shocking words and situations: In the "Modest Proposal" excerpt, the preparing of children as roasting pigs is shocking.

irony to point out faults: In the excerpts from *Battle* and "Verses," people who can't ever see themselves as objects of satire and others too shallow to let the death of a supposed friend interrupt their card playing are treated ironically.

understatement: In the *Tale of a Tub,* the narrator mindlessly accepts the horror of a person being skinned.

The objects of satire are unsympathetic and unfeeling people *(Tale),* people who can't see their own faults *(Battle),* an English society that puts no value on physical labor *(Gulliver),* an English society that thinks so little of the Irish ("Modest"), and people who give little real concern for anyone not intimately connected to them ("Verses").

B Second activity

Possible Responses:

Tale: the fact that the speaker doesn't comprehend the horror, the inhumanity, of what is seen; understatement

Battle: While not particularly funny, this is a clever observation; ironic situation

Gulliver: the fact that something as crucial as mathematics can be deemed of little importance; ironic statement

"Modest": Humor is possibly found only in the ghoulish absurdity of such a sight; shocking situations

"Verses": people weaving news of someone's death into a card-game banter

C Third activity

Students may find that examples of Swift's shocking language are easiest to locate. A good example of this comes from the reference to cannibalism in America, as found in "A Modest Proposal."

Applications

1. **Imitation of Style** Remind students to revisit the Key Aspects box on this page before beginning their imitations.
2. **Changing Style** In preparing this activity, some students may make the discovery that irony gives added impact to strong opinions and makes them more tolerable.
3. **Speaking and Listening** Have students use the following criteria to present their oral interpretations. The student should:
   - make and support a valid interpretation of how Gulliver would react to "A Modest Proposal"
   - use movement and gestures to establish mood and convey meaning
   - use facial expressions to establish mood and convey meaning

Writing Options

1. **Editorial Memo** Remind students that the possible reactions of the audience and of government authorities would be primary concerns of the editor.
2. **Ironic Rebuttal** Encourage students to adopt Swift's tone of well-intentioned and blind altruism. Remind students that, as the speaker, they will believe in the validity of their proposals, but the audience will recognize the irony and satire of their suggestions.
3. **Another Proposal** Students should refer to their responses in question 8 on page 620 (Connect to Life) for possible topics. Invite students to imitate Swift's use of a pseudo-rational voice, perhaps using facts and figures as Swift's narrator did in order to appear scientific and objective.

Activities & Explorations

1. **Town Meeting** You might assign groups of students a particular role as mothers, fathers, children, and so on. Have them write questions that concern the lives and culture of the characters they play. Also encourage them to write questions that reflect their own personal interests in these topics. Students should present their statements clearly with effective appeals that support their claims.
2. **Political Cartoon** Remind students that some people would have taken the proposal seriously and would have been outraged by it.
3. **"Modest" Diagrams** Students should present graphs and figures that clearly communicate Swift's assessment of Ireland's problems and his suggested solutions. Students may find that they list more than one solution for the larger problems Swift identifies.

Choices & CHALLENGES

Writing Options

1. **Editorial Memo** Imagine that you are the editor of an 18th-century periodical. To help your staff decide whether to print "A Modest Proposal," write a memo in which you list the pros and cons of publishing it.

pros & cons

2. **Ironic Rebuttal** In the same spirit of irony, write a response to Swift's proposal in which you argue against his solution to Ireland's problems and propose an equally outrageous one of your own.
3. **Another Proposal** Draft a satiric essay of your own, titled "A Modest Proposal." Offer a ridiculous proposal for reforming a current social or political problem. Place your draft in your **Working Portfolio.**

Writing Handbook
See page 1369: Problem-Solution.

Activities & Explorations

1. **Town Meeting** Pretend you're in Dublin in 1729. In a group, organize a town meeting to discuss Ireland's problems as described in "A Modest Proposal." Include Catholics, Protestants, mothers, fathers, children, landowners, beggars, thieves, and English government officials. You might also include Dean Swift himself. Select a moderator and a record keeper. After the meeting, present a list of problems and proposed solutions. ~ **SPEAKING AND LISTENING**
2. **Political Cartoon** Create a political cartoon that might have appeared in newspapers in response to the original publication of Swift's essay. ~ **ART**
3. **"Modest" Diagrams** Imagine that Jonathan Swift will be presenting his proposal to a committee of English politicians gathered to solve Ireland's problems. He needs some visual aids to display his calculations and help the committee understand the "logic" of his solution. Create a diagram that he could use in his presentation. In addition to a bar graph to show figures, here is a sample diagram that you could use to highlight Swift's "modest" argument. ~ **VIEWING AND REPRESENTING**

Problem
- Who
- What
- When
- Where
- Why

↓

Solution

↓

Projected Results

Inquiry & Research

1. **Literary History** How did readers react to "A Modest Proposal" at the time? Did anyone take the proposed solution seriously? Research the reception of Swift's famous essay. Also, find out why Swift stopped writing anything substantial about Ireland after "A Modest Proposal." Report your findings to the class.
2. **Irish History** Investigate the history of Ireland from the 18th century to the formation of the Irish Republic in 1937. What changes occurred in the relationship between Protestants and Catholics? How did those changes alter the political climate in Ireland? What happened to Ireland's economy? Here are some good places to start your research: a print or online encyclopedia and general histories, such as *History of Ireland* by Edmund Curtis and the *Dictionary of Irish History Since 1800.*
3. **Swift Biography** Find out more about the women in Swift's life: Esther Johnson, whom he called Stella, and Esther Vanhomrigh, whom he referred to as Vanessa. Also look at Swift's works about these women, the series of letters titled *Journal to Stella* and the long poem *Cadenus and Vanessa.* Write a short report on Swift's relationship with these two women.
4. **Swift Online** Check out Swift's web site. Input keyword *Jonathan Swift* in a search engine and see what you find. Write a critical review of online materials about Swift, specifying, for example, what would be useful for students interested in this great 18th-century satirist.

A portrait of Esther Johnson, Swift's Stella

Inquiry & Research

1. **Literary History** Students might begin their research with *Swift: The Critical Heritage* by Kathleen Williams. Students can narrow their focus and follow up on materials cited in this useful text.
2. **Irish History** To **make this assignment more challenging,** suggest students continue to trace the ramifications of those changes in Ireland to the present day. Are there events that occurred in the 18th century or in connection with the formation of the Irish Republic that still trouble Anglo-Irish relations today?
3. **Swift Biography** Students may want to refer to the definitive biography of Jonathan Swift by Irvin Ehrenpreis, *Swift: The Man, His Work, and the Age.*
4. **Swift Online** Students might search under the titles of particular works of Swift.

Vocabulary in Action

EXERCISE: SYNONYMS AND ANTONYMS Decide whether the words in each of the following pairs are synonyms or antonyms. On your paper, write **S** for Synonyms or **A** for Antonyms.

1. **animosity**—admiration
2. **prodigious**—small
3. **perpetual**—temporary
4. **deference**—esteem
5. **expedient**—device
6. **proficiency**—incompetence
7. **deplorable**—wretched
8. **emulation**—cooperation
9. **encumbrance**—asset
10. **rudiment**—basis

Building Vocabulary

For an in-depth lesson on how to use a thesaurus to find a word's synonyms and antonyms, see page 574.

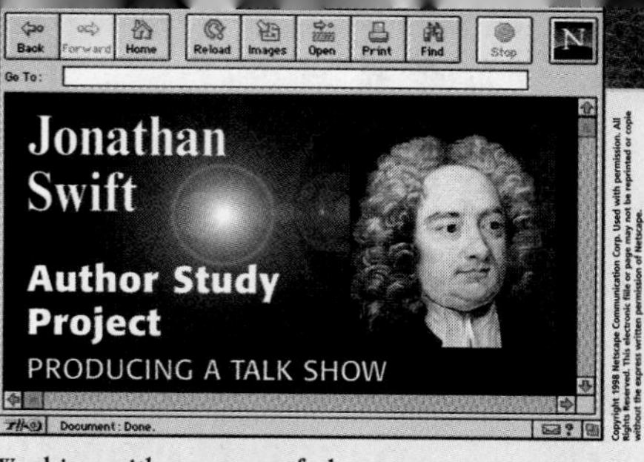

Working with a group of classmates, create a talk show segment with Jonathan Swift as the primary guest. You will need the following people to perform: a talk show host to conduct the interview; someone to play Swift in character (and in costume, if possible); and secondary guests, such as Swift's male friends, Joseph Addison and Alexander Pope, and his female friends, Stella and Vanessa. You will also need researchers, writers, editors, and, most important, a director who organizes everything. If you'd like to videotape the segment, you'll also need someone to operate the camera. Members of your class can act as the studio audience. Make sure they are prepared to participate in the open question-and-answer section of the program.

Print Resources Research biographies and criticisms of Swift's works for important information about him to use in the interview. Also, if you decide to use costumes, look for illustrations of how Swift and his contemporaries dressed. To accurately capture Swift's distinctive "voice," read more of his satire: for example, more of *Gulliver's Travels* and some of his poetry, especially "Verses on the Death of Dr. Swift," which contains Swift's comments about himself.

Video Watch the latest film version of *Gulliver's Travels* available at your local library or video store. Think about how you could use this video in your talk show.

Computers Encyclopedias on CD-ROM and an Internet search could yield valuable current information on Swift.

More Online: Research Starter
www.mcdougallittell.com

Vocabulary in Action

Exercise: Synonyms and Antonyms

1. A	**6.** A
2. A	**7.** S
3. A	**8.** S
4. S	**9.** A
5. S	**10.** S

Author Study Project

PRODUCING A TALK SHOW

Encourage group spontaneity. This can, in some cases, mean that the person chosen to play Swift will not see questions or know of the group's questioning approach beforehand. The person playing the interviewer should ask questions to elicit particular responses as well as to encourage a lively discussion. Remind students to use *who, what, where, when,* and *how* questions. Students acting as Swift who feel that they know his life well enough may want to extend the activity by submitting themselves to the rest of the class for an impromptu interview session.

Print Resources

Help students locate appropriate print and nonprint information by using text resources such as books, encyclopedias, and the Internet.

Video

Highly recommended for its production values is the video release of the 1996 television version of *Gulliver's Travels,* starring Ted Danson.

OVERVIEW

Objectives

1. understand and appreciate a **satire (Literary Analysis)**
2. appreciate the author's use of **humor (Literary Analysis)**
3. recognize shared characteristics of cultures through reading
4. **draw conclusions** about characters to appreciate and understand satire **(Active Reading)**

Summary

Candide, an honest and naive young man, is raised in a magnificent castle. The philosopher Pangloss, Candide's teacher, believes in a philosophy based on the best of all possible worlds. Candide tries to believe in his teacher's theory, but his innocent faith is repeatedly tested. First he is expelled from the castle for kissing a young baroness, and then he is impressed into the Bulgarian army.

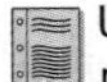 Use **Unit Three Resource Book,** p. 53 for additional support.

Thematic Link

Voltaire uses humorous, sharply ironic satire to criticize many forms of injustice in 18th-century European society and make his **arguments for change.** One of his main targets is the acceptance and rationalization of evil in the world through a naive, philosophical optimism.

5-Minute Warm-Up

Daily Language SkillBuilder

Have students **proofread** the display sentences on page 515l and write them correctly. The sentences also appear on Transparency 15 of **Grammar Transparencies and Copymasters.**

from Candide

Fiction by VOLTAIRE

Comparing Literature of the World

Satirical Commentary Across Cultures

Gulliver's Travels* and *Candide According to Jonathan Swift, satirists hold up a mirror to show society its faults. In both *Gulliver's Travels* and *Candide,* the writers use **satire** to ridicule 18th-century society by revealing its hypocrisies, injustices, and follies.

Points of Comparison As you read the excerpt from *Candide,* compare Voltaire's use of exaggeration as a means to criticize society with Swift's. Notice, too, that both writers present their social commentary by recounting the episodic adventures of impressionable characters.

Build Background

The Best of All Possible Worlds On a literal level, *Candide* tells the story of a naive young man as he wanders through the world. On a philosophical level, the novel deals with the nature of good and evil. Voltaire wrote *Candide* in response to the influential philosophical optimism of Gottfried Leibniz. A German philosopher, mathematician, and scholar, Leibniz believed that God had created the "best of all possible worlds." According to this theory, people should accept evil simply because it is part of the world. Voltaire, who spent much of his life trying to correct the wrongs he saw in the world, found such a philosophy appalling.

In *Candide,* Voltaire creates a world of horrors and folly and a character who enters that world believing fully that it is the best it can possibly be. After seeing and suffering outrageous misfortunes, Candide finally begins to question philosophical optimism and eventually discovers the secret of happiness.

WORDS TO KNOW
Vocabulary Preview
condescend
disposition
doctrine
gauntlet
implicitly

Focus Your Reading

LITERARY ANALYSIS HUMOR **Humor** is the quality possessed by a literary work that entertains by evoking laughter. Humor plays an important part in **satire.** In *Candide,* Voltaire uses a variety of elements to create humor, including exaggeration, absurd reasoning, and irony. Notice the absurdity in the following statement:

> ***Observe, for instance, the nose is formed for spectacles, therefore we wear spectacles.***

As you read the excerpt, look for other examples of humor.

ACTIVE READING DRAWING CONCLUSIONS ABOUT CHARACTERS When you **draw conclusions** about characters in literature, you form opinions about their personalities. You should base your conclusions about a character on the character's speech and actions and on descriptions of the character.

READER'S NOTEBOOK As you read the excerpt from *Candide,* record information about the characters in a chart like the one shown.

	Speech	Action	Description
Candide			a most sweet disposition
Baron			
Pangloss	"It is demonstrable that things . . ."		

LESSON RESOURCES

UNIT THREE RESOURCE BOOK, pp. 53–57

ASSESSMENT RESOURCES

Formal Assessment, pp. 103–104

Teacher's Guide to Assessment and Portfolio Use

Test Generator

SKILLS TRANSPARENCIES AND COPYMASTERS

Reading and Critical Thinking

- Visualizing, T8 (for Active Reading, p. 629)

Grammar

- Diagramming Verbal Phrases, T60 (for Mini Lesson, pp. 626–627)
- Distinguishing Participles, Gerunds, and Verbs, C93 (for Mini Lesson, pp. 626–627)

Writing

- Compare-Contrast, C34 (for Writing Options, p. 630)

INTEGRATED TECHNOLOGY

Audio Library

Visit our website: www.mcdougallittell.com

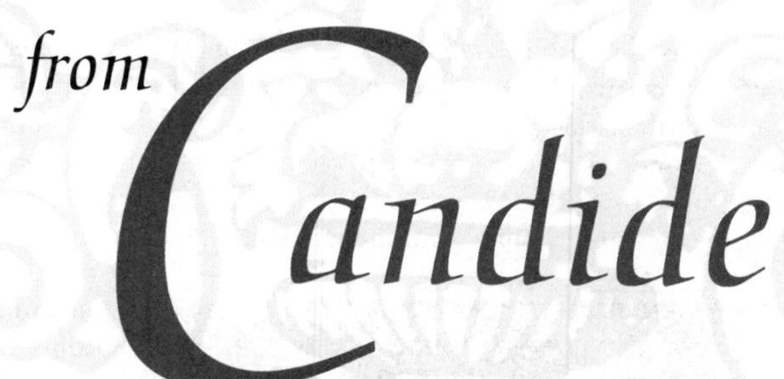

from Candide

TRANSLATED BY TOBIAS SMOLLETT

Chapter I

How Candide was brought up in a magnificent castle, and how he was driven from thence

In the country of Westphalia, in the castle of the most noble Baron of Thunder-ten-tronckh, lived a youth whom nature had endowed with a most sweet disposition. His face was the true index of his mind. He had a solid judgment joined to the most unaffected simplicity, and hence, I presume, he had his name of Candide.[1] The old servants of the house suspected him to have been the son of the Baron's sister, by a mighty good sort of a gentleman of the neighborhood, whom that young lady refused to marry because he could produce no more than threescore and eleven quarterings[2] in his arms; the rest of the genealogical tree belonging to the family having been lost through the injuries of time.

The Baron was one of the most powerful lords in Westphalia, for his castle had not only a gate but even windows, and his great hall was hung with tapestry. He used to hunt with his mastiffs and spaniels instead of greyhounds; his groom served him for huntsman, and the parson of the parish officiated as grand almoner.[3] He was called "My Lord" by all his people, and he never told a story but everyone laughed at it.

My lady Baroness weighed three hundred and fifty pounds, consequently was a person of no small consideration; and then she did the honors of the house with a dignity that commanded universal respect. Her daughter Cunegund was about seventeen years of age fresh colored, comely, plump, and desirable. The Baron's son seemed to be a youth in every respect worthy of his father. Pangloss[4] the preceptor[5] was the oracle of the family, and little Candide listened to his instructions with all the simplicity natural to his age and disposition.

Master Pangloss taught metaphysico-theologo-cosmolo-nigology.[6] He could prove admirably

1. **Candide** (kăn-dēd′): The name is a French word meaning "innocent" or "without guile."
2. **quarterings:** divisions in coat of arms that indicate connections with other noble families. The baron's "threescore and eleven" (71) quarterings are a ridiculously large number.
3. **grand almoner** (ăl′mə-nər): a person in charge of distributing charity to the poor.
4. **Pangloss:** The name of this know-it-all character comes from Greek words meaning "all" and "tongue."
5. **preceptor** (prĭ-sĕp′tər): teacher.
6. **metaphysico-theologo-cosmolo-nigology:** Pangloss teaches a nonsensical subject with a pretentious name. *(Nigology* comes from the French word *nigaud,* meaning "foolish.")

WORDS TO KNOW **disposition** (dĭs′pə-zĭsh′ən) *n.* temperament

625

TEACHING THE LITERATURE

Customizing Instruction

Less Proficient Readers
One of the underlying themes of *Candide* concerns Pangloss's theories about the best of all possible worlds. Candide spends much of the novel trying to decide if he believes the philosopher's teachings. Have students summarize the philosophy of Pangloss. How does Candide initially feel about these ideas?

Students Acquiring English
Explain to students that Westphalia is in modern Germany. Voltaire, who was French, is mocking the sound of the German language with the name of the barony (Thunder-ten-tronckh) and the name of the town (Waldberghoff-trarbk-dikdorff). Have students discuss their opinions of this type of humor. Invite them to share experiences they have had with their primary language being mocked.

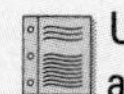
Use **Spanish Study Guide** for additional support, pp. 135–137

Gifted and Talented
Encourage students to view Pangloss from a point of view that is more suspicious than Candide's. Why might Pangloss support a philosophy that justifies the existence of behavior regardless of what it is?

Mini Lesson: Preteaching Vocabulary

USING CONTEXT CLUES

Instruction As students review the WORDS TO KNOW, remind them that they can often rely on the context in which an unfamiliar word is used to determine its meaning. One common context clue is a restatement of the original thought later in the sentence. Demonstrate the strategy using the following model.

Model You should not *condescend* to your sister; just because she is younger than you, does not mean you are better than she.

- Have a student summarize the meaning of the model sentence.
- Have students suggest meanings of the word based on the restatement in the second half of the sentence.

Exercise Read the following sentence, and have students use context clues to understand the meanings of the italicized word.

The kitten trusted his mother *implicitly,* never once doubting she would take care of him.

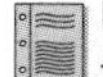
Use **Unit Three Resource Book** p. 56 for additional support.

A lesson on using context clues appears on p. 939 of the Pupil's Edition.

Reading and Analyzing

Literary Analysis HUMOR

A Remind students that authors use humor of situation, humor of character, and humor of language to make their works funny. Ask them what kind of humor is presented in the comments by Pangloss.

Possible Response: Humor of language is the primary kind, as Pangloss's illogical explanations are absurd in the extreme.

Use **Unit Three Resource Book** p. 55 for more exercises.

Active Reading

DRAWING CONCLUSIONS ABOUT CHARACTERS

B Ask students what conclusions they draw about Candide based on his experiences with Cunegund. They must cite evidence from the text and/or their own experience.

Possible Responses: Candide is naive, because he doesn't expect the reaction of the baron.

Use **Unit Three Resource Book** p. 54 for more practice.

Literary Analysis: VERBAL IRONY

C Ask students to pick out examples of verbal irony in the scene with the army recruiters.

Possible Responses: The soldiers proclaim that "mankind were born to assist one another," but they don't want to assist Candide—they want to impress him into the Bulgarian army.

that there is no effect without a cause, and that, in this best of all possible worlds, the Baron's castle was the most magnificent of all castles and my lady the best of all possible baronesses.

"It is demonstrable," said he, "that things cannot be otherwise than they are; for as all things have been created for some end, they must necessarily be created for the best end. Observe, for instance, the nose is formed for spectacles, therefore we wear spectacles. The legs are visibly designed for stockings, accordingly we wear stockings. Stones were made to be hewn, and to construct castles, therefore my lord has a magnificent castle; for the greatest baron in the province ought to be the best lodged. Swine were intended to be eaten; therefore we eat pork all the year round. And they who assert that everything is good do not express themselves correctly; they should
A say that everything is for the best."

The Stolen Kiss (late 1780s), Jean-Honoré Fragonard. Oil on canvas. Hermitage, St. Petersburg, Russia.

Candide listened attentively, and believed implicitly; for he thought Miss Cunegund excessively handsome, though he never had the courage to tell her so. He concluded that next to the happiness of being Baron of Thunder-ten-tronckh, the next was that of being Miss Cunegund, the next that of seeing her every day, and the last that of hearing the doctrine of Master Pangloss, the greatest philosopher of the whole province, and consequently of the whole world.

One day, when Miss Cunegund went to take a walk in a little neighboring wood, which was called a park, . . . she happened to meet Candide; she blushed, he blushed also. She wished him a good morning in a faltering tone; he returned the salute, without knowing what he said. The next day, as they were rising from dinner, Cunegund and Candide slipped behind the screen. She dropped her handkerchief; the young man picked it up. She innocently took hold of his hand, and he as innocently kissed hers with a warmth, a sensibility, a grace—all very extraordinary—their lips met, their eyes sparkled, their knees trembled, their hands strayed. The Baron of Thunder-ten-tronckh chanced to come by; he beheld the cause and effect, and, without hesitation, saluted Candide with some notable kicks on the breech and drove him out of doors. Miss Cunegund fainted away, and, as 1
soon as she came to herself, the Baroness boxed her ears. Thus a general consternation was spread over this most magnificent and most B
agreeable of all possible castles.

WORDS TO KNOW

implicitly (ĭm-plĭs'ĭt-lē) *adv.* without question or doubt
doctrine (dŏk'trĭn) *n.* the ideas taught by an authority

626

Teaching Options

Grammar

DISTINGUISHING PARTICIPLES, GERUNDS, AND VERBS

Instruction A participle is a verb form that ends in *–ing* or often in *-ed.* Participles are used as adjectives in a sentence. A gerund is a verb form that ends in *-ing* and always acts as a noun. The difference between a participle that ends in *-ing* and a gerund is its function in a sentence: a participle always functions as an adjective and a gerund always functions as a noun.

Activity Write on the chalkboard the following excerpts from Voltaire's *Candide.*

"She wished him a good morning in a faltering tone; he returned the salute, without knowing what he said."

"Candide, thus driven out of this terrestrial paradise, wandered a long time, without knowing where he went . . ."

Help students identify the participles and gerunds in the example sentences. *(faltering, participle; knowing, gerund; driven, participle; knowing, gerund)* Explain to students that participles function as adjectives *("faltering" modifies the noun "tone";* "driven" *modifies the noun "Candide")* and

Chapter II

What befell Candide among the Bulgarians

Candide, thus driven out of this terrestrial paradise, wandered a long time, without knowing where he went; sometimes he raised his eyes, all bedewed with tears, toward Heaven, and sometimes he cast a melancholy look toward the magnificent castle where dwelt the fairest of young baronesses. He laid himself down to sleep in a furrow, heartbroken and supperless. The snow fell in great flakes, and, in the morning when he awoke, he was almost frozen to death; however, he made shift to crawl to the next town, which was called Waldberghoff-trarbk-dikdorff, without a penny in his pocket, and half dead with hunger and fatigue. He took up his stand at the door of an inn. He had not been long there before two men dressed in blue fixed their eyes steadfastly upon him.

"Faith, comrade," said one of them to the other, "yonder is a well-made young fellow, and of the right size."

Thereupon they went up to Candide, and with the greatest civility and politeness invited him to dine with them.

"Gentlemen," replied Candide, with a most engaging modesty, "you do me much honor, but, upon my word, I have no money."

"Money, sir!" said one of the men in blue to him. "Young persons of your appearance and merit never pay anything. Why, are not you five feet five inches high?"

"Yes, gentlemen, that is really my size," replied he with a low bow.

"Come then, sir, sit down along with us. We will not only pay your reckoning,[7] but will never suffer such a clever young fellow as you to want money. Mankind were born to assist one another." C

"You are perfectly right, gentlemen," said Candide; "that is precisely the doctrine of Master Pangloss; and I am convinced that everything is for the best."

His generous companions next entreated him to accept a few crowns, which he readily complied with, at the same time offering them his note for the payment, which they refused, and sat down to table.

"Have you not a great affection for—"

"Oh, yes!" he replied. "I have a great affection for the lovely Miss Cunegund."

"Maybe so," replied one of the men, "but that is not the question! We are asking you whether you have not a great affection for the King of the Bulgarians?"

"For the King of the Bulgarians?" said Candide. "Not at all. Why, I never saw him in my life."

"Is it possible! Oh, he is a most charming king! Come, we must drink his health."

"With all my heart, gentlemen," Candide said, and he tossed off his glass.

"Bravo!" cried the blues. "You are now the support, the defender, the hero of the Bulgarians; your fortune is made; you are on the high road to glory." So saying, they put him in irons and carried him away to the regiment. There he was made to wheel about to the right, to the left, to draw his ramrod,[8] to return his ramrod, to present, to fire, to march, and they gave him thirty blows with a cane. The next day he performed his exercise a little better, and they gave him but twenty. The day following he came off with ten and was looked upon as a young fellow of surprising genius by all his comrades.

7. **reckoning:** bill.

8. **ramrod:** a rod used to ram gunpowder and bullets into a musket.

Customizing Instruction

Less Proficient Readers

Ask students the following questions to guide them through the passage.

- What does Candide like about living at the baron's castle?

  Answer: He likes being near the baron, whom he admires, and near Cunegund, whom he finds attractive, and he likes to listen to Pangloss's philosophy.

- Based on Candide's feelings for Cunegund, how do students think their relationship will progress?

  Possible Responses: Some students might think they will become romantically involved or even get married; others might suggest that because of Candide's shyness, nothing will happen between them.

Students Acquiring English

1 Write the phrases "she *came to herself*," "he *made shift* to *crawl*," and "he *tossed off* his glass" on the board. Help students understand the meanings of these idioms. Encourage students to offer analogous idioms from their first language.

Possible Responses: She regained consciousness, he managed to crawl, and he consumed his drink in one mouthful.

Multiple Learning Styles

Visual Learners

Invite students to review Voltaire's descriptions of the baroness, Cunegund, and Candide and to prepare drawings of the characters based on those descriptions. Students should recognize that Voltaire uses exaggeration as a way of creating humor with his characterizations.

gerunds function as nouns *("knowing" is the object of the preposition "without" in both sentences).* Participles are also used with auxiliary verbs to form verb phrases.

Candide was drafted into the Bulgarian army; *("was drafted" is a verb phrase)*

Do not mistake a participle in a verb phrase, which is a verb, for a participle used as an adjective, which is a participle.

Drafted into the Bulgarian army, Candide finds his life utterly changed. *("drafted" is a participle and modifies "Candide")*

Exercise Ask students to underline the participles and gerunds in each sentence. For each participle and gerund have students identify its function in the sentence.

Candide tells the story of a naïve young man wandering through the world. *(participle modifying the noun "man")*

Use **Grammar Transparencies and Copymasters,** p. 93.

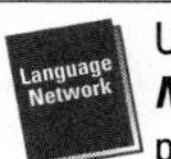

Use McDougal Littell's ***Language Network*** for more instruction in participles, gerunds and verbs.

Reading and Analyzing

Reading Skills and Strategies: DRAWING CONCLUSIONS

A Ask students what happens in this passage and what message is being conveyed by it.

Possible Response: Candide is treated as a criminal for taking a walk. The message is that the military is excessively oppressive and controlling.

Literary Analysis HUMOR

B This passage involves two different humorous techniques, exaggeration and dramatic irony. Have students identify and explain the humor here.

Possible Response: The two alternative punishments are an exaggeration; Candide's belief that he can choose to forego either alternative is an instance of dramatic irony.

Literary Analysis: VERBAL IRONY

C Voltaire is being ironic in the passage "our young hero . . . begged as a favor they would be so obliging as to shoot him through the head." Ask students to explain the irony.

Possible Response: Generally, a person wouldn't consider it a favor to be shot in the head, nor would someone usually beg for such treatment. Candide is saying the opposite of what we would expect in such circumstances.

Literary Analysis: SATIRE

Remind students that satire seeks to criticize social problems. Have students discuss the passage about Candide's court martial. What is Voltaire satirizing?

Possible Response: Voltaire is satirizing excessive restrictions and punishment in the army.

Candide was struck with amazement and could not for the soul of him conceive how he came to be a hero. One fine spring morning, he took it into his head to take a walk, and he marched straight forward, conceiving it to be a privilege of the human species as well as of the brute creation, to make use of their legs how and when they pleased. He had not gone above two leagues[9] when he was overtaken by four other heroes, six feet high, who bound him neck and heels, and carried him to a dungeon. A court-martial[10] sat upon him, and he was asked which he liked best, either to run the gauntlet six and thirty times through the whole regiment, or to have his brains blown out with a dozen musket balls. In vain did he remonstrate to them that the human will is free, and that he chose neither. They obliged him to make a choice, and he determined, in virtue of that divine gift called free will, to run the gauntlet six and thirty times. He had gone through his discipline twice, and the regiment being composed of two thousand men, they composed for him exactly four thousand strokes, which laid bare all his muscles and nerves, from the nape of his neck to his rump. As they were preparing to make him set out the third time, our young hero, unable to support it any longer, begged as a favor they would be so obliging as to shoot him through the head. The favor being granted, a bandage was tied over his eyes, and he was made to kneel down. At that very instant, his Bulgarian Majesty, happening to pass by, inquired into the delinquent's crime, and being a prince of great penetration, he found, from what he heard of Candide, that he was a young metaphysician,[11] entirely ignorant of the world. And, therefore, out of his great clemency, he condescended to pardon him, for which his name will be celebrated in every journal, and in every age. A skillful surgeon made a cure of Candide in three weeks by means of emollient unguents[12] prescribed by Dioscorides.[13] His sores were now skinned over, and he was able to march when the King of the Bulgarians gave battle to the King of the Abares. ❖

Anonymous print (1700s). Recruiting officers in 18th-century Europe often took men by force.

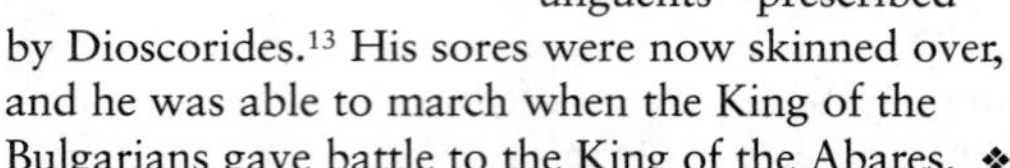

9. **two leagues:** about five or six miles.
10. **court-martial:** military tribunal.
11. **metaphysician** (mĕt′ə-fĭ-zĭsh′ən): one who is skilled in metaphysics, the branch of philosophy that investigates the nature of reality.
12. **emollient unguents** (ĭ-mŏl′yənt ŭng′gwənts): soothing ointments.
13. **Dioscorides** (dī′ə-skôr′ĭ-dēz′): a Greek physician of the first century A.D., who wrote an influential book about the medicinal properties of plants.

WORDS TO KNOW

gauntlet (gônt′lĭt) *n.* a punishment in which a person is forced to run between two lines of people who beat the person as he or she passes

condescend (kŏn′dĭ-sĕnd′) *v.* to do something considered to be beneath one's dignity

628

Teaching Options

Assessment Informal Assessment

CHECKING COMPREHENSION Have students check their comprehension with the following questions:

1. Candide grows up in what kind of household?
   Answer: He's raised by a wealthy baron in a castle.
2. What is Pangloss's philosophy of life?
   Answer: Everything that happens is for the best—even if it is evil.
3. What happens when Candide is caught kissing Cunegund?
   Answer: He is forced to leave the castle.
4. Why is Candide court-martialed and forced either to run the gauntlet or be shot in the head?
   Answer: He takes a walk in the countryside without the army's permission.
5. How does Candide escape his punishment?
   Answer: He is pardoned by the Bulgarian king.

Connect to the Literature

1. **What Do You Think?** What was your reaction to Candide's experiences?

Comprehension Check
- Why is Candide thrown out of the castle by the Baron?
- How is Candide drafted into the Bulgarian army?

Think Critically

2. What happens to Candide when he tries to live according to Master Pangloss's teachings?

THINK ABOUT
- the "cause and effect" Candide engages in with Cunegund
- his assertion to the men in blue that "everything is for the best"
- Candide's decision to "make use of [his] legs" while a soldier in the Bulgarian army

3. Why do you suppose the Baron appreciates Pangloss's philosophy?
4. What is the effect of statements like "Thus a general consternation was spread over this most magnificent and most agreeable of all possible castles"?
5. Do you think that Candide will reject the teachings of Pangloss after his experience with the Bulgarian army? Why or why not?
6. **ACTIVE READING** **DRAWING CONCLUSIONS ABOUT CHARACTERS** With a classmate, discuss the information you recorded in your READER'S NOTEBOOK. Based on this information, what **conclusions** can you draw about the nature of Candide, Pangloss, and other **characters** in the selection?

Extend Interpretations

7. **Connect to Life** Voltaire uses **satire** to point out weaknesses in 18th-century society. What examples can you think of in which writers and filmmakers today use satire to criticize flaws in modern life?
8. **Points of Comparison** Compare Candide's relationship to Pangloss with Gulliver's relationship to the leaders of the Lilliputians and the Brobdingnagians. How are the relationships similar? What do they suggest about Candide and Gulliver?

Literary Analysis

HUMOR There are three basic types of **humor,** all of which may involve exaggeration or irony.

- **Humor of situation** usually involves exaggerated events or **situational irony.** Candide's exaggerated punishment at the hands of the Bulgarian army is an example of this type of humor.
- **Humor of character** often involves exaggerated personality traits or characters who, ironically, don't recognize their own failings. Pangloss, with his self-serving philosophy, reflects this type of humor.
- **Humor of language** may include sarcasm, exaggeration, puns, absurdity, or **verbal irony.** The descriptions of the Baron, the Baroness, and their son are examples of this type of humor.

Paired Activity With a partner, choose a passage of the story that you find particularly funny, and discuss the types of humor it contains. How does the humor contribute to the **satire** in *Candide?* You might use a chart like the one shown to organize your ideas.

Passage	Types of Humor	How Humor Contributes to Satire

GUIDING STUDENT RESPONSE

Connect to the Literature

1. **What Do You Think?**
   Guidelines for student response: Students should provide some detail about their reactions to what befalls Candide. In particular, they should describe what they find appealing about his experiences and what they find disturbing.

Comprehension Check
- The baron catches him kissing Cunegund.
- He is taken away in chains after dining with the recruiters.

 Use Selection Quiz in **Unit Three Resource Book** p. **57**

Think Critically

2. He trusts people too completely, and they take advantage of him.
3. According to Pangloss's philosophy, the baron's wealth and power are justified by their mere existence.
4. The irony of the statement is likely to have a humorous effect on the reader.
5. Responses will vary. Some students might think that Candide will reject the teachings because the world that has used him so harshly cannot be so great. Others will say he will continue to believe because he is so gullible.
6. Possible Responses: Candide is naive and good-natured; Pangloss is pedantic and self-serving; the recruiting officers are sly. Students must cite evidence from the text to support their evidence.

Literary Analysis

Paired Activity In their discussion, students should include ideas about the effect the humor has on the reader and his or her acceptance of the authors' ideas.

Extend Interpretations

Connect to Life Political cartoons offer daily satires of political life, and a book (and movie) such as *Primary Colors* presents a satirical treatment of one presidential campaign. Standup comedians use satire in their commentaries on contemporary life. Comic movies often treat subjects of current interest satirically. For example, *L.A. Story* satirizes lifestyles and problems in Los Angeles, including traffic, drive-by shootings, and status seeking.

Points of Comparison Candide and Gulliver both take the world, and its leaders and teachers, at face value. Both are somewhat naive—Swift and Voltaire adopt an ironic stance toward the world, but their protagonists do not share the authors' critical attitude.

Writing Options

Points of Comparison Remind students that satire ridicules ideas, customs, behaviors, or institutions for the purpose of improving society. Have students make a list of the targets of satire in each work. Are any topics common to both stories? After choosing one or two topics to compare, students should look for examples of irony and humor in the presentation of those topics as a way of comparing the style and effectiveness of the two satires. Remind them that they need a clear topic sentence for each satirical subject they address.

Inquiry & Research

Enlightened Ideas Have students meet in groups and conduct general research on the three writers using encyclopedias and perhaps more specialized collections of biographies of philosophers, scientists, and literary authors. Then have students narrow their focus and choose one or two issues to research for their analysis of Locke's and Newton's influence on Voltaire. For example, what did each of the three writers think about religion? about war? about scientific progress? about human nature? Have students compile written notes on how Voltaire compares to Locke and Newton on one or two of these issues (or other issues). Have students draw conclusions and present their findings to the class.

Vocabulary in Action

Exercise

1. gauntlet
2. doctrine
3. condescend
4. disposition
5. implicitly

Writing Options

Points of Comparison

Think about the use of satire in *Gulliver's Travels* and *Candide.* In which is satire used more effectively? Write an essay explaining your ideas.

Satire in Gulliver

Satire in Candide

Inquiry & Research

Enlightened Ideas

Voltaire was attracted to the ideas of the philosopher John Locke and the scientist Sir Isaac Newton. Learn about Locke's and Newton's ideas and their impact on Voltaire.

Vocabulary in Action

EXERCISE: CONTEXT CLUES Write the vocabulary word that best answers each riddle.

1. I am a group activity that inflicts harm on one person.
2. Some people live their lives in accordance with me.
3. I am what a snob might do.
4. I am different in each person.
5. I am a way in which you might believe or trust.

WORDS TO KNOW		
	condescend	gauntlet
	disposition	implicitly
	doctrine	

Building Vocabulary

For an in-depth study of context clues, see page 938.

Voltaire

1694–1778

Other Works

Philosophical Dictionary
Zadig
Zaïre

Early Success François Marie Arouet chose the pen name Voltaire shortly after *Oedipe,* his first major play, achieved success in 1718. Other successes followed. He became independently wealthy in his early 30s and enjoyed the status of an honored celebrity at the court of King Louis XV.

English Influence Circumstances changed abruptly when Voltaire insulted a young nobleman in 1726. Given the option of imprisonment or exile, Voltaire chose exile in England. During his three years there, Voltaire met the English writers Alexander Pope and Jonathan Swift. After Voltaire returned to Paris in 1729, he wrote a book praising English customs and institutions. However, the book was thought to be critical of the French government, and Voltaire was forced to flee Paris again.

Exile and Return During his years of exile, Voltaire produced a steady flow of books, plays, pamphlets, and letters. Many addressed religious intolerance and persecution. Although Voltaire enjoyed a triumphant return to Paris at age 83, the excitement of the trip proved too much for him and he died shortly thereafter. Because of his criticism of the Catholic Church, Voltaire was denied burial in church ground. However, in 1791, his remains were moved to the Panthéon in Paris, where many of France's most famous citizens are buried.

PREPARING to *Read*

from A Vindication of the Rights of Woman

Essay by MARY WOLLSTONECRAFT

Connect to Your Life

Women's Rights Women's rights have been debated for centuries. From your knowledge of history, what has caused this debate? Do you think that women's rights are still a controversial issue in our society? Why or why not? Jot down your thoughts.

Build Background

Radical Views Although a number of 18th-century British writers discussed the role of women in society, none became as celebrated for their feminist views as Mary Wollstonecraft. Early in her life, Wollstonecraft learned the value of independence and became openly critical of a society that treated females as inferior creatures who were socially, financially, and legally dependent on men. Her concern for humanity was not limited to compassion for downtrodden women; she advocated the equality and independence of all human beings. In 1790, Wollstonecraft had written a defense of the French Revolution entitled *A Vindication of the Rights of Men.* It was controversial not only for its radical ideas but for being a woman's venture into political writing. In 1792, Wollstonecraft continued the controversy with her publication of *A Vindication of the Rights of Woman,* in which she called for an end to the prevailing injustices against females. Although her opinions on women's rights may seem conservative by modern standards, they were radical in 18th-century Britain, where most women accepted their inferior status or at least refrained from expressing their discontent.

WORDS TO KNOW
Vocabulary Preview
affectation
concurring
feign
grovel
ignoble
languid
solicitude
specious
subordinate
vivacity

Focus Your Reading

LITERARY ANALYSIS ARGUMENTATION

Argumentation is speech or writing intended to convince an audience that a proposal should be adopted or rejected. Most argumentation begins with a statement of an idea or opinion, which is then supported with logical evidence. Wollstonecraft states her opinion in the first paragraph of her essay:

> ***. . . the neglected education of my fellow-creatures is the grand source of the misery I deplore. . . .***

As you read this **persuasive essay,** consider the evidence Wollstonecraft uses to support her opinion.

ACTIVE READING RECOGNIZING LOGICAL PERSUASION

In her essay, Wollstonecraft uses persuasive techniques that appeal to logic and reason rather than to emotion. For example, the writer uses the technique of anticipation and rebuttal of opposing views. That is, she foresees the opposition's argument in her **essay** and logically responds to it.

READER'S NOTEBOOK As you read the essay, list in a chart like the one shown opposing views that Wollstonecraft identifies. Jot down briefly how she responds to each view.

Opposing Views	Response

OVERVIEW

This selection is included in the **Grade 12 InterActive Reader.**

Objectives

1. understand and appreciate an **essay** exploring the argument for women's rights **(Literary Analysis)**
2. appreciate the author's use of **argumentation (Literary Analysis)**
3. recognize logical **persuasion** in order to understand *A Vindication of the Rights of Woman* **(Active Reading)**

Summary

Wollstonecraft argues that women's strength and usefulness have been sacrificed in favor of their ability to please men. She agrees that men are physically stronger than women but says that women should cultivate the "manly virtues" of strength, courage, and fortitude. She disputes the idea that women should seek only to be pleasing, especially given that charm fades over time. She concludes that women must be free to develop their own characters and warns that treating women like slaves will sour their virtuous qualities.

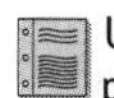
Use **Unit Three Resource Book,** p. 58 for additional support.

Thematic Link

Mary Wollstonecraft believed in the equality and independence of all human beings, including women, and she was critical of a society that treated women as inferior creatures. Her controversial essay, an **argument for change,** also reveals a typical Enlightenment sentiment: the celebration of rational thought.

5-Minute Warm-Up

Daily Language SkillBuilder

Have students **proofread** the display sentences on page 515l and write them correctly. The sentences also appear on Transparency 16 of **Grammar Transparencies and Copymasters.**

LESSON RESOURCES

UNIT THREE RESOURCE BOOK, pp. 58–62

ASSESSMENT RESOURCES
Formal Assessment, p. 105
Teacher's Guide to Assessment and Portfolio Use
Test Generator

SKILLS TRANSPARENCIES AND COPYMASTERS
Reading and Critical Thinking
- Evaluating Argumentation I, T21 (for Active Reading, p. 631)

Grammar
- Diagramming Verbal Phrases, T60 (for Mini Lesson, pp. 634–635)
- Verbals and Verbal Phrases, C94 (for Mini Lesson, pp. 634–635)

Vocabulary
- Roots, C54 (for Mini Lesson, p. 636)

Writing
- Opinion Statement, C35 (for Writing Option 1, p. 638)

Communications
- Interviewing, T9 (for Writing Option 2, p. 638)

INTEGRATED TECHNOLOGY
Audio Library
Visit our website:
www.mcdougallittell.com

Preteaching Vocabulary

If you would like to preteach the WORDS TO KNOW for this selection, use the Mini Lesson p. 632.

TEACHING THE LITERATURE

Reading and Analyzing

Active Reading RECOGNIZING LOGICAL PERSUASION

Students should recognize logic and appeals to reason as a mode of persuasion. Explain that an argument based on logical persuasion uses a series of statements, including personal opinions, that are supported by reasons and evidence. Ask students what opinions Wollstonecraft holds about women and what evidence she uses to support her claims.

Possible Responses: opinion—the education of women is making them mentally weak; evidence—women forego noble ambitions and virtues, wanting only men's love.

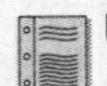 Use **Unit Three Resource Book,** p. 59 for additional support.

Literary Analysis ARGUMENTATION

A Ask students to summarize how Wollstonecraft anticipates and meets opposition in her discussion of physical differences between the sexes and, later, in her description and support of "masculine women."

Possible Response: Wollstonecraft acknowledges that men are physically stronger than women but claims that this fact is no reason to consider women weak in mind and spirit as well.

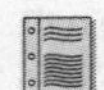 Use **Unit Three Resource Book,** p. 60 for more exercises.

ACTIVE READING

B QUESTION Possible Response: She explains that some "masculine" qualities, such as courage and independence, ennoble the human spirit and would be beneficial to anyone, male or female.

FROM

A VINDICATION OF THE RIGHTS OF WOMAN

MARY WOLLSTONECRAFT

FROM THE INTRODUCTION

After considering the historic page, and viewing the living world with anxious solicitude, the most melancholy emotions of sorrowful indignation have depressed my spirits, and I have sighed when obliged to confess, that either nature has made a great difference between man and man, or that the civilization which has hitherto taken place in the world has been very partial. I have turned over various books written on the subject of education, and patiently observed the conduct of parents and the management of schools; but what has been the result?—a profound conviction that the neglected education of my fellow-creatures is the grand source of the misery I deplore; and that women, in particular, are rendered weak and wretched by a variety of concurring causes, originating from one hasty conclusion. The conduct and manners of women, in fact, evidently prove that their minds are not in a healthy state; for, like the flowers which are planted in too rich

WORDS TO KNOW

solicitude (sə-lĭs'ĭ-to͞od') *n.* care or concern

concurring (kən-kûr'ĭng) *adj.* occurring at the same time; acting together
concur *v.*

632

Teaching Options

Mini Lesson Preteaching Vocabulary

USING A THESAURUS

Instruction Call students' attention to the list of WORDS TO KNOW, and explain that the use of reference materials such as a thesaurus can help determine precise word meanings. Demonstrate how the use of a thesaurus can help build vocabulary with the following activity.

Activity

- Have students find each of the WORDS TO KNOW in the selection and write the sentence, or part of the sentence, in which the word appears.
- Have students use a thesaurus to find a synonym for the word.
- Have students paraphrase the sentence (or part of the sentence) using their word choices from the thesaurus and discuss how the synonym changes the sentence meaning.

Model

1. "After . . . viewing the living world with anxious solicitude . . ." (Wollstonecraft)
2. solicitude: also attentiveness (from thesaurus)
3. After . . . looking at the world with anxious attentiveness . . . (paraphrase)

Use **Unit Three Resource Book,** p. 61 for more practice.

a soil, strength and usefulness are sacrificed to beauty; and the flaunting leaves, after having pleased a fastidious eye, fade, disregarded on the stalk, long before the season when they ought to have arrived at maturity. One cause of this barren blooming I attribute to a false system of education, gathered from the books written on this subject by men who, considering females rather as women than human creatures, have been more anxious to make them alluring mistresses than affectionate wives and rational mothers; and the understanding of the sex has been so bubbled by this specious homage, that the civilized women of the present century, with a few exceptions, are only anxious to inspire love, when they ought to cherish a nobler ambition, and by their abilities and virtues exact respect.

In a treatise,[1] therefore, on female rights and manners, the works which have been particularly written for their improvement must not be overlooked; especially when it is asserted, in direct terms, that the minds of women are enfeebled by false refinement; that the books of instruction, written by men of genius, have had the same tendency as more frivolous productions; and that . . . they are treated as a kind of subordinate beings, and not as a part of the human species, when improvable reason is allowed to be the dignified distinction which raises men above the brute creation, and puts a natural scepter in a feeble hand.

Yet, because I am a woman, I would not lead my readers to suppose that I mean violently to agitate the contested question respecting the quality or inferiority of the sex; but as the subject lies in my way, and I cannot pass it over without subjecting the main tendency of my reasoning to misconstruction, I shall stop a moment to deliver, A in a few words, my opinion. In the government of the physical world it is observable that the female in point of strength is, in general, inferior to the male. This is the law of nature; and it does not appear to be suspended or abrogated[2] in favor of woman. A degree of physical superiority cannot, therefore, be denied—and it is a noble prerogative! But not content with this natural pre-eminence, men endeavor to sink us still lower merely to render us alluring objects for a moment; and women, intoxicated by the adoration which men, under the influence of their senses, pay them, do not seek to obtain a durable interest in their hearts, or to become the friends of the fellow creatures who find amusement in their society.

ACTIVE READING

QUESTION How does Wollstonecraft use **logical persuasion** to respond to those who object to making women more "masculine"?

I am aware of an obvious inference: from every quarter have I heard exclamations against B masculine women; but where are they to be found? If by this appellation men mean to inveigh against their ardor[3] in hunting, shooting, and gaming, I shall most cordially join in the cry; but if it be against the imitation of manly virtues, or, more properly speaking, the attainment of those talents and virtues, the exercise of which ennobles the human character, and which raise females in the scale of animal being, when they are comprehensively termed mankind; all those who view them with a philosophic eye must, I should think, wish with me, that they may every day grow more and more masculine. . . .

My own sex, I hope, will excuse me, if I treat them like rational creatures, instead of flattering their

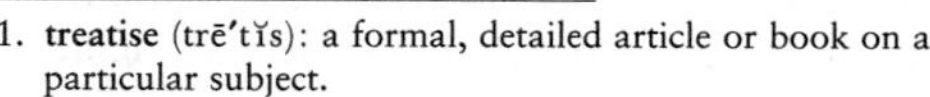

1. **treatise** (trē′tĭs): a formal, detailed article or book on a particular subject.
2. **abrogated** (ăb′rə-gā′tĭd): canceled; repealed.
3. **if by . . . ardor:** if by this word (that is, *masculine*) men mean to condemn some women's enthusiasm.

WORDS TO KNOW
specious (spē′shəs) *adj.* attractive in a deceptive or insincere way
subordinate (sə-bôr′dn-ĭt) *adj.* less important; lower in rank

633

Customizing Instruction

Less Proficient Readers

Set a Purpose Students may find the selection's style difficult, but its message of gender equality will be familiar and accessible. Have students begin a two-column chart with the heading *Problem* in the first column and *Solution* in the second column. As students read, encourage them to write down the problems Wollstonecraft identifies in the first column and the solution, if any, that she suggests in the second column.

Students Acquiring English

Students may have difficulty with usages that they will not find in contemporary English, such as "the historic page" in the first sentence. Alert students to uncommon usages such as *partial* meaning "prejudiced" (rather than "in part"). Students may also benefit from meeting in small groups after reading the selection individually to discuss phrases they did not understand as well as the main idea of each section of the essay.

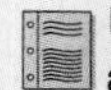

Use **Spanish Study Guide** for additional support, pp. 138–140.

Gifted and Talented

Invite students to imagine additional ways that Wollstonecraft's opponents might have attempted to counter her argument. Then, ask students to add arguments of their own to bolster Wollstonecraft's.

BLOCK SCHEDULING: MANAGING TIME

If your schedule requires that you cover the lesson objectives in a shorter time, use . . .
- Preparing to Read, p. 631
- Thinking Through the Literature, p. 637
- Vocabulary in Action, p. 638

If you want to take advantage of longer class time, use . . .
- TE Teaching Options: Preteaching Vocabulary, p. 632; Grammar, p. 634
- Choices & Challenges, p. 638

Reading and Analyzing

Literary Analysis: ESSAY

Review with students that an essay is a short work of nonfiction that deals with a single subject. Ask students to identify the subject of Wollstonecraft's essay. What is her purpose in writing this piece?

Possible Responses: Her subject is the place of women in her society; her purpose is to persuade her readers that the education of women must change for the better.

Literary Analysis ARGUMENTATION

A Ask students to explain Wollstonecraft's argument against the system of marriage in her society. Why isn't this system beneficial to women?

Answer: Wollstonecraft thinks that women focus on improving their superficial attributes, such as physical beauty, so they can marry but that they are then dependent on their husbands. Such dependence makes them no better than animals or children and renders them incapable of raising and educating children of their own.

Literary Analysis: PARALLELISM

B Ask students what parallel construction is used in the sentence beginning "And this desire . . ."

Answer: "They dress; they paint, and [they] nickname . . . ."

ACTIVE READING

C **ANALYZE** She claims that independence is the key to self-respect and respectability. A woman must first find strength within herself; her ability to please others and to gain the affection of her husband will follow.

fascinating graces, and viewing them as if they were in a state of perpetual childhood, unable to stand alone. I earnestly wish to point out in what true dignity and human happiness consists—I wish to persuade women to endeavor to acquire strength, both of mind and body, and to convince them that the soft phrases, susceptibility of heart, delicacy of sentiment, and refinement of taste, are almost synonymous with epithets[4] of weakness, and that those beings who are only the objects of pity and that kind of love, which has been termed its sister, will soon become objects of contempt. . . .

The education of women has, of late, been more attended to than formerly; yet they are still reckoned a frivolous sex, and ridiculed or pitied by the writers who endeavor by satire or instruction to improve them. It is acknowledged that they spend many of the first years of their lives in acquiring a smattering of accomplishments; meanwhile strength of body and mind are sacrificed to libertine[5] notions of beauty, to the desire of establishing themselves—the only way women can rise in the world—by marriage. And this desire making mere animals of them, when they marry they act as such children may be expected to act: they dress; they paint, and nickname God's creatures. Surely these weak beings are only fit for a seraglio![6] Can they be expected to govern a family with judgment, or take care of the poor babes whom they bring into the world?

If then it can be fairly deduced from the present conduct of the sex, from the prevalent fondness for pleasure which takes place of ambition and those nobler passions that open and enlarge the soul; that the instruction which women have hitherto received has only tended, with the constitution of civil society, to render them insignificant objects of desire—mere propagators of fools!—if it can be proved that in aiming to accomplish them, without cultivating their understandings, they are taken out of their sphere of duties, and made ridiculous and useless when the short-lived bloom of beauty is over, I presume that *rational* men will excuse me for endeavoring to persuade them to become more masculine and respectable.

Indeed the word masculine is only a bugbear:[7] there is little reason to fear that women will acquire too much courage or fortitude; for their apparent inferiority with respect to bodily strength, must render them, in some degree, dependent on men in the various relations of life; but why should it be increased by prejudices that give a sex to virtue, and confound simple truths with sensual reveries?[8]

FROM CHAPTER 2

Youth is the season for love in both sexes; but in those days of thoughtless enjoyment provision should be made for the more important years of life, when reflection takes place of sensation. But Rousseau, and most of the male writers who have followed his steps, have warmly inculcated[9] that the whole tendency of female education ought to be directed to one point: to render them pleasing.

Let me reason with the supporters of this opinion who have any knowledge of human nature, do they imagine that marriage can

4. **epithets:** descriptive terms.
5. **libertine** (lĭb′ər-tēn′): indecent or unseemly.
6. **seraglio** (sə-răl′yō): harem.
7. **bugbear:** an object of exaggerated fear.
8. **confound . . . reveries:** confuse simple truths with sexual daydreams.
9. **inculcated** (ĭn-kŭl′kā′tĭd): taught.

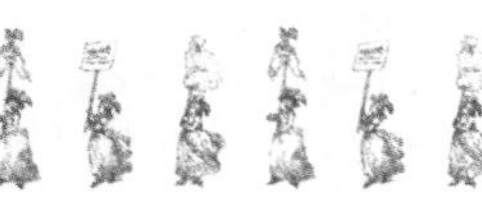

Teaching Options

Grammar

VERBALS AND VERBAL PHRASES

Instruction A verbal is a verb form that is used as a noun, adjective, or an adverb. There are three kinds of verbals: infinitive *(to educate)*, participle *(educating, educated)*, and gerund *(educating)*. When verbals have modifiers and complements, they are called verbal phrases.

Distinguish between a verbal phrase and a verb phrase by reminding students that a verbal phrase consists of a verbal and its modifiers *(Educating all women was her goal)*, while a verb phrase is the main verb of a clause and one or more auxiliary verbs *(Wollstonecraft's works have been educating men and women since the 18th century)*.

Activity Write the following sentences on the chalkboard.

"After considering the historic page, and viewing the living world with anxious solicitude, . . . I have sighed when obliged to confess, that either nature has made a great difference between man and man, or that the civilization which has hitherto taken place in the world has been very partial."

Have students identify the underlined verbals.

1 eradicate the habitude of life? The woman who has only been taught to please will soon find that her charms are oblique sunbeams, and that they cannot have much effect on her husband's heart when they are seen every day, when the summer is passed and gone. Will she then have sufficient native energy to look into herself for comfort, and cultivate her dormant faculties? or, is it not more rational to expect that she will try to please other men; and, in the emotions raised by the expectation of new conquests, endeavor to forget the mortification her love or pride has received? When the husband ceases to be a lover—and the time will inevitably come, her desire of pleasing will then grow languid, or become a spring of bitterness; and love, perhaps, the most evanescent[10] of all passions, gives place to jealousy or vanity.

I now speak of women who are restrained by principle or prejudice; such women, though they would shrink from an intrigue with real abhorrence, yet, nevertheless, wish to be convinced by the homage of gallantry that they are cruelly neglected by their husbands; or, days and weeks are spent in dreaming of the happiness enjoyed by congenial souls till their health is undermined and their spirits broken by discontent. How then can the great art of pleasing be such a necessary study? it is only useful to a mistress; the chaste wife, and serious mother, should only consider her power to please as the polish of her virtues, and the affection of her husband as one of the comforts that render her talk less difficult and her life happier. But, whether she be loved or neglected, her first wish should be to make herself respectable, and not to rely for all her happiness on a being subject to like infirmities with herself.

ACTIVE READING

C **ANALYZE** How does Wollstonecraft suggest that a woman "make herself respectable"?

The worthy Dr. Gregory fell into a similar error. I respect his heart; but entirely disapprove of his celebrated Legacy to his Daughters. . . .

He actually recommends dissimulation,[11] and advises an innocent girl to give the lie to her feelings, and not dance with spirit, when gaiety of heart would make her feet eloquent without making her gestures immodest. In the name of truth and common sense, why should not one woman acknowledge that she can take more exercise than another? or, in other words, that she has a sound constitution; and why, to damp innocent vivacity, is she darkly to be told that men will draw conclusions which she little thinks of? Let the libertine draw what inference he pleases; but, I hope, that no sensible mother will restrain the natural frankness of youth by instilling such indecent cautions. Out of the abundance of the heart the mouth speaketh; and a wiser than Solomon hath said, that the heart should be made clean, and not trivial ceremonies observed, which it is not very difficult to fulfil with scrupulous exactness when vice reigns in the heart.

Women ought to endeavor to purify their heart; but can they do so when their uncultivated understandings make them entirely dependent on their senses for employment and amusement, when no noble pursuit sets them above the little vanities of the day, or enables them to curb the wild emotions that agitate a reed over which every passing breeze has power? To gain the affections of a virtuous man, is affectation necessary? Nature has given woman a weaker frame than man; but, to ensure her husband's

10. **evanescent** (ĕv′ə-nĕs′ənt): quickly vanishing; fleeting.

11. **dissimulation:** a concealing of one's true feelings; pretense.

WORDS TO KNOW

languid (lăng′gwĭd) *adj.* sluggish; weak
vivacity (vĭ-văs′ĭ-tē) *n.* liveliness
affectation (ăf′ĕk-tā′shən) *n.* unnatural behavior; conduct intended to give a false impression

635

Customizing Instruction

Less Proficient Readers

Make sure students understand Wollstonecraft's position regarding women. Use the following questions:

- Does Wollstonecraft think women should cultivate their good looks or their minds, and why?
  Answer: Women should cultivate their reason. Intellectual development is a lasting virtue, while physical beauty and youth eventually fade.
- What was a woman's best option for establishing herself in eighteenth-century society?
  Answer: Women were expected to marry as a way of gaining social status, which they acquired through their husbands.
- What does Wollstonecraft say about the way women in her time are educated?
  Answer: They are educated to be pleasing to men.

Students Acquiring English

1 Help students figure out what the author means by "eradicate the habitude of life." Explain that *eradicate* means "erase." Point out that *habitude* contains the word *habit.* Thus, the phrase means "enable a person to stop doing the things she has done all her life."

Gifted and Talented

Have students imagine that they are giving Mary Wollstonecraft a tour of our twentieth-century society. Students could explain current conventions surrounding marriage and weddings, the positions of men and women in the workplace, contemporary thoughts on education for men and women, and expectations men and women have about domestic responsibility and caring for a family.

(considering–gerund; viewing–gerund; living–participle; to confess–infinitive) Next ask students to identify the verbal phrases. *(considering the historic page; viewing the living world with anxious solicitude. Both are gerund verbal phrases and function as objects of the preposition "After".)*

Exercise Have students identify each underlined verbal phrase as an infinitive, gerund, or participle phrase. Then ask them to name the function each serves in the sentence. Have students meet in cooperative groups to discuss their answers.

1. A woman should learn not to depend on a man's appreciation of her beauty for happiness. *(infinitive phrase; direct object of the verb "learn")*
2. To be independent a woman must be granted the right to be educated like a man. *(infinitive phrase, adjective, modifying the noun "woman"; infinitive phrase, adjective, modifying the noun "right")*

Use **Grammar Transparencies and Copymasters,** p. 94.

Use McDougal Littell's ***Language Network*** for more instruction in verbals and verbal phrases.

Reading and Analyzing

Active Reading

RECOGNIZING LOGICAL PERSUASION

Have students discuss how Wollstonecraft uses her own performance in the essay itself to demonstrate the qualities she advocates for all women.

Possible Response: She encourages women to cultivate their minds and to rely on reason rather than emotion; her essay, which is a persuasive logical argument, relies on appeals to logic instead of feeling.

ACTIVE READING

A **EVALUATE** She condemns marriage in which a wife pretends that she is frail in order to make her husband feel that she is dependent on him and in which the wife has no further goal or ambition once she has gotten married.

Literary Analysis: PARALLELISM

B Ask students to identify the parallel construction that unifies the sentence beginning "If all the faculties . . ."

Answer: "If . . . if . . . but, if . . ."

affections, must a wife, who by the exercise of her mind and body whilst she was discharging the duties of a daughter, wife, and mother, has allowed her constitution to retain its natural strength, and her nerves a healthy tone, is she, I say, to condescend to use art and feign a sickly delicacy in order to secure her husband's affection? Weakness may excite tenderness, and gratify the arrogant pride of man; but the lordly caresses of a protector will not gratify a noble mind that pants for, and deserves to be respected. Fondness is a poor substitute for friendship! . . .

Besides, the woman who strengthens her body and exercises her mind will, by managing her family and practicing various virtues, become the friend, and not the humble dependent of her husband; and if she, by possessing such substantial qualities, merit his regard, she will not find it necessary to conceal her affection, nor to pretend to an unnatural coldness of constitution to excite her husband's passions. . . .

ACTIVE READING

A **EVALUATE** What type of marriage is Wollstonecraft condemning?

If all the faculties of woman's mind are only to be cultivated as they respect her dependence on man; if, when a husband be obtained, she have arrived at her goal, and meanly proud rests satisfied with such a paltry crown, let her grovel contentedly, scarcely raised by her employments above the animal kingdom; B but, if, struggling for the prize of her high calling, she look beyond the present scene, let her cultivate her understanding without stopping to consider what character the husband may have whom she is destined to marry. Let her only determine, without being too anxious about present happiness, to acquire the qualities that ennoble a rational being, and a rough inelegant husband may shock her taste without destroying her peace of mind. She will not model her soul to suit the frailties of her companion, but to bear with them: his character may be a trial, but not an impediment to virtue. . . .

These may be termed Utopian dreams. Thanks to that Being who impressed them on my soul, and gave me sufficient strength of mind to dare to exert my own reason, till, becoming dependent only on him for the support of my virtue, I view, with indignation, the mistaken notions that enslave my sex.

I love man as my fellow; but his scepter, real, or usurped, extends not to me, unless the reason of an individual demands my homage; and even then the submission is to reason, and not to man. In fact, the conduct of an accountable being must be regulated by the operations of its own reason; or on what foundation rests the throne of God?

It appears to me necessary to dwell on these obvious truths, because females have been insulated, as it were; and, while they have been stripped of the virtues that should clothe humanity, they have been decked with artificial graces that enable them to exercise a short-lived tyranny. Love, in their bosoms, taking place of every nobler passion, their sole ambition is to be fair, to raise emotion instead of inspiring respect; and this ignoble desire, like the servility in absolute monarchies, destroys all strength of character. Liberty is the mother of virtue, and if women be, by their very constitution, slaves, and not allowed to breathe the sharp invigorating air of freedom, they must ever languish like exotics,[12] and be reckoned beautiful flaws in nature.

12. **languish like exotics:** wilt like plants grown away from their natural environment.

WORDS TO KNOW
feign (fān) *v.* to give a false appearance of; simulate or counterfeit
grovel (grŏv′əl) *v.* to behave with exaggerated submission or humility
ignoble (ĭg-nō′bəl) *adj.* not noble; degrading; contemptible

Teaching Options

Mini Lesson

Vocabulary Strategy

ROOT WORDS: *Affectation*

Instruction Explain that a **root word** is the simple component that provides the basis of a word. Students can apply the meanings of roots to comprehend unfamiliar words and build vocabulary.

Activity Have students find the root of *affectation,* which is *affect* (a verb meaning "to put on a pretense of"). Then, have students think of other words with this root or other forms of this word, using the dictionary if necessary. Students should use the new words or forms in a sentence.

Model

- affectation = affect (root word)
- new word or form: affected—"pretended; assumed falsely"
- sample sentence: Her manner was extremely *affected* in an effort to impress her boss.

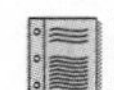 Use **Vocabulary Transparencies and Copymasters,** p. 50.

Connect to the Literature

1. **What Do You Think?** Would you like to hear Wollstonecraft speak on women's rights? Explain why or why not.

Comprehension Check
- How does a woman's lack of education affect her husband and children?
- Why does the author encourage women to strengthen their bodies?

Think Critically

2. In your opinion, what "manly virtues" does Wollstonecraft want women to imitate?

3. How do you think Wollstonecraft would describe a good marriage?

THINK ABOUT
- the kinds of female behavior she criticizes
- her complaints about the attitude of men toward women
- the qualities she would like women to acquire
- her reasons for encouraging women to strengthen their minds

4. Do you think Wollstonecraft believes in the complete equality of men and women?

5. **ACTIVE READING** **RECOGNIZING LOGICAL PERSUASION** With a partner, use the chart in your **READER'S NOTEBOOK** to discuss Wollstonecraft's specific responses to opposing views. Do you think this technique is an effective tool against the opposition? Why or why not?

Extend Interpretations

6. **Comparing Texts** Compare Wollstonecraft's views with those expressed by Defoe in "An Academy for Women" (page 577). How are their attitudes toward women alike? How are they different?

7. **Connect to Life** In your opinion, what social issues would concern Wollstonecraft today? Would she still feel a need to defend women's rights? Discuss your ideas.

Literary Analysis

ARGUMENTATION Writing that seeks to convince readers to adopt or reject an idea or proposal is referred to as **argumentation.** In *A Vindication of the Rights of Woman,* Wollstonecraft attempts to convince her readers that women should receive a better education. The writer supports her proposal with logical evidence. In the following excerpt, for example, Wollstonecraft reasons against limiting a woman's education to the simple goal of rendering her pleasing to a husband.

The woman who has only been taught to please will soon find that her charms are oblique sunbeams, and that they cannot have much effect on her husband's heart when they are seen every day, when the summer is passed and gone.

Cooperative Learning Activity With a small group of classmates, evaluate the evidence Wollstonecraft uses to support her opinion on the education of women. What points do you think are most convincing? What additional points would have strengthened her argument? Use a chart like the one below to keep track of your ideas.

Convincing Evidence	Additional Points

GUIDING STUDENT RESPONSE

Connect to the Literature

1. **What Do You Think?** Guidelines for student response: Some students would undoubtedly like to hear Wollstonecraft speak and others would not. Ask students to provide reasons for their likes and dislikes.

Comprehension Check
- She may be a weak wife and a mother with little judgment in raising her children.
- Strength of body is an important part of a woman's ability to manage her family's affairs and thus earn her husband's respect and friendship.

Use Selection Quiz in **Unit Three Resource Book,** p. 62.

Think Critically

2. Possible Responses: independence, strength of character, rational thought, courage.
3. Possible Response: Wollstonecraft argues for a form of marriage in which the wife cultivates her own inner resources rather than molding herself to her husband's wishes.
4. Some students may say that Wollstonecraft is arguing for as much equality as was conceivable in her time. Others may feel that by granting the physical superiority of men, she is retreating from equality.
5. As students discuss their responses, be sure they indicate how this structure influences their understanding. Some students will find that Wollstonecraft's use of this technique influences them to see her argument as evenhanded, reasonable, and effective; others may feel that this technique limits their understanding because she stacks the deck in her favor by setting up only opposing views that she can convincingly undermine.

Literary Analysis

Cooperative Learning Activity In their critical analysis, students should evaluate the effectiveness of Wollstonecraft's essay.

Extend Interpretations

Comparing Texts Both authors feel that denying education to women wastes their native wit and intelligence. They agree that many people hold women in contempt for being silly and foolish, yet those same people support the current customs that segregate women from rational discourse. Students may differ as to whether the two authors were similarly egalitarian and progressive or whether Defoe still saw women as naturally dependent on men.

Connect to Life Possible responses: inequality in the workplace (for example, women paid less than men for doing the same job), unequal access to education (for example, the existence of all-male military academies), the conflicts faced by women who want both to work outside the home and to raise a family.

Writing Options

1. **Opinion Paper** Encourage students to prewrite using a technique they feel comfortable with, such as freewriting, clustering, or outlining. Next, have students trade papers with a classmate. Tell students to look for clear, logical reasons that support the writer's opinion. Then, have students meet with their partners to discuss each other's reactions. Encourage students to revise their drafts, incorporating their partner's comments.
2. **Questions and Answers** You may want to have students brainstorm questions in small groups. Then they can choose to answer questions that most interest them.

Vocabulary in Action

Exercise

1. phony
2. pep
3. a lie
4. a pat on the shoulder
5. timidly
6. sit on the beach
7. on their knees
8. a real rat
9. putting on airs
10. a scheduling conflict

Writing Options

1. **Opinion Paper** Draft an opinion paper on the importance of cultivating one's mind. Use any of Wollstonecraft's reasons with which you agree, but also add some of your own.
2. **Questions and Answers** Create a set of questions you would like to ask Wollstonecraft, and then write what you think her answers would be.

Vocabulary in Action

EXERCISE: MEANING CLUES Use your knowledge of the boldfaced words to answer the following questions.

1. Are people who **feign** friendship being loyal, being rude, or being phony?
2. Is a person who displays **vivacity** showing conceit, showing pep, or showing wealth?
3. Is a **specious** statement a truth, a mistake, or a lie?
4. Which is a sign of **solicitude**—a salute, a yawn, or a pat on the shoulder?
5. Would a person who feels **subordinate** speak forcefully, moderately, or timidly?
6. Would a person who's feeling **languid** be most likely to want to sit on the beach, to climb a mountain, or to dig at an archaeological site?
7. Are people who **grovel** while asking for something most likely to ask on their knees, with their noses in the air, or while shaking their fists?
8. Is an **ignoble** man most likely to be described as a prince of a fellow, a giant in his field, or a real rat?
9. If you felt that someone was displaying **affectation,** would you say that the person was cracking the whip, was putting on airs, or was looking on the bright side?
10. If you can't take Beginning Art and Advanced Drama because they are **concurring** classes, is your problem due to a scheduling conflict, a lack of training, or a lack of space?

Building Vocabulary
For an in-depth lesson on how to expand your vocabulary, see page 1182.

Mary Wollstonecraft
1759–1797

Other Works
A Vindication of the Rights of Men

Difficult Childhood Mary Wollstonecraft's unusual and difficult childhood taught her to question conventional attitudes about women. Her family moved frequently as her alcoholic father pursued a series of unsuccessful farming ventures in which he used up the family's money, including the money promised to his daughters by their grandfather. In this impoverished, chaotic household, Wollstonecraft received only six or seven years of formal education and was mostly self-taught.

Self-Made Woman At age 19, Wollstonecraft left home to take a job as companion to a rich widow. When she was 22, she opened a private school near London, and although the project was short-lived, it introduced her to important friends who encouraged her to write. Wollstonecraft had taught herself French and German, and in 1787 she was hired as a translator for a journal. She often participated in discussions with the journal's publisher, Joseph Johnson, and his circle of intellectual friends, including political essayist Thomas Paine, the poet William Blake, and the philosopher William Godwin.

Brief Happiness Wollstonecraft later developed a close friendship with Godwin and, at the age of 37, married him. Their happy but brief relationship ended unexpectedly when Wollstonecraft died less than a year later from inept medical care following childbirth. The couple's daughter—the future Mary Wollstonecraft Shelley—was to become famous in her own right as the author of *Frankenstein* and the wife of the poet Percy Bysshe Shelley.

Writing Workshop — Satire

Using Humor to Persuade . . .

A **From Reading to Writing** In "A Modest Proposal," Jonathan Swift uses wit and irony to draw attention to the serious social problems in 18th-century Ireland. Swift was a master of achieving biting social criticism through **satire,** a form of persuasive writing that uses humor to attack human vice or folly. By using satire, a writer can expose problems or argue for change in a way that is powerful but not preachy.

For Your Portfolio

WRITING PROMPT Write a **satire** on the subject of your choice.

Purpose: To persuade and entertain

Audience: Your peers, or a particular group who might be interested in the issues you address.

Basics in a Box

B **Satire at a Glance**

Object of Satire

Takes aim at a particular person, institution, or idea to call attention to a problem, folly, or vice.

Criticism

Uses humor, wit, and irony to attack the problem.

Humor

C **RUBRIC Standards for Writing**

A successful satire should

- poke fun at people, ideas, customs, or institutions to persuade readers to change
- use a tone that matches the goal
- use humor, exaggeration, understatement, and specific examples to reveal the subject in a more critical light
- make clear the object of the satire, but make the reader discover the writer's true perspective on the issue
- use a form that enhances the writer's purpose

Writing Workshop
Satire

Objectives
- write a Satire
- use a written text as a model for writing
- revise a draft for appropriate diction
- use correct pronoun-antecedent agreement

Introducing the Workshop

A **Satire**

Point out that satire is a literary technique used to ridicule the social practices or values of a society, a group, or a prominent individual. Usually, this involves portraying the subject in a way that shows it to be foolish, forcing readers to view the subject in a critical light. Have students name instances of satire with which they are familiar.

Satire is popular in television and film because of its biting humor. Political cartoons on the editorial page of the newspaper are also examples of satires. Their intention is to mock public figures or their political decisions. Point out that through writing a satire, students can ridicule a social or political practice in an amusing way. They can also use satire to call attention to a situation they would like to see changed.

Basics in a Box

B **Using the Graphic**

The graphic representation of a target captures the point of satire: It is created with a specific "target" in mind. The two arrows aimed at the target suggest how criticism and humor are synthesized to create a successful satire.

C **Presenting the Rubric**

To better understand the assignment, students can refer to the Standards for Writing a Successful Satire. You may wish to discuss with them the complete rubric, which describes several levels of proficiency. The rubric may be used as an effective standard for evaluating student writing.

To engage students visually, use **Power Presentation** 5, Satire.

LESSON RESOURCES

USING PRINT RESOURCES

Unit Three Resource Book
- Prewriting, p. 63
- Drafting, p. 64
- Peer Response, pp. 65–66
- Revising, Editing, and Proofreading, p. 67
- Student Models, pp. 68–73
- Rubric, p. 74

Writing Transparencies and Copymasters
- Writing Process Transparencies, pp. 3, 4
- Writing Style Transparencies, p. 13
- Writing Template Copymasters, p. 29

USING MEDIA RESOURCES

LaserLinks

Writing Springboards

See Teacher's SourceBook p. 114 for bar codes.

Writing Coach CD-ROM

Visit our website: www.mcdougallittell.com

For a complete view of Lesson Resources, see page 515g.

Teaching the Lesson

Analyzing the Model

"A New 'Modest Proposal'"

D Discuss the term *welfare* as in *welfare reform.* Explain that the term means financial aid provided to people in need, and that this aid is usually provided by the government. Another term students need to know is *rescind,* which means to repeal or revoke.

The essay students are about to read is a professional writer's response to Congress passing legislation concerning welfare reform.

After students read the model, challenge them to state the serious problem that lies at the heart of the satire and the human consequences of that problem. For example, who will be affected by the problem the writer has identified?

Possible Response The writer feels that Congress made a serious mistake by reforming the welfare system. Children of the poor will suffer because of the decisions of Congress.

Discuss the Rubric in Action. Point out the key words and phrases in the professional model that correspond to the elements mentioned in the Rubric in Action.

2. Explain that satire can be found in many forms. Students need not feel restricted to writing a satirical essay.
3. Point out that the transitional phrase "but now" signals a shift from the brief historical background on childhood to the present reality of welfare reform.
4. Ask students to analyze the irony in the phrase "teensy-weensy reservations."

   Possible Response: It is ironic because the writer means the opposite of what she says. Congress should, in fact, have great reservations about cutting money from the poorest children. Through understatement the writer makes her point that children are very important. Students should evaluate and discuss the model's effectiveness as a satire based on the rubric and other criteria you develop for the writing.

Analyzing a Professional Model

Ellen Goodman
Columnist, the *Boston Globe*

RUBRIC IN ACTION

A New "Modest Proposal"

Now that we have repealed welfare, I have a modest proposal. Let's go all the way and rescind childhood.

Childhood has become far too burdensome for the American public to bear. It isn't good for the country. It isn't even good for children who are captured in an unwholesome and prolonged state of dependency.

The whole idea of childhood, it should be remembered, is nothing but an anachronistic leftover from the original liberals. Before the so-called Enlightenment, before Rousseau, before the left-wing conspiracy of 18th-century do-gooders, the young dressed, worked and were looked upon as short adults.

Children existed, but they didn't have their own 'hood—a place where they were supposed to be educated and nurtured until they reached maturity. Adolescence, for that matter, wasn't invented until the early 20th century. Nor was the concept of juvenile as in delinquency, nor the notion of teen-age as in pregnancy.

But now we are stuck with this useless thing called childhood, a drain on the private and public exchequers. Not to mention a merciless drag on the private and public conscience.

Consider what happened when Congress passed and the president approved the "Personal Responsibility and Work Opportunity Act" (a.k.a. welfare reform). The only teensy-weensy reservations about cutting $56 billion from the poorest Americans, ending the federal guarantee of assistance to poor families and launching them into the unknown, had to do with children.

There are still a handful of people troubled by the fact that America has the highest child poverty rates of any industrialized country and that when this "reform" clicks in, a million more children are expected to become poor.

Why not eliminate all this messy, counterproductive guilt? Why not apply the same principles of "personal responsibility" and "work opportunity" to our youngest citizens?

I am not alone in my plan, though perhaps I am the first to put it quite so baldly. But we are already erasing the line between childhood and adulthood whenever we want to.

❶ Sets a humorous, ironic tone with a seemingly preposterous proposal

❷ This writer uses the form of a persuasive essay.

Another Option:
- Use another format such as a narrative, poem, drama, letter, or cartoon.

❸ Uses exaggeration to make point

❹ This writer introduces the real object of her satire after establishing the overall tone.

Other Option:
- Identify the object of satire up-front.

At the Olympics, we had 14-year-old gymnasts on the "Women's Team." In the states, we now have plans to try 13-year-old lawbreakers as adults. In Congress they are considering doing away with juvenile jails and "mainstreaming" kids with older criminals. Across the world, the "new economy" is using kids as a way to meet global competition.

Most Americans already recognize that childhood is simply not cost-effective. If children were once economic assets, they are now deficits, unlikely to ever pay back our investments. So only a third of our households have anyone under 18 in them today. Communities that once felt a collective responsibility for the next generation now often regard children as private property to be exclusively maintained by their owners.

If we eliminated the entire notion of childhood we wouldn't have to worry about children having children. Or about child care. Or after-school care. Or school. Child labor would become another "work opportunity."

Of course, we could retain childhood as a luxury item for those who could afford it. Sort of like an Ivy League college. The rest, the poor especially, will have to do without childhood the way they do without so much else. . . .

The last great evil in America today is dependency. The last remaining "culture of dependency" is, of course, childhood. Is it any wonder that it has to go?

If my modest proposal seems too harsh, may I remind you of the one Jonathan Swift offered in 1729: "A Modest Proposal for Preventing the Children of Poor People in Ireland from Being a Burden to Their Parents or Country and for Making Them Beneficial to the Public."

Swift proposed, modestly and satirically, that the Irish young be sold and eaten. They would be as well off as growing up in poverty under British policy.

I would never suggest such a thing. But come to think of it, this reckless "reform" is also cutting food stamps by about a fifth. Maybe Swift was just ahead of his time.

5 Cites specific examples to expose the absurdity of the situation

6 Uses exaggeration to reinforce point

7 This writer departs from satire by allowing her own voice to be heard.

Another Option:
- Stay in the satirical mode through the end of the piece.

5. The writer's use of these factual examples lends credibility to her proposal to abolish childhood. It also points out how society is already moving in that direction.
6. Discuss with students the reference here to an Ivy League education. What is she referring to when she says childhood is similarly a "luxury item"?
   Possible Response: An Ivy League education refers to education in elite, expensive colleges and universities. The author feels that the rich are more likely to receive Ivy League educations and the rich also will be more able to afford the luxury of childhood.
7. Ask students to evaluate the effectiveness of the writer's shift into her own voice at the end by using the phrase "reckless 'reform,'" rather than remaining in a satirical voice.
   Possible Responses: Some will say that the shift is effective and that revealing the writer's own voice means the readers will not miss the point of the satire. Others will say that the shift is an intrusion, and the satire could be more effective had the writer kept her own political views hidden.

Guiding Student Writing

Prewriting

Choosing a Topic

If after reading the Idea Bank students are having difficulty choosing their topics, suggest they try the following:

- Collect political cartoons from local and national newspapers to see the kinds of topics that are commonly satirized.
- Complete the following sentence frames for as many topics as come to mind:

  The most ridiculous statement I've ever heard is . . .

  The most ridiculous decision I've ever seen is . . .
- Watch a satirical comedy on television to get a feel for the kinds of subjects that are satirized and the approach that writers take in satirizing them.

Planning the Satire

1. Remind students that when they analyze, they break down a subject into its various parts. Students might make a quick list of features about their subject that they could ridicule.
2. You might consider allowing pairs or small groups of students to work together to create a satirical skit.
3. Have students consider what effect they want their satire to have on their audience. Remind students that the purpose of satire is corrective as well as comic.
4. Point out that understatement is the opposite of exaggeration. Understatement creates emphasis by saying less than what is actually true.

Drafting

Point out that irony—saying the opposite of what the writer intends—is a key element in creating satire. Have students include examples that expose the humor or absurdity of the situation they are satirizing. They may wish to save their most ridiculous example for last. Caution students that satire should not be offensive.

IDEABank

1. Your Working Portfolio
Build on one of the Writing Options you completed earlier in this unit:
- **Persuasive Letter,** p. 583
- **Another Proposal,** p. 622

2. Community Action
With a small group of classmates, make a list of problems in your school or community. Choose one problem as the subject of your satire.

3. Sound Bites
Many magazines and newspapers list "quotes of the week." These are oftentimes ironic or absurd. Choose one of these quotations as the basis for your satire.

Writing Your Satire

❶ Prewriting

What really bugs you? Make a list of everything from your personal pet peeves to global concerns. Include such things as rude drivers, ridiculous dress codes, gender stereotyping, air pollution, and ethnic wars. Scan newspapers and magazines to jog your memory about topics important to you. Then think carefully about each topic on your list. Which topics evoke strong feelings in you? See the **Ideas Bank** for more suggestions. After you select your topic, follow the steps below.

Planning Your Satire

1. **Dissect your victim.** Satire depends on a careful analysis and evaluation of the target subject. Pick apart those aspects of your subject that seem weak or absurd and plan to highlight these in your piece.
2. **Choose a form.** Satire comes in all sizes, shapes, and forms. It can be a letter, a proposal, an advice column, a report, an essay, a speech, or a story. Select a form that you think fits your subject.
3. **Match your tone with your goal.** Do you want to poke gentle fun or offer biting criticism? Your goal should determine your tone.
4. **Flaunt your attitude.** Satire enables writers to go too far. You can make absurd and ridiculous suggestions. You can **exaggerate** the importance of trivial events or facts. You can **understate** critical truths. It's all part of your attitude, and with the right use of satirical techniques you can pull it off.

❷ Drafting

Freewriting can help you discover your satirical **voice.** Just start writing and don't worry about how it sounds yet. Keep going until you begin to develop a sense of who is talking and how your ideas are taking shape. You can go back later and revise your piece so the voice is consistent throughout.

Keep in mind that satire needs to hit the topic hard so your readers have no doubt about the issue you are addressing. You want, however, to be subtle and indirect about where you really stand on this issue. Let your readers mull over your ideas and figure out your true feelings.

Have a question?

See Satire in the Glossary of Literary Terms, p. 1348.

Ask Your Peer Reader

- What subject or issue is being addressed?
- How would you state my true feelings about it?
- Is it clear that the work is satiric? Why or why not?
- What parts work best? How would you improve the piece?

❸ Revising

TARGET SKILL ▶ USING APPROPRIATE DICTION Keep in mind that diction—the words you choose—helps set the tone for your satire. Diction can be formal or informal, technical or general, depending on the purpose. As you revise, choose words that best suit your tone and subject. In general, avoid wordiness, clichés, and jargon. In this model, the writer uses an informal tone.

> The federal government warns us that our national parks are being "loved to death." ~~Each and~~ every [Every] year, more [people] ~~individuals~~ visit the parks. [Campgrounds fill up. Traffic clogs the roads.] ~~Accommodations and transportation facilities are utilized beyond capacity. On the flip side,~~ [Yet] park fees do not bring in enough revenue to pay for park maintenance. ~~Someone has to pay the piper.~~ What to do? It's simple: [Turn the parks over] ~~Give the reins~~ to one of the giant entertainment companies and let it run them.

Need revising help?

Review the **Rubric,** p. 639

Consider **peer reader** comments

Check **Revision Guidelines,** p. 1355.

❹ Editing

TARGET SKILL ▶ PRONOUN-ANTECEDENT AGREEMENT Now check to see that all personal pronouns agree with their antecedents in number (singular or plural), gender (masculine, feminine, or neuter), and person (first, second, or third).

> Just think what a company that runs theme parks could do if [it] ~~they~~ ran the national parks. First, quadruple the entrance fees. Make ~~a~~ visitor[s] think twice before they come to a park. Of course, [people] ~~everyone~~ would expect more than scenery for [their] ~~your~~ money. An entertainment company could add [its] ~~your~~ usual mix of thrilling rides and activities. Imagine the sensation of being whisked down the Grand Canyon on a high-speed roller coaster. Park patrons might miss a bit of the scenery, but that's nothing compared to the thrill [they'll] ~~you'll~~ experience.

Stumped by pronoun-antecedent agreement?

See **Pronoun Agreement,** p. 1398

Publishing IDEAS

- Use your satire as a broadcast news commentary for a classroom radio or TV show.
- Adapt your satire as a comedy skit or make it part of a magazine featuring your class's satires.

More Online: Publishing Options
www.mcdougallittell.com

❺ Reflecting

FOR YOUR WORKING PORTFOLIO How did others respond to your satire? Do you think your writing could help correct the situation you satirized? Why or why not? Attach your answer to your finished work. Save your satire in your **Working Portfolio.**

Revising

USING APPROPRIATE DICTION

Point out that in the example the writer does not have a clear sense of who the audience is. The writer shifts back and forth between formal and informal word choice. The sentence "Accommodations and transportation facilities are utilized beyond capacity" is formal and would be appropriate in a government report. However, the writer follows with informal phrases and clichés, such as "on the flip side," "pay the piper," and "give the reins to."

Have students keep their audience in mind as they choose the words in their own satire. Sometimes it is appropriate for a writer to choose formal words. Other times informal words would work better. Whichever style students choose, remind them to be consistent throughout their writing.

Editing

PRONOUN-ANTECEDENT AGREEMENT

Point out particular problem areas in pronoun-antecedent agreement by reviewing the following rules:

Number These indefinite pronouns are singular:
another, anybody, anyone, anything, each, either, everybody, everyone, everything, neither, nobody, no one, one, somebody, someone

Each player brought *her* own shoes.

Gender When a singular pronoun refers to an antecedent that includes both males and females, the phrase "his or her" can be used.

Each player brought *his or her* own shoes.

Person A personal pronoun must be in the same person as its antecedent. The pronouns *one, everybody,* and *everyone* are in the third person and require a third-person pronoun.

Everyone should turn in *his or her* paper when finished.

Reflecting

As students think about how others responded to their satire, have them consider whether their subject was clear to their readers. Did they leave their readers challenged but not offended? Have students add these self-evaluations to their working portfolios.

Assessment Practice

Before students begin correcting the errors, you might remind them that it is incorrect to use two or more negative words to express a single negative idea.

Answers:

1. B; **2.** D; **3.** A; **4.** A; **5.** D; **6.** D

Assessment Practice Revising & Editing

Read this paragraph from the first draft of a satire. The underlined sections include the following kinds of errors:

- **fragments**
- **double negatives**
- **lack of pronoun-antecedent agreement**
- **misplaced modifiers**

For each underlined phrase or sentence, choose the revision that most improves the writing.

> Computers are no longer just an option for students: those (1) are an essential tool. Today no student can learn without these electronic brains. (2) When is the right time for a first computer? Children should have mastered computer basics. By the time (3) they enter kindergarten. Education specialist Dr. Gwendolyn Flugelhorn states that children should receive their first computers as infants in her published paper. (4) These computers will be lifelong tutors. They (5) will help children think efficiently. Annoying distractions such as daydreams and idle thoughts will no longer be problems. Children raised by this strategy won't hardly even need to go to school. (6)

1. **A.** them
   B. they
   C. those
   D. Correct as is
2. **A.** No student today can fail to learn without these electronic brains.
   B. No student today can hardly learn without these electronic brains.
   C. No students today can learn without these electronic brains.
   D. Correct as is
3. **A.** computer basics by the time
   B. computer basics, by the time
   C. computer basics, basics, by the time
   D. Correct as is
4. **A.** states in her published paper that children should receive their first computers as infants.
   B. states that children in her published paper should receive their first computers as infants.
   C. states that children should receive their first computers in her published paper as infants.
   D. Correct as is
5. **A.** it
   B. them
   C. their
   D. Correct as is
6. **A.** Children raised by this strategy won't barely need to go to school.
   B. Children raised by this strategy will need to go to school.
   C. Children raised by this strategy won't never need to go to school.
   D. Children raised by this strategy will hardly even need to go to school.

Need extra help?

See the **Grammar Handbook**
Writing Complete Sentences, pp. 1408–1409
Pronouns, p. 1398
Misplaced modifiers, p. 1403

Selecting the Right Word

> **The number of souls in this kingdom being usually reckoned one million and a half, of these I calculate there may be about two hundred thousand couple whose wives are breeders.**
> —Jonathan Swift, "A Modest Proposal"

Words have the power to impress and influence people on several different levels. In addition to their precise meanings, called **denotations,** words have implied meanings and overtones, called **connotations.** Writers often choose words with particular connotations in order to elicit emotional responses from readers. For example, what was your reaction to the use of the word *breeders* in the sentence on the left from "A Modest Proposal"?

Although the word *breeder* has the denotation "one that produces offspring," the word's most common application is to livestock, a connotation that Swift exploits throughout his essay. Swift chose the word for its emotional impact, because his purpose in writing the satirical "A Modest Proposal" was to persuade his readers that the policies he was attacking were inhuman.

Strategies for Building Vocabulary

Because readers are influenced by words' connotations as well as their denotations, you need to be aware of the layers of meaning that are implied, but not directly stated, when you read and when you write.

❶ Read Beyond the Literal Meaning Connotations play an important role in revealing a writer's attitude toward his or her subject—that is, in establishing the tone of a work. They can also help in enlisting readers' sympathies. As you read a work, consider the writer's purpose and the audience for which the work was intended. How, for example, does this excerpt from *A Vindication of the Rights of Woman* reveal Mary Wollstonecraft's opinion of the treatment of women in her society?

> **It is acknowledged that they [women] spend many of the first years of their lives in acquiring a smattering of accomplishments.**

Here the word *smattering* was probably chosen for its negative connotations. Wollstonecraft might have used *set* or *collection,* but those words would not have conveyed such associations of triviality. The persuasive power of her sentence would therefore have been diminished.

❷ Choose Words Carefully Although synonyms have similar meanings, they may have very different connotations. When you write, always evaluate the connotations of the words you choose, especially when your purpose is to persuade. To see the full range of synonyms and antonyms of a word, consult a thesaurus. If you wanted, for example, to find a word similar in meaning to *strong* but with a particular connotation, you could choose from the words listed in this entry, adapted from *Roget's II: The New Thesaurus:*

> **strong** ***adjective***
> Having great physical strength: *It takes two strong men to move a piano.*
> **Syns:** brawny, lusty, mighty, potent, powerful, puissant.

If you are still unsure of the connotations of a word, look up the word in a dictionary.

EXERCISE Rewrite each sentence, substituting a synonym for the underlined word. Then, with a partner, decide how the connotations of the new word affect the meaning of the sentence.

1. Landowners used peasants to make their farms profitable.
2. In the 18th century, a woman was expected to defer to her husband in all matters.
3. Wollstonecraft deplored the way women were treated.
4. Swift's proposal is a brilliant example of satire.
5. Both Swift and Wollstonecraft used their writings to encourage social change.

Building Vocabulary

Objectives

- discriminate between denotative and connotative meanings of words
- interpret the connotative power of words

Strategies for Building Vocabulary

EXERCISE

Answers will vary. Possible synonyms are given.

1. Landowners drained peasants to make their farms profitable.
(*Drained* suggests a complete depletion that makes the landowners more actively responsible for controlling peasants' lives.)
2. In the 18th century, a woman was expected to submit to her husband in all matters.
(*Submit* suggests a complete yielding and surrender.)
3. Wollstonecraft lamented the way women were treated.
(*Lamented* suggests an emotional dimension of sorrow as well as disapproval.)
4. Swift's proposal is a clever example of satire.
(*Clever* suggests mentally quick, original, and bright.)
5. Both Swift and Wollstonecraft used their writings to inspire social change.
(*Inspire* suggests an element of exaltation and noble purpose.)

Objectives
- combine ideas in lists in order to produce precise, efficient sentences
- use proper punctuation when making lists and understand parallel structure
- use varied sentence structure to express meanings and achieve desired effect

WRITING EXERCISE
1. The king of Brobdingnag is wise, curious, and gentle.
2. The Lilliputians tie Gulliver down, shoot arrows at him, and realize he is not dangerous.
3. In "A Modest Proposal" Swift wrote that poor Irish children could be seen in cabin doorways, on city streets, and along country roads.
4. Daniel Defoe believed that a women's academy should teach music, dance, speech, history, and foreign languages.
5. A lack of a good education, an emphasis on physical appearance, and a suppression of emotion caused problems for women, according to Mary Wollstonecraft.

GRAMMAR EXERCISE
Student responses may vary. Sample sentences are shown below.
1. Three important people in Lilliput—the emperor, the empress, and the first minister—observe the ceremony of the silken threads.
2. Giant Brobdingnagian flies buzz around Gulliver's ears, spoil his food, and sting him on the nose.
3. Swift's purpose in writing his proposal was to draw attention to England's neglect, mistreatment, and disapproval of the Irish people.
4. Defoe says that women are taught three things—to stitch, sew, and make baubles—during their youth.
5. Wollstonecraft says that men value women for being modest, beautiful, and affectionate.

Sentence Crafting: Using Elements in a Series

Grammar from Literature

One way to include several pieces of information in a single sentence is to link elements—nouns, verbs, modifiers, phrases, or clauses—in a series. A series usually includes three elements, with the items separated by commas and, usually, at least one coordinating conjunction. Notice the examples below. The writers have improved precision and established relationships by listing items in series.

series of nouns
There were shoulders, legs, and loins shaped like those of mutton.
—Jonathan Swift, *Gulliver's Travels*

series of adjectives
Want of discretion . . . makes her conceited, fantastic, and ridiculous.
—Daniel Defoe, *An Academy for Women*

series of prepositional phrases
I think it is agreed by all parties that this prodigious number of children in the arms, or on the backs, or at the heels of their mothers, and frequently of their fathers is . . . a very great additional grievance.
—Swift, "A Modest Proposal"

Using Series in Your Writing Listing items allows you to combine ideas. Look for places where listing will help you reduce repetition. Notice how creating a series eliminates wordiness in the following examples at the top of the next column.

WORDY
Mary Wollstonecraft says that men apply the term *masculine* to women interested or skilled in hunting. This is also true of women good at shooting or gaming.

REVISED
Mary Wollstonecraft says that men apply the term *masculine* to women interested or skilled in hunting, shooting, or gaming.

Usage Tip In a series, items that are parallel in meaning should be parallel in structure.

INCORRECT
adjective adjective
In Brobdingnag, Gulliver is talkative, cooperative,
independent clause
and he entertains the people.

In the sentence above, the last item in the series is not grammatically parallel with the other two items.

CORRECT
adjective adjective
In Brobdingnag, Gulliver is talkative, cooperative,
adjective
and entertaining.

Punctuation Tip When a series interrupts a sentence, you may use dashes to set it off.

Three activities—getting dressed, painting, and naming animals—dominate women's lives, writes Defoe.

WRITING EXERCISE Combine each group of sentences below by creating a sentence containing a series.
1. The king of Brobdingnag is wise. He is curious. Also, he is gentle.
2. The Lilliputians tie Gulliver down. Then they shoot arrows at him, and they realize he is not dangerous.
3. In "A Modest Proposal" Swift wrote that poor Irish children could be seen in cabin doorways. They could also be seen on city streets and along country roads.
4. Daniel Defoe believed that a women's academy should teach music, dance, speech, history. He also thought that the students should learn foreign languages.
5. A lack of a good education caused problems for women, according to Mary Wollstonecraft. So did an emphasis on physical appearance. In addition suppression of emotion was problematic.

GRAMMAR EXERCISE Rewrite the sentences below, correcting any errors in parallelism. Insert dashes where needed.
1. Three important people in Lilliput the emperor, the empress, and the first minister observe the ceremony of the silken threads.
2. Giant Brobdingnagian flies buzz around Gulliver's ears, spoil his food, and they sting him on the nose.
3. Swift's purpose in writing his proposal was to draw attention to England's neglect, mistreatment, and its disapproval of the Irish people.
4. Defoe says that women are taught three things to stitch, sewing, and making baubles—during their youth.
5. Wollstonecraft says that men value women for being modest, their beauty, and acting affectionately.

PART 3 Revelations About Human Nature

In this part of Unit Three, the people of the 18th century come to life in biographical sketches, essays, letters, and poems that offer interesting perspectives on the human condition. The writers of the selections reveal their thoughts on everything from bad habits and other everyday concerns to such universal topics as war, aging, and death. Some even take a humorous look at themselves and the people around them. As you read these writings, you may find yourself confronted with aspects of your own nature.

647

OVERVIEW

Objectives

1. understand and appreciate two **essays** that explore various aspects of human nature **(Literary Analysis)**
2. appreciate the author's use of **aphorism (Literary Analysis)**
3. use **strategies for clarifying meaning** to understand Johnson's essays **(Active Reading)**

Summary

In "On Spring," Johnson observes that some people run away from the beauty of spring. Those people, on the other hand, who do reflect on their natural surroundings will find in nature a limitless source of entertainment, new ideas, religious meditations, and scientific discoveries.

In "On Idleness," after wryly noting that he does not wish to displace pride as the worst of the vices, Johnson proceeds to examine the evil of idleness. He exposes the idleness of those who never get to work because they are too busy planning, preparing, or seeking tools. Others, like his friend Sober, waste their time dabbling in a multitude of crafts, arts, and hobbies.

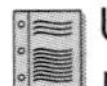 Use **Unit Three Resource Book,** pp. 77–78 for additional support.

Thematic Link

In his journalistic essays, Johnson points out the common human characteristic of looking beyond one's present circumstances for happiness and continually being disappointed. He suggests that one of the great blessings of human life is enjoying the diverse offerings of nature, which provide **revelations about human nature** as well.

5-Minute Warm-Up

Daily Language SkillBuilder

Have students **proofread** the display sentences on page 515m and write them correctly. The sentences also appear on Transparency 16 of **Grammar Transparencies and Copymasters.**

PREPARING to *Read*

On Spring
from The Rambler

On Idleness
from The Idler

Essays by SAMUEL JOHNSON

"Idleness predominates in many lives where it is not suspected."

Connect to Your Life

Human Nature "It's human nature" is an expression often used to justify the behavior of an individual or a group. Describe an experience that gave you valuable insights into human nature. What did the experience tell you about the way people sometimes think or act?

Build Background

The Age of Johnson Among students of English literature, the years 1750–1784 are often called the Age of Johnson—a tribute to the influence of Samuel Johnson, the literary leader of his day. Although known today chiefly for his *Dictionary of the English Language,* Johnson was also a talented poet, essayist, and critic. Perhaps even more famous than Johnson's literary achievements, however, was his witty conversation. He met regularly with a circle of friends, whom he often entertained with his profound wisdom and outrageous opinions. Much of Johnson's own writing was prompted by financial problems. Even while compiling his dictionary, he relied on journalistic writing to help pay his bills. Two of his journalistic **essays,** one from *The Rambler* and one from *The Idler,* appear on the following pages. Johnson launched *The Rambler,* a twice-weekly periodical, in 1750. Each issue consisted of a single essay, often laced with moral instruction. In 1758, he began writing *The Idler,* a weekly feature that appeared for two years in a London newspaper. His keen insights into human nature revealed a recognition of his own shortcomings as well. Many scholars consider the character Mr. Sober to be Johnson's caricature of himself.

LaserLinks: Background for Reading
Biographical Connection

WORDS TO KNOW
Vocabulary Preview

clemency	paradox
languish	procure
malevolence	propitious
obviate	solace
ostentation	suffer

Focus Your Reading

LITERARY ANALYSIS APHORISM An **aphorism** is a brief statement that expresses a general observation about life in a clever or forceful way. The following statement from "On Spring" is an aphorism:

When a man cannot bear his own company there is something wrong.

As you read these essays, be on the lookout for statements that might be regarded as aphorisms.

ACTIVE READING STRATEGIES FOR CLARIFYING MEANING Many of the sentences in Johnson's essays are quite lengthy. His insights into human nature, though perceptive, are often embedded in a series of related thoughts. You might want to approach these selections by using the following strategies:

- Read each sentence slowly, looking for the main idea. **Paraphrase** the main idea in your own words.
- **Take notes** as you read to help unravel the meaning of complex passages.
- Use the **dictionary** to find the meaning of unfamiliar words.
- Read a difficult sentence or passage again, concentrating on phrases or clauses that add meaning to the main point.

READER'S NOTEBOOK Write down two lengthy sentences from each essay that you find challenging. Then use the strategies listed above to decipher the meaning.

LESSON RESOURCES

UNIT THREE RESOURCE BOOK, pp. 77–82

ASSESSMENT RESOURCES
Formal Assessment, pp. 109–110
Teacher's Guide to Assessment and Portfolio Use
Test Generator

SKILLS TRANSPARENCIES AND COPYMASTERS
Reading and Critical Thinking
- Reading for Details, T16 (for Active Reading, p. 648)

Grammar
- Commonly Confused Verbs, C139 (for Mini Lesson, p. 654)

Vocabulary
- Synonyms and Antonyms, C55 (for Mini Lesson, p. 652)

Writing
- Showing, Not Telling, T22 (for Writing Options, p. 657)
- Personality Profile, C25 (for Writing Options, p. 657)

INTEGRATED TECHNOLOGY
Audio Library
LaserLinks
- Biographical Connection: Samuel Johnson. See **Teacher's SourceBook,** p. 38.

Visit our website:
www.mcdougallittell.com

Samuel Johnson

ON Spring

TUESDAY, *April* 3, 1750

ET NUNC OMNIS AGER, NUNC OMNIS PARTURIT ARBOS,
NUNC FRONDENT SILVAE, NUNC FORMOSISSIMUS ANNUS.

VIRGIL, *Eclogues*[1] 3.56–57

Now ev'ry field, now ev'ry tree is green;
Now genial nature's fairest face is seen.[2]

Elphinston

Every man is sufficiently discontented with some circumstances of his present state, to suffer his imagination to range more or less in quest of future happiness, and to fix upon some point of time, in which, by the removal of the inconvenience which now perplexes him, or acquisition of the advantage which he at present wants, he shall find the condition of his life very much improved.

When this time, which is too often expected with great impatience, at last arrives, it generally comes without the blessing for which it was desired; but we solace ourselves with some new prospect, and press forward again with equal eagerness.

It is lucky for a man, in whom this temper prevails, when he turns his hopes upon things wholly out of his own power; since he forbears then to precipitate his affairs,[3] for the sake of the great event that is to complete his felicity,[4] and waits for the blissful hour, with less neglect of the measures necessary to be taken in the mean time.

I have long known a person of this temper, who indulged his dream of happiness with less hurt to himself than such chimerical[5] wishes commonly produce, and adjusted his scheme with such address, that his hopes were in full bloom three parts of the year, and in the other part never

1. *Eclogues* (ĕk'lôgz'): a book of pastoral poems by the Roman poet Virgil.
2. **Now ev'ry . . . is seen:** a free translation of Virgil's lines.
3. **forbears . . . affairs:** refrains from acting rashly or impetuously.
4. **felicity:** happiness.
5. **chimerical** (kī-mĕr'ĭ-kəl): unrealistic and fantastic; fanciful.

WORDS TO KNOW

suffer (sŭf'ər) *v.* to allow; permit
solace (sŏl'ĭs) *v.* to console; comfort

649

TEACHING THE LITERATURE

Customizing Instruction

Less Proficient Readers
Have students name common human faults such as procrastination, tardiness, and talking too much. Ask them why these faults cause problems. Then ask students what solutions they would offer to someone with one of these problems.

Students Acquiring English
Johnson's long sentences and formal diction will daunt many students. Using the first sentence, write the various clauses on the board and have students discuss the meaning of each one.
Possible Response: "Every man is sufficiently discontented with some circumstances of his present state" [Every man (or person) is unhappy enough about something in his present life], "to suffer his imagination to range more or less in quest of future happiness" [so he allows himself to dream of better things to come], "and to fix upon some point of time, in which, by the removal of the inconvenience which now perplexes him, or acquisition of the advantage which he at present wants" [and to look to some time in the future when, because his problem is solved or he has gotten what he wants], "he shall find the condition of his life very much improved" [his life will be much better].

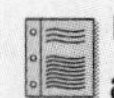
Use **Spanish Study Guide** for additional support, pp. 141–144.

Gifted and Talented
Have students compare the two essays and identify any similarities and contradictions in the themes.

Mini Lesson Preteaching Vocabulary

CONTEXT CLUES

Instruction As students review the WORDS TO KNOW, remind them that they can often rely on the context in which an unfamiliar word is used to determine its meaning. The context clue demonstrated below is cause and effect. Demonstrate how to use cause and effect with the following model.

Model The *ostentation* of her performance overshadowed the other actors.

- Ask students what the effect of her performance was.
  (Answer: *It overshadowed the other actors.*)
- Have students suggest meanings of the word based on the effect of "the ostentation of her performance."
  (Possible Responses: *superiority, showiness*)
- Have students look up *ostentation* in a dictionary to confirm their answer. They should use the same process for the other WORDS TO KNOW.

Use **Unit Three Resource Book,** p. 81 for more practice.

A lesson on context clues appears on p. 939 of the Pupil's Edition.

Reading and Analyzing

Literary Analysis: INFORMAL ESSAY

A An informal essay has a lighter, more personal tone than a formal essay. An informal essay may reflect the writer's feelings, personality, and experiences. Ask students to identify the opinion Johnson expresses in the clause beginning "By long converse . . ."
Possible Response: Johnson enjoys spring greatly.

Active Reading

STRATEGIES FOR CLARIFYING MEANING

B Ask students to paraphrase Johnson's feelings about spring; why does he find it "inexpressibly pleasing"?
Possible Responses: Johnson is pleased to see nature grow and bloom after the bareness of winter. We rejoice over the rebirth of springtime, and we also appreciate that the cold darkness of winter has been banished.

Use **Unit Three Resource Book,** p. 79 for more practice.

Literary Analysis APHORISM

C Remind students that an aphorism is a clever general observation about life or people. Point out the aphorism *"very few men know how to take a walk,"* which is a translation of a French saying that cleverly expresses an observation about life. Ask them to rephrase the saying in their own words.
Possible Responses: Few people can appreciate the natural world; there is an art to something even seemingly so simple as taking a walk.

Use **Unit Three Resource Book,** p. 80 for more exercises.

---

wholly blasted.[6] Many, perhaps, would be desirous of learning by what means he procured to himself such a cheap and lasting satisfaction. It was gained by a constant practice of referring the removal of all his uneasiness to the coming of the next spring; if his health was impaired, the spring would restore it; if what he wanted was at a high price, it would fall in value in the spring.

The spring, indeed, did often come without any of these effects, but he was always certain that the next would be more propitious; nor was ever convinced that the present spring would fail him before the middle of summer; for he always talked of the spring as coming till it was past, and when it was once past, everyone agreed with him that it was coming.

A By long converse with this man, I am, perhaps, brought to feel immoderate pleasure in the contemplation of this delightful season; but I have the satisfaction of finding many, whom it can be no shame to resemble, infected with the same enthusiasm; for there is, I believe, scarce any poet of eminence, who has not left some testimony of his fondness for the flowers, the zephyrs,[7] and the warblers of the spring. Nor has the most luxuriant imagination been able to describe the serenity and happiness of the golden age, otherwise than by giving a perpetual spring, as the highest reward of uncorrupted innocence.

Pocket watch (about 1700), M. Marcou. Musée des Arts Décoratifs, Paris.

B There is, indeed, something inexpressibly pleasing, in the annual renovation of the world, and the new display of the treasures of nature. The cold and darkness of winter, with the naked deformity of every object on which we turn our eyes, make us rejoice at the succeeding season, as well for what we have escaped, as for what we may enjoy; and every budding flower, which a warm situation brings early to our view, is considered by us as a messenger to notify the approach of more joyous days.

The spring affords to a mind, so free from the disturbance of cares or passions as to be vacant to calm amusements, almost every thing that our present state makes us capable of enjoying. The variegated verdure[8] of the fields and woods, the succession of grateful odors, the voice of pleasure pouring out its notes on every side, with the gladness apparently conceived by every animal, from the growth of his food, and the clemency of the weather, throw over the whole earth an air of gaiety, significantly expressed by the smile of nature.

Yet there are men to whom these scenes are able to give no delight, and who hurry away from all the varieties of rural beauty, to lose their hours, and divert their thoughts by cards, or assemblies, a tavern dinner, or the prattle of the day.

It may be laid down as a position which will seldom deceive, that when a man cannot bear his own company there is something wrong. He must fly from himself, either because he feels a

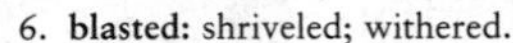

6. **blasted:** shriveled; withered.
7. **zephyrs** (zĕf'ərz): gentle breezes.
8. **variegated verdure** (vâr'ē-ĭ-gā'tĭd vûr'jər): greenery of many hues.

WORDS TO KNOW
procure (prō-kyŏŏr') *v.* to obtain; acquire
propitious (prə-pĭsh'əs) *adj.* favorable; advantageous
clemency (klĕm'ən-sē) *n.* mildness

650

Teaching Options

BLOCK SCHEDULING: MANAGING TIME

If your schedule requires that you cover the lesson objectives in a shorter time, use . . .
- Preparing to Read, p. 648
- Thinking Through the Literature, pp. 652, 656
- Vocabulary in Action, p. 657

If you want to take advantage of longer class time, use . . .
- TE Teaching Options: Preteaching Vocabulary, p. 649; Speaking and Listening, p. 651; Vocabulary Strategy, p. 652; Viewing and Representing, p. 653; Informal Assessment, p. 657; Grammar, p. 654
- Choices & Challenges, p. 657

Sandleford Priory (1744), Edward Haytley. Oil on canvas, The Leger Galleries Ltd., London.

tediousness in life from the equipoise[9] of an empty mind, which, having no tendency to one motion more than another but as it is impelled by some external power, must always have recourse to foreign objects; or he must be afraid of the intrusion of some unpleasing ideas, and, perhaps, is struggling to escape from the remembrance of a loss, the fear of a calamity, or some other thought of greater horror.

Those whom sorrow incapacitates to enjoy the pleasures of contemplation, may properly apply to such diversions, provided they are innocent, as lay strong hold on the attention; and those, whom fear of any future affliction chains down to misery, must endeavor to obviate the danger.

My considerations shall, on this occasion, be turned on such as are burthensome[10] to
1 themselves merely because they want subjects
2 for reflection, and to whom the volume of nature is thrown open, without affording them pleasure or instruction, because they never learned to read the characters.

A French author has advanced this seeming
C paradox, that *very few men know how to take a walk;* and, indeed, it is true, that few know how to take a walk with a prospect of any other pleasure, than the same company would have afforded them at home.

There are animals that borrow their color from the neighboring body, and, consequently, vary their hue as they happen to change their place. In like manner it ought to be the endeavor of every man to derive his reflections from the objects about him; for it is to no purpose that he alters his position, if his attention continues fixed to the same point. The mind should be kept open to the access of every new idea, and so far disengaged from the predominance of particular thoughts, as easily to accommodate itself to occasional entertainment.

A man that has formed his habit of turning every new object to his entertainment, finds in the productions of nature an inexhaustible stock of materials upon which he can employ himself, without any temptations to envy or malevolence; faults, perhaps, seldom totally avoided by those, whose judgment is much exercised upon the works of art. He has always a certain prospect of discovering new reasons for adoring the sovereign

9. **equipoise:** state of balance; lack of direction.
10. **burthensome:** an obsolete spelling of *burdensome*.

WORDS TO KNOW
obviate (ŏb′vē-āt′) *v.* to prevent; avert
paradox (păr′ə-dŏks′) *n.* a statement that appears to be self-contradictory or contrary to common sense but may nevertheless be true
malevolence (mə-lĕv′ə-ləns) *n.* wickedness; ill will

651

Customizing Instruction

Less Proficient Readers

Set a Purpose Ask students to discuss their favorite seasons. Then, have them read to find out what Johnson says about spring.

Students Acquiring English

1 Explain that the word *want* here means "lack" rather than "desire" and that this is an increasingly uncommon usage.

2 Focus on the passage ". . . to whom the volume . . . read the characters." Explain that this is a metaphoric usage, and help students recognize the comparison to opening a book but not understanding because of a lack of familiarity with the written language. Challenge students to identify a metaphor in their first language that conveys the same idea of not being able to understand or appreciate nature.

Multiple Learning Styles

Kinesthetic Learners Help students appreciate Johnson's point here, if possible, by leading them on a short walk outdoors in a natural area. Instruct them to observe "the productions of nature" by using their senses and to imagine what kinds of ideas they might get for activities, writing, and entertainment from what they observe.

Speaking and Listening

MOOD IN ART

Instruction Artists can create a feeling or mood and convey an attitude or tone in a painting by making decisions about such variables as subject matter, medium, color, composition, shadow and light, and line. On pages 651 and 653, students can see and analyze how these choices helped create mood and tone in two typical eighteenth-century English landscape and figure paintings.

Prepare Divide students into **cooperative groups** to discuss how Haytley and Gainsborough created a mood of pleasant idleness in their two pastoral scenes.

Present Have students construct a chart comparing the two painters' use of artistic elements—subject, medium, color, and so forth—to create a mood. Have the groups compare and discuss their interpretations.

BLOCK SCHEDULING This activity is particularly well-suited for longer class periods.

Reading and Analyzing

Reading Skills and Strategies: PARAPHRASING

A The long sentence that makes up the next-to-last paragraph of this essay is a good passage with which students can work to monitor and modify their reading strategies. Encourage them to break the sentence down and work through its parts in detail, investigating the effectiveness of paraphrasing in enhancing their comprehension.

Possible Response: Humanity needs people of many different tastes since life offers and requires a large variety of occupations, and we don't need a country full of nothing but naturalists; but it can't be wrong to point out a new amusement for the sick or dissatisfied, who are looking for a diversion that won't get stale, and to tell all men and women, who feel as though every day is a burden, that they haven't seen it all yet.

Literary Analysis APHORISM

B Ask students to paraphrase the generalization beginning "... vernal flowers, however beautiful ..." that closes the essay.

Possible Response: Accomplishments in youth lay the groundwork for achieving goals in later years.

Thinking Through the Literature

1. Possible Response: He finds it fertile, lively, mild, joyful, and innocent.
2. Accept all reasonable responses.
3. Possible response: He wishes to impress upon young people the importance of preparing themselves for adulthood while they are still young.

author of the universe, and probable hopes of making some discovery of benefit to others, or of profit to himself. There is no doubt but many vegetables and animals have qualities that might be of great use, to the knowledge of which there is not required much force of penetration, or fatigue of study, but only frequent experiments, and close attention. What is said by the chemists of their darling mercury,[11] is, perhaps, true of everybody through the whole creation, that if a thousand lives should be spent upon it, all its properties would not be found out.

A Mankind must necessarily be diversified by various tastes, since life affords and requires such multiplicity of employments, and a nation of naturalists is neither to be hoped, or desired; but it is surely not improper to point out a fresh amusement to those who languish in health, and repine[12] in plenty, for want of some source of diversion that may be less easily exhausted, and to inform the multitudes of both sexes, who are burthened with every new day, that there are many shows which they have not seen.

He that enlarges his curiosity after the works of nature, demonstrably multiplies the inlets to happiness; and, therefore, the younger part of my readers, to whom I dedicate this vernal[13] speculation, must excuse me for calling upon them, to make use at once of the spring of the year, and the spring of life; to acquire, while their minds may be yet impressed with new images, a love of innocent pleasures, and an ardor for useful knowledge; and to remember, that a blighted spring makes a barren year, and that the vernal flowers, however beautiful and gay, are only intended by nature as preparatives to autumnal fruits. ❖ **B**

11. **chemists . . . mercury:** The properties (characteristics) of mercury and its compounds made the silvery liquid metal fascinating to early chemists.
12. **repine:** feel dissatisfied; complain.
13. **vernal:** having to do with spring.

Thinking Through the Literature

1. **Comprehension Check** In Johnson's opinion, why is spring particularly pleasing?
2. What is your overall impression of this essay?
3. Why do you think Johnson, in the last paragraph, dedicates his essay to "the younger part of my readers"? Consider the evidence.

- his recommended approach to life
- the types of behavior he condemns
- the hope he expresses for those in "the spring of life"

WORDS TO KNOW **languish** (lăng′gwĭsh) *v.* to be weak or depressed

652

Teaching Options

Mini Lesson Vocabulary Strategy

WRITING ANALOGIES

Instruction Remind students that synonyms and antonyms are types of analogies. Synonyms are words that have similar meanings; antonyms are words that have opposite meanings. Synonyms and antonyms often rely on connotation (the ideas suggested by the words) to suggest shades of shared meaning (synonyms) and degrees of difference (antonyms).

Exercise Have students write analogy exercises for each of the WORDS TO KNOW, using synonyms and antonyms following the model below.

Model Encourage them to use the dictionary as necessary.

- synonym
  malevolence : malice :: curiosity : inquisitiveness
- antonym
  clemency : harshness :: humor : dullness

Use **Vocabulary Transparencies and Copymasters,** p. 51.

Mr. and Mrs. Andrews (late 1700s), Thomas Gainsborough. National Gallery, London. Bridgeman/Art Resource.

On Idleness

SAMUEL JOHNSON

Saturday, November 18, 1758

1 *Many moralists have remarked, that Pride has of all human*
2 *vices the widest dominion, appears in the greatest multiplicity of forms, and lies hid under the greatest variety of disguises; of disguises, which, like the moon's* veil of brightness, *are both* its luster and its shade, *and betray it to others, though they hide it from ourselves.*

It is not my intention to degrade Pride from this pre-eminence of mischief, yet I know not whether Idleness may not maintain a very doubtful and obstinate competition.

Customizing Instruction

Students Acquiring English

1 Remind students that personification gives human qualities to an object, animal, or idea. Point out that Johnson uses personification to describe pride. Ask them to identify specific details that demonstrate this personification.

Possible Response: "appears in . . . forms," "lies hid," "variety of disguises."

Less Proficient Readers

2 Ask students to paraphrase what Johnson says about pride in the first sentence. Point out that tracing the antecedent of *its/it* can help clarify the meaning of the sentence. (Antecedent is "pride.")

Possible Response: Many moralists have said that pride is the worst of human vices. It appears in many forms and in many disguises. However, those disguises often reveal one's pride to others, while keeping it hidden from oneself.

Viewing and Representing

Mr. and Mrs. Andrews
by Thomas Gainsborough

ART APPRECIATION Gainsborough (1727–1788) was a highly successful portrait painter, but he loved landscape best and combined the two genres in his early period.

Instruction Visual images are sometimes composed of a foreground and a background. The foreground most often is the center of emphasis; however, important details in the background add much to the message of the artwork.

Application Ask students to identify the foreground and background in this composition.

Answer: foreground, portrait; background, landscape.

Discuss students' observations of the foreground and background. Have students analyze the ideas the artist may be trying to express by including certain details of landscape.

Reading and Analyzing

Active Reading STRATEGIES FOR CLARIFYING MEANING

A Ask students to identify specific points Johnson makes to convey the main idea in the third paragraph.
Possible Response: Idleness exists in many people without being noticed, because idleness does not hurt others, as fraud and pride do. Idleness is quiet rather than overly obvious, and it does not bother other people by causing disagreements.

B Encourage students to pause to consider Johnson's meaning in the fourth paragraph on this page.
Possible Response: People often busy themselves with trivialities in order to avoid doing things they should do. Have them ask themselves how a person can be accused of idleness if he or she appears busy most of the time. Point out the following phrases as guides to help students answer their questions: "neglects," "real employment," "crowd his mind," "any thing but what he ought to do."

Literary Analysis APHORISM

C Johnson writes, "Nothing is to be expected from the workman whose tools are forever to be sought." What does this generalization mean?
Possible Response: Excessive preparation for work is a way of avoiding doing the work itself.

There are some that profess Idleness in its full dignity, who call themselves the Idle, as Busiris in the play[1] "calls himself the Proud"; who boast that they do nothing, and thank their stars that they have nothing to do; who sleep every night till they can sleep no longer, and rise only that exercise may enable them to sleep again; who prolong the reign of darkness by double curtains, and never see the sun but to "tell him how they hate his beams"; whose whole labor is to vary the postures of indulgence, and whose day differs from their night but as a couch or chair differs from a bed.

These are the true and open votaries[2] of Idleness, for whom she weaves the garlands of poppies, and into whose cup she pours the waters of oblivion;[3] who exist in a state of unruffled stupidity, forgetting and forgotten; who have long ceased to live, and at whose death the survivors can only say, that they have ceased to breathe.

But Idleness predominates in many lives where it is not suspected; for being a vice which terminates in itself, it may be enjoyed without injury to others; and is therefore not watched like Fraud, which endangers property, or like Pride, which naturally seeks its gratifications in another's inferiority. Idleness is a silent and peaceful quality, that neither raises envy by ostentation, nor hatred by opposition; and therefore nobody is busy to censure or detect it.

As Pride sometimes is hid under humility, Idleness is often covered by turbulence and hurry. He that neglects his known duty and real employment, naturally endeavors to crowd his mind with something that may bar out the remembrance of his own folly, and does any thing but what he ought to do with eager diligence, that he may keep himself in his own favor.

Some are always in a state of preparation, occupied in previous measures, forming plans, accumulating materials, and providing for the main affair. These are certainly under the secret power of Idleness. Nothing is to be expected from the workman whose tools are forever to be sought. I was once told by a great master, that no man ever excelled in painting, who was eminently curious about pencils and colors.

IDLENESS IS A SILENT AND PEACEFUL QUALITY, THAT NEITHER RAISES ENVY BY OSTENTATION, NOR HATRED BY OPPOSITION.

1. **Busiris** (byo͞o-sī′rĭs) **in the play:** a reference to the play *Busiris, King of Egypt* by the English poet Edward Young. A figure in Greek mythology, Busiris put to death all strangers who entered his kingdom and was himself killed by Hercules.
2. **votaries:** worshipers; devotees.
3. **waters of oblivion:** in Greek mythology, the waters of the river Lethe, which produce forgetfulness

WORDS TO KNOW

ostentation (ŏs′tĕn-tā′shən) *n.* a showy display, especially of wealth or knowledge; boastful showiness

Teaching Options

Grammar

COMMONLY CONFUSED VERBS

Instruction The verb pairs *lie* and *lay, rise* and *raise,* and *sit* and *set* can often be confusing because the spelling and meaning of the verbs in each pair are similar.

Activity Write this excerpt from "On Idleness" on the chalkboard.

> Idleness is a silent and peaceful quality, that neither raises envy by ostentation, nor hatred by opposition; and therefore nobody is busy to censure or detect it.

Ask students why *raises* is the correct verb rather than *rises. (In this context, "raise" means "to stir up." "Rise" means "to go upward" which would not make sense here.)* Tell students that "raise" nearly always takes a direct object; whereas, "rise" never does. Ask them to find in the excerpt the direct object of *raises. (envy, hatred)* Have students work in groups to come up with a concise meaning for each pair of verbs: *lie* and *lay, rise* and *raise,* and *sit* and *set. ("lie" – to recline or rest in a flat position; "lay" – to put or place; "rise" – to go upward; "raise" – to lift; "sit" – to occupy a seat; "set" – to put or place)*

There are others to whom Idleness dictates another expedient, by which life may be passed unprofitably away without the tediousness of many vacant hours. The art is, to fill the day with petty business, to have always something in hand which may raise curiosity, but not solicitude, and keep the mind in a state of action, but not of labor.

This art has for many years been practiced by my old friend Sober, with wonderful success. Sober is a man of strong desires and quick imagination, so exactly balanced by the love of ease, that they can seldom stimulate him to any difficult undertaking; they have, however, so
1 much power, that they will not suffer him to lie quite at rest, and though they do not make him sufficiently useful to others, they make him at least weary of himself.

Mr. Sober's chief pleasure is conversation; there is no end of his talk or his attention; to speak or to hear is equally pleasing; for he still fancies that he is teaching or learning something, and is free for the time from his own reproaches.

But there is one time at night when he must go home, that his friends may sleep; and another time in the morning, when all the world agrees to shut out interruption. These are the moments of which poor Sober trembles at the thought. But the misery of these tiresome intervals, he has many means of alleviating. He has persuaded
2 himself that the manual arts are undeservedly overlooked; he has observed in many trades the effects of close thought, and just ratiocination.[4] From speculation he proceeded to practice, and supplied himself with the tools of a carpenter, with which he mended his coalbox very successfully, and which he still continues to employ, as he finds occasion.

He has attempted at other times the crafts of the shoemaker, tinman, plumber, and potter; in all these arts he has failed, and resolves to qualify himself for them by better information. But his daily amusement is chemistry. He has a small furnace, which he employs in distillation,[5] and which has long been the solace of his life. He draws oils and waters, and essences and spirits, which he knows to be of no use; sits and counts the drops as they come from his retort,[6] and forgets that, whilst a drop is falling, a moment flies away.

Poor Sober! I have often teased him with reproof, and he has often promised reformation; for no man is so much open to conviction as the Idler, but there is none on whom it operates so little. What will be the effect of this paper I know not; perhaps he will read it and laugh, and light the fire in his furnace; but my hope is that he will quit his trifles, and betake himself to rational and useful diligence. ❖

---

4. **ratiocination** (răsh′ē-ŏs′ə-nā′shən): systematic and logical thought.

5. **distillation:** the separation of parts of a liquid mixture by condensing and collecting the vapors produced when it is heated.

6. **retort:** a vessel used for distilling liquids.

Customizing Instruction

Less Proficient Readers

Ask students the following questions about the essay.

- Who does Johnson claim are the true worshipers of idleness?
  Answer: those who do nothing.
- What kind of idler is Sober?
  Possible Response: the kind who fills his time with trivial action.
- What does *diligence* mean? What are some synonyms for *diligence*?
  Possible Response: steady and earnest effort; assiduity, steadfastness, perseverance.
- How do idlers disguise their lack of productive work?
  Possible Response: They hurry around; they plan and prepare to work; they talk about working.

Students Acquiring English

Help students with problematic vocabulary.

1 Ask students to identify the WORD TO KNOW that is repeated in the second paragraph and to review its meaning.
Answer: suffer, "to allow; permit."
Instruct students to compare the use of *suffer* here and on p. 649, and encourage them to write their own sentence using the word.

2 Point out Johnson's phrase "the manual arts" near the bottom of the first column. Explain that Johnson is referring to occupations or labor that involves the use of physical skills, primarily the use of the hands. What "manual arts" does Sober try?
Possible Response: carpentry, shoemaking, working with tin, plumbing, pottery.

Exercise Ask students to identify the correct verb form of the two verbs in parentheses.

1. The coming of spring (raised, rose) our spirits and restored our imaginations. (*raised*)
2. Many insatiable people cannot (lie, lay) their wants to rest; they feel it is their duty to improve upon their current situation. (*lay*)
3. By choosing to ignore the beauty of nature, we (have raised, have risen) a barrier that often obstructs new ideas from penetrating our minds. (*have raised*)
4. On the subject of idleness, Johnson sees little difference between whittling away time with fruitless activities and (lying, laying) in bed dormant for days and nights on end. (*lying*)
5. Though Mr. Sober tinkered with many crafts adeptly, he rarely (set, sat) these skills to work for any meaningful goal or purpose. (*set*)

Use McDougal Littell's ***Language Network*** for more instruction and practice in commonly confused verbs.

GUIDING STUDENT RESPONSE

Connect to the Literature

1. **What Do You Think?** Guidelines for student response: Student discussions might begin by relating episodes or incidents of idleness from students' lives, how they coped with it and what they learned from it.

Comprehension Check
- one who does nothing, or one who acts busy but does no true or important work
- idleness

Use Selection Quiz in **Unit Three Resource Book,** p. 82

Think Critically

2. Possible Responses: No, his tone suggests empathy and tolerance for idlers, his examples are amusing, and he calls idleness harmless; yes, his criticisms imply that a love of idleness can seduce one into wasting one's life.
3. Possible Responses: his love of conversation, his fear of being alone, his many and varied interests
4. Some students may say that idle people are harmless because their idleness affects only their own lives; others will say that failure to act can be harmful because responsibilities to others may be neglected.
5. Possible Response: "On Spring" is more formal and earnest; it has a stronger moral message. "On Idleness" is lighter and more forgiving of human weakness.
6. Sentences will vary. Strategies include paraphrasing, breaking a long sentence into several shorter ones, taking notes throughout each essay to keep track of Johnson's points about each subject, and rereading. Johnson's complex sentence structure allows him to connect several related thoughts within one longer sentence, which reinforces the main idea of his sentence.

Literary Analysis

Cooperative Learning Activity In class discussion, encourage students to evaluate the aphorisms by considering their universality and how easily they convey a point.

Connect to the Literature

1. **What Do You Think?** What were your reactions to Johnson's essay "On Idleness"? Discuss with a classmate.

Comprehension Check
- What is Johnson's definition of an idler?
- What quality does Mr. Sober represent?

Think Critically

2. Do you think Johnson views idleness as a serious character flaw?

THINK ABOUT
- the **tone** of the essay
- his examples of idleness
- his expectations regarding Sober's reformation

3. What insights about himself do you think Johnson reveals through the character of Mr. Sober?
4. According to Johnson, idleness is "a vice which terminates in itself" and therefore can be indulged in "without injury to others." Do you agree? Explain your opinion.
5. Would you say that Johnson's **tone** is the same in "On Spring" and "On Idleness"? Support your answer.
6. ACTIVE READING STRATEGIES FOR CLARIFYING MEANING Look again at your  READER'S NOTEBOOK. What sentence in each essay seemed most difficult to understand and what strategies did you use to unravel the meaning? How does Johnson's complex sentence structure reinforce his ideas?

Extend Interpretations

7. **Comparing Texts** Compare these **essays** of Johnson's with the excerpts from Joseph Addison's *Spectator* essays (page 549). Which of Johnson's essays is more similar in tone to Addison's writing? Support your answer with details from the essays.
8. **Different Perspectives** How do you think Mr. Sober might defend idleness? Be specific in your answer.
9. **Connect to Life** What do you think would be good examples of idleness that are common in the world today? Explain.

Literary Analysis

APHORISM Unlike proverbs, which stem from oral folk tradition, **aphorisms** are created by individual authors. Because they are generalizations, aphorisms are meaningful even when taken out of their original contexts. "A blighted spring makes a barren year," in the last sentence of "On Spring," is an example of a statement that is an aphorism. What other aphorisms can you find in these essays?

Cooperative Learning Activity With three or four classmates, try to come up with aphorisms of your own creation. Choose topics that interest the group and then write a couple of aphorisms for each topic. Present your aphorisms to the rest of the class.

REVIEW INFORMAL ESSAY An **informal essay** presents an opinion on a subject, but not in a completely serious or formal tone. Informal essays include a personal approach and a somewhat loose style. They also are often humorous, and they frequently address an unconventional topic. With a partner, look for characteristics of an informal essay in "On Spring" and in "On Idleness." List examples of the characteristics you find, and discuss how effectively you think Johnson uses the informal essay to express his ideas.

Extend Interpretations

Comparing Texts Some students will say that "On Idleness" is more similar to Addison's writing because of its greater readability, its geniality, and its satiric elements. Others will say that "On Spring" is more similar, because it provides encouraging advice on leading a better life.

Different Perspectives Sober might claim that in his activities, such as fixing his coalbox and engaging in his chemical experiments, are useful and potentially beneficial to society.

Connect to Life Possible Responses: cleaning house, washing the car, and brushing the dog instead of doing homework; organizing all the tools and rearranging the garage before working in the yard.

Choices & CHALLENGES

Writing Options

Friendly Anecdote Write an anecdote about someone you know who exhibits one or more of the traits Johnson describes in these essays.

Activities & Explorations

Personality Caricature Draw a caricature portraying one of the personality types described by Johnson in these essays. ~ ART

Vocabulary in Action

EXERCISE A: ANTONYMS For each Word to Know in the first column, write the letter of the best antonym in the second column.

1. **procure**	a. thrive
2. **languish**	b. forbid
3. **obviate**	c. lose
4. **malevolence**	d. permit
5. **suffer**	e. kindness

EXERCISE B: CONTEXT CLUES Write the Word to Know described by each sentence below.

1. "It was the best of times, it was the worst of times" is an example of this.
2. "Red sky at night, sailor's delight" means that a red sunset is a sign of this kind of weather on the next day.
3. "Peacock, look at your legs!" is a reminder that this can be foolish.
4. "When in disgrace with Fortune and men's eyes / I all alone beweep my outcast state" shows that the speaker of the sonnet needs someone to do this to him.
5. "Power can do by gentleness what violence fails to accomplish" indicates that this can be an effective quality.

WORDS TO KNOW			
	clemency	paradox	solace
	ostentation	propitious	

Building Vocabulary
For an in-depth lesson on how to use a thesaurus to find a word's synonyms and antonyms, see page 574.

Samuel Johnson
1709–1784

Other Works
Lives of the Poets
"Preface" in *A Dictionary of the English Language*

Youth and Education Born in Lichfield, England, Samuel Johnson was the son of a prominent but impoverished bookseller. During infancy, he contracted scrofula, a tubercular infection that left him with a disfigured face and impaired vision and hearing. He attended public schools until he was 17 and read widely in his father's shop, but Johnson's family could not afford to give him the higher education he craved. Although a small inheritance of his mother's allowed him to enroll in Oxford University in 1728, he was forced to leave after only 13 months when the money ran out.

Teacher, Translator, Writer For many years, Johnson earned a meager income by teaching and by translating books. Then, at the age of 27, determined to make a name for himself, he walked to London to seek a career in writing. Within a year he had published his first significant poem and had begun to gain recognition as a literary talent.

Literary Achievements Johnson's literary achievements during the next 30 years—particularly his dictionary, an edition of Shakespeare's works, and a series of critical biographies of English poets in which he proves himself a forerunner of modern literary critics—earned him fame, as well as honorary doctorates from Oxford University and Trinity College in Dublin. Nevertheless, he was still on the brink of poverty in 1756, when he was briefly imprisoned for his many debts. In 1762, Johnson's financial woes finally ended when the king awarded him an annual pension.

Writing Options

Friendly Anecdote Suggest that students freewrite to come up with an idea and details for their anecdotes. Encourage them to treat one or two traits in depth rather than dealing with several characteristics superficially. Remind them to introduce their topic clearly: What trait will be considered? They should use humor and specific examples of the characteristic they are discussing. Remind students to consider their tone; they should make their attitude about their subject clear.

Activities & Explorations

Personality Caricature Discuss the concept of caricature—a drawing that exaggerates a person's features for purposes of comic characterization. Have students find examples of caricatures from magazines or newspapers. Then, help them list the personality types Johnson describes, including the idler, the dabbler in hobbies, the discontented person, the person who dreams of future happiness, and the person incapacitated by sorrow or self-hate.

Vocabulary in Action

Exercise A
1. c
2. a
3. d
4. e
5. b

Exercise B
1. paradox
2. propitious
3. ostentation
4. solace
5. clemency

Assessment Informal Assessment

WRITING A PROPOSAL Have students imagine that they are writing a proposal for a book modernizing Johnson's ideas. They will need to include an introduction that states the purpose of the book and an outline that presents the book's scope. Johnson's main ideas should be accessible to modern readers.

RUBRIC

3 **Full Accomplishment** Proposals contain pertinent introductions and outlines that include most of Johnson's main ideas, insightfully and inventively modernized.

2 **Substantial Accomplishment** Proposals include pertinent introductions and outlines that include some of Johnson's ideas, credibly modernized.

1 **Little or Partial Accomplishment** Introductions are only partially relevant to proposal. Outlines show little understanding of Johnson's ideas.

RELATED *Reading*

Primary Source

Objectives
- read and analyze primary sources
- use reference materials such as a dictionary to determine precise word meanings
- discriminate between denotative and connotative meanings of words

Further Background
While a source is any book, document, or person from which information is obtained, a **primary source** is a book document, or person that provides original, firsthand information about a topic.

With the help of six assistants, Johnson worked on his dictionary for more than eight years (1747–1755). When read more than 200 years later, the sample entries at the right reveal some of the dictionary's peculiarities—casual definitions *(fish, river,* and *sun)* existing alongside precise ones *(mould* and *tempest);* and humorous definitions *(dull* and *hiss)* mixed in with standard ones *(amble, miser,* and *warren).*

Reading for Information
Have students notice a few instances where definitions and usage of some words in Johnson's time have substantially changed today: *adult* is a term no longer chiefly associated with medical writing, a novel is no longer a "small tale," and people today no longer think first of a medical prescription when they think of a recipe.

DENOTATION AND CONNOTATION

1. **Determining Denotations**
   Possible Response: The modern meaning of *amble* is an easy gait, a leisurely walk. Johnson's definition seems more general. He refers to movement, not specifically to walking. The two meanings are similar, however, because they both suggest smooth motion.
2. **Archaic Language**
   Have students volunteer any words such as *slubber* that they can think of that are no longer used. Fads are notorious to bringing words into use that end up short-lived.
3. **Clarifying Connotation**
   Possible Response: Students might suggest that tempestuous weather is more violent than stormy weather because a tempest suggests raging, dangerous winds. Stormy weather, while full of turbulence and fury, connotes less intense and damaging activity.

from A Dictionary of the English Language

Samuel Johnson

ADU′LT. A person above the age of infancy, or grown to some degree of strength; sometimes full grown: a word used chiefly by medicinal writers.

❶ **TO A′MBLE.** To move easily, without hard shocks, or shaking.

APE. A kind of monkey remarkable for imitating what he sees.

CORN. The seeds which grow in ears, not in pods; such as are made into bread.

DULL. Not exhilarating; not delightful; as, *to make dictionaries is* dull *work*.

FISH. An animal that inhabits the water.

TO HISS. To utter a noise like that of a serpent and some other animals. It is remarkable, that this word cannot be pronounced without making the noise which it signifies.

LOUSE. A small animal, of which different species live on the bodies of men, beasts, and perhaps of all living creatures.

MI′SER. A wretched person; one overwhelmed with calamity.

MOULD. A kind of concretion on the top or outside of things kept, motionless and damp; now discovered by microscopes to be perfect plants.

MOUSE. The smallest of all beasts; a little animal haunting houses and corn fields, destroyed by cats.

NO′VEL. A small tale, generally of love.

POP. A small smart quick sound. It is formed from the sound.

RE′CIPE. A medical prescription.

RI′VER. A land current of water bigger than a brook.

❷ **TO SLU′BBER.** To do any thing lazily, imperfectly, or with idle hurry.

❸ **SUN.** The luminary that makes the day.

TE′MPEST. The utmost violence of the wind; the names by which the wind is called according to the gradual increase of its force seems to be, a breeze; a gale; a gust; a storm; a tempest.

WA′RREN. A kind of park for rabbits.

Reading for Information

In creating the first comprehensive dictionary in the English language, Johnson compiled 40,000 entries from the most reputable sources of his time. Like every other dictionary, Johnson's dictionary reflects the meaning and usage of words at the time it was written.

DENOTATION AND CONNOTATION

Remember that a word's **denotation** is its literal meaning, whereas its **connotations** are the feelings associated with it. To explore this excerpt from Johnson's dictionary, complete the activities below.

❶ Determining Denotations Look up the word *amble.* How is its definition similar to and different from Johnson's?

❷ Archaic Language Over time, some words may cease to be used at all. Such words are classified as **archaic language**—that is, words that are no longer current. Johnson's word *slubber,* for example, is not included in most modern dictionaries.

❸ Clarifying Connotation The words *tempest* and *storm* have similar denotations but may have different connotations. How would you compare tempestuous weather and stormy weather?

"His mind resembled the vast amphitheater, the Colosseum at Rome."

from The Life of Samuel Johnson

Biography by JAMES BOSWELL

Connect to Your Life

Lives of the Rich and Famous People have always been curious about the lives of famous people. Think of a current celebrity who interests you. What kinds of things would you like to know about this person? Where would you go to find such information? Discuss your ideas with a partner.

Build Background

When Boswell Met Johnson Samuel Johnson was one of the most extraordinary scholars and personalities of his time. Despite years of struggle and hardship, he pursued his literary and intellectual interests and eventually became respected as a poet, essayist, journalist, and critic. He also devoted ten years of his life to compiling a massive dictionary. Though Johnson was a leading figure of his day, his opinions were controversial and often inspired heated reactions.

James Boswell, 31 years younger than Johnson, was a university-trained lawyer from a wealthy Scottish family. He had a lifelong fascination with London and the variety of experiences to be found there. He also had a great desire to meet the famous Samuel Johnson. In 1763, when Boswell was only 22, he was unexpectedly introduced to Johnson in the back room of a bookseller's shop in London. Although Johnson was at first annoyed by Boswell's questions and impertinences, he quickly warmed to the young man.

During the next 21 years, Boswell chronicled in great detail his conversations, experiences, and travels with Johnson. After Johnson's death in 1784, Boswell spent 7 years writing the great man's biography. Unlike earlier biographies, which emphasized the positive aspects of their subjects' lives and were often excessively flattering, Boswell's presents a full and accurate portrait that includes both the good and the bad, giving the reader a vivid sense of Johnson as a real person.

WORDS TO KNOW
Vocabulary Preview

corporal
discernment
impunity
temperate
vehement

Focus Your Reading

LITERARY ANALYSIS **BIOGRAPHY** A **biography** is an account of a person's life written by another person. In a good biography, the presentation of the subject's life is comprehensive, clear, unified, and accurate. As you read these excerpts from Boswell's biography, decide whether each passage creates a clear impression of Johnson.

ACTIVE READING **ANALYZING THE BIOGRAPHER'S PERSPECTIVE**

A biographer's **perspective** may be influenced by his or her own views, prejudices, or relationship to the subject. Boswell's friendship with Johnson helped him gain intimate knowledge of his subject, but it also affected his perception of the man. Evidence of Boswell's perspective is signaled by the following:

- the use of the pronoun *I*
- anecdotes and dialogue that involve the biographer
- the writer's tone

READER'S NOTEBOOK As you read each excerpt, look for evidence of Boswell's perspective. List examples in which Boswell's relationship to Johnson influences the writing.

OVERVIEW

This selection is included in the **Grade 12 InterActive Reader.**

Objectives

1. appreciate excerpts from a classic in the **biography** genre **(Literary Analysis)**
2. appreciate **biography** as a way to explore a person's charachter **(Literary Analysis)**
3. **analyze the biographer's perspective (Active Reading)**

Summary

"On Eating" Boswell recalls that although Johnson often censured gluttony, he relished good eating.
"On Equality of the Sexes" Boswell recalls a conversation in which Mrs. Knowles complains that men have greater liberty than women. Johnson replies that men do women an honor by expecting perfection.
"On the Fear of Death" Boswell recounts Johnson's declarations that the fear of death is natural to humans.
"On Johnson's Physical Courage" Boswell remarks that Johnson, despite his fear of death, separated fighting dogs, discharged a dangerous gun, and fought off four men who attacked him.

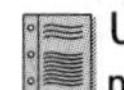
Use **Unit Three Resource Book,** pp. 83–84 for additional support.

Thematic Link

The excerpts from Boswell's biography of Johnson contain topics relevant to all times and societies offering **revelations about human nature.**

5-Minute Warm-Up

Daily Language SkillBuilder

Have students **proofread** the display sentences on page 515m and write them correctly. The sentences also appear on Transparency 16 of **Grammar Transparencies and Copymasters.**

Preteaching Vocabulary

If you would like to preteach the WORDS TO KNOW for this selection, use the Mini Lesson p. 660.

LESSON RESOURCES

UNIT THREE RESOURCE BOOK, pp. 83–88

ASSESSMENT RESOURCES
Formal Assessment, pp. 111–112
Teacher's Guide to Assessment and Portfolio Use
Test Generator

SKILLS TRANSPARENCIES AND COPYMASTERS
Reading and Critical Thinking
- Determining Author's Bias, T23 (for Active Reading, p. 659)

Grammar
- Progressive Verb Forms, C132 (for Mini Lesson,pp. 662–663)
- Subject-Verb Agreement I, C140 (for Mini Lesson, pp. 662–663)

Writing
- Personality Profile, C25 (for Writing Options, p. 665)

Communications
- Identifying and Analyzing Artistic Elements in Literary Texts, T13 (for Activities & Explorations, p. 665)

INTEGRATED TECHNOLOGY
Audio Library
Visit our website:
www.mcdougallittell.com

TEACHING THE LITERATURE

Reading and Analyzing

Active Reading

ANALYZING THE BIOGRAPHER'S PERSPECTIVE

A Remind students that although a biographer presents a subject from a certain point of view, a skilled biographer strives for a balanced treatment, highlighting the subject's weaknesses and strengths, failures and achievements. Ask students to comment on Boswell's perspective on Johnson in the section on eating. Do they think Boswell presents an objective view of Johnson?

Possible Responses: Some students may think Boswell is being objective, because he talks about how Johnson is almost obsessed with his food while he is eating, which is not a very flattering account. Other students may think that Boswell is biased, because while he describes Johnson as an enthusiastic diner, his description of his subject is humorous and basically uncritical.

Use **Unit Three Resource Book,** p. 85 for more practice.

Literary Analysis BIOGRAPHY

Ask students to state several ways a biographer might learn intimate details of the life of the subject.

Possible Responses: A biographer might spend years getting to know the subject; he or she might read previous biographies and articles written about the subject; he or she might interview the subject or the subject's friends and family.

Use **Unit Three Resource Book,** p. 86 for more exercises.

FROM THE LIFE OF

A On Eating (1763)

At supper this night he talked of good eating with uncommon satisfaction. "Some people (said he,) have a foolish way of not minding, or pretending not to mind, what they eat. For my part, I mind my belly very studiously, and very carefully; for I look upon it, that he who does not mind his belly will hardly mind anything else."

He now appeared to me *Jean Bull philosophe,*[1] and he was, for the moment, not only serious but vehement. Yet I have heard him, upon other occasions, talk with great contempt of people who were anxious to gratify their palates; and the 206th number of his *Rambler* is a masterly essay against gulosity.[2] His practice, indeed, I must acknowledge, may be considered as casting the balance of his different opinions upon this subject; for I never knew any man who relished good eating more than he did. When at table, he was totally absorbed in the business of the moment; his looks seemed riveted to his plate; nor would he, unless when in very high company, say one word, or even pay the least attention to what was said by others, till he had satisfied his appetite, which was so fierce, and indulged with such intenseness, that while in the act of eating, the veins of his forehead swelled, and generally a strong perspiration was visible. To those whose sensations were delicate, this could not but be disgusting; and it was doubtless not very suitable to the character of a philosopher, who should be distinguished by self-command. But it must be owned, that Johnson, though he could be rigidly *abstemious,*[3] was not a temperate man either in eating or drinking. He could refrain, but he could not use moderately. He told me, that he had fasted two days without inconvenience, and that he had never been hungry but once. They who beheld with wonder how much he ate upon all occasions when his dinner was to his taste, could not easily conceive what he must have meant by hunger; and not only was he remarkable for the extraordinary quantity which he ate, but he was, or affected to be, a man of very nice discernment in the science of cookery. He used to descant[4] critically on the dishes which had been at table where he had dined or supped, and to recollect very minutely what he had liked. . . .

When invited to dine, even with an intimate friend, he was not pleased if something better than a plain dinner was not prepared for him. I have heard him say on such an occasion, "This was a good dinner enough, to be sure; but it was not a dinner to *ask* a man to." On the other hand, he was wont to express, with great glee, his satisfaction when he had been entertained quite to his mind.

1. ***Jean Bull philosophe*** (zhäɴ′ bo͞ol′ fē-lô-zôf′) *French:* John Bull philosopher. (John Bull is a figure representing the typical Englishman—honest, hearty, and gruff.)
2. **gulosity** (gyo͞o-lŏs′ĭ-tē): excessive appetite; gluttony.
3. **abstemious** (ăb-stē′mē-əs): self-denying; abstinent.
4. **descant** (dĕs′kănt′): speak at length.

WORDS TO KNOW

vehement (vē′ə-mənt) *adj.* forceful in expression or feeling; intense
temperate (tĕm′pər-ĭt) *adj.* moderate; restrained
discernment (dĭ-sûrn′mənt) *n.* good judgment

Teaching Options

Preteaching Vocabulary

USING CONTEXT CLUES

Instruction As students review the WORDS TO KNOW, remind them that they can often determine the meaning of an unfamiliar word by searching for antonyms of the word in the sentence. Demonstrate the strategy using the following model.

Model The dog's *corporal* strength was more impressive than its mental abilities.

- Have a student summarize the meaning of the model sentence.
- Explain that the contrast shown in the sentence tells the reader that *corporal* is the antonym of *mental.*
- Have students suggest meanings of the word based on the overall meaning of the sentence.

Exercise Read the following sentence and have students use an antonym to understand the meaning of the italicized word.

He showed poor judgment rather than his usual *discernment* when he chose to go to the concert instead of studying for the test.

Use **Unit Three Resource Book,** p. 87 for additional support.

A lesson on using context clues appears on p. 939 of the Pupil's Edition.

SAMUEL JOHNSON

JAMES BOSWELL

Oliver Goldsmith, James Boswell, and Dr. Samuel Johnson at the Mitre Tavern, London (19th century), unknown artist. Colored engraving, The Granger Collection, New York.

On Equality of the Sexes (1778)

Mrs. Knowles affected to complain that men had much more liberty allowed them than women.

JOHNSON. "Why, Madam, women have all the liberty they should wish to have. We have all the labor and the danger, and the women all the advantage. We go to sea, we build houses, we do everything, in short, to pay our court to the women."

MRS. KNOWLES. "The Doctor reasons very wittily, but not convincingly. Now, take the instance of building; the mason's wife, if she is ever seen in liquor, is ruined; the mason may get himself drunk as often as he pleases, with little loss of character; nay, may let his wife and children starve."

JOHNSON. "Madam, you must consider, if the mason does get himself drunk, and let his wife and children starve, the parish will oblige him to find security for their maintenance. We have different modes of restraining evil. Stocks for the men, a ducking-stool for women, and a pound for beasts. If we require more perfection from women than from ourselves, it is doing them honor. And women have not the same temptations that we have: they may always live in virtuous company;

Customizing Instruction

Less Proficient Readers
Approach the selection one section at a time. Have students take notes on the main point of each section and make inferences about Johnson's character after they have read each.

Students Acquiring English
Ask students if they have ever read a biography or a biographical article about a famous person from their native culture. Discuss reasons students chose to read about this person and elicit from them reasons people might choose to write about this person.

Use **Spanish Study Guide** for additional support, pp. 145–148.

Gifted and Talented
Encourage students to take notes on and discuss Boswell's biographical techniques and Johnson's character. Then, invite them to write a similar conversational episode—based on one from Boswell's biography—about a present-day individual of their choice. Students may include themselves as participants in their episodes. What makes Boswell's writing effective? Students should evaluate their writing using the same criteria.

BLOCK SCHEDULING: MANAGING TIME

If your schedule requires that you cover the lesson objectives in a shorter time, use . . .
- Preparing to Read, p. 659
- Thinking Through the Literature, p. 664
- Vocabulary in Action, p. 665

If you want to take advantage of longer class time, use . . .
- TE Teaching Options: Preteaching Vocabulary, p. 660; Grammar, p. 662; Speaking and Listening, p. 665
- Choices & Challenges and Author Activity, p. 665

Reading and Analyzing

Active Reading

ANALYZING THE BIOGRAPHER'S PERSPECTIVE

A This section is an extended exchange between the biographer and his subject concerning a difficult issue. Ask students to evaluate the relationship between the two men and to comment on how it shapes the section.

Possible Response: Boswell appears in the role of questioner and Johnson in the role of authority. Boswell continues to ask Johnson about death even though he knows the topic disturbs Johnson. Still, Boswell seems sympathetic about Johnson's fear and is regretful about disturbing him so much.

Literary Analysis BIOGRAPHY

B Boswell's examples of Johnson's daring actions show the importance of detail in biography. Ask students what effect this information has on their appreciation of the selection.

Possible Response: Students may like Johnson better because they see his active, physical side instead of just his wit and sharp thinking.

Literary Analysis: HUMOR

Ask students which of the sections has the most humor. How does Boswell's mix of humor and seriousness affect their impression of him as a biographer?

Possible Responses: The section on eating is funniest, followed by the piece on the equality of women; the section on death is most serious. Boswell appears evenhanded in his presentation of both humorous and serious conversations with Johnson.

Johnson and Boswell (late 1700s), engraving by unknown artist. Copyright © British Museum.

men must mix in the world indiscriminately. If a woman has no inclination to do what is wrong being secured from it is no restraint to her. I am at liberty to walk into the Thames; but if I were to try it, my friends would restrain me in Bedlam,[5] and I should be obliged to them."

MRS. KNOWLES. "Still, Doctor, I cannot help thinking it a hardship that more indulgence is allowed to men than to women. It gives a superiority to men, to which I do not see how they are entitled."

JOHNSON. "It is plain, Madam, one or other must have the superiority. As Shakespeare says, 'If two men ride on a horse, one must ride behind.'"

DILLY. "I suppose, Sir, Mrs. Knowles would have them to ride in panniers,[6] one on each side."

JOHNSON. "Then, Sir, the horse would throw them both."

MRS. KNOWLES. "Well, I hope that in another world the sexes will be equal."

BOSWELL. "That is being too ambitious, Madam. *We* might as well desire to be equal with the angels. *We* shall all, I hope, be happy in a future state, but we must not expect to be all happy in the same degree. It is enough if we be happy according to our several capacities. A worthy carman[7] will get to heaven as well as Sir Isaac Newton.[8] Yet, though equally good, they will not have the same degrees of happiness."

JOHNSON. "Probably not."

A On the Fear of Death (1769)

I mentioned to him that I had seen the execution of several convicts at Tyburn,[9] two days before, and that none of them seemed to be under any concern.

JOHNSON. "Most of them, Sir, have never thought at all."

BOSWELL. "But is not the fear of death natural to man?"

JOHNSON. "So much so, Sir, that the whole of life is but keeping away the thoughts of it."

He then, in a low and earnest tone, talked of his meditating upon the awful hour of his own dissolution,[10] and in what manner he should conduct himself upon that occasion: "I know not (said he,) whether I should wish to have a friend by me, or have it all between God and myself." . . .

When we were alone, I introduced the subject of death, and endeavored to maintain that the fear of it might be got over. I told him that David Hume[11] 1
said to me, he was no more uneasy to think he should *not be* after this life, than that he *had not been* before he began to exist.

JOHNSON. "Sir, if he really thinks so, his perceptions are disturbed; he is mad: if he does not think so, he lies. He may tell you, he holds his finger in the flame of a candle, without feeling pain; would you believe him? When he dies, he at least gives up all he has."

BOSWELL. "Foote,[12] Sir, told me, that when he was very ill he was not afraid to die."

JOHNSON. "It is not true, Sir. Hold a pistol to Foote's breast, or to Hume's breast, and threaten to kill them, and you'll see how they behave."

BOSWELL. "But may we not fortify our minds for the approach of death?"

Here I am sensible[13] I was in the wrong, to bring before his view what he ever looked upon with horror; for although when in a celestial frame, in his "Vanity of Human Wishes," he has supposed death to be "kind Nature's signal for retreat," from this state of being to "a happier seat," his thoughts upon this awful change were in general full of dismal apprehensions. His mind

5. **Bedlam:** a London institution for the mentally ill.
6. **panniers** (păn′yərz): a pair of baskets hung across the back of a pack animal.
7. **carman:** carriage driver.
8. **Sir Isaac Newton:** a famous English mathematician.
9. **Tyburn:** the former site of public hangings in London.
10. **awful . . . dissolution:** awe-inspiring hour of his own death.
11. **David Hume:** a Scottish philosopher and historian.
12. **Foote:** Samuel Foote, an actor and dramatist.
13. **sensible:** aware.

Teaching Options

Grammar

VERBS: USING THE PROGRESSIVE FORM

Instruction The progressive forms of a verb are used to express progressive, or ongoing, actions. They are constructed by combining simple and perfect tenses of *be* with the present participle of a verb. Review with students the following chart showing examples of the six progressive forms.

Present Progressive Boswell is writing a biography.
Past Progressive Boswell was writing a biography.
Future Progressive Boswell will be writing a biography.
Present Perfect Progressive Boswell has been writing a biography.
Past Perfect Progressive Boswell had been writing a biography.
Future Perfect Progressive Boswell will have been writing a biography.

resembled the vast amphitheater, the Colosseum at Rome. In the center stood his judgment, which, like a mighty gladiator, combated those apprehensions that, like the wild beasts of the *Arena,* were all around in cells, ready to be let out upon him. After a conflict, he drove them back into their dens; but not killing them, they were still assailing him. To my question, whether we might not fortify our minds for the approach of death, he answered, in a passion, "No, Sir, let it alone. It matters not how a man dies, but how he lives. The act of dying is not of importance, it lasts so short a time." He added, (with an earnest look,) "A man knows it must be so, and submits. It will do him no good to whine."

I attempted to continue the conversation. He was so provoked, that he said, "Give us no more of this"; and was thrown into such a state of agitation, that he expressed himself in a way that alarmed and distressed me; showed an impatience that I should leave him, and when I was going away, called to me sternly, "Don't let us meet to-morrow."

B

On Johnson's Physical Courage (1775)

. . . No man was ever more remarkable for personal courage. He had, indeed, an awful dread of death, or rather, "of something after death"; and what rational man, who seriously thinks of quitting all that he has ever known, and going into a new and unknown state of being, can be without that dread? But his fear was from reflection; his courage natural. His fear, in that one instance, was the result of philosophical and religious consideration. He feared death, but he feared nothing else, not even what might occasion death. Many instances of his resolution may be mentioned. One day, at Mr. Beauclerk's house in the country, when two large dogs were fighting, he went up to them, and beat them till they separated; and at another time, when told of the danger there was that a gun might burst if charged with many balls, he put in six or seven, and fired it off against a wall. Mr. Langton told me, that when they were swimming together near Oxford, he cautioned Dr. Johnson against a pool, which was reckoned particularly dangerous; upon which Johnson directly swam into it. He told me himself that one night he was attacked in the street by four men, to whom he would not yield, but kept them all at bay, till the watch came up, and carried both him and them to the roundhouse.[14] In the playhouse at Lichfield, as Mr. Garrick informed me, Johnson having for a moment quitted a chair which was placed for him between the side-scenes, a gentleman took possession of it, and when Johnson on his return civilly demanded his seat, rudely refused to give it up; upon which Johnson laid hold of it, and tossed him and the chair into the pit. Foote, who so successfully 2 revived the old comedy, by exhibiting living characters, had resolved to imitate Johnson on the stage, expecting great profits from his ridicule of so celebrated a man. Johnson being informed of his intention, and being at dinner at Mr. Thomas Davies's the bookseller, from whom I had the story, he asked Mr. Davies "what was the common price of an oak stick"; and being answered sixpence, "Why then, Sir, (said he,) give me leave to send your servant to purchase me a shilling one. I'll have a double quantity; for I am told Foote means to *take me off,* as he calls it, and I am determined the fellow shall not do it with impunity." Davies took care to acquaint Foote of this, which effectually checked the wantonness of the mimic. Mr. Macpherson's menaces[15] made Johnson provide himself with the same implement of defense; and had he been attacked, I have no doubt that, old as he was, he would have made his corporal prowess be felt as much as his intellectual. ❖

14. **roundhouse:** jail.

15. **Mr. Macpherson's menaces:** the threats of James Macpherson, a Scottish poet whose "translations" of alleged third-century poems had been exposed as frauds by Johnson.

WORDS TO KNOW

impunity (ĭm-pyo͞o'nĭ-tē) *n.* freedom from punishment or penalty
corporal (kôr'pər-əl) *adj.* bodily; physical

663

Customizing Instruction

Less Proficient Readers

1 Help students clarify the meaning of Hume's comment. Be sure they recognize how the wordplay emphasizes a connection between ceasing to exist and not yet existing while affording a clever way to express the ideas of dying and being born.

2 Explain that Samuel Foote, the comedian against whom Johnson plans to defend himself, was famous for "exhibiting living characters"—that is, he impersonated well-known people in an exaggerated manner onstage. Ask students for their interpretation of the phrase "take me off." What is Johnson worried about?

Possible Responses: The phrase means that Foote will present a humorous and potentially unflattering portrayal of Johnson in the theater. Johnson doesn't want to be humiliated by the comic actor.

Multiple Learning Styles

Interpersonal Learners

Boswell's biography of Johnson is largely a record of social encounters. Encourage volunteers to list three questions that they would like to ask Boswell, Johnson, and Mrs. Knowles.

Activity Write the excerpt from *The Life of Samuel Johnson* on the chalkboard.

"He was so provoked, that he said, "Give us no more of this"; . . . and when I was going away, called to me sternly, "Don't let us meet tomorrow."

Point out that there are many verbs in this excerpt, but only one is in the progressive form. Ask students to identify the verb in the progressive form and its tense. *(was going, past progressive)* Then have students rewrite the phrase *I was going* using the other five progressive forms.

Exercises Ask students to write the correct progressive form of the verb, using the verb and tense named in brackets.

1. Boswell's prodding inquiries concerning death ______ Johnson for quite some time. [agitate - past perfect progressive] *(had been agitating)*
2. If Johnson ______ dinner, Boswell knew better than to interrupt his feast with a petty question. [eat - past progressive] *(was eating)*

Use **Grammar Transparencies and Copymasters,** p. 140.

Use McDougal Littell's ***Language Network*** for more instruction and practice in in the progressive forms of verbs.

GUIDING STUDENT RESPONSE

Connect to the Literature

1. **What Do You Think?**
Guidelines for student response: Students should provide reasons, as well as examples from the text, to explain why they found certain excerpts more interesting.

Comprehension Check

- He loved good food and drink.
- Johnson did not want to talk about death and dying.

Use Selection Quiz in **Unit Three Resource Book** p. 88.

Think Critically

2. Possible Responses: Johnson's opinions are biased or are expressed to provoke argument or show off his verbal skills, rather than based on evidence and fairness; Johnson's opinions are based on his own personal experience and therefore carry a lot of weight.
3. Possible Responses: Johnson was a brave person; he feared death but very little else.
4. Possible Response: Johnson's personal eccentricities played a role in his fame, but his learning and his brilliant, witty conversation were primary factors.
5. Responses will vary. Some students may think Boswell is credible because he gives a detailed and complex view of Johnson; others may think his perspective is colored by hero worship.

Literary Analysis

Cooperative Learning Activity Groups should share their inferences about Johnson's character with one another. Based on these exchanges, students might make a list on the chalkboard of the dominant traits of Johnson's character.

Active Reading Using a biography as a source is appropriate when we want anecdotes about a person or when we want to know what other people thought of the subject. A biography might be an inappropriate source if we want an unbiased account of a person. Boswell, of course, was an eyewitness to some of the events he records.

Thinking through the LITERATURE

Connect to the Literature

1. **What Do You Think?** Which of these excerpts did you find most interesting?

Comprehension Check
- What was Johnson's attitude toward food and drink?
- Why did Johnson become angry with Boswell?

Think Critically

2. Do you think that Johnson's opinions are fair and based on adequate evidence? Support your conclusion with details from the selection.

3. How do you account for Johnson's willingness to risk his life despite his great fear of death?

THINK ABOUT
- Johnson's response to a challenge
- his forcefulness in expressing himself
- Boswell's statement that Johnson's "fear was from reflection; his courage natural"

4. What do you think might account for Johnson's becoming such a well-known figure in his time?

5. **ACTIVE READING** **ANALYZING THE BIOGRAPHER'S PERSPECTIVE** Review the examples you listed in your **READER'S NOTEBOOK** that reveal Boswell's perspective. Do you think Boswell was a credible chronicler of Johnson's life? Why or why not?

Extend Interpretations

6. **Comparing Texts** Compare Johnson's **description** of Mr. Sober in "On Idleness" (page 655) with Boswell's depiction of Johnson. Which characteristics of Mr. Sober do you think could be used to describe Johnson?

7. **Writer's Style** In his **biography** of Samuel Johnson, Boswell recounts many humorous moments and conversations. Look for two or three examples of **humor** in the excerpts you have read. What part does humor seem to play in Boswell's portrayal of Johnson's personality?

8. **Connect to Life** The four subjects treated in these excerpts—eating, the equality of men and women, death, and courage—are still important issues. Choose one of the four subjects and compare the aspects of it that concerned Johnson with the aspects that are most commonly discussed today.

Literary Analysis

BIOGRAPHY In a good **biography,** the reader is provided with a full picture of the subject's personality. The skilled biographer synthesizes information from many sources and strives for a balanced portrayal through detailed anecdotes, reconstructed dialogue, description, quotations, and interpretive passages. Notice how Boswell uses description and interpretation to convey Johnson's attitude toward eating.

- ***When at table, he was totally absorbed in the business of the moment; his looks seemed riveted to his plate. . . .***
- ***He could refrain, but he could not use moderately.***

Cooperative Learning Activity In a small group, discuss some of the details, conversations, and incidents Boswell includes in these excerpts. What can you infer about Johnson's character from these accounts?

ACTIVE READING **EVALUATING SOURCES** For a piece of writing to be a valid source of information, it must be both **credible** and **appropriate.** A work may contain reliable facts about its subject, but the type of information or the way it is presented may not be appropriate for particular research tasks and objectives. Think about the content and how it is presented in Boswell's biography of Johnson. In what situations would the biography be an appropriate source of information? When inappropriate?

Extend Interpretations

Comparing Texts Possible response: Sober enjoys conversation, and clearly Johnson also delighted in talking with others.

Writer's Style Johnson's comments about other people are often humorous as well as critical, and his phrasing is often humorous even on serious topics. When Boswell shows us this humor, he alleviates the impression that Johnson was gloomy or overly serious.

Connect to Life Accept all reasonable, well-supported responses. Possible response: Today we are concerned with good manners, with socializing during a meal, and with keeping up with the latest food trends.

Writing Options

Biography Outline Think about the famous person you identified for the Connect to Your Life on page 659. Write a brief proposal outlining your ideas for a biography of the person.

Activities & Explorations

Scene in Pantomime Work with classmates to present in pantomime one of the scenes from these excerpts. Use gestures and facial expressions to convey the characters' personalities. ~ **VIEWING AND REPRESENTING**

Building Vocabulary
For in-depth study of context clues, see page 938.

Vocabulary in Action

EXERCISE: CONTEXT CLUES Write the word that best completes each sentence.

1. When Johnson was attacked physically or verbally, he was likely to respond in a ________ manner.
2. Surely Johnson's threatening to take a stick to an actor who made fun of him was not the reaction of a ________ man.
3. Johnson frequently used biting sarcasm to attack people who offended him, but at times his attack would be more ________.
4. People quickly found that they could not be rude to Johnson with ________.
5. Clearly, a person with a reasonable amount of ________ would have hesitated to insult or offend Johnson unnecessarily.

WORDS TO KNOW: corporal, discernment, impunity, temperate, vehement

James Boswell
1740–1795

Other Works
The Journal of a Tour to the Hebrides, with Samuel Johnson, LL.D.
Boswell's London Journal: 1762–1763

A Reluctant Lawyer Born in Edinburgh, Scotland, James Boswell was the oldest son of Lord Auchinleck, a wealthy landowner and prominent judge. Under his father's prodding, young Boswell reluctantly took up the study of law, and he did eventually practice law, marry, raise a family, and manage the Auchinleck estate; but his real passion was London—its zest, elegance, and wit. Because he was charming and had a gift for friendship, he became well-known and widely liked in the city.

The Odd Couple His most famous friendship, of course, was with Samuel Johnson, though the two men could not have been more different. Whereas Johnson was learned, deeply religious, and revered for the logic, seriousness, and elegance of his writings, Boswell was gregarious, insatiably curious, and frivolous. Beneath Boswell's apparent superficiality, however, lay a great ability to listen to other people and to record their words and behavior in astonishing detail.

Biographer and Diarist Extraordinaire Boswell began keeping a diary at about the age of 16. It was thought for many years that his personal papers had been destroyed, but during the 1920s and 1930s, in a series of events that read like a detective story, 8,000 pages of Boswell's journal came to light. The diary reveals the extent of Boswell's genius. With a prodigious memory for detail, he described events, recorded impressions, and reconstructed entire conversations with unparalleled immediacy and vividness. Ironically, Boswell died thinking himself a failure, never to know that he would be acclaimed as both the world's greatest biographer and a brilliant diarist.

Author Activity

The Life of James Boswell Locate a copy of Boswell's *Journal* and read some of the entries. What impression do the entries convey of Boswell? How does this impression compare with the image you formed of him after reading the excerpts from *The Life of Samuel Johnson?*

Writing Options

Biography Outline Have students jot down notes from the discussion they had with their partner about the Connect to Your Life. These notes will serve as a good starting point for their outlines. The proposal might have an introduction identifying the celebrity and persuasively setting forth the value of biography and then an outline listing proposed chapters or topics, with some notes on potential details.

Activities & Explorations

Scene in Pantomime Johnson's lack of genteel manners, his lusty eating habits, his gesticulations while speaking, and his threats of violence all would lend themselves to vivid pantomime. Students should present their pantomimes to the class or to small groups, and spectators should provide responses to the performances, perhaps suggesting additional details.

Vocabulary in Action

EXERCISE
1. vehement
2. temperate
3. corporal
4. impunity
5. discernment

Author Activity

The Life of James Boswell For example, the entry for Saturday, 27 November 1762, shows that Boswell knew many prominent people in London. In both his journal and his *Life of Samuel Johnson,* Boswell gives the impression of being well connected and knowledgeable about current issues. In his description of his friends in his journal, we see the same attention to detail found in his biography of Johnson.

Mini Lesson Speaking and Listening

DIALOGUE

Instruction Boswell frequently uses dialogue—between himself and Johnson, between Johnson and other people—as a way of bringing Johnson to life. Point out that Boswell's reconstructed dialogues seem to allow us direct access to Johnson's thoughts, opinions, and personality.

Prepare Divide students into groups or pairs, and have them read the sections of dialogue aloud to get a feel for Boswell's diction and rhythm. Then, have them construct their own dialogues between Johnson and Boswell on a topic of current interest, such as animal rights or television rating systems. Remind students to pay close attention both to Boswell's style as a biographer and to Johnson's wit and love of debate.

Present Have students perform their dialogues for the class, and invite responses from the audience on the effectiveness of the language used and the presentation of Johnson's and Boswell's characters.

BLOCK SCHEDULING This activity is particularly well-suited for longer class periods.

THE LIFE OF SAMUEL JOHNSON 665

OVERVIEW

This selection is included in the **Grade 12 InterActive Reader.**

Objectives

1. understand and appreciate a classic **poem (Literary Analysis)**
2. appreciate the author's use of **personification (Literary Analysis)**
3. **make inferences from details** to appreciate and understand the poem **(Active Reading)**

Summary

The poet begins the poem with a description of the evening, commenting that only sheep, beetles, and an owl break the silence. After revealing that he is in a churchyard, the speaker goes on to discuss the humble but productive lives of the peasants buried there and remarks that the grandeur and ceremony of the upper classes cannot cheat death. He observes that while the rural poor have missed a chance at poetic greatness, they have also avoided the horrors of famous but vice-ridden politicians. An imagined account of the poet's own life and death by one of the peasants follows, and the speaker's own epitaph ends the poem.

Thematic Link

This poem meditates on issues related to death: the sorrow of losing loved ones, death's inevitability and universality, and reflections on life prompted by the acceptance of death. The poem provides moments of profound **revelation about human nature.**

5-Minute Warm-Up

Daily Language SkillBuilder

Have students **proofread** the display sentences on page 515m and write them correctly. The sentences also appear on Transparency 17 of **Grammar Transparencies and Copymasters.**

PREPARING to *Read*

"The paths of glory lead but to the grave."

Elegy Written in a Country Churchyard

Poetry by THOMAS GRAY

Connect to Your Life

Thoughts of Final Things Think about times when you have traveled past or visited a cemetery. What thoughts and feelings did you have? Did you feel sad? Did you wonder about the lives of the people buried there? With a group of classmates, explore your reactions by completing a cluster diagram similar to the one shown.

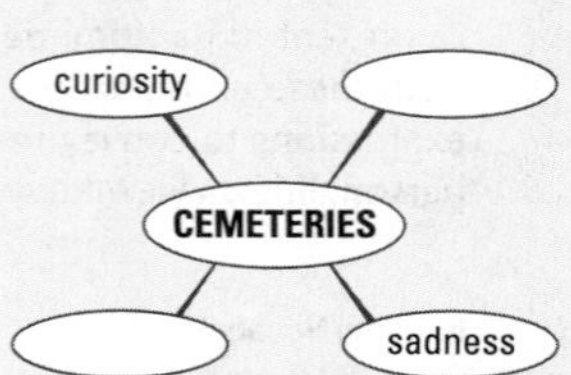

Build Background

A Preromantic Poet Thomas Gray is one of the transitional poets sometimes called preromantic. These poets typically employed the elaborate, stately diction of the neoclassicists but used it to treat different subjects and explore new outlooks. Whereas many neoclassical writers often focused on city life, for example, Gray usually found his subject matter in the country and in nature. Neoclassicists emphasized simplicity and emotional restraint, but Gray dared to describe intense personal feelings.

Gray began "Elegy Written in a Country Churchyard" after his close friend Richard West died at the age of 26. The melancholy and depression Gray suffered as a result of this loss inspired some portions of the elegy, which he spent eight years writing and revising. Although the sense of loss it expresses may be personal, the poem nevertheless clearly has relevance to the lives of all people. This universal appeal has made it one of the most-quoted poems in English literature.

Focus Your Reading

LITERARY ANALYSIS PERSONIFICATION **Personification** is a type of figurative language in which human qualities are attributed to an object, animal, or idea. Notice how Gray personifies the ideas of honor, flattery, and death in the following lines:

Can Honor's voice provoke the silent dust,
Or Flattery soothe the dull cold ear of Death?

As you read this poem, look for other examples of personification used by the poet.

ACTIVE READING MAKING INFERENCES FROM DETAILS You can **make inferences** about the people Gray writes about by paying attention to the **descriptive details** he provides. As you read, notice details related to the following categories:

- the villagers' values—what they believe
- the conditions of their lives
- their dreams and ambitions

READER'S NOTEBOOK Create a list of details about the villagers. Next to each detail, cite the line or lines of the poem that convey the information.

LESSON RESOURCES

UNIT THREE RESOURCE BOOK, pp. 89–90

ASSESSMENT RESOURCES

Formal Assessment, p. 113

Teacher's Guide to Assessment and Portfolio Use

Test Generator

SKILLS TRANSPARENCIES AND COPYMASTERS

Reading and Critical Thinking

- Making Inferences, T7 (for Active Reading, p. 666)

Grammar

- Verbs–Using Correct Verb Forms, T45 (for Mini Lesson, p. 673)
- Emphatic Verb Forms, C131 (for Mini Lesson, p. 673)

Vocabulary

- Using a Dictionary, C56 (for Mini Lesson, p. 667)
- Words with Multiple Meanings, C57 (for Mini Lesson, p. 669)

Writing

- Literary Interpretation, C33 (for Writing Option 1, p. 673)

Communications

- Appreciative Listening, T2 (for Activities & Explorations, p. 673)
- Reading Aloud, T11 (for Activities & Explorations, p. 673)

INTEGRATED TECHNOLOGY

Audio Library

LaserLinks

- Art Gallery: English Hamlets and Churchyards. See **Teacher's SourceBook,** p. 39.

Internet: Research Starter

Visit our website: www.mcdougallittell.com

Elegy Written in a Country Churchyard

Thomas Gray

The curfew tolls the knell of parting day,
    The lowing herd wind slowly o'er the lea,
The plowman homeward plods his weary way,
    And leaves the world to darkness and to me.

Now fades the glimmering landscape on the sight,
    And all the air a solemn stillness holds,
Save where the beetle wheels his droning flight,
    And drowsy tinklings lull the distant folds;

Save that from yonder ivy-mantled tower
    The moping owl does to the moon complain
Of such, as wandering near her secret bower,
    Molest her ancient solitary reign.

GUIDE FOR READING

2 lea (lē): meadow.

667

TEACHING THE LITERATURE

Customizing Instruction

Less Proficient Readers

Set a Purpose Have students read to find out who is buried in this cemetery and how the speaker of the poem feels about them.

Students Acquiring English

Ask students to work in mixed-ability groups to discover the rhyme scheme. Then, ask them to read several lines aloud together and decide how many strong beats, or stressed syllables, there are in each line.

Answer: The rhyme scheme is abab, cdcd, efef, and so on; there are five stressed syllables per line; the meter is iambic pentameter.

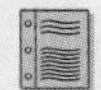

Use **Spanish Study Guide** for additional support, pp. 149–151.

Gifted and Talented

Invite students to discuss and take notes on the poem's content and style. Then, have them write short poems that respond to Gray's "Elegy," using the same style, rhyme scheme, and meter.

Mini Lesson Vocabulary Strategy

USING THE DICTIONARY

Instruction Gray uses many difficult and archaic words in his poem. Because poetry is a streamlined form of writing, context clues often provide less help than they would in prose. A dictionary is often very useful. Have students make a list of unfamiliar words that are not defined in footnotes. Help them discover the precise meanings and usages of those words by using a dictionary.

Activity ***knell*** *(line 1)*

- Definition (from dictionary): an indication that something has ended or died
- "The curfew tolls the knell of parting day" means "The curfew bells signal the end of the day."

Use **Vocabulary Transparencies and Copymasters,** p. 52.

Reading and Analyzing

GUIDE FOR READING

A In a churchyard where elms and yews grow and overhang the gravestones.

Literary Analysis PERSONIFICATION

B Line 17 presents one of many instances of personification in the poem. Ask students to identify the human qualities attributed to morning and what effect this use of personification has on them.

Answer: Morning calls and breathes. Remind students to watch for other instances of personification as they read and to think about why Gray might have used this figure of speech.

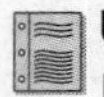

Use **Unit Three Resource Book,** p. 90 for more exercises.

Active Reading

MAKING INFERENCES FROM DETAILS

C Remind students that an inference is a logical guess or conclusion based on information in the text and on experience. Ask what inference students can draw from details presented in lines 25–28.

Possible Response: The peasants work hard and long in the fields but do so with a happy attitude and with strength and competence.

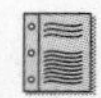

Use **Unit Three Resource Book,** p. 89 for more practice.

GUIDE FOR READING

D He is respectful; he thinks the rich and poor become equal when facing death.

E the hour of death

F Poor people don't necessarily have the opportunity to develop their potential.

Beneath those rugged elms, that yew tree's shade,
    Where heaves the turf in many a moldering heap,
Each in his narrow cell forever laid,
    The rude forefathers of the hamlet sleep.

The breezy call of incense-breathing Morn,
    The swallow twittering from the straw-built shed,
The cock's shrill clarion, or the echoing horn,
    No more shall rouse them from their lowly bed.

For them no more the blazing hearth shall burn,
    Or busy housewife ply her evening care;
No children run to lisp their sire's return,
    Or climb his knees the envied kiss to share.

Oft did the harvest to their sickle yield,
    Their furrow oft the stubborn glebe has broke;
How jocund did they drive their team afield!
    How bowed the woods beneath their sturdy stroke!

Let not Ambition mock their useful toil,
    Their homely joys, and destiny obscure;
Nor Grandeur hear with a disdainful smile
    The short and simple annals of the poor.

The boast of heraldry, the pomp of power,
    And all that beauty, all that wealth e'er gave,
Awaits alike the inevitable hour.
    The paths of glory lead but to the grave.

Nor you, ye proud, impute to these the fault,
    If Memory o'er their tomb no trophies raise,
Where through the long-drawn aisle and fretted vault
    The pealing anthem swells the note of praise.

Can storied urn or animated bust
    Back to its mansion call the fleeting breath?
Can Honor's voice provoke the silent dust,
    Or Flattery soothe the dull cold ear of Death?

16 rude: unsophisticated; rustic. Where is the speaker? **A**

26 glebe: soil; earth.

27 jocund (jŏk'ənd): merry.

32 annals: descriptive records; history. What is the speaker's attitude toward the dead? **D**

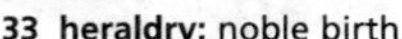

33 heraldry: noble birth.

35 What is meant by "the inevitable hour"? **E**

37 impute . . . fault: assign the blame to them.

38 trophies: sculptures depicting the achievements of the deceased.

39 fretted vault: space enclosed under a decorated arched ceiling.

41 storied . . . bust: an urn for the ashes of the deceased, decorated with scenes from the person's life, or a lifelike portrait sculpture.

43 provoke: call forth.

Teaching Options

BLOCK SCHEDULING: MANAGING TIME

If your schedule requires that you cover the lesson objectives in a shorter time, use . . .
- Preparing to Read, p. 666
- Thinking Through the Literature, p. 672

If you want to take advantage of longer class time, use . . .
- TE Teaching Options: Vocabulary Strategy, pp. 667, 669; Multicultural Link, p. 670; Informal Assessment, p. 671; Grammar, p. 673
- Choices & Challenges and Author Activity, p. 673

Perhaps in this neglected spot is laid
Some heart once pregnant with celestial fire;
Hands that the rod of empire might have swayed,
Or waked to ecstasy the living lyre.

But Knowledge to their eyes her ample page
Rich with the spoils of time did ne'er unroll;
Chill Penury repressed their noble rage,
And froze the genial current of the soul.

Full many a gem of purest ray serene,
The dark unfathomed caves of ocean bear:
Full many a flower is born to blush unseen,
And waste its sweetness on the desert air.

Some village Hampden, that with dauntless breast
The little tyrant of his fields withstood;
Some mute inglorious Milton here may rest,
Some Cromwell guiltless of his country's blood.

The applause of listening senates to command,
The threats of pain and ruin to despise,
To scatter plenty o'er a smiling land,
And read their history in a nation's eyes,

Their lot forbade: nor circumscribed alone
Their growing virtues, but their crimes confined;
Forbade to wade through slaughter to a throne,
And shut the gates of mercy on mankind,

The struggling pangs of conscious truth to hide,
To quench the blushes of ingenuous shame,
Or heap the shrine of Luxury and Pride
With incense kindled at the Muse's flame.

Far from the madding crowd's ignoble strife,
Their sober wishes never learned to stray;
Along the cool sequestered vale of life
They kept the noiseless tenor of their way.

48 lyre: a small harplike musical instrument used in ancient Greece to accompany the singing of poetry and therefore frequently used as a symbol of the poetic art.

51–52 penury (pĕn'yə-rē): extreme poverty; **genial current:** warm, life-giving power. Why has poverty held back their "noble rage" and "genial current"? F

57 Hampden: John Hampden, a 17th-century English politician who opposed the "tyrant" Charles I over unjust taxation.

60 Cromwell: Oliver Cromwell, leader of the Parliamentary forces in the English Civil War and head of the English government from 1653 to 1658.

65 circumscribed: limited; confined.

69 conscious truth: conscience.

72 incense . . . flame: poetic praise.

73 madding: wildly excited; disorderly.

75 sequestered: isolated; secluded.

76 tenor: unwavering course.

Customizing Instruction

Students Acquiring English

1 Ask students to describe the scene in lines 13–16. Point out difficult words and phrases that might obscure the meaning, such as "many a moldering heap" (the mounds of the graves); "narrow cell" (grave); "rude forefathers . . . sleep" (the villagers' ancestors are buried there).

2 Lines 21 and 24 are among many in the poem in which Gray uses inverted word order. Be sure students recognize that this technique is often used in poetry to fit rhyme and meter schemes but that inverted order is extremely uncommon in prose or in speaking. To help students' comprehension, guide them to locate the subject, verb, and object and rephrase the line in that order.

Answer: line 21: "The blazing hearth shall burn for them no more"; line 24: "Or climb his knees to share the envied kiss."

Less Proficient Readers

3 Divide lines 33–36 into smaller phrases and discuss the meaning of each with the class. For example, "the pomp of power" means "the grandeur of important people."

Vocabulary Strategy

MULTIPLE MEANING WORDS

Instruction Explain to students that words often have more than one meaning and that they may have to rely first on dictionaries to discover the various meanings of a word and then on context to determine which meaning is most appropriate.

Exercise Have students identify the multiple meanings of the following words from the poem and select the most appropriate meaning: *molest* (line 12); *homely* (line 30); *swells* (line 40).

Model

pregnant (line 46)

- Various meanings: 1. having possibilities of development or consequence; 2. containing unborn young within the body; 3. abounding in fancy or wit
- Gray is using *heart* in this line in the sense of "spirit" or "soul." Therefore, the first definition fits, but the second does not. The third definition is a possibility, but "fancy or wit" is not generally associated with "celestial fire," or the inspiration of Heaven.
- The first definition is most appropriate.

Use **Vocabulary Transparencies and Copymasters,** p. 52.

ELEGY WRITTEN IN A COUNTRY CHURCHYARD 669

Reading and Analyzing

Literary Analysis: SPEAKER

A Remind students that the speaker is the voice that talks to the reader. The speaker may or may not be the voice of the author, even in a work that uses *I* and *me.* There are potentially several voices in this poem. The primary voice is probably Gray, although it could be that of a person who is visiting the graveyard. Who is the speaker in the last five stanzas of the poem before the epitaph? What is he talking about?
Possible Response: The new speaker is an old peasant who has observed the first speaker's visit to the graveyard. The old man recollects the poet's activities in the countryside and then describes the poet's funeral.

Active Reading
MAKING INFERENCES FROM DETAILS

B According to the peasant's description, what kind of person was the poet? Have students provide details to support their responses.
Possible Responses: The poet was sad and solitary, possibly because of the death of a loved one; he was "drooping," "woeful," and "forlorn"; he seemed depressed and lethargic as he stretched his "listless" body by the brook and stared into the water.

GUIDE FOR READING

C He is modest; he is not famous or rich; he is sad; he is religious; he longs for friendship.

Yet even these bones from insult to protect
　Some frail memorial still erected nigh,
With uncouth rhymes and shapeless sculpture decked,
　Implores the passing tribute of a sigh.

Their name, their years, spelt by the unlettered Muse,
　The place of fame and elegy supply:
And many a holy text around she strews,
　That teach the rustic moralist to die.

For who to dumb Forgetfulness a prey,
　This pleasing anxious being e'er resigned,
Left the warm precincts of the cheerful day,
　Nor cast one longing lingering look behind?

On some fond breast the parting soul relies,
　Some pious drops the closing eye requires;
Even from the tomb the voice of Nature cries,
　Even in our ashes live their wonted fires.

For thee, who mindful of the unhonored dead
　Dost in these lines their artless tale relate;
If chance, by lonely contemplation led,
　Some kindred spirit shall inquire thy fate,

Haply some hoary-headed swain may say,
　"Oft have we seen him at the peep of dawn
Brushing with hasty steps the dews away
　To meet the sun upon the upland lawn.

"There at the foot of yonder nodding beech
　That wreathes its old fantastic roots so high,
His listless length at noontide would he stretch,
　And pore upon the brook that babbles by.

"Hard by yon wood, now smiling as in scorn,
　Muttering his wayward fancies he would rove,
Now drooping, woeful wan, like one forlorn,
　Or crazed with care, or crossed in hopeless love.

81 unlettered Muse: the "inspiration" of the uneducated stonecutters who carved the inscriptions on the tombstones.

85–88 For who . . . behind?: For who has ever accepted that he will be forgotten, leaving the warmth of earthly life without any regret?

90 drops: tears.

92 wonted (wôn′tĭd): accustomed.

93 thee: that is, Gray himself.

97 hoary-headed swain: white-haired peasant.

104 pore: to gaze intently.

Teaching Options

Multicultural Link: African Women Poets

In Gray's time, few European or American women were well-known poets. However, African women have composed poetry as far back as the Eighteenth Dynasty of Egypt. Queen Hatshepsut wrote a poem inscribed on tombs in her mortuary temple at Deir el Bahri. In it, she attributes her power and grandeur to her divine father, Amun. In 1858, Mwana Kupona binti Msham, a Swahili woman, wrote the poem Utendi wa Mwana Kupona (Mwana Kupona's Poem) as an instruction on ethics and etiquette for her daughter, Mwana Hashima binti Sheik. De Sousa, a more modern African poet, played a leading role in the 1940s and 1950s in protest movements against colonialism. In a poem titled "Call," she defies colonial and male African oppression. The poem describes a female villager who sells charcoal and is reduced to poverty by the colonial economy.

"One morn I missed him on the customed hill,
Along the heath and near his favorite tree;
Another came; nor yet beside the rill,
Nor up the lawn, nor at the wood was he;

"The next with dirges due in sad array
Slow through the churchway path we saw him borne.
Approach and read (for thou canst read) the lay,
Graved on the stone beneath yon aged thorn."

111 rill: brook.

113 dirges: funeral hymns.

115 lay: poem.

116 thorn: hawthorn.

The Epitaph

Here rests his head upon the lap of Earth
A youth to fortune and to Fame unknown.
Fair Science frowned not on his humble birth,
And Melancholy marked him for her own.

Large was his bounty, and his soul sincere,
Heaven did a recompense as largely send:
He gave to Misery all he had, a tear,
He gained from Heaven ('twas all he wished) a friend.

No farther seek his merits to disclose,
Or draw his frailties from their dread abode
(There they alike in trembling hope repose),
The bosom of his Father and his God.

117–128 What do you learn about Gray from this epitaph?

Customizing Instruction

Students Acquiring English

1 Help students with poetic and archaic forms such as *e'er* (line 86), *thee* (line 93), and *dost* (line 94), providing replacement words in modern English. *(ever, you,* and *does)*

Less Proficient Readers

Have students check their comprehension. (The correct answer is in boldface.)

- In this poem, the churchyard is a place where people (a) sing hymns; (b) get married; **(c) are buried.**
- The speaker's attitude toward the people in the churchyard is one of **(a) compassion;** (b) envy; (c) anger.
- What the speaker notices most about the people in the churchyard is that they were (a) happy; (b) intelligent; **(c) obscure.**
- The poem is about **(a) the wasting of people's gifts**; (b) the hope of betterment through hard work; (c) the consolation of love.

Gifted and Talented

Invite students to research Gray's life and other works. Have them consider the following questions: Was his background similar to that of the peasants? Was he well educated? Is the strain of melancholy found in this poem predominant in his other works? Gray is known as a poet prone to depression; what events in his life might have contributed to that depression?

Assessment Informal Assessment

WRITING FIRST-PERSON ENTRIES Invite students to write entries in their notebooks using the first-person point of view of the speaker. Their entries should tell about the speaker's experience in the churchyard and should summarize and comment on the scene, thoughts, and feelings in the poem.

RUBRIC

3 Full Accomplishment Journal entries demonstrate understanding of poem's major ideas and feelings.

2 Substantial Accomplishment Journal entries demonstrate awareness that poem is serious meditation on lives and fates of obscure dead.

1 Little or Partial Accomplishment Journal entries do not demonstrate understanding of basic premise of poem.

GUIDING STUDENT RESPONSE

Connect to the Literature

1. **What Do You Think?** Guidelines for student response: Students should support their impressions with evidence from the text. You might discuss with students whether or not they find the speaker admirable.

Comprehension Check
- rural poor
- religious faith

Think Critically

2. Students should support their responses based on information from the text and experience. Students may infer that the people in the poem were poor village folk who made their living farming the land, that they were not educated, that they were not known outside their village, and that they may have had talents that were unfulfilled.
3. Responses will vary. Students might respond that Gray praises the honesty of the rural poor while condemning the corruption of those with power. However, some might think that Gray approves of keeping the harmless peasants in obscurity, away from disorderly, radical influences.
4. Accept all reasonable responses. Students should make specific points of comparison and contrast between their reactions to cemeteries and Gray's reactions.
5. Possible Response: The thought of death depresses him; he fears that he will not have time to live fully before he dies.

Literary Analysis

Paired Activity Possible examples: an owl (lines 10–12), ambition (line 29), grandeur (line 31), memory (line 38), penury (line 51), science (line 119). Personification is useful for poets who want to communicate feelings and abstract ideas in concrete, human terms.

Elegy Possible Response: The poet wants to commemorate the peasants in the churchyard because no one else has remembered them—he is "mindful of the unhonored dead" and relates "their artless tale" (lines 93–94).

Thinking through the LITERATURE

Connect to the Literature

1. **What Do You Think?** What were your impressions of the speaker by the end of the poem?

Comprehension Check
- What kind of people are buried in the churchyard?
- What does the speaker suggest can compensate for unhappiness in life?

Think Critically

2. **ACTIVE READING** **MAKING INFERENCES FROM DETAILS** Review the list of details you made in your  READER'S NOTEBOOK about the people Gray describes. What **inferences** can you make about the lives of the villagers based upon these details? Be specific in your answer.
3. How do you think Gray feels about the society he portrays? Explain your answer.
4. Review the cluster diagram you created for the Connect to Your Life on page 666. How does your reaction to cemeteries compare with Gray's?
5. How would you describe Gray's attitude toward death?

THINK ABOUT
- your answer to question 2
- Gray's description of what someone might say about his own death (lines 98–116)
- his inclusion of his own epitaph

Extend Interpretations

6. **Comparing Texts** Compare the **speakers** of "Elegy Written in a Country Churchyard," Ben Jonson's "On My First Son" (page 459), and Donne's "Holy Sonnet 10" (page 454). Do you notice any similarities or differences in their attitudes toward death? Discuss your observations with your classmates, and compare your ideas with theirs.
7. **Different Perspectives** Consider how different readers might react to this poem. For example, how might the reaction of a 20-year-old reader differ from that of a 70-year-old reader?
8. **Connect to Life** In your opinion, does this poem have relevance to the lives of people today? Why or why not?

Literary Analysis

PERSONIFICATION Gray makes frequent use of **personification** in this poem. In line 117 of the elegy, for example, Earth is personified as a motherly figure upon whose lap the dead may rest their heads. Thus, human qualities of nurturing, affection, and love are attributed to an object.

Paired Activity With a partner, find some other examples of personification in the poem. Make a list of the examples you find and then compare your examples with those found by others. Discuss why you think personification is such a popular figure of speech among poets.

ELEGY Gray's "Elegy Written in a Country Churchyard" is one of the most famous elegies in English literature. An **elegy** is an extended meditative poem in which the speaker reflects upon death—often in tribute to a person who has died recently—or upon an equally serious subject. Most elegies are written in formal, dignified language and are serious in tone. List the purposes you think Gray had for writing his elegy. Give evidence to support your ideas.

Extend Interpretations

Comparing Texts Donne's speaker is defiant in his address to death, while the voice in Jonson's poem is unbearably sad. Gray's speaker is melancholy but does not display extreme anguish or arrogance. All three authors mention their belief in an afterlife, which is a comfort to them.

Different Perspectives A young reader might respond more intellectually to the details of the village, while an older reader might be more emotional, contemplating the meaning of life and death.

Connect to Life Possible Response: The poem is relevant because people still think about whether they have fulfilled their potential; people still think about the nature of death.

Writing Options

1. **Explanatory Paragraph** In a paragraph, explain what you think is meant by "Full many a flower is born to blush unseen, / And waste its sweetness on the desert air" (lines 55–56).

Writing Handbook
See page 1369–1370: Analysis.

2. **Alternative Title** Give the poem a new title that conveys either the poem's mood or an aspect of its subject.

Activities & Explorations

Background Music Create a recording of background music to accompany an oral reading of the poem. For the recording, select an instrumental work or a song (or excerpts from several pieces) that you think complements the poem's mood. Play your recording as you read the poem aloud for your classmates.
~ SPEAKING AND LISTENING

Inquiry & Research

King Charles I Investigate Gray's allusions, in lines 57–60, to events of the reign of Charles I. What circumstances caused the king to be viewed as a "tyrant"? How was he challenged?

More Online: Research Starter
www.mcdougallittell.com

Thomas Gray
1716–1771

Other Works
"Ode on a Distant Prospect of Eton College"
"Ode on the Spring"

Boyhood The only one of his parents' 12 children to survive past infancy, Thomas Gray was rather delicate and frail as a child. Although his mother adored and sheltered her son, his ill-tempered, abusive father frequently vented his rage on the family. Gray was able to escape his uneasy, frightening home life, however, when at the age of 8 he entered boarding school at Eton College. A studious, sensitive boy, he disliked boisterous games and sports and chose friends who shared his scholarly interests. Among these were Horace Walpole—the son of Britain's most prominent Whig leader—and Richard West, a fellow poet.

University and the Grand Tour At about the age of 18, Gray entered Cambridge University. There he embarked upon the study of law, but after several years he abandoned his studies to accompany his friend Walpole on a tour of Europe. The trip ended in a bitter quarrel, which severed their friendship for many years.

A Scholarly Life In 1742, the year of Richard West's early death, Gray returned to Cambridge. There he continued his studies, obtained his degree, and wrote a number of carefully crafted poems. In 1757, the government was ready to offer him the position of poet laureate; however, not wanting to write poems on request and always hesitant to publish his poetry, he declined. Gray remained at Cambridge, rarely leaving its grounds, for the rest of his life. He died at the age of 55 and was buried beside his mother in the rural churchyard at Stoke Poges in Buckinghamshire, the setting of his famous elegy.

Author Activity

A Life of Gray Samuel Johnson, in his *Lives of the Poets,* wrote an essay on Gray. Look at Johnson's essay and find his comments on "Elegy Written in a Country Churchyard." What does Johnson think of the poem? Discuss Johnson's opinions with your classmates.

LaserLinks: Background for Reading
Art Gallery

Writing Options

1. **Explanatory Paragraph** Encourage students to use a topic sentence and to elaborate their responses with examples from the poem and from life. Possible Interpretation: Many beautiful objects live and die without recognition from the world at large.
2. **Alternative Title** Suggest that students look in the poem itself or in other poems they have read for a title. Possible Title: "In Memory of the Unknown."

Activities & Explorations

Background Music Tell students that a requiem is a musical setting of the Mass for the dead, and suggest that they listen to a few requiems written by Mozart, Britten, Brahms, and other composers. Students may also find appropriate popular, religious, or classical songs. Have them select a piece of music that fits well with Gray's poem.

Inquiry & Research

King Charles I Guide students to find appropriate research materials to conduct their investigation of the reign of Charles I. Include both primary sources, such as memoirs, and secondary sources, such as encyclopedias and biographies. Encourage them to link related information and ideas from a variety of sources.

Author Activity

A Life of Gray Although Johnson is less than complimentary about much of Gray's other poetry, he greatly admires "Elegy Written in a Country Churchyard." He says that it is original and expresses sentiments to which every person can relate, which makes it an excellent piece of poetry.

Grammar

VERBS: EMPHATIC FORMS

Instruction The emphatic forms of the present tense and past tense tend to lend force and emphasis to verbs. To form the present emphatic, use the auxiliary *do* or *does* before the present tense of the verb. To form the past emphatic, use the auxiliary *did* before the present tense.

Activity Write on the chalkboard this excerpt from "Elegy Written in a Country Churchyard."

Save that from yonder ivy-mantled tower
The moping owl does to the moon complain
Of such, . . .

Ask students to identify the emphatic form and state whether it is in the present or past tense. *(does complain, present)* Discuss how the use of the emphatic form in poetry adds to a poem's rhythm and tone. Explain that the emphatic form is commonly used in questions and negative statements.

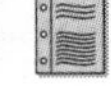

Use **Grammar Transparencies and Copymasters,** p. 134.

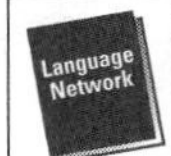

Use McDougal Littell's ***Language Network*** for more instruction in emphatic forms of verbs.

OVERVIEW

Objectives

1. understand and appreciate a **diary entry** in letter form **(Literary Analysis)**
2. appreciate the author's use of **dialogue (Literary Analysis)**
3. understand the effect of **word choice** on tone **(Active Reading)**
4. recognize and compare shared characteristics of cultures through reading

Summary

In this letter to her sister, Burney tells of a party she attends, where she has an unpleasant encounter with the sisters Lady Say and Sele and Lady Hawke. First Burney describes the overdressed and pretentious Lady Say and Sele; then she recalls her introduction to the self-satisfied Lady Hawke, who seems well satisfied to be considered the genius of her family. Burney tells of her momentary escape, only to learn that the two ladies wish to "cultivate her acquaintance"—an entanglement that she avoids by quickly declaring herself "unfortunately engaged."

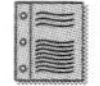
Use **Unit Three Resource Book,** p. 91 for additional support.

Thematic Link

Burney presents a lively and detailed picture of polite British society in the 18th century. Her first-person narrative in the form of a letter provides a humorous **revelation about human nature** in the sometimes pretentious

5-Minute Warm-Up

Daily Language SkillBuilder

Have students **proofread** the display sentences on page 515m and write them correctly. The sentences also appear on Transparency 17 of **Grammar Transparencies and Copymasters.**

from The Diary and Letters of Madame d'Arblay

By FANNY BURNEY

Comparing Literature of the World

The Diary and Letters of Madame d'Arblay and *Memoirs of Madame Vigée-Lebrun*

This lesson and the one that follows present an opportunity for comparing Fanny Burney's personal experiences and observations about life in 18th-century England with those of Madame Vigée-Lebrun about life in 18th-century France. Specific points of comparison in the Vigée-Lebrun lesson will help you note similarities and differences in the writers' comments on human nature and their portrayals of life in their times.

Connect to Your Life

First Impressions Think about your initial conversation with a person you met recently. Did the conversation leave you with a distinct impression of the person? In your opinion, what personality traits can be revealed in a brief conversation? Share your thoughts with your classmates.

Build Background

The Art of Conversation Conversation was a fashionable activity in London throughout the 18th century, but after 1750 the preferred setting for conversation changed from coffeehouses to private homes. Parties intended chiefly as occasions for conversation were often hosted by women, particularly the members of a literary group known as the bluestockings.

One of London's most prominent social hostesses was Hester Thrale, whose prestigious guests included the renowned author Samuel Johnson, the playwright Richard Brinsley Sheridan, the painter Joshua Reynolds, the actor David Garrick, the philosopher Edmund Burke, and a young writer named Fanny Burney. At the age of 26, Burney had anonymously published her first novel, *Evelina,* an instant success.

Although Burney (known after her marriage as Madame d'Arblay) achieved immediate fame through her novels, readers today are more familiar with her **diary,** which she began when she was 15 and wrote in regularly for 70 years. A number of the entries are copies of letters to relatives and close friends, including Burney's sister and best friend, Susan Burney Phillips.

WORDS TO KNOW
Vocabulary Preview

ascribed
complacently
inducement
loquacious
transport

Focus Your Reading

LITERARY ANALYSIS **DIALOGUE** Written conversation between two or more people, in either fiction or nonfiction, is called **dialogue.** Writers use dialogue to bring characters to life and to give readers insights into the characters' qualities, personality traits, and reactions to other people. Notice how the following dialogue brings Lady Say and Sele to life:

> ***"I think it's the most elegant novel I ever read in my life. Such a style! I am quite surprised at it. I can't think where you got so much invention!"***

As you read Burney's letter, be aware of how dialogue reveals the speakers' personalities.

ACTIVE READING **EFFECT OF WORD CHOICE ON TONE** Writers choose words that best convey their ideas, delineate their characters, and set a particular mood. The writer's choice of words also helps establish a work's **tone,** the attitude a writer takes toward a subject. As you read Burney's letter, pay attention to the words she uses to describe the people she meets at the party.

READER'S NOTEBOOK Make a list of all the people Burney encounters. As you read, jot down words used to describe each person.

LESSON RESOURCES

UNIT THREE RESOURCE BOOK, pp. 91–95

ASSESSMENT RESOURCES
Formal Assessment, pp. 115–116
Teacher's Guide to Assessment and Portfolio Use
Test Generator

SKILLS TRANSPARENCIES AND COPYMASTERS
Reading and Critical Thinking
- Analyzing Emotional Appeals, T19 (for Active Reading, p. 679)

Grammar
- Agreement of Subject and Verb, T47 (for Mini Lesson, p. 677)
- Subject-Verb Agreement I, C140 (for Mini Lesson, p. 677)

Writing
- Effective Language, T13 (for Writing Option 1, p. 680)
- The Uses of Dialogue, T24 (for Writing Option 2, p. 680)
- Dramatic Scene, C31 (for Writing Option 1, p. 680)

INTEGRATED TECHNOLOGY
Audio Library
Visit our website:
www.mcdougallittell.com

FROM

The Diary and Letters of MADAME D'ARBLAY

FANNY BURNEY

Letter to Mrs. Phillips, Her Sister

I thank you most heartily for your two sweet letters, my ever dearest Susy, and equally for the kindness they contain and the kindness they accept. And, as I have a frank[1] and a subject, I will leave my *bothers,* and write you and my dear brother Molesworth a little account of a *rout*[2] I have just been at, at the house of Mr. Paradise.

You will wonder, perhaps, in this time of hurry, why I went thither; but when I tell you Pacchierotti[3] was there, you will not think it surprising.

There was a crowd of company; Charlotte and I went together; my father came afterwards. Mrs. Paradise received us very graciously, and led me immediately up to Miss Thrale, who was sitting by the Pac.[4] The Miss Kirwans, you may be sure, were not far off, and so I did pretty well. There was nobody else I knew but Dr. Solander, Mr. Coxe, the traveler, Sir Sampson and Lady Gideon (Streatham acquaintances), Mr. Sastres, and Count Zenobia, a noble Venetian, whom I have often met lately at Mrs. Thrale's.

We were very late, for we had waited cruelly for the coach, and Pac. had sung a song out of *Artaxerxes,*[5] composed for a tenor, which we lost, to my infinite regret. Afterwards he sang "Dolce speme," set by Bertoni, less elegantly than by Sacchini, but more expressively for the words. He sang it delightfully. It was but the second time I have heard him in a room since his return to England.

1. **frank:** an envelope marked by an official so that it can be mailed without postage.
2. **rout:** party.
3. **Pacchierotti** (päk′yĕ-rôt′tē): a well-known operatic singer of the time.
4. **Pac.:** an abbreviation of *Pacchierotti.*
5. ***Artaxerxes*** (är′tə-zûrk′sēz′): an opera by the 18th-century British composer Thomas Arne.

TEACHING THE LITERATURE

Customizing Instruction

CORE OBJECTIVES

1. understand and appreciate a **diary entry** in letter form **(Literary Analysis)**
2. appreciate the author's use of **dialogue (Literary Analysis)**
3. understand the effect of **word choice** on tone **(Active Reading)**
4. recognize and compare shared characteristics of cultures through reading

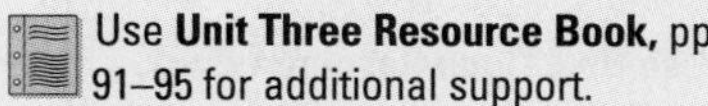
Use **Unit Three Resource Book,** pp. 91–95 for additional support.

ASSESSMENT RESOURCES

- Selection Quiz, Unit Three Resource Book, p. 95
- Formal Assessment, pp. 115–116
- Teacher's Guide to Assessment and Portfolio Use
- Test Generator

BLOCK SCHEDULING: MANAGING TIME

INTEGRATING SKILLS

Grammar

- Mini Lesson, p. 677 Subject and Verb Agreement

Vocabulary

- Mini Lesson, p. 676 Preteaching WORDS TO KNOW

USING MEDIA RESOURCES

Audio Library

Visit our website:
www.mcdougallittell.com

Reading and Analyzing

Active Reading

EFFECT OF WORD CHOICE ON TONE

(A) Remind students that tone is the writer's attitude toward his or her subject matter. Tone is not quantifiable but rather is suggested through the author's choice of words. What is Burney's tone in her description of Lady Say and Sele, and how does her word choice reflect her attitude? Have students describe how Burney's attitude or stance affects the tone.

Possible Response: She is not very impressed with her gaudy dress nor with her overexcited and gushing manner.

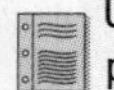 Use **Unit Three Resource Book,** p. 92 for more practice.

Literary Analysis DIALOGUE

(B) Ask volunteers to enact Burney's dialogue with the two sisters (from "Well, and so you wrote this pretty book . . ." to "I was sadly afraid it would not have been . . ."). Discuss what feelings and attitudes Burney implies with her hesitant responses.

Ask students what impression of the two ladies Burney is trying to convey by quoting their rapid-fire dialogue.

Possible Response: She is trying to convey that they are silly, loud, foolish, and pretentious.

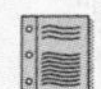 Use **Unit Three Resource Book,** p. 93 for more exercises.

Reading Skills and Strategies:
MAKING JUDGMENTS

(C) Invite students to state and support their opinions of the passage Burney quotes from Lady Hawke's writing.

Possible Response: Some students may be impressed by its complexity, but Burney intends to ridicule it as pretentious and muddled.

The Porten Family, Gawen Hamilton. Museum of Fine Arts, Springfield, Massachusetts, James Philip Gray Collection.

After this he went into another room, to try if it would be cooler; and Mrs. Paradise, leaning over the Kirwans and Charlotte, who hardly got a seat all night for the crowd, said she begged to speak to me. I squeezed my great person out, and she then said,

"Miss Burney, Lady Say and Sele[6] desires the honor of being introduced to you."

(A) Her ladyship stood by her side. She seems pretty near fifty—at least turned forty; her head was full of feathers, flowers, jewels, and geegaws, and as high as Lady Archer's; her dress was trimmed with beads, silver, persian sashes, and all sort of fine fancies; her face is thin and fiery, and her whole manner spoke a lady all alive.

"Miss Burney," cried she, with great quickness, and a look all curiosity, "I am very happy to see you; I have longed to see you a great while; I have read your performance, and I am quite delighted with it. I think it's the most elegant novel I ever read in my life. Such a style! I am quite surprised at it. I can't think where you got so much invention!"

You may believe this was a reception not to make me very loquacious. I did not know which way to turn my head.

"I must introduce you," continued her ladyship, "to my sister; she'll be quite delighted to see you. She has written a novel herself; so you are sister authoresses. A most elegant thing it is, I assure you; almost as pretty as yours, only not quite so elegant. She has written two novels, only one is not so pretty as the other. But I shall insist upon your seeing them. One is in letters, like yours, only yours is prettiest; it's called the *Mausoleum of Julia!*"

What unfeeling things, thought I, are *my* sisters! I'm sure I never heard them go about thus praising *me!*

6. **Lady Say and Sele:** the title of the wife of Baron Say and Sele.

WORDS TO KNOW **loquacious** (lō-kwā′shəs) *adj.* very talkative

676

Teaching Options

 **Preteaching Vocabulary**

USING CONTEXT CLUES

Instruction As students review the WORDS TO KNOW, remind them that they can often rely on context clues to determine the meaning of a word. In particular, they may be able to make inferences from statements following the sentence in which the unfamiliar word is used. These statements may provide clues to the meaning of the word. For example, the exchange between Lady Hawke and Lady Say and Sele following Burney's statement "'I saw Lady Hawke's name ascribed to the play of *Variety*'" on page 677 implies that the newspapers said Lady Hawke wrote the play.

Exercise Have students determine the meaning of the italicized word based on the inferential clues in the second sentence.

The poem has traditionally been *ascribed* to Sappho. However, scholars have recently argued that it was written by an Athenian poet.

 Use **Unit Three Resource Book,** p. 94 for additional support.

A lesson on using context clues appears on p. 939 of the Pupil's Edition.

Mrs. Paradise then again came forward, and taking my hand, led me up to her ladyship's sister, Lady Hawke, saying aloud, and with a courteous smirk, "Miss Burney, ma'am, authoress of *Evelina.*"

"Yes," cried my friend, Lady Say and Sele, who followed me close, "it's the authoress of *Evelina;* so you are sister authoresses!"

Lady Hawke arose and curtsied. She is much younger than her sister, and rather pretty; extremely languishing, delicate, and pathetic; apparently accustomed to be reckoned the genius of her family, and well contented to be looked upon as a creature dropped from the clouds.

I was then seated between their ladyships, and Lady S. and S., drawing as near to me as possible, said,

"Well, and so you wrote this pretty book!—
B and pray did your papa know of it?"

"No, ma'am; not till some months after the publication."

1 "So I've heard; it's surprising! I can't think how you invented it!—there's a vast deal of invention in it! And you've got so much humor, too! Now my sister has no humor—hers is all sentiment. You can't think how I was entertained with that old grandmother and her son!"

I suppose she meant Tom Branghton for the son.

"How much pleasure you must have had in writing it; had not you?"

"Y—e—s, ma'am."

"So has my sister; she's never without a pen in her hand; she can't help writing for her life. When Lord Hawke is traveling about with her, she keeps writing all the way."

"Yes," said Lady Hawke; "I really can't help writing. One has great pleasure in writing the things; has not one, Miss Burney?"

"Y—e—s, ma'am."

"But your novel," cried Lady Say and Sele, "is in
2 such a style!—so elegant! I am vastly glad you made it end happily. I hate a novel that don't end happy."

"Yes," said Lady Hawke, with a languid smile, "I was vastly glad when she married Lord Orville. I was sadly afraid it would not have been."

"My sister intends," said Lady Say and Sele, "to print her *Mausoleum,* just for her own friends and acquaintances."

"Yes," said Lady Hawke, "I have never printed yet."

"I saw Lady Hawke's name," quoth I to my first friend, "ascribed to the play of *Variety.*"

"Did you indeed?" cried Lady Say, in an ecstasy. "Sister! do you know Miss Burney saw your name in the newspapers, about the play!"

"Did she?" said Lady Hawke, smiling complacently. "But I really did not write it; I never wrote a play in my life."

"Well," cried Lady Say, "but do repeat that sweet part that I am so fond of—you know what I mean; Miss Burney *must* hear it,—out of your novel, you know!"

Lady H.—No I can't; I have forgot it.

Lady S.—Oh no! I am sure you have not; I insist upon it.

Lady H.—But I know you can repeat it yourself; you have so fine a memory; I am sure you can repeat it.

Lady S.—Oh, but I should not do it justice! that's all,—I should not do it justice!

Lady Hawke then bent forward, and repeated— C
"'If, when he made the declaration of his love, the sensibility that beamed in his eyes was felt in his heart, what pleasing sensations and soft alarms might not that tender avowal awaken!'"

"And from what, ma'am," cried I, astonished, and imagining I had mistaken them, "is this taken?"

"From my sister's novel!" answered the delighted Lady Say and Sele, expecting my raptures to be equal to her own; "it's in the *Mausoleum,*—did not you know that? Well, I can't think how you can write these sweet novels! And it's all just like that part. Lord Hawke himself says it's all poetry. For my part, I'm sure I never could write so. I suppose, Miss

WORDS TO KNOW

ascribed (ə-skrībd') *adj.* assigned; referred to as a source **ascribe** *v.*
complacently (kəm-plā'sənt-lē) *adv.* in a contented, self-satisfied way; smugly

Customizing Instruction

Multiple Learning Styles

Kinesthetic Learners

To help students understand the action described in the selection, suggest that they stage an informal pantomime of the party as Burney describes it.

Students should take the roles of the various attendees and act as if they are moving about a room, meeting and talking with each other. Encourage them to try to capture their roles' personalities in their pantomime.

Less Proficient Readers

1 Ask students what they think Lady Say and Sele means by "a vast deal of invention" and "all sentiment."

Possible Response: a lot of imagination and creativity; emotion and sentimentality

What details in the text indicate that the comment about invention is a compliment while the comment about sentiment is not?

Answer: The repeated exclamation points show that Lady Say and Sele is enthusiastic as she speaks of Burney's novel; when she speaks of her sister's novel, she begins with a negative comment.

Students Acquiring English

2 Point out the sentence "I hate a novel that don't end happy," and be sure students recognize that this is an incorrect usage in modern English. Have them identify the correct form.

Answer: *don't* should be *doesn't.*

Ask them to find the similar nonstandard usage that appears on the second line of p. 678 and give the correct form.

Answer: *a'n't* should be *aren't.*

Grammar

SUBJECT AND VERB AGREEMENT

Instruction A subject and verb in a sentence must agree in number. *Number* is the term used to indicate whether a word is singular or plural. The subject of a sentence is singular in number when it refers to one person or thing. The subject is plural in number when it refers to more than one person or thing. Singular subjects are used with singular verbs, and plural subjects are used with plural verbs. This is called *agreement.*

Activity Write the following sentence on a chalkboard.

> In "The Diary and Letters of Madame d'Arblay," the author's account of conversations brings characters to life.

Ask students to identify the subject and verb in the sentence. *(account, brings)* Next, ask students what separates the subject and verb in this sentence. *(of conversations)* Explain that a phrase, does not affect the subject and verb agreement.

Use **Grammar Transparencies and Copymasters,** p. 139.

Use McDougal Littell's ***Language Network*** for more instruction in subject and verb agreement.

Reading and Analyzing

Active Reading

EFFECT OF WORD CHOICE ON TONE

A Based on her description, what is Burney's tone regarding Lord Say and Sele? How does he compare to his wife and sister-in-law?

Possible Response: She is unimpressed with the lord—she finds him dull and unimaginative. He is bland compared to the "vehemence" and bold manners of the sisters.

Reading Skills and Strategies: MAKING GENERALIZATIONS

Have students review all the information they have gleaned about the characters (descriptions of clothes, their conversation, facts they reveal about themselves, etc.). Ask for students' overall impressions of the characters. Encourage them to support their responses with details from the text.

Possible Response: Burney is observant, witty, smart, and ironic; she handles herself well with difficult people. We see her disentangle herself from her annoying interlocutors and politely refuse an invitation for a future meeting.

Literary Analysis DIALOGUE

B Ask students what is implied by Burney's concluding statement.

Possible Response: She finds the sisters unbearable. She is obliged to be polite but has no intention of accepting the invitation.

Burney, you are producing another,—a'n't you?"

"No, ma'am."

"Oh, I daresay you are. I daresay you are writing one at this very minute!"

A Mrs. Paradise now came up to me again, followed by a square man, middle-aged, and humdrum, who, I found, was Lord Say and Sele, afterwards from the Kirwans; for though they introduced him to me, I was so confounded by their vehemence and their manners, that I did not hear his name.

"Miss Burney," said Mrs. P., presenting me to him, "authoress of *Evelina*."

"Yes," cried Lady Say and Sele, starting up, "'tis the authoress of *Evelina!*"

"Of what?" cried he.

"Of *Evelina*. You'd never think it,—she looks so young, to have so much invention, and such an elegant style! Well, I could write a play, I think, but I'm sure I could never write a novel."

"Oh yes, you could, if you would try," said Lady Hawke.

"Oh no, I could not," answered she; "I could not get a style—that's the thing—I could not tell how to get a style! and a novel's nothing without a style, you know!"

"Why no," said Lady Hawke; "that's true. But then you write such charming letters, you know!"

"Letters!" repeated Lady S. and S., simpering; "do you think so? Do you know I wrote a long letter to Mrs. Ray just before I came here, this very afternoon,—quite a long letter! I did, I assure you!"

Here Mrs. Paradise came forward with another gentleman, younger, slimmer, and smarter, and saying to me, "Sir Gregory Page Turner," said to him, "Miss Burney, authoress of *Evelina*."

At which Lady Say and Sele, in fresh transport, again arose, and rapturously again repeated—"Yes, she's authoress of *Evelina!* Have you read it?"

"No; is it to be had?"

"Oh dear, yes! it's been printed these two years! You'd never think it! But it's the most elegant novel I ever read in my life. Writ in such a style!"

"Certainly," said he, very civilly; "I have every inducement to get it. Pray where is it to be had? everywhere, I suppose?"

"Oh, nowhere, I hope!" cried I, wishing at that moment it had been never in human ken.[7]

My *square* friend, Lord Say and Sele, then putting his head forward, said, very solemnly, "I'll purchase it!"

His lady then mentioned to me a hundred novels that I had never heard of, asking my opinion of them, and whether I knew the authors; Lady Hawke only occasionally and languidly joining in the discourse: and then Lady S. and S., suddenly arising, begged me not to move, for she should be back again in a minute, and flew to the next room.

I took, however, the first opportunity of Lady Hawke's casting down her eyes, and reclining her delicate head, to make away from this terrible set; and, just as I was got by the piano-forte,[8] where I hoped Pacchierotti would soon present himself, Mrs. Paradise again came to me, and said,

"Miss Burney, Lady Say and Sele wishes vastly to cultivate your acquaintance, and begs to know if she may have the honor of your company to an assembly at her house next Friday?—and I will do myself the pleasure to call for you, if you will give me leave."

"Her ladyship does me much honor, but I am unfortunately engaged," was my answer, with as much promptness as I could command. ❖ B

7. **ken:** range of vision; sight.
8. **piano-forte** (pē-ăn′ō-fôr′tā): piano.

WORDS TO KNOW

transport (trăns′pôrt′) *n.* a state of being carried away by emotion; a state of bliss
inducement (ĭn-dōōs′mənt) *n.* a motive for action; incentive

678

Teaching Options

Mini Lesson: Speaking and Listening

ORAL SUMMARY

Instruction A summary conveys the essential ideas of a work in shortened form. It presents the important points in the same order as the original. It conveys the main idea as well as the tone. An oral summary, especially the retelling of a story or an event, is often less formal than a written summary. A written summary usually reduces the original by deleting unessential details, examples, and anecdotes; an oral summary may retain such elements for entertainment value, depending on the subject and audience.

Prepare Divide students into groups of three. Ask the members of each group to play the roles of Burney and any two of the following characters: Susan Burney Phillips, Lady Say and Sele, Lady Hawke, Lord Say and Sele, Sir Gregory Page Turner, Pacchierotti.

Present Have students take turns retelling the events from the viewpoints of their respective roles.

BLOCK SCHEDULING This activity is particularly well-suited for longer class periods.

Connect to the Literature

1. **What Do You Think?** Jot down your impression of Burney's experience at the party.

Comprehension Check
- Why is Lady Say and Sele so anxious to meet Burney?
- Why does Burney want to escape from Lady Say and Sele and her sister, Lady Hawke?

Think Critically

2. In your opinion, what different aspects of human nature are illuminated by the **dialogue** Burney recounts?

THINK ABOUT
- the reasons for Burney's popularity
- the conduct of Mrs. Paradise
- the sentiments expressed by Lady Say and Sele
- the attitude of Lady Hawke

3. **ACTIVE READING** **EFFECT OF WORD CHOICE ON TONE** Compare your list of descriptive words in your  **READER'S NOTEBOOK** with that of a partner. What **tone** do Burney's word choices help establish? What descriptive words might the writer have used if she had wanted to set an altogether different tone?

4. What kind of person does Fanny Burney seem to be? Cite details from the letter to support your answer.

Extend Interpretations

5. **Comparing Texts** Compare the ways in which Fanny Burney and Samuel Pepys describe social gatherings. How do they differ in the types of details they record? What do the differences reveal about the writers? Justify your answers with examples from their selections in this book.

6. **Different Perspectives** Imagine that Lady Say and Sele writes a gossip column for the society page of her local newspaper. What might she report about her meeting with Fanny Burney? How would her account differ from Burney's?

7. **Connect to Life** Have you ever met or observed a person who behaved like Lady Say and Sele? What do you think motivated the person's behavior?

Literary Analysis

DIALOGUE **Dialogue**—the written conversation between two or more people—helps bring characters to life by providing insights into their qualities and personality traits. It also shows the relationships between characters. Read the following dialogue between Lady Say and her sister:

"Well," cried Lady Say, "but do repeat that sweet part that I am so fond of—you know what I mean; Miss Burney must hear it,—out of your novel, you know!"

Lady H.—No I can't; I have forgot it.

Lady S.—Oh no! I am sure you have not; I insist upon it.

Lady H.—But I know you can repeat it yourself; you have so fine a memory; I am sure you can repeat it.

Lady S.—Oh, but I should not do it justice! that's all,—I should not do it justice!

The dialogue reveals Lady Say's excessive admiration for her sister and her sister's complacent acceptance of it.

Cooperative Learning Activity Do you think Burney's account of the party would have been as effective without dialogue? With a group of classmates, rewrite a scene from the party, replacing the dialogue with description. How does the removal of the dialogue affect your perception of the characters?

GUIDING STUDENT RESPONSE

Connect to the Literature

1. **What Do You Think?**
Accept all reasonable responses. Students may find her experience funny or unbearable; they may think the party sounds interesting or silly.

Comprehension Check
- She wants to appear connected to Burney because Burney is a celebrated author.
- She finds them overbearing and silly.

 Use Selection Quiz in **Unit Three Resource Book,** p. 95.

Think Critically

2. Possible Responses: status seeking, envy, frivolity, showing off, modesty, false modesty, wit, pretension.
3. As students discuss this question, encourage them to think about the effect her tone has on them. Burney's word choices indicate a humorous, amused, and exasperated tone toward her experience at the party. If she had used sharper, more disparaging descriptive words, her tone would have been more serious and critical of the people she met.
4. Possible Response: She is embarrassed by the fuss made over her.

Literary Analysis

Cooperative Learning Activity Many students will say that the account would not have been as effective without dialogue, because the dialogue conveys a great deal of the characterization as well as Burney's attitude. Other students may say that given Burney's skill and wit, she might have found a way to convey those elements through narrative and description. Students might find that removing the dialogue makes the characters more one-dimensional and less lively; others might fill in the characters' physical appearance with more descriptive passages.

Extend Interpretations

Comparing Texts Possible Responses: Pepys and Burney both have encounters with important people; Pepys usually summarizes important points, while Burney brings out telling details; Pepys is willing to let himself look bad at times; Burney is wittier and more willing to mock her acquaintances; Burney's personality intrudes into her diary more than Pepys's into his.

Different Perspectives Encourage students to imagine how Lady Say and Sele sees the world. Her account would probably not include Burney's unflattering picture of Lady Hawke. She might emphasize Burney's celebrity, which would make her meeting with the author more impressive.

Connect to Life Possible Response: People who act like Lady Say and Sele are often motivated by their own insecurity or sense of lack of accomplishment.

Writing Options

1. **Party Script** Students should use Burney's dialogue as the foundation for their scripts, but they might want to trim it and/or add new lines. Have students include cues for entrances and exits and directions for how characters should deliver the lines of dialogue.
2. **Diary Entry** Encourage students to use their own writing style rather than trying to imitate Burney's.

Activities & Explorations

1. **Caricature of a Lady** Remind students that a caricature is a portrait that emphasizes selected features of the subject, usually for comic effect. You might show students some caricatures from political cartoons. Have students review Burney's physical description of Lady Say and Sele.
2. **Photo Essay** Encourage groups of students to work together in looking through a wide variety of magazines in search of photos. Encourage them to write captions or accompanying text intended to evoke certain thoughts and feelings in their readers in response to the photos.

Vocabulary in Action

Exercise

1. transport
2. loquacious
3. ascribed
4. inducement
5. complacently

Writing Options

1. **Party Script** Create a script for the scene Burney describes. Be sure to include any stage directions and director's notes that you think are needed to flesh out the scene.

2. **Diary Entry** Use a conversation that you recently took part in or overheard as the basis for a diary entry written, like Burney's, as a letter to a friend or sibling. Place the entry in your **Working Portfolio.**

Activities & Explorations

1. **Caricature of a Lady** Draw a humorous caricature of Lady Say and Sele, based on the information revealed in this selection. Try to capture her personality as well as her appearance. ~ **ART**

2. **Photo Essay** Create a photo essay called "Conversations." Include pictures that show a variety of facial expressions and gestures. ~ **VIEWING AND REPRESENTING**

Inquiry & Research

Literary Ladies Research the origin of the term *bluestocking.* What role did the bluestockings play in the history of English literature? Did they change society's attitudes toward women?

Vocabulary in Action

EXERCISE: IDIOMS Write the word suggested by each of the following sets of idioms.

1. on cloud nine, walking on air
2. rattle on, run off at the mouth
3. point the finger, give credit where it's due
4. dangle a carrot in front of, light a fire under
5. without batting an eye, not give a hoot

WORDS TO KNOW		
	ascribed	loquacious
	complacently	transport
	inducement	

Building Vocabulary
Several Words to Know in this lesson contain prefixes and suffixes. For an in-depth study of word parts, see page 1104.

Fanny Burney
1752–1840

Timid Child Largely self-taught, Fanny Burney was an avid reader who, by the time she was ten, had begun writing stories, poems, and plays. As a girl, she stood timidly in the background at her father's parties, listening closely to the guests; her remarkable memory allowed her to recall conversations word for word. Even after becoming a successful novelist, she remained modest around her ardent admirers.

Influential Author Burney's novels influenced a number of later female novelists, particularly Jane Austen. *Evelina* was a forerunner of the "novel of manners," a genre in which the customs and conventions of social life occupy a prominent place. None of Burney's other novels had the success of *Evelina,* although Austen was to find both the title and the theme for her *Pride and Prejudice* in Burney's second novel, *Cecilia.*

Working Woman In 1786, Burney's life took a new direction when she reluctantly accepted a position at the court of King George III. It was an unpleasant experience that allowed her little time to write, and she left the court after five years. At age 41, she married Alexandre d'Arblay, a French general who had fled to England during the French Revolution. Although d'Arblay was poor, the proceeds from Burney's third novel, *Camilla,* enabled them to live comfortably. In 1802, a visit to France became a ten-year exile for the d'Arblays and their son when the country suddenly became engaged in war with England. During her later years, back in London, Burney published her father's memoirs. Her own diary was not published until long after her death.

Inquiry & Research

Literary Ladies Refer students to dictionaries or encyclopedias for basic information. Additional resources might include social histories of 18th-century England or reader's encyclopedias.

Have students narrow their focus from the general topic of bluestockings (women who have strong scholarly or literary interests). Students may want to research specific bluestocking women, or perhaps chart the relationship between particular bluestockings and well-known male writers of the time (Mrs. Thrale and Samuel Johnson, for example). Have students work together to narrow their focus and continue their research. Partners should use a variety of sources to compile notes and draw conclusions on their topic.

from Memoirs of Madame Vigée-Lebrun

By ÉLISABETH VIGÉE-LEBRUN (vē-zhā′ lə-brœn′)

Comparing Literature of the World

Personal Narratives Across Cultures

The Diary and Letters of Madame d'Arblay* and *Memoirs of Madame Vigée-Lebrun Like Fanny Burney, Vigée-Lebrun was a keen observer of human nature and offers a unique perspective on some of the famous as well as the ordinary people of her day. Burney and Vigée-Lebrun were writing during the same period, one in England and one in France.

Points of Comparison As you read this memoir, compare how Vigée-Lebrun and Burney paint vivid portraits of their particular time and place through their use of telling detail and attention to daily life.

Build Background

A Painter and Writer In these excerpts from her **memoirs,** Élisabeth Vigée-Lebrun—a gifted artist who painted portraits of the French nobility—recalls events of her own life amidst the turmoil of the French Revolution, which began in 1789. Before the Revolution, France was ruled by a king, who had almost unlimited authority, and by the privileged nobility and clergy. These groups obtained most of the money they needed to maintain their rich lifestyles by taxing peasant farmers and other poor workers. In 1789, the French government's finances were in a shambles. Peasants and farmers were angry because their requests for a voice in government had been denied. Facing economic hardships, they revolted and stormed the Bastille, a Paris fortress-prison that was a hated symbol of royal authority and oppression.

A long period of violence ensued, during which King Louis XVI and his wife, Marie Antoinette, were imprisoned and later executed—the king in January 1793 and the queen in October. The most horrific months of the Revolution, the Reign of Terror, came in late 1793 and 1794, when thousands of citizens were imprisoned and executed.

WORDS TO KNOW
Vocabulary Preview
amiability, consternation, execrable, fortitude, mien

VIDEODISC **LaserLinks:**
Background for Reading
Historical Connection

Focus Your Reading

LITERARY ANALYSIS DESCRIPTION **Description** is writing that helps a reader to picture scenes, events, and characters. Notice, for example, how Vigée-Lebrun describes Marie Antoinette in the following passage:

> ***Her nose was slender and pretty, and her mouth not too large, though her lips were rather thick.***

As you read, be aware of the writer's use of vivid description to bring to life the people and events that she describes.

ACTIVE READING INTERPRETING DETAILS Élisabeth Vigée-Lebrun includes many **details** in her **descriptions.** These details help to create rich and rounded portraits of the various people she encounters in her world.

READER'S NOTEBOOK As you read Vigée-Lebrun's memoirs, use a chart like the one shown to note the details she uses to describe the people whom she encounters.

Person	Details
Marie Antoinette	brilliant complexion

LESSON RESOURCES

UNIT THREE RESOURCE BOOK, pp. 96–100

ASSESSMENT RESOURCES
Formal Assessment, pp. 117–118
Teacher's Guide to Assessment and Portfolio Use
Test Generator

SKILLS TRANSPARENCIES AND COPYMASTERS
Reading and Critical Thinking
- Evaluating Credibility of Information Sources, T43 (for Active Reading, p. 690)

Grammar
- Active and Passive Voice II, C135 (for Mini Lesson, pp. 686–687)

Vocabulary
- Suffixes, C58 (for Mini Lesson, p. 684)

Writing
- Compare-Contrast, C34 (for Writing Options, p. 691)

INTEGRATED TECHNOLOGY
Audio Library
LaserLinks
- Historical Connection: The French Revolution
- Art Gallery: The Art of Vigée-Lebrun. See **Teacher's SourceBook,** pp. 40–41.

Visit our website:
www.mcdougallittell.com

OVERVIEW

Objectives
1. understand and appreciate a **memoir (Literary Analysis)**
2. appreciate the author's use of **description (Literary Analysis)**
3. **interpret details** to appreciate and understand a memoir **(Active Reading)**
4. recognize and compare shared characteristics of cultures through reading

Summary
Élisabeth Vigée-Lebrun recounts some of her experiences with the French aristocracy at the time of the French Revolution. A popular portrait artist, she frequently visited Marie Antoinette, queen of France, finding the queen's beauty, graciousness, and kindness charming. Vigée-Lebrun became frightened by the increasingly aggressive harassment of the nobility by the revolutionaries and resolved to leave France. She and her daughter escaped at night by stagecoach.

Use **Unit Three Resource Book,** p. 96 for additional support.

Thematic Link
Vigée-Lebrun's memoirs contain **revelations about human nature.** They are important social documents, because they provide a detailed account of a notorious period in European history.

5-Minute Warm-Up
Daily Language SkillBuilder

Have students **proofread** the display sentences on page 515m and write them correctly. The sentences also appear on Transparency 17 of **Grammar Transparencies and Copymasters.**

Preteaching Vocabulary
If you would like to preteach the WORDS TO KNOW for this selection, use the Mini Lesson p. 682.

TEACHING THE LITERATURE

Reading and Analyzing

Literary Analysis DESCRIPTION

A Ask students what details Vigée-Lebrun uses to help the reader picture Marie Antoinette.

Possible Responses: "merry and kind" eyes; "rather thick" lips; "brilliant" complexion.

Use **Unit Three Resource Book,** p. 98 for more exercises.

Active Reading
INTERPRETING DETAILS

B Vigée-Lebrun explains that the queen's complexion was so perfect that it was beyond representation. Ask students why the painter would describe the queen this way.

Possible Response: She might be trying to make the queen seem superhuman or divine.

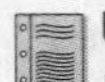
Use **Unit Three Resource Book,** p. 97 for more practice.

Literary Analysis: TONE

C Ask students to pay attention to Vigée-Lebrun's choice of language in these paragraphs. What tone do her words convey?

Answer: Phrasing such as "I had no suspicion of the surprise in store for me," "I can hardly believe that anyone was ever more moved and more grateful than I was," "I was so fortunate," and "I had something of a voice" suggest a modest and flattered attitude.

from MEMOIRS OF MADAME VIGÉE-LEBRUN

It was in the year 1779 that I painted the Queen for the first time; she was then in the heyday of her youth and beauty. Marie Antoinette was tall and admirably built, being somewhat stout, but not excessively so. Her arms were superb, her hands small and perfectly formed, and her feet charming. She had the best walk of any woman in France, carrying her head erect with a dignity that stamped her queen

Teaching Options

Preteaching Vocabulary

USING THE DICTIONARY

Instruction Using the dictionary enables students to check their understanding of words and phrases and to use precise language in their written and oral expression.

Activity Remind students that the dictionary includes listings of all meanings of a word and that usage notes, synonym listings, and example sentences, which are often included, can also be very helpful in determining the proper meaning of a word. Have students use a dictionary to find the WORDS TO KNOW, select the appropriate meaning for each if more than one appears, and then use the words in sentences of their own.

Use **Unit Three Resource Book,** p. 99 for additional support.

in the midst of her whole court, her majestic mien, however, not in the least diminishing the sweetness and amiability of her face. To anyone who has not seen the Queen it is difficult to get an idea of all the graces and all the nobility combined in her person. Her features were not regular; she had inherited that long and narrow oval peculiar to the [A] Austrian nation. Her eyes were not large; in color they were almost blue, and they were at the same time merry and kind. Her nose was slender and pretty, and her mouth not too large, though her lips were rather thick. But the most remarkable [B] thing about her face was the splendor of her complexion. I never have seen one so brilliant, and brilliant is the word, for her skin was so transparent that it bore no umber[1] in the painting. Neither could I render the real effect of it as I wished. I had no colors to paint such freshness, such delicate tints, which were hers alone, and which I had never seen in any other woman.

At the first sitting the imposing air of the Queen at first frightened me greatly, but Her Majesty spoke to me so graciously that my fear was soon dissipated. It was on that occasion that I began the picture representing her with a large basket, wearing a satin dress, and holding a rose in her hand. This portrait was destined for her brother, Emperor Joseph II, and the Queen ordered two copies besides—one for the Empress of Russia, the other for her own apartments at Versailles or Fontainebleau.[2]

I painted various pictures of the Queen at different times. In one I did her to the knees, in a pale orange-red dress, standing before a table on which she was arranging some flowers in a vase. It may be well imagined that I preferred to paint her in a plain gown and especially without a wide hoopskirt. She usually gave these portraits to her friends or to foreign diplomatic envoys. One of them shows her with a straw hat on, and a white muslin dress, whose sleeves are turned up, though quite neatly. When this work was exhibited at the Salon,[3] malignant folk did not fail to make the remark that the Queen had been painted in her chemise,[4] for we were then in 1786, and calumny[5] was already busy concerning her. Yet in spite of all this the portraits were very successful.

Toward the end of the exhibition a little piece was given at the Vaudeville Theater, bearing the title, I think, "The Assembling of the Arts." Brongniart,[6] the architect, and his wife, whom the author had taken into his confidence, had taken a box on the first tier, and called for me on the day of the first performance. As I had no suspicion of the surprise in store for me, judge of my emotion when Painting appeared on the scene and I saw the actress representing that art copy me in the act of painting a portrait of the Queen. The same moment everybody in the parterre[7] and the boxes turned toward me and applauded to bring the roof down. I can hardly believe that anyone was ever more moved and more grateful than I was that evening.

I was so fortunate as to be on very pleasant terms with the Queen. When she heard that I had something of a voice we rarely had a sitting without singing some duets by Grétry[8] together, [C] for she was exceedingly fond of music, although she did not sing very true. As for her conversation, it would be difficult for me to convey all its charm, all its affability. I do not think that Queen Marie Antoinette ever missed an opportunity of saying something pleasant to those who had the honor of being presented to her, and the

1. **umber:** a brown pigment.
2. **Versailles** (vĕr-sī′) . . . **Fontainebleau** (fôN-tĕn-blō′): sites of royal palaces.
3. **Salon:** an annual French art exhibition.
4. **chemise** (shə-mēz′): a woman's loose-fitting undergarment.
5. **calumny** (kăl′əm-nē): the making of false statements intended to injure a person's reputation; slander.
6. **Brongniart** (brôN-nyär′).
7. **parterre** (pär-târ′): the seating area nearest the stage on the main floor of a theater.
8. **Grétry** (grā-trē′): an 18th-century French composer of operas.

WORDS TO KNOW

mien (mēn) *n.* the manner in which one carries and conducts oneself; demeanor

amiability (ā′mē-ə-bĭl′ĭ-tē) *n.* good nature; friendliness

Customizing Instruction

Less Proficient Readers

Encourage students to discuss whatever they know about the French Revolution. Refer them to the time line on pp. 516–517 to help them put the revolution in a historical context.

Set a Purpose Have students read to note the author's observations of Marie Antoinette and her court.

Students Acquiring English

Have students discuss revolutions they know about from their native cultures. Encourage them to talk about the reasons these revolutions took place, and make sure students understand why the French Revolution took place. If necessary, read Build Background on p. 681 aloud and discuss it with students.

To help students understand the English idioms in this selection, discuss the meanings of phrases such as "taken into his confidence," "the surprise in store for me," and "on very pleasant terms with the Queen."

Answer: "told private information," "the surprise that awaited me," and "was friendly with the queen."

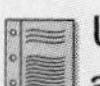

Use **Spanish Study Guide** for additional support, pp. 155–157.

Gifted and Talented

Ask students to consider whether Vigée-Lebrun is a reliable narrator when describing the people she painted. How might one of the "fishwives" who supported the Revolution have described them?

BLOCK SCHEDULING: MANAGING TIME

If your schedule requires that you cover the lesson objectives in a shorter time, use . . .

- Preparing to Read, p. 681
- Thinking Through the Literature, p. 690
- Vocabulary in Action, p. 691

If you want to take advantage of longer class time, use . . .

- TE Teaching Options: Preteaching Vocabulary, p. 682; Vocabulary Strategy, p. 684; Viewing and Representing, pp. 685, 688; Grammar, p. 686; Informal Assessment, pp. 689, 691
- Choices & Challenges, p. 691

Reading and Analyzing

Literary Analysis: **MEMOIR**

A Remind students that memoirs and diaries share some important characteristics. Point out the statement "My heart was beating violently, for I knew that I was in the wrong." Ask students whether this kind of statement might be found in a diary and what characteristic it has that would make it appropriate in that literary form.

Answer: Yes, this is a comment about the writer's emotional state and about a personal observation.

Active Reading

INTERPRETING DETAILS

B Point out Vigée-Lebrun's use of formal diction when she talks to the queen. Ask students what Vigée-Lebrun's reply to the queen reveals about their relationship.

Possible Response: She speaks to the queen in a very humble manner. Even though she is on friendly terms with the monarch, Vigée-Lebrun is still the queen's subject and is worried that the queen is angry with her.

Reading Skills and Strategies: **EVALUATING SOURCES**

C Point out Vigée-Lebrun's description of the queen at Fontainebleau. What impression does she create? Would people of the lower classes agree with the image created by Vigée-Lebrun?

Possible Response: Vigée-Lebrun's words—"diamonds," "brilliant," "dazzling," "goddess"—suggest someone more than human, someone above earthly cares; the lower classes might disagree, seeing self-indulgent extravagance at their expense.

kindness she always bestowed upon me has ever been one of my sweetest memories.

One day I happened to miss the appointment she had given me for a sitting; I had suddenly become unwell. The next day I hastened to Versailles to offer my excuses. The Queen was not expecting me; she had had her horses harnessed to go out driving, and her carriage was the first thing I saw on entering the palace yard. I nevertheless went upstairs to speak with the chamberlains on duty. One of them, M. Campan, received me with a stiff and haughty manner, and bellowed at me in his stentorian voice, "It was yesterday, madame, that Her Majesty expected you, and I am very sure she is going out driving, and I am very sure she will give you no sitting today!" Upon my reply that I had simply come to take Her Majesty's orders for another day, he went to the Queen, who at once had me
1 conducted to her room. She was finishing her toilet,[9] and was holding a book in her hand,
A hearing her daughter repeat a lesson. My heart was beating violently, for I knew that I was in the
2 wrong. But the Queen looked up at me and said most amiably, "I was waiting for you all the morning yesterday; what happened to you?"

B "I am sorry to say, Your Majesty," I replied, "I was so ill that I was unable to comply with Your Majesty's commands. I am here to receive more now, and then I will immediately retire."

"No, no! Do not go!" exclaimed the Queen. "I do not want you to have made your journey for nothing!" She revoked the order for her carriage and gave me a sitting. I remember that, in my confusion and my eagerness to make a fitting response to her kind words, I opened my paint-box so excitedly that I spilled my brushes on the floor. I stooped down to pick them up. "Never mind, never mind," said the Queen, and, for aught I could say, she insisted on gathering them all up herself.

When the Queen went for the last time to C Fontainebleau, where the court, according to custom, was to appear in full gala, I repaired there to enjoy that spectacle. I saw the Queen in her grandest dress; she was covered with diamonds, and as the brilliant sunshine fell upon her she seemed to me nothing short of dazzling. Her head, erect on her beautiful Greek neck, lent her as she walked such an imposing, such a majestic air, that one seemed to see a goddess in the midst of her nymphs. During the first sitting I had with Her Majesty after this occasion I took the liberty of mentioning the impression she had made upon me, and of saying to the Queen how the carriage of her head added to the nobility of her bearing. She answered in a jesting tone, "If I were not Queen they would say I looked insolent, would they not?"

The Queen neglected nothing to impart to her children the courteous and gracious manners which endeared her so to all her surroundings. I once saw her make her six-year-old daughter dine with a little peasant girl and attend to her wants. The Queen saw to it that the little visitor was served first, saying to her daughter, "You must do the honors."

The last sitting I had with Her Majesty was given me at Trianon, where I did her hair for the large picture in which she appeared with her children. After doing the Queen's hair, as well as separate studies of the Dauphin,[10] Madame Royale, and the Duke de Normandie, I busied myself with my picture, to which I attached great importance, and I had it ready for the Salon of 1788. The frame, which had been taken there alone, was enough to 3

9. **toilet:** the process of dressing or grooming oneself.

10. **Dauphin** (dō-făN′): the eldest son of the king of France.

Teaching Options

Vocabulary Strategy

SUFFIXES

Instruction Applying meanings of suffixes can help students expand vocabulary. Explain that the suffixes *-ion* and *-ity* signal that the word is a noun.

Model Write the words *amiable* and *amiability* on the board. Point out the suffix *-ity* and note that it makes an adjective into a noun. Be sure students recognize that in adding a suffix, they occasionally need to adjust the spelling of the root word.

Exercise Have students create nouns from the following list of words by adding *-ion* or *-ity*. They may use a dictionary if needed. Then, have them write the definition of the new word and use it in a sentence.

1. *devote* (devotion)
2. *plural* (plurality)
3. *regulate* (regulation)
4. *passive* (passivity)
5. *propagate* (propagation)
6. *brutal* (brutality)

Use **Vocabulary Transparencies and Copymasters,** p. 53.

Marie Antoinette and Her Children (about 1785), Élisabeth Vigée-Lebrun. Chateau Versailles, France. Giraudon/Art Resource, New York.

evoke a thousand malicious remarks. "That's how the money goes," they said, and a number of other things which seemed to me the bitterest comments. At last I sent my picture, but I could not muster up the courage to follow it and find out what its fate was to be, so afraid was I that it would be badly received by the public. In fact, I became quite ill with fright. I shut myself in my room, and there I was, praying to the Lord for the success of my "Royal Family," when my brother and a host of friends burst in to tell me that my picture had met with universal acclaim. After the Salon, the King, having had the picture transferred to Versailles, M. d'Angevilliers,[11] then minister of the fine arts and director of royal residences, presented me to His Majesty. Louis XVI vouchsafed[12] to talk to me at some length and to tell me that he was very much pleased. Then he added, still looking at my work, "I know nothing about painting, but you make me like it."

The picture was placed in one of the rooms at Versailles, and the Queen passed it going to mass and returning. After the death of the Dauphin, which occurred early in the year 1789, the sight of this picture reminded her so keenly of the cruel loss she had suffered that she could not go through the room without shedding tears. She then ordered M. d'Angevilliers to have the picture taken away, but with her usual consideration she informed me of the fact as well, apprising me of her motive for the removal. It is really to the Queen's sensitiveness that I owed the preservation of my picture, for the fishwives[13] who soon afterward came to Versailles for Their Majesties would certainly have destroyed it, as they did the Queen's bed, which was ruthlessly torn apart.

I never had the felicity of setting eyes on Marie Antoinette after the last court ball at Versailles. The ball was given in the theater, and the box where I was seated was so situated that I could hear what the Queen said. I observed that she was

11. **d'Angevilliers** (däɴzh-vēl-yā').
12. **vouchsafed** (vouch-sāft'): granted in a gracious manner; condescended.
13. **fishwives:** women who sell fish (a derogatory reference to the common women who supported the French Revolution).

Customizing Instruction

Students Acquiring English

1 Students are likely to be confused by the many words in this selection used in relatively uncommon ways. On pages 684–685, point out the word *toilet,* which is footnoted, and also *retire* (leave), *studies* (preparatory sketches for an artwork), and *host* (a huge number). Have students determine other meanings for these words.

Answer: toilet, "commode"; retire, "withdraw from business, take out of circulation"; studies, "branches of knowledge, rooms intended for studying"; host, "one who entertains guests or furnishes facilities for an event."

2 Help students understand the meanings of the idioms "I was in the wrong" and "to appear in full gala" on page 684.

Answer: "I was wrong" and "to appear in formal clothing."

Less Proficient Readers

3 Vigée-Lebrun remarks that the frame for her painting of the queen excited remark from the attendees of the Salon (an annual art exhibition). What does her comment reveal about the mood of the people?

Possible Response: They thought the royal family spent money frivolously, which made them angry.

Gifted and Talented

Invite students to consider the descriptions and anecdotes reported by Vigée-Lebrun from the point of view of the revolutionaries. What would they think of Versailles? How would they feel about the pastimes in which the royal family indulges? Do the actions of the monarchs as presented by Vigée-Lebrun warrant the reaction of the citizens?

Mini Lesson Viewing and Representing

Marie Antoinette and Her Children
by Élisabeth Vigée-Lebrun

ART APPRECIATION For this, the last portrait Vigée-Lebrun painted of Marie Antoinette from life, the queen agreed to pose only for the head. The critic Ilse Bischoff, calling it "one of the greatest pictures at Versailles," says that the queen is shown as "both regal and maternal."

Instruction Remind students that elements of visual design can communicate meanings in much the same way that literary elements can. Tell them that by paying attention to such elements, they can improve their ability to understand and appreciate visual representations.

Application Have students make two lists: one of the regal qualities expressed in the painting, and one of the maternal qualities. Then, have them write descriptive analyses of the painting. Remind students to pay attention to the style of dress, the physical placement and attitude of the figures, and the light and shadow in the painting. How are the elements of design used to invoke the regal and/or maternal side of the queen? Why is it important to have Marie Antoinette represented as a mother and a queen? Have students share their responses in group discussion.

Reading and Analyzing

Literary Analysis DESCRIPTION

A Ask students what this description suggests about Madame Du Barry.

Possible Response: She has had success attracting men by affecting a childish sweetness. Now that she is older, this childishness appears ridiculous.

Reading Skills and Strategies: EVALUATING SOURCES

B Point out the two passages on this page in which Vigée-Lebrun speaks of generosity toward commoners on the part of Madame Du Barry and Louis XV ("She showed herself . . . helped all the poor" and "She was informed . . . her and Louis XV"). What might Vigée-Lebrun's motives be for making these comments? Is she a reliable source of information on this subject?

Possible Responses: She may have wanted to give evidence of fair treatment of commoners by members of the nobility—and of bad treatment of the nobility in return—to argue against the claims of the revolutionaries and to defend the aristocracy. Some students may think she is a good source because of her firsthand knowledge of events; others may find her biased and obviously sympathetic to the aristocracy.

Literary Analysis: TONE

Ask students to describe how the tone of the selection changes as Vigée-Lebrun writes about events during the Revolution.

Possible Response: The tone was light and positive before; here it becomes negative, worried, and horrified.

very excited, asking the young men of the court to dance with her, such as M. Lameth, whose family had been overwhelmed with kindness by the Queen, and others, who all refused, so that many of the dances had to be given up. The conduct of these gentlemen seemed to me exceedingly improper; somehow their refusal likened a sort of revolt—the prelude to revolts of a more serious kind. The Revolution was drawing near; it was, in fact, to burst out before long. . . .

A *It was in 1786* that I went for the first time to Louveciennes,[14] where I had promised to paint Mme. Du Barry. She might then have been about forty-five years old. She was tall without being too much so; she had a certain roundness, her throat being rather pronounced but very beautiful; her face was still attractive, her features were regular and graceful; her hair was ashy, and curly like a child's. But her complexion was beginning to fade. She received me with much courtesy, and seemed to me very well behaved, but I found her more spontaneous in mind than in manner: her glance was that of a coquette,[15] for her long eyes were never quite open, and her pronunciation had something childish which no longer suited her age.

She lodged me in a part of the building where I was greatly put out by the continual noise. Under my room was a gallery, sadly neglected, in which busts, vases, columns, the rarest marbles, and a quantity of other valuable articles were displayed without system or order. These remains of luxury contrasted with the simplicity adopted by the mistress of the house, with her dress and her mode of life. Summer and winter Mme. Du Barry wore only a dressing-robe of cotton cambric or white muslin, and every day, whatever the weather might be, she walked in her park, or outside of it, without ever incurring disastrous consequences, so sturdy had her health become through her life in the country. She had maintained no relations with the numerous court that surrounded her so long. In the evening we were usually alone at the fireside, Mme. Du Barry and I. She sometimes talked to me about Louis XV and his court. She showed herself a worthy person by her actions as **B** well as her words, and did a great deal of good at Louveciennes, where she helped all the poor. Every day after dinner we took coffee in the pavilion which was so famous for its rich and tasteful decorations. The first time Mme. Du Barry showed it to me she said: "It is here that Louis XV did me the honor of coming to dinner. There was a gallery above for musicians and singers who performed during the meal."

When Mme. Du Barry went to England, before the Terror, to get back her stolen diamonds, which, in fact, she recovered there, the English received her very well. They did all they could to prevent her from returning to France. But it was not long before she succumbed to the fate in store for everybody who had some possessions. She was informed against and betrayed by a little Negro called Zamore, who is mentioned in all the memoirs of the period as having been overwhelmed with kindness by her and Louis XV. Being arrested and thrown into prison, Mme. Du Barry was tried and condemned to death by the Revolutionary tribunal at the end of 1793. She was the only woman, among all who perished in those dreadful days, unable to face the scaffold with firmness; **1** she screamed, she sued for pardon to the hideous mob surrounding her, and that mob became moved to such a degree that the executioner hastened to finish his task. This has always confirmed my belief that if the victims of that

14. **Louveciennes** (lo͞ov-syĕn′): an estate given to Madame Du Barry by Louis XV.

15. **coquette** (kō-kĕt′): a woman who tries to get men to notice and admire her; a flirt.

Teaching Options

Grammar

VERBS: ACTIVE AND PASSIVE VOICE

Instruction Explain to students that the "voice" of a verb indicates whether the subject of the verb is the performer or the receiver of the action the verb describes. If the subject is the performer of the action, the verb is in the active voice. If the subject is the receiver of the action the verb is in the passive voice. Using the active voice can make the writing more concise and vivid.

Activity Write the following example on the chalkboard. Underline the verbs as shown.

"This portrait was destined for her brother, Emperor Joseph II, and the Queen ordered two copies besides—one for the Empress of Russia, the other for her own apartments at Versailles or Fontainebleau."

Point out that this is a compound sentence with one verb in the active voice and the other in the passive voice. Ask students to identify the subject of the verb *was destined. (portrait)* Next ask if this subject is the performer or the receiver of the action. *(receiver)* Explain that because the subject is the receiver of the action, the verb is in the *passive* voice. For contrast, point out the verb in the second part of the sentence. Ask students the same questions so that they understand why *ordered* is in the *active voice.*

period of execrable memory had not had the noble pride of dying with fortitude the Terror would have ceased long before it did.

I made three portraits of Mme. Du Barry. In the first I painted her at half length, in a dressing-gown and straw hat. In the second she is dressed in white satin; she holds a wreath in one hand, and one of her arms is leaning on a pedestal. The third portrait I made of Mme. Du Barry is in my own possession. I began it about the middle of September, 1789. From Louveciennes we could hear shooting in the distance, and I remember the poor woman saying, "If Louis XV were alive I am sure this would not be happening." I had done the head, and outlined the body and arms, when I was obliged to make an expedition to Paris. I hoped to be able to return to Louveciennes to finish my work, but heard that Berthier and Foulon[16] had been murdered. I was now frightened beyond measure, and thenceforth thought of nothing but leaving France. The fearful year 1789 was well advanced, and all decent people were already seized with terror. I remember perfectly that one evening when I had gathered some friends about me for a concert, most of the arrivals came into the room with looks of consternation; they had been walking at Longchamps that morning, and the populace assembled at the Étoile gate had cursed at those who passed in carriages in a dreadful manner. Some of the wretches had clambered on the carriage steps, shouting, "Next year you will be behind your carriages and we shall be inside!" and a thousand other insults.

As for myself, I had little need to learn fresh details in order to foresee what horrors impended. I knew beyond doubt that my house in the Rue Gros Chenet, where I had settled but three months since, had been singled out by the criminals. They threw sulphur into our cellars through the airholes. If I happened to be at my window, vulgar ruffians would shake their fists at me. Numberless sinister rumors reached me from every side; in fact, I now lived in a state of continual anxiety and sadness. My health became sensibly affected, and two of my best friends, the architect Brongniart and his wife, when they came to see me, found me so thin and so changed that they besought me to come and spend a few days with them, which invitation I thankfully accepted. Brongniart had his lodgings at the Invalides, whither I was conducted by a physician attached to the Palais Royal, whose servants wore the Orléans livery,[17] the only one then held in any respect. There I was given everything of the best. As I was unable to eat, I was nourished on excellent Burgundy wine and soup, and Mme. Brongniart was in constant attendance upon me. All this solicitude ought to have quieted me, especially as my friends took a less black view of things than I did. Nevertheless, they did not succeed in banishing my evil forebodings. "What is the use of living; what is the use of taking care of oneself?" I would often ask my good friends, for the fears that the future held over me made life distasteful to me. But I must acknowledge that even with the furthest stretch of my imagination I guessed only at a fraction of the crimes that were to be committed. . . .

16. **Berthier** (bĕr-tyā′): a French aristocrat; **Foulon** (fo͞o-lôɴ′): a government minister of war and finance who increased his own wealth at the expense of the poor.

17. **livery:** the uniform of a servant.

WORDS TO KNOW

execrable (ĕk′sĭ-krə-bəl) *adj.* detestable; hateful

fortitude (fôr′tĭ-to͞od′) *n.* the strength to bear misfortune or pain calmly and patiently; firm courage

consternation (kŏn′stər-nā′shən) *n.* a sudden fear or amazement that makes one feel helpless; dismay

Customizing Instruction

Less Proficient Readers
Invite students to share their impressions of the queen, court life, and the author:

- What most impresses Vigée-Lebrun about Marie Antoinette?
  Answer: her graciousness and kindness.
- Do the author's descriptions seem reliable?
  Possible Response: They are factually accurate but probably colored by partisanship.

Set a Purpose Have students read to find out how Vigée-Lebrun and others react to the approach of the Revolution.

1 Ask students what characteristics of Madame Du Barry are revealed by her behavior on the scaffold.
Possible Responses: She's a coward; she wants to cling to life; she has no pride.

Exercise Tell students that the verbs in the sentences below are all in the passive voice. Ask students to underline the verbs and then have them rewrite each sentence changing the passive voice to the active voice.

1. Numerous portraits of Queen Marie Antoinette were painted by Madame Vigée-Lebrun. *(Possible answer: Madame Vigée-Lebrun painted numerous portraits of Queen Marie Antoinette.)*
2. The picture of the Royal Family was hung by a servant in one of the rooms at Versailles. *(Possible answer: A servant hung the picture of the Royal Family in one of the rooms at Versailles.)*
3. Mme. Du Barry was condemned to death by the Revolutionary tribunal. *(Possible answer: The Revolutionary tribunal condemned Mme. Du Barry to death.)*
4. Madame Vigée–Lebrun was frightened by the aggressive harassment of the revolutionaries. *(Possible answer: The aggressive harassment of the revolutionaries frightened Madame Vigée–Lebrun.)*

Use **Grammar Transparencies and Copymasters,** p. 136.

Use McDougal Littell's ***Language Network*** for more instruction in active and passive voice.

Reading and Analyzing

Active Reading

INTERPRETING DETAILS

A Ask students what details Vigée-Lebrun uses to create a vivid picture of the national guardsmen.

Answer: "drunk and shabby," "terrible faces," "coarsest language."

What impression of the men is the author trying to convey with such details?

Possible Response: They are rough, cruel, and out of control.

Literary Analysis: MEMOIR

B What personal details does Vigée-Lebrun reveal in her account of her escape from Paris?

Possible Responses: She reveals her concern for her daughter; she is frightened but courageous in protecting her child from the rough language of one of the passengers in the coach; she enjoys nature.

Literary Analysis DESCRIPTION

C What kind of people does Vigée-Lebrun describe on her journey out of Paris?

Possible Responses: They are from the lower classes; they are dirty and unattractive; one is a thief; they support the Revolution.

Self-Portrait (late 1700s), Élisabeth Vigée-Lebrun. Oil on canvas, Uffizi, Florence, Italy. Scala/Art Resource, New York.

I had made up my mind to leave France. For some years I had cherished the desire to go to Rome. The large number of portraits I had engaged to paint had, however, hindered me from putting my plan into execution. But I could now paint no longer; my broken spirit, bruised with so many horrors, shut itself entirely to my art. Besides, dreadful slanders were pouring upon my friends, my acquaintances and myself, although, Heaven knows, I had never hurt a living soul. I thought like the man who said, "I am accused of having stolen the towers of Notre Dame; they are still in their usual place, but I am going away, as I am evidently to blame." I left several portraits I had begun, among them Mlle. Contat's. At the same time I refused to paint Mlle. de Laborde (afterward Duchess de Noailles),[18] brought to me by her father. She was scarcely sixteen, and very charming, but it was no longer a question of success or money—it was only a question of saving one's head. I had my carriage loaded, and my passport ready, so that I might leave next day with my daughter and her governess, when a crowd of national guardsmen burst into my room with their muskets. Most of them were drunk and shabby, **A** and had terrible faces. A few of them came up to me and told me in the coarsest language that I must not go, but that I must remain. I answered that since everybody had been called upon to enjoy his liberty, I intended to make use of mine. They would barely listen to me, and kept on repeating, "You will not go, citizeness; you will not go!" Finally they went away. I was plunged into a state of cruel anxiety when I saw two of them return. But they did not frighten me, although they belonged to the gang, so quickly did I recognize that they wished me no harm. "Madame," said one of them, "we are your neighbors, and we have come to advise you to leave, and as soon as possible. You cannot live here; you are changed so much that we feel sorry for you. But do not go in your carriage: go in the stage-coach; it is much safer." I thanked them with all my heart, and followed their good advice. I had three places reserved, as I still wanted to take my daughter, who was then five or six years old, but was unable **B** to secure them until a fortnight later, because all who exiled themselves chose the stage-coach, like myself. At last came the long-expected day.

It was the 5th of October, and the King and Queen were conducted from Versailles to Paris surrounded by pikes. The events of that day filled me with uneasiness as to the fate of Their Majesties and that of all decent people, so that I was dragged to the stage-coach at midnight in a dreadful state of mind. I was very much afraid of the Faubourg Saint Antoine, which I was obliged to traverse to reach the Barrière du Trône.[19] My brother and my husband escorted me as far as this gate without leaving the door of the coach for a moment; but the suburb that I was so frightened of was perfectly quiet. All its inhabitants, the workmen and the rest, had been to Versailles after the royal family, and fatigue kept them all in bed.

Opposite me in the coach was a very filthy **C** man, who stunk like the plague, and told me quite simply that he had stolen watches and

18. **Noailles** (nô-ī′).

19. **Faubourg Saint Antoine** (fō-bo͞or′ săN äN-twän′) . . . **Barrière de Trône** (bä-ryĕr′ də trōn′).

Teaching Options

Viewing and Representing

Self-Portrait **by Élisabeth Vigée-Lebrun**

ART APPRECIATION Although the artist was 35 when she painted this self-portrait, she portrays herself as a very young woman. As with so much of her portrait work, she greatly flatters the subject, in this case herself.

Instruction Ask students to point out other details in this portrait and the impressions they convey. Draw a comparison between self-portrait and autobiography. Have students discuss elements that would be common to both forms, such as a focus on activities and events important in the author's/artist's life and personal observations and revelations.

Application Have students draw their own self-portraits. Remind students that they will have to decide how realistic or flattering they want to be in their representations as they determine what features to accentuate or downplay. Students may use a camera with a self-timer to create self-portraits as well.

other things. Luckily he saw nothing about me to tempt him, for I was only taking a small amount of clothing and eighty louis for my journey. I had left my principal effects and my jewels in Paris, and the fruit of my labors was in the hands of my husband, who spent it all. I lived abroad solely on the proceeds of my painting.

Not satisfied with relating his fine exploits to us, the thief talked incessantly of stringing up such and such people on lamp-posts, naming a number of my own acquaintances. My daughter thought this man very wicked. He frightened her, and this gave me the courage to say, "I beg you, sir, not to talk of killing before this child." That silenced him, and he ended by playing at battle with my daughter. On the bench I occupied there also sat a mad Jacobin[20] from Grenoble, about fifty years old, with an ugly, bilious[21] complexion, who each time we stopped at an inn for dinner or supper made violent speeches of the most fearful kind. At all of the towns a crowd of people stopped the coach to learn the news from Paris. Our Jacobin would then exclaim: "Everything is going well, children! We have the baker and his wife safe in Paris. A constitution will be drawn up, they will be forced to accept it, and then it will be all over." There were plenty of ninnies and flatheads who believed this man as if he had been an oracle. All this made my journey a very melancholy one. I had no further fears for myself, but I feared greatly for everybody else—for my mother, for my brother, and for my friends. I also had the gravest apprehensions concerning Their Majesties, for all along the route, nearly as far as Lyons, men on horseback rode up to the coach to tell us that the King and Queen had been killed and that Paris was on fire. My poor little girl got all a-tremble; she thought she saw her father dead and our house burned down, and no sooner had I succeeded in reassuring her than another horseman appeared and told us the same stories.

I cannot describe the emotions I felt in passing over the Beauvoisin[22] Bridge. Then only did I breathe freely. I had left France behind, that France which nevertheless was the land of my birth, and which I reproached myself with quitting with so much satisfaction. The sight of the mountains, however, distracted me from all my sad thoughts. I had never seen high mountains before; those of the Savoy[23] seemed to touch the sky, and seemed to mingle with it in a thick vapor. My first sensation was that of fear, but I unconsciously accustomed myself to the spectacle, and ended by admiring it. A certain part of the road completely entranced me; I seemed to see the "Gallery of the Titans,"[24] and I have always called it so since. Wishing to enjoy all these beauties as fully as possible, I got down from the coach, but after walking some way I was seized with a great fright, for there were explosions being made with gunpowder, which had the effect of a thousand cannon shots, and the din echoing from rock to rock was truly infernal.

I went up Mount Cenis, as other strangers were doing, when a postilion[25] approached me, saying, "The lady ought to take a mule; to climb up on foot is too fatiguing." I answered that I was a work-woman and quite accustomed to walking. "Oh! no!" was the laughing reply. "The lady is no work-woman; we know who she is!" "Well, who am I, then?" I asked him. "You are Mme. Lebrun, who paints so well, and we are all very glad to see you safe from those bad people." I never guessed how the man could have learned my name, but it proved to me how many secret agents the Jacobins must have had. Happily I had no occasion to fear them any longer. ❖

20. **Jacobin:** radical revolutionary.
21. **bilious** (bĭl′yəs): sickly yellow.
22. **Beauvoisin** (bō-vwä-zăɴ′).
23. **the Savoy:** the mountainous region along the border between France and Italy.
24. **Titans:** a group of giants in Greek mythology.
25. **postilion:** a person who helps guide a coach by riding on one of the lead horses.

Customizing Instruction

Less Proficient Readers

Have students discuss their impressions of the author and her experiences around the time of the French Revolution.

- According to Vigée-Lebrun, who was the only woman who did not face execution bravely?
  Answer: Madame Du Barry.
- Why did Vigée-Lebrun become frightened by what she saw happening in France?
  Possible Responses: She felt personally threatened; she was fearful for her life and those of all "decent people."
- What did Vigée-Lebrun do to escape the Reign of Terror?
  Answer: She fled France in a stagecoach and went to Italy.
- Why would Vigée-Lebrun include the comment from the postilion regarding her escape from "those bad people"?
  Possible Response: His remark adds support to her own opinion of the revolutionaries as bad people.

Students Acquiring English

These pages contain several multiple-meaning words that might cause difficulty. Be sure students recognize the sense in which Vigée-Lebrun uses these words: *engaged* (promised, agreed), *effects* (property), *quitting* (leaving), *entranced* (captivated, fascinated). Explain that the two meanings of the last word are signaled by different pronunciations, and encourage students to practice the two pronunciations.

Assessment Informal Assessment

CHECKING COMPREHENSION Have students check their comprehension with the following questions:

1. Did Vigée-Lebrun stay in France during the revolutionary crisis, or did she leave?
   Answer: She left.
2. Describe Vigée-Lebrun's opinion of supporters of the revolution.
   Answer: She thought they were dirty, violent, and uncontrolled.
3. How did the French Revolution affect Vigée-Lebrun's career in France?
   Answer: She turned down commissions and became so ill with fear that she couldn't work.

GUIDING STUDENT RESPONSE

Connect to the Literature

1. What Do You Think?
Guidelines for student response: Students will probably empathize with Vigee-Lebrun's situation as a woman in peril in a chaotic society. You might ask students if they know of countries or societies that have experienced similar social turmoil.

Comprehension Check
- portrait painter
- friendly and admiring

 Use Selection Quiz in **Unit Three Resource Book,** p. 100.

Think Critically

2. She opposes and is frightened by the Revolution, which threatens her livelihood, the lives of her friends, and her own safety. She shows concern for her rich acquaintances and reveals little concern for the poor.
3. Possible Responses: She wanted to describe the queen as a kind, gracious woman; she genuinely admired royalty; staying on the good side of her patrons was in her best interest.
4. Some students will find her sympathetic because they think her descriptions or personality is appealing or because they wish to identify with her; others will find her support of an oppressive aristocracy self-serving and unsympathetic.

Literary Analysis

Paired Activity Students' choices of the most descriptive passage might include the description of Marie Antoinette on pp. 682–683, that of Madame Du Barry on p. 686, or that of the author's flight from Paris on p. 689.

Active Reading Students may think that Vigée-Lebrun was too partial to the king and queen and too interested in defending the monarchy to be a credible source. Other students may find her credible because she observed the crisis in person. Students may find her an appropriate source of information for subjective impressions of the revolutionaries from the royalist point of view, but not an appropriate source for explaining the causes of the people's discontent.

Connect to the Literature

1. **What Do You Think?** As you read, how did you feel about the situation Vigée-Lebrun found herself in? Share your reactions with your classmates.

Comprehension Check
- What was the author's occupation?
- Describe Vigée-Lebrun's relationship with the Queen of France.

Think Critically

2. Explain Vigée-Lebrun's feelings about the French Revolution, as revealed in her comments about the rich and the poor.

THINK ABOUT
- the encounters she has with aristocrats and with revolutionaries
- the terms that she uses to refer to the aristocracy and the revolutionaries
- her acceptance by the French aristocracy

3. ACTIVE READING **INTERPRETING DETAILS** Review the chart in your  READER'S NOTEBOOK that lists **details** about people Vigée-Lebrun encounters. What impression of Marie Antoinette do you think Vigée-Lebrun wished to convey? Why might she have wanted to convey that impression? Use details from the selection to support your opinions.

4. Do you find Vigée-Lebrun a sympathetic person? Why or why not?

Extend Interpretations

5. **Different Perspectives** How do you think Vigée-Lebrun's fellow stagecoach passenger, the "mad Jacobin from Grenoble," would describe her?

6. **Connect to Life** Problems between the rich and the poor continue to exist in modern life. Think about how the rich and the poor view one another in contemporary American society. What do you think would be the best ways of resolving misunderstandings and conflicts between the two groups?

7. **Points of Comparison** Compare this excerpt from Vigée-Lebrun's **memoir** with the excerpt from Fanny Burney's **diary.** What details of daily life does each portray? How do these details affect the **tone** of each work?

Literary Analysis

DESCRIPTION Descriptive writing helps readers understand exactly what someone or something is like by allowing them to picture scenes, events, and characters in their minds. An effective **description** is often like a good painting: it provides visual details of color, size, texture, and shape that give the reader a clear impression of the person, place, object, or event being described.

Paired Activity With a partner, review the excerpt from Vigée-Lebrun's *Memoirs* and decide what descriptive passage in the selection you think is the most effective. Explain your choice.

ACTIVE READING EVALUATING SOURCES In recounting her experiences, Vigée-Lebrun offers a glimpse of life in France at the outbreak of the French Revolution. Do you think her motives for writing the memoirs affect the **credibility** of her account in any way? Do you think her memoirs would be an **appropriate** source of information for understanding the causes and consequences of the French Revolution? List the reasons for your conclusions.

Extend Interpretations

Different Perspectives Remind students that Vigée-Lebrun's fellow passenger would probably regard her as an enemy. Encourage them to freewrite to come up with negative descriptions the passenger might use to characterize someone he would see as a member of the old order.

Connect to Life Encourage students to recall what they know about the ways class conflicts have been addressed in the past in the United States (labor strikes, protests, etc.). Have them consider the methods of the French Revolutionaries as one violent extreme, and have them brainstorm for more peaceful alternatives.

Points of Comparison Each author portrays the pastimes and manners of the aristocracy. Burney's diary presents humorous details concerning dress and conversation; her tone is amused and ironic. Vigée-Lebrun's tone is more earnest and straightforward, especially as she describes events related to the Revolution.

Writing Options

Points of Comparison Write an essay in which you compare the portrayal of people in Fanny Burney's diary with that in Vigée-Lebrun's memoir. As you develop your comparison, consider the techniques used by each author, the relationship of the author to the people being described, and the relative importance of the wider social setting in each work.

Writing Handbook
See page 1367: Compare and Contrast.

Vocabulary in Action

EXERCISE: CONTEXT CLUES On your paper, write the word that best completes each sentence.

1. It was reported that Marie Antoinette, when told that the poor had no bread, responded, "Let them eat cake," and such a response was thought to be truly ________.
2. That story fit the common perception of the queen as haughty and uncaring; Madame Vigée-Lebrun, on the other hand, praises her for her ________.
3. What many of the French people saw as an air of arrogance, Vigée-Lebrun viewed as a majestic ________.
4. Whatever the queen's character, her awareness that her power was gone and that she faced death must have filled her with ________.
5. Even after the king was executed, however, she showed composure and courage in prison—surely a sign of ________.

WORDS TO KNOW		
	amiability	fortitude
	consternation	mien
	execrable	

Building Vocabulary
For an in-depth study of context clues, see page 938.

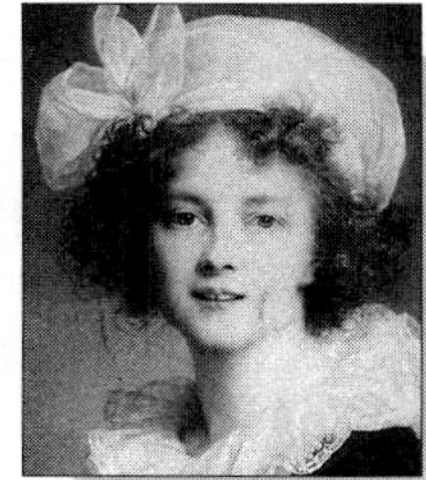

Élisabeth Vigée-Lebrun
1755–1842

A Budding Young Artist As a child, Élisabeth Vigée-Lebrun drew miniature portraits in the margins of her schoolbooks and even on the dormitory walls of the convent school she attended in Paris. She received some instruction from her father, a minor painter, and from artist friends, but she was mainly self-taught. When she was 13, her father died, and Vigée-Lebrun began supporting her mother and brother by painting portraits.

Painter of the Nobility The young artist quickly gained a following, and her reputation as a portrait painter of the nobility was established by the time she was 19. At the age of 24, she was invited to do her first portrait of Marie Antoinette. The many portraits of the queen that followed are among the artist's most famous works.

Painting and Politics Because she painted and mingled with the aristocracy, Vigée-Lebrun felt especially threatened by the events leading up to the French Revolution. After she fled Paris in 1789, she traveled and lived in various parts of Europe and England and was sought as a painter wherever she went. She returned to France in 1810 and published her memoirs in the 1830s.

Portrait of an Age During her long and illustrious career, Vigée-Lebrun created more than 800 paintings, including more than 600 portraits. Although her portraits of women were usually flattering—undoubtedly one reason for her popularity—her talent and the stature of her work are undisputed.

Writing Options

Points of Comparison Encourage students to consider the different historical contexts in which the two pieces were written. In their writing students should interpret the possible influences these historical contexts had on the literary works.

Encourage students to look at the physical descriptions each author gives of her upper-class subjects. Burney uses humorous detail to criticize the women she meets at the party. Vigée-Lebrun's descriptions of the queen, however, are flattering and full of approval. Vigée-Lebrun may feel she has to make her portrayal of the aristocracy very positive to offset the harsh judgments of the revolutionaries. With no apparent threat to their social dominance, the British upper classes can better withstand Burney's unflattering account.

Vocabulary in Action

Exercise
1. execrable
2. amiability
3. mien
4. consternation
5. fortitude

Assessment Informal Assessment

MAKING A TIME LINE Have students prepare a time line that reflects both the historical and the personal events Vigée-Lebrun describes in this essay, beginning with her first portrait of Marie Antoinette and ending with her flight from France.

RUBRIC

3 **Substantial Accomplishment** Students record multiple events for time line, selecting both personal and historical points and showing clear sense of chronology.

2 **Substantial Accomplishment** Students record adequate number of events and show reasonable sense of chronology.

1 **Little or Partial Accomplishment** Students record few events and show little sense of chronology.

Objectives
- reflect on and assess understanding of the unit
- recognize distinctive characteristics of cultures through reading
- understand literary forms such as essays
- understand literary terms such as irony and satire
- assess and build portfolios

Reflecting on the Unit

OPTION 1

A successful response will
- select one writer from Unit Three as a representative of each of the two perspectives.
- note examples from the work of each writer that reveal how people of the day see themselves and others.
- choose which writer had the greater impact on the student's understanding of human nature and society and explain why.

OPTION 2

A successful response will
- identify the kind of writing that a student most enjoys reading and why.
- identify the kind of writing that gives the clearest, more objective view of human nature.
- create a chart listing the literary forms, identify at least one example of each among the unit's selections, and give a strength and weakness of each one.

OPTION 3

You might suggest that each student in a group concentrate on three or four selections and then lead the discussion of those selections.

Self Assessment
Remind students to focus on their own insights rather than recapitulate the writers' perceptions.

The Restoration and Enlightenment

As you read the selections in this unit, what did you learn about the ways people in the 17th and 18th centuries viewed themselves and others? What did they see clearly? In what areas did they have blind spots? Did you learn anything about yourself and the ways people today view themselves and others? Explore these questions by completing one or more of the options in each of the following sections.

Reflecting on the Unit

OPTION 1

Gaining Insights Some of the writers represented in this unit portrayed life as it was in the late 17th century and the 18th century, whereas others portrayed life as they thought it should be. Choose two of the writers—one to represent each perspective. What does the work of each reveal about how people see themselves and others? Which had the greatest impact on your understanding of human nature and society? Explain your choices in one or two paragraphs.

OPTION 2

Examining Form and Content The selections in this unit include essays, poetry, a diary, letters, biography, and autobiography. Which kind of writing did you enjoy reading the most? Which do you think gives the clearest, most objective view of human nature? Make a chart in which you list the literary forms and identify at least one example of each among the selections in this unit. Then jot down one strength and one weakness of each form.

OPTION 3

Evaluating the Issues The selections in this unit reveal a variety of human weaknesses and problems. How clearly did the people of the time understand their own faults and those of others? Which of their concerns seem trivial? Which seem significant? Are any of their concerns important to people today? Get together with some of your classmates to discuss your conclusions.

Self ASSESSMENT

To explore what you have learned about human nature from this unit, create a three-column chart. In the first column, list four insights you have gained into how people view themselves and others; in the second, identify the source of each insight; in the third, rank the insights according to how important each is to you.

Reviewing Literary Concepts

OPTION 1

Analyzing Essays Several of the prose selections in this unit are informal or persuasive essays. Make a chart like the one shown, listing the selections that are essays and identifying each as informal or persuasive. Briefly explain the purpose of each essay and evaluate how effectively the purpose is carried out.

Selection	Type of Essay	Purpose	Effectiveness
from *The Spectator*	informal	entertainment, mild criticism of human weaknesses	enjoyable humor, accurate perceptions of human nature

OPTION 2

Recognizing Irony and Satire Writers often use irony and satire to reveal human defects and weaknesses. Think about the selections that you read from this unit that use these techniques. Which examples are most effective? Why? Compare your choices with those of your classmates and discuss any differences in your opinions.

Self ASSESSMENT

On a piece of paper, copy the following list of literary terms introduced in this unit. Put checks next to those you understand well and question marks next to those that are still unclear to you. Then find a partner and exchange lists. Take turns defining the terms that one of you understands well but the other is having difficulty with. Work together to define any terms whose meanings you are both unsure of.

- diary
- heroic couplet
- iambic pentameter
- fable
- informal essay
- parallelism
- persuasive essay
- fantasy
- satire
- irony
- humor
- argumentation
- aphorism
- biography
- personification
- dialogue
- description

Building Your Portfolio

- **Writing Options** Many of the Writing Options in this unit asked you to observe and comment on aspects of human behavior. Look over your work for these assignments and pick two pieces that you think contain your most perceptive ideas. Write a brief cover note in which you explain why these pieces show particularly clear insights, and add them, along with the note, to your **Presentation Portfolio.**
- **Writing Workshops** In this unit you wrote a Proposal recommending a solution to a problem. You also wrote a Satire that made use of humor to persuade your readers. Reread these pieces and decide which is more successful at convincing your readers to adopt a particular viewpoint. Explain your choice in a note attached to the preferred one. Place the piece in your **Presentation Portfolio.**
- **Additional Activities** Think back to any of the assignments you completed under **Activities & Explorations** and **Inquiry & Research.** Keep a record in your portfolio of any assignments that you would like to do further work on in the future.

Self ASSESSMENT

You are now beginning to build up a variety of writing pieces in your portfolio. Look through them. Do you find a stronger sense of confidence in your more recent writing? What is your favorite piece so far?

Setting GOALS

As you reviewed your work for this unit, you probably noticed some aspects of your writing that are not as strong as others. Identify the weak areas that need continued attention and the skills that need practice. Keep these in mind as you work through the next unit.

Reviewing Literary Concepts

OPTION 1

Use the Unit Three Resource Book, p. 101, to provide students a ready-made, full-depth chart for recording their explanations of purpose in each essay and evaluations of the essays' effectiveness in carrying out their purposes.

OPTION 2

A successful response will
- choose two or three selections that use irony and satire.
- select the most effect examples and explain why.
- involve comparing choices with classmates and discussing differences in opinions with them.

Building Your Portfolio

Students will use their Presentation Portfolios to file what they consider their highest quality work—the very best projects and activities from their Working Portfolios.

For more information on using writing and assessing portfolios, see the *Teacher's Guide to Assessment and Portfolio Use,* p. 53.

The *Electronic Library* is a CD-ROM that contains additional fiction, nonfiction, poetry, and drama for each unit in *The Language of Literature.*

These are the additional selections found in Unit 3 of the *Electronic Library:*

John Dryden
A Song for St. Cecilia's Day, 1687
Alexander's Feast

Robert Burns
To a Mouse
A Red, Red Rose
Afton Water

Encourage students to select one of the titles on this page to enjoy silent sustained reading.

UNIT THREE Extend Your *Reading*

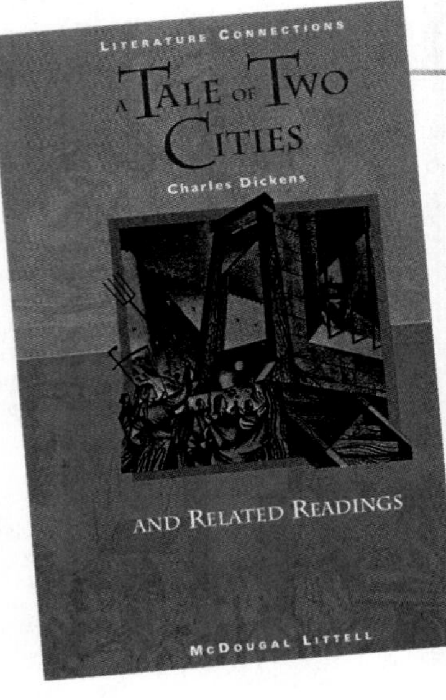

LITERATURE CONNECTIONS

A Tale of Two Cities

CHARLES DICKENS

Set against the raging upheaval of the French Revolution, this novel examines what it means to be a true hero. *A Tale of Two Cities* explores questions about revolutions, the abuse of power, the nature of justice and loyalty, and the ability of love to triumph over hatred.

These thematically related readings are provided along with *A Tale of Two Cities:*

Declaration of the Rights of Man and of the Citizen, August 27, 1789

Declaration of the Rights of Women
BY OLYMPE DE GOUGES

A Last Letter from Prison
BY OLYMPE DE GOUGES

In Defense of the Terror
BY MAXIMILIEN ROBESPIERRE

from **Hind Swarj or Indian Rule**
BY MOHANDAS K. GANDHI

from **Guillotine: Its Legend and Lore**
BY DANIEL GEROULD

Five Men
BY ZBIGNIEW HERBERT

The Pit and the Pendulum
BY EDGAR ALLAN POE

from **Darkness at Noon**
BY SIDNEY KINGSLEY (BASED ON THE NOVEL BY ARTHUR KOESTLER)

The Strike
BY TILLIE OLSEN

And Even *More* . . .

The Letters of James Boswell

EDITED BY C. B. TINKER

Boswell's letters to his friends give the reader a glimpse of the customs, beliefs, and occupations of 18th-century England. In addition to being the biographer of Samuel Johnson, Boswell led a busy life as a lawyer, a literary critic, and a traveler. All in all, his letters provide a richly detailed portrait of an age.

Books

Isaac Newton and the Scientific Revolution
GALE E. CHRISTIANSON
A compelling description of the genius of Isaac Newton and the absolutely central role he played in the history of science.

The Age of Reason Begins
WILL AND ARIEL DURANT
A history of the Enlightenment from 1558 to 1648.

Robinson Crusoe

Daniel Defoe

This riveting tale of shipwreck and survival portrays the adventures of a man isolated on an island for 24 years. Crusoe displays great ingenuity in making the best of his situation. A practical man, he applies his intelligence to contriving various means of improving his physical comfort and security. The novel illustrates the various skills and virtues needed to survive in the face of adversity.

Gulliver's Travels

Jonathan Swift

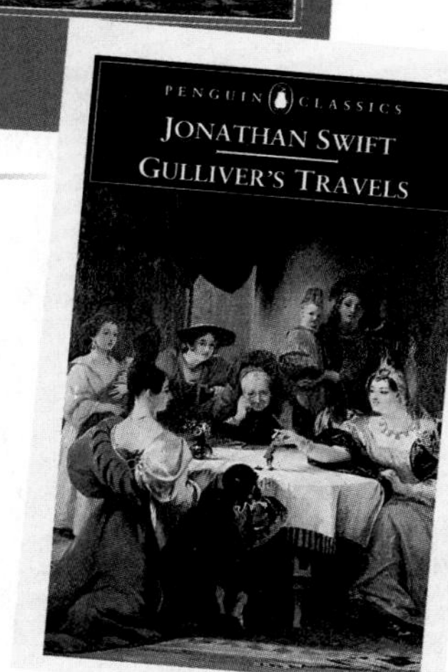

This satiric work traces the travels of a man who encounters strange and fantastic worlds. In addition to the land of Lilliput, populated by tiny people, and Brobdingnag, peopled by giants, Lemuel Gulliver visits a land where the Houyhnhnms (horse-like, rational creatures) rule over Yahoos, who resemble humans. He also encounters Laputa, a flying island ruled by experts and pedants. Fantasy, science fiction, and satire combine in this compelling story of a stranger who visits strange lands.

Johnson and Boswell
Pat Rogers
A dual biography of the most famous pair in English literature, written by one of the leading scholars of the period.

Vindication
Frances Sherwood
Mary Wollstonecraft is portrayed vividly in this fictionalized treatment of her life and times.

Other Media

A Tale of Two Cities
British production of the Dickens classic about the French Revolution, starring Dirk Bogarde. Social Studies School Service.
(videocassette)

Gulliver's Travels
Dove Audio.
(audiocassettes)

The Age of Reason: Europe After the Renaissance
Knowledge Unlimited.
(videocassette)

The Age of Enlightenment
Cambridge Social Studies.
(videocassette)

EXTEND YOUR READING 695

The Flowering of Romanticism

The selections in Unit Four use nature to explore the attitudes, interests, and social concerns of early 19th-century England. The unit is divided into two sections to better represent the romantic emphasis on emotion and the imagination.

Part 1

Seeking Truth The lyric poetry in this part of the unit reflects the romantic love of nature, spontaneity, and individual expression. The poets draw on images from the natural world to communicate their world view. The Comparing Literature selection demonstrates the love of nature shared by the romantics and the writers of Japanese haiku. An Author Study on William Wordsworth permits a broad exposure to the quintessential romantic English poet.

Part 2

Embracing the Imagination The poems in this part reflect the imaginative self-expression of the romantic era. Using images drawn from nature, the poets convey their feelings about such themes as love, death, and eternity. The Comparing Literature selection draws connections between German and English romanticism.

UNIT FOUR

To see a world in a grain of sand
And a heaven in a wild flower,
Hold infinity in the palm of your hand
And eternity in an hour.

William Blake
POET AND ARTIST

The Lake, Petworth: Sunset, Fighting Bucks (about 1828), Joseph Mallord William Turner. Clore Collection, Tate Gallery, London/Art Resource, New York.

696

Mini Lesson Viewing and Representing

The Lake, Petworth: Sunset, Fighting Bucks
by Joseph Mallord William Turner

ART APPRECIATION

Instruction Perhaps the greatest landscape painter of the 19th century, J. M. W. Turner is famous for his use of luminous light and color, which foreshadowed the French Impressionists decades later. Talented even as a child, Turner sold his first painting when he was 12 years old. He was secretive as an adult, living mostly in closely guarded privacy. Turner produced 19,000 images, all of which he left in his will to the "national property" of England.

Petworth is an English village about 40 miles south southwest of London. From 1829 to 1837, Turner was a frequent guest there at the estate of a generous patron, the earl of Egremont. *The Lake, Petworth* probably was painted in the early 1830s.

Ask: What can you infer from this painting about the artist's attitude toward nature?

Possible Response: Turner probably held nature in awe, with reverence for its beauty and life.

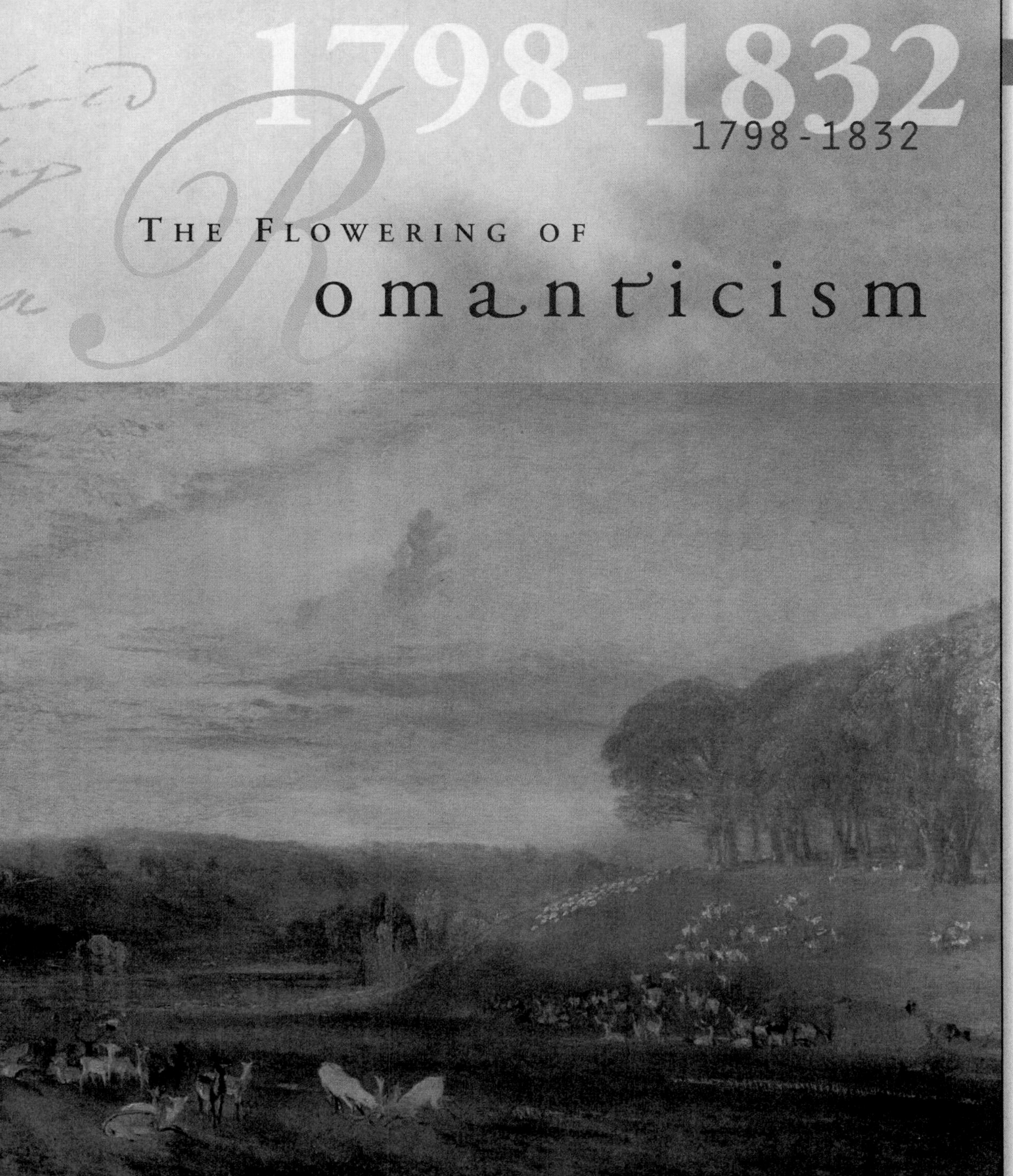

Making Connections

To help students explore the connections among the art, quotation, and the unit theme, have them consider the following questions:

Ask: How would you paraphrase the quotation from Blake, which is the opening stanza of his poem "Auguries of Innocence"?
Possible Response: Blake suggests that a close examination of nature can reveal a great deal about life. The smallest detail of nature can be representative of all life.

Ask: Based on the subject and mood of the painting, what do you think the romantics derived from a contemplation of nature?
Possible Response: an appreciation of beauty and tranquillity; self-knowledge gained through the study of nature
Have students think about the quotation and painting.

Ask: What different kinds of literature do you think you will find in this unit?
Possible Response: There are likely to be imaginative poems about nature and individual expression. Students might also suggest they will find essays about the value of nature and self-expression.

VIDEODISC **LaserLinks**
Historical Literary Connection: The Flowering of Romanticism
Several key historical events and representative artwork of this period are highlighted in this film. Pictures of the American and the French revolutions and paintings by John Constable and J. M. W. Turner are among the images presented. Use this video to help students develop an understanding of the Romantic period.

See Teacher's SourceBook p. 43 for bar codes.

UNIT FOUR

PART 1 SKILLS TRACE

Features and Selections	Literary Analysis	Reading and Critical Thinking	Writing Opportunities
The Flowering of Romanticism **Time Line** **Historical Background/Essay**			
POETRY Selected Poems by William Blake	Symbol, 709, 715	Drawing Conclusions, 709, 715 Test Practice, 711	Blake Critique, 716 Discussion Questions, 716
POETRY Haiku	Haiku, 717, 720	Images and Ideas, 717, 720 Informal Assess., 719	Modern Haiku, 721 Points of Comparison, 721
AUTHOR STUDY **William Wordsworth**			
POETRY Selected Poems	Imagery, 725, 738 Review: Simile, 738	Drawing Conclusions, 725, 738 Informal Assess., 733	Dorothy's Journal, 740 Poem About a Place, 740 Poetic Comparison, 740 Summary, 735
Author's Style Author Study Project	Analysis of Style, 739 Analyzing Sonnet, 739		Imitating Style, 739
POETRY Kubla Khan	Onomatopoeia, 741, 744 Alliteration and Rhyme, 744	Analyzing Structure, 741, 744	
NARRATIVE POETRY The Rime of the Ancient Mariner	Literary Ballad, 745, 766 Review: Simile, 766	Narrative Poetry, 745, 766 Test Practice 760	Poetry of Dreams, 767 Analytical Essay, 767 Informal Assess., 755, 765
Milestones In British Literature Pride & Prejudice			

LEGEND PE instruction shown in black
TE Mini Lessons shown in green

CCL indicates a Cross-Curricular Link
DLS indicates Daily Language SkillBuilder

Speaking and Listening Viewing and Representing	Inquiry and Research	Grammar, Usage, and Mechanics	Vocabulary
Art Appreciation, 696			Prefixes, 700
Ideas Through Art, 716 Art Appreciation, 713 Dramatic Presentation, 714		DLS, 709 Clause From Phrase, 716	Word Origins, 712
	Japanese Art, 721	DLS, 717 Independent and Subordinate Clauses, 721	
Poem in Pictures, 740 **Nature Debate, 740** Art Appreciation, 732 Memorize and Recite, 734 Silhouettes, 736	**Social History, 740**	DLS, 725	Using a Dictionary, 728
Changing Style, 739 **Panel Discussion, 740**		Clauses That Modify Subjects, 739	
		DLS, 741 Noun Clauses, 743	
Choral Reading, 767 **Video Visions, 767** Interview, 752 Art Appreciation, 758 Choral Reading, 759	**Multimedia Report, 767**	DLS, 745 Adjective Clauses, 750	Archaic Verb Forms, 747 Structural Clues, 763
Film Review, 768			

PART 2 SKILLS TRACE

Features and Selections	Literary Analysis	Reading and Critical Thinking	Writing Opportunities
POETRY Selected Poems by George Gordon, Lord Byron	Apostrophe, 773, 779	Comparing Speakers, 773, 779 Informal Assess., 778	Romantic Character, 780 Imaginary Dialogue, 780 Weekly Opinion, 780
POETRY Selected Poems by Percy Bysshe Shelley	Rhythmic Patterns, 781, 790	Drawing Conclusions, 781, 790 Informal Assess., 789	Performance Notes, 791 Travel Brochure, 791
Related Reading *from* A Defense of Poetry	Identifying Persuasive Techniques, 793		
POETRY Comparing Literature of the World The Lotus-Blossom Cowers	Mood, 794, 796 Review: Personification, 796 Review: Rhyme Scheme, 796	Understand and Appreciate, 794, 796	Haiku, Heine, 797 Definition of Love, 797 Points of Comparison, 797
POETRY Selected Poetry by John Keats	Sound Devices, 798, 806 Alliteration, 806 Rhythmic Patterns, 806 Test Practice, 800	Author's Motivation, 798, 806 Test Practice, 800	Seasonal Poetry, 807 Interpretive Essay, 807
Communication Workshop: Perform– ance Presentation Assessment Practice Building Vocabulary Sentence Crafting			
Reflect and Assess	Defining Romanticism, 818 Reviewing Literary Concepts	Analyzing Similarities, 818	Comparing Times, 818 Building Your Portfolio, 819
Reading and Writing for Assessment	Test-Taking Strategies, 822–827 Analyzing Clear Text, 822		Test-Taking Strategies, 822–827

LEGEND PE instruction shown in black
TE Mini Lessons shown in green
CCL indicates a Cross-Curricular Link
DLS indicates Daily Language SkillBuilder

Speaking and Listening Viewing and Representing	Inquiry and Research	Grammar, Usage, and Mechanics	Vocabulary
Illuminated Manuscript, 780 Interview with Poet, 780 Artistic Reflections, 780 Direct Address, 776	Battle of Trafalgar, 780	DLS, 773 Adverb Clauses, 780	Context Clues, 777
Portrait of a King, 791 Poet's Soliloquy, 791 Art Appreciation, 783, 788 Oral Reading, 784	Shelley's Poetic Theories, 791	DLS, 781 Adjective Clauses, 786	Denotation and Connotation, 785
Musical Interp., 797 Art Appreciation, 795	Botany Lesson, 797	DLS, 794 Clauses and Comparisons, 797	
Autumnal Collage, 807 Dramatic Reading, 807 Prose Soliloquy, 802 Art Appreciation, 805	Grecian Art, 807	DLS, 798 Complex Sentences, 807	Word Origins, 804
Analyze Literary Performance, 813 Performance Presentation, 813 Visualizing the Performance, 812		Revising and Editing, 815 Adjective and Noun Clauses, 817	Homonyms, Homophones, and Homographs, 816
		Test-Taking Strategies, 822–827	

UNIT FOUR
RESOURCE MANAGEMENT GUIDE
PART 1

To introduce the theme/literary period of this unit, use Fine Art Transparencies T26–28 in the Communications Transparencies and Copymasters.

	Unit Resource Book	Assessment	Integrated Technology and Media	Additional Support: Literary Analysis Transparencies
from **Songs of Innocence** *from* **Songs of Experience** *pp. 709–716*	• Active Reading p. 4 • Literary Analysis p. 5	• Selection Test, Formal Assessment pp. 129–130 Test Generator	Audio Library LaserLinks, Teacher's SourceBook p. 43	• Romanticism T13 • Symbols in Romantic Poetry T14
Haiku *pp. 717–721*	• Active Reading p. 6 • Literary Analysis p. 7	• Selection Test, Formal Assessment pp. 131–132 Test Generator	Audio Library LaserLinks, Teacher's SourceBook pp. 44–45	• Form and Meaning in Poetry T15
Selected Poems by William Wordsworth *pp. 725–740*	• Active Reading p. 8 • Literary Analysis p. 9	• Selection Test, Formal Assessment pp. 133–134 Test Generator	Audio Library LaserLinks, Teacher's SourceBook p. 46 NetActivities	• Poetic Devices T16
Kubla Khan *pp. 741–744*	• Active Reading p. 10 • Literary Analysis p. 11	• Selection Test, Formal Assessment pp. 135–136 Test Generator	Audio Library LaserLinks, Teacher's SourceBook p. 47 Video: Literature in Performance, Video Resource Book pp. 23–26	• Form and Meaning in Poetry T15
The Rime of the Ancient Mariner *pp. 745–767*	• Summary p. 12 • Active Reading p. 13 • Literary Analysis p. 14 • Selection Quiz p. 15	• Selection Test, Formal Assessment pp. 137–138 Test Generator	Audio Library Research Starter www.mcdougallittell.com	• The Moral Tale, Ballad, Fable, and Folk Tale T23
		Unit Assessment	***Unit Technology***	
		• Unit Four, Part 1 Test, Formal Assessment pp. 139–140 Test Generator • Unit Four Integrated Test, Integrated Assessment pp. 29–37	ClassZone www.mcdougallittell.com Electronic Teacher Tools Electronic Library	

T = Transparency C = Copymaster

	Reading and Critical Thinking Transparencies	Grammar Transparencies and Copymasters	Vocabulary Transparencies and Copymasters	Writing Transparencies and Copymasters	Communications Transparencies and Copymasters
	• Making Inferences T7 • Analyzing Text T18	• Daily Language SkillBuilder T18 • Distinguishing a Clause from a Phrase C106	• Researching Word Origins C59	• Critical Review C32 • Literary Interpretation C33	
	• Visualizing T8	• Daily Language SkillBuilder T18 • Diagramming Subjects, Verbs, and Modifiers T58 • Identifying Independent and Subordinate Clauses C107		• Compare-Contrast C34	
	• Drawing Conclusions T4 • Making Inferences T7 • Venn Diagram T51	• Daily Language SkillBuilder T19 • Identifying Adjective Clauses C109 • Clauses That Modify Subjects C110 • Clauses That Modify Objects C111	• Using a Dictionary C60	• Compare-Contrast C34	• Impromptu Speaking: Debate T15
	• Analyzing Text Structure T17 • Evaluating Argumentation II T22	• Daily Language SkillBuilder T19 • Noun Clauses C117		• Figurative Language and Sound Devices T15	
	• Evaluating Story Elements T6	• Daily Language SkillBuilder T20 • Essential and Nonessential Adjective Clauses C115		• Compare-Contrast C34	• Appreciative Listening T2 • Dramatic Reading T12

STUDENTS ACQUIRING ENGLISH

The **Spanish Study Guide,** pp. 160–177, includes language support for the following pages:
- Family and Community Involvement (per unit)
- Selection Summaries and Vocabulary
- Active Reading
- Literary Analysis

To introduce the theme/literary period of this unit, use Fine Art Transparencies T26–28 in the Communications Transparencies and Copymasters.

Selection	Unit Resource Book	Assessment	Integrated Technology and Media	Additional Support: Literary Analysis Transparencies
She Walks in Beauty **When We Two Parted** *from* **Childe Harold's Pilgrimage** *pp. 773–780*	• Active Reading p. 16 • Literary Analysis p. 17	• Selection Test, Formal Assessment pp. 141–142 Test Generator	Audio Library LaserLinks, Teacher's SourceBook p. 48	• Poetic Devices T16
Ozymandias **Ode to the West Wind** **To a Skylark** *pp. 781–791*	• Active Reading p. 18 • Literary Analysis p. 19	• Selection Test, Formal Assessment pp. 143–144 Test Generator	Audio Library LaserLinks, Teacher's SourceBook p. 49	• Form and Meaning in Poetry T15
The Lotus-Blossom Cowers *pp. 794–797*	• Active Reading p. 20 • Literary Analysis p. 21	• Selection Test, Formal Assessment p. 145 Test Generator	Audio Library	
Selected Poems by John Keats *pp. 798–807*	• Active Reading p. 22 • Literary Analysis p. 23	• Selection Test, Formal Assessment pp. 147–148 Test Generator	Audio Library LaserLinks, Teacher's SourceBook pp. 50–51	• Poetic Devices T16

Communication Workshop: Performance Presentation	Unit Assessment	Unit Technology
Unit Four Resource Book • Planning Your Performance p. 24 • Practicing and Presenting p. 25 • Peer Response Guide pp. 26–27 • Refining Your Performance p. 28 • Student Models pp. 29–34 • Standards for Evaluation p. 35	• Unit Four, Part 2 Test, Formal Assessment pp. 149–150 Test Generator • Unit Four Integrated Test, Integrated Assessment pp. 29–37	INTERNET ClassZone www.mcdougallittell.com Electronic Teacher Tools Electronic Library

T = Transparency C = Copymaster

	Reading and Critical Thinking Transparencies	Grammar Transparencies and Copymasters	Vocabulary Transparencies and Copymasters	Writing Transparencies and Copymasters	Communications Transparencies and Copymasters
	• Compare and Contrast T15 • Organizational Chart: Vertical T53	• Daily Language SkillBuilder T20 • Adverb Clauses C116	• Context Clues C63	• The Uses of Dialogue T24 • Opinion Statement C35	• Interviewing T9
	• Noting Details T9 • Compare and Contrast T15 • Reading for Details T16	• Daily Language SkillBuilder T21 • Adjective Clauses Introduced by Relative Pronouns C112	• Denotation and Connotation C64	• Identifying Writing Variables T2 • Showing, Not Telling T22	• Impromptu Speaking: Dialogue, Role-Play T14
	• Compare and Contrast T15 • Reading for Details T16 • Comparing Authors' Views T24	• Daily Language SkillBuilder T21 • Clauses and Comparisons C119		• Figurative Language and Sound Devices T15 • Compare-Contrast C34	
	• Determining Author's Purpose and Audience T20	• Daily Language SkillBuilder T21 • Compound and Complex Sentences C123	• Word Origins C65	• Figurative Language and Sound Devices T15 • Literary Interpretation C33	• Appreciative Listening T2 • Dramatic Reading T12

STUDENTS ACQUIRING ENGLISH

The **Spanish Study Guide,** pp. 178–189, includes language support for the following pages:

- Family and Community Involvement (per unit)
- Selection Summaries and Vocabulary
- Active Reading
- Literary Analysis

UNIT FOUR
DAILY LANGUAGE SKILLBUILDERS

Selection	SkillBuilder Sentences	Suggested Answers
from Songs of Innocence The Lamb The Little Boy Lost The Little Boy Found *from* Songs of Experience The Tyger The Fly The Sick Rose	**1.** Many writer of the romantic era were inspired by two major wars. the american revolution and, the French Revolution. **2.** both wars were fought to secure what were than referred to as "the rights of man" the freedoms of beleif and expression that we now associate with democracy.	**1.** Many writer**s** of the romantic era were inspired by two major wars**:** the **A**merican **R**evolution and the French Revolution. **2.** **B**oth wars were fought to secure what were th**e**n referred to as "the rights of man"**—**the freedoms of bel**ie**f and expression that we now associate with democracy.
Haiku	**1.** Matsuo Basho was born in japan in 1644 soon after the conclusion of a civil war that has lasted for centuries. **2.** During this long awaited time of peace, many samuri male warriors—turned their energys away from war toward the arts: poetry music and painting	**1.** Matsuo Basho was born in **J**apan in 1644**,** soon after the conclusion of a civil war that **had** lasted for centuries. **2.** During this long**-**awaited time of peace, many samur**ai—**male warriors—turned their energ**ies** away from war toward the arts: poetry**,** music**,** and painting**.**
Selected Poems	**1.** William Wordsworth was born in West Cumberland England, on the northern edge of what is known as the "Lake District. **2.** His mother died when he was eight, and he was sent away to a school near esthwaite lake he boarded with a woman named Ann tyson gave him a simple, comfortable life, and the freedom to rome the country side.	**1.** William Wordsworth was born in West Cumberland**,** England, on the northern edge of what is known as the "Lake District**."** **2.** His mother died when he was eight, and he was sent away to a school near **E**sthwaite **L**ake**. H**e boarded with a woman named Ann **T**yson, **who** gave him a simple, comfortable life and the freedom to ro**am** the **countryside**.

Selection	SkillBuilder Sentences	Suggested Answers
Kubla Khan	**1.** Kubla (or Kublai Khan was a great emporer who lived from A.D. 1215 too 1294 in Mongolia, a region of Asia North of China and South of Russia.	**1.** Kubla (or Kubla**i)** Khan was a great emp**e**r**o**r who lived from A.D. 1215 **to** 1294 in Mongolia, a region of Asia **n**orth of China and **s**outh of Russia.
	2. Kubla Khan like his grandfather Genghis Khan was a skilled conqeror, but he also brought to the Mongolian empire a level of culture unknown before his rule he built cities patronized artists and developed a new form of writing.	**2.** Kubla Khan**,** like his grandfather Genghis Khan**,** was a skilled conqeror, but he also brought to the Mongolian empire a level of culture unknown before his rule**:** he built cities**,** patronized artists**,** and developed a new form of writing.
The Rime of the Ancient Mariner	**1.** Originaly, a ballad was a song intended to accompany a dance it usually had a light uncomplicated rhythm and rhyme sceme.	**1.** Origina**ll**y, a ballad was a song intended to accompany a dance**;** it usually had a light**,** uncomplicated rhythm and rhyme sc**h**eme.
	2. More recently, ballads are thought of as poems that tell a story. And that have short stanza and simple rhymes.	**2.** More recently, ballads are thought of as poems that tell a story **a**nd that have short stanza**s** and simple rhymes.
She Walks in Beauty When We Two Parted *from* Childe Harold's Pilgrimage Ozymandias Ode to the West Wind	**1.** Byron was born in London in 1788 the year before the french Revolution began, to too colorful parents Captain John Byron, a fortune-hunter who squanders the inheritence of two wealthy wives and catherine Gordon of Gight, the last descandent in a line of Scottish nobility.	**1.** Byron was born in London in 1788**,** the year before the **F**rench Revolution began, to **two** colorful parents**:** Captain John Byron, a fortune-hunter who squander**ed** the inheritence of two wealthy wives**,** and **C**atherine Gordon of Gight, the last desc**e**ndent in a line of Scottish nobility.
	2. He became the sixth Lord Byron at the age of ten, when his great-uncle—known to his neighbors as "the Wicked Lord" for his violant behavior died.	**2.** He became the sixth Lord Byron at the age of ten, when his great-uncle—known to his neighbors as "the Wicked Lord" for his viol**e**nt behavior**—**died.

DAILY LANGUAGE SKILLBUILDERS, continued

Selection	SkillBuilder Sentences	Suggested Answers
To a Skylark	**1.** Ramses II—known by the ancient greeks as Ozymandias ruled ancient Egypt for 67-years. **2.** He is remembered for being a great general, in the fifth year of his reign he defended his nation against the hittites, and later he fordged a treaty with them.	**1.** Ramses II—known by the anc**i**ent **G**reeks as Ozymandias**—**ruled ancient Egypt for 67 years. **2.** He is remembered for being a great general**:** in the fifth year of his reign**,** he defended his nation against the **H**ittites, and later he fo**rg**ed a treaty with them.
The Lotus-Blossom Cowers	**1.** The romantic composer Franz Schubert is rembered for bringing the german Lied, or art song to it's highest form. **2.** For his art song, Schubert use verses by many gifted writers, including Goethe Schiller Heine and Shakespeare	**1.** The romantic composer Franz Schubert is rem**em**bered for bringing the **G**erman Lied, or art song**,** to **its** highest form. **2.** For his art song**s**, Schubert use**d** verses by many gifted writers, including Goethe**,** Schiller**,** Heine**,** and Shakespeare**.**
Ode on a Grecian Urn To Autumn When I Have Fears That I May Cease to Be Bright Star, Would I Were Steadfast As Thou Art	**1.** John Keats regarded by many as the more imaginative poet of the 19th-century was born in 1795 in moorfields England. **2.** his father a livery stable manager dies when John was only eight.	**1.** John Keats**,** regarded by many as the most imaginative poet of the 19th century**,** was born in 1795 in **M**oorfields**,** England. **2.** **H**is father**,** a livery stable manager**,** die**d** when John was only eight.

	Unit One	Unit Two	Unit Three	Unit Four	Unit Five	Unit Six	Unit Seven
Grammar Focus by Unit	Parts of a Sentence	Phrases, Part I	Phrases, Part II	Clauses, Part I	Clauses, Part II	Rhetorical Grammar, Part I	Rhetorical Grammar, Part II

The Language of Literature offers several options for integrating grammar instruction and literature.

- Each literature unit has a grammar focus. The Teacher's Edition includes Mini Lessons for each selection that help develop the grammar focus for the unit and spring from the content of the specific literature.
- The Pupil Edition includes several full-page lessons on Sentence Crafting. These lessons are related to both the literature and the grammar focus for the unit and help students use grammar in their own writing.
- Daily Language SkillBuilders in the Teacher's Edition provide students with ongoing proofreading practice and reinforce punctuation, spelling, grammar and usage, and capitalization.
- Grammar Copymasters and Transparencies, which may be used to complement or extend lessons in the Teacher's Edition, present grammar in a traditional, systematic sequence. References to appropriate copymasters or transparencies are included at point of use in the Teacher's Edition Mini Lessons.

TE Mini Lessons shown in green
PE instruction shown in black

Part 1

Using Clauses

Distinguishing a Clause from a Phrase
Blake poems, p. 716

Identifying Independent and Subordinate Clauses
Haiku, p. 721

Identifying Adjective Clauses
"Lines Composed a Few Miles Above Tintern Abbey," p. 730

Clauses That Modify Subjects
"Composed upon Westminster Bridge, September 3, 1802," "The World Is Too Much with Us," p. 739

Clauses That Modify Objects
"It Is a Beauteous Evening," "I Wandered Lonely As a Cloud," p. 740

Essential and Nonessential Adjective Clauses
"The Rime of the Ancient Mariner," p. 750

Noun Clauses
"Kubla Kahn," p. 743

Part 2

Parts of the Sentence

Complete Sentences
Communication Workshop, p. 815

Using Clauses

Identifying Independent and Subordinate Clauses

Identifying Adjective Clauses
Sentence Crafting, p. 817

Adjective Clauses Introduced by Relative Pronouns
Shelley poems, p. 786

Adverb Clauses
Byron poems, p. 780

Noun Clauses
Sentence Crafting, p. 817

Clauses and Comparisons
"The Lotus-Blossom Cowers," p. 797

Clauses in a Complex Sentence: Subordinate Clauses as Nouns
Keats poems, p. 807

Subject-Verb Agreement

Communication Workshop, p. 815

Pronoun Usage

Adjective Clauses Introduced by *Who* or *Whom*
Sentence Crafting, p. 817

Using Modifiers

Misplaced and Dangling Modifiers
Communication Workshop, p. 815

End Marks and Commas

Commas with Nonessential Clauses and Phrases
Sentence Crafting, p. 817

This time line shows important events of the age of romanticism. Further information about some people and events is provided below. Have students explore the historical and cultural context of the literature of the Romantic period by referring back to the time line as they discuss events and their relationships to the literature of the time.

Literature: 1798

A The anonymously published *Lyric Ballads* opened with Coleridge's "The Rime of the Ancient Mariner," followed by three more of Coleridge's poems. Then Wordsworth contributed some verse anecdotes and psychological studies of common people, and the book closed with "Tintern Abbey." While the book was not an immediate revelation for critics, the English essayist William Hazlitt heard Coleridge recite some of the poems and commented that "a sense of a new style and a new spirit in poetry came over [him]" similar to that of "the first welcome breath of spring." Wordsworth published a new edition under his own name in 1800, and in it, he described poetry as "the spontaneous overflow of powerful feelings."

World: 1799

B Few figures have had so remarkable an impact on their time as Napoleon Bonaparte (1769–1821), who rose from an obscure army lieutenant to become emperor of France. During the Italian campaign of 1796–1797, he created an invincible army out of his demoralized, starving troops. In 1799, he led a coup that established a new government in which he served as "first consul" of France. During the next few years, he reduced inflation and created a system of laws known as Code Napoléon. Napoleon and France plagued the English and all of Europe until his defeat at the Battle of Waterloo in 1815.

TIME LINE 1798-1832

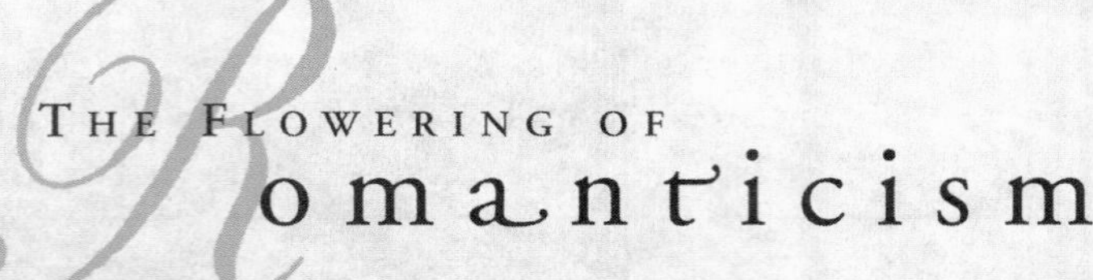

The Flowering of Romanticism

EVENTS IN BRITISH LITERATURE

1790

A **1798** William Wordsworth and Samuel Taylor Coleridge publish "Tintern Abbey" and "The Rime of the Ancient Mariner" anonymously in book *Lyrical Ballads*

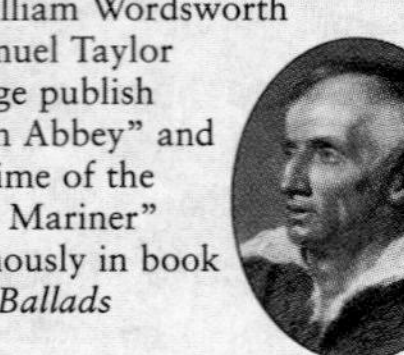

1800

1800 Dorothy Wordsworth begins keeping *Grasmere Journals*

1810

1811 Jane Austen's *Sense and Sensibility* published

1812 Lord Byron wins fame with first two sections of *Childe Harold's Pilgrimage*

D **1813** Jane Austen's *Pride and Prejudice* published

1814 Sir Walter Scott anonymously publishes *Waverly*

EVENTS IN BRITAIN

1790

1799 British diplomats assemble Second Coalition (Britain, Austria, and Russia) hoping to drive Napoleon from power in France

1800

C **1800** Act of Union passed, creating United Kingdom of Great Britain and Ireland

1805 British fleet defeats Napoleon's navy in Battle of Trafalgar off Spanish coast, ending Napoleon's hopes of invading Britain

1807 British slave trade abolished

1810

1811 George III declared permanently insane; eldest son George, Prince of Wales, named regent

1812 Britain fights United States in War of 1812

1815 British and Prussian armies under British leader Wellington defeat Napoleon at Waterloo

EVENTS IN THE WORLD

1790

B **1799** Coup d'état establishes Napoleon dictator of France (crowned emperor in 1804)

1800

1803 U.S. president Jefferson buys Louisiana Territory from France

1804 Haiti gains independence from France

1805 Napoleon begins conquering most of Europe (to 1812); Muhammad Ali begins rule and modernization of Egypt (to 1849)

1808 U.S. abolishes slave trade

1810

1814 Congress of Vienna opens, seeking to remake Europe after Napoleon's downfall and prevent spread of French ideals of democracy (to 1815)

Britain: 1800

C Napoleon's ascension to the French throne made Great Britain uncomfortable. After an unsuccessful French-aided Irish rebellion against English rule in 1798, British statesmen thought that legislative union would solve the Irish threat, and Ireland was made an official part of Britain. (In 1922, after the Irish Free State was established and Northern Ireland stayed with Britain, the latter was officially renamed the United Kingdom of Great Britain and Northern Ireland.)

Literature: 1813

D At her death in 1817, Jane Austen left six complete novels, all notable for their sharp wit and keen perception. Austen herself lived an uneventful life: she never married and lived her life with her family in a small village. Her novels were admired by Sir Walter Scott, but Charlotte Brontë and Elizabeth Barrett Browning found them limited in scope and passion. In the 1990s, filmmakers repopularized Austen, releasing several new movies of her books.

Period Pieces

E Combination night lamp and tea warmer

Iron in which heated brick was inserted

Twelve-month equation clock

1818 Mary Shelley's *Frankenstein* published anonymously (F)

1819 Percy Bysshe Shelley writes "Ode to the West Wind"; John Keats writes "Ode on a Grecian Urn" and "To Autumn"

1821 John Keats, age 25, dies of tuberculosis

1822 Percy Bysshe Shelley, age 32, drowns off coast of Italy

1823 Lord Byron joins Greek war for liberation from Turks

(G) **1824** Byron, age 38, dies of fever

1820 — 1830

1818 Crossing of Atlantic Ocean by steamship

1819 "Peterloo Massacre"—11 killed in St. Peter's Field, Manchester, when cavalry charges social reformers

1820 Regency ends with death of George III and crowning of Prince of Wales as George IV

1821 Engineer George Stephenson begins work on world's first railroad line (passenger service starts in 1825)

1829 First water-purification plant built in London; Catholic Emancipation Act passed, freeing Catholics from restrictions

1830 George IV dies; reign of brother, William IV, begins (to 1837)

1832 First Reform Bill extends voting rights to middle-class men but affects only five percent of population

1820 — 1830

c. 1816 Zulu chief Shaka begins rule over large kingdom in southeastern Africa (to 1828)

1817 Ludwig van Beethoven, nearly deaf, begins composing monumental Ninth Symphony (to 1823)

1821 Spain's Latin American empire begins collapse as Mexico, several Central American states, and Venezuela win independence

1823 U.S. president Monroe issues *Monroe Doctrine* to keep Europe out of Latin America

(H) **1824** Bolivar liberates last Spanish colonies in Latin America

(I) **1830** Greece wins full independence from Ottoman Turks

Period Pieces

E In 1792, the Scottish engineer William Murdock developed the first commercially important gas lamp and a means of distilling the coal gas it burned. By the early 1800s, the streets of London and many other cities were illuminated by gas lamps, which remained the main type of artificial lighting until they were superseded by electric lights in the late 1800s.

Literature: 1818

F The idea for *Frankenstein* was born during the summer of 1816, when, at a house party on the shore of Lake Geneva in Switzerland, Lord Byron suggested that each of his guests, including 18-year-old Mary Shelley, compose a ghost story to entertain the company. In an introduction to her novel, Mary Shelley wrote that she envisioned the monster in a dream, perhaps prompted by a conversation between Percy Shelley and Byron on the possibility of creating life in a laboratory. After Percy's death in Italy in 1922, Mary returned to England and concentrated on publicizing her dead husband's writings. The painting of Mary was created around 1840.

Literature: 1824

G The premature death of Byron was nearly the last act of the playing out of English romanticism. In just a little over seven years, four of its youngest and most promising stars had died (Austen, Keats, Shelley, and Byron), and by 1824 its older major writers such as Blake, Wordsworth, Coleridge, and Scott had either quit writing or were no longer producing significant works.

World: 1824

H The spark for Latin America's wars of independence against Spanish rule came from Napoleon's conquest of Spain in 1808. Rebellion broke out in 1810 in several places on the continent. Venezuela declared independence in 1811, though it had to wait ten years to realize it. Uprisings in Ecuador, Argentina, Chile, and Peru followed, and when Simon Bolívar's army defeated the Spanish at the Battle of Ayacucho in Peru on December 9, 1824, the last Spanish colony in Latin America broke free.

World: 1830

I The Greek war of independence had begun in 1821 and became a popular cause throughout Europe. Volunteers from several nations fought alongside the Greeks. The struggle attracted Lord Byron, who sailed to Greece in 1824 to help train Greek soldiers, caught a fever, and died a few months later. Byron is today considered a Greek national hero.

TIME LINE 699

OVERVIEW

Introduction
This article provides a historical and literary context for the writings presented in Unit Four. In particular students will learn how the period's passions are relected in Britain by the threat of French invasion and by the instituting of sorely needed social reforms.

Teaching Nonfiction

Reading Skills and Strategies

ESTABLISHING A PURPOSE FOR READING
Have students scan the article to establish a purpose for reading. Remind them to adjust their purposes if they encounter unexpected content or difficulty.

USING TEXT ORGANIZERS
If students need more support, have them preview the article, noting the basic text organizers: title, overview, subheads, images and captions, and sidebar commentaries. Ask students to describe what information they would expect to locate in each section. As they read, have students use the subheads to make an outline or graphic organizer. Have them categorize information from the article, sidebars, and timeline with the appropriate heading. Remind students to use text organizers to locate and categorize information as they do independent research.

ANALYZING TEXT STRUCTURE
Have students scan the article and predict how they expect information to be structured. Due to the number of dates, students should expect the basic structure to be chronological. Discuss how this structure influences the way they read and understand the material. Encourage students to note other kinds of relationships (cause / effect and compare / contrast) signaled by text structure and words. Some key relationships: Britain and French Revolution; Britain and Ireland; growth of cities and reform.

IDENTIFYING MAIN IDEAS
The headings form sections that become main ideas. Have students read one section at a time and note how its idea is developed through details.

The Flowering of Romanticism

1798-1832

Great change swept the Western world at the end of the 18th century. A successful revolution in America and an ongoing one in France shattered the political stability of the day. In Britain, revolutions in industry and agriculture rocked the social and economic structure of the nation. Reflecting and responding to these dramatic changes was a movement that came to be called romanticism, which dominated Western intellectual and artistic life in the early 19th century.

A Romanticism was an outgrowth of 18th-century neoclassicism as well as a reaction against it. The spiritual father of the movement was the French Enlightenment thinker Jean Jacques Rousseau. Rousseau's argument that human society is based on a contract between the government and the governed echoed earlier ideas of England's John Locke and helped inspire the French Revolution. B Rousseau attributed evil not to human nature but to society, insisting that in the natural state a human being was essentially good and happy—a "noble savage." This idealization of nature and human beings became basic tenets of romantic thinking. Also basic was an emphasis on the individual, the personal, and the emotional—in sharp contrast to the emphasis on soci-

Top: Portrait of Jean Jacques Rousseau (1753), Maurice Quentin de La Tour. Musée d'Art et d'Histoire, Geneva, Switzerland, Giraudon/Art Resource, New York.
Bottom: Taking of the Bastille on July 14, 1789 (about 1789–1800), unknown French artist. Giraudon/Art Resource, New York.

NOTETAKING
Encourage students to take notes by jotting down important concepts, vocabulary, and terms, or you could use the activity described in Analyzing Text Structure.

ety, science, and reason that had been at the root of neoclassical thought.

Literary romanticism was pioneered in Germany by Johann Wolfgang von Goethe and in Britain by William Wordsworth and Samuel Taylor Coleridge. However, unlike the artistic ideals of neoclassicism, those of romanticism did not reflect the mainstream views of British society. During its peak period from 1798 to 1832, while the political instability and violence emanating from continental Europe prompted a conservative reaction throughout most levels of British society, romanticism flowered mainly as a movement of protest—a powerful expression of a desire for personal freedom and radical reform.

William Pitt the Younger

In the 1780s, before the conservative reaction set in, the need for reform was apparent not only to members of Britain's more liberal Whig party but also to the new Tory prime minister, William Pitt the Younger (son of the prime minister who led Britain through the Seven Years' War). The nation's growing cities were beset with a host of problems, including crime and poor sanitation. Child labor and other factory abuses were not being addressed, the emerging industrial centers in the north and west had no representation in Parliament, and archaic laws denied rights to many religious groups, including the Catholic majority in Ireland. Britain had lost its American colonies, primarily because of incompetent management, and the rest of its overseas empire faced a number of difficulties, ranging from corruption in India to the evils of the slave trade. (C)

Although Pitt came to power as a reformer, his reform plans were pushed aside when the French Revolution erupted in 1789. Initial British sympathy for the revolution soon died down when France's revolutionary moderates fell from power. The Whig politician Edmund Burke, who had supported the American (D)

William Pitt Addressing the House of Commons in 1793, Karl Anton Hickel. Oil on canvas, The Granger Collection, New York.

Development of the English Language

The democratic attitudes of romanticism helped broaden the concept of "acceptable" English and narrow the gap between the language of scholars and aristocrats and that of the common people. In their efforts to create literature based on natural speech, romantic writers sometimes employed regional dialects, colloquialisms, and even slang—to the dismay of more conservative critics. Romantic writers who were interested in capturing the flavor of the legendary past sometimes even used archaic language (*quoth* instead of *said,* for example).

In the aftermath of the American Revolution, British and American English grew further apart. A major figure in the development of American English was Connecticut-born Noah Webster, who patriotically set about proving that the new nation's language was as good as its mother tongue. His *American Spelling Book* went through over 300 editions from 1788 to 1829, and his 1828 *American Dictionary of the English Language* became a national institution. It was in part through Webster's influence that Americans dropped the *k* at the end of words like *publick* and *traffick;* eliminated the *u* in words such as *colour, flavour,* and *splendour* (but not, for some reason, in *glamour*); and changed the British *re* to *er* in words like *centre.*

Making Connections

Philosophy

(A) The works of the Scottish philosopher David Hume (1711–1776) played an important role in paving the way for romanticism. Hume wrote that all human knowledge consists of impressions (the data transmitted by the senses) and ideas, which are formed by the mind's combination and alteration of impressions. His theories supported the romantic notion that all human thought and knowledge of the world is a reflection of sensory experience.

Philosophy

(B) Romanticism's idealization of the natural life and the life of the child was in part due to the influence of Rousseau (1712–1778), and the cult of the "noble savage" led to a sentimentalized perception of Native Americans and Africans by British writers. Frequently at odds with authorities, Rousseau was driven out of Switzerland on one occasion and spent a year in England at Hume's invitation. He eventually developed a persecution mania that kept him from human contact during many of his later years.

Literature

(C) William Blake's poetry contrasts romantic notions of children's innocence with the destructive effects of the Industrial Revolution and urban blight. Many of the poems in Songs of Experience (1794) have urban settings and portray children as hapless victims of poverty and exploitation.

History

(D) The French Revolution had a deep impact on English writers. Afire with republican ideals, the young Wordsworth spent most of the year 1792 in France, but two years later, with the Reign of Terror in full force, he found himself disillusioned with the revolution. Of the many British novels set against the backdrop of the French Revolution, Charles Dickens's *A Tale of Two Cities* (1859), set in London and Paris, is probably the most famous.

Mini Lesson: Development of the English Language

PREFIXES

Tell students that the prefix *neo-* connotes revival. It is commonly applied to a renewed appreciation of a past era—its style or qualities. For example, in the second paragraph of the text above, a reference to 18th-century's neoclassicism means that the 1700s was a time of revived interest in the aesthetics of the simple and balanced forms of the classical era of Greek and Roman cultures. Such revivals often take the form of imitation of the earlier era's trademarks. Music, literature, cinema, painting, and architecture commonly pass through periods of "neo-" influence.

Application Have students identify and define some "neo-" words that they can find in magazines, newspapers, and the like. For example, concert music in the 20th century has gone through neobaroque, neoclassical, and neoromantic periods. Students should be able to unearth and explain several interesting examples.

Making Connections

Sociology

E The growing number of people convicted of crimes (mostly crimes against property) led to the construction of more prisons. An increasing number of convicts were "transported" to Australia, which had been newly discovered by the English and was now used as a gigantic prison colony. Even more oppressive is the fact that about 200 crimes had mandatory death penalties in England. Finally, between 1820 and 1840, the number of crimes punishable by death was reduced, and by 1861 only four such crimes remained on the books.

Music

F Napoleon's hold on the romantic imagination was so great that Beethoven originally planned to dedicate his Third Symphony (1803–1804) to Napoleon, subtitling it *Bonaparte.* However, when Napoleon crowned himself emperor, an enraged Beethoven removed the dedication and subtitled the work *Eroica* (Heroic) and added further words that, translated, mean "Composed to Celebrate the Memory of a Great Man." In 1813, Beethoven composed a *Battle Symphony,* later titled *Wellington's Victory,* to commemorate Wellington's victory over Napoleon in Spain in June of the year; it is possibly the worst music Beethoven ever wrote.

Revolution, was among the first to attack the excesses of the increasingly radical government of France. Burke's attacks created a rift within the Whig party, leaving the party's leader, Charles James Fox, with little support. As the violence of the French radicals increased, so did the British reaction, especially when France began exporting revolution beyond its borders. In 1793, after French troops invaded Holland, Britain entered upon a war with France that would ultimately last for over 25 years. Pitt was forced to succumb to fearful voices equating all reform efforts with revolution and arguing for domestic repression to keep Britain from falling victim to the violence and anarchy seen in France. **E**

Near the end of the century, rebellious Irishmen, encouraged by the promise of French assistance, rose up against their British masters. Though this rebellion was quelled after poor weather prevented a major French landing, the threat of a French invasion of Britain by way of Ireland remained. To combat the threat, Pitt offered to sponsor various reforms, including the granting of voting rights to Roman Catholics, if the Irish Parliament would agree to dissolve itself and join politically with the British Parliament. The passage of the Act of Union in 1800 formalized this arrangement, creating the United Kingdom of Great Britain and Ireland, but George III—still on the throne despite his periodic bouts of madness—refused to allow voting rights for Catholics. Pitt was forced to resign, just when his nation needed him most—when the brilliant Corsican general Napoleon Bonaparte had emerged as the dominant force on the French political scene.

Above: Napoleon Bonaparte Crossing the Alps (about 1801), Jacques Louis David. Chateau de Malmaison, Rueil-Malmaison, France, Giraudon/Art Resource, New York.

Created as a symbol of the union of Great Britain and Ireland, this flag—known as the Union Jack—has served as the national flag of the United Kingdom since 1801. It consists of elements taken from earlier flags of England (red cross on white), Scotland (diagonal white cross on blue), and Ireland (diagonal red cross on white).

The Rise and Fall of Napoleon

In late 1799, when Napoleon had taken control of France's revolutionary government, his charisma and acceptance of democratic principles had won him the admiration of reform-minded intellectuals throughout Europe. Soon, however, his hunger for power became clear. In 1804 he crowned himself **F** emperor of France, and over the next several years his military and political maneuvers allowed him to establish control over most of continental Europe. Called back to power in 1804, Pitt tried to prepare Britain for a seemingly inevitable French invasion. Fortunately, in 1805 the British fleet under Horatio Nelson succeeded in destroying the French navy in the Battle of Trafalgar off the coast of Spain, ending the threat of invasion. The victory was bittersweet, however, for Nelson himself was killed in the battle, and within months Pitt was also gone, dying of overwork at the age of 46.

His plans of invasion thwarted, Napoleon tried to break Britain economically by closing the ports of continental Europe to British trade. Tightening his grip on the Iberian Peninsula (Spain and Portugal), Napoleon deposed the Spanish king and placed his brother Joseph on the throne. In the "Peninsular War" that followed, British troops—commanded first by Sir John Moore (killed in action in 1809) and then by Sir Arthur Wellesley—gradually liberated the Iberian Peninsula from French control.

In 1811, with the Peninsular War in full swing, George III was declared insane and his eldest son and heir—George, Prince of Wales—became Britain's regent, or acting ruler. A spendthrift with loose personal morals, Prince George had been a gambling buddy of the now-deceased Whig leader Charles James Fox and (unlike George III) had always favored the Whigs. Now, however, he abandoned them and sided with the Tories, once again quashing hopes of domestic reform. Anyone who criticized the regent too openly became subject to arrest and imprisonment.

In 1812, Napoleon made the mistake of invading Russia, a nation with which he had enjoyed an uneasy peace. Though his army got as far as Moscow, the brutal Russian winter forced it into a retreat during which starvation, the freezing weather, and Cossack raids managed to kill off most of the French troops. Meanwhile, Wellesley's British forces were closing in on France from the south. At the Battle of Leipzig in 1813, the nations allied against Napoleon dealt him what seemed a death blow. When the allied forces entered Paris a year later, G

Literary History

Although the beginning of Britain's romantic period is traditionally assigned to the year 1798, aspects of romanticism are evident in earlier British literature. H Writing in the dialect of Lowland Scotland, Robert Burns, who died in 1796, produced heartfelt lyrics about love, nature, and the Scottish past, many of which were meant to be sung to familiar tunes. William Blake, who began publishing in the 1780s, expressed his rebellious spirit and his mystical view of the nature of good and evil in such works as *The French Revolution, The Marriage of Heaven and Hell,* and the contrasting poems of *Songs of Innocence* and *Songs of Experience.*

Nevertheless, the real flowering of romanticism came with the 1798 publication of William Wordsworth and Samuel Taylor Coleridge's landmark collection *Lyrical Ballads.* The two men, who had first met in 1795, were united by their shared desire to explore new modes of literary expression. Wordsworth, who had visited France when the revolution began, was deeply committed to the common people and sought to express individual human experiences in a natural language. Coleridge, in poems like "Kubla Khan," focused on more exotic experiences, letting his imagination wander in realms of mystery and the supernatural. Both poets rejected the world of science and industry, feeling that insight into human experience flows most freely from communion with nature. I With Wordsworth's sister, Dorothy—whose diaries reveal much about the two poets' personalities—they spent a good deal of their time in the rural Lake District of northwestern England, so that they and their friend Robert Southey are sometimes referred to as the Lake Poets.

Making Connections

Music

G Events surrounding Napoleon influenced another composer, Peter Ilyich Tchaikovsky. The latter's *1812 Overture* is a prime example of Russian nationalism. The music was premiered in 1882 to commemorate the 70th anniversary of Napoleon's retreat from Russia and quotes *La Marseillaise* as well as the Czarist national anthem. It is meant for outdoor performance, with bells and cannons—hence its attraction, ironically, for Independence Day celebrations in the United States, a country with a War of 1812 that has no connection to Tchaikovsky's famous piece.

Literature

H Many mid-18th-century poets were harbingers of the romantic revolution. Among the best was Thomas Gray, whose "Elegy Written in a Country Churchyard" (1751) became one of the most quoted poems in the English language. The theme of quiet serenity amid rural surroundings also appears in Oliver Goldsmith's *The Deserted Village* (1770), a long meditation on the disappearance of rural life in England that anticipates such romantic poems as Wordsworth's "Michael" (1800). Yet another forerunner of the movement was William Collins, whose "Ode to Evening" (1748) idealized nature.

Literature

I Coleridge's *Biographia Literaria* (1817), a mixture of anecdotal autobiography and theoretical exposition, is a remarkable document of romantic literary criticism. Influenced by Coleridge's interest in 18th-century German philosophy, the work is notable for its theory of imagination and fancy and for its analysis of the psychology of the creative process.

Making Connections

Literature

(J) Given Napoleon's effect on the literary and artistic imagination of 19th-century Europe (to say nothing of its politics), it is not surprising that the Battle of Waterloo became a literary touchstone as well as a political watershed. In *Childe Harold's Pilgrimage,* Byron provides a memorable depiction of it ("There was a sound of revelry by night . . ."), and the battle also plays a pivotal role in William Makepeace Thackeray's novel *Vanity Fair* (1848). The word *waterloo,* has come to mean any decisive, crushing defeat suffered by someone, as in the sentence phrase "to meet one's waterloo."

Above: Early 19th-century improvements in public hygiene included the construction of sewers.

Napoleon was captured and exiled to the island of Elba; but while allied ministers met to decide Europe's fate at the Congress of Vienna, Napoleon escaped and returned to the French throne for the so-called Hundred Days. He was finally defeated at the Battle (J) of Waterloo in Belgium in 1815 and exiled to the more remote island of St. Helena. Wellesley (recently ennobled as the duke of Wellington), who commanded the British troops that bore the brunt of the battle, was the hero of the hour, and "to meet one's Waterloo" became synonymous with "to suffer a decisive defeat."

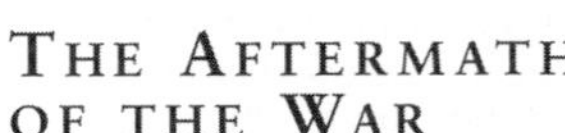

The Aftermath of the War

The end of the war with France did not mean an immediate end to reactionary British domestic policies, for the fear of revolution still remained strong. To Britain's growing mass of restless laborers were added thousands of discharged veter-

In August 1819, workers met in St. Peter's Fields, Manchester, to peacefully demonstrate their discontent with Britain's economic and labor policies and to call for reform. The local militia, ordered to arrest the protest's leader, instead launched an attack that resulted in 11 deaths and hundreds of injuries. The incident, likened to the Battle of Waterloo, became known as the Peterloo Massacre.

ans returning to a nation in which jobs were scarce, wages low, and poverty widespread. Large landowners successfully pressured the Tory government to continue the Corn Laws, which barred cheap foreign grain from British markets and so kept the price of food high. Industry, in contrast, operated under the economic philosophy of laissez-faire capitalism, which held that government should not interfere in private enterprise. Thus, workers remained at the mercy of factory owners. They were even forbidden from banding together in labor unions that might pressure owners into improving work conditions and wages.

The Regency ended in 1820, when George III died and the Prince of Wales officially took the throne as George IV. Over the next several years, the Tories gradually began to institute some of the reforms that the nation so sorely needed. Sir Robert Peel revamped Britain's harsh criminal code and organized the nation's first professional civilian police force. The duke of Wellington, now serving as prime minister, pushed the Catholic Emancipation Act through Parliament in 1829, just in time to allow the newly elected Irish Catholic political leader Daniel O'Connell to take his seat in the House of Commons. Wellington's more conservative fellow Tories opposed the bill, however, and like Pitt before him, he was forced to resign over the issue. Thus, the passage of the Reform Bill of 1832, which more fairly distributed seats in Parliament and extended the vote to middle-class men, would be a Whig effort, not a Tory one. This landmark bill marks the end of the romantic period and the start of the mainstream reform efforts that characterized the dawning Victorian era.

Above: Although certain reforms were made in the education of females, mid-century educational policies were still extremely limiting.

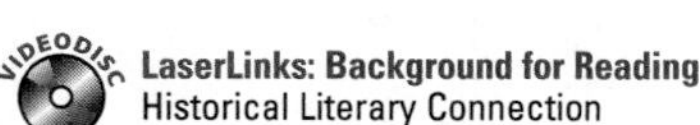

LaserLinks: Background for Reading
Historical Literary Connection

LITERARY HISTORY

Wordsworth and Coleridge belonged to the so-called first generation of romantic writers. The leading poets of the second generation, which rose to prominence during the Regency, were Lord Byron, Percy Bysshe Shelley, and John Keats. Byron, in both his poetry and his personal life, helped popularize the brooding, self-absorbed romantic figure now sometimes known as the Byronic hero. Both he and his friend Shelley, a brilliant lyric poet, were members of the upper class whose radical politics and personal affairs eventually made them figures of scandal, leading to their self-imposed exile from Britain. The equally brilliant John Keats, a less-well-born acquaintance of Shelley's, also left Britain, seeking a cure for his tuberculosis in the warmer climate of Italy. All three poets died young while living abroad.

Though best known for poetry, the romantic period also was a time when many memorable works of prose were produced. The romantic emphasis on personal experience is evident in the fine personal essays of Charles Lamb, William Hazlitt, and Thomas De Quincey, many of which first appeared in literary journals. Sir Walter Scott, the most popular novelist of the day, pioneered the historical novel in his best-selling *Waverley* (1814), set in his native Scotland. Also popular were gothic novels of mystery and horror, such as *Frankenstein* (1818) by Mary Wollstonecraft Shelley, the wife of Percy Bysshe Shelley and the daughter of Mary Wollstonecraft (see page 638). Jane Austen, on the other hand, remained in many ways a neoclassical writer, penning ironic novels of manners such as *Pride and Prejudice* (1813) and *Emma* (1815). Nevertheless, Austen's introduction of more dialogue into fiction helped pave the way for the realistic novels of the Victorian era.

Making Connections

History

K George IV's reign, in contrast to his father's, was relatively short, lasting ten years. While he was on the throne (1820–1830), the power of the monarchy eroded. Then, when his brother William IV succeeded him (1830–1837), the monarchy further lost its ability to influence the operations of the British government.

Literature

L Byron died of fever in 1824 while he was helping Greek forces fight for their country's independence from Turkey. His death might be regarded as an emblem of the romantics' love affair with Greece. Just as the neoclassical writers of the preceding century had looked to Augustan Rome for inspiration, the romantic writers turned to Greece for their ideals of beauty and truth. The arrival of the Elgin marbles—sculptural decorations from the Acropolis in Athens—at the British Museum during the first two decades of the 19th century served as a powerful stimulus for this romantic revival.

Literature

M As the first major writer to portray the lives of ordinary people, Jane Austen is considered to be one of the founders of the modern novel. Her six novels published between 1811 and 1817 brought her a strange kind of fame: she became widely read in that decade but was not known by her own name. All the novels had been published anonymously, and only after her death did her brother reveal her authorship of them.

PART 1 Seeking Truth

The poets of the romantic period turned their attention from the common experience of society in order to focus on the experiences of the individual, believing that emotion was more important than reason as a way of understanding life. Many rejected the formal style of the neoclassicists and instead employed more lyrical poetic forms to express themselves. Romantic poets looked in particular to the natural world as a source of truth and inspiration, as you will see in this part of Unit Four.

706

Romanticism

Have you ever read a poem that had a surprisingly strong impact upon you? Maybe, in an inspired moment, you yourself have written a poem to express your feelings. English poet William Wordsworth described such poetry as the "spontaneous overflow of powerful feelings." The kind of poetry we are most familiar with today reflects many of the qualities in the personal, emotional, and meditative poetry written by Wordsworth and other romantic poets.

According to the romantics, the common man was a worthy subject for poetry.

In the British literary tradition, **romanticism** refers to a historical period dominated by Wordsworth and five other poets: William Blake, Samuel Taylor Coleridge, Lord Byron, Percy Bysshe Shelley, and John Keats. While critics often mark the start of European romanticism around the French Revolution in 1789, they mark the start of the romantic literary movement in England around the publication of the poetry collection *Lyrical Ballads* by Wordsworth and Coleridge in 1798.

Revolt Against Neoclassicism

In his famous Preface to *Lyrical Ballads,* Wordsworth declared the poems as "experiments" in poetic language and subject matter. He deliberately chose language and subjects taken from "common life" instead of upper-class life. The second generation of romantic poets—Byron, Shelley, and Keats—added their unique voices and visions to Wordsworth's foundation, yet took their poetry in slightly different directions. Despite their differences, however, the English romantics were united in rebellion against their Enlightenment forebears, which included John Dryden, Alexander Pope, and Samuel Johnson. Reflecting the revolutionary spirit of the age, the romantics broke neoclassical conventions and expressed a new sensibility of freedom and self-expression. Where the neoclassical writers—also called the Augustans—admired and imitated classical forms, the romantics looked to nature for inspiration. Where the Augustans prized reason, the romantics celebrated strong emotions. Where the Augustans wrote witty satires ridiculing others, the romantics wrote serious lyric poems about their own experiences.

Neoclassical Writers	Romantic Writers
• Stressed reason and common sense	• Stressed emotions and imagination
• Wrote about objective issues that concerned society as a whole, such as politics and religion	• Wrote about subjective experiences of the individual, such as desires, hopes, and dreams
• Respected human institutions of church and state	• Exalted nature in all its creative and destructive forces
• Believed in order in all things	• Believed in spontaneity of thought and action
• Maintained traditional standards	• Believed in experimentatio
• Focused on adult concerns, primarily those of the ruling class	• Reflected on the experiences of childhood, primitive societies, and the common man
• Exercised controlled wit and urbanity	• Celebrated intense passion and vision
• Followed formal rules and diction in poetry	• Sought a more natural poetic diction and form

Romantic Poetry's Defining Features

"There was a mighty ferment in the heads of statesmen and poets, kings and people. . . . It was a time of promise, a renewal of the world," wrote essayist William Hazlitt in 1825 to describe his age of revolution and change. Critics and

OVERVIEW

Objectives

- understand the literary: romanticism
- appreciate shared characteristics of literature across cultures
- recognize themes across cultures

Teaching the Lesson

This lesson will give the students some background on romanticism as a literary movement.

Introducing the Concepts

Although romantic poetry may seem old-fashioned, romanticism emphasized the expression of individual thoughts and feelings, a trend that continues to dominate contemporary poetry, fiction, art, and song lyrics. As students read the poems in this unit, have them consider the following questions:

What themes are most common in these romantic poems?
Possible Responses: nature, daily life, strong emotion, and the supernatural

Does the style of the poems seem outdated? If so, what elements of the style are out of fashion?
Possible Responses: rhyme, elevated diction, and poetic apostrophes

How is the modern relationship with nature similar to or different from that of the romantics?
Possible Response: Answers should recognize the romantics' close, positive relationship with nature and compare or contrast it with modern attitudes.

As they finish reading the romantic selections, students can write reactions to these questions and keep their responses in their Writing Portfolios.

Presenting the Concepts

Read through the strategies aloud or project them on a transparency. Ask students to name a poem or song that they would classify as romantic based on the description of the defining features of romantic poetry on pages 707–708. Discuss the romantic characteristics of the works named. As students read, model how to use the strategies to analyze the poems.

Making Connections

Romanticism Across Cultures

Explain that romanticism began in Germany and spread throughout Europe. Share the following information about romanticism in other countries.

Germany

One of the precursors of romanticism in Germany was Johann Wolfgang von Goethe's (1749–1832) novel *The Sorrows of Young Werther.* It's a story about a sensitive, artistic young man who is unable to reconcile his inner thoughts with the reality of the outside world. He retreats to the countryside where he falls in love with the fiancée of a friend, and torn by love and the emptiness of his life, he commits suicide. Goethe's work greatly influenced German romanticism, which was also known as *Sturm und Drang* (Storm and Stress).

France

The most prominent French romantic writer was Victor Hugo (1802–1885). Hugo felt that a poet should lead the people, and his writing became overtly political toward the end of his life. Another French romantic writer was George Sand (1804–1876), whose novels depict the poor sympathetically. Her novels also show how love can transcend the obstacles of convention and class.

Italy

In January 1816, Madame de Staël (1766–1817), a French-Swiss woman of letters who epitomized European culture of her time, published an article in which she encouraged Italian writers to read foreign literature. Her call was answered by a group of young writers who formed the Italian romantic movement. Most of the members of this movement were patriots who disagreed with the government. By 1821, many had been imprisoned or exiled. The spirit of romanticism continued, however, in the works of such writers as poet Giovanni Prati.

historians have tried to pin down the characteristics of this "mighty ferment" ever since. Here are five features of English romanticism, taken largely from Wordsworth's preface to *Lyrical Ballads.*

A New Concept of Poetry Wordsworth's emphases on personal experience and on the glorification of the individual are very different from earlier poets' emphasis on the greater world of human behavior. To some degree, all romantic poets wrote about the intricate workings of their own minds and the complexities of their emotions.

A New Spontaneity and Freedom Spontaneity is part of Wordsworth's definition of poetry. The romantics were critical of the artificiality they saw in much neoclassical literature, and they placed a high value on emotional outbursts: "I fall upon the thorns of life! I bleed!" wails Shelley in "Ode to the West Wind." This emotional freedom is matched by the free play of imagination. In his poem "Kubla Khan," Coleridge describes an elaborate palace that existed only in his mind.

Love of Nature Romantic poetry is often dubbed "nature poetry" because of its subject matter. But the romantics rarely use nature for its own sake; rather, they look to nature as a stimulus for their own thinking. For instance, a "beauteous evening" for Wordsworth is an occasion for spiritual contemplation.

YOUR TURN Explain some ways that you think nature could stimulate spiritual thoughts.

The Importance of the Commonplace
Wordsworth wanted to enlarge the province of poetry to include "incidents and situations from common life." Although Byron was the only aristocrat among his contemporary poets and didn't quite accept such a lowering of standards, the other romantics often chose humble subjects. They celebrated with Wordsworth the ordinary things—an early morning stroll, a field of daffodils, or a change of seasons.

Fascination with the Supernatural and the Exotic
While Wordsworth concentrated mostly on ordinary life, Coleridge introduced mystery and magic into English romantic poetry. From the wonderfully strange journey in "The Rime of the Ancient Mariner" to the "stately pleasure dome" of "Kubla Khan," Coleridge opened up to poetry the realm of the supernatural and the exotic. A preoccupation with the supernatural already characterized Gothic novels of the 18th century, but the romantic poets added a touch of elegance and alluring beauty to the terrors of the unknown.

YOUR TURN Why do you think the romantics were attracted to the supernatural?

Strategies for Reading: Romantic Poetry

1. Compare the tone and the language used in romantic poetry with comparable elements in Augustan poetry by writers like Alexander Pope.
2. Notice how the romantic poets freely embrace such subjects as life, death, love, and nature.
3. Pay attention to the extensive use of imagery and figurative language.
4. Watch for elements of the supernatural and the exotic in the poetry.
5. **Monitor** your reading strategies and modify them when your understanding breaks down. Remember to use your strategies for Active Reading: **predict, visualize, connect, question, clarify,** and **evaluate.**

Selected Poems

By WILLIAM BLAKE

Comparing Literature of the World

Blake and the Haiku Poets

This lesson and the one that follows present an opportunity for comparing the poetry of two very different cultures: that of William Blake and that of the Japanese haiku poets Bashō and Issa. Specific points of comparison in the lesson on haiku will help you contrast Blake's style and subject matter with that of the two haiku masters.

Connect to Your Life

An Author's Inspiration Have you ever wondered what inspired an author to write a particular story or poem? Briefly describe to the class one of your favorite novels, short stories, or poems. Then share your thoughts and speculations about the source of the author's inspiration.

Build Background

The Visionary World of Blake William Blake was an artist, a poet, and a visionary. His work was so incompatible with the taste of his day that his contemporaries could not appreciate his accomplishments. Some believed him to be inspired but irrational; others thought him to be mad. Throughout his life, Blake saw visions—from angels sitting in a tree to messages from his dead brother—which he attributed not to a supernatural source but to the interaction of his imagination with the world and with infinity, or God. This interaction was the inspiration for both his poetry and his art. His work reflects highly original interpretations of human experience and of the relationship between the human and the divine.

In 1789, using his own method of producing books with hand-colored illustrations, Blake published his first major work, *Songs of Innocence*, a group of poems modeled on the street ballads and rhymes sung by London's children. In 1794, he added to these poems a group of contrasting poems called *Songs of Experience*. Many of the poems in *Songs of Innocence* have matching poems in *Songs of Experience*—for example, "The Lamb" is paired with "The Tyger." In the subtitle for this combined edition of the two collections, Blake indicated that his purpose in putting them together was to show "the two contrary states of the human soul."

Focus Your Reading

LITERARY ANALYSIS SYMBOL A **symbol** is a person, place, object, or activity that stands for something beyond itself. A heart, for example, is a symbol frequently used to stand for love. As you read these examples of Blake's poetry, think about what the subject of each poem might symbolize.

ACTIVE READING DRAWING CONCLUSIONS A reader might be easily tempted to think of Blake's poems as simple descriptions of people and other living things in the natural world. It is important, however, to look beyond the obvious—to try to **draw conclusions** about the possible deeper meaning of Blake's work. As you read, keep in mind the following questions:

- What **details** does Blake include about the subject of each poem?
- What seems to be Blake's **tone,** or attitude, in each poem?
- Why might Blake have chosen a lamb, a tiger, etc., as the subject of each poem?
- What might each subject **symbolize**?

READER'S NOTEBOOK First, read each poem in its entirety. Then go back and read each poem again, pausing after each stanza to jot down any observations you have made about the subject of the poem. See if you can answer any of the above questions.

OVERVIEW

Objectives

1. understand and appreciate **romantic poetry (Literary Analysis)**
2. identify and examine the author's use of **symbols (Literary Analysis)**
3. **draw conclusions** in order to appreciate and understand romantic poetry **(Active Reading)**

Summary

By writing about subjects such as a lamb, a lost child, a tiger, a fly, and a rose, William Blake describes nature while contemplating opposite forces at work in the world.

Thematic Link

In these poems, Blake **seeks truth** as he reflects on the comforting and also mysterious relationships between human beings and God.

5-Minute Warm-Up

Daily Language SkillBuilder

Have students **proofread** the display sentences on page 697i and write them correctly. The sentences also appear on Transparency 18 of **Grammar Transparencies and Copymasters.**

LESSON RESOURCES

UNIT FOUR RESOURCE BOOK, pp. 4–5

ASSESSMENT RESOURCES

Formal Assessment, pp. 129–130

Teacher's Guide to Assessment and Portfolio Use

Test Generator

SKILLS TRANSPARENCIES AND COPYMASTERS

Literary Analysis

- Symbols in Romantic Poetry, T14 (for Literary Analysis, p. 709)

Reading and Critical Thinking

- Making Inferences, T7 (for Active Reading, p. 709)

Grammar

- Distinguishing a Clause from a Phrase, C106 (for Mini Lesson, p. 716)

Vocabulary

- Researching Word Origins, C59 (for Mini Lesson, p. 712)

Writing

- Critical Review, C32 (for Writing Option 1, p. 716)
- Literary Interpretation, C33 (for Writing Option 2, p. 716)

INTEGRATED TECHNOLOGY

Audio Library

LaserLinks

- Art Gallery: The Art of William Blake. See **Teacher's SourceBook,** p. 43.

Visit our website: www.mcdougallittell.com

TEACHING THE LITERATURE

Reading and Analyzing

Active Reading DRAWING CONCLUSIONS

A Ask students what details the poet gives about the lamb in the first stanza. What overall impression might the poet want the reader to have about the lamb?

Possible Response: The poet wants the reader to picture a gentle animal that is a delightful part of the natural world.

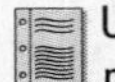 Use **Unit Four Resource Book,** p. 4 for more practice.

Literary Analysis SYMBOL

B Ask with what human conditions the lamb seems to be associated.

Possible Response: Students may say the lamb symbolizes innocent people or children.

Then ask what the poem suggests about God's relationship with these people.

Possible Response: God watches over them like a shepherd watches over sheep.

 Use **Unit Four Resource Book,** p. 5 for more exercises.

Thinking Through the Literature

1. Accept all reasonable responses.
2. Possible Responses: God cares for all innocent creatures; the innocent find wonder in the world.
3. Students who find it appropriate may focus on the lamb's and boy's innocence or on the poems' simple style. Those finding it inappropriate may focus on the father's behavior or the boy's frightening experience.

from Songs of

William Blake

The Lamb

Little Lamb, who made thee?
Dost thou know who made thee?
Gave thee life & bid thee feed,
By the stream & o'er the mead;[1]
A Gave thee clothing of delight,
Softest clothing wooly bright;
Gave thee such a tender voice,
Making all the vales[2] rejoice!
Little Lamb, who made thee?
Dost thou know who made thee?

Little Lamb, I'll tell thee,
Little Lamb, I'll tell thee!
He is callèd by thy name,
For he calls himself a Lamb:[3]
B He is meek & he is mild,
He became a little child:
I a child & thou a lamb,
We are callèd by his name.
Little Lamb, God bless thee.
Little Lamb, God bless thee.

1. **mead:** meadow.
2. **vales:** valleys.
3. In the New Testament, Jesus is sometimes referred to as the Lamb of God.

Teaching Options

BLOCK SCHEDULING: MANAGING TIME

If your schedule requires that you cover the lesson objectives in a shorter time, use . . .

- Preparing to Read, p. 709
- Thinking Through the Literature, p. 715

If you want to take advantage of longer class time, use . . .

- TE Teaching Options: Vocabulary Strategy, p. 712; Viewing and Representing, p. 713; Speaking and Listening, p. 714; Standardized Test Practice, p. 711; Grammar, p. 716
- Choices & Challenges, p. 716

Innocence

The Little Boy Lost

"Father, father, where are you going?
O do not walk so fast.
Speak father, speak to your little boy,
Or else I shall be lost."

The night was dark, no father was there;
The child was wet with dew;
The mire[1] was deep, & the child did weep,
And away the vapor[2] flew.

1. **mire:** wet, swampy ground.
2. **vapor:** mist; fog.

Detail of title page of *Songs of Innocence* (1789), William Blake. The Granger Collection, New York.

The Little Boy Found

The little boy lost in the lonely fen,[1]
Led by the wand'ring light,
Began to cry, but God ever nigh,
Appear'd like his father in white.

He kissed the child & by the hand led
And to his mother brought,
Who in sorrow pale, thro' the lonely dale,
Her little boy weeping sought.

1. **fen:** swamp; marsh.

Thinking Through the Literature

1. What thoughts went through your mind as you were reading these poems? Describe your reactions to a classmate.
2. What ideas about life do you think the speaker expresses?

THINK ABOUT
- his thoughts about the lamb's creation
- what happens to the lost boy

3. Do you think the title *Songs of Innocence* is appropriate for these poems? Explain your answer.

Customizing Instruction

Less Proficient Readers

Suggest that students watch for questions asked by the poet as they read these poems. Explain that some of these are rhetorical questions that the poet uses to make the reader think.

Students Acquiring English

Note that Blake's poems include words and word forms that are rarely used today. Read the poem aloud, providing modern English equivalents such as these examples: *"Dost thou know"* (Do you know); *"bid thee feed"* (told you to eat); *and "thro'"* (through).

Use **Spanish Study Guide** for additional support, pp. 161–163.

Gifted and Talented

Ask students to think about the terms *innocence* and *experience* as opposites as they read the poems. When they have finished reading, have them write a paper explaining how Blake might define these words and comparing his definitions to those used today.

Possible Response: Blake's use of the word *innocence* indicates a sense of youthfulness, trust, or helplessness. *Experience* refers to an awareness of mortality, evil, or the dark side of life. Today, we use this term in a more neutral way to refer to events or occurrences we have lived through.

Assessment Standardized Test Practice

MULTIPLE-CHOICE ITEMS On some standardized tests, multiple-choice items test students' understanding of literary elements. To help prepare students for such items, have them take turns answering these questions. Guide a group discussion of the elements tested (1. mood; 2. theme; 3. speaker; 4. simile) and students' strategies for answering the questions.

1. What is the mood or tone of "The Lamb"?
   - **A.** comforting
   - **B.** suspicious
   - **C.** concerned
   - **D.** mysterious
2. With which statement would the author of "The Little Boy Lost" and "The Little Boy Found" probably agree?
   - **A.** Children who get lost should be punished.
   - **B.** We can all depend on God when we feel lost.
   - **C.** God helps only children when they are in need.
   - **D.** If you cry when you are lost, someone will help you.

Reading and Analyzing

Reading Skills and Strategies:
COMPARING/CONTRASTING

A Ask how this question is like and unlike the opening question in "The Lamb."

Possible Response: It has the same basic meaning, "Who created you?"; however, it is more figurative. For example, the poet includes the image of an "immortal hand or eye" and employs more sophisticated diction.

Literary Analysis: IMAGERY

B Point out the fire imagery in this stanza. Ask students what this imagery suggests about the tiger.

Possible Response: It was created in hell.

Literary Analysis: ALLITERATION AND TONE

C Ask how alliteration helps convey the speaker's attitude toward his subject.

Possible Response: The *d* sounds help capture the stalking, menacing nature of the tiger.

Active Reading
DRAWING CONCLUSIONS

D Ask students what they can conclude about the speaker's attitude toward life from this poem.

Possible Response: We live in a random universe, where tragedy occurs for no reason.

from Songs of SONGS

William Blake

The TYGER

Tyger! Tyger! burning bright
In the forests of the night,
What immortal hand or eye
A Could frame thy fearful symmetry?

In what distant deeps or skies
B Burnt the fire of thine eyes?
On what wings dare he aspire?
What the hand dare seize the fire?

And what shoulder, & what art,
Could twist the sinews of thy heart?
And when thy heart began to beat,
What dread hand? & what dread feet?

What the hammer? what the chain?
In what furnace was thy brain?
C What the anvil? what dread grasp
Dare its deadly terrors clasp?

When the stars threw down their spears
And water'd heaven with their tears,
Did he smile his work to see?
Did he who made the Lamb make thee?

Tyger! Tyger! burning bright
In the forests of the night,
What immortal hand or eye
D Dare frame thy fearful symmetry?

4 symmetry: balance of form.

7 he: the tiger's creator; **aspire:** soar; ascend; aim for something great.

10 sinews (sĭn′yo͞oz): tendons.

Teaching Options

Vocabulary Strategy

RESEARCHING WORD ORIGINS

Instruction Explain that many of the words, word forms, and spellings used in Blake's poems are now archaic, or out of use. Point out that most modern dictionaries contain entries for archaic English words, provide definitions for them, and give information about their origins. Write the word *fen* and its definition on the board:

fen *n.* low, flat, swampy land; bog. [ME [OE *fenn.*]

Explain that the letters "ME" stand for Middle English; *fen* is a Middle English word. Then ask a volunteer to explain the word's origins.

(Answer: *The Middle English word* fen *comes from the Old English word* fenn.)

Activity List the following words on the board: *dost, thee, mead, vale, they, mire, nigh, dread (adj.)*

Have students use a dictionary to look up each word. Ask students to write down the definition, followed by an explanation of the word's origins.

Use **Vocabulary Transparencies and Copymasters,** p. 54.

The Fly

Little Fly,
Thy summer's play
1 My thoughtless hand
Has brush'd away.

Am not I
A fly like thee?
Or art not thou
A man like me?

For I dance
And drink & sing,
Till some blind hand
Shall brush my wing.

If thought is life
And strength & breath,
2 And the want
Of thought is death,

Then am I
A happy fly
If I live
3 Or if I die.

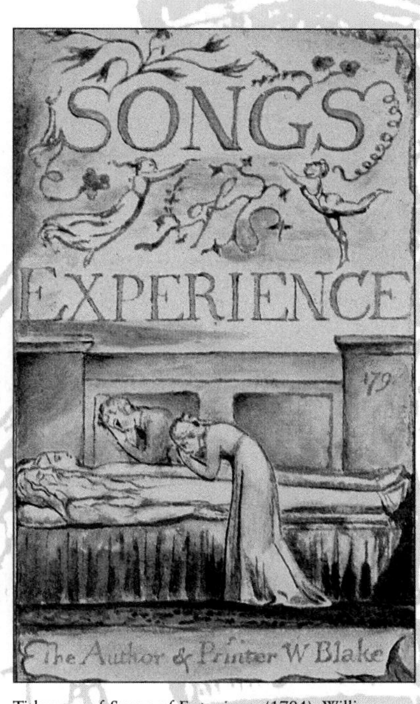

Title page of *Songs of Experience* (1794), William Blake. The Granger Collection, New York.

Customizing Instruction

Students Acquiring English

Make sure students understand the meanings of the following words and phrases: *tyger* (tiger); *distant deeps* (faraway oceans); *burnt* (burned); *furnace* (large oven); *anvil* (a block on which items are set to be hammered); *thy, thee,* and *thou* (your, you, and you).

1 "The Tyger" and "The Fly" make frequent use of inverted sentence structure. Work with students to put these sentences in natural order. For example, lines 1–4 of "The Fly" written in natural order (and in modern English) would read "My thoughtless hand has brushed away your summer's play, little fly."

Less Proficient Readers

2 Have students use context clues to determine what Blake means by *want.* Guide them to see the analogy Blake is constructing: thought : life :: no thought: death.

Answer: lack; absence.

3 To be sure students comprehend the speaker's thoughts, have students paraphrase the entire poem in two or three sentences.

Possible Response: As I brush you away, little fly, might there be some unseen force that will someday brush me away? If to live means to think, and to die means to stop thinking, then perhaps I'll be happy in either state.

Viewing and Representing

Detail of *Songs of Experience* title page, **by William Blake**

ART APPRECIATION

Instruction The designs for the poems in *Songs of Experience* are much more severe than those in *Songs of Innocence.* This design for the title page, with its straight lines and unsoftened figures, demonstrates the difference between the two techniques. (You may want to refer students to the images as shown on page 715.)

Application Ask students what mood this illustration creates.

Possible Response: It depicts desolation; grief; mourning; death.

How is this mood reflected in the *Experience* poems?

Possible Response: The poems are concerned with mortality, loss, the randomness and incomprehensibility of death.

SONGS OF EXPERIENCE 713

Reading and Analyzing

Literary Analysis SYMBOL

A Ask students what they think the rose and the worm might represent.

Possible Responses: The rose might symbolize life or love; the worm might be a symbol of illness or decay.

Reading Skills and Strategies: ANALYZING

B Ask students what is unusual or unexpected about the statement in the last two lines.

Possible Response: Students should observe that in these lines, love—not hate or indifference—is destructive. Have students try to explain the seeming contradiction.

Possible Response: The worm represents jealous, selfish, or smothering love, which can be destructive.

Active Reading DRAWING CONCLUSIONS

Ask students what they can conclude about the speaker's attitude toward love and beauty. Be sure students use evidence from the text and experience.

Possible Response: Love and beauty are fragile and vulnerable, subject to the dark forces of decay and destruction.

from Songs *of* Experience

William Blake

The Sick Rose

O Rose, thou art sick.
The invisible worm
That flies in the night
In the howling storm

Has found out thy bed
Of crimson joy,
And his dark secret love
Does thy life destroy.

Teaching Options

Speaking and Listening

DRAMATIC PRESENTATION

Instruction Blake's *Songs of Innocence* and *Songs of Experience* were modeled on children's rhymes. The poems' strong rhythm and rhyme schemes give them a distinctly musical quality.

Prepare Have students work in groups to prepare a dramatic interpretation of a poem. Encourage them to memorize their poems and to use dramatic effects such as song or sound, lighting, and motion to convey the poem's meaning and heighten its mood.

Present Some students may want to juxtapose "The Lamb" and "The Tyger" to emphasize the contrast. Others may want to do choral readings of "Little Boy Lost" and "Little Boy Found," or narrate one of the poems while others act it out.

Have audience members analyze, evaluate, and critique each performance using the following criteria:

- enhances the mood of the poem
- brings the imagery of the poem to life
- conveys the basic meaning of the poem

This activity is particularly well-suited for longer class periods.

Connect to the Literature

1. **What Do You Think?** Discuss some of the **images** that came to mind as you read "The Tyger," "The Fly," and "The Sick Rose."

Think Critically

2. What view of experience do you think is reflected in these *Songs of Experience*?

- the questions the **speaker** asks about the tiger
- the reasons the speaker compares himself to a fly
- the **image** of the worm in the rose

3. What seems to be the **tone,** or attitude, of the speaker in each of these poems?

4. **ACTIVE READING** DRAWING CONCLUSIONS Review any notes you took in your READER'S NOTEBOOK while reading the poems in *Songs of Experience*. What conclusions can you reach about Blake's choice of a tiger, a fly, and a rose as the subjects of these poems?

Extend Interpretations

5. **Comparing Texts** Compare the attitudes of the speakers in *Songs of Innocence* with those of the speakers in *Songs of Experience*. Consider similarities as well as differences.

6. **Comparing Texts** Compare the views of life expressed in these poems from *Songs of Innocence* and *Songs of Experience* with the views of life presented in the excerpts from the King James Bible in Unit Two. What similarities and differences do you see?

7. **Connect to Life** What do you think might have been the sources of Blake's inspiration for these two sets of poems? Consider feelings and thoughts as well as aspects of the external world.

8. **Art Connection** Look at the two illustrations of Blake's on pages 711 and 713. How do the scenes depicted reflect the themes of innocence and experience?

Literary Analysis

SYMBOL As you know, a person, place, object, or activity that stands for something beyond itself is called a **symbol.** Literary symbols take on meaning within the context of the works in which they occur, and sometimes literary symbols have more than one meaning. For example, the rose in Blake's poem might symbolize goodness, innocence, or all of humanity.

Cooperative Learning Activity In a chart like the one shown, identify the qualities of the lamb and the tiger and tell what you think each animal symbolizes. Then identify any other objects in the six Blake poems that you think might be considered symbols.

Object	Qualities	Symbol of...
Lamb		
Tiger		

GUIDING STUDENT RESPONSE

Connect to the Literature

1. **What Do You Think?**
Guidelines for student response: Students' responses should include details from the poems. For example, students may say that they imagined a tiger prowling through a forest for "The Tyger"; a tiny fly and a big hand for "The Fly"; and a beautiful but decaying red rose for "The Sick Rose."

Think Critically

2. Answers will vary. Some students will feel that Blake focuses on the negative side of human experience; others may say that experience for Blake brings knowledge, mystery, and awe, as well as doubts and fears.
3. Student responses will vary, but may include awed, fearful, puzzled or curious.
4. Students' conclusions will vary, but should be in keeping with the details and tones of the poems. Some may conclude that the tiger is a logical choice for a poem about the marriage of beauty and destructive power. Students may also observe that the fly and the rose were chosen because they are common, everyday objects that people can relate to.

Literary Analysis

Cooperative Learning Activity When students have compiled their list of symbols, have them discuss the effect the symbols had on their understanding of the poem.

Extend Interpretations

Comparing Texts Most students will consider the speakers in *Songs of Innocence* to be simple and childlike, and the speakers in *Songs of Experience* to be more sophisticated, fearful, or doubtful.

Comparing Texts Some students may respond that the views of life are very similar, citing the similarities between the parable of the Prodigal Son and the "The Little Boy Lost" and "The Little Boy Found" poems. Students may note a difference between the affirming views of life in the King James Bible excerpts and the dark tone in "The Sick Rose."

Connect to Life Students may deduce that Blake was inspired by poems and songs remembered from his childhood; by his religious beliefs; by positive and negative experiences in both childhood and adulthood; or by an interest in the natural world.

Art Connection Student responses should note the contrast between the image of comfort and safety and that of loss and grief.

Writing Options

1. **Blake Critique** Student critical analyses will vary, but good responses will support general ideas with specific details from the poems.
2. **Discussion Questions** Good questions will be well written and reflect Blake's major themes and concerns. The best questions will require interpretive responses rather than factual or yes/no responses. **To make this activity easier,** have each student write one discussion question and then discuss possible responses with a partner.

Activities & Explorations

Ideas Through Art Encourage students to take their own photos if they are interested. If photographs are unavailable for use, students can use pictures from magazines or other printed materials.

Choices & CHALLENGES

Writing Options

1. **Blake Critique** Think back to Blake's statement (quoted on page 709) that he paired *Songs of Innocence* with *Songs of Experience* to show "the two contrary states of the human soul." Write a critique of the two groups of poems, in which you evaluate how well they fulfill that purpose. Place the critique in your **Working Portfolio.**

2. **Discussion Questions** Think about some of the issues about life and death that Blake raises in these six poems. Then prepare a set of questions that could be used to lead a discussion of the main themes in *Songs of Innocence* and *Songs of Experience.*

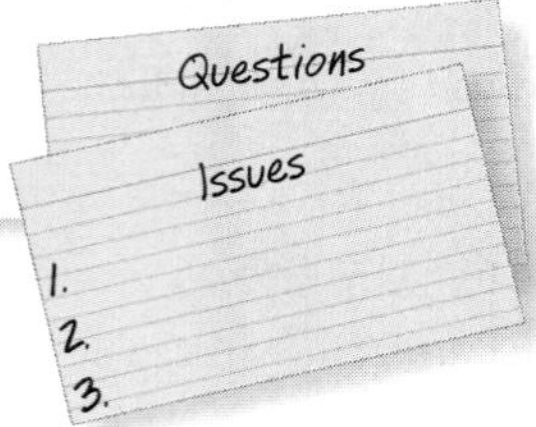

Activities and Explorations

Ideas through Art Create a montage—a composite picture made up of a variety of photos or parts of photos—to illustrate Blake's concept of innocence. Then create a similar montage to illustrate his concept of experience. ~ **ART**

William Blake
1757–1827

Other Works
"Introduction" and "The Chimney Sweeper" in *Songs of Innocence*
"Introduction" and "The Chimney Sweeper" in *Songs of Experience*

Innocence and Experience William Blake's life was at once extraordinary and uneventful. Although his imaginative life was rich and astonishingly creative, his everyday life was lived in obscurity and near poverty. The son of a London clothing merchant, Blake showed an early flair for drawing and began attending art school when he was only 10. He spoke of having visions from the time he was a young child, and he was already writing poetry by the age of 12. When he was 14 he entered a seven-year apprenticeship to an engraver, after which he studied engraving at the Royal Academy of Arts.

Printer and Illustrator When Blake was 24, he married Catherine Boucher, a poor and illiterate young woman. Blake taught her to read, and she later helped him in his engraving and printing work. In 1784, Blake opened his own print shop, where he developed an engraving technique that he called "illuminated printing." The method involved printing both text and illustration on a page at the same time, then coloring the illustration by hand. *Songs of Innocence* was one of the first works he printed in this manner. Because the process was time-consuming, Blake produced only a few copies of each of his books, undoubtedly one of the reasons that his works were not widely known during his lifetime.

Originality and Obscurity Blake's later works were on a grand scale, marked by prophetic and mythic visions, richly illustrated and difficult to understand. These complex works were almost totally ignored by readers in his own day. During his 60s, Blake stopped writing poetry and devoted all his time to pictorial art. He finally gained the recognition of a small group of artists who admired his work, and it was during this period that he created some of his best designs, including illustrations for Dante's *Divine Comedy* and designs for the book of Job. Blake died three months before his 70th birthday, confident of the value of his work but still relatively unknown, his stunning originality as a poet and artist not to be recognized until well into the 20th century.

LaserLinks: Background for Reading
Art Gallery

Teaching Options

Mini Lesson Grammar

DISTINGUISHING A CLAUSE FROM A PHRASE

Instruction The main difference between a clause and a phrase is that a clause has a subject and a predicate while a phrase does not.

Activity Write on the chalkboard the following lines from Blake. Then underline the phrases and clauses as shown.

"Tyger! Tyger! burning bright
<u>In the forests</u> <u>of the night</u>, . . ."
(prep. phrase) (prep. phrase)

"And <u>when thy heart began to beat</u>, . . ."
(subordinate clause)

Point out the two prepositional phrases *(In the forests* and *of the night).* Explain that both of these are phrases because neither one has a subject or a predicate. Then discuss the clause. Ask students to identify the subject and predicate *(heart, began).*

Exercises

1. <u>Although William Blake is a great poet,</u> his contemporaries did not appreciate his work. *(clause; William Blake, is)*
2. <u>Like other romantic poets,</u> Blake regarded the forces of nature to be inspirational. *(phrase)*

Use **Grammar Transparencies and Copymasters,** p. 105.

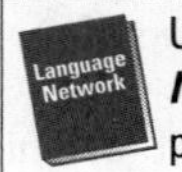

Use McDougal Littell's ***Language Network*** for more instruction and practice in clauses and phrases.

Haiku

Poetry by MATSUO BASHŌ (măt-sŏŏ′ō bä′shō)
and KOBAYASHI ISSA (kō-bä-yä′shē ēs′sä)

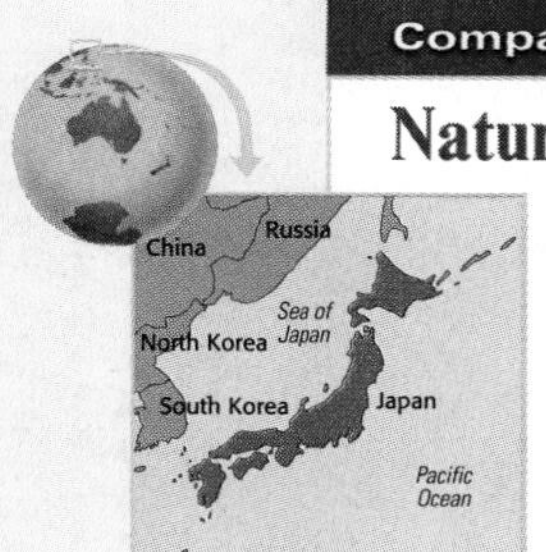

Comparing Literature of the World

Nature Poetry Across Cultures

The Poetry of William Blake and the Haiku Poets Despite differences in location, culture, and time period, the Japanese haiku poets, like William Blake, found nature to be an important source of inspiration.

Points of Comparison As you read the haiku poems in this lesson, compare them with those of Blake. Look for similarities and differences in subject matter, style of writing, ideas expressed, and attitude toward nature.

Build Background

Haiku and Its Masters **Haiku** (hī′ko͞o) is a form of poetry that evolved during the Tokugawa period in Japan (1603–1867). Although it began as a comic style of verse, it eventually became a serious art form, largely due to the efforts and artistry of Matsuo Bashō. Bashō, a 17th-century teacher of haiku, was idolized in his own lifetime and is still regarded as the greatest of all Japanese haiku poets. Kobayashi Issa, who composed nearly 20,000 haiku, achieved fame a century later.

Focus Your Reading

LITERARY ANALYSIS HAIKU **Haiku** is a form of Japanese poetry that embodies three qualities greatly valued in Japanese art: precision, economy, and delicacy. The rules of haiku are strict—in only 17 syllables, arranged in 3 lines of 5, 7, and 5 syllables, the poet must create a clear picture of a single aspect of nature that evokes a strong emotional response in the reader. Although Bashō and Issa followed the strict requirements of the haiku form, the exact number and pattern of syllables in their poems cannot usually be reproduced in English versions, as you may notice when you read these translations.

ACTIVE READING INTERPRETING IMAGES AND IDEAS In order to appreciate the full impact of haiku, make sure to read each poem slowly, allowing a mental **image** to form based on the **details** provided. Then read each poem a second time, stopping to ponder the idea implied.

READER'S NOTEBOOK As you read each haiku, jot down words or phrases that describe your mental image. Also record any ideas that you think the haiku imply.

OVERVIEW

Objectives

1. understand and appreciate Japanese **haiku (Literary Analysis)**
2. appreciate the author's use of haiku to explore universal truths in nature **(Literary Analysis)**
3. recognize and compare distinctive characteristics of cultures through reading **(Literary Analysis)**
4. **interpret images and ideas** in order to appreciate and understand haiku **(Active Reading)**

Summary

In these six poems, the poets share their thoughts about subjects such as a wintry day, a skylark, lotus flowers, and wind.

Thematic Link

The haiku of Basho and Issa express the poets' deep insight into and respect for nature in their **search for the truth.**

5-Minute Warm-Up

Daily Language SkillBuilder

Have students **proofread** the display sentences on page 697i and write them correctly. The sentences also appear on Transparency 18 of **Grammar Transparencies and Copymasters.**

LESSON RESOURCES

UNIT FOUR RESOURCE BOOK, pp. 6–7

ASSESSMENT RESOURCES
Formal Assessment, pp. 131–132
Teacher's Guide to Assessment and Portfolio Use
Test Generator

SKILLS TRANSPARENCIES AND COPYMASTERS
Literary Analysis
- Form and Meaning in Poetry, T15 (for Literary Analysis, p. 717)

Reading and Critical Thinking
- Visualizing, T8 (for Active Reading, p. 717)

Grammar
- Diagramming Subjects, Verbs, and Modifiers, T58 (for Mini Lesson, p. 721)
- Identifying Independent and Subordinate Clauses, C107 (for Mini Lesson, p. 721)

Writing
- Compare-Contrast, C34 (for Writing Option 2, p. 721)

INTEGRATED TECHNOLOGY
Audio Library
LaserLinks
- Cultural Connection: Japanese Printmaking
- Art Gallery: Nature in Japanese Art. See **Teacher's SourceBook,** pp. 44–45.

Visit our website:
www.mcdougallittell.com

TEACHING THE LITERATURE

Reading and Analyzing

Literary Analysis HAIKU

The pattern of five, seven, and five syllables within three lines works well in Japanese, in which no syllable has a marked stress, and the typical syllable is short and uniform. In English, with its marked stresses and long syllables, this pattern does not achieve the same effect. A poem of even fewer syllables would be a closer approximation, which is why these translations have fewer syllables in some lines. Discuss some of the themes compressed into these haiku.

Possible Responses: The haiku express themes of pure sensation; passage of time; harmony with nature; serenity; humanity in conflict with nature.

Use **Unit Four Resource Book,** p. 7 for more exercises.

Active Reading

INTERPRETING IMAGES AND IDEAS

A Ask volunteers to describe the mental image that this poem elicits, using details. What central idea is conveyed through this imagery?

Answer: Nature is soaked or saturated with beauty.

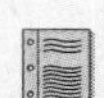
Use **Unit Four Resource Book,** p. 6 for more practice.

Literary Analysis: IMAGE

B Explain that the lotus is a beautiful, fragrant flower. Ask students what the image of these flowers being ploughed under may represent.

Possible Responses: It represents the destruction of beauty; the impractical giving way to the practical; nature giving way to society.

Haiku

Autumn—
even the birds
and clouds look old.

Bashō

Wintry day,
on my horse
a frozen shadow.

Bashō

Skylark
sings all day,
and day not long enough.

Bashō

Teaching Options

BLOCK SCHEDULING: MANAGING TIME

If your schedule requires that you cover the lesson objectives in a shorter time, use . . .

- Preparing to Read, p. 717
- Thinking Through the Literature, p. 720

If you want to take advantage of longer class time, use . . .

- TE Teaching Options: Informal Assessment, p. 719; Grammar, p. 721
- Choices & Challenges, p. 721

Ⓐ Nightingale's song
this morning,
soaked with rain.

I s s a

Ⓑ What a world,
where lotus flowers
are ploughed into a field.

I s s a

Autumn wind—
mountain's shadow
wavers.

I s s a

Translated by Lucien Stryk and Takashi Ikemoto

Customizing Instruction

Less Proficient Readers

Have students read the poems aloud with a partner and then discuss their interpretations.

Students Acquiring English

To help with the elliptical nature of haiku, have students try to supply missing words to turn the poems into sentences.

Use **Spanish Study Guide** for additional support, pp. 164–166.

Gifted and Talented

Have students write a paragraph stating what similar and differing views of the world the haiku reflect. Remind them to include examples to support their ideas.

Possible Response: Students may say that some haiku express the harshness of nature and humanity, while others rejoice in their beauty.

Multiple Learning Styles

Visual Learners

Have students follow the suggestions offered on page 717 under Active Reading. As they read each haiku, have them respond by making a quick sketch with colored pencils.

Assessment Informal Assessment

COMPREHENSION CHECK To check their comprehension of the haiku, have students indicate whether each statement is true or false.

1. None of the haiku explicitly mentions night.
   Answer: t
2. Several of the haiku mention children.
   Answer: f
3. Bashō describes a skylark that sings for only a few minutes every day.
   Answer: f
4. Issa celebrates the ploughing of fields.
   Answer: f
5. Issa describes a forest shaken by the wind.
   Answer: t

GUIDING STUDENT RESPONSE

Connect to the Literature

1. What Do You Think?
Guidelines for student response: As students discuss their favorite haiku, ask questions to help them explore the relationship between the details in the poems and the mental images the poems elicited.

Think Critically

2. Answers will vary. Students may say the overall mood of the haiku poems is peaceful, melancholy, full of wonder or awe, joyful, introspective, or thoughtful.
3. Answers will vary. Students may say that both poets concentrate on tiny details in the natural world; find inspiration and spiritual awareness in nature; and view nature as a teacher of truths about life.
4. Because the haiku's messages are clear and compact, students are likely to find many similarities between their observations.

Literary Analysis

Cooperative Learning Activity As students compare the results of their ratings, have them discuss the aspects of the individual haiku poems that influenced their responses.

Thinking through the LITERATURE

Connect to the Literature

1. **What Do You Think?** Which of these haiku did you enjoy the most? As a class, discuss reasons for your choice.

Think Critically

2. How would you describe the overall **mood** of the haiku poems?
3. What impressions of nature do the two haiku poets seem to share?
4. ACTIVE READING INTERPRETING IMAGES AND IDEAS Review what you recorded in your READER'S NOTEBOOK about the images and ideas you found in the haiku, and compare them with those recorded by a classmate. Are there more similarities or more differences?

Extend Interpretations

5. **What If?** If the two haiku about autumn were about spring instead, what images might be used?
6. **Critic's Corner** Donald Keene, a scholar of Japanese literature, wrote that Bashō was able "to capture at once the eternal and the momentary" in his haiku. Briefly explain what you think Keene meant by this characterization of Bashō's poems. Then explain why you agree or disagree with the comment.
7. **Connect to Life** On the basis of your reading of these poems, do you think haiku have relevance for all cultures and times, or are they more relevant to a specific culture or era? Support your answer with evidence from the poems.
8. Points of Comparison Compare the haiku of Bashō and Issa with the poems of William Blake. Use the following criteria as your points of comparison:

THINK ABOUT
- the subject matter of the poems
- the poets' **style** of writing
- the ideas expressed in the poems

Literary Analysis

HAIKU Through the use of precision, economy, and delicacy, **haiku** poetry has the ability to appeal to both the emotions and intelligence of its readers. The brevity of haiku can be misleading; their powerful effect comes as much from what is suggested as from what is directly said.

Cooperative Learning Activity With two other classmates, rate each haiku on a scale of 1 to 10 (10 being highest)—first, according to its emotional appeal and second, according to its appeal in terms of ideas expressed. Use a chart like the one below to record your ratings. Then compare the ratings with those of other groups. Analyze whether one or two of the poems had particular appeal to the class.

	Emotional Appeal	Ideas Expressed
Bashō		
Autumn . . .		
Wintry day . . .		
Skylark . . .		
Issa		
Nightingale . . .		
Lotus flowers . . .		
Autumn wind . . .		

Extend Interpretations

What If? Possible responses include flowers and rain; spring as a season of rebirth or playfulness. **To make this question more difficult,** have students think of images that might be used in haiku about spring, summer, and winter, *excluding* flowers, sunshine, and snow.

Critic's Corner Students may note that the haiku poems capture momentary images of nature and also eternal truths about human experience. The best responses will point out that the haiku poems contain particular images that point to larger truths.

Connect to Life Students who find haiku generally relevant may focus on the universal wisdom they impart or on their nature subjects. Students who find them relevant to a specific culture may mention their elliptical style or their emphasis on tiny details.

Points of Comparison Students who see similarities may point to the poets' view of nature as a source of inspiration or spiritual guidance and their symbolic use of natural objects to convey broader ideas. Those who see differences may contrast the violence of some of Blake's images with the peaceful depiction of nature in the haiku.

Choices & CHALLENGES

Writing Options

1. **Modern Haiku** Think about various aspects of nature that have strong appeal to you. Then write an original haiku that conveys your reaction to this aspect of nature. Place the poem in your **Working Portfolio.**

2. **Points of Comparison** In a brief essay, discuss whether you think Blake and the haiku poets viewed nature in the same way. Cite evidence to support your opinion.

Inquiry & Research

Japanese Art Explore the Japanese arts of woodblock printing, calligraphy, painting, and pottery. What do these arts have in common with haiku? Create a bulletin-board display to illustrate the connections.

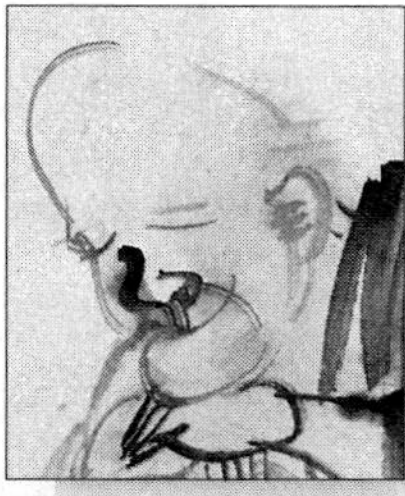

Matsuo Bashō
1644–1694

Humble Beginnings Bashō was born to a family of modest means. Early in life, he became friends with the son of a noble family, whose connections allowed Bashō to study with a prominent teacher of haiku. After his friend died, Bashō pursued a career as a professional haiku poet.

Writer and Teacher Around 1677, Bashō started his own school of haiku and by 1680 was the most famous Japanese poet of his day. In 1684, he began the first of many journeys through Japan—journeys that provided inspiration for much of his poetry. Teaching wherever he traveled, he had more than 2,000 students by the time of his death.

Legendary Figure One day, according to legend, a student announced that he had thought of a poem: "Pluck off the wings of a bright red dragonfly and there a pepper pod will be." Bashō informed him that he would never be a poet. A poet, according to Bashō, would have said: "Add but the wings to a bright red pepper pod and there a dragonfly will be." Whether or not the story is true, it reflects a compassion for living things that, along with his superb technical skills as a poet, has made Bashō a major figure in world literature.

Kobayashi Issa
1763–1828

Promising Student After leaving home at the age of 14, Kobayashi Issa studied under Chikua, a prominent haiku poet. When Chikua died in 1790, Issa took over as head of his school. Issa is known for simple, personal poetry that often touches upon two subjects: his love for insects and small animals and his poverty. Like Bashō, Issa traveled to many parts of Japan and was honored by leading poets of the day.

Poverty and Grief Issa dealt with adversity all his life. In spite of his talent, he lived most of his life in poverty, occasionally being forced to rely on friends for shelter. In 1813, a small inheritance from his family may have given Issa, then in his 50s, the means to marry for the first time. His first four children died in infancy, and his wife eventually died in childbirth. Issa's second marriage ended unhappily, and his only healthy child, the offspring of a third marriage, was born after the poet's death.

LaserLinks: Background for Reading
Cultural Connection
Art Gallery

Writing Options

1. **Modern Haiku** Students' haiku will vary. The best haiku will be brief and terse, and will convey a clear image that evokes a distinct emotion or spiritual insight without directly stating it.
2. **Points of Comparison** Students who think the poets shared a similar view of nature may refer to the way they draw universal meaning out of isolated natural images. Students who think the poets' views of nature differed may say that Blake used nature to reveal truths about God and humanity, while the haiku poets honored nature for its own sake.

Inquiries & Research

Japanese Art Have students work in small groups, with each group focusing on a different traditional art—woodblock printing, calligraphy, painting, pottery, and perhaps others. One group might be in charge of the final display.

Mini Lesson Grammar

IDENTIFYING INDEPENDENT AND SUBORDINATE CLAUSES

Instruction A clause must have a subject and a predicate, whether it is an independent clause or a subordinate clause.

Activity Write the following clauses on the chalkboard.

Subordinate Clause
Although Matsuo Bashō lived during the 17th century

Independent Clause
He is still considered the greatest of all Japanese haiku poets.

Read aloud the subordinate clause. Ask students if it has a subject and a predicate. *(Matsuo Basho, lived)* Underline them as shown. Because it does not express a complete thought, the clause cannot stand alone as a sentence.

Read aloud the independent clause. Have students identify the subject and the predicate. *(He, is)* Underline them as shown. Explain that because this clause expresses a complete thought it is a sentence.

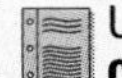
Use **Grammar Transparencies and Copymasters**, p. 106.

Use McDougal Littell's ***Language Network*** for more instruction in independent and subordinate clauses.

An In-Depth Study

OVERVIEW

Objectives
- appreciate the craft of one of England's greatest poets
- interpret the possible influences of the historical context on Wordsworth's romantic poetry
- recognize and discuss themes of romantic poetry across cultures
- gain information about Wordsworth by reading nonfiction

Presenting the Author
This Author Study offers a unique opportunity for students to focus on the work of a major writer. In addition, students can gather information about the life of Wordsworth, gaining insight into the real person behind his famous literary works.

Author Study

William Wordsworth

OVERVIEW

"He is the first poet to try to examine the human mind from a psychological viewpoint."
—Margaret Drabble

England's Greatest Nature Poet

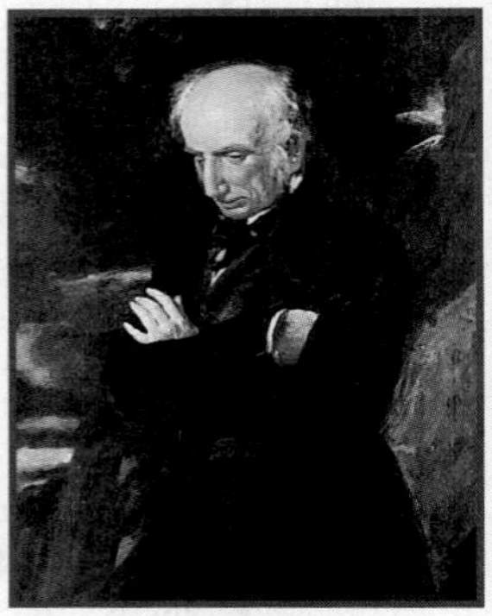

1770–1850

Outliving all the other major English romantic poets, William Wordsworth was a conservative figure by the time of his death in 1850. Yet five decades before, with his friend Samuel Taylor Coleridge, Wordsworth had ushered in a revolution in English poetry, championing the literary philosophy now called romanticism. Viewed as a nature poet, Wordsworth saw nature as a source of spiritual comfort to human beings. His romantic philosophy valued imagination and emotion over reason and stressed the importance of the individual. It also placed poetry at the very center of human experience.

CHILDHOOD TRAGEDY As a child, Wordsworth spent his free time taking in the sights and sounds of the Lake District in northern England, where his father worked as an estate manager. These happy times lasted only until he was seven, when his mother's death began a family breakup that continued with his father's death just five years later. Placed in the care of uncles, the young Wordsworth was sent to the finest schools,

HIS LIFE

1770 **Is born in the Lake District of northern England**

1778 **Death of mother and break up family**

1787 **Begins attending Cambridge University**

S.T. Coleridge

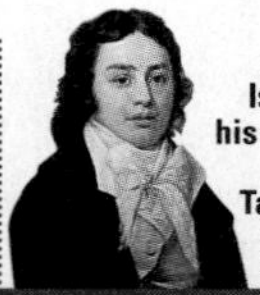

1795 **Is reunited with his sister Dorothy; meets Samuel Taylor Coleridge**

1770 1780 1790

HIS TIMES

1769 **James Watt perfects the steam engine.**

1776 **American colonies declare independence.**

1789 **The French Revolution begins.**

722

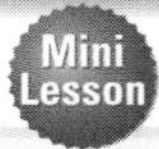

Mini Lesson Reading Nonfiction

USING TEXT ORGANIZERS

Instruction The Author Study begins with a three page article on Wordsworth's Life and Times. Point out The Overview, Table of Contents, the time line, and heads used in this article.

Practice Have students preview the article, noting the text organizers. Discuss the variety of information discussed in three short pages.

After students have read the article, have them create several categories to represent aspects of Wordworth's Life. Have them locate information from the article and insets and categorize it under the appropriate heading. Remind students to locate and categorize information as they do independent research.

including Cambridge University, but he took little joy (A) in them. He had already developed a deep appreciation for nature; by contrast, he found school life stifling and artificial.

ROMANCE AND REVOLUTION During a summer break from Cambridge in 1790, Wordsworth and a friend hiked through France and witnessed firsthand the effects (B) of its recent revolution. Excited by the changes he saw, Wordsworth returned to France a year later, where he fell in love with a young woman named Annette Vallon. But before the two could marry, the outbreak of war between Britain and France forced Wordsworth to return home abruptly. The growing violence and steady erosion of democratic principles in France turned Wordsworth away from his ardent support of the revolution; and with France an enemy nation, for years he could do little to help the child Annette had borne him. The entire situation filled him with guilt and anxiety.

DOROTHY AND DORSETSHIRE One bright spot of Wordsworth's return to England was his reunion with his sister Dorothy, from whom he had been separated since childhood. Resolving not to be parted again, he and Dorothy moved to the western English county of Dorset. They lived near the poet Samuel Taylor Coleridge, whom Wordsworth had recently met. There the two men began

LITERARY *Contributions*

Hugely popular in the decades after his death, Wordsworth is still widely regarded as one of England's finest poets.

Lyric Poems Wordsworth is best known for lyric poetry of moderate length, including

- **"Composed upon Westminster Bridge"**
- **"I Wandered Lonely as a Cloud"**
- **"I Traveled Among Unknown Men"**
- **"It Is a Beauteous Evening"**
- **"Lines Composed a Few Miles Above Tintern Abbey"**
- **"Lines Written in Early Spring"**
- **"London, 1802"** (also called **"To Milton"**)
- **"My Heart Leaps Up"**
- **"Nuns Fret Not"**
- **"Ode: Intimations of Immortality"**
- **"She Dwelt Among the Untrodden Ways"**
- **"She Was a Phantom of Delight"**
- **"A Slumber Did My Spirit Seal"**
- **"The Solitary Reaper"**
- **"Strange Fits of Passion Have I Known"**
- **"Surprised by Joy"**
- **"The Tables Turned"**
- **"Three Years She Grew in Sun and Shower"**
- **"The World Is Too Much with Us"**

Other Works Of Wordsworth's longer works, the most famous probably are the following:

- ***The Excursion*** (philosophical poem)
- ***The Prelude*** (autobiographical poem)
- **Prefaces to *Lyrical Ballads*** (prose)

1798 **Publishes first edition of *Lyrical Ballads* with Coleridge**

1802 **Marries Mary Hutchinson**

1805 **Death by drowning of brother John; begins writing *The Prelude***

1813 **Wins appointment as revenue collector in the Lake District**

1820 **Gains critical and public popularity with *The River Duddon***

1800 — 1810 — 1820

Napoleon Bonaparte

1799 **Napoleon Bonaparte comes to power in France.**

1808 **German romantic poet Goethe publishes first part of *Faust*.**

1815 **Napoleon is defeated at Waterloo; Parliament passes the Corn Laws.**

1816 **Workers protest factory layoffs by destroying machinery.** (C)

1829 **London police force is established.**

LIFE AND TIMES

History

(A) During the time that Wordsworth was a student at Cambridge University, professors were not always concerned with teaching, and students were not always interested in learning. Many professors cared only for their salaries, and wealthy students often spent their time gambling and socializing. Even though students had to pass oral examinations to secure their degrees, these tests were not rigorous and could often be passed without studying.

World Culture

(B) The French Revolution impacted people throughout Europe. In Britain, news of the revolution encouraged people to question the authority of the monarchy, and the British government faced increasing pressure to pass parliamentary reforms. However, as the revolution became violent, many English people turned away from the French Revolution as a model for change in England.

Science

(C) During most of Wordsworth's lifetime, Londoners relied on lamps and candles for light. In 1811, Samuel Clegg invented the watertight gas main and the closed water gasometer, which allowed gas to be delivered to homes and businesses for lighting. In 1812, the German Frederic Albert Winsor founded the Chartered Gas-Light and Coke Company in London. The following year, Westminster Bridge was lit with gas lights.

Science

(D) The first railway in England to use steam power ran between the coastal towns of Stockton and Darlington. George Stephenson developed these steam engines, which were first operated in 1825. However, the developers of the Liverpool-Manchester railroad still considered using gravity to power their trains even after steam engines had been shown to work. They planned to use a combination of inclined planes and cables for uphill portions of the tracks.

History

(E) In August of 1845, a potato blight was noticed on the Isle of Wight. The disease that had hit the potato crop in North America had crossed the Atlantic Ocean. Soon, the blight spread throughout Ireland, where as much as one-third of the population depended on the potato for the sole food in their diet. People not only died of starvation, but diseases such as typhus and scurvy were also common. The famine drove many Irish people to leave Ireland for the New World.

World Culture

(F) As nations became stronger and colonies produced wealth, European cities increased in size. From the years 1600 to 1800, London grew from a city of 200,000 people to almost one million. Grand public buildings were erected as cities competed to see which one could have the most impressive architecture. At the same time, money-hungry landlords turned old houses into tenements, and slums became commonplace.

the famous collaboration that would result in the publication of *Lyrical Ballads.* The poems in the collection, with their simple language and subject matter drawn largely from nature and common life, represented a sharp departure from the more formally crafted poetry of the day. Though now considered a cornerstone of England's romantic movement, *Lyrical Ballads* was praised by only a handful of critics when it was first published in 1798.

BACK TO THE LAKES A year later, Wordsworth and his sister settled in the Lake District of their childhood, with Coleridge for a time taking lodgings nearby. In 1802, Wordsworth married Mary Hutchinson, whom he had known since childhood, and over the next several years he continued to labor to win mainstream acceptance as a poet. Gradually, his reputation improved, enough so that by 1813 he was offered the post of local revenue collector, a patronage job showing appreciation for his literary achievements. By the 1820s, he was hugely popular, and in 1843 he was named Britain's poet laureate, succeeding his friend Robert Southey. Wordsworth died on April 23, 1850, and was buried in the Grasmere Churchyard.

More Online: Author Link
www.mcdougallittell.com

The Lake District

The Lake District, where Wordsworth was born and to which he returned in 1799, is a picturesque hilly area of northern England near the Scottish border. The names of many of the area's small lakes (and the towns on their banks) end in *mere*, from the Old English word for "pond": *Windermere* and *Grasmere,* for example. At the right is a photo of Dove Cottage, the house in Grasmere where Wordsworth lived, first with his sister, Dorothy, and later also with his wife and children.

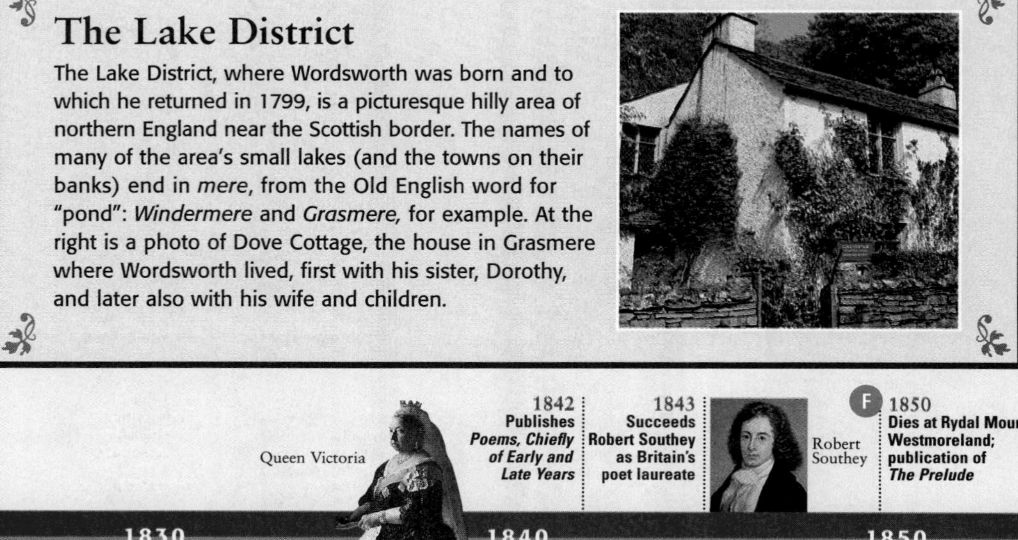

Queen Victoria

1842 **Publishes *Poems, Chiefly of Early and Late Years***

1843 **Succeeds Robert Southey as Britain's poet laureate**

Robert Southey

(F) 1850 **Dies at Rydal Mount, Westmoreland; publication of *The Prelude***

1830 — 1840 — 1850

(D) 1830 **First railway opens between Manchester and Liverpool.**

1832 **First Reform Bill expands voting rights.**

1837 **Victoria becomes queen.**

(E) 1845–46 **Potato famine devastates Ireland.**

PREPARING to *Read*

Selected Poems

By WILLIAM WORDSWORTH

"Nature never did betray / The heart that loved her."

Connect to Your Life

A Sense of Place Think about the places you have visited in your life. Which place made the strongest impression on you? What images leap to mind? Briefly describe the setting that so impressed you and the thoughts and feelings it inspired. Organize your details on a web diagram.

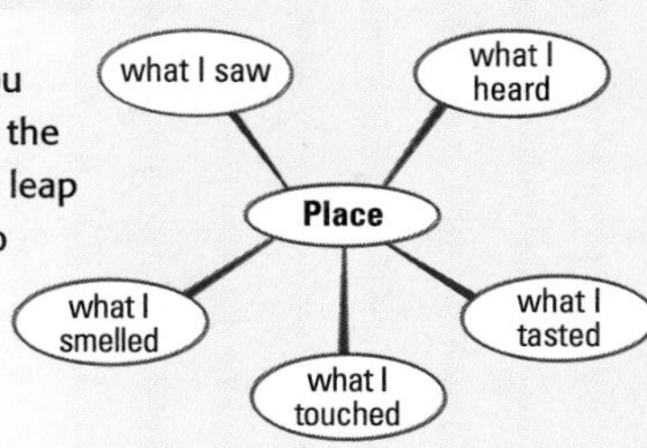

Build Background

Evocative Settings In almost all of the poems on the upcoming pages, Wordsworth describes a specific setting and expresses his thoughts and feelings about it. In "Lines Composed a Few Miles Above Tintern Abbey," he captures an outdoor scene in the Wye River Valley near the English-Welsh border, not far from the ruins of an old abbey. "Composed upon Westminster Bridge" expresses his feelings on seeing the city of London early one morning from a bridge spanning the River Thames. "It Is a Beauteous Evening" also focuses on a specific time of day and the feelings it evokes in the speaker. In "I Wandered Lonely as a Cloud," Wordsworth describes the daffodils he saw on a walk in England's Lake District, not far from the village of Grasmere, where he then lived.

LaserLinks:
Background for Reading
Visual Vocabulary
Art Gallery

Focus Your Reading

LITERARY ANALYSIS IMAGERY To capture the scenes he describes, Wordsworth makes frequent use of **imagery,** words and phrases that create a vivid sensory experience for the reader. The majority of images are visual, but imagery may also appeal to the senses of smell, hearing, taste, and touch. As you read Wordsworth's poetry, look for examples of imagery that help you imagine being in the scene he describes.

ACTIVE READING DRAWING CONCLUSIONS When you **draw conclusions,** you use information you already know as well as details in the poems to make logical statements about themes, attitudes, and feelings that are not directly stated. For example, read Wordsworth's description of London in early morning, when the city seems closest to nature:

This City now doth, like a garment, wear
The beauty of the morning; silent, bare,
Ships, towers, domes, theaters, and temples lie
Open unto the fields, and to the sky;
All bright and glittering in the smokeless air.

The images describing the city's beauty also give you an idea of what London must be like after it has awakened, when the smoke, noise, and bustle of human activity (in the "ships, towers, domes, theaters, and temples") displace the early morning calm. You can then draw conclusions about Wordsworth's attitude toward nature in general and London in particular.

READER'S NOTEBOOK As you read Wordsworth's poems, use details in the poems—especially the imagery—plus your own experience with nature to draw conclusions about Wordsworth's reactions to nature. Record your conclusions.

OVERVIEW

"Lines Composed a Few Miles Above Tintern Abbey" is included in the **Grade 12 InterActive Reader.**

Objectives

1. understand and appreciate **romantic poetry** that explores the effect of landscapes on the poet **(Literary Analysis)**
2. appreciate the author's use of **imagery (Literary Analysis)**
3. **draw conclusions** in order to appreciate and understand **romantic poetry (Active Reading)**

Summary

In these poems, Wordsworth captures feelings evoked by the beauty of nature as seen in a scene near an abbey, from a bridge, at dusk, and in a field of flowers; he also expresses his idea that civilization is at odds with nature.

Thematic Link

Wordsworth's poetry **seeks truth** by exploring the relationships between human beings and the natural world, civilization, and one another.

5-Minute Warm-Up

Daily Language SkillBuilder

Have students **proofread** the display sentences on page 697i and write them correctly. The sentences also appear on Transparency 19 of **Grammar Transparencies and Copymasters.**

LESSON RESOURCES

UNIT FOUR RESOURCE BOOK, pp. 8–9

ASSESSMENT RESOURCES
Formal Assessment, pp. 133–134
Teacher's Guide to Assessment and Portfolio Use
Test Generator

SKILLS TRANSPARENCIES AND COPYMASTERS
Literary Analysis
- Poetic Devices, T16 (for Literary Analysis, p. 738)

Reading and Critical Thinking
- Drawing Conclusions, T4 (for Active Reading, p. 725)

Grammar
- Identifying Adjective Clauses, C109 (for Mini Lesson, pp. 730–731)
- Clauses that Modify Subjects, C110 (for Mini Lesson, pp. 730–731)
- Clauses that Modify Objects, C111 (for Mini Lesson, pp. 730–731)

Vocabulary
- Using a Dictionary, C60 (for Mini Lesson, p. 728)

Writing
- Compare-Contrast, C34 (for Writing Option 3, p. 740)

Communications
- Impromptu Speaking: Debate, T15 (for Activities & Explorations 2, p. 740)

INTEGRATED TECHNOLOGY
Audio Library
Net Activities
LaserLinks
- Visual Vocabulary
- Art Gallery: English Nature Paintings. See **Teacher's SourceBook,** p. 46.

Visit our website:
www.mcdougallittell.com

TEACHING THE LITERATURE

Reading and Analyzing

Literary Analysis IMAGERY

A Ask what mood the images of rolling waters, "soft inland murmur," and "lofty cliffs" help create.

Possible Response: They create a peaceful, pleasant mood.

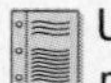

Use **Unit Four Resource Book,** p. 9 for additional support.

Active Reading

DRAWING CONCLUSIONS

B Discuss with students times they have enjoyed nature while alone. Then ask what the "vagrant dwellers" and "Hermit's cave" suggest about the speaker's relationship with nature.

Possible Responses: He likes to be in nature alone; he likes the simplicity of nature.

Use **Unit Four Resource Book,** p. 8 for more practice.

Literary Analysis: SIMILE

C Ask what this comparison suggests about the beauteous forms' effect on the speaker.

Possible Responses: He has seen and can still picture them; they made a strong impression.

Literary Analysis: PASTORAL

D Note that the desire to escape civilization and commune with nature grew more pronounced with the growth of industrial and urban centers in Wordsworth's day. Then ask which details stress this desire.

Possible Response: Students may mention "lonely rooms" and "din of towns and cities."

Lines Composed a Few Miles Above Tintern Abbey

Five years have passed; five summers, with the length
Of five long winters! and again I hear
These waters, rolling from their mountain-springs
(A) With a soft inland murmur. Once again
Do I behold these steep and lofty cliffs,
That on a wild secluded scene impress
Thoughts of more deep seclusion; and connect
The landscape with the quiet of the sky.
The day is come when I again repose
Here, under this dark sycamore, and view
These plots of cottage ground, these orchard tufts,
Which at this season, with their unripe fruits,
Are clad in one green hue, and lose themselves
'Mid groves and copses. Once again I see
These hedgerows, hardly hedgerows, little lines
Of sportive wood run wild; these pastoral farms,
Green to the very door; and wreaths of smoke
Sent up, in silence, from among the trees!
With some uncertain notice, as might seem
(B) Of vagrant dwellers in the houseless woods,
Or of some Hermit's cave, where by his fire
The Hermit sits alone.

These beauteous forms,
(C) Through a long absence, have not been to me
As is a landscape to a blind man's eye;
But oft, in lonely rooms, and 'mid the din
(D) Of towns and cities, I have owed to them,

GUIDE FOR READING

9 repose: lie at rest.

14 copses (kŏp'sĭz): thickets of small trees.

16 pastoral (păs'tər-əl): rural and serene.

20 vagrant: wandering.

Teaching Options

BLOCK SCHEDULING: MANAGING TIME

If your schedule requires that you cover the lesson objectives in a shorter time, use . . .
- Preparing to Read, p. 725
- Thinking Through the Literature, pp. 731, 733, 737, 738

If you want to take advantage of longer class time, use . . .
- TE Teaching Options: Vocabulary Strategy, p. 728; Viewing and Representing, pp. 732, 736; Speaking and Listening, p. 734; Cross Curricular Links, pp. 727, 729, 737; Grammar, pp. 730, 739, 740; Informal Assessment, pp. 733, 735
- The Author's Style, p. 739
- Choices & Challenges and Author Study Project, p. 740

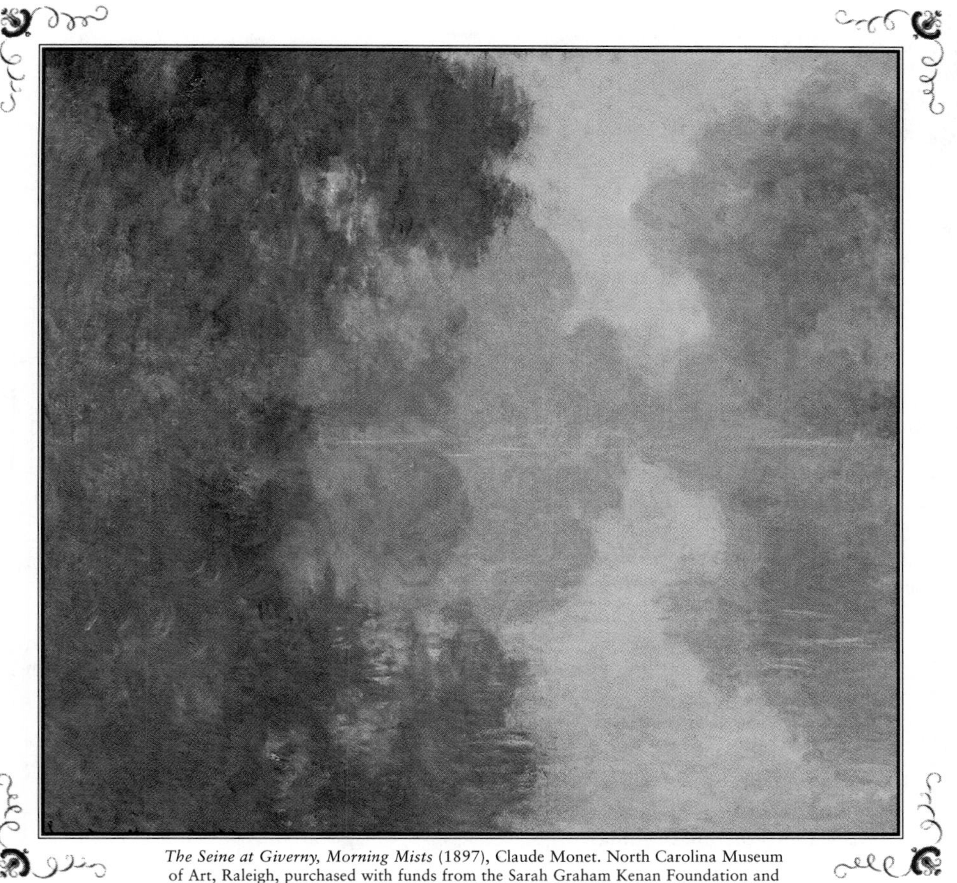

The Seine at Giverny, Morning Mists (1897), Claude Monet. North Carolina Museum of Art, Raleigh, purchased with funds from the Sarah Graham Kenan Foundation and the North Carolina Art Society (Robert F. Phifer Bequest).

Customizing Instruction

Less Proficient Readers

Set a Purpose Have students read to discover the speaker's feelings about the landscape he describes.

Students Acquiring English

To help with the long sentences and extended elaboration on a single thought in the first poem, pair students acquiring English with native English speakers. Have pairs summarize each verse paragraph. Then ask students to continue this process with the other four poems.

Use **Spanish Study Guide** for additional support, pp. 167–169.

Gifted and Talented

As students read the poems, ask them to write in their Reader's Notebook clues that identify the different roles nature plays in the poet's life. Then have them discuss their responses in a small group.

Cross Curricular Link **History**

TINTERN ABBEY Wordsworth had visited the picturesque ruins of Tintern Abbey, located in the Wye River valley near the English-Welsh border, five years before he wrote this poem ("Five years have passed. . . ."). At the time of the poem, he had returned to the site in the company of his sister, Dorothy. Established in 1131, Tintern Abbey was one of many abbeys partly destroyed in the 16th century, when Henry VIII created the Church of England and abolished the Catholic religious orders that had occupied the abbeys. Ask students how, for Wordsworth, the river valley itself serves as a place of worship and what referring to Tintern Abbey might say about his religious beliefs.

Reading and Analyzing

Reading Skills and Strategies: MAKING JUDGMENTS

A Ask if students agree that the acts described in lines 34 and 35 are the "best portion" of a good person's life.
Answer: Students' answers will vary.

Literary Analysis: PASTORAL

B Have students contrast this gift of nature with the gifts in Marlowe's traditional pastoral in Unit 2, "The Passionate Shepherd to His Love" (pages 290–291).
Possible Response: The gifts that Wordsworth speaks of are less materialistic and more complex than those that Marlowe mentions.

Reading Skills and Strategies: ANALYZING

C Have students explain what kind of state Wordsworth describes in lines 43–49.
Possible Responses: He describes a state of deep meditation in which we are connected to nature and all things; a state of spiritual transport in which we sense harmony and joy in the universe.

Then ask how lines 49–50 relate to the previous description.
Possible Response: They express the poet's momentary doubt that there is harmony and joy at the center of everything.

GUIDE FOR READING

D comfort; spiritual renewal

E His awareness of the natural beauty will continue to offer spiritual comfort when he leaves again.

In hours of weariness, sensations sweet,
Felt in the blood, and felt along the heart;
And passing even into my purer mind,
With tranquil restoration—feelings too
Of unremembered pleasure; such, perhaps,
As have no slight or trivial influence
On that best portion of a good man's life,
His little, nameless, unremembered, acts
Of kindness and of love. Nor less, I trust,
To them I may have owed another gift,
Of aspect more sublime; that blessed mood,
In which the burthen of the mystery,
In which the heavy and the weary weight
Of all this unintelligible world,
Is lightened—that serene and blessed mood,
In which the affections gently lead us on—
Until, the breath of this corporeal frame
And even the motion of our human blood
Almost suspended, we are laid asleep
In body, and become a living soul;
While with an eye made quiet by the power
Of harmony, and the deep power of joy,
We see into the life of things.

If this
Be but a vain belief, yet, oh! how oft—
In darkness and amid the many shapes
Of joyless daylight; when the fretful stir
Unprofitable, and the fever of the world,
Have hung upon the beatings of my heart—
How oft, in spirit, have I turned to thee,
O sylvan Wye! thou wanderer through the woods,
How often has my spirit turned to thee!

38 burthen: burden.

43 corporeal (kôr-pôr'ē-əl): bodily.

56 sylvan: located in a wood or forest; **Wye:** a river in Wales and England.

D **22–57** What effect do you think the memory of the "beauteous forms" has on the speaker?

Teaching Options

Vocabulary Strategy

USING A DICTIONARY

Instruction Poets often make frequent use of related words to give their poetry a distinct mood or to evoke particular images and settings. By identifying related words in a poet's works, we can draw conclusions about themes or ideas that are important to a poet.

Write the following words on the chalkboard:

tufts	cataract	sylvan
copse	lea	
hedgerow	vale	

Explain that all the words come from the poems by Wordsworth that appear in the textbook.

Activity Have students use a dictionary or the glossary to locate the definitions of the words on the chalkboard. Ask students to write the definitions, review them, and then decide what the words have in common.

Answer: They are nature words or landscape words.

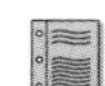 Use **Vocabulary Transparencies and Copymasters,** p. 55.

And now, with gleams of half-extinguished thought
With many recognitions dim and faint,
And somewhat of a sad perplexity,
The picture of the mind revives again;
While here I stand, not only with the sense
Of present pleasure, but with pleasing thoughts
That in this moment there is life and food
For future years. And so I dare to hope,
Though changed, no doubt, from what I was when first
I came among these hills; when like a roe
I bounded o'er the mountains, by the sides
Of the deep rivers, and the lonely streams,
Wherever nature led—more like a man
Flying from something that he dreads than one
Who sought the thing he loved. For nature then
(The coarser pleasures of my boyish days,
And their glad animal movements all gone by)
[3] To me was all in all.—I cannot paint
What then I was. The sounding cataract
Haunted me like a passion; the tall rock,
The mountain, and the deep and gloomy wood,
Their colors and their forms, were then to me
An appetite; a feeling and a love,
That had no need of a remoter charm,
By thought supplied, nor any interest
Unborrowed from the eye.—That time is past,
And all its aching joys are now no more,
[4] And all its dizzy raptures. Not for this
Faint I, nor mourn nor murmur; other gifts
Have followed; for such loss, I would believe,
Abundant recompense. For I have learned
To look on nature, not as in the hour
Of thoughtless youth; but hearing oftentimes
The still, sad music of humanity,
Nor harsh nor grating, though of ample power
To chasten and subdue. And I have felt
A presence that disturbs me with the joy
Of elevated thoughts; a sense sublime
Of something far more deeply interfused,
Whose dwelling is the light of setting suns,
And the round ocean and the living air,
And the blue sky, and in the mind of man:

64–65 E What does the speaker suggest by saying "there is life and food / For future years"?

67 roe: deer.

76 cataract: waterfall.

67–83 Notice how the speaker formerly responded to nature.

88 recompense: compensation. Here the speaker begins to describe what he has received in place of the "aching joys" and "dizzy raptures" of youth.

93 chasten (chā'sən): scold; make modest.

Customizing Instruction

Multiple Learning Styles

Visual Learners

[1] Ask what the art here seems to show.

Answer: It shows a portion of a pillar or column.

Have students explain how, in their opinion, the architectural illustration relates to the poem.

Possible Response: It suggests the abbey ruins and incorporates details from nature.

Less Proficient Readers

[2] Help students overcome the interrupter, and recognize that "sensations sweet" are owed to "them" in line 26 (on page 726). Elicit that "them" refers to the "beauteous forms" of line 22, which in turn refers to the images mentioned earlier.

Students Acquiring English

[3] Have students use the context to determine the meaning of "all in all."

Answer: everything.

[4] Help students understand the meaning of this inverted sentence.

Possible Response: I do not faint, mourn, or murmur for the passage of time.

Multicultural Link: Romantic View of Nature

Wordsworth's attitude toward nature has its parallels in the literature of many times and cultures. In the West it is evident in the pastoral verse of ancient Greece, ancient Rome, and Renaissance writers like Edmund Spenser and Christopher Marlowe. Appreciation of nature runs through Asian literature, and is often evident in the poems of China's Tao Qian (also spelled Tao Chien; A.D. 365–427) and Vietnam's Nguyen Trai (1380–1442), among others, and in the traditional sijo poetry of Korea and the waka and haiku poetry of Japan. The romantic view of nature as a source of truth or guidance is strong in the traditional literature of Africa, including the many proverbs and fables that use examples from nature to offer moral instruction. Respect for nature is also basic to the traditional literature of Native America, and the view of the Americas as a natural paradise is widespread in the writings of early European explorers and settlers in the New World.

Reading and Analyzing

GUIDE FOR READING

A He prays that his sister will continue to remind him of his own youthful passion for nature; he prays that his sister will be inspired and comforted by nature as he has been.

Literary Analysis IMAGERY

B Ask to which senses the images in these lines appeal.
Possible Response: They appeal to sight, feeling or touch, and sound.

Reading Skills and Strategies: MAKING INFERENCES

C Ask to what future occasion the speaker may refer.
Possible Responses: He refers to separation or death.

Thinking Through the Literature

1. Encourage students to describe details of their artworks.
2. Possible Response: Before, the speaker reveled in the sensory beauty of nature; now it lifts him to a higher spiritual plane.
3. Some students may say he wishes he could enjoy nature with the freshness of youth and regrets his inability to experience the scene as before; others may say he is glad he now realizes nature's spiritual value.
4. Most students will conclude that Wordsworth loved his sister and wanted her to enjoy a relationship with nature as meaningful as his own.

A motion and a spirit, that impels
All thinking things, all objects of all thought,
And rolls through all things. Therefore am I still
A lover of the meadows and the woods,
And mountains; and of all that we behold
From this green earth; of all the mighty world
Of eye, and ear—both what they half create,
And what perceive; well pleased to recognize
In nature and the language of the sense
The anchor of my purest thoughts, the nurse,
The guide, the guardian of my heart, and soul
Of all my moral being.

Nor perchance,
If I were not thus taught, should I the more
Suffer my genial spirits to decay:
For thou art with me here upon the banks
Of this fair river; thou my dearest Friend,
My dear, dear Friend; and in thy voice I catch
The language of my former heart, and read
My former pleasures in the shooting lights
Of thy wild eyes. Oh! yet a little while
May I behold in thee what I was once,
My dear, dear Sister! and this prayer I make,
Knowing that Nature never did betray
The heart that loved her; 'tis her privilege,
Through all the years of this our life, to lead
From joy to joy: for she can so inform
The mind that is within us, so impress
With quietness and beauty, and so feed
With lofty thoughts, that neither evil tongues,
Rash judgments, nor the sneers of selfish men,
Nor greetings where no kindness is, nor all
The dreary intercourse of daily life,
Shall e'er prevail against us, or disturb
Our cheerful faith, that all which we behold
Is full of blessings. Therefore let the moon
B Shine on thee in thy solitary walk;
And let the misty mountain winds be free
To blow against thee: and, in after years,
When these wild ecstasies shall be matured
Into a sober pleasure; when thy mind
Shall be a mansion for all lovely forms,
Thy memory be as a dwelling place
For all sweet sounds and harmonies; oh! then,

115 thou my dearest Friend: Wordsworth's sister, Dorothy.

119–120 The speaker sees in his sister's response to nature a mirror of his own youthful response.

121 Note the "prayer" the speaker has made. What does he hope for his sister?

Teaching Options

Grammar

IDENTIFYING ADJECTIVE CLAUSES

Instruction An adjective clause is a subordinate clause that modifies a noun or a pronoun. An adjective clause answers the questions—What kind? or Which one? and usually follows the noun or pronoun it modifies.

Activity Write on the chalkboard the following sentences and underline the adjective clauses.

William Wordsworth, <u>who was one of the Romantic poets</u>, looked to nature for an understanding of life.

A poem <u>that is titled "Lines Composed a Few Miles Above Tintern Abbey"</u> is written in blank verse.

Point out the adjective clauses. Ask students to identify the word or words each one modifies. *(William Wordsworth; poem)* Explain that many adjective clauses begin, as these do, with a relative pronoun*: who, whom, whose, that,* or *which*.

Then ask students if the meaning of the first example changes without the adjective clause. *(no)* Explain that this is a nonessential clause because the clause is not needed to complete the basic meaning of the sentence. Point out that nonessential clauses are always set off by a comma or commas.

C

If solitude, or fear, or pain, or grief
Should be thy portion, with what healing thoughts
Of tender joy wilt thou remember me,
And these my exhortations! Nor, perchance—
If I should be where I no more can hear
Thy voice, nor catch from thy wild eyes these gleams
Of past existence—wilt thou then forget
That on the banks of this delightful stream
We stood together; and that I, so long
1 A worshiper of Nature, hither came
Unwearied in that service; rather say
With warmer love—oh! with far deeper zeal
Of holier love. Nor wilt thou then forget,
That after many wanderings, many years
Of absence, these steep woods and lofty cliffs,
And this green pastoral landscape, were to me
More dear, both for themselves and for thy sake!

146 exhortations: words of encouraging advice.

Thinking Through the Literature

1. Use details provided by the visual imagery to sketch a memorable scene depicted in the poem. Share your sketch with classmates.
2. What effect does nature seem to have on the speaker in the present, and how is that different from its effect in the past? Use details from the poem to support your answer.
3. Do you think the speaker regrets his loss of youth? Explain.

- the way he reacted to nature as a youth in lines 67–83
- his reference to "other gifts" in line 86
- his reaction to his sister's presence

4. Considering what you know about Wordsworth and his feelings expressed in this poem, what conclusions can you draw about his relationship with his sister? Why does showing her the scene a few miles above Tintern Abbey have special meaning for him?

Customizing Instruction

Less Proficient Readers

1 Ask students what has happened to the hustle and bustle of London in the first sonnet?

Possible Response: It is stilled in the early morning.

How does life's hustle and bustle cause the speaker of the next sonnet to feel?

Possible Responses: The speaker feels alienated or sad.

Students Acquiring English

Pair students acquiring English with native English speakers. Have native English speakers paraphrase one or both sonnets, sentence by sentence. Then invite students to discuss and compare the poems.

Explain that the adjective clause in the second example, on the other hand, is an essential clause. It is essential to understanding the sentence. An essential clause is not set off by commas and usually begins with *that*.

Exercise Ask students to underline each adjective clause and identify the noun or pronoun that it modifies. Then have students meet in cooperative groups to discuss whether the clauses are essential or nonessential.

1. William Wordsworth is a 19th-century romantic poet whose poems are still appreciated today. *(poet, nonessential)*
2. In "Lines Composed a Few Miles Above Tintern Abbey," Wordsworth expresses feelings about nature that are universal. *(feelings, essential)*
3. He describes a scene in the Wye River Valley, which you can still see today. *(scene; nonessential)*

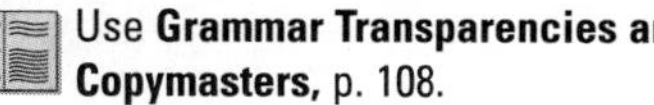
Use **Grammar Transparencies and Copymasters,** p. 108.

Use McDougal Littell's ***Language Network*** for more instruction in placement of adjective clauses.

Reading and Analyzing

Literary Analysis: HYPERBOLE

A Ask what this exaggeration stresses and which other lines exaggerate for similar effects.

Possible Response: It stresses the scene's loveliness; lines 9–11 also contain hyperbole.

Literary Analysis IMAGERY

B Ask students to identify the simile and the things being compared.

Answer: The city wears the beauty of the morning like a garment.

To what sense does this image appeal?

Answer: sight.

Literary Analysis: SONNET

C Ask students to mark the rhyme scheme of this sonnet.

Answer: abba accadedede.

Ask how the final six lines (the sestet) relate or respond to the first eight (the octave).

Remind students that a Petrarchan sonnet presents a problem in the octave and then resolves or comments on the problem in the sestet.

GUIDE FOR READING

D London's vitality; the energy and emotion of London's population.

E materialism; worldliness

F He feels that the ancient Greeks' religion blended divinity with nature better than modern religion does; to see gods in the landscape would give it more meaning and beauty.

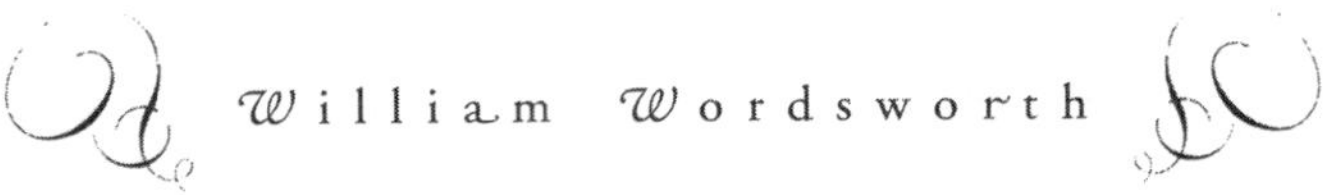

Composed upon Westminster Bridge, September 3, 1802

The Thames Below Westminster (1871), Claude Monet. National Gallery, London, Bridgeman/Art Resource, New York.

(A) Earth has not anything to show more fair: a
Dull would he be of soul who could pass by b
A sight so touching in its majesty; b
(B) This City now doth, like a garment, wear a
The beauty of the morning; silent, bare, a
Ships, towers, domes, theaters, and temples lie c
Open unto the fields, and to the sky; c
All bright and glittering in the smokeless air. a
Never did sun more beautifully steep d
In his first splendor, valley, rock, or hill; e
Ne'er saw I, never felt, a calm so deep! d
The river glideth at his own sweet will: e
Dear God! the very houses seem asleep; d
(C) And all that mighty heart is lying still! e

GUIDE FOR READING

4 this City: London.

9 steep: soak; saturate.

12 the river: the Thames (tĕmz)—the principal river in London.

13 houses: Westminster Bridge is next to the Houses of Parliament; this word may therefore have a double meaning.

14 What do you think "that mighty heart" might be? **D**

Teaching Options

Viewing and Representing

The Thames Below Westminster
by Claude Monet

ART APPRECIATION

Instruction This 1871 painting, one of a series that Monet painted in London, shows a view of the Thames River near Westminster Bridge. The Houses of Parliament and Big Ben are in the background.

Application Ask students if they think the poem or the painting makes the scene more appealing, and why. Have students describe specific aspects of each.

Possible Responses: Some students may be more affected by the interaction of light, shadow, and shade in the painting; others may be inspired by the poem's passionate language and tone.

William Wordsworth

The World Is Too Much with Us

The world is too much with us; late and soon,
Getting and spending, we lay waste our powers;
Little we see in Nature that is ours;
We have given our hearts away, a sordid boon!
This Sea that bares her bosom to the moon,
The winds that will be howling at all hours,
And are up-gathered now like sleeping flowers,
For this, for everything, we are out of tune;
It moves us not.—Great God! I'd rather be
A Pagan suckled in a creed outworn;
So might I, standing on this pleasant lea,
Have glimpses that would make me less forlorn;
Have sight of Proteus rising from the sea;
Or hear old Triton blow his wreathéd horn.

GUIDE FOR READING

2–3 What does the speaker say alienates us from nature?

4 sordid boon: selfish or ignoble gift.

10 a Pagan: a non-Christian (in this case, a worshiper of the gods of ancient Greece). In the following lines, note what the speaker thinks a pagan could do that he cannot.

11 lea: meadow.

13–14 Proteus (prō'tē-əs) . . . **Triton** (trīt'n): sea gods of Greek mythology.

Why do you think the speaker considers it an advantage to be able to see Proteus or hear Triton?

Thinking Through the Literature

1. What words came to mind when you read these two **sonnets?** Discuss your reactions with a partner.
2. In "Composed upon Westminster Bridge," the speaker praises the beauty of the city; but in "The World Is Too Much with Us," the speaker finds more value in the natural world. How do you explain this apparent contradiction?
3. With which of these two poems' speakers do you identify more strongly? Explain your response.

Customizing Instruction

Less Proficient Readers

Ask students what nature provides for the speaker in each of the poems.
Possible Responses: beauty; solace; spirituality.

Ask how the rhythm and tone of the last poem differs from that of the three preceding sonnets.
Possible Response: The rhythm and tone are more singsong, uplifting, cheerful.

Gifted and Talented

Encourage students to read Wordsworth's Preface to *Lyrical Ballads.* This essay-like introduction will give them insight not only into Wordsworth and his poetry, but into much of Romantic poetry.

Thinking Through the Literature

1. Accept all reasonable responses.
2. Possible Responses: He likes the city's vitality and humanity even if it cuts people off from nature; he does not embrace it "in all its glory" but in a quiet time when nature can be appreciated.
3. Students naming the first speaker may cite familiarity with an urban scene that has suddenly become quiet. Those naming the second may identify with the alienation in the first lines.

Assessment Informal Assessment

COMPREHENSION QUESTIONS Use the following items to assess students' understanding of the poem. Write the items on the board. Have students choose the correct word from each pair to complete the sentences.

1. The speaker of "Tintern Abbey" says that five (years, seasons) have passed since he last visited the area.
2. He refers to the scenic details as beauteous (forms, hopes).
3. He claims to have remembered this landscape fondly when he was in (other countries, the city).
4. The speaker says that he (mourns, doesn't mourn) the passing of time.
5. He says that (Nature, his sister) never did betray the heart that loved her.

Reading and Analyzing

Literary Analysis: STYLE

A Point out that, in the first line, the adjectives *calm* and *free* are placed after *evening,* the noun they describe. Ask students what effect the placement of these words has on the reader.

Possible Responses: It has a calming effect; it creates a soothing rhythm; it emphasizes calmness and freedom as two important themes in the poem.

Literary Analysis: SIMILE

B Ask what the comparison to a nun stresses about the evening's beauty.

Possible Response: It stresses the evening's holiness; serenity; spiritual quality.

Literary Analysis IMAGERY

C Ask to what actual motion or sound the speaker refers in these lines.

Possible Response: The speaker refers to the waves crashing to the shore.

Reading Skills and Strategies: MAKING INFERENCES

D Ask to what "Temple" the speaker refers.

Possible Responses: The speaker refers to the shrine of nature; the imagination; the Temple of God.

GUIDE FOR READING

E Because she is a child, she has a divine nature; she can be in tune with nature and therefore with God without being conscious of it.

F The speaker is referring to his memory of the scene.

Mortlake Terrace (1827), Joseph Mallord William Turner. Oil on canvas, 36¼" × 48⅛", National Gallery of Art, Washington, D.C., Andrew W. Mellon Collection. Photo by Richard Carafelli.

It Is a Beauteous Evening

A It is a beauteous evening, calm and free,
B The holy time is quiet as a Nun
Breathless with adoration; the broad sun
Is sinking down in its tranquility;
The gentleness of heaven broods o'er the Sea:
Listen! the mighty Being is awake,
And doth with his eternal motion make
C A sound like thunder—everlastingly.
Dear Child! dear Girl! that walkest with me here,
If thou appear untouched by solemn thought,
Thy nature is not therefore less divine:
Thou liest in Abraham's bosom all the year,
D And worship'st at the Temple's inner shrine,
God being with thee when we know it not.

GUIDE FOR READING

5 broods: hovers protectively.

9 dear Child: Wordsworth's daughter Caroline.

12 in Abraham's bosom: in the presence of God.

10–14 Why does the speaker say that the child's less thoughtful response to the evening does not imply a less divine nature?

Teaching Options

Speaking and Listening

MEMORIZING AND RECITING

Instruction Memorization can make poetry recitation much more immediate for listeners. It also can allow the speaker to concentrate on posture, gesture, eye contact, facial expression, and intonation, and therefore to connect with the audience. Explain that the meter of sonnets, iambic pentameter, is also the meter of English Renaissance drama. Playwrights preferred iambic pentameter because its resemblance to the normal cadences of speech helped the actors remember their lines.

Prepare Have students memorize one of the sonnets in this selection. Before students recite their sonnets, have them work in pairs and give one another feedback.

Present If possible, allow pairs to practice in an empty classroom, with the listener in the back of the room. Have the listener evaluate the speaker's voice projection, expression, posture, and gesture. In a class discussion, have students identify the meter's effect on their ability to memorize.

BLOCK SCHEDULING This activity is particularly well-suited for longer class periods.

William Wordsworth

I WANDERED LONELY AS A CLOUD

1

I wandered lonely as a cloud
That floats on high o'er vales and hills,
When all at once I saw a crowd,
A host, of golden daffodils;
Beside the lake, beneath the trees,
Fluttering and dancing in the breeze.

Continuous as the stars that shine
And twinkle on the milky way,
They stretched in never-ending line
Along the margin of a bay:
Ten thousand saw I at a glance,
Tossing their heads in sprightly dance.

The waves beside them danced; but they
Outdid the sparkling waves in glee;
A poet could not but be gay,
In such a jocund company;
I gazed—and gazed—but little thought
What wealth the show to me had brought:

For oft, when on my couch I lie
In vacant or in pensive mood,
They flash upon that inward eye
Which is the bliss of solitude;
And then my heart with pleasure fills,
And dances with the daffodils.

GUIDE FOR READING

16 jocund (jŏk'ənd): merry.

20 pensive: dreamily thoughtful.

21 What do you think the speaker is referring to when he speaks of "that inward eye"?

Customizing Instruction

Less Proficient Readers

Ask students what nature provides for the speaker in each of the poems.
Possible Responses: beauty; solace; spirituality.
Ask how the rhythm and tone of the last poem differs from that of the three preceding sonnets.
Possible Response: The rhythm and tone are more singsong, uplifting, cheerful.

1 Ask whether the speaker is watching the daffodils now.
Answer: No; he is recalling them.
What details from the speaker's present life contrast with his experience of the daffodils?
Possible Response: He is lying on the couch rather than wandering over hills; he is in a vacant, pensive mood rather than a gay one.

Gifted and Talented

Encourage students to read Wordsworth's Preface to *Lyrical Ballads.* This essay-like introduction will give them insight not only into Wordsworth and his poetry, but into much of Romantic poetry.

Assessment Informal Assessment

WRITING A SUMMARY You can informally assess student's understanding of the selections by asking them to write an introduction summarizing and expressing the main idea of each of the five poems.

RUBRIC

3 Full Accomplishment Students' summaries fully cover developments in poems and convey main ideas with supporting details.

2 Substantial Accomplishment Students' summaries cover most actions in poems and state main ideas.

1 Little or Partial Accomplishment Students' summaries do not cover poems and do not fully or accurately express main ideas.

Teaching the Literature

Build Background

Dorothy Wordsworth (1771–1855), the only girl of five children, was separated from her brothers after their mother died in 1778. However, she and her brother William had a strong bond; she understood him better than anyone else. At age 24, she went to keep house for him, and the two became inseparable, living and traveling together. It was then that they met Samuel Taylor Coleridge (1772–1834), and the three developed a close friendship that has been described as "three persons with one soul." In 1829, she suffered from a severe illness, and she spent the last 20 years of her life both mentally and physically disabled.

Although Dorothy privately circulated her manuscripts and allowed William to publish portions as part of his own prose, she had no real desire to publish her work. Her complete journals did not appear until four decades after her death. Her considerable talent as a diarist is still sometimes overlooked as scholars scan her writing in search of insights into the life and work of her more famous brother. In addition to the *Grasmere Journals,* the *Alfoxden Journal,* Dorothy's record of William's friendship with Coleridge, was the inspiration for *Lyrical Ballads.*

Reading Skills and Strategies: COMPARING AND CONTRASTING

Being able to compare and contrast will help students understand the similarities and differences between two or more things, people, events, or stories. Comparing is discovering how two things are alike, and contrasting is finding out how two or more things are different.

Ask students to compare and contrast Dorothy's journal entry with William's poem. Challenge students to locate images and words that appear in both texts.

Possible Responses: Both texts describe the same scene; both writers are struck by the beauty of the daffodils; both express the idea of the daffodil colony's "simplicity and unity"; both include the words "float," "dance," "glance," and "gay."

DOROTHY WORDSWORTH

from the

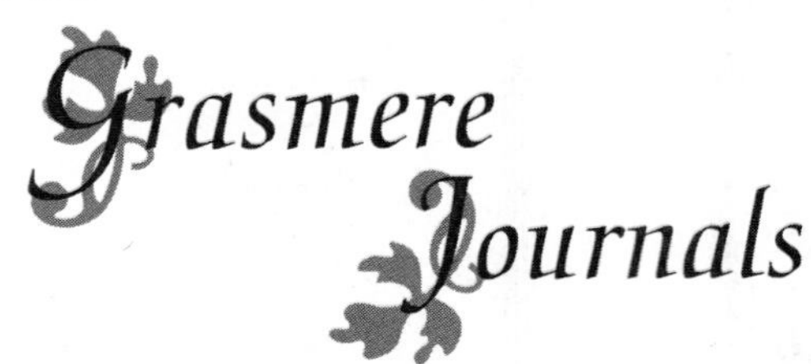

Grasmere Journals

Preparing to Read

Build Background

Much of Wordsworth's inspiration for his poetry came during his frequent walks with his sister Dorothy, first in western England and later in the picturesque Lake District. In her journals, Dorothy recorded her own observations about the sights and sounds they encountered. It was not unusual for Wordsworth to read and borrow from the descriptions in his sister's journal, particularly when he was writing a poem about a scene that they had observed months, or even years, before. This excerpt from Dorothy's journals kept at Grasmere, in the Lake District, records the same scene that inspired Wordsworth's "I Wandered Lonely as a Cloud."

Focus Your Reading

PRIMARY SOURCES | JOURNAL

Private journals, like personal letters, are valuable **primary sources** that offer insights into the everyday lives of historical figures. As you read this journal entry, think about what it tells you about both brother and sister.

Apr. 15.

It was a threatening misty morning—but mild. We [Dorothy and William] set off after dinner from Eusemere.

Mrs. Clarkson went a short way with us but turned back. The wind was furious and we thought we must have returned. We first rested in the large Boat-house, then under a furze Bush opposite Mr. Clarkson's. Saw the plough going in the field. The wind seized our breath the Lake was rough. There was a Boat by itself floating in the middle of the Bay below Water Millock. We rested again in the Water Millock Lane. The hawthorns are black and green, the birches here and there greenish but there is yet more of purple to be seen on the Twigs. We got over into a field to avoid some cows—people working, a few primroses by the roadside, wood-sorrel flower, the anemone, scentless violets, strawberries, and that starry yellow flower which Mrs. C. calls pile wort. When we were in the woods beyond Gowbarrow park we saw a few daffodils close to the water side. We fancied that the lake had floated the seeds ashore and that the little colony had so sprung up. But as we went along there were more and yet more and at last under the boughs of the trees, we saw that there was a long belt of them along the shore, about the breadth of a country turnpike road. I never saw daffodils so beautiful they grew among the mossy stones about and about them, some rested their heads upon these stones as on a pillow for weariness and the rest tossed and reeled and danced and seemed as if they verily laughed at the wind that blew upon them over the lake, they looked so gay ever glancing ever changing. This wind blew directly over the lake to them. There was here and there a little knot and a few stragglers a few yards higher up but they were so few as not to disturb the simplicity and unity and life of that one busy highway. We rested again and again. The Bays were stormy, and we heard the waves at different distances and in the middle of the water like the sea.

Thinking Through the Literature

1. What did you learn about Dorothy Wordsworth while reading her journal entry?
2. What, if any, insights into William Wordsworth did this journal entry give you?
3. **Comparing Texts** How does Dorothy's response to the daffodils compare with her brother's? What similarities do you see in the **imagery** and the feelings expressed?

Thinking Through the Literature

1. Students will probably mention her love of nature and her skills of observation.
2. Students will probably observe that Wordsworth developed some of his ideas by conversing with Dorothy or reading her journal.
3. Students may note that Dorothy wrote a prose description of the scene while William wrote a poem; that both writers are enchanted by the vision of the daffodils; and that both writers described the daffodils dancing happily in the breeze.

GUIDING STUDENT RESPONSE

Connect to the Literature

1. What Do You Think?
Guidelines for student response: Students might describe details in the poems, explain how these images arouse certain senses, and discuss feelings invoked by the poems.

Comprehension Check

- He compares it to a nun.
- The speaker comes across a field of daffodils near a lake.
- The speaker thinks of the flowers when he lies on his couch.

Think Critically

2. Students will likely describe the speakers as idealistic, spiritual, emotional, and nature-loving.
3. Responses will vary. Good responses will observe that Wordsworth's relationship with nature was personal—it served as his friend, teacher, and the object of his affection—or that his devotion to nature was a form of religious or spiritual expression.
4. Students may point out that both poems have a quiet, calm, serene mood and that both take place near water; students may also note that "Beauteous Evening" takes place late in the day and that "Westminster Bridge" takes place at dawn.
5. Both express how the memory of nature sustains the speaker when he is away from it.

Literary Analysis

Cooperative Learning Activity As students share their cooperative activity, have them discuss the effect the imagery had on them as they read.
Review Simile You might ask volunteers to read aloud the similes they have found and explain how they add meaning to the poems

Thinking through the LITERATURE

Connect to the Literature

1. What Do You Think? What images remain in your mind after reading "It Is a Beauteous Evening" and "I Wandered Lonely as a Cloud"?

Comprehension Check

- To what religious figure does Wordsworth compare the beauteous evening?
- What does the speaker come across unexpectedly in "I Wandered Lonely as a Cloud"?
- When does the speaker think of the daffodils again?

Think Critically

2. How would you describe the **speakers** of the two poems?

THINK ABOUT
- each speaker's comments about nature
- the speaker's comments about his daughter in lines 10–14 of "It Is a Beauteous Evening"
- the reference to "that inward eye" in line 21 of "I Wandered Lonely as a Cloud"

3. ACTIVE READING DRAWING CONCLUSIONS Recall the conclusions you reached in your 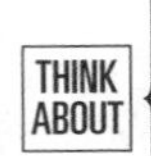 READER'S NOTEBOOK about Wordsworth's reactions to nature. What did nature mean to Wordsworth? Refer to the **imagery, figurative language,** and direct statements in Wordsworth's poems.

4. In what way is the scene described in "It Is a Beauteous Evening" similar to the scene in "Composed upon Westminster Bridge"? How are they different?

5. How is the experience described in the last stanza of "I Wandered Lonely as a Cloud" similar to that in "Lines Composed a Few Miles Above Tintern Abbey"?

Extend Interpretations

6. **Comparing Texts** Compare Wordsworth's treatment of innocence and experience with that of William Blake. How do the two poets differ in their attitudes toward experience and loss of youth?

7. **Critic's Corner** Samuel Taylor Coleridge praised Wordsworth for capturing "the perfect truth of nature in his images and descriptions." Do you agree with this assessment of Wordsworth's writing? Support your answer with examples.

8. **Connect to Life** If Wordsworth were alive today, what do you think he would say about our treatment of the environment and such scientific experiments as cloning? Explain.

Literary Analysis

IMAGERY Among the many tools of poets, few are more important than **imagery,** the use of words and phrases that create vivid sensory experiences for the reader. Imagery can appeal to all five senses: sight, smell, hearing, taste, and touch. Notice how the image in these lines from "Tintern Abbey" appeals to both sight and hearing:

These waters, rolling from their
mountain-springs
With a soft inland murmur.

Cooperative Learning Activity With a small group of classmates, list three examples of imagery from Wordsworth's poems in a chart like the one below. Discuss how the imagery helps create a particular mood or convey a particular idea or emotion.

Image	Poem/Line(s)	Sense(s) Appealed to
These waters . . . inland murmur	"Tintern Abbey"	sight, hearing

REVIEW SIMILE The statement, "I wandered lonely as a cloud," uses a simile to add deeper meaning to the speaker's experience. For example, the simile connects the speaker to nature and emphasizes the harmony between them; the simile also sets up a lighthearted, carefree mood that compliments the pleasurable images and feelings in the poem. Find three more similes in Wordsworth's poems and analyze how they add to the meaning of the poems.

Extend Interpretations

Comparing Texts Student responses will vary. Students may say that both poets idealize youthful innocence and stress its simplicity, but that Blake links it to religious faith while Wordsworth is more of a sensualist/primitivist. Both express regret regarding loss of youth but also recognize that with experience comes powerful new knowledge. **To make this question easier,** have students compare one Blake poem with one Wordsworth poem.

Critic's Corner Students who agree may cite details from the poems that accurately describe nature and images that paint vivid pictures of its splendor. Those who disagree may show evidence of Wordsworth's idealization of nature and/or discuss his disregard for the human suffering that nature sometimes brings. In both cases, students may note details from his sister's journal as part of their proof.

Connect to Life Accept all reasonable, well-supported responses. Most students will speculate that Wordsworth would be saddened at the modern world's neglect of nature and would be opposed to any scientific experiments that diminish the uniqueness of the individual.

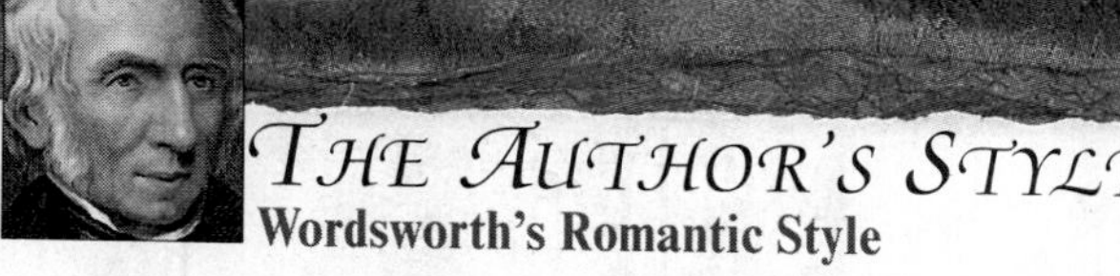

THE AUTHOR'S STYLE

Wordsworth's Romantic Style

Wordsworth stated the poetic philosophy of romanticism in his preface to *Lyrical Ballads* in 1798. In subsequent editions of the book, he continued to revise his preface to further clarify what he was trying to do. The aspects of his style, therefore, come not only from his own poetry but from his statements about poetry as well.

Key Aspects of Wordsworth's Style

- images drawn from nature to show connections between humans and the natural world
- direct statements of emotions
- philosophical statements of personal beliefs
- ordinary experiences, objects, and people transformed by the imagination and presented in an unusual way
- simple diction, or word choice, to express complicated feelings and abstract concepts

Analysis of Style

Study the aspects of Wordsworth's style and read the samples of his poetry at the right. Then complete these activities:

- A • Find examples of each aspect of Wordsworth's style in the samples.
- B • Point out other characteristics in the samples that you think distinguish Wordsworth's poetry from other types of poetry.
- C • Go back through the poems in this Author Study and find further examples that illustrate these key aspects of Wordsworth's style.

Applications

1. **Imitating Style** Imitate Wordsworth's style in either a short poem or a paragraph. Try to capture Wordsworth's simplicity of subject matter and language, while expressing deep emotion and/or thought. Share your work with your classmates.
2. **Changing Style** With a partner, paraphrase, or restate in your own words, three of Wordsworth's philosophical explanations in poems such as "Tintern Abbey," "The World Is Too Much with Us," and "It Is a Beauteous Evening." What gets lost in the paraphrase?
3. **Analyzing Wordsworth's Sonnet Style** All three sonnets in this Author Study are Petrarchan. With a small group of classmates, review the structure of the Petrarchan sonnet on page 308, and then analyze one of Wordsworth's sonnets by (a) tracing the rhyme scheme, (b) paraphrasing the issue or the emotional response set up in the octave, and (c) explaining the conclusions drawn in the sestet.

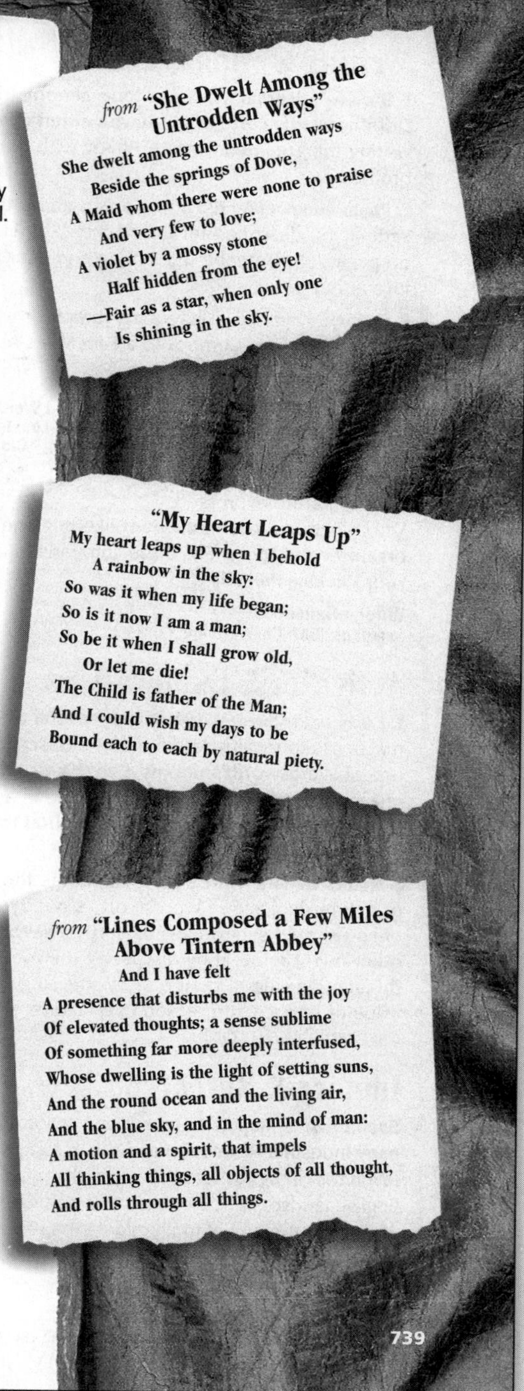

from **"She Dwelt Among the Untrodden Ways"**

She dwelt among the untrodden ways
Beside the springs of Dove,
A Maid whom there were none to praise
And very few to love;
A violet by a mossy stone
Half hidden from the eye!
—Fair as a star, when only one
Is shining in the sky.

"My Heart Leaps Up"

My heart leaps up when I behold
A rainbow in the sky:
So was it when my life began;
So is it now I am a man;
So be it when I shall grow old,
Or let me die!
The Child is father of the Man;
And I could wish my days to be
Bound each to each by natural piety.

from **"Lines Composed a Few Miles Above Tintern Abbey"**

And I have felt
A presence that disturbs me with the joy
Of elevated thoughts; a sense sublime
Of something far more deeply interfused,
Whose dwelling is the light of setting suns,
And the round ocean and the living air,
And the blue sky, and in the mind of man:
A motion and a spirit, that impels
All thinking things, all objects of all thought,
And rolls through all things.

739

The Author's Style

Beyond the elements of romanticism, there are many components to Wordsworth's style. Students will be made aware of his style through the "Key Aspects of Wordsworth's Style" chart and then find examples of the five points in the excerpts in the right margin.

Analysis of Style

A First activity
nature images: She dwelt among the untrodden ways / Beside the springs of Dove; A violet by a mossy stone
emotion: My heart leaps up when I behold; A presence that disturbs me with the joy
personal beliefs: The Child is father of the Man; A motion and a spirit, that impels
imagination: A Maid whom there were none to praise / And very few to love; And the round ocean and the living air
diction: And I could wish my days to be / Bound each to each by natural piety; Whose dwelling is the light of setting suns

B Second activity
In the excerpt from "Lines Composed a Few Miles Above Tintern Abbey," Wordsworth does not rhyme at all. This differs from sonnets, which have specific rhyme conventions. The language in "My Heart Leaps Up" differs from the everyday-language that characterizes metaphysical poetry.

C Third activity
There are many examples of the **key aspects** of Wordsworth's style throughout his poems. For example, in "Lines Composed a Few Miles Above Tintern Abbey," lines 135–142 use imagery to appeal to different senses.

Applications

1. **Imitating Style** Remind students to revisit the Key Aspects box on the page before beginning their creations.
2. **Changing Style** Most students will find that the emotion, mood, and style of the language gets lost in the restatement of the poems' philosophy.
3. **Analyzing Wordsworth's Sonnet Style** The best responses will accurately identify the rhyme scheme, the emotional issue expressed in the octave, and the conclusion drawn in the last six lines.

Mini Lesson Grammar

CLAUSES THAT MODIFY SUBJECTS

Instruction Remind students that adjective clauses can modify the subject of a sentence or clause. Adjective clauses often begin with a relative pronoun: *which, that, who, whom,* or *whose.*

Activity Write the following sentences on the chalkboard.

> The sonnets that Wordsworth wrote were often composed after country walks with his sister Dorothy. When they visited the region whose lakes they both loved, Dorothy wrote of her own observations.

Underline the adjective clauses and have students identify the nouns they modify. *(sonnets; region)* Point out that these are essential clauses—necessary to the meaning of the word they modify—and they are not set off by commas. Then give students this example.

> Sonnets, which Wordsworth wrote, always have fourteen lines.

This adjective clause, in contrast, is a nonessential clause and is set off by commas.

Use **Grammar Transparencies and Copymasters**, p. 110.

Use McDougal Littell's ***Language Network*** for more instruction in clauses.

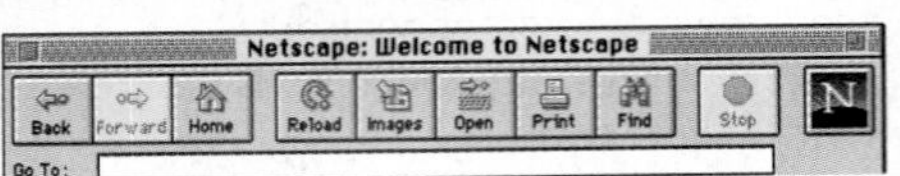

Author Study Project

HOLDING A PANEL DISCUSSION

Be sure each person gets to know their character well enough to answer the questions about Wordsworth. Also, the interviewer should ask questions to elicit particular responses as well as to encourage a lively discussion. Remind students that *who, what, where, when,* and *how* questions are particularly effective. Those who feel they know their person's life well enough may want to extend the activity by submitting themselves to the rest of the class for an impromptu interview session.

MULTIMEDIA PROJECT

Students can turn their panel discussion into a multimedia project by staging it as a television talk show. The groups can add period-appropriate background music, and students can dress in appropriate costumes. Groups of 6–8 students should have enough people for the characters, the host, and a person responsible for coordinating the technical aspects of the project.

Writing Options

1. **Dorothy's Journal** Students' journal entries will vary. Tell students that their responses should use a matter-of-fact tone and simple diction, focusing on description rather than personal emotion or philosophy.
2. **Poem About a Place** Poems will vary. Before they begin writing, remind students to include vivid imagery as well as personal thoughts and feeling. Some students may want to focus on how their attitude toward the place has changed over time.
3. **Poetic Comparison** Comparisons will vary. Some students may conclude that the speaker of "Tintern Abbey" has a much more personal relationship with the setting than does the speaker of "I Wandered Lonely as a Cloud," who is more of an observer than a participant. Students will probably point out that both speakers find solace and comfort in nature, especially when they are separated from it.

Choices & CHALLENGES

Writing Options

1. **Dorothy's Journal** Write the journal entry that Dorothy Wordsworth might have written after visiting the area near Tintern Abbey with her brother.
2. **Poem About a Place** Write a poem about the setting you described for Connect to Your Life on page 725. Describe the setting and your feelings about it.
3. **Poetic Comparison** Write a paragraph or two comparing "Lines Composed a Few Miles Above Tintern Abbey" and "I Wandered Lonely as a Cloud." Discuss the experiences in both poems as well as the view of nature expressed. You might use a Venn diagram like this one to organize your ideas. Place the comparison in your **Working Portfolio.**

Tintern Abbey | I Wandered Lonely as a Cloud

Writing Handbook
See page 1367: Compare and Contrast.

Activities & Explorations

1. **Poem in Pictures** Working with several classmates or alone, illustrate the scene described in one of Wordsworth's poems. Use the visual imagery to help you capture the scene in a drawing, a collage, or even a large mural to decorate your classroom. ~ **ART**
2. **Nature Debate** With a partner, debate the view of nature depicted in Wordsworth's poetry. One of you should support Wordsworth's view; the other might refute it by discussing the more threatening side of nature or by stressing the value of science and reason over nature. ~ **SPEAKING AND LISTENING**

Inquiry & Research

Social History Report Research and report on the early Industrial Revolution and the accompanying revolution in agriculture that were changing the English landscape in Wordsworth's day. Create a poster or other visual to illuminate the romantic poet's turn to nature.

Netscape: Welcome to Netscape

William Wordsworth

Author Study Project

HOLDING A PANEL DISCUSSION

How was *Lyrical Ballads* received by other writers? What did contemporary figures other than writers—such as King George IV, the artist J. M. W. Turner, the influential duke of Wellington, the inventor James Watt, and the political philosopher Jeremy Bentham—think of Wordsworth? Research the answers to these and related questions, and present your findings in a panel discussion in which each participant takes the role of a different person famous in the romantic period (1798–1832). Before the discussion starts, the panelists should introduce themselves and give a brief summary of their achievements. One student should serve as moderator, asking questions when necessary to keep the discussion moving.

Primary Print Sources Consult reviews and other literary criticism of the day, including works by famous romantic prose writers Samuel Taylor Coleridge, William Hazlitt, Thomas De Quincey, and Charles Lamb. Also consider Dorothy Wordsworth's journals and personal writing by later romantic writers, such as Sir Walter Scott, Lord Byron, Percy Bysshe Shelley, Mary Shelley, and John Keats.

Secondary Sources Consult histories, articles in literary journals, historical and biographical entries in reference works, and biographies of different personalities from Wordsworth's era.

Web Sites Reliable Web sites could provide useful information on Wordsworth and the romantic period. Also consider scholarly Web sites maintained by university English departments and established poetry societies.

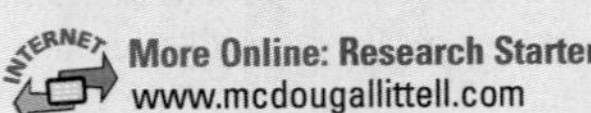

More Online: Research Starter
www.mcdougallittell.com

Activities & Explorations

1. **Poem in Pictures** Suggest that, before they begin, students reread the poem carefully, noting particular details or images they want to include in their illustration.
2. **Nature Debate** Allow students to conduct their debates in front of the class. Encourage audience members to take notes during the debate and refer to them for a question-and-answer session. Students may research points of interest or contention later.

Inquiry & Research

Social History Report Have students work in groups, with different students focusing on different aspects of the Industrial Revolution—important inventions, labor laws, agriculture, and so on. Suggest that students use encyclopedias as well as more specialized reference books, such as *The Oxford Illustrated History of Britain* (Oxford University Press, 1994) and John D. Clare's *Living History: The Industrial Revolution* (Random House, 1994).

PREPARING to *Read*

Kubla Khan

Poetry by SAMUEL TAYLOR COLERIDGE

"In Xanadu did Kubla Khan / A stately pleasure dome decree."

Connect to Your Life

Dream a Little Dream Have you ever had a dream so vivid that you wanted to write it down or tell someone about it? Were you able to recapture the mood of your dream when you described it? Discuss your experience with your classmates.

Build Background

Dream Vision Samuel Taylor Coleridge was an influential poet, critic, and philosopher who, like his good friend William Wordsworth, was a leading figure in the English romantic movement. Like other poets of the era, Coleridge responded to nature with intense emotion. In poems such as "Kubla Khan," he wrote enthusiastically not only about the beauty and serenity of nature but also about its savagery and wildness.

The circumstances surrounding the composition of "Kubla Khan" are almost as well-known as the poem itself. According to Coleridge, he had been reading about the building of a summer palace for Kublai Khan, the great 13th-century Mongol ruler, when he fell asleep in his chair as a result of a painkilling drug he had taken. In his sleep, Coleridge later reported, the images of the poem "rose up before him as *things*, . . . without any sensation or consciousness of effort." When he awoke, he began writing the poem down, but at line 54 he was interrupted by a visitor who needed to see him on business. When he returned to the poem, he was unable to remember the rest of his dream. Coleridge therefore called the lines he had written a "fragment" and "a vision in a dream."

LaserLinks: Background for Reading
Literary Connection

Focus Your Reading

LITERARY ANALYSIS ONOMATOPOEIA **Onomatopoeia** (ŏn′ə-măt′ə-pē′ə) is the use of words whose sounds suggest their meanings—such as *buzz* and *murmur*—or of language that echoes the sound of what is being described. In "Kubla Khan," Coleridge made use of onomatopoeia and many other **sound devices.** As you read, be aware of the musical quality that these devices add to the poem.

ACTIVE READING ANALYZING STRUCTURE **Structure** is the organization of details in a literary work—the way in which the parts of the work are put together. Understanding a work's structure can help you understand its meaning. "Kubla Khan" is divided into three parts, which might be called the **thesis,** the **antithesis,** and the **synthesis:**

- thesis—presents a vision
- antithesis—presents a contrasting vision
- synthesis—pulls together the two visions

READER'S NOTEBOOK As you read, use a diagram similar to the one shown to note where these parts begin and end and what each part of the poem describes.

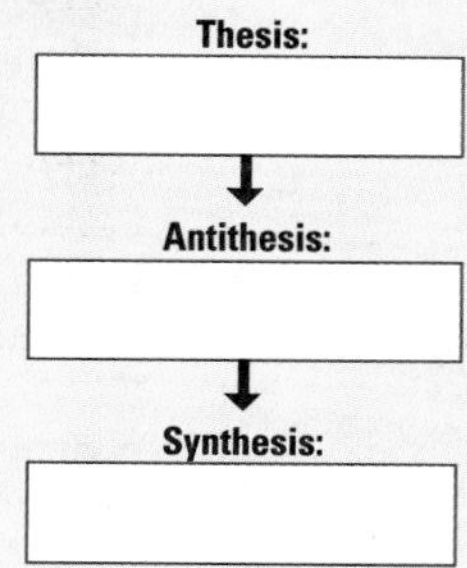

OVERVIEW

Objectives

1. understand and appreciate a **lyric poem** that explores a dream vision **(Literary Analysis)**
2. appreciate the author's use of **onomatopoeia (Literary Analysis)**
3. **analyze structure** to appreciate and understand a lyric poem **(Active Reading)**

Summary

First, Kubla Khan builds a "stately pleasure dome" in the exotic setting of Xanadu. Then the speaker imagines himself at the center of a similar paradise.

Thematic Link

While **seeking truth,** Coleridge expresses his unique relationship to nature by exploring its strange beauty as well as its fierceness.

5-Minute Warm-Up

Daily Language SkillBuilder

Have students **proofread** the display sentences on page 697j and write them correctly. The sentences also appear on Transparency 19 of **Grammar Transparencies and Copymasters.**

LESSON RESOURCES

UNIT FOUR RESOURCE BOOK, pp. 10–11

ASSESSMENT RESOURCES

Formal Assessment, pp. 135–136
Teacher's Guide to Assessment and Portfolio Use
Test Generator

SKILLS TRANSPARENCIES AND COPYMASTERS

Literary Analysis
- Form and Meaning in Poetry, T15 (for Literary Analysis, p. 744)

Reading and Critical Thinking
- Analyzing Text Structure, T17 (for Active Reading, p. 741)

Grammar
- Noun Clauses, C117 (for Mini Lesson, p. 743)

Writing
- Figurative Language and Sound Devices, T15 (for Writing Option 1, p. 767)

INTEGRATED TECHNOLOGY

Audio Library
LaserLinks
- Literary Connection: A Reading of "Kubla Khan." See **Teacher's SourceBook,** p. 47.

Video: Literature in Performance
- "Kubla Khan": a reading with photographs and music. See **Video Resource Book,** pp. 23–26.

Visit our website:
www.mcdougallittell.com

TEACHING THE LITERATURE

Reading and Analyzing

Active Reading

ANALYZING STRUCTURE

A Ask how the description of the land surrounding Xanadu in lines 1–11 contrasts with the description in lines 12–16.

Answer: Lines 1–11 describe a sunny, pleasant place; lines 12–16, a wild, frightening place.

Use **Unit Four Resource Book,** p. 10 for more practice.

Literary Analysis ONOMATOPOEIA

B Clarify that onomatopoeia can refer to groups of words whose combined sounds suggest meaning or mood. Often, rhyme and rhythm, together with alliteration (repeated initial consonant sounds), assonance (repeated internal vowel sounds), and consonance (repeated internal or final consonant sounds) are used to create onomatopoeia. Have students analyze lines 24–25 for elements that help create onomatopoeia.

Possible Response: The repeated *m* suggests the river's lazy, meandering motion, while the *s* and *z*, both sounded like *z*, contribute to the sleepy cadence.

Use **Unit Four Resource Book,** p. 11 for more exercises.

GUIDE FOR READING

C War is in his future; his sanctuary will not safeguard him from conflict.

D He would build the dome. The maid may symbolize an exotic muse or the ability to re-create paradise through art.

E Students may say it would be delightful but dangerous; empowering; transforming.

Samuel Taylor Coleridge

Kubla

In Xanadu did Kubla Khan
A stately pleasure dome decree:
Where Alph, the sacred river, ran
Through caverns measureless to man
Down to a sunless sea.
So twice five miles of fertile ground
With walls and towers were girdled round:
And there were gardens bright with sinuous rills,
Where blossomed many an incense-bearing tree;
And here were forests ancient as the hills,
Enfolding sunny spots of greenery.

But oh! that deep romantic chasm which slanted
Down the green hill athwart a cedarn cover!
A savage place! as holy and enchanted
As e'er beneath a waning moon was haunted
By woman wailing for her demon lover!
And from this chasm, with ceaseless turmoil seething,
As if this earth in fast thick pants were breathing,
A mighty fountain momently was forced:
Amid whose swift half-intermitted burst
Huge fragments vaulted like rebounding hail,
Or chaffy grain beneath the thresher's flail:
And 'mid these dancing rocks at once and ever
It flung up momently the sacred river.
Five miles meandering with a mazy motion
Through wood and dale the sacred river ran,
Then reached the caverns measureless to man,
And sank in tumult to a lifeless ocean:
And 'mid this tumult Kubla heard from far
Ancestral voices prophesying war!
The shadow of the dome of pleasure
Floated midway on the waves;
Where was heard the mingled measure
From the fountain and the caves.
It was a miracle of rare device,
A sunny pleasure dome with caves of ice!

A damsel with a dulcimer
In a vision once I saw:

GUIDE FOR READING

1 Xanadu (zăn′ə-dōō′): Shangdu, one of Kublai Khan's residences in what is now northern China.

8 sinuous rills: winding streams.

13 athwart a cedarn cover: across a grove of cedar trees.

19 momently: at every moment.

20 intermitted: interrupted.

30 What does this line suggest about Kubla's destiny? **C**

35 device: design.

37 dulcimer: a stringed musical instrument played with small hammers.

Teaching Options

Multicultural Link: Great Empires

Kublai (or Kubla) Khan was the grandson of Genghis Khan, ruler of the Mongols of central Asia and one of the great conquerors of history. Kublai himself became *khan,* or ruler, in 1260. At the height of his power, Kublai Khan ruled an empire that stretched from present-day Korea to eastern Poland.

- Alexander the Great, king of the Macedonians, was another great emperor. By the time of his death in 323 B.C., Alexander's empire extended from Greece to India, covering much of what was then considered the civilized world.
- From about the A.D. 300s to the mid-1000s, the Ghana Empire was an important trading state in West Africa. Ghana's greatest period began in the 700s, when tax payments in gold greatly increased the empire's wealth.

Khan

It was an Abyssinian maid,
And on her dulcimer she played,
Singing of Mount Abora.
Could I revive within me
Her symphony and song,
To such a deep delight 'twould win me,
That with music loud and long,
I would build that dome in air,
That sunny dome! those caves of ice!
And all who heard should see them there,
And all should cry, Beware! Beware!
His flashing eyes, his floating hair!
Weave a circle round him thrice,
And close your eyes with holy dread,
For he on honeydew hath fed,
And drunk the milk of Paradise.

39 Abyssinian: from Abyssinia, now called Ethiopia.

41 Mount Abora: a legendary earthly paradise like Kubla Khan's.

46 What would the speaker do if he were able? What do you think the Abyssinian maid symbolizes? 

48 Note in the following lines what effect the speaker's song and appearance will have on others.

53 honeydew: an ideally sweet or luscious substance.

54 What kind of experience would it be to drink "the milk of Paradise"? 

In a Harem Garden (about 1765), attributed to Faiz Allah of Faizabad, Mughal empire. Opaque watercolor on paper. The David Collection, Copenhagen, Denmark.

Customizing Instruction

Less Proficient Readers

Help with the poem's tongue-twisting devices by reading the poem aloud and then having students read it aloud in pairs.

Set a Purpose Ask students what would cause others to fear the speaker.

Possible Responses: Students may mention his ability to build the pleasure dome in air or his otherworldly appearance.

Students Acquiring English

- Help students understand the meaning of difficult words such as *decree* (order), *chasm* (a deep opening), *waning* (decreasing in size), and *thrice* (three times).
- Read the poem aloud, stopping to identify the subject and verb(s) in inverted sentences. Then instruct students to read the poem silently.

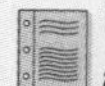 Use **Spanish Study Guide** for additional support, pp. 170–172.

Gifted and Talented

Have students write a paragraph describing how images in the poem might symbolize or relate to the creative process.

Grammar

NOUN CLAUSES

Instruction A **noun clause** is a subordinate clause that is used as a noun in a sentence. It can function as a subject, object, or predicate nominative.

Activity Write on the chalkboard the sentences below.

Xanadu, or Shangdu, is located in what is now northern China.

Where "Kubla Khan" ends is where Coleridge was interrupted in his writing.

Underline the noun clauses and help students to understand how they are used in the examples. In the first sentence, the entire clause is the object of the preposition *in*. The second sentence contains two noun clauses. Ask students to identify the function of each. *(first clause, subject; second clause, predicate nominative)*

On the chalkboard, write these words that often introduce noun clauses: who, *which, that, what, when, where, how.*

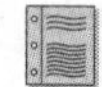 Use **Grammar Transparencies and Copymasters,** p. 115.

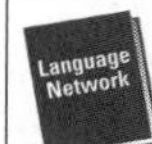

Use McDougal Littell's ***Language Network*** for more instruction in noun clauses.

KUBLA KHAN 743

GUIDING STUDENT RESPONSE

Connect to the Literature

1. **What Do You Think?**
Guidelines for student response: Many students will find the floating pleasure dome of ice the most striking, while others may point to the speaker's fantastic self-portrait in the poem's concluding lines.

Comprehension Check
- Kubla Khan
- war

Think Critically

2. Responses will vary. Some students may describe Xanadu as a paradise where nature is partly tamed and partly wild; others may describe it as a world in which Khan's decree influences society but doesn't change nature or his fate.
3. Responses will vary. Some students may conclude that Coleridge created a mythical, exotic environment in order to explore the mysterious process of creativity or to explore both the beautiful and sinister sides of nature and humanity.
4. Responses will vary. Students citing human effort may argue that the sunny pleasure dome of ice defies the laws of nature; students citing nature may feel that the river, chasm, and caves make a striking setting for the dome.
5. Responses will vary. Some students may say that such a paradise must involve magical, possibly demonic (or dangerous) powers; others will say that someone who experienced such a vision must be mad, or that such a vision is too awe-inspiring for human contemplation.
6. Responses will vary. The best responses will point out that the first part of the poem presents a vision of a paradise, the second provides a sinister and turbulent contrast, and the third pulls together the first two sections with an image of a visionary speaker (or poet) who can overcome the warring elements of nature and human artifice.

Thinking through the LITERATURE

Connect to the Literature

1. **What Do You Think?** What **image** in the poem did you find most striking? Compare your opinion with a classmate's.

Comprehension Check
- Who orders a dome built in Xanadu?
- What do ancestral voices prophesy to Kubla Khan?

Think Critically

2. How would you describe the world of Kubla Khan as it is depicted in this poem?

- the description of the **setting** (lines 1–11)
- the **details** about the chasm (lines 12–16)
- the description of the river (lines 17–28)

3. This poem contains a curious blend of **contrasting images**—images of lush natural beauty and images of sinister, dark mystery. Why do you think the poet used such contradictory images?
4. Which do you think contributes more to the beauty of Kubla Khan's pleasure dome—human effort or nature?
5. Reread lines 37–54. Why would those who heard the speaker's music cry "Beware, beware"?
6. ACTIVE READING ANALYZING STRUCTURE Consult the diagram you created in your READER'S NOTEBOOK. How do the three parts of the poem work together to create a unified whole?

Extend Interpretations

7. **Critic's Corner** Algernon Charles Swinburne, a noted 19th-century English poet and critic, wrote, "In reading it ["Kubla Khan"] we seem rapt into that paradise . . . where music and color and perfume were one, where you could hear the hues and see the harmonies of heaven." Do you agree? Defend your position.
8. **Connect to Life** The world depicted in "Kubla Khan" is strange and exotic, even magical. Think about modern movies, books, and television shows that feature magical or unusual situations. Do you think people are still fascinated by the exotic?

Literary Analysis

ONOMATOPOEIA In its simplest form, **onomatopoeia** is the use of words—such as *crash, groan,* and *boom*—whose sounds suggest their meanings. Onomatopoeia can, however, involve more than the use of such words. Skilled writers, especially poets, choose words whose sounds suggest both their **denotations** and their **connotations.** For example, in this line from "Kubla Khan," the **rhythm** and the repeated *m* and *n* sounds suggest the sound of the lazily winding river that is being described:

Five miles meandering with a mazy motion

Paired Activity With a partner, take turns reading aloud lines 12–24, listening for examples of onomatopoeia. Record your observations, then compare your notes with those of other pairs.

REVIEW ALLITERATION AND RHYME
Find examples of **alliteration**—the repetition of consonant sounds at the beginning of words—in "Kubla Khan." Notice, too, patterns of **rhyme** in the poem. Jot down examples of alliteration, and note the variations you observe in the rhyme. How do these **sound devices** affect your reading of the poem?

Extend Interpretations

Critic's Corner Responses will vary, but students should support their opinions with details from the poem. To make this question easier, have students read the quote and then list details and images from the poem that appeal to the five senses.

Connect to Life Accept all reasonable, well-supported responses. Discuss students' responses as a class. Encourage students to compare and contrast modern exotic movies, books, and TV shows with the poem.

Literary Analysis

Paired Activity Write frequently cited examples of onomatopoeia on the chalkboard.

Review Alliteration and Rhyme Students may say that these devices help carry them forward as they read. Guide students to make a connection between the reading process and the meandering motion of the river.

PREPARING to *Read*

The Rime of the Ancient Mariner

Narrative Poetry by SAMUEL TAYLOR COLERIDGE

*"Alone, alone,
all, all alone, /
Alone on a wide
wide sea!"*

Connect to Your Life

Long Day's Journey Think of the worst trip you ever took. What made the journey so unpleasant? Was it bad traffic, a vehicle breakdown, or something far more dangerous? Whatever it was, how did you feel when you finally reached your destination? Discuss your experience with your classmates.

Build Background

Partners in Rhyme Coleridge and his neighbor William Wordsworth collaborated on the writing of the poems in *Lyrical Ballads.* "It was agreed," Coleridge later wrote, "that my endeavors should be directed to persons and characters supernatural, or at least romantic. . . . Mr. Wordsworth, on the other hand, was to propose to himself as his object, to give the charm of novelty to things of every day." One of the "supernatural" poems that Coleridge created for the book was "The Rime of the Ancient Mariner." According to Wordsworth, "*The Ancient Mariner* was founded on a strange dream, which a friend of Coleridge had, who fancied he saw a skeleton ship, with figures in it. . . . I had very little share in the composition of it." Wordsworth did in fact contribute a few lines to the poem and suggested several details of its plot. The italicized marginal explanations were added by Coleridge in later printings of the poem.

At Sea Before the advent of steamships in the early 19th century, sea voyages were quite dangerous. Traveling at the mercy of winds and currents, sailing ships sometimes took months or even years to reach their destinations. In "The Rime of the Ancient Mariner," an old mariner, or sailor, tells an exciting tale about a perilous voyage in which his ship was blown into waters near the South Pole and then into the Pacific Ocean. To capture the flavor of an earlier era, Coleridge used a number of obsolete words and word forms, such as *stoppeth, swounds,* and *eftsoons.*

Focus Your Reading

LITERARY ANALYSIS LITERARY BALLAD

Originally, a **ballad** was a narrative poem that was intended to be sung. Although traditional **folk ballads** were written by unknown authors and handed down orally, **literary ballads** are the products of writers' conscious efforts to imitate the folk-ballad style. The literary ballad became popular during the romantic period. As you read "The Rime of the Ancient Mariner," listen for its musical qualities.

ACTIVE READING READING NARRATIVE POETRY

Like all ballads, "The Rime of the Ancient Mariner" is a **narrative poem**—a poem that tells a story. It thus contains many of the basic elements of a prose story: **plot, conflict, setting, character, point of view,** and **theme.**

READER'S NOTEBOOK While reading "The Rime of the Ancient Mariner," jot down notes to help you answer the following questions:

- In what **setting** do the events unfold?
- Who are the **characters?**
- From whose **point of view** is the story told?
- How would you summarize the **plot?**
- What are the major **conflicts?**
- What **themes** are central to the poem?

OVERVIEW

An excerpt of this selection is included in the **Grade 12 InterActive Reader.**

Objectives

1. understand and appreciate a **narrative poem (Literary Analysis)**
2. appreciate the author's use of a **literary ballad** to tell a story **(Literary Analysis)**
3. read **narrative poetry** to appreciate and understand "The Rime of the Ancient Mariner" **(Active Reading)**

Summary

An ancient mariner tells a wedding guest the story of his journey at sea. As his ship was drawn by a storm toward the South Pole, an albatross—a sign of hope—visited the crew, but was inexplicably shot by the mariner. As a result, a curse fell on the ship and the mariner was forced to wear the dead albatross around his neck. A skeleton ship appeared, and, upon its vanishing, the mariner's entire crew died and he was left alone. As the mariner watched snakes swimming in the moonlight, he became enchanted by their beauty and blessed them. The albatross fell from his neck, and the ship was helped home by supernatural beings. But, as a penance, the mariner is doomed to spend his days wandering the earth, telling his tale.

Use **Unit Four Resource Book,** p. 12 for additional support.

Thematic Link

Coleridge's narrative poem explores the fragile relationship between human beings and nature as the speaker and the ancient mariner engage in a **search for truth.**

LESSON RESOURCES

UNIT FOUR RESOURCE BOOK, pp. 12–15

ASSESSMENT RESOURCES
Formal Assessment, pp. 137–138
Teacher's Guide to Assessment and Portfolio Use
Test Generator

SKILLS TRANSPARENCIES AND COPYMASTERS
Literary Analysis
- The Moral Tale, Ballad, Fable, and Folk Tale, T23 (for Literary Analysis, p. 745)

Reading and Critical Thinking
- Evaluating Story Elements, T6 (for Active Reading, p. 745)

Grammar
- Essential and Nonessential Adjective Clauses, C115 (for Mini Lesson, pp. 750–751)

Writing
- Compare-Contrast, C34 (for Writing Option 2, p. 767)

Communications
- Appreciative Listening, T2 (for Activities & Explorations 2, p. 767)
- Dramatic Reading, T12 (for Activities & Explorations 1, p. 767)

INTEGRATED TECHNOLOGY
Audio Library
Internet: Research Starter
Visit our website:
www.mcdougallittell.com

5-Minute Warm-Up

Daily Language SkillBuilder

Have students **proofread** the display sentences on page 697j and write them correctly. The sentences also appear on Transparency 20 of **Grammar Transparencies and Copymasters.**

TEACHING THE LITERATURE

Reading and Analyzing

Literary Analysis LITERARY BALLAD

Invite a volunteer to read the first two stanzas of the poem aloud. Ask students to comment on its musical qualities.

Possible Response: Students may mention the *abcb* rhyme scheme, which gives the poem a singsong quality, or the rhythmic quality of the stresses within each line. Ask students to clap out the beat of the stanzas.

 Use **Unit Four Resource Book,** p. 14 for additional support.

Active Reading
READING NARRATIVE POETRY

A Ask students what the mariner's "long grey beard" and "glittering eye" suggest about the main character.

Possible Responses: He is old and wise; he is wizardlike or magical; he is lively, intelligent.

 Use **Unit Four Resource Book,** p. 13 for additional support.

Reading Skills and Strategies:
DRAWING CONCLUSIONS

B Invite students to compare the mariner with the speaker of "Kubla Khan" as he is depicted at the end of the poem.

Possible Response: Both have flashing or glittering eyes; both have hypnotic or supernatural powers.

Based on these two characters, what conclusions can you draw about Coleridge's idea of a poet?

Possible Response: For Coleridge, a poet is a storyteller, a magician, a person of great energy and imagination; a poet also has the power to inspire fear in his audience or to captivate it.

The RIME of the ANCIENT MARINER

Samuel Taylor Coleridge

How a Ship, having first sailed to the Equator, was driven by storms to the cold Country towards the South Pole; how the Ancient Mariner cruelly and in contempt of the laws of hospitality killed a Seabird and how he was followed by many strange Judgments; and in what manner he came back to his own Country.

Engravings by Gustave Doré

Teaching Options

BLOCK SCHEDULING: MANAGING TIME

If your schedule requires that you cover the lesson objectives in a shorter time, use . . .

- Preparing to Read, p. 745
- Thinking Through the Literature, p. 766

If you want to take advantage of longer class time, use . . .

- TE Teaching Options: Vocabulary Strategy, pp. 747, 763; Cross Curricular Links, pp. 748, 749, 756, 757, 762, 764; Grammar, p. 750; Speaking and Listening, pp. 752, 759; Viewing and Representing, pp. 754, 758; Informal Assessment, pp. 755, 765; Standardized Test Practice, p. 760

PART I

It is an ancient Mariner,
And he stoppeth one of three.
"By thy long grey beard and glittering eye,
Now wherefore stopp'st thou me?

The Bridegroom's doors are opened wide,
And I am next of kin;
The guests are met, the feast is set:
May'st hear the merry din."

He holds him with his skinny hand,
"There was a ship," quoth he.
"Hold off! unhand me, grey-beard loon!"
Eftsoons his hand dropped he.

He holds him with his glittering eye—
The Wedding-Guest stood still,
And listens like a three years' child:
The Mariner hath his will.

The Wedding-Guest sat on a stone:
He cannot choose but hear;
And thus spake on that ancient man,
The bright-eyed Mariner.

"The ship was cheered, the harbor cleared,
Merrily did we drop
Below the kirk, below the hill,
Below the lighthouse top.

The Sun came up upon the left,
Out of the sea came he!
And he shone bright, and on the right
Went down into the sea.

Higher and higher every day,
Till over the mast at noon—"
The Wedding-Guest here beat his breast,
For he heard the loud bassoon.

The bride hath paced into the hall,
Red as a rose is she;
Nodding their heads before her goes
The merry minstrelsy.

An ancient Mariner meeteth three Gallants bidden to a wedding feast, and detaineth one.

4 wherefore: why.

12 eftsoons: quickly.

The Wedding Guest is spellbound by the eye of the old seafaring man, and constrained to hear his tale.

23 kirk: church.

The Mariner tells how the ship sailed southward with a good wind and fair weather, till it reached the Line.

30 over . . . noon: The ship has reached the equator, or "Line."

The Wedding Guest heareth the bridal music; but the Mariner continueth his tale.

36 minstrelsy: group of musicians.

Customizing Instruction

Less Proficient Readers

- Encourage students to take note of plot developments as they read.
- Ask students to think about the ancient mariner's credibility as they read. Is he reliable? Why or why not?

Students Acquiring English

Before students begin reading:

- read aloud the summary on page 745 and discuss it with students.
- help students list and define archaic words or word forms.

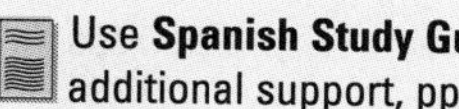

Use **Spanish Study Guide** for additional support, pp. 173–175.

Gifted and Talented

Ask students to consider as they read whether the ancient mariner is an active participant in his fate, a passive one, or both. Then have them discuss this issue in small groups.

Possible Response: Some students may say the mariner commits a crime of his own free will and must therefore suffer the consequences; some may say that he is the victim of unusual or desperate circumstances; others may think the mariner's fate is determined by a combination of choice and circumstance.

Mini Lesson Vocabulary Strategy

ARCHAIC VERB FORMS

Instruction Point out that "The Rime of the Ancient Mariner" contains many archaic verbs and verb forms, such as *spake, bideth,* and *quoth.* Explain that many of these verbs were considered archaic even when Coleridge was writing in the late 18th and early 19th centuries. The verb ending *-eth,* for example, common throughout the Middle English period (1150–1500)—the period during which Chaucer wrote—had been replaced by *-s* by the early 1600s. And verbs with "strong" conjugations, such as *spake,* had for the most part adopted "weak" conjugations *(spoken)* by the same time.

Activity As students read the poem, invite them to note verbs ending in *-th* or *-eth,* as well as verbs with strong conjugations, and to write down their modern equivalents.

Possible Responses: *-th* or *-eth* endings—*stoppeth,* p. 747; *hath,* p. 747 and throughout; *quoth, bideth,* p. 759; *singeth,* p. 762; *doth,* p. 764; *biddeth, loveth,* p. 765; strong conjugations—*spake,* p. 747; *clomb,* p. 752; *smote,* p. 763.

Reading and Analyzing

Literary Analysis:
FIGURATIVE LANGUAGE

A Ask students to identify examples of onomatopoeia and simile in these lines.

Possible Responses: Examples of onomatopoeia are "crack," "growl," "roar," and "howl"; they are compared to noises made by a fainting person; the albatross is welcomed by the crew as if it were a Christian soul.

Literary Analysis: SYMBOL

B Ask students what the albatross might symbolize.

Possible Response: It may represent hope, salvation, good fortune.

Active Reading

READING NARRATIVE POETRY

C Have students summarize the plot developments that occur in Part I.

Possible Response: The ship crosses over the equator and is carried by wind toward the South Pole, where it is surrounded by ice. An albatross appears, the ice splits, and a south wind blows the ship northward. The mariner shoots the albatross.

Ask students what conflicts might arise as a result of the mariner's actions.

Possible Responses: There is the possibility of a conflict between the mariner and crew; an internal conflict between the mariner and his guilty conscience; a conflict between the crew and nature.

The Wedding-Guest he beat his breast,
Yet he cannot choose but hear;
And thus spake on that ancient man,
The bright-eyed Mariner.

"And now the Storm-blast came, and he
Was tyrannous and strong:
He struck with his o'ertaking wings,
And chased us south along.

The ship driven by a storm toward the South Pole.

With sloping masts and dipping prow,
As who pursued with yell and blow
Still treads the shadow of his foe,
And forward bends his head,
The ship drove fast, loud roared the blast,
And southward aye we fled.

And now there came both mist and snow,
And it grew wondrous cold:
And ice, mast-high, came floating by,
As green as emerald.

And through the drifts the snowy clifts
Did send a dismal sheen:
Nor shapes of men nor beasts we ken—
The ice was all between.

The land of ice, and of fearful sounds where no living thing was to be seen.

55 clifts: cliffs.

57 ken: perceive.

The ice was here, the ice was there,
The ice was all around:
A It cracked and growled, and roared and howled,
Like noises in a swound!

62 swound: swoon; fainting fit.

B At length did cross an Albatross,
Thorough the fog it came;
As if it had been a Christian soul,
We hailed it in God's name.

Till a great sea bird, called the Albatross, came through the snow-fog, and was received with great joy and hospitality.

63 Albatross (ăl'bə-trôs'): a large, web-footed ocean bird common in the Southern Hemisphere.

It ate the food it ne'er had eat,
And round and round it flew.
The ice did split with a thunder-fit;
The helmsman steered us through!

1 And a good south wind sprung up behind;
The Albatross did follow,
And every day, for food or play,
Came to the mariners' hollo!

And lo! the Albatross proveth a bird of good omen, and followeth the ship as it returned northward through fog and floating ice.

74 hollo (hă'lō): call.

Teaching Options

Cross Curricular Link Geography

THE SOUTHERN OCEAN The Southern Ocean covers 36 million square kilometers between the Polar Front and the continent of Antarctica. The Polar Front is the point where the cold surface water flowing north from Antarctica meets and sinks below the warm waters flowing south from the tropics. Sailors know when they have reached the Polar Front: conditions become highly unpredictable—often dangerously windy—and waters become very rough. Close to the continent, cold, gravity-driven winds blow down constantly from the icecap. These winds, known as the katabatic winds, can reach speeds unmatched elsewhere in the world, ranging from 80 to 300 kilometers an hour. Sandwiched between these winds and a ring of winds further north lies a region of intense low pressure, which helps to create the stormy conditions typical of the Southern Ocean. The sheer volume of ice also contributes to these hazardous conditions. At its peak in the winter, ice covers as much as 20 million kilometers of the Southern Ocean—57 percent of its total surface.

In mist or cloud, on mast or shroud,
It perched for vespers nine;
Whiles all the night, through fog-smoke white,
Glimmered the white moonshine."

"God save thee, ancient Mariner,
C From the fiends, that plague thee thus!—
Why look'st thou so?"—With my crossbow
2 I shot the Albatross.

75 shroud: one of the ropes that support a ship's mast.

76 vespers nine: nine evenings.

The ancient Mariner inhospitably killeth the pious bird of good omen.

PART II

The Sun now rose upon the right:
Out of the sea came he,
Still hid in mist, and on the left
Went down into the sea.

And the good south wind still blew behind,
But no sweet bird did follow,
Nor any day for food or play
Came to the mariners' hollo!

83 The Sun . . . right: The rising of the sun on the right indicates that the ship is now heading northward.

And I had done a hellish thing,
And it would work'em woe:
For all averred I had killed the bird
3 That made the breeze to blow.
Ah wretch! said they, the bird to slay,
That made the breeze to blow!

His shipmates cry out against the ancient Mariner, for killing the bird of good luck.

93 averred (ə-vûrd'): declared; asserted.

4 Nor dim nor red, like God's own head,
The glorious Sun uprist:
Then all averred I had killed the bird
That brought the fog and mist.
'Twas right, said they, such birds to slay,
That bring the fog and mist.

But when the fog cleared off, they justify the same, and thus make themselves accomplices in the crime.

98 uprist: rose.

The fair breeze blew, the white foam flew,
The furrow followed free;
We were the first that ever burst
Into that silent sea.

The fair breeze continues; the ship enters the Pacific Ocean, and sails northward, even till it reaches the Line.

Down dropped the breeze, the sails dropped down,
'Twas sad as sad could be;
And we did speak only to break
The silence of the sea!
All in a hot and copper sky,

The ship hath been suddenly becalmed.

Customizing Instruction

Multiple Learning Styles

Visual Learners

Have students identify striking visual details in Part I. Invite interested students to include one or more of the details in an illustration of the narrative.

Less Proficient Readers

1 Explain to students that a south wind blows *from* the south, and therefore would propel the ship northward.

2 Have students summarize how the crew reacts to the mariner's shooting of the albatross.

Possible Response: First they accuse him of killing their good luck omen; then they congratulate him for killing the bird "that brought the fog and mist."

Gifted and Talented

3 Ask students what kind of relationship the poem depicts between human beings and nature.

Possible Responses: Human beings regard nature with superstition, reverence, awe, and fear; human beings regard nature as if it were conscious or had divine powers; the actions of human beings can affect or influence nature.

Students Acquiring English

4 Help students paraphrase the inverted clause in lines 97–98.

Possible Response: The sun rose, neither dim nor red—that is, a clear day dawned.

Cross Curricular Link Science

WANDERING ALBATROSS The wandering albatross, native to the Antarctic, is the largest seabird in the world, weighing from 7.7–9.5 kilograms. The albatross is remarkably docile—a young bird will often allow itself to be stroked and handled by human beings. Because albatrosses spend most of their lives at sea, they are clumsy on land; their legs are too far to the rear to provide the central balance needed for walking. Their wingspan, at about 3.5 meters, allows them to soar effortlessly and at high speeds; modern satellite tracking has shown that the albatross can reach 88 kilometers per hour and can fly at an average of 30 kilometers an hour for days at a time. It can even circumnavigate the globe many times during its life, although it prefers to remain in the Southern Hemisphere, where huge expanses of ocean provide enough wind to facilitate the albatross's method of flight. Wandering albatrosses are also known for forming lifelong partnerships with their mates and for their heroic devotion to their young.

Reading and Analyzing

Literary Analysis LITERARY BALLAD

A Ask students to identify examples of repetition in these three stanzas and to explain how the repetition contributes to the mood of the scene.
Possible Response: The repetition of "painted" and "water" emphasizes the monotony and endlessness of the seascape; the repetition of "slimy" emphasizes the horror and the texture of an ocean teeming with creatures.

Literary Analysis: SYMBOL

B Ask students what the albatross now symbolizes.
Possible Responses: It represents guilt, death, and hopelessness.

Reading Skills and Strategies: SUMMARIZING

Have students summarize the events on pages 750 and 751 by summarizing main ideas and supporting details.
Possible Response: The ship is stuck without a breeze at the equator. Parched and angry, the crew hangs the albatross around the mariner's neck as a sign of his guilt. Finally, the mariner spots something on the horizon. As the sun sets, the shape nears.

Reading Skills and Strategies: PREDICTING

Ask students to predict the nature of the approaching vessel, basing their predictions on details in the poem.
Possible Responses: Most students will find the vessel ominous or foreboding because it "plung[es], tack[s], and veer[s]"; because it sails without the wind; because it approaches at sunset; and because it seems to imprison the sun.

1 The bloody Sun, at noon,
Right up above the mast did stand,
No bigger than the Moon.

Day after day, day after day,
We stuck, nor breath nor motion;
As idle as a painted ship
Upon a painted ocean.

Water, water, everywhere,
A And all the boards did shrink;
Water, water, everywhere
Nor any drop to drink.

And the Albatross begins to be avenged.

The very deep did rot: O Christ!
That ever this should be!
Yea, slimy things did crawl with legs
Upon the slimy sea.

About, about, in reel and rout
The death-fires danced at night;
The water, like a witch's oils,
Burnt green, and blue, and white.

127 in reel and rout: with dizzying, unpredictable motion.

128 death-fires: dim flamelike lights reportedly seen above decomposing matter.

And some in dreams assuréd were
Of the Spirit that plagued us so;
Nine fathom deep he had followed us
From the land of mist and snow.

A Spirit had followed them; one of the invisible inhabitants of this planet, neither departed souls nor angels; concerning whom the learned Jew, Josephus, and the Platonic Constantinopolitan, Michael Psellus, may be consulted. They are very numerous, and there is no climate or element without one or more.

133 nine fathom: 54 feet.

And every tongue, through utter drought,
Was withered at the root;
We could not speak, no more than if
We had been choked with soot.

Ah! well a-day! what evil looks
Had I from old and young!
B Instead of the cross, the Albatross
2 About my neck was hung.

The shipmates, in their sore distress, would fain throw the whole guilt on the ancient Mariner: in sign whereof they hang the dead sea bird round his neck.

750

Teaching Options

Grammar

ESSENTIAL AND NONESSENTIAL ADJECTIVE CLAUSES

Instruction An adjective clause is a subordinate clause that is used as an adjective to modify a noun or a pronoun. Adjective clauses may be essential or nonessential. An essential clause is necessary to complete the meaning of a sentence. It is not set off by commas. A nonessential clause, which is set off by commas, adds extra information to a sentence, but is not necessary to the meaning of the sentence. The word *that* usually introduces an essential clause, while *which* often introduces a nonessential clause.

Activity Write the following excerpt from "The Rime of the Ancient Mariner" on the chalkboard or show a transparency.

"Then all averred I had killed the bird
That brought the fog and mist."

Ask students to identify the adjective clause and the noun or pronoun that it modifies. *(That brought the fog and mist; bird)* Ask them whether the clause is essential or nonessential and why. *(essential; without the clause, the sentence would lose important information telling that the sailors now believe the bird brought the fog and mist.)*

PART III

There passed a weary time. Each throat
Was parched, and glazed each eye.
A weary time! a weary time!
How glazed each weary eye!
When, looking westward, I beheld
A something in the sky.

The ancient Mariner beholdeth a sign in the element afar off.

At first it seemed a little speck,
And then it seemed a mist;
It moved and moved, and took at last
A certain shape, I wist.

152 wist: perceived; discerned.

A speck, a mist, a shape, I wist!
And still it neared and neared:
As if it dodged a water-sprite,
It plunged, and tacked and veered.

155 water sprite: a mythical being living in water.

156 tacked and veered: zigzagged.

At its nearer approach, it seemeth him to be a ship; and at a dear ransom he freeth his speech from the bonds of thirst.

With throats unslaked, with black lips baked,
We could nor laugh nor wail;
Through utter drought all dumb we stood!
I bit my arm, I sucked the blood,
And cried, A sail! a sail!

With throats unslaked, with black lips baked,
Agape they heard me call:
Gramercy! they for joy did grin,
And all at once their breath drew in,
As they were drinking all.

A flash of joy;

164 gramercy (grə-mûr'sē): an exclamation of gratitude.

See! see! (I cried) she tacks no more!
Hither to work us weal—
Without a breeze, without a tide,
3 She steadies with upright keel!

And horror follows. For can it be a ship that comes onward without wind or tide?

168 hither to work us weal: in this direction to help us.

The western wave was all aflame,
The day was wellnigh done!
Almost upon the western wave
Rested the broad, bright Sun;
When that strange shape drove suddenly
4 Betwixt us and the Sun.

171 The western wave was all aflame: that is, the water to the west was reflecting the light of the setting sun.

5 And straight the Sun was flecked with bars
(Heaven's Mother send us grace!),
As if through a dungeon-grate he peered
6 With broad and burning face.

It seemeth him but the skeleton of a ship.

178 Heaven's Mother: the Virgin Mary.

Customizing Instruction

Less Proficient Readers

1 Ask students where the ship must be if at noon the sun is standing directly overhead.
Answer: The ship is at the equator.

2 Ask students why the albatross is hung around the mariner's neck.
Possible Responses: It is a sign of his guilt; the crew wants to punish him for bringing bad luck.

3 What is the crew's reaction to the approaching ship?
Answer: First they rejoice, and then they become fearful because the ship is sailing without the help of any wind.

Set a Purpose Have students read to find out if the approaching ship is friend or foe.

Students Acquiring English

4 Explain that the word *betwixt* means "between."

5 Help students by paraphrasing the imagery in this stanza.
Possible Response: When the oncoming ship passes in front of the setting sun, the sun appears to be imprisoned behind the bars of a dungeon, or jail.

Multiple Learning Styles

Visual Learners

6 Invite students to make a series of three sketches of the approaching vessel: one based on the second and third stanzas in Part III, one based on the fourth through the sixth stanzas, and one based on the seventh and eighth stanzas. Encourage students to use color and shading to show corresponding changes in mood.

Exercise Ask students to underline each adjective clause, identify the noun or pronoun the clause modifies, and tell whether the clause is essential or nonessential. Have students work in cooperative groups to explain why each clause is essential or nonessential to the meaning of the sentence.

1. Samuel Taylor Coleridge and William Wordsworth collaborated on a book titled *Lyrical Ballads,* which contained "The Rime of the Ancient Mariner." *(book, nonessential)*
2. The fact that the mariner killed the albatross had a great effect on the voyage. *(fact, essential)*
3. Nineteenth-century sailing ships, which were at the mercy of winds and currents, often remained at sea for months or years. *(ships, nonessential)*
4. It was love for other creatures, the colorful water-snakes, that finally released the mariner from the albatross. *(love, essential)*
5. Part of the mariner's penance, which continued throughout his life, was to tell his tale to those who needed to hear it. *(penance, nonessential)*

Use **Grammar Transparencies and Copymasters,** p. 107.

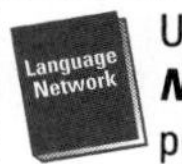

Use McDougal Littell's ***Language Network*** for more instruction and practice in adjective clauses.

THE RIME OF THE ANCIENT MARINER 751

Reading and Analyzing

Literary Analysis: ALLEGORY

A Explain that an allegory is a literary work or an element of a literary work that has both a literal and a symbolic meaning. Have students identify the allegorical character in lines 190–194.
Answer: Life-in-Death.
What does this character do, literally?
Answer: She gambles, apparently for the life of one of the crewmen.

Ask students to predict whose life she has won.
Possible Response: She has won the mariner's life, since we know that he is still alive.

Then ask what the symbolic meaning of Life-in-Death's victory might be.
Possible Responses: The mariner is doomed to live out a deathly life; the mariner is doomed never fully to live or to die.

Literary Analysis LITERARY BALLAD

Remind students that a ballad often focuses on a single event of importance. Ask what important event this ballad is centered around.
Answer: The event is the mariner's shooting of the albatross.

B What does the simile in this stanza compare?
Answer: It compares the flight of the crewmen's souls from their bodies and the flight of the arrow that killed the albatross.

Literary Analysis: SIMILE

C Discuss with students that in romantic poetry, the speaker often strongly identifies with nature or sees himself in nature. Ask what is compared in the simile in lines 226–227.
Answer: The mariner is compared to the ribbed sea-sand.

Alas! (thought I, and my heart beat loud)
How fast she nears and nears!
Are those her sails that glance in the Sun,
Like restless gossameres?

And its ribs are seen as bars on the face of the setting Sun.

184 gossameres (gŏs′ə-mērz′): cobwebs floating in the air.

Are those her ribs through which the Sun
Did peer, as through a grate?
And is that Woman all her crew
Is that a Death? and are there two?
Is Death that Woman's mate?

The Specter-Woman and her Deathmate, and no other on board the skeleton ship.

A

Her lips were red, her looks were free,
Her locks were yellow as gold:
Her skin was as white as leprosy,
The Nightmare Life-in-Death was she,
Who thicks man's blood with cold.

Like vessel, like crew!

192 leprosy (lĕp′rə-sē): a disease marked by spreading patches of discoloration on the skin and by deformities of the limbs and other parts of the body.

The naked hulk alongside came,
And the twain were casting dice;
"The game is done! I've won! I've won!"
Quoth she, and whistles thrice.

Death and Life-in-Death have diced for the ship's crew, and she (the latter) winneth the ancient Mariner.

The Sun's rim dips; the stars rush out:
At one stride comes the dark;
With far-heard whisper, o'er the sea,
1 Off shot the spectre-bark.

No twilight within the courts of the Sun.

202 specter bark: ghost ship.

We listened and looked sideways up!
Fear at my heart, as at a cup,
My life-blood seemed to sip!
The stars were dim, and thick the night,
The steersman's face by his lamp gleamed white;
From the sails the dew did drip—
Till clomb above the eastern bar
The hornéd Moon, with one bright star
Within the nether tip.

At the rising of the Moon,

209 clomb (klōm): climbed.

210 hornéd Moon: crescent moon.

One after one, by the star-dogged Moon,
Too quick for groan or sigh,
Each turned his face with a ghastly pang,
And cursed me with his eye.

One after another,

Four times fifty living men
(And I heard nor sigh nor groan),
With heavy thump, a lifeless lump,
They dropped down one by one.

His shipmates drop down dead.

Teaching Options

Mini Lesson: Speaking and Listening

INTERVIEW

Instruction Explain that an interview is an effective way to get information and to learn about someone's expertise or point of view. Tell students that they are likely to either interview or be interviewed by somebody at some point in their adult lives. Use the following as criteria for evaluating the interviews.

Interviewer:
- Prepare your questions ahead of time.
- Tape-record the interview, if possible, but obtain the interviewee's permission before doing so.
- Ask questions that require explanation or elaboration, rather than "yes-or-no" questions.
- Be prepared to revise questions or follow the interviewee's line of thinking if it is interesting or relevant.
- Be prepared to redirect the conversation if it goes astray.
- Be polite and agreeable. Thank the interviewee for his or her time when the interview is over.

Interviewee:
- Be positive, honest, and responsive.
- If you are asked a question you do not wish to

[B] The souls did from their bodies fly—
They fled to bliss or woe!
And every soul, it passed me by
[2] Like the whizz of my crossbow!

But Life-in-Death begins her work on the ancient Mariner.

PART IV

[3] "I fear thee, ancient Mariner!
I fear thy skinny hand!
[C] And thou art long, and lank, and brown,
As is the ribbed sea-sand.

The Wedding Guest feareth that a Spirit is talking to him;

I fear thee and thy glittering eye,
And thy skinny hand so brown."—
'Fear not, fear not, thou Wedding-Guest!
This body dropped not down.

But the ancient Mariner assureth him of his bodily life, and proceedeth to relate his horrible penance.

Alone, alone, all, all alone
Alone on a wide, wide sea!
And never a saint took pity on
My soul in agony.

The many men, so beautiful!
And they all dead did lie:
And a thousand thousand slimy things
Lived on; and so did I.

He despiseth the creatures of the calm,

I looked upon the rotting sea,
And drew my eyes away;
I looked upon the rotting deck,
And there the dead men lay.

And envieth that they should live, and so many lie dead.

I looked to heaven, and tried to pray;
But or ever a prayer had gushed,
A wicked whisper came, and made
My heart as dry as dust.

I closed my lids, and kept them close,
And the balls like pulses beat;
But the sky and the sea, and the sea and the sky,
Lay like a load on my weary eye,
And the dead were at my feet.

249 balls: eyeballs.

The cold sweat melted from their limbs,
Nor rot nor reek did they:

But the curse liveth for him in the eye of the dead men.

Customizing Instruction

Students Acquiring English

Explain to students the meanings of the following word, phrases, and sentences.

- "thicks man's blood with cold" (line 194)—when a person is frozen with fear or terror, his or her blood is said to run cold.
- "twain" (line 196)—two
- "Fear at my heart, as at a cup, / My life-blood seemed to sip!" (lines 204–205)—My blood seemed to sip fear from my heart, as if it were a cup.
- "nether tip" (line 211)—the lower tip of the crescent moon.

Less Proficient Readers

[1] Ask students what happened to the skeleton ship after Death and Life-in-Death finished their game.

Answer: It shot away.

[2] Have students summarize Part III.

Possible Response: A ship approaches, bearing Death and Life-in-Death. They gamble and Life-in-Death wins. The ship sails away, and soon the mariner's shipmates begin to die. All die except for the mariner himself.

[3] Ask students why the Wedding Guest fears the mariner.

Possible Response: He thinks that the mariner died, too, and so must now be a ghost.

answer, say so politely and simply. Don't become antagonistic.

- Pause for a second or two before you begin responding, to gather your thoughts.
- Answers should be appropriate to the questions asked; avoid tangents.
- Be aware of your interviewer's time limits, if there are any.
- Thank the interviewer when the interview is over.

Prepare Have students role-play interviews with either the Wedding Guest or the Ancient Mariner. Invite students to define the interview situation before they plan the interview. For example, the interview might be for a TV news report, a talk show, a job interview, or a video recording of the wedding.

Present Have students perform their interviews for the class. Encourage students to break one or two of the interview rules, and challenge audience members to analyze the interview and identify which rules were broken and which were followed.

BLOCK SCHEDULING This activity is particularly well suited for longer class periods.

THE RIME OF THE ANCIENT MARINER 753

Reading and Analyzing

Literary Analysis: IMAGE

A Invite students to identify images that appeal to the senses in these three stanzas. Which senses do they appeal to?

Possible Responses: "hoar-frost," touch; "ship's huge shadow," sight; "water burnt alway / A still and awful red," touch and sight; "tracks of shining white . . . the elfish light," sight; "blue, glossy green, and velvet black," sight and touch; "a flash of golden fire," sight.

Ask students to what sense the poem seems most to appeal.

Answer: sight.

Then ask in what more general way the poem is about vision.

Possible Response: Because the story is told from the mariner's point of view, the poet presents the mariner's subjective impressions of the events he describes.

Literary Analysis: SYMBOL

B Ask students what they think the water-snakes symbolize.

Possible Responses: life; the natural world; energy.

Active Reading

READING NARRATIVE POETRY

C Ask students to explain the relationship (1) between the events in these two stanzas and (2) between these events and earlier significant events in the story.

Possible Response: By blessing the snakes, the mariner shows a respect for living creatures that he failed to show when shooting the albatross; he therefore redeems himself and relieves himself of his guilt—symbolically, the albatross.

The look with which they looked on me
Had never passed away.

An orphan's curse would drag to hell
A spirit from on high;
But oh! more horrible than that
1 Is the curse in a dead man's eye!
Seven days, seven nights, I saw that curse,
2 And yet I could not die.

The moving Moon went up the sky,
And nowhere did abide;

Teaching Options

Cross Curricular Link Art

J. M. W. TURNER Joseph Mallord William Turner (1775–1851) was one of the foremost painters of the romantic era, and in many ways his visual artworks parallel Coleridge's poetic ones. Like other romantic artists who combined imagination with nature and science, Turner focused on the elements and forces of nature rather than its forms. He experimented with light and color to depict a wide range of natural subjects, including water, fire, steam, storms, and floods. (See the Turner painting on page 776.) Although he was criticized by William Hazlitt for indulging in "too much abstraction of aerial perspective" and in "representations not properly of the objects of nature as of the medium through which they were seen," he was also regarded as "the ablest landscape painter now living." Like Coleridge and Shelley, Turner was greatly influenced by Joseph Priestley's *History and Present State of Discoveries Relating to Vision, Light, and Colours* (1772). Turner's most famous works include *Calais Pier, Burial at Sea, and Rain, Steam,* and *Speed,* the last of which he researched by putting his head out the window of a speeding train.

Softly she was going up,
And a star or two beside—

In his loneliness and fixedness he yearneth towards the journeying Moon, and the stars that still sojourn, yet still move onward; and everywhere the blue sky belongs to them, and is their appointed rest, and their native country and their own natural homes, which they enter unannounced, as lords that are certainly expected and yet there is a silent joy at their arrival.

Her beams bemocked the sultry main,
Like April hoar-frost spread;
But where the ship's huge shadow lay,
The charméd water burnt alway
A still and awful red.

267 bemocked . . . main: scornfully defied the hot ocean (because the moon's pale light made the sea appear cool).

By the light of the Moon he beholdeth God's creatures of the great calm.

Beyond the shadow of the ship,
I watched the water-snakes:
They moved in tracks of shining white,
And when they reared, the elfish light
Fell off in hoary flakes.

Within the shadow of the ship
I watched their rich attire:
Blue, glossy green, and velvet black,
They coiled and swam; and every track
Was a flash of golden fire.

268 hoar-frost: frozen dew.

276 fell off in hoary flakes: that is, glittered on water droplets falling from the snakes.

Their beauty and their happiness.

O happy living things! no tongue
Their beauty might declare:
A spring of love gushed from my heart,
And I blessed them unaware:
Sure my kind saint took pity on me,
And I blessed them unaware.

He blesseth them in his heart.

The spell begins to break.

The selfsame moment I could pray;
And from my neck so free
The Albatross fell off, and sank
Like lead into the sea.

PART V

O sleep! it is a gentle thing,
Beloved from pole to pole!
To Mary Queen the praise be given!
She sent the gentle sleep from Heaven,
That slid into my soul.

294 Mary Queen: the Virgin Mary.

By grace of the holy Mother, the ancient Mariner is refreshed with rain.

The silly buckets on the deck,
That had so long remained,
I dreamt that they were filled with dew;
And when I awoke, it rained.

Customizing Instruction

Less Proficient Readers

Use these questions to check students' comprehension of the narrative.

1 Under what curse does the mariner suffer?
Answer: the continuous gaze of the dead men upon him.

2 How long does the mariner suffer from this curse?
Answer: It lasts seven days and nights.

3 Why do you think the mariner finds the water-snakes so beautiful?
Possible Response: They are alive and full of motion and light, while he is surrounded by darkness, stillness, and dead men.

Multiple Learning Styles

Visual Learners

Some students may enjoy creating a mobile to illustrate the water-snakes moving on and in the water.

Students Acquiring English

4 Read aloud the following paraphrase to help students understand the sequence of events in these stanzas. Then have them read the stanzas silently.

Paraphrase: Oh happy living things. I could not speak of their beauty, but instead a feeling of love came forth from my heart. It blessed the water-snakes without my knowledge. My kind saint felt sorry for me, and I blessed the snakes without knowing. In that moment, when I prayed, the albatross fell off and sank into the sea.

Assessment

Informal Assessment

WRITE A CONCLUSION You can informally assess students' understanding of events by having them write an introductory summary paragraph of Parts I–IV, and then write an original narrative telling what might happen next. Encourage students to write in verse, if they wish.

RUBRIC

3 Full Accomplishment Student's summary reflects full understanding of events in Parts I–IV; student's original narrative follows logically from earlier events in story.

2 Substantial Accomplishment Student's summary shows general understanding of events in Parts I–IV, but original narrative may not relate to earlier events in meaningful way.

1 Little or Partial Accomplishment Student writing displays little understanding of events in Parts I–IV and does not advance or conclude story in meaningful way.

Reading and Analyzing

Active Reading

READING NARRATIVE POETRY

Explain that literary ballads often contain supernatural events and/or characters. Ask what supernatural events occur on pages 756–757.

Answer: The dead men rise up and begin to sail the ship; later, they sing a beautiful song.

What symbolic meaning might these events have?

Possible Response: The dead men, or the spirits that inhabit their bodies, seem to have forgiven the mariner.

Reading Skills and Strategies: ANALYZING

A Ask students how the meaning of these lines is ambiguous.

Possible Response: The line is ambiguous because it suggests two contrasting meanings: that it would have been strange to see the dead men rise, even in a dream; and that it was strange, even in the dream he was having, to see the dead men rise.

Ask how this ambiguity affects the mood of the poem *or* the credibility of the speaker.

Possible Responses: The ambiguity gives the poem a dreamlike, surreal mood or quality; the ambiguity undercuts the speaker's reliability because it suggests that he is, at best, in a half-dream state, and at worst delusional.

My lips were wet, my throat was cold.
My garments all were dank;
Sure I had drunken in my dreams,
And still my body drank.

I moved, and could not feel my limbs:
I was so light—almost
I thought that I had died in sleep,
And was a blesséd ghost.

And soon I heard a roaring wind:
It did not come anear;
But with its sound it shook the sails,
That were so thin and sere.

He heareth sounds and seeth strange sights and commotions in the sky and the element.

312 sere (sîr): dry.

The upper air burst into life;
And a hundred fire-flags sheen;
To and fro they were hurried about!
And to and fro, and in and out,
The wan stars danced between.

314 fire-flags: probably the aurora australis or southern lights—wavering bands of light in the night sky caused by solar particles entering the earth's magnetic field; **sheen:** bright.

317 wan: pale.

And the coming wind did roar more loud,
And the sails did sigh like sedge;
And the rain poured down from one black cloud;
The Moon was at its edge.

319 sedge: tall grasslike plants that make a rustling sound when blown by the wind.

The thick black cloud was cleft, and still
The Moon was at its side;
Like waters shot from some high crag,
The lightning fell with never a jag,
A river steep and wide.

The loud wind never reached the ship,
Yet now the ship moved on!
Beneath the lightning and the Moon
The dead men gave a groan.

The bodies of the ship's crew are inspirited, and the ship moves on;

They groaned, they stirred, they all uprose,
Nor spake, nor moved their eyes;
It had been strange, even in a dream,
A To have seen those dead men rise.

The helmsman steered, the ship moved on;
Yet never a breeze up-blew;

756

Teaching Options

Cross Curricular Link Science

THE SOUTHERN LIGHTS The deep darkness of an Antarctic winter is sometimes shattered by a spectacle that stopped early explorers in their tracks. When the southern lights, or *aurora australis*, appear, the entire dome of the sky is lit from horizon to horizon with waves of ghostly lights—green, red, orange, and violet. The lights can take many forms, including curtains, arches, bands, and patches. As in rainbows, the lower parts of the arcs and bands are usually more sharply defined than the upper parts. Often the arcs are edged underneath with a red border that may ripple like a curtain—perhaps the "fire-flags" beheld by the mariner. The lights are actually a collection of electrical storms, sparked by charged solar particles (electrons and protons) that enter Earth's atmosphere and interact with its magnetic field. In the pitch black of the winter sky, the southern lights can be brighter than the moon and can last for many hours, often ending as abruptly as they began.

The mariners all 'gan work the ropes,
Where they were wont to do;
They raised their limbs like lifeless tools—
We were a ghastly crew.

The body of my brother's son
Stood by me, knee to knee:
The body and I pulled at one rope,
But he said naught to me.

"I fear thee, ancient Mariner!"
'Be calm, thou Wedding-Guest:
'Twas not those souls that fled in pain,
Which to their corses came again,
2 But a troop of spirits blest:

For when it dawned—they dropped their arms,
And clustered round the mast;
Sweet sounds rose slowly through their mouths,
And from their bodies passed.

Around, around, flew each sweet sound,
Then darted to the Sun;
Slowly the sounds came back again,
Now mixed, now one by one.

Sometimes a-dropping from the sky
I heard the skylark sing;
Sometimes all little birds that are,
How they seemed to fill the sea and air
With their sweet jargoning!

And now 'twas like all instruments,
Now like a lonely flute;
And now it is an angel's song,
That makes the Heavens be mute.

It ceased; yet still the sails made on
A pleasant noise till noon,
A noise like of a hidden brook
In the leafy month of June,
That to the sleeping woods all night
Singeth a quiet tune.

Till noon we quietly sailed on,
Yet never a breeze did breathe:

338 wont: accustomed.

But not by the souls of the men, nor by demons of earth or middle air, but by a blessed troop of angelic spirits, sent down by the invocation of the guardian saint.

348 corses: bodies.

362 jargoning: warbling.

Customizing Instruction

Less Proficient Readers

What good things happen to the mariner on these pages?

Answer: It rains and he is relieved of his thirst; the ship begins to move; the dead men rise up and sail the ship; the dead men sing beautiful songs.

1 What forces have caused the dead men to rise?

Answer: Good spirits have entered the men's bodies.

Students Acquiring English

Define the following words and phrases for students.

- *dank* (line 302)—chilly and wet
- *to and fro* (line 315)—forwards and backwards
- *cleft* (line 322)—split in two
- *crag* (line 324)—a projecting rock or cliff
- *spake* (line 332)—spoke
- *'gan* (line 337)—began to
- *naught* (line 344)—nothing

Gifted and Talented

Challenge students to locate details that relate to a landscape.

Possible Responses: Students may cite the following words and phrases: *sedge, crag, river, skylarks and other birds, a hidden brook, leaves in the month of June, the sleeping woods.*

Ask why the poet may have included such details at this point in the narrative.

Possible Responses: The mariner has been delivered from the horrors of the sea; he is now moving homeward or landward.

Philosophy

COLERIDGE AND THE GERMAN PHILOSOPHERS

Shortly after Coleridge wrote "Kubla Khan" and "The Rime of the Ancient Mariner," he traveled to Germany, where he spent ten months studying the works of Immanuel Kant and other philosophers who had made significant contributions to an intellectual movement known as *naturphilosophie.* In contrast to the speculative, rationalistic sciences of the 18th century, these philosophers did not believe that nature was totally separate from the human mind. Rather, they argued, what the mind perceives as "objective reality," or the external world, is created in part by the imagination—the function of the mind in which sensory perceptions are processed and given meaning. Kant divided the external world into *phenomena,* or appearances, and *noumena,* the causes of these appearances. He argued that all noumena lie outside the human realm of perception and reason. Where reason breaks down, Kant posited, faith must pick up. Coleridge's later critical writings were heavily influenced by German thinkers.

Reading and Analyzing

Literary Analysis LITERARY BALLAD

Have students identify examples of repetition on these pages. Discuss the effect of each repetition on the poem's mood or tone.

Possible Responses: Lines 378 and 403—"the land of mist and snow"—give the story a timeless, fairy-tale quality; lines 386 and 388—"With a short uneasy motion"—bring to life the redundant, rocking motion of the ship and help build suspense before the ship leaps forward.

Literary Analysis: SIMILE

(A) Have students identify the comparison in lines 389–390.

Answer: The ship is compared to a pawing horse who suddenly charges. What qualities not usually associated with a ship does this metaphor provide?

Possible Response: It makes the ship seem alive as if it were eager, restless, or unpredictable.

Active Reading

READING NARRATIVE POETRY

(B) Point out that, like many prose narratives, this narrative poem contains dialogue. Remind students that dialogue can convey information about characters or plot. Then ask what information is revealed in the dialogue between the two voices.

Possible Response: We learn that, in killing the albatross, the mariner has offended the spirit of the South Pole, and that this spirit seeks vengeance on the mariner. We also learn that the ocean itself, or some other nonhuman force, is controlling the ship's speed.

Slowly and smoothly went the ship,
Moved onward from beneath.

Under the keel nine fathom deep,
From the land of mist and snow,
The Spirit slid: and it was he
That made the ship to go.
The sails at noon left off their tune,
And the ship stood still also.

The lonesome Spirit from the South Pole carries on the ship as far as the Line, in obedience to the angelic troop, but still requireth vengeance.

The Sun, right up above the mast,
Had fixed her to the ocean:
But in a minute she 'gan stir,
With a short uneasy motion—

Teaching Options

Viewing and Representing

Illustration **by Gustave Doré**

ART APPRECIATION Ask how the artist's use of line and perspective reflects the mariner's experience or point of view.

Possible Response: The tangled lines and the skewed perspective help re-create the mariner's disorientation and captivity.

Instruction Discuss with students that many poems and other literary works lend themselves to representation in media such as art, film, and video. In these works, visual elements sometimes serve to underscore elements of the literary selections on which they are based. For example, as students look at the engraving on this page, discuss the energetic profusion of diagonal and curved lines. Elicit that these lines create a skewed, unbalanced perspective, which perhaps reflects the mariner's point of view.

Application Tell students that line can also help to support the literary element of mood. Ask them to describe the mood the engraving depicts.

Possible Response: Students may say that the lines create a confused or frightening mood.

Backwards and forwards half her length
With a short uneasy motion.

Then like a pawing horse let go,
She made a sudden bound:
It flung the blood into my head,
And I fell down in a swound.

How long in that same fit I lay,
I have not to declare;
But ere my living life returned,
I heard, and in my soul discerned
Two voices in the air.

394 have not: am not able.

The Polar Spirit's fellow demons, the invisible inhabitants of the element, take part in his wrong; and two of them relate, one to the other, that penance long and heavy for the ancient Mariner hath been accorded to the Polar Spirit, who returneth southward.

"Is it he?" quoth one, "is this the man?
By Him who died on cross,
With his cruel bow he laid full low
The harmless Albatross.

399 him who died on cross: Jesus Christ.

1 The Spirit who bideth by himself
In the land of mist and snow,
2 He loved the bird that loved the man
Who shot him with his bow."

The other was a softer voice,
As soft as honey-dew:
Quoth he, "The man hath penance done,
3 And penance more will do."

408 penance (pĕn′əns): suffering in repayment for a sin.

PART VI

First Voice:
"But tell me, tell me! speak again,
4 Thy soft response renewing—
What makes that ship drive on so fast?
What is the Ocean doing?"

Second Voice:
"Still as a slave before his lord,
The Ocean hath no blast;
5 His great bright eye most silently
Up to the Moon is cast—

If he may know which way to go;
For she guides him smooth or grim.

Customizing Instruction

Students Acquiring English

1 Tell students that *bideth* means "lives."

2 Help students paraphrase lines 404–405.

Possible Response: The albatross loved the mariner, and the Spirit loved the albatross.

Less Proficient Readers

3 Ask students who has given the mariner this penance, and why.

Answer: The Polar Spirit gives the penance because he seeks revenge on the mariner for killing the harmless albatross, whom the Spirit loved.

Multiple Learning Styles

Auditory Learners

4 Invite a pair of students to read aloud lines 410–429, each student taking a different part. After they read, have students summarize the exchange.

Gifted and Talented

5 Ask students what the "great bright eye" of the ocean is.

Answer: It's the reflection of the moon on the ocean's surface.

Then ask students what Coleridge might be saying about the relationship between the human eye, or eyesight, and nature.

Possible Responses: The human eye reflects nature itself; we see ourselves reflected in nature; human eyesight could not exist without nature; humanity and nature are dependent on one another.

Speaking and Listening

CHORAL READING

Instruction Remind students that choral reading is a group recital of a poem, verse, or other writing. Discuss with students the various forms choral reading can take. For example, two groups—high voices and low voices—might alternate lines, verses, or parts; or one group might echo another group at certain points for emphasis.

Prepare Divide students into groups of seven or nine, and invite each group to plan, practice, and perform a choral reading of lines 393–437. Encourage groups to assign one person the part of the mariner (lines 393–397 and 430–437), while the other students take the parts of the First Voice and Second Voice.

Present Remind students to work through the passage, identifying the stresses and beats of each line, and then to coordinate the rhythm and pitch of their delivery. After each choral reading, have audience members comment on the artistic elements within the text and strengths of the performance.

BLOCK SCHEDULING This activity is particularly well suited for longer class periods.

Reading and Analyzing

Literary Analysis: SIMILE

A Have students paraphrase the extended simile in lines 444–451.

Possible Response: As he looks out over the unfamiliar ocean, the mariner feels as if he is walking on a deserted road; sensing that he is being followed, he turns around once and sees nothing, but he doesn't dare turn around again.

Literary Analysis: IMAGE

Ask students to identify images on page 761 that appeal to the senses and then to name the particular sense to which each appeals.

Possible Responses: "It raised my hair, it fanned my cheek," touch; "Sweetly, sweetly, blew the breeze," touch; "I with sobs did pray," hearing; "The harbor-bay was clear as glass," sight; "So smoothly was it strewn," touch; "And on the bay . . . the shadow of the Moon," sight; "The rock shone bright," sight; "moonlight steeped in silentness," hearing; "the bay was white with silent light . . . crimson colors came," hearing and sight.)

See, brother, see! how graciously
She looketh down on him."

First Voice:
"But why drives on that ship so fast,
Without or wave or wind?"

The Mariner hath been cast into a trance; for the angelic power causeth the vessel to drive northward faster than human life could endure.

Second Voice:
"The air is cut away before,
And closes from behind.

Fly, brother, fly! more high, more high!
Or we shall be belated:
For slow and slow that ship will go,
When the Mariner's trance is abated."

I woke, and we were sailing on
As in a gentle weather:
'Twas night, calm night, the Moon was high;
The dead men stood together.

The supernatural motion is retarded; the Mariner awakes, and his penance begins anew.

All stood together on the deck,
For a charnel-dungeon fitter:
All fixed on me their stony eyes,
That in the Moon did glitter.

435 for . . . fitter: more suitable for a burial vault.

The pang, the curse, with which they died,
Had never passed away:
I could not draw my eyes from theirs,
Nor turn them up to pray.

And now this spell was snapped: once more
I viewed the ocean green,
And looked far forth, yet little saw
1 Of what had else been seen—

The curse is finally expiated.

A
Like one that on a lonesome road
Doth walk in fear and dread,
And having once turned round, walks on,
And turns no more his head;
Because he knows a frightful fiend
Doth close behind him tread.

450 fiend: demon.

But soon there breathed a wind on me,
Nor sound nor motion made:

Teaching Options

Assessment Standardized Test Practice

ANALYZING THE RELATIONSHIP AMONG IDEAS For some standardized tests, students will be asked to analyze the relationship among ideas in a piece of writing. One kind of relationship students may encounter is sequence of events. Read aloud or write on the chalkboard the following question. Which of the following lists of events that occur in "The Ancient Mariner" is in the proper chronological sequence?

A. The mariner shoots the albatross; the ship sails into the South Sea; the crewmen die; the mariner wears the albatross around his neck; the mariner blesses the sea creatures; the ship sails homeward.

B. The ship sails into the South Sea; the mariner shoots the albatross; the mariner wears the albatross around his neck; the crewmen die; the mariner blesses the sea creatures; the ship sails homeward.

C. The crewmen die; the ship sails into the South Sea; the mariner blesses the sea creatures; the mariner shoots the albatross; the mariner wears the albatross around his neck; the ship sails homeward.

2 Its path was not upon the sea,
In ripple or in shade.

It raised my hair, it fanned my cheek
Like a meadow-gale of spring—
It mingled strangely with my fears,
Yet it felt like a welcoming.

Swiftly, swiftly flew the ship,
Yet she sailed softly too:
Sweetly, sweetly blew the breeze—
On me alone it blew.

And the ancient Mariner beholdeth his native country.

O dream of joy! is this indeed
The lighthouse top I see?
Is this the hill? is this the kirk?
Is this mine own countree?

We drifted o'er the harbor-bar,
And I with sobs did pray—
O let me be awake, my God!
Or let me sleep alway.

The harbor-bay was clear as glass,
So smoothly it was strewn!
And on the bay the moonlight lay,
And the shadow of the Moon.

3 The rock shone bright, the kirk no less
That stands above the rock:
The moonlight steeped in silentness
The steady weathercock.

479 weathercock: weathervane.

And the bay was white with silent light
Till rising from the same,
Full many shapes, that shadows were,
In crimson colors came.

The angelic spirits leave the dead bodies,

A little distance from the prow
Those crimson shadows were:
I turned my eyes upon the deck—
O Christ! what saw I there!

And appear in their own forms of light.

Each corse lay flat, lifeless and flat,
And, by the holy rood!

489 the holy rood (ro͝od): the cross on which Christ was crucified.

Customizing Instruction

Students Acquiring English

1 Paraphrase lines 444–445 for students.

Possible Response: I looked far into the distance, but didn't see anything familiar.

2 Paraphrase lines 454–455 for students.

Possible Response: The wind did not stir the water or cast a shadow upon it.

Less Proficient Readers

3 Lines 476–483 contain inverted and complex sentences. Help students paraphrase the sentences.

Possible Response: The rock, and the church that stands above the rock, shone brightly. The moonlight made the steady weathervane seem all the more silent. Shadowy, crimson-colored shapes rose from the white, silent bay.

Use the following questions to check students' comprehension of the events described on pages 760–761.

- Why has the mariner been put into a trance?
  Answer: He wouldn't be able to survive the high speed of the ship otherwise.
- When the mariner awakes, by what curse is he bound?
  Answer: He cannot take his eyes from those of the dead men.
- Why do you think the mariner doubts his vision of his homeland?
  Possible Response: He has suffered so much and seen so many unusual and impossible things that he can't trust his own perceptions any longer.

D. The ship sails homeward; the ship sails into the South Sea; the mariner shoots the albatross; the mariner wears the albatross around his neck; the mariner blesses the sea creatures; the crewmen die.

Discuss that all of the choices include events that actually happen in the poem, but that **B** is the only one in which the events are in the correct order.

Reading and Analyzing

Literary Analysis LITERARY BALLAD

A Remind students that the characters in literary ballads are often common people rather than people of nobility or high social status. Ask them to identify the ordinary people introduced in this scene.

Possible Response: The characters include the Pilot, the Pilot's son, and the Hermit.

Active Reading
READING NARRATIVE POETRY

B Ask students what information is conveyed by the dialogue in lines 524–540.

Possible Response: The lines give descriptive information about the boat—its warped planks, its thin and ragged sails, its "fiendish look."

Then ask students to explain whether they consider the Hermit and the Pilot to be reliable or unreliable observers.

Possible Response: They are reliable observers because they are simply describing objectively what they see; they are unreliable because no one on the ship has answered their calls, and they have become afraid.

Remind students that, in fiction, falling action often occurs after the story's climax. Invite students to describe the falling action on pages 762–763.

Possible Responses: The dead men fall dead again; the spirits leave the dead men's bodies; a boat approaches the mariner's ship, promising rescue.

Ask students what previous event they considered to be the climax or the turning point of the story.

Possible Responses: the death and/or resurrection of the crewmen; the high-speed, supernatural sailing of the ship.

A man all light, a seraph-man,
On every corse there stood.

This seraph-band, each waved his hand:
It was a heavenly sight!
They stood as signals to the land,
Each one a lovely light;

This seraph-band, each waved his hand,
No voice did they impart—
No voice; but O, the silence sank
Like music on my heart.

But soon I heard the dash of oars,
I heard the Pilot's cheer;
My head was turned perforce away,
And I saw a boat appear.

The Pilot and the Pilot's boy,
I heard them coming fast:
Dear Lord in Heaven! it was a joy
The dead men could not blast. **A**

I saw a third—I heard his voice:
It is the Hermit good!
He singeth loud his godly hymns
That he makes in the wood.
He'll shrieve my soul, he'll wash away
The Albatross's blood.

490 seraph (sĕr′əf) **man:** angel.

502 perforce: of necessity.

507 blast: destroy.

512 shrieve (shrēv): absolve from sin; pardon.

Teaching Options

Cross Curricular Link Biblical History

SERAPHIM In the biblical tradition, seraphim are supernatural creatures that indicate the presence of God. As described in the Old Testament book of Isaiah, chapter 6 (with which Coleridge was very familiar), each seraph has three pairs of wings: one for flying, one for covering his face, and one for covering his feet. In the Bible, the Hebrew noun *śārāp*, meaning a wild serpent, is often related to the verb *śārap*, meaning to burn. Thus, biblical scholars have proposed that seraphim were fiery, serpentine creatures.

PART VII

This hermit good lives in that wood
Which slopes down to the sea.
How loudly his sweet voice he rears!
He loves to talk with marineres
That come from a far countree.

The Hermit of the Wood

He kneels at morn, and noon, and eve—
He hath a cushion plump.
It is the moss that wholly hides
The rotted old oak-stump.

1 The skiff-boat neared: I heard them talk,
B "Why, this is strange, I trow!
2 Where are those lights so many and fair,
That signal made but now?"

524 trow: believe.

"Strange, by my faith!" the Hermit said—
"And they answered not our cheer!
The planks look warped! and see those sails,
How thin they are and sere!
I never saw aught like to them,
3 Unless perchance it were
Brown skeletons of leaves that lag
My forest-brook along;
When the ivy-tod is heavy with snow,
And the owlet whoops to the wolf below,
That eats the she-wolf's young."

Approacheth the ship with wonder.

535 tod: clump.

"Dear Lord! it hath a fiendish look—
(The Pilot made reply)
I am a-fear'd."—"Push on, push on!"
Said the Hermit cheerily.

4 The boat came closer to the ship,
But I nor spake nor stirred;
The boat came close beneath the ship,
And straight a sound was heard.

Under the water it rumbled on
Still louder and more dread:
It reached the ship, it split the bay;
5 The ship went down like lead.

The ship suddenly sinketh.

Stunned by that loud and dreadful sound,
Which sky and ocean smote,

551 smote: struck.

The ancient Mariner is saved in the Pilot's boat.

Customizing Instruction

Multiple Learning Styles

Kinesthetic Learners

1 Invite small groups of students to act out the mariner's rescue (lines 523–581).

Less Proficient Readers

2 To what lights do the Pilot and his crew refer in line 525?

Answer: They refer to the lights of the seraph-men standing on the deck of the ship.

3 How is the Hermit's description of the ship like other descriptions given in the poem?

Answer: It compares the ship to natural objects.

Students Acquiring English

4 Explain that the *nor . . . nor* construction is archaic, and that it means *neither . . . nor* in contemporary English.

Gifted and Talented

5 Invite students to consider line 549. What other object has sunk "like lead" in the story?

Answer: the albatross.

Ask what the apparent symbolism of these sinking objects is.

Possible Response: They suggest the release of the mariner from various curses.

Then ask students if the mariner is in fact released from these curses. Do the outward symbols of release correspond with the mariner's inward state?

Possible Responses: Some students will say yes, the mariner is released from his guilt, the ship, and the nightmare at sea; others will say no, the mariner remains a captive of his curse, and the symbols will have no meaning until the mariner learns to forgive himself.

Vocabulary Strategy

USING STRUCTURAL CLUES

Instruction Write the words *uprist* and *swound* on the chalkboard. Remind students that unfamiliar or archaic words often contain clues to their own meanings. For example, a word's definition can sometimes be guessed if the meaning of its root, prefix, or suffix is known. Elicit from students that *uprist* contains the root *ris* (rise) and the prefix *up.* Point out that other words may look or sound similar to a familiar word–*swound,* for example, resembles the word *swoon.*

Activity With students, discuss each of the following archaic words or word forms. Have students identify root words, word parts, or similar words whose meanings they know. Have them use this information and context clues to guess the meaning of the archaic word.

eftsoons (line 12) *quickly*
wist (line 148, 149) *perceived; discerned*
betwixt (line 176) *between*
'gan (line 337) *began*
corse (line 348) *bodies*

A lesson on word parts appears on p. 1104 in the Pupil's Edition.

Reading and Analyzing

Literary Analysis: SYMBOL

Have students locate Wordsworth's reference to the Hermit on page 726 (lines 21–22). Ask them what Wordsworth's hermit might symbolize.

Possible Responses: He represents solitude, the human spirit, union with nature.

Then ask what, by contrast, Coleridge's hermit symbolizes.

Possible Responses: He represents holiness; redemption; forgiveness.

How might these characters reflect Wordsworth and Coleridge's ideas about the role of the poet in society?

Possible Response: For Wordsworth, the poet is a loner who communes with nature; for Coleridge, the poet can help transform society.

Active Reading

READING NARRATIVE POETRY

A Coleridge once said that poems should have next to no moral. Ask students if the mariner's "moral" (lines 610–617) is an appropriate or fitting conclusion for the poem.

Possible Responses: Yes, it suggests that the mariner has learned not to harm helpless creatures; no, it seems overly simplified, especially in light of the mariner's harrowing trials.

Reading Strategy: DRAWING CONCLUSIONS

B Ask students why they think the Wedding Guest is described as a "sadder" and a "wiser" man.

Possible Responses: He is saddened by the mariner's captivity and his knowledge of tragedy; he is wiser because he has learned the mariner's lesson.

Like one that hath been seven days drowned
My body lay afloat;
But swift as dreams, myself I found
Within the Pilot's boat.
Upon the whirl, where sank the ship,
The boat spun round and round;
And all was still, save that the hill
Was telling of the sound.

559 telling of: choing.

I moved my lips—the Pilot shrieked
And fell down in a fit;
The holy Hermit raised his eyes,
And prayed where he did sit.

1

I took the oars: the Pilot's boy,
Who now doth crazy go,
Laughed loud and long, and all the while
His eyes went to and fro.
"Ha! ha!" quoth he, "full plain I see
The Devil knows how to row."

And now, all in my own countree,
I stood on the firm land!
The Hermit stepped forth from the boat,
And scarcely he could stand.

2 "O shrieve me, shrieve me, holy man!"
The Hermit crossed his brow.
"Say quick," quoth he, "I bid thee say—
What manner of man art thou?"

575 crossed his brow: made the sign of the cross on his forehead.

The ancient Mariner earnestly entreateth the Hermit to shrieve him; and the penance of life falls on him.

Forthwith this frame of mine was wrenched
With a woeful agony,
Which forced me to begin my tale;
And then it left me free.

Since then, at an uncertain hour,
That agony returns:
And till my ghastly tale is told,
This heart within me burns.

And ever and anon throughout his future life an agony constraineth him to travel from land to land;

I pass, like night, from land to land;
I have strange power of speech;
3 That moment that his face I see,
I know the man that must hear me:
To him my tale I teach.

Teaching Options

Cross Curricular Link Biblical History

CAIN AND ABEL Explain that, since many British romantic poets were revolutionaries or dissidents, they often felt like exiles in their own land, and that the theme of exile was therefore a popular one among these poets. One exile story often alluded to was that of Cain and Abel, told in the book of Genesis. In the story, Cain murders his brother, Abel. In spite of his pleas for mercy, Cain remains unforgiven by God, or Yahweh, who sentences him to wander the earth.

What loud uproar bursts from that door!
The wedding-guests are there:
But in the garden-bower the bride
And bride-maids singing are:
And hark, the little vesper bell,
Which biddeth me to prayer!

O Wedding-Guest! this soul hath been
Alone on a wide, wide sea:
So lonely 'twas, that God Himself
Scarce seemèd there to be.

O sweeter than the marriage-feast,
'Tis sweeter far to me,
To walk together to the kirk
With a goodly company!—

To walk together to the kirk,
And all together pray,
While each to his great Father bends,
Old men, and babes, and loving friends,
And youths and maidens gay!

607 his great Father: God.

Farewell, farewell! but this I tell
To thee, thou Wedding-Guest!
4 He prayeth well, who loveth well
Both man and bird and beast.

A

And to teach, by his own example, love and reverence to all things that God made and loveth.

He prayeth best, who loveth best
All things both great and small;
For the dear God who loveth us,
He made and loveth all.

The Mariner, whose eye is bright,
Whose beard with age is hoar,
Is gone: and now the Wedding-Guest
Turned from the bridegroom's door.

619 hoar: gray.

He went like one that hath been stunned,
And is of sense forlorn:
B A sadder and a wiser man
He rose the morrow morn.

Customizing Instruction

Less Proficient Readers

1 Ask students why they think the Pilot shrieks, the Hermit prays, and the Pilot's son goes crazy?

Possible Responses: The mariner looks so deathly after his trials at sea; the mariner is a madman or a devil.

2 What does the mariner ask the Hermit to do?

Answer: He asks the Hermit to forgive him.

3 What is the mariner compelled to do for the rest of his life?

Answer: He must wander from land to land, telling his tale.

4 Have students paraphrase the "moral" of the story (lines 610–617).

Possible Response: As God loves us, so should we love all creatures, great and small.

Gifted and Talented

Remind students that in romantic poetry, a speaker or character often interacts with nature and, in doing so, resolves a conflict, overcomes a problem, or reaches a higher state of awareness. Have students describer the development of the plot and compare the beginning and the end of "The Rime of the Ancient Mariner." In their view, does the mariner grow, develop, or change in some way? Is a problem or conflict resolved or overcome?

Possible Responses: Yes, the mariner learns respect for nature; no, the mariner—like the poem—begins and ends in the same place, unchanged and unenlightened.

Assessment Informal Assessment

TRAVEL JOURNAL Have students retell the mariner's story using either of the following prompts.

- Imagine that you are the mariner. Write a series of entries in your travel journal describing your voyage to the South Pole.
- Imagine that you are the wedding guest. You also happen to be a writer for a travel magazine. Write an account of the mariner's journey to publish in your magazine. In your article, draw some conclusions about the reliability of the mariner himself.

RUBRIC

3 Full Accomplishment Student writing reflects full understanding of events of narrative.

2 Substantial Accomplishment Student writing shows general understanding of narrative, but may leave out important information or focus too exclusively on certain parts of story while neglecting others.

1 Little or Partial Accomplishment Student writing displays little understanding of narrative, contains inaccurate information, and is not logically organized.

GUIDING STUDENT RESPONSE

Connect to the Literature

1. **What Do You Think?** Guidelines for student response: Students are likely to provide negative adjectives describing the mariner's experience (for example, *harsh, difficult, tragic, brutal)* or adjectives describing the mood of the poem *(surreal, dreamlike, visionary, supernatural).*

Comprehension Check

- The ship travels south.
- The crewmen die.

Use **Unit Four Resource Book,** p. 15 for additional support.

Think Critically

2. Answers will vary slightly. Most will identify the main conflict as that between the mariner and the albatross or between the mariner and the crew after he has killed the albatross. Other conflicts include that between the crew and nature itself, or the internal conflict between the mariner and his own guilty conscience.
3. Answers will vary. Some students will say that the mariner seems not to have any attitude toward the albatross—that the killing is random and unexplained. Others will point out the irony that he regards the albatross as a good omen but then kills it anyway.
4. Answers will vary, but may include the following: when the albatross arrives, it symbolizes hope, salvation, good fortune; its death symbolizes guilt, sin, death, hopelessness; according to the mariner's conclusion, the albatross symbolizes nature, God's creation, life itself.
5. Answers will vary. The best responses will observe that remaining alive is an ambiguous fate for the mariner—part curse, part blessing. Other responses may state that the mariner learns respect for nature through life-in-death.
6. Responses will vary. Some students will note that the joyful wedding event, by contrast, sharpens the misery of the mariner's tale. Others will respond that the wedding gives a sense of urgency or discomfort to the mariner's tale by emphasizing the Wedding Guest's captivity.

Connect to the Literature

1. **What Do You Think?** What adjectives would you use to describe the mariner's voyage?

Comprehension Check

- In what direction does the ship travel after leaving its home port?
- After the mariner kills the albatross, what happens to the rest of the crew?

Think Critically

2. **ACTIVE READING** **READING NARRATIVE POETRY** Look back at the notes you jotted down in your **READER'S NOTEBOOK** in response to the questions listed on page 745. On what **conflicts** do the events of the **plot** focus? How are these conflicts related to the **setting?**
3. What do you think is the mariner's attitude toward the albatross when he kills it?
4. What might the albatross **symbolize,** or represent?

THINK ABOUT

- the effect the arrival of the albatross seems to have on the ship's voyage
- the consequences that follow from the mariner's killing of the bird
- the mariner's statement in lines 612–617

5. What are the consequences of the mariner's being won by Life-in-Death (lines 190–198) rather than by Death? Cite evidence from the poem in your answer.
6. Why do you think the mariner tells his story at a wedding?

Extend Interpretations

7. **Comparing Texts** Since early times, the English have been a seagoing people, and they have a long tradition of poetry about the dangers and mystery of ocean voyaging. Compare "The Rime of the Ancient Mariner" with the Anglo-Saxon poem "The Seafarer" (page 84). How are the experiences and world views of Coleridge's mariner and the Anglo-Saxon seafarer similar? How do they differ?
8. **The Writer's Style** Coleridge used **sensory language** to help the reader visualize the scenes and characters he described. To which of your five senses did the poem appeal most? Cite examples from the poem in your answer.
9. **Connect to Life** From your consideration of the poem's **details,** what do you think the expression "to have an albatross around one's neck" means today?

Literary Analysis

LITERARY BALLAD "The Rime of the Ancient Mariner" is a famous example of a **literary ballad,** a poem by a known writer that imitates the style of an anonymous **folk ballad.** Typically, a folk ballad

- is a brief **narrative poem** intended to be set to music
- opens abruptly
- recounts a single dramatic—often a tragic—episode
- contains supernatural elements
- implies more than it actually tells
- includes dialogue, often without directly stating who is speaking
- contains repetitions of lines or stanzas, sometimes with the wording varied slightly
- is made up of four-line stanzas in which the first and third lines contain four stressed syllables, the second and fourth lines contain three stressed syllables, and the second and fourth lines rhyme

Cooperative Learning Activity With classmates, use the list of ballad characteristics above to determine to what extent "The Rime of the Ancient Mariner" conforms to typical ballad style. Compare your findings with those of other groups.

REVIEW **SIMILE** A **simile** is a **figure of speech** in which the word *like* or *as* is used to make a comparison. Find several particularly effective similes in the poem. Do most of the similes seem to be used to describe characters, to establish settings, or to advance the plot?

Extend Interpretations

Comparing Texts Many students will observe that both poems use strong imagery to describe the harshness of sea life. Both poems also conclude that human beings should "Treat all the world as the world deserves, / With love or with hate but never with harm" ("The Seafarer," lines 111–112), and both concede that God and fate are stronger than mankind. Students may say that the poems differ in form and rhyme scheme, and that, unlike "The Seafarer," Coleridge's poem tells a story. Others may note that the seafarer reveals more about his motives, desires, and regrets than the mariner does.

The Writer's Style Many students will identify sight as the sense most strongly appealed to, but accept all reasonable, well-supported answers. **To make this question easier,** have students look through the poem to find one image for each of the five senses.

Connect to Life Responses will vary slightly. Most students will conclude that "to have an albatross around one's neck" means to feel unrelieved guilt or to struggle with a burden caused by one's own negative behavior.

Choices & CHALLENGES

Writing Options

1. **Poetry of Dreams** Write your own poem or fragment of a poem based on a dream that you remember. Place the poem in your **Working Portfolio.**

2. **Analytical Essay** Write a brief essay in which you compare the attitudes toward the natural and supernatural worlds expressed in "Kubla Khan" and "The Rime of the Ancient Mariner." Be sure to include ample evidence from the poems to support your thesis, or general statement.

Writing Handbook
See page 1367: Compare and Contrast.

Activities & Explorations

1. **Choral Reading** With a group of classmates, prepare a choral reading of a portion of "The Rime of the Ancient Mariner." Perform it for the rest of the class. ~ **SPEAKING AND LISTENING**

2. **Video Visions** View the video of "Kubla Khan," in which the poem is interpreted through oral reading and images. What connections do you see between the imagery in the poem and the images in the video? Do the oral and visual interpretations work well together? With a partner, list what you think are the most effective sections of the video presentation. ~ **VIEWING AND REPRESENTING**

Literature in Performance

Inquiry & Research

Multimedia Report Research the real Kublai Khan, and present your findings in a multimedia report that includes photocopies of artworks illustrating the achievements of his reign.

More Online: Research Starter
www.mcdougallittell.com

Samuel Taylor Coleridge
1772–1834

Other Works
Biographia Literaria
"Christabel"
"Dejection: An Ode"
"Frost at Midnight"
"Work Without Hope"

A Restless Youth As a schoolboy, Coleridge was precocious, reading for amusement the most difficult passages of the ancient Roman poet Virgil. Although already a devoted scholar when he entered Cambridge University, Coleridge did not care for college life and at one point left to enlist in a cavalry unit called the Light Dragoons. When his escapade was discovered by his brothers, he was promptly returned to school; but he left Cambridge in 1794 without having received a degree.

Utopian Dream That year, Coleridge met the author Robert Southey, and together they dreamed about establishing an ideal community on the banks of the Susquehanna River in the United States. Their community was to be a pantisocracy—a society in which all members rule equally. Southey backed out of the project, however, and their dream was never realized.

Literary Friendship In 1795 Coleridge had the extraordinary good fortune to meet William Wordsworth. They became close friends, traveling and writing together and often helping each other with their poetry. *Lyrical Ballads,* the joint collection they published in 1798, included Coleridge's famous poem "The Rime of the Ancient Mariner."

Critic and Sage Most of Coleridge's best poetry was written early in his career. Later, he turned to philosophy and literary criticism, becoming the most influential literary theorist of the romantic movement in Britain. In his later years, Coleridge moved into the home of a Dr. Gilman in Highgate, north of London. The doctor helped him control an addiction to opium, and Coleridge seemed more at peace with himself. His rooms became a center of conversation for an admiring crowd that dubbed him the Sage of Highgate.

Literary Analysis

Cooperative Learning Activity Draw up a chart on the chalkboard listing students' findings about the extent to which the poem conforms to ballad style.

Review Simile Many of the poem's similes describe the setting or characters, but often they advance the plot simultaneously.

Writing Options

1. **Poetry of Dreams** Students' responses will vary, but should contain vivid descriptions of possible dreams.
2. **Analytical Essay** Responses will vary. Good responses will observe that each poem depicts both the natural and the supernatural worlds as powerful, beautiful, awe-inspiring, accessible to human beings, and sometimes cruel, or that each poem depicts a connection or continuum between the natural and the supernatural worlds. Students should support their conclusions with examples from the texts.

Activities & Explorations

1. **Choral Reading** Encourage students to prepare for their reading by working through each line, marking the stressed and unstressed syllables and experimenting with various volumes (loud or soft), pitches (high or low), and rhythms (fast or slow). See the mini-lesson on page 759 for more tips on teaching choral speaking.
2. **Video Visions** Allow students to view the video twice, first for an overall impression of visuals and sound and a second time for note-taking and analysis of the messages those techniques convey. If partners view the video together, encourage them to pause the tape occasionally and discuss the effects. Ask students what they would change if they were producing the video.

Inquiry & Research

Multimedia Report Encourage students to use a variety of reference materials, including history books, art books, and online encyclopedias. You may want to contact a local college library to find out if a version of *Purchas's Pilgrimage* is available on microfilm or microfiche. Coleridge was allegedly reading this book, written by Samuel Purchas in 1613, when he fell asleep and dreamed "Kubla Khan."

Milestones in British Literature

Pride and Prejudice—probably the most popular of Jane Austen's (1775–1817) novels—begins with one of the most famous and ironic opening sentences in literature: "It is a truth universally acknowledged, that a single man in possession of a good fortune must be in want of a wife." Among the greatest of all English novelists, Austen is particularly noted for her ability to create vivid characters—an ability, it has been said, "never excelled among writers of fiction."

Additional Background

JANE AUSTEN

The seventh of eight children (six boys and two girls), Jane Austen lived in the English countryside for most of the first 25 years of her life. When she was 22 years old, having already completed drafts of three novels, she announced her commitment to the art of literature; but in the period 1801–1811, during which she moved from house to house and her father and her best friend died, she practically ceased writing. Only after settling in the country again (at Chawton in Hampshire) did she resume her literary work in earnest, and she was extremely productive until just before her death at the age of 41. Although in her lifetime she never saw her name on the title page of one of her books and had no literary connections, Austen's fame has grown steadily over the years.

Milestones in British Literature

Jane Austen

Pride & Prejudice

Imagine that you are living in England around the turn of the 19th century, standing on the threshold of adulthood. You are a woman, so your only career option is marriage. The match you make will reflect your values and desires—and determine the manner in which you spend the rest of your life.

This is the world of *Pride and Prejudice*, Jane Austen's insightful and clever examination of English manners and morals. The novel centers on the roundabout courtship of a proud young man, Fitzwilliam Darcy, and a spirited but judgmental young woman, Elizabeth Bennet, who fall in dislike at first sight. Elizabeth's and Darcy's friends and families provide a cast of characters whose traits Jane Austen depicts with irony and humor. For example, the silly schemes with which Elizabeth's mother—who has no real understanding of good manners, good breeding, or good sense—tries to ensure that her daughters will marry well cause Elizabeth no end of painful embarrassment. Elizabeth's good-natured

The Cloakroom, Clifton Assembly Rooms, *Rolinda Sharples (1794–1838). City of Bristol Museum and Art Gallery, Bristol, Great Britain.*

Speaking and Listening

ANALYZING AND COMPARING A FILM REVIEW

Many of Jane Austen's books have been translated into films. Use this opportunity to show one or several film versions of *Pride and Prejudice* or other books listed on page 769.

Instruction Introduce this activity by telling students they will see a movie made from one of Jane Austen's novels. After viewing the film, they will locate and analyze a review, and compare the review to their own response.

Prepare After students have seen and discussed the film, have them find a review of the film.

Suggest they use this criteria for analyzing the review:

- identifies the film at the beginning
- includes a general opinion about the film
- includes enough facts, examples, and specifics to support the opinion
- may include a synopsis of the film
- may include a discussion of the craft
- may include the reviewer's personal experience

Painting of Jane Austen by her sister, 1804. Robert Harding Picture Library.

but ineffectual father contributes to the near ruin of the family by neglecting to rein in his wife and younger daughters. Elizabeth's best friend astonishes her when she agrees to marry a pompous suitor of Elizabeth's not for love, or even riches, but for security.

In the course of the novel, Austen exposes the ever-changing nature of public opinion, ridicules the assumed superiority of the upper class, and shows how prejudice can lead to premature and even dangerous conclusions. She gently but firmly chides two young lovers who are so mild and polite in expressing their feelings that they almost lose each other, and she celebrates the independent spirit that leads two unlikely lovers to forge a bond of enduring joy.

Soon after *Pride and Prejudice* was published, critics began comparing Jane Austen to Shakespeare. They admired her command of language, her use of comic fools, and her dramatic presentation of characters in action. In addition, they noticed a kinship between the hard-won affection of Elizabeth and Darcy and the reluctant love of Beatrice and Benedick in Shakespeare's *Much Ado About Nothing*.

Unlike Shakespeare's lovers, however, Austen's characters are not tricked into love. Instead, they hammer out their own romance, allowing for shared values and mutual respect. Their integrity, independence, and well-deserved love has made *Pride and Prejudice* a perennial favorite among novels as well as a classic celebration of joyous love between independent equals.

A Darcy-like character wearing gentleman's clothing typical of the day

LITERARY CHRONOLOGY

The following are publication dates of Austen's six completed novels (the last two were published posthumously):

1811 *Sense and Sensibility*

1813 *Pride and Prejudice*

1814 *Mansfield Park*

1815 *Emma*

1817 (dated 1818) *Northanger Abbey* (written about 1798), *Persuasion* (written 1815–1816)

Present Have students read, analyze, and discuss the review using the above criteria. Have them compare the review to their own response.

Note: Students can find film reviews through *Reader's Guide to Periodical Literature;* in magazines such as *Premier, Film Comment,* and *Entertainment Weekly;* in *infotrac 2000,* a magazine index on CD-ROM and on-line; and major on-line services.

PART 2 Embracing the Imagination

Romantic poets passionately embraced the concept of creative self-expression, giving free rein to their imaginations in an effort to convey their personal visions of love and life. In this part of Unit Four, you will read poems in which writers imagine what it would be like to embody the ocean's majesty, to soar and sing like a bird, and to defy the ravages of time. As you read these poems, consider what images your own imagination might conjure up as a means of creative self-expression.

770

Form and Meaning in Poetry

The Organizing Principles

Hand-colored illustrations from Blake's *Songs of Experience*

Poets from every era have toyed with poetic form and language to create unique expressions of meaning, and the romantic poets were no exception. **Form** in poetry refers to the principles of arrangement in a poem—the ways in which words and images are organized, including the length of lines, the placement of lines, and the grouping of lines.

Some poems follow a **fixed form,** which uses a conventional stanza pattern or a defined rhyme scheme. Other poems follow an **irregular form,** which is not defined by any traditional poetic structure. Samuel Taylor Coleridge wrote extensively about the relationship between content and form in his *Biographia Literaria* (1817). He believed that the form and the content of a poem, like the roots and the leaves of a growing plant, do not develop independently but develop simultaneously. The romantics favored this **organic form**—a form that, as Coleridge explains, "is innate; it shapes, as it develops, itself from within." In other words, the shape of the poem is intimately tied to the poem's meaning.

The Shape of a Poem

The most basic element of poetic form—and the one that first catches the reader's eye—is the physical arrangement of words on the page. Poets use lines and stanzas to shape their poems, and these lines and stanzas can vary significantly, as shown in the examples below.

End-stopped lines are lines in which the end of the line is the end of a thought, a clause, or a sentence. End-stopped lines are signaled by a period, hyphen, or semicolon, as this line from "The World Is Too Much with Us" illustrates:

Getting and spending, we lay waste our powers;

Run-on lines are lines in which the thought continues into the next line or further. Notice the run-on lines in this excerpt from "Lines Composed a Few Miles Above Tintern Abbey":

The day is come when I again repose
Here, under this dark sycamore, and view
These plots of cottage ground, these orchard tufts,
Which at this season, with their unripe fruits,
Are clad in one green hue, and lose themselves
'Mid groves and copses. . . .

YOUR TURN What is the effect of the run-on lines in this stanza?

A **stanza** conveys a particular idea or a set of related ideas and is usually characterized by a common pattern of rhythm, rhyme, and number of lines. Some stanzas are named for the number of lines they contain. For example, a **couplet** is a two-line stanza, a **tercet** is a three-line stanza, a **quatrain** is a four-line stanza, and a **cinquain** is a five-line stanza. The romantics experimented with the verse paragraph form they inherited from the poetry of Dryden and Milton. In a **verse paragraph,** lines of blank verse are grouped according to content, like a paragraph, rather than according to a fixed stanza form. In "Lines Composed a Few Miles Above Tintern Abbey," for example, Wordsworth uses both long and short verse paragraphs: 22 lines in the first stanza, 28 lines in the second, and 9 lines in the third.

LEARNING the Language of LITERATURE

OVERVIEW

Objectives

- understand the following literary terms:
  Form
  Fixed form
  Irregular form
  Organic form
  End-stopped lines
  Run-on lines
  Stanza
  Couplet
  Tercet
  Quatrain
  Cinquain
  Verse paragraph
  Petrarchan sonnet
  Shakespearean sonnet
  Ode
  Sound devices
  Poetic elements
- appreciate shared characteristics of literature across cultures
- recognize themes across cultures

Teaching the Lesson

This lesson will provide background on how form in poetry conveys meaning.

Introducing the Concepts

Students will probably enjoy poetry more if they examine the less obvious elements of form. For example, romantic poets were among the first to tie the form of the poem to its meaning. The trend continues today, and many contemporary poets invent a new form for every poem they write.

Presenting the Concepts

Read through the strategies aloud or project them on a transparency. Ask students to identify the formal elements of a favorite poem, prayer, or song by using the description of poetic form on pages 771–772. Model how to use the strategies to analyze the poems.

Making Connections

Form and Meaning in Poetry Across Cultures

A poem's form and meaning are interrelated, and many poetic forms express the values and ideas of a particular culture, while others, such as the epic, are common to many cultures. Share with students the following descriptions of poetic form in different cultures.

Africa

Many traditional African poems take the form of performances involving music and dance. Poetic forms include the lyric, the ballad, the praise poem, and the sonnet. Africa has a rich tradition of oral epics with subjects that include the history of empires, founders of nations, and heroic quests.

Japan

Two traditional forms of Japanese poetry include the haiku, and the senryū. The haiku developed from the 14th-century tradition of linked verses. Originally, its subject was always an aspect of nature that would evoke an unstated emotional response. However, over time its subject matter broadened, but the basic idea of expressing much in the fewest possible words remains the same. The senryū is a 17-syllable form that uses less formal language than the haiku.

India

Traditional Indian poetic forms include the narasamsi gatha (a ballad in praise of ancestors) along with several oral forms including the purana, the epic, and the vedic hymn. While the epics and puranas constantly evolved and changed with each generation, the vedic hymns could not be altered in the slightest detail. Every word, sound, and accent was sacred. During the last part of the 19th century, Indian writers became familiar with the work of English poets, including Wordsworth, and experimented with such forms as the elegy, the sonnet, and the ode.

Lyric Forms

The romantic poets experimented with a number of traditional lyric forms—including both **Petrarchan** and **Shakespearean** sonnets—and adapted them to suit the contemplative nature of their poetry. For example, Wordsworth followed the Petrarchan sonnet form in "It Is a Beauteous Evening."

Wordsworth, Coleridge, Shelley, and Keats all used the ode form in some of their poems. Originally a choral Greek form that lent itself to dramatic poetry, an **ode** is an exalted, complex lyric that develops a dignified theme and may include an elaborate stanza pattern. In addition, the metrical pattern of an ode quickens and slows to match the emotional intensity of the idea being expressed. The romantic poets favored an irregular form of the ode, which allowed greater freedom of stanza pattern, rhyme scheme, and metrical movement.

The Combination of Poetic Ingredients

The elements of form explained above work together with **sound devices**—such as alliteration, assonance, consonance, onomatopoeia, and repetition—and other **poetic elements** to convey meaning and create a total experience for the reader. This is especially true of the romantic poets. The following excerpt from William Blake's "The Lamb" shows how various literary elements can combine to create meaning—and how form and meaning become an inseparable part of the whole:

Speaker uses figurative language—in this case, personification—in addressing the lamb.

Little Lamb, who made thee?
Dost thou know who make thee?

Short lines reflect simple, almost childlike, speech.

Gave thee life & bid thee feed?
By the stream & o'er the mead;

Imagery in these two lines describes the lamb's appearance.

Gave the clothing of delight,
Softest clothing wooly bright;

Rhythm, rhyme, and repetition create a lyrical, musical quality throughout the entire poem.

YOUR TURN What view of life is presented in the poem, and how is it reinforced by the poem's form?

Strategies for Reading: Form and Meaning in Poetry

1. Read the poem at least three times to clarify the meaning. Also read the poem aloud to hear its music.
2. Analyze the poem's form. Study the way the poet arranges lines and stanzas and uses patterns of rhyme, rhythm, and other sound devices. Is the poem fixed or irregular?
3. Visualize the setting and the situation. As you read, use details and your imagination to help you "see" what is happening.
4. Identify the speaker. Determine whether the poet has created a speaker with a distinctive identity.
5. Determine the theme. What important ideas does the poem convey about life or human nature?
6. **Monitor** your reading strategies and modify them when your understanding breaks down. Remember to use your Strategies for Active Reading: **predict, visualize, connect, question, clarify,** and **evaluate.**

PREPARING to *Read*

Selected Poems

By GEORGE GORDON, LORD BYRON

"I love not Man the less, but Nature more."

Connect to Your Life

The Power of Emotions Think of someone in your family, school, or community who conveys strong emotions when speaking. Does the person usually express the emotions in ordinary conversation, or does he or she do so in speeches, sermons, or other public presentations? Do you think the ability to express powerful emotions is an advantage or a disadvantage? Discuss these questions with a group of classmates.

Build Background

"A Young Gentleman of Tumultuous Passions" During the romantic period, no English poet achieved greater popularity than George Gordon, Lord Byron. Because the heroes he created in many of his works were rebellious, moody figures of great passion and strong will, Byron was viewed during most of the 19th century as the ideal example of the romantic spirit. He attracted admirers throughout Europe, and his influence was felt not only in the poetry of his many imitators but in art and music as well.

Even though Byron became a symbol of romanticism, his poetry was rooted in 18th-century forms, as is evident in the first two poems that you will read. He avoided, and actually scorned, the experimental poetry of his contemporaries; but he was nevertheless decidedly romantic in his emphasis on freedom and the individual and in his expression of powerful emotions. In the words of one of his university instructors, Byron was "a young gentleman of tumultuous passions."

Byron's immense popularity originated with the publication of the first two sections of his poetic travelogue *Childe Harold's Pilgrimage* in 1812. The young poet acquired the material for this work and several other poems during an adventurous two-year excursion through Portugal, Spain, Malta, Greece, and Asia Minor. For 19th-century readers, part of the appeal of *Childe Harold's Pilgrimage* was the excitement of reading about countries or scenery they had never seen.

Focus Your Reading

LITERARY ANALYSIS APOSTROPHE

An **apostrophe** is a figure of speech in which an object, an abstract quality, or an absent or imaginary person is addressed directly, as if present and able to understand. The excerpt from *Childe Harold's Pilgrimage* on the following pages contains an apostrophe to the ocean. As you read it, be aware of this device and contemplate why Byron chose to use it.

ACTIVE READING COMPARING SPEAKERS

The **speaker** in a poem—the voice that "talks" to the reader—is not necessarily the voice of the poet; poets sometimes create a speaker other than themselves in order to achieve a particular effect. For this reason, two poems by the same poet can have speakers that convey different personalities.

READER'S NOTEBOOK As you read each of Byron's poems, keep track of the emotions, thoughts, and wishes of the speaker in a chart similar to the one shown. Be prepared to discuss similarities and differences.

"She Walks in Beauty"		
Emotions	Thoughts	Wishes

OVERVIEW

Objectives

1. understand and appreciate **lyric poetry (Literary Analysis)**
2. appreciate the author's use of **apostrophe (Literary Analysis)**
3. compare speakers to appreciate and understand **lyric poetry (Active Reading)**

Summary

In these three poems, Byron describes a woman's external and internal beauty; his despair over lost love; and feelings of love for the beautiful yet powerful ocean.

Thematic Link

Byron's passionate, exotic poems reveal a person who thrives on feeling, life, art, and **embracing the imagination.**

5-Minute Warm-Up

Daily Language SkillBuilder

Have students **proofread** the display sentences on page 697j and write them correctly. The sentences also appear on Transparency 20 of **Grammar Transparencies and Copymasters.**

LESSON RESOURCES

UNIT FOUR RESOURCE BOOK, pp. 16–17

ASSESSMENT RESOURCES

Formal Assessment, pp. 141–142

Teacher's Guide to Assessment and Portfolio Use

Test Generator

SKILLS TRANSPARENCIES AND COPYMASTERS

Literary Analysis

- Poetic Devices, T16 (for Literary Analysis, p. 773)

Reading and Critical Thinking

- Compare and Contrast, T15 (for Active Reading, p. 773)

Grammar

- Adverb Clauses, C116 (for Mini Lesson, p. 780)

Vocabulary

- Context Clues, C63 (for Mini Lesson, p. 777)

Writing

- The Uses of Dialogue, T24 (for Writing Option 2, p. 780)
- Opinion Statement, C35 (for Writing Option 3, p. 780)

Communications

- Interviewing, T9 (for Activities & Explorations 2, p. 780)

INTEGRATED TECHNOLOGY

Audio Library

LaserLinks

- Author Background: George Gordon, Lord Byron. See **Teacher's SourceBook,** p. 48.

Visit our website: www.mcdougallittell.com

TEACHING THE LITERATURE

Reading and Analyzing

Literary Analysis APOSTROPHE

A Ask students to whom the speaker is addressing himself in "When We Two Parted."

Answer: He addresses his former beloved.

Help them distinguish between the speaker, his audience, the poet, and the poet's audience.

 Use **Unit Four Resource Book,** pp. 17 for more exercises.

Active Reading

COMPARING SPEAKERS

Have students compare and contrast the speakers in the two poems.

Possible Response: The first regards his subject as beautiful, distant, calm, and innocent; the second regards his subject as fickle, hurtful, and unworthy. Both speakers are passionate and intense.

 Use **Unit Four Resource Book,** p. 16 for more practice.

Thinking Through the Literature

1. If students are hesitant to talk about their personal feelings, you may want to discuss other literary characters or characters in films.
2. Possible responses may include admiration and respect in the first poem and passion, shame, and despair in the second.
3. Possible responses: intense; passionate; romantic

SHE WALKS IN BEAUTY

GEORGE GORDON, LORD BYRON

Comus, Disguised as a Rustic, Addresses the Lady in the Wood (1801-1802), William Blake. Henry E. Huntington Library and Art Gallery, San Marino, California.

She walks in beauty, like the night
Of cloudless climes and starry skies;
And all that's best of dark and bright
Meet in her aspect and her eyes:
Thus mellowed to that tender light
Which heaven to gaudy day denies.

One shade the more, one ray the less,
Had half impaired the nameless grace
Which waves in every raven tress,
Or softly lightens o'er her face;
Where thoughts serenely sweet express
How pure, how dear their dwelling place.

And on that cheek, and o'er that brow,
So soft, so calm, yet eloquent,
The smiles that win, the tints that glow,
But tell of days in goodness spent,
A mind at peace with all below,
A heart whose love is innocent!

2 climes: regions; climates.

4 aspect: appearance.

9 tress: lock of hair.

Teaching Options

BLOCK SCHEDULING: MANAGING TIME

If your schedule requires that you cover the lesson objectives in a shorter time, use . . .

- Preparing to Read, p. 773
- Thinking Through the Literature, pp. 775, 779

If you want to take advantage of longer class time, use . . .

- TE Teaching Options: Vocabulary, p. 777; Speaking and Listening, p. 776; Cross Curricular Links, p. 775; Informal Assessment, p. 778; Grammar, p. 780
- Choices and Challenges, p. 780

When We Two Parted

A

When we two parted
In silence and tears,
Half broken-hearted
To sever for years,
Pale grew thy cheek and cold,
Colder thy kiss;
Truly that hour foretold
Sorrow to this.

The dew of the morning
Sunk chill on my brow—
It felt like the warning
Of what I feel now.
Thy vows are all broken,
And light is thy fame;
I hear thy name spoken,
And share in its shame.

They name thee before me,
A knell to mine ear;
A shudder comes o'er me—
Why wert thou so dear?
They know not I knew thee,
Who knew thee too well—
Long, long shall I rue thee,
Too deeply to tell.

In secret we met—
In silence I grieve,
That thy heart could forget,
Thy spirit deceive.
If I should meet thee
After long years,
How should I greet thee?—
With silence and tears.

18 knell: the ringing of a bell to announce a death.

23 rue: remember with feelings of sorrow; regret.

Thinking Through the Literature

1. Did you identify with the situation in one of these poems more than the other? Explain your response.
2. What kinds of relationships does the poet seem to be presenting in the two poems? Support your answer with details from the poems.
3. How would you describe the different emotions expressed by the **speakers** of these poems?

Customizing Instruction

Less Proficient Readers

Set a Purpose Have students write a sentence for each poem describing the speakers' impressions of the poems' subjects, two women and the ocean. Have students use the chart from their Reader's Notebook as reference.

Students Acquiring English

Some of Byron's diction may challenge students. Have students listen to the recording of the poems with a native English speaker. Encourage them to use context clues to define unfamiliar words and to stop the recording to ask their partner for help when necessary.

Use **Spanish Study Guide** for additional support, pp. 176–178.

Gifted and Talented

Have students write a paragraph defining which aspects of romanticism the poems convey.

Possible Response: Students may cite the expression of deep feelings; exotic subject matter; individualism; love of nature and freedom.

Poetry and Music

Note that "She Walks in Beauty" is from Byron's *Hebrew Melodies,* a volume of poems written to be set to Isaac Nathan's adaptations of traditional Jewish tunes. Interest in folk traditions and folk music was part of the Romantic embrace of the common people and the misty past. Robert Burns (1759–1796) adapted many folk songs of his native Scotland. Sir Walter Scott (1771–1832), inspired by similar efforts of German romantics, collected traditional Scottish ballads in *Minstrelsy of the Scottish Border.* Byron's friend Thomas Moore (1179–1852) adapted folk songs of his native Ireland in Irish Melodies.

Today, the preservation of folk songs is very popular in Japan. Folk song preservation societies *(minyo hozon kai)* try to preserve "correct" performances of a single folk song. Japanese folk songs embrace a wide range of styles. This may reflect the long period of Japanese feudalism, which fostered musical variety.

Reading and Analyzing

Literary Analysis: SPEAKER

A Explain that this poem's speaker is a youth named Childe Harold. *Childe* is an archaic term for a young nobleman awaiting knighthood. Ask students what they can glean about the speaker's character from this excerpt.

Possible Responses: He loves adventure; he is critical of man's petty ruthlessness; he loves nature.

Literary Analysis APOSTROPHE

B Ask students to whom the speaker addresses his words.

Answer: the ocean.

How does this affect the reader's mental picture of the ocean?

Possible Responses: It makes the ocean seem alive; it personifies the ocean.

Reading Skills and Strategies: MAKING INFERENCES

C Ask what qualities these images associate with nature.

Possible Responses: Students may cite isolation; wildness; beauty; power.

Literary Analysis: SIMILE

D Discuss that these lines describe a man drowning. Ask students what comparison is made.

Answer: The man is compared to a drop of rain.

What does this comparison suggest about human beings?

Possible Response: They are small and weak compared to the vast, powerful ocean; they are insignificant.

A from Childe Harold's

Snow Storm: Steam-Boat off a Harbour's Mouth (1842), Joseph Mallord William Turner. Clore Collection, Tate Gallery, London/Art Resource, New York.

Teaching Options

Speaking and Listening

DIRECT ADDRESS

Instruction Remind students that, in an apostrophe, an abstract quality or an absent or imaginary person is addressed directly, as if present and able to understand. Discuss with students the similarities and differences between the audiences to which the speakers of "When We Two Parted" and the selection from *Childe Harold* are addressed.

Prepare Invite students to prepare an interpretive reading of "When We Two Parted" or a section of "Apostrophe to the Ocean." As they prepare, encourage students to imagine being in the presence of the addressee.

Present Before students perform for the class, allow them to give practice readings to a partner and then to revise their readings based on their partner's feedback.

BLOCK SCHEDULING This activity is particularly well-suited for longer class periods.

Pilgrimage

George Gordon, Lord Byron

B

Apostrophe to the Ocean

There is a pleasure in the pathless woods,
There is a rapture on the lonely shore,
C There is society where none intrudes,
By the deep Sea, and music in its roar:
I love not Man the less, but Nature more,
From these our interviews, in which I steal
From all I may be or have been before,
To mingle with the Universe, and feel
What I can ne'er express, yet can not all conceal. 1

Roll on, thou deep and dark blue Ocean, roll!
Ten thousand fleets sweep over thee in vain;
Man marks the earth with ruin, his control
Stops with the shore; upon the watery plain
The wrecks are all thy deed, nor doth remain
A shadow of man's ravage, save his own, 
D When, for a moment, like a drop of rain,
He sinks into thy depths with bubbling groan,
Without a grave, unknell'd, uncoffin'd, and unknown.

15 ravage: destruction.

18 unknell'd: with no announcement of his death.

His steps are not upon thy paths, thy fields
Are not a spoil for him,—thou dost arise
And shake him from thee; the vile strength he wields
For earth's destruction thou dost all despise,
Spurning him from thy bosom to the skies,
And send'st him, shivering in thy playful spray
And howling, to his Gods, where haply lies
His petty hope in some near port or bay,
And dashest him again to earth:—there let him lay.

25 haply: perhaps.

Customizing Instruction

Less Proficient Readers

1 Have students summarize lines 5–9.

Possible Response: When I sneak away from my busy life to visit the ocean, I feel an overwhelming love for nature and a connection to the universe; I can't put these feelings into words, but I can't keep them to myself, either.

Students Acquiring English

2 Clarify that *doth* means "does," *there* is implicit after *doth,* and *save* means "except." Ask to whom or what the pronouns *thy* and *his* refer.

Answer: ocean and mankind.

Mini Lesson Vocabulary Strategy

USING CONTEXT CLUES

Instruction Review the following kinds of context clues. **Restatement:** A difficult word or phrase is restated in easier language. **Synonyms or Antonyms:** A synonym or antonym of the unknown word is built into the sentence. **Inferences:** Surrounding text contains clues from which the meaning of the unfamiliar word can be guessed.

Activity Have students use context clues to determine the meaning of each word or phrase. Then have them explain which kind of context clue(s) they used.

1. **gaudy** (page 774, line 6)
   Answer: bright; clues—antonym, tender, or inference from "day"
2. **". . . the vile strength he wields / For earth's destruction thou dost all despise"** (page 777, lines 21–22)
   Answer: you despise his evil, destructive strength; clues—restated in surrounding phrases
3. **armaments** (page 778, line 28)
   Answer: weapons; clues—inference from "thunderstrike the walls"

Use **Vocabulary Transparencies and Copymasters,** p. 56.

Reading and Analyzing

Literary Analysis: RHYME SCHEME

A Ask how the imperfect rhymes (words that do not rhyme exactly) in lines 33, 35, and 36 reflect the content of the lines.

Possible Response: They capture war's harsh, jarring effects.

Reading Skills and Strategies: MAKING INFERENCES

B Ask students what they think these lines might mean. Have them support their responses with evidence from the text and experience.

Possible Responses: Time leaves no mark on the ocean; it rolls now as it did at the beginning of time.

Then ask if they think this remark would still be true today.

Answer: Accept all reasonable, well-supported responses.

The armaments which thunderstrike the walls
Of rock-built cities, bidding nations quake
And monarchs tremble in their capitals,
The oak leviathans, whose huge ribs make
Their clay creator the vain title take
Of lord of thee and arbiter of war,—
These are thy toys, and, as the snowy flake,
They melt into thy yeast of waves, which mar
Alike the Armada's pride or spoils of Trafalgar.

Thy shores are empires, changed in all save thee—
Assyria, Greece, Rome, Carthage, what are they?
Thy waters wash'd them power while they were free,
And many a tyrant since; their shores obey
The stranger, slave, or savage; their decay
Has dried up realms to deserts:—not so thou,
Unchangeable save to thy wild waves' play;
Time writes no wrinkle on thine azure brow;
Such as creation's dawn beheld, thou rollest now.

Thou glorious mirror, where the Almighty's form
Glasses itself in tempests; in all time,
Calm or convulsed—in breeze, or gale, or storm,
Icing the pole, or in the torrid clime
Dark-heaving;—boundless, endless, and sublime—
The image of Eternity—the throne
Of the Invisible; even from out thy slime
The monsters of the deep are made; each zone
Obeys thee; thou goest forth, dread, fathomless, alone.

And I have loved thee, Ocean! and my joy
Of youthful sports was on thy breast to be
Borne, like thy bubbles, onward. From a boy
I wanton'd with thy breakers—they to me
Were a delight; and if the freshening sea
Made them a terror—'t was a pleasing fear,
For I was as it were a child of thee,
And trusted to thy billows far and near,
And laid my hand upon thy mane—as I do here.

31 oak leviathans: large ships.

32 their clay creator: humankind.

33 arbiter: a person with the power of judging or ruling.

35 yeast: turbulent froth.

36 Armada's . . . Trafalgar (trə-făl'gər): The mighty Spanish Armada was defeated by the British fleet in 1588; Trafalgar is a Spanish cape, the site of a great British naval victory over the French and Spanish in 1805.

38 Assyria . . . Carthage: four powerful ancient civilizations.

44 azure (ăzh'ər): sky blue.

47 glasses itself: is reflected.

49 torrid clime: the intensely hot regions near the equator.

53 zone: one of the five climatic regions of the earth.

54 fathomless: too deep to be measured; also, beyond comprehension.

58 wanton'd: frolicked playfully; **breakers:** large waves.

OCEANOS SEPTE

GOUVERNEMENT

Teaching Options

Assessment Informal Assessment

COMPREHENSION CHECK

Use the following questions to gauge students' comprehension of the poems.

1. To what time of day is the woman who "walks in beauty" compared?
   Answer: night.
2. What is her hair color?
   Answer: black or dark brown; "raven."
3. How would the speaker of "When We Two Parted" greet his former beloved if they met now?
   Answer: in silence and tears.
4. Whose strength does Childe Harold despise more: the ocean's or mankind's?
   Answer: the ocean's.
5. When did Childe Harold first come to know the ocean?
   Answer: as a boy.

Thinking through the LITERATURE

Connect to the Literature

1. **What Do You Think?** Describe your reaction to this excerpt from *Childe Harold's Pilgrimage.*

Think Critically

2. What aspects of the ocean do you think the **speaker** admires most? Cite specific examples to support your answer.
3. What different emotions does the ocean seem to inspire in the speaker?

- his **description** of the ocean's relationship to humanity
- what he means when he calls the ocean "the throne / Of the Invisible" (lines 51–52)
- his remembrance of his youth

4. How would you describe the ocean's relationship to other aspects of nature mentioned in the excerpt?
5. **ACTIVE READING** **COMPARING SPEAKERS** Review the charts you created in your **READER'S NOTEBOOK**. What seems to be the main character traits of each speaker? What are their similarities? differences?

Extend Interpretations

6. **The Writer's Style** "She Walks in Beauty" was written to be set to music. What elements of the poem do you think give it a musical quality? Compare your ideas with those of your classmates.
7. **Comparing Texts** Which of the three poems—"She Walks in Beauty," "When We Two Parted," or the excerpt from *Childe Harold's Pilgrimage*—do you think conveys the strongest emotions? Give evidence to support your opinion.
8. **Connect to Life** According to the speaker of *Childe Harold's Pilgrimage,* "Man marks the earth with ruin, his control / Stops with the shore." Do you think a contemporary environmentalist would agree? Why or why not?

Literary Analysis

APOSTROPHE The romantic poets frequently used **apostrophe,** a literary device associated with the expression of powerful emotions. In *Childe Harold's Pilgrimage,* the extended apostrophe addresses the ocean as if it were capable of understanding what is being said and of taking credit for its own characteristics and actions, as the following example illustrates:

Roll on, thou deep and dark blue
Ocean, roll!
Ten thousand fleets sweep over
thee in vain . . .

Paired Activity Reread the excerpt from *Childe Harold's Pilgrimage,* looking for at least two other passages that you think are strong illustrations of apostrophe. Then discuss with your partner why Byron might have chosen to use apostrophe rather than simply describing the ocean's magnificence. In a chart like the one below, record the examples of apostrophe you choose and your explanations of why Byron used apostrophe.

1st passage:
Why Byron used:
2nd passage:
Why Byron used:

GUIDING STUDENT RESPONSE

Connect to the Literature

1. **What Do You Think?**
Guidelines for student response: Accept all reasonable responses that are supported by evidence from the text. Encourage students to share their reactions with the class.

Think Critically

2. Answers will vary. Aspects of the ocean admired by the speaker include power, primitive beauty, elemental nature, permanence, and vastness. Students should support their responses with examples from the poem.
3. Possible Responses include love, fear, faith, exhilaration, and admiration.
4. Some students may say that the ocean, with its vast power and diversity, symbolizes or embodies nature in general; others may feel that the many contrasts between sea, land, human beings, and other creatures suggests that the ocean is the most powerful natural entity of all. Students should support their responses with examples from the poem and experience.
5. Answers will vary. Students are likely to find all three speakers passionate, earnest, expressive, and dramatic. Some may note that the first two speakers are capable of affection for other people, while Childe Harold, a loner, holds humanity in low esteem.

Literary Analysis

Paired Activity On the chalkboard, make a composite chart based on the charts produced by pairs of students.

Extend Interpretations

The Writer's Style Student responses will vary, but may include the following: the short lines of tight iambic tetrameter, with its singsong effect; the prominent rhymes; the assonance (as in "like the night"); and the alliteration (as in "cloudless climes" and "starry skies").

Comparing Texts Accept all reasonable, well-supported responses. **To make this question easier,** have students name one strong emotion expressed by each poem.

Connect to Life Accept all reasonable, well-supported responses. Students are likely to point out that many of today's environmentalists are concerned with the amount of pollution being channeled into the world's oceans, lakes, and rivers.

Choices & CHALLENGES

Writing Options

1. Romantic Character Sketch Write a character sketch conveying your impression of the woman described in "She Walks in Beauty."

2. Imaginary Dialogue Write dialogue for an imaginary conversation between the speaker of "When We Two Parted" and the person he addresses.

3. Weekly Opinion Column As the speaker of *Childe Harold's Pilgrimage,* write an opinion column for a weekly newsmagazine, expressing your views on the foibles of society.

Activities & Explorations

1. Illuminated Manuscript Create border designs for an illuminated manuscript of "She Walks in Beauty." ~ **ART**

2. Interview with the Poet With a partner, plan and conduct an imaginary interview with Lord Byron. Include questions, based on your reading of the excerpt from *Childe Harold's Pilgrimage,* about his attitudes toward society. ~ **SPEAKING AND LISTENING**

Art Connection

Artistic Reflections Look again at the Turner seascape on page 776. What aspects of the excerpt from Childe Harold's Pilgrimage do you see reflected in the painting?

Inquiry & Research

The Battle of Trafalgar Research the Battle of Trafalgar. Who was involved in the battle? What were its causes? What long-range effects did it have? Report your findings to the class.

George Gordon, Lord Byron

1788–1824

Other Works
"So We'll Go No More A-Roving"
"On This Day I Complete My Thirty-Sixth Year"

In Pursuit of Adventure Lord Byron is one of the most handsome and daring figures in literary history. Born into a family of hot-tempered soldiers, seamen, and fighters, he lived a dramatic life. He had a fierce determination to test himself physically—a response, in part, to his having been born with a clubfoot that gave him a slight limp throughout his life. At school, Byron enthusiastically engaged in vigorous sports, including swimming, boxing, riding, and fencing. Later, while traveling in Europe, he frequently sought out dangerous ventures that frightened his companions.

Fame and Fortune At the age of 10, Byron inherited an ancestral estate from his great-uncle—and with it the title of sixth Baron Byron. He was only in his 20s when the first parts of *Childe Harold's Pilgrimage* were published and, as he put it, "I awoke one morning and found myself famous." Unfortunately, he had a reckless and dissipated lifestyle that often left him in debt and suffering from extreme melancholy. He entered into many romantic alliances throughout his life, but his one marriage lasted only a year. The rumors arising from its failure caused a decline in Byron's popularity in England, and in 1816 he left the country for good, living first in Switzerland and then for several years in Italy, where he began work on what was to be his masterpiece, *Don Juan.* In 1823, impelled by his love of the Greek people, he embarked on a mission to help them in their war for independence from Turkish rule. While training soldiers, he contracted a fever and died shortly thereafter, just after his 36th birthday. Byron is still regarded as a national hero in Greece, not for his poetry but for his dedication to the country's revolution.

LaserLinks: Background for Reading
Author Background

Writing Options

1. **Romantic Character Sketch** Sketches should include details that derive logically from the poem.
2. **Imaginary Dialogue** Have students consider the details about both people given in the poem, but remind them that the speaker's point of view may lack objectivity.
3. **Weekly Opinion Column** Have students prewrite by listing the foibles that the poem mentions or hints at. Good student writing will adopt the attitude and express the opinions of Childe Harold as defined in the poem.

Activities & Explorations

1. **Illuminated Manuscript** Before they begin, have students study and discuss examples of illuminated manuscript pages in Unit 1 and in the section on Blake.
2. **Interview with the Poet** In addition to the biographical information on pages 773 and 780, students may want to consult *Byron's Letters and Journals,* edited by Leslie A. Marchand (1975–82), or biographical works such as Peter Manning's *Byron and His Fictions* (1978). Have students draft written questions to prepare for the interview.

Art Connection

Artistic Reflections Both the painting and the poem illustrate the ocean's power, danger, beauty, and mystery.

Inquiry & Research

The Battle of Trafalgar You may wish to expand students' research to include other aspects of the Napoleonic wars, including the Peninsular campaign, the invasion of Russia, the War of 1812, and the Battle of Waterloo. Groups might make their final reports orally or in a graphic presentation, such as a map.

Teaching Options

Grammar

ADVERB CLAUSES

Instruction Adverb clauses modify verbs, adjectives, or other adverbs. They answer the following questions about the words they modify: How? When? Where? Why? To what extent? Under what circumstances? Subordinating conjunctions, such as *before, because, as, so that,* and *where,* usually introduce adverb clauses. Subordinating conjunctions relate the adverb clauses to the words they modify.

Activity Write the following sentence on the chalkboard.

Byron is regarded as a national hero in Greece because he attempted to help the country in its war for independence.

Ask students to identify the adverb clauses and tell what word they modify. *(as a national hero and because he attempted . . ., regarded)* What questions does each clause answer about the word it modifies? *(When? How? Why?)*

Use **Grammar Transparencies and Copymasters,** p. 113.

Use McDougal Littell's ***Language Network*** for more instruction in adverb clauses.

Selected Poems

By PERCY BYSSHE SHELLEY

Comparing Literature of the World

The Poetry of Percy Bysshe Shelley and Heinrich Heine

This lesson and the one that follows present an opportunity for comparing the English romantic poetry of Percy Bysshe Shelley with the German romantic poetry of Heinrich Heine. Specific points of comparison in the Heine lesson will help you contrast Shelley's verse with that of his German contemporary.

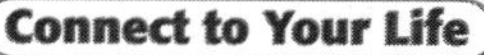

Connect to Your Life

Aiming High What aspirations do people your age tend to have? Survey ten students in your class to find out some of their hopes and dreams for the future. Compare their responses. Are their aspirations practical and realistic? lofty and idealistic? Discuss your findings with your classmates.

Build Background

An Idealistic Life Percy Bysshe Shelley was an idealist and a nonconformist who passionately opposed all injustice and dreamed of changing the world through love, imagination, and poetry. Now ranked among the greatest of the English romantic poets, Shelley was rebuked by his contemporaries for his radical views.

As a young man, Shelley fiercely opposed the oppression and poverty he saw in places like Ireland and Wales. When his efforts at reform met with resistance and failure, however, he turned to poetry as a means of expressing and fulfilling his aspirations. He wrote with the conviction that through the imagination of the poet and the power of love, humanity could perceive and transcend the evils of society.

Shelley was a skillful craftsman who explored a wide array of poetic forms and rhythmic patterns in his work. "Ozymandias" is a **sonnet** in which he experiments with **rhyme** and **rhythm.** "Ode to the West Wind" and "To a Skylark" are examples of the **ode**—an exalted, complex lyric that develops a dignified **theme.**

Focus Your Reading

LITERARY ANALYSIS **RHYTHMIC PATTERNS IN POETRY** Three important terms to keep in mind as you study poetry of this period include the following:

Meter—the regular repetition of a rhythmic unit in a line of poetry
Foot—a unit of meter consisting of one stressed syllable and one or two unstressed syllables
Iambic pentameter—a type of meter in which the line is made up of five feet, each consisting of an unstressed syllable followed by a stressed syllable.

Ĭ mét ă trávĕlĕr fróm ăn antíque lánd

Rhythmic patterns, along with **structural elements** and other **sound devices,** help to complement and enhance a poem's meaning.

ACTIVE READING **DRAWING CONCLUSIONS ABOUT THEME** In order to **draw conclusions** about the **theme** of a poem, use the following strategies:

- Read the poem several times, stopping to ask yourself at the end of each reading what insights you might have gained. Make sure that at least one of your readings is aloud, so that you are able to hear **rhythmic patterns;** these often help to enhance the meaning of the poem.
- Think about the **subject** of the poem. By choosing this particular subject, what theme might the poet be trying to convey?
- Analyze the speaker's **tone,** or attitude toward his or her subject.
- Think about how you would describe the **mood,** or feeling, of the poem; this can also offer clues to the theme.

READER'S NOTEBOOK As you read each poem, jot down notes about rhythmic patterns, subject, tone, and mood. Be ready to discuss your conclusions about theme.

OVERVIEW

"Ozymandias" is included in the **Grade 12 InterActive Reader.**

Objectives

1. understand and appreciate **lyric poetry (Literary Analysis)**
2. appreciate the author's use of **rhythmic patterns** in poetry **(Literary Analysis)**
3. **draw conclusions about theme** to understand lyric poetry **(Active Reading)**

Summary

In the first poem, Shelley analyzes the meaning behind a fallen ancient statue. In the next two poems, he expresses his feelings about wind and compares the song of a bird to other joyful wonders.

Thematic Link

Through his poetry, Shelley **embraced the poetic imagination,** believing it could help enlighten humanity and improve society.

5-Minute Warm-Up

Daily Language SkillBuilder

Have students **proofread** the display sentences on page 697k and write them correctly. The sentences also appear on Transparency 21 of **Grammar Transparencies and Copymasters.**

LESSON RESOURCES

UNIT FOUR RESOURCE BOOK, pp. 18–19

ASSESSMENT RESOURCES
Formal Assessment, pp. 143–144
Teacher's Guide to Assessment and Portfolio Use
Test Generator

SKILLS TRANSPARENCIES AND COPYMASTERS
Literary Analysis
- Form and Meaning in Poetry, T15 (for Literary Analysis, p. 781)

Reading and Critical Thinking
- Noting Details, T9 (for Active Reading, p. 781)

Grammar
- Adjective Clauses Introduced by Relative Pronouns, C112 (for Mini Lesson, pp. 786–787)

Vocabulary
- Denotation and Connotation, C64 (for Mini Lesson, p. 785)

Writing
- Identifying Writing Variables, T2 (for Writing Option 2, p. 791)
- Showing, Not Telling, T22 (for Writing Option 1, p. 791)

Communications
- Impromptu Speaking: Dialogue, Role-Play, T14 (for Activities & Explorations 2, p. 791)

INTEGRATED TECHNOLOGY
Audio Library
LaserLinks
- Cultural Connection: Ancient Egyptian Art
- Art Gallery: Ancient Gallery Art. See **Teacher's SourceBook,** p. 49.

Visit our website:
www.mcdougallittell.com

TEACHING THE LITERATURE

Reading and Analyzing

Active Reading

DRAWING CONCLUSIONS ABOUT THEME

Remind students that a poem's theme is rarely stated in the poem itself. Have them look for clues to the theme of "Ozymandias" as they read the poem.

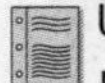

Use **Unit Four Resource Book,** p. 18 for more practice.

Literary Analysis

RHYTHMIC PATTERNS IN POETRY

A Note that while many of the poem's lines are in iambic pentameter, many lines break this pattern. Ask how these variations in meter contribute to the meaning.

Possible Response: The irregular meter reflects the irregular movement and sound of the wind.

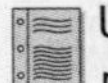

Use **Unit Four Resource Book,** p. 19 for more exercises.

GUIDE FOR READING

B The boast is ironic because the works referred to have vanished with time and because the king's statue is now in ruins.

Thinking Through the Literature

1. the mighty, arrogant ruler of an ancient land
2. Accept all reasonable responses.
3. Possible Responses: The quest for immortality is fruitless, even for the mighty; ruthless tyrants always meet their demise; art outlasts empires.

Percy Bysshe Shelley

Ozymandias

A I met a traveler from an antique land
Who said: Two vast and trunkless legs of stone
Stand in the desert . . . Near them, on the sand,
Half sunk, a shattered visage lies, whose frown,
And wrinkled lip, and sneer of cold command,
Tell that its sculptor well those passions read
Which yet survive, stamped on these lifeless things,
The hand that mocked them, and the heart that fed:
And on the pedestal these words appear:
"My name is Ozymandias, king of kings:
Look on my works, ye Mighty, and despair!"
Nothing beside remains. Round the decay
Of that colossal wreck, boundless and bare
The lone and level sands stretch far away.

GUIDE FOR READING

2 trunkless legs: legs separated from the rest of the body.

4 visage (vĭz′ĭj): face.

6 those passions: that is, Ozymandias' passions.

8 This line may be paraphrased as "The sculptor's hand, which mocked the passions of the king, and the king's heart, which fed those passions."

10 Ozymandias (ŏz′ĭ-măn′dē-əs): the Greek form of "Usermare," a title of the Egyptian pharaoh Rameses II, who reigned from 1304 to 1237 B.C.

11 What is ironic about the boast inscribed on the pedestal? 

Thinking Through the Literature

1. **Comprehension Check** Based on this poem, who was Ozymandias?
2. Does this poem remind you of anything you have seen in your own experience? Explain your response.
3. What **theme,** or message about life, do you think is conveyed in this poem?

- the words Ozymandias had carved on the pedestal
- the aspirations Ozymandias seems to have had
- what has happened to the statue

Teaching Options

BLOCK SCHEDULING: MANAGING TIME

If your schedule requires that you cover the lesson objectives in a shorter time, use . . .
- Preparing to Read, p. 781
- Thinking Through the Literature, pp. 782, 785, 790

If you want to take advantage of longer class time, use . . .
- TE Teaching Options: Vocabulary Strategy, p. 785; Viewing and Representing, pp. 783, 788; Speaking and Listening, p. 784; Informal Assessment, p. 789; Grammar, p. 786
- Choices & Challenges, p. 791

Ode to the West Wind

Percy Bysshe Shelley

Detail of *Cloud Study* (about 1821), John Constable, R.A. Oil on canvas, Victoria and Albert Museum, London/Art Resource, New York.

I

O wild West Wind, thou breath of Autumn's being,
Thou, from whose unseen presence the leaves dead
Are driven, like ghosts from an enchanter fleeing,

Yellow, and black, and pale, and hectic red,
Pestilence-stricken multitudes: O thou,
Who chariotest to their dark wintry bed

The wingéd seeds, where they lie cold and low,
Each like a corpse within its grave, until
Thine azure sister of the Spring shall blow

Her clarion o'er the dreaming earth, and fill
(Driving sweet buds like flocks to feed in air)
With living hues and odors plain and hill:

Wild Spirit, which art moving everywhere;
Destroyer and preserver; hear, oh, hear!

4 hectic: feverish.

9 sister . . . Spring: the reviving south wind of spring.

10 clarion: a trumpet with a clear, ringing tone.

Customizing Instruction

Less Proficient Readers

Set a Purpose

- Tell students that the title of the first poem has the name of a character in it. Then have students read to find out who Ozymandias was.
- Have students read to learn the speaker's emotional state in the second poem.
- Ask students to read to find out what is demanded of the skylark.

Students Acquiring English

Students may have particular difficulty with confusing interrupters or word order. Suggest that they listen to the recording of each poem a few times, noting any language with which they have difficulty. Explain any words or phrases they may not understand. Then discuss with them the theme of each poem, using the steps listed under Active Reading on page 781.

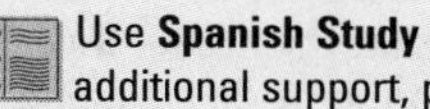

Use **Spanish Study Guide** for additional support, pp. 179–181

Gifted and Talented

Encourage students interested in mythology to read *Prometheus Unbound,* Shelley's verse drama. Other students might be more interested in Mary Wollstonecraft Shelley's *Frankenstein.* Have students present brief oral reports on the works. Then have them propose themes that cross these texts.

Viewing and Representing

Detail of *Cloud Study* by John Constable

ART APPRECIATION

Instruction Constable (1776–1837) was a landscape painter of Britain's romantic age. To capture fleeting light and weather conditions, he made rapid oil sketches, including sky studies like this one.

Application Ask students to describe the clouds in this oil sketch. What mood does the sketch convey? Have students discuss how the ideas in Constable's sketch and Shelley's poem relate.
Possible Response: Both admired the power and beauty of the wind.

Reading and Analyzing

Literary Analysis: APOSTROPHE

Ask students how Shelley uses apostrophe in this poem.

Answer: The poem is addressed directly to the wind.

A Then ask what effect the repetition of the phrase "oh, hear!" (lines 28 and 42) has on the reader.

Possible Response: It builds suspense—what does the speaker want the wind to hear?; it helps the reader to think of the wind in exalted terms.

Literary Analysis: SYMBOL

B Ask what the thorns of life may represent.

Possible Responses: sorrow; despair; pain; hardship.

Active Reading

DRAWING CONCLUSIONS ABOUT THEME

Ask students whether they think the poem's theme is hope or despair, and why.

Possible Responses: It is hope because the speaker seems to trust so fully in the power of the wind; it is despair because the speaker is desperate for assistance from the wind and because the last line suggests uncertainty.

Thinking Through the Literature

1. Accept all reasonable responses.
2. Possible response: He finds it a powerful, almost divine force of nature.
3. Possible responses: to be freed from the trials of life; to be spiritually enlightened; to be inspired; to be a prophet to a sleeping world.

II

Thou on whose stream, mid the steep sky's commotion,
Loose clouds like earth's decaying leaves are shed,
Shook from the tangled bough of Heaven and Ocean,

Angels of rain and lightning: there are spread
On the blue surface of thine aëry surge,
Like the bright hair uplifted from the head

Of some fierce Maenad, even from the dim verge
Of the horizon to the zenith's height,
The locks of the approaching storm. Thou dirge

Of the dying year, to which this closing night
Will be the dome of a vast sepulcher,
Vaulted with all thy congregated might

Of vapors, from whose solid atmosphere
A Black rain, and fire, and hail will burst: oh, hear!

III

Thou who didst waken from his summer dreams
The blue Mediterranean, where he lay,
Lulled by the coil of his crystálline streams,

Beside a pumice isle in Baiae's bay,
And saw in sleep old palaces and towers
Quivering within the wave's intenser day,

All overgrown with azure moss and flowers
So sweet, the sense faints picturing them! Thou
For whose path the Atlantic's level powers

Cleave themselves into chasms, while far below
The sea-blooms and the oozy woods which wear
The sapless foliage of the ocean, know

1 Thy voice, and suddenly grow gray with fear,
And tremble and despoil themselves: oh, hear!

IV

If I were a dead leaf thou mightest bear;
If I were a swift cloud to fly with thee;
A wave to pant beneath thy power, and share

18 angels: messengers.

19 aëry: airy.

20–23 The speaker is saying that the clouds lie in streaks, looking like the streaming hair of a maenad (mē′năd′)—a wildly dancing female worshiper of Dionysus, the Greek god of wine.

23 dirge: funeral song.

25 sepulcher (sĕp′əl-kər): tomb.

31 crystálline (krĭs-tăl′ĭn) **streams:** the different-colored transparent currents of the Mediterranean Sea.

32 pumice (pŭm′ĭs): a light volcanic rock; **Baiae's** (bī′ēz′) **bay:** the Bay of Naples, site of the ancient Roman resort of Baiae.

37 level powers: surface.

Teaching Options

Speaking and Listening

EVALUATING ORAL READING

Instruction Provide students with this list of criteria for the effective oral reading of poetry.

Prepare

The performer:

- varies tone to convey meaning and emotion.
- varies volume to stress key ideas and feelings.
- varies pace but reads slowly enough for content to be absorbed by most listeners.
- pauses only when content or punctuation demands it.
- captures rhythm but avoids a singsong delivery.
- does not overemphasize sound devices like rhyme and alliteration.
- uses body language, gestures, and facial expressions to convey meaning and emotion.

Present Have pairs of students take turns reading Shelley's poems. They should analyze, evaluate, and critique each other's readings, using the criteria. Final performances might be presented to classmates.

This activity is particularly well-suited for longer class periods.

The impulse of thy strength, only less free
Than thou, O uncontrollable! If even
I were as in my boyhood, and could be

The comrade of thy wanderings over Heaven,
As then, when to outstrip thy skyey speed
Scarce seemed a vision; I would ne'er have striven

As thus with thee in prayer in my sore need.
Oh, lift me as a wave, a leaf, a cloud!
B I fall upon the thorns of life! I bleed!

A heavy weight of hours has chained and bowed
2 One too like thee: tameless, and swift, and proud.

V

3 Make me thy lyre, even as the forest is:
What if my leaves are falling like its own!
The tumult of thy mighty harmonies

Will take from both a deep, autumnal tone,
Sweet though in sadness. Be thou, Spirit fierce,
My spirit! Be thou me, impetuous one!

Drive my dead thoughts over the universe
Like withered leaves to quicken a new birth!
And, by the incantation of this verse,

Scatter, as from an unextinguished hearth
Ashes and sparks, my words among mankind!
Be through my lips to unawakened earth

The trumpet of a prophecy! O Wind,
4 If Winter comes, can Spring be far behind?

50 thy skyey (skī'ē) **speed:** the swiftness of clouds moving quickly across the sky.

51 vision: here, something impossible to achieve.

57 lyre: here, a reference to the Aeolian harp, an instrument whose strings make musical sounds when the wind blows over them.

62 impetuous (ĭm-pĕch'o͞o-əs): violently forceful; impulsive.

65 incantation: recitation, as of a magic spell.

Thinking Through the Literature

1. With a partner, discuss the **image** left in your mind after reading "Ode to the West Wind."
2. How would you describe the **speaker's** feelings about the wind? Cite evidence.
3. What aspirations does the speaker appear to have?

THINK ABOUT
- what he means by "the thorns of life" in line 54
- his request in lines 63–67

Customizing Instruction

Students Acquiring English

1 Help students paraphrase each of the two long sentences that make up Section III.

Possible Response: You who wake the Mediterranean Sea from his sleep and from his dreams of summer, of palaces, mosses, and flowers! You who stir up the surface waters and who make the seaweed of the deep tremble with fear: listen!

Less Proficient Readers

2 Ask what the speaker is comparing in these lines.

Answer: He compares himself and the wind—both are "tameless, and swift, and proud."

3 What does the speaker hope the wind will do?

Answer: The speaker hopes the wind will inspire him; carry his words across the world; make his words prophetic.

Gifted and Talented

4 What is the tone of the last line?

Possible Responses: It is hopeful; uncertain.

Why do you think Shelley ended the poem with a question?

Possible Responses: He wanted to emphasize that he is speaking to the wind; to leave the poem unresolved or unanchored like an object flying away on the wind; to engage the reader.

Vocabulary Strategy

DENOTATION AND CONNOTATION

Instruction A word's total meaning consists of its denotation and its connotations. Therefore, although many words are considered synonyms, no two words have *exactly* the same meanings.

Activity Have students give a synonym for each of the following words from "To the West Wind." (Allow students to use dictionaries or thesauruses if needed.) Then have them explain what connotations Shelley may have wanted to evoke by using the word in the poem rather than the synonym.

Possible Responses: Synonyms are given below. Accept all reasonable explanations for Shelley's word choices.

1. *ghosts* (line 3)
   Answer: souls, spirits
2. *clarion* (line 10)
   Answer: trumpet, horn
3. *Heaven* (lines 17, 49)
   Answer: sky
4. *sepulcher* (line 25)
   Answer: tomb, grave

Discuss the overall effect of Shelley's word choices on the poem's mood or theme.

Use **Vocabulary Transparencies and Copymasters,** p. 57.

A lesson on denotation and connotation appears on p. 645 in the Pupil's Edition.

Reading and Analyzing

Literary Analysis: **APOSTROPHE**

Point out that the poem is written *to* a skylark and that the speaker once again addresses his subject directly, as if it can understand.

Literary Analysis

RHYTHMIC PATTERNS IN POETRY

A Have students identify the number of stressed syllables in each stanza's four shorter lines and final longer line.

Answer: three and six.

Ask what purpose this change in line length serves.

Possible Responses: It captures the rhythm of beating wings; the bird's shift from flapping to soaring; the bird's ascent.

Active Reading

DRAWING CONCLUSIONS ABOUT THEME

B Ask students to describe the speaker's tone, or attitude, toward the subject.

Possible Response: Students may say that the speaker expresses wonder at the power of the skylark's song.

C Then ask students what they might conclude about the poem's theme based on the stanza that begins with line 36.

Possible Response: The poem may be about the poet's own desire to produce beautiful sounds, like the skylark does, and to be appreciated for them as the speaker appreciates the skylark.

To a Skylark

PERCY BYSSHE SHELLEY

Hail to thee, blithe Spirit!
Bird thou never wert, **1**
A That from Heaven, or near it,
Pourest thy full heart
In profuse strains of unpremeditated art.

Higher still and higher
From the earth thou springest
Like a cloud of fire;
The blue deep thou wingest,
And singing still dost soar, and soaring ever singest.

In the golden lightning
Of the sunken sun,
O'er which clouds are bright'ning,
Thou dost float and run;
Like an unbodied joy whose race is just begun.

The pale purple even
Melts around thy flight;
Like a star of Heaven,
In the broad daylight
Thou art unseen, but yet I hear thy shrill delight,

Keen as are the arrows
Of that silver sphere,
Whose intense lamp narrows
In the white dawn clear
Until we hardly see—we feel that it is there.

5 unpremeditated (ŭn'prĭ-mĕd'ĭ-tā'tĭd): natural; not planned out ahead of time.

16 even: evening.

22 silver sphere: the planet Venus, often called the morning star because it is visible in the east just before daybreak.

Teaching Options

Grammar

Adjective Clauses Introduced by Relative Pronouns

Instruction An adjective clause is a subordinate clause that modifies a noun or a pronoun. Many adjective clauses begin with the relative pronouns *who, whom, whose, that*, or *which*. These relative pronouns relate the adjective clauses to the words they modify. Adjective clauses beginning with relative pronouns are called "relative clauses."

Activity Write this example from "Ozymandias" on the chalkboard.

". . . its sculptor well those passions read
Which yet survive, stamped on these lifeless
things, . . ."

Have students identify the adjective clause *(Which yet survive)*, the relative pronoun *(Which)*, and the noun or pronoun the clause modifies *(passions)*. Point out that within the adjective clause, *Which* is the subject. Then do the same for these lines from "Ode to a Skylark."

"Teach me half the gladness
That thy brain must know,"

The adjective clause is *That thy brain must know*, the relative pronoun is *That*, and the noun the clause modifies is *gladness*. Tell students that within the adjective clause, *That* is the object of the verb *know*.

All the earth and air
With thy voice is loud,
As, when night is bare,
From one lonely cloud
The moon rains out her beams, and Heaven is overflowed.

B

What thou are we know not;
What is most like thee?
From rainbow clouds there flow not
Drops so bright to see
As from thy presence showers a rain of melody.

C

Like a Poet hidden
In the light of thought,
Singing hymns unbidden,
Till the world is wrought
To sympathy with hopes and fears it heeded not:

Like a high-born maiden
In a palace tower
Soothing her love-laden
Soul in secret hour
With music sweet as love, which overflows her bower:

Like a glowworm golden
In a dell of dew,
Scattering unbeholden
Its aërial hue
Among the flowers and grass, which screen it from the view!

Like a rose embowered
In its own green leaves,
By warm winds deflowered,
Till the scent it gives
Makes faint with too much sweet those heavy-wingéd thieves:

Sound of vernal showers
On the twinkling grass,
Rain-awakened flowers,
All that ever was
Joyous, and clear, and fresh, thy music doth surpass:

45 bower: private room; boudoir.

2

53 deflowered: fully opened.

55 thieves: the warm winds.

56 vernal: spring.

Customizing Instruction

Multiple Learning Styles

Spatial or Graphic Learners

Ask students to predict the speaker's attitude toward the skylark based on the background art.

Possible Responses: He admires it; he idealizes it; he celebrates its simple beauty.

Students Acquiring English

1 Have students use the context to determine the meaning of *wert* and a dictionary to learn what *blithe* means.

Answers: were; carefree.

Less Proficient Readers

2 Ask students what question the speaker is attempting to answer in lines 36–55.

Answer: It is the answer to the question posed in line 32, "What is most like thee?"

Exercise Ask students to complete each sentence with a relative pronoun, underline the adjective clause, and identify the noun or pronoun that the clause modifies. Have students work in cooperative groups to identify the function of each relative pronoun within the adjective clause.

1. Shelley, _____ is one of the greatest romantic poets, was criticized during his lifetime for his radical ideas. *(who, Shelley)*
2. In "Ozymandias," the statue _____ stands in the desert is not as enduring as the forces of nature. *(that, statue)*
3. The ideas for _____ Shelley was criticized included a defense of atheism. *(which, ideas)*
4. The spirit _____ the poet celebrates in "Ode to a Skylark" is a bird. *(whom or that, spirit)*
5. Like most of the romantic poets, Shelley uses many similes, _____ help create images in readers' minds. *(which, similes)*

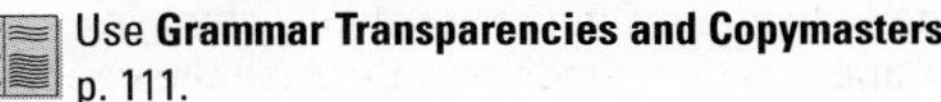

Use **Grammar Transparencies and Copymasters,** p. 111.

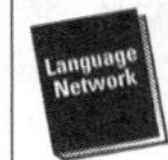

Use McDougal Littell's ***Language Network*** for more instruction and practice in adjective clauses introduced by relative pronouns.

TO A SKYLARK **787**

Reading and Analyzing

Reading Skills and Strategies:
MAKING INFERENCES

A Have students identify characteristics attributed to the skylark by the details in these lines.

Possible Responses: It represents the skylark's immortality; shows that the skylark has instinctive knowledge of spiritual truths.

Reading Skills and Strategies:
MAKING JUDGMENTS

B Have students evaluate the validity of these comments about human nature.

Possible Responses: Most students will probably agree with these sentiments.

Literary Analysis: SYMBOL

C As a "scorner of the ground," what might the skylark symbolize?

Possible Responses: It represents freedom from earthly concerns; soaring to poetic heights; lofty aspirations; bold ventures into spiritual realms.

Active Reading

DRAWING CONCLUSIONS ABOUT THEME

D Have students compare the conclusion of "To a Skylark" with that of "Ode to the West Wind." Then ask what conclusions they can draw about the poems' shared themes.

Possible Responses: A theme of both poems is the poet's desire to be appreciated, heard, and respected by the world; the poet's humility before nature.

Detail of *Cloud Study* (1821), John Constable, R.A. Oil on paper laid on board, 9¾″ × 11⅞″, Yale Center for British Art, Paul Mellon Collection (B1981.25.155).

Teach us, Sprite or Bird,
    What sweet thoughts are thine:
I have never heard
    Praise of love or wine
That panted forth a flood of rapture so divine.

Chorus Hymeneal,
    Or triumphal chant,
Matched with thine would be all
    But an empty vaunt,
A thing wherein we feel there is some hidden want.

1

What objects are the fountains
    Of thy happy strain?
What fields, or waves, or mountains?
    What shapes of sky or plain?
What love of thine own kind? what ignorance of pain?

66 chorus Hymeneal (hī′mə-nē′əl): a wedding song.

69 vaunt: boast.

71 fountains: sources.

Teaching Options

Viewing and Representing

Detail of *Cloud Study*
by John Constable

ART APPRECIATION

Instruction Note that this oil sketch is another of the approximately 50 sky studies that Constable made in trying to capture constantly changing light and weather conditions. Because the conditions changed while he worked, Constable painted quickly—each of these studies took an hour or less to complete.

Application Have students describe this painting's color and mood. Ask them if they think Constable's paintings are suitable illustrations for Shelley's poems, and why.

Possible Responses: They are suitable because they show aspects and elements of the sky; They are not suitable because Shelley describes his subjects as invisible, impossible to illustrate.

With thy clear keen joyance
Languor cannot be:
Shadow of annoyance
Never came near thee:
Thou lovest—but ne'er knew love's sad satiety.

Waking or asleep,
Thou of death must deem
Things more true and deep
Than we mortals dream,
A Or how could thy notes flow in such a crystal stream?

We look before and after,
And pine for what is not:
Our sincerest laughter
With some pain is fraught;
B Our sweetest songs are those that tell of saddest thought.

Yet if we could scorn
Hate, and pride, and fear;
If we were things born
Not to shed a tear,
I know not how thy joy we ever should come near.

Better than all measures
Of delightful sound,
Better than all treasures
That in books are found,
C Thy skill to poet were, thou scorner of the ground!

Teach me half the gladness
That thy brain must know,
D Such harmonious madness
From my lips would flow
2 The world should listen then—as I am listening now.

77 languor (lăng′gər): lack of energy; listlessness.

80 satiety (sə-tī′ĭ-tē): the weariness or disgust caused by having a desire fulfilled to excess.

82 deem: know.

91 if: even if.

Customizing Instruction

Students Acquiring English

1 Have students check a dictionary for the various meanings of *want* and *strain* and then use the context to determine which meaning applies in these lines.
Answer: *Want* means "lack"; *strain* means "a tune; a passage of music."

Less Proficient Readers

2 Summarize what the speaker hopes to learn from the skylark.
Possible Responses: The speaker hopes to learn spiritual contentment, to express soaring vision, to learn how to get the world's attention, and to learn how to reach new imaginative heights.

Use the following questions to check students' comprehension of the three poems in this section.

- Who tells the speaker about Ozymandias's statue?
  Answer: a traveler.
- In what season is the west wind addressed?
  Answer: autumn.
- Who or what is the "blithe Spirit"?
  Answer: the skylark.

Gifted and Talented

Challenge students to analyze the theme of Shelley's poems using either of the following approaches.

- Have students consider what this and the two preceding poems say about the role of the artist (or poet) in the world and the experiences and feelings that inspire him or her.
- Have students compare "Ozymandias" with Shakespeare's "Sonnet 55," focusing on the two poems' themes.

Assessment Informal Assessment

ANOTHER POINT OF VIEW To evaluate students' understanding of the poems, have them complete one of the following options.

- Imagine that you are the "traveler" mentioned in line 1 of "Ozymandias." It is the evening after you viewed the things described in the poem. Write an entry in your travel journal describing the scene and how you felt about it.
- Imagine that you are either the west wind or the skylark. You have heard the poet address you from below. Write a response in which you evaluate his description of you and respond to his requests.

RUBRIC

3 Full Accomplishment Student writing reflects full understanding of poem and makes reference to important details.

2 Substantial Accomplishment Student writing shows general understanding of poem but may lack references to important details or images.

1 Little or Partial Accomplishment Student writing displays little understanding of poem and refers to few important details.

GUIDING STUDENT RESPONSE

Connect to the Literature

1. **What Do You Think?** Guidelines for student response: You may want to suggest that students form small groups to discuss impressions of the poem.

Think Critically

2. Answers will vary, but may include admiring; worshipful; envious; mystified.
3. Responses will vary, but many students will conclude that the speaker would like to escape earthly cares, reach a higher spiritual plane, or create inspired poetry ("harmonious madness") that the world appreciates and heeds.
4. Students are likely to identify themes similar to the following: "Ozymandias"—mortality, the passing of time, human pride; "Ode to the West Wind" and "To a Skylark"—the power, beauty, and mystery of nature; the poet's creative and spiritual aspirations; the poet's desire to overcome his limitations; hope for the future. Encourage students to propose themes that cross texts.

Literary Analysis

Cooperative Learning Activity You might have students write two lines of poetry modeled on the lines they have chosen from one of Shelley's poems.

Connect to the Literature

1. **What Do You Think?** What words or phrases convey your impressions of "To a Skylark"?

Think Critically

2. How would you describe the attitude of the **speaker** toward the skylark? Consider the evidence provided in the poem.

3. How do you think the speaker might like to change his own life?

- the qualities he seems to admire most in the bird
- what he means by "Such harmonious madness / From my lips would flow" (lines 103–104)

4. **ACTIVE READING** DRAWING CONCLUSIONS ABOUT THEME
Review the notes in your READER'S NOTEBOOK. What conclusions did you reach about the **theme** of each poem? What evidence can you cite to support each conclusion? Compare your findings with those of your classmates.

Extend Interpretations

5. **Comparing Texts** Compare "Ozymandias," "Ode to the West Wind," and "To a Skylark." In your opinion, which poem best conveys the power of nature? Defend your position.

6. **Comparing Texts** Compare Shelley's "To a Skylark" with Matsuo Bashō's haiku about a skylark (page 718). Are there any similarities in the poems' **themes?**

7. **Connect to Life** If you were to write a poem that expressed one of your personal aspirations, what element in nature—a tree, a lake, or a season, for example—might you choose as a **symbol?**

Literary Analysis

RHYTHMIC PATTERNS IN POETRY

Meter is the repetition of a regular rhythmic unit in a line of poetry. The meter emphasizes the musical quality of the language and often relates directly to the subject of the poem. Each unit of meter is known as a **foot,** with each foot having one stressed and one or two unstressed syllables. The most common meter used in English poetry is **iambic pentameter,** in which the line is made up of five feet (called **iambs),** each consisting of an unstressed syllable followed by a stressed syllable.

T̆he lóne ănd lévĕl sánds strĕtch fár ăwáy.

"Ozymandias" is written in iambic pentameter. However, poets use different meters, as well as variations within a regular metrical pattern, to create the effects they want and to reinforce meaning. Typically, this involves adding an extra syllable or reversing the stressed and unstressed syllables in a foot.

Cooperative Learning Activity With a group of classmates, choose another line from "Ozymandias" and two lines each from "Ode to the West Wind" and "To a Skylark." Mark the stressed and unstressed syllables, and then compare the meters and variations. Discuss the effects Shelley creates with different rhythmic patterns.

Extend Interpretations

Comparing Texts Accept all reasonable responses. Good responses will provide ample support for stated opinions using details from the selected poem.

Comparing Texts Responses will vary but should be supported by details from both poems. Students may find that one theme of both poems is creative transcendence. **To make this question easier,** have students explain which skylark poem they liked better, and why.

Connect to Life Invite students to explain why they chose a particular symbol. Then ask them to describe what type of poem they would write to express their aspiration. Discuss if they would choose a type of poem from this unit.

Choices & CHALLENGES

Writing Options

1. Performance Notes Think about how you might turn your interpretation of one of Shelley's poems into a performance. Write up your ideas in the form of notes, and place the notes in your **Working Portfolio.**

"To a Skylark"
Play different pieces of music during performance.

2. Travel Brochure Create a travel brochure advertising the desert landmark described in "Ozymandias."

Activities & Explorations

1. Portrait of a King Design and create a clay statue of Ozymandias, based on your impression of the king as he is portrayed in Shelley's poem. ~ **ART**

2. Poet's Soliloquy In the role of either the speaker of "Ode to the West Wind" or the speaker of "To a Skylark," deliver a soliloquy expressing your aspirations and frustrations as a poet. ~ **SPEAKING AND LISTENING**

Inquiry & Research

Shelley's Poetic Theories Do research on Shelley's critical work titled *A Defense of Poetry.* When did he write it? How was the work received by other writers of the day?

Related Reading
An excerpt of *A Defense of Poetry* can be found on page 792.

Percy Bysshe Shelley
1792–1822

Other Works
"Hymn to Intellectual Beauty"/ "The Cloud"/ "To Night"/ "Love's Philosophy"/ "Adonais"

The Early Years Percy Bysshe Shelley led a driven and tumultuous life that ended prematurely. Born into an aristocratic and wealthy family, he was sent away to boarding school at the age of ten. There, he endured bullying and teasing from the other boys, painful experiences that fueled his hatred of injustice. As an adolescent, Shelley embraced many radical views, including atheism, and rejected most of the institutions of society. When he was expelled from Oxford University during his first year for circulating an essay defending atheism, his family was scandalized, especially his father.

Love and Romance In 1811, a few months after leaving Oxford, Shelley eloped to Scotland with Harriet Westbrook, who was only 16. Their relationship was not a strong one, and in 1814, despite the fact that Harriet was expecting their second child, Shelley abandoned her for Mary Wollstonecraft Godwin, the daughter of the philosopher William Godwin and the feminist author Mary Wollstonecraft.

The Poet as Outcast Shelley's radical ideas and personal behavior drew criticism from his family and friends, and he began to view himself as an outcast. In 1818, following the death of Harriet, Shelley finally married Mary Godwin, and they moved permanently to Italy. In 1819, despite his despair at the deaths of his two infant children within a period of nine months, he produced much of his greatest poetry, including "Ode to the West Wind" and his masterpiece, the verse drama *Prometheus Unbound.*

A Tragic Ending The years 1820–1822 were ones of relative stability, during which Shelley wrote many fine lyrics, including "To a Skylark" and "Adonais," an elegy in memory of John Keats. In the last stanza of this poem, he speaks of his spirit as a ship "borne darkly, fearfully, afar." On July 8, 1822, Shelley and a friend were drowned when their boat capsized in a sudden storm. Shelley's ashes were buried in Rome, near the graves of John Keats and Shelley's son William.

LaserLinks: Background for Reading
Cultural Connection

Writing Options

1. **Performance Notes** Have students include notes describing props, costumes, and lighting. Encourage interested students to expand their notes into a script and bring one of their performances to life.
2. **Travel Brochure** Students may want to work in pairs to create their brochures using a computer graphics program. Instruct them to include illustrations and text in their brochures.

Activities & Explorations

1. **Portrait of a King** Allow students with experience in sculpting to advise others working on this assignment.
2. **Poet's Soliloquy** Clarify that a soliloquy is a speech by one character. Remind students to base their soliloquies on details from the poem.

Inquiry & Research

Shelley's Poetic Theories Encourage students to consult a critical biography on Shelley, such as Kenneth Neill Cameron's *Shelley: The Golden Years* (Harvard University Press, 1974), and to review recent editions of the scholarly journal *Shelley and His Circle.* As students discuss their research, encourage them to consider what influences the historical context might have had on Shelley's work and the responses it received.

RELATED *Reading*

Primary Source

Objectives
- read and analyze critical commentary
- read to recognize persuasive techniques
- understand the function of persuasion in critical commentary

Further Background
Critical commentary is often persuasive at its heart, seeking to argue a particular interpretation of a literary topic or work of literature by supporting the interpretation with reasoning and evidence.

The text of Shelley's *A Defense of Poetry* makes its argumentative stance evident from the outset, beginning with the claim stated in its title. The necessity for defending the values and virtues of poetry suggests that poetry has been attacked by critics who support an opposing viewpoint. *A Defense of Poetry* is thus a persuasive argument that seeks to convince readers of the merits of poetry by providing supportive reasoning and evidence.

RELATED *Reading*

from

A DEFENSE OF *Poetry*

Percy Bysshe Shelley

After reading a composition in which a friend and fellow poet jokingly claimed that poetry no longer had a place in society, Percy Bysshe Shelley was troubled. It seemed to him possible that this view was in fact becoming widely held. In response, he wrote *A Defense of Poetry.* As you read this excerpt, note how he made his case for the value of poets and poetry.

1 Poetry is indeed something divine. It is at once the center and circumference of knowledge; . . . Poetry is not like reasoning, a power to be exerted according to the determination of the will. A man cannot say, "I will compose poetry." The greatest poet
2 even cannot say it; for the mind in creation is as a fading coal, which some invisible influence, like an inconstant wind, awakens to transitory brightness; this power arises from within, like the color of a flower which fades and changes as it is developed, and the conscious portions of our natures are unprophetic either of its approach or its departure. . .

1. **potable** (pō′tə-bəl): drinkable.

Percy Bysshe Shelley

Poetry turns all things to loveliness; it exalts the beauty of that which is most beautiful, and it adds beauty to that which is most deformed; it marries exultation and horror, grief and pleasure, eternity and change; it subdues to union under its light yoke all irreconcilable things. It transmutes all that it touches, and every form moving within the radiance of its presence is changed by wondrous sympathy to an incarnation of the spirit which it breathes; its secret alchemy turns to potable[1] gold the poisonous waters which flow from death through life; it strips the veil of familiarity from the world, and lays bare the naked and sleeping beauty which is the spirit of its forms. ❸

Reading for Information

Has something that you feel passionately about been attacked or insulted? If so, you may have tried to defend your position in writing, as Shelley did.

IDENTIFYING PERSUASIVE TECHNIQUES

What techniques can a writer use to persuade others to adopt his or her point of view? To explore Shelley's persuasive techniques, use the questions and activities that follow.

❶ **Hyperbole** is an intentional exaggeration for effect. Shelley's claim that poetry is "something divine" can be seen as hyperbole, but it probably expresses his true opinion. Identify some instances in which you think Shelley was deliberately hyperbolic.

❷ Writers use **figurative language,** which includes **similes** and **metaphors,** to create specific impressions in readers' minds. When Shelley wrote that "the mind in creation is as a fading coal," he used a simile to illuminate the creative forces that shape poetry. How does his use of figurative language contribute to his argument?

❸ **Parallelism** is the repetition of a grammatical structure in order to emphasize an idea or concept, as in Shelley's series of clauses beginning with *it* ("it exalts . . . it adds . . . "). Identify other examples of parallelism in the excerpt.

Reading for Information

Students should attempt to persuade readers of the value and virtue of the topic they are defending with both emotional and logical reasons. In addition, students should find evidence that illustrates the value of the topic they are defending.

Identifying Persuasive Techniques

1. **Possible Responses:** Poetry is "the center and circumference of knowledge"; "poetry turns all things to loveliness"; poetry's "secret alchemy turns to potable gold" that which it touches.
2. **Possible Response:** By using figurative language, Shelley is able to compare poetry to ideas, actions, and concepts that people understand. This particular simile illustrates that poetry is an imaginative creation unsurpassed.
3. **Possible Responses:** Sentences 1–3, each beginning "Poetry is . . . It is . . . [and] Poetry is . . ." ; sentences 4–5, beginning a "man cannot say . . . [and] the greatest poet cannot say. . . ."

Analyzing Aspects of Text

After students have identified Shelley's persuasive techniques, discuss the effects of Shelley's organization and word choice. Ask students if they were persuaded by any of Shelley's techniques. Have them identify which techniques were most effective and explain how they were effective.

OVERVIEW

Objectives

1. understand and appreciate a **lyric poem (Literary Analysis)**
2. appreciate the author's use of **mood (Literary Analysis)**
3. recognize, compare, and discuss themes that cross cultures **(Literary Analysis)**
4. **understand** and **appreciate** poetry **(Active Reading)**

Summary

This poem tells of a lotus flower that comes to life in the moon's glow.

Thematic Link

This poem by Heinrich Heine, by **embracing the imagination,** casts human love in mysterious and imaginative yet natural terms.

5-Minute Warm-Up

Daily Language SkillBuilder

Have students **proofread** the display sentences on page 697k and write them correctly. The sentences also appear on Transparency 21 of **Grammar Transparencies and Copymasters.**

Reading and Analyzing

Literary Analysis MOOD

Ask what mood Heine creates in this poem.

Possible Responses: romantic; mysterious; tender.

 Use **Unit Four Resource Book,** p. 21 for additional support.

Active Reading

UNDERSTANDING AND APPRECIATING POETRY

A Ask students why they think the lotus-blossom feels pain.

Possible Responses: It cannot reach the moon; the moon goes away during the day.

 Use **Unit Four Resource Book,** p. 20 for additional support.

The Lotus-Blossom Cowers

Poetry by HEINRICH HEINE (hīn′rĭk hī′nə)

Comparing Literature of the World

Romanticism Across Cultures

The Poetry of Shelley and Heine Although English poet Percy Bysshe Shelley and German poet Heinrich Heine were from different countries and cultures, both were key figures in the romantic movement during the late 18th and early 19th centuries.

Points of Comparison As you read Heine's poem, compare it with Shelley's poetry in terms of the following:

- the **imagery** used by each poet
- the **tone** each poet conveys in his work
- the **themes** conveyed by each poet about life

Build Background

The Literature of Heinrich Heine In Germany, the romantic period extended from approximately 1790 to 1830. In literature, it was characterized by an interest in folksongs, fables, and medieval romances and by an outpouring of poetry dealing with the themes of love, melancholy, and the beauty of nature.

The early poetry of Heinrich Heine exemplifies the style of the period. In 1827, Heine published *The Book of Songs,* a large collection of lyric poems that includes "The Lotus-Blossom Cowers." Containing love songs, ballads, and sonnets—many of which were later set to music—this volume was responsible for Heine's international reputation as a respected and influential poet.

Eventually, Heine turned from composing love poems to writing poetry and essays about political and social issues. Like the English romantic poet Percy Bysshe Shelley, Heine was an outspoken and often bitter critic of social injustice who was rejected in his homeland for expressing radical and unpopular opinions. Unlike Shelley, however, Heine was not a romantic in spirit. He was skeptical of the power of the imagination and did not believe that romantic idealism was the answer to society's ills. Despite this, his earlier love poems are definitely romantic in style, and in this way are representative of the German romantic movement.

Focus Your Reading

LITERARY ANALYSIS MOOD **Mood** is the feeling or atmosphere that a writer creates for the reader. Notice the mood evoked by the following example:

> ***The lotus-blossom cowers***
> ***Under the sun's bright beams . . .***

As you read Heine's poem, consider which aspects of the poem contribute to the mood it establishes.

ACTIVE READING UNDERSTANDING AND APPRECIATING POETRY When studying a poem, it is important to read the poem more than once. Each time you reread it, you may discover **images** or **ideas** you missed in a previous reading.

READER'S NOTEBOOK In order to understand and fully appreciate "The Lotus-Blossom Cowers," read the poem three times. After each reading, note images and your reactions to specific lines in a chart similar to the one shown.

"The Lotus-Blossom Cowers"
1st Reading:
2nd Reading:
3rd Reading:

LESSON RESOURCES

UNIT FOUR RESOURCE BOOK, pp. 20–21

ASSESSMENT RESOURCES

Formal Assessment, p. 145

Teacher's Guide to Assessment and Portfolio Use

Test Generator

SKILLS TRANSPARENCIES AND COPYMASTERS

Reading and Critical Thinking

- Compare and Contrast, T15 (for Extend Interpretations 7, p. 796)

Grammar

- Clauses and Comparisons, C119 (for Mini Lesson, p. 797)

Writing

- Figurative Language and Sound Devices, T15 (for Writing Option 2, p. 797)
- Compare-Contrast, C34 (for Writing Option 3, p. 797)

INTEGRATED TECHNOLOGY

Audio Library

Visit our website: www.mcdougallittell.com

The Lotus-Blossom Cowers

Heinrich Heine

The lotus-blossom cowers
    Under the sun's bright beams;
Her forehead drooping for hours,
    She waits for the night among dreams.

The Moon, he is her lover,
    He wakes her with his gaze;
To him alone she uncovers
    The fair flower of her face.

She glows and grows more radiant,
    And gazes mutely above;
Breathing and weeping and trembling
   With love—and the pain of love.

Translated by Louis Untermeyer

TEACHING THE LITERATURE

Customizing Instruction

Less Proficient Readers

Set a Purpose Have students read to find out what human emotions are associated with the blossom.

Possible Responses: It is associated with ecstasy; the joy and pain of love.

Students Acquiring English

Explain that *cowers* means "shrinks in fear; cringes." Have volunteers read the poem aloud.

 Use **Spanish Study Guide** for additional support, pp. 182–184

Gifted and Talented

Have students find out more about German Romantics such as Heine. Other well-known writers from this period are Johann Friedrich von Schiller and Johann Wolfgang von Goethe.

Mini Lesson: Viewing and Representing

Bird on a lotus flower

ART APPRECIATION

Instruction This 17th-century Chinese watercolor belonged to Sir Hans Sloane (1660–1753), whose collections formed the basis of the British Museum.

Application Ask students to describe the flower in the painting and how this image corresponds to the lotus in the poem.

Possible Response: It is red, the color of passion; it is radiant and fair.

Ask students to imagine the canvas expanding. How might students add details to express other ideas in the poem, such as the relationship of the sun and moon to the lotus?

Possible Response: The moon could appear above this open lotus.

THE LOTUS-BLOSSOM COWERS 795

GUIDING STUDENT RESPONSE

Connect to the Literature

1. **What Do You Think?**
Guidelines for student response: Some students may find the last stanza poignant and touching, while others may be surprised by the reference to joy and pain.

Think Critically

2. Answers will vary. Good responses will conclude that the speaker recognizes that both joy and pain are necessary parts of love.
3. Answers will vary, but students may point out that the lotus-blossom's beauty, fragility, and mystery make it an apt symbol for romantic love.
4. Specific reactions will vary, but they should be drawn from images and other details in the poem. Have students discuss their findings with a partner.

Literary Analysis

Activity Draw a composite word web on the chalkboard based on students' webs.
Review Personification Volunteers might read their reworking of Heine's poem to the class.
Review Rhyme Scheme The rhyme scheme is ABAB/CDDCD/EFGF.

Thinking through the LITERATURE

Connect to the Literature

1. **What Do You Think?** What is your reaction to the last stanza of the poem?

Think Critically

2. How would you describe the **speaker's** attitude toward love?

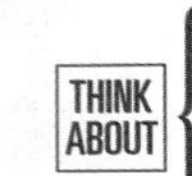

- the way the lotus-blossom responds to the moon
- what the speaker means by "the pain of love" (line 12)

3. Why do you think Heine chose a lotus-blossom as the **subject** of this poem?
4. **ACTIVE READING** **UNDERSTANDING AND APPRECIATING POETRY** Compare the impressions you recorded in your READER'S NOTEBOOK after each reading of the poem. How did they change? After your second the third readings, did you discover any **images** or **ideas** that you hadn't noticed in your first reading? Share your findings.

Extend Interpretations

5. **The Writer's Style** Heine wrote his poems in German, his native language, but they have been translated into English numerous times. What difficulties would you expect a writer to encounter in translating a poem from one language to another? What aspects of a poem might be changed in the process of translation?
6. **Connect to Life** Do you think pain is an integral part of every love relationship? Why or why not?
7. **Points of Comparison** Compare the imagery in "The Lotus-Blossom Cowers" with that in Shelley's "To a Skylark" (page 786). What similarities can you find? In your opinion, which poet paints a more vivid or striking picture? Give reasons for your answer.

Literary Analysis

MOOD The feeling or atmosphere that a writer creates for the reader is referred to as **mood.** One element that contributes to the mood of a poem is **imagery**—the words and phrases that re-create sensory experiences for the reader.

Activity In the center of a word web, describe the mood of Heine's poem. Then, in the surrounding circles, list words or images that contribute to the mood. If you think the poem has more than one mood, complete a word web for each mood you identify.

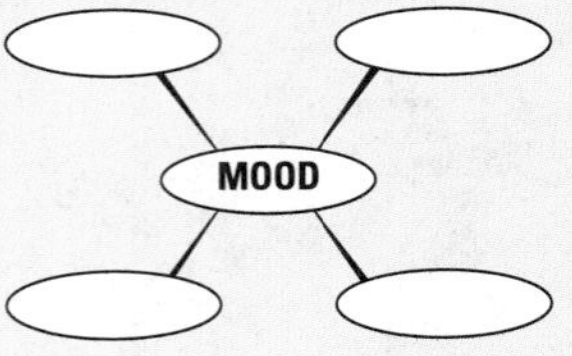

REVIEW **PERSONIFICATION** Heine makes use of **personification** when he gives human qualities to a flower. Working with a partner, rewrite "The Lotus-Blossom Cowers," eliminating all instances of personification. How does the absence of personification change the poem?

REVIEW **RHYME SCHEME** A **rhyme scheme** is the pattern of end rhyme in a poem. Reread "The Lotus-Blossom Cowers," and then chart the poem's rhyme scheme. What is the pattern in the first two stanzas? How does the pattern change in the third stanza? Why do you think it changes?

Extend Interpretations

The Writer's Style Students may mention difficulties with or changes in word connotations, idiomatic expressions, unfamiliar cultural allusions, and sound devices such as meter, rhyme, and alliteration. Before students begin, you might want to point out that in German, all nouns are capitalized; however, the translator chose to capitalize only one noun: Moon.
Connect to Life Accept all reasonable, well-supported answers. Most responses will be based on students' own experience. **As an alternate assignment,** have students describe or summarize a favorite love song that expresses both pain and joy.
Points of Comparison Comparisons will vary, but many students will conclude that both poems express passion or that both use natural objects as symbols for human aspirations or emotions. Students may contrast the direct address of "To a Skylark" with the narrative form of "Lotus-Blossom Cowers," or they may say that Heine's poem is more restrained than Shelley's fervent one.

Choices & CHALLENGES

Writing Options

1. **Haiku, Heine Style** Compose a haiku based on an idea or image in Heine's poem.
2. **A Definition of Love** Imagining yourself to be the speaker of "The Lotus-Blossom Cowers," write your definition of love.
3. **Points of Comparison** Write an essay in which you compare Shelley's and Heine's poems in terms of the tone each poet conveys and the themes about life that each poet imparts to the reader.

Writing Handbook
See page 1367: Compare and Contrast.

Activities & Explorations

Musical Interpretation Look for a musical recording that in your opinion conveys the mood and emotions of the poem. Play the recording for your class.
~ **INTERPRETING**

Inquiry & Research

Botany Lesson As a group, research the habitat and characteristics of the lotus, or water lily. What unique qualities of the plant might have inspired Heinrich Heine to write "The Lotus-Blossom Cowers"? Discuss your findings with the class.

Heinrich Heine
1797–1856

Other Works
The Book of Songs
Poems of Heinrich Heine

Career Pursuits Born in Düsseldorf, Germany (then Prussia), to Jewish parents, Heinrich Heine was greatly influenced by an uncle who tried unsuccessfully to push his nephew into business. When he was 17, Heine began to halfheartedly pursue a series of apprenticeships, but he succeeded at none. His uncle finally agreed to provide him with a university education, and although the young man was more interested in writing poetry, he eventually received a degree in law. Intent on finding a job, Heine reluctantly converted to Protestantism because government positions were not open to Jews at the time; but his conversion was in vain, for he was never offered any of the jobs he desired.

Critic of Society During his university days, Heine became concerned about political and social injustice. Throughout his life, he searched for a solution to such injustice, exploring ideas ranging from various forms of socialism to the communism espoused by his acquaintance Karl Marx. None of these options totally satisfied Heine, however, for he always worried that any radical changes in social order might destroy the literature, art, and music that he so dearly loved.

Ex-Patriot In 1831, Heine moved to Paris, which at the time was a haven for freethinkers. He was heartily welcomed into French social and literary circles, where he found many admirers of his work. In his essays, he began speaking out against the governments of both France and Germany, but these works were poorly received in his homeland. Many Germans considered him unpatriotic, and the government attempted to ban all of his works. This hostility toward Heine lasted for a long time. Many years after his death, efforts to erect memorials to the poet in Germany were met with violent protests that in some cities erupted into riots.

Declining Health In 1848, a serious illness left Heine partially paralyzed, and for eight years the poet was confined to his bed—or as he termed it, his "mattress grave." Although often in tremendous pain, he continued to write until his death, producing some of his best poetry during the last years of his life.

Writing Options

1. **Haiku, Heine Style** Students may want to reexamine the haiku selections on pages 491–495 before they begin. Invite volunteers to read their haiku to the class.
2. **A Definition of Love** You might suggest that students create a word web to help them identify words or images that contribute to the speaker's definition of love. Most students' definitions will include the mysterious nature of love and the joys and pains that come with it.
3. **Points of Comparison** Essays will vary, but many students will find Shelley's tone more exalted and passionate than Heine's and his themes more personal or spiritual.

Activities & Explorations

Musical Interpretation Encourage students to consider music by German Romantic composers such as Beethoven, Franz Schubert, or Johannes Brahms. Schubert, who wrote hundreds of songs, set a great many of Heine's poems to music. After students listen to the recording, have them explain what mood they think the music and the poem share.

Inquiry & Research

Botany Lesson Have students work in small groups to explore multiple sources. You might expand the assignment so that different groups explore different plants—for example, the ancient Egyptian lotus of the poem; other types of water lilies; the Oriental lotus pictured in the art; and less famous plants of the genus *Lotus.* Information on characteristics, habitat, and history can be shared in oral reports or mock garden-book entries.

Mini Lesson Grammar

CLAUSES AND COMPARISONS

Instruction A comparison can be made by using a clause that begins with *than* or an *as . . . as* construction.

Activity Write this sentence on the chalkboard.

Heinrich Heine's earlier poems were more romantic <u>than</u> his later ones were.

Ask students what two things are being compared. *(Heine's earlier and later poetry)*

Sometimes the final clause in a comparison is elliptical; that is, some words are omitted from the clause. Write this sentence on the chalkboard.

Heinrich Heine's earlier poems were more romantic <u>than</u> his later ones.

Ask students if the revised sentence is as clear as the original. Point out that, as with all elliptical clauses, words should only be omitted when there is no possibility that readers will be confused by the omission.

Use **Grammar Transparencies and Copymasters,** p. 115.

Use McDougal Littell's ***Language Network*** for more instruction and practice in clauses and comparisons.

OVERVIEW

"Ode on a Grecian Urn" is included in the **Grade 12 InterActive Reader.**

Objectives

1. understand and appreciate **lyric poetry (Literary Analysis)**
2. appreciate the author's use of **sound devices (Literary Analysis)**
3. **analyze an author's motivation** to appreciate lyric poetry **(Active Reading)**

Summary

In these poems, Keats compares love as depicted on an urn with love in real life; addresses the bountiful season of autumn; and despairs the brevity of life.

Thematic Link

Keats **embraces the imagination** in poetic flights that are aesthetic and sensual, focusing largely on themes of beauty, mortality, and eternity.

Reading and Analyzing

Active Reading
ANALYZING AUTHOR'S MOTIVATION

Ask students why Keats would choose to write about a Grecian urn rather than some other objet d'art. Remind them that although Romanticism was in some ways a reaction against neoclassicism, it also embraced some of its values.

Use **Unit Four Resource Book,** p. 20 for additional support.

Literary Analysis SOUND DEVICES

A Have a student read aloud the first three lines of the poem. Ask students what consonant they hear most often.

Answer: *s.* Point out that Keats's use of *s* is an example of consonance.

Use **Unit Four Resource Book,** p. 21 for additional support.

GUIDE FOR READING

B Many will say the word suggests both meanings.

C **Possible Responses:** Imagination or anticipation is often better than the actual experience.

"Beauty is truth, truth beauty."

Selected Poetry

By JOHN KEATS

Connect to Your Life

Facing Death Think of someone you've either known or heard of who, because of illness, was forced to face death at an early age. What was the person's attitude? How did he or she spend whatever time that was left? Discuss with your classmates.

Build Background

A Brief but Fruitful Life Although John Keats died of tuberculosis at a tragically young age, he was one of the most gifted English romantic poets. Keats began writing poetry at age 18, and by the time of his death at age 25 he had written poems that would establish him as a major poet. In 1819 alone—a year of extreme emotional distress—Keats composed a series of masterpieces, including a narrative poem, numerous sonnets, and five odes. Four of those poems appear on the following pages.

Although his work reflects the powerful emotions typically found in romantic poetry, Keats did not share the social and political concerns of many of his contemporaries. He was not influenced by the revolutionary ideals of the time and did not, like Percy Bysshe Shelley or Heinrich Heine, search for solutions to society's ills. Keats was more concerned with the qualities of beauty and with the private emotions of the individual, such as the joys or pains of love and the anxieties inspired by an uncertain future.

Focus Your Reading

LITERARY ANALYSIS SOUND DEVICES **Assonance** is the repetition of a vowel sound within words—for example, the repetition of the long *e* sound in the following line:

> ***When I have fears that I may cease***
> ***to be***

Consonance is the repetition of consonant sounds within and at the ends of words, like that of the *st* and *z* sounds in this line:

> ***Thou watchest the last oozings***
> ***hours by hours.***

As you read Keats's poems, listen for his use of both sound devices.

ACTIVE READING ANALYZING AN AUTHOR'S MOTIVATION All authors have a reason, or **motivation,** for creating their works, and Keats is no exception. As you read each of the four poems that follow, try to analyze his motivation. Ask yourself: Why did Keats choose this particular **subject?** What seems to be his **tone,** or attitude? What **theme,** or message, is being conveyed? Given what you know about his life, what conclusions might you draw about his motivation?

READER'S NOTEBOOK As you read, jot down notes that reflect your thoughts about Keats's motivation for writing each poem. Also write down specific lines from each poem that you think are evidence of his motivation.

"Ode on a Grecian Urn"
Keats must have been moved by the appearance of the urn.

LESSON RESOURCES

UNIT FOUR RESOURCE BOOK, pp. 22–23

ASSESSMENT RESOURCES

Formal Assessment, pp. 147–148

Teacher's Guide to Assessment and Portfolio Use

Test Generator

SKILLS TRANSPARENCIES AND COPYMASTERS

Literary Analysis
- Poetic Devices, T16 (for Literary Analysis, p. 798)

Reading and Critical Thinking
- Determining Author's Purpose and Audience, T20 (for Active Reading, p. 798)

Grammar
- Compound and Complex Sentences, C123 (for Mini Lesson, p. 807)

Vocabulary
- Word Origins, C65 (for Mini Lesson, p. 804)

Writing
- Figurative Language and Sound Devices, T15 (for Writing Option 1, p. 807)
- Literary Interpretation, C33 (for Writing Option 2, p. 807)

Communications
- Appreciative Listening, T2 (for Mini Lesson, p. 802)
- Dramatic Reading, T12 (for Activities & Explorations 2, p. 807)

INTEGRATED TECHNOLOGY

Audio Library

LaserLinks
- Art Gallery: Ancient Greek Art
- Art Gallery: Country Landscapes. See **Teacher's SourceBook,** pp. 50–51.

Visit our website:
www.mcdougallittell.com

ODE ON A GRECIAN URN

Courtesy of the Keats-Shelley Memorial House, Rome.

John Keats

Thou still unravish'd bride of quietness,
Thou foster-child of silence and slow time,
Sylvan historian, who canst thus express
A flowery tale more sweetly than our rhyme:
What leaf-fring'd legend haunts about thy shape
Of deities or mortals, or of both,
In Tempe or the dales of Arcady?
What men or gods are these? What maidens loath?
What mad pursuit? What struggle to escape?
What pipes and timbrels? What wild ecstasy?

Heard melodies are sweet, but those unheard
Are sweeter; therefore, ye soft pipes, play on;
Not to the sensual ear, but, more endear'd,
Pipe to the spirit ditties of no tone:
Fair youth, beneath the trees, thou canst not leave
Thy song, nor ever can those trees be bare;
Bold lover, never, never canst thou kiss,
Though winning near the goal—yet, do not grieve;
She cannot fade, though thou hast not thy bliss,
For ever wilt thou love, and she be fair!

GUIDE FOR READING

1 Do you think *still* means "as yet" or "motionless" here?

3 sylvan: pertaining to trees or woods.

5 haunts about: surrounds.

7 Tempe (tĕm'pē) . . . **Arcady** (är'kə-dē): two places in Greece that are traditional settings in literary works dealing with idealized rustic life. Tempe is a beautiful valley; Arcady (Arcadia) is a mountainous region.

8 loath: unwilling; reluctant.

10 timbrels: tambourines.

11–12 Why might unheard melodies be sweeter than heard ones?

TEACHING THE LITERATURE

Customizing Instruction

Less Proficient Readers
Suggest that students work with a partner, stopping to summarize each stanza. Then have them read the poems silently.

Students Acquiring English
Review difficult words and phrases with students before they begin reading the poems.

 Use **Spanish Study Guide** for additional support, pp. 185–187.

Gifted and Talented
Have students discuss in small groups what Keats's poems say about the relationship between time and art.

5-Minute Warm-Up

Daily Language SkillBuilder

Have students **proofread** the display sentences and write them correctly.

1. John Keats regarded by many as the more imaginative poet of the 19th-century was born in 1795 in moorfields England.
2. his father a livery stable manager dies when John was only eight.

SUGGESTED ANSWERS

1. John Keats**,** regarded by many as the **most** imaginative poet of the 19th century**,** was born in 1795 in **M**oorfields**,** England.
2. **H**is father**,** a livery stable manager**,** die**d** when John was only eight.

 Use **Grammar Transparencies and Copymasters,** p. 21 to project these sentences.

BLOCK SCHEDULING: MANAGING TIME

If your schedule requires that you cover the lesson objectives in a shorter time, use . . .
- Preparing to Read, p. 798
- Thinking Through the Literature, p. 806

If you want to take advantage of longer class time, use . . .
- TE Teaching Options: Standardized Test Practice: p. 800; Cross Curricular Link, p. 801; Speaking and Listening, p. 802; Viewing and Representing, p. 805; Vocabulary, p. 804; Grammar, p. 807
- Choices & Challenges, p. 807

Reading and Analyzing

GUIDE FOR READING

A The townspeople will forever be elsewhere, at the sacrifice.

B Possible Responses: It lacks the warmth of real life; it is frozen in time; it is literally cold to the touch.

Active Reading

ANALYZING AUTHOR'S MOTIVATION

C Ask what sort of beauty the urn's message refers to and how it may relate to the poet's motivation for writing.

Possible Response: The poet may have wanted to write about the theme of beauty: timeless, transcendent, or spiritual beauty; artistic beauty; the beauty of the imagination.

Literary Analysis: PERSONIFICATION

D Ask students what objects or ideas are personified in the first few lines of "To Autumn."

Answer: autumn and the sun.

Then ask what images are evoked in the reader's mind through this technique.

Possible Response: Autumn and the sun are working closely together, as friends, ensuring the plentiful harvest.

Thinking Through the Literature

1. Possible Responses: its timelessness; its transcendence; its artistic beauty
2. Accept all reasonable, well-supported responses.
3. Possible Responses: Art reflects a higher truth than life; art cannot reproduce the full range of human emotion.

Ah, happy, happy boughs! that cannot shed
1 Your leaves, nor ever bid the spring adieu;
And, happy melodist, unweariéd,
For ever piping songs for ever new;
More happy love! more happy, happy love!
For ever warm and still to be enjoyed,
For ever panting, and for ever young;
All breathing human passion far above,
2 That leaves a heart high-sorrowful and cloy'd,
A burning forehead, and a parching tongue.

29 cloy'd: having had too much of something; oversatisfied.

Who are these coming to the sacrifice?
To what green altar, O mysterious priest,
Lead'st thou that heifer lowing at the skies,
And all her silken flanks with garlands drest?
What little town by river or sea shore,
Or mountain-built with peaceful citadel,
Is emptied of this folk, this pious morn?
And, little town, thy streets for evermore
Will silent be; and not a soul to tell
Why thou art desolate, can e'er return.

38–40 Why do you think the speaker says that the little town will be forever silent and desolate? **A**

O Attic shape! Fair attitude! with brede
Of marble men and maidens overwrought,
With forest branches and the trodden weed;
Thou, silent form, dost tease us out of thought
As doth eternity: Cold Pastoral!
When old age shall this generation waste,
Thou shalt remain, in midst of other woe
Than ours, a friend to man, to whom thou say'st,
C "Beauty is truth, truth beauty,"—that is all
Ye know on earth, and all ye need to know.

41 Attic: pure and classical, in the Athenian style; **brede:** interwoven design.

45 pastoral (păs'tər-əl): an artistic work that portrays rural life in an idealized way. Why do you suppose the speaker calls it "cold"? **B**

Thinking Through the Literature

1. What does the **speaker** seem to admire most about the urn?
2. What role do you think the speaker's imagination plays in his thoughts?

THINK ABOUT
- his reference to unheard melodies
- what has inspired his questions about the "little town"

3. What **themes** about life do you think the poem conveys?

Teaching Options

Assessment **Standardized Test Practice**

MULTIPLE-CHOICE ITEMS For some standardized tests, students will be asked to analyze and critically evaluate texts by completing multiple-choice items. Use the items below to help students practice these skills.

1. With which of the following statements would the author of "Ode on a Grecian Urn" poem probably agree?
   A Art cannot teach us anything because it is cold and dead.
   B One must reflect on art in order to learn from it.
   C Human love brings only joy and contentment.
   D Music is a higher art form than sculpture or poetry.
2. Which words show that the speaker envies the lovers on the urn?
   A ". . . and not a soul to tell / Why thou art desolate, can e'er return."
   B "Ah, happy, happy boughs!"
   C "Bold lover, never, never canst thou kiss, / Though winning near the goal. . . ."
   D ". . . more happy, happy love! / For ever warm and still to be enjoyed. . . ."

To AUTUMN

Autumn Leaves, Sir John Everett Millais (1829–1896). Copyright © Manchester (Great Britain) City Art Galleries.

John Keats

D Season of mists and mellow fruitfulness,
Close bosom-friend of the maturing sun;
Conspiring with him how to load and bless
3 With fruit the vines that round the thatch-eaves run;
To bend with apples the mossed cottage-trees,

GUIDE FOR READING

1 Note the bounty of the harvest the speaker describes in this line and those that follow.

Customizing Instruction

Less Proficient Readers
Discuss the poem's images.

- Why does the speaker envy the lovers depicted on the urn?
  Answer: because they will always be young and in love.
- What scene is depicted on the other side of the urn?
  Answer: a sacrifice.

Students Acquiring English

1 Help students understand that the idiom *to bid adieu* means "to tell goodbye."

2 Help students understand the construction of *high-sorrowful.* Explain that *high* is used as an adverb to intensify the adjective *sorrowful.*

3 Show students a picture or drawing of a house with a thatched roof to illustrate the meaning of *thatch-eaves.*

Multicultural Link: The Ode in Other Cultures

In its original Greek form, an **ode** was performed by a dramatic chorus. The members of the chorus would move from one side of the stage to the other to praise the gods or heroic characters or comment on unfolding actions and emotions. In time, the ode evolved into a complex lyric poem that develops one theme. Odes often praise human achievement or celebrate an aspect of nature.

Odes were also written by pre-Islamic Arabs. These odes, called *qasida,* have a specific pattern. First, the poet speaks of a former lover in the prelude, or *nasib.* The rest of the ode consists of arbitrarily arranged descriptions of the poet's horse or camel and events in the life of a desert nomad. The main theme of the *qasida* is called the *madih.* It is the poet's tribute to himself, his tribe, or his patron and is often disguised in the descriptive passages.

TO AUTUMN **801**

Reading and Analyzing

Literary Analysis SOUND DEVICES

A Have students identify repeated vowel sounds within words and repeated consonant sounds within and at the ends of words in these two lines.

Answer: short e sound in *swell, shells;* long o sound in *core, gourd;* l sound in *fill, all, swell, plump, hazel, shells.*

Ask what sense or feeling these sounds help create.

Possible Response: They create a sense of fullness and ripeness.

GUIDE FOR READING

B autumn

Active Reading

ANALYZING AUTHOR'S MOTIVATION

C Ask students what ideas or concepts Keats wanted to explore in this poem, and why.

Possible Response: He wanted to explore death, isolation, and the passing of time in order to conquer his fears about them, and also to remind himself of the beauty of the present.

GUIDE FOR READING

D "Of an hour" suggests the brevity of life and happiness.

Thinking Through the Literature

1. Accept all reasonable responses.
2. Possible Response: to emphasize that autumn symbolizes a stage of human life
3. Possible Responses: warm, mellow, happy, idyllic

And fill all fruit with ripeness to the core;
To swell the gourd, and plump the hazel shells **1**
With a sweet kernel; to set budding more,
And still more, later flowers for the bees,
Until they think warm days will never cease,
For Summer has o'er-brimmed their clammy cells.

Who hath not seen thee oft amid thy store?
Sometimes whoever seeks abroad may find
Thee sitting careless on a granary floor,
Thy hair soft-lifted by the winnowing wind;
Or on a half-reaped furrow sound asleep,
Drowsed with the fume of poppies, while thy hook
Spares the next swath and all its twinéd flowers:
And sometimes like a gleaner thou dost keep
Steady thy laden head across a brook;
Or by a cider-press, with patient look,
Thou watchest the last oozings hours by hours.

Where are the songs of Spring? Aye, where are they?
Think not of them, thou hast thy music too—
While barred clouds bloom the soft-dying day,
And touch the stubble-plains with rosy hue;
Then in a wailful choir the small gnats mourn
Among the river sallows, borne aloft
Or sinking as the light wind lives or dies;
And full-grown lambs loud bleat from hilly bourn;
Hedge crickets sing; and now with treble soft
2 The redbreast whistles from a garden croft;
And gathering swallows twitter in the skies.

12 Whom does the speaker seem to be addressing? **B**

15 winnowing (wĭn′ō-ĭng): separating chaff from grain by blowing the chaff away.

17 hook: scythe (a tool with a long curved blade used for mowing and reaping).

18 swath: a row of grain to be cut.

28 sallows: willow trees.

30 bourn: region.

32 croft: a small enclosed field.

Thinking Through the Literature

1. What parts of Keats's **description** of autumn appeal most to you?
2. Why do you think Keats addresses autumn as though it were a person?
3. How would you describe the **mood** of this poem?

Teaching Options

Speaking and Listening

PROSE SOLILOQUY

Instruction Review with students that a soliloquy is a dramatic speech in which a character speaks his or her thoughts aloud. Usually the character is alone, not speaking to other characters or consciously addressing the audience. The purpose of a soliloquy is to reveal the speaker's inner thoughts, feelings, and plans to the audience.

Prepare Have small groups turn one of Keats's poems into a prose soliloquy in informal contemporary English.

Present Listeners should use the following criteria to analyze, evaluate, and critique each soliloquy.

- The soliloquy fully reflects the content of the poem
- The feelings expressed in the poems are fully expressed in the performance
- The speaker conveys feeling and meaning using gesture, tone of voice, and expression

BLOCK SCHEDULING This activity is particularly well-suited for longer class periods.

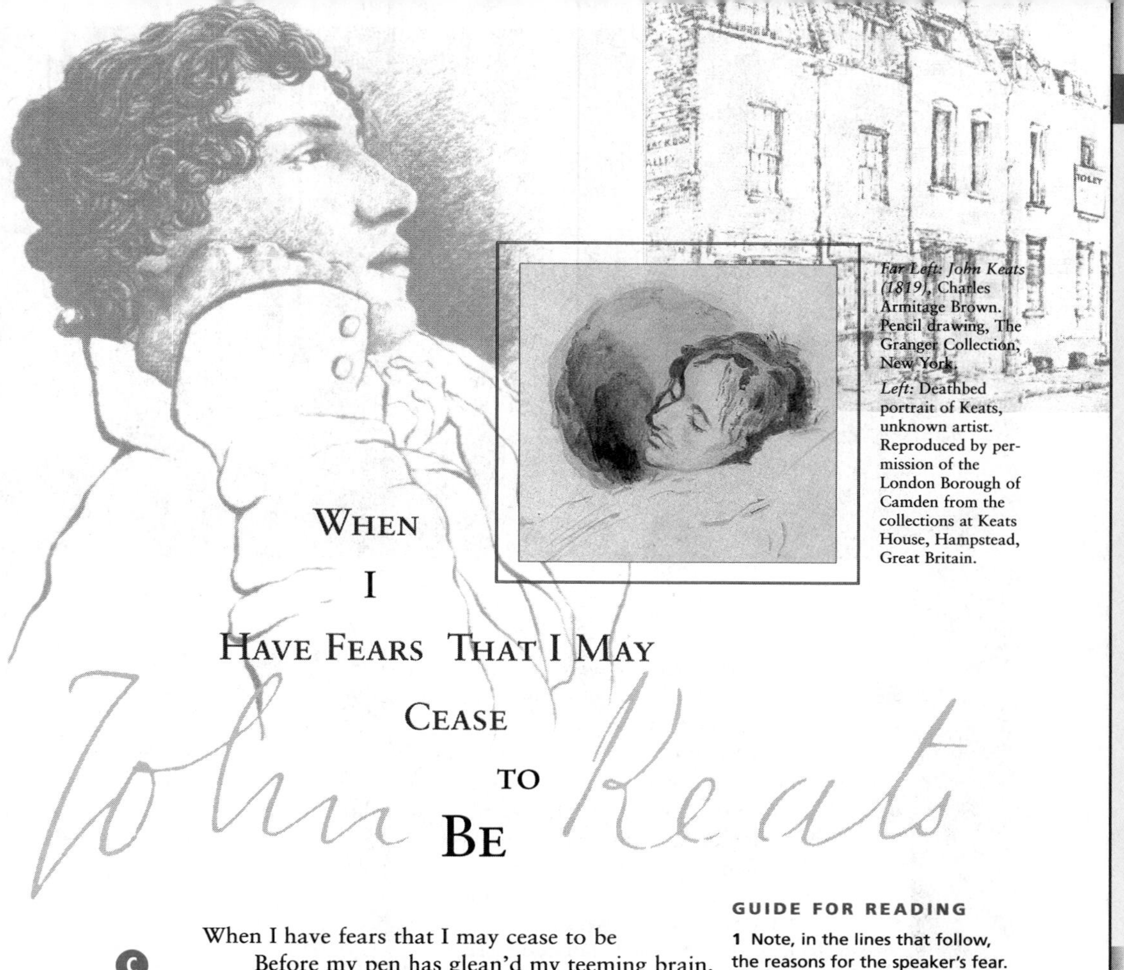

Far Left: John Keats (1819), Charles Armitage Brown. Pencil drawing, The Granger Collection, New York.
Left: Deathbed portrait of Keats, unknown artist. Reproduced by permission of the London Borough of Camden from the collections at Keats House, Hampstead, Great Britain.

When I Have Fears That I May Cease to Be

John Keats

GUIDE FOR READING

1 Note, in the lines that follow, the reasons for the speaker's fear.

3 charactry: handwriting.

4 garners: storage bins.

9 Why is the "fair creature" described as "of an hour"? D

C
When I have fears that I may cease to be
    Before my pen has glean'd my teeming brain,
Before high piled books, in charactry,
    Hold like rich garners the full ripen'd grain;
When I behold, upon the night's starr'd face,
    Huge cloudy symbols of a high romance,
And think that I may never live to trace
    Their shadows, with the magic hand of chance;
And when I feel, fair creature of an hour,
    That I shall never look upon thee more,
3 Never have relish in the fairy power
    Of unreflecting love;—then on the shore
4 Of the wide world I stand alone, and think
Till love and fame to nothingness do sink.

Customizing Instruction

Students Acquiring English

1 Point out to students that *plump* is used as a verb here. Help them understand that it parallels "to swell" at the beginning of the line and that the *to* infinitive marker is understood: "to plump."

2 Make sure students understand the meaning of *redbreast* (a robin).

Less Proficient Readers

How does the author seem to feel about autumn?

Possible Response: He respects it; honors it; appreciates it.

3 What two things will the speaker regret leaving behind when he dies?
Answer: writing and love.

4 What fades away when he realizes he stands alone?
Answer: love and fame.

Gifted and Talented

Have students find out more about tuberculosis, which was epidemic in the 19th century and caused the deaths of not only Keats, but also Emily and Anne Brontë.

Reading and Analyzing

Literary Analysis: BACKGROUND

Keats wrote this sonnet in 1819, two years before he succumbed to tuberculosis. The "bright star" is the North Star, which had inspired the poet during a walking tour of England's Lake District in 1818.

Literary Analysis SOUND DEVICES

(A) Ask students to identify examples of assonance in these lines.
Answer: repeated long u sound in *moving, pure, ablution, human.*

What image in the poem does this repetition bring to life?
Possible Response: Students may say it captures the sound and rhythm of waves washing on the shore.

Reading Skills and Strategies: ANALYZING STYLE

(B) Elicit from students that the poem consists of one long, meandering sentence. Then ask why Keats may have chosen to write the poem in this way.
Possible Responses: He wanted to reflect the stream-of-consciousness thoughts of the speaker; to emphasize the continuity between the stars or the universe and the speaker himself; to reflect the permanence of the star.

Reading Skills and Strategies: MAKING INFERENCES

Ask students what human desires the poem suggests.
Possible Responses: It expresses the speaker's desire for joy not to end; for time to stand still; to be stronger; to be immortal.

Bright STAR, Would I Were Steadfast As Thou Art

JOHN KEATS

[1] Bright STAR, would I were steadfast as thou art—
Not in lone splendor hung aloft the night
And watching, with eternal lids apart,
Like nature's patient, sleepless Eremite,
The moving waters at their priestlike task
(A) Of pure ablution round earth's human shores,
Or gazing on the new soft fallen mask
Of snow upon the mountains and the moors—
No—yet still steadfast, still unchangeable,
Pillowed upon my fair love's ripening breast,
To feel forever its soft fall and swell,
Awake forever in a sweet unrest,
Still, still to hear her tender-taken breath,
(B) And so live ever—or else swoon to death. [2]

4 Eremite (âr′ə-mīt′): hermit.

6 ablution (ə-blo͞o′shən): a ritual washing of the body.

Teaching Options

Vocabulary Strategy

RESEARCHING WORD ORIGINS

Instruction Remind students that word choice reveals a poem's mood or theme, or a writer's values and interests. List the following words used by Romantic poets on the chalkboard.

sylvan	ecstasy	bless	Eremite (hermit)
haunt	melody	creature	swoon

Activity Have students use dictionaries to research the etymologies of the words. Have them write down the origin of the word as well as its original meaning, if given. When students are finished, have them discuss the language of the romantics, responding to these questions.

- From what language(s) did many of the romantics' words come?
  Answer: Latin and Greek.
- What overall themes, moods, or meanings are conveyed through these words?
  Possible Responses: solitude, creation, distress, death, fear, joy, permanence, music.

Use **Vocabulary Transparencies and Copymasters,** p. 58.

A lesson on word origins appears on p. 206 in the Pupil's Edition.

The Starry Night (1889), Vincent van Gogh. Oil on canvas, 29″ × 36¼″. The Museum of Modern Art, New York, acquired through the Lillie P. Bliss Bequest. Photo Copyright © 1995 The Museum of Modern Art, New York.

Customizing Instruction

Students Acquiring English

1 Paraphrase lines 1–2 for students.

Possible Response: Bright star, if only I were as fixed and unchanging as you; not alone, as you are, hanging beautiful in the sky. . . .

2 Define *swoon* as "faint."

Less Proficient Readers

Which qualities of the star does the speaker wish he had?

Answer: He wishes for constancy; permanence; unchangeability.

Which does he not wish to have?

Answer: He doesn't want isolation; loftiness.

Multiple Learning Styles

Visual Learners

Invite students to study van Gogh's painting and then to write a short poem beginning with the words "Bright star," or to create their own drawing or painting of a starry night.

Mini Lesson Viewing and Representing

The Starry Night **by Vincent van Gogh**

ART APPRECIATION

Instruction Vincent Van Gogh (1853–1890), generally considered the greatest Dutch painter after Rembrandt, was a pioneer of Expressionism, which focuses not on outer realities but on the subjective expression of the artist's inner feelings. To capture those feelings, van Gogh often used bold colors and unusual brush strokes over paint applied thickly to the canvas. *The Starry Night,* painted in 1889, is one of his best-known works—so well known that when the American pop singer Don McLean wrote "Vincent," a song about van Gogh, he opened with "starry, starry night."

Application Ask students to describe the shapes and other elements of the painting. What mood does the painting create?

Possible Responses: serene; peaceful; sublime; magical.

GUIDING STUDENT RESPONSE

Connect to the Literature

1. **What Do You Think?**
   Guidelines for student response: Students may say that the poems express moods of fearfulness, yearning, questioning, acceptance.

Think Critically

2. Students may conclude the speaker of "When I Have Fears" is concerned that he will die before he has written down all his ideas or that he will die before his love is fulfilled. Students may conclude that the speaker of "Bright Star" is also concerned with his own mortality. Both speakers express a fear of loneliness.
3. Some students will feel that, in the last line of "When I Have Fears," the speaker gives in to despair; others, that he simply resigns himself to death; still others, that he sees death as a great leveler, revealing the vanity of human concerns. Students may conclude that the last line of "Bright Star" conveys the speaker's desire to live forever or else to die or faint from love.
4. Answers will vary, but many students will find that Keats was motivated by a fascination with death, or by a desire to eternally enjoy the luxuries of life and love. Students may conclude that the tone of the poems is often melancholy, wistful, reflective, or resigned.

Literary Analysis

Paired Activity Have pairs of students share their examples with the rest of the class.

Review Alliteration List the examples of alliteration found by students on the chalkboard.

Review Rhythmic Patterns in Poetry As students discuss Keats's rhythmic patterns, encourage them to explore the effect this technique has on them as readers.

Connect to the Literature

1. **What Do You Think?** How would you describe the **moods** expressed in "When I Have Fears that I May Cease to Be" and "Bright Star, Would I Were Steadfast as Thou Art"? Share your thoughts with a classmate.

Think Critically

2. What specific concerns does each **speaker** appear to have?

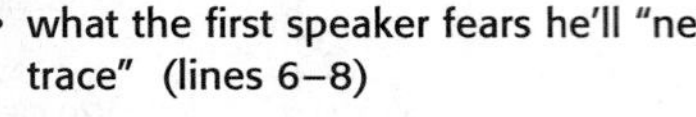

THINK ABOUT
- the first speaker's mention of his pens and books
- what the first speaker fears he'll "never live to trace" (lines 6–8)
- the ways in which the second speaker wishes he were like the star
- each speaker's mention of a loved one

3. How do you interpret the last lines of each poem?
4. **ACTIVE READING** ANALYZING AN AUTHOR'S MOTIVATION Look over the notes you made in your READER'S NOTEBOOK. What conclusions can you reach about Keats's motivation for writing these poems? How does his motivation affect the **tone** of the poems?

Extend Interpretations

5. **Comparing Texts** Compare all four poems by Keats. Do you think any of them convey similar **themes** about life?
6. **Critic's Corner** The famous American writer Edgar Allan Poe praised the work of Keats, saying, "Beauty is always his aim." Cite examples of lines from the four poems that help support this claim.
7. **Connect to Life** Think again about the person you discussed in the Connect to Your Life activity on page 798. How did this person's attitude toward life and death compare with the attitude portrayed by Keats in his poetry?

Literary Analysis

SOUND DEVICES Poets often use **sound devices** to emphasize certain words, impart a musical quality, create a mood, or unify a passage. As you recall, **assonance** is the repetition of a vowel sound within words; **consonance** is the repetition of consonant sounds within and at the ends of words. Consonance is different from **rhyme** in that the vowels preceding or following the repeated consonant differ.

Paired Activity With a partner, find examples of assonance and consonance in the four poems. For each example, discuss what effect the sound device has on the passage.

REVIEW ALLITERATION Keats also uses **alliteration,** or the repetition of consonant sounds at the beginning of words. Find examples of alliteration in the four poems. Of the three devices—alliteration, assonance, and consonance—which is used the most?

REVIEW RHYTHMIC PATTERNS IN POETRY **Meter,** the repetition of a regular rhythmic unit in poetry, emphasizes the musical quality of a poem's language. The poems you have read by Keats are written in **iambic pentameter.** However, the poet used variations in rhythmic patterns to create effects. Look at the rhythmic patterns in each poem. What effect does Keats create with the rhythmic variations he used?

Extend Interpretations

Comparing Texts Responses will vary. Some students may propose that all four poems share the theme of mortality, the passing of time, or the transience of earthly life; others may conclude that several of the poems celebrate art, nature, or love. **To make this question easier,** have students propose and write about a theme that is shared by two of Keats's poems.

Critic's Corner Accept all reasonable, well-supported responses.

Connect to Life Responses will vary. Points of comparison between the student's personal account and Keats's poetry should reflect an accurate understanding of the poet's attitude toward death.

Writing Options

1. **Seasonal Poetry** Rewrite one stanza from "To Autumn," using images that portray another season of the year.
2. **Interpretive Essay** Draft an essay in which you explain your interpretation of the statement "Beauty is truth, truth beauty."

Writing Handbook.
See pages 1369–1370: Analysis.

Activities & Explorations

1. **Autumnal Collage** With a partner, design and create a collage that captures the mood of "To Autumn." You might want to use a variety of forms and materials, including drawings, photographs, leaf rubbings, dried leaves and grasses, nuts, seeds, and so on.
~ **ART**
2. **Dramatic Reading** In a dramatic oral reading of one of the poems, try to convey the intense emotions that might have inspired the poet.
~ **SPEAKING AND LISTENING**

Inquiry & Research

Grecian Art Investigate the art of ancient Greece. Try to locate illustrations of the kinds of vases and sculptures that inspired Keats's "Ode on a Grecian Urn." What kinds of designs typically adorn these early works of art?

John Keats
1795–1821

Other Works
"Ode to a Nightingale"
"Solitude"
"On First Looking into Chapman's Homer"
"La Belle Dame Sans Merci"

A Passionate Beginning John Keats's life was brief but intense. As a young child, he was indifferent to his studies and high-spirited. When he was about 13, however, he developed a passion for reading and within a short time read every book in his school library. He was strongly encouraged by a teacher, Charles Cowden Clarke, who remained a friend and literary influence in his life.

A Career as Poet Keats's father had died when Keats was 8, and his mother died when he was 14. He was then taken out of school by his guardian and apprenticed to a surgeon. When he was 18 he began writing poetry, which became the driving force of his life. Although he qualified to practice surgery, by 1817 he had abandoned medicine for the less certain career of poet. He was not immediately successful. In fact, an early narrative poem, *Endymion,* was savagely attacked by London critics. Although Keats was painfully disappointed, fortunately he did not allow the reviews to deter him from continuing his work.

Illness and Poverty Beginning in 1818, Keats had to confront a series of physical and emotional crises. During the summer he developed the early symptoms of tuberculosis, the same disease that had killed his mother. His brother Tom was also suffering from tuberculosis and died in the autumn of 1818. After his brother's death, Keats moved to a friend's house and fell passionately in love with an 18-year-old neighbor, Fanny Brawne. Although he became engaged to Fanny, he was prevented by poverty and poor health from marrying her, a situation that added greatly to his distress. Amazingly, in the midst of this great emotional turmoil, Keats produced his greatest works, which were received with more favorable critical recognition than *Endymion* had been.

An Early End In the fall of 1820, as his illness progressed, Keats followed the advice of friends and moved to Italy in search of a milder climate. He died less than six months later and was buried in Rome under an epitaph he had composed for himself: "Here lies one whose name was writ in water."

LaserLinks: Background for Reading
Art Gallery

Writing Options

1. **Seasonal Poetry** Encourage students to follow the rhyme scheme and meter of the original stanza, as previously examined in class discussion. Alternately, students might write a free-verse stanza. Have students read their poetry aloud.
2. **Interpretive Essay** Interpretations will vary. Effective, organized essays will begin with a statement of the student's interpretation and then cite details from the poem to support and explain the student's ideas.

Activities & Explorations

1. **Autumnal Collage** Since the poem takes a positive look at autumn, you might suggest that students emphasize the bright, comforting colors of the season. Invite students to explain their designs and inspirations to the class.
2. **Dramatic Reading** You may want to allow students to work in groups and do a choral reading of the poem they choose. After each performance, have audience members identify the dominant emotions expressed in the reading.

Inquiry & Research

Grecian Art Have students work in pairs. Encourage them to visit local museums or consult books on Greek art for examples of urns or vases to study and photocopy. Note that, in addition to the Sosibios Vase shown on page 799, Keats's other likely inspirations included the Townley Vase and urns among the Elgin Marbles at London's British Museum and the Borghese Vase in the Louvre in Paris.

Grammar

Complex Sentences: Subordinate Clauses as Nouns
Instruction A complex sentence is a sentence that has one independent clause and one or more subordinate clauses. The subordinate clause in a complex sentence acts as either a noun or a modifier. When the subordinate clause acts as a noun, it can be the subject, object, complement, or object of a preposition in the independent clause.
Activity Write this excerpt from "Ode on a Grecian Urn" on the chalkboard.

". . . not a soul to tell
Why thou art desolate, can e'er return."

Ask students to identify the subordinate clause. Point out that the subordinate clause functions as the direct object of the verb *to tell* in the independent clause. Then have students compose five complex sentences using subordinate clauses.

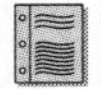
Use **Grammar Transparencies and Copymasters,** p. 122.

Use McDougal Littell's ***Language Network*** for more instruction and practice in complex sentences.

A first novel by a very young woman, *Frankenstein* was something of a sensation when it was published, and it has never since been out of print. The monster and his maker have become a part of Western consciousness and have served as the inspiration for numerous films.

Additional Background

MARY WOLLSTONECRAFT SHELLEY
Daughter of the pioneer feminist Mary Wollstonecraft and the radical political theorist William Godwin, Mary (1797–1851) embraced her parents' beliefs, particularly their convictions about justice and freedom, and lived unconventionally throughout much of her life. She ran away to Europe at the age of 16 to live with the married 21-year-old poet Percy Bysshe Shelley; they were married after the death of his wife in 1816. After her husband's premature death, Mary Shelley prepared editions of various of his works. Her notes on the origin and history of her husband's poems, which appeared in *The Poetical Works of Percy Bysshe Shelley* (1839), are an important contribution to biographical criticism. In addition to *Frankenstein,* she wrote several other novels, including the futuristic *The Last Man,* as well as biographical works, travel books, and a number of poems, articles, and reviews.

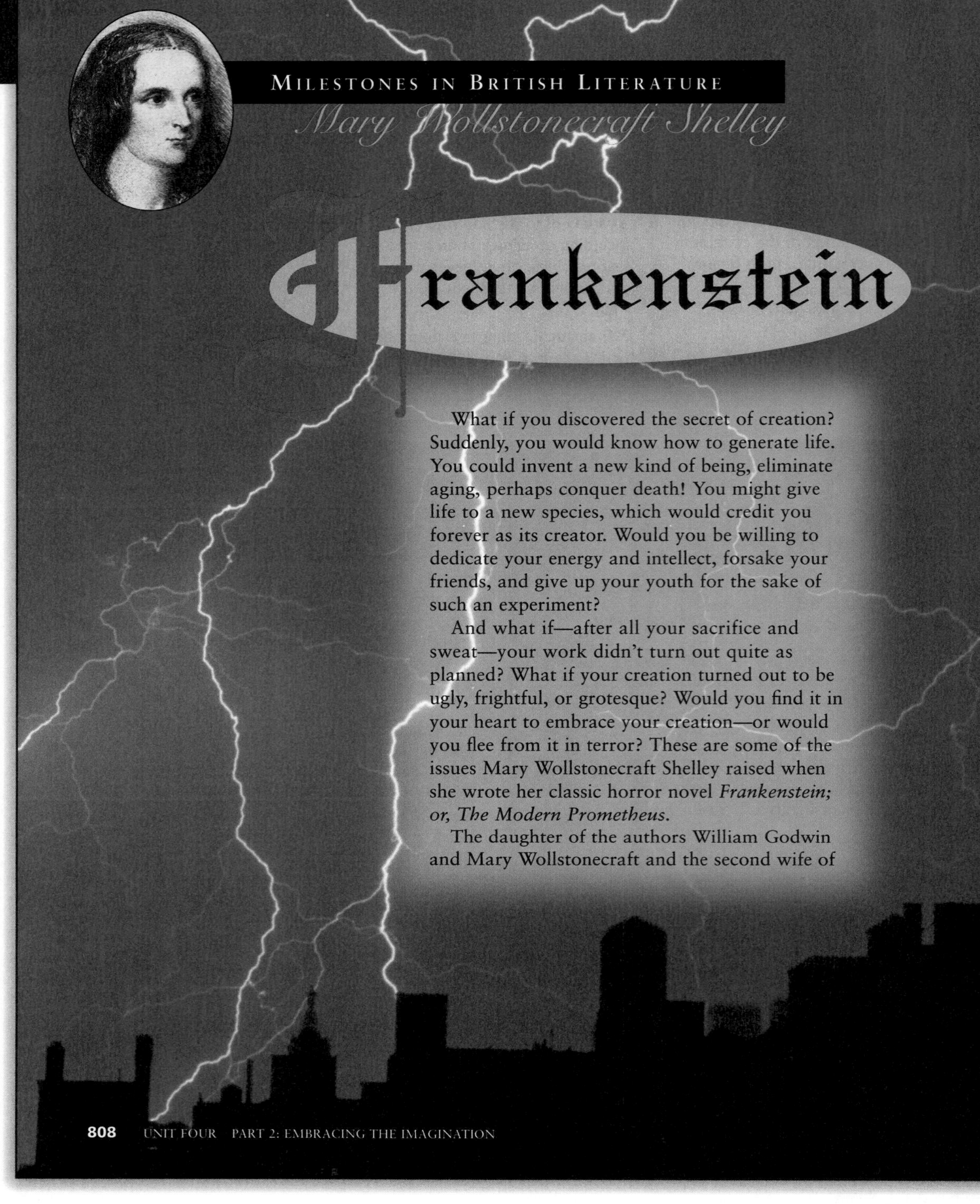
MILESTONES IN BRITISH LITERATURE
Mary Wollstonecraft Shelley
Frankenstein
What if you discovered the secret of creation? Suddenly, you would know how to generate life. You could invent a new kind of being, eliminate aging, perhaps conquer death! You might give life to a new species, which would credit you forever as its creator. Would you be willing to dedicate your energy and intellect, forsake your friends, and give up your youth for the sake of such an experiment?
And what if—after all your sacrifice and sweat—your work didn't turn out quite as planned? What if your creation turned out to be ugly, frightful, or grotesque? Would you find it in your heart to embrace your creation—or would you flee from it in terror? These are some of the issues Mary Wollstonecraft Shelley raised when she wrote her classic horror novel Frankenstein; or, The Modern Prometheus.
The daughter of the authors William Godwin and Mary Wollstonecraft and the second wife of
808 UNIT FOUR PART 2: EMBRACING THE IMAGINATION

the poet Percy Bysshe Shelley, Mary Shelley was keenly aware of the close relationship between life and danger, even death. Her mother had died while giving birth to her. Her own first child, born prematurely, died after two weeks. When Lord Byron first proposed that she write a ghost story, Mary Shelley was only 18 years old, pregnant with her second child, and haunted by suicides in both her husband's family and her own. It is little to be wondered at that she responded by writing a novel of creation gone awry.

Published in 1818, *Frankenstein* received strong, albeit mixed, reviews. One magazine, for example, declared the story "excellent," whereas another called it a "tissue of horrible and disgusting absurdity." Most everyone, however, was struck by the terrifying and pathetic monster created by the scientist Victor Frankenstein. Beginning life as an affectionate creature, the monster became evil only after he was cruelly rejected by Frankenstein and other human beings. Throughout the years, his creator has been compared to Prometheus, Percy Bysshe Shelley, the biblical Adam, and the spirit of science itself.

Today, in our scientific age, Mary Shelley's novel is best known as a tale of scientific horror. Whether on paper or on film, the monster still finds significance and meaning in people's imaginations and hearts.

Top: *Frontispiece from an 1831 edition of Mary Wollstonecraft Shelley's* Frankenstein
Middle: *Charles Ogle as Frankenstein's monster in the first movie version, 1910.* British Film Institute.
Bottom: *Boris Karloff as the monster, 1931.* Photofest.

LITERARY CHRONOLOGY

The following are publication dates of Mary Shelley's three best-known novels. Her journals have been most recently edited by Paula R. Feldman and Diana Scott-Kilvert (1987).

1818 *Frankenstein*

1826 *The Last Man*

1835 *Lodore*

Writing Workshop
Performance Presentation

Objectives
- write a script that supports a valid interpretation of a literary work
- stage a Performance Presentation that enriches the audience's experience of the literary work
- evaluate interpretative choices

Introducing the Workshop

A Performance Presentation
Discuss the differences between reading a text and seeing it performed on stage or in film. Have students give examples of movies based on books. Ask them why film versions are generally more popular than the books. What do books provide that a visual interpretation cannot? How does a script writer know what to include or exclude from a book?

Discuss and categorize elements of movies and dramatic performances that most resemble the intent of the original text. Point out that through a performance presentation, students will be able to communicate to an audience how they envision a literary work. Be sure students understand that they will first need to identify and analyze the artistic elements within the text in order to present a story performance.

Basics in a Box
B Using the Guidelines & Standards
Point out that the Guidelines & Standards present the three broad categories necessary for a performance presentation: script preparation, presentation preparation, and performance preparation. To help students better understand the assignment, discuss with them the elements in each category. You may also wish to discuss with them the complete Standards for Evaluation, which describes several levels of proficiency.

Use McDougal Littell's ***Language Network,*** Chapter 27, for more instruction on oral communication.

To engage students visually, use **Power Presentation** 6, Performance Presentation.

Communication Workshop
Performance Presentation

Interpreting literature through performance . . .

A **From Reading to Performing** The romantic poets let their imaginations soar as they spoke to the ocean, to the wind, to the folly and arrogance of humankind. Poetry is filled with sounds and images that do not always come through fully for the reader who is alone with the text. A **performance presentation,** using some combination of speakers, images, sounds, movement, and props, can reveal and heighten the meaning of a piece of literature and add to the pleasure of those experiencing the work.

For Your Portfolio

WRITING PROMPT Create a script to interpret and present a literary text.

Purpose: To enrich the audience's experience of the text
Audience: Classmates, teachers, families

Basics in a Box

B **Performance Presentation at a Glance**

GUIDELINES & STANDARDS

A useful script will
- present an overall description of the setting, props, and costumes if any
- include stage directions to indicate the specific gestures, movements, and tone of voice performers should use

A successful presentation will
- make and support a valid interpretation of a literary text
- use voice, movement, and facial expressions to enhance the performance and establish a mood
- use props and costumes, if appropriate, to enrich the audience's experience of the literary work

A successful performance presentation needs
- a literary work chosen for its performance possibilities
- a script marked for the performance
- performers committed to a particular interpretation
- optional costumes, props, sound effects, music, and visuals

LESSON RESOURCES

USING PRINT RESOURCES
Unit Four Resource Book
- Planning Your Performance, p. 24
- Practicing and Presenting, p. 25
- Peer Response, pp. 26–27
- Revising, p. 54
- Refining Your Performance, p. 28
- Student Models, pp. 29–34
- Rubric, p. 35

USING MEDIA RESOURCES
LaserLinks
Writing Springboards
See Teacher's SourceBook p. 114 for bar codes.

Writing Coach CD-ROM

Visit our website:
www.mcdougallittell.com

For a complete view of Lesson Resources, see page 697e.

Analyzing a Performance Presentation

Interpretive Reading of *"Ozymandias"*

PROPS

2 large banners suggesting "two vast and trunkless legs of stone" mounted on poles
1 giant, cracked mask showing Ozymandias's sneering face
1 large pedestal
1 drum with drumstick

PERFORMERS

3 speakers: the poet (also plays drum), the traveler, Ozymandias (carries mask)
2 people to carry banners

SCRIPT: "Ozymandias"

Stage is empty except for pedestal.

POET. *(carrying drum, enters stage and speaks)*
Imagine yourself a man who is feared by the world, a man ready to conquer whoever stands in your way. Who can stop you? What can bring you down? After all, you are Ozymandias! And yet . . .

Poet begins to play a soft, steady rhythm on the drum.

POET. I met a traveler from an antique land
Who said:

Traveler and two banner carriers enter. Traveler stands behind pedestal. Banner carriers circle stage, then stand near the pedestal. Banners sway slightly as the traveler speaks.

TRAVELER. *(speaks in a conversational style)*
Two vast and trunkless legs of stone
Stand in the desert . . . Near them, on the sand,
Half sunk, a shattered visage lies, whose frown,
And wrinkled lip, and sneer of cold command,

Ozymandias enters, holding mask, and marches about aggressively. Ozymandias stops, feet apart, between the two banner carriers. Ozymandias faces the audience.

Tell that its sculptor well those passions read
Which yet survive, stamped on these lifeless things,

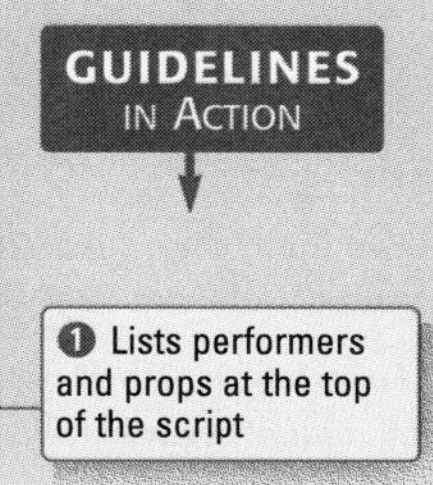

❶ Lists performers and props at the top of the script

❷ Stage directions provide detailed cues for performers to follow.

❸ Performance includes music, movement, and art, based on the interpretation of the literature

Teaching the Lesson

Analyzing the Model

Interpretive Reading of *Ozymandias*

C The model gives clear directions on how to perform a reading of Shelley's poem *"Ozymandias"*. It contains the following elements:
- a list of props
- a list of performers
- stage directions
- words spoken by performers

Have students read aloud the model. Then discuss the Guidelines in Action.

1. Props should contribute to the setting or mood of the literary work or represent characters in the work.
2. Stage directions appear in italics. They indicate what props are used by which characters to perform specific actions, such as playing a soft, steady rhythm on the drum. Point out that stage directions appear throughout the script.
3. Ask students how important Ozymandias' aggressive entry is to the effect of the whole performance.
   Possible Response: Ozymandias' aggressive entry focuses attention on him. It also gives viewers a glimpse of his haughty nature that is later reinforced by the words he speaks.

Ask students to use the standards on page 810 to evaluate the model's effectiveness. You may want students to work on their evaluations in pairs.

4. Based on what students can see from the illustrations of this performance, ask them to think about why the pictured props were chosen. What do they suggest? How do they support the theme of the poem?
Possible Response: The pedestal conveys a setting in ancient times. The mask suggests the shattered visage of Ozymandias. The sneer suggests his haughty nature. The colossal stone feet might represent the power Ozymandias once had. However, the statue of Ozymandias is decaying. His visage and feet are separated from the rest of the statue. Together these props reflect the theme that earthly power is not permanent.
5. Ask students what dramatic effect is achieved by these stage directions.
Possible Response: The crescendo on the drums marks a dramatic build up to the climax— Ozymandias proclaiming his power. The silence, followed by Ozymandias' wilting to the floor is a visual symbol of Ozymandias' powerlessness in death.

❹ Performers use cardboard, fabric, and mop-handle props, with simple staging.

The hand that mocked them, and the heart that fed:
And on the pedestal these words appear:

Poet/Drummer shifts to a steady, heavy beat just before Ozymandias begins to speak, then stops playing suddenly.

OZYMANDIAS. *(speaks in loud, harsh, almost angry voice)*
"My name is Ozymandias, king of kings:
Look on my works, ye Mighty, and despair!"

Poet/Drummer beats out crescendo, then there is silence for a few seconds. Ozymandias wilts to floor. As Traveler begins to speak again, drummer begins playing the soft, steady beat again.

❺ This scriptwriter notes the music, gestures, and tone of voice needed to introduce a dramatic moment.

TRAVELER.
Nothing beside remains. Round the decay
Of that colossal wreck, boundless and bare
The lone and level sands stretch far away.

Poet/Drummer, traveler, Ozymandias, and banner carriers bow.

FADEOUT

812

Mini Lesson Viewing and Representing

VISUALIZING THE PERFORMANCE

Instruction Planning or blocking the sequence of scenes and movements of performers is an important part of organizing a dramatic performance. There should be a clear flow of movement blocked in each scene that puts appropriate elements and performers in foreground and background (upstage, down stage, stage left, stage right).

Activity Have students draw a rectangular graphic of a stage, then use Xs and dotted lines to mark the positions and movements of all characters. Their graphic should represent the basic movement of actors in the scene. If a presentation has more than one scene, students should create a graphic that blocks each scene individually.

Creating Your Performance Presentation

❶ Planning Your Performance

One ought, every day at least, to hear a little song,
read a good poem, see a fine picture, and, if it were possible,
to speak a few reasonable words.
Johann Wolfgang von Goethe, German writer and poet

When choosing a literary work for your performance presentation, you might consider selecting a work that includes one or more of the following:

- dramatic action
- rhythmic or musical language
- opportunities for collaboration with one or more classmates
- compelling characters or setting

See the **Idea Bank** in the margin for more suggestions. Once you have made your choice, follow the steps below.

Developing Your Performance Presentation

1. **Decide on the purpose of your performance.** Is it to add depth to the literature's exact wording? Is it to introduce another point of view? For example, you could present a dialogue between the subject and the writer of "When We Two Parted" to give the woman a chance to defend herself. Or you might want to stage a debate between Truth and Beauty, based on "Ode on a Grecian Urn."
2. **Decide on the mood and texture of the performance.** Do you want your audience to get a sense of anger? joy? beauty? sadness?
3. **Choose strategies for conveying your message.** Will you use props? lighting? music? dance? other forms of communication? How will the strategies you use emphasize your interpretation?
4. **Consider your audience.** What is their level of familiarity with the text? How long is their attention span? What special interests do they have?
5. **Think of what must be included in your script.** For example, if you use music, can you vary the selections or must there be one specific melody? How will you handle entrances and exits if any are needed?

❷ Practicing and Presenting

Follow these steps as you prepare for your performance:

- Memorize your presentation.
- Practice each gesture, tone of voice, facial expression, and movement.
- If your script calls for props, be sure they are available when you practice.
- Time your presentation. Don't wait until you are standing in front of an audience to find out if something is too long, too short, or awkward.

IDEABank

1. Your Working Portfolio
Look for ideas in the **Writing Option** you completed earlier in this unit:
- **Performance Notes,** p. 791

2. Interpretive Movement
Choose a piece of literature—a poem, story, or scene from a novel—and create a dance to accompany a reading of the work.

3. Art Link
Recall a favorite piece of literature from your childhood and develop a slide or video presentation that reflects your interpretation of the piece.

Guiding Student Writing

Planning the Performance

Choosing a Literary Work
If after reading the Idea Bank students are having difficulty choosing a literary work, suggest they try the following:

- Make a list of memorable works of literature. Choose a scene from one of those works that offers intriguing performance possibilities. Identify and analyze the artistic elements within the text that will contribute to a story performance.
- Think of a movie you have seen that is based on a book. Obtain a copy of the book and choose a scene to interpret.

Developing a Performance Presentation

1. You may wish to have students work in groups. Each group can read the work aloud and then discuss the text and the performance possibilities.
2. Visual students may find it helpful to sketch a dominant impression of the scene or poem.
4. If students are producing a single scene from a large work, have them discuss whether they need a stage narrator to provide a synopsis of the action up to this point.
5. Emphasize the importance of clear stage directions. Have students write explicit stage directions for performers as well as for sound and lighting cues.

Practicing and Presenting

Explain that a performance presentation requires careful preparation. Students need ample time to gather props, memorize their parts, prepare and rehearse their scenes, and incorporate peer feedback before their final presentation.

Mini Lesson: Viewing, Representing, Speaking, and Listening

ANALYZING A LITERARY PERFORMANCE
Take this opportunity to have students analyze, evaluate, and critique a literary performance.

Instruction Tell students that this Communication Workshop involves student presentations and evaluations.

Prepare Suggest that students use this criteria for analyzing, evaluating, and critiquing the literary performances.

- makes and supports a valid interpretation of a literary text
- uses voice (volume and tone) to enhance the performance
- uses movement and gesture to enhance the performance
- uses facial expressions to enhance the performance
- uses props and costumes to enhance the performance, if appropriate

Present Have students use the criteria to analyze and evaluate each performance. Students can critique the performances through class discussion or in writing.

Additional activity Have students write reviews of the performances. Encourage them to share their reviews and compare them with their own responses.

Refining Your Performance

EVALUATING YOUR INTERPRETIVE CHOICES

Discuss the effect the changes in stage directions will have on the presentation of Ozymandias.

Possible Response: Hip-hop doesn't fit the theme or the mood of the literary work. Having the banner carriers stomp on stage better reflects Ozymandias' obsession with his own power. Rock music doesn't fit the setting as well as the steady rhythm of drum music.

Reflecting

Have students write brief comments about the effectiveness of their performance presentation and attach it to their script. Have them consider any changes they would make if they were to perform their presentation again.

Have a question?

See the **Communications Handbook** Speaking and Listening, pp.1386–1388

- Practice with the music or other sounds you've planned.
- Get feedback from peers you invite to your practices. If they don't understand your interpretation, you may wish to make some changes before the performance.

With thoughtful planning and adequate practice, your performance presentation will give your audience pleasure and greater understanding of the work.

Ask Your Peer Reviewers

- What is my overall interpretation of this piece?
- What is the most memorable part of my presentation for you?
- What parts of my presentation—sound, movement, voice, props—do I need to change or replace?
- How did your understanding of this piece change as a result of my presentation?

❸ Refining Your Performance

TARGET SKILL ▶ EVALUATING YOUR INTERPRETIVE CHOICES After you have practiced your performance presentation, think about your peer reviewers' comments. Are all the elements you included appropriate for your interpretation of the selection? Do they fit the mood and audience? Make any necessary changes.

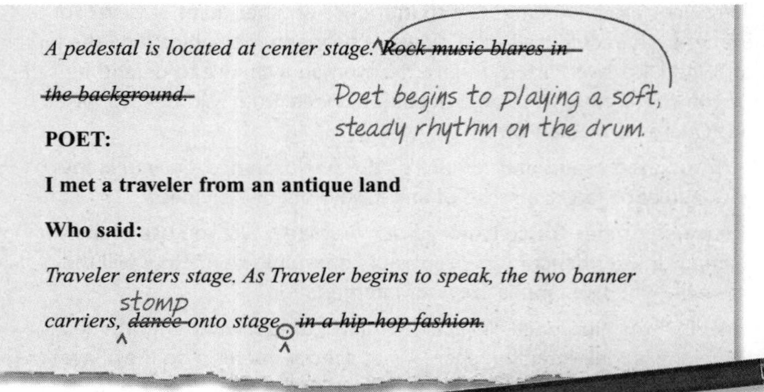

A pedestal is located at center stage. ~~*Rock music blares in the background.*~~ Poet begins to playing a soft, steady rhythm on the drum.

POET:

I met a traveler from an antique land

Who said:

Traveler enters stage. As Traveler begins to speak, the two banner carriers, stomp ~~*dance*~~ *onto stage.* ~~*in a hip-hop fashion.*~~

❹ Reflecting

FOR YOUR WORKING PORTFOLIO How did others respond to your presentation? How did working with the literature affect your appreciation or understanding of it? Attach your answers to your finished work. Save your script in your **Working Portfolio.**

Presentation IDEAS

- Present it to your classmates or videotape it and show it to your families.
- Ask your local library about performing a collection of your classmates' work for your community.
- Present it to your drama club or to other youth groups.

More Online: Publishing Options
www.mcdougallittell.com

TEACHING TIP

You might have students videotape or audiotape the performance rehearsal where they receive peer review. This will help them see the specific points that reviewers address and will also give students the opportunity to evaluate their presentation from the audience's perspective.

Assessment Practice Revising & Editing

Read this paragraph from the first draft of a student essay. The underlined sections may include the following kinds of errors:

- **misplaced modifiers**
- **comma errors**
- **lack of subject-verb agreement**
- **sentence fragments**

For each underlined section, choose the revision that most improves the writing.

Today I attended an interpretive performance of the poem, "Ode on a Grecian Urn," by John Keats. (1) The students' interpretation were (2) wonderful. They used music, costumes, props and movement (3) to dramatize Keats' philosophical musings. The performance began with Keats staring at a large urn and reciting the first few lines of the poem. Then performers danced onto the stage dressed like Greek gods and goddesses. (4) One performer played a simple melody on a penny whistle. As the last stanza was recited. The performers danced off the stage. (5) Finally, Keats was alone again with the urn. Performances like this one make (6) poetry come alive.

1. **A.** the poem, "Ode on a Grecian Urn" by John Keats.
   B. the poem "Ode on a Grecian Urn" by, John Keats.
   C. the poem "Ode on a Grecian Urn" by John Keats.
   D. Correct as is
2. **A.** are
   B. am
   C. was
   D. Correct as is
3. **A.** music costumes, props, and movement
   B. music, costumes, props, and movement
   C. music, costumes, props and movement,
   D. Correct as is
4. **A.** Then, dressed like Greek gods and goddesses, performers danced onto the stage.
   B. Then performers danced, dressed like Greek gods and goddesses, onto the stage.
   C. Then performers dressed like Greek gods and goddesses danced onto the stage.
   D. Correct as is
5. **A.** As the last stanza was recited; the performers danced off the stage.
   B. As the last stanza was recited, the performers danced off the stage.
   C. As the last stanza was recited and the performers danced off the stage.
   D. Correct as is
6. **A.** makes
   B. has made
   C. can makes
   D. Correct as is

Need extra help?

See the **Grammar Handbook**

Correcting Fragments, p. 1409

Punctuation Chart, pp. 1413–1414

Subject-Verb Agreement, p. 1410

Using modifiers correctly, p. 1398

Assessment Practice

Have students read the entire passage first before they correct the errors.

Answers:
1. C; **2.** C; **3.** B; **4.** C; **5.** B; **6.** D

Building Vocabulary

Objectives:
- classify words as homonyms, homophones, or homographs
- use a dictionary to aid in word choice

Sentences will vary.

1. *Mint* (mĭnt), "a place where coins are made," comes from Latin *monēta; mint* (mĭnt), "a plant of the genus *Mentha,*" comes from Latin *menta;* homonyms
   - I plucked some mint to add to my iced tea.
   - My aunt made a mint
2. *Knight* (nīt), "a medieval gentleman soldier," comes from Old English *cniht; night* (nīt), "the period between sunset and sunrise," comes from Old English *niht;* homophones
   - The knight in shining armor is a figure from history.
   - I remember the night I lost my tooth.
3. *Gnome* (nōm), "a dwarflike creature who lives underground," comes from New Latin *gnomus; gnome* (nōm), "an aphorism," comes from Greek *gnōmē;* homonyms
   - Nordic mythology is filled with gnomes.
   - My uncle's witty conversation is filled with gnomes.
4. *Row* (rō)"a series of things arranged in a line," comes from Old English *rāw* or *ræw; row* (rou), "a disturbance or quarrel," is of unknown origin; homographs
   - I put my ducks all in a row.
   - The neighbors had a row last night and woke up everybody.
5. *Complement* (kŏm′ plə-mənt), "something that completes," and *compliment* (kŏm′ plə-mənt), "an expression of praise or admiration," derive ultimately (via different pathways) from Latin *complēre;* homophones
   - I wanted to buy the second volume of the series as a complement to my collection.
   - My brother tends to blush whenever he receives compliments.

Have students discuss the information they found and read their sentences.

Words with Similar Sounds and Spellings

> **Roll on, thou deep and dark blue Ocean, roll!**
> **Ten thousand fleets sweep over thee in vain;**
> **Man marks the earth with ruin, his control**
> **Stops with the shore; upon the watery plain**
> **The wrecks are all thy deed . . .**
>
> —Lord Byron, *Childe Harold's Pilgrimage*

For centuries people have complained about the unsystematic nature of English spelling. Many words with the same spelling have different meanings and different origins, like *bear* and *bear,* while some words that sound the same have different spellings, such as *soul* and *sole.* In the excerpt on the right, which words sound the same as other words with different spellings and meanings?

Words with the same pronunciation but different spellings and meanings are called **homophones.** The word *role,* meaning "the part a character assumes in a play," is a homophone of *roll* in the first line of the excerpt. Other homophones of words in the excerpt include *blew (blue), vein (vain),* and *plane (plain).*

Strategies for Building Vocabulary

In addition to homophones, words called homonyms and homographs further complicate English vocabulary. Use the information below to help you identify and distinguish homophones, homonyms, and homographs.

	Examples	Alike in	Different in
Homophones	*eye* and *I*	pronunciation	spelling and meaning
Homonyms	*strain* (ancestry), *strain* (draw tight), and *strain* (physical or mental tension)	pronunciation and spelling	meaning
Homographs	*tear* (water from the eye) and *tear* (rip)	spelling	meaning and pronunciation

❶ Homophones The word *homophone* comes from two Greek words: *homos,* meaning "same," and *phonē,* meaning "sound." Unfortunately, there is no easy way of remembering the different spellings of homophones. Only familiarity and practice will help you remember the different spellings and meanings of words like *aisle* and *isle, plain* and *plane, sore* and *soar,* and *bough* and *bow.*

❷ Homonyms One effective way to build your knowledge of **homonyms**—words with the same pronunciation and spelling but different meanings—is to use a dictionary. Consider the word *grave* in the lines "The wingéd seeds, where they lie cold and low, / Each like a corpse within its grave" from Percy Shelley's "Ode to the West Wind." If you look up *grave* in a dictionary, you will find several separate entries, each containing a different set of meanings. Some of these words evolved from unrelated words in different languages; others evolved along different paths from a common source. For example, *grave* meaning "burial place" is from Old English *græf,* whereas *grave* meaning "serious" is from Latin *gravis* ("heavy").

❸ Homographs Like sets of homonyms, sets of homographs are found together in a dictionary, at the beginning of separate entries. They can be identified by their different pronunciations. Practice will help you remember the pronunciations and meanings of homographs like *desert* (dĕz′ərt) and *desert* (dĭ-zûrt′) and *live* (lĭv) and *live* (līv).

EXERCISE Look up each pair of nouns in a dictionary, pronounce each word, and identify its meanings and origins. Then classify the pair as homophones, homonyms, or homographs and use each word in a sentence.

1. *mint* and *mint*
2. *knight* and *night*
3. *gnome* and *gnome*
4. *row* and *row*
5. *complement* and *compliment*

Grammar from Literature

Experienced writers use subordinate clauses to make relationships between ideas clear and to achieve vivid description. Subordinate clauses express ideas that are related to, but less important than, the main idea of a sentence. Notice the highlighted passages below. These show two kinds of subordinate clauses: adjective clauses and noun clauses. As you can see, both prose writers and poets use subordinate clauses.

adjective clause
Our sweetest songs are those that tell of saddest thought.
—Percy Bysshe Shelley, "To a Skylark"

noun clauses
We fancied that the lake had floated the seeds ashore and that the little colony had so sprung up.
—Dorothy Wordsworth, *Grasmere Journals*

I have never heard
Praise of love or wine adjective clause
That painted forth a flood of rapture so divine.
—Percy Bysshe Shelley, "To a Skylark"

You may recall that a clause is a group of words containing a subject and a predicate. There are two main types of clauses: independent clauses and subordinate clauses. An independent clause can stand alone as a sentence. A subordinate clause cannot stand alone as a sentence and is usually signaled by a subordinating conjunction such as *who, whom, whose, that,* and *which.*

Using Clauses in Your Writing You can use clauses when you want to join ideas or add detail to a thought. Look at the example at the top of the next column.

SEPARATE
In Greece Byron is celebrated as a hero. He helped Greece win independence.

COMBINED adjective clause
In Greece, Lord Byron is celebrated as a hero who helped Greece win independence.

Usage Tip *Who* is a nominative form pronoun. *Whom* is an objective form. The decision about whether to use *who* or *whom* in a subordinate clause should be based on whether the pronoun is used as a subject or an object within the clause.

subject
Shelley was an idealist who opposed injustice.

direct object
Keats is a poet whom critics admire.

Punctuation Tip An adjective clause that provides information needed to complete the intended meaning of a sentence is called an **essential** adjective clause. An adjective clause that just adds additional information to a sentence in which the meaning is already complete is called **nonessential.** Place a comma before and after a nonessential clause. Do not set off an essential clause with commas.

essential
"Ode on a Grecian Urn" is a poem that is considered one of the most famous works of British literature.

nonessential
"Ode on a Grecian Urn," which John Keats wrote, is one of the most famous works of British literature.

WRITING EXERCISE Combine each pair of sentences into a single sentence by changing one of the sentences into a subordinate clause. Omit underlined words. Follow the directions given in parentheses.

1. "She Walks in Beauty" may have been inspired by Lord Byron's young cousin. She was dressed in a mourning gown. (Change the second sentence into a subordinate clause that begins with the word *who.*)
2. A reader of "Ozymandias" realizes something important. Fame is fleeting. (Change the second sentence into a subordinate clause that begins with the word *that.*)
3. In "Ode on a Grecian Urn," Keats suggests an idea. Perhaps anticipation or imagination is better than actual experience. (Change the second sentence into a subordinate clause that begins with *that.*)
4. The Greek children seem to jump and dance to the music of the merry piper. This is the piper Keats describes. (Change the second sentence into a subordinate clause that begins with *whom.*)
5. Friends surrounded the gravely ill young poet. These people acted like loyal subjects around a dying king. (Change the second sentence into a subordinate clause beginning with *who.* Place the clause after *friends.*)

Sentence Crafting

Objectives
- use adjective and noun clauses to join ideas or add detail
- use punctuation to differentiate between essential and nonessential clauses

WRITING EXERCISE
1. "She Walks in Beauty" may have been inspired by Lord Byron's young cousin who was dressed in a mourning gown.
2. A reader of "Ozymandias" realizes that fame is fleeting.
3. In "Ode on a Grecian Urn," Keats suggests that anticipation or imagination is better than actual experience.
4. The Greek children seem to jump and dance to the music of the merry piper whom Keats describes.
5. Friends who acted like loyal subjects around a dying king surrounded the gravely ill young poet.

Objectives
- reflect on and assess understanding of the unit
- compare text events with the experiences of individuals as well as other readers
- give students the opportunity to assess and build their portfolios

Reflecting on the Unit

OPTION 1

A successful response will
- divide the poems into two groups: those that have no similarity and those that do.
- select five poems from the second group.
- include a discussion of the poems that are similar.
- rank the poems from one (slightly similar) to five (very similar) and use this system to help them fill in their graph. Use the Unit 4 Resource Book, p. 38, to provide students a ready-made, full-depth chart for this activity.

OPTION 2

A successful response will
- identify a specific image in a poem in each part of the unit that may represent a particular contemporary issue.
- include an explanation of how the poem affects the student.
- include an explanation of how the message in the poem relates to contemporary issues.

OPTION 3

Suggest that students create their lists by describing the images and overall effect of the poems in this unit.

Self Assessment
Remind students that a poem's message may be a simple discovery—an insight into nature or love, for example. Studying the figurative language used in a particular poem may help students uncover its message.

The Flowering of Romanticism

What new understanding of the romantic poets have you gained by reading and discussing the poetry in this unit? In your opinion, how do the romantics' views of nature and love compare with the views held by people today? Explore these questions by completing one or more options in each of the following sections.

Reflecting on the Unit

OPTION 1

Analyzing Similarities Recall the quotation from William Blake at the beginning of this unit:

To see the world in a grain of sand
And heaven in a wild flower,
Hold infinity in the palm of your hand
And eternity in an hour.

Working with a small group of classmates, discuss what you think this quotation means. Then, with your group, create a graph indicating how similar the messages of five of the poems in the unit are to the message of Blake's lines.

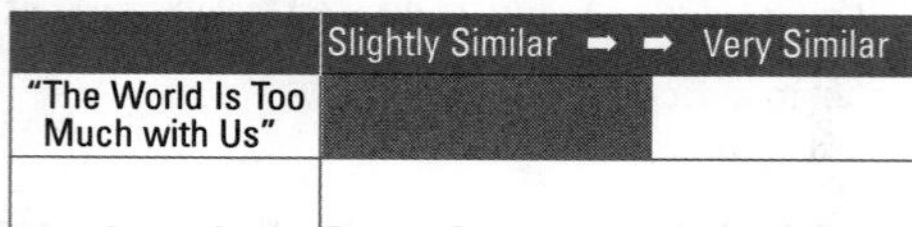

	Slightly Similar ➡ ➡ Very Similar
"The World Is Too Much with Us"	

OPTION 2

Comparing Times Many of the romantic poets were inspired to write about their observations of, and powerful responses to, the natural world. From each part of the unit, select one poem in which the observations and responses are, in your opinion, especially pertinent to issues in today's world. In a paragraph or two, explain how the two poems affected you and how the messages or truths they convey relate to contemporary issues.

OPTION 3

Defining Romanticism How would you define the term *romanticism?* With a group of classmates, create a list of words and phrases that you associate with the romantic movement. Highlight the words and phrases that you think are particularly relevant to the era. Compare your list with those of other groups.

Self ASSESSMENT

READER'S NOTEBOOK

Review your understanding of the poems in this unit by creating a two-column chart. In the first column, list your five favorites among the poems, in order of your preference. In the second, summarize each poem's message and tell why you like the poem.

Reviewing Literary Concepts

OPTION 1

Examining Imagery, Symbol, and Mood The poets represented in this unit all share a purpose: to express themselves through their poetry. Although some of the poems focus on feelings and others on ideas, all of them depend to some degree on imagery—and many depend on symbols—to convey moods and to present the poets' attitudes toward their subjects. Select six or more of the poems in this unit. Decide what mood each evokes, and identify at least two images or symbols that help sustain the mood. Share your conclusions with a partner.

OPTION 2

Appreciating Sound and Meter Think again about some of the elements—such as rhythm, rhyme, alliteration, consonance, and assonance—that work together to create a total experience for readers of poetry. In what passages of the poems in this unit do you think sound and meter are employed in particularly interesting ways? Identify ten noteworthy examples in various poems; then, with a small group, create a list of the five most effective uses of sound and meter.

Self ASSESSMENT

READER'S NOTEBOOK

The following literary terms were discussed in Unit Four. Copy the list in your notebook, circling any terms that you do not completely understand. Use the **Glossary of Literary Terms** (page 1328) to check the definitions of the circled terms.

symbol	haiku
imagery	simile
onomatopoeia	alliteration
assonance	consonance
rhyme	rhythm
literary ballad	form
apostrophe	meter
foot	iambic pentameter

Building Your Portfolio

- **Writing Options** Several Writing Options in this unit asked you to recall your own experiences with nature or your impressions of nature—a particular place, an element of nature, a season. Select two pieces of your writing that you think successfully recreate your impressions or experiences. Write a cover note explaining your choices. Then add the note and the two pieces to your **Presentation Portfolio.**
- **Communication Workshop** Earlier in this unit, you explored your insights into a work of literature by creating an Interpretive Presentation. Evaluate your presentation. If you had to do it over again, what might you change? Respond to this question in a note to be included in your **Presentation Portfolio.**
- **Additional Activities** Reflect on the different assignments you completed from the **Activities & Explorations** and **Inquiry & Research** sections of the lessons in this unit. Which of these projects do you think was most successful? Include a note in your portfolio that explains your choice.

Self ASSESSMENT

Look over the writing that you have chosen for your portfolio so far. Create a list in which you rank the pieces according to how pleased you are with the results. On the list, note any particular writing strengths you have discovered, along with any skills you want to work on in subsequent units. Date your list and add it to your **Presentation Portfolio.**

Setting GOALS

As you worked through this unit, you very likely developed a deeper understanding of the nature of poetry. Are there any poets you studied in this unit whose work you would like to read more of? Do you have any ideas for poetry of your own? Do you still feel that you are reluctant to read poetry? Develop a list of goals for enhancing your own knowledge and appreciation of poetry.

Reviewing Literary Concepts

Self Assessment 

OPTION 1

Tell students to reread each poem and think about how it makes them feel. Then suggest that they look for images and symbols within the poem that help create that particular mood.

OPTION 2

Have the groups take turns sharing their lists. Ask each group member to read aloud one passage and then challenge the class to identify the elements of sound and meter that have been employed.

Building Your Portfolio

Students will use their Presentation Portfolios to file what they consider their highest quality work—the very best projects and activities from their Working Portfolios.

For more information on using writing and assessing portfolios, see the *Teacher's Guide to Assessment and Portfolio Use,* p. 53.

The *Electronic Library* is a CD-ROM that contains additional fiction, nonfiction, poetry, and drama for each unit in *The Language of Literature.*

Suggest students choose one or more of the books described for an opportunity for silent sustained reading.

These are the additional selections found in Unit 4 of the *Electronic Library:*

William Wordsworth
She Was a Phantom of Delight
London, 1802

Charles Lamb
Dream-Children
A Dissertation upon Roast Pig

Lord Byron
from **Don Juan**

John Keats
La Belle Dame Sans Merci
Ode to a Nightingale
On First Looking into Chapman's Homer
Ode on Melancholy

UNIT FOUR Extend Your *Reading*

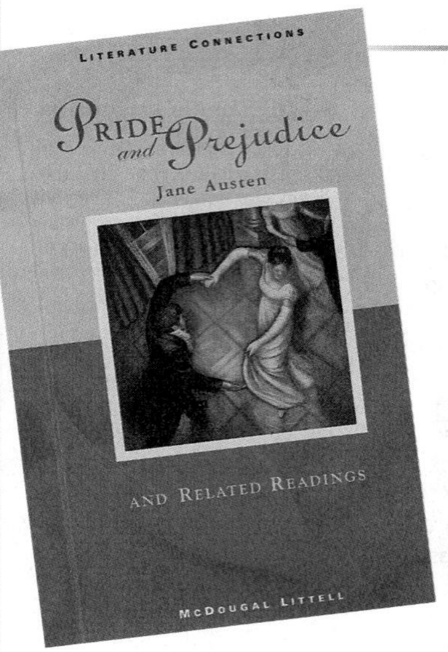

LITERATURE CONNECTIONS

Pride and Prejudice

JANE AUSTEN

In the funniest and sharpest of Jane Austen's novels, strangers who take an instant dislike of one another overcome their first impressions, discover the truth about each other, and fall in love. Austen's deft comic touch and sharp wit are very much on display in this novel.

These thematically related readings are provided along with *Pride and Prejudice:*

from **What Jane Austen Ate and Charles Dickens Knew: From Fox Hunting to Whist—the Facts of Daily Life in 19th-Century England**
BY DANIEL POOL

Mademoiselle Pearl
BY GUY DE MAUPASSANT

You Have What I Look For
BY JAIME SABINES

The Magic Barrel
BY BERNARD MALAMUD

About Marriage
BY DENISE LEVERTOV

from **Jane Austen**
BY VIRGINIA WOOLF

The Princess and the Tin Box
BY JAMES THURBER

And Even *More* . . .

Letters to Alice on First Reading Jane Austen

FAY WELDON

In these fictional letters inspired by letters Austen wrote to her own niece, Weldon tries to teach an 18-year-old how to appreciate Jane Austen's novels.

Books

William Wordsworth: A Biography
MARY MOORMAN
This two-volume work gives full breadth to the life of this great romantic poet.

The Poet Dying: Heinrich Heine's Last Years in Paris
ERNST PAWEL
A vivid and memorable rendering of the remarkable life of one of the great German poets.

Frankenstein

Mary Wollstonecraft Shelley

Victor Frankenstein, a brilliant and precocious scientist, attempts to probe the deepest secrets of nature in order to create life. Toiling in his laboratory, he creates a monster, which is soon loosed upon the world. This tale of fantasy and horror has stimulated the imaginations of generations of readers.

The Letters of John Keats

edited by Robert Gittings

Offering one of the most complete portraits available of any English poet, this collection of letters by Keats reflects the intellect, imagination, and curiosity of his poetic genius. Ideas and opinions fly from the pen of this brilliantly gifted young poet, who was fated to die at the age of 25.

Lord Byron: Selected Letters and Journals
Edited by Leslie Marchand
Byron, the prototype of the romantic hero, comes to life in this collection of his personal prose.

Recollections of the Last Days of Shelley and Byron
Edward J. Trelawny
These two famous friends and fellow poets are examined in this biographical work.

Other Media

Frankenstein: The Making of the Monster: The World of Mary Shelley
Library Video Company.
(videocassettes)

Jane Austen and Her World
Films for the Humanities and Sciences, 1995.
(videocassettes)

Pride and Prejudice
Abridged. Read by Glenda Jackson. Dove Audio, 1995.
(audiocassette)

The Rime of the Ancient Mariner and Other Great Poems
Listening Library, 1987. Narrated by Christopher Plummer and Bramwell Fletcher. Includes "Rime" and "Kubla Khan" by Coleridge as well as poems by Blake, Burns, Wordsworth, Byron, Shelley, and Keats.
(audiocassette)

The Glorious Romantics
Monterey Home Video.
(videocassette)

EXTEND YOUR READING 821

Reading&Writing
for Assessment

OVERVIEW

The Reading & Writing for Assessment feature provides practice in taking standardized tests. As students work through this lesson, they will read a nonfiction passage and answer multiple-choice and essay questions. Boxed strategies located alongside the text will guide students through the activities. These strategies model processes students could use as they take standardized tests.

This feature is based on and will help to prepare students for state assessments, including end-of-course assessments. It will also prepare students for the reading comprehension questions used on such college board examinations as the SAT and the ACT.

Objectives

- understand and apply strategies for reading a test selection
- recognize literary techniques in a test selection
- understand and apply strategies for answering multiple-choice questions about a test selection
- respond to a writing prompt and present ideas in a logical order
- understand and apply strategies for revising and proofreading a test response

Reading & Writing for Assessment

When you studied strategies for reading a test selection on pages 508–513, you practiced techniques for success on reading and writing assessments. These kinds of tests are often important end-of-course examinations.

The following pages will give you more test-taking strategies. You will have a chance to apply them in the practice activities that follow the selection.

PART 1 How to Read a Test Selection

Here are the basic strategies you studied earlier along with several new ones based on a different type of reading selection. Applying these strategies, taking notes, and highlighting or underscoring passages as you read can help you focus on the information you will need to know.

STRATEGIES FOR READING A TEST SELECTION

- **Before you begin reading, skim the questions that follow the passage.** These can help focus your reading.
- **Unlock word meanings.** Use context clues and word parts to help you unlock the meaning of unfamiliar words.
- **Use your active reading strategies such as analyzing, predicting, and questioning.** Make notes in the margin to help you focus your reading. You may do this only if the test directions allow you to mark on the test itself.
- **Look for main ideas.** These are often stated at the beginnings or ends of paragraphs. Sometimes they are implied, not stated. After reading each paragraph, ask "What was this passage about?"
- **Note the literary elements and techniques used by the writer.** You might consider the tone (writer's attitude toward the subject), figurative language, descriptive language, or use of techniques like comparison and contrast. Then ask yourself what effect the writer achieves with each choice.
- **Examine the sequence of ideas.** Are the ideas developed in chronological order, presented in order of importance, or organized in some other way? What does the sequence of ideas suggest about the writer's message?
- **Think about the message and writer's purpose.** What questions does the selection answer? What new questions does it imply? Can you make any generalizations?

822

Teaching Options

Standardized Test Practice

ANALYZING CHARACTERISTICS OF CLEAR TEXT

After students have completed the lesson, have them analyze the model for characteristics of clear text.

Instruction Tell students you want them to analyze the test model from a different point of view. They will reread the model and analyze it for conciseness, completeness, and correctness.

Activity Have students discuss and develop criteria for conciseness, completeness, and correctness. List criteria as students generate them. Then, have them refer to the list as they reread the model. Discuss their responses and questions.

Reading Selection

Why Leaves Turn Color in the Fall
by Diane Ackerman

1 The stealth of autumn catches one unaware. Was that a goldfinch perching in the early September woods, or just the first turning leaf? A red-winged blackbird or a sugar maple closing up shop for the winter? Keen-eyed as leopards, we stand still and squint hard, looking for signs of movement. Early-morning frost sits heavily on the grass, and turns ❶ barbed wire into a string of stars. On a distant hill, a small square of yellow appears to be a lighted stage. At last the truth dawns on us: Fall is staggering in, right on schedule, with its baggage of chilly nights, macabre holidays, and spectacular, heart-stoppingly beautiful leaves. Soon the leaves will start cringing on the trees, and roll up in clenched fists before they actually fall off. Dry seedpods will rattle like tiny gourds. But first there will be weeks of gushing color so bright, so pastel, so confettilike, that people will travel up and down the East Coast just to stare at it—a whole season of leaves.

2 ❷ Where do the colors come from? Sunlight rules most living things with its golden edicts. When the days begin to shorten, soon after the summer solstice on June 21, a tree reconsiders its leaves. All summer it feeds them so they can process sunlight, but in the dog days of summer the tree begins pulling nutrients back into its trunk and roots, pares down, and gradually chokes off its leaves. A corky layer of cells forms at the leaves' slender petioles, then scars over. Undernourished, the leaves stop producing the pigment chlorophyll, and photosynthesis ceases. Animals can migrate, hibernate, or store food to prepare for winter. But where can a tree go? It survives by dropping its leaves, and by the end of autumn only a few fragile threads of fluid-carrying xylem hold leaves to their stems.

3 ❸ A turning leaf stays partly green at first, then reveals splotches of yellow and red as the chlorophyll gradually breaks down. Dark green seems to stay longest in the veins, outlining and defining them. During the summer, chlorophyll dissolves in the heat and light, but it is also being steadily replaced. In the fall, on the other hand, no new pigment is produced, and so we notice the other colors that were always there, right in the leaf, although chlorophyll's shocking green hid them from view. With their camouflage gone, we see these colors for the first time all year, and marvel, but they were always there, hidden like a vivid secret beneath the hot glowing greens of summer.

4 The most spectacular range of fall foliage occurs in the northeastern United States and in eastern China, where the leaves are robustly colored thanks in part to a rich climate. European maples don't achieve the same flaming reds as their

STRATEGIES IN ACTION

❶ **Note literary elements like use of figurative language.**

ONE STUDENT'S THOUGHTS
"The writer uses unusual metaphors—she says that in fall barbed wire looks like a string of stars. She must mean that the frost glistens on the barbs."

YOUR TURN
Find other metaphors in the selection.

❷ **Read actively by questioning.**
"How does this writer answer her own question about the colors?"

YOUR TURN
"Maybe I can make a diagram to help me understand this process."

❸ **Examine the sequence of ideas.**
"This writer is explaining a process—how leaves change color. She seems to be organizing her ideas in the order of the process."

Strategies in Action

Begin by previewing the text. Note the title and identify the subject of the reading selection. Read through the questions and prompts at the end of the text. Ask students what they will need to look for as they read.

Customizing for Less Proficient Readers

1. Use the following questions to help students identify the figurative language in paragraph one.
   - The writer states that "Fall is staggering in, right on schedule, with its baggage . . ." To what is fall being compared and what kind of figurative language is being used?
     Possible Response: a person; personification
   - What does the writer say the changing leaves look like?
     Possible Response: a lighted stage, clenched fists, confetti

YOUR TURN "Keen-eyed as leopards" refers to people who are looking for signs of fall.

2. The writer states the main idea of the paragraph in the form of a question and then answers it by explaining where leaves get their color.

YOUR TURN

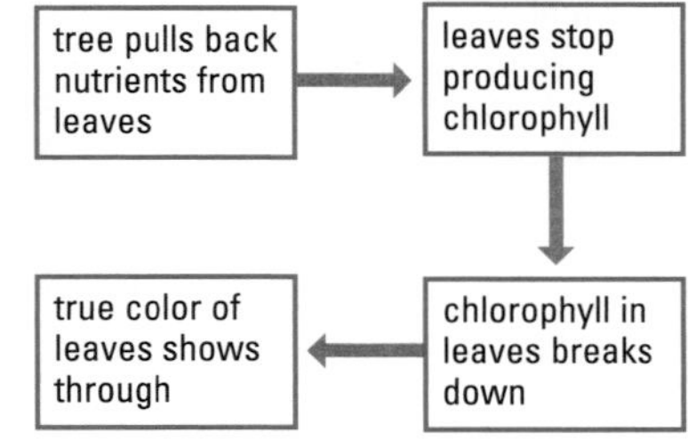

3. If students have difficulty understanding concepts being described in a test selection, they may wish to examine the sequence of ideas by making a diagram similar to the one in activity two.

4. Context clues can help students decipher the meanings of unfamiliar words. However, students should only concentrate on those words that are important to understanding the selection. Ask students whether they need to know the meaning of *anthocyanin* and *carotenoids* to answer the questions at the end.
   Possible Response: Knowing that these are pigments is enough to understand the selection and the questions at the end.

Customizing for Less Proficient Readers

5. To help students identify descriptive language in the paragraph, have them make a chart like the one below and fill it with descriptive words.

	sight	sound	touch
verbs			
adjectives			

6. A piece of writing may contain more than one message or purpose, and students may be tested on it. For example, questions about this selection could test students on how leaves change color in the fall, the beauty of autumn, or the life-cycle of the leaf.

American relatives, which thrive on cold nights and sunny days. In Europe, the warm, humid weather turns the leaves brown or mildly yellow. ❹ Anthocyanin, the pigment that gives apples their red and turns leaves red or red-violet, is produced by sugars that remain in the leaf after the supply of nutrients dwindles. Unlike the carotenoids, which color carrots, squash, and corn, and turn leaves orange and yellow, anthocyanin varies from year to year, depending on the temperature and amount of sunlight. The fiercest colors occur in years when the fall sunlight is strongest and the nights are cool and dry (a state of grace scientists find vexing to forecast). This is also why leaves appear dizzyingly bright and clear on a sunny fall day: The anthocyanin flashes like a marquee. . . .

5 But how do the colored leaves fall? As a leaf ages, the growth hormone, auxin, fades, and cells at the base of the petiole divide. Two or three rows of small cells, lying at right angles to the axis of the petiole, react with water, then come apart, leaving the petioles hanging on by only a few threads of xylem. A light breeze, and the leaves are airborne. They glide and swoop, rocking in invisible cradles. They are all wing and may flutter from yard to yard on small whirlwinds or updrafts, swiveling as they go. Firmly tethered to earth, we love to see things rise up and fly—soap bubbles, balloons, birds, fall leaves. They remind us that the end of a season is capricious, as is the end of life. We especially like the way leaves rock, careen, and swoop as they fall. Everyone knows the motion. Pilots sometimes do a maneuver called a "falling leaf," in which the plane loses altitude quickly and on purpose, by slipping first to the right, then to the left. The machine weighs a ton or more, but in one pilot's mind it is a weightless thing, a falling leaf. She has seen the motion before, in the Vermont woods where she played as a child. Below her the trees radiate gold, copper, and red. Leaves are falling, although she can't see them fall, as she falls, swooping down for a closer view.

6 ❺ At last the leaves leave. But first they turn color and thrill us for weeks on end. Then they crunch and crackle underfoot. They shush, as children drag their small feet through leaves heaped along the curb. Dark, slimy mats of leaves cling to one's heels after a rain. A damp, stuccolike mortar of semidecayed leaves protects the tender shoots with a roof until spring, and makes a rich humus. An occasional bulge or ripple in the leafy mounds signals a shrew or a field mouse tunneling out of sight. ❻ Sometimes one finds in fossil stones the imprint of a leaf, long since disintegrated, whose outlines remind us how detailed, vibrant, and alive are the things of this earth that perish.

STRATEGIES IN ACTION

❹ Unlock word meanings

"*Anthocyanin* and *carotenoids* must be substances that produce color since they are associated with reds and oranges. Besides *carotenoid* looks like it is related to the word *carrot*."

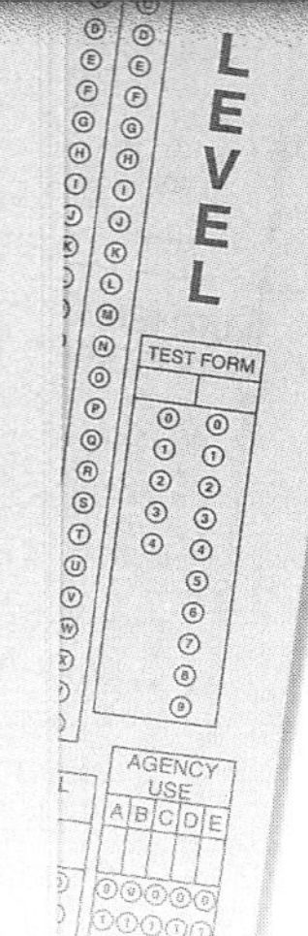

❺ Note literary elements like use of descriptive language.

"The descriptions here are neat. They use the senses like sight, sound, and touch."

❻ Think about the message and writer's purpose.

"The writer seems to suggest that we can learn something about life—and death—by watching the leaves turn color and fall."

Check Your Understanding

Have students use the following questions to test their own understanding of the selection before answering the questions in their texts.

- What were the main ideas in the selection?
- What literary elements does the writer use? How does the writer encourage readers to care about the information presented?
- What structure does the writer use for the selection?
- Did the selection answer all your questions about the subject? If not, what questions remain unanswered?

PART 2 How to Answer Multiple-Choice Questions

Use the strategies in the box and the notes in the side column to help you answer the questions below and on the following pages.

Based on the selection you have just read, choose the best answer for each of the following questions.

1. In paragraph 1, the writer personifies leaves when she says that
   - **A.** they are heart-stoppingly beautiful.
   - **B.** they start cringing on the trees.
   - **C.** their colors will be bright, like confetti.
   - **D.** at first they look like birds perching in the trees.
2. In which of the following passages does the writer adopt a scientific tone?
   - **A.** "Fall is staggering in, right on schedule"
   - **B.** "A corky layer of cells forms at the leaves' slender petioles"
   - **C.** "we see these colors for the first time all year, and marvel"
   - **D.** "a state of grace scientists find vexing to forecast"
3. In paragraph 1, what metaphor does the writer use to suggest what the beginning of fall is like?
   - **A.** a person tiptoeing
   - **B.** a leopard jumping
   - **C.** a lighted stage
   - **D.** a festival
4. What does the writer mean when she says, "Sunlight rules most living things with its golden edicts"?
   - **A.** Most living things could not survive without sunlight.
   - **B.** Most living things enjoy basking in sunlight.
   - **C.** Most living things prefer summer to winter.
   - **D.** The sun determines the actions of plants and animals.
5. Which of the following might be a lesson the writer intends to draw from the falling of leaves?
   - **A.** People should find out more about why leaves change color.
   - **B.** People should try to be more like trees.
   - **C.** Life is a cycle and death is part of life.
   - **D.** Nature appears vibrant but is actually malevolent.

STRATEGIES FOR ANSWERING MULTIPLE-CHOICE QUESTIONS

- **Ask questions** that help you eliminate some of the choices.
- **Pay attention to choices** such as "all of the above" or "none of the above." To eliminate them, all you need to find is one answer that doesn't fit.
- **Skim your notes.** Details you noticed as you read may provide answers.

STRATEGIES IN ACTION

Skim your notes.

ONE STUDENT'S THOUGHTS

"The writer says that we are like leopards as we look for the fall, not that the fall is like a leopard. *So I can eliminate choice B.*"

YOUR TURN

What words does the writer use to describe the beginning of fall?

Ask questions.

Does the writer hope to persuade or describe?

ONE STUDENT'S THOUGHTS

"The writer doesn't seem to be telling people what they should do. She is just describing the process by which leaves fall. *So I can eliminate choices A and B.*"

YOUR TURN

What other choice can you eliminate?

Guilding Student Response

Multiple-Choice Questions

1. B
2. B
3. A

YOUR TURN The writer describes the beginning of fall as "stealthy." She describes people watching and waiting for signs of the approaching fall.

4. A
5. C

YOUR TURN To eliminate choice D, students must note the tone of the selection. For example, the writer uses comparisons to confetti and a flashing marquee to compare autumn to a festival. Even when the writer uses negative images—like that of a tree choking off its leaves—she doesn't describe the tree as malevolent. Instead, she says the tree is doing what it must to survive.

Short-Answer Question

Possible Response: This writer uses figurative language to help readers appreciate the grace of falling leaves. For example, she compares the movements of falling leaves to the rocking of cradles and to a slipping maneuver performed by airplane pilots. These metaphors illustrate the beauty of a falling leaf.

YOUR TURN The writer's comparison of the colors in a leaf to a secret is a simile.

Essay Question

Possible Response: The author uses a poetic tone to describe the leaves changing color. She uses figurative language to compare fall to a punctual guest, sunlight to a ruler, and leaves to birds, soap bubbles, and airplanes. The writer's figurative language conveys her sense that autumn is a wonderful and exciting season. Her tone is scientific when she describes the facts of the color-changing process. She uses scientific terms, such as *petioles, xylem, chlorophyll,* and *photosynthesis,* and she organizes her explanation in a step-by-step process.

YOUR TURN The poetic passages in this selection demonstrate the writer's use of figurative language. For example, "Keen-eyed as leopards, we stand still and squint hard . . ." The scientific passages explain the facts of how leaves turn color and fall. "During the summer, chlorophyll dissolves in the heat and light . . ." Both contain descriptive language, but the poetic passages appeal to emotions, while the scientific passages appeal to reason.

PART 3 How to Respond in Writing

You may also be asked to write answers to questions about a reading passage. **Short-answer questions** usually ask you to answer in a sentence or two. **Essay questions** require a fully developed piece of writing.

Short-Answer Question

STRATEGIES FOR RESPONDING TO SHORT-ANSWER QUESTIONS

- **Identify the key words** in the writing prompt that tell you the ideas to discuss. Make sure you know what is meant by each.
- **State your response** directly and to the point.
- **Support your ideas** by using evidence from the selection.
- **Use correct grammar.**

Sample Prompt

Answer the following question in two or three sentences.

How does this writer use figurative language to help readers understand her subject? Give several examples of figurative language from the essay and explain why use of such language is an effective technique.

STRATEGIES IN ACTION

Identify the key words in the writing prompt.

ONE STUDENT'S THOUGHTS

"The key words are *figurative language, example,* and *explain.* I will have to find examples of figurative language in the selection and then explain why the writer uses them. Maybe I can find a metaphor in the selection to use as one example."

YOUR TURN

Go back to the selection and find a metaphor, simile, or another examples of figurative language.

Essay Question

STRATEGIES FOR ANSWERING ESSAY QUESTIONS

- **Look for direction words** in the writing prompt, such as *essay, analyze, describe,* or *compare* and *contrast,* that tell you how to respond directly to the prompt.
- **List the points** you want to make before beginning to write.
- **Write an interesting introduction** that presents your main point.
- **Develop your ideas** by using evidence from the selection that supports the statements you make. Present the ideas in a logical order.
- **Write a conclusion** that summarizes your points.
- **Check your work** for correct grammar.

Sample Prompt

This writer switches back and forth between a poetic and a scientific tone. Write an essay in which you use examples from the text to compare and contrast the two tones.

Look for direction words.

ONE STUDENT'S THOUGHTS

"The prompt is asking me to *compare* and *contrast* the passages from the selection that have a poetic tone with the ones that sound more scientific. I'll have to explain how the two tones are alike and how they are different."

YOUR TURN

Make a list of scientific passages and poetic passages in this selection. How are they similar? How are they different?

PART 4 How to Revise and Edit a Test Selection

Here is a student's first draft in response to the writing prompt at the bottom of page 826. Read it and answer the multiple-choice questions that follow.

> This writer uses a poetic tone to present her own point of view about the leaves changing color. She uses a scientific tone to describe simple facts. The author uses a poetic tone to describe her feeling that fall tends to sneak upon us. She says that people observing the signs of fall are leopards and fall is a guest staggering in right on schedule and bringing baggage. But she uses scientific language to tell why leaves actually change color giving the names of pigments like anthocyanin and telling us the fact that the presence of anthocyanin depends on the temperature and quantity of sunlight.

1. What is the BEST transition to add to the beginning of the sentence in lines 3–4 ("The author . . . sneak up on us.")?

A. Furthermore,
B. Yet
C. For example,
D. And

2. What is the BEST change, if any, to make to the sentence in lines 4–6 ("She says that . . . bringing baggage.")?

A. Change *the signs of fall* to *leaves.*
B. Add the word *like* between *are* and *leopards.*
C. Delete the words *staggering in right on schedule.*
D. Make no change.

3. What is the BEST change, if any, to make to the sentence in lines 6–10 ("But she uses . . . quantity of sunlight.")?

A. Add a colon after *color.*
B. Add a semicolon after *color.*
C. Add a comma after *color.*
D. Make no change.

STRATEGIES FOR REVISING, EDITING, AND PROOFREADING

- **Read the passage carefully.**
- **Note the parts that are confusing** or don't make sense. What kinds of errors would that signal?
- **Look for errors** in grammar, usage, spelling, and capitalization. Common errors include:
  - run-on sentences
  - sentence fragments
  - lack of subject-verb agreement
  - unclear pronoun antecedents
  - lack of transition words

Answers
1. C
2. B
3. C

Check Your Understanding

Have students reread their own responses to the short-answer and essay questions. Then have students use the following questions to guide themselves as they revise and edit their own work.

- Have I responded directly to the direction words in the writing prompt?
- Have I supported my ideas with evidence from the selection?
- Have I presented my ideas in a logical order?
- Have I included an introduction and a conclusion?
- Have I used correct grammar?

READING AND WRITING FOR ASSESSMENT 827

The Victorians

The selections in Unit Five explore the diversity and variety of Victorian literature, reflecting the period's optimism and conservatism as well as its social pretense and hypocrisy. The unit is divided into two sections to capture the contrasting attitudes of this fascinating era.

Part 1

Personal Relationships The first half of the unit explores the reaction of some famous Victorian writers to the tremendous progress and change of their era. Writers such as Alfred, Lord Tennyson, Charlotte Brontë, and Elizabeth Barrett Browning uphold the power of personal relationships as a mainstay in the midst of the often bewildering social upheaval of the era. Other writers, such as Elizabeth Gleghorn Gaskell, probe the effects of the new social order on human relationships. In the **Comparing Literature** feature, Russian writer Leo Tolstoy examines the values that are of fundamental importance to all people of all times.

Part 2

New Directions The works in this section reveal the wide variety of Victorian literature, from somber poems that probe the human condition to joyful farces that mock its weaknesses. The **Comparing Literature** feature, by Indian poet Rabindranath Tagore, finds that time and the seasons provide a link with his future readers.

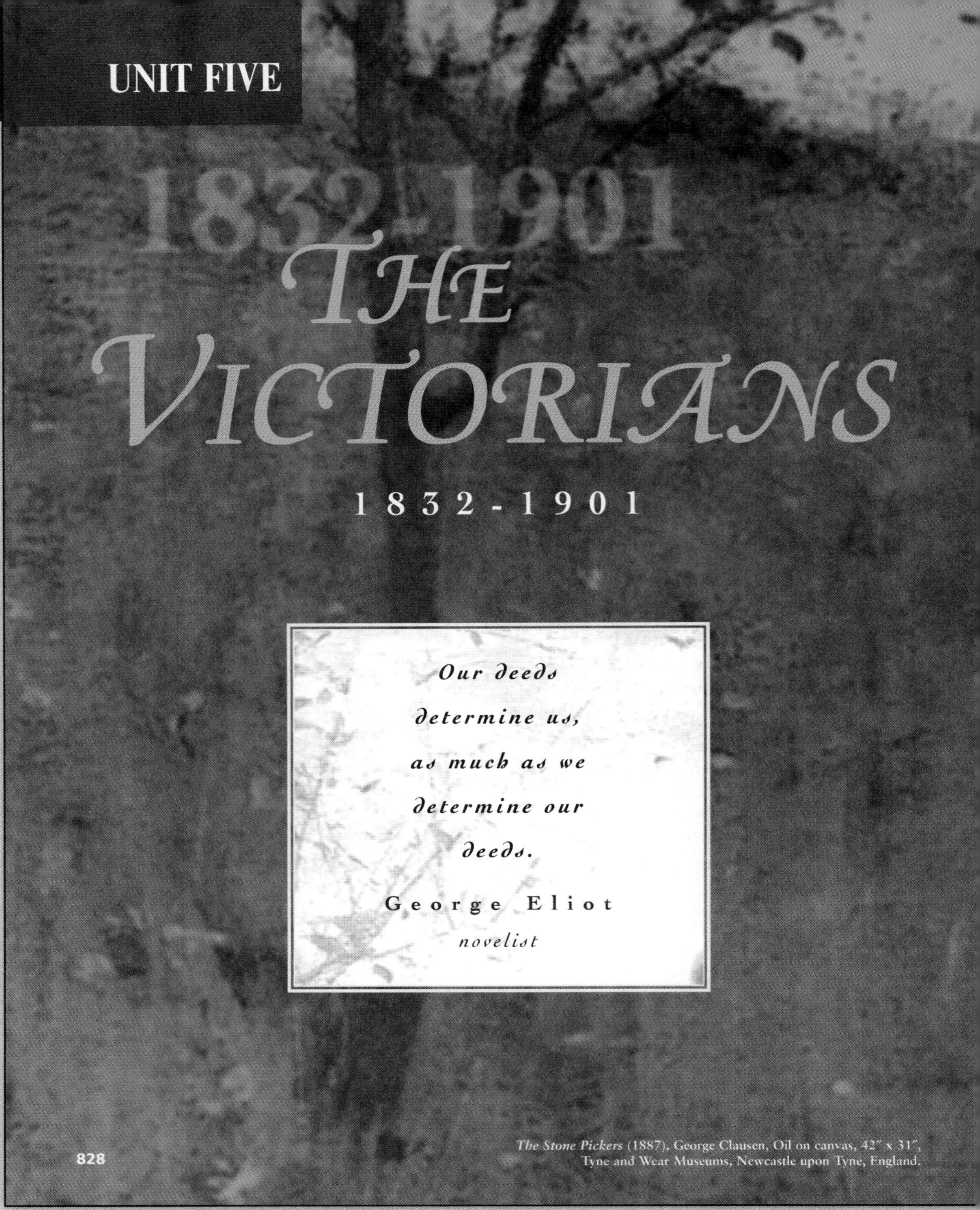

UNIT FIVE

1832–1901

THE VICTORIANS

1832-1901

Our deeds determine us, as much as we determine our deeds.

George Eliot
novelist

The Stone Pickers (1887), George Clausen. Oil on canvas, 42" x 31", Tyne and Wear Museums, Newcastle upon Tyne, England.

828

Viewing and Representing

The Stone Pickers
by George Clausen

ART APPRECIATION

Instruction At the time he rendered *The Stone Pickers* (1887), Clausen (1852–1944) had adopted the plein air (French: "open air") method of painting. That meant he executed his paintings in the open air in front of his subjects. During this period of his life, he went to live in the country, to capture out of doors the life of the agricultural laborer as he or she plowed, harvested, and the like. He sought to capture some insight into these peasant workers.

Ask: **What mood do you think this painting conveys?**

Possible Response: The young woman seems to have a mood of sad resignation, as if she hoped for a better life but realized it was not to be.

Making Connections

To help students explore the connections among the art, quotation, and the unit theme, have them consider the following questions:

The quotation comes from the middle of Chapter 29 of Eliot's 1859 novel of provincial life, *Adam Bede.*

Ask: How would you restate the quotation in your own words?
Possible Response: What people do helps form their characters.

Ask: Based on this quotation, what can you infer about Victorian values?
Possible Responses: Victorians judged people by their deeds or accomplishments. The following were probably important values: duty, social and civic responsibility, moral respectability, a good reputation.

Ask: What does the painting suggest about Victorian society?
Possible Response: It was a period of contrasts, still featuring the hard labor and simpler values of rural life.

Have students study the art, quotation, and the unit title.
Ask: Based on these, what can you infer about Victorian literature?
Possible Response: The literature might reflect strong opinions about duty and moral responsibility, the hardships of the rural way of life, or the relationships among people.

Ask: What deeds or actions do you think define you? Why?
Responses will vary.

VIDEODISC LaserLinks
Historical Literary Connection: The Victorians
The Victorian era was the best of times and the worst of times. Images in this film reflect the expansion of the British industrial empire, the flourishing of the English novel, and the growing prosperity of the British middle and upper classes. The film also conveys the struggles of the lower classes—the unemployment, the crowded slums, and child labor.

See Teacher's SourceBook p. 52 for bar codes.

VIDEODISC LaserLinks
Historical Literary Connection: Upper Class Victorians
The vivid details in these paintings of families and social gatherings of Victorian high society can help students better understand the lives of a group of people often portrayed in stories set in the Victorian age.

See Teacher's SourceBook p. 54 for bar codes.

Features and Selections	Literary Analysis	Reading and Critical Thinking	Writing Opportunities
The Victorians **Time Line** **Historical Background/Essay**			
POETRY The Lady of Shalott Ulysses *from* In Memoriam Crossing the Bar	Speaker, 839, 852 Blank Verse, 852	Speaker and Tone, 839, 852	Analysis Essay, 853 Three Titles, 853 Informal Assess., 842, 851
POETRY My Last Duchess Porphyria's Lover	Dramatic Monologue, 854, 859	Making Inferences, 854, 859	Questions for the Duke, 860 Television Mystery, 860 Informal Assess., 858
POETRY / LETTER Sonnet 43 A Warning Against Passion	Author's Purpose, 861, 866	Comparing Author's Views, 861, 866 Informal Assess., 864	A Letter in Response, 867
Learning the Language of Literature The Growth and Development of Fiction	The Novel, 868	Strategies for Reading, 869	
SHORT STORY Christmas Storms and Sunshine	Third-Person, 872, 883 Plot and Conflict, 883	Causes and Effects, 872, 883 Informal Assess., 879, 882	Letter to Mary's Mother, 884 Mr. Hodgson's Editorial, 884 Dialogue between the Jenkinsens, 884
SHORT STORY The King Is Dead, Long Live the King	Situational Irony, 888, 896 Plot, 896	Predicting, 888, 896 Informal Asses., 891	Letter from Amyas, 897 Obituaries, 897 Informal Assess., 895
SHORT STORY The Miracle of Purun Bhagat	Setting, 900, 912	Analyzing Details, 900, 912 Link to the Workplace, 906 Test Practice, 907 Informal Assess., 911	Obituary, 913 Essay, 913
Comparing Literature of the World What Men Live By	Folk Tale, 914, 929 Author's Purpose, 929 Setting, 929	Summarizing Text, 914, 929 Test Practice, 924 Informal Assess., 927, 928	New Episode, 930 Maxims for Living, 930 Newspaper Report, 930 Analytical Essay, 930 Points of Comparison, 930

LEGEND **PE Instruction shown in black** **TE Mini Lessons shown in green** **CCL indicates a Cross-Curricular Link** **DLS indicates Daily Language SkillBuilder**

Speaking and Listening Viewing and Representing	Inquiry and Research	Grammar, Usage, and Mechanics	Vocabulary
Art Appreciation, 829			Eponyms, 833
Lancelot's Shield, 853 Lady On Film, 853 Art Appreciation, 843, 849 Choral Reading, 848	Grief and Loss, 853	DLS, 839 Adjective Clauses, 846	Connotations, 840 Synonyms, 841
Murder Trial, 860 Portrait of a Madman, 860 Dramatic Reading, 856 Art Appreciation, 857	Roots of Jealousy, 860	DLS, 854 Modifiers, 860	
Imaginary Conversation, 867 Art Appreciation, 865		DLS, 861 Conjunctions, 867	Meaning Clues, 867 Word Origins, 862
Dramatization, 884 Set Design, 884 Improvisation, 884 Character Sketches, 884 Explore Dialect, 876 Art Appreciation, 878	City Life, 884 Victorian Dailies, 884 Author Activity, 885	DLS, 872 Clauses, 884	Context Clues, 884 Context Clues, 874, 880
Dramatic Scene, 897 Create a Dialogue, 892 Art Appreciation, 893 Dramatic Scene, 897	Long Live the Queen, 897	DLS, 888	Meaning Clues, 897 Word Origins, 889 Prefixes, Suffixes, 894
Sculpture Tribute, 913 Dramatic Dialogue, 913 Art Appreciation, 901, 909 Newscasts, 910	Caste System, 913	DLS, 900 Comma Splices, 904	Specialized Vocabulary, 908
Storyboard Illustrations, 930 Newspaper Display, 930 Monument, 930 Alternate Titles, 930 Art Appreciation, 918, 921	Rich and Poor, 930 Angels on the Loose, 930 Reflected Mood, 930 Author Activity, 931	DLS, 914 Complex Sentences, 930	Idioms, 919 Analogies, 925

Features and Selections	Literary Analysis	Reading and Critical Thinking	Writing Opportunities
Writing Workshop: **Subject Analysis** **Assessment Practice** Building Vocabulary Sentence Crafting			Analysis, 935

UNIT FIVE
PART 2 SKILLS TRACE

Features and Selections	Literary Analysis	Reading and Critical Thinking	Writing Opportunities
POETRY Dover Beach To Marguerite—Continued	Controlling Image, 941, 945 Allusion, 945	Mood, 941, 945 Informal Assess., 944	Lecture Notes, 946 Beloved's Diary, 946
POETRY Pied Beauty Spring and Fall: To a Young Child **Related Reading from Journal**	Sprung Rhythm, 947, 950 Alliteration, 951	Coined Words, 947, 950 Author Activity, 951 Understanding Attitudes/Ideas, 952	Nature Poem, 951 Journal Entry, 951 Coined Words, 951
POETRY The Man He Killed Ah, Are You Digging on My Grave? The Convergence of the Twain	Satire in Lyric Poetry, 953, 961 Situational Irony, 961	Making Inferences, 953, 961 Test Practice, 957 Informal Assess., 960	Summary, 962 Epitaph, 962 Poem About Titanic, 962
POETRY When I Was One-and-Twenty To an Athlete Dying Young	Stanza Structure, 963, 967	Inferring Meaning, 963, 967 Author Activity, 968	Personal Anecdote, 968 Essay on Poetry, 968
POETRY **Comparing Literature of the World** 1996	Title, 969, 972	Analyzing Structure, 969, 972	Spring Images, 973 Points of Comparison, 973
Reflect and Assess	Reviewing Literary Concepts, 975	Reflecting, 974	Building Your Portfolio, 975

LEGEND PE Instruction shown in black
TE Mini Lessons shown in green
CCL indicates a Cross-Curricular Link
DLS indicates Daily Language SkillBuilder

Speaking and Listening Viewing and Representing	Inquiry and Research	Grammar, Usage, and Mechanics	Vocabulary
Picturing Text Structure, 933 Informative Messages, 934		Keeping Ideas Parallel/Correct Comparisons, 936 Revising and Editing, 937 Adverb Clauses, 940	Context Clues, 939
Illustration, 946 Set Design, 946	Music and Poetry, 946 Author Activity, 946	DLS, 941 Pronouns and Adverbs, 942	Connotation and Denotation, 946
Nature Mural, 951 Art Appreciation, 948	Natural Patterns, 951	DLS, 947 Punctuation, 951	Connotation, 949
War Poster, 962 Dramatic Reading, 962 Dramatic Monologue, 956	Ship Sinks! 962 Author Activity, 962	DLS, 953 Noun Clauses, 958	Idioms, 954
Rebuttal, 968 Poetic Illustration, 968 Reading for Rhythm, 966	Poetic Soundtracks, 968	DLS, 963 Punctuation, 968	Context, 965
Poetry Anthology, 973 Triptych, 973 Speech, 973	Jewel in the Crown, 973	DLS, 969 Punctuation, 970	
Considering Relationships, 974 Character, 974			

PART 1

To introduce the theme/literary period of this unit, use Fine Art Transparencies T29–31 in the Communications Transparencies and Copymasters.

	Unit Resource Book	Assessment	Integrated Technology and Media	Literary Analysis Transparencies
The Lady of Shalott Ulysses *from* In Memoriam Crossing the Bar *pp. 839–853*	• Summary (The Lady of Shalott) p. 4 • Active Reading p. 5 • Literary Analysis p. 6 • Selection Quiz (The Lady of Shalott) p. 7	• Selection Test, Formal Assessment pp. 151–152 Test Generator	Audio Library LaserLinks, Teacher's SourceBook pp. 55–56 Video: Literature in Performance, Video Resource Book pp. 27–30	• Poetic Devices T16 • Point of View T18
My Last Duchess Porphyria's Lover *pp. 854–860*	• Active Reading p. 8 • Literary Analysis p. 9	• Selection Test, Formal Assessment p. 153 Test Generator	Audio Library LaserLinks, Teacher's SourceBook p. 57	• Point of View T18
Sonnet 43 A Warning Against Passion *pp. 861–867*	• Summary (A Warning Against Passion) p. 10 • Active Reading p. 11 • Literary Analysis p. 12 • Words to Know p. 13 • Selection Quiz (A Warning Against Passion) p. 14	• Selection Test, Formal Assessment pp. 155–156 Test Generator	Audio Library LaserLinks, Teacher's SourceBook p. 58	• Form and Meaning in Poetry T15
Christmas Storms and Sunshine *pp. 872–885*	• Summary p. 15 • Active Reading p. 16 • Literary Analysis p. 17 • Words to Know p. 18 • Selection Quiz p. 19	• Selection Test, Formal Assessment pp. 157–158 Test Generator	Audio Library LaserLinks, Teacher's SourceBook p. 59	• Point of View T18
The King Is Dead, Long Live the King *pp. 888–897*	• Summary p. 20 • Active Reading p. 21 • Literary Analysis p. 22 • Words to Know p. 23 • Selection Quiz p. 24	• Selection Test, Formal Assessment pp. 159–160 Test Generator	Audio Library Research Starter www.mcdougallittell.com	• Verbal, Situational, and Dramatic Irony T17
The Miracle of Purun Bhagat *pp. 900–913*	• Summary p. 25 • Active Reading p. 26 • Literary Analysis p. 27 • Selection Quiz p. 28	• Selection Test, Formal Assessment pp. 161–162 Test Generator	Audio Library LaserLinks, Teacher's SourceBook pp. 60–62 Research Starter www.mcdougallittell.com	• Influences on Plot: Setting and Character T19
What Men Live By *pp. 914–931*	• Summary p. 29 • Active Reading p. 30 • Literary Analysis p. 31 • Selection Quiz p. 32	• Selection Test, Formal Assessment pp. 163–164 Test Generator	Audio Library LaserLinks, Teacher's SourceBook p. 63	• The Moral Tale, Ballad, Fable, and Folk Tale T23

Writing Workshop: Subject Analysis

Unit Five Resource Book
- Prewriting p. 33
- Drafting and Elaboration p. 34
- Peer Response Guide pp. 35–36
- Revising, Editing, and Proofreading p. 37
- Student Models pp. 38–43
- Rubric for Evaluation p. 44

Writing Coach

Writing Transparencies and Copymasters T11, T19, C30

Teacher's Guide to Assessment and Portfolio Use

Unit Assessment

- Unit Five, Part 1 Test, Formal Assessment pp. 165–166

Test Generator

- Unit Five Integrated Test, Integrated Assessment pp. 39–46

Unit Technology

ClassZone www.mcdougallittell.com

Electronic Teacher Tools

Electronic Library

	Reading and Critical Thinking Transparencies	Grammar Transparencies and Copymasters	Vocabulary Transparencies and Copymasters	Writing Transparencies and Copymasters	Communications Transparencies and Copymasters
	• Determining Author's Purpose and Audience T20 • Organizational Chart: Horizontal T52	• Daily Language SkillBuilder T22 • Pronoun Usage–*Who, Whom, Whose* T50 • Adjective Clauses Introduced by *Who* or *Whom* C149	• Connotation C66 • Synonyms C67	• Subject Analysis C30	• Appreciative Listening T2 • Analyze, Evaluate, and Critique: Literary Performance T7
	• Making Inferences T7 • Venn Diagram T51	• Daily Language SkillBuilder T22 • Comparison of Regular and Irregular Adjectives and Adverbs T52 • Comparative Forms C154		• Organizing Your Writing T11	• Evaluating Roles in Groups T8 • Impromptu Speaking: Dialogue, Role-Play T14
	• Comparing Authors' Views T24 • Cluster Diagram T49	• Daily Language SkillBuilder T22 • Subordinating Conjunctions C74	• Word Origins C68	• Subject Analysis C30	• Impromptu Speaking: Dialogue, Role-Play T14
	• Cause and Effect T1	• Daily Language SkillBuilder T23 • Commas with Nonessential Elements T55 • Essential and Nonessential Clauses C114	• Context Clues C69	• The Uses of Dialogue T24 • Opinion Statement C35	• Identifying, Analyzing Artistic Elements in Literary Texts T13 • Impromptu Speaking: Dialogue, Role-Play T14
	• Predicting Outcomes T2	• Daily Language SkillBuilder T23 • Using *That* and *Which* T44 • Correct Use of *That* and *Which* C150	• Prefixes and Suffixes C70	• Levels of Language T12 • Personality Profile C25	• Appreciative Listening T2 • Dramatic Reading T12
	• Noting Details T9	• Daily Language SkillBuilder T23 • Run-on Sentences T43 • Correcting Comma Splices C159		• Personality Profile C25 • Subject Analysis C30	• Impromptu Speaking: Dialogue, Role-Play T14
	• Summarizing T10	• Daily Language SkillBuilder T24 • *If/Then* Complex Sentences C125	• Idioms C72 • Analogies C73	• Achieving Coherence T8 • Subject Analysis C30 • Compare- Contrast C34	• Evaluating Roles in Groups T8

STUDENTS ACQUIRING ENGLISH

The **Spanish Study Guide,** pp. 190–214, includes language support for the following pages:

- Family and Community Involvement (per unit)
- Selection Summaries and Vocabulary
- Active Reading
- Literary Analysis

To introduce the theme/literary period of this unit, use Fine Art Transparencies T29–31 in the Communications Transparencies and Copymasters.	Unit Resource Book	Assessment	Integrated Technology and Media	Literary Analysis Transparencies
Dover Beach **To Marguerite** ***pp. 941–946***	• Active Reading p. 47 • Literary Analysis p. 48	• Selection Test, Formal Assessment pp. 167–168 Test Generator	Audio Library LaserLinks, Teacher's SourceBook p. 64	• Figurative Language T22
Pied Beauty **Spring and Fall: To a Young Child** ***pp. 947–951***	• Active Reading p. 49 • Literary Analysis p. 50	• Selection Test, Formal Assessment pp. 169–170 Test Generator	Audio Library LaserLinks, Teacher's SourceBook p. 65	• Poetic Devices T16 • Figurative Language T22
Selected Poems by Thomas Hardy ***pp. 953–962***	• Active Reading p. 51 • Literary Analysis p. 52	• Selection Test, Formal Assessment pp. 171–172 Test Generator	Audio Library Research Starter www.mcdougallittell.com	• Verbal, Situational, and Dramatic Irony T17
When I Was One-and-Twenty **To an Athlete Dying Young** ***pp. 963–968***	• Active Reading p. 53 • Literary Analysis p. 54	• Selection Test, Formal Assessment pp. 173–174 Test Generator	Audio Library	• Form and Meaning in Poetry T15
1996 ***pp. 969–973***	• Active Reading p. 55 • Literary Analysis p. 56	• Selection Test, Formal Assessment pp. 175–176 Test Generator	Audio Library Research Starter www.mcdougallittell.com	
		Unit Assessment	***Unit Technology***	
		• Unit Five, Part 2 Test, Formal Assessment pp. 177–178 Test Generator • Unit Five Integrated Test, Integrated Assessment pp. 39–46	ClassZone www.mcdougallittell.com Electronic Teacher Tools Electronic Library	

T = Transparency C = Copymaster

Reading and Critical Thinking Transparencies	Grammar Transparencies and Copymasters	Vocabulary Transparencies and Copymasters	Writing Transparencies and Copymasters	Communications Transparencies and Copymasters
• Drawing Conclusions T4 • Noting Details T9	• Daily Language SkillBuilder T24 • Pronouns–Correct Case T41 • Pronoun Usage–*Who, Whom, Whose* T50 • Pronouns–Correct Case T41 • Relative Pronouns and Relative Adverbs C113	• Denotation and Connotation C74	• Opinion Statement C35	
• Comparing Authors' Views T24 • Organizational Chart: Horizontal T52	• Daily Language SkillBuilder T25 • Possessive Nouns T38 • Forming Singular Possessives C163	• Connotation C75	• Sensory Word List T14 • Figurative Language and Sound Devices T15	
• Making Inferences T7 • Summarizing T10	• Daily Language SkillBuilder T25 • Noun Clauses: Common Introductory Words C118		• Sensory Word List T14 • Figurative Language and Sound Devices T15	• Appreciative Listening T2 • Dramatic Reading T12
• Making Inferences T7 • Noting Details T9	• Daily Language SkillBuilder T25 • Possessive Nouns T38 • Forming Plural Possessives C164		• Subject Analysis C30 • Autobiographical Incident C36	• Recognizing Logical Fallacies T3 • Impromptu Speaking: Debate T15
• Analyzing Text Structure T17 • Comparing Authors' Views T24	• Daily Language SkillBuilder T26 • Using Dashes to Introduce an Explanation C162		• Sensory Word List T14 • Compare-Contrast C34	

STUDENTS ACQUIRING ENGLISH

The **Spanish Study Guide,** pp. 215–229, includes language support for the following pages:

- Family and Community Involvement (per unit)
- Selection Summaries and Vocabulary
- Active Reading
- Literary Analysis

UNIT FIVE
DAILY LANGUAGE SKILLBUILDERS

Selection	Skillbuilder Sentences	Suggested Answers
The Lady of Shalott Ulysses *from* In Memoriam Crossing the Bar	**1.** Alfred Lord Tennyson was the poet, whom reflected the feelings of fairly effluent victorians most clear. **2.** Many English peole were poor and worked in factories, Tennyson's poetry has little to do with there lives.	**1.** Alfred**,** Lord Tennyson was the poet **who** reflected the feelings of fairly **a**ffluent **V**ictorians most clear**ly**. **2.** Many English peo**p**le were poor and worked in factories**;** Tennyson's poetry **had** little to do with **their** lives.
My Last Duchess Porphyria's Lover	**1.** Robert browning who often wrote about extreme passions. **2.** Whom has not been afflicted with jealousy?	**1.** Robert **B**rowning often wrote about extreme passions. **2.** **Who** has not been afflicted with jealousy?
Sonnet 43 A Warning Against Passion	**1.** Their are some similarities among the life of Elizabeth barrett Browning and Charlotte Bronte. **2.** For instence both them lost sibling which they loved.	**1.** **There** are some similarities **between** the **lives** of Elizabeth **B**arrett Browning and Charlotte Bronte. **2.** For inst**a**nce**,** both of them lost sibling**s** **whom** they loved.
Christmas Storms and Sunshine	**1.** The story Christmas storms and sunshine like many stories of the victorian era has a strong moral. **2.** The victorians, concerned about what were proper.	**1.** The story **"**Christmas **S**torms and **S**unshine**,"** like many stories of the **V**ictorian era**,** has a strong moral. **2.** The **V**ictorians **were** concerned about what **was** proper.

Selection	Skillbuilder Sentences	Suggested Answers
The King Is Dead, Long Live the King	**1.** In the united states we dont have kings presidents often deal with similar issues of power.	**1.** In the **U**nited **S**tates**,** we don't have kings**, but** presidents often deal with similar issues of power.
	2. It can be difficult for people with power to tell whom there real friends is.	**2.** It can be difficult for people with power to tell **who their** real friends **are**.
The Miracle of Purun Bhagat	**1.** Some believe that success is wealth others power and still others happiness.	**1.** Some believe that success is wealth**;** others**,** power**;** and still others**,** happiness.
	2. Many people like kipling's protagonist have more than one idea of what it mean to be successful.	**2.** Many people**,** like **K**ipling's protagonist**,** have more than one idea of what it mean**s** to be successful.
What Men Live By	**1.** In 1828, Leo Tolstoy was borne into a landowners world of surfs and tutors horses and hunting.	**1.** In 1828, Leo Tolstoy was bor**n** into a landowner**'**s world of s**e**rfs and tutors**,** horses and hunting.
	2. All tho he grew to become a wise and compassionate man as well as a world famous writer his youthful behavior was definately the opposite.	**2.** **Although** he grew to become a wise and compassionate man**,** as well as a world**-**famous writer**,** his youthful behavior was defin**i**tely the opposite.
Dover Beach To Marguerite—Continued	**1.** Why are we reeding pomes by matthew arnold?	**1.** Why are we re**a**ding po**em**s by **M**atthew **A**rnold?
	2. Matthew Arnold was a social and litrary critick.	**2.** Matthew Arnold was a social and lit**e**rary criti**c**.

Selection	Skillbuilder Sentences	Suggested Answers
Pied Beauty Spring and Fall: To a Young Child	**1.** Gerard Manley Hopkins is a famous british poet, who wrote in a verce style he called it sprung rythym.	**1.** Gerard Manley Hopkins is a famous **B**ritish poet who wrote in a ver**s**e style he called sprung rhy**thm**.
	2. In spring and fall, to a young child, the girl who the speaker addresses named Margaret.	**2.** In "**S**pring and **F**all: To a **Y**oung **C**hild," the girl **whom** the speaker addresses **is** named Margaret.
The Man He Killed Ah, Are You Digging on My Grave? The Convergence of the Twain	**1.** Thomas Hardy, he was a prolific writer that published over 40 short storys; 8 volumes of poetry; 14 major novels and a long dramatic piece called: The Dynasts.	**1.** Thomas Hardy was a prolific writer **who** published over 40 short stor**ies**, 8 volumes of poetry**,** 14 major novels**,** and a long dramatic piece called **The Dynasts**.
	2. Much of Hardy's novels were real successful in his day, "Tess of the D'Urbervilles" and "Jude the Obscure" and "The Return of the Native" and they continue to be poplar today.	**2.** **Many** of Hardy's novels were **very** successful in his day—**Tess of the D'Urbervilles**, **Jude the Obscure**, and **The Return of the Native**—and they continue to be pop**u**lar today.
When I Was One-and-Twenty To an Athlete Dying Young	**1.** A.E. Housman studied Classics at Oxford Univ. in the nineteenth Century.	**1.** A.E. Housman studied **c**lassics at Oxford Univ**ersity** in the **19th-c**entury.
	2. In Housman's time, hire education consisted mostly of the study of latin and greek, reports on the validity of this curriculum, is inconclusive.	**2.** In Housman's time, **higher** education consisted mostly of the study of **L**atin and **G**reek; reports on the validity of this curriculum **are** inconclusive.
1996	**1.** Rabindranath Tagore, was born in india in 1861, wrote primarly in his native language which was bengali.	**1.** Rabindranath Tagore, **who** was born in **I**ndia in 1861, wrote primar**i**ly in his native language**,** which was **B**engali.
	2. All though he new the languaje of the British colonist's Tagore didint translate his poems in to english untill he was in his 50's.	**2.** **Although** he **knew** the langua**g**e of the British colonis**ts,** Tagore did**n't** translate his poems **into E**nglish until he was in his **50s**.

	Unit One	Unit Two	Unit Three	Unit Four	Unit Five	Unit Six	Unit Seven
Grammar Focus by Unit	Parts of a Sentence	Phrases, Part I	Phrases, Part II	Clauses, Part I	Clauses, Part II	Rhetorical Grammar, Part I	Rhetorical Grammar, Part II

The Language of Literature offers several options for integrating grammar instruction and literature.

- Each literature unit has a grammar focus. The Teacher's Edition includes Mini Lessons for each selection that help develop the grammar focus for the unit and spring from the content of the specific literature.
- The Pupil Edition includes several full-page lessons on Sentence Crafting. These lessons are related to both the literature and the grammar focus for the unit and help students use grammar in their own writing.
- Daily Language SkillBuilders in the Teacher's Edition provide students with ongoing proofreading practice and reinforce punctuation, spelling, grammar and usage, and capitalization.
- Grammar Copymasters and Transparencies, which may be used to complement or extend lessons in the Teacher's Edition, present grammar in a traditional, systematic sequence. References to appropriate copymasters or transparencies are included at point of use in the Teacher's Edition Mini Lessons.

TE Mini Lessons shown in green
PE instruction shown in black

Part 1

Parts of Speech

Subordinating Conjunctions
"Sonnet 43," "A Warning Against Passion," p. 867
Sentence Crafting, p. 939

Parts of the Sentence

Compound Subjects
Writing Workshop, p. 937

Using Clauses

Essential and Nonessential Clauses
"Christmas Storms and Sunshine," p. 884

Adverb Clauses
Sentence Crafting, p. 939

***If/Then* Complex Sentences**
"What Men Live By," p. 930

Pronoun Usage

Pronoun-Antecedent Agreement
Sentence Crafting, p. 939

Adjective Clauses Introduced by *Who* or *Whom*
Tennyson poems, p. 846

Correct Use of *That* and *Which*
"The King Is Dead, Long Live the King," p. 897

Using Modifiers

Using Correct Comparative Forms
"My Last Duchess," "Porphyria's Lover," p. 860
Writing Workshop, p. 937

End Marks and Commas

Correcting Comma Splices
"The Miracle of Purun Bhagat," p. 904

Other Punctuation

Punctuating Dialogue
Writing Workshop, p. 937

Style

Cohesion: Parallelism
Writing Workshop, p. 937

Part 2

Using Clauses

Relative Pronouns and Relative Adverbs
"Dover Beach," "To Marguerite—Continued," p. 942

Noun Clauses: Common Introductory Words
Hardy poems, p. 958

Other Punctuation

Using Dashes to Introduce an Explanation
"1996," pp. 970–971

Forming Singular Possessives
"Pied Beauty," "Spring and Fall: To a Young Child," p. 951

Forming Plural Possessives
"When I Was One-and-Twenty," "To an Athlete Dying Young," p. 968

This time line shows the major events of the Victorian era. Further information about some people and events is provided below.

Britain: 1832–1848

These painful early years of Britain's industrialization have sometimes been called the Time of Trouble. The British population suffered from widespread unemployment, high bread prices, and food shortages during the 1840s. London's population was 6.5 million by 1845, indicating a dramatic shift from life based on cultivation of land to an economy based on manufacturing.

Britain: 1837

A During Victoria's reign, so vast and widespread were the lands under British control that it was said that the sun never set on the British Empire.

Literature: 1850

B Browning's *Sonnets from the Portuguese* is one of the most beloved collections of love poems. A volume of 44 sonnets written to Browning's husband, Robert, the poems recount the days of their courtship (Elizabeth, an invalid kept nearly a prisoner at home, managed a secret love affair with Robert until her father finally suspected, causing the lovers to elope in 1846) and their married happiness in Italy. The "Portuguese" of the title was Robert's nickname for Elizabeth, derived from her early poem of a Portuguese woman's love for a poet. The collection includes the lines "How do I love thee? Let me count the ways."

World: 1848

C For decades, non-interference from governments spurred on the industrial revolution. Then Karl Marx (a German journalist) and Friedrich Engels (whose father owned a mill in Britain) published the *Communist Manifesto,* written in Brussels. This 23-page pamphlet addressed the gap between rich and poor. It predicted that workers would overthrow business owners, private property would be abolished, and a final phase of pure communism would emerge—with production controlled by workers, the new ruling class. The pamphlet's ideas waited until the 1900s for a practical tryout on the world stage.

TIME LINE 1832–1901

THE VICTORIANS

EVENTS IN BRITISH LITERATURE

1830

1833 Alfred, Lord Tennyson, begins writing long poem *In Memoriam*

1843 Charles Dickens publishes short novel *A Christmas Carol*

1845

1846 Poets Robert Browning and Elizabeth Barrett elope and move to Italy

1847 Charlotte Brontë publishes *Jane Eyre;* sister Emily publishes *Wuthering Heights*

B **1850** Elizabeth Barrett Browning publishes love poems *Sonnets from the Portuguese*

1860

1860 Dickens publishes first magazine installment of *Great Expectations*

1861 George Eliot publishes *Silas Marner*

D **1865** Lewis Carroll publishes *Alice's Adventures in Wonderland*

1868 Gerard Manley Hopkins enters Jesuit religious order and stops writing poetry

EVENTS IN BRITAIN

1830

1833 Factory Act bans factory work for children under nine; slavery abolished in British Empire

A **1837** William IV dies and is succeeded by 18-year-old niece Victoria, ushering in Britain's age of greatest prosperity

1842 Opium War with China settled, with Britain claiming Hong Kong

1845

1845 Irish potato famine begins, killing more than a million people (to 1851)

C **1848** University of London grants admission to women students

1854 Crimean War—in which Britain, Turkey, France, and Austria fight Russia—begins

1859 Charles Darwin publishes *On the Origin of Species*

1860

1860 Florence Nightingale founds school for nurses

1861 Prince Albert dies ➢

1867 Reform Bill doubles number of voters by including working-class men

1870 Local governments establish public schools; Married Women's Act gives women economic rights

EVENTS IN THE WORLD

1830

1839 American Charles Goodyear invents process for making rubber strong and elastic

1844 Samuel F. B. Morse sends first long-distance telegraph message

1845

1848 Ethnic uprisings erupt throughout Europe; Karl Marx and Friedrich Engels publish *Communist Manifesto*

1851 Widespread hunger and government corruption lead to China's Taiping Rebellion (to 1864)

1853 U.S. Commodore Matthew Perry sails four ships into Tokyo harbor, ending Japan's self-imposed isolation

1860

1861 Civil war erupts in United States (to 1865); Alexander II frees serfs in Russia

1862 During American civil war, Abraham Lincoln's Emancipation Proclamation symbolically frees slaves in Confederate territory

1869 Suez Canal opens

E **1874** Alexander Graham Bell develops telephone

Literature: 1865

D Charles Lutwidge Dodge, writing as Lewis Carroll, based *Alice's Adventures in Wonderland* on a delightfully absurd tale with which he amused the young daughter of a family he picnicked with. *Alice* and its sequel, *Through the Looking Glass* (1871), became known collectively as *Alice in Wonderland.* An American composer, David Del Tredici, has based many of his orchestral works on the adventures, including an *Alice Symphony.*

World: 1869

E The Suez Canal through Egypt shortened the sea distance between Britain and India by 6,000 miles, yet the British opposed its construction. Apparently, they feared that other European nations would use this direct Mediterranean to Indian Ocean route to threaten their near monopoly on trade with the East.

Period Pieces

The Benz Viktoria, 1893

Mangle, used to squeeze water from laundry

Big Ben, tower clock installed in Houses of Parliament, 1859 (J)

1875 · 1890 · 1900

(F) **1875** Hopkins resumes writing

1883 Robert Louis Stevenson publishes adventure novel *Treasure Island* ➢

(G) **1887** Sir Arthur Conan Doyle publishes *A Study in Scarlet,* introducing detective Sherlock Holmes

1891 Thomas Hardy publishes *Tess of the D'Urbervilles;* Oscar Wilde's novel, *A Picture of Dorian Gray,* shocks Victorian England with its theme of corruption of wealth

(I) **1895** H. G. Wells publishes landmark science fiction novel *The Time Machine*

1896 Reaction to Thomas Hardy's novel *Jude the Obscure* is so negative that thereafter he writes only poetry

1901 Kipling publishes novel *Kim,* detailing life in India

1875 · 1890 · 1900

1875 Public Health Act expands sanitary laws; new sewer system is installed in London

1876 Disraeli secures title "Empress of India" for Victoria; collective bargaining by trade unions legalized

(H) **1879** Ireland pressures for home rule

1884 Reform Bill gives vote to almost all adult males

(K) **1899** Boer War against Dutch South African settlers begins (to 1902)

1901 Queen Victoria dies after 64-year rule

1875 · 1890 · 1900

1876 Korea becomes independent nation

1879 Thomas Edison invents first practical light bulb

1884 Berlin Conference of 14 European nations sets rules for dividing Africa into colonies

1893 Henry Ford develops gasoline-powered automobile; France conquers Indochina; New Zealand first country to grant women suffrage

1895 Italian Guglielmo Marconi creates first radio

1896 First modern Olympic Games held in Athens, Greece

1898 Spanish-American War begins (to 1899)

1900 German psychiatrist Sigmund Freud publishes *The Interpretation of Dreams*

Literature: 1875

(F) Hopkins (1844–1889), like his contemporary Emily Dickinson, is an amazing example of posthumous discovery. He wrote poetry in his youth, but upon becoming a Jesuit priest in 1868, he burned all his poems. Then in 1875 he resumed writing but died with nothing having been published. Over the next decades, readers discovered his poems in anthologies and notably in a 1918 first collected edition. Hopkins is now considered a true original of verbal subtleties and unique rhythms.

Literature: 1887

(G) Sir Arthur Conan Doyle (1859–1930) set up a medical practice but soon discovered that his real talent was for writing detective stories. His famous creation, Sherlock Holmes, appeared in 56 short stories and 4 novels. When Doyle killed Holmes off in an 1893 story, the public outcry was so great that he brought Holmes back to life for more adventures. The hold on the detective's fans is so great that his fictional address—221B Baker Street—has become a popular tourist site.

Britain: 1879

(H) This year of bad harvests in Ireland intensified a crucial issue of later Victorian times: the future of Ireland, where rampant poverty had fostered hatred of the British. Home rule, or self-government, had been proposed, but the prospect of a Catholic parliament frightened Protestants in Ulster. A hard-line faction of liberals joined with conservatives in the British parliament in defeating two official tries at passing home rule bills in 1886 and 1893.

Literature: 1895

(I) One critic has said that Wells "insisted on the importance of science" at a time when writers "were heinously ignorant of it." *The Time Machine,* one of the first science fiction novels, is the originator of the "time travel" subgenre. Wells's other such classics are *The Invisible Man* (1897) and *The War of the Worlds* (1898), the latter providing a panic in the United States on Halloween of 1938 when the story was adapted as a supposedly live radio broadcast of a Martian invasion of the East Coast.

Period Pieces

(J) Strictly speaking, the name "Big Ben" refers not to the clock but to the bell that peals from the tower. Named to honor Sir Benjamin Hall, commissioner of works in 1859, the 13-ton bell is 7-1/2 feet tall and 9 feet in diameter.

World: 1900

(K) Freud's *The Interpretation of Dreams* ushered in an era of criticism that used the precepts of Freudian theory to psychoanalytically interpret literature. Shakespeare's Hamlet was one of several literary characters "analyzed" in Freud's book.

UNIT FIVE
HISTORICAL BACKGROUND

OVERVIEW

Introduction
This article provides a historical and literary context for the writings presented in Unit Five. In particular students will learn how the period's social and technological advances and spirit of reform was tempered by the anxiety of the age.

Reading Nonfiction

Reading Skills and Strategies

ESTABLISHING A PURPOSE FOR READING
Have students scan the article to establish a purpose for reading. Remind them to adjust their purposes if they encounter unexpected content or difficulty.

USING TEXT ORGANIZERS
If students need more support, have them preview the article, noting the basic text organizers: title, overview, subheads, images and captions, and sidebar commentaries. Ask students to describe the information they would expect to locate in each section. As they read, have students use the subheads to make an outline or graphic organizer. Have them categorize information from the article, sidebars, and timeline with the appropriate heading. Point out that they should use similar text organizers to locate and categorize information when they do independent research and writing.

ANALYZING TEXT STRUCTURE
Have students scan the article and predict how they expect information to be structured. Due to the number of dates, students should expect the basic structure to be chronological. Discuss how this structure influences the way they read and understand the material. Encourage students to note other kinds of relationships (*cause/ and effect and compare/ and contrast*) signaled by text structure and words. Some key relationships: the causes of the reforms, causes and effects of industrial and scientific advances, comparison and contrast of beginning and end of Victorian era.

IDENTIFYING MAIN IDEAS
The headings form sections that become main ideas. Have students read one section at a time and note how its idea is developed through details.

HISTORICAL BACKGROUND

THE VICTORIANS
1832-1901

Britain's Victorian era was a time of overseas expansion and domestic reform. During this period of growth and change, the numbers of the middle class swelled, the lives of the working class improved, and the nation was set on the road to democracy. Its advances included the laying of a transatlantic telegraph cable and the advent of the automobile, electric lighting, and antiseptic medicine. Nevertheless, for many people today the term *Victorian* implies only stuffy complacency, hypocrisy, and prudishness. These characteristics did exist, but they by no means sum up the era.

A Victoria was only 18 when she began her reign in 1837. Mindful of the scandalous conduct of her royal uncles, George IV and William IV, the queen placed great emphasis on moral behavior and was scrupulous in the performance of her royal duties. Ably tutored by the Whig prime minister Lord Melbourne, the young queen accepted—as her predecessors had not—the idea of a constitutional monarchy in which the monarch gave advice rather than orders. B In 1840 Melbourne helped arrange the marriage of Victoria and her German cousin Prince Albert of Saxe-Coburg-Gotha, to whom she became deeply devoted. After Albert died in 1861, Victoria mourned him for the rest of her life, retiring even further from the daily affairs of government. Fortunately, during Victoria's 64-year reign (the longest in British history) she and the nation would be served by a number of talented prime ministers—including, in addition to Melbourne, Sir Robert Peel in the early Victorian years, Lord Palmerston in the mid-Victorian era, and the rival politicians Benjamin Disraeli and William E.

C *Top:* Portrait of Queen Victoria, painted in the year of her marriage
Above: The Great Exhibition of 1851, held in London's Crystal Palace, celebrated industry and technology.
Left: An Indian floral pattern of the sort that had a major influence on Victorian design
Right: Removal of Irish tenants during the potato famine

Gladstone in later Victorian times. These leaders helped guide Britain through a remarkable period of social, economic, and political change.

An Era of Reform

Under Lord Melbourne and the Whigs, who held power throughout much of the 1830s, many long-sought reforms were passed, including the abolition of slavery in the British Empire and the first restrictions on child labor in factories. Nevertheless, the Whigs' goal was not democracy but an enlightened government by an educated upper class. Their best-known achievement, the Reform Bill of 1832, expanded voting rights only to men with a certain amount of property. When members of the working-class movement called Chartism demanded universal male suffrage, the demand went unheeded. D

After the 1841 election brought Sir Robert Peel and the Tories to power, gradual reform continued, with new laws addressing safety in the mines and factories. Peel, however, faced agitation from both Chartists and the Anti-Corn Law League, which sought to repeal the laws protecting British farmers from foreign competition. The league's cause was advanced by the devastating rains of 1845, which ruined England's wheat crop and allowed disease to wipe out Ireland's harvest of potatoes, the staple

Development of the English Language

In Victorian times, as education spread and people entering the middle class attempted to speak "proper" English, the English language became more homogeneous. Increased literacy also stabilized English, since the written language tends to change more slowly than the spoken. The period also saw the beginning of an effort to compile a definitive record of the histories, uses, and meanings of English words, resulting in the massive *Oxford English Dictionary,* the first volume of which was published in 1884. This landmark work, not completed until 1928 and revised several times since, traces each word's changes in meaning from its first recorded use to the present.

Victorian advances in the natural and social sciences spurred the coinage of new words, such as *telephone, photography, psychiatrist,* and *feminist.* As the new fields of study developed their own jargons, their specialized and technical vocabulary began to infiltrate everyday speech. Euphemisms—mild, indirect, or vague terms substituted for ones considered harsh or offensive—also grew more popular as Victorian propriety made certain words taboo. A chicken breast became "white meat"; its legs, "drumsticks." Even words that today seem rather benign—such as *belly, buck,* and *stallion*—were prudishly avoided.

Although "proper" circles frowned on slang, it was widely used among the lower classes as a means of conversing safely in the presence of outsiders, including the police. The Cockneys of London's East End developed an elaborate system of rhyming slang in early Victorian times—using, for example, *loaf* to mean "head" because *loaf* is the first word in the expression *loaf of bread,* which rhymes with *head*. The expression "use your loaf" is still common in the East End today.

Making Connections

History

A Victoria ascended the throne when her uncle, King William IV, died without an heir. The only child of the fourth son of King George III, she ruled until her death in 1901.

History

B When Victoria married the German Albert, some people worried that she would come under the influence of undesirable continental ideas, but Albert turned out to be an impartial adviser. After Albert died of typhoid fever in 1861, a grieving Victoria spent three years in seclusion and dressed in mourning for the remainder of her life. A 1997 film, *Mrs. Brown,* details her later life under the watchful eye of her bodyguard, John Brown. She became a symbol for strict morality and helped involve the crown in public service.

Architecture

C Built for the 1851 Great Exhibition held in London's Hyde Park and covering 19 acres, the Crystal Palace, conceived by a horticulturist, looked like a gigantic greenhouse. It was actually a vast exhibition hall for the wonders of 19th century industry and technology—the unofficial first world's fair. Tables covered with things as diverse as farm machinery and false teeth snaked for eight miles among fountains and live elm trees. The building was constructed from 300,000 panes of glass, 4,500 tons of iron, and six million cubic feet of wood. For its daring, novel construction methods, the Crystal Palace became one of history's most influential buildings.

Labor

D Many families could survive only by sending their young children to work. Boys and girls as young as five toiled in dangerous, exhausting jobs, such as pulling carts of coal out of mines. Some slaved 16 hours a day in dark factories, seeing the sun only on Sundays.

Mini Lesson: Development of the English Language

EPONYMS

Besides its contributions to the English language discussed above, Britain was also a significant source of eponyms, persons whose names are given to new words. (Often it is the new word that is called an eponym.) For example, British officer Henry Shrapnel gave his name to deadly metal fragments released from an exploding bomb. English land agent Charles Boycott gave his name to the act of refusing to use or buy something as an act of protest. The Fourth Earl of Sandwich—what would you guess about his eating habits?

Have students work in pairs to research and present to the class the interesting story behind an eponym. You will need to suggest some additional eponyms, such as the words and phrases *bowdlerize, Braille, cardigan, Celsius, diesel engine, dunce, lynch, mesmerize, ritzy, salmonella, saxophone, sideburns,* and *teddy bear.*

Making Connections

Law

E The Corn Laws (with *corn* used in the British sense of "grain" rather than the American sense of "maize") had been passed between the 1400s and the 1800s to protect British farmers. As industrialization spread, the interests of the farmers were eclipsed by those of factory workers, who were demanding cheaper bread. The Corn Laws were repealed in 1846.

History

F The main objective of Britain and its allies (Turkey, France, and Sardinia) in the Crimean War (1853–1856) was to block Russian expansion in the Black Sea area. The Battle of Balaklava, fought on the Crimean peninsula extending into the sea, formed the basis of Tennyson's stirring 1855 poem "The Charge of the Light Brigade," which commemorated the disastrous charge the year before of the eponymous Seventh Earl of Cardigan's cavalry against a heavily defended Russian position. The war was the first conflict in which British photographers and journalists reported from the front.

Economics

G The British East India Company, along with similar private East India companies supported by the French and the Dutch, had been chartered by Elizabeth I in 1600 as a means of controlling trading activities in India and the Far East. At first, the British company engaged in commerce without trying to acquire land; later, however, it began to take sides in local disputes, and its influence spread rapidly until it was the only surviving East India company. The company was taken over by the British government in 1858 after the Indian mutiny and was officially dissolved in 1873.

food of the Irish poor. With famine stalking Ireland, Peel agreed that foreign grain could ease conditions and introduced a bill to abolish the Corn Laws. The bill passed too late to help most of the Irish, but it did mark the beginning of free trade in Britain. **E**

International Affairs

The free-trade issue divided the Tories and led some of them to join the Whigs to form a new political party, the Liberal party. During this realignment, the dominant political figure was the independent Lord Palmerston, a moderate Whig who served as foreign minister for much of the 1830s and 1840s. In that capacity he had successfully overseen the expansion of Britain's empire—including, in 1840, the annexation of New Zealand and the beginning of a war with China that led to the British acquisition of Hong Kong two years later. Palmerston's clever diplomacy, backed up by the British fleet, had also kept France out of Egypt and Russia out of Turkey. Then, in 1854, with Turkey again threatened and Palmerston out of office, Britain joined the fight against Russia in the Crimean War. **F** By the next year, after a series of British military blunders and defeats, the public was clamoring for change. At this point Palmerston became prime minister, and it was he who received credit for ending the war with the 1856 treaty ensuring Turkish sovereignty. Two years later, following a mutiny by native troops in British India, Palmerston's government attempted to end corruption there by removing control of the colony from the hands of the East India Company. This change had mixed results but was generally applauded in Britain. **G**

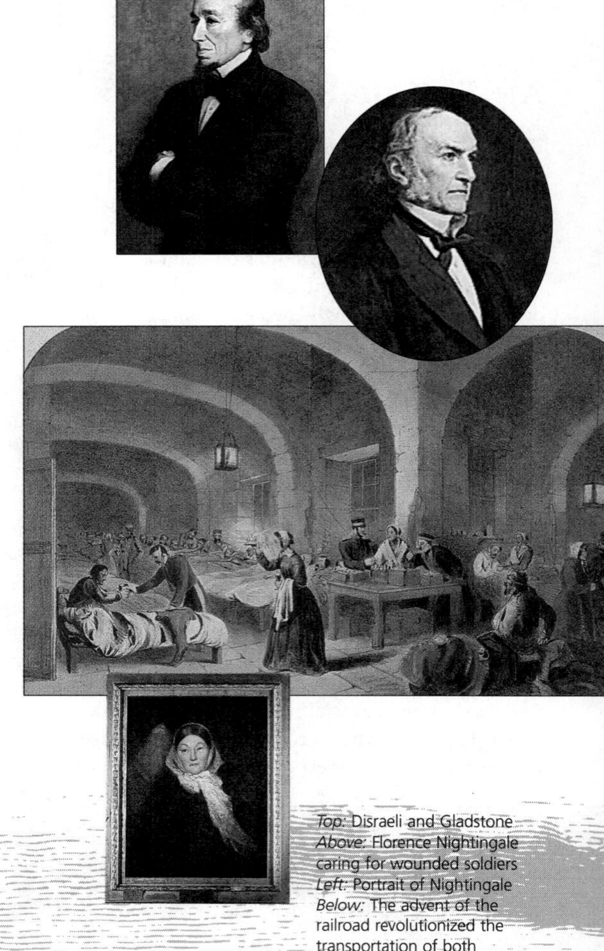

Top: Disraeli and Gladstone
Above: Florence Nightingale caring for wounded soldiers
Left: Portrait of Nightingale
Below: The advent of the railroad revolutionized the transportation of both people and goods.

Prosperity and Advances

Though Palmerston showed little interest in domestic reform, free trade and the expansion of empire helped make the mid-Victorian period a prosperous time in Britain, both for aristocrats and for the growing middle class. Despite the repeal of the Corn Laws, the introduction of the McCormick reaper from America prevented an agricultural decline. Textile exports were booming, and industry in general benefited from Henry Bessemer's new steel-making process. Steamships and railways revolutionized the transportation of goods and people, making travel quicker, cheaper, and far more comfortable than ever before. Communications improved with the advent of the telegraph. Growing literacy and improvements in printing spurred the publication of books, magazines, and newspapers. Advances in medicine included the introduction of antiseptic surgery by Joseph Lister and the founding of the first modern nursing school by Florence Nightingale, who had become famous as a volunteer nurse in the Crimean War.

Nightingale's volunteer spirit was echoed in the foundation of the YMCA, the Salvation Army, and a host of new charitable organizations. In mid-Victorian Britain—a society at once deeply religious and highly materialistic—most people viewed charity as a Christian duty and shared an optimistic faith in humanity's ability to achieve happiness through economic and material progress. John Stuart Mill, the most influential economist of the period, argued for gradual, steady social reform and for the abandonment of the strict laissez-faire (government-noninterference) policies of earlier British liberals. Many of Mill's ideas were put into practice after Palmerston's death, when Gladstone and Disraeli rose on the political scene. H

Gladstone and Disraeli

As head of the new Liberal party, Gladstone wore the mantle of reform, but Disraeli also realized the importance of political and social reforms in attracting working-class support for his revitalized Tory party. Gladstone won passage of bills for land reform in Ireland and for the establishment of public schools and secret balloting in elections. Disraeli won passage of the landmark Second Reform Bill of 1867, which extended the vote to working-class males, as well I

Literary History

Though no longer the radical movement it once was, **romanticism** continued to influence Victorian writing; but a new movement, called **realism,** increasingly began to take hold. Realism sought to capture everyday life as it really was lived. Instead of turning away from science and industry as romanticism had done, realism focused on the effects of the Industrial Revolution, often bringing social problems to public attention. Many early Victorian novels blend romanticism and realism. Charles Dickens, the era's most popular storyteller, produced entertaining novels with farfetched plots that nevertheless exposed real social problems—such as the plight of orphans in *Oliver Twist* (1837–1839) and *Nicholas Nickleby* (1838–1839). In *Wuthering Heights* (1847), Emily Brontë, one of a growing number of women writers, set a melodramatic plot with a Byronic hero against a realistic Yorkshire landscape; in *Jane Eyre* (1847), her sister Charlotte blended gothic elements with realistic social details. Realism is an even stronger element in the novels of William Makepeace Thackeray and Anthony Trollope.

Later in the century, new ideas in the natural and social sciences prompted the style known as **psychological realism,** which focused not on external realities but on the inner realities of the mind, and **naturalism,** an offshoot of realism that viewed nature and society as forces indifferent to human suffering. One of the pioneering psychological realists was the novelist George Meredith. J The beginnings of naturalism are evident in the novels of George Eliot (Mary Ann Evans), but even more strongly naturalistic is the pessimistic fiction of Thomas Hardy, set in the author's native Wessex.

Making Connections

Religion

H The Salvation Army traces its origins to the tent and theater evangelical meetings that William Booth, a Methodist minister, began to conduct in London's East End in 1865. The popularity of these meetings led to Booth's formation of a group known as the Christian Mission, which in 1878 changed its name to the Salvation Army. The new name and use of uniforms of a vaguely military nature were intended to promote the organization's crusade of "warfare against evil."

Politics

I Although working-class men received the right to vote in 1867, women did not. Woman-suffrage petitions had been introduced in Parliament in the 1840s, but no law granting women the right to vote was passed until 1918.

Literature

J One of George Meredith's best-known psychological works is actually a volume of poetry—*Modern Love* (1862), a series of 50 connected poems that chronicle the breakup of a marriage. Published four years after Meredith's wife left him for another man, the poems are semi-autobiographical, recounted in some instances in first person by the husband.

Making Connections

Politics

K One of the domestic issues that greatly concerned William Gladstone (1809–1898) was the Irish problem. Since much of Ireland was Roman Catholic, its people were not loyal to the Church of England. During his first term as prime minister (1868–1874), Gladstone angered Conservatives by ending the requirement of the Irish to pay taxes to the Church of England and supporting legislation that made it more difficult to evict Irish tenants from rented land. In later terms, Gladstone twice introduced the Home Rule Bill (1886, 1893), which would have given the Irish greater control over their country. Each bill, however, was defeated.

Politics

L Benjamin Disraeli (1804–1881) enjoyed politics and high society. He was first elected prime minister in 1868 but lost the office that same year to Gladstone. He was prime minister again from 1874 to 1880. Interestingly, Disraeli was also an author. He wrote numerous novels between 1826 and 1880, many of them using politics as a background.

Philosophy

M Although an optimistic belief in progress characterized the early part of Victorian era, many later Victorians became resistant to new ideas. After Thomas Hardy's novel *Jude the Obscure* was roundly criticized by reviewers, Hardy stated that his critics seemed to be saying, "We Britons hate ideas, and we are going to live up to that privilege of our native country. Your picture may not show the untrue or the uncommon, or even be contrary to the canons of art; but it is not the view of life that we who thrive on conventions can permit to be painted."

as bills that improved housing and sanitation, legalized trade unions, and reformed factory conditions. Where the two rivals differed most was in their personal styles and their attitudes toward British imperialism. A staid, morally righteous figure, Gladstone was a "Little Englander" who believed that Britain should take care of its own problems rather than involve itself in costly expansion abroad. The more flamboyant Disraeli linked prosperity to colonial expansion and patriotically equated imperialism with Britain's destiny. In 1875 he secretly negotiated the British government's purchase of a large interest in the newly completed Suez Canal in Egypt, which cut thousands of miles off the sea trip to India. A year later, he maneuvered Parliament into conferring the title "Empress of India" on Victoria. He also acquired the Mediterranean island of Cyprus and annexed the Transvaal, a South African republic that had been established by the Boers, settlers of mostly Dutch descent. Disraeli's policies enjoyed the support of the queen, who could not conceal her dislike for the self-righteous Gladstone.

Fascinated by the heroic exploits of their explorers, missionaries, and empire builders in Africa and Asia, most British citizens also supported Disraeli's imperialism, although by the time of his death in 1881, that support was waning. Disraeli's effort to prevent a Russian domination of Afghanistan, which threatened British India, resulted in two years of costly warfare there. Similarly, his annexation of the Transvaal led to conflicts with the native Zulu and with the Boers, who regained control of the Transvaal in 1881. Events such as these introduced the nation to the downside of imperialism, much as Gladstone had warned.

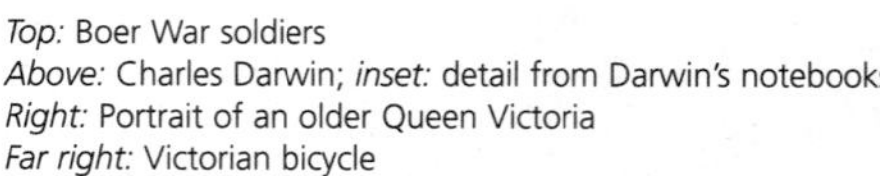

Top: Boer War soldiers
Above: Charles Darwin; *inset:* detail from Darwin's notebooks
Right: Portrait of an older Queen Victoria
Far right: Victorian bicycle

New Directions

During the last decades of the Victorian era, the confident optimism of earlier times was tinged with an undercurrent of anxiety. To be sure, most people patriotically celebrated Victoria's Golden Jubilee, marking 50 years of her rule, in 1887 and her Diamond Jubilee a decade later. Nevertheless, the complacency of mid-Victorian times was beginning to shatter as new ideas took hold. The writings of the scientist Charles Darwin created a rift between liberal Christians, whose interpretation of the Bible allowed the acceptance of Darwin's theory of evolution, and fundamentalist Christians, whose interpretation did not. Applying Darwin's ideas to human society, the philosopher Herbert Spencer coined the phrase "survival of the fittest," which conservatives—called social Darwinists—used to justify a return to government noninterference, saying that nature should be allowed to weed out the "unfit." This thinking brought the social Darwinists into conflict with the increasingly socialist labor movement, which supported industrial reform through government control and ownership. The socialism of the labor movement also frayed its ties to moderate Liberals just as the Liberal party was falling into disarray over the issue of Irish home rule. Then, in 1899, British colonial expansion in Africa resulted in the Boer War, which galvanized public patriotism and further weakened the anti-imperialist Liberal party. A new party formed in 1900—the Labor party— would become a dominant political force in the new century, and the Boer War would be a prelude to the far more devastating warfare of the modern age.

VIDEODISC **LaserLinks: Background for Reading**
Historical Connection

Literary History

Extremely popular in Victorian times, novels often were serialized in magazines aimed at the growing middle class. Toward the 19th century's end the short story also grew popular, in hands such as those of Rudyard Kipling, who championed British imperialism in rousing tales drawn from his experiences in India, and Sir Arthur Conan Doyle, creator of the master detective Sherlock Holmes. The Victorian emphasis on family life also spurred a boom in children's literature, including Lewis Carroll's *Alice's Adventures in Wonderland* (1865) and *Through the Looking Glass* (1872).

Poetry also thrived during Victorian times. Alfred, Lord Tennyson, who became poet laureate in 1850, wrote musical public verse like "The Charge of the Light Brigade," as well as more personal poetry such as that of *In Memoriam* (1850). Elizabeth Barrett Browning produced a bestseller with *Sonnets from the Portuguese* (1850), a volume of love poems to her husband Robert, who himself pioneered the verse form called the dramatic monologue. Poets of the Pre-Raphaelite movement, such as Dante Gabriel Rossetti and his sister Christina, repudiated Victorian excess and sought to return to the clarity of medieval Italian works. The more pessimistic mood of late Victorian times is evident in the verse of Thomas Hardy and A. E. Housman. Gerard Manley Hopkins is noted for his modern experiments in poetic rhythm.

The Victorian era was not an age of great drama, although Oscar Wilde wrote some fine comedies in the 1890s. The era's most enduringly popular stage creations are the comic operas of W. S. Gilbert and Arthur Sullivan, which ridicule social pretense with a vitality that is still admired today.

Making Connections

History

N At the end of the 19th century, Britain found its position of world leadership under increasing challenge. The United States had recently emerged as a major world power, and other European countries' competition with Britain for the rich resources of Africa and China was creating political and military tensions that would culminate in World War I.

Literature

O During the 19th century, many novels first appeared as weekly or monthly installments in magazines and newspapers, with readers waiting eagerly for each installment to appear. Almost all of Dickens's novels first appeared in this form, as did such works as William Makepeace Thackeray's *Vanity Fair,* George Eliot's *Ramola*, Wilkie Collins's *The Woman in White,* and Thomas Hardy's *Tess of the D'Urbervilles* and *Jude the Obscure.*

Music

P The playwright W.S. Gilbert and the composer Arthur Sullivan worked together from 1871 to 1896. During that time they produced 14 operettas, most of which satirize 19th-century British society. Lawyers, judges, military officials, and the aesthetic movement were among their many targets. Some of their most popular works are *H.M.S. Pinafore* (1878), *The Pirates of Penance* (1879), and *The Mikado* (1885). Gilbert and Sullivan's operettas were wildly popular in their own time and are still performed and enjoyed throughout the English-speaking world.

PART 1 Personal Relationships

During the Victorian era, the Industrial Revolution brought increased productivity and economic growth to much of England. However, it also brought poverty, overcrowding, and appalling work conditions to the many people who had flocked to the cities from rural areas, hoping for a better life. As the world became a confusing and often brutal place, personal relationships—love, marriage, friendship—became especially important to the Victorians. Of course, as the writers in this part of Unit Five suggest, not all such relationships provide comfort. Some, twisted by jealousy, turn dark—even criminal. In these selections, you may encounter experiences and questions that continue to concern people.

838

PREPARING to *Read*

The Lady of Shalott
Ulysses
from In Memoriam
Crossing the Bar

Poetry by ALFRED, LORD TENNYSON

" 'Tis better to have loved and lost / Than never to have loved at all."

Connect to Your Life

The Role of the Poet What comes to mind when you think of the word *poet?* Do you imagine someone secluded from the world? Someone who is a popular figure? Someone who expresses deep personal feelings? Discuss your thoughts with some of your classmates.

Build Background

The Voice of His Age Alfred, Lord Tennyson, was a true spokesperson for middle-class Victorians. His poetry reflected many of the prevailing attitudes of the day, especially the moral and religious concerns of individuals living in a universe redefined by scientific discoveries. His output was diverse, ranging from optimistic verse written to please the public, to wistful, melancholy poems expressing his own thoughts and feelings.

In 1833, Tennyson was overwhelmed with grief by the sudden death of his best friend, Arthur Henry Hallam, who had recently become engaged to Tennyson's sister and was just 22 years old. He expressed part of his response to this loss in his poetry. In the two months after his friend's death, Tennyson wrote "Ulysses," in which he describes the restless longing of the now aged hero for one last adventure. He also began writing the lyrics that were to become *In Memoriam,* an elegy mourning the death of a greatly talented man cut off before he is able to fulfill the promise of his youth. Written over a period of 17 years, the poem consists of 132 sections, 3 of which are included in the selection presented here. An early poem, "The Lady of Shalott" is a dreamlike narrative based on the Arthurian legends. "Crossing the Bar" was written by Tennyson near the end of his life; he directed that the poem be printed at the end of all collections of his poetry.

Focus Your Reading

LITERARY ANALYSIS | SPEAKER As you know, the **speaker** in a poem is the voice that "talks" to the reader, like the narrator in fiction. In Tennyson's poetry, the speaking voice varies from poem to poem, from a main character speaking in the first-person point of view to a neutral, objective voice that describes events in the third-person point of view. As you read each of these poems, think about what is revealed about the speaker.

ACTIVE READING | ANALYZING SPEAKER AND TONE
Tennyson's use of a different **speaker** in each poem allows him to convey a different **tone,** or attitude, about the subject matter of each work. In one poem, for example, Tennyson might use a speaker that helps convey a serious tone; in another poem, the speaker might observe the subject matter from a distance and therefore convey a tone of formality.

READER'S NOTEBOOK As you read the four poems, use a chart like the one shown to briefly describe each speaker and the tone that the speaker helps to impart.

Speaker	Speaker's Tone

OVERVIEW

Objectives
1. understand and appreciate classic Victorian **poetry (Literary Analysis)**
2. identify and examine the **speaker** in poetry **(Literary Analysis)**
3. **analyze speaker and tone (Active Reading)**

Summary

"The Lady of Shalott" is about a woman who cannot leave an island. She sees images of the outside world in her mirror and weaves these images into a tapestry. When she sees Lancelot in her mirror, she finally leaves the island for Camelot and dies on the way. In "Ulysses" (the Roman name for Odysseus), Ulysses grows tired of his life as a ruler and wishes for a last adventure at sea. In Section 27 of *In Memoriam,* Tennyson celebrates the human ability to suffer because of love. Section 54 expresses the hope that the universe is guided by a benevolent power. Section 130 contemplates the merging of the loved one with the universe. "Crossing the Bar" is a meditation on death that looks forward to the afterlife and requests that no one mourn the speaker.

Use **Unit Five Resource Book,** p. 4 for additional support.

Thematic Link

In "The Lady of Shalott," the Lady risks death in order to break free of a dull existence. In "Ulysses," Ulysses longs to leave his dull existence, even if it means risking his life. *In Memoriam* asserts the importance of **personal relationships** and their transcendence of death. "Crossing the Bar" deals with death as the inevitable, yet hopeful, conclusion to life.

5-Minute Warm-Up

Daily Language SkillBuilder

Have students **proofread** the display sentences on page 829i and write them correctly. The sentences also appear on Transparency 22 of **Grammar Transparencies and Copymasters.**

LESSON RESOURCES

UNIT FIVE RESOURCE BOOK, pp. 4–7

ASSESSMENT RESOURCES
Formal Assessment, pp. 151–152
Teacher's Guide to Assessment and Portfolio Use
Test Generator

SKILLS TRANSPARENCIES AND COPYMASTERS
Literary Analysis
- Poetic Devices, T16 (for Literary Analysis, p. 852)

Reading and Critical Thinking
- Determining Author's Purpose and Audience, T20 (for Active Reading, p. 839)

Grammar
- Pronoun Usage–*Who, Whom, Whose*, T50 (for Mini Lesson, pp. 846–847)
- Adjective Clauses Introduced by *Who* or *Whom,* C149 (for Mini Lesson, pp. 846–847)

Vocabulary
- Connotation, C66 (for Mini Lesson, p. 840)
- Synonyms, C67 (for Mini Lesson, p. 841)

Writing
- Subject Analysis, C30 (for Writing Option 1, p. 853)

Communications
- Appreciative Listening, T2 (for Activities & Explorations 2, p. 853)
- Analyze, Evaluate, and Critique: Literary Performance, T7 (for Activities & Explorations 2, p. 853)

INTEGRATED TECHNOLOGY
Audio Library
LaserLinks
- Author Background: Alfred, Lord Tennyson
- Art Gallery: Grief and Loss. See **Teacher's SourceBook,** p. 55.

Video: Literature in Performance
- "The Lady of Shalott," a reading with drawings. See **Video Resource Book,** pp. 27–30.

Visit our website: www.mcdougallittell.com

TEACHING THE LITERATURE

Reading and Analyzing

Literary Analysis SPEAKER

Remind students not to assume that the speaker in a poem is the author or the main character. Poets often invent a "voice" to tell a poem. The speaker may have views that are not the author's, and the main character's perspective may differ from the speaker's. Ask students the following questions:

- How can you tell that the speaker in the poem is not the Lady of Shalott?
  Possible Response: The speaker refers to her in the third person.
- What is the speaker's perspective? Is it the same as the Lady of Shalott's?
  Answer: No, the speaker describes the real world in detail; she sees it only in shadowy reflections; the speaker can also report the reapers' reaction to her singing and say what happens after she dies.

Use **Unit Five Resource Book,** p. 6 for more exercises.

Active Reading

ANALYZING SPEAKER AND TONE

A Remind students that a work's tone expresses the speaker's attitude toward the work and its audience. For example, the tone of *Paradise Lost* is formal and serious, while the tone of *Gulliver's Travels* is biting and satiric. Ask students to read Part I and tell what tone they think it has.
Possible Responses: serious; mysterious.

Use **Unit Five Resource Book,** p. 5 for more practice.

The Lady of Shalott

Alfred, Lord Tennyson

Detail, see p. 843.

A PART I

On either side the river lie
Long fields of barley and of rye,
That clothe the wold and meet the sky;
And through the field the road runs by
To many-towered Camelot;
And up and down the people go,
Gazing where the lilies blow
Round an island there below,
　　The island of Shalott.

Willows whiten, aspens quiver,
Little breezes dusk and shiver
Through the wave that runs forever
By the island in the river
　　Flowing down to Camelot.
Four gray walls, and four gray towers,
Overlook a space of flowers,
And the silent isle imbowers
　　The Lady of Shalott.

By the margin, willow-veiled,
Slide the heavy barges trailed
By slow horses; and unhailed
The shallop flitteth silken-sailed
　　Skimming down to Camelot:
But who hath seen her wave her hand?
Or at the casement seen her stand?
Or is she known in all the land,
　　The Lady of Shalott?

3 wold: rolling plain.

7 blow: bloom.

17 imbowers: encloses; surrounds.

22 shallop (shăl′əp): a small open boat.

25 casement: a hinged window that opens outward.

Teaching Options

Vocabulary Strategy

CONNOTATIONS

Instruction Remind students that *connotation* refers to the attitudes or emotions that a word evokes. A word can have positive, negative, or neutral connotations depending on what sense it is being used in. For example, when we use the word *smash* to describe a hit record, it has positive connotations. If we use *smash* (with *against, into,* or *through*) to describe the effect of a violent blow, it can have much harsher connotations. Somewhere in between are the basically neutral connotations of *smash* when used to signify a type of tennis stroke, as in an "overhand smash."

Activity Have students rate the connotative power of the boldface words as positive, negative, or neutral as they appear in the following sentences.

1. The crowd went **wild** when he scored the winning run.
   Answer: positive
2. His pitches were **wild**, and Sparky took him out of the game.
   Answer: negative

Use **Vocabulary Transparencies and Copymasters,** p. 43.

Only reapers, reaping early
In among the bearded barley,
Hear a song that echoes cheerly
From the river winding clearly,
Down to towered Camelot;
And by the moon the reaper weary,
Piling sheaves in uplands airy,
Listening, whispers "'Tis the fairy
Lady of Shalott."

PART II

There she weaves by night and day
A magic web with colors gay.
She has heard a whisper say,
A curse is on her if she stay
To look down to Camelot.
She knows not what the curse may be,
And so she weaveth steadily,
And little other care hath she,
The Lady of Shalott.

And moving through a mirror clear
That hangs before her all the year,
Shadows of the world appear.
There she sees the highway near
Winding down to Camelot;
There the river eddy whirls,
And there the surly village churls,
And the red cloaks of market girls,
Pass onward from Shalott.

Sometimes a troop of damsels glad,
An abbot on an ambling pad,
Sometimes a curly shepherd lad,
Or long-haired page in crimson clad,
Goes by to towered Camelot;
And sometimes through the mirror blue
The knights come riding two and two:
She hath no loyal knight and true,
The Lady of Shalott.

But in her web she still delights
To weave the mirror's magic sights,
For often through the silent nights

52 surly village churls: rude members of the lower class in a village.

55 damsels: young, unmarried women.

56 abbot . . . pad: the head monk in a monastery on a slow-moving horse.

58 page: a boy in training to be a knight.

Customizing Instruction

Less Proficient Readers

Before discussing what the Lady of Shalott represents, have students describe the following:

- her physical isolation
  Possible Responses: She lives on an island, enclosed by "gray" walls and towers; nobody seems aware of her existence except the reapers, who hear her singing before sunup.
- how she relates to the outside world
  Possible Responses: She can't look directly at Camelot because of the spell; she can only look at shadows of the world reflected in a mirror hanging in front of her. She makes art out of these shadows by weaving in her web.

Students Acquiring English

Explain to students that "The Lady of Shalott" draws on the traditions of medieval English romances. The setting is medieval as is the diction (the speaker uses the archaic *-th* to end some verbs, for example), and Lancelot is a legendary hero in many medieval romances.

Use **Spanish Study Guide** for additional support, pp. 191–193.

Gifted and Talented

Tennyson based one of his greatest works, *The Idylls of the King,* on the Arthurian legends. Have students read portions of this poem to gain a better understanding of Tennyson's philosophies and the importance of the Arthurian legends to Victorian culture.

Mini Lesson Vocabulary Strategy

SYNONYMS: DIFFERENT CONNOTATIONS

Instruction Discuss with students the connotative variety among synonyms. Explain that the extra shades of meaning that connotations give to words keep synonyms from having exactly the same meanings.

Activity Have students replace the italicized word in each sentence with the synonym in parentheses that has the most similar connotations. Have students discuss how the sentence meaning has changed.

1. He plays football with a lot of *emotion.* (sentiment, feeling, passion)
   Answer: passion
2. The people *rebelled* against the corrupt regime. (revolted, resisted)
   Answer: revolted
3. You've got a *cozy* place here. (small, intimate)
   Answer: intimate
4. This is a *vintage* car. (classic, old, obsolete)
   Answer: classic

Use **Vocabulary Transparencies and Copymasters,** p. 43.

Reading and Analyzing

Reading Skills and Strategies: **ARCHAIC WORDS**

Discuss with students how specialized activities, such as law and medicine, develop specialized vocabularies. Explain that knighthood had a large specialized vocabulary, and that only some of those words are used today.

Ask students to pick out words in the poem that are part of this archaic vocabulary.
Possible Responses: greaves, baldric, armor.

Literary Analysis: REPETITION

Remind students that one reason authors use repetition is to emphasize an idea, image, or emotion. In this poem, Tennyson repeats not only words and phrases, but also entire lines. Ask students to identify the lines that are repeated on this page and to describe the effect that repetition has on them as readers. (Note: The repetitions do not have to be word-for-word.)
Possible Responses: "As he rode down to Camelot" emphasizes the forcefulness of his impression on the lady and emphasizes her severance from Camelot. "Beside remote Shalott" emphasizes the isolation of the island and the lady, and works ironically to underscore the fact that the Lady is not "remote" at that instant, because she is so strongly attracted to Lancelot.

A funeral, with plumes and lights
And music, went to Camelot;
Or when the moon was overhead,
Came two young lovers lately wed:
"I am half sick of shadows," said
The Lady of Shalott.

1 PART III

A bowshot from her bower eaves,
He rode between the barley sheaves,
The sun came dazzling through the leaves,
And flamed upon the brazen greaves
Of bold Sir Lancelot.
A red-cross knight forever kneeled
To a lady in his shield,
That sparkled on the yellow field,
Beside remote Shalott.

The gemmy bridle glittered free,
Like to some branch of stars we see
Hung in the golden Galaxy.
The bridle bells rang merrily
As he rode down to Camelot;
And from his blazoned baldric slung
A mighty silver bugle hung,
And as he rode his armor rung,
Beside remote Shalott.

All in the blue unclouded weather
Thick-jeweled shone the saddle leather,
The helmet and the helmet-feather
Burned like one burning flame together,
As he rode down to Camelot;
As often through the purple night,
Below the starry clusters bright,
Some bearded meteor, trailing light,
Moves over still Shalott.

His broad clear brow in sunlight glowed;
On burnished hooves his war horse trode;
From underneath his helmet flowed
His coal-black curls as on he rode,
As he rode down to Camelot.
From the bank and from the river

73 bowshot: the distance an arrow can be shot; **bower** (bou′ər) **eaves:** the part of the roof that extends above the lady's private room.

76 brazen greaves: metal armor protecting the legs below the knees.

78–79 red-cross . . . shield: the red cross was a symbol worn by knights who fought in the Crusades, a series of holy wars between European Christians and the Muslim conquerors of Jerusalem and other parts of the Holy Land. Sir Lancelot's shield bears a picture of such a knight kneeling to honor a lady.

82 gemmy: studded with gems.

87 blazoned (blā′zənd) **baldric:** a decorated leather belt, worn across the chest to support a sword, or as in this case, a bugle.

Teaching Options

Assessment **Informal Assessment**

WRITING A PARAGRAPH To assess students' understanding of Lancelot's appearance and their use of side notes, have them write a paragraph describing Lancelot in their own words. You might want to mention that the side notes can help students understand unfamiliar words and terms.

RUBRIC

3 **Full Accomplishment** Paragraph contains all Lancelot's features mentioned in text and shows student used side notes to assist understanding.

2 **Substantial Accomplishment** Paragraph contains most of Lancelot's features mentioned in text and shows student used some of side notes to assist understanding.

1 **Little or Partial Accomplishment** Paragraph contains few of Lancelot's features mentioned in text and shows student used few or none of side notes to assist understanding.

2 He flashed into the crystal mirror,
"Tirra lirra," by the river
Sang Sir Lancelot.

She left the web, she left the loom,
She made three paces through the room,
She saw the water lily bloom,
She saw the helmet and the plume,
She looked down to Camelot.
Out flew the web and floated wide;
The mirror cracked from side to side;
"The curse is come upon me," cried
The Lady of Shalott.

The Lady of Shalott (1888) by J. W. Waterhouse (1849–1917), Tate Gallery, London/Art Resource, New York.

Customizing Instruction

Less Proficient Readers

1 Remind students that formal elements of poems, such as parts or sections, also give the reader information. Point out that Part I of the poem introduces the Lady of Shalott and that Part II describes her life and her curse and expresses her discontent. Ask students to tell why they think Tennyson grouped the stanzas in Part III.

Possible Responses: The stanzas are about the Lady of Shalott falling in love and succumbing to the curse; Tennyson introduces a new character, Lancelot.

Students Acquiring English

Explain that creative writers have poetic license—that is, they can change some of the usual rules of grammar if it suits their purposes. Point out that Tennyson takes liberties with sentence structure, and help students to unscramble the sentences. Share the following examples before having students look for their own:

1. "And down the river's dim expanse . . . Did she look to Camelot" (lines 127, 131). *(And she looked . . . down the river's dim expanse to Camelot.)*
2. "She loosed the chain, and down she lay" (line 133). *(She loosed the chain, and she lay down.)*

Multiple Learning Styles

Visual Learners

2 Ask students to draw a picture of what the Lady of Shalott sees when she views Lancelot in the mirror.

Possible Response: The picture should include Lancelot; the shield with the picture of the knight kneeling before his lady; his bugle, armor and helmet; his beard and long hair curling out from under his helmet; and the dazzling sun if possible.

Viewing and Representing

The Lady of Shalott **by John William Waterhouse**

ART APPRECIATION

Instruction Waterhouse was trained as a classical painter but developed a romantic style over the years. This painting reflects the poem's air of medieval mysticism and romance.

Application Ask students to analyze the painting's message regarding medieval culture. What qualities would a medieval lady represent, according to this painting?

Possible Responses: The elaborateness of the woman's dress and the careful way she has arranged it suggest that a lady should take care about her appearance; the dazzling whiteness of the woman's face and gown suggests that a lady is supposed to be pure; the fact that the woman is not trying to steer or propel the boat suggests that a lady is supposed to be passive.

Reading and Analyzing

Literary Analysis: RHYTHM

Ask students to notice the length of the sentences in Part IV. Ask what effect the long sentences have on the reader.

Possible Responses: They carry the reader along; they give a sense of a swift-flowing river; they lull the reader.

Ask students to read lines 145–148 again, and to think about the effect of the commas and the repetition of "chanted" in the middle of line 146 on the reader.

Possible Responses: The pauses slow the rhythm down; the pauses and the repetition add emphasis and gravity to the lines.

Reading Skills and Strategies: POINT OF VIEW

Remind students that the speaker of this poem is not the Lady of Shalott, and that all the events are being told from the speaker's point of view. Ask students whether the speaker uses the first person or third person to relate events.

Answer: third person.

Explain to students that a speaker using the third person may have a *limited* point of view—in which he or she reports the thoughts, feelings, and observations of only one character—or an *omniscient* point of view—in which he or she may report the thoughts, feelings, and observations of any and all characters. Have students tell which point of view is used in this poem and explain how they know.

Possible Response: omniscient—the speaker reports things that the Lady of Shalott could not know.

PART IV

In the stormy east wind straining,
The pale yellow woods were waning,
The broad stream in his banks complaining,
Heavily the low sky raining
        Over towered Camelot;
Down she came and found a boat
Beneath a willow left afloat,
And round about the prow she wrote
        The Lady of Shalott.

And down the river's dim expanse
Like some bold seër in a trance,
Seeing all his own mischance—
With a glassy countenance
        Did she look to Camelot.
And at the closing of the day
She loosed the chain, and down she lay;
The broad stream bore her far away,
        The Lady of Shalott.

Lying, robed in snowy white
That loosely flew to left and right—
The leaves upon her falling light—
Through the noises of the night
        She floated down to Camelot;
And as the boat-head wound along
The willowy hills and fields among,
They heard her singing her last song,
        The Lady of Shalott.

Heard a carol, mournful, holy,
Chanted loudly, chanted lowly,
Till her blood was frozen slowly,
And her eyes were darkened wholly,
        Turned to towered Camelot.
For ere she reached upon the tide
The first house by the waterside,
Singing in her song she died,
        The Lady of Shalott.

Under tower and balcony,
By garden wall and gallery,
A gleaming shape she floated by,

128 seër (sē′ər): someone who can see into the future; a prophet.

150 ere (âr): before.

Teaching Options

BLOCK SCHEDULING: MANAGING TIME

If your schedule requires that you cover the lesson objectives in a shorter time, use . . .

- Preparing to Read, p. 839
- Thinking Through the Literature, pp. 845, 847, 850, 852

If you want to take advantage of longer class time, use . . .

- TE Teaching Options: Vocabulary Strategies, pp. 840, 841; Informal Assessment, p. 842; Viewing and Representing, pp. 843, 849; Speaking and Listening, p. 848; Grammar, p. 846; Multicultural Link, p. 850, Standardized Test Practice, p. 851
- Choices & Challenges, p. 853

Dead-pale between the houses high,
Silent into Camelot.
Out upon the wharfs they came,
Knight and burgher, lord and dame,
And round the prow they read her name,
The Lady of Shalott.

Who is this? and what is here?
And in the lighted palace near
Died the sound of royal cheer;
And they crossed themselves for fear,
All the knights at Camelot:
But Lancelot mused a little space;
He said, "She has a lovely face;
God in his mercy lend her grace,
The Lady of Shalott."

160 burgher: a middle-class citizen of a town.

Thinking Through the Literature

1. **Comprehension Check** Summarize the main events in the poem's **plot.**
2. What is your impression of the Lady of Shalott?
3. What is her relationship to the outside world?

- what the reapers hear and say
- the curse she lives under
- what she sees in the "mirror clear" (line 46)
- what she weaves in her "magic web" (lines 38, 64–65)

4. Why do you think she says in line 71 that she is "half sick of shadows"?
5. How would you describe her actions after the mirror cracks? Do you think she could have responded differently? Explain your answer.

Thinking Through the Literature

1. The Lady of Shalott, who is under a curse that forbids her from looking out of her secluded living space at Camelot, sees Lancelot riding toward Camelot in her mirror and turns to look after him. The tapestry that is her life's work flies out the window, and the mirror cracks. The Lady of Shalott goes to the river and writes her name on a boat. She lies in it, sets it adrift for Camelot, and dies before reaching the city. It is only then that Lancelot and others of the royal court discover her.
2. Possible Responses: Students may say that she seems sad or pitiful. Some may say that she seems fairly content until she sees the lovers in the mirror. Still others may consider her brave.
3. Possible Responses: The Lady of Shalott is separated from the outside world by a curse. She cannot look at the world directly but only in a mirror that reflects shadowy images, which she weaves into her tapestry, creating a representation of the world for herself.
4. Possible Responses: She is saying that she is tired of only seeing reflections of the world, and not participating in it herself.
5. Possible Responses: Students may describe her actions after the mirror cracks as brave or reckless, inspired by love or by panic. Some may think she could not have acted differently, since the curse was bound to kill her; others may say that if she had stayed on the island, she might have lived.

THE LADY OF SHALOTT 845

Reading and Analyzing

Reading Skills and Strategies: SUMMARIZING

Have students summarize "Ulysses" in one or two sentences. Remind them that summarizing involves providing a shorter version of the text that is in their own words and includes main ideas and supporting details. Make sure they include the following ideas in their summaries: Ulysses' dislike of ruling, his past exploits, his attitude toward his son, and his attitude toward his old companions.

Possible Response: I'm tired of ruling a crowd of people who don't know me. I wish to leave the kingdom in the capable hands of my son and have more adventures like the ones of my youth, with my old companions, who know me well.

Thinking Through the Literature

1. Possible Response: He seems to be adventurous, fearless, and strong-willed.
2. Possible Response: Ulysses believes that his son's role is to civilize his kingdom, while his own role is to be a bold adventurer.
3. Possible Response: Tennyson seems to admire Ulysses, whom he doesn't portray merely as a mindless adventurer but as someone bound to follow knowledge and perform noble deeds.

Alfred, Lord Tennyson

It little profits that an idle king,
By this still hearth, among these barren crags,
Match'd with an aged wife, I mete and dole
Unequal laws unto a savage race,
That hoard, and sleep, and feed, and know not me.
I cannot rest from travel: I will drink
Life to the lees: all times I have enjoy'd
Greatly, have suffer'd greatly, both with those
That loved me, and alone; on shore, and when
Thro' scudding drifts the rainy Hyades
Vext the dim sea: I am become a name;
For always roaming with a hungry heart
Much have I seen and known; cities of men
And manners, climates, councils, governments,
Myself not least, but honor'd of them all;
And drunk delight of battle with my peers,
Far on the ringing plains of windy Troy.
I am a part of all that I have met;
Yet all experience is an arch wherethro'
Gleams that untravell'd world, whose margin fades
For ever and for ever when I move.
How dull it is to pause, to make an end,
To rust unburnish'd, not to shine in use!
As tho' to breathe were life. Life piled on life
Were all too little, and of one to me
Little remains: but every hour is saved
From that eternal silence, something more,
A bringer of new things; and vile it were
For some three suns to store and hoard myself,
And this gray spirit yearning in desire
To follow knowledge like a sinking star,
Beyond the utmost bound of human thought.
This is my son, mine own Telemachus,
To whom I leave the sceptre and the isle—
Well-loved of me, discerning to fulfil
This labor, by slow prudence to make mild
A rugged people, and thro' soft degrees
Subdue them to the useful and the good.
Most blameless is he, centred in the sphere

3 mete (mēt) **and dole:** give and distribute.

7 to the lees: to the dregs or bottom of the cup; completely.

10 scudding drifts: wind-blown rainclouds; **Hyades:** a constellation whose rising was believed to signify the coming of rain.

17 Troy: an ancient city (in what is now Turkey), conquered by the Greeks in the Trojan War in about 1200 B.C. Ulysses (also called Odysseus) was a major character in the *Iliad,* Homer's epic poem about the Trojan War, written in about 800 B.C.

29 three suns: three years.

34 sceptre: a staff held by a king or a queen as a symbol of royal authority.

Above: *Head of Ulysses,* Rhodian Brothers, 1st CE, Sperlonga/Erich Lessing/Art Resource, New York.

Teaching Options

Grammar

Adjective Clauses Introduced by *Who* and *Whom*

Instruction The pronouns *who* and *whom* are often used to introduce adjective clauses—clauses that modify nouns or pronouns. *Who* is in the nominative case and can act as the subject or predicate in a clause. *Whom* is in the objective case and can act as the direct object or the object of a preposition in a clause.

Activity Write on the chalkboard the excerpt from "The Lady of Shalott" and the three steps for determining when to use *who* or *whom.*

". . . And see the great Achilles, (who/whom) we knew."

Answer: whom; the pronoun is the direct object of "we knew"

1. Isolate the adjective clause.
2. Determine how the pronoun is being used in the clause.
3. If the pronoun serves as a subject or predicate pronoun, use *who;* if the pronoun acts as an object, use *whom.*

Ask students to identify the correct pronoun to complete the sentence and explain their choice.

Of common duties, decent not to fail
In offices of tenderness, and pay
Meet adoration to my household gods,
When I am gone. He works his work, I mine.
There lies the port; the vessel puffs her sail:
There gloom the dark broad seas. My mariners,
Souls that have toil'd, and wrought, and thought with me—
That ever with a frolic welcome took
The thunder and the sunshine, and opposed
Free hearts, free foreheads—you and I are old;
Old age hath yet his honor and his toil;
Death closes all: but something ere the end,
Some work of noble note, may yet be done,
Not unbecoming men that strove with Gods.
The lights begin to twinkle from the rocks:
The long day wanes: the slow moon climbs: the deep
Moans round with many voices. Come, my friends,
'Tis not too late to seek a newer world.
Push off, and sitting well in order smite
The sounding furrows; for my purpose holds
To sail beyond the sunset, and the baths
Of all the western stars, until I die.
It may be that the gulfs will wash us down:
It may be we shall touch the Happy Isles,
And see the great Achilles, whom we knew.
Tho' much is taken, much abides; and tho'
We are not now that strength which in old days
Moved earth and heaven; that which we are, we are;
One equal temper of heroic hearts,
Made weak by time and fate, but strong in will
To strive, to seek, to find, and not to yield.

42 meet: appropriate.

47 frolic: merry.

60–61 baths . . . stars: the Ancient Greeks believed the earth was surrounded by an outer ocean or river, into which the stars descended.

63–64 Happy Isles . . . Achilles: the Islands of the Blessed, where the souls of heroes, like Achilles, dwelled after death.

Thinking Through the Literature

1. What type of person does Ulysses seem to be?
   THINK ABOUT
   - his attitude toward his present life
   - his attitude toward aging and death
   - his motive for taking one last voyage
2. What contrast does Ulysses draw between his own role and that of his son, Telemachus?
3. What seems to be Tennyson's **tone,** or attitude, toward Ulysses?

Customizing Instruction

Less Proficient Readers

Help students to paraphrase the following long sentences in the poem.

Lines 1–5

Possible Response: I have no desire to continue as an unhappy, ineffectual ruler over subjects who really don't know me.

Lines 24–32

Possible Response: One life is not enough, and my one life is nearing its end. Every minute of my life is too precious to idle away.

Lines 65–70

Possible Response: We are old and not as strong as we used to be, but we still have the strength of will not to yield.

MULTIPLE LEARNING STYLES

Interpersonal Learners

Group students in pairs. Have one student assume the persona of Ulysses, and the other the persona of a reporter. Have the reporter interview Ulysses and ask the following questions.

- What have you accomplished in your life?
  Possible Response: I have become famous for the heroism I displayed in the Trojan War and on the long voyage home.
- How do you like being king?
  Possible Response: It is too sedentary and removed from life.
- How do you feel about growing older?
  Possible Response: It is depressing to think of all the things I long to do in what little time I have left, but I'm determined not to yield to old age and idleness.

Exercise Ask students to select the correct form of each pronoun and identify its function in the clause.

1. Alfred, Lord Tennyson, (who, whom) Queen Victoria greatly admired, was invited to serve as poet laureate in 1850.
   Answer: whom; direct object.
2. Watching the mirror crack, the Lady of Shalott, (who, whom) spent all of her time weaving a magical web, knew the curse had finally come upon her.
   Answer: who; subject.
3. Ulysses, (who, whom) Tennyson made the subject of his famous poem, is an important figure in Greek mythology.
   Answer: whom; direct object.
4. The Lady of Shalott, on (who, whom) Lancelot gazed, lay motionless before the gathering crowd.
   Answer: whom; object of preposition.

Use **Grammar Transparencies and Copymasters,** p. 82.

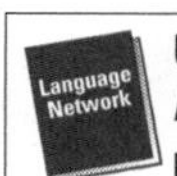

Use McDougal Littell's ***Language Network*** for more instruction and practice in adjective clauses.

Reading and Analyzing

Literary Analysis: ELEGY

Remind students that an elegy is an extended meditative poem in which the speaker reflects on a serious subject—usually someone's death. For an example of an earlier elegy, have students look back at Thomas Gray's "Elegy Written in a Country Courtyard" (page 667). Ask students what the speaker's attitude toward death is in *In Memoriam.*

Possible Responses: that nothing and no one dies in vain; that God has a plan and everything is part of that plan.

Active Reading

ANALYZING SPEAKER AND TONE

A Ask students what the speaker means when he says, "I can but trust that . . . every winter [will] change to spring."

Possible Responses: that something good will come out of every tragic occurrence; that every death will be followed by everlasting life.

B Ask students to describe the tone of section 54: Does it shift at any point?

Possible Responses: grieving but full of faith and hope; some students may say the tone becomes momentarily despondent beginning with line 33, and many of them may also see a return of hope in the second-to-last stanza. The last stanza's triumphant tone is less a shift than the climax of a long buildup

FROM

IN MEMORIAM

ALFRED, LORD TENNYSON

27

I envy not in any moods
The captive void of noble rage,
The linnet born within the cage,
That never knew the summer woods;

I envy not the beast that takes
His license in the field of time,
Unfettered by the sense of crime,
To whom a conscience never wakes;

1 Nor, what may count itself as blest,
The heart that never plighted troth **2**
But stagnates in the weeds of sloth;
Nor any want-begotten rest.

3 I hold it true, whate'er befall;
I feel it, when I sorrow most;
'Tis better to have loved and lost
Than never to have loved at all.

2 void of: lacking in.

3 linnet: a kind of small songbird.

6 license: freedom of action; liberty.

7 unfettered: unrestricted.

9–12 nor, what . . . rest: nor do I envy the supposed peace of mind that arises from remaining sunk in inaction, never pledging one's love, or from any deficiency.

May Day (1960), Andrew Wyeth. Watercolor. Copyright © 1995 Andrew Wyeth.

848

Teaching Options

Speaking and Listening

CHORAL READING

Instruction With its regular rhyme and rhythm, this poem is a good choice for a choral reading. Remind students that a choral reading is a group presentation, but one in which every student does not necessarily read every line.

Prepare The following are some guidelines for choral reading:

- Keep in mind that some lines sound better with a light tone of voice while others sound better with a heavy tone of voice.
- Have some lines read by a few voices or only one, and have other lines read by the whole group.
- Avoid a singsong effect.

Present Have students work in groups to plan a choral reading of the poem. Have them identify the effect of the poem's rhyme and rhythm. After the groups practice, have them make a class presentation.

BLOCK SCHEDULING This activity is particularly well-suited for longer class periods.

Portrait of Lord Tennyson (about 1856–1859), George Frederick Watts. National Gallery of Victoria, Melbourne, Australia.

O, yet we trust that somehow good
Will be the final goal of ill,
To pangs of nature, sins of will,
Defects of doubt, and taints of blood;

That nothing walks with aimless feet;
That not one life shall be destroyed,
Or cast as rubbish to the void,
When God hath made the pile complete;

That not a worm is cloven in vain;
That not a moth with vain desire
Is shriveled in a fruitless fire,
Or but subserves another's gain.

Behold, we know not anything;
I can but trust that good shall fall
At last—far off—at last, to all,
And every winter change to spring.

So runs my dream; but what am I?
An infant crying in the night;
An infant crying for the light,
And with no language but a cry.

19 pangs of nature: physical pain.

20 taints of blood: inherited faults.

23 void: empty space.

25 cloven: split.

28 subserves: promotes or assists.

Customizing Instruction

Students Acquiring English

Remind students that *In Memoriam* was written over a century ago, and that many words have gone out of use, changed their primary meanings, or changed their spellings in that time. Make sure students understand the following words and phrases, as well as those explained in the side notes.

1 blest
Answer: blessed.

2 plighted troth
Answer: To *plight* is to promise, and *troth* is a pledge to be true. The idiom "to plight troth" means to become engaged to marry. *Troth* is the root word in *betrothed*.

3 whate'er
Answer: a contraction of whatever.

Less Proficient Readers

Point out to students that both Section 27 (lines 1–12) and Section 54 (lines 17–28) of *In Memoriam* contain lists. Ask students to complete the lists in their own words.

- things the speaker does not envy
  Possible Responses: living things that are content to live in cages; animals without conscience; a person who has never been in love.
- what the speaker trusts is true
  Possible Responses: that bad things ultimately serve some good; that all living things are guided by a higher power; that all life is sacred; that nothing lives in vain.

Viewing and Representing

Portrait of Lord Tennyson (1856–1859)
by George Frederick Watts

ART APPRECIATION

Instruction Watts typically painted representations of abstract ideals. These paintings are full of symbolism that is obscure to viewers today. Although he professed to dislike portrait painting, he created portraits of many famous people of his time, including Tennyson.

Application Have students study the painting, and then ask them the following questions: What atmosphere or mood does this painting seem to convey? What contributes to this atmosphere? Interest students to describe specific elements in the painting's design to support their answers.

Reading and Analyzing

Literary Analysis: PARADOX

A Remind students that paradox is a form of irony in which a statement seems to contract itself, but actually reveals some element of truth. Ask students to find an example of paradox in the final stanza of *In Memoriam.*

Answer: "Far off thou art, but ever nigh . . ." [line 49].

Then have them explain what deeper truth the paradox reveals.

Possible Response: Even though his friend is no longer physically present, he is always present in spirit.

Thinking Through the Literature

1. Accept all reasonable ideas.
2. Possible Responses: He is glad to have loved his friend even though the friend's death causes him pain; he feels lost and frightened because he can't be sure what happens after death, and therefore all his faith and hope may be misplaced; he trusts that life and death are not in vain; he feels his friend's presence in God and nature.
3. Possible Response: They have become one.
4. Accept all reasonable answers.

130

Thy voice is on the rolling air;
    I hear thee where the waters run;
    Thou standest in the rising sun,
And in the setting thou art fair.

What are thou then? I cannot guess;
    But though I seem in star and flower
    To feel thee some diffusive power,
I do not therefore love thee less.

My love involves the love before;
    My love is vaster passion now;
    Though mixed with God and Nature thou,
I seem to love thee more and more.

A Far off thou art, but ever nigh;
    I have thee still, and I rejoice;
    I prosper, circled with thy voice;
I shall not lose thee though I die.

43 diffusive: scattered about.

49 nigh: nearby.

Thinking Through the Literature

1. With your classmates, discuss your thoughts after reading these sections of *In Memoriam.*
2. What different reactions to grief and loss does the **speaker** seem to experience?

   THINK ABOUT
   - the last stanza of section 27
   - the feelings he expresses in lines 34–36
   - his expression of trust in section 54, especially in lines 30–33
   - his thoughts leading up to the statement, "I have thee still, and I rejoice" in line 50
3. What, in the speaker's mind, is the relationship between the deceased loved one and nature?
4. What is your opinion of the speaker's comment that it is "better to have loved and lost / Than never to have loved at all" (lines 15–16)?

850

Teaching Options

Remembering the Dead

Elegies are just one way to remember and honor the dead. In China, on the festival day of Chi'ng Ming, which means "Clear and Bright," many families pay their respects to their ancestors. Graves are swept and headstone inscriptions repainted. Rice, tea, and other foods are set out. Incense and red candles are lighted. The family kneels out of respect for the dead. Before leaving a grave, the family tucks several pieces of offering paper under a stone on top of the grave, with the ends of the paper situated to flap a little in the wind as a sign that respects have been paid and the dead have not been forgotten.

Fisherman at Sea (1796), J. M. W. Turner, Clore Collection, Tate Gallery, London/Art Resource.

Crossing the Bar

ALFRED, LORD TENNYSON

Sunset and evening star,
    And one clear call for me!
And may there be no moaning of the bar,
    When I put out to sea,

1 But such a tide as moving seems asleep,
    Too full for sound and foam,
When that which drew from out the boundless deep
    Turns again home.

Twilight and evening bell,
    And after that the dark!
And may there be no sadness of farewell,
    When I embark;

For though from out our bourne of Time and Place
    The flood may bear me far,
I hope to see my Pilot face to face
    When I have crossed the bar.

3 moaning of the bar: the sad, mournful sound of the ocean waves pounding against a sand bar at the mouth of a harbor.

9 evening bell: a ship's bell rung to announce the changing of the watch.

13 from out our bourne of Time and Place: beyond the boundary of our lifetimes.

14 flood: ocean.

Customizing Instruction

Less Proficient Readers

1 You may need to help students understand the phrase "But such a tide as moving seems asleep . . ." Remind students that the phrase is part of a sentence that begins at line 1. Have students reread lines 1–5 and then paraphrase line 5.

Possible Response: But a kind of tide that seems asleep although it is moving.

Assessment Informal Assessment

WRITING AN ESSAY You can informally assess students' understanding of important metaphors in the poems by having them write an essay in which they compare and contrast the ways that the sea is used as a metaphor in "Ulysses" and "Crossing the Bar."

RUBRIC

3 Full Accomplishment Response shows full understanding of metaphor and similarities and differences in way it is used in poems.

2 Substantial Accomplishment Response shows general understanding of metaphor or limited understanding of similarities and differences in ways it is used in poems.

1 Little or Partial Accomplishment Response shows little or no understanding of metaphor and similarities and differences in ways it is used in two poems.

GUIDING STUDENT RESPONSE

Connect to the Literature

1. What Do You Think?
Guidelines for student response: Students will probably comment on the note of hopefulness with which the poem concludes.

Comprehension Check
- the seaside
- literally, a sandbar separating a harbor and the sea; figuratively, death

 Use Selection Quiz in **Unit Five Resource Book,** p.7.

Think Critically

2. The extended metaphor of the sea voyage refers to death.
3. God
4. Possible Responses: He believes that death returns us to a spiritual state that is our eternal "home"; he believes that death is a passage like an ocean voyage; he believes that God will guide his soul after death as a pilot guides a boat.
5. Possible Responses: The speaker in "The Lady of Shalott" is not involved in the action, but is narrating events from an omniscient point of view. The tone of the poem is mystical and steeped in romance.
   In "Ulysses," the speaker is the main character, and compared to "The Lady of Shalott," the tone is more realistic, intimate, and intense.
   The speaker in *In Memoriam* seems to be the poet. Because the poet is revealing his thoughts directly to the reader, the tone of this poem is yet more intimate than "Ulysses." The poet's attitude of solemn faith and hope is more evident in the parts of the poem written later than in those written earlier.
   In "Crossing the Bar," the speaker does not emerge as a distinct persona, and seems to be the poet himself. The tone is mature, intimate, spiritual, and peaceful.

Literary Analysis

Cooperative Learning Activity Make up a composite chart on the chalkboard based upon student's responses.
Review Blank Verse "Ulysses" is written in blank verse.

Connect to the Literature

1. **What Do You Think?** With your classmates, discuss your thoughts after reading "Crossing the Bar."

Comprehension Check
- What is the **setting** of the poem?
- What sort of bar is being described?

Think Critically

2. To what does the **extended metaphor** of the sea voyage refer?

   THINK ABOUT
   - the speaker's reference in line 5 to a tide that "as moving seems asleep"
   - the speaker's wish in lines 11–12 that there be no sadness when he embarks
   - the remark in lines 13–14 that the flood may take the speaker beyond "our bourne of Time and Place"
3. Who might the Pilot represent?
4. How would you describe the **speaker's** attitude toward death?
5. **ACTIVE READING** ANALYZING SPEAKER AND TONE Review the chart you created in your 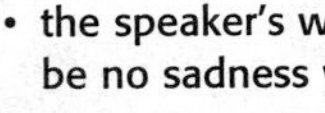 READER'S NOTEBOOK to identify the **speaker** and the **tone** in each poem. How does the tone differ from poem to poem? How does the speaker affect the tone in each case?

Extend Interpretations

6. **Comparing Texts** Compare the excerpts from *In Memoriam* with Ben Jonson's "On My First Son" (page 458). What differences do you see in the two speakers' ways of coping with their grief? Share your thoughts with the class.
7. **Connect to Life** Tennyson wrote both "Ulysses" and *In Memoriam* in response to the death of a friend. Do you think writing a poem or a story or producing other kinds of art would be an effective way of responding to difficulty or loss? Explain your answer.

Literary Analysis

SPEAKER The **speaker** of a poem and the poet are not usually identical, although in some poems the speaker is closely identified with the poet. Often a poet creates a speaker with a distinct identity in order to achieve a particular effect.

Cooperative Learning Activity With a group of classmates, analyze how a different speaker might affect each poem. What if, for example, the speaker of "Ulysses" were his son, Telemachus? Write down your ideas in a chart like the one shown. Then share your conclusions with the rest of the class.

Poem	New Speaker	Effect
"The Lady of Shalott"	Lady of Shalott	
"Ulysses"		
In Memoriam		
"Crossing the Bar"		

REVIEW BLANK VERSE **Blank verse** is unrhymed poetry written in **iambic pentameter.** Because iambic pentameter resembles the natural rhythm of spoken English, it has been considered the most suitable meter for dramatic verse in English. Determine which of Tennyson's four poems is written in blank verse.

Extend Interpretations

Comparing Texts Possible Responses: At the end of *In Memoriam,* Tennyson seems to have accepted his friend's death because the memory of his friend is all around him; further, he believes that it is better to have loved and lost. Jonson, on the other hand, still rues the loss of his son and is having difficulty accepting it—only religion seems to offer him solace.

Connect to Life Accept all reasonable responses. Ask students to come up with examples from contemporary art, literature, or music that show an artist responding to difficulty or loss (such as Eric Clapton's "Tears in Heaven").

Writing Options

1. Analysis Essay Write an essay in which you analyze Ulysses' ideas about what constitutes a good and useful life. As a start, think about these questions: What comparison and contrast does Ulysses draw between his life and that of his son? What moral lessons does the poem seem to be teaching? Place the essay in your **Working Portfolio.**

Writing Handbook
See page 1369: Analysis.

2. Three Titles Write individual titles for the three sections of *In Memoriam.* Make sure that each title reflects the principal theme of the section to which it applies.

Activities & Explorations

1. Lancelot's Shield Draw your interpretation of Lancelot's shield as it is described in the first stanza of Part III of "The Lady of Shalott." ~ **ART**

2. The Lady on Film Watch the video "The Lady of Shalott," which features an oral reading and illustrations of the poem. Discuss how the film helps bring the poem to life. How did the video interpretation help convey the mood of the poem? ~ **VIEWING AND REPRESENTING**

Literature in Performance

Inquiry & Research

Grief and Loss Research current theories of grief and loss. What are the normal stages of the grieving process? Share your findings in a brief oral report to the class.

Alfred, Lord Tennyson
1809–1892

Other Works
"The Charge of the Light Brigade"
Idylls of the King

Childhood The fourth son in a family of twelve children, Alfred Tennyson grew up in Somersby, England, where his father was a clergyman. Even as a child, Tennyson displayed an interest in poetry. He began learning to write poems at age eight by imitating the styles of Milton, Byron, and others. While a teenager, he collaborated with his brother on a collection of poems, which they published in 1826. Although Tennyson's father tutored his children to prepare them for a university education, family life at Somersby was problematic. The Reverend Dr. Tennyson's dissatisfaction with his profession led to periods of drunkenness that caused his family distress. Tensions in the family were increased by the opium addiction of one child and the severe mental illness of another.

University Life In 1827, Tennyson entered Cambridge University, where he won a poetry contest in his first year. His achievements caught the attention of a group of gifted undergraduates who called themselves the Apostles. Under the leadership of Arthur Henry Hallam, the Apostles urged Tennyson to pursue a career as a poet. Unfortunately, lack of funds forced the promising young poet to leave the university in 1831 and return home without taking a degree.

The Writing Life In the following years, Tennyson endured many difficulties, including the calamity of Hallam's death, financial problems, and an engagement complicated by the disapproval of his future wife's father. Throughout this time, however, he persisted with his writing, and in 1850 *In Memoriam* was published to impressive reviews. Tennyson had at last received literary recognition, and later that year he was invited by Queen Victoria to succeed Wordsworth as poet laureate. Tennyson lived a long life, during which he became a living legend—one of the most beloved figures of the Victorian era. In 1884, at the government's urging, he accepted the rank of baron and, along with it, the title *Lord.*

LaserLinks: Background for Reading
Author Background / Art Gallery

Writing Options

1. **Analysis Essay** Remind students that Ulysses was an epic hero, and his values are those you would associate with such a hero. Have them name their own heroes, and ask them if different kinds of heroes represent different kinds of values. To approach the question from the point of view of Ulysses, ask them how he might respond to the suggestion that his son was, or could become, a hero.
2. **Three Titles** Accept all relevant titles.

Activities & Explorations

1. **Lancelot's Shield** Refer students to an encyclopedia to see pictures of knights' shields. Suggest they try looking up the information under "shield," "Middle Ages," or "knights."
2. **The Lady on Film** Accept all reasonable responses.

Inquiry & Research

Grief and Loss To extend the activity, suggest that interested students research what one or more of the world's great religions teach about grief and loss. Students can research Christianity, Islam, Buddhism, or Hinduism. Have students write out their oral report in outline or script form, then rehearse and revise their oral reports with a peer, before presenting in front of the class.

OVERVIEW

"My Last Duchess" is included in the **Grade 12 InterActive Reader.**

Objectives

1. understand and appreciate **dramatic monologues (Literary Analysis)**
2. use strategies for **making inferences (Active Reading)**

Summary

In "My Last Duchess," the speaker is talking with an agent of a count; the speaker is negotiating a marriage with the count's daughter. He shows the agent a portrait of his last wife, talking about her in a fashion that implies he probably killed her out of jealousy. Porphyria's lover strangles her so that she will always be his. She has come to him on a rainy night and announced that, although she loves him, she cannot free herself from "pride" and "vainer ties" to devote herself to him forever. His strangling her represents, in his mind, a way of freeing her from the pride and vainer ties so that she can have her true wish—to be with him.

Thematic Link

These poems show the destructive effect of jealousy on **personal relationships.** On a more reflective level, they deal with the changeable nature of personal relationships and the impossibility of always molding them to our wishes.

5-Minute Warm-Up

Daily Language SkillBuilder

Have students **proofread** the display sentences on page 829i and write them correctly. The sentences also appear on Transparency 22 of **Grammar Transparencies and Copymasters.**

GUIDE FOR READING

A She is dead; she was not his first wife; he intends to marry again.

B He is jealous of others' admiring her; no one is allowed to look at her because she is not in the duke's favor.

C He feels it was a weakness; he feels that her smiles should have been reserved for him alone.

My Last Duchess / Porphyria's Lover

Poetry by ROBERT BROWNING

"That's my last Duchess painted on the wall, / Looking as if she were alive."

Connect to Your Life

Green with Envy Consider the potential consequences of jealousy in a love relationship. Do you think jealousy is normal in such a relationship? Are there different degrees of this emotion? Share your thoughts with classmates.

Build Background

Playwright and Poet Although Robert Browning is best known as one of the greatest of Victorian poets, he actually devoted many years to writing plays. The techniques he learned as a playwright undoubtedly led to his mastery of the **dramatic monologue**—a type of poem in which a fictional speaker addresses a silent listener about a critical experience in his or her life. "My Last Duchess" and "Porphyria's (pôr-fîr'yəz) Lover" are among Browning's best dramatic monologues.

"My Last Duchess" takes place in 16th-century Italy and reflects the esteem for art that characterized the Italian Renaissance. Loosely based on actual events in the life of Alfonso II, duke of Ferrara, the poem presents a single episode in the duke's negotiations to marry the daughter of a powerful count. As the poem begins, the duke is showing a portrait of his former wife to the count's agent. The painting of the duchess "looking as if she were alive" is typical of Renaissance portraits, in which painters endeavored to portray their sitters as accurately and realistically as possible.

"Porphyria's Lover" first appeared with another dramatic monologue under the title *Madhouse Cells,* a title that reveals the poet's fascination with abnormal states of mind. Though Browning was a respectable, well-balanced person, the fictional speakers in his poems—ranging from corrupt bishops to insanely jealous lovers—often display abnormal behavior.

Focus Your Reading

LITERARY ANALYSIS DRAMATIC MONOLOGUE

In a **dramatic monologue,** the speaker describes a crucial experience to one or more listeners who remain silent. As you read these poems, consider how the use of dramatic monologue affects your knowledge of the speakers.

ACTIVE READING MAKING INFERENCES

An **inference** is a logical guess based on evidence. You often need to make inferences to figure out what is unstated yet implied in a literary work. You might, for example, use clues provided by a writer to infer—simply from the way a character acts—that the character is jealous of another character.

READER'S NOTEBOOK As you read each of these poems, use a chart like the one shown to jot down any inferences you make about the speaker, the woman he describes, the setting, or past events.

Inferences		
	"My Last Duchess"	"Porphyria's Lover"
Speaker		
Woman		
Setting		
Past events		

LESSON RESOURCES

UNIT FIVE RESOURCE BOOK, pp. 8–9

ASSESSMENT RESOURCES
Formal Assessment, p. 153
Teacher's Guide to Assessment and Portfolio Use
Test Generator

SKILLS TRANSPARENCIES AND COPYMASTERS
Literary Analysis
- Point of View, T18 (for Think Critically 4, p. 859)

Reading and Critical Thinking
- Making Inferences, T7 (for Active Reading, p. 854)

Grammar
- Comparison of Regular and Irregular Adjectives and Adverbs, T52 (for Mini Lesson, p. 860)
- Comparative Forms, C154 (for Mini Lesson, p. 860)

Writing
- Organizing Your Writing, C30 (for Writing Option 2, p. 860)

Communications
- Impromptu Speaking: Dialogue, Role-Play, T14 (for Activities & Explorations 1, p. 860)

INTEGRATED TECHNOLOGY
Audio Library
LaserLinks
- Film Connection: A Reading of "My Last Duchess"
- Art Gallery: Portraits of Italian Renaissance Ladies. See **Teacher's SourceBook,** p. 57.

Visit our website:
www.mcdougallittell.com

My Last Duchess

Robert Browning

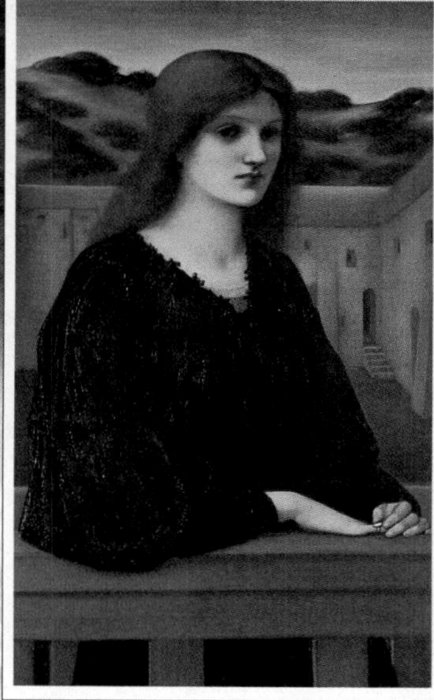

Vespertina Quies (1893), Sir Edward Burne-Jones. Oil on canvas 120.6 cm × 62.2 cm, bequeathed by Miss Maud Beddington, 1940, Tate Gallery, London/Art Resource, New York.

That's my last Duchess painted on the wall,
Looking as if she were alive. I call
That piece a wonder, now: Frà Pandolf's hands
Worked busily a day, and there she stands.
Will't please you sit and look at her? I said
"Frà Pandolf" by design, for never read
Strangers like you that pictured countenance,
The depth and passion of its earnest glance,
But to myself they turned (since none puts by
The curtain I have drawn for you, but I)
And seemed as they would ask me, if they durst,
How such a glance came there; so, not the first
Are you to turn and ask thus. Sir, 'twas not
Her husband's presence only, called that spot
Of joy into the Duchess' cheek: perhaps
Frà Pandolf chanced to say "Her mantle laps
Over my lady's wrist too much," or "Paint
Must never hope to reproduce the faint
Half-flush that dies along her throat": such stuff
Was courtesy, she thought, and cause enough
For calling up that spot of joy. She had
A heart—how shall I say?—too soon made glad,
Too easily impressed; she liked whate'er
She looked on, and her looks went everywhere.

GUIDE FOR READING

1 What can you infer from the duke's use of the word *last*? **A**

3 Frà Pandolf's: of Brother Pandolf, a fictitious friar-painter.

7 countenance: face.

9–10 What might it mean that no one save the duke draws the curtain? **B**

11 durst: dared. (Note the hint that the strangers feel some sense of fear about questioning the duke.)

16 mantle: cloak.

21–24 How do you think the duke feels about the duchess's tendency to be easily pleased? **C**

TEACHING THE LITERATURE

Customizing Instruction

Less Proficient Readers

Set a Purpose Establish the basic sense of lines 6–12; namely, that whenever the speaker shows someone the painting (and *he* is the only person allowed to draw aside the curtain covering it), the person will ask him about the expression on her face.

Students Acquiring English

Since these dramatic monologues are written in rhymed verse, students might tend to read one line at a time. Point out to them the poems' punctuation (how, for example, some periods occur in the middle of lines, and others at the end), and remind them that the sense of each line is not self-contained but runs over from one line to the next.

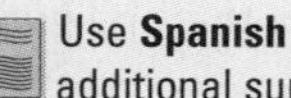

Use **Spanish Study Guide** for additional support, pp. 194–196.

Gifted and Talented

Have students write their own dramatic monologues. Encourage them to model the rhyme scheme and meter of their poems after either "My Last Duchess" or "Porphyria's Lover."

BLOCK SCHEDULING: MANAGING TIME

If your schedule requires that you cover the lesson objectives in a shorter time, use . . .

- Preparing to Read, p. 854
- Thinking Through the Literature, pp. 856 and 859

If you want to take advantage of longer class time, use . . .

- TE Teaching Options: Viewing and Representing, p. 857; Speaking and Listening, p. 856; Informal Assessment, p. 858; Grammar, p. 860
- Choices & Challenges, p. 860

Reading and Analyzing

Literary Analysis DRAMATIC MONOLOGUE

Remind students that in a dramatic monologue we learn about a character in his or her own words.

Use **Unit Five Resource Book,** p. 9 for more exercises.

Active Reading MAKING INFERENCES

Although the speaker in the poem leaves a great deal unsaid, much can be inferred from what he implies. Remind students that *inferring* involves drawing conclusions based on evidence given "between the lines."

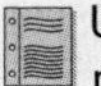
Use **Unit Five Resource Book,** p. 8 for more practice.

GUIDE FOR READING

A He commanded that she be killed; he became such a tyrant that she grew to hate him.

B No—the duke wants to give the impression that such social distinctions are irrelevant to him.

C The duke believed he had to tame his wife.

D He likes possessing things and people.

E Her presence lights and warms the room both physically and emotionally.

F He wants to hear why she has come before he responds; he is mad at her; he has been unhappy without her and wants her to suffer a little too; he is brooding about what to do.

Sir, 'twas all one! My favor at her breast,
The dropping of the daylight in the West,
The bough of cherries some officious fool
Broke in the orchard for her, the white mule
She rode with round the terrace—all and each
Would draw from her alike the approving speech,
Or blush, at least. She thanked men—good! but thanked
Somehow—I know not how—as if she ranked
My gift of a nine-hundred-years-old name
With anybody's gift. Who'd stoop to blame
This sort of trifling? Even had you skill
In speech—(which I have not)—to make your will
Quite clear to such an one, and say, "Just this
Or that in you disgusts me; here you miss,
Or there exceed the mark"—and if she let
Herself be lessoned so, nor plainly set
Her wits to yours, forsooth, and made excuse
—E'en then would be some stooping; and I choose
Never to stoop. Oh sir, she smiled, no doubt,
Whene'er I passed her; but who passed without
Much the same smile? This grew; I gave commands;
Then all smiles stopped together. There she stands
As if alive. Will't please you rise? We'll meet
The company below, then. I repeat,
The Count your master's known munificence
Is ample warrant that no just pretense
Of mine for dowry will be disallowed;
Though his fair daughter's self, as I avowed
At starting, is my object. Nay, we'll go
Together down, sir. Notice Neptune, though,
Taming a sea horse, thought a rarity,
Which Claus of Innsbruck cast in bronze for me!

27 officious: offering unwanted services; meddling.

35 trifling: actions of little importance.

41 forsooth: in truth; indeed.

46 What do you think happened to make the smiles stop? A

49 munificence (myo͞o-nĭf'ĭ-səns): generosity.

50 just pretense: legitimate claim.

51 dowry (dou'rē): a financial settlement given to a groom by the bride's father.

53–54 The count's agent has gestured for the duke, because of his higher social status, to descend first. The duke responds that they will go down together. In your opinion, is the duke's graciousness in ignoring social differences genuine? B

54 Neptune: in Roman mythology, the god of the sea.

55 What comparison can you draw between the duke and duchess's relationship and Neptune's taming the sea horse? C

56 Claus of Innsbruck: a fictitious Austrian sculptor. What can you infer from the last two words of the poem? D

Thinking Through the Literature

1. Describe your reaction to this poem.
2. What do you think happened to the duchess? Why do you suppose the poet never tells us exactly what happened to her?
3. How would you describe the speaker's attitude toward his former wife?

- where he keeps his wife's picture
- his reaction to the courtesy Frà Pandolf shows her
- how he feels about her response to his "gift of a nine-hundred-years-old name" (line 33)
- why he chooses "never to stoop" (line 43)

Thinking Through the Literature

1. Accept all reasonable responses.
2. Possible Response: The speaker probably killed her. The speaker is trying to hide what happened from the envoy so he will be able to marry again.
3. The speaker sees his former wife as a possession.

Teaching Options

Speaking and Listening

DRAMATIC READING

Instruction These two poems are particularly appropriate for a dramatic reading because of their strong plots and characters.

Prepare Share the following strategies with students:

- Read the poem several times until you can make sense of any difficult words or sentence structures.
- Think about what needs to be stressed to make the sense clear, and what needs to be emphasized less.
- Watch for punctuation marks that show where a thought ends.
- Read the poem in a conversational voice, not in a singsong rhythm.
- Use tone, facial expressions, and gestures to convey the speaker's emotions.

Present Have students work in pairs, with one student preparing a dramatic reading of "My Last Duchess" and the other preparing a reading of "Porphyria's Lover."

This activity is particularly well-suited for longer class periods.

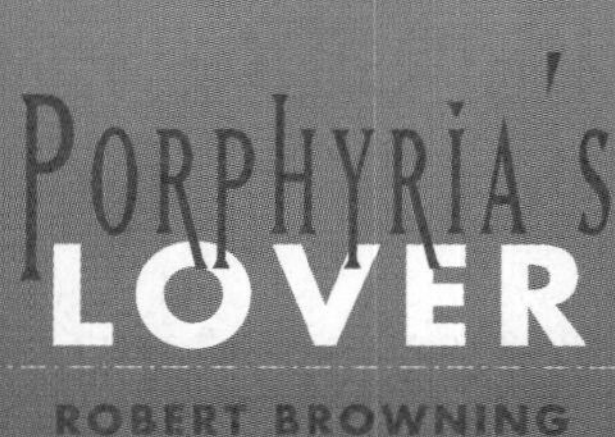

Porphyria's Lover

ROBERT BROWNING

The Model (1939), Georges Braque. Oil on canvas, 100 cm × 100 cm, private collection, New York. Copyright © 1995 Artists Rights Society (ARS), New York/ADAGP, Paris.

The rain set early in tonight,
    The sullen wind was soon awake,
It tore the elm-tops down for spite,
    And did its worst to vex the lake:
    I listened with heart fit to break.
When glided in Porphyria; straight
    She shut the cold out and the storm,
And kneeled and made the cheerless grate
    Blaze up, and all the cottage warm;
    Which done, she rose, and from her form
Withdrew the dripping cloak and shawl,
    And laid her soiled gloves by, untied
Her hat and let the damp hair fall,
    And, last, she sat down by my side
    And called me. When no voice replied,

GUIDE FOR READING

4 vex: to disturb; trouble the surface of.

6 straight: immediately.

6–9 What do you think Porphyria's first actions reveal about her? 

8 grate: fireplace.

15 Although the speaker has heard Porphyria, he does not reply. F Why do you think he remains silent?

Customizing Instruction

Less Proficient Readers

Set a Purpose Have students read "Porphyria's Lover," bearing in mind "My Last Duchess"—another poem about a jealous lover. Suggest that they compare the two men's motivations.

Multiple Learning Styles

Auditory, Kinesthetic, Interpersonal

Ask students to rewrite the poem as a dialogue, with Porphyria voicing all the thoughts her lover attributes to her in the first part of the poem. Then have two students act out the poem, paying particular attention to the unspoken moments in the scene that are so telling.

Possible Response: He doesn't reply to her initial call. She responds by putting his head on her shoulder and covering it with her hair. He then uses her hair to strangle her, props her up, and puts her head on his shoulder.

Mini Lesson Viewing and Representing

The Model **by Georges Braque**

ART APPRECIATION

Instruction This 1939 oil painting by Braque (1882–1963) centers on an interesting combination profile-and-full-face-view. Emphasizing this dual view is the contrast of colors.

Application Ask students what they think the dual views of the model symbolize.

Possible Responses: the oppositions we have inside us between such things as good and evil, the known and the unknown; the difference between being seen head-on by someone we can see, and in profile by someone we aren't aware of.

Reading and Analyzing

GUIDE FOR READING

A She can't make a commitment to the speaker; because she enjoys the admiration of other men—the "vainer ties."

Reading Skills and Strategies: ANALYZING AND INTERPRETING

B Ask students to interpret the speaker's words, "Be sure I looked up at her eyes / Happy and proud; at last I knew / Porphyria worshiped me: surprise / Made my heart swell, and still it grew / While I debated what to do." Their interpretation should help them analyze the speaker's state of mind.

Possible Responses: The choice of the word "proud" echoes Porphyria's use of it to explain her inability to commit to him. His willingness to describe himself as proud underscores the insanity of his action, which seems intended in part to free her from the pride and vanity that distance her from him. The words "worship" and "pride" tell the reader that the speaker's love is of himself and his ego as much as it is of Porphyria; the words "at last" and "surprise" tell the reader that the speaker has long been waiting in vain for his love to be returned.

GUIDE FOR READING

C He is frightened of what he might see.

D that he fulfilled her wish that she be his.

She put my arm about her waist,
  And made her smooth white shoulder bare,
And all her yellow hair displaced,
  And, stooping, made my cheek lie there,
  And spread, o'er all, her yellow hair,
Murmuring how she loved me—she
  Too weak, for all her heart's endeavor,
To set its struggling passion free
  From pride, and vainer ties dissever,
  And give herself to me forever.
But passion sometimes would prevail,
  Nor could tonight's gay feast restrain
A sudden thought of one so pale
  For love of her, and all in vain:
  So, she was come through wind and rain.
B Be sure I looked up at her eyes
  Happy and proud; at last I knew
Porphyria worshiped me: surprise
  Made my heart swell, and still it grew
  While I debated what to do.
That moment she was mine, mine, fair,
  Perfectly pure and good: I found
A thing to do, and all her hair
  In one long yellow string I wound
  Three times her little throat around,
And strangled her. No pain felt she;
  I am quite sure she felt no pain.
As a shut bud that holds a bee,
  I warily oped her lids: again
  Laughed the blue eyes without a stain.
And I untightened next the tress
  About her neck; her cheek once more
Blushed bright beneath my burning kiss:
  I propped her head up as before,
  Only, this time my shoulder bore
Her head, which droops upon it still:
  The smiling rosy little head,
So glad it has its utmost will,
  That all it scorned at once is fled,
  And I, its love, am gained instead!
Porphyria's love: she guessed not how
  Her darling one wish would be heard.
And thus we sit together now,
  And all night long we have not stirred,
  And yet God has not said a word!

22–25 What is Porphyria unable to do? What might the "vainer ties" be? **A**

27–30 Porphyria has left a party in order to be with the speaker.

35 Note that the speaker feels that he must make a decision.

44 In your opinion, why does the speaker open Porphyria's eyes "warily" (cautiously)? **C**

52–55 The speaker here claims that he knows Porphyria's mind.

56–57 What is the speaker claiming? **D**

Teaching Options

Assessment Informal Assessment

WRITING A LETTER Ask students to write a letter from the point of view of a member of the family of either the Duchess or Porphyria telling a friend of the family what happened and how the family member feels about it.

RUBRIC

3 **Full Accomplishment** Letter reflects full understanding of events in poem and family member's probable feelings.

2 **Substantial Accomplishment** Letter reflects general understanding of events in poem and family member's probable feelings.

1 **Little or Partial Accomplishment** Letter reflects little understanding of events in poem and family member's probable feelings.

Connect to the Literature

1. **What Do You Think?** Were you surprised by the events presented in "Porphyria's Lover"? Explain.

Comprehension Check
- How do Porphyria and the speaker feel about each other?
- How does the speaker kill Porphyria?

Think Critically

2. Why do you think the **speaker** kills Porphyria?

- what the speaker expects in a love relationship
- his opinion of Porphyria's activities
- what he hopes to achieve by his action

3. Do you think the speaker feels guilty about what he has done?

- the **tone** in which he speaks
- his reason for strangling Porphyria
- his attempt to make her look as she did before the murder (lines 44–49)
- his comment about God's response to the deed (line 60)

4. How would you describe the **mood** of the speaker throughout the poem?

5. ACTIVE READING | MAKING INFERENCES With a small group of classmates, discuss the chart you completed in your READER'S NOTEBOOK as you read the poems. Use the information to make **inferences** about the love relationships in "My Last Duchess" and "Porphyria's Lover." How are the relationships alike? How are they different?

Extend Interpretations

6. **Comparing Texts** Contrast the speakers of "My Last Duchess" and "Porphyria's Lover" with the speaker of Lord Byron's "She Walks in Beauty" (page 773). How do the speakers differ in their attitudes toward women?

7. **Critic's Corner** The 19th-century novelist George Eliot stated that Browning "sets our thoughts at work rather than our emotions." What do you think she meant? Do you agree with her? Cite evidence from these two poems to support your answer.

8. **Connect to Life** In books and movies, jealous lovers are most often presented in a negative light. Do you think jealousy is ever a positive emotion?

Literary Analysis

DRAMATIC MONOLOGUE

A **dramatic monologue** is a lyric poem in which a speaker describes a crucial experience to a silent or absent listener. The effect on the reader is that of hearing just one side of a conversation. Dramatic monologue allows the poet to take the reader inside the speaker's mind by revealing his or her feelings, personality, and motivations. In "Porphyria's Lover," for example, the following lines reveal the speaker's exultation after Porphyria's declaration of love. They also provide a glimpse of the speaker's obsession and, perhaps, prepare the reader for what is to come.

That moment she was
mine, mine, fair,
Perfectly pure and good. . . .

Paired Activity The speaker of a dramatic monologue often reveals to the reader characteristics or feelings of which the speaker is unaware. For each of these poems, make a Venn diagram like the one shown to compare your own opinion of the speaker with his apparent view of himself. Then share and discuss your diagrams with a partner.

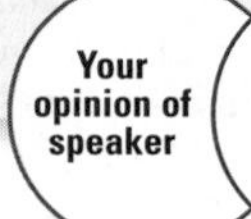

Extend Interpretations

Comparing Texts The speaker of Lord Byron's poem seems to celebrate womanhood. On the other hand, Browning's speakers resent any show by the women of general pleasure or attachment.

Critic's Corner Possible Response: Both of these poems, for example, show the workings of the speakers' *minds* more than anything else.

Connect to Life Accept all reasonable responses.

Literary Analysis

Paired Acitivity Draw a composite Venn diagram on the chalkboard based on student diagrams.

GUIDING STUDENT RESPONSE

Connect to the Literature

1. **What Do You Think?** Guidelines for student response: Few students—in fact few readers—could fail to be somewhat surprised by the ending. The question really raises the issue of whether the murder is believable in light of the details that appear prior to it.

Comprehension Check
- Porphyria feels passion and perhaps even love for the speaker, but not enough to commit herself to him forever. The speaker is obsessed with Porphyria, and she knows this.
- The speaker kills Porphyria by strangling her with her own hair.

Think Critically

2. Possible Response: The speaker kills her so that she can be completely his forever, which he has convinced himself is what she wants as well.
3. The student should take into account the speaker's anxious tone as he reassures the reader (hearer) that she felt no pain, his attempt to justify himself by claiming that in killing her he was granting her wish, his opening of her eyes and propping up of her head, and his comment about God's silence. All indicate that the speaker feels apprehensive and guilty.
4. Students may cite the language the speaker uses to describe the storm, his pretending to be asleep, his reaction when Porphyria tells him she can't be his forever, and/or his claim that he has given her what she wanted, as evidence that his mood is disturbed, desperate, and possibly also triumphant.
5. Possible Responses: The relationships are the same because both speakers were jealous and both caused their beloveds' deaths; the relationships are different because the speaker in "Porphyria's Lover" acted in a moment of passion, while the speaker in "My Last Duchess" possibly acted in cold blood by giving commands to others.

Writing Options

1. **Questions for the Duke** Ask the student to also imagine the speaker's answers to the questions.
2. **Television Mystery** Ask the student to cast his or her television mystery and justify the casting choices.

Activities & Explorations

1. **Murder Trial** Since the speaker is unambiguously guilty of the murder, you might encourage students to have his lawyer use details from the poem to convince the jury of the speaker's insanity. Students should use language skillfully, offering evidence and appeals.
2. **Portrait of a Madman** Encourage students to use color, light, and details to establish the mood and convey the subjects' characteristics.

Inquiry & Research

Roots of Jealousy Have students formulate their own questions to add to those suggested. Students should use writing to organize their ideas and support the conclusions they draw from their research and personal experience. You may also suggest that students view one of the film versions of *Othello,* and have them discuss these questions as they apply to this play.

Author Activity

The Brownings on Film There are two different film versions, one in 1934 that stars Norma Shearer and Fredric March, and one in 1957 that stars Jennifer Jones and John Gielgud. Encourage students to find and analyze reviews of the film and compare them with their own reactions.

Choices & CHALLENGES

Writing Options

1. **Questions for the Duke** Imagine that you are the silent listener in "My Last Duchess" and write a list of questions you would like to ask the speaker.

2. **Television Mystery** Write a synopsis of a television mystery in which the incident described in "Porphyria's Lover" is either the first or the last scene.

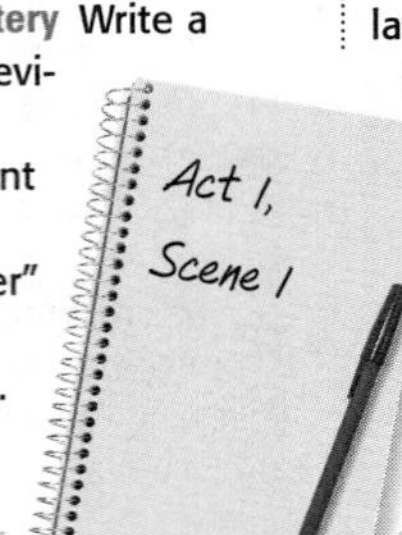

Activities & Explorations

1. **Murder Trial** With a group of classmates, conduct a trial of Porphyria's lover on the charge of murder. Students acting as lawyers should question the defendant, and after deliberating, a jury should deliver their verdict. ~ **SPEAKING AND LISTENING**

2. **Portrait of a Madman** In a pencil or oil portrait, try to convey some of the characteristics of one of the poem's speakers. Your portrait may be realistic or abstract. ~ **ART**

Inquiry & Research

Roots of Jealousy Research theories on jealousy, looking for answers to these questions: What causes some people to be more jealous than others? What is the relationship between jealousy and self-esteem? Can feelings of jealousy be avoided or overcome? Report your findings to the class.

Robert Browning
1812–1889

Other Works
"Count Gismond"
"The Bishop Orders His Tomb at St. Praxed's Church"
"Home Thoughts, from Abroad"
"Prospice"
"The Pied Piper of Hamelin"

Early Criticism Born and raised near London, Robert Browning lived with his parents until he married at the age of 34. Although he attended the University of London for a brief period, his real education took place at home, where he was tutored in literature, history, and music, as well as boxing and horsemanship. At the age of 21 he published his first poem, "Pauline," which was savagely criticized for displaying too much emotion. The criticism embarrassed the young poet, who vowed to keep his writing totally objective, free from personal feelings, in the future. It was at this time that he began to write plays and dramatic monologues. His plays were not well received, and for many years critics claimed that his poetry was too difficult to read.

Happiness and Recognition In 1845, Browning met the poet Elizabeth Barrett, six years his senior, and began a famous romance that has been memorialized in both film and literature. The couple eloped in 1846 and moved to Italy. Although Browning wrote very little during his marriage, he lived happily for the next 15 years. After his wife's death in 1861, he returned to London and concentrated on the writing of *The Ring and the Book,* a series of dramatic monologues based on the records of a 17th-century Roman murder trial. The publication of *The Ring and the Book* made Browning famous and finally obtained for his poetry the recognition it deserved.

LaserLinks: Background for Reading
Film Connection / Art Gallery

Author Activity

The Brownings on Film With a classmate, view one of the films that dramatizes the romance between Browning and Elizabeth Barrett. Then discuss the film by addressing these questions: How does the film portray the two poets? What insight does it provide into their character? their relationship? their writing?

Teaching Options

Grammar

Modifiers: Using Correct Comparative Forms
Instruction Adjectives and adverbs use three forms to show degrees of comparison: the positive *(good),* the comparative *(better),* and the superlative *(best).*
Activity Write the following sentence on the chalkboard. Ask students to select the correct comparative form and explain their choice.

Of the half dozen Robert Browning poems I read, "Porphyria's Lover" was definitely the (more, most) shocking.

Answer: most; superlative is used to compare three or more things.

Exercise Ask students to select the correct word to complete the following sentence and identify the comparative form.

The speaker in Robert Browning's poem "My Last Duchess" believes his first wife's behavior to be (less, least) acceptable than that of his future wife. Answer: less; comparative

Use **Grammar Transparencies and Copymasters,** p. 88.

Use McDougal Littell's ***Language Network*** for more instruction and practice in modifiers.

PREPARING to *Read*

Sonnet 43

Poetry by ELIZABETH BARRETT BROWNING

A Warning Against Passion

Letter by CHARLOTTE BRONTË

"How do I love thee? Let me count the ways."

Connect to Your Life

Reason and Romance The two selections you are about to read express very different attitudes toward romantic relationships. How would you describe your approach to romance? Try judging yourself on the four scales shown. For each pair of opposite qualities, decide at approximately which point of the scale you think your romantic personality falls.

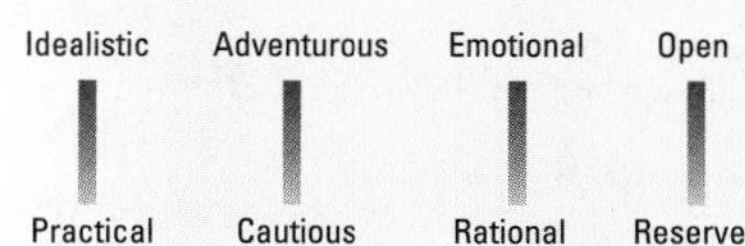

Build Background

Secret Poems Elizabeth Barrett and Robert Browning were one of Victorian England's most famous couples. When they met, Elizabeth, an invalid, was a well-known poet, but Robert—six years her junior—was still struggling to gain recognition. Elizabeth's overprotective father strongly opposed Robert's attentions; the couple, however, married without his knowledge and moved to Italy, where Elizabeth's health improved and her career flourished. During their courtship, Elizabeth had secretly written a group of sonnets, including "Sonnet 43," about her romance with Robert, but she did not show them to him until after they were married. She titled them *Sonnets from the Portuguese* and published them as translations of another poet's work to hide her identity as the author.

Novelist and Letter Writer Charlotte Brontë, the author of the famous romantic novel *Jane Eyre,* reveals some of her attitudes toward love in a personal letter to her close friend Ellen Nussey. Ellen, or Nell, had asked Brontë for advice in handling the attentions of a Mr. Vincent, whom she was thinking of marrying, even though she did not know him well and was not strongly attracted to him. Brontë offers her friend several perspectives on the situation.

WORDS TO KNOW
Vocabulary Preview

deferential
discourse
foible
precept
repugnance

Focus Your Reading

LITERARY ANALYSIS AUTHOR'S PURPOSE

An **author's purpose** may be to entertain, to inform, to express opinions or emotions, or to persuade. The following passage from "A Warning Against Passion" is a direct statement of purpose:

> ***Now, Nell, I am about to write thee a discourse and a piece of advice which thou must take as if it came from thy grandmother. . . .***

As you read these selections, be aware of both explicit statements and more subtle clues that help indicate an author's purpose in writing.

ACTIVE READING COMPARING AUTHOR'S VIEWS

Elizabeth Barrett Browning and Charlotte Brontë had different views of love. To compare two authors' views on the same subject, you need to identify the individual ideas that make up each author's understanding of the subject.

READER'S NOTEBOOK Make a cluster diagram, like the one shown, for each selection. Record the aspects of love that you think would be important elements in each writer's definition of the emotion.

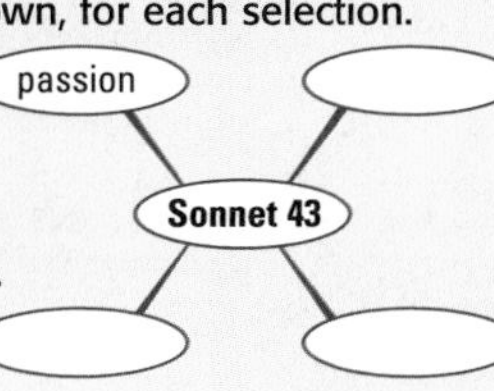

OVERVIEW

Objectives

1. understand a **sonnet** and a **letter** that explore two different attitudes toward romantic relationships
2. identify and examine each **author's purpose (Literary Analysis)**
3. compare **authors' views (Active Reading)**

Summary

"Sonnet 43" lists the different ways the beloved is loved by the speaker. The poem ends on a note of faith: that the love will last—and even deepen—beyond this life and into the next. "A Warning Against Passion" is a letter to Ellen Nussey from Brontë. Brontë gives "Nell" (Ellen's nickname) advice on a suiter named Mr. Vincent. Brontë advises Nell not to wait for "une grande passion" and to accept Mr. Vincent's proposal, taking time to insert a message for Mr. Vincent, encouraging him to be more direct. Her advice to Nell encourages her to be rational and moderate rather than romantic.

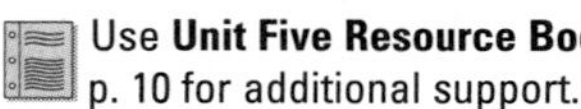
Use **Unit Five Resource Book,** p. 10 for additional support.

Thematic Link

Both works deal with love and personal relationships. "Sonnet 43" expresses the deep, consuming, and abiding love one person can feel for another. "A Warning Against Passion" recommends a cool, cautious, distanced approach to love.

Editor's Note This selection contains material or language that may be considered objectionable.

5-Minute Warm-Up

Daily Language SkillBuilder

Have students **proofread** the display sentences on page 829i and write them correctly. The sentences also appear on Transparency 22 of **Grammar Transparencies and Copymasters.**

Mini Lesson Preteaching Vocabulary

If you would like to preteach the WORDS TO KNOW for this selection, use the Mini Lesson on p. 862.

LESSON RESOURCES

UNIT FIVE RESOURCE BOOK, pp. 10–14

ASSESSMENT RESOURCES

Formal Assessment, pp. 155–156

Teacher's Guide to Assessment and Portfolio Use

Test Generator

SKILLS TRANSPARENCIES AND COPYMASTERS

Literary Analysis
- Form and Meaning in Poetry, T15 (for Literary Analysis, p. 866)

Reading and Critical Thinking
- Comparing Author's Views, T24 (for Active Reading, p. 861)

Grammar
- Subordinating Conjunctions, C74 (for Mini Lesson, pp. 866–867)

Vocabulary
- Word Origins, C68 (for Mini Lesson, p. 862)

Writing
- Subject Analysis, C30 (for Writing Options, p. 867)

Communications
- Impromptu Speaking: Dialogue, Role Play, T14 (for Activities & Explorations, p. 867)

INTEGRATED TECHNOLOGY

Audio Library

Laser Links
- Author Background: Charlotte Brontë. See **Teacher's Sourcebook,** p. 58.

Visit our website:
www.mcdougallittell.com

TEACHING THE LITERATURE

Reading and Analyzing

Literary Analysis
AUTHOR'S PURPOSE

Begin discussion by stating that the author's purpose is the effect the author hopes to have on the reader. Then ask students what reasons people might have for writing letters and poems.
Possible Responses: to inform, to entertain, to express an opinion, or to persuade.

Use **Unit Five Resource Book,** p. 12 for more exercises.

Active Reading
COMPARING AUTHORS' VIEWS

While Brontë states her views about love outright, Barrett Browning's sonnet describes the intensity of the love the speaker feels. Assuming that the speaker is speaking for her, love should be deep, consuming, and abiding.

Use **Unit Five Resource Book,** p. 11 for more practice.

Thinking Through the Literature

1. "How much, and in how many ways, do I love you?"
2. The impression given is of a deep, abiding, and limitless love. (In this connection, it's interesting to note that the entire poem amounts to an assertion by the speaker. The speaker doesn't provide many, if any, details to "support" the assertions.)
3. Possible Responses: Yes, love should be passionate and all-encompassing; possibly, but only if you are loved the same way in return; no, people who claim to love this way have an idealized and unrealistic view of love.
4. At the top.

SONNET 43

Elizabeth Barrett Browning

How do I love thee? Let me count the ways.
I love thee to the depth and breadth and height
My soul can reach, when feeling out of sight
For the ends of Being and ideal Grace.
I love thee to the level of everyday's
Most quiet need, by sun and candlelight.
I love thee freely, as men strive for Right;
I love thee purely, as they turn from Praise.
I love thee with the passion put to use
In my old griefs, and with my childhood's faith.
I love thee with a love I seemed to lose
With my lost saints,—I love thee with the breath,
Smiles, tears, of all my life!—and, if God choose,
I shall but love thee better after death.

Thinking Through the Literature

1. **Comprehension Check** What question does the **speaker** of "Sonnet 43" pose and answer?
2. What is your impression of the romantic relationship described in this sonnet? Share your thoughts with your classmates.
3. Do you think it is desirable to love or be loved in this way? Explain your answer.
4. Look again at the Connect to Your Life on page 861. On each of the scales shown, where would you place the speaker of the sonnet?

Teaching Options

Preteaching Vocabulary

WORD ORIGINS

Instruction Explain to students that English words can change their meaning over time, becoming more specific or more general or even changing parts of speech.

Activity Have students use a dictionary to look up the etymology of each of the following WORDS TO KNOW. Have them write down the original meaning of the word of origin for each and then discuss how the word's meaning has changed.

- **deferential**
  Answer: showing courteous respect–root word *defer*, to submit to another out of respect
- **foible**
  Answer: a relatively minor character flaw–related to feeble, weak
- **repugnance**
  Answer: an extreme dislike or distaste for someone or something–root word *repugn*, to oppose or conflict

Use **Vocabulary Transparencies and Copymasters**, p. 13.

A

Warning Against Passion

Charlotte Brontë

November 20th, 1840.

My dearest Nell,—That last letter of thine treated of matters so high and important I cannot delay answering it for a day—

863

Customizing Instruction

Less Proficient Readers

Ask students to discuss their attitudes toward love and romance. Then have them read the next two selections and compare the writers' approaches to love.

Students Acquiring English

To help students understand "Sonnet 43," point out its listlike structure and have students articulate "the ways" the speaker loves. (See summary above.)

Use **Spanish Study Guide** for additional support, pp. 197–198.

Gifted and Talented

Before students read the sonnet, have them write down their impression of what a "love poem" is. When they are done reading, have them explain the degree to which this poem conforms to their sense of what a "love poem" is—and why.

Possible Response: Most students will probably say that this is exactly the sort of poem they imagine when they think of a "love poem." They may cite the use of the archaic pronoun, the effusive emotion, or the "list" structure. Students who have a different conception of love poetry may cite the abstract and religious nature of the poem.

BLOCK SCHEDULING: MANAGING TIME

If your schedule requires that you cover the lesson objectives in a shorter time, use . . .
- Preparing to Read, p. 861
- Thinking Through the Literature, p. 866
- Vocabulary in Action, p. 867

If you want to take advantage of longer class time, use . . .
- TE Teaching Options: Preteaching Vocabulary, p. 862; Viewing and Representing, p. 865; Informal Assessment, p. 864; Grammar, p. 867
- Choices & Challenges, p. 867

Reading and Analyzing

Literary Analysis: TONE

Point out that there is a mixture of tones in the letter. In some passages, the tone is serious, because the subject—love and marriage—is serious. However, Brontë adds humorous touches by using terms such as *creature* and *worse half* to refer to the prospective husband. Ask students to find other examples of Brontë's humor on this page.

Possible Responses: the imaginary scene with Mr. Vincent; words such as *ninny* and *noodle*.

Reading Skills and Strategies: MAKING JUDGMENTS

A Ask students whether they agree with Brontë's statement that a grand passion is a grand folly.

Possible Responses: Agree—when people let themselves get swept away by love, they often make foolish choices that they later regret; disagree—when a person loves another passionately, the couple can overcome almost any obstacle.

Reading Skills and Strategies: ANALYZING

B Ask students why Brontë, who was actually in her twenties, makes the parenthetical reference to being 60 and a grandmother.

Possible Responses: Brontë wants Nell to take the advice as seriously as if it had come from someone older; she is injecting a little humor into the letter so Nell won't be offended by the advice.

Now, Nell, I am about to write thee a discourse and a piece of advice which thou must take as if it came from thy grandmother—but in the first place—before I begin with thee, I have a word to whisper in the ear of Mr. Vincent and I wish it could reach him.

In the name of St. Chrysostom, St. Simon and St. Jude,[1] why does not that amiable young gentleman come forward like a man and say all that he has to say to yourself personally—instead of trifling with kinsmen and kinswomen? "Mr. Vincent," I say—"walk or ride over to Brookroyd . . . and say, 'Miss Ellen, I want to speak to you.' Miss Ellen will of course civilly answer, 'I'm at your service, Mr. Vincent' and then when the room is cleared of all but *yourself* and *herself* just take a chair near her, insist upon her laying down that silly . . . basketwork, and listening to *you*. Then begin in a clear, distinct, deferential, but determined voice—'Miss Ellen, I have a question to put to you, a very important question—will you take me as your husband, for better for worse? I am not a rich man, but I have sufficient to support us—I am not a great man, but I love you honestly and truly—Miss Ellen, if you knew the world better you would see that this is an offer not to be despised—a kind attached heart, and a moderate competency.'[2] Do this, Mr. Vincent, and you may succeed—go on writing sentimental and love-sick letters to Henry[3] and I would not give sixpence for your suit."[4]

So much for Mr. Vincent—now, Nell, your turn comes to swallow the black bolus[5]—called a friend's advice. . . . Is the man a fool? is he a knave,[6] a humbug, a hypocrite, a ninny, a noodle? If he is any or all of these things, of course there is no sense in trifling with him—cut him short at once—Blast his hopes with lightning rapidity and keenness.

Is he something better than this? has he at least common sense—a good disposition, a manageable temper? Then, Nell, consider the matter. You feel a disgust towards him *now*, an utter repugnance—very likely—but be so good as to remember you don't know him—you have only had three or four days' acquaintance with him—longer and closer intimacy might reconcile you to a wonderful extent. And now I'll tell you a word of truth at which you may be offended or not as you like—From what I know of your character—and I think I know it pretty well—I should say you will never *love before* marriage—After that ceremony is over, and after you have had some months to settle down, and to get accustomed to the creature you have taken for your worse half—you will probably make a most affectionate and happy wife—even if the individual should not prove all you could wish—you will be indulgent towards his little follies and foibles—and will not feel much annoyance at them. This will especially be the case if he should have sense sufficient to allow you to guide him in important matters. Such being the case, Nell, I hope you will not have the romantic folly to wait for the awakening of what the French call "Une grande *passion*"—My good girl, "une grande passion" is "*une* grande *folie*."[7] . . . **A**

> I hope you will not have the romantic folly to wait for the awakening of what the French call "Une grande *passion*" —My good girl, "une grande passion" is "*une* grande *folie*."

1. **St. Chrysostom** (krĭs'əs-təm), **St. Simon, and St. Jude:** saints known for their honesty, sincerity, and courage.
2. **competency:** income or means sufficient to meet one's needs.
3. **Henry:** Ellen Nussey's brother.
4. **suit:** courtship.
5. **black bolus:** a round, bitter medicinal preparation, larger than an ordinary pill.
6. **knave:** an unprincipled, crafty fellow.
7. **"Une grande *passion*"** (ün gränd' pä-syôN') . . . **"*une* grande *folie*"** (ün gränd' fô-lē') *French:* a great passion . . . a great foolishness.

WORDS TO KNOW

discourse (dĭs'kôrs') *n.* a discussion of a subject in speech or writing
deferential (dĕf'ə-rĕn'shəl) *adj.* showing courteous respect
repugnance (rĭ-pŭg'nəns) *n.* an extreme dislike or distaste
foible (foi'bəl) *n.* a minor weakness or character flaw

864

Teaching Options

Assessment **Informal Assessment**

COMPARING ATTITUDES Have students break into small groups and brainstorm words and phrases that capture the tone of each writer's view of love. Then ask them to collaborate on graphics (a chart, a Venn diagram, etc.) that compare the two writers' attitudes about love.

RUBRIC

3 Full Accomplishment Students' graphics appropriate for assignment and reflect excellent grasp of writers' attitudes toward love.

2 Substantial Accomplishment Students have good understanding of writers' attitudes toward love but omit some important ideas.

1 Little or Partial Accomplishment Students' work is sloppy and reflects little or no understanding of writers' attitudes toward love.

Mediocrity[8] in all things is wisdom—mediocrity in the sensations is superlative wisdom. When you are as old as I am, Nell— (I am sixty at least being your grandmother) you will find that the majority of those worldly precepts—whose seeming coldness shocks and repels us in youth—are founded in wisdom. Did you not once say to me in all childlike simplicity, "I thought, Charlotte—no young ladies should fall in love, till the offer was actually made." . . . The maxim is just . . . I will even extend and confirm it—no young lady should fall in love till the offer has been made, accepted—the marriage ceremony performed and the first half year of wedded life has passed away—a woman may then begin to love, but with great precaution—very coolly—very moderately—very rationally—if she ever loves so much that a harsh word or a cold look from her husband cuts her to the heart—she is a fool—if she ever loves so much that her husband's will is her law—and that she has got into a habit of watching his looks in order that she may anticipate his wishes she will soon be a neglected fool.

Couple in a Garden (about 1840), H. Robinson. Engraving after a Daniel Maclise illustration for a Thomas Moore poem, Mary Evans Picture Library, London.

Did I not once tell you of an instance of a relative of mine who cared for a young lady till he began to suspect that she cared more for him and then instantly conceived a sort of contempt for her?[9] . . .

I have two studies—*you* are my study for the success, the credit, and the respectability of a quiet, tranquil character. Mary is my study—for the contempt, the remorse—the misconstruction which follow the development of feelings in themselves noble, warm—generous—devoted and profound—but which being too freely revealed—too frankly bestowed—are not estimated at their real value. . . . I never hope to see in this world a character more truly noble—she would *die* willingly for one she loved—her intellect and her attainments are of the very highest standard, yet I doubt whether Mary will ever marry. . . . ❖

8. **mediocrity** (mē′dē-ŏk′rĭ-tē): a state of being midway between two extremes. (The word is used here without any negative connotation.)

9. **relative of mine . . . contempt for her:** a reference to a failed romance between another friend, Mary Taylor, and Brontë's brother, Branwell.

WORDS TO KNOW **precept** (prē′sĕpt′) *n.* a rule or principle of conduct

Customizing Instruction

Students Acquiring English

Point out to students that Brontë often uses dashes in a very idiosyncratic fashion. Most often, dashes are used after, or in place of, other punctuation such as commas or colons. Ask students to find dashes that are used in an unconventional way, and, if possible, to replace them with standard punctuation.

Possible Response: The first line has an extraneous dash following the personal address and a dash serving as end punctuation in place of a period.

Less Proficient Readers

Help students gain a foothold on the material by asking them the following questions:

- Why is Brontë annoyed with Mr. Vincent?
  Possible Response: He has not spoken directly to Nell but sends letters to her family members.
- What does Brontë say can happen if a woman loves too much?
  Possible Response: The man can begin to neglect her and think her foolish.
- According to Brontë, when should a young woman allow herself to fall in love?
  Possible Response: after being married for six months.

Mini Lesson Viewing and Representing

Couple in a Garden (about 1840), **H. Robinson**

ART APPRECIATION

Instruction This engraving by H. Robinson is based on an illustration by Daniel Maclise for a Thomas Moore poem. Although he is chiefly known for his portraits of famous people of his time and for his two frescoes in the House of Lords, Maclise also illustrated books, including Shakespeare's plays *Hamlet, Richard II, A Midsummer Night's Dream,* and *The Tempest.*

Application Ask students to describe the facial expressions, positioning, and body language of the figures in the engraving. Ask students what they think the figures' relationship is and how they feel about one another.

Possible Response: They are a young, single woman and her suitor. He is interested, but she seems wary and uncomfortable.

Ask students how this engraving relates to Brontë's letter.

Possible Responses: The young woman's trepidation is reminiscent of Nell's feelings toward Mr. Vincent; her caution echoes Brontë's advice about romance.

GUIDING STUDENT RESPONSE

Connect to the Literature

1. What Do You Think?
Guidelines for student response: Accept all reasonable responses that are based on evidence in the text.

Comprehension Check
- He hasn't proposed, and he hasn't spoken directly to Nell but has made his feelings known through letters to others.
- six months after she marries

 Use Selection Quiz in **Unit Five Resource Book,** p. 13..

Think Critically

2. Possible Response: A woman should be rational, level-headed, and cool during courtship and marriage. Students should include main ideas and supporting details as necessary.
3. Possible Responses: She implies that women can remain rational in the pursuit of love but are often their own enemies, showing that they care too much; she implies that men are cowardly and fickle.
4. Possible Responses: Brontë might say that Barrett Browning is too passionate and vocal about her feelings; Barrett Browning might consider Brontë too cold and circumspect.

Extend Interpretations

Comparing Texts Accept all reasonable responses as long as students explain their choices. For example, students who believe that two people in love should accept each other's imperfections are likely to favor Shakespeare's "Sonnet 116."

Different Perspectives Accept all responses that indicate that Barrett Browning would probably encourage Nussey to express her true feelings.

Connect to Life Accept all reasonable, well-supported answers.

Literary Analysis

Paired Activity You might write shared purposes found by students on the chalkboard.

Connect to the Literature

1. **What Do You Think?** What is your opinion of Brontë's advice in "A Warning Against Passion"?

Comprehension Check
- Why is Brontë annoyed with Mr. Vincent?
- According to Brontë, when should a young woman allow herself to fall in love?

Think Critically

2. How would you **summarize** the main points of Brontë's advice about love and marriage?

- her proposed advice to Mr. Vincent
- her view of falling in love
- her view of possible relationships between husbands and wives

3. How would you describe Brontë's views of men and women?

4. **ACTIVE READING** COMPARING AUTHOR'S VIEWS What do you think Brontë and Barrett Browning would say about each other's attitude toward romantic relationships? Look back at the cluster diagrams you created in your READER'S NOTEBOOK to help you identify each writer's attitude.

Extend Interpretations

5. **Comparing Texts** Reread Spenser's "Sonnet 30" (page 297) and Shakespeare's "Sonnet 116" (page 302). Compare these two sonnets with Barrett Browning's "Sonnet 43." Which of the three poems expresses the emotion of love most convincingly for you? Support your opinion.

6. **Different Perspectives** Suppose that Elizabeth Barrett Browning wrote a reply to Ellen Nussey. What advice do you think Barrett Browning would offer Nell?

7. **Connect to Life** Issues relating to love and marriage continue to be of great concern to people. Do you think Brontë's advice has relevance today?

Literary Analysis

AUTHOR'S PURPOSE Although a writer can fulfill a number of **purposes** in a work—to entertain, to inform, to express opinions or emotions, or to persuade—one purpose is usually the most important. In "Sonnet 43," the reader can assume that Barrett Browning's main purpose was to express love. In "A Warning Against Passion," Brontë's main purpose appears to have been to persuade her friend to approach marriage cautiously.

Paired Activity "Sonnet 43" and "A Warning Against Passion" have seemingly different main purposes. However, do they share any purposes? Jot down your ideas. Then discuss and compare your findings with your partner's conclusions.

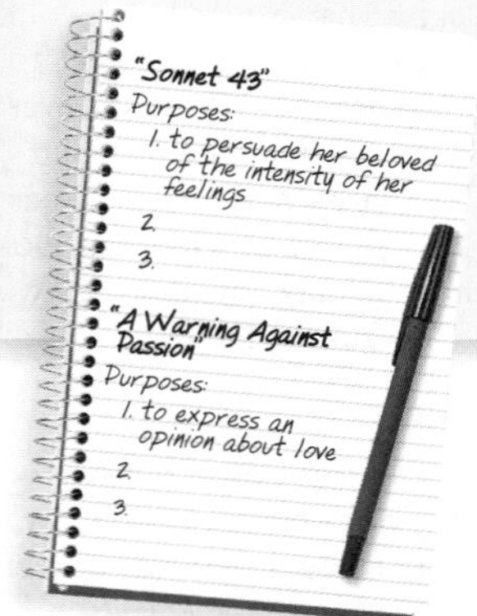

"Sonnet 43"
Purposes:
1. to persuade her beloved of the intensity of her feelings
2.
3.
"A Warning Against Passion"
Purposes:
1. to express an opinion about love
2.
3.

Mini Lesson

Grammar

SUBORDINATING CONJUNCTIONS

Instruction Subordinating conjunctions introduce subordinate clauses—clauses that cannot stand alone as complete sentences. Depending on the conjunction used, the subordinate clause may express condition, manner, place, purpose, reason, or time.

Activity Write the following subordinating conjunctions and the sentence on the chalkboard.

In "A Warning Against Passion," Charlotte Brontë suggests that a woman often is more appealing to a suitor when she pretends to be aloof.

Have students identify the subordinating conjunction in the sentence and tell what idea it expresses.

Answer: when, expresses time

condition: although, as long as, even if, even though, if, provided that, though, unless
manner: as, as if
place: where, wherever
purpose: in order that, so that, that
reason: because, since
time: after, as, as long as, as soon as, before, since, until, when, whenever, while

Writing Options

A Letter in Response Write a letter in which Ellen Nussey responds to Brontë's advice. Tell Charlotte Brontë which ideas of hers you agree with and which you disagree with. Tell her what moral lessons you think you can draw from your experience with Mr. Vincent. Place the letter in your **Working Portfolio.**

Activities & Explorations

Imaginary Conversation With a partner, stage an imaginary conversation between Ellen Nussey and Mr. Vincent after Nussey has read the letter from Brontë. ~ **PERFORMING**

Vocabulary in Action

EXERCISE: MEANING CLUES On your paper, choose the word that is most closely related to each of the following sets.

1. lecture, speech, persuasive essay
2. bowing to a queen, giving someone else first choice of a seat
3. walking out of a movie, boycotting a product
4. "Waste not, want not," "Act in haste, repent at leisure."
5. being late all the time, forgetting to return borrowed items

WORDS TO KNOW		
	deferential	precept
	discourse	repugnance
	foible	

Elizabeth Barrett Browning

1806–1861

Other Works
"Sonnet 22"
The Cry of the Children

Life in Her Parents' House Elizabeth Barrett was the oldest of 11 children in a prosperous family. A precocious child, she read constantly and had her first poem published by the time she was 14. She became ill when she was about 15, and from that time until she eloped with Robert Browning in 1846, she lived the life of an invalid.

Married Life During the 15 years of her marriage, Barrett Browning was intensely happy. She gave birth to a son, wrote a wide variety of poems, and ardently supported such causes as the abolition of slavery, the reform of child labor practices, and women's rights. The Brownings' home in Florence, Italy, became a gathering place for people prominent in politics and the arts. Barrett Browning's most ambitious poem, the verse novel *Aurora Leigh,* was the first work by an Englishwoman in which the main character is herself a writer.

Charlotte Brontë

1816–1855

Other Works
Shirley
Villette

A Writing Family One of six children, Charlotte Brontë grew up in the remote Yorkshire village of Haworth. After the death of her mother and her two oldest sisters, she and her sisters Emily and Anne and her brother, Branwell, became inseparable companions. They wrote constantly through childhood into adulthood, and in 1846 they tried to publish some of their work. Their first efforts received little attention, but when Charlotte's novel *Jane Eyre* appeared in 1847, it was an immediate success.

Decline and Fall Sadly, Charlotte's triumph was soon eclipsed by tragedy. During the next two years, Branwell, Emily, and Anne died, leaving Charlotte heartbroken and lonely. In 1854 she married her father's assistant, but within a year she was dead as a result of pregnancy complications.

LaserLinks: Background for Reading
Author Background

Writing Options

A Letter in Response Have students reread the letter for clues to Nussey's personality. Then discuss the pressure to marry on young women in Victorian times, especially the fate of unmarried older women. Ask students to try to put themselves in Nussey's place.

Activities & Explorations

Imaginary Conversation Before students plan the conversation, have them discuss what kind of man Mr. Vincent likely was. For example, he was apparently in love with Ellen Nussey, yet could not tell her so; he confided in her brother instead. What might that suggest about his personality?

Vocabulary in Action

1. discourse
2. deference
3. repugnance
4. precept
5. foible

Exercise Ask students to complete each sentence by using an appropriate subordinating conjunction and tell what idea the conjunction expresses.

1. ______ Elizabeth Barrett Browning left England for sun-drenched Italy, her health began to improve.
   Possible Responses: As soon as, When, Because; time
2. In the second paragraph of "A Warning Against Passion," Charlotte Brontë invokes the names of three saints ______ she may convince Nell of the serious tone of the letter.
   Possible Responses: so that, in order that; purpose
3. The speaker in Elizabeth Barrett Browning's Sonnet 43 pledges her everlasting fidelity to her lover, ______ she may be—on earth or in heaven.
   Possible Response: wherever; place

Use **Grammar Transparencies and Copymasters,** p. 14.

Use McDougal Littell's ***Language Network*** for more instruction and practice in subordinating conjunctions.

OVERVIEW

Objectives

- understand the following literary terms:
  - novel
  - realism
  - naturalism
- appreciate shared characteristics of literature across cultures
- recognize themes across cultures

Teaching the Lesson

Students will be reading fiction written a century ago. This lesson will give them some background on the development of fiction as a literary form.

Introducing the Concepts

Explain that Victorian fiction ushered in the focus on realistic depictions of life that continues in many art forms today. For example, modern novels, short stories, and even television dramas all attempt to show life as it really is. As students read the selections of fiction in this unit, have them consider the following questions:

Do these stories have another purpose besides depicting the realities of life? If so, what is that purpose?
Possible Response: The stories are meant to affect lives by interesting readers in social reforms and moral living.

How has "real life" as described in these stories changed? In what ways has it stayed the same?
Possible Response: Students may feel that modern life has a complexity of relationships not dreamed of by people in the 19th century, though the basic interconnectedness of life remains a constant.

What values are reflected in the stories? Are these values still held today?
Possible Responses: duty, social and civic responsibility, moral respectability, and maintaining a good reputation; the values remain desirable.

Do the popular genres of Victorian novels—historical, gothic, detective, and Newgate—still exist today? What are some modern genres of the novel?
Possible Response: These genres still exist, though the Newgate is not identified as such today; modern genres include romance, science fiction, techno-thriller, and psychological novels.

As they finish reading the selections of fiction, students can write reactions to these questions and keep their responses in their Working Portfolios.

Presenting the Concepts

Read through the strategies aloud or project them on a transparency. Ask students to name contemporary novels that belong to genres similar to those described on pages 868–869. As students read, model how to use the strategies to analyze the short stories.

The Growth and Development of Fiction

The Novel's Beginning

Although the Internet has been in use for several years, its popularity began to soar in the 1990s. As the general public became more familiar with the Internet, people began to regard it as an "information highway," a new medium of communication that could benefit society. Over a century ago in Victorian England, another medium of communication generated a similar response. English writers began to see this new medium not only as a form of artistic expression, but also as an exciting way to affect the lives of people from all walks of life. It was called the **novel.**

Charles Dickens (1812–1870) used the novel to promote social reform.

The novel as we think of it came into being after Daniel Defoe published *Robinson Crusoe* in 1719. During this time, the novel was viewed primarily as a form of entertainment. In the mid-18th century, a few steps forward in the development of plot and characterization were taken in the novels *Pamela* (1740) and *Clarissa* (1747–1748) by Samuel Richardson and *Tom Jones* (1749) by Henry Fielding. *The Life and Opinions of Tristram Shandy, Gentleman* (1760–1767), a highly original work by Laurence Sterne, focused on characters' conversations and remembrances instead of on action. These writers inspired other writers to take the novel form in new directions.

The Novel Comes of Age

The Victorian period (1832–1901) is often called "the Age of the Novel." Victorian novels are known for their **realism**—the detailed presentation of everyday life. Through the novel, the Victorians wanted to document the lives and the *values* of the English, including the lower classes. As the Victorian era continued, social concerns began playing a greater role in the general society. The novel became a tool for exposing society's ills. No other writer used this tool as effectively as did Charles Dickens. His novels *Oliver Twist* (1838), *A Christmas Carol* (1843), *David Copperfield* (1850), and *Bleak House* (1853), described in riveting detail the troubling state of England's lower classes. (See Milestones in British Literature, pp. 870–871.)

New Forms Emerge

In the 19th century, a remarkable variety of English novels were written, giving rise to new subgenres. Here are several of the most popular forms:

Historical Novels This type of fiction combines historical facts with imagination to recreate the spirit of a past age. Charles Dickens based *A Tale of Two Cities* (1859) on historical accounts of the French Revolution.

Gothic Novel Horror tales became extremely popular in England near the turn of the 19th century. *Frankenstein* (1818) by Mary Shelley is the best known example of gothic fiction.

Detective Novel Mystery is a major ingredient of detective fiction. Sir Arthur Conan Doyle mastered this form in the late 1800s and created Sherlock Holmes, still the world's most famous detective.

Newgate Novel Stories focusing on criminals and their motives found a growing audience. Newgate fiction—which drew its name from a famous London prison—explored the nature of crime and violence. One example of a Newgate novel is Charles Dickens's *Barnaby Rudge* (1841), which looks at the effects of civil unrest and riot on the lives of a host of characters.

YOUR TURN For any of the popular forms described, offer an example of a similar modern-day version.

The Shift to Naturalism

After about 1880, realism began to be replaced by **naturalism**, a movement arising in France that promoted a grimmer, more "scientific" approach to fiction. Naturalistic writing was an attempt to depict the human condition as objectively as scientific writings depicted the processes of nature. In *Tess of the D'Urbervilles* (1891), an example of the naturalistic novel, Thomas Hardy portrayed a hostile world in which only the "fittest" prospered. This movement would extend into the early 20th century.

Women Novelists

Jane Austen
1775–1817
- *Sense and Sensibility*
- *Pride and Prejudice*
- *Emma*

Elizabeth Gaskell
1810–1865
- *Mary Barton*
- *Cranford*
- *North and South*

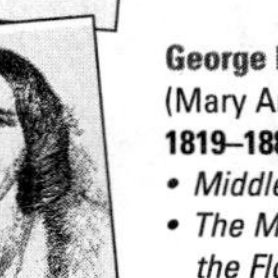

George Eliot
(Mary Ann Evans)
1819–1880
- *Middlemarch*
- *The Mill on the Floss*
- *Silas Marner*

Emily Brontë
(Ellis Bell)
1818–1848
- *Wuthering Heights*

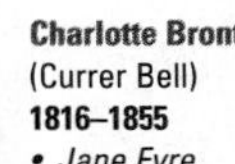

Charlotte Brontë
(Currer Bell)
1816–1855
- *Jane Eyre*
- *The Professor*
- *Shirley*

As the reading public became increasingly female and middle class, female writers emerged. Romantic writer Jane Austen led the way with "novels of manners," works known for their focus on courtship, parental authority, and other "domestic" issues.

Victorian women writers were determined to overcome the commonly accepted view that writing was strictly a man's profession. The topics of many of their works often extended far beyond the home. For example, Elizabeth Cleghorn Gaskell, in both novels and short stories, detailed the plight of the industrial lower class.

Strategies for Reading: Victorian Fiction

1. Connect to the times. Many Victorian writers were middle class, and they wrote fiction for a middle-class audience. Notice what middle-class values the writer seems to uphold.
2. Look for evidence of the writer's social concerns. This might either be expressed directly or be woven into the conflict or characterization.
3. Get a sense of how each of the major characters relates to the plot. Pay particular attention to how characters with different backgrounds and values come into conflict.
4. Judge the work as a whole. What important theme has the Victorian writer conveyed?
5. Try to predict the end of the story as you read along.
6. As you read, list the distinctive qualities that you think characterize the writer's style.
7. **Monitor** your reading strategies and modify them when your understanding breaks down. Remember to use your Strategies for Active Reading: **predict, visualize, connect, question, clarify,** and **evaluate.**

Making Connections

The Novel Across Cultures

Explain that the spread of the novel, with its attention to the details of daily life, helped many people to know what life was like in other countries. As the literary form of the novel has spread to Latin America, India, and Africa, it has continued to encourage understanding among people of different cultures. Share the following information about the development of the novel.

Ireland

Castle Rackrent, published in 1800 by Maria Edgeworth (1767–1849), has been awarded a number of "firsts": first Irish novel, regional novel, socio-historical novel, and saga novel. It tells the story of four generations of an unscrupulous Anglo-Irish landlord family and is said to have inspired Sir Walter Scott's *Waverley* (1814). Another woman, Lady Sydney Morgan (1776–1859), was the next Irish novelist to win fame. The English prejudice against Irish culture strongly affected Irish writers and caused many to deemphasize the setting of their novels. The brothers John and Michael Banim (1798–1842; 1796–1874), however, collaborated on novels that celebrated Irish peasant life.

France

Two popular novel genres in 18th-century France were the fictional autobiography and the epistolary novel (a novel told through the means of letters exchanged between characters). Because fiction was often looked down upon at this time, some writers wanted their books to resemble nonfiction. Influential French novels of the time include the four-volume *Gil Blas de Santillane* (1715–35) by Alain-René Lesage (1668–1747) and *La Nouvelle Héloïse* (1761) by Jean-Jacques Rousseau (1712–1778). These novels set the stage for the great French novelists of the 19th century, such as Honoré de Balzac and Gustave Flaubert.

Russia

During the 18th century, Peter the Great and Catherine the Great encouraged and, in some cases, forced Russians to imitate the societies of Western Europe. Novels were first printed in Russia in 1750, but all were merely translations of foreign writers. The first original Russian novel was printed in 1763, and such works were heavily influenced by French and English writers. Authors such as Mikhail Chulkov (c. 1743–1792), however, made the novel their own by satirizing its conventions. Although none of the early Russian novelists became important or even well-known, the form they developed was adopted by later masters such as Nikolai Gogol, Feodor Dostoyevsky, and Leo Tolstoy.

THE GROWTH AND DEVELOPMENT OF FICTION 869

Few British novelists have equaled Dickens in his ability to evoke both popular and critical acclaim. A number of his characters—such as Mr. Micawber, Uriah Heep, and Ebenezer Scrooge—have become familiar archetypes; his comic zest and verbal inventiveness have lost little of their entertainment value; and his outrage at social injustice remains inspiring.

Additional Background

CHARLES DICKENS

Born in 1812, the second of eight children, Dickens spent happy childhood years in Chatham, a port east of London, where his father was a naval clerk. His adolescence, however, was scarred by the family's move to London. His father was soon arrested and jailed for debt, and a step-cousin found 12-year-old Charles a job—long days of labeling bottles in a boot-polish factory. A small legacy enabled the family to pay its debts several months later, and Dickens received two years of secondary education. At 15, he was an office boy for a lawyer; at 17, a court stenographer; and soon afterward, an expert parliamentary reporter.

By the age of 21, Dickens had turned his talents to writing, and in periodicals his comic pieces began appearing under the pen name Boz, a brother's nickname. In 1836, his fictional chronicles of the Pickwick Club began to appear in serial form, and in 1837 they were published in book form. In 1838 *Oliver Twist* appeared, and Dickens became a recognized writer around the world. He toured the United States in 1842, speaking out against slavery and in favor of international copyright laws. (His books were being widely pirated.)

Thriving under the pressure of monthly or even weekly deadlines, he continued to publish his novels first as serials. While writing novels, he also edited his own magazine, *Household Words,* throughout the 1850s, and founded a second magazine, *All the Year Round,* in 1859. He thrived on highly paid public readings from his works, but the long hours and constant train travel finally took their toll. By 1865, his health began to deteriorate, and he became lame. After an exhaustive public-reading tour in the United States in 1868, he was a physical wreck. He died in 1870, leaving a novel unfinished, and was buried in Westminster Abbey.

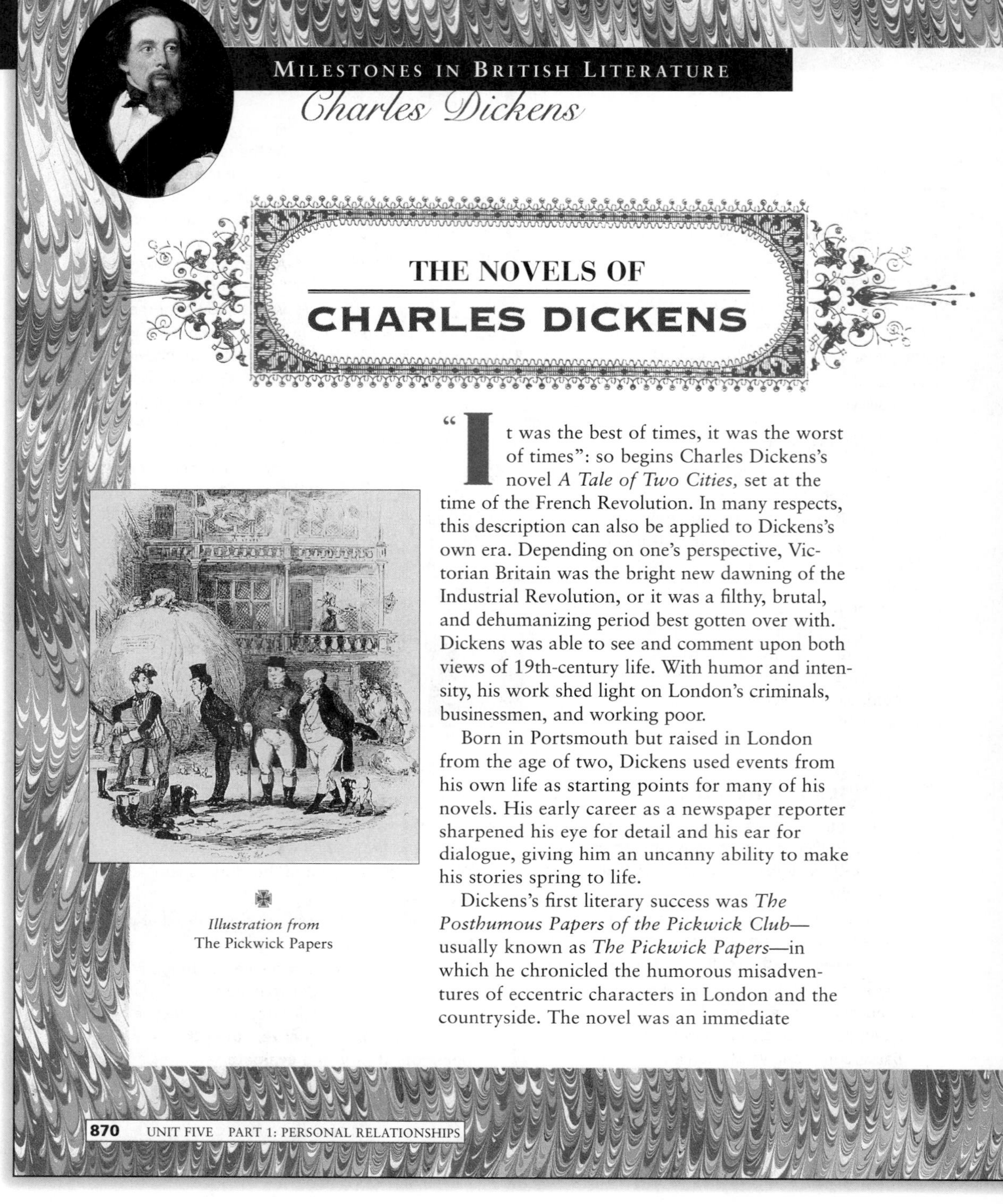

MILESTONES IN BRITISH LITERATURE

Charles Dickens

THE NOVELS OF CHARLES DICKENS

"It was the best of times, it was the worst of times": so begins Charles Dickens's novel *A Tale of Two Cities,* set at the time of the French Revolution. In many respects, this description can also be applied to Dickens's own era. Depending on one's perspective, Victorian Britain was the bright new dawning of the Industrial Revolution, or it was a filthy, brutal, and dehumanizing period best gotten over with. Dickens was able to see and comment upon both views of 19th-century life. With humor and intensity, his work shed light on London's criminals, businessmen, and working poor.

Born in Portsmouth but raised in London from the age of two, Dickens used events from his own life as starting points for many of his novels. His early career as a newspaper reporter sharpened his eye for detail and his ear for dialogue, giving him an uncanny ability to make his stories spring to life.

Dickens's first literary success was *The Posthumous Papers of the Pickwick Club*—usually known as *The Pickwick Papers*—in which he chronicled the humorous misadventures of eccentric characters in London and the countryside. The novel was an immediate

Illustration from The Pickwick Papers

870 UNIT FIVE PART 1: PERSONAL RELATIONSHIPS

W. C. Fields and Freddie Bartholomew in the 1935 film version of David Copperfield

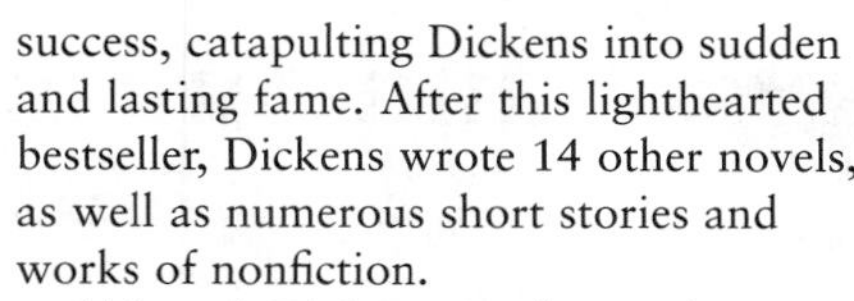

success, catapulting Dickens into sudden and lasting fame. After this lighthearted bestseller, Dickens wrote 14 other novels, as well as numerous short stories and works of nonfiction.

Although Dickens's early novels, including *Oliver Twist* and *Nicholas Nickleby,* address such serious topics as crime, greed, and the mistreatment of children, they are also filled with lighter, humorous moments. His later novels, such as *Bleak House* and *A Tale of Two Cities,* present a grimmer, harsher world, and are etched with irony and satire. In the midst of this later phase of his literary output, however, Dickens also created two celebrated tales of youth and discovery—*David Copperfield,* a largely autobiographical work, and *Great Expectations,* considered by many to be his finest work.

Although Dickens died at the age of 58, his popularity did not. To this day, his works are enjoyed both in their original form and in adaptations as films and plays. An eight-hour stage production of *Nicholas Nickleby* recently enjoyed widespread popularity, and *A Christmas Carol* has become a delightful part of the Christmas tradition in countries around the world. Dickens's novels are an indispensable part of our literary landscape—and our modern social conscience as well.

Upper left:
Dickens's study
Lower left:
Earliest known photograph of Dickens, 1852. Photofest.

LITERARY CHRONOLOGY

The following are book publication dates of Dickens's major works of fiction. In most cases, the book publication immediately followed a serial publication.

1836 *Sketches by Boz*

1837 *The Pickwick Papers*

1838 *Oliver Twist*

1839 *Nicholas Nickleby*

1841 *The Old Curiosity Shop, Barnaby Rudge*

1843 *A Christmas Carol*

1844 *Martin Chuzzlewit*

1846 *The Cricket on the Hearth*

1848 *Dombey and Son*

1850 *David Copperfield*

1853 *Bleak House*

1854 *Hard Times*

1857 *Little Dorrit*

1859 *A Tale of Two Cities*

1861 *Great Expectations*

1865 *Our Mutual Friend*

1870 *The Mystery of Edwin Drood* (unfinished)

OVERVIEW

Objectives

1. understand and appreciate a Victorian **short story (Literary Analysis)**
2. recognize and understand the **third-person omniscient point of view (Literary Analysis)**
3. analyze **causes and effects (Active Reading)**

Summary

In a town somewhere in England ("no matter where"), two local newspapers represent the liberal and conservative opinions of the time. The compositors they employ, Mr. Hodgson and Mr. Jenkins, live in the same building and tend to judge each other severely. On the day before Christmas, Mrs. Jenkins's cat eats Mr. Hodgson's dinner, and the two wives quarrel bitterly. Later that day, however, the Hodgsons' baby suffers an attack of croup. Mrs. Hodgson runs upstairs to ask Mrs. Jenkins for hot water, and after initially refusing, Mrs. Jenkins runs downstairs to help. With a warm bath and a mustard plaster, she saves the baby's life. The next morning, Mrs. Jenkins's cat ruins her Christmas dinner. Mrs. Hodgson takes Mrs. Jenkins some homemade sausages, and the two families have Christmas dinner together. The women become friends, and the men discover mutual interests.

Use **Unit Five Resource Book,** p. 15 for additional support.

Thematic Link

This story shows how our common humanity can forge **personal relationships** even between people who are very different.

5-Minute Warm-Up

Daily Language SkillBuilder

Have students **proofread** the display sentences on page 829i and write them correctly. The sentences also appear on Transparency 23 of **Grammar Transparencies and Copymasters.**

Preteaching Vocabulary

If you would like to preteach the WORDS TO KNOW for this selection, use the Mini Lesson p. 874.

PREPARING to *Read*

Christmas Storms and Sunshine

Short Story by ELIZABETH CLEGHORN GASKELL

"It was a good while since Mrs. Jenkins and Mrs. Hodgson had spoken to each other."

Connect to Your Life

Cold Shoulder Treatment Have you ever given someone you didn't know very well the "cold shoulder"? Think about what might have prompted you to act this way. Were your actions based on sound reasoning? Were they based on a mere first impression of the person or on what someone else had said? Get together with a few other students and share your experiences.

Build Background

Rising Middle Class The early Victorian era was a time of political reform, as the old aristocracy reluctantly gave way to a more democratic system. The First Reform Bill, passed in 1832, gave voting rights to the middle class and, as a result, made the upper class less powerful. The Tories, a political party that had controlled the government for almost 50 years, represented the interests of wealthy landowners and opposed the democratic reforms. The Tories were conservative, and they scorned their opponents, the "Radical" Whigs, for supporting reforms that gradually allowed the middle class to become a major force in England's economy.

Many Victorian writers focused on topics that appealed to the growing number of readers in the newly powerful middle class, writing about the social and personal relationships of ordinary people. The popular Victorian novelist Elizabeth Cleghorn Gaskell wrote about the manners and morals of upper- and middle-class Victorian society as well as the living and working conditions of the lower class. The story you are about to read involves the relationship between two families who rent rooms in the same house.

WORDS TO KNOW
Vocabulary Preview
affronted, allude, mortal, pompous, propensity

LaserLinks: Background for Reading
Historical Connection

Focus Your Reading

LITERARY ANALYSIS THIRD-PERSON OMNISCIENT POINT OF VIEW

Many stories are told from the **third-person point of view**—that is, by a narrator who is outside the action of the story. Occasionally, a story is told from an omniscient, or all-knowing, third-person point of view. In stories told from the **omniscient point of view,** the narrator sees into the minds of more than one character. As you read "Christmas Storms and Sunshine," be aware of the information provided by the story's omniscient narrator.

ACTIVE READING ANALYZING CAUSES AND EFFECTS

Noting the **causes** and **effects** in a narrative helps you understand the relationships between events. In Gaskell's story, many of the events result in particular emotional responses. For example, when the cat eats Mrs. Hodgson's mutton, she feels intense anger. As you read the story, identify the different emotions experienced by Mrs. Hodgson and Mrs. Jenkins. Try to determine the cause of each emotion.

READER'S NOTEBOOK Use a chart like the one shown to record your observations about each character's emotions.

Mrs. Hodgson	
Event (cause)	Emotion (effect)
Cat eats cold mutton.	intense anger

LESSON RESOURCES

UNIT FIVE RESOURCE BOOK, pp. 15–19

ASSESSMENT RESOURCES

Formal Assessment, pp. 157–158

Teacher's Guide to Assessment and Portfolio Use

Test Generator

SKILLS TRANSPARENCIES AND COPYMASTERS

Literary Analysis
- Point of View, T18 (for Literary Analysis, p. 872)

Reading and Critical Thinking
- Cause and Effect, T1 (for Active Reading, p. 872)

Grammar
- Commas with Nonessential Elements, T55 (for Mini Lesson, p. 884)
- Essential and Nonessential Clauses, C114 (for Mini Lesson, p. 884)

Vocabulary
- Context Clues, C69 (for Mini Lesson, p. 880)

Writing
- The Uses of Dialogue, T24 (for Writing Option 3, p. 884)
- Opinion Statement, C35 (for Writing Option 2, p. 884)

Communications
- Identifying, Analyzing Artistic Elements in Literary Texts, T13 (for Activities & Explorations 1, p. 884)
- Impromptu Speaking: Dialogue, Role-Play, T14 (for Activities & Explorations 3, p. 884)

INTEGRATED TECHNOLOGY

Audio Library

LaserLinks
- Historical Connection: The Victorian Era. See **Teacher's SourceBook,** p. 59.

Visit our website:
www.mcdougallittell.com

Christmas Storms and Sunshine

ELIZABETH CLEGHORN GASKELL

In the town of—(no matter where) there circulated two local newspapers (no matter when). Now the *Flying Post* was long-established and respectable—alias bigoted and Tory; the *Examiner* was spirited and intelligent—alias newfangled and democratic. Every week these newspapers contained articles abusing each other, as cross and peppery as articles could be, and evidently the production of irritated minds, although they seemed to have one stereotyped commencement[1]—"Though the article appearing in our

1. stereotyped commencement: a beginning that was repeatedly used without variation.

TEACHING THE LITERATURE

Customizing Instruction

Less Proficient Readers

Set a Purpose Have students read to find out why a quarrel occurs on the day before Christmas.

Students Acquiring English

Tell students that although newspapers strive to report the news objectively, most newspapers have a political leaning, which is most evident on their editorial page. In this story, the *Post* is a conservative newspaper, representing the position of the upper-class establishment. The *Examiner,* in contrast, is a liberal newspaper that represents the interests of the rising middle class.

 Use **Spanish Study Guide** for additional support, pp. 200–202.

Gifted and Talented

Have students learn more about the social problems, such as class conflict and unemployment, that afflicted Victorian society. Some students may be interested in watching episodes of the British television series *Upstairs, Downstairs.*

BLOCK SCHEDULING: MANAGING TIME

If your schedule requires that you cover the lesson objectives in a shorter time, use . . .

- Preparing to Read, p. 872
- Thinking Through the Literature, p. 883
- Vocabulary in Action, p. 884

If you want to take advantage of longer class time, use . . .

- TE Teaching Options: Preteaching Vocabulary, p. 874; Vocabulary Strategy, p. 880; Viewing and Representing, p. 878; Speaking and Listening, p. 876; Cross Curricular Links, pp. 877, 881; Informal Assessment, pp. 879, 882; Grammar, p. 884
- Choices & Challenges and Author Activity, pp. 884–885

Reading and Analyzing

Literary Analysis

THIRD-PERSON OMNISCIENT POINT OF VIEW

Tell students that the third-person omniscient point of view was popular with Victorian authors. Third-person omniscient narrators are less common today, and when they are used they tend to be less "intrusive" than the Victorian narrators were. The narrator of this story, for example, in typically Victorian fashion, not only knows the thoughts of all the characters, but expresses opinions on the characters and situations and even speaks in the first person on occasion. Have students note whenever they come across a passage in which the narrator seems more "intrusive" than is common in contemporary fiction.

Possible Responses: narrator's use of first person in story's third paragraph; the "moral" at the end of the story.

 Use **Unit Five Resource Book,** p. 16 for more exercises.

Active Reading

ANALYZING CAUSES AND EFFECTS

Ask students to jot down, as they read, the cause or causes of the following events in the story:

- Mary being late taking her husband's dinner to the office
  Answer: having to pare the mutton that the cat had chewed; the baby waking up after she slams the door.
- Mary crying
  Answer: her own cruelty to the cat, the quarrel with Mrs. Jenkins, the baby's irritability.
- Mary regaining her good mood
  Answer: the package of sausages from her mother.

 Use **Unit Five Resource Book,** p. 15 for more practice.

last week's *Post* (or *Examiner*) is below contempt, yet we have been induced," &c. &c.; and every Saturday the Radical shopkeepers shook hands together, and agreed that the *Post* was done for by the slashing, clever *Examiner*; while the more dignified Tories began by regretting that Johnson should think that low paper, only read by a few of the vulgar, worth wasting his wit upon; however, the *Examiner* was at its last gasp.

It was not, though. It lived and flourished; at least it paid its way, as one of the heroes of my story could tell. He was chief compositor, or whatever title may be given to the headman of the mechanical part of a newspaper. He hardly confined himself to that department. Once or twice, unknown to the editor, when the manuscript had fallen short, he had filled up the vacant space by compositions of his own; announcements of a forthcoming crop of green peas in December; a grey thrush having been seen, or a white hare, or such interesting phenomena; invented for the occasion, I must confess; but what of that? His wife always knew when to expect a little specimen of her husband's literary talent by a peculiar cough, which served as prelude; and, judging from this encouraging sign, and the high-pitched and emphatic voice in which he read them, she was inclined to think, that an "Ode to an Early Rosebud," in the corner devoted to original poetry, and a letter in the correspondence department, signed "Pro Bono Publico,"[2] were her husband's writing, and to hold up her head accordingly.

I never could find out what it was that occasioned the Hodgsons to lodge in the same house as the Jenkinses. Jenkins held the same office in the Tory Paper as Hodgson did in the *Examiner,* and, as I said before, I leave you to give it a name. But Jenkins had a proper sense of his position, and a proper reverence for all in authority, from the king down to the editor and sub-editor. He would as soon have thought of borrowing the king's crown for a nightcap, or the king's scepter for a walking-stick as he would have thought of filling up any spare corner with any production of his own; and I think it would have even added to his contempt of Hodgson (if that were possible), had he known of the "productions of his brain," as the latter fondly alluded to the paragraphs he inserted, when speaking to his wife.

Jenkins had his wife too. Wives were wanting[3] to finish the completeness of the quarrel which existed one memorable Christmas week, some dozen years ago, between the two neighbors, the two compositors. And with wives, it was a very pretty, a very complete quarrel. To make the opposing parties

2. **"Pro Bono Publico"** (prō bō′nō pŭb′lĭ-kō′): a Latin phrase meaning "for the public good."
3. **wanting:** required; needed.

WORDS TO KNOW — **allude** (ə-lo͞od′) *v.* to make an indirect reference

Teaching Options

Preteaching Vocabulary

USING CONTEXT CLUES Call students' attention to the list of WORDS TO KNOW. Remind students that sometimes they can understand the meaning of a word by examining the context in which the word is used. Use the model sentence to demonstrate the strategy of using context clues that provide inferences to word meanings.

Model Sentence

The gentleman was affronted when the shop clerk spoke to him rudely.

Instruction

- Write the model sentence on the chalkboard.
- Ask a volunteer to summarize the meaning of the sentence.
- Have students use the meaning of the sentence to infer the meaning of the underlined word.
- Ask a volunteer to use the underlined word in a sentence he or she makes up.

still more equal, still more well-matched, if the Hodgsons had a baby ("such a baby!—a poor, puny little thing"), Mrs. Jenkins had a cat ("such a cat! a great, nasty, miowling tom-cat, that was always stealing the milk put by for little Angel's supper"). And now, having matched Greek with Greek, I must proceed to the tug of war.[4] It was the day before Christmas; such a cold east wind! such an inky sky! such a blue-black look in people's faces, as they were driven out more than usual, to complete their purchases for the next day's festival.

Before leaving home that morning, Jenkins had given some money to his wife to buy the next day's dinner.

"My dear, I wish for turkey and sausages. It may be a weakness, but I own I am partial to sausages. My deceased mother was. Such tastes are hereditary. As to the sweets—whether plum-pudding or mince-pies—I leave such considerations to you; I only beg you not to mind expense. Christmas comes but once a year."

And again he called out from the bottom of the first flight of stairs, just close to the Hodgsons' door ("such ostentatiousness," as Mrs. Hodgson observed), "You will not forget the sausages, my dear!"

"I should have liked to have had something above common, Mary," said Hodgson, as they too made their plans for the next day; "but I think roast beef must do for us. You see, love, we've a family."

"Only one, Jem! I don't want more than roast beef, though, I'm sure. Before I went to service,[5] mother and me would have thought roast beef a very fine dinner."

"Well, let's settle it, then, roast beef and a plum-pudding; and now, good-bye. Mind and take care of little Tom. I thought he was a bit hoarse this morning."

And off he went to his work.

Now, it was a good while since Mrs. Jenkins and Mrs. Hodgson had spoken to each other, although they were quite as much in possession of the knowledge of events and opinions as though they did. Mary knew that Mrs. Jenkins despised her for not having a real lace cap, which Mrs. Jenkins had; and for having been a servant, which Mrs. Jenkins had not; and the little occasional pinchings which the Hodgsons were obliged to resort to, to make both ends meet, would have been very patiently endured by Mary, if she had not winced under Mrs. Jenkins's knowledge of such economy. But she had her revenge. She had a child, and Mrs. Jenkins had none. To have had a child, even such a puny baby as little Tom, Mrs. Jenkins would have worn commonest caps, and cleaned grates, and drudged her fingers to the bone. The great unspoken disappointment of her life soured her temper, and turned her thoughts inward, and made her morbid and selfish. **1**

"Hang that cat! he's been stealing again! he's gnawed the cold mutton in his nasty mouth till it's not fit to set before a Christian; and I've nothing else for Jem's dinner. But I'll give it him now I've caught him, that I will!"

So saying, Mary Hodgson caught up her husband's Sunday cane, and despite pussy's cries and scratches, she gave him such a beating as she hoped might cure him of his thievish propensities; when, lo! and behold, Mrs. Jenkins stood at the door with a face of bitter wrath.

"Aren't you ashamed of yourself, ma'am, to abuse a poor dumb animal, ma'am, as knows no better than to take food when he sees it, ma'am?

4. **having matched . . . tug of war:** a reference to the proverb "When Greek meets Greek, then comes the tug of war," meaning that when evenly matched opponents fight, the battle will be fierce.

5. **went to service:** took employment as a servant.

WORDS TO KNOW **propensity** (prə-pĕn′sĭ-tē) *n.* an inclination or tendency

875

Customizing Instruction

Less Proficient Readers

Tell students that the story centers on the relationship between two families: the Hodgsons and the Jenkinses. Mr. Hodgson and Mr. Jenkins work at rival newspapers. Because of the differences in their political ideologies, the families do not get along.

Students Acquiring English

1 Point out the idiomatic phrases "the little occasional pinchings" and "to make both ends meet," and tell students that both phrases have to do with money. Ask them whether they can explain the meaning.

Possible Response: Both phrases refer to people's trying to use little money wisely so that they can pay for what they need.

Gifted And Talented

As a much younger country, the United States lacks England's deep-seated class consciousness. During the Victorian period, class conflict was especially pronounced in England—a fact that is reflected in the relationship between the two families in this story. Have students list the ways that class differences enter into the story and affect the families' relationship.

Possible Responses: Class "markers" include the husbands' political allegiances, Mary's one-time job as a servant, the Hodgson's penny-pinching, and the menus each family plans for Christmas dinner; the families' tendency to let these differences affect their relationship is evident, for example, when Mr. Jenkins calls to his wife "not to mind expense" and Mrs. Hodgson observes "such ostentatiousness."

Exercise Read the following sentences. Ask students to use context clues to determine the meanings of the italicized terms.

1. When the lady asked whether she could borrow a friend's necklace, the friend alluded to previously borrowed and unreturned jewelry.
2. The soldier was relieved to find out that the wound was not mortal.
3. The pompous editor refused to allow slang terms in his publication.
4. His propensity for slang kept the young writer from getting published.

Use **Unit Five Resource Book,** p. 17.

A lesson on context clues appears on page 939 in the Pupil's Edition.

He only follows the nature which God has given, ma'am; and it's a pity your nature, ma'am, which I've heard is of the stingy saving species, does not make you shut your cupboard door a little closer. There is such a thing as law for brute animals. I'll ask Mr. Jenkins, but I don't think them Radicals has done away with that law yet, for all their Reform Bill, ma'am. My poor precious love of a Tommy, is he hurt? and is his leg broke for taking a mouthful of scraps, as most people would give away to a beggar—if he'd take 'em!" wound up Mrs. Jenkins, casting a contemptuous look on the remnant of a scrag end of mutton.

A Mary felt very angry and very guilty. For she really pitied the poor limping animal as he crept up to his mistress, and there lay down to bemoan himself; she wished she had not beaten him so hard, for it certainly was her own careless way of never shutting the cupboard-door that had tempted him to his fault. But the sneer at her little bit of mutton turned her penitence to fresh wrath, and she shut the door in Mrs. Jenkins's face, as she stood caressing her cat in the lobby, with such a bang, that it wakened little Tom, and he began to cry.

Everything was to go wrong with Mary today. Now baby was awake, who was to take her husband's dinner to the office? She took the child in her arms and tried to hush him off to sleep again, and as she sung she cried, she could hardly tell why,—a sort of reaction from her violent angry feelings. She wished she had never beaten the poor cat; she wondered if his leg was really broken. What would her mother say if she knew how cross and cruel her little Mary was getting? If she should live to beat her child in one of her angry fits?

It was of no use lullabying while she sobbed so; it must be given up, and she must just carry her baby in her arms, and take him with her to the office, for it was long past dinner-time. So she pared the mutton carefully, although by so doing she reduced the meat to an infinitesimal quantity, and taking the baked potatoes out of the oven, she popped them piping hot into her basket, with the etceteras of plate, butter, salt, and knife and fork.

It was, indeed, a bitter wind. She bent against it as she ran, and the flakes of snow were sharp and cutting as ice. Baby cried all the way, though she cuddled him up in her shawl. Then her husband had made his appetite up for a potato pie, and (literary man as he was) his body got so much the better of his mind, that he looked rather black at the cold mutton. Mary had no appetite for her own dinner when she arrived at home again. So, after she had tried to feed baby, and he had fretfully refused to take his bread and milk, she laid him down as usual on his quilt, surrounded by playthings, while she sided away, and chopped suet for the next day's pudding. Early in the afternoon a parcel came, done up first in brown paper, then in such a white, grass-bleached, sweet-smelling towel, and a note from her dear, dear mother; in which quaint writing she endeavored to tell her daughter that she was not forgotten at Christmas time; but that, learning that Farmer Burton was killing his pig, she had made interest for some of his famous pork, out of which she had manufactured some sausages, and flavored them just as Mary used to like when she lived at home.

"Dear, dear mother!" said Mary to herself. "There never was any one like her for remembering other folk. What rare sausages she used to make! Home things have a smack with 'em no bought things can ever have. Set them up with their sausages! I've a notion if Mrs. Jenkins had B

Reading and Analyzing

Literary Analysis

THIRD-PERSON OMNISCIENT POINT OF VIEW

A Remind students that the story's narrator is "omniscient" and capable of entering the minds of any of the characters. In this paragraph, the narrator reveals the thoughts and feelings of Mary. Ask students to point out a passage in which the narrator reveals another character's thoughts.

Possible Responses: the passage on page 875 revealing Mrs. Jenkins's desire to have a child; the passages on page 874 describing the men's attitudes toward their work.

Literary Analysis: DIALECT

B Mary's language is not standard English, but dialect. Notice the use of "other folk," "home things," and "a smack with 'em." Ask students why Gaskell chooses to use dialect.

Possible Responses: to establish Mary's social class; it's what characters from a certain place would really say; to make the story seem as if it were really happening.

Literary Analysis: ALLITERATION

C Ask students what effect the alliteration in this passage has.

Possible Response: "Baby was almost black with his gasping breath" emphasizes the urgency of the situation and stresses the problem—difficulty in breathing.

Reading Skills and Strategies: SUMMARIZING

Ask students to explain what the two women quarrel about.

Answer: the cat's theft of the mutton and Mary beating it as punishment.

Teaching Options

Speaking and Listening

EXPLORE DIALECT

Instruction Ask students to consider the value—if any—of dialect in fiction and explain why it might or might not be valuable: It might give a sense of place or to give a sense of the character's background; it might not be valuable because dialect might be difficult to read, it might be seen as a stereotype, or it might be seen as making fun of those who speak it.

Prepare Have a student volunteer to read aloud the passage from "Dear, dear mother!" to ". . . took in just now," using diction the way they think Gaskell intended. Instruct students to listen to decide whether Gaskell intends to make fun of Mary.

Present After the student has finished reading, discuss the class's impressions.

Possible Response: Gaskell is sympathetic toward Mary and does not intend to make fun of her.

This activity is particularly well-suited for longer class periods.

ever tasted mother's she'd have no fancy for them townmade things Fanny took in just now."

And so she went on thinking about home, till the smiles and the dimples came out again at the remembrance of that pretty cottage, which would look green even now in the depth of winter, with its pyracanthus,[6] and its holly-bushes, and the great Portugal laurel that was her mother's pride. And the back path through the orchard to Farmer Burton's, how well she remembered it! The bushels of unripe apples she had picked up there and distributed among his pigs, till he had scolded her for giving them so much green trash!

She was interrupted—her baby (I call him a baby, because his father and mother did, and because he was so little of his age, but I rather think he was eighteen months old,) had fallen asleep some time before among his playthings; an uneasy, restless sleep; but of which Mary had been thankful, as his morning's nap had been too short, and as she was so busy. But now he began to make such a strange crowing noise, just like a chair drawn heavily and gratingly along a kitchen floor! His eyes were open, but expressive of nothing but pain.

"Mother's darling!" said Mary, in terror, lifting him up. "Baby, try not to make that noise. Hush, hush, darling; what hurts him?" But the noise came worse and worse.

"Fanny! Fanny!" Mary called in mortal fright, for her baby was almost black with his gasping breath, and she had no one to ask for aid or sympathy but her landlady's daughter, a little girl of twelve or thirteen, who attended to the house in her mother's absence, as daily cook in gentlemen's families. Fanny was more especially considered the attendant of the upstairs lodgers (who paid for the use of the kitchen, "for Jenkins could not abide the smell of meat cooking"), but just now she was fortunately sitting at her afternoon's work of darning stockings, and hearing Mrs. Hodgson's cry of terror, she ran to her sitting-room, and understood the case at a glance. **C**

"He's got the croup![7] O Mrs. Hodgson, he'll die as sure as fate. Little brother had it, and he died in no time. The doctor said he could do nothing for him—it had gone too far. He said if we'd put him in a warm bath at first, it might have saved him; but, bless you! he was never half so bad as your baby." Unconsciously there mingled in her statement some of a child's love of producing an effect; but the increasing danger was clear enough.

"Oh, my baby! my baby! Oh, love, love! don't look so ill! I cannot bear it. And my fire so low!

6. **pyracanthus** (pī′rə-kăn′thəs): a thorny evergreen shrub.

7. **croup** (kro͞op): a respiratory disease in children, marked by difficulty in breathing and a sharp cough.

WORDS TO KNOW **mortal** (môr′tl) *adj.* intense or severe

877

Customizing Instruction

Less Proficient Readers

Set a Purpose Have students read to find out what happens when Mrs. Hodgson goes to Mrs. Jenkins for help in an emergency.

Gifted And Talented

Ask students to describe the importance that food has played in the story up to this point.

Possible Responses: Both couples make plans for their Christmas dinners. When Mr. Jenkins leaves, he instructs his wife to spare no expense on their sausages, angering Mrs. Hodgson in the process. Then Mrs. Jenkins's cat steals the Hodgson's mutton and is beaten by Mrs. Hodgson, and Mrs. Jenkins pretends to be amazed that someone could get so upset over food that might be turned down by a beggar. Mary's mother sends her homemade sausages.

Cross Curricular Link Science

CROUP Croup is a disease found most commonly in children six months to three years old. It is marked by an inflammation of the passages of the throat and windpipe so that the child wheezes when inhaling, breathes with great difficulty, and coughs with a barking sound. Croup is usually the result of the flu or a cold. Mild cases are treated with bed rest and the use of a vaporizer. Severe cases may require the administering of oxygen or the performing of a tracheotomy—treatments not available at the time of this story. Young children are particularly susceptible to the disease because they have narrow air passages that can easily become blocked.

Reading and Analyzing

Literary Analysis

THIRD-PERSON OMNISCIENT POINT OF VIEW

A Point out that the narrator shares with the reader the thoughts of more than one character. Ask what the impact is of the information imparted here.

Possible Responses: It makes Mrs. Jenkins more sympathetic; it shows she has something in common with Mrs. Hodgson, who also had been reminiscing.

Reading Skills and Strategies: PREDICTING

B Ask students to predict what will happen next, based on everything that has happened up to this point in the story. Will Mrs. Jenkins help Mrs. Hodgson? Will the baby live? Make sure students cite textual evidence for their predictions.

Possible Responses: Mrs. Jenkins will help Mrs. Hodgson and the baby will live because of Mrs. Jenkins's love of children based on her desire for one of her own, the way the carol affects Mrs. Jenkins, the fact that Mrs. Jenkins gives money to the carolers, and the fact that Mrs. Jenkins is remembering the past and her mother; Mrs. Jenkins will not help Mrs. Hodgson and the baby won't live because of Mrs. Jenkins's anger over Mrs. Hodgson beating her cat and the wooden, inflexible look with which Mrs. Jenkins responds to Mrs. Hodgson's request.

Detail, *Newgate* (late 1800s), Frank Holl. Royal Holloway and Bedford Collection, New College, Egham, Surrey, Great Britain. Bridgeman/Art Resource, New York.

Teaching Options

Mini Lesson: Viewing and Representing

Detail from *Newgate* **by Frank Holl**

ART APPRECIATION

Instruction Newgate was a famous prison in central London. Criminals of all types were incarcerated there, from wealthy men imprisoned for debt to common thieves and pickpockets. Men in prison while awaiting trial were permitted to see their families, as Holl depicts here. Holl (1845–1888) was a Londoner and a successful, hard-working painter. Some of his works show melancholy scenes of mothers with children, and Holl was criticized for emphasizing such images. This painting was done at the request of the governor of Newgate Prison.

Application Ask students to analyze the painting and describe what purpose they think Holl was trying to convey when he painted this scene. Make sure students cite elements of the painting to back up their impression.

Possible Response: He wanted to emphasize the suffering of those in prison. The impression of dreariness and suffering is conveyed by the painting's dark shadows, the barely discernible figure of the man behind the bars, and the young woman's shabby clothes, sad expression, and hunched posture, and the way she seems to guard her baby from something.

There, I was thinking of home, and picking currants, and never minding the fire. O Fanny! what is the fire like in the kitchen? Speak."

"Mother told me to screw it up, and throw some slack[8] on as soon as Mrs. Jenkins had done with it, and so I did. It's very low and black. But, oh, Mrs. Hodgson! let me run for the doctor—I cannot abear to hear him, it's so like little brother."

Through her streaming tears Mary motioned her to go; and trembling, sinking, sick at heart, she laid her boy in his cradle, and ran to fill her kettle.

Mrs. Jenkins, having cooked her husband's snug little dinner, to which he came home; having told him her story of pussy's beating, at which he was justly and dignifiedly (?) indignant, saying it was all of a piece with that abusive *Examiner;* having received the sausages, and turkey, and mince pies, which her husband had ordered; and cleaned up the room, and prepared everything for tea, and coaxed and duly bemoaned her cat (who had pretty nearly forgotten his beating, but very much enjoyed the petting); having done all these and many other things, Mrs. Jenkins sat down to get up the real lace cap. Every thread was pulled out separately, and carefully stretched: when—what was that? Outside, in the street, a chorus of piping children's voices sang the old carol she had heard a hundred times in the days of her youth—

"As Joseph was a walking he heard an angel sing,

'This night shall be born our heavenly King.

1 *He neither shall be born in housen nor in hall,* 2

Nor in the place of Paradise, but in an ox's stall.

3 *He neither shall be clothed in purple nor in pall,*

But all in fair linen, as were babies all:

He neither shall be rocked in silver nor in gold,

But in a wooden cradle that rocks on the mould,' " &c.

She got up and went to the window. There, below, stood the group of black little figures, relieved[9] against the snow, which now enveloped everything. "For old sake's sake," as she phrased 4 it, she counted out a halfpenny apiece for the singers, out of the copper bag, and threw them down below.

The room had become chilly while she had been counting out and throwing down her money, so she stirred her already glowing fire, and sat down right before it—but not to stretch her lace; like Mary Hodgson, she began to think over long past days, on softening remembrances of the dead and gone, on words long forgotten, on holy stories heard at her mother's knee. A

"I cannot think what's come over me tonight," said she, half aloud, recovering herself by the sound of her own voice from her train of thought—"My head goes wandering on them old times. I'm sure more texts have come into my head with thinking on my mother within this last half-hour, than I've thought on for years and years. I hope I'm not going to die. Folks says, thinking too much on the dead betokens we're 5 going to join 'em; I should be loth[10] to go just yet—such a fine turkey as we've got for dinner tomorrow too!"

Knock, knock, knock, at the door, as fast as knuckles could go. And then, as if the comer could not wait, the door was opened, and Mary Hodgson stood there as white as death.

"Mrs. Jenkins!—oh, your kettle is boiling, thank God! Let me have the water for my baby, for the love of God! He's got croup, and is dying!"

Mrs. Jenkins turned on her chair with a 6 wooden, inflexible look on her face, that (between ourselves) her husband knew and B dreaded for all his pompous dignity.

---

8. **slack:** fragments of coal.
9. **relieved:** set off by contrast.
10. **loth** (lōth): unwilling; reluctant.

WORDS TO KNOW **pompous** (pŏm′pəs) *adj.* characterized by excessive pride or exaggerated dignity

Customizing Instruction

Students Acquiring English

Make sure students understand the following words and phrases:

1 *housen* (a house)

2 *hall* (the house or castle of a ruler in the Middle Ages)

3 pall (in this context, velvet)

4 *for old sake's sake* (*sake* means "purpose" or "good," and for *old sake's sake* means "for the sake of old times")

5 *betokens* (means)

Multiple Learning Styles

Kinesthetic Learners

6 Tell students that in 19th-century England, no lady would remain seated when another lady came in, and that Mrs. Jenkins deliberately treats Mary as though she were a servant or a social inferior. Have two students enact this short scene for the class.

Assessment Informal Assessment

USING LITERARY DEVICES TO ENHANCE WRITING

Ask students to write a description of Mrs. Jenkins or Mrs. Hodgson, using as many metaphors as possible (or an extended metaphor). Remind students that they must compare the woman with something unlike her, such as an inanimate object or an animal, rather than another person. Help students get started by asking them to list traits of the character they choose and to think of a metaphor for each trait. Have students share their descriptions with the class.

RUBRIC

3 **Full Accomplishment** Characterization is consistent with story, and metaphors contribute significantly to clarity of characterization.

2 **Substantial Accomplishment** Characterization is fairly accurate, but fails to take into account key aspects of her character. Metaphors don't add significantly to clarity of characterization.

1 **Little or Partial Accomplishment** Characterization bears little relationship to story, and metaphor(s) add nothing.

Reading and Analyzing

Reading Skills and Strategies: INFERRING

A Ask students why Mrs. Jenkins brings up the cat-beating episode with her declaration that she is only there to help Tommy in the hope that he will grow up to treat "poor dumb beasts" well.

Possible Responses: Even though Mrs. Jenkins has decided to help, she has not gotten over her anger about Mary's treatment of the cat; Mrs. Jenkins does not know how to give in with grace and generosity; she feels awkward about giving help after her fury over the cat.

Reading Skills and Strategies: DRAWING CONCLUSIONS

B Ask students why they think Mary looks anxiously at her husband.

Possible Responses: Mary wants to accept the invitation but is afraid of what her husband might say; Mary is nervous that her husband might refuse the invitation on ideological grounds; Mary is afraid her husband will argue with Mr. Jenkins if they accept the invitation.

"I'm sorry I can't oblige you, ma'am; my kettle is wanted for my husband's tea. Don't be afeared, Tommy, Mrs. Hodgson won't venture to intrude herself where she's not desired. You'd better send for the doctor, ma'am, instead of wasting your time in wringing your hands, ma'am—my kettle is engaged."

Mary clasped her hands together with passionate force, but spoke no word of entreaty to that wooden face—that sharp, determined voice; but, as she turned away, she prayed for strength to bear the coming trial, and strength to forgive
1 Mrs. Jenkins.

Mrs. Jenkins watched her go away meekly, as one who has no hope, and then she turned upon herself as sharply as she ever did on any one else.

"What a brute I am, Lord forgive me! What's my husband's tea to a baby's life? In croup, too, where time is everything. You crabbed old vixen, you!—any one may know you never had a child!"

She was downstairs (kettle in hand) before she had finished her self-upbraiding;[11] and when in Mrs. Hodgson's room, she rejected all thanks (Mary had not the voice for many words), saying, stiffly, "I do it for the poor baby's sake, ma'am, hoping he may live to have mercy to poor dumb
A beasts, if he does forget to lock his cupboards."

But she did everything, and more than Mary, with her young inexperience, could have thought of. She prepared the warm bath, and tried it with her husband's own thermometer (Mr. Jenkins was as punctual as clockwork in noting down the temperature of every day). She let his mother place her baby in the tub, still preserving the same rigid, affronted aspect, and then she went upstairs without a word. Mary longed to ask her to stay, but dared not; though, when she left the room, the tears chased each other down her cheeks faster than ever. Poor young mother! how she counted the minutes till the doctor should come. But, before he came, down again stalked Mrs. Jenkins, with something in her hand.

"I've seen many of these croup-fits, which, I take it, you've not, ma'am. Mustard plasters[12] is very sovereign,[13] put on the throat; I've been up and made one, ma'am, and, by your leave, I'll put it on the poor little fellow."

Mary could not speak, but she signed her grateful assent.

It began to smart while they still kept silence; and he looked up to his mother as if seeking courage from her looks to bear the stinging pain; but she was softly crying to see him suffer, and her want of courage reacted upon him, and he began to sob aloud. Instantly Mrs. Jenkins's
apron was up, hiding her face: "Peep-bo, baby," 2
said she, as merrily as she could. His little face brightened, and his mother having once got the cue, the two women kept the little fellow amused, until his plaster had taken effect.

"He's better—oh, Mrs. Jenkins, look at his eyes! how different! And he breathes quite softly"—

As Mary spoke thus, the doctor entered. He examined his patient. Baby was really better.

"It has been a sharp attack, but the remedies you have applied have been worth all the Pharmacopoeia[14] an hour later.—I shall send a powder," &c. &c.

Mrs. Jenkins stayed to hear this opinion; and (her heart wonderfully more easy) was going to leave the room, when Mary seized her hand and kissed it; she could not speak her gratitude.

Mrs. Jenkins looked affronted and awkward, and as if she must go upstairs and wash her hand directly.

But, in spite of these sour looks, she came softly down an hour or so afterwards to see how baby was.

---

11. **self-upbraiding:** self-scolding.
12. **mustard plaster:** a paste made of powdered mustard, water, and vinegar that causes localized irritation when applied to the skin and is intended to relieve inflamed tissues.
13. **sovereign** (sŏv′ər-ĭn): effective.
14. **Pharmacopoeia** (fär′mə-kə-pē′ə): all the medicinal drugs listed in the standard reference work on the subject.

WORDS TO KNOW **affronted** (ə-frŭn′tĭd) *adj.* offended **affront** *v.*

880

Teaching Options

Vocabulary Strategy

CONTEXT CLUES

Instruction Remind students that sometimes they can understand the meaning of an unfamiliar word by examining the context in which the word is used.

Activity Ask students to guess the meanings of the boldface words from their context:

1. "I'm sorry I can't **oblige** you, ma'am; my kettle is wanted for my husband's tea."
   Answer: Since this sentence is clearly a refusal, oblige must mean "to comply with a request," or "do someone a favor."
2. "You crabbed old **vixen**, you!"
   Answer: Since this statement occurs in the context of Mrs. Jenkins's self-reproaches and she has just called herself a "brute," it seems likely that she is calling herself a name. More specifically, she is criticizing herself for being quarrelsome and unkind, so *vixen* probably means "quarrelsome and unkind person or thing."

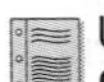
Use **Vocabulary Transparencies and Copymasters,** p. 45.

A lesson on context clues appears on p. 939 in the Pupil's Edition.

The little gentleman slept well after the fright he had given his friends; and on Christmas morning, when Mary awoke and looked at the sweet little pale face lying on her arm, she could hardly realize the danger he had been in.

When she came down (later than usual), she found the household in a commotion. What do you think had happened? Why, pussy had been traitor to his best friend, and eaten up some of Mr. Jenkins's own especial sausages; and gnawed and tumbled the rest so, that they were not fit to be eaten! There were no bounds to that cat's appetite! he would have eaten his own father if he had been tender enough. And now Mrs. Jenkins stormed and cried—"Hang the cat!"

Christmas Day, too! and all the shops shut! "What was turkey without sausages?" gruffly asked Mr. Jenkins.

"O Jem!" whispered Mary, "hearken what a piece of work he's making about sausages—I should like to take Mrs. Jenkins up some of mother's; they're twice as good as bought sausages."

"I see no objection, my dear. Sausages do not involve intimacies, else his politics are what I can no ways respect."

"But, oh, Jem, if you had seen her last night about baby! I'm sure she may scold me forever, and I'll not answer. I'd even make her cat welcome to the sausages." The tears gathered to Mary's eyes as she kissed her boy.

"Better take 'em upstairs, my dear, and give them to the cat's mistress." And Jem chuckled at his saying.

Mary put them on a plate, but still she loitered.

"What must I say, Jem? I never know."

"Say—I hope you'll accept of these sausages, as my mother—no, that's not grammar;—say what comes uppermost, Mary, it will be sure to be right."

So Mary carried them upstairs and knocked at the door; and when told to "come in," she looked very red, but went up to Mrs. Jenkins, saying, "Please take these. Mother made them." And was away before an answer could be given.

Just as Hodgson was ready to go to church, Mrs. Jenkins came downstairs, and called Fanny. In a minute, the latter entered the Hodgsons' room, and delivered Mr. and Mrs. Jenkins's compliments, and they would be particular glad if Mr. and Mrs. Hodgson would eat their dinner with them. 3

"And carry baby upstairs in a shawl, be sure," added Mrs. Jenkins's voice in the passage, close to the door, whither she had followed her messenger. There was no discussing the matter, with the certainty of every word being overheard.

Mary looked anxiously at her husband. She remembered his saying he did not approve of Mr. Jenkins's politics. B

"Do you think it would do for baby?" asked he.

"Oh, yes," answered she eagerly; "I would wrap him up so warm."

Customizing Instruction

Less Proficient Readers

1 Ask students to explain what happens when Mary Hodgson asks Mrs. Jenkins for help. What does Mrs. Jenkins tell Mrs. Hodgson? How does Mary Hodgson respond?

Possible Response: Mrs. Jenkins refuses to let Mary use the hot water for Tommy's bath, because she is going to make tea for her husband. Mary doesn't bother to plead, praying that she will someday be able to forgive Mrs. Jenkins for her heartlessness.

Set a Purpose Tell students to read to find out whether the situation between the two families improves; in other words, if Mrs. Jenkins's kindness has a positive effect on the relationship.

Students Acquiring English

2 Students might find the reference to "Peep-bo" confusing. Tell them that the expression used today is "Peek-a-boo." If warranted, explain that the game is played by hiding one's face and then revealing it suddenly. Discuss the reason Mrs. Jenkins plays it with Tommy.

Answer: to get his mind off his fright and pain, and to show Mary how to interact with him at that moment in a more productive way than acting alarmed.

3 Tell students that *latter* refers to the second person or thing named. An easy way to remember the meaning is to think of the word *later:* The *latter* refers to the person mentioned later, not earlier.

Christmas Around the World

Most students are familiar with the Christmas traditions in the United States, but they might be interested in how people in other countries celebrate Christmas. In Mexico, for example, the nine days before Christmas are important. Called *posadas* ("inns"), the days feature a reenactment of Mary and Joseph searching for a place to stay in Bethlehem. Two children, leading a procession, carry statues of Mary and Joseph and knock on the door of a house. They are first refused but then admitted. After the ceremony, there is a celebration. In both Asia and Africa, the celebration of Christmas is not widespread, because of the smaller number of Christians. However, the Western traditions are generally followed when Christmas is observed. In Ethiopia, though, members of the Coptic Orthodox Church celebrate Christmas on January 7.

Reading and Analyzing

Active Reading

ANALYZING CAUSES AND EFFECTS

Ask students to make a chart of the sequence of causes and effects in the story. The last effect should be the joint Christmas dinner together. Tell students that each effect should be the cause in the row below.

Possible Responses:

Cause Jenkins's cat steals mutton from the Hodgsons.

Effect Mrs. Hodgson beats cat.

Cause Mrs. Hodgson beats cat.

Effect Mrs. Hodgson quarrels with Mrs. Jenkins.

Literary Analysis

THIRD-PERSON OMNISCIENT POINT OF VIEW

Tell students that the word *omniscient* comes from the Latin words *omnis*—which means "all"—and *scientia*—which means "knowledge." Explain that an omniscient narrator knows everything about the story and the characters. Ask students what information in the story proves that the narrator is omniscient.

Possible Responses: the guilt Mary feels after she beats the cat; Mrs. Jenkins's upbraiding herself for not helping with the baby.

"And I've got our room up to sixty-five already, for all it's so frosty," added the voice outside.

Now, how do you think they settled the matter? The very best way in the world. Mr. and Mrs. Jenkins came down into the Hodgsons' room and dined there. Turkey at the top, roast beef at the bottom, sausages at one side, potatoes at the other. Second course, plum pudding at the top, and mince pies at the bottom.

And after dinner, Mrs. Jenkins would have baby on her knee, and he seemed quite to take to her; she declared he was admiring the real lace on her cap, but Mary thought (though she did not say so) that he was pleased by her kind looks and coaxing words. Then he was wrapped up and carried carefully upstairs to tea, in Mrs. Jenkins's room. And after tea, Mrs. Jenkins, and Mary, and her husband, found out each other's mutual liking for music, and sat singing old glees and catches,[15] till I don't know what o'clock, without one word of politics or newspapers.

Before they parted, Mary had coaxed pussy on to her knee; for Mrs. Jenkins would not part with baby, who was sleeping on her lap.

"When you're busy bring him to me. Do, now, it will be a real favor. I know you must have a deal to do, with another coming; let him come up to me. I'll take the greatest of cares of him; pretty darling, how sweet he looks when he's asleep!"

When the couples were once more alone, the husbands unburdened their minds to their wives.

Mr. Jenkins said to his— "Do you know, Burgess tried to make me believe Hodgson was such a fool as to put paragraphs into the *Examiner* now and then; but I see he knows his place, and has got too much sense to do any such thing."

Hodgson said— "Mary, love, I almost fancy from Jenkins's way of speaking (so much civiler than I expected), he guesses I wrote that 'Pro Bono' and the 'Rosebud,'—at any rate, I've no objection to your naming it, if the subject should come uppermost; I should like him to know I'm a literary man."

Well! I've ended my tale; I hope you don't think it too long; but, before I go, just let me say one thing.

If any of you have any quarrels, or misunderstandings, or coolnesses, or cold shoulders, or shynesses, or tiffs, or miffs, or huffs, with anyone else, just make friends before Christmas,—you will be so much merrier if you do.

I ask it of you for the sake of that old angelic song, heard so many years ago by the shepherds, keeping watch by night, on Bethlehem Heights. ❖

15. **glees and catches:** types of unaccompanied part songs for several voices.

Teaching Options

Assessment **Informal Assessment**

CREATING QUESTIONS Have students create five questions about the story and then answer them. If they wish, some of their questions can focus on the technique of the narrator, particularly as it relates to point of view. Writing answers to self-composed questions can help students clarify their thoughts about the story. After they have finished, they can share their questions and answers with a partner.

RUBRIC

3 Full Accomplishment Questions reflect a good understanding of events in story and narrator's point of view.

2 Substantial Accomplishment Questions show a general understanding of events in story and narrator's point of view.

3 Little or Partial Accomplishment Questions show little understanding of events in story and narrator's point of view.

Thinking through the LITERATURE

Connect to the Literature

1. **What Do You Think?** Which character in the story is most appealing to you? Share your thoughts with your classmates.

Comprehension Check
- Why did Mary Hodgson beat Mrs. Jenkins's cat?
- What did Mrs. Hodgson do when her baby got the croup?
- How did Mrs. Jenkins help the baby?

Think Critically

2. How would you describe the characters' first impressions of one another?

THINK ABOUT
- Mr. Hodgson's and Mr. Jenkins's jobs
- the makeup of each family
- the personal opinions and feelings each character reveals
- the social attitudes or class consciousness each character exhibits

3. **ACTIVE READING** ANALYZING CAUSES AND EFFECTS
Compare the chart you created in your READER'S NOTEBOOK for each character and trace how the **characters** and their relationship changed as the story progressed. What event causes each character to change toward the other? After that point, how do their emotions reflect their changing relationship?

4. Do you find the events in the latter part of the story believable? Support your response with details from the story.

Extend Interpretations

5. **Critic's Corner** A student reviewer, Dan Birdsall, thought that "the irony of the ending was cool—it seems like the two families would end up enemies again after a while." Do you agree that the new friendship of the Hodgsons and the Jenkinses is unlikely to last?

6. **What If?** Suppose "Christmas Storms and Sunshine" didn't take place at Christmas. How might the outcome of the story be different? Give reasons for your answer.

7. **Connect to Life** Mr. Jenkins and Mr. Hodgson have opposing political views. Do you think strong political differences always create difficulties in a personal relationship? Support your answer with examples or reasons.

Literary Analysis

THIRD-PERSON OMNISCIENT POINT OF VIEW

In a story told from the **third-person omniscient point of view,** the narrator is all-knowing. This kind of narrator provides the reader with insights into the thoughts, motivations, and responses of all the characters, as well as access to events that may be occurring simultaneously. In the following passage from "Christmas Storms and Sunshine," notice the insight the narrator provides into each character's jealous response to the other:

Mary knew that Mrs. Jenkins despised her for not having a real lace cap, which Mrs. Jenkins had. . . . But she had her revenge. She had a child, and Mrs. Jenkins had none. To have had a child, even such a puny baby as little Tom, Mrs. Jenkins would have worn commonest caps. . . .

Paired Activity The narrator often includes parenthetical remarks about characters and events, as in the clause ". . . I think it would have even added to his contempt of Hodgson (if that were possible) . . ." With a partner, look for other examples of this technique in the story. What kinds of information does the narrator usually convey in parentheses? How does this technique reflect the power of the omniscient narrator?

PLOT AND CONFLICT The events in a narrative's **plot** progress because of a **conflict,** a struggle between opposing forces. What main conflict drives the plot of "Christmas Storms and Sunshine"?

GUIDING STUDENT RESPONSE

Connect To The Literature

1. **What Do You Think?**
Guidelines for student response: Accept all reasonable responses. Have students support their responses with details from the story.

Comprehension Check
- because it ate her mutton
- She called Fanny and went up to Mrs. Jenkins's for hot water.
- She gave Mrs. Hodgson hot water and applied a mustard plaster to the baby. She also showed Mrs. Hodgson how to keep the baby's mind off its fear and discomfort by playing "Peek-a-boo."

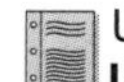
Use Selection Quiz in **Unit Five Resource Book,** p. 18.

Think Critically

2. Possible Response: The Jenkinses think of themselves as superior to the Hodgsons; the Hodgsons think the Jenkinses are snobs.
3. Possible Responses: Mrs. Hodgson begins to change when she regrets beating the cat; Mrs. Jenkins begins to change when she changes her mind about giving Mrs. Hodgson the water. Their ambivalent emotions reflect their changing feelings. Have students comment on the impact the cause-effect text structure had on their understanding.
4. Possible Response: Yes, the quarrel was never serious or deep, and people are often inclined to peace and goodwill at Christmas; no, the resolution is too neat and contrived.

Literary Activity

Paired Activity Have students discuss the effect the narrator's parenthetical remarks have on them as readers.

Plot and Conflict Have students summarize the plot development and identify conflicts and how they are addressed and resolved.

Extend Interpretations

Critic's Corner Agree—Mr. Hodgson seems to invite future discord when he tells his wife she's free to tell the Jenkinses that he invents material for the *Examiner* because near the beginning of the story, the narrator says Mr. Jenkins would probably like Mr. Hodgson even less if he were to find out that Hodgson really did invent such material. Disagree—the fact that they have had dinner together shows that they have overcome their differences.

What If? Possible Responses: The two families might not resolve their differences, since they would not be moved by the "spirit of Christmas" to do so; the details of the story would be different, but the families could come together over something other than a Christmas meal.

Connect to Life Accept all reasonable, well-supported answers.

Writing Options

1. **Letter to Mary's Mother** Before students begin writing, they should review the story for clues to Mary's relationship with her mother. Remind students to adopt a voice appropriate to the period.
2. **Mr. Hodgson's Editorial** Have students make a list of points Mr. Hodgson should include in his editorial.
3. **Dialogue Between the Jenkinses** Have students reread the passage on page 874 in which the narrator states that it would probably have added to Mr. Jenkins's contempt for Hodgson to know that Hodgson used his own compositions. This is the single biggest clue as to how the Jenkinses would respond.

Activities & Explorations

1. **Story Dramatization** Before students assign character roles, they should determine whether they will include the role of a narrator. If they don't use a narrator they will have to go through the story and choose the material that is most "dramatic" (that is, shown and not told). Have students create a script for the performance prior to beginning rehearsal.
2. **Set Design** Students should look in the story for any details, in addition to considering such factors as the differences in the two families' levels of wealth, and the fact that the Hodgsons have a child while the Jenkinses have a cat.
3. **Improvisation** Remind students that since *improvise* means "to create without preparation," the only planning they should do is to determine who will take each role.

Inquiry & Research

City Life Students might like to work in groups to find the information. Each member of the group can research one aspect of Victorian city life (for example, one of the suggestions given), but should use multiple sources. Each group can present its findings to the class.

Victorian Dailies As an extension of the activity, students can use the same questions and apply them to the leading newspapers in England today. Students may compile their written notes into a handout that summarizes their research findings.

Choices & CHALLENGES

Writing Options

1. **Letter to Mary's Mother** Pretend that you are Mary Hodgson. In a letter to your mother, describe the experience you have just had with the Jenkinses.

2. **Mr. Hodgson's Editorial** Imagine that you are Mr. Hodgson and write a brief editorial for the *Examiner.* Based on what you have learned over the Christmas holiday, analyze the importance of living in harmony with your neighbors. Place the paragraph in your **Working Portfolio.**

3. **Dialogue Between the Jenkinses** Suppose that the Jenkinses discover that Mr. Hodgson really does put his own compositions into the *Examiner.* Write the dialogue that might occur between Mr. and Mrs. Jenkins after this revelation.

Activities & Explorations

1. **Story Dramatization** With a partner or group, plan a dramatic interpretation of one or more scenes from the story. Determine how to portray each character and what lines and actions you will use. Then rehearse your presentation, and give your final performance for the entire class. ~ **PERFORMING**

2. **Set Design** Create a drawing or model of the set design you would use for a dramatized version of "Christmas Storms and Sunshine." ~ **ART**

3. **Improvisation** With a partner, improvise a conversation in which Mary Hodgson tells her son, who is now a teenager, about the incidents described in this story. ~ **SPEAKING AND LISTENING**

Inquiry & Research

City Life Look up information on life in English industrial cities—such as Manchester—during the early 19th century. What kind of housing was available? What were the popular social activities? How did life differ for various social classes? What were working conditions like in the factories?

Victorian Dailies Find out what the leading newspapers were in 19th-century England. What were their names, their prices, their political leanings? How were they received by the people of their time?

Art Connection

Character Sketches What thoughts come to mind when you look at the woman in *Newgate* on page 878? How do these thoughts relate to your impression of Mrs. Hodgson in "Christmas Storms and Sunshine"? Discuss your ideas with your classmates.

Vocabulary in Action

EXERCISE: CONTEXT CLUES Write the word that best completes each of the following sentences.

1. Since it is always easier to see things from one's own point of view, Mrs. Hodgson and Mrs. Jenkins have a ________ to blame each other for any quarrel they have.
2. Mrs. Jenkins might be shocked to discover that what she thinks is simple self-respect and good breeding could be seen by Mrs. Hodgson as ________ haughtiness.
3. Mrs. Hodgson might be surprised to find out that while Mrs. Jenkins is behaving coldly and showing ________ indignation, she is really quite worried about the Hodgson baby.
4. After all, the Hodgson baby is in serious, even ________, danger, and Mrs. Jenkins has humanity's normal protective impulses toward helpless babies.
5. A bitter memory makes Mrs. Jenkins ________ to an earlier quarrel by saying, "I do it for the poor baby's sake, ma'am, hoping he may live to have mercy to poor dumb beasts, if he does forget to lock his cupboards."

WORDS TO KNOW		
	affronted	pompous
	allude	propensity
	mortal	

Teaching Options

Grammar

ESSENTIAL AND NONESSENTIAL CLAUSES

Instruction An essential clause is necessary to complete the meaning of a sentence. It is not set off by commas. A nonessential clause, which is set off by commas, adds extra information to a sentence, but is not necessary to the meaning of the sentence. The word *that* usually introduces an essential clause, while *which* often introduces a nonessential clause. *Who* may introduce both essential and nonessential clauses, depending on the context.

Activity Write the following sentences on the chalkboard. Ask students to identify each clause and the word that introduces it. Discuss why each clause is essential or nonessential to the meaning of the sentence.

Every week the two city newspapers, which held opposing political views, published articles critical of the other paper.

Answer: which; nonessential clause. Note that when the clause is removed, the sentence reads well on its own.

The cat *that* Mary punished belonged to Mrs. Jenkins.

Elizabeth Cleghorn Gaskell

1810–1865

Other Works
"My Lady Ludlow"
"Cousin Phillis"
"Half a Life-Time Ago"

Hard Lessons Elizabeth Cleghorn, only 13 months old when her mother died, was taken from her London home to be raised by her mother's sister in a rural village. In this calm, country setting she learned to appreciate and carefully observe all the details of the natural world. At the age of 12, she was sent to boarding school, where she developed a love of reading and a sympathetic nature. Occasionally she saw her father, who had remained in London and remarried, and from his intensive tutoring she gained a proficiency in languages. These early experiences combined to provide her with a lifelong concern for the less fortunate and the desire and skill to write about their lives.

Married Life In 1831, while visiting relatives in Manchester, she met William Gaskell, a Unitarian minister, and the following year they married. As a minister's wife, she devoted much time to helping those in need. She was also kept busy raising and educating four daughters. Her first serious efforts at writing, however, did not occur until she was in her thirties and recovering from the death in 1845 of her infant son.

The Writing Life Gaskell drew upon her firsthand experiences with the poor in writing her first novel, *Mary Barton,* which was extremely successful and won her the approval of such literary figures as Charles Dickens and Charlotte Brontë. On Dickens's urging, Gaskell contributed stories to his new periodical, *Household Words,* in which two of her novels, *Cranford* and *North and South,* would be published in weekly installments. Gaskell and Brontë admired each other's work and eventually became close friends. Shortly after her dear friend's untimely death, and at the request of Brontë's father, Gaskell wrote her first and only biography, *The Life of Charlotte Brontë.* Gaskell herself died quite suddenly at the age of 55, while having tea and conversing with her family at the country home where she planned one day to retire with her husband.

Victorian Crusader Gaskell was committed to raising the social awareness of her readers. Since some Victorians did not consider it proper to discuss or write about social problems, Gaskell created controversy in her time by honestly depicting the appallingly squalid housing of the poor and vividly portraying working-class life.

Author Activity

Fighting for Reforms Find out what reforms Gaskell recommended to improve the living and working conditions of the lower class. What, if any, of her recommendations were eventually adopted? What impact did her writing have on instituting reforms?

Art Connection

Character Sketches Accept all reasonable, well-supported answers.

Vocabulary in Action

1. propensity
2. pompous
3. affronted
4. mortal
5. allude

Author Activity

Fighting for Reforms You might send students to encyclopedia articles about Gaskell, as well as to books on social reform in Victorian England. Students might also search for information about Gaskell on the Internet.

Answer: that, essential clause. Without the clause, the sentence loses its full meaning.

Exercise Ask students to identify the type of clause in each sentence. If the clause is nonessential, have them set it off with commas.

1. Mary gave some Christmas sausages which her mother had made to her neighbor as a gift.
   Answer: nonessential; comma after "sausages" and "made"
2. Mrs. Jenkins who was horrified by her own rude behavior toward Mary rushed to the aid of the ailing baby.
   Answer: nonessential; comma after "Jenkins" and "Mary"
3. The speaker who directly addresses the reader at the end of "Christmas Storms and Sunshine" is the omniscient narrator.
   Answer: essential

Use **Grammar Transparencies and Copymasters,** p. 52.

Use McDougal Littell's ***Language Network*** for more instruction and practice in clauses.

It has been written that in *Jane Eyre* and *Wuthering Heights* "romance . . . in its profoundest sense . . . took to itself this new domain [the novel]." This notion has been confirmed by millions of readers, who have been passionately moved by Jane Eyre and Rochester, Catherine Earnshaw and Heathcliff, and the mysterious, turbulent events in which these characters are caught up. Though Emily's novel was not the immediate success that her sister's was, even some critics who found fault with it confessed to being unable to put it down. One remarked that for sheer imaginative power, it was "one of the greatest novels in the language."

Additional Background

CHARLOTTE AND EMILY BRONTË

Anne (1820–1849) wrote two novels—*Agnes Grey* (1847; published together with Emily's *Wuthering Heights*) and *The Tenant of Wildfell Hall* (1848)—but at her death remained only an author of promise. Charlotte and Emily, however, produced lasting works of fiction.

Emily (1818–1848) wrote only one novel, *Wuthering Heights* (1847), which, though not an immediate success, became an acknowledged masterpiece. Critic Miriam Allen deFord has written that "perhaps no other author in English literature . . . has produced so little and yet has so high a rank. . . . One cannot even say that she died too soon to complete her work. [After *Wuthering Heights*] her work was already completed."

Of the sisters, Charlotte (1816–1855) had slightly more worldly experience. She and Emily studied for a few months in Brussels in 1842, but Charlotte alone returned there in 1843 to teach for a year, falling secretly in love with her married teacher from the previous year. Ignored by the man, Charlotte returned to England, and a couple of years later used the experience as the basis of her first novel, *The Professor.* Though publishers rejected the book, encouraging words moved Charlotte to quickly write *Jane Eyre* (1847), which was immediately accepted.

The Brontës were plagued with a predilection toward fatal diseases, mainly tuberculosis. Though they all died relatively young, in 1854 Charlotte did marry, though she died tragically, while pregnant, within the first year of her marriage.

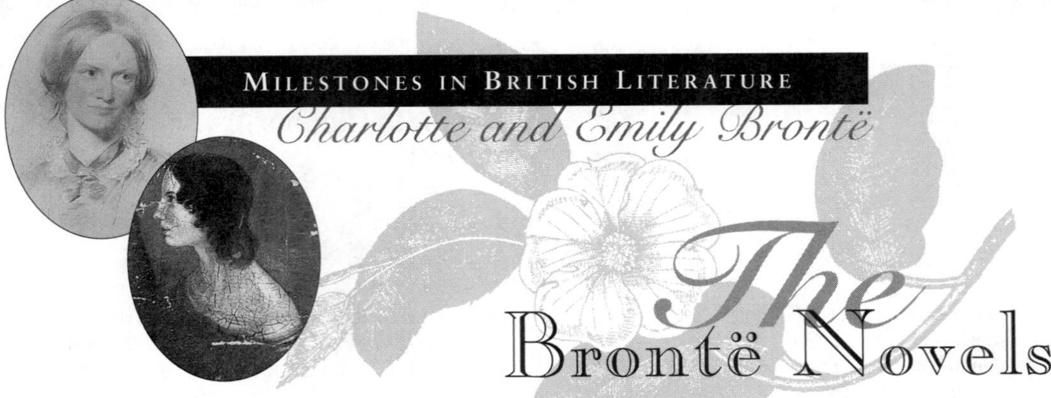

MILESTONES IN BRITISH LITERATURE

Charlotte and Emily Brontë

The Brontë Novels

"*Wuthering Heights* was hewn in a wild workshop, with simple tools, out of homely materials," wrote Charlotte Brontë in an introduction to her sister Emily's novel. The same could be said of Charlotte's masterpiece *Jane Eyre,* for although these novels were published in 1847, when Charlotte was 31 and Emily 29, the imaginations that inspired them were developed at an early age and evident in the childhood games they played in their father's parsonage on the Yorkshire moors. Using wooden soldiers and a toy village, the six Brontë children created a world called the Great Glass Town Confederacy, consisting of tiny kingdoms inhabited by characters based on their favorite heroes. All of them, but especially Charlotte and Emily, wrote everything down—composing stories, essays, and songs about

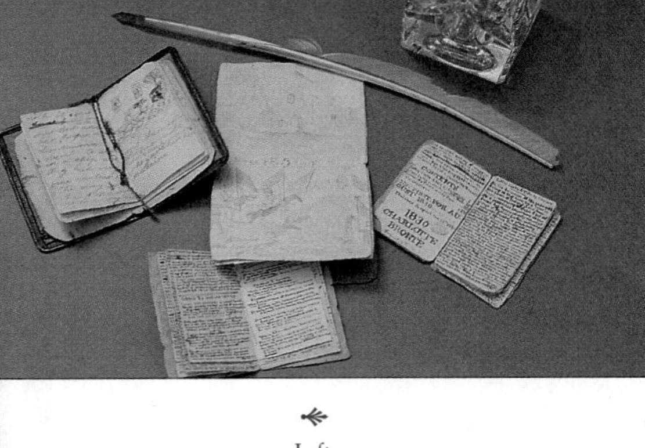

Left:
Photograph of the Yorkshire moor where the Brontë children grew up
Above:
The Brontë children wrote their tiny books by hand on folded sheets of paper measuring about 2 inches by 1½ inches. The covers were made of paper from sugar bags or wrapping paper from local shops.

their kingdoms and binding the writings into tiny books. As the children grew, the Glass Town games fell off, but the Brontë girls continued to write, their works springing from the worlds they continued to create within.

As a young adult, Charlotte discovered a stack of Emily's poems. Elated at their high quality, she convinced Emily and Anne, another sister, to combine their poems with hers in a single volume. The three sisters, adopting the pseudonyms "Currer Bell," "Ellis Bell," and "Acton Bell," published their book in 1846. Although only two copies were sold, the young Brontës were not deterred from continuing to write.

It was with their novels that the sisters would achieve their greatest success, even though when Emily's *Wuthering Heights* was published, it was largely ignored. Nevertheless, this fierce, brooding story—set on the moors—of the star-crossed love between Heathcliff and Catherine eventually came to be considered one of the most original novels of all time. Charlotte's *Jane Eyre* became an immediate critical and popular success as readers fell in love with her noble and passionately independent heroine.

Soon afterward, when Anne published *The Tenant of Wildfell Hall,* rumors circulated that Acton, Currer, and Ellis Bell were all the same man; so the sisters revealed their true identities, and their public literary life began. The triumph was muted, however, by their brother Branwell's sudden death, followed closely by the deaths of Emily and Anne. By the time Charlotte was 33, she was the sole survivor of the six Brontë children. Still, she continued to write.

The Brontës' novels, most notably Charlotte's *Jane Eyre* and Emily's *Wuthering Heights,* have remained popular works of literature for nearly 150 years. Through them, readers can experience the imaginations of two women who, despite the male domination of the Victorian literary world, were able to make their voices heard.

Top:
Painting by Thomas Davidson, depicting the scene from Jane Eyre *in which Jane meets Rochester*
Bottom:
Watercolor by Emily of her pet hawk, 1841. All of the Brontë children drew and painted.

LITERARY CHRONOLOGY

The following are publication dates of the Brontës' major works:

1846 *Poems by Currer* (Charlotte), *Ellis* (Emily), *and Acton* (Anne) *Bell* (Brontë)

1847 *Jane Eyre* (Currer Bell/Charlotte); *Wuthering Heights* (Ellis Bell/Emily); *Agnes Grey* (Acton Bell/Anne)

1848 *The Tenant of Wildfell Hall* (Acton Bell/Anne)

1849 *Shirley* (Charlotte)

1853 *Villette* (Charlotte)

1857 *The Professor* (Charlotte; written c. 1846 and published posthumously)

MILESTONES IN BRITISH LITERATURE 887

OVERVIEW

Objectives

1. understand and appreciate a Victorian **short story (Literary Analysis)**
2. identify and examine **situational irony** in a short story **(Literary Analysis)**
3. **predict** what will happen next in a short story **(Active Reading)**

Summary

Just before he dies, a king hears a voice promising him that if in one hour he can find three people who want him alive, he will be returned to life. He finds that those closest to him see only opportunity in his death; the only ones who wish him alive are a child who misses her parents—who have been in the castle since the king's death—and a man whom the king has condemned to death. At the end of the hour the bedside watchers find the expression on the face of the dead king horribly changed.

 Use **Unit Five Resource Book,** p. 20 for additional support.

Thematic Link

The story presents a portrait of a king who discovers—too late—that his **personal relationships** are all based on hypocrisy and falsehood and that his subjects misunderstand and dislike him.

5-Minute Warm-Up

Daily Language SkillBuilder

Have students **proofread** the display sentences on page 829j and write them correctly. The sentences also appear on Transparency 23 of **Grammar Transparencies and Copymasters.**

The King Is Dead, Long Live the King

Short Story by MARY E. COLERIDGE

"This was his hour, his hour that he had snatched away from death."

Connect to Your Life

Know Thyself How do you think you are perceived by others? Do you think other people's perceptions generally coincide with your own opinion of yourself? Get together with a classmate. While you list words and phrases to describe your partner, your partner should do the same for you. Then trade your lists. Do you think the description is accurate?

Build Background

In the Shadow of Greatness A moderately successful writer during the late 19th century, Mary E. Coleridge is probably better known as the great-grandniece of the romantic poet Samuel Taylor Coleridge. In several of her works—including this story—she, like her more famous relation, touches upon themes of fantasy and the supernatural. Both shared a love for the strange and the unearthly. This similarity once inspired a critic to call Mary Coleridge "the tail of the comet S. T. C."

Although Mary Coleridge was a prolific poet, she never aspired to the great literary world which she believed Samuel Coleridge inhabited. Resigned to live in his shadow, she once wrote: "I have no fairy godmother but lay claim to a fairy great-great-uncle, which is perhaps the reason that I am condemned to wander restlessly around the Gates of Fairyland, although I have never yet passed them."

Royal Rule In a monarchy, the laws of succession attempt to maintain stability: If people know that a monarch will automatically be succeeded by the next family member in line for the throne, they can feel reasonably sure that the transition will be a smooth one. The proclamation "The king is dead, long live the king!" reflects the desire for an orderly succession. The first part announces that one monarch has died; the second honors the new monarch, underscoring the continuity of the monarchy despite the passing of one individual.

WORDS TO KNOW
Vocabulary Preview
malicious, reprieve, malignant, sentiment, presently

Focus Your Reading

LITERARY ANALYSIS SITUATIONAL IRONY **Irony** is a contrast between expectation and reality. **Situational irony** occurs when what happens is not what a character or the reader expects. Suppose, for example, that the detective in a murder mystery turns out to be the murderer. This incongruity is a case of situational irony. Look for examples of situational irony as you read "The King Is Dead, Long Live the King."

ACTIVE READING PREDICTING When you read, you often make **predictions** about what will happen next. The following can help you make predictions:

- details about **characters, setting,** and **events** in the story
- **foreshadowing,** or hints about what is going to happen
- your personal knowledge of human behavior and experiences

READER'S NOTEBOOK As you read Coleridge's story, jot down predictions about what is going to happen each time the king is about to go see a particular person or group of people. In making your predictions, you might use a chart like the one shown.

Person or Group King Is About to See	Your Prediction	Basis of Your Prediction

LESSON RESOURCES

UNIT FIVE RESOURCE BOOK, pp. 20–24

ASSESSMENT RESOURCES
Formal Assessment, pp. 159–160
Teacher's Guide to Assessment and Portfolio Use
Test Generator

SKILLS TRANSPARENCIES AND COPYMASTERS
Literary Analysis
- Verbal, Situational, and Dramatic Irony, T17 (for Literary Analysis, p. 888)

Reading and Critical Thinking
- Predicting Outcomes, T2 (for Active Reading, p. 888)

Grammar
- Using *That* and *Which*, T44 (for Mini Lesson, p. 897)
- Correct Use of *That* and *Which*, C150 (for Mini Lesson, p. 897)

Vocabulary
- Prefixes and Suffixes, C70 (for Mini Lesson, p. 894)

Writing
- Levels of Language, T12 (for Writing Option 2, p. 897)
- Personality Profile, C25 (for Writing Option 2, p. 897)

Communications
- Appreciative Listening, T2 (for Mini Lesson, p. 892)
- Dramatic Reading, T12 (for Activities & Explorations, p. 897)

INTEGRATED TECHNOLOGY
Audio Library
Internet: Research Starter
Visit our website:
www.mcdougallittell.com

THE KING IS DEAD, LONG LIVE THE KING

Mary E. Coleridge

TEACHING THE LITERATURE

Customizing Instruction

Less Proficient Readers

Set a Purpose Have students read to find out who wishes the king to live.

Students Acquiring English

For students learning a language, time shifts can be problematic—especially when used as a device to signal separate narrative stages. Make sure students understand that the king's body remains in his deathbed during the entire story, even when he "comes to" (awakens in the spirit) for an hour, starting at the bottom of page 890. Everything that happens to him in this spiritual state is described in the simple past tense ("Then he sat up with a light laugh"; "This was his hour"); references to his life prior to his illness are in past perfect tense ("He had been a good king;" ". . . he had done very little").

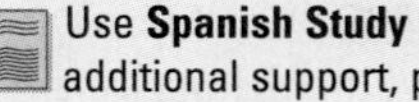

Use **Spanish Study Guide** for additional support, pp. 203–205.

Gifted and Talented

Have students compare this story to others they might have read in which a character gets to find out what others say about him or her after his or her death. You might suggest Charles Dickens's *A Christmas Carol* or Mark Twain's *The Adventures of Tom Sawyer* (in the latter the character is not actually dead, but is believed to be). Ask students to pay close attention to the attitudes of the "dead" characters and of those who react to their deaths.

Mini Lesson: Preteaching Vocabulary

WORD ORIGINS English is a language that borrows heavily from Latin. Learning the Latin origins of English words can help students understand and remember the meanings of those words.

Instruction Write on the chalkboard the following word origins and their definitions.

1. *malignus*: Latin for "wicked" or "harmful"
2. *sentire*: Latin for "to feel"
3. *praeesse*: Latin for "to be present"
4. *malus*: Latin for "bad"
5. *reprehendere*: Latin for "to hold back"

Explain that each of the words is the word of origin of one of the WORDS TO KNOW.

Activity Instruct students to match each WORD TO KNOW with its Latin root.

Answers: 1. malignant; 2. sentiment; 3. presently; 4. malicious; 5. reprieve.

When students have finished, you might have a class discussion on the changes the words' meanings have experienced in their transition from Latin to modern English.

Use **Unit Five Resource Book,** p. 27 for more practice.

A lesson on word origins appears on page 206 in the Pupil's Edition.

Reading and Analyzing

Literary Analysis SITUATIONAL IRONY

Remind students that **situational irony** is found in events themselves, not the language used to talk about them, as in verbal irony. Situational irony generally occurs when a character or the reader expects one thing to happen but something else does or when events are inherently incongruous. Ask students to find examples of situational irony in the selection as they read it.

Possible Responses: The king's best friend is not mourning, as expected, but courting the favor of the new king; the king became fatally ill on a visit to the poor quarters of the kingdom, but the common people don't mourn him and don't appreciate his efforts to help and understand them.

Use **Unit Five Resource Book,** p. 21 for more exercises.

Active Reading PREDICTING

Have students read the first nine paragraphs. Then ask them to predict whether the king will live, basing their predictions on what they have read so far. Instruct students to write down their predictions and revise them as they read.

Use **Unit Five Resource Book,** p. 20 for more practice.

FORESHADOWING

A Remind students that foreshadowing is a writer's use of hints and clues to suggest what will occur later in a narrative. Point out the behavior of those who are in the room with the king. Ask students what their lack of respect might foreshadow.

Possible Responses: a negative attitude toward the king; that the reader will discover he was a bad king.

A It was not very quiet in the room where the king lay dying. People were coming and going, rustling in and out with hushed footsteps, whispering eagerly to each other; and where a great many people are all busy making as little noise as possible, the result is apt to be a kind of bustle, that weakened nerves can scarcely endure.

But what did that matter? The doctors said he could hear nothing now. He gave no sign that he could. Surely the sobs of his beautiful young wife, as she knelt by the bedside, must else have moved him.

For days the light had been carefully shaded. Now, in the hurry, confusion, and distress, no one remembered to draw the curtains close, so that the dim eyes might not be dazzled. But what did that matter? The doctors said he could see nothing now.

For days no one but his attendants had been allowed to come near him. Now the room was free for all who chose to enter. What did it matter? The doctors said he knew no one.

So he lay for a long time, one hand flung out upon the counterpane,[1] as if in search of something. The queen took it softly in hers, but there was no answering pressure. At length the eyes and mouth closed, and the heart ceased to beat.

"How beautiful he looks," they whispered one to another.

When the king came to himself it was all very still—wonderfully and delightfully still, as he thought, wonderfully and delightfully dark. It was a strange, unspeakable relief to him—he lay as if in heaven. The room was full of the scent of flowers, and the cool night air came pleasantly through an open window. A row of wax tapers burned with soft radiance at the foot of the bed on which he was lying, covered with a velvet pall, only his head and face exposed. Four or five men were keeping guard around him, but they had fallen fast asleep.

So deep was the feeling of content which he experienced that he was loth[2] to stir. Not till the great clock of the palace struck eleven, did he so much as move. Then he sat up with a light laugh.

He remembered how, when his mind was failing him, and he had rallied all his powers in one last passionate appeal against the injustice which was taking him away from the world just when the world most needed him, he had heard a voice saying, "I will give thee yet one hour after death. If, in that time, thou canst find three that desire thy life, live!"

This was his hour, his hour that he had snatched away from death. How much of it had he lost already? He had been a good king; he had worked night and day for his subjects: he had nothing to fear, and he knew that it was very pleasant to live, how pleasant he had never known before, for, to do him justice, he was not selfish; it was his unfinished work that he grieved about when the decree went forth against him. **1**
Yet, as he passed out of the room where the watchers sat heavily sleeping, things were changed to him somehow. The burning sense of injustice was gone. Now that he came to think of it, he had done very little. True that it was his utmost, but there were many better men in the world, and the world was large, very large it seemed to him now. Everything had grown larger. He loved his country and his home as well as ever, but in the night it had seemed as if they must perish with him, and now he knew that they were still unchanged.

1. **counterpane:** bedspread.
2. **loth** (lōth): unwilling.

Teaching Options

BLOCK SCHEDULING: MANAGING TIME

If your schedule requires that you cover the lesson objectives in a shorter time, use . . .
- Preparing to Read, p. 888
- Thinking Through the Literature, p. 896
- Vocabulary in Action, p. 897

If you want to take advantage of longer class time, use . . .
- TE Teaching Options: Preteaching Vocabulary, p. 889; Vocabulary, p. 894; Viewing and Representing, p. 893; Speaking and Listening, p. 892; Informal Assessment, pp. 891, 895; Grammar, p. 897
- Choices & Challenges, p. 897

Outside the door he paused a moment, hesitating whither to go first. Not to the queen. The very thought of her

2 grief unnerved him. He would not see her till he could once more clasp her in his arms, and bid her weep tears of joy only because he was come again. After all, he had but an hour to wait. Before the castle clock struck twelve, he would be back again in life, remembering these things only as a dream. He sighed a little to think of it.

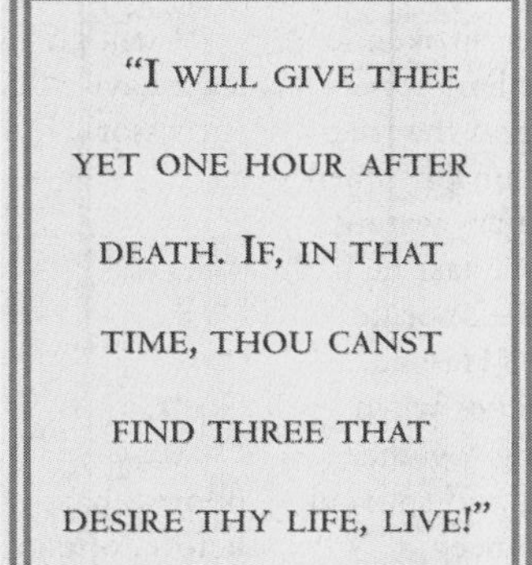
"I WILL GIVE THEE YET ONE HOUR AFTER DEATH. IF, IN THAT TIME, THOU CANST FIND THREE THAT DESIRE THY LIFE, LIVE!"

"All that to do over again some day," he said, as he recalled his last moments.

Almost he turned again to the couch he had so lately left.

"But I have never yet done anything through fear," said the king.

And he smiled as he thought of the terms of the compact. His city lay before him in the moonlight.

"I could find three thousand as easily as three," he said. "Are they not all my friends?"

As he passed out of the gate, he saw a child sitting on the steps, crying bitterly.

"What is the matter, little one?" said the sentinel on guard, stopping a moment.

"Father and mother have gone to the castle, because the king's dead," sobbed the child, "and they've never come back again; and I'm so tired and so hungry! And I've had no supper, and my doll's broken. Oh! I do wish the king were alive again!"

And she burst into a fresh storm of weeping. It amused the king not a little.

"So this is the first of my subjects that wants me back!" he said.

He had no child of his own. He would have liked to try and comfort the little maiden, but there were other calls upon him just then. He was on his way to the house of his great friend, the man whom he loved more than all others. A kind of malicious delight possessed him, as he pictured to himself the deep dejection he should find him in.

"Poor Amyas!" he said. "I know what I should be feeling in his place. I am glad he was not taken. I could not have borne his loss."

As he entered the courtyard of his friend's house, lights were being carried to and fro, horses were being saddled, an air of bustle and excitement pervaded the place. Look where he might, he could not see the face he knew so well. He entered at the open door. His friend was not in the hall. Room after room he vainly traversed —they were all empty. A sudden horror took him. Surely Amyas was not dead of grief?

He came at length to a small private apartment, in which they had spent many a happy, busy hour together; but his friend was not here either, though, to judge by appearances, he could only just have left it. Books and papers were tumbled all about in strange confusion, and bits of broken glass strewed the floor.

A little picture was lying on the ground. The king picked it up, and recognized a miniature of

WORDS TO KNOW **malicious** (mə-lĭsh'əs) *adj.* spiteful; nasty

Customizing Instruction

Students Acquiring English

1 Explain to students that "when the decree went forth against him" refers to the moment when the king knew he was going to die.

Less Proficient Readers

2 Students may not understand why the king does not go to see his wife. Explain that *unnerved* means "made nervous or upset." Then ask them why he decides to postpone his visit until he is restored to life.

Possible Response: He does not want to see her upset over his death; he wants to see her ecstatic over his return.

Mini Lesson Informal Assessment

SUMMARIZING You can informally assess students' understanding of the story so far by having them write a summary of what they have read. Remind students that a summary is a shortened retelling of a text that leaves out all but the most important information. A summary also includes main ideas and supporting details. Then have students summarize "The King is Dead, Long Live the King" from the beginning to "Surely Amyas was not dead of grief?" on p. 891.

RUBRIC

3 **Full Accomplishment** Summary contains all important ideas and details and none of superfluous information.

2 **Substantial Accomplishment** Summary contains most of important ideas and details from selection and little or none of superfluous information.

1 **Little or Partial Accomplishment** Summary contains little or none of important information from passage and consists mostly of superfluous information.

Reading and Analyzing

Literary Analysis: FOLKTALE

Tell students that this story has several elements that are common to folktales. Ask them to find in the story examples of the following folktale elements.

- The number three is important.
  Possible Response: The king has to find three people who want him alive again.
- Supernatural forces are in evidence.
  Possible Response: A voice tells the king he might live again; he is able to visit his kingdom for an hour after his death.
- A bargain is made.
  Possible Response: If the king finds three people who want him alive again, he can go back to his previous existence as the king.

Literary Analysis
SITUATIONAL IRONY

A Draw students' attention to the passage in which the king is still looking for the second person who wants him alive and visits the part of the kingdom where he likely became ill. He expects to find many people there who will want him alive, even though "the houses were as wretched as ever, [and] the people looked as sickly and squalid as ever." What might be considered ironic about this situation?
Possible Responses: The king expects gratitude from the people, even though conditions there are as bad as ever; the people don't appreciate the fact that he is dying because he had visited the poorest sections often—something "remarkable" for a king.

himself, the frame of which had been broken in the fall. He let it drop again, as if it had burnt him. The fire was blazing brightly, and the fragments of a half-destroyed letter lay, unconsumed as yet, in the fender.[3] It was in his own writing. He snatched it up, and saw it was the last he had written, containing the details of an elaborate scheme which he had much at heart. He had only just thrown it back into the flames when two people entered the room, talking together, one a lady, the other a man, booted and spurred as though he came from a long distance.

"Where is Amyas?" he asked.

"Gone to proffer[4] his services to the new king, of course," said the lady. "We are, as you may think, in great anxiety. He has none of the ridiculous notions of his predecessor,[5] who, indeed, hated him cordially. The very favor Amyas has hitherto enjoyed will stand in his way at the new court. I only hope he may be in time to make his peace. He can, with trust, say that he utterly disapproved of the foolish reforms which his late master was bent on making. Of course, he was fond of him in a way; but we must think of ourselves, you know. People in our position have no time for sentiment. He started almost immediately after the king's death. I am sending his retinue[6] after him."

"Quite right," said the gentleman, whom the king now knew as one of his ambassadors. "I shall follow him at once. Between you and me, it is no bad thing for the country. That poor boy had no notion of statesmanship. He forced me to conclude a peace which would have been disastrous to all our best interests. Happily, we shall have war directly now. Promotions in the army would have been at a standstill if he had had his way."

The king did not stay to hear more.

"I will go to my people," he said. "They at least have no interest to make peace with my successor. He will but take from them what I gave."

He heard the clock strike the first quarter as he went. He was, indeed, a very remarkable king, for he knew his way to the poorest part of his dominions. He had been there before, often and often, unknown to any one; and the misery which he had there beheld had stirred and steeled him to attempt what had never before been attempted.

No one about the palace knew where he had caught the malignant fever which carried him off. He had a shrewd suspicion himself, and he went straight to that quarter.

"Fevers won't hurt me now," he said laughing. **A** The houses were as wretched, the people looked as sickly and squalid[7] as ever. They were standing about in knots in the streets, late though it was, talking together about him. His name was in every mouth. The details of his illness, and the probable day of his funeral, seemed to interest them more than anything else.

Five or six men were sitting drinking round a table in a disreputable-looking public-house,[8] and he stopped to overhear their conversation.

"And a good riddance, too!" said one of

3. **fender:** a short metal screen in front of a fireplace.
4. **proffer** (prŏf′ər): to offer for acceptance.
5. **predecessor:** the former holder of an office or position.
6. **retinue** (rĕt′n-o͞o′): a group of attendants; entourage.
7. **squalid** (skwŏl′ĭd): dirty and wretched from poverty or lack of care.
8. **public-house:** tavern.

WORDS TO KNOW
sentiment (sĕn′tə-mənt) *n.* tender or nostalgic feeling
malignant (mə-lĭg′nənt) *adj.* extremely harmful

Teaching Options

Mini Lesson: Speaking and Listening

CREATE A DIALOGUE

Instruction Ask students to imagine that the king could travel with Amyas on part of the journey to the new king's residence.

Prepare Have them write a dialogue between the old king and Amyas. Arrange students in small groups, and have them read their dialogues to one another.

Present Ask each group to respond to each of its dialogues by telling what they think the dialogue says about the relationship between Amyas and the king.

BLOCK SCHEDULING This activity is particularly well-suited for longer class periods.

Romance (about 1924), Maxfield Parrish. Cover lining for *The Knave of Hearts* by Louise Saunders, oil on panel, courtesy of New York Graphic Society Ltd. Photo by Allen Photography.

them, whom he knew well. "What's the use of a king as never spends a farthing more than he can  help? It gives no impetus[9] to trade, it don't. The new fellow's a very different sort. We shall have fine doings soon."

"Ay!" struck in another, "a meddlesome, priggish[10] sort of chap, he was, always aworritting us about clean houses, and such like. What right's he got to interfere, I'd like to know?"

"Down with all kings! says I," put in a third: "but if we're to have 'em, let 'em behave as sich. I like a young fellow as isn't afraid of his missus, and knows port wine from sherry."

"Wanted to abolish capital punishment, he did!" cried a fourth. "Thought he'd get more work out of the poor fellows in prison, I suppose? Depend on it, there's some reason like that at the bottom of it. We ain't so very particular about the lives of our subjects for nothing, we ain't"; an expression of opinion in which all the rest heartily concurred. The clock struck again as the king turned away; he felt as if a storm of abuse from some one he had always hated would be a precious balm[11] just then. He entered the state prison, and made for the condemned cell. Capital punishment was not abolished yet, and in this particular instance he had certainly felt glad of it.

9. **impetus** (ĭm′pĭ-təs): incentive; stimulus.
10. **priggish:** irritatingly concerned with proper behavior.
11. **balm:** something that soothes, heals, or comforts.

Customizing Instruction

Students Acquiring English

1 Explain to students that the common people in this story speak in dialect. Point out that they use incorrect verb agreement ("it don't"; "says I") and some nonstandard vocabulary. Make sure that students understand the following words:

- ay *(yes)*
- chap *(fellow, person)*
- aworritting *(worrying)*
- sich *(such)*

Less Proficient Readers

Ask students to restate the common people's complaints about the king in their own words.

Possible Responses: The king didn't create opportunities for workers and merchants by spending lavishly; he meddled in their lives by trying to get them to clean their houses; he was dominated by his queen; he wanted to get more work out of convicts by abolishing the death penalty.

Mini Lesson Viewing and Representing

Romance **by Maxfield Parrish**

ART APPRECIATION

Instruction A creator of imaginary kingdoms, Maxfield Parrish (1870–1966) has been called one of the most successful American painters of the early 20th century. Many of his paintings focus on mythological heroes, classical women, and lush landscapes.

Application Have students analyze the following elements to determine how they contribute to the painting's romantic feel.

- light and shadow
  Possible Response: The way the light falls on the tower in contrast with the shadows below makes the tower look majestic.
- perspective
  Possible Response: The distance from which the scene is painted places the castle and village in the context of the dramatic landscape and makes them less real and more appealing.
- line and texture
  Possible Response: The irregular surfaces of the tumbled boulders contrasts with the straight lines of the tower to give it a greater appearance of majesty.

Reading and Analyzing

Literary Analysis: CHARACTERIZATION

Remind students that writers build character in a number of ways: by showing the character's actions, words, and thoughts; by having the narrator make direct remarks about the character; and by having other characters say things that provide their perspective on the character. Ask students to find an example of each of these techniques in the story.

Possible Responses: The king's actions, words, and thoughts help characterize him when he cannot find his friend Amyas and thinks Amyas might be "dead of grief"; the narrator describes the king as "remarkable" for visiting the poor quarters; other characters provide their perspectives on the king when the men in the poor quarters describe him as someone who "never spends a farthing more than he can help."

Reading Skills and Strategies: RECORDING DETAILS

A Remind students that the details the narrator provides are important to the judgments readers make about the story's events and characters. Ask students to find telling details in the scene with the condemned man.

Possible Responses: "little haggard man"; the fact that he is writing with the paper on his knee; the man's fear of looking like a coward; the tone of the councillor's voice; the man's stunned look; the man's gesture of passing his hand across his brow; the tears in the man's eyes.

A The cell was tenanted only by a little haggard[12] looking man, who was writing busily on his knee. The king had only seen him once before, and he looked at him curiously.

Presently, the jailer entered, and with him the first councillor, a man whom his late master had greatly loved and esteemed. The convict looked up quickly.

"It was not to be till to-morrow," he said. Then, as if afraid he had betrayed some cowardice, "but I am ready at any moment. May I ask you to give this paper to my wife?"

"The king is dead," said the first councillor gravely. "You are reprieved. His present majesty has other views. You will, in all probability, be set at large to-morrow."

"Dead?" said the man with a stunned look.

"Dead!" said the first councillor, with the impressiveness of a whole board.

The man stood up, passing his hand across his brow.

"Sir," he said earnestly, "I respected him. For all he was a king, he treated me like a gentleman. He, too, had a young wife. Poor fellow, I wish he were alive again!"

There were tears in the man's eyes as he spoke.

The third quarter struck as the king left the prison. He felt unutterably humiliated. The pity of his foe was harder to bear than the scorn of his friends. He would rather have died a thousand deaths than owe his life to

> ALL AT ONCE A SENSE OF LONELINESS THAT CANNOT BE DESCRIBED RUSHED OVER HIM, AND HIS HEART SANK

such a man. And yet, because he was himself noble, he could not but rejoice to find nobility in another. He said to himself sternly that it was not worth what he had gone through. He reviewed his position in no very self-complacent[13] mood. The affection he had so confidently relied upon was but a dream. The people he was fain[14] to work for were not ripe for their own improvement. A foolish little child, a generous enemy, these were his only friends. After all, was it worth while to live? Had he not better go back quietly and submit, making no further effort? He had learnt his lesson; he could "lie down in peace, and sleep, and take his rest." The eternal powers had justified themselves. What matter though every man had proved a liar? The bitterness had passed away, and he seemed to see clearly.

Thick clouds had gathered over the moon, and the cold struck through him. All at once a sense of loneliness that cannot be described rushed over him, and his heart sank. Was there really no one who cared—no one? He would have given anything at that moment for a look, a single word of real sympathy. He longed with sick longing for the assurance of love.

There were yet a few moments left. How had he borne to wait so long? This, at least, he was sure of, and this was all the world to him. He began to find comfort and consolation in the thought; he forgave—indeed he almost forgot—

12. **haggard:** worn and exhausted in appearance.
13. **self-complacent:** self-satisfied; smug.
14. **fain:** ready and willing.

WORDS TO KNOW
presently (prĕz′ənt-lē) *adv.* in a short time; soon
reprieve (rĭ-prēv′) *v.* to cancel a punishment

894

Teaching Options

Mini Lesson Vocabulary Strategy

PREFIXES AND SUFFIXES

Instruction Remind students that many words are made up of a root word in addition to a prefix and/or suffix. Ask students to try to identify the prefixes, suffixes, and roots and their meanings in the words below:

- **unutterably**
  Answer: un, "not" + utter, "speak" + able + ly, adverb suffix
- **reviewed**
  Answer: re, "again" + view, "look at"
- **bitterness**
  Answer: bitter, "resentful, disappointed" + ness, "quality of being"
- **bereavement**
  Answer: bereave, "to cause to be sad or lonely" + ment, "state of being"

Use **Vocabulary Transparencies and Copymasters,** p. 46.

the rest. Yet he had fallen very low, for, as he stood at the door of his wife's room, he hesitated whether to go in. What if this, too, were an illusion? Had he not best go back before he knew?

"But I have never yet done anything through fear," said the king.

His wife was sitting by the fire alone, her face hidden, her long hair falling round her like a veil. At the first sight of her, a pang of self-reproach shot through him. How could he ever have doubted?

She was wearing a ring that he had given her—a ring she wore always, and the light sparkled and flashed from the jewel. Except for this, there was nothing bright in the room.

He ardently desired to comfort her. He wondered why all her ladies had left her. Surely one might have stayed with her on this first night of her bereavement?[15] She seemed to be lost in thought. If she would only speak, or call his name! But she was quite silent.

A slight noise made the king start. A secret door in the wall opened, the existence of which he had thought was known only to himself and his queen, and a man stood before her.

She put her finger to her lips, as though to counsel silence, and then threw herself into his arms.

"You have come," she said— "Oh, I am so glad! I had to hold his hand when he was dying. I was frightened sitting here by myself. I thought his ghost would come back, but he will never come back any more. We may be happy always now," and drawing the ring from her finger, she kissed it, weeping, and gave it to him.

When midnight struck, the watchers wakened with a start, to find the king lying stark and stiff, as before, but a great change had come over his countenance.[16]

"We must not let the queen see him again," they said. ❖

15. **bereavement:** the loss of a loved one to death.

16. **countenance:** face.

Customizing Instruction

Multiple Learning Styles

Visual or Kinesthetic Learners

The king's attitude toward his friends and subjects changes greatly during the story. Assume that as the king lies in bed, the expression on his face changes to reflect each change in his attitude toward his friends and subjects. Have students work in small groups to record the changing expressions, by creating a series of masks, illustrations, photographs, or other representations of the dead king's face. Let the class decide which series most closely captures their mental image of the scene.

Less Proficient Readers

Have students record the king's changing attitudes (described in the Multiple Learning Styles option above) by writing two contrasting poems. Suggest that students pretend they are the king and brainstorm words for two lists. One list should describe how he feels before he sets out on his mission, and the other should describe how he feels after he returns. After students have completed their lists, they can use them to create two "I am" poems. Each line of the poem begins with the words "I am" and ends with a word, or words, from their lists. After their poems are finished, students can present them to the class.

Informal Assessment

WRITING EPITAPHS Ask students to imagine that they are the king's wife or Amyas. Have them write epitaphs that could have been written by the king's wife or Amyas. Have students consider what each person would say about the king. If they have difficulty, suggest they consider the following questions:

- How does each person feel about the king? How do you know?
- What would a queen want her subjects to think of her? Would she be likely to reveal her true feelings?
- Now that someone else is king, what kind of position is Amyas in? Is he apt to praise the former ruler highly?

RUBRIC

3 Full Accomplishment Epitaphs are well thought out and reflect what each person would say about king.

2 Substantial Accomplishment Epitaphs do not entirely reflect what each person would say about king.

1 Little or Partial Accomplishment Epitaphs do not at all reflect what characters would say about king.

GUIDING STUDENT RESPONSE

Connect to the Literature

1. **What Do You Think?**
   Guidelines for student response: Accept all reasonable opinions for which students can provide evidence in the text.

Comprehension Check
- three people who wish he were alive
- the child and his enemy
- She is unfaithful.

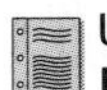
Use Selection Quiz in **Unit Five Resource Book,** p. 23

Think Critically

2. Accept all reasonable responses. Have students give examples of the predictions they made and the kinds of evidence the predictions were based on.
3. Possible Response: The king was a good man. He considers himself someone who did good things for his subjects, and he seems to have been considering reforms that would have benefited the poor. He wants to live so that he can carry out his reforms. His subjects complain about him, but it is clear from their complaints that he was acting for their good.
4. Possible Responses: desperately unhappy; enraged; bewildered. At the end of the first section, the queen announces at his death, "How beautiful he looks." His expression is fearful, then, because it is the opposite of that—something that reflects what he has seen and learned in his hour.
5. Whether students believe the view of human nature coveyed by the story is cynical or realistic, they should be able to find evidence in the text to support their opinions.

Literary Analysis

Cooperative Learning Activity As students discuss the plot development, ask them to identify the story's conflict and how it was addressed and resolved.

Connect to the Literature

1. **What Do You Think?** What did you like best about this story? What did you like least?

Comprehension Check
- What must the king find in the one hour after his death?
- Which two people want him to live?
- What startling discovery does the king make about the queen?

Think Critically

2. ACTIVE READING **PREDICTING** Look over the **predictions** you made about the story in your READER'S NOTEBOOK. How accurate were they? What evidence was most important in making accurate predictions?

3. In your opinion, what kind of person was the king?

- his view of himself and others
- the reason he wants to live
- the reforms he tried to promote during his life
- what others say about him

4. The narrator does not describe the expression on the king's face at the end of the story. How do you think he looks? Give reasons for your response.

5. What view of human nature does the story convey? Do you think this view is overly pessimistic or simply realistic? Cite evidence to support your opinion.

Extend Interpretations

6. **Comparing Texts** Compare and contrast the quest in this story with the knight's quest in "The Wife of Bath's Tale" by Geoffrey Chaucer (page 154). In what ways are the circumstances of the two quests similar and different? How do the outcomes of the quests compare?

7. **What If?** Suppose the king found three people who wanted him to live—and then visited his wife. Do you think he would have chosen to live? Why or why not?

8. **Connect to Life** How do you think people today regard their leaders? Do you think people generally support their elected officials, or do people tend to be cynically suspicious of the leaders' motivations?

Literary Analysis

SITUATIONAL IRONY In **situational irony,** the character or the reader expects one thing to happen, but something else actually occurs. Coleridge's story is filled with situational irony. For example, the king expects Amyas, his closest friend, to be saddened by his death. Instead he finds that Amyas is already busy trying to win favor with the new monarch. On the other hand, the king expects his jailed enemy to be gleeful about his death, but instead he overhears his enemy expressing regret.

Cooperative Learning Activity With a small group of classmates, create a chart like the one below and list the ironic situations in the story. Then discuss the following questions: What do the king's overturned expectations suggest about his relationship with other characters? How does the title help underscore the irony?

Expected Situation	Actual Situation
Amyas mourns king's death.	Amyas is preoccupied with flattering new monarch.

REVIEW **PLOT** As you know, the **plot** in a narrative usually includes the following stages: **exposition, rising action, climax,** and **falling action.** Create a graph in which you identify these stages in "The King Is Dead, Long Live the King."

Extend Interpretations

Comparing Texts Possible Response: The quests are the same in that they both begin because of the protagonist's mistaken idea—the knight's idea that youth and beauty are important, and the king's idea that he was loved by all. Both protagonists are given a set amount of time to complete their quests, and both will die if they fail. The quests are different in that the knight's quest is given to him by a human being, while the king's quest comes from a supernatural being. The quests' outcomes are similar in that both wives turn out to be the opposite of what the protagonists had thought they were, but they are fundamentally different in that the king dies disillusioned, while the knight finds himself married to a lovely and faithful woman.

What If? Accept all reasonable, well-supported answers.

Connect to Life Accept all reasonable, well-supported answers.

Writing Options

1. **Letter from Amyas** Write a letter in which Amyas declares his allegiance to the new king and denounces the dead king.
2. **Obituaries for the King** Compose three obituaries for the king. Write each one from the standpoint of a different character in the story.

Activities & Explorations

Dramatic Scene With a group of classmates, dramatize a scene from the story. Rehearse your scene and then present it to the class.
~ PERFORMING

Inquiry & Research

Long Live the Queen Research the laws of succession for English monarchs, and then study Queen Victoria's ascension to the throne. Use an abbreviated family tree or another graphic to demonstrate how Queen Victoria came to succeed her uncle, William IV.

More Online: Research Starter
www.mcdougallittell.com

Vocabulary in Action

EXERCISE: MEANING CLUES For each boldfaced word, choose the topic in which the word might be used in a discussion

1. **malicious**
a. the king's enemy
b. the king's friend
c. a small child

2. **sentiment**
a. the moat of a castle
b. building a castle
c. admiration for the king

3. **malignant**
a. the queen's maid
b. the king's advisers
c. a deadly disease

4. **presently**
a. winning a war
b. waiting for a doctor's arrival
c. an ancient law

5. **reprieve**
a. a prisoner facing execution
b. a newly appointed minister
c. a royal banner

Mary E. Coleridge
1861–1907

Other Works
Gathered Leaves
The Collected Poems of Mary Coleridge

A Literary Life Although she never achieved the fame of her ancestor, Mary Coleridge was a talented writer in a variety of literary forms, including novels, short stories, poetry, and essays. Born in London, Coleridge received an excellent education at home and, according to one of her friends, could read French, Italian, German, and Hebrew by the time she was 19 years old. Her father was a well-read lawyer who often entertained noted authors, including the poets Tennyson and Browning. Coleridge herself studied both literature and philosophy, eventually obtaining a job as an instructor of English literature at the Working Women's College, a position she held for the last 12 years of her life. She never married and lived with her family until her death at age 45.

A Retiring Writer Coleridge did not publish her first major work until she was in her 30s. Although her first novel, *The Seven Sleepers of Ephesus,* was not generally well received, it was praised by Robert Louis Stevenson, and several of Coleridge's subsequent novels became quite popular. In addition, she regularly contributed stories and essays to various journals, including *Cornhill Magazine* and the *Times Literary Supplement.* As a poet, she was reluctant to publish, or even talk about, her own work. At the urging of a family friend—the poet Robert Bridges—she eventually allowed two small collections of her poems to be published under the pseudonym Anodos. The rest were not made public until after her death. Bridges said of her poems, "They are both beautiful and original, and often exhibit imagination of a very rare kind, conveyed by the identical expression of true feeling and artistic insight."

Writing Options

1. **Letter from Amyas** Before they start, have students review the story for negative things that Amyas could say about the old king.
2. **Obituaries for the King** Make sure students choose characters with different views of the king.

Activities & Explorations

Dramatic Scene To extend the activity, have students write a newspaper style review of the performance. Remind them of the following criteria:
- identifies its subject at the beginning
- open with a general opinion
- includes enough facts, examples, and specifics to support the general opinion
- displays logical organization
- clearly establishes a tone

Have students exchange their reviews and analyze them according to the above criteria. Then have them compare the reviews to their own response.

Inquiry & Research

Long Live the Queen As an alternate activity, have students find out which countries still have monarchies. How many are currently headed by queens or empresses, and how many by kings or emperors?

Vocabulary in Action

1. a
2. c
3. c
4. b
5. a

Mini Lesson Grammar

Correct Use of *That* and *Which*

Instruction Writers are often confused about whether to use *that* or *which* to introduce a clause. The key to choosing the correct pronoun is to decide whether the clause is essential—necessary to the meaning of the sentence—or nonessential. Essential clauses begin with *that.* Nonessential clauses begin with *which* and are set off by commas.

Activity Write the following pair of sentences on the chalkboard. Ask students to combine the pair using an essential or nonessential clause beginning with *that* or *which.*

The king saw a secret meeting between his wife and her lover. It finally destroyed the king's will to live.

Possible Response: It was the secret meeting between his wife and her lover that finally destroyed the king's will to live. (clause essential to meaning of sentence, introduced by "that")

Use **Grammar Transparencies and Copymasters,** p. 830.

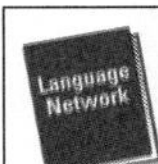
Use McDougal Littell's ***Language Network*** for more instruction and practice in *that* and *which.*

George Eliot's realistic novels of rural life are imbued with a moral seriousness of the sort found in the works of the French novelist Gustave Flaubert and the Russian novelists Leo Tolstoy and Feodor Dostoyevsky.

Additional Background

GEORGE ELIOT

Born in 1819, Mary Ann Evans was raised in an evangelical Methodist family in Warwickshire. Though she rebelled against organized religion in her youth, she retained throughout her life a deep moral sense that found expression in her fiction. When she was 15 years old, her mother died and she left school, undertaking the bulk of the household responsibilities in her family.

Evans began her literary career with an 1846 translation of a German work on the life of Jesus. In 1851, she moved to London and became an assistant editor of the magazine *Westminster Review.* Soon Evans had become acquainted with a number of literary and intellectual figures, including Dickens, John Stuart Mill, Herbert Spencer—and George Henry Lewes, a writer and editor who was separated from his wife. Falling in love, Evans and Lewes lived together unmarried, an arrangement that caused them to be ostracized by much of British society. (Because of certain circumstances, Lewes could not obtain a divorce from his wife under English law.)

Of the shift in her career a few years later, Evans wrote, "September 1856 made a new era in my life, for it was then I began to write fiction." Lewes encouraged Evans to take a male pseudonym for her writing. Evans took "George" from Lewes's name and created "Eliot" with the idea that it was "a good, mouth-filling, easily pronounced word." However, "George Eliot" was never more than Evans's writing name; no one ever called her "Miss Eliot," much less "George."

Evans and Lewes supported themselves and Lewes's three children by writing, so it was fortunate that the Eliot novels were immediately successful with the public. Lewes died in 1878, and in 1880 Evans surprised her friends by marrying John Walter Cross, a man more than 20 years younger than herself. Evans had been ill for much of 1879, and seven months after the wedding, in a weakened condition, she developed pneumonia and died a few days later.

MILESTONES IN BRITISH LITERATURE

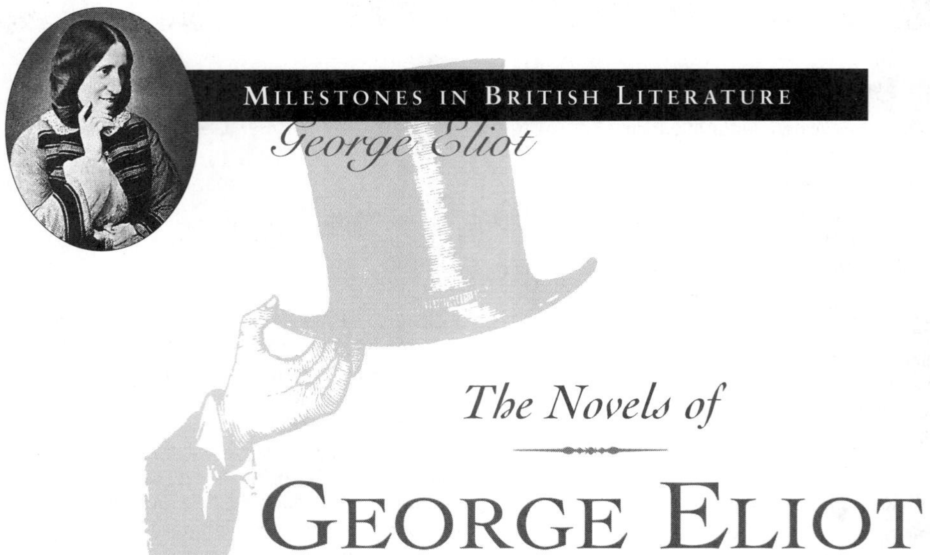

The Novels of GEORGE ELIOT

Who is George Eliot? This question tantalized the literary world and tormented townspeople throughout 1858, the year John Blackwood published Eliot's two-volume *Scenes of Clerical Life.* Critics admired the work; literary figures discussed it; Warwickshire residents were shocked to recognize themselves in print. Then, in 1859, when Blackwood published a novel by Eliot, *Adam Bede,* the rumors fairly flew. Celebrities clamored to know the author, whom critics declared one of the "masters of the art." Townspeople searched for and found a local man to promote as Eliot unmasked.

Meanwhile, the true author, Mary Ann Evans, and her partner George Lewes were doing all they could to keep people off the track. When Blackwood guessed Eliot's identity, she begged him to keep the secret, and he agreed. Evans wanted her work to be judged on its merits, not on the basis of its author's gender. However, the similarities between her characters and real-life people and places made continued anonymity nearly impossible. Within two years, the secret was out.

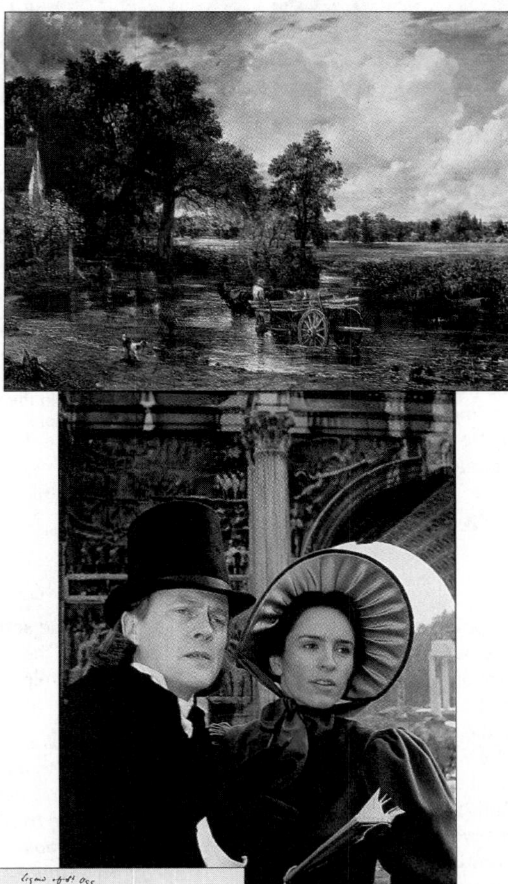

Armed with knowledge of Eliot's gender, critics reexamined her work and found it deeply immoral. One critic even accused George Eliot of destroying "all comfortable notions of right and wrong, true and false." These complaints distressed Eliot, but she had this consolation: although Mary Ann Evans's reviews were terrible, George Eliot's had been good. It's little wonder, therefore, that she retained her pen name.

The complaining critics seem to have been unable to see that Eliot's novels actually have a strong moral tone. In *The Mill on the Floss,* for example, a sister rejected by her judgmental brother nevertheless saves his life at the cost of her own. In *Silas Marner,* an alienated miser adopts a foundling and gains for himself both love and redemption. In *Middlemarch,* one of the greatest novels of the 19th century, a woman who must choose between security and love gives up everything—and finds that she is glad she did. These heroes, torn by conflicting desires, struggle mightily to do what's right, and whether or not they succeed, good always wins in the end.

Now that Eliot's gender is not an issue, critics and readers alike enjoy the power and suspense of her novels. She has become respected and admired for the unfailing idealism and tough realism she showed both in her novels and in her life.

Top:
"My new story," wrote Eliot in 1857, "will be a country story—full of the breath of the cows and the scent of hay." Adam Bede *richly celebrates the vanishing world of the rural community, as depicted by John Constable in his painting* The Hay Wain. The Hay Wain, *(1821) John Constable. National Gallery, London/Bridgeman Art Library, London/Superstock.*
Above:
Scene from the production of Middlemarch *broadcast by PBS in 1994*
Left:
Manuscript page of "Legend of St. Ogg"

LITERARY CHRONOLOGY
The following are publication dates of George Eliot's most important works.

1858 *Scenes of Clerical Life*

1859 *Adam Bede*

1860 *The Mill on the Floss*

1861 *Silas Marner*

1863 *Romola*

1866 *Felix Holt, the Radical*

1872 *Middlemarch*

1876 *Daniel Deronda*

MILESTONES IN BRITISH LITERATURE 899

OVERVIEW

Objectives

1. understand and appreciate a **short story** set in India **(Literary Analysis)**
2. recognize and understand the importance of **setting (Literary Analysis)**
3. **analyze details** in a short story **(Active Reading)**

Summary

Purun Dass, the Brahmin prime minister of an Indian state, establishes schools and railways, improves agriculture, and embraces the English way of life. He gains honor and fame, is knighted, and wins the Grand Cross of the Star of India. At the height of his success, he resigns his position, palace, and power. He renames himself Purun Bhagat, takes up a begging bowl, wanders into the Himalayas, and settles at a deserted shrine. Nearby villagers fill his begging bowl, and the mountain animals become his friends. One stormy night a *langur* and a *barasingh* (stag) come and nudge Purun Bhagat until he understands that the mountain is collapsing. Helped by the animals, Purun hurries into the valley and leads 70 villagers to safety. That night, he dies. The villagers build him a temple and worship him; no one knows that he was once the prime minister who promoted Western ways.

Use **Unit Five Resource Book,** p. 25 for additional support.

Thematic Link

Purun Dass gives up his **personal relationships** when he gives up his post, his power, and his wealth. The new relationships he finds are unusual ones—his closest friends are animals.

5-Minute Warm-Up

Daily Language SkillBuilder

Have students **proofread** the display sentences on page 829j and write them correctly. The sentences also appear on Transparency 23 of **Grammar Transparencies and Copymasters.**

PREPARING to *Read*

The Miracle of Purun Bhagat

Short Story by RUDYARD KIPLING

Comparing Literature of the World

"The Miracle of Purun Bhagat" and "What Men Live By"

This lesson and the one that follows present an opportunity for comparing the moral teachings that can be inferred in Rudyard Kipling's story "The Miracle of Purun Bhagat" with those that can be inferred in Leo Tolstoy's story "What Men Live By." Specific points of comparison in the Tolstoy lesson will help you note similarities and differences in the way each writer develops the moral teachings of his story.

Connect to Your Life

Changing Ways Do you know or have you read about someone who decided to change his or her life in a major way? Perhaps the person took a new job, moved, or married. What kinds of things did this person value most before and after the change in his or her lifestyle? Share your thoughts with your classmates.

Build Background

British India England's first settlements in India were trading posts established during the 1600s. Taking advantage of a weak Indian government, British agents were in control of India by 1774. Although Indian soldiers revolted against foreign rule in 1857, British forces successfully quelled the rebellion. Shortly thereafter, Queen Victoria appointed a viceroy to head India's government and to carry out the wishes of Parliament. Most Indian princes agreed to abide by British law, and government posts were given to a few Indians who supported the British presence. During the late 19th century, the British changed many of India's laws and constructed both railroad and telegraph systems to improve what they viewed as a primitive, or backward, civilization.

A number of British citizens moved to India during its years as a British colony. Among them were the parents of the writer Rudyard Kipling, who was born in India in 1865. Even as a child, Kipling was fascinated by Indian culture and values; later, he would vividly depict Indian life in his stories.

Most Indians are Hindus, and for them Hinduism is not only a religion but a way of life. Hindus are divided into castes, or social classes, and according to Hindu laws, a person can never leave the caste into which he or she is born. Each person's lifestyle—including eating habits, employment, and choice of friends and a marriage partner—is determined by his or her caste.

LaserLinks: Background for Reading
Historical Connection / Visual Vocabulary / Geographical Connection

Focus Your Reading

LITERARY ANALYSIS SETTING The **setting** of a story is the time and place of the action. Setting often plays an important role in a story's events.

> ***. . . he had held before him his dream of peace and quiet—the long, white, dusty Indian road, printed all over with bare feet, the incessant, slow-moving traffic, and the sharp-smelling wood-smoke curling up under the fig-trees in the twilight, where the wayfarers sat at their evening meal.***

As you read this story, be aware of the descriptions of setting and the interaction between the setting and the story's meaning.

ACTIVE READING ANALYZING DETAILS By including many vivid **details,** such as those in the above excerpt, Kipling creates for the reader a strong impression of the different characters, actions, and places in "The Miracle of Purun Bhagat."

READER'S NOTEBOOK As you read this story, notice scenes in the story that stand out vividly. Jot down specific details about the characters, actions, and places in two or three of these scenes.

LESSON RESOURCES

UNIT FIVE RESOURCE BOOK, pp. 25–28

ASSESSMENT RESOURCES
Formal Assessment, pp. 161–162
Teacher's Guide to Assessment and Portfolio Use
Test Generator

SKILLS TRANSPARENCIES AND COPYMASTERS
Literary Analysis
- Influences on Plot: Setting and Character, T19 (for Literary Analysis, p. 900)

Reading and Critical Thinking
- Noting Details, T9 (for Active Reading, p. 900)

Grammar
- Run-on Sentences, T43 (for Mini Lesson, pp. 904–905)
- Correcting Comma Splices, C159 (for Mini Lesson, pp. 904–905)

Writing
- Personality Profile, C25 (for Informal Assessment, p. 911)
- Subject Analysis, C30 (for Writing Option 2, p. 913)

Communications
- Impromptu Speaking: Dialogue, Role-Play, T14 (for Activities & Explorations 2, p. 913)

INTEGRATED TECHNOLOGY
Audio Library
LaserLinks
- Historical Connection: Kipling's India
- Visual Vocabulary
- Geographical Connection: Tibet and the Himalayas. See **Teacher's SourceBook,** p. 60.

Internet: Research Starter
Visit our website: www.mcdougallittell.com

THE MIRACLE OF

PURUN BHAGAT

RUDYARD KIPLING

There was once

a man in India

who was

Prime Minister

of one of the

semi-independent

native States

in the north-western

part of the country.

La coupe de mystère [The chalice of mystery] (1890), Odilon Redon. Oil on paper mounted on linen, 22½" × 14", collection of the Walker Art Center, Minneapolis, Minnesota, gift of Alexander M. Bing, 1953 (53.53).

901

TEACHING THE LITERATURE

Customizing Instruction

Less Proficient Readers

Set a Purpose Tell students that Purun Dass is a person of high standing in the Indian government. He has tried to help his kingdom "take up English progress"—to make it more English in a sense. Have students read to find out what surprising action Purun Dass takes.

Answer: He leaves his job and home and becomes a holy man.

Students Acquiring English

This selection may prove difficult because of both the many references to Indian culture and the relative lack of action. Have students listen to the audiotape, and focus their attention on the main thrust of the narrative: namely, Purun Dass was a powerful and successful Indian who adopted English ways; he gave up his old life to become a holy man.

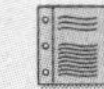 Use **Spanish Study Guide** for additional support, pp. 206–208.

Gifted and Talented

Ask students to consider the possibility that Purun Dass is only playing a "part" during most of his government service. Point out the reference in the first paragraph to "a difficult game" that he "played coolly." Ask students to read the selection with this possibility in mind. If they decide that they do not think he is "faking it" during his time in the government, ask them what they think does happen.

Mini Lesson Viewing and Representing

La coupe de mystère [The chalice of mystery]
by Odilon Redon

ART APPRECIATION Odilon Redon (1840–1916) is known as a Symbolist artist. During the 1890s, when he painted *La coupe de mystère,* Redon was becoming more concerned with spiritual themes.

Instruction Begin by noting that Redon chose the title *The Chalice of Mystery* for this painting. Then have students discuss how the painting might be considered mysterious, taking into account what a chalice is and what sorts of associations it carries.

Application Have students interpret the painting. Tell them to answer the following questions in their interpretations, citing specific details:

- Is the person a man or a woman?
- What is the person wearing?
- What, if anything, is in the bowl?
- What is the significance of the reddish-orange color on the person's shoulders?

Have students share their interpretations with classmates and discuss their differences and similarities.

TEACHING THE LITERATURE

Reading and Analyzing

Literary Analysis SETTING

Have students look for answers to the questions "when?" and "where?" as they read the selection. Encourage them to consider these questions as well:

- How does the setting affect Purun's decisions?
- How does the setting affect the reader's understanding of the story?
- How does the setting relate to the story's themes?
- When the setting changes, how does Purun change?

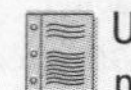 Use **Unit Five Resource Book,** p. 26 for additional support.

Active Reading ANALYZING DETAILS

To help students interpret the actions of Purun Dass, have them look for those details that provide insights into his motivation—and his relationships with the people around him. Have students consider the following questions as they read.

- What details tell us why Purun Dass is able to rise so high in the world?
- How is Purun Dass/Bhagat viewed by the English? by his fellow Indians?
- What effect do the vivid details have on them as readers?

 Use **Unit Five Resource Book,** p. 25 for additional support.

Literary Analysis: SIMILE

A Ask what effect this comparison of Purun Dass's old life to a cloak has on the reader.

Possible Response: It shows that being prime minister was not a personal matter; it shows that the old life has served its purpose and is over.

He was a Brahmin,[1] so high-caste that caste ceased to have any particular meaning for him; and his father had been an important official in the gay-colored tag-rag and bob-tail[2] of an old-fashioned Hindu Court. But as Purun Dass grew up he realized that the ancient order of things was changing, and that if any one wished to get on he must stand well with the English, and imitate all the English believed to be good. At the same time a native official must keep his own master's favor. This was a difficult game, but the quiet, close-mouthed young Brahmin, helped by a good English education at a Bombay University, played it coolly, and rose, step by step, to be Prime Minister of the kingdom. That is to say, he held more real power than his master, the Maharajah.[3]

When the old king—who was suspicious of the English, their railways and telegraphs—died, Purun Dass stood high with his young successor, who had been tutored by an Englishman; and between them, though he always took care that his master should have the credit, they established schools for little girls, made roads, and started State dispensaries[4] and shows of agricultural implements, and published a yearly blue-book on the "Moral and Material Progress of the State," and the Foreign Office and the Government of India were delighted. Very few native States take up English progress without reservations, for they will not believe, as Purun Dass showed he did, that what is good for the Englishman must be twice as good for the Asiatic. The Prime Minister became the honored friend of Viceroys[5] and Governors, and Lieutenant-Governors, and medical missionaries, and common missionaries, and hard-riding English officers who came to shoot in the State preserves, as well as of whole hosts of tourists who travelled up and down India in the cold weather, showing how things ought to be managed. In his spare time he would endow scholarships for the study of medicine and manufactures on strictly English lines, and write letters to the *Pioneer,* the greatest Indian daily paper, explaining his master's aims and objects.

At last he went to England on a visit, and had to pay enormous sums to the priests when he came back; for even so high-caste a Brahmin as Purun Dass lost caste by crossing the black sea. In London he met and talked with every one worth knowing—men whose names go all over the world—and saw a great deal more than he said. He was given honorary degrees by learned universities, and he made speeches and talked of Hindu social reform to English ladies in evening dress, till all London cried, "This is the most fascinating man we have ever met at dinner since cloths were first laid!" **1**

When he returned to India there was a blaze of glory, for the Viceroy himself made a special visit to confer upon the Maharajah the Grand Cross of the Star of India—all diamonds and ribbons and enamel; and at the same ceremony, while the cannon boomed, Purun Dass was made a Knight Commander of the Order of the Indian Empire; so that his name stood Sir Purun Dass, K.C.I.E.

That evening at dinner in the big Viceregal[6] tent he stood up with the badge and the collar of the Order on his breast, and replying to the toast of his master's health, made a speech that few Englishmen could have surpassed.

Next month, when the city had returned to its sun-baked quiet, he did a thing no Englishman would have dreamed of doing, for, so far as the world's affairs went, he died. The jeweled order of his knighthood returned to the Indian Government, and a new Prime Minister was appointed to the charge of affairs, and a great game of General Post[7] began in all the subordinate

1. **Brahmin:** a member of the highest Hindu caste.
2. **tag-rag and bob-tail:** a phrase meaning "a diverse and disorderly assemblage of people."
3. **Maharajah** (mä′hə-rä′jə): an Indian king or prince.
4. **dispensaries:** medical clinics.
5. **Viceroys** (vīs′roiz′): officials ruling as representatives of the sovereign.
6. **Viceregal** (vīs-rē′gəl): belonging to the viceroy.
7. **General Post:** a game in which, at a summons, all players change places.

Teaching Options

BLOCK SCHEDULING: MANAGING TIME

If your schedule requires that you cover the lesson objectives in a shorter time, use . . .

- Preparing to Read, p. 900
- Thinking Through the Literature, p. 912

If you want to take advantage of longer class time, use . . .

- TE Teaching Options: Vocabulary, p. 908; Viewing and Representing, pp. 901, 909; Speaking and Listening, p. 910; Cross Curricular Links, p. 903; Informal Assessment, p. 911; Standardized Test Practice, p. 907; Grammar, p. 904
- Choices & Challenges, p. 913

appointments. The priests knew what had happened and the people guessed; but India is the one place in the world where a man can do as he pleases and nobody asks why; and the fact that Dewan Sir Purun Dass, K.C.I.E., had resigned position, palace, and power, and taken up the begging-bowl
2 and ochre-colored dress of a Sunnyasi[8] or holy man, was considered nothing extraordinary. He had been, as the Old Law recommends, twenty years a youth, twenty years a fighter—though he had never carried a weapon in his life—and twenty years head of a household. He had used his wealth and his power for what he knew both to be worth; he had taken honor when it came his way; he had seen men and cities far and near, and men and cities had stood up and honored him. Now he would let these things go, as
A a man drops the cloak he needs no longer.

> NOW HE WOULD LET THESE THINGS GO, AS A MAN DROPS THE CLOAK HE NEEDS NO LONGER.

Behind him, as he walked through the city gates, an antelope skin and brass-handled crutch under his arm, and a begging-bowl of polished brown *coco-de-mer*[9] in his hand, barefoot, alone, with eyes cast on the ground—behind him they were firing salutes from the bastions[10] in honor of his happy successor. Purun Dass nodded. All that life was ended; and he bore it no more ill-will or good-will than a man bears to a colorless dream of the night. He was a Sunnyasi—a houseless, wandering mendicant,[11] depending on his neighbors for his daily bread; and so long as there is a morsel to divide in India neither priest nor beggar starves. He had never in his life tasted meat, and very seldom eaten even fish. A five-pound note would have covered his personal expenses for food through any one of the many years in which he had been absolute master of millions of money. Even when he was being lionized[12] in London he had held before him his dream of peace and quiet—the long, white, dusty Indian road, printed all over with bare feet, the incessant, slow-moving traffic, and the sharp-smelling wood-smoke curling up under the fig-trees in the twilight, where the wayfarers sat at their evening meal.

When the time came to make that dream true the Prime Minister took the proper steps, and in three days you might more easily have found a bubble in the trough of the long Atlantic seas than Purun Dass among the roving, gathering, separating millions of India.

8. **Sunnyasi** (sŭn-yä′sē).
9. ***coco-de-mer*** (kō′kō-də-mâr′): the shell of a huge nut, resembling two joined coconut shells.
10. **bastions:** projecting parts of a fortification.
11. **mendicant** (mĕn′dĭ-kənt): beggar.
12. **lionized:** treated as a celebrity.

Customizing Instruction

Less Proficient Readers

Check students' understanding with the following questions.

- Who holds more real power, Purun Dass or the Maharajah?
  Answer: Purun Dass.
- What does Purun Dass decide to do after serving as prime minister for many years?
  Answer: He decides to become a holy man.
- What possessions does Purun Dass bring with him when he leaves the city?
  Answer: He brings an antelope skin, a brass-handled crutch, and a begging bowl.

Students Acquiring English

1 Help students understand the phrase "cloths were first laid." Explain that this is a reference to tablecloths being laid on the table—a custom which began long ago. The English ladies are saying that Purun Dass is "the most fascinating man" they have met in years.

2 Show students an ochre-colored object so that they understand that Purun is wearing an orange robe.

Multiple Learning Styles

Visual Learners

Discuss the details of Purun Dass's departure with students—his clothing and possessions, the celebration happening behind him, the dusty road with bare footprints all over it, the travelers sitting around fires under the fig trees. Then, have students sketch the scene. Encourage them to sketch other scenes in the story to help them get a better feel for the setting.

History

EAST INDIA COMPANY

The British East India Company was formed to establish British trade with India. Its first ship reached the Continent in 1608. The English had to compete with the Dutch and the French for Indian trade, and before long the East India Company was empowered to raise its own army and issue its own money. For some time, the main conflict in India was between the English and the French, with Muslim rulers backing each side. Soon, however, the English had the real power in several Indian states, with the Indian or Muslim rulers keeping only the appearance of authority. At last this pretense was dropped, and the East India Company was transformed from a commercial enterprise to a government. In 1858, Parliament passed a bill that transferred the control of India from the East India Company to Queen Victoria.

THE MIRACLE OF PURUN BHAGAT 903

Reading and Analyzing

ACTIVE READING

A ANALYZE **Possible Response:** "mud pillar shrine," "the pitch of the bare grazing-grounds where the flame of his stick fire waked the drowsy camels," "dried bed of the Gugger river."

ACTIVE READING

B CLARIFY **Possible Responses:** Purun Bhagat is seeking the Law of life or happiness; he is searching for inner peace.

Literary Analysis: FIGURATIVE LANGUAGE

C The mountain is compared to a person who is wearing a patchwork apron. Ask students to define patchwork.
Answer: pieces of cloth sewn together.
Then ask them to explain the simile.
Possible Response: He is very far away, and the buildings and fields look like pieces of fabric.

Literary Analysis SETTING

D Ask students what effect is created by this vivid description of Purun Bhagat's country.
Possible Response: It emphasizes the majesty and remoteness of the area in which he is settling.

ACTIVE READING

ANALYZE What **details** in the paragraph help to create a vivid scene? **A**

At night his antelope skin was spread where the darkness overtook him—sometimes in a Sunnyasi monastery by the roadside; sometimes by a mud pillar shrine of Kala Pir, where the Jogis, who are another misty division of holy men, would receive him as they do those who know what castes and divisions are worth; sometimes on the outskirts of a little Hindu village, where the children would steal up with the food their parents had prepared; and sometimes on the pitch of the bare grazing-grounds where the flame of his stick fire waked the drowsy camels. It was all one to Purun Dass—or Purun Bhagat,[13] as he called himself now. Earth, people, and food were all one. But, unconsciously, his feet drew him northward and eastward; from the south to Rohtak; from Rohtak to Kurnool; from Kurnool to ruined Samanah, and then up-stream along the dried bed of the Gugger river that fills only when the rain falls in the hills, till, one day, he saw the far line of the great Himalayas.

Then Purun Bhagat smiled, for he remembered that his mother was of Rajput Brahmin birth, from Kulu way—a Hill-woman, always homesick for the snows—and that the least touch of Hill blood draws a man in the end back to where he belongs.

"Yonder," said Purun Bhagat, breasting the lower slopes of the Sewaliks, where the cacti stand up like seven-branched candlesticks, "yonder I shall sit down and get knowledge"; and the cool wind of the Himalayas whistled about his ears as he trod the road that led to Simla.

The last time he had come that way it had been in state, with a clattering cavalry escort, to visit the gentlest and most affable of Viceroys; and the two had talked for an hour together about mutual friends in London, and what the Indian common folk really thought of things. This time Purun Bhagat paid no calls, but leaned on the rail of the Mall,[14] watching the glorious view of the Plains spread out forty miles below, till a native Mohammedan policeman told him he was obstructing traffic; and Purun Bhagat salaamed[15] reverently to the Law, because he knew the value of it, and was seeking for a Law of his own. Then he moved on, and slept that night in an empty hut at Chota Simla, which looks like the very last end of the earth, but it was only the beginning of his journey. He followed the Himalaya-Thibet[16] road, the little ten-foot track that is blasted out of solid rock, or strutted out on timbers over gulfs a thousand feet deep; that dips into warm, wet, shut-in valleys, and climbs across bare, grassy hill-shoulders where the sun strikes like a burning-glass; or turns through dripping, dark forests where the tree-ferns dress the trunks from head to heel, and the pheasant calls to his mate. And he met Thibetan herdsmen with their dogs and flocks of sheep, each sheep with a little bag of borax on his back,[17] and wandering wood-cutters, and cloaked and blanketed Lamas[18] from Thibet, coming into India on pilgrimage, and envoys[19] of little solitary Hill-states, posting furiously on ring-streaked and piebald ponies, or the cavalcade[20] of a Rajah paying a visit, or else for a long, clear day he would see nothing more than a black bear grunting and rooting down below in the valley. When he first started, the roar of the

ACTIVE READING

CLARIFY What kind of "Law" might Purun Bhagat be seeking? **B**

13. **Bhagat** (bəg′ət): The Hindi word *bhagat* means "a devout person or saint."
14. **Mall:** a major roadway in Simla.
15. **salaamed** (sə-lämd′): bowed deeply, with the right palm pressed to the forehead, to show respect.
16. **Thibet:** a variant form of *Tibet.*
17. **borax on his back:** Tibet was the first important source of borax, a mineral with many industrial uses. In Tibet, sheep are often used as beasts of burden.
18. **Lamas:** Buddhist monks.
19. **envoys** (ĕn′voiz′): government representatives or agents.
20. **cavalcade:** a procession of riders on horseback or in horse-drawn carriages.

904 UNIT FIVE PART 1: PERSONAL RELATIONSHIPS

Teaching Options

Grammar

CORRECTING COMMA SPLICES

Instruction The term "comma splice" describes the incorrect use of a comma to join independent clauses, resulting in a run-on sentence. One way to correct the error is to create a compound sentence by adding a conjunction such as *and* or *but* after the comma or by replacing the comma with a semicolon. Another way is to create two separate sentences by replacing the comma with a period.

Activity Write the following sentences on the chalkboard. Ask students to identify and correct the comma splices.

Purun Dass decided to leave his job as a powerful and respected civil servant, to disguise his true identity, he changed his name to Purun Bhagat. *(There is a comma splice after "servant." Use a period to create two separate sentences, or replace the comma with a semicolon to create a compound sentence.)*

Having become a common beggar, Purun Bhagat journeyed throughout India, heading toward the northern mountains, he eventually found a deserted shrine, there he set up camp.

world he had left still rang in his ears, as the roar of a tunnel rings a little after the train has passed through; but when he had put the Mutteeanee Pass behind him that was all done, and Purun Bhagat was alone with himself, walking, wondering, and thinking, his eyes on the ground, and his thoughts with the clouds.

One evening he crossed the highest pass he had met till then—it had been a two days' climb—and came out on a line of snow-peaks that belted all the horizon—mountains from fifteen to twenty thousand feet high, looking almost near enough to hit with a stone, though they were fifty or sixty miles away. The pass was crowned with dense, dark forest—deodar, walnut, wild cherry, wild olive, and wild pear but mostly deodar, which is the Himalayan cedar; and under the shadow of the deodars stood a deserted shrine to Kali—who is Durga, who is Sitala, who is sometimes worshipped against the smallpox.[21]

Purun Dass swept the stone floor clean, smiled at the grinning statue, made himself a little mud fireplace at the back of the shrine, spread his antelope skin on a bed of fresh pine needles, tucked his *bairagi*—his brass-handled crutch—under his armpit, and sat down to rest.

Immediately below him the hillside fell away, clean and cleared for fifteen hundred feet, to where a little village of stone-walled houses, with roofs of beaten earth, clung to the steep tilt. All round it tiny terraced fields lay out like aprons of
C patchwork on the knees of the mountain, and cows no bigger than beetles grazed between the smooth stone circles of the threshing-floors. Looking across the valley the eye was deceived by the size of things, and could not at first real-
D ize that what seemed to be low scrub, on the opposite mountain-flank, was in truth a forest of hundred-foot pines. Purun Bhagat saw an eagle swoop across the enormous hollow, but the great bird dwindled to a dot ere it was half-way over. A few bands of scattered clouds strung up and down the valley, catching on a shoulder of the hills, or rising up and dying out when they were level with the head of the pass. And "Here shall I find peace," said Purun Bhagat.

Now, a Hill-man makes nothing of a few hundred feet up or down, and as soon as the villagers saw the smoke in the deserted shrine, the village priest climbed up the terraced hillside to welcome the stranger.

When he met Purun Bhagat's eyes—the eyes of a man used to control thousands—he bowed to the earth, took the begging-bowl without a word, and returned to the village, saying, "We have at last a holy man. Never have I seen such a man. He is of the plains—but pale colored—a Brahmin of the Brahmins." Then all the housewives of the village said, "Think you he will stay with us?" and each did her best to cook the most savory meal for the Bhagat. Hill-food is very simple, but with buckwheat and Indian corn, and rice and red pepper, and little fish out of the stream in the little valley, and honey from the flue-like hives built in the stone walls, and dried apricots, and turmeric,[22] and wild ginger, and bannocks[23] of flour, a devout woman can make good things; and it was a full bowl that the priest carried to the Bhagat. Was he going to stay? asked the priest. Would he need a *chela*—a disciple—to beg for him? Had he a blanket against the cold weather? Was the food good?

Purun Bhagat ate, and thanked the giver. It was in his mind to stay. That was sufficient, said the priest. Let the begging-bowl be placed outside the shrine, in the hollow made by those two twisted roots, and daily should the Bhagat be fed; for the village felt honored that such a man—he looked timidly into the Bhagat's face—should tarry among them.

That day saw the end of Purun Bhagat's

21. **Kali . . . smallpox:** In Hinduism, the supreme goddess Devi takes many forms; one of these is Kali, goddess of destruction, who is also identified with the goddesses Durga (another deity of destruction) and Sitala (the deity of smallpox).

22. **turmeric** (tûr′mər-ĭk): a spice made from the roots of the turmeric plant.

23. **bannocks:** flat loaves of unleavened bread.

Customizing Instruction

Less Proficient Readers

Set a Purpose Have students read to find out what Purun Bhagat's life is like in the new place.

Multiple Learning Styles

Visual Learners

Ask students to look up pictures of the Himalayas on the Internet or in the library and to share them with the class. Discuss with the class how such visual images enhance their understanding of the story.

(There are <u>two</u> comma splices—one after "India" and the other after "shrine." The best solution is to replace the commas with periods, creating three complete sentences.)

Exercise Ask students to identify and correct the comma splices in the following sentences. Have students meet in cooperative groups and create three sentences with comma splices. Ask the groups to exchange sentences and correct the splices.

1. Once Purun Bhagat had reached the mountain region near Tibet, he decided to settle down, he set up a shelter in a remote site. *(comma splice between "down" and "he";* Possible answer: *use a period and begin a new sentence)*
2. Every day the people living in the valley brought Purun Bhagat food, he never spoke with the villagers. *(comma splice between "food" and "he"; Possible answers: use a conjunction such as "but" or use a semicolon)*

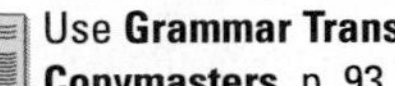
Use **Grammar Transparencies and Copymasters,** p. 93.

Use McDougal Littell's ***Language Network*** for more instruction and practice in comma splices.

Reading and Analyzing

Literary Analysis: FIGURATIVE LANGUAGE

A Ask students to explain the meaning of the metaphor comparing the roofs to gold.

Possible Responses: The roofs are covered with yellow corn that glistens in the sun like gold nuggets; the corn is valuable food, and so it is precious, like gold.

Active Reading ANALYZING DETAILS

Ask students how the details about the animals affect the reader's impressions of them.

Possible Responses: They make the reader feel fond of the animals; they help the reader visualize the animals.

Point out that most of Kipling's readers would never have seen any of these animals. Ask students how this fact might have affected Kipling's choice of details.

Possible Response: Kipling might have described the animals' appearance more carefully than he would have for an audience that was familiar with them.

ACTIVE READING

B **EVALUATE** **Possible Response:** The villagers honor and respect Purun Bhagat and they are proud that this holy man lives near their village. Purun Bhagat relies on the villagers to support him, but he is closer to the animals that visit him and are not in awe of him than he is to the villagers.

wanderings. He had come to the place appointed for him—the silence and the space. After this, time stopped, and he, sitting at the mouth of the shrine, could not tell whether he were alive or dead; a man with control of his limbs, or a part of the hills, and the clouds, and the shifting rain, and sunlight. He would repeat a Name softly to himself a hundred hundred times, till, at each repetition, he seemed to move more and more out his body, sweeping up to the doors of some tremendous discovery; but, just as the door was opening, his body would drag him back, and, with grief, he felt he was locked up again in the flesh and bones of Purun Bhagat.

1 Every morning the filled begging-bowl was laid silently in the crotch of the roots outside the shrine. Sometimes the priest brought it; sometimes a Ladakhi[24] trader, lodging in the village, and anxious to get merit, trudged up the path; but, more often, it was the woman who had cooked the meal overnight; and she would murmur, hardly above her breath: "Speak for me before the gods, Bhagat. Speak for such an one, the wife of so-and-so!" Now and then some bold child would be allowed the honor, and Purun Bhagat would hear him drop the bowl and run as fast as his little legs could carry him, but the Bhagat never came down to the village. It was laid out like a map at his feet. He could see the evening gatherings held on the circle of the threshing-floors, because that was the only level ground; could see the wonderful unnamed green of the young rice, the indigo blues of the Indian corn; the dock-like patches of buckwheat, and, in its season, the red bloom of the amaranth, whose tiny seeds, being neither grain nor pulse,[25] make a food that can be lawfully eaten by Hindus in time of fasts.

A When the year turned, the roofs of the huts were all little squares of purest gold, for it was on the roofs that they laid out their cobs of the corn to dry.
2 Hiving and harvest, rice-sowing and husking, passed before his eyes, all embroidered down there on the many-sided fields, and he thought of them all, and wondered what they all led to at the long last.

Even in populated India a man cannot a day sit still before the wild things run over him as though he were a rock; and in that wilderness very soon the wild things, who knew Kali's Shrine well, came back to look at the intruder. The *langurs,* the big gray-whiskered monkeys of the Himalayas, were, naturally, the first, for they are alive with curiosity; and when they had upset the begging-bowl, and rolled it round the floor, and tried their teeth on the brass-handled crutch, and made faces at the antelope skin, they decided that the human being who sat so still was harmless. At evening, they would leap down from the pines, and beg with their hands for things to eat, and then swing off in graceful curves. They liked the warmth of the fire, too, and huddled round it till Purun Bhagat had to push them aside to throw on more fuel; and in the morning, as often as not, he would find a furry ape sharing his blanket. All day long, one or other of the tribe would sit by his side, staring out at the snows, crooning and looking unspeakably wise and sorrowful.

After the monkeys came the *barasingh,* that big deer which is like our red deer, but stronger. He wished to rub off the velvet of his horns against the cold stones of Kali's statue, and stamped his feet when he saw the man at the shrine. But Purun Bhagat never moved, and, little by little, the royal stag edged up and nuzzled his shoulder. Purun Bhagat slid one cool hand along the hot antlers, and the touch soothed the fretted beast, who bowed his head, and Purun Bhagat very softly rubbed and ravelled off the velvet. Afterwards, the *barasingh* brought his doe and fawn—gentle things that mumbled on the holy man's blanket—or would come alone at night, his eyes green in the fire-flicker, to take his share of fresh walnuts. At last, the musk-deer, the

24. **Ladakhi** (lə-dä′kē): from Ladakh, a region in the upper Indus River valley—at the time, part of northwestern India.

25. **pulse:** the edible seeds of certain pod-bearing plants, such as peas and beans.

Teaching Options

Workplace Link: Managing a Project

Instruction Purun Dass managed many projects. Within the workplace, one person is normally placed in charge of a project. That person, like Purun Dass, is responsible for the following:

- making a workable schedule
- assigning people to different tasks
- answering questions and addressing concerns
- offering guidance
- making sure implementation is smooth

Application Purun Bhagat quickly put together a plan and directed the project when he evacuated the town. Tell students to imagine that they are the civil defense coordinator of a coastal state that, in two days, will most likely take a direct hit from a strong hurricane. They are in charge of the project to protect the citizenry. Have students write a suitable plan. If you wish, you might have them work in small groups.

shyest and almost the smallest of the deerlets, came, too, her big, rabbity ears erect; even brindled, silent *mushick-nabha* must needs find out what the light in the shrine meant, and drop her moose-like nose into Purun Bhagat's lap, coming and going with the shadows of the fire. Purun Bhagat called them all "my brothers," and his low call of *"Bhai! Bhai!"* would draw them from the forest at noon if they were within earshot. The Himalayan black bear, moody and suspicious—Sona, who has the V-shaped white mark under his chin—passed that way more than once; and since the Bhagat showed no fear, Sona showed no anger, but watched him, and came closer, and begged a share of the caresses, and a dole of bread or wild berries. Often, in the still
3 dawns, when the Bhagat would climb to the very crest of the notched pass to watch the red day walking along the peaks of the snows, he would find Sona shuffling and grunting at his heels, thrusting a curious forepaw under fallen trunks, and bringing it away with a *whoof* of impatience; or his early steps would wake Sona where he lay curled up, and the great brute, rising erect, would think to fight, till he heard the Bhagat's voice and knew his best friend.

Nearly all hermits and holy men who live apart from the big cities have the reputation of being able to work miracles with the wild things, but all the miracle lies in keeping still, in never making a hasty movement, and, for a long time, at least, in never looking directly at a visitor. The villagers saw the outlines of the *barasingh* stalking like a shadow through the dark forest behind the shrine; saw the *minaul,* the Himalayan pheasant, blazing in her best colors before Kali's statue; and the *langurs* on their haunches, inside, playing with the walnut shells. Some of the children, too, had heard Sona singing to himself, bear-fashion, behind the fallen rocks, and the Bhagat's reputation as miracle-worker stood firm.

Yet nothing was further from his mind than miracles. He believed that all things were one big Miracle, and when a man knows that much he knows something to go upon. He knew for a certainty that there was nothing great and nothing little in this world; and day and night he strove to think out his way into the heart of things, back to the place whence his soul had come.

So thinking, his untrimmed hair fell down about his shoulders, the stone slab at the side of the antelope-skin was dented into a little hole by the foot of his brass-handled crutch, and the place between the tree-trunks, where the begging-bowl rested day after day, sunk and wore into a hollow almost as smooth as the brown shell itself; and each beast knew his exact place at the fire. The fields changed their colors with the seasons; the threshing-floors filled and emptied, and filled again and again; and again and again, when winter came, the *langurs* frisked among the branches feathered with light snow, till the mother-monkeys brought their sad-eyed little babies up from the warmer valleys with the spring. There were few changes in the village. The priest was older, and many of the little children who used to come with the begging-dish sent their own children now; and when you asked of the villagers how long their holy man had lived in Kali's Shrine at the head of the pass, they answered, "Always."

ACTIVE READING

EVALUATE How would you describe the relationship between the villagers and Purun Bhagat? **B**

Then came such summer rains as had not been known in the Hills for many seasons. Through three good months the valley was wrapped in cloud and soaking mist—steady, unrelenting downfall, breaking off into thunder-shower after thunder-shower. Kali's Shrine stood above the clouds, for the most part, and there was a whole month in which the Bhagat never caught a glimpse of his village. It was packed away under a white floor of cloud that swayed and shifted and rolled on itself and bulged upward, but never broke from its piers—the streaming flanks of the valley.

All that time he heard nothing but the sound of a million little waters, overhead from the trees, and underfoot along the ground, soaking

Customizing Instruction

Less Proficient Readers

1 Have students describe Purun Bhagat's life.

Possible Response: He lives very simply; the village people bring him food each day, and the animals are his friends; he is constantly thinking.

Students Acquiring English

2 Help students find the root word of *hiving.*

Answer: hive.

Then, explain that *hiving* means harvesting honey from beehives.

3 Students might have difficulty with the figurative language in this passage. Point out that *dawns* is plural, and so the narrator means every morning. Ask students what "the red day walking along the peaks of the snows" means.

Answer: the sun rising over the tops of the snow-covered mountains.

Standardized Test Practice

CHOOSING THE BEST ANSWER The following multiple-choice question will help students understand how details support ideas in a story. Using the skills already discussed for analyzing details, have students select the details that support the statement.

1. The villagers honor and respect Purun Bhagat.

- **A.** The village priest climbed up the terraced hillside to welcome Purun Bhagat.
- **B.** The villagers saw the outlines of the *barasingh* stalking like a shadow through the dark forest behind the shrine.
- **C.** The woman who brought Purun Bhagat the meal would murmur, hardly above her breath: "Speak for me before the gods, Bhagat."

Choices A and B do not give any information about how the villagers felt; they are merely facts. Some students may choose A, but explain that the priest's visit is primarily a courtesy. The attitude of the woman in choice C communicates her honor and respect for Purun Bhagat; she calls him "Bhagat" (holy man) and asks him to pray for her. The answer is C.

THE MIRACLE OF PURUN BHAGAT 907

Reading and Analyzing

ACTIVE READING

A PREDICT **Possible Responses:** They are frightened of the storm; something terrible is going to happen, and they are trying to warn Purun Bhagat.

Literary Analysis:
FIGURATIVE LANGUAGE

B Kipling personifies the earth when he writes "the sticky earth below smacked its lips." Ask the students how this personification affects the reader.
Possible Response: It makes the danger very vivid by implying that the earth wants to consume the people and animals.

Active Reading **ANALYZING DETAILS**

C Ask students to note the visual details Kipling provides in this scene. Have them visualize the scene as clearly as they can, and then write down sensory details from their imaginary scene. Use the following cues as prompts:

- sounds
  Possible Responses: the drumming of the rain, the hoof- and paw-beats and snuffling of the animals, the hiss of raindrops in the torch, the rumble of the earth as it prepares to fall.
- smells
  Possible Responses: rain, the sour smell of dampened fire, the smell of wet animals, the smell of the forest.
- feelings
  Possible Responses: the wet fur under Purun Bhagat's hand, the rain streaming over his face, the feeling of his wet hair, the squishing of mud underfoot.

through the pine-needles, dripping from the tongues of draggled fern, and spouting in newly-torn muddy channels down the slopes. Then the sun came out, and drew forth the good incense of the deodars and the rhododendrons, and that far-off, clean smell the Hill People call "the smell of
1 the snows." The hot sunshine lasted for a week, and then the rains gathered together for their last downpour, and the water fell in sheets that flayed off the skin of the ground and leaped back in mud. Purun Bhagat heaped his fire high that night, for he was sure his brothers would need warmth; but never a beast came to the shrine, though he called and called till he dropped asleep, wondering what had happened in the woods.

It was in the black heart of the night, the rain drumming like a thousand drums, that he was roused by a plucking at his blanket, and, stretching out, felt the little hand of a *langur*. "It is better here than in the trees," he said sleepily, loosening a fold of blanket; "take it and be warm." The monkey caught his hand and pulled hard. "Is it food, then?" said Purun Bhagat. "Wait awhile, and I will prepare some." As he kneeled to throw fuel on the fire the *langur* ran to the door of the shrine, crooned, and ran back again, plucking at the man's knee.

"What is it? What is thy trouble, Brother?" said Purun Bhagat, for the *langur's* eyes were full
2 of things that he could not tell. "Unless one of thy caste be in a trap—and none set traps here—I will not go into that weather. Look, Brother, even the *barasingh* comes for shelter."

ACTIVE READING

A **PREDICT** The animals are behaving strangely. What might be happening?

The deer's antlers clashed as he strode into the shrine, clashed against the grinning statue of Kali. He lowered them in Purun Bhagat's direction and stamped uneasily, hissing through his half-shut nostrils.

"Hai! Hai! Hai!" said the Bhagat, snapping his fingers. "Is *this* payment for a night's lodging?" But the deer pushed him towards the door, and as he did so Purun Bhagat heard the sound of something opening with a sigh, and saw two slabs of the floor draw away from each other, while the sticky earth below smacked its lips. B

"Now I see," said Purun Bhagat. "No blame to my brothers that they did not sit by the fire to-night. The mountain is falling. And yet—why should I go?" His eye fell on the empty begging-bowl, and his face changed. "They have given me good food daily since—since I came, and, if I am not swift, tomorrow there will not be one mouth in the valley. Indeed, I must go and warn them below. Back there, Brother! Let me get to the fire."

The *barasingh* backed unwillingly as Purun Bhagat drove a torch deep into the flame, twirling it till it was well lit. "Ah! ye came to warn me," he said, rising. "Better than that we shall do, better than that. Out, now, and lend me thy neck, Brother, for I have but two feet."

He clutched the bristling withers[26] of the C
barasingh with his right hand, held the torch away with his left, and stepped out of the shrine into the desperate night. There was no breath of wind, but the rain nearly drowned the torch as the great deer hurried down the slope, sliding on his haunches. As soon as they were clear of the forest more of the Bhagat's brothers joined them. He heard, though he could not see, the *langurs* pressing about him, and behind them the *uhh! uhh!* of Sona. The rain matted his long white hair into ropes; the water splashed beneath his bare feet, and his yellow robe clung to his frail old body, but he stepped down steadily, leaning against the *barasingh*. He was no longer a holy man, but Sir Purun Dass, K.C.I.E., Prime Minister of no small State, a man accustomed to command, going out to save life. Down the steep plashy path they poured all together, the Bhagat and his brothers, down and down till the deer clicked and stumbled on the wall of a threshing-floor, and snorted because he smelt Man. Now they were at the head of the one crooked village

26. **withers:** the high part of the deer's back, between the shoulder blades.

Teaching Options

Vocabulary Strategy

SPECIALIZED VOCABULARY

Instruction Specialized vocabulary refers to the words and terms associated with a particular topic. This story includes many terms associated with farming as well as words from a foreign language. Suggest that students use the following strategies to help them read texts with specialized vocabulary.

- Look for boldfaced or italicized words—in textbooks, these treatments often signal specialized vocabulary.
- Look for a definition the first time an unfamiliar word is used; specialized vocabulary is often defined when it is introduced.
- Look for footnotes and/or a glossary.
- Keep a personal glossary of terms.

Exercise Have students use context to define each of the following words.

1. *bairagi*
   Answer: a crutch
2. bannocks
   Answer: flat loaves of unleavened bread

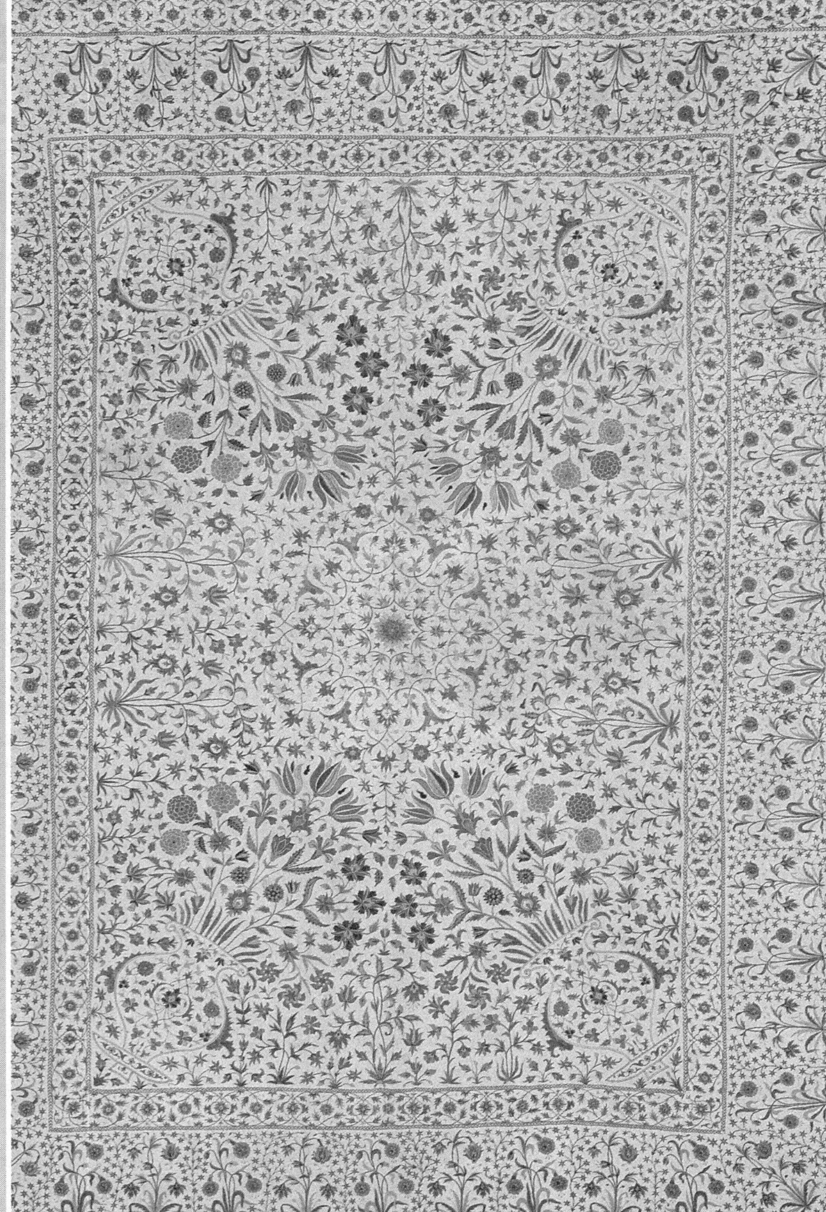

Mughal floorspread (about 1700). Cotton embroidered with silk, 269 cm × 203 cm, Victoria and Albert Museum, London/Art Resource, New York.

Customizing Instruction

Students Acquiring English

Explain to students that some of the language Purun Bhagat uses is archaic. For example, he refers to the animals as "thy" and "ye." Ask students why they think Kipling might have chosen to have Purun Bhagat speak this way.

Possible Responses: to make him seem old; to make him seem holy by bringing to mind language found in the King James Bible.

Less Proficient Readers

1 Have students summarize this sentence in their own words.

Possible Response: The hot sunshine lasted for a week, and then the rains fell again, churning up the topsoil and turning it into mud.

2 Ask students why the *langur* and *barasingh* come to the shrine.

Answer: to warn Purun Bhagat of the landslide.

Mini Lesson Viewing and Representing

Mughal floorspread (about 1700)

ART APPRECIATION

Instruction Tell students that the Mughal empire in India was established by Babur in 1526, and it lasted under his descendants until 1707. The word *mughal* means "Mongol," a name used to describe the Turkic and Mongol peoples who practiced the Islamic faith and conquered India.

Application Ask students to describe the pattern on this floorspread.

Possible Response: highly symmetrical floral patterns, dominated by four pots of flowers—just inside the corners—that are pointing inward.

Compare this pattern with the life Purun Bhagat enters into at this shrine.

Possible Responses: Some students may compare the regular, orderly pattern of this rug with the regular, orderly pattern of the Bhagat's life at the shrine.

Reading and Analyzing

Literary Analysis: THEME

Remind students that the theme of a literary work is its central idea or message. Note that many works have more than one theme, and then ask students what themes are explored in the story.

Possible Responses: the British vs. the Indian way of life; worldly vs. spiritual power; action vs. passivity.

Active Reading ANALYZING DETAILS

Ask students what Purun Bhagat might mean when he says, "Stay—till—I—go!"

Possible Responses: He knows that he is dying and wants the animals to stay with him for company; his strength is waning, and he wants the animals to stay with him until he can gather strength to move on.

street, and the Bhagat beat with his crutch at the barred windows of the blacksmith's house as his torch blazed up in the shelter of the eaves. "Up and out!" cried Purun Bhagat; and he did not know his own voice, for it was years since he had spoken aloud to a man. "The hill falls! The hill is falling! Up and out, oh, you within!"

"It is our Bhagat," said the blacksmith's wife. "He stands among his beasts. Gather the little ones and give the call."

It ran from house to house, while the beasts, cramped in the narrow way, surged and huddled round the Bhagat, and Sona puffed impatiently.

The people hurried into the street—they were no more than seventy souls all told—and in the glare of their torches they saw their Bhagat holding back the terrified *barasingh,* while the monkeys plucked piteously at his skirts, and Sona sat on his haunches and roared.

"Across the valley and up the next hill!" shouted Purun Bhagat. "Leave none behind! We follow!"

Then the people ran as only Hill-folk can run, for they knew that in a landslip you must climb for the highest ground across the valley. They fled, splashing through the little river at the bottom, and panted up the terraced fields on the far side, while the Bhagat and his brethren followed. Up and up the opposite mountain they climbed, calling to each other by name—the roll-call of the village—and at their heels toiled the big *barasingh,* weighted by the failing strength of Purun Bhagat. At last the deer stopped in the shadow of a deep pine-wood, five hundred feet up the hillside. His instinct, that had warned him of the coming slide, told him he would be safe here.

> HIS INSTINCT, THAT HAD WARNED HIM OF THE COMING SLIDE, TOLD HIM HE WOULD BE SAFE HERE.

Purun Bhagat dropped fainting by his side, for the chill of the rain and that fierce climb was killing him; but first he called to the scattered torches ahead, "Stay and count your numbers;" then, whispering to the deer as he saw the lights gather in a cluster: "Stay with me, Brother. Stay—till—I—go!"

There was a sigh in the air that grew to a mutter, and a mutter that grew to a roar, and a roar that passed all sense of hearing, and the hillside on which the villagers stood was hit in the darkness, and rocked to the blow. Then a note as steady, deep, and true as the deep C of the organ drowned everything for perhaps five minutes, while the very roots of the pines quivered to it. It died away, and the sound of the rain falling on miles of hard ground and grass changed to the muffled drums of water on soft earth. That told its own tale.

Never a villager—not even the priest—was bold enough to speak to the Bhagat who had saved their lives. They crouched under the pines and waited till the day. When it came they looked across the valley, and saw that what had been forest, and terraced field, and track-threaded

Teaching Options

Mini Lesson: Speaking and Listening

NEWSCASTS

Instruction Remind students that newscasts can have more than one function. For example, they can be a recap of events or they can alert people to dangerous situations.

Prepare Share these hints for listening.

- Listen for the main elements: who, when, where, what happened, why.
- Listen for any warnings.
- Take notes if you need to remember any of the information.

Present Have students list *Who, When, Where, What,* and *Why* on a sheet of paper. Then have them write the appropriate information next to each heading as you read this "newscast":

Purun Bhagat led Indian villagers to safety this morning. After a week of drenching rains, the hills were saturated. Purun Bhagat, sensing the danger, led the villagers to higher ground before a landslide. Thanks to Purun Bhagat, no one was injured—but he died later that night.

BLOCK SCHEDULING This activity is particularly well-suited for longer class periods.

grazing-ground was one raw, red, fan-shaped smear, with a few trees flung head-down on the scarp.[27] That red ran high up the hill of their refuge, damming back the little river, which had begun to spread into a brick-colored lake. Of the village, of the road to the shrine, of the shrine itself, and the forest behind, there was no trace. For one mile in width and two thousand feet in sheer depth the mountain-side had come away bodily, planed clean from head to heel.

And the villagers, one by one, crept through the wood to pray before their Bhagat. They saw the *barasingh* standing over him, who fled when they came near, and they heard the *langurs* wailing in the branches, and Sona moaning up the hill; but their Bhagat was dead, sitting cross-legged, his back against a tree, his crutch under his armpit, and his face turned to the north-east.

The priest said: "Behold a miracle after a miracle, for in this very attitude must all Sunnyasis be buried! Therefore, where he now is we will build the temple to our holy man."

They built the temple before a year was ended, a little stone and earth shrine, and they called the hill the Bhagat's Hill, and they worship there with lights and flowers and offerings to this day. But they do not know that the saint of their worship is the late Sir Purun Dass, K.C.I.E., D.C.L.,[28] Ph.D., etc., once Prime Minister of the progressive and enlightened state of Mohiniwala, and honorary or corresponding member of more learned and scientific societies than will ever do any good in this world or the next. ❖

27. **scarp:** escarpment—a steep slope or cliff separating two level areas of different elevations.

28. **K.C.I.E., D.C.L.:** abbreviations of the titles *Knight Commander of the Indian Empire* and *Doctor of Civil Law.*

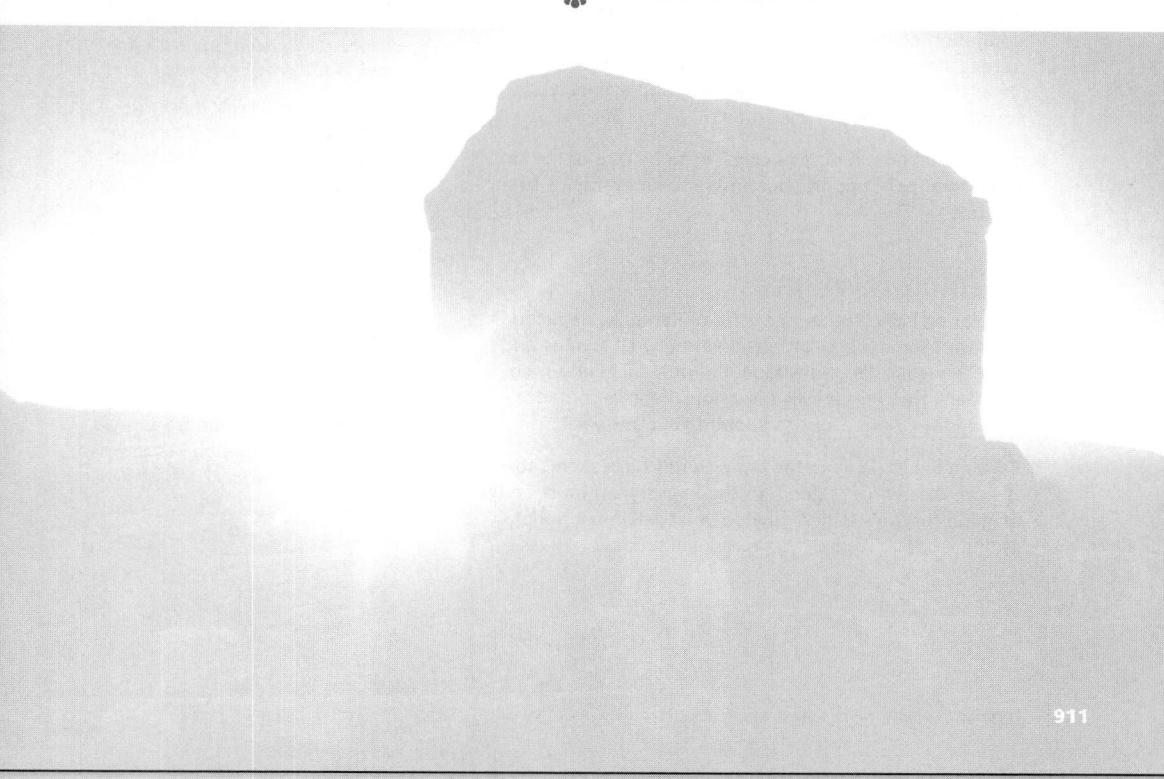

Customizing Instruction

Students Acquiring English

Be sure students understand what is happening to the hill. Tell them that rather than saying "The hill falls," we would probably refer to the event as a landslide. Show students photographs of landslides or mudslides, perhaps those that occurred in California in 1997–1998.

Less Proficient Readers

Ask students how Purun Bhagat repays the villagers.

Answer: He warns them that their hill-side town is about to be engulfed by a landslide, and he leads them to safety.

Gifted and Talented

Ask students to define the word *nirvana* (a state free from pain and worry). Have them discuss whether Purun Bhagat seems to be seeking that state toward the end of the story. Then, ask students whether Purun Bhagat is acting out of a British sense of duty or as a Hindu who is concerned about all living things when he goes to tell the villagers about the impending landslide.

✓ Assessment Informal Assessment

PROFILE SHEET Have students copy the profile sheet below and fill in answers that they believe are consistent with what they know about Purun Bhagat.

- Name: *Purun Dass (or Purun Bhagat)*
- Alias: *Purun Bhagat (or Purun Dass)*
- Address: *the shrine of Kali*
- Former Occupation: *prime minister*
- Hobbies: *Accept all reasonable responses.*
- Favorite Saying: *Accept all reasonable responses.*
- Greatest Achievement: *Accept all reasonable responses.*
- How I Want to Be Remembered: *Accept all reasonable responses.*

GUIDING STUDENT RESPONSE

Connect to the Literature

1. What Do You Think?
Guidelines for student response: Accept all reasonable responses that are rooted in the text and are based upon evidence in the story.

Comprehension Check

- because he is giving up his old life and becoming a holy man
- because part of the mountain is about to fall away

 Use **Unit Five Resource Book,** p. 27 for additional support.

Think Critically

2. Possible Responses: Purun Dass, because few people were able to achieve what he did while walking the fine line between British and Indian culture; Purun Bhagat, because he left material wealth behind in order to search for inner peace.
3. Possible Responses: He feels he has done everything and is ready for a change; he has accomplished much and yet life seems meaningless.
4. Possible Responses: when the time came, he emerged from his spiritual trance to help others; he gave up power and prestige to embrace the life of a man who had nothing
5. Accept all reasonable responses. Vivid details help readers to picture what is happening. Have students cite scenes that seemed vividly described to them.
6. Accept all reasonable, well-supported responses. Students may mention humility, reverence for life, and fulfilling one's duty as important themes.

Literary Analysis

Cooperative Learning Activity As students respond to the activity, be sure they discuss the relevance of the story's setting and time frame to the meaning of the story.

Thinking through the LITERATURE

Connect to the Literature

1. **What Do You Think?** What is your impression of Purun and his actions?

Comprehension Check

- Why does Purun Dass change his name?
- Why do the animals wake Purun Bhagat?

Think Critically

2. Do you admire Purun more in his role as Purun Dass or in his role as Purun Bhagat? Explain your answer.
3. Why do you think Purun changes his life so drastically?

THINK ABOUT
- his cultural heritage
- his values as a young man
- his accomplishments as prime minister
- the values he expresses as he begins his new life

4. What, in your opinion, is the miracle of Purun Bhagat? Share your ideas with your classmates.
5. ACTIVE READING ANALYZING DETAILS Review the details you jotted down in your  READER'S NOTEBOOK. What scenes stand out most vividly in your mind? How do the details describing characters, actions, and events work together to create this vivid effect?
6. What moral lesson do you consider to be one of the story's main **themes?** Support your answer with examples from the text.

Extend Interpretations

7. **Comparing Texts** The heroic code of Rama, as depicted in the *Ramayana* (page 240), is revered by all Hindus and serves as a model of devotion and duty for Hindu men. Do you think that Purun lives his whole life in accordance with that code? Give reasons to support your answer.
8. **Connect to Life** Early in the story, Purun Dass seems to believe that "what is good for the Englishman must be twice as good for the Asiatic." How do you think most people would respond to that type of thinking today?

Literary Analysis

SETTING The time and place of the action of a short story, novel, play, narrative poem, or nonfiction narrative is referred to as the **setting.** Note the details of setting in the following excerpt:

At night his antelope skin was spread where the darkness overtook him—sometimes in a Sunnyasi monastery by the roadside; sometimes by a mud pillar shrine of Kala Pir, where the Jogis, who are another misty division of holy men, would receive him as they do those who know what castes and divisions are worth; sometimes on the outskirts of a little Hindu village, where the children would steal up with the food their parents had prepared; and sometimes on the pitch of the bare grazing-grounds where the flame of his stick fire waked the drowsy camels.

In addition to time and place, setting may include the social and moral environment that form the background for a narrative. Setting is one of the main elements in fiction and often plays an important role in what happens and why.

Cooperative Learning Activity How important do you think the setting of "The Miracle of Purun Bhagat" is? Discuss with your classmates how the events of the story might have been different if Purun Bhagat had become a Sunnyasi but remained in the city. Share your conclusions with the class.

Extend Interpretations

Comparing Texts Possible Response: Yes. Purun is an honorable man who tries to do what is right, whether it is improving the lives of the Maharajah's subjects or saving the mountain villagers from the landslide. He is devoted to the gods and respects the laws.

Connect to Life Accept all reasonable, well-supported responses.

Writing Options

1. Purun Bhagat Obituary Using details from the story, write an obituary of Purun Bhagat for an Indian newspaper.

2. Essay Analyzing Values Write an essay in which you analyze the lifestyle and values chosen by Purun Dass when he becomes Purun Bhagat. What does he give up? What does he gain? Place the essay in your **Working Portfolio.**

Activities & Explorations

1. Sculpture Tribute Create a design or model of a statue that honors Purun by reflecting both phases of his life. ~ **ART**

2. Dramatic Dialogue With a partner, present a dramatic dialogue in which Purun Dass and Purun Bhagat discuss the pros and cons of their lifestyles. ~ **PERFORMING**

Inquiry & Research

Caste System Find out more about India's caste system and its effects on the lifestyle of the Indian people. What constitutes a caste? What kinds of rules govern each caste? Have any low caste members achieved high political office in India? Share your findings with your classmates.

More Online: Research Starter www.mcdougallittell.com

Rudyard Kipling
1865–1936

Other Works
"The Man Who Would Be King"
"The Strange Ride of Morrowbie Jukes"
"The Maltese Cat"
"The King's Ankus"
"The Return of Imray"

A Childhood in England and India Although born in Bombay, Joseph Rudyard Kipling spent many of his childhood years in England, unhappily separated from his family. His English parents had moved to India shortly after their marriage, when his father was assigned to a teaching position at an art school. At that time, it was customary for British residents in India to send their children back to Britain for schooling. When Kipling was 6 years old, therefore, his parents took him and his younger sister to Southsea, England, and placed them in a foster home for the next five years. Kipling felt abandoned and later described his stay in Southsea as a period of extreme unhappiness and anxiety. At the age of 12, Kipling was sent to the United Services College, an inexpensive boarding school in Devon, England. Although Kipling later recalled the bullying and unruliness of the students, his school experiences were generally pleasant enough, and his assignment as editor of the school magazine eventually led him to a career in journalism.

Reporter and Writer In 1882, at the age of 16, Kipling returned to India, where he worked as a newspaper reporter for the next seven years. Many of his early stories were published in a series of paperback books that were sold in train stations. International travelers soon spread word of his work beyond the boundaries of India, and when he returned to England in 1889, his reputation as a great writer had preceded him. He very quickly became one of England's favorite writers.

Marriage and America In 1892, Kipling married an American, Carrie Balestier, and moved with her to the United States. The couple settled in Vermont, but Kipling was never able to adjust to the American way of life. Four years later they were back in England, where Kipling would live the rest of his life. Even though his stay in America was not particularly satisfying, Kipling wrote many of his most famous stories and novels in the United States, including *The Jungle Books* and *Captains Courageous.*

Lifetime Achievement Kipling was an accomplished novelist and poet, as well as the author of over 300 short stories. He is perhaps best known today for his children's stories, particularly the widely read *Just So Stories.* Many of his works—including his most famous novel, *Kim*—reveal his lifelong fascination with the people and animals of India. In 1907, he became the first English writer to be awarded the Nobel Prize for literature.

Writing Options

1. **Purun Bhagat Obituary** If possible, share with students an actual obituary from a local newspaper so that students can use the same style. Have them analyze and discuss the format of this writing. More importantly, make it clear to them that this assignment is really meant to focus their attention on details in the story: specifically, those that relate to Purun Bhagat's biography.
2. **Essay Analyzing Values** Remind students that their essay needs a strong thesis statement. Tell them they should take a stand on the character's life and use evidence from the story to support their view.

Activities & Explorations

1. **Sculpture Tribute** Have students decide whether the statue should show a man with two sides, a man engaged in two activities, or some other aspect.
2. **Dramatic Dialogue** Remind students that a dialogue is an exchange of ideas. Students should list the pros and cons of the two lifestyles and then meet with their partners to determine how best to present the dramatic conversation.

Inquiry & Research

Caste System An encyclopedia is a good starting point for students wanting to find out more about castes. In addition to the suggested questions, students might consider whether Indians living in other countries are governed by the same rules as when they are in India. Students might also write a list of their own questions.

OVERVIEW

Objectives

1. understand and appreciate a Russian **short story (Literary Analysis)**
2. recognize and appreciate the conventions of a **folk tale (Literary Analysis)**
3. recognize and discuss **themes** that cross cultures **(Literary Analysis)**
4. use strategies for **summarizing text (Active Reading)**

Summary

A poor shoemaker named Simon meets a naked, freezing man who will say only that his name is Michael and that God is punishing him. Simon takes the man home and teaches him his trade. One day a gentleman arrives and demands boots that will last a year. Michael makes slippers instead, and soon a messenger delivers the news that the man has died and needs slippers to be buried in. Several years later, a woman orders shoes for her twin girls. She tells how she adopted the girls after their mother died and describes them as the joy of her life. After the woman and the girls leave, Simon and his wife notice light streaming from Michael. He explains that he has been a disobedient angel. When he refused to take the soul of the girls' mother, God sent him to earth to learn what dwells in man, what is not given to man, and what men live by.

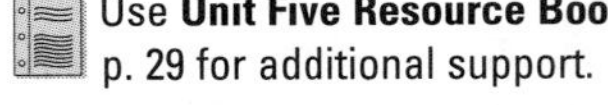
Use **Unit Five Resource Book,** p. 29 for additional support.

Thematic Link

In this folk tale, Tolstoy explores the **personal relationships** between and among humans and between humans and God.

5-Minute Warm-Up

Daily Language SkillBuilder

Have students **proofread** the display sentences on page 829j and write them correctly. The sentences also appear on Transparency 24 of **Grammar Transparencies and Copymasters.**

What Men Live By

Short Story by LEO TOLSTOY

Comparing Literature of the World

Observing Moral Lessons Across Cultures

"The Miracle of Purun Bhagat" and "What Men Live By" Many of Kipling's stories describe his lifelong fascination with India. Most of Leo Tolstoy's stories are set in Russia. Despite the differences in language and setting in the two stories included in this book, both writers deal with the moral issue of what constitutes a good and meaningful life. Further, both stories are concerned with the ways in which a simple life can make virtue more attainable.

Points of Comparison As you read the following story by Tolstoy, compare it with Kipling's story in terms of the moral lesson that can be drawn from it.

Build Background

The Aristocrat and the Peasants During the 19th century, the peasants of Russia were poor and struggling. Russia was still a Christian nation then, and it was ruled by an emperor called the czar. Although the peasants were freed from serfdom, a form of slavery, during the 1800s, their standard of living remained far lower than that of the wealthy landowners.

Even though Leo Tolstoy was himself an aristocrat and a wealthy landowner, he became a leader in the fight to change society and educate the peasant class. Like the British authors Elizabeth Gaskell and Charles Dickens, Tolstoy often used his writing to call attention to social and moral issues—especially the plight of the poor. Toward the end of his writing career, he began writing down and adapting the folk tales through which peasants conveyed **themes** about the meaning of life. He believed that these themes revealed truths that could improve the quality of life for all. In "What Men Live By," you will read about a 19th-century Russian peasant and his encounter with a stranger in need.

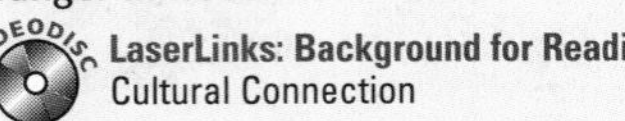
LaserLinks: Background for Reading
Cultural Connection

Focus Your Reading

LITERARY ANALYSIS **FOLK TALE** "What Men Live By" is a version of a Russian **folk tale**—a story that is handed down, usually by word of mouth, from generation to generation. Folk tales often show how the people in a particular region live and what their values are. As you read, be aware of what the story reveals about people's values and way of life.

ACTIVE READING **SUMMARIZING TEXT** Briefly **summarizing** a story can help you to understand the relationships between events and to identify the most important points in a story. It is often useful as you read to pause occasionally and restate the important information in the text.

READER'S NOTEBOOK This story can be divided into four main parts (sections I–V, sections VI–VII, sections VIII–IX, and sections X–XII). As you read, **summarize** briefly the main points of each of these four parts. Include only what you consider to be the most important information.

Part	Summary
I–V	
VI–VII	
VIII–IX	
X–XII	

LESSON RESOURCES

UNIT FIVE RESOURCE BOOK, pp. 29–32

ASSESSMENT RESOURCES

Formal Assessment, pp. 163–164

Teacher's Guide to Assessment and Portfolio Use

Test Generator

SKILLS TRANSPARENCIES AND COPYMASTERS

Literary Analysis
- The Moral Tale, Ballad, Fable, and Folk Tale, T23 (for Literary Analysis, p. 914)

Reading and Critical Thinking
- Summarizing, T10 (for Active Reading, p. 914)

Grammar
- *If-Then* Complex Sentences, C125 (for Mini Lesson, pp. 930–931)

Vocabulary
- Idioms, C72 (for Mini Lesson, p. 919)
- Analogies, C73 (for Mini Lesson, p. 925)

Writing
- Achieving Coherence, T8 (for Writing Option 3, p. 930)
- Subject Analysis, C30 (for Writing Option 4, p. 930)
- Compare-Contrast, C34 (for Writing Option 5, p. 930)

Communications
- Evaluating Roles in Groups, T8 (for Activities & Explorations 4, p. 930)

INTEGRATED TECHNOLOGY

Audio Library

LaserLinks
- Cultural Connection: Tolstoy's World. See **Teacher's SourceBook,** p. 63.

Visit our website:
www.mcdougallittell.com

What Men Live By

LEO TOLSTOY

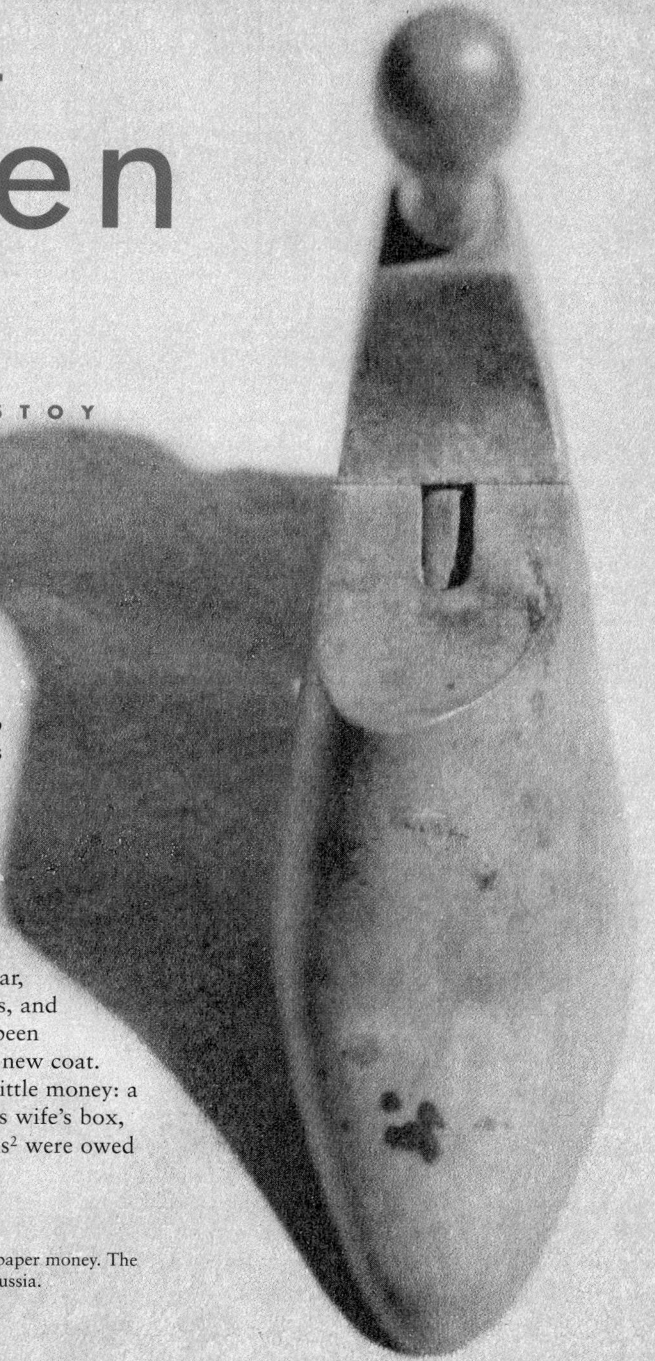

I

A shoemaker named Simon, who had neither house nor land of his own, lived with his wife and children in a peasant's hut and earned his living by his work. Work was cheap but bread was dear, and what he earned he spent for food. The man and his wife had but one sheep-skin coat between them for winter wear, and even that was worn to tatters, and this was the second year he had been wanting to buy sheep-skins for a new coat. Before winter Simon saved up a little money: a three-ruble note[1] lay hidden in his wife's box, and five rubles and twenty kopeks[2] were owed him by customers in the village.

1. **three-ruble** (ro͞o′bəl) **note:** a piece of paper money. The ruble is the main monetary unit of Russia.
2. **kopeks:** one-hundredths of a ruble.

TEACHING THE LITERATURE

Customizing Instruction

Less Proficient Readers

Have students describe the living conditions of the poor peasant, Simon. Elicit that his family has little to eat, has few clothes, and cannot depend on other peasants to pay for Simon's work, since they are just as poor. Tell students that the first two sections of the story concern Simon's attempts to collect what is owed him. Have students read to find out what happens.

Students Acquiring English

You may want to review some of the concepts in the story that may be unfamiliar to students. Ask students what they know about the craft of shoemaking and Russian history. Make sure they understand the information in the Build Background on p. 914.

Explain the meaning of idioms such as "Work was cheap but bread was dear" (wages were low, but food was expensive); "to buy . . . on credit" (to buy something that will be paid for at a later time); "caught the knack" (understood how to do something); "take my measure" (measure someone for clothes or shoes); "the thought they spend on their own welfare" (thinking about their own well-being).

Use **Spanish Study Guide** for additional support, pp. 209–211.

Gifted and Talented

Ask students to consider how each character in the story is rewarded or punished for his or her behavior. How do these consequences support the story's theme?

BLOCK SCHEDULING: MANAGING TIME

If your schedule requires that you cover the lesson objectives in a shorter time, use . . .

- Preparing to Read, p. 914
- Thinking Through the Literature, p. 929

If you want to take advantage of longer class time, use . . .

- TE Teaching Options: Vocabulary, pp. 919, 925; Viewing and Representing, pp. 918, 921; Cross-Curricular Links, pp. 920, 923; Informal Assessment, pp. 927, 928; Standardized Test Practice, p. 924; Grammar, p. 930
- Choices & Challenges and Author Activity, pp. 930–931

Reading and Analyzing

Literary Analysis FOLK TALE

In traditional tales such as this one, the number three often has particular significance. In this story, for example, Michael masters the art of shoemaking in three days. Encourage students as they read to note other instances where the number three is important.

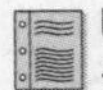
Use **Unit Five Resource Book** p. 30 for more exercises.

Active Reading SUMMARIZING TEXT

Discuss with students what they learn from these first pages or so about the setting and characters. Ask them to summarize the information.

Possible Response: A poor Russian shoemaker named Simon lived with his wife and children in a peasant's hut. He saved money before winter for sheep-skins to make a coat.

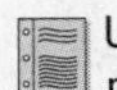
Use **Unit Five Resource Book,** p. 29 for additional support.

Literary Analysis: THEME

Have students think about the theme of this story as they read. Explain that the theme is the central message or idea in a work of literature. It should not be confused with the subject of the work; rather, it is a perception about life or human nature. Have students consider what this story reveals about life and human nature.

ACTIVE READING

A PREDICT Simon knows his wife is going to be unhappy that he is returning without the sheepskins. He says that she won't be pleased that he is bringing along a naked man. Therefore, she probably won't want the young man in her house.

So one morning he prepared to go to the village to buy the sheep-skins. He put on over his shirt his wife's wadded nankeen[3] jacket, and over that he put his own cloth coat. He took the three-ruble note in his pocket, cut himself a stick to serve as a staff, and started off after breakfast. "I'll collect the five rubles that are due to me," thought he, "add the three I have got, and that will be enough to buy sheep-skins for the winter coat."

He came to the village and called at a peasant's hut, but the man was not at home. The peasant's wife promised that the money should be paid next week, but she would not pay it herself. Then Simon called on another peasant, but this one swore he had no money, and would only pay twenty kopeks which he owed for a pair of boots Simon had mended. Simon then tried to buy the sheep-skins on credit, but the dealer would not trust him.

"Bring your money," said he, "then you may have your pick of the skins. We know what debt-collecting is like."

So all the business the shoemaker did was to get the twenty kopeks for boots he had mended and to take a pair of felt boots a peasant gave him to sole with leather.

Simon felt downhearted. He spent the twenty kopeks on vodka and started homewards without having bought any skins. In the morning he had felt the frost; but now, after drinking the vodka, he felt warm even without a sheep-skin coat. He trudged along, striking his stick on the frozen earth with one hand, swinging the felt boots with the other, and talking to himself.

"I'm quite warm," said he, "though I have no sheep-skin coat. I've had a drop and it runs through my veins. I need no sheep-skins. I go along and don't worry about anything. That's the sort of man I am! What do I care? I can live without sheep-skins. I don't need them. My wife will fret, to be sure. And, true enough, it *is* a shame; one works all day long and then does not get paid. Stop a bit! If you don't bring that money along, sure enough I'll skin you, blessed if I don't. How's that? He pays twenty kopeks at a time! What can I do with twenty kopeks? Drink it—that's all one can do! Hard up, he says he is! So he may be—but what about me? You have house, and cattle, and everything; I've only what I stand up in! You have corn of your own growing, I have to buy every grain. Do what I will, I must spend three rubles every week for bread alone. I come home and find the bread all used up and I have to work out another ruble and a half. So just you pay up what you owe, and no nonsense about it!"

By this time he had nearly reached the shrine at the bend of the road. Looking up, he saw something whitish behind the shrine. The daylight was fading, and the shoemaker peered at the thing without being able to make out what it was. "There was no white stone here before. Can it be an ox? It's not like an ox. It has a head like a man, but it's too white; and what could a man be doing there?"

He came closer, so that it was clearly visible. To his surprise it really was a man, alive or dead, sitting naked, leaning motionless against the shrine. Terror seized the shoemaker, and he thought, "Some one has killed him, stripped him, and left him here. If I meddle I shall surely get into trouble."

So the shoemaker went on. He passed in front of the shrine so that he could not see the man. When he had gone some way he looked back, and saw that the man was no longer leaning against the shrine but was moving as if looking towards him. The shoemaker felt more frightened than before, and thought, "Shall I go back to him or shall I go on? If I go near him something dreadful may happen. Who knows who the fellow is? He has not come here for any good. If I go near him he may jump up and throttle me, and there will be no getting away. Or if not, he'd still be a burden on one's hands. What could I do with a naked man? I couldn't give him my last clothes. Heaven only help me to get away!"

So the shoemaker hurried on, leaving the shrine

3. **nankeen:** a sturdy, cotton cloth.

behind him—when suddenly his conscience smote[4] him and he stopped in the road.

"What are you doing, Simon?" said he to himself. "The man may be dying of want, and you slip past afraid. Have you grown so rich as to be afraid of robbers? Ah, Simon, shame on you!"

So he turned back and went up to the man.

II

1 Simon approached the stranger, looked at him and saw that he was a young man, fit, with no bruises on his body, but evidently freezing and frightened, and he sat there leaning back without looking up at Simon, as if too faint to lift his eyes. Simon went close to him and then the man seemed to wake up. Turning his head, he opened his eyes and looked into Simon's face. That one look was enough to make Simon fond of the man. He threw the felt boots on the ground, undid his sash, laid it on the boots, and took off his cloth coat.

"It's not a time for talking," said he. "Come, put this coat on at once!" And Simon took the man by the elbows and helped him to rise. As he stood there, Simon saw that his body was clean and in good condition, his hands and feet shapely, and his face good and kind. He threw his coat over the man's shoulders, but the latter could not find the sleeves. Simon guided his arms into them, and drawing the coat on well, wrapped it closely about him, tying the sash round the man's waist.

Simon even took off his cap to put it on the man's head, but then his own head felt cold and he thought: "I'm quite bald, while he has long curly hair." So he put his cap on his own head again. "It will be better to give him something for his feet," thought he; and he made the man sit down and helped him to put on the felt boots, saying, "There, friend, now move about and warm yourself. Other matters can be settled later on. Can you walk?"

The man stood up and looked kindly at Simon but could not say a word.

"Why don't you speak?" said Simon. "It's too cold to stay here, we must be getting home. There now, take my stick, and if you're feeling weak lean on that. Now step out!"

The man started walking and moved easily, not lagging behind.

As they went along, Simon asked him, "And where do you belong to?"

"I'm not from these parts."

"I thought as much. I know the folks hereabouts. But how did you come to be there by the shrine?"

"I cannot tell."

"Has some one been ill-treating you?"

"No one has ill-treated me. God has punished me."

"Of course God rules all. Still, you'll have to find food and shelter somewhere. Where do you want to go to?"

"It is all the same to me."

Simon was amazed. The man did not look like a rogue, and he spoke gently, but yet he gave no 2
account of himself. Still Simon thought, "Who knows what may have happened?" And he said to the stranger: "Well then, come home with me and at least warm yourself awhile."

So Simon walked towards his home, and the stranger kept up with him, walking at his side. The wind had risen and Simon felt it cold under his shirt. He was getting over his tipsiness by now and began to feel the frost. He went along sniffling and wrapping his wife's coat round him, and he thought to himself: "There now—talk about sheep-skins! I went out for sheep-skins and come home without even a coat to my back, and what is more, I'm bringing a naked man along with me. Matrëna won't be pleased!" And when he thought of his wife he felt sad, but when he looked at the stranger and remembered how he had looked up at him at the shrine, his heart was glad.

ACTIVE READING

PREDICT How do you think Simon's wife will react to the stranger?

4. **smote:** dealt a blow to; sharply affected.

Customizing Instruction

Less Proficient Readers

1 Tell students that as they read this section and the next section, they should pay close attention to Simon's thoughts regarding the naked man. Have students use a chart, such as a flow-chart, to keep track of how Simon's opinion of the naked man changes.

Students Acquiring English

2 Tell students that a *rogue* is a scoundrel, or an unprincipled person. Ask students why Simon at first thinks the man might be a rogue.

Possible Response: By offering so little information about himself, the man appears to have something to hide.

WHAT MEN LIVE BY 917

Reading and Analyzing

Literary Analysis: IRONY

This passage at the beginning of section III is a good example of dramatic irony because the reader knows what Matrëna does not know: Despite her planning, Matrëna cannot make the bread last until Friday because Simon is bringing home someone else to feed.

Reading Skills and Strategies: QUESTIONING

After students have read section III, discuss with them the questions raised so far. The overarching question concerns the identity of the naked man. Have students work in pairs or small groups to create a list of specific questions that have been raised in the story so far.
Possible Responses: Why can't the man tell how he came to the shrine? Why was he naked and freezing? How will Simon and Matrëna survive the winter without a new coat and with no money?

Nightfall at Hradčany (1909–1913), Jakub Schikaneder. Oil on canvas, 33.7″ × 41.9″, National Gallery, Prague, Czech Republic.

III

Simon's wife had everything ready early that day. She had cut wood, brought water, fed the children, eaten her own meal, and now she sat thinking. She wondered when she ought to make bread: now or tomorrow? There was still a large piece left.

"If Simon has had some dinner in town," thought she, "and does not eat much for supper, the bread will last out another day."

She weighed the piece of bread in her hand again and again and thought: "I won't make any more today. We have only enough flour left to bake one batch. We can manage to make this last out till Friday."

So Matrëna put away the bread and sat down at the table to patch her husband's shirt. While she worked she thought how her husband was buying skins for a winter coat.

"If only the dealer does not cheat him. My good man is much too simple; he cheats nobody, but any child can take him in. Eight rubles is a lot of money—he should get a good coat at that price. Not tanned skins, but still a proper winter coat. How difficult it was last winter to get on without a winter coat. I could neither get down to the river nor go out anywhere. When he went out he put on all we had, and there was nothing left for me. He did not start very early today, but still it's time he was back. I only hope he has not gone on the spree!"

Hardly had Matrëna thought this than steps were heard on the threshold and some one entered. Matrëna stuck her needle into her work and went out into the passage. There she saw two men: Simon, and with him a man without a hat and wearing felt boots.

Matrëna noticed at once that her husband smelt of spirits. "There now, he has been drinking," thought she. And when she saw that he was coatless, had only her jacket on, brought no parcel, stood there silent, and seemed ashamed, her heart

Teaching Options

Viewing and Representing

Nightfall at Hradčany **by Jakub Schikaneder**

ART APPRECIATION This oil painting of Old Prague shows the unusual colors of the city's misty sunset.
Instruction Just as writers choose words to convey subtle shades of feeling, artists select colors to do the same. Students might begin to explore this concept by discussing the colors of the sunset in *Nightfall at Hradčany.* The colors an artist combines for a particular painting are called a *palette.*
Application How does the palette affect the mood of this picture?
Possible Response: The muted oranges and misty grays give the painting a distant, dreamlike quality. What is the effect of grouping the figures on one side of the painting and the building's silhouette on the other?
Possible Response: The building seems even more distant by its separation from the woman and the statue on the right. The woman, who stands just right of center, seems at once separate from the building and separate from the statue, which is raised high above her on a pedestal.

was ready to break with disappointment. "He has drunk the money," thought she, "and has been on the spree with some good-for-nothing fellow whom he has brought home with him."

Matrëna let them pass into the hut, followed them in, and saw that the stranger was a young, slight man, wearing her husband's coat. There was no shirt to be seen under it, and he had no hat. Having entered, he stood neither moving nor raising his eyes, and Matrëna thought: "He must be a bad man—he's afraid."

Matrëna frowned, and stood beside the stove looking to see what they would do.

Simon took off his cap and sat down on the bench as if things were all right.

"Come, Matrëna; if supper is ready, let us have some."

Matrëna muttered something to herself and did not move but stayed where she was, by the stove. She looked first at the one and then at the other of them and only shook her head. Simon saw that his wife was annoyed, but tried to pass it off. Pretending not to notice anything, he took the stranger by the arm.

"Sit down, friend," said he, "and let us have some supper."

The stranger sat down on the bench.

"Haven't you cooked anything for us?" said Simon.

Matrëna's anger boiled over. "I've cooked, but not for you. It seems to me you have drunk your wits away. You went to buy a sheep-skin coat but come home without so much as the coat you had on and bring a naked vagabond home with you. I have no supper for drunkards like you."

"That's enough, Matrëna. Don't wag your tongue without reason! You had better ask what sort of man—"

"And you tell me what you've done with the money?"

Simon found the pocket of the jacket, drew out the three-ruble note, and unfolded it.

"Here is the money. Trifonov did not pay, but promises to pay soon."

Matrëna got still more angry; he had bought no sheep-skins but had put his only coat on some naked fellow and had even brought him to their house.

She snatched up the note from the table, took it to put away in safety, and said: "I have no supper for you. We can't feed all the naked drunkards in the world."

"There now, Matrëna, hold your tongue a bit. First hear what a man has to say—!"

"Much wisdom I shall hear from a drunken fool. I was right in not wanting to marry you—a drunkard. The linen my mother gave me you drank; and now you've been to buy a coat—and have drunk it too!"

Simon tried to explain to his wife that he had only spent twenty kopeks; tried to tell how he had found the man—but Matrëna would not let him get a word in. She talked nineteen to the dozen[5] and dragged in things that had happened ten years before.

Matrëna talked and talked, and at last she flew at Simon and seized him by the sleeve.

"Give me my jacket. It is the only one I have, and you must needs take it from me and wear it yourself. Give it here, you mangy dog, and may the devil take you."

Simon began to pull off the jacket, and turned a sleeve of it inside out; Matrëna seized the jacket and it burst its seams. She snatched it up, threw it over her head, and went to the door. She meant to go out, but stopped undecided—she wanted to work off her anger, but she also wanted to learn what sort of a man the stranger was.

IV

Matrëna stopped and said: "If he were a good man he would not be naked. Why, he hasn't even a shirt on him. If he were all right, you would say where you came across the fellow."

"That's just what I am trying to tell you," said

5. **talked nineteen to the dozen:** chattered on excessively.

Customizing Instruction

Less Proficient Readers

Before students continue reading, discuss the first two sections of the story in class.

- Why can't Simon buy sheepskins to make a winter coat?
  Answer: The people who owe him money cannot pay him.
- Whom does Simon see by the shrine?
  Answer: a stranger.
- What does Simon decide to do about the man?
  Answer: After walking past the man, Simon decides to go back and take the stranger home.

Students Acquiring English

1 Point out the idiom *wag your tongue.* Tell students that the expression means "to talk without stopping." Tell students that *hold your tongue* means the opposite of *wag your tongue.* Then ask them what *hold your tongue* means.

Answer: "to say nothing at all."

Gifted and Talented

In section III, Tolstoy explores the contrast between what one expects or believes and what is actually the case. For example, Matrëna thinks that because Simon is late he might have been drinking, when actually he is late for other reasons. Have students construct a chart to show the contrasts between Matrëna's expectations and reality.

Mini Lesson Vocabulary Strategy

IDIOMS

Instruction Every language is made up of idioms—that is, phrases which are not meant to be taken literally, but whose meaning is understood by speakers of that language. For example, one speaker may say she "caught a cold." Another might say that something "caught his eye." Usages like these develop over the years and defy logic.

Activity Have students look for idioms in this story, especially in section III in the conversation between Matrëna and Simon. Ask students to refer to the context to determine what such idioms might mean. One example is given below.

1. "He has drunk the money." (p. 919) Context: Just before Matrëna thought this, she noticed that her husband smelled of spirits, or liquor. She also noticed that he had no parcel, which meant he had not bought the sheep-skins. She assumed that he had collected the money and bought liquor with it—thus the idiom "He has drunk the money."
2. "Don't wag your tongue." (p. 919)
3. "She talked nineteen to the dozen." (p. 919)

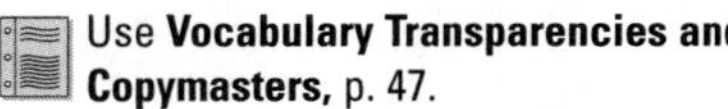
Use **Vocabulary Transparencies and Copymasters,** p. 47.

Reading and Analyzing

Literary Analysis
RUSSIAN SHORT STORY

A Ask students what Simon's anguished question to Matrëna suggests about the couple.
Possible Responses: They are religious; they believe that love of God is synonymous with love of their fellow man; they normally try to do the right thing; they believe that God will reward or punish them according to their actions.

ACTIVE READING

B **QUESTION** **Possible Response:** Simon reminds her of God's role in their lives; she feels genuinely sorry for the stranger; she is curious about his situation; she recognizes he is neither a drunk nor likely to harm them.

Literary Analysis: THEME
Simon is able to get Matrëna to put aside her righteous anger by invoking her love of God. Ask students how this points to the theme of the story.
Possible Response: Simon has reminded Matrëna of her love of God, and this will be Michael's first lesson—that love dwells in people.

Simon. "As I came to the shrine I saw him sitting all naked and frozen. It isn't quite the weather to sit about naked! God sent me to him or he would have perished. What was I to do? How do we know what may have happened to him? So I took him, clothed him, and brought him along. Don't be so angry, Matrëna. It is a sin. Remember, we must all die one day."

1 Angry words rose to Matrëna's lips, but she looked at the stranger and was silent. He sat on the edge of the bench, motionless, his hands folded on his knees, his head drooping on his breast, his eyes closed, and his brows knit as if

A in pain. Matrëna was silent, and Simon said: "Matrëna, have you no love of God?"

Matrëna heard these words, and as she looked at the stranger, suddenly her heart softened towards him. She came back from the door, and going to the stove she got out the supper. Setting a cup on the table, she poured out some kvas.[6] Then she brought out the last piece of bread and set out a knife and spoons.

"Eat, if you want to," said she.

Simon drew the stranger to the table.

"Take your place, young man," said he.

Simon cut the bread, crumbled it into the broth, and they began to eat. Matrëna sat at the corner of the table, resting her head on her hand and looking at the stranger.

And Matrëna was touched with pity for the stranger and began to feel fond of him. And at once the stranger's face lit up; his brows were no longer bent, he raised his eyes and smiled at Matrëna.

When they had finished supper, the woman cleared away the things and began questioning the stranger. "Where are you from?" said she.

"I am not from these parts."

"But how did you come to be on the road?"

"I may not tell."

"Did some one rob you?"

"God punished me."

"And you were lying there naked?"

"Yes, naked and freezing. Simon saw me and had pity on me. He took off his coat, put it on me, and brought me here. And you have fed me, given me drink, and shown pity on me. God will reward you!"

Matrëna rose, took from the window Simon's old shirt she had been patching, and gave it to the stranger. She also brought out a pair of trousers for him.

"There," said she, "I see you have no shirt. Put this on, and lie down where you please, in the loft or on the stove."[7]

ACTIVE READING

QUESTION Why do you think Matrëna's attitude toward the stranger has changed?

The stranger took off the coat, put on the shirt, B
and lay down in the loft. Matrëna put out the candle, took the coat, and climbed to where her husband lay on the stove.

Matrëna drew the skirts of the coat over her and lay down but could not sleep; she could not get the stranger out of her mind.

When she remembered that he had eaten their last piece of bread and that there was none for tomorrow and thought of the shirt and trousers she had given away, she felt grieved; but when she remembered how he had smiled, her heart was glad.

Long did Matrëna lie awake, and she noticed that Simon also was awake—he drew the coat towards him.

"Simon!"

"Well?"

"You have had the last of the bread and I have not put any to rise. I don't know what we shall do tomorrow. Perhaps I can borrow some of neighbor Martha."

"If we're alive we shall find something to eat."

The woman lay still awhile, and then said, "He seems a good man, but why does he not tell us who he is?"

6. **kvas** (kväs): a Russian drink, similar to beer, made from fermented grains.

7. **on the stove:** The large stoves and ovens in Russian peasant homes often had tops large enough to sleep on for extra warmth.

Teaching Options

Multicultural Link: Folktales

Cultures all over the world tell folktales or their variants, the myth and the fable. In many folktales the characters are actually animals, as they are in the African trickster tales. The hare plays the part of trickster in Bantu and western Sudan tales. In West Africa, the spider or the tortoise is the trickster. Sometimes the trickster is a human being, such as in Benin and in Tanzania and among the Zulu. The spider trickster, Anansi, made his way into Jamaican folktales as Anancy.

In one folktale told by the Yoruba of Africa, the tortoise steals a gourd from the gods that contains all the wisdom of the world. He hangs the gourd around his neck, but when he gets to a tree trunk lying in the road, he is unable to climb over it because the gourd gets in his way. The tortoise is so anxious to get home he does not think to put the gourd across his back. Frustrated, the tortoise smashes the gourd. And, so the tale goes, that is why today wisdom is scattered all over the world in tiny pieces.

"I suppose he has his reasons."

"Simon!"

"Well?"

"We give; but why does nobody give us anything?"

Simon did not know what to say; so he only said, "Let us stop talking" and turned over and went to sleep.

In the morning Simon awoke. The children were still asleep; his wife had gone to the neighbor's to borrow some bread. The stranger alone was sitting on the bench, dressed in the old shirt and trousers, and looking upwards. His face was brighter than it had been the day before.

Simon said to him, "Well, friend; the belly wants bread and the naked body clothes. One has to work for a living. What work do you know?"

"I do not know any."

This surprised Simon, but he said, "Men who want to learn can learn anything."

"Men work and I will work also."

"What is your name?"

"Michael."

"Well, Michael, if you don't wish to talk about yourself, that is your own affair; but you'll have to earn a living for yourself. If you will work as I tell you, I will give you food and shelter."

"May God reward you! I will learn. Show me what to do."

Simon took yarn, put it round his thumb and 
began to twist it.

Grain Harvest (1908), Natalia Sergeevna Goncharova. Oil on canvas, 96 cm × 103 cm, The State Russian Museum, St. Petersburg, Russia.

Customizing Instruction

Less Proficient Readers

1 Ask students what happens when Matrëna meets the stranger.

- How does Matrëna react to the stranger at first?
  Answer: She is rude and does not want him in her house.
- What causes Matrëna to have a change of heart?
  Answer: Simon appeals to her love of God.
- What does the stranger do when Matrëna's heart softens toward him?
  Answer: He smiles at her.

Students Acquiring English

2 Be sure students understand that this sentence and the following passages describe Simon's efforts to teach Michael the shoemaking trade.

Multiple Learning Styles

Visual Learners
Bring paintings and photographs of Russian peasants from the late 19th century. Give students an opportunity to study the pictures and to comment on what they learn from them.

Mini Lesson Viewing and Representing

Grain Harvest **by Natalia Sergeevna Goncharova**

ART APPRECIATION

Instruction This 1908 painting shows many of the characteristics of Goncharova's folk art. During summers, she studied the peasants at work at her family's Cotton Factory estate. Their lives and work became a favorite theme of hers.

Application Have students look at the home in the picture. How do the colors and textures affect the meaning of the painting?

Possible Response: The lumpy, rather stark textures emphasize the hard work of the peasants. The bold, natural colors bring out the peasants' close association with nature.

Why would you characterize this work as folk art?

Possible Responses: Its subject is the harvest, a central event in the lives of peasants, or common folk; it appears to have been painted by an untrained artist.

Then, ask students to compare the home in the painting with their image of Simon and Matrëna's home. How do they think the homes are different? How might they be similar?

Possible Responses: This home is painted and has a nice green lawn around it, but Simon and Matrëna's home is probably in worse condition; This home appears to be small, and Simon and Matrëna's home is probably also small.

WHAT MEN LIVE BY 921

Reading and Analyzing

Literary Analysis FOLK TALE

Folktales often incorporate magical features. What aspects of Michael's behavior so far have seemed magical?

Possible Response: Students may point out his ability to learn a craft when he previously knew nothing about work.

Literary Analysis: RUSSIAN SHORT STORY

Mythic tales often involve a challenge to the hero by forces that seem overpowering. Ask students to describe the challenge of making boots that will last a year. Why does this task seem intimidating?

Possible Response: Students may comment that the gentleman seems so large and rough that probably nothing he owns can survive a year of use.

Literary Analysis: IRONY

A After students have read the next section of the story, have them return to the gentleman's words. Ask students what kind of irony is used here.

Answer: situational.

Literary Analysis: FORESHADOWING

B After students have read the next section of the story, have them return to this point. Ask them what function Matrëna's words serve.

Answer: They foreshadow the gentleman's death.

"It is easy enough—see!"

Michael watched him, put some yarn round his own thumb in the same way, caught the knack, and twisted the yarn also.

Then Simon showed him how to wax the thread. This also Michael mastered. Next Simon showed him how to twist the bristle in, and how to sew, and this, too, Michael learned at once.

Whatever Simon showed him he understood at once, and after three days he worked as if he had sewn boots all his life. He worked without stopping and ate little. When work was over he sat silently, looking upwards. He hardly went into the street, spoke only when necessary, and neither joked nor laughed. They never saw him smile, except that first evening when Matrëna gave him supper.

1

VI

Day by day and week by week the year went round. Michael lived and worked with Simon. His fame spread till people said that no one sewed boots so neatly and strongly as Simon's workman, Michael; from all the district round people came to Simon for their boots, and he began to be well off.

One winter day, as Simon and Michael sat working, a carriage on sledge-runners, with three horses and with bells, drove up to the hut. They looked out of the window; the carriage stopped at their door; a fine servant jumped down from the box and opened the door. A gentleman in a fur coat got out and walked up to Simon's hut. Up jumped Matrëna and opened the door wide. The gentleman stooped to enter the hut, and when he drew himself up again his head nearly reached the ceiling and he seemed quite to fill his end of the room.

Simon rose, bowed, and looked at the gentleman with astonishment. He had never seen any one like him. Simon himself was lean, Michael was thin, and Matrëna was dry as a bone, but this man was like some one from another world: red-faced, burly, with a neck like a bull's, and looking altogether as if he were cast in iron.

The gentleman puffed, threw off his fur coat, sat down on the bench, and said, "Which of you is the master bootmaker?"

"I am, your Excellency," said Simon, coming forward.

Then the gentleman shouted to his lad, "Hey, Fédka, bring the leather!"

The servant ran in, bringing a parcel. The gentleman took the parcel and put it on the table.

"Untie it," said he. The lad untied it.

The gentleman pointed to the leather.

"Look here, shoemaker," said he, "do you see this leather?"

"Yes, your honor."

"But do you know what sort of leather it is?"

Simon felt the leather and said, "It is good leather."

"Good, indeed! Why, you fool, you never saw such leather before in your life. It's German and cost twenty rubles."

Simon was frightened and said, "Where should I ever see leather like that?"

"Just so! Now, can you make it into boots for me?"

"Yes, your Excellency, I can."

Then the gentleman shouted at him: "You *can,* can you? Well, remember whom you are to make them for, and what the leather is. You must make me boots that will wear for a year, neither losing shape nor coming unsewn. If you can do it, take the leather and cut it up; but if you can't, say so. I warn you now, if your boots come unsewn or lose shape within a year I will have you put in prison. If they don't burst or lose shape for a year, A
I will pay you ten rubles for your work."

Simon was frightened and did not know what to say. He glanced at Michael and nudging him with his elbow, whispered: "Shall I take the work?"

Michael nodded his head as if to say, "Yes, take it."

Simon did as Michael advised and undertook

Teaching Options

Cross Curricular Link History

NINETEENTH-CENTURY RUSSIA The continuation of a peasant class into the 19th century is one of the distinctive elements of Russian history and culture. The peasant class in Russia was essentially a class of serfs. These people, although not technically slaves, led very slavelike lives.

For centuries in Russia, it was customary for peasants to renegotiate their status with the landowners after the gathering of the harvest, on or about St. George's Day (November 24). Toward the end of the 16th century, however, the power of the nobles and the church over the peasant class was so great that it became nearly impossible for serfs to pay any debts they might owe and leave the land. Their condition degenerated until it began to interfere with the economic development of Russia itself. The Emancipation of 1861 transferred to each serf a portion of the land the serf's family had been cultivating and arranged for the former landowners to be compensated over a period of years.

to make boots that would not lose shape or split for a whole year.

Calling his servant, the gentleman told him to pull the boot off his left leg, which he stretched out.

"Take my measure!" said he.

Simon stitched a paper measure seventeen inches long, smoothed it out, knelt down, wiped his hands well on his apron so as not to soil the gentleman's sock, and began to measure. He measured the sole, and round the instep, and began to measure the calf of the leg, but the paper was too short. The calf of the leg was as thick as a beam.

"Mind you don't make it too tight in the leg."

Simon stitched on another strip of paper. The gentleman twitched his toes about in his sock looking round at those in the hut, and as he did so he noticed Michael.

"Whom have you there?" asked he.

"That is my workman. He will sew the boots."

"Mind," said the gentleman to Michael, "remember to make them so that they will last me a year."

Simon also looked at Michael and saw that Michael was not looking at the gentleman, but was gazing into the corner behind the gentleman, as if he saw some one there. Michael looked and looked, and suddenly he smiled, and his face became brighter.

"What are you grinning at, you fool?" thundered the gentleman. "You had better look to it that the boots are ready in time."

"They shall be ready in good time," said Michael.

"Mind it is so," said the gentleman, and he put on his boots and his fur coat, wrapped the latter round him, and went to the door. But he forgot to stoop, and struck his head against the lintel.[8]

He swore and rubbed his head. Then he took his seat in the carriage and drove away.

When he had gone, Simon said: "There's a figure of a man for you! You could not kill him with a mallet. He almost knocked out the lintel, but little harm it did him."

And Matrëna said: "Living as he does, how should he not have grown strong? Death itself can't touch such a rock as that." B

VII

Then Simon said to Michael: "Well, we have taken the work, but we must see we don't get into trouble over it. The leather is dear, and the gentleman hot-tempered. We must make no mistakes. Come, your eye is truer and your hands have become nimbler than mine, so you take this measure and cut out the boots. I will finish off the sewing of the vamps."[9] 2

Michael did as he was told. He took the leather, spread it out on the table, folded it in two, took a knife and began to cut out.

Matrëna came and watched him cutting and was surprised to see how he was doing it. Matrëna was accustomed to seeing boots made, and she looked and saw that Michael was not cutting the leather for boots, but was cutting it round.

She wished to say something, but she thought to herself: "Perhaps I do not understand how gentlemen's boots should be made. I suppose Michael knows more about it—and I won't interfere."

When Michael had cut up the leather he took a thread and began to sew not with two ends, as boots are sewn, but with a single end, as for soft slippers.

Again Matrëna wondered, but again she did not interfere. Michael sewed on steadily till noon. Then Simon rose for dinner, looked around, and saw that Michael had made slippers out of the gentleman's leather.

"Ah!" groaned Simon, and he thought, "How is it that Michael, who has been with me a whole year and never made a mistake before, should do

8. **lintel:** the horizontal beam at the top of a door frame.

9. **vamps:** the upper parts of shoes or boots, covering the instep or the instep and the toes.

Customizing Instruction

Multiple Learning Styles

Auditory Learners

1 Have volunteers take the parts of Simon, Michael, the gentleman, and the narrator in section VI. Encourage them to read their parts with feeling. Then have students discuss what they have learned about the three characters from how they acted and reacted in this scene. Elicit that Simon now depends on Michael for advice although Simon is still the master craftsman.

Students Acquiring English

2 Students might not understand the expression *your eye is truer.* Explain that Michael is younger than Simon and can see more accurately to measure, cut straight lines, and do the close work required to make perfect boots. Then have students use context clues to determine the meaning of *nimbler.* Point out that the ending *-er* indicates a comparative form meaning "more nimble." Students should be able to infer from Simon's statement that "nimble hands" are more capable, since he is asking Michael to do a difficult and important task. Students may not be able to determine the exact meaning of *nimble (agile* or *graceful)* from context clues, so direct them to a dictionary if necessary.

WHAT MEN LIVE BY 923

Reading and Analyzing

ACTIVE READING

A SUMMARIZE Michael does good work and Simon's business prospers; Michael makes slippers for a gentleman who orders boots—Michael seems to know the gentlemen will die and not need boots but rather slippers for his corpse.

Literary Analysis: SYMBOL

Ask students to describe the light that has come from Michael on three occasions. Ask what the light represents.

Possible Responses: purity; knowledge.

Ask students how Tolstoy's use of this symbol contributes to the meaning of the story.

Possible Response: Students may argue that it is not clear yet how the symbol is being used.

Reading Skills and Strategies: CLARIFYING

How were the twins able to survive after their mother's death?

Answer: They were nursed and raised by the neighbor.

Active Reading SUMMARIZING TEXT

Summarizing is a way of pointing out the most important information in a text. For example, in section VIII, a summary would not include the detail of Matrëna putting away iron pots, but it would emphasize Michael's reaction upon hearing of the woman and the two girls. Have students work in pairs to write a summary of the section. Then have each pair share its summary with the class and receive feedback.

such a dreadful thing? The gentleman ordered high boots, welted,[10] with whole fronts, and Michael has made soft slippers with single soles and has wasted the leather. What am I to say to the gentleman? I can never replace leather such as this."

And he said to Michael, "What are you doing, friend? You have ruined me! You know the gentleman ordered high boots, but see what you have made!"

Hardly had he begun to rebuke Michael, when "rat-tat" went the iron ring hung at the door. Some one was knocking. They looked out of the window; a man had come on horseback and was fastening his horse. They opened the door, and the servant who had been with the gentleman came in.

"Good day," said he.

"Good day," replied Simon. "What can we do for you?"

"My mistress has sent me about the boots."

"What about the boots?"

"Why, my master no longer needs them. He is dead."

"Is it possible?"

"He did not live to get home after leaving you but died in the carriage. When we reached home and the servants came to help him alight, he rolled over like a sack. He was dead already, and so stiff that he could hardly be got out of the carriage. My mistress sent me here, saying: 'Tell the bootmaker that the gentleman who ordered boots of him and left the leather for them no longer needs the boots, but that he must quickly make soft slippers for the corpse. Wait till they are ready and bring them back with you.' That is why I have come."

Michael gathered up the remnants of the leather; rolled them up, took the soft slippers he had made, slapped them together, wiped them down with his apron, and handed them and the roll of leather to the servant, who took them and said: "Good-bye, masters, and good day to you!"

ACTIVE READING

SUMMARIZE Summarize in a sentence or two what happens in sections VI and VII of this story. **A**

VIII

Another year passed, and another, and Michael was now living his sixth year with Simon. He lived as before. He went nowhere, only spoke when necessary, and had only smiled twice in all those years—one when Matrëna gave him food, and a second time when the gentleman was in their hut. Simon was more than pleased with his workman. He never now asked him where he came from and only feared lest Michael should go away.

They were all at home one day. Matrëna was putting iron pots in the oven; the children were running along the benches and looking out of the window; Simon was sewing at one window and Michael was fastening on a heel at the other.

One of the boys ran along the bench to Michael, leant on his shoulder, and looked out of the window.

"Look, Uncle Michael! There is a lady with little girls! She seems to be coming here. And one of the girls is lame."

When the boy said that, Michael dropped his work, turned to the window, and looked out into the street.

Simon was surprised. Michael never used to look out into the street, but now he pressed against the window, staring at something. Simon also looked out and saw that a well-dressed woman was really coming to his hut, leading by the hand two little girls in fur coats and woolen shawls. The girls could hardly be told one from the other, except that one of them was crippled in her left leg and walked with a limp.

The woman stepped into the porch and entered the passage. Feeling about for the entrance she found the latch, which she lifted, and opened the door. She let the two girls go in first, and followed them into the hut.

"Good day, good folk!"

10. **welted:** with a leather strip stitched between the sole and the upper.

Teaching Options

Assessment Standardized Test Practice

IDENTIFYING POINT OF VIEW

Have students write a short essay in response to the following question. Remind them to support their answer with evidence from the story.

Why does Tolstoy tell the story from Simon and Matrëna's point of view, never giving the reader insight into Michael's thoughts and feelings?

RUBRIC

3 Full Accomplishment Students write well-organized essay with evidence from story. They recognize Tolstoy restricts point of view to Simon and Matrëna in order to make Michael a mysterious figure.

2 Substantial Accomplishment Students write logical essay with some evidence from story. They recognize Tolstoy restricts point of view to Simon and Matrëna in order to make Michael a mysterious figure. However, essay may only touch on this point briefly, or it may have distracting spelling, grammar, and usage errors.

1 Little or Partial Accomplishment Students do not recognize Tolstoy restricts point of view to Simon and Matrëna in order to make Michael a mysterious figure. Essay is disorganized and may be somewhat incoherent with many spelling, grammar, and usage errors.

1 "Pray come in," said Simon. "What can we do for you?"

The woman sat down by the table. The two little girls pressed close to her knees, afraid of the people in the hut.

"I want leather shoes made for these two little girls, for spring."

"We can do that. We never have made such small shoes, but we can make them; either welted or turnover shoes, linen lined. My man, Michael, is a master at the work."

Simon glanced at Michael and saw that he had left his work and was sitting with his eyes fixed on the little girls. Simon was surprised. It was true the girls were pretty, with black eyes, plump, and rosy-cheeked, and they wore nice kerchiefs and fur coats, but still Simon could not understand why Michael should look at them like that—just as if he had known them before. He was puzzled but went on talking with the woman and arranging the price. Having fixed it, he prepared the measure. The woman lifted the lame girl on to her lap and said: "Take two measures from this little girl. Make one shoe for the lame foot and three for the sound one. They both have the same-sized feet. They are twins."

Simon took the measure and, speaking of the lame girl, said: "How did it happen to her? She is such a pretty girl. Was she born so?"

"No, her mother crushed her leg."

Then Matrëna joined in. She wondered who this woman was and whose the children were, so she said: "Are not you their mother, then?"

"No, my good woman; I am neither their mother nor any relation to them. They were quite strangers to me, but I adopted them."

"They are not your children and yet you are so fond of them?"

"How can I help being fond of them? I fed them both at my own breasts. I had a child of my own, but God took him. I was not so fond of him as I now am of these."

"Then whose children are they?"

IX

The woman, having begun talking, told them the whole story.

"It is about six years since their parents died, both in one week: their father was buried on the Tuesday, and their mother died on the Friday. These orphans were born three days after their father's death, and their mother did not live another day. My husband and I were then living as peasants in the village. We were neighbors of theirs, our yard being next to theirs. Their father was a lonely man, a wood-cutter in the forest. When felling trees one day they let one fall on him. It fell across his body and crushed his bowels out. They hardly got him home before his soul went to God; and that same week his wife gave birth to twins—these little girls. She was poor and alone; she had no one, young or old, with her. Alone she gave them birth, and alone she met her death.

"The next morning I went to see her, but when I entered the hut, she, poor thing, was already stark and cold. In dying she had rolled on to this child and crushed her leg. The village folk came to the hut, washed the body, laid her out, made a coffin, and buried her. They were good folk. The babies were left alone. What was to be done with them? I was the only woman there who had a baby at the time. I was nursing my first-born—eight weeks old. So I took them for a time. The peasants came together, and thought and thought what to do with them; and at last they said to me: 'For the present, Mary, you had better keep the girls, and later on we will arrange what to do for them.' So I nursed the sound one at my breast, but at first I did not feed this crippled one. I did not suppose she would live. But then I thought to myself, why should the poor innocent suffer? I pitied her and began to feed her. And so I fed my own boy and these two—the three of them—at my own breast. I was young and strong and had good food, and God gave me so much milk that at times it even overflowed. I used sometimes to feed two at a time, while the third was waiting. When one had had enough I nursed

Customizing Instruction

Students Acquiring English

1 Point out the use of the word *pray.* Tell students that they can use cause-and-effect to determine the meaning of the word. After Simon speaks to the woman, she comes inside and sits down by the table. Also, students can infer from the situation and Simon's tone what sort of word *pray* is: The woman is a customer and Simon politely asks, "What can we do for you?" This implies that *pray* is a word used as part of courtesy. In this context, *pray* means "please."

Less Proficient Readers

Ask students the following questions about Michael:

- Why does Simon come to be well off after Michael moves in?
  Answer: Michael becomes an expert shoemaker whose work is valued in the district.
- What does Michael do after the gentleman orders the boots?
  Answer: He uses the leather to make soft slippers.
- Why doesn't Michael suffer any consequences for his decision?
  Answer: The man dies; slippers are needed for his corpse.
- What do you think is the importance to the story of Michael's foreknowledge?
  Possible Responses: Students may recognize that Tolstoy is withholding information that would enable the reader to understand fully.

Vocabulary Strategy

ANALOGIES

Instruction Review with students the meaning of the term *analogy,* focusing on word analogies. Remind students that a word analogy consists of two pairs of words that have the same type of relationship in each pair. The relationship may be cause and effect, part and whole, item to category, characteristic quality, function, synonym, or antonym.

Model Write the following word analogy on the board and then read it aloud.

sycamore : tree :: robin : bird

(*Sycamore* is to *tree* as *robin* is to *bird.)*

Then elicit from students the relationship between each pair of words.

Possible Response: A sycamore is a type of tree as a robin is a type of bird.

Activity Have students complete the following analogy.

shoemaker : boots ::

A. newspaper : printer **C.** athlete : sports
B. architecture : buildings **D.** carpenter : cabinets

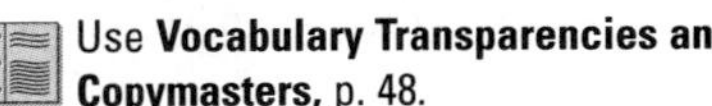
Use **Vocabulary Transparencies and Copymasters,** p. 48.

Reading and Analyzing

ACTIVE READING

A CLARIFY A neighbor woman, who had just had her own baby, took care of them.

Literary Analysis: SYMBOL

B Point out that this is the third time in the story that Michael has smiled. Ask students why this instance might be particularly meaningful.

Possible Response: This time the whole hut lights up, and Michael is gazing toward heaven.

Reading Skills and Strategies: PREDICTING

C Have students stop at this point and make a prediction about why God punished Michael. Urge students to look back at the three times that Michael smiled before they consider their predictions.

Possible Responses: for disobeying God; for doubting God's wisdom and purpose.

ACTIVE READING

D CLARIFY for disobeying God; for acting as if he knew more than God.

Reading Skills and Strategies: MAKING INFERENCES

E Ask students what Michael means when he says that if Matrëna drove him out into the cold, *she* would die.

Possible Responses: that she would have crushed the spirit of love within herself; that her soul would have perished; that she would have condemned herself to eternal damnation because of her sin.

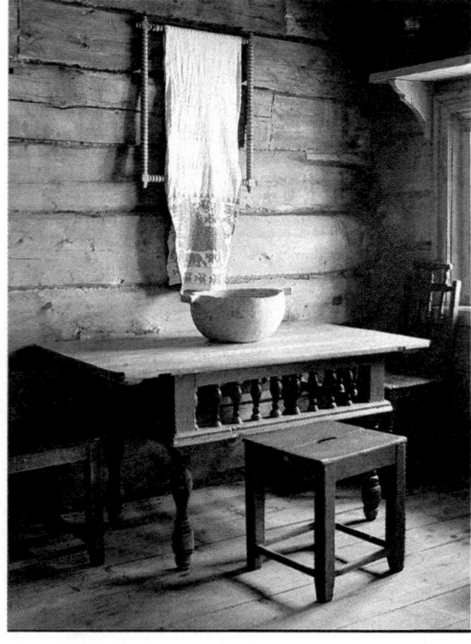

Photo by Kari Haavisto.

the third. And God so ordered it that these grew up, while my own was buried before he was two years old. And I had no more children, though we prospered. Now my husband is working for the corn merchant at the mill. The pay is good and we are well off. But I have no children of my own, and how lonely I should be without these little girls! How can I help loving them! They are the joy of my life!"

ACTIVE READING

A CLARIFY How were the twins able to survive after their mother's death?

She pressed the lame little girl to her with one hand, while with the other she wiped the tears from her cheeks.

And Matrëna sighed, and said: "The proverb is true that says, 'One may live without father or mother, but one cannot live without God.' "

So they talked together, when suddenly the whole hut was lighted up as though by summer lightning from the corner where Michael sat. They all looked towards him and saw him sitting, his hands folded on his knees, gazing upwards and smiling.

The woman went away with the girls. Michael rose from the bench, put down his work, and took off his apron. Then, bowing low to Simon and his wife, he said: "Farewell, masters. God has forgiven me. I ask your forgiveness, too, for anything done amiss."

And they saw that a light shone from Michael. And Simon rose, bowed down to Michael, and said: "I see, Michael, that you are no common man, and I can neither keep you nor question you. Only tell me this: how is it that when I found you and brought you home, you were gloomy, and when my wife gave you food you smiled at her and became brighter? Then when the gentleman came to order the boots, you smiled again and became brighter still? And now, when this woman brought the little girls, you smiled a third time and have become as bright as day? Tell me, Michael, why does your face shine so, and why did you smile those three times?" **B**

And Michael answered: "Light shines from me because I have been punished, but now God has pardoned me. And I smiled three times, because God sent me to learn three truths, and I have learnt them. One I learnt when your wife pitied me, and that is why I smiled the first time. The second I learnt when the rich man ordered the boots, and then I smiled again. And now, when I saw those little girls, I learnt the third and last, and I smiled the third time."

And Simon said, "Tell me, Michael, what did God punish you for? and what were the three truths? that I, too, may know them." **C**

And Michael answered: "God punished me for disobeying him. I was an angel in heaven and disobeyed God. God sent me to fetch a woman's

Teaching Options

Assessment Informal Assessment

COMPARING AND CONTRASTING Have students write an essay comparing and contrasting Matrëna and Mary, the woman with the twins. Have them consider the effect of charity on the women's lives, their maternal feelings, and their views of God. Remind students to support their answers with evidence from the story.

RUBRIC

3 Full Accomplishment Students write well-supported essays that both compare and contrast two women. Students demonstrate thorough understanding of women's character development and discuss effect of charity on their lives, maternal feelings, and views of God. Students may recognize that, in this story, charitable behavior leads to financial prosperity.

2 Substantial Accomplishment Students support answers with evidence from text but may only compare or contrast Matrëna and Mary. Students demonstrate basic understanding of women's character development and discuss at least two of following: effect of charity on women's lives, maternal feelings, and views of God.

soul. I flew to earth and saw a sick woman lying alone who had just given birth to twin girls. They moved feebly at their mother's side but she could not lift them to her breast. When she saw me, she understood that God had sent me for her soul, and she wept and said: 'Angel of God! My husband has just been buried, killed by a falling tree. I have neither sister, nor aunt, nor mother: no one to care for my orphans. Do not take my soul! Let me nurse my babes, feed them, and set them on their feet before I die. Children cannot live without father or mother.' And I hearkened to her. I placed one child at her breast and gave the other into her arms, and returned to the Lord in heaven. I flew to the Lord, and said: 'I could not take the soul of the mother. Her husband was killed by a tree; the woman has twins and prays that her soul may not be taken. She says: "Let me nurse and feed my children, and set them on their feet. Children cannot live without father or mother." I have not taken her soul.' And God said: 'Go—take the mother's soul, and learn three truths: Learn *What dwells in man, What is not given to man,* and *What men live by*. When thou hast learnt these things, thou shalt return to heaven.' So I flew again to earth and took the mother's soul. The babes dropped from her breasts. Her body rolled over on the bed and crushed one babe, twisting its leg. I rose above the village, wishing to take her soul to God, but a wind seized me and my wings drooped and dropped off. Her soul rose alone to God, while I fell to earth by the roadside."

ACTIVE READING

D **CLARIFY** For what was Michael punished?

1

XI

And Simon and Matrëna understood who it was that had lived with them and whom they had clothed and fed. And they wept with awe and with
2 joy. And the angel said: "I was alone in the field, naked. I had never known human needs, cold and hunger, till I became a man. I was famished, frozen, and did not know what to do. I saw, near the field I was in, a shrine built for God, and I went to it hoping to find shelter. But the shrine was locked and I could not enter. So I sat down behind the shrine to shelter myself at least from the wind. Evening drew on, I was hungry, frozen, and in pain. Suddenly I heard a man coming along the road. He carried a pair of boots and was talking to himself. For the first time since I became a man I saw the mortal face of a man, and his face seemed terrible to me and I turned from it. And I heard the man talking to himself of how to cover his body from the cold in winter, and how to feed wife and children. And I thought: 'I am perishing of cold and hunger and here is a man thinking only of how to clothe himself and his wife, and how to get bread for themselves. He cannot help me.' When the man saw me he frowned and became still more terrible and passed me by on the other side. I despaired; but suddenly I heard him coming back. I looked up and did not recognize the same man: before, I had seen death in his face; but now he was alive and I recognized in him the presence of God. He came up to me, clothed me, took me with him, and brought me to his home. I entered the house; a woman came to meet us and began to speak. The woman was still more terrible than the man had been; the spirit of death came from her mouth; I could not breathe for the stench[11] of death that spread around her. She wished to drive me out into the cold, and I knew that if she E
did so she would die. Suddenly her husband spoke to her of God, and the woman changed at once. And when she brought me food and looked at me, I glanced at her and saw that death no longer dwelt in her; she had become alive, and in her too I saw God.

"Then I remembered the first lesson God had set me: *'Learn what dwells in man.'* And I understood that in man dwells Love! I was glad that God had already begun to show me what He had promised, and I smiled for the first time.

11. **stench:** foul smell.

Customizing Instruction

Less Proficient Readers

1 As students read section XI, have them complete a chart that lists the three lessons, under what circumstances Michael learns each lesson, and the students' rephrasing of each lesson.

Multiple Learning Styles

Visual and Spatial Learners

2 Have students illustrate the moment in the story when Simon and Matrëna learn that Michael is an angel. Students should attempt to capture the emotions of awe and joy.

1 **Little or Partial Accomplishment** Students fail to support answers with logical evidence from text. Students do not understand women's character development and may only touch on one of following: effect of charity on women's lives, maternal feelings, and views of God.

Reading and Analyzing

Active Reading SUMMARIZING TEXT

Have students work in pairs to summarize the lessons that Michael learns. Then discuss whether these lessons are useful to us today.

Literary Analysis FOLK TALE

Often in folktales things return to "normal" at the end. This is true of Tolstoy's story. Discuss with students the importance of things returning to "normal" at the end.

Possible Response: By everything returning to normal at the end of the story, the story is essentially finished.

But I had not yet learnt all. I did not yet know *What is not given to man,* and *What men live by.*

"I lived with you and a year passed. A man came to order boots that should wear for a year without losing shape or cracking. I looked at him, and suddenly, behind his shoulder, I saw my comrade—the angel of death. None but me saw that angel; but I knew him, and knew that before the sun set he would take the rich man's soul. And I thought to myself, 'The man is making preparation for a year and does not know that he will die before evening.' And I remembered God's second saying, *'Learn what is not given to man.'*

"What dwells in man I already knew. Now I learnt what is not given him. It is not given to man to know his own needs. And I smiled for the second time. I was glad to have seen my comrade angel—glad also that God had revealed to me the second saying.

"But I still did not know all. I did not know *What men live by.* And I lived on, waiting till God should reveal to me the last lesson. In the sixth year came the girl-twins with the woman; and I recognized the girls and heard how they had been kept alive. Having heard the story, I thought, 'Their mother besought[12] me for the children's sake, and I believed her when she said that children cannot live without father or mother; but a stranger has nursed them and has brought them up.' And when the woman showed her love for the children that were not her own and wept over them, I saw in her the living God, and understood *What men live by.* And I knew that God had revealed to me the last lesson and had forgiven my sin. And then I smiled for the third time."

XII

And the angel's body was bared, and he was clothed in light so that eye could not look on him; and his voice grew louder, as though it came not from him but from heaven above. And the angel said: "I have learnt that all men live not by care for themselves, but by love.

"It was not given to the mother to know what her children needed for their life. Nor was it given to the rich man to know what he himself needed. Nor is it given to any man to know whether, when evening comes, he will need boots for his body or slippers for his corpse.

"I remained alive when I was a man, not by care of myself but because love was present in a passer-by and because he and his wife pitied and loved me. The orphans remained alive not because of their mother's care, but because there was love in the heart of a woman, a stranger to them, who pitied and loved them. And all men live not by the thought they spend on their own welfare, but because love exists in man.

"I knew before that God gave life to men and desires that they should live; now I understood more than that.

"I understood that God does not wish men to live apart, and therefore he does not reveal to them what each one needs for himself; but he wishes them to live united, and therefore reveals to each of them what is necessary for all.

"I have now understood that though it seems to men that they live by care for themselves, in truth it is love alone by which they live. He who has love, is in God, and God is in him, for God is love."

And the angel sang praise to God, so that the hut trembled at his voice. The roof opened, and a column of fire rose from earth to heaven. Simon and his wife and children fell to the ground. Wings appeared upon the angel's shoulders and he rose into the heavens.

And when Simon came to himself the hut stood as before, and there was no one in it but his own family. ❖

Translated by Louise and Aylmer Maude

12. **besought** (bĭ-sôt′): begged.

Teaching Options

Assessment **Informal Assessment**

UNDERSTANDING MAIN IDEA

You can informally assess students' understanding of the story by asking them to summarize in writing the following points:

- the three questions that Michael must answer
- the three answers
- how he arrives at each answer

RUBRIC

3 **Full Accomplishment** Student summaries of each of points are complete and accurate.

2 **Substantial Accomplishment** Student summaries of each of points are largely accurate, but some information is missing.

1 **Little or Partial Accomplishment** Student summaries of each of points are cursory, and some information is inaccurate.

Connect to the Literature

1. **What Do You Think?** What is your reaction to Michael's explanation of what men live by?

Comprehension Check
- Why did Simon need to buy some sheepskins?
- What was Matrëna's initial reaction to Michael?

Think Critically

2. Do you think Simon and Matrëna are basically similar or basically different? Explain your answer.

- their initial reactions to Michael and their later attitudes toward him
- how each of them copes with poverty
- the role of God in each of their lives

3. Do you think Michael has deserved to be punished by God? Give reasons for your opinion.

4. How would you explain the relationship between the three lessons Michael learns?

5. **ACTIVE READING** SUMMARIZING TEXT Review the summaries you created in your READER'S NOTEBOOK. What subtitle would you give to each of the four parts? Compare your subtitles with those of a partner, and discuss which you think are most appropriate.

Extend Interpretations

6. **Connect to Life** What do you think would happen if Michael appeared in your neighborhood as a stranger in need of food, clothing, and shelter? Do you think it would be possible for him to learn the same lessons? Give reasons for your answers.

7. **Points of Comparison** Both Tolstoy's story and Kipling's story "The Miracle of Purun Bhagat" are concerned with the qualities of a good and moral life. What similarities and differences do you think there are between the moral lessons that can be inferred from each story? Do you think the **theme** of either story is valid as a principle for living today? Explain your opinion.

Literary Analysis

FOLK TALE A **folk tale** is a story that is handed down, usually by word of mouth, from generation to generation. In addition to showing how the inhabitants of a region live and what their values are, most folk tales have some or all of the following characteristics:

- They usually suggest or explicitly state a moral.
- Many folk tales involve supernatural elements.
- Often, things happen in threes in folk tales.

Cooperative Learning Activity With three or four classmates, list the elements of folk tales that are featured in Tolstoy's story. Then discuss what elements Tolstoy adds that make this more than just a retelling of a traditional tale.

REVIEW AUTHOR'S PURPOSE Although a writer may fulfill more than one **purpose** in a work, one is usually the most important. What do you think might have been Tolstoy's main purpose for writing "What Men Live By"? What other purposes does the story fulfill?

REVIEW SETTING **Setting,** the time and place of a narrative's action, can have an important impact on what happens and why. Think about the relationship between the setting and the events in "What Men Live By." Do you think the story could have taken place in a large, modern city? Why or why not?

GUIDING STUDENT RESPONSE

Connect to the Literature

1. **What Do You Think?**
Guidelines for student response: Student reactions should be grounded in the text and in their own experience. Students should provide examples to support their opinions.

Comprehension Check
- to make a new winter coat
- negative, suspicious, uncharitable

Use **Unit Five Resource Book,** p. 31 for additional support.

Think Critically

2. Possible Responses: similar, because they both believe in God and want to do the right thing; different, because Simon is willing to help while Matrëna has to be talked into it.
3. Possible Responses: yes, because Michael put his will before God's; no, because Michael felt compassion for a human being.
4. Possible Response: Love dwells within each of us, and we need each other, so it is through living by love that we are fulfilled.
5. Subtitles should reflect the content of the four sections.

Literary Analysis

Cooperative Learning Activity Have students conduct a class discussion in which they share elements of a traditional folktale and those elements added by Tolstoy.

Review Author's Purpose List author's purposes mentioned by students on the chalkboard.

Review Setting Conduct a class discussion on why folktales often have a rural setting.

Extend Interpretations

Connect to Life Accept all reasonable, well-supported answers.

Points of Comparison Responses will vary, but should be supported. Students should recognize that in each story a main character searches for divine knowledge, makes sacrifices, and is rewarded by being able to leave this world of suffering. Have students propose themes that apply to both Tolstoy's and Kipling's stories. This activity can lead to the Points of Comparison writing activity on page 930.

Writing Options

1. **New Episode** Episodes should demonstrate an understanding of the theme of Tolstoy's story and an awareness of Tolstoy's style.
2. **Maxims for Living** Maxims from other cultures may be offered here.
3. **Newspaper Report** Journalistic reports should be true to the details of the story and include quotations from witnesses.
4. **Analytical Essay** Have students brainstorm a list of problems with a partner before they begin writing their essays. Essays should clearly describe problems faced by people today and should offer a well-organized analysis of the difficulties of leading a good life under the circumstances described.
5. **Points of Comparison** Suggest that students organize the points of comparison in a chart or other graphic organizer as a prewriting exercise. Simplicity of life, the nature of the Divine, and essential human nature are all elements to be considered in the comparison.

Activities & Exploration

1. **Storyboard Illustrations** Students might choose to model the style of their art after the style of a contemporary of Tolstoy.
2. **Newspaper Display** Students might also look in magazines for articles.
3. **Commemorative Monument** Students should be urged to look at photographs of various monuments in order to get a feel for the options available to them.
4. **Alternate Titles** Students might look in other sources, such as the Bible or the poetry of John Donne or George Herbert, for ideas.

Inquiry & Research

1. **Rich and Poor** Students might like to work and present their findings in groups of four. After students have finished their research, two students can assume the roles of investigative reporters. They can interview the other two students, who assume the roles of an aristocrat and a peasant.
2. **Angels on the Loose** Encourage students to use the card and online catalogs at the school or local library to search for material related to angels.

Choices & CHALLENGES

Writing Options

1. **New Episode** Write an episode that occurs in the lives of Simon and Matrëna after Michael has left them. Imitate the style of the story, and try to show how Michael has affected the couple's life.

2. **Maxims for Living** Write your own three maxims that embody ideas that might help people lead more meaningful and rewarding lives. Feel free to include ideas that are very different from those in the story.

3. **Newspaper Report** As a reporter for the local newspaper, write a news story on Michael's mysterious ascent to heaven. Include eyewitness accounts from Simon and Matrëna, as well as information from the neighbors and local residents.

4. **Analytical Essay** Write an essay in which you analyze the difficulty of leading a good life in a consumer society. What problems does a person today face in leading a simple life in a materialistic world? Place the essay in your **Working Portfolio.** 

5. **Points of Comparison** Michael learns his lesson while living with a simple peasant family, and Purun Bhagat in Kipling's "The Miracle of Purun Bhagat" deliberately chooses a simple lifestyle. Write an essay in which you compare the ways in which these stories extol the virtues of a simple life. How is simplicity of life connected to the moral lesson of each story?

Writing Handbook
See page 1367: Compare and Contrast.

Activities & Explorations

1. **Storyboard Illustrations** Design a storyboard, or series of sketches, for one part of the story. Each sketch should show the setting and the actions of the characters. Display your storyboard in class. ~ **ART**

2. **Newspaper Display** Near the end of the story, Michael says, "I have learnt that all men live not by care for themselves, but by love." With your classmates, collect and create a display of newspaper columns that could serve to illustrate Michael's comment by showing that people still help one another. ~ **VIEWING AND REPRESENTING**

3. **Commemorative Monument** Design a monument to be placed at the spot where the angel first appeared to Simon. Try to visually convey the lesson that Michael learned during his time with Simon. ~ **ART**

4. **Alternate Titles** The title of a literary work often contains important clues to the content, tone, and theme of the work. In a group, try to come up with alternate titles for Tolstoy's story that manage to convey its central themes. ~ **SPEAKING AND LISTENING**

Inquiry & Research

1. **Rich and Poor** Find out about the differences between the economic conditions of Russian aristocrats and peasants in the 19th century. What were the causes of the huge economic gap between the rich and the poor? Report your findings to the class.

2. **Angels on the Loose** Compile a list of movies, television shows, and works of literature that feature angels who descend to earth. How would you account for the recent increased interest in angels?

Art Connection

Reflected Mood Look again at the painting *Nightfall at Hradčany* on page 918. In your opinion, how closely does this painting reflect the mood of the story?

Teaching Options

Mini Lesson Grammar

IF/THEN COMPLEX SENTENCES

Instruction An "if/then" complex sentence consists of a subordinate clause that begins with *if* and an independent clause that begins with *then.* There is a clear cause-and-effect relationship between the two clauses. If the clauses were separate sentences, the cause-and-effect relationship might still be recognized, but it would not be as clear.

Activity Write the following sentences on the chalkboard.

Simon thought the stranger was in need.

Simon felt that he should help him.

Ask students if the two sentences have a cause-and-effect relationship. *(Yes. The stranger seeming to be in need triggers Simon's feeling that he should help.)* How could the ideas be combined in one "if/then" complex sentence? *(If the stranger were in need, then Simon would have helped him.)* Point out that the compound sentence shows the cause-and-effect relationship more clearly and reads more smoothly.

Exercise Have students combine the following sentences into "if/then" complex sentences.

Leo Tolstoy
1828–1910

Other Works
War and Peace
Anna Karenina
"How Much Land Does a Man Need?"
"Three Questions"
"Two Old Men"
"Alyosha Gorshok"

Youth and Young Adulthood Although Leo Tolstoy was orphaned as a young child, his early years were rather uneventful. He was raised by relatives and lived most of his life on the family estate, Yasnaya Polyana, about 100 miles south of Moscow. At the age of 16, he entered a university, but he returned home after a few years to educate himself. In 1852, determined to change his rather aimless lifestyle, he joined the army and began to spend much of his free time writing. When his stories based on his experiences during the Crimean War were well received, his literary career was launched.

Marriage and the Writing Life In the late 1850s, Tolstoy returned to his family estate and, unhappy with the education available to the peasants there, developed his own school, eliminating all grades, punishments, and rewards. In 1862 he married, and for the next 15 years he devoted his time to his wife, his 13 children, and the writing of his two greatest works, *War and Peace* and *Anna Karenina.* It took him 7 years to complete *War and Peace,* now regarded as one of the greatest novels in world literature.

Spiritual Crisis In spite of his relative success in life, Tolstoy began to suffer a spiritual and emotional crisis during his middle years. He found comfort in Christian principles and decided that he must shed his worldly possessions, give away his wealth, and live the honest, simple life of a Russian peasant. His resolve was not shared by his family, however, and bitter quarrels ensued. To appease them, Tolstoy signed his entire estate over to his wife, thereafter devoting his time to writing essays and stories dealing with religious, social, and moral issues. He dressed in the clothes of a peasant, gave up drinking and smoking, and became a vegetarian. He simplified his life as much as possible but remained unsatisfied. Finally, at the age of 82, accompanied by his youngest daughter and a doctor, Tolstoy left home to search for a simpler existence. He died of pneumonia in a train station a few days later.

Author Activity

War Reporter Research Tolstoy's activities as a reporter during the Crimean War, when Russian forces battled against a coalition of English, French, and Turkish troops. Find out about the outcome of the war, as well as the contribution that Tolstoy's wartime experiences may have made to his ability to write war scenes in his great novel of Napoleon's invasion of Russia, *War and Peace.*

Art Connection

Reflected Mood Possible Responses: very closely, because the mood is somber and relates to the harshness of the peasants' lives; not closely, because the message of the story is love and the painting seems somber.

Author Activity

War Reporter The Crimean War (October 1853–February 1856) was fought between the Russians and the French, British, and Ottoman Turks. A conflict of the great powers in the Middle East and Russian demands to protect the Orthodox subjects of the Ottoman sultan were the major causes of the war. Another factor was the dispute between Russia and France over the Russian Orthodox and Roman Catholic churches' privileges in the Holy Land.

Three days after a successful French attack on a major Russian stronghold in 1855, Russia blew up the forts, sank the ships, and evacuated Sevastopol. Just a few months later, after Austria threatened to join Britain, France, and Ottoman Turkey, Russia accepted preliminary peace terms. The Treaty of Paris was signed on March 30, 1856. Approximately 250,000 men were lost by each side—many to disease.

Tolstoy entered the army in 1851, fighting first the tribes in the Caucasus and then fighting in the Crimean War in that same area. He wrote three stories on the Siege of Sevastopol, which were very well received. The first was actually praised by the czar himself. By the time the war was over, Tolstoy had spent five years in the army.

1. Simon's conscience stopped him. Otherwise, he would have ignored the downtrodden stranger. (*If Simon's conscience hadn't stopped him, then he would have ignored the downtrodden stranger.*)
2. Matrëna almost left the cottage without hearing her husband's explanation. She almost didn't help the stranger. (*If Matrëna had left the cottage without hearing her husband's explanation, then she wouldn't have helped the stranger.*)
3. The peasant woman might not have sheltered the orphaned twins. The girls would likely have died without shelter. (*If the peasant woman hadn't sheltered the orphaned twins, then the girls would likely have died.*)
4. Michael had to learn three truths while living on earth. God would not return him to heaven unless he did. (*If Michael failed to learn three truths while living on earth, then God would not return him to heaven.*)

Use **Grammar Transparencies and Copymasters,** p. 63.

Use McDougal Littell's ***Language Network*** for more instruction and practice in complex sentences.

Objectives
- write a Subject Analysis
- use a written text as a model for writing
- revise a draft to keep similar ideas parallel
- make correct comparisons

Introducing the Workshop

A Subject Analysis Point out that subject analyses are commonly found in textbooks and news articles, as well as in television and news documentaries. Their purpose is to present an overview of the subject, then go into a detailed presentation of the parts to show how these parts contribute to the whole.

Have students name examples of in-depth analyses of current events that they have watched on television or read about in the news. List them on the board. Ask students whether they can identify patterns in the kinds of subjects analyzed or in the approaches to analysis. Point out that writing a subject analysis will allow students to gain an in-depth view of a subject in order to better understand it.

Basics in a Box

B Using the Graphic Like the pieces shown in the pie chart, the elements of a subject analysis focus individually on the parts that make up a whole. This graphic suggests that students move from the overall subject to its component parts and back to the overall subject.

C Presenting the Rubric To better understand the assignment, students can refer to the Standards for Writing a Successful Subject Analysis. You may wish to discuss with them the complete rubric, which describes several levels of proficiency.

Use McDougal Littell's ***Language Network,*** Chapter 20, for more instruction on writing a subject analysis.

To engage students visually, use **Power Presentation** 9, Subject Analysis.

Writing Workshop

Subject Analysis

Examining the parts of a subject . . .

A **From Reading to Writing** Manners and proper social behavior are concerns to people in any age—from the Victorians to present-day experts such as Miss Manners. Although social customs change over time, kindness and courtesy never go out of fashion. The essay on the next page **analyzes** the lack of manners in contemporary society and expresses the writer's concern over this matter. In an analysis the writer breaks down a subject into its individual parts and studies how the parts fit together. Analysis can be applied to various subjects from science to history to literature.

For Your Portfolio

WRITING PROMPT Write an essay in which you present an analysis of the subject of your choice.

Purpose: To explain the parts of a subject and how they work together

Audience: Your classmates, friends, family, or a larger audience

Basics in a Box

Subject Analysis at a Glance

B 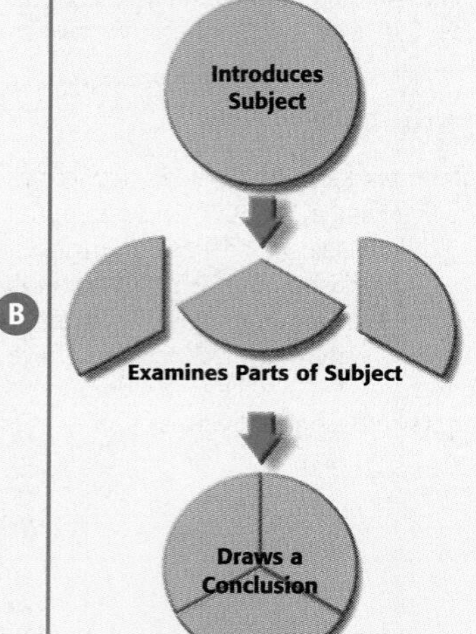

C **RUBRIC Standards for Writing**

A successful subject analysis should
- introduce the subject in an interesting, informative manner
- identify the parts that compose the subject
- examine and explain each part
- present information in a logical order
- show how the parts relate to the whole subject and support the main idea or thesis
- include an effective introduction, body, and conclusion

LESSON RESOURCES

USING PRINT RESOURCES

Unit Five Resource Book
- Prewriting, p. 33
- Drafting, p. 34
- Peer Response, pp. 35–36
- Revising, Editing, and Proofreading, p. 37
- Student Models, pp. 38–43
- Rubrics, p. 44

Writing Transparencies and Copymasters
- Writing Process Transparencies, pp. 3–4
- Writing Template Copymaster, p. 30

USING MEDIA RESOURCES

LaserLinks
Writing Springboards
See Teacher's SourceBook p. 114 for bar codes.

Writing Coach CD-ROM

Visit our website:
www.mcdougallittell.com

For a complete view of Lesson Resources, see page 829e.

Analyzing a Professional Model

L. A. Wilson
Freelance Writer

No One Stops to Say "Thank You" Anymore

I am sitting in a local restaurant offering takeout homestyle meals, surrounded by exhausted but happy shoppers, families out for Friday night dinner, and students taking a break from college exams. The warm room buzzes with conversation. A well-known local homeless man—very scruffy but clean—comes in, places an order, pays for it, then sits quietly waiting for his dinner. All talk stops. No one looks at him and several diners leave. He is aware of the general discomfort his presence has caused. When his takeout is ready, he gathers up his numerous bags and his dinner and, laden down, advances to the door to go back to the streets. Just as he reaches the door and begins to shift bundles to free a hand, a well-dressed man coming to the restaurant steps aside and holds the door for him. The homeless man stops and says, "Thank you very much."

What struck me about this Dickensian encounter was not the wealthier man helping out the less fortunate one. It was the homeless man stopping to thank him despite being desperate to escape a room full of disapproving people. No doubt he also thanked whoever had given him the money to buy dinner. No one had thanked the young people behind the counter who dished up mashed potatoes for them. Had I taken a poll of the room, though, I bet everyone there would have considered themselves as having D more manners than a person who lives on the streets.

But how many of us are truly well mannered? Some observations have been surprising.

When I let someone into my lane of traffic, men almost always acknowledge this courtesy with a wave of the hand; women (the "polite" sex) hardly ever do. More women than men (the "chivalrous" sex) hold open doors for those behind them; teenage boys commit this nicety the least. And I no longer see mothers instructing a child, boy or girl, to hold open a door when several people are approaching—something expected of all boys when I was growing up.

Manners are a tool to remind us of others around us. Our actions affect each other; there is always give and take. However, if youth today are any indication, we are truly destined to become a society of people who think only of themselves. . . .

I have yet to receive an apology from a child who just ran over my foot while chasing a sibling, and only half the time have the parents apologized. Often they simply gather up the children, making no eye contact, and take them to another part of the store to run around. If a child isn't made to deal with a minor situation, how will one ever handle a major *faux pas* (which we all inevitably commit at some point)?

I have noticed that children are not even being schooled in social

RUBRIC IN ACTION

❶ This writer introduces the subject with an interesting anecdote.

Other Options:
- Pose a question.
- Present a startling, unusual or interesting fact.

❷ Uses contrast to examine the meaning in the anecdote

❸ Signals the organizational structure

❹ Identifies the first observation: everyday courtesies

❺ States the main idea or thesis

❻ Examines a second observation—inadequate parenting—and supports the analysis with examples

Viewing and Representing

PICTURING TEXT STRUCTURE

Instruction Explain that logical structure is crucial to the success and effectiveness of a written text.

Activity Have students analyze the text structure of the professional model by constructing an image such as a graphic organizer. The graphic students construct should reflect how the writer has organized her piece. Students might first write a note about each paragraph to see how the paragraphs relate to one another and to the whole topic.

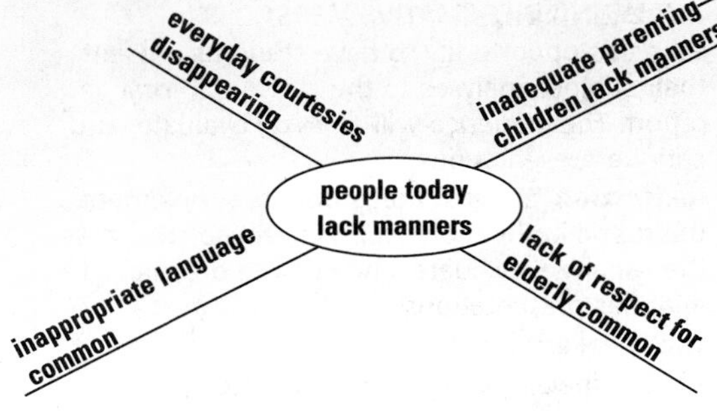

Teaching the Lesson

Analyzing the Model

"No One Stops to Say 'Thank You' Anymore"

D The essay focuses on people's lack of manners in today's society. By using present tense verbs, the writer creates a sense of immediacy.

Have students read the model aloud. Explain that the term "Dickensian encounter" refers to the writing of 19th-century British author Charles Dickens, whose stories frequently depicted homeless, poverty-stricken characters.

Students can take turns reading aloud the Rubric in Action. Point out key words and phrases in the professional model that correspond to the elements mentioned in the Rubric in Action.

1. Have students suggest an alternate opening based on the other options listed.
   Possible Response: How often do you say "thank you"?
2. Ask students to list the contrasts used in this portion of the essay.
   Possible Responses: The contrasts are between the well-dressed man and the homeless man, between the homeless man's thanks and the customers' thanklessness, and between people's perceptions of their manners and the reality of their manners.
4. Ask students what conclusions can be drawn from the observation described in this paragraph.
   Possible Responses: People are rude. Parents no longer teach their children simple courtesies.
5. Ask students to summarize the main idea in one sentence.
   Possible Response: Young people today are not concerned about manners, and they are increasingly self-absorbed.
6. Point out that an analysis will frequently focus on causes that lie behind the subject being analyzed. Ask students to state the reason the author gives to explain the lack of manners in children.
   Possible Response: Parents do not teach their children manners.

Have students evaluate and discuss the model's effectiveness using the standards for writing on page 932 for criteria.

7. The writer concludes that children are rude because their parents are too materialistic and ungrateful.
8. *Blue* vocabulary refers to indecent language.
9. Explain that an ironic situation is one that is contrary to what is expected. While society has progressed in its more equitable treatment of the races, sexes, and economic classes, we are, however, disrespectful to the elderly.
10. Have students suggest an alternate ending based on one of the other options. Compare its effect with the strategy used in the model. **Possible Response:** Our world would be a kinder place if we lived each day with a grateful heart. (Both endings are effective.)

graces. At a Sunday brunch, a clown was making balloon animals for the children. My friend's daughter, Sarah, stood by me waiting her turn. One by one the children grabbed their balloons and—yes—ran. I was the only adult present who prompted "What do you say?" when the clown handed Sarah her balloon. The clown beamed at us, grateful he had actually been acknowledged.

I don't blame the children, however. They emulate what they see. And what they are seeing is a society focused solely on acquisition—be it the dream house or another drink in a restaurant or a space on a crowded freeway—without ever stopping to thank the source.

> 7 Uses a transition to connect the lack of manners in children with poor manners in adults.

Rude language is now so commonplace it is accepted behavior. And I'm not talking about the obviously blue vocabulary in books and movies. I'm referring to inconsiderate word choice. For example, while discussing a story idea with an editor, a very young staff member asked if I was the "chick" who had called for information. I said nothing, knowing that a show of displeasure would have labeled *me* oversensitive rather than *him* rude.

> 8 Examines a third element—inappropriate language.

Most people today feel proud to have built a society that treats the races, sexes, and economic classes more equally than ever before. And, yes, we have made real strides in these areas. But isn't it ironic that these same people don't find it necessary to say "Excuse me" to an older couple walking very slowly in front of them, before zooming around the couple?

> 9 Examines the last part—lack of respect for the aged

It's not necessary to provide yet another analysis of the disintegration of the family or the breakdown of the social fabric or the price of democracy to explain what has happened to our society. The matter at hand is simply to thank the next person who provides a helping hand when needed.

In a crowded world, manners are of vital importance. Small, friendly human interactions help ease the everyday stress of having to hurry, trying to squeeze onto a crowded thoroughfare, standing in one more line to deal with a clerk of some kind, or calling a customer-service representative for the third time about a mistake on a bill. Manners make us aware that everything we have derives from a source. Are we really so pressured that we cannot stop to observe simple courtesy?

> 10 This writer concludes with a question to make the reader think about the issues raised.
>
> **Other Options:**
> - Summarize the parts to explain how they work together.
> - Draw a general conclusion from specific information presented.

934 UNIT FIVE PART 1: PERSONAL RELATIONSHIPS

Speaking and Listening

ANALYZING INFORMATIVE MESSAGES

Take this opportunity to have students present their subject analyses to the class in an oral report. The audience will analyze, evaluate, and critique presentations.

Instruction Suggest that students supplement the rubric in the workshop with these criteria as they analyze, evaluate, and critique the subject analyses presentations.

The speaker:

- has a specific, clearly focused topic
- introduces the subject in an interesting, informative manner
- presents the information objectively
- presents the information in an organized manner
- uses visual aids effectively
- uses uses voice, facial expressions, and gestures effectively

Application Have students use the criteria to analyze (examine in detail) and evaluate (judge) the presentation of each subject analysis.

Writing Your Analysis

❶ Prewriting

There are no dull subjects. There are only dull writers.
H. L. Mencken

You might begin your search for a topic by listing problems or issues that you want to understand better. For example, you might analyze issues that interest you, such as curfew laws, new rules involving teenage drivers, or censorship on the Internet. See the **Idea Bank** for more suggestions. After you have chosen your topic, follow the steps below.

Planning Your Analysis

1. **Explore the topic.** What do you know about the topic? What do you need to know? Make a list of questions about your subject. What are good sources of information—books? magazines? reference materials? interviews?
2. **Think about your purpose and audience.** Do you want to inform readers? prove a point? persuade them to a course of action? What will your audience already know about the subject? What background should you provide? What terms must you define? What tone and voice will be appropriate?
3. **Write a thesis statement.** What is the main idea that you want to communicate? Write one or two sentences that state your main idea.
4. **Break the subject into parts.** When you analyze, you break down the subject into its parts. Will your analysis include steps in a process, characteristics, stages of development, or other elements?

❷ Drafting

To begin your **draft,** try to set down everything you want to say, keeping your overall purpose in mind. You can always add details later or take out what you don't need. You may find that what you write causes you to change your thesis or main idea statement.

Now you are ready to **organize** your ideas. Although your topic will determine how you proceed, follow the steps below to guide the organizational form of your analysis:

- Provide a **provocative introduction** that quickly attracts reader interest.
- **Identify the subject** you plan to analyze in a sentence or short paragraph.
- **Describe the parts** that make up your subject.
- **Examine each part** in relationship to other parts or to the subject as a whole.

Ask Your Peer Reader

- What were the key points of my analysis? Which terms, if any, should I define?
- Describe the structure of my analysis.
- What could I change or add to make my analysis clearer?

IDEA Bank

1. Your Working Portfolio
Build on one of the **Writing Options** you completed earlier in this unit:
- **Analysis Essay,** p. 853
- **A Letter in Response,** p. 867
- **Mr. Hodgson's Editorial,** p. 884
- **Essay Analyzing Values,** p. 903
- **Analytical Essay,** p. 921

2. Virtual Field Trip
Explore a museum site on the Internet. Choose a topic to analyze based on your online visit.

3. Television Guide
Look through your local television guide for programs on scientific or social topics that interest you. Watch one of these shows and jot down ideas for an analysis.

Students can critique (review or discuss critically) orally or in writing.

Refer students to Speaking and Listening in the Communication Handbook on pages 1386-1388.

Guiding Student Writing

Prewriting

Choosing a Subject

If after reading the Idea Bank students are having difficulty choosing their topics, suggest they try the following:

- Create a chart with headings that focus on various problems: Neighborhood Problems, School Problems, City Problems, State Problems, National Problems.
- Find an example of subject analysis to use as a writing model. Evaluate the effectiveness of the model and use the model to generate ideas.
- Review recent copies of news magazines for interesting current-event topics that could be analyzed.

Planning the Analysis

1. Have students jot down notes about their topic by using the "cubing" technique. Instruct them to picture their subject as a cube with each of the six sides representing a different activity: *describe, compare, associate, analyze, apply,* and *argue for or against.* Any side can lead to a topic suggestion.
3. Before students draft their thesis statements, have them work in pairs as they explain their main idea to their partner. The listener should ask questions to help clarify the speaker's thesis statement.
4. Remind students that dividing a topic into subparts for analysis helps make the task manageable. The divisions should be consistent—parts based on the same principle of division—and complete—no important parts should be omitted.

Drafting

The model represents one approach to writing a subject analysis. Remind students that introductions need not be this length nor take this approach. The heart of a subject analysis is the breakdown of the topic into its subparts. Once they choose the subparts of their analysis, students may find it useful to create an outline from which to work. By identifying their subtopics on a topic outline, they can systematically focus their paragraphs.

Revising

KEEPING SIMILAR IDEAS PARALLEL

Have students complete a simple activity to help them revise for parallel structure. Divide the class into groups of three and have each group create four sentences—two that exhibit parallel verb forms and two that do not. Then have groups exchange sentences and quiz each other on identifying parallel and non-parallel examples.

Editing and Proofreading

CORRECT COMPARISONS

Point out that a double comparison can be corrected either by eliminating the modifiers *more/less* and *most/least* or by altering the adjective or adverb. For example, the sentence "Mrs. Smith was *more stricter* as a teacher than Mrs. Jones" can be corrected in two ways: 1) "Mrs. Smith was *stricter* as a teacher than Mrs. Jones," and 2) "Mrs. Smith was *more restrictive* as a teacher than Mrs. Jones." The method students choose may depend on the meaning of the sentence.

Reflecting

As students write their reflections, have them consider how breaking their subject into its parts gave them a more complete understanding of their topic. Have them review their conclusions and draw relevant questions for further study. Have them discuss how they might pursue their current topic further for other projects in other forms.

Option

Managing the Paper Load

Instead of commenting in writing on each student draft before final revisions are turned in, have students meet in groups of four to discuss one another's papers. Ask groups to formulate a brief written response for each paper. When a group has finished, join its discussion, using its written response as a touchstone for your response to each paper. Have students use this feedback and discussion to complete final revisions.

Teaching Tip

When students are proofreading a draft for punctuation errors, encourage them to begin with the last sentence and work backwards through the paper. This enables them to focus strictly on the surface appearance of each sentence without becoming distracted by content.

Think about how you can **elaborate** on your ideas so they are clear to your readers. You might try one or more of the following strategies.

- **Description** Describe each part in detail.
- **Comparison** Show how your subject or one of its parts resembles or differs from another relevant subject. For instance, *a teenager in love is like a traveler on a fog-shrouded street.*
- **Definition** Define key parts, characteristics, or terms for difficult or technical subjects.

Need revising help?

Review the **Rubric,** p. 936

Consider **peer reader** comments

Check **Revision Guidelines,** p.1355.

3 Revising

TARGET SKILL ▶ KEEPING SIMILAR IDEAS PARALLEL As you break down your subject into its components, be sure that sentence parts which are parallel in meaning are also parallel in structure. One error in parallel construction occurs when *and* is used to join unequal constructions. Remember, join nouns with nouns, verbs with verbs, and phrases with phrases.

> Good table manners allow you and your guests to enjoy a meal and ~~be appreciating~~ to appreciate each other's company. It is disrespectful to others to ~~be gobbling~~ gobble your food and rush away from the table while others are still eating. As you dine, remember to eat slowly and ~~no~~ chew~~ing~~ your food with your mouth ~~open~~ closed.

Confused by Comparisons?

See the **Grammar Handbook,** p. 1404

4 Editing and Proofreading

TARGET SKILL ▶ CORRECT COMPARISONS In writing an analysis, you may make a number of comparisons. Be careful to avoid double comparisons. A double comparison results when you use *more* and *-er* or *most* and *-est* together.

> If the phone rings during dinner, you might breifly answer it and politely explain that you'll call back after you finish ~~you're~~ your meal. Perhaps a ~~more~~ better solution is to let the answering machine take the call.

Publishing IDEAS

- Submit your work to your school or community newspaper.
- Make your analysis into a script for a radio interview. Work with a classmate who will be the interviewer and present the interview to your class.

More Online: Publishing Options
www.mcdougallittell.com

5 Reflecting

FOR YOUR WORKING PORTFOLIO How did writing your analysis affect your thinking about your subject? How might you pursue your topic further? Attach your answer to your finished work. Save your analysis in your **Working Portfolio.**

Assessment Practice Revising & Editing

Read this passage from the first draft of a student essay. The underlined sections may include the following kinds of errors:

- **lack of parallel structure**
- **errors in comparative forms**
- **punctuation errors**
- **correctly written sentences that should be combined**

For each underlined phrase or sentence, choose the revision that most improves the writing.

Is free verse poetry? Some critics don't agree. Some poets don't think so. (1) Both groups feel that poetry requires form, rhyme, and structure. (2) Robert Frost said that writing free verse is like tennis without a net. (3) I disagree. Free verse is more like a cage without the bars.

These critics seem to believe that a trite rhyme is more better than no rhyme at all. (4) Personally, I would rather read a poem without rhyme than with a tired old rhyme. (5) In fact, most free verse isn't really free. As T. S. Eliot recommended, The (6) ghost of some simple meter should lurk behind the arras [curtains] in even the 'freest' verse."

1. **A.** Some critics and some poets, too, don't agree.
   B. Some critics don't agree; some poets think not.
   C. Some critics and poets don't agree.
   D. Some don't agree.
2. **A.** forms, rhyming, and structure
   B. form, rhyming, and structuring
   C. forms, rhymes, and structure
   D. Correct as is
3. **A.** writing free verse is like playing tennis without a net.
   B. writing free verse is like doing without a net.
   C. writing free verse is tennis without a net.
   D. Correct as is
4. **A.** more than no rhyme at all.
   B. better than no rhyme at all.
   C. best than no rhyme at all.
   D. Correct as is
5. **A.** a poem without rhyme than a tired old rhyming idea.
   B. a poem without rhyme than a tired old one.
   C. a poem without rhyme than one with a tired old rhyme.
   D. Correct as is
6. **A.** recommended; The
   B. recommended. "The
   C. recommended, "The
   D. Correct as is

Need extra help?

See the **Grammar Handbook**
Punctuation Chart, pp.1418–1419
Structure of Sentences, p. 1413

Assessment Practice

Suggest that students read the passage completely before they begin to correct the errors. Then demonstrate how students can eliminate incorrect choices for the first question.

A. This is not the best choice because it is awkward. It is also unnecessary to repeat the word *some.*

B. This is not the best choice because the sentence sounds awkward. The ideas need to be combined.

D. This choice is incorrect. The ideas in these two sentences need to be combined.

C. This is the best choice. The writer clearly links the two nouns *critics* and *poets* with the conjunction *and.*

Answers:
1. C; **2.** D; **3.** A; **4.** B; **5.** C; **6.** C

Building Vocabulary

Objectives

- use context clues as a strategy for building vocabulary
- recognize and apply a variety of context clues for determining the meaning of a word
- create sentences with context clues to indicate a word's meaning

Strategies for Building Vocabulary

Exercise

Have students use each of the four types of context clues described on page 938. As students are to write five sentences, one type of context clues will be used twice. Allow students to choose which clue they will use twice.

Clues from Context

As you expand the scope of your reading, you are bound to encounter unfamiliar words and terms. Although you can look up an unfamiliar word in a dictionary or glossary, you can often infer its meaning from clues in the words that surround it—that is, its **context.**

Look at the poem on the right. What clues in these opening lines from "Porphyria's Lover" help you understand the meaning of *vex?*

> **The rain set early in tonight,**
> **The sullen wind was soon awake,**
> **It tore the elm-tops down for spite,**
> **And did its worst to vex the lake:**
> —Robert Browning, "Porphyria's Lover"

Browning describes the wind as sullen, destructive, and spiteful. The phrase "did its worst" also has negative implications. Together, these details might lead you to conclude that *vex* means "to upset or disturb." A careful reading of the context provides clues to the meaning of the unfamiliar word.

Strategies for Building Vocabulary

There are a number of different types of context clues. Here are a few.

❶ **Definition or Restatement Clue** This type of clue involves a writer's restating an idea in a different way. Words that signal restatements include *or, that is, in other words,* and *also called.* A restatement clue may also be in the form of an **appositive**–a phrase that redefines a word or idea. Consider, for example, the statement "You feel a disgust towards him *now,* an utter repugnance," from Charlotte Brontë's "A Warning Against Passion." Because the phrase "an utter repugnance" is in apposition to *disgust,* you can conclude that *repugnance* is a synonym of *disgust.*

❷ **Comparison Clue** Sometimes the ideas expressed by unfamiliar words are compared to ideas that are easier to understand. Words that may signal such comparison clues are *like, as, similar to, related,* and *than.* A comparison clue can also be a simile or a metaphor. For example, in the sentence "The landslide left a scarp like a deep, red wound on the mountainside," a simile is used to convey a picture of the aftermath of a landslide. From the simile, you can guess that *scarp* refers to a bare slope of soil or rock produced by erosion.

❸ **Contrast Clue** A contrast clue is the opposite of a comparison clue–it explains an unfamiliar word by means of a contrast with another idea. Contrast clues are often signaled by words such as *but, however, yet, on the other hand, different from,* and *in contrast.* Note the use of the signal word *although* in this sentence: "Although the English had expected the prime minister to be a pompous man, he turned out to be humble and unpretentious." Here *although* signals a contrast between the word *pompous* and the words *humble* and *unpretentious.*

❹ **Inference Clue** A word's meaning can sometimes be deduced from details embedded in the larger context of a sentence or a paragraph. A sensitive reader might also pick up clues from the mood or tone of a passage. What clues in the following passage suggest the meaning of *confer?*

> **When he returned to India there was a blaze of glory, for the Viceroy himself made a special visit to confer upon the Maharajah the Grand Cross of the Star of India.**
> —Rudyard Kipling, "The Miracle of Purun Bhagat"

The tone of this passage is one of triumph: there is a "blaze of glory," the Viceroy makes a "special visit," the Maharajah receives a glorious honor–"the Grand Cross of the Star of India." Together these details suggests that *confer* means "to bestow or award."

EXERCISE Choose five of the Words to Know in this part of Unit Five. For each word, write a sentence containing both the word and a clue to its meaning. Have a classmate identify the context clues that can be used to determine the words' meanings.

Grammar from Literature

Look at the passages below. Notice the kinds of information and detail the highlighted sections provide.

adverb clause showing time
When he first started, the roar of the world he had left still rang in his ears.
—Rudyard Kipling, "The Miracle of Purun Bhagat"

adverb clause showing place
At night his antelope skin was spread where the darkness overtook him.
—Rudyard Kipling, "The Miracle of Purun Bhagat"

adverb clause showing condition
Baby cried all the way, though she cuddled him up in her shawl.
—Elizabeth Cleghorn Gaskell, "Christmas Storms and Sunshine"

The blue sections are adverb clauses: clauses that modify verbs, adjectives, and other adverbs. Writers use adverb clauses to show relationships between ideas. Notice the words that introduce the clauses. They indicate how the information in the clause is related to the rest of the sentence. These introductory words are called **subordinating conjunctions.** In the following list, some subordinating conjunctions are classified according to the relationships they show.

Cause: *because, since, so that*
Condition: *although, as if, if, though, unless*
Place: *where*
Time: *after, as, before, since, until, when, while*

Using Adverb Clauses in Your Writing As you revise, examine how you have shown relationships between ideas. Look for places where an adverb clause with a well-chosen subordinating conjunction would make relationships between ideas clearer.

In "My Last Duchess," the duke was troubled. His wife may have had an eye toward romance elsewhere.

adverb clause
In "My Last Duchess," the duke was troubled because his wife may have had an eye toward romance elsewhere.

Usage Tip When you use a pronoun in a subordinate clause that follows an independent clause, make sure there is no confusion about which noun the pronoun is replacing. In other words, make sure the antecedent of the pronoun is clear.

UNCLEAR
unclear antecedent — pronoun
Ulysses may see Achilles if he reaches the Happy Isles

In the sentence above, it is not clear whether it is Ulysses or Achilles who may reach the Happy Isles. The problem can be solved by restructuring the sentence.

CLEAR
antecedent — pronoun
If Ulysses reaches the Happy Isles, he may see Achilles

WRITING EXERCISE Combine each pair of sentences by changing one into an adverb clause. You may wish to use joining words from the list of subordinating conjunctions above. Follow the directions in parentheses. Omit underlined words.

1. The Lady of Shalott sang her last song. Then she died. (Change the first sentence to an adverb clause showing time.)
2. A silly man went into an orchard. There he broke off a cherry branch for the duchess. (Make the second sentence an adverb clause of place.)
3. Mrs. Hodgson beats the cat. She herself left the cupboard open. (Make the second sentence a clause of condition.)
4. The king must find three people who miss him. Then he can live again. (Make the second sentence a clause of condition.)
5. The Bhagat had given up his important government position. He wanted to live a more spiritual life. (Make the second sentence a clause showing cause.)

GRAMMAR EXERCISE Rewrite the sentences below so that there are no unclear pronoun antecedents.

1. The reapers hear sweet melodies as they approach the island of Shalott.
2. Charlotte Brontë wrote a letter to Nell when she needed advice about marriage.
3. Mr. Hodgson holds Mr. Jenkins in contempt because of his democratic beliefs.
4. The king sees a man enter the queen's room, and she gives him her ring.
5. Purun Dass and the Maharajah made decisions together in the kingdom, where he served as prime minister.

Sentence Crafting

Objectives

- use adverb clauses to show relationships between ideas
- demonstrate control over grammatical elements such as pronoun-antecedent agreement

WRITING EXERCISE

1. After the Lady of Shalott sang her last song, she died.
2. A silly man went into an orchard, where he broke off a cherry branch for the duchess.
3. Mrs. Hodgson beats the cat, although she herself left the cupboard open.
4. If the king finds three people who miss him, he can live again.
5. The Bhagat had given up his important government position because he wanted to live a more spiritual life.

GRAMMAR EXERCISE

1. As the reapers approach the island of Shalott, they hear sweet melodies.
2. When Nell needed advice about marriage, Charlotte Brontë wrote a letter to her.
3. Because Mr. Jenkins has democratic beliefs, Mr. Hodgson holds him in contempt.
4. The king sees the queen give her ring to a man who enters her room.
5. Purun Dass served as prime minister in the kingdom where he and the Maharajah made decisions together.

PART 2 New Voices, New Directions

Industrial growth, social upheaval, and a new interest in science changed the direction of Victorian life. A prosperous middle class emerged even as the problems of the poor increased, and scientific theories challenged traditional religious beliefs. Some poets, reflecting on the loss of old certainties, wrote thoughtful poems about humankind's isolation and the fleeting nature of youth, beauty, and fame. Other writers satirized conventional values and inconsistencies in human behavior. As you read the selections in this part of Unit Five, compare the fears and foibles of Victorian society with those of today's world.

940

PREPARING to *Read*

Dover Beach

To Marguerite—Continued

"Ah, love, let us be true / To one another!"

Poetry by MATTHEW ARNOLD

Connect to Your Life

Lonely Versus Alone What comes to mind when you hear the word *isolation?* Think about situations that might cause a person to experience feelings of isolation. Do you think such feelings occur only when a person is physically separated from other people? Share your thoughts with your classmates.

Build Background

New Science and Old Beliefs In Great Britain, the Victorian era was a time of rapid change in social, economic, and religious life. The growth of industrialization and commercialism created both increasing prosperity and social unrest. The development of new scientific theories challenged traditional beliefs and eroded old assumptions about the nature of the world. Matthew Arnold, who was a social and literary critic as well as a poet, was concerned throughout his life with the questions and struggles of his time. As a critic, he was also disturbed by what he perceived as the complacency of much of society toward the emerging changes and toward the importance of beauty and culture.

In his poetry Arnold deals with the loneliness of humankind in an indifferent universe, bereft of old certainties. Although Arnold thought that religion was an essential part of culture, his poems nonetheless reflect his personal sense of isolation, doubt, and at times even despair. In his poem "Stanzas from the Grande Chartreuse," he speaks of himself as "Wandering between two worlds, one dead, / The other powerless to be born." "Dover Beach," possibly written just after the poet's visit to Dover, England, on his honeymoon in 1851, is probably the most famous of his poems. "To Marguerite—Continued" is one of a series of poems believed to have been written to a woman he met in the 1840s.

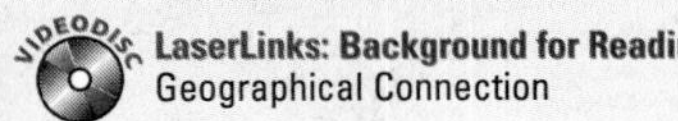

LaserLinks: Background for Reading
Geographical Connection

Focus Your Reading

LITERARY ANALYSIS CONTROLLING IMAGE

A **controlling image** is a single image or comparison that extends throughout a literary work and shapes its meaning. In "Dover Beach," for example, the sound of the sea is an example of imagery that is developed throughout the poem.

But now I only hear
Its melancholy, long, withdrawing
roar. . . .

As you read these poems, be aware of controlling images and how they are elaborated upon in each work.

ACTIVE READING DRAWING CONCLUSIONS ABOUT MOOD

Mood is the feeling, or atmosphere, that a writer creates for the reader. The mood of a poem may be happy, sad, lonely, angry, and so on. **Descriptive details** and careful word choice help a writer create a particular mood.

READER'S NOTEBOOK As you read each of Arnold's poems, record any descriptive details that you find particularly striking. Then draw conclusions about the mood created by each poem.

OVERVIEW

"Dover Beach" is included in the **Grade 12 InterActive Reader.**

Objectives

1. understand and appreciate two Victorian **poems (Literary Analysis)**
2. identify and examine **controlling images** in poetry **(Literary Analysis)**
3. **draw conclusions about mood (Active Reading)**

Summary

In these two lyric poems, the speaker contemplates the nature of human isolation by using sea imagery.

Thematic Link

In these poems, Arnold—**a new voice** expressing a **new direction** in the Victorian period—considers the ways in which humans become isolated from one another.

5-Minute Warm-Up

Daily Language SkillBuilder

Have students **proofread** the display sentences on page 829j and write them correctly. The sentences also appear on Transparency 24 of **Grammar Transparencies and Copymasters.**

LESSON RESOURCES

UNIT FIVE RESOURCE BOOK, pp. 47–48

ASSESSMENT RESOURCES

Formal Assessment, pp. 167–168

Teacher's Guide to Assessment and Portfolio Use

Test Generator

SKILLS TRANSPARENCIES AND COPYMASTERS

Literary Analysis
- Figurative Language, T22 (for Literary Analysis, p. 945)

Reading and Critical Thinking
- Drawing Conclusions, T4 (for Active Reading, p. 941)

Grammar
- Pronouns–Correct Case, T41 (for Mini Lesson, pp. 942–943)
- Pronoun Usage–*Who, Whom, Whose,* T50 (for Mini Lesson, pp. 942–943)
- Relative Pronouns and Relative Adverbs, C113 (for Mini Lesson, pp. 942–943)

Vocabulary
- Denotation and Connotation, C74 (for Active Reading, p. 941)

Writing
- Opinion Statement, C35 (for Writing Option 1, p. 946)

INTEGRATED TECHNOLOGY

Audio Library

LaserLinks
- Geographical Connection: Dover, England
- Film Connection: A Reading of "Dover Beach." See **Teacher's SourceBook,** p. 64.

Visit our website: www.mcdougallittell.com

TEACHING THE LITERATURE

Reading and Analyzing

Literary Analysis

CONTROLLING IMAGE

Explain to students that a controlling image is an image that is found throughout a literary work and determines the nature of the other images in the work. Ask students to identify the controlling image of "Dover Beach."
Possible Responses: the sea; the beach.

Then, ask them to list some images related to the controlling image.
Possible Responses: tide; spray; waves.

 Use **Unit Five Resource Book,** p. 47 for more exercises.

Active Reading

DRAWING CONCLUSIONS ABOUT MOOD

After students have read the entire poem, ask them what the mood is in the first 6 lines.
Possible Responses: tranquil; peaceful.

Ask students what words or phrases create this mood.
Possible Responses: calm; fair; gleams; glimmering; tranquil.

Point out that the mood of the poem changes, and ask students to identify where the change occurs.
Answer: at line 9.

Ask what mood the poem has after this change.

 Use **Unit Five Resource Book,** p. 46 for more practice.

Dover Beach

Matthew Arnold

The sea is calm tonight.
The tide is full, the moon lies fair
Upon the straits—on the French coast the light
Gleams and is gone; the cliffs of England stand,
Glimmering and vast, out in the tranquil bay.
Come to the window, sweet is the night air!
Only, from the long line of spray
Where the sea meets the moon-blanched land,
Listen! you hear the grating roar
Of pebbles which the waves draw back, and fling,
At their return, up the high strand,
Begin, and cease, and then again begin,
With tremulous cadence slow, and bring
The eternal note of sadness in.

3 straits: the Strait of Dover, a narrow channel separating England and France, at the northern end of the English Channel.

8 moon-blanched: shining palely in the moonlight.

13 tremulous cadence: trembling rhythm.

Teaching Options

Grammar

RELATIVE PRONOUNS AND RELATIVE ADVERBS

Instruction Adjective clauses are used as adjectives to modify nouns or pronouns. Many adjective clauses are introduced by the relative pronouns *who, whom, whose, that,* and *which.* These relative pronouns can act as the subject, the direct object, or the object of a preposition in the clause. Some adjective clauses are introduced by the relative adverbs *after, before, since, when, where,* or *why.* Relative adverbs modify the verb within the clause.

Activity Write the following chart and the sentence on the chalkboard.

Relative Pronouns	who, whom, whose, that, which
Relative Adverbs	after, before, since, when, where, why

We drew pictures <u>that illustrate the scene where "Dover Beach" took place</u>.

Ask students to underline the two adjective clauses in the sentence and to identify the word that introduces each clause as relative pronoun or a relative adverb. *(that, relative pronoun; where, relative adverb)* What function does the relative

Sophocles long ago
Heard it on the Aegean, and it brought
Into his mind the turbid ebb and flow
Of human misery; we
Find also in the sound a thought,
Hearing it by this distant northern sea.

The Sea of Faith
Was once, too, at the full, and round earth's shore
Lay like the folds of a bright girdle furled.
But now I only hear
Its melancholy, long, withdrawing roar,
Retreating, to the breath
Of the night wind, down the vast edges drear
And naked shingles of the world.

Ah, love, let us be true
To one another! for the world, which seems
To lie before us like a land of dreams,
So various, so beautiful, so new,
Hath really neither joy, nor love, nor light,
Nor certitude, nor peace, nor help for pain;
And we are here as on a darkling plain
Swept with confused alarms of struggle and flight,
Where ignorant armies clash by night.

15 Sophocles (sŏf'ə-klēz'): an ancient Greek writer of tragic plays.

16 Aegean (ĭ-jē'ən): the Aegean Sea—part of the Mediterranean Sea, between Greece and Turkey.

17 turbid: in a state of turmoil; muddled.

21 Sea of Faith: traditional religious beliefs about God and the world, long viewed as true and unshakable.

23 girdle: a belt or sash worn around the waist.

27 drear: dreary.

28 shingles: pebbly beaches.

Thinking Through the Literature

1. **Comprehension Check** What did the sound of the sea suggest to Sophocles?
2. What **images** stand out in your mind after reading the poem?
3. How would you describe the speaker's view of the world?

- his responses to what he sees and hears at the beach
- what he says about the Sea of Faith
- the images in lines 35–37

4. Why do you think the poem is addressed to the speaker's loved one?

Customizing Instruction

Less Proficient Readers

Suggest that students read each stanza as if it were a paragraph in an essay. Have them read the sentences aloud, from capital letter to period, as if they were reading prose.

Students Acquiring English

Use **Spanish Study Guide** for additional support, pp. 212–214

Gifted and Talented

Have students discuss how effectively these two 19th-century poems reflect 20th-century ideas and attitudes. Ask students what images might be used today to express these ideas.

Thinking Through the Literature

1. The ebb and flow of human misery.
2. Accept all reasonable responses.
3. Possible Responses: bleak; hopeless; losing its faith.
4. Possible Response: needs to believe in faithful love when he has lost faith elsewhere.

pronoun have in its clause? *("That" is the subject of the clause.)* What function does the relative adverb have in its clause? *("Where" modifies the verb "took.")*

Exercise Ask students to underline each adjective clause in the following sentences and identify the word that introduces the clause. Have them tell whether each word is a relative pronoun or relative adverb and what its function is within the clause.

1. The Greek playwright <u>whom Matthew Arnold mentions</u> in his poem "Dover Beach" is Sophocles. (*"Whom" is a relative pronoun and the direct object of the verb "mentions."*)
2. "To Marguerite–Continued" contains references to fictional islands <u>where the sounds of nightingales float from shore to shore</u>. (*"Where" is a relative adverb modifying the verb "float."*)
3. Natural images <u>that the poet conjures up in "Dover Beach"</u> include the ocean, beach, cliffs, and moon. (*"That" is a relative pronoun and the direct object of the verb "conjures."*)

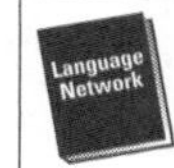

Use McDougal Littell's ***Language Network*** for more instruction in relative pronouns and adverbs.

Reading and Analyzing

Literary Analysis: EXTENDED METAPHOR

Ask students what people are compared to in the poem.

Answer: islands

Then ask them how, according to the poem, people are like islands.

Possible Response: People are isolated from one another, as are islands.

Reading Skills and Strategies: NOTING DETAILS

Draw students' attention to the shift in mood from stanza 1 to stanza 2. Ask them to identify details that set the mood of each stanza.

Possible Response: stanza 1—"shoreless watery wild," "mortal millions," "alone"; stanza 2—"balms of spring," "divinely sing," "lovely notes."

Am Meer [By the sea] (1875), Anselm Feuerbach. Kunstmuseum Düsseldorf im Ehrenhof, Germany.

To Marguerite
—Continued

Matthew Arnold

Yes! in the sea of life enisled,
With echoing straits between us thrown,
Dotting the shoreless watery wild,
We mortal millions live *alone*.
The islands feel the enclasping flow,
And then their endless bounds they know.

But when the moon their hollows lights,
And they are swept by balms of spring,
And in their glens, on starry nights,
The nightingales divinely sing;
And lovely notes, from shore to shore,
Across the sounds and channels pour—

Oh! then a longing like despair
Is to their farthest caverns sent;
For surely once, they feel, we were
Parts of a single continent!
Now round us spreads the watery plain—
Oh might our marges meet again!

Who ordered that their longing's fire
Should be, as soon as kindled, cooled?
Who renders vain their deep desire?—
A God, a God their severance ruled!
And bade betwixt their shores to be
The unplumbed, salt, estranging sea.

1 **enisled** (ĕn-īld′): separated, like islands.

6 **bounds:** limits or boundaries.

8 **balms:** soothing scents and airs.

9 **glens:** valleys.

12 **sounds:** long, wide bodies of water, larger than channels.

18 **marges:** margins.

22 **severance:** separation.

24 **unplumbed:** unmeasured; **estranging** (ĭ-strān′jĭng): alienating.

Teaching Options

Assessment Informal Assessment

UNDERSTANDING THE MAIN IDEA

Have students write two or three sentences that explain the role of the sea in Arnold's poems.

RUBRIC

3 **Full Accomplishment** Responses demonstrate full understanding of Arnold's sea imagery and how it functions in poem.

2 **Substantial Accomplishment** Responses demonstrate significant understanding of Arnold's sea imagery and how it functions in poem.

1 **Little or Partial Accomplishment** Responses demonstrate little or no understanding of Arnold's sea imagery and how it functions in poem.

Connect to the Literature

1. **What Do You Think?** What is your reaction to the speaker in this poem?

Comprehension Check
- Who are the "mortal millions"?
- Who, according to the poem, separates Marguerite from the speaker?

Think Critically

2. What seems to be the **theme,** or message, of this poem?

THINK ABOUT
- the reference to living alone in line 4
- the imagery of islands
- the statement that "a God their severance ruled" (line 22)

3. How do you think the speaker would describe his relationship with Marguerite?

4. ACTIVE READING DRAWING CONCLUSIONS ABOUT MOOD Look back at the notes you recorded in your  READER'S NOTEBOOK. What **descriptive details** contribute to the **mood** of each poem? How would you compare these moods?

Extend Interpretations

5. **Comparing Texts** Compare the attitudes toward life expressed in "Dover Beach" and "To Marguerite—Continued" with the attitude expressed by Tennyson in the excerpt from *In Memoriam* (page 000). In your opinion, which of the three poems reflects the most positive attitude toward the future?

6. **Critic's Corner** In an essay on "Dover Beach," the American poet and novelist James Dickey speaks of the "subtlety, force, and conviction" of the poem. Look for evidence in the poem to support or refute his comments.

7. **Connect to Life** Do you think Arnold would express similar ideas if he were writing poetry today? Explain your opinion.

Literary Analysis

CONTROLLING IMAGE Poets often use a **controlling image** to convey their thoughts or feelings. A controlling image is a single image or comparison that extends throughout a literary work and shapes its meaning. Often, the controlling image is an **extended metaphor,** a comparison of two unlike things at some length and in several ways.

Paired Activity With a partner, reread "To Marguerite—Continued" and identify the extended metaphor that acts as a controlling image. Jot down the extended metaphor, and note what objects and ideas are being compared. Then compare your conclusions with those of another group.

Extended Metaphor:
Objects and ideas being compared:
1.
2.
3.

REVIEW ALLUSION "Dover Beach" contains an **allusion,** or reference, to a well-known literary figure. What is the allusion? What is its function in the poem?

GUIDING STUDENT RESPONSE

Connect to the Literature

1. **What Do You Think?** Guidelines for student response: Student reactions to the speaker should be grounded in evidence from the poem. Ask students to cite examples from the poem to support their opinions.

Comprehension Check
- humankind
- God

Think Critically

2. Possible Responses: Human beings are all isolated from one another; human beings long to return to a state of oneness that may have existed in the past.
3. Possible Response: estranged but longing to be reunited.
4. Possible Response: As students discuss the mood, they should identify the details that contributed to it and the effect the details have on them as readers. Both use descriptive details of sea and land to express similar views about the human condition. The mood of each seems wistful, lonely, philosophical, bewildered, sad. The mood of "Dover Beach" is possibly more hopeful since love helps to soften despair.

Literary Analysis

Paired Activity You might have half of the class perform the activity as written, and half substitute "Dover Beach." Then have them compare results.

Review Allusion The allusion is to the Greek playwright Sophocles. Its function is to lend authority to Arnold's interpretation of the sound of the sea.

Extend Interpretations

Comparing Texts Possible Response: Arnold's poems convey an attitude of isolation and despair, while Tennyson's *In Memoriam* expresses hope. *In Memoriam* reflects the most positive attitude toward the future.

Critic's Corner Student responses will vary, but should be supported with evidence from the poem. Students might cite the last stanza in particular—the figurative language here is forceful, compelling, and memorable.

Connect to Life Accept all reasonable responses. Students should cite examples from today's world to support their opinions about Arnold's ideas.

Writing Options

1. **Lecture Notes** Student responses may hinge on whether they interpret *alone* to be physical or psychological.
2. **Beloved's Diary** Accept all reasonable responses.

Activities & Explorations

1. **Imaginative Illustration** Students might be encouraged to examine *Am Meer* on page 944 before beginning their own projects.
2. **Set Design** You might make this a partner activity in which students who have a background in art work are paired with those who do not.

Inquiry & Research

Music and Poetry Student responses will vary about whether the Barber composition effectively conveys the feelings and ideas expressed in the poem. Have students look for reviews of this work and compare their response to the composition with the reviewers' ideas.

Author Activity

Inspector of Schools Arnold's career lasted 35 years and provided the subject matter of much of his prose writing. He visited the European continent in 1859 and 1865 and came away with ideas about how English education might be improved by adopting European models. Some of his titles are *The Popular Education of France,* 1861; *A French Eton,* 1864; *Schools and Universities on the Continent,* 1868. A biography of Arnold written by Park Honan was published in 1981.

Choices & CHALLENGES

Writing Options

1. **Lecture Notes** Write lecture notes in which you either support or refute the idea, stated in "To Marguerite—Continued," that "we mortal millions live *alone.*"

2. **Beloved's Diary** Imagine that you are the "love" addressed in line 29 of "Dover Beach." Write a diary entry expressing your reaction to what the speaker has said. Place the entry in your **Working Portfolio.**

Activities & Explorations

1. **Imaginative Illustration** Create a drawing or painting to illustrate one of the images in either poem ~ **ART**

2. **Set Design** Make a set design for a dance based on one of the poems. Include brief notes describing the mood you hope to create. ~ **VIEWING AND REPRESENTING**

Inquiry & Research

Music and Poetry Locate and play a recording of the musical composition "Dover Beach" by Samuel Barber, which was based on Arnold's poem. Conduct a class discussion addressing whether the music effectively conveys the feelings and ideas expressed in the poem.

Matthew Arnold

1822–1888

Other Works
"Isolation: To Marguerite"
"The Buried Life"
"Lines Written in Kensington Gardens"
"A Summer Night"

School Days Matthew Arnold grew up under the scholarly influence of his father, a well-known clergyman and renowned headmaster of the distinguished Rugby School. Unlike his father, however, the younger Arnold was high-spirited and mischievous. At Oxford University, he spent more time socializing than studying and, as a result, barely passed his exams. He did, however, win a prestigious award for one of his poems.

Poet and Civil Servant In 1847, Arnold became the private secretary to an English lord. With the help of his employer, he later acquired a job as inspector of schools, a post he held for 35 years. The position required Arnold to travel constantly and gave him the opportunity to observe English culture and society closely. Arnold wrote during his spare time and published his first poems anonymously. His growing reputation as a poet led to his appointment in 1857 as professor of poetry at Oxford, a part-time post that he retained for 10 years.

Writer and Social Critic After 1867, Arnold devoted most of his efforts to writing critical essays on poetry and on problems in English society. He attacked the provincialism of his time and argued for a broader intellectual life and a greater awareness and appreciation of the arts. Arnold also wrote extensively on the religious controversies of his time. He thought that traditional religious views and institutions needed examination. Finally, Arnold made significant efforts to improve English education by visiting schools in Europe and writing forceful reports on his ideas for reform. He died suddenly at the age of 66 and was buried next to three sons who had preceded him in death.

Author Activity

Inspector of Schools Arnold spent most of his working life as an inspector of schools in Great Britain. Do some research in biographies, encyclopedia articles, and on the Internet to find out more about Arnold's career as a civil servant.

Pied Beauty

Spring and Fall: To a Young Child

Poetry by GERARD MANLEY HOPKINS

"Glory be to God for dappled things."

Connect to Your Life

Art Versus Nature Think about a time when you closely examined a single leaf or flower. What unique details do you remember observing? Do you think it is possible to convey the unique qualities of a natural object in a poem or a painting? Share your thoughts with your classmates.

Build Background

Revolutionary Style Gerard Manley Hopkins was an innovator whose poetry was not published or understood until decades after his death. Hopkins developed a revolutionary style, one unlike that of his contemporaries or of any poet before him. He experimented with language and form, inventing new words, using inverted word order, and developing nontraditional rhythmic patterns, which he called **sprung rhythm.** Hopkins is now regarded as a major poet of the Victorian era, whose work became a pivotal influence in the development of modern poetry.

Hopkins responded with intensity to the natural world. He invented a word, *inscape,* to describe the qualities of nature he tried to convey in his poems. Generally, inscape seems to be an inner landscape of meaning, derived from the unique qualities of natural objects, that one can experience through close observation. For almost eight years, Hopkins recorded his impressions of the natural world in a journal, which he illustrated with detailed drawings of flowers and trees. Descriptions from his journal often appeared later in his poetry. Hopkins was an aspiring painter and talented musician as well as a poet, and his talent in both art and music is reflected in his poems.

LaserLinks: Background for Reading
Art Gallery

Focus Your Reading

LITERARY ANALYSIS SPRUNG RHYTHM In order to approximate the rhythms of natural speech in his poetry, Hopkins ignored traditional patterns of rhythm, instead using what he called **sprung rhythm.** The lines of a poem written in sprung rhythm have fixed numbers of stressed syllables but varying numbers of unstressed syllables. As you read the poems, think about which lines come closest to reproducing the rhythms of natural speech.

ACTIVE READING RECOGNIZING COINED WORDS Hopkins frequently coined, or invented, words to capture his impressions of nature's special qualities. In some cases, the coined word is actually a compound made by joining two familiar words in an unfamiliar arrangement, as in "couple-color."

READER'S NOTEBOOK As you read the poems, use a chart like the one shown to make a list of the **coined words** that you discover. Also jot down the **image** or feeling that you think each word conveys. The annotations will help you with the meaning of some words.

Coined Words	Image or Feeling

OVERVIEW

"Pied Beauty" is included in the **Grade 12 InterActive Reader.**

Objectives

1. understand and appreciate two **poems (Literary Analysis)**
2. identify and examine **sprung rhythm (Literary Analysis)**
3. recognize **coined words (Active Reading)**

Summary

In "Pied Beauty," the speaker sings his praise of "dappled things"—whatever is made up of interesting contrasts. In "Spring and Fall: To a Young Child," the speaker addresses Margaret, a young girl. He explains to her that her sadness over nature's impending "death" (the passing of fall into winter), parallels the sorrow she will feel later in life for her own—and all of humanity's—mortality.

Thematic Link

Note the contrasting moods of the two poems. The first can be seen as reflecting the confident optimism of the Victorian period, while in the second we can find evidence of anxiety—also a hallmark of the age—with its fixation on the sorrow and fleeting nature of life. Both poems show evidence of the **new voices and new directions** that came to characterize Victorian poetry.

5-Minute Warm-Up

Daily Language SkillBuilder

Have students **proofread** the display sentences on page 829k and write them correctly. The sentences also appear on Transparency 25 of **Grammar Transparencies and Copymasters.**

LESSON RESOURCES

UNIT FIVE RESOURCE BOOK, pp. 49–50

ASSESSMENT RESOURCES

Formal Assessment, pp. 169–170

Teacher's Guide to Assessment and Portfolio Use

Test Generator

SKILLS TRANSPARENCIES AND COPYMASTERS

Literary Analysis
- Poetic Devices, T16 (for Literary Analysis, p. 950)

Reading and Critical Thinking
- Comparing Authors' Views, T24 (for Extend Interpretations 7, p. 950)

Grammar
- Possessive Nouns, T38 (for Mini Lesson, p. 951)
- Forming Singular Possessives, C163 (for Mini Lesson, p. 951)

Vocabulary
- Connotation, C75 (for Mini Lesson, p. 949)

Writing
- Sensory Word List, T14 (for Writing Option 2, p. 951)
- Figurative Language and Sound Devices, T15 (for Writing Option 1, p. 951)

INTEGRATED TECHNOLOGY

Audio Library

LaserLinks
- Art Gallery: Dappled Things. See **Teacher's SourceBook,** p. 65.

Visit our website: www.mcdougallittell.com

TEACHING THE LITERATURE

Reading and Analyzing

Literary Analysis SPRUNG RHYTHM

A Point out to students that *sprung rhythm* is a term used by Hopkins to describe poetry that has a regular number of stressed syllables per line, but an irregular number of unstressed syllables per line. Have students count the number of stressed and unstressed syllables in the first two lines of "Pied Beauty."

Answer: There are five stressed syllables in each line; the first line has four unstressed syllables, while the second has seven.

Use **Unit Five Resource Book,** p. 49 for more exercises.

Active Reading
RECOGNIZING COINED WORDS

Many of Hopkins's coined words are similar to Old English "kennings." Have students find examples of compounds in the poems by Hopkins.

Possible Responses: in "Pied Beauty": couple-color (line 2), rose-moles (line 3), fresh-firecoal chestnut-falls (line 4), fathers-forth (line 10); in "Spring and Fall": leafmeal.

Use **Unit Five Resource Book,** p. 48 for more practice.

Thinking Through the Literature

1. skies, cows, trout, fallen chestnuts, finches' wings, various landscapes
2. Accept all thoughtful responses.
3. Possible Responses: They show the wonder and diversity of nature; they show the mystery of God's creation.
4. Accept all reasonable responses.

Pied Beauty

GERARD MANLEY HOPKINS

A Glory be to God for dappled things—
For skies of couple-color as a brinded cow;
For rose-moles all in stipple upon trout that swim;
Fresh-firecoal chestnut-falls; finches' wings;
Landscape plotted and pieced—fold, fallow, and plough;
And áll trádes, their gear and tackle and trim.

All things counter, original, spare, strange;
Whatever is fickle, freckled (who knows how?)
With swift, slow; sweet, sour; adazzle, dim;
1 He fathers-forth whose beauty is past change:
Praise him.

1 dappled: spotted or splashed with color.

2 brinded: brindled—streaked or spotted with a darker color.

3 rose-moles . . . stipple: spots of pink in flecks or speckles.

4 fresh-firecoal chestnut-falls: fallen chestnuts that are the color of glowing coals.

5 fold: a pen for animals; **fallow:** land left unseeded.

6 trim: equipment.

7 counter: opposing.

10 fathers-forth: creates.

Thinking Through the Literature

1. **Comprehension Check** What are some of the "dappled things" that Hopkins admires?
2. Describe one **image** that remains in your mind from your reading of "Pied Beauty."
3. Why do you think the speaker is so fascinated by "dappled things"?

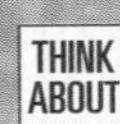

- the details the speaker describes
- the question in parentheses in line 8
- the references to God in lines 1, 10, and 11

4. Why do you think Hopkins includes "all trades" with the details from nature?

Teaching Options

Viewing and Representing

Spring
by Frederick Walker

ART APPRECIATION

Instruction Walker, who often worked in watercolors, was one of a group of mid-Victorian artists who painted figurative subjects in landscapes or domestic scenes.

Application Students may be encouraged to create a watercolor, collage, or web page of images from nature that exhibit the "pied beauty" Hopkins extols. Another direction also presents itself in his second stanza: "All things counter, original, spare, strange." What images might be gathered into a collage to show the opposite and contrasting nature of people, for example? Magazines and newspapers often carry arresting images of this sort of beauty. Ask students to share their findings with the class. Students could create their own photographs depicting the idea of beauty, as well.

Spring (late 1800s), Frederick Walker. Victoria and Albert Museum, London/Art Resource, New York.

SPRING and FALL:

To a Young Child

GERARD MANLEY HOPKINS

Márgarét, are you gríeving
Over Goldengrove unleaving?
Leáves, líke the things of man, you
With your fresh thoughts care for, can you?
Áh! ás the heart grows older
It will come to such sights colder
By and by, nor spare a sigh
Though worlds of wanwood leafmeal lie;
And yet you *will* weep and know why.
Now no matter, child, the name:
Sórrow's spríngs áre the same.
Nor mouth had, no nor mind, expressed
What heart heard of, ghost guessed:
It ís the blight man was born for,
 It is Margaret you mourn for.

1 Hopkins often included stress marks in his poems to indicate the rhythms he intended.

2 unleaving: losing its leaves.

3–4 Leaves . . . can you?: Do you in your innocence grieve about falling leaves as though they were equal to human loss?

8 wanwood: faded woodland; **leafmeal:** dry, ground-up leaves.

12 nor: neither.

13 ghost: spirit; soul.

14 blight: a condition that stops growth and brings withering and death.

Customizing Instruction

Less Proficient Readers

Set a Purpose Ask students to discuss how nature affects their moods. Then have them read both poems to discover two different views of nature.

Then ask students the following questions:

1 In "Pied Beauty," who is referred to (*he* and *him*) in the last two lines?
Answer: God.

2 What does the speaker in "Spring and Fall" mean when he says, "It is Margaret you mourn for"?
Answer: Margaret is, in fact, mourning her own mortality.

Students Acquiring English

Point out to students that many of these words have been invented by the poet and will not be in the dictionary. However, the words are often combinations of words the students may know. Ask them to take terms such as *fathers-forth* and *couple-color* and break them down into their familiar parts to arrive at a possible meaning.

Possible Responses: couple-color—made up of two colors mixed together; fathers-forth—creates.

Use **Spanish Study Guide** for additional support, pp. 215–217.

Gifted and Talented

Have students compare the mood and language of these poems with other nature poems. If they need suggestions, the teacher can suggest that they compare "Pied Beauty" to Percy Bysshe Shelley's "Ode to the West Wind," and "Spring and Fall" to John Keats's "To Autumn."

Mini Lesson Vocabulary Strategy

CONNOTATION

Instruction Ask students to find at least two synonyms for the words listed below, using a thesaurus if necessary. Write their responses on the board.

- weep (line 9)
  Possible Responses: cry; sob
- sorrow (line 11)
  Possible Responses: sadness; grief
- ghost (line 13)
  Possible Responses: apparition; spirit; phantom

Activity Have students discuss why Hopkins chose the words he did instead of some of these synonyms. Ask them to describe the impression made by the words he chose as compared to these synonyms.

Possible Response: With his choice of words, Hopkins is trying to convey a sense of the mournfulness, the sense of loss, that accompanies death. Students can experiment with substituting one or more of the synonyms for the words Hopkins uses in the poem, and then discuss the effects of the substitution on the mood of the poem.

A lesson on denotation and connotation appears on p. 645 in the Pupil's Edition.

GUIDING STUDENT RESPONSE

Connect to the Literature

1. What Do You Think?
Guidelines for student response: Accept all reasonable responses that are rooted in the poem.

Comprehension Check

- She is apparently grieving over the dying leaves and the passage of fall into winter.
- He believes she will be less moved—colder.

Think Critically

2. Possible Response: The speaker seems to care for Margaret as a parent or older relative would. He tries to understand her sorrow and he predicts that age will change her.
3. While Margaret thinks her sorrow is for the change in the trees, the speaker believes it is herself she is grieving for because of the inevitability of death.
4. Possible Response: The tone of the speakers seems contrasting. In the first poem, the speaker is exultant. In the second poem, he is consoling, urging acceptance and reconciliation.
5. Many of the invented words have been pointed out in the footnotes. Appreciation of Hopkins's language will vary. Some students may be inspired to invent their own coinages.

Literary Analysis

Paired Activity You might have pairs of students share their results with the class and discuss any discrepancies from pair to pair.

Review Alliteration Accept all reasonable responses.

Connect to the Literature

1. **What Do You Think?** What impressions of Margaret do you have after reading this poem? Share your reactions with your classmates.

Comprehension Check

- What is Margaret grieving over?
- How does the speaker believe Margaret will react to fall when she grows older?

Think Critically

2. How would you describe the **speaker's** relationship to Margaret?

- the speaker's two questions
- the prediction in lines 5–8
- the statements in lines 9 and 11

3. How does the speaker seem to interpret Margaret's grieving?
4. Compare the speakers of "Pied Beauty" and "Spring and Fall: To a Young Child." What similarities and differences do you find in their **tone,** or attitude?
5. **ACTIVE READING** **RECOGNIZING COINED WORDS** With a small group of classmates, discuss the list of **coined words** you made in your READER'S NOTEBOOK. What **images** or feelings do the words convey? How do the words affect meaning in each poem?

Extend Interpretations

6. **Critic's Corner** One critic has observed that for Hopkins "words are a means of possessing nature." Think about what this statement might mean. Look for words in the two poems that might be a "means of possessing nature."
7. **Comparing Texts** Compare Hopkins's two poems with Wordsworth's "Lines Composed a Few Miles Above Tintern Abbey" (page 725), Shelley's "To a Skylark" (page 786), and Keats's "To Autumn" (page 801). Identify any attitudes toward nature that you think Hopkins shares with the three romantic poets.
8. **Connect to Life** In "Spring and Fall: To a Young Child," Hopkins explores and brings insight into the experience of a young girl. Think of a time, either in your own life or in the life of a **character** in a book or movie, when a childhood experience led to an important understanding of life.

Literary Analysis

SPRUNG RHYTHM Hopkins used **sprung rhythm** to approximate the rhythms of natural speech in his poetry. The lines of a poem written in sprung rhythm have fixed numbers of stressed syllables but varying numbers of unstressed syllables. As in the example below, a line may contain several consecutive stressed syllables, or a stressed syllable may be followed by one, two, or even three unstressed syllables.

Landscape plotted and pieced—
fold, fallow, and plough;

And all trades, their gear and
tackle and trim.

Paired Activity With a partner, read "Pied Beauty" and "Spring and Fall: To a Young Child" aloud. Then work together to mark the stressed and unstressed syllables in one of the poems.

REVIEW **ALLITERATION** Notice the many examples of **alliteration,** or repetition of initial consonant sounds, in both poems. Why do you think Hopkins used alliteration so extensively?

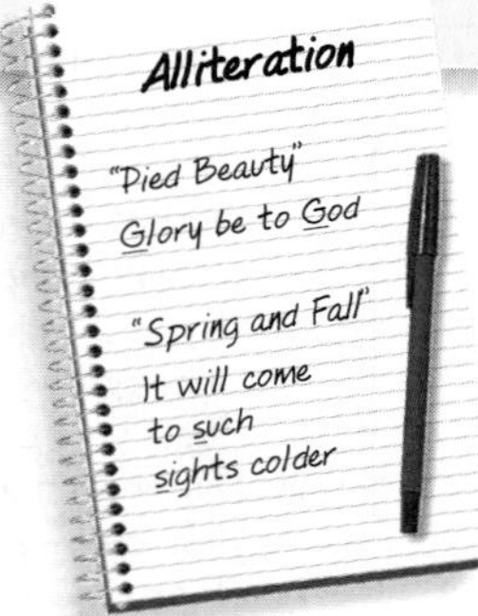

Alliteration
"Pied Beauty"
Glory be to God
"Spring and Fall"
It will come
to such
sights colder

Extend Interpretations

Critic's Corner Students' interpretations of the remark may vary, but they should recognize that it stresses Hopkins's love of nature and desire to capture its wonders.

Comparing Texts Among the poems' similar attitudes toward nature are admiration of nature's diversity, strength, wonder, and beauty; the view of nature as a source of spiritual guidance or comfort; reliance on nature for poetic inspiration; and awareness of nature's cycles and of its destructive as well as nurturing aspects.

Connect to Life Accept all reasonable responses.

Choices & CHALLENGES

Writing Options

1. **Nature Poem** Write a short poem in which you express your enthusiasm for a unique quality or pattern in nature.

2. **Journal Entry** Write an entry for a nature journal, recording your close observations and impressions of one aspect of the natural world. Place the entry in your **Working Portfolio.**

3. **Dictionary of Coined Words** Create a dictionary of your own coined words to describe details related to a particular subject or area of interest, such as music, sport, dance, city life, and so on.

Activities & Explorations

Nature Mural Work with a partner to create a watercolor mural depicting some of the images in these two poems. Display your finished mural in the classroom. ~ **ART**

Inquiry & Research

Natural Patterns Choose an animal or plant characterized by spots or "dappled" splashes of color. What is the function of such markings? Discuss your findings with classmates.

Gerard Manley Hopkins

1844–1889

Other Works
"God's Grandeur"
"Hurrahing in Harvest"
"Binsey Poplars"

Poet and Priest Gerard Manley Hopkins grew up in a family of writers and artists and showed early promise as both a poet and painter. He won a prize for his poetry while still a teenager and continued to write while attending Balliol College at Oxford University, where he was a brilliant student. It was also at Oxford that the deeply religious young man began struggling with his Protestant faith and, in 1866, joined the Roman Catholic Church. This action alienated him from his parents, who could never understand their son's decision. The rift grew even wider when Hopkins joined the Jesuit order and was eventually ordained a priest.

Early Decline Hopkins preached and taught for many years at a number of parishes in England and Scotland. In 1884, he was assigned to teach Greek literature at University College in Dublin, where he would spend his last years. Hopkins did not enjoy his assignment in Ireland, however, because he was overworked and in declining health. At age 44, he died of typhoid fever.

Conflicting Commitments As a young man, Hopkins experienced a continuing conflict between his desire to write poetry and his religious commitment. He burned most of his early poems when he entered the Jesuit order, and he did not write poetry again for seven years, although he did continue to write in his journal. In 1874, Hopkins went to a Jesuit college in rural Wales to study theology. He was deeply happy during his three years there, and with encouragement from his superiors, he eventually returned to writing poetry. When he tried to get his first major poem published, however, it was rejected, and after that he showed his work to only a few friends. A collection of Hopkins's poetry was published in 1918, but it was not until 1930, when a second edition appeared, that his work finally received full recognition.

Author Activity

Word Images Read one or two of Hopkins's other poems and list the coined words he uses in them. Share with the class the images the words convey.

Writing Options

1. **Nature Poem** Encourage students to read their poems aloud to listen for rhythm. Ask them whether the rhythm is regular or sprung.
2. **Journal Entry** Students might be guided to unusual settings, such as nature in the urban landscape.
3. **Dictionary of Coined Words** Words that imitate the sounds they describe are a good source of inspiration. Point out to students that many of Hopkins's coinages are compound words, and that words don't have to be entirely created from scratch.

Activities & Explorations

Nature Mural Students who are not technically skilled or trained artists may be encouraged to use colors or textures to convey the moods or impressions made by the images in the poems. Students may want to document the project on video for classmates, recording the creative process and having student-artists describe the meaning of their images.

Inquiry & Research

Natural Patterns Biology and botany textbooks are unusually good sources for this activity. The concept of protective coloration was developed by naturalists who first noted the efficacy of coloration in helping a species conceal itself from its enemies.

Author Activity

Word Images Other poems by Hopkins that might provide material for this activity are "God's Grandeur," "The Windhover," and "I Wake and Feel the Fell of Dark."

Grammar

PUNCTUATION: FORMING SINGULAR POSSESSIVES

Instruction To form the possessive of a singular noun, add an apostrophe and an -s even if the noun ends in -s. (family's home, Charles's room)

Activity Write on the chalkboard the following sentence.

Bess's essay won the school's first-place prize.

Ask students to identify the nouns that show possession. *(Bess's, school's)*

Remind students that it is the last part of a compound noun that shows possession. *(sister-in-law's gifts)* Add only an apostrophe or an apostrophe and -*s* depending on the form of the word. For nouns such as Secretary of Defense, add an apostrophe and -*s* to the last word (Secretary of Defense's report) In the case of joint ownership, only the last name mentioned takes the possessive case. *(McDermott and Blake's annual report).* However, if possession is not joint, each name takes the possessive form. (Bill's and Robert's motorcycles)

Use **Grammar Transparencies and Copymasters,** p. 99.

Use McDougal Littell's ***Language Network*** for more instruction in forming singular possessives.

Objectives

- read and analyze primary sources
- read in varied sources such as journals
- respond to informational and aesthetic elements in journal entries
- understand a writer's attitude and ideas
- identify the effect of imagery within literary texts

Further Background

A journal is a form of autobiographical writing in which the writer keeps a record of daily events and personal impressions. Journals are generally not as intimate as diaries, but they nevertheless offer a valuable window into a person's thoughts and can thus function as a valuable primary source when seeking insight into a writer's ideas and attitudes.

Reading for Information

Students may say that the most interesting and worthwhile things to record in a journal are unique observations, memorable moments, and responses to events.

UNDERSTANDING A WRITER'S ATTITUDE AND IDEAS

1. **Possible Response:** "Fresh-fire coal chestnut-falls." Leaves fallen in quantity appear in the poem "Spring and Fall."
2. **Possible Response:** In "Pied Beauty," Hopkins describes "rose-moles all in stipple upon trout that swim" and "landscape plotted and pieced–fold, fallow, and plough." Be sure students include main ideas and supporting details in their summaries. Hopkins's attitude toward nature seems to be one of reverence for its beauty and complexity, as inspired by God.

COMPARING TEXTS

Possible Response: Hopkins seemed to rely primarily on the sense of sight in his experience of nature. The examples cited above are all visual, as is the general sense of "dappled things" that he invokes in the opening line of "Pied Beauty."

from

Journal

Gerard Manley Hopkins

The priest and poet Gerard Manley Hopkins diligently kept a journal for eight years. As you read the journal excerpt below, see if you recognize any ideas or language that also appear in his poems.

1 *September 17, 1868*—Fine.—Chestnuts as bright as coals or spots of vermilion.[1]

2 *July 8, 1871*—After much rain, some thunder, and no summer as yet, the river swollen and golden and, where charged with air, like ropes and hills of melting candy, there was this day a thunderstorm on a greater scale—huge rocky clouds lit with livid[2] light, hail and rain that flooded the garden, and thunder ringing and echoing round like brass. . . .

June 16, 1873— . . . I saw [a pigeon] up on the eaves of the roof: as it moved its head a crush of satin green came and went, a wet or soft flaming of the light. . . .

August 9, 1873— . . . From the cliffs I saw the sea paved with wind—clothed and purpled all over with ribbons of wind. . . .

October 17, 1873— . . . At the end of the month hard frosts. Wonderful downpour of leaf: when the morning sun began to melt the frost they fell at one touch and in a few minutes a whole tree was flung of them; they lay masking and papering the ground at the foot. . . .

August 8, 1874— . . . All the west country seems to me to have soft maroon or rosy cocoa-dust-colored handkerchiefs or ploughfields, sometimes delicately combed with rows of green, their hedges bending in flowing outlines and now misted a little by the beginning of twilight run down into it upon the shoulders of the hills; in the bottom crooked rows of rich tall elms. . . .

1. **vermilion:** bright red.
2. **livid:** ashen or pale.

Reading for Information

Of the incidents and thoughts in your everyday experience, what kinds do you think are worth recording? Generally, people keep journals to remember particular events, to recapture feelings, or to record their lives for later generations. Writers often use what they have written in their journals as raw material for their imaginative works.

UNDERSTANDING A WRITER'S ATTITUDE AND IDEAS

Reading a writer's journal can be a revelation. The entries often give you new insight into the sources of ideas and images that you have encountered in the writer's finished works. Use the activities that follow to study the excerpts from Hopkins's journal.

1. In the entry for September 17, 1868, Hopkins remarks on chestnuts "as bright as coals." Find a similar phrase in "Pied Beauty." Locate another instance in which Hopkins used a journal entry as a source of imagery for a poem.
2. In the July 8, 1871, entry, Hopkins described a "river swollen and golden." From the two Hopkins poems you've read, choose three examples of description of nature. Then summarize Hopkins's attitude toward nature.

Comparing Texts After reading Hopkins's journal and poems, which sense would you say he relied on most in his experiencing of nature—sight, hearing, or touch? Cite examples to support your answer.

"Over the mirrors meant / To glass the opulent / The sea-worm crawls."

The Man He Killed

Ah, Are You Digging on My Grave?

The Convergence of the Twain

(Lines on the Loss of the *Titanic*)

Poetry by THOMAS HARDY

Connect to Your Life

Life's Twists and Turns Think about a time, either in your own life, a friend's life, or in current world events, when something unexpected occurred. What happened? What reactions did you or others have to this change? Share your thoughts with your classmates.

Build Background

Novelist and Poet Thomas Hardy is one of the most widely recognized authors of the Victorian era. As a novelist, he focused on the bitter and often disastrous ironies of life. Most of his contemporaries thought he was overly pessimistic, but Hardy once denied the charge, calling himself a "meliorist"—someone who thinks humanity has the ability to make the world better. Although known primarily as a novelist, Hardy was also a gifted poet. After devoting the first 25 years of his literary career to writing fiction, including 14 novels, he turned his attention almost completely to writing poetry. Hardy's life spanned 88 years, and although his novels were composed during the Victorian era, most of his poetry was actually written in the 20th century.

Hardy's **style** of poetry is unlike that of most of his contemporaries. In fact, his departure from the typical language and form of Victorian poetry led some of his contemporaries to complain that his poems seemed more like prose than poetry. Characteristics of the novel that might be observed in some of his poems include the use of **dialogue;** a relaxed narrative style; simple, unadorned language; and the framework of a **plot,** often with interaction between **characters, dramatic moments,** and **unexpected twists.**

Focus Your Reading

LITERARY ANALYSIS SATIRE IN LYRIC POETRY **Satire** is a literary technique in which ideas, customs, behaviors, or institutions are ridiculed for the purpose of improving society. The **tone** of satire may be gently witty, mildly abrasive, or bitterly ironic. As you read these poems, look for the satiric tone in each and try to identify what is being satirized.

ACTIVE READING MAKING INFERENCES ABOUT A SPEAKER'S ATTITUDE As you know, the **speaker** in a poem may be intimately involved in the subject of the poem or may be a detached observer. To understand the speaker's stance, or attitude, you must look not only for what is stated directly but also for what can be **inferred,** or guessed, on the basis of clues in the poems.

READER'S NOTEBOOK As you read each poem, note your impressions of each speaker's attitude by jotting down answers to the following questions and the reasons for your answers.

1. Does the speaker "talk" to the reader in the **first person** or the **third person?**
2. Are any **details** about the speaker's life or personality revealed in the poem?
3. Does the speaker reveal any of his or her emotions?

OVERVIEW

Objectives

1. understand and appreciate three **lyric poems (Literary Analysis)**
2. identify and examine **satire in lyric poetry (Literary Analysis)**
3. make **inferences** about a **speaker's attitude (Active Reading)**

Summary

The first poem is a dramatic monologue in which a soldier imagines that the enemy he has killed would probably have been his friend under different circumstances. In the second poem, the speaker, a dead woman, learns through a dialogue with her little dog, who has been digging on her grave, that everyone, including the dog, is rather indifferent to her passing. The speaker in the third poem juxtaposes the *Titanic,* which he sees as a product of human vanity, with its majestic natural counterpart—the iceberg that destroyed it.

Thematic Link

In these poems, one finds Hardy's typically pessimistic and ironic outlook toward life, an outlook that became increasingly common as the Victorian era gave way to the 20th century. Also evident is naturalism, which viewed nature and society as forces indifferent to the suffering of the individual. In Hardy's poetry, the late 19th century achieves a **new voice and new direction.**

5-Minute Warm-Up

Daily Language SkillBuilder

Have students **proofread** the display sentences on page 829k and write them correctly. The sentences also appear on Transparency 25 of **Grammar Transparencies and Copymasters.**

LESSON RESOURCES

UNIT FIVE RESOURCE BOOK, pp. 51–52

ASSESSMENT RESOURCES

Formal Assessment, pp. 171–172

Teacher's Guide to Assessment and Portfolio Use

Test Generator

SKILLS TRANSPARENCIES AND COPYMASTERS

Literary Analysis
- Verbal, Situational, and Dramatic Irony, T17 (for Literary Analysis, p. 961)

Reading and Critical Thinking
- Making Inferences, T7 (for Active Reading, p. 953)

Grammar
- Noun Clauses: Common Introductory Words, C118 (for Mini Lesson, pp. 958–959)

Writing
- Sensory Word List, T14 (for Writing Option 2, p. 962)
- Figurative Language and Sound Devices, T15 (for Writing Option 3, p. 962)

Communications
- Appreciative Listening, T2 (for Activities & Explorations 2, p. 962)
- Dramatic Reading, T12 (for Activities & Explorations 2, p. 962)

INTEGRATED TECHNOLOGY

Audio Library

Visit our website: www.mcdougallittell.com

TEACHING THE LITERATURE

Reading and Analyzing

Literary Analysis

SATIRE IN LYRIC POETRY

Ask students what is being satirized in this poem.

Possible Responses: war; the duty of soldiers to kill.

Why do you think the poet chose this speaker to address such a serious topic?

Possible Responses: to prompt readers to think about why soldiers shoot at each other; to consider that there may never be a good reason for going to war.

 Use **Unit Five Resource Book,** p. 51 for more exercises.

Active Reading

MAKING INFERENCES ABOUT A SPEAKER'S ATTITUDE

Have students infer the speaker's attitude toward war and toward his own actions in the war. Students might want to begin by making inferences about what sort of person the speaker is.

Possible Responses: The speaker is aware of the irony of having killed a man who might otherwise have been a friend, but his attitude toward the action seems almost blasé, as if he were saying, "I was just a soldier doing my duty"; the speaker is troubled by the war and the killing that it led him to do, although he expresses his trouble in a low-key fashion.

 Use **Unit Five Resource Book,** p. 50 for more practice.

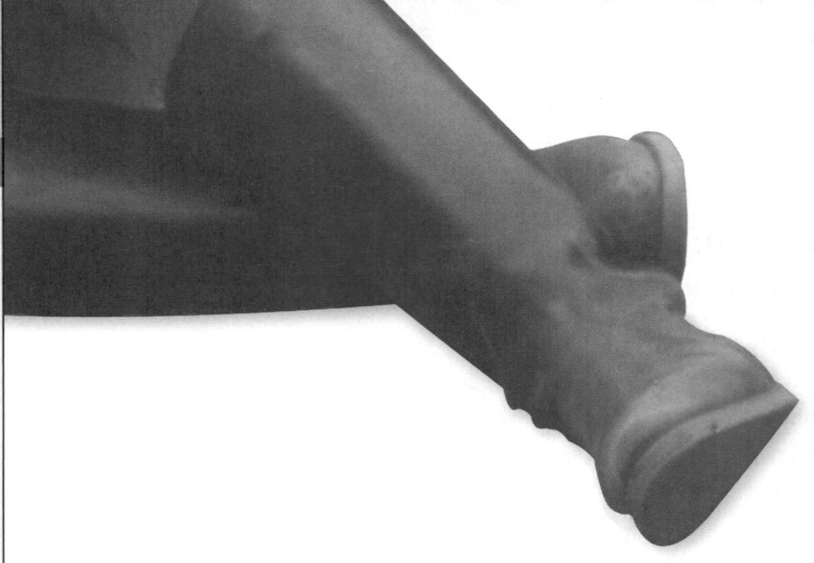

THE MAN HE KILLED

Thomas Hardy

"Had he and I but met
By some old ancient inn,
We should have sat us down to wet
 Right many a nipperkin!

"But ranged as infantry,
And staring face to face,
I shot at him as he at me,
And killed him in his place.

4 nipperkin: a container holding about half a pint of beer or ale.

Teaching Options

Vocabulary Strategy

IDIOMS

Instruction An idiom is an expression that cannot be understood from the meanings of the individual words in that expression. However, context clues can help decipher their meaning.

Activity Have students work in pairs to use context clues to determine the meanings of the following idioms in "The Man He Killed."

to wet . . . a nipperkin (lines 3–4)

Context: The speaker is imagining meeting the man in an *inn* (which here means *tavern*); students know what one does in a bar, and so should be able to surmise that this expression means "to have a drink."

right many (line 4)

Students may be unfamiliar with the modifier *right*. Context: The image of two men in a bar drinking, the idea in the poem that the men would be friends but for war, and the word *many* itself suggest that *right many* must mean "quite a few" or "several."

"I shot him dead because—
Because he was my foe,
Just so: my foe of course he was;
That's clear enough; although

"He thought he'd 'list, perhaps,
Off-hand like—just as I—
Was out of work—had sold his traps—
No other reason why.

"Yes; quaint and curious war is!
You shoot a fellow down
You'd treat if met where any bar is,
Or help to half-a-crown."

13 'list: enlist.

15 traps: personal belongings.

20 half-a-crown: an old British coin.

Thinking Through the Literature

1. Does the **speaker** of this poem react to killing an enemy in a way that you would expect?
2. Do you think the speaker is satisfied with the reason he provides for killing his enemy?

   THINK ABOUT
   - his repetition of the word *because* (lines 9–10)
   - his repetition of his reason for shooting the man (lines 10–11)
   - the emphasis on the word *although* (line 12)
3. Does the **theme,** or message, of this poem have relevance in today's world?

Customizing Instruction

Less Proficient Readers

Set a Purpose Have students read to identify the two important characters in each poem.

1 Ask students what the speaker of "The Man He Killed" says he would have done if he had met the other soldier in an inn.

Answer: had a drink with him.

Students Acquiring English

Students may have problems with Hardy's syntax, particularly his propensity for inverting normal word order. Have students look at the examples of inverted word order in line 11 ("my foe of course he was") and line 17 ("quaint and curious war is"). Then help students work the syntax of these problematic structures into everyday English.

Answers: "Of course he was my foe"; "War is quaint and curious."

Use **Spanish Study Guide** for additional support, pp. 218–220.

Thinking Through the Literature

1. Accept all reasonable responses.
2. Possible Responses: yes, because he doesn't really want to think about it; no, because he identifies with the man and, as can be seen in the third stanza, seems unsure of and uncomfortable with his reason
3. Possible Response: yes, as governments continue to send citizens like the speaker and his "foe" to war

BLOCK SCHEDULING: MANAGING TIME

If your schedule requires that you cover the lesson objectives in a shorter time, use . . .
- Preparing to Read, p. 953
- Thinking Through the Literature, pp. 955, 957, 961

If you want to take advantage of longer class time, use . . .
- TE Teaching Options: Vocabulary, p. 954; Speaking and Listening, p. 956; Standardized Test Practice, p. 957; Grammar, p. 958; Informal Assessment, p. 960
- Choices & Challenges and Author Activity, p. 962

THE MAN HE KILLED 955

Reading and Analyzing

Active Reading

MAKING INFERENCES ABOUT A SPEAKER'S ATTITUDE

Have students examine the questions that begin in stanzas 1–4 and try to make an inference about how the speaker is feeling. What is the speaker's attitude at first? How do the following questions show a change in attitude?

Possible Response: The speaker at first seems hopeful and assured, but this hope gradually diminishes and gives way to resignation.

Reading Skills and Strategies:
POINT OF VIEW

Remind students that first-person point of view uses the pronouns *I, me, my, we, us,* and *our.* Then ask students whether this poem is told in the first person or the third person, or whether the two speakers use different points of view.

Answer: Both the buried woman and the dog are using the first person.

Literary Analysis

SATIRE IN LYRIC POETRY

Ask students what the poet is satirizing in the first two stanzas, which describe the behavior of the woman's lover and kin.

Possible Response: the traditional image of the grief-stricken lover and relatives.

Ask them what similar idea is being satirized in the last stanza.

Possible Response: the idea of dogs as "man's best friend."

Ah, Are You Digging on My Grave?

Thomas Hardy

"Ah, are you digging on my grave,
 My loved one?—planting rue?"
—"No: yesterday he went to wed
One of the brightest wealth has bred.
'It cannot hurt her now,' he said,
 'That I should not be true.' "

2 **rue:** an herb that, because its name is identical to the word *rue* (meaning "sorrow" or "regret"), is often used as a symbol of repentance.

Teaching Options

Speaking and Listening

DRAMATIC MONOLOGUE

Instruction The poem takes place as a conversation between two speakers, the dead woman and her dog.

Prepare Invite students to discuss what changes of mood each speaker experiences in the course of the poem. Then have students form pairs to read the poem aloud, each student taking the part of the woman or the dog.

Present Encourage students to reveal in gesture and vocal quality the drama that unfolds between these two characters. If they wish, allow the pairs to share their performances with the class.

BLOCK SCHEDULING This activity is particularly well-suited for longer class periods.

"Then who is digging on my grave?
My nearest dearest kin?"
—"Ah, no: they sit and think, 'What use!
What good will planting flowers produce?
No tendance of her mound can loose
Her spirit from Death's gin.'"

"But someone digs upon my grave?
My enemy?—prodding sly?"
—"Nay: when she heard you had passed the Gate
That shuts on all flesh soon or late,
She thought you no more worth her hate, 1
And cares not where you lie."

"Then, who is digging on my grave?
Say—since I have not guessed!"
—"O it is I, my mistress dear,
Your little dog, who still lives near,
And much I hope my movements here
Have not disturbed your rest?"

"Ah yes! *You* dig upon my grave . . .
Why flashed it not on me
That one true heart was left behind!
What feeling do we ever find
To equal among human kind
A dog's fidelity!"

"Mistress, I dug upon your grave
To bury a bone, in case
I should be hungry near this spot
When passing on my daily trot.
I am sorry, but I quite forgot
It was your resting place."

11 tendance: attendance; watchful care.

12 gin: a snare or trap.

30 fidelity: faithfulness.

Thinking Through the Literature

1. **Comprehension Check** Who are the two speakers conducting a dialogue in this poem?
2. What was your reaction to the unexpected twist in this poem?
3. What reactions to her death does the first speaker seem to expect?
4. Why do you think the poet conceals the identity of the second speaker until the fourth **stanza?**

Customizing Instruction

Less Proficient Readers

Set a Purpose Have students read to find out to whom the dead woman in "Ah, Are You Digging on My Grave?" speaks?

Answer: her dog.

Students Acquiring English

1 Help students restate line 17 in contemporary American English.

Possible Response: She did not think it was worth the trouble to hate you anymore.

Multiple Learning Styles

Visual Learners

Have students draw a series of sketches depicting the scene in the cemetery between the woman and her dog, including in it what the woman imagines in each stanza and what is actually true.

Thinking Through the Literature

1. The two speakers are a dead woman and her dog.
2. Accept all reasonable responses.
3. She seems to expect that people—even her enemy—will continue to think about her.
4. Possible Responses: to create suspense; to build up to the final irony

Mini Lesson Standardized Test Practice

CHOOSING THE BEST SUMMARY For some standardized tests, students will be asked to choose the best summary of a passage. To provide students with some help in choosing the best summary, read aloud or write on the chalkboard the following question.

Which of the following statements best summarizes "Ah, Are You Digging on My Grave?"

A. A woman learns the depressing truth about her husband and family from her dog.

B. A dead woman finds that her only real friend is her dog.

C. In a dialogue with her dog, a dead woman discovers that nobody she was close to in life really cares about her anymore.

D. A dead woman thinks her dog has come to visit her grave, but he has only come to bury a bone.

Lead students through the process of choosing the best summary. Consider each choice. Point out that the best summary should include the most important information. While *A* and *D* contain accurate information, they are incomplete, and *B* is incorrect. For these reasons, *C* is the best choice.

Reading and Analyzing

Active Reading

MAKING INFERENCES ABOUT A SPEAKER'S ATTITUDE

Ask students to identify the speaker's attitude toward the *Titanic* and to give details or word choices that reveal that attitude.

Possible Response: The speaker seems to have a sort of contempt for the human vanity behind its construction, and chooses details and word choices such as "human vanity" (line 2), the capitalization of "Pride of Life" (line 3), "vaingloriousness" (line 15), the "sea worm" (line 9), and the jewels lying in darkness.

Literary Analysis

SATIRE IN LYRIC POETRY

Ask students what is being satirized in the first five stanzas of the poem.

Possible Responses: human pride; the foolishness of opulence that becomes nothing more than a surface for sea worms to crawl on.

Thomas Hardy

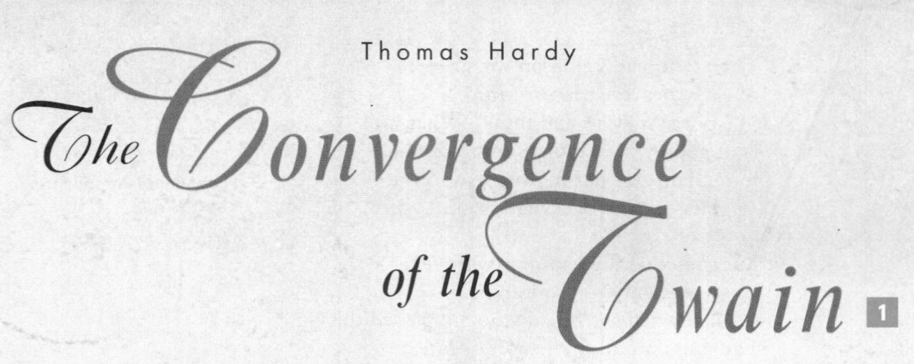

The Convergence of the Twain 1

(LINES ON THE LOSS OF THE *TITANIC*)

1

In a solitude of the sea
Deep from human vanity,
And the Pride of Life that planned her, stilly couches she.

2

Steel chambers, late the pyres
Of her salamandrine fires,
Cold currents thrid, and turn to rhythmic tidal lyres.

3

Over the mirrors meant
2 To glass the opulent
The sea-worm crawls—grotesque, slimed, dumb, indifferent.

3 stilly couches she: quietly she lies.

5 salamandrine fires: extremely hot flames. (The name *salamander* was formerly applied to a mythical lizardlike animal that could live unharmed in fire.)

6 thrid: pass through; thread; **lyres:** stringed instruments of the harp family.

958 UNIT FIVE PART 2: NEW VOICES, NEW DIRECTIONS

Teaching Options

Grammar

Noun Clauses: Common Introductory Words

Instruction A noun clause is a subordinate clause used as a noun in a sentence. Writers use noun clauses just like regular nouns—as subjects, direct and indirect objects, predicate nouns, and objects of prepositions. A noun clause usually begins with a pronoun or a subordinating conjunction. Some of the more commonly used introductory words are shown in the following chart.

Activity Review with students these introductory words and the sentence that follows by writing them on the chalkboard.

Introductory Words for Noun Clauses	
Pronouns:	who, whom, whose, which, that, whoever, whomever, what, whatever
Subordinating conjunctions:	how, if, that, when, where, whether, why

What distinguishes Hardy's poetry from that of his contemporaries is that he incorporates characteristics of a novel in some of his poetry.

Point out to students that this sentence contains two noun clauses. Ask them to identify the intro-

The *Titanic* in Southampton, England, just before sailing on her maiden voyage on 10 April 1912

4

Jewels in joy designed
   To ravish the sensuous mind
Lie lightless, all their sparkles bleared and black and blind.

5

Dim moon-eyed fishes near
   Gaze at the gilded gear
And query: "What does this vaingloriousness down here?". . .

6

Well: while was fashioning
   This creature of cleaving wing,
The Immanent Will that stirs and urges everything

15 vaingloriousness: vain display; ostentation.

18 Immanent Will: Hardy's name for a force that determines the course of events in the world.

Customizing Instruction

Less Proficient Readers

1 Remind students that *twain* means *a set of two.* Ask them to identify the two things that converge or meet in this poem.

Answer: the *Titanic* and the iceberg.

Students Acquiring English

2 Help students use context clues to interpret the unusual verb in stanza 3: "To *glass* the opulent."

Answer: The speaker is describing the mirrors, so students should be able to determine that it means to reflect.

ductory words and the clauses. *(What—What distinguishes Hardy's poetry from that of his contemporaries; that—that he incorporates characteristics of a novel in some of his poetry)* Next ask students how these clauses function as nouns in the sentence. *(subject; predicate nominative)*

Exercise Have students underline each noun clause and identify its function as a noun in the sentence. Have students meet in cooperative groups to identify other types of clauses that may be found in these sentences.

1. *Why people enlist to fight* is a key question raised by Hardy in his poem "The Man He Killed." *(subject)*
2. In "The Man He Killed," the speaker of the poem is affected by what happened to his foe. *(object of the preposition)*
3. The speaker in "Ah, Are You Digging on My Grave?" wonders who could be digging at her grave so soon after her death. *(direct object)*

Use **Grammar Transparencies and Copymasters**, p. 57.

Use McDougal Littell's ***Language Network*** for more instruction and practice in noun clauses.

Reading and Analyzing

Literary Analysis: THEME

One might expect a poem inspired by such a major human tragedy to describe the terror and suffering felt by the passengers, but the speaker provides none of that. Have students discuss how this fits Hardy's view of nature and the place of people in it.

Possible Response: Hardy is more concerned with presenting the indifferent forces at work behind the event rather than the suffering of individual people, which is of little importance in his world, where fate or some other uncaring force has control.

Active Reading

MAKING INFERENCES ABOUT A SPEAKER'S ATTITUDE

How do the phrases "Immanent Will" (line 16) and "Spinner of the Years" (line 31) give clues to the speaker's attitude toward the sinking of the Titanic?

Possible Response: They suggest that the destruction of the Titanic was ordained by some blind force—fate, perhaps—that is neither benevolent nor malevolent, and that the speaker believes humans should be warned that they cannot rise above nature.

Reading Skills and Strategies: ANALYZING CHOICE OF WORDS

Have students discuss the aptness of *welding* (line 27) to describe the idea of the ship's and the iceberg's shared destiny.

Possible Response: The word implies that they are inseparable—that they have been permanently attached to each other.

7

Prepared a sinister mate
For her—so gaily great—
A Shape of Ice, for the time far and dissociate.

8

And as the smart ship grew
In stature, grace, and hue,
In shadowy silent distance grew the Iceberg too.

9

Alien they seemed to be:
No mortal eye could see
The intimate welding of their later history,

10

Or sign that they were bent
By paths coincident
On being anon twin halves of one august event,

11

Till the Spinner of the Years
Said "Now!" And each one hears,
And consummation comes, and jars two hemispheres.

21 dissociate: unrelated.

30 anon: soon; **august:** grand; majestic.

31 Spinner of the Years: a personification of the "Immanent Will" of line 18.

The wreck of the *Titanic* lies on the ocean floor, 13,000 feet beneath the surface of the sea.

Teaching Options

Assessment Informal Assessment

SUMMARIZING

Ask students to write a summary of the events and images that occur in one of the three poems and explain these events in terms of the poem's theme.

RUBRIC

3 Full Accomplishment Students accurately and succinctly summarize each of three poems and relate events and images to theme.

2 Substantial Accomplishment Students summarize three poems, but do not completely relate summaries to theme.

1 Little or Partial Accomplishment Students fail to accurately summarize poems or are unable to grasp themes.

Connect to the Literature

1. **What Do You Think?** What are your thoughts about the sinking of the *Titanic* after reading "The Convergence of the Twain"?

Comprehension Check
- Who or what are the "twain" (two) referred to in the title?
- Who or what crawls over the surface of the ship's mirrors at the bottom of the ocean?

Think Critically

2. What view of human nature do you think Hardy reveals as he describes the sunken *Titanic?*

- the phrase "the Pride of Life that planned her" (line 3)
- the lifestyle suggested by the words *mirrors, jewels,* and *gilded gear*
- the meaning of "vaingloriousness" (line 15)

3. What **extended metaphor** is developed in stanzas 6 through 11? Why do you think Hardy might have chosen to use this metaphor?

4. **ACTIVE READING** MAKING INFERENCES ABOUT A SPEAKER'S ATTITUDE Review the answers you wrote down in your READER'S NOTEBOOK. How would you describe the attitude of each speaker? What differences do you see between the attitudes of the three?

Extend Interpretations

5. **Different Perspectives** In "The Man He Killed," what do you think the man who was killed might say in reply to the speaker of the poem?

6. **Critic's Corner** Lytton Strachey, a well-known biographer and a contemporary of Thomas Hardy, described one of Hardy's poems as depicting a scene that might easily be "the turning point in a realistic psychological novel." Do you think Strachey's description fits any of the Hardy poems you have read? Give reasons to support your answer.

7. **Connect to Life** The sinking of the *Titanic* still shocks and fascinates people, almost 100 years after the event. Think of a major disaster that has occurred in your lifetime. How did people react to it? What do you think are the reasons for how people respond to such events?

Literary Analysis

SATIRE IN LYRIC POETRY **Satire** almost always casts light on foibles and failings that are universal to human experience. These human weaknesses can range from individual actions and attitudes to those belonging to an entire nation. Satire often uses exaggeration to make its point, and it always involves some type of **irony.** Satire can be harsh and biting, as in Jonathan Swift's essay "A Modest Proposal," or it can be quiet and restrained, as in Hardy's poems.

Cooperative Learning Activity With two classmates, compare the object of the satire and the satiric **tone** in each of Hardy's poems. Use a chart like the one shown to list your ideas. Which poem do you think has the most forceful satire? What view of human nature is suggested by the satire in each poem? Share your conclusions with the class.

Title	Object of Satire	Satiric Tone

REVIEW SITUATIONAL IRONY The responses to the questions posed by the first speaker in "Ah, Are You Digging on My Grave?" and the final revelation create a shattering irony in the poem. This is an example of **situational irony**—the reader or a **character** expects one thing to happen but something else happens instead. Look for examples of situational irony in the other two poems. How does the irony contribute to the satire in each poem?

GUIDING STUDENT RESPONSE

Connect to the Literature

1. **What Do You Think?**
Guidelines for student response: Students might amplify their response to the poem with information they have gleaned from the film about the sinking of the Titanic.

Comprehension Check
- the iceberg and the ship
- a sea worm

Think Critically

2. Possible Responses: Human nature is vain and frivolous; humans tend to be blinded by their pride and forget that they are subject to the same laws as the rest of nature.
3. Possible Responses: A coming together of two different mates in a disastrous consummation; also, the formation of the iceberg is compared to the construction of the ship. Hardy is attempting to emphasize the inevitability of their meeting.
4. The speaker of "The Man He Killed" is a soldier who speaks in the first person; the speakers of "Ah, Are You Digging on My Grave" are two—a dead woman and her dog, both speaking in the first person; the speaker of "The Convergence of the Twain" seems an objective observer who speaks in the third person.

Literary Analysis

Cooperative Learning Activity Draw on the chalkboard a composite chart made up of the various responses given by different groups.

Review Situational Irony Have students share their examples of situational irony.

Extend Interpretations

Different Perspectives Answers will vary. Some students may feel that Hardy would have the victim repeat a similarly unreflective response about the "reason" for his death.

Critic's Corner Possible Response: Most students will see that each of the first two poems contains a crucial moment of awareness for its main character. However, in the second poem, the woman cannot have a turning point because her moment of awareness comes after she has died.

Connect to Life Students may recall such events as the 1995 bombing of the federal building in Oklahoma City. Students who have come to the United States as refugees may have different perspectives. Care should be taken with students who may have actually lived through a disaster; they may not feel comfortable talking about it in front of others.

Writing Options

1. Short Story Summary Write a summary of a short story based on the situation described in "The Man He Killed." Include events before and after the time of the poem.

2. Gravestone Epitaph Write the epitaph that the first speaker in "Ah, Are You Digging on My Grave?" might have wished were on her gravestone.

3. Poem About *Titanic* Write your own poem about the sinking of the *Titanic.* You may base your poem on what you know about the sinking of the ship from television documentaries or movies depicting the 1912 disaster. Place the poem in your **Working Portfolio.**

Activities & Explorations

1. War Poster Draw a war poster that the speaker of "The Man He Killed" might have designed. ~ **ART**

2. Dramatic Reading With a partner, practice and present a dramatic reading of "Ah, Are You Digging on My Grave?" in which you try to convey the attitude of each speaker. Be sure to pay attention to the punctuation as an indicator of shifts between speakers. ~ **SPEAKING AND LISTENING**

Inquiry & Research

Ship Sinks! In order to better appreciate the impact of the sinking of the *Titanic,* do some research in magazines and newspapers of the time to read about the famous disaster. Try to find newspaper headlines about the sinking, and make a list of the most dramatic ones. Share your list of headlines with the class.

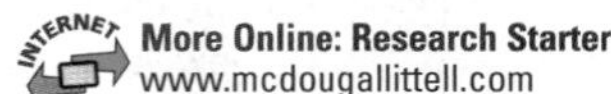

More Online: Research Starter
www.mcdougallittell.com

Thomas Hardy

1840–1928

Other Works
"The Darkling Thrush"
"Channel Firing"
The Return of the Native
Tess of the D'Urbervilles
Jude the Obscure

Architect and Writer The son of a builder, Thomas Hardy was reared and educated in southwestern England, a setting he later used in his novels. Apprenticed to a local architect at the age of 15, he left six years later for London, where he studied and worked as an architect for many years. During his stay in London, he began to write both poetry and fiction, and his first published novel appeared anonymously in 1871. Although the response to it was lukewarm, Hardy continued to write, finally achieving success with *Far from the Madding Crowd,* published in 1874. The popularity of that novel inspired him to give up architecture and devote his life to writing.

Novelist As a novelist, Hardy produced a series of mostly successful works, including *The Return of the Native,* considered one of the best novels in English literature. In 1891, however, his novel *Tess of the D'Urbervilles* was harshly criticized for its sympathetic treatment of what many readers viewed as immoral behavior. His next novel, *Jude the Obscure,* also met with hostility and was censored by one of England's most prominent bookstores. Disgusted by these reactions, Hardy abandoned the novel form altogether and turned to writing poetry.

Poet As a poet, Hardy created ironic anecdotes in verse, often using the rhythm of the ballad to emphasize the timelessness of his themes. His poetry has none of the self-pity so common in Victorian verse; his tone is stern and unflinching, his poetry straightforward and authentic—attributes still admired by critics and readers.

Author Activity

Imaginary County Hardy created an imaginary area called Wessex as the setting for his novels. Find out what you can about what actual county in England Wessex most likely corresponds to and what that part of England is like.

Writing Options

1. **Short Story Summary** Students may be encouraged to account for time, location, and any specific circumstances.
2. **Gravestone Epitaph** Students might be encouraged to visit a local cemetery for inspiration.
3. **Poem About *Titanic*** Students may choose to imitate Hardy's rhyme scheme of *aaa, bbb, ccc.* Encourage them to think of details different from those chosen by Hardy.

Activities & Explorations

1. **War Poster** Since the speaker of Hardy's poem sees his enemy as not so different from himself, the poster should probably not emphasize differences between the two sides or attempt to show one as more evil than the other.
2. **Dramatic Reading** This activity is further explored in the Speaking and Listening activity, page 956.

Inquiry & Research

Ship Sinks! Students will be greatly challenged to find headlines in the newspapers from 1912, especially in school districts where the libraries are more recently created. Some material may be available on microfilm or microfiche. To extend the activity, have students compare and contrast, then critique, coverage of the *Titanic*'s sinking as reported in a newspaper article, on television, and on the Internet. Ask students to distinguish each media's purpose: to entertain, to inform, to advertise, and so forth.

Author Activity

Imaginary County Wessex is Hardy's fictitious name for Dorset, in southwest England, an area running from Dorchester to Swanage Bay. In fact, the novelist's statue stands at the top of High West Street in Dorchester, the "Casterbridge" of Hardy's novel *The Mayor of Casterbridge.* The counterpart of "Kingsbere" in *Tess of the D'Urbervilles* is the nearby town of Bere Regis. The area was also home to T. E. Lawrence, "Lawrence of Arabia," who lived in Clouds Hill until his death in a motorcycle accident in 1935.

When I Was One-and-Twenty

To an Athlete Dying Young

Poetry by A. E. HOUSMAN

Comparing Literature of the World

The Poetry of A. E. Housman and Rabindranath Tagore

This lesson and the one that follows present an opportunity for comparing Housman's role as a poet with the role played by the Indian Nobel Prize-winning poet Rabindranath Tagore. Specific points of comparison in the Tagore lesson will help you contrast the different messages the two poets convey about life and mortality.

Connect to Your Life

Bygone Days Think of conversations you have heard in which older adults, perhaps some of your family members, talked about their youth. What aspects of their younger days did they recall? Share your thoughts with the class.

Build Background

Young Poet, Youthful Themes A. E. Housman composed most of his poems in his early 20s. Although not a prolific poet, he was nevertheless an influential literary figure, admired by many other poets who emulated his concisely crafted short lyrics, and by the public, who appreciated his universal themes and grace of style.

The two poems in this lesson are from Housman's first collection of poetry, *A Shropshire Lad*. In the 63 poems of that book, Housman disguised any autobiographical points by creating an imaginary **speaker**—a young farmer named Terence Hearsay. Like most of Housman's poems, these focus on youth.

Focus Your Reading

LITERARY ANALYSIS STANZA STRUCTURE There are three elements that make up **stanza structure,** the way a group of lines that form a unit in a poem are patterned or organized:

- number of **lines**
- **rhyme scheme,** the pattern of end rhyme
- **meter,** the regular rhythmic pattern in a line

In most poetry, rhythm and rhyme work together to create a particular effect. As you read, notice the stanza structure Housman uses in each poem and the effect created by the rhythm and rhyme in each stanza.

ACTIVE READING INFERRING MEANING When you read a poem, you usually need to **infer** its meaning. An inference about a poem is a guess based on clues in the work. You can make inferences about the subject of a poem by noting the **details** used to describe the subject. The Housman poems deal primarily with the advantages and disadvantages of youth and aging. As you read the poems, look for the details that give you clues about what Housman is saying.

READER'S NOTEBOOK. For each poem, create a chart like the one shown to record details used to describe the advantages and disadvantages of youth and aging.

"When I Was One-and-Twenty"	
Advantages	**Disadvantages**
Youth:	Youth:
Aging:	Aging:

OVERVIEW

Objectives

1. understand and appreciate two **poems (Literary Analysis)**
2. identify and examine **stanza structure (Literary Analysis)**
3. **infer meaning** in poetry **(Active Reading)**

Summary

"When I Was One-and-Twenty" relates advice given to the speaker by a wise man, who advises the speaker not to give away his heart. The speaker ruefully concludes that the wise man's advice is true. "To an Athlete Dying Young" declares that dying young is preferable to outliving fame.

Thematic Link

Both of these poems, as they focus on the fleeting nature of youth, give a new voice and a new direction to English poetry at the turn of the century.

5-Minute Warm-Up

Daily Language SkillBuilder

Have students **proofread** the display sentences on page 829k and write them correctly. The sentences also appear on Transparency 25 of **Grammar Transparencies and Copymasters.**

LESSON RESOURCES

UNIT FIVE RESOURCE BOOK, pp. 53–54

ASSESSMENT RESOURCES

Formal Assessment, pp. 173–174

Teacher's Guide to Assessment and Portfolio Use

Test Generator

SKILLS TRANSPARENCIES AND COPYMASTERS

Literary Analysis
- Form and Meaning in Poetry, T15 (for Literary Analysis, p. 963)

Reading and Critical Thinking
- Making Inferences, T7 (for Active Reading, p. 963)

Grammar
- Possessive Nouns, T38 (for Mini Lesson, p. 968)
- Forming Plural Possessives, C164 (for Mini Lesson, p. 968)

Writing
- Subject Analysis, C30 (for Writing Option 2, p. 968)
- Autobiographical Incident, C36 (for Writing Option 1, p. 968)

Communications
- Recognizing Logical Fallacies, T3 (for Writing Option 2, p. 968)
- Impromptu Speaking: Debate, T15 (for Activities & Explorations 1, p. 968)

INTEGRATED TECHNOLOGY

Audio Library

Visit our website: www.mcdougallittell.com

TEACHING THE LITERATURE

Reading and Analyzing

Active Reading INFERRING MEANING

Explain to students that inferring means drawing logical conclusions based on something that is implied by the writer. Ask them what they can infer from the last two lines of "When I Was One-and-Twenty."

Possible Response: The speaker has foolishly fallen in love.

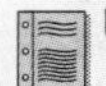

Use **Unit Five Resource Book,** p. 52 for more practice.

Literary Analysis

STANZA STRUCTURE

Ask a volunteer to read aloud the first stanza of each poem. Then ask students to identify the rhyme scheme of each stanza. Have them discuss the effect the rhythm and rhyme have on them as readers.

Possible Response: abcbdeae *and* aabb.

Ask students to state the number of accented syllables per line in each of the two stanzas.

Answer: 3 and 4.

Use **Unit Five Resource Book,** p. 53 for more exercises.

Thinking Through the Literature

1. One's heart (love)
2. Accept all reasonable responses.
3. Possible Response: firsthand experience with the pain of love.
4. Possible Responses: Love can be painful; young people are heedless and overconfident; people learn not from advice but from experience.

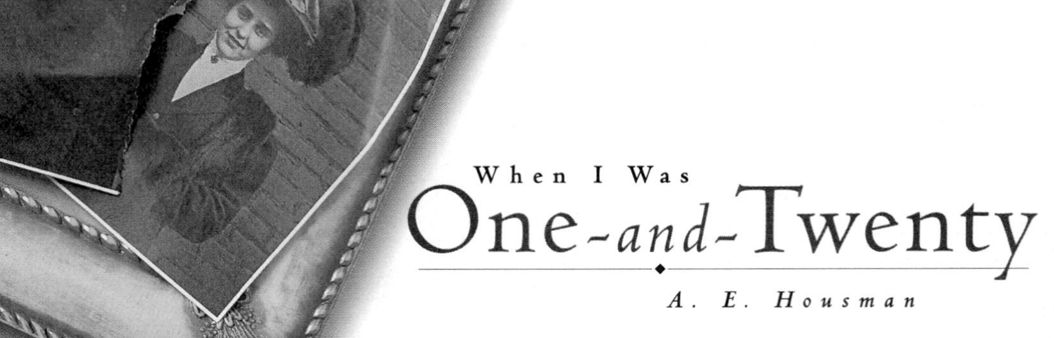

When I Was One-*and*-Twenty

A. E. Housman

When I was one-and-twenty
I heard a wise man say,
"Give crowns and pounds and guineas
But not your heart away;
Give pearls away and rubies
But keep your fancy free."
But I was one-and-twenty,
No use to talk to me.

When I was one-and-twenty
I heard him say again,
"The heart out of the bosom
Was never given in vain;
'Tis paid with sighs a plenty
And sold for endless rue."
And I am two-and-twenty,
And oh, 'tis true, 'tis true.

3 crowns . . . guineas: British units of money.

14 rue: sorrow; regret.

Thinking Through the Literature

1. **Comprehension Check** What does the wise man say is "sold for endless rue"?
2. What is your reaction to the words of the wise man?
3. What do you think could account for the change in the **speaker's** attitude? Give reasons for your answer.
4. What message do you think the speaker is trying to convey?

Teaching Options

BLOCK SCHEDULING: MANAGING TIME

If your schedule requires that you cover the lesson objectives in a shorter time, use . . .

- Preparing to Read, p. 963
- Thinking Through the Literature, pp. 964, 967

If you want to take advantage of longer class time, use . . .

- TE Teaching Options: Vocabulary, p. 965; Speaking and Listening, p. 966; Grammar, p. 968
- Choices & Challenges and Author Activity, p. 968

TO AN ATHLETE DYING YOUNG

A. E. HOUSMAN

The time you won your town the race
We chaired you through the market-place;
Man and boy stood cheering by,
And home we brought you shoulder-high.

Today, the road all runners come,
Shoulder-high we bring you home,
And set you at your threshold down,
Townsman of a stiller town.

Smart lad, to slip betimes away
From fields where glory does not stay
And early though the laurel grows
It withers quicker than the rose.

Eyes the shady night has shut
Cannot see the record cut,
And silence sounds no worse than cheers
After earth has stopped the ears:

2 chaired: carried publicly on a chair or seat, in triumph.

9 betimes: early.

11 laurel: Wreaths made of leaves of the laurel tree were worn by victorious athletes in ancient times as a token of honor and glory.

14 cut: broken.

Customizing Instruction

Less Proficient Readers

Set a Purpose Have students read to learn the two speakers' views on youth. Ask students to look at each stanza as if it were a paragraph in a prose piece. Have them read the sentences aloud, from capital letter to period and then summarize in their own words.

Have students summarize the advice offered by the wise man in "When I Was One-and Twenty."

Possible Response: Do not be so quick to fall in love, because the cost to the emotions is high.

Students Acquiring English

Help students decipher unfamiliar hyphenated compounds, such as *one-and-twenty, shoulder-high,* and *still-defended*, by examining the word parts and context.

Answers: twenty-one; on the shoulders; not yet lost.

Use **Spanish Study Guide** for additional support, pp. 221–223.

Gifted and Talented

Ask students to consider whether the speaker of "When I Was One-and-Twenty" would agree with the ideas presented in "To an Athlete Dying Young."

Vocabulary Strategy

CONTEXT

Instruction Explain to students that poets often rely more on suggestion than direct statement to convey meaning. Housman, for example, tells the reader only in the title of the second poem that the young athlete is dead; the rest of the poem relies on figurative language to get his ideas across. The general context is provided by the title.

Activity Ask students to begin with this general context, and also to consider other context clues within the lines, to decipher the following figurative phrases.

- line 5: "the road all runners come"

Possible Response: a funeral procession; the road to the cemetery; death.

- line 8: "a stiller town"

Possible Response: a cemetery.

- line 13: "the shady night"

Possible Response: death.

A lesson on context clues appears on p. 939 in the Pupil's Edition.

TO AN ATHLETE DYING YOUNG 965

Reading and Analyzing

Literary Analysis: ALLITERATION

(A) Remind students that alliteration is the repetition of initial consonant sounds. Ask students to identify the repeated consonant sound in line 19.
Answer: r.

What effect does this alliteration have on the rhythm of the poem?
Possible Response: It causes the reader to exert more effort, thus slowing down the rhythm.

Point out to students that sometimes writers employ alliteration not for some definite rhythmic purpose, as in line 19, but merely for the sake of musicality, or to provide auditory unity to a line. Ask them to point out other examples of alliteration in lines 21–24.
Possible Responses: So set [line 21]; fleet foot [line 22]; sill . . . shade [line 22]; low lintel [line 23].

Now you will not swell the rout
Of lads that wore their honors out,
(A) Runners whom renown outran
And the name died before the man.

So set, before its echoes fade,
The fleet foot on the sill of shade,
And hold to the low lintel up
The still-defended challenge-cup.

And round that early-laurelled head
Will flock to gaze the strengthless dead,
And find unwithered on its curls
The garland briefer than a girl's.

17 rout (rout): crowd.

22 sill: threshold.

23 lintel: the beam across the top of a door frame.

28 garland: a wreath or woven chain of leaves or flowers.

Teaching Options

Speaking and Listening

READING FOR RHYTHM

Instruction Have one student read the first two lines of "To an Athlete Dying Young" aloud. Ask the other students to scan the lines for rhythm as they listen to the reader. They will probably be able to see that these lines, like the majority of lines in the poem, are written in iambic tetrameter. In this meter, there are four iambic feet (an unstressed followed by a stressed syllable) per line.

Prepare Have another student continue reading, trying to continue with the strict, iambic stress of the first two lines. Students will quickly see that reading a poem this way—certainly this poem—does not work, and in fact makes it sound silly, like a nursery rhyme.

Present Have students take turns reading stanzas aloud, noting which lines are in regular iambic tetrameter, and which are not.

BLOCK SCHEDULING This activity is particularly well-suited for longer class periods.

Connect to the Literature

1. **What Do You Think?** What are your thoughts after reading "To an Athlete Dying Young"? Share them with your classmates.

Comprehension Check
- Why did the townspeople "chair" the athlete through the town in triumph?
- What disappointment does the speaker claim the athlete will never know?

Think Critically

2. How would you describe the **speaker's** response to the young man's death?

THINK ABOUT
- his reference to the athlete as a "smart lad" (line 9)
- what the eyes and ears will not see or hear (lines 13–16)
- his reference to a name's dying "before the man" (line 20)
- the **images** he presents in the last two stanzas

3. Do you agree with the speaker's ideas about fame? Why or why not?

4. **ACTIVE READING INFERRING MEANING** In a small group, discuss the charts you made for the poems in your **READER'S NOTEBOOK**. Based on the details you listed for each one, what can you **infer** about the advantages and disadvantages of youth and aging?

Extend Interpretations

5. **Comparing Texts** Compare and contrast the portrayals of youth in the two Housman poems. Cite lines in each to support your ideas.

6. **Critic's Corner** In 1936, the American poet Conrad Aiken commented that the thoughts expressed in Housman's poetry have an "adolescent note," or "boyishness." Would you use the word *adolescent* or *mature* to describe the thoughts expressed in "To an Athlete Dying Young" and "When I Was One-and-Twenty"? Cite evidence to support your answer.

7. **Connect to Life** Think about how people today typically respond to the untimely death of a famous athlete. Do you think this poem would comfort them?

Literary Analysis

STANZA STRUCTURE A **stanza** is a group of lines that form a unit in a poem. Stanzas are roughly comparable to paragraphs in prose. Each one deals with a single idea that supports the poem's major idea. In "When I Was One-and-Twenty," for example, each stanza tells what the wise man says and gives the speaker's response to it.

The elements of structure in a stanza—the number of **lines, rhyme scheme, rhythm,** and **meter**—work together to reinforce meaning. They may also affect a poem's **mood.** A slow rhythm and longer lines may convey a sad or mysterious mood, for example. A quicker rhythm and shorter lines may create a more lighthearted mood.

Paired Activity Copy the first stanza of each of these poems on a sheet of paper. With a partner, read each stanza aloud, then mark the meter of each. How do the meters of the poems differ? In which poem do you think the rhythm and rhyme are more obvious? What effect do you think the rhythm and rhyme create in each poem? Write down your observations in a chart like the one below.

	Meter	Rhythm and Rhyme
"When I Was One-and-Twenty"		
"To an Athlete Dying Young"		

GUIDING STUDENT RESPONSE

Connect to the Literature

1. **What Do You Think?** Guidelines for student response: Students might connect the ideas and emotions elicited by a reading of this poem to their own experiences in sports and life in general.

Comprehension Check
- because he won the race
- He will never see his own record broken.

Think Critically

2. Possible Responses: comforting; accepting; wistful; cynical. The speaker seems to be an older, wiser man who appreciates the ironic rewards of early death.
3. Students' responses will vary but should recognize the speaker's view that fame is fleeting and that those who experience its loss are often bitterly disappointed.
4. Accept all reasonable responses. Students' charts and ideas should accurately represent the views of the two poems' speakers.

Literary Analysis

Paired Activity As students discuss the paired activity, have them comment on the effect the rhythm and rhyme scheme had on their understanding and appreciation of the poem.

Extend Interpretations

Comparing Texts Possible similarities include the view of youth as fleeting and as a period of hope and confidence that time will soon crush; possible differences include the frivolous concerns of youth discussed in the first poem versus the issue of death in the second.

Critic's Corner Student responses will vary; ask students to articulate their definitions of *mature* and *adolescent.*

Connect to Life Accept all reasonable responses.

Writing Options

1. **Personal Anecdote** Allow students to invent an episode if they cannot recall one or if they prefer to write a fictional anecdote.
2. **Essay on Poetry** Remind students to support their ideas with examples from the works of Housman or other poets.

Activities & Explorations

1. **Rebuttal of Poetic Views** Remind students that a rebuttal is an argument opposing another argument, using evidence to support its claim. Have several students present rebuttals, and ask the rest of the class to evaluate their presentations. Encourage students to use specific, appropriate details to create a strong rebuttal. The class may evaluate arguments according to how skillfully and appropriately a debater used language.
2. **Poetic Illustration** Note that students may illustrate information inferred from the poems, including what happened in the speaker's 22nd year or what event the athlete excelled in.
3. **Sculpture of the Runner** You might wish to make this a cooperative activity in which artistic students are paired with those who do not have a background in art.

Inquiry & Research

Poetic Soundtracks This information is available through catalogs of recordings and indexes of the works of these composers. Encourage students to consult biographies and reference works such as *Grove's Dictionary of Music and Musicians.*

Author Activity

More About Terence Hearsay The poems in *A Shropshire Lad* are marked by the same fatalism found in the two poems here. A common theme is the tragedy of life's brief course. The setting for the poems is mostly rural, or at least provincial England. Nature, love, friendship, and life itself are beautiful, and must be relished during what little time is allotted us. The best of the poems in the collection share the poignancy of "To an Athlete Dying Young."

Choices & CHALLENGES

Writing Options

1. **Personal Anecdote** Reflecting on "When I Was One-and-Twenty," write a personal anecdote in which you describe a time when you did not heed the warning of another person, only to learn later that the warning was justified. Place the anecdote in your **Working Portfolio.**
2. **Essay on Poetry** Echoing the ideas of romanticism, Housman maintained that poetry cannot be explained or analyzed because it is an experience not of intellect but of emotion. Draft an essay explaining whether you agree or disagree with Housman's theory.

Agree: Poetry is felt—an experience for the senses . . .
Disagree: A poem is a tightly constructed piece of writing . . .

Writing Handbook
See page 1367–1370: Explanatory Writing.

Activities & Explorations

1. **Rebuttal of Poetic Views** Practice and present a rebuttal of the views expressed in "When I Was One-and-Twenty." ~ SPEAKING AND LISTENING
2. **Poetic Illustration** Use pencil or charcoal to create a drawing illustrating an image or idea in one of Housman's poems. ~ ART
3. **Sculpture of the Runner** Create a clay or wire sculpture that reflects your impression of the runner described in "To an Athlete Dying Young." ~ ART

Inquiry & Research

Poetic Soundtracks Some of Housman's poems have been set to music by composers such as Ralph Vaughan Williams, George Butterworth, John Ireland, and Arnold Bax. Which poems did they use? How did they happen to write music for these poems? If possible, locate recordings of some of the compositions and play them for the class.

A. E. Housman
1859–1936

Other Works
"Bredon Hill"
"Is My Team Ploughing?"
"Loveliest of Trees"
"On Moonlit Heath and Lonesome Bank"

Early Interests and Setbacks Alfred Edward Housman spent more years working on scholarly Latin translations than writing poetry. His interest in classical studies began in grammar school, where he studied Greek and Latin and developed a skill of creating remarkably clear translations. Although he displayed intellectual prowess early in life, periods of emotional distress plagued his youth and may have contributed to the melancholy later reflected in his poetry. His mother's death when he was just 12 years old upset him greatly. While a student at Oxford University, he faced further personal anxieties that left him in a state of emotional turmoil and caused him to fail his final exams. After leaving the university without a degree, Housman worked in London as a clerk in the patent office for 10 years.

Scholarly Pursuits During his years as a clerk, Housman continued to study Latin on his own, wrote articles for journals, and eventually earned recognition as a brilliant scholar and critic of Latin texts. In 1892, he was made professor of Latin at University College in London, where he taught until 1911. He then became a professor at Cambridge University, teaching there until shortly before his death. In his later years, Housman turned down various awards and honors, including the government's coveted Order of Merit and an appointment as England's poet laureate.

Author Activity

More About Terence Hearsay Read some more poems from *A Shropshire Lad.* How do their images and themes compare with those in "When I Was One-and-Twenty" and "To an Athlete Dying Young"?

Teaching Options

Grammar

Punctuation: Forming Plural Possessives

Instruction To form the possessive of a plural noun that ends in -s, add an apostrophe only. *(the runners' shoes)* To form the possessive of a plural noun that does not end in *-s,* add an apostrophe and *-s. (the people's support)*

Activity Write on the chalkboard the following sentence.

The speakers' thoughts and reflections are often shared by the readers.

Ask students to identify the plural noun that shows possession. *(speakers')*

Exercise Have students select the proper plural possessives in the following sentences.

1. The other (athletes/athlete's/athletes') glory couldn't match those of the lad's. *(athletes')*
2. She broke his heart; his grief lasted for two (month's/months'/months's/months) duration. *(months')*
3. Both (poems/poem's/poems') viewpoints focus on youth. *(poems')*

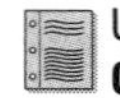

Use **Grammar Transparencies and Copymasters,** p. C164.

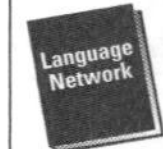

Use McDougal Littell's ***Language Network*** for more instruction and practice in forming plural possessives.

1996

Poetry by RABINDRANATH TAGORE

Comparing Literature of the World

The Role of the Poet Across Cultures

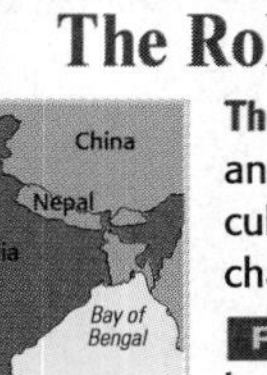

The Poetry of A. E. Housman and Rabindranath Tagore Although A. E. Housman and Indian poet Rabindranath Tagore were separated by both physical and cultural distances, the two lived as contemporaries, each witnessing tremendous change between the 19th and 20th centuries.

Points of Comparison As you read Tagore's poem "1996," think about how he views his role as a poet at the turn of the century. Compare Tagore's view with the role of the poet that Housman seems to imply. Also compare the **themes** used by each poet and the **images** used to help convey these themes.

Build Background

East Meets West During the 19th century, British colonial rule brought dramatic changes to India's educational system as well as its government. Parliament insisted that Indian schools offer instruction not only in the English language but also in English literature. Although this directive displeased many Indians, the people living in the eastern province of Bengal were generally receptive to learning about the culture of their English rulers.

Born in India in 1861, the Bengali poet Rabindranath Tagore was influenced by the works of both English and Bengali authors. Although the Tagore family welcomed the opportunity to study Western culture, they also promoted Bengali arts and traditions. They read widely in English literature, but when writing their own poems, plays, and stories, they wrote in Bengali. It was not until Rabindranath Tagore was in his 50s that he began translating his poems into English, reluctantly honoring a promise he had made to an English admirer. In 1913, shortly after his translations reached the Western world, Tagore was awarded the Nobel Prize in literature, becoming the first Asian to receive that honor.

Tagore looked for the best in every culture and advocated for his own country a balance between the traditions of East and West. He worried about the tensions between cultures and wondered how they would affect the future of the world. It may have been this contemplation of the future that inspired Tagore to write in 1896 the poem you are about to read, called "1996."

Focus Your Reading

LITERARY ANALYSIS TITLE The **title** of a literary work introduces readers to the piece and usually reveals something about its subject or theme. Although some poems are merely identified by their first line, most literary works have been carefully and deliberately titled. Before you read "1996," think about what the poem's **theme** might be. Keep your thoughts and predictions in mind as you read the poem.

ACTIVE READING ANALYZING STRUCTURE
Tagore's "1996" is structured around three questions. The first question occurs in the first two lines of the poem:

> ***Who are you reading curiously this***
> ***poem of mine***
> ***a hundred years from now?***

READER'S NOTEBOOK As you read "1996," notice how Tagore uses questions to structure his poem. Jot down the poem's other two questions and note how the poet responds to each one.

OVERVIEW

Objectives

1. understand and appreciate an Indian **poem (Literary Analysis)**
2. examine the meaning of a poem's **title (Literary Analysis)**
3. **analyze structure** in a poem **(Active Reading)**
4. compare text events with reader's own experience

Summary

In this lyric poem, the speaker sends to his audience 100 years in the future a lovely spring day rendered into verse.

Thematic Link

The poem deals with rebirth by touching on spring with a **new voice and new direction.** By addressing itself to readers and poets 100 years in the future, the poem sends them the thoughts, feelings, and experiences of the poet so that they may be experienced anew in the future.

5-Minute Warm-Up

Daily Language SkillBuilder

Have students **proofread** the display sentences on page 829k and write them correctly. The sentences also appear on Transparency 26 of **Grammar Transparencies and Copymasters.**

LESSON RESOURCES

UNIT FIVE RESOURCE BOOK, pp. 55–56

ASSESSMENT RESOURCES
- **Formal Assessment,** pp. 175–176
- **Teacher's Guide to Assessment and Portfolio Use**
- **Test Generator**

SKILLS TRANSPARENCIES AND COPYMASTERS

Reading and Critical Thinking
- Analyzing Text Structure, T17 (for Active Reading, p. 969)

Grammar
- Using Dashes to Introduce an Explanation, C162 (for Mini Lesson, pp. 970–971)

Writing
- Sensory Word List, T14 (for Writing Option 1, p. 973)
- Compare-Contrast, C34 (for Writing Option 2, p. 973)

INTEGRATED TECHNOLOGY
- **Audio Library**
- **Internet: Research Starter**
- **Visit our website:** www.mcdougallittell.com

TEACHING THE LITERATURE

Reading and Analyzing

Literary Analysis TITLE

A Before students read the poem, ask them to predict what they think it will be about based solely on its title. After they have read the poem, ask them to consider why the poet did not choose to call the poem "1896."

Possible Responses: Tagore wants to emphasize the theme of timelessness and rebirth: the beauty of the spring will be the same 100 years in the future; the focus of the poem is the future (from the speaker's perspective), not the present.

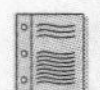
Use **Unit Five Resource Book,** p. 55 for more exercises.

Active Reading
ANALYZING STRUCTURE

Ask students to state the subject of each of the three questions that Tagore asks in lines 1–2, 3–9, and 33–34.

Answer: you [the reader], I [Tagore], the new poet.

Ask students what purpose each of these questions serves in the poem's structure; in other words, how do they organize the poem?

Possible Response: The first question introduces the poem and orients it toward the future. The second question turns the poem to the speaker's present. The third question brings the poem full circle by orienting the poem again toward the future.

Use **Unit Five Resource Book,** p. 54 for more practice.

1996

Rabindranath Tagore

Who are you reading curiously this poem of mine
a hundred years from now?
Shall I be able to send to you
—steeped in the love of my heart—
the faintest touch of this spring morning's joy,
the scent of a flower,
a bird-song's note,
a spark of today's blaze of color
1 a hundred years from now?

Yet, for once, open your window on the south
and from your balcony

Rabindranath Tagore, 1896

Teaching Options

Grammar

Punctuation: Using Dashes to Introduce an Explanation

Instruction Dashes, which are formed by joining two hyphens (–), show an abrupt break in thought, or they signal the addition of nonessential information in a sentence. Dashes show a "looser" connection to the main idea than commas do. Note that the words, clauses, or phrases set off by dashes merely add extra information to an already complete thought.

Activity Write the following sentence on the chalkboard.

Bengali, Tagore's native language, is spoken in the area called the Bengal–the northeastern part of India around the city of Calcutta–and in the adjoining nation of Bangladesh.

Read to the students the statement in the sentence that is set off by the dashes. Ask the students what the main thought is in the sentence. *(The main thought is where Bengali is spoken.)* Then ask what additional information is provided by this statement within the dashes. *(Additional information is given about Bengal's location.)*

gaze at the far horizon.
Then, sinking deep in fancy
think of the ecstasies of joy
that came floating down
from some far heaven of bliss
to touch the heart of the world
a hundred years ago;
think of the young spring day
wild, impetuous and free;
and of the south wind
—fragrant with the pollen of flowers—
rushing on restless wings to paint the earth
with the radiant hues of youth
a hundred years before your day.

And think, how his heart aflame, **2**
his whole being rapt in song,
a poet was awake that day
to unfold like flowers
his myriad thoughts
with what wealth of love!—
one morning a hundred years ago.

A hundred years from now
who is the new poet singing his songs to you?
Across the years I send him
the joyous greeting of this spring.
May my song echo for a while,
on your spring day,
in the beating of your heart,
in the murmur of bees,
in the rustling of leaves,—
a hundred years from today.

February, 1896

20 impetuous (ĭm-pĕch'o͞o-əs): impulsive.

27 rapt: deeply absorbed.

30 myriad (mĭr'ē-əd): countless.

1996 971

Customizing Instruction

Less Proficient Readers

Set a Purpose Have students read to determine what message the speaker has for future readers and poets.

1 Ask students what the speaker would like to send to the readers of this poem.

Possible Response: the beauty of a spring day 100 years before their time.

Students Acquiring English

2 Help students identify the referent for "his" in lines 26–27.

Answer: "a poet" [line 28].

Use **Spanish Study Guide** for additional support, pp. 224–226.

Gifted and Talented

Have students compare this poem to others that are messages to the future (for example, Gray's "Elegy Written in a Country Churchyard"). Ask them to note differences and similarities in themes and concerns. You might have them write their own messages for the future, using either poetry or prose.

Exercise Have students read the following sentences and determine if the dashes are used correctly. If sentences are incorrect, have students rewrite them without the dashes and use proper punctuation where necessary.

1. In "1996" the poet conjures up pleasant images of an early spring day—radiant hues, flowers, the murmur of bees, and the rustling of leaves—to convey what he experienced back in 1896. *(correct; dashes set off parenthetical information)*
2. The poet wants us to think of an early spring day—and recall our first love. *(incorrect; day and recall)*
3. A hundred years from now, will poets continue to write about spring—or will they have lost interest in nature entirely? *(incorrect; spring, or)*
4. Tagore is famous in India for his educational reforms—coeducational classrooms, elimination of class-based schools, etc.—as well as for his writings. *(correct; adds parenthetical information)*

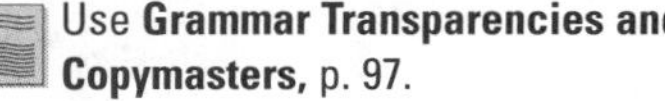
Use **Grammar Transparencies and Copymasters**, p. 97.

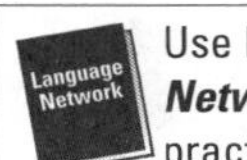

Use McDougal Littell's ***Language Network*** for more instruction and practice in using dashes.

GUIDING STUDENT RESPONSE

Connect to the Literature

1. What Do You Think?
Guidelines for student response: Students might use the photograph of him as well as the poem itself to form an impression of Tagore.

Comprehension Check

- Tagore addresses the reader as well as a future poet, whom he imagines to exist 100 years from the time of his writing.
- The poet hopes that readers of his poem and the poet who "sings" to them will take time to revel in the delights of his spring day 100 years before their time.

Think Critically

2. Accept all reasonable responses. Students should recognize Tagore's optimism and his attempt to communicate with future readers.
3. Possible Responses: happy; hopeful; optimistic
4. Students who feel he expects little change may cite his optimistic attitude or expectation that his ideas and images will be perceived by future readers. Students who feel he expects much change may cite his reliance on universal images of nature to convey his message.
5. Possible Response: The questions relate to each other by dealing with the same subject: the future. They link Tagore, the reader, and the poet by making the reader a reader of Tagore and the poet.

Literary Analysis

Cooperative Learning Activity Have students write a first draft of a poem titled "2096." Have volunteers read their efforts to the class.

Thinking through the LITERATURE

Connect to the Literature

1. **What Do You Think?** What impressions of Rabindranath Tagore do you have after reading this poem?

Comprehension Check
- Who does Tagore address in his poem?
- What does the poet hope will happen in 100 years?

Think Critically

2. How do you think Tagore would explain the **purpose** of his poem?

THINK ABOUT
- what he hopes to "send" to the reader (line 3)
- why he wants the reader to "gaze at the far horizon" (line 12)
- his desire "to unfold like flowers / his myriad thoughts" (lines 29–30)

3. How would you describe the **mood** Tagore creates in his poem?
4. Do you think Tagore expects the world to change much in 100 years? Use evidence from the poem to support your answer.
5. ACTIVE READING ANALYZING STRUCTURE With a classmate, review the notes you wrote down in your READER'S NOTEBOOK about the questions in "1996." How do the questions relate to each other? How do they link Tagore, the reader, and the poet writing "a hundred years from today"?

Extend Interpretations

6. **The Writer's Style** In "1996," Tagore addresses the reader directly. What is your reaction to this technique? What effect do you think the poet is trying to achieve?
7. **Connect to Life** Think about the message that Tagore sends to his future readers. Do you think a contemporary poet might send a similar message to future readers? Why or why not?
8. **Points of Comparison** Compare Housman's message about mortality in "To an Athlete Dying Young" with the **theme** of rebirth in Tagore's poem. What **images** do the poets use to support their themes?

Literary Analysis

TITLE The **titles** of some literary works are straightforward, stating exactly what the reader can expect to discover in the work. Others merely tickle the imagination, perhaps hinting at the subject and forcing the reader to search for deeper meaning. The title of Tagore's poem gives readers a direct clue about its subject. In addition, the text of the poem repeatedly recalls the title with its reference at the end of each stanza to "a hundred years." Deeper understanding of the title is provided by the poem's **theme**—the passage and effect of time—and by its hopeful **tone.**

Cooperative Learning Activity Get together with a small group of your classmates and plan what you would say in a poem titled "2096." In a chart like the one shown here, compare Tagore's "1996" with the poem you would compose. How would your poem differ from Tagore's in theme and tone? Share your ideas with the rest of the class.

	Theme	Tone
Tagore's "1996"		
My "2096"		

Extend Interpretations

The Writer's Style Students' reactions will vary but should be supported by logical reasoning. They may suggest that Tagore is trying to achieve a sense of intimacy with readers or to convey the universality of human experience.

Connect to Life Possible Responses: yes, because people will always be curious about the future; no, because modern poets are more cynical.

Points of Comparison Housman's poem is dominated by images of death and the grave, while Tagore's is dominated by very sensory images of life in springtime.

Writing Options

1. **Spring Images** Jot down some images that come to mind when you think of a spring day. Place a check beside those that might appeal to Tagore.

2. **Points of Comparison** Think again about the poems you've read by Tagore and Housman and the themes these works convey to the reader. If Tagore and Housman had met, would they have had similar ideas about the role of the poet? Freewrite your ideas.

Activities & Explorations

1. **Poetry Anthology** Prepare an anthology of contemporary poetry as an answer to Tagore's question "Who is the new poet?" ~ INTERPRETING

2. **Triptych of Tagore's World** With classmates, prepare a triptych—an artwork in three panels—to illustrate your impressions of the world in Tagore's time, the world today, and the world as it might appear 100 years from now. ~ ART

Inquiry & Research

Jewel in the Crown Research to find out about some of the political, social, and economic changes brought about in India by the British in the 19th century. Share your findings with the class.

More Online: Research Starter www.mcdougallittell.com

Rabindranath Tagore
1861–1941

Other Works
Gitanjali (Song Offerings)
The Crescent Moon
"The Cabuliwallah"
"The Babus of Nayanjore"

A Literary Bent Born into one of the most intellectual and talented Indian families of the time, Rabindranath Tagore wrote his first poem at the age of 8. By the time he was 15, he had published one poem and was reading his work aloud at public gatherings. In spite of his thirst for learning, Tagore disliked his childhood school experiences and rebelled against his rigidly institutionalized education. At the age of 17, he traveled to London, enrolled at University College, and, following his family's wishes, began to study law. Two years later, however, he gave up his studies and returned to India to devote his life to literary pursuits.

Rural Life Although born in the city of Calcutta, Tagore seemed to prefer life in the rural areas of Bengal. He had a fascination with nature that was strengthened during a boyhood trip to northern India and the Himalayas. In later years, he managed his family's estates and composed numerous literary works in rural Bengal, where he eventually founded his own school. In an effort to blend the best of Indian and Western traditions, he introduced many new educational techniques, including coeducation and the elimination of all caste, or class, distinctions. After World War I, he expanded his local school into an international university.

Artist and Activist By the time of his death at the age of 80, Tagore had composed numerous short stories, novels, and plays, as well as 60 volumes of poetry. He was also a gifted painter and musician and had set many of his poems to music. Reflected in some of his best poetry is the intense sadness he experienced after the deaths of his wife, a daughter, and a son within a five-year period. Much of his writing was also inspired by a deep concern for India's poor and by a desire for social and political reforms. Besides being a leader in the arts, Tagore was one of India's leading activists for independence. His death came six years before his country gained its freedom from British rule.

GUIDING STUDENT RESPONSE

Writing Options

1. **Spring Images** Responses may tend to cluster around conventional images of springtime, but in many parts of the country, such as desert areas, signs of spring are more varied. Encourage actual responses based on students' own experiences, rather than conventional responses.
2. **Points of Comparison** Students might expand upon this assignment by making up a chart comparing and contrasting the poets' ideas, or they might write a dialogue between the two about the role of the poet.

Activities & Explorations

1. **Poetry Anthology** Students may want to expand their search for poetry into song lyrics.
2. **Triptych of Tagore's World** Students may want to develop this project as a collage of illustrations and materials from existing sources.

Inquiry & Research

Jewel in the Crown Students may wish to consult books on general Indian history. Some titles to recommend include *Cultural History of India* by A. L. Basham; *India* by Stanley Wolpert; or *India: A Concise History* by Francis Watson.

Mini Lesson: Speaking and Listening

SPEECH

Instruction Point out to students that Tagore's poem does not focus on current issues; rather, the speaker chooses to focus on things he assumes will be timeless (poetry, the beauty of nature), which will therefore allow him to connect to readers of the future.

Prepare Help students to write speeches to a future generation living 100 years from the present. Before students begin writing their speeches, ask them the question Tagore may have asked himself: How can I connect with this future generation? What issues are there that might still concern an audience 100 years from now?

Present Set a limit on the length of the address, perhaps no longer than Tagore's poem. You may want to allow students considerable leeway in style. Students should practice word choice, grammar, and diction, whether they choose to write their speech in the form of a poem like Tagore's, while others may opt for a straightforward address. As the speeches are delivered, have students listen for and write down the main idea or image of each speech.

BLOCK SCHEDULING This activity is particularly well-suited for longer class periods.

Objectives
- reflect on and assess understanding of the unit
- recognize and discuss connections that cross cultures
- understand literary terms as author's purpose and setting
- assess and build portfolios

Reflecting on the Unit

OPTION 1

A successful response will
- identify examples of the three specified kinds of relationships.
- state opinions on which relationships one is most likely to encounter today and explain why.

OPTION 2

A successful response will
- identify two selections that the student finds to be ironic.
- compare those selections, exploring speakers' and narrators' attitudes and circumstances.
- include a student's personal examples of irony.

OPTION 3

Many students will probably respond by choosing characters who performed inspirational, stirring, or dramatic deeds. To prepare for the conversation, tell students to think about what the characters' actions reveal about their personalities.

Self Assessment
You might suggest that students organize their ideas about the Victorians under the following topics:
- roles and obligations
- friendship
- marriage
- death
- society

The Victorians

How has reading the selections in this unit helped you understand the Victorian era? Have you discovered any links between your life and the lives of people you have read about? Choose one or more of the options in each section to help you explore these questions.

Reflecting on the Unit

OPTION 1

Considering Relationships In this unit you have read about many kinds of personal relationships. Which of these relationships did you find the most inspiring? the most frightening? the most saddening? Which of the relationships seemed like ones that you might encounter today? Discuss your opinions with a classmate.

OPTION 2

Reflecting on Life's Ironies In several of the selections in this unit, you encountered speakers and narrators who reflect on life and its ironies. In a paragraph, compare two selections that you found ironic, exploring the speakers' or narrators' attitudes and circumstances. Then reflect on some of the ironies you have experienced in your own life.

OPTION 3

Looking at Character Think about the quotation from George Eliot at the beginning of this unit: "Our deeds determine us, as much as we determine our deeds." With a partner, choose a character or speaker from each part of the unit and brainstorm some ways in which each has been "determined" by his or her deeds. Then, for the class, role-play a conversation in which the two individuals discuss the quotation.

Self ASSESSMENT

READER'S NOTEBOOK

To explore how your understanding of the Victorian era has developed over the course of this unit, make a before-and-after chart. In it, show how your ideas about the lives and relationships of some Victorians have changed as a result of reading the selections.

Reviewing Literary Concepts

OPTION 1

Understanding an Author's Purpose You have learned that an author's purpose may be to entertain, to inform, to express opinions, or to persuade. In a chart like the one shown, group this unit's selections according to their authors' purposes. Do any seem to fall under more than one heading? Are there any headings under which no selection fits? Compare your groupings with a partner's, and discuss any differences between the two.

To Entertain	To Inform	To Express Opinions	To Persuade

OPTION 2

Analyzing Setting In both fiction and poetry, setting often plays an important role—though the settings of poems are frequently implied rather than stated directly. From each part of this unit, choose three selections in which settings are either obvious or implied. List their titles, and describe, next to each, as much as you know about that work's setting. Then rank the selections according to how important you think setting is in them, with 1 representing the selection in which setting plays the most crucial role. Discuss your rankings with the rest of the class.

Self ASSESSMENT

In addition to *setting* and *author's purpose,* the following literary terms were discussed in Unit Five. In your READER'S NOTEBOOK copy the following list. Next to each term, write W (for "well"), S (for "somewhat"), or N (for "not at all") to indicate how well you think you understand it. Review the terms you are not sure about in the **Glossary of Literary Terms** (page 1328).

speaker
blank verse
author's purpose
third-person omniscient point of view
mood
sprung rhythm
satire
title
tone
dramatic monologue
situational irony
setting
folk tale
controlling image
allusion
alliteration
stanza structure

Building Your Portfolio

- **Writing Options** Several Writing Options in this unit asked you to present your responses to the messages, or themes, of selections. Choose one of your pieces in which you think you explored your reactions to themes most thoroughly. Then write a cover note describing why you found the piece particularly insightful, and add the note, along with the piece, to your **Presentation Portfolio.**
- **Writing Workshop** In this unit you chose a topic that interested you and then wrote a Subject Analysis about it. Reread this piece and assess the quality of the writing. Then decide if you would like to keep this piece in your **Presentation Portfolio.**
- **Additional Activities** Review the assignments you completed under **Activities & Explorations** and **Inquiry & Research.** Keep a record in your portfolio of any assignments that you think are representative of your best work.

Self ASSESSMENT

Compare what you have chosen for your **Presentation Portfolio** during Unit Five with what was already in your portfolio. Do you see any progress in your work? In what areas? Jot down your thoughts and observations in your READER'S NOTEBOOK.

Setting GOALS

You have read short stories, poems, and nonfiction in this unit. At this point, which of these genres of literature appeals to you the most, and why? What other works belonging to that genre would you like to read this year? Explore these questions in a paragraph or two.

Reviewing Literary Concepts

OPTION 1

Use the Unit Five Resource Book, p. 56, to provide students a ready-made, full-depth chart for grouping the unit's selections according to their authors' purposes.

OPTION 2

A successful response will
- choose three selections in which settings are either obvious or implied.
- describe as much as each student can about each work's setting.
- rank the selections according to how important each seems.
- involve discussing each student's ranking with classmates.

Building Your Portfolio

Students will use their Presentation Portfolios to file what they consider their highest quality work—the very best projects and activities from their Working Portfolios.

For more information on using writing and assessing portfolios, see the *Teacher's Guide to Assessment and Portfolio Use,* p. 53.

The *Electronic Library* is a CD-ROM that contains additional fiction, nonfiction, poetry, and drama for each unit in *The Language of Literature.*

These are the additional selections found in Unit 5 of the *Electronic Library:*

Alfred, Lord Tennyson
Song of the Lotos-Eaters

Dante Gabriel Rossetti
The Blessed Damozel

Christina Rossetti
Goblin Market

John Stuart Mill and Harriet Taylor Mill
Early Essays on Marriage and Divorce

Gerard Manley Hopkins
God's Grandeur
The Windhover
I Wake and Feel the Fell of Dark

Thomas Hardy
The Darkling Thrush

A. E. Housman
Loveliest of Trees
With Rue My Heart Is Laden
Terence, This Is Stupid Stuff

Have students select one or more of the longer selections mentioned on this spread for sustained silent reading.

UNIT FIVE Extend Your *Reading*

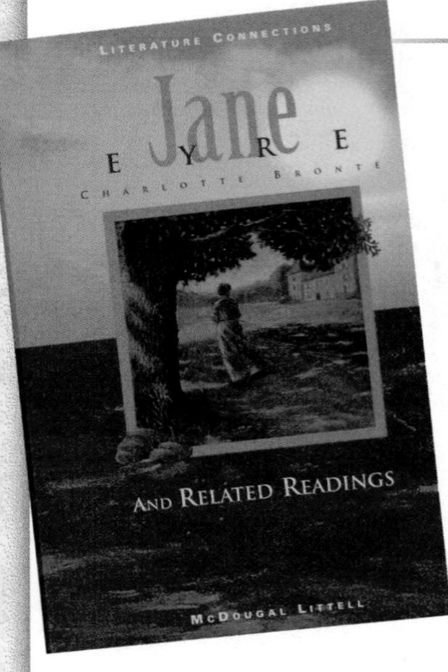

LITERATURE CONNECTIONS

Jane Eyre

CHARLOTTE BRONTË

In 19th-century England, Jane is an orphan, a teacher, and a governess who, although plain in appearance, is fiercely independent and moral in spirit. These qualities are tested and ultimately bring her the happiness she has searched for. Charlotte Brontë was raised on the English moors, and her novel reflects the influence of this dark and brooding landscape.

These thematically related readings are provided along with *Jane Eyre:*

Sonnet 141
BY WILLIAM SHAKESPEARE

Beauty: When the Other Dancer Is the Self
BY ALICE WALKER

The Governess
BY DANIEL POOL

The Little Governess
BY KATHERINE MANSFIELD

I see, I see the crescent moon
BY ANNA AKHMATOVA

Signs and Symbols
BY VLADIMIR NABOKOV

A Home for Hope
BY RON ARIAS

Seventh House
BY R. K. NARAYAN

In the Evening
BY ANNA AKHMATOVA

And Even *More* . . .

The Importance of Being Earnest

OSCAR WILDE

In this classic farce, Oscar Wilde paints a satirical picture of the values and concerns of Victorian England. The play is famous for its witty lines and absurd comic situations in which paradox is used to undermine convention.

Books

Silas Marner
GEORGE ELIOT
This classic novel, described by the author as "a story of old-fashioned village life," portrays a miserly social outcast who comes to adopt a poor orphan and wins redemption.

The Return of the Native
THOMAS HARDY
In this novel, published in 1878, individuals strive through their relationships to overcome the indifferent forces of fate.

LITERATURE CONNECTIONS

Tess of the d'Urbervilles

THOMAS HARDY

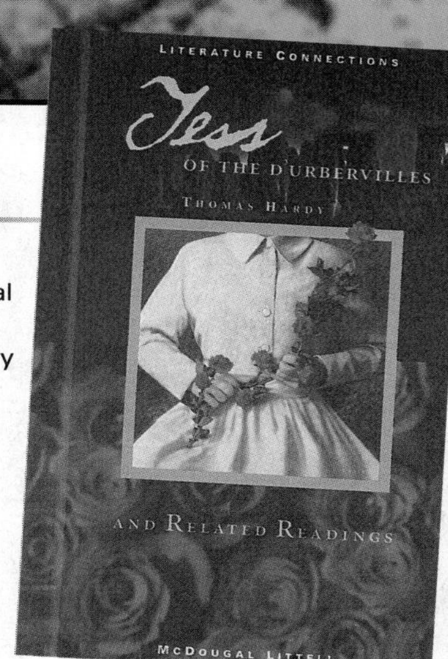

The values of 19th-century society run head-on with the personal life of Tess Durbeyfield, a 16-year-old girl from a poor English family. In this tragic tale of love and betrayal, a father's discovery of his royal ancestry sets in motion a chain of events that spells disaster.

These thematically related readings are provided along with *Tess of the d'Urbervilles:*

Life's Tragedy
BY PAUL LAWRENCE DUNBAR

Disappointment Is the Lot of Woman
BY LUCY STONE

The Paris Gown
BY ESTELA PORTILLO TRAMBLEY

The Ruined Maiden
BY THOMAS HARDY

Yesterday He Still Looked in My Eyes
BY MARINA TSVETAYEVA

A Complaint
BY LADY CHWANG KËANG

The Royal Family
BY GARRISON KEILLOR

Design
BY ROBERT FROST

The Brontës and Their World
PHYLLIS BENTLEY
The work provides a solid introduction to the Brontë sisters.

The Nineteenth Century
ASA BRIGGS
This extensive, encyclopedic work on the period contains hundreds of illustrations.

Other Media

The Victorian Age: Browning, Tennyson and Arnold
Listening Library.
(FILMSTRIP WITH CASSETTE)

Victorian Poetry
Caedmon. Several actors read selections by major poets of the era, including Matthew Arnold, Christina Rossetti, Gerard Manley Hopkins, Thomas Hardy, and A. E. Housman.
(AUDIOCASSETTES)

Jane Eyre
Fox Video. A Hollywood production of the novel, starring Joan Fontaine and Orson Welles.
(VIDEOCASSETTE)

Tess of the d'Urbervilles
Chivers North America. An unabridged reading of the novel by actor Peter Firth, who played Angel Clare in the 1979 film adaptation.
(AUDIOCASSETTES)

EXTEND YOUR READING 977

Emerging Modernism

The selections in Unit Six explore the social, political, and economic changes that helped shape the literature of the modern era. The unit is divided into two sections that present the wide range of themes and literary techniques of this fascinating era.

Part 1

New Images of Reality The selections in this part of the unit reflect the breakdown of the Victorian social structure and the subsequent birth of a modern, alienated society forced to cope with the new conceptions of reality. The selections in the **Author Study** on T. S. Eliot mirror the emerging new reality, and in one instance does so with whimsy. In the **Comparing Literature** feature, a Mexican writer contemplates the role and identity of the writer.

Part 2

Shocking Realities The works in this section explore the devastating effects of the two world wars on people and society. The **Comparing Literature** selection, by a Romanian-born American author, concerns a child caught up in the Holocaust.

UNIT SIX

1901–1950

Emerging Modernism

I feel suddenly attached not to the past but to the **future.**

Virginia Woolf
novelist, critic, and essayist

978

Viewing and Representing

Abstraction on Spectrum (Organization, 5)
by Stanton MacDonald-Wright

ART APPRECIATION

Instruction American painter Stanton MacDonald-Wright (1890–1973) was a pioneer artist of abstraction in the early 20th century. Around 1912, he and one or two others simultaneously and independently developed the notion of using color alone to supply a painting's substance—its form and content—and to create the impression of movement. As a result, color construction eventually became the signature of modern art. *Abstraction on Spectrum* was painted about 1914–17.

Ask: What shapes do you see in this picture? What, if anything, do you think they represent?

Possible Responses: There are overlapping and intersecting circles, arcs, ovals, rectangles, and triangles. They might represent bewilderment, chaos, or a scrambling of one's sense of order.

Abstraction on Spectrum (Organization, 5) (about 1914–1917), Stanton MacDonald-Wright. Oil on canvas, 30 ⅛" × 24 3/16", purchased with funds from the Coffin Fine Arts Trust, Nathan Emory Coffin Collection of the Des Moines (Iowa) Art Center (1962.21).

979

Making Connections

To help students explore the connections among the art, the quotation, and the unit title found in this unit-opening spread, have them consider the following questions:

Ask: The title of this unit is "Emerging Modernism." What does the phrase mean to you?
Possible Response: finding new and improved ways of doing things; rejecting old methods and habits

The quotation is taken from Woolf's essay "Evening Over Sussex: Reflections in a Motor-car," published posthumously in 1942.
Ask: Why might someone feel drawn to the future rather than the past?
Possible Response: The past might be too unbearable to remember; the future offers a new sense of hope and possibility.

Have students look at the painting on this page.
Ask: In what ways is this painting different from most of the art work you have seen in this book?
Possible Response: The picture is abstract and does not show anything that is identifiable. Most of the earlier art work has depicted recognizable people, places, and things.

Ask: Based on these opening pages, what kinds of experiences do you expect to read about in this unit?
Possible Response: selections that try to make sense of a confusing modernistic era and find optimism in the future; selections that deal with a whole spectrum of social and personal issues

VIDEODISC **LaserLinks**
Historical Literary Connection: Emerging Modernism
This montage focuses on the two world wars and their impact on the art and literature of the period. The film can be used to enhance the historical overview and the time line in the student anthology.

See Teacher's SourceBook p. 68 for bar codes.

UNIT SIX

PART 1 SKILLS TRACE

Features and Selections	Literary Analysis	Reading and Critical Thinking	Writing Opportunities
Emerging Modernism **Time Line** **Historical Background/Essay**			
POETRY The Second Coming Sailing to Byzantium	Symbols, 988, 992 Imagery, 992	Clarifying Meaning, 988, 992	Stanza Titles, 993 Symbolic Description, 993 Informal Assess., 991
DRAMA The Rising of the Moon	Suspense, 994, 1002	Analyzing Dialect, 994, 1002 Test Practice, 1001	Dramatic Scene, 1003 Story Outline, 1003 Political Ballad, 1003
Learning the Language of Literature Irony	Irony, 1004	Strategies for Reading, 1005	
SHORT STORY The Rocking-Horse Winner	Foreshadowing, 1006, 1019 Irony, 1019	Drawing Conclusions, 1006	Advice Column, 1020 Alternative Ending, 1020 Detective's Report, 1020 Workplace Link, 1014
SHORT STORY Araby	Point of View, 1022, 1029 Setting, 1029	Making Inferences, 1022, 1029	Childhood Diary, 1030 Biographical Sketch, 1030 Explanatory Para., 1030 Informal Assess., 1028
SHORT STORY A Cup of a Tea	Realism, 1034, 1042 Tone, 1042	Analyzing Plot, 1034, 1042	Concluding Para., 1043 Missing Scene, 1043 Informal Assess., 1043
Milestones in British Literature **The Novels of Virginia Woolf**		Analyzing and Comparing a Film Review, 1044	
SHORT STORY The Duchess and the Jeweller	Style, 1046, 1054 Figurative Language, 1054	Making Inferences, 1046, 1054	Alternative Ending, 1055 Profile of Oliver, 1055 Imaginary Dialogue, 1055 Paragraph Analysis, 1055 Test Practice, 1053
Related Reading *from* Virginia Woolf		Summarizing and Evaluating, 1057	
AUTHOR STUDY **T. S. Eliot**			
LYRIC POEMS Selected Poems	Rhythm, 1064, 1073 Mood, 1073	Strategies for Reading Modern Poetry, 1064, 1073 Choosing the Best Restatement, 1069	Dramatic Skit, 1075 Analysis, 1075
The Author's Style Author Study Project	Analysis of Style, 1074		Changing Style, 1074 Imitating Style, 1074 Comparing Styles, 1074
POETRY Musée des Beaux Arts The Unknown Citizen	Irony, 1076, 1081	Drawing Conclusions, 1076, 1081	Editorial, 1082 Comparison, 1082
POETRY What I Expected	Imagery, 1083, 1085 Free Verse, 1085	Major Ideas, 1083	Diary Entries, 1086 Opinion Paper, 1086

LEGEND **PE instruction shown in black** **TE Mini Lessons shown in green** **CCL indicates a Cross-Curricular Link** **DLS indicates Daily Language SkillBuilder**

Speaking and Listening Viewing and Representing	Inquiry and Research	Grammar, Usage, and Mechanics	Vocabulary
Art Appreciation, 979			Acronyms, 983
Dance Interpretation, 993 Sculpture Design, 993 Discussion, 990	Byzantine Art, 993	DLS, 988 Verbs, 993	Denotation and Connotation, 989
Debate, 1003 Poster, 1003 Performance, 999 Art Appreciation, 1000	A Divided Nation, 1003	DLS, 994 Verbs, 1003	Dialect, 998
Radio Play, 1020 Story to Movie, 1020 Abstract Painting, 1020 Sports Announcing, 1012 Art Appreciation, 1010	Horse racing, 1020	DLS, 1006 Verbs, 1020	Assessment Practice, 1020 Synonyms and Antonyms, 1007 Test Practice, 1016
Pantomime, 1030 Araby Ad, 1030 Photo Gallery, 1030 Photo Images, 1030 Art Appreciation, 1023	Irish History, 1030 Author Activity, 1031	DLS, 1022 Adverbials, 1030	Meaning Clues, 1031 Synonyms, 1024 Greek Roots in English, 1027
Contemporary Version, 1043 Party Invitation, 1043 Art Appreciation, 1038 Dramatic Presentation, 1039	Class in Britain, 1043 Author Activity, 1043	DLS, 1034 Rhythm, 1036, 1040	
Caricature, 1055 Soliloquy, 1055 Discussion of Greed, 1055 Art Appreciation, 1050 Speech, 1052	Bloomsbury Group, 1055 Precious Jewels, 1055	DLS, 1046 Parallelism, 1056	Meaning Clues, 1055 Using the Dictionary, 1049 Using Context Clues, 1051
		Pronouns, 1074	
Poetic Collage, 1075 Dramatic Reading, 1075 Dramatic Reading, 1068	Urban Poverty, 1075 Contemporary Issues, 1075	DLS, 1064 Pronouns, 1074	Using Dictionaries, 1070 Prefixes, 1071
	Dramatizing a Day in the Life, 1075		
Interview, 1082 Census Forms, 1082 Art Appreciation, 1079	The 1930s, 1082	DLS, 1076 Adverbials, 1082	Meanings of -ing Endings, 1078
Dramatic Reading, 1086 Interpretive Montage, 1086 Visual-Verbal Images, 1086	Crystals, 1086 Author Activity, 1086	Gerund, 1086	Applying Meanings of Suffixes, 1084

UNIT SIX
PART 1 SKILLS TRACE

Features and Selections	Literary Analysis	Reading and Critical Thinking	Writing Opportunities
POETRY Do Not Go Gentle into That Good Night In My Craft or Sullen Art	Consonance and Assonance, 1087, 1092 Villanelle, 1092	Visualizing Setting, 1087, 1092	Letter, 1093 Interpretive Notes, 1093 Test Practice, 1091
POETRY **Comparing Literature of the World** Writing/Escritura	Paradox, 1094, 1096	Analyzing Poetic Language, 1096, 1096	Definition, 1097 Monologue, 1097 Points of Comparison, 1097
Writing Workshop: **Dramatic Scene** **Assessment Practice** Building Vocabulary Sentence Crafting			Dramatic Scene, 1101

UNIT SIX
PART 2 SKILLS TRACE

Features and Selections	Literary Analysis	Reading and Critical Thinking	Writing Opportunities
POETRY An Irish Airman Foresees His Death The Soldier Dreamers	Speaker, 1107, 1111	Making Inferences, 1107, 1111	Epitaphs, 1112 Letter, 1112 Multimedia Notes, 1112 Bumper Stickers, 1112 Informal Assess., 1110
MEMOIR *from* Testament of Youth	Memoir, 1114, 1124 Theme, 1124	Distinguishing Fact from Opinion, 1114, 1124	Letter, 1125 Words of Advice, 1125 War Poem, 1125 Letters, 1121
SPEECH The Speeches, May 19, 1940	Persuasion, 1127, 1133	Evaluating Persuasive Language, 1127, 1133 Test Practice, 1131	Web Site Page, 1134
AUTOBIOGRAPHY **Comparing Literature of the World** *from* Night **Related Reading** *from* Letters from Westerbork	Style, 1135, 1141 Tone	The Effect of the War Across Cultures, 1135 Prior Knowledge, 1141 Analyzing Primary Sources, 1143	Rewritten Version, 1142 Points of Comparison, 1142
ESSAY Words and Behavior	Diction, 1145, 1155 Persuasion, 1155	Analyzing Patterns of Organization, 1145, 1155 Test Practice, 1149	Analysis, 1156 Informal Assess., 1154
SHORT STORY The Demon Lover	Setting and Suspense, 1157, 1164 Surprise Ending, 1164	Analyzing Flashback, 1157, 1164 Test Practice, 1163	The Next Scene, 1165 Missing-Person Report, 1165 Explanatory Para., 1165
PERSONAL ESSAY A Hanging	Personal Essay, 1167, 1174 Irony, 1174	Inferring the Author's Perspective, 1167	Diary, 1175 Informal Assess., 1173
Communication Workshop: **Website** **Assessment Practice** Building Vocabulary Sentence Crafting			Web Site, 1178
Reflect and Assess	Tracking Sudden Changes, 1184 Irony, 1185 Analyzing Style, 1185	Comparing Perspectives, 1184 Evaluating Public and Private Realities, 1184	Building Your Portfolio, 1185

LEGEND **PE instruction shown in black** **TE Mini Lessons shown in green** **CCL indicates a Cross-Curricular Link** **DLS indicates Daily Language SkillBuilder**

Speaking and Listening Viewing and Representing	Inquiry and Research	Grammar, Usage, and Mechanics	Vocabulary
Speech, 1093 The Poet's Voice, 1093 Art Appreciation, 1089	Welsh Literary Tradition, 1093 Author Activity, 1093	DLS, 1087 Cohesion, 1093	Word Origins, TE 1090
Stamp Design, 1097 Multimedia Presentation, 1097	Translating Poetry, 1097 Author Activity, 1097	Ending the Sentence, 1097	
		Revising and Editing, 1103 Creating Sentence Closers, 1105	Identifying Parts of a Word, 1104
Role Play, 1112 Soldier Rating, 1112 Choral Reading, 1112 War Diorama, 1112 Author Activity, 1113 Art Appreciation, 1108 Discussion, 1109	World War I, 1112	DLS, 1107 Adverbs, 1112	
Book Jacket, 1125 Class Survey, 1125 Newscasts, 1120 Art Appreciation, 1123	Chemical Warfare, 1125 World War I, 1125 Author Activity, 1125	DLS, 1114 Verbs, 1125	Meaning Clues, 1125 Context Clues, 1116 Prefixes, 1122
Debate, 1134 Art Appreciation, 1132	Western Europe, 1134 Author Activity, 1134	DLS, 1127 Passive Voice, 1134	Assessment Practice, 1134 Connotations, 1128
Holocaust Monument, 1142 Movie Review, 1142 Art Appreciation, 1136 Expressing an Opinion, 1139	Author Activity, 1142	DLS, 1135 Verbs, 1142	Researching Word Origins, 1138
Debate, 1156 Art Appreciation, 1150 Speech, 1152	Propaganda, 1156	DLS, 1145 Style, 1156	Synonyms, 1156 Synonyms, 1146 Prefixes, 1151
Dramatic Performance, 1165 Movie Poster, 1165 Journalists' Meeting, 1165 Moody Image, 1165 Art Appreciation, 1161	London During the War, 1165 Author Activity, 1166	DLS, 1157 Sentence Fragments, 1165	Meaning Clues, 1165 Dictionary, 1158
Still Life, 1175 Art Appreciation, 1171 Debate, 1172	End of British Rule, 1175	DLS, 1167 Run-on Sentences, 1175	Context Clues, 1175 Context Clues, 1168
		Revising and Editing, 1181 Creating Sentence Openers, 1183	Ways to Develop Your Vocabulary, 1182

UNIT SIX

RESOURCE MANAGEMENT GUIDE PART 1

To introduce the theme/literary period of this unit, use Fine Art Transparencies T32–34 in the Communications Transparencies and Copymasters.

	Unit Resource Book	Assessment	Integrated Technology and Media	Additional Support: Literary Analysis Transparencies
The Second Coming Sailing to Byzantium *pp. 988–993*	• Active Reading p. 4 • Literary Analysis p. 5	• Selection Test, Formal Assessment pp. 179–180 Test Generator	Audio Library LaserLinks, Teacher's SourceBook pp. 68–69 Research Starter www.mcdougallittell.com	• Figurative Language T22
The Rising of the Moon *pp. 994–1003*	• Summary p. 6 • Active Reading p. 7 • Literary Analysis p. 8 • Selection Quiz p. 9	• Selection Test, Formal Assessment pp. 181–182 Test Generator	Audio Library LaserLinks, Teacher's SourceBook, pp. 70–71	• External Conflicts/ Societal Conflicts T20
The Rocking-Horse Winner *pp. 1006–1021*	• Summary p. 10 • Active Reading p. 11 • Literary Analysis p. 12 • Words to Know p. 13 • Selection Quiz p. 14	• Selection Test, Formal Assessment pp. 183–184 Test Generator	Audio Library LaserLinks, Teacher's SourceBook p. 72 Video: Literature in Performance, Video Resource Book pp. 31–36	• Verbal, Situational, and Dramatic Irony T17
Araby *pp. 1022–1031*	• Summary p. 15 • Active Reading p. 16 • Literary Analysis p. 17 • Words to Know p. 18 • Selection Quiz p. 19	• Selection Test, Formal Assessment pp. 185–186 Test Generator	Audio Library	• Point of View T18
A Cup of Tea *pp. 1034–1043*	• Summary p. 20 • Active Reading p. 21 • Literary Analysis p. 22 • Selection Quiz p. 23	• Selection Test, Formal Assessment pp. 187–188 Test Generator	Audio Library LaserLinks, Teacher's SourceBook p. 72	• Verbal, Situational, and Dramatic Irony T17
The Duchess and the Jeweller *pp. 1046–1056*	• Summary p. 24 • Active Reading p. 25 • Literary Analysis p. 26 • Words to Know p. 27 • Selection Quiz p. 28	• Selection Test, Formal Assessment pp. 189–190 Test Generator	Audio Library LaserLinks, Teacher's SourceBook p. 73 Research Starter www.mcdougallittell.com	• Figurative Language T22 • Style, Tone, and Mood T24
Selected Poems by T. S. Eliot *pp. 1064–1075*	• Active Reading p. 29 • Literary Analysis p. 30	• Selection Test, Formal Assessment pp. 191–192 Test Generator	LaserLinks, Teacher's SourceBook p. 74 Research Starter www.mcdougallittell.com NetActivities	• Poetic Devices T16
Musée des Beaux Arts The Unknown Citizen *pp. 1076–1082*	• Active Reading p. 31 • Literary Analysis p. 32	• Selection Test, Formal Assessment pp. 193–194 Test Generator	Audio Library LaserLinks, Teacher's SourceBook p. 75	• Verbal, Situational, and Dramatic Irony T17
What I Expected *pp. 1083–1086*	• Active Reading p. 33 • Literary Analysis p. 34	• Selection Test, Formal Assessment pp. 195–196 Test Generator	Audio Library LaserLinks, Teacher's SourceBook p. 76	• Figurative Language (Imagery) T22
Do Not Go Gentle into That Good Night In My Craft or Sullen Art *pp. 1087–1093*	• Active Reading p. 35 • Literary Analysis p. 36	• Selection Test, Formal Assessment pp. 197–198 Test Generator	Audio Library	• Poetic Devices T16

T = Transparency C = Copymaster

Reading and Critical Thinking Transparencies	Grammar Transparencies and Copymasters	Vocabulary Transparencies and Copymasters	Writing Transparencies and Copymasters	Communications Transparencies and Copymasters
• Organizational Chart: Vertical T53	• Daily Language SkillBuilder T26 • Verbs–Using Correct Verb Forms T45 • Verbs: Diction C167	• Denotation and Connotation C78	• Figurative Language and Sound Devices T15	• Reading Aloud T11 • Identifying and Analyzing Artistic Elements in Literary Texts T13
• Using an Outline T44 • Organizational Chart: Horizontal T52	• Daily Language SkillBuilder T27 • Avoiding Shifts in Tense T46 • Simple and Perfect Tenses of Verbs C130	• Dialect C79	• Dramatic Scene C31	• Impromptu Speaking: Debate T15
• Drawing Conclusions T4 • Sequencing T13	• Daily Language SkillBuilder T27 • Agreement of Subject and Verb T47 • Subject-Verb Agreement II C141	• Synonyms and Antonyms C55	• Identifying Writing Variables T2	• Analyze, Evaluate, and Critique: Literary Performance T7 • Evaluating Roles in Groups T8 • Dramatic Reading T12
• Making Inferences T7	• Daily Language SkillBuilder T27 • Commas with Nonessential Elements T55 • Adverbials: Subordinate Clauses C169	• Synonyms C67 • Greek Roots C80	• Personality Profile C25 • Dramatic Scene C31 • Literary Interpretation C33	
• Generating Research Questions T27 • Sequence Chain T50	• Daily Language SkillBuilder T28 • Rhythm: Power Words C171 • Controlling Rhythm C172		• The Uses of Dialogue T24 • Dramatic Scene C31	• Appreciative Listening T2 • Evaluating Roles in Groups T8 • Impromptu Speaking: Dialogue, Role-Play T14
• Making Inferences T7 • Sequence Chain T50	• Daily Language SkillBuilder T28 • Parallelism T57 • Parallelism C175	• Context Clues C81	• The Uses of Dialogue T24 • Personality Profile C25 • Literary Interpretation C33	• Appreciative Listening T2 • Evaluating Roles in Groups T8 • Impromptu Speaking: Dialogue, Role-Play T14
• Compare and Contrast T15 • Analyzing Text T18	• Daily Language SkillBuilder T28 • Pronoun-Antecedent Agreement T48 • Pronouns: Vague Antecedents C147	• Using Specialized Dictionaries C82	• Subject Analysis C30 • Dramatic Scene C31	• Appreciative Listening T2 • Dramatic Reading T12
• Drawing Conclusions T4 • Compare and Contrast T15	• Daily Language SkillBuilder T29 • Comparison of Regular and Irregular Adjectives and Adverbs T52 • Adverb Qualifiers C153	• Meanings of *-ing* Endings C84	• Compare-Contrast C34 • Opinion Statement C35	• Interviewing T9 • Impromptu Speaking: Dialogue, Role-Play T14
• Drawing Conclusions T4 • Analyzing Text T18	• Daily Language SkillBuilder T29 • Diagramming Verbal Phrases T60 • Gerunds and Gerund Phrases II C104	• Suffixes (Verbals) C85	• Opinion Statement C35	• Dramatic Reading T12
• Visualizing T8 • Compare and Contrast T15	• Daily Language SkillBuilder T29 • Repetition vs. Redundancy C176	• Word Origins C86	• Literary Interpretation C33	• Appreciative Listening T2 • Formal Presentations T10

UNIT SIX PART 1 CONTINUED

	Unit Resource Book	Assessment	Integrated Technology and Media	Additional Support: Literary Analysis Transparencies
Writing/Escritura *pp. 1094–1097*	• Active Reading p. 37 • Literary Analysis p. 38	• Selection Test, Formal Assessment pp. 199–200 Test Generator	Audio Library	

Writing Workshop: Dramatic Scene

Unit Six Resource Book
- Prewriting p. 39
- Drafting and Elaboration p. 40
- Peer Response Guide pp. 41–42
- Revising, Editing, and Proofreading p. 43
- Student Models pp. 44–49
- Rubric for Evaluation p. 50

Writing Coach

Writing Transparencies and Copymasters T11, T19, C31

Teacher's Guide to Assessment and Portfolio Use

Unit Assessment
- Unit Six, Part 1 Test, Formal Assessment pp. 201–202
- Test Generator
- Unit Six Integrated Test, Integrated Assessment pp. 47–58

Unit Technology
- ClassZone www.mcdougallittell.com
- Electronic Teacher Tools
- Electronic Library

UNIT SIX PART 2

To introduce the theme/literary period of this unit, use Fine Art Transparencies T32–34 in the Communications Transparencies and Copymasters.

	Unit Resource Book	Assessment	Integrated Technology and Media	Additional Support: Literary Analysis Transparencies
An Irish Airman Forces His Death **The Soldier, Dreamer** *pp. 1107–1113*	• Active Reading p.53 • Literary Analysis p. 54	• Selection Test, Formal Assessment pp. 203–204 Test Generator	Audio Library LaserLinks, Teacher's SourceBook p. 77	• Poetic Devices T16
from **Testament of Youth** *pp. 1114–1126*	• Summary p. 55 • Active Reading p. 56 • Literary Analysis p. 57 • Words to Know p. 58 • Selection Quiz p. 59	• Selection Test, Formal Assessment pp. 205–206 Test Generator	Audio Library LaserLinks, Teacher's SourceBook p. 78 Research Starter www.mcdougallittell.com	• Point of View T18
from **The Speeches, May 19, 1940** *pp. 1127–1134*	• Summary p. 60 • Active Reading p. 61 • Literary Analysis p. 62 • Words to Know p. 63 • Selection Quiz p. 64	• Selection Test, Formal Assessment pp. 207–208 Test Generator	Audio Library LaserLinks, Teacher's SourceBook p. 79 Research Starter www.mcdougallittell.com	
from **Night** *pp. 1135–1142*	• Summary p. 65 • Active Reading p. 66 • Literary Analysis p. 67 • Selection Quiz p. 68	• Selection Test, Formal Assessment pp. 209–210 Test Generator	Audio Library Research Starter www.mcdougallittell.com	• Style, Tone, and Mood T24
Words and Behavior *pp. 1145–1156*	• Summary p. 69 • Active Reading p. 70 • Literary Analysis p. 71 • Words to Know p. 72 • Selection Quiz p. 73	• Selection Test, Formal Assessment pp. 211–212 Test Generator	Audio Library LaserLinks, Teacher's SourceBook p. 81	
The Demon Lover *pp. 1157–1166*	• Summary p. 74 • Active Reading p. 75 • Literary Analysis p. 76 • Words to Know p. 77 • Selection Quiz p. 78	• Selection Test, Formal Assessment pp. 213–214 Test Generator	Audio Library	• Influences on Plot: Setting and Character T19
A Hanging *pp. 1167–1175*	• Summary p. 79 • Active Reading p. 80 • Literary Analysis p. 81 • Words to Know p. 82 • Selection Quiz p. 83	• Selection Test, Formal Assessment pp. 215–216 Test Generator	Audio Library	• Verbal, Situational, and Dramatic Irony T17

Communication Workshop: Web Site

Unit Six Resource Book
- Planning the Context p. 84
- Planning the Design p. 85
- Peer Response Guide pp. 86–87
- Revising, Editing, and Proofreading p. 88
- Standards for Evaluation p. 89

Unit Assessment
- Unit Six, Part 2 Test, Formal Assessment pp. 217–218
- Test Generator
- Unit Six Integrated Test, Integrated Assessment pp. 47–58

Unit Technology
- ClassZone www.mcdougallittell.com
- Electronic Teacher Tools
- Electronic Library

T = Transparency C = Copymaster

Reading and Critical Thinking Transparencies	Grammar Transparencies and Copymasters	Vocabulary Transparencies and Copymasters	Writing Transparencies and Copymasters	Communications Transparencies and Copymasters
• Analyzing Text T18 • Comparing Authors' Views T24	• Daily Language SkillBuilder T30 • Ending the Sentence C177		• Compare-Contrast C34	• Evaluating Roles in Groups T8

STUDENTS ACQUIRING ENGLISH

The **Spanish Study Guide,** pp. 230–265, includes language support for the following pages:
- Family and Community Involvement (per unit)
- Selection Summaries and Vocabulary
- Active Reading
- Literary Analysis

Reading and Critical Thinking Transparencies	Grammar Transparencies and Copymasters	Vocabulary Transparencies and Copymasters	Writing Transparencies and Copymasters	Communications Transparencies and Copymasters
• Making Inferences T7	• Daily Language SkillBuilder T30 • Avoiding Misplaced and Dangling Modifiers T51 • Adverbials: *Only* C71		• Effective Language T13 • Personality Profile C25	• Reading Aloud T11 • Impromptu Speaking: Dialogue, Role-Play T14
• Fact vs. Opinion T3	• Daily Language SkillBuilder T30 • Verbs–Using Correct Verb Forms T45 • Passive Voice C136	• Prefixes C87	• Identifying Writing Variables T2 • Sensory Word List T14 • Figurative Language and Sound Devices T15	• Interviewing T9
• Identifying Persuasive Techniques T25 • Analyzing Persuasive Techniques T26	• Daily Language SkillBuilder T31 • Passive Voice: Weak Subjects C168	• Connotation C90	• Generating Writing Ideas T1	• Impromptu Speaking: Debate T15
• Making Inferences T7 • Compare and Contrast T15	• Daily Language SkillBuilder T31 • Avoiding Shifts in Tense T46 • Verbs: Tense Shifts C133	• Word Origins C91	• Point of View T23 • Compare-Contrast C34	• Analyze, Evaluate, and Critique: Entertainment T5
• Analyzing Argumentation II T22	• Daily Language SkillBuilder T31 • Commas with Nonessential Elements T55 • Rhythm and the Comma C173	• Prefixes C89 • Synonyms C96	• Subject Analysis C30	• Impromptu Speaking: Debate T15
• Chronological Order T11 • Organizational Chart: Horizontal T52	• Daily Language SkillBuilder T32 • Sentence Fragments T42 • Complete Sentences C76	• Using Specialized Dictionaries C82	• Personality Profile C25 • Literary Interpretation C33	• Evaluating Roles in Groups T8 • Dramatic Reading T12
• Determining Author's Bias: Effect of Stance and Tone on Structure T23 • Cluster Diagram T49	• Daily Language SkillBuilder T32 • Run-on Sentences T43 • Complete Sentences C76 • Run-on Sentences C126	• Using Context to Understand Dialect C93	• Showing, Not Telling T22	• Impromptu Speaking: Debate T15

STUDENTS ACQUIRING ENGLISH

The **Spanish Study Guide,** pp. 266–286, includes language support for the following pages:
- Family and Community Involvement (per unit)
- Selection Summaries and Vocabulary
- Active Reading
- Literary Analysis

DAILY LANGUAGE SKILLBUILDERS

Selection	SkillBuilder Sentences	Suggested Answers
The Second Coming Sailing to Byzantium	**1.** William butler Yeats knew early in his life that he wanted to become an Author. **2.** Yeats was an irishman of British descent he spent part of his childhood in Sligo, on the northwest cost of Ireland.	**1.** William **B**utler Yeats knew early in his life that he wanted to become an **a**uthor. **2.** Yeats was an **I**rishman of British descent. **He** spent part of his childhood in Sligo, on the northwest co**a**st of Ireland.
The Rising of the Moon	**1.** The Abbey Theatre in Dublin was home of the Irish national Theatre society for 47 yrs. **2.** W.b. Yeats and Lady Gregory worked together to found the theater. In response to strong national feelings in Ireland.	**1.** The Abbey Theatre **(or Theater)** in Dublin was home of the Irish **N**ational Theatre **(or Theater)** **S**ociety for 47 **years**. **2.** W.**B.** Yeats and Lady Gregory worked together to found the theater **i**n response to strong national feelings in Ireland.
The Rocking-Horse Winner	1. David herbert Lawrence was born to a coal-miner father and Schoolteacher mother in an industrial area of england. **2.** the educational and social gap among his parents is reflected in many of Lawrences' works.	**1.** David **H**erbert Lawrence was born to a coal-miner father and **s**choolteacher mother in an industrial area of **E**ngland. **2.** **T**he educational and social gap **between** his parents is reflected in many of Lawrence**'s** works.
Araby	**1.** James Joyce, who was the older of ten children was born on Febrary 2, 1998, at 41 Brighton square in rathgar, Ireland. **2.** John Joyce James's father, lost his job as a tax Collector when he was 42 years old. He didn't hold no job again, and his poverty-stricken family moves often to avoid creditors.	**1.** James Joyce, who was the old**est** of ten children**,** was born on Febr**u**ary 2, 1998, at 41 Brighton **S**quare in **R**athgar, Ireland. **2.** John Joyce**,** James's father, lost his job as a tax **c**ollector when he was 42 years old. He didn't hold **a** job again, and his poverty-stricken family move**d** often to avoid creditors.
A Cup of Tea	**1.** Borne in Wellington, New, Zealand as a young girl, Katherine Mansfield studied in London and later moved their. **2.** she began to write, short stories, in 1911, drawing upon her observations of the middle-class life she observed around her noting societys' hypocrisies she created stories that focused on the real relationships between people.	**1.** Bor**n** in Wellington, New Zealand**,** Katherine Mansfield studied in London **as a young girl** and later moved **there**. **2.** **S**he began to write short stories in 1911, drawing upon her observations of the middle-class life she observed around her. **N**oting society**'s** hypocrisies**,** she created stories that focused on the real relationships between people.
The Duchess and the Jeweller	**1.** Like most victorian women Virginia Woolf received little formal education. **2.** The confident incisive and intellectual tone of her writing testify to her successful efforts to educate herself.	**1.** Like most **V**ictorian women**,** Virginia Woolf received little formal education. **2.** The confident**,** incisive**,** and intellectual tone of her writing testif**ies** to her successful efforts to educate herself.

Selection	SkillBuilderSentences	Suggested Answers
The Hollow Men	**1.** After World War I many writers werent no longer certan about the old certantees. **2.** Many solders, returned from the trentches, broken in body or mind, victims of poison gas or suffaring from shellshock.	**1.** After World War I, many writers **were** no longer certain about the old certainties. **2.** Many soldiers returned from the trenches broken in body or mind, victims of poison gas or suffering from shellshock.
Musée des Beaux Arts The Unknown Citizen	**1.** Auden like Eliot switched his nationality and is considered both an english and an american poet. **2.** Auden became an American citizen in 1946 while Eliot became a British citizen in 1927.	**1.** Auden, like Eliot, switched his nationality and is considered both an **E**nglish and an **A**merican poet. **2.** Auden became an American citizen in 1946, while Eliot became a British citizen in 1927.
What I Expected	**1.** The great depression which began with the 1929 stock market crash in America spread to the rest of the World and severly effected Great britains economic stability. **2.** In Great britain Factory Workers were loosing there jobs and often there sense of wellbeing in the harsh econmic climate of the 1930's.	**1.** The **G**reat **D**epression, which began with the 1929 stock market crash in America, spread to the rest of the **w**orld and sever**e**ly **a**ffected Great **B**ritain's economic stability. **2.** In Great **B**ritain, **f**actory **w**orkers were **los**ing **their** jobs and often **their** sense of well-being in the harsh econ**o**mic climate of the 19**30s**.
Do Not Go Gentle into That Good Night In My Craft or Sullen Art	**1.** Some people consider Dylan Thomases' poetry depressing others find it uplifting. **2.** By sharing personal feelings Thomas express important aspects of the human condition.	**1.** Some people consider Dylan Thoma**s's** poetry depressing; others find it uplifting. **2.** By sharing personal feelings, Thomas express**es** important aspects of the human condition.
Writing/Escritura	**1.** Octavio paz, a Nobel prize-winning poet and essaist, was born in Mexico City Mexico, on march 31, 1914. **2.** Because of the Mexican revolution, Pazs family hadn't no money. As their house was falling apart the family members moved their furniture into rooms that had not yet collapsed.	**1.** Octavio **P**az, a Nobel **P**rize-winning poet and essa**y**ist, was born in Mexico City, Mexico, on **M**arch 31, 1914. **2.** Because of the Mexican **R**evolution, Paz's family **had** no money. As their house was falling apart, the family members moved their furniture into rooms that had not yet collapsed.
An Irish Airman Foresees His Death	**1.** The Grate War was a clash, among the Allied Powers and the Central Powers. **2.** At the beginning of the war, the Allies included France, Belgium, great Britain, Russia, Serbia and, Montenegro	**1.** The Gr**ea**t War was a clash **between** the Allied Powers and the Central Powers. **2.** At the beginning of the war, the Allies included France, Belgium, **G**reat Britain, Russia, Serbia, and Montenegro.

DAILY LANGUAGE SKILLBUILDERS

Selection	SkillBuilderSentences	Suggested Answers
The Soldier Dreamers *from* Testament of Youth	**1.** In the first half of the 20th Century the following events occurred two world wars a worldwide depression, the Holocaust, and to drop the first atomic bomb. **2.** Its not no suprize that these events profoundly effected english life and literature.	**1.** In the first half of the 20th Century**,** the following events occurred**:** two world wars**,** a worldwide depression, the Holocaust, and **the dropping of** the first atomic bomb. **2.** It's no sur**p**rise that these events profoundly affected **E**nglish life and literature.
from The Speeches, May 19, 1940	**1.** Many People may not know that Winston Churchills Mother was American. **2.** Early in his career welfare reforms were supported by Churchill.	**1.** Many **p**eople may not know that Winston Churchill's **m**other was American. **2.** Early in his career**, Churchill supported welfare** reforms.
from Night	**1.** Hasidism is a Jewish spiritual movement founded in the 1,700s in the region near the carpathian mountains. **2.** Hasidism emphasizes devotion more than study. And enthusiasm more than an intellectual approach.	**1.** Hasidism is a Jewish spiritual movement founded in the **1700**s in the region near the **C**arpathian **M**ountains. **2.** Hasidism emphasizes devotion more than study **a**nd enthusiasm more than an intellectual approach.
Words and Behavior	**1.** Some 20th century writers rise questions about the possible affects of trends in the modern world **2.** In 1932 aldous huxley published Brave new World, a novel about a future society controled by technology.	**1.** Some 20th**-**century writers **raise** questions about the possible **e**ffects of trends in the modern world**.** **2.** In 1932**, A**ldous **H**uxley published **Brave New World**, a novel about a future society control**l**ed by technology.
The Demon Lover	**1.** Elizabeth bowen an only child was tended to by a Governess, taken to church on sundays, and taught to have good manners. **2.** Her Mother instructed her daughters' caretakers not to teach her to read until she was seven.	**1.** Elizabeth **B**owen**,** an only child**,** was tended to by a **g**overness, taken to church on **S**undays, and taught to have good manners. **2.** Her **m**other instructed her daughter**'s** caretakers not to teach her to read until she was seven.
A Hanging	**1.** George Orwell is one of the 20th-century writers who rised questions about the possible affects of trends in the modern world. **2.** Born Eric Blair Orwell chose to live in poverty in Paris France and london, England and the worte a book about it.	**1.** George Orwell is one of the 20th-century writers who **raised** questions about the possible **e**ffects of trends in the modern world. **2.** Born Eric Blair Orwell**, he** chose to live in poverty in Paris**,** France**,** and **L**ondon, England**,** and **then wrote** a book about it.

INTEGRATING GRAMMAR AND LITERATURE: GRAMMAR PLANNER

	Unit One	Unit Two	Unit Three	Unit Four	Unit Five	Unit Six	Unit Seven
Grammar Focus by Unit	Parts of a Sentence	Phrases, Part I	Phrases, Part II	Clauses, Part I	Clauses, Part II	Rhetorical Grammar, Part I	Rhetorical Grammar, Part II

The Language of Literature offers several options for integrating grammar instruction and literature.

- Each literature unit has a grammar focus. The Teacher's Edition includes Mini Lessons for each selection that help develop the grammar focus for the unit and spring from the content of the specific literature.
- The Pupil Edition includes several full-page lessons on Sentence Crafting. These lessons are related to both the literature and the grammar focus for the unit and help students use grammar in their own writing.
- Daily Language SkillBuilders in the Teacher's Edition provide students with onging proofreading practice and reinforce punctuation, spelling, grammar and usage, and capitalization.
- Grammar Copymasters and Transparencies, which may be used to complement or extend lessons in the Teacher's Edition, present grammar in a traditional, systematic sequence. References to appropriate copymasters or transparencies are included at point of use in the Teacher's Edition Mini Lessons.

TE Mini Lessons shown in green
PE instruction shown in black

Part 1

Parts of Speech

Possessives with Proper Nouns That End in *-s*
Writing Workshop, p. 1103

Using Phrases

Gerund and Its Subject
"What I Expected," p. 1086

Using Clauses

Run-on Sentences
Writing Workshop, p. 1103

Verb Usage

Simple vs. Perfect Tenses
The Rising of the Moon, p. 1003

Subject-Verb Agreement

"The Rocking-Horse Winner," p. 1020

Pronoun Usage

Pronoun-Antecedent Agreement
Writing Workshop, p. 1103

Vague Antecedents
Eliot poems, p. 1074

Using Modifiers

Adverbials: The Qualifiers
"Musée des Beaux Arts," "The Unknown Citizen," p. 1082

End Marks and Commas

Correcting Comma Splices
Writing Workshop, p. 1103

Style

Verbs: Choosing Precise Diction
"The Second Coming," "Sailing to Byzantium," p. 993

Adverbials: Function and Placement
"Araby," p. 1030

Power Words
"A Cup of Tea," p. 1036

Cohesion: Parallelism
"The Duchess and the Jeweller," p. 1056

Cohesion: Repetition vs. Redundancy
"Do Not Go Gentle into That Good Night," "In My Craft or Sullen Art," p. 1093

Ending the Sentence
"Writing/Escritura," p. 1097
Sentence Crafting, p. 1105

Part 2

Parts of Speech

Adverbials: *only*
"An Irish Airman Foresees His Death," "The Soldier," "Dreamers," p. 1112

Parts of the Sentence

Complete Sentences
Communication Workshop, p. 1181

Using Clauses

Run-on Sentences
"A Hanging," p. 1175

Verb Usage

Avoiding Unnecessary Shifts in Tense
from *Night,* p. 1142

Passive Voice
from *Testament of Youth,* p. 1125

Subject-Verb Agreement

Communication Workshop, p. 1181

Using Modifiers

Misplaced and Dangling Modifiers
Sentence Crafting, p. 1183

Style

Verbs: Weak Subjects
from *The Speeches, May 19, 1940,* p. 1134

Rhythm and the Comma
"Words and Behavior," p. 1156

Word Order
"The Demon Lover," pp. 1165–1166

Cohesion: Repetition vs. Redundancy
Communication Workshop, p. 1181

Word Order Variation
Sentence Crafting, p. 1183

This time line shows some major events of emerging modernism in Britain. Have students speculate about events in Britain or in other parts of the world might have influenced events in British literature. Further information about selected people and events is provided below.

Britain: 1903

A Pankhurst's most important work began with this founding of the WSPU. She defied politicians by disrupting party rallies, marching and smashing store windows, and going on hunger strikes when jailed. During World War I Pankhurst's tactics changed, and she won support for her cause by helping the war effort. In 1918, Parliament voted women age 30 or older the right to vote, and in 1928 voting age was lowered to 21 years old.

World: 1912

B China's Qing Dynasty was slow to modernize and underestimated the nationalism sweeping China after the unsuccessful 1900 Boxer Rebellion against foreign interference in Chinese affairs. Sun Yixian (Sun Yat-sen) and his revolutionary alliance threw out China's last emperor, and the country went through a prolonged period of political turmoil until the Communists achieved supremacy in 1949.

Literature: 1914

C No novel has had the history of Joyce's revolutionary *Ulysses*. Initially judged obscene, early editions subjected to confiscation and book burning, long banned in England and the United States, *Ulysses* found its exalted stature confirmed in controversy in 1998 when it was chosen the best English-language novel of the 20th century by an editorial board of the Modern Library, a division of Random House publishers.

World: 1914

D Since recent wars had been small-scale conflicts, a generation of patriotic young British men eagerly enlisted to fight Germany when war broke out; however, trench warfare was a new reality, and by war's end, 908,000 men from the British Empire had been killed.

TIME LINE 1901–1950

Emerging Modernism

EVENTS IN BRITISH LITERATURE

1900 — 1920

1902 Joseph Conrad's novella, *Heart of Darkness*, published

1913 George Bernard Shaw's play *Pygmalion* produced

C **1914** James Joyce begins writing controversial novel *Ulysses* (to 1921)

1921 T. S. Eliot writes groundbreaking long poem *The Waste Land*

E **1922** Katherine Mansfield's *The Garden Party and Other Stories* published; Virginia Woolf's experimental *Jacob's Room* published

1926 D. H. Lawrence writes "The Rocking-Horse Winner"

EVENTS IN BRITAIN

1900 — 1920

1901 Queen Victoria dies and is succeeded by son Edward VII

A **1903** Emmeline Pankhurst founds Women's Social and Political Union to promote women's suffrage in Britain

1907 Britain, France, and Russia form alliance known as Triple Entente to counter Germany

1910 Edward VII dies and is succeeded by son George V

1912 More than 1,500 drown when Titanic sinks in Atlantic

D **1914** Britain enters World War I after Germany invades Belgium

1918 British military deaths total about 750,000 at World War I's end; British women over 30 allowed to vote

F **1921** Irish Free State established, while Northern Ireland remains in union with Great Britain

1926 General strike protests national lockout of coal miners

1932 At depth of global depression, British unemployment rate is 23 percent

EVENTS IN THE WORLD

1900 — 1920

1903 U.S. Wright brothers fly first engine-powered airplane

1905 Russian soldiers fire on petitioning citizens in St. Petersburg, starting brief first Russian Revolution

B **1912** Last emperor of Qing Dynasty, rulers of China since 1644, overthrown

1913 Ford revolutionizes auto industry with assembly-line production

1914 Assassination of Archduke Franz Ferdinand sparks World War I

1917 V. I. Lenin leads Bolshevik Revolution that topples Russian czar

1918 Allies, with U.S. help, defeat Central Powers, ending World War I; Bolsheviks renamed Communist Party

1919 Allies and Germany sign Treaty of Versailles; Gandhi becomes leader of Indian independence movement

1920 Hitler takes control of new National Socialist German Workers' (Nazi) Party; American women gain right to vote

1927 Charles Lindbergh flies solo from New York to Paris; first "talking" movie released in U.S.

1928 Joseph Stalin becomes dictator of Communist Russia

1929 U.S. stock market crashes, initiating global depression

980 UNIT SIX EMERGING MODERNISM (1901–1950)

Literature: 1922

E With the publication of this book, Mansfield achieved front rank among British authors. Exclusively a writer of short stories, Mansfield had a style that was unique at the time, emphasizing subtlety and small but telling insights over broad plot developments. Mansfield suffered several personal tragedies in her short, 35-year life, and her death from tuberculosis in 1923 silenced a potentially masterful hand.

Britain: 1921

F In 1918, members of Sinn Fein—a militant group begun in 1905 by Irish Catholics—proclaimed Ireland a republic with themselves as its head, and Sinn Fein supporters and other Irish nationalists waged a guerrilla war against British troops. The passage of the Home Rule Bill of 1920 divided Ireland into two sections. The six Protestant counties of Ulster, designated Northern Ireland, remained part of the United Kingdom.

PERIOD PIECES

California Clipper, mid-1930s

Telephone, 1920s–1930s

Clock in style known as Art Deco, c. 1935

J

1940

G **1927** Yeats's "Sailing to Byzantium" published; T. S. Eliot becomes British citizen

1932 Aldous Huxley's novel *Brave New World,* warning of scientifically controlled future society, published

1934 Dylan Thomas, 20-year-old Welsh poet, publishes *Eighteen Poems*

1940 W. H. Auden publishes poem "Musée des Beaux Arts"

1941 Depression and despair drive Woolf to suicide

1945 George Orwell publishes classic anti-utopian fable *Animal Farm;* Elizabeth Bowen publishes short-story collection *The Demon Lover*

1946 Auden becomes U.S. citizen

1949 Orwell publishes *1984,* nightmarish vision of future totalitarian England

1940

H **1936** George V dies; son Edward VIII renounces throne; Edward's younger brother becomes king as George VI

1937 Prime minister claims "peace in our time" after giving Hitler part of Czechoslovakia

1939 Britain joins France in declaring war on Germany

I **1940** Britain suffers daily German bombing but is unconquered in Battle of Britain (to 1941)

1945 At end of war, British military and civilian losses total 360,000; socialist program creates British welfare state (to 1951)

1947 India and Pakistan given independence

K **1949** Britain helps found NATO; Irish Free State becomes Republic of Ireland

1940

1930 Nationalists and Communists begin civil war in China (to 1949)

1932 Kingdom of Saudi Arabia declared

1933 Hitler and Nazis seize dictatorial control of Germany

1937 Japan invades China

1939 Germany invades Poland and World War II begins

1941 Attack on Pearl Harbor in Hawaii causes U.S. to declare war on Japan

1942 Nazis initiate "Final Solution" stage of murdering unwanted civilians, mostly Jews (to 1945)

1945 World War II ends; United Nations formed

L **1946** Cold War between U.S. and Soviet Union begins (to 1991)

1948 Israel becomes nation; South African policy of apartheid begins

1949 Communists win civil war to gain control of China

TIME LINE 981

Literature: 1927

G Eliot blurred his national identification by becoming a British citizen. However, the St. Louis-born, Harvard-educated poet early on "was English in everything but accent and citizenship" according to his college classmates. "He smoked a pipe, liked to be alone, carefully avoided slang, and dressed with the studied carelessness of a dandy."

Britain: 1936

H Edward VIII became the subject of one of the most popular love stories of the 20th century. After becoming king in 1936, he announced his intention to marry an American divorcée. When the British government objected to this, Edward abdicated after only 325 days as king, the first person ever to voluntarily relinquish the British throne. With the woman he loved, Edward VIII (1894–1972) lived out his days known as the duke of Windsor.

Britain: 1940

I To combat the despair brought on Britons by almost daily German air attacks, prime minister Winston Churchill used stirring words to rally the people to stand defiant. He declared that Britain would "wage war, by sea, land, and air, with all our might and with all the strength that God can give us . . . against monstrous tyranny."

PERIOD PIECES

J The term *Art Deco* derives from the name of a 1925 Paris exhibit—the Exposition Internationale des Arts Décoratifs et Industriels Modernes. This style is marked by geometric shapes and smooth lines suggesting elegance and sophistication. New York City's Empire State Building is a famous example of Art Deco architecture.

World: 1946

L In a speech in 1946, delivered in the United States, Winston Churchill coined the phrase "iron curtain" as he warned of the threat posed by the Soviet Union, which a year earlier had been an ally in the defeat of Hitler. The United States quickly took the lead in containing communism's post-war expansion, and this Cold War became a fact of international life for the next 45 years.

Literature: 1949

K George Orwell, the pen name of Eric Blair, carried a lifelong "horror of politics" and concern for human freedom. This was transferred in his writings into two landmark books—*Animal Farm* (1945) and *1984* (1949), the former bitterly predicting the downfall of communism and the latter warning of what he saw as a trend toward totalitarian dominance by governments.

OVERVIEW

Introduction
This article provides a historical and literary context for the writings presented in Unit Six. In particular students will learn how the era in Britain was dominated by growing nationalistic feelings among its colonies and by Germany's drive for continental superiority.

Reading Nonfiction

Reading Skills and Strategies

ESTABLISHING A PURPOSE FOR READING
Have students scan the article to establish a purpose for reading. Remind them to adjust their purposes if they encounter unexpected content or difficulty.

USING TEXT ORGANIZERS
Have students preview the article, noting the basic text organizers: title, overview, subheads, images and captions, and sidebar commentaries. Ask them to describe what information they would expect to locate in each section. As they read, have students use the subheads to make an outline or graphic organizer. Have them categorize information from the article, sidebars, and timeline with the appropriate heading. Remind students to use text organizers to locate and categorize information as they do independent research.

ANALYZING TEXT STRUCTURE
Have students scan the article and predict how they expect information to be structured. Due to the number of dates, students should expect the basic structure to be chronological. Discuss how this structure influences the way they read and understand the material. Encourage students to note other kinds of relationships such as cause and effect and compare and contrast, that are signaled by text structure and words. Key cause and effect relationships are easy to identify in each section of the article. Encourage students to note relationships between the historical events and literary history.

IDENTIFYING MAIN IDEAS
The headings form sections that in which main ideas are developed. Have students read one section at a time and note how its idea is developed through details..

Emerging Modernism

1901-1950

Far left: George V, Victoria, Edward VII, and Edward VIII. *Above:* Women demanding the right to vote.

From the accession of Edward VII in 1901 until the outbreak of World War I, Britain remained the dominant political, economic, and military power in the world. **A** The world, however, was rapidly changing. Recent advances, including electric power and the automobile, were completely transforming everyday life. Through strikes and the emergence of the Labor party, British workers were obtaining economic and political power. **B** Women were growing increasingly vocal in public demonstrations, demanding the right to vote. In Ireland, as well as India and other British colonies, nationalist movements were gaining momentum. At the same time, colonial and commercial rivalries were driving European powers into competing alliances, such as the Triple Entente of Britain, France, and Russia, formed in 1907. These rivalries would escalate into World War I, shattering the Victorian way of life forever.

World War I

Known at the time as the Great War, World War I was precipitated by the assassination of Archduke Francis Ferdinand, heir to the throne of Austria-Hungary, by a Serbian nationalist in Sarajevo on June 28, 1914. Austria's demands for satisfaction from Serbia were impossibly harsh, and when Serbia was unable to meet them, Austria declared war on Serbia. The Russian czar came to the aid of his fellow Slavs in Serbia, mobilizing troops along the border of Austria's strongest ally,

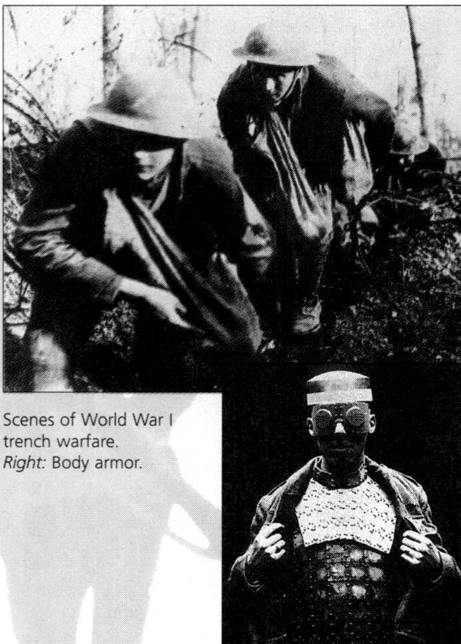

Scenes of World War I trench warfare. *Right:* Body armor.

Mini Lesson: Development of the English Language

ACRONYMS
Modern warfare's new words (see the language sidebar above) include a type of word derived from the initial letter or letters of a name—an acronym. *Radar* (radio detecting and ranging, 1941) is one of the most famous acronyms of the era. Others include POW (prisoner of war, c. 1919), AWOL (absent without leave, 1919), Wave (Women Accepted for Volunteer Emergency Service, 1942), GI (government issue, 1943), Wac (Women's Army Corps, 1943), MIA (missing in action, 1944), and sonar (sound navigation ranging, 1945). Even the word *acronym* did not identify such words until 1943.

Have students work in pairs toidentify, research, and present to the class stories behind other, more modern acronyms they discover, such as AIDS (1982), CB (1959), DNA (1944), IQ (1920), laser (1960), scuba (1952), TNT (1915), and UFO (1953). After students present the story behind an acronym without revealing the acronym itself, other class members can identify the acronym.

Germany, which proceeded to declare war on Russia and France. A German invasion of neutral Belgium prompted Britain, already committed by the Triple Entente, to join the war on the side of France and Russia. After British and French forces halted the Germans' westward advance at the First Battle of the Marne in September 1914, both sides dug in, locked together in bloody trench warfare—a chaos of mud, barbed wire, exploding shells and hand grenades, machine guns, tanks, and poison gas. This stalemate would drag on for four years, with massive propaganda intensifying the bitterness and leaders refusing to admit that the carnage and devastation were in vain. C

In 1917 disillusionment with the failures of the war effort led to revolution in Russia. A moderate government was formed to replace the czar, but it was soon overthrown by Lenin's Bolsheviks, who promptly established a Communist state, agreed to a separate peace with Germany, and withdrew from the war. By then, however, the United States had entered it, tipping the balance in favor of Britain and France and forcing Germany to sue for peace. In the subsequent negotiations, French fears and anti-German sentiment resulted in the highly punitive Treaty of Versailles. To help defuse future crises, the treaty established the League of Nations, brainchild of the U.S. president Woodrow Wilson. The moderating U.S. influence was lost, however, when Congress refused to sign the treaty and join the league. D

Aftermath of the War

Through the provisions of the Treaty of Versailles, Britain acquired several former German colonies in Africa and became "trustee" of large chunks of the Middle East that had been part of the Turkish (or Ottoman) Empire, a German ally. With France a war-torn shambles, Russia ravaged by internal conflict, and the United States abandoning the international scene, Britain seemed to be the war's greatest victor. However, the nation had lost almost an

Development of the English Language

In the 20th century, the English language has increasingly reflected the fads and fancies of popular culture. The horrors of World War I made the delicacies of Victorian usage seem inappropriate, and by the 1920s a spirit of "anything goes" had made slang and colloquial language far more acceptable. Modern warfare generated new words—*blimp* and *camouflage* in World War I, for example, and *radar* and *blitz* in World War II—as did new technologies, the terminologies of which sometimes differed from one side of the Atlantic to the other. Thus, what Americans called the *phonograph* and the *radio* were known as the *gramophone* and the *wireless* by their British counterparts. Later, when Americans watched *TV*, Britons were watching the *telly*. Despite these verbal differences, the main effect of the two world wars and the communications revolution was to bring speakers of English even closer together. In Britain, U.S. soldiers, Hollywood films, and recordings of American music all helped to spread American popular culture, including its distinctive vocabulary.

Making Connections

Politics

A Because Queen Victoria was long-lived and occupied the throne until her death, Edward VII, her oldest son, was already 59 years old when he became king. The years of his relatively short reign (1901–1910), known as the Edwardian era, were a time when Britain's upper classes enjoyed their wealth, casting off the shackles of the rigid moral code that had prevailed under Victoria.

History

B The trade-union movement gained strength and momentum during the years preceding World War I. Between 1901 and 1911—when, according to studies of economic and social conditions, nearly 30 percent of British people were living in poverty—membership in unions swelled from 2 million to 4.1 million. Strikes began to affect the country in 1910, and a general railway strike occurred in 1911. The trade unions also helped increase support for the Labor Party.

Military History

C The tank was a British invention during World War I. After knocking down the barbed wire that protected a system of trenches, a tank could be driven over the trenches so that the men in the tank could gun down enemy soldiers as they attempted to flee.

Military History

D Leaders of Germany wanted a friendly Russian government that would allow Germany to unify its army currently split up fighting on eastern and western fronts. So Germany helped V. I. Lenin, a Russian revolutionary living in exile in Switzerland, return to his country. A short time later, Lenin took control of Russia and made the desired separate peace with Germany. German troops fighting Russia in the east were then able to move west and join the battles against France and Britain.

HISTORICAL BACKGROUND 983

Making Connections

Sociology

E World War I did not lead to a classless society in Britain, but it did cause a blurring of the lines between groups. Members of the upper class fought in the trenches alongside their lower-class countrymen, and their casualties were great. Moreover, many lower- and middle-class people, who blamed the upper class for getting Britain involved in the war, resolved to have a greater say in how they were governed in the future.

Politics

F Gandhi, who was called Mahatma ("Great Soul") by the people of India, was determined to free his country from British rule by relying on a policy of nonviolent resistance that was based on courage, truth, and a belief that people's behavior is more important than their achievements. His efforts were rewarded in 1947, when British India was granted its independence, though the country was split into two countries to accommodate the area's warring religious factions—Hindu (India) and Muslim (Pakistan).

Literature

G In his poem "Easter 1916," W. B. Yeats celebrated the abortive attempt of the Irish nationalists—some of whom he knew personally—to free their country from British domination. From 1922 to 1928, Yeats was a senator of the Irish Free State.

"Never in the field of human conflict was so much owed by so many to so few."

E entire generation of young men—over 750,000 killed and more than twice as many wounded—including a disproportionate number from the upper class, which had traditionally provided military leadership.

The casualties resulting from trench warfare had been so great, in fact, that halfway through the war the British government had been forced to make military service compulsory for the first time. Meanwhile, with so many of the nation's men fighting in France, British women had been forced to take on traditionally male jobs. Their contribution was acknowledged in 1918, when women over 30 were granted the right to vote.

Also acknowledged after the war was the military support supplied by Canada, Australia, New Zealand, and South Africa. By 1931, these former colonies, already largely self-governing, had been granted equal footing with Britain in the British Commonwealth of Nations. F Britain moved more slowly with India, however, where nonviolent resistance to British rule, under the direction of the spiritual leader Mohandas K. Gandhi, was making Britain look bad in the eyes of the world. Britain did reach a compromise of sorts with Ireland, however. During the G war, Irish republican extremists had courted German support, and on Easter Monday, 1916, they had launched an armed rebellion, seizing the General Post Office in Dublin. Although the rebellion had quickly been crushed, the British government's brutal punishment of its leaders led to widespread sympathy for their cause. In 1921, Britain succeeded in negotiating a partition with a group of Irish delegates, establishing the Irish Free State but allowing northern Ireland, with its Protestant majority loyal to the crown, to remain in the United Kingdom. The Irish Free State later became the Republic of Ireland.

While Britain was facing these problems, political turmoil was rocking nations dissatisfied with the terms of the Treaty of Versailles. Italy fell into the hands of the dictator Benito Mussolini, whose Fascist movement was based on an ideal of military glory. In the Soviet Union—the Communist successor of the Russian empire—another dictator, Joseph Stalin, came to power. The fear and confusion caused by the global economic depression

Come and help with the
VICTORY HARVEST
You are needed in the fields!
APPLY TO NEAREST EMPLOYMENT EXCHANGE FOR LEAFLET & ENROLMENT FORM OR WRITE DIRECT TO THE DEPARTMENT OF AGRICULTURE FOR SCOTLAND 15 GROSVENOR STREET, EDINBURGH.

Top to bottom: Winston Churchill giving "victory" sign; World War II Spitfires; war poster asking for volunteers in war effort; London residents with gas masks

that began in 1929 also favored the rise of dictators. Germany's postwar experiment with democracy ended abruptly in 1933, when its parliament gave dictatorial powers to Adolf Hitler, leader of the Nazi party and advocate of German racial and military supremacy. Soon Hitler was rebuilding the German army (in violation of the Treaty of Versailles) and constructing concentration camps where he secretly planned to exterminate Jews and other "racial undesirables."

In the wake of World War I, the Western democracies had little stomach for further violent confrontations. In 1931, when Japan invaded the Chinese region of Manchuria, China's appeals to the West were largely ignored. Four years later, when Italy invaded Ethiopia, the League of Nations invoked only mild economic sanctions. In the Spanish civil war of 1936, Fascists aided by Italy and Germany defeated the democratic loyalists, whose pleas for formal aid from the Western democracies went unheeded. Two years later, when Hitler forcibly annexed Austria and marched into Czechoslovakia, Britain and France maintained their policy of appeasement. Only when Hitler—after signing a secret pact with Stalin—invaded Poland on September 1, 1939, did Britain and France declare war on Germany. Italy and Japan soon allied themselves with Germany. World War II had begun.

World War II

H For a year after the fall of France in June 1940, Britain stood alone. With its entire population mobilized, civilian volunteers acted as plane spotters, firefighters, and rescue workers. All citizens endured severe shortages and rationing. Londoners slept in subways while bombs rained on the city above. During this period, known as the Battle of Britain, a handful of well-trained fighter pilots battered away at the German bombers. Prime Minister Winston Churchill praised these heroes of the Royal

Literary History

I During the first decade of the 20th century—known as the Edwardian era—the major literary movements of Victorian times continued to flourish. The novelists John Galsworthy and Arnold Bennett; the short story writers W. Somerset Maugham, P. G. Wodehouse, and Saki; and the playwright George Bernard Shaw, among others, explored the changes and conflicts in the British class system in a realistic and often witty style. At the same time, a strong romantic spirit marked the work of Rupert Brooke, John Masefield, and other Edwardian poets. Romanticism was also evident in the early poetry of William Butler Yeats, the writings of Lady Gregory, and other works of the Irish Literary Renaissance—a movement propelled by the growing Irish nationalism and a renewed interest in the Celtic myths and legends of Ireland's past.

Shaw

Yeats

Mansfield

Lawrence

J By 1910, however, Victorian ideas were yielding to the spirit of modernism, the movement that would dominate Western literature in the first half of the 20th century. Modernists stressed innovation as they attempted to create a new kind of literature for a new age. Such modernist poets as T. S. Eliot—and later Yeats—abandoned traditional patterns of stanza and meter for the more natural flow of **free verse.** Influenced by the French symbolists, they discarded the refined sentiment of the 19th century, preferring to convey emotions by means of strong images and unusual symbols. The works of modernist fiction writers—including Joseph Conrad, Katherine Mansfield, E. M. Forster, and D. H. Lawrence—began to reflect the new psychological theories of Sigmund Freud and Carl Jung.

Making Connections

History

H During World War II, each side made extensive use of espionage to obtain information about the plans of the other. Early in the war, Britain obtained a German code machine from a Polish spy, and after British mathematicians managed to crack the code, the machine was used to decipher German communications. The British acted on the decoded knowledge they gained so selectively that the Germans never realized that the code had been broken.

Literature

I Although steeped in Victorian traditions, Edwardian writers looked at existing institutions with a critical eye and questioned moral authority. That English literature was moving away from its earlier orientation can be seen, according to C. Hugh Holman, "by the fact that in the Edwardian Age the best dramatist was an Irishman, Shaw; the best poet an Irishman, Yeats; the best novelist an expatriate Pole, Conrad; and the figure with the greatest promise for the future an Irishman, Joyce."

Literature

J War literature tended to be cynical and angry. Wilfred Owen's works, often cited as the finest and most powerful poetry to come from the war, were stylistically experimental and thematically insistent on the cruelty and horror of war. His poetic manifesto, used as an epigraph in his *Collected Poems,* was "My subject is War, and the pity of War. The Poetry is in the pity." A company commander during World War I, Owen (1893–1918) was killed fighting in France, just one week shy of the end of hostilities.

Making Connections

Literature

(K) George Orwell's novel *1984,* a grim portrait of a world dominated by three warring superpowers, was published in 1949. In the novel, totalitarian regimes rule a bleak world in which there is no personal liberty. The book is famous for its catch phrase, "Big Brother is watching you."

Military History

(L) The main thrust of the Battle of Britain lasted from August 8 until October 31, 1940, as the Germans strove to weaken the British will to fight and to make a land invasion easier. After focusing their attacks on shipping ports and industries, in September the German air forces began to bomb London itself. Although the Royal Air Force was vastly outnumbered, the British proved to be superior to the Germans in technical and tactical prowess. By the time Hitler finally stopped the heaviest air attacks on Britain, Germany had lost 2,300 planes, whereas Britain had lost only 900. German planes continued sporadic bombings into May of 1941.

Politics

(M) The Labor Party, led by Clement Attlee, regained power in 1945 and instituted many changes in the fabric of British society. The government nationalized the Bank of England and many industries, began a program of socialized medicine, and accepted aid from the United States (under the Marshall Plan) in order to rebuild the economy. When Churchill was restored to power in 1951, he denationalized the Bank of England and some of the nationalized industries.

Literary History

Psychology also had a major impact on the pioneering fiction of James Joyce and Virginia Woolf. In different ways, each became a master of **stream of consciousness,** a narrative technique that attempts to depict the leaps and associations of the human mind.

The excitement of early modernism, however, crumbled into disillusionment for many of the writers who survived the devastation of World War I. In the aftermath of the war, writers tended to see the world as bleak and fragmentary—a Waste Land like that presented by T. S. Eliot in his most famous poem. The tone of many writers became bitter, expressing the cynicism of what has come to be called the Lost Generation. Others turned away from society altogether, exploring private concerns, personal experience, and the role of the artist.

Thomas

Auden

In the 1930s and 1940s, the growth of fascism and communism and the trauma of World War II prompted many British writers to focus again on social concerns. W. H. Auden and Stephen Spender examined and criticized society in much of their poetry; Aldous Huxley, Graham Greene, and George Orwell did likewise in their fiction. (K) Aspects of modernism were increasingly accepted as they became more familiar, and mere novelty played a less important role in literature than before. Free verse remained popular, but such poets as Auden and Dylan Thomas were equally at home with more traditional forms. In fiction, the use of the stream-of-consciousness technique became more widespread and less obscure.

Air Force, stating that "never in the field of human conflict was so much owed by so many to so few." (L)

In 1941, Hitler broke his pact with Stalin and invaded the Soviet Union. Later that year Japan bombed Pearl Harbor, and the United States entered the war. With these new allies, Britain was able to persevere until the war ended in 1945. Nearly 50 million people died in World War II, including over 10 million in concentration camps and almost a quarter million British civilians. The war also drained Britain financially.

After the war, devastated by widespread poverty and in desperate need of refashioning their social order, Britons turned to the nation's young liberals, electing a Parliament overwhelmingly dominated by Labor members. Over the next few years, the Labor government transformed Britain into a welfare state, setting up a national health-care system and nationalizing such industries as steel, coal, and railroads. (M) Britain also began slowly to relinquish its colonies. In the climate of the cold war, with the United States assuming a leading role in international affairs, Britain was no longer to be the world's greatest power.

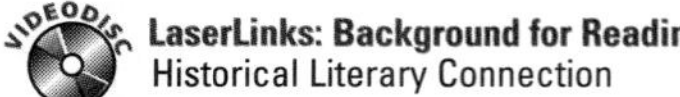

LaserLinks: Background for Reading
Historical Literary Connection

Through his non-violent resistance to British rule, Mohandas K. Gandhi helped win independence for India in 1947.

PART 1 New Images of Reality

The profound changes of the first half of the 20th century gave rise to a sharpened anxiety and sense of irony. In this part of Unit Six, you will encounter writers who began to experiment with new and highly personal forms to express these feelings. As you read, consider whether their new images of reality express any ideas similar to your own.

987

OVERVIEW

 These selections are included in the **Grade 12 InterActive Reader.**

Objectives

1. understand and appreciate **modern poetry (Literary Analysis)**
2. appreciate the author's use of **symbols (Literary Analysis)**
3. **clarify meaning in poetry** in order to understand Yeats's poems **(Active Reading)**

Summary

"The Second Coming" presents Yeats's apocalyptic vision of the breakdown of society. "Sailing to Byzantium" is Yeats's look at one of the great empires of the ancient world.

Thematic Link

Yeats's visions of the past, present, and future represent the **new images of reality** in the early 20th century.

5-Minute Warm-Up

Daily Language SkillBuilder

Have students **proofread** the display sentences on page 979i and write them correctly. The sentences also appear on Transparency 26 of **Grammar Transparencies and Copymasters.**

Reading and Analyzing

Literary Analysis SYMBOLS

(A) After students read the first stanza, ask them what they think the falcon and falconer might represent.

Possible Response: human beings and God.

 Use **Unit Six Resource Book,** p. 5 for additional support.

Active Reading

CLARIFYING MEANING IN POETRY

After students have read each poem once, guide them through problematic lines, using the technique listed on p. 988.

 Use **Unit Six Resource Book,** p. 4 for additional support.

PREPARING to *Read*

The Second Coming
Sailing to Byzantium

Poetry by WILLIAM BUTLER YEATS

"Things fall apart; the center cannot hold."

Connect to Your Life

Hopes and Fears Most people have concerns and questions about the future—both their own and the world's. What are your main hopes and fears for the future? Do your friends and relatives have similar hopes and fears? Share some of your thoughts with your classmates.

Build Background

Yeats's Beliefs William Butler Yeats, considered by many the greatest poet of the 20th century, was a visionary who developed his own set of beliefs to answer his questions about life and help him interpret the uncertainties of the future. Among these beliefs was the view that history occurs in 2,000-year cycles and that as each era comes to an end, another era—its opposite—is ushered in by a momentous occurrence. Yeats wrote "The Second Coming" at what might be seen as such a time of upheaval in world history—he wrote the poem in January 1919, not long after the Russian Revolution of 1917 and the end of World War I in 1918. In the poem, Yeats employed a cyclical view of history to explain what he and many others saw as a breakdown of society at the beginning of the 20th century.

In the 1920s, Yeats became fascinated with the history and art of medieval Byzantium. This interest is reflected in his 1926 poem "Sailing to Byzantium," one of his most celebrated and closely studied poems. He later commented, "Byzantium was the center of European civilization and the source of its spiritual philosophy, so I symbolize the search for spiritual life by a journey to that city."

Focus Your Reading

LITERARY ANALYSIS SYMBOLS **Symbols**—persons, places, objects, or actions that stand for things beyond themselves—are a central element in Yeats's poetry. In the two poems you are about to read, there are a number of symbols including a falcon, a beast, fire, and gold. As you read the poems, consider what these and other symbols might represent.

ACTIVE READING CLARIFYING MEANING IN POETRY When reading complex poems, you may encounter some unfamiliar ideas and images. If a poem seems obscure, it may help to read it several times. Use the following steps as strategies for your reading:

- On your first reading, refer to the explanations in the notes and think about each poem's **subject.**
- The next time you read the poem, note any **images** that stand out in your mind.
- On subsequent readings, be aware of any **lines** that you think are especially difficult.

Don't expect to understand a complex poem immediately, but do expect to discover new insights each time you read it.

READER'S NOTEBOOK As you read, use the strategies listed above to clarify the meaning of the two poems. Using a chart like the one shown, briefly describe the general subject of each poem. Then jot down images and lines that you want to focus on.

Title:

Subject:	
Images	Lines

LESSON RESOURCES

UNIT SIX RESOURCE BOOK, pp. 4–5

ASSESSMENT RESOURCES

Formal Assessment, pp. 179–180

Teacher's Guide to Assessment and Portfolio Use

Test Generator

SKILLS TRANSPARENCIES AND COPYMASTERS

Literary Analysis
- Figurative Language, T22 (for Literary Analysis, p. 988)

Reading and Critical Thinking
- Organizational Chart: Vertical, T53 (for Active Reading, p. 988)

Grammar
- Verbs—Using Correct Verb Forms, T45 (for Mini Lesson, p. 993)
- Verbs—Diction, C167 (for Mini Lesson, p. 993)

Vocabulary
- Denotation and Connotation, C78 (for Mini Lesson, p. 989)

Writing
- Figurative Language and Sound Devices, T15 (for Writing Option 2, p. 993)

Communications
- Reading Aloud, T11 (for Activities & Explorations 1, p. 993)
- Identifying and Analyzing Artistic Elements in Literary Texts, T13 (for Activities & Explorations 2, p. 993)

INTEGRATED TECHNOLOGY

Audio Library

LaserLinks
- Author Background: William Butler Yeats
- Art Gallery: Byzantine Art. See **Teacher's SourceBook,** p. 68.

Internet: Research Starter

Visit our website: www.mcdougallittell.com

William Butler Yeats

THE SECOND COMING

Turning and turning in the widening gyre
The falcon cannot hear the falconer;
Things fall apart; the center cannot hold;
Mere anarchy is loosed upon the world,
The blood-dimmed tide is loosed, and everywhere
The ceremony of innocence is drowned;
The best lack all conviction, while the worst
Are full of passionate intensity.

Surely some revelation is at hand;
Surely the Second Coming is at hand.
The Second Coming! Hardly are those words out
When a vast image out of *Spiritus Mundi*
Troubles my sight: somewhere in sands of the desert
A shape with lion body and the head of a man,
A gaze blank and pitiless as the sun,
Is moving its slow thighs, while all about it
Reel shadows of the indignant desert birds.
The darkness drops again; but now I know
That twenty centuries of stony sleep
Were vexed to nightmare by a rocking cradle,
And what rough beast, its hour come round at last,
Slouches towards Bethlehem to be born?

1 gyre (jīr): spiral. (Yeats, however, pronounced this word with a hard *g* [gīr].)

2 falcon: a hawklike bird of prey; **falconer:** a person who uses trained falcons to hunt small game.

6 ceremony of innocence: the rituals (such as the rites of baptism and marriage) that give order to life.

10 Second Coming: Christ's return to earth, predicted in the New Testament as an event preceded by a time of terror and chaos.

12 *Spiritus Mundi* (spĭr′ĭ-to͝os mo͝on′dē) *Latin:* Spirit of the World. Yeats used this term to refer to the collective unconscious, a supposed source of images and memories that all human beings share.

14 This image suggests the Great Sphinx in Egypt, built more than 40 centuries ago.

20 rocking cradle: a reference to the birth of Christ.

Thinking Through the Literature

1. Describe the image from this poem that remains most vivid in your mind.
2. What concerns does the poem's speaker seem to be expressing?
3. How would you describe the speaker's view of the future?

- the speaker's apparent attitude toward the Second Coming
- the speaker's feelings about the "rough beast"
- the effect of the rocking cradle

Customizing Instruction

Less Proficient Readers

Before students begin reading, have them make predictions about the content of each poem based on its title. Then, as they read, have students restate the text in their own words at each terminal punctuation mark.

Students Acquiring English

Have students describe beliefs or myths about the end of the world from their primary cultures. Then, invite them to discuss ancient cultures that have special significance to them––for example, the Aztecs or Maya.

Use **Spanish Study Guide** for additional support, pp. 230–232.

Thinking Through the Literature

1. Accept all reasonable responses.
2. Possible responses: loss of faith or moral compass, anarchy, uncontrolled violence, warfare, lack of restraint, strong preying on the weak. Responses should make some reference to the historical context. If necessary, students should refer to the opening essay or Build Background.
3. Accept all reasonable responses.

Mini Lesson

Vocabulary Strategy

DENOTATION AND CONNOTATION

Instruction Connotation refers to the attitudes and feelings people associate with a word; denotation, on the other hand, is the literal or dictionary meaning of a word. (Point out to students that "denotation" begins with a "d," just as "dictionary" does. This mnemonic device will help them distinguish between the two terms.)

The connotation of a word may be positive or negative. For example, *beast* and *creature* have similar denotative meanings, but *beast* usually has a more negative connotation, bringing to mind violent or uncivilized behavior. Thus, Yeats's use of *beast* in line 21 of "The Second Coming" creates a stronger negative image.

Activity Have students compare the positive and negative connotations of everyday words such as *home, school, pet.* Then, have students cite words with negative connotations from "The Second Coming" and words with positive connotations from "Sailing to Byzantium." Encourage students to offer explanations as to why Yeats might have chosen these particular words.

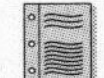

Use **Vocabulary Transparencies and Copymasters**, p. 50.

A lesson on denotations and connotations appears on p. 645 in the Pupil's Edition.

Reading and Analyzing

Literary Analysis SYMBOLS

A Have students note the repeated use of "gold" in stanzas III and IV. Discuss what the gold may represent.

Possible Responses: that which is truly valuable, great art, faith, imagination, immortality—in contrast to mortal flesh.

Literary Analysis: RHYME SCHEME

Have students identify the rhyme scheme of each stanza.

Answer: ababcc.

Ask them what effect the final couplet in each stanza has on the poem as a whole.

Possible Response: It gives the poem a complete, rounded structure that is both optimistic and serene.

Reading Skills and Strategies: DRAWING INFERENCES

B Refer students to lines 20–24. Ask to what "dying animal" they think the speaker's heart is fastened.

Possible Response: his elderly body.

Why might being attached to a body keep the heart from knowing what it is (line 23)?

Possible Responses: Emphasis on worldly issues may interfere with eternal values; bodily concerns can overshadow artistic or immortal ones.

William Butler Yeats

SAILING TO BYZANTIUM

That is no country for old men. The young
In one another's arms, birds in the trees
—Those dying generations—at their song,
The salmon-falls, the mackerel-crowded seas,
Fish, flesh, or fowl, commend all summer long
Whatever is begotten, born, and dies.
Caught in that sensual music all neglect
Monuments of unaging intellect.

An aged man is but a paltry thing,
A tattered coat upon a stick, unless
Soul clap its hands and sing, and louder sing
For every tatter in its mortal dress,
Nor is there singing school but studying
Monuments of its own magnificence;
And therefore I have sailed the seas and come
To the holy city of Byzantium.

4 salmon-falls: the rapids in rivers that salmon swim up to spawn.

13 but: except for.

14 its: the soul's.

16 Byzantium (bĭ-zăn'shē-əm): a city of southeastern Europe (now Istanbul, Turkey) that was a center of European civilization, especially art and religion, in the Middle Ages.

Teaching Options

Speaking and Listening

HOLDING A DISCUSSION

Instruction Have students work in small groups to engage in a formal discussion of "Sailing to Byzantium." Every group member must contribute to the discussion and respond appropriately to the contributions of other members.

Prepare Tell each group to choose a "speaking staff," an item that will signify that it is a particular person's turn to speak. A person must have the speaking staff in hand before he or she can offer an opinion or interpretation.

Present Provide each group with one of the following prompts to stimulate their discussions.

- Why does the speaker's soul need to be taught to sing (lines 13, 20)?
- What sort of desire has made the speaker's heart sick (lines 21–23)?
- Why does the speaker want to shun the form of natural things (line 26)?

This activity is particularly well-suited for longer class periods.

Saint Mark arriving in Venice (about A.D. 800–1000). Byzantine mosaic from San Marco, Venice, Italy, Scala/Art Resource, New York.

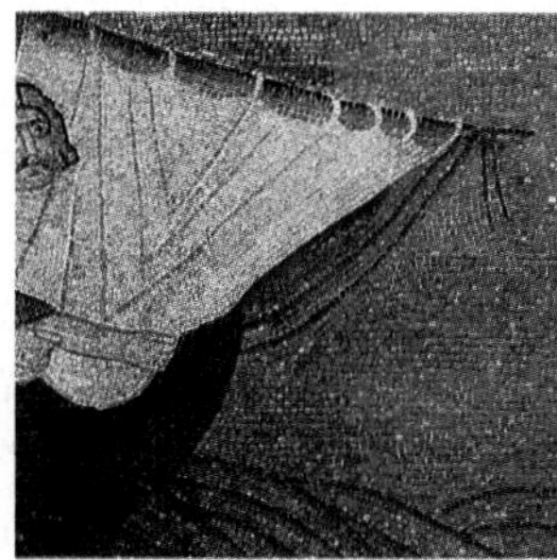

O sages standing in God's holy fire
As in the gold mosaic of a wall,
Come from the holy fire, perne in a gyre,
And be the singing-masters of my soul.
Consume my heart away; sick with desire
And fastened to a dying animal
It knows not what it is; and gather me
Into the artifice of eternity.

Once out of nature I shall never take
My bodily form from any natural thing,
But such a form as Grecian goldsmiths make
Of hammered gold and gold enameling
To keep a drowsy Emperor awake;
Or set upon a golden bough to sing
To lords and ladies of Byzantium
Of what is past, or passing, or to come.

17 sages: wise people; saints.

18 gold mosaic of a wall: artwork in an ancient church.

19 perne (pûrn) **in a gyre:** whirl in a spiral.

23 it: the speaker's heart.

24 artifice: skilled craftsmanship.

29 Emperor: the ninth-century Byzantine emperor Theophilus, said to have possessed a golden sculpture of a tree with mechanical singing birds on its branches.

Customizing Instruction

Less Proficient Readers

Check students' understanding with the following questions.

- To what country is Yeats referring in line 1?
  Answer: the country he is living in now.
- What do the people of this country value most?
  Possible Responses: pleasure; life.
- What does the speaker ask the sages to do?
  Possible Responses: become his singing-masters; consume his heart; gather him into eternity.

Students Acquiring English

Make sure students understand the sidenote for "salmon-falls," as they may be unfamiliar with the verb *spawn.*

Help them understand the literal meaning and the larger meaning of "Fish, flesh, and fowl" (line 5).

Answer: fish, animals, and birds; all living things.

Suggest that students first try to determine the meaning of unfamiliar words from context clues before turning to the sidenotes or to a dictionary.

Gifted and Talented

To encourage students to make connections between different literary works, you might give them a copy of Robert Frost's "Nothing Gold Can Stay." Have them read the poem independently and then break into small groups to discuss the symbolic value of gold in Frost's poem compared to Yeats's use of it. If students have read *The Great Gatsby*, have them draw upon Fitzgerald's negative view of gold.

Assessment Informal Assessment

WRITING AN ESSAY Write the following quote from T. S. Eliot on the chalkboard: "Born into a world in which the doctrine of 'Art for Art's sake' was generally accepted, and living on into one in which art has been asked to be instrumental to social purposes, he [Yeats] held firmly to the right view which is between these, though not in any way a compromise between them . . . ."
Have students evaluate Eliot's observations about Yeats's poetry, using the two poems here as the basis for their evaluations.

RUBRIC

3 **Full Accomplishment** Students evaluate social and personal/artistic concerns in both poems, showing full understanding of Yeats's attitudes and concerns.

2 **Substantial Accomplishment** Students demonstrate understanding of Yeats. However, they may discuss only social concerns in both poems or they may discuss social and artistic concerns in only one poem.

1 **Little or Partial Accomplishment** Students provide superficial evaluation, showing little or no in-depth understanding of Yeats or of Eliot's comment.

SAILING TO BYZANTIUM 991

GUIDING STUDENT RESPONSE

Connect to the Literature

1. What Do You Think?
Guidelines for student response: Encourage students to draw parallels between Yeats's view of growing older and the ways in which contemporary society treats the aged.

Comprehension Check
- old
- wise people and saints

Think Critically

2. Possible Responses: feels too old for the society in which he lives; envies youth its place in his world but also sees that world's flaws; needs to go where his soul can thrive or "sing"
3. Possible Responses: feels out of place in his society; longs for something more permanent; admires its artistic and intellectual achievements
4. Possible Responses: immortality, peace, death
5. Possible Responses: Each speaker is critical of his own society, although the first speaker focuses on its violence, anarchy, and lack of morals, while the second focuses on the emphasis on sexual experience and neglect of intellectual or artistic pursuits. The first speaker offers only uncertainty about the Second Coming; the second offers a clearer and more clearly positive alternative world.
6. After students have exchanged ideas with a partner, take a tally to see if the students show any consistency in the images they chose.

Literary Analysis

Activity To help students with another of Yeats's recurring symbols, that of Byzantium, refer them to his comment in the Build Background on page 988. Tell students what Byzantium might represent in terms of art and imagination. Then have students complete the activity.

Review Imagery The students are expected to use their analysis of visual images as they discuss the impact on the poem's meaning and the reader.

Connect to the Literature

1. **What Do You Think?** What impressions of growing old do you have after reading "Sailing to Byzantium"?

Comprehension Check
- Is the speaker young or old?
- To whom does the speaker go for spiritual guidance?

Think Critically

2. What **conflict** does the speaker seem to be facing at the start of the poem?
3. Why do you think the speaker decides to go to Byzantium?

   THINK ABOUT
   - what the speaker might mean by "monuments of unaging intellect"
   - the possible meanings of *singing*
   - the references to sages, holy fire, and gold mosaic
4. What do you think the speaker expects from the future?
5. Compare and contrast the ways in which the speakers of "The Second Coming" and "Sailing to Byzantium" view the future. Do they share any attitudes or expectations? Explain your answer.
6. ACTIVE READING CLARIFYING MEANING IN POETRY Review the charts you completed in your READER'S NOTEBOOK. Choose an **image** or **line** from each poem that you think is particularly striking or important to the meaning of the poem. Explain your choice to a partner.

Extend Interpretations

7. **Writer's Style** Yeats once wrote, "I tried to make the language of poetry coincide with that of passionate, normal speech." Keeping in mind the importance of both **word choice** and **rhythm,** comment on how successful you think Yeats was in his attempt to reflect "passionate, normal speech" in these two poems.
8. **Connect to Life** Some people see uncertainty and change as a challenge; others, as a threat. What kinds of uncertainties and changes do you think people will face in the 21st century? Do you think these two poems offer any perspectives that might be useful in today's world?

Literary Analysis

SYMBOLS Yeats uses **symbols**—persons, places, objects, or actions that stand for things beyond themselves—to convey major ideas and themes in his poetry. One of his most important symbols is the *gyre,* or spiral, which he uses to express his view of history and his belief that life repeats itself even as it moves forward.

Activity In a chart like the one below, list other possibly symbolic details in the two poems, noting what each symbol might represent.

"The Second Coming"		"Sailing to Byzantium"	
Symbol	What It Represents	Symbol	What It Represents
gyre	repetition in life		

REVIEW IMAGERY As you know, **imagery** refers to words or phrases that create vivid sensory experiences. With a partner, read through each poem, making a list of the visual images that you think are essential to the poem's meaning. Decide what feelings or ideas each image conveys and how it contributes to the meaning of the whole poem. Then discuss your list and thoughts with the whole class. Be prepared to defend your interpretation of the images you selected from the text.

Extend Interpretations

Writer's Style Possible examples of everyday language include "Things fall apart," "Surely some revelation is at hand," "slouches," and "That is no country for old men." Students will offer differing opinions on Yeats's success, but they should offer specific evidence from the poems as support.

Connect to Life Accept all reasonable, well-supported responses. You might suggest to students that they think about these questions in the context of developing technology—technology can be both a problem and a solution to a problem. Other problems technology cannot address or solve. Discuss the role of technology with students in the context of the questions raised.

Choices & CHALLENGES

Writing Options

1. Stanza Titles Compose subtitles for the four stanzas of "Sailing to Byzantium." Try to make each subtitle reflect your interpretation of the stanza it applies to.

2. Symbolic Description Write a symbolic description of a major event or change in the world or in your life. Use an original symbol that you think captures the intensity or significance of the event.

Activities & Explorations

1. Dance Interpretation Work with a partner to prepare a reading-and-dance presentation of one of these poems. As one of you reads the poem, the other should use gesture and movement to interpret the images and the development of ideas in the poem. ~ **PERFORMING**

2. Sculpture Design Draw a design for a sculpture that conveys your interpretation of part or all of either poem. ~ **ART**

Inquiry & Research

Byzantine Art Research the art of medieval Byzantium. What was the style of Byzantine art like? What materials were used? Look in art history books for photographs of Byzantine art, and share some of the best examples with the class. Discuss why you think Yeats felt drawn to this culture.

More Online: Research Starter
www.mcdougallittell.com

William Butler Yeats

1865–1939

Other Works
"No Second Troy"
"A Prayer for My Daughter"
"Byzantium"
"Under Ben Bulben"

Early Years Born in Dublin of Protestant parents, William Butler Yeats was educated in large part by his father, a portrait painter. After a brief period at an art school, Yeats decided to write instead of paint. He published his first poems in 1885, and from that time until the end of his life, he was constantly writing—producing drama and criticism as well as poetry.

Patriotic Feelings Yeats was passionately committed to Ireland—its people, culture, and political destiny. At the age of 24, he met and fell in love with the actress Maud Gonne, a fiery Irish patriot. Although Gonne refused to marry him, she inspired some of his finest lyrics and deepened his commitment to Irish nationalism. In 1896, he met Lady Gregory, an Irish aristocrat; together they worked to create a national drama for Ireland, founding Dublin's Abbey Theatre in 1904. Their work was vital to the 20th-century revival of Irish literature.

Yeats's Mysticism Throughout his life, Yeats had an intense interest in mysticism and the supernatural—an interest that received a fresh impetus after his marriage in 1917, when he discovered that his wife could apparently convey "spirit messages" by means of automatic writing. Yeats used the metaphors and symbols he found in these messages to pursue new directions in his poetry and to create his mythological system. Many of his best works were produced in the following decade.

Resting Place In 1923, Yeats received the Nobel Prize in literature. He died in France in January 1939, but after World War II his remains were reburied in Ireland, as he had wished.

Author Activity

Mystical Beliefs Find out more about Yeats's beliefs in mysticism. What elements of these beliefs are reflected in the poems you have just read?

LaserLinks: Background for Reading
Author Background
Art Gallery

Writing Options

1. **Stanza Titles** Students might work in small groups to complete this exercise.
2. **Symbolic Description** Students' descriptions may take the form of poetry or prose. You might ask students to exchange papers and try to interpret each other's symbolic descriptions.

Activities & Explorations

1. **Dance Interpretation** Clarify that dance interpretations should be performed to the spoken poem rather than to music, although students might include music before or after reading the poem.
2. **Sculpture Design** If students have trouble generating ideas, they can sketch a sculpture of the widening gyre of "The Second Coming," perhaps with a falcon or falconer inside or a sculpture of the golden tree with mechanical birds described in the last stanza of "Sailing to Byzantium."

Inquiry & Research

Byzantine Art Have students work in small groups, with each member exploring a different aspect of the subject—mosaics, metalwork, architecture, sculpture, and so on.

Final presentations might be oral reports with graphics, art displays with captions, or videotaped museum visits.

Author Activity

Mystical Beliefs Elements of mysticism that students may identify in "The Second Coming" include Yeats's cyclical view of history and the vision of the creature coming out of the desert (lines 11–17). Elements of mysticism in "Sailing to Byzantium" include the reverence of "sages" and the ability to prophesy the future (line 32).

Grammar

VERBS: CHOOSING PRECISE DICTION

Instruction A message is most effective when diction is correct, wording is concise, and verbs are precise. Remind students to consider each of these factors when writing.

Diction refers to word choice. Select words that are appropriate in degree of formality and in style, considering both the subject and the audience.

Concise means "brief; free from unnecessary words." Avoid idioms and other phrases when a single word is more effective. *Precise* verbs are those that describe, or create an image, as well as convey a general meaning.

Activity Write the following sentence on the chalkboard. Have the students identify and correct any problems with the underlined words.

The stuff that Yeats went on and on about in "The Second Coming" is worth trying to understand. *("stuff"—inappropriate diction; replace with "ideas . . . are"; "went on and on about"—inappropriate and wordy; replace with "writes about" or "explores")*

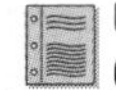

Use **Grammar Transparencies and Copymasters,** p. 1050.

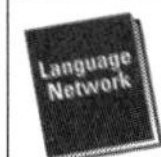

Use McDougal Littell's ***Language Network*** for more instruction and practice in choosing precise verbs.

OVERVIEW

Objectives

1. understand and appreciate a **one-act play (Literary Analysis)**
2. appreciate the author's use of **suspense (Literary Analysis)**
3. **analyze dialect** to appreciate and understand the play **(Active Reading)**

Summary

While guarding a quay where a fugitive rebel may make his escape, a police sergeant in British-ruled Ireland is approached by a ragged balladeer. After mentioning his firsthand knowledge of the dangerous fugitive, the singer offers to help stand watch. To pass the time, he sings anti-British ballads whose lyrics the sergeant seems to know. Songs and conversation soon make the sergeant recall that, much like the fugitive, he also dreamed of fighting to free Ireland. When the singer reveals himself as the fugitive, the sergeant hides the man's identity from the other police officers and lets the man escape.

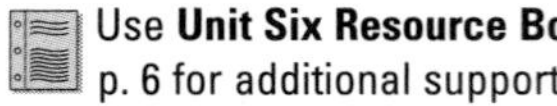

Use **Unit Six Resource Book,** p. 6 for additional support.

Thematic Link

In this play, **reality** is not what it at first appears to be: A ragged balladeer is revealed to be a fugitive rebel, and a police sergeant goes against the law he serves to assist the Irish cause.

5-Minute Warm-Up

Daily Language SkillBuilder

Have students **proofread** the display sentences on page 979i and write them correctly. The sentences also appear on Transparency 27 of **Grammar Transparencies and Copymasters.**

The Rising of the Moon

Drama by LADY ISABELLA AUGUSTA GREGORY

"Maybe, Sergeant, you'll be on the side of the country yet."

Connect to Your Life

Facing a Dilemma This play focuses on a moral dilemma—a man must choose between two opposing sides, each of which seems to be right. Think of a time when you had to make a hard choice between two sides of an issue. Describe your experience and tell how you made your decision.

Build Background

Fight for Independence When *The Rising of the Moon* was first performed in 1907, the Irish were struggling to gain independence from Great Britain, and individual citizens found themselves in the position of having to take sides. Some patriots worked for gradual change through peaceful means; others were willing to use violence to obtain an immediate separation from Great Britain. Set in the late 1800s, this play is about the search for an Irish rebel who has plotted to overthrow the British.

Two popular revolutionary songs are important in the play. The song "The Rising of the Moon" celebrates a famous Irish rebellion in 1798. It describes a gathering of rebels at moonrise, armed and ready to fight, and ends with thanks to God that there are still men "who would follow in their footsteps at the rising of the moon." In the other song, "Granuaile" (grăn′o͝o-āl′), Ireland is portrayed as a maiden who has been brutalized by the "ruffian band" of the English. At one time, when the English outlawed even the speaking of the name of Ireland, *Granuaile* was one of the many metaphorical names that Irish patriots applied to their homeland.

Focus Your Reading

LITERARY ANALYSIS | SUSPENSE A writer may purposely leave readers uncertain about what will happen in a story or play in order to create **suspense**—that is, a feeling of tension or excitement. For example, reading this passage from the play, the reader wonders what the character has heard out on the moonlit water and what might follow:

Sergeant. Oh! What's that? . . . I thought it might be a boat.

As you read, look for other statements and events that add to the suspense.

ACTIVE READING | ANALYZING DIALECT This play reflects the **dialect** of County Galway in western Ireland. In this dialect, longer vowel sounds and differences in grammar, sentence structure, and idiom—such as the use of *me* for *my*—give a musical quality to the language. A writer may use dialect to make **dialogue** seem authentic or to give a musical quality to the language. Dialect can also be used to give clues about **characters'** backgrounds and beliefs.

READER'S NOTEBOOK As you read this play about a man who takes sides in the Irish-English conflict, use a chart like the one below to jot down interesting examples of dialect.

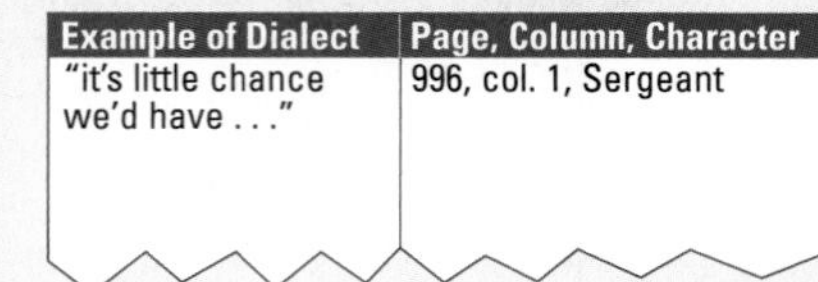

Example of Dialect	Page, Column, Character
"it's little chance we'd have . . ."	996, col. 1, Sergeant

LaserLinks: Background for Reading
Historical Connection
Literary Connection

LESSON RESOURCES

UNIT SIX RESOURCE BOOK, pp. 6–9

ASSESSMENT RESOURCES
Formal Assessment, pp. 181–182
Teacher's Guide to Assessment and Portfolio Use
Test Generator

SKILLS TRANSPARENCIES AND COPYMASTERS
Literary Analysis
- External Conflicts/Societal Conflicts, T20 (for Think Critically 2, p. 1002)

Reading and Critical Thinking
- Using an Outline, T44 (for Active Reading, p. 994)

Grammar
- Avoiding Shifts in Tense, T46 (for Mini Lesson, p. 1003)
- Simple and Perfect Tenses of Verbs, C130 (for Mini Lesson, p. 1003)

Vocabulary
- Dialect, C79 (for Mini Lesson, p. 998)

Writing
- Dramatic Scene, C31 (for Writing Option 1, p. 1003)

Communications
- Impromptu Speaking: Debate, T15 (for Activities & Explorations 1, p. 1003)

INTEGRATED TECHNOLOGY
Audio Library
LaserLinks
- Historical Connection: Irish Rebellion, Early 1900s. See **Teacher's SourceBook,** p. 70.

Visit our website:
www.mcdougallittell.com

THE RISING OF THE MOON

Lady Isabella Augusta Gregory

CAST OF CHARACTERS

Sergeant
Policeman X
Policeman B
A Ragged Man

Scene: *Side of a quay*[1] *in a seaport town. Some posts and chains. A large barrel. Enter three policemen. Moonlight.* Sergeant, *who is older than the others, crosses the stage to right and looks down steps. The others put down a pastepot and unroll a bundle of placards.*[2]

1. **quay** (kē): a landing place for boats; wharf.
2. **placards** (plăk′ärdz′): posters.

TEACHING THE LITERATURE

Customizing Instruction

Less Proficient Readers
Students may experience some difficulty with the dialect in the play. Reading aloud will often help them to understand the unusual syntax and Irish slang that characterize the dialogue. Emphasize that stage directions often provide guidelines for interpreting character motivation and emotion.

Students Acquiring English
Read the Build Background on p. 994 with students to ensure their understanding of the play's setting. Discuss the current situation in Northern Ireland, and explain, if necessary, the religious aspect of the conflict. Invite students to share their knowledge or experience of civil conflicts in their native cultures.

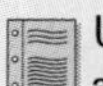 Use **Spanish Study Guide** for additional support, pp. 233–235.

Gifted and Talented
As students read the play, have them consider the various meanings of the title.
Possible Responses: It uses the name of a famous rebel song to reflect content and theme; it stresses the suspenseful night setting; it suggests the new light in which the sergeant comes to view himself and his politics; it suggests the new light in which the rebel views the sergeant.

BLOCK SCHEDULING: MANAGING TIME

If your schedule requires that you cover the lesson objectives in a shorter time, use . . .
- Preparing to Read, p. 994
- Thinking Through the Literature, p. 1002

If you want to take advantage of longer class time, use . . .
- TE Teaching Options: Cross Curricular Links, pp. 996, 997; Vocabulary, p. 998; Grammar, p. 1003; Speaking and Listening, p. 999; Viewing and Representing, p. 1000; Standardized Test Practice, p. 1001
- Choices & Challenges and Author Activity, p. 1003

Reading and Analyzing

Literary Analysis SUSPENSE

Ask students how foreshadowing can contribute to suspense, the quality of being anxious about what will happen in a dramatic work.

Possible Response: Foreshadowing heightens the reader's/audience's awareness of particular details and makes them want to find out why the author has focused on a particular place or event.

Use **Unit Six Resource Book,** p. 8 for more exercises.

Active Reading ANALYZING DIALECT

Point out that a play consists largely of dialogue. Ask students why they think an author would choose to write a play in dialect.

Possible Response: Spoken language is often more informal than written language. By writing in dialect, the author can show how people speak to each other in their everyday lives.

Use **Unit Six Resource Book,** p. 7 for more practice.

Reading Skills and Strategies: SPECULATING

A Ask students why they think the author decided not to give her characters actual names.

Possible Responses: The characters are symbols rather than real people; a variety of people could fill the roles that the characters suggest; the characters represent all people rather than specific individuals.

Literary Analysis: FORESHADOWING

B Ask what the sergeant's focus on the flight of steps suggests may happen later in the play.

Possible Response: It suggests that some crucial activity or event may occur there.

A **Policeman B.** I think this would be a good place to put up a notice. (*He points to barrel.*)

Policeman X. Better ask him. (*calls to* Sergeant) Will this be a good place for a placard? (*no answer*)

Policeman B. Will we put up a notice here on the barrel? (*no answer*)

B **Sergeant.** There's a flight of steps here that leads to the water. This is a place that should be minded well. If he got down here, his friends might have a boat to meet him; they might send it in here from outside.

Policeman B. Would the barrel be a good place to put a notice up?

Sergeant. It might; you can put it there. (*They paste the notice up.*)

Sergeant (*reading it*). Dark hair—dark eyes, smooth face, height five feet five—there's not much to take hold of in that—It's a pity I had no chance of seeing him before he broke out of jail. They say he's a wonder, that it's he makes all the plans for the whole organization. There isn't another man in Ireland would have broken jail the way he did. He must have some friends among the jailers.

Policeman B. A hundred pounds is little enough for the Government to offer for him. You may be sure any man in the force that takes him will get promotion.

Sergeant. I'll mind this place myself. I wouldn't wonder at all if he came this way. He might come slipping along there (*points to side of quay*), and his friends might be waiting for him there (*points down steps*), and once he got away it's little chance we'd have of finding him; it's maybe under a load of kelp[3] he'd be in a fishing boat, and not one to help a married man that wants it to the reward.

Policeman X. And if we get him itself, nothing but abuse on our heads for it from the people, and maybe from our own relations.

Sergeant. Well, we have to do our duty in the force. Haven't we the whole country depending on us to keep law and order? It's those that are down would be up and those that are up would be down, if it wasn't for us. Well, hurry on, you have plenty of other places to placard yet, and come back here then to me. You can take the lantern. Don't be too long now. It's very lonesome here with nothing but the moon.

Policeman B. It's a pity we can't stop with you. The Government should have brought more police into the town, with *him* in jail, and at assize[4] time too. Well, good luck to your watch. (*They go out.*)

Sergeant (*walks up and down once or twice and looks at placard*). A hundred pounds and promotion sure. There must be a great deal of spending in a hundred pounds. It's a pity some honest man not to be the better of that. (*A ragged man appears at left and tries to slip past.* Sergeant *suddenly turns.*)

Sergeant. Where are you going?

Man. I'm a poor ballad singer, your honor. I thought to sell some of these (*holds out bundle of ballads*) to the sailors. (*He goes on.*)

Sergeant. Stop! Didn't I tell you to stop? You can't 1
go on there.

Man. Oh, very well. It's a hard thing to be poor. All the world's against the poor!

Sergeant. Who are you?

Man. You'd be as wise as myself if I told you, but I don't mind. I'm one Jimmy Walsh, a ballad singer.

Sergeant. Jimmy Walsh? I don't know that name.

Man. Ah, sure, they know it well enough in Ennis. Were you ever in Ennis, Sergeant?

Sergeant. What brought you here?

Man. Sure, it's to the assizes I came, thinking I might make a few shillings here or there. It's in

3. **kelp:** a seaweed used to keep fish fresh until they get to market.

4. **assize** (ə-sīz′): in Britain, a court session held periodically in a county.

Teaching Options

Cross Curricular Link **History**

POLICING IRELAND One point of conflict that the Irish had with British rule at this time was the British-run police force stationed in Ireland. In 1822, Robert Peel, then the Home Secretary of Britain, introduced the Constabulary Act into British Parliament. This act established a British-controlled police force in Ireland. Robert Peel also established London's metropolitan police—nicknamed "bobbies" in his honor—in 1829. The more derogatory nickname, "peelers," was widely used in Ireland, where the police force was highly unpopular.

The peelers were only one objection that the Irish had to British rule. They struggled to gain independence from Great Britain for many years, and in 1922, most of Ireland finally did gain its freedom.

the one train with the judges I came.

Sergeant. Well, if you came so far, you may as well go farther, for you'll walk out of this.

Man. I will, I will; I'll just go on where I was going. (*goes toward steps*)

Sergeant. Come back from those steps; no one has leave to pass down them tonight.

Man. I'll just sit on the top of the steps till I see will some sailor buy a ballad off me that would give me my supper. They do be late going back to the ship. It's often I saw them in Cork carried down the quay in a handcart.

Sergeant. Move on, I tell you. I won't have anyone lingering about the quay tonight.

Man. Well, I'll go. It's the poor have the hard life! Maybe yourself might like one, Sergeant. Here's a good sheet now. (*turns one over*) "Content and a pipe"—that's not much. "The Peeler[5] and the Goat"—you wouldn't like that. "Johnny Hart"—that's a lovely song.

Sergeant. Move on.

Man. Ah, wait till you hear it. (*sings*)

There was a rich farmer's daughter lived near the town of Ross;
She courted a Highland soldier, his name was Johnny Hart;
Says the mother to her daughter, "I'll go distracted mad
If you marry that Highland soldier[6] dressed up in Highland plaid."

Sergeant. Stop that noise. (Man *wraps up his ballads and shuffles toward the steps.*)

Sergeant. Where are you going?

Man. Sure you told me to be going, and I am going.

Sergeant. Don't be a fool. I didn't tell you to go that way; I told you to go back to the town.

Man. Back to the town, is it?

Sergeant (*taking him by the shoulder and shoving him before him*). Here, I'll show you the way. Be off with you. What are you stopping for?

Man (*who has been keeping his eye on the notice, points to it*). I think I know what you're waiting for, Sergeant.

Sergeant. What's that to you?

Man. And I know well the man you're waiting for—I know him well—I'll be going. (*He shuffles on.*)

Sergeant. You know him? Come back here. What sort is he?

Man. Come back is it, Sergeant? Do you want to have me killed?

Sergeant. Why do you say that?

Man. Never mind. I'm going. I wouldn't be in your shoes if the reward was ten times as much. (*goes on offstage to left*) Not if it was ten times as much.

Sergeant (*rushing after him*). Come back here, come back. (*drags him back*) What sort is he? Where did you see him?

Man. I saw him in my own place, in the County Clare. I tell you you wouldn't like to be looking at him. You'd be afraid to be in the one place with him. There isn't a weapon he doesn't know the use of, and as to strength, his muscles are as hard as that board. (*slaps barrel*)

Sergeant. Is he as bad as that?

Man. He is then.

Sergeant. Do you tell me so?

2 **Man.** There was a poor man in our place, a sergeant from Ballyvaughan.[7]—It was with a lump of stone he did it.

Sergeant. I never heard of that.

Man. And you wouldn't, Sergeant. It's not everything that happens gets into the papers. And

5. **Peeler:** policeman (from the name of the British politician Robert Peel, who established the Irish constabulary in the early 1800s).

6. **If you marry that Highland soldier:** Scottish soldiers were hated by the Irish because of Scotland's close ties to England.

7. **Ballyvaughan** (băl′ē-vôn′).

Customizing Instruction

Less Proficient Readers

Set a Purpose Have students recall scenes in television programs and movies in which the police are searching for a particular criminal or suspect. Then have students read to discover for whom the police are searching.

Students Acquiring English

1 Although students will probably be able to determine the meaning of *stop* in this context, explain that the use of this word to mean "stay" or "remain" is uncommon in American English.

Less Proficient Readers

2 Ask students what they think happened to the sergeant from Ballyvaughn.

Possible Response: He was hit and probably killed with a stone.

Who did this to the sergeant?

Answer: the fugitive.

Multicultural Link: National Theater

Lady Gregory helped to found Dublin's Abbey Theatre in 1904. Over the centuries, many societies have supported theaters that preserved cultural traditions. A famous example is the Noh theater of Japan, developed in the 14th century. *Noh* means "talent" or "ability" in Japanese, and Noh theater blends many talents and abilities, including music, dance, poetry, costume and set design, and acting. Performances are highly stylized, with masked actors (traditionally male) reciting and singing lines of verse that tell stories of patriotism, warfare, romance, obsession, or religious faith. The form influenced later Japanese drama, such as puppet theater and kabuki, as well as Western modernists of the 20th century, especially the American poet Ezra Pound and Lady Gregory's Abbey Theatre colleague, William Butler Yeats.

Reading and Analyzing

Literary Analysis SUSPENSE

A Ask students what effect the man's speech about the fugitive's possible movements has on the sergeant.
Possible Responses: It frightens him; it creates more uncertainty about what will happen.
Then ask students why they think the man is doing this.
Possible Responses: He is sincerely concerned about the sergeant; he sympathizes with the rebel.

Reading Skills and Strategies: MAKING INFERENCES

B Ask students why the man insists that the sergeant watch the quay while the man lights his pipe.
Possible Responses: The man doesn't want the sergeant to get a clear view of him; the man fears the sergeant would recognize him; the man is the fugitive.

Literary Analysis: CHARACTER

C Ask students what the sergeant's correcting the lyrics of the man's song tells them about the sergeant.
Possible Response: This suggests that the sergeant had an anti-British upbringing or sympathies.
Then ask why the man might have deliberately omitted the line.
Possible Responses: to test the sergeant; to find out if the sergeant knew the words.

---

there was a policeman in plain clothes, too . . .
1 It is in Limerick he was. . . . It was after the time of the attack on the police barrack at Kilmallock. . . . Moonlight . . . just like this . . . waterside. . . . Nothing was known for certain.

Sergeant. Do you say so? It's a terrible county to belong to.

Man. That's so, indeed! You might be standing there, looking out that way, thinking you saw him coming up this side of the quay (*points*),
A and he might be coming up this other side (*points*), and he'd be on you before you knew where you were.

Sergeant. It's a whole troop of police they ought to put here to stop a man like that.

Man. But if you'd like me to stop with you, I could be looking down this side. I could be sitting up here on this barrel.

Sergeant. And you know him well, too?

Man. I'd know him a mile off, Sergeant.

Sergeant. But you wouldn't want to share the reward?

Man. Is it a poor man like me, that has to be going the roads and singing in fairs, to have the name on him that he took a reward? But you don't want me. I'll be safer in the town.

Sergeant. Well, you can stop.

Man (*getting up on barrel*). All right, Sergeant. I wonder, now, you're not tired out, Sergeant, walking up and down the way you are.

Sergeant. If I'm tired I'm used to it.

Man. You might have hard work before you tonight yet. Take it easy while you can. There's plenty of room up here on the barrel, and you see farther when you're higher up.

Sergeant. Maybe so. (*Gets up beside him on barrel, facing right. They sit back to back, looking different ways.*) You made me feel a bit queer with the way you talked.

Man. Give me a match, Sergeant (*He gives it and* Man *lights pipe.*); take a draw yourself? It'll quiet you. Wait now till I give you a light, but you needn't turn round. Don't take your eye off B
the quay for the life of you.

Sergeant. Never fear, I won't. (*Lights pipe. They both smoke.*) Indeed it's a hard thing to be in the force, out at night and no thanks for it, for all the danger we're in. And it's little we get but abuse from the people, and no choice but to obey our orders, and never asked when a man is sent into danger, if you are a married man with a family.

Man (*sings*).

As through the hills I walked to view the hills 2
and shamrock plain,
I stood awhile where nature smiles to view the
rocks and streams,
On a matron fair I fixed my eyes beneath a
fertile vale,
As she sang her song it was on the wrong of
poor old Granuaile.

Sergeant. Stop that; that's no song to be singing in these times.[8]

Man. Ah, Sergeant, I was only singing to keep my heart up. It sinks when I think of him. To think of us two sitting here, and he creeping up the quay, maybe, to get to us.

Sergeant. Are you keeping a good lookout?

Man. I am; and for no reward too. Amn't I the foolish man? But when I saw a man in trouble, I never could help trying to get him out of it. What's that? Did something hit me? (*rubs his heart*)

Sergeant (*patting him on the shoulder*). You will get your reward in heaven.

Man. I know that. I know that, Sergeant, but life is precious.

Sergeant. Well, you can sing if it gives you more courage.

8. **that's no song . . . these times:** "Granuaile" is an anti-British revolutionary anthem.

Teaching Options

Vocabulary Strategy

DIALECT

Instruction To help students see how context can help them understand words from an unfamiliar dialect of English, write the following sentences on the board:
He leaned the ladder against the house.
She was self-conscious about the ladder in her stockings.
Even though most students are probably unaware of the British use of "ladder" to mean "run" or "snag," students will quickly infer this meaning from the context of the second sentence. Explain that dialects can vary in vocabulary, pronunciation, usage, and word order.

Activity Have students form groups of four or five, and assign each group one page of the play to examine. Students can identify dialect differences in vocabulary and usage, determine the meaning of each unfamiliar word or usage by using context clues, and list the context clues that enabled them to decipher each meaning. Have groups share their results with the class.

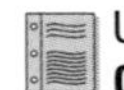
Use **Vocabulary Transparencies and Copymasters,** p. 51.

Man (*sings*).

Her head was bare, her hands and feet with iron bands were bound,
Her pensive[9] strain and plaintive[10] wail mingles with the evening gale,
And the song she sang with mournful air, I am old Granuaile.
Her lips so sweet that monarchs kissed . . .

Sergeant. That's not it. . . . "Her gown she wore
C was stained with gore." . . . That's it—you missed that.

Man. You're right, Sergeant, so it is; I missed it. (*repeats line*) But to think of a man like you knowing a song like that.[11]

Sergeant. There's many a thing a man might know and might not have any wish for.

Man. Now, I daresay, Sergeant, in your youth, you used to be sitting up on a wall, the way you are
3 sitting up on this barrel now, and the other lads beside you, and you singing "Granuaile"? . . .

Sergeant. I did then.

Man. And the "Shan Bhean Bhocht"?[12] . . .

Sergeant. I did then.

Man. And the "Green on the Cape"?

Sergeant. That was one of them.

Man. And maybe the man you are watching for tonight used to be sitting on the wall, when he was young, and singing those same songs. . . . It's a queer world.

4 **Sergeant.** Whisht! . . . I think I see something coming. . . . It's only a dog.

Man. And isn't it a queer world? . . . Maybe it's one of the boys you used to be singing with that time you will be arresting today or tomorrow, and sending into the dock.[13]

Sergeant. That's true indeed.

Man. And maybe one night, after you had been singing, if the other boys had told you some plan they had, some plan to free the country, you might have joined with them . . . and maybe it is you might be in trouble now.

Sergeant. Well, who knows but I might? I had a great spirit in those days.

Man. It's a queer world, Sergeant, and it's little any mother knows when she sees her child creeping on the floor what might happen to it before it has gone through its life, or who will be who in the end.

Sergeant. That's a queer thought now, and a true thought. Wait now till I think it out. . . . If it wasn't for the sense I have, and for my wife and family, and for me joining the force the time I did, it might be myself now would be after breaking jail and hiding in the dark, and it might be him that's hiding in the dark and that got out of jail would be sitting up where I am on this barrel. . . . And it might be myself would be creeping up trying to make my escape from himself, and it might be himself would be keeping the law, and myself would be breaking it, and myself would be trying maybe to put a bullet in his head, or to take up a lump of a stone the way you said he did . . . no, that myself did. . . . Oh! (*gasps; after a pause*) What's that? (*grasps* Man's *arm*)

Man (*jumps off barrel and listens, looking out over water*). It's nothing, Sergeant.

Sergeant. I thought it might be a boat. I had a notion there might be friends of his coming about the quays with a boat.

Man. Sergeant, I am thinking it was with the people you were, and not with the law you were, when you were a young man.

---

9. **pensive:** thoughtful in a serious or sad way.
10. **plaintive:** mournful; melancholy.
11. **to think of . . . song like that:** Since the sergeant is a police officer, paid to uphold British laws, the man is surprised that he is familiar with an anti-British song.
12. **"Shan Bhean Bhocht"** (shăn′ văn′ vôKHt′): a revolutionary song from the 1798 rebellion. Its title (meaning "the poor old woman"), like that of "Granuaile," is a reference to Ireland.
13. **dock:** the place where the accused person stands in a criminal court.

Customizing Instruction

Students Acquiring English

1 Explain that many dialects of English spoken in Ireland use grammatical structures drawn from Gaelic, Ireland's native Celtic language. The British ban on the use of Gaelic almost wiped out the language in the late 19th century. Point out a sentence such as "It is in Limerick he was," and ask students to rephrase it in American English.

Possible Response: He was in Limerick.

Gifted and Talented

2 Have students investigate the origin of the verse form known as a "limerick." They can report to the class as a whole on the structure of a limerick and how and why the form is connected to the town of Limerick, Ireland. You might have students write original limericks as well.

Less Proficient Readers

3 Have students state what the sergeant reveals about his youth.

Possible Response: He used to know and sing the rebel ballads, and he considered joining the rebels in trying to free Ireland from British rule.

Students Acquiring English

4 Help students determine the meaning of *whisht* in "Whisht! . . . I think I see something coming . . . ." Have them visualize the immediate situation so they understand that the sergeant is telling the man to be quiet or be still so that he can better see and hear the approaching figure.

Speaking and Listening

DRAMATIC PERFORMANCE

Instruction Once students have investigated some of the dialect differences between the language in the play and standard American English, have them prepare a performance of one section of the play. Select one group of students to perform a section as it is written, with efforts to reproduce the Irish dialect as well as possible. Select a second group to rewrite, and then perform, the play in standard American English, substituting American vocabulary, usage, and pronunciation for Irish idioms.

Prepare Appropriate sections to assign might include pages 996–997; page 998, from the sergeant's comment, "Never fear, I won't" to page 999, when the man says, "Sergeant, I am thinking it was with the people you were . . ."; or pages 1000–1001.

Present Have students who are not performing act as drama critics, evaluating not only the performances but also the "translation" into American English.

BLOCK SCHEDULING This activity is particularly well-suited for longer class periods.

THE RISING OF THE MOON 999

Reading and Analyzing

Literary Analysis SUSPENSE

A Ask students how the arrival of the boat increases the tension.

Possible Response: The audience knows something important is about to happen but does not know what either the sergeant or the balladeer will do.

Reading Skills and Strategies: CLARIFYING

B Make sure students understand that the whistler from below answers the ragged man by whistling the same tune. Then ask them why this song is an appropriate signal.

Possible Responses: The song is about Irish rebels; it uses the words "signal" and "whistle."

Reading Skills and Strategies: MAKING INFERENCES

Why does the man put his hand to his breast?

Possible Response: He had hoped to persuade the sergeant through dialogue, but now he's reaching for his gun.

Active Reading ANALYZING DIALECT

When students have finished reading, have them discuss the effect of the dialect on their understanding of the play. Did the dialect enhance the setting? Did it help them relate to the characters? Or, did they find it distracting and difficult to read? Have students make a list of the pros and cons of using dialect in a play.

Captain Ned Bishop with Officers on the Bridge of the SS Eagle (1969), David Blackwood. Original etching.

Sergeant. Well, if I was foolish then, that time's gone.

Man. Maybe, Sergeant, it comes into your head sometimes, in spite of your belt and your tunic, that it might have been as well for you to have followed Granuaile.

Sergeant. It's no business of yours what I think.

Man. Maybe, Sergeant, you'll be on the side of the country yet.

Sergeant (*gets off barrel*). Don't talk to me like that. I have my duties and I know them. (*looks round*) That was a boat; I hear the oars. (*goes to the steps and looks down*) **A**

Man (*sings*).

Oh then tell me, Shawn O'Farrell,
Where the gathering is to be.
In the old spot by the river
Right well known to you and me!

Sergeant. Stop that! Stop that, I tell you!

Man (*sings louder*).

One word more, for signal token,
Whistle up the marching tune,
With your pike upon your shoulder,
At the Rising of the Moon.

Sergeant. If you don't stop that, I'll arrest you. (*A whistle from below answers, repeating the air.*) **B**

Sergeant. That's a signal. (*stands between him and steps*) You must not pass this way. . . . Step farther back. . . . Who are you? You are no ballad singer.

Man. You needn't ask who I am; that placard will tell you. (*points to placard*)

Sergeant. You are the man I am looking for.

Man (*takes off hat and wig.* Sergeant *seizes them*). I am. There's a hundred pounds on my head. There is a friend of mine below in a boat. He knows a safe place to bring me to.

Sergeant (*looking still at hat and wig*). It's a pity!

Teaching Options

Viewing and Representing

Captain Ned Bishop with Officers on the Bridge of the SS Eagle
by David Blackwood

ART APPRECIATION

Instruction This color lithograph is by a contemporary printmaker. Lithography is a process in which a flat metal surface is treated so that portions forming an image retain ink while the rest of the surface repels it. The image can then be reproduced over and over.

Application What mood does the lithograph convey? Is it consistent with the mood established in the play? Why or why not?

Possible Response: The deep shadows of the lithograph give it a somber mood. This agrees with the mood of the play, which deals with the serious subjects of loyalty and betrayal.

It's a pity. You deceived me. You deceived me well.

Man. I am a friend of Granuaile. There is a hundred pounds on my head.

Sergeant. It's a pity, it's a pity!

Man. Will you let me pass, or must I make you let me?

Sergeant. I am in the force. I will not let you pass.

Man. I thought to do it with my tongue. (*puts hand in breast*) What is that?

(*Voice of* Policeman X *outside*) Here, this is where we left him.

Sergeant. It's my comrades coming.

Man. You won't betray me . . . the friend of Granuaile. (*slips behind barrel*)

(*Voice of* Policeman B) That was the last of the placards.

Policeman X (*as they come in*). If he makes his escape it won't be unknown he'll make it. (Sergeant *puts hat and wig behind his back.*)

Policeman B. Did anyone come this way?

Sergeant (*after a pause*). No one.

Policeman B. No one at all?

Sergeant. No one at all.

Policeman B. We had no orders to go back to the station; we can stop along with you.

Sergeant. I don't want you. There is nothing for you to do here.

Policeman B. You bade us to come back here and keep watch with you.

Sergeant. I'd sooner be alone. Would any man come this way and you making all that talk? It is better the place to be quiet.

Policeman B. Well, we'll leave you the lantern anyhow. (*hands it to him*)

Sergeant. I don't want it. Bring it with you.

Policeman B. You might want it. There are clouds coming up and you have the darkness of the night before you yet. I'll leave it over here on the barrel. (*goes to barrel*)

Sergeant. Bring it with you I tell you. No more talk.

Policeman B. Well, I thought it might be a comfort to you. I often think when I have it in my hand and can be flashing it about into every dark corner (*doing so*) that it's the same as being beside the fire at home, and the bits of bogwood blazing up now and again. (*flashes it about, now on the barrel, now on* Sergeant)

Sergeant (*furious*). Be off the two of you, yourselves and your lantern! (*They go out.* Man *comes from behind barrel. He and* Sergeant *stand looking at one another.*)

Sergeant. What are you waiting for?

Man. For my hat, of course, and my wig. You wouldn't wish me to get my death of cold? (Sergeant *gives them.*)

Man (*going toward steps*). Well, good night, comrade, and thank you. You did me a good turn tonight, and I'm obliged to you. Maybe I'll be able to do as much for you when the small rise up and the big fall down . . . when we all change places at the Rising (*waves his hand and disappears*) of the Moon.

Sergeant (*turning his back to audience and reading placard*). A hundred pounds reward! A hundred pounds! (*turns toward audience*) I wonder, now, am I as great a fool as I think I am?

Customizing Instruction

Less Proficient Readers

Use the following questions to help students understand the play:

- What happens after the boat arrives?
  Answer: A signal comes from the boat. The balladeer signals back and reveals to the sergeant that he is the fugitive. The sergeant lets the fugitive escape.
- Why does the sergeant let the man escape?
  Possible Responses: He has much in common with fugitive; as an Irishman, he sympathizes with the cause of Irish independence.

Multiple Learning Styles

Visual Learners

Have students prepare a three-column chart to help them analyze the sergeant's conflicting loyalties. In the first column, have students list the reasons he has for turning in the man; in the second, have them list the reasons he has for letting the man escape. Have students use the third column to record their opinions about the validity of the reasons.

Multiple Learning Styles

Auditory Learners

Encourage students to listen to recordings of Irish ballads. "The Rising of the Moon" is on the Clancy Brothers and Tommy Makem's CDs *Ain't It Grand Boys* and *Irish Songs of Rebellion; "Granuaile,"* spelled "Gran Waile" is on the Wolfe Tones' cassette, *Irish to the Core.*

 **Assessment**

Standardized Test Practice

CHOOSING THE BEST SUMMARY For some standardized tests, students will be asked to choose the best summary of a passage. To provide students with some help in choosing the best summary, read aloud or write on the chalkboard the following question.

Which of the following statements best summarizes the conversation between the sergeant and the balladeer before the arrival of the boat?

A. The balladeer sings songs that reveal his loyalties to the Irish cause.

B. The balladeer admits that he knows the fugitive and describes the fugitive's actions.

C. The sergeant admits his knowledge of the balladeer's songs and that he too once felt loyalty to the Irish cause.

Lead students through the process of choosing the best summary. Consider each choice. Point out that, while all the statements contain accurate information about the story, the best summary should include the most important information. For that reason, **C** is the best choice.

GUIDING STUDENT RESPONSE

Connect to the Literature

1. What Do You Think?
Guidelines for student response: You might have students compare their lists of words and phrases to see if there were certain common reactions to the play.

Comprehension Check
- an escaped Irish rebel
- the escaped rebel

Use Selection Quiz in **Unit Six Resource Book,** p. 9.

Think Critically

2. Possible Responses: Yes, because the man is fighting for Irish freedom; no, because the sergeant's job is to uphold the law; no, because the sergeant's family needs the money, and he will be in trouble if anyone finds out he let the man escape.
3. Possible Responses: The best strategy is helping the sergeant see that he himself could have become a freedom fighter; the best strategy is appealing to the sergeant's love of Ireland.
4. Possible Responses: the "ragged man" for his courage and dedication to his cause; the sergeant for his compassion, ability to change, and courage in risking punishment.
5. Possible Responses: The writer uses dialect to give an accurate picture of the Irish people of the time; she uses dialect to show the author's connection to and feelings for Irish heritage.
6. Possible responses should include some understanding and interpretation of the historical context. Her purpose was to show the divided loyalties of the Irish people; to stress the comradeship and shared experience of all the Irish; to inspire all Irish to support the cause of freedom; to show that one's heritage and upbringing often outweigh professional responsibilities.

Literary Analysis

Paired Activity Make up a composite chart on the chalkboard based on the charts produced by the pairs of students.

Connect to the Literature

1. **What Do You Think?** Jot down words and phrases that describe your reaction to this play.

Comprehension Check
- Who are the policemen looking for?
- Who does the singer reveal himself to be?

Think Critically

2. Do you think the sergeant does the right thing by allowing the man to escape?

- Policeman X's statement that "the people" might give them "nothing but abuse" if they catch the man
- what the reward might do for the sergeant's family
- the sergeant's duty to enforce the law

3. Think about the different strategies the man uses to persuade the sergeant to let him go. Which do you think works best?

- the man's stories about the dangerousness of the escapee
- the songs he sings
- how he compares the sergeant to himself

4. Which of the two characters do you admire more? Give reasons for your answer.

5. **ACTIVE READING** ANALYZING DIALECT Look back at the examples of dialect you noted in your READER'S NOTEBOOK. Why do you think the writer uses dialect in this play? Explain your answer.

6. What would you say was Lady Gregory's **purpose** in writing this play?

Extend Interpretations

7. **What If?** Imagine that Policeman B discovers the revolutionary's disguise and hiding place. How do you think the play might end if this were so?

8. **Connect to Life** The sergeant breaks the law by letting the man escape. What are your feelings about breaking the law for the sake of a cause?

Literary Analysis

SUSPENSE **Suspense**—the tension or excitement readers feel as they are drawn into a story—is created when a writer purposely leaves readers uncertain or apprehensive about what will happen. Writers rely on suspense to entertain their audiences and to hold the audiences' interest. Lady Gregory uses suspense-building techniques such as the interactions between the sergeant and the unidentified man, unexpected sounds and actions, and the songs the man sings.

Paired Activity With a partner, make a chart like the one shown below. Look through the play for other statements and events that add to the suspense. Then for each one, note why the statement or event is suspenseful.

Statement/Event	Why Statement/Event Is Suspenseful
The man sings "Granuaile."	The man's singing of outlawed ballads makes us wonder about his identity.

Extend Interpretations

What If? Encourage students to discuss whether Policeman B would be sympathetic to the fugitive's cause or if his desire for the reward money would determine his actions.

Connect to Life Accept all reasonable, well-supported responses. You might discuss this question in terms of an episode in American history, such as the civil-rights movement, or in European history, such as those Germans who broke the law to help Jews escape Hitler's murderous tyranny.

Choices & CHALLENGES

Writing Options

1. **Dramatic Scene** Write a scene in which the sergeant tells his wife about his encounter with the man. Try to convey his concern for his family as well as for the nationalist cause. Place the scene in your **Working Portfolio.**

2. **Story Outline** What might the future hold for the two main characters? Will the sergeant's life go on as usual? Will the man stay out of trouble? Write an outline of a short story that explains what happens to each man in the weeks following their encounter.

3. **Political Ballad** Write an original ballad that tells the story of the sergeant and the rebel.

Activities & Explorations

1. **Classroom Debate** Stage a debate in which you present arguments about whether the sergeant was right or wrong to let the man get away. ~ **SPEAKING AND LISTENING**

2. **First Night Poster** *The Rising of the Moon* opened in 1907 at the Abbey Theatre in Dublin. Create an advertising poster for the play. Draw an appropriate picture and write an attention-getting caption. ~ **VIEWING AND REPRESENTING**

Inquiry & Research

A Divided Nation Although much of Ireland gained independence in 1922, organizations such as Sinn Fein and the Irish Republican Army have continued to fight for the independence of Northern Ireland, which is still part of the United Kingdom. Research the recent activities of these groups and the current status of English-Irish relations. Share your findings with the class.

Lady Isabella Augusta Gregory
1852–1932

Other Works
Spreading the News
The Workhouse Ward

Late Starter The pastoral life of a titled Irish gentlewoman seems far removed from Isabella Gregory's eventual achievements as a dramatist, Irish partisan, and "godmother" of Dublin's Abbey Theatre. Lady Gregory did not take an active interest in literature until after the death of her husband in 1892. When her son told her that he wanted to learn to speak with the people who lived on their estate, she began to study Gaelic (gā′lĭk), the language of the Celtic people of Ireland, and became fascinated with Gaelic myths, legends, and folk tales.

Irish Literary Revival Her interest in Irish traditions led her to a close friendship with William Butler Yeats, Ireland's foremost poet. The two became leading figures in the Irish Literary Revival, which sought to preserve and renew the country's cultural traditions. It was her son whom Yeats commemorated in his poem "An Irish Airman Foresees His Death" (page 1107). Together, Lady Gregory and Yeats helped found the Abbey Theatre expressly for the purpose of staging works such as *The Rising of the Moon*. The theater provided a forum for works celebrating the speech, history, and spirit of the Irish people.

Prolific Career After writing her first play at the age of 52, Lady Gregory went on to write or translate 40 more plays. She also published three collections of Irish oral histories and legends, based on what she called her "imperfect, stumbling" knowledge of Gaelic. These efforts to bring Irish tales and legends to English-speaking readers met with high critical acclaim when they were published and are still highly regarded today.

Author Activity

Abbey Theatre Find out more about Lady Gregory's involvement with the Abbey Theatre. Share your findings with your classmates.

Grammar

Verbs: Simple vs. Perfect Tenses
Instruction The tense of a verb shows the time of the action. The three simple tenses are present, past, and future. The three perfect tenses are present perfect, past perfect, and future perfect. These three perfect tenses use different forms of the auxiliary verb *to have* before the past participle of a verb.
Activity Write the chart on the chalkboard.

Present
I *see* him.

Present Perfect
I *have seen* him.

Past
I *saw* him.

Past Perfect
I *had seen* him when you arrived.

Future
I *will see* him.

Future Perfect
I *will have seen* him when you arrive.

Have students identify the tenses of the underlined verbs in the following sentence.

The wanted man masqueraded as a ballad singer. *(past)*

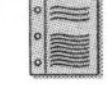

Use **Grammar Transparencies and Copymasters,** p. 72.

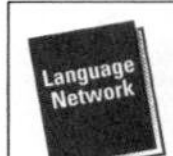

Use McDougal Littell's ***Language Network*** for more instruction and practice in verbs.

Writing Options

1. **Dramatic Scene** You might make this a cooperative activity in which two students write a scene and then perform it for classmates.
2. **Story Outline** Have interested students write stories from their outlines and share them with the class.
3. **Political Ballad** Before students begin writing, you might review the characteristics of the ballad form as explained in the Literary Terms section in the back of this textbook and in the lessons on Old English ballads on pages 192–199.

Activities & Explorations

1. **Classroom Debate** Although you may not want to require formal debate procedure, outline certain requirements for students. Have them make an opening statement, followed by rebuttal, followed by response. Encourage them to support their point of view with well-explained reasons and examples rather than with emotional appeals.
2. **First Night Poster** Interested students can research the original production to learn the opening date (March 9, 1907) or other details to include on their posters.

Inquiry & Research

A Divided Nation Students should use print and electronic resources to research recent activities in Northern Ireland. This could be an ideal project for using the Internet. Students could search using key words mentioned in the activity.

Author Activity

Abbey Theatre Lady Gregory helped to back the Abbey Theatre financially. Her plays were among the most popular in the first years of the theater. In addition, she often helped settle disputes among her fiery-tempered colleagues at the Abbey.

LEARNING the Language of LITERATURE

OVERVIEW

Objectives
- understand the following literary terms:
  - Verbal irony
  - Situational irony
  - Dramatic irony
- appreciate shared characteristics of literature across cultures
- recognize themes across cultures

Teaching the Lesson

Students will be reading short stories written approximately a century ago. This lesson will give them some background on irony in modern literature.

Introducing the Concepts
Ask students to identify stories, television shows, or movies that contain irony and have them discuss the purpose of irony in these examples. As students read the short stories in this unit, have them consider the following questions:

What concerns and values do the characters in the stories share with people today?
Possible Responses: the desire for money and possessions; the desire to impress others

What did you find ironic in each of the stories?
Possible Responses: "The Rocking-Horse Winner": Paul kills himself in the pursuit of luck; "Araby": the narrator makes a great effort to go to the bazaar but arrives too late to buy anything

As they finish reading the short stories, students can write reactions to these questions and keep their responses in their Working Portfolios.

Presenting the Concepts
Read through the strategies aloud or project them on a transparency. Using the definitions of the types of irony on page 1004, ask students to give examples of each type of irony from stories, movies, television, or real life. Model how to use the strategies to analyze students' examples.

LEARNING the Language of Literature

Irony in Modern Literature

Unsinkable Irony

To think about irony, let's consider the *Titanic* at three points in history: first, in 1912 when the magnificent ship went down in the North Atlantic and 1,500 lives were tragically lost; second, in 1986 with the exciting discovery of the *Titanic's* wreckage; and third, in 1997 with the release of the blockbuster movie *Titanic,* the largest-grossing motion picture to date. The ghost of irony continues to haunt the great ship in several respects. It is ironic that the largest, strongest ship ever built would be brought down by an iceberg—and on its maiden voyage. It is also ironic that this tragedy at the beginning of the century would become, by the end of the century, a source of popular entertainment and titanic sums of money. Such is the nature of modern irony.

As with irony, there is more to an iceberg than what appears on the surface.

Irony as a Literary Technique

Irony in literature works very much like irony in everyday life. Simply put, irony is the contrast, often great, between expectation or appearance and reality. Generally, irony in literature is classified in three ways:

Verbal irony occurs when a writer says one thing but means another. Jonathan Swift's title for his satiric essay, "A Modest Proposal" (p. 611), is an example.

Situational irony occurs when a character or the reader expects one thing to happen but something entirely different happens. In Mary Coleridge's story, "The King Is Dead, Long Live the King" (p. 888), the king discovers the opposite of what he and the reader expect: his trusted friends and his wife are hypocrites and his enemy is a friend.

Dramatic irony is the difference between what a character knows and what the reader or audience knows. This type of irony is commonly used in drama: think of Duncan's expression of trust in Macbeth, just after the audience has heard Macbeth's desire to murder him. Dramatic irony also occurs in fiction when a character has a limited view of the events (or no view at all), but the reader is fully aware of what is going on.

A Short History of Irony

Irony has been present in European literature since ancient times. You can find examples of verbal, situational, and dramatic irony in Homer's *Odyssey,* the great Greek dramas, *Beowulf,* and the Old Testament. But ironically, the concept was not really named until the 18th century. The great 18th-century satirists primarily defined irony as a figure of speech: "saying the opposite of what you mean." You can see how Swift relies primarily on verbal irony in his satire.

At the end of the 18th century and the beginning of the 19th century, the concept of irony began to take on new meaning. This shift was consistent with the philosophical shift in worldview from the Enlightenment to the Romantic Age. The former meaning of irony as primarily verbal (an intentional manipulation of language) now took on the added idea that irony is something that happens in life (something unintentional but real). For example, in the 18th century, Swift used verbal irony in "A Modest Proposal" to ridicule British policy in Ireland. In the 19th century, Shelley used situational irony in "Ozymandias" (p. 781) to expose the vanity of tyrants by contrasting the "colossal wreck" of the ruler's statue with its arrogant inscription—"Look on my works, ye Mighty, and despair!"

Modern Irony: Less Is More

Over the last century, irony has again undergone a transformation in meaning. For modernist writers—W. B. Yeats, T. S. Eliot, D. H. Lawrence, James Joyce, Virginia Woolf, and others—irony became something larger than a literary technique; it became an attitude infusing the whole of a novel, a story, a poem, or a play.

This new ironic attitude of the modernists is seen as detached and questioning. Its source was the uncertainty that many felt at the core of modern life. Modernists refused to assume an all-knowing attitude. Instead, they aimed for complete objectivity in presenting ideas without commenting on meaning. Modernists regarded such restraint as an appropriate response to the complexities of modern life.

YOUR TURN With a couple of classmates, brainstorm ironic situations that you've encountered in your daily life.

A Study in Contrasts: Shelley and Yeats

Percy Bysshe Shelley

Readers of Shelley's "Ozymandias" understand the irony because of the clear contrast between Ozymandias's arrogant expectation and the inevitability of what actually happens. Shelley, like Swift before him, speaks with the authority of righteousness on his side, and readers agree that Ozymandias gets what he deserves. The irony in W. B. Yeats's "Sailing to Byzantium" is not so easily grasped. The poet's certainty is gone. In one way, the old man in Yeats's poem is similar to Ozymandias in his desire for "unaging" monuments. Yet, the old man is not a tyrannical king but a "tattered coat upon a stick." The reader tends to sympathize with him because he is lost and defeated by the reality around him. The contrast is not so much between expectation and reality, but between different aspects of reality—the living (and therefore "dying") generations of humanity and the monuments of the past (art, religion, and history).

William Butler Yeats

Notice that Yeats's irony is much more paradoxical, or contradictory, and less emotionally satisfying than Shelley's. In much of Yeats's poetry and the modernist literature that follows in this unit, irony is not just something that occasionally happens; it has become the nature of reality itself.

Strategies for Reading: Irony in Modern Literature

1. Be alert to anything in a work that seems contradictory or inconsistent with your expectations.
2. Keep the date of the work in mind. Consider how the early decades of the 20th century, with World War I and technological changes, may have shaped the views of a modern writer.
3. Draw conclusions about the type of irony that is used. Is the irony obvious so that you can point it out, or is the irony more subtle and a matter of tone and atmosphere?
4. Question what is actually the object of the writer's concern. Is the writer mocking or sympathetic to one attitude or behavior? Or, does he or she seem to be looking at things from multiple perspectives?
5. **Monitor** your reading strategies and modify them when your understanding breaks down. Remember to use your Strategies for Active Reading: **predict, visualize, connect, question, clarify,** and **evaluate.**

Making Connections

Irony Across Cultures

Originally, irony referred to a figure of speech. However, the German literary critic Friedrich Schlegel (1772–1829) changed the meaning of irony when he used it to describe the mood of works by Boccaccio, Cervantes, Sterne, and Goethe. Schlegel's usage was accepted, and today many books and stories are written from an ironic point of view. Share with students the following information about masters of irony.

Spain

The tradition of irony in Spain began early (at the end of the 16th century) with Cervantes's (1547–1616) famous parody of chivalry, *Don Quixote.* In this novel, the insane Don Quixote believes that he is a great knight on a romantic quest. In the modern era, Jacinto Benavente y Martínez, known for his sparkling dialogue, wrote plays that satirized Madrid society and political corruption, among other topics.

Russia

Russia's most famous ironist was Nikolai Gogol (1809–1852). His novel *Dead Souls,* published in 1842, concerns a nobleman with an extraordinary plan to make his fortune. This plan involves buying dead serfs, or "souls," and pawning them to raise money. This novel satirizes both the institution of serfdom and the bureaucracy of feudal Russia.

France

Eugène Ionesco (1912–1994) was a French playwright and a founder of the Theater of the Absurd. His farcical plays confront audiences with the emptiness of modern life. Two of his famous early plays, *La Cantatrice Chauve (The Bald Singer)* and *La Leçon (The Lesson),* portray this human emptiness.

OVERVIEW

This selection is included in the **Grade 12 InterActive Reader.**

Objectives

1. understand and appreciate a **short story (Literary Analysis)**
2. appreciate the author's use of **foreshadowing in fiction (Literary Analysis)**
3. **draw conclusions** about "The Rocking-Horse Winner" **(Active Reading)**

Summary

Paul's parents live beyond their means. His mother blames their troubles on bad luck—especially the father's. Anxiety about money is so rampant that Paul can even hear the house whispering, "There must be more money." Deeply disturbed, he feverishly rides his rocking horse, hoping to go where luck is. His rides reveal to him the names of winning racehorses. He shares these with the gardener, Bassett, and his uncle Oscar, who bets on the winners and funnels the money to Paul's mother. Despite these winnings, the house grows even more anxious. A lull in his luck makes Paul frantic, and one night his mother finds him riding the rocking horse in a frenzy, screaming a horse's name. Oscar bets a huge sum on the horse, winning a fortune for Paul's mother—but the strain of this last ride (revelation) costs Paul his life.

Thematic Link

Told somewhat in the manner of a fairy tale, this story presents a **new image of reality** in order to probe the psychological issues that are indispensable to a full understanding of Paul's homelife.

Use **Unit Six Resource Book,** p. 10 for additional support.

5-Minute Warm-Up

Daily Language SkillBuilder

Have students **proofread** the display sentences on page 979i and write them correctly. The sentences also appear on Transparency 27 of **Grammar Transparencies and Copymasters.**

PREPARING to *Read*

The Rocking-Horse Winner

Short Story by D. H. LAWRENCE

Connect to Your Life

Best of Luck What do you think of when you hear the word *luck?* Are good luck and bad luck always what they appear to be? With a group of classmates, discuss your thoughts about luck, sharing any notable examples of good luck or bad luck you can think of.

Build Background

Horseracing In England, where this story is set, horseracing dates back more than 800 years. Two of the five great annual horseraces in England are the St. Leger Stakes and the Derby. Other notable English races mentioned in this story are the Grand National, the Ascot Gold Cup, and the Lincolnshire.

Large sums of money are bet on horseraces. The amount a bettor can win depends on the odds. The odds on each horse are expressed as a ratio—3 to 1, for example—and are determined by what proportion of the total amount bet on the race is bet on that horse. The more money bet on a horse, the lower the odds and the lower the payoff. For example, the odds on a "favorite" (a horse that many people have bet on) might be 2 to 1; if that horse wins, each person who has bet on the horse receives 2 dollars for every dollar bet. The odds on a "long shot" (a horse that few people have bet on) might be 20 to 1; if that horse wins, each person who has bet on the horse wins 20 dollars for every dollar bet.

Bettors can wager on horses to win, to place, or to show. A holder of a win ticket collects only if the horse finishes first. A holder of a place ticket collects if the horse comes in first or second, and a holder of a show ticket collects if the horse comes in first, second, or third; but holders of place and show bets on a winning horse receive smaller payoffs than holders of win tickets.

LaserLinks: Background for Reading
Cultural Connection

WORDS TO KNOW
Vocabulary Preview
career
inconsiderable
obscure
parry
remonstrate

Focus Your Reading

LITERARY ANALYSIS FORESHADOWING IN FICTION In a short story a writer may use hints or clues at one point in the narrative to suggest events that will occur later. This technique, called **foreshadowing,** creates suspense and prepares readers for what is to come. As you read, look for clues about what will occur later in the story.

ACTIVE READING DRAWING CONCLUSIONS In "The Rocking-Horse Winner," luck plays a significant role in the characters' lives, though Lawrence does not always explicitly state that role. To **draw conclusions** about the role of luck in the story, you must combine the facts that are stated in the text, the facts you must **infer,** and your own **prior knowledge.**

READER'S NOTEBOOK Use a chart like the one shown to note both the stated facts and the inferred facts about each character's experiences with luck.

Characters	Stated Facts	Inferred Facts
Paul		
Paul's mother		
Oscar		

LESSON RESOURCES

UNIT SIX RESOURCE BOOK, pp. 10–14

ASSESSMENT RESOURCES

Formal Assessment, pp. 183–184

Teacher's Guide to Assessment and Portfolio Use

Test Generator

SKILLS TRANSPARENCIES AND COPYMASTERS

Literary Analysis
- Verbal, Situational, and Dramatic Irony, T17 (for Literary Analysis, p. 1019)

Reading and Critical Thinking
- Drawing Conclusions, T4 (for Active Reading, p. 1006)

Grammar
- Agreement of Subject and Verb, T47 (for Mini Lesson, p. 1020)
- Subject-Verb Agreement II, C141 (for Mini Lesson, p. 1020)

Vocabulary
- Synonyms and Antonyms, C55 (for Mini Lesson, p. 1007)

Writing
- Identifying Writing Variables, T2 (for Writing Option 3, p. 1020)

Communications
- Analyze, Evaluate, and Critique: Literary Performance, T7 (for Activities & Explorations 2, p. 1020)
- Evaluating Roles in Groups, T8 (for Activities & Explorations 1, p. 1020)

INTEGRATED TECHNOLOGY

Audio Library

LaserLinks
- Cultural Connection: Horseracing in England. See **Teacher's SourceBook,** p. 72.

Video: Literature in Performance
- from *The Rocking Horse Winner,* a film adaptation. See **Video Resource Book,** pp. 31–36.

Visit our website:
www.mcdougallittell.com

There must be more money! There must be more money!
There must be more money!

The Rocking-Horse WINNER

D. H. Lawrence

There was a woman who was beautiful, who started with all the advantages, yet she had no luck. She married for love, and the love turned to dust. She had bonny[1] children, yet she felt they had been thrust upon her, and she could not love them. They looked at her coldly, as if they were finding fault with her. And hurriedly she felt she must cover up some fault in herself. Yet what it was that she must cover up she never knew. Nevertheless, when her children were present, she always felt the center of her heart go hard. This troubled her, and in her manner she was all the more gentle and anxious for her children, as if she loved them very much. Only she herself knew that at the center of her heart was a hard little place that could not feel love, no, not for anybody. Everybody else said of her: "She is such a good mother. She adores her children." Only she herself, and her children themselves, knew it was not so. They read it in each other's eyes.

1. bonny: pretty.

TEACHING THE LITERATURE

Customizing Instruction

Less Proficient Readers

Set a Purpose Ask students whether they consider themselves lucky. Then have them read to discover what "luck" means in Paul's house.

Students Acquiring English

Generally, the vocabulary of this story is fairly accessible. However, students might have difficulty with the British idioms. In places where a footnote does not explain a British idiom, encourage students to apply context clues to clarify the meaning.

Use **Spanish Study Guide** for additional support, pp. 236–238.

Gifted and Talented

Ask students to keep the first paragraph in mind as they read the rest of the story. What is revealed in this paragraph? How might it be important to the story's conflict?

Preteaching Vocabulary

SYNONYMS AND ANTONYMS

Instruction Draw students' attention to the word *career,* which they probably know only as a noun. Then write the following phrases on the board:

- to move slowly
- to agree with
- to accept
- easily recognizable
- important

Tell students that each of these phrases is an antonym for one of the words to know. Have students correctly match the antonym to the vocabulary word. *(career, remonstrate, parry, obscure, inconsiderable)* Point out how some words, such as *parry,* do not have exact antonyms or synonyms. To clarify the meaning of the word, explain what a *parry* is in the sport of fencing. *(to deflect or ward off a thrust from an opponent)*

Activity Working in pairs or small groups, have students use a thesaurus to compile a list of synonyms and antonyms for the WORDS TO KNOW.

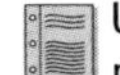

Use **Unit Six Resource Book,** p. 13 for additional support.

Reading and Analyzing

Active Reading

DRAWING CONCLUSIONS

Remind students that making inferences is an important part of drawing conclusions about events or characters in a literary work. Ask students what they infer about the mother based on the initial descriptions of her background, marriage, and relationship to her children.

Possible Response: She's been relatively privileged, but is never satisfied with her lot in life.

What conclusions can be drawn about how the mother will fare in the story?

Possible Response: She will continue to blame others for her unhappiness and will remain discontented with her life.

Use **Unit Six Resource Book,** p. 11 for additional support.

Literary Analysis

FORESHADOWING IN FICTION

A The foreshadowing in "The Rocking-Horse Winner" is tied in with the story's conflict. At the beginning of the story, for example, Lawrence points to a number of things that create conflict and could easily grow worse. Ask students what the details about the family situation might foreshadow.

Possible Response: The mother's lack of love for her children might affect their behavior; the family's habit of spending beyond their means might cause problems.

B Ask students what later events might be foreshadowed by Paul's frenzied ride and his sister's unease.

Possible Response: Something bad may happen to Paul as a result of his frenzied rocking-horse riding.

Use **Unit Six Resource Book,** p. 12 for additional support.

There were a boy and two little girls. They lived in a pleasant house, with a garden, and they had discreet servants, and felt themselves superior to anyone in the neighborhood.

Although they lived in style, they felt always an anxiety in the house. There was never enough money. The mother had a small income, and the father had a small income, but not nearly enough for the social position which they had to keep up. The father went into town to some office. But though he had good prospects, these prospects never materialized. There was always the **A** grinding sense of the shortage of money, though the style was always kept up.

At last the mother said: "I will see if *I* can't make something." But she did not know where to begin. She racked[2] her brains, and tried this thing and the other, but could not find anything successful. The failure made deep lines come into her face. Her children were growing up, they would have to go to school. There must be more money, there must be more money. The father, who was always very handsome and expensive in his tastes, seemed as if he never *would* be able to do anything worth doing. And the mother, who had a great belief in herself, did not succeed any better, and her tastes were just as expensive.

And so the house came to be haunted by the unspoken phrase: *There must be more money! There must be more money!* The children could hear it all the time, though nobody said it aloud. They heard it at Christmas, when the expensive and splendid toys filled the nursery. Behind the shining modern rocking-horse, behind the smart doll's house, a voice would start whispering: "There *must* be more money! There *must* be more money!" And the children would stop playing, to listen for a moment. They would look into each other's eyes, to see if they had all heard. And each one saw in the eyes of the other two that they too had heard. "There *must* be more money! There *must* be more money!"

It came whispering from the springs of the still-swaying rocking-horse, and even the horse, bending his wooden, champing head, heard it. The big doll, sitting so pink and smirking in her new pram,[3] could hear it quite plainly, and seemed to be smirking all the more self-consciously because of it. The foolish puppy, too, that took the place of the teddy bear, he was looking so extraordinarily foolish for no other reason but that he heard the secret whisper all over the house: "There *must* be more money!"

Yet nobody ever said it aloud. The whisper was everywhere, and therefore no one spoke it. Just as no one ever says: "We are breathing!" in spite of the fact that breath is coming and going all the time.

"Mother," said the boy Paul one day, "why don't we keep a car of our own? Why do we always use uncle's, or else a taxi?"

"Because we're the poor members of the family," said the mother.

"But why *are* we, mother?"

"Well—I suppose," she said slowly and bitterly, "it's because your father has no luck."

The boy was silent for some time.

"Is luck money, mother?" he asked, rather timidly.

"No, Paul. Not quite. It's what causes you to have money."

"Oh!" said Paul vaguely. "I thought when Uncle Oscar said *filthy lucker,* it meant money."

"*Filthy lucre*[4] does mean money," said the mother. "But it's lucre, not luck."

"Oh!" said the boy. "Then what *is* luck, mother?"

"It's what causes you to have money. If you're lucky you have money. That's why it's better to

2. **racked:** strained; tortured.
3. **pram:** baby carriage (a shortened form of *perambulator*).
4. **filthy lucre** (lo͞o′kər): money, especially that obtained through fraud or greed (an expression from the King James Bible [Titus 1:11] that has passed into familiar usage).

Teaching Options

BLOCK SCHEDULING: MANAGING TIME

If your schedule requires that you cover the lesson objectives in a shorter time, use . . .
- Preparing to Read, p. 1006
- Thinking Through the Literature, p. 1019
- Vocabulary in Action, p. 1020

If you want to take advantage of longer class time, use . . .
- TE Teaching Options: Preteaching Vocabulary, p. 1007; Viewing and Representing, p. 1010; Speaking and Listening, p. 1012; Cross-Curricular Links, pp. 1009, 1011; Workplace Link, p. 1014; Standardized Test Practice, p. 1016; Grammar, p. 1020
- Choices & Challenges and Author Activity, pp. 1020–1021

be born lucky than rich. If you're rich, you may lose your money. But if you're lucky, you will always get more money."

"Oh! Will you? And is father not lucky?"

"Very unlucky, I should say," she said bitterly.

The boy watched her with unsure eyes.

"Why?" he asked.

"I don't know. Nobody ever knows why one person is lucky and another unlucky."

"Don't they? Nobody at all? Does *nobody* know?"

"Perhaps God. But He never tells."

"He ought to, then. And aren't you lucky either, mother?"

"I can't be, if I married an unlucky husband."

"But by yourself, aren't you?"

"I used to think I was, before I married. Now I think I am very unlucky indeed."

"Why?"

"Well—never mind! Perhaps I'm not really," she said.

The child looked at her to see if she meant it. But he saw, by the lines of her mouth, that she was only trying to hide something from him.

"Well, anyhow," he said stoutly,[5] "I'm a lucky person."

"Why?" said his mother, with a sudden laugh.

He stared at her. He didn't even know why he had said it.

1 "God told me," he asserted, brazening it out.

"I hope He did, dear!" she said, again with a laugh, but rather bitter.

"He did, mother!"

"Excellent!" said the mother, using one of her husband's exclamations.

The boy saw she did not believe him; or rather, that she paid no attention to his assertion. This angered him somewhere, and made him want to compel her attention.

He went off by himself, vaguely, in a childish way, seeking for the clue to "luck." Absorbed, taking no heed of other people, he went about with a sort of stealth, seeking inwardly for luck. He wanted luck, he wanted it, he wanted it. When the two girls were playing dolls in the nursery, he would sit on his big rocking-horse, charging madly into space, with a frenzy that made the little girls peer at him uneasily. Wildly the horse careered, the waving dark hair of the boy tossed, his eyes had a strange glare in them. The little girls dared not speak to him. B

When he had ridden to the end of his mad little journey, he climbed down and stood in front of his rocking-horse, staring fixedly into its lowered face. Its red mouth was slightly open, its big eye was wide and glassy-bright.

"Now!" he would silently command the snorting steed. "Now, take me to where there is luck! Now take me!"

And he would slash the horse on the neck with the little whip he had asked Uncle Oscar for. He *knew* the horse could take him to where there was luck, if only he forced it. So he would mount again and start on his furious ride, hoping at last to get there. He knew he could get there. 2

"You'll break your horse, Paul!" said the nurse.

"He's always riding like that! I wish he'd leave off!" said his elder sister Joan.

But he only glared down on them in silence. Nurse gave him up. She could make nothing of him. Anyhow, he was growing beyond her.

One day his mother and his Uncle Oscar came in when he was on one of his furious rides. He did not speak to them.

"Hallo, you young jockey! Riding a winner?" said his uncle.

"Aren't you growing too big for a rocking-horse? You're not a very little boy any longer, you know," said his mother.

But Paul only gave a blue glare from his big, rather close-set eyes. He would speak to nobody

5. **stoutly:** bravely; firmly.

WORDS TO KNOW **career** (kə-rîr') *v.* to move at full speed; rush

Customizing Instruction

Students Acquiring English

1 Make sure students know the meaning of "asserted," then have them use the context to determine the meaning of "brazening it out."

Answer: facing something boldly and defiantly.

Less Proficient Readers

2 Help students identify ways in which the author's word choice affects interpretation of the story. For example, point out the phrase "slash the horse" and tell them that using "slash" suggests more violent behavior than a neutral phrase such as "waved the whip." Have them find other ways word choice affects interpretation.

Cross Curricular Link Sociology

PUBLIC SCHOOLS Point out that most upper-class British parents send their children to costly "public schools" (a confusing term, since they are equivalent to private schools in the United States). Eton, mentioned on page 1015, is, along with Harrow, the most aristocratic of Britain's public schools. The name of an upper-class boy like Paul would often be put on the admissions list soon after his birth. The course of study is rigorous and stresses sports and the classics (Latin and Greek). Private home tutors often help prepare youngsters for public schools.

Reading and Analyzing

Reading Skills and Strategies: MAKING INFERENCES

A Note that when Lawrence says Paul's blue eyes are still "flaring" when he stops his horse, it is only one of many references to Paul's eyes, which are often described as glaring. References to eyes abound in the story, such as when the children and the mother are said to read in each other's eyes their shared knowledge about her lack of love (on p. 1007). Ask the students why Lawrence puts so much emphasis on this facial feature?

Possible Responses: Eyes often reveal a person's character or emotional state; Paul's frenzy is reflected in his eyes; the family members are suspicious of one another, and it emphasizes their mutual scrutiny.

Point out to students that repeated references to "eyes" also help to foreshadow Paul's eventual mental collapse.

Literary Analysis: SETTING

B Clarify that the story takes place soon after World War I. Its criticism of middle-class values is typical of the disillusionment many writers felt in those postwar years.

Literary Analysis: SIMILE

C Have students identify the simile used to describe Bassett.

Answer: His seriousness is compared to that of a church.

Why is this a fitting comparison?

Possible Response: because he regards racing as a form of religion.

when he was in full tilt.[6] His mother watched him with an anxious expression on her face.

At last he suddenly stopped forcing his horse into the mechanical gallop and slid down.

A "Well, I got there!" he announced fiercely, his blue eyes still flaring, and his sturdy long legs straddling apart.

"Where did you get to?" asked his mother.

"Where I wanted to go," he flared back at her.

"That's right, son!" said Uncle Oscar. "Don't you stop till you get there. What's the horse's name?"

"He doesn't have a name," said the boy.

"Gets on without all right?" asked the uncle.

"Well, he has different names. He was called Sansovino last week."

"Sansovino, eh? Won the Ascot. How did you know his name?"

"He always talks about horse races with Bassett," said Joan.

B The uncle was delighted to find that his small nephew was posted with all the racing news. Bassett, the young gardener, who had been wounded in the left foot in the war and had got his present job through Oscar Cresswell, whose batman[7] he had been, was a perfect blade of the "turf."[8] He lived in the racing events, and the small boy lived with him.

Oscar Cresswell got it all from Bassett.

"Master Paul comes and asks me, so I can't do more than tell him, sir," said Bassett, his face terribly serious, as if he were speaking of religious matters.

1 "And does he ever put anything on a horse he fancies?"

"Well—I don't want to give him away—he's a young sport,[9] a fine sport, sir. Would you mind asking him himself? He sort of takes a pleasure in it, and perhaps he'd feel I was giving him away, sir, if you don't mind."

C Bassett was serious as a church.

The uncle went back to his nephew and took him off for a ride in the car.

"Say, Paul, old man, do you ever put anything on a horse?" the uncle asked.

The boy watched the handsome man closely.

"Why, do you think I oughtn't to?" he parried.

6. **in full tilt:** moving at full speed.
7. **batman:** in Britain, a soldier who acts as an officer's servant.
8. **blade of the "turf":** one who is very knowledgeable about horseracing.
9. **sport:** good fellow.

WORDS TO KNOW **parry** (păr′ē) *v.* to respond by turning aside or evading (a question or argument)

1010

Teaching Options

Mini Lesson

Viewing and Representing

The Races at Longchamp **by Edouard Manet**

ART APPRECIATION

The French artist Edouard Manet (1832–1883) was a precursor of Impressionism, a late 19th-century movement, in which the artist created a visual impression of a scene instead of capturing it in precise detail. Longchamp Racecourse is a famous Paris track that opened in 1857.

Instruction Tell students that impressionist painters tried to paint in a way that was more spontaneous than traditional. They often went outdoors and attempted to capture a fleeting scene, for example, instead of sitting in a studio and painting a still life or a posed model.

Application Ask the students to describe details that make *The Races at Longchamp* seems especially spontaneous or "impressionistic."

Possible Responses: The visible brushstrokes in the painting give a sensation of movement rather than the precise detail of a horserace; the outlines of the objects in the painting are not clearly defined, as if the entire scene were grasped at a glance.

The Races at Longchamp (1866), Édouard Manet. Oil on canvas, 43.9 cm × 84.5 cm, The Art Institute of Chicago, Mr. and Mrs. Potter Palmer Collection (1922.424). Photo Copyright © 1994 The Art Institute of Chicago, all rights reserved.

"Not a bit of it! I thought perhaps you might give me a tip for the Lincoln."

The car sped on into the country, going down to Uncle Oscar's place in Hampshire.

"Honor bright?"[10] said the nephew.

"Honor bright, son!" said the uncle.

"Well, then, Daffodil."

"Daffodil! I doubt it, sonny. What about Mirza?"

"I only know the winner," said the boy. "That's Daffodil."

"Daffodil, eh?"

There was a pause. Daffodil was an obscure horse comparatively.

"Uncle!"

"Yes, son?"

"You won't let it go any further, will you? I promised Bassett."

"Bassett be damned, old man! What's he got to do with it?"

10. **honor bright:** an expression meaning "on your (or my) honor."

WORDS TO KNOW

obscure (ŏb-skyŏŏr') *adj.* not well-known; undistinguished

Customizing Instruction

Less Proficient Readers

Ask students the following questions about the story:

- What is the financial situation of Paul's family?
  Answer: always overspending; in debt
- What does the mother value most and why?
  Answer: luck, because she believes lucky people always have money
- Where does Paul hope his rocking horse will take him?
  Answer: where there is luck

Set a Purpose Have students read to see if riding the rocking horse brings Paul luck. Remind students that being lucky is more than just having money. People often consider themselves lucky when they enjoy good health, for example, or are surrounded by loved ones. Tell students to consider different ways a person can be considered lucky when they decide whether Paul has been lucky.

Students Acquiring English

1 Have students use the context to determine the meaning of *fancies*.
Answer: "desires," "likes"

Gifted and Talented

Critics have noted similarities between this story's plot and the plot of other stories (such as *Faust,* or certain fairy tales) in which the hero strikes a bargain with an evil, supernatural force in order to acquire power, knowledge, or some personal advantage. Ask students to predict what will happen to Paul based on what they know about stories with this plot.

Multicultural Link: Horses

The modern breeds of horses descend from a migratory stream that swept from Central Asia across India, Iran, and Arabia and into North Africa. These so-called "Oriental" horses, with names like Arabian and Barb (from North Africa's Barbary coast) reflecting their origins, were brought to Europe by the ancient Greeks and Romans. Christian crusaders returning from the Holy Land and Muslims who controlled areas of Europe such as Spain, which was famous for fine horses, imported more horses into Europe during the Middle Ages. Spanish conquerors, in turn, brought these horses to the New World, where the animals became the chief ancestors of mustangs and other wild horses roaming the prairies and pampas of the Americas. Though horseracing was popular for centuries, modern thoroughbred racing began in early 18th-century Britain, where the Byerly Turk, the Darley Arabian, and the Godolphin Barb were brought over to strengthen British racehorses' deteriorated bloodlines. Today, thoroughbreds the world over all trace their male lineage back to these three breeds.

Reading and Analyzing

Reading Skills and Strategies: ANALYZING

A Ask students why Paul's gaze makes Uncle Oscar uneasy.

Possible Responses: The boy is too intense; the uncle senses Paul's obsession; the uncle senses that Paul's interest in horseracing is unhealthy; the uncle may feel that he should not be encouraging Paul in this pastime.

Literary Analysis: IRONY

B Have students compare Paul's behavior at the racetrack with that of the Frenchman. Ask them to identify the irony in the two characters' conflicting behavior.

Possible Response: The reader would probably expect the young boy to display such excitement, rather than the grown man.

What does Paul's behavior reveal about him?

Possible Response: further evidence of his intensity

Literary Analysis: REPETITION

C Point out the repetition of "honor bright" throughout Paul's conversation with Oscar. Then ask students why they think Lawrence uses the expression so many times.

Possible Responses: The childish expression contrasts ironically with the boy's adult pursuits and cares; the repetition touchingly reminds readers that Paul is a young boy; the phrase suggests the purity of Paul's motives in trying to get money for his parents.

"We're partners. We've been partners from the first. Uncle, he lent me my first five shillings,[11] which I lost. I promised him, honor bright, it was only between me and him; only you gave me that ten-shilling note I started winning with, so I thought you were lucky. You won't let it go any further, will you?"

A The boy gazed at his uncle from those big, hot, blue eyes, set rather close together. The uncle stirred and laughed uneasily.

"Right you are, son! I'll keep your tip private. Daffodil, eh? How much are you putting on him?"

"All except twenty pounds,"[12] said the boy. "I keep that in reserve."

The uncle thought it a good joke.

"You keep twenty pounds in reserve, do you,
1 you young romancer? What are you betting, then?"

"I'm betting three hundred," said the boy gravely. "But it's between you and me, Uncle Oscar! Honor bright?"

The uncle burst into a roar of laughter.

"It's between you and me all right, you young Nat Gould,"[13] he said, laughing. "But where's your three hundred?"

"Bassett keeps it for me. We're partners."

"You are, are you! And what is Bassett putting on Daffodil?"

"He won't go quite as high as I do, I expect. Perhaps he'll go a hundred and fifty."

"What, pennies?" laughed the uncle.

"Pounds," said the child, with a surprised look at his uncle. "Bassett keeps a bigger reserve than I do."

Between wonder and amusement Uncle Oscar was silent. He pursued the matter no further, but he determined to take his nephew with him to the Lincoln races.

"Now, son," he said, "I'm putting twenty on Mirza, and I'll put five on for you on any horse you fancy. What's your pick?"

"Daffodil, uncle."

"No, not the fiver on Daffodil!"

"I should if it was my own fiver," said the child.

"Good! Good! Right you are! A fiver for me and a fiver for you on Daffodil."

The child had never been to a race-meeting before, and his eyes were blue fire. He pursed his mouth tight and watched. A Frenchman just in front had put his money on Lancelot. Wild with excitement, he flayed his arms up and down, yelling *"Lancelot! Lancelot!"* in his French accent. B

Daffodil came in first, Lancelot second, Mirza third. The child, flushed and with eyes blazing, was curiously serene. His uncle brought him four five-pound notes, four to one.

"What am I to do with these?" he cried, waving them before the boy's eyes.

"I suppose we'll talk to Bassett," said the boy. "I expect I have fifteen hundred now; and twenty in reserve; and this twenty."

His uncle studied him for some moments.

"Look here, son!" he said. "You're not serious about Bassett and that fifteen hundred, are you?"

"Yes, I am. But it's between you and me, uncle. Honor bright?"

"Honor bright all right, son! But I must talk to Bassett." C

"If you'd like to be a partner, uncle, with Bassett and me, we could all be partners. Only, you'd have to promise, honor bright, uncle, not to let it go beyond us three. Bassett and I are lucky, and you must be lucky, because it was your ten shillings I started winning with. . . ."

Uncle Oscar took both Bassett and Paul into Richmond Park for an afternoon, and there they talked.

---

11. **shillings:** coins formerly used in Britain. (There were 20 shillings in a pound.)
12. **twenty pounds:** the equivalent of about $1,000 in today's dollars. (In the mid-1920s, a pound was worth about $5, and the purchasing power of a dollar was about 10 times what it is now.)
13. **Nat Gould:** a well-known British horseracing authority and writer.

Teaching Options

Speaking and Listening

SPORTS ANNOUNCING

Instruction Make the following points about sports announcers:

- The announcer's job is to help the audience follow the action and share in the excitement of a sporting event.
- To follow the event, some audiences require more information than others. Radio listeners, for example, need many details to help them visualize the action, as do horserace spectators, whose viewing is hindered by the size and speed of the event and obstacles on the course itself.
- The announcer must be well versed in the sport and its traditions, including its jargon and the achievements of particular participants.
- A good announcer speaks clearly while adjusting tone, volume, and pacing to communicate excitement. The event's length may also determine pacing; in horseracing, most races last only a few minutes, so announcers must speak fairly rapidly.

Prepare Have students give mock announcements of the horserace that Daffodil wins. They

"It's like this, you see, sir," Bassett said. "Master Paul would get me talking about racing
2 events, spinning yarns, you know, sir. And he was always keen on knowing if I'd made or if I'd
3 lost. It's about a year since, now, that I put five shillings on Blush of Dawn for him: and we lost. Then the luck turned, with that ten shillings he had from you: that we put on Singhalese. And since that time, it's been pretty steady, all things considering. What do you say, Master Paul?"

"We're all right when we're sure," said Paul. "It's when we're not quite sure that we go down."

"Oh, but we're careful then," said Bassett.

"But when are you *sure?*" smiled Uncle Oscar.

"It's Master Paul, sir," said Bassett in a secret, religious voice. "It's as if he had it from heaven. Like Daffodil, now, for the Lincoln. That was as sure as eggs."[14]

"Did you put anything on Daffodil?" asked Oscar Cresswell.

"Yes, sir. I made my bit."

"And my nephew?"

Bassett was obstinately silent, looking at Paul.

"I made twelve hundred, didn't I, Bassett? I told uncle I was putting three hundred on Daffodil."

"That's right," said Bassett, nodding.

"But where's the money?" asked the uncle.

"I keep it safe locked up, sir. Master Paul he can have it any minute he likes to ask for it."

"What, fifteen hundred pounds?"

"And twenty! And *forty,* that is, with the twenty he made on the course."

"It's amazing!" said the uncle.

"If Master Paul offers you to be partners, sir, I would, if I were you: if you'll excuse me," said Bassett.

Oscar Cresswell thought about it.

"I'll see the money," he said.

They drove home again, and, sure enough, Bassett came round to the garden-house with fifteen hundred pounds in notes. The twenty pounds reserve was left with Joe Glee, in the Turf Commission deposit.[15]

"You see, it's all right, uncle, when I'm *sure!* Then we go strong, for all we're worth. Don't we, Bassett?"

"We do that, Master Paul."

"And when are you sure?" said the uncle, laughing.

"Oh, well, sometimes I'm *absolutely* sure, like about Daffodil," said the boy; "and sometimes I have an idea; and sometimes I haven't even an idea, have I, Bassett? Then we're careful, because we mostly go down."

"You do, do you! And when you're sure, like about Daffodil, what makes you sure, sonny?"

"Oh, well, I don't know," said the boy uneasily. "I'm sure, you know, uncle; that's all."

"It's as if he had it from heaven, sir," Bassett reiterated.

"I should say so!" said the uncle.

But he became a partner. And when the Leger was coming on Paul was "sure" about Lively Spark, which was a quite inconsiderable horse. The boy insisted on putting a thousand on the horse, Bassett went for five hundred, and Oscar Cresswell two hundred. Lively Spark came in first, and the betting had been ten to one against him. Paul had made ten thousand.

"You see," he said, "I was absolutely sure of him."

Even Oscar Cresswell had cleared two thousand.

"Look here, son," he said, "this sort of thing makes me nervous."

"It needn't, uncle! Perhaps I shan't be sure again for a long time."

14. **as sure as eggs:** absolutely certain (a shortened form of the expression "as sure as eggs is eggs").

15. **Turf Commission deposit:** a bank where bettors keep money for future bets.

WORDS TO KNOW **inconsiderable** (ĭn'kən-sĭd'ər-ə-bəl) *adj.* not worth consideration; insignificant

Customizing Instruction

Students Acquiring English

1 Be sure students understand that "in reserve" refers to money saved rather than risked on bets.

2 Clarify that "spinning yarns" means "telling tales" and that one meaning of *yarn* is "a long or elaborate story."

3 Make sure students understand that to "put [something] on" a horse means to bet money on that horse.

can invent past achievements for horses and jockeys but should try to use real racing jargon.

Present Have students rate the performance of each "announcer" on clarity of speech, authenticity of vocabulary, and the ability to create a visual image of the race for the listening audience.

This activity is particularly well-suited for longer class periods.

Reading and Analyzing

Literary Analysis: SYMBOL

Remind students that a symbol is a person, place, object, or activity that stands for more than it literally says. Within a single work, a symbol can evoke numerous nonliteral meanings.

A Ask students what all the worsening whispers may symbolize.

Possible Responses: bigger debts, looming disaster, the truth breaking through the family's veil of secrecy

Active Reading

DRAWING CONCLUSIONS

B Ask students why the voices in the house scream for more money.

Possible Responses: The 5,000 pounds just triggered wild spending and a desire for more money to cover those expenses; the house—and its screams—reflect Paul's deteriorating state of mind.

Literary Analysis

FORESHADOWING IN FICTION

C Return to the issue of "eyes" first raised on page 1010. Remind students how references to Paul's eyes are used to draw attention to his emotional state. Ask what his "madness" over the Derby might foreshadow.

Possible Responses: a big win or big loss; Paul's actual descent into madness; his death.

"But what are you going to do with your money?" asked the uncle.

"Of course," said the boy, "I started it for mother. She said she had no luck, because father is unlucky, so I thought if I was lucky, it might stop whispering."

"What might stop whispering?"

"Our house. I *hate* our house for whispering."

"What does it whisper?"

"Why—why"—the boy fidgeted—"why, I don't know. But it's always short of money, you know, uncle."

"I know it, son, I know it."

"You know people send mother writs,[16] don't you, uncle?"

"I'm afraid I do," said the uncle.

"And then the house whispers, like people laughing at you behind your back. It's awful, that is! I thought if I was lucky—"

"You might stop it," added the uncle.

The boy watched him with big blue eyes, that had an uncanny cold fire in them, and he said never a word.

"Well, then!" said the uncle. "What are we doing?"

"I shouldn't like mother to know I was lucky," said the boy.

"Why not, son?"

"She'd stop me."

"I don't think she would."

"Oh!"—and the boy writhed in an odd way—"I *don't* want her to know, uncle."

"All right, son! We'll manage it without her knowing."

They managed it very easily. Paul, at the other's suggestion, handed over five thousand pounds to his uncle, who deposited it with the family lawyer, who was then to inform Paul's mother that a relative had put five thousand pounds into his hands, which sum was to be paid out a thousand pounds at a time, on the mother's birthday, for the next five years.

"So she'll have a birthday present of a thousand pounds for five successive years," said Uncle Oscar. "I hope it won't make it all the harder for her later."

Paul's mother had her birthday in November. The house had been "whispering" worse than ever lately, and, even in spite of his luck, Paul could not bear up against it. He was very anxious to see the effect of the birthday letter, telling his mother about the thousand pounds. **A**

When there were no visitors, Paul now took his meals with his parents, as he was beyond the nursery control. His mother went into town nearly every day. She had discovered that she had an odd knack of sketching furs and dress materials, so she worked secretly in the studio of a friend who was the chief "artist" for the leading drapers.[17] She drew the figures of ladies in furs and ladies in silk and sequins for the newspaper advertisements. This young woman artist earned several thousand pounds a year, but Paul's mother only made several hundreds, and she was again dissatisfied. She so wanted to be first in something, and she did not succeed, even in making sketches for drapery advertisements.

She was down to breakfast on the morning of her birthday. Paul watched her face as she read her letters. He knew the lawyer's letter. As his mother read it, her face hardened and became more expressionless. Then a cold, determined look came on her mouth. She hid the letter under the pile of others, and said not a word about it.

"Didn't you have anything nice in the post for your birthday, mother?" said Paul.

"Quite moderately nice," she said, her voice cold and absent.

She went away to town without saying more.

But in the afternoon Uncle Oscar appeared. He said Paul's mother had had a long interview

16. **writs:** legal documents (in this case, demands for the payment of debts).

17. **drapers:** in Britain, dealers in cloth and dry goods.

Teaching Options

Workplace Link Portfolios

Note that the job Paul's mother has as a fashion illustrator is one of many careers that require the keeping of a portfolio, a collection of work samples to show prospective employers. For example, a composer's portfolio could include cassettes of the composer's compositions as well as written musical scores. Make these general points about compiling a portfolio:

- Choose your finest and most impressive work. For example, in an actor's portfolio, a good review from a famous critic may be more impressive than a spectacular review from an unknown critic.
- Select samples that illustrate an appropriate range of skills.
- Include recent work when possible.
- Label and date everything clearly.

Have students organize portfolios of the writing samples they might select if they were seeking a job writing descriptive copy for a catalog advertising clothing. Encourage students with artistic, theatrical, or athletic skills to compile portfolios reflecting these interests and abilities.

with the lawyer, asking if the whole five thousand could not be advanced at once, as she was in debt.

"What do you think, uncle?" said the boy.

"I leave it to you, son."

"Oh, let her have it, then! We can get some more with the other," said the boy.

"A bird in the hand is worth two in the bush, laddie!" said Uncle Oscar.

"But I'm sure to *know* for the Grand National; or the Lincolnshire; or else the Derby. I'm sure to know for *one* of them," said Paul.

So Uncle Oscar signed the agreement, and Paul's mother touched[18] the whole five thousand. Then something very curious happened. The voices in the house suddenly went mad, like a chorus of frogs on a spring evening. There were certain new furnishings, and Paul had a tutor. He was *really* going to Eton, his father's school, in the following autumn. There were flowers in the winter, and a blossoming of the luxury Paul's mother had been used to. And yet the voices in the house, behind the sprays of mimosa and almond-blossom, and from under the piles of iridescent[19] cushions, simply trilled and screamed in a sort of ecstasy: "There *must* be more money! Oh-h-h; there *must* be more money. Oh, now, now-w! Now-w-w—there *must* be more money!—more than ever! More than ever!" B

It frightened Paul terribly. He studied away at his Latin and Greek with his tutor. But his intense hours were spent with Bassett. The Grand National had gone by: he had not "known," and had lost a hundred pounds. Summer was at hand. He was in agony for the Lincoln. But even for the Lincoln he didn't "know," and he lost fifty pounds. He became wild-eyed and strange, as if something were going to explode in him.

"Let it alone, son! Don't you bother about it!" urged Uncle Oscar. But it was as if the boy couldn't really hear what his uncle was saying.

"I've got to know for the Derby! I've got to know for the Derby!" the child reiterated, his big blue eyes blazing with a sort of madness. C

His mother noticed how overwrought he was.

"You'd better go to the seaside. Wouldn't you like to go now to the seaside, instead of waiting?

18. **touched:** took.

19. **iridescent** (ĭr′ĭ-dĕs′ənt): shining with a rainbowlike display of colors.

Spotted rocking horse, late 1800s. Wood with polychrome, 29″ × 53″, courtesy of Ricco Moresca Gallery.

Customizing Instruction

Less Proficient Readers
Check students' understanding of the story using the following questions:

- How has Paul made some money?
  Answer: by betting on horseraces
- Why has Paul been betting?
  Possible Responses: to stop the house from whispering about money; to get his mother to love him

Set a Purpose Have students read to see if Paul manages to help his mother and stop the house from whispering.

Reading and Analyzing

Literary Analysis: IRONY

A Ask why the mother's remarks are ironic.

Possible Responses: She criticizes Paul's interest in gambling but fails to recognize her own weaknesses regarding money; Paul at least has been successful in his financial gambits, although she does not know this.

Literary Analysis: CHARACTER

B Draw students' attention to the mother's sudden anxiety about her son. Then ask them what attending a big party suggests about her character.

Possible Response: She is not strong enough to curtail her social pursuits or pleasure seeking, even though she is worried about her son.

Literary Analysis: SUSPENSE

C Ask students how Lawrence builds suspense when Paul's mother stands outside her son's door.

Possible Response: He describes her mounting anxiety, her delay in opening the door, and the familiar yet unidentified noise.

What do students think she will see when she opens the door?

Possible Response: Paul on the rocking horse; Paul gone mad

Literary Analysis: SYMBOL

D Point out that Paul's eyes and his mother's heart both turn to stone. Ask what this symbolizes.

Possible Responses: the end of his madness and obsession; his mother's inability to love; the stoniness is shared by them, but the connection comes too late and is negative

I think you'd better," she said, looking down at him anxiously, her heart curiously heavy because of him.

But the child lifted his uncanny blue eyes.

"I couldn't possibly go before the Derby, mother!" he said. "I couldn't possibly!"

"Why not?" she said, her voice becoming heavy when she was opposed. "Why not? You can still go from the seaside to see the Derby with your Uncle Oscar, if that's what you wish. No need for you to wait here. Besides, I think you care too much about these races. It's a bad sign. My family has been a gambling family, and you won't know till you grow up how much damage it has done. But it has done damage. I shall have to send Bassett away, and ask Uncle Oscar not to talk racing to you, unless you promise to be reasonable about it: go away to the seaside and forget it. You're all nerves!" **A**

"I'll do what you like, mother, so long as you don't send me away till after the Derby," the boy said.

"Send you away from where? Just from this house?"

"Yes," he said, gazing at her.

"Why, you curious child, what makes you care about this house so much, suddenly? I never knew you loved it."

He gazed at her without speaking. He had a secret within a secret, something he had not divulged, even to Bassett or to his Uncle Oscar.

But his mother, after standing undecided and a little bit sullen for some moments, said:

"Very well, then! Don't go to the seaside till after the Derby, if you don't wish it. But promise me you won't let your nerves go to pieces. Promise you won't think so much about horse-racing and *events,* as you call them!"

"Oh no," said the boy casually. "I won't think much about them, mother. You needn't worry. I wouldn't worry, mother, if I were you."

"If you were me and I were you," said his mother, "I wonder what we *should* do!"

"But you know you needn't worry, mother, don't you?" the boy repeated.

"I should be awfully glad to know it," she said wearily.

"Oh, well, you *can,* you know. I mean, you *ought* to know you needn't worry," he insisted.

"Ought I? Then I'll see about it," she said.

Paul's secret of secrets was his wooden horse,
that which had no name. Since he was emanci- 1
pated from a nurse and a nursery-governess, he had had his rocking-horse removed to his own bedroom at the top of the house.

"Surely you're too big for a rocking-horse!" his mother had remonstrated.

"Well, you see, mother, till I can have a *real* horse, I like to have *some* sort of animal about," had been his quaint answer.

"Do you feel he keeps you company?" she laughed.

"Oh yes! He's very good, he always keeps me company, when I'm there," said Paul.

So the horse, rather shabby, stood in an arrested prance in the boy's bedroom.

The Derby was drawing near, and the boy grew more and more tense. He hardly heard what was spoken to him, he was very frail, and his eyes were really uncanny. His mother had sudden strange seizures of uneasiness about him. Sometimes, for half an hour, she would feel a sudden anxiety about him that was almost anguish. She wanted to rush to him at once, and know he was safe.

Two nights before the Derby, she was at a big party in town, when one of her rushes of anxiety about her boy, her first-born, gripped her heart till she could hardly speak. She fought with the feeling, might and main,[20] for she believed in common sense. But it was too strong. She had to **B**

20. **might and main:** with all her strength.

WORDS TO KNOW **remonstrate** (rĭ-mŏn′strāt′) *v.* to protest or object

1016

Teaching Options

Assessment **Standardized Test Practice**

TAKING OBJECTIVE TESTS: ANALOGIES

Explain that analogies in objective tests are double comparisons that follow the pattern "A : B :: C : D," which means "A is to B as C is to D." This mini-lesson follows the common practice of giving students one pair of terms and asking them to choose a word that completes a second pair so that it expresses a relationship similar to the first. For example:

Rocking horse: racehorse :: doll: ______
a. toy b. person c. wood d. rocking chair

The answer is *b, person;* just as a rocking horse represents a real horse, a doll represents a real person.

Application Have students identify the relationship between the first pair of words and then select the letter of the word that forms the same relationship in the second pair. Tell them to check the story for clues about the meanings of unfamiliar words.

1. nickel : dollar :: shilling : ______
a. penny **b.** metal **c.** peso **d.** pound

leave the dance and go downstairs to telephone to the country. The children's nursery-governess was terribly surprised and startled at being rung up in the night.

"Are the children all right, Miss Wilmot?"

"Oh yes, they are quite all right."

"Master Paul? Is he all right?"

"He went to bed as right as a trivet.[21] Shall I run up and look at him?"

"No," said Paul's mother reluctantly. "No! Don't trouble. It's all right. Don't sit up. We shall be home fairly soon." She did not want her son's privacy intruded upon.

"Very good," said the governess.

It was about one o'clock when Paul's mother and father drove up to their house. All was still. Paul's mother went to her room and slipped off her white fur cloak. She had told her maid not to wait up for her. She heard her husband downstairs, mixing a whisky and soda.

And then, because of the strange anxiety at her heart, she stole upstairs to her son's room. Noiselessly she went along the upper corridor. Was there a faint noise? What was it?

She stood, with arrested muscles, outside his door, listening. There was a strange, heavy, and yet not loud noise. Her heart stood still. It was a soundless noise, yet rushing and powerful. Something huge, in violent, hushed motion. What was it? What in God's name was it? She ought to know. She felt that she knew the noise. She knew what it was.

Yet she could not place it. She couldn't say what it was. And on and on it went, like a madness.

Softly, frozen with anxiety and fear, she turned the door handle.

The room was dark. Yet in the space near the window, she heard and saw something plunging to and fro. She gazed in fear and amazement.

Then suddenly she switched on the light, and saw her son, in his green pajamas, madly surging on the rocking-horse. The blaze of light suddenly lit him up, as he urged the wooden horse, and lit her up, as she stood, blonde, in her dress of pale green and crystal, in the doorway.

"Paul!" she cried. "Whatever are you doing?"

"It's Malabar!" he screamed in a powerful, strange voice. "It's Malabar!"

His eyes blazed at her for one strange and senseless second, as he ceased urging his wooden horse. Then he fell with a crash to the ground, and she, all her tormented motherhood flooding upon her, rushed to gather him up.

But he was unconscious, and unconscious he remained, with some brain-fever. He talked and tossed, and his mother sat stonily by his side.

"Malabar! It's Malabar! Bassett, Bassett, I *know!* It's Malabar!"

So the child cried, trying to get up and urge the rocking-horse that gave him his inspiration.

"What does he mean by Malabar?" asked the heart-frozen mother.

"I don't know," said the father stonily.

"What does he mean by Malabar?" she asked her brother Oscar.

"It's one of the horses running for the Derby," was the answer.

And, in spite of himself, Oscar Cresswell spoke to Bassett, and himself put a thousand on Malabar: at fourteen to one.

The third day of the illness was critical: they were waiting for a change. The boy, with his rather long, curly hair, was tossing ceaselessly on the pillow. He neither slept nor regained consciousness, and his eyes were like blue stones. His mother sat, feeling her heart had gone, turned actually into a stone.

In the evening, Oscar Cresswell did not come, but Bassett sent a message, saying could he come up for one moment, just one moment? Paul's mother was very angry at the intrusion, but on second thoughts she agreed. The boy was the same. Perhaps Bassett might bring him to consciousness.

21. **as right as a trivet:** in perfect condition.

Customizing Instruction

Students Acquiring English

1 Have students use the context to determine the meaning of *emancipated.*
Answer: freed

2 Make clear to students that *rung up* means "called on the telephone."

3 Some of the students might be confused by the idiom to "sit up" with someone. Explain to them that the mother is telling the governess not to stay awake until they get home.

Gifted and Talented

4 Ask students to describe how a sound can be "heavy" and "soundless."
Possible Responses: The description of the sound as *heavy* suggests it weighs heavily on the mother, because it indicates to her that something bad is happening. The word *soundless* is an overstatement that emphasizes how faint the sound is.

2. frail : weak :: obstinate : ____
a. casual **b.** stubborn **c.** anxious **d.** uncanny

3. rocking horse : toy :: ivy : ____
a. plant **b.** sequin **c.** furnishing **d.** turf

Answers: 1. d., smaller/larger currency units 2. b., synonyms 3. a., specific/general

Reading and Analyzing

Reading Skills and Strategies: ANALYZING

Ask students why Paul tells his mother at this point about his rocking-horse riding, which he had been keeping secret from her.

Possible Responses: because now he knows for certain that he's lucky; because he knows he's dying; because he's made a fortune for her.

Why is it important to Paul that his mother think him lucky?

Possible Response: because he wants her to love him, and she doesn't love unlucky people

Reading Skills and Strategies: NOTING DETAILS

Point out to students that Paul's mother is incorrect when she tells him that he has never told her that he was lucky (see p. 1009). Ask students if they think she is consciously lying to him, and if so what is the significance of her lie.

Possible Responses: She knows he's told her before, but she wants to be agreeable, given his condition; she doesn't remember he said it, because she didn't take him seriously before; she denies he said it to avoid drawing attention to the fact that she never questioned where the 5,000 pounds came from; she is keeping one last secret from him even as he tells her his big secret.

The gardener, a shortish fellow with a little brown mustache and sharp little brown eyes, tiptoed into the room, touched his imaginary cap to Paul's mother, and stole to the bedside, staring with glittering, smallish eyes at the tossing, dying child.

"Master Paul!" he whispered. "Master Paul! Malabar came in first all right, a clean win. I did as you told me. You've made over seventy thousand pounds, you have; you've got over eighty thousand.[22] Malabar came in all right, Master Paul."

"Malabar! Malabar! Did I say Malabar, mother? Did I say Malabar? Do you think I'm lucky, mother? I knew Malabar, didn't I? Over eighty thousand pounds! I call that lucky, don't you, mother? Over eighty thousand pounds! I knew, didn't I know I knew? Malabar came in all right. If I ride my horse till I'm sure, then I tell you, Bassett, you can go as high as you like. Did you go for all you were worth, Bassett?"

"I went a thousand on it, Master Paul."

"I never told you, mother, that if I can ride my horse, and *get there,* then I'm absolutely sure—oh, absolutely! Mother, did I ever tell you? I *am* lucky!"

"No, you never did," said his mother.

But the boy died in the night.

And even as he lay dead, his mother heard her brother's voice saying to her: "My God, Hester, you're eighty-odd thousand to the good, and a poor devil of a son to the bad. But, poor devil, poor devil, he's best gone out of a life where he rides his rocking-horse to find a winner." ❖

22. **eighty thousand:** the equivalent of about $4 million in today's dollars.

Connect to the Literature

1. **What Do You Think?** What scene or image in the story did you find most memorable?

Comprehension Check
- What happens when Paul rides his rocking horse?
- What does he do with his winnings?
- Why doesn't Paul want to leave before the Derby?

Think Critically

2. Why do you think Paul becomes obsessed with horseracing?

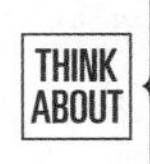

- his mother's attitude toward money
- the "voices" in the house
- what happens when he rides the rocking horse

3. How would you describe the relationship between Paul and his mother?

- his mother's view of herself and her family
- what she says about luck
- what Paul wants to do for his mother

4. Why do you think the voices get louder after Paul's mother receives the 5,000 pounds?

5. Who, if anyone, do you think is to blame for Paul's death? Support your answer with evidence from the story.

6. ACTIVE READING DRAWING CONCLUSIONS Based on the chart in your READER'S NOTEBOOK, what **conclusions** would you draw about the role of luck in the lives of Paul, his mother, and his uncle Oscar? For each **character,** is luck a negative, a positive, or a neutral force?

Extend Interpretations

7. **What If?** How might the outcome of the story have been different if Paul's predictions had started to fail?

8. **Connect to Life** Popular culture today is full of suggestions that people can achieve happiness by acquiring possessions. What do you think of this approach to life?

Literary Analysis

FORESHADOWING IN FICTION
A writer's use of hints or clues that suggest events and consequences that will appear later in a narrative is known as **foreshadowing.** The use of foreshadowing points readers to significant developments in the story and creates a **mood** of suspense. Early in "The Rocking-Horse Winner," the strange frenzy with which Paul rides his rocking horse foreshadows the tragedy of his final ride.

Cooperative Learning Activity Working with a small group of classmates, use a chart like the one shown to list other examples of foreshadowing in the story. Note how each one prepares readers for the tragic ending.

Example of Foreshadowing	How Suggests Ending
Paul charging madly on his horse while his sisters watch	Foreshadows final mad ride

REVIEW IRONY Lawrence uses **irony**—a contrast between expectation and reality—to explore the meaning of luck for the story's characters. For example, Paul's mother's statement "If you're lucky you have money" (page 1008) is ironic when read in the light of the story's ending. List other examples of irony, explaining how each contributes to Lawrence's exploration of luck.

GUIDING STUDENT RESPONSE

Connect to the Literature

1. **What Do You Think?**
Guidelines for student response: Accept all reasonable responses. You might ask students to draw or illustrate the scene they find most memorable.

Comprehension Check
- He goes into a frenzy and hears names of winning horses.
- His Uncle Oscar funnels them to his mother without saying where they come from.
- He wants to ride on his rocking horse so he can pick the winner.

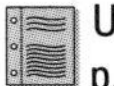
Use **Unit Six Resource Book,** p. 14 for additional support.

Think Critically

2. Possible Responses: He believes what his mother says about luck being the source of money; wants to please his mother; wants to create a happy, loving family; after winning, obsessed with winning more.
3. Possible Responses: Paul loves her, but she has difficulty returning his love; the parent-child relationship is reversed with Paul trying to care for a self-centered mother careless of his needs.
4. Possible Responses: Having come into some money, the mother spends even more lavishly; having money creates the desire for more.
5. Students may blame Paul's mother. Others may believe Paul caused his own death. Responses should be supported with textual evidence.
6. Possible Responses: Paul has the best and worst luck, coming up with the names of the winning horses but then dying due to the strain of the effort; Paul's mother has similar luck, because she gains a fortune but loses a child; Oscar provides the money for the first winning bet, goes on to make considerable money, but he loses a nephew of whom he seems quite fond.

Extend Interpretations

What If? Possible Response: He would not have continued riding his rocking horse and therefore might not have died at the end.
Connect to Life Students might discuss what they believe are keys to a happy life.

Literary Analysis

Cooperative Learning Activity Additional examples include the uncle's nervousness about Paul's uncanny talents, the house's whispers suddenly going mad, the mother's remark about Paul caring too much about the races, and her anxiety for Paul near the end.
Review Irony Examples of irony: Paul's efforts to aid his mother is situational irony, because it reverses the parent-child relationship; Paul's assertions that he is "lucky" are instances of dramatic irony and, in some respects, verbal irony because the reader understands that he has a dysfunctional family and is collapsing mentally.

Writing Options

1. **Advice Column** Tell students to have the mother include details from those scenes where Lawrence describes her becoming aware of Paul's state.
2. **Alternative Ending** Remind students that the ending of the story should resolve the plot conflict. Suggest that they write down the conflict(s) and then jot down two or three different resolutions before writing the ending.
3. **Detective's Report** Remind students to make sure the statements of the witnesses (Paul's mother, Oscar, Bassett, the nurse, his sisters) are consistent with their characters. The evidence they cite should only be those things important to the crime (Paul's winnings, the rocking horse, writs and other evidence of the family's debt).

Activities & Exploration

1. **Radio Play** Students without access to tape recorders might perform their radio dramatizations live for classmates. Tell students to try to capture the tone and mood of the story in their dramatization.
2. **Story to Movie** Encourage all reasonable responses. Remind students that various media communicate differently. Ask them to look for changes that were made to convey the story in a visual format as opposed to a written one.
3. **Abstract Painting** Make sure that students understand the meaning of "abstract." Tell them that artists often choose abstract methods because they want to emphasize emotion, and not factual accuracy. One method to convey strong emotion is to use broad, dark strokes. Ask volunteers to share their work and explain the effect they intended.

Inquiry & Research

Horseracing Allow students to make their final reports orally, in writing, or in a visual presentation such as a videotape.

Choices & CHALLENGES

Writing Options

1. **Advice Column** Imagine you are Paul's mother. Write a letter to an advice columnist, asking for advice about Paul's odd behavior. Then write the columnist's response.
2. **Alternative Ending** Write a new ending for this story, in which Paul does not predict the winner of the Derby and does not die.
3. **Detective's Report** As a police detective, write a report of your investigation into Paul's death. Include statements from witnesses and a list of evidence gathered at the scene, as well as your own conclusions about the death.

Activities & Explorations

1. **Radio Play** Work with a small group of classmates to rewrite a scene from this story in the form of a radio dramatization. Remember that a radio dramatization relies heavily upon dialogue, and be sure to include sound effects. You might also include descriptive passages for a narrator to read. Collaborate with other groups to tape-record a performance of the entire story. ~ **PERFORMING**
2. **Story to Movie** Watch the video of an excerpt from a movie adaptation of Lawrence's story. What elements of the story have been changed? Discuss why you think the filmmakers might have made the changes they did. ~ **VIEWING AND REPRESENTING**

Literature in Performance

3. **Abstract Painting** Think about the emotions you had as you read this story. Create an abstract painting that expresses one or more of your feelings. Use colors that convey the intensity of your emotions. ~ **ART**

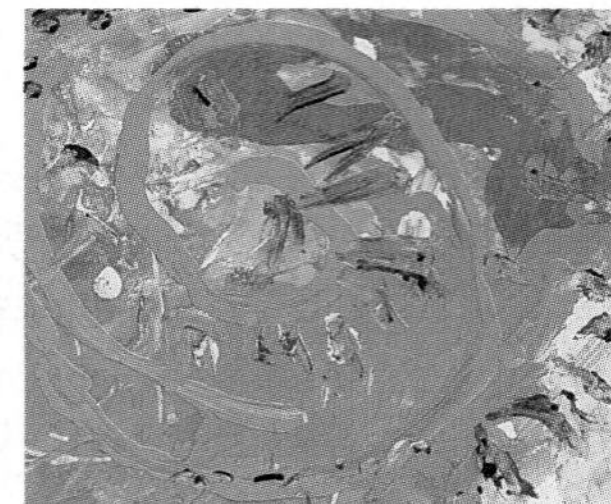

Inquiry & Research

Horseracing Research the career of a professional jockey. Find out what physical characteristics, skills, and education a jockey must have. You could investigate the entrance of women into the profession. Report your findings to the class.

Vocabulary in Action

EXERCISE A: ASSESSMENT PRACTICE For each pair of words, indicate whether the words are **synonyms** or **antonyms.**

1. **remonstrate**—agree
2. **career**—speed
3. **parry**—avoid
4. **obscure**—illustrious
5. **inconsiderable**—outstanding

EXERCISE B In groups of five, take turns pantomiming the meaning of each Word to Know. Choose the person who you think best conveyed the meaning of his or her word. Challenge members of other groups to guess which word is being pantomimed as the person repeats the performance.

WORDS TO KNOW	career	inconsiderable	obscure	parry	remonstrate

Building Vocabulary
For an in-depth lesson on how to use a thesaurus to find a word's synonyms and antonyms, see page 574.

Teaching Options

Grammar

VERBS: SUBJECT-VERB AGREEMENT

Instruction The verb must agree with the subject in number. For example, in the sentence, "Daffodil and Lively Spark were the winners," the compound subject, *Daffodil and Lively Spark*, is plural so the verb, *were,* is plural.

When two subjects of different numbers are joined by *either/or* or *neither/nor,* the subject closer to the verb determines the number of the verb. In the sentence, "Either Paul and Bassett or Uncle Oscar wins the bet," the singular verb, *wins,* agrees with the singular subject, *Uncle Oscar,* which is closer to the verb.

Explain that there are other special cases. Pronouns such as *everybody* and *anyone* are singular and take singular verbs. Collective nouns such as *team* and *group* take singular verbs unless the emphasis is on the individual members. Phrases that refer to a single quantity such as *twenty-five cents* or *five hours* also take singular verbs.

Activity Write on the chalkboard the following sentence.

"Nobody ever knows why one person is lucky

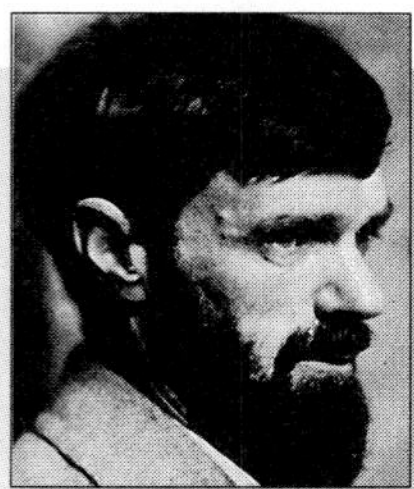

D. H. Lawrence
1885–1930

Other Works
Sons and Lovers
Women in Love
"Tickets, Please"
"Odor of Chrysanthemums"

A Miner's Son One of five children, David Herbert Lawrence was born in a coal-mining village in the central English county of Nottinghamshire. His early semiautobiographical novel *Sons and Lovers* (1913) is set in this region and reflects the conflict between his mother, who had been a teacher and poet, and his father, an uneducated miner. Lawrence was often ill as a child, and his mother, determined to keep him out of the mines, encouraged him in school, where he remained until he was 15, when financial problems forced him to take a job as a clerk and then as an elementary school teacher. After earning a teaching certificate at the University of Nottingham, he taught school in London for four years. He had already begun writing poetry and fiction, and his first novel, *The White Peacock,* was published when he was 26.

Controversy Strikes Although Lawrence was recognized as brilliant and imaginative, the passionate, sensual nature of his work made him one of the most controversial writers of the early 20th century. He not only broke literary conventions but also fought against the restrictive social, political, and moral conventions of his day. Many of his novels, short stories, and books of poetry were destroyed or had their publication delayed because censors objected to his treatment of relationships between men and women.

The "Here and Now" of Life Despite censorship, chronic poverty, and advancing tuberculosis, Lawrence wrote a remarkable number of stories, poems, and novels. He and his wife, Frieda, lived all over the world, trying to discover a better way to relate, live, and grow with other people. Later in his life, Lawrence wrote that "the magnificent here and now of life in the flesh is ours, and ours alone, and ours only for a time. We ought to dance with rapture that we should be alive." Today, Lawrence is studied and admired for the fresh perspective and style he brought to literature and living.

Author Activity
Questioning Conventions Critics have observed that much of Lawrence's fiction expresses a dissatisfaction with the values and limited viewpoint of conventional middle-class people. What evidence for this attitude can you find in "The Rocking-Horse Winner"?

Author Activity
Questioning Conventions Possible Responses: Lawrence criticizes the middle class (and especially the upper middle class) for their desire for social prestige, their lack of passion and inability to love or relate to others meaningfully, their lack of spirituality, and their single-minded striving after material possessions.

Vocabulary in Action
Exercise A
1. antonyms
2. synonyms
3. synonyms
4. antonyms
5. antonyms

Exercise B
Responses will vary.

and another unlucky."

Ask students to identify the subject and the verb and say whether they are singular or plural and whether or not the sentence is correct. *(subject, Nobody; verb, knows; singular; correct)* Point out that *person* and *is* in the dependent clause also agree in number.

Exercise Have students identify the subject and verb in each sentence. Ask them to explain which sentences are correct and to correct those that have faulty subject-verb agreement.

1. Voices in the house became louder. *(Voices, became; correct; both plural)*
2. Everybody except the children were fooled by the woman's behavior. *(Everybody, were; incorrect; for singular pronoun use singular "was")*
3. Neither the mother nor the children seem to be happy. *(children, seem; correct; plural subject is closer to verb)*

Use **Grammar Transparencies and Copymasters,** p. 79.

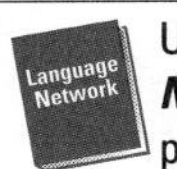

Use McDougal Littell's ***Language Network*** for more instruction and practice in subject-verb agreement.

OVERVIEW

 This selection is included in the **Grade 12 InterActive Reader.**

Objectives

1. understand and appreciate a modern **short story (Literary Analysis)**
2. appreciate the author's use of **point of view (Literary Analysis)**
3. **make inferences** to understand and interpret "Araby" **(Active Reading)**

Summary

The narrator describes his childhood crush on his friend Mangan's sister. The narrator promises to bring the girl something from a bazaar she is unable to go to herself. On the day of the bazaar, the boy must wait for his uncle to come home to give him money for the bazaar. The uncle is late, and by the time the boy arrives at the bazaar, most of the stalls are closed, and those that remain open have items too expensive for the boy.

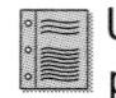 Use **Unit Six Resource Book,** p. 15 for additional support.

Thematic Link

Joyce draws heavily upon his own childhood experiences and relationships to present a **new image of reality** in the archetypal coming-of-age experience. Joyce, like his contemporaries, is more involved in the psychological, rather than physical, ramifications of the experience.

5-Minute Warm-Up

Daily Language SkillBuilder

Have students **proofread** the display sentences on page 979i and write them correctly. The sentences also appear on Transparency 27 of **Grammar Transparencies and Copymasters.**

Preteaching Vocabulary

If you would like to preteach the WORDS TO KNOW for this selection, use the Mini Lesson on p. 1024.

PREPARING to *Read*

Araby

Short Story by JAMES JOYCE

"She asked me was I going to Araby."

Connect to Your Life

Moment of Truth Try to recall a time in your childhood or adolescence when you came to a sudden realization about yourself or someone close to you. Perhaps you discovered that you had a hidden talent, or maybe you suddenly understood why a friend was treating you a certain way. Share the insight with your classmates, explaining the impact it had on you.

Build Background

Joyce's Dublin The Irish writer James Joyce is best known for his novel *Ulysses,* published in 1922. (See pages 1032–1033.) In writing it and his other works, Joyce called upon his own remembrances of Dublin at the turn of the century. Financial problems forced the Joyce family to move frequently, each time to a poorer and shabbier section of the city, and Joyce thus became acquainted with many facets of Dublin society. As a young man, Joyce was critical of the "paralysis," or immobility, of the Irish people, and he left the country to live abroad. Nevertheless, his mind was preoccupied with the people of Dublin, and the life of the city became the focal point of all his fiction. For example, there actually was a charity bazaar called *Araby* which came to Dublin when Joyce was a child.

"Araby" is one of a series of short stories that Joyce began writing in 1904 and that were eventually published in the collection *Dubliners.* The events in each story lead up to what Joyce called an **epiphany**—an ordinary moment or situation in which an important truth about a character's life is suddenly revealed.

WORDS TO KNOW
Vocabulary Preview
garrulous, luxuriate, imperturbable, pervade, litany

Focus Your Reading

LITERARY ANALYSIS | POINT OF VIEW **Point of view** refers to the narrative method used in a literary work. "Araby" is told from the **first-person point of view**—the **narrator** is a character in the story and so participates in the events he recounts. Readers see everything through the narrator's eyes, and his comments and descriptions convey the intensity of his situation.

> ***I could not call my wandering thoughts together. I had hardly any patience with the serious work of life. . . .***

As you read, be aware of what Joyce's use of the first-person point of view reveals about the narrator.

ACTIVE READING | MAKING INFERENCES **Making inferences** about **characters** involves using clues in the text and "reading between the lines" to understand why characters think and act as they do.

READER'S NOTEBOOK As you read this story, try to infer how the narrator feels during the various events he recalls. Use a chart similar to the one shown here.

Narrator's Situation	Narrator's Feelings
before talking to Mangan's sister	longing, amazement
during conversation with Mangan's sister	
at school	

LESSON RESOURCES

UNIT SIX RESOURCE BOOK, pp. 15–19

ASSESSMENT RESOURCES
Formal Assessment, pp. 185–186
Teacher's Guide to Assessment and Portfolio Use
Test Generator

SKILLS TRANSPARENCIES AND COPYMASTERS
Literary Analysis
- Point of View, T18 (for Literary Analysis, p. 1022)

Reading and Critical Thinking
- Making Inferences, T7 (for Active Reading, p. 1022)

Grammar
- Commas with Nonessential Elements, T55 (for Mini Lesson, p. 1030)
- Adverbials: Subordinate Clauses, C169 (for Mini Lesson, p. 1030)

Vocabulary
- Synonyms, C67 (for Mini Lesson, p. 1024)
- Greek Roots, C80 (for Mini Lesson, p. 1027)

Writing
- Personality Profile, C25 (for Writing Option 3, p. 1030)
- Dramatic Scene, C31 (for Writing Option 2, p. 1030)
- Literary Interpretation, C33 (for Writing Option 4, p. 1030)

INTEGRATED TECHNOLOGY
Audio Library
Visit our website:
www.mcdougallittell.com

ARABY

JAMES JOYCE

North Richmond Street, being blind, was a quiet street except at the hour when the Christian Brothers' School set the boys free. An uninhabited house of two stories stood at the blind end, detached from its neighbors in a square ground.

1023

TEACHING THE LITERATURE

Customizing Instruction

Less Proficient Readers

Set a Purpose Have students read to discover what Araby is, and then what happens when the narrator at last visits it.

Students Acquiring English

Ask students from different ethnic backgrounds what areas of the world their respective cultures would consider exotic. Have them share their views with the class, and encourage them to describe these exotic images.

Use **Spanish Study Guide** for additional support, pp. 239–241.

Gifted and Talented

Have students note Joyce's use of light and dark throughout the story. Ask them to trace the various images of light and shadow throughout the story and then interpret how these images define the boy's feelings at each point.

Viewing and Representing

St. Patrick's Close
by Walter Frederick Osborne

ART APPRECIATION The Irish painter Osborne (1859–1903) depicts the *close,* or dead-end alley, adjoining the Dublin cathedral. Refer students to p. 1028 for a better view of the close.

Instruction Point out to students that the painting depicts a dead-end street in Dublin, as does the opening paragraph of "Araby."

Application Ask students what the street scene suggests about the life of the people portrayed.

Possible Response: The people are living in tight quarters, crowded and perhaps noisy.

Ask students how the scene in the painting differs from that in the opening of "Araby."

Possible Response: The painting's street looks crowded and noisy, while the street in the story is described as mainly quiet.

Reading and Analyzing

Literary Analysis POINT OF VIEW

Ask students to list advantages and disadvantages of a first-person narrator.

Possible Response: can know and perhaps relate own feelings with some accuracy, would have knowledge of things he or she has experienced; would not be able to see the broader implications of an action or event, would be unable to communicate events he or she does not participate in.

Use **Unit Six Resource Book** p. 17 for more exercises.

Active Reading MAKING INFERENCES

Ask students what they think the setting of the story will be, judging from the picture and the opening passage.

Possible Response: a city, possibly around the turn of the century.

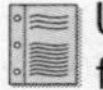
Use **Unit Six Resource Book** p. 16 for more practice.

Literary Analysis: SETTING

Note that Joyce describes an actual street and house where he once lived. Ask what details make the setting (place and time frame) seem especially realistic.

Possible Responses: musty air, useless paper, actual books, apple trees, straggling bushes.

Ask students to describe Dublin as it is presented in these opening paragraphs.

Possible Response: crowded, impoverished, working-class, coarse, shabby, colorful.

• • •

The other houses of the street, conscious of decent lives within them, gazed at one another with brown imperturbable faces.

The former tenant of our house, a priest, had died in the back drawing-room. Air, musty from having been long enclosed, hung in all the rooms, and the waste room behind the kitchen was littered with old useless papers. Among these I found a few paper-covered books, the pages of which were curled and damp: *The Abbot,* by Walter Scott, *The Devout Communicant* and *The Memoirs of Vidocq.*[1] I liked the last best because its leaves were yellow. The wild garden behind the house contained a central apple-tree and a few straggling bushes under one of which I found the late tenant's rusty bicycle-pump. He had been a very charitable priest; in his will he had left all his money to institutions and the furniture of his house to his sister.

When the short days of winter came dusk fell before we had well eaten our dinners. When we met in the street the houses had grown somber. The space of sky above us was the color of ever-changing violet and towards it the lamps of the street lifted their feeble lanterns. The cold air stung us and we played till our bodies glowed. Our shouts echoed in the silent street. The career of our play brought us through the dark muddy lanes behind the houses where we ran the gantlet[2] of the rough tribes from the cottages, to the back doors of the dark dripping gardens where odors arose from the ashpits, to the dark odorous stables where a coachman smoothed and combed the horse or shook music from the buckled harness. When we returned to the street light from the kitchen windows had filled the areas. If my uncle was seen turning the corner we hid in the shadow until we had seen him safely housed. Or if Mangan's sister came out on the doorstep to call her brother in to his tea we watched her from our shadow peer up and down the street. We waited to see whether she would remain or go in and, if she remained, we left our shadow and walked up to Mangan's steps resignedly. She was waiting for us, her figure defined by the light from the half-opened door. Her brother always teased her before he obeyed and I stood by the railings looking at her. Her dress swung as she moved her body and the soft rope of her hair tossed from side to side.

Every morning I lay on the floor in the front parlor watching her door. The blind was pulled down to within an inch of the sash so that I could not be seen. When she came out on the doorstep my heart leaped. I ran to the hall, seized my books and followed her. I kept her brown figure always in my eye and, when we came near the point at which our ways diverged, I quickened my pace and passed her. This happened morning after morning. I had never spoken to her, except for a few casual words, and yet her name was like a summons to all my foolish blood.

When she came out on the doorstep my heart leaped.

Her image accompanied me even in places the most hostile to romance. On Saturday evenings when my aunt went marketing I had to go to carry some of the parcels. We walked through the flaring streets, jostled by drunken men and bargaining women, amid the curses of laborers, the shrill litanies of shopboys who stood on guard by the barrels of pigs' cheeks, the nasal chanting of street-singers, who sang a *come-all-*

1. ***The Abbot . . . Vidocq*** (vē-dôk'): three widely varying 19th-century works—the first a historical novel, the second a book of religious instruction, and the third an autobiography of a French police detective.
2. **ran the gantlet:** passed through an area of hostility or attack. (A gantlet [or gauntlet] is a punishment in which a person is made to run between two rows of people who strike him with clubs.)

WORDS TO KNOW
imperturbable (ĭm'pər-tûr'bə-bəl) *adj.* not easily disturbed; calm
litany (lĭt'n-ē) *n.* a repetitive chant or recital

1024

Teaching Options

Mini Lesson: Preteaching Vocabulary

SYNONYMS

Instruction Write the following sentences on the chalkboard:

1. The cold, muddy plowman was grateful to indulge in a hot bath.
2. Behind the couch, the serene cat continued to ignore its owner's calls and fell asleep.
3. The customer waited impatiently for the gabby clerk to get off the phone.
4. In a short time, the smell of spaghetti sauce managed to fill the room.
5. At any provocation, the child would launch into a lengthy recitation of the birthday gifts she wanted.

Each underlined word above is a synonym for one of the WORDS TO KNOW.

Exercise Match each WORD TO KNOW with the sentence that contains its synonym.

Answers: 1. luxuriate; 2. imperturbable; 3. garrulous; 4. pervade; 5. litany.

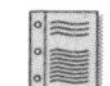
Use **Unit Six Resource Book,** p. 18 for more practice.

you about O'Donovan Rossa, or a ballad about the troubles in our native land. These noises converged in a single sensation of life for me: I imagined that I bore my chalice safely through a throng of foes. Her name sprang to my lips at moments in strange prayers and praises which I myself did not understand. My eyes were often full of tears (I could not tell why) and at times a flood from my heart seemed to pour itself out into my bosom. I thought little of the future. I did not know whether I would ever speak to her or not or, if I spoke to her, how I could tell her of my confused adoration. But my body was like a harp and her words and gestures were like fingers running upon the wires.

One evening I went into the back drawing-room in which the priest had died. It was a dark rainy evening and there was no sound in the house. Through one of the broken panes I heard the rain impinge[3] upon the earth, the fine incessant needles of water playing in the sodden beds. Some distant lamp or lighted window gleamed below me. I was thankful that I could see so little. All my senses seemed to desire to veil themselves and, feeling that I was about to slip from them, I pressed the palms of my hands together until they trembled, murmuring: *O love! O love!* many times.

At last she spoke to me. When she addressed the first words to me I was so confused that I did not know what to answer. She asked me was I going to *Araby*. I forgot whether I answered yes or no. It would be a splendid bazaar, she said; she would love to go.

—And why can't you? I asked.

While she spoke she turned a silver bracelet round and round her wrist. She could not go, she said, because there would be a retreat that week in her convent. Her brother and two other boys were fighting for their caps and I was alone at the railings. She held one of the spikes, bowing her head towards me. The light from the lamp opposite our door caught the white curve of her neck, lit up her hair that rested there and, falling, lit up the hand upon the railing. It fell over one side of her dress and caught the white border of a petticoat, just visible as she stood at ease.

—It's well for you, she said.

—If I go, I said, I will bring you something.

What innumerable follies laid waste my waking and sleeping thoughts after that evening! I wished to annihilate the tedious intervening days. I chafed against the work of school. At night in my bedroom and by day in the classroom her image came between me and the page I strove to read. The syllables of the word *Araby* were called to me through the silence in which my soul luxuriated, and cast an Eastern enchantment over me. I asked for leave to go to the bazaar on Saturday night. My aunt was surprised and hoped it was not some Freemason[4] affair. I answered few questions in class. I watched my master's face pass from amiability to sternness; he hoped I was not beginning to idle. I could not call my wandering thoughts together. I had hardly any patience with the serious work of life which, now that it stood between me and my desire, seemed to me child's play, ugly monotonous child's play.

On Saturday morning I reminded my uncle that I wished to go to the bazaar in the evening. He was fussing at the hallstand,

3. **impinge** (ĭm-pĭnj'): hit; strike.

4. **Freemason:** having to do with the Free and Accepted Masons, a worldwide charitable and social organization. (Freemasonry has often been opposed by Roman Catholics and other religious groups, in part because of its secret rituals and signs.)

WORDS TO KNOW **luxuriate** (lŭg-zho͝or'ē-āt') *v.* to take great delight

Customizing Instruction

Multiple Learning Styles

Kinesthetic Learners

1 Encourage students to pair up and present a pantomime presentation of the conversation.

Less Proficient Readers

Use the following questions to monitor students' reading.

- Where does the narrator live?
  Answer: on North Richmond Street, a dead-end street in Dublin.
- Summarize the narrator's attitude toward Mangan's sister.
  Possible Response: He idealizes her but is shy about actually talking to her.
- What does he promise to do for her if he goes to the bazaar?
  Answer: to bring back something for her.

BLOCK SCHEDULING: MANAGING TIME

If your schedule requires that you cover the lesson objectives in a shorter time, use . . .

- Preparing to Read, p. 1022
- Thinking Through the Literature, p. 1029
- Vocabulary in Action, p. 1031

If you want to take advantage of longer class time, use . . .

- TE Teaching Options: Preteaching Vocabulary, p. 1024; Viewing and Representing, p. 1023; Multicultural Link, p. 1026; Vocabulary, p. 1027; Informal Assessment, p. 1028; Grammar, p. 1030
- Choices & Challenges and Author Activity, pp. 1030–1031

Reading and Analyzing

Literary Analysis: CHARACTERIZATION

A Ask what the aunt's remark to the narrator, "I'm afraid you may put off your bazaar for this night of Our Lord" shows about her relationship with her nephew.

Possible Responses: She does not understand him; she is insensitive to his emotions.

Literary Analysis: ALLUSION

B "The Arab's Farewell to His Steed" is a once-popular sentimental poem by 19th-century British author and feminist Caroline Norton, granddaughter of the Irish playwright Richard Brinsley Sheridan. Why would Joyce have the uncle allude to the poem?

Possible Responses: to give a sense of time and place to the story; to suggest that the uncle has had too much to drink; to demonstrate the uncle's attempts to communicate with his nephew by referring to something with "Arab" in the title.

Teaching Options

Multicultural Link **Araby**

Clarify that Araby is an archaic and poetic term for Arabia, which geographically applies to the peninsula in Southwest Asia between the Red Sea and the Persian Gulf but culturally applies more broadly to all areas of the Middle East in which Arabic is the primary language. Located just east of Arabia and sharing in many aspects of Arabian culture is Iran, formerly called Persia, where Farsi, the modern descendent of Persian, is the chief language.

From Persian, English borrowed the word *bazaar* to refer to the open-air markets common throughout the region—colorful, bustling markets consisting of streets lined with shops and stalls. By Joyce's time, the word's meaning had expanded to refer to any fair or sale, often for charitable purposes, at which people or organizations sell miscellaneous goods.

looking for the hat-brush, and answered me curtly:

—Yes, boy, I know.

As he was in the hall I could not go into the front parlor and lie at the window. I left the house in bad humor and walked slowly towards the school. The air was pitilessly raw and already my heart misgave[5] me.

When I came home to dinner my uncle had not yet been home. Still it was early. I sat staring at the clock for some time and, when its ticking began to irritate me, I left the room. I mounted
1 the staircase and gained the upper part of the house. The high cold empty gloomy rooms liberated me and I went from room to room singing. From the front window I saw my companions playing below in the street. Their cries reached me weakened and indistinct and, leaning my forehead against the cool glass, I looked over at the dark house where she lived. I may have stood there for an hour, seeing nothing but the brown-clad figure cast by my imagination, touched discreetly by the lamp-light at the curved neck, at the hand upon the railings and at the border below the dress.

When I came downstairs again I found Mrs. Mercer sitting at the fire. She was an old <u>garrulous</u> woman, a pawnbroker's widow, who collected used stamps for some pious purpose. I had to endure the gossip of the tea table. The meal was prolonged beyond an hour and still my uncle did not come. Mrs. Mercer stood up to go: she was sorry she couldn't wait any longer, but it was after eight o'clock and she did not like to be out late, as the night air was bad for her. When she had gone I began to walk up and down the room, clenching my fists. My aunt said:

—I'm afraid you may put off your bazaar for this night of Our Lord. A

At nine o'clock I heard my uncle's latchkey in the hall-door. I heard him talking to himself and heard the hall-stand rocking when it had received the weight of his overcoat. I could interpret these signs. When he was midway through his dinner I asked him to give me the money to go to the bazaar. He had forgotten.

—The people are in bed and after their first sleep now, he said.

I did not smile. My aunt said to him energetically:

—Can't you give him the money and let him go? You've kept him late enough as it is.

My uncle said he was very sorry he had forgotten. He said he believed in the old saying: *All work and no play makes Jack a dull boy.* He asked me where I was going and, when I had told him a second time he asked me did I know *The Arab's Farewell to His Steed.* B When I left the kitchen he was about to recite the opening lines of the piece to my aunt.

I held a florin[6] tightly in my hand as I strode down Buckingham Street towards the station. The sight of the streets thronged with buyers and glaring with gas[7] recalled to me the purpose of my journey. I took my seat in a third-class carriage of a deserted train. After an intolerable delay the train moved out of the station slowly. It crept onward among ruinous houses and over the twinkling river. At Westland Row Station a crowd of people pressed

5. **misgave:** caused to feel doubt or anxiety.

6. **florin:** a former British coin worth 2 shillings (24 pence).

7. **gas:** gaslight.

WORDS TO KNOW **garrulous** (găr′ə-ləs) *adj.* rambling in speech; tiresomely talkative

Customizing Instruction

Students Acquiring English

1 Point out to students that "gain" is used in an unfamiliar way here. Have them look up "gain" in a good dictionary and choose the definition that makes the most sense in this sentence. **Answer:** to reach; to arrive at.

Vocabulary Strategy

GREEK ROOTS IN ENGLISH

Instruction The Greek root "phan-" (also "phen-"), used in the word *epiphany*, means "to show, appear, or shine." It is the basis for many English words, among them *phantom* and *diaphanous.* By extension, the root has come to mean "that which appears or shows from the imagination" and, ultimately, "imagination" itself. Our word *fantasy* stems from the same root.

Exercise Write the following words on the board:

1. *phantasmagoria*
2. *phenomenon*
3. *fantastic*

Have students consult a dictionary to look up the definition of each word. Lead students in a discussion of how each word relates to appearance or imagination. Have students comment on how knowing the word origin helps them understand the word's meaning.

Possible Response: 1. A *phantasmagoria* is a rapid series of things seen or imagined; 2. a *phenomenon* is an observable event; 3. A *fantastic* thing is one that exists in the imagination or seems as if it should exist in the imagination.

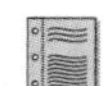 Use **Vocabulary Transparencies and Copymasters,** p. 54.

Reading and Analyzing

Active Reading MAKING INFERENCES

A Ask students to pay close attention to the narrator's actions and descriptions in these last few paragraphs, and then ask them to infer the narrator's reason for not buying anything.

Possible Response: The items are too expensive.

Literary Analysis: EPIPHANY

B Explain that *epiphany* comes from the Greek word for "a manifestation or a showing forth." It was familiar to Joyce from the Christian festival of Epiphany, which commemorates the arrival of the Magi to visit the Christ child. Joyce popularized the word as a literary term meaning an event in which the true nature of something is suddenly understood. Ask students to identify an epiphany in this story.

Possible Response: the moment at the end in which the narrator realizes that he is "a creature driven and derided by vanity."

to the carriage doors; but the porters moved them back, saying that it was a special train for the bazaar. I remained alone in the bare carriage. In a few minutes the train drew up beside an improvised wooden platform. I passed out on to the road and saw by the lighted dial of a clock that it was ten minutes to ten. In front of me was a large building which displayed the magical name.

I allowed the two pennies to fall against the sixpence in my pocket.

I could not find any sixpenny entrance and, fearing that the bazaar would be closed, I passed in quickly through a turnstile, handing a shilling to a weary-looking man. I found myself in a big hall girdled at half its height by a gallery. Nearly all the stalls were closed and the greater part of the hall was in darkness. I recognized a silence like that which pervades a church after a service. I walked into the center of the bazaar timidly. A few people were gathered about the stalls which were still open. Before a curtain, over which the words *Café Chantant*[8] were written in colored lamps, two men were counting money on a salver.[9] I listened to the fall of the coins.

Remembering with difficulty why I had come

A I went over to one of the stalls and examined porcelain vases and flowered tea-sets. At the door of the stall a young lady was talking and laughing with two young gentlemen. I remarked their English accents and listened vaguely to their conversation.

—O, I never said such a thing!

—O, but you did!

—O, but I didn't!

—Didn't she say that?

—Yes. I heard her.

—O, there's a . . . fib!

Observing me the young lady came over and asked me did I wish to buy anything. The tone of her voice was not encouraging; she seemed to have spoken to me out of a sense of duty. I looked humbly at the great jars that stood like eastern guards at either side of the dark entrance to the stall and murmured:

—No, thank you.

The young lady changed the position of one of the vases and went back to the two young men. They began to talk of the same subject. Once or twice the young lady glanced at me over her shoulder.

I lingered before her stall, though I knew my stay was useless, to make my interest in her wares seem the more real. Then I turned away slowly and walked down the middle of the bazaar. I allowed the two pennies to fall against the sixpence in my pocket. I heard a voice call from one end of the gallery that the light was out. The upper part of the hall was now completely dark.

Gazing up into the darkness I saw myself as a creature driven and derided by vanity; and my eyes burned with anguish and anger. ❖ B

8. *Café Chantant* (kä-fā' shäN-täN'): a café providing musical entertainment.

9. **salver:** serving tray.

St. Patrick's Close, Dublin (1887), Walter Frederick Osborne. Oil on canvas, 27 ¼" × 20". National Gallery of Ireland, Dublin.

WORDS TO KNOW **pervade** (pər-vād') *v.* to spread throughout; completely fill

Teaching Options

Assessment **Informal Assessment**

ALTERNATIVE ENDING

You can informally assess students' understanding of the selection by having them write an alternative ending in which the boy is able to buy something at the bazaar and takes it to the girl.

RUBRIC

3 **Full Accomplishment** Response reflects full understanding of events in story and of main character.

2 **Substantial Accomplishment** Response reflects general understanding of events in story but may not reflect full understanding of main character.

1 **Little or Partial Accomplishment** Response shows little or no understanding of events in story or of main character.

Connect to the Literature

1. **What Do You Think?** Do you agree with the narrator's opinion that he was "driven and derided by vanity"? Why or why not?

Comprehension Check
- What is Araby?
- Why does the narrator want to go there?
- Why doesn't the narrator buy anything?

Think Critically

2. How would you describe the relationship between the narrator and Mangan's sister?
3. What aspects of this story do you think might be considered **ironic**?

- the way the narrator expresses his feelings for Mangan's sister
- his expectations and excitement about going to the bazaar
- his experiences at the bazaar

4. What epiphany, or sudden awareness, does the narrator seem to experience?
5. ACTIVE READING MAKING INFERENCES Review the chart you completed in your READER'S NOTEBOOK. Consider the narrator's emotions at different points of the story, what can you infer about him? Support your answer with examples.

Extend Interpretations

6. **Critic's Corner** According to the American poet and critic Ezra Pound, one of Joyce's merits is that "he carefully avoids telling you a lot that you don't want to know." Similarly, Eva Tanner, a student reviewer, praised "Araby" for its "simplicity" and thoughtful use of **detail.** Do you agree that Joyce is frugal in his use of detail? Use evidence from this story to support your opinion.
7. **Comparing Texts** Compare and contrast the portrayals of adults in "Araby" and D. H. Lawrence's "The Rocking-Horse Winner."
8. **Connect to Life** Do you think the narrator's actions and feelings are typical of a boy's behavior? Why or why not?

Literary Analysis

POINT OF VIEW A literary work's **point of view** is the perspective from which it is told. "Araby" is told from a **first-person point of view;** that is, by a narrator who participates in the story's action. First-person narration imparts an immediacy to the narrative and usually leads to involvement with the narrating **character.**

Paired Activity With a partner, look through the story and choose a passage that you find particularly revealing about the narrator. Rewrite the passage from a third-person point of view. What effect on the passage do you think the shift in point of view has? Then discuss why you think Joyce wrote the story from the first-person point of view.

Every morning he lay on the floor in the front parlor watching her door.

REVIEW SETTING The importance of **setting**—the time and place in which a story's action occurs—varies from story to story. It may play a major role in what happens, contributing to the story's **mood, tone,** or **theme,** or it may be only incidental. Think about the different settings described in "Araby," and discuss what they add to the story.

Extend Interpretations

Critic's Corner Opinions will vary but should be supported by story details. Have students consider the information Joyce allows the reader to infer.

Comparing Texts Possible Responses: The adults in both stories behave selfishly; Lawrence's adults are more destructive and more directly involved in the young protagonist's unhappiness; Lawrence's adults seem less realistic; their flaws exaggerated, in keeping with the less realistic nature of his story.

Connect to Life Accept all reasonable, well-supported responses.

GUIDING STUDENT RESPONSE

Connect to the Literature

1. **What Do You Think?** Guidelines for student response: Students should find evidence in the text to support their opinions.

Comprehension Check
- a bazaar set up in Dublin
- to buy a gift for his friend's sister, whom he loves
- The bazaar is closing, and he is unable to afford anything at the one booth he manages to visit.

 Use Selection Quiz in **Unit Six Resource Book** p. 19

Think Critically

2. Possible Responses: romantic; awkward; unspoken; idealized; exaggerated; exists mainly in the narrator's own head
3. The story is ironic because he is excited to go to the bazaar but ends up disappointed; he intends to purchase something for Mangan's sister but fails to buy anything; his romantic dreams are sullied by the bazaar.
4. Possible Responses: that the bazaar is dull and tawdry makes him aware of his own foolishness in thinking that the bazaar would be glamorous and exotic; his worship of Mangan's sister is overly romantic and fanciful recognition of the drab realities of life.
5. Possible Response: The narrator seems young, passionate, hopeful, romantic at the beginning of the story; by the end he seems disillusioned.

Literary Analysis

Paired Activity Have volunteers read their rewritten third-person passages to the class.

Review Setting As students analyze the various settings and what they add to the story, be sure they discuss both place and time frame.

Writing Options

1. **Childhood Diary** Have students focus on the narrator's inner feelings, his insights, and his observations at the bazaar. Remind them that the boy is probably younger than they are.
2. **Dramatic Scene** You might have students perform their scenes for their classmates.
3. **Biographical Sketch** Students can elaborate on details provided in the selection. You may want to have them use peer readers to help in revising.
4. **Explanatory Paragraph** Ask students to describe their initial reactions to the imagery in "Araby." Has their response changed over time?

Activities & Explorations

1. **Interpretation in Pantomime** Have students work in small groups to create their pantomimes.
2. **Araby Ad** You might group students without artistic training or skills with those who have them. Encourage those without artistic training or skills to act as "idea people."
3. **Photo Gallery** Along with each photograph, students might include a brief oral explanation of what the photo depicts and why they chose it.

Art Connection

Photo Images Have students compare their responses to the full picture of the boy (p. 1027) with their responses to this close-up. What details do they notice in his face that they might not have commented on in the earlier activity?

Inquiry & Research

Irish History You might have students split into small groups and have each group research a particular topic (class structure, schooling, clothing, and so forth). Direct students to Internet sites about Joyce or about Dublin that might contain information about Dublin at that time. Also encourage students to explore print information through the library.

Choices & CHALLENGES

Writing Options

1. **Childhood Diary** Imagine that you are the narrator. Write a diary entry in which you express your thoughts after arriving home from the bazaar.

2. **Dramatic Scene** Write a dramatic scene showing the narrator's next encounter with Mangan's sister. Place the scene in your **Working Portfolio.** 

The next day I saw her leave her house.

3. **Biographical Sketch** Write a biographical sketch of the narrator as a child, based on the information given about him and his family in the story. Feel free to add missing pieces of information.

4. **Explanatory Paragraph** The images that Joyce uses add a rich layer of intensity and interest to his stories. Sometimes a single image will occur several times in a story. Choose your favorite images in "Araby," and write a brief explanation of why you selected them and what impact you think they have on the story.

Writing Handbook
See pages 1369–1370: Analysis.

Activities & Explorations

1. **Interpretation in Pantomime** Practice and perform a pantomime of the narrator's actions on the day and evening of the bazaar. ~ **PERFORMING**

2. **Araby Ad** Design an advertisement for Araby that reflects the narrator's anticipation of what the bazaar will be like. ~ **ART**

3. **Photo Gallery** Look through books to find photographs illustrating your impression of the early-20th century city life portrayed in "Araby." Display them in the classroom. ~ **VIEWING AND REPRESENTING**

Inquiry & Research

Irish History Find out more about Dublin life in the early 1900s. Write a brief report describing the class structure, schooling, clothing, housing, occupations, religious practices, and transportation of the city's residents.

Art Connection

Photo Images Look again at the photograph of the boy on page 1027. Does his appearance match your mental image of the narrator of this story? Discuss your impressions with a partner.

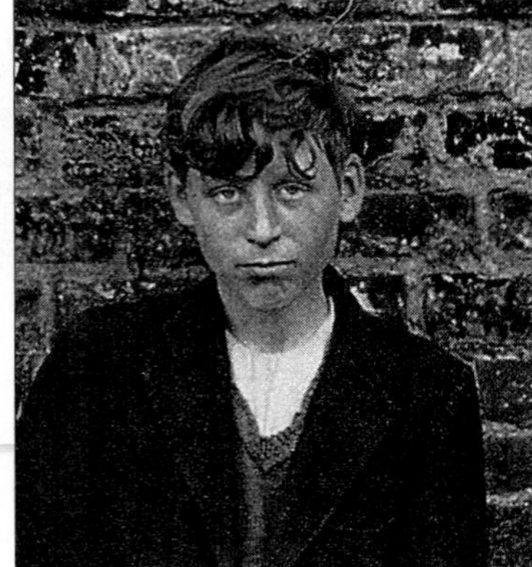

Teaching Options

Mini Lesson **Grammar**

Adverbials: Subordinate Clauses

Instruction A clause is a group of words with a subject and a predicate that may or may not be a sentence. If the words can stand independently, they are a sentence. However, if the clause begins with a subordinating conjunction—such as *since, where, because, although, so that,* or as *if*—then it is subordinate, or dependent. Often a subordinate clause adds adverbial information. Because a subordinate clause does not express a complete thought, it must be attached to an independent clause in order to make sense. Subordinating conjunctions show the relationship of a subordinate clause to an independent clause. Such a relationship may be one of time, place, cause, condition, purpose, or manner. The following example is from "Araby."

Activity Write the following example on the chalkboard.

> "When she came out on the doorstep my heart leaped."

The underlined part of the sentence is a subordinate clause used as an adverb. Its relationship to the independent clause is one of time; it tells *when* the boy's heart leaped. (You may wish to remind students that in current American style, a

Vocabulary in Action

EXERCISE : MEANING CLUES Write the word that is best described by each clue.

1. Joy, light, or a fragrance can do this to a group or a place.
2. A person who is this is someone you don't want to have a conversation with when you're in a hurry.
3. You might do this in a hot bath on a cold day or in a cool lake on a hot day.
4. It can require great patience not to interrupt this, because you're tempted to say, "So you've said . . . and said and said!"
5. A person who is this might gaze serenely from the stands while the rest of the fans are leaping to their feet to cheer a home run.

WORDS TO KNOW garrulous imperturbable litany luxuriate pervade

Building Vocabulary
For an in-depth study of context clues, see page 938.

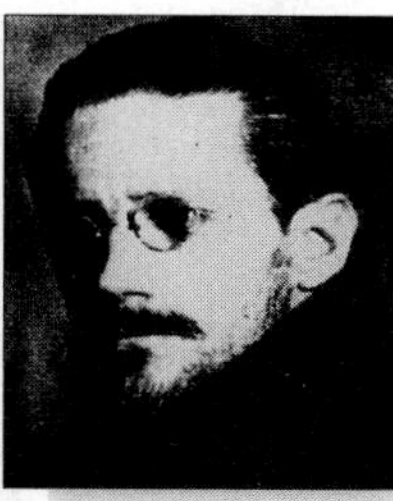

James Joyce
1882–1941

Other Works
Ulysses
Dubliners
Finnegans Wake
"An Encounter"
"The Sisters"
"Eveline"
"Counterparts"

A Childhood of Poverty James Joyce overcame many handicaps to become one of the greatest novelists of the 20th century. Born into a large Dublin family, he began feeling the effects of poverty as a young child. His father was extremely irresponsible and drank heavily, and during Joyce's childhood the family sank further and further into debt. The children grew accustomed to bill collectors, frequent moves, and the loss of family possessions. At one point, Joyce was forced to leave a grammar school when his parents could no longer afford the tuition. After two years of trying to educate himself at home, he finally had his tuition fees waived so that he might finish his formal education.

His Varied Career In 1902, Joyce graduated from University College in Dublin, where he first began to write seriously. Writing, however, was not the only interest that Joyce pursued—he had a fine voice and as a young man considered a singing career. When he finally did focus his attention on writing, he knew that it was an uncertain profession and that he would probably need another source of income. He began the study of medicine but quickly abandoned it because he had neither the tuition nor the proper educational background. During his lifetime, he tried his hand at various other jobs and enterprises, including teaching, banking, and the movie-theater business.

Self-imposed Exile In June 1904, Joyce met Nora Barnacle, a young girl from Galway, and a few months later the couple moved to Austria-Hungary. Over the next few years, they lived in several European cities—including Trieste, Paris, and Zurich—but never returned to Ireland. Throughout much of his adult life, Joyce faced financial disaster but managed to continue writing with assistance from friends. He also faced serious problems with his vision, undergoing eye surgery 25 times between 1917 and 1930. While working on his last novel, *Finnegans Wake,* he was occasionally forced to write in crayon on large sheets of paper in order to see his own work.

Author Activity

Life in Literature The house in "Araby" is based on one in which Joyce lived as a boy. Find out more about the author's early life to learn what other elements in "Araby," or other short stories by Joyce, are drawn from the author's own life.

Vocabulary in Action

1. pervade
2. garrulous
3. luxuriate
4. litany
5. imperturbable

Author Activity

Life in Literature The setting descriptions in "Araby" correspond to the real-life details of 17 North Richmond Street in Dublin, where the Joyce family moved in 1894. Earlier, Joyce had briefly attended the Christian Brothers' School on the same street. Owing in part to its negative depiction of his home city, Joyce had great difficulty publishing *Dubliners,* although the work was finally published in England in 1915.

comma always follows a subordinate clause at the beginning of a sentence.)

Exercise Ask students to underline each subordinate clause and to tell whether its relationship to the main clause is one of time, place, cause, condition, purpose, or manner.

1. The boys hid in the shadow until the uncle had gone into the house. *(time)*
2. Although the boy passed the girl each morning he never spoke to her. *(condition)*
3. Although he tried to conceal the depth of his feelings when his uncle was late in returning, the boy was disappointed. *(condition; time)*
4. His mother was concerned because she thought the bazaar might be a Freemason affair. *(cause)*
5. At the bazaar stall the boy tried to behave as if he were really interested in the wares. *(manner)*

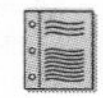

Use **Grammar Transparencies and Copymasters,** p. 54.

Use McDougal Littell's ***Language Network*** for more instruction and practice in subordinate clauses.

Ulysses was first published in Paris on February 2, 1922—Joyce's 40th birthday—by Sylvia Beach, the American owner of a bookstore called Shakespeare & Co. It aroused such a storm of controversy that it was banned in both Britain and the United States. The first U. S. edition did not appear until 1934, after a court finally ruled that the book was not obscene.

Additional Background

JAMES JOYCE

Even though James Joyce (1882–1941) left Ireland to escape what he considered the provincialism of its inhabitants, the people of Ireland were those he knew best, and he continued to write about them for the rest of his life. In fact, his first collection of short stories was called *Dubliners*. Some critics have suggested that Joyce left his homeland so that his everyday experiences there would not interfere with his objectivity.

Joyce's first novel, *A Portrait of the Artist as a Young Man,* is in part autobiographical. It focuses on the relationship between the artist, in the person of the young Stephen Dedalus, and society. At the novel's end, Dedalus makes the decision Joyce himself had made, choosing to leave Ireland.

After completing *Ulysses*, Joyce spent 17 years writing the massive, dreamlike *Finnegans Wake*—a "book of the night" to balance his account of a single day in the earlier work. Intending to reflect the whole of human civilization in his last novel, Joyce wove a dense tapestry of allusions, multilingual puns, distorted language and syntax, and metamorphoses of characters and events that has baffled many readers but constitutes what is perhaps his greatest work.

MILESTONES IN BRITISH LITERATURE

James Joyce

ULYSSES

Above:
Images of Dublin, early 20th century

Is it possible to write an epic set in the modern world? Where could one find characters of suitably heroic dimensions? The Irish writer James Joyce faced these questions after leaving his homeland, which he believed to be too narrow in its cultural and religious views, to live in self-imposed exile in Trieste, Zurich, and Paris. From 1914 to 1921, impoverished and struggling to support his family, he produced his masterwork, *Ulysses,* probably the most influential novel of the 20th century.

On one level the plot of *Ulysses* reflects the events recounted in Homer's *Odyssey*—the return of the Greek hero Odysseus (in Latin, Ulysses) to his faithful wife, Penelope, and his son,

Telemachus, after ten years of wandering throughout the Mediterranean after the Trojan War. In typical Joycean fashion, however, the Greek epic is turned on its ear. The hero of *Ulysses* is Leopold Bloom, a middle-aged advertising salesman who lives in Dublin with his unfaithful wife, Molly. He wanders about the city on a single day—June 16, 1904—beginning and ending his journey at his home in Eccles Street. During the course of his wanderings, he encounters Stephen Dedalus, a 22-year-old poet who was the protagonist of Joyce's first novel, *A Portrait of the Artist as a Young Man.* As their lives intersect, the two men form a bond, and in a way Stephen becomes a son to Bloom—a Telemachus to Bloom's Odysseus.

What elevates the story to truly epic proportions is Joyce's presentation of the amazing inner life of his characters through interior monologues. Their thoughts, including the most intimate ones, come rushing by in a stream of consciousness. In the following passage, for example, Bloom, having just attended the funeral of Patrick Dignam, is in a pub, deciding what to have for lunch. Notice how, in the space of a few lines, his thoughts range from sensory experience to a biblical pun to an advertising slogan to Dignam's corpse to a flight of fancy:

> Sardines on the shelves. Almost taste them by looking. Sandwich? Ham and his descendants musterred and bred there. Potted meats. What is home without Plumtree's potted meat? Incomplete. What a stupid ad! Under the obituary notices they stuck it. All up a plumtree. Dignam's potted meat. Cannibals would with lemon and rice. . . .

In addition to the Homeric parallels, allusions to Shakespeare and Dante abound, along with references to the Roman Catholic Church, music, psychology, philosophy, pulp fiction, and a multitude of other topics. Every imaginable aspect of a day in the life of a 20th-century Odysseus, Penelope, and Telemachus is captured in exacting detail, as if their thoughts were our very own.

It is ironic that Joyce, a man who spent his lifetime wandering about Europe, searching for a home, should have spent so much time writing about the very homeland he rejected. Once, when asked if he had plans to return to Ireland at some point, Joyce replied, "Have I ever left?"

Below:
Ulysses and the Sirens *(third century A.D.), unknown artist. Musée National du Bardo, Le Bardo, Tunisia, Giraudon/Art Resource, New York.*

1033

LITERARY CHRONOLOGY

Although Joyce also published poetry and a play, he is best known for his short stories and novels. The following are their publication dates:

1914 *Dubliners*

1916 *A Portrait of the Artist as a Young Man*

1922 *Ulysses*

1939 *Finnegan's Wake*

OVERVIEW

Objectives

1. understand and appreciate a modern **short story (Literary Analysis)**
2. appreciate the author's use of **realism (Literary Analysis)**
3. **analyze plot** in "A Cup of Tea" **(Active Reading)**

Summary

After visiting a London shop and examining a costly trinket, the rich and fashionable Rosemary Fell meets a woman who asks for money for a cup of tea. Instead, Rosemary takes the woman home and serves her tea. Rosemary is full of plans for her new protégée, Miss Smith, until Rosemary's husband, Philip, comments that Miss Smith is quite pretty. Rosemary then gives Miss Smith three pounds and sends her away. After redoing her hair and make-up, Rosemary rejoins Philip, asks him whether she can buy the expensive trinket, and whispers, "Am I pretty?"

Use **Unit Six Resource Book,** p. 20 for additional support.

Thematic Link

Like Joyce and Lawrence, Mansfield focuses her gaze on the milieu in which she was raised in order to discover **new images of reality.** Her observations of modern middle-class behavior provide insight into the social mores of her time, and of ours.

5-Minute Warm-Up

Daily Language SkillBuilder

Have students **proofread** the display sentences on page 979i and write them correctly. The sentences also appear on Transparency 28 of **Grammar Transparencies and Copymasters.**

PREPARING to *Read*

A Cup of Tea

Short Story by KATHERINE MANSFIELD

"Would you let me have the price of a cup of tea?"

Connect to Your Life

A Touch of Class Although class distinctions based on wealth are not as pronounced in the United States as they once were, they do still exist. Make three lists, noting what seem to you to be (1) typically upper-class, (2) typically middle-class, and (3) typically lower-class places, events, and institutions. Discuss your lists with classmates.

Build Background

British Society In the early 1900s, when "A Cup of Tea" was written, class distinctions were quite evident in Britain. The best schools and neighborhoods were typically reserved for the rich, who also tended to shop in separate stores on exclusive streets and to avoid contact with people of lower classes whenever possible. An upper-class wife never worked, either inside or outside the home—instead spending her days shopping, visiting, and entertaining. It was considered improper for her to associate with people of lower classes unless they were serving her in some way. In "A Cup of Tea," Mansfield portrays a character named Rosemary who belongs to this pampered upper class.

Focus Your Reading

LITERARY ANALYSIS REALISM "A Cup of Tea" is a work of **realism**—that is, one that attempts to give a truthful representation of actual life, without sentimentality or idealism. Mansfield's portrayal of the wealthy Rosemary and her lifestyle employs many details of daily life that were contemporary when the story was written. As you read, be aware of the realistic elements in Mansfield's depiction of Rosemary's character and lifestyle.

ACTIVE READING ANALYZING PLOT Most **plots** include the following stages:

- The **exposition** introduces the characters, setting, and major conflict.
- In the **rising action,** complications develop.
- The **climax** is the turning point of the story.
- The **falling action**—sometimes called the **resolution**—consists of the events after the climax.

READER'S NOTEBOOK As you read the story, plot the sequence of events, using a diagram like the one shown. Identify the most important events, and note where you think the four stages of the plot occur.

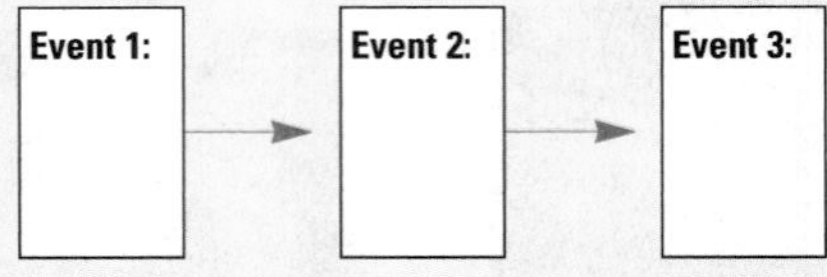

LESSON RESOURCES

UNIT SIX RESOURCE BOOK, pp. 20–23

ASSESSMENT RESOURCES

Formal Assessment, pp. 187–188

Teacher's Guide to Assessment and Portfolio Use

Test Generator

SKILLS TRANSPARENCIES AND COPYMASTERS

Literary Analysis

- Verbal, Situational, and Dramatic Irony, T17 (for Think Critically 5, p. 1042)

Reading and Critical Thinking

- Generating Research Questions, T27 (for Inquiry & Research, p. 1043)

Grammar

- Rhythm: Power Words, C171 (for Mini Lesson, pp. 1036–1037)
- Controlling Rhythm, C172 (for Mini Lesson, pp. 1036–1037)

Writing

- The Uses of Dialogue, T24 (for Writing Option 2, p. 1043)
- Dramatic Scene, C31 (for Writing Option 2, p. 1043)

Communications

- Appreciative Listening, T2 (for Activities & Explorations 1, p. 1043)
- Evaluating Roles in Groups, T8 (for Activities & Explorations 1, p. 1043)
- Impromptu Speaking: Dialogue, Role-Play, T14 (for Activities & Explorations 1, p. 1043)

INTEGRATED TECHNOLOGY

Audio Library

LaserLinks

- Art Gallery: Women of Wealth & Leisure. See **Teacher's SourceBook,** p. 72.

Visit our website: www.mcdougallittell.com

A Cup of Tea

Katherine Mansfield

Rosemary Fell was not exactly beautiful. No, you couldn't have called her beautiful. Pretty? Well, if you took her to pieces . . . But why be so cruel as to take anyone to pieces? She was young, brilliant, extremely modern, exquisitely well dressed, amazingly well read in the newest of the new books, and her parties were the most delicious mixture of the really important people and . . . artists—quaint creatures, discoveries of hers, some of them too terrifying for words, but others quite presentable and amusing.

TEACHING THE LITERATURE

Customizing Instruction

Less Proficient Readers

Set a Purpose Have students read to find out what Rosemary Fell does when a young woman asks her for a handout.

Students Acquiring English

In this selection, students will come across some British usages with which they might not be familiar. Help students understand the following words as they are used in the story:

oughtn't (p. 1037) contraction of "ought not"; means "should not"

daren't (p. 1039) contraction of "dare not"

frightfully (p. 1040) used as an intensifier; means "very"

 Use **Spanish Study Guide** for additional support, pp. 242–244.

Gifted and Talented

Ask students to compare Rosemary and Miss Smith as they read. Ask students how the two women's situations are similar, and how easy or difficult it would be for them to change places.

BLOCK SCHEDULING: MANAGING TIME

If your schedule requires that you cover the lesson objectives in a shorter time, use . . .

- Preparing to Read, p. 1034
- Thinking Through the Literature, p. 1042

If you want to take advantage of longer class time, use . . .

- TE Teaching Options: Grammar, pp. 1036, 1040; Viewing and Representing, p. 1038; Speaking and Listening, p. 1039; Informal Assessment, p. 1041
- Choices & Challenges and Author Activity, p. 1043

Reading and Analyzing

Active Reading ANALYZING PLOT

Explain to students that the opening paragraphs of this story provide exposition. Remind students that they should focus on details in the exposition, such as setting and characters. What initial details does Mansfield provide?

Possible Responses: that Rosemary is "young, brilliant, extremely modern, exquisitely well-dressed"; that she has parties with people both "important" and "quaint"; how she shops for flowers.

 Use **Unit Six Resource Book** p. 21 for more practice.

Literary Analysis REALISM

Ask students what elements of the opening paragraphs indicate that this story will be realistic.

Possible Responses: "not exactly beautiful"; the description of the parties, in which "too terrifying for words" is balanced with "quite presentable and amusing"; details of her marriage to Michael and her shopping habits.

 Use **Unit Six Resource Book** p. 22 for more exercises.

Literary Analysis: TONE

After students have read the first two paragraphs of the story, ask them to describe their tone.

Possible Responses: humorous; casual; ironic.

Literary Analysis: CHARACTERIZATION

A Ask students what Rosemary's response to the shopkeeper's flattery reveals about her character.

Possible Responses: She's vain and self-centered; even though she knows the flattery might be insincere, she likes it.

Rosemary had been married two years. She had a duck[1] of a boy. No, not Peter—Michael. And her husband absolutely adored her. They were rich, really rich, not just comfortably well off, which is odious and stuffy and sounds like one's grandparents. But if Rosemary wanted to shop she would go to Paris as you and I would go to Bond Street.[2] If she wanted to buy flowers, the car pulled up at that perfect shop in Regent Street, and Rosemary inside the shop just gazed in her dazzled, rather exotic way, and said: "I want those and those and those. Give me four bunches of those. And that jar of roses. Yes, I'll have all the roses in the jar. No, no lilac. I hate lilac. It's got no shape." The attendant bowed and put the lilac out of sight, as though this was only too true; lilac was dreadfully shapeless. "Give me those stumpy little tulips. Those red and white ones." And she was followed to the car by a thin shopgirl staggering under an immense white paper armful that looked like a baby in long clothes. . . .

One winter afternoon she had been buying something in a little antique shop in Curzon Street. It was a shop she liked. For one thing, one usually had it to oneself. And then the man who kept it was ridiculously fond of serving her. He beamed whenever she came in. He clasped his hands; he was so gratified he could scarcely speak. Flattery, of course. All the same, there was something . . . (A)

"You see, madam," he would explain in his low respectful tones, "I love my things. I would rather not part with them than sell them to someone who does not appreciate them, who has not that fine feeling which is so rare. . . ." And, breathing deeply, he unrolled a tiny square of blue velvet and pressed it on the glass counter with his pale fingertips.

Today it was a little box. He had been keeping it for her. He had shown it to nobody as yet. An exquisite little enamel box with a glaze so fine it looked as though it had been baked in cream. On the lid a minute creature stood under a flowery tree, and a more minute creature still had her arms around his neck. Her hat, really no bigger than a geranium petal, hung from a branch; it had green ribbons. And there was a pink cloud like a watchful cherub[3] floating above their heads. Rosemary took her hands out of her long gloves. She always took off her gloves to examine such things. Yes, she liked it very much. She loved it; it was a great duck. She must have it. And, turning the creamy box, opening and shutting it, she couldn't help noticing how charming her hands were against the blue velvet. The shopman, in some dim cavern of his mind, may have dared to think so too. For he took a pencil, leaned over the counter, and his pale bloodless fingers crept timidly towards those rosy, flashing ones, as he murmured gently: "If I may venture to point out to madam, the flowers on the little lady's bodice."[4] 1

"Charming!" Rosemary admired the flowers. But what was the price? For a moment the shopman did not seem to hear. Then a murmur reached her. "Twenty-eight guineas,[5] madam."

"Twenty-eight guineas." Rosemary gave no sign. She laid the little box down; she buttoned her gloves again. Twenty-eight guineas. Even if one is rich . . . She looked vague. She stared at a plump teakettle like a plump hen above the shopman's head, and her voice was dreamy as she answered: "Well, keep it for me—will you? I'll . . ." 2

But the shopman had already bowed as though keeping it for her was all any human being could ask. He would be willing, of course, to keep it for her forever.

1. **duck:** in British usage, a darling person or thing.
2. **Bond Street:** one of London's main business streets.
3. **cherub:** an angel depicted as a chubby child with wings.
4. **bodice** (bŏd′ĭs): the upper part of a dress.
5. **guineas** (gĭn′ēz): units of British money (equal to 21 shillings each), used mainly for pricing luxury items.

Teaching Options

Grammar

RHYTHM: POWER WORDS

Instruction Well-chosen adjectives and adverbs, especially those that carry an emotional charge, have the power to draw attention to themselves. Such power words change the rhythm of a sentence.

> The *staggering* problem of feeding the town's poor has become an *overwhelming* concern for the mayor.

Words like *staggering* and *overwhelming* in this sentence carry a sense of urgency and importance. These power words can influence the reader's opinion, but they can also cause the reader to stop and question: Is the problem truly staggering? Is the mayor really overwhelmed? Is the writer exaggerating? Power words can often change a statement of fact into an arguable proposition, a proposition that the writer may or may not persuasively demonstrate. The best writers use such adjectives and adverbs sparingly. In this way power words achieve maximum effect.

Point out that writers sometimes use adjectives and adverbs for ironic effect as well. In "A Cup of Tea," Katherine Mansfield describes Rosemary as *charming,* but the reader probably doesn't find her charming, and neither does the writer.

The discreet door shut with a click. She was outside on the step, gazing at the winter afternoon. Rain was falling, and with the rain it seemed the dark came too, spinning down like ashes. There was a cold bitter taste in the air, and the new-lighted lamps looked sad. Sad were the lights in the houses opposite. Dimly they burned as if regretting something. And people hurried by, hidden under their hateful umbrellas. Rosemary felt a strange pang.[6] She pressed her muff to her breast; she wished she had the little box, too, to cling to. Of course, the car was there. She'd only to cross the pavement. But still she waited. There are moments, horrible moments in life, when one emerges from shelter and looks out, and it's awful. One oughtn't to give way to them. One ought to go home and have an extra-special tea. But at the very instant of thinking that, a young girl, thin, dark, shadowy—where had she come from?—was standing at Rosemary's elbow and a voice like a sigh, almost like a sob, breathed: "Madam, may I speak to you a moment?"

"Speak to me?" Rosemary turned. She saw a little battered creature with enormous eyes, someone quite young, no older than herself, who clutched at her coat-collar with reddened hands, and shivered as though she had just come out of the water.

"M-madam," stammered the voice. "Would you let me have the price of a cup of tea?"

"A cup of tea?" There was something simple, sincere in that voice; it wasn't in the least the voice of a beggar. "Then have you no money at all?" asked Rosemary.

"None, madam," came the answer.

"How extraordinary!" Rosemary peered through the dusk, and the girl gazed back at her. How more than extraordinary! And suddenly it seemed to Rosemary such an adventure. It was like something out of a novel by Dostoyevsky,[7] this meeting in the dusk. Supposing she took the girl home? Supposing she did do one of those things she was always reading about or seeing on the stage, what would happen? It would be thrilling. And she heard herself saying afterwards to the amazement of her friends: "I simply took her home with me," as she stepped forward and said to that dim person beside her: "Come home to tea with me."

The Mirror (1890), Dennis Miller Bunker. Oil on canvas, 50⅜" × 40⅜", Terra Foundation for the Arts, Daniel J. Terra Collection (43.1980). Photo Copyright © 1995 courtesy of Terra Museum of American Art, Chicago.

The girl drew back startled. She even stopped shivering for a moment. Rosemary put out a hand and touched her arm. "I mean it," she said, smiling. And she felt how simple and kind her smile was. "Why won't you? Do. Come home with me now in my car and have tea."

"You—you don't mean it, madam," said the girl, and there was pain in her voice.

6. **pang:** a sudden sharp pain or feeling.
7. **Dostoyevsky** (dŏs′tə-yĕf′skē): Feodor Dostoyevsky, a 19th-century Russian writer of novels and short stories. He wrote a number of works dealing with the lives of the poor and the underprivileged.

Customizing Instruction

Students Acquiring English

1 Help students differentiate between the homographs *minute,* referring to a measurement of time, and *minute* (pronounced "my NOOT"), meaning "very small." Ask students which meaning is intended in this passage.
Answer: very small.

Multiple Learning Styles

Logical/Mathematical Learners

2 A guinea was worth one pound, one shilling. Inform students that 20 shillings made a pound. Then ask them how much the box costs in pounds and shillings.
Answer: 29 pounds, 8 shillings.

Activity Write the following sentence on the chalkboard. Ask students to identify and discuss the power word in this sentence from the story.

"However . . . I think you're making a ghastly mistake." *(ghastly)*

Exercise Ask students to identify power words in each of the following sentences and determine which ones change statements of fact into arguable propositions.

1. Rosemary and her husband were immensely rich. *(immensely)*
2. Rosemary's delightful spirit of adventure stirred her to take the poor girl home. *(delightful; arguable)*
3. The terrified girl feared that Rosemary would take her to the police. *(terrified)*
4. The girl was astonishingly pretty. *(astonishingly; arguable)*
5. Katherine Mansfield's writing career was tragically short. *(tragically; arguable)*

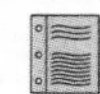

Use **Grammar Transparencies and Copymasters,** p. 107.

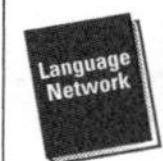

Use McDougal Littell's ***Language Network*** for more instruction and practice in power words.

Reading and Analyzing

Literary Analysis: IRONY

A Point out that Rosemary exclaims, "Why should I be so cruel?" when the young woman expresses her fear of the police. Ask students to explain why Rosemary's question is ironic.

Possible Response: By treating the girl as a possession or acquisition, Rosemary is already being cruel.

Literary Analysis: CHARACTER

B Ask students why Rosemary feels triumphant after she has "netted" the girl.

Possible Responses: She sees the episode as an adventure that will help fill a few empty moments; she needs the girl's cooperation if she is to play the benefactor; she is doing this more for herself than for the girl.

C What does Rosemary's fantasy of herself as a fairy godmother suggest?

Possible Response: She sees the episode as a Cinderella story; her perception of this event is romanticized and unrealistic.

Reading Skills and Strategies: MAKING INFERENCES

D Ask students why the girl might stagger.

Possible Responses: She is weak from hunger; she is ill.

Then ask what Rosemary's reaction suggests about Rosemary.

Possible Response: She is self-centered; she is insensitive to the needs of others; she is ignorant of real-world problems.

The First Cloud (1887), Sir William Quiller Orchardson. Tate Gallery, London/Art Resource, New York.

"But I do," cried Rosemary. "I want you to. To please me. Come along."

The girl put her fingers to her lips and her eyes devoured Rosemary. "You're—you're not taking me to the police station?" she stammered.

"The police station!" Rosemary laughed out. (A) "Why should I be so cruel? No, I only want to make you warm and to hear—anything you care to tell me."

Hungry people are easily led. The footman held the door of the car open, and a moment later they were skimming through the dusk.

"There!" said Rosemary. She had a feeling of (B) triumph as she slipped her hand through the velvet strap. She could have said, "Now I've got you," as she gazed at the little captive she had netted. But of course she meant it kindly. Oh, more than kindly. She was going to prove to this girl that—wonderful things did happen in life, that—fairy godmothers were real, that—rich (C) people had hearts, and that women *were* sisters. She turned impulsively, saying: "Don't be frightened. After all, why shouldn't you come back with me? We're both women. If I'm the more fortunate, you ought to expect . . ."

But happily at that moment, for she didn't know how the sentence was going to end, the car stopped. The bell was rung, the door opened, and with a charming, protecting, almost embracing movement, Rosemary drew the other into the hall. Warmth, softness, light, a sweet scent, all those things so familiar to her she never even thought about them, she watched that other receive. It was fascinating. She was like the little

Teaching Options

Viewing and Representing

The First Cloud **by Sir William Quiller Orchardson**

ART APPRECIATION

Instruction The Scottish painter Orchardson (1832–1910) is noted for his portraits, of which this scene is a typical example. Fellow artist Tom Graham served as the model for the husband.

Application Ask students how the room in this picture compares with their image of Rosemary's room. What details in the painting correspond to their mental image of Rosemary's room, and what details do not? What might the artist intend to convey with these details?

rich girl in her nursery with all the cupboards to open, all the boxes to unpack.

"Come, come upstairs," said Rosemary, longing to begin to be generous. "Come up to my room." And, besides, she wanted to spare this poor little thing from being stared at by the servants; she decided as they mounted the stairs she would not even ring for Jeanne, but take off her things by herself. The great thing was to be natural!

And "There!" cried Rosemary again, as they reached her beautiful big bedroom with the curtains drawn, the fire leaping on her wonderful lacquer furniture, her gold cushions and the primrose and blue rugs.

The girl stood just inside the door; she seemed dazed. But Rosemary didn't mind that.

"Come and sit down," she cried, dragging her big chair up to the fire, "in this comfy chair. Come and get warm. You look so dreadfully cold."

"I daren't, madam," said the girl, and she edged backwards.

"Oh, please,"—Rosemary ran forward—"you mustn't be frightened, you mustn't, really. Sit down, and when I've taken off my things we shall go into the next room and have tea and be cozy. Why are you afraid?" And gently she half pushed the thin figure into its deep cradle.

But there was no answer. The girl stayed just as she had been put, with her hands by her sides and her mouth slightly open. To be quite sincere, she looked rather stupid. But Rosemary wouldn't acknowledge it. She leaned over her, saying: "Won't you take off your hat? Your pretty hair is all wet. And one is so much more comfortable without a hat, isn't one?"

There was a whisper that sounded like "Very good, madam," and the crushed hat was taken off.

"Let me help you off with your coat, too," said Rosemary.

The girl stood up. But she held on to the chair with one hand and let Rosemary pull. It was quite an effort. The other scarcely helped her at all. She seemed to stagger like a child, and the thought came and went through Rosemary's mind, that if people wanted helping they must respond a little, just a little, otherwise it became very difficult indeed. And what was she to do with the coat now? She left it on the floor, and the hat too. She was just going to take a cigarette off the mantelpiece when the girl said quickly, but so lightly and strangely: "I'm very sorry, madam, but I'm going to faint. I shall go off, madam, if I don't have something." D

"Good heavens, how thoughtless I am!" Rosemary rushed to the bell.

"Tea! Tea at once! And some brandy immediately!"

The maid was gone again, but the girl almost cried out. "No, I don't want no brandy. I never drink brandy. It's a cup of tea I want, madam." And she burst into tears.

It was a terrible and fascinating moment. Rosemary knelt beside her chair.

"Don't cry, poor little thing," she said. "Don't cry." And she gave the other her lace handkerchief. She really was touched beyond words. She put her arm round those thin, birdlike shoulders.

Now at last the other forgot to be shy, forgot everything except that they were both women, and gasped out: "I can't go on no longer like this. I can't bear it. I shall do away with myself. I can't bear no more."

"You shan't have to. I'll look after you. Don't cry anymore. Don't you see what a good thing it was that you met me? We'll have tea and you'll tell me everything. And I shall arrange something. I promise. *Do* stop crying. It's so exhausting. Please!"

The other did stop just in time for Rosemary to get up before the tea came. She had the table placed between them. She plied the poor little creature with everything, all the sandwiches, all the bread and butter, and every time her cup was

Customizing Instruction

Less Proficient Readers

Use the following questions to help students summarize the plot.

- How does Rosemary spend her day before meeting the poor woman?
  Answer: shopping in an antique shop.
- What does Rosemary decide to do when the poor woman asks for money for a cup of tea?
  Answer: take her home for tea.

Students Acquiring English

Point out to students that *tea* in British usage refers not only to the beverage but also to a late-afternoon snack, usually consisting of sandwiches and cakes.

Speaking and Listening

DRAMATIC PRESENTATION

Instruction Many new films are remakes and updates of existing stories, with changes in setting or costuming or perhaps language to make the story contemporary. Discuss with students the advantages and disadvantages of such an approach, particularly with works of authors such as Dickens and Shakespeare.

Prepare Have students work in groups of four or five to write a contemporary dramatic presentation of "A Cup of Tea." Encourage them to place the story in their own community or in another area they know fairly well.

Have them write stage directions for familiar settings and create believable, contemporary dialogue for Rosemary, Philip, and Miss Smith.

Present As each group presents its performance, have the class analyze and evaluate how accurately and easily the story transfers from England in the early 20th century to the United States in the early 21st century.

BLOCK SCHEDULING This activity is particularly well-suited for longer class periods

Reading and Analyzing

Literary Analysis: **IRONY**

A Ask students why it is ironic that Rosemary calls the girl her friend.

Possible Response: She does not even know the girl's name.

Active Reading ANALYZING PLOT

B Ask students to identify the turning point or climax of the story.

Possible Response: The turning point occurs when Philip mentions how lovely Miss Smith is.

Literary Analysis REALISM

C Ask students why Rosemary is so surprised to hear Philip call Miss Smith pretty.

Possible Response: Up to that time, the woman hasn't been real to Rosemary; she's startled to realize that Philip could look at a lower-class woman and find her pretty; she's jealous.

Have students describe the relationship between Rosemary and Philip.

Possible Responses: unequal; he treats her as if she were a pampered child.

empty she filled it with tea, cream and sugar. People always said sugar was so nourishing. As for herself she didn't eat; she smoked and looked away tactfully so that the other should not be shy.

And really the effect of that slight meal was marvelous. When the tea table was carried away a new being, a light, frail creature with tangled hair, dark lips, deep, lighted eyes, lay back in the big chair in a kind of sweet languor,[8] looking at the blaze. Rosemary lit a fresh cigarette; it was time to begin.

"And when did you have your last meal?" she asked softly.

But at that moment the door-handle turned.

"Rosemary, may I come in?" It was Philip.

"Of course."

He came in. "Oh, I'm so sorry," he said, and stopped and stared.

"It's quite all right," said Rosemary smiling.

A "This is my friend, Miss—"

"Smith, madam," said the languid figure, who was strangely still and unafraid.

"Smith," said Rosemary. "We are going to have a little talk."

"Oh, yes," said Philip. "Quite," and his eye caught sight of the coat and hat on the floor. He came over to the fire and turned his back to it. "It's a beastly afternoon," he said curiously, still looking at that listless figure, looking at its hands and boots, and then at Rosemary again.

"Yes, isn't it?" said Rosemary enthusiastically. "Vile."[9]

Philip smiled his charming smile. "As a matter of fact," said he, "I wanted you to come into the library for a moment. Would you? Will Miss Smith excuse us?"

The big eyes were raised to him, but Rosemary answered for her. "Of course she will." And they went out of the room together.

"I say," said Philip, when they were alone. "Explain. Who is she? What does it all mean?"

Rosemary, laughing, leaned against the door and said: "I picked her up in Curzon Street. Really. She's a real pick-up. She asked me for the price of a cup of tea, and I brought her home with me."

"But what on earth are you going to do with her?" cried Philip.

"Be nice to her," said Rosemary quickly. "Be frightfully nice to her. Look after her. I don't know how. We haven't talked yet. But show her—treat her—make her feel—"

"My darling girl," said Philip, "you're quite mad, you know. It simply can't be done."

"I knew you'd say that," retorted Rosemary. "Why not? I want to. Isn't that a reason? And besides, one's always reading about these things. I decided—"

"But," said Philip slowly, and he cut the end of a cigar, "she's so astonishingly pretty." B

"Pretty?" Rosemary was so surprised that she blushed. "Do you think so? I—I hadn't thought about it." C

"Good Lord!" Philip struck a match. "She's absolutely lovely. Look again, my child. I was bowled over when I came into your room just now. However . . . I think you're making a ghastly mistake. Sorry, darling, if I'm crude and all that. But let me know if Miss Smith is going to dine with us in time for me to look up *The Milliner's Gazette*."[10]

"You absurd creature!" said Rosemary, and she went out of the library, but not back to her bedroom. She went to her writing-room and sat down at her desk. Pretty! Absolutely lovely! Bowled over! Her heart beat like a heavy bell. Pretty! Lovely! She drew her checkbook towards her. But no, checks would be no use, of course. She opened a drawer and took out five pound notes, looked at them, put two back, and holding the three squeezed in her hand, she went back to her bedroom.

8. **languor** (lăng′gər): a dreamy, lazy mood.
9. **vile:** unpleasant; highly disagreeable.
10. ***The Milliner's Gazette:*** an imaginary newsletter for working-class women. (A milliner is a maker of women's hats.)

Teaching Options

Grammar

RHYTHM: CONTROLLING RHYTHM

Instruction The reader expects wording in a sentence to follow a familiar pattern. When that pattern is changed, the "inner ear" reacts, and the reader's thought process is interrupted. A speaker can control rhythm by varying the tone of voice, but a writer must rely on sentence structure. The writer can control emphasis by placing words in rhythmically strategic places in the sentence. In a common type of sentence rhythm known as **end focus,** the reader's "inner ear" recognizes the final or semifinal position in the sentence as the focal point. In other words, this is where the reader expects to find new or important information.

Activity Write the following sentences from "A Cup of Tea" on the chalkboard. The first sentence illustrates end focus.

"Her heart beat like a heavy bell."

"She had a feeling of triumph as she slipped her hand through the velvet strap."

Point out that in the first sentence the emphasis falls on "heavy bell," the writer's simile for a beating heart, and the natural stresses in the sentence

Half an hour later Philip was still in the library, when Rosemary came in.

"I only wanted to tell you," said she, and she leaned against the door again and looked at him with her dazzled exotic gaze, "Miss Smith won't dine with us tonight."

Philip put down the paper. "Oh, what's happened? Previous engagement?"

Rosemary came over and sat down on his knee. "She insisted on going," said she, "so I gave the poor little thing a present of money. I couldn't keep her against her will, could I?" she added softly.

Rosemary had just done her hair, darkened her eyes a little, and put on her pearls. She put up her hands and touched Philip's cheeks.

"Do you like me?" said she, and her tone, sweet, husky, troubled him.

"I like you awfully," he said, and he held her tighter. "Kiss me."

There was a pause.

Then Rosemary said dreamily, "I saw a fascinating little box today. It cost twenty-eight guineas. May I have it?"

Philip jumped her on his knee. "You may, little wasteful one," said he.

But that was not really what Rosemary wanted to say.

"Philip," she whispered, and she pressed his head against her bosom, "am I *pretty?*" ❖

Customizing Instruction

Less Proficient Readers

Make sure students understand what happens between Rosemary and Miss Smith by asking them the following questions.

- What does Rosemary at first not notice about her guest's state?
  Possible Response: that the girl is weak with hunger.
- What does Philip praise about Miss Smith?
  Answer: her prettiness.
- What does Rosemary do after hearing Philip's praise of Miss Smith?
  Answer: She gives Miss Smith money and sends her off.

(**heart, beat, heavy, bell**) reinforce the impression of heartbeats. End focus, of course, is not the only way to create emphasis. Writers may use many different techniques to make their emphasis unmistakable. For example, in the second sentence, the emphasis falls on "feeling of triumph," which comes near the beginning of the sentence, following the subject and verb.

Exercise Ask students to study each sentence below, let the underlined words be the focus, and rewrite the sentence for better emphasis. Answers will vary; possible answers are given.

1. <u>Rosemary's wealth</u> causes the shopkeeper to behave in an awe-stricken manner. *(The shopkeeper is in awe of Rosemary's wealth.)*
2. Rosemary thinks that she is being <u>noble and generous</u> when she makes her gesture toward the girl. *(Rosemary's gesture toward the girl allows her to see herself as noble and generous.)*

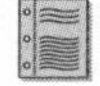 Use **Grammar Transparencies and Copymasters**, p. 108.

 Use McDougal Littell's ***Language Network*** for more instruction and practice in controlling rhythm.

GUIDING STUDENT RESPONSE

Connect to the Literature

1. **What Do You Think?**
Guidelines for student response: Encourage students to speculate on the motive behind her question. Is she asking for something else from her husband, such as reassurance?

Comprehension Check
- Rosemary plans to take care of the girl.
- He thinks she is pretty.
- money

Use Selection Quiz in **Unit Six Resource Book,** p. 23

Think Critically

2. Possible Responses: whim; naiveté; wants to act out events from novels; treats people as objects and views Miss Smith as just another "trinket"
3. Possible Response: Philip's comment on Miss Smith's beauty. Everything seems to be falling into place for Rosemary until her husband notices Miss Smith's beauty. Rosemary becomes jealous, and her "plan" changes course.
4. Possible Response: Rosemary asks her to leave. Rosemary's jealousy at her husband's remark and her selfishness lend themselves to this interpretation.
5. Possible Response: Rosemary claims that Miss Smith insisted on going, but the reader knows that Rosemary sent her away.
6. Possible Responses should have students apply inductive thinking, from the details to the conclusion. Rosemary is entirely dependent on Philip, who treats her like a spoiled child; Rosemary is superficial and vain, while Philip is amused by her; their lifestyle is lavish, frivolous, pointless.

Literary Analysis

Activity Hold a class discussion in which students share their views on realism in this story.

Review Tone Have students analyze the effect the details had on them as they formulate a description of the tone.

Thinking through the LITERATURE

Connect to the Literature

1. **What Do You Think?** What is your reaction to Rosemary's question at the end of the story? Share your thoughts with a classmate.

Comprehension Check
- What plans for Miss Smith does Rosemary have at first?
- How does Philip react toward Miss Smith?
- What does Rosemary give to Miss Smith?

Think Critically

2. Why do you think Rosemary invites Miss Smith home?

- Rosemary's mood when she meets Miss Smith
- her thoughts when Miss Smith asks her for money
- the reasons she gives to Miss Smith and to Philip

3. **ACTIVE READING ANALYZING PLOT** Review the plot sequence chart you made in your **READER'S NOTEBOOK.** Which event do you think is the **climax,** or turning point, of the story? Explain your choice.
4. Why do you think Miss Smith doesn't stay for dinner? Support your answer with evidence from the story.
5. How might Rosemary's conversation with Philip at the end of the story be considered an example of **dramatic irony?** Explain your answer.
6. What is your opinion of Rosemary, Philip, and the upper-class lifestyle presented in this story?

Extend Interpretations

7. **Different Perspectives** How do you think Miss Smith would describe her encounter with Rosemary? Bear in mind what might have made the strongest impression on Miss Smith, the differences between her and Rosemary, and the separate worlds they inhabit.
8. **Connect to Life** Some people help others out of a true sense of compassion, whereas others have strictly self-serving motives for lending a helping hand. With a partner, discuss which motive you think is more prevalent.

Literary Analysis

REALISM **Realism** in fiction is a truthful representation of actual life. In a realistic work, ordinary, everyday events are presented in clear, direct prose. Detailed **characterization,** focusing on characters' thoughts and values, is also an important element of realism. John Middleton Murry, the critic who became Katherine Mansfield's husband, praised her work for its realism, recalling the judgment of a printer who remarked after reading a manuscript of hers, "But these kids are real!"

Activity Do you agree with this view of the realism in Mansfield's work? Why or why not? Find two or three passages from "A Cup of Tea" to support your answer.

REVIEW TONE **Tone** is the expression of a writer's attitude toward his or her subject. Throughout "A Cup of Tea," Mansfield suggests her view of Rosemary through her choice of words and through details describing Rosemary's appearance, actions, and thoughts. After looking through the story to find details that reveal Mansfield's attitude, try to formulate a description of the story's overall tone.

Extend Interpretations

Different Perspectives Accept all reasonable responses that show an understanding of the differences between Miss Smith and Rosemary. Students' answers should accurately relate story details and reflect Miss Smith's point of view.

Connect to Life Accept all reasonable, well-supported responses. What are some instances in which helping someone else is more self-serving than altruistic?

Writing Options

1. Concluding Paragraph The story ends before Philip answers Rosemary's final question. Write a concluding paragraph in which he gives an answer. Try to match Mansfield's writing style and Philip's manner of speech.

2. Missing Scene Write a brief dramatic scene showing what takes place between Rosemary and Miss Smith just before Miss Smith leaves. Try to make the dialogue reflect the social class of each character. Place the scene in your **Working Portfolio.**

Activities & Explorations

1. Contemporary Version With a small group of classmates, brainstorm ideas for a contemporary version of the scene in which Rosemary first meets Miss Smith. You could begin by writing a list of what details would make the scene a work of realism set in modern times. Choose two students to play the characters and have them perform the scene for the class. ~ **SPEAKING AND LISTENING/PERFORMING**

2. Party Invitation Imagine that, having decided to make Miss Smith her protégée, Rosemary wants to throw a party to introduce the woman to her rich friends. Design an invitation she might send, including a description of Miss Smith and of the evening's entertainment. ~ **ART**

Inquiry & Research

Class in Britain Research and report on the British class system today. Is it as rigid as it was at the time of this story? If not, how has it changed?

Katherine Mansfield
1888–1923

Other Works
Bliss and Other Stories
Something Childish and Other Stories
The Garden Party and Other Stories

Around the World Although she lived to be only 34 years old, Katherine Mansfield was a master of the short story who developed a distinctive prose style characterized by mood and suggestion rather than dramatic action. Born Kathleen Mansfield Beauchamp in Wellington, New Zealand, she published her first story when she was 9. In 1903 she was sent to college in London, where she played the cello and edited the college literary magazine. On her return to New Zealand, she was so unhappy that her father sent her back to London, where her interest quickly shifted from music to literature. She married in 1909 but left her husband after a few days and began reviewing and writing short stories.

Married Life In 1911, Mansfield met the English critic John Middleton Murry, and they began a creative but stormy relationship. In 1919, after she obtained a divorce from her first husband, she and Murry were married. The couple stayed some weeks with Frieda and D. H. Lawrence, and Lawrence loosely based the main characters in his novel *Women in Love* on the four of them.

Early Death Mansfield suffered from ill health and traveled often in search of a favorable climate. During her last years, although she was at the height of her powers as a writer, she lived as an invalid, fighting a losing battle with tuberculosis. Despite the shortness of her writing career, she is considered a major contributor to the form and style of the modern short story.

Author Activity

Mansfield and Lawrence Find out more about the friendship, and later falling-out, between Mansfield and D. H. Lawrence. How did Lawrence portray Mansfield and her husband when he used them as models for characters in *Women in Love*?

LaserLinks: Background for Reading
Art Gallery

Writing Options

1. **Concluding Paragraph** Remind students that they must continue to use the third-person limited point of view. Responses should be consistent with Philip's character and his relationship with Rosemary.
2. **Missing Scene** Scenes should accurately relate story details and reflect Rosemary's uneasiness with the new "twist" presented to her as well as Miss Smith's reaction.

Activities & Explorations

1. **Contemporary Version** Students might begin by considering the specific points they will need to update—for example, where Rosemary will shop, and what she will consider buying. Students might wish to make this scene part of the Speaking and Listening activity suggested earlier. The group should move from brainstorming to drafting and revising the scene before rehearsing.
2. **Party Invitation** Have students first determine the tone Rosemary would use to write such an invitation. How would she describe Miss Smith to her friends? What would constitute the evening's entertainment?

Inquiry & Research

Class in Britain Allow students to work in pairs and make their final reports orally, in writing, or in a group panel discussion.

Author Activity

Mansfield and Lawrence You might suggest that students see *Katherine Mansfield: A Secret Life* by Claire Tomalin or Mansfield's *Collected Letters* edited by V. O'Sullivan and M. Scott.

Informal Assessment

WRITING AN ARTICLE
To assess students' understanding of the story, you might set up this scenario:

Imagine that you are gossip columnist for a London newspaper or tabloid. Write an article in which you describe Rosemary's visit to the Curzon Street shop and her subsequent "good deed" involving Miss Smith.

Have students work on their articles alone or in pairs and then share them with classmates.

RUBRIC

3 **Full Accomplishment** Students accurately describe story events and capture aspects of Rosemary's personality in style suitable to gossip column.

2 **Substantial Accomplishment** Students accurately describe story events and capture some aspects of Rosemary's personality and behavior.

1 **Little or Partial Accomplishment** Students have difficulty with story events, omitting some or placing them in wrong sequence. They show little understanding of Rosemary's personality and behavior.

Although Graham Greene wrote short stories, plays, children's books, and nonfiction, he is best known for his psychological novels and thrillers, a number of which have been made into award-winning films.

Additional Background

GRAHAM GREENE

Graham Greene (1904–1991) was brought up in the Church of England, but he converted to Roman Catholicism in 1926, making himself a member of a very small religious minority in Britain. A man to whom spiritual matters were profoundly important, he wrestled with the problems of sin, guilt, and redemption in many of his more serious novels.

Greene's first novel, a thriller titled *Stamboul Train* (1932; U. S. edition titled *Orient Express)* was successful with the public and was made into a film two years later. He followed this work with other fast-paced novels of crime and intrigue, including *This Gun for Hire* and *Our Man in Havana.*

In 1948, Greene published *The Heart of the Matter,* his first major critical success. This novel also established his reputation as a Catholic writer, a label to which Greene objected. In his view, only a few of his books–*Brighton Rock, The Power and the Glory, The End of the Affair,* and *The Heart of the Matter*–had religious overtones.

Greene was a private man who kept his personal life to himself. He once wrote, "If anybody ever tries to write a biography of me, how complicated they are going to find it and how misled they are going to be." According to one writer, Greene "did his best to remain personally invisible, covering his trail with practical jokes, exaggerations, lies, evasions, and legal suits in an effort to confuse and confound his trackers."

Graham Greene

The Novels of Graham Greene

A stranger arrives in Vienna, or Vietnam, or Cuba—a scene of conflict and intrigue. He intends to live quietly, but trouble soon finds him. Torn between conscience and friendship, duty and love, evidence and faith, the stranger must betray one or the other. Which will he choose?

Situations such as this fascinated Graham Greene, who used them as frameworks for many of his novels. First and foremost, Greene saw himself as an entertainer, even characterizing some of his books as "entertainments" rather than novels. A number of his works, including *Our Man in Havana* and *Brighton Rock,* have been made into films; one, *The Third Man,* was actually conceived as a film before it was published as a novel. Greene's style is itself basically cinematic, sometimes displaying a wide view from a distance, sometimes zooming in for a close-up of details. It is a style that has had a tremendous influence on other writers, especially writers of the spy novel—brimming with suspense, danger, and international intrigue—a form of which Greene was a master.

The settings of Greene's novels tend to be the world's trouble spots, including such far-flung places as Africa, Mexico, London, South America, and Haiti. Most of these exotic locales are places Greene knew well. *The Ministry of Fear* grew out of his wartime service in West Africa, and *The Heart of the Matter* evolved from his experiences

Speaking, Listening, Viewing and Representing

ANALYZING AND COMPARING A FILM REVIEW

Many of Jane Graham Greene's books have been translated into films. Use this opportunity to show one of the films mentioned in this article.

Introduce this activity by telling students that, after viewing a film version of one of Graham Greene's novels, they will locate and analyze a review, and compare the review to their own response.

Instruction After students have seen and discussed the film, have them find a review of it. Students can find film reviews through *Readers' Guide to Periodical Literature;* in magazines such as *Premier, Film Comment,* and *Entertainment Weekly;* in *infotrac, 2000,* a magazine index on CD-ROM and on-line; and major on-line services. Suggest they use the following criteria for analyzing the review.

The review:

- identifies the film at the beginning
- includes a general opinion about the film
- includes enough facts, examples and specifics to support the opinion

in Freetown, Sierra Leone. Similarly, a visit to Vienna resulted in *The Third Man,* and trips to Vietnam, Cuba, and South America provided material for *The Quiet American, Our Man in Havana,* and *The Honorary Consul.*

Like his settings, the themes of Greene's novels spring from personal experience. The web of conflicting loyalties in which his characters are caught resembles his own boyhood sense of dual loyalty—to his headmaster father on the one hand and to his school chums on the other. His concern with moral dilemmas reflects his personal interest in spiritual growth as well as his conversion to Roman Catholicism. His political themes reflect his lifelong involvement in world affairs and his experience as a spy.

Recognizing these various influences, critics have labeled Graham Greene a Catholic novelist, a political novelist, and a spy novelist. He is all of these, of course, and more. Despite their varied themes and settings, Greene's novels essentially center on complex, unpredictable people. Like real people, they refuse to be classified or pigeonholed. Instead, they live as best they know how in a world that is in turmoil.

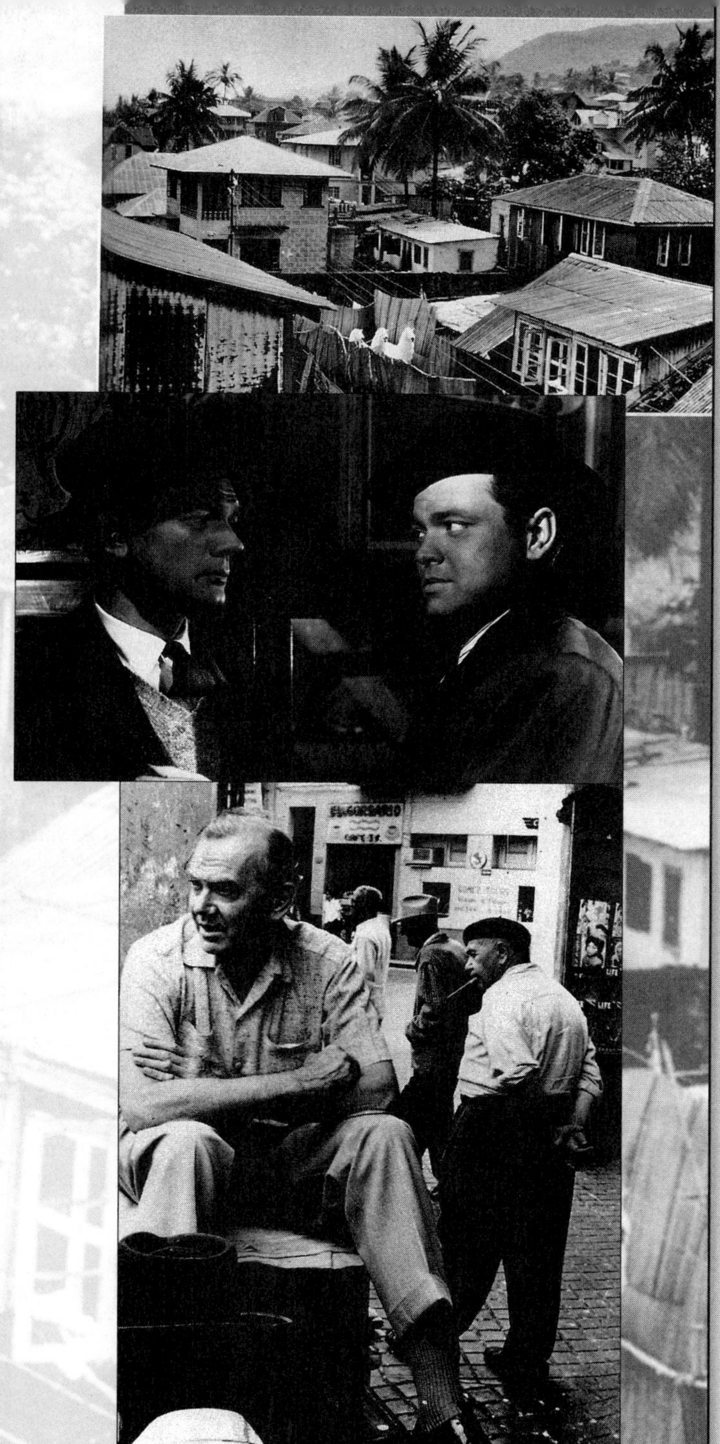

Far top left:
The giant Ferris wheel in Vienna used in filming The Third Man. *Photofest.*
Top right:
Freetown, Sierra Leone, one of the many places Greene lived in and wrote about.
Middle right:
Joseph Cotton and Orson Welles in The Third Man. *Photofest.*
Bottom right:
Greene in Havana.

LITERARY CHRONOLOGY

The following are publication dates of some of Greene's best-known novels:

1938 *Brighton Rock*

1940 *The Power and the Glory*

1943 *The Ministry of Fear*

1948 *The Heart of the Matter*

1950 *The Third Man*

1951 *The End of the Affair*

1955 *The Quiet American*

1958 *Our Man in Havana*

1973 *The Honorary Consul*

- may include a synopsis of the film
- may include a discussion of the craft used to produce the film
- may include the reviewer's personal experience

Present Have students read, analyze, and discuss the review using the above criteria. Have them compare the review to their own response.

OVERVIEW

 This selection is included in the **Grade 12 InterActive Reader.**

Objectives

1. understand and appreciate a **short story (Literary Analysis)**
2. appreciate the author's use of **style (Literary Analysis)**
3. **make inferences** to understand and interpret Woolf's story **(Active Reading)**

Summary

Oliver Bacon began life as a poor alley kid, but he has become the richest jeweller in London. He lives well and moves in the highest social circles, but he feels something lacking in his life. One day the duchess of Lambourne visits his shop. She wants to sell Bacon some pearls to raise money to pay off gambling debts. Bacon wonders whether the pearls are real or fake. However, he is in love with the duchess's daughter, Diana, and does not want to offend the mother. Just as Bacon is about to order the pearls to be tested, the duchess invites him to a weekend party at her home with many important guests and Diana. The jeweller then writes a sizable check to the duchess for her pearls. After she leaves, he examines the pearls and discovers they are fake.

 Use **Unit Six Resource Book,** p. 24 for additional support.

Thematic Link

In this story, Virginia Woolf presents a **new image of reality** in which the vanity of social position, whether achieved by birth or wealth, is evident.

5-Minute Warm-Up

Daily Language SkillBuilder

Have students **proofread** the display sentences on page 979i and write them correctly. The sentences also appear on Transparency 28 of **Grammar Transparencies and Copymasters.**

The Duchess and the Jeweller

Short Story by VIRGINIA WOOLF

"'Tears!' said Oliver, looking at the pearls."

Connect to Your Life

Hard Bargain Have you ever agreed to do something unpleasant in return for a favor? What was the driving force that moved you to accept the bargain? Looking back on the situation, do you think you made the right decision? Explore your thoughts with a classmate.

Build Background

Woolf and the Bloomsbury Group Virginia Woolf was one of the most celebrated members of the Bloomsbury group, a circle of intellectual writers, painters, and philosophers who met and conversed frequently from about 1907 to 1930. Many in the group lived in the Bloomsbury district of London, and they often met in Woolf's house. Members questioned existing ideas and sought ways of improving not only their literary and artistic expression but society in general. They rejected many 19th-century views about literature, art, politics, and social issues and supported writers and artists who were breaking new ground.

Woolf continually experimented with the form of the novel and excelled at revealing the inner thoughts and feelings of her characters. In her essay "Modern Fiction," she wrote that "everything is the proper stuff of fiction, every feeling, every thought; every quality of brain and spirit is drawn upon; no perception comes amiss." Her brilliantly original fiction has won wide acclaim from prominent literary figures, including the novelist E. M. Forster (also a member of the Bloomsbury group), whose comments on Woolf appear on page 1057.

WORDS TO KNOW
Vocabulary Preview

arrogance · astute · forge · lissome · obsequiously

Focus Your Reading

LITERARY ANALYSIS STYLE An important element of Woolf's **style** is her use of **stream of consciousness,** a technique of presenting, in a series of loosely connected associations, the flow of thoughts and sensations in a character's mind:

> ***He looked past her, at the backs of the houses in Bond Street. But he saw not the houses in Bond Street, but a dimpling river; and trout rising and salmon; and the Prime Minister; and himself too; in white waistcoats; and then, Diana.***

As you read, be aware of Woolf's use of this stylistic technique.

ACTIVE READING MAKING INFERENCES
Understanding what impels a **character** is often the key to understanding an entire story. Sometimes the character's **motivation**—the driving force behind his or her thoughts, feelings, and actions—is obvious; at other times it must be **inferred** from clues buried within the story.

READER'S NOTEBOOK As you read Woolf's story, record the motivations of both the duchess and the jeweller in a diagram like the one shown here.

Character: Jeweller
↓
Action: Reflects on his past
↓
Motivation: ?

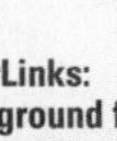 **LaserLinks: Background for Reading** Geographical Connection

LESSON RESOURCES

UNIT SIX RESOURCE BOOK, pp. 24–28

ASSESSMENT RESOURCES
Formal Assessment, pp. 189–190
Teacher's Guide to Assessment and Portfolio Use
Test Generator

SKILLS TRANSPARENCIES AND COPYMASTERS
Literary Analysis
- Figurative Language, T22 (for Literary Analysis, p. 1054)

Reading and Critical Thinking
- Making Inferences, T7 (for Active Reading, p. 1046)

Grammar
- Parallelism, T57 (for Mini Lesson, p. 1056)
- Parallelism, C175 (for Mini Lesson, p. 1051)

Vocabulary
- Context Clues, C81 (for Mini Lesson, p. 1056)

Writing
- The Uses of Dialogue, T24 (for Writing Option 3, p. 1055)
- Personality Profile, C25 (for Writing Option 2, p. 1055)
- Literary Interpretation, C33 (for Writing Option 4, p. 1055)

Communications
- Evaluating Roles in Groups, T8 (for Activities & Explorations 2, p. 1055)
- Impromptu Speaking: Dialogue, Role-Play, T14 (for Activities & Explorations 1, p. 1055)

INTEGRATED TECHNOLOGY
Audio Library
LaserLinks
- Geographical Connection: London, Early 1900s. See **Teacher's SourceBook,** p. 73.

Internet: Research Starter
Visit our website: www.mcdougallittell.com

Virginia Woolf

The Duchess and the Jeweller

1047

TEACHING THE LITERATURE

Customizing Instruction

Less Proficient Readers
Help students focus on the psychological subtleties of the story by summarizing for them in advance the jeweller's situation: He is a wealthy man who grew up poor and made his fortune by outsmarting his aristocratic clients.

Set a Purpose Have students predict how someone in the jeweller's position might feel toward his aristocratic clients and what conflicts he might feel. Have them read the selection to check their predictions.

Students Acquiring English
Students may not be familiar with the British class system and its sharp division between the landed aristocracy of inherited wealth and everyone else. Point out that people such as the jeweller, who earn their wealth through business and rise up from poverty, are never considered the social equals of the aristocracy, even if the people in "trade" have more money.

 Use **Spanish Study Guide** for additional support, pp. 245–247.

Gifted and Talented
Have students infer Woolf's attitude toward the British class system in general and aristocrats such as the duchess in particular. Have them compare her attitude with that of P. G. Wodehouse as shown in "The Truth About George."

BLOCK SCHEDULING: MANAGING TIME

If your schedule requires that you cover the lesson objectives in a shorter time, use . . .

- Preparing to Read, p. 1046
- Thinking Through the Literature, p. 1054
- Vocabulary in Action, p. 1055

If you want to take advantage of longer class time, use . . .

- TE Teaching Options: Preteaching Vocabulary, p. 1049; Vocabulary, p. 1051; Grammar, p. 1056; Viewing and Representing, p. 1050; Speaking and Listening, p. 1052; Cross-Curricular Links, p. 1048; Standardized Test Practice, p. 1053
- Choices & Challenges and Author Activity, pp. 1055–1056

Reading and Analyzing

Literary Analysis STYLE

Remind students that many elements, including word choice, sentence length, tone, figurative language, use of dialogue, and point of view, combine to make up a writer's style. Ask students to pay close attention to these elements as they read. You might want to list them on the board for easy reference.

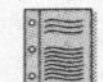 Use **Unit Six Resource Book** p. 26 for more exercises.

Active Reading MAKING INFERENCES

Remind students that an inference is a logical guess made from clues in the text. Tell students that the motivations of the story's main character are not openly stated, and must be inferred. As they read, ask students to write down facts they think might be clues to the later actions of the characters.

 Use **Unit Six Resource Book** p. 25 for more practice.

Literary Analysis: CHARACTER

Point out to students that in these pages Woolf introduces readers to Oliver as an adult and Oliver as a child. Ask students to work in groups to list characteristics of the adult Oliver and of the young Oliver. Then have them compare the lists and decide in what ways Oliver has changed and in what ways he is the same.

Possible Response: adult Oliver—wealthy, insecure, ambitious; young Oliver—poor, insecure, ambitious; changed—now wealthy; same—still insecure and ambitious.

Oliver Bacon lived at the top of a house overlooking the Green Park. He had a flat; chairs jutted out at the right angles—chairs covered in hide. Sofas filled the bays of the windows—sofas covered in tapestry. The windows, the three long windows, had the proper allowance of discreet net and figured satin.[1] The mahogany sideboard bulged discreetly with the right brandies, whiskeys and liqueurs. And from the middle window he looked down upon the glossy roofs of fashionable cars packed in the narrow straits of Piccadilly.[2] A more central position could not be imagined. And at eight in the morning he would have his breakfast brought in on a tray by a manservant; the manservant would unfold his crimson dressing gown; he would rip his letters open with his long pointed nails and would extract thick white cards of invitation upon which the engraving stood up roughly from duchesses, countesses, viscountesses[3] and Honorable Ladies. Then he would wash; then he would eat his toast; then he would read his paper by the bright burning fire of electric coals.

"Behold Oliver," he would say, addressing himself. "You who began life in a filthy little alley, you who . . ." and he would look down at his legs, so shapely in their perfect trousers; at his boots; at his spats. They were all shapely, shining; cut from the best cloth by the best scissors in Savile Row.[4] But he dismantled himself[5] often and became again a little boy in a dark alley. He had once thought that[6] the height of his ambition—selling stolen dogs to fashionable women in Whitechapel.[7] And once he had been done.[8] "Oh, Oliver," his mother had wailed. "Oh, Oliver! When will you have sense, my son?" . . . Then he had gone behind a counter; had sold cheap watches; then he had taken a wallet to Amsterdam. . . . At that memory he would chuckle—the old Oliver remembering the young. Yes, he had done well with the three diamonds; also there was the commission on the emerald. After that he went into the private room behind the shop in Hatton Garden;[9] the room with the scales, the safe, the thick magnifying glasses. And then . . . and then . . . He chuckled. When he passed through the knots of jewellers in the hot evening who were discussing prices, gold mines, diamonds, reports from South Africa, one of them would lay a finger to the side of his nose and murmur, "Hum–m–m," as he passed. It was no more than a murmur; no more than a nudge on the shoulder, a finger on the nose, a buzz that ran through the cluster of jewellers in Hatton Garden on a hot afternoon—oh, many years ago now! But still Oliver felt it purring down his spine, the nudge, the murmur that meant, "Look at him—young Oliver, the young jeweller—there he goes." Young he was then. And he dressed better and better; and had, first a hansom cab;[10] then a car; and first he went up to the dress circle,

1. **discreet net and figured satin:** curtains made of lace that is not showy and satin with a design woven into it.
2. **Piccadilly** (pĭk′ə-dĭl′ē): one of London's main business streets.
3. **viscountesses** (vī′koun′tĭs-ĭz): noblewomen ranking below duchesses and countesses but above baronesses.
4. **Savile** (săv′ĭl) **Row:** a London street in which many exclusive men's clothing stores are located.
5. **dismantled himself:** took himself apart (that is, mentally removed the outer symbols of success in order to see the person he once was).
6. **that:** The word is used as a pronoun here, referring to the selling of stolen dogs mentioned later in the sentence.
7. **Whitechapel:** a seedy area in eastern London.
8. **done:** British slang meaning "arrested and charged with a crime."
9. **Hatton Garden:** the center of London's jewelry trade.
10. **hansom cab:** a two-wheeled horse-drawn carriage.

Teaching Options

Cross Curricular Link History

SOUTH AFRICAN COLONISTS The Dutch were the first Europeans to colonize South Africa. After gold and diamonds were discovered there in 1886, however, British colonists flocked to South Africa to make their fortunes. The result was the Boer War (1899–1902), which the British won after three years of fighting the Dutch colonists, or Boers.

then down into the stalls.[11] And he had a villa at Richmond, overlooking the river, with trellises of red roses; and Mademoiselle used to pick one every morning and stick it in his buttonhole.

"So," said Oliver Bacon, rising and stretching his legs. "So . . ."

And he stood beneath the picture of an old lady on the mantelpiece and raised his hands. "I have kept my word," he said, laying his hands together, palm to palm, as if he were doing homage to her. "I have won my bet." That was so; he was the richest jeweller in England; but his nose, which was long and flexible, like an elephant's trunk, seemed to say by its curious quiver at the nostrils (but it seemed as if the whole nose quivered, not only the nostrils) that he was not satisfied yet; still smelt something under the ground a little further off. Imagine a giant hog in a pasture rich with truffles;[12] after unearthing this truffle and that, still it smells a bigger, a blacker truffle under the ground further off. So Oliver snuffed always in the rich earth of Mayfair[13] another truffle, a blacker, a bigger further off.

Now then he straightened the pearl in his tie, cased himself in his smart blue overcoat; took his yellow gloves and his cane; and swayed as he descended the stairs and half snuffed, half sighed through his long sharp nose as he passed out into Piccadilly. For was he not still a sad man, a dissatisfied man, a man who seeks something that is hidden, though he had won his bet?

For was he not still a sad man, a dissatisfied man, a man who seeks something that is hidden, though he had won his bet?

He swayed slightly as he walked, as the camel at the zoo sways from side to side when it walks along the asphalt paths laden with grocers and their wives eating from paper bags and throwing little bits of silver paper crumpled up on to the path. The camel despises the grocers; the camel is dissatisfied with its lot; the camel sees the blue lake and the fringe of palm trees in front of it. So the great jeweller, the greatest jeweller in the whole world, swung down Piccadilly, perfectly dressed, with his gloves, with his cane; but dissatisfied still, till he reached the dark little shop, that was famous in France, in Germany, in Austria, in Italy, and all over America—the dark little shop in the street off Bond Street.[14]

As usual he strode through the shop without speaking, though the four men, the two old men, Marshall and Spencer, and the two young men, Hammond and Wicks, stood straight behind the counter as he passed and looked at him, envying him. It was only with one finger of the amber-colored glove, waggling, that he acknowledged their presence. And he went in and shut the door of his private room behind him.

Then he unlocked the grating that barred the window. The cries of Bond Street came in; the purr of the distant traffic. The light from reflectors at the back of the shop struck upwards. One tree waved six green leaves, for it was June. But Mademoiselle had married Mr. Pedder of the local brewery—no one stuck roses in his buttonhole now.

"So," he half sighed, half snorted, "so . . ."

Then he touched a spring in the wall and slowly the paneling slid open, and behind it were the steel safes, five, no, six of them, all of burnished steel. He twisted a key; unlocked one; then another. Each was lined with a pad of deep

11. **dress circle . . . stalls:** In a theater or concert hall, the dress circle is a section of seats—usually in the first balcony—that are expensive but available to all. The stalls are seats near the stage that are usually reserved for royalty or others of very high rank.
12. **truffles:** edible fungi that grow underground, considered a rare delicacy. (Hogs are often used to sniff them out.)
13. **Mayfair:** a fashionable residential section of London.
14. **Bond Street:** a main business street passing through the jewelers' district in London.

Customizing Instruction

Multiple Learning Styles

Visual Learners

Have students browse through photo guides and tour guides of London to find pictures of Piccadilly, Savile Row, Whitechapel, Hatton Garden, Mayfair, and Bond Street. Have them locate these landmarks on a map of London.

Mini Lesson Preteaching Vocabulary

USING THE DICTIONARY

Instruction Cite some examples of unusual, exotic, or unfamiliar words from this story.

Activity Have students look up the WORDS TO KNOW in a good dictionary and write down the meaning for each word.

- arrogance
  Possible Response: haughtiness or self-importance
- astute
  Possible Response: shrewd
- forge
  Possible Response: to give form to by careful effort
- lissome
  Possible Response: able to move with ease
- obsequiously
  Possible Response: fawningly; compliantly

 Use **Unit Six Resource Book** p. 27 for additional support.

Reading and Analyzing

Literary Analysis: FIGURATIVE LANGUAGE

A Tell students that the jeweller's remarks ("Tears! . . . Heart's blood! . . . Gunpowder!") express three implied metaphors. Ask what the metaphors reveal about his feelings.

Possible Responses: He relishes his success and sense of power, but he is also a frustrated and angry man. He may feel he has sacrificed part of himself to accumulate his wealth, and yet he does not feel a part of the fashionable world he moves in and he resents it.

Literary Analysis: STREAM OF CONSCIOUSNESS

B Ask students what they think the stream of associations from the last paragraph on p. 1050 through the first paragraph on p. 1051 reveals about the jeweller's past experiences and their relevance to his present attitudes.

Possible Responses: Images of his deprived and powerless past are never far from his mind; he now savors being able to assert his power over his aristocratic clients.

Reading Skills and Strategies: MAKING JUDGMENTS

C Ask students whether they think what the narrator says about the duchess opening her private heart to the jeweller is true.

Answer: Accept all reasonable responses.

A Dinner Table at Night (The Glass of Claret) (1884), John Singer Sargent. Oil on canvas, 20¼" × 26¼", The Fine Arts Museums of San Francisco, gift of the Atholl McBean Foundation (73.12).

crimson velvet; in each lay jewels—bracelets, necklaces, rings, tiaras, ducal coronets;[15] loose stones in glass shells; rubies, emeralds, pearls, diamonds. All safe, shining, cool, yet burning, eternally, with their own compressed light.

A "Tears!" said Oliver, looking at the pearls.

"Heart's blood!" he said, looking at the rubies.

"Gunpowder!" he continued, rattling the diamonds so that they flashed and blazed.

"Gunpowder enough to blow up Mayfair—sky high, high, high!" He threw his head back and made a sound like a horse neighing as he said it.

The telephone buzzed obsequiously in a low muted voice on his table. He shut the safe.

B "In ten minutes," he said. "Not before." And he sat down at his desk and looked at the heads of the Roman emperors that were graved[16] on his sleeve links. And again he dismantled himself and became once more the little boy playing marbles in the alley where they sell stolen dogs on Sunday. He became that wily astute little boy, with lips like wet cherries. 1

15. **ducal** (do͞o'kəl) **coronets:** small crowns worn by dukes and duchesses.

16. **graved:** engraved.

WORDS TO KNOW

obsequiously (ŏb-sē'kwē-əs-lē) *adv.* in a subservient or fawning manner

astute (ə-sto͞ot') *adj.* clever; shrewd

1050

Teaching Options

Viewing and Representing

A Dinner Table at Night (The Glass of Claret) **by John Singer Sargent**

ART APPRECIATION

Instruction The American painter Sargent (1856–1925) was a highly successful painter of society portraits in both England and America.

Application Ask students whether they would like to be in the place of the woman in the painting; and why or why not.

Answer: Accept all reasonable responses.

Ask students to describe specific elements of the painting that makes them feel the way they do.

Possible Responses: Students who would like to be in the woman's place might point out her elegant clothing and the gleaming tableware as well as her facial expression; students who would not like to be in the woman's place might point out the picture's gloom, the woman's solitude, and the lack of warmth in the painting.

He dabbled his fingers in ropes of tripe;[17] he dipped them in pans of frying fish; he dodged in and out among the crowds. He was slim, lissome, with eyes like licked stones. And now—now—the hands of the clock ticked on. One, two, three, four . . . The Duchess of Lambourne waited his pleasure; the Duchess of Lambourne,
2 daughter of a hundred Earls. She would wait for ten minutes on a chair at the counter. She would wait his pleasure. She would wait till he was ready to see her. He watched the clock in its shagreen[18] case. The hand moved on. With each tick the clock handed him—so it seemed—pâté de foie gras;[19] a glass of champagne; another of fine brandy; a cigar costing one guinea. The
B clock laid them on the table beside him, as the ten minutes passed. Then he heard soft slow footsteps approaching; a rustle in the corridor. The door opened. Mr. Hammond flattened himself against the wall.

"Her Grace!" he announced.

And he waited there, flattened against the wall.

And Oliver, rising, could hear the rustle of the dress of the Duchess as she came down the passage. Then she loomed up, filling the door, filling the room with the aroma, the prestige, the arrogance, the pomp, the pride of all the Dukes
3 and Duchesses swollen in one wave. And as a wave breaks, she broke, as she sat down, spreading and splashing and falling over Oliver Bacon the great jeweller, covering him with sparkling bright colors, green, rose, violet; and odors; and iridescences;[20] and rays shooting from fingers, nodding from plumes, flashing from silk; for she was very large, very fat, tightly girt[21] in pink taffeta, and past her prime. As a parasol with many flounces,[22] as a peacock with many feathers, shuts its flounces, folds its feathers, so she subsided and shut herself as she sank down in the leather armchair.

"Good morning, Mr. Bacon," said the Duchess. And she held out her hand which came through the slit of her white glove. And Oliver bent low as he shook it. And as their hands touched the link was forged between them once more. They were friends, yet enemies; he was master, she was mistress; each cheated the other, each needed the other, each feared the other, each felt this and knew this every time they touched hands thus in the little back room with the white light outside, and the tree with its six leaves, and the sound of the street in the distance and behind them the safes.

"And today, Duchess—what can I do for you today?" said Oliver, very softly.

The Duchess opened; her heart, her private C
heart, gaped wide. And with a sigh, but no words, she took from her bag a long wash-leather pouch—it looked like a lean yellow ferret.[23] And from a slit in the ferret's belly she dropped pearls—ten pearls. They rolled from the slit in the ferret's belly—one, two, three, four—like the eggs of some heavenly bird.

"All that's left me, dear Mr. Bacon," she moaned. Five, six, seven—down they rolled, down the slopes of the vast mountainsides that fell between her knees into one narrow valley—the eighth, the ninth, and the tenth. There they lay in the glow of the peach-blossom taffeta. Ten pearls.

17. **tripe:** the stomach lining of a cow or calf, used as a food.
18. **shagreen** (shə-grēn′): untanned leather, often dyed green.
19. **pâté de foie gras** (pä-tā′ də fwä grä′): a delicacy made from goose liver.
20. **iridescences** (ĭr′ĭ-dĕs′ən-sĭz): brilliant displays of changing, rainbowlike colors.
21. **girt:** wrapped; encircled.
22. **parasol with many flounces:** umbrella with many ruffles.
23. **ferret:** a small weasel-like mammal.

WORDS TO KNOW
lissome (lĭs′əm) *adj.* easy and graceful in movement
arrogance (ăr′ə-gəns) *n.* overbearing pride; exaggerated self-importance
forge (fôrj) *v.* to form, shape, or produce

Customizing Instruction

Less Proficient Readers

1 Make sure students understand that these lines are Oliver's reverie—that he returns to his childhood in thought while the duchess waits.

Students Acquiring English

Help students to understand the figurative language of the following passages.

2 Tell students that each minute he keeps the duchess waiting is as enjoyable to him as fine food, wine, or a cigar.

3 Explain that Woolf compares the duchess to a wave to express her overwhelming presence.

Multiple Learning Styles

Kinesthetic Learners

Have students design a costume for the duchess. They might sketch it, make a small version for a doll, or make a costume to wear.

Vocabulary Strategy

USING CONTEXT CLUES

Instruction Remind students that the context of a word usually includes a word or a phrase with a similar meaning.

Activity Ask students to look at the context of each of the following WORDS TO KNOW and to find the words or phrases with meanings similar to the WORDS TO KNOW.

- obsequiously
  Answer: in a low muted voice
- astute
  Answer: wily
- lissome
  Answer: dodged in and out
- arrogance
  Answer: pride

Use **Vocabulary Transparencies and Copymasters,** p. 55.

Reading and Analyzing

Literary Analysis:
FIGURATIVE LANGUAGE

A Ask students what other precious jewels have been compared to tears in the story.

Answer: pearls.

Ask students why they think tears in the story are compared to diamonds and pearls.

Possible Response: They end up costing the jeweller a great deal of money; the emotion they represent is of greater value than material possessions.

Literary Analysis:
STREAM OF CONSCIOUSNESS

B Ask what associations the mention of Diana's name arouses in the jeweller.

Possible Response: images of the aristocratic surroundings in which she lives, and finally, of her.

Then ask why these associations create conflict for him.

Possible Response: He wants Diana and wants to be part of her world, but to please her mother, he may have to let himself be duped.

Reading Skills and Strategies:
DRAWING CONCLUSIONS

Ask students whether they think Oliver will ever get the satisfaction he desires. Make sure students support their answers with evidence from the text.

Possible Responses: Yes, Oliver will get what he wants. He was willing to be taken in so he could go to the duchess's for the weekend. No, Oliver will not get what he wants. It is clear from the way the duchess treats him that the aristocrats will never consider him their equal.

"From the Appleby cincture,"[24] she mourned. "The last . . . the last of them all."

Oliver stretched out and took one of the pearls between finger and thumb. It was round, it was lustrous. But real was it, or false? Was she lying again? Did she dare?

She laid her plump padded finger across her lips. "If the Duke knew . . ." she whispered. "Dear Mr. Bacon, a bit of bad luck . . ."

Been gambling again, had she?

"That villain! That sharper!"[25] she hissed.

The man with the chipped cheek bone? A bad 'un. And the Duke was straight as a poker; with side whiskers; would cut her off, shut her up down there if he knew—what I know, thought Oliver, and glanced at the safe.

"Araminta, Daphne, Diana," she moaned. "It's for *them.*"

The Ladies Araminta, Daphne, Diana —her daughters. He knew them; adored them. But it was Diana he loved.

"You have all my secrets," she leered. Tears slid; **A** tears fell; tears, like diamonds, collecting powder in the ruts of her cherry-blossom cheeks.

"Old friend," she murmured, "old friend."

"Old friend," he repeated, "old friend," as if he licked the words.

"How much?" he queried.

She covered the pearls with her hand.

"Twenty thousand," she whispered.

But was it real or false, the one he held in his hand? The Appleby cincture—hadn't she sold it already? He would ring for Spencer or Hammond. "Take it and test it," he would say. He stretched to the bell.

"You will come down tomorrow?" she urged, she interrupted. "The Prime Minister—His Royal Highness . . ." She stopped. "And Diana," she added.

Oliver took his hand off the bell.

He looked past her, at the backs of the houses in Bond Street. But he saw, not the houses in Bond Street, but a dimpling river; and trout rising and salmon; and the Prime Minister; and himself too; in white waistcoats; and then, **B** Diana. He looked down at the pearl in his hand. But how could he test it, in the light of the river, in the light of the eyes of Diana? But the eyes of the Duchess were on him.

"Twenty thousand," she moaned. "My honor!"

24. **cincture** (sĭngk′chər): an ornamental belt.

25. **sharper:** a cheating gambler.

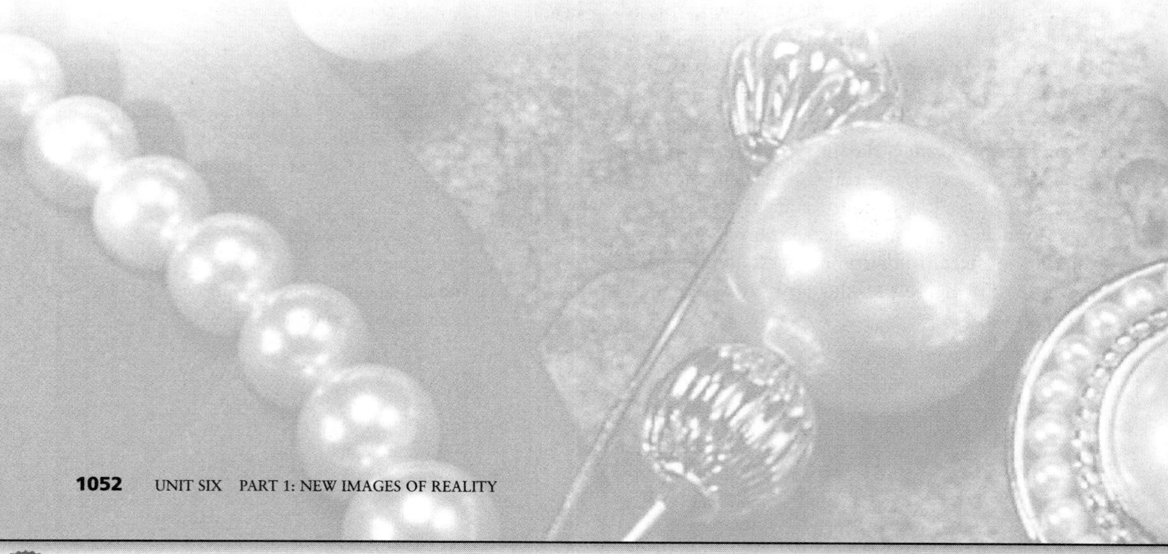

Teaching Options

Speaking and Listening

MAKING A SPEECH

Instruction Ask students to imagine that the portrait of Oliver's mother can speak. Have them write a speech from her to Oliver.

Present Ask selected students to deliver these speeches to the class. Have the class listen to see which speeches best fit the idea of Oliver's mother they got from the story.

BLOCK SCHEDULING This activity is particularly well-suited for longer class periods.

The honor of the mother of Diana! He drew his checkbook towards him; he took out his pen.

"Twenty," he wrote. Then he stopped writing. The eyes of the old woman in the picture were on him—of the old woman, his mother.

"Oliver!" she warned him. "Have sense! Don't be a fool!"

"Oliver!" the Duchess entreated—it was "Oliver" now, not "Mr. Bacon." "You'll come for a long weekend?"

Alone in the woods with Diana! Riding alone in the woods with Diana!

"Thousand," he wrote, and signed it.

"Here you are," he said.

And there opened all the flounces of the parasol, all the plumes of the peacock, the radiance of the wave, the swords and spears of Agincourt,26 as she rose from her chair. And the two old men and the two young men, Spencer and Marshall, Wicks and Hammond, flattened themselves behind the counter envying him as he led her through the shop to the door. And he

The eyes of the old woman in the picture were on him —of the old woman, his mother.

waggled his yellow glove in their faces, and she held her honor—a check for twenty thousand pounds with his signature—quite firmly in her hands.

"Are they false or are they real?" asked Oliver, shutting his private door. There they were, ten pearls on the blotting paper on the table. He took them to the window. He held them under his lens to the light. . . . This, then, was the truffle he had routed out of the earth! Rotten at the center—rotten at the core! 1

"Forgive me, oh my mother!" he sighed, raising his hands as if he asked pardon of the old woman in the picture. And again he was a little boy in the alley where they sold dogs on Sunday.

"For," he murmured, laying the palms of his hands together, "it is to be a long weekend." ❖

26. **Agincourt** (ăj'ĭn-kôrt'): a French village where, in 1415, Henry V's English forces defeated a much larger French army in what is considered one of England's most glorious victories.

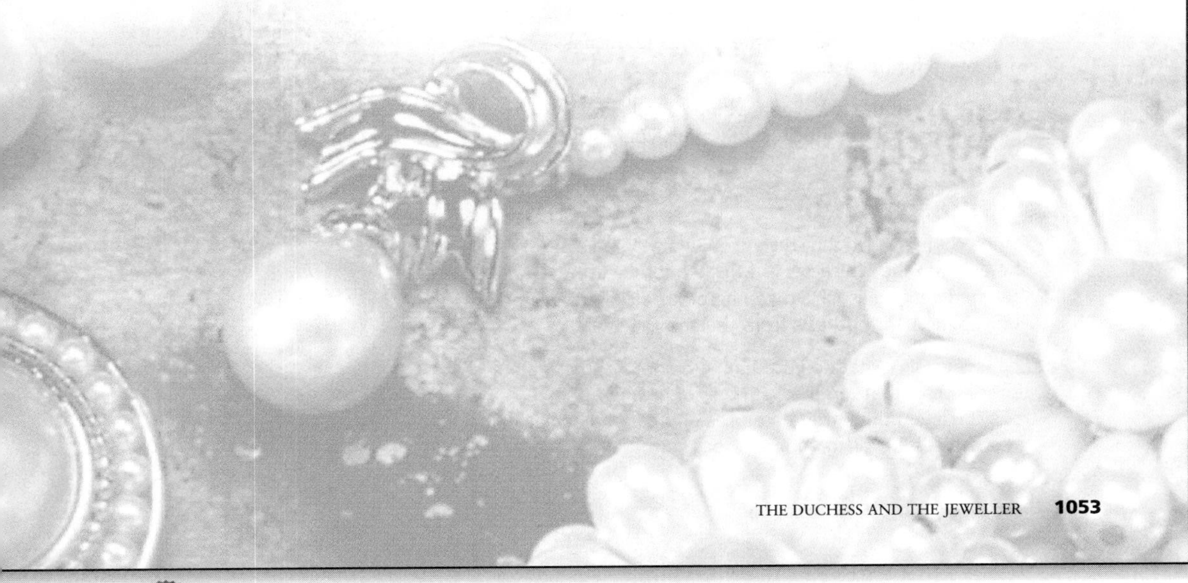

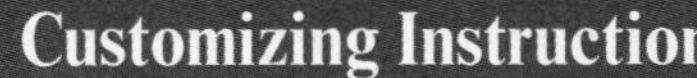

Customizing Instruction

Less Proficient Readers

1 Make sure students understand what is meant by the statement that "the truffle he had routed out of the earth" was "Rotten at the center–rotten at the core!"

Answer: The pearls are fake.

Gifted and Talented

Suggest that students write a continuation of the short story showing Oliver's weekend at the duchess's. Have students attempt to duplicate Woolf's style.

Mini Lesson Standardized Test Practice

WRITING AN ESSAY Have students write a five-paragraph essay attempting to prove that one of the characters, the duchess or the jeweller, is the more deceitful. Then ask students to switch essays with a partner and assess whether their partner's essay is persuasive.

RUBRIC

3 Full Accomplishment Essay reflects full understanding of story's facts. Facts from story are used to prove topic sentence of each paragraph.

2 Substantial Accomplishment Essay reflects partial understanding of story's facts. Facts from story are used to prove topic sentence of most paragraphs.

1 Little or Partial Accomplishment Essay reflects poor understanding of facts of story. Facts from story are not used consistently to prove topic sentence of each paragraph.

GUIDING STUDENT RESPONSE

Connect to the Literature

1. **What Do You Think?**
   Guidelines for student response: Accept all reasonable responses that are based on evidence found in the text. The reasons students give to support their responses should have some connection with the text.

Comprehension Check

- a poor one—he had little money and little guidance
- He hopes to be accepted into the duchess's social circle and to win the love of her daughter, Diana.
- that they are fake

Use **Unit Six Resource Book,** p. 28 for additional support.

Think Critically

2. Possible Responses: All his wealth has not brought him love or happiness; material things by themselves cannot fill his emptiness.
3. Possible Responses: His mother is the only person he's ever really loved; he feels cut off from his past and doesn't feel at home in the aristocratic circles in which he travels.
4. Possible Response: They are adversaries, each trying to gain power over the other, each resenting their interdependence.
5. Possible Responses: The jeweller wants to gain acceptance from the aristocrats; the duchess wants to hide her gambling debts from her husband.
6. Possible Responses: Though he gets what he wanted, a weekend with Diana, he has paid an absurdly high price for it; his final line hints that he will turn the weekend to good account, marry Diana, and thus outwit the Duchess.

Literary Analysis

Paired Activity Have pairs of students share with the class what their stream-of-consciousness examples tell about Oliver Bacon's consciousness.

Review Figurative Language You might chart on the chalkboard the examples of similes and metaphors cited by students.

Thinking through the LITERATURE

Connect to the Literature

1. **What Do You Think?**
   Is the jeweller someone you would like to know? Give reasons for your response.

Comprehension Check

- What kind of childhood did Oliver have?
- Why does he buy the pearls without having them tested?
- What does he discover about the pearls?

Think Critically

2. Why do you think the jeweller is dissatisfied with his life?

THINK ABOUT

- what has been the driving force in his life
- the image of him as a hog searching for truffles
- the references to Mademoiselle and the red roses

3. Why do you think the jeweller keeps thinking about his mother and his past?

4. How would you describe the relationship between the jeweller and the duchess?

THINK ABOUT

- what motive he might have for making her wait ten minutes
- his concerns about the pearls
- what motivates her to mention the prime minister and Diana

5. **ACTIVE READING** **MAKING INFERENCES** Review the diagrams you made in your **READER'S NOTEBOOK.** In a single sentence, how would you describe the jeweller's motivation for his actions in the story? the duchess's motivation for her actions?

6. Would you call the jeweller a winner or a loser in his transactions with the duchess? Support your answer.

Extend Interpretations

7. **Critic's Corner** A student reviewer, Sarah Slezak, said that she enjoyed the **characters** in this story because they "seemed very realistic." Do you agree or disagree? Support your opinion with **details** from the story.

8. **Connect to Life** What do you think are some of the main driving forces that motivate successful businesspeople today? Do you think there are pros and cons to achieving great success? Explain your answer.

Literary Analysis

STYLE The **style** of a literary work is the distinctive way in which it is written—not what is said but how it is said. Many elements contribute to style, including **word choice, tone, figurative language,** and **point of view.** Virginia Woolf uses with great skill a style of writing called **stream of consciousness,** which presents the flow of thoughts and sensations in a character's mind. In this kind of writing, ideas and images occur as loosely connected associations rather than in a logical progression. A character's stream of consciousness is often expressed as an **interior monologue,** a record of the total workings of the character's mind and emotions.

Paired Activity Find a passage in "The Duchess and the Jeweller" (other than the one identified in Focus Your Reading on page 1046) that records Oliver Bacon's stream of consciousness. What does it tell you about his character?

REVIEW **FIGURATIVE LANGUAGE** **Similes** and **metaphors** are types of **figurative language** in which basically unlike things are compared. Look through the story to find at least three examples of similes and metaphors involving animals. What two things are compared in each figure of speech? How does each influence your understanding of the story?

Extend Interpretations

Critic's Corner Possible Response: The characters' mixed motives, childhood memories, and stream of changing associations are realistic and common to most people.

Connect to Life Students might discuss whether the price of success is too high.

Writing Options

1. **Alternative Ending** Write a new ending for this story—one that the jeweller's mother might prefer.

2. **Profile of Oliver** Imagine that you are the jeweller's psychologist. Write a psychological profile for your records, in which you describe the forces motivating him and the conflicts in his personality.

3. **Imaginary Dialogue** Compose a dialogue in which the duchess tells her daughter Diana the truth about her encounter with the jeweller and advises Diana how to behave during his impending visit.

4. **Paragraph Analysis** Woolf uses many precise details in her descriptions of the characters. Choose one descriptive passage and discuss how the use of detail contributes to your understanding of the character.

Writing Handbook
See pages 1369–1370: Analysis.

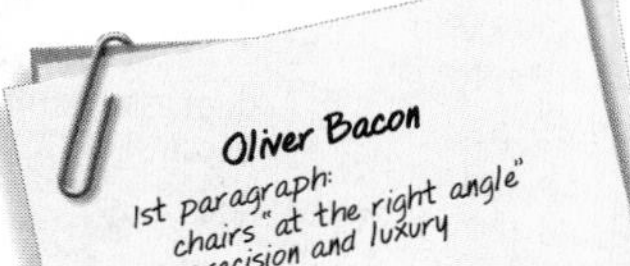

Oliver Bacon
1st paragraph:
chairs "at the right angle"
precision and luxury

Activities & Explorations

1. **Caricature of a Shrewd Pair** Draw a caricature that depicts the duchess and the jeweller conducting their business deal. Share your work with the class. ~ ART

2. **Duchess's Soliloquy** As the duchess, deliver a stream-of-consciousness soliloquy in which you reveal your thoughts and feelings as you wait to see the jeweller. ~ SPEAKING AND LISTENING/PERFORMING

3. **Discussion of Greed** With a small group of classmates, hold a roundtable discussion in which you consider whether the jeweller is a greedy person. ~ SPEAKING AND LISTENING

Inquiry & Research

1. **Bloomsbury Group** Locate more information on the Bloomsbury group, and find the names of three of its members (other than Virginia Woolf, Leonard Woolf, and E. M. Forster). Share your findings with the class, briefly describing the contributions each of the three persons made to society.

More Online: Research Starter
www.mcdougallittell.com

2. **Precious Jewels** Collect information on the production and sale of precious jewels. Research the production process from the finding of the raw stones to the creation of the highest-quality jewels for sale. Include information about the characteristics that make some gems more valuable than others, as well as details about famous jewels of the past and present. Report to the class on your findings.

Vocabulary in Action

EXERCISE A: MEANING CLUES Use your knowledge of the Words to Know to answer the following questions.

1. If you **forge** an agreement, are you making it, breaking it, or shaking it?
2. Is an **astute** person one who is conceited, one who is honest, or one who is bright?
3. Is being **lissome** most necessary for a lawyer, for a gymnast, or for a weight lifter?
4. Would someone known for **arrogance** be considered appealing, obnoxious, or wise?
5. Does a person who behaves **obsequiously** give the impression of being proud, of being meek, or of being trustworthy?

EXERCISE B Work with four classmates to develop a short scene involving five characters. The scene can deal with any situation—the important thing is to portray the characters in such a way that, by the end of the scene, each has become associated with one of the five vocabulary words. Do not use the words themselves in the scene; develop the associations through the characters' actions and dialogue.

WORDS TO KNOW		
	arrogance	lissome
	astute	obsequiously
	forge	

Building Vocabulary
For an in-depth study of context clues, see page 938.

Writing Options

1. **Alternative Ending** If students need help getting started, point out the jeweller's apology to his mother on the last page. Help them infer how his mother might prefer to deal with the duchess.
2. **Profile of Oliver** Point out that many psychologists focus on how relationships and painful incidents from childhood can continue to influence people into adulthood.
3. **Imaginary Dialogue** Before students write, have them decide whether Diana loves the jeweller, feels sorry for him, or shares her mother's contempt for him.
4. **Paragraph Analysis** Before students write, have them form small groups and discuss what details of dress, language, and action cause them to form opinions about people.

Activities & Explorations

1. **Caricature of a Shrewd Pair** Have students skim the selection looking for physical details of each character. Tell them that a caricature exaggerates physical characteristics for comic or satiric effect.
2. **Duchess's Soliloquy** Have students study the jeweller's stream of consciousness on pages 1050–1051 as he keeps the duchess waiting. Then have them imagine how the duchess feels, perhaps in freewriting.
3. **Discussion of Greed** Have students list points in the story that prove his greed or lack thereof.

Inquiry & Research

1. **Bloomsbury Group** Students can consult general encyclopedias or literary references such as *Benet's Reader's Encyclopedia.* Encourage them to research any cross-references they find in the article on Bloomsbury.
2. **Precious Jewels** In addition to consulting print sources, students can interview a jeweller in the community.

Vocabulary in Action

Exercise A
1. making
2. bright
3. gymnast
4. obnoxious
5. meek

Exercise B
Have the groups of students perform their scenes for the rest of the class, and let class members identify the word each character is associated with.

Author Activity

Landmark Essay Virginia Woolf kept diaries through much of her life and was also a prolific writer of letters. Her diaries, published in five volumes, reveal her powers of observation, sharp insights into people, and original ideas. Her letters, published in six volumes, give a detailed picture of the rich and complex relationships she had with a wide variety of people. Both the diaries and the letters are marked by her characteristic style and reveal a full and often fascinating view of her life and times. You may ask students to look in the diaries or letters to gain further insight into the Author Activity.

Virginia Woolf
1882–1941

Other Works
A Haunted House and Other Short Stories
To the Lighthouse
A Room of One's Own
Flush

Unusual Education Childhood experiences greatly influenced the path Virginia Woolf would take as an adult. Born Adeline Virginia Stephen and raised in a cultured upper-middle-class family, whose friends included leading artists and thinkers of the late Victorian era, she was writing by the time she was nine. Although her parents encouraged her literary efforts, they adhered to the Victorian custom of sending only their sons to school. While her brothers went off to private schools and to Cambridge University, she remained at home with tutors. Although she would never forget this injustice, she fortunately had free access to her father's vast library and was continually exposed to the brilliant ideas and conversation of the family's intellectual friends. Through these avenues, she managed to gain an education that was rich and varied, though unusual.

Literary First As a young woman, Woolf rejected the restrictions of Victorian society and eagerly embraced the free-thinking ideas of her brothers' university friends, who eventually formed the nucleus of the Bloomsbury group. In 1912 she married Leonard Woolf, a member of the group, with whom she founded the Hogarth Press and began to publish her own fiction as well as the poetry of T. S. Eliot and the short stories of Katherine Mansfield. Throughout her life, Woolf was also an articulate feminist. Her long essay *A Room of One's Own* is considered by many to be the first major literary achievement in the movement for female equality in England.

Battle with Illness The death of Woolf's mother when Woolf was 13 contributed to the first of many battles with mental illness that the author would face during her lifetime. At the start of World War II, her anxieties about a German invasion of England compounded her already deteriorating mental health. In 1941, deeply depressed and fearful that she was going insane, Woolf drowned herself in the river Ouse at the age of 59.

Author Activity

Landmark Essay Find and read a copy of Woolf's essay *A Room of One's Own.* Why do you think some people consider this essay a landmark in the British movement for female equality?

Teaching Options

Mini Lesson Grammar

PARALLELISM

Instruction Good writers balance related ideas in a sentence by giving them parallel structure. For example, the sentence "You can travel by car, by train, or by plane" is easier to follow than "You can travel by car, take a train, or you can fly."

Activity Write the following on the chalkboard.

Oliver's flat had furniture set at the right angles, windows covered with the proper allowance of fabric, and a mahogany cabinet was stocked with the right liquors.

Ask students to correct the sentence so that all three elements are parallel. *(Eliminate "was.")*

Exercise Ask students to read the following sentence and make corrections for parallelism as needed.

Shoppers in London may choose to visit clothing stores in Piccadilly, Savile Row where there are many small shops, or jewellers in Hatton Garden. *(. . . clothing stores in Piccadilly, small shops in Savile Row, or jewellers in Hatton Garden.)*

Use **Grammar Transparencies and Copymasters,** p. 111.

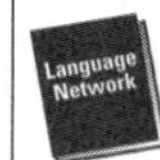

Use McDougal Littell's ***Language Network*** for more instruction and practice in parallelism.

from

Virginia Woolf

by E. M. Forster

E. M. Forster was, like Virginia Woolf, a member of the Bloomsbury group. He built his fame as a novelist and a writer of literary criticism. Shortly after Woolf died, Forster wrote a critical review of her work. In this excerpt he describes her process of writing.

1 She liked receiving sensations—sights, sounds, tastes—passing them through her mind, where they encountered theories and memories, and then bringing them out again, through a pen, on to a bit of paper. 2 Now began the higher delights of authorship. For these penmarks on paper were only the prelude to writing, little more than marks on a wall. They had to be combined, arranged, emphasized here, eliminated there, new relationships had to be generated, new penmarks born, and out of the interactions, something, one thing, one, arose. This one thing, whether it was a novel or an essay or a short story or a biography or a private paper to be read to her friends, was, if it was successful, itself analogous to a sensation. Although it was so complex and intellectual, although it might be large and heavy with facts, it was akin to the very simple things which had started it off, to the sights, sounds, tastes. It could be best 3 described as we describe them. For it was not about something. It was something.

Reading for Information

For an author like Virginia Woolf, whose work is often viewed as difficult, critical commentary can provide another way to look at the author's work.

SUMMARIZING AND EVALUATING

Summarizing is the process of condensing a work into fewer words. This process will help you better understand and remember what you read. Use the following suggestions and activities as you explore Forster's comments.

1. **Identifying Main Ideas** Forster explains that Woolf absorbed sensations that ultimately found expression in her writing. But what happened to the sensations along the way? You might think of the process like this:

   New sensations
   \+ Woolf's knowledge ("theories") and memories
   = **a literary work**

2. Forster writes, "Now began the higher delights of authorship." According to Forster, what seems to have delighted Woolf about writing?
3. **Summarizing** Summarize the review in a few sentences.

Evaluating involves making judgments about a work. How accurately do you think Forster's comments apply to "The Duchess and the Jeweller"(p. 1046)?

RELATED *Reading*

Primary Source

Objectives
- read and analyze critical commentary
- read to identify, summarize, and evaluate main ideas
- understand elements of authorship

Further Background
Critical commentary reflects the critic's interpretation of a literary work. It is the critic's job to offer readers pathways to understanding and appreciality a piece of literature.

Reading for Information
Ask students to consider evidence in Forster's commentary that might lead them to conclude that Virginia Woolf's writing might be difficult.

Possible Responses: Students may point out that the level of complexity Forster describes could contribute to the difficulty of Woolf's texts. Also, the fact that her writing is so much like "receiving sensations" suggests that, like sensations, Woolf's writing does not explain itself but merely presents itself.

SUMMARIZING AND EVALUATING

1. **Possible Response:** As sensations interact with "theories and memories," they are transformed into a literary work that both includes and extends these sensations.
2. **Possible Response:** For Woolf, the delight in writing seems to have come from her creative response of arranging and rearranging words in a way that provides new relationships or insights. For her, "authorship" was a process of exploring materials by crafting them in ways that deepen and develop them.
3. **Possible Response:** Student summaries should include main ideas and supporting details. For Virginia Woolf, writing was a process of exploring sensations, combining them with experiences and memories, and then bringing this mixture out with words. She then would rework her writing to achieve the desired outcome–a sensation.

Evaluating
Possible Response: Students may say that Forster's comments are accurate insofar as Woolf's story re-creates the experience of life.

Although Virginia Woolf grew up in the Victorian era, most of her works belong to the modern age rather than to the world of the 19th century. Her novels represent a departure from the Victorian tradition in form (her use of interior monologue and stream of consciousness) and in content (her treatment of such subjects as feminism, sexuality, and insanity).

Additional Background

VIRGINIA WOOLF

Virginia Woolf (1882–1941) was born into a family that encouraged the study of art and literature. Each of her parents had been married before—her father, Leslie Stephen, brought one child to the second marriage and her mother, Julia, brought three. Together, the couple had four more children—Vanessa, Thoby, Virginia, and Adrian.

Woolf drew on her family life and her own early experiences when writing her novels. For example, the main character in *Night and Day* is, like Woolf herself, an anxious writer from a literary family. *To the Lighthouse* is probably based in part on Woolf's memories of childhood summers spent at St. Ives, Cornwall. *Orlando* was inspired by her relationship with her friend Vita Sackville-West. Her avant-garde novel *The Waves* at one point focuses on the characters' reactions to the unexpected death of a young man, recalling the sudden death of her own brother Thoby at the age of 26.

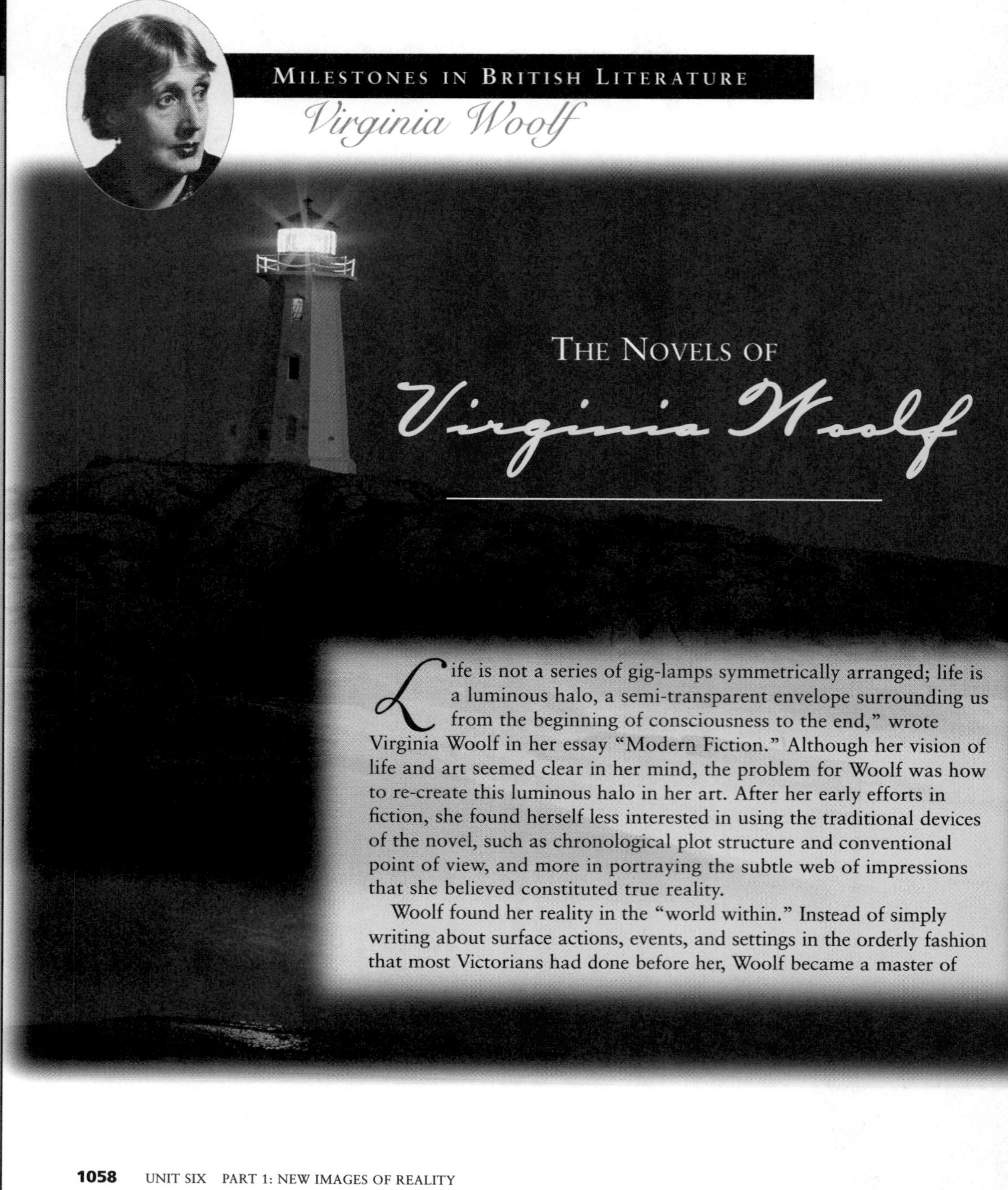
MILESTONES IN BRITISH LITERATURE
Virginia Woolf
THE NOVELS OF
Virginia Woolf
"Life is not a series of gig-lamps symmetrically arranged; life is a luminous halo, a semi-transparent envelope surrounding us from the beginning of consciousness to the end," wrote Virginia Woolf in her essay "Modern Fiction." Although her vision of life and art seemed clear in her mind, the problem for Woolf was how to re-create this luminous halo in her art. After her early efforts in fiction, she found herself less interested in using the traditional devices of the novel, such as chronological plot structure and conventional point of view, and more in portraying the subtle web of impressions that she believed constituted true reality.
Woolf found her reality in the "world within." Instead of simply writing about surface actions, events, and settings in the orderly fashion that most Victorians had done before her, Woolf became a master of
1058 UNIT SIX PART 1: NEW IMAGES OF REALITY

interior monologue and stream of consciousness in order to "record the atoms [of thought] as they fall upon the mind." Believing that one flash of insight could be a more powerful reflection of reality than line after line of literal description, she wove the evocative details and flowing rhythms of lyric poetry into her fiction.

Mrs. Dalloway was the first novel in which Woolf displayed mastery of this distinctive prose style. It depicts a single day in the life of a middle-class Englishwoman preparing to give a party. The novel's reality, however, is composed of the characters' memories and thoughts about life, loved ones, and even strangers—thoughts that create a delicate montage of impressions as they rise to the surface. In similar fashion, *To the Lighthouse* explores the thoughts of a family and their friends on holiday. In the process, one glimpses aspects of daily life that reveal subtle truths about love, death, and art.

In the novel *Orlando,* employing a very different time span, Woolf displays her fascination with male and female identity and with the interplay of past and present. At the opening of the novel, Orlando is a young man in Elizabethan times, but by the work's midpoint, Orlando has become a young woman in the 1920s. *The Waves,* Woolf's most experimental novel, consists almost entirely of interior monologues representing the thoughts of its six major characters from childhood through old age.

In addition to these and other novels, Woolf's literary contributions included numerous reviews and critical essays, as well as the journals that she kept throughout her life. Her most remarkable offerings, however, were undoubtedly her novels, which challenged the existing structures and traditions of literature and inspired future generations of writers to share in her luminous vision of reality.

Top:
The recent film version of the novel Orlando *used lush visuals, music, and voice-overs to convey Orlando's inner life.* Photofest.
Middle:
Leonard and Virginia Woolf.
Left:
Cover of Woolf's novel Mrs. Dalloway

LITERARY CHRONOLOGY

The following are publication dates of Woolf's novels:

1915 *The Voyage Out*

1919 *Night and Day*

1922 *Jacob's Room*

1925 *Mrs. Dalloway*

1927 *To the Lighthouse*

1928 *Orlando*

1931 *The Waves*

1933 *Flush*

1937 *The Years*

1941 *Between the Acts*

MILESTONES IN BRITISH LITERATURE **1059**

OVERVIEW

Objectives

- appreciate the craft of one of the most influential poets of the 20th century
- interpret the interaction between modern poetry and the society in which it is produced
- gain information about Eliot by reading nonfiction

Presenting the Author

This Author Study offers a unique opportunity for students to focus on the work of a major writer. In addition, students can gather information about the life of Eliot, gaining insight into the real person behind his famous poems.

Reading Skills and Strategies

Establishing a Purpose for Reading

Have students scan pages 1060–1063 and establish a purpose for reading

Discuss the wide array of information presented on these pages. Remind students that they may choose to adjust their purposes as they encounter different presentations and information.

Author Study

T. S. Eliot

OVERVIEW

"Mr. Eliot does not write for the lazy, the stupid, or the gross. Literature is to him a serious affair."

—E. M. Forster

T. S. Eliot

HIS LIFE
HIS TIMES

A Modern Voice

Claimed by his native America as well as his adopted homeland of Britain, T. S. Eliot was one of the giants of 20th-century literature. As a poet, playwright, and influential literary critic, Eliot helped to define the contours of modern poetry in the early 20th century.

1888–1965

AN INTERNATIONAL EDUCATION Thomas Stearns Eliot grew up in St. Louis, Missouri, where his grandfather had founded Washington University. Education was a top priority in his family, and he was sent to private schools in Missouri and Massachusetts before attending Harvard University, where he obtained his bachelor's degree in three years. Pursuing further studies at the Sorbonne in Paris and Oxford University in England, he was caught in Europe when World War I broke out, and he eventually married and settled in

1888 **Is born in St. Louis, Missouri**

Eliot's birthplace in St. Louis, Missouri

1898 **Enters Smith Academy in St. Louis**

1906 **Begins attending Harvard University**

1890 1895 1900 1905

1893 **Karl Benz builds his first four-wheel car.**

1899 **Sigmund Freud publishes *The Interpretation of Dreams.***

1906 **Pablo Picasso experiments with cubism.**

1060

England. A quiet, cultured man, Eliot supported himself and his wife by working successively as a teacher, a bank clerk, and an editor at a London publishing firm while trying to make a name for himself as a writer.

A **MAKE IT NEW!** The years leading up to World War I were a time of social, scientific, and economic changes that radically altered everyday life. This transition into the modern age was both difficult and invigorating. B Many European artists and writers, including Eliot, lamented the alienating effects of modern industrial society, with its masses of people crowded into cities C and working in monotonous factory jobs. At the same time, however, they energetically seized the opportunity to cast off 19th-century traditions and find new forms of expression to mirror the new realities of modern life. In Paris, Pablo Picasso and Georges Braque developed cubism in painting by breaking up images into geometric parts, sometimes showing different sides of a face in a single portrait. Eliot's American friend and fellow poet Ezra Pound headed a group of poets called the imagists, who aimed at the creation of clear, precise images rather than at the presentation of ideas in their poems. "Make it new!" was Pound's rallying cry for his generation.

LITERARY *Contributions*

Modernist Poetry With Ireland's William Butler Yeats and America's Ezra Pound, T. S. Eliot is considered by many to be one of the three most influential 20th-century poets in English. His most famous poems include

- **"Ash Wednesday"**
- ***Four Quartets***
- **"Gerontion"**
- **"The Hollow Men"**
- **"Journey of the Magi"**
- **"The Love Song of J. Alfred Prufrock"**
- **"Preludes"**
- **"Rhapsody on a Windy Night"**
- **"Sweeney Among the Nightingales"**
- ***The Waste Land***
- **"Whispers of Immortality"**

On Stage After 1930, Eliot also won fame as a dramatist. Among his plays are

- ***The Cocktail Party***
- ***Murder in the Cathedral***

Literary Criticism Eliot's literary essays had an enormous influence on the literary criticism of the 20th century. They include

- **"Hamlet and His Problems"**
- **"The Metaphysical Poets"**
- **"Tradition and the Individual Talent"**

1910 **Studies at the Sorbonne in Paris**

Ezra Pound

1914 **Meets the poet Ezra Pound**

1915 **Marries Vivien Haigh-Wood**

1917 **Publishes *Prufrock and Other Observations***

1922 **Publishes *The Waste Land***

1927 **Joins the Church of England and becomes a British citizen**

1910 1915 1920 1925

1913 **Igor Stravinsky's modernist ballet *The Rite of Spring* premieres in Paris.**

1914 **World War I begins.**

1917 **Russian Revolution brings Communists to power.**

1922 **Irish author James Joyce publishes the modernist novel *Ulysses*.**

LIFE AND TIMES

Science

A In 1895, Guglielmo Marconi sent a radio signal through the air. Prior to this, the only ways in which people could send long-distance messages quickly were by telegraph and telephone, both of which depended on wires to carry information. The invention of the triode vacuum tube by Lee De Forest a few years later made the development of the radio possible. In 1910, experimental radio broadcasts began. The "wireless" was soon used to communicate with ships at sea and airplanes in flight.

Science

B The early 1900s saw a revolution in physics. In 1905, Einstein used the ideas of Max Planck (1858–1947) to show that light consists of particles of energy that act like waves. Niels Bohr demonstrated how atoms radiate light in 1913. In the mid-1920s, Erwin Shrödinger and Werner Heisenburg began the first steps towards the development of the theory of quantum mechanics.

History

C During Eliot's life, the British government began to regulate the conditions of factory work, especially for children. Beginning in 1825, workers were granted a short day on Saturdays. In 1833, a new law gave children Christmas, Good Friday, and four other days as holidays. In 1844, the workday for children aged eight to thirteen was limited to six and a half hours per day, and by 1918 the minimum working age was raised to fourteen years old.

Science

(D) Much of the destruction of World War I was made possible by advances in technology. Tanks, personnel carriers, and other motorized vehicles improved mobility. Airplanes were used for purposes ranging from bombing to delivering supplies. During the war, fighter planes and anti-aircraft guns were developed to target enemy planes.

World Culture

(E) The years preceding World War II resulted in the end of monarchies in much of western Europe. In 1918, Social Democrats proclaimed a German republic now known as the Weimar Republic. In 1920, army officers attempted a coup of this unstable republic. Other uprisings followed, setting the stage for the rise of Hitler. In Italy, the fascist Benito Mussolini sent an army to occupy Rome in 1922, seizing power from the constitutional monarch. In the chaos following the Russian Revolution and the deposition of the czar, Lenin emerged as the communist dictator of the Soviet Union.

Author Study: T. S. Eliot

A VAST WASTELAND Although Eliot was never called upon to fight, World War I (D) seemed to him a total breakdown of 2,000 years of European civilization. The war destroyed the old order that had held European culture together, and Eliot had little faith that the technological and social changes of the 20th century were going to improve the situation. He felt that modern life was a shattered confusion, without a center. William Butler Yeats's prophesy in "The Second Coming"—"Things fall apart; the center cannot hold"—seemed to have come true. "The ordinary man's experience is chaotic, irregular, and fragmentary," Eliot wrote in an essay in 1921. It was, he thought, up to the poet to bring the fragments together into a meaningful whole.

BUILDING A LEGACY In 1917, encouraged by Ezra Pound, Eliot published his first collection of poems, *Prufrock and Other Observations,* which included the now famous poems "The Love Song of J. Alfred Prufrock" and "Preludes." The volume's revolutionary impact has been compared to that of Wordsworth and Coleridge's publication in 1798 of *Lyrical Ballads,* in that it ushered a new era of poetry.

Still working at his "day job" as a bank clerk to support himself and his wife, Eliot poured all his other energies into his writing. In 1919 he published another volume of verse, and the next year saw the publication of *The Sacred Wood,* a book of literary criticism in which he explained his view of modern poetry. In 1921, he completed most of *The Waste Land,* a long, highly complex poem. Published in 1922 with Pound's help, the poem's expression of the spiritual infirmities of the age echoed throughout the literary world. Today, it is still viewed as one of the definitive modernist statements of the human condition.

REDEMPTION AND RENEWAL Eliot gradually put the disillusionment expressed in *The Waste Land* and in poems such as "The Hollow Men" behind him and turned to religion for spiritual comfort. In 1927 he joined the Church of England; he also became a British citizen, officially adopting England's cultural heritage as well as its state religion. Thereafter, religious themes and symbols came to pervade Eliot's work, notably in "Ash Wednesday" (1930) and *Four Quartets* (1943). *Murder in the Cathedral,* one of Eliot's best-known plays, also reflected his

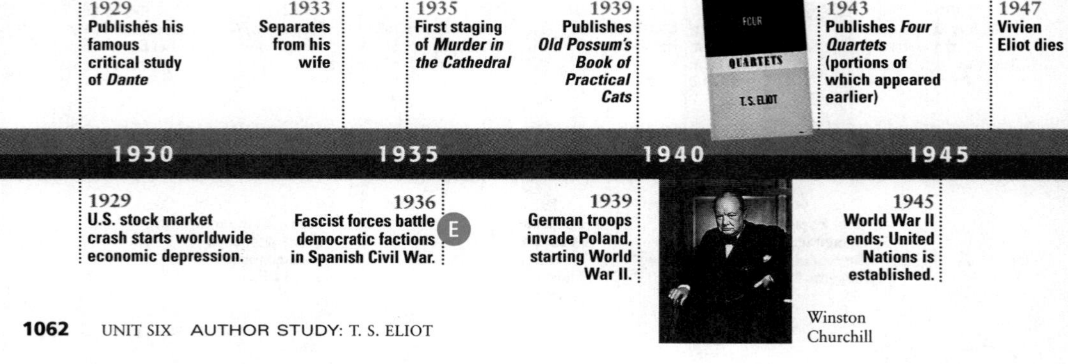

1929 Publishes his famous critical study of *Dante*
1933 Separates from his wife
1935 First staging of *Murder in the Cathedral*
1939 Publishes *Old Possum's Book of Practical Cats*
FOUR QUARTETS T.S. ELIOT
1943 Publishes *Four Quartets* (portions of which appeared earlier)
1947 Vivien Eliot dies
1930
1935
1940
1945
1929 U.S. stock market crash starts worldwide economic depression.
1936 Fascist forces battle democratic factions in Spanish Civil War. (E)
1939 German troops invade Poland, starting World War II.
1945 World War II ends; United Nations is established.

Winston Churchill

newfound religious convictions. A verse drama first staged in 1935, it presents the story of the slaying of Thomas à Becket, the archbishop of Canterbury whose shrine was visited by Chaucer's pilgrims.

FINAL HONORS In 1925, Eliot became an editor in the London publishing house of Faber & Faber and from that position wielded extensive influence on the English literary scene. After World War II, he was awarded one of literature's highest honors, the Nobel Prize.

More Online: Author Link
www.mcdougallittell.com

Modernism: Without Rhyme or Reason

Still Life, first state (1925), Fernand Legér. The Menil Collection, Houston.

Eliot's modernist poetry differs from most 19th-century poetry as greatly as Picasso's cubism differs from Monet's impressionism:

- Eliot often wrote free verse, without regular patterns of rhyme and rhythm—perhaps the poetic equivalent of modern art's break from the limits of realism.
- Eliot's poetry, like much modern art, isn't pretty. He took his images from the gritty urban streets rather than the pastoral lakes and woods favored by most romantic poets.
- Both Eliot's poetry and modern art are hard for most people to understand. Like the imagist poets, Eliot eliminated connections between his images and gave the reader no explanation of the images' meaning.

Eliot on Broadway

The London and Broadway musical *Cats* is based on Eliot's surprisingly witty *Old Possum's Book of Practical Cats* and some of his other poetry. The play contains a musical version of the poem "The Naming of Cats" (page 1070), as well as the popular song "Memory," which features images and lines from "Preludes" (page 1065) and other Eliot poems.

(F) **1948** Wins the Nobel Prize for literature

1949 Enjoys popular success with his play *The Cocktail Party*

1957 Marries Valerie Fletcher

1965 Dies in London on Jan. 4

1950 — 1955 — 1960 — 1965

1949 Communist government is established in mainland China.

1952 Irish-born Samuel Beckett's "absurdist" play *Waiting for Godot* premieres in Paris. (G)

1961 Beatles become a popular rock 'n' roll band in Liverpool, England.

History

(F) The Nobel Prize, which Eliot received in 1925, was first awarded in 1901. This prize was founded by Alfred Nobel (1833–1896), the inventor of dynamite. It is supposed to be awarded to people who have made valuable contributions to the "good of humanity." Nobel left his estate to fund prizes in physics, chemistry, medicine, literature, and international peace. A prize in economics was added in 1969.

World Culture

(G) The French Theater of the Absurd was an influential movement that flourished in the 1950s and 1960s. Such playwrights as Artaud, Beckett, Ionesco, Adamov, Genet, Arrabal, and Pinter challenged audiences to see the emptiness and absurdity of their lives by presenting unrealistic plays without linear plots or rounded characters. One of the most famous absurdist plays is Beckett's *Waiting for Godot*.

LIFE AND TIMES 1063

OVERVIEW

"Preludes" is included in the **Grade 12 InterActive Reader.**

Objectives

1. understand and appreciate **modern poetry (Literary Analysis)**
2. appreciate the author's use of **rhythm in modern verse (Literary Analysis)**
3. use **strategies** for reading modern verse to understand and interpret Eliot's poems **(Active Reading)**

Summary

The four sections of "Preludes" present a series of city images that depict modern urban life as dismal and dreary. "The Hollow Men" is made up of five free-verse poems. This sequence thematically joins together allusions to a variety of sources, including myth, religion, literature, and even a nursery rhyme. "The Naming of Cats" is a comic rhymed poem that details the claim that cats have three names, with each performing a specific and important function in the cat's life.

Thematic Links

Eliot's poetry evokes the **new images of reality** in the 20th century—a reality full of alienation, emptiness, and despair.

GUIDE FOR READING

A bleak; cold; run-down; working-class; lonely

B The speaker projects his experience onto the morning to distance himself from an alienating world.

5-Minute Warm-Up

Daily Language SkillBuilder

Have students **proofread** the display sentences on page 979j and write them correctly. The sentences also appear on Transparency 28 of **Grammar Transparencies and Copymasters.**

PREPARING to *Read*

Selected Poems

Lyric Poetry by T. S. ELIOT

"You had such a vision of the street / As the street hardly understands."

Connect to Your Life

A Failure to Communicate People today often speak of being alienated from one another. Many people don't know their neighbors, for example, and commuters spend hours with strangers on planes, trains, and buses. Create a chart, like the one shown here, to explore the causes and consequences of alienation today. Then discuss your observations with your classmates.

Examples of Alienation	Causes of Alienation	Immediate Consequences	Long-Term Effects
bus riders ignoring each other	fear of strangers	tension, nervousness	feeling of isolation

Build Background

The Urban Wasteland The first two of the poems you are about to read—"Preludes" and "The Hollow Men"—reflect Eliot's alienation during World War I and his despair at the decay of Western civilization. In both, Eliot used a patchwork of images and allusions to capture his sense of modern life, replacing the authoritative voice of the 19th-century poet with a speaker who is suffering the same spiritual losses as the rest of society. When reading "Preludes," keep in mind that a prelude is a short musical piece based on a recurrent theme.

The last poem, "The Naming of Cats," shows the whimsical, witty side of T. S. Eliot after he came to terms with the modern age. Always fond of the humorous verse of Lewis Carroll and Edward Lear, Eliot tried his hand at humor in a series of cat poems published as *Old Possum's Book of Practical Cats,* from which "The Naming of Cats" is taken.

Focus Your Reading

LITERARY ANALYSIS RHYTHM IN MODERN VERSE Rhythm is the pattern of stressed and unstressed syllables in a line of poetry. When such a pattern is repeated throughout a poem, the poem is said to have a meter. T. S. Eliot and other modernist poets felt that the demands of writing in a meter too often forced poets to dilute their meaning. They began experimenting with free verse, poetry with no fixed rhythmic pattern, as in these lines:

Wipe your hand across your mouth, and laugh;
The worlds revolve like ancient women
Gathering fuel in vacant lots.

As you read Eliot's poetry, think about the rhythm of each poem. Do any of the poems have a meter? In which of the free-verse poems is the rhythm especially strong, even if it is not regular?

ACTIVE READING STRATEGIES FOR READING MODERN VERSE Modern poetry can be difficult to understand. Follow these guidelines as you read Eliot's poems.

- Read each section of the poem aloud, lingering over images that engage your attention or evoke strong feelings in you.
- Try to make connections between the images by noticing which ones are similar, which are contrasting, and which are repeated.
- Use the sidenotes to help you understand unfamiliar allusions.
- Try paraphrasing passages that you find puzzling.
- Reread the poem several times, and discuss your impressions with your classmates.

READER'S NOTEBOOK After using the guidelines above, jot down ideas you form about the poems' interpretations.

LESSON RESOURCES

UNIT SIX RESOURCE BOOK, pp. 29–30

ASSESSMENT RESOURCES

Formal Assessment, pp. 191–192

Teacher's Guide to Assessment and Portfolio Use

Test Generator

SKILLS TRANSPARENCIES AND COPYMASTERS

Literary Analysis

- Poetic Devices, T16 (for Literary Analysis, p. 1073)

Reading and Critical Thinking

- Compare and Contrast, T15 (for Extend Interpretations 7, p. 1073)

Grammar

- Pronoun-Antecedent Agreement, T48 (for Mini Lesson, p. 1067)
- Pronouns: Vague Antecedents, C147 (for Mini Lesson, p. 1067)

Vocabulary

- Using Specialized Dictionaries, C82 (for Mini Lesson, p. 1070)

Writing

- Subject Analysis, C30 (for Writing Option 2, p. 1075)
- Dramatic Scene, C31 (for Writing Option 1, p. 1075)

Communications

- Appreciative Listening, T2 (for Activities & Explorations 2, p. 1075)
- Dramatic Reading, T12 (for Activities & Explorations 2, p. 1075)

INTEGRATED TECHNOLOGY

Net Activities

LaserLinks

- Art Gallery: Fear and Terror in Art. See **Teacher's SourceBook,** p. 74.

Internet: Research Starter

Visit our website:
www.mcdougallittell.com

PRELUDES

T. S. ELIOT

I

The winter evening settles down
With smell of steaks in passageways.
Six o'clock.
The burnt-out ends of smoky days.
And now a gusty shower wraps
The grimy scraps
Of withered leaves about your feet
And newspapers from vacant lots;
The showers beat
On broken blinds and chimney-pots,
And at the corner of the street
A lonely cab-horse steams and stamps.
And then the lighting of the lamps.

GUIDE FOR READING

2 steaks: In the early 20th century, steaks (usually cheap cuts from low-grade beef) were primarily a food of the working class.

7 As you read, note how pronouns are used and how they affect the point of view.

10 What picture do you have of the place being described? A

II

The morning comes to consciousness
Of faint stale smells of beer
From the sawdust-trampled street
With all its muddy feet that press
To early coffee-stands.
With the other masquerades
That time resumes,
One thinks of all the hands
That are raising dingy shades
In a thousand furnished rooms.

14 Why do you think morning is personified? B

18 early coffee-stands: stands of venders who cater to early-morning pedestrians.

23 furnished rooms: one-room apartments with furniture included, usually cheap and rundown.

TEACHING THE LITERATURE

Customizing Instruction

Less Proficient Readers

Note that Eliot's patchwork style is meant to reflect the fragmentary experience of modern life. Ask students to look for shifts in point of view and other irregularities that create a sense of disorder.

Students Acquiring English

Warn students about Eliot's use of sentence fragments and the lack of transitions—grammatical and logical—between sentences, lines, and sections. As they read, have them list questions they have about the poems. Then, have them meet in small groups to discuss their questions and brainstorm answers or solutions.

Use **Spanish Study Guide** for additional support, pp. 248–250.

Gifted and Talented

Ask students to consider a possible paradox of Eliot as they read: His distaste for modernity seems romantic and conservative, but his technique is avant garde. Does this seem incongruous? Why or why not?

BLOCK SCHEDULING: MANAGING TIME

If your schedule requires that you cover the lesson objectives in a shorter time, use . . .

- Preparing to Read, p. 1064
- Thinking Through the Literature, pp. 1066, 1071, 1073

If you want to take advantage of longer class time, use . . .

- TE Teaching Options: Multicultural Link, p. 1066; Speaking and Listening, p. 1068; Standardized Test Practice, p. 1069; Vocabulary, pp. 1070, 1071; Grammar, p. 1074
- Choices & Challenges and Author Activity, p. 1075

PRELUDES **1065**

Reading and Analyzing

Active Reading

STRATEGIES FOR READING MODERN VERSE

Warn students against trying to read these poems as narratives. Tell them to concentrate on the imagery and tone of the poems.

Use **Unit Six Resource Book,** p. 29 for more practice.

Literary Analysis

RHYTHM IN MODERN VERSE

To emphasize the importance of rhythm and musicality in free verse, have students note words repeated at the beginnings of lines and sound devices (e.g., rhymes, consonance, and alliteration).

Use **Unit Six Resource Book,** p. 30 for more exercises.

GUIDE FOR READING

(A) Accept all reasonable, well-supported responses.

(B) fancies implicitly compared to fingers or to paper curlers from line 36

(C) nurturing; struggling to survive; unceasing and routine

Thinking Through the Literature

1. Accept all reasonable, well-supported responses.
2. poor; shabby; dull; urban.
3. Negative images of poor, struggling people leading tiresome existence; hopeful images of the lamps and humanity struggling to survive.

III

You tossed a blanket from the bed,
You lay upon your back, and waited;
You dozed, and watched the night revealing
The thousand sordid images
Of which your soul was constituted;
They flickered against the ceiling.
And when all the world came back
And the light crept up between the shutters
And you heard the sparrows in the gutters,
You had such a vision of the street
As the street hardly understands;
Sitting along the bed's edge, where
You curled the papers from your hair,
Or clasped the yellow soles of feet
In the palms of both soiled hands.

27 sordid: wretched; dirty; morally degraded.

33–38 Lines 35–36 suggest that the person being addressed is a woman. What kind of vision do you think she had? (A)

IV

His soul stretched tight across the skies
That fade behind a city block,
Or trampled by insistent feet
At four and five and six o'clock;
And short square fingers stuffing pipes,
And evening newspapers, and eyes
Assured of certain certainties,
The conscience of a blackened street
Impatient to assume the world.

I am moved by fancies that are curled
Around these images, and cling:
The notion of some infinitely gentle
Infinitely suffering thing.

Wipe your hand across your mouth, and laugh;
The worlds revolve like ancient women
Gathering fuel in vacant lots.

39 his: the street's. Think about why the street is personified.

42 A reference to afternoon and early evening.

48–49 What metaphor is used here? (B)

50–51 Note the rhythm of these lines.

53–54 What aspect of the women's activity is focused on in this simile? (C)

Thinking Through the Literature

1. Jot down any questions that this poem raised in your mind.
2. How would you describe the **setting** of the poem?
3. What impressions do you have of the people mentioned in the poem?

Teaching Options

Symbolists

The symbolists were a school of late-19th-century French poets, including Stéphane Mallarmé, Arthur Rimbaud, Paul Valéry, and Paul Verlaine. Among the earlier writers who influenced them were America's Edgar Allan Poe, author of darkly romantic verse and highly symbolic horror fiction, as well as Charles Baudelaire, who was himself influenced by Poe. In his poetry, Baudelaire tried to capture what he saw as the dark, confusing "forest of symbols" beneath the physical world that human beings inhabit. Drawing on Poe's and Baudelaire's ideas, the symbolists identified art's basic role as communication of unique personal emotions that they felt could be conveyed only indirectly through a complex set of highly personal symbols. Mood and music are important elements in symbolist poetry, and the movement had close ties to aestheticism, the late-19th-century artistic credo associated with Oscar Wilde. The symbolist poets had great impact on many modernist writers, including Rainer Maria Rilke, William Butler Yeats, James Joyce, Ezra Pound, and T. S. Eliot.

THE Hollow MEN

T. S. Eliot

Mistah Kurtz—he dead.
A penny for the Old Guy

I

1 We are the hollow men
We are the stuffed men
Leaning together
Headpiece filled with straw. Alas!
Our dried voices, when
We whisper together
Are quiet and meaningless
As wind in dry grass
Or rats' feet over broken glass
In our dry cellar

Shape without form, shade without colour,
Paralysed force, gesture without motion;

Those who have crossed
With direct eyes, to death's other Kingdom
Remember us—if at all—not as lost
Violent souls, but only
As the hollow men
The stuffed men.

II

Eyes I dare not meet in dreams
In death's dream kingdom
These do not appear:
There, the eyes are
Sunlight on a broken column
There, is a tree swinging
And voices are
In the wind's singing
More distant and more solemn
Than a fading star.

GUIDE FOR READING

[Epigraphs] **Mistah . . . dead:** a quotation from Joseph Conrad's *Heart of Darkness,* in which Kurtz is a character whose descent into evil makes him akin to the "lost violent souls" mentioned in lines 15–16 of the poem; **A penny . . . Guy:** a cry that English children use when collecting money to buy fireworks for Guy Fawkes Day—a yearly celebration of the failure of an attempt, by Guy Fawkes and other conspirators, to blow up Parliament in 1605. The celebration also traditionally includes the burning of straw effigies of Fawkes.

4 headpiece . . . straw: The speaker likens himself and his companions, with their empty and meaningless lives, to the straw effigies prepared for Guy Fawkes Day. 2

14 death's other Kingdom: perhaps heaven (as opposed to hell, where the "lost violent souls" go).

Customizing Instruction

Students Acquiring English

1 Explain that the words *hollow* and *empty* are used metaphorically in idiomatic English to refer to spiritual (and emotional) emptiness.

2 Help students understand that an effigy (mentioned in the sidenote for line 4) is a crude representation of a person. It is usually destroyed (often burned), a symbol of that person's death. Try to elicit the phrase "burned in effigy."

Less Proficient Readers

Guide students to recognize that "voices" appears in lines 5 and 25; "eyes" appears in lines 14, 19, and 22. Encourage them to make connections among the contexts in which the words appear and to speculate on what these words might symbolize.

Possible Response: "Voices" might symbolize communication and "eyes" might symbolize sight or the ability to perceive reality vs. the dream world.

Multiple Learning Styles

Auditory Learners

Have students read the poem a number of different ways. For example, since the hollow men speak in unison, you could have several students read as a chorus, using deadpan voices. You might also ask for a volunteer to read dramatically, pausing at places where the sense demands it, and emphasizing the rhythmic variations between the short, declarative lines and the long, syntactically involved ones.

Grammar

PRONOUNS: VAGUE ANTECEDENTS

Instruction When a pronoun refers to a specific word (a noun or another pronoun), that word is the *antecedent* of the pronoun. Antecedents should be clear and definite. The number, gender, and person of a pronoun must be the same as that of its antecedent. Students may need these reminders:

- *One, everyone,* and *everybody* are third-person singular; the pronouns that refer to these words are *he, his, him, she, her,* and *hers.*
- Singular subjects joined by *or* or *nor* require a singular pronoun.
- Pronouns such as *anybody, few,* and *most,* which do not refer to a definite person or thing, often need no antecedents.

Activity Write the following example on the chalkboard.

Giroux and Eliot met in 1946, and he recounted their conversation.

Ask students to reword the first sentence to clarify the antecedent of *he.* *(. . . 1946, and Giroux recounted . . .)*

Use **Grammar Transparencies and Copymasters,** p. 81.

Use McDougal Littell's ***Language Network*** for more instruction and practice in antecedents.

Reading and Analyzing

Literary Analysis: IMAGERY

(A) Ask students to explain what each of the images of the dead land conveys.

Possible Responses: "cactus land" conjures up a picture of a lifeless desert; "stone images" brings to mind inanimate sacred objects unable to answer prayers; "stone images" could also refer to city buildings that house people indifferent to the pleas of another (dead) man; the fading star implies that the dead land is soon-to-be-gone.

Active Reading

STRATEGIES FOR READING MODERN VERSE

Suggest that students keep track of repeated concepts or images as they read and examine each occurrence for its relationship to other occurrences. One repeated image is the fading star (lines 28 and 44). Repeated concepts include sight (or eyes) (lines 14, 19, 22, 52, 53, 61, 62) and speech (or voices) (lines 5, 6, 25, 56, 59).

GUIDE FOR READING

(B) Since they are sightless, their only hope is the intervention of those who have crossed to death's other Kingdom.

(C) The shadow symbolizes the failure of will or the inability to commit to anything; the shadow could also echo the darkness that comes from being sightless.

Let me be no nearer
In death's dream kingdom
Let me also wear
Such deliberate disguises
Rat's coat, crowskin, crossed staves
In a field
Behaving as the wind behaves
No nearer—

Not that final meeting
In the twilight kingdom

III

(A)

This is the dead land
This is cactus land
Here the stone images
Are raised, here they receive
The supplication of a dead man's hand
Under the twinkle of a fading star.

Is it like this
In death's other kingdom
Waking alone
At the hour when we are
Trembling with tenderness
Lips that would kiss
Form prayers to broken stone.

IV

The eyes are not here
There are no eyes here
In this valley of dying stars
In this hollow valley
This broken jaw of our lost kingdoms

In this last of meeting places
We grope together
And avoid speech
Gathered on this beach of the tumid river

Sightless, unless
The eyes reappear
As the perpetual star
Multifoliate rose
Of death's twilight kingdom
The hope only
Of empty men.

33 staves: poles—here, those used as a support for a scarecrow.

43 supplication: begging; plea.

60 tumid (to͞o′mĭd): swollen.

64 multifoliate (mŭl′tĭ-fō′lē-ĭt) **rose:** a reminiscence of the multifoliate (many-petaled) rose formed by the souls of the blessed in Dante's *Divine Comedy*

61–67 What hope is possible for the hollow men? (B)

Teaching Options

Mini Lesson: Speaking and Listening

DRAMATIC READING

Instruction "The Hollow Men" lends itself to dramatic performance. Help students prepare a dramatic presentation of the poem.

Prepare Have them work in cooperative groups to prepare a choral reading that emphasizes the hopelessness and repetitiveness of the hollow men's existence, as well as other interpretive elements that they wish to bring out. Have them consider the rhythm, pitch, tone, volume, and speed that will best convey this.

Present Student groups can decide how they will present the dramatic reading. Students who are audience members should evaluate how the performance increases their appreciation and understanding of the plight of the hollow men.

This activity is particularly well-suited for longer class periods.

V

2 *Here we go round the prickly pear*
Prickly pear prickly pear
Here we go round the prickly pear
At five o'clock in the morning.

Between the idea
And the reality
Between the motion
And the act
Falls the Shadow
3 *For Thine is the Kingdom*

Between the conception
And the creation
Between the emotion
And the response
Falls the Shadow
Life is very long

Between the desire
And the spasm
Between the potency
And the existence
Between the essence
And the descent
Falls the Shadow
For Thine is the Kingdom

For Thine is
4 Life is
For Thine is the

This is the way the world ends
This is the way the world ends
This is the way the world ends
Not with a bang but a whimper.

68–71 Here . . . morning: a variation of the children's rhyme "Here We Go Round the Mulberry Bush" appropriate to the "cactus land" of line 40. (A prickly pear is a type of cactus.)

77 For . . . Kingdom: the beginning of a sentence appended to the Lord's Prayer by many Christians. The "Kingdom" referred to is the kingdom of God.

90 How do you interpret the "Shadow" mentioned here and in lines 76 and 82? C

Thinking Through the Literature

1. Which lines and **images** in this poem do you find the most memorable? Describe your reactions.
2. How would you describe the lives of the "hollow men"?
3. How do you interpret part V of the poem? What do you think keeps the hollow men from fulfillment on earth and salvation after death?

Customizing Instruction

Students Acquiring English

1 Help students understand the meaning of *perpetual.*
Answer: eternal, lasting forever.

2 Show students a photograph or drawing of a prickly pear, a cactus that grows an edible fruit that is covered with spines.

3 If possible, provide students with a copy of the Lord's Prayer in their native language to help them understand this allusion.

Less Proficient Readers

4 Guide students to recognize that lines 92–94 repeat the first few words of lines 77, 83, and 91. Ask them why Eliot might have broken off these phrases right before the last four lines of the poem.
Possible Responses: to show that when the world ends, it will interrupt everything; to emphasize the contrast between "For Thine is the Kingdom," which embraces eternal life, and "Life is very long," which makes existence sound bleak and undesirable

Thinking Through the Literature

1. Accept any reasonable response as long as students specify lines and images and give reactions to them.
2. Possible Responses: unfulfilled, lonely, boring, meaningless
3. Possible Responses: A lack of belief, faith, or commitment prevents the hollow men from doing anything of value; unable to conceive of immortality, they live bland lives that simply end.

Assessment Standardized Test Practice

CHOOSING THE BEST RESTATEMENT
For some standardized tests, students will be asked to choose the best restatement of a poem or an aspect of a poem. The following exercise will let students practice choosing the best restatement.

Which of these statements best describes the setting in which the hollow men exist?

A. It is a place of twilight, roses, and perpetually shining stars.
B. It is a dead land, sterile and inhospitable, a land of broken idols.
C. It is a land of sunlight and trees, where the wind sings.

Lead students through the process of choosing the best restatement. Consider each choice. Point out that, while all of the statements reflect elements mentioned in the poem, both **A** and **C** describe the setting of "death's other kingdom," not the land of the hollow men. Only **B** describes the "dream kingdom" where the hollow men exist.

THE HOLLOW MEN 1069

Reading and Analyzing

Literary Analysis: SOUND DEVICES

Have students analyze the poem's rhyme scheme.

Answer: ababcbcbdbdbefefghghijijk-bkbllb

Active Reading

STRATEGIES FOR READING MODERN VERSE

A Most of this humorous verse is an explanation about cats, but in line 25 there is a description of the cat. Ask students to describe what they visualize.

Possible Response: a cat curled up, oblivious to everything around it

Literary Analysis: STYLE

Guide students to note how Eliot achieves an informal style with the use of contractions, of silly names like Quaxo, of many simple words. Ask them how words like *perpendicular, profound meditation, rapt contemplation, ineffable,* and *inscrutable* work in this style.

Possible Response: Because this more sophisticated vocabulary is used in the context of a poem whose content and mood is silly, it provides a nice contrast and highlights the mock seriousness of its claim that cats need three names.

from The Book of Practical Cats

The Naming of Cats

T. S. Eliot

The Naming of Cats is a difficult matter,
It isn't just one of your holiday games;
You may think at first I'm as mad as a hatter
When I tell you, a cat must have THREE DIFFERENT NAMES.
First of all, there's the name that the family use daily,
Such as Peter, Augustus, Alonzo or James,
Such as Victor or Jonathan, George or Bill Bailey—
All of them sensible everyday names.
There are fancier names if you think they sound sweeter,
Some for the gentlemen, some for the dames:
Such as Plato, Admetus, Electra, Demeter—
But all of them sensible everyday names.
But I tell you, a cat needs a name that's particular,
A name that's peculiar, and more dignified,
Else how can he keep up his tail perpendicular,
Or spread out his whiskers, or cherish his pride?
Of names of this kind, I can give you a quorum,
Such as Munkustrap, Quaxo, or Coricopat,
Such as Bombalurina, or else Jellylorum—
Names that never belong to more than one cat.
But above and beyond there's still one name left over,
And that is the name that you never will guess;
The name that no human research can discover—
But THE CAT HIMSELF KNOWS, and will never confess.
When you notice a cat in profound meditation,
The reason, I tell you, is always the same:
His mind is engaged in a rapt contemplation
Of the thought, of the thought, of the thought of his name:
His ineffable effable
Effanineffable
Deep and inscrutable singular Name.

Peter
Augustus
Alonzo
James
Victor
Jonathan
George
Bill Bailey
Plato
Admetus
Electra
Demeter
Munkustrap
Quaxo
Coricopat
Bombalurina
Jellylorum

Teaching Options

Vocabulary Strategy

USING DICTIONARIES

Instruction Explain to students that they can use specialized dictionaries to help them discover the meanings of allusions. Biographical dictionaries will help them understand references to historical figures, dictionaries of mythology will help them understand allusions to myths and heroes, and dictionaries of foreign terms can help them understand phrases from other languages.

Activity Have students work with a partner in the library to locate specialized dictionaries that will help them understand the allusions in "The Naming of Cats." Make sure they define Plato, Admetus, Electra, and Demeter. Then ask students what these allusions add to the poem.

Answers: Plato was a Greek philosopher; Admetus was the king of Thessaly who allowed his wife to die in his place so that he could live forever; Electra, the daughter of Clytemnestra and Agamemnon, helped her brother Orestes avenge the death of her father by killing her mother; Demeter is the Greek goddess of the seasons and the harvest.

Use **Vocabulary Transparencies and Copymasters,** p. 56.

Preparing to Read

Build Background

In 1917 the English novelist May Sinclair wrote a review of Eliot's first poetry collection, *Prufrock and Other Observations* (which included "Preludes"). In her review, she compared the poetry of the relatively unknown Eliot with the Victorian poetry of Robert Browning and W. E. Henley.

Focus Your Reading

LITERARY ANALYSIS **BOOK REVIEW**

A **book review** is a kind of opinion essay. In a careful review, well-informed arguments are supported with appropriate examples. A good reviewer is not afraid to be outspoken and leaves no doubt in the reader's mind about his or her opinion of the book being reviewed. As you analyze this excerpt from Sinclair's review, compare her opinion of Eliot's poetry with your own.

from

"Prufrock and Other Observations": A Criticism

Book Review by MAY SINCLAIR

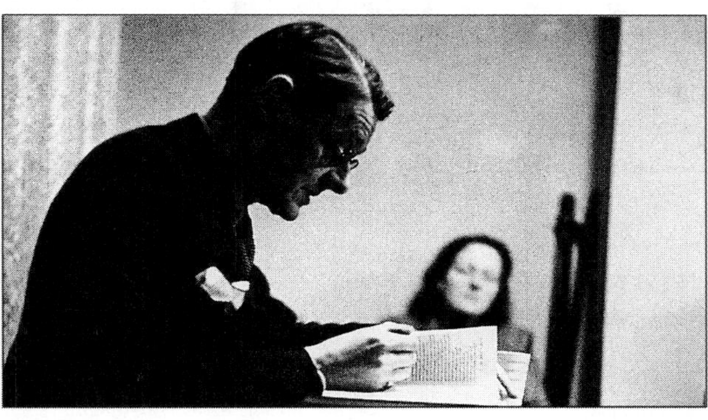

Mr. Eliot is not in any tradition at all; not even in Browning's and Henley's tradition. . . . His difference is twofold; a difference of method and technique; a difference of sight and aim. He does not see anything between him and reality, and he makes straight for the reality he sees; he cuts all his corners and his curves; and this directness of method is startling and upsetting to comfortable, respectable people accustomed to going superfluously in and out of corners and carefully round curves. Unless you are prepared to follow with the same nimbleness and straightness you will never arrive with Mr. Eliot at his meaning. . . .

The comfortable and respectable mind loves conventional beauty, and some of the realities that Mr. Eliot sees are not beautiful. He insists on your seeing very vividly, as he sees them, the streets of his "Preludes" and "Rhapsody." . . . And these things are ugly. The comfortable mind turns away from them in disgust. It identifies Mr. Eliot with a modern tendency; it labels him securely "Stark Realist," so that lovers of "true poetry" may beware.

It is nothing to the comfortable mind that Mr. Eliot is

. . . moved by fancies that are curled
Around these images, and cling:
The notion of some infinitely gentle
Infinitely suffering thing.

It is nothing to it that the emotion he disengages from his ugliest image is unbearably poignant. His poignancy is as unpleasant as his ugliness, disturbing to comfort.

Teaching the Literature

Build Background

Because Sinclair (1865–1946) was a writer who delved into psychology and experimented in technique, she was quite capable of grasping the uniqueness and worth of young Eliot's poetry. Critical opinion of Eliot at that time was still quite mixed. Ezra Pound, in *The Egoist,* was calling him a genius, while critics for English magazines such as *The New Statesman* and *Quarterly* had just called Eliot, respectively, an "insignificant phenomenon" and "a drunken Helot."

Sinclair brings up the names of Robert Browning and William Henley because of their influences on young poets of the day. Browning's poetry sometimes employs such devices as stream of consciousness, giving attention to psychological insights and aspects of modern life. Henley (1849–1903), author of a poem with the famous line "I am the master of my fate;/I am the captain of my soul," is a noted pioneer of free-verse in poetry.

The title "Rhapsody" is a reference to "Rhapsody on a Windy Night," another poem in the *Prufrock* collection.

Teaching Nonfiction

Reading Skills and Strategies

REVIEW

Reviews of literature—like those of art, movies, concerts, and the theater—are critical assessments. Opinions often involve specific, strong commentary on the various aspects of the work or performance being examined. The **Focus Your Reading** activity asks students to analyze Sinclair's review of Eliot's poetry for the purpose of comparing it to their own responses to Eliot. Students should not feel intimidated by the eloquent and metaphoric manner of Sinclair's expression and should concentrate on comparing opinions.

Mini Lesson Vocabulary Strategy

PREFIXES

Instruction The last paragraph of Sinclair's review includes the words *disengages, unbearably,* and *unpleasant.* Remind students that there are many negative prefixes in English: *un-, mis-, dis-, a-, im-, in-, il-, ir-,* and so on. These prefixes negate the meaning of the word to which they are appended.

Activity Have students identify the meanings of the three words with negative prefixes.

***dis*engages:** to detach, release, or withdraw
***un*bearably:** something that cannot be endured
***un*pleasant:** displeasing, not agreeable

Have students find words in Sinclair's book review that can take one of the negative prefixes. Have them rewrite the sentence in which the word(s) occur by attaching the negative prefixes to the word(s).

Example:

The comfortable and respectable mind loves conventional beauty.

becomes

The *un*comfortable and *un*respectable mind loves *un*conventional beauty.

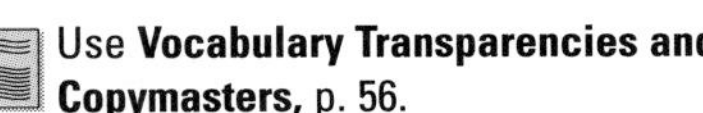

Use **Vocabulary Transparencies and Copymasters,** p. 56.

Teaching the Literature

Build Background

As an editor in 1946, Giroux corrected, adapted, and revised (as needed) original manuscript submitted by authors, often in direct consultation with them. There is a stereotype that writers resent the work of editors, who are seen as people who fuss and tinker with writers' words in the name of "improvement." This tug-of-war between writers and editors has led to an age-old view of editors as being failed creative writers.

Teaching Nonfiction

Reading Skills and Strategies

Anecdote

If students seem unsure of the nature of an anecdote, inform them that it is a short narrative telling an interesting or humorous event, often detailing something ironic. Ask students to characterize this anecdote.

Encounter with T. S. Eliot

Anecdote by **Robert Giroux**

Preparing to Read

Build Background

This anecdote—recorded in 1966 by Robert Giroux, then editor in chief of the New York publishing firm of Farrar, Straus & Giroux—provides a personal glimpse of T. S. Eliot. When he first met Eliot, Giroux was a struggling young editor with Eliot's American publisher, and Eliot was both a world-famous author and an influential editor in the London publishing world.

I first met T. S. Eliot in 1946, when I was an editor at Harcourt, Brace, under Frank Morley. I was just past thirty, and Eliot was in his late fifties. . . .

We went across the street to the old Ritz-Carlton. It was a lovely spring day and the courtyard restaurant—I think it was called the Japanese Garden—had just been opened for the season. For some reason I was astonished at the sight of newly hatched ducklings swimming in the center pond, perhaps because they seemed to embody the odd and improbable quality the occasion had for me.

Eliot could have not found a kinder, or more effective, way of putting me at my ease. As we sat down, he said, "Tell me, as one editor to another, do you have much author trouble?" I could not help laughing, he laughed in return—he had a *booming* laugh—and that was the beginning of our friendship. His most memorable remark of the day occurred when I asked him if he agreed with the definition that most editors are failed writers, and he replied: "Perhaps, but so are most writers."

Connect to the Literature

1. **What Do You Think?** Would you have thought it likely that "The Naming of Cats" was the work of the same person who wrote "Preludes" and "The Hollow Men"? Why or why not?

Comprehension Check
- According to the poem, how many names must a cat have?
- What are the different uses of the names?

Think Critically

2. What impression of cats do you think Eliot wanted to convey?

- the names given as examples
- the feline activities mentioned in lines 15–16
- cats' "deep and inscrutable" secret names

3. How does Eliot's **diction,** or word choice, contribute to the poem's humor?

4. In what way are the details in this poem like and unlike the details in the other two Eliot poems?

5. ACTIVE READING READING MODERN POETRY Review the poems' interpretations in your READER'S NOTEBOOK. How did you use the Active Reading guidelines on page 1064 to help you develop those interpretations? Share your experiences with classmates.

Extend Interpretations

6. **Critic's Corner** A conservative man, Eliot characterized himself as "classicist in literature, royalist in politics, and Anglo-Catholic in religion." Yet the British author Anthony Burgess observed that Eliot "was most radical when he was most conservative." How do you think Burgess's comment might apply to the form and content of Eliot's poems?

7. **Comparing Texts** Compare "Preludes" and "The Hollow Men" with William Wordsworth's poems on pages 725–735. How different are they in **imagery, subject matter, mood, tone,** and **form?**

8. **Connect to Life** Is the worldview underlying "Preludes" and "The Hollow Men" relevant today? Explain why or why not.

Literary Analysis

RHYTHM IN MODERN POETRY

In the early 20th century, many poets abandoned the strictures of regular rhythms, or **meters,** to produce **free verse**—poetry with no fixed rhythm.

By writing lines that corresponded to natural units of thought, they hoped to emphasize the meanings, rather than just the sounds, of their words. Notice, for example, how the lines in this passage of "Preludes" represent natural units of thought and highlight the shifts from image to image:

The morning comes to
consciousness
Of faint stale smells of beer
From the sawdust-trampled street
With all its muddy feet that press
To early coffee-stands.

Paired Activity With a partner, examine the rhythm of one section of "The Hollow Men," focusing on the lengths of the lines and the patterns of stressed syllables in them. Does the irregular rhythm contribute to the poem's meaning? How does the rhythm of "The Naming of Cats" differ from that of "The Hollow Men"? Discuss the different effects of irregular and regular rhythmic patterns.

REVIEW MOOD The **imagery** in a poem usually contributes to its **mood**—the feeling or atmosphere the writer creates. How would you describe the mood of "Preludes"? of "The Hollow Men"? How is the mood of "The Naming of Cats" different from the other two poems' moods?

GUIDING STUDENT RESPONSE

Connect to the Literature

1. **What Do You Think?** Guidelines for student response: Students should make comparisons and contrasts among the poems in order to support their opinions.

Comprehension Check
- three
- an everyday name for use by the family (humans); a name to express the cat's unique personality; a mysterious name known only to the cat

Think Critically

2. Possible Response: Each cat is unique and unfathomable, even though at one level the cat may seem ordinary and approachable.
3. Much of the language is playful, as in his transformation of *ineffable.* Likewise, the names he claims for cats sound both unlikely and inappropriate.
4. Possible Response: This poem is like the others because many of the details are allusions, such as some of the cat names. Also, the details draw from the whole range of culture: children's literature ("mad as a hatter"), classical culture (Augustus, Plato), myth (Electra, Demeter), and popular culture (Bill Bailey). The details in this poem are unlike those in the others because many seem frivolous or exist purely for their sound.
5. Accept all reasonable responses.

Literary Analysis

Paired Activity As students discuss the activity, be sure they discuss the effect the regular and irregular rhythmic patterns had on them as readers and on their response to the poems.

Extend Interpretations

Critic's Corner Possible Response: Eliot's attack on the modern world in "Preludes" and "The Hollow Men" is very conservative. Despite their content, though, both poems are very radical in their fragmented, innovative form. In contrast, the content of "The Naming of the Cats" is *less* conservative, but its form is *more* conservative.

Comparing Texts Students' responses may note that the historical contexts influenced both Wordsworth and Eliot; that is, Wordsworth's concerns about the effects of industrialization foreshadow some of Eliot's discomfort with modern life. Accept all well-supported responses that address imagery, subject matter, mood, tone, and form.

Connect to Life Ask students to summarize Eliot's world-view presented in the two poems.

The Author's Style

T. S. Eliot's unique style marks the beginning of modern poetry. Students will be made aware of Eliot's style through the "Key Aspects of Eliot's Style" chart and then find examples of the five points in the excerpts in the right margin.

Analysis of Style

A First activity

openness of language: one-night cheap hotels; the interjection "Oh"; And drank coffee, and talked for an hour

ordinary, unpleasant experiences: "The Love Song of J. Alfred Prufrock" talks of wandering the streets

free verse: "The Love Song of J. Alfred Prufrock" and "The Waste Land" are both written in free verse

symbols: Like a patient etherized upon a table; Winter kept us warm

allusions: April is the cruelest month, breeding / Lilacs out of the dead land, mixing / Memory and desire

B Second activity

openness of language: "Preludes": Of faint stale smells of beer; "The Hollow Men": Gathered on this beach of the tumid river

ordinary, unpleasant experiences: "Preludes": From the sawdust-trampled street / With all its muddy feet that press / To early coffee-stands; "The Hollow Men": We are the hollow men / We are the stuffed men

free verse: Both poems are examples

symbols: "Preludes": Or clasped the yellow soles of feet / In the palms of both soiled hands; "The Hollow Men": / In death's other kingdom / Walking alone

allusions: "Preludes": One thinks of all the hands / That are raising dingy shades / In a thousand furnished rooms; "The Hollow Men": There are no eyes here / In this valley of dying stars

C Third activity

The "Naming of Cats" is much lighter and more humorous than the other two poems. It also has a more traditional rhyme scheme.

Applications

1. Changing Style Have students go through the entire writing process for this activity—prewriting, drafting, editing, and publishing. Encourage them to choose manageable sections of no more than 20 lines.

2. Imitating Style Remind students to revisit the Key Aspects box on the page before beginning their creations.

3. Comparing Styles Students may want to read other poems by Yeats and Eliot to get a better idea of the poets' distinct styles.

The Author's Style

Eliot's Modernist Style

Before the 20th century, most British poetry had regular patterns of rhyme and rhythm, dealt with their subjects in a "realistic" way, and contained easily understood images and direct statements of ideas and emotions. T. S. Eliot, as a pioneer of modernism, often broke with these traditions.

Key Aspects of Eliot's Style

- an openness to everyday language, including slang and references to popular culture
- a focus on ordinary, often unpleasant, experiences
- a frequent use of free verse, in which the rhythms fall into no fixed pattern
- the conveying of ideas and feelings by means of complex images and symbols, rather than by means of explicit statements
- a patchwork of images, symbols, and allusions, in which the reader must supply the connections

from **"The Love Song of J. Alfred Prufrock"**

Let us go then, you and I,
When the evening is spread out against
the sky
Like a patient etherized upon a table;
Let us go, through certain half-deserted
streets,
The muttering retreats
Of restless nights in one-night cheap hotels
And sawdust restaurants with oyster-shells:
Streets that follow like a tedious argument
Of insidious intent
To lead you to an overwhelming
question . . .
Oh, do not ask, "What is it?"
Let us go and make our visit.

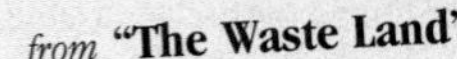

Analysis of Style

At the right are the opening lines of two of Eliot's most famous poems. Study the list of stylistic features above, and read each excerpt carefully. Then complete the following activities:

- **A** Find examples of each aspect of Eliot's style in the two excerpts.
- **B** Reread "Preludes" and "The Hollow Men," noting examples of each stylistic feature.
- **C** Explain how "The Naming of Cats" differs in style from the other two poems and from the two excerpts.

from **"The Waste Land"**

April is the cruelest month, breeding
Lilacs out of the dead land, mixing
Memory and desire, stirring
Dull roots with spring rain.
Winter kept us warm, covering
Earth in forgetful snow, feeding
A little life with dried tubers.
Summer surprised us, coming over the
Starnbergersee
With a shower of rain; we stopped in the
colonnade,
And went on in sunlight, into the Hofgarten,
And drank coffee, and talked for an hour.

Applications

1. Changing Style Choose a section of "Preludes" or "The Hollow Men," and rewrite it—either as poetry or as prose—in a different style. You could, for example, recast the section in rhyming couplets. Your rewriting should express the same ideas as the original passage. Read your version aloud to your classmates.

2. Imitating Style Working with a partner, imitate Eliot's style by writing an additional section for "Preludes" or "The Hollow Men."

3. Comparing Styles Compare Eliot's style with that of his older contemporary William Butler Yeats. Review Yeats's poems on pages 989–991, and compare his style to Eliot's.

Mini Lesson Grammar

PRONOUNS: VAGUE ANTECEDENTS

Instruction When a pronoun refers to a specific word (a noun or another pronoun), that word is the *antecedent* of the pronoun. Antecedents should be clear and definite. The number, gender, and person of a pronoun must be the same as that of its antecedent.

A common error is to construct a sentence with a vague pronoun, one that has more than one possible antecedent. Pronouns such as *this, that,* or *which* often have unclear antecedents.

Activity Write the following example on the chalkboard.

Giroux and Eliot met in 1946, and he recounted their conversation.

Ask students to reword the sentence to clarify the antecedent of *he. (. . . 1946, and Giroux recounted . . .)*

Use **Vocabulary Transparencies and Copymasters,** p. 147.

Choices & CHALLENGES

Writing Options

1. **Dramatic Skit** Write a short dramatic work based on one of Eliot's poems. For example, you might create characters to reveal the personalities behind some of the names in "The Naming of Cats." Place the dramatic skit in your **Working Portfolio.**

2. **Armchair Analysis** Write an essay explaining the worldview underlying "Preludes" and "The Hollow Men." Use a graphic like this one to note specific lines from each poem.

Writing Handbook
See pages 1369–1370: Analysis.

Name of Poem	Revealing Lines	Worldview Expressed

Activities & Explorations

1. **Poetic Collage** Capture the fragmentary nature of "Preludes" or "The Hollow Men" by creating a collage of images corresponding to the images in the poem. ~ ART

2. **Dramatic Reading** With two or three classmates, rehearse and perform a dramatic reading of one of the three Eliot poems in a manner appropriate to its mood and tone. ~ SPEAKING AND LISTENING

Inquiry & Research

1. **Urban Poverty** Research the living conditions in the poorer sections of London in Eliot's day. In a written report, compare them to the conditions in poor neighborhoods today.

2. **Contemporary Issues** Find songs and poems that comment on life in America or Britain today. How do the images and issues in the works compare with those in Eliot's poems? Present your conclusions in a panel discussion before the class.

LaserLinks: Background for Reading
Art Gallery

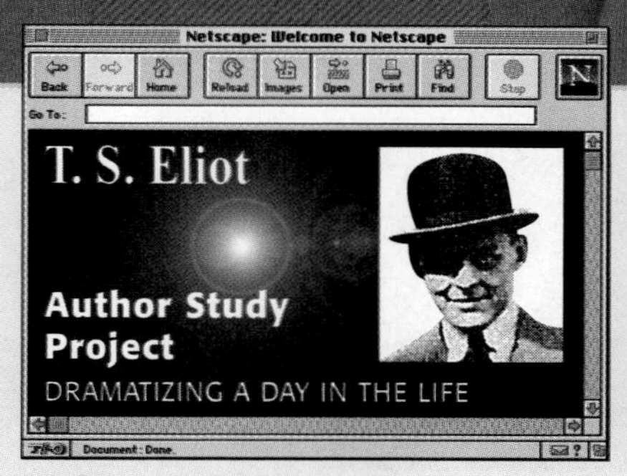

What was life like for Eliot as an expatriate American living in England in the early 20th century? Who were his friends and acquaintances? What kind of social life did he have? What was his courtship and marriage like? With a group of classmates, research the answers to these and related questions. Present your findings in a dramatization of a typical day, a revealing incident, or an important conversation in Eliot's life during the period 1910–1930. One group member should play T. S. Eliot; the others should play important figures in Eliot's life, such as his wife Vivien, Bertrand Russell, Ezra Pound, and Virginia Woolf.

Primary Print Sources Consult newspaper and magazine articles, and perhaps even fiction set in the period. Consider investigating memoirs, diaries, autobiographies, and collections of letters by such writers as Ezra Pound, Bertrand Russell, E. M. Forster, Virginia Woolf, James Joyce, Ford Madox Ford, Wyndham Lewis, I. A. Richards, and Eliot himself.

Secondary Print Sources Consult biographies and historical and biographical entries in reference works. Also look in the 20th-century sections of literary histories of England and America.

Computer Resources Reliable Web sites can provide useful information on Eliot and the modernists. Consider sites maintained by university English departments and by established poetry societies.

More Online: Research Starter
www.mcdougallittell.com

Writing Options

1. **Dramatic Skit** Student responses will vary, but should reflect the tone and mood of the poem they chose. If the students choose to dramatize "Preludes" or "The Hollow Men," you might suggest that they think of the speaker as someone wandering the streets of a city—alienated, lonely, searching for meaning.
2. **Armchair Analysis** Students might be interested in looking into secondary sources to get a fuller understanding of Eliot's views. They might also consider reading some of his essays on Christianity and culture.

Activities & Explorations

1. **Poetic Collage** You might underline the similarities between the patchwork nature of Eliot's poetry and a collage. The artwork itself will vary depending on the poem chosen, which should be obvious from the images in the collage.
2. **Dramatic Reading** See the Speaking and Listening mini-lesson on page 1068 for tips on preparing students for oral presentations.

Inquiry & Research

1. **Urban Poverty** Remind students that Eliot lived from 1888–1965, during which time urban conditions changed dramatically. Students may want to research one particular decade.
2. **Contemporary Issues** Encourage students to locate at least one poem for every song. Appoint a student to act as the moderator for the panel discussion.

Author Study Project

DRAMATIZING A DAY IN THE LIFE

This project will give you an opportunity to explore with students the research process from beginning to end. Use as much of the following as time permits. Make the following suggestions to students:

- Meet in groups to generate questions about Eliot's time to open their minds and focus their research.
- Explore a wide array of print and nonprint resources. Abundant text sources (primary and secondary sources) and technical resources (databases and internet) are available on this subject.
- use study and reading skills to help determine the relevance and usefulness of material.
- evaluate the credibility and appropriateness of the materials. Checking a writer's credentials and sources is one way to determine credibility. Students can check appropriateness by checking any new information against the questions they are pursuing.
- While gathering information, record and organize material by taking notes, outlining, and converting information to new forms.
- At the conclusion, identify areas for further investigation by generating questions related to research findings and conclusions.

As support for the research process, refer students to the following resources: Writing Handbook: Research Report Writing, 1373–1378; Communication Handbook: Research and Inquiry, 1381–1390.

OVERVIEW

"Musée des Beaux Arts" is included in the **Grade 12 InterActive Reader.**

Objectives

1. understand and appreciate **modern poetry (Literary Analysis)**
2. appreciate the author's use of **irony** in modern poetry **(Literary Analysis)**
3. **draw conclusions** about Auden's poetry **(Active Reading)**

Summary

"Musée des Beaux Arts" looks at the indifference with which suffering is often met. The poem's speaker illustrates this indifference with a reference to Brueghel's painting *Landscape with the Fall of Icarus.* "The Unknown Citizen" gives a brief overview of the life of a citizen named only as JS/07/M/378. The speaker calls the citizen a "saint"—a judgment based on the fact that he had the "right" views, an exemplary work record, and was a model consumer, among other things.

Thematic Link

The **new images of reality** that Auden describes in these poems are harsh and critical. In his view, human beings are essentially self-centered and unable to relate to one another, particularly in the modern world.

5-Minute Warm-Up

Daily Language SkillBuilder

Have students **proofread** the display sentences on page 979j and write them correctly. The sentences also appear on Transparency 29 of **Grammar Transparencies and Copymasters.**

"The sun shone as it had to."

Musée des Beaux Arts
The Unknown Citizen

Poetry by W. H. AUDEN

Connect to Your Life

Who Cares? Create a bar graph like the one shown, indicating the extent to which you think other people are concerned about your personal well-being. In addition to groups with whom you are both directly involved—family members, friends, teachers, coaches, employers, doctors—include some with whom you are involved more indirectly, such as store clerks or bus drivers.

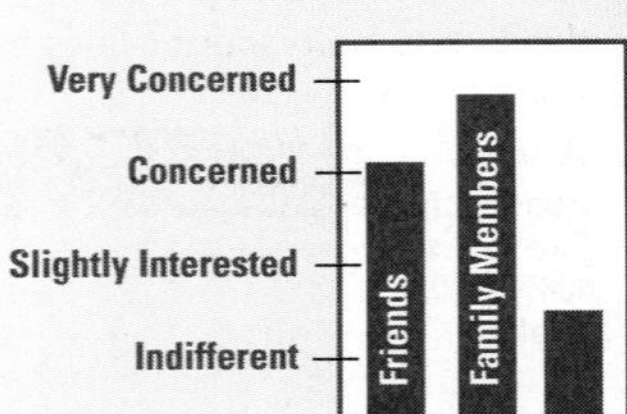

Build Background

Auden's Poetry Generally regarded as one of the foremost modern English poets, W. H. Auden produced a large and complex body of work. At times obscure, his poetry defies easy description or categorization, for it is at times religious, at times lyrical, and frequently satirical. His interest in the problems of modern society and the psychological aspects of human existence is revealed throughout his writing.

Auden, who wanted the style of his poetry to reflect his concern for the common person, strove to write simply and avoid the finery of "grand poetry." He believed that his role as a poet was to present ordinary aspects of human existence in a way that readers could understand and relate to their lives.

The two poems you are about to read reveal Auden's knack for simplicity of style and biting satire. "Musée des Beaux Arts" was inspired by a trip to Brussels, where Auden viewed the paintings in the Royal Museum of Fine Arts, including several by the 16th-century Flemish artist Pieter Breughel (broi'gəl) the Elder. In "The Unknown Citizen," Auden explores the quality of life in the 20th century.

Focus Your Reading

LITERARY ANALYSIS IRONY IN MODERN POETRY Both of the poems you are about to read contain ironic elements.

- **Situational irony** is a contrast between what readers expect and what actually happens.
- **Verbal irony** is a speaker's or writer's saying one thing and meaning another.

As you read these poems, watch for examples of irony.

ACTIVE READING DRAWING CONCLUSIONS A work's **theme** is a central idea or message that conveys a perception about life or human nature. Poems do not usually state their themes explicitly, but you can discover theme by paying attention to poetic elements that help to convey it—for example, **imagery** and **tone.** In order to **draw conclusions** about a poem's theme, you need to combine what is implied or stated in the poem with your own prior knowledge.

READER'S NOTEBOOK As you read each poem, note down phrases, images, or lines that you think help to convey Auden's ideas about human nature and life.

LESSON RESOURCES

UNIT SIX RESOURCE BOOK, pp. 31–32

ASSESSMENT RESOURCES

Formal Assessment, pp. 193–194

Teacher's Guide to Assessment and Portfolio Use

Test Generator

SKILLS TRANSPARENCIES AND COPYMASTERS

Literary Analysis
- Verbal, Situational, and Dramatic Irony, T17 (for Literary Analysis, p. 1081)

Reading and Critical Thinking
- Drawing Conclusions, T4 (for Active Reading, p. 1076)

Grammar
- Comparison of Regular and Irregular Adjectives and Adverbs, T52 (for Mini Lesson, p. 1082)
- Adverb Qualifiers, C153 (for Mini Lesson, p. 1082)

Vocabulary
- Meanings of *-ing* Endings, C84 (for Mini Lesson, p. 1078)

Writing
- Compare-Contrast, C34 (for Writing Option 2, p. 1082)
- Opinion Statement, C35 (for Writing Option 1, p. 1082)

Communications
- Interviewing, T9 (for Activities & Explorations 1, p. 1082)
- Impromptu Speaking: Dialogue, Role-Play, T14 (for Activities & Explorations 1, p. 1082)

INTEGRATED TECHNOLOGY

Audio Library

LaserLinks
- Art Gallery: Nameless Men. See **Teacher's SourceBook,** p. 75.

Visit our website:
www.mcdougallittell.com

Landscape with the Fall of Icarus (about 1560), Pieter Brueghel the Elder. Musée Royaux des Beaux Arts de Belgique, Brussels, Belgium/Superstock.

Musée des Beaux Arts

W. H. AUDEN

About suffering they were never wrong,
The Old Masters: how well they understood
Its human position; how it takes place
While someone else is eating or opening a window or just walking dully along;
How, when the aged are reverently, passionately waiting
For the miraculous birth, there always must be

2 Old Masters: great European artists of the 16th–18th centuries.

TEACHING THE LITERATURE

Customizing Instruction

Less Proficient Readers
Have students read the poems individually and then meet in small groups to discuss them. Monitor the discussions and answer questions as needed.

Students Acquiring English
Help students with the syntax of the first poem. Have volunteers reword statements and identify antecedents of pronouns where necessary. In the second poem, help students recognize the qualities of the speaker's language that identify it as bureaucratese.

 Use **Spanish Study Guide** for additional support, pp. 251–253.

Gifted and Talented
Have students consider what each poem suggests about individuality.

BLOCK SCHEDULING: MANAGING TIME

If your schedule requires that you cover the lesson objectives in a shorter time, use . . .
- Preparing to Read, p. 1076
- Thinking Through the Literature, pp. 1078, 1081

If you want to take advantage of longer class time, use . . .
- TE Teaching Options: Vocabulary Strategy, p. 1078; Viewing and Representing, p. 1079; Cross-Curricular Link, p. 1080; Grammar Mini Lesson, p. 1082
- Choices & Challenges, p. 1082

MUSÉE DES BEAUX ARTS 1077

Reading and Analyzing

Active Reading

DRAWING CONCLUSIONS

Ask students whether they believe the painting shown on p. 1077 could relate to the theme of "Musée des Beaux Arts." If necessary, refer them to the credit line. Then ask students what other elements of a poem besides those listed on p. 1076 could help them draw conclusions about a poem's theme.

Possible Responses: the poem's title; allusions; literary elements such as irony and symbolism

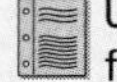 Use **Unit Six Resource Book** p. 31 for more practice.

Literary Analysis

IRONY IN MODERN POETRY

Ask students whether lines 1–4 are ironic.

Possible Responses: No, Auden does not want the reader to see any incongruity in the coexistence of suffering and indifference; yes, the first two lines raise the expectation that the Old Masters had a special empathy for suffering, then lines 3–4 describe their view as something nearly the opposite: an endorsement of indifference toward suffering.

A Ask students why the bystanders' reaction to Icarus's fall is ironic.

Possible Response: Their indifference is incongruous with a tragic event.

 Use **Unit Six Resource Book** p. 32 for more exercises.

Thinking Through the Literature

1. Icarus's fall after escaping from imprisonment, using wax-and-feather wings made by his father
2. Accept all reasonable responses.
3. Accept all reasonable, well-supported responses.
4. Possible Responses: ironic, serio-comic, pragmatic

Children who did not specially want it to happen, skating
On a pond at the edge of the wood:
They never forgot
That even the dreadful martyrdom must run its course
Anyhow in a corner, some untidy spot
Where the dogs go on with their doggy life and the
torturer's horse
Scratches its innocent behind on a tree.

In Breughel's *Icarus*, for instance: how everything turns 
away
Quite leisurely from the disaster; the ploughman may
Have heard the splash, the forsaken cry,
But for him it was not an important failure; the sun shone (A)
As it had to on the white legs disappearing into the green
Water; and the expensive delicate ship that must have seen
Something amazing, a boy falling out of the sky,
Had somewhere to get to and sailed calmly on.

14 Breughel's *Icarus* (ĭk′ər-əs): the painting *Landscape with the Fall of Icarus* by Pieter Brueghel (also spelled *Bruegel* and *Breughel*). In Greek mythology, Icarus and his father, Daedalus (dĕd′l-əs), escape imprisonment by flying away on wings crafted of wax and feathers. When Icarus flies too near the sun, the wax melts and he falls into the sea and drowns.

Thinking Through the Literature

1. **Comprehension Check** What incident in the Icarus legend is depicted in Breughel's painting and alluded to by the **speaker** of the poem?
2. What words or phrases best describe your reaction to this poem?
3. Do you agree with the speaker's ideas about suffering and indifference? Give reasons for your answer.
4. How would you describe the **tone** of this poem?

Teaching Options

Vocabulary Strategy

MEANINGS OF *-ing* ENDINGS: *eating, opening, walking, waiting, skating, disappearing, falling*

Instruction Ask students to look at the list of words above. Remind them that the *-ing* ending is used for the present progressive form of a verb, and that using the present progressive gives a distinctive feel to the action. Ask students to describe the effect of the *-ing* words in the poem.

Possible Response: They impart a feeling of timelessness, because the verb form does not establish a time frame for events.

Exercise Have students identify other important verb forms used in the poem and their impact.

Answer: The present tense verbs *go, scratches,* and *turns* emphasize the sense of immediacy already established by the *-ing* words. The past tense verbs *was, shone, had,* and *sailed* give a sense of finality to the rejection of the incident as being important.

 Use **Vocabulary Transparencies and Copymasters,** p. 57.

Golconde [Golconda] (1953), René Magritte. Oil on canvas, 31½″ × 39½″, The Menil Collection, Houston. Photo by Hickey-Robertson.

THE Unknown Citizen

(To JS/07/M/378
This Marble Monument
Is Erected by the State)

W. H. AUDEN

2 He was found by the Bureau of Statistics to be
One against whom there was no official complaint,
And all the reports on his conduct agree
3 That, in the modern sense of an old-fashioned word, he was a saint,
For in everything he did he served the Greater Community.
Except for the War till the day he retired
He worked in a factory and never got fired,
But satisfied his employers, Fudge Motors Inc.
Yet he wasn't a scab or odd in his views,

9 scab: a worker who refuses to support a union strike and crosses a picket line.

Customizing Instruction

Less Proficient Readers

1 Have students locate a complete retelling of the myth of Daedalus and Icarus. Then explain to them that Icarus's fall is not merely a myth but also a moral tale. Daedalus warned his son not too fly too high, but Icarus, with a young man's overconfidence, ignored his father's warning. Historically, the myth has often been used to illustrate the limitations of technology and why young people should listen to their parents.

Students Acquiring English

2 Explain that the construction "He was found . . . to be" refers to the results (i.e., "findings") of whatever inquiries were made by the Bureau of Statistics into his records.

Less Proficient Readers

Ask students these questions:

- Who is the speaker in this poem?
- Why does the speaker refer to the citizen as a saint?

Possible Responses: a government bureaucrat speaking for the state (see "we" in line 29); the speaker is pleased with the citizen's conformity and service but indifferent to who he really was.

Gifted and Talented

3 Have students discuss the irony created by the use of the word *saint* in line 4.

Possible Response: The word *saint* usually refers to a devout religious person who stands out for his or her holiness and remarkable good deeds. Calling someone a saint simply because he behaves responsibly and predictably creates an ironic contrast.

Mini Lesson Viewing and Representing

Golconde and *La grande guerre*
by René Magritte

ART APPRECIATION

Instruction The paintings on this page and the following are by René Magritte (1898–1967), a Belgian artist associated with the international movement known as Surrealism, whose revolutionary practices changed the subject matter and stylistic practices of much modern art.

Application Have students deconstruct *Golconde.* Note the highly symmetrical diagonals that the men in bowler hats are arranged in. Then ask students what view of modern life the painting conveys.

Possible Responses: Conformity forces people to dress alike and act alike; something extraordinary lurks behind everyday ordinariness.

Next, have students look at *La grande guerre* [*The Great War*] on p. 1080. Why might Magritte have hidden the man's face behind the apple?

Possible Response: By placing the apple in front of the man's face, Magritte seems to be emphasizing the facelessness of humanity in modern life.

THE UNKNOWN CITIZEN 1079

Reading and Analyzing

Literary Analysis: TONE

A Note the difference between *mood* and *tone* (that is, mood is the feelings created by the poem; tone is the poet's attitude toward the material). Ask students to describe the tone of these lines.

Possible Response: satiric—buying on the installment plan in fact creates debt and fosters a dependence on materialism

Active Reading

DRAWING CONCLUSIONS

B Ask students what Auden is suggesting about the value placed on independent thinking.

Possible Response: Conformity is highly valued, and opposing opinions are considered unacceptable.

Literary Analysis: SPEAKER

C Ask students what the speaker's attitude toward the unknown citizen is.

Possible Responses: pleased with his conformity and service; patronizing; indifferent to his real needs

Literary Analysis: STYLE

Have students discuss the purpose of capitalizing words such as *Union, Press,* and *Public Opinion.*

Possible Responses: It conveys the power and authority of these organizations and concepts. It also suggests an ironic attitude toward these organizations.

For his Union reports that he paid his dues,
(Our report on his Union shows it was sound)
And our Social Psychology workers found
That he was popular with his mates and liked a drink.
The Press are convinced that he bought a paper every day
And that his reactions to advertisements were normal in
every way.
Policies taken out in his name prove that he was fully insured,
And his Health-card shows he was once in hospital but left it cured.
Both Producers Research and High-Grade Living declare
He was fully sensible to the advantages of the Installment Plan
And had everything necessary to the Modern Man,
A phonograph, a radio, a car and a frigidaire.
Our researchers into Public Opinion are content
That he held the proper opinions for the time of year;
When there was peace, he was for peace; when there was
war, he went.
He was married and added five children to the population,
Which our Eugenist says was the right number for a parent
of his generation,
And our teachers report that he never interfered with their
education.
Was he free? Was he happy? The question is absurd:
Had anything been wrong, we should certainly have heard.

21 frigidaire: refrigerator.

26 Eugenist (yo͞o'jə-nĭst): a scientist who tries to improve the human race by controlling hereditary factors.

La grande guerre [The great war] (1964), René Magritte. Private collection, Giraudon/Art Resource, New York. Copyright © 1996 Herscovici/Artists Rights Society (ARS), New York.

Teaching Options

Cross Curricular Link Art

DUTCH AND FLEMISH PAINTERS *Flemish* refers to the Dutch-related language and people of Flanders, a historical region now mainly in Belgium. Dutch and Flemish cultures are strongly intertwined. Early in the Renaissance, Flemish artist Jan van Eyck pioneered techniques of modern oil painting, while Dutchman Hieronymus Bosch painted busy scenes of people mingling with grotesque symbolic figures. Pieter Brueghel (or Breughel) the Elder was much influenced by Bosch, although Brueghel's more earthbound landscapes were usually peopled by lively Flemish peasants. Peter Paul Rubens, also Flemish, was a master of the baroque, the dominant art style from about 1550 to 1700, noted for curving figures and elaborate ornamentation. Holland's Jan Vermeer is famous for vividly realistic interior scenes that brilliantly use light and color, while another Dutch master, Rembrandt van Rijn, is unmatched in portraying human emotions in historical and religious scenes as well as in portraits and self-portraits.

Thinking through the LITERATURE

Connect to the Literature

1. **What Do You Think?** What is your opinion of the person memorialized in "The Unknown Citizen"? Share your thoughts with your classmates.

Think Critically

2. How would you describe the **tone** of the poem?

- the dedication in parentheses at the beginning of the poem
- the types of accomplishments cited by the speaker
- the speaker's conclusions

3. Do you think the unknown citizen was free and happy? Explain why or why not.

4. **ACTIVE READING** **DRAWING CONCLUSIONS** Review the notes you made in your READER'S NOTEBOOK relating to the theme of each poem. What perception about life or human nature do you think is conveyed in each of these poems?

5. After reading "Musée des Beaux Arts" and "The Unknown Citizen," how would you describe Auden's view of the average person?

Extend Interpretations

6. **Critic's Corner** The literary critic Richard Hoggart has remarked on the conversational **style** of Auden's poems, saying that reading them is like "listening to the poet thinking aloud." Do you agree with Hoggart? Cite examples from both poems to support your answer.

7. **Connect to Life** Refer to the graph you created on page 1076. Compare any indifference you noted with the types of indifference portrayed in the two poems. Do you think indifference is an inevitable fact of life?

8. **Art Connection** Look at the reproduction of Brueghel's painting *Landscape with the Fall of Icarus* on page 1077. Why do you think Auden chose this particular painting as the focus of "Musée des Beaux Arts"?

Literary Analysis

IRONY IN MODERN POETRY In a literary work, **situational irony** is a contrast between what readers expect and what actually happens. **Verbal irony** is a character's or writer's saying one thing and meaning another.

Paired Activity Jot down examples of situational irony in "Musée des Beaux Arts" and verbal irony in "The Unknown Citizen." Then give your interpretation of Auden's use of irony in both poems, citing lines from each one to support your ideas. With your partner, speculate on how the two poems might be different if they contained no irony.

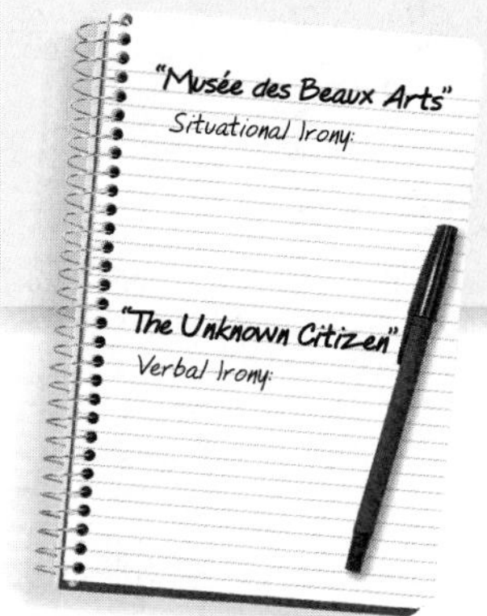

GUIDING STUDENT RESPONSE

Connect to the Literature

1. **What Do You Think?** Guidelines for student response: Students should react both to the characteristics detailed by the speaker and to the context of the person's life.

Think Critically

2. Possible Responses: author ironic, mocking; satiric; speaker indifferent, patronizing.
3. Possible Responses: yes, so deadened he does not know what he is missing; no, experiences only illusion of happiness and freedom.
4. Possible Responses: In "Musée des Beaux Arts," Auden suggests that suffering is a part of life; or, in "Musée des Beaux Arts" people are so involved in trite and habitual acts of life that they are (tragically) indifferent to suffering; in "The Unknown Citizen," the lack of concern for the citizen's individual freedom and happiness is similar to everyone's indifference to Icarus's suffering in the first poem.
5. Possible Responses: Both poems mourn the lack of importance the average person has in the general scheme of things; the first poem celebrates the average person by showing the endurance of everyday life; the second poem harshly criticizes institutions that rob the average person of his or her freedom and happiness.

Literary Analysis

Paired Activity Conduct a class discussion, based upon the findings of the student pairs, of the function of irony in these poems.

Extend Interpretations

Critic's Corner Those who feel Auden has a conversational style may cite, in the first poem, the irregular word order and double subject in lines 1–2, the chatty long lines such as 4 and 12, and the use of informal *doggy* in line 12; in the second poem, the informal wordiness of line 4 and the use of the slang term *mates* in line 13.

Connect to Life Accept any reasonable, well-considered response.

Art Connection The painting itself is ironic, barely showing poor Icarus; it stresses those who ignore Icarus's suffering; it captures the calm pleasure of everyday life despite Icarus's woes.

Writing Options

1. **Newspaper Editorial** Student responses will vary, but they should address both indifference to human suffering and the idea that modern society is dehumanizing.
2. **Comparison of Workers** Many student comparisons will be based on their experience with entry-level jobs in the service or retail sectors. Ask them to also consider changes in the workplace fostered by the computer and the "information economy."

Activities & Explorations

1. **Police Interview** The student role-playing the police officer should choose appropriate questions to collect information in an accident case. To make this assignment more challenging, have the student role-playing the officer conduct the interviews in order to prepare to press charges under "failure to render aid" or the "Good Samaritan" law because the witness did nothing to respond to the emergency situation.
2. **Census Forms** If possible, provide sample census forms for the class to examine before beginning the activity. You might want to have students work in pairs or small groups to create their census forms.

Inquiry & Research

The 1930s Encyclopedia yearbooks for the 1930s might provide a good starting point for students. Have them interpret the possible influence of historical context (1930s) on the poems.

Choices & CHALLENGES

Writing Options

1. **Newspaper Editorial** Write an editorial in which you urge average citizens to cast aside the kinds of indifference portrayed in these two poems.
2. **Comparison of Workers** Draft a short essay in which you compare Auden's depiction of the unknown citizen with your impression of workers in today's society.

Writing Handbook
See page 1367: Compare and Contrast.

Activities & Explorations

1. **Police Interview** With a partner, role-play an interview in which a police officer asks either the plowman or the captain of the ship in Brueghel's *Landscape with the Fall of Icarus* for more details about the boy's accident. ~ **PERFORMING**
2. **Census Forms** Create two census forms for the Bureau of Statistics—one that seeks only the kind of information presented in "The Unknown Citizen" and one that might elicit a more in-depth picture of people. ~ **SOCIOLOGY**

Inquiry & Research

The 1930s Working with a small group of classmates, research political and social developments in the world during the 1930s. Then list some ideas expressed in these poems that readers in the 1930s may have seen as reflections of new realities.

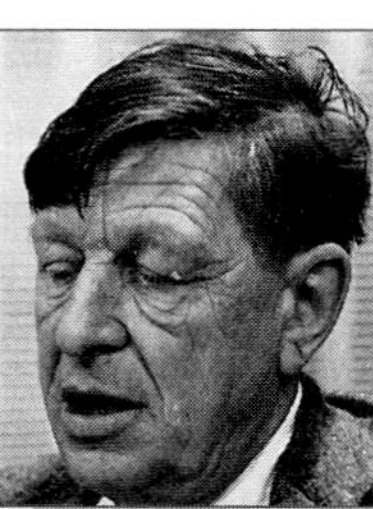

W. H. Auden
1907–1973

Other Works
"On This Island"
"Their Lonely Betters"
"In Praise of Limestone"

Early Life Wystan Hugh Auden was born in York, England, the son of a doctor. His earliest interest was science, and as a boy he planned to become a mining engineer. From his mother, who loved music, he derived a lifelong interest in many kinds of music, particularly opera. At the age of 15, however, he discovered his talent for writing poetry; thereafter, he knew that writing would be his career.

Oxford Years While a student at Oxford University, Auden exerted a significant influence on a group of young writers who would become the literary leaders of the 1930s. Later known as the Auden Generation, this group included Stephen Spender, who in 1928 printed Auden's first published book of poems on a hand-operated press. Auden's genius was also encouraged by the poet T. S. Eliot, then an editor at the publishing firm of Faber & Faber.

American Years Auden assumed various other roles during his lifetime, including those of teacher, playwright, documentary filmmaker, critic, and editor. In 1939 he moved to New York City, becoming a U.S. citizen in 1946. He spent most of his literary career in the United States, where he regularly taught and lectured at colleges and universities, including Yale, Swarthmore, Penn State, and the University of Michigan.

Eccentric Lifestyle Even after becoming a renowned literary figure who mingled with the rich and famous, Auden chose to live the life of an eccentric, residing in messy, rundown apartments; dressing in shabby attire; and frequently appearing in public wearing jeans and bedroom slippers. Although disordered in his daily life, he maintained a strict sense of order in his poetry.

Return to Oxford Auden never had a family of his own, but he appreciated home life and liked to be surrounded by friends and their families. Extremely clever and witty, he hosted parties that were attended by guests from all walks of life. In 1972, a year before his death, his college at Oxford offered him a rent-free residence, and he returned to England to live his remaining days in security and comfort on the Oxford campus.

LaserLinks: Background for Reading
Art Gallery

Teaching Options

Grammar

ADVERBIALS: QUALIFIERS

Instruction Qualifiers are words that limit or intensify adjectives and adverbs. Overusing qualifiers such as *very, really,* and *little* results in weak sentences; substituting a precise adjective or adverb makes the qualifier unnecessary. For example, such phrases as *very nice breeze* and *rather strange appearance* might be rewritten effectively as *gentle breeze* or *bizarre appearance.* Point out that sometimes a qualifier weakens an already strong word—*extraordinary,* for example, is stronger than *very extraordinary.* In addition, "absolute" words such as *unique* or *totally* should not have qualifiers—*fairly unique* is a contradiction in terms.

Activity Write this sentence on the board.

In "The Unknown Citizen," Auden created a character who was very average in every way.

Have students replace the underlined words with a more precise word. *("unexceptional" or "ordinary")*

Use **Grammar Transparencies and Copymasters,** p. 87.

Use McDougal Littell's ***Language Network*** for more instruction in adverbials.

"Expecting always / Some brightness to hold in trust"

What I Expected

Poetry by STEPHEN SPENDER

Connect to Your Life

Dashed Hopes Recall a time when what you hoped or dreamed for didn't turn out the way you wanted. How did you react to the disappointment? What realities were you forced to face? Share your thoughts with a classmate.

Build Background

The Auden Generation When he entered Oxford University in 1928, Stephen Spender had already decided that he wanted to be a famous poet. There, he showed his poems to W. H. Auden, a slightly older student who had already achieved recognition within the school for his poetic genius. Auden approved of Spender's work, and a famous literary alliance was formed. The two poets were key members of a small group of Oxford students—the so-called Auden Generation—who became prominent literary figures during the 1930s. In addition to Auden and Spender, the group included the poets Louis MacNeice and C. Day Lewis and the novelist Christopher Isherwood.

The 1930s were turbulent years in European history—the time of the Great Depression, the Spanish civil war, and the start of World War II. Many English writers, particularly those of the Auden Generation, were appalled by what they saw taking place in the world. Sharing a hatred of war and a disgust for the deplorable living conditions endured by the swelling ranks of England's unemployed, they believed that it was their job to reflect the political and social concerns of the time in their writings. Although Spender did notable work as a critic, editor, translator, and travel writer, it is for his political poetry that he is best known. In "What I Expected," written during the early 1930s, he deals with the realities he faced during that period.

Focus Your Reading

LITERARY ANALYSIS IMAGERY IN MODERN POETRY

A striking element of "What I Expected" is its **imagery.** Images such as "smoke before wind" and "the faceted crystal" create vivid sensory experiences for the reader. As with much modern poetry, the poem uses patterns of imagery that imply meaning rather than state it. As you read the poem, consider the meaning and effect of each image.

ACTIVE READING DETERMINING MAJOR IDEAS IN POETRY

The vivid **images** of "What I Expected" help to convey the poem's major ideas. Some of these images describe the speaker's expectations; others describe the realities the speaker must face. As you read the poem, consider why each image is being used.

READER'S NOTEBOOK In a chart like the one shown, distinguish between the images that express the speaker's expectations and those that express the reality the speaker has had to face. Decide what different impressions the two types of images convey.

Images That Describe Expectations	Images That Describe Reality
1.	1.
2.	2.

LaserLinks: Background for Reading
Historical Connection

OVERVIEW

Objectives

1. understand and appreciate a **poem (Literary Analysis)**
2. appreciate the author's use of **imagery** in modern poetry **(Literary Analysis)**
3. **determine major ideas in poetry** to understand Spender's poem **(Active Reading)**

Summary

The youthful expectation of a life filled with accomplishment and ease turns to disillusionment when the speaker of Spender's poem confronts life's harsh realities. The speaker finds that the aging process weakens the body and the spirit. The compromises of the soul necessary to survive modern life's impermanence and injustice turn idealism into bitterness and regret.

Customizing Instruction

Less Proficient Readers

Ask students to make two columns, one "What I expected" and the second "What I had not foreseen," and under the headings list verbals that appear in the first two stanzas. Ask what two ideas are contrasted by the two lists.

Answers: (1) "expected": fighting, climbing, straining (suggest strength); (2) "not foreseen": weakening, leaking, fading (suggest weakness).

Students Acquiring English

Explain that poetry uses words that have double meanings, and that poets often will use such words to give double meanings to lines of a poem. Point out the line "The wearing of Time" as an example, and explain that "wearing" can mean "intending for wear" (such as clothing), "tiring," or "gradually diminishing."

Use **Spanish Study Guide** for additional support, pp. 257–259.

LESSON RESOURCES

UNIT SIX RESOURCE BOOK, pp. 33–34

ASSESSMENT RESOURCES

Formal Assessment, pp. 195–196

Teacher's Guide to Assessment and Portfolio Use

Test Generator

SKILLS TRANSPARENCIES AND COPYMASTERS

Literary Analysis
- Figurative Language (Imagery), T22 (for Literary Analysis, p. 1085)

Reading and Critical Thinking
- Drawing Conclusions, T4 (for Think Critically 5, p. 1085)

Grammar
- Diagramming Verbal Phrases, T60 (for Mini Lesson, p. 1086)
- Gerunds and Gerund Phrases II, C104 (for Mini Lesson, p. 1086)

Vocabulary
- Suffixes (Verbals), C85 (for Mini Lesson, p. 1084)

Writing
- Opinion Statement, C35 (for Writing Option 2, p. 1086)

Communications
- Dramatic Reading, T12 (for Activities & Explorations 1, p. 1086)

INTEGRATED TECHNOLOGY

Audio Library

Laser Links
- Historical Connection: Spender and England of the 1930s. See **Teacher's SourceBook,** p. 76.

Visit our website:
www.mcdougallittell.com

5-Minute Warm-Up

Daily Language SkillBuilder

Have students **proofread** the display sentences on page 979j and write them correctly. The sentences also appear on Transparency 29 of **Grammar Transparencies and Copymasters.**

TEACHING THE LITERATURE

Reading and Analyzing

Active Reading

DETERMINING MAJOR IDEAS IN POETRY

A Remind students that the major ideas in modern poems are suggested through a poem's images. An image describing the speaker's expectations is "the rocks would shake," while "The wearing of Time" (line 17) is an image describing the realities the speaker faces. Have students think of images the speaker might have used to describe what he expected that are "answered" by the images of the smoke and the cripples.

Possible Response: The speaker might have expected fire, but got smoke; he might have expected beauty, but got only the grotesque.

Use **Unit Six Resource Book,** p. 33 for more practice.

Literary Analysis

IMAGERY IN MODERN POETRY

B Point out to students that images used in modern poetry are often quite brutal. Ask students to visualize the image suggested by "limbs shaped like questions / In their odd twist." Ask them what the speaker might be trying to evoke with this image.

Possible Responses: The image is deliberately grotesque; the twisted bodies might suggest mental as well as physical suffering.

Use **Unit Six Resource Book** p. 34 for more exercises.

WHAT I EXPECTED

Stephen Spender

What I expected, was
Thunder, fighting,
Long struggles with men
And climbing.
After continual straining
I should grow strong;
A Then the rocks would shake
And I rest long.

What I had not foreseen
Was the gradual day
Weakening the will
Leaking the brightness away,
The lack of good to touch,
The fading of body and soul
Smoke before wind,
Corrupt, unsubstantial.

The wearing of Time,
And the watching of cripples pass
B With limbs shaped like questions
In their odd twist,
The pulverous grief
Melting the bones with pity,
The sick falling from earth—
These, I could not foresee.

Expecting always
Some brightness to hold in trust
Some final innocence
Exempt from dust,
That, hanging solid,
Would dangle through all
Like the created poem,
Or the faceted crystal.

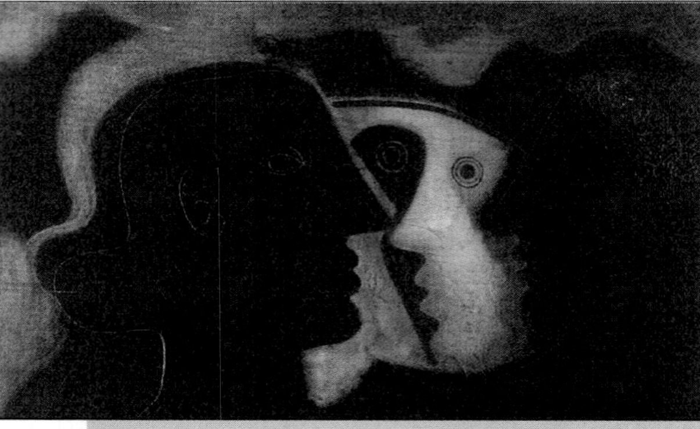

Detail of *1933 (St. Rémy-Provence)* (1933), Ben Nicholson. Copyright © 1995 Mrs. Angela Verren-Taunt/Licensed by VAGA, New York/DACS, London.

21 pulverous: devastating; crushing.

32 faceted: having flat, smooth surfaces.

Teaching Options

Mini Lesson Vocabulary Strategy

APPLYING MEANINGS OF SUFFIXES (VERBALS)

Instruction Remind students that verbals are most commonly nouns or adjectives that are derived from verbs or have the form of verbs. The most common types are *gerunds,* which are verbals ending in *-ing* and used as nouns, and *participles,* which are verbals ending in either the present or past participle and used as adjectives.

Activity Have students find the verbals in the poem and determine whether they are gerunds or participles. If a verbal is a participle, have them find the word that it refers to.

- First stanza: *fighting, climbing, straining* (all gerunds, as they are used as nouns)
- Second stanza: *weakening, leaking* (participles that refer to *day*), *fading* (gerund)
- Third stanza: *wearing, watching* (gerunds), *shaped* (participle that refers to *limbs*), *melting* (participle that refers to *grief*), *falling* (participle that refers to *the sick*)
- Fourth stanza: *expecting* (participle that refers to the speaker), *created* (participle that refers to *poem*), *faceted* (participle that refers to *crystal*)

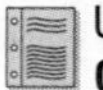

Use **Vocabulary Transparencies and Copymasters,** p. 58.

Use McDougal Littell's ***Language Network*** for more instruction in applying the meaning of suffixes (verbals).

Connect to the Literature

1. **What Do You Think?** Which **images** from "What I Expected" linger in your mind?

Think Critically

2. Summarize what you think the **speaker** expected to feel at this point in his life. Cite details from the poem to support your ideas.
3. In your own words, tell what you think the speaker "had not foreseen." Compare your thoughts with those of your classmates.
4. **ACTIVE READING** DETERMINING MAJOR IDEAS IN POETRY
With a partner, review the contrasting **images** chart you created in your READER'S NOTEBOOK. In what ways do the images contribute to the poem's major ideas?
5. In your opinion, what **theme,** or message, is expressed in this poem?

- the speaker's reference to fighting (lines 2–7)
- what the speaker says about "brightness" (lines 12 and 26)
- the **image** of "smoke before wind" (line 15)
- the reference to "Time" (line 17)

Extend Interpretations

6. **Comparing Texts** Do you think the speaker of Gerard Manley Hopkins's "Spring and Fall: To a Young Child" (page 947) would agree with the depiction of reality in "What I Expected"? Why or why not?
7. **Critic's Corner** The critic Geoffrey Thurley considers "What I Expected" to be one of Spender's best poems. He says that Spender conceived the poem "as an act, rather than as a statement" and that for this reason the reader "experiences the poem." Explain what you think Thurley means and tell how you experienced the poem.
8. **Connect to Life** Think of the realities that the speaker acknowledges in the poem. Do you think most people come to similar realizations during the course of their lives?

Literary Analysis

IMAGERY IN MODERN POETRY
The term **imagery** refers to words and phrases that create vivid sensory experiences for the reader. Most images are visual, but imagery may also appeal to the senses of smell, hearing, taste and touch.

Activity Look again at the imagery charts you created on page 1083. Select two or three images that you find especially striking or powerful. In a chart like the one shown, list the senses each one appeals to. Then explain to your classmates why you find these images effective.

Image	Senses
cripples with twisted limbs	

REVIEW FREE VERSE Most of Spender's poems are written in **free verse**—verse without regular patterns of **rhythm** and **rhyme.** Although free verse lacks conventional meter, it may contain various rhythmic effects and other sound effects—such as recurring syllables or words. Free verse can also contain rhyme, but if so, it is used with great freedom. How would you characterize the overall rhythm of "What I Expected"? How does the rhythm relate to the content of the poem?

GUIDING STUDENT RESPONSE

Connect to the Literature

What Do You Think?

1. Guidelines for students responses: Accept all thoughtful responses. You might have students compare the images they found most memorable.

Think Critically

2. Possible Responses: a feeling of strength, accomplishment, and confidence; a restful ease with life
3. Possible Responses: the disillusionment of youthful ideals; the cruel realities of life
4. Responses will vary, but students should be aware that the contrasting images serve to point out the contrast between what the speaker expected and what he actually experienced.
5. Possible Responses: Life is a continuing struggle that never gets easier; aging weakens not only the body but also the spirit; only in art can we find any hope for deliverance from the grim reality of life.

Literary Analysis

Activity Students should recognize that the first and last stanzas describe the speaker's expectations, while the second and third describe the realities he has had to face. The images in these stanzas correspond to those ideas.

Review Free Verse The short lines seem to be stacked on top of each other, giving an impression of things piling up on the speaker, perhaps wearing him down in the process. Other students may find that the conversational rhythm adds reality to the speaker's world-weariness.

Extend Interpretations

Comparing Texts Possible Responses: yes, because Hopkins's speaker also muses on a person's deepening, more personal understanding of mortality and grief as the person grows older; no, because Hopkins's speaker is less despairing about and more accepting of mortality.

Critic's Corner Possible Response: Students may say that the vivid imagery of the poem creates a series of strong action scenes in their minds, some representing youthful experience and some representing disappointment and death. The point of the poem is made through these images.

Connect to Life Accept all thoughtful, well-supported responses.

Writing Options

1. **Diary Entries** Suggest that students keep a written record of their reactions to poetry they read. Freewriting reactions in a journal is good preparation for this activity and can be turned into the kind of diary entry suggested.
2. **Opinion Paper** Suggest students try writing their paper in the form of a poem. Have them create their own images to argue against Spender's.

Activities & Explorations

1. **Dramatic Reading** You might suggest that the backdrop present different images in the poem, or have the performers simultaneously read different parts of the poem so that their dramatic reading suggests the cacophony of the modern world.
2. **Interpretive Montage** In addition to using computer graphics, another effective way to present a poem is to cut words out of magazines for the words of the poem in the text part of the montage.

Art Connection

Visual-Verbal Images Have a student volunteer make a list of comparisons between the painting and the poem's images, then present the list to the class for further discussion. This strategy would be particularly effective for visual learners.

Inquiry & Research

Crystals This activity might be appropriate for students with a scientific bent. Have students present information on the chemical properties of crystal for extra credit.

Author Activity

Propaganda War Researching the Spanish Civil War might be a good activity for Gifted and Talented students. Have them research the ideals that were at stake in Spain and the reasons for the large number of foreigners who participated in the war.

Choices & CHALLENGES

Writing Options

1. **Diary Entries** Imagine that you are the speaker of "What I Expected." Rewrite each stanza as an individual diary entry.

2. **Opinion Paper** Write an opinion paper in which you disagree with the speaker's attitude toward life. Be sure to support your opinions with reasons.

Activities & Explorations

1. **Dramatic Reading** With a small group of classmates, stage and present a dramatic reading of the poem for your class. Select appropriate background music and prepare a simple cloth backdrop or screen to enhance your performance. ~ **PERFORMING**

2. **Interpretive Montage** Create a montage that conveys your interpretation of "What I Expected." Include lines from the poem as well as illustrations or photographs. If you have access to a computer, use it to create designs or to set lines of the poem in different sizes and fonts. ~ **ART**

Art Connection

Visual-Verbal Images In your opinion, how do the visual images in the painting *1933 (St. Rémy-Provence)* on page 1084 relate to the verbal images in "What I Expected"?

Inquiry & Research

Crystals Read about the properties of crystals. What significant qualities, shapes, and uses do they have? In the last lines of "What I Expected," the speaker equates a "created poem" with a "faceted crystal." How do you think the properties of a crystal might be like those of a poem?

Stephen Spender
1909–1995

Other Works
"The Vase of Tears"
"Two Armies"
"Moving Through the Silent Crowd"
"Dark and Light"
"Fall of a City"

Social Writer Throughout his career, Stephen Spender had a reputation for creating humanistic works that struck a balance between bleak pessimism and unfailing optimism. A modest and sometimes shy man, Spender nevertheless enjoyed a camaraderie with his fellow writers. He eagerly accepted invitations to visit the gatherings of London's numerous literary circles, where he met such writers as Virginia Woolf and T. S. Eliot. In later years his reputation for witty conversation made him a popular guest in the homes of the socially prominent both in Britain and in the United States.

Cultural Ambassador Spender's strong interest in humanity was reflected not only in his writing but in his other activities. For approximately 20 years, he acted as a cultural ambassador, lecturing throughout the world on the importance of the artistic and intellectual dimensions of life. From 1970 to 1975, he was a full-time professor of English at University College in London, and he also served as a visiting professor at many universities in the United States and as poetry consultant to the Library of Congress. In 1983 Spender was knighted for his many contributions to literature.

Author Activity

Propaganda War During the Spanish civil war, Spender did propaganda work for the democratic forces that remained loyal to the Spanish Republic and fought against General Franco's Fascist rebels. Find out more about this conflict and the part Spender played in it. How might the war have affected Spender's outlook?

Teaching Options

Grammar

GERUND AND ITS SUBJECT

Instruction A gerund is a verb form ending in *-ing* that is used as a noun. It can be used in a sentence as a subject, object, predicate nominative, or appositive, just as a noun can. It can also have a subject of its own, just as a verb can. When the subject of the gerund is a pronoun or a proper noun, the subject takes the possessive case.

Activity Write this sentence on the chalkboard.

I appreciated my friend helping me understand this poem.

Ask students to identify the gerund (helping) and its subject (friend). Ask what the case of the noun friend should be. (possessive, "friend's")

Exercise Ask students to underline the gerund in the following sentence, and identify the subject if the gerund has one.

Our expecting brightness from life does not guarantee that we will receive it. *(subject of "expecting" is "Our")*

Use **Grammar Transparencies and Copymasters,** p. 44.

Use McDougal Littell's ***Language Network*** for more instruction in gerunds.

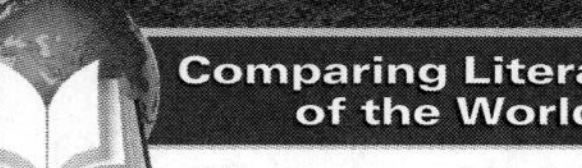

Do Not Go Gentle into That Good Night
In My Craft or Sullen Art

Poetry by DYLAN THOMAS

Comparing Literature of the World

The Poetry of Dylan Thomas and Octavio Paz

This lesson and the one that follows offer an opportunity to compare poems about the nature and process of writing poetry by the Welsh poet Dylan Thomas and the Mexican poet Octavio Paz. Specific points of comparison in the Paz lesson will help you note similarities and differences in the poets' perceptions of their desire to write and the directions they take.

Connect to Your Life

Source of Inspiration If you were a poet, what topics would you be inspired to write about? What personal events would motivate you to take pen in hand? As you read these two poems by Dylan Thomas, compare your own ideas about topics for poems with the topics that he treats.

Build Background

One-of-a-Kind Poet The poetry of Dylan Thomas has provoked strong and widely divergent reactions. The style of his poems, which are unique and difficult to classify but also quite lyrical and moving, seemed bold, unconventional, and unfamiliar to readers in the 1930s and 1940s and aroused responses ranging from adoration to contempt.

In the late 1940s and early 1950s, while critics argued over the merit of his writing, adoring fans flocked to hear the poet read his works. Not all of them fully understood his poetry, but they loved to listen to it—to hear its sounds. In explaining why he began writing, Thomas once said, "I wanted to write poetry in the beginning because I had fallen in love with words. . . . What the words stood for, symbolized, or meant, was of very secondary importance. What mattered was the sound of them." Like the 19th-century poet Gerard Manley Hopkins, Thomas frequently experimented with language, playing with sound devices, coining new words, and creating fresh images.

Thomas wrote about the things closest to his heart, calling his poetry "the record of my individual struggle from darkness towards some measure of light." He was motivated not by social and political issues but by his own experiences, writing about topics such as childhood, holidays, nature, and death. The intensely personal nature of his writing is revealed in both of the poems that you are about to read. In "Do Not Go Gentle into That Good Night," Thomas reacts to his father's deteriorating health; in "In My Craft or Sullen Art," he explores his fundamental motivation for writing.

Focus Your Reading

LITERARY ANALYSIS CONSONANCE AND ASSONANCE The following line from "Do Not Go Gentle into That Good Night" illustrates Thomas's love of the sound of words:

> ***Blind eyes could blaze like meteors and be gay . . .***

The repetition of the final *z* sound in *eyes, blaze,* and *meteors* is an example of **consonance**, the repetition of consonant sounds within and at the ends of words. The line also provides examples of **assonance**, a repetition of vowel sounds in words—the long *i* in *blind, eyes,* and *like* and the long *a* in *blaze* and *gay.* As you read the poems, look for other examples of these techniques.

ACTIVE READING VISUALIZING SETTING IN POETRY Although neither of these poems is what would normally be considered a narrative poem, each poem's topic implies a **setting.** As you read these poems, try to visualize a time and place for each speaker. Consider the relevance of the settings to the meaning of the poems.

READER'S NOTEBOOK Jot down words and phrases that you think suggest the setting of each poem.

OVERVIEW

"Do Not Go Gentle into That Good Night" is included in the **Grade 12 InterActive Reader.**

Objectives
1. understand and appreciate two **poems (Literary Analysis)**
2. appreciate the author's use of **consonance** and **assonance (Literary Analysis)**
3. **visualize settin**g in poetry to appreciate Thomas's poems **(Active Reading)**

Summary
In "Do Not Go Gentle into That Good Night," the speaker entreats his father not to accept death without a struggle. In "In My Craft or Sullen Art," the speaker describes his purpose for writing and the audience for whom he writes.

Thematic Link
The **new image of reality** Dylan Thomas portrays in his poems is one in which the human spirit struggles against the inevitable.

5-Minute Warm-Up
Daily Language SkillBuilder

Have students **proofread** the display sentences on page 979j and write them correctly. The sentences also appear on Transparency 29 of **Grammar Transparencies and Copymasters.**

LESSON RESOURCES

UNIT SIX RESOURCE BOOK, pp. 35–36

ASSESSMENT RESOURCES
Formal Assessment, pp. 197–198
Teacher's Guide to Assessment and Portfolio Use
Test Generator

SKILLS TRANSPARENCIES AND COPYMASTERS
Literary Analysis
- Poetic Devices, T16 (for Literary Analysis, p. 1092)

Reading and Critical Thinking
- Visualizing, T8 (for Active Reading, p. 1087)

Grammar
- Repetition vs. Redundancy, C176 (for Mini Lesson, p. 1093)

Vocabulary
- Word Origins, C86 (for Mini Lesson, p. 1090)

Writing
- Literary Interpretation, C33 (for Writing Option 2, p. 1093)

Communications
- Appreciative Listening, T2 (for Activities & Explorations 1, p. 1093)
- Formal Presentations, T10 (for Inquiry & Research, p. 1093)

INTEGRATED TECHNOLOGY
Audio Library
Visit our website: www.mcdougallittell.com

TEACHING THE LITERATURE

Reading and Analyzing

Literary Analysis

CONSONANCE AND ASSONANCE

A Ask students to identify examples of consonance in line 1 and assonance in line 2.

Possible Responses: consonance—*not, gentle, into. that, night*; assonance—*age, rave, day*)

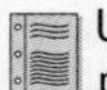
Use **Unit Six Resource Book** p. 36 for more exercises.

Active Reading

VISUALIZING SETTING IN POETRY

Have students list the images of nature in the poem.

Possible Responses: sunset, lightning, a green bay, the sun, meteors.

Ask students to extrapolate the setting of the poem from these images and to think about why Thomas chose this setting.

Possible Responses: The poem is set in the natural universe that the dying are about to leave; the poem is set on the earth, which is the stage for the actions of the living.

Use **Unit Six Resource Book** p. 35 for more practice.

Do Not Go Gentle into That Good Night

Dylan Thomas

Do not go gentle into that good night,
Old age should burn and rave at close of day;
Rage, rage against the dying of the light.

Though wise men at their end know dark is right,
Because their words had forked no lightning they
Do not go gentle into that good night.

Good men, the last wave by, crying how bright
Their frail deeds might have danced in a green bay,
Rage, rage against the dying of the light.

Wild men who caught and sang the sun in flight,
And learn, too late, they grieved it on its way,
Do not go gentle into that good night.

Grave men, near death, who see with blinding sight
Blind eyes could blaze like meteors and be gay,
Rage, rage against the dying of the light.

And you, my father, there on the sad height,
Curse, bless, me now with your fierce tears, I pray.
Do not go gentle into that good night.
Rage, rage against the dying of the light.

Teaching Options

BLOCK SCHEDULING: MANAGING TIME

If your schedule requires that you cover the lesson objectives in a shorter time, use . . .

- Preparing to Read, p. 1087
- Thinking Through the Literature, pp. 1089, 1092

If you want to take advantage of longer class time, use . . .

- TE Teaching Options: Viewing and Representing, p. 1089; Vocabulary, p. 1090; Standardized Test Practice, p. 1091; Grammar, p. 1093
- Choices & Challenges and Author Activity, p. 1093

Portrait of Father III (1972), Leon Kossoff. Oil on board, 60″ × 48″, private collection.

Thinking Through the Literature

1. **Comprehension Check** What does the **speaker** mean by the phrase "that good night"?
2. Jot two or three phrases that convey your reaction to this poem.
3. How would you describe the speaker's attitude toward death? Give evidence from the poem to support your answer.
4. What can you **infer** about the relationship between the speaker and his father?

Customizing Instruction

Students Acquiring English

Explain to students that these poems will employ figurative language, and that most images should not be taken literally. Have students find an example of figurative language in "Do Not Go Gentle into That Good Night."

Possible Responses: "their words had no forked lightning" (line 5); "caught and sang the sun in flight" (line 10).

 Use **Spanish Study Guide** for additional support, pp. 257–259.

Less Proficient Readers

Set a Purpose Have students read the poems to find out what motivates Thomas to write poetry.

Ask students to whom, specifically, the poem is addressed?

Answer: the speaker's father.

Gifted and Talented

Have students decide, as they read both poems, what Thomas thought were the important purposes of poetry.

Thinking Through the Literature

1. death
2. Accept all reasonable responses.
3. Possible Responses: pugnacious, illustrated by title; sad, illustrated by lines 16–17; fatalistic, illustrated by lines 4–5.
4. Possible Responses: close; loving; guilty; regretful.

Mini Lesson Viewing and Representing

Portrait of Father III **by Leon Kossoff**

ART APPRECIATION

Instruction Kossoff was born in London in 1926. His father, portrayed here, was a frequent subject in Kossoff's early work. Kossoff has become especially noted for his cityscapes and his scenes of everyday life.

Application Ask students to look at the painting to determine what kind of man Kossoff's father was.

Possible Responses: bold; powerful; capable; hard-working; stern.

Then ask students what design elements helped them come to those conclusions.

Possible Responses: the bold brushstrokes; the way the figure fills the canvas; the very large hands; the harsh, dark lines.

Reading and Analyzing

Literary Analysis: SPEAKER

Ask students who the speaker of this poem seems to be.

Possible Response: the poet.

Have students list the things the speaker reveals about himself.

Possible Responses: He writes late at night; he doesn't write for ambition or money or for the dead or to impress people; he writes for the lovers who don't pay any attention to his poetry.

Ask students whether someone who is writing about himself is a reliable speaker and why or why not.

Possible Responses: Yes, because the writer knows his own thoughts and feelings best; no, because the writer might want to control the impression he makes on the reader.

Reading Skills and Strategies: CLARIFYING

Break students into small groups and ask them to discuss what they think Thomas means when he says that the lovers hold all their own griefs and the griefs of the ages in their arms.

Possible Responses: that love often brings grief; that the greatest cause of grief is the fact that our loved ones will die.

Then ask students why they think Thomas writes only for the lovers.

Possible Responses: because he thinks love is important; because their lack of regard for his poetry frees him to write however he wishes.

In My Craft or Sullen Art

Dylan Thomas

In my craft or sullen art
Exercised in the still night
When only the moon rages
And the lovers lie abed
With all their griefs in their arms,
I labor by singing light
Not for ambition or bread
Or the strut and trade of charms
On the ivory stages
But for the common wages
Of their most secret heart.

Not for the proud man apart
From the raging moon I write
On these spindrift pages
Nor for the towering dead
With their nightingales and psalms
But for the lovers, their arms
Round the griefs of the ages,
Who pay no praise or wages
Nor heed my craft or art.

14 spindrift: spray blown up from the sea by the wind.

Teaching Options

Vocabulary Strategy

WORD ORIGINS

Instruction Remind students that even a single word in a poem carries a great deal of meaning.

Activity Have students look up the word *sullen* in at least one good dictionary and pay close attention to its etymology. Ask students how what they learned enhanced their understanding of the word in the poem.

Possible Response: *Sullen* comes originally from the Latin *solus,* alone. Thomas seems to intend the meaning of "solitary" rather than "sulky."

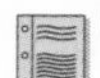
Use **Vocabulary Transparencies and Copymasters,** p. 59.

Les amoureux aux fleurs [Lovers with flowers] (1927), Marc Chagall. Israel Museum (IDAM), Jerusalem, Israel, Giraudon/Art Resource, New York. Copyright © 1996 Artists Rights Society (ARS), New York/ADAGP, Paris.

Customizing Instruction

Less Proficient Readers

Ask students what irony the speaker recognizes about the lovers he says are his audience.

Answer: They pay no attention to his verse.

Gifted and Talented

Have students discuss whether there are similar themes between the first and second poems.

Possible Responses: No, the first poem is about death, while the second poem deals with lovers. Yes, both poems express deep love—as Thomas exhorts his father to relish life in the same way the lovers in the second poem do; both poems focus on conveying similar emotions.

Standardized Test Practice

WRITING A PARAGRAPH Ask students to write a paragraph showing how one of the elements of Thomas's poetry, such as rhyme, consonance, assonance, or choice of images, contributes to the meaning of one of the poems.

RUBRIC

3 **Full Accomplishment** Paragraph accurately identifies one of elements of poetry and demonstrates its contribution to valid meaning of poem.

2 **Substantial Accomplishment** Paragraph accurately identifies one of elements of poetry and partially demonstrates its contribution to valid meaning of poem.

1 **Little or Partial Accomplishment** Paragraph does not accurately identify one of elements of poetry and does not demonstrate its contribution to valid meaning of poem.

GUIDING STUDENT RESPONSE

Connect to the Literature

1. **What Do You Think?**
   Guidelines for student response: You might make a list on the chalkboard of the images mentioned by students and then have them write a poem of their own using these images.

Comprehension Check

- writing poetry
- for lovers

Think Critically

2. Possible Responses: intense; introspective; lonely; emotional
3. Possible Responses: He places importance on strong, immediate emotions and on communicating them in his poetry.
4. Accept all reasonable responses. Some students may suggest a deathbed scene in the first poem and a poet at his desk, working late into the night in the second.

Literary Analysis

Paired Activity Have a volunteer from each pair read the examples of assonance and consonance they have found aloud to the class.
Villanelle Thomas's poem contains all the features of the villanelle form.

Thinking through the LITERATURE

Connect to the Literature

1. **What Do You Think?**
   What **images** linger in your mind after your reading of "In My Craft or Sullen Art"?

Comprehension Check

- To what practice does the title of "In My Craft or Sullen Art" refer?
- For whom does the speaker say he practices his craft?

Think Critically

2. How would you describe the speaker?

   THINK ABOUT
   - why he refers to writing as his "sullen art"
   - his use of the words *labor* (line 6) and *wages* (line 10)
   - his fascination with lovers
   - what he might mean by "the towering dead / With their nightingales and psalms" (lines 15–16)

3. The verb *rage* appears in both "Do Not Go Gentle into That Good Night" and "In My Craft or Sullen Art." Why do you think Thomas chose to include this word in both poems?

4. **ACTIVE READING** **VISUALIZING SETTING IN POETRY**
   Review the notes about **setting** that you made in your **READER'S NOTEBOOK**. How would you describe the setting of each poem? Do you consider the setting important? Explain your answer.

Extend Interpretations

5. **Comparing Texts** Do you think the speaker of A. E. Housman's "To an Athlete Dying Young" (page 000) shares the attitude toward life expressed by the speaker of "Do Not Go Gentle into That Good Night"? Why or why not?

6. **Critic's Corner** According to the poet and critic Karl Shapiro, Thomas's poems are characterized by "a fatal pessimism . . . offset by a few bursts of joy and exuberance." Do you detect pessimism, joy, or exuberance in these poems—or perhaps all three? Support your answer with examples.

7. **Connect to Life** Think back to the Connect to Your Life activity on page 1087. How do the topics of these poems compare with your own notions of topics that might inspire a poet?

Literary Analysis

CONSONANCE AND ASSONANCE Thomas's love of the sound of words is reflected in his use of **consonance** (a repetition of consonant sounds within and at the ends of words) and **assonance** (a repetition of vowel sounds in words). He uses both assonance and consonance to emphasize particular words, to create **mood,** and to add a musical quality to poems.

Paired Activity In both poems, find examples of consonance and assonance that you think are particularly effective. Practice reading the lines aloud. Then explain to your partner why you chose the examples you did.

VILLANELLE "Do Not Go Gentle into That Good Night" is an example of an intricate verse form of French origin called the **villanelle.** Its structure includes the following characteristics:

- It is a 19-line poem comprised of five **tercets,** or three-line stanzas, followed by a **quatrain,** or four-line stanza.
- The **rhyme scheme** is *aba* for each tercet and then *abaa* for the quatrain.
- Line 1 is repeated as a **refrain** at the ends of the second and fourth stanzas. The last line of the first stanza is repeated at the ends of the third and fifth stanzas. Both lines reappear at the final two lines of the poem.
- Villanelles in English often use **iambic pentameter.**

How closely does Thomas's poem follow the villanelle form? How effective is the form in conveying ideas and emotions?

Extend Interpretations

Comparing Texts Accept all reasonable, well-supported responses.
Critic's Corner Possible Response: The poems are exuberant in their power and passion, although their tone is not cheerful. They might be considered pessimistic in their emphasis on death and human sorrow, but this does not accurately describe the overall impression they make. Expressions of joy occur in individual lines, such as lines 8, 10, and 14 in the first poem.
Connect to Life Accept all reasonable responses.

Writing Options

1. Letter to the Poet Write a letter to Dylan Thomas, explaining your opinion of the view of death expressed in "Do Not Go Gentle into That Good Night."

2. Interpretive Notes Reread the poems, writing down any words, phrases, or sentences that you think are used in unusual or ambiguous ways—for example, "spindrift pages" in line 14 of "In My Craft or Sullen Art." Then write a brief interpretation of each word, phrase, or sentence, based on its use in the poem. Share your interpretations with the class.

Activities & Explorations

1. Inspiring Speech Write and deliver a speech that the speaker of "In My Craft or Sullen Art" might give to a class of aspiring poets. ~ **SPEAKING AND LISTENING**

2. The Poet's Voice Locate a recording of Dylan Thomas reading his poetry. After playing the recording for the class, discuss the effect of hearing the works in the poet's own voice. ~ **SPEAKING AND LISTENING**

Inquiry & Research

Welsh Literary Tradition Wales has a long and rich literary history. Although Dylan Thomas did not speak the Welsh language, his work is part of a poetic tradition that began in the sixth century. Find out more about Wales's literary history and traditions. Report your findings to the class.

Dylan Thomas
1914–1953

Other Works
"And Death Shall Have No Dominion"
"Fern Hill"
"Poem in October"
Portrait of the Artist as a Young Dog
Under Milk Wood
A Child's Christmas in Wales

Welsh Roots Dylan Thomas was considered by many the most original English poet since Yeats and Eliot. He was born in Swansea in southwestern Wales, and his writing is rooted in the countryside and culture of his homeland. Although he did not learn to speak the Welsh language, he captured its cadences and word sequences in both his poetry and prose.

Teenage Poet Thomas attended Swansea Grammar School, where his father taught English and where Thomas performed poorly in every subject but literature. At the age of 16, he quit school and went to work as a newspaper reporter. Already, he had become a prolific poet. By the time he was 20, his first book of poems had been published.

Money Trouble In the late 1930s, Thomas moved to London to look for more lucrative writing assignments and began writing fewer poems and more short stories, radio scripts, and screenplays. Unfortunately, Thomas had no business sense and was always in dire financial straits. He fell behind on his taxes and had to borrow money to support his wife and family. In 1949, Thomas and his family moved back to Wales. The following year, in an attempt to improve his finances, he booked his first series of poetry readings in the United States.

Self-Destructive Streak Thomas captivated audiences with dramatic readings of his own works as well as those of earlier poets. To his many fans in America and Great Britain, he personified the typical image of the bohemian poet—reckless and romantic. Sadly, he was also self-destructive. Thomas had a serious drinking problem, and at the age of 39, in the midst of his fourth American tour, he died in a hotel room from complications of alcoholism. He nevertheless left a legacy of innovative, lyrical work that helped set a new standard for modern poetry.

Author Activity

Celebrated Reader When Thomas began visiting American colleges, he soon became renowned for his dramatic readings. Find out whose poetry he performed in addition to his own work. Why do you think he chose these poets?

Writing Options

1. **Letter to the Poet** Tell students to be explicit about what they think is the main view of death that Thomas expresses in the poem.
2. **Interpretive Notes** Encourage students to refer to a dictionary and a thesaurus to sharpen their understanding of the words they have chosen and to revise their choices if needed.

Activities & Explorations

1. **Inspiring Speech** Encourage students to deliver their speeches to classmates.
2. **The Poet's Voice** Many public libraries have recordings of Thomas reading his poetry. Students might also obtain, listen to, and discuss the noted readings of Thomas's verse by the Welsh actor Emlyn Williams; the 1988 production of *A Child's Christmas in Wales,* narrated by Denholm Elliott and available on videocassette; or perhaps the 1973 film adaptation of *Under Milk Wood* starring Peter O'Toole, Elizabeth Taylor, and the Welsh actor Richard Burton, also on videocassette.

Inquiry & Research

Welsh Literary Tradition Suggest students begin their search by looking in the *Oxford Companion to the Literature of Wales.*

Author Activity

Celebrated Reader Thomas read the poetry of Yeats, Auden, and other contemporary British poets.

Mini Lesson Grammar

Cohesion: Repetition vs. Redundancy

Instruction Writers often use repetition to add emphasis or to create a mood. Repeating parallel structure can create a sense of drama, as when Dylan Thomas writes, "Not for ambition or bread . . . Not for the proud man apart . . . Nor for the towering dead." To give cohesion to their work, poets may repeat consonant sounds, vowel sounds, words, or even entire lines.

Less experienced writers sometimes have the problem of redundancy—using more words than necessary. They repeat ideas that they have already expressed. To correct this, replace redundant material with supporting ideas.

Activity Write this sentence on the chalkboard.

Dylan Thomas writes about death in "Do Not Go Gentle into That Good Night," and the theme of the poem is how to face death.

Ask students to reword the sentence so that it is no longer redundant. *(The theme of Dylan Thomas's poem "Do Not Go Gentle into That Good Night" is how to face death.)*

Use **Grammar Transparencies and Copymasters,** p. 112.

Use McDougal Littell's ***Language Network*** for more instruction and practice in avoiding redundancy.

OVERVIEW

Objectives

1. understand and appreciate a modern **Latin American poem (Literary Analysis)**
2. appreciate the author's use of **paradox (Literary Analysis)**
3. **analyze poetic language** to appreciate and understand Paz's poem **(Active Reading)**
4. recognize and discuss themes that cross cultures

Summary

Octavio Paz, a noted Mexican poet, considers the writing process, and what part of him controls the writing and the judgment of it.

TEACHING THE LITERATURE

Reading and Analyzing

Active Reading ANALYZING POETIC LANGUAGE

A Discuss with students what they think the shore might be.

Possible Responses: the process of writing, the poet.

Then ask students what emotions the images in lines 6 and 7 evoke.

Possible Response: The images evoke wonder, fear, and joy.

Use **Unit Six Resource Book,** p. 37 for additional support.

Literary Analysis PARADOX

B Ask how the judge can be the victim.

Possible Response: Since the writer himself is his own critic, he suffers from his self-criticism.

Use **Unit Six Resource Book,** p. 38 for additional support.

5-Minute Warm-Up

Daily Language SkillBuilder

Have students **proofread** the display sentences on page 979j and write them correctly. The sentences also appear on Transparency 30 of **Grammar Transparencies and Copymasters.**

Writing/Escritura

Poetry by OCTAVIO PAZ

Comparing Literature of the World

Poetry Across Cultures

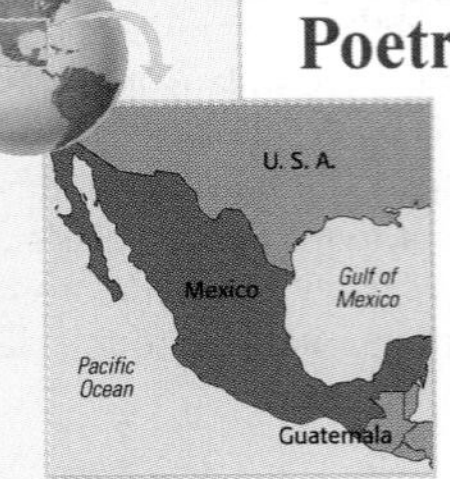

Poems of Dylan Thomas and Octavio Paz In their writing, both Octavio Paz and Dylan Thomas have reflected upon their own cultures—Mexican and Welsh respectively. However, both poets explore subjects that reflect the universal human condition and so have appealed to people in all countries.

Points of Comparison As you read Paz's poem, compare it with Dylan Thomas's poetry in terms of the following:

- the use of **imagery**
- each poet's **purpose** for writing poetry
- each poet's view of the creative process

Build Background

Writing About Writing Although the history of English poetry extends back many centuries, poetry did not become a popular literary genre in the Spanish-speaking countries of Latin America until the late 19th century and did not flourish until after World War I. In 1933, when a 19-year-old Mexican writer named Octavio Paz published his first volume of poetry, he began a literary career that spanned more than 60 years. Paz achieved widespread recognition for both his poetry and his prose, including the 1990 Nobel Prize in literature.

In his writing, Paz explores the creative process—what it means to be a poet and what steps lead to a finished work. According to Paz, the meaning of a poem depends entirely on the way a reader interprets the work; thus, the reader's response is a part of the creative process.

Focus Your Reading

LITERARY ANALYSIS PARADOX "Writing/Escritura" contains examples of **paradoxes**—statements that seem contradictory but nevertheless express truths. Because a paradox is often surprising, it draws the reader's attention to what is being said. As you read Paz's poem, look for seeming contradictions. Consider the meaning and effect of each one.

ACTIVE READING ANALYZING POETIC LANGUAGE In addition to paradox, Paz integrates opposites in a number of other ways in his work. For example, he frequently juxtaposes contrasting **images,** such as fire and ice. As you read, be aware of the poet's use of contrast.

READER'S NOTEBOOK Look for examples of contrasting images in "Writing/Escritura." Note them in a chart similar to the one below.

Image	Contrasting Image
fire	ice

LESSON RESOURCES

UNIT SIX RESOURCE BOOK, pp. 37–38

ASSESSMENT RESOURCES

Formal Assessment, pp. 199–200

Teacher's Guide to Assessment and Portfolio Use

Test Generator

SKILLS TRANSPARENCIES AND COPYMASTERS

Reading and Critical Thinking

- Analyzing Text, T18 (for Active Reading, p. 1094)

Grammar

- Ending the Sentence, C177 (for Mini Lesson, p. 1097)

Writing

- Compare-Contrast, C34 (for Writing Option 3, p. 1097)

Communications

- Evaluating Roles in Groups, T8 (for Activities and Explorations 2, p. 1097)

INTEGRATED TECHNOLOGY

Audio Library

Visit our website: www.mcdougallittell.com

Writing

Octavio Paz

When over the paper the pen goes writing
in any solitary hour,
who drives the pen?
To whom is he writing, he who writes for me,
this shore made of lips, made of dream,
a hill of stillness, abyss,
shoulder on which to forget the world forever?

Someone in me is writing, moves my hand,
hears a word, hesitates,
halted between green mountain and blue sea.
With icy fervor
contemplates what I write.
All is burned in this fire of justice.
But this judge is nevertheless the victim
and in condemning me condemns himself:
He writes to anyone, he calls nobody,
to his own self he writes, and in himself forgets,
and is redeemed, becoming again me.

Translated by Muriel Rukeyser

11 fervor: heat; intensity of feeling.

Customizing Instruction

Less Proficient Readers

If students have difficulty with this poem, have them use reading strategies that have worked for them in the past, such as rereading, paraphrasing, and taking notes as they read.

Students Acquiring English

Encourage native Spanish speakers to share their own translations of Paz's poem with the class. Lead a discussion of the differences and similarities between their translations and Muriel Rukeyser's.

Gifted and Talented

Have students do a close reading of this poem and then compare its imagery to that in other modernist poetry.

Escritura

Octavio Paz

Cuando sobre el papel la pluma escribe,
a cualquier hora solitaria,
¿quién la guía?
¿A quién escribe el que escribe por mí,
orilla hecha de labios y de sueño,
quieta colina, golfo,
hombro para olvidar al mundo para siempre?

Alguien escribe en mí, mueve mi mano,
escoge una palabra, se detiene,
duda entre el mar azul y el monte verde.
Con un ardor helado
contempla lo que escribo.
Todo lo quema, fuego justiciero.
Pero este juez también es víctima
y al condenarme, se condena:
no escribe a nadie, a nadie llama,
a sí mismo se escribe, en sí se olvida,
y se rescata, y vuelve a ser yo mismo.

Multicultural Link: *Modernismo*

Although the Spanish *modernismo* means "modernism," in Latin American letters the term is often applied only to the years 1888–1910. Especially influential in this period was the Nicaraguan-born Rubén Darío, whose powerful, often elliptical imagery, akin to that of the symbolists, had great impact on subsequent Spanish-language verse on both sides of the Atlantic. Like Oscar Wilde and the symbolists, Darío rejected romanticism as too sentimental or melodramatic, and realism and naturalism as too localized or ugly, focusing instead on the artistic sensibility and the creation of "art for art's sake." His identification with fellow artists the world over was shared by later modernists (in the broader sense) such as Argentine writers Jorge Luis Borges and Julio Cortázar. The rise of fascism and the Spanish Civil War had a profound effect on many younger Spanish-language writers, however. In the poetry of Octavio Paz and Chile's Pablo Neruda, for example, the role of the artist shares equal billing with political and social concerns.

WRITING / ESCRITURA 1095

GUIDING STUDENT RESPONSE

Connect to the Literature

1. What Do You Think?
Guidelines for student response: Students might compare the words and phrases they come up with to see if their responses share anything in common.

Comprehension Check

- The speaker answers that someone in him is writing.

Think Critically

2. Possible Responses: hill and abyss; mountain and sea; fire and ice; judge and victim. Accept any reasonable explanation of why students found the opposites they chose most striking.
3. Possible Responses: intense; liberating; self-critical; vital to his existence
4. Possible Response: He finds it intense and sometimes painful, but ultimately rewarding.

Literary Analysis

Cooperative Learning Activity Write on the chalkboard a composite chart made up of the examples of paradox found by the student groups.

Connect to the Literature

1. What Do You Think? What words or phrases best describe your response to this poem?

Comprehension Check

- What answer does the speaker give to the question, "Who drives the pen?"

Think Critically

2. ACTIVE READING ANALYZING POETIC LANGUAGE Review the chart in your READER'S NOTEBOOK about contrasting **images** and words. Which juxtaposition of opposites in the poem do you find the most striking? Explain why you think it is effective.

3. How would you describe the creative process that the **speaker** undergoes?

   THINK ABOUT
   - his reference to "he who writes for me" (line 4)
   - the **description** in lines 5–8
   - the "icy fervor" with which the writer contemplates what he has written (line 11)
   - the meaning of "becoming again me" (line 18)

4. What would you say is the speaker's attitude toward this process?

Extend Interpretations

5. **Critic's Corner** The critic John M. Fein has suggested that Octavio Paz's poetry might seem "unconcluded" to a reader who does not realize that Paz "invites him to feel his own version of the poem." Explain what you think Fein means and why you agree or disagree with him.

6. **Connect to Life** Over the centuries, many poets have written about writing. Why do you think this is so?

7. **Points of Comparison** Compare the ideas conveyed in "Writing" and in Dylan Thomas's "In My Craft or Sullen Art." Do you think their **purpose** for writing poetry is similar? Use evidence from the poems to support your answer.

Literary Analysis

PARADOX The use of **paradox**—a statement that seems to contradict itself but, in fact, reveals some element of truth—is one way in which Paz integrates opposites. For example, in the following lines, how can the judge be the victim?

But this judge is nevertheless the victim / and in condemning me condemns himself

This important component of Paz's literary style enables him to express ideas in a concise and memorable way.

Cooperative Learning Activity Working with a small group of classmates, look back at the poem for other examples of paradox. Complete a chart, similar to the one below, in which you note the paradoxical statement and give your interpretation of the truth it expresses. When you have completed the chart, discuss with your classmates how effective you consider this stylistic device to be.

Paradox	Meaning
this judge is . . . the victim (l. 14)	the writer is his own critic; he suffers from self-criticism

Extend Interpretations

Critic's Corner Accept all reasonable, well-supported responses.

Connect to Life Possible Response: Most people are interested in their own work; poets are by nature introspective and that part of their self-examination naturally involves their art.

Points of Comparison Possible Responses: Some students may find the purposes similar because both poets focus on personal expression. Others may feel that whereas Thomas focuses on personal expression of strong emotion, Paz never specifies what poetry should express and seems more cerebral. Still others may focus on differences in audience.

Writing Options

1. Creative Definition Write a definition of the word *creativity* from the perspective of this poem's speaker.

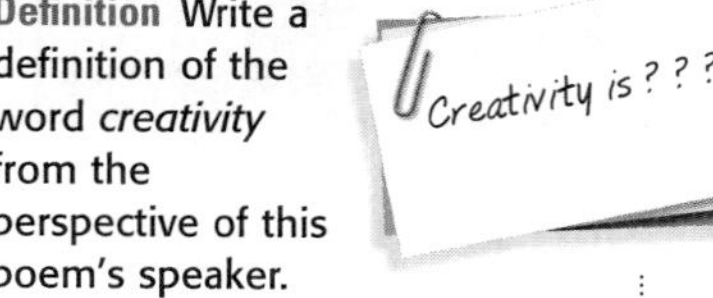

2. Interior Monologue Write a monologue to represent the thoughts of the poem's "he" during the creative process.

3. Points of Comparison Basing your views on the ideas expressed in "In My Craft or Sullen Art" and "Writing/Escritura," write the draft for an essay in which you discuss whether or not Paz and Dylan Thomas share a similar vision of the creative process.

Writing Handbook
See page 1367: Compare and Contrast.

Activities & Explorations

1. Stamp Design Create a design for a postage stamp commemorating the art of writing. ~ **ART**

2. Multimedia Presentation With a group of classmates, look for books, essays, and interviews in which well-known writers explore the creative process. Then create a flowchart plan for a multimedia presentation called "Writers on Writing," in which you include inspirational quotations from those works. ~ **TECHNOLOGY/SPEAKING AND LISTENING**

Inquiry & Research

Translating Poetry In an essay entitled "On Translation," Paz wrote that "to a certain extent every translation is an original invention and thus constitutes a unique text." Locate the work of several different translators who have translated Paz's poems. If possible, find different translations of the same poems. Compare the translations, and, in the light of your comparison, discuss your thoughts about Paz's statement.

Octavio Paz
1914–1998

Other Works
"Two Bodies"
"Wind and Water and Stone"
"Fable"
"The Spoken Word"
"Nightfall"

Mexican Heritage Octavio Paz was born on the outskirts of Mexico City during the Mexican Revolution. The war left his family in financial ruin, and Paz remembers that as a child he lived in a large house that was gradually crumbling to the ground. In spite of these circumstances, he had a fairly pleasant childhood, spending many hours in his grandfather's extensive library. After attending the National Autonomous University of Mexico, he traveled extensively in Spain, France, and the United States, becoming immersed in the literature, history, art, and philosophy of other nations. His experiences are reflected in his writing, which embraces a diversity of topics, including politics, Eastern philosophy, psychology, art, and anthropology. Despite his interest in travel and other cultures, however, Paz never forgot his heritage: his first book of prose, *The Labyrinth of Solitude,* was an exploration of Mexican culture and thought. Published in 1950, it was well-received and brought Paz international recognition.

Varied Career Paz also worked as an ambassador, editor, and teacher. In 1946, he joined the Mexican diplomatic corps and served for 22 years in such countries as France, Switzerland, Japan, and India. He founded and was editor of several literary magazines and, after resigning from his diplomatic post in 1968, taught at various universities, including the Universities of Texas and California, Harvard, and Cambridge.

Author Activity

Cultural Interests Paz was interested in pre-Columbian Mexican history, and this interest is reflected in his work. Find out about his long poem, *Piedra de Sol*, which is about the Aztec calendar. Present your findings to the class in an oral report.

Writing Options

1. **Creative Definition** Responses will vary. Students' definitions, like those in a dictionary, could contain several numbered parts.
2. **Interior Monologue** Remind students that an interior monologue often makes free associations, leaping from thought to thought in a stream of consciousness.
3. **Points of Comparison** Encourage students to use a graphic organizer such as a chart or a Venn diagram to help them explore Thomas's and Paz's visions of the creative process.

Activities & Explorations

1. **Stamp Design** You might want to have students work in small groups to complete this activity, emulating the committee process of choosing a stamp design.
2. **Multimedia Presentation** Have each group focus its presentation on a particular culture or time period. In addition to using quotes from books, essays, and interviews about writing, students might include poems about poetry.

Inquiry & Research

Translating Poetry Translators of Paz's poetry into English include Muriel Rukeyser and Charles Tomlinson.

Author Activity

Cultural Interests Bring in to class a picture of the huge carved stone that depicts the Aztec calendar. The original is on display in the Anthropological Museum in Mexico City.

Grammar

ENDING THE SENTENCE

Instruction The last word or words of a sentence, the sentence closer, can leave an indelible impression on the mind of the reader. For an effective ending, choose words, phrases, or clauses that deliver the mood and the intensity, as well as the information, that you want to give to the reader.

Activity Write on the chalkboard the following excerpt from "Writing/Escritura" by Octavio Paz.

"Someone in me is writing, <u>moves my hand, hears a word, hesitates, halted between green mountain and blue sea</u>."

Ask students to identify the sentence closer. What does the sentence closer add to the sentence as a whole? *(gives life to the inner person doing the writing; builds intensity)*

Use **Grammar Transparencies and Copymasters,** p. 1130

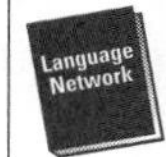

Use McDougal Littell's ***Language Network*** for more instruction and practice in sentence endings.

Objectives
- write a dramatic scene
- use a written text as a model for writing
- revise a draft to use dialogue effectively
- use proper formats for scripts

Introducing the Workshop

A Dramatic Scene Point out that the heart of a drama is the story of engaging characters confronting and overcoming difficulties. Typically, there is a conflict that confronts a sympathetic character who engages in action to resolve the conflict.
Have students list engaging dramatic scenes from movies and television involving sympathetic characters. What characteristics do these scenes and characters have in common? Point out that writing a dramatic scene will enable students to portray an interesting character struggling to resolve a conflict.

Basics in a Box

B Using the Graphic As the graphic indicates, an effective dramatic scene involves bringing all elements of the drama together simultaneously. The writer, however, works by giving attention to discrete elements, refining them to create unity during the process of revision.

C Presenting the Rubric To better understand the assignment, students can refer to the Standards for Writing a Successful Dramatic Scene. You may wish to discuss with them the complete rubric, which describes several levels of proficiency.

Use McDougal Littell's ***Language Network,*** Chapter 22, for more instruction on writing a dramatic scene.

To engage students visually, use **Power Presentation** 8, Dramatic Scene.

Writing Workshop — Dramatic Scene

Literature through performance . . .

A **From Reading to Writing** In *The Rising of the Moon,* Lady Gregory chose to tell her story in the form of a **drama,** or play. Plays have many of the same elements as narratives—characters, setting, plot, conflict. But in a play, dialogue and stage directions are used to reveal character traits and setting, and to move the plot forward. Drama is the format used for skits, television programs, theater productions, and movies.

For Your Portfolio

WRITING PROMPT Write a dramatic scene based on a piece of fiction or on an incident you create.

Purpose: To entertain

Audience: Your classmates or anyone who will read it or see it performed

Basics in a Box

Dramatic Scene at a Glance

B

C **RUBRIC Standards for Writing**

A successful dramatic scene should
- introduce the setting and characters in the opening stage directions
- use the setting and characters to create a convincing world
- develop a clear and interesting situation or conflict
- reveal the personalities of the characters through the dialogue
- use actions as well as dialogue to advance the story
- include stage directions as necessary

LESSON RESOURCES

USING PRINT RESOURCES

Unit Six Resource Book
- Prewriting, p. 39
- Drafting, p. 40
- Peer Response, p. 41
- Revising, Editing, and Proofreading, p. 42
- Student Models, pp. 43–49
- Rubric, p. 50

Writing Transparencies and Copymasters
- Writing Process Transparencies, p. 3
- Writing Style Transparencies, p. 24
- Writing Template Copymasters, p. 31

USING MEDIA RESOURCES

LaserLinks
Writing Springboards
See Teacher's SourceBook p. 114 for bar codes.

Writing Coach CD-ROM

Visit our website:
www.mcdougallittell.com

For a complete view of Lesson Resources, see page 979e.

Analyzing a Student Model: Dramatic Scene

Ana Woody
Gobles High School

RUBRIC IN ACTION

Two Characters on a Bus

Characters: **Josh** *is a sixteen-year-old runaway;*
Gretta *is an uneducated older woman traveling alone.*

Setting: *It is summer, and Josh and Gretta are strangers seated next to each other on a cross-country bus. Gretta is going to visit a friend. Josh is headed north to his great-aunt's house. As lights come up, Josh and Gretta are in the middle of a conversation.*

➊ Introduces the characters and setting in the opening stage directions

Gretta. Where ya goin' all by yourself? (*Josh doesn't answer.*) Well, ya know we're goin' t'be together on this bus for a long time, boy. Why don't ya just tell me why ya look so sad. It's not hard once ya start.

Josh. (*quietly*) It's about my family, my so-called family. But I don't really want to talk about it.

Gretta. (*pats his leg*) Sometimes it helps to talk 'bout it to someone. I may be old, but I got good ears to listen with and a quick mind to understand.

➋ This writer has the character reveal information about herself through dialogue.

Other Options:
- Reveal information through the character's actions.
- Reveal information through a narrator or another character.

Josh. (*sad*) After my mom left, my dad was mad all the time. At me, at everyone. He wouldn't talk to me. He said he wished my "no good mother" would've taken me with her. But she couldn't.

D

Gretta. (*softly*) Why couldn't she take ya with her?

Josh. She didn't have a job, and she was goin' to live with her aunt. She promised to come and get me when she could. It's already been over a year, and I can't wait any longer. Not with him. He's just too mean to live with. (*Gretta hands him a tissue. Josh blows his nose.*)

Josh. Yesterday I told him I was goin' to stay at my friend's house and he got so mad. He yelled that I couldn't go anywhere. When I asked why, he just started mumbling to himself that I was just like my mother. (*hesitates*)

Gretta. (*puts hand on his knee*) Go on, child, it hurts, but it'll help.

➌ Uses the stage directions to indicate attitudes and body movements

Josh. I went upstairs to my room and packed all the stuff I could in my bag and snuck out last night. I had some money saved for a car, so I took that along with the money he had stashed for going out on the weekends.

Gretta. (*nodding*) And ya bought a bus ticket with it.

Josh. I had to get away. I just hate the way he acts.

Gretta. (*with a concerned smile*) What're ya gonna do, Josh? You're too young to be out in the world all alone.

Josh. Well, I plan to go to my great-aunt's house and find out where my mother is and what she's doing. If I tell my great-aunt what I've been dealin' with, she won't send me back. At least I hope not.

Gretta. I'm sure she won't, honey. If'n she's a good-hearted woman, she'll do what she can to help ya.

Teaching the Lesson

Analyzing the Model

D "Two Characters on a Bus"

The model introduces two characters as an unlikely pair. The setting of a bus suggests the possibility that the characters are leaving something behind.

Have students read aloud the model. Use the rubric to discuss and evaluate the model. Point out key words and phrases in the student model that correspond to the elements mentioned in the Rubric in Action.

1. Point out that the stage directions provide ample background to establish character and setting in a way that suggests potential conflict. Ask students to predict the central conflict based on the information provided in the opening stage directions.
   Possible Responses: Josh is unable to get along with his parents; Josh is orphaned.
2. Ask students to summarize the information revealed about Gretta in this passage and to describe how it could be revealed using one of the other options suggested.
   Possible Response: We learn that Gretta is helpful and understanding. Alternatively, we could see Gretta responding helpfully and appropriately to Josh.
3. Ask students what these stage directions indicate about the characters of both Josh and Gretta.
   Possible Response: They indicate that Josh is hesitant and unsure of whom he can trust, and that Gretta is safe, nurturing, and supportive.

4. Point out that a dramatist must rely on three things to reveal a character: 1) the character's actions; 2) the character's words; and 3) what other characters say about the character. Ask students which of these three techniques are being used here. Ask students to provide examples.
   Possible Response: actions—Gretta laughs; what the character says—Gretta describes unusual things she's seen.
5. Ask students what important advance in the story is made in this dialogue.
   Possible Response: Josh comes to an important realization about his relationship with his father.
6. Ask students to characterize the scene's ending. Is it hopeful or despairing? What actions and dialogue support their conclusion?
   Possible Response: It is a hopeful ending. Gretta concludes with a statement of pride, which indicates that she likes the way things turned out. Josh closes by waving to Gretta's smiling face.

Josh. (*smiles for the first time*) I never told anyone about my dad. I just hope he's okay. (*pauses for a beat*) What about you, Gretta? What's your life like?

Gretta. (*laughs a little*) I've had a pretty quiet life, I guess. (*closes eyes*) I ain't seen any real trouble, but I seen a good many beautiful and unexplainable things.

Josh. (*encouragingly*) Like what?

Gretta. (*opens eyes*) Oh, flowers in the middle of a snowy field, rainbows on dry days, green waterfalls, angels in my garden, and such.

Josh. (*amazed*) Wha-at? How? Why?

Gretta. (*wistfully*) I guess the good Lord saw fit to show me those things along with other things. I never really had anyone on earth to guide me on my life's path, so I figure heaven stepped in. Maybe so I could guide others.

❹ Develops the character through specific details

Josh. (*shakes head*) I wish my life was like yours.

Gretta. Ya got it wrong if'n ya think it's easy. This world can be a hard place. Ya got ta make do with what ya have, and share what ya can. It's hard work bein' a good person to more than just yourself.

Josh. Do you think it got too hard for my dad to be good to me? When I was young, I thought he was the greatest man alive. But now I see him differently. Maybe he's just a normal person with problems, and no one to help him. No one to listen.

Gretta. (*nods*) I think ya just might have learned somethin'. How did ya feel when ya got on this bus?

Josh. I felt bad, like I hated my life. And lonely. I hated my dad, too. Well, thought I did, anyway. You know the right things to say. I feel older. Is that strange?

Gretta. (*looking for something in her bag*) No, honey, it ain't strange. It's just sad. You shouldn't have to worry about your dad and his problems. Sometimes people have to grow up a little faster than normal. Happens to the best of us. (*puts bag on floor, smiles*)

❺ Advances story entirely without action

Josh. Yeah, I get it. . . . Maybe everything is gonna work out.

(*The bus driver's voice booms out from offstage: Everybody out for Clarksburg!*)

Josh. Here's where I get off. (*stands up to leave*) Thanks for listening. I won't forget you.

Gretta. I'm proud to hear that. Remember, be a good listener and ask the right questions. A fool always has somethin' to say and a wise man hardly speaks. (*laughs again*) Ya take care of ya self.

Josh. (*waves as he steps off the bus*)

Gretta. (*moves over to the window seat, smiling*)

❻ Uses action, stage directions, and dialogue to resolve the situation

Writing Your Dramatic Scene

❶ Prewriting

The secret of playwriting can be given in two maxims: stick to the point and whenever you can, cut.
W. Somerset Maugham, British novelist and playwright

Begin by thinking about a character or situation that interests you and involves a problem or conflict. Another option is to adapt material from books, movies, magazines, or even songs. For example, you could retell a well-known myth in dramatic form. See the **Idea Bank** in the margin for more suggestions. After you select an idea for your scene, follow the steps below.

Planning Your Dramatic Scene

1. **Consider the basic elements of your scene.** Fill out a chart like the one below to help you identify the elements you need to include.

Characters	Setting	Plot	Stage Directions
Who are the characters? How do they interact?	When and where does the scene take place?	What events will happen? In what sequence will they occur?	How will the characters speak? What is the pace of the scene?

2. **Think about your audience.** Who will read or view your dramatic scene? What language is appropriate for them? What background will they need to understand the setting, characters, and action?
3. **Decide on a mood.** What general emotional atmosphere do you want to convey? What basic elements of character, setting, and action will help contribute to that mood?
4. **Explore your scene.** How will your characters interact and speak? You might write an outline of your scene or jot down bits of dialogue.

❷ Drafting

As you write a script for your dramatic scene, keep the following points in mind:

- Introduce the **characters** and establish the **setting** of your scene. You might begin by putting a character in a situation and having him or her talk with another character.
- Use **dialogue** and **action** to advance the plot. You might collaborate with a partner to think of various actions and situations you could include.

IDEABank

1. Your Working Portfolio
Build on one of the **Writing Options** you completed earlier in this unit:
- **Dramatic Scene,** p. 1030.
- **Missing Scene,** p. 1043.
- **Dramatic Skit,** p. 1075.

2. From the Headlines
Borrow an idea for your scene from the headlines, or check a newspaper for human interest stories or news events.

3. Conflict Chart
List conflicts that you or people you know have experienced. Build your scene around one of these conflicts.

Guiding Student Writing

Prewriting

Choosing a Topic

If after reading the Idea Bank students are having difficulty choosing their subjects, suggest they try the following:

- Have students create three headings on a sheet of paper—*Character, Conflict,* and *Resolution*. Under each heading, have students list real and imagined examples of each based on situations they know.
- Have students begin by thinking of themes that express opposing ideas or conflicting emotions. Themes could include Trust/Mistrust, Acceptance/Rejection, and Success/Failure. Then ask them to think of situations that might illustrate these themes.
- Have students skim magazines looking for interesting stories that might lead to the creation of a character and a scene.

Planning the Dramatic Scene

1. One way students can establish unique identities for a character is to give their character habitual phrases or gestures.

3. Encourage students to think of scenes from movies and television shows that conveyed the mood that they wish to convey. Ask them to list elements of those scenes that contributed to the mood.
4. Visual learners may find it useful to create charts, clusters, sketches, or time lines to explore their scenes. Auditory learners may feel more comfortable extemporizing dialogue. Kinesthetic learners may benefit from acting out characters and conflicts with partners and then listing the ideas that surface. They might also benefit from using simple props that they make or gather.

Drafting

If students are having trouble getting started, suggest that they place their characters in a situation and have them start talking to one another. The scene will grow out of what the characters say. Encourage students to experiment with different ways of moving their plot forward through dialogue and action.

Revising

USING DIALOGUE EFFECTIVELY

In the revised sample, point out that the writer makes changes in dialogue to reflect Gretta's lack of education.

Have students work in pairs to read their dialogues aloud, revising for the rhythm and feel of spoken language. Have one student read a line of dialogue, then have the second student answer without reading the script. Compare the second student's response with the written response, making adjustments if necessary.

Editing and Proofreading

FORMATS FOR SCRIPTS

Have students review scripts by bringing in examples of screenplays or examining plays in the textbook. Have students look for examples that correspond to each of the guidelines.

Reflecting

Encourage students to describe and evaluate the way in which they approached the writing assignment. Ask them to discuss the prewriting and drafting strategies that worked most effectively. Have them add these self-evaluations to their working portfolios.

- Use **dialogue** to reveal details about the characters—personalities, interests, attitudes, and beliefs.
- Use **stage directions** to describe setting, costumes, lighting, sound effects, and props. Stage directions can also indicate mood through use of gestures, tone of voice, and characters' body movements.

Ask Your Peer Reader

- What do you think of the way the scene begins? How could this be improved?
- How would you describe the characters?
- Which part of the scene, if any, is not clear to you?

❸ Revising

Need help with dialogue?

See the **Writing Handbook**, p. 1365

TARGET SKILL ▸ USING DIALOGUE EFFECTIVELY Your characters' words should sound natural when spoken, so read your dialogue aloud. Use contractions and sentence fragments to mimic actual speech. Indicate tone of voice or emotion with precise stage directions, such as *mumbles, with a sob,* or *thoughtfully.*

(laughs a little). I've pretty I guess. ain't
Gretta. ~~I have~~ had a ~~fairly~~ quiet life. *(closes eyes)* I ~~have never~~
a good
seen any real trouble, but I ~~have~~ seen many beautiful and unexplainable things.

(encouragingly) Like what?
Josh. ~~What kinds of things have you seen?~~

❹ Editing and Proofreading

TARGET SKILL ▸ FORMATS FOR SCRIPTS Although the format for stage scripts differs from the format for television and film scripts, there are some common conventions to follow.

- Dialogue does not have quotation marks.
- The name of each speaker is set off so actors can find their lines easily.
- Speaking directions follow the name of the character.
- Directions for movements appear in the script where the action happens.
- General directions for props, lighting, or sound effects for a whole scene appear in a separate paragraph.

Publishing IDEAS

- Choose several scenes from your class to produce and present to other classes.
- Videotape your scene to show to family members and friends.

More Online: Publishing Options
www.mcdougallittell.com

❺ Reflecting

FOR YOUR WORKING PORTFOLIO What did you learn about writing dialogue for a dramatic scene? How could you make your characters and situation more realistic next time? Attach your answers to your finished work. Save your dramatic scene in your **Working Portfolio.**

Option
Spot Check

Circulate among students as they are working on their drafts to see how effectively they integrate dialogue and stage directions. Check to see that students are actively aware of the following resources to move their plots and dramatic scenes forward: stage directions, sound effects, a narrator, and dialogue.

Assessment Practice Revising & Editing

Read this paragraph from the first draft of a drama review. The underlined sections may include the following kinds of errors:

- **lack of pronoun-antecedent agreement**
- **run-on sentences**
- **punctuation errors**
- **incorrect possessive forms**

For each underlined section, choose the revision that most improves the writing.

The Littletown Community Players (1) current revue, *Watch It!*, is an irreverent and playful look at time. The set is elegantly simple, a large clock hangs over the stage. (2) As the show opens, the clock chimes six A.M. The cast of four engaging performers wake up and begin his or her day. (3) This is a convenient device for the cast to sing some old standby songs about time. My favorites included "Rock Around the Clock," "Five O'clock World," and "Nine to Five." (4) The show closes with a sensational performance by Martha Ryan. The entire audience was caught up in Ryans' (5) stirring version of "Time After Time". (6)

1. **A.** Players's
   B. Player's
   C. Players'
   D. Correct as is
2. **A.** The set is elegantly simple a large clock hangs over the stage.
   B. The set is elegantly simple; a large clock hangs over the stage.
   C. The set is elegantly simple a large clock, hangs over the stage.
   D. The set is elegantly simple. A large clock hangs, over the stage.
3. **A.** The cast of four engaging performers wake up and begin their day.
   B. Each member of the engaging cast wakes up and begin their day.
   C. The cast of four, each an engaging performer, wakes up and begins his or her day.
   D. Correct as is
4. **A.** My favorites included "Rock Around the Clock, Five O'clock World, and Nine to Five."
   B. My favorites included "Rock Around the Clock," Five O'clock World, and "Nine to Five."
   C. My favorites included Rock Around the Clock, Five O'clock World, and Nine to Five.
   D. Correct as is
5. **A.** Ryan's
   B. Ryans
   C. Ryan'
   D. Correct as is
6. **A.** "Time After Time.".
   B. Time After Time.
   C. "Time After Time."
   D. "Time After Time"

Need extra help?

See the **Grammar Handbook**

Possessive Nouns, p. 1392

Pronoun Agreement, p. 1393

Punctuation Chart, pp. 1413–1414

Correcting run-on Sentences, p. 1409

Assessment Practice

Have students read the entire passage before they correct the errors.

Answers:
1. C; **2.** B; **3.** C **4.** D; **5.** A; **6.** C

WRITING WORKSHOP **1103**

Objectives

- understand how to use word parts to build vocabulary
- identify, classify, and research the meanings of affixes

Strategies for Building Vocabulary

INSTRUCTION

Have students find the meaning of the root or base words in a dictionary. Discuss how the prefix or suffix alters the punction or meaning of the root or base word.

EXERCISES

1. Base word *satisfy;* prefix *dis-,* meaning "not;" inflectional suffix *-ed,* indicating past tense
2. Base word *ordinary;* prefix *extra-,* meaning "beyond;" derivational adverb suffix *-ly,* indicating a certain manner
3. Base word *history;* prefix *pre-,* meaning "before;" derivational adjective suffix *-ic,* meaning "relating to"
4. Base word *dark;* prefix *semi-,* meaning "half" or "partial;" derivational noun suffix *-ness,* meaning "condition of"
5. Base word *consider;* prefix *in-,* meaning "not;" derivational adjective suffix *-able,* meaning "worthy of"

Building New Words

Part of what makes English a flexible language is the ease with which new words can be created by adding word parts to the beginning or end of existing words. The lines from William Butler Yeats's "The Second Coming" at the right contain an example—*falconer.*

Knowing the meaning and function of the word part *-er* can help you understand the word *falconer.* One meaning of *-er* is "one who," signifying a person occupationally associated with the thing named by the word to which it is attached. A falconer, therefore, is someone who works with falcons.

> **Turning and turning in the widening gyre**
> **The falcon cannot hear the falconer;**
> —W. B. Yeats, "The Second Coming"

Strategies for Building Vocabulary

Roots and base words form the foundation of almost all complex words. **Roots** are core word parts that cannot stand alone, like *dict,* a Latin root meaning "speak." **Base words** are simple complete words, like *turn.* In order to produce words with various meanings, word parts called affixes, such as *anti-* and *-er,* are added to roots and base words. Learning the meanings of affixes can help you decode unfamiliar words and create new words.

1 Look for Prefixes Affixes added to the beginning of base words and roots are called **prefixes.** For example, adding the prefix *anti-,* meaning "against," to the base word *social* creates the word *antisocial,* meaning "shunning the society of others."

Prefixes Expressing Direction

Prefix	Meaning	Words
ab-	away from	abscond, abhor, abstract
circum-	around	circumference, circumspect
inter-	among, between	interject, intercede

Prefixes Expressing Quantity

Prefix	Meaning	Words
equi-	equal	equinox, equilibrium
over-	too much	overbearing, overindulge
poly-	many	polyglot, polyester

2 Look for Suffixes Affixes added to the end of roots and base words are called **suffixes.** There are two types of suffixes: inflectional suffixes and derivational suffixes. An **inflectional suffix** shows a change in number (*falcon/falcons*), tense (*reiterate/reiterated*), or degree of comparison (*livelier/liveliest*). A **derivational suffix** changes a word's part of speech and may add meaning. For example, adding the negative suffix *-less* to the noun *expression* creates the adjective *expressionless,* meaning "without expression."

Noun Suffixes

Suffix	Meaning	Words
-ance	state or action of	repentance
-ation	process of	indoctrination, emancipation
-mony	product of	testimony, ceremony

Adjective Suffixes

Suffix	Meaning	Words
-ent	causing	absorbent, fraudulent
-ose	full of, having a quality of	comatose, verbose
-ous	characterized by	contemptuous, fallacious

Verb Suffixes

Suffix	Meaning	Words
-ate	to engage in the action of	decimate, infiltrate
-fy	to make	amplify, stultify
-ize	to treat as	dramatize, marginalize

EXERCISE Identify the base word in each word below. Then use a dictionary to identify the meanings of the affixes. Classify each suffix as inflectional or derivational.

1. dissatisfied
2. extraordinarily
3. prehistoric
4. semidarkness
5. inconsiderable

Creating Sentence Closers'

Grammar from Literature

Writers use sentence closers for a variety of reasons.

- To provide concrete details.
- To produce sentence variety and interesting sentence rhythms.

A sentence closer can be a word, phrase, or clause. It is called a closer because it appears at the end of a sentence—after the main idea. Many types of words, phrases, and clauses can be used as closers. Some types of closers are shown below, in examples from D. H. Lawrence's "The Rocking-Horse Winner."

single word
"That's right," said Bassett, nodding.

prepositional phrase
"Oh, well, sometimes I'm absolutely sure, like about Daffodil."

So he would mount again and start on his furious ride,
participial phrase
hoping at last to get there.

adverb clause
He became wild-eyed and strange, as if something were going to explode in him.

Writers sometimes combine several elements in closers.

appositive
He had a secret within a secret, something he had not
adverbial phrase
divulged, even to Bassett or to his Uncle Oscar.

adverb prepositional phrase
He went off by himself, vaguely, in a childish way,
participial phrase
seeking for the clue to "luck."

Using Sentence Closers in Your Writing Sentence closers provide a way to add detail to your writing and to vary your sentence structures. Sometimes during revision, you may think of an additional word or phrase that, added as a closer, will make an idea clearer. At other times, you may notice that you can express an idea in fewer words if you create a sentence closer by combining two sentences.

ORIGINAL
She invited the young woman to her home.

REWRITTEN
She invited the young woman to her home, but not out of total selflessness.

ORIGINAL
The Derby is named for the twelfth Earl of Derbyshire. The earl founded the race in 1780.

REWRITTEN
The Derby is named for the twelfth Earl of Derbyshire, who founded the race in 1780.

Usage Tip As you add closers to your sentences, be sure to use the word *like* properly. *Like* may be used to introduce a prepositional phrase. *Like* may not be used to introduce a clause. Use *as,* or as *if,* to introduce a clause.

CORRECT
I enjoy stories with a touch of suspense, like **this story.**

INCORRECT
The mother tries to act like **she adores her children.**

CORRECT
The mother tries to act as if **she adores her children.**

WRITING EXERCISE Combine each sentence pair, adding the underlined portion as a closer to the first sentence. Omit words in italics. Punctuate correctly.

1. The voices in the house grow louder. *They were so loud they were* <u>frightening Paul.</u>
2. Paul worries about his mother. *He can see that she is* <u>a bitter, unhappy woman.</u>
3. Paul rides the rocking horse. *He moves* <u>as if he were in a trance.</u>
4. Paul believes Bassett is someone who is *trustworthy. Bassett is* <u>trustworthy enough to keep the money.</u>
5. At the end Paul dies. *Clearly, he is* <u>exhausted.</u>

GRAMMAR EXERCISE Rewrite the sentences below, correcting errors involving the use of the word *like.* If there is no error, write *Correct.*

1. Like Paul's mother says, the family has had no luck.
2. Voices in the house make it seem like the house were alive.
3. Children like Paul should not have to worry about money.
4. At first Uncle Oscar acts like Paul can't know anything about horse racing.
5. Paul is lucky to have a loyal friend like Bassett.

Sentence Crafting

Objectives

- use sentence openers to add detail, improve sentence variety, and increase reader interest
- revise sentences by correcting dangling modifiers

WRITING EXERCISE

Answers will vary. Possible responses are given.

1. The voices in the house grow louder, <u>frightening Paul</u>.
2. Paul worries about his mother, <u>a bitter, unhappy woman</u>.
3. Paul rides the rocking horse <u>as if he were in a trance</u>.
4. Paul believes Bassett is someone who is <u>trustworthy enough to keep the money</u>.
5. At the end Paul dies, <u>exhausted</u>.

GRAMMAR EXERCISE

1. <u>As</u> Paul's mother says, the family has had no luck.
2. Voices in the house make it seem <u>as if</u> the house were alive.
3. *Correct*
4. At first Uncle Oscar acts <u>as if</u> Paul can't know anything about horse racing.
5. *Correct*

PART 2 Shocking Realities

The first half of the 20th century was one of the most violent times in human history. The bloodshed and atrocities of two world wars shocked people everywhere and altered the course of British life. Throughout the century, many writers have explored the purposes, experiences, and consequences of war. The selections in this part of Unit Six will challenge you to define your own views and beliefs.

1106

An Irish Airman Foresees His Death

Poetry by WILLIAM BUTLER YEATS

The Soldier

Poetry by RUPERT BROOKE

Dreamers

Poetry by SIEGFRIED SASSOON

"In the great hour of destiny they stand."

Connect to Your Life

Call to Arms What if your country were suddenly engaged in a full-scale war with another country? Would you volunteer for military service? Would your decision depend on what caused the war, where it was fought, or who the enemy was? Share your thoughts.

Build Background

World War I At the start of the 20th century, the British were for the most part optimistic. Few anticipated a major conflict. However, a feverish sense of nationalism—the belief that loyalty to one's nation comes before all other loyalties—had led the British government and the governments of other nations to stockpile weapons and to issue increasingly alarming threats to their rivals. Tension mounted between countries with opposing goals, and the assassination of an Austrian archduke in 1914 ignited a war that quickly pulled in all the major powers of Europe. The war, known at the time as the Great War and later as World War I, was a devastating four-year conflict that spread to the Middle East, Africa, Asia, and the Pacific, although most of the major battles were fought in Europe. The casualty count was enormous—more than 8.5 million soldiers killed and approximately 21 million wounded.

Perhaps because World War I affected a large portion of the British population, it inspired an abundance of British literature. The military ranks included not only professional soldiers like those who had fought in previous wars but also civilian volunteers and draftees, most of whom were unprepared for the grim realities of warfare. Many experienced changes in attitude during the course of the war, with the patriotism and enthusiasm of the first two years turning into disillusionment and despair as the war dragged on. Rupert Brooke and Siegfried Sassoon were among those who set off to defend their nation.

Focus Your Reading

LITERARY ANALYSIS | SPEAKER As you know, the **speaker** of a poem—the voice that "talks" to the reader—may be either a distant observer not directly involved in the situation he or she describes or a participant in the situation presented in the poem. In either case, the speaker should not necessarily be identified with the poet. As you read, be aware of details that indicate how involved each speaker is with the situation described.

ACTIVE READING | MAKING INFERENCES These poems present three different perspectives on World War I, though the speakers do not directly state their attitudes. To fully appreciate these perspectives, you must read between the lines, or **make inferences,** about what each speaker says.

READER'S NOTEBOOK Create a chart like the one shown, recording words and phrases that you think help to convey each speaker's attitude toward war.

Poem	Attitude Toward War
"An Irish Airman . . ."	
"The Soldier"	
"Dreamers"	

LaserLinks: Background for Reading
Historical Connection

OVERVIEW

Objectives

1. understand and appreciate three **poems about World War I (Literary Analysis)**
2. appreciate authors' uses of **speakers (Literary Analysis)**
3. **make inferences** to understand poems by Yeats, Brooke, and Sassoon **(Active Reading)**

Summary

In these three poems, soldiers fighting for Britain ponder the meanings of life and death during World War I. Yeats's Irish airman ponders his probable death and the reasons—impulse, glory, a desire for adventure—for his participation in a cause that is not his own. Brooke's soldier speaks of his love of England, and the speaker in Sassoon's poem reflects on the contrast between a soldier's existence in the trenches and the home he dreams about.

Thematic Link

By showing the **shocking realities** of the early 20th century and World War I warfare through the voices of individual soldiers, these three poems stand on the cusp between the Edwardian age and full-blown modernism.

5-Minute Warm-Up

Daily Language SkillBuilder

Have students **proofread** the display sentences on page 979j and write them correctly. The sentences also appear on Transparency 30 of **Grammar Transparencies and Copymasters.**

LESSON RESOURCES

UNIT SIX RESOURCE BOOK, pp. 53–54

ASSESSMENT RESOURCES

Formal Assessment, pp. 203–204

Teacher's Guide to Assessment and Portfolio Use

Test Generator

SKILLS TRANSPARENCIES AND COPYMASTERS

Literary Analysis
- Poetic Devices, T16 (for Extend Interpretations 6, p. 1111)

Reading and Critical Thinking
- Making Inferences, T7 (for Active Reading, p. 1107)

Grammar
- Avoiding Misplaced and Dangling Modifiers, T51 (for Mini Lesson, p. 1112)
- Adverbials: *Only*, C71 (for Mini Lesson, p. 1112)

Writing
- Effective Language, T13 (for Writing Option 2, p. 1112)
- Personality Profile, C25 (for Writing Option 1, p. 1112)

Communications
- Reading Aloud, T11 (for Activities & Explorations 3, p. 1112)

INTEGRATED TECHNOLOGY

Audio Library

LaserLinks
- Historical Connection: World War I. See **Teacher's SourceBook,** p. 77.

Visit our website:
www.mcdougallittell.com

TEACHING THE LITERATURE

Reading and Analyzing

Literary Analysis SPEAKER

Have students consider the following questions as they read the poems.

- Is the speaker directly involved in the action described in the poem?
- What information does the poem provide about the speaker?
- Is the speaker's voice that of a soldier or that of a poet?

Use **Unit Six Resource Book,** p. 54 for more exercises.

Active Reading MAKING INFERENCES

To help students make inferences about the speakers' attitudes toward war, suggest that they consider specific elements such as diction, meter, and rhyme scheme, as well as the overall impression left by the poem.

Use **Unit Six Resource Book,** p. 53 for more practice.

Literary Analysis: TONE

Have students analyze the speaker's tone in "The Soldier."

Possible Responses: The tone is very gentle, considering that the speaker is a combat soldier; the tone is romantic, presenting an idealized view of death.

Thinking Through the Literature

1. Possible Responses: young; fatalistic; thrill seeker
2. Possible Response: fearful but excited; he claims to feel "a lonely impulse of delight"; he feels free of all duties and pressures to conform.
3. Possible Response: duty; desire for excitement; desire to leave home.

Detail of *The Bombing of El-Afuleh Railway Junction*, C. R. Fleming-Williams. Imperial War Museum, London.

William Butler Yeats

An Irish Airman Foresees His Death

I know that I shall meet my fate
Somewhere among the clouds above;
Those that I fight I do not hate,
Those that I guard I do not love;
My country is Kiltartan Cross,
My countrymen Kiltartan's poor,
No likely end could bring them loss
Or leave them happier than before.
Nor law, nor duty bade me fight,
Nor public men, nor cheering crowds.
A lonely impulse of delight
Drove to this tumult in the clouds;
I balanced all, brought all to mind,
The years to come seemed waste of breath,
A waste of breath the years behind
In balance with this life, this death.

4 Those that I guard . . . love: Many of the Irish—even those who fought beside the English against the Germans—resented their English rulers.

5 Kiltartan: a district in the west of Ireland.

Thinking Through the Literature

1. Jot down words that come to mind when you think about the **speaker** of this poem.
2. How do you think the speaker feels each time he gets into his plane?
3. What factors may have influenced the speaker's decision to go to war?

Teaching Options

Mini Lesson: Viewing and Representing

Detail of *The Bombing of El-Afuleh Railway Junction* **by C. R. Fleming-Williams**

ART APPRECIATION

Instruction This picture shows a group of World War I bombers, the types of planes flown by pilots such as the speaker of Yeats's poem. Fleming-Williams attempts to portray the bombing with pictorial realism, a style of art that had gone out of fashion by 1919 and had been replaced by such movements as Fauvism, Cubism, and Futurism.

Application Ask students in what ways the realistic style of the detail of *The Bombing of El-Afuleh Railway Junction* romanticizes war. Compare the emotions the picture communicates with those of Yeats's poem.

Possible Response: The photorealism that Fleming-Williams employs in his work makes the bombing look exciting and the piloting of the bombers thrilling work. The viewer experiences only the excitement of aerial warfare. Yeats's poem, however, communicates a sense of futility and despair; the airman puts on a gallant face, but he actually feels doomed.

The Soldier

Rupert Brooke

Wounded in the Chest: "Just Out of the Trenches near Arras," Sir William Orpen. Imperial War Museum, London.

If I should die, think only this of me,
That there's some corner of a foreign field
That is forever England. There shall be
In that rich earth a richer dust concealed,
A dust whom England bore, shaped, made aware,
Gave, once, her flowers to love, her ways to roam,
A body of England's, breathing English air,
Washed by the rivers, blest by suns of home.

And think, this heart, all evil shed away,
A pulse in the Eternal mind, no less
Gives somewhere back the thoughts by England given,
Her sights and sounds; dreams happy as her day;
And laughter, learnt of friends; and gentleness,
In hearts at peace, under an English heaven.

Thinking Through the Literature

1. After reading this poem, what thoughts or questions do you have?
2. How would you describe the **tone** of the poem?
3. In your opinion, would the sentiments expressed in this poem console the speaker's loved ones? Explain your view.

Customizing Instruction

Less Proficient Readers

Set a Purpose Help students to understand the context of each of the poems: a pilot flying high in the clouds; a soldier contemplating a possible grave site; and soldiers dreaming of home.

Students Acquiring English

Students may not be familiar enough with Irish history to understand lines 3–7. Remind them of Britain's treatment of the Irish during modern times.

Use **Spanish Study Guide** for additional support, pp. 260–262.

Gifted and Talented

Students might be interested in how a poet's reputation changes with literary fashion. Have students research Rupert Brooke's work by looking up critical writings on him in the *Humanities Index.* Have them compare critics' reception of Brooke's poetry in the 1920s with the critical writing on him today.

Thinking Through the Literature

1. Accept all reasonable responses to the poem.
2. Possible Responses: patriotic, idealistic, blithe
3. Possible Responses: yes, because the speaker would have died willingly for a cause he believed in; no, because noble sentiments cannot console a person on the loss of a loved one

Speaking and Listening

CLASS DISCUSSION

Instruction The three poems allude to issues of war and peace that are as relevant today as during World War I. Remind students that the 20th century has revolved around two major world wars and that issues of war and peace have stirred passionate public debate throughout the century.

Prepare Divide the class into three groups. Tell each group to appoint a moderator, a scribe, and a timekeeper. Ask the groups to discuss the justification of war for the individual soldier, using the views and precise details expressed in the three poems as a point of reference. Have them discuss the question of how the individual soldier justifies the taking of human lives during wartime.

Present Remind students to respect each other's opinions and to participate actively in the group's discussion, even if they are serving as the moderator, scribe, or timekeeper. Then, have the scribe of each group present the group's views to the class.

BLOCK SCHEDULING This activity is particularly well-suited for longer class periods.

THE SOLDIER 1109

Reading and Analyzing

Literary Analysis SPEAKER

Ask students to characterize the speaker in each of the three poems. How are they alike, and how are they different?

Possible Response: All are soldiers, roughly the same age, although the soldier in the third poem might be older. The soldier in the first poem is fatalistic, the soldier in the second is patriotic, and the one in the third poem is wistful, perhaps even bitter.

Literary Analysis: PARALLELISM

Have students identify elements of parallelism in "Dreamers."

Answer: Lines 1, 5, and 7 begin with "Soldiers are . . ." and lines 10, 12, and 14 begin with "And."

Reading Skills and Strategies: ANALYZING

A Have students analyze the first two lines closely. Ask them what the speaker implies by stating that soldiers are "citizens of death's gray land."

Possible Responses: that they are not citizens of their native country anymore; that they all belong to the same country on the fields of war.

Then ask students what they think line 2 means.

Possible Response: that soldiers exist only in the here and now.

Dreamers

Siegfried Sassoon

A Soldiers are citizens of death's gray land,
Drawing no dividend from time's tomorrows.
In the great hour of destiny they stand,
Each with his feuds, and jealousies, and sorrows.
Soldiers are sworn to action; they must win
Some flaming, fatal climax with their lives.
Soldiers are dreamers; when the guns begin
They think of firelit homes, clean beds and wives.

I see them in foul dugouts, gnawed by rats,
And in the ruined trenches, lashed with rain,
Dreaming of things they did with balls and bats,
And mocked by hopeless longing to regain
Bank holidays, and picture shows, and spats,
And going to the office in the train.

1110

Teaching Options

Assessment Informal Assessment

WRITE AN ESSAY

You can informally assess students' understanding of the three poems by having them write an essay discussing the characteristics of the speaker of each poem.

RUBRIC

3 **Full Accomplishment** Essay displays keen understanding of characteristics of each speaker.

2 **Substantial Accomplishment** Essay displays basic understanding of characteristics of each speaker.

1 **Little or Partial Accomplishment** Essay reveals student has not been able to differentiate among speakers.

Thinking through the LITERATURE

Connect to the Literature

1. **What Do You Think?** What images were left in your mind after you read "Dreamers"?

Comprehension Check
- What do the soldiers dream about?

Think Critically

2. What contrasts are made in "Dreamers"? How do you think these contrasts contribute to the poem's impact?
3. Do you think the **speaker** expects that the soldiers' dreams will be fulfilled? Give reasons to support your opinion.
4. ACTIVE READING MAKING INFERENCES Based on the chart you created in your READER'S NOTEBOOK, explain how you think the speakers' attitudes toward war differ in these three poems.
5. Which poem, "The Soldier" or "Dreamers," was most likely written at the start of the war? Cite evidence to support your answer.

Literary Analysis

SPEAKER In each of these three poems, the **speaker** is intimately involved with the situation being described. In two of the poems, the speakers speculate on their own fates, as in the opening lines of "An Irish Airman Foresees His Death":

I know that I shall meet my fate / Somewhere among the clouds above;

As you know, the speaker is not necessarily to be identified with the poet. Yeats himself was not an airman; he modeled the speaker after a real pilot he knew.

Paired Activity Create a chart like the one shown and note details about each speaker. Then compare your chart with a partner's. How important is the identity of each speaker? How would each poem be different if the speaker were a distant observer?

Poem	Speaker's Identity	Speaker's Participation in Events	Speaker's Character
"An Irish Airman Foresees His Death"			
"The Soldier"			
"Dreamers"			

Extend Interpretations

6. **Writer's Style** All three of these poems contain parallelism—the use of similar grammatical structures to express related or equally important ideas—and repetition. Find examples of parallelism or repetition in the three poems. Compare and contrast the ways in which these devices contribute to the overall effect of each poem.
7. **Comparing Texts** In your opinion, which speaker in these three war poems would be most likely to share the feelings expressed by the speaker of Thomas Hardy's "The Man He Killed" (page 953)? Give reasons for your choice.
8. **Connect to Life** Do you think any of the thoughts expressed in these three poems would be relevant to soldiers fighting in wars today? Explain your opinion.

GUIDING STUDENT RESPONSE

Connect to the Literature

1. **What Do You Think?**
Guidelines for student response: You might list the images volunteered by students on the chalkboard.

Comprehension Check
- the simple pleasures of a peaceful life, such as holidays, cricket games, movies, and work

Think Critically

2. Possible Response: The horrors of war are contrasted with the simple pleasures of home, such as clean beds, loving wives, and holidays. These contrasts make the poem's antiwar message even more powerful.
3. Possible Response: no, because he believes their longings for home are hopeless; yes, eventually the war will end and at least some men's longings will be fulfilled.
4. Accept all reasonable, well-supported responses. Students may find that Yeats and Sassoon have more realistic attitudes about the horrors of war.
5. Accept all reasonable, well-supported responses. Tell students that "The Soldier" was, in fact, written near the start of the war. Note the more romantic view of war in "The Soldier," as compared with the sadder tone in the other poems.

Literary Analysis

Paired Activity Draw up a composite chart on the chalkboard based upon the charts done by pairs of students.

Extend Interpretations

Writer's Style Students may mention any of several examples of parallelism and repetition in all three poems. In the first poem, these devices contribute to the sense of futility and waste; in the second, these devices create an ideal image of England; in the third, they stress the destructiveness of war.

Comparing Texts The speaker of "Dreamers" would be most likely to share the sentiments of the speaker of "The Man He Killed," since both poems convey a grim view of war.

Connect to Life Accept all reasonable, well-supported responses.

Writing Options

1. **Wartime Epitaphs** Remind students that epitaphs present the "last word" on the subject's life; they are the kinds of statements that might be written on tombstones.
2. **Letter to a Soldier** Generally, soldiers in the field appreciate news from home, treats of food or candy, small practical items such as socks, and recreational items such as books or decks of cards.
3. **Multimedia Notes** Encourage interested students to share their flowcharts with the class.
4. **Bumper Stickers** Point out to students that a bumper sticker should be pithy, capturing a vivid opinion in a few words.

Activities & Explorations

1. **Role Play** One student should play the role of the counselor and the other, the speaker. Remind students to consider the different attitudes toward war and death held by the two speakers.
2. **Soldier Rating** Remind students to listen politely to the opinions of others and tell them that all group members should contribute to the discussion. To facilitate this, you might want to have students begin by each group member stating one quality that each speaker has.
3. **Choral Reading** Have students divide the responsibilities of the presentation equally among group members. For example, two students could read the poem while two others manage the lighting, sound, and props.
4. **War Diorama** Set aside an area in the classroom to display dioramas created by the students.

Inquiry & Research

World War I Songs Most popular songs of World War I, such as "Pack Up Your Troubles in Your Old Kit Bag (and Smile, Smile, Smile)" and "It's a Long Way to Tipperary," convey a wistful, but patriotic "keep a stiff upper lip" "smile through the face of adversity" message that would have given the wartime public comfort through empathy.

Choices & CHALLENGES

Writing Options

1. **Wartime Epitaphs** Compose brief epitaphs for the speakers of "An Irish Airman Foresees His Death," "The Soldier," and "Dreamers." In each epitaph, include details that convey the unique qualities of the individual who is its subject.

2. **Letter to a Soldier** If you were sending a "CARE package" to one of the speakers, what might you include in it? Write a letter to accompany the package, explaining what you are sending and why you chose those things.

3. **Multimedia Notes** Make notes for an online multimedia presentation on poetry about World War I. Sketch a flowchart that shows how the different parts of your presentation would be connected. Place the notes and chart in your **Working Portfolio.**

4. **Bumper Stickers** If the speakers of these three poems chose to express their attitudes toward war on bumper stickers, what sentiments might they express? Write messages for three different bumper stickers, one for each speaker.

Activities & Explorations

1. **Role Play** With a partner, role-play a counseling session in which you offer advice to the speaker of either "An Irish Airman Foresees His Death" or "Dreamers." ~ **PERFORMING**

2. **Soldier Rating** With a group of classmates, discuss the qualities—both strengths and weaknesses—of the speaker of each poem, and decide how those qualities might affect his performance as a soldier. In an informal vote, choose the speaker you think would make the best soldier; then give a brief rationale for your choice.
~ **SPEAKING AND LISTENING**

3. **Choral Reading** With a small group of classmates, plan and present a dramatic choral reading of the three poems. Use special effects—such as lighting, background music, and costumes—to help convey the moods and messages of the poems.

As you are preparing, work with your classmates to develop criteria for evaluating a literary performance. After the choral reading, have classmates use the criteria to analyze, evaluate, and critique your performance.
~ **SPEAKING AND LISTENING**

4. **War Diorama** Create a miniature diorama depicting the setting presented in one of the three poems. ~ **ART**

Inquiry & Research

World War I Songs Locate printed versions or recordings of songs that were popular during World War I. Read the lyrics or play a few of the songs for the class. As you listen to the lyrics of each song, try to answer these questions: What message about war does the song convey? How might wartime listeners have reacted to the message?

Teaching Options

Mini Lesson Grammar

Adverbs: *Only*

Instruction *Only* is an adverb that helps the reader to focus on an important part of the sentence. However, if placed incorrectly, *only* can cause confusion for the reader. For clarity, *only* should be placed immediately before the word or words it qualifies.

Activity Write on the chalkboard this example from "The Soldier."

"If I should die, think only this of me,
That there's some corner of a foreign field
That is forever England."

Ask students what the soldier means by the word *only* here. *(He wants us to remember just this one thing—that in death as in life he is part of England.)* Have students consider what the meaning would be if *only* were placed after the word *this*. *(It would qualify "of me" rather than "this," and so would mean "of me alone and not of anyone else.")*

William Butler Yeats 1865–1939

A biography of William Butler Yeats appears on page 993.

Rupert Brooke

1887–1915

Other Works
"The Dead"
"Peace"
"Safety"
"The Old Vicarage"
"Grantchester"

Youthful Promise Rupert Brooke, an extraordinarily handsome and intelligent young man who excelled at both athletics and academics while attending Cambridge University, was regarded as one of Britain's most promising poets. During his brief life, he mingled with such prominent figures as Virginia Woolf and Winston Churchill. At the outbreak of World War I, he joined the Royal Navy and began training for combat. During this time he wrote *1914,* a series of five war sonnets that included "The Soldier."

Victim of War The young poet saw very little wartime action, however, for he fell victim to blood poisoning on the way to his first major conflict. He died at the age of 27 on a hospital ship in the Aegean Sea and was buried on the Aegean island of Skíros. Upon learning of Brooke's death, Churchill, then first lord of the admiralty, recalled that the poet-soldier was "joyous, fearless, versatile . . . all one could wish England's noblest sons to be."

Author Activity

Poet of Youth In an essay written in 1919, the British poet Walter de la Mare referred to the "life-giving youthfulness" of Brooke's poetry. Read several of Brooke's other poems, and discuss what you think of de la Mare's assessment.

Siegfried Sassoon

1886–1967

Other Works
"Absolution"
"To Victory"
"To My Brother"
"Golgotha"
"A Working Party"

From Student to Soldier Although Siegfried Sassoon began writing poetry as a child, he was more interested in sports than in scholastic achievement. Born to a prosperous family in Kent, he attended Cambridge University but left without a degree. He joined the army just a few days before England declared war and, while serving as an infantry officer in France, was wounded several times and received the Military Cross for bravery.

From Soldier to Pacifist Sassoon's experiences in trench warfare affected him profoundly, however, and his early idealism turned to bitter disillusionment as the war progressed. In 1917, having become a pacifist, he wrote his commanding officer a letter protesting the continuation of the war. The letter might have led to a court-martial, but Sassoon was instead briefly hospitalized for shell shock, then sent back to the battlefield, where he was wounded in the head. His wartime experiences were not easily forgotten, and he continued to write about them long after the conflict ended.

Author Activity

Brothers in Arms Find out more about Sassoon's influence on another poet who wrote about World War I, Wilfred Owen. How did the two meet? What part did Sassoon play in securing public recognition of Owen's poetry?

Author Activity

Poet of Youth Brooke died of blood poisoning at the age of 27, before he ever reached the battlefield. His poems, which were published posthumously and therefore are of a voice eternally frozen at age 27, are eternally idealistic and innocent in their view of patriotic war. He never had to experience war's harsh reality—or, indeed, life's harsh realities. His poems could always maintain their youthful naiveté and romanticism.

Brothers in Arms Sassoon belonged to a socially prominent British family and was able to help and encourage Owen's writing and publication. Sassoon met Owen during the war, and Owen, before his death in 1918, came to share Sassoon's contempt for the war, for nationalism, and for the class system that perpetuated the need for both.

Exercise Ask students to place the *only* in each of these sentences immediately before the word or words it should modify.

1. The Irish airman says that the "impulse of delight" only led him to soar among the clouds. *(only the "impulse of delight")*
2. The soldier in Rupert Brooke's poem only thought of England. *(thought only)*
3. Soldiers may dream, though they are only sworn to action. *(sworn only)*
4. The war poets only tried to explain the feelings of soldiers on the front. *(Only the war poets)*
5. Among the three war poets, Sassoon only invokes the horrors of war. *(only Sassoon)*

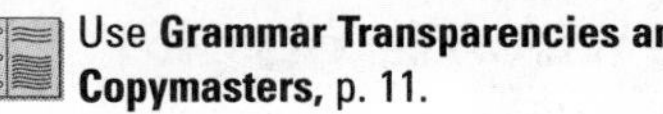
Use **Grammar Transparencies and Copymasters,** p. 11.

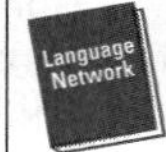

Use McDougal Littell's ***Language Network*** for more instruction and practice in the adverb *only.*

OVERVIEW

Objectives

1. understand and appreciate a **memoir** that explores the realities of battle and the home front **(Literary Analysis)**
2. **distinguish fact from opinion** in a memoir **(Active Reading)**

Summary

Brittain writes about her experiences as a British nurse in France during World War I. She receives a summons from her father to return to England and take care of her parents. Feeling torn between duty to her country and to her family, Brittain writes to her brother, Edward, who is stationed in Italy. After much agonizing, she returns to England. Her frustration and fear for Edward build as the war in Italy escalates. The family finally receives word that Edward has been killed, and Brittain's mourning for her brother, fiancé, and friends killed in the war redirect her life toward working for peace.

 Use **Unit Six Resource Book**, p. 55 for additional support.

Thematic Link

Vera Brittain experienced many **shocking realities** of war, which she reveals to us through her memoirs. Brittain details the horrors of war, the reality of her brother Edward's death, and the sharp contrast between trivial concerns and life-and-death situations on the battlefront.

5-Minute Warm-Up

Daily Language SkillBuilder

Have students **proofread** the display sentences on page 979k and write them correctly. The sentences also appear on Transparency 30 of **Grammar Transparencies and Copymasters.**

Preteaching Vocabulary

If you would like to preteach the WORDS TO KNOW for this selection, use the Mini Lesson p. 1116.

from Testament of Youth

Memoir by VERA BRITTAIN

Connect to Your Life

Weighing Obligations Most of us live in a web of relationships. We have ties to our families, to friends, to the communities in which we live, and to society as a whole. How committed are you to your family? your friends? society? yourself? Make a bar graph like the one shown, rating your senses of obligation to the different groups in your life. Then, with your classmates, discuss times when a person might experience conflicting obligations.

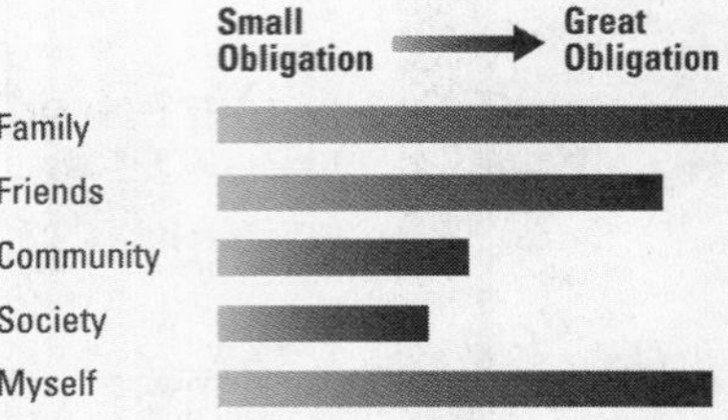

Build Background

Brittain's Life Vera Brittain's autobiographical *Testament of Youth* is a rare account of World War I from the perspective of a young woman. Brittain lived at a time when options for women were limited. Her childhood was sheltered and comfortable, yet she grew up to find few opportunities for personal and professional growth. Although she had a close relationship with her brother, Edward, Brittain was well aware that many choices open to him were denied to her. For example, Brittain's father—like many people of the time—thought that a university education was valuable for a son but wasted on a daughter. Yet Brittain convinced her father to let her attend Somerville College at Oxford University. She entered in 1914, shortly after World War I broke out in Europe.

Although the war seemed somewhat remote to Brittain at first, it soon changed her life. After her fiancé, Roland Leighton, was sent to the front lines, and then as news of war casualties began to come through, Brittain felt a sense of obligation to join the war effort. She interrupted her education to train as an army nurse—nursing being one of the few war-related jobs available to women. In 1915, while caring for wounded soldiers in London, Brittain learned that her fiancé had been killed by enemy fire. In 1916, she requested duty near the front lines, and she was eventually assigned to a field hospital near Étaples (ā-täp' lə), France. This selection begins during Brittain's time in Étaples.

WORDS TO KNOW
Vocabulary Preview

awry	incessant
bravado	insoluble
dissipation	quiescence
ethereal	semblance
excruciating	travesty

Focus Your Reading

LITERARY ANALYSIS MEMOIR *Testament of Youth* is a **memoir**—a form of autobiographical writing in which a person recalls significant events in his or her life. Brittain's memoir deals with an important historical event—World War I—but this is presented from the writer's personal perspective. For example, instead of simply giving facts about bombing raids, Brittain writes:

> ***I knew that I was more frightened than I had ever been in my life, yet all the time a tense, triumphant pride . . . held me to the semblance of self-control.***

As you read, be aware of the writer's personal perspective.

ACTIVE READING DISTINGUISHING FACT FROM OPINION Because memoirs often include the writers' feelings and opinions about historical events, they give readers insight into the impact of history on people's lives. Be sure to distinguish Brittain's feelings and opinions from the historical facts she presents.

READER'S NOTEBOOK Keep two lists as you read this selection. In one, record the historical information that Brittain provides; in the other, record Brittain's personal feelings and opinions.

LaserLinks: Background for Reading
Biographical Connection

LESSON RESOURCES

UNIT SIX RESOURCE BOOK, pp. 55–59

ASSESSMENT RESOURCES

Formal Assessment, pp. 205–206

Teacher's Guide to Assessment and Portfolio Use

Test Generator

SKILLS TRANSPARENCIES AND COPYMASTERS

Literary Analysis

- Point of View, T18 (for Literary Analysis, p. 1124)

Reading and Critical Thinking

- Fact vs. Opinion, T3 (for Active Reading, p. 1114)

Grammar

- Verbs–Using Correct Verb Forms, T45 (for Mini Lesson, p. 1125)
- Passive Voice, C136 (for Mini Lesson, p. 1125)

Vocabulary

- Prefixes, C87 (for Mini Lesson, p. 1122)

Writing

- Identifying Writing Variables, T2 (for Writing Option 1, p. 1125)
- Sensory Word List, T14 (for Writing Option 3, p. 1125)
- Figurative Language and Sound Devices, T15 (for Writing Option 3, p. 1125)

Communications

- Interviewing, T9 (for Activities & Explorations 2, p. 1125)

INTEGRATED TECHNOLOGY

Audio Library

LaserLinks

- Biographical Connection: Vera Brittain. See **Teacher's SourceBook,** p. 78.

Internet: Research Starter

Visit our website: www.mcdougallittell.com

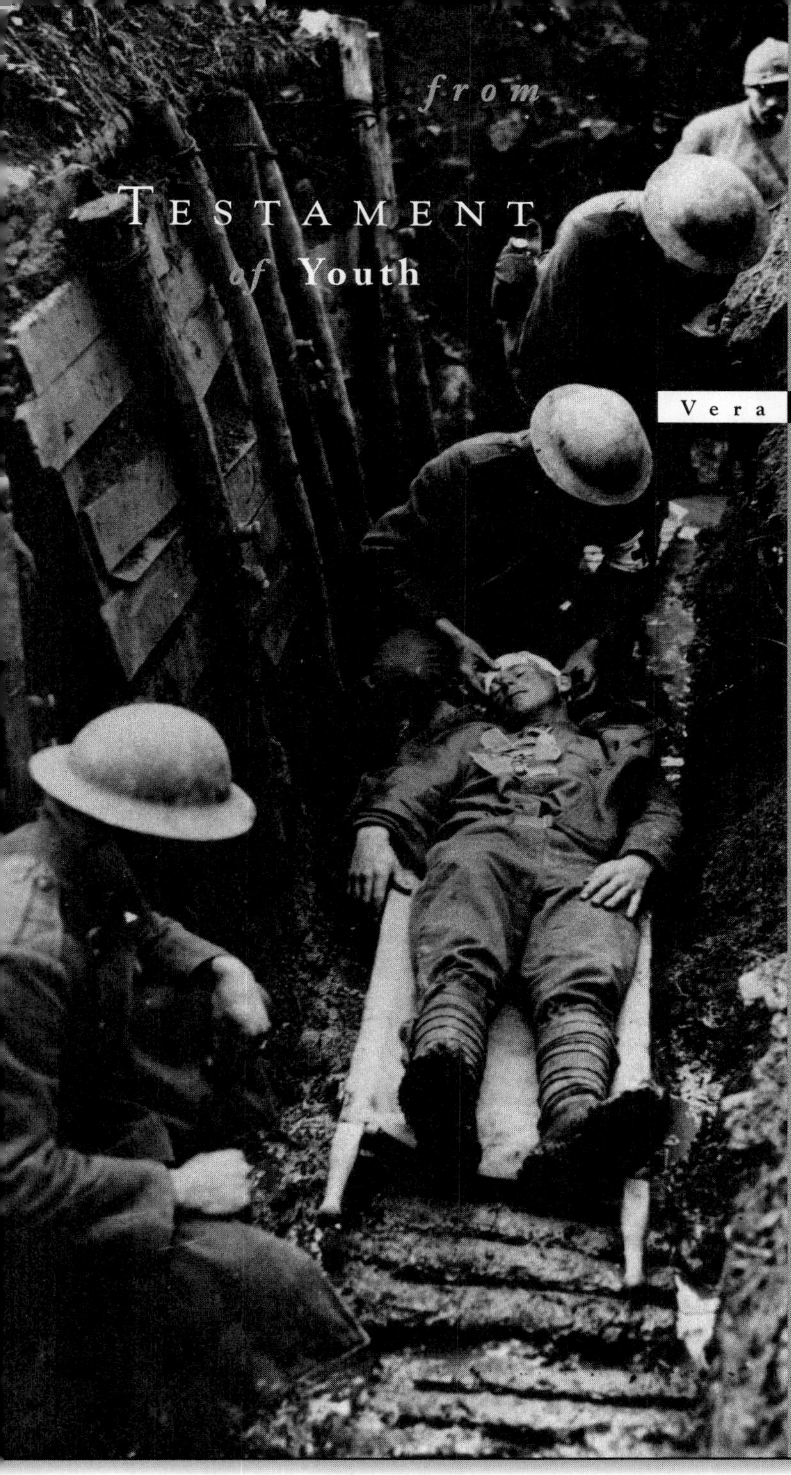

from

TESTAMENT *of* Youth

Vera Brittain

After days of continuous heavy duty and scamped,[1] inadequate meals, our nerves were none too reliable, and I don't suppose I was the only member of the staff whose teeth chattered with sheer terror as we groped our way to our individual huts in response to the order to scatter. Hope Milroy and I, thinking that we might as well be killed together, sat glassy-eyed in her small, pitch-black room. Suddenly, intermittent flashes half blinded us, and we listened frantically in the deafening din for the bugle call which we knew would summon us to join the night staff in the wards if bombs began to fall on the hospital.

1. scamped: hurried.

TEACHING THE LITERATURE

Customizing Instruction

Students Acquiring English
Point out that this selection contains many long sentences. Encourage students to break these sentences into smaller, meaningful chunks as they read. You might wish to model this procedure yourself, using the opening sentences of the selection.

 Use **Spanish Study Guide** for additional support, pp. 263–265.

Less Proficient Readers
Set a Purpose Have students read to find out why Vera Brittain's wartime experience had such a lasting effect on her.

Gifted and Talented
Encourage students to imagine the events narrated by Brittain from the perspectives of other characters, such as Brittain's father; her brother, Edward; and her friends. Have students write brief monologues in which these characters express their responses to her actions.

BLOCK SCHEDULING: MANAGING TIME

If your schedule requires that you cover the lesson objectives in a shorter time, use . . .
- Preparing to Read, p. 1114
- Thinking Through the Literature, p. 1124
- Vocabulary in Action, p. 1125

If you want to take advantage of longer class time, use . . .
- TE Teaching Options: Preteaching Vocabulary, p. 1116; Cross Curricular Link, p. 1118 ; Multicultural Link, p. 1119; Speaking and Listening, p. 1120; Informal Assessment, p. 1121; Vocabulary, p. 1122; Viewing and Representing, p. 1123; Grammar, p. 1125
- Choices & Challenges and Author Activity, pp. 1125–1126

Reading and Analyzing

Active Reading

DISTINGUISHING FACT FROM OPINION

Remind students that facts are verifiable pieces of information (the time and date are facts) and opinions express subjective responses and feelings ("Reading literature is fun," is an opinion). Encourage students to distinguish Brittain's feelings and opinions from the historical facts she presents.

Use **Unit Six Resource Book,** p. 56 for more practice.

Literary Analysis MEMOIR

Brittain's memoir deals with an important historical event—World War I—but this is presented from the writer's personal perspective. Remind students that a memoir is a form of autobiographical writing in which a person recalls significant events in his or her life. As students read, stress the importance of looking for the writer's personal perspective.

Review with students the definition of a memoir. Ask them what features of a memoir they can find on pages 1116–1117 that help support this definition. **Possible Responses:** narrative, first-person point of view, actual events recounted, newsworthy items with significance beyond the personal life of the writer, the presentation of feelings and opinions

Use **Unit Six Resource Book,** p. 57 for more exercises.

One young Sister,[2] who had previously been shelled at a Casualty Clearing Station, lost her nerve and rushed screaming through the Mess;[3] two others seized her and forcibly put her to bed, holding her down while the raid lasted to prevent her from causing a panic. I knew that I was more frightened than I had ever been in my life, yet all the time a tense, triumphant pride that I was not revealing my fear to the others held me to the semblance of self-control.

When a momentary lull came in the booms and the flashes, Hope, who had also been under fire at a C.C.S., gave way to the sudden bravado of rushing into the open to see whether the raiders had gone; she was still wearing her white cap, and a dozen trembling hands instantly pulled her indoors again, a dozen shakily shrill voices scolded her indiscretion. Gradually, after another brief burst of firing, the camp became quiet, though the lights were not turned on again that night. Next day we were told that most of the bombs had fallen on the village; the bridge over the Canche,[4] it was reported, had been smashed, and the train service had to be suspended while the engineers performed the exciting feat of mending it in twelve hours. . . .

. . . Within the next few weeks a good night's rest proved impossible for most of us. The liability to be called up for late convoys[5] had already induced a habit of light, restless dozing, and the knowledge that the raiders meant business and might return at any moment after sunset did not help us to settle down quietly and confidently during the hours of darkness. Whenever a particularly tiring day had battered our exhausted nerves into indifference, the lights went out as the result of alarming reports from Abbeville or Camiers[6] and revived our apprehensions. Rumor declared that we were all to be issued with steel helmets, and further spasmodic efforts were made to provide us with trenches in case of emergency.

Three weeks of such days and nights, lived without respite or off-duty time under the permanent fear of defeat and flight, reduced the staffs of the Étaples hospitals to the negative conviction that nothing mattered except to end the strain. England, panic-stricken, was frantically raising the military age to fifty and agreeing to the appointment of Foch[7] as Commander-in-Chief, but to us with our blistered feet, our swollen hands, our wakeful, reddened eyes, victory and defeat began—as indeed they were afterwards to prove—to seem very much the same thing. . . .

Just when the Retreat had reduced the strip of coast between the line and the sea to its narrowest dimensions, the summons came that I had subconsciously dreaded ever since my uncomfortable leave.

> Victory and defeat began—as indeed thay were afterwards to prove—to seem very much the same thing. . . .

Early in April a letter arrived from my father
to say that my mother had "crocked up" and 1
had been obliged, owing to the inefficiency of the domestic help then available, to go into a nursing home. What exactly was wrong remained unspecified, though phrases referred to

2. **Sister:** nurse.
3. **Mess:** mess hall—the place where people in the armed forces eat meals.
4. **Canche** (känsh): the river on which Étaples is located.
5. **convoys:** groups of vehicles traveling with protective escorts (here, they are bringing wounded soldiers).
6. **reports from Abbeville** (äb-vēl′) **or Camiers** (kä-myā′): In March 1918, the Germans were advancing on these French towns, which lie directly between Étaples and Paris. As the British retreated toward the coast, it was feared that Étaples itself might be captured or cut off.
7. **Foch** (fôsh): Ferdinand Foch, a French general who in March 1918 became commander of all Allied forces on the western front.

WORDS TO KNOW

semblance (sĕm′bləns) *n.* an outward appearance

bravado (brə-vä′dō) *n.* a reckless or false show of courage

Teaching Options

Preteaching Vocabulary

USING CONTEXT CLUES Call students' attention to the list of WORDS TO KNOW. Remind them that sometimes they can understand the meaning of an unfamiliar word by examining the context in which the word is used and inferring its meaning. Use the model sentence to demonstrate the strategy of using context clues that provide hints that allow readers to infer the word meaning.

Model Sentence

Agnes looked in the dining room and found everything *awry:* chairs overturned, the cloth pulled halfway off the table, water glasses toppled, and silverware on the floor.

Instruction

- Write the model sentence on the chalkboard.
- Ask a volunteer to summarize the meaning of the sentence.
- Have students use the meaning of the sentence to infer a meaning of the word *awry.*
- Ask a volunteer to use the word *awry* in a new sentence.

Exercises Read the following sentences. Ask students to use context clues to determine the meanings of the italicized terms.

1. Our mathematics teacher forgot to include part of the information in the problem we were

"toxic heart" and "complete general breakdown." My father had temporarily closed the flat and moved into a hotel, but he did not, he told me, wish to remain there. "As your mother and I can no longer manage without you," he concluded, "it is now your duty to leave France immediately and return to Kensington."[8]

I read these words with real dismay, for my father's interpretation of my duty was not, I knew only too well, in the least likely to agree with that of the Army, which had always been singularly unmoved by the worries of relatives. What was I to do? I wondered desperately. There was my family, confidently demanding my presence, and here was the offensive, which made every pair of experienced hands worth ten pairs under normal conditions. I remembered how the hastily imported VADs had gone sick at the 1st London[9] during the rush after the Somme;[10] a great push was no time in which to teach a tyro[11] her job. How much of my mother's breakdown was physical and how much psychological—the cumulative result of pessimism at home? It did not then occur to me that my father's sense of emergency was probably heightened by a subconscious determination to get me back to London before the Germans reached the Channel ports,[12] as everyone in England felt certain they would. I only knew that no one in France would believe a domestic difficulty to be so insoluble; if I were dead, or a male, it would have to be settled without me. I should merely be thought to have "wind-up,"[13] to be using my mother's health as an excuse to escape the advancing enemy or the threatening air raids.

Half-frantic with the misery of conflicting obligations, I envied Edward his complete powerlessness to leave the Army whatever happened at home. . . . What exhausts women in wartime is not the strenuous and unfamiliar tasks that fall upon them, nor even the hourly dread of death for husbands or lovers or brothers or sons; it is the incessant conflict between personal and national claims which wears out their energy and breaks their spirit.

That night, dizzy from work and indecision, I sat up in bed listening for an air raid and gazing stupidly at the flickering shadows cast by the candle lantern which was all the illumination that we were now allowed. Through my brain ran perpetually a short sentence which—having become, like the men, liable to sudden light-headed intervals—I could not immediately identify with anything that I had read.

" 'The strain all along,' " I repeated dully, " 'is very great . . . very great.' " What exactly did those words describe? The enemy within shelling distance—refugee Sisters crowding in with nerves all awry—bright moonlight, and airplanes carrying machine guns—ambulance trains jolting noisily into the siding, all day, all night—gassed men on stretchers, clawing the air—dying men, reeking with mud and foul green-stained bandages, shrieking and writhing in a grotesque travesty of manhood—dead men with fixed, empty eyes and shiny, yellow faces. . . . Yes, perhaps the strain all along *had* been very great. . . . **2**

Then I remembered; the phrase came out of my father's letter, and it described, not the offensive in France, but the troubles at home. The next day I went to the Matron's[14] office and interviewed the successor to the friendly Scottish Matron who had

8. **Kensington:** a residential section of London.
9. **VADs . . . at the 1st London:** Voluntary Aid Detachment nurses at another Étaples hospital.
10. **the Somme** (sŏm): In July 1916, the Allies had launched what turned into a devastating, months-long battle along the Somme River; it resulted in more than a million casualties.
11. **tyro** (tī′rō): beginner.
12. **Channel ports:** seaports on the English Channel.
13. **"wind-up"** (wĭnd′ŭp′): a British slang term meaning "nervousness" or "anxious excitement."
14. **Matron's:** head nurse's.

WORDS TO KNOW

insoluble (ĭn-sŏl′yə-bəl) *adj.* incapable of being solved
incessant (ĭn-sĕs′ənt) *adj.* never ceasing; constant
awry (ə-rī′) *adj.* twisted; faulty; disordered
travesty (trăv′ĭ-stē) *n.* a distorted, bizarre imitation

1117

Customizing Instruction

Multiple Learning Styles

Visual and Graphic Learners

Have students find maps of England and continental Europe, preferably from the early 20th century (during the time of World War I). Encourage students to chart on the maps the whereabouts of the narrator, her brother, and her family in France, Italy, and England.

Students Acquiring English

1 Explain that the present-day American equivalent of "crocked up" is *cracked up,* "to have suffered an emotional breakdown, or a nervous breakdown." Invite students to offer equivalent phrases from their native languages.

2 Make sure students understand that "the strain" refers to the pressures of war. The sensory details in these sentence fragments describe particular scenes of strain. Have students identify some of the images mentioned here that contribute to the strain of war as Brittain experiences it through her senses.

Possible Responses: the sounds of airplanes attacking them at night, of ambulances arriving with wounded men, of soldiers screaming in pain; the smell of mud and bandages; the sight of dead men's faces.

working on, and the omission made the problem *insoluble,* so none of us had an answer.

2. Although really scared during the flood, the new volunteer on the rescue squad put on a show of *bravado,* hoping it would be calming for others.
3. Because of her deep compassion for the pain of others, Beverly found the movie depicting the suffering during the war *excruciating* to watch.
4. Some people believe that good manners require us to show a *semblance* of delight upon receiving an unwanted gift, while others think people should always display their true emotions.
5. The *incessant* blowing of the foghorn, which continued day and night until the light was fixed, heralded the danger caused by the failure of the lighthouse.

Use **Unit Six Resource Book,** p. 58 for more practice.

A lesson on context clues appears on page 939 in the Pupil's Edition.

Reading and Analyzing

Reading Skills and Strategies:
RELEVANT DETAILS

A Ask students to find details that support the conclusion that Brittain was dissatisfied with life at home.

Possible Responses: Sentences such as "I returned to a society where no one discussed anything but the price of butter . . ." and "The agony of the last few weeks in France appeared not to interest London in comparison with . . ."

Reading Skills and Strategies:
MAKING INFERENCES

B Ask students to think about a time when they avoided thinking about something. Then ask them why they think the agony of France didn't interest people in London.

Possible Response: They did not want to think about the possibility of their loved ones dying in France or of their own country being invaded.

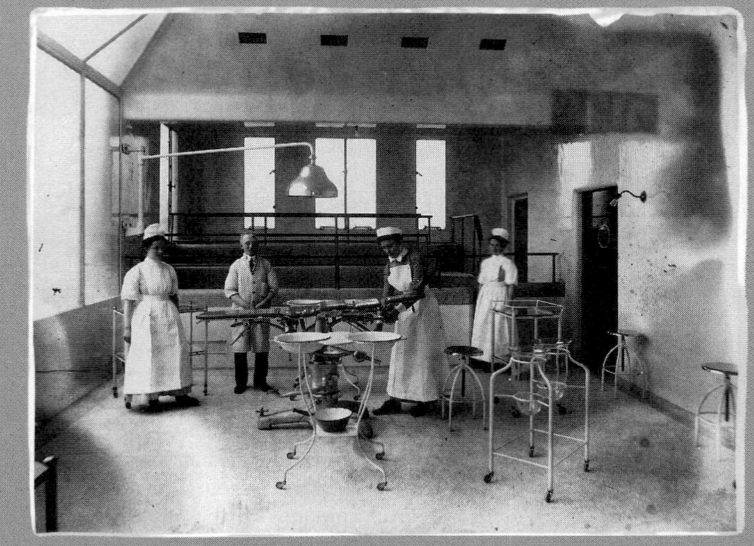

sent me on leave, and whose health had obliged her to leave Étaples and return to the calmer conditions of home service. The new Matron was old and charitable, but she naturally did not welcome my problem with enthusiasm. The application for long leave which I had hoped to put in would have, she said, no chance at all while this push was on; the only possibility was to break my contract, which I might be allowed to do if I made conditions at home sound serious enough.

"I'm giving you this advice against my will," she added. "I'm already short of staff and I can't hope to replace you."

So, with a sinking heart, I asked for leave to break my contract owing to "special circumstances," and returned to my ward feeling a cowardly deserter. Only to Edward could I express the explosive misery caused by my dilemma, and he replied with his usual comprehending sympathy.

"I can well understand how exasperating it must be for you to have to go home now . . . when you have just been in the eddying backwater of the sternest fight this War has known; it is one of those little ironies which life has ready to offer at a most inopportune moment. I suppose that the Armentières[15] push will have affected you more nearly still as it is not so very far away. . . ."

I was glad that my orders did not come through until almost the end of April, when the offensive against the British had slackened, and we knew for certain that we had not yet lost the War.

Early one morning I bade a forlorn farewell to my friends and went down alone in an ambulance to the station. . . . As the train passed through Hardelot,[16] I noticed that the woods on either side of the line were vivid with a golden green latticework of delicate leaves. For a whole month in which off-duty time had been impossible, I had ceased to be aware of the visible world of the French countryside; my eyes had seen nothing but the wards and the dying, the dirt and dried blood, the obscene wounds of

15. **Armentières** (är-mäN-tyĕr′): a town, only 40 miles from Étaples, taken by the Germans in April 1918.

16. **Hardelot** (är-də-lō′).

Teaching Options

Cross Curricular Link History

STRATEGIES OF WAR Paul von Hindenburg, having promised the German people that he would reach Paris by April 1, was determined to overrun the Allies before the Americans were fully involved. The Central Powers' April 1918 offensive was followed by a summer offensive, known as the Second Battle of the Marne, which was successfully stopped before the Germans crossed the Marne River to reach Paris. The success in rebuffing the Germans was due in part to the unified command of the Allies given to Marshall Ferdinand Foch, who became Commander-in-Chief of the Allied Armies in France in April.

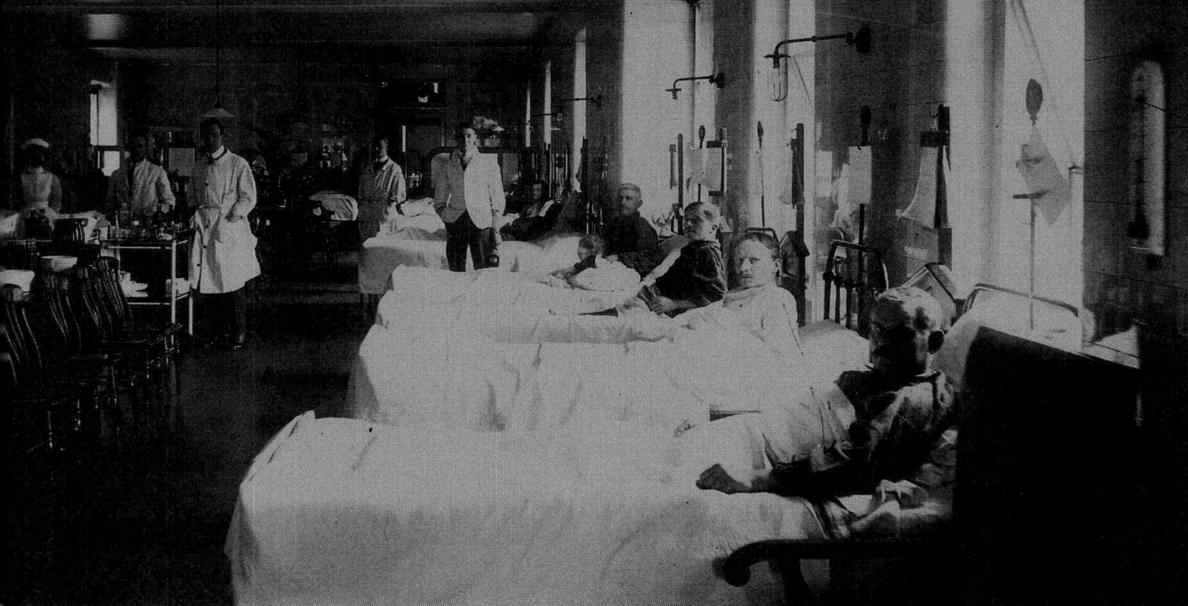

mangled men and the lotions and lint with which I had dressed them. Looking, now, at the pregnant buds, the green veil flung over the trees and the spilt cream of primroses in the bright, wet grass, I realized with a pang of astonishment that the spring had come.

I can look back more readily, I think, upon the War's tragedies—which at least had dignity—than upon those miserable weeks that followed my return from France. From a world in which life or death, victory or defeat, national survival or national extinction, had been the sole issues, I returned to a society where no one discussed anything but the price of butter and the incompetence of the latest "temporary."[17]. . . A

Keyed up as I had been by the month-long strain of daily rushing to and fro in attendance on the dying, and nightly waiting for the death which hovered darkly in the sky overhead, I found it excruciating to maintain even an appearance of interest and sympathy. Probably I did not succeed, for the triviality of everything drove me to despair. The old feeling of frustration that I had known . . . came back a thousand times intensified; while disasters smashed up the world around me I seemed to be marooned in a kind of death-in-life, with the three years' experience that now made me of some use to the Army all thrown away. 1

. . . Most bitterly of all I resented the constant dissipation of energy on what appeared to me to be nonessentials. My youth and health had mattered so much when the task was that of dragging wounded men back to life; I believed that the vitality which kept me going had helped others who had lost their own to live, and it seemed rather thrown away when it was all exploded upon persuading the grocer to give us a pot of jam. The agony of the last few weeks in France appeared not to interest London in comparison with the struggle to obtain sugar; the latter was discussed incessantly, but no one wanted even to hear about the former. . . . B

17. **temporary:** a domestic servant hired for a short time.

WORDS TO KNOW

excruciating (ĭk-skro͞o'shē-ā'tĭng) *adj.* intensely painful; agonizing
dissipation (dĭs'ə-pā'shən) *n.* a wasteful expenditure of resources

1119

Customizing Instruction

Students Acquiring English

1 Encourage students to use context clues to infer the meaning of the phrase "death-in-life."

Possible Response: a meaningless, unfulfilling life

Less Proficient Readers

Ask volunteers to review the relevant details about Brittain's wartime experience.

- What was the author's role in the war?
  Answer: nurse near the front lines
- What did her father want her to do?
  Answer: return home to England
- Why did her father ask her to return?
  Answer: Her mother had suffered a breakdown.

Help students set a purpose for reading by suggesting they read to find out what happened to Brittain at home and how the war continued to affect her.

Nursing Around the World

The activities of nursing have long been performed in many cultures in a variety of ways. St. Vincent de Paul (1580?-1660), a French priest, founded the Sisters of Charity and encouraged women to train in nursing. The improvement of mental facilities throughout Canada and the United States can be credited to a nurse named Dorthea Dix. Dix was a superintendent of Union army nurses during the American Civil War. Florence Nightingale (1820-1910), who is considered the founder of modern nursing, established the first nursing school in Britain at St. Thomas's Hospital, London, in 1860. In China, nursing has been linked to traditional Chinese medicine for centuries. No matter how nursing may have originated in various parts of the world, the nursing profession has the same goal in common—to provide help and healing to individuals. International Nurses Week is celebrated around the world during the week of May 12th, Florence Nightingale's birthday.

Reading and Analyzing

Reading Skills and Strategies:
MAKING INFERENCES

A Sometimes the answers to questions don't have to be given because we can figure them out. This is true in writing as well as in conversation. Ask students to infer the answers to the questions Brittain asks herself after receiving the letter from Norah.
Possible Response: She shouldn't have considered returning to an academic environment when her friends were at risk; the waste of her mind was insignificant; her decision to return home had been swayed by emotion rather than reason.

Reading Skills and Strategies:
MAKING CONNECTIONS

B Deep grief affects people differently, depending on their personalities and the context. Ask students how they reacted to Brittain's response to the news of her brother's death.
Answer: Students may think her "mechanical" reaction is due to shock.

I was no better reconciled to staying at home when I read in *The Times* a few weeks after my return that the persistent German raiders had at last succeeded in their intention of smashing up the Étaples hospitals, which, with the aid of the prisoner-patients, had so satisfactorily protected the railway line for three years without further trouble or expense to the military authorities.

It was clear from the guarded *communiqué*[18] that this time the bombs had dropped on the hospitals themselves, causing many casualties and far more damage than the breaking of the bridge over the Canche in the first big raid. Hope Milroy, I was thankful to remember, had been moved to Havre[19] a fortnight earlier, but a few days later a letter from Norah filled in the gaps of the official report. The hospital next door, she told me, had suffered the worst, and several Canadian Sisters had been killed. At 24 General one of the death-dealing bombs had fallen on
1 Ward 17, where I had nursed the pneumonias on night duty; it had shattered the hut, together with several patients, and wounded the VAD in charge, who was in hospital with a fractured skull. The Sisters' quarters were no longer safe after dark, she concluded, and they all had to spend their nights in trenches in the woods.

More than ever, as I finished her letter, I felt myself a deserter, a coward, a traitor to my patients and the other nurses.

A How could I have played with the idea—as I had, once or twice lately—of returning to Oxford[20] before the end of the War? What did the waste of an immature intellect matter, when such things could happen to one's friends? My comrades of the push had been frightened, hurt, smashed up—and I was not there with them, skulking[21] safely in England. Why, oh why, had I listened to home demands when my job was out there?

A brief note that came just afterwards from Edward seemed an appropriate—and fear-provoking—comment on the news from Étaples.

"Ma chère," he had written just before midnight on May 12th, *"la vie est brève*[22]—usually too short for me to write adequate letters, and likely to be shorter still."

For some time now, my apprehensions for his safety had been lulled by the long quiescence of the Italian front, which had seemed a haven of peace in contrast to our own raging vortex.[23] Repeatedly, during the German offensive, I had thanked God and the Italians who fled at Caporetto[24] that Edward was out of it, and rejoiced that the worst I had to fear from this particular push was the comparatively trivial danger that threatened myself. But now I felt the familiar stirrings of the old tense fear which had been such a persistent companion throughout the War. . . .

On Sunday morning, June 16th, I opened the *Observer,* which appeared to be chiefly concerned with the new offensive—for the moment at a standstill—in the Noyon-Montdidier[25] sector of the Western Front, and instantly saw at the head of a column the paragraph for which I had looked so long and so fearfully:

ITALIAN FRONT ABLAZE
GUN DUELS FROM MOUNTAIN TO SEA
BAD OPENING OF AN OFFENSIVE

. . . There was nothing to do in the midst of one's family but practice that concealment of fear which the long years of war had instilled,

18. ***communiqué*** (kô-mü-nē-kā′) *French:* an official communication.
19. **Havre** (hä′vrə): Le Havre, a French seaport used as an Allied troop and supply base.
20. **Oxford:** Oxford University.
21. **skulking:** hiding out.
22. ***Ma chère, . . . la vie est brève*** (mä shĕr′ lä vē′ ā brĕv′) *French:* My dear, . . . life is short.
23. **vortex:** whirl of activity.
24. **Caporetto** (kăp′ə-rĕt′ō): a 1917 battle near the Italian–Austro-Hungarian border that resulted in a major Allied defeat. (Edward was stationed in Italy.)
25. **Noyon-Montdidier** (nwä-yôN′ môN-dē-dyā′).

WORDS TO KNOW
quiescence (kwē-ĕs′əns) *n.* a state of quiet, stillness, or rest; inactivity

1120

Teaching Options

Speaking and Listening

NEWSCASTS

Instruction Even when a newscast presents no explicit opinions, it may slant a news story through the reporter's choice of details, through the use of loaded language, and through the editor's cutting and splicing of footage to construct the story. Listeners and viewers should be on the lookout for evidence of potential bias in newscasts.

Prepare Ask students to watch a television newscast at home. They should take notes on the presentation of the story.

Present Have students prepare reports for the class that present a general summary of the story and then an assessment of the report's objectivity or bias. They might want to describe or imitate the reporter's tone of voice and/or facial expressions as examples of potential subjective bias. Invite the other students to offer alternative angles to the story under discussion.

BLOCK SCHEDULING This activity is particularly well-suited for longer class periods.

thrusting it inward until one's subconscious became a regular prison house of apprehensions and inhibitions which were later to take their revenge. My mother had arranged to stay with my grandmother at Purley[26] that week in order to get a few days' change from the flat; it was the first time that she had felt well enough since her breakdown to think of going away, and I did not want the news from Italy to make her change her plans. At length, though with instinctive reluctance, she allowed herself to be prevailed upon to go, but a profound depression hung over our parting at Charing Cross.[27]

A day or two later, more details were published of the fighting in Italy, and I learnt that the Sherwood Foresters[28] had been involved in the "show" on the plateau.[29] After that I made no pretense at doing anything but wander restlessly round Kensington or up and down the flat, and, though my father retired glumly to bed every evening at nine o'clock, I gave up writing the semi-fictitious record which I had begun of my life in France. Somehow I couldn't bring myself even to wrap up the *Spectator* and *Saturday Review* that I sent every week to Italy, and they remained in my bedroom, silent yet eloquent witnesses to the dread which my father and I, determinedly conversing on commonplace topics, each refused to put into words.

By the following Saturday we had still heard nothing of Edward. The interval usually allowed for news of casualties after a battle was seldom so long as this, and I began, with an artificial sense of lightness unaccompanied by real conviction, to think that there was perhaps, after all, no news to come. I had just announced to my father, as we sat over tea in the dining room, that I really must do up Edward's papers and take them to the post office before it closed for the weekend, when there came the sudden loud clattering at the front-door knocker that always meant a telegram.

For a moment I thought that my legs would not carry me, but they behaved quite normally as I got up and went to the door. I knew what was in the telegram—I had known for a week—but because the persistent hopefulness of the human heart refuses to allow intuitive certainty to persuade the reason of that which it knows, I opened and read it in a tearing anguish of suspense.

"Regret to inform you Captain E. H. Brittain M.C.[30] killed in action Italy June 15th."

"No answer," I told the boy mechanically, and handed the telegram to my father, who had followed me into the hall. As we went back into the dining room I saw, as though I had never seen them before, the bowl of blue delphiniums on the table; their intense color, vivid, ethereal, seemed too radiant for earthly flowers. **B** Then I remembered that we should have to go down to Purley and tell the news to my mother.

> I knew what was in the telegram—I had known for a week—

Late that evening, my uncle brought us all back to an empty flat. Edward's death and our sudden departure had offered the maid—at that time the amateur prostitute—an agreeable opportunity for a few hours' freedom of which she had taken immediate advantage. She had not even finished the household handkerchiefs, which I had washed that morning and intended to iron after tea; when I went into the kitchen I found them still hanging, stiff as boards, over the clotheshorse near the fire where I had left them to dry.

---

26. **Purley:** a town south of London.
27. **Charing Cross:** Charing Cross Station, a railway terminal in central London.
28. **Sherwood Foresters:** the British regiment to which Edward belonged.
29. **"show" on the plateau:** battle on the Asiago Plateau in northeastern Italy.
30. **M.C.:** holder of the Military Cross, a medal of honor.

WORDS TO KNOW

ethereal (ĭ-thîr'ē-əl) *adj.* delicate; heavenly

Customizing Instruction

Students Acquiring English

1 Ask students to guess whom "the pneumonias" are.

Answer: patients suffering from pneumonia, an illness of the lungs.

Students who speak Romance languages may know words in their native languages that contain the prefix *pneumo-*, meaning "having to do with the lungs."

Assessment Informal Assessment

WRITING LETTERS

The selection refers to letters by Brittain's father, her brother, Edward, Brittain herself, and her friend Norah. Ask students to write letters to Vera Brittain expressing their responses to the selection.

RUBRIC

3 Full Accomplishment Letters reflect full understanding and insight into selection. Responses might show empathy for Brittain's conflicts and losses, and discuss her views on war.

2 Substantial Accomplishment Letters reflect general understanding of basic events and conflicts of selection.

1 Little or Partial Accomplishment Letters reflect little understanding of central events and conflicts of selection, or respond to them in ways that are obviously inappropriate.

Reading and Analyzing

Active Reading

DISTINGUISHING FACT FROM OPINION

Ask students to scan the page for facts and opinions within Brittain's writings. Remind students that while facts can be proven true or false, opinions are beliefs or judgments that cannot be proven. Many times, an opinion contains judgment words. *Ought, should, better, horrible,* and *lovely* are some examples of judgment words.

Possible Responses: Edward had suffered more than his friends, because he had to watch them die; stopping people who want to wage war is a better fight than war itself.

Literary Analysis: THEME

A Remind students that a theme is a central idea or message in a work of literature. The question at the beginning of the paragraph states one possible theme of the selection. Invite students to paraphrase it.

Possible Response: Life goes on.

Long after the family had gone to bed and the world had grown silent, I crept into the dining room to be alone with Edward's portrait. Carefully closing the door, I turned on the light and looked at the pale, pictured face, so dignified, so steadfast, so tragically mature. He had been through so much—far, far more than those beloved friends who had died at an earlier stage of the interminable War, leaving him alone to mourn their loss. Fate might have allowed him the little, sorry compensation of survival, the chance to make his lovely music[31] in honor of their memory. It seemed indeed the last irony that he should have been killed by the countrymen of Fritz Kreisler, the violinist whom of all others he had most greatly admired.

And suddenly, as I remembered all the dear afternoons and evenings when I had followed him on the piano as he played his violin, the sad, searching eyes of the portrait were more than I could bear, and falling on my knees before it I began to cry "Edward! Oh, Edward!" in dazed repetition, as though my persistent crying and calling would somehow bring him back.

The loss of Brittain's fiancé, brother, and friends in the war, as well as the death and suffering she witnessed in the hospitals, shaped the rest of her life. She became a pacifist and worked tirelessly to oppose war and to urge the resolving of differences through rational and peaceful means. Testament of Youth *was published in 1933, the same year Adolf Hitler became the head of government in Germany. Brittain wrote in the foreword to the book that her object was "to challenge that too easy, too comfortable relapse into forgetfulness which is responsible for history's most grievous repetitions." The following paragraph comes near the end of the book and gives her perspective on war several years after the end of World War I.*

. . . In spite of the War, which destroyed so much hope, so much beauty, so much promise, life is still here to be lived; so long as I am in the world, how can I ignore the obligation to be part of it, cope with its problems, suffer claims and interruptions? The surge and swell of its movements, its changes, its tendencies, still mold me and the surviving remnant of my generation whether we wish it or not, and no one now living will ever understand so clearly as ourselves, whose lives have been darkened by the universal breakdown of reason in 1914, how completely the future of civilized humanity depends upon the success of our present halting endeavors to control our political and social passions, and to substitute for our destructive impulses the vitalizing[32] authority of constructive thought. To rescue mankind from that domination by the irrational which leads to war could surely be a more exultant fight than war itself, a fight capable of enlarging the souls of men and women with the same heightened consciousness of living, and uniting them in one dedicated community whose common purpose transcends the individual. Only the purpose itself would be different, for its achievement would mean, not death, but life. ❖ A

31. **his lovely music:** Edward was an accomplished musician.
32. **vitalizing:** life-giving; invigorating.

Teaching Options

Vocabulary Strategy

PREFIXES

Instruction Sometimes knowing the meaning of a prefix helps make unfamiliar words become more familiar. When Brittain writes about incessant conflict, she means the conflict never ceases. The prefix "in" means "not." Other words with the same prefix are: *insoluble, involuntary, insecure,* and *infinite.*

Activity Have students work in pairs to find the meanings of the prefixes "dis" and "ex". Ask them to list words with each prefix and use them in sentences. What do the words in each list have in common? Students can infer the meaning of each prefix by looking for patterns in the word meanings.

Possible Responses: "Dis" means "away " or "not." Students can infer this meaning from words like dislike, disobedience, or disassemble. "Ex" means "away" or "from." Students can infer this meaning from words like expatriate, exhale, or excommunicate.

Use **Vocabulary Transparencies and Copymasters,** p. 61.

. . . In spite of the War, which destroyed so much hope, so much beauty, so much promise, life is still here to be lived.

1123

Customizing Instruction

Students Acquiring English

Make sure students understand that irony occurs when a situation turns out to be the opposite of, or different from, what one expected. Ask students why it is ironic that Edward, an accomplished violinist, is killed in the war by the Austrian Army.

Possible Response: Fritz Kreisler, the violinist Edward admired above all others, was born in Austria.

Gifted and Talented Students

Invite students to read other memoirs or novels about World War I, such as E. E. Cummings's *The Enormous Room,* Robert Graves's *Goodbye to All That,* and Erich Maria Remarque's *All Quiet on the Western Front.* They might want to prepare a comparative report on different personal responses to the war.

Mini Lesson Viewing and Representing

ART APPRECIATION

Instruction Personal belongings and their placement, arrangement, and care can often reveal information about the feelings and personality of their owners. Point out the various items on the bureau. Ask how the items and their arrangement reveal the family's feelings about Edward.

Possible Response: The arrangement may be a memorial to Edward: his photograph, reading glasses atop a book, and medals earned in the war. Perhaps the Brittain family wanted to make sure they would always remember Edward.

Application Ask students to consider how the pieces would be treated when the room was dusted. What care is implied by the leaning of the picture against the mirror? by the presentation on lace? What might be in the box?

Possible Response: All the elements put together show great care: The mirror is carefully balanced and must be rebalanced every time the bureau is dusted; the glasses must be treated with delicacy as well. The lace highlights the picture and gives the picture an added personal touch. The box might contain valuable memorabilia and trinkets.

GUIDING STUDENT RESPONSE

Connect to the Literature

1. What Do You Think?
Guidelines for student response: Students should supply evidence from the text to support their opinions of Vera Brittain. Responses should also show some understanding of the hard experiences that she had lived through.

Comprehension Check
- He asks Brittain to return home.
- She breaks her contract.
- He dies in the war.

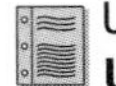 Use Selection Quiz in **Unit Six Resource Book,** p. 59.

Think Critically

2. Possible Response: She did the right thing in obeying her parents and fulfilling the expectations of her culture; she should have been more self-assertive, for the sake of the soldiers who needed her, for the sake of women, and for the sake of her own fulfillment.
3. The facts Brittain includes about the war give her account credibility and authority; the reader thinks Brittain knows what she's talking about. Her grief for the people she lost and her constant concern about the fighting show that she understands the gravity and potential consequences of the conflict.
4. Possible Responses: the loss of her brother; her inability to help the soldiers; her feelings of guilt for leaving her comrades.
5. Students who disagree may believe that it is more in our nature to be at war than to work for peace.

Literary Analysis

Paired Activity Have students brainstorm the differences between memoir and fiction. Remind them that although fiction may include elements of truth, memoirs are usually assumed to be entirely true.

Review Theme Students may want to think about themes from different angles: family relations, national crises, war, personal growth, and so on.

Connect to the Literature

1. **What Do You Think?** What did you think of Vera Brittain when you finished reading?

Comprehension Check
- What does Brittain's father request in his letter?
- How does Brittain manage to leave the war?
- What happens to Edward?

Think Critically

2. What is your opinion of the way Brittain handled her conflicting obligations?

THINK ABOUT
- her responsibilities at the field hospital
- her parents' situation and expectations
- the position of women in society at the time
- what she most wanted for herself

3. ACTIVE READING DISTINGUISHING FACT FROM OPINION According to the writer Carolyn Heilbrun, Brittain's memoirs are effective because she "understood the terror of the world she lived through." In the light of this statement, review the lists you made in your  READER'S NOTEBOOK. How do you think the historical facts and the feelings and opinions presented in the memoir support Heilbrun's claim?

4. What do you think was hardest for Brittain to deal with after she returned to England?

5. Reread the last paragraph of the selection. Do you agree with Brittain's ideas about humanity and war? Explain your opinion.

Extend Interpretations

6. **What If?** What might have happened if Brittain had not returned to England when she did?

7. **Different Perspectives** If Brittain had been a man, how would her sense of obligation have been different during World War I?

8. **Connect to Life** Do you think that women today face conflicting obligations similar to those experienced by Brittain? Support your answer with examples.

Literary Analysis

MEMOIR Most **memoirs**—autobiographical writing in which a person recalls significant events in his or her life—share the following characteristics:

- They usually are structured as narratives told by the writers themselves, using the **first-person point of view.**
- They are true accounts of actual events.
- Although basically personal, they may deal with events having a significance beyond the writers' lives.
- Unlike strictly historical accounts, they often include the writers' feelings and opinions about historical events.

Paired Activity At one point, Brittain planned to fictionalize her war experiences in a long novel. With a partner, discuss how the selection's being a memoir rather than a fictionalized account affects its impact. Keep in mind the characteristics of a memoir as you discuss your ideas.

REVIEW THEME **Theme** is an idea or message communicated by a work of literature. It is a perception about life or human nature. Some themes are stated directly, and some are implied; but every theme is an expression of the significance of the story being told. Certain works contain more than one theme. With a group of classmates, determine the theme or themes of Brittain's memoir. State each one in a single sentence.

Extend Interpretations

What If? Students may pursue several avenues: for example, that Brittain might have died in France or that her feelings about the bombing and her brother's death would not have been mingled with feelings of shame, self-doubt, and cowardice.

Different Perspectives She might not have felt obligated to return to England to care for her parents. A man would have had a more clearly defined sense of duty to the war, because men were expected to put obligations to the country ahead of obligations to family.

Connect to Life Students may believe women today struggle more than ever to balance their career, family, and personal life. Others might feel these conflicting roles are less pronounced.

Writing Options

1. Letter to Father If Brittain had decided to remain in France, how might she have explained her decision to her father? Imagine you are Brittain and write a letter to your father, explaining why you are not returning to England.

2. Words of Advice After returning to England, Brittain felt herself to be "a deserter, a coward, a traitor to my patients and the other nurses." Make notes of what you might say to her in response to these feelings.

3. War Poem Create a poem that conveys Brittain's thoughts and emotions about the bombing raids, about the death of her brother, or about war's effects on humanity.

Activities & Explorations

1. Book Jacket Design an eye-catching book jacket for Vera Brittain's *Testament of Youth.* Illustrate a scene from her memoir, and write a brief advertising message that would appeal to people of Brittain's generation. ~ **ART**

2. Class Survey Conduct a class survey to determine how many people think Brittain's decision to return home at her father's request was the right one. Tabulate the results and discuss why people responded as they did. ~ **SPEAKING AND LISTENING**

Inquiry & Research

1. Chemical Warfare Research and report on the development of chemical warfare during World War I. What chemical weapons and other technologies used in World War I were new? How did the technological developments affect the nature of war?

More Online: Research Starter www.mcdougallittell.com

2. World War I On a map of the world, mark the battlefronts of World War I. Use encyclopedias or books about the war as resources. Be sure to identify the area of France where Vera Brittain served as a nurse and the area of Italy where her brother was killed.

Vocabulary in Action

ACTIVITY: MEANING CLUES On your paper, write the word that is described by each clue below.

1. Recyclers and conservationists oppose this in people's use of nature.
2. A person who wears expensive clothes may be wealthy only in this.
3. It would be foolish to expect to find this in an emergency room or a basketball game.
4. One's clothing might be this after a wrestling match, as might one's emotions after an argument.
5. Dentists use Novocain and other anesthetics to keep their treatments from being this.
6. Most people will quit working on a problem that seems this.
7. This is a harsh misrepresentation of what it copies.
8. Rain during a monsoon, cold at the North Pole, and complaints about taxes can all be said to be this.
9. Certain otherworldly works of art might be called this.
10. This is what a dog demonstrates by barking fiercely at a bigger dog that is safely on the other side of a sturdy fence.

WORDS TO KNOW

awry	excruciating	semblance
bravado	incessant	travesty
dissipation	insoluble	
ethereal	quiescence	

Building Vocabulary
Several Words to Know in this lesson contain prefixes and suffixes. For an in-depth study of word parts, see page 1104.

Mini Lesson Grammar

VERBS: PASSIVE VOICE

Instruction When the subject of a sentence is *acted upon,* the sentence is in the passive voice. Explain that the passive voice is useful when the person or thing doing the action is unknown or when a writer wants to emphasize the person or thing receiving the action.

Activity Write on the chalkboard:

Vera Brittain was trained as an army nurse.

Her fiancé and her brother were killed by enemy fire.

Ask students to identify the voice in these sentences. *(passive)* In the first sentence, is the identity of the person or thing who performed the action stated? *(no)* In the second sentence? *(yes, enemy fire)* Is it important to emphasize enemy fire by making it the subject of the sentence, "Enemy fire killed her fiancé and her brother"? *(no)* Therefore, there is no need to change either of these sentences to the active voice.

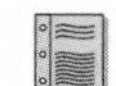

Use **Grammar Transparencies and Copymasters,** p. 101.

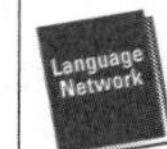

Use McDougal Littell's ***Language Network*** for more instruction and practice in passive voice.

Writing Options

1. **Letter to Father** Remind students that this letter should not only fit into the persuasive writing category, but must also show sensitivity and compassion for Brittain's father and his dilemma as well.
2. **Words of Advice** Before students begin, encourage them to pick a persona in which they will pretend to speak to Brittain, to help them focus what they would say and how they would say it.
3. **War Poem** You may want to make this exercise more challenging by having students find and discuss some of the poems written by British citizens who fought in World War I (Rupert Brooke, Wilfred Owen, Siegfried Sassoon, etc.) and follow the style or form of one of them.

Activities & Explorations

1. **Book Jacket** Encourage students to examine the jackets of several memoirs and novels about war, especially World War I classics such as *All Quiet on the Western Front.*
2. **Class Survey** Encourage students to list the criteria they used to make their decisions.

Inquiry & Research

1. **Chemical Warfare** Mustard gas, the major chemical weapon used in World War I, is a colorless, oily, sweet-smelling gas whose burning effects on the skin resemble those of mustard oil. It causes severe blistering and eye inflammation, often leading to blindness, and damages the respiratory tract and lungs if inhaled.

More Online: Research Starter www.mcdougallittell.com

2. **World War I** Encourage students to learn about changes in European borders that have occurred since World War I. Students should use writing to compile and explore their research.

Vocabulary in Action

1. dissipation
2. semblance
3. quiescence
4. awry
5. excruciating
6. insoluble
7. travesty
8. incessant
9. ethereal
10. bravado

Author Activity

Worker for Peace Students may find these sources helpful

- *Testament of Youth: An Autobiographical Study of the Years 1900–1925* (Penguin, 1994).
- *Testament of Youth* (Penguin Audiobooks, 1996).
- *Testament of a Peace Lover: Letters from Vera Brittain,* 1991.
- *Vera Brittain's Diary: 1939–1945* (Ulverscroft, 1993).

Vera Brittain

1893–1970

Other Works
Testament of Friendship
Testament of Experience

The Great War Vera Brittain was reared in a comfortable middle-class home in northern England. She grew up, fell in love, and expected to live a rather conventional life—except for attending college, which few women of her time could do—but World War I got in the way of her plans. By the time she entered Oxford University's Somerville College in 1914, the war was already underway in Europe, and in 1915 she decided to postpone her studies to serve in the war like her brother, her fiancé, and her friends. From 1915 to 1919, she worked as a Red Cross nurse in several British army hospitals.

Birth of a Pacifist Brittain lost her fiancé, two friends, and her brother in the war. She also lost her youth. "My work and experiences during the war," she wrote, "turned me from an ordinary patriotic young woman into a convinced pacifist." Yet when Brittain finally returned to college after the war, she found herself serving as an unwelcome reminder of the war that her fellow students longed to forget.

Something of Value Throughout the war years, Brittain had recorded her experiences in a diary. At first, she attempted to fictionalize her experiences, but finding that her efforts rang false, she began writing a personal account of the war in the hope that she could "rescue something that might be of value . . . from the smashing up of my own youth by the war." She also hoped to remind her readers of the great suffering caused by war and to convince them to work for peace. First published in 1933, *Testament of Youth* became an immediate success, with more than 167,000 copies sold in the first year. It was acclaimed as "a moving elegy to a lost generation."

Groundbreaker Brittain continued to write memoirs about her experiences; she also continued to break new ground for women by persisting in her career after marrying. Throughout her life, Brittain was active in peace movements, for she firmly believed that "war, which is man-created, can be man-prevented."

Author Activity

Worker for Peace Brittain was a committed pacifist. Find out more about her long involvement in antiwar movements.

PREPARING to *Read*

from The Speeches, May 19, 1940

Speech by WINSTON CHURCHILL

Comparing Literature of the World

Winston Churchill's Speeches and Elie Wiesel's *Night*

The world would never be the same again after World War II. This lesson and the one that follows present an opportunity for examining two different voices and the challenges they faced during this bleak chapter of history. Specific points of comparison in the Wiesel lesson will help you understand the differences in experience and perspective of the two writers.

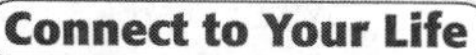

Connect to Your Life

Moving Words Think about the most memorable speech you have ever heard. It may be one delivered by a classmate or a politician, or it may be one in a play or movie. Jot down words and phrases that describe your most vivid memories of the speech. Your description may touch on powerful statements made by the speaker, details of the speaker's tone of voice and body language, emotions you felt during the speech, or the reaction of the audience. Share your experience with some classmates.

Build Background

World War II World War II began in Europe two years before the United States became involved. Between September 1939 and May 1940, Germany—which had already annexed Austria and most of Czechoslovakia—conquered Poland, Denmark, and Norway. Just nine days before Churchill's speech, Hitler's army invaded Holland and Belgium, sweeping through those countries on its way into France. By May 19, 1940, the British troops that had been fighting in western Europe had been backed up against the ocean, ready to retreat to England.

Winston Churchill, who had just been chosen prime minister, had only three hours to prepare this speech for delivery on a BBC (British Broadcasting Corporation) radio broadcast. Although Churchill had been in politics for years, his wartime speeches made him famous and inspired the British people working on the home front to greater efforts. The spirit and determination of these workers, both male and female, during the darkest moments of the war are reflected in Churchill's speeches.

WORDS TO KNOW
Vocabulary Preview
animate, dogged, gravity, indomitable, retaliate

Focus Your Reading

LITERARY ANALYSIS PERSUASION Churchill made this radio speech at a time when the Germans appeared to be winning World War II. His goal was to persuade the British people not to lose heart. **Persuasion**—the technique of convincing an audience to adopt an opinion, perform an action, or both—generally involves two elements:

- **logical appeals** that put forward reasons and evidence to support opinions
- **emotional appeals** that stir feelings within the audience

As you read Churchill's speech, consider how well he balances these persuasive techniques.

ACTIVE READING EVALUATING PERSUASIVE LANGUAGE In making emotional appeals to an audience, a speaker or writer may use **loaded language**—words and phrases with strong emotional content. Loaded language may be used legitimately to reinforce arguments, or it may be used inappropriately to mislead by manipulating the feelings of the audience. Be on the lookout for loaded language in persuasive writing and consider its impact.

READER'S NOTEBOOK In a chart like the one shown, note examples of loaded language in the speech. Record the information they convey, the ideas they suggest, and the emotions they inspire.

Loaded Word or Phrase	Information Provided	Ideas Suggested	Emotions Inspired

LESSON RESOURCES

UNIT SIX RESOURCE BOOK, pp. 60–64

ASSESSMENT RESOURCES
Formal Assessment, pp. 207–208
Teacher's Guide to Assessment and Portfolio Use
Test Generator

SKILLS TRANSPARENCIES AND COPYMASTERS
Reading and Critical Thinking
- Identifying Persuasive Techniques, T25 (for Active Reading, p. 1127)

Grammar
- Passive Voice: Weak Subjects, C168 (for Mini Lesson, p. 1134)

Vocabulary
- Connotation, C90 (for Mini Lesson, pp. 1128–1129)

Writing
- Generating Writing Ideas, T1 (for Writing Options, p. 1134)

Communications
- Impromptu Speaking: Debate, T15 (for Activities & Explorations, p. 1134)

INTEGRATED TECHNOLOGY
Audio Library
LaserLinks
- Author Background: Winston Churchill. See **Teacher's SourceBook,** p. 79.

Internet: Research Starter
Visit our website:
www.mcdougallittell.com

OVERVIEW

This selection is included in the **Grade 12 InterActive Reader.**

Objectives

1. understand and appreciate a **persuasive speech (Literary Analysis)**
2. appreciate the author's use of **persuasion (Literary Analysis)**
3. **evaluate persuasive language** in Churchill's speech **(Active Reading)**

Summary

In his first speech as prime minister, Churchill informs the British people of the German invasion of France and the impending attack upon England. He describes the formidable French army and the heroism of the English Air Force but reminds his listeners that a long ordeal is ahead. Churchill promises that England will fight to the end, which "can only be glorious." He vows that England and France will never surrender and adds that the British and French will "rescue not only Europe but mankind from the foulest and most soul-destroying tyranny which has ever darkened and stained the pages of history."

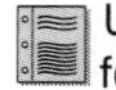

Use **Unit Six Resource Book,** p. 60 for additional support.

Thematic Link

In an effort to motivate England to defeat the **shocking reality** of Hitler's aggression, Churchill wrote this speech and others, which underline the theme of sacrificing oneself for the good of one's country

5-Minute Warm-Up

Daily Language SkillBuilder

Have students **proofread** the display sentences on page 979k and write them correctly. The sentences also appear on Transparency 31 of **Grammar Transparencies and Copymasters.**

Preteaching Vocabulary

If you would like to preteach the WORDS TO KNOW for this selection, use the Mini Lesson on p. 1128.

TEACHING THE LITERATURE

Reading and Analyzing

Literary Analysis PERSUASION

Lead a discussion with students about speeches they have heard. Some students may have heard or viewed recordings of Martin Luther King, Jr.'s "I Have a Dream" speech. Ask students which aspect of the speeches they found most persuasive—the overall message, the delivery, or the specific arguments.

Use **Unit Six Resource Book** p. 62 for more exercises.

Active Reading
EVALUATING PERSUASIVE LANGUAGE

After students have read p. 1129, have them share some examples of loaded language that they recorded in their Reader's Notebooks. Ask them why they thought these were examples of persuasive language—what emotions did they evoke, what images did they conjure, and so on.

Use **Unit Six Resource Book** p. 61 for more practice.

Literary Analysis: PARALLELISM

Explain that speakers often use parallelism—the repetition of similar grammatical structures to express related ideas—to stir emotions, control pace, and create connections among ideas. Have students find examples of parallelism on p. 1129.

Possible Responses: the repeated "if" structure in the second paragraph; "No officer or man, no brigade or division" in the third paragraph

from

The SPEECHES

May 19, 1940

UPI/Bettmann.

1128

Teaching Options

Preteaching Vocabulary

CONNOTATIONS OF WORDS

Instruction Explain that Churchill's persuasive writing style includes many words and phrases with strong connotations—that is, words and phrases loaded with strong feelings, associations, or even judgments. Here are some of the "loaded" terms that appear in the first two paragraphs of his speech:

- battle is raging
- ravaging the open country
- penetrated deeply
- magnificent efforts
- genius for recovery
- dogged endurance

Point out that in each instance, Churchill could have chosen another word or term to create a different, less extreme effect. For example, *ravaging the open country* and *penetrated deeply*—as opposed to *advancing across the fields* and *caused damage*—make us think of terrorism and violation, which is Churchill's intent.

Exercises Have students replace the underlined word in each sentence with one of the WORDS TO KNOW.

Winston Churchill

I speak to you for the first time as Prime Minister in a solemn hour for the life of our country, of our Empire, of our Allies, and, above all, of the cause of Freedom. A tremendous battle is raging in France and Flanders.[1] The Germans, by a remarkable combination of air bombing and heavily armored tanks, have broken through the French defenses north of
1 the Maginot Line, and strong columns of their armored vehicles are ravaging the open country, which for the first day or two was without defenders. They have penetrated deeply and spread alarm and confusion in their track. Behind them there are now appearing infantry in lorries,[2] and behind them, again, the large masses are moving forward. The regroupment of the French armies to make head against, and also to strike at, this intruding wedge has been proceeding for several days, largely assisted by the magnificent efforts of the Royal Air Force.

We must not allow ourselves to be intimidated by the presence of these armored vehicles in unexpected places behind our lines. If they are behind our Front, the French are also at many points fighting actively behind theirs. Both sides are therefore in an extremely dangerous position. And if the French Army, and our own Army, are well handled, as I believe they will be; if the French retain that genius for recovery and counterattack for which they have so long been famous; and if the British Army shows the dogged endurance and solid fighting power of which there have been so many examples in the past—then a sudden transformation of the scene might spring into being.

It would be foolish, however, to disguise the gravity of the hour. It would be still more foolish to lose heart and courage or to suppose that well-trained, well-equipped armies numbering three or four millions of men can be overcome in the space of a few weeks, or even months, by a scoop, or raid of mechanized vehicles, however formidable. We may look with confidence to the stabilization of the Front in France, and to the general engagement of the masses, which will enable the qualities of the French and British soldiers to be matched squarely against those of their adversaries. For myself, I have invincible confidence in the French Army and its leaders. Only a very small part of that splendid army has yet been heavily engaged; and only a very small part of France has yet been invaded. There is good evidence to show that practically the whole of the specialized and mechanized forces of the enemy have been already thrown into the battle; and we know that very heavy losses have been inflicted upon them. No officer or man, no brigade or division, which grapples at close quarters with the enemy, wherever encountered, can fail to make a worthy contribution to the general result. The Armies must cast away the idea of resisting behind concrete lines or natural obstacles, and must realize that mastery can only be regained by furious and unrelenting assault. And this spirit must not only animate the High Command, but must inspire every fighting man.

In the air—often at serious odds—often at odds hitherto thought overwhelming—we have

1. **Flanders:** western Belgium.
2. **lorries:** the British term for motor trucks.

WORDS TO KNOW
dogged (dô′gĭd) *adj.* persistent; stubborn
gravity (grăv′ĭ-tē) *n.* seriousness; importance
animate (ăn′ə-māt′) *v.* to encourage; motivate

1129

Customizing Instruction

Less Proficient Readers
Read aloud the first three paragraphs of the speech. Ask students which of Churchill's points they find encouraging and which they find discouraging.

Set a Purpose Ask students to look for additional points of encouragement or discouragement as they read.

Students Acquiring English
The long sentences in this speech may challenge students. Encourage them to break long sentences into shorter ones. In addition, tell them to keep a dictionary close at hand while reading the speech, because Churchill uses many difficult and uncommon words.

Use **Spanish Study Guide** for additional support, pp. 266–268.

Gifted and Talented
Have students listen to tapes of Churchill speaking. Ask them to analyze his style of delivery and to draw comparisons to the styles of other famous speakers.

Multiple Learning Styles
Visual Learners

1 Remind students that the Maginot Line was a system of heavy fortifications that guarded the eastern border of France, from Belgium to Switzerland. Have students locate a map showing the Maginot Line. Then, help them trace the route of the German army, who outflanked the Maginot Line by entering France through Belgium.

1. My mother's *stubborn* efforts to repair the air conditioner were to no avail.
   Answer: dogged
2. When the medic determined the *seriousness* of the soldier's injury, she immediately contacted the base camp.
   Answer: gravity
3. The captain's brave actions inspired his troops.
   Answer: animated
4. Lady Capulet wanted her husband to strike back against the Montagues for the death of Tybalt.
   Answer: retaliate
5. The irrepressible politician ran for mayor once again.
   Answer: indomitable

Use **Unit Six Resource Book** p. 63 for more practice.

A lesson on connotation appears on page 645 in the Pupil's Edition.

Reading and Analyzing

Reading Skills and Strategies: SUMMARIZING

A Have students summarize the status of the war as Churchill has described it up to this point.

Possible Response: Germany has invaded France by entering through Belgium. The French armies are counterattacking, aided by the Royal Air Force. There have been a number of air battles between Britain and Germany, in which the Royal Air Force has done well. The heavy British bombers have also damaged German oil refineries.

Literary Analysis PERSUASION

B Ask students whether Churchill's argument for more munitions is based on logic or emotion.

Possible Response: logic, because it sets forth a cause-effect connection without regard to emotion

C Ask students whether the passage on fighting to the end is an appeal to logic or to emotion.

Answer: emotion

Literary Analysis: ALLUSION

D Remind students that an allusion is a reference to a historical or fictional person, place, or event with which the reader is assumed to be familiar. Churchill's allusion to "the long history of France and England" is a reference to such events as the Hundred Years' War (1337–1453), in which France successfully resisted British attempts at conquest; the Napoleonic Wars; and World War I, in which the two nations were allies. Have students find other examples of allusion on these pages.

Possible Responses: Trinity Sunday, the Bible verse

Our task is not only to win the battle—but to win the War.

been clawing down three or four to one of our enemies; and the relative balance of the British and German Air Forces is now considerably more favorable to us than at the beginning of the battle. In cutting down the German bombers, we are fighting our own battle as well as that of France. My confidence in our ability to fight it
A out to the finish with the German Air Force has been strengthened by the fierce encounters which have taken place and are taking place. At the same time, our heavy bombers are striking
1 nightly at the taproot of German mechanized power, and have already inflicted serious damage upon the oil refineries on which the Nazi effort to dominate the world directly depends.

We must expect that as soon as stability is reached on the Western Front, the bulk of that hideous apparatus of aggression which gashed Holland into ruin and slavery in a few days, will be turned upon us. I am sure I speak for all when I say we are ready to face it; to endure it; and to retaliate against it—to any extent that the unwritten laws of war permit. There will be many men, and many women, in this island who when the ordeal comes upon them, as come it will, will feel comfort, and even a pride—that they are sharing the perils of our lads at the Front—soldiers, sailors and airmen, God bless 2

WORDS TO KNOW **retaliate** (rĭ-tăl'ē-āt') *v.* to take revenge; pay back in kind

Teaching Options

Cross Curricular Link History

VICHY France surrendered to Germany on June 22, 1940, and an occupation government with headquarters in Vichy was set up. The Vichy regime is often referred to as collaborationist because it cooperated with the Nazis, going so far as turning over French Jews to the Germans. However, the French Resistance, an underground organization, and the Free French forces under General Charles de Gaulle continued to oppose the Nazis. After D-Day—the Allied landing in Normandy—the French Resistance rose up and began to fight the Germans garrisoned in Paris. De Gaulle and the French felt that the liberation of Paris was of utmost importance. The city was officially liberated on August 24, 1944, and became a symbol of the impending Allied victory.

them—and are drawing away from them a part at least of the onslaught they have to bear. Is not this the appointed time for all to make the utmost exertions in their power? If the battle is to be won, we must provide our men with ever-increasing quantities of the weapons and ammunition they need. We must have, and have quickly, more airplanes, more tanks, more shells, more guns. There is imperious[3] need for these B vital munitions. They increase our strength against the powerfully armed enemy. They replace the wastage of the obstinate struggle; and the knowledge that wastage will speedily be replaced enables us to draw more readily upon our reserves and throw them in now that everything counts so much.

Our task is not only to win the battle—but to win the War. After this battle in France abates its force, there will come the battle for our island—for all that Britain is, and all that Britain means. That will be the struggle. In that supreme emergency we shall not hesitate to take every step, even the most drastic, to call forth from our people the last ounce and the last inch of effort of which they are capable. The interests of property, the hours of labor, are nothing compared with the struggle for life and honor, for right and freedom, to which we have vowed ourselves.

I have received from the Chiefs of the French Republic, and in particular from its indomitable Prime Minister, M. Reynaud,[4] the most sacred pledges that whatever happens they will fight to the end, be it bitter or be it glorious. Nay, if we fight to the end, it can only be glorious.

Having received His Majesty's commission, I have found an administration of men and women of every party and of almost every point of view. We have differed and quarreled in the past; but now one bond unites us all—to wage C war until victory is won, and never to surrender ourselves to servitude and shame, whatever the cost and the agony may be. This is one of the most awe-striking periods in the long history of France and Britain. It is also beyond doubt the most sublime. Side by side, unaided except by their kith and kin[5] in the great Dominions[6] and by the wide Empires which rest beneath their shield—side by side, the British and French peoples have advanced to rescue not only Europe but mankind from the foulest and most soul-destroying tyranny which has ever darkened and stained the pages of history. Behind them—behind us—behind the armies and fleets of Britain and France—gather a group of shattered States and bludgeoned races: the Czechs, the Poles, the Norwegians, the Danes, the Dutch, the Belgians—upon all of whom the long night of barbarism will descend, unbroken even by a star of hope, unless we conquer, as conquer we must; as conquer we shall.

Today is Trinity Sunday.[7] Centuries ago words D were written to be a call and a spur to the faithful servants of Truth and Justice: "Arm yourselves, and be ye men of valor, and be in readiness for the conflict; for it is better for us to perish in battle than to look upon the outrage of our nation and our altar. As the Will of God is in Heaven, even so let it be."[8] ❖

---

3. **imperious** (ĭm-pîr′ē-əs): urgent; pressing.
4. **M. Reynaud:** Paul Reynaud, who had long argued, like Churchill, for firmness toward Germany and for a close British-French alliance. (*M.* is an abbreviation of *Monsieur,* "Mister.")
5. **kith and kin:** friends and relatives.
6. **Dominions:** self-governing nations within the British Commonwealth.
7. **Trinity Sunday:** the eighth Sunday after Easter, dedicated to the Trinity (Father, Son, and Holy Spirit).
8. **"Arm yourselves . . . let it be":** a quotation from 1 Maccabees 3:58–60. This book of the Apocrypha (found in only some versions of the Bible) tells of the heroism of the Maccabees, a Jewish family, in preventing the destruction of Judaism by the Syrians during the second century B.C.

WORDS TO KNOW **indomitable** (ĭn-dŏm′ĭ-tə-bəl) *adj.* not easily discouraged or defeated; unconquerable

Customizing Instruction

Students Acquiring English

1 Help students understand the literal meaning of *taproot.*

Answer: the long root of a plant or a tree that reaches down toward the water table.

Then, ask them how Churchill is using this word figuratively.

Possible Responses: to compare the oil refineries to a taproot; to emphasize the importance of the object of the British attack.

2 Point out that Churchill's use of the word "lads" reflects his British culture, and that we would say "boys" or "men."

Less Proficient Readers

Have students paraphrase Churchill's long sentences in their own words to aid understanding. Also encourage them to break these long sentences into shorter ones and replace difficult or uncommon words with ones that are more familiar.

Gifted and Talented

Explain that the Battle of Britain was a series of German attacks on England from August to October 1940. Although greatly outnumbered, the Royal Air Force prevented a German invasion of England and lost 900 planes to the German Luftwaffe's 2,300. After their failure in the air, the Germans tried bombing English cities at night—the "blitz"—but that did not break the British will. The Battle of Britain was the first major defeat of the Nazis; history's first wartime use of radar helped make it possible. Have groups of students do some research on the Battle of Britain and present brief reports to the class on different aspects of the battle.

Assessment Standardized Test Practice

IDENTIFYING EMOTIONAL APPEALS

To provide students with some help in answering multiple choice questions, read aloud or write on the chalkboard the following question.

Which of the following statements from Churchill's essay best shows emotional appeal?

A. They have penetrated deeply and spread alarm and confusion in their track.

B. Both sides are therefore in an extremely dangerous position.

C. In cutting down the German bombers, we are fighting our own battle as well as that of France.

D. We have differed and quarreled in the past; but now one bond unites us all—to wage war until victory is won, and never to surrender ourselves to servitude and shame, whatever the cost and the agony may be.

Guide students to understand that, although all sentences are persuasive, only D clearly reflects emotional appeal. The language in A, B, and C is very terse, implying logic and fact. In contrast, the language in D is designed to evoke strong emotions in the listener.

Reading and Analyzing

Literary Analysis: SIMILE

Have students find similes in the first stanza and tell what is being compared.

Possible Responses: "as huge as Asia"—mother and Asia; "Irresistible as Rabelais"—mother and Rabelais; "like a little dog following a brass band"—follower and little dog, mother and brass band

Literary Analysis: ALLUSION

A Have students find out who Rabelais was. What does the reference to Rabelais indicate about the author's mother?

Answer: He was a late medieval French writer of fantastic, humorous tales with a great appetite for life. The reference to Rabelais is an indication that the author's mother has an irresistible sense of humor and outlook.

To My MOTHER

George Barker

Portrait of Mrs. B. (1937), Edwin Dickinson. The Baltimore (Maryland) Museum of Art, Thomas E. Benesch Memorial Collection (BMA 1974.5).

Most near, most dear, most loved and most far,
Under the window where I often found her
Sitting as huge as Asia, seismic with laughter,
Gin and chicken helpless in her Irish hand,
 Irresistible as Rabelais, but most tender for
The lame dogs and hurt birds that surround her,—
She is a procession no one can follow after
But be like a little dog following a brass band.

She will not glance up at the bomber, or condescend
To drop her gin and scuttle to a cellar,
But lean on the mahogany table like a mountain
Whom only faith can move, and so I send
O all my faith, and all my love to tell her
That she will move from mourning into morning.

Teaching Options

Mini Lesson: Viewing and Representing

Portrait of Mrs. B. **by Edwin Dickinson**

ART APPRECIATION

Instruction Dickinson's wife has identified this portrait as that of a woman named Mrs. Byrd or Bird. The drawing was rejected by the client and remained in the artist's collection.

Application Ask students whether the woman in this portrait matches their idea of the mother described in Barker's poem. How do the textures and colors in the portrait affect their opinion?

Possible Responses: No, the portrait does not illustrate the mother in the poem. The woman in the portrait looks very serious and tired and the woman in the poem sounds happy and energetic. Yes, the woman in the poem sounds imperturbable and self-confident, as does the woman in the portrait.

Connect to the Literature

1. **What Do You Think?** If you had been in England at the time of this speech, would Churchill's words have inspired you to help the war effort? Why or why not?

Comprehension Check
- What was the situation in France at the time Churchill made the speech?
- What economic task does Churchill ask the British people to perform?
- What does Churchill expect to happen after the fighting in France eases up?

Think Critically

2. In your opinion, which parts of the speech are most effective? Support your answer with details from the speech.

3. ACTIVE READING **EVALUATING PERSUASIVE LANGUAGE** Review the chart and examples you noted in your READER'S NOTEBOOK. Does Churchill use **loaded language** to reinforce logical arguments in his speech? Do you think he is justified in his use of loaded language? Explain your answers.

4. How would you describe Churchill's attitudes toward the English, the French, and the Germans? Cite words and phrases that suggest those attitudes.

Extend Interpretations

5. **Comparing Texts** Reread George Barker's poem "To My Mother" on page 1132. How do you think the speaker's mother would react to Churchill's speech?

6. **Writer's Style** Churchill's speech features the use of **parallelism**—the repetition of similar grammatical structures to express related ideas. Find two or three examples of parallelism in the speech. What do they add to the speech's effectiveness?

7. **Connect to Life** If Churchill were to give his speech today, it would be televised. How might he change it? Do you think the speech would be more or less powerful on television? Why?

Literary Analysis

PERSUASION Churchill's speech is considered one of the greatest persuasive speeches of all time because it stirred the British people to hold out against the German assault on their homeland. Effective **persuasion**—the technique of convincing an audience to adopt an opinion, perform an action, or both—appeals to both the intellect and the emotions.
- Appeals to the intellect involve putting forward **reasons** and **evidence** to support opinions.
- Appeals to the emotions involve stirring feelings within the audience.

In most good persuasive writing, emotional appeals are used to add to the impact of logical arguments.

Cooperative Learning Activity Reread the speech, or have one member of your group read it aloud. Discuss how effectively you think Churchill's speech balances intellectual and emotional appeals. Use a chart like the one shown to organize your thoughts.

Intellectual Appeals	Emotional Appeals

Extend Interpretations

Comparing Texts Most students will say that she would be moved and inspired.

Writer's Style Students' examples of parallelism will vary, but they should each show the repetition of similar grammatical structures to express related ideas.

Possible examples: No officer or man, no brigade or division; to face it, to endure it, and to retaliate against it; and more airplanes, more tanks, more shells, more guns.

Students may say parallelism strengthens the point Churchill is making.

Connect to Life Accept all reasonable, well-supported responses.

GUIDING STUDENT RESPONSE

Connect to the Literature

1. **What Do You Think?** Guidelines for student response: If students have trouble identifying with the condition of Britons during World War II, you might update the situation to present-day America and ask them to consider what they would do if the U.S. were threatened by invasion.

Comprehension Check
- France had been invaded by the Germans.
- He asks them to supply more ammunition and munitions for the war effort.
- that the island of England will be attacked

 Use **Unit Six Resource Book**, p. 64 for additional support.

Think Critically

2. Some students may find the appeals to emotion most effective because they are persuasive, while others may find appeals to reason most effective. Specific examples will vary.
3. Perhaps the most obvious example in the speech of loaded language is Churchill's description of Nazi Germany as "the foulest and most soul-destroying tyranny which has ever darkened and stained the pages of history." His use of loaded language helped to mobilize the British people to meet the challenge posed by Hitler and the German armed forces.
4. Possible Responses: Churchill is glowingly patriotic about the English *(magnificent efforts of our Royal Air Force; my confidence in our ability)*, respectful of the French *(that genius for recovery and counterattack; splendid army)*, and wary and contemptuous of the Germans *(that hideous apparatus of aggression; the foulest and most soul-destroying tyranny)*.

Literary Analysis

Cooperative Learning Activity Have a class discussion about current issues that might elicit both intellectual and emotional appeals from people on both sides.

Writing Options

Web Site Page Encourage students to be creative with their visual and factually accurate in their introductory paragraph. Accept all reasonable responses.

Activities & Explorations

War Debate Enforce the formal standards of a debate with time limits. Alternatively, you may want to engage students in a class discussion and write their arguments on the chalkboard in two columns, for and against.

Inquiry & Research

Western Europe in World War II Students can begin their research by looking in a card catalogue under World War II and under specific countries. The *New York Times Index* for the war years will guide students to the newspaper coverage of the war. Encourage students to use multiple sources.

Vocabulary in Action

1. a
2. c
3. b
4. b
5. c

Author Activity

Inspiring Words You may want to extend this activity by having students listen to recordings of Franklin Delano Roosevelt's World War II speeches. Have students compare the styles of the two speakers. Ask them whether they think the differences could be partially due to the men coming from different countries and cultures.

Choices & CHALLENGES

Writing Options

Web Site Page Prepare notes for the first screen of a Web site presentation about World War II or about Churchill's role in the war. Your screen should include an introductory paragraph, an idea for a visual, and the contents of the rest of the presentation. Place the notes in your **Working Portfolio.**

Activities & Explorations

War Debate Churchill ends his speech by quoting a statement that "it is better for us to perish in battle than to look upon the outrage of our nation and our altar." Stage a debate in which you argue for and against this statement. ~ **SPEAKING AND LISTENING**

Inquiry & Research

Western Europe in World War II Find out what happened in western Europe during the six months following Churchill's speech. Write a documentary news report explaining your findings.

More Online: Research Starter
www.mcdougallittell.com

Vocabulary in Action

EXERCISE: ASSESSMENT PRACTICE For each group of words below, write the letter of the word that is an antonym of the boldfaced word.

1. **animate:** (a) stifle, (b) appreciate, (c) liberate
2. **gravity:** (a) height, (b) clearness, (c) insignificance
3. **dogged:** (a) respectable, (b) nonchalant, (c) friendly
4. **retaliate:** (a) praise, (b) forgive, (c) discourage
5. **indomitable:** (a) angry, (b) strong, (c) vulnerable

Building Vocabulary
For an in-depth study on how to use a thesaurus to find a word's antonyms, see page 574.

Winston Churchill
1874–1965

Other Works
The Gathering Storm
Blood, Sweat, and Tears
Their Finest Hour
History of the English-Speaking Peoples (4 volumes)
The Second World War (6 volumes)

Military Career The son of a noble English father and an American mother, Winston Churchill received a traditional English secondary education. Because his school record was not particularly distinguished, he did not go on to a university, instead entering the Royal Military College at Sandhurst at the age of 18 and then joining the military. There he found his niche, serving both as a war correspondent and as an officer.

A Nation's Leader Churchill entered politics in 1900, and 40 years later he became a compromise prime minister in a deeply divided government. With his public-speaking ability and talent at working with opposing forces, he was able to unite the British people and lead them to victory over the Germans in World War II. Despite his lifetime involvement in politics, Churchill never stopped writing. He was awarded the Nobel Prize in literature in 1953.

Author Activity

Inspiring Words Churchill's radio speeches had a tremendous impact on the British people. Search the Internet or your local library to find an audio recording of Churchill's speeches. Listen to them with your class, and discuss what you think his delivery adds to the speeches' effectiveness.

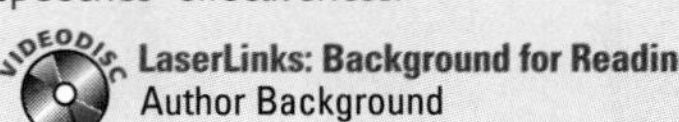

LaserLinks: Background for Reading
Author Background

Teaching Options

Mini Lesson Grammar

PASSIVE VOICE: WEAK SUBJECT

Instruction One type of weak subject can occur when a noun is created from a verb, such as *appearance* from *appear.* "He appeared suddenly, frightening us" is a stronger sentence than "His appearance was sudden and caused us to be frightened."

Activity Write this excerpt from Churchill's speech on the chalkboard.

"We must expect that as soon as stability is reached on the Western Front, the bulk of that hideous apparatus of aggression . . . will be turned upon us. . . . If the battle is to be won, we must provide our men with ever-increasing quantities of the weapons and ammunition they need."

Point out that in the first sentence, changing the verb *expect* to a noun and using it as the subject weakens the force of the sentence. In the second sentence, changing *provide* to a verb phrase and using it as the subject has the same weakening effect.

Use **Grammar Transparencies and Copymasters,** p. 103.

Use McDougal Littell's ***Language Network*** for more instruction and practice in passive voice.

from Night

Autobiography by ELIE WIESEL (vē-zĕl')

Comparing Literature of the World

The Effect of the War Across Cultures

Churchill's Speeches and Wiesel's *Night* Winston Churchill's World War II speeches rallied the British in part by reminding them of the dark forces they were fighting. In *Night,* a victim of those dark forces gives a firsthand account of the terror he experienced after his homeland was overrun by Nazi Germany.

Points of Comparison As you read the excerpt from *Night,* think about the evidence it provides to support Churchill's description of Nazi Germany as "the foulest and most soul-destroying tyranny which has ever darkened and stained the pages of history."

Build Background

Nightmare Years As the leader of the Nazi Party, Adolf Hitler promoted racist nationalism and a policy of military expansion intended to make Germany a world empire. After he became chancellor of Germany in 1933, he began a huge military buildup; he also set up a private army, called the SS, and a secret police force, called the Gestapo, to crack down on opposition of any kind. His launching of an invasion of Poland in 1939 was the beginning of World War II.

In his quest for German supremacy, Hitler was determined to rid his empire of Jews, whom he blamed for every evil in the world. In Germany and all the European nations the Nazis invaded, Jews were rounded up and sent—usually by train—to concentration camps, where many were killed in gas chambers, were shot by firing squads, or died of torture, starvation, and disease. The dead were cremated in huge ovens.

Auschwitz-Birkenau, in Poland, was the largest of these death camps. Its director, Rudolf Hess, later testified that 2 million people were executed there and another half-million starved to death. Among those taken to Auschwitz was a Jewish teenager named Elie Wiesel, who survived the death camps and was eventually able to write about his experiences. It was Wiesel who first used the term *holocaust* to refer to the Nazis' mass slaughter.

Focus Your Reading

LITERARY ANALYSIS **STYLE IN NONFICTION** **Style** is the way in which a work is written—not what is said but how it is said. Elements that contribute to a writer's style include **word choice; sentence length, structure,** and **variety; tone; imagery;** and the use of **dialogue.** As you read, notice how these elements contribute to Wiesel's style, and consider the relationship between Wiesel's style and his subject matter.

ACTIVE READING **USING PRIOR KNOWLEDGE TO INTERPRET TEXTS** Most readers come to Wiesel's account with **prior knowledge** about the Holocaust. For example, though the name of the train's final stop—Auschwitz—is unfamiliar to Wiesel and his fellow prisoners when they arrive there, its significance is almost always known to readers. As you read the excerpt, look for other moments when your knowledge of historical events allows you to understand the wider implications of events described in Wiesel's account.

READER'S NOTEBOOK As you read, take notes about events or details that your prior knowledge makes meaningful to you. Pay special attention to details whose significance is clear to most readers but not to the prisoners on the train.

Objectives

1. understand and appreciate an **autobiography (Literary Analysis)**
2. appreciate the author's **style** in nonfiction **(Literary Analysis)**
3. use **prior knowledge** to interpret texts **(Active Reading)**
4. recognize and discuss connections that cross cultures

Summary

Wiesel tells how, as a teenager, he was taken in a crowded boxcar from his Romanian village to a concentration camp. The trip is a series of shocks: the deportees are going further away than they thought; German officers threaten them, demanding valuables; the doors are nailed shut. Madame Schächter, a former neighbor, has seemingly gone mad. Every night, waking and terrifying the others, she screams that she sees fire or flames. The others restrain and even hit her. Then they reach Birkenau, where there is a fiery furnace, producing foul smells.

Use **Unit Six Resource Book,** p. 65 for additional support.

Thematic Links

Madame Schächter's night visions seem to be madness, but they foreshadow the **shocking reality** that will face the Jews at the concentration camp. No one believes her—until they see the flames of the furnaces with their own eyes.

5-Minute Warm-Up

Daily Language SkillBuilder

Have students **proofread** the display sentences on page 979k and write them correctly. The sentences also appear on Transparency 31 of **Grammar Transparencies and Copymasters.**

LESSON RESOURCES

UNIT SIX RESOURCE BOOK, pp. 65–68

ASSESSMENT RESOURCES

Formal Assessment, pp. 209–210

Teacher's Guide to Assessment and Portfolio Use

Test Generator

SKILLS TRANSPARENCIES AND COPYMASTERS

Literary Analysis
- Style, Tone, and Mood, T24 (for Literary Analysis, p. 1135)

Reading and Critical Thinking
- Making Inferences, T7 (for Active Reading, p. 1135)

Grammar
- Avoiding Shifts in Tense, T46 (for Mini Lesson, p. 1142)
- Verbs: Tense Shifts, C133 (for Mini Lesson, p. 1142)

Vocabulary
- Word Origins, C91 (for Mini Lesson, p. 1138)

Writing
- Point of View, T23 (for Writing Option 1, p. 1142)
- Compare-Contrast, C34 (for Writing Option 2, p. 1142)

Communications
- Analyze, Evaluate, and Critique: Entertainment, T5 (for Activities & Explorations 2, p. 1142)

INTEGRATED TECHNOLOGY

Audio Library

Internet: Research Starter

Visit our website: www.mcdougallittell.com

TEACHING THE LITERATURE

Reading and Analyzing

Active Reading

USING PRIOR KNOWLEDGE TO INTERPRET TEXTS

Have students write a brief description of what they know about Nazi Germany's treatment of Jews during World War II, particularly at Auschwitz.

Possible Response: Most students will know that the Nazis transported, treated inhumanely, and killed 6 million Jews in their camps. Some may know that the worst of the camps was Auschwitz, accounting for some 4 million deaths, many burned in its furnaces.

Use **Unit Six Resource Book** p. 66 for more practice.

Literary Analysis

STYLE IN NONFICTION

Remind students that elements of style enhance the effect of a clearly written work. Ask them to describe elements of the author's style as shown on these two pages, such as word choice, tone, point of view, sentence length, and sentence structure.

Possible Responses: Students may mention Wiesel's use of fairly simple, accessible vocabulary; a journalistic, "you are there" reporting tone; a first-person participant's point of view; varied sentence length (short sentences punctuate or shock, long ones lull or describe); and repetition of sentence structures for effect ("Our terror was . . . Our nerves were . . . Our flesh was. . . ").

Use **Unit Six Resource Book** p. 67 for more exercises.

From NIGHT

ELIE WIESEL

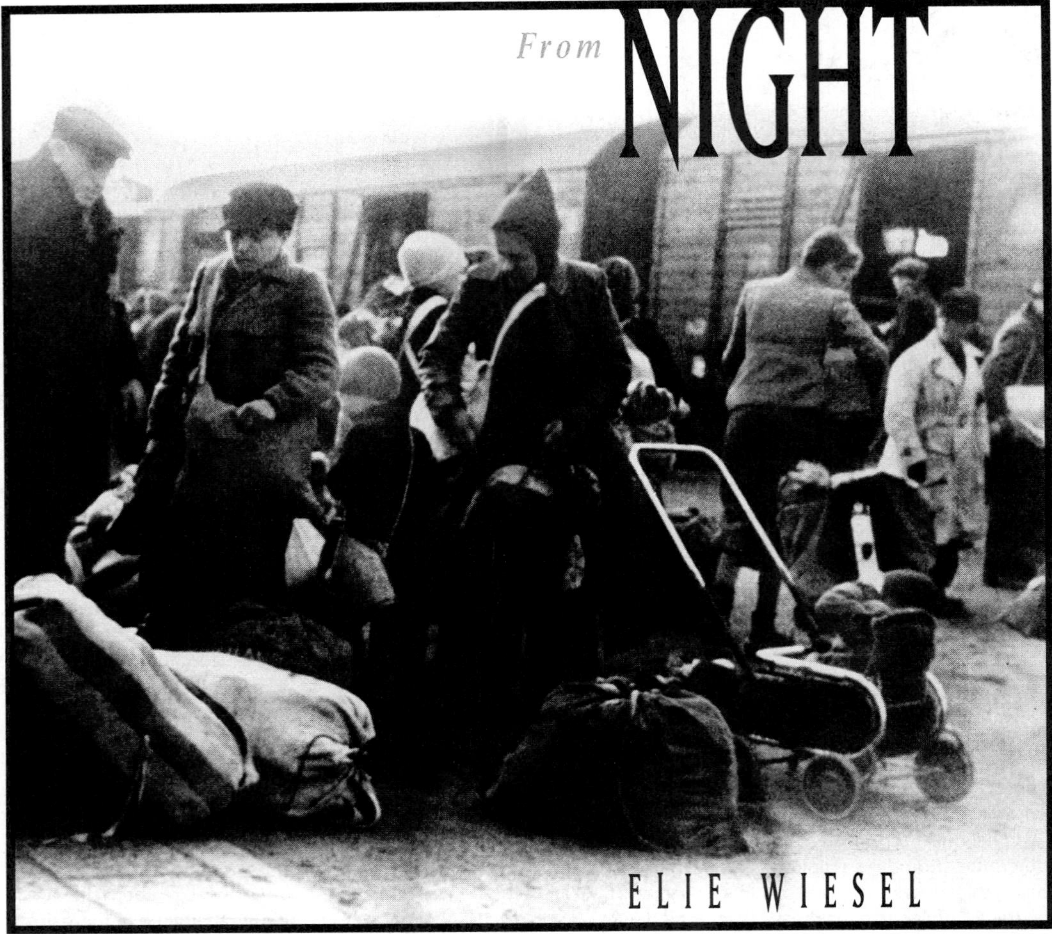

Deportation of Jews from Westerbork transit camp in the Netherlands to a Nazi death camp in Poland

The train stopped at Kaschau, a little town on the Czechoslovak frontier.[1] We realized then that we were not going to stay in Hungary. Our eyes were opened, but too late.

The door of the car slid open. A German officer, accompanied by a Hungarian lieutenant-interpreter, came up and introduced himself.

"From this moment, you come under the authority of the German army. Those of you who still have gold, silver, or watches in your possession must give them up now. Anyone

Teaching Options

Mini Lesson: Viewing and Representing

ART APPRECIATION

Instruction Point out to students the photograph on this page. Have students indicate details in this photo that suggest how the prisoners may not yet have realized what's ahead for them.

Possible Response: Some have loaded belongings on a small cart as if the worst they had to fear was weariness from carrying their things. Others have packed belongings into large sacks difficult to carry. The prisoners may not even be allowed to take these belongings with them, as the boxcars were typically jammed full of people.

Application Ask students to identify details that show how the four photos accompanying this selection relate to the prisoners' journey.

Possible Response: The bundled, scanty belongings and the open, waiting boxcars indicate the start of the journey. One photo on 1139 shows unhappy looking people crowded onto a railroad car; the other shows an eerily empty camp with many austere bunkhouses for the prisoners and a menacing perimeter of barbed wire and guard towers. On page 1140 is a photo of the entry gates of Auschwitz.

who is later found to have kept anything will be shot on the spot. Secondly, anyone who feels ill may go to the hospital car. That's all."

The Hungarian lieutenant went among us with a basket and collected the last possessions from
1 those who no longer wished to taste the bitterness of terror. "There are eighty of you in the wagon," added the German officer. "If anyone is missing, you'll all be shot, like dogs . . . ."

They disappeared. The doors were closed. We were caught in a trap, right up to our necks. The doors were nailed up; the way back was finally cut off. The world was a cattle wagon hermetically[2] sealed.

We had a woman with us named Madame Schächter. She was about fifty; her ten-year-old son was with her, crouched in a corner. Her husband and two eldest sons had been deported with the first transport by mistake. The separation had completely broken her.

I knew her well. A quiet woman with tense, burning eyes, she had often been to our house. Her husband, who was a pious man, spent his days and nights in study, and it was she who worked to support the family.

Madame Schächter had gone out of her mind. On the first day of the journey she had already begun to moan and to keep asking why she had been separated from her family. As time went on, her cries grew hysterical.On the third night, while we slept, some of us sitting one against the other and some standing, a piercing cry split the silence:

"Fire! I can see a fire! I can see a fire!"

There was a moment's panic. Who was it who had cried out? It was Madame Schächter. Standing in the middle of the wagon, in the pale light from the windows, she looked like a withered tree in a cornfield. She pointed her arm toward the window, screaming:

"Look! Look at it! Fire! A terrible fire! Mercy! Oh, that fire!"

Some of the men pressed up against the bars. There was nothing there; only the darkness.

The shock of this terrible awakening stayed with us for a long time. We still trembled from it. With every groan of the wheels on the rail, we felt that an abyss was about to open beneath our bodies. Powerless to still our own anguish, we tried to consol ourselves:

"She's mad, poor soul. . . ."

Someone had put a damp cloth on her brow, to calm her, but still her screams went on:

"Fire! Fire!"

Her little boy was crying, hanging onto her skirt, trying to take hold of her hands. "It's all right, Mummy! There's nothing there . . . Sit down . . . " This shook me even more than his mother's screams had done.

Some women tried to calm her. "You'll find your husband and your sons again . . . in a few days. . . ."

She continued to scream, breathless, her voice broken by sobs. "Jews, listen to me! I can see a fire! There are huge flames! It is a furnace!"

It was as though she were possessed by an evil spirit which spoke from the depths of her being.

We tried to explain it away, more to calm ourselves and to recover our own breath than to comfort her. "She must be very thirsty, poor thing! That's why she keeps talking about a fire devouring her.

"But it was in vain. Our terror was about to burst the sides of the train. Our nerves were at breaking point. Our flesh was creeping. It was as though madness were taking possession of us all. We could stand it no longer. Some of the young men forced her to sit down, tied her up, and put a gag in her mouth.

Silence again. The little boy sat down by his mother, crying. I had begun to breathe normally again. We could hear the wheels churning out that monotonous rhythm of a train traveling through the night. We could begin to doze, to rest, to dream. . . .

1. **Czechoslovak** (chĕk′ə-slō′väk) **frontier:** the border of Czechoslovakia, a former European country occupied by Germany during World War II.
2. **hermetically** (hər-mĕt′ĭ-klē): in an airtight manner; thoroughly.

Customizing Instruction

Less Proficient Readers

Have students read to decide if Madame Schächter's visions mean she really has lost her mind.

Students Acquiring English

1 Help students understand the meaning of the expression "taste the bitterness of terror." In context, the prisoners yielding up their last precious things are the ones who are panicked by the threat that they will be executed if they are caught hiding anything valuable. The "taste" Wiesel vividly describes is the back-of-the-throat sensation of fear-induced nausea.

Use **Spanish Study Guide** for additional support, pp. 269–271.

Gifted and Talented

Remind students that dramatic irony is the contrast between a character's lack of knowledge and the greater knowledge of the reader. In this piece the reader's sense of dramatic irony is partly dependent on prior knowledge about what awaits the characters at the concentration camp. Have students identify instances of irony on these two pages.

Possible Response: In the first paragraph, "Our eyes were opened," in reference to the prisoners' discovery that they are being sent far away, is ironic because the situation is much worse than they even now know. Madame Schächter's ". . . huge flames! It is a furnace!" is ironic; her neighbors think her mad, but she is all too horribly right about what is ahead.

BLOCK SCHEDULING: MANAGING TIME

If your schedule requires that you cover the lesson objectives in a shorter time, use . . .

- Preparing to Read, p. 1135
- Thinking Through the Literature, p. 1141

If you want to take advantage of longer class time, use . . .

- TE Teaching Options: Viewing and Representing, p. 1136; Vocabulary, p. 1138; Speaking and Listening, p. 1139; Cross-Curricular Link: History, p. 1140; Grammar, p. 1142
- Choices & Challenges and Author Activity, p. 1142

Reading and Analyzing

Active Reading

USING PRIOR KNOWLEDGE TO INTERPRET TEXTS

A Tell students to evaluate the effects prior knowledge has on their understanding. Ask them to analyze how they would understand this passage and how they would feel when reading it if they had no knowledge of Auschwitz.

Possible Response: For those who know what it means, this passage has dramatic irony. For those who know little about what happened at Auschwitz, this passage creates curiosity about what the prisoners' arrival at their destination is going to mean. The reader and the prisoners are in suspense.

Reading Skills and Strategies: CLARIFYING

B Point out that after stating repeatedly that Madame Schächter is out of her mind and that the other prisoners use force to silence her, the people again heed her alarmed cries "The fire! The furnace!" Ask students what this might mean about the people's relationship to Madame Schächter and the effects of the people's experiences and fears.

Possible Response: Although there is much evidence that Madame Schächter is mad, the people feel trapped in a nightmare world where anything bad can happen. Madame Schächter is known to them, even if she seems to be crazy. Her cry of danger expresses their denied fears.

An hour or two went by like this. Then another scream took our breath away. The woman had broken loose from her bonds and was crying out more loudly than ever:

"Look at the fire! Flames, flames everywhere . . . ."

Once more the young men tied her up and gagged her. They even struck her. People encouraged them:

"Make her be quiet! She's mad! Shut her up! She's not the only one. She can keep her mouth shut. . . ."

They struck her several times on the head—blows that might have killed her. Her little boy clung to her; he did not cry out; he did not say a word. He was not even weeping now.

An endless night. Toward dawn, Madame Schächter calmed down. Crouched in her corner, her bewildered gaze scouring the emptiness, she could no longer see us.

She stayed like that all through the day, dumb, absent, isolated among us. As soon as night fell, she began to scream: "There's a fire over there!" She would point at a spot in space, always the same one. They were tired of hitting her. The heat, the thist, the pestilential[3] stench, the suffocating lack of air—these were as nothing compared with these screams which tore us to shreds. A few days more and we should all have started to scream too.

But we had reached a station. Those who were next to the windows told us its name: "Auschwitz."[4] **A**

No one had ever heard that name.

The train did not start up again. The afternoon passed slowly. Then the wagon doors slid open. Two men were allowed to get down to fetch water. When they came back, they told us that, in exchange for a gold watch, they had

3. **pestilential** (pĕs′tə-lĕn′shəl): disease-bearing; noxious.

4. **Auschwitz** (oush′vĭts′): a town in southern Poland, near the site of the Auschwitz-Birkenau extermination camp, where between 1 million and 4 million people (mostly Jews from Germany and eastern Europe) were systematically murdered by the Nazis between 1942 and 1945.

View of the Birkenau concentration camp, February 1945

Teaching Options

Mini Lesson Vocabulary Strategy

RESEARCHING WORD ORIGINS: *Pestis, Ominari, Truncus*

Instruction The word *pestilential* comes from the Latin *pestis,* "plague or disease" and means "causing serious illness or disease." Related words are *pest, pesticide, pestilence, pestilent.* The word *abominable* comes from the Latin roots *ab* "from" + *ominari* "to regard as a (bad) omen," and it means "very disagreeable or unpleasant." Related words are *omen, ominous, abominate, abomination.* The word *truncheon* comes from the Latin root *truncus* or "cut-off portion" and refers to a short wooden club or staff. Related words are *trunk* (human torso or tree trunk), *truncate, truncated.*

Activity Have students work in pairs to find the meanings of *pesticide, pestilence, ominous, abominate,* and *truncated.* Ask them to use each word in a sentence. Then ask students to describe how they can use knowledge of these three word roots to remember the meanings of these and the other closely related words.

Use **Vocabulary Transparencies and Copymasters,** p. 63.

A lesson on word origins appears on p. 206 in the Pupil's Edition.

discovered that this was the last stop. We would be getting out here. There was a labor camp.
1 Conditions were good. Families would not be split up. Only the young people would go to work in the factories. The old men and invalids would be kept occupied in the fields.

The barometer of confidence soared. Here was a sudden release from the terrors of the previous nights. We gave thanks to God.

Madame Schächter stayed in her corner, wilted, dumb, indifferent to the general confidence. Her little boy stroked her hand.

As dusk fell, darkness gathered inside the wagon. We started to eat our last provisions. At ten in the evening, everyone was looking for a convenient position in which to sleep for a while, and soon we were all asleep. Suddenly: "The fire! The furnace!
B Look, over there!. . ."

Waking with a start, we rushed to the window. Yet again we had believed her, even if only for a moment. But there was nothing outside save the darkness of night. With shame in our souls, we went back to our places, gnawed by fear, in spite of ourselves. She continued to scream, they began to hit her again, and it was with the greatest difficulty that they silenced her.

The man in charge of our wagon called a German officer who was walking about on the platform, and asked him if Madame Schächter could be taken to the hospital car.

"You must be patient," the German replied. "She'll be taken there soon."

Jewish captives from the ghetto in Lublin, Poland, being transported to a death camp

Customizing Instruction

Multiple Learning Styles

Visual Learners

Have students use a map of Europe to locate the places connected with this selection and try to trace the general route taken by the prisoners. Countries mentioned include Romania, Hungary, Germany, the former Czechoslovakia, and Poland. Specific locations, include Wiesel's village of Sighet (in the Transylvanian region of Romania), Kaschau (on the Czechoslovak border), Auschwitz (in Poland).

Less Proficient Readers

1 This passage refers to the prisoners' suppositions about conditions at Auschwitz. Explain that the camp had a sign over the gate (shown in photo on page 1140) that said, in German, "Arbeit macht frei," meaning "Work makes you free."

- Ask why the prisoners feel relieved and give thanks to God.
  Possible Response: They are glad that the journey has ended. They can understand a labor camp; at least it would mean that they are to be of some use and thus will be housed and fed. They are all anxious about family members from whom they were separated and hope that they will be reunited in the camp.
- Ask why the prisoners' response to another outcry by Madame Schächter causes them "shame in their souls"; how do they treat her?
  Possible Response: Their rushing to see what prompted her outburst proves that, deep down, they are still very fearful. Some people hit Madame Schächter. One man summons a German officer and tries to get her taken out of the boxcar.

Mini Lesson Speaking and Listening

EXPRESSING AN OPINION

Instruction Help students prepare a persuasive statement to protest the treatment of the people in the boxcar, particularly the difficulties that seem to have affected Madame Schächter's sanity.

Prepare Have students work in cooperative groups, gathering details about the difficulties and discomforts the people, particularly Madame Schächter, have endured on their journey. Have students find details in Wiesel's account that reveal conditions in the boxcar for sleeping, eating, sanitary needs, and so on.

Present Student groups can decide how they wish to present their statements. For example, each group may tell about a specific aspect of the journey. Students who are audience members should evaluate how the statements increase their understanding of the hardships faced by the people in Wiesel's account. Audience members might also play the role of an after-the-war tribunal judging appropriate punishment for the cruelty of the Nazi captors.

BLOCK SCHEDULING This activity is particularly well-suited for longer class periods.

Reading and Analyzing

Reading Skills and Strategies: SUMMARIZING

After students have finished reading, have them summarize the sequence of events that involved Madame Schächter. Ask them whether or not, in the end, they think Madame Schächter was irrational. If they think she wasn't, ask them to explain her behavior based on the selection and their prior knowledge.

Possible Response: Madame Schächter was clearly distraught and, during the journey, seemed to be reacting to visions of fire that were not there. However, in the end, her warnings about "The fire! The furnace!" proved to be true and seem to have been premonitions of the horrors ahead for those on the journey.

Entrance to the concentration camp in Auschwitz. The sign in German above the gate says "Work makes you free."

Toward eleven o'clock, the train began to move. We pressed against the windows. The convoy was moving slowly. A quarter of an hour later, it slowed down again. Through the windows we could see barbed wire; we realized that this must be the camp.

We had forgotten the existence of Madame Schächter. Suddenly, we heard terrible screams:"

"Jews, look! Look through the window! Flames! Look!"

And as the train stopped, we saw this time that flames were gushing out of a tall chimney into the black sky.

Madame Schächter was silent herself. Once more she had become dumb, indifferent, absent, and had gone back to her corner.

We looked at the flames in the darkness. There was an abominable odor floating in the air. Suddenly, our doors opened. Some odd-looking characters, dressed in striped shirts and black trousers leapt into the wagon. They held electric torches[5] and truncheons.[6] They began to strike out to right and left, shouting:

"Everybody get out! Everyone out of the wagon! Quickly!"

We jumped out. I threw a last glance toward Madame Schächter. Her little boy was holding her hand. In front of us flames. In the air that smell of burning flesh. It must have been about midnight. We had arrived—at Birkenau, reception center for Auschwitz.

5. **electric torches:** flashlights.

6. **truncheons** (trŭn′chənz): small clubs, like those carried as weapons by police officers.

Teaching Options

Cross Curricular Link History

PERSECUTION DURING WORLD WAR II

Although Jews were the victims of the Nazi regime's most notorious persecution during World War II, other groups suffered at the hands of Hitler's forces. Six million Jews died by the end of the war, and 2,000,000 others, including Communists, people with alleged physical and mental disabilities, Catholics, Slavs in the Soviet Union, and Gypsies also perished. Gypsies, in particular, were systematically exterminated—almost half a million were killed during the war. Gypsies have been convenient scapegoats in other countries throughout history because of their preference for living a nomadic, rather than settled, lifestyle. The issue of war crimes and accountability links the past with the present through the current investigation of Switzerland's financial dealings with the Nazi's during the war. Holocaust victims whose assets were confiscated by the Nazis and deposited in Swiss banks are slowly being reimbursed by special funds from the Swiss government.

Connect to the Literature

1. **What Do You Think?** What are your thoughts after reading this excerpt?

Comprehension Check
- What recurring vision frightens Madame Schächter?
- What do the Jews see when they get off the train?

Think Critically

2. What is your opinion of the way the other prisoners treat Madame Schächter? Why do you think they treat her so harshly?

3. What do you think is the most likely explanation for Madame Schächter's visions?

4. How do you think the **settings** described in this excerpt contribute to its **mood?** Give examples to support your answer.

5. ACTIVE READING USING PRIOR KNOWLEDGE TO INTERPRET TEXTS Review the notes you jotted down in your  READER'S NOTEBOOK and discuss any details whose significance you understood because of your **prior knowledge** of relevant historical events. How did your prior knowledge affect your reading of the excerpt?

6. What do you think is the significance of the title *Night?*

THINK ABOUT
- the physical descriptions of the train and the concentration camp
- the behavior of the prisoners and their captors
- the ultimate fate of the Jews
- what *night* might symbolize

Extend Interpretations

7. **Connect to Life** Do you think something like the Holocaust could happen today to people of a particular race or religion or to some other group? Why or why not?

8. Points of Comparison Consider Winston Churchill's speech of May 19, 1940 (page 000), in the light of the information that Wiesel provides. How do the details of Wiesel's experience add impact to the reasons Churchill gives for Britain's fight against Nazi Germany?

Literary Analysis

STYLE IN NONFICTION A writer's **style**—the unique way he or she handles elements such as **word choice, sentence length** and **variety, imagery,** and **dialogue**—is influenced in part by the ideas he or she wants to convey. In *Night,* Wiesel employs a style having the following characteristics:

- a reliance on simple words and short sentences
- an occasional use of imagery, as when Madame Schächter is described as looking "like a withered tree in a cornfield"
- a use of dialogue to show how the Jews on the train react to their situation

Cooperative Learning Activity Work with a group of three or four classmates to find passages that illustrate these characteristics of Wiesel's style. Record your findings in a chart like the one shown. How do you think Wiesel's style reinforces the ideas he wants to convey about his subject?

Element of Style	Example
Simple words	
Short sentences	
Imagery	
Dialogue	

REVIEW TONE A writer's choice of words and details is in part determined by the **tone,** or attitude toward his or her subject, that the writer wants to convey. A work might, for example, have a sad tone, an angry tone, or a matter-of-fact tone. How would you describe the tone of this excerpt from *Night?* What effect does the tone have on you?

Extend Interpretations

Connect to Life Although there are too many instances of humans being inhuman to others in the world, there are many people worldwide who, after the Holocaust, vowed that this type of atrocity would never be allowed to happen again. The UN and other multinational organizations attempt to publicize and prevent such abuses. Nonetheless, in the Balkans, in Cambodia, and in Rwanda there are examples of whole classes or groups of people being murdered because of their identity.

Points of Comparison As Wiesel's account illustrates, the Nazis represented what Churchill described as a "soul-destroying tyranny." Not only did the Nazis treat others inhumanely, they forced people into circumstances where they treated each other inhumanely.

GUIDING STUDENT RESPONSE

Connect to the Literature

1. **What Do You Think?** Guidelines for student response: Students might share their responses to this harrowing excerpt.

Comprehension Check
- Fire, flames, and a furnace
- Flames and a furnace

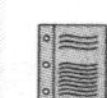 Use **Unit Six Resource Book,** p. 68 for additional support.

Think Critically

2. Possible Response: Others treat her harshly because they are terrified about their circumstances and want to avoid drawing the guards' attention. Their frustration erupts into violence against a person who seems weaker and over whom, perhaps, they feel they can exercise control.
3. Accept all reasonable responses, including the possibility that she had an actual vision of what lay ahead.
4. Possible Response: The stench and discomfort of the boxcar, sight of flames, smell of strange odors at Birkenau are details that contribute to a mood of impending doom.
5. Possible Response: Knowing the historical context allows the reader to see the dramatic irony; not knowing allows the reader to discover the horrors of the situation as those experiencing it do.
6. Possible Response: *Night* may simply refer to the setting: almost all of Madame Schächter's terrible visions take place at night, as does the train's arrival at Auschwitz (midnight). *Night* connotes "darkness, evil" and may refer to the inhumane behavior of the Nazis, as well as the behavior of those in the boxcar to Madame Schächter. *Night* can also connote "death" and may refer to the ultimate fate of millions of Jews at Auschwitz.

Literary Analysis

Cooperative Learning Activity As students analyze the characteristics of Wiesel's style, have them also consider Wiesel's intended audience.

Review Tone Lead a class discussion on Wiesel's tone in this selection and the effect it creates.

Writing Options

1. **Rewritten Version** Students should use an effective narrative style in covering the sequence of events as Wiesel's account outlined them and reflect what they imagine was Madame Schächter's state of mind.
2. **Points of Comparison** Responses will vary, but in comparing the two works, students should either analyze all points about one piece and then consider the other, or they should move back and forth on point-to-point comparison between the two pieces. Emphasize the importance of using transitional words and organization to make the essay clear. **To make this assignment more challenging,** ask students to explain why one piece had a more profound effect than the other, given the characteristics of both selections and their own preferences as readers.

Activities & Explorations

1. **Holocaust Monument** Accept all reasonable responses. Some students' responses to the abuse of the concentration camp victims may be very graphic. Be sensitive to the fact that some students may come from families directly affected by the Holocaust and that some may have relatives who are Holocaust survivors.
2. **Movie Review** Encourage students to watch the movie without interruption if possible. You may also want to suggest that they may be more comfortable if they watch it with others and have a "debriefing session" together after their viewing, or you may watch the movie as a class.

Inquiry & Research

The Holocaust Student reports should specify that it was Soviet troops who liberated the Auschwitz-Birkenau camp near the end of the war in January 1945.

Author Activity

Human Rights Champion Wiesel continues to bear witness around the world to the horrors of the Holocaust not only in his writings but also in lectures.

Choices & CHALLENGES

Writing Options

1. **Rewritten Version** Rewrite this excerpt, narrating the events from Madame Schächter's point of view. Place your rewritten version in your **Working Portfolio.**
2. **Points of Comparison** Write an essay in which you compare and contrast the effects on you of Churchill's speech and the excerpt from *Night.* In your opinion, which work's portrayal of the evils of Nazism evokes a more powerful reaction? Explain your answer.

Writing Handbook
See page 1367: Compare and Contrast.

Activities & Explorations

1. **Holocaust Monument** Create a design for a monument memorializing the victims of the Holocaust. ~ **ART**
2. **Movie Review** Obtain and view a videotape of *Schindler's List,* the Oscar-winning 1993 film about an industrialist who helped more than a thousand Jews to escape the Holocaust. Discuss the impact of the film in an oral review. ~ **VIEWING AND REPRESENTING**

Inquiry & Research

The Holocaust Investigate and prepare an oral report on the conditions at the Auschwitz-Birkenau concentration camp and on the camp's liberation near the end of the war.

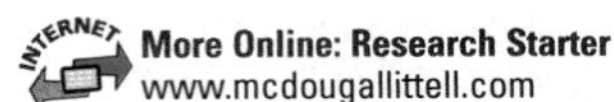
More Online: Research Starter
www.mcdougallittell.com

Elie Wiesel
1928–

Other Works
The Accident
Dawn
Legends of Our Time
The Oath
One Generation After

A Cut-Off Village Elie Wiesel was born in Sighet (sĕ′gĕt), a town in the Romanian region of Transylvania (the town was annexed by Hungary during World War II but later returned to Romania). Raised as a devout orthodox Jew, Wiesel was just 15 when, in the spring of 1944, the Nazis ordered the deportation of Sighet's 15,000 Jews, shipping them on a cattle train to Auschwitz in Poland. The Jews of Sighet, cut off by the war from most communication, had no idea where they were going. Although they had been warned of Nazi atrocities by a man passing through the town, who told them to run for their lives, they had taken the man for a madman and refused to believe him.

Into the Night Wiesel's mother and one of his three sisters were murdered at Auschwitz. Separated from the women in the family, Wiesel and his father were eventually sent to the Buchenwald concentration camp in Germany, where Wiesel's father died of starvation and dysentery less than three months before the camp was liberated. When Wiesel was freed, he vowed to remain silent about the Holocaust for ten years, writing nothing about his experiences even though he worked as a journalist and writer. "I didn't want to use the wrong words," he later explained. "I was afraid that words might betray it."

Bearing Witness Wiesel's first attempt at writing about the Holocaust was an 800-page autobiographical account in Yiddish, the language of his childhood. He then wrote a French version of the account, condensed to just over 100 pages, which was published as *La Nuit* in 1958. Two years later, the English version, *Night,* appeared. Since then Wiesel has written numerous histories, novels, and stories bearing witness to the Holocaust. He has also worked tirelessly to call attention to human rights violations around the world, winning the 1986 Nobel Peace Prize for his efforts.

Author Activity

Human Rights Champion Find out more about Wiesel's involvement in battling human rights violations and genocide in Cambodia, Rwanda, Bosnia, and other places around the world.

Teaching Options

Grammar

VERBS: TENSE SHIFTS

Instruction Have students review the two grammar lessons for Selection 3. Shifts in tense are sometimes necessary, but they must make sense. When a sentence contains two or more actions occurring at the same time, use the same tense for each verb showing the actions. When a sentence presents a sequence of events, or shows the relationship of one event to another, use tenses appropriate to the time of each event. Avoid illogical tense shifts.

Activity Write this sentence on the chalkboard.

Elie Wiesel's experiences <u>formed</u> the basis for the selection we <u>are reading</u> now.

Ask the students to state the tenses of the underlined verbs *(past; present progressive).* Explain that these tenses show the time relationship of one event to the other.

Use **Grammar Transparencies and Copymasters,** p. 75.

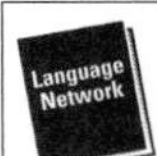
Use McDougal Littell's ***Language Network*** for more instruction and practice in verb tense shifts.

from

Letters from Westerbork

by Etty Hillesum

1 24 August 1943

I have told you often enough that no words and images are adequate to describe nights like these. But still I must try to convey something of it to you. One always has the feeling here of being the ears and eyes of a piece of Jewish history, but there is also the need sometimes to be a still, small voice. We must keep one another in touch with everything that happens in the various outposts of this world, each one contributing his own little piece of stone to the great mosaic that will take shape once the war is over. . . . 2

In the afternoon I did a round of the hospital barracks one more time, going from bed to bed. Which beds would be empty the next day? The transport lists are never published until the very last moment, but some of us know well in advance that our names will be down. A young girl called me. She was sitting bolt upright in her bed, eyes wide open. This girl has thin wrists and a peaky little face. She is partly paralyzed, and has just been learning to walk again, between two nurses, one step at a time. "Have you heard? I have to go." We look at each other for a long moment. It is as if her face has disappeared; she is all eyes. Then she says in a level, gray little voice, "Such a pity, isn't it? That everything you have learned in life goes for nothing." And, "How hard it is to die." Suddenly the unnatural rigidity of her expression gives way and she sobs, "Oh, and the worst of it all is having to leave Holland!" And, "Oh, why wasn't I allowed to die before . . ." Later, during the night, I saw her again, for the last time. 3

There was a little woman in the washhouse, a basket of dripping clothes on her arm. She grabbed hold of me; she looked deranged. A flood of words poured over me: "That isn't right, how can that be right? I've got to go and I won't even be able to get my washing dry by tomorrow. And my child is sick, he's feverish, can't you fix things so that I don't have to go? And I don't have enough things for the child, the rompers they sent me are too small, I need the bigger size, oh, it's enough to drive you mad. . . ."

Reading for Information

During World War II, more than 100,000 Dutch Jews were sent by the Nazis to the transit camp of Westerbork, from which most were transported to the death camp at Auschwitz in Poland. After being sent to Westerbork in 1943, Etty Hillesum worked in the hospital barracks. She also kept a diary and wrote many letters to friends outside the camp. In this excerpt from one of her letters, Hillesum describes the preparations for transporting prisoners by train to Auschwitz.

ANALYZING PRIMARY SOURCES

Letters are important primary sources because they reveal the feelings and attitudes of real people. As eyewitness accounts of the operations of a concentration camp, Etty Hillesum's letters are especially valuable. When you analyze letters as primary sources, consider when they were written and what they can tell you about life during those times. Use the activities below to analyze this letter.

1. Recall what you already know about the situation in Europe in August 1943. The unit time line on pages 980–981 can help you.
2. Notice Hillesum's awareness of her important role in history. How do you think this awareness influenced her choice of what to write about?
3. When you read a primary source, you need to evaluate the reliability of its writer. In other words, can the writer be trusted

continued on p. 1144

RELATED *Reading*

Primary Source

Objectives

- read and analyze primary sources
- understand how letters reveal dimensions of history
- evaluate the credibility of sources of information
- note how a writers' motivation affects credibility
- evaluate the appropriateness of information sources.

Further Background

In this excerpt of her letter, Etty Hillesum provides a detailed account of the human suffering she observed in the transit camp at Westerbork. Rather than writing a letter that simply summarizes her own thoughts, feelings, and experiences, Hillesum writes a letter that describes in detail the people and circumstances that surround her. The result is a letter that functions as a chronicle of events, grounded in a description that provides readers with a close-up perspective.

Reading for Information

Ask students to summarize Hillesum's larger purpose in writing letters, as stated in the opening paragraph.
Possible Response: to document the experience of the Jews in World War II.

Analyzing Primary Sources

1. **Possible Responses:** Major events prior to August 1943 include England's survival of the Battle of Britain, the Nazi invasion of the Soviet Union, the entry of the United States into the war, the beginning of the "Final Solution" by the Nazis, and the Allied invasion of Sicily.
2. **Possible Response:** Her role as a historian of human experience and her desire to document the depths of this human suffering led her to write about the terror, fear, and anguish of women about to be shipped to the death camps.
3. **Possible Response:** Yes, she is a credible source. Her role as a nurse at Westerbork enabled her to closely observe the people and the conditions in the camp.

4. **Possible Response:** These details suggest that life in the barracks was emotionally traumatic and physically rough.
5. **Possible Response:** Information is spread by rumor and gossip, probably based on reports of other people's experiences that have filtered back.
6. **Possible Response:** It describes the dehumanizing conditions and suggests that prisoners were treated like animals being transported in cattle cars.
7. **Possible Response:** Her statement that the process has continued for over a year suggests that the number of people sent to the death camps was high.

Comparing Texts
Possible Response: Both accounts are equally vivid and personal in their descriptions of a tragic and horrifying human experience.

Reading Skills and Strategies
Evaluating Appropriateness of Sources
Have students evaluate whether or not Hillesun's account would be an appropriate source for a paper on the Holocaust.

LaserLinks
Historical Connection
See Teacher's SourceBook p. 80 for bar codes.

❹ You really can't tell who is going and who isn't this time. Almost everyone is up, the sick help each other to get dressed. There are some who have no clothes at all, whose luggage has been lost or hasn't arrived yet. Ladies from the "Welfare" walk about doling out clothes, which may fit or not, it doesn't matter so long as you've covered yourself with something. Some old women look a ridiculous sight. Small bottles of milk are being prepared to take along with the babies, whose pitiful screams punctuate all the frantic activity in the barracks. . . . The little woman with the wet washing is on the point of hysterics. "Can't you hide my child for me? Go on, please, won't you hide him, he's got a high fever, how can I possibly take him along?" She points to a little bundle of misery with blond curls and a burning, bright-red little face. The child tosses about in his rough wooden cot. The nurse wants the mother to put on an extra woolen sweater, tries to pull it over her dress. She refuses. "I'm not going to take anything along, what use would it be? . . .
❺ my child." And she sobs, "They take the sick children away and you never get them back. . . ."

Slowly but surely six o'clock in the morning has arrived. The train is due to depart at eleven, and they are starting to load it with people and luggage. . . . The camp has been cut in two halves since yesterday by the
❻ train: a depressing series of bare, unpainted freight cars in the front, and a proper coach for the guards at the back. Some of the cars have paper mattresses on the floor. These are for the sick. . . .

My God, are the doors really being shut now? Yes, they are. Shut on the herded, densely packed mass of people inside. Through small openings at the top we can see heads and hands, hands that will wave to us later when the train leaves. . . .

❼ The tide of helpers gradually recedes; people go back to their sleeping quarters. So many exhausted, pale, and suffering faces. One more piece of our camp has been amputated. Next week yet another piece will follow. This is what has been happening now for over a year, week in, week out. . . .

Translated by Arnold J. Pomerans

to tell the truth, and was he or she in a position to know the truth? Do you think Hillesum is a credible source of information about life in Westerbork? Explain your conclusion.

❹ What does this paragraph tell you about life inside the barracks?

❺ This woman's statement, like Hillesum's earlier statement that some people know that their names are going to appear on a transport list, suggests that not everything in the camp could be kept secret. How do you think information was spread in the camp?

❻ What does this description tell you about the conditions under which prisoners were transported?

❼ From Hillesum's statements, what impression do you get about the number of people transported to the death camp? (Etty Hillesum herself was transported to Auschwitz, where she died on November 30, 1943.)

Comparing Texts How does Hillesum's account of the Holocaust compare with Elie Wiesel's account in the excerpt from *Night?*

LaserLinks: Background for Reading
Historical Connection

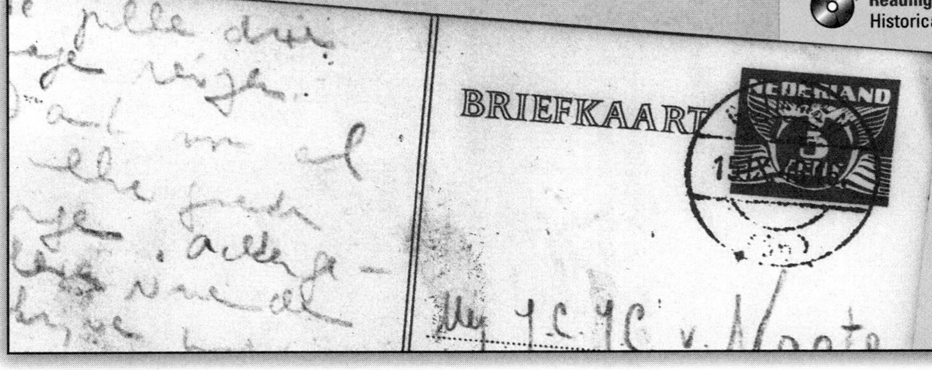

This card, thrown out of the train by Etty on 7 September, was found by farmers outside Westerbork camp and posted by them.

"Now, language is, among other things, a device which men use for suppressing and distorting the truth."

Words and Behavior

Essay by ALDOUS HUXLEY

Connect to Your Life

Breaking the News Suppose that you accidentally backed the family car into a tree, causing serious damage to the vehicle. How would you break the news to your parents? Would you describe the damage accurately and completely, or would you try to conceal or gloss over the facts? Share your thoughts with classmates.

Build Background

Social and Political Writings Throughout his life, the English novelist Aldous Huxley was concerned with social and political issues. His earliest novels satirize the vanity and foolishness of English society, and his later works reflect his skepticism about the direction in which the world was headed. Today, Huxley is best known for his 1932 novel *Brave New World,* which was viewed as a satiric warning of how dismal the world could become as a result of technology and political manipulation.

In the late 1930s, Huxley became alarmed at the turmoil that seemed to be leading up to a second world war. During the 20th century, most governments at war, or about to enter into a war, have naturally been concerned about the manner in which their activities are reported to the general public. Often, they have formed special bureaus to control the type and amount of information released to the public. The information that has been released has usually been presented in carefully worded language designed to evoke feelings of patriotism and to diminish antiwar sentiment. A few years before the start of World War II, Huxley wrote the essay "Words and Behavior," in which he reflects upon the nature of wartime communication.

WORDS TO KNOW
Vocabulary Preview

ardent	inexorable
balefully	inherently
diabolical	iniquity
embellish	odious
euphemism	vitiate

Focus Your Reading

LITERARY ANALYSIS DICTION As you would expect in an essay with this title, Huxley chooses his words very carefully. Most of the **diction,** or choice of words, in this essay is rather formal. As you read, be aware of Huxley's formal diction and the impact it has on the effectiveness of his arguments.

ACTIVE READING ANALYZING PATTERNS OF ORGANIZATION

Writers may present logical arguments in two ways:

- A **deductive argument** begins with a generalization, or premise, and then presents facts and evidence that support it and lead to a conclusion.
- An **inductive argument** begins with examples or facts and builds toward a generalization on the basis of them.

To support his main premise about the nature of language, Huxley presents **deductive arguments** about two linguistic areas—the language of war and the language of politics.

READER'S NOTEBOOK As you read Huxley's essay, complete a deductive reasoning frame, like the one shown, to track Huxley's arguments about the language of war and the language of politics. In the first box, summarize Huxley's generalization. In the smaller boxes, list the examples he uses to illustrate the generalization.

Language of War

Generalization:

Example 1:

Example 2:

Example 3:

LaserLinks: Background for Reading
Historical Connection

OVERVIEW

Objectives

1. understand and appreciate an **essay (Literary Analysis)**
2. appreciate the author's use of **diction (Literary Analysis)**
3. analyze **patterns of organization** to understand Huxley's essay **(Active Reading)**

Summary

Huxley suggests that military and political speech uses words to hide the truth and obscure reality. Using inappropriate or incorrect words prevents people from knowing the truth of a situation. Ignorance of the truth makes it difficult for people to respond appropriately and enables people to tolerate situations that in reality are intolerable. Huxley believes that to behave well, people need to avoid the temptation to hide the truth by using incorrect words.

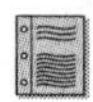

Use **Unit Six Resource Book,** p. 69 for additional support.

Thematic Link

Huxley wrote this essay in the period between the two world wars. Still horrified by the violence and atrocities of World War I, he wrote in an attempt to make people recognize the **shocking reality** of war, rather than obscure it through the power of words.

5-Minute Warm-Up

Daily Language SkillBuilder

Have students **proofread** the display sentences on page 979k and write them correctly. The sentences also appear on Transparency 31 of **Grammar Transparencies and Copymasters.**

Mini Lesson **Preteaching Vocabulary**

If you would like to preteach the WORDS TO KNOW for this selection, use the Mini Lesson on p. 1146.

LESSON RESOURCES

UNIT SIX RESOURCE BOOK, pp. 69–73

ASSESSMENT RESOURCES
Formal Assessment, pp. 211–212
Teacher's Guide to Assessment and Portfolio Use
Test Generator

SKILLS TRANSPARENCIES AND COPYMASTERS
Reading and Critical Thinking
- Analyzing Argumentation II, T22 (for Active Reading, p. 1145)

Grammar
- Commas with Nonessential Elements, T55 (for Mini Lesson, p. 1156)
- Rhythm and the Comma, C173 (for Mini Lesson, p. 1156)

Vocabulary
- Prefixes, C89 (for Mini Lesson, p. 1151)
- Synonyms, C96 (for Mini Lesson, pp. 1146–1147)

Writing
- Subject Analysis, C30 (for Writing Options, p. 1156)

Communications
- Impromptu Speaking: Debate, T15 (for Activities & Explorations, p. 1156)

INTEGRATED TECHNOLOGY
Audio Library
LaserLinks
- Historical Connection: Wartime Propaganda. See **Teacher's SourceBook,** p. 81.

Visit our website:
www.mcdougallittell.com

TEACHING THE LITERATURE

Reading and Analyzing

Literary Analysis DICTION

Explain to students that diction is a writer's choice of words and that Huxley's essay can be described as having formal diction. Explain to students that this essay is argumentative; in other words, it is trying to convince you of something. Ask students why a writer of an argumentative essay might choose to use formal diction.
Possible Response: to sound intelligent and serious.

Use **Unit Six Resource Book** p. 71 for more exercises.

Active Reading

ANALYZING PATTERNS OF ORGANIZATION

Explain to students that all writers of fiction and nonfiction choose a pattern of organization, or structure, for presenting their information, arguments, or stories. Review with students the explanation of a deductive argument given on p. 1145. For each of Huxley's deductive arguments, have students fill in a deductive reasoning frame like the one on p. 1145.

Use **Unit Six Resource Book** p. 70 for more practice.

ACTIVE READING

A CLARIFY **Possible Response:** Ignorance allows people to evade the dictates of their consciences.

Words and Behavior

ALDOUS HUXLEY

1146

Teaching Options

Preteaching Vocabulary

SYNONYMS

Instruction Tell students that identifying a word's synonym can be helpful in learning how to use a word. Remind students that synonyms are words with the same or similar meanings.

Activity Write on the chalkboard the following sentences. Instruct students to find the WORD TO KNOW that is a synonym for the underlined word in each sentence.

1. The song's rise in popularity was unrelenting, and soon it was heard everywhere. (Answer: inexorable)
2. The mongoose maliciously approached the cobra. (Answer: balefully)
3. The speaker did his best to adorn his speech with flowery phrasing. (Answer: embellish)
4. His wrongdoing led to his downfall. (Answer: iniquity)

Words form the thread on which we string our experiences. Without them we should live spasmodically and intermittently. Hatred itself is not so strong that animals will not forget it, if distracted, even in the presence of the enemy. Watch a pair of cats, crouching on the brink of a fight. Balefully the eyes glare; from far down in the throat of each come bursts of a strange, strangled noise of defiance; as though animated by a life of their own, the tails twitch and tremble. With aimed intensity of loathing! Another moment and surely there must be an explosion. But no; all of a sudden one of the two creatures turns away, hoists a hind leg in a more than fascist salute[1] and, with the same fixed and focused attention as it had given a moment before to its enemy, begins to make a lingual toilet.[2] Animal love is as much at the mercy of distractions as animal hatred. The dumb creation lives a life made up of discrete[3] and mutually irrelevant episodes. Such as it is, the consistency of human characters is due to the words upon which all human experiences are strung. We are purposeful because we can describe our feelings in rememberable words, can justify and rationalize our desires in terms of some kind of argument. Faced by an enemy we do not allow an itch to distract us from our emotions; the mere word "enemy" is enough to keep us reminded of our hatred, to convince us that we do well to be angry. Similarly the word "love" bridges for us those chasms of momentary indifference and boredom which gape from time to time between even the most ardent lovers. Feeling and desire provide us with our motive power; words give continuity to what we do and to a considerable extent determine our direction. Inappropriate and badly chosen words vitiate thought and lead to wrong or foolish conduct. Most ignorances are vincible,[4] and in the greater number of cases stupidity is what the Buddha pronounced it to be, a sin. For, consciously, or subconsciously, it is with deliberation that we do not know or fail to understand—because incomprehension allows us, with a good conscience, to evade unpleasant obligations and responsibilities, because ignorance is the best excuse for going on doing what one likes, but ought not, to do. Our egotisms are incessantly fighting to preserve themselves, not only from external enemies, but also from the assaults of the other and better self with which they are so uncomfortably associated. Ignorance is egotism's most effective defense against that Dr. Jekyll[5] in us who desires perfection; stupidity, its subtlest stratagem. If, as so often happens, we choose to give continuity to our experience by means of words which falsify the facts, this is because the falsification is somehow to our advantage as egotists.

ACTIVE READING

CLARIFY According to Huxley, how do people use ignorance as a defense? 

Consider, for example, the case of war. War is enormously discreditable to those who order it to be waged and even to those who merely tolerate its existence. Furthermore, to developed sensibilities the facts of war are revolting and horrifying. To falsify these facts, and by so doing to make war seem less evil than it really is, and our own responsibility in tolerating war less heavy, is doubly to our advantage. By suppressing and distorting the truth, we protect our sensibilities and preserve our self-esteem. Now, language is, among other things, a device which men use for suppressing and distorting the

1. **fascist** (făsh′ĭst) **salute:** a salute, used in Nazi Germany, in which the arm is rigidly extended forward, slightly above the horizontal.
2. **make a lingual toilet:** clean itself with its tongue.
3. **discrete:** separate; distinct.
4. **vincible** (vĭn′sə-bəl): capable of being overcome.
5. **Dr. Jekyll:** in Robert Louis Stevenson's novel *The Strange Case of Dr. Jekyll and Mr. Hyde,* an idealistic medical researcher who is transformed by an experimental drug into the murderously evil Mr. Hyde.

WORDS TO KNOW

balefully (bāl′fə-lē) *adv.* in a menacing way; wickedly
ardent (är′dnt) *adj.* passionate
vitiate (vĭsh′ē-āt′) *v.* to destroy the quality of; corrupt; debase

1147

Customizing Instruction

Less Proficient Readers

Set a Purpose Have students read to find out why people use language that distorts the truth.

Students Acquiring English

Students will probably have difficulty with Huxley's formal diction. You might want to have students get together in small groups to discuss the essay and any questions that arise from reading it. Remind them to make use of the footnotes and WORDS TO KNOW definitions.

Use **Spanish Study Guide** for additional support, pp. 272–274.

Gifted and Talented

Ask students to convene a roundtable discussion to consider the complementary theories that language influences thought and that thought influences language. Have them give several examples of each theory. Suggest that students address the question of whether both theories can hold true or whether only one can be true.

5. Her use of equivocation made it difficult to understand what she was trying to say. (Answer: euphemism)
6. To see a real Babylonian ziggurat was his most heartfelt desire. (Answer: ardent)
7. The car gave out a huge, disgusting cloud of stinking exhaust. (Answer: odious)
8. The story is not intrinsically that good; the way it is told makes it entertaining. (Answer: inherently)
9. Greed began to spoil the investor's judgment. (Answer: vitiate)
10. The fiendish king threw his country into a state of revolt. (Answer: diabolical)

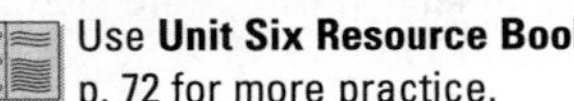

Use **Unit Six Resource Book** p. 72 for more practice.

Reading and Analyzing

Literary Analysis: Persuasion

A Invite students to point out emotional appeals in this paragraph.
Possible Responses: the assertion that war kills and injures innocent people; the use of loaded language such as "monstrous" and "to murder or be murdered."

Active Reading

ANALYZING PATTERNS OF ORGANIZATION

B Direct students' attention to the paragraph beginning "The language of strategy and politics . . . ," and tell them that it presents a generalization that will be supported by the following paragraphs. Be sure students recognize that Huxley's organizational pattern is not always signaled by paragraph breaks. Challenge them to identify the supporting points using a deductive reasoning frame.

truth. Finding the reality of war too unpleasant to contemplate, we create a verbal alternative to that reality, parallel with it, but in quality quite different from it. That which we contemplate thenceforward is not that to which we react emotionally and upon which we pass our moral judgments, is not war as it is in fact, but the fiction of war as it exists in our pleasantly falsifying verbiage. **1** Our stupidity in using inappropriate language turns out, on analysis, to be the most refined cunning.

A The most shocking fact about war is that its victims and its instruments are individual human beings, and that these individual human beings are condemned by the monstrous conventions of politics to murder or be murdered in quarrels not their own, to inflict upon the innocent and, innocent themselves of any crime against their enemies, to suffer cruelties of every kind.

Language

B The language of strategy and politics is designed, so far as it is possible, to conceal this fact, to make it appear as though wars were not fought by individuals drilled to murder one another in cold blood and without provocation, but either by impersonal and therefore wholly non-moral and impassible forces, or else by personified abstractions.

Here are a few examples of the first kind of falsification. In place of "cavalrymen" or "foot soldiers" military writers like to speak of "sabers" and "rifles." Here is a sentence from a description of the Battle of Marengo:[6] "According to Victor's report, the French retreat was orderly; it is certain, at any rate, that the regiments held together, for the six thousand Austrian sabers found no opportunity to charge home." The battle is between sabers in line and muskets in échelon[7]—a mere clash of ironmongery.[8]

On other occasions there is no question of anything so vulgarly material as ironmongery. The battles are between Platonic ideas,[9] between the abstractions of physics and mathematics. Forces interact; weights are flung into scales; masses are set in motion. Or else it is all a matter of geometry. Lines swing and sweep; are protracted or curved; pivot on a fixed point.

Alternatively the combatants are personal, in the sense that they are personifications. There is "the enemy," in the singular, making "his" plans, striking "his" blows. The attribution of personal characteristics to collectivities,[10] to geographical expressions, to institutions, is a source, as we shall see, of endless confusions in political thought, of innumerable political mistakes and crimes. Personification in politics is an error which we make because it is to our advantage as egotists to be able to feel violently proud of our country and of ourselves as belonging to it, and to believe that all the misfortunes due to our own mistakes are really the work of the Foreigner. It is easier to feel violently toward a person than toward an abstraction; hence our habit of making political personifications. In some cases military personifications are merely special instances of political personifications. A particular collectivity, the army or the warring nation, is given the name and, along with the name, the attributes of a single person, in order that we may be able to love or hate it more intensely than we could do if we thought of it as what it really is: a number of diverse individuals. In other cases personification

6. **Battle of Marengo:** a battle fought in 1800, in which French troops led by Napoleon Bonaparte defeated an Austrian army near the town of Marengo in northern Italy.
7. **échelon** (ĕsh′ə-lŏn′): an arrangement of groups of soldiers in a steplike formation.
8. **ironmongery** (ī′ərn-mŭng′gə-rē): hardware.
9. **Platonic ideas:** in the thought of Plato (a Greek philosopher of the fourth century B.C.), immaterial realities that all actual things are copies of.
10. **collectivities:** groups of people.

Teaching Options

BLOCK SCHEDULING: MANAGING TIME

If your schedule requires that you cover the lesson in a shorter time, use . . .

- Preparing to Read, p. 1145
- Thinking Through the Literature, p. 1155
- Vocabulary in Action, p. 1156

If you want to take advantage of longer class time, use . . .

- TE Teaching Options: Preteaching Vocabulary, pp. 1146–1147; Viewing and Representing, p. 1150; Speaking and Listening, p. 1152; Standardized Test Practice, p. 1149; Vocabulary, p. 1151; Multicultural Link, p. 1153; Informal Assessment, p. 1154; Grammar, p. 1156
- Choices & Challenges, p. 1156

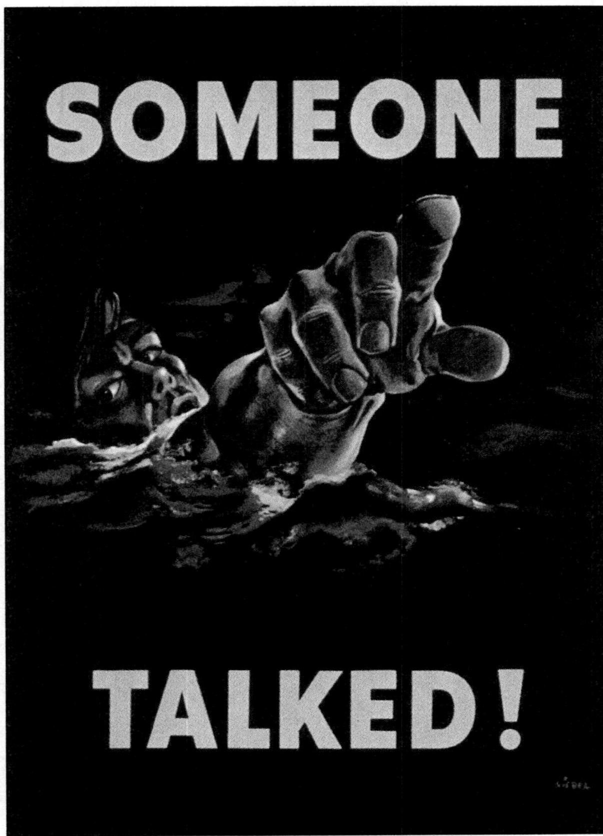

Official Photograph, United States Air Force, courtesy of Sam. R. Quincey.

is used for the purpose of concealing the fundamental absurdity and monstrosity of war. What is absurd and monstrous about war is that men who have no personal quarrel should be trained to murder one another in cold blood. By personifying opposing armies or countries, we are able to think of war as a conflict between individuals. The same result is obtained by writing of war as though it were carried on exclusively by the generals in command and not by the private soldiers in their armies. ("Rennenkampf had pressed back von Schubert.") The implication in both cases is that war is indistinguishable from a bout of fisticuffs[11] in a bar room. Whereas in reality it is profoundly different. A scrap between two individuals is forgivable; mass murder, deliberately organized, is a monstrous <u>iniquity</u>. We still 2
choose to use war as an instrument of policy; and to comprehend the full wickedness and absurdity of war would therefore be inconvenient. For, once we understood, we should have to make some effort to get rid of the abominable thing. Accordingly, when we talk about war, we use a language which conceals or <u>embellishes</u> its reality. Ignoring the facts, so far as we possibly can, we imply that battles are not fought by soldiers, but by things, principles, allegories, personified collectivities, or (at the most human) by opposing commanders, pitched against one another in single combat. For the same reason, when we have to describe the processes and the results of war, we employ a rich variety of <u>euphemisms</u>. Even the most violently patriotic and militaristic are reluctant to call a spade by its own name. To conceal their inten- 3
tions even from themselves, they make use of picturesque metaphors. We find them, for example, clamoring for war planes numerous and powerful enough to go and "destroy the hornets in

11. **fisticuffs** (fĭs′tĭ-kŭfs′): fighting with the fists.

WORDS TO KNOW

iniquity (ĭ-nĭk′wĭ-tē) *n.* immorality; wickedness
embellish (ĕm-bĕl′ĭsh) *v.* to add ornamental or fictitious details to; decorate
euphemism (yo͞o′fə-mĭz′əm) *n.* a mild or vague term used in place of a blunt or offensive one

Customizing Instruction

Students Acquiring English

1 Help students understand that "pleasantly falsifying verbiage" means "words that tell pleasant lies." Ask students what Huxley claims these pleasant lies cause us to think about.
Possible Response: the fiction rather than the reality of war.

Less Proficient Readers

2 Ask students whether they agree with Huxley's opinion that war is mass murder and never justified.
Answer: Responses will vary.

How do they think, as Huxley suggests, we could "get rid of the abominable thing"?
Answer: Responses will vary.

Students Acquiring English

3 Help students understand the phrase "to call a spade by its own name."
Answer: to call something by its rightful name; to be honest.

Standardized Test Practice

CHOOSING THE BEST SUMMARY Some standardized tests require students to find the best summary of a passage. To help students practice this skill, write on the chalkboard the following question and multiple-choice options:
Which of the following statements best summarizes the argument of Huxley's essay?

A. The use of deceptive language allows people to disguise the fact that war and politics lead to murder, hate, and cruelty.
B. By using deceptive wording, we often think of war as disagreements between individuals.
C. Language is a subject that is often not helpful during war.

Guide students to understand that although all three sentences pertain to the passage, only **A** summarizes the most important information.

Reading and Analyzing

ACTIVE READING

A CLARIFY **Possible Response:** Abstract words can be substituted for concrete words, thus concealing the fact that people suffer and die in war.

Reading Skills and Strategies: **PARAPHRASING**

B Ask students to put into their own words Huxley's distinction between the force used by the police and that used during war.
Possible Response: Police force is used against guilty people; that used in time of war is used against innocent people.

Literary Analysis: **DICTION**

C Ask students why Huxley chooses to replace "force" with phrases including the words *thermite, high explosives,* and *vesicants.*
Possible Response: These are concrete terms that realistically convey war's destructive power.

war

their nests"—in other words, to go and throw thermite,[12] high explosives and vesicants[13] upon the inhabitants of neighboring countries before they have time to come and do the same to us. And how reassuring is the language of historians and strategists! They write admiringly of those military geniuses who know "when to strike at the enemy's line" (a single combatant deranges the geometrical constructions of a personification); when to "turn his flank"; when to "execute an enveloping movement." As though they were engineers discussing the strength of materials and the distribution of stresses, they talk of abstract entities called "man power" and "fire power." They sum up the long-drawn sufferings and atrocities of trench warfare in the phrase, "a war of attrition";[14] the massacre and mangling of human beings is assimilated to the grinding of a lens.[15] A dangerously abstract word, which figures in all discussions about war, is "force." Those who believe in organizing collective security by means of military pacts against a possible aggressor are particularly fond of this word. "You cannot," they say, "have international justice unless you are prepared to impose it by force." "Peace-loving countries must unite to use force against aggressive dictatorships." "Democratic institutions must be protected, if need be, by force." And so on.

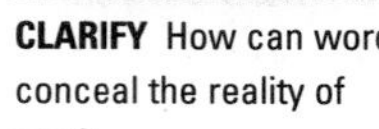

ACTIVE READING

A **CLARIFY** How can words conceal the reality of war?

Now, the word "force," when used in reference to human relations, has no single, definite meaning. There is the "force" used by parents when, without resort to any kind of physical violence, they compel their children to act or refrain from acting in some particular way. There is the "force" used by attendants in an asylum when they try to prevent a maniac from hurting himself or others. There is the "force" used by the police when they control a crowd, and that other "force" which they use in a baton charge.[16] And finally there is the "force" used in war. This, of course, varies with the technological devices at the disposal of the belligerents, with the policies they are pursuing, and with the particular circumstances of the war in question. But in general it may be said that, in war, "force" connotes violence and fraud used to the limit of the combatants' capacity. **B**

Variations in quantity, if sufficiently great, produce variations in quality. The "force" that is war, particularly modern war, is very different from the "force" that is police action, and the use of the same abstract word to describe the two dissimilar processes is profoundly misleading. (Still more misleading, of course, is the explicit assimilation of a war, waged by allied League-of-Nations powers against an aggressor, **1** to police action against a criminal. The first is the use of violence and fraud without limit against innocent and guilty alike; the second is the use of strictly limited violence and a minimum of fraud exclusively against the guilty.)

Reality is a succession of concrete and particular situations. When we think about such situations we should use the particular and concrete words which apply to them. If we use abstract words which apply equally well (and equally badly) to other, quite dissimilar situations, it is certain that we shall think incorrectly.

Let us take the sentences quoted above and translate the abstract word "force" into language

12. **thermite:** a mixture of chemicals that burns very intensely, used in certain kinds of bombs.
13. **vesicants** (vĕs′ĭ-kənts): chemical agents, such as mustard gas, that cause inflammation and blistering of the skin and internal tissues.
14. **attrition:** a gradual process of wearing down.
15. **assimilated . . . lens:** likened to the process by which glass is ground into lenses.
16. **baton charge:** the beating back of a mob by policemen wielding wooden clubs.

Teaching Options

Mini Lesson: Viewing and Representing

War Posters
ART APPRECIATION

Instruction Explain that the use of language or symbols to manipulate people is called propaganda. Nations at war use various forms of propaganda to manipulate their citizens' feelings and behavior. Direct students' attention to the posters reproduced on pp. 1149, 1151, 1153, and 1154. Explain that these are all posters issued by governments and aimed at persuading citizens to support the war effort.

Application Tell students that, just as in writing, visual persuasive techniques can be deceptive. Divide students into groups, and assign each group one of the posters. Have each group examine its image to distinguish its purpose, to get the main idea of its content, and to evaluate and critique its persuasive techniques.

Possible Response: The image on p. 1153 aims to persuade Englishmen to enlist in the armed forces. Its main idea is that being a soldier is the highest calling an Englishman could aspire to. Its persuasive techniques include the appeal to Englishmen's patriotism.

that will render (however inadequately) the concrete and particular realities of contemporary warfare.

"You cannot have international justice, unless you are prepared to impose it by force." Translated, this becomes: "You cannot have international justice unless you are prepared, with a view to imposing a just settlement, to drop thermite, high explosives and vesicants upon the inhabitants of C 2 foreign cities and to have thermite, high explosives and vesicants dropped in return upon the inhabitants of your cities." At the end of this proceeding, justice is to be imposed by the victorious party—that is, if there is a victorious party. It should be remarked that justice was to have been imposed by the victorious party at the end of the last war. But, unfortunately, after four years of fighting, the temper of the victors was such that they were quite incapable of making a just settlement. The Allies are reaping in Nazi Germany what they sowed at Versailles.[17] The victors of the next war will have undergone intensive bombardments with thermite, high explosives and vesicants. Will their temper be better than that of the Allies in 1918? Will they be in a fitter state to make a just settlement? The answer, quite obviously, is: No. It is psychologically all but impossible that justice should be secured by the methods of contemporary warfare.

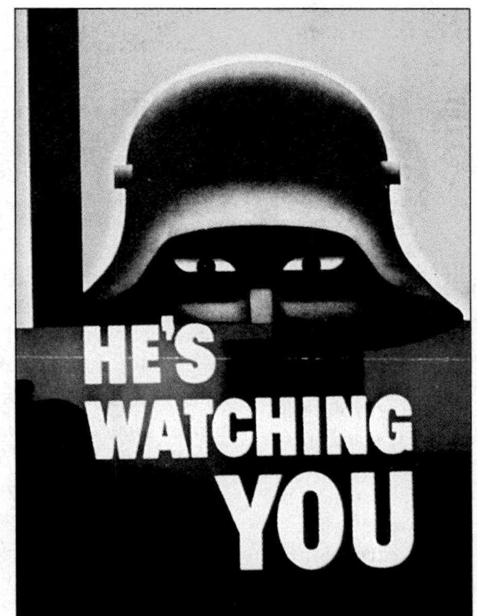

He's Watching You (1942), Glenn Grohe. American World War II poster, The Granger Collection, New York.

The next two sentences may be taken together. "Peace-loving countries must unite to use force against aggressive dictatorships. Democratic institutions must be protected, if need be, by force." Let us translate. "Peace-loving countries must unite to throw thermite, high explosives and vesicants on the inhabitants of countries ruled by aggressive dictators. They must do this, and of course abide the consequences, in order to preserve peace and democratic institutions." Two questions immediately propound[18] themselves. First, is it likely that peace can be secured by a process calculated to reduce the orderly life of our complicated societies to chaos? And, second, is it likely that democratic institutions will flourish in a state of chaos? Again, the answers are pretty clearly in the negative.

By using the abstract word "force," instead of terms which at least attempt to describe the realities of war as it is today, the preachers of collective security through military collaboration disguise from themselves and from others, not only the contemporary facts, but also the probable consequences of their favorite policy. The attempt to secure justice, peace and democracy by "force" seems reasonable enough until we realize, first, that this noncommittal word stands, in the circumstances of our age, for activities which can hardly fail to result in social chaos; and second, that the

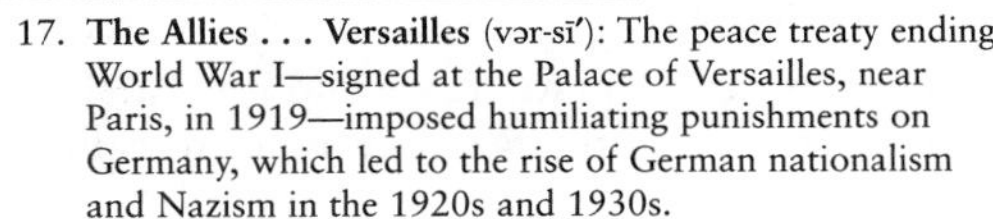

17. **The Allies . . . Versailles** (vər-sī′): The peace treaty ending World War I—signed at the Palace of Versailles, near Paris, in 1919—imposed humiliating punishments on Germany, which led to the rise of German nationalism and Nazism in the 1920s and 1930s.

18. **propound:** to put forward for consideration; pose.

Customizing Instruction

Gifted and Talented

1 Invite interested students to research World War I and the League of Nations. An understanding of the outcome of World War I and the alliances formed out of it will greatly enhance students' understanding of the essay. Suggest that students work together to create a brief group presentation of the historical context of this essay to deliver for the whole class.

Less Proficient Readers

2 Explain that Huxley repeats words to emphasize his message. Then ask students why Huxley repeats the words *thermite, high explosives,* and *vesicants.*

Possible Response: to emphasize his message that abstract terms are misleading and wrong and to underscore the horrors of war.

Mini Lesson Vocabulary Strategy

PREFIXES

Instruction Explain to students that a prefix may have several different meanings. Point out that the WORDS TO KNOW *inexorable, inherently,* and *iniquity* begin with the same prefix. That prefix, *in–,* however, means "in" or "not" depending on to which word it is attached.

Activity Have students use a dictionary to determine the meaning of each of the three words, then have them determine whether each word's prefix means "in" or "not."

Answer: inexorable–"not"; inherently–"in"; iniquity–"not"

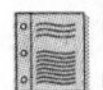
Use **Vocabulary Transparencies and Copymasters,** p. 65.

WORDS AND BEHAVIOR **1151**

Reading and Analyzing

Active Reading

ANALYZING PATTERNS OF ORGANIZATION

A Ask students what generalization Huxley uses to support his argument that language is used to conceal the truth.

Possible Response: In politics, language is used to arouse and justify certain emotional attitudes.

Literary Analysis DICTION

B Tell students that Huxley began his literary career as a poet, and direct their attention to these lines. Ask them what impact this diction has in Huxley's essay.

Possible Response: The passage adds eloquence and dignity to the essay and makes it seem more earnest and effective.

Reading Skills and Strategies: SUMMARIZING

C Remind students that a summary is a shortened version of a text, put in the reader's own words, which leaves out everything but the most important information. Have students summarize this paragraph.

Possible Response: Speaking about certain people in abstract terms obscures their individuality and humanity and allows hateful characteristics to be attached to them so that moral concerns can be avoided.

consequences of social chaos are injustice, chronic warfare and tyranny. The moment we think in concrete and particular terms of the concrete and particular process called "modern war," we see that a policy which worked (or at least didn't result in complete disaster) in the past has no prospect whatever of working in the immediate future. The attempt to secure justice, peace and democracy by means of a "force," which means, at this particular moment of history, thermite, high explosives and vesicants, is about as reasonable as the attempt to put out a fire with a colorless liquid
1 that happens to be, not water, but petrol.

What applies to the "force" that is war applies in large measure to the "force" that is revolution. It seems inherently very unlikely that social justice and social peace can be secured by thermite, high explosives and vesicants. At first, it may be, the parties in a civil war would hesitate to use such instruments on their fellow-countrymen. But there can be little doubt that, if the conflict were prolonged (as it probably would be between the evenly balanced Right and Left of a highly industrialized society), the combatants would end by losing their scruples.

The alternatives confronting us seem to be plain enough. Either we invent and conscientiously employ a new technique for making revolutions and settling international disputes; or else we cling to the old technique and, using "force" (that is to say, thermite, high explosives and vesicants), destroy ourselves. Those who, for whatever motive, disguise the nature of the second alternative under inappropriate language, render the world a grave disservice. They lead us into one of the temptations we find it hardest to resist—the temptation to run away from reality, to pretend that facts are not what they are. Like Shelley (but without Shelley's acute awareness of what he was doing) we are perpetually weaving

A shroud of talk to hide us from the sun
Of this familiar life.

Politics

We protect our minds by an elaborate system of abstractions, ambiguities, metaphors and similes from the reality we do not wish to know too clearly; we lie to ourselves, in order that we may still have the excuse of ignorance, the alibi of stupidity and incomprehension, possessing which we can continue with a good conscience to commit and tolerate the most monstrous crimes: A

The poor wretch who has learned his only prayers
From curses, who knows scarcely words enough
To ask a blessing from his Heavenly Father,
Becomes a fluent phraseman, absolute
And technical in victories and defeats,
And all our dainty terms for fratricide;[19]
Terms which we trundle smoothly o'er our tongues
Like mere abstractions, empty sounds to which
We join no meaning and attach no form! B
As if the soldier died without a wound:
As if the fibers of this godlike frame
Were gored without a pang: as if the wretch
Who fell in battle, doing bloody deeds,
Passed off to Heaven translated and not killed;
As though he had no wife to pine for him,
No God to judge him.

The language we use about war is inappropriate, and its inappropriateness is designed to conceal a reality so odious that we do not wish to know it. The language we use about politics is also inap-

19. **fratricide** (frăt′rĭ-sīd′): the killing of one's brother or sister.

WORDS TO KNOW
inherently (ĭn-hîr′ənt-lē) *adv.* essentially; naturally
odious (ō′dē-əs) *adj.* disgusting; hateful

1152

Teaching Options

Speaking and Listening

MAKING A SPEECH

Instruction Explain to students that the wartime communication techniques outlined by Huxley are very effective even though they are misleading. Point out that Huxley's own methods of honesty and directness can also be very persuasive.

Prepare Divide students into small groups. Ask students to act as though the government is pushing for the U.S. to enter a war. Have half of the groups write a speech in support of war, using the techniques of depersonifying persons, personifying abstractions, and using euphemisms; have the other half write a speech opposed to war, using direct, honest, specific words.

Present Have each group work together to write its speech, and have each group select a volunteer to read it to the class. Guide the class in a discussion of the effectiveness of each of the speeches and their techniques.

BLOCK SCHEDULING This activity is particularly well-suited for longer class periods.

propriate; but here our mistake has a different purpose. Our principal aim in this case is to arouse and, having aroused, to rationalize and justify such intrinsically[20] agreeable sentiments as pride and hatred, self-esteem and contempt for others. To achieve this end we speak about the facts of politics in words which more or less completely misrepresent them. . . .

C The evil passions are further justified by another linguistic error—the error of speaking about certain categories of persons as though they were mere embodied abstractions. Foreigners and those who disagree with us are not thought of as men and women like ourselves and our fellow-countrymen; they are thought of as representatives and, so to say, symbols of a class. In so far as they have any personality at all, it is the personality we mistakenly attribute to their class—a personality that is, by definition, intrinsically evil. We know that the harming or killing of men and women is wrong, and we are reluctant consciously to do what we know to be wrong. But when particular men and women are thought of merely as representatives of a class, which has previously been defined as evil and personified in the shape of a devil, then the reluctance to hurt or murder disappears. Brown, Jones and Robinson are no longer thought of as Brown, Jones and Robinson, but as heretics, gentiles, Yids, niggers, barbarians, Huns, communists, capitalists, fascists, liberals[21]—whichever the case may be. When they have been called such names and assimilated to the accursed class to which the names apply, Brown, Jones and Robinson cease to be conceived as what they really are—human persons—and become for the users of this fatally inappropriate language mere vermin or, worse, demons whom it is right and proper to destroy as thoroughly and as painfully as possible. Wherever persons are present, questions of morality arise. Rulers of nations and leaders of parties find morality embarrassing. That is why they take such pains to depersonalize their opponents. All propaganda directed against an opposing group has but one aim: to substitute diabolical abstractions for concrete persons. The propagandist's purpose is to make one set of people forget that certain other sets of people are human. By robbing them of their per-

The Only Road for an Englishman (1914), Gerald Spencer Pryse. Imperial War Museum, London.

20. **intrinsically** (ĭn-trĭn′zĭk-lē): inherently; essentially.
21. **heretics . . . liberals:** terms used to disparage groups of people. (*Yid* is an offensive term for a Jew, and *Huns* was what some British people called the Germans during World War I.)

WORDS TO KNOW

diabolical (dī′ə-bŏl′ĭ-kəl) *adj.* extremely wicked or cruel; devilish

Customizing Instruction

Students Acquiring English

1 Ask a volunteer what Americans would say instead of *petrol.*

Answer: gasoline.

Less Proficient Readers

Ask students to explain the analogy comparing the use of a colorless liquid to put out a fire to the use of explosives to secure justice.

Possible Response: If the colorless liquid were gasoline, it would just feed the flames. Likewise, explosives would only strengthen the enemy's resolve.

Multicultural Link: Native American Code Talkers

Words, during wartime, have other uses than as propaganda. They are also changed into codes to transmit crucial information between military units.

Near the end of World War I, fourteen Choctaw "Code Talkers" in the Army's 36th Division used their native language as an unbreakable code, helping the AEF win several key battles against the Germans. The Choctaw language was also used in World War II, again with great success.

Other "Code Talkers" in World War II were a small group of Comanches in the Signal Corps and a large number of Navajos with the Marines in the Pacific.

The Navajo Code Talkers began with 29 men but eventually included 400. Using the complex syntax and tonal qualities of Navajo, the code talkers sent thousands of messages, of which not one was deciphered by the Japanese. They were especially successful at Iwo Jima, where the entire landing was communicated in Navajo by the Navajo Code Talkers.

Reading and Analyzing

ACTIVE READING

A ANALYZE **Possible Response:** to allow people to support their nations' war effort; to foster nationalism; to encourage hatred of the opponent.

Literary Analysis: PERSUASIVE ESSAY

Point out that most of the text on this page is the conclusion of Huxley's essay. Ask students to list ways Huxley strengthens his argument in the conclusion.
Possible Responses: by restating his main point about the use of abstractions to represent concrete reality; by introducing a thought-provoking comparison between internal and external politics; by using connotatively rich words such as "stupidity" and "self-interest"; by making an appeal to morality.

Reading Skills and Strategies: SUMMARIZING

Ask students what main generalizations the author uses to support his argument.
Possible Response: He says the language used to describe war and that used by political leaders to describe opponents both use abstractions in place of concrete words, in the first place to conceal the reality that war is mass murder and atrocity and in the second place to support political leaders' self-interest and to allow people to act in immoral ways.

sonality, he puts them outside the pale of moral obligation. Mere symbols can have no rights—particularly when that of which they are symbolical is, by definition, evil.

ACTIVE READING

A **ANALYZE** What **argument** does Huxley give for why rulers "depersonalize their opponents"?

Politics can become moral only on one condition: that its problems shall be spoken of and thought about exclusively in terms of concrete reality; that is to say, of persons. To depersonify human beings and to personify abstractions are complementary errors which lead, by an inexorable logic, to war between nations and to idolatrous worship of the State, with consequent governmental oppression. All current political thought is a mixture, in varying proportions, between thought in terms of concrete realities and thought in terms of depersonified symbols and personified abstractions. In the democratic countries the problems of internal politics are thought about mainly in terms of concrete reality; those of external politics, mainly in terms of abstractions and symbols. In dictatorial countries the proportion of concrete to abstract and symbolic thought is lower than in democratic countries. Dictators talk little of persons, much of personified abstractions, such as the Nation, the State, the Party, and much of depersonified symbols, such as Yids, Bolshies,[22] Capitalists. The stupidity of politicians who talk about a world of persons as though it were not a world of persons is due in the main to self-interest. In a fictitious world of symbols and personified abstractions, rulers find that they can rule more effectively, and the ruled, that they can gratify instincts which the conventions of good manners and the imperatives of morality demand that they should repress. To think correctly is the condition of behaving well. It is also in itself a moral act; those who would think correctly must resist considerable temptations. ❖

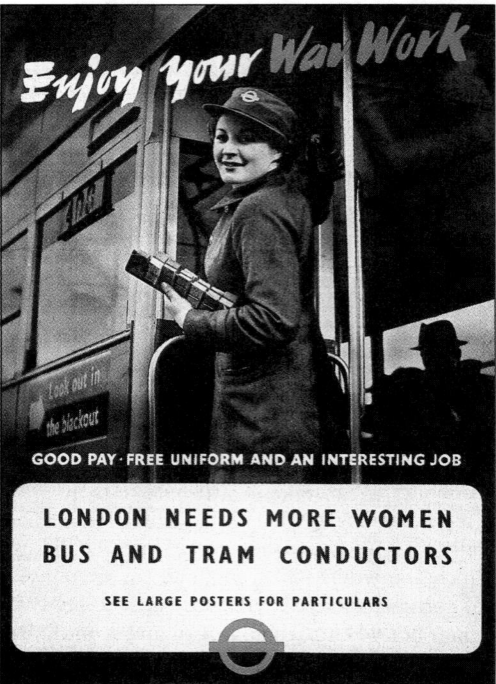

Enjoy Your War Work (1941), unknown artist. London Transport Museum.

22. **Bolshies:** Communists (after *Bolshevik,* the name of the Russian Communist faction that came to power in the 1917 revolution).

WORDS TO KNOW **inexorable** (ĭn-ĕk'sər-ə-bəl) *adj.* unyielding; relentless

1154

Teaching Options

Mini Lesson Informal Assessment

WRITING ABOUT WORDS AND BEHAVIOR

Have students write a brief essay in which they discuss what they learned from the selection about the relationship between words and behavior.

RUBRIC

3 **Full Accomplishment** Essay touches on and displays full understanding of all of selection's major points regarding relationship between words and behavior.

2 **Substantial Accomplishment** Essay touches on and displays adequate understanding of most of selection's major points regarding relationship between words and behavior.

1 **Little or Partial Accomplishment** Essay touches on few or none of selection's major points regarding relationship between words and behavior and displays little or no understanding of those points.

Connect to the Literature

1. **What Do You Think?** What is your overall reaction to Huxley's ideas in this essay?

Comprehension Check

- According to Huxley, why do military powers talk about "lines" and "forces" instead of "soldiers"?
- What does Huxley think people must do in order to behave well?

Think Critically

2. Adopting the role of Aldous Huxley, explain what you hoped to achieve by writing this **essay.**

3. If Huxley were asked to describe the worst effect of using **euphemisms** and **abstractions** to gloss over the facts of war, what do you think he would say?

- the examples of euphemisms and abstractions that he gives
- the reasons people use euphemisms
- the dangers of using abstractions

4. **ACTIVE READING** **ANALYZING PATTERNS OF ORGANIZATION** Review the deductive reasoning frame you made in your **READER'S NOTEBOOK**. What are Huxley's main points about the language of war and of politics? Which of his examples do you think best illustrate these two main points?

5. Do you think Huxley's arguments are objective and convincing? Explain your answer.

Extend Interpretations

6. **Comparing Texts** How do you think Huxley might have reacted to Winston Churchill's speech of May 19, 1940 (page 1127)? Cite specific passages in your answer.

7. **Connect to Life** If people always spoke as directly as possible and never used euphemisms or abstractions to gloss over facts, what do you think would be the results? Be specific in your answer.

Literary Analysis

DICTION One important element of any writer's style is **diction,** or choice of words. Diction includes both **vocabulary** (individual words) and **syntax** (the order or arrangement of words). A writer's diction may be described as formal or informal, as technical or ordinary, as abstract or concrete. Most of the language in Huxley's essay is formal, as in the sentence beginning "Our egotisms are incessantly fighting to preserve themselves . . ." (page 1147).

Activity Rewrite the sentence cited above in informal language. Then find two other examples of formal diction in the essay and rewrite them as well. How do you think the use of less formal diction affects the sentences' impact on the reader?

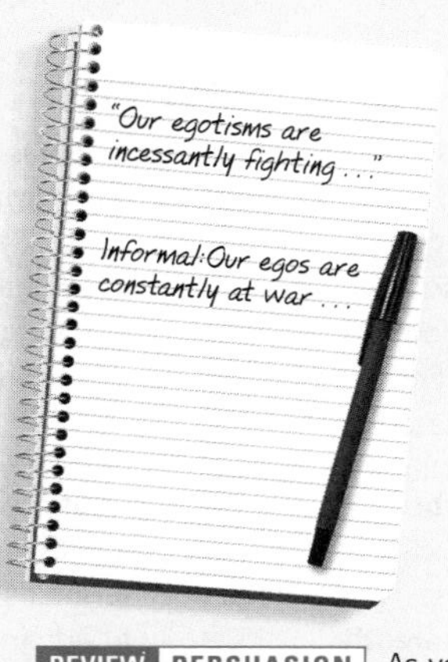

"Our egotisms are incessantly fighting . . ."
Informal: Our egos are constantly at war . . .

REVIEW **PERSUASION** As you recall, **persuasion**—the technique of convincing an audience to adopt an opinion, perform an action, or both—may use both logical appeals and emotional appeals. Does Huxley use both of these approaches in his essay? Explain your answer.

GUIDING STUDENT RESPONSE

Connect to the Literature

1. **What Do You Think?** Guidelines for student response: You might have students relate Huxley's ideas to political life today.

Comprehension Check

- to depersonify their opponents
- They must think correctly by using concrete language that doesn't disguise the truth.

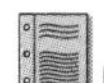 Use Selection Quiz in **Unit Six Resource Book** p. 73.

Think Critically

2. Possible Responses: I hoped to change the way those in power misuse language; I hoped to help people recognize the true horror of war.
3. Possible Response: Euphemisms and abstractions used in reference to war hide its horrors and allow people to rationalize and tolerate war.
4. Accept all reasonable, well-supported responses.
5. Make sure students who find his argument unconvincing point out the places they think Huxley's reasoning is flawed.

Literary Analysis

Activity Have volunteers read their rewritings of Huxley's sentences in less formal language. Student rewrites should show awareness of the importance of vocabulary and syntax in achieving an informal tone.
Review Persuasion Have students cite examples from Huxley of both logical and emotional appeals to support their answers.

Extend Interpretations

Comparing Texts Possible Responses: Huxley would consider Churchill's speech the epitome of what he was attacking in his essay; Huxley would have approved of Churchill's concrete diction and his avoidance of using words that depersonalize opponents.

Connect to Life Possible Responses: People would be offended by what others say about them; people would not have to guess at what others were thinking.

Writing Options

Analysis of Persuasion Encourage students to discuss euphemisms and the specific political contexts in which they might be used. Students might work in pairs to discuss the content and design of the posters before they write. Accept all reasonable, well-supported responses.

Activities & Explorations

Debate on the Language of War You might have small groups of students engage in the debate, rather than pairs. Students on each side of the issue should get together and discuss their ideas before the debate begins.

Inquiry & Research

Propaganda In addition to an encyclopedia and library catalog system, students might find academic journals in the disciplines of communications and rhetoric to be helpful.

Vocabulary in Action

EXERCISE: SYNONYMS

1. f
2. g
3. i
4. a
5. d
6. h
7. e
8. b
9. j
10. c

Writing Options

Analysis of Persuasion Look at the posters that illustrate Huxley's essay. What modes of persuasion—valid and faulty—do you see reflected in the words and images? List examples of logical, deceptive, and faulty modes of persuasion used in the posters.

Activities & Explorations

Debate on the Language of War With a partner, conduct a debate in which the two of you argue for and against the use of euphemisms and abstract language during wartime. Support your position. ~ **SPEAKING AND LISTENING**

Inquiry & Research

Propaganda Find out about the uses of propaganda during the 20th century—for example, in Nazi Germany or during the Cold War. Report your findings to the class, and discuss what insights your research has given you into Huxley's essay.

Vocabulary in Action

EXERCISE: SYNONYMS For each phrase in the first column, write the letter of the synonymous phrase in the second column.

1. **odious** poultry
2. **ardent** protection
3. a fiendish romp
4. **vitiate** the efforts
5. destined to **embellish**
6. direct **balefully**
7. sayin' "powder room"
8. **inherently** harmonious
9. an unrelenting power
10. an evil from the past

a. spoil the toil
b. naturally matchable
c. an **iniquity** from antiquity
d. born to adorn
e. usin' a **euphemism**
f. sickening chicken
g. intense defense
h. administer sinisterly
i. a **diabolical** frolic
j. an **inexorable** force

Building Vocabulary
For an in-depth lesson on how to use a thesaurus to find a word's synonyms, see page 574.

Aldous Huxley
1894–1963

Other Works
Crome Yellow
Point Counter Point
Brave New World
Brave New World Revisited
Island

Changing Paths Aldous Huxley was born in Surrey, England, into a family of gifted intellectuals, including scientists, educators, and writers. As a student at Eton College, a prestigious English prep school, he was pursuing studies in science when he contracted keratitis, an eye disease that resulted in near-blindness. Although he had to abandon any hope of a career in science or medicine, he learned Braille in order to continue his education. He studied English literature at Oxford University, where his sight improved, and he was awarded an honors degree in 1916. During the same year, he published his first book, a collection of poetry.

Literary Rebel After working as a teacher and as a journalist for a literary magazine, Huxley concentrated on his own writing, moving away from poetry to fiction and essays. The witty skepticism of his first two novels, published in the 1920s, established his reputation and also brought him a certain popularity as a rebel. During the 1930s, Huxley's writing focused on political and cultural trends that he felt to be alarming.

Go West Huxley and his wife, Maria, had been traveling extensively since the mid-1920s, and in 1937 they settled in California, where both the climate and new medical treatments improved Huxley's vision. His later work, which reflected his wide range of interests, included film scripts and explorations of mysticism and parapsychology. Huxley endured a painful battle with cancer at the end of his life, but he continued to write, relentless in his attention to the problems facing society.

Teaching Options

Grammar

STYLE: RHYTHM AND THE COMMA

Instruction The skilled writer develops his or her message with the occasional use of interrupters—words, phrases, and clauses that not only add to the message but may also serve to stress important words in the sentence. Interrupters include such parenthetical expressions as *I believe* or *first of all.* They are set off by commas.

Activity Write the following sentence on the chalkboard.

Huxley believed, as many others did, that the language of politics promoted war.

Have a volunteer read the sentence aloud for the class. Students should notice the stress that naturally falls on the word *believed.*

Among the most useful interrupters for controlling rhythm and meaning are conjunctive adverbs, such as *furthermore, of course, however, nevertheless, therefore, in fact,* and *also.* These, too, are set off by commas when they are used parenthetically in a sentence.

Use **Grammar Transparencies and Copymasters,** p. 109.

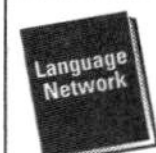

Use McDougal Littell's ***Language Network*** for more instruction and practice in style.

PREPARING to *Read*

The Demon Lover

Short Story by ELIZABETH BOWEN

"'I shall be with you,' he said, 'sooner or later.'"

Connect to Your Life

The Unexplained Most people are intrigued by unexplained events—mysterious occurrences or strange coincidences that seem outside the limits of ordinary life. Jot down descriptions of any events of this sort that you have read about, heard about, or experienced yourself. Discuss these events with your classmates.

Build Background

London During World War II
During World War II, German aircraft bombed British cities for more than four years. From September 1940 to May 1941, Germany hit London with a series of nightly air attacks—known as the Blitz—designed to force Britain to surrender. Londoners sought safety in subway tunnels and air-raid shelters during the bombings. Those who could afford to do so left the city and moved to the countryside.

Mrs. Drover, the main character in this story, lived with her family in the wealthy Kensington district of London before moving to the country to escape the Blitz. As the story begins, she is returning to her Kensington home to reclaim some valued personal belongings.

WORDS TO KNOW
Vocabulary Preview
assent
emanate
impassively
precipitately
prosaic

Focus Your Reading

LITERARY ANALYSIS SETTING AND SUSPENSE As the plot develops in "The Demon Lover," Bowen builds **suspense,** making the reader increasingly eager to find out what will happen. One technique she uses to create suspense is her description of **setting,** as in the following example:

> ***The room looked over the garden and other gardens: the sun had gone in; as the clouds sharpened and lowered, the trees and rank lawns seemed already to smoke with dark.***

As you read, look for other examples in which description of the time and place of the story's action contributes to the building of suspense.

ACTIVE READING ANALYZING FLASHBACK "The Demon Lover" is set during World War II, but the story involves a **flashback** to events 25 years earlier. A flashback is an account of a conversation, an episode, or an event that happened before the main sequence of events in a story. Flashbacks often reveal significant thoughts, experiences, or events in characters' lives, and may contain **foreshadowing,** or hints of what is to come. As you read "The Demon Lover," identify where the flashback begins and ends, and consider what the use of this technique adds to Bowen's story.

READER'S NOTEBOOK In a chart like the one shown, identify important details presented in flashback. Note what significant information you think each detail reveals about Mrs. Drover or her former fiancé. Then jot down possible outcomes that the flashback might foreshadow.

Flashback Detail	Mrs. Drover	Fiancé	Possible Outcomes

OVERVIEW

Objectives
1. understand and appreciate a **short story (Literary Analysis)**
2. appreciate the author's use of **setting** and **suspense (Literary Analysis)**
3. analyze **flashback** in order to understand Bowen's story **(Active Reading)**

Summary
During World War II, the Drover family moves out of London to be safe from air raids. One day, however, Mrs. Drover returns to the city house to pick up some items and notices a mysterious note on a table, which confirms an appointment she had made 25 years earlier to meet her former fiancé on this date. She becomes fearful as she recalls her strange fiancé and his coldness toward her, the threatening way he said he would be with her "sooner or later," and her relief upon hearing he was presumed to have been killed in World War I.

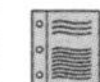
Use **Unit Six Resource Book,** p. 74 for additional support.

Thematic Link
Mrs. Drover faces the **shocking reality** of a mysterious and surprising encounter with her former fiancé, who reportedly had died during World War I.

5-Minute Warm-Up

Daily Language SkillBuilder

Have students **proofread** the display sentences on page 979k and write them correctly. The sentences also appear on Transparency 32 of **Grammar Transparencies and Copymasters.**

Preteaching Vocabulary
If you would like to preteach the WORDS TO KNOW for this selection, use the Mini Lesson on p. 1158.

LESSON RESOURCES

UNIT SIX RESOURCE BOOK, pp. 74–78

ASSESSMENT RESOURCES
Formal Assessment, pp. 213–214
Teacher's Guide to Assessment and Portfolio Use
Test Generator

SKILLS TRANSPARENCIES AND COPYMASTERS
Literary Analysis
- Influences on Plot: Setting and Character, T19 (for Literary Analysis, p. 1157)

Reading and Critical Thinking
- Chronological Order, T11 (for Active Reading, p. 1157)

Grammar
- Sentence Fragments, T42 (for Mini Lesson, p. 1164)
- Complete Sentences, C76 (for Mini Lesson, p. 1164)

Vocabulary
- Using Specialized Dictionaries, C82 (for Mini Lesson, p. 1158)

Writing
- Personality Profile, C25 (for Writing Option 2, p. 1165)
- Literary Interpretation, C33 (for Writing Option 3, p. 1165)

Communications
- Evaluating Roles in Groups, T8 (for Activities & Explorations 3, p. 1165)
- Dramatic Reading, T12 (for Activities & Explorations 1, p. 1165)

INTEGRATED TECHNOLOGY
Audio Library
Visit our website:
www.mcdougallittell.com

TEACHING THE LITERATURE

Reading and Analyzing

Active Reading

ANALYZING FLASHBACK

Have students review the definition of flashback on p. 1157 and remind them to be on the lookout for a flashback as they read the story. Have them discuss what clues they can use to recognize when a flashback begins.

Possible Response: There might be a change in setting as the character recalls the past experience; new characters might be introduced in the flashback that had not appeared yet in the main story.

Use **Unit Six Resource Book** p. 75 for more practice.

Literary Analysis

SETTING AND SUSPENSE

Explain that *setting* is usually defined as "the time and place of the action of a short story." In addition to time and place, however, setting may include the social and moral environment that form the background and atmosphere for a narrative. Ask students to describe the setting of this story in terms of:

- time

Answer: August 1941 during World War II

- place

Answer: the wealthy Kensington district of London

- social environment

Possible Response: house has been deserted—eerie and menacing—because of war

Use **Unit Six Resource Book** p. 76 for more exercises.

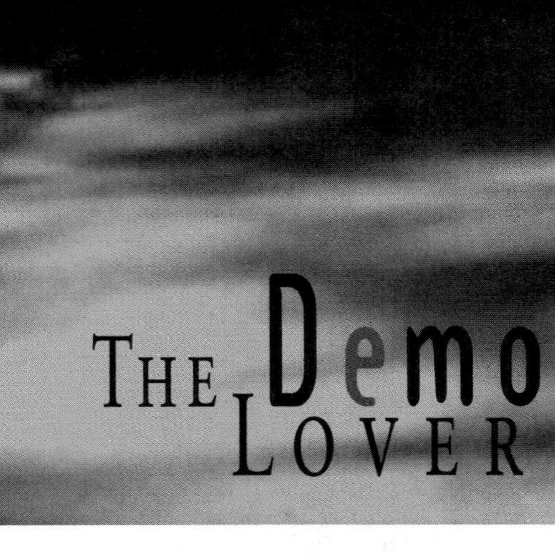

Elizabeth Bowen

THE Demon LOVER

Towards the end of her day in London Mrs. Drover went round to her shut-up house to look for several things she wanted to take away. Some belonged to herself, some to her family, who were by now used to their country life. It was late August; it had been a steamy, showery day: at the moment the trees down the pavement glittered in an escape of humid yellow afternoon sun. Against the next batch of clouds, already piling up ink-dark, broken chimneys and parapets stood out. In her once familiar street, as in any unused channel, an unfamiliar queerness had silted up;[1] a cat wove itself in and out of railings, but no human eye watched Mrs. Drover's return. Shifting some parcels under her arm, she slowly forced round her latchkey in an unwilling lock, then gave the door, which had warped, a push with her knee. Dead air came out to meet her as she went in.

The staircase window having been boarded up, no light came down into the hall. But one door, she could just see, stood ajar, so she went quickly through into the room and unshuttered the big window in there. Now the prosaic woman, looking about her, was more perplexed than she knew by everything that she saw, by traces of her long former habit of life—the yellow smoke stain up the white marble mantelpiece, the ring left by a vase on the top of the escritoire;[2] the bruise in the wallpaper where, on the door being thrown open widely, the china handle had always hit the wall. The piano, having gone away to be stored, had left what looked like claw marks on its part of the parquet.[3] Though not much dust had seeped in, each object wore a film of another kind; and, the only

1. **silted up:** piled up, like sediment deposited in a river channel.
2. **escritoire** (ĕs′krĭ-twär′): a writing desk or table.
3. **parquet** (pär-kā′): a wood floor made of small blocks laid in a geometric pattern.

WORDS TO KNOW **prosaic** (prō-zā′ĭk) *adj.* commonplace; ordinary; dull

1158

Teaching Options

Preteaching Vocabulary

USING A DICTIONARY Explain that a dictionary can help students develop word knowledge based on order of meanings from most common to least common. Archaic meanings, usage notes, word origins, and synonym listings will also be found in a dictionary.

Instruction Ask students to find the word *prosaic* on page 1158 and then to choose a meaning from the choices below that best describes the way the word is used in the story.

a. characteristic of prose as distinguished from poetry

b. factual, unimaginative

c. everyday, ordinary

Because the word is used to describe Mrs. Drover, the correct response is **c.**

Activity Have students find the following words in a dictionary and write down all the meanings. As they find these words while reading the short

ventilation being the chimney, the whole drawing room smelled of the cold hearth. Mrs. Drover put down her parcels on the escritoire and left the room to proceed upstairs; the things she wanted were in a bedroom chest.

She had been anxious to see how the house was—the part-time caretaker she shared with some neighbors was away this week on his holiday, known to be not yet back. At the best of times he did not look in often, and she was never sure that she trusted him. There were some cracks in the structure, left by the last bombing, on which she was anxious to keep an eye. Not that one could do anything—

A shaft of refracted daylight now lay across the hall. She stopped dead and stared at the hall table—on this lay a letter addressed to her.

She thought first—then the caretaker *must* be back. All the same, who, seeing the house shuttered, would have dropped a letter in at the box? It was not a circular, it was not a bill. And the post office redirected, to the address in the country, everything for her that came through the post. The caretaker (even if he *were* back) did not know she was due in London today—her call here had been planned to be a surprise—so his negligence in the manner of this letter, leaving it to wait in the dusk and the dust, annoyed her. Annoyed, she picked up the letter, which bore no stamp. But it cannot be important, or they would know . . . She took the letter rapidly upstairs with her, without a stop to look at the writing till she reached what had been her bedroom, where she let in light. The room looked over the garden and other gardens: the sun had gone in; as the clouds sharpened and lowered, the trees and rank lawns seemed already to smoke with dark. Her reluctance to look again at the letter came from the fact that she felt intruded upon—and by someone contemptuous of her ways. However, in the tenseness preceding the fall of rain she read it: it was a few lines.

Dear Kathleen: You will not have forgotten that today is our anniversary, and the day we said. The years have gone by at once slowly and fast. In view of the fact that nothing has changed, I shall rely upon you to keep your promise. I was sorry to see you leave London, but was satisfied that you would be back in time. You may expect me, therefore, at the hour arranged. Until then . . . K.

Mrs. Drover looked for the date: it was today's. She dropped the letter onto the bedsprings, then picked it up to see the writing again—her lips, beneath the remains of lipstick, beginning to go white. She felt so much the change in her own face that she went to the mirror, polished a clear patch in it and looked at once urgently and stealthily in. She was confronted by a woman of forty-four, with eyes starting out under a hat brim that had been rather carelessly pulled down. She had not put on any more powder since she left the shop where she ate her solitary tea. The pearls her husband had given her on their marriage hung loose round her now rather thinner throat, slipping in the V of the pink wool jumper her sister knitted last autumn as they sat round the fire. Mrs. Drover's most normal expression was one of controlled worry, but of assent. Since the birth of the third of her little boys, attended by a quite serious illness, she had had an intermittent muscular flicker to the left of her mouth, but in spite of this she could always sustain a manner that was at once energetic and calm.

Turning from her own face as precipitately as she had gone to meet it, she went to the chest where the things were, unlocked it, threw up the lid and knelt to search. But as rain began to come crashing down she could not keep from looking over her shoulder at the stripped bed on which the letter lay. Behind the blanket of rain the clock of the church that still stood struck six—with rapidly heightening apprehension she counted each of the slow strokes. "The hour

WORDS TO KNOW

assent (ə-sĕnt') *n.* agreement; acceptance
precipitately (prĭ-sĭp'ĭ-tĭt-lē) *adv.* hurriedly; suddenly

Customizing Instruction

Less Proficient Readers

Invite students to discuss their favorite suspense stories, films, or TV programs. Then have them read to find out what frightens Mrs. Drover when she goes to her house in London.

Students Acquiring English

Bowen's formal diction and syntax and sophisticated vocabulary will be difficult for some students. As they read the story, encourage them to keep a list of unfamiliar words and phrases. Then have students get together with a partner who can help them translate the phrases into informal English.

Use **Spanish Study Guide** for additional support, pp. 275–277.

Gifted and Talented

Ask students to consider the role of fate in the story. Do they think the ending was predestined? Was there anything Mrs. Drover could have done differently to alter her fate, or would her fiancé have found her anyway?

story, ask them to underline the meaning most appropriate to the passage in which each word is used.

- assent
- precipitately
- emanate
- impassively

Use **Unit Six Resource Book** p. 77 for more practice.

Reading and Analyzing

Active Reading

ANALYZING FLASHBACK

A Explain that a flashback is an account of a conversation, an episode, or an event that happened before the beginning of a story. Have students identify where the flashback begins. Then ask them who the soldier is.

Answer: the writer of the letter.

What does the dark setting suggest about the soldier?

Possible Response: He is mysterious, sinister, and threatening.

Literary Analysis: FORESHADOWING

B Ask students what the words "sinister troth" suggest will happen later in the story.

Possible Response: The soldier will find Mrs. Drover and hold her to her promise.

Literary Analysis

SETTING AND SUSPENSE

Explain that suspense is the tension or excitement readers feel as they are drawn into a story and become increasingly eager to learn the outcome of the plot. Ask them to explain how the last line on page 1161 helps to build the suspense.

Possible Response: By locking the door of the empty house, Mrs. Drover reveals that she is genuinely afraid for her safety, and the reader begins to anticipate some harm coming to her.

arranged . . . My God," she said, "*what* hour? How should I . . . ? After twenty-five years . . ."

A The young girl talking to the soldier in the garden had not ever completely seen his face. It was dark; they were saying goodbye under a tree. Now and then—for it felt, from not seeing him at this intense moment, as though she had never seen him at all—she verified his presence for these few moments longer by putting out a hand, which he each time pressed, without very much kindness, and painfully, onto one of the breast buttons of his uniform. That cut of the button on the palm of her hand was, principally, what she was to carry away. This was so near the end of a leave from France that she could only wish him already gone. It was August 1916. Being not kissed, being drawn away from and looked at, intimidated Kathleen till she imagined spectral[4] glitters in the place of his eyes. Turning away and looking back up the lawn she saw, through branches of trees, the drawing-room window alight: she caught a breath for the moment when she could go running back there into the safe arms of her mother and sister, and cry: "What shall I do, what shall I do? He has gone."

Hearing her catch her breath, her fiancé said, without feeling: "Cold?"

"You're going away such a long way."

"Not so far as you think."

"I don't understand?"

"You don't have to," he said. "You will. You know what we said."

"But that was—suppose you—I mean, suppose."

"I shall be with you," he said, "sooner or later. You won't forget that. You need do nothing but wait."

Only a little more than a minute later she was free to run up the silent lawn. Looking in through the window at her mother and sister, who did not for the moment perceive her, she already felt that unnatural promise drive down between her and the rest of all humankind. No other way of having given herself could have made her feel so apart, lost and foresworn.[5] She could not have plighted a more sinister troth.[6] B

Kathleen behaved well when, some months later, her fiancé was reported missing, presumed killed. Her family not only supported her but were able to praise her courage without stint[7] because they could not regret, as a husband for her, the man they knew almost nothing about. They hoped she would, in a year or two, console herself—and had it been only a question of consolation things might have gone much straighter ahead. But her trouble, behind just a little grief, was a complete dislocation from everything. She did not reject other lovers, for these failed to appear: for years she failed to attract men—and with the approach of her thirties she became natural enough to share her family's anxiousness on this score. She began to put herself out, to wonder; and at thirty-two she was very greatly relieved to find herself being courted by William Drover. She married him, and the two of them settled down in this quiet, arboreal[8] part of Kensington:[9] in this house the years piled up, her children were born and they all lived till they were driven out by the bombs of the next war. Her movements as Mrs. Drover were circumscribed,[10] and she dismissed any idea that they were still watched.

As things were—dead or living the letter-writer sent her only a threat. Unable, for some minutes, to go on kneeling with her back exposed to the empty room, Mrs. Drover rose from the chest to sit on an upright chair whose back was firmly against the wall. The desuetude[11] of her former bedroom, her married London home's whole air

4. **spectral:** ghostly; phantomlike.
5. **foresworn:** guilty of perjury.
6. **plighted . . . troth:** made a more ominous promise of marriage.
7. **stint:** limitation or restriction.
8. **arboreal** (är-bôr′ē-əl): tree-filled.
9. **Kensington:** a residential section of London.
10. **circumscribed:** restricted; confined.
11. **desuetude** (dĕs′wĭ-to͞od′): disuse.

Teaching Options

BLOCK SCHEDULING: MANAGING TIME

If your schedule requires that you cover the lesson objectives in a shorter time, use . . .

- Preparing to Read, p. 1157
- Thinking Through the Literature, p. 1164
- Vocabulary in Action, p. 1165

If you want to take advantage of longer class time, use . . .

- TE Teaching Options: Preteaching Vocabulary, p. 1158; Viewing and Representing, p. 1161; Cross Curricular Links, p. 1162; Standardized Test Practice, p. 1163; Grammar, p. 1165
- Choices & Challenges and Author Activity, pp. 1165-1166

of being a cracked cup from which memory, with its reassuring power, had either evaporated or leaked away, made a crisis—and at just this crisis the letter-writer had,
1 knowledgeably, struck. The hollowness of the house this evening canceled years on years of voices, habits and steps. Through the shut windows she only heard rain fall on the roofs around. To rally herself, she said she was in a mood—and for two or three seconds shutting her eyes, told herself that she had imagined the letter. But she opened them—there it lay on the bed.

On the supernatural side of the letter's entrance she was not permitting her mind to dwell. Who, in London, knew she meant to call at the house today? Evidently, however, this had been known. The caretaker, *had* he come back, had had no cause to expect her: he would have taken the letter in his pocket, to forward it, at his own time, through the post. There was no other sign that the caretaker had been in—but, if not? Letters dropped in at doors of deserted houses do not fly or walk to tables in halls. They do not sit on the dust of empty tables with the air of certainty that they will be found. There is needed some human hand—but nobody but the caretaker had a key.
2 Under circumstances she did not care to consider, a house can be entered without a key. It was possible that she was not alone now. She might be being waited for, downstairs. Waited for—until when? Until "the hour arranged." At least that was not six o'clock: six has struck.

She rose from the chair and went over and locked the door.

Interior with Seated Woman (1908), Vilhelm Hammershøi. Oil on canvas, 76 cm × 66 cm, Aarhus (Denmark) Kunstmuseum.

Customizing Instruction

Students Acquiring English

1 Explain that "the hollowness" of Mrs. Drover's house and its "shut windows" establish a mood. Ask students to describe the mood the writer is trying to portray.

Possible Response: a feeling of abandonment, isolation.

Less Proficient Readers

Review the events students have read about so far:

- What does Mrs. Drover find in her London home?
  Answer: a letter.
- What is Mrs. Drover's reaction when she finds this item?
  Answer: She is shocked and upset.

Set a Purpose Have students read to find out how Mrs. Drover's past comes back to haunt her.

Gifted and Talented

2 Ask students to discuss how a house can be entered without a key. What are the "circumstances" Mrs. Drover does not care to consider?

Possible Responses: A house can be broken into or entered by supernatural means; she may not want to consider either possibility. Who does Mrs. Drover think might be waiting for her downstairs?

Answer: her former fiancé.

Mini Lesson Viewing and Representing

Interior with Seated Woman **by Vilhelm Hammershøi**

ART APPRECIATION Explain that Hammershøi, a Danish painter (1864–1916), traveled extensively throughout Europe. His work was influenced by the American painter James McNeill Whistler and by the Dutch artist Jan Vermeer. Hammershoi produced most of his best work between 1899 and 1909.

Instruction Explain that just as a writer creates *mood,* a feeling or atmosphere for the reader, so do visual artists create mood in their art. Whereas the use of details, dialogue, imagery, figurative language, foreshadowing, and setting can help set the mood of a story, so can elements of art, such as line, color, space, and texture, set the mood of an artwork.

Application Have the class identify lines, colors, spaces, and textures in the painting and discuss how the use of these elements helps establish the mood of the painting. Then ask them to draw a parallel between the mood of the painting and the mood of the short story.

Reading and Analyzing

Literary Analysis: FORESHADOWING

A Ask students what events are foreshadowed by Mrs. Drover's inability to remember her fiancé's face.

Possible Responses: She will meet him but not recognize him; she will not have enough time to get away from him.

Reading Skills and Strategies: SUMMARIZING

B Remind students that summarizing a short story is retelling it, or a portion of it, in fewer words, while emphasizing the most important parts. Ask students to summarize Mrs. Drover's actions from the time she leaves the house until her arrival at the taxi rank.

Possible Response: She walks quickly, looking behind her to see if she is being followed.

Literary Analysis
SETTING AND SUSPENSE

C Ask students how the author builds suspense in this setting.

Answer: She describes the draft created by someone leaving the house.

Why is this description suspenseful?

Possible Responses: The reader is left wanting to know who was in the house; the author leaves the reader uncertain about what will happen next.

The thing was, to get out. To fly? No, not that: she had to catch her train. As a woman whose utter dependability was the keystone of her family life she was not willing to return to the country, to her husband, her little boys and her sister, without the objects she had come up to fetch. Resuming work at the chest she set about making up a number of parcels in a rapid, fumbling-decisive way. These, with her shopping parcels, would be too much to carry; these meant a taxi—at the thought of the taxi her heart went up and her normal breathing resumed. I will ring up the taxi now; the taxi cannot come too soon: 1 I shall hear the taxi out there running its engine, till I walk calmly down to it through the hall. I'll ring up—But no: the telephone is cut off . . . She tugged at a knot she had tied wrong.

The idea of flight . . . He was never kind to me, not really. I don't remember him kind at all. Mother said he never considered me. He was set on me, that was what it was—not love. Not love, not meaning a person well. What did he do, to make me promise like that? I can't remember—But she found that she could.

She remembered with such dreadful acuteness that the twenty-five years since then dissolved like smoke and she instinctively looked for the weal[12] left by the button on the palm of her hand. She remembered not only all that he said and did but the complete suspension of *her* existence during that August week. I was not myself—they all told me so at the time. She remembered—but with one white burning blank as where acid has dropped on a photograph: *under no conditions* could she remember his face. **A**

So, wherever he may be waiting, I shall not know him. You have no time to run from a face you do not expect.

The thing was to get to the taxi before any clock struck what could be the hour. She would **B** slip down the street and round the side of the square to where the square gave on the main road. She would return in the taxi, safe, to her own door, and bring the solid driver into the house with her to pick up the parcels from room to room. The idea of the taxi driver made her decisive, bold: she unlocked her door, went to the top of the staircase and listened down.

She heard nothing—but while she was hearing nothing the *passé*[13] air of the staircase was disturbed by a draft that traveled up to her face. **C** It emanated from the basement: down there a door or window was being opened by someone who chose this moment to leave the house.

The rain had stopped; the pavements steamily shone as Mrs. Drover let herself out by inches from her own front door into the empty street. The unoccupied houses opposite continued to meet her look with their damaged stare. Making towards the thoroughfare and the taxi, she tried not to keep looking behind. Indeed, the silence was so intense—one of those creeks of London silence exaggerated this summer by the damage of war—that no tread could have gained on hers unheard. Where her street debouched[14] on the square where people went on living, she grew conscious of, and checked, her unnatural pace. Across the open end of the square two buses impassively passed each other: women, a

12. **weal:** a mark or ridge raised on the skin.
13. ***passé*** (pä-sā') *French:* old; stale; past its prime.
14. **debouched** (dĭ-boucht'): emerged.

WORDS TO KNOW
emanate (ĕm'ə-nāt') *v.* to come forth; flow out
impassively (ĭm-păs'ĭv-lē) *adv.* without feeling or emotion

1162

Teaching Options

Cross Curricular Link History

BATTLE OF THE SOMME During World War I, the Battle of the Somme was fought from July to November 1916 on the Somme River in northern France. To relieve pressure on Verdun, which was under devastating German attack in February 1916, the Battle of the Somme was begun on July 1 by British ground troops led by officers optimistic about their chances to advance uncontested across ground cleared of defenders by artillery. This optimism was misguided, however, as the British infantry—60,000 men advancing in precise formation with over 60 pounds of equipment each—was mowed down by German machine guns. The day's casualties were the heaviest ever sustained by a British army. The French forces, who had more guns than the British, did a better job against weaker forces in a different area of the battle, but little could be done to mount any real advance on the German army. Tanks were used for the first time in battle in September, but they made little difference. In the end, only about 7 miles had been gained, at the cost of half a million casualties for the Germans and over half a million for the British and French.

perambulator,[15] cyclists, a man wheeling a barrow signalized, once again, the ordinary flow of life. At the square's most populous corner should be—and was—the short taxi rank. This evening, only one taxi—but this, although it presented its blank rump, appeared already to be alertly waiting for her. Indeed, without looking round the driver started his engine as she panted up from behind and put her hand on the door. As she did so, the clock struck seven. The taxi faced the main road: to make the trip back to her house it would have to turn—she had settled back on the seat and the taxi *had* turned before she, surprised by its knowing movement, recollected that she had not "said where." She leaned forward to scratch at the glass panel that divided the driver's head from her own.

The driver braked to what was almost a stop, turned round and slid the glass panel back: the jolt of this flung Mrs. Drover forward till her face was almost into the glass. Through the aperture[16] driver and passenger, not six inches between them, remained for an eternity eye to eye. Mrs. Drover's mouth hung open for some seconds before she could issue her first scream. After that she continued to scream freely and to beat with her gloved hands on the glass all round as the taxi, accelerating without mercy, made off with her into the hinterland of deserted streets. ❖

15. **perambulator:** baby carriage.

16. **aperture** (ăp′ər-chər): opening.

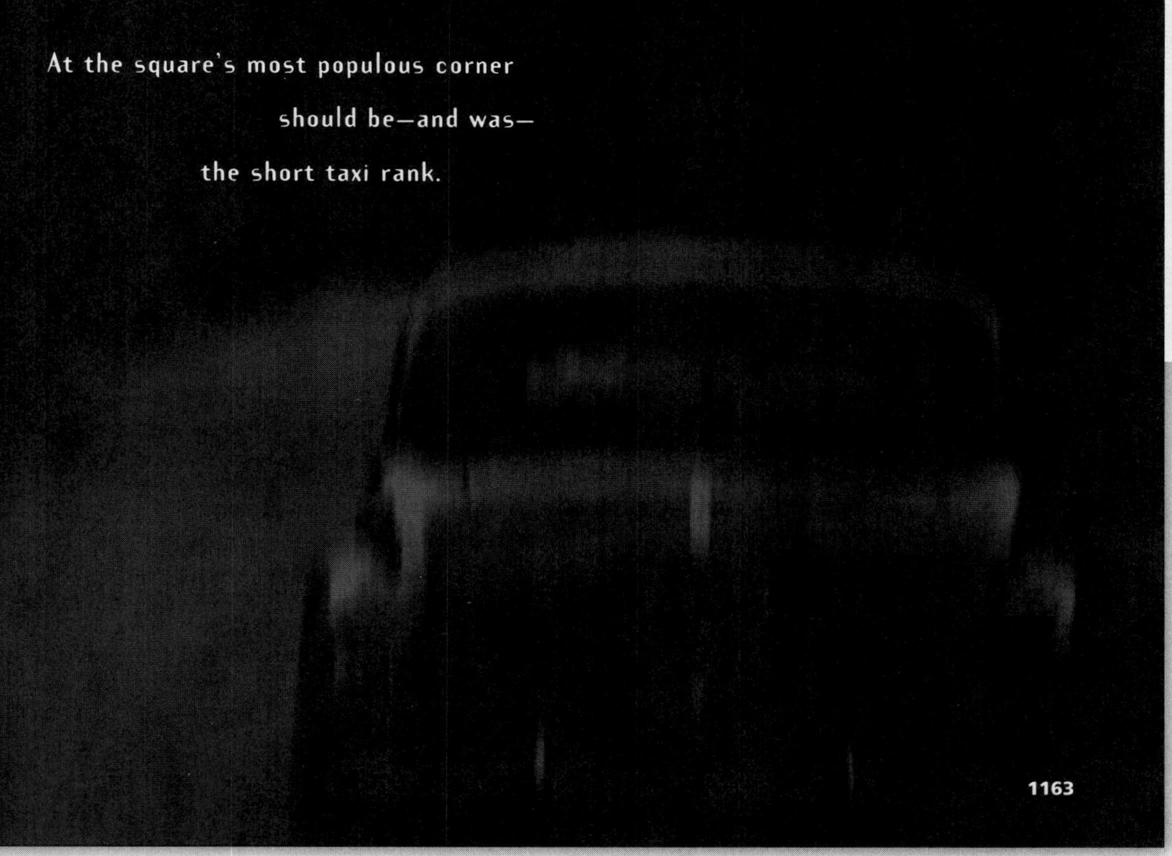
At the square's most populous corner
should be—and was—
the short taxi rank.

Customizing Instruction

Students Acquiring English

1 Point out that this passage reveals Mrs. Drover's own thoughts. Then ask them what the inner dialogue reveals about her state of mind.

Possible Response: She is frightened but trying to calm herself down.

Less Proficient Readers

Check students' understanding of the story using the following questions.

- Who wrote the letter Mrs. Drover found in her home?
  Answer: her former fiancé.
- Why is she anxious to get to a taxi?
  Answer: She thinks she'll be safe if another person is with her.
- What happens when Mrs. Drover settles into the taxi?
  Answer: Her fiancé drives off with her.

Multiple Learning Styles

Auditory Learners

Ask students to create sound effects for the passage that describes the moment Mrs. Drover leaves the house until the end of the story. They may describe sounds or bring in recordings to illustrate this scene.

Assessment Standardized Test Practice

MAKING A STORY MAP Some standardized tests will assess students' reading skills by asking them to organize and summarize information for study purposes. Have students create a story map for "The Demon Lover." Remind them to identify the story's elements, including its main conflict, climax, and resolution.

RUBRIC

3 **Full Accomplishment** Students accurately identify story's elements. They correctly trace story's rising and falling action.

2 **Substantial Accomplishment** Students identify most of story's elements. With some inaccuracy, they trace story's rising and falling action.

1 **Little or Partial Accomplishment** Students are unable to identify many of story's elements. They cannot trace story's rising and falling action.

GUIDING STUDENT RESPONSE

Connect to the Literature

1. **What Do You Think?**
   Guidelines for student response: Student speculations about Mrs. Drover's former fiancé should be based on evidence in the text.

Comprehension Check

- She is going to look for some things she wants to take away for herself and her family.
- She finds a letter.
- She is frightened.

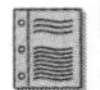
Use **Unit Six Resource Book,** p 78 for additional support.

Think Critically

2. Possible Responses: He is a strange, cold, frightening person.
3. Possible Responses: Mrs. Drover is frightened and nervous; she is trying to be brave.
4. Possible Response: Mrs. Drover is afraid of her fiancé, who behaves in a controlling and sinister way and says he will return to her. This flashback foreshadows the real event at the end of the story, in which he returns to her as the taxi driver.
5. Possible Response: The story wouldn't be as powerful in chronological order because knowing about the letter near the beginning sets the stage for suspense.
6. Possible Response: objective, detached, sinister
7. Possible Responses: Some students may say that the fiancé survived World War I; others may say that there is no rational explanation—the fiancé is a supernatural being come to claim Mrs. Drover.

Literary Analysis

Activity Use the chart to help students analyze the relevance of setting and time frame to the story's suspense and meaning.

Surprise Ending Plot twist: Mrs. Drover thinks she will be safe when she gets into the taxi. However, her former fiancé is the taxi driver, and he carries her away.

Thinking through the LITERATURE

Connect to the Literature

1. **What Do You Think?** Do you think that Mrs. Drover's former fiancé is still alive? Why or why not?

Comprehension Check

- Why does Mrs. Drover return to the house in London?
- What does she find in the house?
- How does she feel at the prospect of seeing her fiancé?

Think Critically

2. What conclusions can you draw about Mrs. Drover's former fiancé?

   THINK ABOUT
   - his words and actions during their 1916 farewell meeting
   - her reactions to him during their farewell
   - her current memories of him

3. How would you describe Mrs. Drover's emotions during the course of the story?
4. **ACTIVE READING** ANALYZING FLASHBACK Review the chart you made in your  READER'S NOTEBOOK. What do you learn about Mrs. Drover and her former fiancé in the **flashback?** In what ways do you think the flashback **foreshadows** the story's outcome?
5. Would the story be as powerful if the events were told in chronological order? Why or why not?
6. How would you describe the **tone** of the story's narrator?
7. Do you think there is a rational explanation for the events in this story?

Extend Interpretations

8. **Writer's Style** Bowen creates a **mood** of foreboding by choosing words carefully. Such phrases as "no human eye" (page 1158) and "spectral glitters" (page 1160) add to this mood. Look for other examples of words and phrases that have similar effects. How important do you think **word choice** is in making the action of this story convincing?
9. **Connect to Life** Bowen does not offer an explanation for the events at the end of the story, and the reader may interpret the ending in several ways. In general, what is your opinion of stories that are open to more than one interpretation in this way? Support your answer with examples of stories or movies that you know.

Literary Analysis

SETTING AND SUSPENSE The **setting**—the time and place in which a story's action occurs—may play a significant role in creating **suspense** (the tension readers feel as they are drawn into a story). In "The Demon Lover," the setting of war-torn London and Mrs. Drover's empty house—abandoned because of the Blitz—contributes to building suspense by conveying a sense of uncertainty and fear.

Activity Use a chart like the one shown to record your thoughts about the relationship between setting and suspense in Bowen's story.

Details of Setting	How Details Create Suspense
"Dead air came out to meet her as she went in."	Detail creates atmosphere of apprehension and fear.

SURPRISE ENDING A **surprise ending** is an unexpected twist at the end of a story's **plot.** The surprise may be a sudden turn in the action or a revelation that provides a different perspective on the entire story. The last paragraph of "The Demon Lover" reveals an unexpected turn in the action. Identify the twist in the plot, and explain what contributes to making it a surprise.

Extend Interpretations

Writer's Style Other examples include: "Dead air came out to meet her"; "rain began to come crashing down"; and "sinister troth." Words evoking a particular mood can better help the reader understand what a character feels or experiences.

Connect to Life Accept all reasonable, well-supported responses.

Vocabulary in Action

Exercise A

1. nodding
2. shrugging
3. fragrance
4. routine
5. quick

Exercise B

Responses will vary.

Writing Options

1. The Next Scene The story ends with Mrs. Drover screaming and pounding her fists on the windows of a speeding taxi. What do you think happens next? Write a new scene to add to the end of the story.

Writing Handbook
See pages 1365–1366: Narrative Writing.

2. Missing-Person Report Using evidence from the story, write a missing-person report about Mrs. Drover. Describe her appearance, actions, and state of mind before her disappearance.

3. Explanatory Paragraph Explain what you think Bowen's purpose for writing this story might have been. Support your ideas with evidence from the story.

Activities & Explorations

1. Dramatic Performance Work with classmates to select music, create sound effects, and develop lighting for a dramatic reading of the story. Cast different people to read the soldier's letter, the thoughts of Mrs. Drover, and the narration. Rehearse and perform the reading. ~ PERFORMING

2. Movie Poster Suppose that a movie version of this story has been made. Draw or paint a poster, depicting the taxi scene, to advertise the movie. ~ ART

3. Journalists' Meeting You are the editor in chief of a sensational tabloid newspaper. Choose several classmates to act as reporters and editors, and role-play a staff meeting to discuss how you want to cover Mrs. Drover's disappearance.
~ SPEAKING AND LISTENING

Art Connection

Moody Image Do you think the painting *Interior with Seated Woman*, reproduced on page 1161, is a suitable image to accompany this story? Explain your answer, commenting on the mood of the painting.

Inquiry & Research

London During the War Research what life was like in London during World War II. Prepare a report that includes copies of photos of wartime London, as well as quotations from people who experienced the Blitz.

Vocabulary in Action

EXERCISE A: MEANING CLUES Answer the following questions.

1. Would you be most likely to signal **assent** by nodding your head up and down, yawning and stretching, or holding your nose?
2. Would a person who is reacting **impassively** be laughing, gasping, or shrugging?
3. What **emanates** from a bouquet of roses—fragrance, thorns, or roots?
4. Would a **prosaic** lifestyle tend to be full of excitement, routine, or danger?
5. If you needed to act **precipitately,** would you be cautious, quick, or sneaky?

EXERCISE B Work with four classmates to describe a fictional school or social event, using the five vocabulary words. One student should begin the description and keep going until he or she has used one of the words; then another student should continue the description, using a second vocabulary word; and so on until all the words have been used.

Building Vocabulary
For an in-depth study of context clues, see page 938.

WORDS TO KNOW: assent, emanate, impassively, precipitately, prosaic

Mini Lesson Grammar

SENTENCE FRAGMENTS

Instruction A sentence fragment is a group of words that is only part of a sentence. A sentence has a subject and a verb, and it expresses a complete thought. A fragment may be any part of a sentence, but it is often a phrase—a few words that would require the addition of a subject, a verb, or both to express a complete thought. To correct a fragment, you need to identify what is missing.

Activity Write this fragment on the chalkboard.

Went to look for several things.

Ask students what is missing here. *(subject)* Have them correct the fragment. *(The woman went to look for several things.)*

Students may observe that experienced writers occasionally use sentence fragments to achieve special effects. You may wish to remind them that it is best to demonstrate mastery before bending the rules.

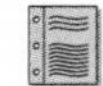

Use **Grammar Transparencies and Copymasters,** p. 66.

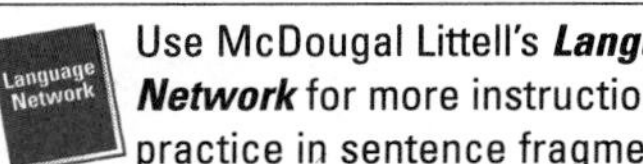

Use McDougal Littell's ***Language Network*** for more instruction and practice in sentence fragments.

Writing Options

1. **The Next Scene** Allow students to work on their scene in small groups. Invite them to recall horror stories they have read or seen on screen to stimulate ideas.
2. **Missing-Person Report** Tell students the reports should concentrate on factual information. They might quote "witnesses" who saw Mrs. Drover hurry from her home and enter the taxi.
3. **Explanatory Paragraph** Students may say that entertainment and self-expression are Bowen's main purposes for writing this story. Encourage students to think of more specific purposes, such as to describe the psychological trauma of living under the Blitz.

Activities & Explorations

1. **Dramatic Performance** Students should divide the roles of directors, readers, sound and light effects people, and photographers. Remind them that the effects and narration should reflect the story's mood.
2. **Movie Poster** You might tell students not to give away too much in the illustration. They might limit themselves to drawing a taxi on an empty street, for example.
3. **Journalists' Meeting** Tell students that a tabloid newspaper would probably emphasize supernatural explanations or would play up the strange circumstances of the past love affair between Mrs. Drover and her fiancé.

Art Connection

Moody Image Answers will vary. If students have other ideas for other, more suitable illustrations, you might ask them to draw a sketch of their ideas.

Inquiry & Research

London During the War Suggest Victoria Glendinning's biography, *Elizabeth Bowen* (Knopf), and Bowen's novel, *The Heat of the Day*. Although fictional, the novel provides images of London life during the war. Students should use multiple sources and may work on the written report in small groups.

Author Activity

War Duties During her wartime years in the Ministry of Information, Bowen assessed Irish attitudes on the war—Ireland was a neutral nation during World War II. In a 1941 writers' conference, she was also involved in helping writers in the Axis nations. Later, during the Blitz, Bowen volunteered as an air-raid warden. Her home was bombed, as was the hotel in which she and her husband took refuge.

Elizabeth Bowen

1899–1973

Other Works
The Death of the Heart
The Heat of the Day
Collected Stories

Neither English Nor Irish Born in Dublin, Ireland, of Anglo-Irish parents, Elizabeth Bowen spent her early childhood at Bowen's Court, an estate that had been in the family since the 17th century. Although her early childhood was happy, her later childhood years were difficult. When she was seven, her father suffered a nervous breakdown, and she was sent to England with her mother and a governess. Six years later, her mother died after a three-year battle with cancer. Bowen then attended a boarding school for a few years, increasingly feeling herself part of neither England nor Ireland. During the last year of World War I, she returned to Dublin and nursed soldiers suffering from shell shock.

London Years In 1918 Bowen returned to London, where she began writing stories. She later wrote of that time, "From the moment that my pen touched paper, I thought of nothing but writing, and since then I have thought of practically nothing else. . . . [W]hen I have nothing to write, I feel only half alive." In 1923, she married Alan C. Cameron, an educator, and published her first collection of stories, *Encounters.* Her first novel, *The Hotel,* appeared in 1927, when she also inherited Bowen's Court, becoming the first woman owner of the estate, although she did not move there until 1952.

Bowen's Fiction Bowen had a prolific career, publishing more than 20 novels and volumes of short stories. Her fiction, which deals primarily with the upper middle class, is beautifully crafted, with finely drawn characters and detailed, evocative descriptions of setting. Many of her best works are set in wartime London, a setting she presents with realism and force.

Diverse Career Bowen's career was diversified as well as distinguished. She was a reviewer for the *Tatler* in 1941 and worked for the Ministry of Information during the early years of World War II. In addition to short stories and novels, she published *Bowen's Court* (a history of her family) and nonfiction works dealing with her life and writing. She is considered a major 20th-century British writer.

Author Activity

War Duties During the early years of World War II, Bowen worked for the Ministry of Information. Find out what she did and why her Anglo-Irish background made her particularly suited to the work.

PREPARING to *Read*

A Hanging

Personal Essay by GEORGE ORWELL

"Till that moment I had never realized what it means to destroy a healthy, conscious man."

Connect to Your Life

Crime and Punishment Do you believe that some crimes merit the death penalty, or do you oppose any use of capital punishment? With a small group of classmates, discuss your views on capital punishment.

Build Background

British Burma Orwell's essay is set in Burma, a Southeast Asian country now known as Myanmar. In a series of wars in the 19th century, the British gradually gained control of the country, which in 1886 was made a province of British India. The Burmese people deeply resented British rule, under which they endured poverty, a lack of political freedom, and religious restrictions. It was into this atmosphere of discontent that Eric Blair—later to assume the pen name George Orwell—came in 1922.

Born in India but educated in England, Orwell arrived in Burma as an assistant superintendent in the Indian Imperial Police. He and his fellow British officers, many of whom were inexperienced in police work, led a native-born police force 13,000 men strong. Orwell became increasingly disillusioned with his role as a police officer and with British colonialism in general, and he later gave a scathing account of British society in Burma in his novel *Burmese Days.* His classic essays "A Hanging" and "Shooting an Elephant" also focus on his experiences of and reactions to British colonial rule.

WORDS TO KNOW
Vocabulary Preview
anecdote
formality
genially
oscillate
timorously

Focus Your Reading

LITERARY ANALYSIS PERSONAL ESSAY **Personal essays** allow writers to express their viewpoints on subjects by reflecting on events or incidents in their own lives. Such essays tend to contain more descriptive details than formal and objective essays do—like this detail in "A Hanging":

And once, in spite of the men who gripped him by each shoulder, he [the prisoner] stepped slightly aside to avoid a puddle on the path.

As you read Orwell's essay, look for other descriptive passages that reveal the writer's observations.

ACTIVE READING INFERRING THE AUTHOR'S PERSPECTIVE A writer's view of his or her subject is called the **author's perspective.** A perspective can be a result of a political standpoint or of an attitude, a belief, or a feeling that affects a writer's treatment of a topic. To identify the author's perspective in a personal essay, you have to **infer** it from clues such as the following:

- **details** that the author chose to include
- **opinions,** as when Orwell says that he suddenly realized the "unspeakable wrongness" of the execution
- **language** that reveals the author's emotions about the events he or she describes

READER'S NOTEBOOK Use a cluster diagram like the one shown to keep track of details, opinions, and language that reveal Orwell's perspective.

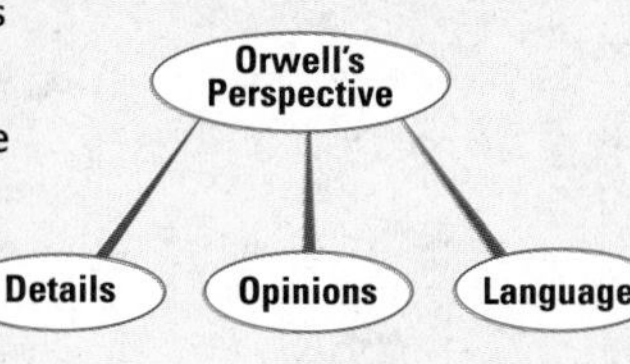

LESSON RESOURCES

UNIT SIX RESOURCE BOOK, pp. 79–83

ASSESSMENT RESOURCES
Formal Assessment, pp. 215–216
Teacher's Guide to Assessment and Portfolio Use
Test Generator

SKILLS TRANSPARENCIES AND COPYMASTERS
Literary Analysis
- Verbal, Situational, and Dramatic Irony, T17 (for Review, p. 1174)

Reading and Critical Thinking
- Determining Author's Bias: Effect of Stance and Tone on Structure, T23 (for Active Reading, p. 1167)

Grammar
- Run-on Sentences, T43 (for Mini Lesson, p. 1175)
- Complete Sentences, C76 (for Mini Lesson, p. 1175)
- Run-on Sentences, C126 (for Mini Lesson, p. 1175)

Vocabulary
- Using Context to Understand Dialect, C93 (for Mini Lesson, pp. 1168–1169)

Writing
- Showing, Not Telling, T22 (for Writing Options, p. 1175)

Communications
- Impromptu Speaking: Debate, T15 (for Mini Lesson, p. 1172)

INTEGRATED TECHNOLOGY
Audio Library
Visit our website:
www.mcdougallittell.com

OVERVIEW

Objectives

1. understand and appreciate a **personal essay** containing social and political commentary **(Literary Analysis)**
2. **infer the author's perspective** in order to understand Orwell's essay **(Active Reading)**

Summary

At a prison in Burma, Orwell and other officials are waiting to attend the hanging of a Hindu prisoner. The prisoner remains passive as guards tie his arms and march him to the gallows, followed by the assembled officials. Orwell, watching the prisoner's back, realizes for the first time how wrong it is to destroy a healthy human being.

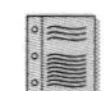

Use **Unit Six Resource Book,** p. 79 for additional support.

Thematic Link

Watching the prisoner being led to the gallows, Orwell realizes for the first time the **shocking reality** of capital punishment—the planned death of a healthy, conscious human being.

5-Minute Warm-Up

Daily Language SkillBuilder

Have students **proofread** the display sentences on page 979k and write them correctly. The sentences also appear on Transparency 32 of **Grammar Transparencies and Copymasters.**

Mini Lesson **Preteaching Vocabulary**

If you would like to preteach the WORDS TO KNOW for this selection, use the Mini Lesson on p. 1168.

TEACHING THE LITERATURE

Reading and Analyzing

Active Reading

INFERRING THE AUTHOR'S PERSPECTIVE

Tell students that in addition to the specific clues listed on p. 1167, they can also rely on more general clues to infer the author's perspective. For example, the overall impression that the text leaves as well as the plot and setting can be valuable clues.

Use **Unit Six Resource Book** p. 80 for more practice.

Literary Analysis PERSONAL ESSAY

Remind students that personal essays have some characteristics that differentiate them from other, more formal essays. Ask them to identify characteristics that they find on p. 1169 that help them identify this as a personal essay.
Possible Response: It has a first-person point of view; the author uses irony to express his opinion, a technique unlikely to be used in a formal essay.

Use **Unit Six Resource Book** p. 81 for more exercises.

Reading Skills and Strategies:
CLARIFYING DETAILS

Ask students to list words and phrases Orwell uses to describe the prisoner.
Answer: Hindu; puny wisp of a man; shaven head; vague liquid eyes; thick, sprouting moustache, absurdly too big for his body; quite unresisting; limply.
Then ask students what effect these descriptions have on the reader's impression of the prisoner.
Possible Responses: They make him seem pitiable, helpless, and harmless.

A Hanging

George Orwell

Teaching Options

Preteaching Vocabulary

USING CONTEXT CLUES Call students' attention to the list of WORDS TO KNOW on p. 1167. Remind them that sometimes the suffix on an unfamiliar word will give them a clue to its part of speech. Knowing a word's part of speech and how it functions in a sentence are the necessary first steps in using context clues to determine the meaning of a word.

Model Sentence

Paul already knew that he had won the award, so the ceremony was merely a *formality*.

Instruction

- Write the model sentence on the chalkboard. Point out the word *formality.*
- Ask a volunteer to identify the base word and the suffix.

Answer: formal + ity

- Have students think of other words with the same suffix to determine the part of speech of *formality*.

Possible Responses: intensity, curiosity, monstrosity

It was in Burma, a sodden morning of the rains. A sickly light, like yellow tinfoil, was slanting over the high walls into the jail yard. We were waiting outside the condemned cells, a row of sheds fronted with double bars, like small animal cages. Each cell measured about ten feet by ten and was quite bare within except for a plank bed and a pot of drinking water. In some of them brown silent men were squatting at the inner bars, with their blankets draped round them. These were the condemned men, due to be hanged within the next week or two.

One prisoner had been brought out of his cell. He was a Hindu, a puny wisp of a man, with a shaven head and vague liquid eyes. He had a thick, sprouting moustache, absurdly too big for his body, rather like the moustache of a comic man on the films. Six tall Indian warders[1] were guarding him and getting him ready for the gallows. Two of them stood by with rifles and fixed bayonets, while the others handcuffed him, passed a chain through his handcuffs and fixed it to their belts, and lashed his arms tight to his sides. They crowded very close about him, with their hands always on him in a careful, caressing grip, as though all the while feeling him to make sure he was there. It was like men handling a fish which is still alive and may jump back into the water. But he stood quite unresisting, yielding his arms limply to the ropes, as though he hardly noticed what was happening.

Eight o'clock struck and a bugle call, desolately thin in the wet air, floated from the distant barracks. The superintendent of the jail, who was standing apart from the rest of us, moodily prodding the gravel with his stick, raised his head at the sound. He was an army doctor, with a grey toothbrush moustache and a gruff voice. "For God's sake hurry up, Francis," he said irritably. "The man ought to have been dead by this time. Aren't you ready yet?"

Francis, the head jailer, a fat Dravidian[2] in a white drill suit and gold spectacles, waved his black hand. "Yes sir, yes sir," he bubbled. "All iss satisfactorily prepared. The hangman iss waiting. We shall proceed."

"Well, quick march, then. The prisoners can't get their breakfast till this job's over."

We set out for the gallows. Two warders marched on either side of the prisoner, with their rifles at the slope; two others marched close against him, gripping him by arm and shoulder, as though at once pushing and supporting him. The rest of us, magistrates and the like, followed behind. Suddenly, when we had gone ten yards, the procession stopped short without any order or warning. A dreadful thing had happened—a dog, come goodness knows whence, had appeared in the yard. It came bounding among us with a loud volley of barks, and leapt round us wagging its whole body, wild with glee at finding so many human beings together. It was a large, wooly dog, half Airedale, half pariah.[3] For a moment it pranced round us, and then, before anyone could stop it, it had made a dash for the prisoner, and jumping up tried to lick his face. Everyone stood aghast, too taken aback even to grab at the dog.

"Who let that bloody brute in here?" said the superintendent angrily. "Catch it, someone!"

A warder, detached from the escort, charged clumsily after the dog, but it danced and gamboled[4] just out of his reach, taking everything as part of the game. A young Eurasian jailer picked up a handful of gravel and tried to stone the dog away, but it dodged the stones and came after us again. Its yaps echoed from the jail walls. The prisoner, in the grasp of the two warders, looked on incuriously, as though this was another formality of the hanging. It was several minutes

1. **warders:** prison guards.
2. **Dravidian** (drə-vĭd'ē-ən): a member of a dark-skinned people of southern India.
3. **pariah:** a wild or domesticated mongrel dog.
4. **gamboled** (găm'bəld): jumped about playfully.

WORDS TO KNOW

formality (fôr-măl'ĭ-tē) *n.* a procedure that is required or customary in performing a particular activity

1169

Customizing Instruction

Less Proficient Readers

You may wish to have students use paired reading for this brief essay. Have students find partners and take turns reading one or two paragraphs, either silently or aloud to each other, and then have them discuss what they just read.

Students Acquiring English

Prepare students for the use of irony in the piece by pointing out examples after they have read p. 1169. Orwell's irony comes mainly from exaggeration, incongruous juxtaposition, and the unexpected. For example, when he writes "a dreadful thing has happened" speaking of the appearance of the dog, it is ironic that the disturbance by the dog should be considered "dreadful," but the death of a human being is not.

Use **Spanish Study Guide** for additional support, pp. 278–280.

Gifted and Talented

Have students discuss whether capital punishment benefits or harms society. Who benefits from the hanging, and who suffers?

Multiple Learning Styles

Visual Learners

Have students stage a tableau vivant, or living tableau, to illustrate this scene. Have the entire class work together to determine the position of each person, and then have them assume roles and positions. Encourage the use of costumes and props, as these are essential features of a tableau vivant.

Make sure students understand that the suffix *-ity* changes an adjective to a noun.

- Then have students infer from context clues the meaning of *formality* in this sentence.

Answer: procedure or customary practice

Exercise Read the following sentences. Ask students to identify the root word and suffix (if any) of each italicized word. Then have them use that information and the sentence's syntax to determine the word's part of speech. Finally, tell them to infer the word's meaning from context clues.

1. The talk show host smiled *genially* at the contestants, putting them at ease.
   Answer: genial + ly; adverb; in a friendly manner
2. The dog at the animal shelter approached its new owner *timorously,* creeping with its belly to the ground and whining.
   Answer: timorous + ly; adverb; in a frightened manner

Use **Unit Six Resource Book** p. 82 for more practice.

A lesson on context clues appears on page 939 in the Pupil's Edition.

Reading and Analyzing

Active Reading

INFERRING THE AUTHOR'S PERSPECTIVE

A Point out to students that the style of Orwell's essay changes dramatically with the paragraph beginning "It is curious . . ." as Orwell introduces a personal reflection on the events. Ask them what they inferred about his perspective from that paragraph.

Possible Responses: that Orwell is horrified by the hanging; that this essay is not just about the hanging but also about its injustice

Literary Analysis: THEME

B Point out to students that themes are often announced in the title or final words of an essay, but not always. Ask them to consider how the final sentence of the paragraph beginning "It is curious . . ." might be considered thematic.

Possible Response: The last six words, which imply that the loss of a single human being is an irreplaceable and irreconcilable loss, might be Orwell's theme.

Reading Skills and Strategies: MAKING CONNECTIONS

C The sentence "minutes seemed to pass" is marked as hyperbole by the word *seemed.* Ask students to recall situations when time seemed to stand still. Have them explain, in the light of their reflections, what they think was going on in the minds and hearts of the spectators during this brief time.

before someone managed to catch the dog. Then we put my handkerchief through its collar and moved off once more, with the dog still straining and whimpering.

It was about forty yards to the gallows. I watched the bare brown back of the prisoner marching in front of me. He walked clumsily with his bound arms, but quite steadily, with that bobbing gait of the Indian who never straightens his knees. At each step his muscles slid neatly into place, the lock of hair on his scalp danced up and down, his feet printed themselves on the wet gravel. And once, in spite of the men who gripped him by each shoulder, he stepped slightly aside to avoid a puddle on the path.

A It is curious, but till that moment I had never realized what it means to destroy a healthy, conscious man. When I saw the prisoner step aside to avoid the puddle, I saw the mystery, the unspeakable wrongness, of cutting a life short when it is in full tide. This man was not dying, he was alive just as we were alive. All the organs of his body were working—bowels digesting food, skin renewing itself, nails growing, tissues forming—all toiling away in solemn foolery. His nails would still be growing when he stood on the drop, when he was falling through the air with a tenth of a second to live. His eyes saw the yellow gravel and the grey walls, and his brain still remembered, foresaw, reasoned—reasoned even about puddles. He and we were a party of men walking together, seeing, hearing, feeling, understanding the same world; and in two minutes, with a sudden snap, one of us would be gone—one mind less, one world less. **B**

The gallows stood in a small yard, separate from the main grounds of the prison, and overgrown with tall prickly weeds. It was a brick erection like three sides of a shed, with planking on top, and above that two beams and a crossbar with the rope dangling. The hangman, a grey-haired convict in the white uniform of the prison, was waiting beside his machine. He greeted us with a servile[5] crouch as we entered.

5. **servile:** slavelike; cringing.

George Orwell at the police training school at Mandalay, Burma, in 1922. Photo courtesy of Roger Beadon. Orwell is circled.

1170

Teaching Options

BLOCK SCHEDULING: MANAGING TIME

If your schedule requires that you cover the lesson objectives in a shorter time, use . . .

- Preparing to Read, p. 1167
- Thinking Through the Literature, p. 1174
- Vocabulary in Action, p. 1175

If you want to take advantage of longer class time, use . . .

- TE Teaching Options: Preteaching Vocabulary, pp. 1168–1169; Viewing and Representing, p. 1171; Speaking and Listening, p. 1172; Informal Assessment, p. 1173; Grammar, p. 1175
- Choices & Challenges, p. 1175

At a word from Francis the two warders, gripping the prisoner more closely than ever, half led, half pushed him to the gallows and helped him clumsily up the ladder. Then the hangman climbed up and fixed the rope round the prisoner's neck.

WE stood waiting, five yards away. The warders had formed in a rough circle round the gallows. And then, when the noose was fixed, the
1 prisoner began crying out to his god. It was a high, reiterated cry of "Ram! Ram! Ram! Ram!"[6] not urgent and fearful like a prayer or a cry for help, but steady, rhythmical, almost like the tolling of a bell. The dog answered the sound with a whine. The hangman, still standing on the gallows, produced a small cotton bag like a flour bag and drew it down over the prisoner's face. But the sound, muffled by the cloth, still persisted, over and over again: "Ram! Ram! Ram! Ram! Ram!"

The hangman climbed down and stood ready, holding the lever. Minutes seemed to pass. The C

6. **Ram** (räm): a form of *Rama,* the name of an incarnation of Vishnu, one of the three main Hindu gods.

Customizing Instruction

Gifted and Talented

1 Explain to students that the name of Ram is customarily used as a mantra to call upon the gods. "Ram, Ram," was the last thing Gandhi said before he died, to tell the gods that he was coming. Have students look for other foreign words in the essay. Then have them evaluate the effect of including these words, particularly on the setting.

Multiple Learning Styles

Visual Learners
Have students create a map of the prison's grounds, adding as many details as possible from the essay.

Mini Lesson Viewing and Representing

George Orwell at the police training school at Mandalay, Burma, in 1922

ART APPRECIATION

Instruction Point out that in a grouping of people it is natural to look for similarities and differences. Ask students to name some similarities and differences among the thirteen men.

Possible Response: all in uniform; stand/sit in different postures; some, but not all, have hats and sticks; one has a dog; eyes focused in different places; mostly Caucasian; some clean shaven, others not.

Application Tell students that observations about photographs can be used to create cultural/social interpretations. Ask what they can conclude from their observations.

Possible Response: While the officers all wear the same uniform, a closer glance shows a wide variety of attitudes.

Reading and Analyzing

Literary Analysis: IRONY

Remind students that Orwell used irony in the beginning of this essay. Ask them to find examples on these pages.

Possible Responses: "dead silence"; "dead as a stone"; "He's all right"; "homely, jolly scene"; "our friend"; "think of all the pain and trouble you are causing to us"; "everyone was laughing"

Reading Skills and Strategies: INFERRING MOOD

A As everyone watching the hanging changes color, ask students how they think the mood changes at that moment.

Possible Response: As the guards realize what they are about to do, the mood becomes tense and uncomfortable.

Reading Skills and Strategies: SUMMARIZING

B Have students summarize what has occurred during this section of the essay, which begins with "We stood waiting" on p. 1171.

Possible Response: The prisoner, with the noose around his neck, repeatedly cries out "Ram! Ram! Ram!" This chant unnerves the spectators. Finally, the prisoner is hanged and everyone feels relieved. The warders then feed the other prisoners breakfast and the officers begin chatting happily.

steady, muffled crying from the prisoner went on and on, "Ram! Ram! Ram!" never faltering for an instant. The superintendent, his head on his chest, was slowly poking the ground with his stick; perhaps he was counting the cries, allowing the prisoner a fixed number—fifty, perhaps, or a hundred. Everyone had changed color. (A) The Indians had gone grey like bad coffee, and one or two of the bayonets were wavering. We looked at the lashed, hooded man on the drop, and listened to his cries—each cry another second of life; the same thought was in all our minds: oh, kill him quickly, get it over, stop that abominable noise!

Suddenly the superintendent made up his mind. Throwing up his head he made a swift motion with his stick. "Chalo!"[7] he shouted almost fiercely.

There was a clanking noise, and then dead silence. The prisoner had vanished, and the rope was twisting on itself. I let go of the dog, and it galloped immediately to the back of the gallows; but when it got there it stopped short, barked, and then retreated into a corner of the yard, where it stood among the weeds, looking timorously out at us. We went round the gallows to inspect the prisoner's body. He was dangling with his toes pointed straight downwards, very slowly revolving, as dead as a stone.

The superintendent reached out with his stick and poked the bare body; it oscillated, slightly. "*He's* all right," said the superintendent. He backed out from under the gallows, and blew out a deep breath. The moody look had gone out of his face quite suddenly. He glanced at his wristwatch. "Eight minutes past eight. Well, that's all for this morning, thank God."

The warders unfixed bayonets and marched away. The dog, sobered and conscious of having misbehaved itself, slipped after them. We walked out of the gallows yard, past the condemned cells with their waiting prisoners, into the big central yard of the prison. The convicts, under the command of warders armed with lathis,[8] were already receiving their breakfast. They squatted in long rows, each man holding a tin pannikin,[9] while two warders with buckets 1
marched round ladling out rice; it seemed quite a homely, jolly scene, after the hanging. An enormous relief had come upon us now that the job was done. One felt an impulse to sing, to break into a run, to snigger. All at once everyone began chattering gaily. (B)

THE Eurasian boy walking beside me nodded towards the way we had come, with a knowing smile: "Do you know, sir, our friend (he meant the dead man), when he heard his appeal had been dismissed, he pissed on the floor of his cell. From fright.—Kindly take one of my cigarettes, sir. Do you not admire my new silver case, sir? From the boxwallah,[10] two rupees eight annas.[11] Classy European style."

Several people laughed—at what, nobody seemed certain.

Francis was walking by the superintendent, talking garrulously:[12] "Well, sir, all hass passed off with the utmost satisfactoriness. It wass all finished—flick! like that. It iss not always so—oah, no! I have known cases where the doctor

7. **Chalo!** (chä′lō) *Hindi:* Go!
8. **lathis** (lä′tēz): heavy bamboo sticks bound with iron, used as weapons by the police in India.
9. **pannikin:** a small pan or shallow cup.
10. **boxwallah:** in India, a peddler.
11. **rupees** (ro͞o-pēz′) . . . **annas** (ä′nəz): Indian units of money. (Annas, which are no longer used, were coins worth $\frac{1}{16}$ of a rupee.)
12. **garrulously** (găr′ə-ləs-lē): in a wordy, long-winded manner.

WORDS TO KNOW
timorously (tĭm′ər-əs-lē) *adv.* in a fearful or apprehensive way; timidly
oscillate (ŏs′ə-lāt′) *v.* to swing back and forth

1172

Teaching Options

Speaking and Listening

DEBATE INSTRUCTION

Instruction Remind students of the format of a formal debate. Make sure students understand that, in a formal debate, the debaters may or may not personally agree with the team's position. The point is to present logical, solid arguments that are persuasive yet factually correct.

Prepare Divide the class into two groups. Have one side argue for capital punishment and the other side argue against it. Act as the moderator, enforcing time limits and behavior. Have students meet in teams to discuss arguments.

Present If possible, arrange the classroom in two aisles so that the debating teams face one another. Have each team state its position and then move into the phase of rebuttals and replies. If students get too emotional, take a recess to remind them that a debate is not a shouting match but an exercise in persuasive techniques, logic, and fairly expressing one's views.

BLOCK SCHEDULING This activity is particularly well-suited for longer class periods.

wass obliged to go beneath the gallows and pull the prisoner's legs to ensure decease. Most disagreeable!" **2**

"Wriggling about, eh? That's bad," said the superintendent.

"Ach, sir, it iss worse when they become refractory![13] One man, I recall, clung to the bars of hiss cage when we went to take him out. You will scarcely credit, sir, that it took six warders to dislodge him, three pulling at each leg. We reasoned with him. 'My dear fellow,' we said, 'think of all the pain and trouble you are causing to us!' But no, he would not listen! Ach, he wass very troublesome!"

I found that I was laughing quite loudly. Everyone was laughing. Even the superintendent grinned in a tolerant way. "You'd better all come out and have a drink," he said quite genially. "I've got a bottle of whisky in the car. We could do with it."

We went through the big double gates of the prison, into the road. "Pulling at his legs!" exclaimed a Burmese magistrate suddenly, and burst into a loud chuckling. We all began laughing again. At that moment Francis's anecdote seemed extraordinarily funny. We all had a drink together, native and European alike, quite amicably.[14] The dead man was a hundred yards away. ❖

13. **refractory:** hard to manage; stubborn.
14. **amicably:** in a friendly manner.

WORDS TO KNOW
genially (jēn′yə-lē) *adv.* in a friendly manner
anecdote (ăn′ĭk-dōt′) *n.* a brief account of an interesting or humorous incident

Customizing Instruction

Less Proficient Readers

Check students' understanding with the following questions.

- Who is Francis?
  Answer: the head jailer
- How is the prisoner executed?
  Answer: He is hanged by the neck until dead.
- What is the spectators' reaction to the prisoner's repeated cry of "Ram! Ram!"?
  Possible Responses: It makes them very uncomfortable; it makes them want the hanging to be finished.
- What time is the prisoner hanged?
  Answer: at 8:08 A.M.
- What do the superintendent, warders, and other officers do after the hanging?
  Answer: They have a drink together.

Students Acquiring English

1 Explain to students that the suffix *-(i)kin* indicates a diminutive, comparable to the Spanish *-ito/a.* Ask them to think of other English words with this suffix. If necessary, have them look up the suffix in a good dictionary.
Possible Responses: mannikin, bodkin, napkin, lambkin

Less Proficient Readers

2 Explain that death is not always instantaneous when a person is hanged. The doctor had to pull on the prisoner's legs either to break his neck or to hasten strangulation.

Assessment Informal Assessment

WRITING FROM ANOTHER POINT OF VIEW
Ask students to write a brief story based on the essay but narrated from another participant's point of view. Students may wish to write from the first-person perspective of an Indian warder, the superintendent, another prisoner, the hangman, or the hanged man himself.

RUBRIC
3 **Full Accomplishment** Students' stories accurately reflect first-person perspective of character. Stories display imagination and narrative skill.
2 **Substantial Accomplishment** Students use first-person point of view of character other than Orwell. Stories display good grasp of basic narrative elements.
1 **Little or Partial Accomplishment** Students' stories are not based on recognizable person from essay. Stories are lacking key narrative elements.

GUIDING STUDENT RESPONSE

Connect to the Literature

1. What Do You Think?
Guidelines for student response: Look for student responses to include emotional elements as well as views about capital punishment.

Comprehension Check

- the appearance of the dog
- They watch as the superintendent checks to see that the man is dead, then walk away together, chatting.

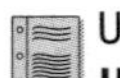

Use Selection Quiz in **Unit Six Resource Book** p. 83.

Think Critically

2. Possible Responses: They want to forget what happened; their relief makes them giddy; they are callous and heartless.
3. Possible Response: The dog provides grotesque comic relief that only heightens the participants' tension.
4. Possible Response: It makes the man seem more like a victim because we cannot label him as a "thief," "blackmailer," or other criminal type.
5. Accept all reasonable, well-supported responses. After students have made a statement about the author's position, ask them to describe how his perspective affected the essay's tone.

Literary Analysis

Paired Activity Have a class discussion in which pairs of students share their ideas about Orwell's purpose and theme in this essay.

Review Irony in Nonfiction Perhaps the central irony in this piece is that Orwell, as a representative of the colonial power enforcing the death sentence, does not believe in the justice of what he is doing.

Connect to the Literature

1. **What Do You Think?** What is your reaction to the events described in "A Hanging"? Discuss your thoughts with a classmate.

Comprehension Check

- What event disrupts the procession to the gallows?
- What do the men do after the hanging takes place?

Think Critically

2. How would you account for the men's laughter and chatter after the hanging?
3. How do you think the intrusion of the dog affects the **mood** of this essay?

- the moods of the prisoner and the warders
- the behavior of the dog
- the warders' struggle to catch the dog

4. Orwell does not tell the reader what the condemned man's crime was. Why do you think he chose not to include this information?
5. **ACTIVE READING** **INFERRING THE AUTHOR'S PERSPECTIVE** Review the cluster diagram you made in your **READER'S NOTEBOOK**. What can you **infer** about Orwell's **perspective** on the subject of the essay?

Extend Interpretations

6. **Different Perspectives** How might the essay be different if it were written by one of the Indian warders or by one of the prisoners in the condemned cells?
7. **Connect to Life** Think back to your discussion of capital punishment for the Connect to Your Life feature on page 000. Has reading "A Hanging" altered your view on the subject of the death penalty? Share your thoughts with a classmate.

Literary Analysis

PERSONAL ESSAY Whereas a formal essay usually presents carefully structured arguments, a **personal essay** is a brief nonfiction work that expresses a writer's thoughts, feelings, and opinions on a subject in a less systematic way. Frequently, a personal essay is (like "A Hanging") a reflection on an episode in the writer's life.

Most personal essays are written with more than one **purpose** in mind. Identifying the writer's main purpose for writing can help you to determine an essay's **theme**—the message that the writer conveys about the events described.

Paired Activity Bearing in mind your thoughts about Orwell's perspective, answer the following questions:

- What do you think was Orwell's main purpose in writing this essay?
- What do you think is the main theme of the essay?

Jot down your thoughts, and discuss them with a partner. How might Orwell have conveyed the same theme in a formal essay?

REVIEW **IRONY IN NONFICTION** As you know, **irony** involves a contrast between what is expected and what actually happens. In works of nonfiction, irony can be used to reveal and reinforce important ideas. What details or statements in "A Hanging" might be considered ironic? What effect do you think Orwell's use of irony has on the **tone** of the essay? How does irony relate to the essay's main **theme?**

Extend Interpretations

Different Perspectives Two key features of Orwell's essay are the change in perspective he has undergone since the event took place and the use of irony to convey this change; both of these features might be absent. In addition, neither of the suggested authors might be willing to convey their true feelings, given their situations.

Connect to Life Accept all reasonable responses. You might choose to conduct an informal class discussion or a more formal debate on the subject of capital punishment.

Writing Options

Orwell's Diary Imagine you are George Orwell. Write a diary entry describing the day of the hanging. Remember, a diary writer, unlike the writer of a personal essay, is not writing for an audience.

Activities & Explorations

Still Life In "A Hanging," the setting and several events are described in great detail. Draw a picture of a key scene in the work, relying as much as possible on the details Orwell provided. ~ **ART**

Inquiry & Research

End of British Rule Research the final decades of British rule in Burma. Find out about the country's nationalist movement, its fate during World War II, and its gaining of independence in 1948. Present your findings to the class in an oral report.

Vocabulary in Action

EXERCISE: CONTEXT CLUES On your paper, write the Word to Know that best completes each sentence.

1. The condemned man ________ observed the noose.
2. His guards treated him ________, as if they were all on a picnic.
3. The hanging was a strange combination of a ceremonial ________ and a sudden killing.
4. The noose began to ________ in the breeze.
5. After the prisoner was dead, one of the guards told an amusing ________.

Building Vocabulary

For an in-depth lesson on how to expand your vocabulary, see page 1182.

WORDS TO KNOW		
	anecdote	oscillate
	formality	timorously
	genially	

George Orwell

1903–1950

Other Works

"Shooting an Elephant"
"How the Poor Die"
Animal Farm
Nineteen Eighty-Four

Voluntary Poverty "George Orwell" was the pen name of Eric Arthur Blair, who was born in the Indian province of Bengal, where his father was serving in the Indian civil service. In 1922 Orwell joined the Indian Imperial Police and left for Burma, which was at that time under British rule. When Orwell discovered how much the Burmese disliked British rule, however, he became disenchanted with Britain's imperialist policies. He eventually quit his job and, at the age of 25, decided to live the life of the poor and downtrodden, for whom he had deep, abiding sympathies. Working as a dishwasher and a day laborer, he tramped through the countryside with the homeless. Out of these experiences came his first book, *Down and Out in Paris and London,* published in 1933.

Speaking Out for Justice and Freedom Throughout his short life, Orwell continued to sympathize with the underdog and to speak out against social and political injustice. Like many other young writers, he left England to fight with the anti-Fascist forces in Spain's civil war. He was wounded in the fighting, but his experiences provided him with the material for his book *Homage to Catalonia.* Near the end of World War II, he completed the first of his famous novels—*Animal Farm,* a satire in which he warned prophetically of the dangers of dictatorships. In 1949 he published *Nineteen Eighty-Four,* focusing on the appalling possibilities of life in a totalitarian state. Orwell completed *Nineteen Eighty-Four* while battling tuberculosis, from which he died at the peak of his career.

Writing Options

Orwell's Diary Students' entries will vary but should address the contradiction in Orwell's response at the time: that he realized what it was to kill a man, and yet joined in the laughter and made no move to stop the proceedings.

Activities & Explorations

Still Life This activity gives students the opportunity to present the actual death of the man or not, as they choose. Respect should be shown to students' choices, both in what they portray and in how they portray it. Students who oppose capital punishment and who consider the man's death to be a murder may choose to use striking graphic images to convey their viewpoint. Allow students to use computer graphics and drawing software, if available.

Inquiry & Research

End of British Rule You might want to have students work in small groups so as to maximize class time. Set a time limit, such as 10 minutes, for each oral report. Encourage students to use visual aids such as time lines or maps.

Vocabulary in Action

1. timorously
2. genially
3. formality
4. oscillate
5. anecdote

Grammar

RUN-ON SENTENCES

Instruction A run-on sentence is two or more sentences written as one sentence. You can correct run-on sentences in any of several ways:

- Use a period and a capital letter to separate the sentences.
- Use a comma and a coordinating conjunction such as *and.*
- Use a semicolon, or a semicolon and a conjunctive adverb such as *however,* followed by a comma.
- Combine the ideas in a compound sentence.

Activity Write this run-on sentence on the chalkboard.

George Orwell was a policeman in Burma he became disillusioned with the job.

Ask students to tell what the two sentences are and to suggest different ways to correct the run-on. *(George Orwell was a policeman in Burma, but he became disillusioned with the job.)*

Use **Grammar Transparencies and Copymasters,** p. 68.

Use McDougal Littell's ***Language Network*** for more instruction and practice in run-on sentences.

Objectives

- create a Web site
- use a written text as a model for writing
- revise a draft to eliminate clutter
- edit and proofread for complete sentences

Introducing the Workshop

A Web Site Explain that one of the most revolutionary aspects of the World Wide Web is the way information is so richly connected to other information. With a simple Hypertext link, users are immediately connected to related sources that can provide background information for an idea. Have students compare an advertising billboard to a home page on the Web. Discuss the differences in these two forms of communication.

Establish some criteria for what makes a good home page on the Web. Point out that by creating a personal Web site, students will be able to introduce themselves and subjects they care about to Internet users. They can use Hypertext links to establish a richly connected "web" of information.

Basics in a Box

B Using the Graphic The graphic lists three necessary components of an effective Web site: verbal information, visual information, and hypertext links.

C Presenting the Guidelines and Standards To better understand the assignment, students can refer to the Guidelines and Standards for a Successful Web Site. You may wish to discuss each standard individually. These six guidelines will aid students in preparing effective Web sites.

Use McDougal Littell's ***Language Network,*** Chapter 29, for more instruction on creating a web site.

To engage students visually, use **Power Presentation** 9, Web Site.

Communication Workshop
Web Site

Reaching out through the Web . . .

A During World Wars I and II, people around the world tuned in their radios to learn how the war was progressing and to listen to political leaders such as Winston Churchill deliver important speeches. Radio broadcasting revolutionized communication by allowing people to learn about events as they happened. Today, the World Wide Web allows more people to communicate faster than ever before. The Web contains millions of **Web sites** that offer news and information about individuals, companies, and organizations.

For Your Portfolio

PROMPT Create a Web site that gives information about yourself, an area that interests you, or an issue you feel is important.

Purpose: To share information about you and your interests

Audience: The diverse users of the Web

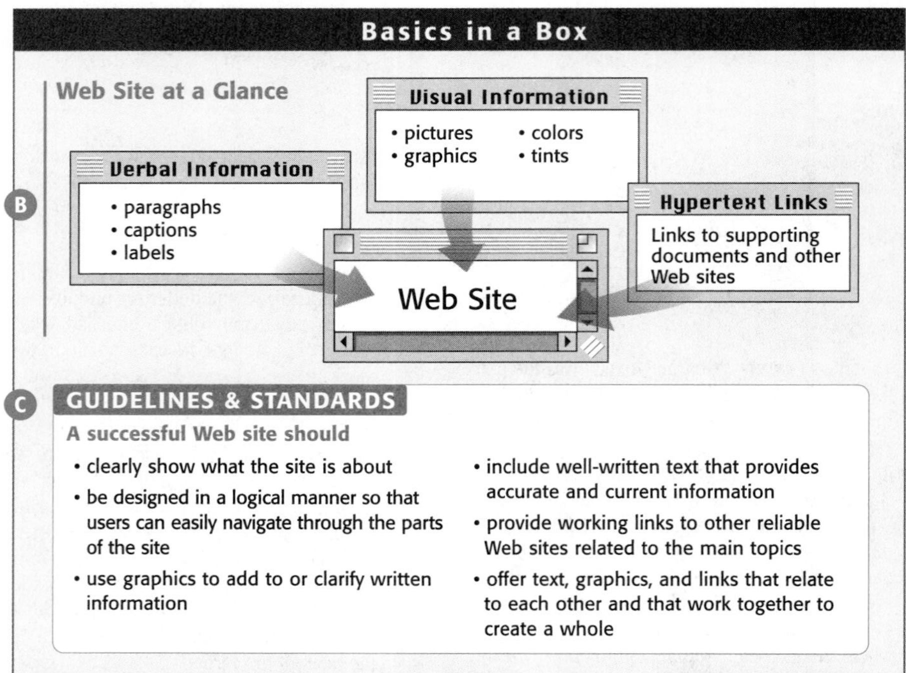

C **GUIDELINES & STANDARDS**

A successful Web site should

- clearly show what the site is about
- be designed in a logical manner so that users can easily navigate through the parts of the site
- use graphics to add to or clarify written information
- include well-written text that provides accurate and current information
- provide working links to other reliable Web sites related to the main topics
- offer text, graphics, and links that relate to each other and that work together to create a whole

LESSON RESOURCES

USING PRINT RESOURCES

Unit Six Resource Book

- Planning the Content, p. 84
- Planning the Design, p. 85
- Peer Response, pp. 86–87
- Revising, Editing, and Proofreading, p. 88
- Standards for Evaluation, p. 89

USING MEDIA RESOURCES

LaserLinks

Writing Springboards

See Teacher's SourceBook p. 114 for bar codes.

Writing Coach CD-ROM

Visit our website:
www.mcdougallittell.com

For a complete view of Lesson Resources, see page 979e.

Analyzing a Model Web Site

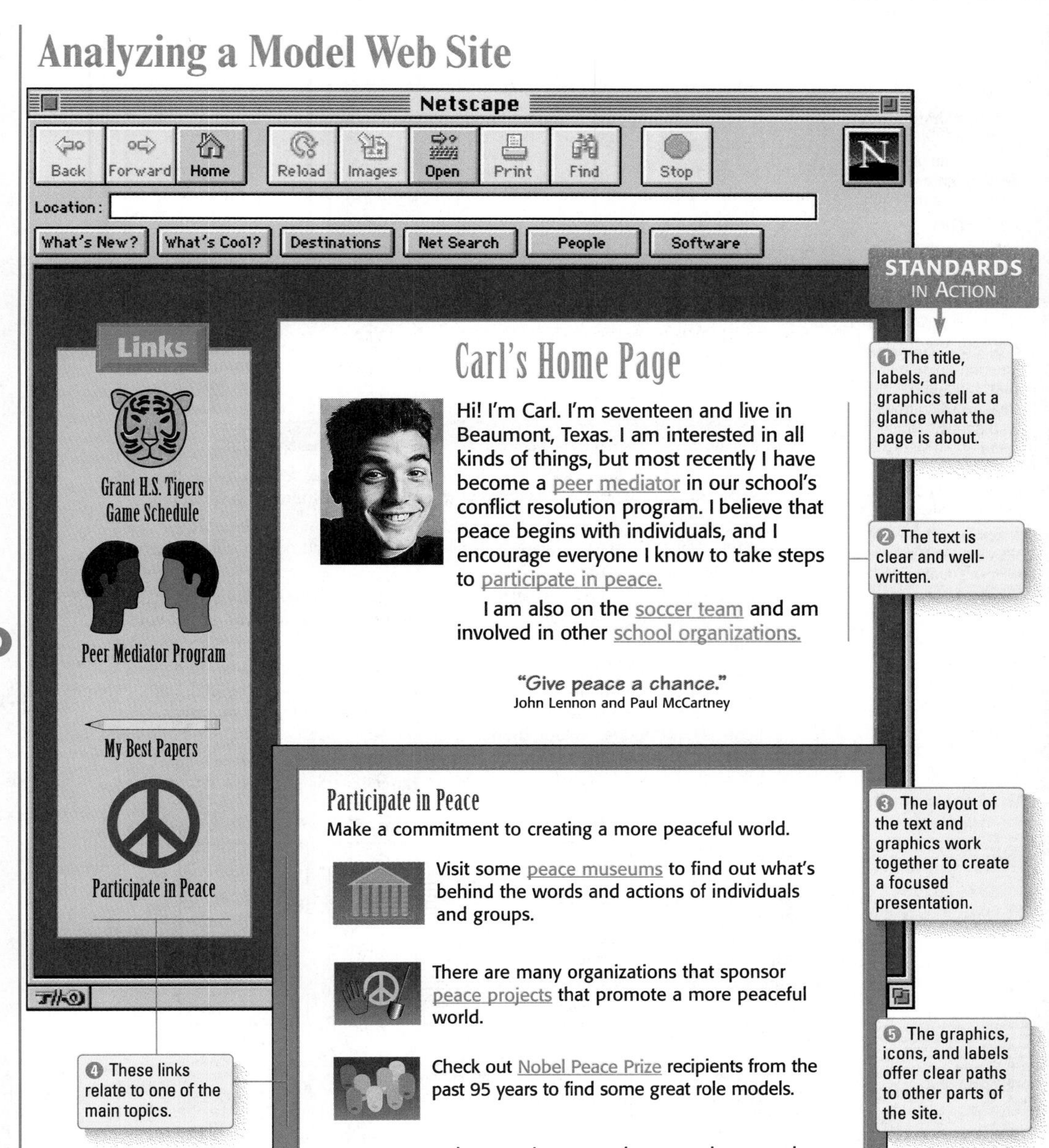

D

Teaching the Lesson

Analyzing the Model

"Carl's Home Page"

D The student model introduces its creator, Carl, through a casual, conversational introduction. By the end of the home page, students have a basic idea of Carl's interests and the kind of person he is. Have students read the model aloud. Then ask them to list Carl's interests.

Possible Response: peace, soccer, school organizations

Students can take turns reading aloud the Standards in Action. Point out key words and phrases in the student model that correspond to the elements mentioned in the Standards in Action.

2. Point out that while the opening of Carl's Home Page is informal in tone, it doesn't waste words with irrelevant conversation. Notice how Carl includes descriptive noun phrases that give a concise idea of his interests.
3. Tell students that in an effective graphic layout, the text works to support graphic information rather than to repeat it. The words give additional information that the graphics cannot express.
4. Point out that links are an important way to streamline a graphic design and still provide readers with vital information. For instance, if readers need to know more about the Nobel Peace Prize, Carl shows them how to get that information. If readers don't need to know more, Carl's Web page is not burdened with unnecessary text.
5. Tell students that identifying pathways is one of the fun parts of creating a Web page. The links provide readers access to additional information. Links can also be updated, added, and changed as students maintain their Web site.

Guiding Student Writing

Planning the Site

If after reading the Idea Bank students are having difficulty planning their sites, suggest they try the following:

- What interests you most? history? cars? new technology? music videos? Choose one of your favorite interests and create a Web site based on that interest.
- What issues are you most concerned with in your community? Choose one and center your Web site around that issue.

Text: Planning the Content

1. Have students work in pairs to narrow their subject lists to three or four interesting choices. Then have them examine those subjects for the following qualities: Interesting to Others, Most Revealing About Me, Most Interesting to Me, Provides Interesting Links.
2. Have students create a two-column chart with the headings "What I Know" and "What I Want to Know." In the appropriate columns, students can fill in information under each heading. Encourage them to research those things they do not know. Remind students to list any Web resources they use as possible links.
3. Have students create a schematic for each page of their Web site as well as a rough plan for the space that is to be allotted to items on that page.
4. The home page design shown here may provide a helpful orientation.
5. Have students explore the Web itself in search of resources for and examples of Web site design.

Teaching Tip

Throughout the planning and design process, have students keep a "Links Idea List" on which they jot down ideas for Hypertext links. Later, they can decide which ideas are worth developing.

IDEABank

1. Your Working Portfolio
Build on one of the **Writing Options** you completed earlier in this unit:

- **Multimedia Notes,** p. 1112
- **Web Site Page,** p. 1134

2. Student Web Pages
Conduct an online search using the keywords "student web pages." Study some of the Web pages you find to get ideas for your own Web site.

3. Surfing
Visit our Web site at www.mcdougallittell.com

Creating Your Web Site

❶ Planning the Site

Don't be overwhelmed by the technology involved in publishing on the Web. The first step in creating your Web site is deciding what you want to publish. Your site might include:

- a brief description of who you are
- information about your hobbies, interests, talents, job, or school
- your stories, poems, and school essays

See the **Idea Bank** in the margin for more suggestions.

Your Web site will integrate text, graphics, and Hypertext links to other Web sites. Follow the planning steps below.

Text: Planning the Content

1. **Choose your subject or subjects.** Stick with three or four subjects that you think are interesting and that you would like to share with others.
2. **Develop the subjects or issues that you will include.** Make some notes about all that you already know and all that you might want to include about each subject.
3. **Decide how many pages to include in your site.** How many pages will you need to clearly cover the content? Use the notes you made about your subjects to help you figure this out.
4. **Organize your home page.** How will you set up your page? Most Web sites cluster around various topics. You will need to decide on the order of topics on your first page and how to encourage users to try out the various possibilities you are offering them.
5. **Look for resources.** Books or the Web itself will give you information on planning your Web site. You may find diagrams like this one helpful.

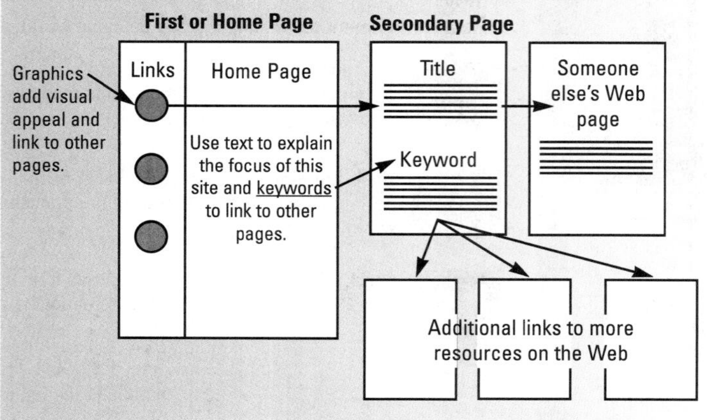

Graphics: Planning the Design

1. **Focus on the first page, or home page, of your Web site.** Visitors to your home page should be able to learn quickly what the site is about, who created it, and what links are available.
2. **Think about the balance of graphics and text.** How many illustrations or visual aids will you provide? How much text will you include? Make several sketches to help you achieve the right balance.
3. **Keep it simple.** Make sure the elements of your site work together to create a clear presentation. Don't crowd your screen with unnecessary colors or visuals. Also avoid using large or complicated illustrations that take a long time to download. Visitors to your site will be frustrated by this.
4. **Compile an annotated list of Hypertext links.** Make a list of several other Web sites that offer additional information about your topics. Be sure these other sites contain reliable information. Jot down a brief description of each site. Later, you can decide which ones to link to from your site.

TECHTutor

The Web is your best source of information on the technical skills required for creating a Web page. Spend some time working through one of the excellent on-line tutorials or workshops that give you step-by-step guidance in creating a Web page. Your teacher may provide the addresses for tutorials or you can find them by doing a search using the keywords "creating web pages."

❷ Developing the Site

Maintain a clear focus on your goals as you develop your content. Follow the steps below.

- First, write the text. This can include short paragraphs that introduce the site and labels or captions for the graphics, as well as other paragraphs that provide more in-depth information on a topic.
- Next, arrange the text and graphics so that the organization of each page in your site is clear. Use your planning sketch as a guide. Remember that space is limited. The more text you use, the smaller the graphics need to be.
- Finally, add your links. Review your annotated planning list of links and select those that are most relevant. Make sure you haven't connected your site to any bad links—links that don't work.

Ask Your Peer Reviewer

- Which parts of the site, if any, were confusing? Why?
- What are the most interesting parts?
- What problems did you have in navigating through my site?

❸ Revising

TARGET SKILL ▶ ELIMINATING CLUTTER Visual clutter can make a Web site hard to understand. Delete any text or graphics that seem to distract viewers from the main points of your page.

WEBShortcuts

A basic template is provided for this lesson on the McDougal Littell Web site. You can avoid much of the HTML coding if you choose to use this template. Access the Web site at this address: www.mcdougallittell.com

Graphics: Planning the Design

1. Encourage students to focus on graphic images that tell visitors something about the site.
2. Point out that graphics should support text, not replace it. Encourage students to keep images simple and identifiable and to let text explain any complex ideas.
3. Encourage students to leave white space—an area empty of text or design—on the page so as not to overload their screen with information.

Developing the Site

The student model represents one approach to designing a personal Web site. Once students grasp the basics, they can experiment with their own approach.

Revising

ELIMINATING CLUTTER

As students compare Model 1 to Model 2, point out that bullets set off the major points in the text without deleting any words.

Have students work in pairs to eliminate clutter from their Web pages. Partners should read each other's Web pages, noting any passages, words, or images that are unnecessary. Partners might also make suggestions on how to visually present the information more effectively.

Editing and Proofreading

COMPLETE SENTENCES

Have students review each other's Web sites, noting sentence fragments, punctuation errors, and capitalization errors.

Reflecting

On their Web pages, students might also include a "Comments and Feedback" prompt with an electronic mailing address. Students can evaluate the effectiveness of their Web pages by analyzing the responses they receive. Have students comment on these suggestions, and add their responses to their working portfolios.

Encourage students to consider the effect that creating a Web page had on their perceptions of the World Wide Web.

Need revising help?

Review the **Guidelines and Standards,** p. 1176

Consider **peer reader** comments

Check **Revision Guidelines,** p. 1355

Make sure that every heading, picture, color, and background contributes to the clarity of the page. Review your site and note any long paragraphs that look hard to read. Can these be shortened? One technique that makes reading on the Web easier is to use bulleted lists to set off the major points in a text.

Model 1

Make a commitment to creating a more peaceful world. Visit some Peace Museums to find out what's behind the words and actions of individuals and groups. There are many organizations that sponsor peace projects that promote a more peaceful world.

Model 2

Make a commitment to creating a more peaceful world.

- Visit some Peace Museums to find out what's behind the words and actions of individuals and groups.
- There are many organizations that sponsor peace projects that promote a more peaceful world.

❹ Editing and Proofreading

TARGET SKILL ▶ COMPLETE SENTENCES Your Web site will create a better impression if you take the time to edit your text. Reread captions and paragraphs to check that you have written complete sentences. Be sure that each sentence contains a subject and a predicate. Rewrite any fragments you find. Check for errors in punctuation and capitalization too.

Have a question?

See the **Communications Handbook**
Inquiry and Research, pp. 1381–1383
Viewing and Representing, pp. 1388–1390

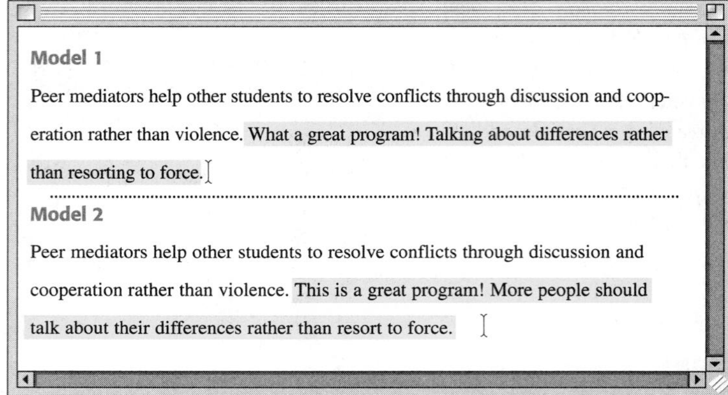

Model 1
Peer mediators help other students to resolve conflicts through discussion and cooperation rather than violence. What a great program! Talking about differences rather than resorting to force.
Model 2
Peer mediators help other students to resolve conflicts through discussion and cooperation rather than violence. This is a great program! More people should talk about their differences rather than resort to force.

❺ Reflecting

FOR YOUR WORKING PORTFOLIO What did you learn about writing for the Web? How is the writing process different in this media? What new skills would you like to develop to help you with future online writing projects? Attach your responses to a print-out of your Web site. Save these in your **Working Portfolio.**

Assessment Practice Revising & Editing

Read this excerpt from a Web page. The underlined sections may include the following kinds of errors:

- **redundant or unnecessary phrases**
- **sentence fragments**
- **comma errors**
- **lack of subject-verb agreement**

For each underlined section, choose the revision that most improves the writing.

> Welcome to *Words of Peace.* On this Web page you will find a selection of my favorite quotations about peace, which I especially like. (1) Together they present an inspiring survey of feelings, and ideas (2) about this important topic. People who have not experienced war. Peace is often taken for granted. (3) Young people today may believe that peace is something hippies talked about in the 1960s. Perhaps some people believes (4) peace is a worn-out idea; maybe they find it embarrassing. At this point in time, these attitudes are (5) dangerous and irresponsible. I hope these quotations will help readers abandons (6) such cynical points of view.

1. A. which I like a lot.
B. that I especially like.
C. Delete phrase and add period after *peace.*
D. Correct as is

2. A. feelings, and, ideas
B. feelings and ideas
C. feelings and, ideas
D. Correct as is

3. A. People who have not experienced war often take peace for granted.
B. People who have not experienced war they often take peace for granted.
C. People who have not experienced war, they often take peace for granted.
D. Correct as is

4. A. some peoples believe
B. some peoples believes
C. some people believe
D. Correct as is

5. A. At this point in time—these attitudes are
B. Nowadays these attitudes are
C. At this point in time. These attitudes are
D. Correct as is

6. A. readers abandoned
B. readers abandon
C. reader abandon
D. Correct as is

Need extra help?

See the **Grammar Handbook**
Correcting fragments, p. 1409
Punctuation chart, pp. 1413–1414
Subject-verb agreement, p. 1410

Assessment Practice

Review the list of possible errors the passage may contain. Remind students to carefully read all the choices in each question before they select the correct answer.

Answers:
1. C; **2.** B; **3.** A; **4.** C; **5.** B; **6.** B

Objectives
- develop strategies for deciphering word meaning
- understand how to apply strategies to decipher meaning and build vocabulary

Strategies for Building Vocabulary

EXERCISE

Answers will vary, but students should follow the format used in the Pupil Edition.

Clues to Word Meaning

> **From a world in which life or death, victory or defeat, national survival or national extinction, had been the sole issues, I returned [home] to a society where no one discussed anything but the price of butter. . . .**
>
> **Keyed up as I had been by the month-long strain of daily rushing to and fro in attendance on the dying, and nightly waiting for the death which hovered darkly in the sky overhead, I found it excruciating to maintain even an appearance of interest and sympathy.**
>
> —Vera Brittain, *Testament of Youth*

There are many ways of deciphering the unfamiliar words that you encounter when you read. In the excerpt on the left, Vera Brittain describes her sense of alienation upon returning home to England from the battlefields of France. How might you figure out the meaning of *excruciating,* a word whose meaning provides an insight into Brittain's feelings?

Note that Brittain contrasts the "life or death, victory or defeat" concerns of those fighting the war with the trivial, "price of butter" problems of those at home. Then imagine yourself just home from the front-lines, trying to sympathize with civilians who have not experienced the intensity of war. By examining context clues and putting yourself in a character's place, you can make a good guess that Brittain's efforts to cope might be extremely painful—that is, *excruciating.*

Strategies for Building Vocabulary

Using context clues is just one strategy that can be used to decipher the meaning of a word. Other strategies include comparing the unfamiliar word with a known word and noting familiar word parts. The chart on this page demonstrates how those strategies can be applied to the deciphering of meanings.

❶ **Plan Your Attack** Read this excerpt from George Orwell's "A Hanging." Note the word *servile.* Then study the chart.

> **The hangman, a grey-haired convict in the white uniform of the prison, was waiting beside his machine. He greeted us with a servile crouch as we entered.**
>
> —George Orwell, "A Hanging"

Step	Example
1. Think of Similar Words	*Serve* and *servant* are like *servile.*
2. Compare Roots	All three words are so similar; I think their roots must be the same. They might be part of the same word family.
3. Analyze the Context	The hangman is a prisoner, and he greets the officers in a crouch, as a servant afraid of displeasing his master might.
4. Develop a Meaning	So *servile* has something to do with serving and with fear; it must mean something like "behaving fearfully, like a powerless servant."
5. Check a Dictionary	*Servile* means "slavish in character or attitude," so my definition was good. The word's etymology indicates that it is related to *servant* and *serve.*

❷ **Record and Use the Word** To make the word a part of your permanent vocabulary, write it down and make a point of using it in class discussions or other conversations during the next few days.

EXERCISE Choose five unfamiliar words from the selections in Unit Six, and apply the deciphering strategies outlined above to each word.

Grammar from Literature

Experienced writers sometimes use special structures called sentence openers to begin their sentences. A **sentence opener** is a word or phrase that calls attention to certain details. The main idea in a sentence always comes after the sentence opener. Using sentence openers allows a writer to add concrete detail, to improve sentence variety and rhythm, and to increase readers' interest by building suspense. Look at the examples of sentence openers below.

single word
Annoyed, **she picked up the letter, which bore no stamp.**
—Elizabeth Bowen, "The Demon Lover"

infinitive phrase
To conceal their intentions even from themselves, **they make use of picturesque metaphors.**
—Aldous Huxley, "Words and Behavior"

adverb clause
Long after the family had gone to bed and the world had grown silent, **I crept into the dining room to be alone with Edward's portrait.**
—Vera Brittain, *Testament of Youth*

A writer may use grammatical structures of more than one kind in an opener.

infinitive phrase / prepositional phrase
To conceal their intentions even from themselves, **they make use of picturesque metaphors.**
—"Words and Behavior"

prepositional phrase / adjective clause
In spite of the War, which destroyed so much hope, so much beauty, so much promise, **life is still here to be lived.**
—*Testament of Youth*

Using Sentence Openers in Your Writing Professional writers take advantage of the impact of sentence openers, and so can you. Openers offer not only the opportunity to add detail and improve sentence variety, they also provide a way to hold your reader's attention. By placing detail in the opener, you intentionally delay the main idea. You control your reader's focus. Study the effect of the opener in the example below.

Original
The Germans bombed Britain.

Rewritten
Almost nightly from August to October 1940, **the Germans bombed Britain.**

Usage Tip Avoid dangling modifiers when writing periodic sentences. A **dangling modifier** does not clearly modify any noun or pronoun in the sentence. Make sure the sentence opener clearly modifies a word in the sentence.

Incorrect — participial phrase
Having contracted blood poisoning early in the war, **Rupert Brooke's** poems **were published posthumously because he died.**

Correct — participial phrase
Having contracted blood poisoning early in the war, Rupert Brooke **died, and his poems were published posthumously.**

In the first example above, although the opener appears to modify *poems,* it does not clearly modify any noun in the sentence. In the second example, the opener clearly modifies *Rupert Brooke.*

WRITING EXERCISE Rewrite each sentence by adding a sentence opener of the type named in parentheses.

1. The young airman spoke of the wastefulness of war. (single word)
2. Winston Churchill gave powerful radio speeches. (infinitive phrase)
3. Patients often found it difficult to sleep at the hospital. (participial phrase)
4. The plane returned to the base in England. (adverb clause)
5. The soldier's mother stared at the photograph of her son. (prepositional phrase)

GRAMMAR EXERCISE Rewrite these sentences, correcting any errors in punctuation and usage. If a sentence is correct, write *Correct.*

1. With a surprise ending, the reader is unprepared for the last paragraph of "The Demon Lover."
2. Wounded several times in combat, World War I affected Siegfried Sassoon for the rest of his life.
3. In "The Demon Lover," Elizabeth Bowen tells the story of Kathleen Drover.
4. Trying to get her packages to the train station, a taxi picks up Drover and takes her on a terrifying ride.
5. Ending with a reference to the dead prisoner who "was a hundred yards away," Orwell underscores the horror of the hanging.

Sentence Crafting

Objectives

- use sentence openers to add detail, improve sentence variety, and increase reader interest
- revise sentences by correcting dangling modifiers

WRITING EXERCISE

Answers will vary. Possible responses are given.

1. Discouraged, the young airman spoke of the wastefulness of war.
2. To improve the morale of the British people, Winston Churchill gave powerful radio speeches.
3. Disturbed by the noise, patients often found it difficult to sleep at the hospital.
4. After each target had been bombed, the plane returned to the base in England.
5. With a broken heart, the soldier's mother stared at the photograph of her son.

GRAMMAR EXERCISE

1. With a surprise ending, "The Demon Lover" leaves the reader unprepared for the last paragraph.
2. **Possible Response:** Wounded several times in combat, Siegfried Sassoon was affected by World War I for the rest of his life.
3. *Correct*
4. **Possible Response:** Trying to get her packages to the train station, Drover gets into a taxi and takes a terrifying ride.
5. *Correct*

Objectives
- reflect on and assess their understanding of the unit
- compare text events with his/her own and other readers' experiences
- understand such literary concepts and devices as suspense and style
- assess and build their portfolios

Reflecting on the Unit

OPTION 1

A successful response will
- choose two selections from the unit in which writers give a differing perspective on a topic or event.
- include a chart which lists the topic or event, the important points each writer makes, and a summary of his or her opinion, with details that support the opinion.
- identify which perspective most closely matches the student's.

OPTION 2

A successful response will
- choose four or five selections in which these shifts occur.
- explain how the speakers or characters react to the changes.
- explain how this change has altered the characters' understanding of the world or other people.
- evaluate whether these changes have led to important insights into reality.

OPTION 3

Have students select one work from each part to evaluate. Ask them to identify the public issue or event in each selection and then determine what the characters think about the issue and how they are affected by it. You might also ask partners to discuss how a current issue has affected them.

Self Assessment
Some students might jot down words or phrases that reflect the pessimism in literature, as illustrated in the works of Orwell and Lawrence. Others may use words or phrases that reflect a guarded optimism, as demonstrated by the works of Churchill and Lady Gregory. Encourage students to support their ideas with supporting evidence from the selections.

Emerging Modernism

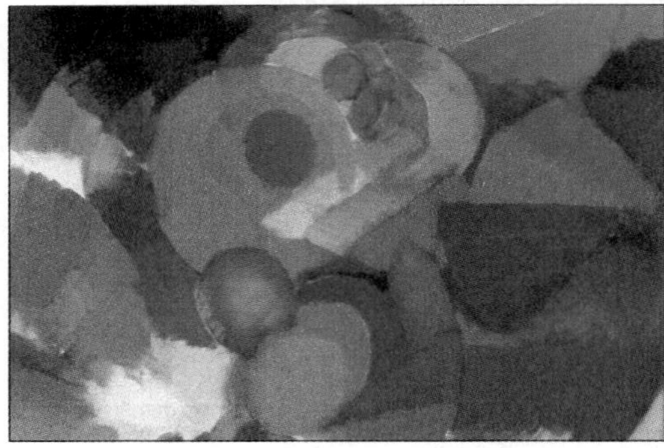

What important issues of the first half of the 20th century can you identify from your reading of the selections in this unit? In what ways do you think your life has been influenced by these issues? To explore these questions, choose one or more options in each of the following sections.

Reflecting on the Unit

OPTION 1

Comparing Perspectives In these works from the first half of the 20th century, the writers approach various aspects of reality—war, love, motivation, truth—from different perspectives. Pick two selections from the unit, in which writers offer differing interpretations of some topic or experience. In a chart, identify the topic or experience, list the important points each writer makes, and summarize the opinion of each. Then comment on which perspective matches your own most closely.

OPTION 2

Tracking Sudden Changes In many selections in this unit, circumstances take unexpected turns, or actions have unforeseen consequences. With a small group of classmates, choose four or five selections in which such shifts occur. How do the speakers or characters react to the new developments? What effect do they have on the speakers' or characters' understanding of the world and other people? Discuss whether you think such sudden changes can lead to important insights into reality.

OPTION 3

Evaluating Public and Private Realities Some of the writers represented in this unit address public issues, and some deal with private concerns. Work with a partner to identify the main focus of each selection as public or private. Then look for relationships between the public and the private: How do the larger issues of public life affect people's private lives? How do people's personal experiences and viewpoints affect their interpretation of public events? Summarize your conclusions and then present them to the class.

Self ASSESSMENT

READER'S NOTEBOOK

To explore how your understanding of modern literature has developed over the course of this unit, jot down words and phrases that you associate with literature from the first half of the 20th century. Then get together with a group of classmates and compare and assess your lists. As a group, identify the pieces of literature from this unit that you think most contributed to your impressions.

Reviewing Literary Concepts

OPTION 1

Identifying Irony Irony plays a major role in modern literature. Review the three types of irony identified on pages 1004–1005: verbal irony, situational irony, and dramatic irony. Then look over the selections in this unit and find at least one example of each type of irony. Which type of irony seems to be most prevalent in the literature of this unit?

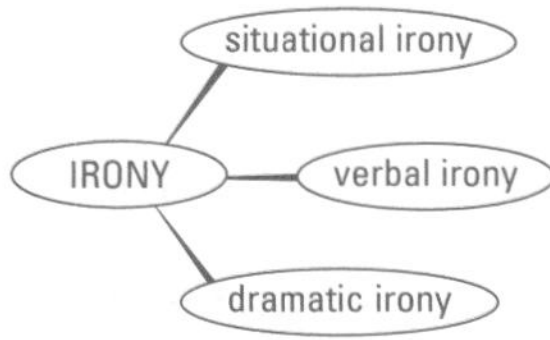

OPTION 2

Analyzing Style Writers convey their ideas and attitudes in part through details of style. From this unit, choose two selections that you think have particularly interesting or forceful styles. List the main characteristics of each style, and then make notes about how the styles work to express the writers' thoughts and feelings.

Self ASSESSMENT

READER'S NOTEBOOK

Some of the literary terms presented in this unit relate to only one genre, but many relate to two or more. Copy the following list of terms, and use the letters F (for "fiction"), P (for "poetry"), N (for "nonfiction"), and D (for "drama") to identify the genres each term relates to. Exchange lists with a partner and discuss any terms you categorized differently.

symbols	imagery
imagery	free verse
suspense	consonance
foreshadowing	assonance
irony	villanelle
point of view	paradox
setting	speaker
realism	memoir
tone	theme
style	persuasion
figurative language	diction
rhythm	surprise ending
mood	personal essay

Building Your Portfolio

- **Writing Options** Of the Writing Options you completed for this unit, choose the one in which you think you displayed the most creativity. Write a brief note explaining your choice, and place it with the piece in your **Presentation Portfolio.**
- **Writing and Communication Workshops** During this unit, you created a Dramatic Scene and explored ways to develop a Web site. Which of these assignments would you like to continue developing? Write up your explanation, and place it in your **Presentation Portfolio.**
- **Additional Activities** Think about the various assignments you completed under **Activities & Explorations** and **Inquiry & Research.** Keep a record in your portfolio of any assignments that you think are representative of your best work.

Self ASSESSMENT

Presentation Portfolio

By now you have put together a substantial collection of pieces. Decide if there are any that you would like to replace. Which ones do you think are the most outstanding examples of your work?

Setting GOALS

In this unit, you undoubtedly noted some significant events and viewpoints that influenced the literature of the first half of the 20th century. Jot down some questions and ideas that you would like to explore as you read works from the later part of the century in Unit Seven.

Reviewing Literary Concepts

OPTION 1

Use the Unit 6 Resource Book, p. 92, to provide students a ready-made, full-depth chart for examining irony.

OPTION 2

To expand this assignment, have students examine the styles of all the writers in the unit.

Building Your Portfolio

Students will use their Presentation Portfolios to file what they consider their highest quality work—the very best projects and activities from their Working Portfolios.

For more information on using writing and assessing portfolios, see the *Teacher's Guide to Assessment and Portfolio Use,* p. 53.

The *Electronic Library* is a CD-ROM that contains additional fiction, nonfiction, poetry, and drama for each unit in *The Language of Literature.*

These are the additional selections found in Unit 6 of the *Electronic Library:*

Virginia Woolf
Professions for Women

D. H. Lawrence
The Horse Dealer's Daughter

William Butler Yeats
The Lake Isle of Innisfree
The Wild Swans at Coole

James Joyce
The Boarding House

Liam O'Flaherty
Spring Sowing

W. H. Auden
The Shield of Achilles

Katherine Mansfield
Miss Brill

Have students select one of the longer titles mentioned on this spread to enjoy through silent sustained reading.

UNIT SIX Extend Your *Reading*

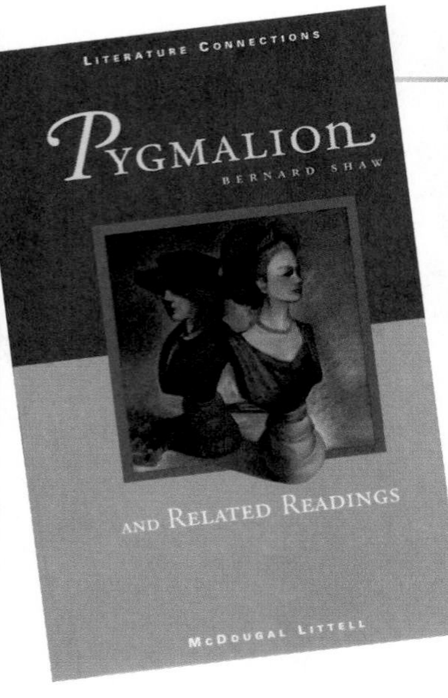

LITERATURE CONNECTIONS

Pygmalion

BERNARD SHAW

One of the most entertaining and best-loved modern British plays, *Pygmalion* explores human relations and the complex modern social order. Shaw, born in Dublin, moved to London at age 20, where he wrote many brilliant and witty plays, including *Major Barbara, Heartbreak House, Caesar and Cleopatra,* and *Man and Superman,* but *Pygmalion* remains his most popular play.

These thematically related readings are provided along with *Pygmalion:*

The Story of Pygmalion *from* The Metamorphoses
BY OVID

***Excerpt from* My Fair Lady**
BY ALAN JAY LERNER

Her First Ball
BY KATHERINE MANSFIELD

The London Language *from* The Story of English
BY ROBERT MCCRUM, WILLIAM CRAN, AND ROBERT MACNEIL

Mother Tongue
BY AMY TAN

Two Words
BY ISABEL ALLENDE

The Model
BY BERNARD MALAMUD

Words
BY VERN RUTSALA

And Even *More* . . .

Schindler's List

THOMAS KENEALLY

This book, which won Britain's Booker Prize in 1983, tells the true story of Oskar Schindler, a German war profiteer who came to save thousands of Jews from unspeakable deaths during the Holocaust. Steven Spielberg directed a film version of the book, which won Academy Awards for best picture and best director in 1993.

Books

Dubliners
JAMES JOYCE
This collection of related stories, first published in 1914, asks probing questions about Irish history, identity, and culture.

Mrs. Dalloway
VIRGINIA WOOLF
A montage of thoughts and images help paint a day in the life of Clarissa Dalloway, a middle-aged English society woman. This was the first of Woolf's novels to make use of her unique style of stream-of-consciousness.

LITERATURE CONNECTIONS

1984

GEORGE ORWELL

In this book, Orwell portrays a fictional future world in which a totalitarian government controls individual thought and even reality itself. A modern classic, *1984* remains timely and continues to stir the imagination while asking important questions about human nature.

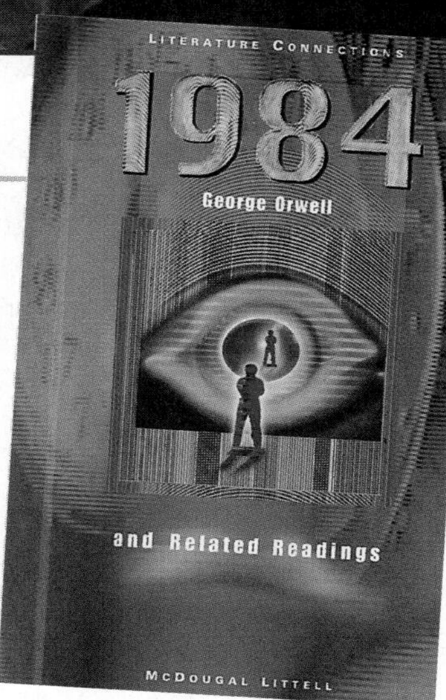

These thematically related readings are provided along with *1984*:

What Can They
BY JULIA HARTWIG

End Game
BY J. G. BALLARD

The Spy
BY BERTOLT BRECHT

***from* Politics and the English Language**
BY GEORGE ORWELL

No One Died in Tiananmen Square
BY WILLIAM LUTZ

The Invasion of Privacy
BY REED KARAIM

The IWM 1000
BY ALICIA YÁÑZ COSSÍO

Thumbprint
BY EVE MERRIAM

Testament of Youth
VERA BRITTAIN
Brittain's gripping memoir of her experiences during World War I echo with poignancy the realities of this painful chapter of history. It has been called "a moving elegy to a lost generation."

The Guns of August
BARBARA TUCHMAN
Barbara Tuchman has been praised for her ability to make history come alive. This narrative on the outbreak of World War I, published in 1962, won the Pulitzer Prize.

Other Media

The Great War: 1918
PBS Video, 1989. World War I is examined through the letters and diaries of U.S. soldiers.
(VIDEOCASSETTE)

Upstairs, Downstairs
London Weekend Television, 1971; A&E Home Video. This series presents the life and times of the Bellamy household in England in the early years of this century.
(VIDEOCASSETTES)

We Must Never Forget: The Story of the Holocaust
Society for Visual Education, 1994.
(VIDEOCASSETTE)

The Wasteland and Other Poems
Listening Library.
(AUDIOCASSETTE)

EXTEND YOUR READING 1187

Contemporary Voices

The selections in Unit Seven explore the growing diversity of British life and literature in the contemporary period. The writers focus on people's inner lives as well as the social problems evident throughout the British Commonwealth during the period. The unit is divided into two sections to represent the wide range of British literature currently being produced.

Part 1

Appearance and Reality The selections in this part of the unit focus on characters who, mostly by chance, deal with disquieting realities that lead to powerful insights into life. In the **Comparing Literature** feature, Polish writer Czeslaw Milosz reflects on what he perceives in his mind's eye when he hears a piece of music.

Part 2

Culture and Conflict The works in this section represent voices from the British Commonwealth: Ireland, the Caribbean islands, Nigeria, and South Africa. The stories and poems reveal the conflicts that sometimes result when people from different cultures try to co-exist. In the **Comparing Literature** selection, Latin American writer Isabel Allende claims that writing provides a means to communicate with people and overcome differences.

UNIT SEVEN

CONTEMPORARY VOICES

1950 – PRESENT

IT WAS A BRIGHT COLD DAY IN APRIL, AND THE CLOCKS WERE STRIKING THIRTEEN.

George Orwell
novelist, essayist, and critic

1188

Viewing and Representing

Invasion
by Carel Weight

ART APPRECIATION

Instruction British artist Carel Weight (1908–1997) served in World War II and was an Official War Artist in 1945. After the war, he taught painting at the Royal College of Art (1947–1973). Many of his works, according to one critic, are "imaginative figure compositions" with "idiosyncratic perspective effects." They are "strange human dramas, producing an effect that is sometimes humorous and sometimes menacing." Weight himself has written that his paintings reflect the basic emotions of hate, love, loneliness, and fear.

Ask: What mood do you think this painting conveys?

Possible Response: The overall mood is one of gentle amusement. The fear expressed on the faces of the two fleeing boys (town bullies?) is offset by the apparent source of their fear: the "invasion" of genial, circuslike performers floating harmlessly, if surrealistically, overhead.

Invasion (1987–1988), Carel Weight. Oil on canvas, 48″ × 60″, The Saatchi Collection, London.

Making Connections

To help students explore the connections among the art, the quotation, and the unit title found in this unit-opening spread, have them consider the following questions:

Ask: How do you define "contemporary" literature?
Possible Responses: literature written in the past 50 years; literature about current topics and concerns; literature that uses innovative techniques

The quotation is the attention-grabbing opening sentence from Orwell's novel *1984.*
Ask: What does the quotation suggest to you about contemporary life?
Possible Response: Contemporary life is surprising, absurd, and perhaps even frighteningly illogical.

Ask: What does the painting suggest about the nature of contemporary life?
Possible Response: Life today is full of conflict and bizarre behavior; life can contain frightening yet wondrous events.

Ask: Based on the unit title, painting, and quotation, what topics do you expect to read about in this unit?
Possible Response: the frightening aspects of everyday life; absurd and ironic events; social issues

VIDEODISC **LaserLinks**
Historical Literary Connection: Contemporary Voices
See Teacher's SourceBook p. 84 for bar codes.

UNIT SEVEN
PART 1 SKILLS TRACE

Features and Selections	Literary Analysis	Reading and Critical Thinking	Writing Opportunities
Contemporary Voices **Time Line** **Historical Background/Essay**			
Learning The Language of Literature Point of View	Point of View, 1197	Strategies for Reading, 1198	Mistaken Identity, 1198
SHORT STORY At the Pitt-Rivers	Setting, 1199, 1207	Conclusions About Narrator, 1199, 1207	Narrator's Poem, 1208 Character Sketch, 1208 Short Story Plot, 1208 Museum Description, 1208 Informal Assess.,1206
SHORT STORY A Sunrise on the Veld	Kinesthetic Imagery, 1210, 1217 Third-Person Limited, 1217	Character Development, 1210, 1217 Informal Assess., 1216	Diary Entry, 1218 Story Sequel, 1218 Nature Log, 1218
SHORT STORY The First Year of My Life	Point of View, 1220, 1227	Analyzing Satire, 1220, 1227 Test Practice, 1226	Letter to Asquith, 1228
POETRY The Moment	Theme in Poetry, 1229, 1232	Analyzing Structure, 1229, 1232	Dialogue b/t Opposites, 1233 Personal Essay, 1233
POETRY Digging The Horses	Sound Devices, 1234, 1239	Interpreting Imagery, 1234, 1239 Test Practice, 1238	Comparison Booklet, 1240 Descriptive Paragraph, 1240
SPEECH **Related Reading** *from* Crediting Poetry	Analyzing a Speech, 1241		
POETRY **Comparing Literature of the World** In Music	Imagery and Mood, 1244, 1246	Analyzing Structure, 1244, 1246	Letter to a Friend, 1247 Points of Comparison, 1247
POETRY The Frog Prince Not Waving But Drowning	Diction in Poetry, 1248, 1252	Major Ideas, 1248,1252	Fairy Tale Poem, 1253 Diary Entry, 1253
DRAMA That's All	Dialogue in a Play, 1254, 1258	Unconventional Works, 1254, 1258	Second Scene Dialogue, 1259 Drama Review, 1259 Informal Assess., 1257

LEGEND PE instruction shown in black
TE Mini Lessons shown in green
CCL indicates a Cross-Curricular Link
DLS indicates Daily Language SkillBuilder

Speaking and Listening Viewing and Representing	Inquiry and Research	Grammar, Usage, and Mechanics	Vocabulary
Art Appreciation, 1188, 1194			
Dramatic Conversation, 1208 Silent Movie, 1208 Museum, 1208 Role Playing, 1203 Art Appreciation, 1204	Museum Origins, 1208 Author Activity, 1209	DLS, 1199 Types of Sentences, 1208	Synonyms, 1208 Analogies/Antonyms, 1200
Veld Collage, 1218 Soundtrack, 1218 Interior Monologue, 1218 Setting the Mood, 1218 Art Appreciation, 1214	Independent Africa, 1218 Preserving Nature, 1218 Author Activity, 1219	DLS, 1210 Movable Adjectives, 1218	Idioms, 1218 Word Origins, 1211
Parliament Debate, 1228 Presenting a Speech, 1224		DLS, 1220 Participial Phrases, 1223	Word Meaning, 1228 Latin Roots, 1221
Musical Reading, 1233 Art Appreciation, 1230	Canadian Literature, 1233 Multicultural Link, 1231	DLS, 1229 Relative Clauses, 1233	
Scene Illustrations, 1240		DLS, 1234 Fragments, 1240	Connotation, 1235
Association Game, 1247 Dramatic Reading, 1247 Art Appreciation, 1245	Author Activity, 1247	DLS, 1244 Appositive Phrase, 1247	
Frog Prince, 1253 Author Activity, 1253 Art Appreciation, 1251	Artistic Mind Games, 1253	DLS, 1248 Style: Appositives, 1253	Word Origins, 1249
Set Design, 1259 Mood Music, 1259 Dramatic Scene, 1256	Real Versus Absurd, 1259 Author Activity, 1259	DLS, 1254 Possessives, 1259	Idioms, 1255

PART 2 SKILLS TRACE

Features and Selections	Literary Analysis	Reading and Critical Thinking	Writing Opportunities
Learning the Language of Literature Literature as Social Criticism	Social Criticism, 1261	Strategies for Reading, 1262	
SHORT STORY The Distant Past	Conflict, 1263, 1272 Setting, 1272	Cause and Effect, 1263, 1272	Paragraph Critique, 1273 Informal Assess., 1271
SHORT STORY Civil Peace	Dialect, 1274, 1279 Conflict, 1279	Judgments About Characters, 1274, 1279 Author Activity, 1280	Job Recommendation, 1280 Front Page News, 1280 Test Practice, 1278
POETRY Telephone Conversation *from* Midsummer	Tone in Satire, 1281, 1286	Compare and Contrast, 1281, 1286	Critical Review, 1287 Advice Column, 1287 Guest Editorial, 1287 Informal Assess., 1285
SHORT STORY Six Feet of Country	Point of View, 1289, 1299 Imagery, 1299 Informal Assess., 1298	Predicting, 1289, 1299 Author Activity, 1301 Test Practice, 1292	Story Review, 1300 Memo for Teacher, 1300 Letter to Authorities, 1300
ESSAY **Comparing Literature of the World** *from* Writing as an Act of Hope	Essay, 1302, 1308	Main Ideas/Details, 1302, 1308	Explanatory Paragraph, 1309 Letter to Allende, 1309 Anecdote, 1309 Points of Comparison, 1309
Writing Workshop: **Critical Review** **Assessment Practice** Building Vocabulary Sentence Crafting			Critical Review, 1314
Reflect and Assess	Reviewing Literary Concepts, 1320	Applying a Quotation, 1319	Building Your Portfolio, 1320

LEGEND PE instruction shown in black
TE Mini Lessons shown in green

CCL indicates a Cross-Curricular Link
DLS indicates Daily Language SkillBuilder

Speaking and Listening Viewing and Representing	Inquiry and Research	Grammar, Usage, and Mechanics	Vocabulary
Social Critics Speak, 1262			
Role-Play, 1273 Art Appreciation, 1267, 1269	Author Activity, 1273	DLS, 1263 Reflexive Pronouns, 1266 Reciprocal Pronouns, 1270	Word Meanings, 1273 Analogies, 1265
Oral Reading, 1280 Book Jacket Design, 1280 C.A.R.E. Package, 1280	Nigeria, 1280	DLS, 1274 Indefinite Pronouns, 1280	Context/Dialect, 1277
T-Shirt Design, 1287 Mock Trial, 1287 Scrapbook, 1287 Summer and Shadow, 1287 Art Appreciation, 1284	Civil Rights Laws, 1287	DLS, 1281 Elliptical Clauses, 1287	Connotation, 1283
Monument, 1300 Improvised Dialogue, 1300 Portrait, 1300 Mood in Art, 1300 Making A Speech, 1294 Art Appreciation, 1296	New Leader, 1300 On the Map, 1300	DLS, 1289 Elliptical Clause, 1300	Synonymous Phrases, 1301 Word Origins, 1291 Connotation, 1297
Speech, 1309 Collage, 1309 Poster, 1309 Illustrated Ideas, 1309 Art Appreciation, 1305	Allende's Home, 1309	DLS, 1302 Modifiers, 1309	Context Clues, 1310 Synonyms, 1304
		Using Appositives/Modifier Replacement, 1315 Assessment Practice, 1316 Subject-Verb Splits, 1318	Understanding Analogies, 1317
Appearance and Reality, 1319 Comparing/Contrasting, 1319			

UNIT SEVEN
RESOURCE MANAGEMENT GUIDE
PART 1

To introduce the theme/literary period of this unit, use Fine Art Transparencies T35–37 in the Communications Transparencies and Copymasters.

Selection	Unit Resource Book	Assessment	Integrated Technology and Media	Additional Support: Literary Analysis Transparencies
At the Pitt-Rivers *pp. 1199–1209*	• Summary p. 4 • Active Reading p. 5 • Literary Analysis p. 6 • Words to Know p. 7 • Selection Quiz p. 8	• Selection Test, Formal Assessment pp. 219–220 Test Generator	Audio Library LaserLinks,Teacher's SourceBook pp. 85–86	• Influences on Plot: Setting and Character T19
A Sunrise on the Veld *pp. 1210–1219*	• Summary p. 9 • Active Reading p. 10 • Literary Analysis p. 11 • Words to Know p. 12 • Selection Quiz p. 13	• Selection Test, Formal Assessment pp. 221–222 Test Generator	LaserLinks,Teacher's SourceBook pp. 87–88 Research Starter www.mcdougallittell.com	• Characterization T21
The First Year of My Life *pp. 1220–1228*	• Summary p. 14 • Active Reading p. 15 • Literary Analysis p. 16 • Words to Know p. 17 • Selection Quiz p. 18	• Selection Test, Formal Assessment pp. 223–224 Test Generator	Audio Library LaserLinks,Teacher's SourceBook pp. 89–90	• Point of View T18
The Moment *pp. 1229–1233*	• Active Reading p. 19 • Literary Analysis p. 20	• Selection Test, Formal Assessment pp. 225–226 Test Generator	Audio Library LaserLinks,Teacher's SourceBook p. 91	• Theme T9
Digging **The Horses** *pp. 1234–1240*	• Active Reading p. 21 • Literary Analysis p. 22	• Selection Test, Formal Assessment p. 227 Test Generator	Audio Library	• Poetic Devices T16
In Music *pp. 1244–1247*	• Active Reading p.23 • Literary Analysis p. 24	• Selection Test, Formal Assessment p. 229 Test Generator	Audio Library LaserLinks,Teacher's SourceBook p. 92	• Style, Tone, and Mood T24
The Frog Prince **Not Waving but Drowning** *pp. 1248–1253*	• Active Reading p.25 • Literary Analysis p. 26	• Selection Test, Formal Assessment pp. 231–232 Test Generator	Audio Library	• Poetic Devices T16
That's All *pp. 1254–1259*	• Summary p. 27 • Active Reading p. 28 • Literary Analysis p. 29 • Selection Quiz p. 30	• Selection Test, Formal Assessment pp. 233–234 Test Generator	Audio Library	
		Unit Assessment • Unit Seven, Part 1 Test, Formal Assessment pp. 235–236 Test Generator • Unit Seven Integrated Test, Integrated Assessment pp. 59–68	***Unit Technology*** ClassZone www.mcdougallittell.com Electronic Teacher Tools Electronic Library	

T = Transparency C = Copymaster

	Reading and Critical Thinking Transparencies	Grammar Transparencies and Copymasters	Vocabulary Transparencies and Copymasters	Writing Transparencies and Copymasters	Communications Transparencies and Copymasters
	• Drawing Conclusions T4 • Classification Tree T59	• Daily Language SkillBuilder T32 • Diagramming Subjects, Verbs, and Modifiers T58 • Varying Types of Sentences C179	• Analogies C73	• Sensory Word List T14 • Personality Profile C25	• Impromptu Speaking: Dialogue, Role-Play T14
	• Compare and Contrast T15 • Reading for Details T16	• Daily Language SkillBuilder T33 • Avoiding Misplaced and Dangling Modifiers T51 • Movable Adjectives C91	• Word Origins C91	• Sensory Word List T14 • Showing, Not Telling T22	• Impromptu Speaking: Dialogue, Role-Play T14
	• Organizational Chart: Horizontal T52	• Daily Language SkillBuilder T33 • Commas with Nonessential Elements T55 • Essential and Nonessential Participial Phrases C101		• Opinion Statement C35	• Impromptu Speaking: Debate T15
	• Analyzing Text T18	• Daily Language SkillBuilder T33 • Commas with Nonessential Elements T55 • Relative Clauses C108 • Identifying Adjective Clauses C109		• The Uses of Dialogue T24 • Autobiographical Incident C36	• Reading Aloud T11
	• Comparing Authors' Views T24 • Observation Chart T47	• Daily Language SkillBuilder T34 • Sentence Fragments T42 • Deliberate Fragments C127	• Connotation C95	• Sensory Word List T14 • Compare-Contrast C34	
	• Analyzing Text T18	• Daily Language SkillBuilder T34 • Commas with Nonessential Elements T55 • Style: The Appositive Phrase C180		• Compare-Contrast C34	• Dramatic Reading T12
	• Paraphrasing and Summarizing T42	• Daily Language SkillBuilder T34 • Commas with Nonessential Elements T55 • Essential and Nonessential Appositives C170	• Word Origins C91	• Effective Language T13 • Sensory Word List T14	
		• Daily Language SkillBuilder T35 • Possessive Nouns T38 • Possessives with Proper Nouns That End in *s* C63	• Idioms C92	• Dramatic Scene C31 • Critical Review C32	• Dramatic Reading T12

STUDENTS ACQUIRING ENGLISH

The **Spanish Study Guide,** pp. 287–313, includes language support for the following pages:

- Family and Community Involvement (per unit)
- Selection Summaries and Vocabulary
- Active Reading
- Literary Analysis

To introduce the theme/literary period of this unit, use Fine Art Transparencies T35–37 in the Communications Transparencies and Copymasters.

Selection	Unit Resource Book	Assessment	Integrated Technology and Media	Additional Support: Literary Analysis Transparencies
The Distant Past *pp. 1263–1273*	• Summary p. 31 • Active Reading p. 32 • Literary Analysis p. 33 • Words to Know p. 34 • Selection Quiz p. 35	• Selection Test, Formal Assessment pp. 237–238 Test Generator	Audio Library LaserLinks,Teacher's SourceBook pp. 93–94	• External Conflicts/ Societal Conflicts T20
Civil Peace *pp. 1274–1280*	• Summary p. 36 • Active Reading p. 37 • Literary Analysis p. 38 • Selection Quiz p. 39	• Selection Test, Formal Assessment pp. 239–240 Test Generator	Audio Library LaserLinks,Teacher's SourceBook pp. 95–96 Research Starter www.mcdougallittell.com	• External Conflicts/ Societal Conflicts T20
Telephone Conversation *from* **Midsummer** *pp. 1281–1288*	• Active Reading p. 40 • Literary Analysis p. 41	• Selection Test, Formal Assessment pp. 241–242 Test Generator	Audio Library LaserLinks,Teacher's SourceBook pp. 97–98 Research Starter www.mcdougallittell.com	• Horatian vs. Juvenalian Satire T12 • Style, Tone, and Mood T24
Six Feet of the Country *pp. 1289–1301*	• Summary p. 42 • Active Reading p. 43 • Literary Analysis p. 44 • Words to Know p. 45 • Selection Quiz p. 46	• Selection Test, Formal Assessment pp. 243–244 Test Generator	Audio Library LaserLinks,Teacher's SourceBook p. 99 Research Starter www.mcdougallittell.com	• Point of View T18
from **Writing as an Act of Hope** *pp. 1302–1310*	• Summary p. 47 • Active Reading p. 48 • Literary Analysis p. 49 • Words to Know p. 50 • Selection Quiz p. 51	• Selection Test, Formal Assessment pp. 245–246 Test Generator	Audio Library LaserLinks,Teacher's SourceBook pp. 100–101 Research Starter www.mcdougallittell.com	• Characteristics of the Essay T11

Writing Workshop: Critical Review

Unit Seven Resource Book
- Prewriting p. 52
- Drafting and Elaboration p. 53
- Peer Response Guide pp. 54–55
- Revising, Editing, and Proofreading p. 56
- Student Models pp. 57–62
- Rubric for Evaluation p. 63

Writing Coach

Writing Transparencies and Copymasters T11, T19, C32

Teacher's Guide to Assessment and Portfolio Use

Unit Assessment
- Unit Seven, Part 2 Test, Formal Assessment pp. 247–248
- End-of-Year Test, Formal Assessment pp. 249-259

Test Generator
- Unit Seven Integrated Test, Integrated Assessment pp. 59–68
- End-of-Year Integrated Assessment pp. 69–92

Unit Technology

ClassZone www.mcdougallittell.com

Electronic Teacher Tools

Electronic Library

T = Transparency C = Copymaster

Reading and Critical Thinking Transparencies	Grammar Transparencies and Copymasters	Vocabulary Transparencies and Copymasters	Writing Transparencies and Copymasters	Communications Transparencies and Copymasters
• Cause and Effect T1 • Making Inferences T7	• Daily Language SkillBuilder T35 • Pronouns–Personal, Reflexive, and Intensive T39 • Reflexive Pronouns C143 • Reciprocal Pronouns C148	• Analogies C73	• Literary Interpretation C33	• Impromptu Speaking: Dialogue, Role-Play T14
• Making Judgments T5 • Organizational Chart: Vertical T53	• Daily Language SkillBuilder T35 • Indefinite Pronouns T40 • Indefinite Pronouns C145	• Using Context to Understand Dialect C93	• Showing, Not Telling T22	• Dramatic Reading T12
• Venn Diagram T51	• Daily Language SkillBuilder T36 • Avoiding Misplaced and Dangling Modifiers T51 • Elliptical Subordinate Clauses C121	• Denotation and Connotation C94	• Critical Review C32 • Opinion Statement C35	• Impromptu Speaking: Debate T15
• Predicting Outcomes T2	• Daily Language SkillBuilder T36 • Elliptical Clause of Comparison C122	• Word Origins C91 • Synonyms C96	• Critical Review C32 • Opinion Statement C35	• Impromptu Speaking: Dialogue, Role-Play T14
• Main Idea and Supporting Details T12	• Daily Language SkillBuilder T36 • Avoiding Misplaced and Dangling Modifiers T51 • Avoiding Misplaced and Dangling Modifiers C157	• Synonyms C96	• Literary Interpretation C33 • Compare-Contrast C34 • Autobiographical Incident C36	• Formal Presentations T10

STUDENTS ACQUIRING ENGLISH

The **Spanish Study Guide**, pp. 314–329, includes language support for the following pages:

- Family and Community Involvement (per unit)
- Selection Summaries and Vocabulary
- Active Reading
- Literary Analysis

DAILY LANGUAGE SKILLBUILDERS

Selection	SkillBuilderSentences	Suggested Answers
At the Pitt-Rivers	**1.** The Pitt-Rivers museum that you can found on the campus of "Oxford university" is devoted to Anthropology and Arkeology.	**1.** The Pitt-Rivers **M**useum, **which can be** found on the campus of Oxford **U**niversity**,** is devoted to **a**nthropology and **arch**eology.
	2. The Pitt-Rivers museum contains artafacts, which have been colected from all over the world. Including real old tool's and weapon's.	**2.** The Pitt-Rivers **M**useum contains art**i**facts **that** have been co**ll**ected from all over the world**,** **i**ncluding old too**ls** and weapo**ns**.
A Sunrise on the Veld	**1.** The purpose of this story might be to show what life is like on the veld in southern Africa, entertaining the reader, and an illustration of a life lesson.	**1.** The purpose of this story might be to show what life is like on the veld in southern Africa, **to entertain** the reader, and **to illustrate** a life lesson.
	2. Although, Doris Lessing was british, she grew up in africa.	**2.** Althoug**h** **D**oris Lessing was **B**ritish, she grew up in **A**frica.
The First Year of My Life	**1.** To put it mildly; world war I was a violent brutish and catastrophic affair.	**1.** To put it mildly**,** **W**orld **W**ar I was a violent**,** brutish**,** and catastrophic affair.
	2. Facing with the options of either fighting or fleeing, the uncle chose the safest route and run.	**2.** **Faced** with the optio**n** of either fighting or fleeing, the uncle chose the saf**er** route and **ran**.
The Moment	**1.** Margaret Atwood a Canadian writer naturaly has a place in a discussion of British Literature.	**1.** Margaret Atwood**,** a Canadian writer**,** natura**ll**y has a place in a discussion of British Literature.
	2. The Canadian writing tradition has been slow to emerge in the world of literature Atwood was instrumental in presenting Canadas own cultural identity through her works.	**2.** The Canadian writing tradition has been slow to emerge in the world of literature**;** Atwood was instrumental in presenting Canada**'**s own cultural identity through her works.
Digging The Horses	**1.** Seamus heaneys early influences include ted hughes, and the american poet robert frost.	**1.** Seamus **H**eaney**'**s early influences include **T**ed **H**ughes and the **A**merican poet **R**obert **F**rost.
	2. Born to margaret and Patrick heaney, Seamus was raised on the family farm in county derry.	**2.** Born to **M**argaret and Patrick **H**eaney, Seamus was raised on the family farm in **C**ounty **D**erry.

Selection	SkillBuilderSentences	Suggested Answers
In Music	**1.** An independant Poland was created by the Allies after world war I. **2.** In 1939, Germany and the Soviet union attacks and invades Poland.	**1.** An independ**e**nt Poland was created by the Allies after **W**orld **W**ar I. **2.** In 1939, Germany and the Soviet **U**nion attack**ed** and invad**ed** Poland.
The Frog Prince Not Waving but Drowning	**1.** I like poetry better than her. **2.** The poets who the reading public takes to it's heart are not always great poets.	**1.** I like poetry better than **she**. **2.** The poets **whom** the reading public takes to **its** heart are not always great poets.
That's All	**1.** Many contemporary works invites the reader to look behind appeerences to the hidden reality. **2.** Because contemporary writers rarely tell the reader what to think there works can be challenging.	**1.** Many contemporary works invit**e** the reader to look behind appear**a**nces to the hidden reality. **2.** Because contemporary writers rarely tell the reader what to think**,** **their** works can be challenging.
The Distant Past	**1.** Writers often choose as subjects events and situations that moves or concerns them. **2.** In many cases fiction give the reader information news reports didn't.	**1.** Writers often choose as subjects events and situations that mov**e** or concer**n** them. **2.** In many cases**,** fiction give**s** the reader information news reports **don't**.
Civil Peace	**1.** The story Civil peace, told from the main characters point of view. **2.** The character's point of view are not always the same as the writers'.	**1.** The story **"**Civil **P**eace**"** is told from the main character**'s** point of view. **2.** The character's point of view **is** not always the same as the writer**'s**.

Selection	SkillBuilderSentences	Suggested Answers
Telephone Conversation *from* Midsummer	**1.** Some poems have a clear narrative others depend more on images for there affect.	**1.** Some poems have a clear narrative**;** others depend more on images for **their e**ffect.
	2. In fact it is sometimes difficult to tell the difference between a long poem and short stories.	**2.** In fact**,** it is sometimes difficult to tell the difference between a long poem and **a** short stor**y**.
Six Feet of the Country	**1.** Some white south Africans supported apartheid others however opposed it.	**1.** Some white **S**outh Africans supported apartheid**;** others**,** however**,** opposed it.
	2. Nadine Gordimer was opposed to apartheid as reflected in her writing.	**2.** Nadine Gordimer was opposed to apartheid**,** as reflected in her writing.
from Writing as an Act of Hope	**1.** In this essay Allende tries to explain why she was writing.	**1.** In this essay**,** Allende tries to explain why she **writes**.
	2. Essays are not just for school they can influence opinions around the world	**2.** Essays are not just for school—they can influence opinions around the world.

INTEGRATING GRAMMAR AND LITERATURE: GRAMMAR PLANNER

	Unit One	Unit Two	Unit Three	Unit Four	Unit Five	Unit Six	Unit Seven
Grammar Focus by Unit	Parts of a Sentence	Phrases, Part I	Phrases, Part II	Clauses, Part I	Clauses, Part II	Rhetorical Grammar, Part I	Rhetorical Grammar, Part II

The Language of Literature offers several options for integrating grammar instruction and literature.

- Each literature unit has a grammar focus. The Teacher's Edition includes Mini Lessons for each selection that help develop the grammar focus for the unit and spring from the content of the specific literature.
- The Pupil Edition includes several full-page lessons on Sentence Crafting. These lessons are related to both the literature and the grammar focus for the unit and help students use grammar in their own writing.
- Daily Language SkillBuilders in the Teacher's Edition provide students with ongoing proofreading practice and reinforce punctuation, spelling, grammar and usage, and capitalization.
- Grammar Copymasters and Transparencies, which may be used to complement or extend lessons in the Teacher's Edition, present grammar in a traditional, systematic sequence. References to appropriate copymasters or transparencies are included at point of use in the Teacher's Edition Mini Lessons.

TE Mini Lessons shown in green
PE instruction shown in black

Part 1

Parts of Speech

Possessives with Proper Nouns That End in *-s*
That's All, p. 1259

Using Phrases

Movable Adjectives
"A Sunrise on the Veld," pp. 1218–1219

Essential and Nonessential Participial Phrases
"The First Year of My Life," p. 1223

Using Clauses

Relative Clauses
"The Moment," p. 1233

Deliberate Fragments
"Digging," "The Horses," p. 1240

Style

Essential vs. Nonessential Appositives
"The Frog Prince," "Not Waving but Drowning," p. 1253

Varying Types of Sentences
"At the Pitt-Rivers," pp. 1208–1209

The Appositive Phrase
"In Music," p. 1247

Part 2

Using Clauses

Adverbial: Elliptical Subordinate Clauses
"Telephone Conversation," from *Midsummer,* pp. 1287–1288

Elliptical Clause of Comparison
"Six Feet of the Country," pp. 1300–1301

Subject-Verb Agreement

Sentence Crafting, p. 1318

Pronoun Usage

Reflexive Pronouns
"The Distant Past," p. 1266

Indefinite Pronouns
"Civil Peace," p. 1280

Reciprocal Pronouns
"The Distant Past," p. 1270

Using Modifiers

Misplaced and Dangling Modifiers
from *Writing as an Act of Hope,* pp. 1309–1310
Writing Workshop, p. 1316

Capitalization

Proper Nouns and Adjectives
Writing Workshop, p. 1316

End Marks and Commas

Commas with Nonessential Clauses and Phrases
Writing Workshop, p. 1316
Sentence Crafting, p. 1318

Other Punctuation

Forming Singular Possessives
Writing Workshop, p. 1316

Style

Rhythm and the Comma
Sentence Crafting, p. 1318

This time line shows some important events in British political, social, and literary history during the period 1950 to 1997. Further information about selected people and events is provided below.

Literature: 1953

A Revered soldier and orator Winston Churchill (1874–1965) was also a journalist and historian. For his writings, especially for his six-volume *The Second World War,* published 1948–53, he won this Nobel Prize. His four-volume *A History of the English-speaking People* appeared from 1956–58, and the two history sets were said to have been outsold in Churchill's later life only by the Bible. In 1954, Churchill was acclaimed by Queen Elizabeth "the greatest living Briton," and in 1963 an Act of the U.S. Congress made him an honorary U.S. citizen.

Britain: 1956

B In 1956, the Egyptians nationalized the Suez Canal, which had been under Anglo-French control. On October 31, 1956, claiming that the ongoing Israeli-Egyptian war constituted a threat to the canal, the British and French sent forces in an attempt to seize it. Because of negative world opinion, however, the invasion ended after only one week.

Literature: 1956

C Hughes' marriage to American poet Sylvia Plath awakened his dormant career. Hughes has said that the two of them "would write poetry every day. It was all we were interested in, all we ever did." His first volume of poetry appeared in 1957. The death-haunted Plath committed suicide in 1963, and Hughes ceased writing for almost three years. Thereafter he resumed his career, becoming one of Britain's leading poets and, in 1984, poet laureate.

TIME LINE 1950–PRESENT

CONTEMPORARY VOICES

EVENTS IN BRITISH LITERATURE

1950 | 1960

1952 Samuel Beckett's play *Waiting for Godot* published

A **1953** Winston Churchill wins Nobel Prize in literature

1954 William Golding's *Lord of the Flies* published

C **1956** South African Nadine Gordimer's *Six Feet of the Country and Other Stories* published; poet Ted Hughes and American poet Sylvia Plath marry

1957 Harold Pinter's first one-act play, *The Room,* produced

1962 Anthony Burgess's satirical *A Clockwork Orange* published

1965 Doris Lessing's *African Stories* published

1966 Poet Seamus Heaney publishes first collection, *Death of a Naturalist*

EVENTS IN BRITAIN

1950 | 1960

1952 George VI dies and is succeeded by daughter, Elizabeth II; Britain becomes atomic power

B **1956** British troops sent to Egypt in Suez crisis

1957 Britain grants independence to Gold Coast (now Ghana), first African colony south of Sahara to achieve such status **D**

1961 South Africa withdraws from British Commonwealth

E **1963** Britain's attempt to join Common Market rejected

1964 Beatles enjoy huge international popularity in rock music

1969 Violence erupts in Northern Ireland following attempt to grant civil rights to Catholic minority

EVENTS IN THE WORLD

1950 | 1960

1950 Korean War begins (to 1953)

1953 First television broadcasting in color begins in the U.S.

1955 Soviets counter NATO with Warsaw Pact alliance of Eastern European countries

1956 Revolutions against Communist rule in Poland and Hungary crushed

1957 Soviets launch Sputnik, first artificial space satellite; European Economic Community (known as Common Market) forms to provide tariff-free trading

1959 Fidel Castro takes control of Cuba after ouster of dictator

1961 Soviet Yuri Gargarin first human to orbit Earth

1962 Cuban missile crisis ends with removal of Soviet missiles from Cuba

1965 U. S. becomes lead player in Vietnam War (to 1975)

1967 Israel claims Jerusalem, Golan Heights, and West Bank after Six-Day War with Arab states

1968 Soviets crush Czech uprising

1969 First human walks on moon

Britain: 1957

D Britain's granting of independence to the Gold Coast signaled not only the rapid decline of the British Empire but for all of colonial rule by European countries in Africa. Like many former British colonies, Ghana joined the Commonwealth of Nations, Britain's voluntary association for consultation, development, and trade agreements.

Britain: 1963

E Britain's attempt to join the Common Market, an economic union of European countries highlighted by the dropping of tariff barriers and intended to evolve into political union, is vetoed by France principally because of Britain's desire for special status for its Commonwealth.

Period Pieces

The Concorde, a supersonic passenger plane

1950s television

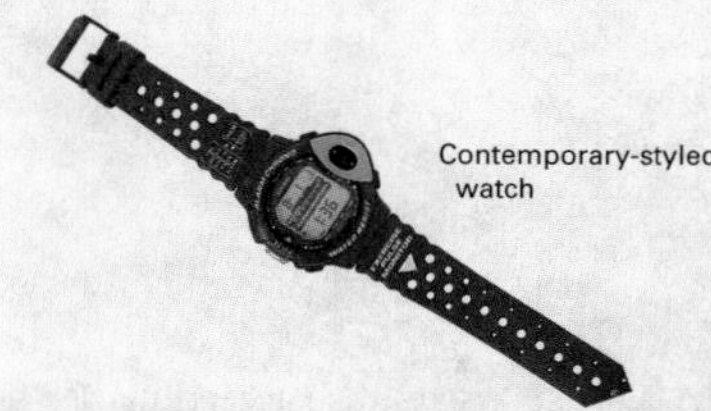
Contemporary-styled watch

1970

1972 Stevie Smith's illustrated *Collected Poems* published

1977 Penelope Lively, former children's author, publishes first adult fiction

1980

(G) **1983** Golding wins Nobel Prize in literature

1984 Ted Hughes named poet laureate

1990

1991 Gordimer wins Nobel Prize in literature

(H) **1995** Heaney wins Nobel Prize in literature; Margaret Atwood's first poetry collection in ten years, *Morning in the Burned House,* published

1970

1970 Equal Pay Act ensures that British women's wages will equal those of men with same jobs

1973 Britain and Ireland allowed into Common Market (now European Union or EU)

1979 Margaret Thatcher becomes first female prime minister (F)

1980

1981 Racial tensions and unemployment lead to riots in London; Charles, heir to British throne, marries Lady Diana Spencer

1982 Britain defeats Argentina in Falklands War

1987 Construction begins on 31-mile long "chunnel" joining Britain to France under English Channel (to 1994)

1990

1991 Britain joins with United States and other nations in Persian Gulf War

(I) **1997** Britain returns Hong Kong to China after 155 years of colonial rule; Princess Diana dies in Paris auto accident

1970

1972 SALT talks between U. S. and Soviet Union limit missiles

1973 Arab attack surprises Israel but fails

1977 First practical home computer, Apple II, hits market

1978 Camp David accords unite Israel and Egypt in peace

1979 Shah flees Iran and Muslims take U.S. hostages (to 1981); Soviets invade Afghanistan

1980

1985 Mikhail Gorbachev comes to power in Soviet Union and initiates reforms

1989 Berlin Wall falls, uniting two Germanys; students demonstrating for Chinese democracy killed in Beijing's Tiananmen Square

1990

1991 Soviet Union breaks up into 15 republics; Iraq invades Kuwait, prompting short Persian Gulf War

1993 Oslo Peace agreements signed between Israelis and Palestinians

(J) **1994** Nelson Mandela becomes South African president in nation's first all-race election

World: 1994

(J) For decades minority white rule made South Africa an outcast among nations, and in the 1970s the United Nations urged members not to trade with the country. A new era began in 1990 with the release of protest leader Nelson Mandela, in jail since 1963. Racial barriers were overturned by law, and in 1994 all races voted in South Africa for the first time, electing Mandela president.

Britain: 1979

(F) Margaret Thatcher (b. 1925), head of Britain's Conservative party, became Britain's first woman prime minister. She brought greater privatization to Britain, moving the government to sell some of its interests in industries. She served to 1990 and then resigned, having served in the post longer than any other person in the 20th century.

Literature: 1983

(G) The first published novel of William Golding (b. 1911) was *Lord of the Flies* (1954), which along with J.D. Salinger's *The Catcher in the Rye,* became a cult classic among students. *Lord of the Flies* was not immediately popular; only after its publication in paperback in 1959 was it widely read. In awarding its prize to Golding, the Nobel committee acknowledged that his books are entertaining but also present situations "in which odd people are tempted to reach beyond their limits, thereby being bared to the very marrow."

Literature: 1995

(H) Seamus Heaney won the Nobel Prize for literature for "works of lyrical beauty and ethical depth," works "which exalt everyday miracles and the living past." However, a critic for the *New York Times Book Review* saw politics behind his selection, believing that Heaney was chosen "to nudge the peace talks between London and the IRA."

Britain: 1997

(I) Hong Kong, with a mere 399 square miles in southeast China, was occupied by Great Britain after the 1839–42 Opium War with China. Britain retained control of the tiny region throughout the 19th century and in 1898 signed a 99-year lease for it. On July 1, 1997, Great Britain handed the former colony back to China, which promised to respect its economy and civilian liberties.

TIME LINE **1191**

INTRODUCTION

This article provides a historical and literary context for the writings presented in Unit Seven. In particular, students will learn that the second half of the 20th century in Britain was one of a weakening economy, continuing controversy over the status of Northern Ireland, and, after 1979, dominance by prime minister Margaret Thatcher.

Reading Nonfiction

Reading Skills and Strategies

ESTABLISHING A PURPOSE FOR READING

Have students scan the article to establish a purpose for reading. Remind them to adjust their purposes if they encounter unexpected content or difficulty.

USING TEXT ORGANIZERS

As students preview the article, have them note the basic text organizers. Ask students to describe the information they would expect to locate in each section. As they read, have students use the subheads to make an outline or graphic organizer. Have them organize information from the article, sidebars, and timeline under the appropriate headings. Remind students to use text organizers to locate and categorize information as they do independent research.

ANALYZING TEXT STRUCTURE

Have students suggest how the text is structured. Due to the number of dates, students should expect the basic structure to be chronological. Discuss how this structure influences the way they read and understand the material. Encourage students to note other kinds of relationships (cause and effect and compare and contrast) signaled by text structure and words. Key cause and effect relationships are easy to identify in each section of the article. Encourage students to note relationships between the historical events and literary history.

IDENTIFYING MAIN IDEAS

The section headings relate to the main idea in each section Have students read one section at a time and note how its idea is developed through details.

CONTEMPORARY VOICES

1950 – PRESENT

A In 1953, a year after succeeding her father, George VI, as Britain's monarch, Elizabeth II was crowned in a glorious ceremony in Westminster Abbey. To many, the coronation symbolized a return of hope after the enormous loss and suffering of World War II, yet even though the ceremony recalled Britain's long tradition of greatness, there was no question that Britain was a greatly altered nation. The political power of the working class had been firmly established, and the influence of the upper class substantially diminished. The economic instability caused by Britain's huge war debt, which affected all classes, had prompted a series of nationwide strikes and other crises. B The Labor government's social welfare programs and nationalization of industries, begun just after the war to address the dire economic situation, had continued even when the Conservatives returned to power in the 1950s. The dismantling of the empire was also continuing, with Britain—in response to both economic and nationalistic pressures—relinquishing control of most of its colonies in Asia, Africa, and the West Indies. C At the same time, immigration from the former colonies was transforming what had formerly been a homogeneous population, creating racial and ethnic tensions on a scale never before known in Britain.

Top: Queen Elizabeth II at her coronation ceremony, 1953. *Center:* Newly built row houses in postwar England. *Above left* and *above:* Increasing religious and ethnic diversity is shown in two London photographs, one of a Hindu temple and the other of spectators watching a cricket match between a team of West Indians and a police team. *Right:* The Beatles, 1966.

A SHIFT IN POWER AND LEADERSHIP

During the international political struggle that dominated the postwar decades—the so-called cold war between Western democracies and Communist nations—the United States became the chief champion of the West. Britain, though it became an atomic power and an important member of both the United Nations and the North Atlantic Treaty Organization (NATO), generally followed the lead of its powerful American ally. One exception was the Suez crisis of the mid-1950s, in which Britain joined with France in an unsuccessful military effort to reverse the Egyptian government's nationalization of the Suez Canal. Although the United States criticized the policy, the differences were soon smoothed over, and Britain retained its position as one of the United States' closest allies.

The new international supremacy of the United States extended beyond the political arena. As the world's most powerful nation and richest market, the United States became the center of Western technological development, particularly in the decades preceding the full recovery of the Japanese and German economies. Britain made valuable contributions in such areas as DNA research and fiber optics but clearly had lost the preeminent position in science and technology that it had once enjoyed. During the "brain drain" of the early 1960s, many of Britain's top scientists and engineers emigrated to the United States, lured by greater opportunities and financial resources. Similarly, the worldwide dominance of U.S. popular culture attracted much of Britain's entertainment talent to American shores.

Britain's greatest international success in the sphere of popular culture came in the 1960s, with the "British invasion" of the American rock-music scene. Led by the Beatles and the Rolling Stones, British rock groups not only dominated international pop music but also launched a teenage craze for long hair (D)

Development of the English Language

Since the 1960s, the women's movement has left its mark on the English language, promoting existing alternatives and new coinages as replacements for terms perceived as sexist. For example, the title *Ms.* was introduced, and efforts were made to secure acceptance of such gender-neutral terms as *humanity* and *firefighter* in place of *mankind* and *fireman.* Technology, however, has proved the greatest source of vocabulary expansion. From space exploration have come a host of new or rejuvenated terms, including *liftoff, astronaut,* and *A-OK;* the spread of computer technology has given us such terms as *software, floppy disk,* and *user-friendly.* (E)

At the same time, satellite broadcasting, computer modems, FAX machines, and other advances in communications have helped turn the world into a "global village" in which English—spread originally by British and more recently by American influence—has become a universal language. If a Greek does business with someone in Japan, or a Norwegian diplomat negotiates with an Israeli, they are likely to communicate in English, a second language common to both. In such former British colonies as India and Malaysia, English bridges the gaps between dozens of native languages and dialects.

Literary History

British writers have responded in several ways to the changes of the contemporary era. During the 1950s, a group of young poets called the Movement—including Ted Hughes, Thom Gunn, Elizabeth Jennings, and Philip Larkin—achieved recognition by rejecting complex styles and producing clear, rational, understated poetry on subjects

Making Connections

Architecture

(A) The present Westminster Abbey is an enlargement of a church and was constructed primarily between 1245 and 1269. Miraculously, German air raids in World War II damaged only parts of the building, which were then restored. The abbey has been the site of almost every English coronation since it was constructed.

Politics

(B) The Labor and Conservative parties are the two major political parties in Parliament. The Labor party has its roots in socialist doctrine and has traditionally been supported by trade unions. As successor to the Tory party, the Conservative party customarily favors the preservation of existing forms of government and other institutions.

Sociology

(C) Needing unskilled labor after World War II, Britain made room for a million immigrants. Many people also migrated from the Irish Free State and, after 1950, from the West Indies. The arrival of almost 140,000 immigrants, 1949 to 1959, led to major racial tensions.

Music

(D) Although they were together for less than ten years, the Beatles revolutionized popular music in the 1960s and 1970s. Their songs are still popular, and each member individually has become an icon.

Language

(E) To some people, the influence of political considerations and technology on the English language is eerily reminiscent of the government-controlled language Newspeak in George Orwell's novel *1984.* In Newspeak, all descriptive and subjective words were eliminated, along with words for concepts that people were no longer allowed to think about, such as freedom and love.

Making Connections

Fashion

F In 1960, the British designer Mary Quant was the first to introduce dresses with hemlines above the knee, and in 1962 she designed outfits in which bellbottomed slacks were worn with matching cardigans. After the miniskirt, the most important women's fashion trend of the 1960s was the increasing popularity of the pantsuit.

Politics

G The Conservative politician Edward Heath became prime minister in 1970. He oversaw a reduction in income taxes, a tight monetary policy (which worsened unemployment), and passage of a law making it harder for workers to strike. He also secured Britain's entry into the Common Market in 1973. Preparations for this, such as raising British food prices to Common Market levels, brought hardships and anger to the working class, precipitating a strike by coal miners. Heath lost the general election of 1974, and Harold Wilson, the Labor leader, became prime minister.

Military History

H The Falklands War was fought for control of the Falkland Islands, a small cluster in the Atlantic Ocean about 300 miles east of Argentina. It has been an issue between the two countries since British explorer John Strong first landed on the islands in 1690. In 1833, the British deported Argentines living there. In 1982, Argentina made a surprise invasion, taking the islands and stationing 10,000 troops there. Ten weeks later the Argentine forces surrendered to British forces after air, sea, and land battles. For her forceful, swift action, Thatcher's prime ministry received a public-opinion boost.

F and for things British—British TV shows, British slang, and the "mod" fashions of London's Carnaby Street, for example.

Although prominence in the pop-culture scene had its economic rewards, the weaknesses of the British economy required far more extensive remedies. One was provided by the discovery in 1969 of oil beneath the North Sea off the Scottish coast; in the next 12 years, Britain would be transformed from an oil-importing nation to one self-sufficient in energy. Another solution to the nation's economic problems, according to some Britons—particularly members of the Conservative party—lay in joining the European Community (EC), or Common Market, which several Western European nations had established in 1957. Opponents of this view, mainly in the Labor party, felt that EC membership would weaken trade ties within the British Commonwealth, entangle Britain in continental politics, and threaten the nation's sovereignty and agricultural interests. Since the Labor party held sway for most of the 1960s, British efforts to join the Common Market were not vigorously pursued during those years. **G** Soon after the Conservative party returned to power in 1970, however, Britain's application for membership was accepted.

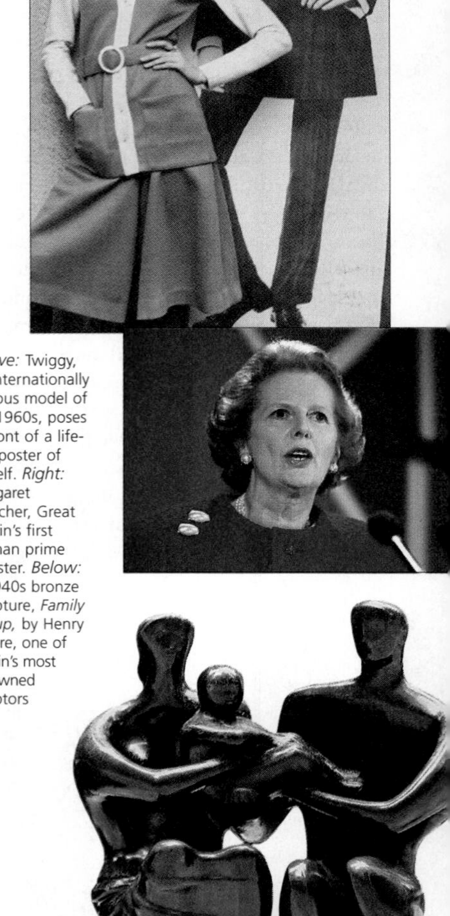

Above: Twiggy, an internationally famous model of the 1960s, poses in front of a life-size poster of herself. *Right:* Margaret Thatcher, Great Britain's first woman prime minister. *Below:* A 1940s bronze sculpture, *Family Group*, by Henry Moore, one of Britain's most renowned sculptors

THE THATCHER ERA

In 1975, following defeats in two general elections the year before, the Conservative party elected a new leader who four years later would become Britain's first woman prime minister. The daughter of a small-town grocer, Margaret Thatcher had risen in the ranks of Britain's new "meritocracy," in which success was attained not through birth or wealth but through hard work and talent. Her 11 years as prime minister (1979–1990), known as the Thatcher Era, left their mark on both Britain and the rest of the world. **H** A pragmatist in the fight against communism, Thatcher was the first Western leader to recognize and promote the changes that were occurring in the Soviet Union, and she encouraged President Ronald Reagan to do the same. Under her leadership, Britain successfully waged the Falklands War of 1982 and joined the victorious U.S.-led coalition in the Persian Gulf War of 1991. Meanwhile, on the domestic front, Thatcher was leading her country in a new economic direction. Insisting that Britain become a "wealth-producing" rather than merely a "wealth-redistributing" nation, she began privatizing the previously nationalized industries and instituting other changes to make British industry more

Mini Lesson Viewing and Representing

Family Group
by Henry Moore

ART APPRECIATION

Instruction British sculptor Henry Moore (1898–1986) sculpted *Family Group* in the 1940s for the front lawn of an English school that offered weekend classes for parents. It is meant to symbolize the parent-student relationship. Moore cast 4 copies of the sculpture in bronze, at 5 feet high, and the edition pictured above is found at the Museum of Modern Art in New York City, where it sits among tables and chairs in an outdoor museum garden.

Have students notice the sculpture's almost surreal look: wide, scooped shoulders and nearly featureless simple heads.

Ask: Why do you think that the detail on the figures is so vague?

Possible Response: Keeping details on the people at a minimum allows the viewer to concentrate on the work's message of family togetherness, with the baby forming a knotlike center uniting the family.

competitive.

A significant problem faced by Thatcher and her successor, John Major, was the ongoing conflict in Northern Ireland. A decade before Thatcher took office, Northern Ireland's Roman Catholic minority had begun a civil-rights movement, calling for an end to discrimination against Catholics there. When clashes broke out between Catholics and Protestants, the British government sent in troops that the Catholics perceived as favoring the Protestants. Before long, Irish Republican Army (IRA) extremists had gained prominence over the civil-rights moderates among the Catholics, and Protestant extremists had formed militant groups of their own, including the Ulster Defense League (UDL). For over two decades, violence between these factions rocked Northern Ireland and spilled over, in the form of bombings and other terrorist attacks, into other parts of the United Kingdom. A peace effort led by two Northern Irish women, Mairead Corrigan and Betty Williams, earned them the Nobel Peace Prize but failed to end the violence. Finally, in 1994, both the IRA and the UDL agreed to a cease-fire, and British and Irish officials began peace negotiations that seemed more promising than past efforts. I

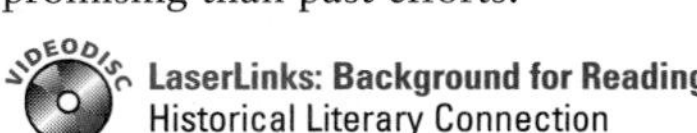

LaserLinks: Background for Reading
Historical Literary Connection

Street scene in Northern Ireland, 1991

LITERARY HISTORY

drawn from everyday experience. Even more simple in style was the work of Stevie Smith, who—like Dylan Thomas before her—helped popularize the oral reading of poetry for modern audiences.

The 1950s also gave birth to the fiction of the so-called Angry Young Men and to the "kitchen sink" school of drama. Works like John Osborne's play *Look Back in Anger* (1956) and Alan Sillitoe's story collection *The Loneliness of the Long Distance Runner* (1959) expressed the contempt for authority and middle-class values felt by British working-class and student radicals. The social radicalism of these works was matched by the stylistic radicalism of the plays of Samuel Beckett and others associated with the "theater of the absurd," who abandoned realism, plot, and characterization in order to focus on the isolation and absurdity of contemporary life—themes that have also reverberated in the plays of Harold Pinter. J Meanwhile, some contemporary dramatists have drawn on British tradition: in *A Man for All Seasons* (1960), for example, Robert Bolt dramatized the life of the Renaissance hero Thomas More, and in *Rosenkrantz and Guildenstern Are Dead* (1967), Tom Stoppard retold Shakespeare's *Hamlet* from the viewpoint of two minor characters.

Another significant contemporary trend is the increasingly favorable reception given to regional and commonwealth writers, broadening the concept of "English" literature. Seamus Heaney (Northern Ireland), Muriel Spark (Scotland), Nadine Gordimer (South Africa), Chinua Achebe (Nigeria), Margaret Atwood (Canada), Judith Wright (Australia), and Derek Walcott (St. Lucia and Trinidad) are just a few of the talented writers who have enriched English letters with their unique perceptions of human experience. K

Religion

I In Northern Ireland, most Protestants support the country's status as part of the United Kingdom, whereas most Roman Catholics want it to be reunited with the Republic of Ireland.

Philosophy

J Irish-born Samuel Beckett (1896–1989) and other absurdist writers did not accept an absolute, universal reality, believing that the only thing humankind can be sure of is that it exists. According to their philosophy, life has no meaning that we can discover with any certainty. In Beckett's most famous play, *Waiting for Godot* (1952, first published in French), the theater of the absurd's first success, two men await the arrival of the mysterious Godot, who may provide enlightenment on their condition, but who never arrives. To Beckett, this senseless waiting epitomizes the essence of life.

Literature

K Another commonwealth writer is V.S. Naipaul (b. 1932), born in Trinidad in the West Indies. Much of Naipaul's work explores the destruction of the small cultures of the West Indies by outside cultural forces. He first achieved international acclaim with his novel *A House of Mr. Biswas* (1961), an epic account of a Trinidadian family. In *In a Free State* (1971), he suggests that all people are "colonial," existing in what is ironically called a "free state." He was knighted in 1990.

PART 1 Appearance and Reality

In the second half of the 20th century, many writers have explored the disquieting realities and startling insights lying beneath the surface of ordinary life. In a world in which technological development has threatened to depersonalize society, these writers have probed the significance of passing moments in individual experience. As you read the selections in this part of Unit Seven, look for the ways in which hidden realities and meaning emerge from seemingly ordinary times in life.

1196

Point of View in Contemporary Fiction

The Narrative Lens

Like a photographer who switches lenses to vary the view of an object, a writer chooses a method of narration that can reveal, to varying degrees, what is happening within a story. In contemporary fiction of the 20th century, writers have made use of narrators with various **points of view,** or vantage points. The choice of a particular point of view determines *what* is presented to the reader and *how* it is presented. There are three basic types of point of view:

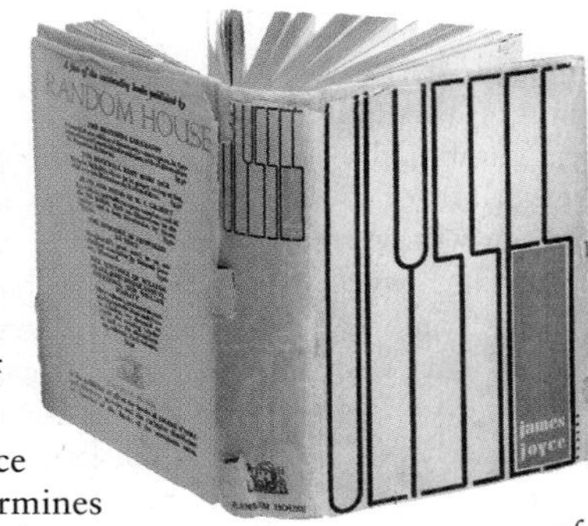

James Joyce's *Ulysses* (published in novel form in 1922) is noted for its stream-of-consciousness technique.

POINTS OF VIEW
First-Person Narrator • Narrator is a major or a minor character who tells the story. • Narrator can be actively involved or merely an observer.
Third-Person Omniscient • Narrator can see into the past and into the future. • Narrator relates characters' thoughts and comments on events. • Writer can make "editorial" comments about the characters and their motivations.
Third-Person Limited • The narrator is not a participant in the story, but relates events from one character's viewpoint. • All the reader knows is what the narrator reveals of that character's thoughts, feelings, observations, and experiences.

Traditional Points of View

The **third-person omniscient** point of view is the most established type of narration, used by Chaucer in the 14th century and by the early novelists of the 18th century. The third-person omniscient narrator allows the writer the freedom to reveal a variety of information about a number of characters or events. In William Trevor's "The Distant Past" (page 1263), for example, the narrator is able to show the shifting thoughts and feelings of several townspeople during a time of political and religious conflicts.

Traditional **first-person narrators** are popular with authors because they can provide a firsthand account of events, but also appeal to contemporary writers' love of irony. Nadine Gordimer's "Six Feet of Country" (page 1289), for example, demonstrates how a first-person narrator can tell a story that is ironic insofar as he is not aware of the effect on readers of his own part in the story.

Perhaps the most common use of point of view in contemporary fiction is the **third-person limited** point of view. Its limitations, ironically, are what make it attractive to contemporary writers. For one thing, the writer can focus primarily on the development of one character. Events are related from the perspective of that character, who rarely "editorializes" (or comments) on events. In addition, the restriction of the focus to a single character makes the fiction seem more realistic. The advantages of this point of view are evident in Doris Lessing's "A Sunrise on the Veld" (page 1210), which "looks over the shoulder" of a young South African on a day he is witness to an event that changes his attitude about life.

The Experimenters

In contemporary fiction of the early 20th century, Virginia Woolf, James Joyce, and other "modernist" writers were known for their innovative use of point of view. They experimented with **stream of consciousness,** a technique that departs from literal description

OVERVIEW

Objectives

- understand the following literary terms:
  - point of view
  - third-person omniscient
  - first-person narrator
  - third-person limited
  - stream of consciousness
  - multiple narrator
- appreciate shared characteristics of literature across cultures
- recognize themes across cultures

Teaching the Lesson

This lesson will give students some background on point of view in contemporary literature.

Motivating the Students

The omniscient point of view is not often used by contemporary Western writers. Discuss with students the ideas or beliefs of our society that might make omniscience less acceptable. As students read the short stories in this unit, have them consider the following question.

In which story did you feel closest to the main character and why? From what point of view was the story written?
Possible Response: "A Sunrise on the Veld," told from the third-person limited point of view, reveals the South African boy's every thought.

As they finish reading the short stories, students can write reactions to these questions and keep their responses in their Working Portfolios.

Presenting the Concepts

Read through the strategies aloud or project them on a transparency. Using the Points of View table, ask students to write three different versions of a one-page story: one in first person, one in third-person omniscient, and one in third-person limited. Model how to use the strategies to analyze students' stories.

Point of View Across Cultures

Many contemporary writers experiment with point of view. The point of view often relates to the theme of the work and contributes to its meaning. Share with students the following writers' use of point of view.

India

Salman Rushdie (b. 1947) wrote his novel *Midnight's Children* in 1981. The main character, who was born at the stroke of midnight on the exact moment of Indian independence, can hear the voices of all of the other 1,000 children born within the first hour of that time, a telepathic discovery he makes at age nine. This character's first-person account becomes a story not just of his own life but of the hopeful birth and disappointing maturity of independent India itself.

France

In his 1957 novel, *La Jalousie* (Jealousy), Alain Robbe-Grillet (b. 1922) uses an extremely limited point of view. Because the reader is told nothing directly about the character from whose point of view the events are presented, the reader must make inferences to deduce that he is a jealous husband who spies on his wife.

Mexico

One of the themes of the 1962 novel *La muerte de Artemio Cruz* (The Death of Artemio Cruz) by Carlos Fuentes (b. 1928) is the multiplicity of the self. Fuentes reinforces this theme by dividing the point of view of a dying man into three monologues, each using a different narrative person: I, you, and he.

to reveal the flow of a character's thoughts. These experimenters also used multiple narrators.

Woolf's **multiple-narrator** technique was quite inventive. Passages of her writing combined both spoken and unspoken observations of different characters—many of whom were never actually identified. (See "Milestones in British Literature" on page 1058.) Although some readers might find it challenging to figure out who's who, the advantage of this technique lies in the amount of information and insight it allows Woolf to reveal.

Many contemporary British writers have returned to a more traditional style of writing, but that does not mean they have abandoned experimentation altogether. A case in point is Muriel Spark's use of a first-person narrator in "The First Year of My Life" (page 1220). A first-person point of view is, by definition, limited to what can be known by a single character. Spark's first-person narrator, however, is an imaginative departure from ordinary narrators. She creates an unusual first-person narrator who has the omniscience of a third-person narrator.

Cases of Mistaken Identity

Actors and actresses often complain that fans confuse them with the characters they play. In a similar fashion, writers are often confused with the narrators they have invented. This error is probably easiest to make when the story is related by an omniscient, impersonal voice that has no characteristics that set it apart from the writer.

A practiced reader will resist the temptation to assume the narrator really is the writer. After all, the writer is deliberately telling a story. Nonfiction would be the better choice for a writer who wants to convey a direct connection to information he or she presents. In creating a work of fiction, the writer removes him- or herself from the events and puts on a kind of mask in the form of the narrator. As Oscar Wilde noted, "Give a man a mask and he will tell you the truth."

YOUR TURN What characters from books, TV shows, and films have you identified with closely? What do you think the writers did to breathe life into those characters? Discuss your responses with a partner.

Strategies for Reading: Point of View

1. Remember that in the first-person point of view, the narrator's account of events will reflect his or her knowledge and experiences within the story, as well as possible bias.
2. See what insights you gain about a narrator by observing how other characters respond to him or her.
3. Be aware of the possibility that the point of view may shift during the story.
4. Draw conclusions about the narrator. For example, is the narrator always reliable? What personal flaws or ulterior motives might the narrator reveal, even unconsciously?
5. Infer why the writer chose a particular point of view. Challenge yourself to explore how the story might be different if told from another perspective.
6. **Monitor** your reading strategies and modify them when your understanding breaks down. Remember to use your Strategies for Active Reading: **predict, visualize, connect, question, clarify,** and **evaluate.**

At the Pitt-Rivers

Short Story by PENELOPE LIVELY

"As a matter of fact I've been in love myself twice."

Connect to Your Life

Other Lives Recall a time when you became completely engrossed in the conversation or activities of strangers you observed in a park, restaurant, or other public place. What attracted your attention to these people? Did you begin to speculate about their lives or situations? Share your thoughts with classmates.

Build Background

Fact Behind the Fiction "At the Pitt-Rivers" takes place in 20th-century Oxford, a city northwest of London. More specifically, it takes place in the Pitt-Rivers, an actual museum located on the campus of Oxford University. The Pitt-Rivers Museum was established in 1883 when a collection of early weapons, tools, pottery, and other artifacts was donated to the university by an English soldier and archaeologist, Lieutenant-General Pitt-Rivers. He believed that by sharing his treasures with the public, he could give ordinary people a better understanding of their ancestors. The Pitt-Rivers Museum is well-known for its exhibits in anthropology (the study of the origin and development of human beings) and archaeology (the excavation and study of items belonging to ancient cultures). It also contains an extensive collection of musical instruments from around the world.

Penelope Lively, the award-winning author of "At the Pitt-Rivers," has a personal link to the setting of her story, being a graduate of Oxford University, with a degree in modern history. In many of her stories, Lively reveals her preoccupation with history, especially its ability to change one's perspective on life. She frequently relates experiences in which a child matures greatly as a result of a new awareness about history or humanity. In the following story, a teenage boy gains insights into life by observing the relationship of two adults.

WORDS TO KNOW
Vocabulary Preview
benign, bleak, compulsory, explicit, pretentious

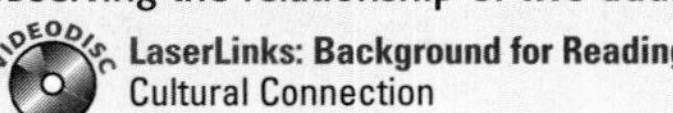
LaserLinks: Background for Reading
Cultural Connection

Focus Your Reading

LITERARY ANALYSIS SETTING **Setting** is the time and place of the action of a short story or other literary work. In addition to time and place, however, setting may include the social and moral environment that form the background for a narrative. As you read this story, be aware of the way in which the setting of two adjoining museums in Oxford contributes to the plot.

ACTIVE READING DRAWING CONCLUSIONS ABOUT THE NARRATOR

When you **draw conclusions** about characters in literature, you form opinions about them on the basis of their actions, speech, and appearance. In addition, you can draw conclusions about the **narrator** of a story on the basis of the thoughts and feelings he or she expresses. The narrator of this story encounters a couple three times on his trips to the museum. On each occasion, as he describes the couple, he reveals something about himself.

READER'S NOTEBOOK In a chart like the one shown, briefly describe what the boy tells about the couple he encounters and what he reveals about himself.

	The Couple	The Boy
1st Visit		
2nd Visit		
3rd Visit		

OVERVIEW

Objectives

1. understand and appreciate the role of **setting** in a short story **(Literary Analysis)**
2. appreciate the relationship between **setting** on the one hand, and **plot, character,** and **theme** on the other **(Literary Analysis)**
3. **draw conclusions about the narrator (Active Reading)**

Summary

The narrator, a boy of 16, goes frequently to the Pitt-Rivers Museum to write poetry. One day, the boy spots a woman who is not beautiful, but nevertheless has a radiance about her. On subsequent visits to the museum, he sees the woman in the company of a man. She is clearly in love with him. The narrator begins to look for the couple whenever he goes to the museum.

Use **Unit Seven Resource Book,** p. 4 for additional support.

Thematic Link

In "At the Pitt-Rivers," the narrator can only observe appearances because he cannot hear the couple's conversations. However, he speculates on the reality of their relationship, eventually digging deeper into his own experiences and learning the difference between **appearance and reality.**

5-Minute Warm-Up

Daily Language SkillBuilder

Have students **proofread** the display sentences on page 1189i and write them correctly. The sentences also appear on Transparency 32 of **Grammar Transparencies and Copymasters.**

Mini Lesson Preteaching Vocabulary

If you would like to preteach the WORDS TO KNOW for this selection, use the Mini Lesson on p. 1200.

LESSON RESOURCES

UNIT SEVEN RESOURCE BOOK, pp. 4–8

ASSESSMENT RESOURCES
Formal Assessment, pp. 219–220
Teacher's Guide to Assessment and Portfolio Use
Test Generator

SKILLS TRANSPARENCIES AND COPYMASTERS
Literary Analysis
- Influences on Plot: Setting and Character, T19 (for Literary Analysis, p. 1207)

Reading and Critical Thinking
- Drawing Conclusions, T4 (for Active Reading, p. 1199)

Grammar
- Diagramming Subjects, Verbs and Modifiers, T58 (for Mini Lesson, pp. 1208–1209)
- Varying Types of Sentences, C179 (for Mini Lesson, pp. 1208–1209)

Vocabulary
- Analogies, C73 (for Mini Lesson, pp. 1200–1201)

Writing
- Sensory Word List, T14 (for Writing Option 1, p. 1208)
- Personality Profile, C25 (for Writing Option 2, p. 1208)

Communications
- Impromptu Speaking: Dialogue, Role-Play, T14 (for Activities & Explorations 1, p. 1208)

INTEGRATED TECHNOLOGY
Audio Library
LaserLinks
- Cultural Connection: At Natural History Museums
- Art Gallery: Observations on Couples. See **Teacher's SourceBook,** pp. 85–86.

Visit our website:
www.mcdougallittell.com

TEACHING THE LITERATURE

Reading and Analyzing

Literary Analysis SETTING

The narrator describes the setting in detail in the first two paragraphs. Have students describe the atmosphere inside a museum, giving special consideration to the narrator's description of a place where one "can learn a lot . . . about what people get up to: it makes you think." Have them discuss why a narrator might choose such a place to begin a story.

Possible Responses: Perhaps the action of the story will take place there; it is an unusual setting that will grab the reader's attention.

Have students identify the two different areas within the story's setting and to define their position in relation to one another.

Answer: The Natural History Museum and the Pitt-Rivers are adjacent museums; the former, which leads to the latter, is the "bigger draw" and is where the narrator first sees the woman.

Use **Unit Seven Resource Book** p. 6 for more exercises.

Active Reading

DRAWING CONCLUSIONS ABOUT THE NARRATOR

Suggest that students keep a list of facts they learn about the narrator as they read. They can use this list, as well as the chart in their Reader's Notebook, as a basis for drawing conclusions about the narrator's character.

Use **Unit Seven Resource Book** p. 5 for more practice.

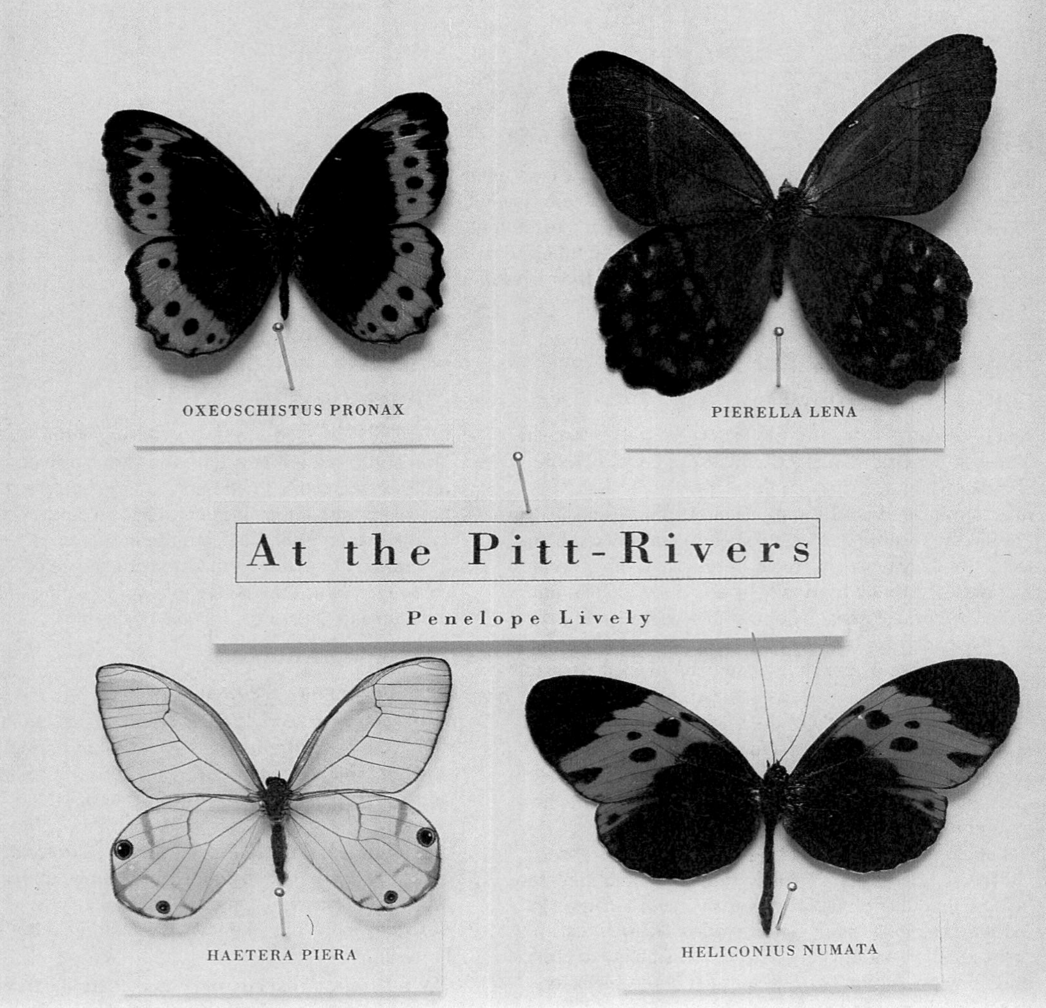

1200 UNIT SEVEN PART 1: APPEARANCE AND REALITY

Teaching Options

Preteaching Vocabulary

ANALOGIES/ANTONYMS On standardized tests, analogies are often presented in the form of word pairs. Students must determine the relationship between one pair of words and then apply that relationship to another word pair.

Model

soiled : clean :: careless : ______

Instruction

- Write the model on the chalkboard.
- Explain to students that the proper way to read this analogy is "*Soiled* is to *clean* as *careless* is to *blank*."
- Next, have students identify the relationship between the first pair of words. In this case, the first two words are antonyms.
- Remind students that the relationship between the second pair of words should be the same. Then have them provide an antonym for *careless,* such as *careful.*
- Remind students that analogies often illustrate other relationships between words, including synonyms, cause and effect, characteristic quality, part and whole, location, and classification.

They've got this museum in Oxford,[1] called the Pitt-Rivers; I spend a lot of time there. It's a weird place, really weird, stuff from all over the world crammed into glass cases like some kind of mad junk-shop—native things from New Guinea and Mexico and Sumatra and wherever you like to think of. Spears and stone axes and masks and a thousand different kinds of fish-hook. And bead jewelry and peculiar musical instruments. And a great totem from Canada. You can learn a lot there about what people get up to: it makes you think. Mostly it's pretty depressing—umpteen different nasty ways of killing each other.

I didn't start going there to learn anything; just because it was a nice quiet place to mooch around and be on my own, Saturdays, or after school. It got to be a kind of habit. There aren't often people there—the odd art student, a few kids gawping at the shrunken heads, one or two serious-looking blokes[2] wandering around. The porter's[3] usually reading the *Sun* or having a snooze; there's not a lot of custom.[4] The Natural History Museum is a bigger draw; you have to go through that to get into the Pitt-Rivers. You'll always get an audience for a dinosaur and a few nasty-looking jellyfish in formalin.[5] Actually I'm partial to the Natural History Museum myself; that makes you think, too. All those fossils, and then in the end you and me. I had a go at reading *The Origin of Species* last term, not that I got very far. There's a room upstairs in the museum where Darwin's friend—Huxley[6]—had this great argument with that bishop and the rest of them. It says so on the door. I like that, it seems kind of respectful. Putting up a plaque to an argument, instead of just JOE SOAP WAS BORN HERE or whatever. It should be done more often.

It was in the Natural History Museum—underneath the central whale—that I first saw her, and since my mind was on natural selection I thought she wasn't all that good an example of it. I remember thinking that it was funny it doesn't seem to operate with girls, so you got them getting prettier and prettier, because good-looking girls have a better deal than bad-looking ones, you've only got to observe a bit to see that. I always notice girls, to see if they're pretty or not, and she wasn't. She wasn't specially ugly; just very ordinary—you wouldn't look at her twice. She was sitting on a bench, watching the entrance.

All the girls I know—at school or round where I live—are either attractive or they're not. If they're attractive they have lots of blokes after them and if they're not they don't. It's as simple as that. If they're attractive just looking at them makes you think of all sorts of things, imagine what it would be like and so forth, and if they're not then it doesn't really occur to you, except in so far as it occurs to you a good deal of the time,

1. **Oxford:** a city in England that is the site of Oxford University, the world's oldest English-speaking university.
2. **blokes:** British slang meaning "fellows," "guys."
3. **porter:** a British term for a doorman.
4. **custom:** the customers or patrons of a business or store. (The narrator is saying that there are usually not many visitors in the museum.)
5. **formalin** (for′mə-lĭn): a solution of formaldehyde in water, used as a preservative.
6. **Huxley:** One of the main supporters of Darwin's theory of evolution was Thomas Henry Huxley (1825–1895), a British biologist.

Customizing Instruction

Less Proficient Readers

Set a Purpose Have students read the first paragraph of the story, visualizing the displays that the narrator sees in the museum. Then have them read on to find out why the narrator goes to the museum and whom he sees there.

Students Acquiring English

Tell students that they will encounter many idioms and slang expressions in this story. Help them distinguish expressions that are still used by Americans, such as *as a matter of fact,* from strictly British expressions, such as *bloke.* Help students understand the meanings of idioms and slang expressions that cannot be deciphered from their context.

Use **Spanish Study Guide** for additional support, pp. 290–292.

Gifted and Talented

Encourage students to write brief essays or journal entries about the inner struggles of adolescence that are implicit in the story.

Exercise Have students use a thesaurus and a dictionary, if necessary, to help them complete the following antonym analogies that use the WORDS TO KNOW. Answers may vary, but each response should be an antonym and match the part of speech of the word with which it is paired.

1. **benign** : malicious :: best : _____
   Possible Response: worst
2. tired : energetic :: **bleak**: _____
   Possible Response: cheery
3. fame : obscurity :: **compulsory** : _____
   Possible Response: optional
4. **explicit** : vague :: profit : _____
   Possible Response: loss
5. rich : poor :: **pretentious** : _____
   Possible Response: modest

Use **Unit Seven Resource Book** p. 7 for more practice.

Reading and Analyzing

Literary Analysis SETTING

A When the narrator first sees the woman, he notices that she is "very ordinary—you wouldn't look at her twice." When he comes nearer, however, he notices that "she glowed . . . it made you feel good just to look at her." Have students discuss what the narrator's reaction might have been had he encountered the woman elsewhere: in a shopping mall, on the street, or even a library.

Possible Response: He probably would not have noticed her, but in a museum, where one examines things more closely, he notices her immediately.

Literary Analysis: CHARACTERIZATION

B Invite students to discuss what they know about the narrator so far and what impressions they have formed of him.

Possible Responses: He is sensitive and intellectual; he probably hasn't dated much, but seems to be romantically inclined; he is ordinary looking; his background is one that seems to encourage his poetry writing.

actually. This girl was definitely not attractive. In the first place she was in fact quite old, not far off thirty, I should think, and in the second she hadn't got a nice figure; her legs were kind of dumpy and she didn't have pretty hair or anything like that. I gave her a look, just automatically, to check, and then didn't bother with her.

. . . she had the most beautiful expression I've ever seen in my life. She glowed; that's the only way I can put it.

Until I came alongside, where I could see her face clearly, and then I looked again. And again. She still wasn't pretty, but she had the most beautiful expression I've ever seen in my life. She glowed; that's the only way I can put it. She sat there with her hands in her lap, watching the door, and radiating away so that in a peculiar fashion it made you feel good just to look at her, a bit like you were joining in how she felt. Stupid, I daresay, but that's how it was. **A**

And I thought to myself: oh ho . . . I mean, I've seen films and I've read books and I know a bit about things.

As a matter of fact I've been in love myself twice. The first time was with a girl in my class at school and I suppose it was a bit of a trial run, really, I mean I'm not altogether sure how much I was feeling it but it seemed quite important when it was going on. The second time was last year, when I was fifteen. She came to stay with her married sister who lives round the corner from us and though it's months and months ago now I still feel quite faint and weak when I go past the house. **B**

Oh ho, I thought. I felt kindly—sort of benign—and a bit curious to see what the bloke would be like. I thought he couldn't be much because of her not being pretty. I mean, in films you can always tell who's going to fall for who because they'll be the two good-lookers and while I'm not saying real life's like that there is a way people match each other, isn't there, you've only got to look round at married people. Let me hasten to say that I'm not all that good-looking myself, only about B+. Not too bad, but not all that marvelous, either.

But he didn't show up and I wanted to get on into the Pitt-Rivers, so I left her there, waiting. What I haven't said is that one of the things I go to the Pitt-Rivers for is to write poetry. I write quite a lot of poetry. I could do it at home—I often do—and it's not that I'm coy or anything, my parents know about it and they're quite interested, but I just like the idea of having a special place to go to. It's quiet there, and a bit odd like I've said, and nobody takes any notice of me. 1

Sometimes I feel I'm getting somewhere with this poetry, and other times it looks to me pretty awful. I showed a few poems to our English master[7] and he was very helpful: he said what was good and pointed out where I'd used words badly, or not worked out what I was thinking very well, so that was quite encouraging. He's a nice bloke. I like his lessons. He's very good at explaining poetry. I mean, I think poetry's amazingly difficult: sometimes you read a thing again and again and you just can't see what . . . the person's getting at. He reads all sorts of poetry to us, our English master, and you really get the hang of it after a bit—hard stuff like Hopkins and *The Hound of Heaven*,[8] and Donne. He read us some of those Donne poems about love the other day which are all very explicit and I must say first time round I hadn't quite got the point—"License my roving hands . . ." and so forth—but he wasn't embarrassed or anything, our English master, and when you realize that it's not geography he's talking about, the poet, then as a matter of fact I think that 2

7. **English master:** English teacher.
8. ***The Hound of Heaven:*** a poem by the English poet Francis Thompson (1859–1907).

WORDS TO KNOW
benign (bĭ-nīn') *adj.* gentle; mild
explicit (ĭk-splĭs'ĭt) *adj.* clear and fully expressed

Teaching Options

BLOCK SCHEDULING: MANAGING TIME

If your schedule requires that you cover the lesson objectives in a shorter time, use . . .
- Preparing to Read, p. 1199
- Thinking Through the Literature, p. 1207
- Vocabulary in Action, p. 1208

If you want to take advantage of longer class time, use . . .
- TE Teaching Options: Preteaching Vocabulary, p. 1200; Speaking and Listening, p. 1203; Viewing and Representing, p. 1204; Multicultural Link, p. 1205; Informal Assessment, p. 1206; Grammar, p. 1208
- Choices & Challenges and Author Activity, pp. 1208–1209

poem's lovely. I got a bit fed up with the way some of my mates were sniggering about it, being all-knowing; truth to tell I doubt if they know any more than I do, it's all just show. And that's a beautiful poem: I mean, if anything makes it clear that there's nothing wrong about sex, that poem does, they ought to make it compulsory reading for some people.

Anyway, I went on into the Pitt-Rivers and I was up on the first floor, in a favorite corner of mine among the arrow-heads, when I saw her again, and I must say I got quite a shock. Because the man with her was an old bloke: he
3 was older than my father, fiftyish and more, he must have been at least twenty years older than her. So I reckoned I must have made a mistake. Not that at all.

They were talking, though I couldn't hear what they were saying because they were on the far side of the gallery. They stopped in front of a case and I could see their faces quite clearly. They stood there looking at each other, not talking any more, and I realized I hadn't made a mistake after all. Absolutely not. They didn't touch each other, they just stood and looked; it seemed like ages. I don't imagine they knew I was there.

And that time I was shocked. Really shocked. I don't mind telling you, I thought it was disgusting. He was an ordinary-looking person—he might have been a schoolmaster or something, he wore those kind of clothes, old trousers and sweater, and he had greyish hair, a bit long. And there was she, and as I've said she wasn't pretty, not at all, but she had this marvelous look about her, and she was years and years younger.

It was because of him, I realized, that she had that look.

I didn't like it at all. I got up, from where I was sitting, with quite a clatter to make sure they heard me and I went stumping off out of the museum. I wasn't going to write any more poetry that day, I could see. I went off home and truth to tell I didn't really think much more about them, that man and the girl, mainly because of being rather disgusted, like I said.

A couple of weeks later they were there again. They were on the ground floor, at the back, by the rush matting[9] and ceremonial gear for with-it tribesmen, leaning up against a glass case that they weren't looking into, and talking. At least he was talking, quiet and serious, and she was listening, and nodding from time to time. I was busy with some thinking I wanted to do, and I tried not to take any notice of them; I mean, they were neither here nor there as far as I was concerned, none of my business, though I still thought it was a bit creepy. I couldn't see *why*, frankly. You fancy people your own age, and that's all there is to it, is what I thought. What I'd always thought.

So I ignored them, except that I couldn't quite. I kept sneaking a look, every now and then, and the more I did the more I felt kind of friendly towards them; I liked them. Which was a bit weird considering they didn't know I even existed—they certainly weren't interested in *me*—so it was a pretty one-sided kind of relationship. I thought he seemed like a nice bloke, whatever you thought about him and her and all that. It was something about the way he smiled, and the way he told her things (not that I ever heard a word they said, I wasn't eavesdropping, not ever, let's be quite clear about that) that made her look interested and say things back and so on. I thought it was obvious they liked talking to each other, quite apart from anything else. I thought that was nice.

I only took out that girl I mentioned—the one who came to stay with her sister—once, and

9. **rush matting:** mats made from the stems of stiff marsh plants called rushes.

WORDS TO KNOW **compulsory** (kəm-pŭl'sə-rē) *adj.* required; mandatory

Customizing Instruction

Less Proficient Readers

1 Invite students to explain what the narrator does and sees at the Pitt-Rivers. What is the boy doing in the museum?

Answer: writing poetry.

What does he see that surprises him?

Answer: A youngish woman and a fiftyish man, apparently lovers, meet. Have students continue reading to find out what else the boy notices about the couple and how it affects him; in particular, have them read to find out what it is about them that causes him to change his attitude towards their relationship.

Students Acquiring English

2 Ask a volunteer to provide a synonymous expression for *as a matter of fact.*

Possible Responses: in fact; to be honest with you.

3 Point out the suffix *-ish* (as in *fiftyish*), and ask a volunteer what it means.

Answer: about, approximately, sort of.

Ask another volunteer to guess what *fiftyish* means.

Answer: about fifty years old

Tell students to look for the same suffix elsewhere in the story.

Answer: *Greyish* appears in column one, third paragraph, page 1203, and *latish* on page 1206, first column, eighth line.

Mini Lesson Speaking and Listening

ROLE-PLAYING

Instruction In role-playing a story with no dialogue, students must be particularly imaginative in exploring how the characters move and the facial expressions they have. If they should decide to have the narrator interact with the characters, they must decide how the characters would respond, what they might say to each other, and the language they would use. Reviewing the story, perhaps in small discussion groups, making notes, and writing and rehearsing dialogue are important preliminary tasks.

Prepare Have groups of three choose one of the encounters in the museum between the narrator and the couple for a role-play activity.

Present As students perform, have others in the class critique their performance, noting whether the actions and dialogue are true to the characters and setting of the story.

BLOCK SCHEDULING This activity is particularly well-suited for longer class periods.

Reading and Analyzing

Literary Analysis: CHARACTERIZATION

A Ask students what the narrator's idea that the "best part [of his being in love with the girl] was just thinking about her" reveals about him.

Possible Responses: He is immature; he prefers the ideal to the real; he is not really in love with the girl.

Reading Skills and Strategies: SUMMARIZING

B Have students summarize the realization the narrator comes to in this paragraph.

Possible Response: In trying to imagine what the man must feel when he realizes the profound and happy effect he has on the woman, the narrator realizes that he does not really know anything about them.

Literary Analysis: THEME

C Have students discuss how the narrator's observation in this paragraph ("nobody wants to go on being a child all their lives") and the poem that he is working on might relate to the theme of the story.

Possible Responses: The narrator identifies with the so-called primitive people, who according to the boy are like children, simply not understanding how things work. The narrator himself does not want to go on being a child, and so he observes this couple to try to learn how to be a grown-up; the poem is also a reference to the theme of maturing: the boy and the old man are the same person, which represents how the boy grows out of his initial naiveté and attains some degree of maturity.

Portrait of Scott (1968), Robert Vickrey. Collection of Remson Scott Vickrey.

Teaching Options

Viewing and Representing

Portrait of Scott **by Robert Vickrey**

ART APPRECIATION Robert Vickrey is known for his experimentation with *egg tempera,* a painting process that uses egg yolk to bind pigments. This type of paint cracks when applied to canvas, so a wooden panel is used instead. The panel is sealed with glue and covered with five to eight coats of a plasterlike substance called *gesso.* The surface of the panel is then sanded to a smooth finish that looks like ivory. An ink underpainting is then applied to this surface, after which the artist applies the tempera paint in minute hatch marks that allow the white of the gesso to be preserved in successive layers of paint.

Instruction Ask students to describe the mood of the subject and how the artist conveys that mood.

Possible Responses: Both the expression on the subject's face—the tilt of the head, the downcast eyes, the sad mouth—and the artist's use of shadow help to convey a mood of brooding introspection.

Application Have students discuss whether this portrait could function as a portrait of the narrator.

Possible Responses: The boy is of approximately the right age and his serious expression matches the narrator's introspective personality.

as a matter of fact we couldn't find much to talk about. I was still in love with her—no doubt about that—but it was a bit sticky, I don't mind admitting. In fact I was quite glad when it was time to take her back to
A her sister's. In many ways the best part was just thinking about her.

I found myself imagining what it must be like being able to feel that you've made someone look like that.

Every time I looked at the girl—the Pitt-Rivers one, that is—I found myself
1 imagining what it must be like being able to feel that you've made someone look like that. Radiant, like she was. Which is what that bloke must have been able to feel. I found myself putting myself in his place, as it were, and wondering. I've done a lot of wondering about things like that—everybody does, I suppose—but mostly it's been
B more kind of basic. Now, I began to think I didn't really know anything. Looking at those two—watching them, if you like—was a bit like seeing something go on behind a thick glass window, so it was half removed from you. You could see but not hear, hear but not touch, or whatever. I could see, but I didn't know.

2 I suppose you could say I was envious, in a funny kind of way. I don't mean jealous in that I fancied the girl, or anything like that. As I've said already, she wasn't pretty, or even attractive. And I wasn't envious like you might be envious of someone for being happier than you are, because I'm not specially unhappy, as it happens. I think I was envious of them for being what they were—as though one fossil creature might be envious of a more evolved kind of fossil creature, which of course is a stupid idea.

When I was in the Pitt-Rivers again I looked for them, quite deliberately, but they weren't there. I was disappointed, though I pretended to myself it really didn't matter. I wondered about why they went there in the first place; I mean, people have to meet each other somewhere but why *there?* It doesn't exactly spring to mind as a romantic spot. I supposed there were reasons they didn't want to meet somewhere obvious and public: maybe he was married, I thought, or maybe she was, even. I wondered if that was the only place they met, or did they have others. Once walking through the botanical gardens, I found myself looking for them in the big glasshouses there.

I know the inside of the Pitt-Rivers pretty well by now. Considering it's not anthropology or ethnology[10] or whatever I went there for in the first place, it's quite surprising what a lot I could tell you about the things people believe and do. Primitive people, that is—what the Pitt-Rivers calls primitive people. And I think it's all very sad, actually: sad because it's like children, not understanding how things work and getting it all wrong, and carving each other up because of it a lot of the time. It does actually make you feel things get better—wars and bombs and everything notwithstanding. Nobody wants to go on being a child all their lives. C

I was thinking about this—looking at a case full of particularly loony stuff to do with witchcraft—when I saw them again. At least I saw her first, standing by the totem with her hands in her coat pockets, and I didn't have to look at the door to know he'd arrived: her face told you that. He came up to her and gave her a kind of hug—arm round her shoulders and then quickly off again—and they wandered away up the stairs, heads together, talking.

I didn't follow them; it had been nice to see them again, and know they were there, and that was it. I was busy on a poem I'd been writing and unpicking and rewriting for some time. It was a poem about an old man sitting on a bench in a park and getting into conversation with a boy—someone around my age—and they swap 3
opinions and observations (it's all dialogue, this poem, like a long conversation) and it's not till the end you realize they're the same person. It sounds

10. **ethnology** (ĕth-nŏl′ə-jē): the branch of anthropology that involves the study and comparison of human cultures.

Customizing Instruction

Less Proficient Readers

1 Ask students how the man makes the woman feel, according to the narrator.

Answer: very happy; radiant

Students Acquiring English

2 Point out to students that the verb *fancy* means "attracted to" here.

Gifted and Talented

3 Have students imagine the content of the poem that the narrator is working on, and then try to write it as they imagine the narrator would have.

Multicultural Link — Anthropology

The narrator takes issue with the museum's use of the term *primitive.* As applied to nonliterate or nonindustrial cultures, the term is no longer widely accepted in the field of anthropology, which has come to view all cultures as valid adaptations to their own specific circumstances, which may include environment, history, beliefs, and cross-cultural interactions. In the 19th and early 20th centuries, anthropologists did much of their most significant work among tribal peoples, such as the Nuer of the Sudan, the Bushmen of South Africa, the aborigines of Australia, the Trobriand Islanders of the South Pacific, and the natives of both American continents. More recently, the scope of anthropology has widened to include the study of peasant villages, such as those of Mexico or India, and of ethnic groups in the industrial world, such as the Amish or the Hasidic Jews of the United States.

AT THE PITT-RIVERS **1205**

Reading and Analyzing

Literary Analysis: CLIMAX

A Remind students that the climax is the point in the story where the action reaches its height, or the conflict reaches a turning point and is decided one way or another. The climax usually results in some change in the characters or a solution to the conflict. The resolution usually shows the effects of the climax on the main character or characters, or it may simply tie up loose ends. Have students identify the climax of the story and explain its resolution.

Possible Response: The climax occurs when the narrator realizes that the couple are breaking up. The woman is devastated; the narrator is disappointed, perhaps disillusioned, realizes that he has learned something from the experience, and decides to tear up his poem.

Active Reading

DRAWING CONCLUSIONS ABOUT THE NARRATOR

B Have students read the last paragraph carefully to decide why the narrator tears up his poem.

Possible Responses: He no longer feels that people of different ages can understand each other; he realizes that there is still much about life he does not understand, and so he believes the poem to be inadequate or immature; he is disillusioned about life and love and his own feelings about them.

I don't know what had happened. I never will.

either corny, or pretentious, I know; and what I could never decide was whether to have it as though the old man's looking back, or the boy's kind of projecting forward—imagining himself, as it were. So I went on fiddling about with this, and didn't really think much about the man and the girl, until I saw it was latish and there was no one else in the museum except me and some feet on the wooden floor of the gallery overhead, walking round and round, round and round. Two pairs of feet. They'd been doing that for ages, I realized; I'd been hearing them without registering.

I saw them go past—just their heads, above the glass cases—and something wasn't right. They weren't talking. She had her arm through his, and she was looking straight in front of her, and when I saw her face I had a nasty kind of twinge in my stomach. Because she was miserable. Once, she looked at him, and they both managed a bleak sort of smile. And then they walked on, round the gallery again, and next time past they still weren't talking, just holding on to each other like that, like people who're ill, or very old. And then the attendant rang the bell, and I heard them come down the stairs, and they came past me and went out into the Natural History Museum.

I went after them. I saw them stop—under the central whale, just where I first saw her—and then they did say something to each other. I couldn't see her face; she had her back to me. He went off then, on his own, out through the main entrance, quickly, and she sat down on a bench. For a moment or two she just sat staring at that wretched whale, and then she felt in her bag and got out a comb and did her hair, as though that might help. And then she dropped the comb and didn't seem to have noticed, even, because she just sat; she didn't bother to pick it up or anything. I could see her face then, and I hope I don't ever see anyone look so unhappy again. I truly hope that. **A**

I don't know what had happened. I never will. Somehow, I don't think they were ever going to see each other again, but why . . . well, that's their concern, just like the rest of it was, except that in this peculiar way I'd come to feel it was mine too. I didn't think there was anything disgusting about them any more, or creepy—I hadn't for a long time. I suppose you could say I'd learned something else in the Pitt-Rivers, by accident. I never did go on with that poem. I tore it up, as far as it had got; I wasn't so sure any more about that conversation, that there could even be one, or not like I'd been imagining, anyway. ❖ **B**

WORDS TO KNOW

pretentious (prĭ-tĕn'shəs) *adj.* marked by an artificial display intended to impress others

bleak (blēk) *adj.* gloomy; hopeless

Teaching Options

Assessment Informal Assessment

WRITING AN ESSAY

Have students write a multiparagraph essay in which they perform the following tasks:

- Summarize the plot of "At the Pitt-Rivers."
- Discuss the importance of the setting as it relates to the theme of the story.
- Describe the narrator and what insight into life he acquires.

RUBRIC

3 Full Accomplishment Response effectively and succinctly summarizes plot, showing complete understanding of events of story, and communicates full understanding of setting, characterization, and theme.

2 Substantial Accomplishment Response effectively summarizes plot and shows general understanding of setting and character, but may only partially explain theme or fail to relate it to setting or character.

1 Little or Partial Accomplishment Response is incomplete or overly detailed summary and shows little understanding of setting, character, or theme.

Thinking through the LITERATURE

Connect to the Literature

1. **What Do You Think?** Did you like the narrator in this story? Why or why not?

Comprehension Check
- Why is the narrator surprised that the man and woman are a couple?
- What happens to the couple at the end of the story?

Think Critically

2. Why do you think the **narrator** becomes so interested in the woman at the museum?

3. How would you explain the narrator's reaction to the couple the first time he observed them?

4. The narrator says that he "learned something else in the Pitt-Rivers, by accident." What do you think he learned?

5. Why do you think the narrator tore up his poem at the end of the story?

- how the narrator's opinion of the couple has changed
- how he feels when he sees the woman's unhappy face
- what the narrator means when he says, "I wasn't so sure any more about that conversation"

6. **ACTIVE READING** **DRAWING CONCLUSIONS ABOUT THE NARRATOR** Based on the information you recorded in the chart in your **READER'S NOTEBOOK**, what conclusions can you draw about the **narrator** and about the couple he encounters? Did your opinion of the couple or of the boy change as you read the story?

Extend Interpretations

7. **Critic's Corner** Critic John Mellors said of Lively: "She is particularly good at showing how one generation looks at, or ignores, the activities and preoccupations of another." Describe how this comment applies to "At the Pitt-Rivers." Use evidence from the story to support your opinion.

8. **Connect to Life** Consider the narrator's thoughts, feelings, and interests. In your estimation, is he a believable teenager? In other words, does he seem like a real person, like someone you might know? Why or why not?

Literary Analysis

SETTING Setting is one of the main elements in fiction and often plays an important role in what happens and why. In many stories, the setting, or time and place of the action, is critical to a complete understanding of the plot and characters. In other stories, the setting plays a more subtle role, perhaps supporting or enhancing the theme. In the following passage from "At the Pitt-Rivers," notice how the museum setting reflects the relationship between the couple and the narrator:

A couple of weeks later they were there again. They were on the ground floor, at the back, by the rush matting and ceremonial gear for with-it tribesmen, leaning up against a glass case that they weren't looking into, and talking. . . . I kept sneaking a look, every now and then, and the more I did the more I felt kind of friendly towards them. . . .

Paired Activity Consider both the atmosphere and the function of the Pitt-Rivers Museum. Why do you think Lively chose it as the setting for this story? With a partner, complete a diagram like the one shown. Briefly describe the story's setting, and then note ways in which the setting connects to the plot, characters, and theme of the story.

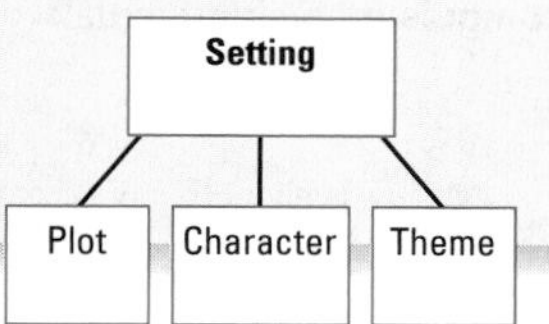

GUIDING STUDENT RESPONSE

Connect to the Literature

1. **What Do You Think?** Guidelines for student response: Students may choose to connect characteristics of the narrator with personality traits they have encountered in their own real-life experience.

Comprehension Check
- because the man is so much older than the woman
- They appear to break up.

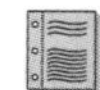 Use Selection Quiz in **Unit Seven Resource Book** p. 8.

Think Critically

2. Possible Response: Her radiant expression arouses his interest.
3. Possible Responses: He finds their age difference shocking; he is fascinated or he wouldn't be observing them so closely.
4. Possible Responses: that he had a lot to learn about love; that love is not limited to certain ages or to "beautiful" people; that love can be bitter as well as sweet
5. Possible Response: He felt embarrassed by his previous naiveté and immaturity.
6. Accept all thoughtful responses. Students should note that the boy's responses change over time.

Extend Interpretations

Critic's Corner Possible Response: the younger generation (the boy) observes the activities of the older generation (the couple), who ignore him.

Connect to Life Accept all reasonable, well-supported responses.

Literary Analysis

Paired Activity Some students may say that the setting of an anthropology museum is appropriate, since the boy is acquiring knowledge of his culture's customs by observing the couple. Others may see a contrast between what the boy goes to the museum intending to do and what he actually does there.

AT THE PITT-RIVERS 1207

Writing Options

1. **Narrator's Poem** Students may write in free verse or in traditional forms. Encourage them to write in the narrator's first-person voice.
2. **Character Sketch** Allow students to write either from the narrator's first-person point of view or from an omniscient third-person point of view.
3. **Short Story Plot** Students may work independently or in pairs or small groups. Encourage them to read their summaries aloud.
4. **Museum Description** Remind students to describe the ambiance of the museum as well as physical details.

Activities & Explorations

1. **Dramatic Conversation** Encourage students to prepare by discussing the characters, writing either a dialogue script or detailed notes, and then rehearsing. Encourage several pairs to present their interpretations to the class.
2. **Silent Movie** In addition to standard filmmaking roles such as director, actors, and camera operator, students may wish to write subtitles, take charge of costumes and props, and put together a musical score.
3. **Natural History Museum** Encourage students to visit a local museum or take an online virtual tour of a museum for ideas. Stress to them that the exhibits in their museum should be relevant to their local community.

Inquiry & Research

Museum Origins If students are writing about a local museum, encourage them to visit it as part of their research. Students might start at the information desk and, after explaining their purpose, visit the office of a museum official. Students might also telephone or use electronic mail or the World Wide Web as part of their research.

Vocabulary in Action

1. c
2. d
3. b
4. e
5. a

Writing Options

1. **Narrator's Poem** As the narrator of this story, write a poem expressing your feelings about the couple.
2. **Character Sketch** Write a character sketch of the narrator based on what he reveals about himself and on your own judgment of his attitudes.
3. **Short Story Plot** Unravel the mystery of the couple at the Pitt-Rivers Museum. Outline the plot for a short story that focuses on their relationship.
4. **Museum Description** Write a two-paragraph description of a museum you have enjoyed visiting. Be sure to tell what kind of museum it was, what sorts of exhibits it had, and where it is located. Use the narrator's description of the Pitt-Rivers as a model for your description.

Activities & Explorations

1. **Dramatic Conversation** With a partner, rehearse and present a dramatization of a conversation the narrator might have had with the woman in the story. ~ **PERFORMING**
2. **Silent Movie** Plan and shoot a silent movie that depicts a variety of relationships and conversations between couples of all ages. Stage your film with friends or family members role-playing the different couples. Share your work with the class. ~ **VIEWING AND REPRESENTING**
3. **Natural History Museum** Imagine that you are in charge of designing and planning a natural history museum for your community. What sorts of exhibitions would you want to present? Draw up a floor plan for your museum and sketch in the sorts of exhibits you would mount. ~ **ART**

Inquiry & Research

Museum Origins Research the origins of a famous museum or a museum in your community. Find out why the museum was founded, who funded it, and what its early collections consisted of. Share your information with the class in an oral report.

Vocabulary in Action

EXERCISE: SYNONYMS

For each phrase in the first column, write the letter of the synonymous phrase from the second column.

1. **pretentious** nonsense	a. mandatory story
2. **explicit** counsel	b. **benign** design
3. harmless scheme	c. **phony** baloney
4. dreary pinnacle	d. precise advice
5. **compulsory** bedtime ritual	e. **bleak** peak

Building Vocabulary
For an in-depth lesson on how to use a thesaurus to find a word's synonyms, see page 575.

WORDS TO KNOW: benign bleak compulsory explicit pretentious

Teaching Options

Grammar

VARYING TYPES OF SENTENCES

Instruction A sentence can be one of four structural types: simple, compound, complex, or compound-complex. A simple sentence contains one independent clause (a clause that can stand alone). A compound sentence has two or more independent clauses joined together. A complex sentence contains one independent clause and one or more subordinate clauses (clauses that cannot stand on their own). A compound-complex sentence has two or more independent clauses and one or more subordinate clauses. Remind students that a skillful writer uses all of these types.

Activity Write the following sentences on the chalkboard.

"You'll always get an audience for a dinosaur and a few nasty-looking jellyfish in formalin."

"If they're attractive they have lots of blokes after them and if they're not they don't."

"But he didn't show up and I wanted to get on into the Pitt-Rivers, so I left her there, waiting."

"The second time was last year, when I was fifteen."

Penelope Lively

1933–

Other Works
"Customers"
"Miss Carlton and the Pop Concert"
"A World of Her Own"
"Yellow Trains"
"Black Dogs"

Egyptian Childhood In a memoir of her childhood called *Oleander, Jacaranda,* Penelope Lively describes what it was like growing up in Egypt—a culture that included mosquito netting, water buffalo, pyramids, and annual visits from the snake charmer. Although her parents were English, Lively was born in Egypt, which at that time was a protectorate of the British government. Her father had moved from England as a young man to accept a position with the National Bank of Egypt. Lively's world was vastly different from that of her English contemporaries, but it was a world she would desperately miss when forced to leave Cairo at the age of 12.

School in England While living in Egypt, Lively was educated at home by her governess, who used a program designed for teaching English children living in foreign countries. In 1945, after the divorce of her parents, she was sent to England and enrolled in a boarding school. For a long time, Lively was an unhappy exile, living in an unfamiliar country and attending a school where success was equated with athletic and social skills rather than intellectual ability. It was a family friend who eventually sparked Lively's interest in history, an interest she later pursued at Oxford University.

Writing Career Lively has earned considerable recognition as a versatile author. She has successfully woven her historical knowledge into numerous books for younger readers, including *The Ghost of Thomas Kempe* and *A Stitch in Time.* In the late 1970s, after writing juvenile literature for about ten years, the author turned her energies to adult fiction, writing both novels and short stories.

Author Activity

Growing Up in Egypt Get a copy of *Oleander, Jacaranda* at a library and find out more about Lively's childhood in Egypt. Choose one or two incidents that you find especially interesting and share them with the class.

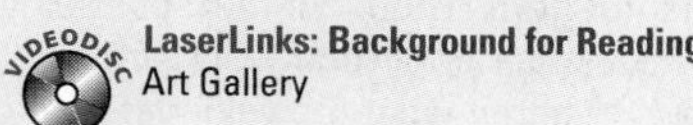

LaserLinks: Background for Reading
Art Gallery

Author Activity

Growing Up in Egypt You might also suggest gathering photographs and magazine articles dealing with Egypt.

Have students identify each type of sentence. *(simple, compound-complex, compound, complex)*

Exercise Ask students to identify each type of sentence. Have students meet in cooperative groups to change each sentence to a different type of sentence.

1. When the narrator first saw the girl, she was in the Natural History Museum. *(complex)*
2. The girl met an older man, and they walked around the museum gallery together. *(compound)*
3. At first the narrator, who was uncomfortable with the couple, left the museum, but when the couple returned two weeks later, he stayed and watched them. *(compound-complex)*
4. Eventually the narrator deliberately looked for the couple in the museum. *(simple)*

Use **Grammar Transparencies and Copymasters,** p. 118.

Use McDougal Littell's ***Language Network*** for more instruction in types of sentences.

OVERVIEW

This selection is included in the **Grade 12 InterActive Reader.**

Objectives

1. appreciate the author's use of **kinesthetic imagery (Literary Analysis)**
2. appreciate and understand the author's use of the **third-person limited point of view (Literary Analysis)**
3. **analyze character development (Active Reading)**

Summary

A boy in southern Africa considers himself invincible and fully in control of all aspects of his existence. One morning when he is out on his customary rumble through the veld, he sees an injured buck being killed and eaten by a swarm of ants. The painful and ignominious death of the graceful creature punctures the boy's sense of invincibility and forces him to contemplate mortality.

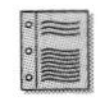

Use **Unit Seven Resource Book,** p. 9 for additional support.

Thematic Link

In this story, the main character looks past **appearances into reality** and catches a glimpse of his own mortality.

5-Minute Warm-Up

Daily Language SkillBuilder

Have students **proofread** the display sentences on page 1189i and write them correctly. The sentences also appear on Transparency 33 of **Grammar Transparencies and Copymasters.**

"There was nothing he couldn't do, nothing!"

A Sunrise on the Veld

Short Story by DORIS LESSING

Connect to Your Life

Changing Your Mind Consider how easy or hard it is for you to change your ideas and viewpoints. How do you respond when an experience leads you to new insights? Do you enjoy being challenged to see the world in a new way or to think about your life from a different perspective? Jot down some of your thoughts.

Build Background

Growing Up on the Veld Doris Lessing grew up on a farm in the African country of Southern Rhodesia (rō-dē′zha), today known as Zimbabwe (zĭm-bäb′wē). The farm was situated on the edge of the veld (fĕlt), a vast grassy land having only a few bushes and almost no trees, but a land that teemed with wildlife in the years of Lessing's childhood. She spent her youth exploring her surroundings and later claimed that her real education came not from school but from observing nature on the veld. In her nonfiction work *African Laughter,* she wrote about what the veld was like for her and her brother:

> ***Lying in our blankets under the trees on the sandveld of Marandellas, or in the house on the farm in Banket, the shrilling, clamoring, exulting of the birds as the sun appeared was so loud the ears seemed to curl up and complain before . . . we leaped up into the early morning, to become part of all that tumult and activity.***

Not surprisingly, the same veld that taught Lessing so much about nature and life became the setting for many of her stories, including "A Sunrise on the Veld."

WORDS TO KNOW
Vocabulary Preview

fastidious
incredulously
myriad
superfluity
vigilant

LaserLinks: Background for Reading
Zoological Connection

Focus Your Reading

LITERARY ANALYSIS KINESTHETIC IMAGERY

In addition to using **imagery** that relates to the five senses—sight, hearing, taste, touch, and smell—Lessing employs **kinesthetic imagery.** Kinesthetic imagery re-creates the tension felt through muscles, tendons, or joints in the body, as in the following description from "A Sunrise on the Veld":

> ***As soon as he stepped over the lintel, the flesh of his soles contracted on the chilled earth. . . .***

Look for other examples of kinesthetic imagery.

ACTIVE READING ANALYZING CHARACTER DEVELOPMENT **Characters** frequently change over the course of a narrative. A key event often precipitates this change. Being aware of a character's thoughts and actions can help you figure out what event causes a character to change and how the character develops as a result.

READER'S NOTEBOOK As you read "A Sunrise on the Veld," fill out a chart like the one shown, listing the boy's thoughts and actions.

Thoughts	Actions

LESSON RESOURCES

UNIT SEVEN RESOURCE BOOK, pp. 9–13

ASSESSMENT RESOURCES
Formal Assessment, pp. 221–222
Teacher's Guide to Assessment and Portfolio Use
Test Generator

SKILLS TRANSPARENCIES AND COPYMASTERS

Literary Analysis
- Characterization, T21 (for Active Reading, p. 1210)

Reading and Critical Thinking
- Compare and Contrast, T15 (for Extend Interpretations 7, p. 1217)

Grammar
- Avoiding Misplaced and Dangling Modifiers, T51 (for Mini Lesson, pp. 1218–1219)
- Movable Adjectives, C91 (for Mini Lesson, pp. 1218–1219)

Vocabulary
- Word Origins, C91 (for Mini Lesson, p. 1211)

Writing
- Sensory Word List, T14 (for Writing Option 3, p. 1218)
- Showing, Not Telling, T22 (for Writing Option 1, p. 1218)

Communications
- Impromptu Speaking: Dialogue, Role-Play, T14 (for Activities & Explorations 3, p. 1218)

INTEGRATED TECHNOLOGY

LaserLinks
- Zoological Connection: The African Veld
- Science Connection: Army Ants. See **Teacher's SourceBook,** pp. 87–88.

Internet: Research Starter
Visit our website:
www.mcdougallittell.com

A SUNRISE ON THE VELD

DORIS LESSING

Every night that winter he said aloud into the dark of the pillow: Half-past four! Half-past four! till he felt his brain had gripped the words and held them fast. Then he fell asleep at once, as if a shutter had fallen; and lay with his face turned to the clock so that he could see it first thing when he woke.

It was half-past four to the minute, every morning. Triumphantly pressing down the alarm-knob of the clock, which the dark half of his mind had outwitted, remaining vigilant all night and counting the hours as he lay relaxed in sleep, he huddled down for a last warm moment under the clothes, playing with the idea of lying abed for this once only. But he played with it for the fun of knowing that it was a weakness he could defeat without effort; just as he set the alarm each night for the delight of the moment when he woke and stretched his limbs, feeling the muscles tighten, and thought: Even my brain—even that! I can control every part of myself.

Luxury of warm rested body, with the arms and legs and fingers waiting like soldiers for a word of command! Joy of knowing that the precious hours were given to sleep voluntarily!—for he had once stayed awake three nights running, to prove that he could, and then worked all day, refusing even to

WORDS TO KNOW **vigilant** (vĭj′ə-lənt) *adj.* ever watchful and alert

1211

TEACHING THE LITERATURE

Customizing Instruction

Less Proficient Readers
Set a Purpose Have students read to find out why the boy is rising so early.

Students Acquiring English
Lessing's descriptive style may confuse some students. Help clarify meanings by reading examples of imagery and description aloud. Suggest that students try to describe the boy's emotion in their own words.

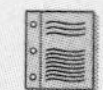
Use **Spanish Study Guide** for additional support, pp. 293–295.

Gifted and Talented
Ask students to come up with as many plausible reasons as possible to explain why the boy desires to exert so much self-control over his mind and body. Have them discuss whether that much self-control is a positive or negative attribute, both in this story and in everyday life.

Preteaching Vocabulary

WORD ORIGINS
Instruction Call students' attention to the WORDS TO KNOW. Point out to them that finding the origins of a word can be quite interesting, can sometimes help in understanding a word better, and can often give insight into the meanings of words with similar spellings derived from the same parent word.

Activity Have students use a dictionary to find the origins of each of the WORDS TO KNOW. Have them write the earliest form of the word and what language it came from.

Use **Unit Seven Resource Book** p. 12 for more practice.

A lesson on word origins appears on page 206 in the Pupil's Edition .

Reading and Analyzing

Active Reading

ANALYZING CHARACTER DEVELOPMENT

Ask students to discuss what sort of person the boy might be, based on what they see in the first paragraphs of the story.

Possible Responses: He seems very confident of himself; he is very disciplined; he might be overly proud of his self-discipline.

Have students read to find out whether this initial impression holds up as the story progresses and whether the boy changes in any way by the end of the story.

 Use **Unit Seven Resource Book** p. 10 for more practice.

Literary Analysis

KINESTHETIC IMAGERY

Have students read to find examples of kinesthetic imagery in the opening pages. Allow a liberal interpretation of the term so that they will be receptive to the more explicit examples of it that occur later in the story.

Possible Responses: "his brain gripped the words"; "huddled down for a last warm moment"; "luxury of warm rested body, with the arms and legs and fingers waiting like soldiers."

Ask students why an author might want to use this type of imagery.

Possible Response: to make the reader experience the story more fully.

 Use **Unit Seven Resource Book** p. 11 for more exercises.

admit that he was tired; and now sleep seemed to him a servant to be commanded and refused.

The boy stretched his frame full-length, touching the wall at his head with his hands, and the bedfoot with his toes; then he sprung out, like a fish leaping from water. And it was cold, cold.

He always dressed rapidly, so as to try and conserve his night-warmth till the sun rose two hours later; but by the time he had on his clothes his hands were numbed and he could scarcely hold his shoes. These he could not put on for fear of waking his parents, who never came to know how early he rose.

THE AIR SMELLED OF MORNING AND THE STARS WERE DIMMING.

As soon as he stepped over the lintel,[1] the flesh of his soles contracted on the chilled earth, and his legs began to ache with cold. It was night: the stars were glittering, the trees standing black and still. He looked for signs of day, for the greying of the edge of a stone, or a lightening in the sky where the sun would rise, but there was nothing yet. Alert as an animal he crept past the dangerous window, standing poised with his hand on the sill for one proudly fastidious moment, looking in at the stuffy blackness of the room where his parents lay.

Feeling for the grass-edge of the path with his toes, he reached inside another window further along the wall, where his gun had been set in readiness the night before. The steel was icy, and numbed fingers slipped along it, so that he had to hold it in the crook of his arm for safety. Then he tiptoed to the room where the dogs slept, and was fearful that they might have been tempted to go before him; but they were waiting, their haunches crouched in reluctance at the cold, but ears and swinging tails greeting the gun ecstatically. His warning undertone kept them secret and silent till the house was a hundred yards back: then they bolted off into the bush, yelping excitedly. The boy imagined his parents turning in their beds and muttering: Those dogs again! before they were dragged back in sleep; and he smiled scornfully. He always looked back over his shoulder at the house before he passed a wall of trees that shut it from sight. It looked so low and small, crouching there under a tall and brilliant sky. Then he turned his back on it, and on the frowsting[2] sleepers, and forgot them.

He would have to hurry. Before the light grew strong he must be four miles away; and already a tint of green stood in the hollow of a leaf, and the air smelled of morning and the stars were dimming.

He slung the shoes over his shoulder, veld *skoen*[3] that were crinkled and hard with the dews of a hundred mornings. They would be necessary when the ground became too hot to bear. Now he felt the chilled dust push up between his toes, and he let the muscles of his feet spread and settle into the shapes of the earth; and he thought: I could walk a hundred miles on feet like these! I could walk all day, and never tire!

He was walking swiftly through the dark tunnel of foliage that in day-time was a road. The dogs were invisibly ranging the lower travelways of the bush, and he heard them panting. Sometimes he felt a cold muzzle on his leg before they were off again, scouting for a trail to follow. They were not trained, but free-running companions of the hunt, who often tired of the long stalk before the final shots, and went off on their own pleasure. Soon he could see them, small and wild-looking in a wild

1. **lintel:** used here to mean "threshold" (the wood or stone sill at the bottom of a doorway).
2. **frowsting** (frou'stĭng): a British term for lounging about.
3. ***skoen*** (sko͞on) *Afrikaans:* shoes.

WORDS TO KNOW **fastidious** (fă-stĭd'ē-əs) *adj.* displaying meticulous attention to detail

1212

Teaching Options

BLOCK SCHEDULING: MANAGING TIME

If your schedule requires that you cover the lesson objectives in a shorter time, use . . .
- Preparing to Read, p. 1210
- Thinking Through the Literature, p. 1217
- Vocabulary in Action, p. 1218

If you want to take advantage of longer class time, use . . .
- TE Teaching Options: Preteaching Vocabulary, p. 1211; Viewing and Representing, p. 1214; Cross Curricular Link, p. 1215; Informal Assessment, p. 1216; Grammar, p. 1218
- Choices & Challenges and Author Activity, pp. 1218–1219

strange light, now that the bush stood trembling on the verge of color, waiting for the sun to paint earth and grass afresh.

The grass stood to his shoulders; and the trees were showering a faint silvery rain. He was soaked; his whole body was clenched in a steady shiver.

Once he bent to the road that was newly scored with animal trails, and regretfully straightened, reminding himself that the pleasure of tracking must wait till another day.

He began to run along the edge of a field, noting jerkily how it was filmed over with fresh spiderweb, so that the long reaches of great black clods seemed netted in glistening grey. He was using the steady lope he had learned by watching the natives, the run that is a dropping of the weight of the body from one foot to the next in a slow balancing movement that never tires, nor shortens the breath; and he felt the blood pulsing down his legs and along his arms, and the exultation and pride of body mounted in him till he was shutting his teeth hard against a violent desire to shout his triumph.

Soon he had left the cultivated part of the farm. Behind him the bush was low and black. In front was a long vlei,[4] acres of long pale grass that sent back a hollowing gleam of light to a satiny sky. Near him thick swathes of grass were bent with the weight of water, and diamond drops sparkled on each frond.

The first bird woke at his feet and at once a flock of them sprang into the air calling shrilly that day had come; and suddenly, behind him, the bush woke into song, and he could hear the guinea fowl[5] calling far ahead of him. That meant they would now be sailing down from their trees into thick grass, and it was for them he had come: he was too late. But he did not mind. He forgot he had come to shoot. He set his legs wide, and balanced from foot to foot, and swung his gun up and down in both hands horizontally, in a kind of improvised exercise, and let his head sink back till it was pillowed in his neck muscles, and watched how above him small rosy clouds floated in a lake of gold.

Suddenly it all rose in him: it was unbearable. He leapt up into the air, shouting and yelling wild, unrecognizable noises. Then he began to run, not carefully, as he had before, but madly, like a wild thing. He was clean crazy, yelling mad with the joy of living and a superfluity of youth. He rushed **1** down the vlei under a tumult of crimson and gold, while all the birds of the world sang about him. He ran in great leaping strides, and shouted as he ran, feeling his body rise into the crisp rushing air and fall back surely on to sure feet; and thought briefly, not believing that such a thing could happen to him, that he could break his ankle any moment, in this thick tangled grass. He cleared bushes like a duiker,[6] leapt over rocks; and finally came to a dead stop at a place where the ground fell abruptly away below him to the river. It had been a two-mile-long dash through waist-high growth, and he was breathing hoarsely and could no longer sing. But he poised on a rock and looked down at stretches of water that gleamed through stooping trees, and thought suddenly, I am fifteen! Fifteen! The words came new to him; so that he kept repeating them wonderingly, with swelling excitement; and he felt the years of his life with his hands, as if he were counting marbles, each one hard and separate and compact, each one a wonderful shining thing. That was what he was: fifteen years of this rich soil, and this slow-moving water, and air that smelt like a challenge whether it was warm and sultry at noon, or as brisk as cold water, like it was now.

There was nothing he couldn't do, nothing! A vision came to him, as he stood there, like when a child hears the word "eternity" and tries to understand it, and time takes possession of the mind. He felt his life ahead of him as a great and wonderful thing, something that was his; and he

4. **vlei** (flā): low, swampy land.
5. **guinea fowl:** pheasantlike birds that have dark gray bodies flecked with white.
6. **duiker** (dī′kər): small African antelope.

WORDS TO KNOW
superfluity (so͞o′pər-flo͞o′ĭ-tē) *n.* excess; overabundance; oversupply

Customizing Instruction

Less Proficient Readers

Make sure that students understand how the boy tries to exercise control over himself. Ask them what he does every morning to prove he has control over his mind.

Answer: He wakes himself up at exactly 4:30 without using an alarm clock. How does his ability to control his mind and body make him feel?

Possible Responses: triumphant; in control; superior to his parents and perhaps everyone else.

Students Acquiring English

1 Invite students to try to understand this description of the boy's emotion by thinking about different ways they have heard the word *clean* used. Have them discuss the meaning of the phrases "clean sweep" and "clean out of luck." Ask students what *clean* means in this sentence.

Answer: completely, thoroughly.

Multiple Learning Styles

Visual Learners

Invite students to create a map of the boy's journey based on the description provided in the story. Students can include drawings of the places depicted such as the boy's house, the river gorge, and the site of the buck's death, as well as markings to indicate the end of the cultivated farmland and the beginning of the wild veld.

Reading and Analyzing

Literary Analysis: SUSPENSE

A Ask students to point out elements of the situation that create suspense.

Possible Response: the awareness that he is alone; the strange scream; the beating of his heart; his sudden caution as compared to his previous recklessness; the mention of a leopard.

Reading Skills and Strategies: SUMMARIZING

B Have students briefly summarize the boy's feelings from the paragraph beginning with "It came into his mind . . ." to the paragraph ending with ". . . the sweat of the other creature's pain."

Possible Response: The boy tries to convince himself that what happens to the buck is natural and right, and that he should not care or interfere. Just as he feels "satisfied with his new stoicism," he finds himself crying over the buck's fate.

Horned Forms (1944), Graham Sutherland. Tate Gallery, London/Art Resource, New York.

said aloud, with the blood rising to his head: all the great men of the world have been as I am now, and there is nothing I can't become, nothing I can't do; there is no country in the world I cannot make part of myself, if I choose. I contain the world. I can make of it what I want. If I choose, I can change everything that is going to happen: it depends on me, and what I decide now.

The urgency, and the truth and the courage of what his voice was saying exulted him so that he began to sing again, at the top of his voice, and the sound went echoing down the river gorge. He stopped for the echo, and sang again: stopped and shouted. That was what he was!—he sang, if he chose; and the world had to answer him.

And for minutes he stood there, shouting and singing and waiting for the lovely eddying[7] sound of the echo; so that his own new strong thoughts came back and washed round his head, as if someone were answering him and encouraging him; till the gorge was full of soft voices clashing back and forth from rock to rock over the river. And then it seemed as if there was a new voice. He listened, puzzled, for it was not his own. Soon he was leaning forward, all his nerves alert, quite still: somewhere close to him there was a noise that was no joyful bird, nor tinkle of falling water, nor ponderous[8] movement of cattle.

There it was again. In the deep morning hush that held his future and his past, was a sound of pain, and repeated over and over: it was a kind of shortened scream, A
as if someone, something, had no breath
to scream. He came to himself, looked 1
about him, and called for the dogs. They did not appear: they had gone off on their own business, and he was alone. Now he was clean sober, all the madness gone. His heart beating fast, because of that frightened screaming, he stepped carefully off the rock and went towards a belt of trees. He was moving cautiously, for not so long ago he had seen a leopard in just this spot.

At the edge of the trees he stopped and peered, holding his gun ready; he advanced, looking steadily about him, his eyes narrowed. Then, all at once, in the middle of a step, he faltered, and his face was puzzled. He shook his head impatiently, as if he doubted his own sight.

There, between two trees, against a background of gaunt black rocks, was a figure from a dream, a strange beast that was horned and drunken-legged, but like something he had never even imagined. It seemed to be ragged. It looked like a small buck

7. **eddying** (ĕd′ē-ĭng): moving contrary to the main current; circling.

8. **ponderous:** clumsy because of heaviness and size.

Teaching Options

Viewing and Representing

Horned Forms **by Graham Sutherland**

ART APPRECIATION Born in England in 1903, Graham Sutherland started as an engraver, but turned to painting in the 1930s. He took little interest in the prevailing surrealist movement, developing instead a highly individual, often abstract style, of which this painting is a typical example.

Instruction Have students discuss how the image, while unnatural, still conveys a distinct impression or emotion. Ask students to describe this impression.

Possible Response: The painting resembles the carcass of an unknown creature and carries with it feelings of death, desolation, and loneliness.

Application Ask students which part of the story has the closest relation to the art, and how the painting's colors help convey this connection.

Possible Response: The death of the buck has the closest connection to the painting. The dark, angular shape recalls the destructive capabilities of the ants, while the white horns recall the carcass of the buck. The reds and yellows call to mind the sands and grasses of the veld.

that had black ragged tufts of fur standing up irregularly all over it, with patches of raw flesh beneath . . . but the patches of rawness were disappearing under moving black and came again elsewhere; and all the time the creature screamed, in small gasping screams, and leaped drunkenly from side to side, as if it were blind.

Then the boy understood: it *was* a buck. He ran closer, and again stood still, stopped by a new fear. Around him the grass was whispering and alive. He looked wildly about, and then down. The ground was black with ants, great energetic ants that took no notice of him, but hurried and scurried towards the fighting shape, like glistening black water flowing through the grass.

And, as he drew in his breath and pity and terror seized him, the beast fell and the screaming stopped. Now he could hear nothing but one bird singing, and the sound of the rustling, whispering ants.

He peered over at the writhing blackness that jerked convulsively with the jerking nerves. It grew quieter. There were small twitches from the mass that still looked vaguely like the shape of a small animal.

It came into his mind that he should shoot it and end its pain; and he raised the gun. Then he lowered it again. The buck could no longer feel; its fighting was a mechanical protest of the nerves. But it was not that which made him put down the gun. It was a swelling feeling of rage and misery and protest that expressed itself in the thought: if I had not come it would have died like this: so why should I interfere? All over the
B bush things like this happen; they happen all the time; this is how life goes on, by living things dying in anguish. He gripped the gun between his knees and felt in his own limbs the myriad swarming pain of the twitching animal that could no longer feel, and set his teeth, and said over and over again under his breath: I can't stop it. I can't stop it. There is nothing I can do.

He was glad that the buck was unconscious and had gone past suffering so that he did not have to make a decision to kill it even when he was feeling with his whole body: this is what happens, this is how things work.

It was right—that was what he was feeling. *It was right and nothing could alter it.*

The knowledge of fatality, of what has to be, had gripped him and for the first time in his life; and he was left unable to make any movement of brain or body, except to say: "Yes, yes. That is what living is." It had entered his flesh and his bones and grown in to the furthest corners of his brain and would never leave him. And at that moment he could not have performed the smallest action of mercy, knowing as he did, having lived on it all his life, the vast unalterable, cruel veld, where at any moment one might stumble over a skull or crush the skeleton of some small creature.

Suffering, sick, and angry, but also grimly satisfied with his new stoicism,[9] he stood there leaning on his rifle, and watched the seething black mound grow smaller. At his feet, now, were ants trickling back with pink fragments in their mouths, and there was a fresh acid smell in his nostrils. He sternly controlled the uselessly convulsing muscles of his empty stomach, and reminded himself: the ants must eat too! At the same time he found that the tears were streaming down his face, and his clothes were soaked with the sweat of that other creature's pain.

The shape had grown small. Now it looked like nothing recognizable. He did not know how long it was before he saw the blackness thin, and bits of white showed through, shining in the sun—yes, there was the sun, just up, glowing over the rocks. Why, the whole thing could not have taken longer than a few minutes.

He began to swear, as if the shortness of the time was in itself unbearable, using the words he had heard his father say. He strode forward, crushing ants with each step, and brushing them

9. **stoicism** (stō′ĭ-sĭz′əm): calm acceptance of events as inevitable. This viewpoint is identified with ancient Greek Stoic philosophy.

WORDS TO KNOW **myriad** (mĭr′ē-əd) *adj.* made up of many different elements or parts

Customizing Instruction

Less Proficient Readers

Set a Purpose Have students read to find an incident that brings the boy out of his happy, confident state.

Students Acquiring English

1 Help students understand the expression "came to himself" and point out that the phrasal verb *come to* is usually used to mean "to regain consciousness." Ask students what "came to himself" means.

Possible Response: "regained his senses."

Cross Curricular Link Science

DRIVER ANTS The driver ants of Africa are similar in habits to the army ants of tropical America. The ants live in huge colonies of a million or more. Unlike other ants, driver ants do not construct nests; rather, the nests are the ants themselves, as they cluster together and actually form walls by fastening onto each other using their jaws and the claws on their legs. Driver ants are carnivorous: they feed mostly on other insects and actually hunt as a group, capturing insects in well-organized raids. The ants described by Lessing are *swarm raiders,* which swarm across the ground in a fan-shaped array of columns, flushing out prey as they go. They have been known to kill and dismember livestock and wild animals, such as the bush buck in this story, if the animals have been injured and are unable to escape. Driver ants are also migratory; they have to be to satisfy their feeding needs. Large colonies require as much as 100,000 other insects per day.

Reading and Analyzing

Literary Analysis: SYMBOL

A Ask students what the ants seem to represent to the boy.

Possible Response: the inevitability of death.

Ask students why the author might have chosen ants as the vehicle by which the boy gains insight into mortality and the ability to control destiny.

Possible Response: Because ants are such small and seemingly unlikely killers, they provide an especially shocking reminder of the susceptibility of all creatures to death.

Active Reading

ANALYZING CHARACTER DEVELOPMENT

B Ask students what change has occurred in the boy's character as a result of his encounter with the buck and the ants. Ask them what it is that "he had to think out."

Possible Response: The boy is no longer so confident of his ability to control himself and his environment. He has encountered firsthand the reality of mortality and the cruelty of life, and this has caused him to reassess his youthful attitude of being in absolute control of his destiny.

off his clothes, till he stood above the skeleton, which lay sprawled under a small bush. It was clean-picked. It might have been lying there years, save that on the white bone were pink fragments of gristle. About the bones ants were ebbing away, their pincers full of meat.

The boy looked at them, big black ugly insects. A few were standing and gazing up at him with small glittering eyes.

A "Go away!" he said to the ants, very coldly. "I am not for you—not just yet, at any rate. Go away." And he fancied that the ants turned and went away.

He bent over the bones and touched the sockets in the skull; that was where the eyes were, he thought incredulously, remembering the liquid dark eyes of a buck. And then he bent the slim foreleg bone, swinging it horizontally in his palm.

That morning, perhaps an hour ago, this small creature had been stepping proud and free through the bush, feeling the chill on its hide even as he himself had done, exhilarated by it. Proudly stepping the earth, tossing its horns, frisking a pretty white tail, it had sniffed the cold morning air. Walking like kings and conquerors it had moved through this free-held bush, where each blade of grass grew for it alone, and where the river ran pure sparkling water for its slaking.[10]

And then—what had happened? Such a swift surefooted thing could surely not be trapped by a swarm of ants?

The boy bent curiously to the skeleton. Then he saw that the back leg that lay uppermost and strained out in the tension of death, was snapped midway in the thigh, so that broken bones jutted over each other uselessly. So that was it! Limping into the ant-masses it could not escape, once it had sensed the danger. Yes, but how had the leg been broken? Had it fallen, perhaps? Impossible, a buck was too light and graceful. Had some jealous rival horned it?

What could possibly have happened? Perhaps some Africans had thrown stones at it, as they do, trying to kill it for meat, and had broken its leg. Yes, that must be it.

Even as he imagined the crowd of running, shouting natives, and the flying stones, and the leaping buck, another picture came into his mind. He saw himself, on any one of these bright ringing mornings, drunk with excitement, taking a snap shot at some half-seen buck. He saw himself with the gun lowered, wondering whether he had missed or not; and thinking at last that it was late, and he wanted his breakfast, and it was not worth while to track miles after an animal that would very likely get away from him in any case.

For a moment he would not face it. He was a small boy again, kicking sulkily at the skeleton, hanging his head, refusing to accept the responsibility.

Then he straightened up, and looked down at the bones with an odd expression of dismay, all the anger gone out of him. His mind went quite empty: all around him he could see trickles of ants disappearing into the grass. The whispering noise was faint and dry, like the rustling of a cast snakeskin.

At last he picked up his gun and walked homewards. He was telling himself half defiantly that he wanted his breakfast. He was telling himself that it was getting very hot, much too hot to be out roaming the bush.

Really, he was tired. He walked heavily, not looking where he put his feet. When he came within sight of his home he stopped, knitting his brows. There was something he had to think out. B The death of that small animal was a thing that concerned him, and he was by no means finished with it. It lay at the back of his mind uncomfortably.

Soon, the very next morning, he would get clear of everybody and go to the bush and think about it. ❖

10. **slaking:** quenching of thirst.

WORDS TO KNOW **incredulously** (ĭn-krĕj′ə-ləs-lē) *adv.* in a manner showing disbelief

1216

Teaching Options

Informal Assessment

UPDATING THE STORY

You can informally assess students' understanding of the selection's plot by having them update the story so that it takes place in the United States. Have them write a plot summary for their story. Encourage students to share and discuss their updated versions.

RUBRIC

3 Full Accomplishment Plot summary comprehensively and imaginatively translates plot and themes of story into present-day American setting, and reflects full understanding of events that lead to boy's character development.

2 Substantial Accomplishment Plot summary is competently translated to present-day American setting, but may not reflect complete understanding of boy's insight or character development.

1 Little or Partial Accomplishment Plot outline is sketchy and unimaginative, and shows little understanding of boy's character development.

Connect to the Literature

1. **What Do You Think?** What was your reaction to the events of this story? Share your thoughts with your classmates.

Comprehension Check
- Why does the boy exult as he runs through the veld?
- What sight puts an end to his exultation?

Think Critically

2. Why do you think it is so important to the boy to go out on the veld each morning?

THINK ABOUT
- his attitude toward his abilities and powers
- his attitude toward his parents
- the scene on the veld at sunrise

3. Why do you think the buck's death upsets the boy so much?

4. ACTIVE READING ANALYZING CHARACTER DEVELOPMENT Get together with a classmate and compare the charts you made in your  READER'S NOTEBOOK of the boy's thoughts and actions. How does the experience with the buck affect the character's view of the world and of himself?

5. Would you have reacted to the buck's death in the same way as the boy in the story? Explain your answer.

Extend Interpretations

6. **Critic's Corner** Critics have noted that Lessing has a remarkable ability to understand **characters** and to interpret their thoughts, feelings, and motivations. Think about the boy in "A Sunrise on the Veld." What are some of the important things you learn about him that make him believable and worth your attention?

7. **Comparing Texts** In both "At the Pitt-Rivers" by Penelope Lively (page 1199) and "A Sunrise on the Veld," the main character is a teenage boy. Compare the attitudes of the two boys. How do they view themselves, others, and the world? Which boy do you think changes the most from the beginning to the end of the story? Explain your answer.

8. **Connect to Life** For what different reasons do people around the world hunt wild animals? Do you think hunting is an acceptable activity? Why or why not?

Literary Analysis

KINESTHETIC IMAGERY Imagery that conveys the tension and movement of muscles, tendons, and joints is called **kinesthetic imagery.** In "A Sunrise on the Veld," Lessing uses this type of imagery to describe the boy, his dogs, and the veld wildlife. Notice the images conveyed by the following examples:

The boy stretched his frame full-length, touching the wall at his head with his hands, and the bedfoot with his toes. . . .

. . . he let the muscles of his feet spread and settle into the shapes of the earth. . . .

. . . he ran, feeling his body rise into the crisp rushing air and fall back surely on to sure feet. . . .

Cooperative Learning Activity With a small group of classmates, find other examples of kinesthetic imagery in the story. Discuss why you think Lessing uses this kind of imagery. Be specific in your answer.

THIRD-PERSON LIMITED POINT OF VIEW When a writer uses the **third-person limited point of view,** the narrator tells the story from only one character's perspective. In Lessing's story, the reader learns only what the boy thinks, feels, observes, and experiences. The reader sees the boy, his parents, and the veld through the boy's eyes. How does this narrative point of view affect your perception of the boy at the beginning of the story? at the end of the story?

GUIDING STUDENT RESPONSE

Connect to the Literature

1. **What Do You Think?** Accept all reasonable responses.

Comprehension Check
- He believes he is in complete control of his body and his mind.
- the sight of the dying buck

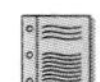 Use Selection Quiz in **Unit Seven Resource Book** p. 13.

Think Critically

2. Possible Responses: to test and revel in his physical and mental strength; to separate himself from his parents; to enjoy the wild beauty of the veld.
3. Possible Responses: because he could do nothing to stop the buck's suffering; because he realizes for the first time the power of forces beyond his control; because he realizes that his actions might have caused the animal to suffer and die.
4. Possible Response: The meeting with the buck destroys the boy's belief that he can control all the events in his world, and makes him question the scope of events beyond his ability to change.
5. Accept all thoughtful responses.

Literary Analysis

Cooperative Learning Activity Remind students that kinesthetic imagery helps the reader imagine physical sensations felt by the characters.
Third-Person Limited Point of View Have students compare their feelings for this boy with the first-person narrator of "At the Pitt-Rivers."

Extend Interpretations

Critic's Corner Possible Responses: that he is capable of adult emotions; that he is intelligent; that he is capable of growth; that he is self-aware; that he is strong-willed

Comparing Texts Students may say that the boys in both stories are changed by what they witness. The boy in "Sunrise on the Veld" views himself as powerful and in control until he witnesses the death of the buck. The attitudes of the boy in "At the Pitt-Rivers" continually shifts as a result of the scene he witnesses in the museum. Encourage students to discuss the connections they see across these two cultures and to propose theme statements that apply to both selections.

Connect to Life Accept all reasonable, well-supported responses.

Writing Options

1. **Diary Entry** Accept all reasonable responses.
2. **Story Sequel** If students wish, encourage them to write their sequels from first-person point of view.
3. **Nature Log** Encourage students to use figurative language to present the images in greater detail.

Activities & Explorations

1. **Veld Collage** Students may find pictures for their collages in travel brochures and nature and wildlife magazines.
2. **Soundtrack of the Veld** Students can use the author's description of the sounds heard on the veld as inspiration for their soundtracks.
3. **Interior Monologue** You might have students choose one scene in the story as the inspiration for their monologues.

Inquiry & Research

1. **Independent Africa** Students might want to go back as far as 1914 to discover that all of Africa except for Liberia, Ethiopia, and Egypt, which was a British protectorate, was under European colonial rule. This status remained virtually unchanged until the 1950s.
2. **Preserving the Balance of Nature** Encourage students to use as a point of departure the boy's decision not to interfere in the death of the buck.

Art Connection

Setting the Mood Accept all reasonable responses. You might ask students to suggest other colors and shapes that might have worked as well.

Vocabulary in Action

1. superfluity
2. myriad
3. fastidious
4. vigilant
5. incredulously

Choices & CHALLENGES

Writing Options

1. **Diary Entry** Imagine that you are the boy in this story. Write a diary entry describing your thoughts and feelings after witnessing the buck's death. Place the entry in your **Working Portfolio.**
2. **Story Sequel** Write a short sequel to "A Sunrise on the Veld," describing the boy's thoughts, feelings, and actions the next morning.
3. **Nature Log** With a partner, take a walk in a nature preserve. Keep a log of things you see, hear, smell, or feel and of your reaction to each. You may want to continue keeping your log over a period of time, recording experiences with nature in other settings, such as your own yard or parks.

Activities & Explorations

1. **Veld Collage** The boy in the story experiences both the beauty and the cruelty of nature on the veld. Make a collage of pictures that illustrates these two opposing views of life on the veld. ~ **ART**
2. **Soundtrack of the Veld** Using voice, musical instruments, sound effects, and brief passages from recordings, create a soundtrack expressing your impression of the veld. Record your sound landscape on tape and present it to the class. ~ **MUSIC**
3. **Interior Monologue** Use what you learn about the boy's thoughts and feelings in the story to create an interior monologue that reveals the inner workings of his mind. Practice the monologue, and present it to the class. ~ **SPEAKING AND LISTENING**

Inquiry & Research

1. **Independent Africa** Locate two political maps of Africa, one from about 1955 and one from the present. List all the countries that were once colonies and are now independent nations; include their former and current names. What European countries held colonies in Africa? Approximately how much of the continent was colonized? Summarize your information for the class.

More Online: Research Starter
www.mcdougallittell.com

2. **Preserving the Balance of Nature** With a small group, research the importance of balance within an ecosystem. Explain what an ecosystem is, how the balance of nature is maintained, and what can happen if the balance is upset. Present your findings to the rest of the class.

Art Connection

Setting the Mood Look again at the painting *Horned Forms* on page 1214. Note especially the colors and shapes used. In what ways does the painting convey the **mood** and **themes** of the story?

Vocabulary in Action

EXERCISE: IDIOMS Write the vocabulary word that is suggested by each set of idioms below.

1. over and above; too much of a good thing; the icing on the cake; money to burn
2. countless as the sands of the sea; more than you can count; a thousand and one; everything but the kitchen sink
3. be a fussbudget; cross all t's and dot all i's; be persnickety
4. be on the lookout; stay on one's toes; keep one ear to the ground; look alive
5. have to pinch oneself; that'll be the day; take with a grain of salt

WORDS TO KNOW fastidious incredulously myriad superfluity vigilant

Building Vocabulary
For an in-depth study of context clues, see page 938.

Teaching Options

Grammar

MOVABLE ADJECTIVES

Instruction A single noun is often modified by two or more adjectives or by an adjective and an intensifying adverb like *highly* or *extremely.* Such adjectives or adjective/adverb combinations are called movable adjectives. Movable adjectives can either precede or follow the noun they modify. Their placement affects the rhythm of the sentence and the emphasis they are given.

Activity Write the following sentences on the chalkboard.

The suffering, sick, and angry boy watched the black mound of ants grow smaller.

Suffering, sick, and angry, the boy watched the black mound of ants grow smaller.

The boy, suffering, sick, and angry, watched the black mound of ants grow smaller.

Point out the placement of the adjective phrase (underlined) in each sentence. Have students read the sentences aloud and notice how they vary in rhythm. Ask students where they think the emphasis is in each sentence—on the subject *(boy),* on the adjective phrase, or equally on both

Doris Lessing

1919–

Other Works
"The Old Chief Mshlanga"
"No Witchcraft for Sale"
"Through the Tunnel"
"Homage for Isaac Babel"
"A Mild Attack of Locusts"
African Laughter

Getting Started Doris Lessing was born in Persia (now Iran), but when she was 5, her British parents moved to Southern Rhodesia, where her father bought a farm. Lessing was not interested in socializing with other British settlers—a part of life that was important to her mother—and she disliked school intensely, much preferring to wander the lonely veld. Rebelling against her parents' wishes, Lessing left school at the age of 14 and worked for several years as a nursemaid, a typist, and a telephone operator in Salisbury, Southern Rhodesia. During these years, she read a great deal, especially the works of 19th-century novelists, and began to write fiction. When she was in her mid-20s, she quit her job in a lawyer's office to write what turned out to be her first major novel. Lessing was married and divorced twice, and in 1949 she moved to Great Britain with her youngest child, Peter. The publication of her novel *The Grass Is Singing* in the following year marked the beginning of her professional career.

Author and Activist Lessing has been a prolific writer—publishing more than 30 works in several genres—and is considered by many to be one of the most important novelists of the 20th century. Her early fiction was based on her own life and on her intimate knowledge of the culture and people of Southern Rhodesia, especially the problems between blacks and whites. Because of her outspoken criticism of racism and her radical political sympathies, Lessing was banned for many years from her homeland and from South Africa.

Works in Progress Lessing's fiction has become increasingly more complex and ambitious, ranging from novels of social realism to science fiction. Her most widely read and controversial work is *The Golden Notebook,* a novel exploring women's concerns and experiences that is written in the form of a conventional narrative interwoven with a writer's notebooks. Lessing feels that contemporary society is in the midst of monumental change and crisis and that the writer must speak with integrity, imagination, and a clear sense of moral responsibility. Her work continues to evolve as she develops new formats and addresses the dilemmas of contemporary life.

Author Activity

Coming Home Find out about Doris Lessing's relationship to her homeland since Zimbabwe gained its independence. Has she been allowed to return to her homeland? Does she approve of the country's new government? What does she think of the changes that have taken place in Zimbabwe since 1949?

LaserLinks: Background for Reading
Science Connection

Author Activity

Coming Home Students may want to consult Lessing's two-volume autobiography *Under My Skin* (1994) and *Walking in the Shade* (1997) to get her views on these issues.

the subject and the adjective phrase.

Exercise Ask students to identify the movable adjectives in each sentence and to rewrite the sentence, placing the adjectives in a different position. Have students work in cooperative groups to discuss how the emphasis has changed in the rewritten sentences.

1. The boy slung his crinkled, stiff shoes over his shoulder and walked barefoot. *(Possible answer: The boy slung his shoes, crinkled and stiff, over his shoulder and walked barefoot.)*
2. He walked through the foliage, dark, damp, and unfamiliar, and finally came to a vlei. *(Possible answer: He walked through the dark, damp, and unfamiliar foliage and finally came to a vlei.)*
3. Highly alert, the boy listened for the noise. *(Possible answer: The boy, highly alert, listened for the noise.)*
4. A buck, convulsing and screaming, was being attacked by fierce ants. *(Possible answer: A convulsing and screaming buck was being attacked by fierce ants.)*

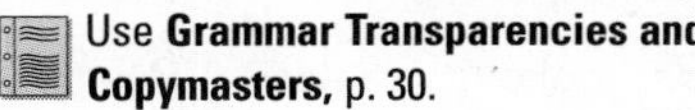
Use **Grammar Transparencies and Copymasters,** p. 30.

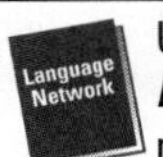

Use McDougal Littell's ***Language Network*** for more instruction in movable adjectives.

OVERVIEW

Objectives

1. appreciate and understand the author's use of **point of view** in a story **(Literary Analysis)**
2. analyze how the author merges two different **points of view** in this story **(Literary Analysis)**
3. **analyze satire** in order to appreciate a story that exposes the faults of society **(Active Reading)**

Summary

Born during the last year of World War I, the speaker says she never once smiled during her first year of life because she was omniscient and was therefore aware of and able to understand all of the grim occurrences connected to World War I in 1918.

Use **Unit Seven Resource Book,** p. 14 for additional support.

Thematic Link

Spark's experiment with narrative voice—an omniscient first-person narrator, an infant no less—is an effective device for contrasting **appearance and reality,** and is typical of the exploration of point of view found in much modern and contemporary literature.

5-Minute Warm-Up

Daily Language SkillBuilder

Have students **proofread** the display sentences on page 1189i and write them correctly. The sentences also appear on Transparency 33 of **Grammar Transparencies and Copymasters.**

Preteaching Vocabulary

If you would like to preteach the WORDS TO KNOW for this selection, use the Mini Lesson on p. 1221.

Reading and Analyzing

ACTIVE READING

PREDICT

Since this new school of psychology will establish "that all of the young of the human species are born omniscient," we can assume that this narrator, even though she is an infant, will be totally aware of all the events that are happening in the world.

"I was known as the baby whom nothing and no one could make smile."

The First Year of My Life

Short Story by MURIEL SPARK

Connect to Your Life

Baby Talk What kind of baby were you, according to your parents and other relatives? Were you happy? cranky? Did you seem interested in the world around you or indifferent to it? Briefly describe yourself at that point in your life. Then, as you read this story, compare yourself with the rather astonishing baby being depicted.

Build Background

World War I The story you are about to read is set in 1918, the final year of World War I. By that time, the bloodshed and devastation of the Great War, as it was then called, had reached levels never seen in any previous conflict. The use of advanced weaponry and poison gas in the brutal stalemate of trench warfare had resulted in heavy casualties, and many families across Europe suffered the loss of loved ones. The war also left deep political and economic scars on almost every European country—scars that eventually led to the eruption of World War II only two decades later.

In her account of her life as an infant, the narrator of this story provides an unusual perspective on the final year of World War I. Although the premise of the story is pure fantasy, the narrator makes allusions to many individuals who actually lived during the time, including figures famous in history and the arts.

WORDS TO KNOW
Vocabulary Preview
authenticity, omniscient, demented, seditious, discern

Focus Your Reading

LITERARY ANALYSIS | POINT OF VIEW In a story that is told from the **first-person point of view,** the narrator is the "I" who is speaking. In a story that is told from the **third-person omniscient point of view,** the narrator is outside the story and can see into the minds of the characters. As you read this story, be aware of the way in which the writer merges these two points of view in order to provide an unusual perspective on events.

ACTIVE READING | ANALYZING SATIRE **Satire** is a literary technique in which criticism is mixed with humor in order to expose the faults of society. The **tone** of a satirical work may be gently witty, mildly abrasive, or even bitterly critical. As you read "The First Year of My Life," look for specific instances of satire and decide what effects are created by the narrator's unusual **point of view.** Note passages in which you think the satire is particularly effective.

READER'S NOTEBOOK List some of the individuals and groups that are satirized in this story. Then identify what fault the narrator finds with each one. Use a chart like the one shown to record their faults.

Individual/Group	Fault

LESSON RESOURCES

UNIT SEVEN RESOURCE BOOK, pp. 14–18

ASSESSMENT RESOURCES

Formal Assessment, pp. 223–224

Teacher's Guide to Assessment and Portfolio Use

Test Generator

SKILLS TRANSPARENCIES AND COPYMASTERS

Literary Analysis

- Point of View, T18 (for Literary Analysis, p. 1220)

Reading and Critical Thinking

- Organizational Chart: Horizontal, T52 (for Active Reading, p. 1220)

Grammar

- Commas with Nonessential Elements, T55 (for Mini Lesson, p. 1223)
- Essential and Nonessential Participial Phrases, C101 (for Mini Lesson, p. 1223)

Writing

- Opinion Statement, C35 (for Writing Options, p. 1228)

Communications

- Impromptu Speaking: Debate, T15 (for Activities & Explorations, p. 1228)

INTEGRATED TECHNOLOGY

Audio Library

LaserLinks

- Historical Connection: 1918—The Year in Pictures. See **Teacher's SourceBook,** pp. 89–90.

Visit our website: www.mcdougallittell.com

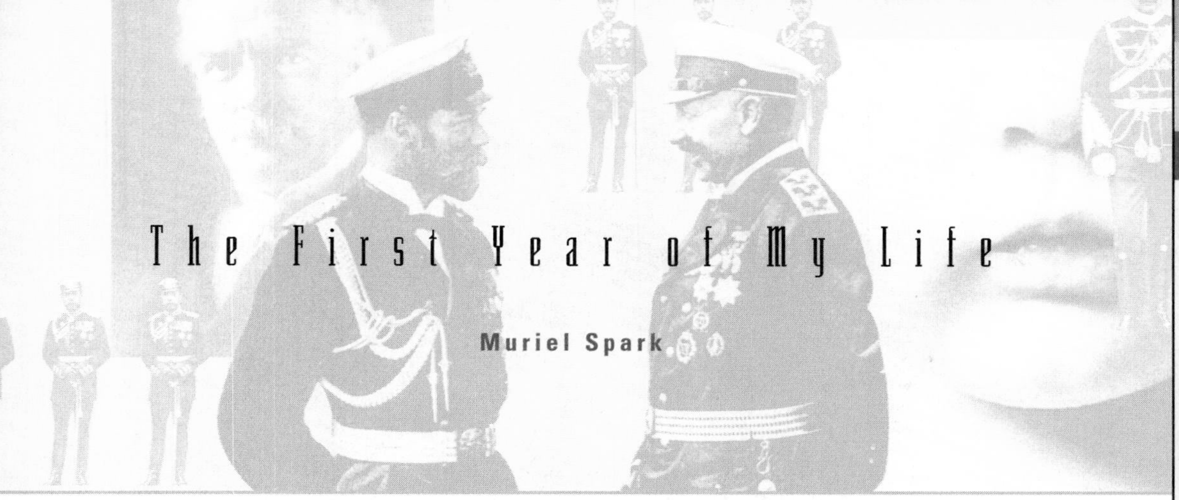

The First Year of My Life

Muriel Spark

I was born on the first day of the second month of the last year of the First World War, a Friday. Testimony abounds that during the first year of my life I never smiled. I was known as the baby whom nothing and no one could make smile. Everyone who knew me then has told me so. They tried very hard, singing and bouncing me up and down, jumping around, pulling faces. Many times I was told this later by my family and their friends; but, anyway, I knew it at the time.

You will shortly be hearing of that new school of psychology, or maybe you have heard of it already, which after long and far-adventuring research and experiment has established that all of the young of the human species are born omniscient. Babies, in their waking hours, know everything that is going on everywhere in the world; they can tune in to any conversation they choose, switch on to any scene. We have all experienced this power. It is only after the first year that it was brainwashed out of us; for it is demanded of us by our immediate environment that we grow to be of use to it in a practical way. Gradually, our know-all brain-cells are blacked out, although traces remain in some individuals in the form of E.S.P., and in the adults of some primitive tribes.

It is not a new theory. Poets and philosophers, as usual, have been there first. But scientific proof is now ready and to hand. Perhaps the final touches are being put to the new manifesto[1] in some cell[2] at Harvard University. Any day now it will be given to the world, and the world will be convinced.

Let me therefore get my word in first, because

ACTIVE READING

PREDICT What will this information about a "new school of psychology" have to do with the events in the story?

1. **manifesto:** a declaration of principles.
2. **cell:** a small group forming a unit of a larger organization.

WORDS TO KNOW

omniscient (ŏm-nĭsh′ənt) *adj.* having complete knowledge; all-knowing

TEACHING THE LITERATURE

Customizing Instruction

Less Proficient Readers

Set a Purpose Invite students to discuss what they know about World War I. Then ask them to pay close attention to the ways in which the war affects this story's narrator. How does she feel? How do we know she feels this way? Explain that the narrator is troubled by the war, which is why she does not want to smile.

Students Acquiring English

This selection is challenging because of its many allusions to historical events and literary figures and its elevated diction. You may wish to have partners read and discuss the story together. Inform students that almost all proper names mentioned are either famous writers or important political figures of World War I, and that the context should help them understand which is which.

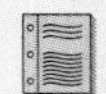 Use **Spanish Study Guide** for additional support, pp. 290–292.

Gifted and Talented

Have students consider why the narrator makes so many references to literary figures and to literature. Ask them what they think Spark might be suggesting about the effectiveness of writers and the written word.

Mini Lesson Preteaching Vocabulary

LATIN ROOTS

Instruction Remind students that the root of a word might be broken down further into a prefix and another root word.

Activity Have students use a dictionary to research word origins as a way to understand derivation of the WORDS TO KNOW. They should be able to come up with the following:

- **authenticity:** from *authenticus,* meaning " genuine"; from a Greek root *authenes,* meaning "perpetrator" or "author"
- **demented:** from *demens,* meaning "mad"; consists of the prefix *de-* + the root *mens* (mind)
- **discern:** from *discernere,* meaning "to separate by sifting"; prefix *dis-* (meaning here "in different directions") + *cernere* (separate)
- **omniscient:** from *omnisciens,* meaning "all knowing"; prefix *omni-* (all) + *sciens* (knowing)
- **seditious:** from *sedito,* meaning "a going apart"

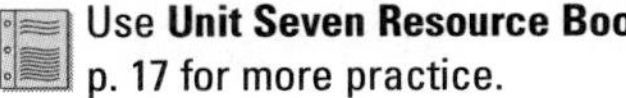 Use **Unit Seven Resource Book** p. 17 for more practice.

A lesson on Latin roots appears on page 432 in the Pupil's Edition.

Reading and Analyzing

Active Reading ANALYZING SATIRE

Remind students that satire is a literary technique in which ideas, customs, behaviors, or institutions are ridiculed. Ask them what targets might be the objects of ridicule in a story with an omniscient baby as a narrator.

Possible Response: adult behavior; the idea that babies are completely sweet, innocent, and oblivious to what is going on around them; the field of psychology.

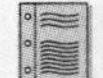 Use **Unit Seven Resource Book** p. 15 for more practice.

Literary Analysis POINT OF VIEW

After reviewing the information on point of view on page 1220, have students identify what the point of view in the story is.

Possible Response: Students should immediately recognize that the story is told by a first-person narrator. They may surmise at this point that the point of view will be unusual in that the first-person narrator is also omniscient.

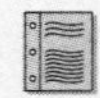 Use **Unit Seven Resource Book** p. 16 for more exercises.

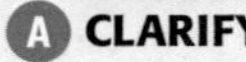

ACTIVE READING

A CLARIFY

The women are dressed in black because black is the traditional color for mourning, and the women have lost "their husbands and brothers."

ACTIVE READING

B ANALYZE

The main target of satire is the folly of humanity and the horror of war.

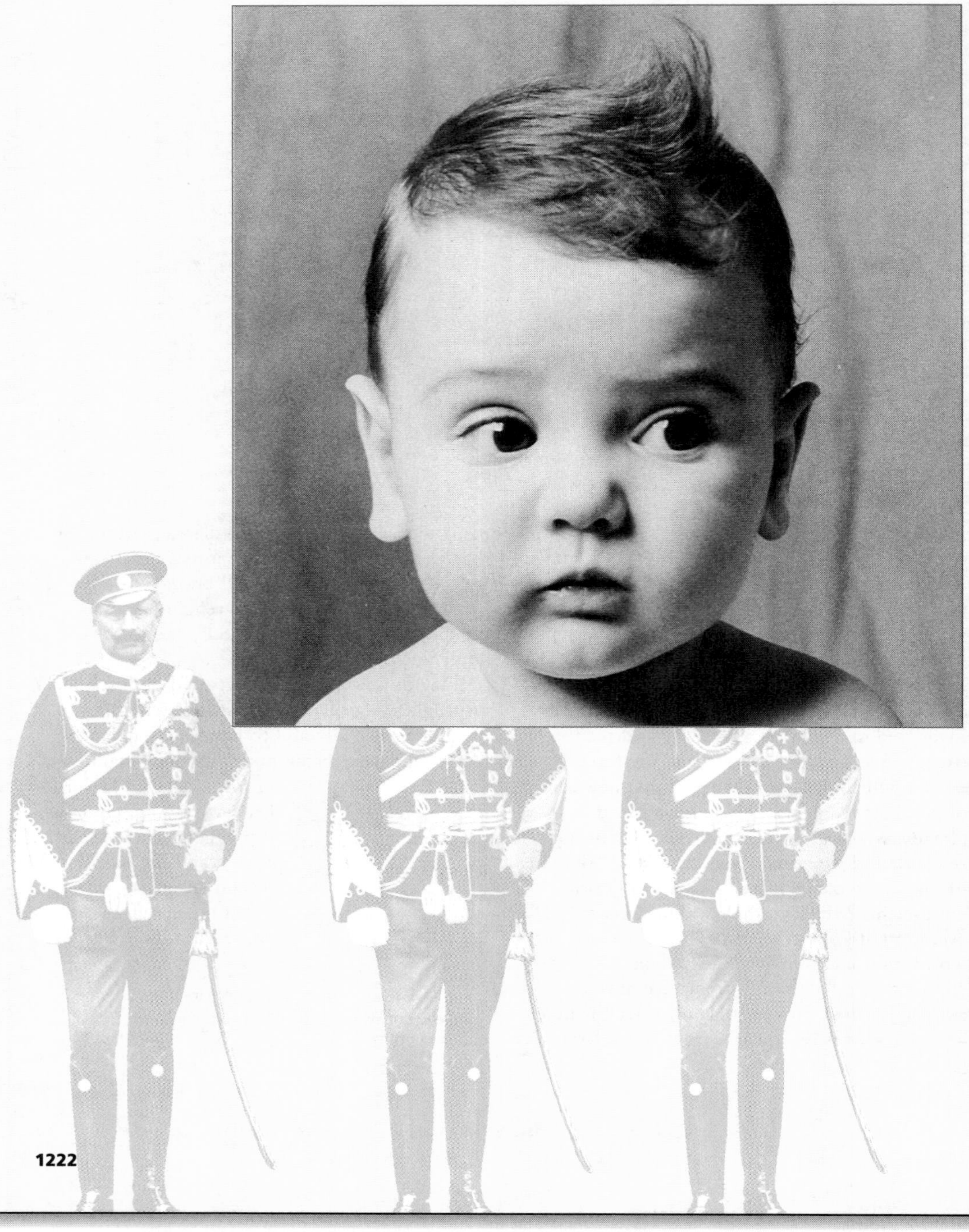

1222

Teaching Options

BLOCK SCHEDULING: MANAGING TIME

If your schedule requires that you cover the lesson objectives in a shorter time, use . . .

- Preparing to Read, p. 1220
- Thinking Through the Literature, p. 1227
- Vocabulary in Action, p. 1228

If you want to take advantage of longer class time, use . . .

- TE Teaching Options: Preteaching Vocabulary, p. 1221; Grammar, p. 1223; Speaking and Listening, p. 1224; Cross Curricular Links, p. 1225; Standardized Test Practice, p. 1226
- Choices & Challenges, p. 1228

I feel pretty sure, now, about the authenticity of my remembrance of things past. My autobiography, as I very well perceived at the time, started in the very worst year that the world had ever seen so far. **1** Apart from being born bedridden and toothless, unable to raise myself on the pillow or utter anything but farmyard squawks or police-siren wails, my bladder and my bowels totally out of control, I was further depressed by the curious behavior of the two-legged mammals around me. There were those black-dressed people, females of the species to which I appeared to belong, saying they had lost their sons. I slept a great deal. Let them go and find their sons. It was like the special pin for my nappies[3] which my mother or some other hoverer dedicated to my care was always losing. These careless women in black lost their husbands and their brothers. Then they came to visit my mother and clucked and crowed over my cradle. I was not amused.

ACTIVE READING

A **CLARIFY** Why are the women dressed in black?

"Babies never really smile till they're three months old," said my mother. "They're not *supposed* to smile till they're three months old."

My brother, aged six, marched up and down with a toy rifle over his shoulder:

The grand old Duke of York
He had ten thousand men;
He marched them up to the top of the hill
And he marched them down again.

And when they were up, they were up.
And when they were down, they were down.
And when they were neither down nor up
They were neither up nor down.

"Just listen to him!"

"Look at him with his rifle!"

I was about ten days old when Russia stopped fighting. I tuned in to the Czar,[4] a prisoner, with the rest of his family, since evidently the country had put him off his throne and there had been a revolution not long before I was born. Everyone was talking about it. I tuned in to the Czar. "Nothing would ever induce me to sign the treaty of Brest-Litovsk,"[5] he said to his wife. Anyway, nobody had asked him to.

At this point I was sleeping twenty hours a day to get my strength up. And from what I discerned in the other four hours of the day I knew I was going to need it. The Western Front[6] on my frequency was sheer blood, mud, dismembered bodies, blistering crashes, hectic flashes of light in the night skies, explosions, total terror. Since it was plain I had been born into a bad moment in the history of the world, the future bothered me, unable as I was to raise my head from the pillow and as yet only twenty inches long. "I truly wish I were a fox or a bird," D. H. Lawrence was writing to somebody. . . .

ACTIVE READING

ANALYZE What is the main target of the **satire** in the paragraph? **B**

Red sheets of flame shot across the sky. It was 21st March, the fiftieth day of my life, and the German Spring Offensive[7] had started before my morning feed. Infinite slaughter. I scowled at the scene, and made an effort to kick out. But the

3. **nappies:** the British term for diapers.
4. **Czar:** Nicholas II, the last czar of Russia, who was forced from power in the Russian Revolution of 1917.
5. **treaty of Brest-Litovsk:** the treaty—signed on March 3, 1918—by which the new Communist government of Russia made peace with Germany, withdrawing from World War I eight months before its end.
6. **Western Front:** a 450-mile-long battlefront across Belgium and northeastern France, along which the Allies and Germany were locked in bloody trench warfare from 1914 to 1918.
7. **German Spring Offensive:** In late March 1918, after its peace treaty with Russia ended the fighting on the eastern front, Germany began a major push to win the war on the western front.

WORDS TO KNOW
authenticity (ô'thĕn-tĭs'ĭ-tē) *n.* genuineness
discern (dĭ-sûrn') *v.* to observe; perceive

Customizing Instruction

Less Proficient Readers

1 Have students read to find out why the narrator calls her first year of life "the very worst year that the world had ever seen."

Multiple Learning Styles

Linguistic Learners

Ask students to write a brief monologue in which the baby in the photograph on page 1222 reveals his or her thoughts. Encourage students to detail thoughts and desires that match the baby's expression.

Grammar

ESSENTIAL AND NONESSENTIAL PARTICIPIAL PHRASES

Instruction A participle is a verb form that functions as an adjective, modifying a noun or a pronoun. A present participle ends in *-ing (showing),* while a past participle usually ends in *-ed (showed).* A participial phrase consists of a participle, its modifiers, and its complements. A participial phrase can be essential or nonessential. An essential participial phrase is necessary to complete the meaning of a sentence. It is not set off by commas. A nonessential participial phrase, which is set off by commas, adds additional information to an already clear and complete sentence.

Activity Write the following sentences on the chalkboard. Have students identify the participial phrase as essential or nonessential.

I stretched and kicked for exercise, <u>seeing that I had a lifetime before me</u>. *(nonessential)*

The men <u>fighting in the war</u> sometimes did not return. *(essential)*

Have students compose five sentences using participial phrases.

Use **Grammar Transparencies and Copymasters,** p. 41.

Use McDougal Littell's ***Language Network*** for more instruction and practice in participial phrases.

Reading and Analyzing

Reading Skills and Strategies: **MAKING INFERENCES**

A Have students read the whole paragraph and then infer why the baby finds the song, "The Grand Old Duke" so silly. Ask them how the baby's point of view creates a satiric effect.

Possible Response: The song is silly because it glorifies war, and the author implies that glorifying war is so wrong that even a baby can perceive it.

Literary Analysis: **TONE**

B Invite students to describe the tone of the narrator's comments about her uncle and Marshall Foch, and what kind of tone her repetition of Foch's exhortation *(Tout le monde a la bataille)* gives to the story.

Possible Response: The tone is scornful: "the old swine." Foch gives the orders but, unlike her uncle, is not in the trenches himself. There is bitter irony in her repetition of the exhortation in the midst of her description of frivolous activities.

Literary Analysis: **CHARACTERIZATION**

C Have students describe the character of the narrator as revealed by the comments about the House of Commons and the Western Front.

Possible Response: cynical, realistic. Ask them what is humorous about this characterization of the baby.

Possible Response: Babies are usually thought to be innocent.

attempt was feeble. Furious, and impatient for some strength, I wailed for my feed. After which I stopped wailing but continued to scowl.

The grand old Duke of York
He had ten thousand men . . .

They rocked the cradle. I never heard a sillier song. Over in Berlin and Vienna the people were starving, freezing, striking, rioting and yelling in the streets. In London everyone was bustling to work and muttering that it was time the whole . . . business was over.

The big people around me bared their teeth; that meant a smile, it meant they were pleased or amused. They spoke of ration cards[8] for meat and sugar and butter.

"Where will it all end?"

I went to sleep. I woke and tuned in to Bernard Shaw[9] who was telling someone to shut up. I switched over to Joseph Conrad[10] who, strangely enough, was saying precisely the same thing. I still didn't think it worth a smile, although it was expected of me any day now. I got on to Turkey. 1 Women draped in black huddled and chattered in their harems; yak-yak-yak. This was boring, so I came back to home base.

In and out came and went the women in British black. My mother's brother, dressed in his uniform, came coughing. He had been poison-gassed in the trenches. *"Tout le monde à la bataille!"*[11] declaimed Marshal Foch[12] the old swine. He was now Commander-in-Chief of the Allied Forces. My uncle coughed from deep within his lungs, never to recover but destined to return to the Front. His brass buttons gleamed in the firelight. I weighed twelve pounds by now; I stretched and kicked for exercise, seeing that I had a lifetime before me, coping with this crowd. I took six feeds a day and kept most of them down by the time the *Vindictive* was sunk in Ostend harbor,[13] on which day I kicked with special vigor in my bath.

In France the conscripted[14] soldiers leapfrogged over the dead on the advance and littered the fields with limbs and hands, or drowned in the mud. The strongest men on all fronts were dead before I was born. Now the sentries used bodies for barricades and the fighting men were unhealthy from the start. I checked my toes and fingers, knowing I was going to need them. *The Playboy of the Western World*[15] was playing at the Court Theatre in London, but occasionally I beamed over to the House of Commons[16] which made me drop off gently to sleep. Generally, I preferred the Western Front where one got the true state of affairs. It was essential to know the worst, blood and explosions and all, for one had to be prepared, as the boy scouts said. Virginia Woolf yawned and reached for her diary. Really, I preferred the Western Front.

8. **ration cards:** cards entitling the bearers to limited amounts of certain foods and other goods that were in short supply during the war.
9. **Bernard Shaw:** George Bernard Shaw, an Irish-born British playwright and social critic.
10. **Joseph Conrad:** a Polish-born British novelist.
11. ***Tout le monde à la bataille!*** (to͞o′ lə môɴd′ ä lä bä-tī′) *French:* The whole world into the battle!
12. **Marshal Foch** (fôsh): Ferdinand Foch, a French general who in March 1918 became commander of all Allied forces on the western front.
13. ***Vindictive* . . . Ostend harbor:** In May 1918, a crew of Allied volunteers sunk the ship *Vindictive* to block the entrance of the harbor of Ostend, Belgium, which the Germans had been using as a submarine base.
14. **conscripted:** drafted into military service.
15. ***The Playboy of the Western World:*** a controversial drama by the Irish playwright John Millington Synge.
16. **House of Commons:** the lower house of the British parliament.

1224

Teaching Options

Speaking & Listening

PRESENTING A SPEECH

Instruction Have students work in cooperative groups to prepare an antiwar speech based on the views presented by the baby.

Prepare They can begin by listing the baby's ideas and beliefs about the war, politicians, writers, and family members. Decide which points are the most persuasive, and what would be the best way to express them.

Present Students can decide who will present their group's speech. Audience members can discuss how closely the speech expressed the baby's viewpoints.

BLOCK SCHEDULING This activity is particularly well-suited for longer class periods.

In the fifth month of my life I could raise my head from my pillow and hold it up. I could grasp the objects that were held out to me. Some of these things rattled and squawked. I gnawed on them to get my teeth started. "She hasn't smiled yet?" said the dreary old aunties. My mother, on the defensive, said I was probably one of those late smilers. On my wavelength Pablo Picasso[17] was getting married and early in that month of July the Silver Wedding of King George V and Queen Mary was celebrated in joyous pomp at St. Paul's Cathedral. They drove through the streets of London with their children. Twenty-five years of domestic happiness. A lot of fuss and ceremonial handing over of swords went on at the Guildhall where the King and Queen received a check for £53,000 to dispose of for charity as they thought fit. *Tout le monde à la bataille!* Income tax in England had reached six shillings in the pound. Everyone was talking about the Silver Wedding; yak-yak-yak, and ten days later the Czar and his family, now in Siberia, were invited to descend to a little room in the basement. Crack, crack, went the guns; screams and blood all over the place, and that was the end of the Romanoffs.[18] I flexed my muscles. "A fine healthy baby," said the doctor; which gave me much satisfaction.

Tout le monde à la bataille! That included my gassed uncle. My health had improved to the point where I was able to crawl in my playpen. Bertrand Russell[19] was still cheerily in prison for writing something seditious about pacifism. Tuning in as usual to the Front Lines it looked as if the Germans were winning all the battles yet losing the war. And so it was. The upper-income people were upset about the income tax at six shillings to the pound. But all women over thirty got the vote. "It seems a long time to wait," said one of my drab old aunts, aged twenty-two. The speeches in the House of Commons always sent me to sleep which was why I missed, at the actual time, a certain oration by Mr. Asquith[20] following the armistice on 11th November.[21] Mr. Asquith was a greatly esteemed former prime minister later to be an Earl, and had been ousted by Mr. Lloyd George.[22] I clearly heard Asquith, in private, refer to Lloyd George as "that . . . Welsh goat."

The armistice was signed and I was awake for that. I pulled myself on to my feet with the aid of the bars of my cot. My teeth were coming through very nicely in my opinion, and well worth all the trouble I was put to in bringing them forth. I weighed twenty pounds. On all the world's fighting fronts the men killed in action or dead of wounds numbered 8,538,315 and the warriors wounded and maimed were 21,219,452. With these figures in mind I sat up in my high chair and banged my spoon on the table. One of my mother's black-draped friends recited:

I have a rendezvous with Death
At some disputed barricade,
When spring comes back with rustling shade
And apple blossoms fill the air—
I have a rendezvous with Death.[23]

Most of the poets, they said, had been killed. The poetry made them dab their eyes with clean white handkerchiefs.

17. **Pablo Picasso:** a Spanish painter and sculptor.
18. **Romanoffs:** the ruling family of Russia from 1613 to 1917.
19. **Bertrand Russell:** a British philosopher, mathematician, and writer.
20. **Mr. Asquith:** Herbert Henry Asquith, prime minister of Britain from 1908 to 1916.
21. **armistice on 11th November:** the agreement that marked the end of fighting in World War I.
22. **Lloyd George:** David Lloyd George, prime minister of Britain from 1916 to 1922.
23. ***I . . . Death:*** the beginning of "I Have a Rendezvous with Death" by the American poet Alan Seeger, who was killed in action during World War I. (Another quotation from the poem appears three paragraphs farther on.)

WORDS TO KNOW

seditious (sĭ-dĭsh'əs) *adj.* stirring up discontent or rebellion

Customizing Instruction

Students Acquiring English

1 Point out to students that "yak" is a slang expression for idle, meaningless conversation. Ask them what point the narrator is making by using this expression here.

Possible Response: The people are engaged in trivial conversation while millions are dying.

Less Proficient Readers

2 Have students discuss why the narrator has not smiled yet.

Possible Response: She is too upset by the misery in the world.

Cross Curricular Link History

WORLD WAR World War I is the name commonly given to the war of 1914–1918, which began in Europe and was fought principally on that continent but eventually involved all the continents of the world. It was a "world war" because, for the first time, all the great powers of the world were engaged at once: Austria-Hungary, Germany, and the Ottoman Empire against France, Great Britain, Italy, and Russia in Europe; Japan in Asia; and the United States in North America. In addition, many other countries were involved, to the extent that by the end of the war nearly 90 percent of the world's population was in some degree involved. The narrator's estimate of casualties is rather conservative: Most estimates put the figure killed at over 10 million. The United States did not enter the war until April 1917, but had casualties of 126,000 killed and over 200,000 wounded, most of which came in the last eight months of the war. France lost half its men—from all walks of life—between the ages of 20 and 32, and the figures in Britain were similar.

Reading and Analyzing

Literary Analysis: CHARACTERIZATION

Ask students what the narrator reveals about Mr. Asquith's character in the first paragraph, and why she includes that information.

Possible Response: She wants to show the frivolity and lack of integrity characteristic of the leaders of the war.

Literary Analysis: TONE

Have students explain the narrator's attitude towards Asquith's speech, and the tone that her smile gives to the story.

Possible Response: She feels so amused by the absurdity of this comment that she smiles for the first time. The tone is satirical, and might best be described as contemptuous amusement.

Next February on my first birthday, there was a birthday-cake with one candle. Lots of children and their elders. The war had been over two months and twenty-one days. "Why doesn't she smile?" My brother was to blow out the candle. The elders were talking about the war and the political situation. Lloyd George and Asquith, Asquith and Lloyd George. I remembered recently having switched on to Mr. Asquith at a private party where he had been drinking a lot. He was playing cards and when he came to cut the cards he tried to cut a large box of matches by mistake. On another occasion I had seen him putting his arm around a lady's shoulder in a Daimler[24] motor car, and generally behaving towards her in a very friendly fashion. Strangely enough she said, "If you don't stop this nonsense immediately I'll order the chauffeur to stop and I'll get out." Mr. Asquith replied, "And pray, what reason will you give?" Well anyway it was my feeding time.

The guests arrived for my birthday. It was so sad, said one of the black widows, so sad about Wilfred Owen who was killed so late in the war, and she quoted from a poem of his:

What passing-bells for these who die as cattle?
Only the monstrous anger of the guns.[25]

The children were squealing and toddling around. One was sick and another wet the floor and stood with his legs apart gaping at the puddle. All was mopped up. I banged my spoon on the table of my high chair.

But I've a rendezvous with Death
At midnight in some flaming town;
When spring trips north again this year,
And I to my pledged word am true,
I shall not fail that rendezvous.

More parents and children arrived. One stout man who was warming his behind at the fire, said, "I always think those words of Asquith's after the armistice were so apt . . ."

They brought the cake close to my high chair for me to see, with the candle shining and flickering above the pink icing. "A pity she never smiles."

"She'll smile in time," my mother said, obviously upset.

"What Asquith told the House of Commons just after the war," said that stout gentleman with his backside to the fire, "—so apt, what Asquith said. He said that the war has cleansed and purged the world. . . . I recall his actual words: 'All things have become new. In this great cleansing and purging it has been the privilege of our country to play her part . . .' "

That did it. I broke into a decided smile and everyone noticed it, convinced that it was provoked by the fact that my brother had blown out the candle on the cake. "She smiled!" my mother exclaimed. And everyone was clucking away about how I was smiling. For good measure I crowed like a demented raven. "My baby's smiling!" said my mother.

"It was the candle on her cake," they said.

. . . Since that time I have grown to smile quite naturally, like any other healthy and house-trained person, but when I really mean a smile, deeply felt from the core, then to all intents and purposes it comes in response to the words uttered in the House of Commons after the First World War by the distinguished, the immaculately dressed and the late Mr. Asquith. ❖

24. **Daimler** (dīm′lər): a German automobile-manufacturing company.
25. ***What . . . guns:*** the beginning of Owen's "Anthem for Doomed Youth."

WORDS TO KNOW
demented (dĭ-mĕn′tĭd) *adj.* insane

1226

Teaching Options

Standardized Test Practice

IDENTIFYING A WRITER'S PURPOSE

On some standardized tests, students will be asked to pick a sentence that best describes the writer's purpose. Read aloud or write on the chalkboard the following question.

Which of the following best describes the writer's purpose?

A. She is attempting to show that all babies are omniscient.

B. The story shows the horrors of war, but the death of the Romanovs illustrates the sad necessity of warfare.

C. She wants to show the pointless carnage of war between countries and the foolishness of those countries' leaders.

Lead students through the process of choosing the best answer. Consider each choice. Point out that while all of the statements contain some accurate information, the best answer should include information that is both verifiable and completely true. For that reason, **C** is the best choice.

Connect to the Literature

1. **What Do You Think?** What is your reaction to the story? Share your thoughts with your classmates.

Comprehension Check
- Why is the narrator's mother worried about her baby?
- Why do the relatives think the baby smiles?

Think Critically

2. Why do you think Muriel Spark chose to tell the story from the unusual perspective of a baby?

3. Why do you think the **narrator** finally smiles after hearing Asquith's postwar remarks?

- her opinion of world figures and the people around her
- her reactions to news about the war
- Asquith's reference to the war as "this great cleansing and purging"

4. ACTIVE READING ANALYZING SATIRE Review the chart that you completed in your READER'S NOTEBOOK. What do you think is the main point of the **satire** in this story? How does the unusual **point of view** of the narrator contribute to creating the satire?

Extend Interpretations

5. **Critic's Corner** The critic Michiko Kakutani has remarked that Spark presents a "distinctly dark view of human nature" in her stories. Do you think her comment can be applied to this story?

6. **Comparing Texts** How do you think Vera Brittain, author of the excerpt from *Testament of Youth* (page 1114), would respond to this story? Explain your answer.

7. **Connect to Life** If an author chose to tell a similar story from the perspective of a baby living today, what people and events might the baby "tune in to"?

Literary Analysis

POINT OF VIEW Many stories are told from a **first-person point of view,** by narrators who participate in the stories' action. Another common narrative point of view is the **third-person omniscient** (all-knowing) **point of view,** in which the narrator is outside the story's action but can see into the minds of more than one character. It is unusual, however, for these two narrative techniques to be merged in a **first-person omniscient point of view** like that used in "The First Year of My Life."

Cooperative Learning Activity With a group of three or four classmates, look through the story and choose a passage that you find particularly amusing. Rewrite the passage, telling the events from either a first-person or a third-person limited point of view. What changes do you notice in the **tone** of the passage?

At this point, the
baby was sleeping
twenty hours a day.

GUIDING STUDENT RESPONSE

Connect to the Literature

1. **What Do You Think?**
Accept all reasonable responses.

Comprehension Check
- She is worried because the baby won't smile.
- The relatives think the baby smiles in response to her brother blowing out the candle on her birthday cake.

 Use Selection Quiz in **Unit Seven Resource Book** p. 18.

Think Critically

2. This unusual perspective allows the author to satirize events more effectively by contrasting the baby's wisdom with the adults' foolishness.
3. She finally smiles because of Asquith's inane comments in which he describes the war as "this great cleansing and purging," while she has spent the first year of her life aware of all the death and destruction caused by the war.
4. Responses will vary. Students should understand that the story satirizes the terrible, pointless nature of war, and that the unusual point of view is meant to enhance the satire.

Extend Interpretations

Critic's Corner Possible Response: The "dark view" may refer to the tone of Spark's stories and her use of satire. This comment could be applied here, because this story is a commentary on the foolishness of people who accept and even celebrate war.

Comparing Texts Accept all reasonable responses. Vera Brittain would probably find this story sympathetic, since both writers point out the futility and utter waste of war.

Connect to Life Responses will vary. The baby may tune in to crime in the streets, the strife in the Balkans, or the bombing of the U. S Embassies in Kenya and Tanzania.

Literary Analysis

Cooperative Learning Activity Students may find that the tone becomes less satirical and mocking.

THE FIRST YEAR OF MY LIFE 1227

Writing Options

Letter to Asquith Responses will vary, but the overall tone should be sarcastic, mocking, or contemptuous.

Activities & Explorations

Parliament Debate Students might be encouraged to select one student to play Asquith, and imagine what he might say in response.

Vocabulary in Action

1. crazy
2. fool
3. mutiny
4. truth (in the sense of trustworthiness or genuineness)
5. camouflage

Writing Options

Letter to Asquith As the narrator of this story, write a letter to Mr. Asquith, giving your opinion of his comments to the House of Commons.

Activities & Explorations

Parliament Debate Imagine that you were in the House of Commons when Asquith made his remarks about the results of the war. Role-play a scene in which other members of Parliament take issue with Asquith and dispute his comments. ~ **SPEAKING AND LISTENING**

Vocabulary in Action

EXERCISE: WORD MEANING Answer the following questions.

1. If you called someone **demented,** would you mean that the person was insulting, powerful, or crazy?
2. If you were **omniscient,** would someone find it difficult to see you, to soothe you, or to fool you?
3. What cannot be successful without the involvement of **seditious** people—a contest, a mutiny, or a charity fundraiser?
4. If you questioned the **authenticity** of something, would you be doubting its truth, its safety, or its legality?
5. What do soldiers sometimes use to make it difficult for the enemy to **discern** them—radar, helmets, or camouflage?

Building Vocabulary
Several Words to Know in this lesson contain prefixes and suffixes. For an in-depth study of word parts, see page 1104.

Muriel Spark
1918–

Other Works
"The Twins"
"The Ormolu Clock"
"Miss Pinkerton's Apocalypse"
"You Should Have Seen the Mess"
"The Playhouse Called Remarkable"

Early Adventures Born in Edinburgh, Scotland, Muriel Spark attended James Gillespie's Girls' School in that city, where her literary efforts were encouraged and she was considered the school's "poet and dreamer." In 1937, at the age of 19, she moved to Central Africa, marrying there shortly afterward. Although her African venture provided her with excellent material for some of the stories she would later publish, her marriage was not successful; after a divorce, she returned to Great Britain in 1944. In order to have a closer view of the realities of World War II, which was then raging, she decided to live in London rather than Edinburgh. There she worked for the Intelligence Service's anti-Nazi propaganda department until the war's end.

A Writing Career Spark remained in London for more than a decade after the war, writing poetry, short stories, and biographies and working as an editor. In 1957, she published the first of her many novels, *The Comforters.* A few of her best-known works, including *The Prime of Miss Jean Brodie,* have been made into movies.

A People Watcher Many of the characters in Spark's stories are based on real people who have touched her life. In her autobiography, *Curriculum Vitae,* she states, "I can't remember a time when I was not a person-watcher, a behaviorist." Of her very early years, she remarks, "People were far more important to me than toys or nature."

LaserLinks: Background for Reading
Historical Connection

PREPARING to *Read*

The Moment

Poetry by MARGARET ATWOOD

"No, they whisper.
You own nothing."

Connect to Your Life

Moments of Revelation Think about a moment when you were struck by a new awareness or had an important insight into something you didn't understand or recognize before. What prompted the revelation? What effect, if any, did the insight have on you? Discuss your insight with a classmate.

Build Background

Canadian Literature Since 1867, Canada has functioned as a British Dominion, one of a group of nations allied under the British Crown. Although the reigning English monarch is the official head of state, Canada is self-governing. British influence is seen in the structure of Canada's government, which is modeled after British Parliament, but Canada has developed its own heritage and is a blend of distinctly different cultures, of which English is only one.

Canadian literature did not begin to flourish until the 1960s, when a sense of nationalism spurred efforts to promote Canadian culture. One of the most effective promoters of Canadian literature, and one of its most talented contributors, is Margaret Atwood.

Atwood began her writing career as a poet. She went on to write many successful novels and short stories but, unlike many who have achieved success in fiction, she has continued to write poetry. Atwood's writing in both genres is characterized by her use of vivid images and precise language. Her poem "The Moment" appears in *Morning in the Burned House,* a collection of her poetry published in 1995.

Focus Your Reading

LITERARY ANALYSIS THEME IN CONTEMPORARY POETRY

Themes, or central ideas, in contemporary poetry are usually implied rather than stated and can therefore be difficult to understand. Read "The Moment" slowly, paying attention to the ideas suggested. Then read the poem a second time in order to see what further insights can be gained.

ACTIVE READING ANALYZING STRUCTURE **Structure** in poetry involves the arrangement of words and lines to produce a desired effect and emphasize certain aspects of content. "The Moment" is organized into three free-verse stanzas of six lines each. As you read the poem, notice the structure of each stanza and the relationship between the stanzas.

READER'S NOTEBOOK Using a chart like the one shown, **summarize** each stanza's major idea and then jot down what you notice about the structure of each stanza.

Stanza	Major Idea	Details About Structure
attribute 1		
attribute 2		
attribute 3		

OVERVIEW

Objectives

1. appreciate and understand the poet's use of **theme** in a contemporary poem **(Literary Analysis)**
2. appreciate the poet's use of **personification (Literary Analysis)**
3. **analyze structure** in a contemporary poem **(Active Reading)**

Summary

The narrator feels, in the first stanza, a moment of strong ownership of place. Instantly, in the second stanza, all nature in that place responds, withdrawing and rejecting the human claimant. In the third stanza, nature speaks. It tells the human that it is not to be owned and that, rather than the person owning or discovering nature, the reverse is true.

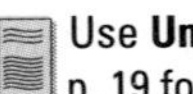
Use **Unit Seven Resource Book,** p. 19 for additional support.

Thematic Link

In the moment described in this poem, Atwood describes a discrepancy between **appearance and reality.** Sensitivity to relationships is prominent in Margaret Atwood's work, and in "The Moment," she gives nature a voice to explain that gifts of the natural world are shared with, not owned by, humans.

5-Minute Warm-Up

Daily Language SkillBuilder

Have students **proofread** the display sentences on page 1189i and write them correctly. The sentences also appear on Transparency 33 of **Grammar Transparencies and Copymasters.**

LESSON RESOURCES

UNIT SEVEN RESOURCE BOOK, pp. 19–20

ASSESSMENT RESOURCES

Formal Assessment, pp. 225–226

Teacher's Guide to Assessment and Portfolio Use

Test Generator

SKILLS TRANSPARENCIES AND COPYMASTERS

Literary Analysis
- Theme, T9 (for Literary Analysis, p. 1229)

Reading and Critical Thinking
- Analyzing Text, T18 (for Active Reading, p. 1229)

Grammar
- Commas with Nonessential Elements, T55 (for Mini Lesson, p. 1233)
- Relative Clauses, C108 (for Mini Lesson, p. 1233)
- Identifying Adjective Clauses, C109 (for Mini Lesson, p. 1233)

Writing
- The Uses of Dialogue, T24 (for Writing Option 1, p. 1233)
- Autobiographical Incident, C36 (for Writing Option 2, p. 1233)

Communications
- Reading Aloud, T11 (for Activities & Explorations, p. 1233)

INTEGRATED TECHNOLOGY

Audio Library

LaserLinks
- Author's Background: Margaret Atwood. See **Teacher's SourceBook,** p. 91.

Visit our website:
www.mcdougallittell.com

TEACHING THE LITERATURE

Reading and Analyzing

Active Reading

ANALYZING STRUCTURE

Ask students how the three-stanza structure emphasizes the sequence of events the poet wants to depict as occurring in a moment of time. Have students consider how the speakers, stanza breaks, and use of italics contribute to the meaning of the poem.

Possible Responses: Each stanza is a sequential step: first, the human speaker claims ownership; second, the speaker experiences nature's reaction; third, nature speaks in rebuttal (italics). The three perspectives of the same moment become almost a chorus of voices that produces one shared experience.

Use **Unit Seven Resource Book,** p. 20 for more practice.

Literary Analysis

THEME IN CONTEMPORARY POETRY

Ask students to explain the literary theme of the poem and to support their ideas by citing the text.

Possible Responses: human urge to possess or claim ownership, line 6; human interaction with nature, lines 7–12; transience of humans, line 14.

Use **Unit Seven Resource Book,** p. 21 for more exercises.

Literary Analysis: PERSONIFICATION

Point out to students that Atwood uses personification, portraying nature as a character. Have them draw conclusions about how this personification supports the theme and structure of the poem.

Possible Responses: By personifying nature, Atwood strengthens the theme of nature's resistance to being owned.

1230

Teaching Options

Viewing and Representing

Untitled (painting of Helga Testorf)
by Andrew Wyeth

Art Appreciation This is one of the Helga pictures, a series of 240 paintings and sketches of a woman who was a neighbor of the New England painter Andrew Wyeth that Wyeth completed over a 15-year period.

Instruction Have students comment on how the depiction of the person and the landscape relate to the poem's theme.

Possible Responses: The human fills only a bit of the picture; nature fills the rest. The woman seems to have come to this place "after many years of hard work." In the setting, she looks confident and comfortable enough to claim, "I own this," but the dominance of the natural details refutes such a claim.

Application Ask how details in the painting show the relationship between the human and the natural setting.

Possible Response: The woman stands close to the tree, implying her sense of connection with it. Several details of her "body language" are echoed—and dwarfed—by the setting.

Autumn, 1984. Watercolor, 21″ × 291/2″. Collection of Mr. and Mrs. Andrew Wyeth. Copyright Andrew Wyeth.

The Moment

MARGARET ATWOOD

The moment when, after many years
of hard work and a long voyage
you stand in the centre of your room,
house, half-acre, square mile, island, country,
knowing at last how you got there,
and say, *I own this,*

is the same moment the trees unloose
their soft arms from around you,
the birds take back their language,
the cliffs fissure and collapse,
the air moves back from you like a wave
and you can't breathe.

No, they whisper. *You own nothing.*
You were a visitor, time after time
climbing the hill, planting the flag, proclaiming.
We never belonged to you.
You never found us.
It was always the other way round.

10 fissure (fĭsh′ər): to crack; split apart

Customizing Instruction

Less Proficient Readers

Point out that there are several characters in this short poem. Have students identify and explain the role each plays in the scene Atwood creates.

Possible Responses: the person who speaks to claim ownership of the natural world; the natural world, which speaks its reply; the speaker/narrator who describes the interaction between the two interlocutors

Students Acquiring English

Explain that the first two stanzas are one long sentence. Atwood breaks the sentence into two parallel phrases in order to collapse two moments into one. Help students simplify each phrase and have them offer a simple paraphrase of the entire sentence.

Possible Response: The moment when you feel like you are finally in command of nature is the same moment that nature retreats from you.

 Use **Spanish Study Guide** for additional support, pp. 293–295.

Gifted and Talented

Invite students to consider the concept of ownership applied to elements of the natural world, such as natural resources (the ocean, national parks, oil, etc.), animals (including pets and zoos), even their own physical person. Have them think about whether it is possible or desirable to "own" these things, and encourage them to do additional research (on environmental issues or animals rights, for example).

Multicultural Link: Reverence for Nature

Although Western cultures tend to view nature as divided into human and nonhuman (a cultural inheritance from the Greeks), other cultures emphasize the oneness of humans and nature. Students may know of such beliefs among Native American peoples, but may not know of other cultural traditions, such as *Shinto* in Japan. Central to *Shinto* is the idea of *kami,* the essential and unique spirit found in all creatures and things in nature. This sense of respect, reverence, and connection with nature is reflected in Japanese culture. For instance, Japan had a tradition of landscape art centuries before the West. Japanese architecture also pays close attention to the landscape. Traditional Japanese structures are inspired and carefully situated in their surroundings, mingling indoors and outdoors by using only thin paper screens as walls and doors.

For further exploration, encourage students to research the beliefs of Native American peoples. Have students focus on how belief in the unity of humans with nature manifests itself in cultural myths, hunting rituals, funeral customs, art, and architecture.

GUIDING STUDENT RESPONSE

Connect to the Literature

1. **What Do You Think?**
Guidelines for student response: Make a cluster diagram on the chalkboard of the images that students mention.

Comprehension Check

- Possible Responses: success, the purchase of location, a return to the place of a fond memory
- Possible Response: The place withdraws the support that led the person to a feeling of possession.

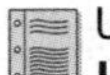 Use Selection Quiz in **Unit Seven Resource Book,** p. 22.

Thinking Critically

2. Possible Responses: travels, experiences, or path toward a goal
3. Possible Responses: After the human's declaration of ownership, nature recoils; it rejects one that it once embraced; it denies ever belonging to or being "found" by that person.
4. Possible Response: The speakers are representatives of nature, addressing the human visitor. Whispering is the "natural language" of trees and wind; it also implies reverence.
5. Students should note that the first stanza establishes the setting, the second stanza personifies it, and the third gives it voice in order to counter, in formal sentences, the first two stanzas' free-form structure and ideas.

Literary Analysis

Activity Have students share their ideas in a class discussion about Atwood's use of theme, imagery, and figurative language.

Thinking through the LITERATURE

Connect to the Literature

1. **What Do You Think?** What **image** lingers in your mind after reading this poem?

Comprehension Check

- What has the person being addressed in the poem apparently accomplished?
- What happens after the person says, "I own this"?

Think Critically

2. What do you think is meant by "the voyage" in line 2?
3. How would you explain the events described in the second stanza?

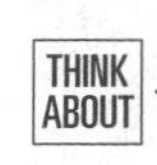
THINK ABOUT
- the declaration made in line 6
- the description of the person being addressed as "a visitor" in line 14
- the statement made in line 16

4. What do you think the speakers in the last stanza mean when they say, "It was always the other way round"?

THINK ABOUT
- who the speakers are
- who they are addressing
- why they whisper

5. **ACTIVE READING** ANALYZING STRUCTURE Look over the summaries and details you wrote down in the chart in your READER'S NOTEBOOK. How is the structure in the third stanza different from that of the first two stanzas? What is the effect of this change in structure?

Extend Interpretations

6. **Critic's Corner** According to critic John Bemrose, "Atwood's hallmark as a poet has always been a combination of startling, razor-sharp images held in tight control." Do you think the images in "The Moment" are "startling" and "razor-sharp"? Why or why not? In what way are they held in "tight control"?
7. **Comparing Texts** Compare the attitude toward nature expressed in this poem with that in William Wordsworth's "The World Is Too Much with Us" on page 725.
8. **Connect to Life** In your opinion, are possessiveness and territoriality part of human nature? If so, do you think people should try to curb their desire to own material goods and land?

Literary Analysis

THEME IN CONTEMPORARY POETRY

The **theme** or themes in a contemporary poem can often be conveyed by the sensory experiences created through **imagery.** What senses does this line from "The Moment" appeal to?

the cliffs fissure and collapse

Theme can also be understood by examining the effects created by the **figurative language** in a poem. Atwood uses both **simile** and **personification** to express her ideas. Personification is a type of figurative language in which human qualities are attributed to an object, an animal, or an idea. Think about the effect created by personification in the following lines from the poem:

. . . the trees unloose
their soft arms from around you

What ideas and emotions do these examples of imagery and figurative language suggest?

Activity Notice the relationship between theme, imagery, and figurative language in Atwood's poem, paying particular attention to her use of personification. Write down some of the themes in the poem. Beside each theme you identify, list the images and figurative language that are used to develop it. Then answer the following questions: What is the impact of the poem's imagery? Why does Atwood use personification to convey theme?

Extend Interpretations

Critic's Corner Students might include images of trees and air drawing away as "startling" or "sharp." Atwood holds tight control in the poem's structure, with three stanzas of six lines each.
Comparing Texts Possible Responses: Both speak to the detachment of humans from the natural world. *(". . . we are out of tune; / It moves us not.")* Both personify nature. *("bosom to the moon . . .")* Differences are seen in Wordsworth's comments that *"Little we see in Nature that is ours,"* which could indicate his view that nature is separate from "our" human concerns.
Connect to Life Accept all reasonable responses.

Writing Options

1. Dialogue Between Opposites Write a dialogue between the "you" and the "they" in the poem. Have both sides explain and defend their positions.

2. Personal Essay Write a personal essay about the insight you recalled in Connect to Your Life on page 1229. Place the essay in your **Working Portfolio.**

Activities & Explorations

Musical Reading Choose a piece of music to accompany a dramatic reading of "The Moment." The music should evoke the images and convey the mood in the poem. Play the background music while you read the poem to the class.
~ **PERFORMING/MUSIC**

Inquiry & Research

Canadian Literature Find out more about Canadian literature. In addition to Margaret Atwood, who are some of the country's major contemporary writers? What subjects or themes do they deal with in their work? What, if anything, have these writers done to promote Canadian culture? Present your findings in an oral report.

Margaret Atwood

1939–

Other Works
The Circle Game
Wilderness Tips
Alias Grace

Child of the Wilderness During much of her childhood, Margaret Atwood and her family spent six or seven months of every year living in the Canadian bush, the sparsely populated areas of northern Quebec and Ontario. These trips were an important part of her father's job as an entomologist, a scientist who collects and studies insects. For Atwood, the trips provided vast knowledge of the natural world, knowledge that would appear in her writing many years later.

Supportive Family Atwood began writing poems at age 5, and by age 16, she knew that writing was her sole ambition. She has credited her parents for their supportive role in her early pursuits. Although they did not urge her to become a writer, they did expect her to put her intelligence and creative talent to good use. Atwood grew up in a highly educated family of readers and storytellers who believed that girls as well as boys should acquire all the education they could. In this respect, her parents were unlike many of their contemporaries during the 1950s, when society generally pushed young women toward marriage and often discouraged them from other pursuits.

Academic Life In 1961, Atwood graduated with honors in English from Victoria College at the University of Toronto, where she had displayed her creativity not only in writing but also in drama and art. That same year, her first collection of poetry was published. She received a Master of Arts degree in English from Radcliffe College at Harvard University in 1962 and later began working toward a doctorate at Harvard. She has taught English literature and creative writing in universities in Canada, Australia, Germany, and the United States.

Accolades and Adulation By the 1970s, Atwood's writing had gained worldwide attention, and by 1982, her work had been published in 14 different languages. She is especially popular in her native Canada, where she has gained the status usually accorded only to movie stars and musicians. Atwood was honored for her first book of poems and has been receiving awards for both her poetry and her prose ever since. She has twice been the recipient of the Governor General's Award, Canada's most prestigious literary honor.

LaserLinks: Background for Reading
Author Background

Writing Options

1. **Dialogue Between Opposites** Student responses will vary, but should contain a succinct statement of main ideas on each side. **To create a more challenging writing option,** have students create a play between these two opposites, with suggested stage directions. This dialogue can be read aloud with the class.
2. **Personal Essay** Responses will vary, but students should cite specific details to support their insight.

Activities & Explorations

Musical Reading You may wish to request a written or oral explanation from the student for the musical choice.

Inquiry & Research

Canadian Literature Students might use general studies of contemporary Canadian culture to become familiar with Canada's artistic traditions, and then move on to more specific sources like anthologies of Canadian poetry, prose, or drama. Encourage students to read the work of several authors and to focus on one or two writers in whom they are particularly interested.

Mini Lesson Grammar

RELATIVE CLAUSES

Instruction An adjective clause functions as an adjective to modify a noun or a pronoun. A relative clause is an adjective clause that begins with either the relative pronoun *that, which, who, whose,* or *whom,* or with the relative adverb *after, before, since, when, where,* or *why.* Within the clause, a relative pronoun can act as the subject, the direct object, the object of a preposition, or a modifier; a relative adverb always modifies the verb within the clause. If a relative clause is not essential to the meaning of the sentence, it should be set off with commas.

Activity Write the following sentence on the chalkboard. Have students identify the relative clause and relative pronoun or relative adverb. Ask what function the relative pronoun or relative adverb has within the clause.

The speaker of the poem, <u>who is not necessarily the author herself</u>, has a powerful message. *(who, relative pronoun; subject of the linking verb "is")*

Use **Grammar Transparencies and Copymasters,** p. 51.

Use McDougal Littell's ***Language Network*** for more instruction and practice in relative clauses.

OVERVIEW

Objectives

1. understand and appreciate how two modern poets use **sound devices (Literary Analysis)**
2. **interpret imagery** to understand and appreciate two modern poems **(Active Reading)**

Summary

In "Digging," the speaker sits, pen in hand, preparing to write. He hears his father digging in the flowerbeds outside his window. He looks out, sees his father, and flashes back 20 years. In his memory, he sees his father planting potatoes, and then he has an earlier memory of his father's father cutting peat on the bog. He admires both men's skill with a spade and recognizes that he will continue the family tradition symbolically by digging with his pen.

In "The Horses," the speaker recalls an early morning walk through the British moors where he encountered ten horses standing in the gray morning. He recalls the calmness and silence. In the end, he relates his hope of recalling this solitary memory as he walks through his daily life on the busy streets of a city.

Thematic Link

Both of the poems, "Digging" and "The Horses," deal with different aspects of the contrast between **appearance and reality.**

Editor's Note This selection contains language that may be considered objectionable.

5-Minute Warm-Up

Daily Language SkillBuilder

Have students **proofread** the display sentences on page 1189i and write them correctly. The sentences also appear on Transparency 34 of **Grammar Transparencies and Copymasters.**

Digging

Poetry by SEAMUS HEANEY (shā′məs hā′nē)

The Horses

Poetry by TED HUGHES

Comparing Literature of the World

The Poetry of Seamus Heaney, Ted Hughes, and Czeslaw Milosz

This lesson and the one that follows present an opportunity for comparing lyric poems by the Irish poet Seamus Heaney, the English poet Ted Hughes, and the Polish poet Czeslaw Milosz. Specific points of comparison in the Milosz lesson will help you note similarities and differences in the poets' reflections on ordinary experiences and the larger meanings of those experiences.

Connect to Your Life

Lasting Impressions Think about the kinds of experiences that have made lasting impressions on you. Did those experiences involve ordinary events or extraordinary moments? Jot down some of your lasting impressions and your thoughts about them.

Build Background

Two Gifted Poets The Irish poet Seamus Heaney grew up on a farm in Northern Ireland. Although much of Heaney's work is concerned with the political unrest in his native land, there is also a concern with the poet as a craftsman who interacts with the force and mystery of language. Heaney's poems are characterized by themes and images taken from the natural world and rural life. His early poems, in particular, reflect the land and experiences of his childhood. His work shows the influence of both William Wordsworth and Gerard Manley Hopkins. "Digging" was the opening poem in his first book, *Death of a Naturalist,* published in 1966. In describing the poem, Heaney once said, "This was the first place where I felt I had done more than make an arrangement of words: I felt that I had let down a shaft into real life."

As a young man, Heaney was inspired by the writing of a slightly older contemporary, the English poet Ted Hughes. Many of Hughes's poems describe wild natural settings. He frequently focused on the savage, predatory aspects of animals and sometimes used animals to probe the instinctual, nonrational side of human life. Hughes's fascination with nature began during his youth, when he loved to hunt. Gradually, his passion shifted from literal hunting to searching for the essential qualities and energies of animals and writing about his discoveries in poetry. "The Horses," one of Hughes's earliest poems, appeared in his first book, *The Hawk in the Rain,* published in 1957.

Focus Your Reading

LITERARY ANALYSIS SOUND DEVICES Poets employ various **sound devices.** These include the following:

- **repetition**—the repeated use of words and phrases
- **alliteration**—the repetition of consonant sounds at the beginning of words
- **consonance**—the repetition of consonant sounds within words
- **assonance**—the repetition of vowel sounds within words

As you read these poems, be aware of the various sound devices used by the two poets.

ACTIVE READING INTERPRETING IMAGERY Read through each poem and look for **imagery** that appeals to one or more of the five senses—sight, hearing, smell, taste, touch. Note how images help the reader to visualize and otherwise bring to mind the characters, settings, or events being described and how they relate to the meaning of the poem.

READER'S NOTEBOOK List the images from each poem. Then indicate which senses each image appeals to.

LESSON RESOURCES

UNIT SEVEN RESOURCE BOOK, pp. 21–22

ASSESSMENT RESOURCES

Formal Assessment, p. 227

Teacher's Guide to Assessment and Portfolio Use

Test Generator

SKILLS TRANSPARENCIES AND COPYMASTERS

Literary Analysis
- Poetic Devices, T16 (for Literary Analysis, p. 1234)

Reading and Critical Thinking
- Comparing Authors' Views, T24 (for Extend Interpretations 6, p. 1239)

Grammar
- Sentence Fragments, T42 (for Mini Lesson, p. 1240)
- Deliberate Fragments, C127 (for Mini Lesson, p. 1240)

Vocabulary
- Connotation, C95 (for Mini Lesson, p. 1235)

Writing
- Sensory Word List, T14 (for Writing Option 2, p. 1240)
- Compare-Contrast, C34 (for Writing Option 1, p. 1240)

INTEGRATED TECHNOLOGY

Audio Library

Visit our website: www.mcdougallittell.com

DIGGING

SEAMUS HEANEY

Between my finger and my thumb
The squat pen rests; snug as a gun.

Under my window, a clean rasping sound
When the spade sinks into gravelly ground:
My father, digging. I look down

Till his straining rump among the flowerbeds
Bends low, comes up twenty years away
Stooping in rhythm through potato drills
Where he was digging.

8 drills: furrows for planting seeds.

TEACHING THE LITERATURE

Customizing Instruction

Less Proficient Readers
Ask what the speaker might mean by saying that his father, bending down, comes up *twenty years away?*
Possible Response: Although the speaker is writing in the present tense, he travels through time and remembers when his father was a younger man. He is remembering his father from twenty years ago, rather than seeing him physically as he is today.

Students Acquiring English
Help students understand that alliteration (the repetition of consonant sounds at the beginning of words) often can illustrate the meaning of the words. Have students pick out the alliterative words in line 4 and help them understand how the sounds contribute to the meaning of the line.
Possible Response: *spade* and *sinks; gravelly* and *ground;* the repeated *s* sounds like the slick movement of the spade, and the repeated *gr* sounds like the friction caused by digging gravelly ground.

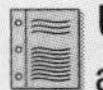
Use **Spanish Study Guide** for additional support, pp. 296–298.

Gifted and Talented
Students who are interested in Ireland may want to research the agrarian history of the island, especially the roles that potatoes, peat, and the land have played in the lives of the Irish.

Vocabulary Strategy

CONNOTATION
Instruction Remind students that **denotation** is the dictionary definition, or literal meaning, of the word. **Connotation** refers to the ideas or feelings a word suggest, or the emotions a word evokes.
Activity Point out the word *coarse* in line 10 of "Digging." Ask students what connotations that word has for them. Invite them to think of a synonym for *coarse* and substitute that word in the poem. Does the sense of the line change?

After reading the two poems, have students work in pairs to identify at least two more words from "Digging" and two words from "The Horses" that have a particular connotation. Have them identify the connotation and suggest synonyms that would change the words' connotative meaning. Then ask them to discuss the connotative power of the words Heaney chooses.

Use **Vocabulary Transparencies and Copymasters,** p. 72.

A lesson on denotation and connotation appears on page 645 in the Pupil's Edition.

DIGGING **1235**

Reading and Analyzing

Literary Analysis SOUND DEVICES

Which consonant and vowel sounds does Hughes use repeatedly in the first 12 lines? Encourage students to discuss the effect of these repeated sounds on the poem's mood.

Possible Response: the consonants *w, f, d, g, b, h,* and *m,* and the vowel sounds *oo, ay,* and *eh*

Use **Unit Seven Resource Book** p. 24 for more exercises.

Active Reading

INTERPRETING IMAGERY

Have students consider the poet's phrase *living roots awaken in my head.* What visual image is evoked here? What other meanings can the word *roots* have?

Possible Response: The poet's image evokes the idea of a plant or tree, perhaps a family tree. *Roots* can also refer to one's ancestry.

Use **Unit Seven Resource Book** p. 23 for more practice.

Thinking Through the Literature

1. The father is a potato farmer; the grandfather is a peat cutter.
2. The speaker admires them. He feels guilty for departing from their way of life, and he feels he must live up to their examples.
3. The kind of digging the speaker plans to do is digging in memory and history. It is his way of following in his forefather's footsteps; therefore, the past is very important to him.

The coarse boot nestled on the lug, the shaft
Against the inside knee was levered firmly.
He rooted out tall tops, buried the bright edge deep
To scatter new potatoes that we picked
Loving their cool hardness in our hands.

By God, the old man could handle a spade.
Just like his old man.

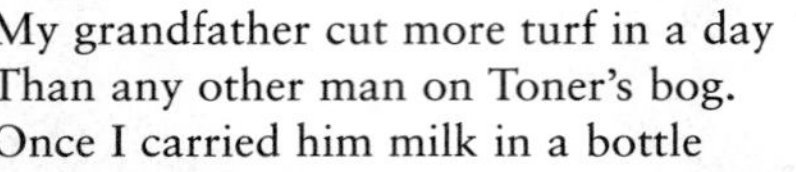

My grandfather cut more turf in a day
Than any other man on Toner's bog.
Once I carried him milk in a bottle
Corked sloppily with paper. He straightened up
To drink it, then fell to right away
Nicking and slicing neatly, heaving sods
Over his shoulder, going down and down
For the good turf. Digging.

The cold smell of potato mold, the squelch and slap
Of soggy peat, the curt cuts of an edge
Through living roots awaken in my head.
But I've no spade to follow men like them.

Between my finger and my thumb
The squat pen rests.
I'll dig with it.

10 lug: a widening at the top of a shovel blade to support the foot.

17–18 Turf, or peat—partially decayed vegetable matter found in wet areas called bogs—was cut in blocks, called sods, and used as fuel in Ireland.

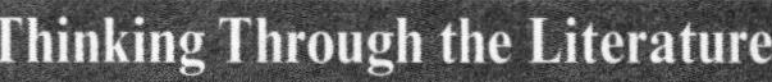

Thinking Through the Literature

1. **Comprehension Check** What do the speaker's father and grandfather do for a living?
2. How would you describe the relationship between the **speaker** and his father and grandfather? Be specific in your answer.
3. How important are the lasting impressions of the past to the speaker's understanding of his future?

THINK ABOUT
- how his father "buried the bright edge deep" (line 12)
- his grandfather "heaving sods" (line 22) and "going down and down" (line 23)
- what kind of digging the speaker plans to do

Teaching Options

BLOCK SCHEDULING: MANAGING TIME

If your schedule requires that you cover lesson objectives in a shorter time, use . . .
- Preparing to Read, p. 1234
- Thinking Through the Literature, pp. 1236, 1239

If you want to take advantage of longer class time, use . . .
- TE Teaching Options: Vocabulary, p. 1235; Cross Curricular Links, p. 1237; Standardized Test Practice, p. 1238; Grammar, p. 1240
- Choices & Challenges, p. 1240

THE HORSES

TED HUGHES

I climbed through woods in the hour-before-dawn dark.
Evil air, a frost-making stillness,

Not a leaf, not a bird—
A world cast in frost. I came out above the wood

Where my breath left tortuous statues in the iron light.
But the valleys were draining the darkness

Till the moorline—blackening dregs of the brightening gray—
Halved the sky ahead. And I saw the horses:

Huge in the dense gray—ten together—
Megalith-still. They breathed, making no move,

With draped manes and tilted hind-hooves,
Making no sound.

I passed: not one snorted or jerked its head.
Gray silent fragments

Of a gray silent world.

5 tortuous: winding or twisting.

7 moorline: the horizon at the edge of a moor, a large area of high, open land; **dregs:** small amounts left over.

10 megalith: a very large stone of the sort used in various prehistoric formations, such as Stonehenge in England.

1237

Customizing Instruction

Less Proficient Readers

Have students keep these things in mind as they read:

- Who the speakers are in each poem
- What the speakers are doing at the beginning of the poem
- How the setting shifts in the poems

Students Acquiring English

Although the syntax in these two poems is generally clear, the diction, which is specific and concrete, is denser than colloquial speech. Explain, for example, that compound adjectives consist of two or more words joined with a hyphen (or hyphens) and are used to modify nouns. Have students pick out the compound adjectives in the first 10 lines of "The Horses," and help them understand the modifiers' meanings.

Possible Responses: "hour-before dawn"; "frost-making"; "megalith-still"; point out that "hind-hooves" (line 11) functions as a noun, not a modifier.

Gifted and Talented

Encourage students to compare and contrast contemporary nature poetry with older nature poetry they have read, such as that of Wordsworth or Hopkins. Wordsworth's poem "Tintern Abbey," in particular, deals with a theme also found in Hughes's poem: both poets want to preserve experiences in nature, so they can draw comfort from their recollections when they are in the city.

Cross Curricular Link Music

LYRIC A **lyric** is a short poem in which a single speaker expresses personal thought and feelings. The word *lyric* comes from the Greek word *lyre,* a musical instrument that was used to accompany songs. In modern poetry, lyrics are not usually intended for singing, but they are characterized by strong, melodic rhythms. Lyric poems can be in a variety of forms and cover many subjects, from life to death to everyday experience. Most poems, other than dramatic and narrative poems, are lyric poems.

Discuss what makes "Digging" and "The Horses" lyric poems. If these poems were songs or were read with background music, what style of music would appropriately match the mood of the poems? What sorts of instruments would work well with these words and rhythms?

Reading and Analyzing

Literary Analysis SOUND DEVICES

A Ask students to review lines 24–28 and find sounds that are repeated.

Possible Responses: *st, m, e, d, s, l*

Encourage students to discuss the effect of these repeated sounds on the poem's idea or mood.

Literary Analysis: REPETITION

B Invite students to find four words or phrases in lines 29–32 that repeat earlier passages.

Possible Responses: *draped stone manes, tilted hind-hooves, made no sound, not one snorted*

Have students discuss the effect of these repetitions.

Possible Responses: They create a mood of frozen stillness—of a moment preserved.

Reading Skills and Strategies: ANALYZING

C Ask what the last four lines imply about the speaker's feelings about the horses.

Possible Responses: They are symbols of freedom for civilization, symbols of communion with nature.

I listened in emptiness on the moor-ridge.
The curlew's tear turned its edge on the silence.

Slowly detail leafed from the darkness. Then the sun
Orange, red, red, erupted

Silently, and splitting to its core tore and flung cloud,
Shook the gulf open, showed blue,

And the big planets hanging.
I turned,

Stumbling in the fever of a dream, down toward
The dark woods, from the kindling tops,

A And came to the horses.
There, still they stood,
But now steaming and glistening under the flow of light,

B Their draped stone manes, their tilted hind-hooves
Stirring under a thaw while all around them

The frost showed its fires. But still they made no sound.
Not one snorted or stamped,

Their hung heads patient as the horizons,
High over valleys, in the red leveling rays—

C In din of the crowded streets, going among the years, the faces,
May I still meet my memory in so lonely a place

Between the streams and the red clouds, hearing curlews,
Hearing the horizons endure.

17 curlew: a large, brownish, long-legged shore bird with a long, slender, downward-curving bill.

1238

Teaching Options

Assessment Standardized Test Practice

IDENTIFYING THE WRITER'S PURPOSE For some standardized tests, students will be asked to choose the best answer regarding the author's purpose for writing. To provide students practice in choosing the best answer, read aloud or write on the chalkboard the following question.

Which of the following statements best describes Ted Hughes's purpose in writing "The Horses"?

A. Hughes wishes to recall the silence and serenity of his experience when his busy life overwhelms him.

B. Hughes wishes to protest the capture and exploitation of horses.

C. Hughes wishes to convince his readers that the horses were in a dream he had while living in the city.

Lead students through the process of choosing the best answer. Consider each choice. Point out that while all of the answers contain some element that is referenced in the poem, the best answer is **A.**

Connect to the Literature

1. **What Do You Think?** Did you find the mood in "The Horses" appealing? Why or why not?

Comprehension Check
- Where, and at what time of day, does the scene take place?
- What are the horses doing?

Think Critically

2. Why do you think the horses made such an impression on the **speaker?**

- the phrase "a world cast in frost"
- his references to darkness and silence
- his descriptions of the horses after sunrise

3. How would you describe the relationship between the speaker and the horses?

4. ACTIVE READING INTERPRETING IMAGERY Look at the list of images you made in your READER'S NOTEBOOK. What images in each of these two poems do you think are the most forceful? How do these images help convey the ideas and experiences being expressed in each poem?

5. Compare the speakers' experiences as described in "Digging" and "The Horses." Which experience had the stronger effect on you as a reader?

Extend Interpretations

6. **Comparing Texts** Both Dylan Thomas in "Do Not Go Gentle into That Good Night" (page 1087) and Seamus Heaney in "Digging" write about their fathers. What kinds of feelings and attitudes toward the father does each poet express? Compare the impression of the father that each poet leaves with the reader.

7. **Connect to Life** Which of the speakers in these two poems seems to deal more with issues and concerns similar to your own? Explain your opinion.

Literary Analysis

SOUND DEVICES Both Heaney and Hughes experiment with **sound devices** such as the **repetition** of words and phrases, **alliteration** (the repetition of consonant sounds at the beginning of words), **consonance** (the repetition of consonant sounds within words), and **assonance** (the repetition of vowel sounds within words). For example, look at the use of **alliteration** (*s* and *gr*) and **consonance** (*n, d,* and *nd*) in these lines from "Digging":

Under my window, a clean
rasping sound

When the spade sinks into a
gravelly ground . . .

Activity Look for at least one example of each technique in each of the poems. Make a list of your examples and discuss them with the class. Explain how each example provides focus or reinforces meaning.

	"Digging"	"The Horses"
Repetition		
Alliteration		
Consonance		
Assonance		

GUIDING STUDENT RESPONSE

Connect to the Literature

1. **What Do You Think?**
Guidelines for student response: Accept all appropriate responses related to students' feelings about the mood. Some possible descriptions of mood: bleak, grim, gloomy, enchanted, lurid, exciting.

Comprehension Check
- a British moor at sunrise
- They are standing in the forest, still and silent.

Use Selection Quiz in **Unit Seven Resource Book** p. 25.

Think Critically

2. Possible Response: The speaker found the horses and the surrounding landscape strange and unexpected.
3. Possible Responses: The speaker identifies with the horses; he wishes he were among the horses.
4. Accept all responses with appropriate citations.
5. Some students might be more affected by "Digging," because it is a personal reflection about family. Other students will find the powerful and majestic natural images of "The Horses" awe-inspiring.

Literary Analysis

Activity Have students work in pairs so that they can compare their choices and note any differences in their examples. They may also find it useful to read their examples aloud to each other in order to hear the various sound techniques being used. As a conclusion to the activity have students discuss the effect sound devices have on them as they read the poems.

Extend Interpretations

Comparing Texts This question is well suited for gifted and talented students. Possible Responses: Thomas expresses feelings of anger and sadness, while Heaney remembers his father's life with respect and love. Thomas leaves us with the impression of a dying father, resigned to his fate. Heaney's father is still healthy, working in the flowerbeds.

If you wish to make the question easier, have students consider these questions regarding only "Digging."

Connect to Life Accept all responses with appropriate support for opinions. Students may feel that "Digging" deals more with issues in their lives, such as making decisions about what to do as adults, or considering whether to go into a different field than their parents. "The Horses" may appeal more to those students who feel overwhelmed by the busy-ness of life.

Writing Options

1. **Comparison Booklet** Students' similes will vary. Accept all reasonable comparisons. To extend this activity, suggest that students illustrate their similes.
2. **Descriptive Paragraph** You might focus the paragraph for students by suggesting that they write about their most memorable experience with an animal.

Activities & Explorations

Scene Illustrations Extend this lesson by having students find works of art—paintings, photographs, or sculptures—that would be appropriate illustrations for the poems. Students may want to break the poems into sections and illustrate each section; for example, a student might develop a set of illustrations for the speaker, one for the father, and one for the grandfather in "Digging."

Choices & CHALLENGES

Writing Options

1. **Comparison Booklet** In "Digging" the speaker implies that, figuratively, he'll use his writing to "dig," just as his father and grandfather dug with a spade. Develop as many comparisons as you can think of that equate writing with other actions. Then, with other students, combine your comparisons in a booklet titled "Writing Is Like . . ."
2. **Descriptive Paragraph** In a descriptive paragraph, try to capture the images of an experience that made a lasting impression on you. Place the paragraph in your **Working Portfolio.**

Activities & Explorations

Scene Illustrations Create a series of drawings to illustrate three or more scenes from either "Digging" or "The Horses." ~ **ART**

Seamus Heaney
1939–

Other Works
"Blackberry-Picking"
"Follower"
"Personal Helicon"
"A Drink of Water"

Youth and First Writing Seamus Heaney was the oldest of nine children. He went to Queen's University in Belfast on a scholarship and, while there, became interested in poets who wrote about their local surroundings. The work of these poets affirmed for Heaney the validity of his own background, and after graduating in 1961, he began to write poetry regularly. His first book was published when he was 27.

Teacher and Poet Heaney took a teaching position at Queen's University and later lectured at other universities in Ireland and at universities in England and the United States. In 1969, violent conflicts erupted in Northern Ireland between the Irish Protestant allies of England and the Irish Republican Army. Shortly thereafter, Heaney, a Catholic, left Queen's and eventually settled near Dublin.

Nobel Prize Winner Today, Heaney divides his time between Dublin and Cambridge, Massachusetts, where he has taught at Harvard since 1982. Although Heaney is not comfortable being viewed as a political poet, he has dealt with the tensions and devastation of the Irish struggles with deep feeling and power. Many consider him to be the most important Irish poet since W. B. Yeats. Heaney won the Nobel Prize in literature in 1995.

Ted Hughes
1930–

Other Works
"Thistles"
"Hawk Roosting"
"The Thought-Fox"
"Wind"
"A March Calf"

Youth and Marriage Ted Hughes grew up in Yorkshire, England, and began writing poetry when he was 15. After serving in the Royal Air Force, he went to Cambridge University, where he first studied English and then anthropology and archaeology. In 1956 he met and married the American poet Sylvia Plath, and for two years they lived in the United States, where Hughes taught at the University of Massachusetts. Hughes's first book of poetry, *The Hawk in the Rain,* was published in 1957 to critical acclaim.

Poet Laureate Hughes and Plath returned to England in late 1959, and his second book, *Lupercal,* was published the next year, establishing his reputation as an important new poet. In 1962 Hughes and Plath separated, and in 1963 Plath committed suicide; for nearly three years, Hughes wrote no poetry at all. When he began writing again, however, he was prolific, producing numerous works for adults and children that included poetry, drama, short stories, and criticism. Hughes has received many awards for his literary achievements and in 1984 was named England's poet laureate.

Teaching Options

Grammar

STYLE: DELIBERATE FRAGMENTS

Instruction Experienced writers occasionally use sentence fragments for emphasis, to mark a transition, or to answer a question. Using sentence fragments can be risky, however, and if students are writing in a formal style, it is best to avoid fragments completely.

Activity Write the following sentences on the chalkboard. For each example, have students identify the fragment and tell why it is used.

"By God, the old man could handle a spade. <u>Just like his old man</u>." *(fragment emphasizes the connection between the men in the poem)*

<u>So much for the past</u>. Now we should think about the future. *(fragment marks a transition)*

Why does the speaker remember the horses? <u>Because they made such a profound impression</u>. *(fragment answers a question)*

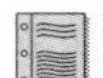

Use **Grammar Transparencies and Copymasters,** p. 67.

Use McDougal Littell's ***Language Network*** for more instruction and practice in fragments.

from

Crediting *Poetry*

THE NOBEL LECTURE

Speech by Seamus Heaney

Seamus Heaney won the 1995 Nobel Prize in literature for, in the words of the Nobel committee, "works of lyrical beauty and ethical depth, which exalt everyday miracles and the living past." This is an excerpt from the speech Heaney gave in Stockholm, Sweden, when he accepted the prize.

When I first encountered the name of the city of Stockholm, I little thought that I would ever visit it, never mind end up being welcomed to it as a guest of the Swedish Academy and the Nobel
1 Foundation. At that particular time, such an outcome was not just beyond expectation: it was simply beyond conception. In the nineteen-forties, when I was the eldest child of an ever-growing family in rural County Derry, we crowded together in the three rooms of a traditional thatched farmstead and lived a kind of den life which was more or less emotionally and intellectually proofed against the outside world. It was an intimate, physical, creaturely existence in which the night sounds of the horse in the stable beyond one bedroom wall mingled with the sounds of adult conversation from the kitchen beyond the other. We took in everything that was going on, of course—rain in the trees, mice on the ceiling, a steam train rumbling along the railway line one field back from the house—but we took it in as if we were in the doze of hibernation. Ahistorical, pre-sexual, in suspension between the archaic and the modern, we were as susceptible and impressionable
2 as the drinking water that stood in a bucket in our scullery: every time a passing train made the earth shake, the surface of that water used to ripple delicately, concentrically, and in utter silence.

But it was not only the earth that shook for us: the air around and above us was alive and signaling as well. When a wind stirred in the beeches, it also stirred

Nobel Medal

Reading for Information

What would you expect to hear in a speech by someone accepting an important prize? Heaney expresses gratitude and discusses poetry and personal experiences.

ANALYZING A SPEECH

A person giving a speech can use tones of voice, body language, and timing to make his or her meaning clear to the audience; but when the audience is a reader, those clues are lost. Nevertheless, in a well-written speech, the following devices can help convey ideas to readers as well as listeners:

- **parallel construction,** a use of like grammatical structures to make connections clear
- **repetition** of words and phrases for emphasis and clarification
- **sound devices,** such as rhythm, alliteration, and onomatopoeia (the use of words whose sound echoes their meaning), which can draw attention to concepts and descriptions
- strong **imagery** that helps the audience visualize scenes
- **figurative language** that illustrates concepts

Use the activities below to analyze this speech.

1 **Parallelism** Notice the balance created by the parallel phrasing of the two parts of this sentence. Find another sentence in which Heaney achieves a similar balance.

2 **Figurative Language** In this simile, what features of the bucket of water are likened to characteristics of Heaney's family?

RELATED *Reading*

Primary Source

Objectives

- read and analyze primary sources
- read to recognize parallel structures, repetition, sound devices, imagery, and figurative language
- understand the function of rhetorical devices in a speech

Further Background

The Nobel Prize in literature has resulted in acceptance speeches by prize winners that are noteworthy for their power, clarity, and strength as literary statements in and of themselves. Rather than delivering a standard "thank-you" speech, Seamus Heaney presents a narrative story of his experience of growing up in rural Ireland and the unlikely path that poetry created for him, unlocking the larger world of language that eventually led him to Stockholm and the Nobel Prize. His narrative style is at once distinctive in its creativity and powerful in its vivid image of the world he experienced.

Reading for Information

Students may expect a humble expression of gratitude and a sense of thankfulness. The prize winner would be gracious and perhaps would acknowledge a larger spiritual source.

Analyzing a Speech

1. **Possible Response:** "If there was something ominous in the newscaster's tones, there was something torpid about our understanding of what was at stake; and if there was something culpable about such political ignorance in that time and place, there was something positive about the security I inhabited as a result of it."
2. **Possible Response:** The similarity between the water in the bucket and Heaney's family is the simpleness and isolation of their existence; both existed in state of primitiveness—pliable and open to influence from any and all contacts with the outside world.

3. **Possible Response:** *burbles* and *squeaks*
4. **Possible Response:** The imagery appeals to the sense of hearing, an important sense because sound is a major poetic medium.
5. **Possible Response:** The parallel structure gives equal weight to the opposing situations and clarifies how Heaney was spared the terrors of World War II: (1) the ominousness of world events did not affect his neighborhood because it failed to comprehend what was truly happening, and (2) though his neighborhood could be blamed for this ignorance, at least its naivety allowed it to remain secure. (Students who did not correctly interpret the meaning of the initial *Ifs* will probably have difficulty in understanding that Heaney is talking about counterbalanced situations.)

Seamus Heaney accepting the Nobel Prize

an aerial wire attached to the topmost branch of the chestnut tree.
3 Down it swept, in through a hole bored in the corner of the kitchen window, right on into the innards of our wireless set, where a little pandemonium of burbles and squeaks would suddenly give way to the voice of a BBC newsreader speaking out of the unexpected like a deus ex machina.[1] And that voice too we could hear in our bedroom, transmitting from beyond and behind the voices of the adults in the kitchen; just as we could often hear, behind and
4 beyond every voice, the frantic, piercing signaling of Morse code.

We could pick up the names of neighbors being spoken in the local accents of our parents, and in the resonant English tones of the newsreader the names of bombers and of cities bombed, of war fronts and army divisions, the numbers of planes lost and of prisoners taken, of casualties suffered and advances made; and always, of course, we would pick up too those other, solemn, and oddly bracing words "the enemy" and "the allies." But even so, none of the news of these world spasms entered me as terror. If there was something ominous in the newscaster's tones, there was something
5 torpid[2] about our understanding of what was at stake; and if there was something culpable[3] about such political ignorance in that time and place, there was something positive about the security I inhabited as a result of it.

The wartime, in other words, was pre-reflective time for me. Pre-literate too. Pre-historical in its way. Then as the years went on and my listening became more deliberate, I would climb up on an arm of our big sofa to get my ear closer to the wireless speaker. But it

1. **deus ex machina** (dā′əs ĕks mä′kə-nə): in ancient Greek and Roman drama, a god suddenly lowered onto the stage to resolve a conflict.
2. **torpid:** sluggish.
3. **culpable:** blameworthy.

3 **Sound Devices** What instances of onomatopoeia can you find in this sentence?

4 **Imagery** Which of the five senses does the imagery in this speech mainly appeal to? Why do you think that sense is important to Heaney?

5 **Repetition and Parallelism** Notice the repetition of the phrase "there was something" in this long sentence. Read the sentence aloud to hear the rhythm of the language. How do repetition and parallelism help to clarify the sentence's meaning?

was still not the news that interested me; what I was after was the thrill of story, such as a detective serial about a British special agent called Dick Barton or perhaps a radio adaptation of one of Captain W. E. Johns's adventure tales about an RAF flying ace called Biggles. Now that the other children were older and there was so much going on in the kitchen, I had to get close to the actual radio set in order to concentrate my hearing, and in that intent proximity to the dial I grew familiar with the names of foreign stations, with Leipzig and Oslo and Stuttgart and Warsaw and, of course, with Stockholm.

I also got used to hearing short bursts of foreign languages as the dial hand swept round from BBC to Radio Eireann, from the intonations of London to those of Dublin, and even though I did not understand what was being said in those first encounters with the gutturals and sibilants of European speech, I had already begun a journey into the wideness of the world. This in turn became a
6 journey into the wideness of language, a journey where each point of arrival—whether in one's poetry or one's life—turned out to be a stepping-stone rather than a destination, and it is that journey which has brought me now to this honored spot. And yet the platform here feels more like a space station than a stepping-stone, so that is why, for once in my life, I am permitting myself the luxury of walking on air.

I credit poetry for making this space walk possible. I credit it immediately because of a line I wrote fairly recently encouraging myself (and whoever else might be listening) to "walk on air against your better judgement." But I credit it ultimately because poetry can make an order as true to the impact of external reality and as sensitive to the inner laws of the poet's being as the ripples that rippled in and rippled out across the water in that scullery bucket fifty years ago. An order where we can at last grow up to that which
7 we stored up as we grew. An order which satisfies all that is appetitive[4] in the intelligence and prehensile[5] in the affections. I credit poetry, in other words, both for being itself and for being a help, for making possible a fluid and restorative relationship between the mind's center and its circumference, between the child gazing at the word "Stockholm" on the face of the radio dial and the man facing the faces that he meets in Stockholm at this most privileged moment. I credit it because credit is due to it, in our time and in all time, for its truth to life, in every sense of that phrase. . . .

4. **appetitive** (ə-pĕt′ĭ-tĭv): desirous.

5. **prehensile** (prē-hĕn′səl): perceptive; insightful.

6 Repetition Heaney packs a lot of meaning into the sentence that begins "This in turn . . . ," using repetition to help the audience keep its bearings. Read the sentence aloud, employing pauses, changes in tone of voice, or gestures in a way that would help listeners understand it.

7 In this paragraph, Heaney returns to many of the devices he has used earlier in the speech. Identify some of these devices, and explain how they help him sum up the ideas he has been expressing.

Comparing Texts Reread Heaney's poem "Digging" on page 1234. Now that you have learned more about Heaney by reading this excerpt of his Nobel Prize acceptance speech, what new insights do you have about the poem?

6. Encourage students to read the sentence aloud several times, giving emphasis in a different pattern each time through.

7. Possible Responses: Parallelism and repetition ("I credit . . . I credit . . . But I credit . . . I credit . . . I credit" and "an order . . . An order . . . "An order") Sound Devices of onomatopoeia ("ripples that rippled in and rippled out") and of alliteration ("restorative relationship" and "face . . . facing the faces"). These devices emphasize his love and devotion to poetry.

Comparing Texts

Possible Response: The poem "Digging" illustrates the depths of connection that Heaney feels with ancestors and tradition, a connection that is equally expressed in the Nobel Prize acceptance speech.

OVERVIEW

Objectives
1. appreciate the poet's use of **imagery** in "In Music" **(Literary Analysis)**
2. understand the poet's creation of **mood** in a poem **(Literary Analysis)**
3. recognize and discuss **themes** that cross cultures **(Literary Analysis)**
4. **analyze structure** to understand transitions within a poem **(Active Reading)**

Summary
While listening to music, the speaker imagines a wedding procession. The procession disappears, but the music triumphantly endures as a reminder of ordinary lives.

Thematic Link
The wedding procession has the **appearance of reality** until it is revealed that the scene has been imagined by the speaker.

5-Minute Warm-Up
Daily Language SkillBuilder

Have students **proofread** the display sentences on page 1189j and write them correctly. The sentences also appear on Transparency 34 of **Grammar Transparencies and Copymasters.**

Reading and Analyzing

Active Reading
ANALYZING STRUCTURE

Ask students what it is that the second stanza reveals about the first.

Answer: The scene of the first stanza has been imagined by the narrator.

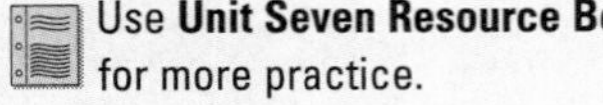

Use **Unit Seven Resource Book** p. 23 for more practice.

Literary Analysis
IMAGERY AND MOOD

Ask students to cite wedding imagery.

Possible Responses: "much white satin" (line 4); "festively stiff" [line 6]

Ask students to cite village imagery.

Possible Responses: "the hills, parched" (line 7); "dry mounds of manure" (line 8).

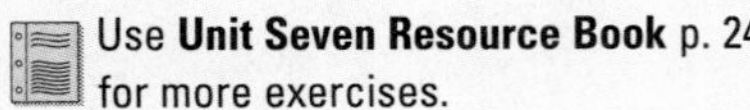

Use **Unit Seven Resource Book** p. 24 for more exercises.

In Music

Poetry by CZESLAW MILOSZ (chĕ'släv mē'wŏsh')

Comparing Literature of the World

Poetic Contemplations Across Cultures

"Digging," "The Horses," and "In Music" Contemporary lyric poetry is often reflective, focusing on impressions and moments of experience that yield insights about life. Ted Hughes in England, Seamus Heaney in Ireland, and Czeslaw Milosz in Poland and the United States all have written poems that use a particular event or image as the occasion for contemplating the meaning and significance of certain aspects of life.

Points of Comparison As you read the following poem by Milosz, compare it with those of Heaney and Hughes in terms of the following:
- the experience that each poet is responding to
- how each experience is portrayed
- the insights revealed in each poem

Build Background

Poetry in Exile Like Seamus Heaney and many other contemporary poets, Czeslaw Milosz frequently examines the past and its associations as he searches for insights into life's experiences. Sometimes called the greatest poet in Poland, he has not lived in that country since 1951, the year he defected to the West. Even after moving to the United States in 1960, Milosz continued writing in his native language, but in the 1970s he began translating his own poetry into English with the help of some of his graduate students. When his *Selected Poems* was published in 1973, his readership and his international reputation grew rapidly. In 1980 he was awarded the Nobel Prize in literature.

Focus Your Reading

LITERARY ANALYSIS IMAGERY AND MOOD Milosz makes extensive use of **imagery** in this poem, and the images shape the overall **mood** of the piece. Although many images are visual, some appeal to the sense of smell, hearing, taste, or touch. As you read, look for words and phrases that create vivid sensory experiences. Be aware of the mood that these images help to create.

ACTIVE READING ANALYZING STRUCTURE The **structure** of a poem can reflect important transitions from one thought, perspective, or image to another. These transitions are often quick and subtle, particularly in poetry, where ideas are usually expressed briefly and compactly. The two-part structure of "In Music" reflects a major transition in the poet's development of his impressions and ideas in the poem.

READER'S NOTEBOOK As you read "In Music," look for the transition that occurs between the first and second stanzas. In a chart such as the one shown, note what is described in each of the poem's stanzas.

LESSON RESOURCES

UNIT SEVEN RESOURCE BOOK, pp. 23–24

ASSESSMENT RESOURCES
Formal Assessment, p. 229
Teacher's Guide to Assessment and Portfolio Use
Test Generator

SKILLS TRANSPARENCIES AND COPYMASTERS
Literary Analysis
- Style, Tone, and Mood, T24 (for Literary Analysis, p. 1244)

Reading and Critical Thinking
- Analyzing Text, T18 (for Active Reading, p. 1244)

Grammar
- Commas with Nonessential Elements, T55 (for Mini Lesson, p. 1247)
- Style: The Appositive Phrase, C180 (for Mini Lesson, p. 1247)

Writing
- Compare-Contrast, C34 (for Writing Option 2, p. 1247)

Communications
- Dramatic Reading, T12 (for Activities & Explorations 2, p. 1247)

INTEGRATED TECHNOLOGY
Audio Library
LaserLinks
- Author Background: Czeslaw Milosz. See **Teacher's SourceBook,** p. 92.

Visit our website: www.mcdougallittell.com

In Music

Czeslaw Milosz

Wailing of a flute, a little drum.
A small wedding cortege accompanies a couple
Going past clay houses on the street of a village.
In the dress of the bride much white satin.
How many pennies put away to sew it, once in a lifetime.
The dress of the groom black, festively stiff.
The flute tells something to the hills, parched, the color of deer.
Hens scratch in dry mounds of manure.

I have not seen it, I summoned it listening to music.
The instruments play for themselves, in their own eternity.
Lips glow, agile fingers work, so short a time.
Soon afterwards the pageant sinks into the earth.
But the sound endures, autonomous, triumphant,
For ever visited by, each time returning,
The warm touch of cheeks, interiors of houses,
And particular human lives
Of which the chronicles make no mention.

Translated by the poet
and Robert Hass

2 cortege (kôr-tĕzh'): a ceremonial procession, as at a funeral or wedding.

Wedding Procession. Elek Győry. Hungarian National Gallery, Budapest.

Customizing Instruction

Less Proficient Readers

Ask the following questions to ensure students' comprehension of the poem.

- What is the major event in the first stanza?

  Answer: A village couple gets married.

Students Acquiring English

Ask students what makes line 4 a sentence fragment.

Answer: It does not have a verb.

Ask students to supply the missing verb.

Answer: is

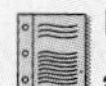 Use **Spanish Study Guide** for additional support, pp. 299–301.

Gifted and Talented

Invite students to compare and contrast Milosz's lyrical use of contemplative moments with Hearney's and Hughes's.

Mini Lesson Viewing and Representing

Wedding Procession **by Elek Györya**

ART APPRECIATION Hungarian painter Györy (1905–1957) came from a long line of blacksmiths. Although he learned the family trade, he began painting scenes from his village in 1932. In 1940, he began formal study of painting. His paintings have been shown all over the world.

Instruction Point out that the wedding procession itself occupies only about one-fourth of the painting; the rest depicts hills planted with crops. Ask what students think the artist intends to convey by dividing his painting in this way.

Possible Response: The central part of these people's lives is farming; the wedding is a brief respite from this occupation.

Application Compare and contrast this wedding procession with that described in the poem.

Possible Responses: Both occur in rural, hilly communities; both are outdoors. The hills in the poem are parched, but those in the painting are fertile; no village is depicted in the painting.

Thinking through the LITERATURE

Connect to the Literature

1. **What Do You Think?** What are your thoughts after reading this poem?

Comprehension Check
- Summarize what you think has happened in the poem.

Think Critically

2. What aspects of life seem to concern the **speaker**?

THINK ABOUT
- the scene he describes in the first **stanza**
- the kinds of **details** he notices
- what he means by "particular human lives / Of which the chronicles make no mention" (lines 16–17)

3. What contrasts does the poet make within each stanza? What ideas are conveyed through these contrasts?

4. **ACTIVE READING** ANALYZING STRUCTURE Review the chart you completed in your  READER'S NOTEBOOK. What is the transition that occurs between the two stanzas in the poem? Do you think the poem's two-part **structure** conveys this transition clearly? Explain your answer.

Extend Interpretations

5. **Connect to Life** What different effects can music have on its listeners? Base your response on your own experience or observations.

6. **Comparing Texts** Compare "In Music" with Thomas Gray's "Elegy Written in a Country Churchyard" (page 666). Can you find any similarities in the framework of the two poems or in the thoughts expressed about humanity? Cite lines from the poems to help you explain your answer.

7. **Points of Comparison** Compare the poems by Heaney, Hughes, and Milosz. In your opinion, which offers the most meaningful insight into life? Explain your answer.

Literary Analysis

IMAGERY AND MOOD **Imagery** refers to words and phrases that create vivid sensory experiences for the reader. As you know, imagery may appeal to the senses of sight, smell, hearing, taste, and touch. For example, in Milosz's poem the line "Hens scratch in dry mounds of manure" appeals to the senses of sight, hearing, and smell. The imagery that a writer uses can help set a poem's **mood,** the feeling or atmosphere the work creates for the reader.

Paired Activity With a partner, come up with a word or phrase that seems to capture the mood of the poem. Then make a list of images that contribute to the overall mood. Share your description of mood and list of images with the class.

GUIDING STUDENT RESPONSE

Connect to the Literature

1. **What Do You Think?**
Guidelines for student response: Accept all reasonable responses.

Comprehension Check
- Possible Response: The speaker is listening to music, which inspires him to imagine a wedding procession in a village and to think about larger ideas.

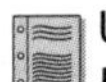 Use Selection Quiz in **Unit Seven Resource Book** p. 28.

Think Critically

2. Possible Response: The speaker seems concerned about the major events of life—such as weddings—and the small, everyday moments—such as sewing and listening to music. The people he seems to care about are poor or obscure.
3. Possible Response: In the first stanza, the poet contrasts everyday things (the village) and special things (the wedding apparel). This stanza also contrasts nature (the hills) and culture (the wedding). In the second stanza, the mortality of human life (the fading of the wedding scene) is contrasted with the immortality of art (the music the poet hears).
4. Answer: The transition that occurs is between the description of a village wedding and the revelation by the poet that the wedding has occurred only in his imagination.
Possible Responses: No; the transition is not clear because it is too sudden. Yes; the transition is clear because of the change in point of view from third person to first person.

Literary Analysis

Paired Activity You might draw a word web on the chalkboard that shows the main word or phrase that students have come up with to identify the mood, along with the images that support the mood.

Extend Interpretations

Connect to Life Music can have a variety of effects; students may mention excitement, tranquillity, inducement to dance, the evoking of memories, and the stirring of romantic feelings.

Comparing Texts In both poems, sensitive, pensive speakers find their thoughts turning toward eternal subjects after the inspiration of either art or nature. Both speakers are concerned with the lives and fates of obscure people and with finding consolation for obscurity and mortality. Accept all reasonable responses.

Points of Comparison Accept all reasonable responses.

Writing Options

1. **Letter to a Friend** In a letter to a friend, explain how a certain song affected you and what thoughts it suggests. Place the letter in your **Working Portfolio.**

2. **Points of Comparison** In an essay, compare and contrast the sights and sounds that inspire the poems by Heaney, Hughes, and Milosz. How effectively do these sights and sounds contribute to the main ideas of each poem?

Writing Handbook
See page 1367: Compare and Contrast.

Activities & Explorations

1. **Association Game** With a group of classmates, play an association game in which everyone responds independently to various pictures of people, places, or objects. As each picture is shown to your group, write down your associations. Then discuss your responses with those of other group members. ~ **SPEAKING AND LISTENING**

2. **Dramatic Reading** Plan and present for your class a dramatic reading of the poem, accompanied by flute and drum music. Students who play in your school band or orchestra could provide live music, or you could play a recording. ~ **PERFORMING**

Czeslaw Milosz

1911–

Other Works
"Song on Porcelain"
"Rivers"
"Incantation"
"Earth"
"Should, Should Not"

Multicultural Beginnings Czeslaw Milosz was born in Lithuania, a country that once existed as a Polish-Lithuanian confederation. Long before Milosz's birth, the confederation collapsed and was taken over by Russia. As a result, the poet, during his early years, was exposed to the language and customs of three different cultures.

The Outbreak of War Milosz attended the Stefan Batory University in Wilno (now called Vilnius), where he studied law and published his first book of poems at the age of 21. At the university, he also became involved with a group of poets called the Catastrophists, who predicted the outbreak of World War II. After the war erupted, Milosz moved to Nazi-occupied Warsaw, where he helped the Polish Resistance movement by contributing anti-Nazi writings and by promoting the cultural activities of the Polish underground. In order to have access to books, he worked as a janitor in a university library that had been closed to the general public.

Ambassador and Refugee When the war ended, Poland's new Communist government rewarded Milosz with a job in the foreign service. He was assigned as a cultural ambassador first to the United States and then to France. Milosz became disillusioned with Poland's totalitarian government, however, and in 1951 he asked the French government for political asylum. That same year he began writing his prose work *The Captive Mind,* an explanation of his reasons for defecting and of the effects of communism on creativity.

American Experience In 1960, Milosz moved to the United States to accept a teaching position at the University of California in Berkeley. Ten years later, he became an American citizen. His poetry and political writings reflect his diverse life experiences, and his recent poetry also probes aspects of American culture.

Author Activity

Milosz's Life Story In *Native Realm,* Milosz wrote an autobiography that covered his life from childhood up to the 1950s. Locate a copy of the book at a library and find out more about Milosz's experiences during World War II. Write a summary of his anti-Nazi activities during the war and present it to the class.

LaserLinks: Background for Reading
Author Background

Writing Options

1. **Letter to a Friend** Encourage students to elaborate on their responses to music by using examples, anecdotes, and descriptive details.
2. **Points of Comparison** Remind students to support their ideas with specific examples from each of the three poems.

Activities & Explorations

1. **Association Game** Remind students that there are no right or wrong answers in this exercise. Instead, the game attempts to illustrate how people's minds will offer wildly differing responses in such situations.
2. **Dramatic Reading** You may wish to have groups of students work independently of one another to find background music for the reading and then join together to listen to the music and choose what works best.

Author Activity

Milosz's Life Story Emphasize to students that summaries should be written in their own words and should not be taken directly from the text.

Mini Lesson Grammar

Style: The Appositive Phrase

Instruction Remind students that an appositive is a noun or pronoun that identifies or gives more information about a word that it usually follows. An appositive phrase is a noun phrase consisting of an appositive and its modifiers. It can be placed just before or after the noun or pronoun it modifies. Experienced writers use appositive phrases to combine related ideas in an interesting way.

Activity Write the following sentences on the chalkboard. Have students identify each appositive phrase and the noun or pronoun it modifies.

In this poem, a work of only seventeen lines, the speaker describes a vision. *(poem)*

A simple but festive occasion, the wedding that the speaker imagines takes place in a small village. *(wedding)*

Music lasts long beyond its creation by performers, the people who play musical instruments. *(performers)*

Use **Grammar Transparencies and Copymasters,** p. 120.

Use McDougal Littell's ***Language Network*** for more instruction in appositive phrases.

OVERVIEW

Objectives

1. understand and appreciate two **poems (Literary Analysis)**
2. appreciate the poet's use of **diction** in poetry **(Literary Analysis)**
3. **summarize a poem's major ideas (Active Reading)**

Summary

In her poem "The Frog Prince," Stevie Smith takes a familiar fairy tale and shifts the focus, which is traditionally on the handsome prince and beautiful princess, to the frog—a frog that now expects the quiet contentment he has known for a hundred years to become, hopefully, a *heavenly* existence.

"Not Waving but Drowning" also scrutinizes perception. What on-lookers thought was a man impishly waving to them from outside the social mainstream was really a man frantically signaling for the help that would bring him back into the warmth of society.

Thematic Link

Both poems deal cleverly with contemporary issues of individuality and the frequent tension between **appearance and reality.** The frog in "The Frog Prince" anticipates leaving his solitary, enchanted life and welcomes the *heavenly* but disenchanted life the princess offers. The individual in "Not Waving but Drowning" drowns in his singular approach to life, and others who misunderstood that individual did not even know to come to his aid.

5-Minute Warm-Up

Daily Language SkillBuilder

Have students **proofread** the display sentences on page 1189j and write them correctly. The sentences also appear on Transparency 34 of **Grammar Transparencies and Copymasters.**

The Frog Prince
Not Waving but Drowning

Poetry by STEVIE SMITH

"I was much too far out all my life"

Connect to Your Life

Can You Believe Your Eyes? Get together with a partner and examine the image on the right. What do you see? Look at it longer. Do you see something different? This type of image is sometimes referred to as an optical illusion; what you see on the surface at first glance becomes something different as you look longer. Literature, too, can have this effect, as you will see in the poems you are about to read.

Build Background

Her Own Style During her early years as a writer, Florence Margaret Smith—better known as Stevie Smith—read widely in older works of literature, avoiding the poetic works of her contemporaries for fear that their influence would keep her from developing her own style. She did indeed achieve a distinctive style, and critics have therefore found her work hard to compare with that of other poets. At first glance, her poems appear simple both in subject matter and in their use of conventional rhyme, but closer scrutiny often reveals deep insights in her supposedly "light" verse.

Although Smith did not consider herself a visual artist, she illustrated many of her poems with drawings—she called them doodles—that she thought helped readers to understand the poetry. The drawing that appears on page 1253 is the one Smith chose to print with "The Frog Prince."

Focus Your Reading

LITERARY ANALYSIS **DICTION IN POETRY** Stevie Smith's style is distinguished by her use of a simple, straightforward **diction,** or choice of words. This simplicity can be deceiving, however. Smith often uses words with multiple meanings to convey her messages. She also depends on a word's **connotation**—the attitudes or feelings associated with the word—to develop meaning. As you read these poems, think about the layers of meaning in the words Smith uses.

ACTIVE READING **SUMMARIZING A POEM'S MAJOR IDEAS** Poetry, even poetry with relatively simple diction, can be hard to understand. As you read Smith's poems, it may be useful to try to **summarize** the major idea in each stanza or selected group of lines.

READER'S NOTEBOOK "The Frog Prince" can be divided into four sections. Use a chart like the one shown to summarize the major idea in each section. Make a similar chart for "Not Waving but Drowning," and summarize the major idea of each stanza.

"The Frog Prince"	
Lines	**Major Idea**
1–9	Speaker identifies himself as prince-turned-frog who is waiting for princess to kiss him and break spell.
10–29	
30–42	
43–48	

LESSON RESOURCES

UNIT SEVEN RESOURCE BOOK, pp. 25–26

ASSESSMENT RESOURCES

Formal Assessment, pp. 231–232

Teacher's Guide to Assessment and Portfolio Use

Test Generator

SKILLS TRANSPARENCIES AND COPYMASTERS

Literary Analysis

- Poetic Devices, T16 (for Literary Analysis, p. 1252)

Reading and Critical Thinking

- Paraphrasing and Summarizing, T42 (for Active Reading, p. 1248)

Grammar

- Commas with Nonessential Elements, T55 (for Mini Lesson, p. 1253)
- Essential and Nonessential Appositives, C170 (for Mini Lesson, p. 1253)

Vocabulary

- Word Origins, C91 (for Mini Lesson, p. 1249)

Writing

- Effective Language, T13 (for Writing Option 2, p. 1253)
- Sensory Word List, T14 (for Writing Option 1, p. 1253)

INTEGRATED TECHNOLOGY

Audio Library

Visit our website:
www.mcdougallittell.com

The Frog Prince

STEVIE SMITH

I am a frog,
I live under a spell,
I live at the bottom
Of a green well.

And here I must wait
Until a maiden places me
On her royal pillow,
And kisses me,
In her father's palace.

The story is familiar,
Everybody knows it well,
But do other enchanted people feel as nervous
As I do? The stories do not tell,

Ask if they will be happier
When the changes come,
As already they are fairly happy
In a frog's doom?

I have been a frog now
For a hundred years
And in all this time
I have not shed many tears,

I am happy, I like the life,
Can swim for many a mile
(When I have hopped to the river)
And am for ever agile.

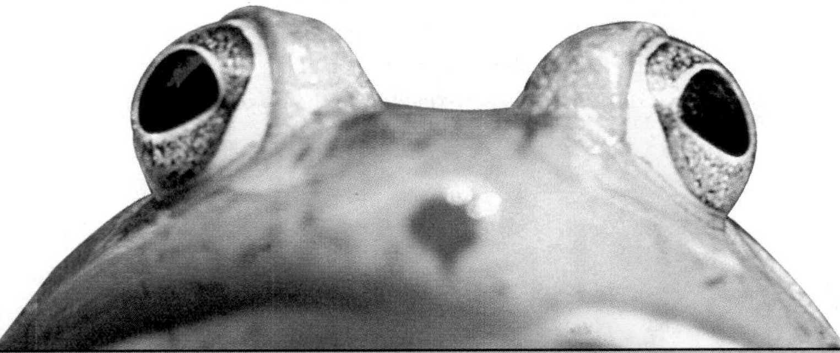

TEACHING THE LITERATURE

Customizing Instruction

Less Proficient Readers
Point out that magical transformations are common in literature. For example, in Homer's *Odyssey,* Circe transforms Odysseus' men into swine; in Franz Kafka's *The Metamorphosis,* Gregor Samsa is transformed into a giant insect. Invite students to share examples of transformations from literature, fairy tales, myths and legends, and popular culture. Then have them read to find out what transformation the frog expects to undergo.

Students Acquiring English
Point out the word "doom" in line 17 and explain that although "doom" usually means "a sentence of condemnation" or "ruin," it can also mean "fate or destiny" without such negative connotations. Have students discuss which meaning makes more sense in this context.

Possible response: "Doom" meaning "destiny" without the negative overtones makes more sense, because the frog says that frogs generally are happy.

Use **Spanish Study Guide** for additional support, pp. 302–304.

Gifted and Talented
Point out that the frog is having a debate in his mind about the pros and cons of trading his happy, solitary life for a "heavenly," royal life. Have students rewrite the frog's debate for a modern audience struggling with similar issues.

Mini Lesson Vocabulary Strategy

RESEARCHING WORD ORIGINS: ***enchant***

Instruction The word *enchant* is based upon the Latin *incantare : in-* against + *cantare* to sing. "To enchant," therefore, was originally "to sing against." Have students consider this view of "enchantment" when they reread the "The Frog Prince."

Activity Have students pick out each use of "enchant" (or "disenchant") in the poem, then have them discuss whether the original Latin meaning of "enchant" still fits the Frog Prince.

Possible Responses: Those who think it does might mention that he is being sung against for being a frog in a well rather than a prince in a palace. He appears to feel "up against" the pressure of changing. The princess will be a disenchanter—one who will now sing with him—and the frog is uncertain about leaving his quiet world.

Use **Vocabulary Transparencies and Copymasters,** p. 73.

A lesson on word origins appears on p. 206 in the Pupil's Edition.

Reading and Analyzing

Active Reading

SUMMARIZING A POEM'S MAJOR IDEAS

Ask students to read through the poems, silently or orally, then write down a sentence summary of each poem's content. Read each poem a second time out loud. Ask for students' summary statements to create a thorough overview of the poems.

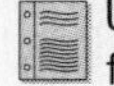
Use **Unit Seven Resource Book** p. 29 for more practice.

Literary Analysis

DICTION IN POETRY

Diction is the poet's word choice. Since the words are not difficult in these selections, ask students what might have been Smith's desired effect in using this vocabulary.

Possible Response: It allows for a play on words, and the associations the language brings to mind influence understanding. It makes the poem accessible to readers.

Use **Unit Seven Resource Book** p. 30 for more exercises.

Thinking Through the Literature

1. The frog is waiting for *disenchantment* and is anxious about what it might bring.
2. Accept all reasonable answers.
3. Most students will reply that the frog's nervousness comes from his contentment with the life he has been living for a hundred years, and a fear of the unknown.
4. Students may suggest that the solitary life is quiet and comfortable, but not as valuable ("royal") as a life shared with someone.

And the quietness,
Yes, I like to be quiet
I am habituated
To a quiet life,

But always when I think these thoughts
As I sit in my well
Another thought comes to me and says:
It is part of the spell

To be happy
To work up contentment
To make much of being a frog
To fear disenchantment

Says, It will be *heavenly*
To be set free,
Cries, *Heavenly* the girl who disenchants
And the royal times, *heavenly,*
And I think it will be.

Come, then, royal girl and royal times,
Come quickly,
I can be happy until you come
But I cannot be heavenly,
Only disenchanted people
Can be heavenly.

Thinking Through the Literature

1. **Comprehension Check** What is the frog in the poem waiting for?
2. What is your opinion of this poem? Explain your answer.
3. Why do you think the frog prince is nervous?

- what his life is like now
- what changes he anticipates

4. What do you think is the underlying **theme** of this poem?

Teaching Options

BLOCK SCHEDULING: MANAGING TIME

If your schedule requires that you cover the lesson objectives in a shorter time, use . . .
- Preparing to Read, p. 1248
- Thinking Through the Literature, p. 1250

If you want to take advantage of longer class time, use . . .
- TE Teaching Options: Vocabulary Strategy, p. 1249; Viewing and Representing, p. 1251; Grammar, p. 1253
- Choices & Challenges and Author Activity, p. 1253

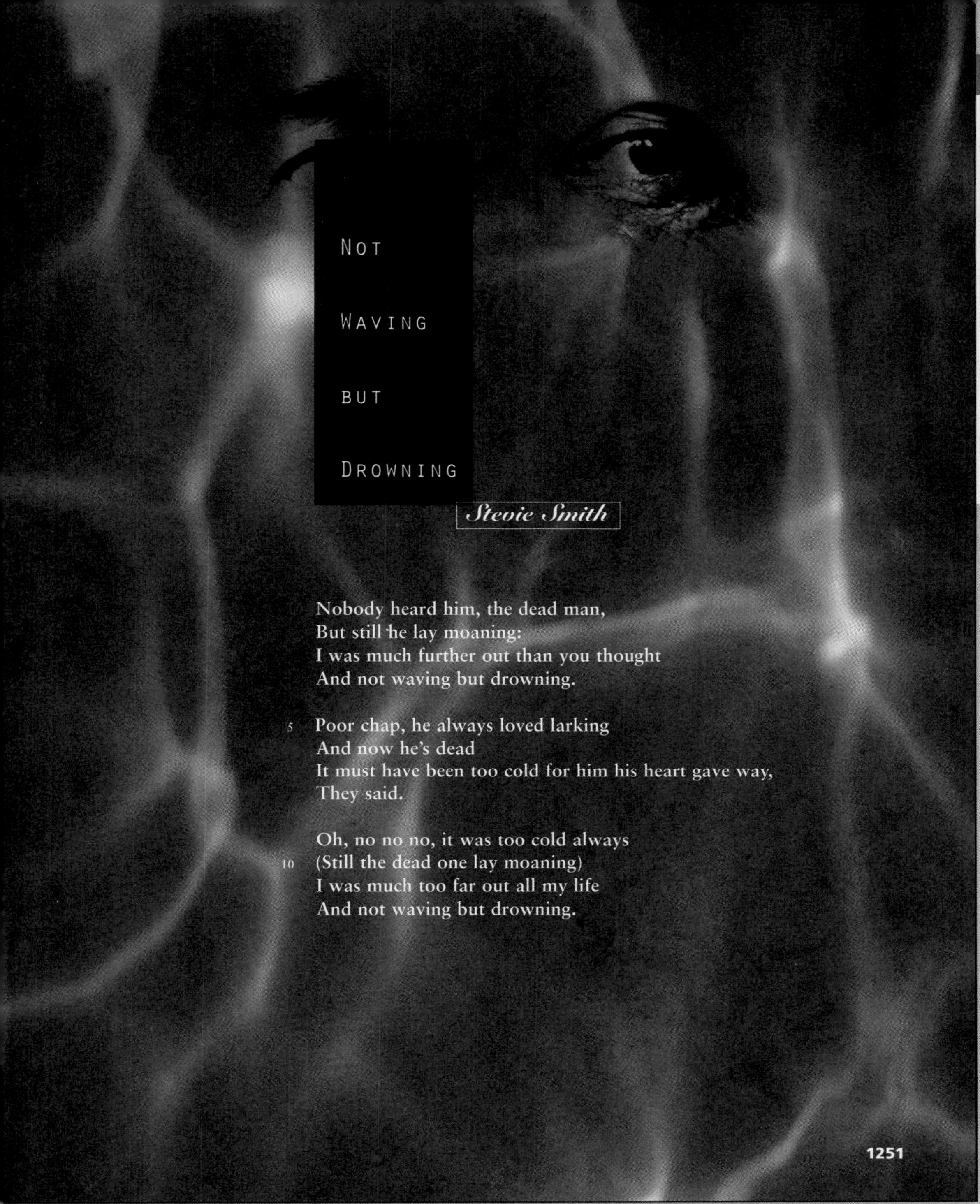

Not Waving but Drowning

Stevie Smith

Nobody heard him, the dead man,
But still he lay moaning:
I was much further out than you thought
And not waving but drowning.

Poor chap, he always loved larking
And now he's dead
It must have been too cold for him his heart gave way,
They said.

Oh, no no no, it was too cold always
(Still the dead one lay moaning)
I was much too far out all my life
And not waving but drowning.

Customizing Instruction

Less Proficient Readers
Point out that their are several voices in this short poem. Have students identify the speakers in the first stanza.
Possible Response: A third-person narrator speaks the first two lines, and the subject of the poem—the man who drowned—speaks the last two lines.

Students Acquiring English
Help students understand that "larking" (line 5) is a form of the verb "to lark," which means to frolic, play, and have a merry time. Explain that, although there is also a bird called a lark, the verb here comes from a root word meaning "to hop."

Viewing and Representing

ART APPRECIATION

Instruction Draw students' attention to the photograph of a frog on page 1249 and the Stevie Smith doodle of a frog on page 1253. Remind students that different media (that is, a subjective drawing versus a representational photograph) make different contributions to the interpretation of a text.

Application Ask students to consider how these visual images of frogs affect their impressions of "The Frog Prince." How does the photograph differ from Smith's drawing?

Possible Response: Smith's drawing humanizes the frog, which corresponds to the human concerns and voice the frog has in the poem; the photograph, however, reminds us that we are, in fact, reading about a frog and that the poem is about a fairy tale.

You may wish to remind students that writers other than Smith, such as James Thurber (page 417), complemented their work with their own drawings.

GUIDING STUDENT RESPONSE

Connect to the Literature

1. What Do You Think?
Guidelines for student response: Have students compare their responses. You might write the words and phrases suggested by the students on the chalkboard.

Comprehension Check

- He drowned.
- He was too far out; they thought he was waving, not drowning.

Thinking Critically

2. Possible Responses: a narrator, a dead man, spectators, an anonymous public
3. Possible Responses: Some students might find it has an ironic tone because even as the drowning man explains himself in the first stanza, he is misunderstood in the second by others' comments. Some students may also notice a matter-of-fact tone that seems to be conveyed by the diction of the voices in the poem.
4. Possible Response: This situation of drowning, being overwhelmed by life, is not a new one for the man. He has been cold, alone, and drowning for some time but his actions were misinterpreted, and others did not hear or heed his cry for help.
5. Accept all summaries that are supported with textual evidence.

Literary Analysis

Paired Activity Have volunteers read their lines aloud to the class. Volunteers might identify the poem to which they are adding lines or they might have the class guess after they have heard the new lines.

Thinking through the LITERATURE

Connect to the Literature

1. **What Do You Think?** What emotions did "Not Waving but Drowning" evoke in you?

Comprehension Check

- Why did the man die?
- Why didn't anyone try to rescue him?

Think Critically

2. What different voices, or **speakers,** do you hear in the poem?
3. Although the poem has more than one speaker, it has a single overall **tone.** How would you describe the tone?

   THINK ABOUT
   - the attitude of the first speaker
   - the fact that a dead man speaks
   - what the dead man says
   - the fact that the dead man is heard by no one
4. What do you think the speaker means in the last stanza?
5. ACTIVE READING **SUMMARIZING A POEM'S MAJOR IDEAS** Get together in a small group and discuss the summary charts you created in your 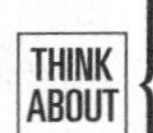 **READER'S NOTEBOOK.** Identify specific lines in each poem where the ideas progress from simple to complex. Taking these complex ideas into account, how would you **summarize** each poem's major idea?

Extend Interpretations

6. **Critic's Corner** Muriel Spark once wrote that Smith's "style is comic and her vision melancholy but dry-eyed." Do you think Smith displays both a comic style and a melancholy vision in "The Frog Prince" and "Not Waving but Drowning"? Support your opinion with details from the two poems.
7. **Connect to Life** Smith once called the time period in which she was living and writing an "age of unrest." Do you think her poetry also speaks to your generation? Explain your opinion.

Literary Analysis

DICTION IN POETRY **Diction** is a writer's choice of words. The diction in Stevie Smith's poetry is deceptively simple. The poet relies on **wordplay**—a clever use of the multiple meanings of words—to express ambiguities. In "The Frog Prince," for instance, she plays with the different meanings of *disenchantment* and *heavenly* to give added depth to the poem and its message. In "Not Waving but Drowning," Smith uses the different meanings of such words as *far out* and *cold* to create an image of the speaker as misunderstood and alone. The connotations of words in Smith's poems also influence meaning. For example, you may find as you read "The Frog Prince" that your reaction to words like *frog* and *spell* has changed.

Paired Activity With a partner, discuss your ideas for adding your own lines to one of Smith's poems. For example, in "The Frog Prince," you might tell what happens when the princess finally kisses the frog. In "Not Waving but Drowning," you might explain in what way the speaker was "much too far out" all his life. Be sure to maintain Smith's simple diction, but at the same time try to use wordplay and the connotations of words to express deeper meaning and insights.

Extend Interpretations

Critic's Corner Smith's comic style is suggested by her use of irony and by her speakers, a frog and dead man; a melancholy vision is suggested by the sad, disillusioned mood of the poems.

Connect to Life Students may think that Smith's poetry speaks to their generation, because it deals with issues such as the search for happiness and the isolation that can come from being overwhelmed by life, which are themes that can affect everyone.

Writing Options

1. **Fairy Tale Poem** Following the style of "The Frog Prince," write your own poem based on a famous fairy tale or nursery rhyme. Try to give the original story a humorous twist while at the same time conveying an insight about life. Place the poem in your **Working Portfolio.**
2. **Diary Entry** As the man in "Not Waving but Drowning," write a diary entry in which you explain why it's been "too cold always" and you've been "not waving but drowning."

Activities & Explorations

Drawings of the Frog Prince With a partner, create a series of drawings depicting the frog prince as he sits in his well. Be sure to convey his various thoughts about his impending "disenchantment." Add your drawings to a class display, and discuss any similarities and differences between them and Stevie Smith's frog "doodle" shown here. ~ **ART**

Inquiry & Research

Artistic Mind Games The image next to Connect to Your Life on page 1248 is by M. C. Escher, a 20th-century Dutch graphic artist. Find other examples of Escher's work. Then get together with a small group of classmates to share what you've found.

Stevie Smith
1902–1971

Other Works
"There Is an Old Man"
"Tender Only to One"
"The New Age"
"Pretty"
"Is It Wise?"

New Name Florence Margaret Smith acquired her nickname in the early 1930s, while horseback riding. Alluding to a well-known jockey named Steve Donaghue, some boys jokingly called her Steve; her friends picked up the name, changing it to "Stevie." Smith loved the nickname and continued to use it the rest of her life.

Restricted Family Circle For most of her life, Smith lived in a house in Palmers Green, a northern suburb of London, having moved there at the age of three with her mother, her sister, and a favorite aunt (whom she affectionately called the Lion Aunt) shortly after her father deserted the family. After her mother died and her sister left home, Smith and her best friend, the Lion Aunt, continued to live together until the older woman died at the age of 96.

Filling in Free Time In grammar school and high school, Smith was an average student. Instead of going on to college, she entered a secretarial school and then worked for the next 30 years as secretary to a magazine publisher. She found the job boring, but it did afford her ample free time to write stories and poems. Her first published work was a novel she wrote on the yellow paper used in her office, to which she gave the title *Novel on Yellow Paper.*

Recognition and Achievement Although she first gained recognition as a novelist, Smith is known primarily for her achievements as a poet. She was awarded the Cholmondeley Poetry Award in 1966, and in 1969 Queen Elizabeth II personally presented Smith with the Queen's Gold Medal for Poetry. She undoubtedly would have received many more honors for her unique work, but she died in 1971, at the height of her popularity. A few years later, her life and literary achievements became the subject of a stage play and a movie, both entitled *Stevie.*

Author Activity

Life on Film View a video recording of *Stevie,* the movie about Stevie Smith's life. Share several anecdotes or interesting scenes from the film with your classmates.

Writing Options

1. **Fairy Tale Poem** To assist students in this activity, brainstorm with the class as a whole or in small groups on fairy tales, myths, and legends. List these on the board. It may be helpful to have a number of books on hand for reference. The students' poems should, like Stevie Smith's, shift the focus or perspective of the tale.
2. **Diary Entry** Student responses will vary but should contain a tone appropriate to the dead man described. Remind students that others thought him out for a lark and failed to see his actions as cries for help.

Activities & Explorations

Drawings of the Frog Prince **To make this assignment more challenging,** suggest that students rewrite the poem and place these illustrations next to the stanzas where appropriate.

Inquiry & Research

Artistic Mind Games Students may want to show each other their illustrations at a distance before presenting them for closer inspection. They can then compare their descriptions and interpretations of Escher's work from both perspectives.

Author Activity

Life on Film In the 1978 film version, Stevie Smith is played by the distinguished British actress Glenda Jackson. Have students write reviews or find reviews of the film and compare their personal responses with those of the reviewer.

Grammar

STYLE: ESSENTIAL VS. NONESSENTIAL APPOSITIVES

Instruction An appositive is a noun or pronoun that identifies or gives more information about a word that it usually follows. When an appositive is needed to make the meaning clear, it is an essential appositive and should not be set off with commas. When an appositive adds extra meaning to a sentence that is already clear, it is nonessential and should be set off with commas.

Activity Write the following sentences on the chalkboard. Have students identify each appositive and tell whether or not it should be set off with commas.

The poet Stevie Smith wrote the poem "The Frog Prince." *(Do not add commas.)*
The speaker of the poem a frog lives in a well. *(Add a comma after "poem" and "frog.")*
The poem expresses discontentment Smith's main theme. *(Add a comma after "discontentment.")*

Use **Grammar Transparencies and Copymasters,** p. 96.

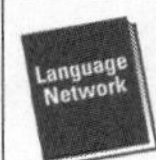

Use McDougal Littell's ***Language Network*** for more instruction in appositives.

OVERVIEW

Objectives

1. understand and appreciate a **drama (Literary Analysis)**
2. appreciate the author's use of **dialogue (Literary Analysis)**
3. develop techniques for **reading unconventional works (Active Reading)**

Summary

Mrs. A has a conversation with Mrs. B about an unnamed "she," who used to visit Mrs. A on Wednesdays. After "she" moved, "she" changed her visiting day to Thursday to coincide with her trips to the butcher. Mrs. A dominates the halting conversation while Mrs. B's responses consist of one, two, or three words until the end of the play when Mrs. B asks whether "she" still visits. Mrs. A replies that "she" does, but not "so much. That's all."

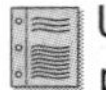 Use **Unit Seven Resource Book,** p. 27 for additional support.

Thematic Link

In this short play, the audience is invited to consider the difference between **appearance and reality** as it listens to an everyday conversation between two women to understand the shallowness of their relationship and the emptiness of their lives.

5-Minute Warm-Up

Daily Language SkillBuilder

Have students **proofread** the display sentences on page 1189j and write them correctly. The sentences also appear on Transparency 35 of **Grammar Transparencies and Copymasters.**

PREPARING to *Read*

That's All

Drama by HAROLD PINTER

"I always put the kettle on about that time."

Connect to Your Life

Small Talk What kinds of conversations do people engage in most of the time? Do you think people typically talk about important issues, or do most conversations consist of small talk about everyday routines and events? Discuss your responses to these questions with your classmates.

Build Background

Distinctive Style Harold Pinter began writing plays in the late 1950s, when various new styles were emerging in British drama. Some critics saw similarities between Pinter's style of writing and that of the "kitchen sink" school of realists, with its focus on the language and lifestyle of the working class. Others likened his plays to those of the "theater of the absurd," in which disjointed, seemingly meaningless dialogue was used to convey the absurdity of many of life's circumstances.

Pinter, however, has never belonged to a single school. Instead, he has drawn from various dramatic styles to create his own distinctive approach—a style sometimes referred to as Pinteresque. Typically, a Pinter play involves just one setting, only two or three characters, and a minimal amount of action. The dialogue tends to be very simple—sometimes even ordinary and conversational—but it usually conveys a level of meaning beyond the literal meanings of the words that are spoken. According to Pinter, "The speech we hear is an indication of that which we don't hear."

That's All, written in 1959, is one of Pinter's early works. It is a short dramatic sketch intended to be performed either as one segment of a variety show or as a short radio skit.

Focus Your Reading

LITERARY ANALYSIS DIALOGUE IN A PLAY In drama, **dialogue** is the main means of characterization and the main vehicle for conveying events and **themes.** One characteristic of Pinter's dialogue is repetition; another is the use of pauses, always indicated by **stage directions.** As you read the play, note Pinter's use of repetition and pauses.

ACTIVE READING READING UNCONVENTIONAL WORKS The play you are about to read is unconventional both in subject matter and in the style of the dialogue. As you read it, try to abandon your expectations of typical dramatic works so that you can experience Pinter's unique brand of humor.

READER'S NOTEBOOK Jot down your reactions to the play while you are reading. Make a note if something strikes you as funny, sad, confusing, or annoying. Also write down any questions or comments triggered by the play.

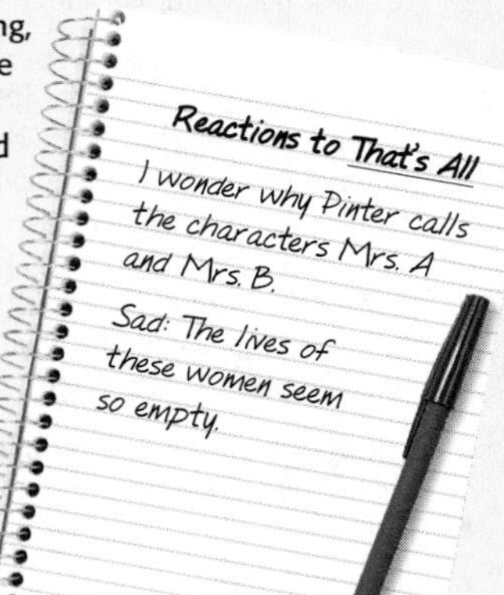

Reactions to That's All
I wonder why Pinter calls the characters Mrs. A and Mrs. B.
Sad: The lives of these women seem so empty.

LESSON RESOURCES

UNIT SEVEN RESOURCE BOOK, pp. 27–30

ASSESSMENT RESOURCES

Formal Assessment, pp. 233–234

Teacher's Guide to Assessment and Portfolio Use

Test Generator

SKILLS TRANSPARENCIES AND COPYMASTERS

Grammar

- Possessive Nouns, T38 (for Mini Lesson, p. 1259)
- Possessives with Proper Nouns That End in *s*, C63 (for Mini Lesson, p. 1259)

Vocabulary

- Idioms, C92 (for Mini Lesson, p. 1255)

Writing

- Dramatic Scene, C31 (for Writing Option 1, p. 1259)
- Critical Review, C32 (for Writing Option 2, p. 1259)

Communications

- Dramatic Reading, T12 (for Mini Lesson, p. 1256)

INTEGRATED TECHNOLOGY

Audio Library

Visit our website: www.mcdougallittell.com

THAT'S ALL

Mrs. A. I always put the kettle on about that time.

Mrs. B. Yes. (*pause*)

Mrs. A. Then she comes round.

Mrs. B. Yes. (*pause*)

Mrs. A. Only on Thursdays.

Mrs. B. Yes. (*pause*)

Mrs. A. On Wednesdays I used to put it on. When she used to come round. Then she changed it to Thursdays.

Mrs. B. Oh yes.

Mrs. A. After she moved. When she used to live round the corner, then she always came in on Wednesdays, but then when she moved she used to come down to the butcher's on Thursdays. She couldn't find a butcher up there.

TEACHING THE LITERATURE

Customizing Instruction

Less Proficient Readers

To help students understand the playwright's spare style, invite volunteers to read the first page and then compare Pinter's language to their own everyday speech.

Set a Purpose Ask students to read to find the subject of the two characters' conversation.

Students Acquiring English

The British diction of the play may be challenging to students. Review some of the British expressions Pinter uses, such as *put the kettle on* and *comes round.* Ask students to give American equivalents of these expressions.

Answers: have a cup of tea or coffee; stops by.

Use **Spanish Study Guide** for additional support, pp. 311–313.

Gifted and Talented

Ask students to consider the object of the play's satire as they read the selection. Who or what is Pinter ridiculing? How does he distance himself from his subject?

Mini Lesson Vocabulary Strategy

IDIOMS

Instruction Remind students that an idiom is an informal expression that cannot be completely understood from the meanings of its individual words. Explain that idioms are often specific to certain dialects. For example, the phrase *keeps a stiff upper lip* is an idiom of British English meaning "does not show emotion."

Activity Ask students to find the idioms in this selection and define them based on context.

- put the kettle on
  Possible Response: to have a teatime snack
- come round
  Possible Response: to visit
- stick to
  Possible Response: stay with, continue to patronize
- slip in
  Possible Response: make a quick trip
- that's all
  Possible Response: there's nothing more to the matter

Use **Vocabulary Transparencies and Copymasters,** p. 74.

Reading and Analyzing

Literary Analysis
DIALOGUE IN A PLAY

Tell students that Pinter once commented: "One way of looking at speech is to say that it is a constant stratagem to cover nakedness." To find out what "nakedness" the characters might be trying to cover, invite students to read between the lines by noticing what the characters fail to say.

Possible Responses: the shallowness of their relationship; the emptiness of their lives

Use **Unit Seven Resource Book** p. 34 for more exercises.

Active Reading
READING UNCONVENTIONAL WORKS

Ask students what connotations the word *unconventional* has for them.

Possible Responses: shocking, rebellious.

Ask students to keep these connotations in mind as they read to see if the play meets their expectations of *unconventional.* Explain that some unconventional works may be considered so because they are very ordinary.

Use **Unit Seven Resource Book** p. 33 for more practice.

Reading Skills and Strategies:
WRITING QUESTIONS OR COMMENTS

Explain that it is especially important to write down questions and comments when reading unconventional works. Have students review their questions and comments when they have finished reading and then read the play again to look for answers.

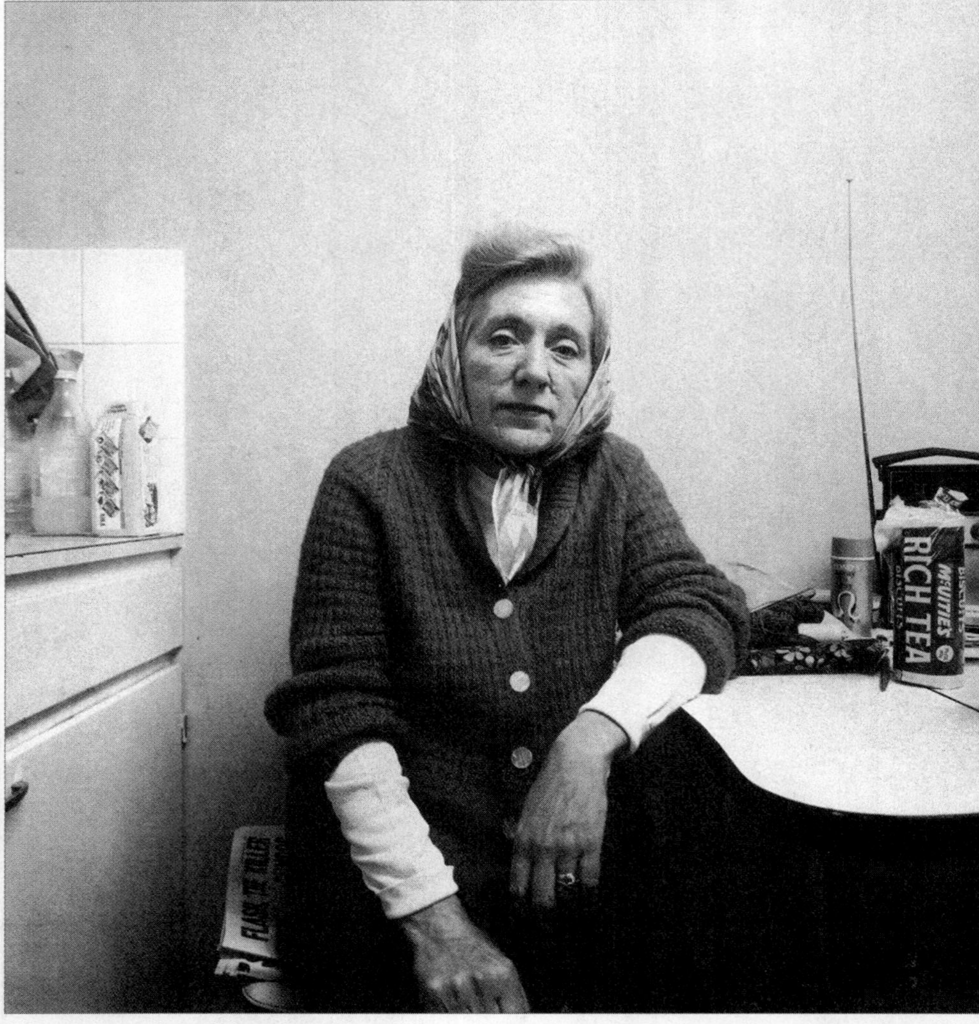

May Shield (1974), Nancy Hellebrand. Copyright © 1974 Nancy Hellebrand.

Teaching Options

Speaking and Listening

DRAMATIC SCENE

Instruction Help students to prepare a dramatic scene based on an everyday conversation taken from their own lives. Students may work in cooperative groups.

Prepare Have students attempt to recall the tone, pitch, volume, and speed of the conversation as well as its dialogue. Suggest that students consider the physical interactions of the speakers: Do they gesture as they talk? Do they look at each other? What does their posture indicate? What facial expressions do they use?

Present Before students present their dramatic scenes, have them determine the criteria by which the audience will evaluate each scene. Have groups present their scenes to the class. Students who are audience members should act as drama critics and evaluate whether the performances seem to portray authentic conversation.

BLOCK SCHEDULING This activity is particularly well-suited for longer class periods.

Mrs. B. No.

Mrs. A. Anyway, she decided she'd stick to her own butcher. Well, I thought, if she can't find a butcher, that's the best thing.

Mrs. B. Yes. (*pause*)

Mrs. A. So she started to come down on Thursdays. I didn't know she was coming down on Thursdays until one day I met her in the butcher.

Mrs. B. Oh yes.

Mrs. A. It wasn't my day for the butcher, I don't go to the butcher on Thursdays.

Mrs. B. No, I know. (*pause*)

Mrs. A. I go on Friday.

Mrs. B. Yes. (*pause*)

Mrs. A. That's where I see you.

Mrs. B. Yes. (*pause*)

Mrs. A. You're always in there on Fridays.

Mrs. B. Oh yes. (*pause*)

Mrs. A. But I happened to go in for a bit of meat, it turned out to be a Thursday. I wasn't going in for my usual weekly on Friday. I just slipped in, the day before.

Mrs. B. Yes.

Mrs. A. That was the first time I found out she couldn't find a butcher up there, so she decided to come back here, once a week, to her own butcher.

Mrs. B. Yes.

Mrs. A. She came on Thursday so she'd be able to get meat for the weekend. Lasted her till Monday, then from Monday to Thursday they'd have fish. She can always buy cold meat, if they want a change.

Mrs. B. Oh yes. (*pause*)

Mrs. A. So I told her to come in when she came down after she'd been to the butcher's and I'd put a kettle on. So she did. (*pause*)

Mrs. B. Yes. (*pause*)

Mrs. A. It was funny because she always used to come in Wednesdays. (*pause*) Still, it made a break. (*long pause*)

Mrs. B. She doesn't come in no more, does she? (*pause*) 1

Mrs. A. She comes in. She doesn't come in so much, but she comes in. (*pause*)

Mrs. B. I thought she didn't come in. (*pause*)

Mrs. A. She comes in. (*pause*) She just doesn't come in so much. That's all.

Customizing Instruction

Students Acquiring English

1 Point out the double-negative in the line "She doesn't come in no more, does she?" Stress that double-negatives are heard in some dialects of English but that double-negatives are not standard English. Ask students whether double-negatives are standard in their native language. Encourage students to provide examples.

Multiple Learning Styles

Visual and Kinesthetic Learners
Ask students to create a list or make sketches of props that might be used in staging this play. Suggest that students actually create a set and costumes for the play.

Mini Lesson Informal Assessment

ANALYTICAL PARAGRAPH
Ask students to write a paragraph explaining what they think is the intended meaning of the play. Remind students to include a thesis sentence as well as supporting details from the play.

RUBRIC

3 Full Accomplishment Thesis of paragraph is plausible and supported by at least three details from play.

2 Substantial Accomplishment Thesis of paragraph is plausible and supported by one or more details from play.

1 Little or Partial Accomplishment Thesis of paragraph is not plausible and not supported by details from play.

THAT'S ALL 1257

GUIDING STUDENT RESPONSE

Connect to the Literature

1. What Do You Think?
Guidelines for student response: Student responses might be placed on the chalkboard in a cluster diagram.

Comprehension Check
- The two women discuss a third, unnamed woman who used to visit on Wednesdays but changed her visiting day to Thursdays after she moved.
- Mrs. B thinks that the woman doesn't come in anymore. Mrs. A says that the woman does come in, but not as much.

 Use Selection Quiz in **Unit Seven Resource Book** p. 35.

Think Critically

2. Possible Response: It differs in subject matter, the conversational style of the dialogue, and plot. The subject (a conversation about a woman's visiting days) seems trivial, the dialogue circular and one-sided, and the plot nonexistent.
3. Possible Response: The women are lonely and bored.
4. Possible Response: Pinter's purpose was to show that many people lead empty, meaningless lives; to show that people often fail to communicate with each other.
5. Possible Response: He used this title to indicate that such a conversation is all that these women, and perhaps most people, can expect when they try to communicate.

Literary Analysis

Dialogue in a Play The repetition seems to reduce life and communication to a few meaningless phrases. The pauses underscore the fact that there is nothing to say; the silent pauses communicate as much as the women's words.

Cooperative Learning Activity
Encourage students to experiment with styles ranging from subtle, understated performances to broader, more exaggerated styles. Then ask them to decide which style is more appropriate to the play.

Connect to the Literature

1. **What Do You Think?** What word best describes your impression of this play? Compare it with the words suggested by your classmates.

Comprehension Check
- What do the two women in the play talk about?
- What misunderstanding does Mrs. A clear up at the end of the play?

Think Critically

2. How does *That's All* differ from other dramas or skits you have encountered? Cite details in your answer.

3. What emotions do you think lie beneath the women's mundane **dialogue**?

   THINK ABOUT
   - the subject matter of the characters' conversation
   - the way the characters interact

4. ACTIVE READING | READING UNCONVENTIONAL WORKS With a group of classmates, share the reactions, questions, and comments you recorded in your READER'S NOTEBOOK. What do you think was Pinter's **purpose** in writing this play?

5. Why do you think Pinter chose to use Mrs. A's last remark, "That's all," as the **title** of his play?

Extend Interpretations

6. **Critic's Corner** The critic Alrene Sykes has written that Pinter tends to establish a "lack of communication between his characters" at the beginning of each of his plays. Do you see any evidence of this in *That's All?* Support your answer.

7. **Connect to Life** Do you think the conversation in this play is typical of small talk between friends? Why or why not?

Literary Analysis

DIALOGUE IN A PLAY In *That's All,* Pinter communicates his message by using **dialogue** filled with repetition and frequent pauses, as seen in the following lines from the play:

Mrs. B. ***She doesn't come in no more, does she?*** **(pause)**

Mrs. A. ***She comes in. She doesn't come in so much, but she comes in.*** **(pause)**

Mrs. B. ***I thought she didn't come in.*** **(pause)**

Mrs. A. ***She comes in.*** **(pause)** ***She just doesn't come in so much.***

What effect do you think Pinter creates by having his characters repeat certain words and phrases? What effects does he achieve with pauses?

Cooperative Learning Activity How dialogue is read or performed will determine to a great extent the reactions of the reader or audience to the play. Work with a small group of classmates to give several dramatic readings of the play, taking turns in the roles of Mrs. A and Mrs. B and experimenting with inflections, facial expressions, and ways of observing the pauses. Then discuss how different ways of reading the play can affect its meaning.

Extend Interpretations

Critic's Corner Students should note the confusing nature of the dialogue at the beginning of the play and the pointlessness and repetition of it throughout.

Connect to Life Some students may think the conversation is typical because most people have superficial daily interactions, even with close friends; others will argue that most people communicate on deeper, more meaningful levels.

Writing Options

1. Second Scene Dialogue Compose dialogue and stage directions for a second scene in the encounter between Mrs. A and Mrs. B. Then, with a partner, perform your scene for your classmates.

2. Drama Review Write a review of *That's All,* stating your overall opinion of the play and pointing out its strengths and weaknesses. Place the review in your **Working Portfolio.**

Activities & Explorations

1. Set Design Create a three-dimensional model of the set design you would use for a production of *That's All.* ~ **ART**

2. Mood Music Select several pieces of music that you think reflect the characters and mood in *That's All.* Bring in the recordings and play two or three for the class. Explain your selections. ~ **MUSIC**

Inquiry & Research

Real Versus Absurd Find out more about the "kitchen sink" school of realists and the theater of the absurd. Which playwrights lead or belong to these movements? Which plays are representative of each one?

Harold Pinter

1930–

Other Works
Last to Go
Trouble in the Works
The Black and White
The Birthday Party
The Dumb Waiter
The Caretaker

Early Memories Harold Pinter was born and educated in a working-class neighborhood of London's East End. Though he was a child during World War II, he vividly recalls the German bombing raids that took him away from his parents for a year, when he was evacuated to the country along with other London children. A son of Jewish parents, he also recalls the anti-Jewish sentiment that was widespread in some sectors of British society during and after the war. On many occasions, he found himself involved in fistfights as a result of attacks by unruly neighborhood thugs.

Acting Days As a teenager, Pinter acted in plays and wrote poetry for a school magazine, but he also showed his proficiency in sports. He played soccer, broke a school record in sprinting, and received an award for his accomplishments in cricket, a sport that he continued to play into adulthood. At the age of 18, he received a grant to study at London's Royal Academy of Dramatic Art, but he left the school after only a few months. Later, he studied acting with more success at the Central School of Speech and Drama, and he spent his early and middle 20s acting in various productions and repertory theaters throughout England.

Prolific Playwright During his years as an actor, Pinter continued to write, but all his early works were poetry and fiction. In 1957, he composed his first play—a one-act drama called *The Room,* which he wrote in four days. In explaining how he started writing plays, Pinter has stated, "I went into a room one day and saw a couple of people in it. . . . I started off with this picture of the two people and let them carry on from there. . . . It was quite a natural movement." Pinter has since written scripts for television and movies as well as for the theater and has won numerous literary prizes, including a Tony Award.

Author Activity

Pinter's Roles Research Pinter's acting career. Find out what roles he played and whether his efforts were reviewed favorably.

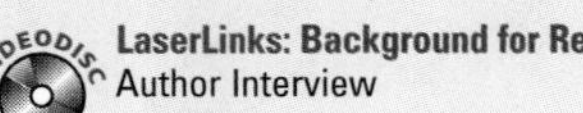

LaserLinks: Background for Reading
Author Interview

Writing Options

1. **Second Scene Dialogue** Remind students to maintain the play's tone and to use understatement when they compose new dialogue. Students might consider writing a scene that includes the third woman, the "she" of the play.
2. **Drama Review** Guide students to start by establishing criteria for evaluating the play, such as theme, humor, and characterization.

Activities & Explorations

1. **Set Design** Guide students to capture the mood of the play in the stage design and to check their interpretation by rereading the play. Students should also create their model to scale, such as one inch equals one foot.
2. **Mood Music** Have students start by writing down adjectives that describe how the play makes them feel. Then have them consider what kind of music gives them the same feeling.

Inquiry & Research

Real Versus Absurd The Theater of the Absurd consists of dramatists in the 50s and early 60s, such as Samuel Beckett ("Waiting for Godot"), Eugene Ionesco ("The Bald Soprano"), Jean Genet, Arthur Adamov, and Harold Pinter.
Students might find copies of absurdist plays for discussion in their local video store.

Author Activity

Pinter's Roles Suggest that students read another absurdist play and draw basic philosophical parallels with "That's All."

Mini Lesson Grammar

POSSESSIVES WITH PROPER NOUNS THAT END IN -S

Instruction Remind students that the possessive of most nouns, both common and proper, is formed by adding -*'s* to the noun. *(family's, Jason's)* This rule also applies to most proper nouns ending in *-s,* such as *Bess's and Charles's.* However, in the following instances the possessive of a proper noun is formed by adding just an apostrophe: with a name that has more than one syllable and an unaccented ending pronounced *-eez (Achilles', Euripides');* with a plural name that ends in *-s (Joneses');* and with the names *Jesus* and *Moses.*

Activity Write the following on the chalkboard.

Socrates lessons, like Pinter *That's All,* were usually written in the form of a dialogue.

In Alrene Sykes opinion, Pinter characters fail to communicate at the beginning of his plays.

Have students identify each proper noun and tell how its plural should be formed. *(Socrates', Pinter's, Sykes's, Pinter's)*

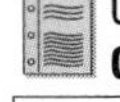

Use **Grammar Transparencies and Copymasters,** p. 3.

Use McDougal Littell's ***Language Network*** for more instruction and practice in possessives.

PART 2 Culture and Conflict

England has had complex relationships with other countries–especially the other parts of the United Kingdom and the countries that were once British colonies, some of which still belong to the British Commonwealth. Political conflicts have ravaged Northern Ireland, and citizens of former colonies find themselves caught in transition within their own countries and faced with the tensions of culture clash when they immigrate to England. Some of the writers represented in this part of Unit Seven describe struggles for peace and justice in their homelands, whereas others detail the prejudice many immigrants experience in England. As you read the selections, think about how you would react in similar situations.

Literature as Social Criticism

When Life Is Unfair

If you've ever been critical of the way things are—something as small as roadside littering, for example, or as large as race discrimination—then you've probably engaged in social criticism. **Social criticism** is also a term used to distinguish literature that addresses specific political, social, and sometimes religious and economic issues. Jonathan Swift's fantasy *Gulliver's Travels* can be classified as social criticism because it broadly satirizes, or pokes fun at, ideas and practices that Swift felt were either wrong or downright ridiculous.

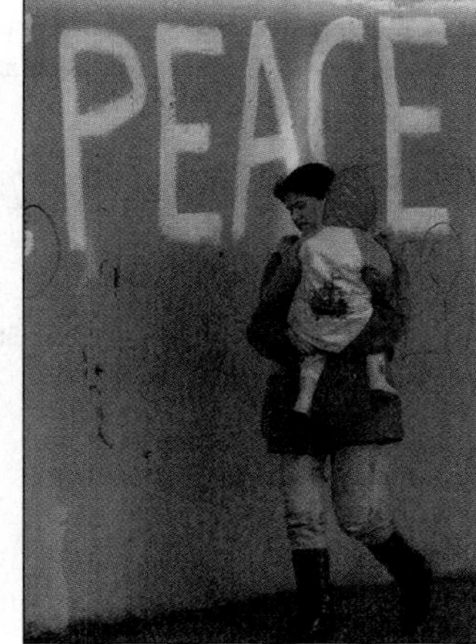

In Northern Ireland, a place suffering from decades of turmoil, a mother carries her child past a peace sign.

Throughout the history of English literature, writers have focused on social and political issues. In the 19th century, for example, the novelist Charles Dickens addressed the darker side of England's industrial development, while in the early 20th century, English poet Siegfried Sassoon graphically depicted the horrors of World War I. Since World War II, social criticism has achieved widespread exposure in the literature of writers throughout the world.

Writer's Purposes

Unlike journalists or political writers, most fiction writers don't set out to write social criticism; their primary purpose is to tell a story, express a feeling, or create an impression. South African writer Nadine Gordimer has written about the reality and the evils of apartheid, the rigid system of racial segregation that governed her country until the 1990s. In her words, "What else can an honest writer do but draw on the life around him?"

Typically, the writers who include social criticism in their works hope to do more than merely entertain readers. Although their reasons for addressing political and social problems may vary, most writers feel a responsibility to make readers aware of certain facts. Sometimes a writer's motives may be personal, based on direct experiences; in other instances, the writer may simply be presenting thoughts on a problem that has bothered his or her conscience.

In her essay "Writing As an Act of Hope" (page 1302), Chilean writer Isabel Allende expresses the goal to change "the conscience of some readers." This goal separates the literature of social criticism from other forms of social criticism, such as propaganda, which aims to stir people to direct action.

The Active Ingredients

Fiction writers differ in the way they introduce social criticism into their work. One or many of the following elements may be evident in a single work of social criticism.

Treatment of Issue In some stories, a political or social issue may dominate the entire plot and become the central theme around which all actions revolve. In other stories, the social criticism is less direct, and the political or social issue serves as a backdrop for another situation.

Use of Tone Other writers convey their views through the use of tone. Nadine Gordimer, in her story "Six Feet of the Country" (page 1289), sharpens her social criticism with irony and casts a critical eye on her main character.

OVERVIEW

Objectives

- understand the following literary term: social criticism
- appreciate shared characteristics of literature across cultures
- recognize themes across cultures

Teaching the Lesson

Motivating the Students

As students read the pieces in this unit, have them consider the following questions:

What attitudes do the writers have toward their characters?

How do the writers use irony to point out social injustice?

Are the issues that the writers address still relevant today? Have these issues changed?

As they finish reading the pieces, students can write reactions to these questions and keep their responses in their Working Portfolios.

Presenting the Concepts

Read through the strategies aloud or project them on a transparency. Using The Active Ingredients listed on page 1261, ask students to identify social problems that they think would make good subjects for stories. Have a class discussion about how to use the "active ingredients" to make these social problems compelling. Use the class discussion to model how to use the strategies.

Reading Skills and Strategies:
READING TO TAKE ACTION

Students can be inspired to take action by reading, listening, observing, and participating. The selections that follow this article will expose students to writers who have chosen to express their concerns about social conditions through their writings. As an additional activity for this unit, encourage students to identify a social condition about which they are concerned and locate material that expresses their attitude or broadens their information base. Have them share their information with the class.

Making Connections

Literature as Social Criticism Across Cultures

In every society, fiction writers serve as witnesses to corruption and injustice. Because literature can have such a strong emotional impact on the reader, stories, novels, and poems addressing social problems can shape public opinion. Share the following information about fiction writers of social criticism.

South Africa

Although the writer Alan Paton (1903–1988) was of European ancestry, he was born in South Africa and cared deeply about its problems. In his novel *Cry, the Beloved Country* (1948), he tells the story of a rural Zulu pastor who journeys to Johannesburg to search for his son, who has killed a white man. The novel vividly portrays the racism and danger of Johannesburg under apartheid, as well as the breakdown of traditional African values.

Russia

Aleksandr Solzhenitsyn (b. 1918) was arrested in 1945 for a comment in a personal letter that appeared to criticize Stalin. He was sentenced to eight years in a labor camp as a result. He drew on this experience for his 1962 novella *One Day in the Life of Ivan Denisovich,* which recounts a single day of a camp inmate who is subjected to brutal "corrective labor" for 10 years merely because he had allowed himself to be taken prisoner by the German army in World War II.

Peru

Mario Vargas Llosa (b. 1936) is a prolific author of novels aimed mainly at exposing the tyrannies of the political left and right, that so often tear at Latin America. His 1969 novel *Conversacion en la catedral* (Conversation in the Cathedral) concerns corruption "in virtually all the shapes and spheres you can imagine," wrote one critic, while another considered it "one of the most scathing denunciations ever written on the corruption and immorality of Latin America's ruling classes." His 1984 novel Guerra (published in English as *The War of the End of the World*) is set in 19th-century Brazil and concerns an apocalyptic religious movement. The author has written that it examines the "fanaticism [that] is the root of violence in Latin America." Using Brazil as a microcosm of all Latin America, Vargas Llosa's novel reflects his contemporary criticism of both at rightist dictatorships and communist guerrillas. Vargas Llosa believes that any Latin American writer, privileged by virtue of his education, has a "moral obligation" to speak out on politics and civic activities.

Involvement of Readers Like George Orwell, most writers of social criticism ask their readers to bear witness to the wrongs they expose.

Focus on Individuals Typically, writers cast their characters as ordinary individuals caught up in the context of larger world issues. The reader then observes how the larger issues affect the motives, behaviors, and destinies of real people. Both William Trevor's "The Distant Past" (page 1263) and Chinua Achebe's "Civil Peace" (page 1274) portray the lingering effects of civil war on neighbors. Some writers simply dramatize a demeaning personal experience in order to shed light on a larger social problem—such as Wole Soyinka in his poem "Telephone Conversation" (page 1281), which portrays a man trying to rent an apartment.

Often the best examples of social criticism in fiction are those in which writers present the truth about situations without injecting their personal beliefs, thereby allowing readers to form their own opinions. In "The Distant Past" (on page 1263), William Trevor captures how a large problem—the growing hostility between Protestants and Catholics in Northern Ireland—affects people's daily lives.

Regardless of their methods, however, all writers appeal to the readers' sense of humanity. The communion between writer and reader lasts only as long as the act of reading; then it is up to the reader to live with what he or she has learned.

Social Critics Speak

George Orwell — Targets Totalitarianism

VIEWPOINT *"When I saw the prisoner step aside to avoid the puddle, I saw the mystery, the unspeakable wrongness, of cutting a life short when it is in full tide."*

from "A Hanging"

Nadine Gordimer — Targets Apartheid

VIEWPOINT *"I am not a preacher or a politician. It is simply not the purpose of a novelist. I am totally opposed to apartheid and all the cruel and ugly things it stands for, and have been so all my life. But my writing does not deal with my personal convictions; it deals with the society I live and write in . . ."*

Isabel Allende — Targets Political Turmoil

VIEWPOINT *"I feel that writing is an act of hope, a sort of communion with our fellow men. The writer of good will carries a lamp to illuminate the dark corners. Only that, nothing more—a tiny beam of light to show some hidden aspect of reality, to help decipher and understand it and thus to initiate, if possible, a change in the conscience of some readers."*

from "Writing as an Act of Hope"

YOUR TURN On the basis of these statements, which of these social critics would you like to explore further? Discuss your choice with a classmate.

Strategies for Reading: Social Criticism

1. Consider the context of the work. If necessary, refer to the Build Background section accompanying each selection.
2. Pay attention to how great historical, political, and social forces affect people's everyday lives.
3. Evaluate what you read. Don't hesitate to judge characters.
4. Be aware of how writers use irony and figurative language to uncover truths.
5. Draw conclusions about themes, which tend to be unstated in works of social criticism.
6. **Monitor** your reading strategies and modify them when your understanding breaks down. Remember to use your Strategies for Active Reading: **predict, visualize, connect, question, clarify,** and **evaluate.**

The Distant Past

Short Story by WILLIAM TREVOR

"In the town and beyond it they were regarded as harmlessly peculiar."

Connect to Your Life

Living in the Past Do you know someone who seems to live in the past—who likes to think and talk about events that happened long ago? What do you think might make such a person dwell on past experiences? Share your thoughts with classmates.

Build Background

A Divided Ireland Conflicts between the English and the Irish extend back to the 12th century, when England first succeeded in gaining control of part of Ireland. Later, when the English tried to establish Protestantism as the sole religion in the predominantly Roman Catholic land, they naturally met with resistance and considerable anti-English sentiment. In the late 1800s, Irish Catholics began demanding self-rule, but the mostly Protestant settlements in northern Ireland opposed the plan.

In 1920, Britain divided Ireland into two countries with some powers of self-government. Northern Ireland, with its Protestant majority, readily accepted the decision. The Catholics in the rest of Ireland, however, wanted complete independence. In 1921 southern Ireland agreed to become a self-governing dominion called the Irish Free State. By 1949, the nation had severed all ties with Great Britain, becoming the independent Republic of Ireland. Meanwhile, dissension between Protestants and Catholics in Northern Ireland continued, and in the late 1960s the Irish Republican Army (IRA), an outlawed group of Catholic militants, began a series of terrorist attacks aimed at removing the British from that country as well.

The author William Trevor was born in 1928 to a Protestant family living in the Irish Free State. Many of Trevor's stories are set in Ireland, and his characters are often forced to confront the realities of a long history of violence and hatred.

WORDS TO KNOW **Vocabulary Preview**
adversity, convivial, regime, anachronism, perversity

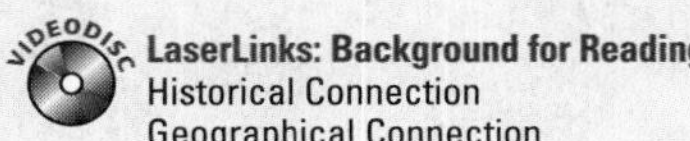

LaserLinks: Background for Reading
Historical Connection
Geographical Connection

Focus Your Reading

LITERARY ANALYSIS CONFLICT

Many contemporary short stories revolve around a character's **internal conflicts**—the inner struggles a character wrestles with. In other stories, however, the **plot** and **themes** develop primarily out of **external conflicts,** which involve outside forces. As you read, be aware of the conflicts in this story, and note whether they are internal or external.

ACTIVE READING INFERRING CAUSE AND EFFECT

During the course of this story, the events that the narrator describes affect the characters, causing changes in their attitudes about themselves, others, and important events in their lives.

READER'S NOTEBOOK Make two columns, one labeled **Causes** and one labeled **Effects.** As you read, list events from the story in the first column. Then, in the second column, list the effects of each event on the attitudes and relationships of the Middletons and the townspeople.

OVERVIEW

Objectives

1. understand and appreciate the author's use of **conflict** in a short story **(Literary Analysis)**
2. **infer cause and effect** in order to understand a **short story (Active Reading)**

Summary

The Middletons, a brother and sister, are proud heirs to Carraveagh, a once-glorious estate in Ireland. As the years go by, they remain loyal to each other, to the remains of their estate, and to the British crown. For most of these years, the townspeople are tolerant and even fond of the Middletons. By the late 1960s, however, the distant past proves to be not so distant after all.

When terrorism and bombings in Northern Ireland begin to disrupt the town's economy, the townspeople begin to deny the Middletons even the most basic civilities. The Middletons look ahead to a friendless death.

Use **Unit Seven Resource Book,** p. 35 for additional support.

Thematic Link

"The Distant Past" shows how political **conflicts affect cultures** and the ordinary people who are part of them.

5-Minute Warm-Up

Daily Language SkillBuilder

Have students **proofread** the display sentences on page 1189j and write them correctly. The sentences also appear on Transparency 35 of **Grammar Transparencies and Copymasters.**

Mini Lesson **Preteaching Vocabulary**

If you would like to preteach the WORDS TO KNOW for this selection, use the Mini Lesson on p. 1265.

Editor's Note:
This selection contains language that may be considered objectionable.

LESSON RESOURCES

UNIT SEVEN RESOURCE BOOK, pp. 31–35

ASSESSMENT RESOURCES

Formal Assessment, pp. 237–238

Teacher's Guide to Assessment and Portfolio Use

Test Generator

SKILLS TRANSPARENCIES AND COPYMASTERS

Literary Analysis
- External Conflicts/Societal Conflicts, T20 (for Literary Analysis, p. 1263)

Reading and Critical Thinking
- Cause and Effect, T1 (for Active Reading, p. 1263)

Grammar
- Pronouns—Personal, Reflexive, and Intensive, T39 (for Mini Lesson, p. 1266)
- Reciprocal Pronouns, C148 (for Mini Lesson, p. 1270)

Vocabulary
- Analogies, C73 (for Mini Lesson, p. 1265)

Writing
- Literary Interpretation, C33 (for Writing Options, p. 1273)

Communications
- Impromptu Speaking: Dialogue, Role-Play, T14 (for Activities & Explorations, p. 1273)

INTEGRATED TECHNOLOGY

Audio Library

LaserLinks
- Historical Connection: Conflict in Northern Ireland
- Geographical Connection: Scenes of Ireland. See **Teacher's SourceBook,** pp. 93–94.

Visit our website:
www.mcdougallittell.com

TEACHING THE LITERATURE

Reading and Analyzing

Literary Analysis CONFLICT

Explain to students that the most common external conflicts are between
• two characters
• a character and a group or society
• two groups or societies
• a character and a force of nature

Then ask students what conflicts (internal and external) they see in the beginning of the story.

Possible Responses: external—conflict between Protestants and Catholics; conflict between nationalists and British loyalists; internal—conflict between present reality and Middletons' loyalties; conflict within townspeople between their liking for the Middletons and distrust of their political views.

Use **Unit Seven Resource Book,** p. 33 for more exercises.

Active Reading
INFERRING CAUSE AND EFFECT

Explain to students that writers do not always use words such as *since* or *because* to signal cause-and-effect relationships. Sometimes you must infer causes and effects by asking yourself how the situation came to be and what the possible results of events might be. Ask students to trace the chain of causes and effects in the story so far.

Possible Response: The father's mortgaging his estate caused the Middletons to lose money. The lack of money increased their pride in Carraveagh and caused them to blame the new government and their father's mistress.

Use **Unit Seven Resource Book,** p. 32 for more practice.

The Distant Past

William Trevor

The Distant Past

1264

Teaching Options

BLOCK SCHEDULING: MANAGING TIME

If your schedule requires that you cover the lesson objectives in a shorter time, use . . .
• Preparing to Read, p. 1263
• Thinking Through the Literature, p. 1272
• Vocabulary in Action, p. 1273

If you want to take advantage of longer class time, use . . .
• TE Teaching Options: Vocabulary, p. 1265; Grammar, pp. 1266, 1270; Viewing and Representing, pp. 1267, 1269; Cross Curricular Link, p. 1268; Informal Assessment, p. 1271
• Choices & Challenges and Author Activity, p. 1273

In the town and beyond it they were regarded as harmlessly peculiar. Odd, people said, and in time this reference took on a burnish[1] of affection.

They had always been thin, silent with one another, and similar in appearance: a brother and sister who shared a family face. It was a bony countenance, with pale blue eyes and a sharp, well-shaped nose and high cheek-bones. Their father had had it too, but unlike them their father had been an irresponsible and careless man, with red flecks in his cheeks that they didn't have at all. The Middletons of Carraveagh the family had once been known as, but now the brother and sister were just the Middletons, for Carraveagh didn't count any more, except to them.

They owned four Herefords,[2] a number of hens, and the house itself, three miles outside the town. It was a large house, built in the reign of George II,[3] a monument that reflected in its glory and later decay the fortunes of a family. As the brother and sister aged, its roof increasingly ceased to afford protection, rust ate at its gutters, grass thrived in two thick channels all along its avenue. Their father had mortgaged his inherited estate, so local rumor claimed, in order to keep a Catholic Dublin woman in brandy and jewels. When he died, in 1924, his two children discovered that they possessed only a dozen acres. It was locally said also that this adversity hardened their will and that because of it they came to love the remains of Carraveagh more than they could ever have loved a husband or a wife. They blamed for their ill-fortune the Catholic Dublin woman whom they'd never met and they blamed as well the new national regime, contriving in their eccentric way to relate the two. In the days of the Union Jack[4] such women

1 would have known their place: wasn't it all part and parcel?

Twice a week, on Fridays and Sundays, the Middletons journeyed into the town, first of all in a trap[5] and later in a Ford Anglia car. In the shops and elsewhere they made, quite gently, no secret of their continuing loyalty to the past. They attended on Sundays St. Patrick's Protestant Church, a place that matched their mood, for prayers were still said there for the King whose sovereignty[6] their country had denied. The revolutionary regime would not last, they quietly informed the Reverend Packham: what sense was there in green-painted pillar-boxes and a language that nobody understood?[7]

On Fridays, when they took seven or eight dozen eggs to the town, they dressed in pressed tweeds and were accompanied over the years by a series of red setters, the breed there had always been at Carraveagh. They sold the eggs in Keogh's grocery and then had a drink with Mrs. Keogh in the part of her shop that was devoted to the consumption of refreshment. Mr. Middleton had whisky and his sister Tio Pepe.[8] They enjoyed the occasion, for they liked Mrs. Keogh and were liked by her in return. Afterwards they shopped, chatting to the shopkeepers about whatever news there was, and then they went to Healy's Hotel for a few more drinks before driving home.

Drink was their pleasure and it was through it that they built up, in spite of their loyalty to the past, such convivial relationships with the people of the town. Fat Driscoll, who kept the butcher's shop, used even to joke about the past when he

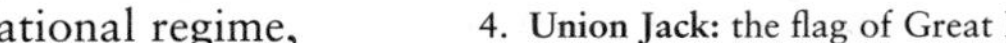

1. **burnish:** a smooth, polished finish.
2. **Herefords** (hûr′fərdz): cattle of a breed raised for beef.
3. **George II:** king of Great Britain, 1727–1760.
4. **Union Jack:** the flag of Great Britain.
5. **trap:** a light two-wheeled carriage.
6. **sovereignty:** royal authority.
7. **green-painted . . . understood:** mailboxes painted Irish green (instead of red British mailboxes) and Gaelic—also known as Irish—the traditional language of Ireland's Celtic inhabitants and one of the official languages of the Republic of Ireland.
8. **Tio Pepe:** a brand of Spanish sherry.

WORDS TO KNOW
adversity (ăd-vûr′sĭ-tē) *n.* hardship; misfortune
regime (rā-zhēm′) *n.* a government in power
convivial (kən-vĭv′ē-əl) *adj.* characterized by friendly companionship; sociable

1265

Customizing Instruction

Less Proficient Readers

Be sure students realize that the story is set in the Republic of Ireland, which had gained its independence from Great Britain at the time of the story.

Explain that this story focuses on the Middletons, a brother and sister, who live in Ireland but feel loyal to Britain long after British rule had been overthrown.

Students Acquiring English

1 Help students understand the idiom *part and parcel,* which means "part of the same thing." In this context, the idiom means that the Middletons connect the new national regime with their father's spending his fortune on a (low-class) Catholic mistress, both symptoms of the decline of values or of the proper order of things.

Use **Spanish Study Guide** for additional support, pp. 314–316.

Gifted and Talented

Have students consider what Carraveagh, the Middletons' home, might symbolize throughout the story.

Mini Lesson Preteaching Vocabulary

ANALOGIES Call students' attention to the list of WORDS TO KNOW. Remind them that a word analogy compares two pairs of words that have the same relationship. Discuss with students some of the kinds of relationships the words can have: characteristic quality, part to whole, specific to general, task and tool, antonym, synonym, and cause/effect. Use the model to demonstrate how to approach analogies.

Model

club : organization :: monarchy : write-on line

Instruction

- Have a volunteer read the model aloud: *"Club* is to *organization as monarchy* is to *blank."*
- Have students identify the relationship between the first pair of words (specific to general).
- Then have students use the first pair of words in a sentence that expresses their relationship; for example, "A club is a type of organization."
- Guide students to create a second sentence for the incomplete pair and then fill in the blank with a WORD TO KNOW: "A monarchy is a type of *regime."*

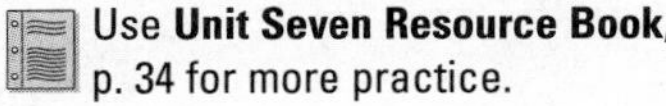
Use **Unit Seven Resource Book,** p. 34 for more practice.

A lesson on analogies appears on page 1317 in the Pupil's Edition.

Reading and Analyzing

Literary Analysis CONFLICT

A Ask students to identify the external struggle that ensues after Reverend Packham dies.

Possible Response: conflict between the Middletons and the new minister, the Reverend Bradshaw, who does not share their loyalty to Great Britain and the monarchy; increasing conflict between the Middletons and contemporary society.

What does this struggle suggest may happen to the Middletons?

Possible Response: They will become more isolated.

Literary Analysis: CHARACTERIZATION

Discuss with students how writers develop character by showing the character's thoughts, words, and actions. Ask students what the following details tell about the Middletons:

- their suspicions of the German couple
  Possible Responses: It shows how isolated the Middletons were, since they did not know the couple well enough to know they were harmless.
- their decision to display the Union Jack in their car
  Possible Responses: It shows that they were not sensitive to their neighbors' feelings.

Active Reading
INFERRING CAUSE AND EFFECT

Have students think about what effects the Middletons' actions of rising to their feet when the radio played "God Save the King" and of displaying the Union Jack might be expected to have.

Possible Responses: It might make the townspeople angry; it might make the townspeople dislike them.

stood with them in Healy's Hotel or stood behind his own counter cutting their slender chops or thinly slicing their liver. "Will you ever forget it,
1 Mr. Middleton? I'd ha' run like a rabbit if you'd lifted a finger at me." Fat Driscoll would laugh then, rocking back on his heels with a glass of stout in his hand or banging their meat on to his weighing-scales. Mr. Middleton would smile. "There was alarm in your eyes, Mr. Driscoll," Miss Middleton would murmur, smiling also at the memory of the distant occasion.

Fat Driscoll, with a farmer called Maguire and another called Breen, had stood in the hall of Carraveagh, each of them in charge of a shotgun. The Middletons, children then, had been locked with their mother and father and an aunt into an upstairs room. Nothing else had happened: the expected British soldiers had not, after all, arrived and the men in the hall had eventually relaxed their vigil. "A massacre they wanted," the Middletons' father said after
2 they'd gone. "Damn bloody ruffians."

The Second World War took place. Two Germans, a man and his wife called Winkelmann who ran a glove factory in the town, were suspected by the Middletons of being spies for the Third Reich.[9] People laughed, for they knew the Winkelmanns well and could lend no credence to the Middletons' latest fantasy: typical of them, they explained to the Winkelmanns, who had been worried. Soon after the War the Reverend
A Packham died and was replaced by the Reverend Bradshaw, a younger man who laughed also and regarded the Middletons as an anachronism. They protested when prayers were no longer said for the Royal Family in St. Patrick's, but the Reverend Bradshaw considered that their protests were as absurd as the prayers themselves had been. Why pray for the monarchy of a neighboring island when their own island had its chosen President now? The Middletons didn't reply to that argument. In the Reverend Bradshaw's presence they rose to their feet when the BBC[10] played "God Save the King," and on the day of the coronation of Queen Elizabeth II[11] they drove into the town with a small Union Jack propped up in the back window of their Ford Anglia. "Bedad, you're a holy terror, Mr. Middleton!" Fat Driscoll laughingly exclaimed, noticing the flag as he lifted a tray of pork-steaks from his display shelf. The Middletons smiled. It was a great day for the Commonwealth of Nations, they replied, a remark which further amused Fat Driscoll and which he later repeated in Phelan's public house. "Her Britannic Majesty," guffawed[12] his friend Mr. Breen.

Situated in a valley that was noted for its beauty and with convenient access to rich rivers and bogs over which game-birds flew, the town benefited from post-war tourism. Healy's Hotel changed its title and became, overnight, the New Ormonde. Shopkeepers had their shop-fronts painted and Mr. Healy organized an annual Salmon Festival. Even Canon[13] Kelly, who had at first commented severely on the habits of the tourists, and in particular on the summertime dress of the women, was in the end obliged to confess that the morals of his flock remained unaffected. "God and good sense," he proclaimed, meaning God and his own teaching. In time he even derived pride from the fact that people with other values came briefly to the town and that the values esteemed by his parishioners were in no way diminished.

9. **Third Reich** (rīk): Nazi-controlled Germany.
10. **BBC:** British Broadcasting Corporation.
11. **the day . . . Queen Elizabeth II:** June 2, 1953—more than four years after Ireland withdrew from the British Commonwealth of Nations, severing all official ties with England.
12. **guffawed:** laughed loudly.
13. **Canon:** the title of certain Roman Catholic priests.

WORDS TO KNOW
anachronism (ə-năk'rə-nĭz'əm) *n.* something out of keeping with a specified time; especially, something proper to a former age but not to the present

Teaching Options

Grammar

REFLEXIVE PRONOUNS

Instruction A reflexive pronoun is a pronoun with the suffix *-self* or *-selves* that is used as the direct or indirect object of an action. Remind students that the reflexive pronoun is used only when the object of a sentence is identical with the subject.

Activity Write the following sentences on the chalkboard.

Twice a week the Middletons took themselves into town.

"Canon Kelly looked in as a rule and satisfied himself that all was above board."

In time, Mrs. O'Brien couldn't bring herself to reply when the Middletons addressed her.

Have students identify each reflexive pronoun and the noun to which it refers. *(themselves, Middletons; himself, Canon Kelly; herself, Mrs. O'Brien)*

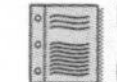
Use **Grammar Transparencies and Copymasters,** p. 6.

Use McDougal Littell's ***Language Network*** for more instruction and practice in reflexive pronouns.

A Self-Portrait (about 1965), William Leech. National Gallery of Ireland, Dublin.

The town's grocers now stocked foreign cheeses, brie and camembert and Port Salut, and wines were available to go with them. The plush Cocktail Room of the New Ormonde set a standard: the wife of a solicitor, a Mrs. O'Brien, began to give six o'clock parties once or twice a year, obliging her husband to mix gin and Martini in glass jugs and herself handing round a selection of nuts and small Japanese crackers. Canon Kelly looked in as a rule and satisfied himself that all was above board. He rejected, though, the mixture in the jugs, retaining his taste for a glass of John Jameson.[14]

From the windows of their convent the Loretto nuns[15] observed the long, sleek cars with G.B. plates; English and American accents drifted on the breeze to them. Mothers cleaned up their children and sent them to the Golf Club to seek employment as caddies. Sweet shops sold holiday mementoes. The brown, soda and currant breads of Murphy-Flood's bakery were declared to be delicious. Mr. Healy doubled the number of local girls who served as waitresses in his dining-room, and in the winter of 1961 he had the builders in again, working on an extension for which the Munster and Leinster Bank had lent him twenty-two thousand pounds.

14. **John Jameson:** a brand of Irish whiskey.

15. **Loretto nuns:** members of a Roman Catholic religious order founded near Dublin in 1822.

Customizing Instruction

Gifted and Talented

Tell students that the Republic of Ireland remained neutral during World War II. Then ask them why the Middletons might have thought the Winkelmanns were spies but the townspeople did not.

Possible Response: The Middletons' suspicions were a result of their overidentification with the British, who were at war with the Germans. The townspeople, whose country was not at war with Germany, had no reason to be suspicious of the Winkelmanns.

Less Proficient Readers

Help students to infer why Fat Driscoll and the others came to Carraveagh with shotguns. Point out that since they were waiting there for British soldiers, they must have thought that the Middletons were opening their home to British troops. Since no troops came, we can infer that this belief was wrong.

Students Acquiring English

1 Help students understand the contractions Fat Driscoll uses here. Remind them that *I'd* is the contraction for either *I had* or *I would.* In this case, it is the contraction for *I would.* In contrast, *you'd* is the contraction for *you had.* Explain that the abbreviated *ha'* is dialect for *have.*

2 Explain that *bloody* is a curse word in British and Irish English.

Mini Lesson Viewing and Representing

A Self-Portrait **by William Leech**

ART APPRECIATION Leech (1881–1968) grew up in Dublin and lived as an adult in London and France. This is one of a series of self-portraits he painted two years before he died.

Instruction Point out the contrast between the broad, flat leaves in the background and the highly detailed figure. Ask students why they think the artist created this contrast.

Possible Response: to focus the viewer's attention on the figure

Application Ask students in what ways this portrait reflects the description and/or their perception of Mr. Middleton.

Possible Response: It shows an older man, rather conservatively dressed, who looks out at the viewer with a suspicious expression.

Reading and Analyzing

Literary Analysis: SYMBOL

A Ask what the portrait of their father may symbolize to the Middletons.
Possible Responses: the past; their family's former glory; their connection to England; the way things should be.

Literary Analysis: IRONY

B You might have students return to the paragraph after they have finished the story and discuss the irony of the townspeople's attitude.
Possible Responses: The old wounds had not healed when the townspeople feel they must take sides over the conflict in Northern Ireland; they are as suspicious of the Middletons as the latter were of the Winkelmanns; the people have not "lived and learned."

Reading Skills and Strategies: SUMMARIZING INTERNAL AND EXTERNAL CONFLICTS

Ask students to list the conflicts in the story so far. Use the following prompts.

- external
  Possible Responses: British loyalists vs. republicans; Catholic vs. Protestant
- internal—the Middletons
  Possible Response: their need for friendship vs. their loyalty to Britain
- internal—the townspeople
  Possible Response: their fondness for the Middletons vs. their suspicion of them

But as the town increased its prosperity Carraveagh continued its decline. The Middletons were in their middle-sixties now and were reconciled to a life that became more uncomfortable with every passing year. Together they roved the vast lofts of their house, placing old paint tins and flowerpot saucers beneath the drips from the roof. At night they sat over their thin chops in a dining-room that had once been gracious and which in a way was gracious still, except for the faded appearance of furniture that was dry from lack of polish and of a wallpaper that time had rendered colorless. In the hall their father gazed down at them, framed in ebony and gilt, in the uniform of the Irish Guards. He had conversed with Queen Victoria, and even in their middle-sixties they could still hear him saying that God and Empire and Queen formed a trinity unique in any worthy soldier's heart. In the hall hung the family crest, and on ancient Irish linen the Cross of St. George.[16]

The dog that accompanied the Middletons now was called Turloch, an animal whose death they dreaded for they felt they couldn't manage the antics of another pup. Turloch, being thirteen, moved slowly and was blind and a little deaf. He was a reminder to them of their own advancing years and of the effort it had become to tend the Herefords and collect the weekly eggs. More and more they looked forward to Fridays, to the warm companionship of Mrs. Keogh and Mr. Healy's chatter in the hotel. They stayed longer now with Mrs. Keogh and in the hotel, and idled longer in the shops, and drove home more slowly. Dimly, but with no less loyalty, they still recalled the distant past and were listened to without ill-feeling when they spoke of it and of Carraveagh as it had been, and of the Queen whose company their careless father had known.

The visitors who came to the town heard about the Middletons and were impressed. It was a pleasant wonder, more than one of them remarked, that old wounds could heal so completely, that the Middletons continued in their loyalty to the past and that, in spite of it, they were respected in the town. When Miss Middleton had been ill with a form of pneumonia in 1958 Canon Kelly had driven out to Carraveagh twice a week with pullets and young ducks that his housekeeper had dressed. "An upright couple," was the Canon's public opinion of the Middletons, and he had been known to add that eccentric views would hurt you less than malice. "We can disagree without guns in this town," Mr. Healy pronounced in his Cocktail Room, and his visitors usually replied that as far as they could see that was the result of living in a Christian country. That the Middletons bought their meat from a man who had once locked them into an upstairs room and had then waited to shoot soldiers in their hall was a fact that amazed the seasonal visitors. You lived and learned, they remarked to Mr. Healy.

The Middletons, privately, often considered that they led a strange life. Alone in their two beds at night they now and again wondered why they hadn't just sold Carraveagh forty-eight years ago when their father had died: why had the tie been so strong and why had they in perversity encouraged it? They didn't fully know, nor did they attempt to discuss the matter in any way. Instinctively they had remained at Carraveagh, instinctively feeling that it would have been cowardly to go. Yet often it seemed to them now to be no more than a game they played, this worship of the distant past. And at other times it seemed as real and as important as the remaining acres of land, and the house itself.

16. **Cross of St. George:** horizontal and vertical red bars crossing on a white background—an ancient flag of England.

WORDS TO KNOW

perversity (pər-vûr′sĭ-tē) *n.* a stubborn determination to act in an inappropriate or unexpected way

1268

Teaching Options

Cross Curricular Link Social Studies

PEACE ACCORD IN NORTHERN IRELAND On May 22, 1998, the people of Northern Ireland voted in a referendum to pass a peace agreement. Under this agreement, Northern Ireland remains part of the United Kingdom, but the agreement calls for a new assembly whose members would be elected by the people. The agreement also sets up a council to work with government officials of the Irish Republic and another council to meet with governing bodies in Scotland, Wales, the Irish Republic, and England. The agreement is an attempt to address the concerns of both sides in the struggle.

Au Cinquième [On the fifth floor]: *A Portrait of the Artist's Wife* (about 1940), William Leech. Oil on canvas, 74 cm × 60 cm, National Gallery of Ireland, Dublin.

"Isn't that shocking?" Mr. Healy said one day in 1967. "Did you hear about that, Mr. Middleton, blowing up them post offices in Belfast?"[17]

Mr. Healy, red-faced and short-haired, spoke casually in his Cocktail Room, making midday conversation. He had commented in much the same way at breakfast-time, looking up from the *Irish Independent*. Everyone in the town had said it too: that the blowing up of sub–post offices in Belfast was a shocking matter.

"A bad business," Fat Driscoll remarked, wrapping the Middletons' meat. "We don't want that old stuff all over again."

"We didn't want it in the first place," Miss Middleton reminded him. He laughed, and she laughed, and so did her brother. Yes, it was a game, she thought: how could any of it be as real or as important as the afflictions and problems of the old butcher himself, his rheumatism and his reluctance to retire? Did her brother, she wondered, privately think so too?

"Come on, old Turloch," he said, stroking the flank of the red setter with the point of his shoe, and she reflected that you could never tell what he was thinking. Certainly it wasn't the kind of thing you wanted to talk about. 1

"I've put him in a bit of mince," Fat Driscoll said, which was something he often did these 2

17. **blowing up . . . in Belfast:** In Northern Ireland, Belfast (the capital) and the town of Londonderry were sites of terrorist attacks by members of the IRA.

Customizing Instruction

Less Proficient Readers

Have students summarize the relationship between the Middletons and the townspeople.

Possible Response: The townspeople think the Middletons are odd because they cling to their old, British past; they are fond of the pair, nonetheless.

Set a Purpose Have students read to find out what happens to the relationship between the townspeople and the Middletons.

Students Acquiring English

1 Make sure students understand that Mr. Middleton says, "Come on, old Turloch," not Fat Driscoll.

2 Explain to students that the mince the butcher gives the Middletons for their dog is chopped meat.

Viewing and Representing

Au Cinquième: A Portrait of the Artist's Wife
by William Leech

ART APPRECIATION When Leech exhibited this portrait of his wife in Ireland in 1967, he was disappointed "that none of the critics mentioned *Au Cinquième.* I suppose it was badly hung. I think it one of my best things."

Instruction Point out the X created in the painting by the angle of the woman's body and the sharp diagonal of the windowsill. Ask students what mood Leech creates in the painting by the play of light and the subject's occupation.

Possible Response: The sharp contrast of light and shadow gives the painting a feel of arrested movement emphasized by the woman's drowsing. The mood is one of serenity in the midst of action or chaos.

Application Ask students how this mood compares with that of Carraveagh. How does it compare with the mood of the town?

Possible Response: This mood closely matches the mood at Carraveagh and in the town. Carraveagh exists in a sort of time warp, and the town is a haven from the violence in the North.

Reading and Analyzing

Active Reading

INFERRING CAUSE AND EFFECT

A Discuss with students the effects of the unrest in the North of Ireland on the town and its inhabitants.

Possible Responses: Tourism declines, which causes the town's prosperity to ebb; the townspeople become suspicious of the Middletons because they have always supported Britain; the townspeople stop being friendly to the Middletons; the Middletons go into mourning because the *modus vivendi* has ceased to exist.

Literary Analysis: IRONY

Ask students what seems ironic now about the title "The Distant Past."

Possible Responses: The past is very much present in everyone's minds; the past and everyone's actions are being revised to suit events in the present; the people are reliving the past; the past has become the present.

Literary Analysis: SYMBOL

B Ask students what the Middletons symbolize to the townspeople now.

Possible Responses: the enemy; the British; oppression

days, pretending the mince would otherwise be thrown away. There'd been a red setter about the place that night when he waited in the hall for the soldiers: Breen and Maguire had pushed it down into a cellar, frightened of it.

1 "There's a heart of gold in you, Mr. Driscoll," Miss Middleton murmured, nodding and smiling at him. He was the same age as she was, sixty-six: he should have shut up shop years ago. He would have, he'd once told them, if there'd been a son to leave the business to. As it was, he'd have to sell it and when it came to the point he found it hard to make the necessary arrangements. "Like us and Carraveagh," she'd said, even though on the face of it it didn't seem the same at all.

Every evening they sat in the big old kitchen, hearing the news. It was only in Belfast and Derry,[18] the wireless[19] said; outside Belfast and Derry you wouldn't know anything was happening at all. On Fridays they listened to the talk in Mrs. Keogh's bar and in the hotel. "Well, thank God it has nothing to do with the South," Mr. Healy said often, usually repeating the statement.

The first British soldiers landed in the North of Ireland, and soon people didn't so often say that outside Belfast and Derry you wouldn't know anything was happening. There were incidents in Fermanagh and Armagh, in Border villages and towns. One Prime Minister resigned and then another one. The troops were unpopular, the newspapers said; internment[20] became part of the machinery of government. In the town, in St. Patrick's Protestant Church and in the Church of the Holy Assumption, prayers for peace were offered, but no peace came.

"We're hit, Mr. Middleton," Mr. Healy said one Friday morning. "If there's a dozen visitors this summer it'll be God's own stroke of luck for us."

"Luck?"

"Sure, who wants to come to a country with all that malarkey[21] in it?"

"But it's only in the North."

"Tell that to your tourists, Mr. Middleton." A

The town's prosperity ebbed. The Border was more than sixty miles away, but over that distance had spread some wisps of the fog of war. As anger rose in the town at the loss of fortune so there rose also the kind of talk there had been in the distant past. There was talk of atrocities and counter-atrocities, and of guns and gelignite[22] and the rights of people. There was bitterness suddenly in Mrs. Keogh's bar because of the lack of trade, and in the empty hotel there was bitterness also.

On Fridays, only sometimes at first, there was a silence when the Middletons appeared. It was as though, going back nearly twenty years, people remembered the Union Jack in the window of their car and saw it now in a different light. It wasn't something to laugh at any more, nor were certain words that the Middletons had gently spoken, nor were they themselves just an old, peculiar couple. Slowly the change crept about, all around them in the town, until Fat Driscoll didn't wish it to be remembered that he had ever given them mince for their dog. He had stood with a gun in the enemy's house, waiting for soldiers so that soldiers might be killed: it was better that people should remember that. B

One day Canon Kelly looked the other way when he saw the Middletons' car coming and

18. **Derry:** another name for Londonderry.
19. **wireless:** radio.
20. **internment:** confinement or imprisonment, especially in wartime.
21. **malarkey:** foolishness.
22. **gelignite** (jĕl′ĭg-nīt′): a powerful explosive.

Teaching Options

Grammar

RECIPROCAL PRONOUNS

Instruction *Each other* and *one another* are reciprocal pronouns. A reciprocal pronoun refers to the individual parts of a plural antecedent. *Each other* is ordinarily used when there are two antecedents, and *one another* is ordinarily used with three or more antecedents.

Activity Write the following sentences on the chalkboard.

The townspeople didn't laugh with ______ anymore when they remembered the Union Jack in the Middletons' car.

The brother and sister told ______, "It is worse than before."

Have students decide whether *each other* or *one another* should complete each sentence and explain why. *("one another," many townspeople; "each other," two people)*

Exercise Ask students to complete the sentence with the appropriate reciprocal pronoun.

The Middletons and Mrs. Keogh enjoyed chatting with ______ on Fridays. *(one another)*

Use **Grammar Transparencies and Copymasters,** p. 104.

Use McDougal Littell's ***Language Network*** for more instruction and practice in pronouns.

they noticed this movement of his head, although he hadn't wished them to. And on another day Mrs. O'Brien, who had always been keen to talk to them in the hotel, didn't reply when they addressed her.

2 The Middletons naturally didn't discuss these rebuffs but they each of them privately knew that there was no conversation they could have at this time with the people of the town. The stand they had taken and kept to for so many years no longer seemed ridiculous in the town. Had they driven with a Union Jack now they would, astoundingly, have been shot.

"It will never cease." He spoke disconsolately one night, standing by the dresser where the wireless was.

She washed the dishes they'd eaten from, and the cutlery. "Not in our time," she said.

"It is worse than before."

"Yes, it is worse than before."

They took from the walls of the hall the portrait of their father in the uniform of the Irish Guards because it seemed wrong to them that at this time it should hang there. They took down also the crest of their family and the Cross of St. George, and from a vase on the drawing-room mantelpiece they removed the small Union Jack that had been there since the Coronation of Queen Elizabeth II. They did not remove these articles in fear but in mourning for the *modus vivendi*[23] that had existed for so long between them and the people of the town. They had given their custom[24] to a butcher who had planned to shoot down soldiers in their hall and he, in turn, had given them mince for their dog. For fifty years they had experienced, after suspicion had seeped away, a tolerance that never again in the years that were left to them would they know.

One November night their dog died and he said to her after he had buried it that they must not be depressed by all that was happening. They would die themselves and the house would become a ruin because there was no one to inherit it, and the distant past would be set to rest. But she disagreed: the *modus vivendi* had been easy for them, she pointed out, because they hadn't really minded the dwindling of their fortunes while the town prospered. It had given them a life, and a kind of dignity: you could take a pride out of living in peace.

He did not say anything and then, because of the emotion that both of them felt over the death of their dog, he said in a rushing way that they could no longer at their age hope to make a living out of the remains of Carraveagh. They must sell the hens and the four Herefords. As he 3
spoke, he watched her nodding, agreeing with the sense of it. Now and again, he thought, he would drive slowly into the town, to buy groceries and meat with the money they had saved, and to face the silence that would sourly thicken as their own two deaths came closer and death increased in another part of their island. She felt him thinking that and she knew that he was right. Because of the distant past they would die friendless. It was worse than being murdered in their beds. ❖

23. ***modus vivendi*** (mō′dəs vĭ-vĕn′dē) *Latin:* way of life.

24. **custom:** business; trade.

Customizing Instruction

Students Acquiring English

1 Explain that *heart of gold* is an idiom that means "good-hearted" or "generous."

2 Help students understand that *rebuff* means "a blunt refusal; a snub."

Less Proficient Readers

3 Ask students why the Middletons decide to sell their hens and cattle now.

Possible Responses: because the townspeople will probably refuse to conduct business with them; because the townspeople are no longer their friends; because events in Northern Ireland have isolated them from the townspeople.

Less Proficient Readers

Check students' understanding with the following questions.

- How has Fat Driscoll's relationship with the Middletons changed over the years?
  Possible Response: First he planned to shoot down British soldiers in their hall, then he was very friendly toward them, then he became their enemy again.
- What is the political situation in Ireland at the end of the story?
  Possible Responses: There is a lot of unrest; people are committing acts of terrorism; the British army is patrolling border towns and occupying Northern Ireland.
- How do the townspeople feel about the Middletons at the end of the story?
  Possible Responses: They dislike them; they are suspicious of them; they no longer want to tolerate the Middletons' loyalty to Britain.

Mini Lesson Informal Assessment

WRITE A LETTER Have students get together with a partner and write two letters. One student should write a letter from Miss or Mr. Middleton's point of view, discussing what's happening in the town. The other student should write a reply, expressing one of the townspeople's point of view.

RUBRIC

3 Full Accomplishment Letters accurately express characters' points of view, which are developed using many specific details from story.

2 Substantial Accomplishment Letters generally reflect characters' points of view, which are developed using several details from story.

1 Little or Partial Accomplishment Letters do not reflect characters' points of view and do not refer to specific details in story.

GUIDING STUDENT RESPONSE

Connect to the Literature

1. **What Do You Think?**
Guidelines for student response: Students might relate the events in the story to the current political situation in Ireland. They might consider how and in what ways the situation has or has not changed.

Comprehension Check

- Fat Driscoll is the town butcher; he was one of the men who locked the Middletons in a room and waited to kill British soldiers.
- brother and sister

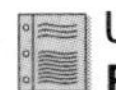
Use Selection Quiz in **Unit seven Resource Book,** p. 35.

Think Critically

2. Possible Response: When the father was alive, the people were openly hostile. After his death, as political issues subsided, the people gradually accepted the Middletons and seemed to like them. Once politics became an issue again, the people snubbed the Middletons.
3. Possible Responses: the Middletons' continuing to show loyalty to the British; the increase in political tensions, signaled by the bombing of the post office; the town's economic decline.
4. Possible Responses: yes, because the Middletons never completely put the past behind them; no, because the Middletons have done nothing to provoke their ill will.
5. Possible Responses: The Middletons feel sentimental about the past, yet they also resent it because it has led to Carraveagh's decline. At the end of the story, the Middletons' longing for the past is over, and they realize that the distant past and their part in it will cause them to die friendless.

Literary Analysis

Paired Activity Student answers should reflect an understanding of the relevance of the setting to the story's meaning.

Thinking through the LITERATURE

Connect to the Literature

1. **What Do You Think?** What parts of the story did you find most thought-provoking? Share your reactions with a partner.

Comprehension Check

- Who is Fat Driscoll?
- What is the relationship between the Middletons?

Think Critically

2. How would you describe the relationship between the Middletons and the people of the town?

THINK ABOUT
- how the townspeople felt about the Middletons' parents
- the Middletons' behavior
- the changing feelings of all involved
- the political loyalties of all involved

3. **ACTIVE READING** INFERRING CAUSE AND EFFECT What events do you think have the most significant effect on the relationship between the Middletons and the townspeople? Review the lists you created in your 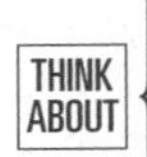 READER'S NOTEBOOK to help you answer this question.
4. Do you think the townspeople are justified in their behavior? Why or why not?
5. How would you describe the Middletons' feelings about the past, and how do these feelings change at the end of the story?

Extend Interpretations

6. **Writer's Style** Throughout the story, Trevor repeats the word *past* and the phrase "the distant past." How does this **repetition** reinforce the **themes** in the story?
7. **Comparing Texts** Compare the characters in "The Distant Past" with those in Lady Gregory's *The Rising of the Moon* (page 994). What conflicts do they share? Are those conflicts resolved in either selection?
8. **Connect to Life** Do you think that a situation similar to the one depicted in "The Distant Past" could occur in your own community? Defend your position.

Literary Analysis

CONFLICT As you know, a **conflict** is a struggle between opposing forces that moves a plot forward. The conflict provides the interest or suspense in a short story. Conflict may be **external,** with a character being pitted against some outside force—another person, a physical obstacle, nature, or society. Conflict may also be **internal,** occurring within a character. In "The Distant Past," the Middletons experience internal conflicts, primarily in their relationship to the values of the past. However, most of the conflicts in the story are external. Some of them are between individual characters, while others involve factions in the society at large.

Paired Activity With a partner, list the conflicts between characters and the conflicts in the larger society. How are the two kinds of conflicts related? Are any of the conflicts resolved? Could any of the conflicts have been avoided? Discuss your conclusions with other classmates.

Conflicts Between Characters	Conflicts in Society

REVIEW SETTING **Setting** can refer not only to the time and place of a story but also to the social and moral environment that forms the background of a narrative. All of these aspects of setting contribute to the development of the **plot, characters,** and **themes.** Think about the setting of "The Distant Past." Briefly describe how it relates to the plot, characters, and themes in the story.

Extend Interpretations

Writer's Style The word *past* recurs in the story, just as the events of the past recur in the minds of the characters. The repetition of the word does not allow the reader to forget the past, just as the characters cannot forget it.

Comparing Texts Accept all reasonable responses. Students may say that since the police sergeant protects the revolutionary, the conflict is somewhat resolved in *The Rising of the Moon,* whereas the characters in "The Distant Past" never truly resolve their conflict over the past.

Connect to Life Accept all reasonable responses.

Choices & CHALLENGES

Writing Options

Paragraph Critique In a paragraph, discuss the effectiveness of the last sentence of the story: "It was worse than being murdered in their beds." Consider such questions as the following: What responses does the sentence draw from the reader? How does the statement relate to the lives of the Middletons? to the political climate of the times? Why do you think Trevor ended the story with this comment? Place the paragraph in your **Working Portfolio.**

Activities & Explorations

Role-Play Conversations With a partner, role-play two different conversations between Fat Driscoll and Mrs. Keogh, one during the 1950s and one in the late 1960s, after the British soldiers land in Northern Ireland. ~ **SPEAKING AND LISTENING**

Vocabulary in Action

EXERCISE: WORD MEANINGS Write the word suggested by each of the following descriptions.

1. An example of this might be a Neanderthal man in modern Berlin or a helicopter hovering over King Arthur and his Round Table.
2. More exasperating than mere misbehavior and harder to deal with than simple stubbornness, this is a trait found in real brats and people we call ornery.
3. This may or may not change when there's a national election, but it does change when there's a successful revolution.
4. This word describes the guests we are happiest to entertain and most likely to invite again.
5. If you retire to a bed of thorns after having a hard row to hoe, your life has a good deal of this in it.

WORDS TO KNOW			
	adversity	convivial	regime
	anachronism	perversity	

Building Vocabulary

For an in-depth lesson on how to expand your vocabulary, see page 1182.

William Trevor

1928–

Other Works

"Mrs. Silly"
"Autumn Sunshine"
"The Tennis Court"
Mrs. Acland's Ghosts

An Irregular Education William Trevor was born William Trevor Cox in County Cork, Ireland. During his childhood, his family relocated often, moving from town to town throughout southern Ireland as his father pursued a career in banking. As a result, Trevor's education was somewhat irregular; he went to 13 different grammar schools and, at times, no school at all. Later, he attended St. Columba's College and Trinity College in Dublin. Immediately after receiving a degree from Trinity, he accepted a position as a history teacher in Northern Ireland. In 1952, he moved to England, where he taught art and began a career as a sculptor.

A Late Bloomer As a youth, Trevor never entertained thoughts of a writing career. In fact, he always assumed that he would someday enter the business world, perhaps working in a store or a bank. He did not publish his first novel until 1958, and not until he was in his mid-30s did he abandon art in order to write full-time. The numerous novels, plays, and short stories he has published since then have been commended for their restrained style, subtle humor, and compassionate characterization. Although his writing often deals with the people, culture, and history of his native Ireland, he has continued to reside and work in England.

Author Activity

Trinity College, Dublin William Trevor was educated at Trinity College, also called the University of Dublin. It is the oldest university in Ireland, having been founded by Queen Elizabeth I in 1591. Many famous writers have attended this university. Do some research and draw up a list of names of writers who have graduated from Dublin's Trinity College.

Writing Options

Paragraph Critique Use these prompts to help students get started.

- Do you agree with the opinion expressed in the last line?
- What does the last line lead you to expect for the characters' future?
- Considering what you know of the Irish conflict, do you think the writer meant the reader to take seriously the possibility the line expresses of the Middletons being murdered?

Activities & Explorations

Role-Play Conversations Suggest that students reread parts of the story that reveal the feelings of Fat Driscoll and Mrs. Keogh. If students prefer, they can add the role of a third character, a tourist who visits the town and asks questions about the elderly couple.

Vocabulary in Action

1. anachronism
2. perversity
3. regime
4. convivial
5. adversity

Author Activity

Trinity College, Dublin Suggest that, in addition to Internet and library sources, students send away for Trinity College's catalog and read the material on the college's history.

OVERVIEW

This selection is included in the **Grade 12 InterActive Reader.**

Objectives

1. understand and appreciate the author's use of **dialect (Literary Analysis)**
2. **make judgments about characters** in order to understand a short story. **(Active Reading)**

Summary

Jonathan Iwegbu considers himself lucky to have survived the Nigerian civil war with five of his six family members still alive. However, the night after Jonathan has received 20 pounds from the government, thieves knock at his door demanding his money. Jonathan hands the money to them. The next day, Jonathan assures his neighbors that the loss of the money is unimportant, dismissing the incident with his characteristic refrain, "Nothing puzzles God."

Use **Unit Seven Resource Book,** p. 36 for additional support.

Thematic Link

Achebe shows the physical and emotional effects of civil war and makes it clear that **cultures in conflict** can also cause devastation in times of peace.

5-Minute Warm-Up

Daily Language SkillBuilder

Have students **proofread** the display sentences on page 1189j and write them correctly. The sentences also appear on Transparency 35 of **Grammar Transparencies and Copymasters.**

Editor's Note

This selection contains language that may be considered objectionable.

Civil Peace

Short Story by CHINUA ACHEBE (chĭn′wä ä-chā′bā)

"Nothing puzzles God."

Connect to Your Life

Life After War Think about articles or books you have read that describe the aftermath of war. What is life typically like for ordinary civilians after a war has been fought on their land? Share your knowledge with classmates.

Build Background

War and Independence Chinua Achebe often writes about the conflicts and transitions in his native Nigeria, a former British colony on the western coast of Africa. After more than 100 years of British influence, Nigeria finally gained its independence in 1960. Although English is the country's official language, over 250 ethnic groups, each with its own language and customs, live there. The three largest of these are the Hausa, the Yoruba, and the Ibo.

Throughout the 1960s, various ethnic groups struggled, often violently, for control of Nigeria's government. The principal opponents were the Ibo and the Hausa. In 1967, the Ibo in the eastern part of the country seceded from Nigeria and formed their own republic, called Biafra. A period of civil war followed, lasting until 1970 and causing massive hardship and devastation—especially in Biafra, which suffered from a lack of supplies. It is estimated that over 1.5 million Biafrans starved to death before their leaders surrendered. Chinua Achebe was a tireless spokesperson for the Biafran cause, but in the war's aftermath he just as diligently joined in the long process of unifying and rebuilding the country.

LaserLinks: Background for Reading
Historical Connection
Cultural Connection

Focus Your Reading

LITERARY ANALYSIS | DIALECT A **dialect** is a form of a language that is spoken in one place by a certain group of people. Here are some examples of words from one dialect of English found in "Civil Peace," along with the meanings of the words:

na ("is" or "it is") soja ("soldiers")
commot ("leave") am ("it")
wetin ("what") katakata ("trouble")

As you read the story, try to decipher the meanings of other words in dialect.

ACTIVE READING | MAKING JUDGMENTS ABOUT CHARACTERS When you read a narrative, you make judgments about characters based on their speech, thoughts, feelings, and reactions to events. In "Civil Peace," the narrator says that Jonathan Iwegbu considers himself very lucky. As you read the story, think about whether you agree with this assessment.

READER'S NOTEBOOK To assess Jonathan's luck, make a chart like the one shown here and record what you consider to be his losses and blessings.

Jonathan's Luck	
Losses	Blessings

LESSON RESOURCES

UNIT SEVEN RESOURCE BOOK, pp. 36–39

ASSESSMENT RESOURCES

Formal Assessment, pp. 239–240

Teacher's Guide to Assessment and Portfolio Use

Test Generator

SKILLS TRANSPARENCIES AND COPYMASTERS

Literary Analysis
- External Conflicts/Societal Conflicts, T20 (for Review, p. 1279)

Reading and Critical Thinking
- Making Judgments, T5 (for Active Reading, p. 1274)

Grammar
- Indefinite Pronouns, T40 and C145 (for Mini Lesson, p. 1280)

Vocabulary
- Using Context to Understand Dialect, C93 (for Mini Lesson, p. 1277)

Writing
- Showing, Not Telling, T22 (for Writing Option 2, p. 1280)

Communications
- Dramatic Reading, T12 (for Activities & Explorations 1, p. 1280)

INTEGRATED TECHNOLOGY

Audio Library

LaserLinks
- Historical Connection: The Nigerian Civil War
- Cultural Connection: Nigeria Today. See **Teacher's SourceBook,** pp. 95–96.

Internet: Research Starter

Visit our website: www.mcdougallittell.com

CIVIL PEACE

Chinua Achebe

Jonathan Iwegbu counted himself extraordinarily lucky. "Happy survival!" meant so much more to him than just a current fashion of greeting old friends in the first hazy days of peace. It went deep to his heart. He had come out of the war with five inestimable blessings—his head, his wife Maria's head and the heads of three out of their four children. As a bonus he also had his old bicycle—a miracle too but naturally not to be compared to the safety of five human heads.

The bicycle had a little history of its own. One day at the height of the war it was commandeered "for urgent military action." Hard as its loss would have been to him he would still have let it go without a thought had he not had some doubts about the genuineness of the officer. It wasn't his disreputable rags, nor the toes peeping out of one blue and one brown canvas shoes, nor yet the two stars of his rank done obviously in a hurry in biro,[1] that troubled Jonathan; many good and heroic soldiers looked the same or worse. It was rather a certain lack of grip and firmness in his manner. So Jonathan, suspecting he might be amenable to influence, rummaged in his raffia[2] bag and produced the two pounds with which he had been going to buy firewood which his wife, Maria, retailed to camp officials for extra stock-fish and corn meal, and got his bicycle back. That night he buried it in the little clearing in the bush where the dead of the camp, including his own youngest son, were buried. When he dug it up again a year later after the surrender all it needed was a little palm-oil greasing. "Nothing puzzles God," he said in wonder.

He put it to immediate use as a taxi and accumulated a small pile of Biafran money ferrying camp officials and their families across the four-mile stretch to the nearest tarred road. His standard charge per trip was six pounds and those who had the money were only glad to be rid of some of it in this way. At the end of a fortnight he had made a small fortune of one hundred and fifteen pounds.

Then he made the journey to Enugu[3] and found another miracle waiting for him. It was unbelievable. He rubbed his eyes and looked again and it was still standing there before him. But, needless to say, even that monumental blessing must be accounted also totally inferior to the five heads in the family. This newest miracle was his little house in Ogui Overside. Indeed nothing puzzles God! Only two houses away a huge concrete edifice some wealthy contractor had put up just before the war was a mountain of rubble. And here was Jonathan's little zinc house[4] of no regrets built with mud blocks quite intact! Of course the doors and windows were missing and five sheets off the roof. But what was that? And anyhow he had returned to Enugu early enough to pick up bits of old zinc and wood and soggy sheets of card-board lying around the neighborhood before thousands more came out of their forest holes looking for the same things. He got a destitute carpenter with one old hammer, a blunt plane and a few bent and rusty nails in his tool bag to turn this assortment of wood, paper and metal into door and window shutters for five Nigerian shillings or fifty Biafran pounds. He paid the

1. **biro** (bîr′ō) a British term for a ballpoint pen. (The officer's insignia, that is, had been drawn in ink.)
2. **raffia:** a palm fiber used for weaving such items as mats, baskets, and hats.
3. **Enugu** (ā-no͞o′go͞o): a city in southeastern Nigeria.
4. **zinc house:** a house roofed with sheets of galvanized metal.

TEACHING THE LITERATURE

Customizing Instruction

Less Proficient Readers

Set a Purpose Have students read to find out why Jonathan Iwegbu counts himself a lucky man.

Students Acquiring English

Remind students that in this story they will encounter many dialect words. Point out to them the list of dialect words on p. 1274, and remind them of the footnotes throughout the story, which will help them understand many of the dialect words. Have students keep a list of dialect words they encounter as they read, along with their definitions.

Use **Spanish Study Guide** for additional support, pp. 317–319.

Gifted and Talented

Invite students to compare this story with others dealing with the effects of war on civilian populations. You might suggest that they read *The Clay Marble* by Minfong Ho or *Farewell to Manzanar* by Jeanne Wakatsuki Houston and James D. Houston.

BLOCK SCHEDULING: MANAGING TIME

If your schedule requires that you cover the lesson objectives in a shorter time, use . . .
- Preparing to Read, p. 1274
- Thinking Through the Literature, p. 1279

If you want to take advantage of longer class time, use . . .
- TE Teaching Options: Cross Curricular Link, p. 1276; Vocabulary, p. 1277; Standardized Test Practice, p. 1278; Grammar, p. 1280
- Choices & Challenges and Author Activity, p. 1280

Reading and Analyzing

Literary Analysis DIALECT

Explain to students that a dialect is a regional variety of a language. Ask students why a writer might use dialect in fiction.

Possible Responses: to be realistic; to show differences between characters such as class, education, or region.

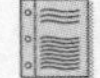
Use **Unit Seven Resource Book,** p. 38 for more exercises.

Active Reading

MAKING JUDGMENTS ABOUT CHARACTERS

Point out to students that readers judge characters in fiction in some of the same ways that people judge others in life: by evaluating their words and actions. Ask students what advantages a reader of fiction might have over a person in a real-life encounter in terms of judging character

Possible Responses: access to a character's thought; narrator's remarks.

Tell students to look for Jonathan's words, actions, and thoughts and the narrator's remarks about him as they form judgments about his character.

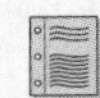
Use **Unit Seven Resource Book,** p. 37 for more practice.

Literary Analysis: REPETITION

Ask students to state the effect of the repetition of the line "Nothing puzzles God."

Possible Responses: It emphasizes Iwegbu's philosophy; it operates as a comforting refrain for the story's chaotic events.

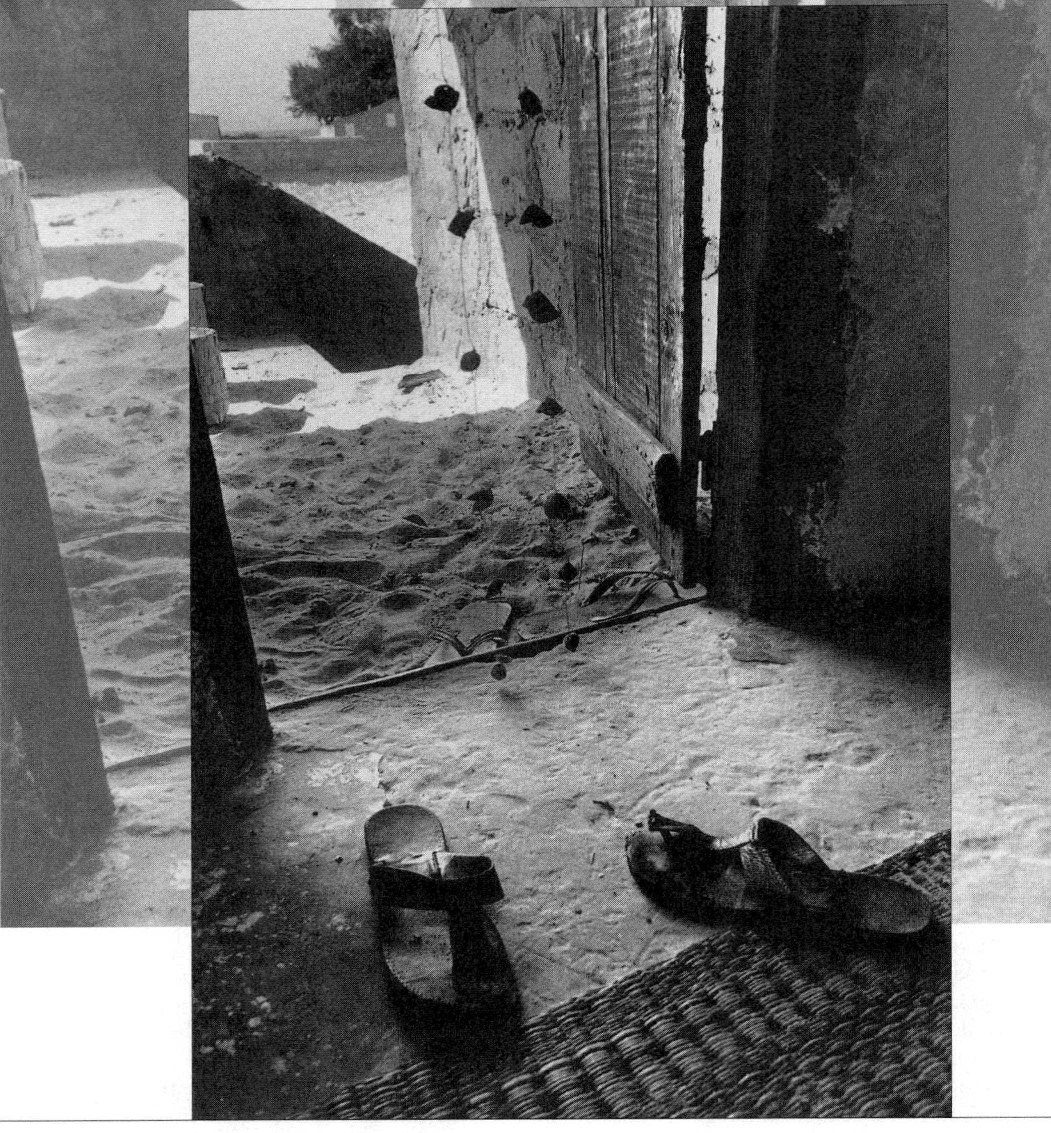

pounds, and moved in with his overjoyed family carrying five heads on their shoulders.

His children picked mangoes near the military cemetery and sold them to soldiers' wives for a few pennies—real pennies this time—and his wife started making breakfast akara[5] balls for neighbors in a hurry to start life again. With his family earnings he took his bicycle to the villages around

5. **akara** (ä-kä'rä) **balls:** bean cakes.

Teaching Options

Cross Curricular Link **History**

NIGERIAN CIVIL WAR The Nigerian Civil War began with a coup d'etat (military takeover of the government) on January 14, 1966. Major General Johnson Aguiyi-Ironsi established control and set up a military administration. Aguiyi-Ironsi's government didn't last. On July 28, there was another coup d'etat. General Yakubu Gowon emerged as the leader, but he was unable to impose order on the military. Most Ibos chose to flee to the East. Despite the attempts of Gowon and other leaders to find a viable way to govern Nigeria, the East seceded from Nigeria and declared itself the Republic of Biafra. The Nigerian government saw this as rebellion and began to take military action against Biafra. The next two years saw heavy military and civilian casualties.

and bought fresh palm-wine which he mixed generously in his rooms with the water which had recently started running again in the public tap down the road, and opened up a bar for soldiers and other lucky people with good money.

At first he went daily, then every other day and finally once a week, to the offices of the Coal Corporation where he used to be a miner, to find out what was what. The only thing he did find out in the end was that that little house of his was even a greater blessing than he had thought. Some of his fellow examiners who had nowhere to return at the end of the day's waiting just slept outside the doors of the offices and cooked what meal they could scrounge together in Bournvita tins. As the weeks lengthened and still nobody could say what was what Jonathan discontinued his weekly visits altogether and faced his palm-wine bar.

But nothing puzzles God. Came the day of the windfall when after five days of endless scuffles in queues[6] and counter-queues in the sun outside the Treasury he had twenty pounds counted into his palms as ex-gratia[7] award for the rebel money he had turned in. It was like Christmas for him and for
1 many others like him when the payments began. They called it (since few could manage its proper official name) *egg-rasher*.

As soon as the pound notes were placed in his palm Jonathan simply closed it tight over them and buried fist and money inside his trouser pocket. He had to be extra careful because he had seen a man a couple of days earlier collapse into near-madness in an instant before that oceanic crowd because no sooner had he got his twenty pounds than some heartless ruffian picked it off him. Though it was not right that a man in such an extremity of agony should be blamed yet many in the queues that day were able to remark quietly on the victim's carelessness, especially after he pulled out the innards of his pocket and revealed a hole in it big enough to pass a thief's head. But of course he had insisted that the money had been in the other pocket, pulling it out too to show its comparative wholeness. So one had to be careful.

Jonathan soon transferred the money to his left hand and pocket so as to leave his right free for shaking hands should the need arise, though by fixing his gaze at such an elevation as to miss all approaching human faces he made sure that the need did not arise, until he got home.

He was normally a heavy sleeper but that night he heard all the neighborhood noises die down one after another. Even the night watchman who knocked the hour on some metal somewhere in the distance had fallen silent after knocking one o'clock. That must have been the last thought in Jonathan's mind before he was finally carried away himself. He couldn't have been gone for long, though, when he was violently awakened again.

"Who is knocking?" whispered his wife lying beside him on the floor.

Who is knocking?

Who is knocking?

"I don't know," he whispered back breathlessly.

The second time the knocking came it was so loud and imperious that the rickety old door could have fallen down.

"Who is knocking?" he asked then, his voice parched and trembling.

"Na tief-man and him people," came the cool reply. "Make you hopen de door." This was followed by the heaviest knocking of all.

Maria was the first to raise the alarm, then he followed and all their children.

"Police-o! Thieves-o! Neighbors-o! Police-o! We are lost! We are dead! Neighbors, are you asleep? Wake up! Police-o!"

This went on for a long time and then stopped suddenly. Perhaps they had scared the thief away. There was total silence. But only for a short while.

"You done finish?" asked the voice outside. "Make we help you small. Oya, everybody!"

"Police-o! Tief-man-o! Neighbors-o! we done loss-o! Police-o! . . ."

---

6. **queues** (kyo͞oz): lines of waiting people.
7. **ex-gratia** (ĕks′grā′shə): given as a favor rather than as a legal obligation.

Customizing Instruction

Students Acquiring English

1 Pronounce *ex-gratia* for students (ex GRAY-sha). Point out the similarity in sound to *egg-rasher.* Explain that a *rasher* is a slice of bacon.

Less Proficient Readers

Use the following questions to make sure students understand the story so far.

- Where did Jonathan and his family live during the civil war?
  Answer: in a camp
- What job did Jonathan have before the civil war?
  Answer: He was a coal miner.
- How does he earn a living after the war?
  Answer: He opens a palm-wine bar.
- Where does Jonathan get the 20 pounds?
  Answer: from the government in return for his Biafran money

Vocabulary Strategy

USING CONTEXT TO UNDERSTAND DIALECT

Instruction Tell students that some of the unfamiliar dialect words they will encounter in this story can be understood because they are restated in more familiar terms. On the chalkboard, write the word *tief-man.* Ask students to what this word refers.

Answer: the person knocking on the door.

Ask students what other words refer to this same person.

Answer: "Thieves-o" and "thief"

Then ask students what *tief-man* means.

Answer: "thief"

Write the answer on the chalkboard, next to *tief-man*

Activity Have students read through the encounter between Jonathan's family and the thieves on pp. 1277–1278, looking for dialect words that are clarified by restatement and giving definitions of the dialect words based on the restatements.

Possible Responses: frien—"friend"; guitar-boy—"automatic gun"; missisi—"woman" or "wife"

Use **Vocabulary Transparencies and Copymasters,** p. 76.

TEACHING THE LITERATURE

Reading and Analyzing

Literary Analysis DIALECT

Have students paraphrase the thieves' dialect. Suggest they try to re-create the tone, as well as the meaning, of the words. Ask students to share their paraphrases with the class and to tell why they chose the words they did.

Possible Response: "My friend, why you no de talk again. I de ask you say you wan make we call soja?" might be paraphrased "My friend, why don't you say something? I asked you whether you want us to call the soldiers."

Reading Skills and Strategies: DRAWING INFERENCES

Point out that the interaction between the thieves and Jonathan is unusual, because the thieves knock on the door (rather than breaking in) and they refer to Jonathan as "friend." Ask students what they can infer about the thieves based on their somewhat deferential treatment of the person they want to rob.

Possible Response: They don't really want to be outlaws and terrorize their neighbors, but the war has left them destitute and they feel they have no choice but to steal from others.

Literary Analysis: THEME

A Remind students that a story's theme is its central idea or message. Ask what insight about life is inferred by the repetition of the line "nothing puzzles God."

Possible Responses: People do not control their own fate; life is full of surprises, both good and bad.

There were at least five other voices besides the leader's.

Jonathan and his family were now completely paralyzed by terror. Maria and the children sobbed inaudibly like lost souls. Jonathan groaned continuously.

The silence that followed the thieves' alarm vibrated horribly. Jonathan all but begged their leader to speak again and be done with it.

"My frien," said he at long last, "we don try our best for call dem but I tink say dem all done sleep-o. . . . So wetin we go do now? Sometaim you wan call soja? Or you wan make we call dem for you? Soja better pass police. No be so?"

"Na so!" replied his men. Jonathan thought he heard even more voices now than before and groaned heavily. His legs were sagging under him and his throat felt like sand-paper.

"My frien, why you no de talk again. I de ask you say you wan make we call soja?"

"No."

"Awrighto. Now make we talk business. We no be bad tief. We no like for make trouble. Trouble done finish. War done finish and all the katakata wey de for inside.[8] No Civil War again. This time na Civil Peace. No be so?"

"Na so!" answered the horrible chorus.

"What do you want from me? I am a poor man. Everything I had went with this war. Why do you come to me? You know people who have money. We . . ."

"Awright! We know say you no get plenty money. But we sef no get even anini.[9] So derefore make you open dis window and give us one hundred pound and we go commot. Orderwise we de come for inside now to show you guitar-boy like dis . . ."

A volley of automatic fire rang through the sky. Maria and the children began to weep aloud again.

"Ah, missisi de cry again. No need for dat. We done talk say we na good tief. We just take our small money and go nwayorly. No molest. Abi we de molest?"

"At all!" sang the chorus.

"My friends," began Jonathan hoarsely. "I hear what you say and I thank you. If I had one hundred pounds . . ."

"Lookia my frien, no be play we come play for your house. If we make mistake and step for inside you no go like am-o. So derefore . . ."

"To God who made me; if you come inside and find one hundred pounds, take it and shoot me and shoot my wife and children. I swear to God. The only money I have in this life is this twenty-pounds *egg-rasher* they gave me today . . ."

"OK. Time de go. Make you open dis window and bring the twenty pound. We go manage am like dat."

There were now loud murmurs of dissent among the chorus: "Na lie de man de lie; e get plenty money. . . . Make we go inside and search properly well. . . . Wetin be twenty pound? . . ."

"Shurrup!" rang the leader's voice like a lone shot in the sky and silenced the murmuring at once. "Are you dere? Bring the money quick!"

"I am coming," said Jonathan fumbling in the darkness with the key of the small wooden box he kept by his side on the mat.

At the first sign of light as neighbors and others assembled to commiserate with him he was already strapping his five-gallon demijohn[10] to his bicycle carrier and his wife, sweating in the open fire, was turning over akara balls in a wide clay bowl of boiling oil. In the corner his eldest son was rinsing out dregs of yesterday's palm wine from old beer bottles.

"I count it as nothing," he told his sympathizers, his eyes on the rope he was tying. "What is *egg-rasher*? Did I depend on it last week? Or is it greater than other things that went with the war? I say, let *egg-rasher* perish in the flames! Let it go where everything else has gone. Nothing puzzles God." ❖ **A**

8. **wey de for inside:** Nigerian dialect for "that went with it."

9. **anini** (ä-nē′nē): a small coin worth less than a penny.

10. **demijohn** (dĕm′ē-jŏn′): a large bottle with a narrow neck, usually encased in wicker.

Teaching Options

Standardized Test Practice

WRITE A DIALOGUE For some standardized tests, students will be asked to demonstrate their ability to communicate effectively in writing on a specified topic. Ask students to invent a character who overheard the robbery. Have students write a dialogue in which the new character talks with another character about the robbery.

RUBRIC

3 Full Accomplishment Student's dialogue shows complete understanding of events and characters in story.

2 Substantial Accomplishment Student's dialogue shows some understanding of events and characters in story.

1 Little or Partial Accomplishment Student's dialogue shows little or no understanding of events and characters in story.

Connect to the Literature

1. **What Do You Think?** How did you react to the events in this story? Discuss your reaction with several classmates.

Comprehension Check
- How does Jonathan and his family make money after the war?
- What happens to the ex-gratia award money Jonathan receives?

Think Critically

2. How would you describe Jonathan's approach to life?

THINK ABOUT
- the value he places on "the safety of five human heads"
- his ways of earning money
- his reaction to the thieves
- what he means when he says "Nothing puzzles God"

3. What **ironies** did you find in this story?

4. ACTIVE READING **MAKING JUDGMENTS ABOUT CHARACTERS** With a partner, look at the charts you created in your READER'S NOTEBOOK to assess Jonathan's luck. Based on what you identified as losses and blessings, do you agree with Jonathan's view of himself as lucky? Why or why not?

5. What ideas about the aftermath of war do you think the story conveys?

Extend Interpretations

6. **Comparing Texts** Compare Jonathan in "Civil Peace" with Miss Middleton in "The Distant Past" (page 1263). What similarities and differences can you find in their attitudes toward life? Which character is more prepared to cope with hardship?

7. **What If?** Suppose the thieves had robbed one of Jonathan's neighbors. Do you think Jonathan would have ignored his neighbor's cry for help, or do you think he would have done something to stop the robbery? Support your opinion.

8. **Critic's Corner** The student reviewer Carrie Mitchell indicated that the **suspense** in "Civil Peace" kept her attention and that she "couldn't read fast enough" to discover the outcome of Jonathan's encounter with the thieves. Did you experience a similar feeling during your reading? Explain your answer.

9. **Connect to Life** Do you think Jonathan's attitude in the wake of the war's destruction and tragedy is common among the survivors of wars? Give reasons for your opinion.

Literary Analysis

DIALECT **Dialect** reflects the pronunciations, vocabulary, and grammatical rules that are typical of a region. In "Civil Peace," Chinua Achebe actually uses two dialects of English, the Nigerian dialect of the thieves and the near-standard dialect of Jonathan and his family. The Nigerian dialect is first used when Jonathan asks who is knocking on his door and the thief answers as follows:

"Na tief-man and him people," came the cool reply. "Make you hopen de door."

Jonathan's own dialect is evident in this passage, when he and his family raise the alarm about the thieves:

"Police-o! Thieves-o! Neighbors-o! Police-o! We are lost! We are dead! Neighbors, are you asleep? Wake up! Police-o!"

Cooperative Learning Activity Get together in small groups and read other passages that contain dialect. Discuss any words or phrases you have trouble understanding. Then answer these questions: What does the use of dialect add to the story? Why do you think Achebe chose to include both dialects?

REVIEW CONFLICT **Conflict,** a struggle between opposing forces, provides the interest or suspense in a literary work. Are the conflicts in "Civil Peace" primarily **external** or **internal?** What is the main conflict in the story? How does Jonathan deal with it?

Extend Interpretations

Comparing Texts Students might point out that although Jonathan and Miss Middleton both accept their fates, he is flexible and resourceful, while she resists change.

What If? Accept all reasonable, well-supported responses.

Critic's Corner Accept all reasonable, well-supported responses.

Connect to Life Accept all reasonable, well-supported responses.

GUIDING STUDENT RESPONSE

Connect to the Literature

1. What Do You Think?
Guidelines for student response: Accept all reasonable responses. You might have students compare their reactions by summing them up in a word or phrase and putting their reactions in a word web on the chalkboard

Comprehension Check
- They sell mangoes, akara balls, and palm wine.
- Thieves come and steal it.

Use Selection Quiz
Unit Seven Resource Book, p. 39.

Think Critically

2. Possible Responses: He accepts fate; he's resourceful; he values his family's welfare over material things.
3. Possible Responses: Jonathan calls small blessings "miracles"; his good fortune at receiving 20 pounds actually puts him and his family in danger; he is terrorized not during war but during "civil peace"; he and the thieves refer to each other as "friends."
4. Possible Responses: Yes, because he and his family are able to survive better than many others; no, because Jonathan and his family have few material possessions, and the little money they get is taken from them.
5. Possible Response: The aftermath of war presents hardships and problems that are almost as severe as those faced during the war itself. Student responses should interpret the effect of historical context on the work.

Literary Analysis

Cooperative Learning Activity
Have students share their groups' findings about dialect in a class discussion.

Writing Options

1. **Job Recommendation** Suggest that students first note how Jonathan deals with war and its aftermath. Then have them determine what his actions reveal about his strengths and weaknesses.
2. **Front Page News** Encourage students to look at the front pages of various newspapers to see what should be included. Tell them that their report of the robbery should answer the questions *who, what, where, when, why,* and *how* in the first paragraph.

Activities & Explorations

1. **Oral Reading** Encourage students to make sure they understand all that is being said in the dialogue. It might be helpful for them to translate the dialogue into standard English.
2. **Book Jacket Design** Suggest that students choose an illustration or design that reflects a major event or theme in the story. The back and inside flaps might give some background information, tell a little about the plot of the story, and relate information about the author.
3. **C.A.R.E. Package** Students might consider the kind of items usually collected for disaster relief. Suggest that students make a list of items that Jonathan and his family can use. Have them consider what the family's living conditions are and the problems they face.

Inquiry & Research

Nigeria's Past and Present Make sure students know how to do an online periodical search at their local library. Ask each student to bring to class one newspaper or magazine article about life in Nigeria today.

Author Activity

Rulers and Ruled Achebe quotes "The Second Coming" by W. B. Yeats.

Choices & CHALLENGES

Writing Options

1. **Job Recommendation** Write a job recommendation for Jonathan, telling a prospective employer what you consider to be his strengths and weaknesses.
2. **Front Page News** With a group of classmates, plan and write the front page of a newspaper for the residents of Jonathan's town. Include a report of the robbery and other articles based on newsworthy details in the story. If a desktop-publishing program is available to you, use it to design your page. Make copies of your work to share with classmates.

Activities & Explorations

1. **Oral Reading** With a small group of classmates, practice and perform an oral reading of the robbery scene. Use appropriate tones of voice to convey the characters' emotions, and try to reproduce the thieves' dialect. ~ **SPEAKING AND LISTENING**
2. **Book Jacket Design** Imagine that "Civil Peace" is to be published as a small book. Design a book jacket that might entice people to read the story. Display your work in the classroom. ~ **ART**
3. **C.A.R.E. Package** Using pictures or real objects, put together a package of items that you might send Jonathan and his family to help them adjust to life after the war. ~ **INTERPRETING**

Inquiry & Research

Nigeria's Past and Present Find out more about Nigeria's history. What economic, political, and social progress has Nigeria made since 1970? What problems still beset the nation?

More Online: Research Starter www.mcdougallittell.com

Chinua Achebe

1930–

Other Works
"Marriage Is a Private Affair"
"Vengeful Creditor"
"The Sacrificial Egg"
"Dead Men's Path"
Things Fall Apart

Educational Achievements A son of Ibo missionaries in eastern Nigeria, Chinua Achebe was raised a Christian and attended British-run schools, studying first in the Ibo language and later in English. A gifted student, Achebe became one of the few 14-year-olds chosen to attend Government College, one of the best high schools in Nigeria. At the age of 18, he left high school with a scholarship to study medicine at the University of Ibadan in western Nigeria. Achebe quickly changed his course of study, however, and it was in English literature that he received his degree in 1953.

Impact of War After teaching for a year, Achebe went to work for the Nigerian Broadcasting Corporation in Lagos, where he eventually became the director of external broadcasting. In 1966, amidst the often violent strife between the Ibo and other ethnic groups, Achebe felt that he and his family were no longer safe in Lagos. He quit his job and returned to eastern Nigeria, where he became an outspoken advocate of—and fundraiser for—the Biafran cause. He also started a publishing company with the poet Christopher Okigbo, who was later killed in the war.

Writer and Lecturer In addition to short stories, Achebe has written novels, essays, poems, and children's books. His first novel, *Things Fall Apart* (1958), focuses on the effects of European colonialism in Nigeria. Many of his other works focus on problems associated with Nigeria's emergence as a modern nation. Throughout his literary career, Achebe has taught and lectured at universities in both Nigeria and the United States.

Author Activity

Rulers and Ruled Read excerpts from *Things Fall Apart.* Note how the European colonialists are portrayed and how native Nigerians react to European rule. What poem does Achebe quote in the book's title?

Teaching Options

Grammar

INDEFINITE PRONOUNS

Instruction When a pronoun has an indefinite pronoun as its antecedent, the pronoun must agree with the indefinite pronoun in number. If the antecedent is the indefinite pronoun *all, some, any, most,* or *none,* the pronoun can be either singular or plural. Whether it is singular or plural depends on the prepositional phrase following the antecedent. If the prepositional phrase refers to members of a collective group as individuals, the pronoun is plural; if the prepositional phrase refers to a group to as a single entity, the pronoun is singular.

Activity Write the following on the chalkboard.

"Some of his fellow examiners . . . just slept outside the doors of the offices and cooked what meal they could scrounge together. . . ."

Have students identify the indefinite pronoun that is the antecedent in the sentence and the pronoun that refers to the antecedent. *(Some, they)*

Use **Grammar Transparencies and Copymasters,** p. 85.

Use McDougal Littell's ***Language Network*** for more instruction and practice in indefinite pronouns.

Telephone Conversation

Poetry by WOLE SOYINKA (wō′lĕ shô-yĭng′kə)

from Midsummer

Poetry by DEREK WALCOTT

"I hate a wasted journey—I am African."

Connect to Your Life

Prejudice Recall a time when you read about or witnessed an obvious display of prejudice against someone because of his or her race, gender, nationality, or religion. What was your reaction? Do you think any form of prejudice exists in your school or community? Share your thoughts with classmates.

Build Background

Two Nobel Prize Winners A native of Nigeria, on the west coast of Africa, Wole Soyinka was awarded the 1986 Nobel Prize in literature, becoming the first African to receive that honor. In 1992, Derek Walcott—born on St. Lucia, a small island in the West Indies—became the first native Caribbean author to receive the Nobel literature prize. For many years, the now-independent countries of Nigeria and St. Lucia were British colonies, and both Soyinka's and Walcott's works draw upon the often antagonistic African and English cultures that have played such a significant role in their lives.

Both authors include social criticism—on racial prejudice and other issues—in their writing, undoubtedly in an attempt to enlighten their readers and encourage change. According to Soyinka, writers must become "a part of that machinery that will actually shape events." He often speaks out against political corruption and violations of human rights and is frequently at odds with government leaders in his own country. Walcott, while appreciating the literary traditions of England, often voices opposition to the neglect of West Indian culture by the islands' British colonizers and by present-day tourists. Acknowledging his own diverse cultural background, Walcott from time to time contemplates his own identity and role as a poet. In his Nobel Prize acceptance speech, he stated that "the process of poetry is one of excavation and of self-discovery."

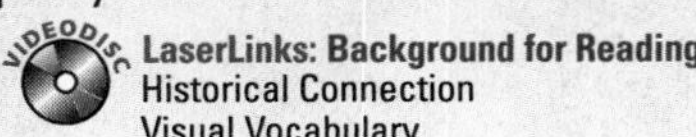

LaserLinks: Background for Reading
Historical Connection
Visual Vocabulary

Focus Your Reading

LITERARY ANALYSIS TONE IN SATIRE **Tone** is a writer's attitude toward a subject. Tone plays an important part in **satire,** writing that combines criticism with wit and humor for the purpose of improving some aspect of society. Tone in satiric works can range from light and humorous to bitter and harsh. "Telephone Conversation" and the excerpt from *Midsummer* are both satires. As you read, try to identify the tone in each.

ACTIVE READING COMPARING AND CONTRASTING POEMS Wole Soyinka and Derek Walcott are each writing about racial prejudice. However, they use very different **speakers,** situations, language, and **imagery** in their poems to express their ideas. Comparing and contrasting the ways the poets use these four elements can help you understand the ideas in each poem.

READER'S NOTEBOOK Make a Venn diagram like the one shown for each of the four elements listed above. As you read, note the similarities and differences for each element in each poem.

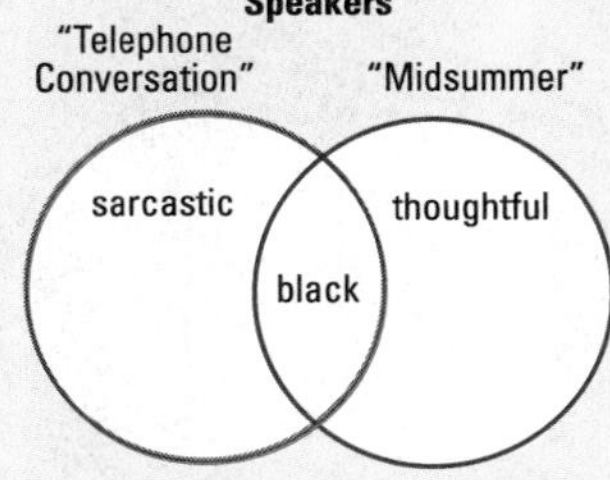

OVERVIEW

Objectives

1. understand and appreciate the **tone** in two poems **(Literary Analysis)**
2. understand and appreciate **satire** in poetry **(Literary Analysis)**
3. **compare and contrast** two poems **(Active Reading)**

Summary

In "Telephone Conversation," the speaker, an African man, is trying to rent an apartment over the telephone. When he reveals to the landlady that he is black, she asks how dark his skin is. The speaker responds to this by making fun of her.

In the excerpt from *Midsummer,* Derek Walcott compares the people of an area in London to the leaves of a tree in autumn and links the racist statement that blacks can't do Shakespeare to race riots.

Thematic Link

These poems show different ways of responding to **cultural conflict.** The excerpt from *Midsummer* illustrates both more subtle and violent cultural conflict.

5-Minute Warm-Up

Daily Language SkillBuilder

Have students **proofread** the display sentences on page 1189k and write them correctly. The sentences also appear on Transparency 36 of **Grammar Transparencies and Copymasters.**

LESSON RESOURCES

UNIT SEVEN RESOURCE BOOK, pp. 40–41

ASSESSMENT RESOURCES
Formal Assessment, pp. 241–242
Teacher's Guide to Assessment and Portfolio Use
Test Generator

SKILLS TRANSPARENCIES AND COPYMASTERS
Literary Analysis
- Horatian vs. Juvenalian Satire, T12 (for Literary Analysis, p. 1281)

Reading and Critical Thinking
- Venn Diagram, T51 (for Active Reading, p. 1281)

Grammar
- Avoid Misplaced and Dangling Modifiers, T51 (for Mini Lesson, p. 1287)
- Elliptical Subordinate Clauses, C121 (for Mini Lesson, p. 1287)

Vocabulary
- Denotation and Connotation, C94 (for Mini Lesson, p. 1283)

Writing
- Critical Review, C32 (for Writing Option 1, p. 1287)

Communications
- Impromptu Speaking: Debate, T15 (for Activities & Explorations 2, p. 1287)

INTEGRATED TECHNOLOGY
Audio Library
LaserLinks
- Historical Connection: Civil Strife in Britain
- Visual Vocabulary. See **Teacher's SourceBook,** pp. 97–98.

Internet: Research Starter
Visit our website: www.mcdougallittell.com

TEACHING THE LITERATURE

Reading and Analyzing

Literary Analysis TONE IN SATIRE

Explain that in satire, the speaker or main character is usually calm and does not react emotionally to the situation. This gives satire a detached tone. Ask students how the poem would be different if the speaker had had a strong emotional reaction to the situation.

Possible Responses: The poem would have had an angry tone; the focus of the poem would be the speaker's reaction rather than the woman's prejudice.

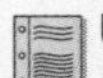

Use **Unit Seven Resource Book,** p. 41 for more exercises.

Active Reading

COMPARING AND CONTRASTING POEMS

Set a Purpose Suggest that students read the next poem to discover its similarities to and differences from "Telephone Conversation." Ask students to compare the following aspects:

- subject
  Possible Response: Both poems are about prejudice.
- tone
  Possible Response: The tone of Soyinka's poem is humorous, while Walcott's tone is serious.
- use of imagery
  Possible Response: "Telephone Conversation" uses dialogue and witty images to convey meaning, while the excerpt from *Midsummer* relies mostly on arresting images.

Use **Unit Seven Resource Book,** p. 42 for more practice.

TELEPHONE CONVERSATION

WOLE SOYINKA

The price seemed reasonable, location
Indifferent. The landlady swore she lived
Off premises. Nothing remained
But self-confession. "Madam," I warned,
"I hate a wasted journey—I am African."
Silence. Silenced transmission of
Pressurized good-breeding. Voice, when it came,
Lipstick-coated, long gold-rolled
Cigarette-holder pipped. Caught I was, foully.

"HOW DARK?" . . . I had not misheard . . . "ARE YOU LIGHT
"OR VERY DARK?" Button B. Button A. Stench
Of rancid breath of public hide-and-speak.
Red booth. Red pillar-box. Red double-tiered
Omnibus squelching tar. It *was* real! Shamed
By ill-mannered silence, surrender
Pushed dumbfoundment to beg simplification.
Considerate she was, varying the emphasis—

12 rancid (răn′sĭd): smelling of decay; rotten.

13 pillar-box: a pillar-shaped mailbox.

Teaching Options

BLOCK SCHEDULING: MANAGING TIME

If your schedule requires that you cover the lesson objectives in a shorter time, use . . .

- Preparing to Read, p. 1281
- Thinking Through the Literature, pp. 1283, 1286

If you want to take advantage of longer class time, use . . .

- TE Teaching Options: Vocabulary, p. 1283; Viewing and Representing, p. 1284; Informal Assessment, p. 1285; Grammar, p. 1287
- Choices & Challenges, pp. 1286–1287

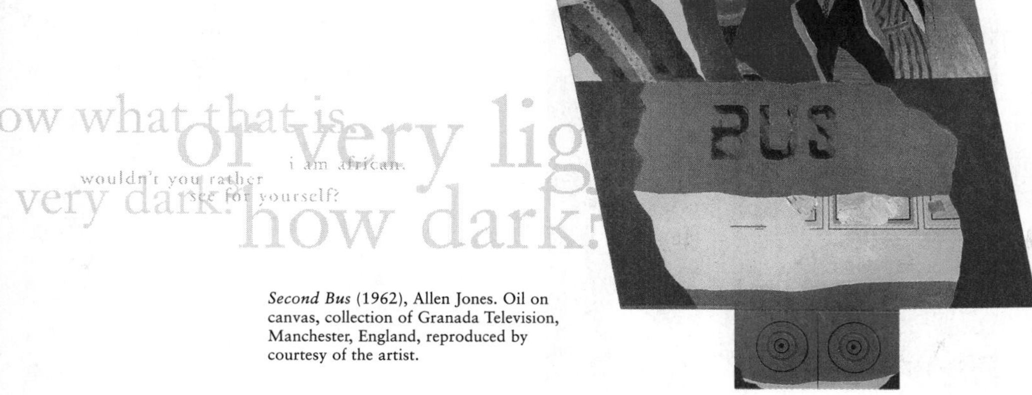

ow what that is
or very light
i am african.
wouldn't you rather
see for yourself?
very dark?
how dark?
BUS

Second Bus (1962), Allen Jones. Oil on canvas, collection of Granada Television, Manchester, England, reproduced by courtesy of the artist.

"ARE YOU DARK? OR VERY LIGHT?" Revelation came.
"You mean—like plain or milk chocolate?"
Her assent was clinical, crushing in its light
Impersonality. Rapidly, wave-length adjusted,
I chose, "West African sepia"—and as an afterthought,
"Down in my passport." Silence for spectroscopic
Flight of fancy, till truthfulness clanged her accent
Hard on the mouthpiece "WHAT'S THAT?", conceding,
"DON'T KNOW WHAT THAT IS." "Like brunette."

"THAT'S DARK, ISN'T IT?" "Not altogether.
"Facially, I am brunette, but madam, you should see
"The rest of me. Palm of my hand, soles of my feet
"Are a peroxide blonde. Friction, caused—
"Foolishly, madam—by sitting down, has turned
"My bottom raven black.—One moment madam!"—sensing
Her receiver rearing on the thunder clap
About my ears—"Madam," I pleaded, "wouldn't you rather
"See for yourself?"

22 sepia (sē′pē-ə): a dark yellow brown or olive brown.

23 spectroscopic: here, pertaining to the analysis of colors. (A spectroscope is an instrument that separates light into its various wavelengths—colors—for scientific study.)

Thinking Through the Literature

1. **Comprehension Check** Why does the landlady hesitate to rent the speaker an apartment?
2. What is your impression of the landlady?
3. How and why does the **speaker's** attitude change as the poem progresses? Cite evidence to support your answer.
4. How would you describe the **tone** of this poem?

Customizing Instruction

Students Acquiring English

Point out to students that in this poem Soyinka often leaves out words, especially articles and the verb "to be." Help students supply the missing words. For instance, "Silenced transmission of / Pressurized good-breeding" might be paraphrased, "There was a silenced transmission of pressurized good breeding."

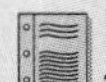 Use **Spanish Study Guide** for additional support, pp. 320–321.

Less Proficient Readers

Set a Purpose Ask students how they would react if someone refused to rent them an apartment because of their race, gender, nationality, or religion. Then have them read "Telephone Conversation" to discover how the speaker deals with this problem.

Gifted and Talented

As students read the poems, have them consider which speaker's response to prejudice is more likely to bring about social change.

Thinking Through the Literature

1. Because he is African and she is prejudiced against blacks.
2. Responses will vary.
3. Possible Response: He is polite at first, but when he encounters bigotry, he becomes sarcastic.
4. Possible Response: playfully critical, humorous, mocking

Vocabulary Strategy

CONNOTATION AND DENOTATION

Instruction Point out to students that words we think of as negative may seem that way because they name something unpleasant in itself or because the word has developed a negative connotation

Activity Ask students to decide whether the following words name unpleasant things or have unpleasant connotations.

- stench *(names something unpleasant)*
- rancid *(names something unpleasant)*
- clinical *(has a negative connotation)*
- impersonality *(has a negative connotation)*

Discuss the power these words have in the poem and the impact they have on the reader.

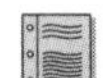 Use **Vocabulary Transparencies and Copymasters,** p. 77.

Reading and Analyzing

Literary Analysis: IMAGERY

A Ask students what the Brixton riots are being compared to in these lines
Possible Responses: lemmings, leaves.

B What image is created by the reference to water hoses?
Possible Responses: police turning hoses on rioters; leaves being hosed into a gutter.

Reading Skills and Strategies: EVALUATING SPEAKER'S RESPONSE TO PREJUDICE

C Ask students what the speaker was doing and feeling during the Brixton riots.
Answer: He was acting in Shakespearean plays, and the praise he earned blunted his anger.

Ask students to think about what feelings are expressed by the images of the poem. Do they express the same feelings the speaker describes himself as having?
Possible Response: No, the images don't describe the same feelings the speaker discusses. The images express anger, while the speaker reveals a sense of complacency.

Reading Skills and Strategies: CLARIFYING

Ask students to explain how Walcott uses the statement that "blacks can't do Shakespeare" to satirize prejudice.
Possible Response: He says that the skinheads, who are rioting against the acceptance of other races, quote Shakespeare when they abuse the police who are trying to keep them under control.

The Sniper (1987), R. B. Kitaj. Oil on canvas, 120" × 36". The Saatchi Collection, London.

Teaching Options

Viewing and Representing

The Sniper **by R. B. Kitaj**

ART APPRECIATION Upon leaving high school, Cleveland-born painter R(obert) B(rooks) Kitaj (1932–) became a merchant seaman and journeyed to the Caribbean and South America. He came to England in 1958 and became a naturalized British citizen.

Instruction Have students study and describe the composition of the painting, paying special attention to the placement of the figures.
Possible Response: The painting is rendered in a narrow, vertical space; the figures of the sniper and the people in the street are small, while the victim is large.

Application Why does Kitaj paint the scene in a narrow stripe on the canvas? How does the position of the passers-by affect the tone of the work?
Possible Responses: The narrow scene surrounded by blank space makes the viewer feel as though he or she is peeking at the scene as a sniper would; the distortion of the figures in the foreground, in contrast with the normal appearance of the background, gives an impression of violence. The tone is bleak, because the people in the street seem to be ignoring this violent scene.

from # Midsummer

Derek Walcott

With the stampeding hiss and scurry of green lemmings,
A midsummer's leaves race to extinction like the roar
of a Brixton riot tunneled by water hoses;
they seethe toward autumn's fire—it is in their nature, B
being men as well as leaves, to die for the sun.
The leaf stems tug at their chains, the branches bending
like Boer cattle under Tory whips that drag every wagon
1 nearer to apartheid. And, for me, that closes
the child's fairy tale of an antic England—fairy rings,
thatched cottages fenced with dog roses,
a green gale lifting the hair of Warwickshire.
I was there to add some color to the British theater.
"But the blacks can't do Shakespeare, they have no experience."
C This was true. Their thick skulls bled with rancor 2
when the riot police and the skinheads exchanged quips
you could trace to the Sonnets, or the Moor's eclipse.
Praise had bled my lines white of any more anger,
and snow had inducted me into white fellowships,
while Calibans howled down the barred streets of an empire
3 that began with Caedmon's raceless dew, and is ending
in the alleys of Brixton, burning like Turner's ships.

1 lemmings: small rodents whose migrations in northern Europe sometimes end in mass drownings.

3 Brixton: an area in London.

7 Boer (bōr): belonging to South Africans of Dutch ancestry.

8 apartheid (ə-pärt'hīt'): the official policy of racial segregation formerly practiced in South Africa.

11 Warwickshire (wär'ĭk-shîr'): the English county where Shakespeare was born.

14 rancor (răng'kər): bitter resentment; ill will.

15 skinheads: young British working-class hoodlums—typically having hair cut very short—who are known for their use of violence against members of minority groups.

16 Sonnets: Shakespeare's 154 sonnets; **Moor's eclipse:** a reference to the downfall of the black hero of Shakespeare's *Othello.*

19 Calibans: beastlike human beings (from the name of a grotesque slave in Shakespeare's *The Tempest).*

20 Caedmon (kăd'mən): a seventh-century Anglo-Saxon poet.

21 Turner's ships: burning ships in paintings by the 19th-century British artist J. M. W. Turner.

Customizing Instruction

Less Proficient Readers

Point out to students that it is necessary to read carefully to discover the antecedents of many of Walcott's pronouns. Ask students to identify the antecedents of the following pronouns.

1 *that* (apartheid in South Africa)

2 *their* (the blacks)

3 *that* (an empire)

Gifted and Talented

Discuss Walcott's choice of images and allusions with students. Ask them to think about what culture the images belong to.

Answer: British.

Then ask them why Walcott chose to use British images and allusions in this poem.

Possible Responses: to show that possession of British cultural heritage is not restricted by skin color; to expose the evils of prejudice in the oppressor's own language.

Students Acquiring English

Help students follow this complex poem by making sure they read the side notes and by explaining each of the poem's images.

Informal Assessment

WRITE A LETTER

Have students write a letter home from the point of view of the poem's speaker. Ask students to describe what the speaker is doing in England, what he has seen, and what he feels.

RUBRIC

3 Full Accomplishment Letters indicate that speaker is in England to act in Shakespeare's plays. They state he has been told that "blacks can't do Shakespeare," and he has seen riot in Brixton. They express feelings of disillusionment.

2 Substantial Accomplishment Letters include most of ideas above.

1 Little or Partial Accomplishment Letters include few or none of ideas above.

Connect to the Literature

1. **What Do You Think?** What **image** in the excerpt from *Midsummer* made the greatest impression on you?

Think Critically

2. With what specific social issues does the **speaker** of this poem seem to be most concerned?

- his comparison of leaves to human beings
- his references to historical events and works of art
- the quotation about blacks in the theater

3. What message about the English, or about European culture in general, do you think the speaker is trying to convey?

4. How does the speaker appear to feel about his own role in society? Cite evidence from the poem to support your answer.

5. **ACTIVE READING** COMPARING AND CONTRASTING POEMS
In what ways are these poems most alike? most different? How would you summarize what each poem conveys about the realities and consequences of racial prejudice? Look back at the Venn diagrams you created in your READER'S NOTEBOOK to help you answer these questions.

Extend Interpretations

6. **Critic's Corner** The critic Sven Birkerts has written that in Walcott's *Midsummer* "sharply etched **descriptions** give way to dark surges." What do you think he meant by this statement? Support your answer with examples from the excerpt in this book.

7. **Comparing Texts** Do you think either of these poems share any **themes** about humanity with W. H. Auden's "The Unknown Citizen" (page 1076)? Explain your opinion.

8. **Connect to Life** Do you think there will ever be a time when the majority of the world's people accept cultural and racial differences? Why or why not?

Literary Analysis

TONE IN SATIRE The **tone** of a work is established in part by the writer's choice of words and details. In a satiric work, the tone is also influenced by what the writer is satirizing—the fault or foible that is being exposed for criticism and correction. If, for example, the object of the **satire** is a minor annoyance, such as the tendency of some people to dominate a conversation, the tone might be humorous and playful. On the other hand, if—as in "Telephone Conversation" and the excerpt from *Midsummer*—the object of the satire is a serious human failing, the tone is likely to be much more biting and harsh.

Cooperative Learning Activity Both of these poems satirize racist attitudes and behavior, but they do not use an identical tone. With three or four classmates, decide what the tone of each poem is and list all the aspects of the poem that contribute to creating it. Then take turns reading each poem aloud, paying particular attention to conveying the tone. Do you gain any more insights into the tone of each poem as you read it aloud or listen to it being read?

GUIDING STUDENT RESPONSE

Connect to the Literature

1. What Do You Think?
Guidelines for student response: Responses will vary. You might write the images suggested by students on the chalkboard to create a word web.

Think Critically

2. Possible Responses: prejudice, injustice, cultural assimilation
3. Possible Response: Dominant cultures treat minorities as inferiors and feel justified in oppressing them.
4. Possible Responses: The speaker is frustrated by his secondary role in society and angered that he has yielded to assimilation.
5. Possible Response: The poems are alike in that they deal with prejudice against blacks; they are different in that Soyinka deals with a humiliating social situation, while Walcott describes violence against blacks.

Literary Analysis

Cooperative Learning Activity
"Telephone Conversation"—The tone is humorous, but with an undercurrent of desperation and anger.
Midsummer—The tone is serious and somewhat detached.

Extend Interpretations

Critic's Corner Students might assert that the "dark surges" refer to Walcott's use of violent images, including "Boer cattle under Tory whips," "thick skulls bled with rancor," and "burning like Turner's ships."

Comparing Texts Student responses should include theme statements for all three poems and a discussion of themes that cross any two or three poems. Some students might find little commonality between Auden's poem dealing with an impersonal society and these dealing with racial prejudice; others might feel that in all three poems, the individual is brutalized by an increasingly inhumane society.

Connect to Life Responses will vary.

Writing Options

1. Critical Review In an essay, evaluate how effectively you think each poem satirizes the effects of racial prejudice in a society. Cite evidence from the poems to support your conclusions. Place the paper in your **Working Portfolio.**

2. Advice Column With a partner, create an advice column, writing letters in which the speakers of these poems seek help in dealing with the issues presented in the poems. Then write responses to each letter.

3. Guest Editorial Write a guest editorial for your school paper, expressing your concerns about a specific violation of human rights that you have either read about or witnessed.

Activities & Explorations

1. T-Shirt Design Create a design for a T-shirt that promotes what one or both of the speakers might consider an ideal society. Display your work in the classroom. ~ **ART**

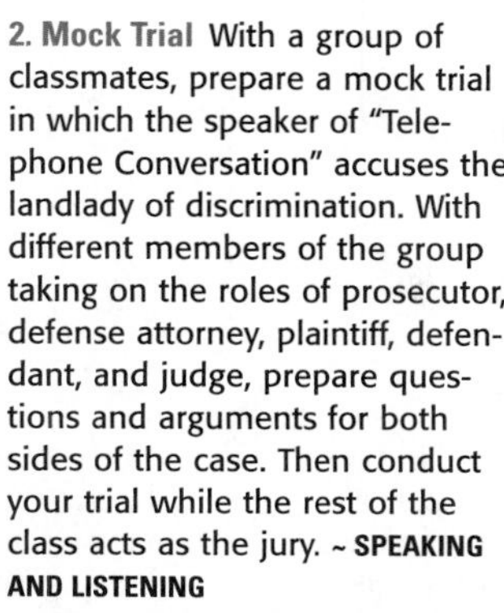

2. Mock Trial With a group of classmates, prepare a mock trial in which the speaker of "Telephone Conversation" accuses the landlady of discrimination. With different members of the group taking on the roles of prosecutor, defense attorney, plaintiff, defendant, and judge, prepare questions and arguments for both sides of the case. Then conduct your trial while the rest of the class acts as the jury. ~ **SPEAKING AND LISTENING**

3. Scrapbook of Social Issues Create a scrapbook of photographs, political cartoons, news articles, and other items that you think reflect the social issues dealt with in these poems. ~ **SOCIAL STUDIES**

Inquiry & Research

Civil Rights Laws Investigate the history of civil rights legislation in the United States since 1950. What civil rights laws have been enacted? What events led to their enactment? How have the laws affected race relations?

More Online: Research Starter
www.mcdougallittell.com

Art Connection

Summer and Shadow Look again at the painting *The Sniper* on page 1284. What thoughts come to mind when you look at the scene? How do these thoughts relate to the social issues raised in the excerpt from *Midsummer?* Discuss your ideas with your classmates.

Mini Lesson Grammar

ELLIPTICAL SUBORDINATE CLAUSES

Instruction A subordinate clause is a clause that cannot stand on its own as a sentence. One kind of subordinate clause is the elliptical clause, in which a word or phrase is deleted. The most common elliptical clauses begin with *while* and *when.* Emphasize to students that the missing subject of the elliptical clause must also be the subject of the independent clause.

Activity Write the following on the chalkboard.

When referring to Shakespeare, many of the characters from the plays are discussed.

Help students understand that the sentence is incorrect because the subjects of the elliptical and independent clauses are not the same. The subject of the elliptical clause is Derek Walcott, but the subject of the main clause is *many.* Have students suggest ways to rewrite the sentence. *(When referring to Shakespeare, Walcott discusses many characters from the plays.)*

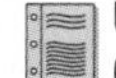

Use **Grammar Transparencies and Copymasters,** p. 59.

Use McDougal Littell's ***Language Network*** for more instruction and practice in subordinate clauses.

Writing Options

1. **Critical Review** Help students evaluate the poems by asking the following questions.
   - Which poem seemed to reflect the reality of life under a system of racial prejudice more accurately?
   - Which poem made the impact of prejudice on everyday life clearer?
2. **Advice Column** Encourage students to look at newspaper advice columns for style and content. As a prewriting activity, have them list issues raised in the poems that would be appropriate for the column.
3. **Guest Editorial** Before students write, they should consider possible solutions to the human-rights violation.

Activities & Explorations

1. **T-Shirt Design** Ask students to consider what changes in society the speakers would like to see. Encourage students to use images, symbols, and colors in their design that capture the essence of this utopia.
2. **Mock Trial** Suggest that each side do research to prepare their case, finding accounts of similar cases if possible.
3. **Scrapbook of Social Issues** Suggest that students make a list of the social issues dealt with in the poems and to have this list handy as they search for items to include in the scrapbook.

Inquiry & Research

Civil Rights Laws Have students work in pairs. You might have one pair research one particular civil rights law, concentrating on the events leading to its enactment and how it has affected racial prejudice. The pairs can then share their findings with the entire class.

Art Connection

Summer and Shadow Possible Response: Thoughts that come to mind are official indifference to violence and the way violence alters reality; the painting is literally a "narrow view" of people; the painting captures the ugliness of violence.

Wole Soyinka

Soyinka once explained that the African artist "has always functioned as the record of the mores and experience of his society." Soyinka's works reflect this, recording the political unrest in 20th-century Africa as well as the conflict between old customs and contemporary ideas. Soyinka's works appeal to all cultures because he writes about universal themes. Biographer Eldred Jones says of Soyinka: "The essential ideas which emerge from a reading of Soyinka's work are not specially African ideas, although his characters and mannerisms are African. His concern is with man on earth."

Derek Walcott

Walcott describes himself as a "divided child." He is a Methodist living in a Catholic country, a black man with a white grandfather, and a middle-class man with a European education existing in the midst of poverty. It is no wonder that the major preoccupation of Walcott's works is the conflict between races and cultures. The poet J. D. McClatchy recognizes that Walcott's "mixed state" contributes to his unique style, which combines British and island features "without indulging in either ethnic chic or imperial drag."

Discussion

Have students refer to Building Background, the Author Biographies, and Literary Analysis. Ask them to consider the following:

- How does each author's motivation, stance, or position affect the tone of the poem?
- How would you interpret the influence of historical context on each poem?
- The two writers grew up in different cultures. What themes or connections do you see that cross their two cultures?

Wole Soyinka

1934–

Other Works
"After the Deluge"
"Your Logic Frightens Me, Mandela"
"Massacre, October 66"
"Civilian and Soldier"

Between England and Nigeria Though his travels extend far beyond Nigeria, Wole Soyinka's main interest is in promoting his native Yoruba culture. Like his Nigerian contemporary Chinua Achebe, Soyinka attended high school at Government College and then entered the University of Ibadan. Later, he studied at the University of Leeds in England, graduating with honors in English. His early jobs included work as a bricklayer and a nightclub bouncer, but a job as play reader for London's Royal Court Theatre proved more suitable to his temperament. In 1960, he returned to Nigeria and launched his own theater company, called The 1960 Masks.

Playwright Soyinka is probably best known as a playwright. His first major play, *A Dance of the Forests,* was commissioned as a salute to Nigeria's independence in 1960. Since then, his works have been presented in cities throughout the world. In addition, he has produced, directed, and acted in plays and films—both in English and in his native Yoruba language—has organized theater groups at various schools in Nigeria, and has lectured at universities in Britain and the United States.

Politics and Poetry Like Achebe, Soyinka was actively involved in the Nigerian civil war of the late 1960s. Accused of helping the Biafrans secede, he was arrested by the Nigerian government and imprisoned for over two years. His confinement did not stifle his writing voice, however; in 1969, while he was still incarcerated, his volume *Poems from Prison* was published.

Derek Walcott

1930–

Other Works
"A Far Cry from Africa"
"A Sea Change"
"The Liberator"
"Port of Spain"
"Hurucan"

A Cultural Spokesman Derek Walcott's interest in the arts was inspired by his parents. His mother was a teacher on St. Lucia and acted in a local theater group, and his father, who died when Walcott was just a baby, was an aspiring painter and poet. Walcott once said, "I have felt from my boyhood that I had one function and that was somehow to articulate, not my own experience, but what I saw around me." While hoping to preserve his own culture through his writing, the witty and outgoing writer also relishes cultural diversity. His closest friends include two other Nobel Prize winners featured in this book—the Irish poet Seamus Heaney and the Polish poet, essayist, and novelist Czeslaw Milosz.

The Young Writer Walcott's literary talent developed early. He recalls that as a child he rejected sports for reading, writing, and playing with puppets. At the age of 18, he borrowed $200 from his mother to publish his first book of poems and then sold copies on the street to pay back the loan. At the age of 20, he and his twin brother organized a theater group in St. Lucia and staged a play that Walcott had written. While still a student at the University of the West Indies in Jamaica, he published several works, among them a play.

Teaching Career After studying drama in New York for a year, Walcott moved to Trinidad, where he recruited and trained the first professional West Indian acting troupe. Since 1970, he has taught at various schools in the United States—including Yale, Columbia, and Boston University—in recent years dividing his time between homes in Boston, Trinidad, and St. Lucia.

Six Feet of the Country

Short Story by NADINE GORDIMER

Comparing Literature of the World

Six Feet of the Country and *from* Writing as an Act of Hope

This lesson and the one that follows present an opportunity for comparing Nadine Gordimer's examination of the effects of South African apartheid with Isabel Allende's observations on the political unrest and economic hardship in Chile. Specific points of comparison in the Allende lesson will help you contrast the two writers' portrayals of the people and conditions in their homeland.

Connect to Your Life

Lip Service Have you ever encountered a situation in which a person claimed to understand and respect another race or culture but really showed little understanding or respect? Discuss your experiences and insights with your classmates.

Build Background

Separate but Unequal Nadine Gordimer writes about the people of her South African homeland and reveals how the system of apartheid has affected their lives. The term *apartheid*—which means "separateness" in Afrikaans, the language of the Dutch settlers of South Africa—refers to an official system of racial separation enforced by the South African government from 1948 to 1991. During the first 20 years of that period, laws were enacted that segregated education and housing, restricted the movement and voting rights of nonwhites, and gave the government far-reaching police powers to ensure compliance with apartheid. In 1961, South Africa withdrew from the United Nations after other member nations severely criticized its racial policies.

In the 1970s and 1980s, the government of South Africa, responding to years of national and international protest, began to repeal some apartheid laws and to open public facilities and transportation systems to all races. Many apartheid regulations remained, however, as did segregation of schools and neighborhoods. Finally, in 1991, the government granted full rights to nonwhites, repealing the last of the discriminatory laws that had formed the basis of apartheid. Although apartheid has now been officially dismantled, its economic and social effects are likely to linger for some time.

From the first days of apartheid, many white South Africans opposed the system for its inhumanity and lack of respect for people of other cultures. A few, like Nadine Gordimer, openly expressed their disapproval of the system. In "Six Feet of the Country," first published in the 1950s, she examines the experiences and attitudes of a white British couple—a businessman and a former actress—who have moved to the South African countryside.

LaserLinks: Background for Reading
Cultural/Historical Connection

WORDS TO KNOW
Vocabulary Preview

attenuated	inane
enamor	laconic
expostulate	stint
extraneous	submissive
imbue	untainted

Focus Your Reading

LITERARY ANALYSIS POINT OF VIEW

As you know, the term ***point of view*** refers to the narrative method used in a literary work. "Six Feet of the Country" is told from the **first-person point of view** of a narrator who is also the story's **main character.** As you read, keep in mind that the events and other characters in the story are described from the main character's personal perspective.

ACTIVE READING PREDICTING

When you make a **prediction,** you try to figure out what will happen next. Historical knowledge about a narrative's subject and even the story's title can help you make predictions. Use the information provided in the Build Background and the title "Six Feet of the Country" to predict what the story will be about.

READER'S NOTEBOOK Write your prediction about the story in your notebook. Then, at key moments in the story, continue to jot down your predictions about what will happen next.

OVERVIEW

This selection is included in the **Grade 12 InterActive Reader.**

Objectives

1. understand and appreciate the author's use of **point of view** in a short story **(Literary Analysis)**
2. appreciate the author's use of **imagery (Literary Analysis)**
3. **make predictions** to understand the unfolding of a short story **(Active Reading)**

Summary

The narrator and his wife, a British couple living on a farm in South Africa, find that an illegal immigrant and brother to one of their workers has died on their property. Government officials bury the body. Petrus, the brother of the dead man, wishes to have the body back. He pays a large sum, but the body returned is the wrong one. At Petrus's insistence, the narrator first attempts to get the correct body, then when that proves fruitless, to get the money back. Petrus receives neither his brother's body nor his money.

Thematic Link

This story shows how a man is drawn into a **conflict between cultures.**

5-Minute Warm-Up

Daily Language SkillBuilder

Have students **proofread** the display sentences on page 1189k and write them correctly. The sentences also appear on Transparency 36 of **Grammar Transparencies and Copymasters.**

LESSON RESOURCES

UNIT SEVEN RESOURCE BOOK, pp. 42–46

ASSESSMENT RESOURCES

Formal Assessment, pp. 243–244

Teacher's Guide to Assessment and Portfolio Use

Test Generator

SKILLS TRANSPARENCIES AND COPYMASTERS

Literary Analysis
- Point of View, T18 (for Literary Analysis, p. 1289)

Reading and Critical Thinking
- Predicting Outcomes, T2 (for Active Reading, p. 1289)

Grammar
Elliptical Clause of Comparison, C122 (for Mini Lesson, p. 1300)

Vocabulary
- Word Origins, C91 (for Mini Lesson, p. 1291)
- Synonyms, C96 (for Vocabulary in Action, p. 1301)

Writing
- Critical Review, C32 (for Writing Option 1, p. 1300)
- Opinion Statement, C35 (for Writing Option 3, p. 1300)

Communications
- Impromptu Speaking: Dialogue, Role-Play, T14 (for Activities & Explorations 2, p. 1300)

INTEGRATED TECHNOLOGY

Audio Library

LaserLinks
- Cultural/Historical Connection: Apartheid in South Africa, 1948–1991. See **Teacher's SourceBook,** p. 99.

Internet: Research Starter

Visit our website: www.mcdougallittell.com

Mini Lesson **Preteaching Vocabulary**

If you would like to preteach the WORDS TO KNOW for this selection, use the Mini Lesson on p. 1291.

Editor's Note

This selection contains language that may be considered objectionable.

TEACHING THE LITERATURE

Reading and Analyzing

Literary Analysis POINT OF VIEW

Ask students what effect is created by having a first-person narrator.

Possible Response: The reader knows what the character is thinking and feeling; the reader can more easily identify with the main character.

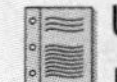 Use **Unit Seven Resource Book,** p. 44 for more exercises.

Active Reading PREDICTING

Remind students that in short stories, the main character's beliefs about his life are often proved to be false. Ask students to read the opening passage, stopping at ". . . but more comfortable all round." Then ask them to predict how the narrator's evaluation of his situation might be reversed or changed as the story progresses.

Possible Response: The racial tensions of the city will begin to surface on his farm.

 Use **Unit Seven Resource Book,** p. 43 for more practice.

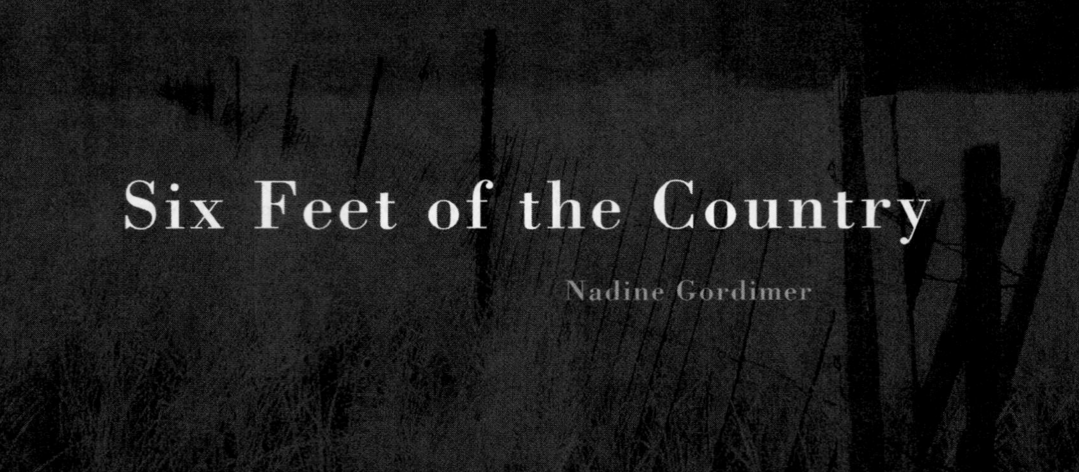

Six Feet of the Country

Nadine Gordimer

My wife and I are not real farmers—not even Lerice, really. We bought our place, ten miles out of Johannesburg on one of the main roads, to change something in ourselves, I suppose; you seem to rattle about so much within a marriage like ours. You long to hear nothing but a deep, satisfying silence when you sound a marriage. The farm hasn't managed that for us, of course, but it has done other things, unexpected, illogical. Lerice, who I thought would retire there in Chekhovian sadness for a month or two, and then leave the place to the servants while she tried yet again to get a part she wanted and become the actress she would like to be, has sunk into the business of running the farm with all the serious intensity with which she once imbued the shadows in a playwright's mind. I should have given it up long ago if it had not been for her. Her hands, once small and plain and well-kept—she was not the sort of actress who wears red paint and diamond rings—are hard as a dog's pads.

WORDS TO KNOW

imbue (ĭm-byōō') *v.* to fill with a quality; saturate

Teaching Options

BLOCK SCHEDULING: MANAGING TIME

If your schedule requires that you cover the lesson objectives in a shorter time, use . . .

- Preparing to Read, p. 1289
- Thinking Through the Literature, p. 1299
- Vocabulary in Action, p. 1301

If you want to take advantage of longer class time, use . . .

- TE Teaching Options: Preteaching Vocabulary, p. 1291; Standardized Test Practice, p. 1292; Speaking and Listening, p. 1294; Multicultural Link, p. 1295; Viewing and Representing, p. 1296; Vocabulary Strategy, p. 1297; Informal Assessment, p. 1298; Grammar, p. 1300
- Choices & Challenges and Author Activity, pp. 1300–1301

I, of course, am there only in the evenings and at week-ends. I am a partner in a luxury-travel agency, which is flourishing—needs to be, as I tell Lerice, in order to carry on the farm. Still, though I know we can't afford it, and though the sweetish smell of the fowls Lerice breeds sickens me, so that I avoid going past their runs, the farm is beautiful in a way I had almost forgotten—especially on a Sunday morning when I get up and go out into the paddock and see not the palm trees and fish pond and imitation-stone bird-bath of the suburbs but white ducks on the dam, the lucerne[1] field brilliant as window-dresser's grass, and the little, stocky, mean-eyed bull, lustful but bored, having his face tenderly licked by one of his ladies. Lerice comes out with her hair uncombed, in her hand a stick dripping with cattle-dip. She will stand and look dreamily for a moment, the way she would pretend to look sometimes in those plays. "They'll mate tomorrow," she will say. "This is their second day. Look how she loves him, my little Napoleon." So that when people come out to see us on Sunday afternoon, I am likely to hear myself saying, as I pour out the drinks, "When I drive back home from the city every day, past those rows of suburban houses, I wonder how the devil we ever did stand it. . . . Would you care to look around?" And there I am, taking some pretty girl and her young husband stumbling down to our river-bank, the girl catching her stockings on the mealie-stooks[2] and stepping over cow-turds humming with jewel-green flies while she says, ". . . the *tensions* of the damned city. And you're near enough to get into town to a show, too! I think it's wonderful. Why, you've got it both ways!"

And for a moment I accept the triumph as if I *had* managed it—the impossibility that I've been trying for all my life—just as if the truth was that you could get it "both ways," instead of finding yourself with not even one way or the other but a third, one you had not provided for at all.

But even in our saner moments, when I find Lerice's earthy enthusiasms just as irritating as I once found her histrionical[3] ones, and she finds what she calls my "jealousy" of her capacity for enthusiasm as big a proof of my inadequacy for her as a mate as ever it was, we do believe that we have at least honestly escaped those tensions peculiar to the city about which our visitors speak. When Johannesburg people speak of "tension" they don't mean hurrying people in crowded streets, the struggle for money, or the general competitive character of city life. They mean the guns under the white men's pillows and the burglar bars on the white men's windows. They mean those strange moments on city pavements when a black man won't stand aside for a white man.

Out in the country, even ten miles out, life is better than that. In the country, there is a lingering remnant of the pretransitional stage; our relationship with the blacks is almost feudal.[4] Wrong, I suppose, obsolete, but more comfortable all round. We have no burglar bars, no gun. 1
Lerice's farm-boys have their wives and their piccanins[5] living with them on the land. They brew their sour beer without the fear of police raids. In fact, we've always rather prided ourselves that the poor devils have nothing much to fear, being with us; Lerice even keeps an eye on their children, with all the competence of a woman who has never had a child of her own, and she certainly doctors

1. **lucerne** (lo͞o-sûrn′): a British term for alfalfa.
2. **mealie-stooks:** a South African term for cornstalks.
3. **histrionical:** theatrical; dramatic.
4. **feudal** (fyo͞od′l): characteristic of feudalism—the medieval European economic, political, and social system in which the serfs who worked the land were protected by, and owed allegiance to, their overlords.
5. **piccanins** (pĭk′ə-nĭnz′): in South Africa, a term (usually considered derogatory) for native African children.

Customizing Instruction

Students Acquiring English

1 Tell students that British English is spoken in South Africa and that the characters in this story will therefore employ some unfamiliar usage. Point out the word "round." Ask students what word would be used in its place in American English
Answer: around.

Encourage students to watch for other British usages in the story.

Use **Spanish Study Guide** for additional support, pp. 323–325.

Less Proficient Readers

Set a Purpose Have students read to find out the narrator's feelings about country life and his workers.

Gifted and Talented

As students read the selection, ask them to identify the techniques the writer uses to characterize the narrator. What is the effect of these techniques on the reader?

Mini Lesson Preteaching Vocabulary

WORD ORIGINS

Have students match the following WORDS TO KNOW with their appropriate word origins.

1. attenuated — a. Middle English *stinten,* "cease"
2. enamor — b. Greek *Lakonikos,* "spartan"
3. expostulate — c. Latin *amor,* "love"
4. extraneous — d. Latin *submittere,* "send down"
5. imbue — e. old French *ataint,* "touched"
6. inane — f. Latin *extra,* "outside"
7. laconic — g. Latin *attenuare,* "make thin"
8. stint — h. Latin *inanis,* "empty"
9. submissive — i. Latin *postulare,* "demand"
10. untainted — j. Latin *imbuere,* "soak"

(Answers: 1. g.; 2. c.; 3. i.; 4. f.; 5. j.; 6. h.; 7. b.; 8. a.; 9. d.; 10. e.)

Use **Unit Seven Resource Book,** p. 45 for more practice.

A lesson on word origins appears on page 206 in the Pupil's Edition.

SIX FEET OF THE COUNTRY 1291

TEACHING THE LITERATURE

Reading and Analyzing

Literary Analysis: IMAGERY

A Remind students that images are words and phrases that create vivid sensory experiences for the reader. Ask students to list details that make the scene with the dead man vivid.
Possible Response: the iron bedstead; the brick stilts; the light, cold sweat on his forehead; the warmth of the body

ACTIVE READING

PREDICT

B Since the dead man is clearly a stranger to the main character, students should realize that the man is not a worker on the farm. Before students read the next two paragraphs, ask them to predict who the dead man will turn out to be. Then have them read ahead to check their predictions.
Answer: The dead man is Petrus's brother.

Literary Analysis: IRONY

C Ask students how the word *paradise* is used ironically in this passage.
Possible Response: The word is in no way appropriate to describe a slum township.

them all—children and adults—like babies whenever they happen to be sick.

It was because of this that we were not particularly startled one night last winter when the boy Albert came knocking at our window long after we had gone to bed. I wasn't in our bed but **B** sleeping in the little dressing-room-cum-linen room next door, because Lerice had annoyed me, and I didn't want to find myself softening toward her simply because of the sweet smell of the talcum powder on her flesh after her bath. She came and woke me up. "Albert says one of the boys is very sick," she said. "I think you'd better go down and see. He wouldn't get us up at this hour for nothing."

"What time is it?"

"What does it matter?" Lerice is maddeningly logical.

I got up awkwardly as she watched me—how is it I always feel a fool when I have deserted her bed? After all, I know from the way she never looks at me when she talks to me at breakfast the next day that she is hurt and humiliated at my not wanting her—and I went out, clumsy with sleep.

1 "Which of the boys is it?" I asked Albert as we followed the dance of my torch.

"He's too sick. Very sick, *Baas*,"[6] he said.

"But who? Franz?" I remembered Franz had had a bad cough for the past week.

Albert did not answer; he had given me the path, and was walking along beside me in the tall dead grass. When the light of the torch caught his face, I saw that he looked acutely embarrassed. "What's this all about?" I said.

He lowered his head under the glance of the light. "It's not me, *Baas*. I don't know. Petrus he send me."

Irritated, I hurried him along to the huts. And there, on Petrus's iron bedstead, with its brick stilts, was a young man, dead. On his forehead there was still a light, cold sweat; his body was **A** warm. The boys stood around as they do in the kitchen when it is discovered that someone has broken a dish—uncooperative, silent. Somebody's wife hung about in the shadows, her hands wrung together under her apron.

ACTIVE READING

PREDICT Who do you think the dead man is?

I had not seen a dead man since the war. This was very different. I felt like the others—extraneous, useless.

"What was the matter?" I asked.

The woman patted at her chest and shook her head to indicate the painful impossibility of breathing.

He must have died of pneumonia.

I turned to Petrus. "Who was this boy? What was he doing here?" The light of a candle on the floor showed that Petrus was weeping. He followed me out the door.

When we were outside, in the dark, I waited for him to speak. But he didn't. "Now come on, Petrus, you must tell me who this boy was. Was he a friend of yours?"

"He's my brother, *Baas*. He come from Rhodesia to look for work."

The story startled Lerice and me a little. The young boy had walked down from Rhodesia to look for work in Johannesburg, had caught a chill from sleeping out along the way, and had lain ill in his brother Petrus's hut since his arrival three days before. Our boys had been

6. *baas* (bäs) *Afrikaans:* master; boss (formerly used as a term of address by black South Africans when speaking to a white man).

WORDS TO KNOW

extraneous (ĭk-strā′nē-əs) *adj.* not relevant; inessential

1292

Teaching Options

Mini Lesson Standardized Test Practice

CHOOSING THE BEST SUMMARY For some standardized tests, students will be asked to choose the best summary of a passage. To provide students with some help in choosing the best summary, read aloud or write on the chalkboard the following questions.

Which of the following statements best summarizes the passage from "The story startled Lerice . . ." (p. 1292) to ". . . my morning drive to town" (p. 1293)?

A. The narrator decides that, since the cause of the illegal immigrant's death is not known, he must notify the health authorities.

B. The narrator thinks that other illegal immigrants have undoubtedly been kept in secret on his farm.

C. Lerice acts offended that Petrus did not tell her or her husband about his sick brother.

Lead students through the process of choosing the best summary. Consider each choice. Point out that, while all of the statements contain accurate information about the passage, the best summary should include the most important information. For that reason, **A** is the best choice.

frightened to ask us for help for him because we had not been intended ever to know of his presence. Rhodesian natives are barred from entering the Union[7] unless they have a permit; the young man was an illegal immigrant. No doubt our boys had managed the whole thing successfully several times before; a number of relatives must have walked the seven or eight hundred miles from poverty to the paradise of zoot suits,[8] police raids, and black slum townships that is their *Egoli,*[9] City of Gold—the Bantu name for Johannesburg. It was merely a matter of getting such a man to lie low on our farm until a job could be found with someone who would be glad to take the risk of prosecution for employing an illegal immigrant in exchange for the services of someone as yet untainted by the city.

Well, this was one who would never get up again.

"You would think they would have felt they could tell *us,*" said Lerice next morning. "Once the man was ill. You would have thought at least—" When she is getting intense over something, she has a way of standing in the middle of a room as people do when they are shortly to leave on a journey, looking searchingly about her at the most familiar objects as if she had never seen them before. I had noticed that in Petrus's presence in the kitchen, earlier, she had the air of
2 being almost offended with him, almost hurt.

In any case, I really haven't the time or inclination any more to go into everything in our life that I know Lerice, from those alarmed and pressing eyes of hers, would like us to go into. She is the kind of woman who doesn't mind if she looks plain, or odd; I don't suppose she would even care if she knew how strange she looks when her whole face is out of proportion with urgent uncertainty. I said, "Now, I'm the one who'll have to do all the dirty work, I suppose."

She was still staring at me, trying me out with those eyes—wasting her time, if she only knew.

"I'll have to notify the health authorities," I said calmly. "They can't just cart him off and bury him. After all, we don't really know what he died of."

She simply stood there, as if she had given up—simply ceased to see me at all.

I don't know when I've been so irritated. "It might have been something contagious," I said. "God knows?" There was no answer.

I am not enamored of holding conversations with myself. I went out to shout to one of the boys to open the garage and get the car ready for my morning drive to town.

As I had expected, it turned out to be quite a business. I had to notify the police as well as the health authorities, and answer a lot of tedious questions: How was it I was ignorant of the boy's presence? If I did not supervise my native quarters, how did I know that that sort of thing didn't go on all the time? Et cetera, et cetera. And when I flared up and told them that so long as my natives did their work, I didn't think it my right or concern to poke my nose into their private lives, I got from the coarse, dull-witted police sergeant one of those looks that come not from any thinking process going on in the brain but from that faculty common to all who are possessed by the master-race theory—a look of insanely inane certainty. He grinned at me with a mixture of scorn and delight at my stupidity.

Then I had to explain to Petrus why the health authorities had to take away the body

7. **Union:** Union of South Africa—the South African state preceding the formation of the Republic of South Africa in 1961.
8. **zoot suits:** flashy men's suits with broad padded shoulders and baggy trousers.
9. ***Egoli*** (ā-gō'lē).

WORDS TO KNOW
untainted (ŭn-tān'tĭd) *adj.* not contaminated; unspoiled
enamor (ĭ-năm'ər) *v.* to inspire with love; fascinate
inane (ĭn-ān') *adj.* foolish; senseless

Customizing Instruction

Students Acquiring English

1 Tell students that *torch* is the British term for "flashlight."

Less Proficient Readers

Set a Purpose Have students read to find out what the worker wants done with the body.

Multiple Learning Styles

Interpersonal and Auditory Learners

2 Remind students that the thoughts revealed by the main character affect the reader's perceptions. Have two students perform the scene on this page between the main character and Lerice. Tell them to leave out the main character's thoughts and use just the actions and dialogue. Have the class write down the characters' emotions and character traits as they listen and discuss their findings.

Possible Responses: Students may say that Lerice is childish and self-involved; they may say that the main character is self-important, rigid, and cold.

Reading and Analyzing

Literary Analysis: CHARACTERIZATION

A Ask students what this description of Petrus reveals about the narrator's feelings.

Possible Response: He may feel guilty because he thinks he should try to help Petrus but he doesn't really want to help.

ACTIVE READING

CLARIFY

B **Possible Response:** The narrator thinks that money should be spent on everyday needs; he is surprised that people with so little in life would sacrifice to raise money to bury someone.

Literary Analysis POINT OF VIEW

C What does the narrator reveal about himself in his description of his reaction to Lerice's project?

Possible Response: He expects to have things his way; he puts his wants before his wife's.

for a post-mortem[10]—and, in fact, what a post-mortem was. When I telephoned the health department some days later to find out the result, I was told the cause of death was, as we had thought, pneumonia, and that the body had been suitably disposed of. I went out to where Petrus was mixing a mash for the fowls and told him that it was all right, there would be no trouble; his brother had died from that pain in his chest. Petrus put down the paraffin tin and said, "When can we go to fetch him, *Baas?*"

"To fetch him?"

"Will the *Baas* please ask them when we must come?"

I went back inside and called Lerice, all over the house. She came down the stairs from the spare bedrooms, and I said, *"Now* what am I going to do? When I told Petrus, he just asked calmly when they could go and fetch the body. They think they're going to bury him themselves."

"Well, go back and tell him," said Lerice. "You must tell him. Why didn't you tell him then?"

When I found Petrus again, he looked up politely. "Look, Petrus," I said. "You can't go to fetch your brother. They've done it already—they've *buried* him, you understand?"

"Where?" he said, slowly, dully, as if he thought that perhaps he was getting this wrong.

"You see, he was a stranger. They knew he wasn't from here, and they didn't know he had some of his people here, so they thought they must bury him." It was difficult to make a pauper's grave sound like a privilege.

"Please, *Baas,* the *Baas* must ask them?" But he did not mean that he wanted to know the burial-

place. He simply ignored the incomprehensible machinery I told him had set to work on his dead brother; he wanted the brother back.

"But Petrus," I said, "how can I? Your brother is buried already. I can't ask them now."

"Oh *Baas!"* he said. He stood with his bran-smeared hands uncurled at his sides, one corner of his mouth twitching.

"Good God, Petrus, they won't listen to me! They can't, anyway. I'm sorry, but I can't do it. You understand?"

He just kept on looking at me, out of his knowledge that white men have everything, can do anything; if they don't, it is because they won't. **A**

And then, at dinner Lerice started. "You could at least phone," she said.

"Christ, what d'you think I am? Am I supposed to bring the dead back to life?"

But I could not exaggerate my way out of this ridiculous responsibility that had been thrust on me. "Phone them up," she went on. "And at least you'll be able to tell him you've done it and they've explained that it's impossible."

She disappeared somewhere into the kitchen quarters after coffee. A little later she came back to tell me, "The old father's coming down from Rhodesia to be at the funeral. He's got a permit and he's already on his way."

Unfortunately, it was not impossible to get the body back. The authorities said that it was somewhat irregular, but that since the hygiene conditions had been fulfilled, they could not refuse permission for exhumation.[11] I found out that, with the undertaker's charges, it would cost twenty pounds. Ah, I thought, that settles it. On five pounds a month, Petrus won't have twenty pounds—and just as well, since it couldn't do the dead any good. Certainly I should not offer it to him myself. Twenty pounds—or anything else within reason, for that matter—I would have spent without grudging it on doctors or medicines that might have helped the boy when he was alive. Once he was dead, I had no intention of encouraging Petrus to throw away, on a gesture, more than he spent to clothe his whole family in a year.

When I told him, in the kitchen that night, he said, "Twenty pounds?"

10. **post-mortem:** an examination of a corpse to determine the cause of death.

11. **exhumation** (ĕg′zyo͞o-mā′shən): the removal of a corpse from a grave.

Teaching Options

Mini Lesson

Speaking and Listening

MAKING A SPEECH

Instruction Ask students to close their books and listen as two people read the interactions between the narrator and Petrus on pages 1294 and 1295.

Prepare Have them listen to decide what Petrus's motives, values, and concerns are. Then ask each student to write a short speech from Petrus's point of view asking for his brother's body back.

Present Have students present their speeches to the class.

This activity is particularly well-suited for longer class periods.

I said, "Yes, that's right, twenty pounds."

For a moment, I had the feeling, from the look on his face, that he was calculating. But when he spoke again I thought I must have imagined it. "We must pay twenty pounds!" he said in the far-away voice in which a person speaks of something so unattainable that it does not bear thinking about.

"All right, Petrus," I said in dismissal, and went back to the living-room.

The next morning before I went to town, Petrus asked to see me. "Please *Baas,*" he said, awkwardly handing me a bundle of notes. They're so seldom on the giving rather than the receiving side, poor devils, that they don't really know how to hand money to a white man. There it was, the twenty pounds, in ones and halves, some creased and folded until they were soft as dirty rags, others smooth and fairly new—Franz's money, I suppose, and Albert's, and Dora the cook's, and Jacob the gardener's, and God knows who else's besides, from all the farms and small holdings round about. I took it in irritation more than in astonishment, really—irritation at the waste, the uselessness of this sacrifice by people so poor. Just like the poor everywhere, I thought, who stint themselves the decencies of life in order to insure themselves the decencies of death. So incomprehensible to people like Lerice and me, who regard life as something to be spent extravagantly and, if we think about death at all, regard it as the final bankruptcy.

ACTIVE READING

B **CLARIFY** Why is the narrator so surprised by the farm hands' efforts?

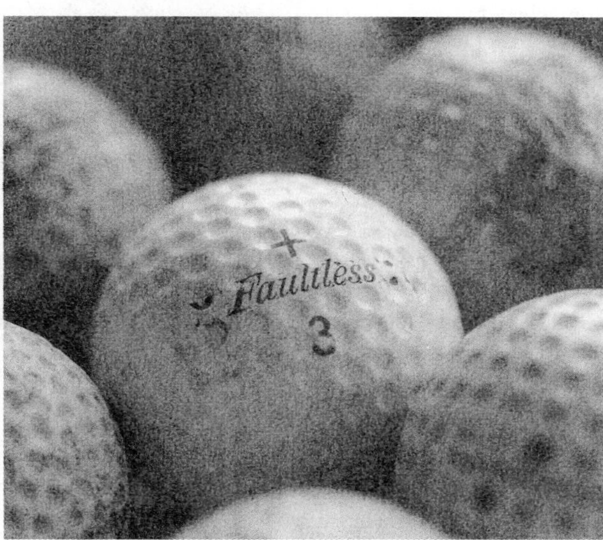

The servants don't work on Saturday afternoon anyway, so it was a good day for the funeral. Petrus and his father had borrowed our donkey-cart to fetch the coffin from the city, where, Petrus told Lerice on their return, everything was "nice"—the coffin waiting for them, already sealed up to save them from what must have been a rather unpleasant sight after two weeks' interment. (It had taken all that time for the authorities and the undertaker to make the final arrangements for moving the body.) All morning, the coffin lay in Petrus's hut, awaiting the trip to the little old burial-ground, just outside the eastern boundary of our farm, that was a relic of the days when this was a real farming district rather than a fashionable rural estate. It was pure chance that I happened to be down there near the fence when the procession came past; once again Lerice had forgotten her promise to me and had made the house uninhabitable on a Saturday afternoon. I had come home and been infuriated to find her in a pair of filthy old slacks and with her hair uncombed since the night before, having all the varnish scraped off the living-room floor, if you C

WORDS TO KNOW

stint (stĭnt) *v.* to limit to a small amount; give sparingly

1295

Customizing Instruction

Students Acquiring English

1 Explain that "incomprehensible machinery" in this case refers to elaborate government rules and policies.

Less Proficient Readers

Ask students the following questions to check their comprehension.

- What do the health authorities do with the body?
  Answer: bury it in a pauper's grave.
- What does Petrus want to do with his brother's body?
  Answer: have a proper funeral.
- How does Petrus raise the money to exhume the body?
  Answer: His friends all chip in.

Multicultural Link

Funeral Ceremonies

Funeral ceremonies vary from culture to culture. In some Islamic traditions, four people place the four corners of the bier, or platform, that supports the body on their shoulders. While transporting the body, the carriers repeat *"Allah Akbar"* ("God is great") and pray for blessing. The grave should face Mecca, the birthplace of Muhammad. During the burial, the mourners gather to pray and ask God for forgiveness. No conversation occurs, just praying and crying, because it is believed that weeping releases sorrow.

A traditional Jewish funeral service begins with the tearing of a garment or a black ribbon, symbolizing the deceased being "rent" (torn) from loved ones. The reading of psalms precedes a eulogy by the rabbi, offering personal words about the deceased. Following the chanting of *el molei rachamim,* a slow dirge, the mourners proceed to the cemetery where additional prayers are recited. As the final act of the service, the family recites *kaddish,* an ancient prayer praising God as the author of life.

Reading and Analyzing

A Literary Analysis: POINT OF VIEW

Ask students how the narrator's description of the funeral procession is colored by his personal perspective.

Possible Response: He's concerned with the "awkwardness" of his own situation rather than the solemnity of the funeral procession.

ACTIVE READING

QUESTION

B Possible Response: He is not accustomed to showing any respect to blacks; he may feel ashamed for his lack of compassion or the incongruity of his playing golf while others mourn.

Literary Analysis: ALLUSION

C Point out that references to the donkey in the Bible indicate that it was valued for its strength and endurance. Ask students to explain the ways the allusion to the donkey might be related to black South Africans living under apartheid.

Possible Response: Black South Africans were forced to submit to white South Africans and had to be strong and patient to endure their fate.

please. So I had taken my No. 8 iron and gone off to practice my approach shots. In my annoyance I had forgotten about the funeral, and was reminded only when I saw the procession coming up the path along the outside of the fence toward me; from where I was standing, you can see the graves quite clearly, and that day the sun glinted on bits of broken pottery, a lopsided homemade cross, and jam-jars brown with rain-water and dead flowers. **A**

Funeral Procession (1940), Ellis Wilson. Armistad Research Center, Tulane University, New Orleans, Louisiana.

I felt a little awkward, and did not know whether to go on hitting my golf ball or stop at least until the whole gathering was decently past. The donkey-cart creaks and screeches with every revolution of the wheels and it came along in a slow, halting fashion somehow peculiarly suited to the two donkeys who drew it, their little potbellies rubbed and rough, their heads sunk between the shafts, and their ears flattened back with an air submissive and downcast; peculiarly suited, too, to the group of men and women who came along slowly behind. The patient ass. Watching, I thought, you can see now why the creature became a Biblical symbol. **C** Then the procession drew level with me and stopped, so I had to put down my club. The coffin was taken down off the cart—it was a shiny, yellow-varnished wood, like cheap furniture—and the donkeys twitched their ears against the flies. Petrus, Franz, Albert and the old father from Rhodesia hoisted it on their shoulders and the procession moved on, on foot. It was really a very awkward moment. I stood there rather foolishly at the fence, quite still, and slowly they filed past, not looking up, the four men bent beneath the shiny wooden box, and the straggling troop of mourners. All of them were servants or neighbors' servants whom I knew as casual, easygoing gossipers about our lands or kitchen. I heard the old man's breathing.

ACTIVE READING

B QUESTION Why does the narrator feel awkward as the funeral passes?

I had just bent to pick up my club again when there was a sort of jar in the flowing solemnity of their processional mood; I felt it at once, like a wave of heat along the air, or one of those sudden currents of cold catching at your legs in a placid stream. The old man's voice was muttering

WORDS TO KNOW **submissive** (səb-mĭs'ĭv) *adj.* yielding to the control of another

Teaching Options

Viewing and Representing

Funeral Procession **by Ellis Wilson**

ART APPRECIATION

Instruction In this oil painting, Ellis Wilson (1899–1977) focuses the viewer's attention on the mourners, most of whom are shown in profile. The artist stresses the dignity and solemnity of the occasion.

Application Ask students to think about Wilson's use of color. Ask students what they think the contrast between the bright colors of the foliage and flowers and the dark colors of the people and earth might represent.

Possible Responses: the contrast between life and death; the way that the fact of death makes life more vivid; joy in the midst of sorrow

Ask students why they think Wilson has shown the procession as a circle with vegetation in the middle.

Possible Response: He wants to show that life is surrounded by death; he wants to show that life flourishes in the midst of death.

something, and they bumped into one another, some pressing to go on, others hissing at them to be still. I could see that they were embarrassed, but they could not ignore the voice; it was much the way that the mumblings of a prophet, though not clear at first, arrest the mind. The corner of the coffin the old man carried was sagging at an angle; he seemed to be trying to get out from under the weight of it. Now Petrus expostulated with him.

The little boy who had been left to watch the donkeys dropped the reins and ran to see. I don't know why—unless it was for the same reason people crowd round someone who has fainted in a cinema—but I parted the wires of the fence and went through, after him.

Petrus lifted his eyes to me—to anybody—with distress and horror. The old man from Rhodesia had let go of the coffin entirely, and the three others, unable to support it on their own, had laid it on the ground, in the pathway. Already there was a film of dust lightly wavering up its shiny sides. I did not understand what the old man was saying; I hesitated to interfere. But now the whole seething group turned on my silence. The old man himself came over to me, with his hands outspread and shaking, and spoke directly to me, saying something that I could tell from the tone, without understanding the words, was shocking and extraordinary.

"What is it, Petrus? What's wrong?" I appealed.

Petrus threw up his hands, bowed his head in a series of hysterical shakes, then thrust his face up at me suddenly.

"He says, 'My son was not so heavy.'"

Silence. I could hear the old man breathing; he kept his mouth a little open as old people do.

"My son was young and thin," he said, at last, in English.

Again silence. Then babble broke out. The old man thundered against everybody; his teeth were yellowed and few, and he had one of those fine, grizzled, sweeping moustaches that one doesn't often see nowadays, which must have been grown in emulation of early Empire builders.[12] It seemed to frame all his utterances with a special validity, perhaps merely because it was the symbol of the traditional wisdom of age—an idea so fearfully rooted that it carries still something awesome beyond reason. He shocked them; they thought he was mad, but they had to listen to him. With his own hands he began to prise the lid off the coffin and three of the men came forward to help him. Then he sat down on the ground; very old, very weak, and unable to speak, he merely lifted a trembling hand toward what was there. He abdicated, he handed it over to them; he was no good any more.

They crowded round to look (and so did I), and now they forgot the nature of this surprise and the occasion of grief to which it belonged, and for a few minutes were carried up in the astonishment of the surprise itself. They gasped and flared noisily with excitement. I even noticed the little boy who had held the donkeys jumping up and down, almost weeping with rage because the backs of the grown-ups crowded him out of his view.

In the coffin was someone no one had ever seen before: a heavily built, rather light-skinned native with a neatly stitched scar on his forehead—perhaps from a blow in a brawl that had also dealt him some other, slower-working injury which had killed him.

I wrangled with the authorities for a week over that body. I had the feeling that they were shocked, in a laconic fashion, by their own mistake, but that in the confusion of their anonymous dead **1** they were helpless to put it right. They said to me, "We are trying to find out," and "We are still making enquiries." It was as if at any moment they might conduct me into their mortuary and say, "There! Lift up the sheets; look for him—your poultry boy's brother. There are so many black faces—surely one will do?"

12. **Empire builders:** British colonizers.

WORDS TO KNOW
expostulate (ĭk-spŏs′chə-lāt′) *v.* to reason earnestly in an effort to correct or dissuade
laconic (lə-kŏn′ĭk) *adj.* making use of few words

Customizing Instruction

Students Acquiring English

1 Explain that by "anonymous dead" the narrator means those bodies that no one has identified or tried to identify.

Less Proficient Students

Ask students the following questions to make sure they understand the selection.

- Why did the narrator feel that he had to put down his golf club?
  Answer: to show respect to the funeral procession.
- Why did the procession stop?
  Answer: because the old man said that the body they were carrying wasn't his son.
- How did the old man know it was not his son?
  Answer: The coffin was too heavy.

Vocabulary Strategy

CONNOTATION

Instruction Remind students that in addition to designating things or ideas, words carry judgments.

Activity Ask students what judgments are expressed by the following words used by the narrator to describe the mourners.

- straggling
  Possible Response: The procession is disorganized and halfhearted.
- muttering
  Possible Response: The old man is incoherent, and what he is saying is nonsensical and unimportant.
- seething
  Possible Response: The procession is like a force of nature.
- babble
  Possible Responses: The mourners' talk is senseless.

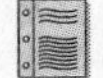
Use **Vocabulary Transparencies and Copymasters,** p. 79.

A lesson on denotation and connotation appears on p. 645 in the Pupil's Edition.

Reading and Analyzing

Reading Skills and Strategies: DRAWING INFERENCES

A Because the story is told from the narrator's point of view, readers must infer Lerice's feelings from her words and actions. Ask students to examine Lerice's words and actions in this paragraph and the one following. Ask them what they can infer that Lerice thinks of her husband's search and his motives.

Possible Responses: She thinks his "matter of principle" has more to do with him than with Petrus and Petrus's father; she suspects that her husband has selfish motives; she thinks he is doing too little too late.

Active Reading QUESTION

B **Possible Response:** They may look alike in the way they look at him, perhaps showing disappointment or a lack of understanding when he tries to explain the problem.

Literary Analysis: IRONY

C Ask students to think about the power of the story's last paragraph. Ask them what makes this statement ironic.

Possible Response: The old man is not better off than he had been. His son is dead and the body has been lost.

And every evening when I got home Petrus was waiting in the kitchen. "Well, they're trying. They're still looking. The *Baas* is seeing to it for you, Petrus," I would tell him. "God, half the time I should be in the office I'm driving around the back end of town chasing after this affair," I added aside, to Lerice, one night.

She and Petrus both kept their eyes turned on me as I spoke, and, oddly, for those moments they looked exactly alike, though it sounds impossible: my wife, with her high, white forehead and her attenuated Englishwoman's body, A and the poultry boy, with his horny bare feet below khaki trousers tied at the knee with string and the peculiar rankness of his nervous sweat coming from his skin.

> ACTIVE READING
>
> B **QUESTION** Why do Lerice and Petrus look alike to the narrator at this point?

"What makes you so indignant, so determined about this now?" said Lerice suddenly.

I stared at her. "It's a matter of principle. Why should they get away with a swindle? It's time these officials had a jolt from someone who'll bother to take the trouble."

She said, "Oh." And as Petrus slowly opened the kitchen door to leave, sensing that the talk had gone beyond him, she turned away too.

I continued to pass on assurances to Petrus every evening, but although what I said was the same, and the voice in which I said it was the same, every evening it sounded weaker. At last, it became clear that we would never get Petrus's brother back, because nobody really knew where he was. Somewhere in a graveyard as uniform as a housing scheme, somewhere under a number that didn't belong to him, or in the medical school, perhaps, laboriously reduced to layers of muscles and strings of nerves? Goodness knows. He had no identity in this world anyway.

It was only then, and in a voice of shame, that Petrus asked me to try and get the money back.

"From the way he asks, you'd think he was robbing his dead brother," I said to Lerice later. But as I've said, Lerice had got so intense about this business that she couldn't even appreciate a little ironic smile.

I tried to get the money; Lerice tried. We both telephoned and wrote and argued, but nothing came of it. It appeared that the main expense had been the undertaker, and, after all, he had done his job. So the whole thing was a complete waste, even more of a waste for the poor devils than I had thought it would be.

The old man from Rhodesia was about Lerice's father's size, so she gave him one of her father's old suits and he went back home rather better off, for the winter, than he had come. ❖ C

WORDS TO KNOW **attenuated** (ə-tĕn′yo͞o-ā′tĭd) *adj.* slender; thin **attenuate** *v.*

1298

Teaching Options

Informal Assessment

STORY MAP Ask students to create a story map charting the events in "Six Feet of the Country." Remind them to include the story's elements—characters, setting, and plot—in the map.

RUBRIC

3 Full Accomplishment Students accurately identify all narrative elements and place important events in order.

2 Substantial Accomplishment Students list most narrative elements and place most important events in order.

1 Little or Partial Accomplishment Students are unable to identify most narrative elements and omit important events.

Connect to the Literature

1. **What Do You Think?** How did you react to the ending of this story? Share your impressions with your classmates.

Comprehension Check
- What happens to Petrus's brother?
- What does Petrus ask the narrator to do for him?
- How does Petrus's father know that the wrong body is in the coffin?

Think Critically

2. **ACTIVE READING PREDICTING** Get together with a classmate and compare the **predictions** you each wrote down in your  READER'S NOTEBOOK with what actually happens in the story. How accurate were your predictions? With your partner, discuss the clues and information you used to make your predictions. What helped you the most?
3. Could the **narrator** have done anything differently in dealing with the mix-up of the corpses?
4. How would you describe the relationship between the narrator and Lerice?

   THINK ABOUT
   - how he describes their marriage
   - each **character's** values and interests
   - the effect of this incident on their relationship
5. What do you consider the most powerful **conflict** in this story? Give reasons for your opinion.
6. What do you think of the narrator's comment, in the last sentence of the story, that the old man "went back home rather better off . . . than he had come"?

Extend Interpretations

7. **Different Perspectives** Think about the events in the story from Petrus's perspective. How do you think he feels when he discovers that his brother's body is not in the coffin? How do you think he views the narrator? Support your answers with details from the story.
8. **Connect to Life** Despite poverty and extreme hardship, Petrus and his neighbors are resourceful, strong, and supportive to one another. Do you think it is possible to form such a close-knit group in contemporary American society? Why or why not?

Literary Analysis

POINT OF VIEW "Six Feet of the Country" is narrated from the **point of view** of the main character. All we know about the characters and the story's events is based on his observations and thoughts, which may be colored or distorted by his personal perspective. Notice the narrator's attitude toward nonwhites in the following observation:

They're so seldom on the giving rather than the receiving side, poor devils, that they don't really know how to hand money to a white man.

The comment reveals the narrator's narrow view of the world. He doesn't seem to realize that people like Petrus receive very little and are constantly "giving."

Cooperative Learning Activity With a small group of classmates, choose a passage that has a particularly strong effect on you. Then rewrite the passage, telling the events from a **third-person point of view.** Discuss the two versions. Why do you think Gordimer chose to use the **first-person point of view?**

REVIEW IMAGERY **Imagery** refers to the words and phrases that create vivid sensory experiences for the reader. Notice how the following description appeals to several senses:

And there I am, taking some pretty girl and her young husband stumbling down to our river-bank, the girl catching her stockings on the mealie-stooks and stepping over cow-turds humming with jewel-green flies. . . .

How does the imagery in the story affect your impressions of the characters and events?

Extend Interpretations

Different Perspectives Possible Responses: Petrus's gestures show that he is horrified, frustrated, and heartbroken that after all that effort and money, they still don't have his brother's body; the fact that Petrus stops responding to the narrator's assurances that the body will be found shows that he is disappointed in the narrator.

Connect to Life Possible Responses: Some students may say that the demands of work, the distractions of TV, and individual transportation would keep contemporary Americans from forming such a close-knit community; others may cite examples of close-knit communities based on neighborhoods, workplaces, churches, or other groups.

GUIDING STUDENT RESPONSE

Connect to the Literature

1. **What Do You Think?**
   Guidelines for student response: Students might come up with alternate endings for the story as a way of testing their reactions to the ending provided by Gordimer.

Comprehension Check
- He dies of pneumonia. The narrator calls the health authorities, and they take the body and bury it.
- Petrus asks the narrator to get the body back so he can bury it.
- The body is too heavy.

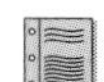 Use Selection Quiz in **Unit Seven Resource Book** p. 51.

Think Critically

2. Accept all reasonable responses.
3. Possible Responses: Yes, he could have been more insistent that the government find the right body; no, the authorities lost the body, and no amount of pressure by the narrator would have helped.
4. Possible Responses: strained; fraught with misunderstanding
5. Possible Responses: the conflict between Petrus and a society that views him as inferior; the conflict between the unfeeling narrator and the people around him
6. Possible Responses: It reflects the narrator's insensitivity to situation; it is ludicrous to think that a suit of clothes could comfort a bereaved father.

Literary Analysis

Cooperative Learning Activity Gordimer chose to use the first-person point of view to show how those who look down on other ethnic groups think; she wanted to show that the self-justifications of such people are wrong.

Review Imagery The imagery makes the events seem real; it shows the reader a reality colored by the narrator's perspective.

Writing Options

1. **Story Review** Remind students that the narrator is an unreliable observer and recorder of events. Encourage them to examine the behavior of Petrus and his father to find details that demonstrate the writer's respect for other cultures.
2. **Memo for the Teacher** Ask students to consider what information the story conveys about South Africa and apartheid that cannot be found in a textbook.
3. **Letter to the Authorities** Encourage students to mention in the letter all relevant information from the story, such as the money paid and the government's blunder.

Activities & Explorations

1. **Monument Design** Encourage students to use pictures, symbols, and designs that capture the plight of black South Africans living under apartheid.
2. **Improvised Dialogue** Before they improvise their dialogue, students might wish to consider how each character reacts to the plight of Petrus and his family.
3. **Character Portrait** Encourage students to take into consideration not only the character's physical description, but also the character's personality traits.

Inquiry & Research

1. **New Leader** Students might work in small groups to locate and summarize articles about South Africa. One student might do the research, another might write the summary, and a third might present the information to the class in the form of an oral report.
2. **On the Map** Encourage students to use different colors and symbols to represent different features. A legend accompanying the map should explain these symbols. Students should also draw their maps to scale and provide a mileage scale.

Art Connection

Mood in Art The processions are the same in that they are both slow and dignified; the order of the painting is very different from the disorder of the procession in the story after the discovery.

Writing Options

1. **Story Review** Nadine Gordimer has been praised for her ability to convey the importance of respecting other cultures. Write a critical review of "Six Feet of the Country" in which you explain how the story demonstrates this idea. Place the review in your **Working Portfolio.**
2. **Memo for the Teacher** Compose a memo to a history teacher, recommending that Gordimer's story be required reading for a unit on South Africa.
3. **Letter to the Authorities** Write a letter to the South African health authorities, demanding that the body of Petrus's brother be found.

Activities & Explorations

1. **Monument Design** Create a design for a monument to Petrus's brother, symbolizing the plight of his family and others like them. ~ **ART**
2. **Improvised Dialogue** With a classmate, improvise a dialogue in which the narrator and Lerice, after the old man's departure, talk over the events of the story. Try to convey the nature of their marital relationship, as well as the reactions of each to the events. ~ **SPEAKING AND LISTENING**
3. **Character Portrait** Choose one of the main characters of the story—the narrator, Lerice, Petrus, or Petrus's father—and draw a portrait of the character. ~ **ART**

Inquiry & Research

1. **New Leader** As a result of the April 1994 election in South Africa, in which blacks were permitted to vote for the first time, Nelson Mandela became the leader of the nation. Use the *Readers' Guide to Periodical Literature* to locate recent articles on Mandela and events in South Africa. Summarize the articles and share the information with the class.

More Online: Research Starter
www.mcdougallittell.com

2. **On the Map** Using a reliable atlas as a resource, draw a map of South Africa, outlining its four provinces and highlighting the one in which this story is set. Be sure to indicate the main cities and physical features of each province.

Art Connection

Mood in Art What mood is conveyed by *Funeral Procession,* the painting on page 1296? How does the mood in the painting compare with that created by the procession described in the story—both before and after the terrible discovery?

Teaching Options

Mini Lesson **Grammar**

ELLIPTICAL CLAUSE OF COMPARISON

Instruction An elliptical clause is an adverb clause from which a word or words have been omitted. One type of elliptical clause is the elliptical clause of comparison in which two people or things are compared using *than* or *as*. Often the verb or the subject and verb are omitted in an elliptical clause that shows a comparison.

Activity Write the following sentences on the chalkboard.

"... the farm is beautiful in a way I had almost forgotten—especially ... when I ... see ... the lucerne field brilliant as window-dresser's grass ..."

"Out in the country, even ten miles out, life is better than that."

"I had not seen a dead man since the war. ... I felt like the others—extraneous, useless."

Have students identify each elliptical clause of comparison and add the word or words that are

Vocabulary in Action

EXERCISE A: SYNONYMOUS PHRASES For each phrase in the first column, write the letter of the synonymous phrase in the second column.

1. **laconic** account
2. idiotic chorus
3. manageable sibling
4. infatuated faltering
5. pure pigment
6. **stint** the stallion
7. **expostulate** on the way
8. permeate with sadness
9. **attenuated** agent
10. variety of unnecessary things

a. dispute en route
b. **untainted** paint
c. short report
d. **inane** refrain
e. delicate delegate
f. **enamored** stammering
g. **submissive** sister
h. **imbue** with the blues
i. **extraneous** miscellany
j. underfeed the steed

EXERCISE B Work with a partner to come up with an appropriate phrase—such as "**extraneous** details" or "**inane** chatter"—for each vocabulary word. Then challenge another pair of students to compete with each other to guess one of the phrases, allowing them to suggest letters one by one (as in the game hangman or the TV show *Wheel of Fortune).* When one has guessed the phrase, compete with your partner to guess a phrase that they have written.

WORDS TO KNOW			
	attenuated	imbue	submissive
	enamor	inane	untainted
	expostulate	laconic	
	extraneous	stint	

Building Vocabulary

For an in-depth lesson on how to use a thesaurus to find a word's synonyms, see page 574.

Nadine Gordimer

1923–

Other Works
Burger's Daughter
July's People
Jump and Other Stories

Solitary Writer Nadine Gordimer is known for her beautifully crafted novels and short stories dealing with themes of exile, alienation, and life's missed opportunities. Born into a white middle-class family in the Transvaal province of South Africa, she spent much of her childhood in solitude, which she relieved by visiting her local library. She began to write while still a child, publishing her first short story at the age of 15.

Reflections on Society At first Gordimer concentrated on writing short stories, but as her subject matter grew increasingly complex, she turned to the novel. Almost from the beginning, critics noted her precise ear for spoken language, her sensitivity to the rhythm of the spoken word, her keen sense of social satire, and the strong moral purpose of her work. Since much of her writing is set in South Africa, her characters have inevitably been shaped by the political situation there; yet even as she has used her talents and influence to oppose apartheid, she has refused to let her writing become propaganda. Instead, she has said, she strives simply to portray the society in which she lives: "I thrust my hand as deep as it will go, deep into the life around me, and I write about what comes up."

Accolades and Achievements In 1974 Gordimer won the Booker Prize for her novel *The Conservationist,* and in 1991 she received the Nobel Prize in literature. She has been called "one of the most gifted practitioners of the short story anywhere in English."

Author Activity

Building Character Read a short story by Nadine Gordimer that takes place after the abolition of apartheid laws. Compare the characters in the story with those in "Six Feet of the Country." In what ways has the relationship between whites and blacks changed in the more recent story? What, if anything, has not changed?

Vocabulary in Action

Exercise A

1. c
2. d
3. g
4. f
5. b
6. j
7. a
8. h
9. e
10. i

Exercise B

Phrases will vary.

Author Activity

Building Character If students are interested in looking at a longer work of Gordimer's, you might suggest *The House Gun.* Students may also look for the address of Nadine Gordimer's publishers and write a letter to the author.

missing from the clause. *(as window-dresser's grass is brilliant; than that is; like the others felt)*

Exercise Ask students to identify the elliptical clause in each sentence and add the word(s) that are missing or understood.

1. I think Lerice is more compassionate in the story than the narrator. *(than the narrator is compassionate)*
2. She seems to like Petrus better than him. *(than she likes him [the narrator])*
3. She seems to like Petrus better than he. *(than he [the narrator] likes Petrus)*
4. Petrus collects as much money as possible from all the workers. *(as it is possible for him to collect)*
5. Petrus's feelings mean less to the narrator than to her. *(than they mean to her)*

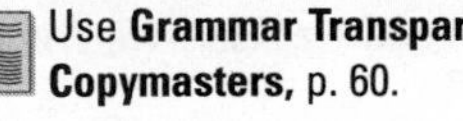

Use **Grammar Transparencies and Copymasters,** p. 60.

Use McDougal Littell's ***Language Network*** for more instruction and practice in elliptical clauses.

OVERVIEW

Objectives

1. appreciate and understand an **essay (Literary Analysis)**
2. distinguish between **informative** and **persuasive essays (Literary Analysis)**
3. **determine main ideas and supporting details (Active Reading)**

Summary

Allende explains that her first novel began as a letter to her grandfather, which she wrote for a full year without any plan and which she continued to write after her grandfather's death. Through the process of writing her first novel, she discovered that writing makes life more comprehensible and the world more tolerable for her. Another reason to write, she adds, is to preserve memories. The novel is the form most suited to this task for Latin American writers, who draw on such rich and varied sources of contrast and violence in their own land. Allende concludes that, in times of crisis and grave social inequality in Latin America, writing is an act of hope.

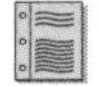 Use **Unit Seven Resource Book,** p. 47 for additional support.

Thematic Link

Allende explains that the process of writing helps her to live with ongoing **cultural conflicts** in Latin America as well as to celebrate Latin American culture.

5-Minute Warm-Up

Daily Language SkillBuilder

Have students **proofread** the display sentences on page 1189k and write them correctly. The sentences also appear on Transparency 36 of **Grammar Transparencies and Copymasters.**

Preteaching Vocabulary

If you would like to preteach the WORDS TO KNOW for this selection, use the Mini Lesson p. 1304.

from Writing as an Act of Hope

Essay by ISABEL ALLENDE (ä-yĕn′dā)

Comparing Literature of the World

Politics and Literature Across Cultures

"Six Feet of the Country" and *from* "Writing as an Act of Hope" Both Gordimer and Allende write about the social, political, and economic inequalities in their homeland. In "Six Feet of the Country," Gordimer uses a white man's biased perspective to reveal the injustices perpetuated by apartheid in South Africa. In the excerpt from "Writing as an Act of Hope," Allende examines what she calls the "contrasts" and violence in Latin America.

Points of Comparison As you read Allende's essay, compare her observations of the people and conditions in Latin America with those shown in Gordimer's story.

Build Background

A Woman's Voice Like South African literature, the literature of Latin America—where political unrest and economic hardship have been facts of life during much of the past century—is characterized by a good deal of social commentary. Since the 19th century, many Latin American writers, even those living in exile elsewhere, have had a strong reason for writing—to speak out about the social and political problems of their homelands. Until recently, however, the handling of such issues was the exclusive domain of male writers. In the region's male-dominated culture, female writers were discouraged from engaging in political or intellectual commentary, even in fiction. It was the Chilean author Isabel Allende who, in the 1980s, became the first Latin American female to produce a widely read novel that focuses on the effects of social and political turmoil.

Allende's writing is inspired principally by her Chilean roots and her family's experiences. In all of her novels, she skillfully interweaves **realism** and **fantasy**—so much so that she herself claims to find it difficult to distinguish reality from the inventions of her mind in her writing.

 **LaserLinks: Background for Reading**
Cultural Connection

WORDS TO KNOW
Vocabulary Preview

cataclysm	narcissistic
exorcising	pathological
hyperbole	pretension
illusory	rancor
imperialist	repression

Focus Your Reading

LITERARY ANALYSIS ESSAY An **essay** is a brief work of nonfiction that offers an opinion on a subject. The writer of an essay may seek to express ideas and feelings, to analyze, to inform, to entertain, or to persuade. In an **informative essay,** the writer's purpose is to reveal information on a subject about which he or she is particularly knowledgeable or concerned. In a **persuasive essay,** the writer's intent is to persuade readers to adopt a particular opinion or to perform a certain action. As you read Allende's essay, try to determine whether it is informative or persuasive.

ACTIVE READING DETERMINING MAIN IDEAS AND SUPPORTING DETAILS At the beginning of her essay, Allende states the two questions she will try to answer: "Why do I write?" and "Who do I write for?" The answers to these questions can help you determine the essay's **main ideas** and identify the **supporting details** for each idea.

READER'S NOTEBOOK As you read the excerpt from Allende's essay, write down all the answers you can find for each question.

1302 UNIT SEVEN PART 2: CULTURE AND CONFLICT

LESSON RESOURCES

UNIT SEVEN RESOURCE BOOK, pp. 47–51

ASSESSMENT RESOURCES

Formal Assessment, pp. 245–246

Teacher's Guide to Assessment and Portfolio Use

Test Generator

SKILLS TRANSPARENCIES AND COPYMASTERS

Literary Analysis
- Characteristics of the Essay, T11 (for Literary Analysis, p. 1302)

Reading and Critical Thinking
- Main Idea and Supporting Details, T12 (for Active Reading, p. 1302)

Grammar
- Avoiding Misplaced and Dangling Modifiers, T51 (for Mini Lesson, p. 1309)
- Avoiding Misplaced and Dangling Modifiers, C157 (for Mini Lesson, p. 1309)

Vocabulary
- Synonyms, C96 (for Mini Lesson, p. 1304)

Writing
- Literary Interpretation, C33 (for Writing Option 2, p. 1309)
- Compare-Contrast, C34 (for Writing Option 4, p. 1309)
- Autobiographical Incident, C36 (for Writing Option 3, p. 1309)

Communications
- Formal Presentations, T10 (for Activities & Explorations 1, p. 1309)

INTEGRATED TECHNOLOGY

Audio Library

LaserLinks
- Cultural Connection: Allende's Latin America. See **Teacher's SourceBook,** pp. 100–101.

Internet: Research Starter

Visit our website: www.mcdougallittell.com

FROM

Writing as an Act of Hope

ISABEL ALLENDE

In every interview during the last few years I encountered two questions that forced me to define myself as a writer and as a human being: Why do I write? And who do I write for? Tonight I will try to answer those questions.

In 1981, in Caracas, I put a sheet of paper in my typewriter and wrote the first sentence of *The House of the Spirits:* "Barabbas came to us by sea." At that moment I didn't know why I was doing it, or for whom.

TEACHING THE LITERATURE

Customizing Instruction

Students Acquiring English

Students may be challenged by Allende's extensive use of imagery. Call attention to difficult passages and explain their meaning.

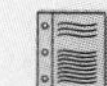

Use **Spanish Study Guide** for additional support, pp. 326–328.

Less Proficient Readers

Set a Purpose Invite students to discuss a favorite book or story. Why do they think the author wrote it? For whom did the author write it? Then have students read to find out what Allende discovered after she completed her first novel.

Gifted and Talented

Lead students to discuss whether they believe that writing can have any real effect on readers.

BLOCK SCHEDULING: MANAGING TIME

If your schedule requires that you cover the lesson objectives in a shorter time, use . . .

- Preparing to Read, p. 1302
- Thinking Through the Literature, p. 1308
- Vocabulary in Action, p. 1310

If you want to take advantage of longer class time, use . . .

- TE Teaching Options: Preteaching Vocabulary, p. 1304; Viewing and Representing, p. 1305; Cross Curricular Link, p. 1306; Informal Assessment, p. 1307; Grammar, p. 1309
- Choices & Challenges and Author Activity, pp. 1309–1310

Reading and Analyzing

Literary Analysis ESSAY

Set a Purpose Ask students to read to discover what Allende has expressed in the essay that would have been difficult to express in fiction.

Possible Response: She can express her motivations for writing and her opinions about her culture without them being confused with the motives and opinions of her fictional characters.

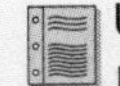
Use **Unit Seven Resource Book,** p. 49 for more exercises.

Active Reading

DETERMINING MAIN IDEAS AND SUPPORTING DETAILS

Remind students that the main idea may be stated at the beginning or end of a paragraph, or may even be unstated and have to be inferred from the supporting details. Suggest that as students read, they try to identify the main idea and supporting details of each paragraph. Have them describe how this text structure helps them understand the essay.

Use **Unit Seven Resource Book,** p. 48 for more practice.

Literary Analysis ESSAY

Ask students why they think Allende describes how she came to write her first novel.

Possible Response: She wants to convey the importance of writing as a way of preserving the past.

How did writing make Allende's life seem more comprehensible?

Possible Response: Writing forced her to realize and to organize what she wanted to say.

In fact, I assumed that no one would ever read it except my mother, who reads everything I write. I was not even conscious that I was writing a novel. I thought I was writing a letter—a spiritual letter to my grandfather, a formidable old patriarch,[1] whom I loved dearly. He had reached almost one hundred years of age and decided that he was too tired to go on living, so he sat in his armchair and refused to drink or eat, calling for Death, who was kind enough to take him very soon.

I wanted to bid him farewell, but I couldn't go back to Chile, and I knew that calling him on the telephone was useless, so I began this letter. I wanted to tell him that he could go in peace because all his memories were with me. I had forgotten nothing. I had all his anecdotes, all the characters of the family, and to prove it I began writing the story of Rose, the fiancée my grandfather had had, who is called Rose the Beautiful in the book. She really existed; she's not a copy from García Márquez,[2] as some people have said.

1 For a year I wrote every night with no hesitation or plan. Words came out like a violent torrent. I had thousands of untold words stuck in my chest, threatening to choke me. The long silence of exile was turning me to stone; I needed to open a valve and let the river of secret words find a way out. At the end of that year there were five hundred pages on my table; it didn't look like a letter anymore. On the other hand, my grandfather had died long before, so the spiritual message had already reached him. So I thought, "Well, maybe in this way I can tell some other people about him, and about my country, and about my family and myself." So I just organized it a little bit, tied the manuscript with a pink ribbon for luck, and took it to some publishers.

The spirit of my grandmother was protecting the book from the very beginning, so it was refused everywhere in Venezuela. Nobody wanted it—it was too long; I was a woman; nobody knew me. So I sent it by mail to Spain, and the book was published there. It had reviews, and it was translated and distributed in other countries.

2 In the process of writing the anecdotes of the past, and recalling the emotions and pains of my fate, and telling part of the history of my country, I found that life became more comprehensible and the world more tolerable. I felt that my roots had been recovered and that during that patient exercise of daily writing I had also recovered my own soul. I felt at that time that writing was unavoidable—that I couldn't keep away from it. Writing is such a pleasure; it is always a private orgy, creating and recreating the world according to my own laws, fulfilling in those pages all my dreams and exorcising some of my demons.

But that is a rather simple explanation. There are other reasons for writing.

Six years and three books have passed since *The House of the Spirits*. Many things have changed for me in that time. I can no longer pretend to be naïve, or elude questions, or find refuge in irony. Now I am constantly confronted

1. **patriarch** (pā′trē-ärk′): a respected old man, especially one who is head of a family, clan, or tribe.
2. **García Márquez** (gär-sē′ə mär′kĕs): Gabriel García Márquez (1928–), a Colombian novelist and short story writer.

WORDS TO KNOW **exorcising** (ĕk′sôr-sī′zĭng) *adj.* driving out (an evil spirit) by prayer, ceremony, or command **exorcise** *v.*

Teaching Options

Preteaching Vocabulary

SYNONYMS Call students' attention to the list of WORDS TO KNOW. Remind students that no two words have exactly the same meaning, but may have meanings that are similar.

Model Sentence

Gentle winds often blew over the island.

Instruction

- Write the model sentence on the chalkboard.
- Ask volunteers to name synonyms for *gentle.*
- Have students look up the word *gentle* and its synonyms in a dictionary.
- Discuss shades of meaning among these words.

Exercise Ask students to match the WORDS TO KNOW with their synonyms.

1. cataclysm	a. overstatement
2. hyperbole	b. affectation
3. illusory	c. diseased
4. pathological	d. disaster
5. pretension	e. hallucinatory

Use **Unit Seven Resource Book,** p. 50 for more practice.

Sin título [Untitled] (1985), Rocío Maldonado. Acrylic with collaged elements on canvas with painted frame, 69″ × 85″ × 6″, courtesy of Gallery OMR, Mexico City.

Customizing Instruction

Students Acquiring English

1 Explain to students that in this passage Allende is comparing the ideas and emotions that she needed to express to water trapped in a confined space ("violent torrent"; "river of secret words") and to something caught in her throat ("untold words stuck in my chest").

Less Proficient Readers

2 Have students summarize why Allende enjoys writing.

Possible Response: When she writes, she can make the world the way she wants it to be.

Multiple Learning Styles

Visual Learners

Have students sketch images suggested by the essay. Encourage them to draw either an abstract or a realistic interpretation of the images.

Mini Lesson: Viewing and Representing

***Sin título [Untitled]* by Rocío Maldonado**

ART APPRECIATION Maldonado was born in Mexico in 1951. Critics have commented that her canvases suggest puppet shows or trunks full of fragmented memories. Her collages include a variety of textures, such as cardboard, cloth, and cord.

Instruction Point out that some of the images are cut off by the edge of the canvas. Ask students what effect this technique has.

Possible Responses: It encourages you to complete the artwork in your mind, drawing you into the artistic process. It suggests violence—that the images have been sliced and cut off by the artist.

Application Allende says many people think she makes up fantastic events for her novels, but that she is just reflecting the reality in which she lives. Ask students what reality they think Maldonado might be reflecting in *Sin título.* How does this reality compare to the one Allende describes in her essay?

Possible Responses: In Maldonado's representation of reality, things are disconnected and out of control; everything is mixed together. Both Allende and Maldonado draw on their memories to describe the past.

Reading and Analyzing

Literary Analysis: SIMILE

A Ask students to identify the simile in this sentence.
Answer: Allende compares a novel to an open window.

Ask what this comparison suggests about writing a novel.
Possible Response: Just as a window may reveal "an infinite landscape," anything can be included in a novel.

Reading Skills and Strategies: CONTRASTING

B Ask students to discuss the contrast that Allende uses to describe the opposing realities of Latin America.
Answer: Allende describes two faces—one "legal," the other "dark and tragic."

What idea does Allende suggest by using this technique?
Possible Response: By saying that the legal face has "a certain pretension," she suggests that the dark, tragic face is more real.

C Ask students to explain this contrast between two worlds.
Possible Response: Officials put a deceptively positive light on conditions in their countries, while the truth is that people are suffering there.

Literary Analysis ESSAY

D Ask students what opinion Allende is trying to persuade the reader to adopt in this passage.
Possible Response: Serious writers have an obligation to provide social commentary with the goal of helping their fellow human beings.

by my readers, and they can be very tough. It's not enough to write in a state of trance, overwhelmed by the desire to tell a story. One has to be responsible for each word, each idea. Be very
1 careful: the written word cannot be erased. . . .

Maybe the most important reason for writing is to prevent the erosion of time, so that memories will not be blown away by the wind. Write to register history, and name each thing. Write what should not be forgotten. But then, why write novels? Probably because I come from Latin America, a land of crazy, illuminated people, of geological and political cataclysms—a land so large and profound, so beautiful and frightening, that only novels can describe its fascinating complexity.

A A novel is like a window, open to an infinite landscape. In a novel we can put all the interrogations, we can register the most extravagant, evil, obscene, incredible or magnificent facts—which, in Latin America, are not hyperbole, because that is the dimension of our reality. In a novel we can give an illusory order to chaos. We
2 can find the key to the labyrinth of history. We can make excursions into the past, to try to understand the present and dream the future. In a novel we can use everything: testimony, chronicle, essay, fantasy, legend, poetry and other devices that might help us to decode the mysteries of our world and discover our true identity.

For a writer who nourishes himself or herself on images and passions, to be born in a fabulous continent is a privilege. In Latin America we don't have to stretch our imaginations. Critics in Europe and the United States often stare in disbelief at Latin American books, asking how the authors dare to invent those incredible lies of young women who fly to heaven wrapped in linen sheets; of black emperors who build fortresses with cement and the blood of emasculated bulls; of outlaws who die of hunger in the Amazon with bags full of emeralds on their backs; of ancient tyrants who order their mothers to be flogged naked in front of the troops and modern tyrants who order children to be tortured in front of their parents; of hurricanes and earthquakes that turn the world upside down; of revolutions made with machetes, bullets, poems and kisses; of hallucinating landscapes where reason is lost.

It is very hard to explain to critics that these things are not a product of our pathological imaginations. They are written in our history; we can find them every day in our newspapers. We hear them in the streets; we suffer them frequently in our own lives. It is impossible to speak of
Latin America without mentioning violence. We 3
inhabit a land of terrible contrasts and we have to survive in times of great violence.

Contrast and violence, two excellent ingredients for literature, although for us, citizens of that reality, life is always suspended from a very fragile thread.

The first, the most naked and visible form of violence is the extreme poverty of the majority, in contrast with the extreme wealth of the very few. In my continent two opposite realities coexist. One is a legal face, more or less comprehensible and with a certain pretension to dignity and civilization. The other is a dark and tragic face, which we do not like to show but which is always threatening us. There is an apparent B

WORDS TO KNOW
cataclysm (kăt'ə-klĭz'əm) *n.* a violent change or sudden upheaval
hyperbole (hī-pûr'bə-lē) *n.* an exaggeration used for emphasis or effect
illusory (ĭ-lo͞o'sə-rē) *adj.* unreal; deceptive
pathological (păth'ə-lŏj'ĭ-kəl) *adj.* diseased; unhealthy
pretension (prĭ-tĕn'shən) *n.* a claim or aspiration

1306

Teaching Options

Cross Curricular Link History

CHILEAN REVOLUTION From the 16th century to the early 19th century, Chile was a Spanish colony. Then, in 1808, Napoleon Bonaparte invaded Spain and seized power. Chileans had been waiting for just such an opportune moment. The citizens of Chile revolted against Spain and established their own government. However, this government itself was soon overthrown by soldiers that remained loyal to Spain. Bernardo O'Higgins, one of the leaders of the revolt and the son of an Irish immigrant, escaped to Argentina. He returned with an Argentine army and defeated the Spanish loyalists in 1817. O'Higgins, the first leader of the independent nation of Chile, established schools and a library, abolished titles of nobility, and tried to weaken the power of large landholders.

world and a real world—nice neighborhoods where blond children play on their bicycles and servants walk elegant dogs, and other neighborhoods, of slums and garbage, where dark children play naked with hungry mutts. There are offices of marble and steel where young executives discuss the stock market, and forgotten villages where people still live and die as they did in the Middle Ages. There is a world of fiction created by the official discourse, and another world of blood and pain and love, where we have struggled for centuries. C

In Latin America we all survive on the borderline of those two realities. Our fragile democracies exist as long as they don't interfere with imperialist interests. Most of our republics are dependent on submissiveness. Our institutions and laws are inefficient. Our armed forces often act as mercenaries[3] for a privileged social group that pays tribute to transnational enterprises. We are living in the worst economic, political and social crisis since the conquest of America by the Spaniards. There are hardly two or three leaders in the whole continent. Social inequality is greater every day, and to avoid an outburst of public rancor, repression also rises day by day. Crime, drugs, misery and ignorance are present in every Latin American country, and the military is an immediate threat to society and civil governments. We try to keep straight faces while our feet are stuck in a swamp of violence, exploitation, corruption, the terror of the state and the terrorism of those who take arms against the status quo.

BUT Latin America is also a land of hope and friendship and love. Writers navigate in these agitated waters. They don't live in ivory towers; they cannot remove themselves from this brutal reality. In such circumstances there is no time and no wish for narcissistic literature. Very few of our writers contemplate their navel in self-centered monologue. The majority want desperately to communicate.

I feel that writing is an act of hope, a sort of communion with our fellow men. The writer of good will carries a lamp to illuminate the dark corners. Only that, nothing more—a tiny beam of light to show some hidden aspect of reality, to help decipher and understand it and thus to initiate, if possible, a change in the conscience of some readers. This kind of writer is not seduced by the mermaid's voice of celebrity or tempted by exclusive literary circles. He has both feet planted firmly on the ground and walks hand in hand with the people in the streets. He knows that the lamp is very small and the shadows are immense. This makes him humble. ❖ D

3. **mercenaries** (mûr′sə-nĕr′ēz): soldiers who will do anything for money.

WORDS TO KNOW

imperialist (ĭm-pîr′ē-ə-lĭst′) *adj.* pertaining to a government's domination of the economic or political affairs of a weaker nation

rancor (răng′kər) *n.* bitter resentment; ill will

repression (rĭ-prĕsh′ən) *n.* the act of subduing or keeping down by force

narcissistic (när′sĭ-sĭs′tĭk) *adj.* characterized by excessive self-love or self-involvement

1307

Customizing Instruction

Gifted and Talented

1 Ask students to discuss what Allende might mean when she says that "the written word cannot be erased."

Possible Response: Once an idea has been put in writing, it cannot be taken back; it is there for all to see.

Ask students if they agree with Allende's statement and to give examples to support their opinion.

Students Acquiring English

2 Explain that a labyrinth is any confusing or complicated state of affairs.

3 Explain that "violence" refers here not only to harmful physical force but also to injustice and inequality.

Mini Lesson: Informal Assessment

WRITE A PARAGRAPH Ask students to write a paragraph analyzing Allende's use of contrast to describe Latin American life. Tell students to cite several examples of her use of contrast and to explain why she uses this technique. Encourage students to consider the following questions: What does Allende's use of contrast clarify about Latin America? What ideas does the technique help emphasize? What emotional response, if any, does Allende's use of contrast elicit?

RUBRIC

3 Full Accomplishment Response reflects full understanding of why Allende uses contrast in her description and cites several specific examples of use of contrast.

2 Substantial Accomplishment Response may cite one or more examples of Allende's use of contrast, but reflects only general understanding of why technique is used.

1 Little or Partial Accomplishment Response shows little understanding of how and why contrast is used.

GUIDING STUDENT RESPONSE

Connect to the Literature

1. What Do You Think?
Students can compare and contrast their responses to Allende's ideas about the writing life and the responsibilities of the writer.

Comprehension Check
- She wanted to record her memories of her grandfather.
- Possible Response: She uses the words "fabulous continent," "a land of terrible contrasts," and "a land of hope and friendship and love."
- She sees their role as shedding light on the dark corners of Latin American life and initiating change.

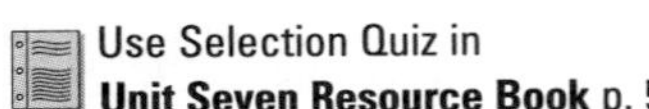
Use Selection Quiz in **Unit Seven Resource Book** p. 51.

Think Critically

2. Possible Responses: Writing makes life more comprehensible and the world more tolerable; she feels that the novel can record the truth, even if the truth is multifaceted; therefore, it can "give an illusory order to chaos." Latin America is a land full of such contrasting truths. Most people live in extreme poverty while a minority live in luxury. Allende believes that writing is an act of hope in that a writer's words may open the eyes of the reader to the injustices of the world. After students identify the main ideas and supporting details, have them summarize the essay.
3. Possible Responses: moral, considerate, conscientious, and humane.
4. Possible Responses: sincerity, courage, humanity; writers who give hope to their readers are not tempted by fame or literary success.
5. Possible Responses: Yes, she believes that a piece of writing should affect its audience in some way; no, it is enough to create and re-create the world according to one's own laws.
6. Accept all reasonable, well-supported responses.

Thinking through the LITERATURE

Connect to the Literature

1. What Do You Think? Discuss your response to this excerpt from "Writing as an Act of Hope" with your classmates.

Comprehension Check
- Why did Allende write her first novel?
- What words does she use to describe Latin America?
- What role does she see for Latin American writers?

Think Critically

2. ACTIVE READING DETERMINING MAIN IDEAS AND SUPPORTING DETAILS With a partner, discuss the answers you wrote down in your  READER'S NOTEBOOK. Based on these answers, what do you think are the **main ideas** of Allende's essay? What **details** does the writer use to support her ideas?

3. On the basis of this **essay,** how would you describe Allende?

THINK ABOUT
- her reasons for writing
- her relationship with her family
- her feelings of responsibility to her readers

4. What qualities do you think Allende most admires in other writers? Cite evidence to support your answer.

5. Do you think Allende feels that it is important for a writer to be able to answer the questions "Why do I write?" and "Whom do I write for?" Give reasons to support your answer.

6. Does reading this essay make you want to read Allende's fiction? Why or why not?

Extend Interpretations

7. **Connect to Life** What "hidden aspect of reality" do you think should be exposed in American society? Which writers have tried to shed some light on the problem?

8. **Points of Comparison** Compare Allende's description of the contrast between rich and poor in Latin America with Gordimer's depiction of the narrator and Petrus in "Six Feet of the Country." What connections do you see between the realities in Latin America and South Africa?

Literary Analysis

ESSAY An **essay**—whether intended to inform, to persuade, or to entertain—serves to express the opinions of its writer. Allende's essay contains aspects of both an **informative** and a **persuasive essay.** In the following passage from the essay, the author tells the reader that violence is a fact of life in Latin America:

The first, the most naked and visible form of violence is the extreme poverty of the majority, in contrast with the extreme wealth of the very few.

In this next passage, Allende tries to convince the reader that a writer should try to "illuminate the dark corners":

Only that, nothing more—a tiny beam of light to show some hidden aspect of reality, to help decipher and understand it and thus to initiate, if possible, a change in the conscience of some readers.

Notice that throughout her essay, Allende uses facts, reasons, and examples that support her opinions.

Cooperative Learning Activity Get together with a small group of classmates to discuss the following question: Would you describe Allende's essay as primarily informative or as primarily persuasive? Back up your opinion with reasons. Then decide what details would need to be added to make the essay more informative or more persuasive.

Extend Interpretations

Connect to Life Have students research a social or political issue that they feel strongly about. Then encourage them to write an article on the issue, highlighting its positive aspects.

Points of Comparison Possible Response: In both South Africa and Latin America, there is a huge gulf between the rich and the poor, the powerful and the powerless, the educated and the unschooled.

Literary Analysis

Cooperative Learning Activity Some students may indicate that the essay is informative, citing the information Allende reveals about her motivations; others may find the essay persuasive, since Allende tries to convince the reader that a writer has an obligation to humanity. Some students may analyze the essay for completeness and not add details. Others may find details necessary.

Writing Options

1. **Explanatory Paragraph** In a paragraph, identify your favorite passage in this selection, giving reasons for your choice.

2. **Letter to Allende** Write a letter to Isabel Allende, in which you evaluate the ideas expressed in her essay. Tell Allende whether or not you agree with her views on the role of a writer as a social critic. Place the letter in your **Working Portfolio.**

3. **Anecdote About a Memory** Write an anecdote—either fictional or nonfictional—in which you capture an important memory involving a parent or grandparent. Write a brief introduction, addressed to the older person, telling the person what you are trying to do.

4. **Points of Comparison** Write an essay explaining which selection—"Writing as an Act of Hope" or "Six Feet of the Country"—you think presents the social, political, and economic inequalities of the writer's homeland more forcefully and convincingly. Cite evidence from the selections to support your opinions.

Activities & Explorations

1. **Nomination Speech** Deliver a speech in which you nominate Allende for an award on the basis of her ideas about writing. ~ **SPEAKING AND LISTENING**

2. **Collage of Contrasts** Create a collage of pictures to illustrate some of the contrasts that, according to Allende's essay, exist in Latin America. ~ **ART**

3. **Poster Promoting Speech** "Writing as an Act of Hope" originated as a lecture that Allende gave at the New York Public Library—part of a series of lectures by writers on particular aspects of the craft of writing. Allende was one of a group of writers who were asked why they wrote political novels. Design a poster advertising Allende's speech, being sure to include all pertinent information and to make the poster interesting and eye-catching. ~ **ART**

Inquiry & Research

Allende's Home Work with a group of classmates to prepare an oral report on Chile, Allende's native country. Individual group members can investigate different aspects of Chile's culture and history—for example, its geography, its early history, the military coup of 1973, and the current political and social conditions in the country. Where appropriate, use slides, pictures, maps, charts, and graphs in presenting your report to the class.

More Online: Research Starter www.mcdougallittell.com

Art Connection

Illustrated Ideas Look at the painting on page 1305. What ideas or details in the essay does the painting help illustrate?

Writing Options

1. **Explanatory Paragraph** Encourage students to reread the essay looking for their favorite passage. Have them consider what about the passage appeals to them and why.
2. **Letter to Allende** Suggest that students note questions they would like to ask Allende and then organize these into a cohesive letter. Encourage students to mail their letters to Allende in care of her publisher.
3. **Anecdote About a Memory** Help students get started by having them make a list of the person's character traits. Suggest that they pick a specific trait and try to think of a story that illustrates it.
4. **Points of Comparison** Some students may say that "Writing as an Act of Hope" presents these issues more forcefully because it gives more information about them; other students may say that "Six Feet of the Country" presents these issues more forcefully because it allows the reader to become involved with characters who are affected by them.

Activities & Explorations

1. **Nomination Speech** Have students prepare and deliver a speech that nominates Allende and gives valid reasons for including her as a nominee.
2. **Collage of Contrasts** Encourage students to review the essay, jotting down the contrasts cited by Allende on a chart. They can then use the chart as they search for appropriate pictures for the collage.
3. **Poster Promoting Speech** Suggest that students include pictures, symbols, and colors that capture the essence of Allende's work in their poster.

Inquiry & Research

Allende's Home Each student in a group should be assigned a different aspect of Chile's culture and history to research. Invite groups to share their findings with the class.

Art Connection

Illustrated Ideas Possible responses: It helps to illustrate disconnection, violence, and a chaotic reality.

Mini Lesson Grammar

Avoiding Misplaced and Dangling Modifiers

Instruction When a modifier is separated from the word it modifies in such a way as to cause confusion, it is misplaced. A dangling modifier is one that does not seem to be related to any word in the sentence.

Activity Write the following sentences on the chalkboard.

For writing, Allende says that the most important reason is to prevent the erosion of time. *(misplaced; . . . the most important reason for writing is . . .)*

Writing every night for a year, Allende's book took shape. *(dangling; As Allende wrote every night for a year, her book took shape.)*

Have students tell whether the modifier in each sentence is misplaced or dangling. Then, ask them to rewrite the sentences.

Use **Grammar Transparencies and Copymasters,** p. 91.

Use McDougal Littell's ***Language Network*** for more instruction and practice in misplaced and dangling modifiers.

Vocabulary in Action

Exercise A
1. hyperbole
2. repression
3. rancor
4. cataclysm
5. imperialist

Exercise B
1. b
2. a
3. a
4. c
5. c

Vocabulary in Action

EXERCISE A: CONTEXT CLUES Write the word that best completes each sentence.

1. "The pen is mightier than the sword" is not a ________; it is quite true.
2. Thomas Paine's widely read pamphlet *Common Sense* spoke so harshly against British ________ of the American colonists that it helped to inspire the American Revolution.
3. The novel *Uncle Tom's Cabin,* written by an abolitionist, created so much antislavery ________ that it is considered one of the causes of the Civil War.
4. Not every change that a book or article may help to bring about is a ________; some are more gradual and subtle alterations of people's perceptions of reality.
5. Rudyard Kipling's writings, which made the British presence in India look both appealing and righteous, were influential in perpetuating Great Britain's ________ attitude toward its colonies.

EXERCISE B: ASSESSMENT PRACTICE Write the letter of the word that is a synonym of each boldfaced word.

1. **exorcise:** (a) maneuver, (b) expel, (c) glorify
2. **pretension:** (a) claim, (b) ability, (c) decision
3. **illusory:** (a) imaginary, (b) evasive, (c) flexible
4. **pathological:** (a) skillful, (b) lasting, (c) sick
5. **narcissistic:** (a) numb, (b) addictive, (c) self-centered

WORDS TO KNOW

cataclysm, exorcising, hyperbole, illusory, imperialist, narcissistic, pathological, pretension, rancor, repression

Building Vocabulary
For an in-depth study of context clues, see page 938.

Isabel Allende
1942–

Other Works
The House of the Spirits
Of Love and Shadows
Eva Luna
The Stories of Eva Luna

Family Ties Isabel Allende traveled extensively as a child. Born in Peru, she moved to Chile with her mother after her parents' divorce. Although she lost contact with her father, she remained close to his family—especially to her uncle, a prominent politician. After her mother remarried, the family moved again, first to Bolivia, then to Europe and the Middle East, and finally, when Allende was 15, back to Chile. Allende's mother nurtured her creativity by encouraging her to record all her thoughts in a notebook and to draw anything she wanted on a bedroom wall.

Upheaval and Exile A rebellious teenager, Allende quit school early, married, and eventually found a job as a journalist, writing and reporting for television and magazines. By the time she was 30, she felt settled and expected to spend the rest of her life in Chile, but a military coup in 1973 changed her plans dramatically. The Chilean government was overthrown, and Allende's uncle, who was then president, was assassinated. In spite of the widespread violence in Chile, she remained there for a time, secretly helping those who opposed the new regime. After her own life was threatened, however, she fled to Venezuela, where she lived in exile for 13 years before coming to the United States. She currently resides near San Francisco.

Body of Work Allende was in her late 30s before she started writing fiction. After gaining worldwide attention with her first novel, *The House of the Spirits,* she has continued to write in Spanish, but her work has been translated into 27 languages, including English. In 1994, she published an autobiography, entitled *Paula* in memory of her daughter who had died a year earlier.

Writing Workshop

Critical Review

Evaluating a literary work . . .

From Reading to Writing How do you decide what movies to see, what books to read, or what concerts to attend? You might read a **critical review,** an essay in which a writer expresses a personal opinion of a literary or artistic work by referring to some of the elements of that work. The word *critical* does not mean that the writer must find fault; it means that the writer evaluates a work based on certain criteria. (A)

For Your Portfolio

WRITING PROMPT Write a critical review of a literary work based on criteria you establish.

Purpose: To interpret and evaluate

Audience: Persons interested in the work you are reviewing

Basics in a Box

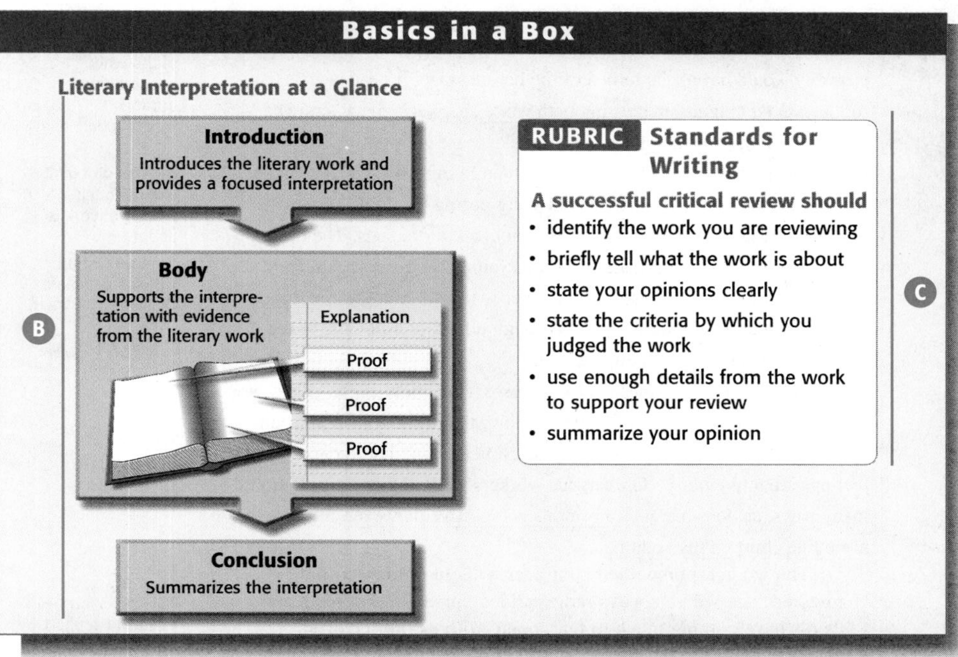

Literary Interpretation at a Glance
Introduction
Introduces the literary work and provides a focused interpretation
Body
Supports the interpretation with evidence from the literary work
Explanation
Proof
Proof
Proof
Conclusion
Summarizes the interpretation
B

RUBRIC Standards for Writing

A successful critical review should
- identify the work you are reviewing
- briefly tell what the work is about
- state your opinions clearly
- state the criteria by which you judged the work
- use enough details from the work to support your review
- summarize your opinion

(C)

LESSON RESOURCES

USING PRINT RESOURCES

Unit Seven Resource Book
- Prewriting, p. 52
- Drafting, p. 53
- Peer Response, p. 54
- Revising, Editing, and Proofreading, p. 55
- Student Models, pp. 56–62
- Rubric, p. 63

Writing Transparencies and Copymasters
- Writing Process Transparencies, pp. 1–4
- Writing Style Transparencies, p. 19
- Writing Template Copymasters, p. 32

USING MEDIA RESOURCES

LaserLinks
Writing Springboards
See Teacher's SourceBook p. 114 for bar codes.

Writing Coach CD-ROM

Visit our website:
www.mcdougallittell.com

For a complete view of Lesson Resources, see page 1189e.

Objectives
- write a Critical Review
- use a written text as a model for writing
- revise sentences using appositives
- place modifiers close to the words they modify

Introducing the Workshop

(A) **Critical Review** Explain that a critical review offers readers an analysis of a subject, such as a movie, play, concert, or book and suggests whether seeing it, listening to it, or reading it would be worthwhile. For instance, a critical review might evaluate a movie based on the following criteria: special effects, suspenseful plot, character development, and theme. Point out to students that every time they make judgments about the movies and television shows they watch and the books they read, they play the role of a critical reviewer.

Discuss reviews students have read in newspapers and magazines or heard on the radio. Ask why they read or listen to reviews. Point out that the skills they will learn in this workshop will help them establish criteria for evaluating a literary work. In turn, their literary review will inform others and help them decide whether or not to read a particular literary work.

Basics in a Box

(B) **Using the Graphic** The graphic suggests three important elements of a successful critical review: an introduction that identifies the work and states an opinion of it; a body that names the criteria for evaluation and tells how well the work satisfies those criteria; and a conclusion that summarizes the opinion and may make a recommendation about it.

(C) **Presenting the Rubric** To better understand the assignment, students can refer to the Standards for Writing a Successful Critical Review. You may wish to discuss with them the complete rubric, which describes several levels of proficiency.

You may remind students that you will use these standards to evaluate their writing.

Teaching the Lesson

Analyzing the Model

"Six Feet of the Country"

D Explain that the system of apartheid was an official policy of racial segregation established by law in the Republic of South Africa but is now abolished. Point out that in this review, the student writer is not directly evaluating apartheid itself but is evaluating a story about apartheid.

Have students read the student model and then discuss the Rubric in Action. Point out key words and phrases in the student model that correspond to the elements mentioned in the Rubric in Action.

2. Ask students to state the writer's criteria in their own words.
   Possible Response: The criteria is how effectively the writer illustrates the racial attitudes of her society.
3. Have students summarize the writer's opinion of the short story.
   Possible Response: The writer feels that the story succeeds because Gordimer does not oversimplify the characters and their racial attitudes but shows their complexities.
5. Ask students to evaluate the effectiveness of the evidence used to support the claim that the narrator believes the workers "are more like children than adults."
   Possible Response: The evidence is effective. The narrator condescendingly refers to his workers as "poor devils" whom he and his wife must protect, suggesting the narrator's parental attitude toward the workers. Lerice also treats the workers as dependents—even "babies"—when she doctors their illnesses.

Use McDougal Littell's ***Language Network,*** Chapter 19, for more instruction on writing a critical review.

To engage students visually, use **Power Presentation** 10, Critical Review.

Analyzing a Student Model

Ali Nagib
New Trier High School

"Six Feet of the Country"

"Six Feet of the Country" is a politically and personally based short story written by Nadine Gordimer. In the story, the author draws on her experience as a white woman during the time of apartheid in South Africa to examine the many flaws and injustices inherent in that system. Gordimer wrote this story before apartheid was ever significantly challenged. Because her society's racial attitudes are at the forefront of her story, the story must be judged on how effectively she illustrates them. Her story succeeds because, while bringing the problems of her society to light, she gives her characters very human dimensions. They are neither totally good nor totally evil but mixtures of good intentions, blindness to injustice, and petty concerns. Had Gordimer preached about the injustice of apartheid, people probably would have been turned off by her message. Instead, she uses subtlety and ambiguity in creating both white and black characters. She presents an engaging story—not a sermon. D

The main character, the narrator, is a man living with his wife on an isolated farmstead outside of Johannesburg during the 1950s. His wife manages the farm with the help of several black farmhands. The narrator commutes to Johannesburg and is home evenings and weekends. In the narrator, Gordimer has created a character with whom any white South African of the time could identify. Through him, Gordimer shows the attitudes of many white South Africans.

The narrator is by no means an oppressor. He is not a slave-owner, nor is he a cruel master. In fact, Gordimer shows that the scenario in South Africa was not treacherous, only unjust. Nonetheless, the narrator's true feelings are ambiguous. He treats his workers well, and he helps them in many ways, as does his wife. From his perspective, however, they are more like children than adults:

> [The workers] brew their sour beer without the fear of police raids. In fact, we've always rather prided ourselves that the poor devils have nothing much to fear, being with us; Lerice even keeps an eye on their children, with all the competence of a woman who has never had a child of her own, and she certainly doctors them all—children and adults—like babies whenever they happen to be sick.

RUBRIC IN ACTION

1. Identifies the work being reviewed
2. States the criteria
3. States a general opinion of the work based on the criteria
4. This writer begins to tell what the work is about.
   Another Option:
   - Give a complete summary of the work.
5. Uses short quotes to support the statements about the narrator's view of the workers

He acts within the system of apartheid and believes in its values. In response to dealing with the dead body of Petrus's brother, the narrator laments, "Now, I'm the one who'll have to do all the dirty work, I suppose." He is obviously annoyed with the system, but he accepts its injustice and makes no attempt to change it. By highlighting this attitude, Gordimer is clearly trying to inspire change.

6 Uses details from the work to support the review

While creating a sympathetic narrator with whom readers can identify, the author also shows him the white South Africans' misguided belief that what they were doing was perfectly all right, and even moral. They treated the blacks as lower-class citizens and never questioned the inequity they perpetuated. In Gordimer's story, it is hard to tell if a white South African is a bigot or a well-meaning, ignorant person. "There are so many black faces—surely one will do?" asks the health official when the narrator tries to retrieve the real body of Petrus's brother. Is this a complete lack of respect bred of hatred, or a pathetic ignorance arising from a long-standing cultural bias? By showing the racial attitudes without comments, Gordimer effectively leads readers to see the injustice for themselves.

7 Provides evidence that the author effectively illustrates the society's racial attitudes

Another issue that Gordimer brings out is how the blacks' fear and distrust due to oppression have made them seemingly accept their status. She portrays the main black character, Petrus, as a simple-minded worker who has lived under oppression for so long that he feels he can do nothing to change it. Gordimer illustrates the blacks' mistrustful attitude when the workers won't ask their employers for help even to save a man's life. "You would think they would have felt they could tell *us*," exclaims Lerice in response to the workers' fear. Gordimer shows how neither group understands the other.

8 Uses a quote to support a statement about the work

In "Six Feet of the Country," Gordimer successfully creates interesting, realistic characters. She also effectively illustrates the injustice of apartheid. Finally, she expresses a larger theme relevant to all readers: It is easy to accept the status quo, even a harmful or unjust one. But it can be detrimental to individuals and society to do so.

9 Restates the writer's original opinion that Gordimer's writing is successful

Another Option:
- Summarize the points of the review.

6. Point out that the details here show the character attempting to be helpful while displaying a shockingly insensitive attitude. The contrast creates an ambiguous character who means well but is unwittingly unjust.

7. Ask students to explain how the underlined sentence links directly to the criteria and thesis established in the first paragraph.

Possible Response: The underlined sentence refers to ideas mentioned in the first paragraph—that Gordimer uses "subtlety and ambiguity" to create her characters, and that her story is not preachy. Gordimer shows racial injustice by illustration rather than explanation.

8. Point out that the quote also illustrates the naiveté of Lerice in particular and white South Africans in general regarding their lack of understanding of black South Africans. This quote illustrates the complexity of character.

9. Have students use the other option of summarizing the points of the review.

Possible Response: In "Six Feet of the Country," Gordimer creates a sympathetic narrator who participates in an unjust system and creates oppressed characters who participate in their subjugation; Gordimer thereby illustrates the injustices of apartheid.

Have students assign a grade or overall evaluation to the model based on how well the writing achieved its purpose.

Guiding Student Writing

Prewriting

Choosing a Topic

If after reading the Idea Bank students are having difficulty choosing their subjects, suggest they try the following:

- Write the following categories on a page and list specific titles that fit under each: poem, short story, historical fiction, mystery, novel, essay, drama, magazine article, autobiography, biography.
- Make a list of your favorite authors, then look in the library for individual titles by those authors.
- Create a list of subjects that interest you, then use the library to look for literary titles dealing with those topics.

Planning Your Critical Review

1. Suggest that students use a literature textbook or a literary reference book to familiarize themselves with critical elements of the genre they plan to review.
3. Visual learners may find a cluster map to be a less constraining format than a linear chart. Have them write each claim in the center of a page and circle it. Then students can reread the story, making additions to the cluster map as they proceed.
4. To help students decide which elements to focus on, they might consider the following questions: Which make the most interesting analysis? Which have the most supporting evidence? Which represent the most accurate and thorough analysis of the story?

Drafting

You might tell students to let the genre guide the organization of their review. For a play, they might first describe the plot, then discuss the merits and flaws of the script and stage directions.

Remind students that they need not write their introduction first. They might begin by writing the body and later return to writing the introduction.

IDEABank

1. Your Working Portfolio
Build on one of the **Writing Options** you completed earlier in this unit:

- **Paragraph Critique,** p. 1273
- **Critical Review,** p. 1287
- **Story Review,** p. 1300
- **Letter to Allende,** p. 1309

2. Your Preferences
What types of literature do you enjoy most? science fiction? stories with a foreign setting? plays? poetry? Choose from a type of literature that you like to read.

3. Critics' Conference
Discuss the work you chose with a small group of classmates. Find out how others reacted to it and why.

Writing Your Critical Review

The critic should describe, and not prescribe.
Eugène Ionesco

❶ Prewriting

Begin by choosing a literary work about which you have a strong opinion. You might choose a work you like or one you strongly dislike. See the **Idea Bank** in the margin for more suggestions. After you choose a work to review, follow the steps below.

Planning Your Critical Review

1. **Identify key elements of your subject.** Consider the theme, characters, plot, and setting of a story you plan to review. If you choose a poem or a drama, you will want to examine such elements as the rhythm and language of a poem or the dialogue and actions of a drama.
2. **Establish criteria for evaluation.** How do you decide what makes an element especially strong or weak? By stating that you believe the theme is expressed clearly through the actions of the characters, for example, you are establishing criteria.
3. **Analyze each element of your subject.** Now examine each element and make some notes about the way the literary work handled that element. As you make your notes, be sure to list specific things in the work that support your opinion. You might make a chart like this one.

Element	Critique	Support
plot		
character		

4. **Choose a focus.** Your review doesn't need to evaluate every element in the work. After you have examined most elements, you can choose to focus on one or two. Look for strengths and weaknesses in each area you choose.

❷ Drafting

Begin writing even if you haven't worked out all the details of your opinion about the work. Some of your ideas will become clearer as you draft. Just keep going. You can add details and refine your ideas as you revise.

Start out by identifying the title, author, and type of work, and state a general **opinion** of it. Once you are comfortable with your ideas, begin reworking your material into a more formal review format.

In the body of the review, let your subject guide your **organization.** For a story, you might **summarize** the plot and then state the **criteria** by which you measured the work. Then **evaluate** the various elements of the work that fit your criteria. For a poem, you could **describe the work as a whole,** state the criteria for evaluation, and then address those specific elements in turn. Always **support your opinions** with specific details or examples. End by summing up your opinion.

Ask Your Peer Reader

- How would you summarize my opinions about this work?
- What elements of this work did I analyze? Should I have analyzed any other elements?
- Which supporting example is most convincing?

❸ Revising

TARGET SKILL ▶ USING APPOSITIVES You can use appositive phrases in your review to include important details without being wordy. An appositive phrase renames a noun by clarifying it or giving additional information about the noun.

> The main character ~~is~~ the narrator, ~~He~~ is a man living with his wife on an isolated farmstead outside of Johannesburg during the 1950s.

❹ Editing and Proofreading

TARGET SKILL ▶ MODIFIER PLACEMENT Modifiers can help make your review specific and interesting. Some modifiers function as adjectives and some function as adverbs. Be sure to place each modifier, whether it is a word or a phrase, close to the word it modifies. Beware of dangling modifiers, which do not clearly modify anything in a sentence or appear to modify words that they cannot sensibly modify.

> By showing the racial attitudes without comments, Gordimer leads readers to see the injustice for themselves effectively.
>
> Another issue that Gordimer brings out is how the blacks' fear and distrust have made them seemingly ~~except~~ accept their status due to oppression. She offers a mirror to the black south africans of the system and tries to convince them to change it.

❺ Reflecting

FOR YOUR WORKING PORTFOLIO Would you recommend the story you reviewed? How would your audience affect your recommendation? Attach your answers to your finished work. Save your critical review in your **Working Portfolio.**

Mystified by modifier placement?

See the **Grammar Handbook**
Using Modifiers Correctly, pp. 1399–1400

Publishing IDEAS

- Meet with classmates who wrote reviews of the same work. Compare your classmates' reviews to your own reactions.
- Submit your review to an online Web site about the author or to the school newspaper or literary magazine.

More Online: Publishing Options
www.mcdougallittell.com

Revising

USING APPOSITIVES

Tell students that appositive phrases can be used to include important details without excessive wordiness. Ask a volunteer to create a simple sentence. Then have students suggest appositives to describe the subject. As a class, compare the initial sentence with the final sentence.

Editing and Proofreading

MODIFIER PLACEMENT

In the first sentence of the example, it sounds as though the *readers* are showing the racial attitudes when, in fact, the writer means that *Gordimer* is showing the racial attitudes. Also, the word *effectively* modifies the verb leads and should be moved closer to the word it modifies. In the second sentence, the phrase *due to oppression* modifies *fear* and *mistrust,* not *status.* In the third sentence, the prepositional phrase of the *system* modifies the word *mirror.*

Reflecting

As students write their reflections, they might also describe a problem they encountered in writing their critical review, and explain how they solved it. Have them examine all of their earlier planning notes and drafts as they complete this reflection. They can add these reflections to their working portfolios.

Publishing Ideas

- As students meet with classmates to compare reviews, have them analyze the reviews using the criteria on page 1311. Then have them compare their responses to the same work.

Assessment Practice

Demonstrate how students can eliminate incorrect answers for the first question.

A. This choice is incorrect because the words *born* and *artist* should not be capitalized.

B. This choice is incorrect because the word *artist* should not be capitalized.

D. This choice is incorrect because the word *British* is a proper adjective and should be capitalized.

C. This choice is correct because just the proper adjectives and proper nouns are capitalized.

Answers:
1. C; **2.** C; **3.** D; **4.** A; **5.** B; **6.** A

Assessment Practice Revising & Editing

Read this paragraph from the first draft of a critical review. The underlined sections may include the following kinds of errors:

- **comma errors**
- **capitalization errors**
- **misplaced modifiers**
- **incorrect possessive forms**

For each underlined section, choose the revision that most improves the writing.

> The painting *Caesar Asks for Fries with His Hot Dog* is representative of the work by the Irish-born british artist Francis Kelly. (1) Kelly a retired history teacher often (2) depicts historical figures in modern situations. In *Caesar,* Kelly depicts the Roman emperor in line at a fast-food restaurant. As in many of Kelly's (3) paintings, humor and pathos are essential elements. In this painting, Caesar appears undecided as he addresses the cashier wearing a toga and sandals. (4) The cashier, a teenaged girl seems (5) bored to tears as she waits. The paintings (6) humor makes it impossible to look at the image without smiling.

1. **A.** Irish-Born British Artist Francis Kelly
   B. Irish-born British Artist Francis Kelly
   C. Irish-born British artist Francis Kelly
   D. Correct as is

2. **A.** Kelly, a retired history teacher often
   B. Kelly a retired history teacher, often
   C. Kelly, a retired history teacher, often
   D. Correct as is

3. **A.** Kellys
   B. Kellie's
   C. Kellys'
   D. Correct as is

4. **A.** In this painting Caesar, wearing a toga and sandals, appears undecided as he addresses the cashier.
   B. In this painting, wearing a toga and sandals, Caesar appears undecided as he addresses the cashier.
   C. In this painting, Caesar appears undecided, wearing a toga and sandals, as he addresses the cashier.
   D. Correct as is

5. **A.** The cashier a teenaged girl seems
   B. The cashier, a teenaged girl, seems
   C. The cashier a teenaged girl, seems
   D. Correct as is

6. **A.** painting's
   B. paintings'
   C. paintings
   D. Correct as is

Need extra help?

See the **Grammar Handbook**
Capitalization Chart, p. 1415
Possessive Nouns, p. 1392
Punctuation Chart, pp. 1413–1414
Using Modifiers Correctly, pp. 1399–1400

The Logic of Words

Good writers are always drawing our attention to connections that we may not have noticed between things, people, and experiences. One way they do so is by making comparisons, or **analogies.** In the following excerpt from the poem "Digging," for example, Seamus Heaney draws an analogy between the work and tools of a turf cutter and the work and tools of a poet. The speaker says that the poet's pen is analogous, or similar, to the turf cutter's spade.

The cold smell of potato mold, the
squelch and slap
Of soggy peat, the curt cuts of an edge
Through living roots awaken in my head.
But I've no spade to follow men like them.

Between my finger and my thumb
The squat pen rests.
I'll dig with it.

—Seamus Heaney, "Digging"

Strategies for Building Vocabulary

A word analogy states that the relationship between one pair of words or things is similar to the relationship between another pair. Word analogies are often stated as formulas. Here is the formula for Heaney's analogy:

PEN : POET :: spade : turf cutter

This analogy is based on the relationship of tools to the workers who use them. To read the formula, you would say, "A pen *is to* a poet *as* a spade *is to* a turf cutter."

1 Solve Test Analogies Word analogies often appear in standardized tests. One type of test analogy consists of a formula in which one word is missing, as in this example:

THERMOMETER : TEMPERATURE :: odometer : ______

(a) heat, (b) automobile, (c) distance, (d) numerals

To solve such an analogy, first identify the relationship between the first pair of words. In this example, the relationship is one of measure, since a thermometer measures temperature. Then ask yourself, What does an odometer measure? The answer is (c) *distance.*

In another type of test analogy, you must select a pair of words to complete the analogy:

EXHIBIT : MUSEUM ::
(a) marsupial : mammal, (b) enthrall : captivate, (c) clean : immaculate, (d) merchandise : store

To solve an analogy of this type, identify the relationship between the first two words, and then find the corresponding relationship among the answer choices. In this case, an exhibit is found in a museum; so the relationship is one of location. Which pair of words also shows a location relationship? The answer is (d) because merchandise is found in a store.

2 Distinguish Among Types of Analogies The chart below identifies some other relationships you might encounter in test analogies.

Common Relationships in Analogies

Type	Example	Relationships
Cause to Effect	DROUGHT : FAMINE	is the cause of
Part to Whole	KNOB : DOOR	is a part of
Antonyms	OVERT : COVERT	is opposite in meaning to
Degree of Intensity	JOY : EXULTATION	is less (or more) intense
Manner	WORK : ASSIDUOUSLY	how
Characteristic to Object (or Person)	STINGINESS : MISER	is a quality of
Classification	LATIN : LANGUAGE	is a type of
Location	DESK : OFFICE	is found in

EXERCISE Complete each analogy, identifying the relationship between the words in each pair.

1. SUBMISSIVE : SERVANT :: rebellious : _____
2. POSITIVE : NEGATIVE :: laconic : _____
3. NILE : AFRICA :: Mississippi : _____
4. TRANSPARENCY : GLASS :: fluidity : _____
5. GRANITE : STONE :: cedar : _____

Building Vocabulary

Objectives
- read and understand analogies
- understand how analogies are used in literary language
- solve analogy problems that appear on standardized tests
- analyze the relationships between words to complete analogies

EXERCISE
1. **Possible Response:** rebel (is a quality of)
2. **Possible Response:** wordy (is opposite in meaning to)
3. **Possible Response:** North America (is found in)
4. **Possible Response:** water (is a quality of)
5. **Possible Response:** wood (is a type of)

Objectives
- use varied sentence structure to express meanings and achieve desired effect
- demonstrate control over grammatical elements such as subject-verb agreement
- revise sentences to correct errors in punctuation and agreement

WRITING EXERCISE
1. "The Distant Past," a story by William Trevor, deals with conflict in Ireland.
2. The story, which covers a period of about 40 years, is set in an area not far from Northern Ireland.
3. The Middletons, remaining loyal to Britain, become unpopular with their neighbors.
4. "The First Year of My Life," which is written from an infant's viewpoint, is a humorous example of satire.
5. Muriel Spark, after some sarcastic comments about war, goes on to make fun of politicians.

GRAMMAR EXERCISE
1. Ireland, the birthplace of many famous writers, has had a history of conflict with Great Britain.
2. These conflicts, at the cost of many lives, have had an important influence on Irish literature.
3. In the 1920s an Irish writer named Sean O'Casey wrote powerful plays about civil war in Ireland.
4. Modern British writers, including Muriel Spark, inspire readers with moving stories about war.

Grammar from Literature

Sentences can be expanded in a number of ways. Writers sometimes add words between the subject and the verb. The inserted structure is called an interrupter, and it creates what is known as a subject-verb split. Writers use subject-verb splits to add detail, explain relationships, and create sentence variety and rhythm. The examples below from William Trevor's "The Distant Past" illustrate the variety of structures that may be used in subject-verb splits.

adverb
The Middletons, naturally, didn't discuss these rebuffs.

prepositional phrase
The brown, soda and currant breads of Murphy-Flood's bakery were declared to be delicious.

appositive
The Middletons, children then, had been locked with their mother and father and an aunt into an upstairs room.

participial phrase
Mr. Healy, red-faced and short-haired, spoke casually in his Cocktail Room, making midday conversation.

adjective clause
The visitors who came to town heard about the Middletons and were impressed.

Using Subject-Verb Splits in Your Writing Look for opportunities in your own writing to vary sentence structure and add detail by inserting information as a subject-verb split. Sometimes, you can streamline wording by combining sentences, inserting information from one sentence as a subject-verb split into an another sentence.

ORIGINAL
Often writers hope to do more than entertain. This is true of those who comment on social issues.

REVISED
Often writers who comment on social issues hope to do more than entertain.

Usage Tip When using a subject-verb split, make sure that the verb agrees with the subject in number. Nouns in an interrupter do not affect subject-verb agreement.

INCORRECT subject noun
The pro-British stand of the Middletons
verb
were often unpopular in the community.

CORRECT subject noun
The pro-British stand of the Middletons
verb
was often unpopular in the community.

The subject, *stand,* is singular, so *was* is the correct verb.

Punctuation Tip Nonessential interrupters should be set off with commas; essential interrupters should not. A nonessential interrupter adds extra detail to a sentence in which the meaning is already complete. An essential interrupter is part of the main idea of a sentence.

nonessential
Fat Driscoll, the town butcher, was the man who liked to joke around with the Middletons.

essential
The man who liked to joke around with the Middletons was Fat Driscoll.

WRITING EXERCISE Combine each pair of sentences. Add the information in the second sentence to the first as a subject-verb split of the type indicated in parentheses. Eliminate words as necessary.

1. "The Distant Past" deals with conflict in Ireland. It is a story by William Trevor. (appositive)
2. The story is set in an area not far from Northern Ireland. The story covers a period of about 40 years. (adjective clause)
3. The Middletons become unpopular with their neighbors. The Middletons remain loyal to Britain. (participial phrase)
4. "The First Year of My Life" is a humorous example of satire. The story is written from an infant's viewpoint. (adjective clause)
5. Muriel Spark goes on to make fun of politicians. First, she makes some sarcastic comments about war. (adverb phrase)

GRAMMAR EXERCISE Rewrite the sentences below, correcting any errors in punctuation and usage.

1. Ireland, the birthplace of many famous writers, have had a history of conflicts with Great Britain.
2. These conflicts at the cost many lives have had an important influence on Irish literature.
3. In the 1920s an Irish writer, named Sean O'Casey, wrote powerful plays about civil war in Ireland.
4. Modern British writers, including Muriel Spark, inspires readers with moving stories about war.

Contemporary Voices

The selections in this unit depict contemporary conflicts, characters, and speakers who gain insights into life by observing the world. How did you respond to the perspectives presented? Which of the selections caused you to think more about particular problems or to change your own attitudes? Choose one or more of the options in each of the following sections to help you answer these questions and further analyze your reactions as a reader.

Reflecting on the Unit

OPTION 1

Analyzing Appearance and Reality Get together with a group of classmates and discuss how the Part 1 title "Appearance and Reality" applies to each selection in this part. Compare your conclusions with those of other groups.

OPTION 2

Comparing and Contrasting The selections in Part 2 of this unit focus on social and political issues, revealing how individuals are affected by conflict. Select two of these individuals that you find most memorable. With a partner, role-play a conversation in which the two reflect on their experiences with conflict. You may also want to have them comment on each other's words and actions, as depicted in the selections.

OPTION 3

Applying a Quotation Think about the quotation from George Orwell's novel *1984* that introduces this unit: "It was a bright cold day in April, and the clocks were striking thirteen." Which selection in the unit do you think best reflects the tone and mood of Orwell's sentence? Write a paragraph explaining your opinion.

Self ASSESSMENT

READER'S NOTEBOOK

Recall the thoughts and impressions that the selections in this unit conveyed to you. Then, working with a small group of classmates, create a cluster diagram for each part of the unit—"Appearance and Reality"and "Culture and Conflict." In each diagram, record the messages, ideas, and insights you and your group members received from the selections.

Objectives
- reflect on and assess understanding of the unit
- compare text events with his/her own and other readers' experiences
- understand such literary terms as point of view and style
- assess and build portfolios

Reflecting on the Unit

OPTION 1

Use the Unit Seven Resource Book, p. 66, to provide students a ready-made, full-depth chart for recording how appearance and reality applies to each selection.

OPTION 2

A successful response will
- recreate a realistic conversation between two memorable characters from Part 2.
- reveal how each character dealt with conflict.
- allow each role-play character to comment the words and actions of the other.
- entertain and interest whatever audience looks on.

OPTION 3

Before students begin writing, you might have a class discussion of the Orwell quotation, which opens his novel *1984.* Students will probably be able to apply the quotation to absurdist selections such as *That's All* and "The Happy Man." However, you might encourage students to consider ways that some of the more conventional selections reflect Orwell's sentence.

Self Assessment
Suggest that students review the table of contents to help them recall their thoughts and impressions of the selections in this unit. As students share their ideas, have them make rough diagrams summarizing those ideas. The final cluster diagram can be developed from these rough sketches.

Reviewing Literary Concepts

OPTION 1

A successful response will
- include an explanation as to why the writer chose that particular point of view.
- show how the story would change if another point of view were used.

OPTION 2

A successful response will
- identify the style of each author in this unit.
- illustrate that style by challenging another group to identify a writer and work based on a quotation from it.

Building Your Portfolio

Students will use their Presentation Portfolios to file what they consider their highest quality work—the very best projects and activities from their Working Portfolios.

For more information on using writing and assessing portfolios, see the *Teacher's Guide to Assessment and Portfolio Use,* p. 53

Reviewing Literary Concepts

OPTION 1

Examining Point of View With a group, review the fictional works in this unit and list the point of view used in each. Why do you think each writer chose that particular point of view? If the point of view were changed in each story, how would this alter its effectiveness? Discuss these questions with your group members.

OPTION 2

Analyzing Style A writer's style is an expression of his or her individuality. Although writers may have similar styles, there are usually certain characteristics that distinguish each writer's work from the work of others. With a small group of classmates, review the selections in this unit, choosing from each a passage that you think exemplifies the writer's style. Then quiz other groups by reading each a passage and asking them to identify the writer and the selection. Allow groups to glance over the Table of Contents if they need help recalling the names of the writers and selections.

Self ASSESSMENT

READER'S NOTEBOOK

Copy the following list of literary terms covered in this unit. Put a question mark next to each term that you do not fully understand. Then consult the **Glossary of Literary Terms** (page 1328) to clarify meanings of the terms you've marked.

setting	consonance
kinesthetic imagery	assonance
point of view	imagery
theme	mood
repetition	diction
alliteration	dialogue

Building Your Portfolio

- **Writing Options** Some of the Writing Options in this unit asked you to reflect on experiences and people's reactions to them—either your own or those of characters or speakers in the selections. Look over your responses and select one or two pieces that you think give the best accounts of experiences and reactions. Write a short note explaining why you think those pieces are successful. Add the pieces and the note to your **Presentation Portfolio.**
- **Writing Workshop** In this unit, you wrote a Critical Review in response to a piece of literature. Reread your review and assess the quality of your writing. What do you see as the strengths of the review? the weaknesses? Attach a note indicating your evaluation, and place the writing in your **Presentation Portfolio.**
- **Additional Activities** Reflect on any assignments you completed under **Activities & Explorations** and **Inquiry & Research.** Keep a record in your portfolio of any assignments that you think are worth expanding into a more comprehensive project.

Self ASSESSMENT

READER'S NOTEBOOK

At this stage, the contents of your portfolio should represent the work of an entire year. Review the pieces in your portfolio and choose three of your best works—one done in the fall, one in the winter, and one in the spring. Write a note explaining what these works reveal about your progress and abilities as a writer.

Setting GOALS

Reflect on all the goals that you set for yourself during the course of the year. Which goals did you reach? Which goals seem nearly within your reach? Which goals seem as far away as ever? Write an evaluation of your progress this year, and identify three goals for the future.

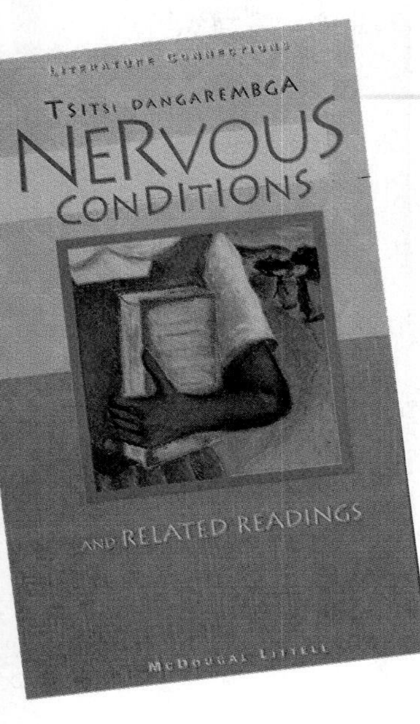

LITERATURE CONNECTIONS

Nervous Conditions

TSITSI DANGAREMBGA

A young girl must choose between her own African heritage and the education provided by the British in Zimbabwe in the 1960s. The oldest daughter of a native Shona family living in the British colony of Rhodesia (now Zimbabwe), Tambudzai is intent on getting an education and developing her independence. To do so, she must overcome the autocratic authority exercised by the men in her family and the racism and patriarchy of the colonial culture.

These thematically related readings are provided along with *Nervous Conditions:*

Professions for Women
BY VIRGINIA WOOLF

Back to School
BY ANDREA LEE

***from* Hunger of Memory**
BY RICHARD RODRIGUEZ

Losing a Language
BY W. S. MERWIN

Points of View
BY LUCINDA ROY

The Old Chief Mshlanga
BY DORIS LESSING

Young Africa's Plea
BY DENNIS OSADEBAY

And Even More . . .

When Rain Clouds Gather

BESSIE HEAD

In this novel from Botswana, the characters' personal feelings of love, bitterness, and hope reveal themselves in the midst of a village's efforts to survive and prosper. This book is also part of the *Literature Connections* series published by McDougal Littell.

Books

July's People
NADINE GORDIMER
This novella is set in an unspecified future time when, in an ironic reversal, white people are servants of black people.

African Laughter: Four Visits to Zimbabwe
DORIS LESSING
In this book, the author recounts her observations and experiences during four visits to Zimbabwe between 1982 and 1992.

The *Electronic Library* is a CD-ROM that contains additional fiction, nonfiction, poetry, and drama for each unit in *The Language of Literature.*

These are the additional selections found in Unit Seven of the *Electronic Library:*

V. S. Pritchett
The Fly in the Ointment

Margaret Drabble
A Voyage to Cythera

Sustained Silent Reading
Encourage students to select one of these books to read as an opportunity for sustained silent reading.

EXTEND YOUR READING 1321

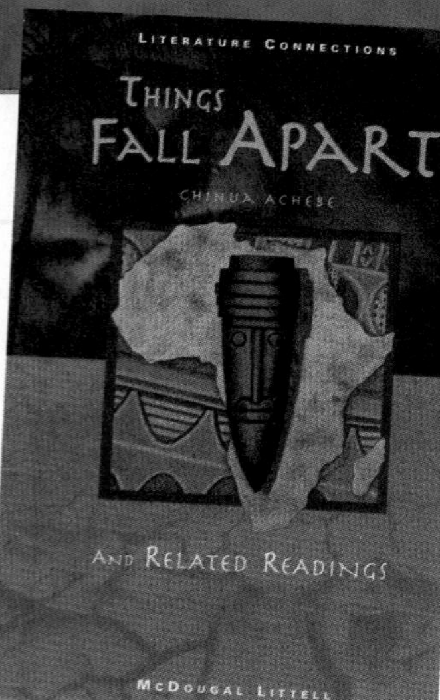

Literature Connections

Things Fall Apart

Chinua Achebe

Set in an Ibo village in Nigeria at the turn of the century, the story of Okonkwo unfolds like a Greek tragedy, as traditional Ibo customs are challenged by new European ways. When Okonkwo, through a series of incidents, finds himself alienated from his clansmen, he is plunged into despair. The novel is a profound meditation on the psychological disintegration that occurs as the ties of kinship unravel in a traditional society.

These thematically related readings are provided along with *Things Fall Apart:*

The Second Coming
by William Butler Yeats

Genesis 22: 1–19 The Sacrifice of Isaac
the Bible

Mother Was a Great Man
by Catherine Obianuju Acholonu

Prayer to Masks
by Leopold Sedar Senghor

Shooting an Elephant
by George Orwell

The Significance of a Veteran's Day
by Simon Ortiz

Able, Baker, Charlie, Dog
by Stephanie Vaughn

Exiles
by Mark Strand

And Even *More* . . .

Books

The Caretaker
Harold Pinter
This classic play combines absurdity and reality to reveal the tensions and struggles of its characters.

Death of a Naturalist
Seamus Heaney
In this volume of Heaney's early poems, the poet celebrates different aspects of rustic life and reveals his strong tie to the farmlands of his youth.

Other Media

Doris Lessing Reads Her Short Stories
Jeffrey Norton Publishers.
(audiocassette)

The Poetry and Voice of Ted Hughes
Caedmon.
(audiocassette)

A World of Ideas
PBS Video, 1988. Bill Moyers interviews Chinua Achebe.
(videocassette)

The House of the Spirits
Live Home Video, 1993. Film adaptation of Isabel Allende's novel.
(videocassette)

Student *Resource Bank*

Words to Know: Access Guide

1324 WORDS TO KNOW: ACCESS GUIDE

F

G

H

I

L

M

N

O

1326 WORDS TO KNOW: ACCESS GUIDE

Pronunciation Key

Symbol	Examples	Symbol	Examples	Symbol	Examples
ă	at, gas	m	man, seem	v	van, save
ā	ape, day	n	night, mitten	w	web, twice
ä	father, barn	ng	sing, anger	y	yard, lawyer
âr	fair, dare	ŏ	odd, not	z	zoo, reason
b	bell, table	ō	open, road, grow	zh	treasure, garage
ch	chin, lunch	ô	awful, bought, horse	ə	awake, even, pencil,
d	dig, bored	oi	coin, boy		pilot, focus
ĕ	egg, ten	o͝o	look, full	ər	perform, letter
ē	evil, see, meal	o͞o	root, glue, through		
f	fall, laugh, phrase	ou	out, cow	**Sounds in Foreign Words**	
g	gold, big	p	pig, cap	KH	*German* ich, auch;
h	hit, inhale	r	rose, star		*Scottish* loch
hw	white, everywhere	s	sit, face	N	*French* entre, bon, fin
ĭ	inch, fit	sh	she, mash	œ	*French* feu, cœur;
ī	idle, my, tried	t	tap, hopped		*German* schön
îr	dear, here	th	thing, with	ü	*French* utile, rue;
j	jar, gem, badge	*th*	then, other		*German* grün
k	keep, cat, luck	ŭ	up, nut		
l	load, rattle	ûr	fur, earn, bird, worm		

Stress Marks

′ This mark indicates that the preceding syllable receives the primary stress. For example, in the word *language,* the first syllable is stressed: lăng′gwĭj.

´ This mark is used only in words in which more than one syllable is stressed. It indicates that the preceding syllable is stressed, but somewhat more weakly than the syllable receiving the primary stress. In the word *literature,* for example, the first syllable receives the primary stress, and the last syllable receives a weaker stress: lĭt′ər-ə-cho͝or´.

WORDS TO KNOW: ACCESS GUIDE 1327

Glossary of Literary Terms

Allegory An allegory is a story in verse or prose in which characters are used to personify abstract qualities. Like a fable or parable, an allegory is often used to express generalizations about human existence and teach religious or moral lessons.

Example: The best-known allegory in the English language is John Bunyan's *Pilgrim's Progress.* Christian, the hero of Bunyan's work, represents all people. Other allegorical characters include Mr. Worldly Wiseman, Faithful, and Hopeful. The allegory traces Christian's efforts to achieve a godly life.

Alliteration Alliteration is the repetition of consonant sounds at the beginning of words.

> **Out from the marsh, from the foot of misty**
> **Hills and bogs, bearing God's hatred,**
> **Grendel came,**
> **—from *Beowulf***

Writers use alliteration to emphasize certain words, to heighten mood, to establish a musical effect, to unify a passage, and to help create meaning. Often alliteration is reinforced by repeating the same consonant sound within and at the end of other words. Look for examples of alliteration in the following lines:

> **In Xanadu did Kubla Khan**
> **A stately pleasure dome decree:**
> **Where Alph, the sacred river, ran**
> **Through caverns measureless to man**
> **Down to a sunless sea.**
> **—Samuel Taylor Coleridge, from "Kubla Khan"**

See pages 63, 96, 300, 744, 806, 950, 1239.
See also **Assonance; Consonance.**

Allusion An allusion is a reference to a historical or fictional person, place, or event with which the reader is assumed to be familiar. Understanding the allusions in a work can give the reader a better understanding of it.

Examples: In Thomas Gray's "Elegy Written in a Country Churchyard," the speaker alludes to Milton, the famous English poet, and Cromwell, the leader of the Puritan revolt in the 17th century. These allusions to two of the most well-known figures in English life emphasize the poet's ideas about what the lives of the obscure people buried in the churchyard might have been like had they had different opportunities. In the excerpt from Derek Walcott's poem *Midsummer,* allusions contribute to the satiric tone of the poem.

See pages 479, 945.

Analogy An analogy is a comparison between two dissimilar things made to clarify a point or create an image.

Example: In his essay "On Spring," Samuel Johnson compares animals that can blend in with their surroundings to people who are able to appreciate and be inspired by the objects around them.

Anglo-Saxon Poetry Anglo-Saxon poetry, which was written between the 7th and 12th centuries, is characterized by a strong rhythm, or cadence, that makes it easily chanted or sung. It was originally recited by **scops,** poet-singers who traveled from place to place. Lines of Anglo-Saxon poetry are unified through alliteration and through use of the same number of accented syllables in each line. Typically, a line is divided by a **caesura,** or pause, into two parts, with each part having two accented syllables. Usually, one or both of the accented syllables in the first part alliterate with an accented syllable in the second part. This passage illustrates some of these characteristics:

> **He took what he wanted, // all the**
> **treasures**
> **That pleased his eye, // heavy plates**
> **And golden cups // and the glorious**
> **banner,**
> **Loaded his arms // with all they could**
> **hold.**
> **—from *Beowulf***

1328 GLOSSARY OF LITERARY TERMS

Another characteristic of Anglo-Saxon poetry is the use of **kennings,** metaphorical compound words or phrases substituted for simple nouns.

Examples: Kennings from "The Seafarer" include "whales' home" for the sea and "givers of gold" for rulers or emperors. Examples from *Beowulf* include "shepherd of evil" for Grendel, and "folk-king" for Beowulf.

See page 96.

Antagonist The antagonist of a novel, short story, drama, or narrative poem is the character or force against which the main character, or **protagonist,** is pitted. The antagonist may be another character, some aspect of society or nature, or an internal force within the protagonist.

Examples: In *Sir Gawain and the Green Knight,* the antagonist is the Green Knight, who challenges Sir Gawain. In Doris Lessing's "A Sunrise on the Veld," the antagonist is the natural world, which confronts the boy with his limits.

See also **Conflict; Protagonist.**

Antithesis Antithesis is a figure of speech in which sharply contrasting words, phrases, clauses, or sentences are juxtaposed to emphasize a point. In a true antithesis, both the ideas and the grammatical structures are balanced. An example is the second line of the following couplet:

> **Regard not then if wit be old or new,**
> **But blame the false, and value still the true.**
> **—Alexander Pope, from *An Essay on Criticism***

See page 741.

Aphorism An aphorism is a brief statement that expresses a general observation about life in a witty, pointed way. Unlike proverbs, which may stem from oral folk tradition, aphorisms originate with specific authors. "A blighted spring makes a barren year," from Samuel Johnson's essay "On Spring," is an example of an aphorism.

See page 656.

Apostrophe Apostrophe is a figure of speech in which an object, an abstract quality, or an absent or imaginary person is addressed directly, as if present and able to understand. Writers use apostrophe to express powerful emotions, as in this apostrophe to the ocean:

> **Roll on, thou deep and dark blue Ocean, roll!**
> **Ten thousand fleets sweep over thee in vain;**
> **Man marks the earth with ruin, his control**
> **Stops with the shore; upon the watery plain**
> **The wrecks are all thy deed, nor doth remain**
> **A shadow of man's ravage, save his own,**
> **When, for a moment, like a drop of rain,**
> **He sinks into thy depths with bubbling groan,**
> **Without a grave, unknell'd, uncoffin'd, and unknown. . . .**
> **—George Gordon, Lord Byron,**
> **from *Childe Harold's Pilgrimage***

See page 779.

Argumentation Argumentation is speech or writing intended to convince an audience that a proposal should be adopted or rejected. Most argumentation begins with a statement of an idea or opinion, which is then supported with logical evidence. Another technique of argumentation is the anticipation and rebuttal of opposing views.

Examples: One example of argumentation is the excerpt from *A Vindication of the Rights of Woman,* in which Mary Wollstonecraft argues for the rights of women and argues against views that would subjugate women. Another example is Margaret Cavendish's "Female Orations," in which seven women present their arguments for and against women's rights.

See pages 500, 637.

Aside In drama, an aside is a remark spoken in an undertone by a character, either to the audience or to another character. A traditional dramatic convention, the aside is heard by the audience but supposedly not by the other characters on stage. Asides can be used to express characters' feelings, opinions, and reactions, so they function as a method of characterization.

GLOSSARY OF LITERARY TERMS 1329

> Macbeth. [*Aside*] If chance will have me King,
> why, chance may crown me,
> Without my stir.
> —William Shakespeare, from *Macbeth*

See page 324.
See also **Drama.**

Assonance Assonance is the repetition of a vowel sound in two or more stressed syllables that do not end with the same consonant. Poets use assonance to emphasize certain words, to impart a musical quality, to create a mood, or to unify a passage. An example of assonance is the repetition of the long *e* sound in the following lines. Note that the repeated sounds are not always spelled the same.

> When I have fears that I may cease to be
> Before my pen has glean'd my teeming brain
> —John Keats, from "When I Have Fears That I May Cease to Be"

See pages 806, 1092, 1239.
See also **Alliteration; Consonance; Rhyme.**

Author's Purpose An author's purpose may be to entertain, to inform, to express opinions, or to persuade. Although a writer can fulfill more than one of these purposes in a work, one is usually the most important. The purposes of the excerpt from the Venerable Bede's *A History of the English Church and People* are to inform and to persuade.

See pages 866, 929.

Autobiography An autobiography is a writer's account of his or her own life. Autobiographies often convey profound insights as writers recount past events from the perspective of greater understanding and distance. A formal autobiography involves a sustained, lengthy narrative of a person's history, but other autobiographical narratives may be less formal and briefer. Under the general category of autobiography fall such writings as diaries, journals, memoirs, and letters. Both formal and informal autobiographies provide revealing insights into the writer's character, attitudes, and motivations, as well as some understanding of the society in which the writer lived. *The Book of Margery Kempe* is an autobiography.

See page 256.
See also **Diary; Memoir.**

Ballad A ballad is a narrative poem that was originally intended to be sung. Traditional folk ballads, written by unknown authors and handed down orally, usually depict ordinary people in the midst of tragic events and adventures of love and bravery. They tend to begin abruptly, focus on a single incident, use dialogue and repetition, and suggest more than they actually state. They often contain supernatural elements.

Typically, a ballad consists of four-line stanzas, or quatrains, with the second and fourth lines of each stanza rhyming. Each stanza has a strong rhythmic pattern, usually with four stressed syllables in the first and third lines and three stressed syllables in the second and fourth lines. The rhyme scheme is usually *abcb* or *aabb.* "Barbara Allan," "Sir Patrick Spens," and "Get Up and Bar the Door" are ballads. Notice the rhythmic pattern in the following stanza:

> O slowly, slowly rase she up, *a*
> To the place where he was lyin', *b*
> And when she drew the curtain by: *c*
> "Young man, I think you're dyin'." *b*
> —from "Barbara Allan"

A **literary ballad** is a ballad with a single author. Modeled on the early English and Scottish folk ballads, literary ballads became popular during the romantic period. Samuel Taylor Coleridge's "The Rime of the Ancient Mariner" is a romantic literary ballad.

See pages 198, 766.
See also **Narrative Poem; Quatrain.**

Biography A biography is an account of a person's life written by another person. In a good biography, the presentation of the subject's life is comprehensive, unified, and accurate. The skilled biographer synthesizes information from sources such as letters, journals, interviews, and documents and strives for a balanced portrayal through detailed anecdotes, reconstructed dialogue, description,

1330 GLOSSARY OF LITERARY TERMS

quotations, and interpretive passages. An outstanding example of a biography is James Boswell's *The Life of Samuel Johnson.*

Although full-length biographies cover the life history of a person from birth to death, less extensive writings also may be considered biographical. These include the anecdote, which relates a revealing incident in a person's life, and the character sketch, a brief descriptive essay that highlights certain qualities of the subject.

See page 664.

Blank Verse Blank verse is unrhymed poetry written in iambic pentameter. Because iambic pentameter resembles the natural rhythm of spoken English, it has been considered the most suitable meter for dramatic verse in English. Shakespeare's plays are written largely in blank verse, as is Milton's epic *Paradise Lost.* Blank verse has also been used frequently for long poems, as in the following:

> **Ănd nów, wĭth gleáms ŏf hálf-**
> **ĕxtinǵuĭshed thoúght**
> **Wĭth mány̆ récŏgńitiŏns dím ănd**
> **faínt,**
> **Ănd somḗwhăt óf ă sád pĕrpléxĭtý,**
> **Thĕ píctŭre óf thĕ mínd rĕvívĕs**
> **ăgaín;**
> **—William Wordsworth, from "Lines Composed a Few Miles Above Tintern Abbey"**

See pages 324, 491, 852.
See also **Iambic Pentameter; Meter.**

Caesura *See* **Anglo-Saxon Poetry.**

Character Characters are the people who participate in the action of a work. The most important characters are the **main characters.** Less prominent characters are known as **minor characters.** In Katherine Mansfield's "A Cup of Tea," Rosemary and the girl are main characters, and the shopman is a minor character.

Whereas some characters are two-dimensional, with only one or two dominant traits, a fully developed character possesses many traits, mirroring the psychological complexity of a real person. In longer works of fiction, main characters often undergo change as the plot unfolds. Such characters are called **dynamic characters,** as opposed to **static characters,** who remain the same. In D. H. Lawrence's story "The Rocking-Horse Winner," Paul is a dynamic character because he becomes increasingly absorbed by his obsession to get money for his mother. Uncle Oscar is a static character who primarily observes and responds to Paul's actions.

See also **Characterization.**

Characterization Characterization refers to the techniques that writers use to develop characters. There are four basic methods of characterization:

1. A writer may describe the physical appearance of a character. In William Trevor's "The Distant Past," the narrator describes the Middletons: "They had always been thin, silent with one another, and similar in appearance: a brother and sister who shared a family face. It was a bony countenance, with pale blue eyes and a sharp, well-shaped nose and high cheek-bones."
2. A character's nature may be revealed through his or her own speech, thoughts, feelings, or actions. In Trevor's story, the reader learns about the kind of life the Middletons lead: "Together they roved the vast lofts of their house, placing old paint tins and flowerpot saucers beneath the drips from the roof. At night they sat over their thin chops in a dining-room that had once been gracious . . ."
3. The speech, thoughts, feelings, and actions of other characters can be used to develop a character. The attitudes of the townspeople to the Middletons help the reader understand the old couple better: "'An upright couple,' was the Canon's public opinion of the Middletons, and he had been known to add that eccentric views would hurt you less than malice."
4. The narrator can make direct comments about the character's nature. The narrator in Trevor's story comments, "The Middletons were in their middle-sixties now and were reconciled to a life that became more uncomfortable with every passing year."

See pages 111, 237.
See also **Character.**

GLOSSARY OF LITERARY TERMS 1331

Climax *See* **Plot.**

Comedy A comedy is a dramatic work that is light and often humorous in tone, usually ending happily with a peaceful resolution of the main conflict. A comedy differs from a farce by having a more believable plot, more realistic characters, and less boisterous behavior. Shakespeare's *A Midsummer Night's Dream* is a comedy.

See also **Drama; Farce.**

Comic Relief Comic relief is a humorous scene, incident, or speech that is included in a serious drama to provide respite from emotional intensity. Because it breaks the tension, comic relief allows an audience to internalize preceding plot events and to prepare emotionally for events to come. The sharp contrasts afforded by comic relief may intensify the themes of a literary work.

Example: In many of Shakespeare's plays, a scene involving a fool or humorous interplay among common folks provides comic relief. Comic relief in *Macbeth* is provided by Macbeth's garrulous, vulgar porter at the beginning of Act II, Scene 3, just after Duncan's murder. This scene is needed to relax the tension built up in the preceding scenes.

Conceit *See* **Extended Metaphor**.

Conflict A conflict is a struggle between opposing forces that moves a plot forward. The conflict provides the interest or suspense in a short story, drama, novel, narrative poem, or nonfiction narrative. Conflict may be **external,** with a character being pitted against some outside force—another person, a physical obstacle, nature, or society. Conflict may also be **internal,** occurring within a character.

Examples: In Elizabeth Gaskell's "Christmas Storms and Sunshine," Mrs. Hodgson is in a running conflict with Mrs. Jenkins. The sergeant in Lady Gregory's *The Rising of the Moon* faces an external conflict with the escaped prisoner and an internal conflict involving his double loyalties.

See pages 190, 883, 1272.
See also **Plot.**

Connotation *Connotation* refers to the attitudes and feelings associated with a word, in contrast to **denotation,** which is the literal or dictionary meaning of a word. The connotation of a word may be positive or negative. For example, *enthusiastic* has positive associations, but *rowdy* has negative ones. Connotations of words can have an important influence on style and meaning and are particularly important in poetry.

Example: In W. B. Yeats's poem "Sailing to Byzantium," the connotations of the words *paltry* and *tattered* in the lines "An aged man is but a paltry thing, / A tattered coat upon a stick, . . ." help to create the image of a thin, ragged scarecrow.

See page 1252.

Consonance *Consonance* is the repetition of consonant sounds within and at the ends of words, as in "lonely afternoon." Consonance is unlike rhyme in that the vowels preceding or following the repeated consonant sounds differ. Sometimes the repeated sounds have different spellings, as in *hours* and *squeeze.* Consonance is often used together with alliteration, assonance, and rhyme to create a musical quality, to emphasize certain words, or to unify a poem. The repetition of the *l* sound in the following lines reinforces the meaning of *leisurely* and helps create a slow pace:

> **In Breughel's *Icarus*, for instance: how**
> **everything turns away**
> **Quite leisurely from the disaster; the**
> **ploughman may**
> **Have heard the splash, the forsaken cry,**
> **But for him it was not an important failure; . . .**
> **—W. H. Auden, from "Musée des Beaux Arts"**

See pages 806, 1092, 1239.
See also **Assonance.**

Contrast Contrast is a stylistic device in which one element is put into opposition with another. The opposing elements might be contrasting structures, such as sentences of varying lengths or stanzas of different configurations. They could also be contrasting ideas or images juxtaposed within phrases, sentences, paragraphs, stanzas, or sections of a

1332 GLOSSARY OF LITERARY TERMS

longer work of literature. Writers use contrast to clarify or emphasize ideas and to elicit emotional responses from the reader.

Example: Part of the force of Siegfried Sassoon's poem "Dreamers" lies in the contrast between images of war, such as "death's gray land," and images of ordinary life, such as "firelit homes."

See page 534.

Controlling Image *See* **Extended Metaphor; Imagery.**

Couplet A couplet is a rhymed pair of lines. A simple couplet may be written in any rhythmic pattern. The following couplet is written in iambic tetrameter (lines of four iambs):

> **Hăd wé bŭt wórld enóugh, ănd tíme,**
> **Thĭs cóyneŝs, lády̆, wére nŏ críme.**
> **—Andrew Marvell, from "To His Coy Mistress"**

A **heroic couplet** consists of two rhyming lines written in iambic pentameter. The term *heroic* comes from the fact that English poems having heroic themes and elevated style have often been written in iambic pentameter. Alexander Pope's masterful use of the heroic couplet made it a popular verse form during the neoclassical period. The following lines are one of many possible examples from his work:

> **Ăvóid ĕxtrémes; ănd shŭn thĕ fáult**
> **ŏf súch,**
> **Whŏ stíll ăre pléased tŏo líttlĕ ór**
> **tŏo múch.**
> **—Alexander Pope, from *An Essay on Criticism***

See page 538.

Denotation *See* **Connotation.**

Denouement *See* **Plot.**

Description Description is writing that helps a reader to picture scenes, events, and characters. It helps the reader understand exactly what someone or something is like. To create description, writers often use sensory images—words and phrases that enable the reader to see, hear, smell, taste, or feel the subject described—and figurative language. Effective description also relies on precise nouns, verbs, adjectives, and adverbs, as well as carefully selected details. The following passage contains clear details and images:

> **Air, musty from having been long enclosed, hung in all the rooms, and the waste room behind the kitchen was littered with old useless papers. Among these I found a few paper-covered books, the pages of which were curled and damp. . . . The wild garden behind the house contained a central apple-tree and a few straggling bushes under one of which I found the late tenant's rusty bicycle-pump.**
> **—James Joyce, from "Araby"**

See page 690.

Dialect Dialect is a particular variety of language spoken in one place by a distinct group of people. A dialect reflects the colloquialisms, grammatical constructions, distinctive vocabulary, and pronunciations that are typical of a region. At times writers use dialect to establish or emphasize settings, as well as to develop characters.

Example: The thieves in Chinua Achebe's story "Civil Peace" speak in a Nigerian dialect of English, which highlights the contrast between the thieves and Jonathan Iwegbu.

See page 1279.

Dialogue Written conversation between two or more people, in either fiction or nonfiction, is called dialogue. Writers use dialogue to bring characters to life and to give readers insights into the characters' qualities, personality traits, and reactions to other people. Realistic, well-paced dialogue also advances the plot of a narrative.

Dialogue in drama is critical to an understanding of the playwright's story or message. How the dialogue is read or performed will determine to a great extent the reactions of the reader or audience to the play. Dramatists use **stage directions** to indicate how they intend the dialogue to be interpreted by the actors. In Lady Gregory's play *The Rising of the Moon,* the words *gasps* and *furious* are stage directions

GLOSSARY OF LITERARY TERMS 1333

used to indicate how the Sergeant is supposed to react and speak at two different times. In Harold Pinter's play *That's All,* the frequent pauses and breaks in conversation are indicated by stage directions.

Although dialogue is most common in novels, short stories, and dramas, it is also used in other forms of prose as well as in poetry. Fanny Burney's account of the party in the excerpt from *The Diary and Letters of Madame d'Arblay* makes effective use of dialogue.

See pages 679, 1258.
See also **Characterization; Drama.**

Diary A diary is a writer's personal day-to-day account of his or her experiences and impressions. Most diaries are private and not intended to be shared. Some, however, have been published because they are well written and provide useful perspectives on historical events or on the everyday life of particular eras. The excerpt from *The Diary of Samuel Pepys* is an example of a well-written diary of great historical interest.

See page 532.
See also **Autobiography.**

Diction Diction is a writer's choice of words, a significant component of style. Diction encompasses both vocabulary (individual words) and syntax (the order or arrangement of words). Diction can be described with terms such as *formal* or *informal, technical* or *common, abstract* or *concrete.*

Examples: Much of the diction in Aldous Huxley's essay "Words and Behavior" is formal, which is appropriate to the seriousness of his subject. The lofty, elevated diction in John Milton's *Paradise Lost* befits the poem's exalted subject and themes. By contrast, the blandness of the diction in W. H. Auden's "The Unknown Citizen"—for example, the words *employers, advertisements, advantages,* and *population*—helps establish the detached, ironic tone of the poem.

See pages 491, 1155, 1252.
See also **Connotation; Style.**

Drama Drama is literature that develops plot and character through dialogue and action; in other words, drama is literature in play form. Dramas are meant to be performed by actors who appear on a stage, before radio microphones, or in front of television or movie cameras.

Unlike other forms of literature, such as fiction and poetry, a drama requires the collaboration of many people in order to come to life. In an important sense, a drama in printed form is an incomplete work of art. It is a skeleton that must be fleshed out by a director, actors, set designers, and others who interpret the work and stage a performance. When the members of an audience become caught up in a drama and forget to a degree the artificiality of the play, the process is called the "suspension of disbelief."

Most plays are divided into acts, with each act having an emotional peak, or climax, of its own. The acts sometimes are divided into scenes; each scene is limited to a single time and place. Shakespeare's plays have five acts. Contemporary plays usually have two or three acts, although some, such as Lady Gregory's *The Rising of the Moon* and Harold Pinter's *That's All,* have only one.

All plays have **stage directions,** instructions included in the script to help performers and directors put on the play or to help readers visualize the action. Stage directions can describe setting, lighting, sound effects, the movement of actors, or the way in which dialogue is spoken.

See page 325.
See also **Aside; Dialogue; Plot; Soliloquy.**

Dramatic Irony *See* **Irony.**

Dramatic Monologue A dramatic monologue is a lyric poem in which a speaker addresses a silent or absent listener in a moment of high intensity or deep emotion, as if engaged in private conversation. The speaker proceeds without interruption or argument, and the effect on the reader is that of hearing just one side of a conversation. This technique allows the poet to focus on the feelings, personality, and motivations of the speaker—in a sense, taking the reader

1334 GLOSSARY OF LITERARY TERMS

inside the speaker's mind. Robert Browning's poems "Porphyria's Lover" and "My Last Duchess" are both dramatic monologues.

See page 859.

Elegy An elegy is an extended meditative poem in which the speaker reflects upon death—often in tribute to a person who has died recently—or on an equally serious subject. Most elegies are written in formal, dignified language and are serious in tone. Alfred, Lord Tennyson's *In Memoriam,* written in memory of his friend Arthur Henry Hallam, is a famous elegy.

Elizabethan (Shakespearean) Sonnet *See* **Sonnet.**

End Rhyme *See* **Rhyme.**

English (Shakespearean) Sonnet *See* **Sonnet.**

Epic An epic is a long narrative poem on a serious subject, presented in an elevated or formal style. It traces the adventures of a great hero. Most epics share some or all of the following characteristics:

1. The hero is a figure of high social status and often of great historical or legendary importance.
2. The actions of the hero often determine the fate of a nation or group of people.
3. The hero performs exceedingly courageous, sometimes even superhuman, deeds that reflect the ideas and values of the era.
4. The plot is complicated by supernatural beings and events.
5. The setting is large in scale, involving more than one nation and often a long and dangerous journey through foreign lands.
6. Long formal speeches are often given by the main character.
7. The poem treats universal ideas, such as good and evil, life and death.

Beowulf, the *Iliad,* the *Ramayana,* and *Paradise Lost* are all epics.

See pages 28, 63, 250.

Epic Simile *See* **Simile.**

Epigram The epigram is a literary form that originated in ancient Greece. It developed from simple inscriptions on monuments into a literary genre—short poems or sayings characterized by conciseness, balance, clarity, and wit. A classic epigram is written in two parts, the first establishing the occasion or setting the tone and the second stating the main point. A few lines taken from a longer poem can also be an epigram. Epigrams are used for many purposes, including the expression of friendship, grief, criticism, praise, and philosophy. Many passages in Pope's *An Essay on Criticism* constitute epigrams, as in the following example:

> **Good nature and good sense must ever join;**
> **To err is human, to forgive, divine.**
> **—Alexander Pope, from *An Essay on Criticism***

Epitaph An epitaph is an inscription on a tomb or monument to honor the memory of a deceased person. The term *epitaph* is also used to describe any verse commemorating someone who has died. Although a few humorous epitaphs have been composed, most are serious in tone. Ben Jonson's "On My First Son" is sometimes called an epitaph.

See page 461.

Epithet An epithet is a brief phrase that points out traits associated with a particular person or thing. Homer's *Iliad* contains many examples of epithets, such as the references to Achilles as "the great runner" (line 34) and to Hector as "killer of men" (line 328).

Essay An essay is a brief work of nonfiction that offers an opinion on a subject. The purpose of an essay may be to express ideas and feelings, to analyze, to inform, to entertain, or to persuade. In a **persuasive essay,** a writer attempts to convince readers to adopt a particular opinion or to perform a certain action. Most persuasive essays present a series of facts, reasons, or examples in support of an opinion or proposal. Sir Francis Bacon's "Of Studies" and "Of Marriage and Single Life" are good examples of the persuasive essay.

GLOSSARY OF LITERARY TERMS 1335

Essays can be formal or informal. A **formal essay** examines a topic in a thorough, serious, and highly organized manner. An **informal essay** presents an opinion on a subject, but not in a completely serious or formal tone. Characteristics of this type of essay include humor, a personal or confidential approach, a loose and sometimes rambling style, and often a surprising or unconventional topic. Daniel Defoe's essay "An Academy for Women" is a formal essay, meant to analyze and persuade. Joseph Addison's essays from *The Spectator* are informal, meant to express observations, ideas, and feelings and to entertain with gentle humor and wit.

A **personal essay** is a type of informal essay. Personal essays allow writers to express their viewpoints on subjects by reflecting on events or incidents in their own lives. George Orwell's "A Hanging" is an example of a personal essay.

See pages 447, 552, 582, 1174, 1308.

Exaggeration *See* **Hyperbole.**

Exposition *See* **Plot.**

Extended Metaphor Like any metaphor, an extended metaphor is a comparison between two essentially unlike things that nevertheless have something in common. It does not contain the word *like* or *as.* In an extended metaphor, two things are compared at length and in various ways—perhaps throughout a stanza, a paragraph, or even an entire work. The likening of God to a shepherd in Psalm 23 is an example of an extended metaphor.

Like an extended metaphor, a **conceit** parallels two essentially dissimilar things on several points. A conceit, though, is a more elaborate, formal, and ingenious comparison than the ordinary extended metaphor. Sometimes a conceit forms the framework of an entire poem, as in John Donne's "A Valediction: Forbidding Mourning," in which the poet describes his own and his lover's souls as the two legs of a mathematician's compass.

See pages 456, 945.
See also **Figurative Language; Metaphor; Simile.**

External Conflict *See* **Conflict.**

Fable A fable is a brief tale, in either prose or verse, told to illustrate a moral or teach a lesson. Often, the moral of a fable appears in a distinct and memorable statement near the tale's beginning or end. Jean de La Fontaine's "The Acorn and the Pumpkin" and "The Value of Knowledge" are both fables.

See page 544.

Falling Action *See* **Plot.**

Fantasy *Fantasy* is a term applied to works of fiction that display a disregard for the restraints of reality. The aim of a fantasy may be purely to delight or may be to make a serious comment. Some fantasies include extreme or grotesque characters. Others portray realistic characters in a realistic world who only marginally overstep the bounds of reality.

Examples: In *Gulliver's Travels,* Jonathan Swift creates imaginary worlds to present his satire of 18th-century England. Mary Coleridge uses fantasy to underscore the situational irony in her short story "The King Is Dead, Long Live the King." In Muriel Spark's "The First Year of My Life," the presentation of events from the perspective of an infant is an element of fantasy.

See page 607.

Farce A farce is a type of exaggerated comedy that features an absurd plot, ridiculous situations, and humorous dialogue. The main purpose of a farce is to keep an audience laughing. The characters are usually stereotypes, or simplified examples of different traits or qualities. They may seem reasonable at the start but soon become far-fetched. Comic devices typically used in farces include mistaken identity, deception, wordplay—such as puns and double meanings—and exaggeration.

See also **Stereotype.**

Fiction *Fiction* refers to imaginative works of prose, primarily the novel and the short story. Although fiction sometimes draws on actual events and real people, it springs mainly from the imagination of the writer. The purpose of fiction is to entertain, but it also enlightens by providing a deeper understanding of the human

1336 GLOSSARY OF LITERARY TERMS

condition. The basic elements of fiction are plot, character, setting, and theme.

See page 868.

See also **Character; Fable; Fantasy; Novel; Plot; Setting; Short Story; Theme.**

Figurative Language Language that communicates meanings beyond the literal meanings of the words is called figurative language. A figurative expression is not literally true, but rather creates an impression in the reader's mind. Writers use figurative language to create effects, to emphasize ideas, and to evoke emotions. Figurative language is used in both prose and poetry, as well as in oral expression. Special types of figurative language, called figures of speech, include simile, metaphor, personification, hyperbole, and apostrophe.

Examples: In his poem "Preludes," T. S. Eliot uses four kinds of figurative language: (1) simile—"The worlds revolve like ancient women / Gathering fuel in vacant lots"; (2) metaphor—"The burnt-out ends of smoky days"; (3) personification—"The morning comes to consciousness"; (4) hyperbole—"The thousand sordid images." An example of apostrophe is in Milton's *Paradise Lost,* line 6, "Sing, Heavenly Muse . . ."

See pages 306, 1054.

See also **Apostrophe; Hyperbole; Metaphor; Personification; Simile.**

First-Person Point of View *See* **Point of View.**

Flashback A flashback is an account of a conversation, an episode, or an event that happened before the beginning of a story. By revealing significant thoughts, experiences, or events in a character's life, a flashback can help readers understand a character's present situation. Flashbacks may take the form of reminiscences, dream sequences, or descriptions by third-person narrators; they usually interrupt the chronological flow of a story. Flashbacks may contain foreshadowing or other clues to the outcome of a story.

Examples: The use of flashback in Virginia Woolf's "The Duchess and the Jeweller" helps to reveal the conflicting emotions and motivations of the jeweller. The use of flashback in William Trevor's "The Distant Past" provides important background for understanding the relationship of the Middletons to the townspeople.

See page 1157.

Foil A foil is a character who provides a striking contrast to another character. By using a foil, a writer can call attention to certain traits possessed by a main character or simply enhance a character by contrast.

Folk Ballad *See* **Ballad.**

Folk Tale A folk tale is a story that is handed down, usually by word of mouth, from generation to generation. Folk tales reflect the unique characteristics of the regions they come from, showing how the inhabitants live and what their values are. Many involve supernatural events, and most suggest morals. Often, things happen in threes in folk tales. Leo Tolstoy's "What Men Live By" is a version of a Russian folk tale.

See page 929.

Foreshadowing Foreshadowing is a writer's use of hints or clues that suggest what events will occur later in a narrative. The use of foreshadowing creates suspense while preparing readers for what is to come.

Example: In "The Rocking-Horse Winner," the strange mad frenzy with which Paul rides his rocking horse early in the story foreshadows the tragedy of his final ride.

See pages 324, 1019.

Form When applied to poetry, the term *form* refers to all the principles of arrangement in a poem—the ways in which the words and images are organized and patterned to produce a pleasing whole, including the length and placement of lines and the grouping of lines into stanzas. Elements of form—such as the sound devices of rhythm, rhyme, alliteration, consonance, and assonance—work together with elements such as figurative language and imagery to shape a poem, convey meaning, and create a total experience for the reader. The term *form* can also refer to a type of poetry,

GLOSSARY OF LITERARY TERMS 1337

such as the sonnet or the dramatic monologue. William Wordsworth's "The World Is Too Much with Us," "It Is a Beauteous Evening," and "I Wandered Lonely As a Cloud" all provide good examples of the poet's artful use of form.

See page 771.
See also **Structure.**

Frame Story A frame story exists when a story is told within a narrative setting or frame—hence creating a story within a story.

Examples: The collection of tales in Chaucer's *The Canterbury Tales,* including "The Pardoner's Tale" and "The Wife of Bath's Tale," are set within a frame story. The frame is introduced in "The Prologue," in which 30 characters on a pilgrimage to Canterbury agree to tell stories to pass the time. "Federigo's Falcon" and the other tales in Boccaccio's *Decameron* are set within a similar framework. The frame, or outer story, is about ten characters fleeing plague-ravaged Florence, Italy, who decide to amuse themselves by telling stories.

See page 154.

Free Verse Free verse is verse that does not contain regular patterns of rhythm and rhyme. The lines in free verse often flow more naturally than do rhymed, metrical lines and thus achieve a rhythm more like that of everyday speech. Although free verse lacks conventional meter, it may contain various rhythmic and sound effects, such as repetitions of syllables or words. Free verse can also contain rhyme, although the rhyme will not follow predictable patterns. Much 20th-century poetry, such as Stephen Spender's "What I Expected" and T. S. Eliot's "The Hollow Men," is written in free verse.

See pages 1073, 1085.

Haiku Haiku is a form of Japanese poetry that embodies three qualities greatly valued in Japanese art: precision, economy, and delicacy. Nature is a particularly important source of inspiration for Japanese haiku poets, and details from nature are often the subject of their poems. The rules of haiku are strict—in only 17 syllables, arranged in 3 lines of 5, 7, and 5 syllables, the poet must create a clear picture that will evoke a strong emotional response in the reader. The poems of Matsuo Bashō and Kobayashi Issa are examples of haiku.

See page 720.

Hero A hero, or **protagonist,** is a central character in a work of fiction, drama, or epic poetry. A traditional hero possesses good qualities that enable him or her to triumph over an antagonist who is bad or evil in some way.

The term ***tragic hero,*** first used by the Greek philosopher Aristotle, refers to a central character in a drama who is dignified or noble. According to Aristotle, a tragic hero possesses a defect, or tragic flaw, that brings about or contributes to his or her downfall. This flaw may be poor judgment, pride, weakness, or an excess of an admirable quality. The tragic hero, Aristotle noted, recognizes his or her flaw and its consequences, but only after it is too late to change the course of events. The characters Macbeth and Hamlet in Shakespeare's tragedies are tragic heroes.

A **cultural hero** is a hero who represents the values of his or her culture. Such a hero ranks somewhere between ordinary human beings and the gods. The role of a cultural hero is to provide a noble image that will inspire and guide the actions of mortals. Beowulf is a cultural hero.

In more recent literature, heroes do not necessarily command the attention and admiration of an entire culture. They tend to be individuals whose actions and decisions reflect personal courage. The conflicts they face are not on an epic scale but instead involve moral dilemmas presented in the course of living. Such heroes are often in a struggle with established authority because their actions challenge accepted beliefs. The sergeant in Lady Gregory's play *The Rising of the Moon* might be viewed as such a hero.

See also **Epic; Protagonist; Tragedy.**

Heroic Couplet *See* **Couplet.**

Historical Writing Historical writing is the systematic telling, often in narrative form, of the past of a nation or group of people. Historical writing generally has the following

1338 GLOSSARY OF LITERARY TERMS

characteristics: (1) it is concerned with real events; (2) it uses chronological order; and (3) it is usually an objective retelling of facts rather than a personal interpretation. The Venerable Bede's *A History of the English Church and People* is an example of historical writing.

See page 104.

Humor In literature there are three basic types of humor, all of which may involve exaggeration or irony. **Humor of situation** is derived from the plot of a work. It usually involves exaggerated events or situational irony, which occurs when something happens that is different from what was expected. **Humor of character** is often based on exaggerated personalities or on characters who fail to recognize their own flaws, a form of dramatic irony. **Humor of language** may include sarcasm, exaggeration, puns, or verbal irony, which occurs when what is said is not what is meant. In *Candide,* Voltaire uses all three kinds of humor, including absurd situations, ridiculous characters, and ironic descriptions.

See page 629.

Hyperbole Hyperbole is a figure of speech in which the truth is exaggerated for emphasis or for humorous effect. Notice the jarring effect created by this hyperbole:

> **"Through the aperture driver and passenger, not six inches between them, remained for an eternity eye to eye."**
> **—Elizabeth Bowen, from "The Demon Lover"**

The following example of hyperbole has a humorous effect:

> **"A court-martial sat upon him, and he was asked which he liked best, either to run the gauntlet six and thirty times through the whole regiment, or to have his brains blown out with a dozen musket balls."**
> **—Voltaire, from *Candide***

See page 468.
See also **Figurative Language.**

Iambic Pentameter Iambic pentameter is a metrical line of five feet, or units, each of which is made up of two syllables, the first unstressed and the second stressed. Iambic pentameter is the most common form of meter used in English poetry; it is the meter used in blank verse, the heroic couplet, and the sonnet. The following line is an example of iambic pentameter:

> **Hŏw sóon hăth Tíme, thĕ súbtlĕ thiéf**
> **ŏf yóuth**
> **—John Milton, from "How Soon Hath Time"**

Iambic pentameter is also the meter Milton used in his epic *Paradise Lost.*

See page 790.
See also **Blank Verse; Couplet; Meter; Sonnet.**

Imagery The term *imagery* refers to words and phrases that create vivid sensory experiences for the reader. The majority of images are visual, but imagery may also appeal to the senses of smell, hearing, taste, and touch. In addition, images may re-create sensations of heat (thermal), movement (kinetic), and bodily tension (kinesthetic). Effective writers of both prose and poetry frequently use imagery that appeals to more than one sense simultaneously. For example, in John Keats's ode "To Autumn," the image "Thy hair soft-lifted by the winnowing wind," appeals to two senses—sight and touch.

When an image describes one sensation in terms of another, the technique is called **synesthesia.** For example, the phrase "cold smell of potato mold" from Seamus Heaney's poem "Digging" is an image appealing to smell described in terms of touch (temperature).

A poet may use a **controlling image** to convey thoughts or feelings. A controlling image is a single image or comparison that extends throughout a literary work and shapes its meaning. A controlling image sometimes is an **extended metaphor.** The image of the Greek vase in Keats's "Ode on a Grecian Urn" and the image of digging in Heaney's poem "Digging" are controlling images.

See pages 738, 945, 992, 1085, 1246, 1299.
See also **Kinesthetic Imagery.**

GLOSSARY OF LITERARY TERMS 1339

Glossary of Literary Terms

Informal Essay *See* **Essay.**

Interior Monologue *See* **Stream of Consciousness.**

Internal Conflict *See* **Conflict.**

Internal Rhyme *See* **Rhyme.**

Irony Irony is a contrast between expectation and reality. This incongruity often has the effect of surprising the reader or viewer. The techniques of irony include hyperbole, understatement, and sarcasm. Irony is often subtle and easily overlooked or misinterpreted.

There are three main types of irony. **Situational irony** occurs when a character or the reader expects one thing to happen but something else actually happens. In Mary Coleridge's story "The King Is Dead, Long Live the King," the king's—and the reader's—expectations are repeatedly overturned. In Thomas Hardy's poem "Ah, Are You Digging on My Grave?" the speaker questions who is digging on her grave and why. The responses to her questions and the final revelation shock the speaker and create a shattering irony in the poem.

Verbal irony occurs when a writer or character says one thing but means another. An example of verbal irony is the title of Jonathan Swift's essay "A Modest Proposal." The reader soon discovers that the narrator's proposal is outrageous rather than modest and unassuming.

Dramatic irony occurs when the reader or viewer knows something that a character does not know. In Muriel Spark's story "The First Year of My Life," the characters in the final scene think that the baby smiles because her brother blows out the candle on her birthday cake. The reader knows, however, that she smiles in response to hearing someone quote a prominent politician.

See pages 324, 620, 896, 961, 1004, 1019, 1081, 1174.

Italian (Petrarchan) Sonnet *See* **Sonnet.**

Kenning *See* **Anglo-Saxon Poetry.**

Kinesthetic Imagery Kinesthetic imagery re-creates the tension felt through muscles, tendons, or joints in the body.

Example: An example of kinesthetic imagery is the following description from Doris Lessing's "A Sunrise on the Veld": "he felt the chilled dust push up between his toes."

See page 1217.

See also **Imagery.**

Letters *Letters* refers to the written correspondence exchanged between acquaintances, friends, or family members. Most such letters are private and not designed for publication.

Examples: *The Paston Letters,* the correspondence of a family in Norfolk, England, is a famous collection of letters. Other well-known letter writers include Lord Chesterfield, Lady Mary Wortley Montagu, Fanny Burney, and John Keats. Letters provide an invaluable source of information about the social, historical, and political conditions of the period in which they were written.

See page 180.

Literary Ballad *See* **Ballad.**

Lyric A lyric is a short poem in which a single speaker expresses personal thoughts and feelings. Most poems other than dramatic and narrative poems are lyrics. In ancient Greece, lyrics were meant to be sung—the word *lyric* comes from the word *lyre,* the name of a musical instrument that was used to accompany songs. Modern lyrics are not usually intended for singing, but they are characterized by strong, melodic rhythms. Lyrics can be in a variety of forms and cover many subjects, from love and death to everyday experiences. They are marked by imagination and create for the reader a strong, unified impression.

Examples: "The Wife's Lament," Shakespeare's sonnets, Keats's odes, and Margaret Atwood's "The Moment" are all lyrics. Sir Thomas Wyatt's "My Lute, Awake!" is an example of a lyric that was written to be set to music.

See also **Poetry.**

Major Character *See* **Character.**

1340 GLOSSARY OF LITERARY TERMS

Memoir A memoir is a form of autobiographical writing in which a person recalls significant events in his or her life. Most memoirs share the following characteristics: (1) they usually are structured as narratives told by the writers themselves, using the first-person point of view; (2) though some names may be changed to protect privacy, memoirs are true accounts of actual events; (3) although basically personal, memoirs may deal with newsworthy events having a significance beyond the confines of the writers' lives; (4) unlike strictly historical accounts, memoirs often include the writers' feelings and opinions about historical events, giving the reader insight into the impact of history on people's lives. Vera Brittain's *Testament of Youth* is a memoir from the period of World War I.

See page 1124.
See also **Autobiography.**

Metaphor A metaphor is a figure of speech that makes a comparison between two things that are basically unlike but have something in common. Unlike a simile, a metaphor does not contain the word *like* or *as.* In the following poem, the phrase "Time's wingéd chariot" is a metaphor in which the swift passage of time is compared to a speeding chariot:

> **But at my back I always hear**
> **Time's wingéd chariot hurrying near**
> **—Andrew Marvell, from "To His Coy Mistress"**

See pages 468, 474.
See also **Extended Metaphor; Figurative Language; Simile.**

Metaphysical Poetry Metaphysical poetry is a style of poetry written by a group of 17th-century poets, of whom John Donne was the first. The metaphysical poets rejected the conventions of Elizabethan love poetry, with its musical quality and themes of courtly love. Instead, they approached subjects such as religion, death, and even love by analyzing them logically and philosophically. The metaphysical poets were intellectuals who, like the ideal Renaissance man, were well-read in a broad spectrum of subjects. The characteristics of metaphysical poetry include more than just an intellectual approach to subject matter, however. Instead of the lyrical style of most Elizabethan poetry, metaphysical poets used a more colloquial, or conversational, style. In spite of the simplicity of the words, the ideas may seem obscure or confusing at first, because metaphysical poets loved to play with language. Donne's writing is filled with surprising twists: unexpected images and comparisons, as well as the use of **paradox,** seemingly contradictory statements that in fact reveal some element of truth. Donne's poem "A Valediction: Forbidding Mourning" contains many characteristics of metaphysical poetry.

See page 449.
See also **Paradox.**

Meter Meter is the repetition of a regular rhythmic unit in poetry. The meter of a poem emphasizes the musical quality of the language. Each unit of meter is known as a **foot,** consisting of one stressed syllable and one or two unstressed syllables. In representations of meter, a stressed syllable is often indicated by the symbol ´, an unstressed syllable by the symbol ˘. The four basic types of metrical feet are the **iamb,** an unstressed syllable followed by a stressed syllable (˘ ´); the **trochee,** a stressed syllable followed by an unstressed syllable (´ ˘); the **anapest,** two unstressed syllables followed by a stressed syllable (˘ ˘ ´); and the **dactyl,** a stressed syllable followed by two unstressed syllables (´ ˘ ˘).

Two words are used to identify the meter of a line of poetry. The first word describes the predominant type of metrical foot in the line. The second word describes the number of feet in the line: dimeter (two feet), trimeter (three feet), tetrameter (four feet), pentameter (five feet), hexameter (six feet), and so forth. The meter in this poem is iambic tetrameter:

> **Ĭ hóld ĭt trúe, whăte'ér bĕfáll;**
> **Ĭ féel ĭt, whén Ĭ sórrŏw móst;**
> **'Tĭs béttĕr tó hăve lóved ănd lóst**
> **Thăn névĕr tó hăve lóved ăt áll.**
> **—Alfred, Lord Tennyson, from *In Memoriam***

Glossary of Literary Terms

GLOSSARY OF LITERARY TERMS 1341

Poets use variations within a regular metrical pattern—adding an extra syllable or reversing the stressed and unstressed syllables in a foot—to create the effects they want and to reinforce meaning. In his poem "Still to Be Neat," Ben Jonson also uses iambic tetrameter, but he frequently changes iambs to trochees to achieve emphasis and to create interesting rhythmic effects:

> **Still to be neat, still to be dressed,**
> **As you were going to a feast;**
> **Still to be powdered, still perfumed;**
> **Lady, it is to be presumed,**
> **Though art's hid causes are not found,**
> **All is not sweet, all is not sound.**
> **—Ben Jonson, from "Still to Be Neat"**

See page 790.
See also **Free Verse; Iambic Pentameter; Rhythm.**

Minor Character *See* **Character.**

Miracle Play *See* **Mystery Play.**

Monologue *See* **Dramatic Monologue; Soliloquy.**

Mood Mood is the feeling, or atmosphere, that a writer creates for the reader. The use of connotation, details, dialogue, imagery, figurative language, foreshadowing, setting, and rhythm can help set the mood.

Example: The mood of Rudyard Kipling's "The Miracle of Purun Bhagat" is one of peace and reflection, created in part by the descriptions of the main character and his relationships with other people, the land, and the animals.

See pages 796, 1246.
See also **Tone.**

Morality Play *See* **Mystery Play.**

Motif A motif is a recurring word, phrase, image, object, idea, or action in a work of literature. Motifs function as unifying devices and often relate directly to one or more major themes. Motifs in "The Prologue" to *The Canterbury Tales,* for example, include images of earthly love along with images of spiritual devotion. In *Macbeth,* references to blood, sleep, and water form motifs in the play.

Mystery Play A mystery play is a drama, written in the Middle Ages, that portrays a biblical story. Mystery plays were first performed in churches but were later staged outdoors. Closely related to mystery plays were miracle plays, which dramatized saints' lives, and morality plays, which dramatized moral conflicts through allegory; the characters in morality plays were allegorical figures, such as Vice, Mercy, Death, and Good Deeds. These types of plays became increasingly elaborate and popular, and some were performed well into the Renaissance period.

Narration *See* **Narrative; Narrator; Point of View.**

Narrative A narrative is any type of writing that is primarily concerned with relating an event or a series of events. A narrative can be imaginary, like a short story or a novel, or it can be factual, like a newspaper account or a work of history. *Memoirs of Madame Vigée-Lebrun* and Penelope Lively's story "At the Pitt-Rivers" are both narratives.

Narrative Poem A narrative poem tells a story. Like a short story or a novel, a narrative poem has the following elements: characters, setting, plot, and point of view, all of which combine to develop a theme.

Examples: Epics, such as *Beowulf* and the *Iliad,* are narrative poems, as are ballads. Samuel Taylor Coleridge's *The Rime of the Ancient Mariner* is also a narrative poem.

See page 745.

Narrator The narrator of a literary work is the person or voice that tells the story. The narrator can be a character in the story or a voice outside the action.

Examples: In Nadine Gordimer's "Six Feet of the Country," the narrator participates in the incidents he recounts. The narrator of Elizabeth Gaskell's "Christmas Storms and Sunshine," is, on the other hand, observant but detached.

See page 167.

Naturalism An extreme form of realism, naturalism in fiction involves the depiction of

1342 GLOSSARY OF LITERARY TERMS

life objectively and precisely, without idealizing. Like the realist, the naturalist accurately portrays the world. However, the naturalist creates characters who are victims of environmental forces and internal drives beyond their comprehension and control. Naturalistic fiction conveys the belief that everything that exists is part of the scheme of nature, explainable entirely by natural and physical causes.

Example: Doris Lessing's "A Sunrise on the Veld," which depicts a boy who encounters death and brutality in nature, has naturalistic aspects.

See also **Realism.**

Neoclassicism *Neoclassicism* refers to the attitudes toward life and art that dominated English literature during the Restoration and the 18th century. Neoclassicists respected order, reason, and rules and viewed humans as limited and imperfect. To them, the intellect was more important than emotions, and society was more important than the individual. Imitating classical literature, neoclassical writers developed a style that was characterized by strict form, logic, symmetry, grace, good taste, restraint, clarity, and conciseness. Their works were meant not only to delight readers but also to instruct them in moral virtues and correct social behavior. Among the literary forms that flourished during the neoclassical period were the essay, the literary letter, and the epigram. The heroic couplet was the dominant verse form, and satire and parody prevailed in both prose and poetry. For examples of neoclassical works, see the selections by Alexander Pope, Jonathan Swift, and Samuel Johnson.

See also **Romanticism.**

Nonfiction Nonfiction is prose writing that is about real people, places, and events. Unlike fiction, nonfiction is largely concerned with factual information, although the writer selects and interprets the information according to his or her purpose and viewpoint. Although the subject matter of nonfiction is not imaginative, the writer's style may be individualistic and innovative. Types of nonfiction include autobiographies, biographies, letters, essays, diaries, journals, memoirs, and speeches. Examples include *The Paston Letters* and Winston Churchill's speeches.

See page 546.
See also **Autobiography; Biography; Diary; Essay; Memoir.**

Novel A novel is an extended work of fiction. Like a short story, a novel is essentially the product of a writer's imagination. The most obvious difference between a novel and a short story is length. Because the novel is considerably longer, a novelist can develop a wider range of characters and a more complex plot.

Octave *See* **Sonnet.**

Ode An ode is an exalted, complex lyric that develops a serious and dignified theme. Odes appeal to both the imagination and the intellect, and many commemorate events or praise people or elements of nature. Examples of odes that celebrate an element of nature are Percy Bysshe Shelley's "Ode to the West Wind" and "To a Skylark."

Off Rhyme *See* **Rhyme.**

Omniscient Point of View *See* **Point of View.**

Onomatopoeia Onomatopoeia is the use of words whose sounds echo their meanings, such as *buzz, whisper, gargle,* and *murmur.* Onomatopoeia as a literary technique goes beyond the use of simple echoic words, however. Skilled writers, especially poets, choose words whose sounds in combination suggest meaning. In the following lines, the poet uses onomatopoeia to help convey the images and meanings he wants to express:

> **Whatever is fickle, freckled (who knows how?)**
> **With swift, slow; sweet, sour; adazzle, dim**
> **—Gerard Manley Hopkins, from "Pied Beauty"**

See pages 744, 766.

Oxymoron *See* **Paradox.**

Parable A parable is a brief story that is meant to teach a lesson or illustrate a moral truth. A parable is more than a simple story,

Glossary of Literary Terms

GLOSSARY OF LITERARY TERMS 1343

however. Each detail of the parable corresponds to some aspect of the problem or moral dilemma to which it is directed. The story of the prodigal son in the Bible is a classic parable.

Paradox A paradox is a statement that seems to contradict itself but, in fact, reveals some element of truth. Paradox is found frequently in the poetry of the 16th and 17th centuries. The first line of the following couplet contains two examples of paradox:

> **I am and not, I freeze and yet am burned,**
> **Since from myself another self I turned.**
> **—Elizabeth I, from "On Monsieur's Departure"**

A special kind of concise paradox is the **oxymoron,** which brings together two contradictory terms. Examples are "cruel kindness" and "brave fear."

See pages 451, 1096.
See also **Metaphysical Poetry.**

Parallelism Parallelism is the use of similar grammatical constructions to express ideas that are related or equal in importance. The parallel elements may be words, phrases, sentences, or paragraphs. In Lady Mary Montagu's letters, the writer frequently uses parallelism to reflect the relationship between ideas:

> **It seemed your business to learn how to live in the world, as it is hers to know how to be easy out of it.**
> **—Lady Mary Wortley Montagu, from "Letter to Her Daughter"**

See page 564.
See also **Repetition.**

Parody A parody imitates or mocks another work or type of literature. Like caricature in art, parody in literature mimics a subject or a style. The purpose of a parody may be to ridicule through broad humor. On the other hand, a parody may broaden understanding of or add insight to the original work. Some parodies are even written in tribute to a work of literature. ***Example:*** Shakespeare's "Sonnet 130" is in part a parody of love poetry of other Renaissance poets. The sonnet mocks some of the characteristics of the traditional beautiful woman praised in the earlier poems.

Pastoral A pastoral is a poem presenting shepherds in rural settings, usually in an idealized manner. The language and form of pastorals are artificial. The supposedly simple, rustic characters tend to use formal, courtly speech, and the meters and rhyme schemes are characteristic of formal poetry. Renaissance poets were drawn to the pastoral as a means of conveying their own emotions and ideas, particularly about love. Christopher Marlowe's "The Passionate Shepherd to His Love" is a pastoral.

See page 293.

Personal Essay *See* **Essay.**

Personification Personification is a figure of speech in which human qualities are attributed to an object, animal, or idea. Writers use personification to communicate feelings and images in a concise, concrete way. In line 117 of Thomas Gray's "Elegy Written in a Country Churchyard," for example, the earth is personified: "Here rests his head upon the lap of Earth." In these lines, time is personified:

> **Love's not Time's fool, though rosy lips and cheeks**
> **Within his bending sickle's compass come,**
> **—William Shakespeare, from "Sonnet 116"**

See pages 672, 796.
See also **Figurative Language; Metaphor; Simile.**

Persuasion Persuasion is a technique used by speakers and writers to convince an audience to adopt a particular opinion, perform an action, or both. Effective persuasion appeals to both the intellect and the emotions. The most common form of persuasion is the oration, or speech, as in Winston's Churchill's speech of May 19, 1940.

See pages 1133, 1155.
See also **Essay.**

Persuasive Essay *See* **Essay; Persuasion.**

Persuasive Speech *See* **Persuasion.**

1344 GLOSSARY OF LITERARY TERMS

Petrarchan (Italian) Sonnet *See* **Sonnet.**

Plot Plot is the sequence of actions and events in a narrative. Usually, the events of a plot progress because of a conflict, or struggle between opposing forces. Most plots include the following stages:

1. The **exposition** lays the groundwork for the plot and provides the reader with essential background information. Characters are introduced, the setting is described, and the major conflict is identified. Although the exposition generally appears at the opening of a work, it may also occur later in the narrative.
2. In the **rising action,** complications usually arise, causing difficulties for the main characters and making the conflict more difficult to resolve. As the characters struggle to find solutions to the conflict, suspense builds.
3. The **climax** is the turning point of the action, the moment when interest and intensity reach their peak. The climax of a work usually involves an important event, decision, or discovery that affects the final outcome.
4. The **falling action** consists of the events that occur after the climax. Often, the conflict is resolved, and the intensity of the action subsides. Sometimes this phase of the plot is called the **resolution** or the **denouement** (dā'nōō-mäɴ'). *Denouement* is from a French word that means "untying"—in this stage the tangles of the plot are untied and mysteries are solved.

See pages 177, 883, 896.
See also **Conflict.**

Poetry Poetry is an arrangement of lines on the page in which form and content fuse to suggest meanings beyond the literal meanings of the words. Like other forms of literature, poetry attempts to re-create emotions and experiences. Poetry, however, is usually more compressed and suggestive than prose. Because poetry frequently does not include the kind of explanation common in the short story or the novel, it tends to leave more to the reader's imagination.

Many poems are divided into stanzas. The stanzas of a poem may contain the same number of lines, or they may vary in length. Some poems have definite patterns of meter and rhyme. Others, especially poems of the 20th century, rely more on the sounds of words and less on fixed rhythms and rhyme schemes. Characteristic of poetry is the use of imagery, language that appeals to the senses. Poetry is also rich in connotative words and figurative language.

See also **Figurative Language; Form; Free Verse; Imagery; Meter; Repetition; Rhyme; Rhythm; Stanza.**

Point of View *Point of view* refers to the method of narrating a short story, novel, narrative poem, or work of nonfiction. The three most common points of view are first-person, third-person omniscient, and third-person limited. The point of view that a writer employs determines to a great degree the reader's view of the action and the characters; manipulation of point of view creates many striking effects in fiction.

In **first-person point of view,** the narrator is a character in the work, narrating the action as he or she perceives and understands it. First-person narration imparts an immediacy to the narrative and usually leads to involvement with the narrating character. Two short stories using first-person narration are "Araby" by James Joyce and "At the Pitt-Rivers" by Penelope Lively. Almost all autobiographies have first-person narration.

In **third-person point of view,** events and characters are described by a narrator outside the action. In **third-person omniscient point of view,** the narrator is omniscient, or all-knowing, and can see into the mind of more than one character. The use of a third-person omniscient narrator gives the writer great flexibility and provides the reader with access to all the characters' motivations and responses and to events that may be occurring simultaneously. In D. H. Lawrence's "The Rocking-Horse Winner," the use of a third-person omniscient narrator allows for psychological complexity and depth that would not be possible with a first-person narrator.

When a writer uses **third-person limited point of view,** the narrator tells the story from the perspective of only one of the characters. The reader learns only what that character thinks, feels, observes, and experiences. Doris Lessing's "A Sunrise on the Veld" is told from a

GLOSSARY OF LITERARY TERMS 1345

third-person limited point of view. Lessing's use of this point of view allows the reader to see how the boy's character changes as the story develops.

See pages 883, 1029, 1197, 1217, 1227, 1299.
See also **Narrator.**

Primary Source A primary source is a book, document, or person that provides original, firsthand information about a topic. Primary sources for an event or period of history might include letters, wills, diaries, tape recordings, and government records. A person can be a primary source for events that he or she has experienced or witnessed. Etty Hillesum's letters are a primary source for information about the Holocaust.

Prop The word *prop,* an abbreviation of *property,* refers to any physical object that is used in a stage production. In Lady Gregory's *The Rising of the Moon,* the props include placards and a hat and wig.

See also **Drama.**

Prose Generally, *prose* refers to all forms of written or spoken expression that are organized and that lack regular rhythmic patterns. Prose is characterized by logical order, continuity of thought, and individual style. Prose style varies from one writer to another, depending on such elements as word choice, sentence length and structure, use of figurative language, and tone.

Examples: Examples of the variety of prose styles can be seen in John Donne's religious meditations from the 17th century, Samuel Johnson's essays from the 18th century, Elizabeth Gaskell's fiction from the 19th century, and Katherine Mansfield's fiction from the 20th century.

See also **Poetry.**

Protagonist The central character in a story, novel, or play is called the protagonist. The protagonist is always involved in the main conflict of the plot and often changes during the course of the work. The force or person who opposes the protagonist is the antagonist.

Examples: In Boccaccio's story "Federigo's Falcon," the protagonist is Federigo, who considers himself opposed by Fortune. In 20th-century fiction and drama, the conflict may be subtle, and the protagonist is not always opposed by an antagonist. In Penelope Lively's story "At the Pitt-Rivers," for example, the main character changes in his perceptions as the story develops, but he is not opposed by another character or by an outside force.

See also **Antagonist; Hero.**

Quatrain A quatrain is a four-line stanza, or unit, of poetry. The most common stanza in English poetry, the quatrain can display a variety of meters and rhyme schemes. The following quatrain follows a typical *abab* rhyme scheme:

Gather ye rosebuds while ye may, ***a***
Old time is still a-flying; ***b***
And this same flower that smiles today ***a***
Tomorrow will be dying. ***b***
—Robert Herrick, from "To the Virgins, to Make Much of Time"

See also **Ballad; Form; Sonnet; Stanza.**

Realism As a general term, *realism* refers to any effort to offer an accurate and detailed portrayal of actual life. In this sense, realism has been a significant element in almost every school of writing in human history. Thus, critics praise Geoffrey Chaucer's realistic descriptions of people from all social classes and analyze Shakespeare's realistic portrayals of character.

Realism also refers to a literary method developed in the 19th century. The 19th-century realists based their writing on careful observations of ordinary life, often focusing on the middle or lower classes. They attempted to present life objectively and honestly, without the sentimentality or idealism that had characterized earlier literature, particularly fiction. Typically, the realists developed settings in great detail in an effort to re-create specific times and places for the reader. Modern realists focus on characterization and avoid contrived plot structures.

Examples: Elements of realism can be found in the novels of Jane Austen and Charles Dickens, but it is not fully developed until the fiction of George Eliot. James Joyce's story "Araby" and

1346 GLOSSARY OF LITERARY TERMS

Nadine Gordimer's "Six Feet of the Country" are examples of 20th-century realistic fiction.

See page 1042.
See also **Naturalism.**

Repetition Repetition is a technique in which a sound, word, phrase, or line is repeated for emphasis or unity. The use of repetition often helps to reinforce meaning and to create an appealing rhythm. *Repetition* is a general term that includes specific devices associated with both prose and poetry, such as alliteration and parallelism. Examples of effective repetition can be found in William Blake's "The Lamb" and "The Tyger" and in Elizabeth Barrett Browning's "Sonnet 43."

See pages 440, 461, 1239.
See also **Alliteration; Assonance; Consonance; Parallelism; Rhyme; Rhyme Scheme.**

Resolution *See* **Plot.**

Rhyme Words rhyme when the sounds of their accented vowels and all succeeding sounds are identical, as in *amuse* and *confuse.* For true rhyme, the consonants that precede the vowels must be different. Rhyme that occurs at the end of lines of poetry is called **end rhyme,** as in Thomas Hardy's rhyming of *face* and *place* in "The Man He Killed." End rhymes that are not exact but approximate are called **off rhyme,** or **slant rhyme,** as in the words *come* and *doom* in Stevie Smith's "The Frog Prince." Rhyme that occurs within a single line is called **internal rhyme:**

> **Give crowns and pounds and guineas**
> **—A. E. Housman, from "When I Was One-and-Twenty"**

Rhyme Scheme A rhyme scheme is the pattern of end rhyme in a poem. A rhyme scheme is charted by assigning a letter of the alphabet, beginning with *a,* to each line. Lines that rhyme are given the same letter—in the following poem, for example, the rhyme scheme of each stanza is *aabab:*

> **Vengeance shall fall on thy disdain** *a*
> **That makest but game on earnest pain.** *a*
> **Think not alone under the sun** *b*
> **Unquit to cause thy lovers plain,** *a*
> **Although my lute and I have done.** *b*
> **—Sir Thomas Wyatt, from "My Lute, Awake!"**

See page 287.
See also **Ballad; Rhyme; Sonnet; Spenserian Stanza; Villanelle.**

Rhythm Rhythm is a pattern of stressed and unstressed syllables in a line of poetry. Poets use rhythm to bring out the musical quality of language, to emphasize ideas, to create mood, to unify a work, and to heighten emotional response. Devices such as alliteration, rhyme, assonance, consonance, and parallelism often contribute to creating rhythm. The slow rhythms of the following lines help to convey the mysterious mood of the poem:

> **I listened in emptiness on the**
> **moor-ridge.**
> **The curlew's tear turned its edge on**
> **the silence.**
> **—Ted Hughes, from "The Horses"**

See page 790.
See also **Anglo-Saxon Poetry; Ballad; Meter; Spenserian Stanza; Sprung Rhythm.**

Rising Action *See* **Plot.**

Romance The romance has been a popular narrative form since the Middle Ages. Generally, the term *romance* refers to any imaginative adventure concerned with noble heroes, gallant love, a chivalric code of honor, daring deeds, and supernatural events. Romances usually have faraway settings, depict events unlike those of ordinary life, and idealize their heroes as well as the eras in which the heroes lived. Medieval romances are often lighthearted in tone, usually consist of a number of episodes, and often involve one or more characters in a quest.

Example: Thomas Malory's *Le Morte d'Arthur* is an example of a medieval romance. Its stories of kings, knights, and ladies relate many

GLOSSARY OF LITERARY TERMS 1347

adventures, tales of love, superhuman feats, and quests for honor and virtue.

See pages 222, 237.

Romanticism *Romanticism* refers to a literary movement that flourished in Britain and Europe throughout much of the 19th century. Romantic writers looked to nature for their inspiration, idealized the distant past, and celebrated the individual. In reaction against neoclassicism, their treatment of subjects was emotional rather than rational, imaginative rather than analytical. The romantic period in English literature is generally viewed as beginning with the publication of *Lyrical Ballads,* poems by William Wordsworth and Samuel Taylor Coleridge.

See page 707.
See also **Neoclassicism.**

Sarcasm Sarcasm, a type of verbal irony, refers to a remark in which the literal meaning is complimentary but the actual meaning is critical. One such contemptuous remark is this one:

> **You have clearly proved that ignorance, idleness, and vice are the proper ingredients for qualifying a legislator.**
> **—Jonathan Swift, from *Gulliver's Travels***

See also **Irony.**

Satire Satire is a literary technique in which ideas, customs, behaviors, or institutions are ridiculed for the purpose of improving society. Satire may be gently witty, mildly abrasive, or bitterly critical, and it often uses exaggeration to force readers to see something in a more critical light. Often, a satirist will distance himself or herself from a subject by creating a fictional speaker—usually a calm, and often a naive, observer—who can address the topic without revealing the true emotions of the writer. The title character of Voltaire's *Candide* is an example of such an observer. Whether the object of a satiric work is an individual person or a group of people, the force of the satire will almost always cast light on foibles and failings that are universal to human experience.

There are two main types of satire, named for the Roman satirists Horace and Juvenal; they differ chiefly in tone. Horatian satire is playfully amusing and seeks to correct vice or foolishness with gentle laughter and sympathetic understanding. Joseph Addison's essays are examples of Horatian satire. Juvenalian satire provokes a darker kind of laughter. It is biting and criticizes corruption or incompetence with scorn and outrage. Jonathan Swift's "A Modest Proposal" is an example of Juvenalian satire.

See pages 584, 607, 961, 1286.
See also **Irony.**

Scripture Scripture is literature that is considered sacred—that is, it is used in religious rituals of worship, initiation, celebration, and mourning. Such literature is usually preserved in what are considered holy books. The hymns, chants, prayers, myths, and other forms passed down through generations and combined as a body of scripture express the core beliefs of a group of people. The excerpts from the King James Bible are examples of scripture gathered from the Jewish and Christian traditions.

Sestet *See* **Sonnet.**

Setting *Setting* is usually defined as "the time and place of the action of a short story, novel, play, narrative poem, or nonfiction narrative." In addition to time and place, however, setting may include the social and moral environment that form the background for a narrative. Setting is one of the main elements in fiction and often plays an important role in what happens and why. Sometimes it serves as a source of conflict, as in Doris Lessing's story "A Sunrise on the Veld."

See pages 912, 929, 1029, 1164, 1207.
See also **Fiction.**

Shakespearean (English) Sonnet *See* **Sonnet.**

Short Story A short story is a work of fiction that can be read in one sitting. Generally, a short story develops one major conflict. The basic elements of a short story are setting, character, plot, and theme.

A short story must be unified; all the elements must work together to produce a total effect. This unity of effect is reinforced through

1348 GLOSSARY OF LITERARY TERMS

an appropriate title and through the use of symbolism, irony, and other literary devices.

See also **Fiction.**

Simile A simile is a figure of speech that compares two things that are basically unlike yet have something in common. Unlike a metaphor, which implies or suggests a comparison, a simile states it by means of the word *like* or *as.* Both poets and prose writers use similes to intensify emotional response, stimulate vibrant images, provide imaginative delight, and concentrate the expression of ideas. In her story "The Duchess and the Jeweller," Virginia Woolf uses similes to describe the duchess as she sits down:

> **As a parasol with many flounces, as a peacock with many feathers, shuts its flounces, folds its feathers, so she subsided and shut herself as she sank down in the leather armchair.**
> **—Virginia Woolf, from "The Duchess and the Jeweller"**

An **epic simile** is a long comparison that often continues for a number of lines. It does not always contain the word *like* or *as.* Here is an example of an epic simile:

> **Conspicuous as the evening star that comes,**
> **amid the first in heaven, at fall of night,**
> **and stands most lovely in the west, so shone**
> **in sunlight the fine-pointed spear**
> **Achilles poised in his right hand. . . .**
> **—Homer, from the *Iliad***

See pages 81, 306, 738, 766.
See also **Figurative Language; Metaphor.**

Situational Irony *See* **Irony.**

Slant Rhyme *See* **Rhyme.**

Soliloquy A soliloquy is a speech in a dramatic work in which a character speaks his or her thoughts aloud. Usually the character is on the stage alone, not speaking to other characters and perhaps not even consciously addressing the audience. (If there are other characters on stage, they are ignored temporarily.) The purpose of a soliloquy is to reveal a character's inner thoughts, feelings, and plans to the audience. Soliloquies are characteristic of Elizabethan drama; *Macbeth* has several soliloquies. Following is part of Macbeth's most famous soliloquy.

> **Life's but a walking shadow, a poor player,**
> **That struts and frets his hour upon the stage**
> **And then is heard no more. It is a tale**
> **Told by an idiot, full of sound and fury,**
> **Signifying nothing.**
> **—William Shakespeare, from *Macbeth***

See page 324.

Sonnet A sonnet is a lyric poem of 14 lines, commonly written in **iambic pentameter.** For centuries the sonnet has been a popular form because it is long enough to permit development of a complex idea yet short and structured enough to challenge any poet's skills. Sonnets written in English usually follow one of two forms.

The **Petrarchan,** or **Italian, sonnet,** introduced into English by Sir Thomas Wyatt, is named after Petrarch, the 14th-century Italian poet. This type of sonnet consists of two parts, called the **octave** (the first eight lines) and the **sestet** (the last six lines). The usual rhyme scheme for the octave is *abbaabba.* The rhyme scheme for the sestet may be *cdecde, cdccdc,* or a similar variation. The octave generally presents a problem or raises a question, and the sestet resolves or comments on the problem. John Milton's sonnets are written in the Petrarchan form.

The **Shakespearean,** or **English, sonnet** is sometimes called the **Elizabethan sonnet.** It consists of three quatrains, or four-line units, and a final couplet. The typical rhyme scheme is *abab cdcd efef gg.* In the English sonnet, the rhymed couplet at the end of the sonnet provides a final commentary on the subject developed in the three quatrains. Shakespeare's sonnets are the finest examples of this type of sonnet.

A variation of the Shakespearean sonnet is the **Spenserian sonnet,** which has the same structure but uses the interlocking rhyme scheme *abab bcbc cdcd ee.* Spenser's "Sonnet 30" is an example.

Some poets have written a series of related sonnets that have the same subject. These are

GLOSSARY OF LITERARY TERMS 1349

called **sonnet sequences,** or **sonnet cycles.** Toward the end of the 16th century, writing sonnet sequences became fashionable, with a common subject being love for a beautiful but unattainable woman. Francesco Petrarch, Edmund Spenser, and Elizabeth Barrett Browning wrote sonnet sequences.

See pages 295, 300, 306, 311, 479.
See also **Iambic Pentameter; Lyric; Meter; Quatrain.**

Sound Devices *See* **Alliteration; Assonance; Consonance; Meter; Onomatopoeia; Repetition; Rhyme; Rhyme Scheme; Rhythm.**

Speaker The speaker in a poem is the voice that "talks" to the reader, like the narrator in fiction. The speaker is sometimes a distant observer and at other times intimately involved with the experiences and ideas being expressed in the poem. The speaker and poet are not necessarily identical. Often a poet creates a speaker with a distinct identity in order to achieve a particular effect.

Examples: The speaker of Alfred, Lord Tennyson's poem "The Lady of Shalott" is neutral and objective, as though merely recording observations. The speaker in Tennyson's "Ulysses," on the other hand, is passionately involved in the ideas and feelings he is expressing.

See pages 852, 1111.

Spenserian Stanza The Spenserian stanza (named for Edmund Spenser, who invented it for his romance *The Faerie Queene*) consists of nine iambic lines rhyming in the pattern *ababbcbcc.* Each of the first eight lines contains five feet, and the ninth contains six. The rhyming pattern helps to create unity, and the six-foot line, called an **alexandrine,** slows down the stanza and so gives dignity and allows for reflection on the ideas in the stanza. Byron used the Spenserian stanza in *Childe Harold's Pilgrimage.*

See also **Stanza.**

Sprung Rhythm In order to approximate the rhythms of natural speech in poetry, the poet Gerard Manley Hopkins developed what he called sprung rhythm. The lines of a poem written in sprung rhythm have fixed numbers of stressed syllables but varying numbers of unstressed syllables. A line may contain several consecutive stressed syllables, or a stressed syllable may be followed by one, two, or even three unstressed syllables. The following lines are written in sprung rhythm:

> **Lándscăpe plóttĕd ănd piéced—fóld,**
> **fállŏw, ănd plóugh;**
> **Ănd áll trádes, thĕir geár ănd tácklĕ**
> **ănd trím.**
> **—Gerard Manley Hopkins, from "Pied Beauty"**

See page 950.

Stage Directions *See* **Drama.**

Stanza A stanza is a group of lines that form a unit in a poem. The stanza is roughly comparable to the paragraph in prose. In traditional poems, the stanzas usually have the same number of lines and often have the same rhyme scheme and meter. In the 20th century, poets have experimented more freely with stanza form, sometimes writing poems that have no stanza breaks at all.

Examples: The quatrains in Richard Lovelace's "To Lucasta, Going to the Wars," are a traditional stanza form. The two stanzas of W. B. Yeats's "The Second Coming," one 8 lines long and the other 14 lines long, are an example of an unconventional stanza form.

See page 967.
See also **Quatrain; Spenserian Stanza; Villanelle.**

Stereotype In literature, simplified or stock characters who conform to a fixed pattern or are defined by a single trait are called stereotypes. Such characters do not usually demonstrate the complexities of real people.

Examples: Familiar stereotypes in popular literature include the absent-minded professor, the busybody, and the merciless villain. The figure of the rejected lover in many ballads is another example of a stereotype.

Stream of Consciousness *Stream of consciousness* refers to a style of fiction that takes as its subject the flow of thoughts,

1350 GLOSSARY OF LITERARY TERMS

responses, and sensations of one or more characters. A stream-of-consciousness narrative is not structured as a coherent, logical presentation of ideas. Rather, the connections between ideas are associative, with one idea suggesting another.

A character's stream of consciousness is often expressed as an interior monologue, a record of the total workings of the character's mind and emotions. An interior monologue may reveal the inner experience of the character on many levels of consciousness, often represented through a sequence of images and impressions. Virginia Woolf and James Joyce make extensive use of stream of consciousness in their fiction.

See also **Characterization; Point of View; Style.**

Structure Structure is the way in which the parts of a work of literature are put together. Paragraphs are a basic unit in prose, as are chapters in novels, acts and scenes in plays, and stanzas and lines in poems. A prose selection can be structured by idea or incident, like most essays, short stories, narrative poems, and one-act plays. Structure in poetry involves the arrangement of words and lines to produce a desired effect; a poem's structure takes into account the sounds in the poem as well as the ideas.

The structure of a poem, short story, novel, play, or work of nonfiction usually emphasizes certain important aspects of content. For example, the division of T. S. Eliot's poem "Preludes" into sections enables him to shift between different times of day and between the interior of a room and the street outside. The structure of each stanza in Margaret Atwood's poem "The Moment" and the relationship between the stanzas help convey the theme that nature cannot be possessed.

Structure is also a means through which a writer adds layers of psychological complexity to characters. Katherine Mansfield's story "A Cup of Tea" begins and ends with questions about whether Rosemary is pretty. This framework suggests the element in Rosemary's character—her vanity—that proves to be the crux of the story.

See pages 741, 1229.
See also **Form.**

Style Style is the particular way in which a piece of literature is written. Style is not what is said but how it is said. It is the writer's uniquely individual way of communicating ideas. Many elements contribute to style, including word choice, sentence length, tone, figurative language, use of dialogue, and point of view. A literary style may be described in a variety of ways, such as *formal, conversational, journalistic, wordy, ornate, poetic,* or *dynamic.*

Examples: The interior monologue and detailed, evocative imagery in Virginia Woolf's "The Duchess and the Jeweller" are important elements of the style of the story. In the excerpt from Elie Wiesel's *Night,* the author uses simple words, short sentences, imagery, and dialogue to convey his horrifying experiences.

See pages 1054, 1141.

Supernatural Elements *See* **Supernatural Tale.**

Supernatural Tale A supernatural tale is a story that goes beyond the bounds of reality, usually by involving **supernatural elements—** beings, powers, or events that are unexplainable by known forces or laws of nature. In Valmiki's Indian epic *Ramayana,* Ravana's brother Kumbakarna is a supernatural being. In Sir Thomas Malory's romance *Le Morte d'Arthur,* Sir Launcelot uses supernatural powers in his battles against Sir Gawain.

In many supernatural tales, **foreshadowing—** hints or clues that point to later events—is used to encourage readers to anticipate the unthinkable. Sometimes readers are left wondering whether a supernatural event has really taken place or is the product of a character's imagination. In an effective supernatural tale, the writer manipulates readers' feelings of curiosity and fear to produce a mounting sense of excitement. Elizabeth Bowen's "The Demon Lover" is a supernatural tale.

See page 250.

Surprise Ending A surprise ending is an unexpected twist in the plot at the end of a story. The surprise may be a sudden turn in the action or a revelation that gives a different perspective to the entire story.

GLOSSARY OF LITERARY TERMS 1351

Example: The final paragraph of "The Demon Lover," which sets off a new direction in the plot instead of bringing it to its expected conclusion, is an example of a surprise ending.

See page 1164.
See also **Plot.**

Suspense Suspense is the tension or excitement readers feel as they are drawn into a story and become increasingly eager to learn the outcome of the plot. Suspense is created when a writer purposely leaves readers uncertain or apprehensive about what will happen.

Example: In *The Rising of the Moon,* Lady Gregory uses suspense-building techniques when she describes the sounds the sergeant hears in the dark.

See pages 1002, 1164.

Symbol A symbol is a person, place, object, or activity that stands for something beyond itself. Certain symbols are commonly used in literature, such as a journey to represent life or night to represent death. Other symbols, however, acquire their meanings within the contexts of the works in which they occur.

Examples: In Boccaccio's story "Federigo's Falcon," the falcon comes to symbolize the passionate and consuming love of Federigo for Monna Giovanna. In Tennyson's "The Lady of Shalott," the lady symbolizes the poet. Sometimes a literary symbol has more than one possible meaning. For example, the rose in Blake's poem "The Sick Rose" might symbolize goodness, innocence, or all of humanity.

See pages 715, 992.

Synecdoche Synecdoche is a figure of speech in which the name of a part is used to refer to a whole—for example, the use of *wheels* to mean "automobile."

Example: T. S. Eliot uses synecdoche in his poem "Preludes" when he uses words for body parts to refer to people, as in line 17, where "muddy feet" refers to early-morning crowds of people going to work.

Synesthesia *See* **Imagery.**

Theme A theme is a central idea or message in a work of literature. Theme should not be confused with subject, or what the work is about. Rather, theme is a perception about life or human nature shared with the reader. Sometimes the theme is directly stated within a work; at other times it is implied, and the reader must infer the theme. There may be more than one theme in a work. In *Macbeth,* for example, the themes include the corrupting effect of unbridled ambition, the corrosiveness of guilt, the lure and power of inscrutable supernatural forces, and the tragedy of psychological disintegration. The theme of Coleridge's "The Rime of the Ancient Mariner" has been interpreted as the transformation of the human personality through a loss of innocence and youth; another interpretation of the theme concerns the effects of sin and spiritual redemption.

One way to discover the theme of a literary work is to think about what happens to the central characters. The importance of those events, stated in terms that apply to all human beings, is the theme. In poetry, imagery and figurative language also help convey theme. In Chaucer's "The Pardoner's Tale," what happens to the three young men illustrates the theme "The love of money is the root of all evil."

See pages 324, 468, 474, 1124, 1232.

Third-Person Point of View *See* **Point of View.**

Title The title of a literary work introduces readers to the piece and usually reveals something about its subject or theme. Although works are occasionally untitled or, in the case of some poems, merely identified by their first line, most literary works have been deliberately and carefully named. Some titles are straightforward, stating exactly what the reader can expect to discover in the work. Others suggest possibilities, perhaps hinting at the subject and forcing the reader to search for interpretations.

Examples: "1996," the title of a poem by Rabindranath Tagore, gives the reader a direct clue about the subject of the poem, as does "Writing," the title of a poem by Octavio Paz. On the other hand, "Dover Beach," the title of a

1352 GLOSSARY OF LITERARY TERMS

poem by Matthew Arnold, is open to interpretation, and the reader has to work through the significance of the title in relation to the poem.

See page 972.

Tone Tone is an expression of a writer's attitude toward a subject. Unlike mood, which is intended to shape the reader's emotional response, tone reflects the feelings of the writer. The writer's choice of words and details helps establish the tone, which might be serious, humorous, sarcastic, playful, ironic, bitter, or objective. To identify the tone of a work, you might find it helpful to read the work aloud. The emotions you convey in reading should give you clues to the tone of the work.

Examples: The tone of Jonathan Swift's "A Modest Proposal" is searingly ironic; the tone of Katherine Mansfield's "A Cup of Tea" is amused and ironic. In "The Prologue" from *The Canterbury Tales,* Chaucer's restrained, detached tone accounts for much of the work's humor.

See pages 137, 190, 1042, 1141, 1286.
See also **Mood.**

Tragedy A tragedy is a dramatic work that presents the downfall of a dignified character who is involved in historically or socially significant events. The main character, or **tragic hero,** has a **tragic flaw,** a quality that leads to his or her destruction. The events in a tragic plot are set in motion by a decision that is often an error in judgment caused by the tragic flaw. Succeeding events are linked in a cause-and-effect relationship and lead inevitably to a disastrous conclusion, usually death. A tragic hero evokes both pity and fear in readers or viewers: pity because readers or viewers feel sorry for the character, and fear because they realize that the problems and struggles faced by the character are perhaps a necessary part of human life. At the end of a tragedy, a reader or viewer generally feels a sense of waste, because humans who were in some way superior have been destroyed. Shakespeare's plays *Macbeth, Hamlet, Othello,* and *King Lear* are famous examples of tragedies.

See page 321.

Tragic Flaw *See* **Hero; Tragedy.**

Tragic Hero *See* **Hero; Tragedy.**

Understatement Understatement is a technique of creating emphasis by saying less than is actually or literally true. Understatement is the opposite of hyperbole, or exaggeration. One of the primary devices of irony, understatement can be used to develop a humorous effect, to create biting satire, or to achieve a restrained tone. Understatement is an important element in the dramas of Harold Pinter, as in his one-act play *That's All.*

Verbal Irony *See* **Irony.**

Villanelle The villanelle is an intricately patterned French verse form, planned to give the impression of simplicity. A villanelle has 19 lines, composed of 5 tercets, or 3-line stanzas, followed by a quatrain. The first line is repeated as a refrain at the end of the second and fourth stanzas. The last line of the first stanza is repeated at the end of the third and fifth stanzas. Both lines reappear as the final two lines of the poem. The rhyme scheme of a villanelle is *aba* for each tercet and then *abaa* for the quatrain. Dylan Thomas's "Do Not Go Gentle into That Good Night" is an example of a villanelle.

See page 1092.
See also **Quatrain; Stanza.**

Wordplay Wordplay is the intentional use of more than one meaning of a word to express ambiguities, multiple interpretations, and irony.

Examples: In the excerpt from Derek Walcott's poem *Midsummer,* the poet achieves some of his irony through the use of wordplay—for example, through his use of the words *color* and *white.* In Stevie Smith's poem "Not Waving but Drowning," the poet plays with the different meanings of *far out* and *cold* to give added meaning to her poem.

See page 1252.

GLOSSARY OF LITERARY TERMS 1353

1 The Writing Process

Different writers use different processes. Try out different strategies and figure out what works best for you. For some assignments, it is best to start by figuring out what you need to end up with, make a plan or outline, and stick to it. Other writing assignments may be more successful if you start by writing everything you know about the topic, allow things to get messy, and then reshape and revise the writing so it fits the assignment. Try both approaches and get to know yourself as a writer.

Also consider whether the assignment is high-stakes or low-stakes writing. When the success of the piece is very important, such as in a test, you might choose to focus on meeting the requirements or criteria of the assignment. When the purpose of the writing is to develop your ideas, there is more opportunity to experiment and take risks. Take into account the time factor as well. In a timed writing test, you may not have time to explore and revise.

Correct grammar and spelling are very important in your final product. You don't need to focus on these as you shape your ideas and draft your piece, but be sure you allow time for a careful edit before turning in your final piece.

1.1 Prewriting

In the prewriting stage, you explore your ideas and discover what you want to write about.

Finding Ideas for Writing

Try one or more of the following techniques to help you find a writing topic.

Personal Techniques

- Practice imaging, or trying to remember mainly sensory details about a subject—its look, sound, feel, taste, and smell.
- Complete a knowledge inventory to discover what you already know about a subject.
- Browse through magazines, newspapers, and on-line bulletin boards for ideas.
- Start a clip file of articles that you want to save for future reference. Be sure to label each clip with source information.

Sharing Techniques

- With a group, brainstorm a topic by trying to come up with as many ideas as you can without stopping to critique or examine them.
- Interview someone who knows a great deal about your topic.

Writing Techniques

- After freewriting on a topic, try looping, or choosing your best idea for more freewriting. Repeat the loop at least once.
- Make a list to help you organize ideas, examine them, or identify areas for further research.

Graphic Techniques

- Create a pro-and-con chart to compare the positive and negative aspects of an idea or a course of action.
- Use a cluster map or tree diagram to explore subordinate ideas that relate to your general topic or central idea.

Determining Your Purpose

Your purpose for writing may be to express yourself, to entertain, to describe, to explain, to analyze, or to persuade. To clarify it, ask questions like these:

- Why did I choose to write about my topic?
- What aspects of the topic mean the most to me?
- What do I want others to think or feel after they read my writing?

LINK TO LITERATURE One purpose for writing is to clarify a subject. For example, the Nigerian writer

1354 WRITING HANDBOOK

Chinua Achebe, author of "Civil Peace," page 1274, wrote to correct the errors and misunderstandings about Africans in European literature and to show the value of African cultures.

Identifying Your Audience

Knowing who will read your writing can help you focus your topic and choose relevant details. As you think about your readers, ask yourself questions like these:

- What does my audience already know about my topic?
- What will they be most interested in?
- What language is most appropriate for this audience?

 Drafting

In the drafting stage, you put your ideas on paper and allow them to develop and change as you write.

Two broad approaches in this stage are discovery drafting and planned drafting.

Discovery drafting is a good approach when you are not quite sure what you think about your subject. You just plunge into your draft and let your feelings and ideas lead you where they will. After finishing a discovery draft, you may decide to start another draft, do more prewriting, or revise your first draft.

Planned drafting may work better for research reports, critical reviews, and other kinds of formal writing. Try making a writing plan or a scratch outline before you begin drafting. Then, as you write, you can fill in the details.

LINK TO LITERATURE Sometimes the creative process is accelerated out of necessity. Harold Pinter, author of *That's All,* page 1254, wrote his first play, *The Room,* in just four afternoons while he was working as an actor. Spending mornings in rehearsal and evenings in performance, he wrote the play for a group of college drama students.

 Revising, Editing, and Proofreading

The changes you make in your writing during this stage usually fall into three categories: revising for content, revising for structure, and proofreading to correct mistakes in mechanics.

Use the questions that follow to assess problems and determine what changes would improve your work.

Revising for Content

- Does my writing have a main idea or central focus? Is my thesis clear?
- Have I incorporated adequate detail? Where might I include a telling detail, revealing statistic, or vivid example?
- Is any material unnecessary, irrelevant, or confusing?

WRITING TIP Be sure to consider the needs of your audience as you answer the questions under Revising for Content and Revising for Structure. For example, before you can determine whether any of your material is unnecessary or irrelevant, you need to identify what your audience already knows.

Revising for Structure

- Is my writing unified? Do all ideas and supporting details pertain to my main idea or advance my thesis?
- Is my writing clear and coherent? Is the flow of sentences and paragraphs smooth and logical?
- Do I need to add transitional words, phrases, or sentences to make the relationships among ideas clearer?
- Are my sentences well constructed? What sentences might I combine to improve the grace and rhythm of my writing?

Proofreading to Correct Mistakes in Grammar, Usage, and Mechanics

When you are satisfied with your revision, proofread your paper, looking for mistakes in grammar, usage, and mechanics. You may want

WRITING HANDBOOK 1355

to do this several times, looking for different types of mistakes each time. The following checklist may help.

Sentence Structure and Agreement

- Are there any run-on sentences or sentence fragments?
- Do all verbs agree with their subjects?
- Do all pronouns agree with their antecedents?
- Are verb tenses correct and consistent?

Forms of Words

- Do adverbs and adjectives modify the appropriate words?
- Are all forms of *be* and other irregular verbs used correctly?
- Are pronouns used correctly?
- Are comparative and superlative forms of adjectives correct?

Capitalization, Punctuation, and Spelling

- Is any punctuation mark missing or not needed?
- Are all words spelled correctly?
- Are all proper nouns and all proper adjectives capitalized?

WRITING TIP For help identifying and correcting problems that are listed in the Proofreading Checklist, see the Grammar Handbook, pages 1391–1420.

You might wish to mark changes on your paper by using the proofreading symbols shown in the chart below.

Proofreading Symbols

Symbol	Meaning	Symbol	Meaning
∧	Add letters or words.	/	Make a capital letter lowercase.
⊙	Add a period.	¶	Begin a new paragraph.
≡	Capitalize a letter.	⌐	Delete letters or words.
⌒	Close up space.	∿	Switch the positions of letters or words.
∧	Add a comma.		

1.4 Publishing and Reflecting

Always consider sharing your finished writing with a wider audience. Reflecting on your writing is another good way to bring closure to a project.

Creative Publishing Ideas

Following are some ideas for publishing and sharing your writing.

- Post your writing on an electronic bulletin board or send it to others via e-mail.
- Create a multimedia presentation and share it with classmates.
- Publish your writing in a school newspaper or literary magazine.
- Present your work orally in a report, a speech, a reading, or a dramatic performance.
- Submit your writing to a local newspaper or a magazine that publishes student writing.
- Form a writing exchange group with other students.

WRITING TIP You might work with other students to publish an anthology of class writing. Then exchange your anthology with another class or another school. Reading the work of other student writers will help you get ideas for new writing projects and find ways to improve your work.

Reflecting on Your Writing

Think about your writing process and whether you would like to add what you have written to your portfolio. You might attach a note in which you answer questions like these:

- What did I learn about myself and my subject through this writing project?
- Which parts of the writing process did I most and least enjoy?
- As I wrote, what was my biggest problem? How did I solve it?
- What did I learn that I can use the next time I write?

1356 WRITING HANDBOOK

1.5 Using Peer Response

Peer response consists of the suggestions and comments your peers or classmates make about your writing.

You can ask a peer reader for help at any point in the writing process. For example, your peers can help you develop a topic, narrow your focus, discover confusing passages, or organize your writing.

Questions for Your Peer Readers

You can help your peer readers provide you with the most useful kinds of feedback by following these guidelines:

- Tell readers where you are in the writing process. Are you still trying out ideas, or have you completed a draft?
- Ask questions that will help you get specific information about your writing. Open-ended questions that require more than yes-or-no answers are more likely to give you information you can use as you revise.
- Give your readers plenty of time to respond thoughtfully to your writing.
- Encourage your readers to be honest when they respond to your work. It's OK if you don't agree with them—you always get to decide which changes to make.

Tips for Being a Peer Reader

Follow these guidelines when you respond to someone else's work:

- Respect the writer's feelings.
- Make sure you understand what kind of feedback the writer is looking for, and then respond accordingly.
- Use "I" statements, such as "I like . . . ," "I think . . . ," or "It would help me if . . . ." Remember that your impressions and opinions may not be the same as someone else's.

WRITING TIP Writers are better able to absorb criticism of their work if they first receive positive feedback. When you act as a peer reader, try to start your review by telling something you like about the piece.

The chart below explains different peer-response techniques to use when you are ready to share your work.

Peer-Response Techniques

Sharing Use this when you are just exploring ideas or when you want to celebrate the completion of a piece of writing.

- *Will you please read or listen to my writing without criticizing or making suggestions afterward?*

Summarizing Use this when you want to know if your main idea or goals are clear.

- *What do you think I'm saying? What's my main idea or message?*

Replying Use this strategy when you want to make your writing richer by adding new ideas.

- *What are your ideas about my topic? What do you think about what I have said in my piece?*

Responding to Specific Features Use this when you want a quick overview of the strengths and weaknesses of your writing.

- *Are the ideas supported with enough examples? Did I persuade you? Is the organization clear enough for you to follow the ideas?*

Telling Use this to find out which parts of your writing are affecting readers the way you want and which parts are confusing.

- *What did you think or feel as you read my words? Would you show me which passage you were reading when you had that response?*

WRITING HANDBOOK 1357

Writing Handbook

2 Building Blocks of Good Writing

Whatever your purpose in writing, you need to capture your readers' interest, organize your ideas well, and present your thoughts clearly. Giving special attention to some particular parts of a story or an essay can make your writing more enjoyable and more effective.

2.1 Introductions

When you flip through a magazine trying to decide which articles to read, the opening paragraph is often critical. If it does not grab your attention, you are likely to turn the page.

Kinds of Introductions

Here are some introduction techniques that can capture a reader's interest.

- Make a surprising statement
- Provide a description
- Pose a question
- Relate an anecdote
- Address the reader directly
- Begin with a thesis statement

Make a Surprising Statement Beginning with a startling statement or an interesting fact can capture your reader's curiosity about the subject, as in the model below.

MODEL

Since it was first published in 1883, Robert Louis Stevenson's *Treasure Island* has never been out of print, and it has been translated into languages as diverse as Welsh, Zulu, and Ukrainian. This unusual success attests to the universal appeal of Stevenson's storytelling skills.

Provide a Description A vivid description sets a mood and brings a scene to life for your reader. Here, details about visitors at Ellis Island set the tone for an essay about immigration to the United States.

MODEL

The visitors to the museum at Ellis Island wander almost reverently through rooms filled with photos and memorabilia. The walls seem to reverberate with countless stories—many long since forgotten—of immigrants who passed through this island.

Pose a Question Beginning with a question can make your reader want to read on to find out the answer. The following introduction asks a significant question about the careers of two women writers.

MODEL

George Eliot and George Sand were both successful writers in the 19th century; both were also women. At this time in history, why did they need to use male pen names?

Relate an Anecdote Beginning with a brief anecdote, or story, can hook readers and help you make a point in a dramatic way. The anecdote below introduces an essay about gangsters in the 1920s.

MODEL

The man, in an immaculate suit with broad lapels, narrowed his eyes against the sun as he stepped from the shadowy doorway. Pulling his hat down, he tossed a dime to the dazed, grubby boy standing before him. "Go get me a coupla Cokes, willya?—and step on it, kid!" So it was that my grandfather met Al Capone.

1358 WRITING HANDBOOK

Address the Reader Directly Speaking directly to readers establishes a friendly, informal tone and involves them in your topic.

> MODEL
> **If you are concerned about the appearance of our community, you should learn how you can participate in the Adopt-a-Street program that begins this April.**

Begin with a Thesis Statement A thesis statement expressing a paper's main idea may be woven into both the beginning and the end of nonfiction writing. The following is a thesis statement that introduces a literary analysis.

> MODEL
> **In "Words and Behavior," Aldous Huxley argues that language must be used carefully. He shows that its misuse can establish and perpetuate great evil.**

WRITING TIP In order to write the best introduction for your paper, you may want to try more than one of the methods and then decide which is the most effective for your purpose and audience.

 Paragraphs

A paragraph is made up of sentences that work together to develop an idea or accomplish a purpose. Whether or not it contains a topic sentence stating the main idea, a good paragraph must have unity and coherence.

Unity

A paragraph has unity when all the sentences support and develop one stated or implied idea. Use the following techniques to create unity in your paragraphs.

Write a Topic Sentence A topic sentence states the main ideas of the paragraph; all other sentences in the paragraph provide supporting details. A topic sentence is often the first sentence in a paragraph. However, it may also appear later in the paragraph or at the end, to summarize or reinforce the main idea, as shown in the model that follows.

> MODEL
> **Magnesium is a mineral found in food sources such as beans, nuts, meats, and dairy products. This mineral is necessary for the breakdown of nutrients in cells and is important to the stimulation of muscles and nerves. A healthy body effectively conserves magnesium. Insufficient amounts of the mineral, however, are related to various health problems. Dietary magnesium is clearly vital to human health.**

Relate All Sentences to an Implied Main Idea A paragraph can be unified without a topic sentence as long as every sentence supports the implied, or unstated, main idea. In the model below, all the sentences work together to create a unified impression of an impending storm.

> MODEL
> **All morning the wind had gently rustled the branches of trees and tossed back curtains from open windows. By early afternoon, however, it had picked up a force that tore green leaves from the trees and pushed thick and menacing clouds across the sky.**

Coherence

A paragraph is coherent when all its sentences are related to one another and flow logically from one to the next. The following techniques will help you achieve coherence in paragraphs.

- Present your ideas in the most logical order.
- Use pronouns, synonyms, and repeated words to connect ideas.
- Use transitional devices to show the relationships among ideas.

In the model below, the writer used some of these techniques to create a unified paragraph.

> MODEL
> **Most people know that the gravitational pull of the moon causes tides in the ocean. Are you aware, though, that the moon exerts the same pull on the solid part of the earth? Unlike ocean tides, however, earth tides are deformations of as much as a foot in the earth's surface. The extent to which its surface bulges is greatest during full moon and new moon because the gravitational pull of the moon combines with that of the sun.**

WRITING HANDBOOK 1359

2.3 Transitions

Transitions are words and phrases that show the connections between details. Clear transitions help show how your ideas relate to each other.

Kinds of Transitions

Transitions can help readers understand several kinds of relationships:

- Time or sequence
- Spatial relationships
- Degree of importance
- Compare and contrast
- Cause and effect

Time or Sequence Some transitions help to clarify the sequence of events over time. When you are telling a story or describing a process, you can connect ideas with such transitional words as *first, second, always, then, next, later, soon, before, finally, after, earlier, afterward,* and *tomorrow.*

> MODEL
> **Before a blood donation can be used, it must be processed carefully. First, a sample is tested for infectious diseases and identified by blood type. Next, preservatives are added. Finally, a blood cell separator breaks up the blood into its parts, such as red blood cells, platelets, and plasma.**

Spatial Relationships Transitional words and phrases, such as *in front, behind, next to, along, nearest, lowest, above, below, underneath, on the left,* and *in the middle,* can help readers visualize a scene.

> MODEL
> **A theater-in-the-round stage is constructed in the middle of the theater space, with the audience sitting around the entire stage. To create a more intimate setting, the seats nearest the stage are often only a few feet away.**

Degree Transitional words, such as *mainly, strongest, weakest, first, second, most important, least important, worst,* and *best,* may be used to rank ideas or to show degree of importance.

> MODEL
> **Cory made several New Year's resolutions. Most important, he decided to cut back on watching TV.**

Compare and Contrast Words and phrases such as *similarly, likewise, also, like, as, neither . . . nor,* and *either . . . or* show similarity between details. *However, by contrast, yet, but, unlike, instead, whereas,* and *while* show difference. Note the use of both types of transitions in the model below.

> MODEL
> **Like running and bicycling, swimming helps you maintain aerobic fitness; however, swimming has the added benefit of exercising muscles throughout your body.**

WRITING TIP Both *but* and *however* may be used to join two independent clauses. When *but* is used as a coordinating conjunction, it is preceded by a comma. When *however* is used as a conjunctive adverb, it is preceded by a semicolon and followed by a comma.

Cause and Effect When you are writing about a cause-and-effect relationship, use transitional words and phrases, such as *since, because, thus, therefore, so, due to, for this reason,* and *as a result,* to help clarify that relationship and to make your writing coherent.

> MODEL
> **Because the temperature dropped to 28 degrees after it rained for five hours, car door locks froze.**

1360 WRITING HANDBOOK

 Conclusions

A conclusion should leave readers with a strong final impression. Try any of these approaches.

Kinds of Conclusions

Here are some effective methods for bringing your writing to a conclusion:

- Restate your thesis
- Ask a question
- Make a recommendation
- Make a prediction
- Summarize your information

Restate Your Thesis A good way to conclude an essay is by restating your thesis, or main idea, in different words. The conclusion below restates the thesis introduced on page 1359.

> MODEL
> **Aldous Huxley's "Words and Behavior" clearly warns of the danger of misusing language to manipulate and control. Unless we begin using concrete words and plain language, he maintains, we may ultimately destroy our civilization.**

Ask a Question Try asking a question that sums up what you have said and gives readers something new to think about. The question below concludes an appeal to halt funding for space exploration.

> MODEL
> **Given all the evidence, can you imagine that continued investment in the space program will benefit future generations more than the same investment in the basic needs of those living now?**

Make a Recommendation When you are persuading your audience to take a position on an issue, you can conclude by recommending a specific course of action.

> MODEL
> **Voting is a vital way to influence your world. Add voter registration to your birthday plans.**

Make a Prediction Readers are concerned about matters that may affect them and therefore are moved by a conclusion that predicts the future.

> MODEL
> **If we continue to overuse antibiotics, we will speed the development of infections that resist treatment. Such infections will kill millions despite the best medical science.**

Summarize Your Information Summarizing reinforces the writer's main ideas, leaving a strong, lasting impression. The model below concludes with a statement that summarizes a review of a book.

> MODEL
> **James Gurney's book *Dinotopia* appeals to adult readers, as well as to children, with its imaginative adventures, its fascinating drawings of dinosaurs, and its timeless theme of cooperation in a diverse community.**

2.5 Elaboration

Elaboration is the process of developing a writing idea by providing specific supporting details that are relevant and appropriate to the purpose and form of your writing.

- **Facts and Statistics** A fact is a statement that can be verified, while a statistic is a fact stated in numbers. Make sure the facts and statistics you supply are from a reliable, up-to-date source. As in the model below, the facts and statistics you use should strongly support the statements you make.

> MODEL
> **The decade from 1900 to 1910 saw 8,795,000 immigrants come to the United States. Then Congress passed the Emergency Quota Act of 1921. Between 1921 and 1930, only 4,107,000 immigrants entered the United States. The law had cut immigration by more than half.**

WRITING HANDBOOK 1361

- **Sensory Details** Details that show how something looks, sounds, tastes, smells, or feels can enliven a description, making readers feel they are actually experiencing what you are describing. Which senses does the writer appeal to in this paragraph?

MODEL
Gina wasn't sure she enjoyed her first hayride. As the wagon bumped along the furrows, she clumsily bounced between Marty and Deanna. She tried to imagine she was having fun as she shivered under the scratchy wool blankets that smelled of straw and dust.

- **Incidents** From our earliest years, we are interested in hearing "stories." One way to illustrate a point powerfully is to relate an incident or tell a story as shown in the example below.

MODEL
Reforms often do not happen until a significant tragedy brings a problem to public attention. The deaths of 146 women workers in a fire at New York City's Triangle Shirtwaist factory in 1911 led to tougher protective labor laws in New York State and a national awareness of unsafe management practices.

- **Examples** An example can help make an abstract or a complex idea concrete or can provide evidence to clarify a point for readers.

MODEL
There was a time when many of the foods eaten around the world today were found only in North, Central, and South America. For example, tomatoes, potatoes, beans, and corn all originated in the Americas.

- **Quotations** Choose quotations that clearly support your points and be sure that you copy each quotation word for word. Remember always to credit the source.

MODEL
Technological advances in the design of tennis rackets have changed the nature of the sport, but many players lament the passing of the wood racket. In his article "The Feel of Wood," Marshall Fisher states that after he switched to an aluminum racket in college competition, he concluded that the unavoidable "march of technology had degraded tennis."

2.6 Using Language Effectively

Effective use of language can help readers to recognize the significance of an issue, to visualize a scene, or to understand a character. Keep these particular points in mind.

The specific words and phrases that you use have everything to do with how effectively you communicate meaning. This is true of all kinds of writing, from novels to office memos.

- **Specific Nouns** Nouns are specific when they refer to individual or particular things. If you refer to a *city*, you are being general. If you refer to *London*, you are being specific. Specific nouns help readers identify the *who, what,* and *where* of your message.
- **Specific Verbs** Verbs are the most powerful words in sentences. They convey the action, the movement, and sometimes the drama of thoughts and observations. Verbs such as *trudged, skipped,* and *sauntered* provide a more vivid picture of the action than the verb *walked*.
- **Specific Modifiers** Use modifiers sparingly, but when you use them, make them count. Is the building *big* or *towering*? Are your poodle's paws *small* or *petite*? Once again, it is the more specific word that carries the greater impact.

1362 WRITING HANDBOOK

3 Descriptive Writing

Descriptive writing allows you to paint word pictures about anything and everything in the world, from events of global importance to the most personal feelings. It is an essential part of almost every piece of writing, including essays, poems, letters, field notes, newspaper reports, and videos.

RUBRIC **Standards for Writing**

A successful description should
- have a clear focus and sense of purpose.
- use sensory details and precise words to create a vivid image, establish a mood, or express emotion.
- present details in a logical order.

3.1 Key Techniques

Consider Your Goals What do you want to accomplish in writing your description? Do you want to show why something is important to you? Do you want to make a person or scene more memorable? Do you want to explain an event?

Identify Your Audience Who will read your description? How familiar are they with your subject? What background information will they need? Which details will they find most interesting?

Think Figuratively What figures of speech might help make your description vivid and interesting? What simile or metaphor comes to mind? What imaginative comparisons can you make? What living thing does an inanimate object remind you of?

MODEL
Her laughter was a powerful potion that soothed the hurt feelings and damaged egos of the dinner guests. She was the antidote to her husband's rude and dismissive behavior, and she knew it.

Gather Sensory Details Which sights, smells, tastes, sounds, and textures make your subject come alive? Which details stick in your mind when you observe or recall your subject? Which senses does it most strongly affect?

MODEL
The stowaways were wedged between the rough-hewn crates deep in the bowels of the creaking ship. Through the blackness of the dank and putrid air, a thin shaft of light was their only measure of day and night.

You might want to use a chart like the one shown here to collect sensory details about your subject.

Sights	Sounds	Textures	Smells	Tastes

Create a Mood What feelings do you want to evoke in your readers? Do you want to soothe them with comforting images? Do you want to build tension with ominous details? Do you want to evoke sadness or joy?

MODEL
The heavy gray sky hung above the vast expanse of empty plains. The families, exhausted from too much travel and precious little rest, trudged beside their tattered wagons containing those few but cherished treasures from their former lives. They lived in the present. Remembering life before this journey was too painful. The uncertainty of life after this journey was too frightening.

WRITING HANDBOOK 1363

3.2 Options for Organization

Spatial Order Choose one of these options to show the spatial order of a scene.

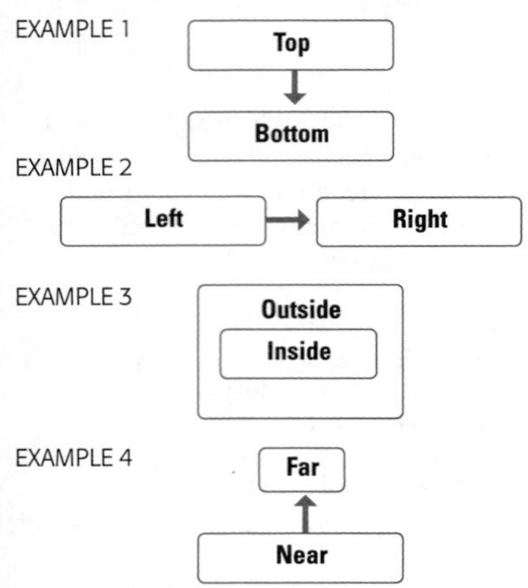

MODEL
Detective Malloy surveyed the scene. Just inside the ruined door, a torn letter lay on the floor. In the middle of the room stood a large oak desk, neatly organized except for a lamp that hung off the edge. Behind the desk, a chair lay against the far wall.

WRITING TIP Use transitions that help the reader picture the relationship among the objects you describe. Some useful transitions for showing spatial relationships are *behind, below, here, in the distance, on the left, over,* and *on top.*

Order of Impression Order of impression is how you notice details.

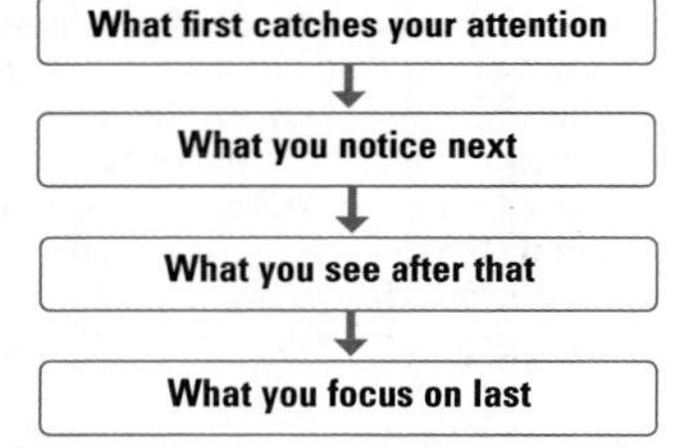

MODEL
First, we heard the screech of a car braking before our house. Next came the slam of a car door and then the staccato clicking of a woman's high heels as she ran up the cobblestone walk. It was already late in the evening, and we couldn't imagine who it could be.

WRITING TIP Use transitions that help readers understand the order of the impressions you are describing. Some useful transitions are *after, next, during, first, before, finally,* and *then.*

Order of Importance You might want to use order of importance as the organizing structure for your description.

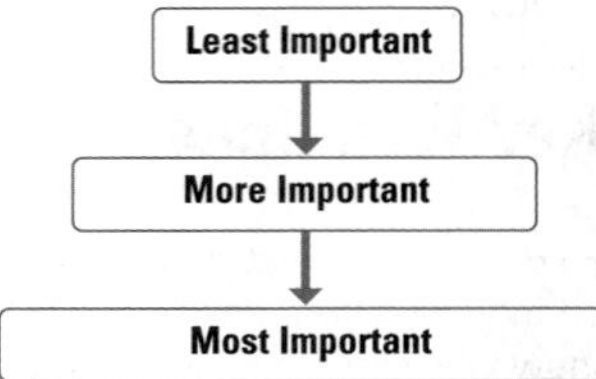

MODEL
All the Thanksgiving fixings were there: the perfectly browned, steaming turkey, the cranberry sauce glistening like rubies in the candlelight, the mounds of mashed potatoes like fluffy snowdrifts. The dining room resounded with chatter and laughter, but an emptiness clung to the corners and a silence cut through the conversation. Grandma wasn't with us.

WRITING TIP Use transitions that help the reader understand the order of importance that you attach to the elements of your description. Some useful transitions are *first, second, mainly, more important, less important,* and *least important.*

1364 WRITING HANDBOOK

4 Narrative Writing

Narrative writing tells a story. If you write a story from your imagination, it is a fictional narrative. A true story about actual events is a nonfictional narrative. Narrative writing can be found in short stories, novels, news articles, and biographies.

RUBRIC Standards for Writing

A successful narrative should

- include descriptive details and dialogue to develop the characters, setting, and plot.
- have a clear beginning, middle, and end.
- have a logical organization with clues and transitions to help the reader understand the order of events.
- maintain a consistent tone and point of view.
- use language that is appropriate for the audience.
- demonstrate the significance of events or ideas.

4.1 Key Techniques

Identify the Main Events What are the most important events in your narrative? Is each event part of the chain of events needed to tell the story? In a fictional narrative, this series of events is the story's plot.

MODEL

Event 1 — **The morning after my grandfather's funeral, I go to the cemetery.**

Event 2 — **I stare at his grave and become angry and frustrated.**

Event 3 — **A cool rain reminds me of my grandfather's love of nature.**

Event 4 — **At the beach, I sit on the piece of driftwood near where my grandfather and I used to walk.**

Describe the Setting When do the events occur? Where do they take place? How can you use setting to create mood and to set the stage for the characters and their actions?

MODEL

The morning after the funeral, my grandfather's grave is covered with flowers and wreaths that are just starting to wilt from the cold.

Depict Characters Vividly What do your characters look like? What do they think and say? How do they act? What vivid details can show readers what the characters are like?

MODEL

I stand shivering in my black sweatshirt before my grandfather's grave. My cold stare and stony face mask the anger and frustration that is welling up inside me. A muffled cry escapes, and the question "Why?" echoes in the emptiness of the cemetery.

WRITING TIP Dialogue is an effective way of developing characters in a narrative. As you write dialogue, choose words that express your characters' personalities and show how they feel about one another and about the events in the plot.

MODEL

I could just hear my grandfather say, "Boy, smell that salty wind. You just can't get a whiff of boiling nature like that any old where!"

I'd look at him and say, "Yeah, I know." But I might be thinking that I'd like a whiff of juicy hot dogs and even bus fumes back in the city.

Then he'd pull me into his world—our world—with something like "You and I, Boy. We're just alike. We love the water and the wind."

WRITING HANDBOOK 1365

4.2 Options for Organization

Option 1: Chronological Order One way to organize a piece of narrative writing is to arrange the events in chronological order, as shown below.

Introduction *characters and setting*

MODEL

The morning after my grandfather's funeral, I wake up early and walk to the cemetery.

Event 1

I stand by his grave and become angry and frustrated.

Event 2

I want to find some place where I can remember my grandfather and all the good times we had together.

End *perhaps show the significance of the events*

On the beach, I sit on the huge piece of driftwood where my grandfather and I used to sit. The cool lake wind and the noise of the waves bring back my favorite memories of him.

Option 2: Flashback It is also possible in narrative writing to arrange the order of events by starting with an event that happened before the beginning of the story.

Flashback
Begin with a key event that happened before the time in which the story takes place.

↓

Introduce characters and setting.

↓

Describe the events leading up to the conflict.

Option 3: Focus on Conflict When the telling of a fictional narrative focuses on a central conflict, the story's plot may follow the model shown below.

Describe the main characters and setting

MODEL

The brothers arrive at the school gym long before the rest of the basketball team. Although the twins are physically identical, their personalities couldn't be more different. Mark is outgoing and impulsive, while Matt is thoughtful and shy.

Present the conflict

Matt realizes his brother is missing shots on purpose and believes they will lose the championship.

Relate the events that make the conflict complex and cause the characters to change

- Matt has a chance at a basketball scholarship if they win the championship.
- Mark needs money to buy a car.
- Matt and Mark have stood by each other no matter what.

Present the resolution or outcome of the conflict

Matt retells a family story in which their grandfather chose honor and integrity over easy money. Mark plays to win.

1366 WRITING HANDBOOK

5 Explanatory Writing

Explanatory writing informs and explains. For example, you can use it to evaluate the effects of a new law, to compare two movies, to analyze a piece of literature, or to examine the problem of greenhouse gases in the atmosphere.

5.1 Types of Explanatory Writing

There are many types of explanatory writing. Think about your topic and select the type that presents the information most clearly.

Compare and Contrast How are two or more subjects alike? How are they different?

> MODEL
> **King Arthur and Sir Launcelot share similar qualities that lead to their friendship, but they also share weaknesses that ensure their deaths.**

Cause and Effect How does one event cause something else to happen? Why do certain conditions exist? What are the results of an action or a condition?

> MODEL
> **King Arthur dies in battle with Sir Modred because he adheres too closely to the honor of knighthood and believes too much in the knights of his court.**

Analysis How does something work? How can it be defined? What are its parts?

> MODEL
> **Legends, such as the story of King Arthur, change over time as they are retold and take on new interpretations.**

Problem-Solution How can you identify and state a problem? How would you analyze the problem and its causes? How can it be solved?

> MODEL
> **Arthur has to choose between honor and friendship—two values that are equally desirable until they conflict.**

5.2 Compare and Contrast

Compare-and-contrast writing examines the similarities and differences between two or more subjects. You might, for example, compare and contrast two short stories, the main characters in a novel, or two movies.

RUBRIC Standards for Writing

Successful compare-and-contrast writing should
- clearly identify the subjects that are being compared and contrasted.
- include specific, relevant details.
- follow a clear plan of organization dealing with the same features of both subjects under discussion.
- use language and details appropriate to the audience.
- use transitional words and phrases to clarify similarities and differences.

Options for Organization

Compare-and-contrast writing can be organized in different ways. The examples that follow demonstrate feature-by-feature organization and subject-by-subject organization.

WRITING HANDBOOK 1367

Option 1: Feature-by-Feature Organization

MODEL

Feature 1 — **I. Noble qualities**

Subject A. **Arthur: admires Launcelot as great knight, so is reluctant to fight him**

Subject B. **Launcelot: respects Arthur as his liege, so is reluctant to fight him**

Feature 2 — **II. Weaknesses**

Subject A. **Arthur: trusts his knights' judgment over his own**

Subject B. **Launcelot: love for Arthur's wife stronger than respect for Arthur**

Option 2: Subject-by-Subject Organization

MODEL

Subject A — **I. Arthur:**

Feature 1. **Noble quality: admires Launcelot as great knight, so is reluctant to fight him**

Feature 2. **Weakness: trusts his knights' judgment over his own**

Subject B — **II. Launcelot:**

Feature 1. **Noble Quality: respects Arthur as his liege, so is reluctant to fight him**

Feature 2. **Weakness: love for Arthur's wife stronger than respect for Arthur**

WRITING TIP Remember your purpose for comparing and contrasting your subjects, and support your purpose with expressive language and specific details.

 Cause and Effect

Cause-and-effect writing explains why something happened, why certain conditions exist, or what resulted from an action or a condition. You might use cause-and-effect writing to explain a character's actions, the progress of a disease, or the outcome of a war.

RUBRIC Standards for Writing

Successful cause-and-effect writing should

- clearly state the cause-and-effect relationship.
- show clear connections between causes and effects.
- present causes and effects in a logical order and use transitions effectively.
- use facts, examples, and other details to illustrate each cause and effect.
- use language and details appropriate to the audience.

Options for Organization

Your organization will depend on your topic and purpose for writing.

- If you want to explain the causes of an event such as the closing of a factory, you might first state the effect and then examine its causes.

Option 1: Effect to Cause Organization

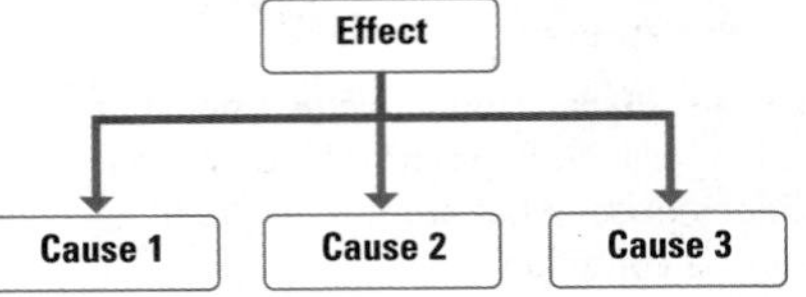

- If your focus is on explaining the effects of an event, such as the passage of a law, you might first state the cause and then explain the effects.

Option 2: Cause to Effect Organization

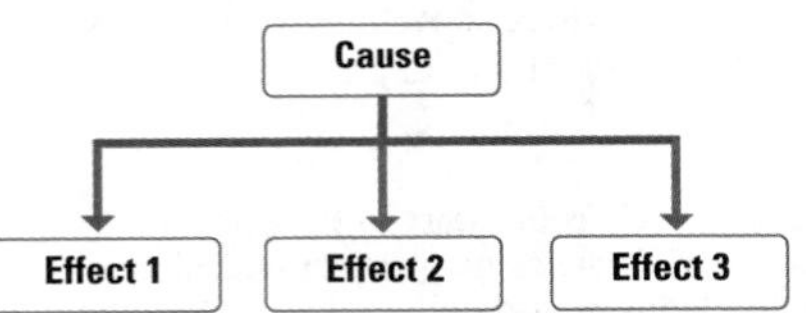

- Sometimes you'll want to describe a chain of cause-and-effect relationships to explore a topic such as the disappearance of tropical rain forests or the development of home computers.

1368 WRITING HANDBOOK

Option 3: Cause-and-Effect Chain Organization

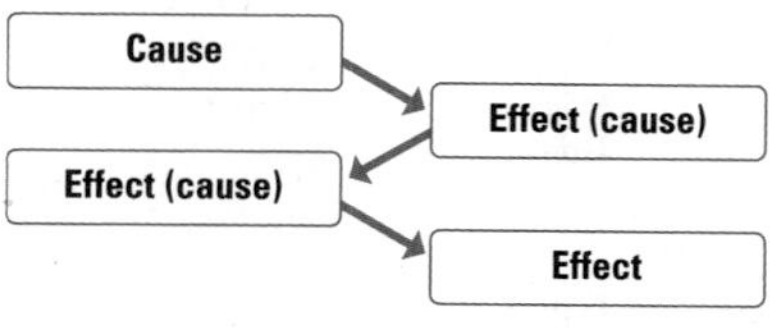

WRITING TIP Don't assume that a cause-and-effect relationship exists just because one event follows another. Look for evidence that the later event could not have happened if the first event had not caused it.

 5.4 Problem-Solution

Problem-solution writing clearly states a problem, analyzes the problem, and proposes a solution to the problem. It can be used to identify and solve a conflict between characters, analyze a chemistry experiment, or explain why the home team keeps losing.

RUBRIC Standards for Writing

Successful problem-solution writing should

- identify the problem and help the reader understand the issues involved.
- analyze the causes and effects of the problem.
- integrate quotations, facts, and statistics into the text.
- explore possible solutions to the problem and recommend the best one(s).
- use language, tone, and details appropriate to the audience.

Options for Organization

Your organization will depend on the goal of your problem-solution piece, your intended audience, and the specific problem you choose to address. The organizational methods that follow are effective for different kinds of problem-solution writing.

Option 1: Simple Problem-Solution

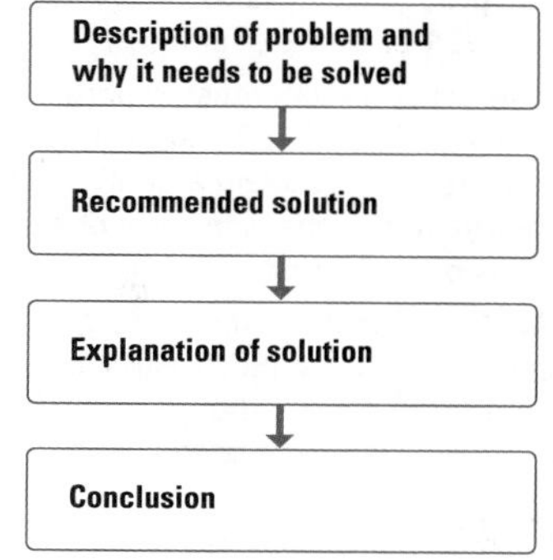

Option 2: Deciding Between Solutions

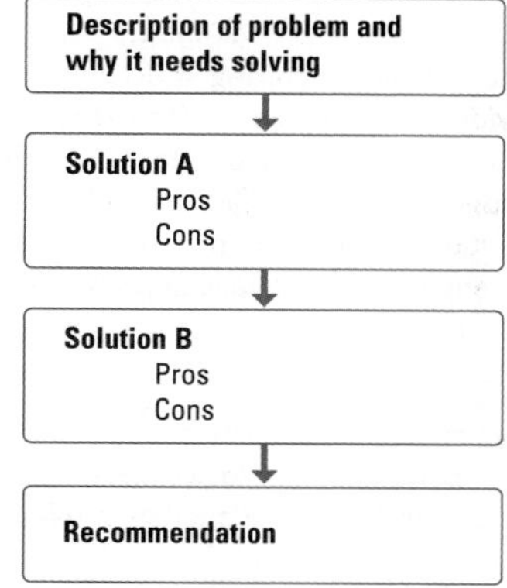

WRITING TIP Have a classmate read and respond to your problem-solution writing. Ask your peer reader: Is the problem clearly stated? Is the organization easy to follow? Do the proposed solutions seem logical?

5.5 Analysis

In writing an analysis, you explain how something works, how it is defined, or what its parts are. The details you include will depend upon the kind of analysis you write.

Process Analysis What are the major steps or stages in a process? What background information does the reader need to know—such as definitions of terms or a list of needed

WRITING HANDBOOK 1369

equipment—to understand the analysis? You might use process analysis to explain how to program a VCR or prepare for a test.

Definition What are the most important characteristics of a subject? You might use definition analysis to explain a quality, such as honor or loyalty, the characteristics of a sonnet, or the skills of a physicist.

Parts Analysis What are the parts, groups, or types that make up a subject? Parts analysis could be used to explain the makeup of King Arthur's army or the parts of the brain.

RUBRIC **Standards for Writing**

A successful analysis should

- hook the readers' attention with a strong introduction.
- clearly state the subject and its parts.
- use a specific organizing structure to provide a logical flow of information.
- show connections among facts and ideas through subordinate clauses and transitional words and phrases.
- use language and details appropriate for the audience.

Options for Organization

Organize your details in a logical order appropriate for the kind of analysis you're writing.

Option 1: Process Analysis A process analysis is usually organized chronologically, with steps or stages in the order they occur.

MODEL

Introduction	**Arthurian legends reinterpreted**
Background	**British ruler in 500s**
Explain Steps	**Step 1: Around 1469 *Le Morte d'Arthur* is compiled.**
	Step 2: Between 1842 and 1885 *Idylls of the King* is published.
	Step 3: In 1960 the musical *Camelot* opens.

Option 2: Definition Analysis You can organize the details in a definition or parts analysis in order of importance or impression.

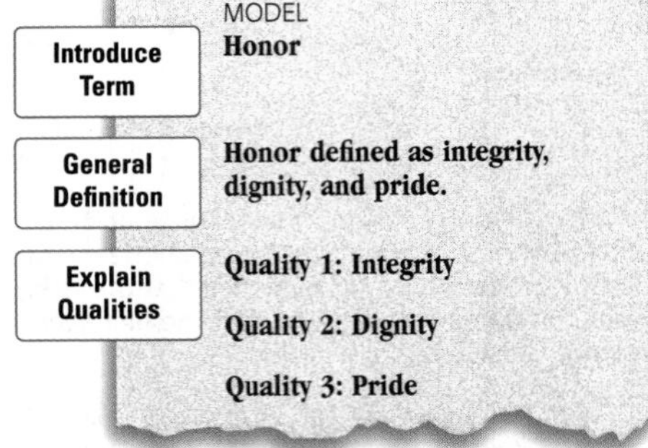

MODEL
Introduce Term
Honor
General Definition
Honor defined as integrity, dignity, and pride.
Explain Qualities
Quality 1: Integrity
Quality 2: Dignity
Quality 3: Pride

Option 3: Parts Analysis The following parts analysis explores three elements of a medieval knight's code of chivalry.

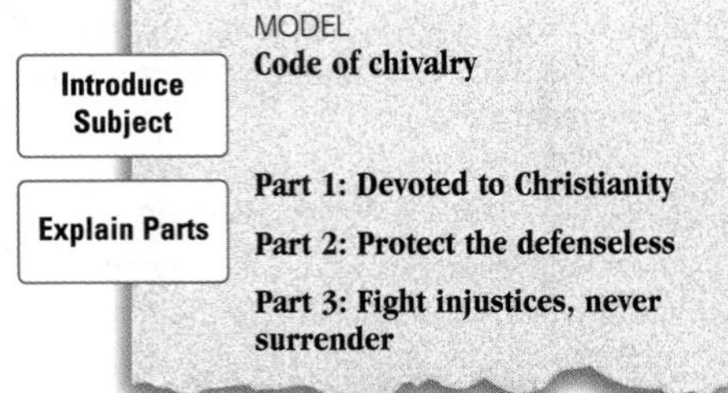

MODEL
Introduce Subject
Code of chivalry
Explain Parts
Part 1: Devoted to Christianity
Part 2: Protect the defenseless
Part 3: Fight injustices, never surrender

WRITING TIP Try to capture your readers' interest in your introduction. You might begin with a vivid description or an interesting fact, detail, or quotation. For example, an exciting excerpt from the narrative could open the process analysis.

An effective way to conclude an analysis is to return to your thesis and restate it in different words.

1370 WRITING HANDBOOK

6 Persuasive Writing

Persuasive writing allows you to use the power of language to inform and influence others. It can take many forms including speeches, newspaper editorials, billboards, advertisements, and critical reviews.

RUBRIC **Standards for Writing**

Successful persuasion should

- state the issue and the writer's position.
- give opinions and support them with facts or reasons.
- have a reasonable and respectful tone.
- answer opposing views.
- use sound logic and effective language.
- conclude by summing up reasons or calling for action.

6.1 Key Techniques

Clarify Your Position What do you believe about the issue? How can you express your opinion most clearly?

MODEL

We must find ways to depend less on the use of paper communication in order to save the forests.

Know Your Audience Who will read your writing? What do they already know and believe about the issue? What objections to your position might they have? What additional information might they need? What tone and approach would be most effective?

MODEL

We must take responsibility for using fewer of the products that come from trees. Meanwhile, we need to take a hard look at the chip mill practices which wipe out whole sections of forests.

Support Your Opinion Why do you feel the way you do about the issue? What facts, statistics, examples, quotations, anecdotes, or opinions of authorities support your view? What reasons will convince your readers? What evidence can answer their objections?

MODEL

Each mill can cause the clear-cutting of 10,000 acres of forest land in one year. The *St. Louis Post-Dispatch* quotes a member of the Department of Natural Resources that the clear-cutting of the Ozark forests has "had a well-documented, widespread, and devastating effect."

Ways to Support Your Argument	
Statistics	Facts that are stated in numbers
Examples	Specific instances that explain your point
Observations	Events or situations you yourself have seen
Anecdotes	Brief stories that illustrate your point
Quotations	Direct statements from authorities

Begin and End with a Bang How can you hook your readers and make a lasting impression? What memorable quotation, anecdote, or statistic will catch their attention at the beginning or stick in their minds at the end? What strong summary or call to action can you conclude with?

BEGINNING

Our forests are being cut down. The chip mill industry, which supplies the raw material for making so-called "high quality" paper, has tripled in the southwest United States in the last decade.

CONCLUSION

It's time to stop the rapid devastation of the forests. If it means less slick paper for magazines and computer printouts, so be it. Write the Conservation Department, the Forest Service, and especially your state's members of Congress.

WRITING HANDBOOK 1371

6.2 Options for Organization

In a two-sided persuasive essay, you want to show the weaknesses of other opinions as you explain the strengths of your own.

The example below demonstrates one method of organizing your persuasive essay to convince your audience.

Option 1: Reasons for Your Opinion

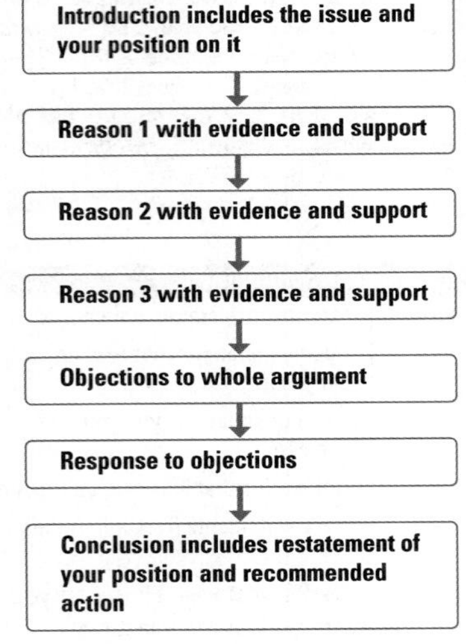

Introduction includes the issue and your position on it
Reason 1 with evidence and support
Reason 2 with evidence and support
Reason 3 with evidence and support
Objections to whole argument
Response to objections
Conclusion includes restatement of your position and recommended action

Option 2: Point-by-Point Basis

In the organization that follows, each reason and its objections are examined on a point-by-point basis.

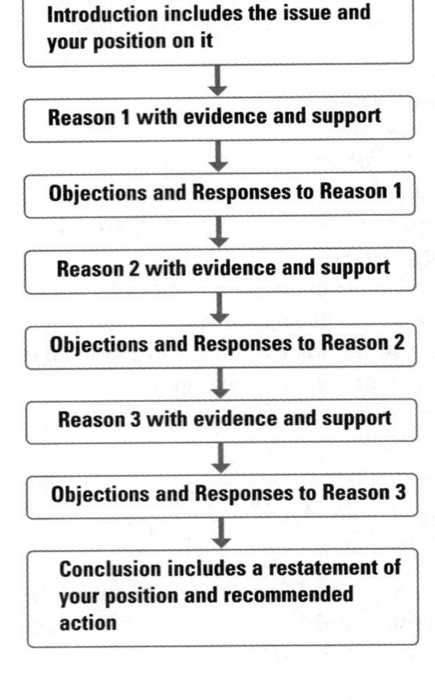

Beware of Illogical Arguments Be careful about using illogical arguments. Opponents can easily attack your argument if you present illogical material.

Circular reasoning—trying to prove a statement by just repeating it in different words

> The forests are disappearing because the trees are being cut down.

Either-or fallacy—stating that there are only two alternatives when they are many

> Either we quit using slick paper for magazines, or the forests will die.

Over-generalization—making a statement that is too broad to prove

> The chip-mill companies don't care about trees.

Cause-and-effect fallacy—falsely assuming that because one event follows another the first event caused the second

> Chip mills are needed because we read so many magazines.

1372 WRITING HANDBOOK

7 Research Report Writing

A research report explores a topic in depth, incorporating information from a variety of sources.

RUBRIC **Standards for Writing**

An effective research report should
- clearly state the purpose of the report in a thesis statement.
- use evidence and details from a variety of sources to support the thesis.
- contain only accurate and relevant information.
- document sources correctly.
- develop the topic logically and include appropriate transitions.
- include a properly formatted Works Cited list.

 Key Techniques

Develop Relevant, Interesting, and Researchable Questions Asking thoughtful questions is an ongoing part of research. Begin with a list of basic questions that are relevant to your topic. Focus on getting basic facts that answer the *who, what, where, when,* and *why* of your topic. If you were researching the social context of Dickens's novels, you might develop a set of questions like these.

MODEL
What were living conditions like in London during the 1800s?
What happened to orphans?

As you become more familiar with your topic, think of questions that might provide an interesting perspective that makes readers think.

MODEL
How did the legal system reflect society's values?

Check that your questions are researchable. Ask questions that will uncover facts, statistics, case studies, and other documentable evidence.

Clarify Your Thesis A thesis statement is one or two sentences clearly stating the main idea that you will develop in your report. A thesis may also indicate the organizational pattern you will follow and reflect your tone and point of view.

MODEL
In *Oliver Twist,* instead of drawing clear lines between the dark underworld of London and the light of the more civilized world, Charles Dickens blurs the distinction, making good and evil in society difficult to define.

Document Your Sources You need to document, or credit, the sources where you find your evidence. In the example below, the writer uses and documents a quotation from the novel.

MODEL
In *Oliver Twist,* Dickens shows the intertwining of good and evil in the world. The narrator states, "Men who look on nature . . . and cry that all is dark and gloomy, are in the right; but the somber colours are reflections from their own jaundiced eyes and hearts. The real hues . . . need a clearer vision." (Pool 256–257)

Support Your Ideas You should support your ideas with relevant evidence—facts, anecdotes, and statistics—from reliable sources. In the example below, the writer includes a fact about the conditions of workhouses.

MODEL
Oliver is condemned to a workhouse. The living conditions in workhouses were deliberately worse than in prisons in order to discourage the poor from depending on the publicly funded institutions. (Pool 245)

WRITING HANDBOOK 1373

7.2 Gathering Information: Sources

You will use a range of sources to collect the information you need to develop your research paper. These will include both print and electronic resources.

General Reference Works To clarify your thesis and begin your research, consult reference works that give quick, general overviews on a subject. General reference works include encyclopedias, almanacs and yearbooks, atlases, and dictionaries.

Specialized Reference Works Once you have a good idea of your specific topic, you are ready to look for detailed information in specialized reference works. In the library's reference section, specialized dictionaries and encyclopedias can be found for almost any field. For example, in the field of literature, you will find specialized reference sources such as *Contemporary Authors* and *Twentieth-Century Literary Criticism.*

Periodicals Journals and periodicals are a good source for detailed, up-to-date information. Periodical indexes, found in print and on-line catalogs in the library, will help you find articles on a topic. The *Readers' Guide to Periodical Literature* indexes many popular magazines. More specialized indexes include the *Humanities Index* and the *Social Sciences Index.*

Electronic Resources **Commercial information services** offer access to reference works such as dictionaries and encyclopedias, databases, and periodicals.

The **Internet** is a vast network of computer networks. News services, libraries, universities, researchers, organizations, and government agencies use the Internet to communicate and to distribute information. The Internet gives you access to the World Wide Web, which provides information on particular topics and links you to related topics and resources.

A **CD-ROM** is a research aid that stores information on a compact disk. Reference works on CD-ROMs may include text, sound, images, and video.

Databases are large collections of related information stored electronically. You can scan the information or search for specific facts.

RESEARCH TIP To find books on a specific topic, check the library's on-line catalog. Be sure to copy the correct call numbers of books that sound promising. Also look at books shelved nearby. They may relate to your topic.

7.3 Gathering Information: Validity of Sources

When you find source material, you must determine whether it is useful and accurate.

Credibility of Authorship Check whether an author has written several books or articles on the subject and has published in a well-respected newspaper or journal.

Objectivity Decide whether the information is fact, opinion, or propaganda. Reputable sources credit other sources of information.

Currency Check the publication date of the source to see whether the information is current.

Credibility of Publisher Seek information from a respected newspaper or journal, not from a tabloid newspaper or popular-interest magazine.

WEB TIP Be especially skeptical of information you locate on the Internet since virtually anyone can post anything there. Read the URL, or Internet address. Sites sponsored by a government agency (*.gov*) or an educational institution (*.edu*) are generally more reliable.

7.4 Taking Notes

As you find useful information, record the bibliographic information of each source on a separate index card. Then you are ready to take notes on your sources. You will probably use these three methods of note-taking.

1374 WRITING HANDBOOK

Writing Handbook

Paraphrase, or restate in your own words, the main ideas and supporting details of the passage.

Summarize, or rephrase in fewer words, the original materials, trying to capture the key ideas.

Quote, or copy word for word, the original text, if you think the author's own words best clarify a particular point. Use quotation marks to signal the beginning and the end of the quotation.

For more details on making source cards and taking notes, see the Research Report Workshop on pages 423–430.

 7.5 Options for Organization

Begin by reading over your note cards and sorting them into groups. The main-idea headings may help you find connections among the notes. Then arrange the groups of related note cards so that the ideas flow logically from one group to the next.

Option 1: Topic Outline

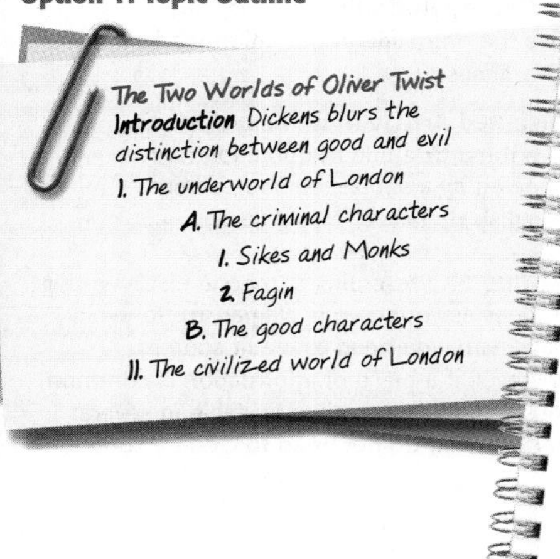

Like other forms of writing, research reports can be organized in several different ways. Some subjects may fit in chronological order. For other subjects, you may want to compare and contrast two topics. Other possibilities are a cause-and-effect organization or least-important to most-important evidence. If your material does not lend itself to any of the above organizations, try a general-to-specific approach.

Whatever your organizational pattern, making an outline can help guide the drafting process. The subtopics that you located in sorting your note cards will be the major topics of your outline, preceded by Roman numerals. Make sure that items of the same importance are parallel in form. For example, in the Option 1 Topic Outline below, topics I and II are both phrases. So are subtopics A and B.

A second kind of outline, shown below in Option 2, uses complete sentences instead of phrases for topics and subtopics.

Option 2: Sentence Outline

The Two Worlds of Oliver Twist

Introduction Dickens blurs the distinction between good and evil.

I. Dickens depicts the underworld of London by showing both evil criminal characters and those who commit crimes due to poverty or misfortune.

  A. The criminal characters are cruel and brutal.

    1. Sikes and Monks are characterized as men who will do anything to get what they want.

    2. Fagin's amorality is shown in his manipulating children into committing crimes.

  B. The good characters have believable human weaknesses and failings.

II. The civilized world of London is populated with people who are far from perfect.

WRITING HANDBOOK 1375

Writing Handbook

7.6 Documenting Sources

When you quote, paraphrase, or summarize information from a source, you need to credit that source. Parenthetical documentation is the accepted method for crediting sources. You may choose to name the author in parentheses following the information along with the page number on which the information is found.

MODEL
Workhouses were purposely made "as grim and forbidding as possible" (Pool 245).

In parenthetical documentation, you may also use the author's name in the sentence along with the information. If so, enclose, in parentheses after the sentence, only the page number on which the information is found.

MODEL
According to Pool, many poor children like Oliver Twist populated London in the 1800s (31).

In either case, your reader can find out more about the source by turning to your Works Cited page, which lists complete bibliographical information for each source.

PUNCTUATION TIP When only the author and page number appear in parentheses, there is no punctuation between the two items. Also notice that the parenthetical citation comes after the closing quotation marks of a quotation, if there is one, and before the end punctuation of the sentence.

The examples above show citations for books with one author. The list that follows shows the correct way to write parenthetical citations for several kinds of sources.

Guidelines for Parenthetical Documentation

Work by One Author
Put the author's last name and the page reference in parentheses: **(Pool 191).**

If you mention the author's name in the sentence, put only the page reference in parentheses: **(191)**

Work by Two or Three Authors
Put the authors' last names and the page reference in parentheses:
(Mitchell and Deane 42).

Work by More Than Three Authors
Give the first author's last name followed by et al and the page reference: **(Bentley et al. 122).**

Work with No Author Given
Give the title or a shortened version and (if appropriate) the page reference:
("Hurried Trials" 742).

One of Two or More Works by Same Author
Give the author's last name, the title or a shortened version, and the page reference:
(Dunn, "But We Grow" 54).

Selection from a Book of Collected Essays
Give the name of the author of the essay and the page reference: **(Bayley 54).**

Dictionary Definition
Give the entry title in quotation marks:
("Workhouse").

Unsigned Article in an Encyclopedia
Give the article title in quotation marks followed by a shortened source title:
("English Literature," World Book).

WRITING TIP Presenting someone else's writing or ideas as your own is plagiarism. To avoid plagiarism, you need to credit sources. However, if a piece of information is common knowledge—information available in several sources—you do not need to credit a source.

7.7 Following MLA Manuscript Guidelines

The final copy of your report should follow the Modern Language Association (MLA) guidelines for manuscript preparation.

- The heading in the upper left-hand corner of the first page should include your name, your teacher's name, the course name, and the date, each on a separate line.
- Below the heading, center the title on the page.
- Number all the pages consecutively in the upper right-hand corner, one-half inch from the top. Also, include your last name before the page number.
- Double-space the entire paper.
- Except for the margins above the page numbers, leave one-inch margins on all sides of every page.

The Works Cited page at the end of your report is an alphabetized list of the sources you have used and documented. In each entry all lines after the first are indented an additional one-half inch.

WRITING TIP When your report includes a quotation that is longer than four lines, set if off from the rest of the text by indenting the entire quotation one inch from the left margin. In this case, you should not use quotation marks.

Works Cited

Models for Works Cited Entries

Works Cited

Bayley, John. "Oliver Twist: 'Things as They Really Are.'" Dickens and the Twentieth Century. Ed. John Gross and Gabriel Pearson. London: Routledge, 1962. 49–64.

Bentley, Nicholas, et al. The Dickens Index. Oxford: Oxford UP, 1988.

Collins, Philip, ed. Sikes and Nancy: A Facsimile. London: Dickens, 1982.

Dickens, Charles. Oliver Twist. New York: Bantam, 1981.

Dunn, Richard J. "'But We Grow Affecting: Let Us Proceed.'" Dickensian 62 (1966): 53–55.

__. Oliver Twist: Whole Heart and Soul. New York: Twayne, 1993.

Mitchell, B. R., and Phyllis Deane. Abstract of British Historical Statistics. Cambridge: Cambridge UP, 1962.

1. Selection from a book of collected essays; note that publishers' names are shortened.
2. Book with more than three authors
3. Book with editor but no single author
4. Book with one author
5. Article in scholarly journal
6. Second work by same author
7. Work with two authors

WRITING HANDBOOK 1377

Writing Handbook

7.8 MLA Documentation: Electronic Sources

As with print sources, information from electronic sources such as CD-ROMs or the Internet must be documented on your Works Cited page. You may find a reference to a source on the Internet and then use the print version of the article. If so, document it as you do other printed works. However, if you read or print out an article directly off the Internet, document it as shown below for an electronic source. Although electronic sources are shown separately below, they should be included on the Works Cited page with print sources.

Internet Sources Works Cited entries for Internet sources include the same kind of information as those for print sources. They also include the date you accessed the information and the electronic address of the source. Some of the information about the source may be unavailable. Include as much as you can. For more information on how to write Works Cited entries for Internet sources, see the MLA guidelines posted on the Internet or access this document through the McDougal Littell website.

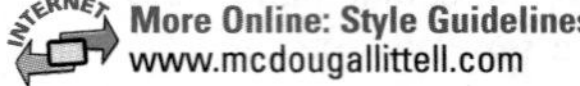

More Online: Style Guidelines
www.mcdougallittell.com

CD-ROMs Entries for CD-ROMs include the publication medium (CD-ROM), the distributor, and the date of publication. Some of the information shown may not be always available. Include as much as you can.

Works Cited

Models for Works Cited entries for electronic sources

Works Cited

"Charles Dickens." Britannica Online. Vers. 98.2. Apr. 1998. Encyclopaedia Britannica. 17 Sept. 1998 <http://www.eb.com:180>

1 Encyclopedia entry from online version

Dickens, Charles. Oliver Twist. London: Chapman & Hall. 1897. University of Virginia Library Electronic Text Center. 14 June 1998. <http:// etext.lib.virginia.edu/etcbin/browse-mixed-new?id=DicOliv&tag=public&images=images/modeng&data=/texts/english/modeng/parsed>

2 The complete text of the novel, available on the Internet; includes access date

The Dickens Page. Nagoya U. 14 June 1998 <http://lang.nagoya-u.ac.jp/~matsuoka/ Dickens.html>

3 Scholarly site; shows date you accessed it

Rosenberg, Brian. "Character and Contradiction in Dickens." Nineteenth Century Literature—Electronic Edition 47.2 (1992): 18 pp. 15 June 1998 <http://www-ucpress.berkeley.edu:8080/scan/ncl-e/472/articles/rosenberg.art472.html>

4 Article in a scholarly journal available on the Internet; includes number of pages and access date

"Workhouse." Oxford English Dictionary. 2nd ed. CD-ROM. Oxford: Oxford UP, 1992.

5 Dictionary entry from CD-ROM version

1378 WRITING HANDBOOK

8 Business Writing

The ability to write clearly and succinctly is an essential skill in the business world. As you prepare to enter the job market, you will need to know how to create letters, memos, and resumes.

RUBRIC

Standards for Writing

Successful business writing should

- have a tone and language geared to the appropriate audience.
- state the purpose clearly in the opening sentences or paragraph.
- use precise words and avoid jargon.
- present only essential information.
- present details in a logical order.
- conclude with a summary of important points.

8.1 Key Techniques

Think About Your Purpose Why are you doing this writing? Do you want to "sell" yourself to a college admissions committee or a job interviewer? Do you want to order or complain about a product? Do you want to set up a meeting or respond to someone's ideas?

Identify Your Audience Who will read your writing? What background information will they need? What questions might they have? What tone or language is appropriate?

Support Your Points What specific details clarify your ideas? What reasons do you have for your statements? What points most strongly support them?

Finish Strongly How can you best sum up your statements? What is your main point? What action do you want others to take?

8.2 Key Techniques

Model 1: Letter

223 Harvest Way
Austin, TX 78712
May 2, 19__

Heading *Where the letter comes from and when*

Ms. Anne Shields, Department Head
Theater Department
Parker State University
Tulsa, OK 74133

Inside Address *To whom the letter is being sent*

Dear Ms. Shields:

Salutation *Greeting*

I am a high school senior. I am considering attending Parker State University and majoring in theater. I attended a performance of *Our Town* last fall and was very impressed with your production.

Could you please send me any available information about your department, including requirements for a major and a list of the year's productions?

Thank you very much.

Body *Text of the message*

Sincerely yours,
Jason Woemack

Closing

WRITING HANDBOOK 1379

Model 2: Memo

Heading *Whom the memo is to and from, what it's about, and when it's being sent*	To: Mark From: Anne Shields Re: Student Request Date: 5/12/__
Body	Mark, I'm attaching a copy of a letter from a high school student. Please send him a department bulletin and a performance calendar. Also put him on our mailing list of prospective students.

Model 3: Resume A well-written resume is invaluable when you apply for a part-time or full-time job or for college. It should highlight your skills, accomplishments, and experience. Proofread your resume carefully to make sure it is clear and accurate and free of errors in grammar and spelling. It is a good idea to save a copy of your resume on your computer or on a disk so that you can easily update it.

State your purpose. *This resume is for a job application. A modified style can be used for a college application.*

List your previous employment experience *in reverse chronological order.*

Extracurricular activities and hobbies *can give a fuller picture of you and point out special job-related skills.*

MARY LLANOS
6642 W. Water Street, Denver, CO 80201
(303)555-8842

Objective	A part-time position as a teacher's assistant
Qualifications	Talent and interest in working with children Skills in arts and crafts activities Ability to cooperate with others
Work Experience	*Summers 1999–Present: Handicamp, Denver, CO* Was counselor for 9- and 10-year-olds at camp for handicapped children; planned arts and crafts activities for all age groups *1999–Present: Learn with Llanos, Denver, CO* Tutored a total of twelve children in English and math
Education	*Lakeland High School, Class of 2000* • Honor Roll • Three years of Art • One semester of Children's Literature
Extra Curricular Activities	• Treasurer, Future Teachers of America • Vice President, Art Club • Soccer Team
Hobbies	Reading, arts and crafts, gardening
References	Available upon request

1380 WRITING HANDBOOK

1 Inquiry and Research

In this age of seemingly unlimited information, the ability to locate and evaluate resources efficiently can spell the difference between success and failure—in both the academic and the business worlds. Make use of print and nonprint information sources.

 Finding Sources

Good research involves using the wealth of resources available to answer your questions and raise new questions. Knowing where to go and how to access information can lead you to interesting and valuable sources.

Reference Works

Reference works are print and nonprint sources of information that provide quick access to both general overviews and specific facts about a subject. These include

Dictionaries—word definitions, pronunciations, and origins

Thesauruses—lists of synonyms and antonyms for each entry

Glossaries—collections of specialized terms, such as those pertaining to literature, with definitions

Encyclopedias—detailed information on nearly every subject, arranged alphabetically (*Encyclopaedia Britannica*). Specialized encyclopedias deal with specific subjects, such as music, economics, and science (*Encyclopedia of Economics*).

Almanacs and Yearbooks—current facts and statistics (*World Almanac, Statistical Abstract of the United States*)

Atlases—maps and information about weather, agricultural and industrial production, and other geographical topics (*National Geographic Atlas of the World*)

Specialized Reference Works—biographical data (*Who's Who, Current Biography*), literary information (*Contemporary Authors, Book Review Digest, Cyclopedia of Literary Characters, The Oxford Companion to English Literature*), and quotations (*Bartlett's Familiar Quotations*)

Electronic Sources—Many of these reference works and databases are available on CD-ROMs, which may include text, sound, photographs, and video. CD-ROMs can be used on a home or library computer. You can subscribe to services that offer access to these sources on-line.

Periodicals and Indexes

One kind of specialized reference is a periodical.

- Some periodicals, such as *Atlantic Monthly* and *Psychology Today,* are intended for a general audience. They are indexed in the *Readers' Guide to Periodical Literature.*
- Many other periodicals, or journals, are intended for specialized or academic audiences. These include titles and subject matter as diverse as *American Psychologist* and *Studies in Short Fiction.* These are indexed in the *Humanities Index* and the *Social Sciences Index.* In addition, most fields have their own indexes. For example, articles on literature are indexed in the *MLA International Bibliography.*
- Many indexes are available in print, CD-ROM, and on-line forms.

Internet

The Internet is a vast network of computers. News services, libraries, universities, researchers, organizations, and government agencies use the Internet to distribute information and to communicate. The Internet can provide links to library catalogs, newspapers, government sources, and many of the reference sources described above. The Internet includes two key features:

World Wide Web—source of information on specific subjects and links to related topics

Electronic mail (e-mail)—communications link to other e-mail users worldwide

COMMUNICATION HANDBOOK 1381

Other Resources

In addition to reference works found in the library and over the Internet, you can get information from the following sources: corporate publications, lectures, correspondence, and media such as films, television programs, and recordings. You can also observe directly, conduct your own interviews, and collect data from polls or questionnaires that you create yourself.

1.2 Evaluating Sources

Not all information is equal. You need to be a discriminating consumer of information and evaluate the credibility of the source, the reliability of the specific information included, and its value in answering your research needs.

Credibility of Sources

You must determine the credibility and appropriateness of each source in order to write an effective report or speech. Ask yourself the following questions:

Is the writer an authority? A writer who has written several books on a subject or whose name is included in many bibliographies may be considered an authoritative source.

Is the source reliable and unbiased? What is the author's motivation? For example, a defense of an industry in which the author has a financial interest may be biased. A profile of a writer or scientist written by a close relative may also be biased.

WEB TIP Be especially skeptical of information you locate on the Internet, since virtually anyone can post anything there. Read the URL, or Internet address. Sites sponsored by a government agency (*.gov*) or an educational institution (*.edu*) are generally more reliable.

Is the source up to date? It is important to consult the most recent material, especially in fields, such as medicine and technology, that undergo constant research and development. Some authoritative sources have withstood the test of time, however, and should not be overlooked.

Is the source appropriate? What audience is the material written for? In general, look for information directed at the educated reader. Material geared to experts or to popular audiences may be too technical or too simplified and therefore not appropriate for most research projects.

Distinguishing Fact from Opinion

As you gather information, it is important to recognize facts and opinions. A **fact** can be proven to be true or false. You could verify the statement "Congress rejected the bill" by checking newspapers, magazines, or the *Congressional Record.* An **opinion** is a judgment based on facts. The statement "Congress should not have rejected the bill" is an opinion. To evaluate an opinion, check for evidence presented logically and validly to support it.

Recognizing Bias

A writer may have a particular bias. This does not automatically make his or her point of view unreliable. However, recognizing an author's bias can help you evaluate a source. Recognizing that the author of an article about immigration is a Chinese immigrant will help you understand that author's bias. On the other hand, an author may have a hidden agenda that makes him or her less than objective about a topic. To avoid relying on information that may be biased, check an author's background and gather a variety of viewpoints.

1.3 Collecting Information

People use a variety of techniques to collect information during the research process. Try out several of those suggested below and decide which ones work best for you.

Paraphrasing and Summarizing

You can adapt material from other sources by quoting it directly or by paraphrasing or summarizing it. A paraphrase involves restating the information in your own words. It is often a simpler version but not necessarily a shorter

1382 COMMUNICATION HANDBOOK

version. A summary involves extracting the main ideas and supporting details and writing a shorter version of the information.

Remember to credit the source when you paraphrase or summarize. See the Writing Handbook—Research Report, pp. 1373–1378.

Strategies for Paraphrasing
1. Select the portion of the article you want to record.
2. Read it carefully and think about those ideas you find most interesting and useful to your research. Often these will be the main ideas.
3. Retell the information in your own words.

Strategies for Summarizing
1. Read the article carefully. Determine the main ideas.
2. In your own words, write a shortened version of these main ideas.

Avoiding Plagiarism

Plagiarism is copying someone else's ideas or words and using them as if they were your own. This can happen inadvertently if you are sloppy about collecting information and documenting your sources. Plagiarism is intellectual stealing and can have serious consequences.

How to Avoid Plagiarism

1. When you paraphrase or summarize, be sure to change entirely the wording of the original by using your own words.
2. Both in notes and on your final report, enclose in quotation marks any material copied directly from other sources.
3. Indicate in your final report the sources of any ideas that are not general knowledge—including those in the visuals—that you have paraphrased or summarized.
4. Include a list of Works Cited with your finished report. See the Writing Handbook—Research Report, pp. 1373–1378.

2 Study Skills and Strategies

As you read an assignment for the first time, review material for a test, or search for information for a research report, you use different methods of reading and studying.

2.1 Skimming

When you run your eyes quickly over a text, paying attention to overviews, headings, topic sentences, highlighted words, and graphic features, you are skimming.

Skimming is a good technique for previewing material in a textbook or other source that you must read for an assignment. It is also useful when you are researching a self-selected topic. Skimming a source helps you determine whether it has pertinent information. For example, suppose you are writing a research report on three protagonists of Charles Dickens: Pip, Oliver Twist, and David Copperfield. Skimming an essay or a book on Dickens can help you quickly determine whether any part of it deals with your topic.

2.2 Scanning

To find a specific piece of information in a text, use scanning. To scan, place a card under the first line of a page and move it down slowly. Look for key words and phrases that signal the information you are looking for.

Scanning is useful in reviewing for a test or in finding a specific piece of information for a paper. Suppose you are looking for a discussion of Pip's relationship with Estella for your research report. You can scan a book chapter or an essay, looking for the key names *Pip* and *Estella.*

COMMUNICATION HANDBOOK 1383

Communication Handbook

2.3 In-Depth Reading

When you must thoroughly understand the material in a text, you use in-depth reading.

In-depth reading involves asking questions, taking notes, looking for main ideas, and drawing conclusions as you read slowly and carefully. For example, in researching your report on Dickens's characters, you may find an essay on how Pip's relationship with Estella affects his life. Since this is closely related to your topic, you will read it in depth and take notes. You also should use in-depth reading for reading textbooks and literary works.

2.4 Outlining

Outlining is an efficient way of organizing ideas and is useful in taking notes.

Outlining helps you retain information as you read in depth. For example, you might outline a chapter in a history textbook, listing the main subtopics and the ideas or details that support them. An outline can also be useful for taking notes for a research report or in reading a piece of literature. The following is an example of a topic outline, which uses short phrases, that summarizes part of a chapter.

MAIN IDEA: **Oliver Twist is compared to Pip and David Copperfield.**

I. Pip and David Copperfield
- **A. Independent**
- **B. Have growing self-awareness**
- **C. Tell own stories**

II. Oliver Twist
- **A. Dependent on outside forces**
- **B. Described by third-person narrator**

2.5 Identifying Main Ideas

To understand and remember any material you read, identify its main idea.

In informative material, the main idea is often stated. The thesis statement of an essay or article and the topic sentence of each paragraph often state the main idea. In other material, especially literary works, the main idea is implied. After reading the piece carefully, analyze the important parts, such as characters and plot. Then try to sum up in one sentence the general point that the story makes.

2.6 Taking Notes

As you listen or read in depth, take notes to help you understand the material. Look and listen for key words that point to main ideas.

One way to help you summarize the main idea and supporting details is to take notes in modified outline form. In using a modified outline form, you do not need to use numerals and letters. Unlike a formal outline, a modified outline does not require two or more points under each heading, and headings do not need to be grammatically parallel. Yet, like a formal outline, a modified outline organizes a text's main ideas and related details. The following modified outline describes social classes in nineteenth-century England.

House of Lords
Peerage
- **Dukes**
- **Barons**
- **Viscounts**
- **Earls**
- **Marquises**

Church of England clergy
- **Bishops**
- **Archbishops**

"Gentry"
- **upper middle class**
- **Baronets**
- **Knights**

Use abbreviations and symbols to make note taking more efficient. Following are some commonly used abbreviations for note taking.

w/	with	re	regarding
w/o	without	=	is, equals
#	number	*	important
&, +	and	def	definition
>	more than	Amer	America
<	less than	tho	although

1384 COMMUNICATION HANDBOOK

3 Critical Thinking

Critical thinking includes the ability to analyze, evaluate, and synthesize ideas and information. Critical thinking goes beyond simply understanding something. It involves making informed judgments based on sound reasoning skills.

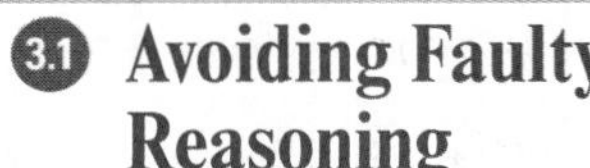

3.1 Avoiding Faulty Reasoning

When you write or speak for a persuasive purpose, you must make sure your logic is valid. Avoid these mistakes in reasoning, called **logical fallacies.**

Overgeneralization

Conclusions reached on the basis of too little evidence result in the fallacy called overgeneralization. A person who saw three cyclists riding bicycles without helmets might conclude, "Nobody wears bicycle helmets." That conclusion would be an overgeneralization.

Circular Reasoning

When you support an opinion by simply repeating it in different terms, you are using circular reasoning. For example, "Sport utility vehicles are popular because more people buy them than any other category of new cars." This is an illogical statement because the second part of the sentence simply uses different words to restate the first part of the sentence.

Either-Or Fallacy

Assuming that a complex question has only two possible answers is called the either-or fallacy. "Either we raise the legal driving age or accidents caused by teenage drivers will continue to increase" is an example of the either-or fallacy. The statement ignores other ways of decreasing the automobile accident rate of teenagers.

Cause-and-Effect Fallacy

The cause-and-effect fallacy occurs when you say that event B was caused by event A just because event B occurred after event A. A person might conclude that, because a city's air quality worsened two months after a new factory began operation, that new factory caused the air pollution. However, this cause-and-effect relationship would have to be supported by more specific evidence.

3.2 Identifying Modes of Persuasion

Understanding persuasive techniques can help you evaluate information, make informed decisions, and avoid persuasive techniques intended to deceive you. Some modes of persuasion appeal to your various emotions.

Loaded Language

Loaded language is words or phrases chosen to appeal to the emotions. It is often used in place of facts to shape opinion or to evoke a positive or negative reaction. For example, you might feel positive about a politician who has a *plan.* You might, however, feel negative about a politician who has a *scheme*.

Bandwagon

Bandwagon taps into the human desire to belong. This technique suggests that "everybody" is doing it, or buying it, or believing it. Phrases such as "Don't be the only one . . ." and "Everybody is . . . " signal the bandwagon appeal.

Testimonials

Testimonials offer well-known people or satisfied customers to promote and endorse a product or idea. This technique taps into the appeal of celebrities or into people's need to identify with others just like themselves.

COMMUNICATION HANDBOOK 1385

Communication Handbook

3.3 Logical Thinking

Persuasive writing and speaking require good reasoning skills. Two ways of creating logical arguments are deductive reasoning and inductive reasoning.

Deductive Arguments

A deductive argument begins with a generalization, or premise, and then advances with facts and evidence that lead to a conclusion. The conclusion is the logical outcome of the premise. A false premise leads to a false conclusion; a valid premise leads to a valid conclusion provided that the specific facts are correct and the reasoning is correct.

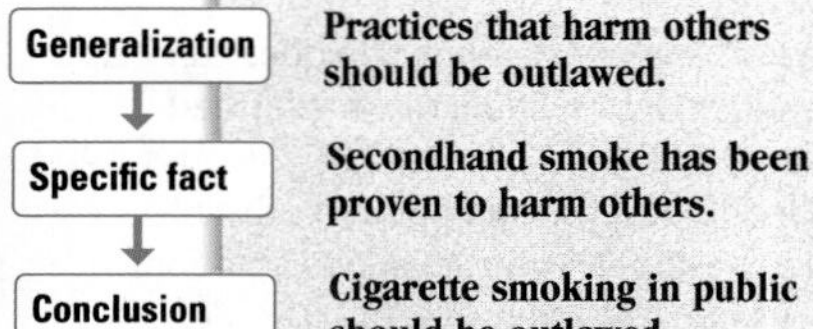

Generalization
Practices that harm others should be outlawed.
Specific fact
Secondhand smoke has been proven to harm others.
Conclusion
Cigarette smoking in public should be outlawed.

You may use deductive reasoning when writing a persuasive paper or speech. Your conclusion is the thesis of your paper. Facts in your paper supporting your premise should lead logically to that conclusion.

Inductive Arguments

An inductive argument begins with specific evidence that leads to a general conclusion.

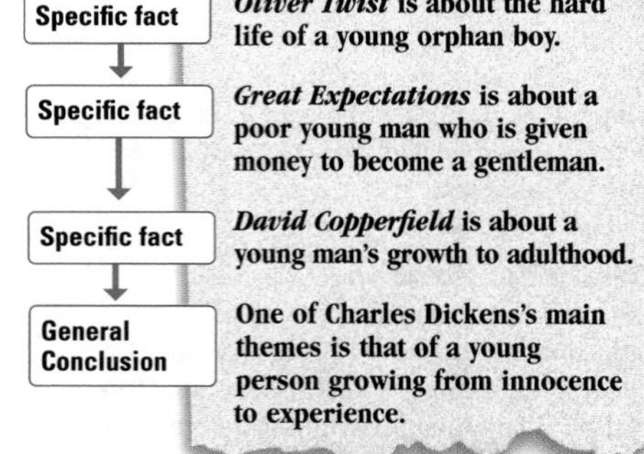

Specific fact
Oliver Twist is about the hard life of a young orphan boy.
Specific fact
Great Expectations is about a poor young man who is given money to become a gentleman.
Specific fact
David Copperfield is about a young man's growth to adulthood.
General Conclusion
One of Charles Dickens's main themes is that of a young person growing from innocence to experience.

The conclusion of an inductive argument often includes a qualifying term such as *some, often,* or *most.* This usage helps to avoid the fallacy of overgeneralization.

4 Speaking and Listening

Good speakers and listeners do more than just talk and hear. They use specific techniques to present their ideas effectively, and they are attentive and critical listeners.

4.1 Giving a Speech

In school, in business, and in community life, giving a speech is one of the most effective ways of communicating. Whether to persuade, to inform, or to entertain, you may often speak before an audience.

Analyzing Audience and Purpose

In order to speak effectively, you need to know to whom you are speaking and why you are speaking. When preparing a speech, think about how much knowledge and interest your audience has in your subject. A speech has one of two main purposes: to inform or to persuade. A third purpose, to entertain, is often considered closely related to these two purposes.

A speech **to inform** gives the audience new information, provides a better understanding of information, or enables people to use information in a new way. An informative speech is presented in an objective way.

In a speech **to persuade,** a speaker tries to change the actions or beliefs of an audience.

1386 COMMUNICATION HANDBOOK

Preparing and Delivering a Speech

There are four main methods of preparing and delivering a speech:

Manuscript When you speak from **manuscript,** you prepare a complete script of your speech in advance and use it to deliver your speech.

Memory When you speak from **memory,** you prepare a written text in advance and then memorize it so you can deliver it word for word.

Impromptu When you speak **impromptu,** you speak on the spur of the moment without any special preparation.

Extemporaneous When you give an **extemporaneous** speech, you research and prepare your speech and then deliver it with the help of notes.

Points for Effective Speech Delivery

- Avoid speaking either too fast or too slow. Vary your **speaking rate** depending on your material. Slow down for difficult concepts. Speed up to convince your audience that you are knowledgeable about your subject.
- Speak loud enough to be heard clearly, but not so loud that your voice is overwhelming.
- Use a **conversational tone.**
- Use a change of **pitch,** or inflection, to help make your tone and meaning clear.
- Let your **facial expression** reflect your message.
- Make **eye contact** with as many audience members as possible.
- Use **gestures** to emphasize your words. Don't make your gestures too small to be seen. On the other hand, don't gesture too frequently or wildly.
- Use **good posture**—not too relaxed and not too rigid. Avoid nervous mannerisms.

4.2 Analyzing, Evaluating and Critiquing a Speech

Evaluating speeches helps you make informed judgments about the ideas presented in a speech. It also helps you learn what makes an effective speech and delivery. Use these criteria to help you analyze, evaluate, and critique speeches.

CRITERIA How to Evaluate a Persuasive Speech

- Did the speaker have a clear goal or argument?
- Did the speaker take the audience's biases into account?
- Did the speaker support the argument with convincing facts?
- Did the speaker use sound logic in developing the argument?
- Did the speaker use voice, facial expression, gestures, and posture effectively?
- Did the speaker hold the audience's interest?

CRITERIA How to Evaluate an Informative Speech

- Did the speaker have a specific, clearly focused topic?
- Did the speaker take the audience's previous knowledge into consideration?
- Did the speaker cite sources for the information?
- Did the speaker communicate the information objectively?
- Did the speaker present the information in an organized manner?
- Did the speaker use visual aids effectively?
- Did the speaker use voice, facial expression, gestures, and posture effectively?

COMMUNICATION HANDBOOK 1387

4.3 Using Active Listening Strategies

Listeners play an active part in the communication process. A listener has a responsibility just as a speaker does. Listening, unlike hearing, is a learned skill.

As you listen to a public speaker, use the following active listening strategies:

- Determine the **speaker's purpose.**
- Listen for the **main idea** of the message and not simply the individual details.
- **Anticipate the points** that will be made based on the speaker's purpose and main idea.
- Listen with an open mind, but **identify faulty logic, unsupported facts,** and **emotional appeals.**

4.4 Conducting Interviews

Conducting a personal interview can be an effective way to get information.

Preparing for the Interview

- Read any articles by or about the person you will interview. This background information will help you get to the point during the interview.
- Prepare a list of questions. Think of more questions than you will need. Include some yes/no questions and some open-ended questions. Order your questions from most important to least important.

Participating in the Interview

- Listen interactively. Be prepared to follow up on a response you find interesting.
- Avoid arguments. Be tactful and polite.

Following Up on the Interview

- Summarize your notes while they are still fresh in your mind.
- Send a thank-you note to the interviewee.

5 Viewing and Representing

In our media-saturated world, we are immersed in visual messages that convey ideas, information, and attitudes. To understand and use visual representations effectively, you need to be aware of the techniques and the range of visuals that are commonly used.

5.1 Understanding Visual Messages

Information is communicated not only with words but with graphic devices. A **graphic device** is a visual representation of data and ideas and the relations among them.

Reading Charts and Graphs

A chart organizes information by arranging it in rows and columns. It is helpful in showing complex information clearly. When interpreting a chart, first read the title. Then analyze how the information is presented. Charts can take many different forms. The following chart compares two English literary eras.

A Comparison of Neoclassicism and Romanticism

Neoclassicism	Romanticism
Focus on society	Focus on individual
Emphasis on intellect	Emphasis on emotions
Emphasis on science	Emphasis on humanity
Reflected mainstream views	Reflected radical protest against society
Formal style	Personal, natural style

1388 COMMUNICATION HANDBOOK

Communication Handbook

There are several different types of **graphs,** visual aids that are often used to display numerical information.

- A **circle graph** shows proportions of the whole. The following circle graph shows the kinds of plays Shakespeare wrote.

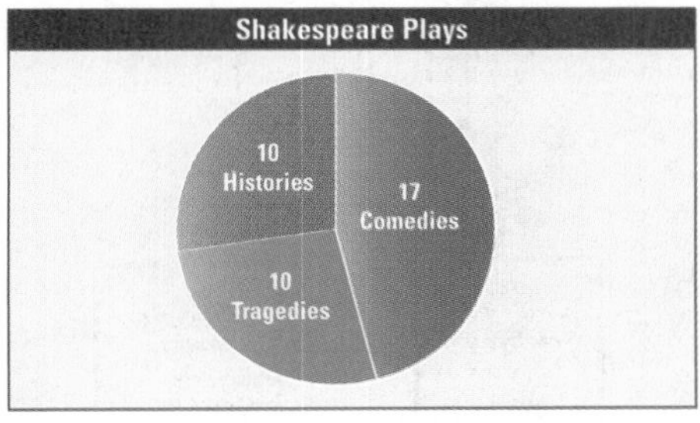

- A **line graph** shows the change in data over a period of time.
- A **bar graph** compares amounts. The following bar graph shows how many plays Shakespeare wrote in each period of his artistic development.

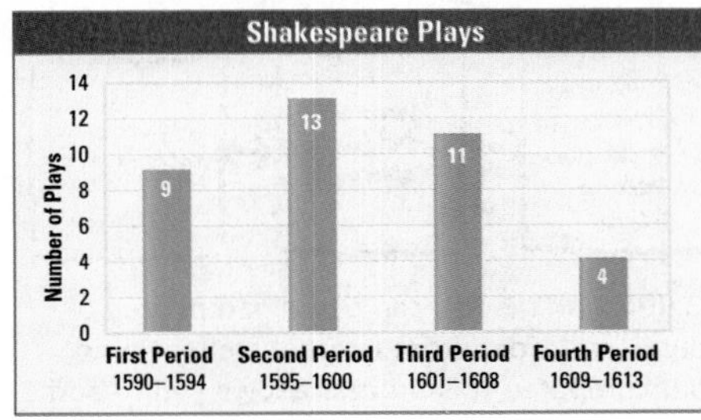

Interpreting Images

Speakers and writers often use visual aids to inform or persuade their audiences. These aids can be invaluable in helping you understand the information being communicated. However, you must interpret visual aids critically, as you do written material.

- **Examine photographs critically.** Does the camera angle or the background in the photo intentionally evoke a positive or negative response? Has the image been altered or manipulated?
- **Evaluate carefully the data presented in charts and graphs.** Some charts and graphs may exaggerate the facts. For example, a circle graph representing a sample of only ten people may be misleading if the speaker suggests that this data represents a trend.

5.2 Evaluating Visual Messages

When you view images, whether they are cartoons, advertising art, photographs, or paintings, there are certain elements to look for.

CRITERIA **How to Analyze Images**

- Is color used realistically? Is it used to emphasize certain objects? To evoke a specific response?
- What tone is created by color and by light and dark in the picture?
- Do the background images intentionally evoke a positive or negative response?
- What is noticeable about the picture's composition, that is, the arrangement of lines, colors, and forms? Does the composition emphasize certain objects or elements in the picture?
- For graphs and charts, does the visual accurately represent the data?

5.3 Using Visual Representations

Tables, graphs, diagrams, pictures, and animations often communicate information more effectively than words alone do.

Use visuals with written reports to illustrate complex concepts and processes or to make a page look more interesting. Computer programs, CD-ROMs, and on-line services can help you generate

- **graphs** that present numerical information;
- **charts** and **tables** that allow easy comparison of information;
- **logos** and **graphic devices** that highlight important information;
- **borders** and **tints** that signal different kinds of information;

COMMUNICATION HANDBOOK 1389

Communication Handbook

- **clip art** that adds useful pictures;
- **interactive animations** that illustrate difficult concepts.

You might want to explore ways of displaying data in more than one visual format before deciding which will work best for you.

 5.4 Making Multimedia Presentations

A multimedia presentation is an electronically prepared combination of text, sound, and visuals such as photographs, videos, and animation. Your audience reads, hears, and sees your presentation at a computer, following different "paths" you create to lead the user through the information you have gathered.

Planning Presentations

To create a multimedia presentation, first choose your topic and decide what you want to include. Then plan how you want your user to move through your presentation. For a multimedia presentation on the changing faces of heroes through the ages, you might include the following items:

- text defining *hero* and discussing heroic qualities
- taped reading from *Beowulf*
- taped reading from Malory's Arthurian tales
- chart comparing heroic qualities of Arthur and a modern superhero
- video interview with a scholar on the mythic origins of modern heroes
- video from *Batman* or Bond film
- photo of real-life modern hero

You can choose one of the following ways to organize your presentation:

step by step, with only one path, or order, in which the user can see and hear the information

a branching path that allows users to make some choices about what they will see and hear, and in what order

A flow chart can help you figure out the paths a user can take through your presentation. Each box in the flow chart that follows represents something about heroes for the user to read, see, or hear. The arrows on the flow chart show the possible paths the user can follow.

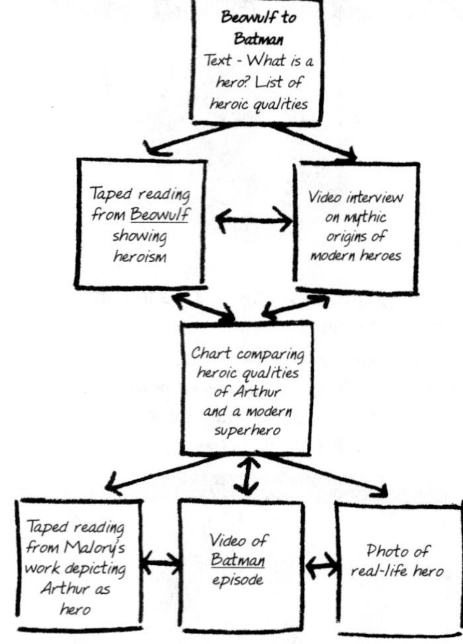

TECHNOLOGY TIP You can download photos, sound, and video from Internet sources onto your computer. This process allows you to add to your multimedia presentation various elements that would usually require complex editing equipment.

Guiding Your User

Your user will need directions to follow the path you have planned for your multimedia presentation.

Most multimedia authoring programs allow you to create screens that include text or audio directions that guide the user from one part of your presentation to the next.

If you need help creating your multimedia presentation, ask your school's technology adviser. You may also be able to get help from your classmates or your software manual.

1390 COMMUNICATION HANDBOOK

Grammar Handbook

1 Quick Reference: Parts of Speech

Part of Speech	Definition	Examples
Noun	Names a person, place, thing, idea, quality, or action.	Beowulf, England, boxes, liberty, kindness, hiking
Pronoun	Takes the place of a noun or another pronoun.	
Personal	Refers to the one speaking, spoken to, or spoken about.	I, me, my, mine, we, us, our, ours, you, your, yours, she, he, it, her, him, hers, his, its, they, them, their, theirs
Reflexive	Follows a verb or preposition and refers to a preceding noun or pronoun.	myself, yourself, herself, himself, itself, ourselves, yourselves, themselves
Intensive	Emphasizes a noun or another pronoun.	(Same as reflexives)
Demonstrative	Points to specific persons or things.	this, that, these, those
Interrogative	Signals questions.	who, whom, whose, which, what
Indefinite	Refers to person(s) or thing(s) not specifically mentioned.	both, all, most, many, anyone, everybody, several, none, some
Relative	Introduces subordinate clauses and relates them to words in the main clause.	who, whom, whose, which, that
Verb	Expresses action, condition, or state of being.	
Action	Tells what the subject does or did, physically or mentally.	run, reaches, listened, consider, decides, dreamt
Linking	Connects subjects to that which identifies or describes them.	am, is, are, was, were, sound, taste, appear, feel, become, remain, seem
Auxiliary	Precedes and introduces main verbs.	be, have, do, can, could, will, would, may, might
Adjective	Modifies nouns or pronouns.	**strong** women, **two** epics, **enough** time
Adverb	Modifies verbs, adjectives, or other adverbs.	walked **out**, **really** funny, **far** away
Preposition	Relates one word to another (following) word.	at, by, for, from, in, of, on, to, with
Conjunction	Joins words or word groups.	
Coordinating	Joins words or word groups used the same way.	and, but, or, for, so, yet, nor
Correlative	Join words or word groups used the same way and are used in pairs.	both . . . and, either . . . or, neither . . . nor
Subordinating	Joins word groups not used the same way.	although, after, as, before, because, when, if, unless
Interjection	Expresses emotion.	wow, ouch, hurrah

GRAMMAR HANDBOOK 1391

GRAMMAR PRACTICE ANSWERS

1. common, concrete
2. common, concrete; common, abstract
3. proper, concrete; common, abstract
4. common, concrete; proper, concrete; common, abstract
5. common, concrete
6. common, concrete; common, abstract; common, abstract
7. proper, concrete; common, concrete
8. common, abstract
9. common, abstract; common, abstract; common, concrete
10. common, abstract; common, abstract

11–15. compound nouns: roof boards, footprints, fire dragon; collective nouns: group, society

16. Hrothgar's
17. Danes'
18. heroism's
19. family's
20. darkness's
21. oceans'
22. army's
23. warrior's
24. scop's
25. companions'

2 Nouns

A noun is a word used to name a person, place, thing, idea, quality, or action. Nouns can be classified in several ways. All nouns can be placed in at least two classifications. They are either common or proper. All are also either abstract or concrete. Some nouns can be classified as compound, collective, and possessive as well.

2.1 ***Common Nouns*** are general names, common to an entire group.

EXAMPLES: *author, poem, valor, battle*

2.2 ***Proper Nouns*** name specific, one-of-a-kind things. (See Capitalization, page 1415.)

EXAMPLES: *Denmark, Beowulf, Viking*

2.3 ***Concrete Nouns*** name things that can be perceived by the senses.

EXAMPLES: *bird, scream, Troy, Homer*

2.4 ***Abstract Nouns*** name things that cannot be observed by the senses.

EXAMPLES: *intelligence, fear, joy, loneliness*

	Common	Proper
Abstract	bravery	Middle Ages
Concrete	monster	Denmark

2.5 ***Compound Nouns*** are formed from two or more words but express a single idea. They are written as single words, as separate words, or with hyphens. Use a dictionary to check the correct spelling of a compound noun.

EXAMPLES: *kingmaker, mead hall, ring-giver*

2.6 ***Collective Nouns*** are singular nouns that refer to groups of people or things. (See Subject-Verb Agreement, page 1410.)

EXAMPLES: *army, flock, class, species*

2.7 ***Possessive Nouns*** show who or what owns something. Consult the chart below for the proper use of the possessive apostrophe.

Category	Possessive Nouns Rule	Examples
All singular nouns	Add apostrophe plus *-s*	Beowulf's witness's, city's father-in-law's
Plural nouns not ending in *-s*	Add apostrophe plus *-s*	children's women's people's
Plural nouns ending in *-s*	Add apostrophe only	witnesses' churches' males' Johnsons'

GRAMMAR PRACTICE

A. For each underlined noun, first tell whether it is common or proper. Then tell whether it is concrete or abstract.

1. The story of Beowulf is a great epic.
2. Warriors praised his heroism.
3. Grendel was a powerful force.
4. The roof boards swayed, and the Danes shook with terror.
5. Their footprints were bloody.
6. The group had high hopes of victory.
7. Beowulf killed the fire dragon.
8. In doing so, he defeated evil.
9. Heroism is a common theme of great literature.
10. Is there any similarity to today's society?

B. 11–15. From the sentences above, write three compound nouns and two collective nouns.

C. Write the possessive forms of the following nouns.

16. Hrothgar	**21.** oceans
17. Danes	**22.** army
18. heroism	**23.** warrior
19. family	**24.** scop
20. darkness	**25.** companions

❸ Pronouns

A pronoun is a word that is used in place of a noun or another pronoun. The word or word group to which the pronoun refers is called its antecedent.

3.1 ***Personal Pronouns*** are pronouns that change their form to express person, number, gender, and case. The forms of these pronouns are shown in the chart that follows.

	Nominative	Objective	Possessive
Singular			
First Person	I	me	my, mine
Second Person	you	you	your, yours
Third Person	she, he, it	her, him, it	her, hers, his, its
Plural			
First Person	we	us	our, ours
Second Person	you	you	your, yours
Third Person	they	them	their, theirs

3.2 ***Pronoun Agreement*** Pronouns should agree with their antecedents in number and person. Singular pronouns are used to replace singular nouns. Plural pronouns are used to replace plural nouns. Pronouns must also match the gender (masculine, feminine, or neuter) of the nouns they replace.

3.3 ***Pronoun Case*** Personal pronouns change form to show how they function in a sentence. This change of form is called *case.* The three cases are **nominative, objective,** and **possessive.**

A nominative pronoun is used as the subject or the predicate nominative of a sentence.

An objective pronoun is used as the direct or indirect object of a sentence or as the object of a preposition.

SUBJECT **OBJECT**

He will lead them to us.

OBJECT OF PREPOSITION

A possessive pronoun shows ownership. The pronouns *mine, yours, hers, his, its, ours,* and *theirs* can be used in place of nouns.

EXAMPLE: *This horse is mine.*

The pronouns *my, your, her, his, its, our,* and *their* are used before nouns.

EXAMPLE: *This is my horse.*

USAGE TIP To decide which pronoun to use in a comparison, such as *He tells better tales than (I* or *me),* fill in the missing words: *He tells better tales than I tell.*

WATCH OUT! Many spelling errors can be avoided if you watch out for *its* and *their.* Don't confuse the possessive pronoun *its* with the contraction *it's*, meaning *it is* or *it has*. The homonyms *they're* (contraction for *they are*) and *there* (a place or an expletive) are often mistakenly used for *their.*

3.4 ***Reflexive and Intensive Pronouns*** These pronouns are formed by adding *-self* or *-selves* to certain personal pronouns. Their forms are the same, and they differ only in how they are used.

Reflexive pronouns follow verbs or prepositions and reflect back on an earlier noun or pronoun.

EXAMPLES: *He likes himself too much. She is now herself again.*

Intensive pronouns intensify or emphasize the nouns or pronouns to which they refer.

EXAMPLES: *They themselves will educate their children. You did it yourselves.*

GRAMMAR HANDBOOK 1393

GRAMMAR PRACTICE ANSWERS

1. hisself = himself
2. them = those
3. their = his or her
4. myself = I
5. theirselves = themselves

Grammar Handbook

Singular	
First Person	myself
Second Person	yourself
Third Person	herself, himself, itself
Plural	
First Person	ourselves
Second Person	yourselves
Third Person	themselves

WATCH OUT! Avoid using *hisself* or *theirselves.* Standard English does not include these forms.

> **NONSTANDARD:** *John enjoyed hisself at the play.*
> **STANDARD:** *John enjoyed himself at the play.*

USAGE TIP Reflexive and intensive pronouns should never be used without antecedents.

> **INCORRECT:** *Read a tale to my brother and myself.*
> **CORRECT:** *Read a tale to my brother and me.*

3.5 ***Demonstrative Pronouns*** point out things and persons near and far.

	Singular	Plural
Near	this	these
Far	that	those

WATCH OUT! Avoid using the objective pronoun *them* in place of the demonstrative *those.*

> **INCORRECT:** *Let's dramatize one of them tales.*
> **CORRECT:** *Let's dramatize one of those tales.*

3.6 ***Indefinite Pronouns*** do not refer to specific persons or things and usually have no antecedents. The chart shows some commonly used indefinite pronouns:

Singular	Plural	Singular or Plural	
each	both	all	half
either	few	any	plenty
neither	many	more	none
another	several	most	some

Here is another set of indefinite pronouns, all of which are singular. Notice that, with one exception, they are spelled as one word:

anyone	everyone	no one	someone
anybody	everybody	nobody	somebody
anything	everything	nothing	something

USAGE TIP Since all these are singular, pronouns referring to them should be singular.

> **INCORRECT:** *Did everybody play their part well?*
> **CORRECT:** *Did everybody play his or her part well?*

If the antecedent of the pronoun is both male and female, *his or her* may be used as an alternative, or the sentence may be recast:

> **EXAMPLES:** *Did everybody play his or her part well?*
> *Did all the students play their parts well?*

GRAMMAR PRACTICE

Write the correct form of all incorrect pronouns in the sentences below.

1. Chaucer hisself appears as a pilgrim in one tale.
2. Each student selected one of them tales to read aloud.
3. Did everybody have their turn?
4. My best friend and myself read "The Pardoner's Tale."
5. After the performance, the students treated theirselves to a medieval supper.

3.7 ***Interrogative Pronouns*** tell a reader or listener that a question is coming. The interrogative pronouns are *who, whom, whose, which,* and *what.*

> **EXAMPLES:** *Who is going to rehearse with you?*
> *From whom did you receive the script?*

USAGE TIP *Who* is used for subjects, *whom* for objects. To find out which pronoun you need to use in a question, change the question to a statement:

> **QUESTION:** *(Who/Whom?) did you meet there?*
> **STATEMENT:** *You met (?) there.*

Since the verb has a subject *(you)*, the needed word must be the object form, *whom.*

> **EXAMPLE:** *Whom did you meet there?*

WATCH OUT! A special problem arises when you use an interrupter such as *do you think* within a sentence:

EXAMPLE: *(Who/Whom) do you think will win?*

If you eliminate the interrupter, it is clear that the word you need is *who.*

3.8 ***Relative Pronouns*** relate, or connect, clauses to the words they modify in sentences. The noun or pronoun that the clause modifies is the antecedent of the relative pronoun. Here are the relative pronouns and their uses:

Replacing:	Subject	Object	Possessive
Persons	who	whom	whose
Things	which	which	whose
Things/Persons*	that	that	whose

* *That* generally will not replace specific names, such as *Geoffrey Chaucer.*

Often short sentences with related ideas can be combined using relative pronouns to create a more effective sentence.

SHORT SENTENCE: *Chaucer was the father of English poetry.*
RELATED SENTENCE: *Chaucer wrote* The Canterbury Tales.
COMBINED SENTENCE: *Chaucer, who wrote* The Canterbury Tales, *was the father of English poetry.*

GRAMMAR PRACTICE

Choose the appropriate interrogative or relative pronoun from the words in parentheses.

1. Can you name most of the characters (who, whom) Chaucer portrayed?
2. The pilgrims, (who/whom) were traveling to Canterbury, told tales to one another.
3. The Pardoner, (which/ whose) greed is exceptional, is not a sympathetic character.
4. (Who/Whom) do you think is the most sympathetic character?
5. Chaucer portrays himself as a somewhat foolish man (who/whom) others might overlook.

4 Verbs

A verb is a word that expresses an action, a condition, or a state of being. There are two main kinds of verbs: action and linking. Other verbs, called auxiliary verbs, are sometimes used with action verbs and linking verbs.

4.1 ***Action Verbs*** tell what action someone or something is performing, physically or mentally.

PHYSICAL ACTION: *You hit the target.*
MENTAL ACTION: *She dreamed of me.*

4.2 ***Linking Verbs*** do not express action. Linking verbs link subjects to complements that identify or describe them. Linking verbs may be divided into two groups:

FORMS OF *TO BE*: *She is our queen.*
VERBS THAT EXPRESS CONDITION: *The writer looked thoughtful.*

4.3 ***Auxiliary Verbs,*** sometimes called helping verbs, precede action or linking verbs and modify their meanings in special ways. The most commonly used auxiliary verbs are parts of the verbs *be, have,* and *do.*

Be: *am, is, are, was, were, be, being, been*
Have: *have, has, had*
Do: *do, does, did*

Other common auxiliary verbs are *can, could, will, would, shall, should, may, might,* and *must.*

EXAMPLES: *I always have admired her.*
You must listen to me.

4.4 ***Transitive and Intransitive Verbs***
Action verbs can be either transitive or intransitive. A transitive verb directs the action towards someone or something. The transitive verb has an object. An intransitive verb does not direct the action towards someone or something. It does not have an object. Since linking verbs convey no action, they are always intransitive.

Transitive: *The storm sank the ship.*
Intransitive: *The ship sank.*

Grammar Handbook

GRAMMAR PRACTICE ANSWERS
1. whom
2. who
3. whose
4. who
5. whom

4.5 ***Principal Parts*** Action and linking verbs typically have four principal parts, which are used to form verb tenses. The principal parts are the *present*, the *present participle*, the *past*, and the *past participle*.

If the verb is a regular verb, the past and past participle are formed by adding the ending *-d* or *-ed* to the present part. Here is a chart showing four regular verbs:

Present	Present Participle	Past	Past Participle
risk	(is) risking	risked	(have) risked
solve	(is) solving	solved	(have) solved
drop	(is) dropping	dropped	(have) dropped
carry	(is) carrying	carried	(have) carried

Note that the present participle and past participle forms are preceded by a form of *be* or *have.* These forms cannot be used alone as main verbs and always need an auxiliary verb.

EXAMPLES: *The rescuers were risking their lives. The doctor has solved the problem.*

The past and past participle of irregular verbs are not formed by adding *-d* or *-ed* to the present; they are formed in irregular ways.

Present	Present Participle	Past	Past Participle
begin	(is) beginning	began	(have) begun
break	(is) breaking	broke	(have) broken
bring	(is) bringing	brought	(have) brought
choose	(is) choosing	chose	(have) chosen
go	(is) going	went	(have) gone
lose	(is) losing	lost	(have) lost
see	(is) seeing	saw	(have) seen
swim	(is) swimming	swam	(have) swum
write	(is) writing	wrote	(have) written

4.6 ***Verb Tense*** The tense of a verb tells the time of the action or the state of being. An action or state of being can occur in the present, the past, or the future. There are six tenses, each expressing a different range of time.

Present tense expresses an action that is happening at the present time, occurs regularly, or is constant or generally true. Use the present part.

EXAMPLES
NOW: *That ballad sounds great.*
REGULAR: *I read every day.*
GENERAL: *The sun rises in the east.*

Past tense expresses an action that began and ended in the past. Use the past part.

EXAMPLE: *The storyteller finished his tale.*

Future tense expresses an action (or state of being) that will occur. Use *shall* or *will* with the present part.

EXAMPLE: *They will attend the next festival.*

Present perfect tense expresses action (1) that was completed at an indefinite time in the past or (2) that began in the past and continues into the present. Use *have* or *has* with the past participle.

EXAMPLE: *Poetry has inspired readers throughout the ages.*

Past perfect tense shows an action in the past that came before another action in the past. Use *had* before the past participle.

EXAMPLE: *The messenger had traveled for days before he delivered his knight's response.*

Future perfect tense shows an action in the future that will be completed before another action in the future. Use *shall have* or *will have* before the past participle.

EXAMPLE: *They will have finished the novel before seeing the movie version of the tale.*

4.7 ***Progressive Forms*** The progressive forms of the six tenses show ongoing action. Use a form of *be* with the present participle of a verb.

PRESENT PROGRESSIVE: *She is rehearsing her lines.*
PAST PROGRESSIVE: *She was rehearsing her lines.*
FUTURE PROGRESSIVE: *She will be rehearsing her lines.*

1396 GRAMMAR HANDBOOK

PRESENT PERFECT PROGRESSIVE: *She has been rehearsing her lines.*
PAST PERFECT PROGRESSIVE: *She had been rehearsing her lines.*
FUTURE PERFECT PROGRESSIVE: *She will have been rehearsing her lines.*

WATCH OUT! Do not shift tense needlessly. Watch out for these special cases.

- In most compound sentences and in sentences with compound predicates, keep the tenses the same.

  INCORRECT: *We work hard, and they paid us well.*
  CORRECT: *We work hard, and they pay us well.*

- If one past action happens before another, do shift tenses—from the past to the past perfect:

  INCORRECT: *They wished they started earlier.*
  CORRECT: *They wished they had started earlier.*

GRAMMAR PRACTICE

Identify the tense of the verb(s) in each of the following sentences. If you find an unnecessary tense shift, correct it.

1. Many consider *Le Morte d' Arthur* one of the greatest legends in Western culture.
2. King Arthur himself led his knights into battle.
3. While King Arthur is fighting in France, Sir Modred usurped his throne.
4. After Launcelot had defeated the French army, he settled in France.
5. A terrible struggle began, and each knight wounds the other.

4.8 *Active and Passive Voice*

The voice of a verb tells whether the subject of a sentence performs or receives the action expressed by the verb. When the subject performs the action, the verb is in the active voice. When the subject is the receiver of the action, the verb is in the passive voice.

Compare these two sentences:

ACTIVE: *Launcelot beat Gawain in the battle.*
PASSIVE: *Gawain was beaten by Launcelot in the battle.*

To form the passive voice use a form of *be* with the past participle of the main verb.

WATCH OUT! Use the passive voice sparingly. It tends to make writing less forceful and less direct. It can also make the writing awkward.

AWKWARD: *An oath of allegiance was sworn by the knights.*
CORRECT: *The knights swore an oath of allegiance.*

There are occasions when you will choose to use the passive voice because

- you want to emphasize the receiver: *The king was shot.*
- the doer is unknown: *My books were stolen.*
- the doer is unimportant: *French is spoken here.*

4.9 *Mood*

The mood identifies the manner in which the verb expresses an idea. There are three moods.

The indicative mood states a fact or asks a question. You use this mood most often.

EXAMPLE: *His trust was shattered by the betrayal.*

The imperative mood is used to give a command or make a request.

EXAMPLE: *Be there by eight o'clock sharp.*

The subjunctive mood is used to express a wish or a condition that is contrary to fact.

EXAMPLE: *If I were you, I wouldn't get my hopes up.*

GRAMMAR PRACTICE

Identify the verbs as active or passive.

1. *Le Morte d'Arthur* has influenced many other Arthurian stories.
2. It was written by Sir Thomas Malory, the son of a gentleman.
3. Malory did not live a settled life.
4. He was put in prison for his various offenses.
5. Malory was buried near Newgate, in a chapel at the Grey Friars.

Grammar Handbook

GRAMMAR PRACTICE ANSWERS

Column 1

1. consider = present
2. led = past
3. is fighting = present progressive
   usurped = past
   usurped > usurps
4. had defeated = past perfect
   settled = past
5. began = past
   wounds = present
   wounds > wounded

Column 2

1. active
2. passive
3. active
4. passive
5. passive

GRAMMAR PRACTICE ANSWERS

6. subjunctive
7. indicative
8. indicative
9. indicative
10. subjunctive

Grammar Handbook

For the following items, identify the boldfaced verb as indicative or subjunctive in mood.

6. If Malory **were** alive today, he'd probably be writing romance fiction.
7. Scholars **have praised** the style of *Le Morte d'Arthur* very highly.
8. The stories **were printed** by William Caxton in 1485.
9. Malory's knights **were** chivalrous.
10. If there **were** female knights then, would they have slain dragons?

5 Modifiers

Modifiers are words or groups of words that change or limit the meanings of other words. The two kinds of modifiers are adjectives and adverbs.

5.1 ***Adjectives*** An adjective is a word that modifies a noun or pronoun by telling *which one, what kind, how many,* or *how much.*

WHICH ONE: *this, that, these, those*
EXAMPLE: *Those shoes need new soles.*

WHAT KIND: *small, ugly, brave, black*
EXAMPLE: *The brave knight won the battle.*

HOW MANY: *some, few, thirty, none, both, each*
EXAMPLE: *Each village paid a tax for protection.*

HOW MUCH: *more, less, enough, scarce*
EXAMPLE: *Food was scarce.*

The **articles** *a, an,* and *the* are usually classified as adjectives. These are the most common adjectives that you will use.

EXAMPLES: *The bridge was burned before the attack.*
A group of peasants led the procession in the town.

5.2 ***Predicate Adjectives*** Most adjectives come before the nouns they modify, as in the examples above. Predicate adjectives, however, follow linking verbs and describe the subject.

EXAMPLE: *My friends are very intelligent.*

Be especially careful to use adjectives (not adverbs) after such linking verbs as *look, feel, grow, taste,* and *smell.*

EXAMPLE: *The weather grows cold.*

5.3 ***Adverbs*** modify verbs, adjectives, or other adverbs by telling *where, when, how,* or *to what extent.*

WHERE: *The children played outside.*
WHEN: *The author spoke yesterday.*
HOW: *We walked slowly behind the leader.*
TO WHAT EXTENT: *He worked very hard.*

Unlike adjectives, adverbs tend to be mobile words; they may occur in many places in sentences.

EXAMPLES: *Suddenly the wind shifted. The wind suddenly shifted. The wind shifted suddenly.*

Changing the position of adverbs within sentences can vary the rhythm in your writing.

5.4 ***Adjective or Adverb*** Many adverbs are formed by adding *-ly* to adjectives.

EXAMPLES: *sweet, sweetly; gentle, gently*

However, *-ly* added to a noun will usually yield an adjective.

EXAMPLES: *friend, friendly; woman, womanly*

5.5 ***Comparison of Modifiers*** The form of an adjective or adverb indicates the degree of comparison that the modifier expresses. Both adjectives and adverbs have three forms, or degrees: the positive, comparative, and superlative.

The positive form is used to describe individual things, groups, or actions.

EXAMPLES: *Arthur's jousting team is strong. The new weapons are useful.*

The comparative form is used to compare two things, groups, or actions.

EXAMPLES: *Arthur's jousting team is stronger than theirs. The new weapons are more useful than Stone Age clubs.*

The superlative form is used to compare more than two things, groups, or actions.

EXAMPLES: *Arthur's jousting team is the strongest in the land. The new weapons are the most useful they have ever had.*

5.6 *Regular Comparisons* One-syllable and some two-syllable adjectives and adverbs form their comparative and superlative forms by adding *-er* or *-est.* All three-syllable and most two-syllable modifiers form their comparative and superlative by using *more* or *most.*

Positive	Comparative	Superlative
small	smaller	smallest
thin	thinner	thinnest
sleepy	sleepier	sleepiest
useless	more useless	most useless
precisely	more precisely	most precisely

WATCH OUT! Note that spelling changes must sometimes be made to form the comparative and superlative of modifiers.

EXAMPLES: *friendly, friendlier* (change *y* to *i* and add the ending)
sad, sadder (double the final consonant and add the ending)

5.7 *Irregular Comparisons* Some commonly used modifiers have irregular comparative and superlative forms. You may wish to memorize them.

Positive	Comparative	Superlative
good	better	best
bad	worse	worst
far	farther or further	farthest or furthest
little	less or lesser	least
many	more	most
well	better	best
much	more	most

5.8 *Using Modifiers Correctly* Study the tips that follow to avoid common mistakes.

Farther* and *Further *Farther* is used for distances; use *further* for everything else.

Avoiding double comparisons You make a comparison by using *-er/-est* or by using *more/most.* Using *-er* with *more* or using *-est* with *most* is incorrect.

INCORRECT: *I like her more better than she likes me.*
CORRECT: *I like her better than she likes me.*

Avoiding illogical comparisons An illogical or confusing comparison results if two unrelated things are compared or if something is compared with itself. The word *other* or the word *else* should be used in a comparison of an individual member with the rest of the group.

ILLOGICAL: *Sir Walter Raleigh was as interesting as any English explorer.* (Was Raleigh an English explorer?)
LOGICAL: *Sir Walter Raleigh was as interesting as any other English explorer.*

Bad* vs. *Badly *Bad,* always an adjective, is used before nouns or after linking verbs to describe the subject. *Badly,* always an adverb, never modifies a noun. Be sure to use the right form after a linking verb.

INCORRECT: *Ed felt badly after his team lost.*
CORRECT: *Ed felt bad after his team lost.*

Good* vs. *Well *Good* is always an adjective. It is used before nouns or after a linking verb to modify the subject. *Well* is often an adverb meaning "expertly" or "properly." *Well* can also be used as an adjective after a linking verb, when it means "in good health."

INCORRECT: *Helen writes very good.*
CORRECT: *Helen writes very well.*
CORRECT: *Yesterday I felt bad; today I feel well.*

GRAMMAR HANDBOOK 1399

GRAMMAR PRACTICE ANSWERS

1. The author of "Female Orations" enjoyed more freedom than almost any other Englishwoman of her time.
2. Her education and position allowed her to travel farther than many men.
3. Many feel that women of the 17th century had the hardest lives.
4. The life of a farmer's wife was particularly difficult, especially when important crops failed badly.
5. Farmers forced to leave their land didn't have anywhere to go.
6. It is hard to tell whether a farmer's wife or an aristocratic lady had the more interesting life.
7. Although Cavendish wrote well on a number of subjects, some people thought she was mad.

Grammar Handbook

Double negatives If you add a negative word to a sentence that is already negative, the result will be an error known as a double negative. When using *not* or *-n't* with a verb, use "any-" words, such as *anybody* or *anything,* rather than "no-" words, such as *nobody* or *nothing,* later in the sentence.

INCORRECT: *I don't have no money.*
CORRECT: *I don't have any money.*

INCORRECT: *We haven't seen nobody.*
CORRECT: *We haven't seen anybody.*

Using *hardly, barely*, or *scarcely* after a negative word is also incorrect.

INCORRECT: *They couldn't barely see two feet ahead.*
CORRECT: *They could barely see two feet ahead.*

Misplaced modifiers A misplaced modifier is one placed so far away from the word it modifies that the intended meaning of the sentence is unclear. Place modifiers as close as possible to the words they modify.

MISPLACED: *We found the child in the park who was missing.* (The child was missing, not the park.)

CLEARER: *We found the child who was missing in the park.*

GRAMMAR PRACTICE

Rewrite these sentences, correcting mistakes in modifiers.

1. The author of "Female Orations" enjoyed the most freedom than almost any other Englishwoman of her time.
2. Her education and position allowed her to travel further than many men.
3. Many feel that women of the 17th century had the most hardest lives.
4. The life of a farmer's wife was particularly difficult, especially when important crops failed bad.
5. Farmers forced to leave their land didn't have nowhere to go.
6. It is hard to tell whether a farmer's wife or an aristocratic lady had the most interesting life.
7. Although Cavendish wrote good on a number of subjects, some people thought she was mad.

6 Prepositions, Conjunctions, and Interjections

6.1 *Prepositions* A preposition is a word used to show the relationship between a noun or a pronoun and another word in the sentence.

Commonly Used Prepositions

above	down	near	through
at	for	of	to
before	from	on	up
below	in	out	with
by	into	over	without

The preposition is always followed by a word or group of words which serve as its object. The preposition, its object, and modifiers of the object are called the **prepositional phrase.** In each example below, the prepositional phrase is underlined and the object of the preposition is in boldface type.

EXAMPLES:
*The future of the entire **kingdom** is uncertain.*
*We searched through the deepest **woods.***

Prepositional phrases may be used as adjectives or as adverbs. The phrase in the first example is used as an adjective modifying the noun *future*. In the second example, the phrase is used as an adverb modifying the verb *searched*.

WATCH OUT! Prepositional phrases must be as close as possible to the word they modify.

MISPLACED: *We have clothes for leisure wear of many colors.*
CLEARER: *We have clothes of many colors for leisure wear.*

6.2 *Conjunctions* A conjunction is a word used to connect words, phrases, or sentences. There are three kinds of conjunctions: **coordinating conjunctions, correlative conjunctions,** and **subordinating conjunctions.**

Coordinating conjunctions connect words or word groups that have the same function in a sentence. These include *and, but, or, for, so, yet,* and *nor.*

Coordinating conjunctions can join nouns, pronouns, verbs, adjectives, adverbs, prepositional phrases, and clauses in a sentence.

These examples show coordinating conjunctions joining words of the same function:

EXAMPLES:

I have many friends but few enemies. (two noun objects)

We ran out the door and into the street. (two prepositional phrases)

They are pleasant yet seem aloof. (two predicates)

We have to go now, or we will be late. (two clauses)

Correlative conjunctions are similar to coordinating conjunctions. However, correlative conjunctions are always used in pairs.

Correlative Conjunctions		
both . . . and	neither . . . nor	whether . . . or
either . . . or	not only . . . but also	

Subordinating conjunctions introduce subordinate clauses—clauses that cannot stand by themselves as complete sentences. The subordinating conjunction shows how the subordinate clause relates to the rest of the sentence. The relationships include time, manner, place, cause, comparison, condition, and purpose.

SUBORDINATING CONJUNCTIONS	
TIME	*after, as, as long as, as soon as, before, since, until, when, whenever, while*
MANNER	*as, as if*
PLACE	*where, wherever*
CAUSE	*because, since*
COMPARISON	*as, as much as, than*
CONDITION	*although, as long as, even if, even though, if, provided that, though, unless, while*
PURPOSE	*in order that, so that, that*

In the example below, the boldface word is the conjunction, and the underlined words are called a subordinate clause:

EXAMPLE: *I whistle a happy tune **whenever** I feel afraid.*

I whistle a happy tune is an independent clause because it can stand alone as a complete sentence. *Whenever I feel afraid* cannot stand alone as a complete sentence; it is a subordinate clause.

Conjunctive adverbs are used to connect clauses that can stand by themselves as sentences. Conjunctive adverbs include *also, besides, finally, however, moreover, nevertheless, otherwise,* and *then.*

EXAMPLE: *She loved the fall; however, she also enjoyed winter.*

6.3 *Interjections* are words used to show strong emotion, such as *wow* and *cool.* Often followed by an exclamation point, they have no grammatical relationship to the rest of a sentence.

EXAMPLE: *Whew! It's really hot outside.*

GRAMMAR PRACTICE

Label each of the boldface words as a preposition, conjunction, or interjection.

1. Fanny Burney went to the party **because** she wished to hear the great tenor sing.
2. **After** Burney arrived, she greeted her hosts **and** listened to the singer perform.
3. **Because of** the great heat in the crowded room, the singer decided to move **into** another one.
4. Lady Say and Sele accosted Burney **before** the writer could escape.
5. **"Oh!"** cried Lady S. and S. "'Tis the authoress of *Evelina.*"

Grammar Handbook

GRAMMAR PRACTICE ANSWERS

1. preposition
2. preposition, conjunction
3. preposition, preposition
4. conjunction
5. interjection

Grammar Handbook

7 Quick Reference: The Sentence and Its Parts

The diagrams that follow will give you a brief review of the essentials of the sentence—subjects and predicates—and of some of its parts.

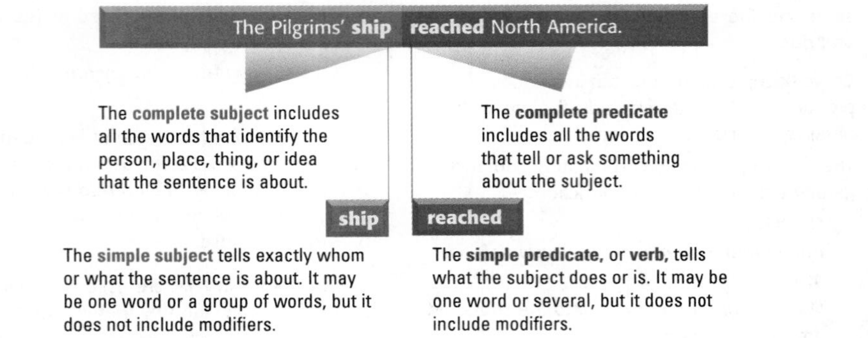

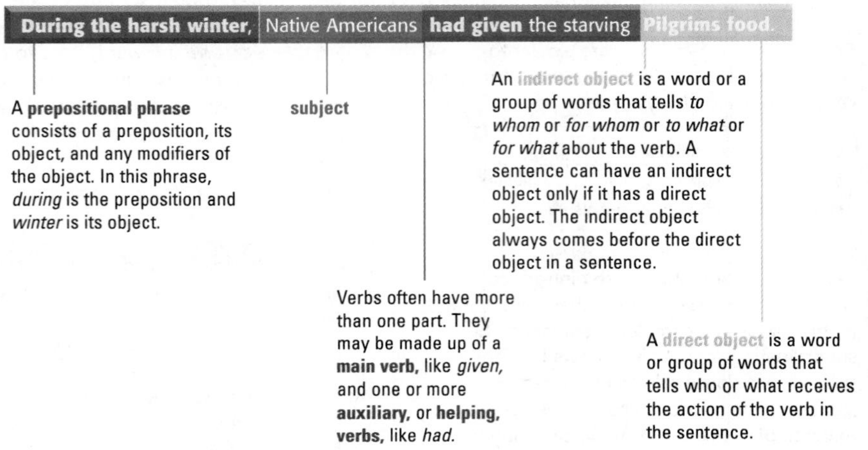

The Pilgrims' **ship** **reached** North America.

The **complete subject** includes all the words that identify the person, place, thing, or idea that the sentence is about.

The **complete predicate** includes all the words that tell or ask something about the subject.

ship

The **simple subject** tells exactly whom or what the sentence is about. It may be one word or a group of words, but it does not include modifiers.

reached

The **simple predicate**, or **verb**, tells what the subject does or is. It may be one word or several, but it does not include modifiers.

During the harsh winter, Native Americans **had given** the starving **Pilgrims food.**

A **prepositional phrase** consists of a preposition, its object, and any modifiers of the object. In this phrase, *during* is the preposition and *winter* is its object.

subject

An **indirect object** is a word or a group of words that tells *to whom* or *for whom* or *to what* or *for what* about the verb. A sentence can have an indirect object only if it has a direct object. The indirect object always comes before the direct object in a sentence.

Verbs often have more than one part. They may be made up of a **main verb,** like *given,* and one or more **auxiliary,** or **helping, verbs,** like *had.*

A **direct object** is a word or group of words that tells who or what receives the action of the verb in the sentence.

1402 GRAMMAR HANDBOOK

8 The Sentence and Its Parts

A sentence is a group of words used to express a complete thought. A complete sentence has a subject and predicate.

8.1 *Kinds of Sentences*

Sentences make statements, ask questions, give commands, and show feelings. There are four basic types of sentences.

Type	Definition	Example
Declarative	states a fact, wish, intent, or feeling	I read Malory's poem recently.
Interrogative	asks a question	Did you read his poem?
Imperative	gives a command, request, or direction	Read the poem or else.
Exclamatory	expresses strong feeling or excitement	This writer is good!

WRITING TIP One way to vary your writing is to employ a variety of different types of sentences. In the first example below, each sentence is declarative. Notice how much more interesting the revised paragraph is.

SAMPLE PARAGRAPH: *You have to see Niagara Falls in person. You can truly appreciate their awesome power in no other way. You should visit them on your next vacation. They are a spectacular sight.*

REVISED PARAGRAPH: *Have you ever seen Niagara Falls in person? You can truly appreciate their awesome power in no other way. Visit them on your next vacation. What a spectacular sight they are!*

WATCH OUT! Conversation frequently includes parts of sentences, or **fragments.** In formal writing, however, you need to be sure that every sentence is a complete thought and includes a subject and predicate. (See Correcting Fragments, page 1409.)

8.2 *Complete Subjects and Predicates*

A sentence has two parts: a subject and a predicate. The complete subject includes all the words that identify the person, place, thing, or idea that the sentence is about. The complete predicate includes all the words that tell what the subject did or what happened to the subject.

Complete Subject	Complete Predicate
The poets of the time	wrote about nature.
This new approach	was extraordinary.

8.3 *Simple Subjects and Predicates*

The simple subject is the key word in the complete subject. The simple predicate is the key word in the complete predicate. In the examples that follow they are underlined.

Simple Subject	Simple Predicate
The poets of the time	wrote about nature.
This new approach	was extraordinary.

8.4 *Compound Subjects and Predicates*

A compound subject consists of two or more subjects that share the same verb. They are typically joined by the coordinating conjunction *and* or *or*.

EXAMPLE: *The knight and his horse rode into the forest.*

A compound predicate consists of two or more predicates that share the same subject. They, too, are usually joined by the coordinating conjunction *and, but,* or *or*.

EXAMPLE: *Sir Gawain beheaded the Green Knight but did not kill him.*

8.5 *Subjects and Predicates in Questions*

In many interrogative sentences, the subject may appear after the verb or between parts of a verb phrase.

INTERROGATIVE: *Was Gawain living by the code of chivalry?*

INTERROGATIVE: *Why is this story very popular?*

Grammar Handbook

GRAMMAR HANDBOOK 1403

GRAMMAR PRACTICE ANSWERS

1. The Old English alliterative tradition emerged about 1350.
2. There were four texts in the manuscript.
3. None of the four texts originally had a title.
4. The last of the four texts was Sir Gawain and the Green Knight.
5. It may well be the greatest Arthurian romance in English.
6. Twelve rough illustrations accompanied the original texts.
7. The Pearl Poet evidently was not an artist.
8. [you] Think about the way that the Green Knight tests Gawain's virtues.
9. Why has the code of chivalry disappeared?
10. The knights of King Arthur's court have all become legendary figures.

Grammar Handbook

8.6 ***Subjects and Predicates in Imperative Sentences*** Imperative sentences give commands, requests, or directions. The subject of an imperative sentence is the person spoken to, or *you*. While it is not stated, it is understood to be *you*.

EXAMPLE: *(You) Please tell me what you're thinking.*

8.7 ***Subjects in Sentences That Begin with* There *and* Here** When a sentence begins with *there* or *here*, the subject usually follows the verb. Remember that *there* and *here* are never the subjects of a sentence. The simple subjects in the example sentences are underlined.

EXAMPLES

Here is the solution to the mystery.

There is no time to waste now.

There were too many passengers on the boat.

GRAMMAR PRACTICE

Copy each of the following sentences. Then draw one line under the complete subject and two lines under the complete predicate.

1. The Old English alliterative tradition emerged about 1350.
2. There were four texts in the manuscript.
3. None of the four texts originally had a title.
4. The last of the four texts was *Sir Gawain and the Green Knight.*
5. It may well be the greatest Arthurian romance in English.
6. Twelve rough illustrations accompanied the original texts.
7. The Pearl Poet evidently was not an artist.
8. Think about the way that the Green Knight tests Gawain's virtues.
9. Why has the code of chivalry disappeared?
10. The knights of King Arthur's court have all become legendary figures.

8.8 ***Complements*** A complement is a word or group of words that completes the meaning of the sentence. Some sentences contain only a subject and a verb. Most sentences, however, require additional words placed after the verb to complete the meaning of the sentence. There are three kinds of complements: **direct objects, indirect objects,** and **subject complements.**

Direct objects are words or word groups that receive the action of action verbs. A direct object answers the question *what?* or *whom?* In the examples that follow the direct objects are underlined.

EXAMPLES

The students asked many questions. (asked what?)

The teacher quickly answered them. (answered what?)

The school accepted girls and boys. (accepted whom?)

Indirect objects tell *to* or *for whom* or *what* the action of the verb is performed. Indirect objects come before direct objects. In the examples that follow the indirect objects are underlined.

EXAMPLES

My sister usually gave her friends good advice. (gave to whom?)

Her brother sent the post office a heavy package. (sent to what?)

His kind grandfather mailed him a new tie. (mailed to whom?)

Subject complements come after linking verbs and identify or describe the subject. Subject complements that name or identify the subject of the sentence are called **predicate nominatives.** These include **predicate nouns** and **predicate pronouns.** In the examples that follow the subject complements are underlined.

EXAMPLES

My friends are very hard workers.

The best writer in the class is she.

Other subject complements describe the subject of the sentence. These are called **predicate adjectives.**

EXAMPLE: *The pianist appeared very energetic.*

GRAMMAR PRACTICE

Write all of the complements in the following sentences and label them as direct objects, indirect objects, predicate nouns, predicate pronouns, or predicate adjectives.

1. William Wordsworth inaugurated the English Romantic period.
2. With Samuel Taylor Coleridge, he published *Lyrical Ballads* in 1798.
3. That volume quickly became immensely popular.
4. The last poem in *Lyrical Ballads* was "Lines Composed a Few Miles Above Tintern Abbey."
5. Wordsworth wrote the poem after a walking tour in June 1798.
6. In 1800, while living at Dove Cottage near Grasmere, Wordsworth and his friend enlarged their famous collection.
7. In that edition, Wordsworth gave the world his famous "Preface."
8. He stated his convictions and intentions about poetry.
9. He would draw his material from nature and everyday events.
10. Wordsworth offered readers a radical new philosophy.

9 Phrases

A phrase is a group of related words that does not have a subject and predicate and functions in a sentence as a single part of speech.

9.1 *Prepositional Phrases* A prepositional phrase is a phrase that consists of a preposition, its object, and any modifiers of the object. Prepositional phrases that modify nouns or pronouns are called **adjective phrases.** Prepositional phrases that modify a verb, an adjective, or another adverb are **adverb phrases.**

ADJECTIVE PHRASE: *The central character of the story is a wicked villain.*
ADVERB PHRASE: *He reveals his nature in the first scene.*

9.2 *Appositives and Appositive Phrases* An appositive is a noun or pronoun that usually comes directly after another noun or pronoun and identifies or provides further information about that word. An appositive phrase includes the appositive and all its modifiers. In the following examples, the appositive phrases are underlined.

EXAMPLES

We were discussing Mary Shelley, my hero.

Mary Wollstonecraft, the famous feminist, was considered a radical.

Occasionally, an appositive phrase may precede the noun it tells about.

EXAMPLE: *A great feminist, Mary Wollstonecraft wrote many essays.*

10 Verbals and Verbal Phrases

A verbal is a verb form that is used as a noun, an adjective, or an adverb. A verbal phrase consists of a verbal, all its modifiers, and all its complements. There are three kinds of verbals: infinitives, participles, and gerunds.

10.1 *Infinitives and Infinitive Phrases* An infinitive is a verb form that usually begins with *to* and functions as a noun, adjective, or adverb. The infinitive and its modifiers constitute an infinitive phrase. The examples that follow show several uses of infinitives and infinitive phrases. Each infinitive phrase is underlined.

NOUN: *To know her is my only desire.* (subject)

She wrote to voice her opinions. (direct object)

Her goal was to promote women's rights. (predicate nominative)

Grammar Handbook

GRAMMAR PRACTICE ANSWERS

1. period = direct object
2. *Lyrical Ballads* = direct object
3. popular = predicate adjective
4. "Lines Composed a Few Miles Above Tintern Abbey" = predicate noun
5. the poem = direct object
6. collection = direct object
7. world = indirect object
   "Preface" = direct object
8. convictions and intentions = direct object
9. material = direct object
10. readers = indirect object
    philosophy = direct object

GRAMMAR PRACTICE ANSWERS

1. participial phrase
2. appositive phrase
3. infinitive phrase, gerund phrase
4. gerund phrase
5. appositive phrase
6. infinitive phrase
7. appositive phrase

ADJECTIVE: *We saw his need to be loved.* (adjective modifying *need*)

ADVERB: *I'm planning to walk with you.* (adverb modifying *planning*)

Like verbs themselves, infinitives can take objects (*her* in the first noun example), be made passive (*to be loved* in the adjective example), and take modifiers (*with you* in the adverb example).

Because *to*, the sign of the infinitive, precedes infinitives, it is usually easy to recognize them. However, sometimes *to* may be omitted.

EXAMPLE: *Let no one dare [to] enter this shrine.*

10.2 Participles and Participial Phrases

A participle is a verb form that functions as an adjective. Like adjectives, participles modify nouns and pronouns. Most participles use the present participle form, ending in *-ing*, or the past participle form, ending in *-ed* or *-en*. In the examples below the participles are underlined.

MODIFYING A NOUN: *The dying man had a smile on his face.*

MODIFYING A PRONOUN: *Frustrated, everyone abandoned the cause.*

Participial phrases are participles with all their modifiers and complements.

MODIFYING A NOUN: *The dogs searching for survivors are well trained.*

MODIFYING A PRONOUN: *Having approved your proposal, we are ready to act.*

10.3 Dangling and Misplaced Participles

A participle or participial phrase should be placed as close as possible to the word that it modifies. Otherwise the meaning of the sentence may not be clear.

MISPLACED: *The boys were looking for squirrels searching the trees.*

CLEARER: *The boys searching the trees were looking for squirrels.*

A participle or participial phrase that does not clearly modify anything in a sentence is called a **dangling participle.** A dangling participle causes confusion because it appears to modify a word that it cannot sensibly modify.

Correct a dangling participle by providing a word for the participle to modify.

CONFUSING: *Running like the wind, my hat fell off.* (The hat wasn't running.)

CLEARER: *Running like the wind, I lost my hat.*

10.4 Gerunds and Gerund Phrases

A gerund is a verb form ending in *-ing* that functions as a noun. Gerunds may perform any function nouns perform.

SUBJECT: *Running is my favorite pastime.*

DIRECT OBJECT: *I truly love running.*

SUBJECT COMPLEMENT: *My deepest passion is running.*

OBJECT OF PREPOSITION: *Her love of running keeps her strong.*

Gerund phrases are gerunds with all their modifiers and complements. The gerund phrases are underlined in the following examples.

SUBJECT: *Wishing on a star never got me far.*

OBJECT OF PREPOSITION: *I will finish before leaving the office.*

APPOSITIVE: *Her avocation, flying airplanes, finally led to full-time employment.*

GRAMMAR PRACTICE

Identify the underlined phrases as appositive phrases, infinitive phrases, participial phrases, or gerund phrases.

1. Concerned about the injustices in Ireland, Swift wrote his satiric essay "A Modest Proposal."
2. Irony, a contrast between expectations and reality, can be an effective literary device.
3. Swift's modest proposal to prevent the children of Ireland from becoming a burden is ironic.
4. Referring to people as a commodity is a strong insult.
5. Was Swift a misanthrope, someone who mistrusts mankind?
6. What can be done to change the abhorrent conditions of the Irish poor?
7. *Gulliver's Travels,* an English satire, has many admiring readers.

⑪ Clauses

A clause is a group of words that contains a subject and a verb. There are two kinds of clauses: independent clauses and subordinate clauses.

11.1 *Independent and Subordinate Clauses* An independent clause can stand alone as a sentence, as the word *independent* suggests.

INDEPENDENT CLAUSE: *The English are noted for their independence.*

A sentence may contain more than one independent clause.

EXAMPLE: *The English are noted for their independence, and they are proud of their history of leadership in the Western world.*

In the example above the coordinating conjunction *and* joins the two independent clauses.

A subordinate clause cannot stand alone as a sentence. It is subordinate, or dependent, on the main clause.

EXAMPLE: *The English are known for their independence, although they are also very willing to work with others.*

Although they are also very willing to work with others cannot stand by itself.

11.2 *Adjective Clauses* An adjective clause is a subordinate clause used as an adjective. It usually follows the noun or pronoun it modifies.

EXAMPLE: *William Wordsworth is someone whom millions have read.*

Adjective clauses are typically introduced by the relative pronouns *who, whom, whose, which,* and *that* (see Relative Pronouns, page 1395). In the examples that follow, the adjective clauses are underlined.

EXAMPLES

A person who wants friends should be a friend.

Mary Ann Evans, whose pen name was George Eliot, wrote several great novels.

I read novels that let me escape from daily life.

WATCH OUT! The relative pronouns *whom, which,* and *that* may sometimes be omitted when they are objects of their own clauses.

EXAMPLE: *William Wordsworth is someone [whom] millions admire.*

11.3 *Adverb Clauses* An adverb clause is a subordinate clause that is used as an adverb to modify a verb, an adjective, or another adverb. It is introduced by a subordinating conjunction (see Subordinating Conjunctions, page 1401).

Adverb clauses typically occur at the beginning or end of sentences. The clauses are underlined in these examples.

MODIFYING A VERB: *When we need you, we will call.*
MODIFYING AN ADVERB: *I'll stay here where there is shelter from the rain.*
MODIFYING AN ADJECTIVE: *Roman felt good when he finished his essay.*

11.4 *Noun Clauses* A noun clause is a subordinate clause that is used in a sentence as a noun. A noun clause may be used as a subject, a direct object, an indirect object, a predicate nominative, or an object of a preposition. Noun clauses are often introduced by pronouns such as *that, what, who, whoever, which,* and *whose,* and by subordinating conjunctions, such as *how, when, where, why,* and *whether.* (See Subordinating Conjunctions, page 1401.)

USAGE TIP Because the same words may introduce adjective and noun clauses, you need to consider how the clause functions within its sentence.

To determine if a clause is a noun clause, try substituting *something* or *someone* for the clause. If you can do it, it is probably a noun clause.

EXAMPLES: *I know whose woods these are.* ("I know something." The clause is a noun clause, direct object of the verb know.)

Give a copy to whoever wants one. ("Give a copy to someone." The clause is a noun clause, object of the preposition to.)

GRAMMAR HANDBOOK 1407

GRAMMAR PRACTICE ANSWERS

1. noun clause
2. adverb clause
3. adjective clause
4. noun clause
5. adjective clause

Grammar Handbook

GRAMMAR PRACTICE

Identify each underlined clause as an adjective clause, an adverb clause, or a noun clause.

1. Some people think that John Keats is the best Romantic poet.
2. When I read the last line of "Ode on a Grecian Urn," I cried.
3. Did Keats, who wrote "When I Have Fears That I May Cease to Be," have a premonition of his own early death?
4. At first, Keats could not decide whether he wanted to be a poet or a surgeon.
5. He made the fateful decision, which the world welcomed, at about the age of 21.

12 The Structure of Sentences

When classified by their structure, there are four kinds of sentences: simple, compound, complex, and compound-complex.

12.1 ***Simple Sentences*** A simple sentence is a sentence that has one independent clause and no subordinate clauses. The fact that they are called "simple" does not mean that such sentences are uncomplicated. Various parts of simple sentences may be compounded, and they may contain grammatical structures such as appositives and verbals.

EXAMPLES

Lord Byron, a symbol of romanticism, has influenced poets, composers, and artists. (appositive and compound direct object)

Percy Bysshe Shelley, best known for writing poetry, was also an essayist. (participial and gerund phrases)

12.2 ***Compound Sentences*** A compound sentence has two or more independent clauses. The clauses are joined together with a comma and a coordinating conjunction (*and, but, or, nor, yet, for*), a semicolon, or a conjunctive adverb with a semicolon. Like simple sentences, compound sentences do not contain any dependent clauses.

EXAMPLES

I love Shelley's poem "Ozymandias," yet I don't admire Ozymandias himself.

Jane Austen lived a relatively quiet life; however, that did not prevent her from writing great novels.

WATCH OUT! Do not confuse compound sentences with simple sentences that have compound parts.

EXAMPLE: *A subcommittee drafted a document and immediately presented it to the entire group.* (here *and* signals a compound predicate, not a compound sentence)

12.3 ***Complex Sentences*** A complex sentence has one independent clause and one or more subordinate clauses. Each subordinate clause can be used as a noun or as a modifier. If it is used as a modifier, a subordinate clause usually modifies a word in the main clause and the main clause can stand alone. However, when a subordinate clause is a noun clause it is a part of the independent clause; the two cannot be separated.

MODIFIER: *One should not complain, unless she or he has a better solution.*

NOUN CLAUSE: *We sketched pictures of whomever we wished.* (noun clause is the object of the preposition *of* and cannot be separated from the rest of the sentence)

12.4 ***Compound-Complex Sentences*** A compound-complex sentence has two or more independent clauses and one or more subordinate clauses. Compound-complex sentences are, simply, both compound and complex. If you start with a compound sentence, all you need to do to form a compound-complex sentence is add a subordinate clause.

COMPOUND: *All the students knew the answer, yet they were too shy to volunteer.*

COMPOUND-COMPLEX: *All the students knew the answer that their teacher expected, yet they were too shy to volunteer.*

GRAMMAR PRACTICE

Tell whether each sentence is a simple sentence, a compound sentence, a complex sentence, or a compound-complex sentence.

1. Keats is my favorite romantic poet.
2. His life was tragically short, but he produced a remarkable body of work.
3. Although he became engaged to Fanny Brawne, poverty and poor health prevented him from marrying her.
4. Despite his illness, he produced many great works.
5. As his illness progressed, Keats moved to the milder climate of Italy, but he died six months later.

13 Writing Complete Sentences

A sentence is a group of words that expresses a complete thought. In writing that you wish to share with a reader, try to avoid both sentence fragments and run-on sentences.

13.1 ***Correcting Fragments*** A sentence fragment is a group of words that is only part of a sentence. It does not express a complete thought and may be confusing to the reader or the listener. A sentence fragment may be lacking a subject, a predicate, or both.

FRAGMENT: *waited for the boat to arrive* (no subject)
CORRECTED: *We waited for the boat to arrive.*
FRAGMENT: *people of various races, ages, and creeds* (no predicate)
CORRECTED: *People of various races, ages, and creeds gathered together.*
FRAGMENT: *near the old cottage* (neither subject nor predicate)
CORRECTED: *The burial ground is near the old cottage.*

In your own writing, fragments are usually the result of haste or incorrect punctuation. Sometimes fixing a fragment will be a matter of attaching it to a preceding or following sentence.

FRAGMENT: *We saw the two girls. Waiting for the bus to arrive.*
CORRECTED: *We saw the two girls waiting for the bus to arrive.*
FRAGMENT: *Newspapers appeal to a wide audience. Including people of various races, ages, and creeds.*
CORRECTED: *Newspapers appeal to a wide audience, including people of various races, ages, and creeds.*

13.2 ***Correcting Run-on Sentences***
A run-on sentence is made up of two or more sentences written as though they were one. Some run-ons have no punctuation within them. Others may use only a comma where a conjunction or stronger punctuation is necessary. Use your judgment in correcting run-on sentences, as you have choices. You can make two sentences if the thoughts are not closely connected. If the thoughts are closely related, you can keep the run-on as one sentence by adding a semicolon or a conjunction.

RUN-ON: *We found a place by a small pond for the picnic it is three miles from the village.*
MAKE TWO SENTENCES: *We found a place by a small pond for the picnic. It is three miles from the village.*
RUN-ON: *We found a place by a small pond for the picnic it was perfect.*
USE A SEMICOLON: *We found a place by a small pond for the picnic; it was perfect.*
ADD A CONJUNCTION: *We found a place by a small pond for the picnic, and it was perfect.*

WATCH OUT! When you add a conjunction, make sure you use appropriate punctuation before it: a comma for a coordinating conjunction, a semicolon for a conjunctive adverb. (See Conjunctions, page 1401.) A very common mistake is to use a comma instead of a conjunction or an end mark. This error is called a **comma splice**.

INCORRECT: *He finished the apprenticeship, then he left the village.*
CORRECT: *He finished the apprenticeship, and then he left the village.*

GRAMMAR PRACTICE ANSWERS

1. simple sentence
2. compound sentence
3. complex sentence
4. complex sentence
5. compound-complex sentence

GRAMMAR HANDBOOK 1409

GRAMMAR PRACTICE ANSWERS

Rudyard Kipling was born in India, where his father was a teacher at the University of Bombay. When he was only six years old, he was sent to school in England. There, at an early age, he wrote verses. Some of them were very good. He turned many of his earlier experiences to literary use in such works as *The Light That Failed.*

GRAMMAR PRACTICE

Rewrite the following paragraph, correcting all fragments and run-ons.

Rudyard Kipling was born in India. Where his father was a teacher at the University of Bombay. When he was only six years old. He was sent to school in England. There, at an early age, he wrote verses, some of them were very good. He turned many of his earlier experiences to literary use. In such works as *The Light That Failed.*

14 Subject-Verb Agreement

The subject and verb of a sentence must agree in number. Agreement means that when the subject is singular, the verb must be singular; when the subject is plural, the verb must be plural.

14.1 *Basic Agreement* Fortunately, agreement between subject and verb in English is simple. Most verbs show the difference between singular and plural only in the third person present tense. The present tense of the third person singular ends in *-s.*

Present Tense Verb Forms

Singular	Plural
I sleep	we sleep
you sleep	you sleep
she, he, it sleeps	they sleep

14.2 *Agreement with* Be The verb *be* presents special problems in agreement because this verb does not follow the usual verb patterns.

Forms of *Be*

Present Tense Singular	Present Tense Plural	Past Tense Singular	Past Tense Plural
I am	we are	I was	we were
you are	you are	you were	you were
she, he, it is	they are	she, he, it was	they were

14.3 *Words Between Subject and Verb* A verb agrees only with its subject. When words come between a subject and its verb, ignore them when considering proper agreement. Identify the subject and make sure the verb agrees with it.

EXAMPLES

A story in the newspapers tells about the 1890s.

Dad as well as Mom reads the paper daily.

14.4 *Agreement with Compound Subjects* Use a plural verb with most compound subjects joined by the word *and.*

EXAMPLE: *My father and his friends (they) read the paper daily.*

You could substitute the plural pronoun *they* for *my father and his friends*. This shows that you need a plural verb.

If the compound subject is thought of as a unit, you use the singular verb. Test this by substituting the singular pronoun *it.*

EXAMPLE: *Peanut butter and jelly [it] is my brother's favorite sandwich.*

Use a singular verb with a compound subject that is preceded by *each, every,* or *many a*.

EXAMPLE: *Each novel and short story seems grounded in personal experience.*

With *or, nor,* and the correlative conjunctions *either . . . or* and *neither . . . nor*, make the verb agree with the noun or pronoun nearest the verb.

EXAMPLES

Cookies or ice cream is my favorite dessert.

Either Cheryl or her friends are being invited.

Neither ice storms nor snow is predicted today.

14.5 *Personal Pronouns as Subjects* When using a personal pronoun as a subject, make sure to match it with the correct form of the verb *be*. (See the chart in 14.2.) Note especially that the pronoun *you* takes the verbs *are* and *were*, regardless of whether it is referring to the singular *you* or to the plural *you.*

WATCH OUT! *You is* and *you was* are nonstandard forms and should be avoided in writing and speaking. *We was* and *they was* are also forms to be avoided.

INCORRECT: *You was my best friend. They was going away.*
CORRECT: *You were my best friend. They were going away.*

14.6 *Indefinite Pronouns as Subjects*

Some indefinite pronouns are always singular; some are always plural. Others may be either singular or plural.

Singular Indefinite Pronouns			
another	either	neither	other
anybody	everybody	nobody	somebody
anyone	everyone	no one	someone
anything	everything	nothing	something
each	much	one	

EXAMPLES
Each of the writers was given an award.
Somebody in the room upstairs is sleeping.

The indefinite pronouns that are always plural include *both, few, many*, and *several*. These take plural verbs.

EXAMPLES
Many of the books in our library are not in circulation.

Few have been returned recently.

Still other indefinite pronouns may be either singular or plural.

Singular or Plural Indefinite Pronouns			
all	enough	most	plenty
any	more	none	some

The number of the indefinite pronouns *any* and *none* depends on the intended meaning.

EXAMPLES
Any of these topics has potential for a good article. (any singular topic)

Any of these topics have potential for a good article. (any of the many topics)

The indefinite pronouns *all, some, more, most,* and *none* are singular when they refer to a quantity or part of something. They are plural when they refer to a number of individual things. Context will usually give a clue.

EXAMPLES
All of the flour is gone. (referring to a quantity)

All of the flowers are gone. (referring to individual items)

14.7 *Inverted Sentences*

Inverted Sentences Problems in agreement often occur in inverted sentences beginning with *here* or *there*; in questions beginning with *why, where*, and *what*; and in inverted sentences beginning with a phrase. Identify the subject—wherever it is—before deciding on the verb.

EXAMPLES
There clearly are far too many cooks in this kitchen.

What is the correct ingredient for this stew?

Far from the embroiled cooks stands the master chef.

GRAMMAR PRACTICE

Locate the subject of each sentence. Then choose the correct verb.

1. Many writers have been controversial, but few (is/are) as controversial as D. H. Lawrence.
2. Neither his novels nor that shocking short story (is/are) censored today, however.
3. Nearly everybody who has read him either (love/loves) him or (hate/hates) him.
4. There (is/are) no opinions in between.
5. He and his wife Frieda searched for new ways to relate to people; they (was/were) a remarkable couple.

Grammar Handbook

GRAMMAR PRACTICE ANSWERS

1. few > are
2. novels nor short story > is
3. everybody > loves, hates
4. opinions > are
5. they > were

GRAMMAR HANDBOOK 1411

GRAMMAR PRACTICE ANSWERS

1. doesn't
2. entertains
3. hear
4. attract
5. is
6. were
7. doesn't
8. votes
9. was
10. has

Grammar Handbook

14.8 *Sentences with Predicate Nominatives*

When a predicate nominative serves as a complement in a sentence, use a verb that agrees with the subject, not the complement.

EXAMPLES

The novels of Dickens are a milestone in British literature. (*Novels* is the subject, not *milestone,* and it takes the plural verb *are.*)

A milestone in British literature is the novels of Dickens. (The subject is the singular noun *milestone.*)

14.9 Don't *and* Doesn't *as Auxiliary Verbs*

The auxiliary verb *doesn't* is used with singular subjects and with the personal pronouns *she, he*, and *it*. The auxiliary verb *don't* is used with plural subjects and with the personal pronouns *I, we, you*, and *they*.

SINGULAR

He doesn't know Elizabeth Barrett Browning's famous "Sonnet 43."
Doesn't the young man read very much?

PLURAL

I don't know what time it is now.
Novelists don't necessarily write short stories.

14.10 *Collective Nouns as Subjects*

Collective nouns are singular nouns that name a group of persons or things. *Team*, for example, is the collective name of a group of individuals. A collective noun takes a singular verb when the group acts as a single unit. It takes a plural verb when the members of the group act separately.

EXAMPLES

Our team usually wins. (the team as a whole wins)

Our team vote differently on most issues. (the individual members vote)

14.11 *Relative Pronouns as Subjects*

When a relative pronoun is used as a subject of its clause—*who, which,* and *that* can serve as subjects—the verb of the clause must agree in number with the antecedent of the pronoun.

SINGULAR: *I didn't read the book on trees that was given to me, but I did leaf through it.*

The antecedent of the relative pronoun *that* is the singular *book*; therefore, *that* is singular and must take the singular verb *was*.

PLURAL: *D. H. Lawrence and James Joyce, who were very different from each other, are both outstanding novelists.*

The antecedent of the relative pronoun *who* is the plural compound subject *D. H. Lawrence and James Joyce*. Therefore, *who* is plural, and it takes the plural verb *were*.

GRAMMAR PRACTICE

Choose the correct verb for each of the following sentences.

1. "The Rocking-Horse Winner" (don't/doesn't) end happily.
2. Nevertheless, it is a story that (entertain/entertains) most readers.
3. Even a collection of toys (hear/hears) the secret whisper.
4. The boy asked why some people (attract, attracts) luck.
5. Paul (are/is) partners with the older men.
6. What do you think the voices in the house that (were/was) speaking to Paul symbolize?
7. Why is it that Paul's horse (don't/doesn't) have a name?
8. Our class (vote/votes) on each story we read.
9. Lawrence's story about Paul's family, which (were/was) read last week, was a big winner in our poll.
10. A group of students (have/has) decided to dramatize it.

Grammar Handbook

Quick Reference: Punctuation

Punctuation	Function	Examples
End Marks period, question mark, exclamation point	to end sentences	It was the best time of my life. Was it the best time for you? What an architect Inigo Jones was!
	initials and other abbreviations	Dr. Robert Boyle, I. M. Pei, McDougal Littell Inc., A.M., B.C., yds., ft., Ave., St.
	items in outlines	I. Volcanoes A. Central-vent 1. Shield
	exception: P.O. states	NE (Nebraska), NV (Nevada)
Commas	before conjunction in compound sentence	I have never disliked poetry, but now I really love it.
	items in a series	She is brave, loyal, and kind. The slow, easy route is best.
	words of address	"Bright star, would I were steadfast . . . ." We need to solve this problem, men.
	parenthetical expressions	Well, just suppose that we can't? Hard workers, as you know, don't quit. I'm not a quitter, believe me.
	introductory phrases and clauses	In the beginning of the day, I feel fresh. While she was out, I was here. Having finished my chores, I went out.
	nonessential phrases and clauses	Ed Pawn, captain of the chess team, won. Ed Pawn, who is the captain, won. The two leading runners, sprinting toward the finish line, ended in a tie.
	in dates and addresses	Send it by June 20, 1998, to Maple Industry, 22 Spring Street, York, PA
	in letter parts	Dear Jim, Sincerely yours,
	for clarity, or to avoid confusion	By noon, time had run out. What the minister does, does matter. While cooking, Jim burned his hand.
Semicolons	in compound sentences that are not joined by coordinators *and,* etc.	The last shall be first; the first shall be last. I read the Bible; however, I have not memorized it.
	with items in series that contain commas	We invited my sister, Jan; her friend, Don; my uncle Jack; and Mary Dodd.
	in compound sentences that contain commas	After I ran out of money, I called my parents; but only my sister was home, unfortunately.

GRAMMAR HANDBOOK 1413

Grammar Handbook

Punctuation	Function	Examples
Colons	to introduce lists	**Correct:** Those we wrote were the following: Dana, John, and Will. **Incorrect:** Those we wrote were: Dana, John, and Will.
	before a long quotation	Winston Churchill wrote: "It would be foolish, however, to disguise the gravity of the hour. It would be still more foolish to lose heart."
	after the salutation of a business letter	To Whom It May Concern: Dear Prime Minister:
	with certain numbers	1:28 P.M., Genesis: 2–5
Dashes	to indicate an abrupt break in thought	I was thinking of my mother—who is arriving tomorrow—just as you walked in.
Parentheses	to enclose less important material	Like Dave (but without his English accent), Fran told many funny stories. Big Ben (Have you ever seen it?) is really big!
Hyphens	with a compound adjective before nouns	I come from a line of big-boned Englishmen.
	in compounds with *all-, ex-, self-, -elect*	She's an ex-MP but all-British. Our senator-elect is too self-important.
	in compound numbers (to *ninety-nine*)	Today, I turn twenty-one.
	in fractions used as adjectives	My cup is one-third full.
	between prefixes and words beginning with capital letters	Who was the best pre-Elizabethan poet? The weather was good in mid-May.
	when dividing words at the end of a line	Churchill won the Nobel Prize in litera-ture in 1953.
Apostrophes	to form possessives of nouns and indefinite pronouns	my friend's book, my friends' book, anyone's guess, somebody else's problem
	for omitted letters in numbers/contractions	don't (omitted **o**); he'd (omitted **woul**) the class of '99 (omitted **19**)
	to form plurals of letters and numbers	I had two A's and no 2's on my report card.
Quotation Marks	to set off a speaker's exact words	Sara said, "I'm finally ready." "I'm ready," Sara said, "finally." Did Sara say, "I'm ready"? Sara said, "I'm ready!"
	for titles of stories, short poems, essays, songs, book chapters	I liked Joyce's "Araby," Brooke's "The Soldier," and Orwell's "A Hanging." My favorite is the Beatles' "Yesterday."
Ellipses	for material omitted from a quotation	"It would be foolish . . . to disguise the gravity of the hour. . . ."
Italics	for titles of books, plays, magazines, long poems, operas, films, names of ships	*Pride and Prejudice, Macbeth, Time, The Rime of the Ancient Mariner, Carmen, Titanic,* HMS *Queen Elizabeth II*

1414 GRAMMAR HANDBOOK

Quick Reference: Capitalization

Grammar Handbook

Category/Rule	Examples
People and Titles	
Names and initials of people	**I**sabel **A**llende, **A**. **E**. **H**ousman
Titles with names or in place of them	**P**rofessor **H**olmes, **S**enator **L**ong The **S**enator has arrived.
Deities and members of religious groups	**J**esus, **A**llah, the **B**uddha, **Z**eus, **B**aptists, **R**oman **C**atholics
Names of ethnic and national groups	**H**ispanics, **J**ews, **A**frican **A**mericans
Geographical Names	
Cities, states, countries, continents	**L**ondon, **A**von, **I**reland, **A**ustralia
Regions, bodies of water, mountains	the **F**ar **W**est, **L**och **L**omond, **M**ount **I**da
Geographic features, parks	**G**reat **P**lains, **K**ensington **G**ardens
Streets and roads, planets	55 **W**est **T**hird **A**venue, **G**reen **L**ane, **M**ars, **S**aturn
Organizations and Events	
Companies, organizations, teams	**M**axwell **I**ndustries, the **M**asons
Buildings, bridges, monuments	**B**larney **C**astle, **W**estminster **B**ridge, **V**ietnam **W**ar **M**emorial
Documents, awards	**M**agna **C**arta, **D**istinguished **F**lying **C**ross
Special named events	**S**uper **B**owl, **W**orld **S**eries
Governmental bodies, historical periods and events	the **H**ouse of **L**ords, **P**arliament, the **E**lizabethan **A**ge, **W**orld **W**ar **I**
Days and months, holidays	**F**riday, **M**ay, **E**aster, **G**uy **F**awkes **D**ay
Specific cars, boats, trains, planes	**MG**, *Titanic, Orient Express*
Proper Adjectives	
Adjectives formed from proper nouns	**S**ocratic method, **I**rish cooking, **C**haucerian age, **A**tlantic coast
First Words and the Pronoun *I*	
The first word in a sentence or quote	**T**his is it. **H**e said, "**L**et's go."
Complete sentence in parentheses	(**C**onsult the previous chapter.)
Salutation and closing of letters	**D**ear **M**adam, **V**ery truly yours,
First lines of most poetry The personal pronoun, I	**T**hen am **I** **A** happy fly **I**f **I** live **O**r if **I** die.
First, last, and all important words in titles	***A T**ale of **T**wo **C**ities,* "**T**he **W**orld **I**s **T**oo **M**uch with **U**s"

GRAMMAR HANDBOOK 1415

Grammar Handbook

Little Rules That Make A Big Difference

Sentences

Avoid sentence fragments. Make sure all your sentences express complete thoughts.

A sentence fragment is a group of words that does not express a grammatically complete thought. It may lack a subject, a predicate, or both. Fragments may be corrected by adding the missing element(s) or by changing the punctuation to make the fragment part of another sentence.

FRAGMENT: *We admire George Eliot. A woman who prevailed over many prejudices of her time.*

COMPLETE: *We admire George Eliot. She was a woman who prevailed over many prejudices of her time.* (adding a subject and a predicate)

COMPLETE: *We admire George Eliot, a woman who prevailed over many prejudices of her time.* (changing the punctuation)

Avoid run-on sentences. Make sure all clauses in a sentence have the proper punctuation and/or conjunctions between them.

A run-on sentence consists of two or more sentences written as though they were one or separated only by a comma. Correct run-ons by making two separate sentences, using a semicolon, adding a conjunction, or rewriting the sentence.

RUN-ON: *James Galway is a great musician, he plays the flute.*

CORRECT: *James Galway is a great musician. He plays the flute.*

CORRECT: *James Galway is a great musician; he plays the flute.*

CORRECT: *James Galway, who plays the flute, is a great musician.*

Use end marks correctly. Use a period, not a question mark, at the end of an indirect question.

An indirect question is a question that does not use the exact words of the original speaker. Note the difference between the following sentences, and observe that the second sentence ends in a period, not a question mark.

DIRECT: *Lou asked, "What is that?"*

INDIRECT: *Lou asked what it was.*

Do not use quotation marks with indirect quotations within a sentence.

A direct quotation uses the speaker's exact words. An indirect quotation puts the speaker's words in other words. Compare these sentences:

DIRECT: *Jean said, "I'm going to be up all night writing my essay."* (quotation marks appropriate)

INDIRECT: *Jean said that she was going to be up all night writing her essay.* (no quotation marks)

Phrases

Place participial and prepositional phrases as close as possible to the words they modify. Participial and prepositional phrases are modifiers; that is, they tell about some other word in a sentence. To avoid confusion, they should be placed as close as possible to the word that they modify.

INCORRECT: *Tiny microphones are planted by agents called bugs.*

CORRECT: *Tiny microphones called bugs are planted by agents.*

Avoid dangling participles. Make sure a participial phrase does modify a word in the sentence.

INCORRECT: *Disappointed in love, a hermit's life seemed attractive.* (Who was disappointed?)

CORRECT: *Disappointed in love, the man became a hermit.*

1416 GRAMMAR HANDBOOK

Clauses

Use commas to set off nonessential adjective clauses.

Do you need the clause in order to indicate precisely who or what is meant? If not, it is nonessential and should be set off by commas.

USE COMMAS: *Nadine Gordimer, who is a great role model for young writers, received the 1991 Nobel Prize in literature.*

NO COMMAS: *A writer who is a great role model for young writers received the 1991 Nobel Prize in literature.*

Verbs

Don't use past tense forms with an auxiliary verb or past participle forms without an auxiliary verb. (See Auxiliary Verbs, page 1395.)

INCORRECT: *I have saw her somewhere before.* (*saw* is past tense and shouldn't be used with *have*)

CORRECT: *I have seen her somewhere before.*

INCORRECT: *I seen her somewhere before.* (*seen* is a past participle and shouldn't be used without an auxiliary)

Shift tense only when necessary.

Usually, when you are writing in present tense, stay in present tense; when you are writing in past tense, stay in past tense.

INCORRECT: *When my grandmother tells stories, everybody listened.*

CORRECT: *When my grandmother told stories, everybody listened.*

Sometimes a shift in tense is necessary to show a logical sequence of actions or the relationship of one action to another.

CORRECT: *After he had told his story, everybody went to sleep.*

Subject-Verb Agreement

Make sure subjects and verbs agree in number.

INCORRECT: *The Brontë sisters of England was great writers.*

CORRECT: *The Brontë sisters of England were great writers.*

INCORRECT: *Charlotte, as well as her sisters, were reserved.*

CORRECT: *Charlotte, as well as her sisters, was reserved.*

INCORRECT: *Emily and Anne was dead before 1850.*

CORRECT: *Emily and Anne were dead before 1850.*

Use a singular verb with nouns that look plural but have singular meaning.

Some nouns that end in *-s* are singular, even though they look plural. Examples are *measles, news, Wales,* and the names ending in *-ics* when they refer to a school subject, science, or general practice.

EXAMPLES: *Measles is a serious disease.*
Politics was the bane of Daniel Defoe.

Use a singular verb with titles.

EXAMPLE: Scenes of Clerical Life *was published in 1858.*
"At the Pitt-Rivers" was written by Penelope Lively.

Rule: Use a singular verb with words of weight, time, and measure.

EXAMPLES: *Seven years is the length of time Joyce took to write* Ulysses.
Fifty pounds was a great deal of money in the 1800s.

Pronouns

Use personal pronouns correctly in compounds.

Don't be confused about case when *and* joins a noun and a personal pronoun; the case of the pronoun still depends upon its function.

Grammar Handbook

GRAMMAR HANDBOOK 1417

Grammar Handbook

INCORRECT: *Him and his friends went to a Renaissance festival.*

CORRECT: *He and his friends went to a Renaissance festival.*

INCORRECT: *The teacher recommended John Donne's poetry to Lisa and I.*

CORRECT: *The teacher recommended John Donne's poetry to Lisa and me.*

INCORRECT: *Give Mary and they some flowers.*

CORRECT: *Give Mary and them some flowers.*

Usually, if you remove the noun and *and,* the correct pronoun will be obvious.

Use *we* and *us* correctly with nouns.

When a noun directly follows *we* or *us*, the case of the pronoun depends upon its function.

INCORRECT: *Us readers enjoy romantic poetry.*

CORRECT: *We readers enjoy romantic poetry.* (*we* is the subject)

INCORRECT: *The teacher read Kipling's "If" to we students.*

CORRECT: *The teacher read Kipling's "If" to us students.* (*us* is the object of *to*)

Avoid unclear pronoun reference.

The reference of a pronoun is ambiguous when the reader cannot tell which of two preceding nouns is its antecedent. The reference is indefinite when the idea to which the pronoun refers is only weakly or vaguely expressed.

AMBIGUOUS: *Homer, not Hesiod, wrote the* Iliad, *and he* [who?] *wrote the* Odyssey *too.*

CLEARER: *Homer, not Hesiod, wrote the* Iliad, *and Homer wrote the* Odyssey *too.*

INDEFINITE: *The Nobel Prize was won by Seamus Heaney in 1995, which is given to the greatest writers.*

CLEARER: *The Nobel Prize, which is given to the greatest writers, was won by Seamus Heaney in 1995.*

Avoid change of person.

If you are writing in third person—using pronouns such as *she, he, it, they, them, his, her, its*—do not shift to second person—*you*.

INCORRECT: *The feudal laborer had to obey his lord, and you needed to obey the king as well.*

CORRECT: *The feudal laborer had to obey his lord, and he needed to obey the king as well.*

Use correct pronouns in elliptical comparisons.

An elliptical comparison is a comparison from which words have been omitted. In order to choose the proper pronoun, fill in the missing words. Note the difference below:

EXAMPLES: *I know my math teacher better than* (I know) *him. I know my math teacher better than he* (knows my math teacher).

Don't confuse pronouns and contractions.

Personal pronouns are made possessive without the use of an apostrophe, as is the relative pronoun *whose*. Whenever you are unsure whether to write *it's* or *its*, *who's* or *whose*, ask if you mean *it is/has* or *who is/has*. If you do, write the contraction. Do the same for *you're* and *your*, *they're* and *their*, except that the contraction in this case is for the verb *are*.

Modifiers

Avoid double comparisons.

A double comparison is a comparison made twice. In general, if you use *-er* or *-est* on the end of a modifier, you would not also use *more* or *most* in front of it.

INCORRECT: *I like Shakespeare more better since I've read* Macbeth.

CORRECT: *I like Shakespeare better since I've read* Macbeth.

INCORRECT: *He's the most greatest playwright in the world.*

CORRECT: *He's the greatest playwright in the world.*

1418 GRAMMAR HANDBOOK

Avoid illogical comparisons.

Can you tell what is wrong with the following sentence?

Plays are more entertaining than any kind of performance art.

This sentence is difficult to understand. To avoid such illogical comparisons, use *other* when comparing an individual member with the rest of the group.

Plays are more entertaining than any other kind of performance art.

To avoid another kind of illogical comparison, use *than* or *as* after the first member in a compound comparison.

ILLOGICAL: *Josh baked as many tasty pies if not more than Marsha.* (Did he bake as many pies or as many tasty pies?)

CLEARER: *Josh baked as many tasty pies as Marsha, if not more.*

Avoid misplacing modifiers.

Modifiers of all kinds must be placed as close as possible to the words they modify. If you place them elsewhere, you risk being misunderstood.

MISPLACED: *The Parson is "a holy man of good renown" in Chaucer's* Canterbury Tales.

CLEARER: *The Parson in Chaucer's* Canterbury Tales *is "a holy man of good renown."*

It is the particular parson in Chaucer's poem who is "a holy man of good renown."

Words Not to Capitalize

Do not capitalize *north, south, east,* and *west* when they are used to tell direction.

EXAMPLES: *London is east and south of Oxford.*

Leeds is located in West Yorkshire. (West Yorkshire is the name of a county in the United Kingdom.)

Do not capitalize *sun* and *moon,* and capitalize *earth* only when it is used with the names of other planets.

EXAMPLES: *The sun and the moon are heavenly bodies in a solar system that includes Mars, Jupiter, and the Earth.*

We now live on the earth, not in heaven.

Do not capitalize the names of seasons.

EXAMPLE: *One of Gerard Manley Hopkins's best poems alludes to the seasons of spring and fall.*

Do not capitalize the names of most school subjects.

School subjects are capitalized only when they name a specific course, such as World History I. Otherwise, they are not capitalized.

EXAMPLE: *I'm taking physics, social studies, and a foreign language this year.*

Note: English and the names of other languages are always capitalized.

EXAMPLE: *Everybody takes English and either Spanish or French.*

GRAMMAR PRACTICE

Rewrite each sentence correctly.

1. The professor, a renowned authority on Shakespeare.
2. A modern version of *King Lear* is *A Thousand Acres* by Jane Smiley, an award-winning novel.
3. The tragedies of Shakespeare is more popular than his histories.
4. When *Macbeth* was performed, the tickets are impossible to get.
5. Make sure to reserve tickets for Mark and I.
6. Several productions of *A Midsummer Night's Dream* are performed on warm Summer nights in Central Park.
7. Having written both plays and sonnets, millions of readers admire the work of Shakespeare.
8. I like *West Side Story* more better than *Romeo and Juliet.*
9. The cast held a workshop for we students.
10. Founded in 1599, people still enjoy performances of Shakespeare's plays in the Globe Theatre.

GRAMMAR PRACTICE ANSWERS

1. The professor is a renowned authority on Shakespeare.
2. A modern version of *King Lear* is *A Thousand Acres,* an award-winning novel by Jane Smiley.
3. The tragedies of Shakespeare are more popular than his histories.
4. When *Macbeth* was performed, the tickets were impossible to get.
5. Make sure to reserve tickets for Mark and me.
6. Several productions of *A Midsummer Night's Dream* are performed on warm summer nights in Central Park.
7. Having written both plays and sonnets, Shakespeare is admired by millions of people.
8. I like *West Side Story* better than *Romeo and Juliet.*
9. The cast held a workshop for us students.
10. People still enjoy performances of Shakespeare's plays in the Globe Theater, which was founded in 1599.

Grammar Handbook

Commonly Confused Words

accept/except	The verb *accept* means "to receive or believe"; *except* is usually a preposition meaning "excluding."	The ticket office accepted all forms of payment except personal checks.
advice/advise	*Advise* is a verb; *advice* is a noun naming that which an *adviser* gives.	How did the witches advise Macbeth? Did they give him good advice?
affect/effect	As a verb *affect* means "to influence." *Effect* as a verb means "to cause." If you want a noun, you will almost always want *effect*.	Did the passionate shepherd's plea affect his beloved? It may effect a change in her attitude. Its effect is unknown.
all ready/already	*All ready* is an adjective meaning "fully ready." *Already* is an adverb meaning "before or by this time."	Two hours later, they were all ready to leave. I had already read Sonnets 116 and 130.
allusion/illusion	An *allusion* is an indirect reference to something. An *illusion* is a false picture or idea.	T. S. Eliot makes many allusions to the literary works of others. It's an illusion to believe you are always right.
among/between	*Between* is used when you are speaking of only two things. *Among* is used for three or more.	I had to choose between chocolate and vanilla. The "Rubáiyát" is among my favorite poems.
bring/take	*Bring* is used to denote motion toward a speaker or place. *Take* is used to denote motion away from such a person or place.	Bring the books over here, and I will take them to the library.
fewer/less	*Fewer* refers to the number of separate, countable units. *Less* refers to bulk quantity.	We have less literature and fewer selections in this year's curriculum.
leave/let	*Leave* means "to allow something to remain behind." *Let* means "to permit."	The librarian will leave some books on display but will not let us borrow any.
lie/lay	To *lie* is "to rest or recline." It does not take an object. To *lay* always takes an object.	Dogs love to lie in the sun. We always lay some bones next to him.
loose/lose	*Loose* (loos) means "free, not restrained"; *lose* (looz) means "to misplace or fail to find."	Who turned the horses loose? I hope we won't lose any of them.
precede/proceed	*Precede* means "to go or come before." Use *proceed* for other meanings.	The Anglo-Saxon period precedes Middle English. The teacher proceeded to read to the class.
than/then	Use *than* in making comparisons; use *then* on all other occasions.	Marlowe is better than Raleigh; We read one, and then the other.
two/too/to	*Two* is the number. *Too* is an adverb meaning "also" or "very." Use *to* before a verb or as a preposition.	Meg had to go to town, too. We had too much reading to do. Two chapters is too much.

1420 GRAMMAR HANDBOOK

Grammar Glossary

This glossary contains various terms you need to understand when you use the Grammar Handbook. Used as a reference source, this glossary will help you explore grammar concepts and the ways they relate to one another.

Abbreviation An abbreviation is a shortened form of a word or word group; it is often made up of initials. (B.C., A.M., *Maj.*)

Active voice. *See* **Voice.**

Adjective An adjective modifies, or describes, a noun or pronoun. (*happy* camper, she is *small*)

A ***predicate adjective*** follows a linking verb and describes the subject. (The day seemed *long.*)

A ***proper adjective*** is formed from a proper noun. (*Jewish* temple, *Alaskan* husky)

The ***comparative*** form of an adjective compares two things. (*more alert, thicker*)

The ***superlative*** form of an adjective compares more than two things. (*most abundant, weakest*)

What Adjectives Tell	Examples
How many	*some* writers *much* joy
What kind	*grand* plans *wider* streets
Which one(s)	*these* flowers *that* star

Adjective phrase. See **Phrase.**

Adverb An adverb modifies a verb, an adjective, or another adverb. (Clare sang *loudly.*)

The ***comparative*** form of an adverb compares two actions. (*more generously, faster*)

The ***superlative*** form of an adverb compares more than two actions. (*most sharply, closest*)

What Adverbs Tell	Examples
How	climb *carefully* chuckle *merrily*
When	arrived *late* left *early*
Where	climbed *up* moved *away*
To what extent	*extremely* upset *hardly* visible

Adverb, conjunctive. *See* **Conjunctive adverb.**

Adverb phrase. *See* **Phrase.**

Agreement Sentence parts that correspond with one another are said to be in agreement.

In ***pronoun-antecedent agreement,*** a pronoun and the word it refers to are the same in number, gender, and person. (*Bill* mailed *his* application. The *students* ate *their* lunches.)

In ***subject-verb agreement,*** the subject and verb in a sentence are the same in number. (*A child cries* for help. *They cry* aloud.)

Ambiguous reference An ambiguous reference occurs when a pronoun may refer to more than one word. (Bud asked his brother if *he* had any mail.)

Antecedent An antecedent is the noun or pronoun to which a pronoun refers. (If *Adam* forgets *his* raincoat, he will be late for school. *She* learned *her* lesson.)

Appositive An appositive is a noun or phrase that explains one or more words in a sentence. (Cary Grant, an *Englishman,* spent most of his adult life in America.)

An ***essential appositive*** is needed to make the sense of a sentence complete. (A comic strip inspired the musical *Annie.*)

A ***nonessential appositive*** is one that adds information to a sentence but is not necessary to its sense. (O. Henry, a *short-story writer,* spent time in prison.)

Article Articles are the special adjectives *a, an,* and *the.* (*the* day, *a* fly)

The ***definite article*** (the word *the*) is one that refers to a particular thing. (*the* cabin)

An ***indefinite article*** is used with a noun that is not unique but refers to one of many of its kind. (*a* dish, *an* otter)

Auxiliary verb. *See* **Verb.**

Clause A clause is a group of words that contains a verb and its subject. (*they slept*)

An ***adjective clause*** is a subordinate clause that modifies a noun or pronoun. (Hugh bought the sweater *that he had admired.*)

An ***adverb clause*** is a subordinate clause used to modify a verb, an adjective, or an adverb. (Ring the bell *when it is time for class to begin.*)

GRAMMAR HANDBOOK 1421

Grammar Handbook

A ***noun clause*** is a subordinate clause that is used as a noun. (*Whatever you say* interests me.)

An ***elliptical clause*** is a clause from which a word or words have been omitted. (We are not as lucky as *they.*)

A ***main (independent) clause*** can stand by itself as a sentence. (the *flashlight flickered*)

A ***subordinate (dependent) clause*** does not express a complete thought and cannot stand by itself. (*while the nation watched*)

Clause	Example
Main (independent)	The hurricane struck
Subordinate (dependent)	while we were preparing to leave.

Collective noun. *See* **Noun.**

Comma splice A comma splice is an error caused when two sentences are separated with a comma instead of a correct end mark. (*The band played a medley of show tunes, everyone enjoyed the show.*)

Common noun. *See* **Noun.**

Comparative. *See* **Adjective; Adverb.**

Complement A complement is a word or group of words that completes the meaning of a verb. (The kitten finished the *milk.*) *See also* **Direct object; Indirect object.**

An ***objective complement*** is a word or a group of words that follows a direct object and renames or describes that object. (The parents of the rescued child declared Gus a *hero.*)

A ***subject complement*** follows a linking verb and renames or describes the subject. (The coach seemed *anxious.*) *See also* **Noun (predicate noun); Adjective, (predicate adjective).**

Complete predicate The complete predicate of a sentence consists of the main verb plus any words that modify or complete the verb's meaning. (The student *produces work of high caliber.*)

Complete subject The complete subject of a sentence consists of the simple subject plus any words that modify or describe the simple subject. (*Students of history* believe that wars can be avoided.)

Sentence Part	Example
Complete subject	The man in the ten-gallon hat
Complete predicate	wore a pair of silver spurs.

Compound sentence part A sentence element that consists of two or more subjects, verbs, objects, or other parts is compound. (*Lou* and *Jay* helped. Laura *makes* and *models* scarves. Jill sings *opera* and *popular music.*)

Conjunction A conjunction is a word that links other words or groups of words.

A ***coordinating conjunction*** connects related words, groups of words, or sentences. (*and, but, or*)

A ***correlative conjunction*** is one of a pair of conjunctions that work together to connect sentence parts. (*either . . . or, neither . . . nor, not only . . . but also, whether . . . or, both . . . and*)

A ***subordinating conjunction*** introduces a subordinate clause. (*after, although, as, as if, as long as, as though, because, before, if, in order that, since, so that, than, though, till, unless, until, whatever, when, where, while*)

Conjunctive adverb A conjunctive adverb joins the clauses of a compound sentence. (*however, therefore, yet*)

Contraction A contraction is formed by joining two words and substituting an apostrophe for a letter or letters left out of one of the words. (*didn't, we've*)

Coordinating conjunction. *See* **Conjunction.**

Correlative conjunction. *See* **Conjunction.**

Dangling modifier A dangling modifier is one that does not clearly modify any word in the sentence. (*Dashing for the train,* the barriers got in the way.)

Demonstrative pronoun. *See* **Pronoun.**

Dependent clause. *See* **Clause.**

Direct object A direct object receives the action of a verb. Direct objects follow transitive verbs. (Jude planned the *party.*)

Direct quotation. *See* **Quotation.**

Divided quotation. *See* **Quotation.**

Double negative A double negative is the incorrect use of two negative words when only one is needed. (*Nobody didn't care.*)

End mark An end mark is one of several punctuation marks that can end a sentence. See the punctuation chart on page 1413.

Fragment. *See* **Sentence fragment.**

Future tense. *See* **Verb tense.**

Gender The gender of a personal pronoun indicates whether the person or thing referred to is male, female, or neuter. (My cousin plays the tuba; *he* often performs in school concerts.)

Gerund A gerund is a verbal that ends in *-ing* and functions as a noun. (*Making* pottery takes patience.)

Helping verb. *See* **Verb (auxiliary verb).**

Illogical comparison An illogical comparison is a comparison that does not make sense because words are missing or illogical. (My computer is *newer than Kay.*)

Indefinite pronoun. *See* **Pronoun.**

Indefinite reference Indefinite reference occurs when a pronoun is used without a clear antecedent. (My aunt hugged me in front of my friends, and *it* was embarrassing.)

Independent clause. *See* **Clause.**

Indirect object An indirect object tells to whom or for whom (sometimes to what or for what) something is done. (Arthur wrote *Kerry* a letter.)

Indirect question An indirect question tells what someone asked without using the person's exact words. (*My friend asked me if I could go with her to the dentist.*)

Indirect quotation. *See* **Quotation.**

Infinitive An infinitive is a verbal beginning with *to* that functions as a noun, an adjective, or an adverb. (He wanted *to go* to the play.)

Intensive pronoun. *See* **Pronoun.**

Interjection An interjection is a word or phrase used to express strong feeling. (*Wow! Good grief!*)

Interrogative pronoun. *See* **Pronoun.**

Intransitive verb. *See* **Verb.**

Inverted sentence An inverted sentence is one in which the subject comes after the verb. (*How was the movie? Here come the clowns.*)

Irregular verb. *See* **Verb.**

Linking verb. *See* **Verb.**

Main clause. *See* **Clause.**

Main verb. *See* **Verb.**

Modifier A modifier makes another word more precise. Modifiers most often are adjectives or adverbs; they may also be phrases, verbals, or clauses that function as adjectives or adverbs. (*small* box, smiled *broadly,* house *by the sea,* dog *barking loudly*)

An ***essential modifier*** is one that is necessary to the meaning of a sentence. (Everybody *who has a free pass* should enter now. None *of the passengers* got on the train.)

A ***nonessential modifier*** is one that merely adds more information to a sentence that is clear without the addition. (We will use the new dishes, *which are stored in the closet.*)

Noun A noun names a person, a place, a thing, or an idea. (*auditor, shelf, book, goodness*)

An ***abstract noun*** names an idea, a quality, or a feeling. (*joy*)

A ***collective noun*** names a group of things. (*bevy*)

A ***common noun*** is a general name of a person, a place, a thing, or an idea. (*valet, hill, bread, amazement*)

A ***compound noun*** contains two or more words. (*hometown, pay-as-you-go, screen test*)

A ***noun of direct address*** is the name of a person being directly spoken to. (*Lee,* do you have the package? No, *Suki,* your letter did not arrive.)

A ***possessive noun*** shows who or what owns or is associated with something. (*Lil's* ring, a *day's* pay)

A ***predicate noun*** follows a linking verb and renames the subject. (Karen is a *writer.*)

A ***proper noun*** names a particular person, place, or thing. (*John Smith, Ohio, Sears Tower, Congress*)

Number A word is **singular** in number if it refers to just one person, place, thing, idea, or action, and **plural** in number if it refers to more than one person, place, thing, idea, or action. (The words *he, waiter,* and *is* are singular. The words *they, waiters,* and *are* are plural.)

Object of a preposition The object of a preposition is the noun or pronoun that follows a preposition. (The athletes cycled along the *route.* Jane baked a cake for *her.*)

GRAMMAR HANDBOOK 1423

Object of a verb The object of a verb receives the action of the verb. (Sid told *stories.*)

Participle A participle is often used as part of a verb phrase. (had *written*) It can also be used as a verbal that functions as an adjective. (the *leaping* deer, the medicine *taken* for a fever)

The ***present participle*** is formed by adding *-ing* to the present form of a verb. (*Walking* rapidly, we reached the general store.)

The ***past participle*** of a regular verb is formed by adding *-d* or *-ed* to the present form. The past participles of irregular verbs do not follow this pattern. (*Startled,* they ran from the house. *Spun* glass is delicate. A *broken* cup lay there.)

Passive voice. *See* **Voice.**

Past tense. *See* **Verb tense.**

Perfect tenses. *See* **Verb tense.**

Person Person is a means of classifying pronouns.

A ***first-person*** pronoun refers to the person speaking. (*We* came.)

A ***second-person*** pronoun refers to the person spoken to. (*You* ask.)

A ***third-person*** pronoun refers to some other person(s) or thing(s) being spoken of. (*They* played.)

Personal pronoun. *See* **Pronoun.**

Phrase A phrase is a group of related words that does not contain a verb and its subject. (*noticing everything, under a chair*)

An ***adjective phrase*** modifies a noun or a pronoun. (The label *on the bottle* has faded.)

An ***adverb phrase*** modifies a verb, an adjective, or an adverb. (Come *to the fair.*)

An ***appositive phrase*** explains one or more words in a sentence. (Mary, *a champion gymnast,* won gold medals at the Olympics.)

A ***gerund phrase*** consists of a gerund and its modifiers and complements. (*Fixing the leak* will take only a few minutes.)

An ***infinitive phrase*** consists of an infinitive, its modifiers, and its complements. (*To prepare for a test,* study in a quiet place.)

A ***participial phrase*** consists of a participle and its modifiers and complements. (*Straggling to the finish line,* the last runners arrived.)

A ***prepositional phrase*** consists of a preposition, its object, and the object's modifiers. (The Saint Bernard does rescue work *in the Swiss Alps.*)

A ***verb phrase*** consists of a main verb and one or more helping verbs. (*might have ordered*)

Possessive A noun or pronoun that is possessive shows ownership or relationship. (*Dan's* story, *my* doctor)

Possessive noun. *See* **Noun.**

Possessive pronoun. *See* **Pronoun.**

Predicate The predicate of a sentence tells what the subject is or does. (The van *runs well even in winter.* The job *seems too complicated.*) *See also* **Complete predicate; Simple predicate.**

Predicate adjective. *See* **Adjective.**

Predicate nominative A predicate nominative is a noun or pronoun that follows a linking verb and renames or explains the subject. (Joan is a computer *operator.* The winner of the prize was *he.*)

Predicate pronoun. *See* **Pronoun.**

Preposition A preposition is a word that relates its object to another part of the sentence or to the sentence as a whole. (Alfredo leaped *onto* the stage.)

Prepositional phrase. *See* **Phrase.**

Present tense. *See* **Verb tense.**

Pronoun A pronoun replaces a noun or another pronoun. Some pronouns allow a writer or speaker to avoid repeating a proper noun. Other pronouns let a writer refer to an unknown or unidentified person or thing.

A ***demonstrative pronoun*** singles out one or more persons or things. (*This* is the letter.)

An ***indefinite pronoun*** refers to an unidentified person or thing. (*Everyone* stayed home. Will you hire *anybody?*)

An ***intensive pronoun*** emphasizes a noun or pronoun. (The teacher *himself* sold tickets.)

An ***interrogative pronoun*** asks a question. (*What* happened to you?)

A ***personal pronoun*** shows a distinction of person. (*I* came. *You* see. *He* knows.)

A ***possessive pronoun*** shows ownership. (*My* spaghetti is always good. Are *your* parents coming to the play?)

A ***predicate pronoun*** follows a linking verb and renames the subject. (The owners of the store were *they.*)

A ***reflexive pronoun*** reflects an action back on the subject of the sentence. (Joe helped *himself.*)

A ***relative pronoun*** relates a subordinate clause to the word it modifies. (The draperies, *which* had been made by hand, were ruined in the fire.)

Pronoun-antecedent agreement. *See* **Agreement.**

Pronoun forms

The ***subject form*** of a pronoun is used when the pronoun is the subject of a sentence or follows a linking verb as a predicate pronoun. (*She* fell. The star was *she*.)

The ***object form*** of a pronoun is used when the pronoun is the direct or indirect object of a verb or verbal or the object of a preposition. (We sent *him* the bill. We ordered food for *them*.)

Proper adjective. *See* **Adjective.**

Proper noun. *See* **Noun.**

Punctuation Punctuation clarifies the structure of sentences. See the punctuation chart below.

Quotation A quotation consists of words from another speaker or writer.

A ***direct quotation*** is the exact words of a speaker or writer. (Martin said, *"The homecoming game has been postponed."*)

A ***divided quotation*** is a quotation separated by words that identify the speaker. (*"The homecoming game,"* said Martin, *"has been postponed."*)

An ***indirect quotation*** reports what a person said without giving the exact words. (*Martin said that the homecoming game had been postponed.*)

Reflexive pronoun. *See* **Pronoun.**

Regular verb. *See* **Verb.**

Relative pronoun. *See* **Pronoun.**

Run-on sentence A run-on sentence consists of two or more sentences written incorrectly as one. (*The sunset was beautiful its brilliant colors lasted only a short time.*)

Sentence A sentence expresses a complete thought. The chart at the top of the next page shows the four kinds of sentences.

A ***complex sentence*** contains one main clause and one or more subordinate clauses. (*Open the windows before you go to bed. If she falls, I'll help her up.*)

A ***compound sentence*** is made up of two or more independent clauses joined by a conjunction, a colon, or a semicolon. (*The ship finally docked, and the passengers quickly left.*)

A ***simple sentence*** consists of only one main clause. (*My friend volunteers at a nursing home.*)

Punctuation	Uses	Examples
Apostrophe (')	Shows possession Indicates a contraction	Lou's garage Alva's script I'll help you. The baby's tired.
Colon (:)	Introduces a list or quotation Divides some compound sentences	three colors: red, green, and yellow This was the problem: we had to find our own way home.
Comma (,)	Separates ideas Separates modifiers Separates items in series	The glass broke, and the juice spilled all over. The lively, talented cheerleaders energized the team. We visited London, Rome, and Paris.
Exclamation point (!)	Ends an exclamatory sentence	Have a wonderful time!
Hyphen (-)	Joins parts of some compound words	daughter-in-law, great-grandson
Period (.)	Ends a declarative sentence Indicates most abbreviations	Swallows return to Capistrano in spring. min. qt. Blvd. Gen. Jan.
Question mark (?)	Ends an interrogative sentence	Where are you going?
Semicolon (;)	Divides some compound sentences Separates items in series that contain commas	Marie is an expert dancer; she teaches a class in tap. Jerry visited Syracuse, New York; Athens, Georgia; and Tampa, Florida.

GRAMMAR HANDBOOK 1425

Grammar Handbook

Sentence fragment A sentence fragment is a group of words that is only part of a sentence. (*When he arrived. Merrily yodeling.*)

Kind of Sentence	Example
Declarative (statement)	Our team won.
Exclamatory (strong feeling)	I had a great time!
Imperative (request, command)	Take the next exit.
Interrogative (question)	Who owns the car?

Simple predicate A simple predicate is the verb in the predicate. (John *collects* foreign stamps.)

Simple subject A simple subject is the key noun or pronoun in the subject. (The new *house* is empty.)

Split infinitive A split infinitive occurs when a modifier is placed between the word *to* and the verb in an infinitive. (*to quickly speak*)

Subject The subject is the part of a sentence that tells whom or what the sentence is about. (*Lou* swam.) *See* **Complete subject; Simple subject.**

Subject-verb agreement. *See* **Agreement.**

Subordinate clause. *See* **Clause.**

Superlative. *See* **Adjective; Adverb.**

Transitive verb. *See* **Verb.**

Unidentified reference An unidentified reference usually occurs when the word *it, they, this, which,* or *that* is used. (In California *they* have good weather most of the time.)

Verb A verb expresses an action, a condition, or a state of being.

An ***action verb*** tells what the subject does, has done, or will do. The action may be physical or mental. (Susan *trains* guide dogs.)

An ***auxiliary verb*** is added to a main verb to express tense, add emphasis, or otherwise affect the meaning of the verb. Together the auxiliary and main verb make up a verb phrase. (*will* intend, *could have* gone)

A ***linking verb*** expresses a state of being or connects the subject with a word or words that describe the subject. (The ice *feels* cold.) Linking verbs include *appear, be* (*am, are, is, was, were, been, being*), *become, feel, grow, look, remain, seem, smell, sound,* and *taste.*

A ***main verb*** expresses action or state of being; it appears with one or more auxiliary verbs. (will be *staying*)

The ***progressive form*** of a verb shows continuing action. (She *is knitting.*)

The past tense and past participle of a ***regular verb*** are formed by adding *-d* or *-ed.* (*open, opened*) An ***irregular verb*** does not follow this pattern. (*throw, threw, thrown; shrink, shrank, shrunk*)

The action of a ***transitive verb*** is directed toward someone or something, called the object of a verb. (Leo *washed* the windows.) An ***intransitive verb*** has no object. (The leaves *scattered.*)

Verb phrase. *See* **Phrase.**

Verb tense Verb tense shows the time of an action or the time of a state of being.

The ***present tense*** places an action or condition in the present. (Jan *takes* piano lessons.)

The ***past tense*** places an action or condition in the past. (We *came* to the party.)

The ***future tense*** places an action or condition in the future. (You *will understand.*)

The ***present perfect tense*** describes an action in an indefinite past time or an action that began in the past and continues in the present. (*has called, have known*)

The ***past perfect tense*** describes one action that happened before another action in the past. (*had scattered, had mentioned*)

The ***future perfect tense*** describes an event that will be finished before another future action begins. (*will have taught, shall have appeared*)

Verbal A verbal is formed from a verb and acts as another part of speech, such as a noun, an adjective, or an adverb.

Verbal	Example
Gerund (used as a noun)	Lamont enjoys *swimming.*
Infinitive (used as an adjective, an adverb, or a noun)	Everyone wants *to help.*
Participle (used as an adjective)	The leaves *covering the drive* made it slippery.

Voice The voice of a verb depends on whether the subject performs or receives the action of the verb.

In the ***active voice*** the subject of the sentence performs the verb's action. (We *knew* the answer.)

In the ***passive voice*** the subject of the sentence receives the action of the verb. (The team *has been eliminated.*)

Index of Fine Art

INDEX OF FINE ART **1427**

1428 INDEX OF FINE ART

278 *top*	*Edward VI as a Child* (about 1538), Hans Holbein the Younger.
278 *center*	*Queen Mary I of England* (1544), Master John.
280 *top*	*Portrait of James I,* unknown artist.
280 *bottom*	*Charles I on Horseback* (1637), Anthony Van Dyck.
281 *left*	*Sailing of the Pilgrims from Plymouth, England* (1941), Charles Shimmin.
281 *right*	*Oliver Cromwell* (about 1649), Robert Walker.
283	*The Huguenot* (1893), Sir John Everett Millais.
286	Portrait of Queen Elizabeth I of England as a princess (about 1542–1547), unknown artist.
290	*The Hireling Shepherd* (1851), William Holman Hunt.
295	*Henry Percy, Ninth Earl of Northumberland* (about 1595), Nicholas Hilliard.
304	*Anne of Gonzaga* (16th century), Nathaniel Hatch.
305	*Catherine Howard* (16th century), John Hoskins.
310	*Portrait of a Man and Woman at a Casement* (about 1440–1445), Fra Filippo Lippi.
316 *bottom left*	*King James I,* John de Critz the Elder.
382	*The Three Witches* (1783), Henry Fuseli.
400 *bottom right*	*Ellen Terry as Lady Macbeth* (1889), John Singer Sargent.
436	The labors of July, illumination from the *Trés riches heures du duc de Berry* (about 1415), Limbourg brothers.
438	*Return of the Prodigal Son* (1667–1668), Rembrandt van Rijn.
443	Detail of *Still Life with Old Books* (17th century), unknown French artist.
449	*John Donne* (about 1595), unknown artist.
458	Portrait said to be of Ben Jonson and Shakespeare playing chess (1603), Karel van Mander.
459	Detail of *The Graham Children* (1742), William Hogarth.
460	*Portrait of Frances Howard, Countess of Essex and Somerset,* Isaac Oliver.
465	*The Proposal* (1872), Adolphe William Bouguereau.
467	*Sir Philip Sidney* (about 1576), unknown artist.
472	Joy of Wine fresco (Persian).
475 *top right*	Manuscript painting of Majnun visited in the desert by his mother and Salim, from the *Khamsa* of Nizami (1595).
480	*The Expulsion from Paradise* (about 1424–1427), Masaccio.
481	*The Blind Milton Dictating to His Daughters* (1878), Mihály von Munkácsy.
494	*Young Woman Standing at a Virginal* (about 1670), Jan Vermeer.
498	Detail of *Adam Tempted by Eve* (1517), Hans Holbein the Younger.
503 *top*	Illustration for *The Pilgrim's Progress*, William Blake.
516 *left*	*James II* (1684), Sir Godfrey Kneller.
516 *right*	*Portrait of Anne, England's Last Stuart Monarch* (about 1694), unknown artist.
518 *top right*	*Charles II* (1661), John Michael Wright.
519 *top*	*William III* (1677), after a painting by Sir Peter Lely.
519 *bottom*	*Queen Mary II, Wife of William III,* William Wissing.
520 *top*	*King George I of England* (1716), Sir Godfrey Kneller.
520 *bottom*	*George III, Queen Charlotte and Their Six Eldest Children,* Johann Zoffany.
521	*The Boston Massacre, March 5, 1770* (1770), Paul Revere, after a drawing by Henry Pelham.
522 *top*	*Sir Isaac Newton* (about 1726), John Vanderbank.
522 *center*	*The Ladies Waldegrave* (about 1780), Sir Joshua Reynolds.
522 *bottom*	*Mr. Healey's Sheep,* W. H. Davis.
526	*Samuel Pepys* (1666), John Hayls.
529	*The Great Fire of London, 1666,* Dutch school.
536	*The Sense of Touch* (about 1615–1616), Jusepe de Ribera.
550	*Patience in a Punt* (1792), Henry William Bunbury.
555	*George Morland* (about 1785–1810), Thomas Rowlandson.
560	*Lady Mary Wortley Montagu* (about 1725), Jonathan Richardson.

INDEX OF FINE ART **1429**

1430 INDEX OF FINE ART

INDEX OF FINE ART **1431**

Index of Skills

Literary Concepts

1432 INDEX OF SKILLS

INDEX OF SKILLS **1433**

1434 INDEX OF SKILLS

Reading and Critical Thinking Skills

INDEX OF SKILLS **1435**

1436 INDEX OF SKILLS

INDEX OF SKILLS **1437**

Vocabulary Skills

Grammar, Usage, and Mechanics

1438 INDEX OF SKILLS

INDEX OF SKILLS **1439**

1440 INDEX OF SKILLS

Writing Skills, Modes, and Formats

INDEX OF SKILLS **1441**

1442 INDEX OF SKILLS

INDEX OF SKILLS **1443**

Inquiry and Research

1444 INDEX OF SKILLS

INDEX OF SKILLS **1445**

Speaking and Listening

Viewing and Representing

1446 INDEX OF SKILLS

Assessment

INDEX OF SKILLS **1447**

Index of Titles and Authors

Page numbers that appear in italics refer to biographical information.

1448 INDEX OF TITLES AND AUTHORS

INDEX OF TITLES AND AUTHORS **1449**

1450 INDEX OF TITLES AND AUTHORS

Acknowledgments *(continued)*

Rosanna White Norton: "The Wife's Lament," from *The Women Poets in English,* edited by Ann Stanford. Reprinted by permission of Rosanna White Norton, trustee.

Penguin Books Ltd: Excerpts from *A History of the English Church and People* by Bede, translated by Leo Sherley-Price, revised translation by R. E. Latham (Penguin Classics 1955, revised edition 1968); Copyright © 1955, 1968 by Leo Sherley-Price. Excerpts from "The Prologue," "The Pardoner's Prologue," "The Pardoner's Tale," "The Wife of Bath's Prologue," and "The Wife of Bath's Tale" from *The Canterbury Tales* by Geoffrey Chaucer, translated by Nevill Coghill. (Penguin Classics 1951, fourth revised edition 1977). Copyright © 1951, 1958, 1960, 1975, 1977 by Nevill Coghill. Excerpts from Chapter 1 from *The Book of Margery Kempe,* translated by B. A. Windeatt (Penguin Classics, 1985); Copyright © 1985 B. A. Windeatt. Reproduced by permission of Penguin Books Ltd.

The Folio Society: Excerpts from *The Pastons: A Family in the Wars of the Roses,* edited by Richard Barber (The Folio Society 1981; Boydell Press [Woodbridge, U.K., and Rochester, NY] 1993). Reprinted by permission of The Folio Society.

Jennifer Yu: "Her Three Inch Feet," from the Niskayuna High School (NY) Web Page, by Jennifer Yu. Reprinted with the permission of Jennifer Yu.

University of Chicago Press: Excerpts from *Sir Gawain and the Green Knight,* translated by John Gardner. Copyright © 1965 by The University of Chicago. Reprinted by permission of The University of Chicago Press.

Northwestern University Press: From the preface by William Caxton from *Le Morte d'Arthur,* parts seven and eight by Sir Thomas Malory, edited by D. S. Brewer. Copyright © 1968 by D. S. Brewer. Reprinted by permission.

Viking Penguin: "The Siege of Lanka" and "Rama and Ravana in Battle" from *The Ramayana,* translated by R. K. Narayan. Copyright © 1972 by R. K. Narayan. Used by permission of Viking Penguin, a division of Penguin Putnam Inc.

Mustang Publishing: "Whomp!" from *Essays That Worked: 50 Essays from Successful Applications to the Nation's Top Colleges,* edited by Boykin Curry & Brian Kasbar. Copyright © 1986. Reprinted by permission of Mustang Publishing.

Unit Two

University of Alabama Press: Sonnet 169 and Sonnet 292 from *Petrarch: Selected Poems,* English translation by Anthony Mortimer, Copyright © 1977 by The University of Alabama Press. Used by permission of The University of Alabama Press.

Barbara Hogenson Agency: "The Macbeth Murder Mystery" by James Thurber, from *My World—And Welcome to It.* Copyright © 1942 by James Thurber. Copyright © renewed 1970 by Helen Thurber and Rosemary A. Thurber. Reprinted by arrangement with Rosemary A. Thurber and the Barbara Hogenson Agency.

The New York Times: "Network Helps Children Cope with Serious Illness" by Catherine Greenman, from *The New York Times,* May, 28, 1998. Copyright © 1998 by *The New York Times.* Reprinted by permission.

Unit Three

University of California Press: Excerpts from *Diary of Samuel Pepys,* edited by Robert Latham and William Matthews. Copyright © 1972–1986 by The Master, Fellows and Scholars of Magdalen College, Cambridge, Robert Latham, and the Executors of William Matthews. Reprinted by permission of the University of California Press, Berkeley, California.

University of Illinois Press: "The Acorn and the Pumpkin" and "The Value of Knowledge" from *The Fables of La Fontaine,* translated by Norman R. Shapiro.

ACKNOWLEDGMENTS 1451

Copyright © 1985, 1988 by Norman R. Shapiro. Used with the permission of the author and of the University of Illinois Press.

The Washington Post: "A New Modest Proposal" by Ellen Goodman, from *The Boston Globe,* August, 1996. Copyright © 1996, *The Washington Post.* Reprinted with permission of The Washington Post Writers Group.

Unit Four

Lucien Stryk: Selected haiku from *Penguin Book of Zen Poetry,* edited and translated by Lucien Stryk and Takashi Ikemoto. London: Penguin Books Ltd., 1977. Reprinted by permission of the author.

Harcourt Brace & Company: "The Lotus-Blossom Cowers," from *Heinrich Heine: Paradox and Poet, The Poems* by Louis Untermeyer, copyright 1937 by Harcourt Brace & Company and renewed 1965 by Louis Untermeyer, reprinted by permission of the publisher.

Random House, Inc.: "Why Leaves Turn Color in the Fall," from *A Natural History of the Senses* by Diane Ackerman. Copyright © 1990 by Diane Ackerman. Reprinted by permission of Random House, Inc.

Unit Five

L. A. Wilson: "No One Stops to Say 'Thank You' Anymore" by L. A. Wilson, from *The Humanist,* November/December 1997. Copyright © 1997 by L. A. Wilson. Reprinted with the permission of the author.

Henry Holt and Company, Inc., and The Society of Authors: "To an Athlete Dying Young" and "When I Was One-and-Twenty," from *The Collected Poems of A. E. Housman* by A. E. Housman. Copyright 1939, 1940 by Henry Holt & Co., Inc. Copyright © 1967 by Robert E. Symons. Reprinted by permission of Henry Holt and Company, Inc., and The Society of Authors as the literary representative of the Estates of A. E. Housman.

Unit Six

Simon & Schuster, Inc.: "Sailing to Byzantium" by William Butler Yeats, Copyright 1928 by Macmillan Publishing Company, renewed 1956 by Georgie Yeats, and "The Second Coming" by William Butler Yeats, Copyright 1924 by Macmillan Publishing Company, renewed 1952 by Bertha Georgie Yeats, from *The Poems of W. B. Yeats: A New Edition,* edited by Richard J. Finneran. Reprinted with the permission of Simon & Schuster, Inc.

Viking Penguin and Laurence Pollinger Ltd.: "The Rocking-Horse Winner" by D. H. Lawrence; Copyright 1933 by the Estate of D. H. Lawrence, renewed © 1961 by Angelo Ravagli and C. M. Weekley, Executors of the Estate of Frieda Lawrence Ravagli. From *Complete Short Stories of D. H. Lawrence* by D. H. Lawrence. Used by permission of Viking Penguin, a division of Penguin Putnam Inc., and Laurence Pollinger Ltd.

Alfred A. Knopf, Inc. and The Society of Authors: "A Cup of Tea," from *The Short Stories of Katherine Mansfield* by Katherine Mansfield. Copyright 1923 by Alfred A. Knopf, Inc., and renewed 1951 by John Middleton Murry. Reprinted by permission of the publisher and The Society of Authors.

Harcourt Brace & Company and The Hogarth Press: "The Duchess and the Jeweller," from *A Haunted House and Other Short Stories* by Virginia Woolf; Copyright 1944 and renewed 1972 by Harcourt Brace & Company, reprinted by permission of the publisher and the Hogarth Press.

Cambridge University Press: Excerpt from *Virginia Woolf* by E. M. Forster. Reprinted with the permission of Cambridge University Press.

1452 ACKNOWLEDGMENTS

University of the South: "A Personal Memoir" by Robert Giroux, from *The Oxford Book of Literary Anecdotes.* First published in *The Sewanee Review,* vol. 74, no. 1, Winter 1966. Copyright © 1966 by the University of the South. Reprinted with the permission of the editor.

Harcourt Brace & Company and Faber and Faber Limited: "Preludes" from *Collected Poems 1909–1962* by T. S. Eliot, copyright 1936 by Harcourt Brace & Company, copyright © 1963, 1964 by T. S. Eliot, reprinted by permission of the publisher and Faber and Faber Limited.
"The Hollow Men" by T. S. Eliot, from *Collected Poems 1909–1962.* Copyright 1936 by Harcourt Brace & Company, copyright © 1964, 1963 by T. S. Eliot. "The Naming of Cats" by T. S. Eliot, from *Old Possum's Book of Practical Cats.* Copyright 1939 by T. S. Eliot and renewed 1967 by Esme Valerie Eliot. Reprinted by permission of Harcourt Brace & Company and Faber and Faber Limited.

Random House, Inc.: "Musée des Beaux Arts" and "The Unknown Citizen," from *W. H. Auden: Collected Poems* by W. H. Auden, edited by Edward Mendelson. Copyright © 1940 and renewed 1968 by W. H. Auden. Reprinted by permission of Random House, Inc.

Random House, Inc., and Faber and Faber Ltd.: "What I Expected," from *Selected Poems* by Stephen Spender. Copyright © 1934 and renewed 1962 by Stephen Spender. Reprinted by permission of Random House, Inc., and Faber and Faber Ltd.

New Directions Publishing Corporation and David Higham Associates: "Do Not Go Gentle into That Good Night" and "In My Craft or Sullen Art," from *The Poems of Dylan Thomas* by Dylan Thomas. Copyright 1946 by New Directions Publishing Corporation, Copyright 1952 by Dylan Thomas. Reprinted by permission of New Directions Publishing Corporation and David Higham Associates.

Indiana University Press and Fondo de Cultura Económica: "Writing/Escritura" from *Selected Poems of Octavio Paz,* edited and translated by Muriel Rukeyser. Copyright © 1963 by Octavio Paz and Muriel Rukeyser. Reprinted by permission of Indiana University Press and Fondo de Cultura Económica, Mexico.

Penguin Putnam Inc. and G. T. Sassoon: "Dreamers," from *Collected Poems of Siegfried Sassoon* by Siegfried Sassoon. Copyright 1918, 1920 by E. P. Dutton. Copyright 1936, 1946, 1947, 1948 by Siegfried Sassoon. Used by permission of Viking Penguin, a division of Penguin Putnam Inc., and George Sassoon.

Paul Berry, Literary Executor, and Virago Press, London: Excerpts from *Testament of Youth* by Vera Brittain are included with the permission of Paul Berry, literary executor for Vera Brittain, Victor Gollanez and The Virago Press, London.

Curtis Brown Ltd.: "Be Ye Men of Valour," from *Blood, Toil, Tears and Sweat* by Winston Churchill. Reproduced with permission of Curtis Brown Ltd., London, on behalf of the Estate of Sir Winston S. Churchill. Copyright © the Estate of Sir Winston S. Churchill.
"The Demon Lover," from *The Collected Stories of Elizabeth Bowen* by Elizabeth Bowen. Copyright © 1941 by Elizabeth Bowen.
Reproduced by permission of Curtis Brown Ltd., London.

Faber and Faber Limited: "To My Mother" from *Collected Poems* by George Barker. Copyright © 1987 by George Barker. Reprinted by permission of Faber and Faber Ltd.

Hill and Wang: Excerpt from *Night* by Elie Wiesel. Copyright © 1960 by MacGibbon & Kee. Copyright © 1988 by The Collins Publishing Group. Reprinted by permission of Hill and Wang, a division of Farrar, Straus & Giroux, Inc.

Pantheon Books: Excerpts from *Letters from Westerbork* by Etty Hillesum, translated by Arnold J. Pomerans. Translation copyright © 1986 by Random House, Inc. Reprinted by permission of Pantheon Books, a division of Random House, Inc.

Reece Halsey Agency: Excerpt from "Words and Behavior," from *Collected Essays* by Aldous Huxley. Reprinted by permission of Dorris Halsey, as agent for the Aldous

ACKNOWLEDGMENTS **1453**

Huxley Literary Estate.

Harcourt Brace & Company: "A Hanging," from *Shooting an Elephant and Other Essays* by George Orwell, copyright 1950 by Sonia Brownell Orwell and renewed 1978 by Sonia Pitt-Rivers. Reprinted by permission of Harcourt Brace & Company.

Unit Seven

Grove/Atlantic, Inc., and Murray Pollinger: "At the Pitt-Rivers," from *Pack of Cards and Other Stories* by Penelope Lively. Copyright © 1986 by Penelope Lively. Used by permission of Grove/Atlantic, Inc., and Murray Pollinger, Literary Agent.

Simon & Schuster and Jonathan Clowes Ltd.: "A Sunrise on the Veld," from *African Stories* by Doris Lessing. Copyright © 1965 by Doris Lessing; Copyright renewed © 1993 by Doris Lessing. Reprinted by permission of Simon & Schuster, Inc., and of Jonathan Clowes Limited, London, on behalf of Doris Lessing.

Georges Borchardt, Inc.: "The First Year of My Life," from *The Stories of Muriel Spark* by Muriel Spark. (New York: E. P. Dutton, 1985) Copyright © 1985 by Copyright Administration. Reprinted by permission of Georges Borchardt, Inc. and David Higham Associates on behalf of Muriel Spark. This story originally appeared in *The New Yorker.*

Houghton Mifflin Company and McClelland & Stewart, Inc.: "The Moment" from *Morning in the Burned House* by Margaret Atwood. Copyright © 1995 by Margaret Atwood. Reprinted by permission of Houghton Mifflin Company and McClelland & Stewart, Inc., the Canadian Publishers. All rights reserved.

Farrar, Straus & Giroux, Inc., and Faber and Faber Ltd.: "Digging," from *Poems* 1965–1975 by Seamus Heaney. Copyright © 1980 by Seamus Heaney. Used by arrangement with Farrar, Straus & Giroux, Inc., and Faber and Faber Ltd. All rights reserved.

Faber and Faber Ltd.: "The Horses," from *The Hawk in the Rain* by Ted Hughes. Reprinted by permission of Faber and Faber Ltd.

Farrar, Straus & Giroux, Inc.: Excerpt from *Crediting Poetry: The Nobel Lecture* by Seamus Heaney. Copyright © 1995 by The Nobel Foundation. Reprinted by permission of Farrar, Straus & Giroux, Inc.

The Ecco Press: "In Music" from *Provinces* by Czeslaw Milosz. Copyright © 1991 by Czeslaw Milosz Royalties Inc. First printed by The Ecco Press in 1991. Reprinted by permission of The Ecco Press.

New Directions Publishing Corp.: "The Frog Prince" and "Not Waving but Drowning" from *Collected Poems* by Stevie Smith. Copyright © 1972 by New Directions Publishing Corp. Reprinted by permission of New Directions Publishing Corp.

Grove/Atlantic, Inc., and Faber and Faber Ltd.: "That's All" from *Revue Sketches* by Harold Pinter. Copyright © 1966 by H. Pinter Ltd. Used by permission of Grove/Atlantic, Inc., and Faber and Faber Ltd.

Viking Penguin: "The Distant Past," from *Angels at the Ritz and Other Stories* by William Trevor. Copyright © 1975 by William Trevor. Used by permission of Viking Penguin, a division of Penguin Putnam Inc.

Doubleday and Harold Ober Associates: "Civil Peace," from *Girls at War and Other Stories* by Chinua Achebe. Copyright © 1972, 1973 by Chinua Achebe. Used by permission of Doubleday, a division of Bantam Doubleday Dell Publishing Group, Inc., and Harold Ober Associates Incorporated.

Wole Soyinka: "Telephone Conversation" by Wole Soyinka, first published in *Reflections: Nigerian Prose and Verse,* edited by Frances Ademola. Copyright © Wole Soyinka. Reprinted by permission of Wole Soyinka.

1454 ACKNOWLEDGMENTS

Farrar, Straus & Giroux, Inc.: "XXIII" from *Midsummer* by Derek Walcott. Copyright © 1984 by Derek Walcott. Used by arrangement with Farrar, Straus & Giroux, Inc. All rights reserved.

Russell & Volkening, Inc.: "Six Feet of the Country" from *Six Feet of the Country and Other Stories* by Nadine Gordimer. Copyright © 1956 by Nadine Gordimer, Copyright © renewed 1984 by Nadine Gordimer. Reprinted by permission of Russell & Volkening as agents for the author.

Agencia Literaria Carmen Balcells, S.A.: Excerpts from "Writing as an Act of Hope" by Isabel Allende in *Paths of Resistance,* edited by William Zinsser. Copyright © 1989 by Isabel Allende. Reprinted by permission of the author's agent.

The editors have made every effort to trace the ownership of all copyrighted material found in this book and to make full acknowledgment for its use. Omissions brought to our attention will be corrected in a subsequent edition.

Art Credits

Cover, Frontispiece

Illustration copyright © 1997 David Bowers.

Front Matter

x *left* Detail of the Bayeux Tapestry (late 11th–early 12th century). Musée de la Tapisserie, Bayeux, France. Giraudon/Art Resource, New York; *right* The Granger Collection, New York; **xi** Stock Montage/SuperStock; xii Photograph from *Angkor* by Michael Freedman and Roger Warner, edited and designed by David Larkin. Photographs copyright © 1990 by Michael Freedman. Reprinted by permission of Houghton Mifflin Company. All rights reserved; **xiii** *left* Ashburnham watch (mid-7th century). Courtesy of the Bickersteth family, Ashburnham, England; *right* Detail of the altarpiece of the Virgin of the Navigators (16th century), unknown artist. Reales Alcázares, Seville, Spain; **xiv** *top* The Granger Collection, New York; *bottom* Photofest; **xv** Detail of nativity of Christ. Stained glass. Abbey Ste. Foy, Conques, France. Giraudon/Art Resource, New York; **xvi** *left* Carved day bed (1695). Private collection. Bridgeman/Art Resource, New York; *right, Spring Gardens, Ranelagh,* Thomas Rowlandson. Victoria & Albert Museum, London/SuperStock; **xvii** The Granger Collection, New York; **xviii** Pocket watch (about 1700), M. Marcou. Musée des Arts Décoratifs, Paris; **xix** *left* Victoria & Albert Museum, London/Art Resource, New York; *right, The Lake, Petworth: Sunset, Fighting Bucks* (about 1828), Joseph Mallord William Turner. Clore Collection, Tate Gallery, London/Art Resource, New York; **xx** *top* The Granger Collection, New York; *bottom* Copyright © British Museum; **xxii** *left* Photo by Peter Roberts; *right, The Stone Pickers* (1887), George Clausen. Oil on canvas, 42″ × 31″. Tyne and Wear Museums, Newcastle upon Tyne, England; **xxiv** *Abstraction on Spectrum (Organization, 5)* (about 1914–1917), Stanton MacDonald-Wright. Oil on canvas, 30⅛″ × 24³⁄₁₆″. Des Moines (Iowa) Art Center, Nathan Emory Coffin Collection, purchased with funds from the Coffin Fine Arts Trust (1962.21); **xxv** Detail of *Portrait of T. S. Eliot,* Sir Gerald Kelly. Oil on canvas, 45⅛″ × 37″. National Portrait Gallery, Smithsonian Institution/Art Resource, New York; **xxvii** *top, Invasion* (1987–1988), Carel Weight. Oil on canvas, 48″ × 60″. The Saatchi Collection, London; *bottom* Copyright © 1971 John Dommers/Photo Researchers, Inc.; **xxviii** *Funeral Procession* (1940), Ellis Wilson. Amistad Research Center, Tulane University, New Orleans, Louisiana; **2** *right* Photofest; **3** *left* Photofest; *right, L'Ange du Destin,* Odilon Redon. Private collection. Bridgeman Art Library, London/New York; **6–7** Photofest.

ACKNOWLEDGMENTS **1455**

Unit One

16 *Hadrian's Wall* Nawrocki Stock Photo, Inc.; *helmet* The Granger Collection, New York; **17** *sandals* Museum of London; *candlestick* Photo copyright © British Museum; *sundial* R. Krubner/H. Armstrong Roberts; *Prioress* Ellesmere manuscript of *The Canterbury Tales* (1410), The Huntington Library, San Marino, California; *Battle of Crécy* Bibliothèque Nationale, Paris. Giraudon/Art Resource, New York; **18** *top left* Excavation site at Sutton Hoo (seventh century). The Granger Collection, New York; *bottom left* Gundestrup cauldron (Celtic, about 100 B.C.), detail from inner plate depicting the god Teutates accepting human sacrifice from warriors. Embossed silver, gilded, probably from Gaul. National Museum, Copenhagen, Denmark. Erich Lessing/Art Resource, New York; *right* Illustration by John Sandford; **19** *left* M. Berman/H. Armstrong Roberts; *right* Silver groat of King Henry VI of England. Ancient Art and Architecture Collection, London; **20** *background* Illustration by John Sandford; *center* Portrait of St. John with the tools of a scribe, from the Book of Kells, fol. 291v. Trinity College Library, by permission of the Board of Trinity College, Dublin; *bottom* Beginning of the Gospel of St. Luke, from the Lindisfarne Gospels (about A.D. 698), MS Cott. Nero D.IV, fol. 139. British Library, London. Bridgeman/Art Resource, New York; **21** *background* Knudsens-Giraudon/Art Resource, New York; *bottom left* Alfred the Great in majesty, late-9th-century jewel worked in cloisonné enamel. The Granger Collection, New York; **22** *left* By permission of The British Library, London; *right* John Bethell Photography; **23** MS Douce 383, fol. 16. The Bodleian Library, Oxford, U.K.; **24** *bottom left, top right, bottom right* Bibliothèque Nationale, Paris; *top center* Suit of armor for George IV of Puchheim (about 1515). Kunsthistorisches Museum, Vienna, Austria. Erich Lessing/Art Resource, New York; *center right* The Magna Carta of Liberties (1215). Department of the Environment, London. Bridgeman/Art Resource, New York; **25** The Bettmann Archive, New York; **26** *top* Edimedia, Paris; *bottom* Illustration from the Mary Evans Picture Library, London; **28** The Granger Collection, New York; **29** Photofest; **32–33** Illustration by Stephen Johnson; **34** Knudsens-Giraudon/Art Resource, New York; **37** Courtesy Museet ved Trelleborg, Denmark. Photo by Georg Hemmingsen; **40** The Granger Collection, New York; **45, 46** Illustration by Stephen Johnson; **47** Copyright © Statens Historiska Museum, Stockholm, Sweden; **49** Courtesy of the Royal Ontario Museum, Toronto, Canada; **50** Copyright © British Museum; **52** *top* Illustration by Rebecca McClellan; *center* The Granger Collection, New York; **53, 54–55** Illustration by Rebecca McClellan; **56, 57** The Granger Collection, New York; **59** Giraudon/Art Resource, New York; **60** By permission of the British Museum. Photograph copyright © Michael Holford, showing a previous restoration, recently reconstructed by the experts of the museum. See *The Sutton Hoo Ship Burial* by Angela Evans (1974); **61, 62** Copyright © Stephanie Berger. All rights reserved; **64** Copyright © British Museum; **65** MS Cott. Vitellius A.XV, fol. 132. By permission of the British Library; **67** Ancient Art and Architecture Collection, London; **73** Copyright © George Hunter/H. Armstrong Roberts; **77** Scala/Art Resource, New York; **82** *right* Copyright © SuperStock; **83** The Bettmann Archive, New York; **85** *top, center left* Copyright © Mapfile/Westlight; **85** *bottom right,* **86** Details of the Whale, MS Ashmole 1511, fol. 86v. The Bodleian Library, Oxford, U.K.; **94** The Pierpont Morgan Library/Art Resource, New York; **97** *left* Reproduced by kind permission of *The Times,* London. Copyright; *right* Copyright © Sonia Halliday Photographs; **98** Erich Lessing/Art Resource, New York; **99** Trinity College MS R.17.1, fol. 283v. The Master and Fellows of Trinity College, Cambridge, U.K.; **107–111** *border* Photo by Sharon Hoogstraten; **107** *signature* The Granger Collection, New York; *portrait* Stock Montage/SuperStock; **108** *left* National Portrait Gallery, London/SuperStock; *bottom right,* upper Nicolò Orsi Battaglini/Art Resource, New

1456 ACKNOWLEDGMENTS

York; *bottom right, lower* Copyright © Sonia Halliday & Laura Lushington; **109** The Granger Collection, New York; 110 *top* Charles Duke of Orleans, Tower of London, MS Royal 16.F.11, fol. 73. By permission of The British Library; *bottom* Copyright © Museum of London; **113–136, 142–151, 155–166** Calligraphy by Sharon D. Siegel; **115, 116, 117, 119, 122, 123, 129, 130** From the 1911 facsimile edition of the Ellesmere manuscript. Bridgeman Art Library, London; **139** Detail of V*isscher's View of London.* By permission of the Folger Shakespeare Library; **141, 142** Detail of the Pardoner. From the Ellesmere manuscript of Chaucer's *Canterbury Tales,* EL 26.C.9, fol. 138r. The Huntington Library, San Marino, California; **144** Nawrocki Stock Photo; **147** Detail from the *Psalter and Prayer Book of Bonne of Luxembourg, Duchess of Normandy* (French, Paris, 14th century), fol. 321v. Grisaille, color, gilt, and brown ink on vellum, $4\frac{15}{16}'' \times 3\frac{9}{16}''$. The Metropolitan Museum of Art, New York, The Cloisters Collection (69.86). Photograph copyright © 1991 The Metropolitan Museum of Art; **150** The Metropolitan Museum of Art, New York, The Cloisters Collection (69.86). Photograph copyright © 1991 The Metropolitan Museum of Art; **155** From the 1911 facsimile edition of the Ellesmere manuscript. Bridgeman Art Library, London; **159** Detail from *Le roman de Lancelot du lac* (early 14th century), MS M. 805, fol. 48. The Pierpont Morgan Library, New York/Art Resource, New York; **160** MS Douce 195, fol. 105r. The Bodleian Library, Oxford, U.K.; **162** Duomo, Florence, Italy. Scala/Art Resource, New York; **166** MS Douce 195, fol. 155r; The Bodleian Library, Oxford, U.K.; **167–170** *border* Photo by Sharon Hoogstraten; **168** Stock Montage/SuperStock; **169** *top* Christie's Images, London; *bottom* Copyright © David H. Endersbee/Tony Stone Worldwide; **170** *Chaucer portrait* The Granger Collection, New York; **178** Miniature from Codex Manesse (about 1300), unknown artist. Universitätsbibliothek Heidelberg, Germany. Photo by Lossen Foto; **179** The Granger Collection, New York; **180** July sheep shearing, from a book of hours by Simon Benninck. British Library. Bridgeman/Art Resource, New York; **182** *background* With permission of the Trustees of the British Library; *foreground left* Detail of women defending a castle with bow and crossbow (about 1326–1327). Manuscript illumination from *De nobilitatibus, sapientiis, et prudentiis regum* by Walter de Milemete, MS CH.CH.92, fol. 4r. By permission of the Governing Body of Christ Church, Oxford, U.K.; *foreground right,* The Governing Body of Christ Church, Oxford, U.K.; **183, 184, 185** *left,* **186** The Governing Body of Christ Church, Oxford, U.K.; **187** Letter from Richard Calle to Margery Paston, MS Add. 34889, fol. 78v–79v. By permission of The British Library; **188** *left background* With permission of the Trustees of the British Library; *right* The Governing Body of Christ Church, Oxford, U.K.; **189** The Governing Body of Christ Church, Oxford, U.K.; **191** *right* Gaia Caecilia, from MS Royal 16.G.V, fol. 56 Det. By permission of the British Library; **194** Illustration by Gordon Grant; **199** Copyright © Paul Merideth/Tony Stone Worldwide; **200–204** Photos by Sharon Hoogstraten; **209, 210, 215, 216, 218** *shield device* Illustration by Rebecca McClellan; **210–211, 216–217, 218–219, 221** Illustrations by Lorraine Silvestri; **210, 211, 215, 216, 217, 218** Calligraphy by Sharon D. Siegel; **223** *right* Armor (16th century), anonymous, attributed to Chevalier Bayard. Musée de l'Armée, Paris. Giraudon/Art Resource, New York; **235** MS Add. 10294, fol. 94 Det. By permission of the British Library; **241, 242, 243, 244, 246, 248, 249** Photograph from *Angkor* by Michael Freedman and Roger Warner, edited and designed by David Larkin. Photographs copyright © 1990 by Michael Freedman. Reprinted by permission of Houghton Mifflin Co. All rights reserved; **252** Victoria & Albert Museum, London/Art Resource, New York; **253, 254** Woman tending fire and reading, from the Bruges illuminated manuscript, Royal 15.D.1, fol. 18. By permission of the British Library; **258** *top left* By permission of the Folger Shakespeare Library, Washington, D.C.; *top right* Illustration from *Romance of Alexander* (Flemish, about 1340). The Granger Collection, New York; **259** *bottom* By permission of the British Library;

ACKNOWLEDGMENTS **1457**

260–264 Photos by Sharon Hoogstraten; **268** Detail of the Bayeux Tapestry (late 11th–early 12th century). Musée de la Tapisserie, Bayeux, France. Giraudon/Art Resource, New York.

Unit Two

274 *map of Utopia* The Granger Collection, New York; *Henry VIII* (1518), unknown artist. The Granger Collection, New York; *Queen Elizabeth* (about 1588), attributed to George Cower. The Granger Collection, New York; **275** *household items* Two basting spoons, an Elizabeth I apostle spoon (1561), and a William III spoon (late 17th century). Christie's Images, London; *microscope* (about 1675) used by Robert Hooke. Science & Society Picture Library, London; *floral clock* Ashburnham watch (mid-17th century). Courtesy of the Bickersteth family, Ashburnham, England; **276** *top, Portrait of Henry VIII* (about 1540), Hans Holbein the Younger. Galleria Nazionale d'Arte Antica, Rome. Scala/Art Resource, New York; *bottom* Self-portrait, number 15741, Leonardo da Vinci. Biblioteca Reale, Turin, Italy. Scala/Art Resource, New York; **277** *top* Derrick E. Witty/The National Trust Photographic Library, London; *bottom* The Granger Collection, New York; **278** *top, Edward VI as a Child* (about 1538), Hans Holbein the Younger. Oil on panel, 22⅜″ × 17⅜″. National Gallery of Art, Washington, D.C., Andrew W. Mellon Collection. Photo by Richard Carafelli; *center, Queen Mary I of England* (1544), Master John. The Granger Collection, New York; *bottom* Gold medal of Queen Elizabeth I, commemorating defeat of the Spanish Armada in 1588. The Granger Collection, New York; **279** Map of the English Channel from *The Mariner's Mirrour.* By permission of the Folger Shakespeare Library, Washington, D.C.; **280** *top* Portrait of James I. The Royal Collection, copyright © Her Majesty Queen Elizabeth II; *bottom, Charles I on Horseback* (1637), Anthony Van Dyck. Canvas, 367 cm × 292.1 cm. National Gallery, London; **281** *left, Sailing of the Pilgrims from Plymouth, England* (1941), Charles Shimmin. Woolaroc Museum, Bartlesville, Oklahoma; *right* The Granger Collection, New York; **283** *The Huguenot* (1893), Sir John Everett Millais. Christie's, London. Bridgeman/Art Resource, New York; **286** Queen Elizabeth I of England as a princess (about 1542–1547), unknown artist. The Granger Collection, New York; **288** *left* The Granger Collection, New York; *right* North Wind Picture Archives; **289, 291, 292** Details of *The Hireling Shepherd* (1851), William Holman Hunt. Manchester (U.K.) City Art Gallery. A.K.G., Berlin/SuperStock; **294** *left* The Granger Collection, New York; *right* North Wind Picture Archives; **295** *Henry Percy, Ninth Earl of Northumberland* (about 1595), Nicholas Hilliard. Bodycolor on vellum stuck to a playing card. Fitzwilliam Museum, University of Cambridge, U.K./Bridgeman Art Library, London; **299** Copyright © Dave Bjorn/Tony Stone Worldwide; **301** North Wind Picture Archives; **303, 304–305** *chain* Photo by Sharon Hoogstraten; **307** *top, Anne of Gonzaga,* Nathaniel Hatch. Victoria & Albert Museum, London/Art Resource, New York; *bottom, Catherine Howard,* John Hoskins. Victoria & Albert Museum, London/Art Resource, New York; **312** Copyright © Culver Pictures; **314–325** *border* Photo by Sharon Hoogstraten; **314** *Shakespeare signature and portrait* The Granger Collection, New York; *bottom, upper* Camerique/H. Armstrong Roberts; *bottom, lower* The Granger Collection, New York; **315** Special Collections Department, Colgate University; **316** *left, right* The Granger Collection, New York; **317** North Wind Picture Archives; **318** Mansell Collection, Time/Life Syndication; **319** *right* By permission of the Folger Shakespeare Library; **320** AP/Wide World Photos/ROTA; *inset* Copyright © Jacqueline Arzt/AP/Wide World Photos; **321** Photofest; **322** *left* National Museum, Athens; *right* Copyright © 1996 20th Century Fox. Photo by Merrick Morton; **323** *top left* Shakespeare Centre Library, Stratford-upon-Avon, U.K., photo copyright © Angus McBean; **326** Licensed by the

1458 ACKNOWLEDGMENTS

Estate of Orson Welles. All rights reserved. Represented by Thomas A. White, Beverly Hills, California. The Kobal Collection; **328** Photofest; **332** *top* British Film Institute; *bottom* Photofest; **342** Photofest; **344** Licensed by the Estate of Orson Welles. All rights reserved. Represented by Thomas A. White, Beverly Hills, California. Photofest; **347** *clockwise from top left* Copyright © Hulton Getty Picture Collection/Tony Stone Images; Shakespeare Centre Library, Stratford-upon-Avon, U.K., photo copyright © Angus McBean; British Film Institute; Photofest; **349** Photofest; **351** *top* Copyright © Donald Cooper/Photostage; *bottom* Deutsches Institut für Filmkunde, Frankfurt am Main, Germany; **354** Copyright © Culver Pictures; **366** Photofest; **369** *top* Copyright © Shooting Star; *bottom* Shakespeare Centre Library, Stratford-upon-Avon, U.K., photo copyright © Angus McBean; **373** Licensed by the Estate of Orson Welles. All rights reserved. Represented by Thomas A. White, Beverly Hills, California. The Kobal Collection; **382** Erich Lessing/Art Resource, New York; **385** The Kobal Collection; **389** Licensed by the Estate of Orson Welles. All rights reserved. Represented by Thomas A. White, Beverly Hills, California. Archive Photos; **400** *clockwise from top* Photofest; Photofest; Tate Gallery, London/Art Resource, New York; Photofest; **402** *top* Copyright © Reg Wilson; *bottom* Photofest; **406** Licensed by the Estate of Orson Welles. All rights reserved. Represented by Thomas A. White, Beverly Hills, California. The Kobal Collection; **411** Photofest; **413** *top, bottom* Copyright © Shooting Star; **419** Reprinted by arrangement with Rosemary A. Thurber and the Barbara Hogenson Agency; **420–422** *border* Photo by Sharon Hoogstraten; **421, 422** Shakespeare portrait North Wind Picture Archives; **423–430** Photos by Sharon Hoogstraten; **441** Detail of *Return of the Prodigal Son* (1667–1668), Rembrandt van Rijn. The Hermitage Museum, St. Petersburg, Russia. Bridgeman Art Library, London/SuperStock; **442, 445** *center* Copyright © Shoji Yoshida/The Image Bank; **448, 449** The Granger Collection, New York; **455** *top left* Camerique/H. Armstrong Roberts; *top right* H. Abernathy/H. Armstrong Roberts; **457** Copyright © Culver Pictures; **458** Portrait said to be of Ben Jonson and Shakespeare playing chess (1603), Karel van Mander. Courtesy of Frank de Heyman, Brooklyn, New York; **459** background Copyright © Arnulf Husmo/Tony Stone Worldwide; **462** Copyright © Culver Pictures; **464–465** *background,* **466** *The Genus Rosa,* Ellen Willmott. Royal Horticultural Society, Lindley Library; **467** *background* Erich Lessing/Art Resource, New York; **469** Detail of *The Proposal* (1872), Adolphe William Bouguereau. Oil on canvas, 64⅜″ × 44″. The Metropolitan Museum of Art, New York, gift of Mrs. Elliot L. Kamen in memory of her father, Bernard R. Armour, 1960 (60.122); **470** *left* North Wind Picture Archives; *right* The Granger Collection, New York; **472–73** *top background* Copyright © Suzanne and Nick Geary/Tony Stone Worldwide; **475** *top* Courtesy of the Trustees of the British Museum; *bottom* Copyright © Culver Pictures; **476** The Granger Collection, New York; **477** Copyright © 1989 Barry Seidman/The Stock Market; **480** *The Expulsion from Paradise,* Masaccio (before restoration). Brancacci Chapel, S. Maria del Carmine, Florence, Italy. Scala/Art Resource, New York; **482, 488** Copyright © Stock Montage; **492** Copyright © Culver Pictures; **499** *Detail of Adam Tempted by Eve* (1517), Hans Holbein the Younger. Öffentliche Kunstsammlung Basel, Switzerland (313); **501** The Granger Collection, New York; **502** *top, bottom* The Granger Collection, New York; **503** *top* Copyright © The Frick Collection, New York; *bottom* The Granger Collection, New York; **504** Detail of the altarpiece of the Virgin of the Navigators (16th century), unknown artist. Reales Alcázares, Seville, Spain; **508–510** Photos by Sharon Hoogstraten.

Unit Three

516 *James II* (1684), Sir Godfrey Kneller. Courtesy of the National Portrait Gallery, London; *Anne, England's Last Stuart Monarch* (about 1694), unknown artist. Courtesy of the National Portrait Gallery, London; **517** *washstand* Cooper-Bridgeman Library;

ACKNOWLEDGMENTS **1459**

carved day bed (1695). Private collection. Bridgeman/Art Resource, New York; *painted watch* Copyright © British Museum; *British coin commemorating capture of Quebec* Copyright © Hulton Deutsch Collection Ltd.; **518** *left* Perspective view of the garden and chateau, Versailles, France, by Pierre Patel. Giraudon/Art Resource, New York; *center* Museum of London; *top right, Charles II,* John M. Wright. The Royal Collection, copyright © Her Majesty Queen Elizabeth II; *bottom right* Copyright © R. Korh/H. Armstrong Roberts; **519** *top, William III* (1677), unknown artist, after Sir Peter Lely. The Granger Collection, New York; *bottom, Queen Mary II, Wife of William III,* William Wissing. National Portrait Gallery, Edinburgh, U.K. Bridgeman/Art Resource New York; **520** *top, King George I of England* (1716), Sir Godfrey Kneller. Oil on canvas. The Granger Collection, New York; *frame* Photo by Sharon Hoogstraten; *bottom, George III, Queen Charlotte and Their Six Eldest Children,* Johann Zoffany. The Royal Collection, copyright © Her Majesty Queen Elizabeth II; **521** *The Boston Massacre, March 5, 1770,* Paul Revere, after a drawing by Henry Pelham. The Granger Collection, New York; **522** *top, Sir Isaac Newton* (about 1726), John Vanderbank. The Granger Collection, New York; *center, The Ladies Waldegrave,* Sir Joshua Reynolds. National Gallery of Scotland; *bottom, Mr. Healey's Sheep,* W. H. Davis. Lincoln (U.K.) Museum and Art Galleries/E.T. Archive, London; **533** The Granger Collection, New York; **538** Detail of *The Sense of Touch* (around 1615–1616), Jusepe de Ribera. Oil on canvas, 45⅝″ × 34¾″. The Norton Simon Foundation, Pasadena, California; **539** The Granger Collection, New York; **541** J. Nettis/H. Armstrong Roberts; **545** The Granger Collection, New York; **546** *bottom left* The printer's workshop, from a woodcut by Jost Amman in Hartmann Schopper's *Panoplia* (Frankfurt am Main, 1568). Ann Ronan Picture Library; **553** The Granger Collection, New York; **554** *Lady Mary Wortley Montagu* (about 1725), Jonathan Richardson. Private collection. Courtesy of the Earl of Harrowby; **565** *left, right* The Granger Collection, New York; **566** *top, Daniel Defoe* (1706), unknown artist, after Michiel van der Gucht. Colored engraving. The Granger Collection, New York; *bottom, Rio de Janeiro Bay* (1864), Martin Johnson Heade. Canvas, 17⅞″ × 35⅞″. National Gallery of Art, Washington, D.C., gift of the Avalon Foundation; **567** *top right* Illustration from *A Field Guide to Eastern Birds,* copyright © 1980 by Roger Tory Peterson. Reprinted by permission of Houghton Mifflin Company. All rights reserved; **568–572** Photos by Sharon Hoogstraten; **582** Detail of *Portrait of a Young Woman, Called Mademoiselle Charlotte du Val d'Ognes* (about 1800), unknown French artist. Oil on canvas, 63½″ × 50⅝″. The Metropolitan Museum of Art, bequest of Isaac D. Fletcher, 1917, Mr. and Mrs. Isaac D. Fletcher Collection (17.120.204). Copyright © 1989 The Metropolitan Museum of Art; **583** The Granger Collection, New York; **584** The Granger Collection, New York; **585** Copyright © 1977 Charles E. Martin/The New Yorker Collection, from cartoonbank.com. All rights reserved; **586–590** *border* Photo by Sharon Hoogstraten; **586** *signature, top, bottom* The Granger Collection, New York; *portrait frame* Photo by Sharon Hoogstraten; **587** The Granger Collection, New York; **588** *top* The Granger Collection, New York; *bottom* North Wind Picture Archives; **589** *top* British Museum, London/E.T. Archive, London; *bottom* H. Sutton/H. Armstrong Roberts; **591, 600** The Granger Collection, New York; **601** Victoria & Albert Museum, London/E.T. Archive, London; **605** The Granger Collection, New York; **607–608** *border* Photo by Sharon Hoogstraten; **609** North Wind Picture Archives; **611** *border* Photo by Sharon Hoogstraten; **614, 618** Details of *Industry and Idleness: The Idle 'Prentice Executed at Tyburn* (1747), William Hogarth. The Granger Collection, New York; **620–623** *border* Photo by Sharon Hoogstraten; **621** *top* The Granger Collection, New York; *frame* Photo by Sharon Hoogstraten; **622** National Gallery of Ireland; **623** *Swift portrait* The Granger Collection, New York; **626** Erich Lessing/Art Resource, New York; **628** Mansell

1460 ACKNOWLEDGMENTS

Collection; **630** Copyright © Culver Pictures; **631, 632, 633, 634–635** Copyright © Hulton Deutsch Collection Ltd.; **638** The Granger Collection, New York; **639–643** Photos by Sharon Hoogstraten; **648** Detail of *Sandleford Priory* (1744), Edward Haytley. Oil on canvas. The Leger Galleries Ltd., London; **649** *Solanum macrocarpum,* G. van Spa'ndonck. Courtesy of the Natural History Museum, London; **657** The Granger Collection, New York; **665** The Granger Collection, New York; **667–671** *background* Photo by Allan I. Ludwig; **673** The Granger Collection, New York; **675–678** Copyright © Phil Brodatz. Reproduction and publication rights reserved; **675, 678** Details of *The Porten Family,* Gawen Hamilton. Museum of Fine Arts, Springfield, Massachusetts, James Philip Gray Collection; **680** The Granger Collection, New York; **682** *foreground* Copyright © Editions d'Art Lys, Versailles, France; *background* Department of Rare Books and Special Collections, University of Rochester Library; **685, 686, 687, 689** Copyright © Editions d'Art Lys, Versailles, France; **691** The Granger Collection, New York; **692** Detail of *Spring Gardens, Ranelagh,* Thomas Rowlandson. Victoria & Albert Museum, London/SuperStock; **695** *top* From *Robinson Crusoe* (jacket cover) by Daniel Defoe. Copyright. Used by permission of Bantam Books, a division of Bantam Doubleday Dell Publishing Group, Inc.; *bottom, Gulliver's Travels* by Jonathan Swift, Penguin Books Ltd. Published in Penguin English Library 1967, reprinted in Penguin Classics 1985.

Unit Four

698 *William Wordsworth* (1818), Benjamin Robert Haydon. Courtesy of the National Portrait Gallery, London; **699** *night lamp* (about 1820). Victoria & Albert Museum, London/Art Resource, New York; *early-19th-century iron* From *Everyday Life Through the Ages,* copyright © 1992 Reader's Digest; *twelve-month equation clock* (1830), Charles Edward Viner. Collection of L. A. Mayer Memorial Institute for Islamic Art, Jerusalem, Israel; *Mary Shelley* (1841), Richard Rothwell. The Granger Collection, New York; **702** *bottom* The Granger Collection, New York; **704** *top* Courtesy Barnaby's Picture Library; *bottom* Manchester heroes, September 1819. E.T. Archive, London; **705** *The Circulating Library,* Issac Cruikshank. Pen, ink, watercolor, and wash on woven paper, 6⅞″ × 8 7/16″. Yale Center for British Art, Paul Mellon Collection (B1975.4.867); **707** *Sleeping Shepherd—Morning* (about 1857), Samuel Palmer. Watercolor. Fitzwilliam Museum, University of Cambridge, U.K. Bridgeman Art Library, London/New York; **709** The Granger Collection, New York; **710–711** *background* Copyright © Linda Dufurrena/Grant Heilman Photography, Inc.; **712** Tiger in Africa. Mark Newman/Adventure Photo & Film; **714** Photo by Sharon Hoogstraten; **715** *top, bottom* The Granger Collection, New York; **716** Copyright © Culver Pictures; **718–719** Illustrations by Rebecca McClellan; **721** *left, Portrait of Bashō,* Suzuki Manrei. New Orleans (Louisiana) Museum of Art, anonymous donor; *right* Heibonsha Ltd., Tokyo; **722–725** *border* Photo by Sharon Hoogstraten; **722** *signature, top, bottom* The Granger Collection, New York; **723** Photo by Soalhat/Sipa Press, New York; **724** *top* Copyright © David Ball/Tony Stone Images; *bottom left, bottom right* The Granger Collection, New York; **725** Detail of *Mortlake Terrace* (1827), Joseph Mallord William Turner. Oil on canvas, 36¼″ × 48⅛″. National Gallery of Art, Washington, D.C., Andrew W. Mellon Collection. Photo by Richard Carafelli; **736** Silhouette of Dorothy Wordsworth, unknown artist. The Wordsworth Trust; **737** Photo by Sharon Hoogstraten; **738–740** *border* Photo by Sharon Hoogstraten; **739, 740** *Wordsworth portrait* Copyright © Culver Pictures; **741** Detail of *In a Harem Garden* (about 1765), attributed to Faiz Allah of Faizabad (Mughal empire). Opaque watercolor on paper. The David Collection, Copenhagen, Denmark; **745, 746, 748, 749, 750, 754, 756, 758, 760, 762, 765** Copyright © Stock Montage; **767** Copyright © Culver Pictures; **768** *top, Jane Austen* (about 1810), Cassandra Austen. Pencil and watercolor. The Granger Collection, New York; **769** *bottom* From *The Repository of Arts, Literature,*

ACKNOWLEDGMENTS **1461**

Commerce, Manufacture, Fashions and Politics, published by R. Ackerman (London, 1809–1828); **771** *The Sick Rose,* from *Songs of Experience* by William Blake. Library of Congress, Washington, D.C. Bridgeman Art Library, London/New York; **773** Detail of *Comus, Disguised as a Rustic, Addresses the Lady in the Wood* (1801–1802), William Blake. Henry E. Huntington Library and Art Gallery, San Marino, California; **775** *Lone Tree in the Snow,* D. Petku/H. Armstrong Roberts; **780** The Granger Collection, New York; **782** *top center* Abu Simbel, Egypt. R. Benson/ H. Armstrong Roberts; *left border* Calendar of Elephantine, with Egyptian hieroglyphs. Musée du Louvre, Paris. Giraudon/Art Resource, New York; *background* Original manuscript of Shelley's "Ozymandias." The Bodleian Library, Oxford, U.K. (MS Shelley e.4, fol. 85r); **791, 793** The Granger Collection, New York; **795** *background* Copyright © William Thompson/Tony Stone Images; **797** German Information Center, New York; **798** Detail of *John Keats* (1821), Joseph Severn. Oil on canvas. The Granger Collection, New York; **799** *background* Copyright © Jerry Schad/Science Source/Photo Researchers; **801** *background* Illustration by Rebecca McClellan; *signature* The Granger Collection, New York; **802** Illustration by Rebecca McClellan; **803** *signature,* **804** *signature,* **807** The Granger Collection, New York; **808** *top* The Granger Collection, New York; *background* Copyright © SuperStock; **810–814** Photos by Sharon Hoogstraten; **818** Detail of *The Lake, Petworth: Sunset, Fighting Bucks* (about 1828), Joseph Mallord William Turner. Clore Collection, Tate Gallery, London/Art Resource, New York; **821** *top, L'Ange du Destin,* Odilon Redon. Private collection. Bridgeman Art Library, London/New York; *bottom, John Keats* (1819), Joseph Severn. Courtesy of the National Portrait Gallery, London; **822–824** Photos by Sharon Hoogstraten.

Unit Five

828 Detail of *The Stone Pickers* (1887), George Clausen. Oil on canvas, 42″ × 31″. Tyne and Wear Museums, Newcastle upon Tyne, England; **830** *Prince Albert* (1867), F. X. Winterhalter. Oil on canvas. The Granger Collection, New York; **831** *Benz Viktoria* Photo by Peter Roberts; *mangle* Copyright © Marshall Cavendish; *Big Ben* Copyright © Geoffrey C. Garner/SuperStock; *Treasure Island illustration, Israel Hands* (1911), N. C. Wyeth. Oil on canvas, 47¼″ × 38½″. New Britain (Connecticut) Museum of American Art, Harriet Russell Stanley Fund. Photo by Michael Agee; **832** *top, Queen Victoria* (1840), Aaron Edwin Penley. By courtesy of the National Portrait Gallery, London; *bottom, Great Exhibition, 1851: Waiting for the Queen at Coalbrookdale Gates,* Joseph Nash. Lithograph. Guildhall Library, London. Bridgeman/Art Resource, New York; *background* Floral patterns. Victoria and Albert Museum, London/Art Resource, New York; **833** From *The Illustrated London News,* xiii, 1848; **834** *top left* Detail of Benjamin Disraeli, Sir John Everett Millais. The Granger Collection, New York; *top right, William E. Gladstone* (1879), Sir John Everett Millais. Oil on canvas. The Granger Collection, New York; *center, Sketch of a Ward at the Hospital at Scutari,* Joseph-Austin Benwell. Greater London Council, London. Bridgeman/Art Resource, New York; *bottom, Florence Nightingale,* Sir William Blake Richmond (1842–1921). Claydon House, U.K. Bridgeman/Art Resource, New York; **836** *top* Copyright © Hulton Deutsch Collection Ltd.; *bottom, Charles Darwin* (1894), John Collier. Oil on canvas. The Granger Collection, New York; *bottom inset* By permission of the Syndics of Cambridge (U.K.) University Library; **837** *bottom left* Copyright © Hulton Deutsch Collection Ltd.; **839** Detail of *May Day* (1960), Andrew Wyeth. Watercolor. Copyright © 1995 Andrew Wyeth; **840** Detail of *The Lady of Shalott,* John William Waterhouse. Tate Gallery, London/Art Resource, New York; **853** Stock Montage; **854** Detail of *Vespertina Quies* (1893), Sir Edward Burne-Jones. Oil on canvas, 120.6 cm × 62.2 cm. Tate Gallery, London, bequeathed by Miss Maud Beddington,

1462 ACKNOWLEDGMENTS

1940. Art Resource, New York; **860** The Granger Collection, New York; **861, 862** Copyright © 1995 G. Heck/Panoramic Images, Chicago; **863** Photo by Sharon Hoogstraten; **867** *left* Courtesy of Armstrong Browning Library, Baylor University, Waco, Texas; *right* The Granger Collection, New York; **868** *top* Library of Congress; *bottom* The Granger Collection, New York; **869** *top to bottom* Stock Montage; Copyright © Culver Pictures; Stock Montage; Copyright © Culver Pictures; Stock Montage; **870** *top, Portrait of Charles Dickens* (1859), William Powell Frith. Victoria and Albert Museum, London. Bridgeman/Art Resource, New York; *bottom* Sam Weller's first appearance in Dickens's *The Pickwick Papers.* Illustration by Phiz; **871** *top* Photofest; *center* Mansell Collection; *bottom* Copyright © Hulton Deutsch Collection Ltd.; **872, 874, 877, 881** Illustrations by John Leach; **884** Detail of *Newgate* (late 1800s), Frank Holl. Royal Holloway and Bedford Collection, New College, Egham, Surrey, U.K. Bridgeman/Art Resource, New York; **885** The Granger Collection, New York; **886** *top left* Detail of *Charlotte Brontë* (1850), G. Richmond. Chalk drawing. The Granger Collection, New York; *top right, Emily Brontë* (about 1833), Patrick Branwell Brontë. Oil on canvas. The Granger Collection, New York; *bottom left* Copyright © Simon Warner; *bottom right* Copyright © The Brontë Society; **887** *top, The First Meeting of Jane Eyre and Mr. Rochester,* Thomas Davidson. Copyright © The Brontë Society; *bottom, Merlin Hawk,* Emily Brontë. Watercolor. Copyright © The Brontë Society; **898** The Granger Collection, New York; **899** *center* Photofest; *bottom* From the Castle Howard Archives, by kind permission of the Honorable Simon Howard and Mr. Jonathan Ouvry; **901** *background,* **903, 910, 911** Roloff Beny/National Archives of Canada/1986-009; **913** The Granger Collection, New York; **915** Copyright © Greg Heck/Montresor; **916–928** *border* Photo by Sharon Hoogstraten; **930** Detail of *Nightfall at Hradčany* (1909–1913), Jakub Schikaneder. Oil on canvas, 33.7″ × 41.9″. National Gallery, Prague, Czech Republic; **931** The Granger Collection, New York; **932–934** Photos by Sharon Hoogstraten; **941** Detail of *Am Meer* [By the sea] (1875), Anselm Feuerbach. Kunstmuseum Düsseldorf im Ehrenhof, Germany; **942** Copyright © Masao Ota/Photonica; **946** The Granger Collection, New York; **947, 948** Copyright © Ross Hamilton/Tony Stone Images; **948** *background* Copyright © E. Cooper/H. Armstrong Roberts; **951** The Granger Collection, New York; **953** Copyright © H. Abernathy/H. Armstrong Roberts; **954** Copyright © Hulton Deutsch Collection Ltd.; **956–957** Copyright © H. Abernathy/H. Armstrong Roberts; **958–959** The Granger Collection, New York; **960** *Sunken Titanic,* Ken Marschall. By permission of Madison Press Ltd.; **962** The Granger Collection, New York; **964** H. Armstrong Roberts. Photo by Sharon Hoogstraten; **965, 966** The Bettmann Archive; **968** The Granger Collection, New York; **973** The Bettmann Archive; **974** *The Stone Pickers* (1887), George Clausen. Oil on canvas, 42″ × 31″. Tyne and Wear Museums, Newcastle upon Tyne, England.

Unit Six

978 Illustration by Rebecca McClellan; **980** Underwood Collection/The Bettmann Archive, New York; **981** *California Clipper* Pan American Airways/H. Armstrong Roberts; *woman on telephone* H. Armstrong Roberts; *art deco clock* From *Pastime* by Phillip Collins. Copyright © 1993, published by Chronicle Books; *1984* by George Orwell. Copyright © 1949 by Harcourt Brace Jovanovich. Used by permission of Harcourt Brace & Company; **982** *left, bottom right* Copyright © Hulton Deutsch Collection Ltd.; *top right* The Bettmann Archive; *center right, background* Imperial War Museum, London; **983** *left* Imperial War Museum, London; *right* Copyright © Hulton Deutsch Collection Ltd.; **984** *top, center, bottom left* Copyright © Hulton Deutsch Collection Ltd.; *bottom right* Imperial War Museum, London; **985** *top left* Copyright © Hulton Deutsch Collection Ltd.; *top right* The Granger Collection, New York; *bottom left, David Herbert Lawrence* (1920), Jan Juta. By courtesy of the

National Portrait Gallery, London; *bottom right* The Granger Collection, New York; **986** *top left, Portrait of Dylan Thomas,* Augustus John. National Museum of Wales, Cardiff, U.K. Bridgeman/Art Resource, New York; *bottom left* Copyright © Hulton Deutsch Collection Ltd.; *right, Gandhi* (1946), Margaret Bourke-White. *Life* magazine. Copyright © Time Inc.; **988** Detail of Saint Mark arriving in Venice, Byzantine mosaic from San Marco, Venice, Italy (about A.D. 800–1000). Scala/Art Resource, New York; **989** Copyright © M. Thonig/H. Armstrong Roberts; **993** Copyright © Hulton Deutsch Collection Ltd.; **994, 995** H. Armstrong Roberts; **1003** The Bettmann Archive; **1004** Copyright © Geraldine Prentice/Tony Stone Worldwide; **1005** *left, right* The Granger Collection, New York; **1006** Detail of *The Races at Longchamp* (1866), Édouard Manet. Oil on canvas, 43.9 cm × 84.5 cm. The Art Institute of Chicago, Mr. and Mrs. Potter Palmer Collection (1922.424). Photo Copyright © 1994 The Art Institute of Chicago, all rights reserved; **1018** *left* Copyright © William S. Nawrocki, all rights reserved; *right* Photo by Sharon Hoogstraten; **1020** Photo by Sharon Hoogstraten; **1021** The Granger Collection, New York; **1022, 1023** *St. Patrick's Close, Dublin* (1887), Walter Frederick Osborne. Oil on canvas, 27¼″ × 20″. National Gallery of Ireland, Dublin; **1024, 1025, 1030** *top* Details of *St. Patrick's Close, Dublin* (1887), Walter Frederick Osborne. Oil on canvas, 27¼″ × 20″. National Gallery of Ireland, Dublin; **1026, 1027, 1030** *bottom* Copyright © Evelyn Hofer, courtesy of The Witkin Gallery, Inc., New York; **1031** UPI/Bettmann; **1032** *top, Portrait of James Joyce* (1935), Sean O'Sullivan. Red chalk and charcoal with white highlights on gray paper, 21⁷⁄₁₆″ × 15″. National Gallery of Ireland, Dublin; *bottom left* O'Connell Bridge and Sackville Street, Dublin. National Library of Ireland; *bottom center* The Slide File; *bottom right* Trinity College Library, Dublin; **1033** *left* From the collections of the Library of Congress; **1034** Photo by Sharon Hoogstraten; **1035** Copyright © 1994 Photonica; **1036, 1039, 1041** Photos by Sharon Hoogstraten; **1043** The Granger Collection, New York; **1044** *Greene portrait* The Bettmann Archive; **1044–1045** *background,* **1045** *top right* Photo of Freetown, Sierra Leone, by Islay Lyons; *bottom right* Graham Greene in Cuba. Peter Stackpole, *Life* magazine. Copyright © Time Inc.; **1046, 1047, 1049, 1051, 1052–1053** Copyright © 1994 Rita Maas/The Image Bank; **1056** Copyright © Archive Photos; **1057** Copyright © Mrs. Vinogradoff; **1058–1059** *background* Copyright © SuperStock; **1058** *top left* Virginia Woolf. Photo by Man Ray. Copyright © 1996 Artists Rights Society (ARS), New York/ADAGP/Man Ray Trust, Paris; **1059** *center* Leonard Woolf and Virginia Woolf at Asheham House. By permission of Mrs. Angelica Garnett; *bottom* Cover of *Mrs. Dalloway* by Virginia Woolf, a Harvest Book, copyright © 1990 Harcourt Brace & Company. By permission of Harcourt Brace & Company; **1060–1064** *border* Photo by Sharon Hoogstraten; **1060** *signature* The Granger Collection, New York; *top, Portrait of T. S. Eliot,* Sir Gerald Kelly. Oil on canvas, 45⅛″ × 37″. National Portrait Gallery, Smithsonian Institution/Art Resource, New York; *bottom* By permission of the Houghton Library, Harvard University; **1061** The Granger Collection, New York; **1062** *top* The Granger Collection, New York; *bottom* Woodfin Camp & Associates; **1063** *left* Photofest; **1064** Musée de la Publicité, Paris; **1071** Copyright © Hulton Getty Collection/Tony Stone Images; **1072** By permission of the Houghton Library, Harvard University (AC9.E1464.Zzx Box 2, env. 6); **1073–1075** *border* Photo by Sharon Hoogstraten; **1074** The Granger Collection, New York; **1075** *Eliot portrait* By permission of the Houghton Library, Harvard University (AC9.E1464.Zzx Box 2, env. 6); **1076** *La grande guerre* [The great war] (1964), René Magritte. Private collection. Giraudon/Art Resource, New York. Copyright © 1996 Herscovici/Artists Rights Society (ARS), New York; **1078** Detail of *Landscape with the Fall of Icarus* (about 1560), Pieter Brueghel the Elder. Musée Royaux des Beaux Arts de Belgique, Brussels, Belgium/SuperStock; **1081** *Landscape with the Fall of Icarus* (about 1560), Pieter Brueghel the Elder. Musée Royaux des

Beaux Arts de Belgique, Brussels, Belgium/SuperStock; **1082** Copyright © Hulton Deutsch Collection Ltd.; **1086** *top* The Granger Collection, New York; *bottom* Detail of *1933* (St. Rémy-Provence) (1933), Ben Nicholson. Copyright © 1995 Mrs. Angela Verren-Taunt/Licensed by VAGA, New York/DACS, London; **1093** The Granger Collection, New York; **1097** Copyright © Globe Photos; **1098–1102** Photos by Sharon Hoogstraten; **1110** *top left* Roger-Viollet, Paris; *top right* Copyright © Robert Tardio/Graphistock; *center* Courtesy Martin Middlebrook, author of *The First Day on the Somme; bottom left* Troops of the Canadian Fourth Division, 1917. Imperial War Museum, London; *bottom right* UPI/Bettmann **1112** Copyright © Culver Pictures; **1113** *left, right* The Granger Collection, New York; **1115** National Archives; **1118, 1118–1119** Copyright © Hulton Deutsch Collection Ltd.; **1123** Photo by Sharon Hoogstraten; **1125** West Point Museum; **1126** Copyright © Hulton Deutsch Collection Ltd.; **1130–1131** *background* UPI/Bettmann; **1134** Woodfin Camp & Associates; **1136** State Institute for War Documentation, Netherlands; **1138–1139** Sovfoto/Eastfoto; **1139** Zydowski Instytut Historyczny Instytut Naukowo-Badawczy, courtesy of USHMM Photo Archives; **1140** Main Commission for the Investigation of Nazi War Crimes in Poland, courtesy of USHMM Photo Archives; **1142** Magnum Photos; **1143** *background,* **1144** Collection Jewish Historical Museum, Amsterdam, Netherlands; **1146** Official photograph, United States Air Force, courtesy of Sam R. Quincey; **1156** The Granger Collection, New York; **1157, 1158** Copyright © 1994 Alain Choisnet/The Image Bank; **1161** *top* Courtesy Martin Middlebrook, author of *The First Day on the Somme;* **1162** Copyright © 1992 Color Box/FPG International; **1163** Copyright © 1994 Masaru Suzuki/Photonica; **1165** Detail of *Interior with Seated Woman* (1908), Vihelm Hammersh¿i. Oil on canvas, 76 cm × 66 cm. Aarhus (Denmark) Kunstmuseum; **1166** Copyright © Elliott Erwitt/Camera Press/Globe Photos; **1167** George Orwell at the police training school at Mandalay, Burma, in 1922. Photo courtesy of Roger Beadon; **1168, 1173** Photo by Sharon Hoogstraten; **1175** Copyright © Globe Photos; **1176** Photo by Sharon Hoogstraten; **1177** Photo copyright © Ron Krisel/Tony Stone Images; **1184** Detail of *Abstraction on Spectrum (Organization, 5)* (about 1914–1917), Stanton MacDonald-Wright. Oil on canvas, 30⅛″ × 24 3/16″. Des Moines (Iowa) Art Center, Nathan Emory Coffin Collection, purchased with funds from the Coffin Fine Arts Trust (1962.21).

Unit Seven

1190 *Queen Elizabeth II* Hulton Getty/Gamma-Liaison Agency; *Sputnik 1* Tass/Sovfoto; **1191** *Concorde, television* Copyright © H. Armstrong Roberts; *watch* Casio Pulse Monitor Watch by Casio, Inc.; *Ted Hughes* Copyright © Michael Blackman/Camera Press London/Globe Photos; *Nelson Mandela* Copyright © 1994 John Harrington/Black Star; **1192** *top* Copyright © R. B. Goodman/National Geographic Society Image Collection; *center left* Alistair Berg FSP/Gamma Liaison; *center right, bottom* Copyright © Hulton Deutsch Collection Ltd.; **1193** Copyright © Hulton Deutsch Collection Ltd.; *background* Photo by Sharon Hoogstraten; **1194** *top* Copyright © Hulton Deutsch Collection Ltd.; *center* Copyright © Peter Jordan/Gamma Liaison; *bottom, Family Group* (1945–1949), Henry Moore. Bronze (cast 1950), 59¼″ × 46½″ x 29⅞″. The Museum of Modern Art, New York, A. Conger Goodyear Fund. Photo copyright © 1996 The Museum of Modern Art, New York; **1195** Copyright © 1991 Peter Stone/Black Star; **1197** Photo by permission of Chronicle Books. *Ulysses* cover by permission of Random House; **1199, 1200** Photos by Sharon Hoogstraten; **1208** Copyright © The British Museum; **1209** Copyright © Jane Brown/Camera Press/Globe Photos; **1218** Detail of *Horned Forms* (1944), Graham Sutherland. Tate Gallery, London/Art Resource, New York; **1219** Copyright © Globe Photos; **1220** Copyright © Hulton Deutsch Collection Ltd.; **1221** *right background (baby)* Copyright © A. Kachaturian/Photonica; *other images* The Bettmann Archive; **1222** Copyright ©

ACKNOWLEDGMENTS **1465**

A. Kachaturian/Photonica; *background* The Bettmann Archive; **1223, 1224, 1226** The Bettmann Archive; **1228** AP/Wide World Photos; **1229** Detail of *Autumn* (1984), Andrew Wyeth. Watercolor, 21″ × 29½″. Collection of Mr. and Mrs. Andrew Wyeth. Copyright © Andrew Wyeth; **1233** Copyright © Layle Silbert; **1235** Copyright © Michael La Monica/Graphistock; **1237, 1238** Copyright © Tim Davis/Tony Stone Images; **1240** *left* Copyright © Billet Potter/Camera Press/Globe Photos; *right* Copyright © Fay Godwin/Camera Press/Globe Photos; **1241** Copyright © The Nobel Foundation/AP/Wide World Photos; **1242** Eric Roxfelt/AP/Wide World Photos; **1247** AP/Wide World Photos; **1248** *left* Copyright © 1971 John Dommers/Photo Researchers, Inc.; *right* Copyright © 1995 M. C. Escher/Cordon Art, Baarn, Holland. All rights reserved; **1249** *bottom,* **1250** *bottom* Copyright © 1971 John Dommers/Photo Researchers, Inc.; **1251** *eyes* Copyright © Elma Garcia/Photonica; *water* Copyright © Howard Schatz/Graphistock; **1253** *left* Hulton Deutsch Collection Ltd.; *right* Reproduced by permission of New Directions Publishing Corp., agents for the estate of Stevie Smith; **1254** Detail of *May Shield* (1974), Nancy Hellebrand. Copyright © 1974 Nancy Hellebrand; **1255, 1256** *background* Copyright © J. Hohmann/H. Armstrong Roberts; **1257** Copyright © H. Armstrong Roberts; **1259** Copyright © Globe Photos; **1261** Photo attributed to Hulton Deutsch Collection Ltd., photographer unknown; **1262** *top to bottom* Copyright © Globe Photos; Reuters/Bettmann; Copyright © R. Drinkwater/Camera Press/Globe Photos; **1263** *Au Cinquième: A Portrait of the Artist's Wife* (about 1940), William Leech. Oil on canvas, 74 cm × 60 cm. National Gallery of Ireland, Dublin; **1264** Copyright © 1991 Steve McCurry/Magnum Photos, Inc.; **1267** *background,* **1269** *background,* **1271** Portal at Clonfert. Department of Art History, Trinity College, Dublin; **1273** Copyright © Jane Brown/Camera Press/Globe Photos; **1274** Photo by Sharon Hoogstraten; **1280** The Schomburg Center for Research in Black Culture, The New York Public Library, Astor, Lenox and Tilden Foundations; **1287** *left* Copyright © Bruce Davidson/Magnum Photos; *right, The Sniper* (1987), R. B. Kitaj. Oil on canvas, 120″ × 26″. The Saatchi Collection, London; **1288** *left* Copyright © Globe Photos; *right* Copyright © Layle Silbert; **1290, 1292** Copyright © Joshua Sheldon/Photonica; **1295** Copyright © 1995 Mel Curtis/Photonica; **1296** *background,* **1298** Copyright © Joshua Sheldon/Photonica; **1300** *Funeral Procession* (1940), Ellis Wilson. Amistad Research Center, Tulane University, New Orleans, Louisiana; **1301** Reuters/Bettmann; **1309** *Sin título* [Untitled] (1985), Rocío Maldonado. Acrylic with collaged elements on canvas with painted frame, 69″ × 85″ × 6″. Courtesy of Gallery OMR, Mexico City; **1310** Copyright © R. Drinkwater/Camera Press/Globe Photos; **1311–1313** Photos by Sharon Hoogstraten; **1319** Detail of *Invasion* (1987–1988), Carel Weight. Oil on canvas, 48″ × 60″. The Saatchi Collection, London.

1466 ACKNOWLEDGMENTS

Multicultural Advisory Board *(continued)*

Noreen M. Rodriguez, Trainer for Hillsborough County School DistrictÕs Staff Development Division, independent consultant, Gaither High School, Tampa, Florida

Olga Y. Sanmaniego, English Department Chairperson, Burges High School, El Paso, Texas

Liz Sawyer-Cunningham, Los Angeles Senior High School, Los Angeles, California

Michelle Dixon Thompson, Seabreeze High School, Daytona Beach, Florida

Teacher Review Panels *(continued)*

Sandi Capps, Dwight D. Eisenhower High School, Alding Independent School District

Judy Chapman, English Department Chairperson, Lawrence D. Bell High School, Hurst-Euless-Bedford School District

Dana Davis, English Department Chairperson, Irving High School, Irving Independent School District

Pat Fox, Grapevine High School, Grapevine-Colley School District

Susan Fratcher, Cypress Creek High School, Cypress Fairbanks School District

Yolanda Garcia, Abilene High School, Abilene Independent School District

Patricia Helm, Lee Freshman High School, Midland Independent School District

Joanna Huckabee, Moody High School, Corpus Christi Independent High School

LaVerne Johnson, McAllen Memorial High School, McAllen Independent School District

Josie Kinard, English Department Chairperson, Del Valle High School, Ysleta Independent School District

Donna Matsumura, W. H. Adamson High School, Dallas Independent School District

Ruby Mayes, Waltrip High School, Houston Independent School District

Mary McFarland, Amarillo High School, Amarillo Independent School District

Gwen Rutledge, English Department Chairperson, Scarborough High School, Houston Independent School District

Bunny Schmaltz, English Department Chairperson, Ozen High School, Beaumont Independent School District

Adrienne Thrasher, A. N. McCallum High School, Austin Independent School District

Michael Urick, A. N. McCallum High School, Austin Independent School District

OHIO

Joseph Bako, English Department Chairperson, Carl Shuler Middle School, Cleveland City School District

Glyndon Butler, English Department Chairperson, Glenville High School, Cleveland City School District

Deb Delisle, Language Arts Department Chairperson, Ballard Brady Middle School, Orange School District

Ellen Geisler, English/Language Arts Department Chairperson, Mentor Senior High School, Mentor School District

Dr. Paulette Goll, English Department Chairperson, Lincoln West High School, Cleveland City School District

1467

Dr. Mary Gove, English Department Chairperson, Shaw High School, East Cleveland School District

Loraine Hammack, Executive Teacher of the English Department, Beachwood High School, Beachwood City School District

Sue Nelson, Shaw High School, East Cleveland School District

Mary Jane Reed, English Department Chairperson, Solon High School, Solon City School District

Nancy Strauch, English Department Chairperson, Nordonia High School, Nordonia Hills City School Dictrict

Ruth Vukovich, Hubbard High School, Hubbard Exempted Village School District

FLORIDA

Judith H. Briant, English Department Chairperson, Armwood High School, Hillsborough County School District

Beth Johnson, Polk County English Supervisor, Polk County School District

Sharon Johnston, Learning Resource Specialist, Evans High School, Orange County School District

Eileen Jones, English Department Chairperson, Spanish River High School, Palm Beach County School District

Jan McClure, Winter Park High School, Orange County School District

Wanza Murray, English Department Chairperson (retired), Vero Beach Senior High School, Indian River City School District

Shirley Nichols, Language Arts Curriculum Specialist Supervisor, Marion County School District

Debbie Nostro, Ocoee Middle School, Orange County School District

Barbara Quinaz, Assistant Principal, Horace Mann Middle School, Dade County School District

CALIFORNIA

Steve Bass, 8th Grade Team Leader, Meadowbrook Middle School, Ponway Unified School District

Cynthia Brickey, 8th Grade Academic Block Teacher, Kastner Intermediate School, Clovis Unified School District

Karen Buxton, English Department Chairperson, Winston Churchill Middle School, San Juan School District

Bonnie Garrett, Davis Middle School, Compton School District

Sally Jackson, Madrona Middle School, Torrance Unified School District

Sharon Kerson, Los Angeles Center for Enriched Studies, Los Angeles Unified School District

Gail Kidd, Center Middle School, Azusa School District

Myra LeBendig, Forshay Learning Center, Los Angeles Unified School District

Corey Lay, ESL Department Chairperson, Chester Nimitz Middle School, Los Angeles Unified School District

Dan Manske, Elmhurst Middle School, Oakland Unified School District

Joe Olague, Language Arts Department Chairperson, Alder Middle School, Fontana School District

Pat Salo, 6th Grade Village Leader, Hidden Valley Middle School, Escondido Elementary School District

1468

Manuscript Reviewers *(continued)*

Jacqueline Anderson, James A. Foshay Learning Center, Los Angeles, California

Kathleen M. Anderson-Knight, United Township High School, East Moline, Illinois

Anita Arnold, Thomas Jefferson High School, San Antonio, Texas

Cassandra L. Asberry, Justin F. Kimball High School, Dallas, Texas

Jolene Auderer, Pine Tree High School, Longview, Texas

Don Baker, English Department Chairperson, Peoria High School, Peoria, Illinois

Beverly Ann Barge, Wasilla High School, Wasilla, Alaska

Louann Bohman, Wilbur Cross High School, New Haven, Connecticut

Rose Mary Bolden, J. F. Kimball High School, Dallas, Texas

Lydia C. Bowden, Boca Ciega High School, St. Petersburg, Florida

Angela Boyd, Andrews High School, Andrews, Texas

Judith H. Briant, Armwood High School, Seffner, Florida

Hugh Delle Broadway, McCullough High School, The Woodlands, Texas

Stephan P. Clarke, Spencerport High School, Spencerport, New York

Dr. Shawn Eric DeNight, Miami Edison Senior High School, Miami, Florida

JoAnna R. Exacoustas, La Serna High School, Whittier, California

Linda Ferguson, English Department Head, Tyee High School, Seattle, Washington

Ellen Geisler, Mentor Senior High School, Mentor, Ohio

Ricardo Godoy, English Department Chairman, Moody High School, Corpus Christi, Texas

Meredith Gunn, Secondary Language Arts Instructional Specialist, Katy, Texas

Judy Hammack, English Department Chairperson, Milton High School, Alpharetta, Georgia

Robert Henderson, West Muskingum High School, Zanesville, Ohio

Martha Watt Hosenfeld, English Department Chairperson, Churchville-Chili High School, Churchville, New York

Janice M. Johnson, Assistant Principal, Union High School, Grand Rapids, Michigan

Eileen S. Jones, English Department Chair, Spanish River Community High School, Boca Raton, Florida

Paula S. L'Homme, West Orange High School, Winter Garden, Florida

Bonnie J. Mansell, Downey Adult School, Downey, California

Linda Maxwell, MacArthur High School, Houston, Texas

Ruth McClain, Paint Valley High School, Bainbridge, Ohio

Rebecca Miller, Taft High School, San Antonio, Texas

Deborah Lynn Moeller, Western High School, Fort Lauderdale, Florida

Bobbi Darrell Montgomery, Batavia High School, Batavia, Ohio

Bettie Moody, Leesburg High School, Leesburg, Florida

1469

Margaret L. Mortenson, English Department Chairperson, Timpanogos High School, Orem, Utah

Marjorie M. Nolan, Language Arts Department Head, William M. Raines Sr. High School, Jacksonville, Florida

Julia Pferdehirt, freelance writer, former Special Education teacher, Middleton, Wisconsin

Cindy Rogers, MacArthur High School, Houston, Texas

Pauline Sahakian, English Department Chairperson, San Marcos High School, San Marcos, Texas

Jacqueline Y. Schmidt, Department Chairperson and Coordinator of English, San Marcos High School, San Marcos, Texas

David D. Schultz, East Aurora High School, East Aurora, New York

Milinda Schwab, Judson High School, Converse, Texas

John Sferro, Butler High School, Vandalia, Ohio

Brad R. Smedley, English Department Chairperson, Hudtloff Middle School, Lakewood, Washington

Faye S. Spangler, Versailles High School, Versailles, Ohio

Rita Stecich, Evergreen Park Community High School, Evergreen Park, Illinois

GayleAnn Turnage, Abiline High School, Abiline, Texas

Ruth Vukovich, Hubbard High School, Hubbard, Ohio

Kevin J. Walsh, Dondero High School, Royal Oak, Michigan

Charlotte Washington, Westwood Middle School, Grand Rapids, Michigan

Tom Watson, Westbridge Academy, Grand Rapids, Michigan

Linda Wetaherby, Deerfield High School, Deerfield, Illinois

1470